REMEMBERING FOR THE FUTURE

Titles of related interest

ALMOG/Antisemitism Through the Ages

ARAD et al/Documents on the Holocaust

BAUER/Dry Bones: The Impact of American Jewry on Post-Holocaust Jewish Europe

ECKARDT & ECKARDT/Long Night's Journey into Day: A Revised Retrospective on the Holocaust

GILBERT/Atlas of the Holocaust

HEIFETZ/Oral History and the Holocaust: A collection of poems from interviews with survivors of the Holocaust

KATZ/Origins of the Yiddish Language

KATZ/Dialects of the Yiddish Language

LIBOWITZ/Faith & Freedom: A Tribute to Franklin H. Littell

NETTLER/Past Trials & Present Tribulations: A Muslim Fundamentalist's View of the Jews

STEFANESTI/Portrait of a Romanian Shtetl

WIESEL & FRIEDLANDER/ The Six Days of Destruction: Meditations towards Hope

YADLIN/Antisemitism in Contemporary Egypt

Journals of related interest

Holocaust and Genocide Studies

Yad Vashem Studies

REMEMBERING FOR THE FUTURE

Papers to be presented at an International Scholars' Conference
to be held in Oxford

10–13 July, 1988

THEME I

Jews and Christians During and After the Holocaust

PERGAMON PRESS
OXFORD . NEWYORK . BEIJING . FRANKFURT
SÃO PAULO . SYDNEY . TOKYO . TORONTO

U.K.	Pergamon Press plc, Headington Hill Hall, Oxford OX3 0BW, England
U.S.A.	Pergamon Press Inc., Maxwell House, Fairview Park, Elmsford, New York 10523, U.S.A.
PEOPLE'S REPUBLIC OF CHINA	Pergamon Press, Room 4037, Qianmen Hotel, Beijing, People's Republic of China
FEDERAL REPUBLIC OF GERMANY	Pergamon Press GmbH, Hammerweg 6, D-6242 Kronberg, Federal Republic of Germany
BRAZIL	Pergamon Editora Ltda, Rua Eça de Queiros 346, CEP 04011, Paraiso, São Paulo, Brazil
AUSTRALIA	Pergamon Press Australia Pty Ltd., P.O. Box 544, Potts Point, N.S.W. 2011, Australia
JAPAN	Pergamon Press, 5th Floor, Matsuoka Central Building, 1-7-1 Nishishinjuku, Shinjuku-ku, Tokyo 160, Japan
CANADA	Pergamon Press Canada Ltd., Suite No. 271, 253 College Street, Toronto, Ontario, Canada M5T 1R5

Remembering for the Future Conference logo designed by Shigeo Fukuda of Japan.

Printed in Great Britain by Hazell Watson & Viney Limited Member of BPCC plc Aylesbury, Bucks, England

THEME I

Jews and Christians During and After the Holocaust

Christian attitudes and responses to the Jewish plight in Central Europe 1933–1945 and after

CHAIRPERSON **Dr F. Burton Nelson**

RAPPORTEUR **Dr David Bankier**

Christian attitudes and responses to the Jewish plight in Eastern Europe 1933–1945 and after

CHAIRPERSON **Professor Ronald Modras**

RAPPORTEUR **Dr David Kranzler**

Christian attitudes and responses to the Jewish plight in Southern and Western Europe and by the Vatican 1933–1945

CHAIRPERSON **Dr Asher Cohen**

RAPPORTEUR **Professor Eva Fleischner**

*These papers are being translated and will appear in the supplementary volume.

Christian attitudes and responses to the Jewish plight in English-speaking countries 1933–1945 and after

CHAIRPERSON **Dr Robert Everett**

RAPPORTEUR **Professor Richard Pierard**

Helpers and rescuers: Ethical, psychological and religious factors

CHAIRPERSON **Mr Douglas Huneke**

RAPPORTEUR **Dr Mordecai Paldiel**

*These papers are being translated and will appear in the supplementary volume.

The challenge to the Christian and Jewish communities: Faith, theology and life after the Holocaust (Christian-Jewish relations)

CHAIRPERSON **Dr Beverly Asbury**

RAPPORTEUR **Dr Franz von Hammerstein**

*These papers are being translated and will appear in the supplementary volume.

The challenge to the Christian community with emphasis on theology and ethics

CHAIRPERSON **Professor John T. Pawlikowski**

RAPPORTEUR **Professor Larry Axel**

*These papers are being translated and will appear in the supplementary volume.

The challenge to the Christian community with emphasis on early Christianity and overall historical considerations

CHAIRPERSON **Professor Frederick Schweitzer**

RAPPORTEUR **Dr Jacobus Schoneveld**

The challenge to the Jewish community: Religion, life and the state of Israel

CHAIRPERSON **Rabbi Albert Friedlander**

RAPPORTEUR **Dr Dina Porat**

The challenge to the Jewish community: Religion, life and the State of Israel

CHAIRPERSON **Dr Normon Solomon**

RAPPORTEUR **Professor Edward Alexander**

The survivors' challenges and contributions

CHAIRPERSON **Mr Ze'ev Mancowitz**

RAPPORTEUR **Dr Abraham Peck**

THEME II

The Impact of the Holocaust on the Contemporary World

The universities and other teaching institutions

CHAIRPERSON **Professor Yaffa Eliach**

RAPPORTEUR **Professor David Weinberg**

The legal, medical and psychology professions

CHAIRPERSON **Professor Jack Boozer**

RAPPORTEUR **Professor Roger Errera**

*These papers are being translated and will appear in the supplementary volume.

Political aspects and responsibilities

CHAIRPERSON **Dr Stephen Roth**

RAPPORTEUR **Dr William Korey**

Fiction and poetry

CHAIRPERSON **Professor Alan Berger**

RAPPORTEUR **Professor John Felstiner**

Art, drama and the cinema

CHAIRPERSON **Professor Ziva Amishai-Maisels**

RAPPORTEUR **Professor Geoffrey Hartman**

Art, drama and the cinema

Philosophical and moral implications

CHAIRPERSON **Professor Lyman Legters**

RAPPORTEUR **Professor Zev Garber**

*These papers are being translated and will appear in the supplementary volume.

Identifying genocidal signals: Antisemitism, terrorism, denials of the Holocaust

CHAIRPERSON **Professor Randolf Braham**

RAPPORTEUR **Professor Harry James Cargas**

The social sciences (Historiography)

CHAIRPERSON **Professor Christopher Browning**

RAPPORTEUR **Mr Robert Wolfe**

*These papers are being translated and will appear in the supplementary volume.

Methodologies in the Social Sciences: Problems of the Holocaust

CHAIRPERSON **Professor Herbert Strauss**

RAPPORTEUR **Dr Shmuel Almog**

Christian attitudes and responses to the Jewish plight in Central Europe 1933–1945 and after

CHAIRPERSON **Dr F. Burton Nelson**

RAPPORTEUR **Dr David Bankier**

THE ROLE OF THE NORWEGIAN LUTHERAN CHURCH DURING WORLD WAR II

PROFESSOR SAMUEL ABRAHAMSEN

Brooklyn College and The Graduate Center, The City University of New York, 33 West 42nd Street, New York, NY 10036

As a result of the Treaty of Kiel between Sweden and Denmark on January 14, 1814, Norway was ceded from Denmark to Sweden without the consent of Norway's population. As a protest against this action, a Constituent Assembly was called together at Eidsvold on April 10, 1814. On May 17, the delegates adopted a Constitution, known as *Norges Grunnlov* or Norway's Fundamental Acts. Article 2 stated that:[1]

> "The Evangelical-Lutheran Religion shall be maintained and constitutes the established Church of the Kingdom. The inhabitants who profess the same religion are obligated to educated their children in the same. Jesuits and Monastic orders shall not be tolerated. Jews are still excluded from admission to the Kingdom."

The first two sentences of Article 2 established religious principles which became crucial in the fight of the Norwegian Lutheran Church against the Quisling-Nazi regime during World War II. It became a national fight for human rights and for spiritual liberty against the foreign invasion of Nazi-Germany which was bent on destroying the judicial system, the democratic way of life, the church and the schools. The means used were terrorism and propagation of the Aryan race supremacy which was utterly alien to the moral and religious traditions of the Norwegian people. The aim of the German occupation force was to consistently nazify the Norwegian way of life. Thus the Norwegian people did not only have a military front, but also cultural and religious fronts to fight on. During the occupation, the fight of the Norwegian Church concentrated mainly on moral values: justice, humanity and freedom of conscience. The church became a focal organization in guiding the Norwegian resistance Movement. The role of the church became crucial; it was to protect the Christian values which the Nazis aimed at destroying. The Nazis had proved experts at transforming their own society and made a determined effort to do the same in Norway. They knew exactly what their was and how to achieve it: by controlling all institutions through terrorism and by nazifying the population through schools, youth and trade organizations, and the churches.

Throughout the occupation, it was the pulpit that became the most commonly utilized means of communication through consistent opposition to Nazism. On some occasions, the churches were the main institution protesting against brutalities, such as the deportation of the Norwegian Jews in the Fall of 1942.[2] Another courageous example was the church's protest against the German mobilization of Norwegian youth to join the German war effort. In these instances, the church spoke on behalf of the nation. The fight of the Norwegian Church became identical with the fight for the national concept of freedom, and it waged this fight, not on the periphery, but in the middle of the battles to be fought.

For this battle, the churches were theoretically well prepared. They provided an ideal basis for resistance because the congregations were spread all over Norway. In addition, the church, which represented all social classes, had access to the intellectual elite as well as to the working class. It had the population support needed to organize an effective opposition.[3]

The reactions of the German Lutheran Church to the rise of Nazism was, of course, followed with great interest in the "Motherland of Protestantism." It was disturbing for Norwegian clergy to notice that supporters of Nazism within the German Protestant Church also supported anti-Jewish legislation. What was noticed with satisfaction was Niemøller's dissident Bekkenntniskirche[4] which defended the rights of Christians of Jewish origin within the church. Its memorandum to Adolf Hitler in 1936 was also duly noted. Here it was stated that "when, in the framework of the National-Socialist ideology antisemitism is forced on the Christian, obliging him to hate Jews, he has nonetheless the divine commandment to love his neighbor."[5]

One Norwegian who took up the fight against the Nazi ideology at an early stage was Bishop Eivind Josef Berggrav (1884-1959), who played a prominent role in the Norwegian Resistance Movement.[6] He followed very closely the events in Germany, being completely fluent in German but opposed to the Nazi ideology and mentality.[7] In 1933, Berggrav refused an invitation to participate in the inauguration of the Nazi Bishop, Miller, in Germany; nor did the other Scandinavian Bishops participate in these festivities.

There had, for centuries, been confrontations between the Norwegian Lutheran State Church and the many opposing Lutheran lay churches.[8] A joint proposal in 1939, designed to bring about cohesion between liberal and conservative church elements during a unique era in Norwegian history, presaged the liberal Bishop Berggrav's preeminence and his intellectual leadership in during the coming Nazi occupation.[9]

Opposition to Nazism did not start on the day of invasion, April 9, 1940. Rather, it grew gradually throughout the first few months until differences became crystallized.[10] The Church had benefitted from a period of Nazi non-interference following Reichskommisar Josef Terboven's speech of September 25, 1940, promising to respect the Hague Convention "regarding full religious freedom in the occupied regions."[11] In fact, Terboven's speech became the signal to increase the Norwegian Resistance Movement when it became clear that the price for peace was to support the Quisling regime through his Nazi party, Nasjonal Samling,[12] a party which had never been able to elect a single representative to the Storting (Parliament). In this speech Terboven expounded the Nazi policy of total nazification of the Norwegian people. In doing so he challenged the very foundations of Norwegian culture. The church was ready to do battle and Bishop Berggrav became its leading spokesman.[13]

At a meeting on October 28, 1940 in Carlmeyergatens Misjonhus (Mission House), the first major consolidation of the Church opposition to the Nazi regime took place with the establishment of an organization, "Kristent Samråd for den norske kirke" (Christian Joint Council for the Norwegian Church). Now, in the hour of danger, the Norwegian church was united into a single front where important events were discussed in detail and decisions made.

eighteen of the leading churchmen including the seven Bishops, stated that the Joint Council would follow "the inspired words of God according to the Lutheran Confession of our Church.[14]

On December 12, 1940, the members of Norway's Supreme Court resigned in protest against Terboven's terror-regime in disregarding the 1907 Hague Convention where it was stated that the occupying power must "respect the valid laws in the country unless there are absolute hindrances for this."[15] The Norwegian Supreme Court insisted that an independent court, i.e., the Norwegian Supreme Court, must judge whether the occupying power actually adhered to the law. Terboven's reply was that the occupying power itself must have that right. The Supreme Court answered that it could not continue to function under these lawless circumstances, and the judges relinquished their offices. The resignation of the Supreme Court was the most dramatic and effective action so far to mobilize the Norwegian people against establishing a Nazi lawless society. The Supreme Court had shown the road as to the principles of justice, and by resigning, it had given the direction which the home front was to follow.[16] The unity, reached within the Joint Council, had proven to be of inestimable importance for th resistance movement, which had suffered the mob rule by the young men in the Hird, which had been very aggressive and brutal.

On January 15, 1941, the Norwegian Bishops addressed a document to the Acting Head of the Department of Church and Education, Mr. Ragnar Skancke. This pastoral letter changed the relationship between state and church. The Bishops called attention to the fact that the foundation of the Norwegian Church was based on a definite constitutional relationship to the state and on the assumption that the duty of the state was to uphold justice and righteousness in accordance with the word of God. Now the lines were clearly drawn. The church challenged the state on the basis of the Norwegian Constitution which stated that the Lutheran religion shall be the official religion of Norway and emphasized the importance of the state accepting and honoring the legal and moral obligations contained in the Articles of Faith and in the Bible. Bishop Berggrav had consulted widely with other resistance leaders and they were now prepared to fight the lawlessness which the Nazi Quisling government had introduced.

Specifically, three instances were mentioned in the document: namely, the systematic rule of terror by the Norwegian Nazi stormtroopers (Hird); secondly, the resignation of the Supreme Court of Norway; and thirdly, the interference of the state with the ministers' Oath of Silence. These three items were thoroughly documented. The main emphasis, however, was on the last point, whereby a minister could not pledge complete silence to a confessor as long as the state was empowered to force him to break his oath.

The Bishops quoted Article 16 of the Augustana Confession of Faith of the Church, which clearly defined the legitimate relationship between Church and State, especially as to the duty and right of church officials to speak up on topics vital to the church. The Bishops stated that one of the most vital concerns was the order given to the Police Department, whereby the Oath of Silence could be abolished by the police.[17] The letter concluded by saying that it was of utmost importance for the population to have full and unqualified confidence in the pastoral Oath of Silence: "To abolish this Magna Carta of Conscience is an attack upon the very heart of the church. It is an attack which takes on an especially serious character by the fact that Article 5 empowers police to imprison an offending pastor and force him to talk without having been taken before a court of law."[18]

The letter ended with a demand for a reply to clarify the issues, but no reply arrived. The three bishops, Berggrav, Støøren and Marone went in person to see the Minister of Church and Education,[19] and presented him with an additional letter[20] expressing in even sharper terms the role of the church in a lawless society. Three days later, an unsatisfactory reply was received from Minister Ragnar Skancke. At this time the Bishops decided to "go public" by sending the correspondence as a pastoral letter to be read in the churches all over the country. The following excerpt is especially pertinent:[21]

> "When those in authority in the society tolerate violence and injustice and oppress the souls of men, then the Church is the guardian of men's conscience ... On that account, the bishops of the Church had laid before the Minister some of the facts and official announcements concerning the administration of our society which the Church finds to be in conflict with the law of God."

This episcopal letter was not only read from the pulpits in the Norwegian churches; it found its way to London from where it was broadcast throughout the world.[22] The wide distribution and the reading from the pulpits of the episcopal letter in February 1941 led to open disagreement between state and church in occupied Norway. But further actions were being planned by Quisling to completely nazify the Church. The dramatic high point of this struggle took place on February 1, 1942. The background for this incident was a follows:

On Sunday, February 1, 1942, the Nazi Reichkommissar Terboven appointed Quisling as "Minister President" with a solemn "Act of State" at the old fortress of Akershus in Oslo. In this connection, a high mass was scheduled on that day to be conducted at 11:00 A.M. by a Nazi minister, the Reverend Blessing Dahle, in the main National Cathedral, Nidarosdomen, in the City of Trondheim. The Bishops had protested this usurpation of power, since the regular minister, Dean (later, Bishop) Arne Fjellbu, was still in office. He could not be prevented legally from conducting a High Mass, which was to take place at 2:00 P.M.[23] The police, however, reacted by forbidding this Divine Service to take place and actually closed the doors after a few hundred persons had entered the church. Several thousand of the congregants had assembled in the cold weather outside to support their church. An eye witness, Pastor Bang-Hanssen, said: "We froze so that our teeth chattered, but we could not part from each other. From the easterly part of the place, I suddenly heard a voice starting Luther's old hymn. All of us took off our hats and joined in the singing of "A mighty fortress is our God, a trusty shield and weapon." While we were standing there with uniformed and armed policemen in front of us, the old song carried by thousands of voices sounded prouder and mightier than I have ever heard. Then came Blix's 'National Hymn' and after that Norway's National Anthem. Nothing else was sung, nothing else spoken. I was standing almost in front of the crowd beside some girls fifteen the twenty years old. When I looked at them, I saw that they were crying convulsively. And all of us had difficulty in restraining our tears.""[24]

Using force, the police pushed the masses back and informed everyone that the Divine Service had been called off. People were ordered to go home quietly, since then would be waiting in vain. The masses, however, did not disburse.

What took place inside the cathedral is told by Dean Fjellbu in his book, Minner fra krigsårene (Memoirs from the War Years):[25]

> "I hid in the cathedral early Sunday morning so that no one should find me. I found this very sensible. Upon prearrangement with the architect, Mr.

This, I hid in his office in the cathedral yard. From there a secret stairway extends through the workshops to the cathedral and from the workshops I could, unnoticed, come in to the west front of the cathedral. From my hiding place I had a good view of the open space before the cathedral and the main door to the church. When Blessing Dahle's service was over, they came up and reported. My wife brought food. People began to stream in for my service which was to begin at 2:00, but at 1:15 I saw that disturbances were beginning at the entrance. There were police in front of the door and at 1:25 I was informed that the police had closed the church. It had been my intention to proceed at once to the pulpit, but my wife advised me to go before the altar; if I were to be arrested it ought to occur at the most sacred spot. I found this entirely right. I went directly from the altar to the pulpit and gave my sermon without intimating that anything extraordinary had happened."

There were serious consequences of this courageous protest. On February 19, 1942, Dean Fjellbu was dismissed and on February 24th, the seven Bishops of Norway decided unanimously to "cease administrative cooperation with a State which practices violence against the Church," although they maintained the right to exercise the spiritual vacation given them by ordination at the Lord's altar.[26] There was thus no <u>single</u> act by the state that caused the resignations, but the Norwegian clergy had been subject to police hearings, arrests, confiscation of property, threats of deportation and even the death penalty. Nonetheless, the Church could not be frightened and continued to protest Quisling's efforts at encroachment, stressing that its aim was not of a political but of a spiritual nature. Indeed, it was stated that the Lutheran Church was not interested in destroying the State Church, but was fighting for its mission to preach the word of God and to be able to perform their duties in ministering to the needs of the congregations. Therefore, in spite of the resignation, the clergy continued to serve in their capacities as churchmen, regardless of the changed situation of the state.

The clergy also insisted that the councils of the congregation would have to continue regardless of whether the clergy was dismissed by the state.

The issuance, on April 5, 1942, of a declaration known as "The Foundation of the Church," (Kirkens Grunn) constituted a definite break with the Nazi state. This document is of lasting value in drawing the lines between the obedience due to the state and the cases where protest and opposition must be used in terms of non-violent resistance. This declaration was read from the pulpits and emphasized the sovereignty of God above all ideologies. Having read this document from the pulpits, the ministers resigned from their positions as civil servants, but continued to do their work as clergymen. Out of a total of 699 ministers, 645 resigned and only 54 chose to remain in their positions. This protest showed that the Norwegian Lutheran Church was almost unanimous in this opposition to the Nazi Government. Those who remained in their positions became isolated, both from their colleagues and from their congregations. The Church had taken the motto: "Fear not those who destroy the body, but are not able to destroy the soul, but rather fear him who is able to destroy the body and the soul." It was like an echo from Worms when Luther spoke the definitive works: "Here I stand. I cannot do otherwise. So help me God. Amen."

The complete title of the declaration was "The Foundation of the Church. A Confession and a Declaration." It was divided into six parts:

1. Regarding the Freedom of God's Word and our obligation to the Word.

2. Regarding the Church and the Ordination.

3. Regarding the Sacred Solidarity of the Church.

4. Regarding parents and their rights and obligations as to children's education.

5. Regarding the correct attitude of Christians and the Church to the state authorities.

6. Regarding the state church.

One of the main points in this document was the insistence on the independence of the Church over the State in spiritual matters, and of the Word of God as sovereign over all ideologies.[27] Eight prominent Nazi clergymen, however, issued a statement published in the controlled press on June 30, 1942.[28] Here they maintained that those who opposed state authority also opposed the sovereignty of God. They based these assertions on "The Epistle of Paul to the Romans," Chapter 13:2: "Whosoever therefore resisteth the power, resisteth the ordinance of God; and they that resist shall receive the themselves damnation."[29] Needless to say, the "Berggrav Church," as his opponents called it, disagreed sharply with this interpretation. The state was to be considered a divine creation only if it did not force on to act against God's commandments. Only a state based on justice could demand obedience. This was a new interpretation of the Lutheran concept of State.[30]

The "Foundation of the Church," formulated to protect endangered Christianity in Norway under Nazi rule, concluded with:[31]

> "We ordained men ... declare that we herewith, for reasons of conscience, lay down our offices, but intend to continue to do all the work and services in our flock which can be done by a non-official, in keeping with the Holy Scriptures, the Church's Confession, and the Service Book of the Norwegian Church."

During Easter, 1942, the leaders of the Church were arrested: Bishop Berggrav and the three ministers, Indrebø, Carlsen and Wisløff.

Quisling, appointed by Terboven as Minister President on February 1, 1942, had usurped the power as "Norway's Supreme Bishop." He now boasted that he had taken over the earlier functions of the King, the Parliament, the Church and the Government. According to the Constitution, the King is Norway's Supreme Bishop. Thus, Quisling had become a sort of "Führer-bishop." He reacted violently to the resignation of the clergy, characterizing it as and "Act of insurrection directed against Norway's liberty and independence." The law stipulated many years of imprisonment or even death for an individual found guilty of insurrection. The threats were serious, especially against Bishop Berggrav who was told that he had committed treason three times and, according to Quisling, warranted triple execution. Despite these threats from Quisling who, with great justification regarded Bishop Berggrav as the arch-enemy of his party, the Bishop received only a short stay in prison and was kept under "house arrest" in his own home is Asker for the next three years.

Much speculation has been offered to explain this leniency afforded Bishop Berggrav. One plausible explanation has been suggested by Professor Arvid Brodersen in his book, Between the Fronts.[32] He traced the relationship between Norwegian and German resistance groups through such leaders as Theodore Steltzer, Helmuth James von Moltke and Carl Friedrisch Goerdler. Major Steltzer was with the Oberkommando der Wehrmacht in Oslo under General Falkenhorst. There was no love lost between him and Terboven, who received orders, probably from Himmler through Borman, to go easy on the Norwegian Church, and especially not to harm Bishop Berggrav. The reasoning offered was that the "Wehrmacht" did not want additional difficulties among the Norwegian population.

The Norwegian clergy had now severed all relations with the Nazi Quisling state from whom they could expect no further economic help. It was up to the local congregations to support their churches and church leaders. The reaction of the Norwegian people to these arrests was one of extreme indignation. The population responded with generous financial support and made it possible for the ministers to continue holding Divine Services. The issues were now very clear. The Norwegian Church was no longer a state church, but had separated itself from a state with which it could not cooperate.

After Easter 1942, there were really two churches in Norway, namely the State Church of the Department of Church and Education, which had appointed Nazi Bishops and Ministers, and the "Free Church." The two churches constituted a chasm which separated the population. Very few attended the services conducted by the Nazis. They preached to empty seats. The other churches were filled to capacity. During this period there was a spiritual revival, led by the resisting Norwegian clergymen who enjoyed great respect and veneration throughout the occupation.[33]

Since the church leaders had to go underground, a separate organization was created on July 26, 1942 called "The Temporary Church Leadership" (D.M.K., Den Midlertidige Kirkeledelsen). This now functioned as the highest church leadership council; i.e., a leadership refusing to accept control by the Quisling government. The latter had declared the Temporary Church Leadership unconstitutional and illegal, to be dissolved as of August 7, 1942. The leadership, however, replied in a letter on August 15th that they could not dissolve themselves and that they intended to continue their active opposition "come what may." It did not take long before the next outrageous event took place. That was the persecution of the Jews, a process which had started in 1940 but not came to a sudden climax in the fall of 1942. The murder of half of Norway's Jewry , executed with the cooperation of Norwegian police and German authority constitutes the biggest crime committed during the German occupation. These murders differed from all the other forms of terrorism inasmuch as they were directed towards an innocent religious group which was being exterminated, not for any criminal acts, but for having been born Jews. As one Norwegian author put it: "Other Norwegians did not have to feel they were threatened."[34] This fanatical racism took its own murderous path, "no matter how big the cost, no matter how small the yield, the Germans had to strike."[35]

Ever since the invasion on April 9, 1940, the Nazis had managed to make life extremely difficult for the Jews. Their radios were confiscated in May 1940 and the display windows of Jewish stores were painted over with anti-Semitic slogans: "Jews are not tolerated in Norway."[36] On March 29, 1941, Vidkun Quisling gave an anti-Jewish speech at the Institute for the Exploration of the Jewish Question in Frankfurt am Main. After the German invasion of the USSR in June 1941, Jews in Northern Norway were arrested. In November, Jewish property was registered, Jewish firms confiscated and mass arrests of Jews took place. Jews had been dismissed from professional and civil services.

On January 10, 1942, Jonas Lie, Minister of Police, issued an order to have a "J" for Jøde (Jew) stamped into identification cards and passports of Jews by the Norwegian police. On March 12, 1942, the 1814 Constitutional prohibition of admission of Jews to Norway was re-introduced. Marriage laws were changed so that a non-Jewish spouse, through a Jewish marriage, became a

Jew. The persecutions increased dramatically with the arrival of Hauptsturmführer Wilhelm Artur Konstantin Wagner to take charge of the Gestapo Headquarters in Oslo. A wholesale arrest of male Jews took place on October 26, 1942, the arrest of women and children took place on November 26. The men were transported to concentration camps to await deportation aboard the troop transport S/S Donau; the women and children were boarded directly on the same ship, which left the same day "towards an unknown destination." We know today, this destination was Auschwitz.

Sympathy mingled with courage as the Norwegians protested these acts, undertaking rescue of Norway's Jews to Sweden. Organizations and individuals spontaneously brought Jews and half-Jews out of the country. Many risked their lives to do this. Some of the most active in the rescue efforts had to escape the Sweden across borders guarded by the German police; others committed suicide. It was something of a miracle that a stream of Jewish refugees, about 850 could be brought safely to Sweden during 1942 and 1943. The Norwegians did have some warning of the Nazi plans through secret contacts with the Wehrmacht through Helmuth James von Moltke who had mentioned in September 1942, during a visit to Oslo, that actions against the Jews in Norway were being contemplated, but he could give neither the exact plans not the times for arrest and deportation.

If any evidence was needed to prove that the Church's opposition to Nazism was not weakening during the occupation, it came in November 1942. The Temporary Church Leadership, supported by many other religious groups of other denominations, sent directly to Minister President Quisling a sharp protest against the Jewish persecution that wan then being carried out by the Nazis. It was the voice of the Norwegian Church speaking out forcefully. It should be noted, however, that prior to this protest, little had been done by the Church to stem the tide of rising anti-Semitism in Norway. When the Quisling National Union Party accused the Jews in March 1942 of "poisoning the soul of the Norwegian people," the Church had remained silent.[40] But public opinion had been aroused by the brutal treatment, arrests and deportation of Jews, and this sense of agony was articulated by the Norwegian Lutheran Church.

In their letter of November 10, 1942, the seven dismissed Bishops stated that Jews had had a legal right for 91 years to reside and to earn a livelihood in Norway, but that they had now been deprived of their properties without warning.[41] Furthermore, Jews were being punished as the worst criminals, wholly and solely because they were Jews. The Bishops pointed out that Quisling had, on various occasions, emphasized that his party would protect the basic Christian values, and one of them was now being endangered: the Christian commandment to "love they neighbor," the most elementary right for any human being. The Bishops stated: "When we now appeal to you, Mr. Minister President, it is not to defend whatever wrongs the Jews may have committed. If they have committed crimes, they shall be tried, judged and punished according to Norwegian law, just as all other citizens. But those who have committed no crime shall enjoy the protection of our country's justice." The letter went on the say the protest was caused by the deepest dictates of conscience, because silence in view of the legalized injustice against Jews would make the Church co-guilty in this injustice.

> "The Church has God's call and full authority to proclaim God's law and God's Gospel. Therefore, it cannot remain silent when God's commandments are being trampled underfoot. And now it is one of Christianity's basic values which is being violated; the commandment of God which is fundamental to all society, namely law and justice ... Stop the persecution of the Jews and stop the race hatred which, through the press, is being spread in our land."

The Bishops emphasized in closing that this appeal had nothing to do with politics. Before worldly authorities the Church maintained that obedience in temporal matters must follow God's word. This protest was supported by theology scholars, nineteen church organizations and six non-state -church religious societies. A total of over sixty signatures from all sections of Norway's Protestant community endorsed the protest.

The Catholic Church, however, did not participate in this protest. Bishop Jacob Mangers, who was in charge of the Catholic Church during the occupation, had sent a letter to the Department of Church and Education on November 10, the same day the Protestant Church sent its protest. The Bishop, had written, not to protest the Jewish persecutions, but to secure the release of five baptized Jewish families.[42] The Bishop thought it would be inappropriate to send another letter before he had received a reply to the first one.[43] A letter dated November 10, 1942, from Bishop Mangers to Ole Hallesby, a leader of the Protestant protest and Chairman of the Temporary Church Leadership, stated that "another letter on my part will undoubtedly lead to no consideration for the first one, and thus harm Christians of Jewish descent."[44]

While the protests and prayers of the Norwegian Lutheran Church did not stop the deportation of the Jews, the vigorous protest made a deep impression in Norway and abroad. Additional protests were made by the Swedish Bishops, the British Broadcasting Corporation, and by many countries throughout the free world. The fight of the Norwegian Lutheran Church to resist nazification had become identical with the fight for national freedom. The majority of the population realized, as Ferdinand Schjelderup expressed it, that resistance would pay off "cost what it may -- to the bitter end!"[45]

The Germans tried to minimize the effectiveness of the Church protest. For example, the daily reports of December 1942 mentioned that the Norwegian churches had pleaded for the Norwegian Jews, but "the radical solution of the Jewish question will be forgotten by the egoistic Norwegians."[46]

The protest reflected the contest between Church and State in Norway: "The State cannot enact any law or decree which is in conflict with the Christian faith or the Church's Confession." The attitude of the Lutheran Churches in Germany had been explained by recalling Luther's conception of the two dominions through which God rules this world: the spiritual one, or the Church, and the secular one, or the "worldly authorities." The people, according to Luther, do not have the right to resist the authorities; only princes have.[47] The Lutheran Church of Norway did not accept this interpretation, but quoted the Confession (Augustana) and Luther in order to stress that it was "the Church's God-given duty as the conscience of the State to object" to the anti-Semitic measures. The letter of protest won a response throughout the country. It was read in the churches on the 6th and 13th of November, 1942, at which time prayers were said for the persecuted Jews.

The fight of the Norwegian Church became a subject of great interest to the world press. This was not surprising since the activities and opposition of the Norwegian Church took place in the open, whereas many of the Home Front's other activities had to be carried out in secret. The reaction in Sweden to the deportation of Norway's Jews was strong. The Swedish Bishops quoted the protest of the Norwegian Bishops and referred to it in pastoral letters. The noted theologian, Nataniel Beskow, stated on the occasion of a large protest meeting in Stockholm:[48]

> "A ship that left Oslo harbour had a freight of anguish on board. We can not imagine how much these human beings, men, women and children are

suffering....We can not call them back. They go to their death or to slavery....If we can do nothing else we can try to be the voice of the condemned...and through us call forth their anguish and accusations...."

Domprost Olle Nystedt stated on Sunday, November 22, 1942, at the Gothenburg Cathedral that "the churches in Sweden cannot remain silent when such things happen on our borders. If we are silent the stones will cry out. We are shaken to our innermost thinking by the suffering of the unfortunates. This is a break of God's law and a violation of the basic values of our civilization."[49]

The Swedish press was almost unanimous in condemning the brutal treatment of Norway's Jews and quoted the protest in full. Ture Newman, editor of Trots Allt (In Spite of Everything), wrote that "the beastialities which Nazism commits in Norway is nothing new, but it is shocking that it is happening so close by. We protest against the treatment of Norway's Jews."[50]

In addition, the Swedish women's organizations published a protest expressing their anger at the persecutions of Jews in Norway: "Persecutions of people belonging to another race is against the Nordic concept of justice and has, until now, been unknown in Nordic countries."[51]

There was a protest within Quisling's party as well. The party journal, N.S. Månedshefte (National Union Monthly Journal), stated on December 15, 1942 that:[52]

"...we must not forget that this ÆJewishÅ problem is not only a racial one, but also a national and, above all, a human one. The Norwegian people have never regarded Jews as countrymen...since the people is too healthy for that, but they have always been regarded as human beings and, at that, as miserable human beings....We have to guard ourselves against transgression of feelings of justice within ourselves. It does not help to win the whole world if one harms one's own soul."

Bishop Lars Frøyland, a Bishop of Oslo appointed by Quisling, wrote in 1943 that the Norwegian people were shamed by:[53]

"...our behavior towards a people of another race and another belief within our own borders. I feel bound by my conscience to say this. And I do this even if it shall cost me ever so much. Is it correct to judge everyone the same way, and to punish the guilty with the innocent? We are, after all, Norwegians! We are, after all, Christians!"

The leader of the Nazi Party, however, defended the deportation. In a speech in Trondheim on December 6, 1942, Vidkun Quisling commented:[54]

"I want to make one point quite clear top you while touching on th subject of the Jews....The Jew is no Norwegian; he is an oriental and does not belong in Europe. He has nothing to do in Norway. He is an international element of destruction."

On February 22, 1943, Quisling announced the Labor Conscription Act; i.e., a general mobilization of the civilian population. Men, ages 18 to 55 and women ages 21 to 40 were forced to register under threat of losing their ration cards. Those who did not report willingly were rounded up by police. To start with, thirty-five thousand men were to be used for road and railroad building and for the "Organization Todt" which had charge of military installations in Norway.[55] Again, the Church was the only Norwegian institution to speak up publicly against this breach of the Hague Convention of 1907. On May 8, 1943, the Temporary Church Leadership (DMK) condemned this act in a letter to the Minister President as a purely military undertaking whereby Norwegians were forced against their conscience to participate in the building of military fortifications under German command and in German uniforms. The letter stated:[56]

> "As Christians we look upon our land as a gift from God entrusted to our people by God. He has called upon the church to be the guardian of conscience when force threatens the soul. Therefore we must ask the Minister President to withhold the registration of Norwegians contrary to people's conscience and sense of right. Against such violation of conscience, the church cannot remain silent."

The consequences of this attack on Quisling and the German administration were predictable. Those who had signed the letter, Hallesby and Hope, were arrested on May 13, 1943 and interned at Grini Concentration Camp. Hope was released in August 1944, but Hallesby had to wait until the end of the occupation to be set free.[57]

The Church did not speak again publicly during the remainder of the occupation but went underground as all the other anti-Nazi organizations had had to do. But the terror was not over. Hundreds of ministers were deported from their homes to other parts of the country or to German concentration camps. At the end of the war, 35 Norwegian ministers and one bishop were in jails or concentration camps. Two ministers died there.[58]

The Church could, however, be proud that the losses both in human life and material had not been in vain. The Lutheran Church had been victorious. It did not lose its soul during these tragic years. Neither did the various dissenting sects in Norway refrain from protesting Jewish persecutions. At the risk of arrest, they joined in the various protests against the Nazi regime and lent their support against the ruthless treatment and other injustices suffered during the occupation.[59] In this way the Norwegian Protestant Churches created a strong moral front against the inhuman treatment of human beings.

CONCLUSIONS

The Second World War, with its five years of Nazi-German occupation (1940-1945), had a profound impact on all aspects of life in Norway, including the religious. The Church of Norway was a bastion of resistance, under the leadership of Bishop Eivind Berggrav, who established the leadership of the "Joint Christian Council" (Kristent Samråd). The courage and high purpose of the leaders of th Norwegian Church would have been of little avail in the fight against Nazism had they failed to retain the support of the people of Norway. The majority of the population showed repeatedly, by word and act, their complete and uncompromising opposition to Hitler and Quisling in their attempts to establish a Nazi-Norwegian church.

There were basically five major events in the conflict between the Norwegian Lutheran Church and the Quisling-Nazi State:

1. The protest on January 15, 1941 against lawlessness under Nazism and the Quisling regime.

2. The protest on February 1, 1941 at the Nidaros Cathedral in Trondheim.

3. The issuance of the <u>Foundation of the Church</u> (Kirkens Grunn) on April 5, 1942, constituting the definitive break with the Quisling government.

4. The protest against the Jewish persecutions of November 1942.

5. The protest against the Labor Conscription Act of February 22, 1943, after which time the Church had to go underground.

Crisis after crisis found the people's loyalty to the Church and its leaders unshaken, just as their loyalty to King Haakon never wavered. The people remained loyal and grateful to their Church which, for the first time in Norwegian history, became a self-administering free church without any connection with the state. This break of relations, however, was not a break with the principle of a state-church, as such. Indeed, it was not a struggle for or against any particular form of church organization; it merely marked the end of relations with a lawless government. This took its toll. Two pastors died in concentration camps, many more were jailed, and fifty-five were banished to an island. Following liberation of the country in 1945, all bishops and ministers were restored to office in the State Church. The document, The Church's Foundation (Kirkens Grunn), a fundamental statement of principle concerning the connection between state and church, marked the formal break between the Norwegian Lutheran Church and the Nazi state. It stated: "The word of God is sovereign over all ideologies." The people made the Church's fight their own fight; and the Nazis learned that in attacking the Church, or any of its representatives, they in fact attacked the people of Norway.

The record of the European Lutheran Churches in their opposition to Nazism is uneven and puts the credibility of Christianity in doubt in many country. This is not true in Norway. Many Christians in other countries failed to resist the ideas and ideologies of Nazism, but there were church leaders who rendered a clear witness to the reality of the Christian faith in their outspoken anti-Nazi attitudes.[60] Among them were the majority of the clergy of the Lutheran Churches in Norway.

FOOTNOTES

[1]Kongeriget Norges brundlov Given I rigsforsamlingen paa Eidsvold den 17de mai 1814, Oslo: H. Aschehoug & Co., 1964, p. 1.

[2]Einar Molland, "Kirkens Kamp," in Sverre Steen (ed.), Norges Krig, 1940-1945, Oslo: Gyldendal Norsk Forlag, 1950, p. 36.

[3]Helen Fein, Accounting for Genocide, New York: The Free Press, 1979, p. 71.

[4]Carl Fr. Wisløff, Norske Kirkehistorie, Oslo: Lutherstiftelsen, 1971, Vol. III, P. 415.

[5]Guenter Lewy and John M. Snoek, "The Christian Churches," in Holocaust, Jerusalem: Keter Publishing, 1974, P. 139.

[6]Rolf Kluge, Hjemmefrontledelsen tar form -- Kretsen dannes sommeren 1941, Olso: Universitetsforlaget 1970, pp. 78-79.

[7]Ingvald B. Carlsen, Kirkens kamp i Norge, København: P. Haase & søns Forlag, 1946, p. 24.

[8]Carl C. Rasmussen, What About Scandinavia?, Philadelphia: The Muhlenberg Press, 1948, pp. 102-104.

[9]Einar Molland, Fra Hans Nielsen Hauge til Eivind Berggrav, Oslo: Gyldendal, 1972, p. 87.

[10]Eivind Berggrav, Da kampen kom. Noen blad fra startåret, Oslo: Land Og kirke, 1945, pp. 80-81.

[11]Bjarne Høye and Trygve Ager, The Fight of the Norwegian Church Against Nazism, New York: The Macmillan Company, 1943, pp. 5-6.

[12]Sverre Kjellstadli, Hjemmestyrkene. Hovedtrekk av den militære motstanden under okkupasjonen, Oslo: H. Aschehough & Co., 1959, pp. 25-26.

[13]Torleiv Austad, Kirkens Grunn. Analyse av en kirkelig bekjennelse fra okkupasjonstiden 1940-45, Oslo: Luther Forlag, 1974, p. 63.

[14]Carlsen, op. cit., p. 22.

[15]Edvard Bull, "Motstand. Fettsikkerhet mot terror," in Knut Mykland, Norges Historie, Vol. 13, Oslo: J.W. Cappelens Forlag, n.d., pp. 387-388.

[16]Chr. R. Christensen, "Hjemmefronten," in Våre Falne 1939-1945, Oslo: 1948, Vol. III, p. 16.

[17] Berggrav, op. cit., p. 132.

[18]Høye and Ager, op. cit., pp. 156-158. Underlined in text.

[19]Ture Nerman, Norsk Front, Stockholm: Federativs, 1941, p. 115.

[20]Berggrav, op. cit., pp. 134-136.

[21]Ibid., p. 8.

[22]Gjelsvik, op. cit., p. 35.

[23]Chr. R. Christensen, Vårt folks historie, Oslo: Aschehoug, 1961, Vol. IX, P. 303.

[24]Arne Fjellbu, Memories from the War Years, Minneapolis: Augsburg Publishing House, 1947, p. 141.

[25]Ibid., pp. 138-140.

[26]John M. Snoek, The Grey Book, Assen, The Netherlands: Van Gorcum & Co., 1969, p. 116.

[27]Molland, op. cit., p. 54. The English translation of "The Foundation of the Church" is found in Høye and Ager, op. cit., pp. 172-180.

[28]The Nazi clergymen were G. Chr. Falck-Hansen, Lars Frøyland, H.O. Hagen, O.J.B. Kvasnes, Einar Lothe, J.E. Sivertsen, L Daae Zwilgemeyer and Dagfinn Zwilgemeyer, as cited in Arne Hasiing, The Nazi Church in Occupied Norway, unpublished manuscript.

[29]The New Testament, American Bible Society, p. 166.

[30]Austad, op. cit., p. 176: "Bare rettstaten har krav på lydighet."

[31]Høye and Ager, op. cit., p. 180.

[32]Arvid Brodersen, Mellom Frontene, Oslo: Cappelen, 1979, pp. 88ff.

[33]Frederick Hale, "An Embattled Church, Scandinavian Review, Vol. 69, No. 1, (1981): 55.

[34]Edvard Bull, op. cit., p. 398.

[35]Raul Hilberg, The Destruction of the European Jews, Chicago: Quadrangle Books, 1961, p. 355.

[36]Chr. A.R. Christensen, op. cit., p. 348.

[37]Ludvig Schübeler, Kirkekampen slik jeg så den, Oslo: Lutherstiftelsens Forlag, 1946, p. 211: "... ekteskapslovgivningen var endret for å motvirke blandede ekteskaper. En jødes ektefelle ble i kraft av sitt ekteskap selv jøde."

[38]Samuel Abrahamsen, "The Holocaust in Norway," in Contemporary Views on the Holocaust, Randolph L. Braham (ed.), Boston, The Hague: Kluwer-Nijhoff Publishing, 1983, pp. 109-142.

[39]Brodersen, op. cit., pp. 67-68.

[40]Torleiv Austad, "Fra Statskirke til selvadministrert folkekirke. Den norske kirken under krigen," in Stein Ugelvik Larsen and Igun Montgomery (eds.) Kirken, Krisen og Krigen, Oslo-Bergen-Tromsø: Universitetsforlaget, 1982, p. 346.

[41]"Kirken Protesterer mot Jødeforfølgelsene," Norske Tidend, London, November 28, 1942, as reprinted in Johan M. Snoek, op. cit., p. 346.

[42]The baptized Jews were Dr. Ernest Adler, Samuel B. Jaffe, Hans Huszar, the family Neubauer and Adolf Neumann.

[43]Personal communication to author from Pastor John J. Duin of Hamar Bishopric, dated February 22, 1982.

[44]Letter of November 10, 1942 from Bishop Mangers to Professor Hallesby, Archives, Hamar Bishopric, Norway: See also, Gottlieb W. Rieber-Mohn, "Vi var med. Glimt av den katolske kirke i Norge under Okkupasjonen," St. Olav, No. 57, 1945, p. 94.

[45]Ferdinand Schjelderup, På Bred Front, Oslo: Grøndahl & Søns, Forlag, 1947, p. 301.

[46]Anlage 120 zum Tatigkeitbericht December 1942 Abt Ic Niederschrift uber die Ic-Besprechung beim AOK Norwegen in der Zeit vom 8.-11.12 1942: 1. Tag 8.12.1942: "3. Einzelnes. Die Gesamtikirche Norwegens hat fur die Juden Interpelliert, als bekannt wird, dass die Juden zum Osten transportiert wurden. Die radikale Løsung der Judenfrage wird jedoch der egoistiche Norweger vergessen."

[47]Snoek, op. cit., 119.

[48]Protest Meeting, Stockholm, December 2, 1942, Yad Vashem Archives, 0/54/38.

[49]Nordiska Röster mot Judeforföljelse och Vald. Dokument och Kommentar, Stockholm: Judish Tiddskrift, 1943, p. 14. Yad Vashem Archives, 85.2952.

[50]Ture Nerman, in Trots Allt, December 4, 1942.

[51]Norske Tidend, December 9, 1942: "Forfølgelsen av folk tilhørende en annen rase er i strid med den nordiske rettsoppfatning og har hittil vaert ukjent i nordiske land."

[52]As quoted by Johan Scharffenberg, Morgenbladet, Oslo, September 15, 1952: "Protester mot Quislings jødeforfølgelse."

[53]Lars Frøland, I Korsets Tegn (By the Sign of the Cross), Oslo: Viking Forlag, 1943, pp. 43-44.

[54]Fritt Folk, December 7, 1942, as quoted from Memorandum (Dispatch N. 1408), February 11, 1943, the American Legation, Stockholm, National Archives, Washington, D.C., NND 730032.

[55] Gjelsvik, op. cit., p. 94.

[56] News of Norway, July 23, 1943. The Norwegian text is found in Ingval B. Carlsen, Kirkens Kamp i Norge, p. 137.

[57] Francis Bull, Minner om mennesker, Oslo: Gyldendal Norsk Forlag, 1962, pp. 148ff.

[58] Carlsen, op. cit., p. 185.

[59] Amanda Johnson, Norway, Her Invasion and Occupation, Decatur, GA: Bowen Press, 1948, p. 258.

[60] W. A. Visser't Hooft, The Ecumenical Movement in the Radical Problem, Paris, 1954, p. 40, as quoted in Snoek, op. cit., p. 289.

THE RESPONSE OF GERMAN CONSERVATIVE EXILES TO NAZI ANTISEMITISM

David Bankier

Institute of Contemporary Jewry
The Hebrew University
Jerusalem

The position of the German exiles as regards antisemitism in the Third Reich has not yet been subjected to a comprehensive study. After several years' work on the subject, I published a number of articles which constitute the partial results of my inquiry into the reactions of communist and socialist exiles to the Jewish question in the Third Reich.[1]

In this lecture, I shall try and broaden this perspective and deal with an issue that still warrants further research, namely the reactions of exiles of a Christian-conservative orientation. The discussion will not deal with the viewpoint of conservatives who remained in Nazi Germany, as this topic deserves a separate study.

One centre of Christian-conservative, anti-Nazi publicity was the Vita Nova publishing house in Switzerland. Its publications provide an important source of material for the subject at hand. Not only German exiles who took shelter in Switzerland, but also other opponents of Nazism, with a Christian orientation, found the Vita Nova helpful in spreading their anti-Nazi viewpoints. In 1935, for example, it published the Die Gefaehrdung des Christentums durch Rassenwahn und Judenverfolgung, an anthology to which almost all the Christian professions contributed: Anglican, Greek-Orthodox, Protestant and Catholic. The latter stream was represented in this collection of articles by Aloisius Scheiwiler, the bishop of Saint Gallen, one of Switzerland's leading campaigners against Nazism. A note of scorn, coupled with a vigorous anti-Nazi line, runs through all the articles. In no uncertain terms, the authors denounce Nazi racial theory with its stamp of vulgar materialism marked by a mystical, naturalist determinism which, in their eyes, is worse even than the Marxist theory of class struggle. According to Marx, after all, the consciousness of the bourgeoisie could be changed, whereas racial doctrine allowed no room for change. The viewpoint of the authors can be summed up in Scheiwiler's closing remark: not mincing his words, he pronounces in the strongest terms that whoever claimed that Judaism and Christianity contradicted one another, undermined the basis of the New Testament and the writings of the Apostles, and whoever tried to sever Judaism from Christianity, so clearly bound together, attacked Jesus' doctrine. He reminds his readers that Jesus had declared that salvation was to come from the Jews, and that the Popes had condemned the persecution of Jews. Therefore, he concludes, it is a Christian duty to love Jews not only because of the injunction to love one's neighbour as oneself, but because of the importance of the Jews to the doctrine of Christian salvation.

One of the exiles who found a literary home in Vita Nova was the Catholic dramatist, Eugen Guersten. Prior to his emigration, he had been the chief playwright of the state theatre in Hessen, a post he relinquished when the Nazis came to power. Under the pseudonym Herrmann Steinhausen, he discusses the Jewish question in a work entitled "Die Judenfrage eine Christenfrage".[2] In a serious attempt to get to the root of the matter, he arrives at the conclusion that antisemitism did not simply cast shame on society, but was tantamount to an earthquake for Western civilization as a whole. And because it undermines the framework of Christianity, hatred of the Jews could bring the entire Christian edifice tumbling down. The persecution of the Jews indicates and symbolizes the crossing of a threshold into a frightening era. And what is more, it perforce changes the life of every Christian, even if he does not take part in it, neither as a victim nor a victimizer. For, of necessity, the freedom of the Christian is limited as long as the freedom of the Jew is limited. When it becomes impossible for him to observe the precept of loving the other, he loses his freedom.

Another forum that served the conservative exiles was Die Erfuellung, a periodical edited by Johannes Maria Oesterreicher, who had earned his reputation as the head of the Pauluswerke, the Viennese missionary organization. This organization was at the forefront of the battle against racism and antisemitism in the Austrian, Christian community. Oesterreicher, himself, discussed the Jewish question in numerous articles and books both in Austria and in the United States, where he arrived as an exile following the Anschluss. A look at any of these opens a window onto his overall attitude on the subject. Of special interest is his Racisme Antisemitisme Antichristianisme, published in New York in 1943, which sums up his study of the question.[3] This book, written in 1939, denounces Nazism in the spirit of the Christian interpretation of Nazi racial and antisemitic phenomena. To Oesterreicher mind, Nazism is a revolutionary force, born in reaction to communism, and the two set up a chain reaction inevitably leading to war. In the typical Catholic interpretation, Nazism was perceived as a secular religion born of the religious and moral value crisis of modern civilization, the direct consequence of which was atheism. Not by chance, then, does Oesterreicher stress that the forces and energies previously directed at, and finding a home in religion, were now, in the new era, channelled into a torrent carrying Nazi totalitarianism forward. The movement has taken the place of the Church. The attempt to lump together Nazism and Bolshevism and point out the parallels and similarities between them was also typical of the Catholic perception of Nazism. Both are global doctrines, striving for an inhuman humanism, whether in the materialistic humanism of the dictatorship of the proletariat or in the biological humanism of blood and race. Nevertheless, Oesterreicher writes, this common ground does not obscure the differences between the two ideologies. Whereas communism strives to establish a noxious regime and a new culture outside of the framework of bourgeois civilization, Nazism seeks to remain within the framework of historical development, to preserve the bourgeoisie and fight within it to create a destructive revolutionary dynamism. Oesterreicher felt it his duty to sound the alarm, particularly against racial theory which lent Nazism its special dimension. He emphatically states that racism posed a threat not only to the Jews but to all men as it quickly endangered the very essence and role of the Church. Racial theory stands in direct opposition to science and Church dogma, to reason and revelation. And because racism denies the gospel, it is, ideologically, a rebellion against God. In rebelling against the chosenness of Israel, racism constitutes the Antichrist on earth and one cannot, therefore, remain neutral towards it but must oppose it vigorously. Moreover, if antisemitism stems also from hatred of Christianity, then hating the Jews is concomitant with hating Christianity. In Oesterreicher's view, antisemitism combines a mixture of ideological - inherently pathological - and utilitarian elements. Antisemitism is a mythomania, deriving from morbid fear and hatred of the Jews but it is also useful, serving political ends. For trampling the Jews diverts attention, captures the imagination and drills into the public consciousness the existence of a single foe: the Jewish scapegoat. Oesterreicher's perspicacity is worth noting, for like Harnack, he saw fit to point to the persistence and influence of the Manichaean idea embedded in Western civilization. The basic conception underlying this trend was the perception of Christianity not as the successor of Judaism but as its antithesis. According to him, one of its ascendant trends leads from gnosticism to Nazism, from Marcian to Hitler. This matter, it seems to me, is neither purely hypothetical nor totally unfounded and certainly deserves closer study.

Two other exiles who dealt with the Jewish question in their writings were Alexander Emmerich and Hermann Rauschning. The publicist, Emmerich, who wrote under the name of Edgar Alexander, forcefully attacked Nazism, from the Catholic viewpoint, in his book Der Mythus Hitler. While Rauschning, who had been associated with Nazism and the head of the senate in Danzig, wrote numerous works, the most relevant to our purposes being The Revolution of Nihilism.[4] Alexander's book,[5] burning with an anti-Nazi fervour, views Nazism as void of ideological content, the fruit of social resentment and a political inferiority complex. Its antisemitic theory is a principle of fanatical hatred and in his hatred for the Jews, Hitler remains faithful to his overall approach which calls for the brutal and merciless destruction of the enemy, regardless of who he is. Here, too, we find a conception of Nazism as some form of secular religion. To Alexander, Nazism is not merely a political stream but a Weltanschauung, some kind of new religious reformation. The Nazi myth advocates the return to the pre-Christian primitivism of European culture. Nor does Alexander content himself with a theoretical discussion of the Nazi phenomenon; he lashes out against the representatives of the Church who lacked the courage to combat the Nazi heresy. He clearly and repeatedly explains that the struggle against Nazism was not to be taken lightly. The battle is not over the fate of the Jews but over the truth of Christian gospel. In this context, he cites Faulhaber's sermon from the end of 1933, "Christentum Germanentun, Judentum", as the only instance in which a church leader stepped forward to defend Christianity against Nazi hostility instead of swallowing it in silence.

Alexander's approach was closely related to the views expressed by Rauschning. This statesman maintained contact with exiles from the conservative Right, such as Gottfried Treviranus, Albert Kluthe and Heinrich Bruening, sharing an intellectual kinship with them. He, too, claimed that Nazism had no ideology, as a movement was unfaithful to any idea whatsoever, and was sustained purely by the lust for power. This led him to regard it as a pretext for a nihilistic revolution, as denoted by the title of his book. Its dynamism, he notes, can be maintained only so long as it can point to foes, thereby creating a situation of constant revolution. And if it were able to do so - by destroying the principles of law and order, freedom and personal safety - Nazism would pave the way for mass revolution and rebellion. As regards antisemitism, Rauschning asserts that Christianity could not be understood in isolation from its Jewish legacy, whereas Hitler's mythical world turned the Jew into the principle of absolute evil. And yet, although he perceived the Jewish factor as central to Nazi doctrine, Rauschning nevertheless put the emphasis on the manipulative value of antisemitism; that is, on its systematic and methodical exploitation in order to unleash the brutal instincts of the masses.

We have seen how Nazi antisemitism was treated in the writings of Christian-conservative orientated exiles. For the most part, however, though they recognized the dominance of the Jewish element in Nazi doctrine, they saw the threat posed by antisemitism as a political weapon no less dangerous to Christianity than to the Jews. Let us now see to what extent the question of antisemitism disturbed or preoccupied the regular press of the conservative exiles, by examining several such newspapers. We shall look first at _Deutsche Briefe_, which actually did not represent any specific group but was chiefly the mouthpiece of two figures who came together in exile in Switzerland, Waldemar Gurian and Otto Michael Knab.

Gurian came from a wealthy Jewish St. Petersburg family that had immigrated to Germany and converted to Catholicism. He worked as a journalist, publishing several books on political themes. When Hitler came to power, he emigrated to Switzerland and lived there until 1937 when he made his final move, this time to the United States.[6] Knab, too, left Germany for Swiss exile, in 1934, where he lived more or less in Gurian's shadow. A number of other exiles - such as Karl Thieme, who had been one of the editors of the Catholic youth magazine _Junge Front_ until he left Germany in 1935 - also contributed to _Deutsche Briefe_. But these, as already noted, were secondary contributors; most of the articles in _Deutsch Briefe_ were composed by Gurian who set the pace and was the driving force behind its operations.[7] Apart from editing and writing for this periodical, he contributed also to other publications which provided a podium for the anti-Nazi, Christian front in Europe: _Die Erfuellung_, _Der Christliche Staendestaat_ and _Der Deutsche in Polen_.

Like the other publications of anti-Nazi exiles, also the pages of the _Deutsche Briefe_ were filled with reports of the living drama unfolding in the Third Reich. Its importance, however, lay not in the information it provided but in the quality of its analysis of the reported events, an analysis informed by Gurian's insight into the nature of Nazism and the consequences of its policy. He spared no words in exposing the true face of Nazism, dealing primarily with the cultural struggle being waged in Germany between the Nazi regime and the Church. In reviews of articles and books on Nazism, published both inside and outside of Germany, he spoke out heatedly against the regime of the Third Reich and its racial theory. His assault, for the most part, was directed against Streicher's publications - _Der Stuermer_ and _Fraenkische Tageszeitung_ - and the SS publication, _Das Schwarze Korps_. Remarkably well-reasoned, his articles were written in the light of the Christian-conservative interpretation of Nazism and it is to his credit that he was among the first to discern the similarities between Bolshevism and National Socialism, despite the ostensible gulf between the two. His contribution to the comparative study of the two types of totalitarianism, an approach which has been accepted by various researchers, is without a doubt an important link in the historiography of Nazism.

The basis for his comparison of the two totalitarian regimes is his analysis of the absolutist nature of the party and its doctrine. He argues that this phenomenon is unprecedented in human history, that modern trends sustain both types of regime which, in function, serve as a substitute for religion (_Ersatzreligion_). Their similarity lies both in their ideological base and in the form of regime they wish to establish. Insofar as their intellectual infrastructure is concerned, both rest on vulgar materialism: Bolshevism, on economic materialism and Nazism, on the materialism of the blood, deriving from its irrational ethos and its cult of vital instincts. Nazi materialism is the worse of the two because it seeks to enslave man to his basest instincts and irrational impulses. In exposing the vulgarity of Nazism and its low cultural level, Gurian did not simply wish to make it ridiculous to his readers, as did most of the emigrant literature. In his view, Nazism is the most dangerous adversary of Western civilization, not because it is a political movement, but because of its totalitarian ambitions. Its aspiration to change the spirit of man and mould humanity in its totalitarian guise, lends it the aspect of a heretical movement. Furthermore, the _Gleichschaltung_ that is the expression of its totalitarian will, the terror that turns men into nihilists, as exemplified by the SS, makes Nazism the most dangerous heresy ever known to Western civilization. This analysis leads Gurian to conclude that since the fateful confrontation is between Nazism and the whole of Western civilization based on Christianity, the war against Nazism transcends individual, political duty. It is not enough to resist one policy or another; an all-out war must be waged, inspired by the religious and moral values of Western man. If it is a Christian duty to reject all compromise with Bolshevism, this duty is even more urgent with respect to Nazism. In the context of this discussion of the nature and dangers of Nazism, Gurian took issue with racial theory in articles occupying a central place in Deutsche Briefe. He emphasizes the perversion of racial theory, denying as it does the spiritual nature of man who, according to Christianity, was created in God's image and is the prototype of divine substance. With reference to the pseudo-religious and pseudo-messianic nature of Nazism, he examines the anti-Christian elements of Nazi antisemitism that made blood a fundamental category for rating people. There is no doubt in his eyes that the sharpening conflict between Christianity and Nazism is a confrontation between two contradictory theories of salvation: between racial theory which views the Jews as the chief obstacle to the reign of its messianic era, when man will be reunited with nature and submit to its laws, and the Christian doctrine of salvation which accords Jews a central role in the Second Coming. In other words, Christianity and its Heilsgeschichte, in which the Jews serve as a theological catalyst, instrumental in bringing on salvation, are the antithesis of Nazi racism. Nazism, then, is clearly some kind of political demon to be eliminated without mercy. Racism and its principles create a naturalistic worldview, and must serve a warning to the Church, for its consequences are awesome and far-reaching, well beyond the harm done the Jews. Gurian was to clarify this point in a memorandum published in 1937 on the Church's attitude towards the Jews, which shall be discussed below.

While the significance of Nazism and the repercussions of racial theory from the theological point of view occupied a considerable place in Gurian's articles, only a small portion of Deutsche Briefe was devoted to antisemitism itself. Gurian was content with reporting on the articles appearing in Der Stuermer, the legal judgments illustrating the difficulties of the Jews, the restriction of Jewish rights, and the regime's punitive actions against Germans who lent a helping hand to Jews.[8] On his own role in assisting Jews, we have no information. This is not so with respect to converts. We know, for instance, that he intervened on behalf of his convert friend, Ernst Kamnitzer, and also appealed to Maritain to use his influence with the Pope and present Gurian's plea that places of work be established for converts who had been forced to leave Germany or that the possibility of their settling in Palestine be investigated.[9] However, since his practical measures do not concern us here, we shall proceed to his analysis of Nazi antisemitism.

His systematic analysis of antisemitism rests on Christian thinkers, particularly the well-known neo-Thomist Jacques Maritain. Maritain and those who shared his views saw antisemitism as a pathological manifestation deriving from the change in the Christian consciousness of modern man. Seen from this angle, hatred of the Jews is an expression of anti-Christian resentment, dangerous not merely because of the harm done the Jews, but chiefly because of its political potential which can be utilized to achieve goals beyond the blow dealt the Jews. In the light of this approach which viewed antisemitism as a political instrument to incite the public or divert its attention, he analyses the sharpening tone of the Nazi regime's antisemitic propaganda at the end of 1934.[10] Within the same context, he explains the intensification of the public debate on the Jewish question as an attempt on the part of the regime to extricate itself from the political stalemate created in Germany between the trends of consolidation represented by the conservative elements in the government and the impulse for radicalization represented by the extremists in the Nazi party. To his mind, the call for antisemitic agitation is thus a tactic to divert public attention from the internal troubles plaguing the regime. Only the proclamation of the Nuremberg Laws in September 1935 provided him with the proper opportunity to deal with the subject in greater depth, and he reverted to the familiar argument as to the contradiction between Nazism and Christianity. The laws, he felt, defied both the law of nature and the Christian ethic because they dismissed the validity of the sacrament of baptism, thereby blocking the path to salvation from the Jews. They also defied Christian doctrine as their purpose was the destruction of the Jews, rather than their conversion. The purpose of the laws, he writes, is to trample the Jews and make their life in Germany intolerable: to close most professions to them, to make it difficult for them to exist economically in the country and to pressure them into emigrating. Beyond this analysis, however, which did not deviate from the accepted oppositionist stance towards Nazism, he showed a rare acumen with respect to the consequences of these laws, unlike most of his contemporaries. The Jewish establishment in Germany, as is well known, saw the laws on race and citizenship as a basis for possible Jewish existence in the Third Reich. Thus, for example, the National Representation of German Jewry declared that the laws were meant to "create a basis which would allow tolerable relations between the German people and the Jewish people", whereas others, including Leftist exiles, saw them as a diversionary maneuver. Gurian's extraordinary interpretation is even more striking in the light of these attitudes. In an almost prophetic vein, he writes that the laws constitute "a way-station on the road to the total, physical extermination of Judaism... the racial legislation is a campaign of annihilation" (eine Etappe auf dem Wege... einer voelligen physischen Vernichtung des Judentums...die Ariergesetzgebung ist ein Ausrottungsfeldzug...).[11]

In further writings on Nazi antisemitism, he nevertheless returned to the standard conception of it being a diversionary maneuver, or more dangerous to Christianity than to the Jews themselves. Thus, in his discussion of the policy of Aryanization, he again resorted to the accepted view that the crux of the matter was not the fate of the Jews, but the fate of Christianity.

A better understanding of his conception of antisemitism can be gained perhaps from a look at the articles he devoted to the subject in forums outside of Deutsche Briefe. Particularly pertinent to our purposes is the memorandum he composed together with Karl Thieme, Die Kirche Christi und die Judenfrage.[12] The memorandum was published in Die Erfuellung in 1937, at the initiative of Joseph Wirth, who had served as chancellor of Germany, representing the Catholic Zentrum party. Wirth apparently had planned to publish a number of essays on contemporary political issues in his campaign against the Nazi regime, but it seems that only the aforementioned memorandum was in fact published. The document which bore the signatures of 14 prominent Catholic personalities, world-wide, dealt with the theological and political aspects of the Jewish question. It begins by noting that racial theory rejects the idea of the uniformity of mankind in Creation, in original sin and in salvation, and is consequently the mortal enemy of Christianity and Christian gospel. Anyone who comes to terms with it, will therefore share in the responsibility for the consequences of implementing racial theories in Nazi policy. Racism is a naturalist world-view, incompatible with the Church. On the Jewish question, specifically, the memorandum asserts that as the guardian of the spiritual image of mankind, the Church cannot remain silent about the violation of the rights of Jews as people. For these rights derive from God's will and, thus, Gurian adds, the defence of the Jews cannot be seen merely as the defence of a persecuted minority but also as concern for those who will come after the Jews. With uncanny intuition, Gurian predicts that once the persecution of the Jews is legitimized in the nation's consciousness, the Nazi regime will be able to institute additional measures such as naturalistic methods of breeding, euthanasia, the elimination of the incurably ill, severance from Christianity and the establishment of a new religion and moral system.

In another article on the Jewish question, which also appeared in Die Erfuellung, Gurian arrived at conclusions far in advance of the state of research on antisemitism in the Thirties. In an essay entitled "Das Judentum und die Aufklaerung des 19 Jahrhunderts", from 1934, he analyses the writings of Eugen Duehring, Karl Marx and Bruno Bauer, substantiating the conception adopted by many researchers today, who seek to attribute the roots of modern antisemitism to the Enlightenment, primarily to the influence of Voltaire and Reimarus on 19th century antisemites such as Chamberlain and Bruno Bauer.[13] His conclusions were clearly inspired by his Christian-conservative outlook which accorded the Jews a special status in history under the wings of the Church. According to this conception, the Jewish people were indeed chosen, but in the negative sense: their rejection of the Messiah is to serve as a warning to all the nations. At the same time, Judaism's kinship with Christianity was advantageous for the Jews and their physical survival enjoyed the protection of the Church. The hope of converting the Jews and the idea of returning them to the faith as formulated in Paul's letter to the Romans, ensured their protection from annihilation throughout the Middle Ages; whereas the secularization of Western society and the displacement of the hope for salvation from the theological to the historical sphere, from divine to human action, removed the Church's protection from the Jews, exposing them to the whims of political and social movements. These movements, in the nature of things, do not regard the solution to the Jewish problem as something to be left to the end of days and the hand of God but seek to bring about a solution by the hands of man. Viewing Judaism as a superstition, as an ancient vestige that must be destroyed by and for mankind, they obviously threaten its existence and endanger its proponents. The secularization of state and society did pave the way for the emancipation of the Jews but it also led to their being perceived as an anti-race. Further on, Gurian examines the status of the Jews in the modern era. Despite Wirth's request, he refused to include in the memorandum a declaration that the Church had erred in legislating anti-Jewish laws, counter to the spirit of the gospel. Indeed, he threatened to wash his hands of the memorandum should such a declaration be included.[14] This legislation, he felt, had been reasonable and had conformed with the spirit of the times and the character of the order of the Middle Ages when society as a whole accepted the normative order determined by the Church. In any other context, such legislation becomes impossible since it is both infeasible and unthinkable to restore a single feature of medieval legislation - the status of the Jews - while the rest of society is guided by laws and norms deriving their authority from trends of modernization. In a society that has cut itself off from Christianity, there is no choice but to preserve the principle of equality between Jews and non-Jews and it is therefore the practical duty of every Christian to expose the prevailing errors about the Jews, to oppose their vilification and persecution and, most of all, to help non-Aryan Christians.

He expanded his analysis of modern antisemitism in two articles written in the Forties in the United States.[15] The 19th century antisemitic literature and the antisemitic trends in various sectors of German society could not in themselves determine the fate of German Jewry, he writes. Only the transformation in the political situation and the social fabric, following World War I, changed the social role and historical weight of the hatred for the Jews. Especially, as during this period, Hitler and Nazism appeared on the scene. Gurian's analysis of Hitler's role is influenced by Burckardt's remarks on Muhammed. He sees Hitler as a fanatical simplifier, like Muhammed, whose political eclecticism offered something to everyone. And akin to Rauschning and Alexander in analytical method, Gurian, too, identifies Hitler as unifying - through simplification - different, even opposite, trends in German political culture. As regards antisemitism, Gurian returns to the basic conception he had developed in the Thirties, noting its instrumentalist and manipulative nature. To his mind, Nazism succeeded because of its use of antisemitism as a weapon of protest, a tool with which to radically oppose the existing political and social order. Hitler turned antisemitism into a double-edged sword to be used in social criticism to focus feelings of hatred, and as a device with which to create the Volksgemeinschaft myth. Hitler was well aware of the central role antisemitism could play as a factor of political integration and he understood that antisemitic motifs could unite varying political streams in a single front. For this reason, in order to enlist anti-communist and anti-capitalist elements in a common front, he portrayed the Jews as both Bolsheviks and capitalists and this tag became one of Nazism's key mottos. Antisemitism also succeeded in bringing together other sectors of the society under one roof. It was what created the common ground for mass enlistment and turning German liberal nationalism into totalitarianism. It captivated the masses who by nature are not prone to delve too deeply into matters, and attracted the conservatives whose image of Nazism was that of a protest movement against the odious Weimar republic and they saw the opposition to Nazism as a Jewish affair.

Other periodicals representing conservative exiles or serving as a forum for their views dealt with the Jewish question infrequently and only in the context of specific antisemitic state policy such as the Nuremberg Laws or Crystal Night. This can be clearly seen from a glance at the pages of Der Deutsche in Polen, the official publication of the Deutsche Christliche Volkspartei, edited by Karl Maier Hultschin and representing the German minority in Poland. Indeed, this newspaper took a firm anti-Nazi stand and as such opposed antisemitic policy. Nevertheless, its treatment of the Jewish question was the exception rather than the rule. In its 12th issue, for example, which appeared in April 1936, it reported the condemnation of antisemitism made by the leader of the German minority in Poland, Professor Eduard Pant. Pant's case rests on the argument that antisemitism is more detrimental to Christianity than to the Jews, a criticism with which we are already well acquainted from the writings of Catholic circles. On another occasion, following the promulgation of the Nuremberg Laws, the newspaper reprinted Gurian's article from Deutsche Briefe, which we discussed above. On the whole it did not deviate from the general view that antisemitism was an instrument of political integration. This is particularly obvious from the article it published after Crystal Night. According to its author, the annexation of the Sudeten did not raise the morale of the German population as the Nazi regime had expected and it therefore resorted to rallying the masses through an antisemitic campaign. This incidental treatment of the Jewish question in a newspaper which consistently fought against Nazism, treatment more noticeable by its absence, is even more striking in Der Deutsche Weg. The latter weekly appeared between 1934 and 1940 and was the official publication of the Catholic Germans in Holland. Through underground routes it made its way into Germany and was read also by the Catholic public in the western regions of the Reich. It was headed by two of the most prominent Christian exiles, Joseph Steinhage and Friedrich Muckermann. Muckermann had been closely associated with the Austrian chancellor, Schuschnigg, and was the leader of the conservative anti-Nazi movement Deutsche Freiheitspartei.[16] He had believed at the start of the Nazi regime in the possibility of cooperation between Nazism and Catholicism within the framework of the struggle for German national regeneration but he very soon recognized the true face of Hitler's regime and left Germany. In his overall approach to Nazism, as reflected in his newspaper articles, he takes the line common in Christian circles. Nazism is characterized as neo-paganism, which leads from the worship of God to the worship of the German nation, except that its worldview has the features of a religion. If, however, we were to ask how he dealt with the issue of antisemitism, we would find, as stated above, that the Jewish question received only marginal treatment in his writings; so much so, that in the September 22, 1935 issue, he devotes an entire page to the Nazi party convention in Nuremberg with reference to the struggle of Nazism against Christianity, and says not a word about the significance of the laws adopted for the Jews.[17] The whole discussion of the laws revolves around clarifying the relation between religion and state. It concludes with an attack on the Nazi regime for having interfered in a sphere rightfully belonging to the Church by deciding the validity or invalidity of marriage between Jews and Germans. The Jewish question comes up in his writings only within the context of the discussion of the pornographic nature of Der Stuermer, which is an admixture of perversion and the vilification of the Jews. Even more interesting, though hardly surprising, is the remark that follows his pronouncement that the antisemitism of the Stuermer's must be combatted. This position, he writes, is warranted not only by pro-Jewish feelings but by Christianity, for in demanding rights for the Jews, he is demanding rights which derive their authority not from the idealism of the French revolution but from Christian philosophy which does not view these rights as contingent on one's membership in a particular class or race. The Jews are as worthy of Christian love as anyone else and, as a Christian, therefore, he must protest against their persecution. And between this date and Crystal Night, the Jewish question received no mention in the newspaper except in its October 1936 issue, which published an article from the Erfuellung by Franziskus Stratman, "Die Judenfrage als Friedenfrage", giving the stereotyped Christian conception of the issue. Only Crystal Night, as already stated, earned the subject prime place in the newspaper. After this unprecedented shock to his system, Muckermann could no longer confine his censure to the damage done to Church institutions during the rioting. A considerable number of articles on Streicher and in condemnation of racism, such as the severe exposition "Gotesfrevel im dritten Reich", compare the burning of synagogues in Germany to the burning of churches in Spain. In the strongest terms, he again points out the barbarism of both acts, the one committed by Red Bolshevism, the other by Brown Bolshevism.

Muckermann's basic perspective that the persecution of the Jews must be opposed in principle as demanded by Christianity, regardless of the character of the Jews, found explicit expression not in his newspaper but in an interview he gave on January 23, 1938, to the Austrian newspaper, Reichspost. Reacting to a caricature in the SS Schwarze Korps which described Christianity and Judaism as the foes of Nazism, he stated that the persecution of anyone demanded a protest from Christians even if they were aware of the part played by Jews in the Bolshevik persecution of the Church.[18]

The marginal treatment accorded the Jewish question in the Third Reich, apart from a few exceptional instances, applied also to Der Christliche Staendstaat.[19] This weekly was edited by Dietrich von Hildebrand who left Germany in 1933 and Austria in 1938 and its campaign against Nazism sometimes included articles on antisemitism. In his article, "Katholische Theologie und Judenfrage", for example, Peter B. Lacombe condemns antisemitism as a fraud sustained by sinful man vis-a-vis God.[20] A similar criticism was raised by Von Hildebrand himself who saw antisemitism as the harshest slap on the cheek dealt Jesus since the Passion.[21] Apart from condemning antisemitism out of Christian humanist motives, however, the position that emerges from the publication is the basic Christian conception of the nature of the Jewish problem in modern times and the Christian-conservative version of a solution that we found in Gurian's writings. The rise of liberalism and secularization left the Jews exposed to the dangers of modernization trends in Western society and removed Christian protection for the physical survival of the Jews. The various solutions offered to the Jewish problem in the modern era all suffer from drawbacks; assimilation is impractical as it is impossible to organically penetrate a people; Zionism, on the other hand, is inappropriate as it denies the character of the Jews as "a people in the family of man" (menscheitsvolk), while political Zionism's aim to return to Palestine removes the Jews from the Western Christian world and puts the Jewish question on a modern national voelkisch plane. This is a form of spiritual suicide as it denies the meaning and essence of Jewish existence which is functional to Christianity. Consequently, the only solution he sees is conversion to Christianity.[22] Hildebrand and his Christian-conservative circle spoke out on the Jewish question also at other forums, as well as before the Jewish audience of the Wiener Kulturbund. On the latter occasion, he expressed the view that while Jews could be accorded the status of a minority they could not be obliged to adopt such status and any attempt to restrict their rights was an anti-Christian act.[23] In a similar vein, Paul Schiemann, president of the Deutscher Verband zur nationalen Befriedung Europas, writes that belonging to a people was a matter of self-definition deriving from the individual's freedom of decision.[24] At first glance, this position of the Christian conservatives unequivocally repudiates the restriction of Jewish rights; but their widespread support for a Christian corporative state necessarily leads to an infringement of the civil rights of Jews. This becomes clear from the article by the Catholic publicist, Hugo Diwald, for instance, which deals with the attitude of the Christian class state towards the Jews. Diwald (his real name was Alfred Missong) asserts that the Jews certainly deserve state protection and the state should not force the Jews to become a minority, but they can define themselves as such of their own free will. At the same time, the state, as a Christian state, can demand of the Jews that they refrain from any act that would undermine Christian life. The Jewish community must see to it that none of its members be active in the press, the arts and the economy in such a way as would be detrimental to Christian citizens. The Jews must understand that the key positions in state leadership would be held exclusively by Christians, a policy which does not emanate from the introduction of the Numerus Clausus or antisemitism but from the logical consistency of the translation of the idea of a Christian state into practice. The creation of this form of social and political reality would benefit the Jews as well, as in their attempt to penetrate places which are not meant for them, they hamper the Christians in their attempt to treat them with a humanitarian attitude and Christian love![25]

Let us look at these views in greater detail as they found expression in various organizations established by the Christian conservatives. One such organization was the Deutsche Front gegen das Hitler System, a coalition of Right-wing, anti-Nazi forces, set up in 1937, with the aim of constituting an alternative to the popular front of the Leftist parties. It included various revolutionary conservative, Christian and nationalist groups such as the German Catholic Youth, the League for German Federalism (a Monarchist movement from southern Germany), the Revolutionary Peasants (formerly the Nazi nationalist movement from the north and Silesia), the Circle of United Youth of the Young Germans (made up of students and members of the scouts movement), the Black Steel Helmets and the Black Front. To these were added also the People's Socialists, the right flank of the German socialist party as well as a group of Jews who called themselves the Gruppe Juedischer Widerstand.[26] The position of the organization with respect to the Jewish question is not sufficiently clear though some inkling may be had of its overall trend from the stance taken by the People's Socialists. The latter were conservative socialists who came under the influence of Belgian and French neo-socialists such as Mans, Berger, Deat, Renaudels. They had broken with the tradition of Marx and Kautsky, which ignored the centrality of the national factor, and this led them to recognize Judaism as a nationality. Hans Jaeger, head of the movement, expressed its position on the Jewish question in the statement he issued following Crystal Night and in the party platform published in November 1939. Mostly, it acknowledged the existence of the Jewish problem which it attributed to the sociological composition of Jewish society and the function filled by Jews in human history. Without going into the question of what the Jews are - whether a race or a people - he suggested that the problem be solved within the framework of a federation of nations to constitute the basis of Europe after Hitler. Since the roots of the problem were social, economic planning would enable the Jews to undergo vocational retraining, thus solving the problem of the surplus of Jewish intellectuals. As far as their status was concerned, those who wanted to would come under the law on minorities, Jaeger said, while the rest of the Jews would have to assimilate.[27] Though there are certain interesting analytical elements in this viewpoint, particularly insofar as it concerns the relationship between the image of the Jews and the suggestions Jaeger offers for a solution, the organization occupied a borderline position between socialism and conservatism and further discussion on this subject would not serve our purposes. We shall look instead at movements or organizations with a clearly identifiable conservative worldview.

The London-centred Deutsche Freiheitspartei, established in late 1936, was not - despite its name - a party but an organization of German exiles holding to conservative political views. Its prominent leaders were August Weber and Albert Kluthe in London, and Otto Klepper and Karl Spiecker in Paris. It maintained contacts in Germany with civil servants, the army, the Church and economic circles, directing its anti-Nazi propaganda at these conservative circles.[28] From a reading of its publications, it becomes apparent that it almost totally ignored the Jewish issue. A notable exception was its condemnation of the events of Kristallnacht in a clandestine leaflet entitled "Deutsche Freiheitsbriefe"; its periodical, Das Wahre Deutschland, however, did not mention the November pogrom in as a much as a word. Moreover, as Kluthe's papers reveal, an article sent to him for publication by Alfred Hinzelmann,[29] sharply criticizing the barbaric incident, was not published. I found only one instance in which this organization reacted to the situation of the Jews in Germany. This, however, did not appear in the periodical aimed at its conservative readership but in the publication aimed at the English public. One of the issues of "Uncensored Germany. Letters and News Sent Secretly from Germany to the German Freedom Party", published in London in 1940, quoted a letter allegedly sent from Berlin in June 1939. In it, the writer describes the tragic fate of German Jews, queuing up in front of a local pawnshop. The sight of by-passers jeering at a waiting woman led someone to remark loudly enough to be heard: "It is a disgrace to be German". Although it seems that the Jewish question was intentionally avoided in its open publications in German, its attitude to the Jews can perhaps be inferred from the correspondence between Albert Kluthe, the leader of the movement, and a Jewish conservative exile, Joachim Schoeps, who shared the views of the gentile conservatives.

In his letter to Schoeps, dated 17 June 1939, Kluthe notes that the German exiles ignore the Jewish question, believing that it would be solved with the removal of Hitler. Although he himself adopted this attitude, he considered it both foolish and dangerous. Let us recall for a moment who Schoeps was and what his ideology was.[30] He had been the leader of the Deutsche Vortrupp (the German Vanguard), a Jewish conservative movement, and had left Germany for Sweden in 1938. The Deutsche Vortrupp, founded in February 1933 by a group of Jewish university students led by Schoeps, started with some 150 people. Its numbers gradually declined until it was finally dissolved by the Gestapo in December 1935. It had been a curious attempt on the part of its members to retain their Jewish religious identity while emphasizing their profound bond with German culture. Wishing to participate as a Jewish political movement in the "German national regeneration", it advocated authoritarian leadership also within the Jewish community. As ultra-patriotic Germans, the Deutscher Vortrupp had a highly negative attitude towards Eastern European Jews and opposed Zionism, Marxism and Liberalism. Jewish religious observance, however, was part of its program. It opposed Zionism because it stressed the idea of being a nation like all nations, while it believed that Jews belonged to the German Volk, differentiated from other Germans only by the specificity of their religion. Schoeps had been deeply influenced by the proponents of a conservative revolution and he defined himself as a conservative Prussian Jew. Grounding his peculiar worldview in the writings of Friedrich Julius Stahl and Franz Rosenzweig, he maintained that Prussianism and the Jewish religion were based on common values, and he developed a conservative, German nationalist ideology, fusing it with Judaism. He failed to comprehend the racist basis of Nazism and believed that the Third Reich would develop as a corporate state, in which the Jews could be integrated. Small wonder than that he found a common language with Kluthe.

In his response to Kluthe, Schoeps returns to the concept of the second or new emancipation, a theory developed by certain circles of German Jews in a desperate attempt to adapt Judaism to the conditions created by the Third Reich. They believed that the proper integrational framework was as a Jewish corporation in the totalitarian Nazi state. Schoeps maintains that prior to Hitler's assumption of power, the Jews were German nationalists and conservatives and they had been forced to turn to the Left only because of the misguided policy of the right-wing parties. After Hitler defeat, the Jews who recognize the distinction between Germany and Hitler would become reintegrated. This reintegration would be preconditioned by the attitude of both parties: on the one hand, the Jews should unequivocally affirm their adherence to the German nation; on the other hand, the attitude of the new Germany must be determined by certain considerations. The Jewish issue should be dealt with by a future state secretary of Jewish origin and the new policy should be based on the following:

1. the abolition of all antisemitic legislation enacted since January 1933; the equalization of Jewish rights and duties with those of the rest of the German population; the return of all confiscated property; full religious liberty; and in the event that Germany was to be a corporate state, the establishment of a *Deutsche Judenschaft* was to be considered.
2. To guarantee a friction-free symbiosis between the German nation and the Jewish minority, and to eliminate the causes of antisemitism, it would be necessary to introduce a *numerus clausus*, *"wird fuer den Anteil der Juden am beruflichen Leben der totale Numerus Clausus eingefuehrt"*. The *numerus clausus* would limit the participation of the Jews in public life to double their percentage in the population. The return of German Jews forced to emigrate after 1933, would be regulated by a yearly quota, with priority being given to those able and willing to be artisans and farmers. Incentives would be offered for the returning immigrants to move to small cities, villages and rural towns. And the re-immigration of non-German Jews would depend on state interests.

In his response, Kluthe declares that he is totally opposed to racial prejudice, but agrees that one must allow for the fact that public opinion has been poisoned; he therefore supports the introduction of the undesirable *numerus clausus* and though he hopes that it would be a temporary measure, its abolition would depend on the behaviour of the Jews. Schoeps' proposal and Kluthe's response are a distinct reflection of the basic stand of these circles on the Jewish question. To be sure, they were definitely opposed to Nazi antisemitism. At the same time, however, they agreed on discriminatory measures against the Jews.[31]

These views were the rule rather than the exception in the future solution of the Jewish question envisaged by German conservative exiles. Let us look at two other conservative groups: the Black Front and the Freies Deutschland Bewegung, both led by the former Nazi, Otto Strasser. They, too, advocated a restricted Jewish participation in German life with the addition, however, of a new element: the support for Jewish national aspirations. Since this may well sound odd, let us examine the reasons behind this support in more detail.

Strasser's general political doctrine on the essence of the German revolution is formulated in his *Aufbau des Deutschen Sozialismus*, published in 1932.[32] All his subsequent; articles and books, written during his years of exile in Vienna and Prague, are simply the development and elaboration of subjects discussed in the above work.

His general political conception was based on a theory termed "the law of trinal polarity" (Gesetz der dreieinige Polaritaet) which holds that two socio-philosophical systems constantly alternate: the system of freedom (System der Freiheit) in the form of liberalism, rationalism and capitalism; and the system of relationship (System der Gebundenheit) in the form of conservatism, nationalism and Voelkisch idealism. In his view, the German revolution was a concrete expression of the transition to the system of relationship. Since the systems are contraposed, their polarization highlights the dialectic tension between the instinct for individual existence in liberalism, and the instinct for community existence in conservatism. The era of liberalism and its source of authority - reason - were now being replaced by a new era ruled by the principle of organic law which emphasizes the differences between peoples and creates the need for their self-determination as national entities. On this point, tension arises between two contradictory principles: the principle of organic law creates political, social and cultural differences between nations; the principle of self-determination accords the individual the right to choose the collective entity to which he wishes to belong, even if he does not share the majority's historical and ethnic-racial qualities. Disassociating himself from racial theory which emphasizes biological determinism, he is explicit in his contention that the human spirit can surmount the obstacles created by the objective elements which define a nation and a race. The individual is thus able to assimilate into any national group, even that of a different race. In keeping with this general view, Strasser suggests that, politically speaking, all German residents whose racial origins differ from the majority's have three possible solutions: (a) they can be defined as foreigners; (b) they can be seen as constituting national minorities; or (c) they can be incorporated into the main body of the nation through assimilation. All three options, he says, are equally feasible and equally honourable with the proviso that every adult, of a racial stock different to that of the majority, have the right to decide which option to adopt. His solution to the Jewish question derived from the same principle. In his books, as well as in his periodical, Die Deutsche Revolution,[33] Strasser notes that from the point of view of Nazism, antisemitism was "justified" by a sort of pseudo-philosophy. The Jews were designated as an inferior race, and their extermination was alleged to be a law of self-preservation. He rejects this position, both from the perspective of simple justice and of Christianity, particularly the latter. He sees the underlying cause of antisemitism not in religious or economic motives but in the problem of incorporating Jews into the state and the secondary problem of incorporating them into society. This problem, he says, has prevailed since the beginnings of the Jewish Diaspora, chiefly because of the attitude of the Jews themselves.

In his attempt to analyse the status of the Jewish people, Strasser declares that most Jews and gentiles agree that the Jews are a distinct people who nonetheless have a religion of their own. They are neither a race, nor a nation. In contrast to all the other peoples of Europe, the Jews have stubbornly resisted assimilating into the state or even any attempt to clarify their status. They have refused, on the one hand, to allow themselves to become assimilated and, on the other, to form a state of their own. As a solution to the problem of incorporating the Jewish people into the constitutional and social life of Europe - and, he adds, of America, for sooner or later the problem will crop up there as well - he offers two alternatives: assimilation into the state majority, or the development of a Jewish nation. Whoever chooses the former solution must realize that his assimilation has to be genuine, not merely formal.

In the particular case of Germany, the Jews should be divided into three groups: Nationaljuden, Volkstumjuden and Assimilanten. The first group would be represented by the Zionist movement which provides some sort of framework until the establishment of a Jewish state. Legally, they would enjoy the same status as other foreigners living outside of their homeland. The second group, the Volkstumjuden, would be considered a national minority, and subject to the European laws governing minorities. This temporary solution is necessary since it would be difficult for many European Jews - namely, the older generation - to choose either the category of emigrating to Palestine or that of assimilation. Moreover, it accommodates the Jewish communities who have lived in Europe for hundreds of years, consider themselves attached to their host countries, but are not prepared to relinquish their national religion or social identity. After the collapse of the Third Reich, the Volkstumjuden would be state citizens (Staatsbuerger), though not Reichsbuerger (citizens enjoying full rights), as the political leadership, the state institutions and the military corps would all be entrusted in the hands of Germans. Of the third group, those who assimilate, Strasser demands a declaration that they are no longer Jews and that they wish to cease to exist as an independent religious and social group; they must renounce their separateness and dissolve their organizational frameworks.[34]

However sincere Strasser was in his endeavour to solve the Jewish problem, however fair his solutions may appear, the fact remains - as is evident from his correspondence - that he disliked Jews. In many of his letters, particularly to his brother Bernhard and to his representative in South America, Bruno Fricke, he condemned "Jews and communists" in the same breath. And when he referred to a paper or group as "Jewish", the connotation was clearly derogatory, implying that its aims and methods could be neither honest, nor decent. Strasser's attitude to the Jews, together with his attitude to communism, was one of the chief sources of attack against him and led to his virtual ostracism by almost all the anti-Nazi organizations, particularly on the American continent.[35]

Let us now examine the attitudes to the Jewish question as reflected in the writings of another conservative circle, this time not in Europe but in Latin America.

The Christian-conservative anti-Nazi movements Das Wahre Deutschland, the Frei Deutschland Bewegung and the Service National Autrichien were represented in Uruguay by a group of exiles who rallied around the publication Die Zeit, founded by Erico Schonemann at the end of 1934, as a newsletter of the German anti-Nazi community in Montevideo. In his search for a political roof in the major exile centres in England and in the United States, Schonemann always tended towards the Christian-conservative Right which in Latin America was reflected by the anti-Nazi movements mentioned above. Die Zeit's attitude towards the Jewish question was ambivalent. On the one hand, it tried more than other exile groups in Uruguay to draw nearer to the Jewish public, particularly to the German-Jewish community, the Nueva Comunidad Israelita. In his efforts to pave a path to the Jews, Schonemann presented himself as the defender of the Jewish public. Indeed, he added a subtitle to Die Zeit which read: "The organ of the German popular front in Uruguay against National-Socialism and antisemitism". His desire to win favour with the Jews at times took the form of biting criticism against newspapers with an antisemitic slant which appeared in Uruguay during this period. The same motive, it may be assumed, prompted him to devote a significant number of his articles in Die Zeit to the war against antisemitism and in support of Zionism. On the other hand, however, Schonemann's approach was neither purely utilitarian, nor devoid of ideology. His condemnation of antisemitism and his pro-Zionist stand went hand in hand with a vigorous opposition to Jewish particularism. In the internal battles between the camps of exiles, Schonemann aspired to the crown of leadership of the anti-Nazi front in South America and he may well have hoped for the support of the Jews to daunt his competitors. But it would be wrong to assume that his criticism of Judaism sprung from dashed hopes in this direction and his failure to win the coveted prize. His opposition to Jewish particularism was fundamental and cannot be attributed wholly to opportunistic motives. Schonemann accused the Jews of cleaving to an independent identity as a community with organized frameworks and institutions to help immigrants, while "avoiding the anti-Nazi struggle in the expectation that others would do the work". In his writings on the Jewish question, Schonemann takes the familiar view that particularism is reasonable only on religious grounds. Any other form of sectarianism - whether social or cultural - is thus illegitimate and harmful to both Jewish and general interests. Openly demanding that the Jews give up their group existence and dismantle their organizational frameworks, he charges the Jews of Uruguay, who have recently arrived from Germany, with having learned nothing from their experience. In Uruguay, too, they continue to constitute a "state within a state", publishing their own newspapers, maintaining their own banks and clubs "in which they danced while Europe suffered", he adds demagogically. Antisemitism is thus partially the result of their own behavior and can be lain at their door. His criticism contained also another familiar motif: the problems of the Jews stemmed not only from their unwillingness to adapt and assimilate but also from their obtrusiveness: "Jews need not deny their Jewishness," he writes, "but it is imprudent to highlight it, certainly in these tense times". To substantiate this, he cites evidence from the very same anti-Jewish press against which he fought, such as an editorial demanding that Jewish immigration be stopped because the country "needs races that assimilate, not Israelites who will always stick out, thereby creating more antisemitism". His tone, at times, is threatening. Those who do not take part in the current struggle, he says - the allusion being to the Jews - will not reap the fruits of the future after Hitler. Schonemann's writings are reminiscent of the criticism voiced by circles which ostensibly defended the Jews but, in fact, demanded that they voluntarily renounce their group identity and vanish.[36]

To sum up, the views expressed by most conservative exile movements on the Jewish question continued trends that developed in the Second Reich, demanding that emancipation - in the sense perceived by the Jews - be revoked: whether by legally segregating the Jews and distancing them, as proposed by advocates of the Christian state, or through assimilation and merging, as demanded by national liberals such as Theodor Mommsen. These views were polarized between two contesting trends: conservatism and modernism. It was understood that since the state was to be both Christian and constitutional, all its citizens would have to be granted equal rights. But Jews who wished to be citizens and maintain their Judaism would have to accept an inferior status. Being unable to meet the objectives of a Christian state, the Jews would be relegated to positions that did not affect the essence of a Christian state.

Conservative elements that expressed their sympathy for the Zionist solution of the Jewish problem voiced opinions which were popular among both conservatives and nationalists in Germany and Austria. Convinced that Jewish particularism was very difficult to eradicate, they now and then supported Zionism or other schemes to concentrate the Jews outside of Europe. They also reflected the popular trends stressing anti-liberal, anti-democratic national ideologies of order and authoritarianism, such as that found in Emmerich Czermak's Ordnung in der Judenfrage.[37] This evaluated Jewish nationalism in a positive light because it rejected all possibility of Jewish integration, but it denied the Jews the status of equal citizens in the state he envisaged. Other Christian conservatives, like Oesterreicher or Hildebrand, continued to believe in their missionary duty and opposed Zionism or secular assimilation as they still hoped to convert the Jews, and saw conversion as the only viable solution to the Jewish question.

Notes

1. See my articles, 'The German Communist Party and Nazi Antisemitism, 1933-1938', Year Book of the Leo Baeck Institute 32 (1987), pp. 325-340; 'Exiles and Refugees: Jews and Germans in Argentina and Uruguay in the Forties', Yahadut Zemanenu, Contemporary Jewry, A Research Annual 4 (1987) pp.253-268: 'Leftist Opposition and the Jews in the Third Reich', in M. Zimmermann (ed.), Opposition to National-Socialism, Jerusalem 1986 pp.94-120; 'El movimiento Alemania Libre y la communidad judia de Mexico', Proceedings of the 9th World Congress of Jewish Studies, Jerusalem 1986, Division B, Vol. 3, pp.329-336.
2. Herrmann Steinhausen, Die Judenfrage eine Christenfrage, Luzern 1939.
3. J.M. Oesterreicher, Racisme-Antisemitisme Antichristianisme, New York 1943.
4. H. Rauschning, Die Revolution des Nihilismus, Kulisse und Wirklichkeit im Dritten Reich, Zurich 1938; idem, Hitler Speaks. A Series of Political Conversations with Adolf Hitler on his Real Aims, London 1939.
5. Edgar Alexander, Der Mythus Hitler, Zurich 1937.
6. On Gurian see: H. Huerten, Waldemar Gurian, Mainz 1972.
7. On the Deutsche Briefe, see: M.A. Fitzsimons, 'Die Deutschen Briefe: Gurian and the German Crisis', Review of Politics 17 (1955), pp. 47-72.
8. See for example, Deutsche Briefe (hereafter DB), 1 January 1935; 26 July 1935.
9. H. Huerten, op. cit. p.122.
10. DB, 30 November 1934.
11. ibid., 27 September 1935.
12. W. Gurian, 'Die Kirche Christi und Die Judenfrage', Die Erfuellung 2 (1936/7), pp. 73-101.
13. idem, 'Das Judentum und die Aufklaerung des 19 Jahrhunderts', Die Erfuellung I (1934/5), pp. 26-34.
14. H. Huerten, op. cit., pp. 128-129.
15. W. Gurian, 'The Sources of Hitler's Power', Review of Politics 4 (1942), pp. 379-408; idem, 'Antisemitism in Modern Germany', in K. S. Pinson (ed.), Essays on Antisemitism, New York 1946.
16. On Muckermann see: Heinz Huerten, '"Der Deutsche Weg". Katholische Exilpublizistik und Auslandsdeutschtum. Ein Hinweis auf Friedrich Muckermann', Exilforschung 4 (1986), pp. 115-129.
17. 'Der Turmbau zu Babel in Nuerenberg', Der Deutsche Weg, 22 September 1935.
18. Muckermann's utterance on 23 January 1938 was reprinted in, 'Ein christliches Wort zur Judenfrage', Der Deutsche Weg, 24 April 1938.
19. On this periodical see: R. Ebneth, Die Oesterreichische Wochenschrift "Der Christliche Staendestaat", Mainz 1976.
20. P.B. Lacombe, 'Katholische Theologie und Judenfrage', Der Christliche Staendestaat (hereafter CS), 10 May 1936.
21. CS, 9 May 1937.
22. 'Die Juden und das Christliche Abendland', Die Erfuellung 3 (1/2) Juni 1937, pp. 9-32.
23. Reported in Gerechtigkeit, 4 February 1937.
24. P. Schiemann, 'Minderheitenbewegung und Judenfrage', CS, 26 April 1936.
25. H. Diwald, 'Der christliche Staendestaat', CS, 3 October 1937.
26. On this movement see: F.M. Cahén, Men against Hitler, Indianapolis 1939.
27. H. Jager, Diktatur-Pogrom-Krieg, Den Haag 1939; idem, Die Volkssozialisten und die Judenfrage. Ein Entwurf in sechs Thesen, Wiener Library Archives, antinazi pamphlets P 121.
28. B. Bouvier, Die deutsche Freiheitspartei (DFP). Ein Beitrag zur Geschichte der Opposition gegen den Nationalsozialismus, Ph.D. Diss., Frankfurt 1972.
29. Hinzelmann to Kluthe, 12 November 1938, Bundesarchiv Koblenz (hereafter BA, NL 162/27.
30. On Schoeps see: C.J. Rheins, 'Deutscher Vortrupp, Gefolgschaft Deutscher Juden 1933-1935', Yearbook of the Leo Baeck Institute 26 (1981), pp. 207-239.
31. Kluthe to Schoeps, 17 June 1939, BA, NL 162/27; Schoeps proposal and Kluthe's response, ibid., NL 162/45.

32. Otto Strasser, Aufbau des deutschen Sozialismus, Leipzig 1932.
33. See for example the articles in Strasser's periodical Die deutsche Revolution: 'Die Eingliederung der Juden in das neue Deutschland', 19 November 1935; 'Manifest ueber die Stellung der Juden in kommenden Deutschland', 9 August 1936.
34. For a detailed study of Strasser's attitude on the Jewish question see my: 'Otto Strasser und die Judenfrage', Bulletin des Leo Baeck Instituts 60 (1981), pp. 3-20.
35. See also Philadelphia Daily News, 25 March 1942, which presents an article by Otto Strasser stating that propaganda to Germany should not be written by Jews and Marxists.
36. 'Was ist Antisemitismus', Die Zeit, 15 April 1938; Cf. ibid., 15 February 1939; 'Wir und der Antisemitismus' ibid. 1; 15 October 1939.
37. On the attitude of Czermak to the Jews as a national minority in a country led by non-Jews exclusively, E. Czermak, 'Verstaendigung mit dem Judentum', in E. Czermak-O. Karbach, Ordnung in der Judenfrage, Vienna 1934, pp. 59-61, 67; Cf. Sylvia Maderegger, Die Juden im oesterreichischen Staendestaat 1934-1938, Wien-Salzburg 1973.

THE HOLOCAUST AND THE HUMAN SITUATION IN PRE-HITLER GERMANY

Moral and Philosophical Implications

FRED J. BLUM

New Era Centre
The Abbey
Sutton Courtenay
Abingdon, OX 14 4AF
England

In order to understand the moral and philosophical implications of the Holocaust we must explore it in the light of the historical situation prevailing in Germany when Hitler came to power, and in a depth which allows us to go beyond a limited cause-effect thinking to deeper underlying reasons. Such an approach poses the question: How was it at all possible that the Holocaust could happen in a civilized country on the European continent? For it was in Germany, a country often referred to as "the country of poets and thinkers", that crimes of hitherto unheard of proportions were committed.

In this paper I endeavour to show that we can understand the Holocaust only as we explore it in the light of long-term movements which underlie the historical process. In particular we must explore the relationship between history and a transcending universal reality. Only such an approach will enable us to see the moral and philosophical implications of the Holocaust in their true significance. At the same time such an approach makes it possible for us to live and work for a transformation which would make it impossible for the events which culminated in the Holocaust in the 1940's to repeat themselves.

Hitler rose at a time when the world view which had come to life in the 16th and 17th centuries - marked by the Renaissance and the Enlightenment - was nearing its end, indeed entering into a phase of decadence. This era had begun with hope for renewal and the conviction that the elevation of reason as the new goddess would throw new light on the human situation and the potentialities of human development. Seen in historical perspective such a hope was certainly justified since the flowering of the medieval world had come to an end and its limitations had become apparent. The conception of the world as a hierarchical order ruled by God and a divine law alive in a universal truth manifested itself most gloriously in the majesty and beauty of the Gothic Cathedral. But in its declining phase the negative aspects of the medieval world - its superstition and its witch-hunting for example - and its closedness to the then emerging new potentials of human development became decisive. Hence the potentials of the new world view became ever more strongly felt. While the medieval world elevated the symbol to the central place in human awareness, the postmedieval era (from about 1500 to our time) made the mathematical sign the key to unlock the secrets of the universe. This it did indeed, by conquest of as yet unknown countries on this planet as well as by opening our minds to a rationality which made it possible to develop a new technology finding its practical application in the assembly line.

An essential characteristic of this new world view was its dualism: spirit and matter, feeling and thought, inner and outer, value and facts, faith and science, were all understood and experienced as belonging to separate and indeed clearly separable realms of experience. Indeed the various spheres of life - religion, the economy, politics, were all separated, each having its own values. When the postmedieval world came into its own, these separations made it possible to explore a hitherto unchartered world and signified an important landmark in the evolution of thought and life. It opened the doors for a new understanding of life, throwing light on phenomena which hitherto could not be satisfactorily explained. It opened not only new vistas but also new energies for a creative transformation. Modern industrial development and the rising standards of living which it made possible would not have been feasible without such a world view. Its implications and consequences were far-reaching, ranging from an inner division in the Western world to a separation of "East" and "West", "North" and "South", particularly of the industrialized world of Europe and North America and the pre-industrial cultures of Asia and South America.

While fully recognizing the achievements, indeed the glory of this age initiated by the Enlightenment, we must also see clearly its shortcomings: its inherent dualism dividing those who had the power to organize work and those who did not have the power because they had to sell their labour power on a market without having the means to become entrepreneurs. While this condition was alleviated as trade unions became more powerful, rationality became more and more emptied of true reason and was replaced by a purely formal understanding of achieving a given purpose with the most efficient means - regardless of any ethical meaning or implications. This marked the decline of an era. Starting in the twilight of freedom of entrepreneurship and what Blake called "satanic mills", it ended with concentration camps whose organization was as rational as any factory. Auschwitz had its oven and chimney and the logic of the assembly line devoid of any trace of humanity was pushed to its ultimate conclusion.

II

Three major historical events were a precondition for Hitler to come into power: the last war of 1914-1918 the reparations and the occupation of the Ruhr, the inflation of 1922-23 and the worldwide crisis of 1929.

The loss of the war led to the end of the monarchy which symbolised the power of the aristocracy, the landed interests and a middle class which prospered as standards of living increased and the economy expanded. The treaty of Versailles, opened more wounds than healing them. It was more a result of revenge for suffering than of the ideals of Wilson, the President of the United States who returned home greatly disheartened from Versailles. Followed by the occupation of the Ruhr the treaty enhanced the sense of injustice mingled with the bitterness of defeat while undermining the economic basis of a true recovery.

The second historical event without which the nationalsocialist movement could never have gained the following it did was the inflation of 1922-23. It was not an inflation as we have been using the word during the past years. It was a complete breakdown of the monetary system which was at least partly a result of the reparations Germany had to pay according to the Treaty of Versailles and of the cost of the occupation of the Ruhr. The value of the mark devalued so quickly that if a worker was paid on a Friday afternoon he or his wife had to go shopping before the shops closed in the evening and spend all the money because by the next morning it would have bought so little. When all was over, one new Mark was equal in value to 1 billion old Marks. I still remember that my own pocket money, equivalent to about 50 Pfennig or 10 pence, amounted to 2 million Mark at the height of the inflation. The result was nothing less than the destruction of the wealth of the middle classes who had saving accounts or owned shares and bonds rather than real estate.

The third event without which the rise of nationalsocialism would have been impossible was the Great Depression of 1929. At that time unemployment rose to six million people in a total population of about sixty millions. At the time when inflation had reached its zenith and hopelessness if not despair were spreading throughout the country, the chancellor of a coalition government, Heinrich Brüning, a member of the largely Roman Catholic party, gave a speech in the Reichstag. The essence of what he had to say may be summed up thus: The economy is sick, it has a high fever. We must wait for the natural energies alive in the body social to overcome this fever. There is not much else we can do.

It was assumed that any intervention would only interfere with the healing process directed by what Adam Smith called the "invisible hand" - a synonym for God or for the energies in the universe which bring about harmony. The faith that the actually existing social-economic order was a true reflection of a harmonious world order, was so strong that the resistance to the ever rising waves of nationalsocialism was totally ineffective. There is no doubt that without the ravages of the Great Depression of 1929 Hitler could not have come to power. This depression, in turn, could not have happened unless the prevailing mode of consciousness had lost touch with a universal truth and reality. As long as the economy was expanding and capitalism yielded increasing standards of living, its inner contradictions could be, if not healed, at least overlaid due to the general improvement in the conditions of life and the glamour of the ever increasing stream of goods and services to be sold and bought. Granted that in the political sphere a powerful countermovement arose in the form of marxism. But as we will see soon, this weakened rather than strengthened the Republic born in 1918 in Weimar - the hallowed place where Goethe lived. The impact of Marxism undoubtedly strengthened the trade union movement. But it remained powerless in the face of the depression of 1929. The reason for this was ultimately the prevailing faith in the universal harmony of a market economy combined with blindness to the reduction of labour to a means in a labour market due to the historically unique organization of the economy. This alienation from a universal truth was the ultimate reason which made it possible for Hitler to seize power. People's hearts were marked by despair because they were unable to comprehend a world which pronounced the harmony of a market economy while millions were without work after millions of others had lost their hard-earned savings which for many was all they ever had.

III

The lack of clarity about the fundamental causes of the spiritual crisis which was rooted in an inability to relate to the universal truth in a way which would have made it a power of transformation was clearly expressed in the political situation enabling Hitler to come to power. Ranged from left to right, the main parties were: the communists, the social democrats, the Centre party, the Volkspartei, the German nationalist and the National socialist party.

The communist party was an important remnant of the radical marxist tradition. It united a truly utopian vision of a classless society transcending the injustices of the existing social order with the idea of a class struggle leading to a classless society marked by true harmony and equality. Yet such a vision of a classless society became more an ideology than a living reality nurtured by a universal quest. Hate often vitiated the hope for a social order which truly gave equal opportunities to every human being. The idea of a planned economy implied in fact a more radical deprivation of freedom than that due to the inner divisions of a capitalist society. Rosa Luxemburg and Karl Liebknecht had a consistent vision of a true order but they were murdered - their deep longings nevertheless were preserved in the drawings of Käthe Kollwitz. The mixture of radicalism and the inability to be witnesses of a universal truth of justice and equality - which alone has the power of true transcendence - made the communist party a powerful but ultimately ineffective opposition to the rising tides of national socialism.

The socialdemocratic party had in effect given up the basic tenets of its marxist origin. Radical in its birth and early history during the days of the monarchy, it became essentially a party of reform rather than revolution. This was in some ways a positive development had it not failed to ground itself on that rock which is the foundation of truth: the ability to clearly distinguish between what is true in a universal sense and what is historically unique and hence needing continual renewal if not transformation to remain in a living creative relationship to its universal foundation. It reformed the market economy and counteracted the inequality between those who had been given the power to organize work and those who had to gain some compensating power through trade unions. But it did not touch the ultimate denial of the equality of opportunity understood as the recognition of the potentialities alive in all human beings. Hence it failed to come to grips with the fundamental problems of a capitalist society which manifested in the depression of 1929. Its basic failure was to have lost a living relationship with a universal truth which would have given it the power of transforming what was false while strengthening the universal truth of a free market economy.

The same - though in a different way - is true of the parties of the centre - primarily the Roman Catholic Centre party and the largely protestant "People's party". Both had a deep intuitive awareness of the truth of a free society as well as of the universal truth of a free market economy. Their faith in a free enterprise fostered the spirit of true entrepreneurship. But they either closed their eyes or were simply unable to see that the truth was vitiated by a dualism which was divisive and which ultimately undermined the universal truth of their work and lives. The chancellor Brüning, already mentioned, is a typical example of the deep faith in the harmony of a free society and at the same time a tragic reminder that the natural law tradition of the Roman Catholic Church did not become a power of transformation. This had manifold reasons which we can not explore in this paper. But the fact that deeply devout people were unable to have a transforming impact was of far-reaching importance. It was a major factor for creating an atmosphere of hopelessness among those who were the victims of the inflation and depression. It also meant that the very centre of the political spectrum lost its power to overcome the existing crisis thus expressing in more than symbolic ways the root cause of the possibility for Hitler to obtain power: the failure to offer a truly transcending alternative. This was indeed a tragic failure since the ingredients for such a transcendence were present yet they could not come to fruition because they were not understood with a clarity which would have made it possible to realize their universal truth free from outmoded ways.

The party to the right of the Volkspartei was the German National Party. It was the party of the landed aristocracy, particularly of the Eastern parts of Germany, indeed of those with aristocratic roots who were the mainstay of the old empire. They were people of tradition and conviction rooted in a pre-industrial society. Hence the German Nationalist party was a refuge allowing them to hibernate in a Republic alien to their traditions. They were vainly hoping that Spring might come again. How great the hope then, when a silver lining appeared on the horizon in the form of a possibility to resume power - even if it had to be shared with an alien ideology! They themselves had a true sense of values but it was intermingled with a longing for their realization in ways which were outmoded. Yet they clung to these forms, partly out of tradition, partly in reaction to those aspects of the parties to the left - the communists and social democrats - which they experienced as destructive of their notions without being able to see the truth alive in them. In their ideology the German National Party was remote from the spirit which animated the National Socialist Party of Hitler. Yet they shared an important existential situation: they were the dispossessed, not by any radical socialist or other action but by a lost war and the ensuing formation of the Republic.

It is, therefore, no accident of history that Auschwitz became a possibility through a coalition of the arch-conservative German Nationalist party and the National Socialist Party of Hitler. It is important to know that Hitler did not have a majority in the Reichstag when he came to power. Indeed, he had lost an election in one of the LÄNDER shortly before he was asked by the president of the Republic to form a coalition government with the German Nationalist Party. At a first glance one could hardly imagine a more unlikely combination: Hitler and Hindenburg, a discontented or disinherited citizen and a man steeped in an old established aristocratic tradition. Yet when we look more closely at what first appears as a strange chance event we get a deeper understanding of the real causes which were not only present in Germany in the 20's and early 30's of this century, but which marked this whole epoch in the development of consciousness.

IV

The motives of those who directly or indirectly supported Hitler varied. We can distinguish three main groups: The first consisted mainly of young people who felt lost and found a refuge in a "return" to nature - as they understood the slogan of "blood and soil". The people in this group were the first ones to be disappointed and disillusioned once Hitler had come to power and revealed the true face of nationalsocialism. The second group consisted of people belonging to the middle classes who had suffered from the inflation. Some had lost all their savings and were in danger of losing also their jobs as well as their status as the great crisis undermined their economic position. They chose the National Socialist party without developing much enthusiasm for its antisemitic policies while feeling relieved from competitors. The third group were those who became ideologically nationalsocialist and whose antisemitism took various forms of virulence. Yet no matter in which group a particular person may have been, there was a common denominator which affected all those who were drawn to the nationalsocialist party: a movement towards the collective undifferentiated aspects of our psyche.

To be human means to go through certain predetermined stages of development. When we are born we are close to powerful energies as well as to the opposites of good and evil, light and darkness, love and hate. We do not yet have an effective centre which enables us to guide and direct our own lives. Hence we are very sensitive and vulnerable. Slowly the energies which at first are relatively undifferentiated become woven into an ever finer pattern expressing our true nature.

The centre of such a constellation is our true self - an expression of energies which manifest the kind of person we essentially - and hence truly - are, as well as our relationships to other people, to the social order and to the world in which we are living. The development and unfolding of our true selfhood is a slow process: we have to go through a number of stages and must master the challenges of each stage to be able to move successfully to an adulthood and maturity which is rooted in trust and enables us to be free to give as well as receive, to love as well as to be loved, aware of our true identity as women, men, friends, citizens, and members of a human community.

As we grow and develop we must make choices, particularly whenever we are confronted with a critical situation. We must choose whether to meet it with the deepest and truest in us and thus grow in insight and establish deeper relationships to our fellow human beings and to Life, or whether to regress to a lower level of awareness by adjusting to a given situation at the expense of our true selfhood. To choose the first way presupposes a living relationship to the universal ground of all life from which springs true energy for renewal and transformation. To choose the second way is dangerous since it may activate destructive energies which pull us ever more deeply into a maelstrom of energies threatening us with dissociation if not breakdown. Yet this is what happened in Germany ravaged by a lost War, an inflation of hitherto unheard of proportions and the Great Depression of 1929. Many people regressed to a mode of consciousness which was molded by the power of the opposites combined with negative instincts and intuitions. As a result a vicious downward spiral was activated. The collapse of the Weimar republic was thus preceded by the activation of negative energies unbalancing and eventually bringing about a collapse of the then existing mode - and level - of awareness. Hopelessness and despair were major factors in this situation.

Almost any mass meeting of the faithful and their fellow travellers illustrates this situation and shows vividly how Hitler could attract a mass following and why people could experience him as their saviour in a desperate situation: People entering a great hall in which thousands had gathered were enveloped by one mass of human beings. Being greeted by martial music enhanced the experience of merging into something greater than the sum of the individuals. In the evocation of such an oceanic feeling, the sense of loneliness indeed lostness and disintegration vanished. A sense of community came alive, of being part of something great and life-giving which relieved the tensions of everyday life and channelled energy towards the glorious future - symbolically labelled "The Empire which will last a thousand years". This sense of community was of course illusory, as people were lost in a collective mass rather than finding a creative true-self assertion. Yet it brought to a halt the pull of those energies which threatened to destroy the very integrity of a person.

The rhetoric of a mass assembly revealed the deeper reasons why Hitler could gain a mass following. Cut off from those energies which would have made it possible to meet a critical situation by moving to a deeper and higher awareness of life people were pulled to lower levels of adjustment. The danger inherent in such a situation, namely to fall into a bottomless pit, was counteracted by collective identification corresponding to a sense of unity on a primitive but powerful level.

Given this situation there was no choice but to cling to a spurious but effective "salvation" through being close to instincts which have taken a negative expression while projecting the negativity on those marked as an outgroup - the Jews. Among those who for whom antisemitism was a major avenue of escaping from their own unresolved inner pressures and negative feelings we find the most powerful and undifferentiated relapse into undifferentiated emotions. The tragedy of such a relapse to a less than truly human level of awareness at which the energies for true self realization have become wholly inoperative, is the inability to free oneself once a certain threshold of false self-abandonment has been transgressed.

V

The era which started in the 16th and 17th centuries, - and which is now coming to an end - was marked at its beginning by a deep religious conviction motivating those who became the pioneers of the new social order: the Puritan ethic was indeed an ethic of restraint and moderation centred in a true love of God. It manifested itself in a striving to develop our capacities and potentialities. But as capitalism developed, the original notion of self interest - which had a positive foundation in an awareness of true human potentialities - was more and more emptied of its meaning and became a selfish pursuit of wealth and power rather than a vehicle for a true-Self centred interest. The ethic prevailing at the beginning of the 20th century was indeed a rationalistic ethic of maximizing profits while God - inasmuch as he had not died in the hearts of men - had a safe place in a church which more often than not was either identified with the existing order or oblivious of its problems. Ethics was often reduced to the simple precept of a moral if not moralistic nature, while neither the profound ethics of the New Testament pertaining to true personal growth and relationships, nor the "natural law" tradition of the Church which was grounded on an understanding of universal energies and a universal truth, was alive.

In the absence of such a deeper awareness many people clung to the original meaning and truth of a free market economy based on faith in the freedom of the individual to make the basic choices about what to do and how to do it, as well as faith that a free market would bring into harmony these individual choices resulting from the free actions of millions of people each pursuing a more or less enlightened self-interest. A steady upward trend in production, consumption - and in happiness - was the expected final result. Many people clung to such a faith though the harmony which it expressed had vanished more and more from the reality of daily life. Unable to actualize the underlying universal truth, the invisible hand remained in fact powerless to bring harmony into the social body, powerless to awaken those energies for transformation which are activated whenever a truth rooted in the depth of our being is touched. Eventually this truth became an ideology, a rationalization which has lost touch with a true ratio, an illusion which made people impotent in the face of the rising tide of national socialism. For those who clung to the true liberal tradition, Hitler was simply incomprehensible. They saw him as one who had grasped power temporarily. They believed Hitler would honour the rules of the democratic game and did not expect him to last for more than a short time as the chancellor of a democratically elected government. This is the deeper reason for the ineffectiveness of their opposition to the rise of nationalsocialism.

There always remained a true core in the liberal world view. But in the actual world in which Hitler won his following the invisible hand did not and could not cure the fever manifest in the greatest depression in the history of Germany. The markets had lost contact with the universal truth and harmony which constituted their core. Hitler despised the liberal world view and was determined to make an end of it without regard to the rules of the liberal game.

This situation, tragic in its meaning and implications, was only possible because the liberal world already contained an inner contradiction when capitalism first arose and divided humankind on the one hand into people who had the money and the power to become entrepreneurs - or gain power in other ways - enabling them to benefit from the underlying harmony of markets, and on the other hand into a proletariat cut off from the power to give to their lives a form expressing their true selfhood. This split was ultimately due to the dualism which undermined the moral and ethical foundation of society since it gave to one person or group what it denied to the other. In theory there was complete freedom to move from being an employee - from being a seller of one's energy or time on the labour market - to becoming an employer. But in reality this was only open to a relatively small number of people with the freedom of power over their own lives. And in the crisis of 1929 even this small number was threatened with extinction.

VI

The Holocaust is a crime behond human comprehension. As human beings we can enter deeply into the loss of a person close to us, even a number of people. We can also share in the suffering of others, but it is not possible to realize fully that six million human beings entered the gas chambers of Auzchwitz after having been stripped of all outer signs of human dignity, without the solemnity due to a passage from this life into another, often with their children crying in fear and panic, somehow knowing the horror expecting them. If we are true to ourselves we must admit that figures of such magnitude are utterly beyond our comprehension, indeed in the deepest sense of "comprehend", for they surpass our ability to "take in" without being destroyed ourselves.

It could be argued that the Holocaust was the work of a small group of people of which the vast majority of people - in Germany as well as abroad - knew nothing. There is undoubtedly more than a grain of truth in this. But it does not answer the basic question, which we asked at the beginning of this paper: How was it at all possible for the Holocaust to happen? We have already indicated a variety of reasons or contributing factors. Ultimately the rise of national-socialism and its assumption of power was only possible because of the inadequacy if not outright failure to live a universal Truth which is inscribed in the hearts of all human beings, and to apply it consistently to the human community and organized society.

A knowledge and yearning for this Truth is alive in all human beings. But it may be covered up to the point of virtual - though not ultimate - extinction at certain times and in certain situations. In post World War I Germany, in the days preceding the victory of Hitler, it was not dead inasmuch as it somehow lived on in the hearts and minds of millions of people. But it died inasmuch as it was inoperative as a power of transformation since it was not clearly recognized in its meaning and was confused in its application. The mixture of hallowing the Truth of a free market economy with a denial of Truth exemplified by reducing human beings to mere means for the purposes of others - which constitutes the very essence of a "labour market" - was the root cause making the rise of nationalsocialism possible.

I have known communists animated by a deep love for human beings and a yearning for social justice - indeed for the kingdom of God on earth. I have known socialdemocrats combining a deep humanitarian feeling with an awareness of the need for basic reforms. I have known members of the Centry party whose soul was yearning to live in the kingdom of God in their personal as well as in their political relationships. I have known members of the Volkspartei who truly felt free enterprise to be the source and guarantee of freedom. I have known members of the German nationalist party who deeply loved their country and felt its true virtues were being endangered. And I have known nationalsocialists who truly felt that only a radical departure, a return to a world which had been lost, could bring salvation.

They all had a glimpse of the Truth and yet all were wrong. Wrong because they could not clearly distinguish between a universal timeless truth and its timebound manifestation. Wrong because they actually confused a partial realization of Truth in history with a timeless universal truth. Wrong because in their confusion they had lost contact with the universal source of all Life and all Truth. Instead of living for a true Utopia they became victims of an inadequate Ideology.

Had the connection with the universal source of life remained open and alive, Hitler could never have seized power in Germany. Yet without such a recognition the massacre of the innocent of the proportions of the Holocaust became a possibility. The arsenal of atombombs stored on this planet for "defence" could bring disaster of a proportion which does not surpass the Holocaust in terms of inhumanity - but will surpass it in the number of people wantonly killed. Hence the ultimate conclusion of a person sensitive to the possibility of alienation from our true self and the suffering this implies, instead of pointing the finger at anybody, can only say: "There but for the grace of God, go I". And in saying this we must also commit ourselves to do our utmost in developing a human community and society which recognises and respects the true humanity of every human being.

Joseph Mayer and the Missing Memo:
A Catholic Justification for Euthanasia

Donald J. Dietrich

Department of History
University of Wisconsin-Stevens Point
Stevens Point, WI 54481
USA

ABSTRACT

In the modern era, the Catholic Church has condemned eugenic euthanasia. During the Third Reich, however, Joseph Mayer, a Catholic moral theologian, provided Albert Hartl (SD) with a memo justifying euthanasia. This memo, presumed lost or destroyed, has now been found and is analyzed in this study. Mayer's basic theme is that the welfare of the community supersedes that of the individual.

KEYWORDS

Eugenics: euthanasia: common welfare and eugenics.

1.

After World War I, German Catholics were faced with acute political problems. Not only did they have to function in what some felt was a detestable liberal, democratic order, but they also had to analyze and critique the eugenics movement that had been gaining strength since the late nineteenth century and that proposed a biological solution for socioeconomic and political problems (Blacker, 1931; Lifton, 1986; Kevles, 1985; Proctor, 1982; Gassman, 1971). Making the theological and political situation particularly involved was the fact that the Nazi nationalist and anti-Marxist assault on Weimar Germany could be supported by an array of varied individuals and groups, even though the Nazi radical eugenic theories were anathema to most Catholic leaders. Initially, seeking political stability, patriotic German Catholics offered their support to Hitler after he became Chancellor in 1933 (Lewy, 1964; Zahn, 1969). Historical politicization, highlighted by the Kulturkampf, and subsequently combined with the pressures of the Gleichschaltung, placed Catholics in the position of opposing Nazi biologically racist principles and simultaneously supporting Hitler's political policies (Dietrich, 1988). Catholics, for example, might well be religiously, but not racially, anti-Semitic. They generally opposed the compulsory eugenic policies of the Nazis and their predecessors, since such intrusions into the private spheres of human relations seemed to interfere with God's creative plans and so were felt to be unnatural. Nazi sterilization legislation in July 1933, for example, had support among many non-Catholics, and could be handled through moral casuistry by Catholics who were determined to remain good Germans throughout the history of the Third Reich (Lewy, 1964, pp. 258-263; Lilienthal, 1979; Amir, 1977). Euthanasia, however, was a life and death issue and left less room for probabilism.

2.

In 19th century in Germany, the movement for voluntary euthanasia was concentrated around the Monistenbund, a liberally oriented, atheistic-agnostic association of scientists, led by the famous biologist Ernest Haeckel, who felt that eugenic policies, including euthanasia, were means to make natural selection more organized and less chaotic. The liberal psychiatrist, Professor Alfred Hoche, whose ideas were to play a decisive role in the formulation of the Nazi program, was a member of this Monistenbund (Ehrhardt, 1965, pp. 10,53). With the appearance of the work of Karl Binding and Hoche (1920), the question of involuntary euthanasia turned into a widely discussed subject in German medical circles. Horrified by the casualties of the First World War, they proposed that in specific circumstances those suffering from incurable and severely crippling handicaps and injuries, so-called burdens on the community, should be killed. This proposal assumed that an outside agency had the right to define which individual life was "worthless" and that an individual actually had to justify his existence according to criteria imposed from outside. These assumptions were rooted in the biological and collectivist approach to human life that had long been debated (Noakes, 1985, p. 16), and had given rise to the German eugenic socio-moral milieu (Lepsius, 1973, pp. 56-80; Chickering, 1984, pp. 240-243; Glass, 1981, pp. 357-367).

Biological determinism, far from labeling the individual guiltless, extended the "guilt" to those irresponsible and innocent (children, the insane, the malformed) and even more generally to all members of specified inferior or dangerous races. Such Spencerian biological determinism influenced both eugenics in Europe and the United States as well as Nazi racism. Preaching the improvement race, eugenicists claimed that defective births could be prevented through large scale compulsory castration, sterilization, or separation of the sexes. Within such an intellectual milieu even such leading racial hygienists as Fritz Lenz had begun to identify with the Nazi movement by 1930. Hitler himself had set the tone: "A people is a body, too. A people, too, must have the will to live and to preserve bodily health and muster up the strength to overcome illness and infectious diseases" (Amir, 1977, pp. 22-23, 26-30; Dörner, 1967; Turner, 1985). The sterilization law of 1933 was the first move in an elaborate policy for "improving the racial health" of the German people, a policy which was institutionalized along with the measures against the Jews and which prepared the way for the euthanasia programme against the handicapped, which began in 1939. Sterilization can be seen as a direct prelude to mass murder; a program that prohibited bearing "unworthy" children eventually expanded into the wholesale murder of unworthy people, and euthanasia was a step along the way (Bock, 1983, p. 415).

Both the eugenics programme to improve German racial hygiene and the policy of anti-Semitism ultimately derived from the basic perspective which viewed man and society in biological terms (Mann, 1973; Webster, 1981). In the mid-1930s Hitler told Reichsärzteführer Dr. Gerhard Wagner that in the event of a war he would initiate a program of euthanasia. The reasoning for the timing was a lessening in wartime of the influence of the churches, from which he expected opposition. Nazi party slogans presumably would prepare the way. The Gemeinnutz (common need) always was to have precedence over Eigennutz (self-interest). An emphasis on Volk, Vaterland, and Heimat helped set the stage for the community dominance over the individual (National Archives, M887, Roll 4, p. 2402). Hitler asserted that every sick and impoverished member of the organic community affected the health of the whole body and thus detracted from the nation's economic vitality and military potential (Reher, 1938; Hilgenfeldt, 1937). Destruction of "life unworthy to be lived", then, had been a policy discussed within the government and the academic and medical professions (Amir, 1977, pp. 81 ff.; Proctor, 1982, p. 531 ff.). The euthanasia order itself, given in October 1939, was backdated to September 1, thus indicating its intimate connection to the war and the dramatic fulfillment of the Nazi Lebensraum and racial programs.

3.

Euthanasia had certainly been debated by Catholics long before the advent of the Third Reich. The parameters of the debate were shaped by two issues: voluntary and involuntary mercy killing. Early Catholic speculative thought opposed both forms. But scholastic philosophy broke with the classical tradition by rejecting suicide (voluntary euthanasia) when the purpose was solely to preserve individual dignity. Group survival was considered a mitigating condition (Wilson, 1975, p. 23). The fundamental change that occurred in the Medieval era was that "quality" of life came to be measured by ethical and societal criteria, instead of the essentially subjective criterion of the dignity of the individual. From the 1920s onward Catholic moral theologians increasingly grappled with the issues imbedded within eugenics as a medical and social policy. Was it wrong, they asked, for example, to intervene surgically to prevent the proliferation of undesirable stock and so save the race from degeneration? Defending the traditional position that sterilization was forbidden by both the Christian and the natural moral law was Professor Franz Hürth of the Jesuit Theological Seminary and later of the Pontifical Gregorian University. As the controversy continued, Hürth was ultimately vindicated by the Holy See and universally supported by the German bishops as well. In his 1930 encyclical, Casti Connubi (On Christian Marriage) Pius XI had insisted that the body of man was inviolable and that the state had no right to sterilize unless for restricted medical reasons or as a punishment for crime; purely eugenic reasons would not suffice (Amir, 1977, pp. 4-5; Niedermeyer,

1937; Niedermeyer, 1949-52, 4:222; Just, 1932). Even the encyclical, however, did not close the issue. Trying to reconcile opposites, and not really understanding Nazi goals, such scholars as Albert Niedermeyer (1937) , for example, stated that Casti Connubi was eugenics in the best sense of the word.

Hürth's foremost antagonist, however, Professor Joseph Mayer of the Paderborn Academy, defended sterilization itself as probably licit and certainly an unresolved issue. Mayer had taken his first tentative steps onto this path in the late 1920s in his book (1927) against Hürth. Unconvinced by Casti Connubi and the proliferation of pronouncements from Church leaders, Mayer continued to defend not only sterilization but abortion as well (Dietrich, 1988, Chap. 7). In 1933, Mayer's position (1933a) on the varied aspects of the eugenics issue was equally consistent; his views were consonant with those of the regime, and he seemed as obsessed with the "good of society" as his Nazi patrons. That such a prominent theologian was not specifically and publicly corrected by the Church could do nothing but confuse German Catholics. Opposing Hürth and others, Mayer insisted that the chief issue promoted by his opponents in the 1933 sterilization controversy was that the sterilized, according to canon law, would not really have been capable of a proper marital relationship.

Even during the 1920s, marriage, Mayer felt, was not a union designed exclusively for procreation, but for sanctifying the souls of the partners. The only question that could logically be asked was whether sterilization intended either an individual or societal moral good. He concluded that neither private morality nor the moral world order was endangered through the sterilization of the mentally ill. The healing and well-being of the community, he concluded, was more important than the physical integrity of the individual. Stressing that Thomas Aquinas accepted castration for sex offenders and that an extensive literature had developed emphasizing that the common good supersedes the individual benefit, Mayer asserted that the state does have the right to control the mentally and medically ill from "haphazard breeding." Since the goal of marriage, he insisted, was not just to beget children, sterilized individuals may certainly be allowed to marry and enjoy the other pleasures of connubial bliss. Mayer was very quick to point out that, conducted properly, legal sterilization measures would not lead to excess (Mayer, 1927, pp. 113, 121, 124-25, 128, 352, 373-86, 422). In his scholarly treatises, then, he asserted that it would be licit for the state to enforce sterilization for eugenic reasons. A person, for example, who is incapable of educating children should have no right to beget them (Mayer, 1929). Mayer also argued that in case of necessity an abortion may be procured and opposed Hürth who had rejected this view with the traditional Catholic position: "Catholic moral theology sees in the life of a fully innocent person an inviolable good that is immune from a direct human attack by a private person or by the public authority" (Mayer, 1933b; 1933c).

Mayer's public theological position on eugenics has been analyzed by Robert Graham (1976) and Kurt Nowak (1978), but his most controversial product, a Gutachten (opinion) commissioned by Albert Hartl of the SD (Sicherheitsdienst), until recently has been presumed lost or destroyed. The contents of Mayer's memo were initially introduced by the 1947 interrogation testimony of Albert Hartl, a former SS officer and Gestapo official in charge of gathering information on the Catholic Church. In 1967 Hartl insisted that on Hitler's order he had commissioned from Mayer a memorandum on the subject in 1939. Mayer, he said, had responded with a 100+ page theological opinion in favor of euthanasia. Hartl allegedly circulated the document to those engaged in the euthanasia program, since the theologian apparently anticipated no fundamental objection from the Church. In Hartl's words, "Only then did Hitler decide to begin the 'mercy killing' program" (Süddeutsche Zeitung, 15 February 1967). A Catholic moral theologian, he insisted, had eased the political consciences of the responsible Nazis at the very inception of this eugenics program. With the name of an Erich Warmund of Vienna and a 1940 date on the cover page, a memo "Euthanasie im Lichte der katholischer Moral und Praxis" identical to that described by Hartl in his postwar interrogation (National Archives, RG 238, CI-FIR/123) and in his 1967 testimony has recently been found. In 1967 Hartl stated that the memo had been written in 1939. In his Interrogation Report of 1947 he stated that it was written in 1940. The descriptions of the content of the memo in the Hartl testimonies are identical, leading one to assume that the 1940 memo could have been a revised copy of the original or the original with a new cover page or the original itself and that Hartl had confused the dates, a common problem reflected in his other interrogation testimony. In a letter to me (2 May 1983) Christopher Browning indicated that he had found the memo and was trying to verify its legitimacy. In 1982 Hartl died the day Browning wrote to verify the memo. In a letter (24 September 1984) to me, Robert Graham, S J. asserted that the memo from Warmund appears to be that written by Joseph Mayer. Before Hartl died he had confided to a colleague of Graham's that this memo was written by Johannes Holnsteiner of Vienna. According to Graham, Holnsteiner, employed by Hartl in the SD, had no qualifications for this type of work, and Hartl himself had already insisted in his 1947 testimony that Mayer wrote the memo in 1940, which would be more likely than 1939, since by 1940 the euthanasia program was being attacked by religious leaders and the regime may have felt the need for support from some Catholic experts (Lewy, 1964, p. 264; Amir, 1977, pp. 262-264; National Archives, RG 238, Cl-FIR/123, pp. 42-43). Whether the date on the memo was 1939 or the more likely date of 1940 when Hartl, according to the interrogation notes, was attempting to secure opinions to support his Führer, the memo exposes the extent that völkisch and Nazi values had permeated theological circles and were undermining Catholic moral positions, although the Church had officially denounced euthanasia on more than one occasion (Dietrich, 1988, Chap. 7; Dietrich, 1987).

4.

Certainly Mayer could have provided such an opinion. His views on sterilization and abortion had already predisposed him for such an eugenic conclusion and had probably provided the reason why he was approached by the Nazis. If Hartl hoped to offer his Nazi colleagues reliable information on the real views of the bishops, however, he misled them. The reactions of the German bishops indicate that Mayer's opinion was completely out of line with Catholic doctrine. Hitler, moreover, certainly was not the type to rely on the Pfaffen before proceeding on his course. Professor Mayer himself ultimately left the Paderborn Academy after 1945 and ceased writing on moral issues. The reasons for his departure are not completely known, but perhaps suggest the truth in the accusation that he apparently not only supplied scholarly opinions to the Nazis, but also communicated other information as well (National Archives, RG 238, Cl-FIR/123, pp. 16-18).

His memo, at times rambling and ignoring logical steps of development, offers a good example of moral theology tailored to a diseased political milieu. Mayer's speculation also suggests that under specific conditions there can be a logical development from sterilization to euthanasia to Auschwitz. Like most ideas, eugenics, he felt, could be traced at least as far back as the ancient Greeks. Indeed, Plato's Republic could be read as an eugenics tract. Mayer cited Plato's viewpoint that the state was the individual writ large. The healthy state or political community was used to understand the "good" man. Through the state or polis man first became in body and soul that which he was destined to be according to the Idea. If the actualized ideal of man was understood by comprehending the "true" state, then the statesman seemed justified in removing unhealthy elements from the body politic. In essence, Mayer defended the policies of the polis in terms of the development of the natural body. Each was used to understand the other (Mayer, 1940, p. 1). Plato was, of course, interested in the morally good life and thus he philosophically used the ideal organic state as a reflection to help his reader understand the ideal man. In this context, the community could be seen as a metaphor. Under the influence of romanticism, however, for Mayer the state had become a real, organic being.

Following Plato, not surprisingly, Aristotle next was cited. Naturally Mayer pointed to Aristotle's comment that the acceptable newborn should possess a superb physical constitution. No crippled child should be raised. Mayer concluded in this section that classical philosophers advised euthanasia as a mechanism to produce and then to maintain their polis composed of genetically healthy citizens. Such a position was modified by the early Church fathers. These men definitely wanted to avoid making the welfare of the state or political authority the measure of moral worth. The sick were to be accepted and nurtured. Simlutaneously, they retained as much as possible the norms and values of Plato and Aristotle. Hence, the early Christian commentators continued the vigorous philosophical and now theological debates on the socio-political, economic, and medicinal issues of the day (Mayer, 1940, pp. 3-5). Although the evidence is not overwhelmingly conclusive, Mayer insisted, of course, that the issue, as he understood it, had been addressed from earliest Christian times to the present, and so clearly it was still an open question.

Administering eugenic policies could be the function of the government or of a private facility under political authority, which could employ euthanasia for the purposes of controlling criminals or for social hygiene. From antiquity onward the support of the public welfare rather than private needs had been a foremost consideration. Moral theories similar in the classical and the Christian eras, have appeared in the ongoing Catholic debates on the declaration of war, capital punishment, and immunization, according to Mayer. The issue was still being debated, insisted Mayer, as he introduced the works of such contemporary scholars as Franz Walther (1935), who scarcely mentioned politically mandated euthanasia, but rather focused on the private variety as if this were the major issue. Walther's premise was that euthanasia as such was murder and so all such acts were barbarian, nonhuman, and unchristian. Mayer countered that Walther failed to make the appropriate distinctions with which theologians as professionals should be concerned. Theologians were supposed to distinguish among the specific circumstances that would allow the state to intervene. Abstract principles should be analyzed along with historical political regimes. For centuries political power had been wielded by Christian laity, by bishops, and even by the Pope, and so research should be able to provide the guidelines and the criteria that Christians could apply when moral issues relating to the welfare of the community were addressed (Mayer, 1940, pp. 12-15).

The first type of euthanasia Mayer dealt with was "Gesetzliche Abkürzung lebensunwerten Lebens." Within the historical context of a body of literature, he hoped to analyze euthanasia for idiots and the mentally ill. The practice of the Church had been shaped by the moral theory dealing with the individual in society. Certainly, Christ did not confront the problem of euthanasia, because it was not a pressing issue in his time and social milieu. If one looked at the Church's official teaching on a less significant issue, moreover, Mayer insisted that the issue even of sterilization was not decisively addressed until Casti Connubi, which Mayer reminded his readers was not an infallible encyclical. Pius XI had not supported his line of argument either with revelation per se or with the decisions of past councils, but cited texts from Thomas Aquinas, since after Leo XIII Thomistic philosophy had become for some identical with Church teaching. Mayer maintained, of course, that Thomistic scholasticism was not infallible, but was merely a useful methodology for speculatively organizing Catholic teaching (Mayer, 1940, pp. 15-19). Anyway, Thomas could be used by Mayer as well.

Thomas, for example, maintained that political power was to extend over the individual's life and property, since this authority theoretically had a moral basis. The individual, for example, could be removed from the community when he posed a danger, just as, analogously, a diseased organ could be surgically removed from the body. The community was not considered a real physical organism, of course, but was composed of human personalities which had a special sanctity due to their organized existence. As a result, the state or secular ruler of the political community had a right of disposition against criminals, because such persons had denigrated human dignity and had reduced themselves to the level of the non-rational beast. Thomas emphasized that a criminal was one who menaced the common welfare. Mayer maintained that one particular argument of Thomas, i.e., no punishment without guilt, had continued to be controversial. Thomas tried to make a distinction between punishment for wrongdoing and punishment used as a means for healing the community. In the latter case personal guilt was not involved. Neither Thomas nor Pius XI, Mayer noted, supported their analysis of public welfare on the words of Christ or on natural law. Thomas based his argument on Roman Law in which punitive measures could not be applied to the innocent citizen. Physical punishments (death, torture, etc.) could only be practiced against animals and slaves, not against free men, unless a trial or an established normative process had deprived them of their human dignity as citizens contributing to the community (Mayer, 1940, pp. 19-26).

Mayer, of course, wanted to focus on the issue of the community versus the mentally ill which, for example, could include epileptics. Along with Walther and several other theologians, he pointed out that the difference between paganism and Christianity lay precisely in the fact that, ideally, Christians were to care for the crippled and the sick. Mayer contended, however, that scholars had to know not only what theologians teach, but also how Christians had historically dealt with a problem in a practical sense, since only the deed can really illuminate the teaching (Mayer, 1940, pp. 27-28; Walther, 1935).

In the ancient world, Mayer insisted, it was felt that the mentally ill were possessed by the gods. Christianity suggested that the mentally ill were possessed by evil demons, not gods. In principle, Christ, who talked about casting out devils, had the same goal as Plato, i.e., to free the community of the unhealthy. Both wanted to cleanse the community of sickness in body and soul. Plato would use expurgation. Christ preferred sanctification, and the early Church relied heavily on exorcism. As long as possession existed, a person could not be baptized and so could not become part of the Christian community, the people of God. Exorcism was a sign that God supported the early Church. For nearly two millenia people continued to identify possession and mental illness. Mayer himself expanded on the theme that earlier commentators felt that mental illness and sin were causally connected. If a person were baptized, for example, and then became mentally ill, that individual would not be allowed communion and so would be excluded from full participation in the Christian community. If this condition persisted, of course, such a person would ultimately be excluded from heaven itself. Naturally this called into question the entire issue of individual guilt. One might have to presume, then, the guilt of the parents in order to handle this conundrum. Mental illness was thought to be caused by demonic possession, especially if it proved impervious to healing. Only grace could save the person from eternal damnation. Mayer here cited Clement and Origin who said that through sin demons gained entrance into the human body (Mayer, 1940, pp. 28, 32-39). In this concrete fashion, then, natural sickness was rooted in a spiritual disorder.

Moral speculation in modern times, of course, would maintain that the state should not be permitted to injure physically the guiltless citizen. That was fine, but Mayer insisted that the mentally ill in earlier centuries were not viewed as guiltless. The mentally ill were excluded from the community because they could not be baptized. Early Christians maintained Plato's ideal in a similar fashion by insisting that the religious community itself should be kept free of epileptics and the mentally ill even though that meant "eternal damnation" imposed by the Church as an institution that was supposed to be promoting salvation (Mayer, 1940, pp. 40-43). Confronted with functioning in the world, the Church expanded the label of "guilt," so that what now might be considered as "innocent" persons were shifted into the category of the guilty. The Church did this to handle those who could not be included in the spiritual community (Mayer, 1940, pp. 47-48).

The "inhuman" treatment of the mentally ill in the Middle Ages is public knowledge. The ill were locked up in so-called witch towers, starved, driven into the forests, tortured, and even burned as witches. Based on a theological-metaphysical foundation, the mentally ill were frequently also classified as sorcerers and heretics and then sadistically punished by priests, judges, and princes. The brutality was so exceptional that in hindsight many of these jurists, theologians, princes, bishops, and popes today might even be analyzed as psychopaths. Times change, and in 1886 Sigmund Freud, for example, had noted that in Medieval Europe a woman, who today would be diagnosed as hysterical, would have been judged and condemned at that time as a witch or as possessed by the devil. Mentally ill or physically deformed newborns as well could be drowned since they were not viewed as human, but as products of the devil. In general, both Church and state rigorously punished those afflicted with mental illness, since they interfered with the integral community (Mayer, 1940, pp. 48-50; McGrath, 1986, p. 165; Trachtenberg, 1943).

Medieval theologians asserted that the mentally ill were possessed by the devil and so were to be defined as criminals, a thesis accepted by secular judges as well. Officials from the Church (inquisitors) and secular judges subjected these persons to a physically brutal investigation, not to a procedurally ordered process. According to Mayer, witches, whom some might diagnose as mentally ill women, were burned. The basis of this punitive behavior was the fusion of mental illness, sin, and the devil in such a way that each was the cause or result of the other. Here even Thomas did not follow the more rational pagan, Aristotle. Thomas could not free himself from astrologers or from those who fostered a belief in demonology. In fact, it seems clear that Thomas directly or indirectly afforded explanations and support for demonology although not for the witchcraft delusion in most of its 14th and 15th century features. (Cohn, 174) His theories were later extended to give credence to witchhunts. Citing Chrysostomus, Gratian, and medieval penitential manuals, Mayer was able to conclude that essentially the Christian tradition perceived mental illness as the result of sin. Penitential manuals saw sin as the chief cause of illness and so forbade Christian doctors from treating a patient who had not confessed his sins. The use of this pastoral approach toward the mentally ill was naturally catastrophic, since those who were sick could not rationally confess their sins. The mentally ill, moreover, were frequently classified as witches with subsequently gruesome results. Witches were judged as a danger threatening the socio-political order, which both the state and Church had a duty to defend. After the great witchhunts in early modern Europe, the mentally ill continued to be confined as wild animals until relatively recent times. Ultimately, then, during the Middle Ages there occurred a fusion of insanity, witchcraft, and heresy into one concept (Mayer, 1940, pp. 50-59; Szasz, 1970, p. 76).

In the Middle Ages, Mayer insisted, the mentally ill were considered the "devil's vomit." Still, there were exceptions. Some cloisters cared for the mentally ill as the early Christian communities had cared for the possessed and for penitents. Due to their primitive lack of comprehension, it would be senseless to condemn the practices prevalent in medieval Europe. But it would also be unjust to assert that the contemporary humane care of the insane was essentially the result of Christianity. Medieval thinkers wanted to expurgate the insane and so maintain the integrity of the community. This barbarous activity was not solely the result of Christianity, but was due to the acceptance of the natural selection approach which was characteristic of the early barbarian tribes (Mayer, 1940, pp. 62-63), who considered physical deformity dangerous as well.

Here Mayer used the word Missgeburt to label those born deformed, i.e., he designated them as non-humans. In the Middle Ages, such "monsters" were annihilated, generally drowned. If only slightly misformed, they could be considered orphans. Germanic law had traditionally given the father the right to reject legally a child, and theology provided the moral underpinning, since demonic influences, it was thought, had created the half-human, half-animal creature. Such creatures could not be baptized, and so were excluded from the community; their death was not viewed as murder by the Church or secular rulers. When the newborn creature was misformed, medieval theorists insisted that the parents had sinned and so concluded that Satan had a role in the conception. From the Mosaic law to Isidor of Seville there emerged a thematic continuum, for example, that children conceived during the menstruation cycle were demonically possessed and most likely to be deformed. Albert the Great, Thomas Aquinas, and Scotus all believed that a child conceived during this period had to be deformed because of the mother's blood and the demonically influenced male seed. Sexual sins lead to the corruption of the male seed, resulting in the creation of a being part human and part animal, but lacking a spiritual soul. Elimination of such a creature from the community was seen as neither a murder nor a sin (Mayer, 1940, pp. 64-67).

Mayer reminded his readers that the legalistic issue of the spiritual and moral relationship of the individual to the political regime was a completely modern concept. In the Middle Ages, for example, the individual was in a specific guild or socio-economic group and so did not have those civic rights we associate with modern relationships. The modern, abstract state did not exist and neither did abstract individual rights. According to Plato and Aristotle and similarly in Medieval Europe, the community was more than the sum of all parts and had precedence before all components. This organic state or political community was a unique reality. The Medieval community could be viewed analagously as a type of organism, which was in fact superior to its parts. This was generally accepted until Leo XIII, under the pressure of French Catholic democrats, had to make certain concessions to the atomistic and democratic Rousseauean political theory, a decision obviously condemned by Mayer. In Mayer's opinion, Staat, understood properly, had developed from the speculation of Aristotle and Thomas into a morally complete person which in essence, structure, and goal was far more important than the individual with specific political rights and duties (Mayer, 1940, pp. 68-69).

Ignoring the Medieval Weltanschauung, which certainly had no modern concept of race, Mayer also asked how the scholastics viewed the relation between the political power and the race. Adopting the Platonic ideal, Thomas had insisted the type (Art) is eternal and unchangeable. The scholastic expression Art was identical to what today would be designated as race, at least according to Mayer. He thought that the achievement of common cultural goals was a duty for the state. These included the normal material and spiritual welfare as well as the health of the family. To perpetuate the Art, the state was to continue as a healthy, prosperous entity with a right to execute individuals who lived outside the purview of the integral and organic community (Mayer, 1940, pp. 70-71).

From this point Mayer could and did develop the theme that the individual person should work for the whole according to Platonic as well as Christian thought. According to Meyer's interpretation of Thomas, "love of the fatherland" (community) would necessitate that the welfare of the organic whole means that the individual welfare must be subordinated to that of the community. The individual was to be a part of the Volk, Mayer's creative translation of the Medieval Latin term multitudo. In nature and human society sacrifices were to be made for the welfare of the whole, and laws, which regulate such actions, would have to bind in conscience (Mayer, 1940, pp. 70-72). In his memo, Mayer clearly attempted to impose twentieth century meanings on thirteenth century terminology, leading to results as erroneous the reverse would.

Although the medieval Church controlled the souls and moral perspectives of its members and certainly misused this power more than once for political goals, Popes and others maintained, at least abstractly, that political organizations should not become the objects of theological critiques and certainly not be punished for the fulfillment of political duties. There was to be a separation between Church and state, although the former was considered hierarchically superior to the latter. The Church accepted the regulations of the political authority as morally binding and frequently justified by practical necessity. There was no recognition of the personal sovereignty inherent in the individual, which became customary during the Enlightenment. In the Middle Ages the individual Christian obeyed the state just as analagously a Catholic was to conform to the ordinances of the Roman Curia (Mayer, 1940, pp. 72-73).

Since the Medieval Christian community practiced neither social-hygenic nor preventative measures to develop healthy populations, medieval rulers consigned all these "eugenic" issues to the legal processes, administered by the state and Church, which focused on exclusion. The incomplete, they insisted, was to be governed by the complete according to Thomas' hierarchical viewpoint. Hence, animals could be killed by man. Amputation was permitted for the health of the entire body. In the same line of thought, each person was to be ordered to the entire community. If an individual, as a sinner or as one possessed, interfered with the organic and hierarchical structure of the community, he could be executed, since the common welfare was to remain intact. In Medieval thought, Mayer reminded his readers, the state or kingdom was viewed as a holistic entity, to which individuals were completely subordinated. The prince was, of course, responsible for implementing God's law. Insofar as individuals belonged to the community, they stood exclusively in a relationship to the members of the whole organism. The unique secular source of law was that much cited common welfare which was an earthly reflection of the transcendent good. As such, the common welfare possessed the greatest authority in itself because its source was God. The common good in the Middle Ages was seen as the equivalent of a divine law or a divine commandment and Gemeinwohl was a dictate of logical and social necessity, originating from God's created natural order. In recent times, Viktor Cathrein, S.J. and Leo XIII had acknowledged as well this foundation for all states (Mayer, 1940, pp. 73-76).

According to both Thomas and Aristotle, the asocial creature as lawbreaker or sinner was either an animal or a God. Those possessed by demons, of course, lost their human dignity and sank to the animal level. According to the scholastics, the possessed were subsumed under the concept of sinner. Even though they may not have acted freely and may have been the results of parental sinful acts, they could be punished by both the state and the Church. Answering the question, "Is it permitted to execute the possessed sinner?" Thomas responded that the sorcerer should not be allowed to live. Sorcerer in this context was the later equivalent of witch. Petrus Binsfeldius and others later contended that execution for sorcerers or witches was justified, since Thomas had subordinated sinners to the common good. The designation of persons as sorcerers and witches as heretics was used as a spiritual reason for the execution of the mentally ill. A creature of this nature was subhuman and was not only comparable to an animal but was worse than an animal. Mayer emphasized that Thomas and the scholastics did not oppose the brutal assault on the body or the life of the mentally ill individual who had ceased to be an intact member of the community. In the later Middle Ages witchcraft and possession were judged by special courts, which entertained nameless denunciations and used torture to extract confessions. Medieval morality accepted the employment of torture in order to obtain proof for the guilt of witches and the possessed. From Thomas to the Enlightenment, no one objected to these tortures. Innocent IV (1252) and Canon Law in general accepted torture for heretics and witches. Only in early modern times were clergy and nobles exempted from torture. God's judgement induced through water and fire were used to indict witches or others dangerous to the community. In this way, presumably, God spoke, and the courts administered (Mayer, 1940, pp.77-83; Midelfort, 1972; Cohn, 1975). The Medieval Church supported the political regime by excommunicating an individual prior to execution. Those possessed by the devil, whom today authorities would designate as mentally ill, were excommunicated as sinners. The possessed were cast from the community of the Church and delivered to Satan.

In another context of ethical speculation, European moral philosophers after 1492 even considered slavery as a consequence and punishment for earlier sins and crimes or at least as one consequence of original sin for certain groups on earth. Similarly, Aristotle had held that some peoples were by nature inferior to others. Sensitive to the political reality, Paul III (1537) proclaimed that the fate of slaves in lands possessed by Christians need not be made mild, and the slave trade was not eliminated. Only most recently did Leo XIII in connection with the non-Christian, humanitarian movements take a decisive position that contributed to the elimination of slavery. In earlier eras when it had political influence, the Church never acted, since the norms of the European communities seemed to uphold slavery (Mayer, 1940, pp. 84-88).

The Church historically supported political authorities in the elimination (Ausmerzung) of the mentally ill and of idiotic children. In the reality of current medical advances, they were innocent, but theologians declared they were guilty through their parents. Only in modern times has the medical profession denied the so-called demonic possession of the mentally ill. This resulted in charitable Christians accepting idiot-children, epileptics, and the mentally ill (Mayer, 1940, pp. 93-94). Since the 19th century, according to Mayer, moral theology has opted for the absolute protection of the lives of those who were insane rationalism had initially caused this perversion of nature. Thus, common good lost its preeminence to private need. Historically, the principles of Christianity had opposed this. The Enlightenment emphasized universal human rights as an absolute value, and so common welfare lost its legal force and was replaced by a politically alien individualism. If life makes sense for the individual, for the community, and for the Church, and the resources exist, Mayer stated, then every effort should be made to preserve life. But given the limited resources of society, young and healthy lives should not be neglected for those who are dying or lost. Realizing economic limitations, a movement counter to sterile humanitarianism began to emerge in the late nineteenth century. In the United States for the past 25 years, Mayer indicated, there had existed sterilization laws for checking and controlling the hereditarily ill in order to support natural selection through legal means. The eugenic movement, Mayer insisted, became stronger as the peoples of Europe, following the catastrophic World War I, awakened to the new challenges of a healthy population-politics. Insane asylums during the war had been almost emptied through starvation; states now felt called upon to help in the rebirth of a healthy population to stem their political decline. Scientists and statesmen rightly felt that they should perhaps not engage in preventative measures artificially to prolong life. Mayer agreed with Alfred Ploetz, a prominent proponent of eugenics, who had earlier warned against medical care for the infirm, since this allowed those individuals to survive and reproduce, who otherwise, without the intervention of doctors, would never have survived (Mayer, 1940, pp. 102-103; Proctor, 1982, p. 424; Weiss, 1987).

Those outside the Church and Pius XI himself in Casti Connubi had already urged that the health of peoples was to be preserved through a properly arranged and healthy Christian and has rejected euthanasia as an instrument to protect the community. Clearly, Mayer insisted, opinions change.

As late as 1832, mentally ill, illegitimate, and depraved children still shared the same quarters with criminals, the same dungeon, the same chains, and the same treatment. These persons were being treated as criminals and so were being punished. The metamorphosis in the handling of the mentally ill did not originate from Christianity, which only adapted to contemporary conditions, but from the medical profession. Mayer acknowledged the works of Vincent dePaul and the various orders that mitigated the injustices practiced against the mentally ill, but they did not change the traditional basic principle. The mentally ill person was still to be isolated from the community, but not to be abused (Mayer, 1940, pp. 93-96).

The official Church did not initially work for the amelioration of these brutal conditions. From the Enlightenment onward, non-Christian rationalism urged treatment of the mentally ill, based on so-called human dignity and utilizing state intervention. In the French Revolution Dr. Philipp Pinel, who believed that the so-called witches should be classified as mentally ill, unchained these unfortunate persons and sought to quiet their ravings through medicinal means. This was, Mayer maintains, the beginning of psychiatry. Not through Christianity but despite Christianity was the life of the mentally ill person made safe. Freethinking doctors and not Catholic moralists saw in the mentally ill only sick individuals who should be cared for. It was the unique characteristic of the Enlightenment which began to see "man in himself" (human essence) in the criminal and in the mentally ill. From this abstract concept of life developed rationalistic philosophy supporting individualism,, jurisprudence, and modern medicine. In the Middle Ages the ordering of society was conceptualized in terms of divine grace. In recent times institutional psychiatry had replaced the Inquisition to protect the group from those suffering mental illness (Szasz, 1970, p. 13). Thus, theologians tailored theology to accord with modern thought, just as they had always done. Increasingly, the ideal was to save and lengthen human life. The sick should be nursed in the family and in the Volk community, even though such individuals had lost the true essence of a rational life. What nature had allowed to be destroyed, until recently medical science had sought to save. With this attitude and the rise of social hygiene and care, artificial prolongation of life became in the 19th century a universally accepted norm. Thousands of insane persons have been kept alive, who in past centuries would have been eliminated. More food and better medicine made all this possible. Given the number of current inmates in institutions, for example, Germans were supporting an additional 1.2 million years of these spiritually and vegetable-like persons (Mayer, 1940, pp. 98-100).

Briefly, according to Mayer, the Enlightenment and the Church itself stressed political rights and the absolute value of human life and so resulted in an irresponsible invasion into the wise rule of the natural processes of selection, which in less sentimental times had been used by the Church and state to preserve the organic Ordo. Not Christianity, but marriage, in which precautions could be taken to insure genetically well bred stock. Following his unorthodox interpretation of Casti Connubi, Mayer emphasized that in mental institutions the inhabitants were more lumps of flesh than men and were not images of God. Thus the injunction to "increase and multiply" could not apply to such creatures since it was not God's will to have propagated distortions of his image in the course of generations. Sterilization attempts as also legal measures for shortening purely vegetative life, which are subhuman reflections of human forms, had already gained support in the United States. In Italy, France, England, Switzerland, Belgium just as in Germany, medical, judicial authorities, and some theologians had already supported legislation designed to preserve the people (Volk) and to care for the healthy young men and women in each society (Mayer, 1940, pp. 104-105).

Mayer developed his theme that contemporary issues were not really new problems. The contemporary state no less than the medieval kingdom had the right to regulate society for the common welfare. Only in modern times had the Church abandoned its traditional support of the common good. Legal regulations and medical professionals had the duty and power to abolish any abcess on the body-politic. To oppose such regulations would be conceivable only if his contemporaries had not accepted the current conception of the state with its obligation toward the Volk. Public welfare, implemented through Volkshygiene and not seen as legal punishment, must be the guiding principle. The health of the Volk was again to be the highest ideal (Mayer, 1940, p. 107).

Theology, Mayer insisted, should re-dedicate its speculation to some serious and traditional issues. First, theologians should not assume that they automatically have as much influence as they had in the Middle Ages and so can shape the functioning of the contemporary state as effectively as they did in Medieval Europe. The Church, which has consistently adapted, should not insist that it possesses eternal, Christian, and unchangeable moral guidelines or it will be mauled by the wheels of history. Because of numerous, fateful errors through the centuries, moral theology has been guilty of indescribable horrors in the political and social lives of men, justified by the Church as it implemented its moral interpretations. Theologians, Mayer insisted, should clarify their basic principles, which historically developed over centuries and were only changed following the Enlightenment, before they try again to claim that they have the right to act as the world conscience and assume a responsible role in contemporary German culture (Mayer, 1940, pp. 108-109).

Finally, Mayer indicated that current theology had to respond to the secularized state in the spirit of Cardinal Bellarmine's suggestion, which was certainly reminiscent of Plato's axiom: "The state is in a certain measure man enlarged...the ruler is in the same measure the head of the body." From this organic idea would arise the political duty to maintain the whole, to preserve the common good opposed to the individual member, and to stabilize itself even through the death of selected "lebensunwerten" persons. The duty of the political leader, to whom the protection of the common good was entrusted, was to ensure that the parts do not injure the organic political community. Because of this, he must, if he cannot support all parts inviolate, eliminate one segment so that the common good may be more thoroughly preserved. Just as farmers cut branches and tendrils which are damaging the trees or the vines and the doctor removes limbs and organs which are poisoning the entire body, Mayer concluded, the political ruler has both a right and duty to eliminate those elements undermining the healthy integrity of the state. But the ruler must operate under modern legal, moral, and medical strictures. Both the witch and the Jew, then, have been hunted and persecuted as demonic aliens in the Christian cultural community. As conspiracies, both have been viewed as threats to the social and political order of Europe (Mayer, 1940, pp. 109-110; Arnold, 1934; Ruether, 1975).

5.

The Nazi campaign to indoctrinate the German people against the racially inferior used exactly the same arguments as those against the biologically inferior. The Final Solution, euthanasia, and sterilization all belong to the same politically biological policy. The goal was the maintenance of the health and integrity of the Aryan community, and Germany had to defend itself against those of foreign races as well as against the unhealthy elements within her own people. Thus the common roots of the extermination of the insane and that of the Jews can be found in the very justification of killing itself: destruction of individual life to foster the well-being of the racial community. Even though bound by a common eugenic ideology, the two extermination programs were not totally identical. A close institutional connection existed in part due to the similar aspects and technical problems of the two murder plans. But certainly the failure of the euthanasia program did not result in the establishment of the Final Solution. Both operations were distinct, but proceeded on parallel paths toward the same goal. There was, of course, an outcry against euthanasia, although not against the Final Solution. In the case of the Final Solution, the Jew was still "the other," while in the euthanasia program the victim could be the significant other. Through an accident or merely the aging process, any German could turn into a "useless eater," although he could never become a Jew (Amir, 1977, pp. 323-333, 346-47; Dörner, 1967, p. 148). Both the Jew and the "useless eater" threatened the community welfare.

The euthanasia program itself was a logical escalation based on the sterilization laws. Once a human hierarchy was established, and the exclusion of the Untermensch from procreation decided, the next logical step was his exclusion from life and for the Jew to be viewed as a sick or diseased creature (Wagner, 1935, p. 432; Günther, 1929; Proctor, 1982, pp. 542-550). The Third Reich's policy toward the ill and those "unworthy" to live stands as a frightful warning both against the application of "valueless-science" to social problems and against the rationalization of social prejudices in terms of science. Even more to the point, the example of Mayer's adaptation of moral theology to political authority warns those who naively may think that theologians are the guardians of sacrosanct moral principles and are impervious to their political environment. Along with others, they should also beware of applying consistently the moral "truths" of one era to a completely different situation.

REFERENCES

Amir, A. (1977). "Euthanasia in Nazi Germany," Ph.D. dissertation, State University of New York - Albany.

Arnold, F.X. (1934). Die Staatslehre des Kardinals Bellarmin. Ein Beitrag zur Rechts-und Staatsphilosophie des konfessionellen Zeitalters, H. Hueber, Munich.

Bindung, K. and A. Hoche. (1920). Die Freigabe der Vernichtung lebensunwerten Lebens, Ihr Mass und Ihre Form, E. Strache, Leipzig.

Blacker, C.P. (1931). "The Sterilization Proposals." The Eugenics Review. 22: 239-247.

Bock, G. (1983). "Racism and Sexism in Nazi Germany: Motherland, Compulsory Sterilization and the State." Signs. 8: 400-421.

Chickering, R. (1984). We Men Who Feel Most German: A Cultural Study of the Pan-German League, 1886-1914, George Allen and Unwin, Boston.

Cohn, N. (1975). Europe's Inner Demons: An Enquiry Inspired by the Great Witch Hunt, Basic Books, New York.

Dietrich, D.J. (1988). Catholic Citizens in the Third Reich: Psycho-Social Principles and Moral Reasoning, Transaction Press, New Brunswick, NJ.

Dietrich, D.J. (1987). "Catholic Theologians in the Third Reich." Journal of Church and State. 29: 19-46.

Dörner, K. (1967). 'Nationalsozialismus und Lebensvernichtung." Vierteljahrshefte für Zeitgeschichte. 15: 121-152.

Ehrhardt, H. (1965). Euthanasie und Vernichtung "lebensunwerten" Lebens, Enke, Stuttgart.

Gasman, D. (1971). The Scientific Origins of National Socialism: Social Darwinism in Ernst Haeckel and the German Monist League, American Elsevier, New York.

Glass, B. (1981). "A Hidden Chapter of German Eugenics between the Two World Wars." Proceedings of the American Philosophical Society. 125: 357-367.

Graham, R. (1976). "The 'Right to Kill' in the Third Reich. Prelude to Genocide." The Catholic Historical Review. 62: 56-76.

Günther, H.F.K. (1929). Rassenkunde des Juedischen Volkes, Eher, Munich. Hilgenfeldt, E. (1937). Aufgaben den nationalsozialistischen Wohlfahrtspflege, Eher, Munich.

Just, K. (1932). Eugenik und Weltanschauung, Reichert, Berlin.

Kevles, D. (1985). In the Name of Eugenics: Genetics and the Uses of Human Heredity, Knopf, New York.

Lepsius, M.R. (1973). "Parteisystem und Sozialstruktur: Zum Problem der Demokratisierung der deutschen Gesellschaft." In Ritter, G. (ed.), Deutsche Parteien vor 1918, Kiepenheuer und Witsch, Cologne.

Lewy, G. (1964). The Catholic Church and Nazi Germany, McGraw Hill, New York.

Lifton, R.J. (1986). The Nazi Doctors: Medical Killing and the Psychology of Genocide, Basic Books, New York.

Lilienthal, G. (1979). "Rassenhygiene im Dritten Reich." Medizinhistorisches Journal. 14: 114-132.

McGrath, W.C. (1986). Freud's Discovery of Psychoanalysis: The Politics of Hysteria, Cornell University Press, Ithaca.

Mann, G. (ed.) (1973). Biologismus im 19. Jahrhundert. Vorträge eines Symposiums von 30. bis 31 Oktober 1970 in Frankfurt am Main, Enke, Stuttgart.

Mayer, J. (1933a). "Eugenische Sterilisierung?" Schonere Zukunft. 34: 814-815, 837-839.

Mayer, J. (1940) "Euthanasie im Lichte der katholischen Moral und Praxis." 1940. (Staatsarchiv Nürnberg, KV-Anklage Dokumente Nr. Zz-266 Rep. 502)

Mayer, J. (1933b). "Zum Gesetz gegen erbkranken Nachwuchs." Germania, 13 August

Mayer, J. (1927). Gesetzliche Unfruchtbarmachung Geisteskranken, Herder, Freiburg.

Mayer, J. (1929). "Sexualprobleme zur Strafrechtsreform." Theologie und Glaube. 21: 137-162.

Mayer, J. (1933c). "Vorschläge für ein eugenisches Aufbauprogram." Schönere Zukunft. 37: 814-815, 837-839.

Midelfort, H.C.E. (1972). Witch Hunting in Southwestern Germany, 1562-1684: The Social and Intellectual Foundations, Stanford University Press, Stanford.

Niedermeyer, A. (1937). "Die Bedeutung der Enzyklika 'Casti Connubi' für Eugenik in Wissenschaft und Praxis." In Kleineidam, E. and Kuss, O. (eds.). Die Kirche und die Welt. Beiträge zur christlichen Besinnung in der Gegenwart, Pustet, Salzburg, pp. 357-389.

Niedermeyer, A. (1949-52). Handbuch der speziallen Pastoralmedizin, 4 Vols., Herder, Vienna.

Noakes, J. (1985). "Social Outcasts in Nazi Germany. History Today. 35: 15-19.

Nowak, K. (1978). Euthanasie und Sterilisierung im Dritten Reich. Die Konfrontation der Evangelischen und Katholischen Kirche mit dem "Gesetz zur Verhütung erbkranken Nachwuchses" und der "Euthanasie" - Aktion, Vandenhoeck und Ruprecht, Göttingen.

Proctor, R. (1982). "Pawns or Pioneers? The Role of Doctors in the Origins of Nazi Racial Science," Ph.D. dissertation, Harvard.

Reher, W. (1938). Social Welfare in Germany, Terramare, Berlin.

Ruether, R. (1975). "Witches and Jews: The Demonic Alien in Christian Culture." In Ruether, R. (ed.), New Woman, New Earth: Sexist Ideologies and Human Liberation, The Free Press, New York, pp. 89-114.

Szasz, T. (1970). The Manufacture of Madness: A Comparative Study of the Inquisition and the Mental Health Movement, Harper & Row, New York.

Trachtenberg, J. (1943). The Devil and the Jews: The Medieval Conception of the Jew and Its Relation to Modern Anti-Semitism, Yale University Press, New Haven.

Turner, H.A. (ed.), (1985). Hitler-Memoirs of a Confidant, trans. Ruth Hein, Yale University Press, New Haven.

Wagner, G. (1935). "Unser Reichsarzteführer Spricht." Ziel und Weg. 19: 430-437.

Walther, F. (1935). Die Euthanasie und die Heiligkeit des Lebens. Die Lebensvernichtung im Dienste der Medizin und Eugenik nach christlicher und monistischer Ethik, Kaiser, Munich.

Webster, C. (1981). Biology, Medicine, and Society: 1840-1940. Cambridge University Press, Cambridge.

Weiss, S.F. (1987). Race Hygiene and the Rational Management of National Efficiency: Wilhelm Schallmayer and the Origins of German Eugenics, 1890-1920. University of California Press, Berkeley.

Wilson, J.B. (1975). Death by Decision: The Medical, Moral, and Legal Dilemmas of Euthanasia, Philadelphia.

Zahn, Gordon. (1969). German Catholics and Hitler's Wars: A Study in Social Control, E.P. Dutton & Co., Inc., New York.

GERMAN VIEWS OF THE HOLOCAUST AS REFLECTED IN MEMOIRS

Julie D. Freeman

State University of New York at Buffalo, Department of History, Faculty of Social Sciences, Park Hall, Buffalo, New York, USA, 14260.

The issue this paper addresses is that of German public opinion toward the Holocaust. The question of German public opinion in the Third Reich as a whole has recently gained interest for historians.(1) Except for a few instances, the German people seldom expressed their opinion openly under the Nazi dictatorship. This is, of course, natural to any terrorist state. But silence under such conditions cannot be taken as aquiesence or dissent and we need to know what Germans thought and how they felt about the policies and actions of the regime which governed them, especially with respect to the crimes committed in their name.

Because of a lack of direct information on public opinion, data must be gleaned from other sources. Historians have been assiduous in exploiting official and unofficial sources.(2) A largely untapped source however is memoir literature. This source has its limitations. Memoir literature has to be used cautiously because of the flaws inherent in it: faulty memories, a tendency of the author to overstate his or her importance or centrality to events, the author's tendency to minimize faults while magnifying virtues, our inability to check the accuracy of authors who are not public figures, and so on. Keeping this in mind, memoir literature is still a useful source of information on the thoughts and reactions of ordinary people. At least they supply direct testimony rather than the perceptions of others.

This paper uses memoir literature in conjunction with secondary sources to explore German public opinion on Nazi anti-Semitic actions, and also to attempt briefly to determine how much the German public knew of the "Final Solution" in the East. As a preliminary report, this paper does not cover all memoir literature, and, overall, memoirs taken together would not be representative enough to allow for fully ironclad conclusions, or even generalizations. Used with the secondary sources however, the memoirs can perhaps test their conclusions.

Memoir literature is by nature ecclectic. To guide us through it we may draw on various theories of human behavoir. One that seems directly applicable to the issue of German responses to the Holocaust is the "bystander theory".

The response of the German people to the persecution of the Jews was limited to three possiblities, or combinations of them. A minority aided, sustained, and protected Jews, at great personal risk. Another minority were involved in the exploitation and persecution of Jews, especially if they were active members of the Nazi movement, particularly the SS. The vast majority of Germans however, and those to be examined principally here, fell between these two extremes. They were what social psychologists call 'bystanders', and they reacted with apathy to the plight of the Jews. Why?

There exists an articulated theory on the "bystander" phenomenon, which I have used in this paper. Applying this theory to a whole country may be somewhat risky because most psychological studies investigating the phenomenon deal with individuals and small groups, not entire nations. But, assuming that basic human motivation is an underlying constant factor irrespective of the size of the group being studied, the bystander theory seems particularly appropriate to the theme of this paper.

According to the theory a bystander must pass through three stages before he decides to intervene in an emergency. The bystander must first notice that something out of the ordinary is occuring. Next he must interpret the situation as an emergency requiring intervention. Finally, the bystander must decide that he has a personal responsibility to act. Studies have determined that people in large groups are less likely to intervene than lone individuals because personal responsibility is diffused throughout the entire group. Bystanders are more likely to act if the victim is personally known to them.(3)

We can apply this theory to the situation on the Third Reich only by including the additional factor of fear. There can be no doubt that the actions of people during the Hitler regime were conditioned by fear of the brutality of the Nazis. Despite this, the bystander theory might help to explain the lack of intervention on the part of the German people.

People could not have failed to notice that something out of the ordinary was happening to the Jews of Germany. Nazi anti-Semitic propaganda, "legal actions", and violent acts against Jews were not kept secret. But, recognizing the situation of the Jews as an emergency requiring intervention might have eluded many people, even including some Jews. In that case, accepting personal responsibility for the Jews would have been impossible for the bystanders.

Since most Jews lived in, or migrated to, large cities during the Third Reich, they were then poorly situated geographically to recieve the assistance of bystanders. In large cities, bystanders are less likely to be alone when they witness a scene of harassment or persecution. Bystanders would not have come to the aid of their Jewish neighbors because personal responsibility would have been greatly diffused.

A final factor in applying the bystander theory to the situation in Nazi Germany is the size of the Jewish population. Because it was so small, less than one per cent of the total German population, most Gentiles did not personally know any Jews. Again, this decreased the likelihood of bystanders intervening in a crisis.

Other factors need to be considered in explaining the apathy of the German people to the plight of the Jews. One of these is propaganda. Recent studies related to the success of Nazi propaganda, in many different areas, all indicate its failure to influence and manipulate Germans. Propaganda can confuse and blind people to the truth, but it cannot radically alter the fundemental moral convictions of individuals.(4) The terror/indimidation system was much more effective in altering behavoir. These two observations are supported again in the area of German public opinion toward the persecution of the Jews: propaganda was much less decisive than terror. Seventeen year old Hiltgunt Zassenhaus recorded her inpression of a speech given by Hitler at a rally by writing: "The loudness of his voice can silence you but it cannot convince."(5)

Nazi anti-Semitic propaganda dealt in generalizations, stereotypes, and abstractions about the Jews. But,there was in actuality, no such thing as "the Jews". Jewish Germans were largely integrated into the non-Jewish communities in which they lived as neighbors, friends, local businessmen, and so on. Some did not even consider themselves Jewish.(6) It was one thing to listen to propaganda about the "evil Jews", the "World Jewish Conspiracy", "Jewish Bolshevism" and so on, but it was quite another thing to apply this to the old woman who lived next door, or the family doctor, or local shopkeeper. This phenomenon is described well by Melita Maschmann in her memoir:

> Rosel Cohen was a Jewish classmate of ours, but I did not really connect her with the 'The Jews'. Those Jews were and remained something mysteriously menacing and

> anonymous. They were not the sum of all Jewish indivduals who included yourself (the Jewish friend for whom the book was supposedly written) or old Herr Lewy: they were an evil power, something with the attributes of a spook. One could not see it, but it was there, an active force for evil. (7)

The success, or acceptance, of anti-Semitic propaganda in the Third Reich was strongly related to the relationship between Jews and Gentiles before 1933. This can be regarded as a constant factor. Naturally this factor would have varied from area to area. Ian Kershaw's study of Bavaria and Francis Henry's study of a small town in southern Germany, which she calls "Sonderburg", indicate the variance of pre-existing relationships between Jews and Gentiles during the Third Reich.(8)

Francis Henry's study of her home town of "Sonderburg" presents a picture of tolerence and harmony between Jews and Gentiles. Although she describes the Jews of "Sonderburg" as 'accomodated' rather than 'assimilated', relationships were good,without hostility or tension. Schoolchildren formed close relationships since there were not enough Jewish children to form segregated groups. Close relationships also formed between neighbors. Friends shared in each other's religiousholidays. In short, there was extensive contact there but, a weak undercurrent of anti-Semitismitic attidudes existed.

This harmony did not exist in all parts of Germany however. Ian Kershaw's study shows that in many areas of Bavaria for example, anti-Semitic violence and hostility was traditional The desecration of Jewish burial grounds, physical violence toward individual Jews and Jewish property, and even the occasional burning of a synagogue had been common in Bavaria in the ninteenth century. This type of anti-Semitism was more akin to Nazi anti-Semitism than the social anti-Semitism of "Sonderburg". But, there was still a major difference. Nineteenth century Bavarian anti-Semitism had been directed against individuals whom one actually knew and had contact with. This was not necessary with Nazi anti-Semitism .(10) Also in contrast with Nazi anti-Semitism, any violence against the Jews was likely to be openly condemned by public officials and opinion leaders, especially as the century wore on.

If the pre-existing relations between Jews and Gentiles in a general sense is a constant factor, then so is individual relationships. Did existing friendships with Jews condition the response of individual Germans to Nazi anti-Semitic measures?

One of the first "legal" actions taken against the Jews by the Nazis was the boycott of 1 April 1933. When critisms of the new regime began to appear in the foreign press, the Nazis claimed that it had been initiated by the Jews, who wished to discredit the Nazis. The boycott was said to be in response to this.(11) It was actually a measure designed to satisfy the SA's desire for violent revolution following the seizure of power. The SA had implemented its own independent anti-Jewish campaign in March involving boycotts and personal attacks on Jews.(12) These acts threatened the appearance of legality which Hitler was attempting to create.

The effect of the boycott according to the memoir sources, indicated that it was an embarrassment to the Nazis. The public's response showed a lack of support and a lack of awareness of the new status of the Jews in the Third Reich. While some Germans were intimidated by the SA thugs blocking the entrances of Jewish businesses, most simply ignored them.(13) There were even some outward signs of sympathy shown towards Jews.(14) Ingeborg Hecht, a "half-breed, second class" in Nazi terminology, meaning a child of a Jewish/Gentile marriage, noted that many shoppers were willing to "run the Brownshirts' gauntlet...".(15) Many regarded the whole thing as an intrusion on their daily lives. Hecht believed that the idea of a national boycott was too new and too sudden to be taken seriously by many Germans.(16)

The boycott was successful in one respect however, and that was in identifying the Jews in each community. It began the process of isolating the Jews from the rest of Germany. This isolation, combined with the apathy and psychological denial of the later years of the regime, sealed the fate of Germany's Jews. But, from 1933 to 1935, relationships could and very often did continue as they had previously with only minor pressure and intimidation. Propaganda abounded but, as indicated above, this did not radically alter the attitudes, values, and habits of non-Nazi Germans. It was with the implementation of the Nuremberg Laws in 1935 that this began to change. The prohibitions against the Jews increased simultaneously with increased pressure, through intimidation, on Gentiles to break off their relationships with Jews. As fear increased, many Germans abandoned former Jewish aquaintances. The Jews interviewed by Francis Henry told her that the most common response among Gentiles was refusing to acknowledge former Jewish friends on the street.(17) The growth of public humiliation, threats of retribution, and physical violence, began to cause the disintegration of friendships.

Martha Dodd, daughter of the American Ambassador to Germany, wrote:

> I have seen the doors of German homes closed to them. I have seen them all wince with pain at social snubs, not to mention more fundemental restrictions upon their personal lives and property.... Some former so-called Christian friends through fear avoid their Jewish friends, cross the street rather than speak or chat with them....(18)

In certain ways the German people reacted favourably to the Nuremberg Laws. The laws brought a measure of state control and some sense of legal order to the volitile and violent situation of the Jews, which made most Germans uncomfortable. Everyone now knew where they stood, what was legal and what was not. Many hoped that the spontaneous violence and harassment would now end. This had actually been the intention of the regime. With the upcoming Olymic Games (1936), and the need to stabilize the new regime, the Nazis needed a period of calm and order.(19)

The general response to the Nuremberg Laws, according to Ian Kershaw, was indifference. Germans might not have liked the race laws on principle, but they were preferable to the lawless violence which they found so distasteful. Also in 1935 the Nazis launched a second anti-Jewish boycott. Like the first boycott of 1 April 1933, this was also a failure. These actions were attempts by the regime to simultaneously squeeze the Jews economically while breaking the ties between Jews and Gentiles.

The boycotts failed largely because the Jews did not live in an economic vacuum and many non-Jews were indirectly threatened by the boycotts. "Aryan" employees did not want to lose their jobs if their Jewish employers went out of business. Tourist areas were afraid of the economic repercussions of the persecution of the Jews.(20) But, the German response must be qualified. While the boycotts caused hostility towards the regime, they did not necessarily cause sympathy for the Jews; a distinction which needs to be considered.(21)

The trade boycott of 1936-1937 had similar results. This action was meant to break the business and agricultural relations between Jews and Gentiles. This boycott also failed. Economic self-interest proved to be a stronger factor than the Nazis had considered. This was also true of rural relations where peasants and Jews continued interacting as before.(22)

Although direct, specific anti-Jewish measures, such as the boycotts, generally met with indifference, the effect of the constant bombardment of propaganda,(23) and several years of intimidation and fear began to take its toll. By 1937 many German Jews had been forced out of business and Jews began migrating to the larger cities seeking anonymity and a chance to continue earning a living, or emigrating out of Germany all together.(24)As life became more difficult for the Jews, many people helped to support their friends and neighbors, providing food, safeguarding possessions, helping them to emigrate, and so on. But the effect of the increased terror and intimidation must have caused many Germans to weigh the risk of their actions. The Nuremberg Laws outlined, very specifically, the legal position of the Jews in Germany. They also brought some clarity to the relationships between Jews and Gentiles. To overstep the boundaries was to break the law. This was one factor which conditioned the response of Germans. The terror system threatened not only those who aided Jews but their friends and families as well. This was a second consideration for those helping Jews. The violent nature of the regime, revealled to all throughout the 1930's, must have caused many to want to stay out of trouble at all costs, even if that meant turning their backs of former friends and neighbors in trouble. Here fear must be added to the bystander theory to explain the lack of response of the Germans.

Informal and socially reinforced terror proved to be much more effective than legal terrorism in conditioning the actions of Germans. Hiltgunt Zassenhaus, who tried to resist the Third Reich, wrote about the atmosphere of fear and mistrust which permeated life in the Third Reich.

> We had learned to fear the ringing of the doorbell after dark. Friends had disappeared; picked up by the Gestapo in the middle of the night. They had not returned, but we had seen the letters from the Gestapo - form letters informing the families that death had ensued due to "sudden illness".
> We knew better - many knew. (25)

Zassenhaus believed that by targeting specific groups for persection, Hitler "apparently sensed human behavoir patterns and exploited them. He counted on the apathy of the individual who would react only if he himself were endangered."(26)

Heinrich Böhl, an adolescent during the Nazi era, similarly noted the effect of the fear.

> The nonsymbolic purges were visible and audible, were tangible: Social Democrats disappeared...as did politicans of the Catholic Party and, needless to say, Communists...; expressions such as "protective custody" and "shot while trying to escape" became familiar. Paralysis spread, an atmosphere of fear prevailed.... (27)

Fear and lack of trust isolated people from each other. It isolated the persecuted from the non-persecuted. It isolated Jewish Germans from Gentile Germans. In this state of isolation, it would have been difficult, or impossible for bystanders to be fully aware of the crisis facing the Jews. They might have been aware that something unusual was happening to the Jews, but, as the statement by Bohl above indicates, others were being persected as well.

<u>Kristallnacht</u>, November 9/10, 1938, is seen by historians as a turning point in Jewish-Gentile relations. It was an unprecedented event in Nazi Germany. During that night two hundred synagogues were burned, seventy-five hundred businesses were destroyed, ninety-one Jews were killed, and twenty-six thousand Jews were arrested. Many of these were sent to concentration camps; most were subsequently released .(28) The overt violence and the destruction of property shocked the German public. The event should have made people more aware of the seriosness of the Jewish situation.

Paul Hagan, pseudonym of a member of the Socialist underground organization "New Beginnings", wrote of <u>Kristallnacht</u>: "Great numbers of the workers, the middle class, and professional people of Germany, even some Nazis, were deeply ashamed by this cowardly demonstration against a defenseless minority." (29) He also noted that many incidents of "active solidarity with the persecuted Jews have been reported."(30) Ruth Andreas-Friedric was a member of an underground, anti-Nazi group based in Berlin called <u>Onkel Emil</u>. Andreas-Friedric was riding to work on the bus on the morning of November 10 and she observed the other passengers. She noted:"Everyone's expression seems somehow to be asking forgiveness."(31) Friedrich Reck-Malleczewen believed that through <u>Kristallnacht</u>, Hitler was bringing "misery and immeasurable shame" to Germany. (32)

Germans were ashamed of <u>Kristallnacht</u>. Many saw it as too similar to a barbaric Russian pogrom, unfitting the German people. The destruction of private property was abhorent to many Germans. The destruction of synagogues offended religious sensibilites. The blatant disregard for law and order shocked others. A few rejected anti-Semitism on ideological and philosophical grounds.(33)

In his memoirs, Horst Krüger noted the very strong memories he had of Kristallnacht. He remembered streets littered with broken glass and storm-troopers standing amid the destruction. "We walked past in embarassment and silence....Thoughtful faces at home, silent indignation: Does the Führer know about this?"(34)

Andreas-Friedric noted that everybody felt guilty and ashamed, and blamed the actions on others. But, she wondered, if no one admitted to participation, who did destroy the synagogues? "Then who is X, the great unknown?"(35) Zassenhaus wrote:"I could not tell what they thought or felt, but I heard no open protest."(36)

All of these observations by witnesses record feelings of shame, embarassment, and indignation. None of these feelings equal the recognition of a crisis requiring intervention. They certainly do not equal a sense of personal responsibility, the third condition of the bystander theory. Also, it might be possible to recognize a crisis but supress the knowledge through denial. For example, twenty year old Melita Maschmann, living in Berlin at the time, saw the destruction the following morning. She realized that something "terrible" had happened. "But almost at once I switched over to accepting what had happened as over and done with and avoided critical reflection." (37)

Was this reaction of remaining aloof, or denying responsibility, unique to this young woman, or was it shared by other bystanders? Furthermore, Maschmann admits that this became her standard reaction to events in the Third Reich: "...I forced the memory of it (Kristallnacht) out of my consciousness as quickly as possible. As the years went by I grew better and better at switching off quickly in this manner on similar occasions."(38)

Kristallnacht was the first really critical test of the German public with regard to Nazi anti-Semitic violence. Jews were suddenly in need of immediate help and protection. Andreas-Friedric's apartment became a haven for many of her Jewish friends, and also strangers, in the days following Kristallnacht. Hundreds of others also took in Jews in Berlin.(39) It is likely that the anonymity of the big city lessened the risk people felt in helping Jews. In small towns and rural areas Jews, and those who would help them, were much more visible and, therefore, the risk was greater. These people who aided Jews felt a personal responsibility to intervene on behalf of those in trouble. The memoirs do not really explain the motivation of these people in the terms of the bystander theory. Those who acted do not really tell you why they did what they did.(40)

Kershaw concluded that Catholics were more likely to help Jews than Protestants. Of course, Bavaria is a region where Catholics predominated. Traditional Catholic values could not be eroded by propaganda. But, this conclusion cannot be drawn too far. Catholics were more opposed to the regime in general and their reaction to anti-Jewish action was an extension of this. Neither Church took an official stance on Kristallnacht and, except for a few individual clergymen, most said and did nothing.(41)

The economic restrictions of the Nuremberg Laws, and the loss of property following Kristallnacht, caused increasing impoverishment for Germany's Jews. Emigration increased rapidly after 1938. By 1938 one hundred and forty-nine thousand of Germany's original five hundred thousand Jews (1933) had emigrated. For those who could not, or would not, leave, life became an increasingly difficult struggle for survival. H.K. Smith, an American correspondent in Germany, thought that it would have been hard for outsiders to appreciate the fear Jews lived with during these years. "They live on the terror of expectancy which is always more horrible than actual persecution itself."(42)

During these years Jews were dependant on non-Jews for food, clothing, information, what money they could still make, and protection when crises arose. Evidence exists that people ceased to be bystanders. Francis Henry's father was sent to Dachau during Kristallnacht. She and her mother moved in with neighbors for protection, and a local washerwoman left food for them everyday.A Gentile relative lent the family money to have the father released. (43) The shopkeepers of "Sonderburg" still sold food to the Jews, often after hours, despite the "Jews not wanted here" signs in their windows. They also allowed Gentile customers to buy extra food that the shopkeepers knew was actually for Jews.(44) The civil servants of"Sonderburg" often assisted Jews through the emigration process, telling them how to get around rules and regulations,who to bribe and with how much, and so on.(45)

As commendable as all this was, one must remember that by 1939 there were only twelve Jews left in "Sonderburg", two of whom were Henry's grandparents. Why were these people willing to help these elderly Jews despite the risk involved in a small town where privacy is customarily rare? One answer might be that while there is generally less risk in the anonymity of the big cities, what happened in small towns depended on the nature of the town's Nazis. In "Sonderburg" no one was harassed by the local Nazis for helping the Jews, although people certainly acted discretely.

Throughout December 1938 and January 1939 many Jews caught in the roundups following Kristallnacht began to return to their homes. They told people of their cruel treatment, inhumane living conditions, torture, and death. On 16 January 1939 Andreas-Friedric wrote in her journal, "Gradually they're all coming back - the ones from Buchenwald and the ones from Sachsenhausen, with shaven skulls and eyes overfull of suffering."(46) Onkel Emil now became involved in helping Jews to leave Germany. There could be no more denial of the crisis. Because of the restrictive baggage allowance Jews had to leave most of their possessions behind. Members of Onkel Emil took trips on which they brought out Jewish possessions to the exiles. They also checked in on the relatives whom the emigrees had left behind. "The great plague has infected us all - victims and the lucky ones alike." Andreas-Friedric wrote.(47)

On 1 September 1941 the Yellow Star Decree was issued requiring all remaining Jews to wear a yellow Star of David on their clothing. It made the Jews instantly identifiable and was a prelude to the final solution in the East. Historian Marlis Steinert, using SD reports, concluded that the German response to the decree was largely positive.(48) But H.K. Smith, the journalist, reported that "the new campaign was a flop from the day of its birth."(49) The German public knew that the inpoverished, mostly elderly Jews remaining in Germany were not responsible for the disappearance of food, or the failure of the Russian campaign, as Goebbels had said they were. Out of a sense of shame, non-Jews bowed their heads to Jews wearing the star. Some called it the "yellow badge of honour".(50) Even some party members opposed the decree. One told Smith that he thought it was cowardly. Anonymous leaflets circulated calling tha decree an act of treason against the German people.(51) Andreas-Friedric wrote:

> Thank God the greater part of the people are not pleased with the new decree. Almost everyone is as much ashamed as we....The yellow star makes segregation easier. It lights the way into the darkness - the darkness called the ghetto. (52)

Yet there was no outspoken opposition against the decree despite these indications of sympathy for the Jews. Like the reaction to Kristallnacht, sympathy for the Jews did not mean willingness to act.

Following the Yellow Star Decree, the final roundup of the Jews of Germany began. Nowhere (excepting one recorded instance - see below) did the process meet with interference or any disturbances from the German people. In "Sonderburg" the final roundup took place on 25 July 1942. The night before, SS men visited the homes of the remaining Jews and ordered them to assemble the following morning in front of the synagogue. All were sent to Theresianstadt where they all died. When asked by Henry how they felt about the roundup, those who remembered it said that it saddened them to watch the truck take away their Jews, but what could they have done to stop it, they asked.(53) Granted, interference with the SS in their duty would have been an exceptionally dangerous thing to do. Here we see how fear must be considered when applying the bystander theory to the situation in Nazi Germany.

In Berlin, many Jews grasped their final opportunity for survival and went underground. In a city as large as Berlin, this was possible, but only for the very strong as life on the run was a nightmarishly precarious existence. To survive, these Jews were dependant on non-Jews for their survival.(54) One by one the Jewish friends of Andreas-Friedric were seized and deported. She was one of the few who questioned where they were sent." 'To Jewish concentration camps in Poland', some say. 'To certain death', say others."(55) On 19 June 1942 Andreas-Friedric wrote in her journal: "Stone by stone, fragment by fragment, they're crumbling away, being washed off the solid bank and out into the raging torrent."(56) This indicates her clear awareness of the Jewish crisis.

H.K.Smith believed that the roundups "stank even in the dullest nostrils of their own people."(57) Those who were left to be seized were mostly old people, "raw from much suffering and able to feel, with double sensitivity, each blow."(58) The German public also did not like the way in which these Jews were taken, usually at night, with very little warning. But dislike did not necessarily lead to interaction except in the following case which is a good illustration of personal responsibility.

On Sunday, 7 March 1943 the single example of an active demonstration against the deportation of Jews occured. On February 27 the final roundup of the Jews of Berlin began. Many of the men seized were "privileged Jews", Jewish men with Gentile wives. After the roundup these protected Jews were seperated from the others and sent to a holding center on the Rossenstrasse. Expecting their release, the mens' wives waited outside the building and were soon joined by sympathizers until a mob of thousands stood in the street. The women began chanting "We want our men", and they could not be scattered.(59)

Andreas-Friedric witnessed this unusual demonstration. "Six thousand women called for their husbands, screamed for their husbands, howled for their husbands, and stood like a wall, hour after hour, night after day."(60) After several days of this, the men were finally set free to be "incorporated into the national community."(61)

This extrodinary event only accentuates the fact that all over Germany the Jews disappeared quietly with no intervention from most of the German people. Why was the German public so apathetic to the deportation of the Jews? Ian Kershaw believes that the burden of war caused their concern for themselves to outweigh their concern for the Jews. Moral principles weakened under the strain of food shortages, air raids, and so on, and people did not worry about what was happening to the Jews.(62) Marlis Steinert however, believes that people did worry about the Jews. The deportation relieved them of this worry.(63) And, as stated above, most Germans had no actual contact with the small number of Jews in Germany, especially if they lived outside of the major cities where the Jews were concentrated. For these people the "Final Solution", like the "Jewish Question" in general, was an abstract concept.(64)

For those Germans who did know Jews, contact with friends and neighbors would have been lost if most of the Jews had emigrated, as was the case in "Sonderburg". The migration to large cities, or the retreat into anonymity also broke the contact between Jews and non-Jews. This would indicate that the loss of personal contact is the important element.A bystander is more likely to act if the victim is personally known to them, as in the case of the wives of the "privileged Jews" of Berlin.

How much did the German people know of the genocide that was taking place in the East? Many, if not most Germans today claim that they knew nothing, or that they heard rumours which they did not believe.(65) Raul Hilberg points out that many measures were taken to ensure the secrecy of the Holocaust. All camp personal were sworn to secrecy. Visitors to the camps were carefully controlled. And, the whole operation was covered up by "verbal camoflage".(66) These attempts to cover up their actions implies that the regime was not confident about possible responses of the German public. The negative response to Kristallnacht, expressed by the German people, indicated that violent treatment of the Jews would have to be hidden from them. For this reason, the fate of the Jews was handed over to the SS who decided that the Jews should be taken out of Germany to be murdered.(67)

Despite the attempt at concealment, the SS could not prevent information from leaking out. Auschwitz, for example, was also an industrial complex resulting in "a constant stream of incoming and outgoing corporate officials, engineers, construction men, and other temporary personnel, all excellent carriers of gossip to the farthest corners of the Reich."(68) The soldiers who participated in the mass shootings knew, and sometimes took pictures. They brought information home to their families when on leave. Rumours began to spread.(69) Arvid Freborg was a Swedish journalist in Berlin from 1941 to 1943. In his memoirs (written in 1944), he wrote about the slaughter in the East, estimating that two million Jews had been executed at mass graves they had dug themselves. He wrote of "special trains" and gas chambers.(70) Edward Schulte, a German industrialist, had friends in high military and diplomatic circles. He was one of the first Germans to try to get information about the Holocaust to the outside world.(71)

Reck-Malleczewen was told by a friend who had witnessed the execution of thirty thousand Jews in a single day. When the bullets ran out, flamethrowers were used.(72) Andreas-Friedric also knew about the mass execution and the gas chambers. "The horror is so inconcievable that imagination rebels at grasping it as reality.... Is it cowardice that makes us think so, ostrich behavoir, a shunning of responsibility?"(73)

It might be suggested that many people knew generally that something terrible was happening in the East, but did not know details. Whatever knowledge the German people had, there is no way to measure what they believed. Bombarded for years by propaganda, people might have stopped believeing in rumours. Isolated from each other by intimidation, people probably were afraid to speak to each other. They were not likely to discuss the tales they heard with others. An interesting example of this is the number of memoir writers who listened to the BBC. It seems that many people did this, but no one admitted. They did not know how many shared this crime.

When all is considered, it must be concluded that the Jews of Europe were murdered against the will of the German people. Anti-Semitism existed in Germany prior to the Third Reich, as it did in most of Europe. But Nazi anti-Semitism was something unique. The absurd racial theories of the Nazis were believed by only a small number of fanatics. Nazi propaganda failed to convince the German people that the Jews were the cause of German's problems. It would never have convinced them that the Jews of Europe should be brutally exterminated. But, the long-term effect of the bombardment of propaganda, the terror and intimidation, and the effects of war caused people to withdraw into themselves, thus eliminating virtually all possibility of active opposition and concerted demonstrations against the treatment of the Jews. So, most Germans did nothing to help the Jews, no matter what their opinion was. A suprisingly large number of memoirs fail to even mention the Jews.

The small number who aided and protected Jews did so out of a sense of responsibility to their fellow Germans and out of a deep hostility to the regime in general. Their actions took a great deal of courage because of the risk involved. As Zassenhaus put it: "They were marching without guns or boots, and their only weapon was the deed done in secret. All odds were against them." (74) This is a degree of courage which we would like to think we possess, but the reality of life in a terror regime is something most of us have not lived with. So we cannot condemn those who failed to act. The few Germans who helped Jews were not morally different from the rest. Except for the minority of fanatics, Germans believed that what happened to the Jews was wrong. But, only a few had the opportunity, the freedom, the skill, and the courage to do something about it.

This preliminary study hopefully shows the usefullness of memoir literature for discovering the motives of the German people during the Third Reich. We need to analize the circumstances that some memoirs take for granted. Why did some act and not others? What conditioned their responses? What was their opinion on the anti-Semitic policies and actions of the Nazis? The bystander theory is a useful aid in answering these questions. The theory is perhaps too simplistic to apply it to the situation in Nazi Germany, and modfications are necessary. Factoring in the effect of fear is a crucial modification. Historians need to systematically exploit memoir sources. They contain information about life in Nazi Germany which can add to our understanding of the very complicated problem of the Holocaust.

NOTES

1. See for example, W.S. Allen, "The German Popular Response to Kristallnacht: Value Hierarchies versus Propaganda" in Lyman H. Legters (ed.), Western Society After the Holocaust (Bolder, Colorado: 1983): Sarah Gordon, Hitler, Germans and the "Jewish Question"(Princeton: 1984); Ian Kershaw, Popular Opinion and Political Dissent in the Third Reich (Oxford: 1983) and "The Persecution of the Jews and the German Public in the Third Reich", Publications of the Leo Baeck Yearbook, XXVI (London: 1981): and Marlis Steinert, Hitler's War and the Germans: Public Mood and Attitude During the Second World War (Athens, Ohio: 1977).
2. For example, Steinert used official government and police reports, see Heinz Boberach (comp.), Meldunden aus dem Reich: Auswahl aus den Geheimen Lagerberichten des Sicherhiestdeinstes der SS, 1939-1944 (Neuweid: 1965); Kershaw used, among other sources, Deutshland Berichtes der Sopade.
3. Bibb Latane and John M. Darley, The Unresponsive Bystander: Why doesn't he help? (New York: 1970).
4. Allen. "German Popular Response", 77.
5. Hiltgunt Zassenhaus, Walls: Resisting the Third Reich - One Woman's Story (Boston:1974), 12.
6. See, for example, John S. Conway, "Letters of the Brandt-Meyer Family from Berlin in Livia Rothkirchen (ed.) Yad Vashem Studies, XI (Jerusalem: 1976).
7. Melita Maschmann, Account Rendered: A Dossier on My Former Self (London: 1964), 40.
8. Kershaw. Popular Opinion; and Francis Henry, Victims and Neighbors: A Small Town in Nazi Grmany Remembered (Massachusettes: 1984).
9. Henry. Victims and Neighbors, 53-59.
10. Kershaw. Popular Opinion, 228-230.
11. Helmut Krausnick and Martin Broszat, Anatomy of the SS State (London: 1982), 40; and Lawrence D. Stokes, "The German People and the Destruction of the European Jews", Central European History, 6, (1973), 172.
12. Karl A. Schleunes, The Twisted Road to Auschwitz: Nazi Policy Toward the Jews, 1933-1939 (London: 1970), 71-73.
13. Schleunes. The Twisted Road to Auschwitz, 88-89; and Stokes, "The German People", 173; and Krausnick and Broszat. Anatomy of the SS State, 42-43.
14. Schleunes. The Twisted Road to Auschwitz, 88-89.
15. Ingeborg Hecht, Invisible Walls: A German Family under the Nuremberg Laws (New York and London: 1985), 13-14. For another memoir by a so-called half-breed see, Ilse Koehn, Mischling, Second Degree: My Childhood in Nazi Germany (London: 1978).

16. Hecht. Invisible Walls, 18.
17. Henry. Victims and Neighbors, 95-95.
18. Martha Dodd, Through Embassy Eyes (New York: 1939), 308.
19. Kershaw. Popular Opinion, 239-240.
20. Kershaw. "Persecution of the Jews", 266-267; and Schleunes. The Twisted Road to Auschwitz, 80-86.
21. Kershaw. Popular Opinion, 235.
22. Ibid., 240-243.
23. Allen concluded that while propaganda cannot alter fundemental moral convictions, it can confuse and blind people to the truth. In the long term, this must have affected Germans' attitudes about their society, causing withdrawal and isolation from others.
24. Kershaw. Popular Opinion, 245-246; and Kershaw, "Persecution of the Jews", 268.
25. Zassenhaus. Walls, 22.
26. Ibid.
27. Heinrich Böhl, What's To Become of the Boy? or: Something to do With Books (New York: 1985), 12-13.
28. Gordon. Hitler, 123-124.
29. Paul Hagan, Will Germany Crack? A Factual Report on Germany from Within (New York: 1942), 220.
30. Ibid.
31. Ruth Andreas Friedric, Berlin Underground, 1939-1945 (London: 1948), 25.
32. Friedrich Percyval Reck-Malleczewen, Diary of a Man in Dispair (New York: 1970), 70.
33. Allen. "German Popular Response", 72-75.
34. Horst Krüger. A Crack in the Wall: Growing Up under Hitler (New York: 1982), 35-36.
35. Andreas-Friedric. Berlin Underground, 25.
36. Zassenhaus. Walls, 23.
37. Maschmann. Account Rendered, 56.
38. Ibid.
39. Andreas-Friedric. Berlin Underground, 28-30.
40. Kershaw. "Persecution of the Jews", 227.
41. Kershaw, Popular Opinion, 251-255. Kershaw believes that there are several reasons for the Churches' silence. Fear and intimidation was more acute for the clergy because of their exposed position. Adegree of latent anti-Semitism among their parishoners was recognized by the parish clergy who followed general attitudes rather than molding them. And, finally, the Churches regarded Kristallnacht as a political issue, not a religious one, and they did not get involved in political issues.
42. Howard K. Smith, Last Train from Berlin (New York: 1942), 186-187.
43. Henry. Victims and Neighbors, 3.
44. Ibid., 97.
45. Ibid., 76-77.
46. Andreas-Friedric. Berlin Underground, 37.
47. Ibid., 41.
48 Steinert. Hitler's War, 134-135.
49. Smith. Last Train, 195.
50. Ibid., 196.
51. Ibid.
52. Andreas-Friedric. Berlin Underground, 65.
53. Henry. Victims and Neighbors, 119-121.
54. See, Leonard Gross, The Last Jews in Berlin (New York: 1982).
55. Andreas-Friedric. Berlin Underground, 65.
56. Ibid., 71.
57. Smith. Last Train, 187.
58. Ibid., 188.
59. Gross. Last Jews, 71-72.
60. Andreas-Friedric. Berlin Underground, 82.
61. Ibid., 83.
62. Kershaw. "Persecution of the Jews", 281.
63. Steinert. Hitler's War, 136.
64. Steinert. Hitler's War, 136; Kershaw. Popular Opinion, 226 and "Persecution of the Jews", 266.

65. For an interesting collection of responses to questions about the Holocaust see, Walter Kemposki, Haben Sie davon Gewusst? Deutsche Antworten (Hamburg: 1979).
66. Raul Hilburg, The Destruction of the European Jews (New York: 1961), 619-622.
67. Allen. "German Popular Response", 79.
68. Hilburg. Destruction of the European Jews, 623.
69. Steinert. Hitler's War, 140-141.
73. Arvid Fredborg. Behind the Steel Wall: A Swedish Journalist in Berlin, 1941-1943 (New York: 1944), 233-234.
71. See Walter Laquer and Richard Breitman, Breaking the Silence (New York: 1986).
72. Reck-Malleczewen. Man in Dispair, 166.
73. Andreas-Friedric. Berlin Underground, 102.
74. Zassenhaus. Walls, 129.

GERMAN CHRISTIAN NATIONALISM: ITS CONTRIBUTION TO THE HOLOCAUST

Arlie J. Hoover

Department of History, Abilene Christian University, ACU Station, Abilene, Texas 79699, USA

"How could such a thing happen in a modern, civilized nation like Germany?"

One frequently hears this question when searching for an explanation of the Holocaust. But then someone usually responds: "We mustn't blame the entire nation. The Germans as a whole weren't responsible." Edmund Burke is often cited as an authority: "I do not know the method of drawing up an indictment against a whole people."

This observation contains both a truth and a falsehood. For example, if we had a town where there was an excess of crime we would say call in the police and clean it up. But even after we cleaned up the crime we would still have some nagging questions. Why were the crimnals so numerous in that town? And more puzzling, why did they have so free a hand?

It is the same with Germany and the Holocaust. After the crime of attempted genocide was stopped, we were still wrestling with the question, why was anti-Semitism so strong in Germany and why did it have so free a hand? The answer comes in several pieces but I suggest that one piece is the special brand of religious nationalism that had been developing since the early nineteenth century, and I suggest, further, that German Protestant pastors, especially those of World War I, made a significant contribution to that nationalism. This paper will explore the contribution of German Christian nationalism to the Holocaust.

The primary sources for this study are patriotic sermons, what the Germans call Kriegspredigten or "war sermons." Most were delivered in the First World War (1914-18), but a few come from the War of Liberation (1813-15) and the Franco-Prussian War (1870-71). Clerics saw the hand of God in German national history as the fatherland defeated Napoleon I and Napoleon III and unified the Germans into the great Reich of Bismarck. But they viewed the Great War as the most decisive struggle of all German history.

The phrase "German Christian nationalism" may sound like an oxymoron, since Christianity is supposed to be universal. The German clergy stoutly insisted that there was no contradiction between Christian universalism and German nationalism, because nationalism was a legitimate sense of identity held by a legitimate group, the nation or Volk. What is a nation? The safest definition one could give would be "a subdivision of the human race," but our churchmen would hasten to add one qualification: a nation is a divinely-ordained subdivision of the human race.

A nation is not an accident of nature, a fortuitous result of soil, climate, genetics, and history. God may use such secondary causes to mold a nation but the primary cause of all ethnicity is the Almighty himself, who uses nations to accomplish his purpose in history. Christian patriots love St. Paul's statement in Acts 17:26: "He made from one every nation of men to live on all the face of the earth, having determined allotted periods and the boundaries of their habitation, that they might seek God" (Hoover, 59).

Man is a social being. Individualism, especially atomistic individualism, is a great error because man does not live alone in this world. Man has a will to love, a drive to personal relationships; he must always be reaching forth beyond himself. This drive, however, stops with the nation; it does not extend to "the human race"--a concept that German nationalists considered a mischievous abstraction. Just as Aristotle warned us to beware of "watery friendships," German churchmen warned against such nebulous ideas as internationalism, cosmopolitanism, or "good Europeanism." To be a good fruit, reasoned Harnack, you must be a good specific fruit, like a good pear or apple. "A culture without a national character is bland, watery, and insipid" (Harnach, 318). Otto Dibelius agreed: "Everything great, everything truly holy and noble is native, growing up from the ground of a sound nationality" (Dibelius, 6). In another sermon he warned:

> Whoever fights for his nationality and offers everything for his nationality fulfills God's command. . . . Anyone who tries to further international culture at the expense of the nation is guilty of high treason against mankind; there stands against him the curse of the God who is not mocked. Whoever wants to be a Christian must esteem his nation higher than all else in the world (Pressel, 6).

Friedrich Rittelmeyer explained to his parishioners that, "When one gets an inkling of the splendor of German spiritual gifts, he will feel a deep pleasure in being a German and will believe that it must be a joy for God to see himself mirrored in the German soul" (Rittelmeyer, 1915:17). Elsewhere he said, "If I could have had the choice of time and place in which to be born, I would have chosen no other nation but Germany. . . . Indeed, every individual among us has been personally entrusted with a German soul" (Rittelmeyer, 1916:24).

This concept of nationality owes much to the romantic movement, the intellectual climate that prevailed in Europe when German nationalism was born in the early nineteenth century. One could say that romanticism was a birthmark of German nationalism. National diversity is a good instance, we are told, of the "principle of plentitude," an idea that was given popular expression by Johann Gottfried Herder (1744-1803), sometimes called the father of German nationalism. Variety is the spice of the creation. Each nation represents, as it were, a plant of unique growth in the great garden of God's universe, where each Volk pursues its course according to its innate instincts and character. The same notion was championed during the War of Liberation by the dean of all German patriotic preachers, Frederick Schleiermacher (1768-1834). "Each nation," he claimed, "was designed to illustrate a special aspect of the image of God, in its own peculiar setting and by its own specially determined position in the world" (Schleiermacher, 228).

Perhaps the best statement of this romantic-Christian nationalism came from the pen of theologian, Paul Althaus (1888-1966), who wrote in 1937:

> The belief that God has created me includes also my nation. Whatever I am and have, God has given me out of the wellspring of my nation: the inheritance of blood, the corporeality, the soul, the spirit. God has determined my life from its outermost to its innermost elements through my nation, through its blood, through its history, but especially through its spiritual style, which especially endows and stamps me in the language. This womb of my being is God's method, his order, by which to create me and endow me. . . . He created this special style of a nation and therefore for us it is holy (Althaus, 3-5).

History has a stern justice about it. This nationalism sounds harmless at first but after a while thinkers begin to discover disquieting corollaries to it and press them into action. For example, if a nation is a unique divine creation, it follows logically that each Volk will have not only a Volkstum, a national essence, but also a Volksgeist, a national spirit or soul. Now this national mind will be as unique as the nation itself and thus we are driven to the conclusion that each nation will have a special perspective on nearly all questions. This style of nationalism will eventually lead to a volkish epistemology, to an ethnic relativism in all knowledge, all disciplines. Truth will cease to be absolute and will become a matter of perspective, with the national perspective being the most crucial. Even "eternal" truths, like those of mathematics and science, will become colored by the volkish viewpoint. Universal reason or the general mind will become, like the human race, mischievous abstractions.

But if the notion of humanity is an abstraction, then the notion of universal law is also an abstraction. There is no common conscience, no general norm for good and evil, no Tao. One is driven to agree with Nietzsche, that there are no moral facts, only a moral interpretation of the facts. Morality becomes merely a volkish prejudice, an ethnic perspective. When you reach this point, it becomes much easier for you to commit genocide with a clear conscience.

We may conclude, therefore, that a radical volkish nationalism could easily produce a relativism in ethics that would prepare a nation for an event as terrible as the Endlösung.

In the Great War certain thinkers began to press this relativism as a necessary implication of Christian nationalism. In a passage praising nationality, Walter Lehmann went so far as to say that we cannot have an objective picture of Jesus Christ, since each of the four gospels--Matthew, Mark, Luke, and John--was written from a special ethnic perspective and, on top of that, each German viewed this four-fold picture from his unique ethnic perspective. Thus, concluded Lehmann, "an absolutely valid picture of Christ is absolutely impossible." Each nation will have its own unique perspective on Christ and hence it makes a great deal of sense to speak of deutsche Frömmigkeit--German piety or German religion (Lehmann, 1917:5-6).

Dr. Hans von Schubert, a high church official and professor of theology at the University of Heidelberg, wrote a book in 1916 called The Education of our Nation to a World Nation, in which he affirmed the existence of a "German Christianity" in Europe, a unique version of the gospel that had become just as legitimate as Greek or Roman Christianity. Christianity, he argued, is not a cold, simple, mathematical formula that passes from generation to generation without alteration, but a living thing that takes on the traits of the people who believe and practice it. We speak of the "Hellenizing" of Christianity in the East and the "Romanizing" of Christianity in the West and we are now compelled by the history of Europe since Luther to speak of the "Germanizing" of Christianity in the North (Schubert, 21-27).

It is not surprising to hear Protestant churchmen affirm that God had been preparing Germany since the Reformation for her role in world history. Bruno Doehring was typical of those pastors who emphasized Luther and the German Bible as the indispensable key to German history and German nationality:

> I must confess, I cannot imagine our German nation without its Bible! What I mean is this: we should have passed out of existence long ago if God had not given us the gift of the Bible through the German, Martin Luther! What the south European Renaissance with its humanism was not able to do was accomplished by the faith of a German and his Bible! . . . Luther and his Bible made our German nation possible; they molded the German form of nobility and nurtured the powers with which we have defied half the world (Doehring, 1916:181).

The idea of Germany as God's select nation seemed confirmed by the events of 1914. When the Great War broke out, German clergymen were astounded at the world-historical Reichstag meeting of August 4, 1914. They pronounced it one of the greatest "revelation-hours" of all German history. On that day the Riechstag approved by a unanimous vote an initial war credit of five million marks for the war effort. In an earlier caucus the delegates of the SPD, the largest party and the one expected to oppose war credits, voted 96 to 14 in favor of them. Later, in the final vote, all 110 Socialist deputies voted for credits. Without a single dissenting deputy, the Reichstag stood united behind the government of the Kaiser. The "house divided against it" now seemed united. William II gloated: "I recognize no more parties, I recognize only Germans!" (Hoover, 50).

Protestant clergymen also gloated. They saw August 4 as the clearest gesture of divine favor. God had again destroyed the provincial spirit in time of Germany's greatest need, just as he had done in 1813 and 1870. Germans could once again boast of their solidarity: ein Volk, ein Reich, ein Kaiser, ein Gott. Afolf Deissmann called it a "spiritual mobilization" and confessed that he had lived in Germany several decades and had never seen a Rogation Day like that one in August, 1914. What was before only an idealistic dream was now achieved through a miracle: "A nation united down to the last man, assembled because its holiest possessions are threatened. A world-historical transformation: emperor and people exchange vows and clasp hands" (Deissmann, 1915:120).

The events of August were so unusual that many German pastors declared it to be the coming of the Holy Spirit on the German people, just like the first Pentacost that witnessed the very beginning of the Christian Church (Acts 2:1-4). In a sermon on Pentacost, 1915, Gustav Freybe of Hanover described the "mobilization Pentacost" in words that paralleled almost exactly the passage in the second chapter of Acts:

> When the day of mobilization had fully come, there were Germans all together in unity--villagers and city dwellers, conservatives and freethinkers, Social Democrats and Alsatians, Welfs and Poles, Protestants and Catholics. Then suddenly there occurred a rushing from heaven. Like a powerful wind it swept away all party strife and fraternal bickering. . . . The apostles of the Reich

> stood together united on the fourth of August, and the Kaiser gave this unanimity the most appropriate expression: "I see no more parties, I see only Germans!" (Pressel, 17-18)

Chaplain Fritz Philippi go so carried away with this theme that he became a universalist! "Have we not recovered a common sanctuary for all our parties? No, for all Germans! Do we not have a home again in which we can pray to the same God? Catholic, Protestant, and Jew? Yes, even more, Christians and freethinkers can feel the same Holy Spirit for the fatherland" (Philippi, 54).

Nietzsche once quipped that bad music and bad arguments all seem to sound good in wartime. One could add bad theology to that list, bad sermons, bad exegesis. For many churchmen, God's Holy Spirit had become merely a German Volksgeist, as one can see from this ecstatic sermon by Walter Lehmann:

> The God of the Germans has come to life! This God is perhaps not entirely orthodox Christian. He belongs to no particular confession, he swears to no special dogma, and he does not always hold to the Second Article. He is rather an inwardly spiritual, undogmatic, interconfessional piety. Catholics and Protestants, Liberals and Orthodox stand together. In the German religion everything dogmatic and confessional becomes of secondary importance while the most valuable things in Christianity remain. To recognize and describe these things in all their depth is not easy. The most valuable features of Christianity have been strongly and firmly united with the unique character of the German nationality. Especially noteworthy is the belief in a moral world order and the victory of truth, purity, and right (Lehmann, 1914:106,113).

We see here one of the most dangerous aspects of German Christian nationalism, the idea that God reveals himself in national history. This immanental notion would make August 4, 1914, equal in revelatory value to the Exodus or the Resurrection. Churchmen were deeply convinced that God had disclosed himself in great moments of German history, like 1517, 1813, 1870, and especially 1914. August Showalter, military pastor for the province of Antwerp, claimed that "whoever has not experienced God in the history of his nation will not experience him in the church or in the creed" (Showalter, i-ii).

It was not just the Holy Spirit but spirit in general--Geist--that filled the war sermons of 1914-18. Germany would win World War I with Geist, not with material or numbers, which were against her. According to the odds makers of the world, Germany could not last long in 1914, outnumbered as she was four to one and caught between the British navy and the Russian steamroller. But the odds makers all through history have been materialists, realists, and pragmatists, like the British, petty men who calculate the percentages and play the averages. They never reckon with the spirit, or the will, or faith, or the unseen factors in a struggle. They calculate by the slogan of Napoleon who said that "God is on the side of the strongest battalions." They reason like Stalin who asked of the pope, "How many divisions does he have?"

But then, against the odds, Germany began to win victories in August and September, 1914. The fortresses of Belgium gradually yielded to German arms; the Schlieffen Plan pressed to within a few miles of Paris; the Russians scattered at Tannenberg. German soldiers pressing forward singing "A might fortress in our God" seemed irresistible. Chaplain Reetz boasted, "Nations are not numbers and God is not bound by the laws of mathematics" (Hoover, 123). In a sermon on the power of faith, Dibelius made this point well:

> According to mathematical necessity Germany should have been crushed in 1914 by superior power--and she is still alive! By mathematical necessity our munitions should have been exhausted by the beginning of 1915 for the lack of raw materials--and we are still shooting! By mathematical necessity we all should have starved in the summer of 1915--and we are still eating and drinking! There is a reality that evades sober calculation, and the strongest part of this reality is the power of faith (Pressel, 275).

The favorite Biblical illustration for the power of Geist was the case of David and Goliath (1 Sam.17). Here a small Jewish shepherd boy, with God on his side, killed the heavily-armed giant of the Philistines with a small stone fired from a humble weapon, the slingshot. Many preachers compared David to Germany and Goliath to England, a clear case of faith versus mass. They also likened the slingshot to the submarine, the "secret weapon" of the fatherland, whereby 20 men could send 2000 men to their death. With this instrument Germany would bring the British giant crashing down to his well-deserved destruction. Truly, as John Knox said, "One plus God is a majority!" Or, as the old German proverb has it: viel Feind, viel Ehr--

"many enemies, much honor" (Hoover, 122).

The magnitude of events in 1914 convinced most clergymen that their fatherland stood on the threshold of its greatest kairos. They felt that German history was reaching an extraordinary culmination, an Omega Point, to which it had been travelling for many centuries. Germany was not going to perish in the this war; this strong belief turned them to David's statement in Psalm 118:17, "I shall not die, but I shall live and recount the deeds of the Lord." Dozens of war sermons used this psalm as a text. Luther had called it his very own; he not only recited it many times but also wrote it on the wall of his room during the Augsburg Reichstag (1630). Preachers applied it to Germany, the nation that would not die but would live to tell the deeds of God in her history. Many times in the history of Germany it seemed as if God had abandoned the fatherland; there were dark times when destruction seemed certain from Romans, Huns, Magyars, Turks, Swedes, Spanish, Frenchmen, and now Englishmen and Russians. But God had always given Germany the inner strength to resist these enemies. Typical were the words of Dr. Paul Kirmss:

> We may become frightened, but the history of our nation steps before us and consoles us: "You will not die, but live; you will not perish, but be preserved." Only have courage, you land of the Teutons! Only have courage, you sons and daughters of Germany! Endure! Stand fast! The God of old still lives, the God who has so many times brought storms to our country. He is with you. He will not forsake you. Only do not forsake him. You will not die, but live (Kirmss, 5).

One notable condition that heightened this sense of historical destiny in the Great War was the cluster of major anniversaries that coincided with the conflict, e.g. (1) 1913, the centennial of the War of Liberation and the victory over Napoleonic France, (2) 1915, the 500-year anniversary of the arrival of the Hohenzollerns, (3) 1915, the centennial of Bismarck's birth, and (4) 1917, the 400-year anniversary of the Lutheran Reformation. With so many anniversaries of so many wonderful events falling so close together it was easy to flow with the feeling that the war was a culmination of German history. The period 1914-18 seemed to be a giant ganglion of historical threads. Perhaps the most ecstatic expression of this culmination belief came from the pulpit of Franz Rhode of Kalrsruhe, whose Kingdom of God was almost identical to the geopolitical abstraction, Mitteleuropa:

> Now it must come! The great dual empire [Germany and Austria-Hungary] that will be washed by the blue tide of the Adriatic and the North Sea, a central kingdome, undivided, German forever, a bulwark of peace, crouched in peaceful stubbornness like a lion against the tide of the national chaos in the east [Russia] and the restless neighbor in the west [France] and the envious sea-ruling shopheeper on his isle of security [Britain]. Now it must come--the empire that the most noble among the people have been anticipating for a long time. It must come, the completion of the meaning of German history. The old Red Beard [Frederick Barbarossa] climbs again out of the Kyffhäuser and beholds the flight of the ravens around the German hearth and his eyes are gleaming because his people in the north and in the south have drawn the sword in a fellowship of arms for the Holy German Empire of the German nation (Rhode, 19).

Many pastors quoted the familiar words of Schiller in expressing the importance of the Great War: "Every nation has its day in history, but the day of the Germans will be the harvest of the entire world." The British held the conviction that Germany was in a period of temporary insanity, but the truth was that Germany was reaching her harvest, the culmination of her history. She was facing the greatest crisis of her national life, a struggle that would install her as the leading nation of Europe.

If one believes that his Volk was brought into being by God, then he will feel that all its national institutions are divinely ordained and holy. Germans felt this way about the dynasty of the Hohenzollerns, whose 500-year anniversary they celebrated in the second year of the Great War. This celebration gave many preachers the chance to expatiate on the providential care of the ruling family. God had chosen and directed Germany and the Hohenzollerns just as surely as he had chosen Abraham and guided the destinies of Israel. The sudden victory over France in 1870 was interpreted by the clerics of that generation as certain proof that God had put his stamp on the dynasty. During World War I William II was eulogized as the most fortunate of the dynasty for being Kaiser at the culmination of German history. The general motif of such sermons went like this:

In the year 1415, when the Hohenzollerns began their rule in Berlin, no one would have dreamed that the dynasty would someday dominate most of central Europe. The German cause had just five years before received a mortal blow from the Poles at the Battle of Tannenberg (1410). God nevertheless called the Hohenzollerns from south to north Germany, just as he once summoned Abraham from Ur to Canaan, without telling him the purpose of his migration (Gen.12: 1-3). It took a lot of faith for the chosen family to pick up everything and move into the Mark Brandenburg, a land so sandy and infertile that it was called "the sand box of the Holy Roman Empire."

Under God's guidance, this special family produced a line of remarkable rulers, twenty in all, including nine kings and three emperors, most of whom displayed the godly, Prussian-German virtues of frugality, gravity, responsibility, and devotion to duty. The family produced Frederick the Great, who penned a treatise called Anti-Machiavelli, extolling the philosophy that the prince is the "first servant of the state," a ruler who must look first of all, not to himself, but to the welfare of his people. The family produced serious, religious men like the Great Elector, whose last words were, "Come, Lord Jesus, I am ready."

In the plan of God, the Hohenzollerns adopted the Protestant faith and helped to spread it over most of northern Europe. They defeated both Napoleon I and Napoleon III, leaders of that godless nation, France, thus stemming the spread of a rotten culture. They united most of the Germans into the great Bismarckian Reich of 1871. And now, in the fullness of time, as it were, in 1914, Germany is the leading nation of Europe militarily, economically, culturally, religiously, and intellectually, poised to take its place as la grande nation. Truly, the mills of the gods grind slowly but they grind exceeding fine (Hoover, 43,55). In one such sermon Johann Kessler summed up:

> We believe in a world calling for our nation. A nation that God has equipped with such gifts of the spirit and such depths of mind, that he called to be a bearer of the gospel in the days of the Reformation, that he chose in the War of Liberation to be a harbinger of the new era, a nation to which God has given a Luther and a Lessing, a Goethe and a Schiller, a Kant and a Bismarck--this nation cannot be cast aside. God has great things in store for such a nation. Such a nation could defy a world of enemies and still triumph (Kessler, 83).

Defending the Kaiser and extolling the Hohenzollern dynasty gave many pastors an excellent chance to expound on the virtues of monarchism and the evils of republicanism. Albert Lorenz testified that the war had opened his eyes on this topic: "I believe that the war has shown us what a republic is--example France. What a sham monarchy is--example England and Italy. What a capricious autocracy is--example Russia. We give thanks to God in heaven that he has given us the strong and righteous government of the Hohenzollerns" (Lorenz, 10).

Most German churchmen labored under the assumption that German civilization, as God had developed it through history, was all of one piece. It was unitary, almost like an animal species. Hohenzollerns, Protestantism, kaisers, monarchy, militarism--it was all meant to hang together, to be a unique mosaic of features defining the peculiar German nation with its unique Volkstum or national essence. To remove the Kaiser or the principle of monarchy from the gestalt would be as shameful as removing the Torah from Judaism. What God had joined together by historical development man should not put asunder.

Perhaps the most startling aspect of German clerical nationalism was the clergy's unabashed defense of Prussian-German militarism. One would think that disciples of the Christ who said "Blessed are the peacemakers" would find little to extol in militarism. German churchmen, however, said that foreigners could not possibly understand German militarism because it was a national peculiarity. The English, protested Deissmann, cannot even get the words right when discussing the topic, because they translated allgemeine Wehrpflicht as "compulsory service" (which should be rendered Zwangdienst) instead of "general military duty." By this linguistic trick they distorted the voluntary aspect of German military service and perpetuated the myth that Germans had to be rounded up by the police and driven like cattle to the front (Deissmann, 1915:18-20).

Many clergymen insisted that there was a genuine connection between militarism and the moral strength of Germany. Military training develops discipline, obedience, frugality, loyalty, self-control, love, and comradeship. The soldier and the monk and the saint all have many key virtues in common. As one pastor explained, "The German nation has surpassed every nation in the world in extolling the command of duty in its national education, in its professional work, in its civic spirit, and in its great poets and philosophers. . . . Our children become great in the consciousness that each person has his duty to fulfill" (Hoover, 91).

If God had developed this special German Volk to be a tool in implementing his will, how did it come about that Germany was in such a precarious situation in 1914, with most of the great powers of Europe against her? German pastors were stunned by the attack of the Entente Powers (most of them probably did not know that Germany attacked first), but they had a ready answer: God's chosen vessels often excite jealousy in evil people. To be chosen of God does not mean that a nation is exempt from hardship. Like Jesus, Germany could say, "They hated me without a cause."

The truth was that foolish diplomacy had gotten Germany into the dangerous military-diplomatic situation of August, 1914, but the truth is injurious to the national ego so German leaders had to search for a scapegoat. Who was most responsible for the fatherland's precarious condition? England! The clergy followed their Kaiser and their leaders in laying all the blame at the feet of Britain, Albion, who was proving to be "perfidious" indeed. Scarcely a dark chapter of British history was left unmentioned as the German churchmen called the roll of Albion's perfidy: the oppression of the American colonists, the taking of slaves from Africa, the subjugation of India, the seizure of South American trade during the Napoleonic period, the Opium Wars against China, the crushing of the Boers in South Africa, the massacre of natives under Kitchener in the Sudan, and so on. But the crowning blow came when Germanic, Protestant England went to war against her racial and religious brother--Germany!

Pastors were appalled at the anti-German propaganda coming out of Britain, lies about Germany and her policies, falsehoods about German domestic life, atrocity stories about her soldiers in Belgium. They referred to the "international lie press," the "lie bureau," the "lie machine," and the "lie factory." They insisted that this moral flaw had been concealed from them in the past, before the infallible searchlight of war revealed it.

Pastors accused Britain of betrayal and compared her to Judas Iscariot, the man who delivered the innocent Son of God to his enemies (John 13:30). Britain betrayed Christianity, especially Protestant Christianity, by attacking Germany in concert with Roman Catholic France and Orthodox Russia. She betrayed the white race by bringing in all kinds of colored soldiers from her colonies to throw into the trenches of the western front. She betrayed European culture or western civilization by attacking Germany in alliance with Asiatic Russia and Japan. Ministers of the gospel are sometimes uncertain about the will of God but Tolzien was dogmatic about the will of God in this matter:

> Can it be the will of God that Russian barbarism, Mongolian heathenism, and English crimnality will destroy beautiful Europe? . . . It cannot be the will of God that the heathen peoples of Asia should get a foothold in Europe, the ancient, holy, mother soil of the Christian religion! It cannot be the will of God that this our German nation--the most efficient and most thorough, the most loyal and the most honorable of all nations--should be crushed. No, that cannot be the will of God! (Tolzien, V,30).

Harnack felt keenly the future threat of Russia to European civilization. In a speech to a group of Americans he told his audience that the common German-American culture rested on respect for the individual personality, an entity unknown to Russian history. In Russia, on the contrary, you have the "culture of the herd" or the "culture of the heap," ruled patriarchically, massed and held together like a pile of sand by a strange, incoherent Byzantine-Mongolian-Muscovite framework. Great Britain was trying to break the dam that protected western Europe from the desert sands of the Asiatic Unkultur (non-culture) of Russia. Germans, therefore, must take up the cry of the Kaiser: "People of Europe, protect your most holy possessions!" Ironically, noted Harnack, Germans are fighting for Great Britain, though she is ignorant of this great truth. If Germany should fall, he concluded, "the day that Great Britain broke the dam will never be forgotten in world history" (Harnack, 287, 295).

For the purpose of understanding the Holocaust, however, the most important aspect of the clerical attack on Britain was the charge of materialism and commercialism. In 1915, Werner Sombart, distinguished German economist and authority on modern capitalism, wrote a withering indictment of England called Händler und Helden, which translates roughly as "shopkeepers and heroes" or, to render the sense of the book, "peddlers and heroes." Sombart argued that the British were a nation of sordid, petty shopkeepers while the Germans were a nation of deep, spiritual heroes. The Englishman was incredibly narrow, he claimed, totally incapable of rising above the superficial reality of the cash nexus worshipped by his commercial civilization. A glance at English philosophers from Bacon to Spencer will show in a minute how superficially empirical is the English mentality. The tradesman is guilty of the reductive fallacy on a grand scale: he reduces everything to a series of monetary transactions--life, art, religion, science, war. The entire British Empire is a giant trading enterprise and its wars are merely wars of pecuniary calculation. But the Germans will never be conquered by this damning taint of commercialism and their special Geist will stamp it from the world (Pressel, 150; Hammer, 124).

The Protestant clergy took up Sombart's theme of England as the land of the Krämergeist, the petty, shopkeeper's mentality. They echoed the view of the Kaiser, who said that the war was a Kulturkampf, a struggle between civilizations or worldviews, the German versus the Anglo-Saxon. It was a conflict between mammon and nobility. These two cultures, said Doehring, must fight to the death--no diplomatic settlement could terminate such a war. If the British should win, "then gold, power, and brutality" would become the ruling principles of the world and the entire globe would become "a loathsome department store" in which men would be merely machines and the powerful would rule the weak (Doehring, 1919:140,144).

But what exactly was this petty, ignoble spirit? It comes out in a number of small ways. For example, the Englishman shows his innate selfishness and individualism by capitalizing the personal pronoun, while the German spells ich with small letters. The Englishman demonstrates his incredibly narrow mentality by using the slogan, "My country, right or wrong!" Yet he also illustrates his personal cupidity with the saying, "My fatherland is wherever it goes well with me." The Germans say, "We will fight to the last drop of blood," but the English say, "We will fight to the last penny." All through his history the Englishman has supplied the pennies but he usually finds someone else to do his actual fighting for him, like the French or the Russians or the colonials. He is essentially a spineless coward, not a brave knight, and the crowning proof of his cowardice is the naval blockade. He does not have the courage to fight like a man so he uses starvation. He wars against women and children. Karl König spoke for many when he formulated the fall of Britain into a German war aim:

> We cannot change English jealousy or the cold policy of England which fills their entire political character, but our determined will must be to shatter this jealousy and the means of power connected with this political egoism. . . . It will not do any good to humble France; it will help nothing to smash Russia. The evil spirit of Europe is that cold, English power politics, which is bereft of any noble feeling (König, 4).

In searching out the historical roots of this defective British mentality, German thinkers divined a crucial difference between the British and the German moral philosophies, a difference that had momentous implications in many areas. It could be reduced to a struggle between Kant and Bentham, between duty and utilitarianism.

To understand British behavior, it was argued, you must grasp the direction of British moral thinking for several centuries, which had been in the direction of what we call Utilitarianism. If you wish to go very far back, you could start the apostolic line with Pelagius (360-420), who misunderstood the doctrine of salvation by grace and thought rather too much of free will. Certainly the empirical school goes back as far as Roger and Francis Bacon and William of Occam, and then comes through Hobbes, Locke, Berkeley, Hume, Bentham, and Mill. Out of the school of empirical epistemology emerges finally the Benthamite "principle of utility," which asserts that good and evil are merely matters of pain and pleasure. All men seek to maximize pleasure and minimize pain. Pleasure is good and pain is evil, so whatever leads to pleasure is good and whatever leads to pain is evil. All moral norms, therefore, are grounded solely in human usage and physical consequences. Such thinking will lead eventually to the maxim, "the greatest happiness for the greatest number." Utilitarianism finally degenerates into a cow's morality, where simple fleshly euphoria is the summum bonum. It seems ludicrous on its face because most people will be caught at some time in their lives deliberately doing things that cause pain, e.g. a mother running into a burning house to save her child.

Utilitarianism is easy to refute if you define it simplistically, which is what the German preachers did. They had fun contrasting this patently selfish view with the (alleged) German view illustrated so beautifully by their great moralist, Immanuel Kant. Kant insisted that only confusion could result from the premise that morality must terminate in pleasant consequences, in "personal happiness." One must do his duty, regardless of the consequences; he must do what is right, though the heavens fall. If one seeks happiness directly he will end up neglecting true values in life. One does his duty, he pursues the good as apprehended by reason, and then perhaps he may find happiness, he may be "surprised by joy." But he will certainly find no true happiness if he pursues it directly.

Utilitarianism on the personal level may seem harmless, but when it becomes writ large in the style of an entire nation, said Arthur Titius, the results can be especially frightening. When an entire Volk implements this hedonism, "The goal turns out to be: if we can secure greater happiness and greater profit for England, then let us pursue a reckless, brutal, business morality (Geschäftsmoral), even if it be at the cost of faith and loyalty" (Titius, 41).

What is so interesting about this critique of British hedonism is that it sounds very similar to the Nazi critique of the Jewish mentality (Mosse, 106). It pits German Geist, depth, profundity, and nobility against the Geldmensch, against hedonism, commercialism, and materialism. It contrasts the rootless peddler with the rooted knight. When the anti-Semites of the Third Reich began to analyze the defective Jewish Volksgeist it must have sounded vaguely fimiliar to those who had already heard it in the anti-British propaganda of the Great War.

As we bring all these threads together, it should now be apparent how German Christian nationalism contributed to the advent of the Third Reich, and later, to the Holocaust. We are not saying that the pastors of World War I would all have voted for Hitler or implemented the Final Solution. We are simply saying that some key religious ideas propounded in the Great War helped create a climate of opinion that made the Third Reich possible, maybe even probable. One could develop a good case for the thesis that the first "German Christians" were not the pro-Nazi Protestants of the 30s but the religious patriots of the First World War.

It is but a short step from this romantic-religious nationalism of the war to the volkish-romantic Pangermanism of the Third Reich. All you need to do is add racism and deepen the immanental thrust of the theology until you have God revealing himself directly through national events like Hitler and the movement of National Socialism. God had already revealed himself in August 4, 1914, had he not? God made all the nations radically different and charged them to cultivate their diversity, did he not? With all these doctrines you can easily prepare a people to accept Gleichschaltung, or "coordination." People already had a firm notion of the national essence, backed up with theological sanctions; all you need to do is add blood and race to define the Volk and you are close to Nazi racism. Would anyone in the Third Reich have disagreed with Troeltsch in this statement from 1915?

> We fight not only for what we are, but also for what we will and must become. . . . Our faith is not just that we can and must defend our state and homeland but that our nationality contains an inexhaustible richness and value that are inexpressibly important for mankind, a value that the Lord and God of history has entrusted to our protection and development. The German faith is a faith in the inner moral and spiritual content of Germanness, the faith of the Germans in themselves, in their future, in their world mission. . . . This is a belief in the divine ruler and world reason that has allowed us to become a great world nation, that will not forsake us or deny us because our spirit comes from its spirit (Troeltsch, 19).

Such a view fosters a spirit of intolerance. It implies that pluralism is a sin against God, that a nation must be monolithic culturally. If a certain group does not fit with the national "style" it must be removed. German Christian theology played into the hands of the radical nationalists when it put God behind such an ethnic monism.

German Christian nationalism was at the crossroads in 1919. Defeat should have destroyed the war theology of the religious patriots but it did not. Most of them joined the unrepentant patriots in pushing the stab-in-the-back legend, which said that Germany lost the war on the home front, not the battlefield. The Christian Church could have helped to shepherd the nation through this crisis and point it in a direction that would have led to sanity, moderation, and recovery, but it did not. It was a fateful missed opportunity.

To speak candidly, by the twentieth century German nationalism had become a menace to civilization. It was born in the Napoleonic era and carried the birthmark of romanticism from then on. It matured in that strange period called the Second Reich with its sundry delusions about racism, imperialism, eugenics, and Social Darwinism. In its first century it picked up some rather unpleasant traits. By 1914 it was narrow, petty, racist, arrogant, immature, hypersensitive, paranoid, and resentful. In other words--sick. The Christian clergy gave a religious justification, a theological underpinning, to a sick nationalism.

The Holocaust opened a lot of eyes, including those of many churchmen. Let us hope that the Church has learned a valuable lesson. Christian clergymen should be careful never to give unconditional support to *any* nationalism . . . but certainly not to a sick nationalism.

REFERENCES

Althaus, Paul. Völker vor und nach Christus. Leipzig, 1937.

Deissmann, Adolf. Deutsche Schwertsegen: Kräfte der Heimat fürs reisige Heer. Stuttgart, 1915.

_____. Inneres Aufgebot: Deutsche Worte im Weltkrieg. Berlin, 1915.

Dibelius, Otto. Gottes Ruf in Deutschlands Schicksalstunde. Berlin-Lichterfelde, 1915.

Doehring, Bruno. Gott und Wir Deutsche: Gedanker zur Gegenwart. Berlin, 1916.

_____. Ihr habt nicht gewollt. Berlin, 1919.

Hammer, Karl. Deutsche Kriegstheologie, 1870-1918. Munich, 1971.

Harnack, Adolf von. Aus der Friedens- und Kriegsarbeit. Giessen, 1916.

Hoover, Arlie J. The Gospel of Nationalism: German Patriotic Preaching from Napoleon to Versailles. Stuttgart, 1986.

Kessler, Johann. Unser Glaube ist Sieg. Dresden, 1915.

Kirmss, Paul. Kriegspredigten. Berlin, 1914.

König, Karl. Neue Kriegspredigten. Jena, 1915.

Lehmann, Walter. Deutsche Frömmigkeit: Stimmen deutscher Gottesfreunde. Jena, 1917.

_____. Vom deutschen Gott: Vierzehn Predigten aus den Kriegsmonaten August, September, und Oktober. Ulm, 1914.

Lorenz, Albert. Warum blüht der Honehzollern Krone? Bonn, 1915.

Phillippi, Fritz. An der Front: Feldpredigten. Wiesbaden, 1916.

Pressel, Wilhelm. Die Kriegspredigt 1914-1918 in der evangelischen Kirche Deutschlands. Göttingen, 1967.

Rittelmeyer, Friedrich. Von der religiösen Zukunft des deutschen Geistes. Nuremberg, 1915.

_____. Deutschlands religiöser Weltberuf. Nuremberg, 1916.

Rhode, Franz. Kriegspredigten. Karlsruhe, 1914.

Schleiermacher, Friedrich. Predigten. Berlin, 1834-36.

Schubert, Hans von. Die Erziehung unseres Volkes zum Weltvolk. Berlin, 1916.

Showalter, August. Der Krieg in Predigten. Barmen, 1915.

Titius, Arthur. Unser Krieg: Ethische Betrachtungen. Tübingen, 1915.

Tolzien, Gerhard. Kriegspredigten im Dom zu Schwerin gehalten. Vol.V. Schwerin, 1914-19.

Troeltsch, Ernst. Deutsche Glaube und Deutsche Sitte in unserem grossen Krieg. Berlin, n.d.

ANTI-SEMITISM IN THE AMIABLE GUISE OF THEOLOGICAL PHILO-SEMITISM IN KARL BARTH'S ISRAEL THEOLOGY BEFORE AND AFTER AUSCHWITZ.

DR.HANS JANSEN
Patrijzenhof 136
3755 EV EEMNES
THE NETHERLANDS

I

Karl Barth is sometimes rightly called the Church Father of the twentieth century. Since the works of this Swiss dogmatist, in particular, have to this day played such a significant role in many designs of a new Israel theology in Europe, I should like to outline in the present context how Karl Barth over the years before and after Auschwitz formulated his Israel theology with ever increasing clarity. I have given my paper the title 'Anti-Semitism in the amiable guise of theological philo-Semitism in Karl Barth's Israel theology before and after Auschwitz', by which I hope to have provided an insight into the reason why, on the one hand, many members of the Jewish community experience certain statements of Christian theologians as anti-semitic while, on the other hand, these theologians themselves - sometimes deeply shocked by such reactions from Jewish circles - believe they can declare in all honesty that their Israel theology is philo-Semitic. I think that both are partly right and partly wrong. I hope to show Christians, in particular, that certain models of an Israel theology betray a dangerous ambivalence, which a not inconsiderable number of members of the Jewish community experience as a threat to their religion and its adherents.

II

In Barth's 'Der Römerbrief'('The Epistle to the Romans) of 1919(1)Israel and the Church are synonymous concepts. Barth protests against the deeply rooted theological view that the writings of the Old Testament do not belong in the canon and that Israel has nothing to do with the Church. Both advocates of the emancipation of the Jews and anti-Semites had defended this thesis: Adolf von Harnack and Friedrich Schleiermacher on the one hand and Paul de Lagarde on the other. Adolf von Harnack wrote:'Marcion's rejection of the Old Testament in the second century was rightly denounced by the the official Church of the day; the Reformation's adherence to the Old Testament in the sixteenth century was a fate from which it could not escape at the time; Protestantism's desire since the nineteenth century to maintain the Old Testament as a canonical document is the result of a religious and ecclesiastical paralysis'(2).

Israel and the Church are never in their entirety the object of God's judgment. God never rejects all. In the second edition of 'Der Römerbrief' Barth gives the following interpretation of Romans 11:4 about Elias and the 7,000 still faithful men:'The 7,000 are, however paradoxical and in conflict with the text itself this may seem, not members of a silent minority that Elias could have found here and there and recognised as still faithful. Not as 7,000 psychological individuals but as a group of 7,000 who in an overwhelming crowd invisibly step into the breach for the lonely Elias, as a mere 7,000 who in a disappearing minority invisibly step into the breach for the whole people of Israel(chosen as such, while others were rejected), as the invisible Church of Jacob amidst the Church of Esau, that is how those 7,000 just men stand before God himself, for God alone, that is to say as His people that He has not rejected'.

In 'Der Römerbrief' Barth wrote:'Christ is the Christ of Israel, of the Church. Israel has placed itself outside and next to Christ. The Church has crucified Christ'(3). The Church is Isreal and Israel is the Church: Israel 'kata pneuma'(= Israel according to the spirit) and Israel 'kata sarka'(= Israel according to the flesh) belong together, in accordance with the principal of the Reformation 'simul iustus et peccator'(= just and sinning at the same time). As there is a dialectical affinity between the two(i.e. between the 'spirit' and the 'flesh'), we may never identify Israel exclusively with the Israel 'according to the flesh' and the Church never exclusively with the Ecclesia 'according to the spirit'. In Paul's writings, the concept of 'pneuma'(= spirit) refers to God-orientated human existence, i.e. the altruistic, desinterested Church, while on the other hand the concept of 'sarka'(= flesh) refers to human existence not orientated towards God, namely the egoistic, covetous Israel. Here Barth protests against a deeply rooted theological conviction in which Israel is viewed as the egoistic and greedy woman who is not orientated towards God and the Church, in contrast, as the altruistic and desinterested woman who is orientated to God.

In the mirror of Israel, the Church sees itself: its own election and its own fall, and reversely Israel sees itself in the mirror of the Church. The Church does not exist in a way different from Israel. For throughout history the Church has also been miraculously preserved. For throughout history the Church has also a nation of strangers, and the annoyance which anti-Semites feel towards Israel is the same as that which the Church will necessarily generate in the world. In the fall of Israel the Church recognises its own fall. The Church can only be an 'Israelitic makeshift Church'. The whole history of the Church is identical to that of Israel, a history of repeated unfaithfulness, alienation, violation, and betrayel. The Church has something of Dostoyevsky's grand inquisitor, but the grand inquisitor is kissed by Christ on his bloodless, ninety-year-old lips. Dostoyevsky writes:'That was all he gave as an answer', to which Barth adds:'That there was nothing more, that this was all he gave as an answer, therein lies the hope of the Church'. And he gives the same answer to Israel, however hardened and obstinate, for the Church <u>is</u> Israel.

Barth's Epistle to the Romans, in which he made an urgent appeal to the Church to see itself in the mirror of an Israel temporarily rejected by God, was experienced as a provocation by many contemporaries, New Testament scholars and theologians alike. Adolf Jülicher and Adolf Schlatter reproached him for unjustifiably identifying the Church with Israel on the basis of Chapters 9-11 of his Epistle to the Romans, because Paul does not speake here of a temporary rejection of the Church but(indeed very clearly) of a temporary casting away of Israel(4).In the twenties the Church, fully in accordance with the tradition, did not place itself beside Israel, in its guilt and its lot. On the contrary. The Dutch theologian Miskotte, who was profoundly influenced by Barth's Israel theology, wrote in his diary, a few years after Barth had published his commentary:'Israel! In the year 70(Titus) we witnessed a judgment of God, but we forgot that Israel still has a future on earth. But who sees <u>our</u> destructions as a judgment of God? What a cataract of judgments, rejections, admonitions. Why did the Church not place itself <u>beside</u> Israel in its guilt and in its lot? Humility vis-à-vis the rejected Israel would have saved us'(5).

III

On 17 February 1933 Barth wrote an uncharacteristically long letter to the Jewish scholar Hans Joachim Schoeps, from which I quote the following:'I am interested in your discussion of the "Sinai Revelation" - it is remarkable that Barth puts "Sinai Revelation" in quotation marks - and of the works of the Jewish scholar Steinheim; I am also considerably interested in your attempt at designing a systematic theology of Judaism and, finally, in your Israelitic impetuosity. The Christian Church regards itself, as you know, as the lawful heir of the Synagogue. It considers the "Sinai Revelation" as annulled, in fact as annulled in Christ. This is the very reason why the Church will forever be bound up with her - still living as Synagogue today (according to the Church's belief: in an as such impossible way) - in a community such as would be impossible between two other religions'(6). In the same letter, Barth continues as follows:'A systematic theology of Judaism, also and particularly in our time, cannot but lead to the proof that Jesus had to be crucified', which corresponds exactly to that astounding sentence in his'Church Dogmatics':'From whom else would the world and the Church have to learn by whom, for whom and why Jesus Christ had to be crucified than from . . . the Synagogue which hears the Word of God and which in spite of this is still without belief'(7).

A month after 13 November 1933, when the macabre 'Sportpalast-Kundgebung' of 'German Christians' had taken place in Berlin - whereby Jewish Christians were cast out of the official Church - Karl Barth preached in Bonn on 10 December to students and professors on the meaning of a fragment from Paul's Epistle to the Romans(15:5-13). Barth gave particular attention to the words:'Jesus Christ was a minister of the circumcision for the truth of God'. From his sermon I wish to quote the following:'Christ belonged to the Jewish people. The blood of this people flowed in His veins as the blood of the Son of God. He adopted the nature of this people when He became man, not for the sake of this people, not because He would have had a preference for the blood of this race, but for the sake of truth, that is, to show His truthfulness and loyality. Because God had made a covenant with this people, and with this people alone - an obstinate and wicked people - with the Jews of all peoples, and had offered His presence and the promise of a unique redemption, not to reward the Jews but in order to fulfil this free, merciful promise made to the Patriarchs. This is the sole reason why Jesus was a Jew'(8).

A few years ago the New Testament scholar Lothar Steiger of the University of Heidelberg said in one of his lectures that in the situation of 1933 Barth should in the circumstances obtaining at the time have said exactly the opposite, namely that Jesus had become a Jew himself and that the blood of the Jews came under the protection of the election by God and of the truth of the Patriarchs who were also the Patriarchs of the Gentiles Christians. That is what Barth should have said in his exegesis because in 1933 the Jews were being singled out solely because of their race and blood. Instead of saying this, Barth allows himself to be misled by traditionally anti-Jewish motives as he defends the Jews in such an unclear manner that his audience could very easily hear the exact opposite of what he actually meant to say. For Barth continues as follows:'The Jew, in his so enigmatically strange and also in his so enigmatically indestructible existence amidst all other nations, is the living proof that God is free to elect whomsoever He wants. It is quite possible that the all too passionate agitations against the Jews today are tantamount to turning against the God of free grace. The Jewish people have rejected their Redeemer and crucified Him not in foolish overhaste and not because of a misunderstanding but as an exact, deliberate continuation of the way in which they always behaved vis-à-vis their God'. Like all Church fathers from the east and the west, Barth also regarded Israel's history as one long 'cronique scandaleuse'. And in the same sermon he continues:'My people, as God had so often called this people, showed itself, for a last and decisive time, as "not-My-people". This is why Jews living today stand under both judgment and grace of God'(9).

It is evident that in his polemically coloured exegesis Barth protests against the discrimination of the Jews. On the other hand, from 1933 a decisive change emerges in Barth's Israel theology. In 1982 the Prague theologian Dieter Kraft, an expert on Karl Barth's Israel theology, wrote of this radical change among other things:'In the face of the escalation of anti-Semitism, Barth's argumentation became increasingly philo-Semitic from 1933 onwards. But where he tries to provide a theological basis for philo-Semitism, this theological philo-Semitism is dominated by an objective dialectic to such an extent that it is hardly distinguishable from the cynism of anti-Semitism'(10). In other words Barth speaks of his own unbelief in the good done by the Jews in such an offensive and embarassing manner that he expresses this unbelief in mild mocekery and sometimes even sarcasm. In correspondence with one of his pupils, Friedrich-Wilhelm Marquardt, Barth himself in fact admitted this. I quote:'I am definitely not a "philo-Semite" inasmuch as in my personal contacts with Jews(also with Jewish Christians!) I have always, for as long as I can remember, had to supress something of a fully <u>irrational aversion</u> - of course I had to suppress this immediately because of all my views and managed to totally conceal it in all my statements - but it was nevertheless there. I ought to be ashamed of myself, is all I can say to this personal, somewhat allergic reaction! But the fact is that it was and is there. It is a good thing that this objectionable instinct is quite alien to my sons and to other people better than I(e.g.you). And yet: it could be that my Israel theology has to some extent been affected by this objectionable instinct too'(11). The first traces of the abovementioned shift in Barth's thinking were already discernible in his sermon of 1933, in particular where he speaks of 'the Jew' without further comment.

IV

In a lecture which Barth delivered on 5 december 1938 he formulated the 'mystery of Christ' as an inextricable link between Jesus as the Messiah of Israel and the Jewish people. He stated, among other things:'What would we be, indeed what are we, without Israel? For who rejects and persecutes the Jew rejects and persecutes Him who died for our sins. Who is a fundamental enemy of the Jews thereby shows that he is a fundamental enemy of Jesus Christ. Anti-Semitism means the rejection of God's grace'(12). The Church ought to see itself in the mirror of the temporarily rejected Synagogue in order not to be rejected itself. Anti-Semitism is objectionable because of the solidarity in sin connecting both Israel and the Synagogue. In this lecture Barth resumed the underlying argument expounded in his Epistle to the Romans. The Church is the Church because it emerged from Israel. The Elected One(the Church) knows the Rejected One(Israel) not only as a stranger vis-à-vis itself but also as an equal, a sister within and beside it. If the Church detaches itself from Israel, it places itself outside life and outside reality. And this is what happens time and again whenever the Church covers up its own failures by indicting the Jews.

It is particularly in his standard work 'Church Dogmatics', which from 1932 on appeared in numerous volumes, that Barth started giving an ever more negative view of the position of the Synagogue in Christian society, even though in particular in the first volumes of this major work - which continues to profoundly influence Israel theology in Europe today - the principal motif from his Epistle to the Romans is still clearly present.

In Church Dogmatics 1-2, which appeared in 1938(13), Barth dwelt at length on the Old Testament as the 'time of expectation' and of the New Testament as the 'time of fulfilment'. I should like to quote the following from this volume:'The Old Testament does not say as such and for itself that and how its own enigma is solved. The Old Testament does not yet as such and for itself know the truly hidden God. It does not yet know God who had become a hidden God unto Himself. And it therefore does not know the truly revealed God either. But this Old Testament is as such and for itself not a reality at all, but a "Jewish abstraction"'. And in another passage in the same volume one reads:'In that time after Christ the Synagogue was that more than tragic, sombre and anguished figure blindfolded and with a broken staff, as can be seen on the outside of Strasbourg cathedral. We must remember that also the Church, even though it carries the New Testament in its hands, can be a figure with eyes blindfolded and its staff broken. And if the Church is not, this is owing to God's grace alone. Through the secret of God's free, unmerited grace, the Church of the New Testament is inextricably linked with the people that, as witnessed by the Old Testament, is blessed with grace in so far as it awaited Jesus Christ. And it is this very secret that not only separates but also links the Church and the Synagogue(which like the obstinate sister could see but did not want to see)'.

In Church Dogmatics II-1, which appeared in 1940, Barth observed that Israel was not wholly destroyed by God's judgment, 'but some remnant always lives on'. While the 'Final Solution' to the Jewish question was unfolding in Germany, Barth evolved his teachings on the election. In Church Dogmatics II-2 he wrote at great length of the 'eternal election of Israel' which despite all Gentile arrogance remains in force. However, he speaks of this election in a very strange, ambivalent manner. He introduces a new concept into his Israel theology, viz. that of 'Gemeinde'(=community). The 'chosen community' exists as the people of Israel and at the same time as the Church of Jews and Gentiles. Israel and the Church are both figures within the chosen community. This Barth wrote in 1942, on the eve of the genocide of European Jewry. To all anti-Semites he says that 'the fundaments of the Church are at stake' if even one single Israelite were yielded to destruction and that anti-Semitism is the 'unforgivable sin' because 'whosoever believes in Jesus . . . must include them(the Jews). Otherwise he cannot include Jesus the Jew either'. The strong bond between Christians and Jews is not primarily an ethical imperative but forms part of the fundamental structure of the Church itself. The Church has a twofold link with Israel:'She lives from Israel and Israel lives in Her', which implies that 'the Church cannot have a life of its own beside and opposite Israel'.
As we can see, Barth theologises more and more philo-Semitically. This approach enables him, as Dieter Kraft wrote, 'to erect a theological dike against the Fascist and clerical-Nazist policy of extermination'(14), but he does not succeed in preserving the underlying concept of his commentary on the Epistle to the Romans, i.e. that Israel may not be exclusively identified with the mirror of God's judgment and the Church not exclusively with the mirror of God's mercy. Unfortunately, this dangerous identification clearly come to the fore in Barth's work of 1942: Israel is destined to be 'the mirror of God's judgment' and the Church has become destined to be 'the mirror of God's mercy'. Barth writes:'This one community of God has to serve as the representation of God's judgment in the shape of Israel and of God's mercy in the shape of the Church'(15). The 'special duty' which Israel is destined to fulfil within the 'chosen community' consists in having to be the mirror of God's judgment. In contrast with the Church as 'the mirror of God's mercy' Israel must, as an example to all, represent and embody human need and misery consequent upon sin: human suffering, human wasting and human death. That is why Barth writes such horrible things when he analyses the identity of the Synagogue within Christian society. Let me quote what Barth wrote of the Synagogue: The Synagogue is the 'imposing shady side of the history of Israel', the 'disobedient, idol-worshipping Israel of all times', the 'Synagogue of death', the 'hearing but despite all this hearing still unbelieving Synagogue'; the 'tragic, pitiable figure with covered eyes', it is the 'fossilized personification of the outdated Old Testament as such and in abstracto', it is the 'organization of a humanity racing towards an empty future', it is the 'image of the unbelieving', the 'phenomenon of the recalcitrant Synagogue', it is characterised by 'conceited lying', and by 'nationalistic and legalistic dreaming of the coming of the Messiah', it shows itself in a 'ghostly shape'; Barth calls its members 'wretched members of the Synagogue' and he adds that the 'Synagogue Jews do not belong to the obedient Jews'; the Synagogue is 'the Israel that has become ungenuine', it stands there before us as the 'enemy of God' and has 'as yet no part in the fulfilment of the promise it was given'; it has a 'disconsulate chronology', it lives out of a 'carnal hope' and has 'sworn a promise of carnal faith unto itself'; the Synagogue 'puts into practise Jewish rigidity, melancholy, capriciousness and fanaticism'; in short it presents a picture of a 'half venerable, half terrifying relic, an oddly conservative antiquity'. Then, in a single sentence, Bart sums up his view that God's curse lies upon the Synagogue:'Thus it punishes itself'. Barth further lists the following characteristics of the Synagogue: 'activist', 'vain' and 'illusionistic'. The 'messianic activism' of

Judas was its model. And the epithet of 'wandering' in the sense of eternal searching - the opposite of settling down - is in his view characteristic of 'Jewish conduct'(16)

In exactly the same way the Synagogue is a mirror of God's judgment. The history of Israel does not continue after the crucifixion of Jesus, and Jesus 'may be regarded as marking the conclusion of God's history with the people of Israel'. Whoever is offended by this 'half venerable, half terrifying relic, an oddly conservative antiquity' is in fact offended firstly by the Jew and secondly by God's mirror of His judgment.

The abovementioned Prague theologian Dieter Kraft wondered whether, if it is true that Israel (as Barth puts in, 'in the full extent of its history in past and future') must by way of example represent and embody human guilt and distress, human suffering and death, need we then be at all surprised that 'this Israël - in a particular sense also by way of example - meets its death once more in the gas chambers of Auschiwtz?'(17). Of course Barth did not accept this logic; but neither did he refute it. On the contrary, where, in the next volumes of his Church Dogmatics and in a radio lecture of 1950(18), he speaks extensively about anti-Semitism, he confirms, according to Dieter Kraft, the plausibility of this logic in a dangerous fashion.

V

In the third part of his Church Dogmatics(chapter 3), Barth deals extensively with 'the history of the Jews'(19). In the aforementioned radio broadcast(20) he gave a brief summary of this chapter. On the one hand he writes:'The Jewish people could and can disappear just as little as God's fathfulness can come to an end, just as little as we can cancel out what happened to that one Jew while he was on the earth. The Jews can be despised and hated and oppressed and persecuted and even assimilated, but they cannot really be touched; they cannot be exterminated; they cannot be destroyed. They are the only people that necessarily continues to exist, with the same certainty as that God is God'. On the other hand he writes:'What are the Jews?', he asks first of all. And he goes on:'People speak of the Jews as if they knew who or what is understood by this term. A nation? But what one usually understands by "nation" is in fact exactly what they are not. The Jews do not have a language of their own, for among them Hebrew has long since become a scholarly language of a handful of theologians; and the fact that in the present State of Israel it is used again, like a kind of Esperanto, merely proves that the Jews who have come together there in fact speak other, foreign languages. Since the year 70 AD the Jews have played an important part in the formation and also the destruction of all kinds of foreign cultures, but there has never been a specifically Jewish culture of any significance. Moreover, one cannot possibly speak of a religion common to the Jews. And in all earnest one may well ask whether since 70 AD there can be said to have been a common history of the Jews'. According to Barth, the 'actual history of the Jews' started in 70 AD as the 'negative side of the redeeming death of Christ, after God had granted them forty more years since the death of Jesus as a final 'period of grace'.

'Are the Jews a nation? Perhaps a nation that is not a nation? Or not a nation, and yet a nation? The Christian answer will focus on this odd contradiction: yes, they are a nation, which, incomprehesively enough, is totally different from all other nations; its special nature lies in its being so anonymous(Barth italicises 'anonymous'), so lacklustre and without any specificity of its own. But it has lost its specificity, it used to have its own specificity, raising it high above all other nations. It did not acknowledge this but cast it away. This happened when that one Jew died on the cross outside the walls of Jerusalem. This did not undo God's election. It did not remove God's grace from this people. Is it not almost palpable that, quite the contrary, it is God's mercy which has made it endure? But now not as a figure, but as only the shadow of a figure(Barth italicises 'the shadow of a figure'), now as the unwilling witness of the Son of God and the Son of Man who came from their midst'

Then he goes on to wonder where anti-Semitism actually came from. I quote:'It is self-evident that, in all its stupid and wicked forms, it is the product of human blindness. And yet, how can one explain the fact that, like the plague, it erupted time and again and could once again erupt - and worse than ever- in the middle of our enlightened age? What do people have against the Jews? It is beyond question that the Jews are no worse than all other people. But it stings us that they are like a mirror held up to us to see who or what we all are. Wherever God's grace shines, it becomes visible that man does not merit it, that he is a transgressor and a rebel. The sun that shines upon the Jews brought and brings to light the condition of us all. But what good is it to reverse the mirror or dash it? We still remain the same people as those we saw in the mirror. But this foolish reversing and dashing of the mirror is at any rate the only sensible thing in the great nonsense which is anti-Semitism'. 'One can', Barth continues, 'understand anti-Semitism only as a disease. It cannot be denied that mankind suffers from this disease and one cannot but acknowledge that this disease cannot be fought with any rational or moral argument, because it annoys us - and it does not matter whether we are aware of this - that we are shown and recognize only too clearly our own nature in them(i.e.the Jews), and in their nature'. In the Jews we can see as in a mirror held up to us all'how bad we all are'. That, according to Barth, is the fundamental and most profound reason for'the insuppressible dislike which all people, all nations feel towards the Jews'. And Barth continues:'In the eyes of all of us the Jew stands before us in order to represent what every human being basically is. In the Jew the original rebellion, the unbelief, the disobedience of every man comes to light. And this is why the Jews do not make us happy at all. On the contrary, we turn away from the Jews and make them even more wicked than they are'. But since the Jews are 'God's chosen people, they must serve as such a mirror, and as their election is the original model for the election of all peoples and all mankind this mirror can and will never be taken away and all men will have to look in it time and again so as to see what they look like themselves'.

We need to wonder whether such a definition of anti-Semitism is not in fact tantamount to driving out the devil with Beelzebub. Does this not make the Jew into the archetype of all evil? Dieter Kraft observed in this context:'If Anti-Semitism is an insuppressible dislike of man for Jewish nature, if it is a fatal illness that has infected everyone and that cannot be combated, if in the Jew the nature of the non-Jew, i.e. of man, bursts forth incessantly, compulsively and unavoidably, if this is really so, woe the Jews who have survived Auschwitz, for eventually this fatal disease will also strike them, like a plague. Quite understandly so. For is it not just and fair that man should dash the mirror in which he is forced to behold his own primeval revolt? Must man not hate the Jews when what he hates in them is what he abhors in himself? And so on. But would it were not so!'(21).

Trough such a definition of anti-Semitism, which follows logically from the way in which Barth, in his second part of 'Church Dogmatics', depicts Israel as the 'mirror of God's judgment', he has unwillingly contributed more to perpetuating than overcoming anti-Semitism. For here Judaism becomes an 'existential', spiritual archetype. Here, the Jews are neither a race nor a nation and even less a legally recognized religious community. He regards Judaism as first and foremost a spiritual orientation, a psychical state, which reveals itself in every human being but which has found in historical Judaism its highest and most tragic realisation. As people only hate those by whom they are unpleasantly reminded of themselves, non-Jews will time and again necessarily and compulsively reverse and dash the mirror. Whoever hates this spiritual archetype(the Jews) hates primarily what he recognizes in himself; the fact that he persecutes it in others is merely an attempt to liberate himself of it. He attemps to overcome this psychical state in himself by localizing it completely in the Jews, enabling him to feel free of it himself for a short or longer period. I repeat: by the presence of the Jews in our midst man is unpleasantly reminded of himself in all places and at all times, and he therefore cannot but abhor and hate them.

Finally, Dieter Kraft points out that Barth's Israel theology and his definition of anti-Semitism may have horrific consequences:'Barth's confrontation of man with the Jews(what a remarkable opposition!) inevitably always had to lead to Auschwitz'(22). In his opinion, Barth himself had also been afraid that his Israel theology could become a fertile breeding ground for anti-Semitism because he knew only too well that the history of the Church showed that the Christians usually prefered to reverse and dash Israel as the mirror of God's judgment. Where, in his later works and letters, Barth writes of the 'Jew-hostile attitude of the old, medieval and modern Church'(23), he characterises this as one of the darkest chapters of the history of the Church. The fact that in the same period Barth takes a pro-Zionist stand with increasing clarity would, according to Dieter Kraft, have sprung from the same fear. For if the past showed that the Church time and again dashed Israel as the mirror of God's judgment, what reason would we have now to expect that in the near and distant future the Church would for once leave the mirror alone? In this connection, Dieter Kraft observed:'For of course Barth cannot but fear that even after the defeat of Fascism anti-Semitism would erupt again sometime, somewhere. And woe unto the Jew who would then not live behind the protective borders of a State of Israel'(24).

VI

There is yet another way in which the Jews are like a mirror into which we have to look in order to be saved eventually. Barth wrote:'In the perdition and endurance of Jewish existence this Other looks us in the face: that one Jew on the cross in Whom there is salvation for all men. Outside Him there is no salvation for any man. This we reject. And this is also rejected by many who nevertheless do not want to be anti-Semites. This is also rejected by the Jews themselves. But they should note that this is in fact the other sense in the great nonsense which is anti-Semitism, this is the other root of anti-Semitism. He who rejects this should beware that he does not become an anti-Semite to boot, for he is well on the way to becoming one'(25). In other words, Jews and non-Jews who reject Jesus - who looks at all men in the perdition and endurance of Jewish existence - as the Messiah of Israel should beware not to become anti-Semites as well:'they are well on the way to becoming one!' And Barth continues as follows **'What is it that separates us from the Jews? Strangely enough it is the same thing** that links us with them: the Jew, the Jew on the cross on Golgotha, Whom we recognise as the fulfilment of the promise made to Israel and thus as the Saviour of the whole world. The Jews do not recognise this one Jew, although they should have been the first to do so. This is why they are so completely unwilling to be satisfied that they may live solely by God's grace, indeed to live. This is why the Jews to this day are such an arrogant people, an arrogance only too similar to that of the anti-Semites. Such is the true, lasting, terrible enigma of Jewish existence'(26).

VII

In Church Dogmatics, Vol.1V-3, Barth wrote about Jesus Christ as the content and the conclusion of Israel's history. 'The history of Israel and its prophecy can therefore have no continuation after the coming of Jesus Christ, in which it has reached its fulfilment'(27). Barth then dwells at lenght on the end of Israel. We may clarify from four angles what Barth means exactly when writing of the end of Israel. When he writes about the end of Israel and the end of Israel's history, he means Israel as a witness. Israel's status of being a witness determines its identity very precisely. Now that the trial in which Israel acted as a witness(as we can read in the Gospels) has taken place and the sentence has been passed in the form of the resurrection of Jesus, the witness has nothing new to say. In this respect, Israel has reached its end and there will never again be a new testimony of Israel. But does it not imply that the testimony given is outdated? 'How could it become oudated?' Till the end of time, when Jesus Christ shall come again, Israel will have to continue to bear witness that the end of Israel is identical with the completion of Israel in Jesus Christ. But there is a continuation of the history of Israel after Christ, although merely in 'abstract memories', 'remarkably haunting and barren', of so-called Judaism. Barth fully recognises that Judaism is a historic reality. But this Judaism is purely a reality of 'world history' of which no further testimony, no more words of truth are to be expected. However, Barth does not fully maintain this stark rejection of a testimony by Judaism. He writes:'To this day the history of the Jews was and is a history in which the Old Testament is partly updated, because this history is largely a unique tale of humiliations and disappointments, a history of suffering. This history is, as the Old Testament itself provisionally shows, an a posteriori testimony of that which was fulfilled in that one Israelite: Jesus'. In the most passive form possible, i.e. in suffering, Judaism is the witness of Jesus. A testimony without words; the words come from the Scriptures and from the Church.

This approach to the history is extremely negative. But for Barth this negative view is the reverse of very positive happenings and therefore also of a very positive evaluation. For the end of Israel is the completion of Israel in Jesus Christ. It is particularly in his Church Dogmatics that it becomes clear that Barth theologises very traditionally and classically. If'Jesus Christ is the eschatalogical execution of the Divine Will in Israel and in all mankind', Israel's mission and calling is fulfilled and consequently Israel's history had ended. The principal lines of Barth's thinking re-emerge in this volume in his observations on the relationship of Christendom 'to the Jews, to the Synagogue, to Israel'. While Jesus, by His delivery into the hands of Pilate the Roman, became the Saviour of the world, the Synagogue is still merely 'the organization of a humanity heading for an empty future'. Christendom has no calling to evangelise among the Jews. For the decisions were already taken when Israel handed over its king, thereby making Him into our king. 'What is there to evangelise? God's judgment in God's love is there to behold and to fear in ardent participation . . . What, therefore, is the use in the long run of any discussion?' The sole expectation we can and may entertain for the future of Israel is that of God's own intervention. Barth thinks of the future of Israel as a people of God, i.e. in no respect with an eye to 'later historical developments' but only from the angle of the decisions taken - those of Israel and those of God - and from the angle of the end of time when God Himself will intervene to save the Jewish people. In the meantime, there can be no discussion with and no evangelising among the Jews. In his Church Dogmatics, Barth persist in this view. Discussions with Jewish philosophers and theologians are therefore completely absent from all his works. This 'shortcoming' - all the more remarkable when we see how extensively Barth can enter into debates with contemporaries and predecessors - can be understood only within this theological frame of reference.

VIII

Many in the Church and in society have come to take it for granted that any form of anti-Semitism will have to be combated. In this combat Christians will continually have to be reminded of the words of Dutch-Jewish author Abel Herzberg, who once observed that it is the privilege of the Jews to decide what constitutes anti-Semitism. Many in the Church and in society will hopefully also come to recognise that in view of the survival of the Jewish people it is a sacred duty and one of the first goals of research at our theological faculties of the universities to unmask certain forms of theological philo-Semitism as amiable guises of anti-Semitism. Who, for instance, could deny that the notably ambivalent Israel theology of Karl Barth, may be a fertile breeding-ground for anti-Semitism?(28). Indeed, Barth himself pointed to this danger when, in his radio talk of 1950, he observed:'But this foolish reversal and dashing of the mirror is at any rate the only sensible thing in the great nonsense which is anti-Semitism', by which he himself in a certain sense legitimatised anti-Semitism.

Footnotes

1 Karl Barth, Der Römerbrief, Bern 1919, München 1922^{2}.
2 Adolf von Harnack, Marcion: Das Evangelium vom fremden Gott. Eine Monographie zur Geschichte der Grundlegung der Katholischen Kirche. Zweite, verbesserte und vermehrte Auflage, Leipzig 1924, 217.
3 Karl Barth, Der Römerbrief, 267,269.
4 Adolf Jülicher in: Ein moderner Paulus-Ausleger, in: Anfänge der dialektischen Theologie. Teil I, hrsg.von J.Moltmann, München 1962,96; Adolf Schlatter, Karl Barths Römerbrief, 144.
5 K.H.Miskotte, Uit de dagboeken 1917-1930. Verzameld werk 4, Kampen 1985, 447.
6 B.Klappert, Israel und die Kirche, 1980, 27-29.
7 Karl Barth, Kirchliche Dogmatik(=KD), II,2, par.34,3.
8 Karl Barth, Theologische Existenz heute, Heft 5, München 1933, 13,14,16.
9 Karl Barth, KD I,2, 556; KD III,3,238.
10 Dieter Kraft,'Israel in der Theologie Karl Barths' in: Communio Viatorum. A Theological Quarterly, ished by Ecumenical Institute of Comenicus Faculty, XXVII,1-2, 1984, 59-72(64).
11 Hans Jansen, Christelijke theologie na Auschwitz. Nieuwtestamentische wortels van het antisemitisme, Deel 2, Band 2, Den Haag 1985, 742.
12 Hans Jansen, Christelijke theologie na Auschwitz. Nieuwtestamentische wortels van het antisemitisme, Deel 2, Band 1, Den Haag 1985, 193.
13 Karl Barth, KD 1,2,77-111; KD II,2,215-336.
14 Dieter Kraft, Israel in der Theologie Karl Barths, l.c., 64.
15 Karl Barth, KD II,2,215,227,231.
16 Karl Barth, KD I,2,513,517; KD II,2, 271,289,377; KD IV,1, 182.
17 Dieter Kraft, Israel in der Theologie Karl Barths, l.c.67.
18 Karl Barth, KD III,3,238-256; Karl Barth, 'Die Judenfrage und ihre christliche Beantwortung. Rundfunkansprache' in: Die Juden und wir Christen, Hrsg. H.Kahlenbach, Schriftenreihe der Ev.Akademie Hessen, Heft 5, Frankfurt am Main, 1950, 9.
19 Karl Barth, KD III,3,238-256.
20 Karl Barth, Die Judenfrage und ihre christliche Beantwortung, l.c.
21 Dieter Kraft, Israel in der Theologie Karl Barths, l.c., 70.
22 Dieter Kraft, Israel in der Theologie Karl Barths, l.c., 71.
23 Karl Barth, Briefe 1961-1968, Hrsg. Jürgen Fagmeier und Hinrich Stoevesandt, Zürich 1975,40.
24 Dieter Kraft, Israel in der Theologie Karl Barths, l.c., 71.
25 Karl Barth, Die Judenfrage und ihre christliche Beantwortung, l.c.
26 Karl Barth, Die Judenfrage und ihre christliche Beantwortung, l.c.
27 Karl Barth, KD IV,1, 31,35,191; KD IV,3,76.
28 Hans Jansen, Christelijke theologie na Auschwitz. Theologische en kerkelijke wortels van het antisemitisme, Den Haag 1981, idem, Christelijke theologie na Auschwitz. Nieuwtestamentische wortels van het antisemitisme, Den Haag 1985.

"THE BEST OF THE GERMAN GENTILES:
DIETRICH BONHOEFFER AND THE
RIGHTS OF JEWS IN HITLER'S GERMANY"

JAMES PATRICK KELLEY,
Lynchburg College
Lynchburg, VA 24501-3199 U.S.A.

The complexity of recalling the Holocaust must be acknowledged.

Personal reactions color and distort memories. Eyewitnesses, especially those whø have suffered, must be respected, but in a very special way. Such respect extends also to remembrances of those who sought to prevent the Holocaust. Eberhard Bethge, for example, acknowledges that even sheltering or otherwise aiding victims and publicly resisting the Hitler regime do not exempt one from feeling the horror of these events.[1] The subtlety of so many different kinds of complicity[2] in the acts of the Hitler regime requires of all who would remember this time the most serious, self-critical contemplation. No one prevented the Holocaust. No one stands, finally, as a hero where it is remembered.

How we contemplate such testimony is also supremely important. Our remembering cannot be oriented completely toward the past.[3] Furthermore, as we remember, we must seek to face particular, concrete realities, above all addressing with new urgency what our theological traditions have said and can say now about handling political and social power. Finally, we must seek the highest accuracy and detail of which we are capable in our assessments of these matters.

Dietrich Bonhoeffer has long been acknowledged as one from the "other Germany" which at least sought to replace the Nazi regime.[4] Furthermore, he is one who acted from a continuing, conscious dialogue within the Christian tradition. Eva Fleischner has accurately called him "one of the most courageous opponents of Nazism, and a great Christian".[5] At the same time, she and others have taken him to task as the most "graphic illustration of how deeply the teaching of contempt had taken root [in Christian theology]".[6] Part of our remembering here ought to seek clarifications of both the strengths and shortcomings of this man, who was undoubtedly one of the best of the German gentiles.[7]

This paper traces briefly Bonhoeffer's view of what political action was required by Christian ethics (mainly as he expressed this in two works from the first months of the Hitler regime), indicates some strengths and shortcomings of his position, and lodges some suggestions about what one can learn about theological assessment of social and political power from Bonhoeffer's example.[8]

Bonhoeffer's "Führer" Essay

Immediately after Hitler's appointment as Reichskanzler on January 30, 1933, Bonhoeffer spoke on Berlin radio concerning the "Changes in the Concept of the Leader in the Younger Generation".

The address was presented later on February 23 in an expanded, somewhat changed version as a public lecture at the Technische Hochschule, where Bonhoeffer had been serving as Chaplain to Protestant Students since 1931, under the title "The Leader and the Individual in the Younger Generation". It was published, March 6, in a still later version given at the Hochschule für Politik, which apparently included revisions made in light of Hindenburg's

"Order...for the Protection of People and State" (February 28), exacted by Hitler from the President after the Reichstag fire the previous night. This act, to be in effect until further notice (in fact until the collapse of the Hitler regime in 1945), nullified the fundamental civil rights guaranteed by the Weimar Constitution on the basis that an emergency threatened the state's very existence. Bonhoeffer made no further revisions after the so-called "Enabling Act" of March 24 had made it completely clear that Hitler's plan was not only to sweep away all Germans' constitutional rights, but also to replace any remnant of parliamentary government, once and for all, with a new dictatorship led solely by the Reichskanzler and the Nazi Party.[9]

In this address and its subsequent revisions given in Berlin in the next weeks Bonhoeffer drew upon detailed information and insights into the Weimar Republic's recent political and legal process. This data had been supplied over the preceding two years by his family and friends, especially Gerhard Leibholz and Hans von Dohnanyi.[10] The result was a remarkably clear series of statements, immediately assessing from a theological standpoint the earliest acts leading to the Hitler state.

Those who are interested in Bonhoeffer's theological development are struck by the formative concepts first presented in this little essay and later developed in the drafts of his projected Ethik.[11]

He began by contrasting the quite different groups included in the "younger generation".[12] Detailed descriptions of each segment were added in the longer versions of the address. Those who had served in World War I retained a sense of ultimate questions and ideals, although this had been hardened and reformed—by their experience of extreme suffering and stupidity—into a deep appreciation of concrete acts of personal loyalty and courage in the face of death itself. Their younger brothers shared their cynicism about abstract ideals, but they also regarded any talk about ultimate matters as empty. For them life was pervasively problematic: "...the ultimate questions of life are answered [by them] with silence." They are preoccupied with "...dumb involvement with reality in sport, travel, work and politics [which] deters curiosity and sensation." What amounts to a "metaphysic of reality" drives them to engage all conditions as occasions for a "political activism", which seeks always to transform the world from what it is to what it ought to be. A still younger group, born after 1910, has allied their immediately older brothers' "metaphysic of reality" and political activism with a recognition of the urgent, concrete needs of those who are unemployed or otherwise hopeless, producing a kind of "political-chiliastic" outlook, shorn of the more cynical realism of their older brothers. The mass of these youngest ones dare to dream and to act boldly![13]

In contrast to their elders, however, all three younger groups stand together. They have inherited a world in which the established forms of Western civilization were nearly totally lost. In their lifetimes, realism could only seek a rescue of some of its components as supports against utter collapse. Thus three crucial clarifications motivated all of them: (1) recognition that machines had triumphed over their inventors, who were defenseless hostages of their own creations; (2) acknowledgment that previous ideologies—political, philosophical, or religious—were powerless; and (3) an overwhelming impression that "masses"—whether they be casualties, revolutionary activists, or simply unemployed—have dull power, while "the individual" is doomed to solitude and insignificance. This resulted in their passionate, unified call for "authority...association...community".[14]

Bonhoeffer proceeds next to present his own account of the changes in the concept of the leader[15] among this composite, younger generation.

Earlier generations saw teachers, statesmen, and, above all, their fathers, as models for their understanding of leadership. Such figures were not leaders apart from their position in some fixed social order. Their offices in such social structures defined and limited what they were properly able to do when they led. Their commitment to fulfilling the functions of these offices and accepting the limits they imposed on their personal choices were part and parcel of their being leaders.

Among the younger generation, however, the true leader is a supremely independent figure, able to do whatever he wishes—without limit in office or law—so long as he can carry along those followers who chose him as their leader. These followers are finally his only source of continued authority and leadership.

Here Bonhoeffer is adapting some details of a political analysis of the German situation made earlier by his brother-in-law, Gerhard Leibholz.[16] In contrast to those who see the Nazis' so-called "leader principle" as producing an exclusively downward flow of authority "from above" in a totalitarian state structure, Leibholz and Bonhoeffer held to a more paradoxical account. Formerly, leaders were free to act in a way that was not always popular and pleasant to those whom they led, so long as the impersonal, neutral responsibilites of their offices required such unpopular actions. Leibholz and Bonhoeffer assert that any political leader who fits the new definition exercises only a purely personal authority which is rooted completely in his followers' acceptance of each of his acts. Such a leader's fundamental concern must always be to maintain his personal popularity among his followers.

Bereft of any appeal to external restraints of law or office, this new leader can only govern a state in which power and authority actually flow "from below", from his personal popularity with the masses. According to this account, the new leader will always be hampered in his ability to lead when this requires some act which is not immediately perceived by the masses as in their interests. They can easily choose another leader. This new kind of leader is, therefore, not only inherently limited, as were earlier leaders. The confidence placed in him by those who have chosen to be led by him is also itself predisposed to its own frustration. Desiring a leader, the masses themselves actually have to provide in this way their own leadership.[17] Such a new totalitarian state is, finally, "populist" or "volkisch".

Bonhoeffer's specifically theological assessment of this situation follows. "The Leader is set at a tremendous distance from those...he leads, but—and this is...decisive...—...is Leader only as the one chosen by those...he leads."[18] Especially the third sub-group among the younger generation, those born after 1910 and 23 years old or younger in 1933, clearly represent this new situation. What had been even for their older brothers concrete, pragmatic questions of a purely political kind of authority, have become for this segment of the younger generation an amalgam of religious and practical factors. What was "political authority" has become "the political-messianic concept of the Leader" into which streams all the religious consciousness of the masses. The "spirit of the people"[19] becomes a "divinized, metaphysical value". And the leader, who incarnates this Volksgeist, becomes in the most definite way "the Messiah" whose appearance brings about "the fulfillment of ultimate hope".[20] Were this present outlook to be joined to the traditional "pietistic ideal of community", one could call this a new form of the recurrent quest for building a "universal kingdom of God upon the earth", expressed earlier in communities of religious "enthusiasts" and in the French Revolution, as well as in other groups. However, the German younger generation decisively rejects such an identification of what Bonhoeffer here calls its "political-messianic Leader".

Divisions among the segments of the younger generation, and also the inherent paradox of their redefinition of leadership so that a leader is not finally free to lead, combine to prevent their giving widespread support to any positive definition of power or authority. When those who reject the former leaders' limitations imposed by office and law seek to define what their new leader will stand for, deep disagreements and divisions open up.[21]

Careful definition of a conceptual structure which might suggest the realism and concretion of Christian revelation had been a pervasive concern of Bonhoeffer's previous theological study.[22] From this base he next projected a crushing critique of the new concept of the leader as "an unreal phantasy". Precisely where concretion, particularity, and respect for the relevant evidence are most required, their new leader is described by those who seek to follow him in ways that remain totally abstract and imaginary. He is, as it were, their mirage, which preoccupies their rhetoric and consciousness when they ought to be speaking realistically. In contrast to their claims

> ...the authority of the [new] Leader is utterly at...risk...every moment...in the hands of his followers....I subordinate myself to the authority of the Leader, [whereas] I stand [already] under the authority of father and teacher [examples of the old kind of limited "leadership", which was responsible to exercise an office whether it is pleasing or not]...Anyone who expects otherwise is not looking at reality, he is dreaming.[23]

In the name of realism, Bonhoeffer says, the leader must himself always remain conscious of the clear limits upon his power, constantly reminding his followers both of his limits and of their responsibility. Otherwise, he will simply become a seducer (Verführer). Those among his followers who do not feel themselves to be "mature, strong, responsible enough", especially "young men", will not be inclined to face realities. One cannot realistically expect it of them. Therefore, the "...true Leader must always...disillusion." He must "...refuse to become...the idol,...the ultimate authority of those...he leads." He must lead his followers away from an unrealistic and unstable leadership, rooted in a kind of personality cult, and help them acknowledge, however unwillingly, that the "authority of orders and offices", which limit any actual leader's freedom and at the same time set him free to do what is unpopular, is, therefore, essential to real leadership. If the leader does so, "...his service can be of incomparable value. But only so long as he keeps strictly in his place." He may accept, but only as a temporary trust, responsibility turned over to him by his followers. But he must finally lead them to see that they themselves also must bear responsibility for his leadership. This means that "...he has to lead the individual into his own maturity."[24] Anything less is unrealistic and unstable.

One special point has been obscured by the English version of this essay, which inexplicably omits the one sentence which in the manuscripts contained an underscored (in fact twice-underscored!) term. In a new way it addresses directly those in the German civil administration. After his remarks calling upon the leader to provide genuine leadership, not false seduction, for his followers, Bonhoeffer notes:

> However, even here humanity is not yet seen as it actually is. If it can be that the individual has rights over against an office, then the office is not a final authority. Where can the individual become conscious of rights over against the office? Only where he sees that the office is a penultimate authority over against a final authority of which one cannot speak, the authority of God.[25]

Here the danger that the vaunted German civil administration itself may be corrupted by the new regime is specifically addressed in terms similar to the general question of the national political leadership.

The fact that Bonhoeffer speaks on a clearly theological basis of these political details is underscored in his conclusion.

> The fearful danger of the present time is that above the cry for authority, be it of the Leader or of an office, we forget that man stands alone before the ultimate authority and that anyone who lays violent hands on man here is infringing eternal laws and taking upon himself superhuman authority which will eventually crush him....Leaders or offices which set themselves up as gods mock God and the individual who stands alone before him, and must perish. Only the Leader who himself serves the penultimate and the ultimate authority can find faithfulness.[26]

Here in the name of Christian faith is a clear protest against the extremism of pseudo-religious political ideologies and the entitlements to violence against those perceived as opponents to which such extremist outlooks lead. Bonhoeffer set it forth publicly and unequivocally in the first days of the Hitler administration.

In the various forms of this essay Bonhoeffer is addressing the Nazi Party and its new Chancellor Hitler, as well as those others who must choose now either to support or to oppose this new leadership. These latter include both the mass of German people and the then critically-important group who serve in the civil administration. He seeks to lay out for them a picture of the confusing events of the day with a clarity for which he was indebted to those in his family and close circle of friends who had been trained in law and civil administration, especially Leibholz. He appeals to his German audience to face reality and not be led by their impulses to remain aloof, holding to illusory hopes or entrusting to others their own responsibilities in the confusing, sometimes desperate political and economic situation they faced. The basis of his appeal is always theological—all must avoid the forms of idolatry which sustain both false religious and unrealistic political views. In contrast, he calls upon those who will hear what he has to say to remain in touch with reality, because God himself, in the Christian view, remains indissolubly in touch with reality.

Against some others' views,[27] his Christological norm was clearly intended to bestow only a relative authority upon the state or its leaders. But the concept he used at this point for the state and other social institutions in their theological reality, "orders of preservation" ("Erhaltungsordnungen"), was still open to different interpretations which attributed direct and positive christological significance to such human "orders". He would, therefore, later abandon all talk about divine "orders" to guard against such misunderstandings.[28] Above all, according to Bonhoeffer's consistent view, the state and its leaders must be understood by Christians as concrete, limited, human realities, even if they claim more than this in their own behalf.

What is special about this work? Surely it is not that Bonhoeffer is presenting an essay in theological ethics or that he is addressing broader social and political questions in such a discussion. The special tone it sounds derives from the politically-informed way he addresses the details of such questions from such a theological perspective. For this reason, it is worthy of our special attention.

"The Church Facing the Jewish Question"[29]

In March, 1933, the political crisis deepened, and major new steps were taken on the road to a solidification of Hitler's control over the German state. Having successfully suspended the constitutional guarantees of personal civil rights on February 28, Hitler moved to force a self-liquidation of the weakened constitutional powers of the Reichstag by the so-called "Enabling Act", passed by a new Reichstag itself on March 24 after elections called by Hitler.[30]

April then brought the administration's initiatives, unencumbered by laws either protecting the rights of citizens or reserving certain powers to the Reichstag, to enact as state policies the long-proclaimed antisemitism of the Nazi Party. The general boycott of Jewish businesses began on April 1. The first Reichstagung of the so-called "German Christians", who sought to "restore" both what they judged to be "true Christianity" and also sweeping, uncritical nationalism, had convened April 3-5. With their virulent "Christian antisemitism", led by soon-to-be Reichsbischof Müller, the "German Christians" were a kind of corps of Christian cheerleaders for the Nazi rise to power and became the administration's allies in their first efforts to impose the implications of party doctines upon the German churches. Then the so-called "Law for the Restoration of the Civil Service" decreed on April 7 the forced dismissals of all "non-Aryans" and other state employees whose past political activity called into question their full loyalty to the new state administration.[31] Those who had read the "unalterable program of the NSDAP" or Mein Kampf but retained some doubts about Hitler's actual goals now had plenty of reason to conclude that he was indeed serious about the antisemitism already clearly recorded there.

Bonhoeffer had earlier prepared six theses concerning "church membership and persons of Jewish ancestry" for discussion in a circle of younger Berlin pastors. After these decrees, he added a discussion of the church's responsibility for their victims to a typescript of about double the length of the first version. After much hand-written revision of this text, quotations from Luther were added at the beginning and the end, and a long passage also at the end of the first section. Dated April 15, this essay was published in Der Vormarsch in June.[32] In this work Bonhoeffer made full use of the detailed theological ethic opposed to Nazism, which he had clarified in February and March while his "Führer Essay" was being presented and revised in the midst of the crisis of the earliest months of the Hitler regime. What is new here is his first direct, specific treatment of the rights of German Jews in light of his theological ethic.[33]

The first sections of the published version cite two passages from Luther, the first from 1546, another from 1523. The later quotation identifies conditions for accepting Jews as brothers. According to Luther, Jews should simply convert, "leave their usury, and accept Christ". They will be acceptable only as Christians! Earlier, however, Luther had at least strongly condemned Christian gentiles for their treatment of Jews, if only because mistreatment hampers their conversion. Since the

> ...Apostles, who also were Jews,...acted in such a brotherly way towards us, we in turn should act in a brotherly way towards the Jews so that we might convert some of them. For we are not yet fully their equals, much less their superiors.[34]

Luther states that even here force should not be used against the Jews, since it would not be likely to produce genuine conversions. Christians' forbidding the Jews the right to work and live in fellowship with Christians in fact drives them to practice usury. So all such oppressive practices should be rejected. Doubtless, Luther later was more explicit in rejecting Jews as those who deny the true faith. Only by conversion can they be accepted into the community.[35] But he had earlier simply put a somewhat more subtle face on the same attitude. Some responsibility for the Jews' deficient, single vocation ("usury"!) must be borne by the Christian gentiles who exclude them from normal community life and work. Persuasion by indoctrination and example, not force, is commended as the means to convert the Jews. But Luther's more restrained earlier strategy is directed to achieve the same goal as the more simplistic outlook enunciated later: the Jews become fully acceptable only by conversion to Christianity.

Exclusion of the "old people of God" from the "new Israel" and the displacement of the "old covenant" by the "new" are Luther's controlling assumptions. We might anticipate that Bonhoeffer, beginning with such quotations, will go on to express similar views.[36]

Bonhoeffer's own definition of the occasion for the essay is presented immediately after the Luther materials. A unique event has occurred: "...the Jew has been made subject to special laws by the state solely because of the race to which he belongs...quite apart from his religious beliefs..."[37] He seems quickly conscious of the novelty of "political antisemitism", which had now made "non-Aryan" status virtually a biological trait without regard for religious faith. This is different from the "religious antisemitism" of Luther. Bonhoeffer then notes that two questions are here raised for the theologian: first, "what should the church's attitude toward this action be, and what actions should it take in light of the state decrees?", and, secondly, what should be the church's attitude toward its own members who are "non-Aryan"? Both questions are not to be considered now in political or practical terms, but in light of a "true concept of the church".

Part one treats the first questions. Bonhoeffer again appears to be on a predictable course when he acknowledges at the outset that the church of the Reformation has no "right to address the state directly in its specifically political actions".[38] The state is here again an "order of preservation" (Erhaltungsordnung), which has been granted by God to control a godless world. It needs no approval or criticism from "a humanitarian point of view". Its methods are not those of the church or of a humanitarian association. Christians may speak out, assessing state actions from a moral point of view. But, in such cases, they can speak only as individuals or as members of such humanitarian associations. The church itself, however, cannnot properly speak out on the basis of some humanitarian, moral ideal and remain true to her task, the proclamation of a divine gospel.

The church must, therefore, accept both the "absolute necessity of the use of force in this world" and also "the moral injustice" of state actions. Furthermore, the church "cannot in the first place exert direct political action," since it does not know what is the necessary course to follow in history. Furthermore, all this remains applicable "...even today in the Jewish question..."[39]

However, this does not mean that the church remains completely disinterested and idle when the state acts. Precisely "...because it does not moralize in individual instances..." the church must "continually ask the state whether its action can be justified as legitimate..., i.e. as action which leads to law and order,...not to lawlessness and disorder."[40]

Here Bonhoeffer first sounds a drastically-changed note in his theological view of political acts. The church must ask the state if it is acting legally or illegitimately, not if it is "moral" or "immoral", according to some debatable, human standard. But this is precisely the question that no one was asking in Germany. Since the February 28 order suspending all civil rights guaranteed by the Weimar Constitution, the Nazis' "legal revolution" had repeatedly violated any real claim to legitimacy. The constitution clearly guaranteed equality before the law to all Germans, regardless of birth or social class, and provided protection for all religious communities and for the free practice of all religions.[41] The Supreme Court had already held in 1932 that no unqualified suspension of freedom of press or assembly could legally occur, even in a time of emergency which threatened the state, as in the brief Prussian Putsch.[42] No protests against the illegality of such sweeping nullifications, however, were heard in February or March of 1933—from the President, the army, the cabinet (which still included more non-Nazi Ministers than members of the NSDAP), leaders of other political parties or trade unions, or from the courts themselves.

Here Bonhoeffer contends that the church's total concern is to address only this one question to the state.[43] The church "...is called to put this question with great emphasis...[and] quite clearly today in the matter of the Jewish question."[44]

He then goes on to declare that the criterion for genuine church opposition to the state by direct political action is whether or not the state is maintaining order through law. If the state were to create disorder and lawlessness through its acts, it would be no longer an effective state. Then the church itself, not merely individual Christians, would have to engage in direct action against such a derelict state.

Bonhoeffer spells out, again drawing upon Leibholz' political theory,[45] two more detailed criteria for the sort of illegitimate state acts which would require church opposition. The state can lose its legitimacy, he says, either by too little or too much law and order. Too little law and order would be produced when a state acts to empower a "group of men" to "lawless" acts. Bonhoeffer admits the ambiguity of this criterion, since the understanding of what the law requires and what is lawless changes. The church accepted slavery, he points out, for eighteen centuries. In fact, it was only outlawed when non-ecclesiastical powers and interests came into political control. "Even in slavery a minimum of law and order was preserved, and yet...re-introduction of slavery would mean...lawlessness."[46] Too much law and order would certainly result if a state "...deprives Christian preaching and...faith...of their rights..." Again, the church must act to reject such a state as no longer controlled by its own legal fundamentals.[47]

Bonhoeffer admits, in summary, that three possibilities are open for the church in response to the state: (1) to throw the state back upon its own responsibilities by asking it whether it is true to its own legal basis, as he had presented this in detail; (2) to aid victims of state action, and (3) to engage in direct political action against the state, if it has created too little or too much law and order by its actions. He contends that, "In the Jewish problem the first two posssibilities will be the compelling demands..." for the present. However, he holds open the possibility that an "Evangelical Council" could meet "at any time" to debate and decide collectively whether either condition for direct political action was at hand.

The church's responsibility in April, 1933, includes, then, (1) calling the state to task if it has violated its own legal basis, and (2) aiding victims of state action. In the wake of the first "anti-non-Aryan" decrees he asserts, "The church has an unconditional obligation to the victims of any order, even if they do not belong to the Christian community."[48] His keyword is "unconditional". What he has in mind cannot be fulfilled by some underfinanced, minimal effort. And the victims to whom such "unconditional" aid is owed are obviously not only Christians of "non-Aryan" ancestry. The church owes this "unconditional" aid to all affected by the "anti-non-Aryan" decrees, including the Jews.

The situation after the first "anti-non-Aryan" decrees produced Bonhoeffer's immediate call for the church to challenge the Hitler state to justify the legality of its clearly illegal acts against Jews and others and also to give itself unstintingly to relieve the suffering of all victims of the state's actions.

However, he did not at that time also call for the church to engage in acts of political opposition to the Hitler state, although he admitted this was a possibilty, if not included in the "first course" of church responses to state actions. Individuals who are called of conscience to such deeds must not be restricted from this course by church actions. But only open debate in a representative "Evangelical Council" could assess for the church the criteria of whether too much law or too little law was actually produced by the acts of the Hitler regime. If either situation were to be declared by such a council, the church would indeed have an obligation "...not just to bandage the victims run over by the wheel, but to throw themselves into the spokes."[49]

For Bonhoeffer, the First Confessing Church Synod in Barmen, May, 1934, was clearly an "Evangelical Council" which declared that "too much law" had been produced by Müller's "German Christian" Church Administration." Through this structure the state had restricted the church's freedom so severely that it could no longer proclaim the gospel. The Reichskirche sought to impose the "anti-non-Aryan" decrees within the church; to produce segregated congregations for all "non-Aryan" church members; and to adopt unbiblical or unconfessional norms related to race, people, social class, and the like, for church proclamation or practice.[50] But all such policies were incompatible with the church's fundamental claim that "...all [are] one in Christ Jesus." From that time onward Bonhoeffer stood uncompromisingly against every claim that the Reichskirche could truly be the church in Germany. He was willing repeatedly to defy all acts of the government which required obedience to the leadership of the Reichskirche.

Did he also believe that the escalating state actions against the Jews and others, producing too little law and order through authorized, but illegal actions against Germans who happened to be untrustworthy to the regime or "non-Aryan", were also included in the decrees of the Confessing Church Synods? We shall return to this issue in the concluding part of this paper.

At the end of this section Bonhoeffer again seeks to lay out the proper attitude of the church toward the Jews in light of the recent decrees against "non-Aryans".

> The church...has never lost sight of the thought that the 'chosen people', who nailed the redeemer of the world to the cross, must bear the curse for its action through a long history of suffering.[51]

But, he adds, "...this people, loved and punished by God, stands under the sign of the final homecoming of the people of Israel to its God."

His identification of this homecoming with the conversion of Israel to Christianity places Bonhoeffer himself in support of the attitude expressed in the Luther quotations with which the section began. His outlook is that of "theological antisemitism", presupposing the displacement of the old covenant and people with a new counterpart. Jews, currently part of the displaced people and covenant, must reject their identity and heritage, since God has rejected them. Only the "...conversion of Israel...is to be the end of the people's...suffering."[52] So far, Bonhoeffer is here quite consistent with Luther in his "theological antisemitism".

Then comes this striking passage:

> From here the Christian church sees the history of the people of Israel with trembling as God's own, free, fearful way with his people. He knows that no nation of the world can be finished with this mysterious people, because God is not yet finished with it. Each new attempt to "solve the Jewish problem" comes to nothing on the saving-historical significance of this people; nevertheless, such attempts must continually be made. This consciousness on the part of the church of the curse that bears down upon this people, raises it far above any cheap moralizing; instead, as it looks at the rejected people, it humbly recognizes itself as a church continually unfaithful to its Lord and looks full of hope to

> those who have come home, to those who have come to believe in the one true God in Christ, and knows itself to be bound to them in brotherhood.[53]

Here there are at least some first hints of a less exclusively-antisemitic understanding of the relationship between the church and Israel, one that will be stressed in some portions of Bonhoeffer's later, incomplete work on Ethics.

At this point in 1933 Bonhoeffer still says that the primary attitude of the church towards Jews should be that of seeking their conversion—for their own benefit. Still, he also asserts, no effort at a final solution to the Jewish problem, through conversion or pogrom, can succeed, since God himself is not finished with Israel. Above all, the church cannot look down upon Jews from a superior moral position. Instead, the Jews' very rejection reminds the church of its own unfaithfulness. The church is also, like its Lord and the Jews, suffering in the world. So the simplistic "displacement" model is not totally controlling Bonhoeffer's outlook here, even if it remains predominant. Israel and the church are in some ways together, even while the church continues to seek to convert Jews to Christian faith.

In his later work on ethics Bonhoeffer would write, after the "ultimate solution" was underway,

> Jesus Christ was the promised Messiah of the Israelite-Jewish people, and for that reason the line of our fathers goes back beyond the appearance of Jesus Christ to the people of Israel. Western history is, by God's will, indissolubly linked with the people of Israel, not only in terms of origins, but also in a genuinely uninterrupted relationship. The Jew keeps open the question of Christ. He is the sign of God's free and merciful choice and of the repudiating wrath of God....An expulsion of the Jews from the West must necessarily bring with it the expulsion of Christ; for Jesus Christ was a Jew.[54]

Here there is no clear sign of even mild "theological antisemitism" or the "displacement theory". Instead, Bonhoeffer presents a view that the messianic tradition is shared in different ways which are "indissolubly linked...in a genuinely uninterrupted relationship." Western history is also bound by this linkage, determined by God's will itself. Bonhoeffer appears here to suggest that Christian faith cannot be reduced to a position which is held with pure, unquestioning commitment and without any doubt. For such reasons, the Jewish faith, by rejecting Jesus' messiahship in the sense held by Christians, is essential to preserve Christian faith as a real faith rather than some kind of human certainty.

According to this view, the Jews' questioning what Christians believe is the essential other side of their faith. The impossible expulsion of the Jews would destroy Christianity itself, since Christ himself was a Jew. It would also remove "the sign" of the necessary dialogue of commitment and doubt which is essential to faith, falsely resolve in a final way "the question of Christ", and make authentic faith in Christ impossible even for Christians. Here is a dialectic, both a difference and an indissoluble linkage between its two forms. For Bonhoeffer at this time, such a relation characterizes the two covenants and the two "peoples of God". Obviously, Bonhoeffer's later view would only strengthen the grounds for the church's necessary opposition to any action against the Jews.

Part two of Bonhoeffer's 1933 essay, not the section discussed above, confines its attention to the more restricted question of what the church should do about its own members who, because they had one or more Jewish grandparents, were affected by the decrees of April 7. His answer is unequivocal: "...exclusion of Jews by race from the German church...remains impossible for the church."[55] This would treat Jews as "political antisemitism" has come to view them—not as a religious, but as a pseudo-biological group. Since the church's task is to view all things from its special theological perspective, it cannot adopt this patently human, political view as its standard. If anyone

> ...feels unable to tolerate church fellowship with Christians of Jewish race...[,]...it must be made clear to him with the utmost seriousness that he is thus loosing himself from the place on which the church of Christ stands...[56]

In the form in which it was published in June, Bonhoeffer's essay closed with another quotation from Luther, again more ambiguous as a criterion of who actually belongs to the "people of God" than any simple "displacement theory" would permit. On Psalm 110.3 Luther had said that the sole test of whoever belongs to the people of God or the church is whether or not that person is part of the little group who accept, teach, and confess the Lord's word against those who persecute them, and suffer as they should. Do those who so honor God's word in their suffering include or exclude those who do not accept the special messianic status of Jesus? Here is the crucial question, whose answer admits or excludes any form of "theological antisemitism". Christian theology will be vulnerable to being a collateral support for "social or political antisemitism" or not, depending upon its answer. But neither Bonhoeffer in this essay nor Luther provided a clear answer which totally excluded any co-opting of theology for personal or political antisemitic programs.

Some Assessments

Bonhoeffer developed views of the necessary solidarity between Christians and non-Christians, including especially the Jews, only later. In the early months of 1933 he only hints that what we have called "theological antisemitism" is not an adequate expression of Christians' understanding of Judaism. At this time he still made statements which presupposed a "displacement" of the "old covenant" and "Israel" by the church as the "new people of God" with its different, "new covenant". And these latter set the more dominant tone.

But such views did not, he asserted even at this time, soften the church's responsibility to make public objections to the "anti-non-Aryan" acts of the Hitler administration: simply because they were "lawless" acts, violating the constitutional rights of all Germans. The church's single task is to question the state constantly and publicly regarding its illegal act until they are rescinded. Such a questioning, pursued as the central issue, should have been enough to kindle massive opposition to the acts of the Hitler administration at any time after the sweeping, arbitrary, and clearly illegal nullification of consitutional rights on February 28. All subsequent decrees against "non-Aryans" and others whose loyalty to the regime was suspect could not be part of a "legal revolution" at all.

The fact that Jews were in need of religious salvation, according to Bonhoeffer's theological outlook at this time, also does not release the church in any way from what he saw as its unconditional obligation to aid the victims of any state action, regardless of their religious faith or lack of it.

Finally, he held even at this point that the church may decide at any time that the state has, by acting to provide too little law and order to protect its citizens from lawlessness or too much law by interfering with limits upon the freedom of the church to proclaim its gospel, forfeited its claim to be a legitimate state. If such a decision were to be reached by an "Evangelical Council", the church would have thereafter to engage in direct political action against the state, sacrificing itself to make such political orders ineffective.

Had Bonhoeffer's views, then, been persuasive for more Christians, the Hitler state could never have become firmly established and certainly not able to eventually enact the whole program which Hilberg has vividly called "the destruction of the European Jews". This is true in spite of Bonhoeffer's continuing to hold at this period to some "theological antisemitism".

Bonhoeffer's theological ethic here reflects the liberal values of his family and their friends. They were part of a special circle of privileged professional academics and civil administrators. For all of them, a minimum from the Weimar Constitution had to be salvaged at all costs, no matter what other changes might be necessary in the critical social, economic, and political conditions of early 1933. This minimum was equitable protection by irrevocable law of <u>all</u> Germans from arbitrary acts of the government. By holding this view, Bonhoeffer and his circle opposed many others in their class[57] and other segments of German society who were not upset by the sweeping, arbitrary, and permanent suspension of such fundamental laws on February 28.

What, then, was their failure?

Probably one needs to admit that their very liberal tradition was itself a handicap, restraining their efforts to oppose the Nazis' opportunistic push for "legal revolution" and "national revolution" just when decisive opposition had the greatest chances of successfully checking the Hitler regime. The Nazis depended at this point, as later also, upon the technical expertise of the professionals in commerce, the civil agencies, the army, and manufacturing industries. In these months forceful strikes or other refusals to cooperate with the increasingly illegal thrust of Hitler's initiatives to solidify his control of the state stood a good chance of success in restraining him. But their commitment to reason and evidence, law and humanity, confined Bonhoeffer and his colleagues to particular niches only in the German social structure. The universities, research institutes, and informal networks of interested collaborators who held crucial administrative offices were their familiar forum. They quite naturally concentrated their considerable efforts at this time within this sphere. Even Bonhoeffer's venture into radio was only a brief flirtation. In any case, all such mass media were soon closely controlled by the Hitler regime. What was needed, however, was an ability to communicate across the lines dividing German society into class and functional segments. A challenge which would appeal to different interests which were hurt by the sweeping withdrawal of civil rights might still in these months have welded a sufficient coalition of opposition to control the Nazis. Had they been able to communicate more broadly, the special circle of which Bonhoeffer was a part might have been more effective. But Goebbels, not Leibholz, von Dohnanyi, or Bonhoeffer, was the expert on mass communication with the new media. And Goebbels served another master.

Other factors outside Germany must also be noted as significant deterrents to the effectiveness of what we might call the incipient Resistance. The inactivity of France at the time of the reoccupation of the Rhineland, when the Wehrmacht was poised to intervene, supporting a Putsch against the Nazis, and of Britain at the time of the Munich Pact, when German opposition to Hitler's recklessness was strong again, simply failed to provide occasions for the German Resistance to act. Repeated, unpredictable combinations of improbable circumstances prevented their assassination of Hitler when their strongly-backed and well-coordinated plan for a Putsch in March, 1943, might well have succeeded. Their intellectualism and liberalism were surely not the only reasons for the German Resisters' failure to prevent the Holocaust and also the impending self-destruction of their nation. If more of the social elite of Germany had supported such views, these liberals might well have succeeded in stopping the Hitler regime.

Whatever their failures, they were only partly redeemed when some suffered later martyrdoms for the Resistance. Bonhoeffer and his circle, if they did demonstrate that an "other Germany" existed even during the Hitler time, did not prevent the near annihilation of Europe's Jews.

However, it should be clear in light of the present analysis that one can no longer justly claim that Bonhoeffer should be respected as one who was personally better than his theology, since "...theologically his fight was only on behalf of non-Aryan Christians."[58] Surely in light of the evidence here presented it is time also to cease repeating: "I know of no writing of Bonhoeffer which seeks to lay out the relation between Judaism and Christianity."[59] Bonhoeffer's undeniable, early rejection of "lawless acts" of state against defenseless groups, his call for "unconditional" aid from the church to victims of state acts without regard to their religious status, and the evidence that his ambiguous early "theological antisemitism" was later replaced by some kind of indissoluble solidarity between the two covenant peoples, should all make it clear also that the following statement is grossly oversimplified and distorted:

> ...the only interest a Bonhoeffer Christian can have in Judaism is the individual conversion of its erstwhile adherents. This, it seems to me, is Bonhoeffer's initial position, e.g. in The Community [sic!] of Saints, and he maintains it throughout his life with admirable consistency.[60]

The situation is far less simple than is stated here. Even when Bonhoeffer still affirmed in 1933 what we can identify as "theological antisemitism", he was calling upon all Christians to protect the Jews' legally-guaranteed rights and upon the church to aid them and other victims "unconditionally" without regard for their religious views.

One cannot deny the moral fervor, but certainly can question the respect for relevant evidence reflected in the flat assertion: "Hitler and Bonhoeffer were united in seeking a world without Jews."[61]

What, then, about Bonhoeffer's role in response to the first "anti-non-Aryan" laws enacted on April 7, 1933? He was certainly right to object to their illegality. He was also right to call upon the church to aid the victims "unconditionally". He was right to indicate that individual Christians, singly or in humanitarian organizations, should not be restricted by the church from voicing their moral protests against such acts. He was right to claim already at that time that the church could convene an "Evangelical Council" to determine if the state was producing either too little or too much law. And he was entitled to identify a positive act by such a council as the occasion when the church itself must intervene through direct political action. His continued support for "theological antisemitism" at this point, however, left his theology open to being co-opted as a support for the "social and political antisemitism" of the Nazis, their supporters, and those who were simply not troubled enough over the fate of the Jews to intervene.

Again, Bethge has spoken clearly to the point of assessing what Bonhoeffer's shortcomings and strengths in the Hitler time were, along with others who belong in the category of the "best of the German gentiles". His summary is: "We [Christians] resisted by confessing, but we did not confess by resisting!"[62] Accurately defining just what this deficiency of the best German gentiles is—and what it is not—ought to be at least part of our concern as we remember for the future.

NOTES

[1]Cf. "The Holocaust and Christian Anti-Semitism: Perspectives of a Christian Survivor," Union Seminary Quarterly Review, 32.3-4 (Spring and Summer, 1977), pp. 141-142.

[2]Renate Bethge has characterized the attitude of many Germans, who after the end of World Ward II discovered with surprise what had happened to the Jews, as simply standing by, "knowing enough to know they did not want to learn any more."

[3]Elie Wiesel, Nobel laureate and survivor, has asked in The Oath (New York, 1983), among other places, if it might not be better to honor the victims themselves simply to keep silence in the fact of such unspeakable evil. His decision is that the story of countless deaths must be told if this might mean that even one life might be saved in the future.

[4]Bonhoeffer was executed on April 9, 1945 along with a small number of others who had

been centrally-engaged in the German Resistance. Bethge's Dietrich Bonhoeffer (München, 1967; E.T.: London and New York, 1970) is, in addition to a biography of his friend and associate, a definitive source of information also about the Church Struggle in Germany, as well as the Resistance, especially as Christians engaged in it.

[5]Judaism in German Christian Theology since 1945: Christianity and Israel Considered in terms of Mission (Metuchen, New Jersey, 1975), p. 24f.

[6]ibid.

[7]Bethge addressed these issues with care in "Bonhoeffer and the Jews" in Ethical Responsibility: Bonhoeffer's Legacy to the Churches (New York and Toronto, 1981), ed. John D. Godsey and Geffrey B. Kelly, pp. 43-96 [cf. "Dietrich Bonhoeffer und die Juden (24. Oktober, 1979)" in Konsequenzen: Dietrich Bonhoeffers Kirchenverständnis he... hrsg. Ernst Feil und Ilse Tödt (München, 1980), S. 171-214]. Since that time, however, new, detailed studies have been made by the Bonhoeffer Project of the Theological Faculty of Ruprecht-Karls-Universität of Heidelberg. They trace the emergence in Bonhoeffer's theology of an ethic of unrelenting opposition to Nazism's decrees suspending constitutional guarantees of personal civil rights of all Germans, but especially of Jews after the first "anti-non-Aryan" laws. See, above all, the unpublished dissertation of Christoph Strohm, "Theologische Ethik des Politischen in der Auseinandersetzung mit dem National-sozialismus. Dietrich Bonhoeffers Weg in den Widerstand im Gespräch mit seinen als Juristen tätigen Freunden" (1987) [publication by Christian Kaiser Verlag, 1989]. During 1932 and early 1933, influences from a circle of his family and friends who were legal scholars or political administrators trained as lawyers provided increasing specificity and detail for Bonhoeffer's theological perspective upon political affairs.

[8]Above all, today a clarification of Bonhoeffer's actual position is needed to correct some errors and misunderstandings which persist among those who have sought seriously to remember the Holocaust.

[9]The last version, incorporating the changes and additions without notation, is the published form.

[10]Cf. Strohm, especially chapters one and two.

[11]For example, the basic distinction between the "ultimate and the penultimate" in ethics and the notion of "worldliness".

[12]"The Leader and the Individual in the Younger Generation," in No Rusty Swords: Letters, Lectures and Notes from the Collected Works of Dietrich Bonhoeffer, I, ed. Edwin H. Robertson and tr. by Robertson and John Bowden (London and New York, 1965), pp. 190-191 [Gesammelte Schriften, II, "Der Führer und der einzelne in der jungen Generation," S. 22-23].

[13]ibid., pp. 191-193.

[14]ibid., pp. 193-194.

[15]In the later forms of the paper associated changes in the concept of "the individual" are also traced.

[16]Especially in "Die Auflösung der liberalen Demokratie in Deutschland und das autoritäre Staatsbild," Wissenschaftliche Abhandlungen und Reden zur Philosophie, 12 (München und Leipzig, 1933).

[17]NRS, pp. 193-199. Cf., among others, Franklin Littell: "The Protestant Churches and Totalitarianism (Germany, 1933-1948)" in Totalitarianism, ed. Karl Friedrich (Cambridge MA, 1954), pp. 108-119.

[18]NRS, p. 199.

[19]Here the "populism" of movements expressing the new "Leader" concept is explicit and fundamental in the National Socialists' outlook.

[20]NRS, p. 199. [English slightly altered by the present author]

[21]ibid., p.200.

[22]Kelley has traced this process from some of Bonhoeffer's earliest student papers, first published in 1987 (Dietrich Bonhoeffer Werke, I), through its later formulations in "Revelation and the Secular in the Theology of Dietrich Bonhoeffer" (unpublished Ph. D. dissertation, Yale University, 1980). See also works by Bethge, James Burtness, Ernst Feil, Clifford Green, Robin Lovin, Geffrey Kelly, Strohm, and Heinz Eduard Tödt.

[23]NRS, p. 201. The crucial sentence is: "Wer etwas anderes erwartet, sieht nicht die Wirklichkeit, ist Phantast." (GS, II, S. 44-45)

[24]ibid., p. 202.

[25]The present author's translation of: "Aber auch hier ist der Mensch noch nicht als das gesehen, was er ist. Denn es **kann** sein, daß der einzelne recht hat gegen das Amt, das Amt ist nicht letzte Autorität. [Wo kann der einzelne das Recht gegen das Amt vernehmen?] Nirgends als dort, wo er sieht, daß das Amt vorletzte Autorität ist gegenüber einer letzten, unsagbaren Autorität, gegenüber der Autorität Gottes." (GS, II, pp. 36-37. The sentence in brackets is from the manuscript and omitted in the published German version.) The truncated translation in No Rusty Swords is: "Even here, however, man is not yet seen as he is. Only when a man sees that office is a penultimate authority in the face of an ultimate, indescribable authority, in the face of the authority of God has the real situation been reached." (p. 203)

[26]ibid., pp. 203-204.

[27]Gogarten and Brunner are clearly in view, although many other spokesmen for Christian ethics agreed with them.

[28]Cf. the "mandates" of God in his later Ethics.

[29]"Die Kirche vor der Judenfrage", GS, II, pp. 44-53; English as "The Church and the Jewish Question," NRS, pp. 221-229.

[30]The Reichstag passed on this date, to become effective immediately and to remain so until April 1, 1937, a bill which permitted the administration to enact laws and ratify treaties without act or consent of the Reichstag, even if these laws "deviate from the constitution", provided they do not affect the "position of the Reichsrat and Reichstag". On January 30, 1937, this law was extended by an act of the Reichstag, then sitting with only Nazi members as deputies, for an additional four years. Hitler personally extended the act indefinitely on May 10, 1943.

[31]Exemptions were provided, partly on pressure from President von Hindenburg, for those employed prior to August 1, 1914, for combat veterans who fought for Germany or her allies in World War I, and for fathers or sons of soldiers who died in the war. "Non-Aryan descent" was defined in an additional decree three days later as including anyone who had one or more Jewish grandparents. The political undesirables and others who had been employed after November 9, 1918, and who remained untrained were to be summarily dismissed with three months' pay. In some hardship cases, where such persons were supporting destitute relatives, an annuity of up to one third of their salaries might be granted, although it might also not be provided and in any case could be withdrawn at any time. Arbitrary transfers and reductions in rank, as well as forced retirements, were also authorized without legal redress. "Non-Aryans" and those whose loyalty was suspect on the basis of their previous political activity were to be retired or dismissed with no pensions unless they had completed at least ten years' service. All this, when unemployment stood at about 45% of the labor force with many of those who were still working only employed two or three days per week!

[32]3.6, S. 171-176.

[33]Some blatantly mistaken claims have been made about Bonhoeffer's stance in this essay (Cf. below). Therefore, a careful reading of the text itself is here required.

[34]NRS, p 222; cf. GS, II, s. 44.

[35]In his notorious late treatise "On the Jews" Luther did advocate force, imprisonments, expropriations of property, virtually all elements of the Nazis' program short of a "final solution" by extermination.

[36]Franklin Littell, among others, has written in many works with clarity and precision about the different, but related forms of "theological", "religious", "social", and "political antisemitism". Robert Everett has spoken recently of a "theology of oppression", which can be more or less explicit. Both Littell and Everett agree that Christians must today seek a form of understanding their faith which cannot support oppression or antisemitism. For both this means totally rejecting the "displacement" relation between the two covenants and peoples as unbiblical and unconscionable.

[37]NRS, pp. 222.

[38]ibid.

[39]ibid., p.223.

[40]ibid.

[41]See Part II of the Weimar Constitution.

[42]Cf. among many authorities Karl Dietrich Bracher, "The Technique of the National Socialist Seizure of Power" in The Path to Dictatorship, 1918-1933: Ten Essays by German Scholars, tr. John Conway (Garden City NY, 1966), p.121.

[43]Bracher notes that a large part of Hitler's success in this crucial period, when his new state control could have been limited by opposition, is simply that he "...knew what he wanted." (ibid., p. 120) Most others simply did not know what question they wanted to raise or policy they wanted to pursue in the desperate circumstances of early 1933. Bonhoeffer appears exceptional in his dogged concentration of the church's attention upon the one crucial question, ignoring as irrelevant all other aspects of the complex issues to be faced in those stormy months.

[44]NRS, pp. 223-224.

[45]Cf. Strohm, pp. 171ff.

[46]NRS, pp. 223-224.

[47]ibid.

[48]ibid., p. 225.

[49]Translated by the present author: "...nicht nur die Opfer unter dem Rad zu verbinden, sondern dem Rad selbst in die Speichen zu fallen." (GS, II, s. 48) Cf. NRS, 225.

[50] On February 26, 1932-1933, Bonhoeffer said at Holy Trinity Church in a Service At the end of the Wintersemester in his "Gideon Sermon" on Judges 6.15-16; 7.2; 8,23, his first since the Machtergreifung [cf. Dietrich Bonhoeffer: Predigten -Auslegungen - Meditationen,

1925-1945: I: 1925-1935. Herausgegeben von Otto Dudzus. München: Christian Kaiser Verlag, 1984. S. 349-358]: "In the church we have only one altar,...the altar of the Most High...to whom alone is due honor and adoration...We have no auxiliary altars for the adoration of men. The worship of God, not of man, happens here at the altar of the church. Anyone who wants anything else may stay away." (p. 127)

[51]NRS, p. 226.

[52]ibid.

[53]ibid., pp. 226-227.

[54]Bethge: "Bonhoeffer and the Jews", p.78. Partly retranslated by Bethge from Ethik, p. 95, with emphasis added by the translator. Cf. Ethics, pp. 89-90.

[55]NRS, p. 228.

[56]ibid., p 229.

[57]Cf., among others, the sad stories of Paul Althaus, Gerhard Kittel, and Emanuel Hirsch (Robert P. Ericksen: Theologians Under Hitler [New Haven and London: 1985]).

[58]Emil Fackenheim to the English Language Section of the International Bonhoeffer Society in 1979, cited in Bethge, "Bonhoeffer and the Jews," pp. 44-45. Fackenheim went on to say that Bonhoeffer's deficiency is "...hardly surprising in view of what little of the facts of the Holocaust he could have known." (ibid., p. 45.) The Heidelberg researchers have shown that Bonhoeffer was well-informed from the very first through the last stages about the steps of increasing persecution of Jews. Fackenheim is, at this point, too kind to Bonhoeffer. However, as deficient as his theological fight with Nazism may have been in 1933 in light of its "theological antisemitism" which he was only to disavow later in his Ethik, obviously Bonhoeffer never sought to defend only the rights of "non-Aryan Christians". Fackenheim's claim here is simply wrong.

Fackenheim later aptly noted the paradox that "...in Berlin lived two great Christians..., Niemöller and Bonhoeffer. [Yet] I do not think it ever occurred to either of them to pick up the phone and speak to their fellow Berliner, my own teacher, Leo Baeck. And I often wonder how different it might have been within the Christian resistance in Germany, if dialogue between Jews and Christians had existed." ("Discussion," in Littell: American Protestantism and Antisemitism, [Jerusalem, 1985], pp. 30-31.) The tragedy of the German Resistance to Hitler is precisely its lack of coordination of cells of opposition. This remains the decisive failure of Bonhoeffer and other gentiles from the "other Germany" in the months here surveyed. The implication of this later observation by Fackenheim hits the mark squarely!

[59]Walter Harrelson in his 1962 essay, "Bonhoeffer and the Bible," in The Place of Bonhoeffer, ed. Martin Marty, p. 139, published three years before "The Church Before the Jewish Question" appeared in English.

[60]Stanley R. Rosenbaum, "Dietrich Bonhoeffer: A Jewish View," in Journal of Ecumenical Studies, 18.2 (Spring, 1981), p. 305. Rosenbaum goes on to commend Bonhoeffer for his "courageous" statement quoted above from Ethics, but wonders why euphemisms for Jews were necessary in such a manuscript in the last years of the Third Reich and also calls Bonhoeffer to task because the statement "...was not published in Bonhoeffer's lifetime." Bonhoeffer was forbidden to publish anything by the Security Police on March 27, 1941, before this manuscript could be completed!

[61]Clarke Williamson, Has God Rejected His People?, p. 103. Williamson asserts that Bonhoeffer's response to the anti-Aryan laws was hampered by two theological assumptions, which he characterizes as: (1) "...the Lutheran claim that the state's ordinances were 'based on the sustaining will of God amidst the chaotic godlessness of the world...", and (2) "...very much a part of Bonhoeffer's theological outlook...anti-Judaism." (ibid., p. 103).

[62]"The Confessing Church Then and Now," in Newsletter of the International Bonhoeffer Society—English Language Section, 33 (October, 1986), p. 6.

Roman Catholicism and the Nazis : A Review of the Attitude of the Church during the Persecutions of the Jews in Hitler's Europe .

Ukachukwu Chris MANUS (Ph.D Louvain)
Senior Lecturer, Dept. of Religious Studies
Obafemi Awolowo University
Ile - Ife, NIGERIA .

Abstract :

The claim of ethnic and cultural superiority of the Aryans over other races and its consequent diffusion of particularist racialist ideology culminated into a cataclysm that gripped the whole of christian Europe under the Nazi regime (1939 - 1945) . These racists, among other things, sought the explanation of their economic malaise on the Jews . The resultant brutal extermination of millions of Jewish people in Nazi Germany and the mass murders in squalid concentration camps on east European soil amidst official Church silence has left such a sordid scar on the history of mankind such that European Christianity still remains culpable for her acquiescence . This horrendous attempt at a ' final solution ' of the so - called'Jewish problem' could not have been the achievement of one man alone . Inspite of the secular overtones of the Nazi pogrom, religious anti - semitism paved the way for racial anti - semitism; the consequences which are reflected in the horrors of Auschwitz .

Based on information arising from this preview, this paper explores the historical antecedents that fertilized the soil on which the seed of Nazism germinated as an ideological plant that later bore the fruits of hatred and racism . Adolf Hitler 's rise to power and the role of his lieutenants, men like Alfred Rosenberg who legitimated the philosophy of Nazism and Franz von Papen, that shrewd diplomat, are briefly x-rayed .

The intra-ecclesial discord which prevailed in the ranks of the German episcopacy of the time paralized the efforts of the Church - leaders to settle for a concerted confrontation with the Nazis and their genocidal crimes against the Jews . The paper considers the gravity of this disunity on the events of the period . It describes the tussle between Cardinal Betram of Breslau and Bishop Gröbe; the Bishops' inability to raise some protests against the excesses of the *Reich* and the later squabble between Betram and Cardinal Konrad von Preysing of Berlin .

The scope of Hitler's ' Total War' is studied in the context of his *Blitzkrieg* campaign of 1938 - 1941 aimed at subjugating all Europe and the eventual inauguration of the political and racial *Weltanschauung* of the Third *Reich*. Anti - Judaic crimes perpetrated against the Jews during the campaign are looked at from the social and psychological stand-points .

The *Reichskristallnacht* and its consequences to Jewish business and enterprise represents in practical terms an evidence of anti - Judaic oppression of the Third *Reich*. The costs in men and material are discussed and analytically judged in the light of the *Reich*'s programmatic racial laws .

The role of the Vatican during the period constitutes a central ' kernel ' in the plot of the paper . The data is objectively examined, analysed and judged.

It is the contention of the paper that Pope Pius XII and the German Bishops were rather more mindful of the security of Church rights, her institutional and professional concerns than of the fate of the Jews in their midst .

The conclusion presents a brief summary of the discussion with some personal reflections . A five - point concern deemed pertinent to the spirit of " The Remembering for the Future " conference is articulated . These provide caveats I consider urgent for our future in a world almost on the brink of a more serious global economic recession when scapegoats can always be found om any group of people .

As a whole, the paper makes a number of submissions : the history of the events leading to the Holocaust provide too important a lesson for humanity which ought to be handed down from generation to generation . The memory of this tragedy should make us all sober and should provide us a time to ask God's forgiveness and mercy . Above all, it should enkindle in Europe's young generation, tomorrow's leaders, the need to refrain from temptations to join in the increasing and resurgent anti - Judaic currents in parts of today's Europe . To gurantee better and meaningful contacts with Jews and to ensure a better, more human and more truly God - centred world in which racism and religious bigotry are eschiewed; the Church should show remorse and repentance and should ask for forgiveness from our Jewish friends .

Introduction

Among several cruces that confront a contemporary African historian investigating the horrendous events leading to the near destruction of European Jewry by the Nazis is the problem of man's inhumanity to man . In other words, why would people in the so - called higher civilization wilfully engage in such acts of barbarism and bestiality against another race? And viewed critically from the perspective of contemporary western church history, the same homo Africanus; a homo religiousus himself is compelled to raise a number of queries with special reference to the attitude of the Catholic Church in that savage event which saw the extermination of a third of the Jewish people; namely what had occured in German social history that seemed to have fuelled the thirst and mass support for war? How had subsequent events in Church polity been responsible for the dreadful consequences of the Nazi war? Could it still be maintained that the Church was acquiescent or tacitly supportive of the horrors of the Holocaust? What precisely is meant when opinio consensus holds that the Church did not take a clear - cut position against Adolf Hitler by preventing the rise of Nazism?

Whether the facts can rightly be judged as " complicity " or as one of " collective guilt " as had rather been often acknowledged; it is my contention that concrete historical data from dependable sources must be scrutinized and their findings considered objectively so that they can throw more light on the role of the German Episcopacy and that of the Papacy under Pius XII . My starting-point in this paper is a discussion on the emergence of the National Socialism in the midst of the socio - political - economic upheavals of those times .

The second section offers insight into the disunity which developed in the ranks of the German Roman Catholic Bishops and its implications for the Jewish condition during and after the war . My third section looks at Hitler's grand design - the Total War (1938 - 1941); its geographical extent; its social implications and its obvious pathological consequences . The tragic events of the Reichskristallnacht (Nov 9 - 10, 1938) is briefly sketched in the fourth section . The fifth part summarily examines the attitude of Pope Pius XII towards the persecutions of millions of Jews during the war years . My conclusion attempts to offer a rapid overview of the main thrust of the paper and to articulate some concerns I consider quite pertinent to the " Remembering for the Future Conference .

The Emergence of the National Socialism

Even though the status of the Jews in Germany became roughest in the period 1939 - 1945, the history of their oppression would be incomplete without a review of events leading to Adolf Hitler's rise to power and the birth of the National Socialism as an ideological system . November 3, 1918 has been generally recognized as the date of the abdication of the Kaiser which was forced on him by workers' uprising .[1] On February 6, 1919, the Constitution of the Weimar Republic was drafted . From the outset, the Republic was beset with enormous hardships and difficulties . The Treaty of Versailles, known to the Germans as " ein Diktat " caused general disaffection; the Germans lost land and had to pay huge sums of money as compensation for war damages. They were forbidden to possess big army in the Rhineland, not to mention the vindictive Ruhr war . All these social problems compounded matters for the new Republic . The days of the Republic were further marred by violent strikes as a result of widespread economic depression . Unemployment galore (6 million persons jobless) precipitated several attempts to tople the Government. In fact, instability marked everyday business of the government; twenty three different governments were known to have succeeded each other from 1918 to 1923 . Even Field Marshall Paul von Hindenburg (1847 - 1934) could not bring stability and discipline in the elections of 1925 . Germany by this time tottered on the brink of collapse and the danger of Communist take - over starred her on the face.[2]

There gradually developed a process of left - right polarization with the Nazis on the extreme right and the hapless Catholic organisation, the Zentrumpartei (Centre Party) in the middle . With the eventual weakening of the other parties, the National Socialism, being the only opposition party enjoyed free play though with no state responsibility at that stage . National Socialism originally known as the Deutsche Arbeiter Partei (DAP) was born in the city of Munich of the state of Bavaria in 1919 . Two years later, Adolf Hitler headed the Party and attempted a coup d' etat in Bavaria the following year . The putsch failed and he was immediately arrested and incacerated for five years but released after ten months. In 1925 the Party was renamed the Nationalsozialistische Deutsche Arbeiter Partei (NSDAP) . The Party attracted thousands of people partly because of the attraciveness of its slogans and partly because of its support for big business in the private sector of the economy . And moreover the para-military structures of the Party attracted millions of Germans who looked up to militaristic adventures in order to affirm themselves . After the 1931 Presidential polls, Paul von Hindenburg recognizing the massive support Hitler had received nominated him Chancellor (Prime Minister).[4] The Parliamentary elections of July 31, 1932 when the Nazis won 230 out of 608 seats signalled the downfall of the Centre Party controlled by the Catholics and their clerics especially in the person of Monsignor Kaas .[5] In fact, the Party's demise marked the triumph of extremism as long as the NSDAP and the Communists controlled a majority in the parliament . But because the NSDAP would not accept the Communists as bed - fellows, the Centre Party, at the initiative of Hindenburg, arranged a coalition with the enigmatic NSDAP . As time went on, the Centre Party became unable to curb the excesses of Hitler and his party agents. It later opted for its self - dissolution with the approval of the German Bishops . At this juncture, Hitler's dream for one party, one state, one people with himself as the Führer was becoming a reality . By this time, the NSDAP had become the " alleinige Tragerin des politischen Willens des deutsche Volkes " - the unique bearer of the political will of the German people . It was at this time that the German Bishops had been lured into believing that the National Socialism would have been able to renew the State and to fight Bolshevism . But unexpectedly the Party tended towards totalitarianism. Even in the period 1930 - 1931, there was told, among some party stalwarts, the policy of maintaining purity of blood, race and soil; issues which later brought the Jewish race into perfidy .

As of that time there was no complete unanimity among the Bishops on the powers claimed by the National Socialism . Some church leaders denounced Catholics who joined the Nazi party but the vast majority in the corridor of ecclesiatical powers kept mut .[6]
An interesting figure in the centre of the looming crisis between the Church and the Nazi government at that time was Franz von Papen (1879 - 1969), a catholic himself and a former member of the Centre Party . Von Papen became Hitler's personal adviser . In 1933, von Papen as vice - Kanzler got the Führer agree to demonstrate some signs of loyalty and re-assurance to the Bishops . Consequently in his first public policy statement, Hitler announced that he wanted Christianity and the Church to provide the foundational ideology for the State . He pledged to fight Communism and affirmed his willingness to uphold the family as the central cell of German society . The Bishops responded positively by stating that without any derogation to their condemnation of some religious and moral lapses found in former public utterances of the Führer, they agreed

that they could express confidence that their warnings against Nazism were no longer necessary . This was the result of von Papen's diplomacy .[7] Apparently this state of affairs made it possible for the Roman Pontiff, Pope Pius XI to speak in praise of Hitler during the secret consistory of March 13, 1933.[8] The Bishops issued the Denkschrift in a further laudatio for the Führer . The National Socialism who did not care so much for the content of the document all the more considered it as good propaganda for the Führer who did not hesitate to propound his own Manifesto part of which included " die entpolitisierung des Klerus " . Many people appeared quite apprehensive of the events of the period . Unfortunately the Church and even some Catholic theologians attempted to give theological legitimation to Nazi socialist ideology . Great names like Professor Eschweiler in Braunsberg in their theologizing sought an agreement with Nazi ideology and Barion, a canonist, thorized on the compatibility of the law on sterilization and the Papal Encyclical, Casti Connubi (1930).[9] Indeed ideas rule the world . The propositions of those theologians culminated in the infamous declaration of March 23, 1933 at Fulda by the German Bishops retracting most of their hardline denunciations against National Socialism . Matters became compounded as the two main Bishops' Conferences at Fulda and Munich were undecided as to whether Hitler's declarations should be proscribed or not . While Cardinal Betram of Fulda was the more pushful towards the idea of proposing sanctions, Cardinal Faulhaber of Munich displayed a laissez - faire attitude. When matters got almost to a crisis - point, the Bishops accepted Hitler's offer for peace, thus implicitly recognizing him as the Führer . Von Papen continued his game of duplicity in the events of those days . He got Nazi government and Hitler to support negotiations towards the arrangement of a Concordat . Archbishop Gröber of Freiburg, the man in the lead at the time, kept the German Episcopate constantly informed of the progress of the negotiations . Gröber sought a modus vivendi with the National Socialism . The Concordat was initialled on July 8, 1933 and signed by Eugenio Cardinal Pacelli for the Vatican and Franz von Papen, vice Chancellor for the Reich on the 20th . The Document was officially published by both the Vatican and the Third Reich on September 18, 1933 .[10]

To conclude this section some questions need to be raised : could this event not be read as an act of international recognition of a totalitarian regime by the Church? Certainly as a compromise arrangement, the Concordat had its negative sides . Did the Church not by this singular act sign away most of her public and political influence? How did the Church in its over - protectionist zeal not recognize that the terms of the Concordat were open to limitless exploitation by a government that had so manifested abject lack of conscience? Did the Church not realize the ambiguity inherent in Article 32 (the exclusion of the clergy from party politics) of the Concordat? Why did the Holy See not refuse being drawn to conclude a Concordat with the Nazis who later used its terms against the moral teachings of the Church?

I am under the impression that the Church was acting on selfish grounds . For me, here is a third costly mistake on the part of the German Church vis a vis the events of the time . As a matter of fact, the unholy wedlock between the Centre Party and the NSDAP; the disbandment of the Centre Party with the approval of the Church leaders and this time, the acceptance of the Concordat compounded matters,thus making it uneasy for one to completely exonerate the Catholic Church whose population counted over one - third of the nation from co - responsibility in the events of the years ahead. Moreover, 1933 when the Concordat was signed was the actual year the Nazis made racism legal yet the Bishops made no protests about those savage practices . They were rather concerned with the defense of their own institutions, rights, social and professional interests than the plight of the Jews in their midst .

The Discord Among the German Bishops

In this section, I wish to explore the confusion that erupted in the ranks of the German Bishops and its implications for the triumph of the plans of the National Socialism . The terms of the Concordat broke down quite rapidly . Hitler thereupon began his systematic attack on the Church. He accused the Church of representing other worldviews . Alfred Rosenberg's contoversial work, Mythus des 20 - Jahrhundert (1930), appeared about this period . The book contributed towards the sagging Church - State relations at that time . Rosenberg portrayed the Church as believing in a Weltanschauung of the past .[11] In his view, Nazi philosophy championed the question between being " a Christian or a German ", and publically proclaimed it in such slogans as :

> " Right is what Aryans think right ".
> " The vital strength of the race must be preserved and taken care of by all and any means ... whatever is useful is lawful and right " .
> " Religion is subject to the command of the race, and it must adapt itself to that command " .

Even such ideas were disseminated into the Hitler Youth Movement.[12] One of the songs which swept off the feet of many able - bodied young Germans went as follows :

> Now the time of the Cross is past,
> the Wheel of the Sun will rise,
> We 'll be done with God,
> So as to honour the Fatherland .

With this type of philosophy, it could have become clear that the National Socialism posed a danger to Catholic and general christian values. Protests were heard from some quarters . But as early as possible, Franz von Papen nipped them in the bud . He proposed that a committee be set up to examine the greviances and status of Catholics in the events of the time . His Action Commission of Catholic Germans (Aktionsgemeinschaft katholischer Deutscher) produced nothing but chaos and the Bishops were pitted in squabbles against themselves . Cardinal Betram of Breslau disassociated himself quite early from the committee . Bishop Gröbe of Freiburg embraced it fully and became von Papen's mouthpiece. When von Papen advised the Church to disband the Catholic Youth groups in order to restore confidence in the Führer who had promised to guarantee spiritual care to the youth of the church, Gröber went ahead and concluded an arrangement on behalf of the Church without consulting Rome or the president of the Bishops' Conference . He invited the representatives of the youth organisations to Freiburg to discuss the matter, but some were surprised at the naivety of the Bishops faith in von Papen's role . The discord among the Bishops continued to linger on till the general elections of November 12, 1933 such that the Bishops failed to take a unified stand against the totalitarian tendencies of the National Socialism .

Even Cardinal Betram who was the more vocal prelate among the rest of his confreres believed in doing things through traditional diplomacy . But was such a diplomacy useful in dealing with a totalitarian regime? It was recognized that Betram never spoke against the Nazis in the pulpit .[13] As relations continued to be strained, von Papen arranged a meeting between the influencial Cardinal Schulte and Hitler . The meeting produced no meaningful result . Hitler evaded every question put before him . He accused the Bishops of trumping up falsehood against the Reich . Life became almost unbearable for Catholic organisations and catholic members in general . Tension grew from the demands of being a catholic and from that of the family . A catholic father or mother lost his job if he or she did not belong to any organisation of the National Socialism . The Bishops decided on the publication of a Pastoral Letter to the faithful and to send a copy to Hitler . The Government caught wind of the prelates' plan and summoned a deligation of the Bishops to Berlin . As soon as they received the invitation, the church - men quickly abandoned their plan presuming a favourable outcome of the meeting which never came . Hitler even demanded that the Bishops repeal Article 31 of the Concordat;namely the protection of Catholic organisations and societies which pursue only cultural or religious objectives .

The Berlin Meeting signalled Hitler's unwillingness to bind himself to the stipulations of the Concordat . Like the previous mistake, the Bishops' failure to have published their Pastoral Letter, even to have handed it down to Hitler or to his representatives at the Meeting reveals yet another weakness of the German Roman Catholic Church to keep abreast with developments immediately preceding the Holocaust . The moderate views of Cardinal Faulhaber and his concession to disband Catholic Youth Associations in order to save the abrogation of the Concordat which Hitler was not respecting anyway represented, to my own way of thinking, a misreading of the real intentions of Hitler and his regime . If this is not credible, did the German Bishops not realize, on the part of the clerics, by the end of 1934, the utter hopelessness of their negotiations? Was there not a crisis of confidence in the Bishops' union already felt by the catholic faithful ? When the Führer 's troops, in order to realize their expansionist dreams, annexed Austria on March 13, 1938 for purposes of restoring the so - called " law and order " and to effect the Anschluss; was it not Cardinal Innitzer of Vienna who made another unexpected optimistic remarks about the credibility of the National Socialism and its government .[14]

Even in the war years the division existing in the ranks of the German hierarchy made it quite impossible for the Church to mount a concerted resistance. In the words of the German Foreign minister, Joachim von Ribbentrop (1893 - 1946), the Vatican maintained neutrality in the face of the events of those years; a neutrality which I think was encouraged by the attitude of some German Bishops .

In 1939 when Hitler celebrated his fiftieth birthday Cardinal Betram single-handedly sent him a congratulatory telegram which surprised the faithful . In 1940 when he did it a second time on Hitler's fifty - first birthday, Cardinal Konrad von Preysing, who had in 1939 expressed serious reservations, did not hesitate to reprimand Betram . It was Pope Pius XII whose timely intervention made the two prelates patch up their quarrels yet that did not heal the division already created in the German hierarchy. The disunity made it impossible for the Bishops to have taken a common and united stand on the matters of the moment and to have issued a challenging Pastoral Letter in which they should have registered their protest against such Nazi crimes as euthanasia and mass deportations of the Jews to Eastern Europe . The absence of unity in the hierarchy made the Bishops unable to decide on the prompt publication of an Apostolic Letter from the Pope . Besides, Cardinal Betram 's conservative attitude was still felt during the period of the war . Betram's vacillations delayed the publication of another planned pastoral letter based on the Ten Commandments in which the crimes of the government would have been denounced . His preference " to do things " through diplomatic channels doomed the chances of the Church to protest . Betram's failure to comprehend the fact that Germany of his day had undergone a radical evolution from a constitutional democracy to a totalitarian regime was unfortunate . Neither did he realize that the totalitarian ambitions of the National Socialism would never compromise with anything that was not prepared to allow itself to be assimilated into its philosophy .

These reflections, no doubt, compel me to draw the conclusion that most Bishops in both Germany and Austria, even Rome, by their procastination and silence were culpable in the emergence of a climate of hatred and injustice that made the tragedy of the Holocaust possible .

Hiter 's Total War (1938 - 1941)

By this period, the Nazi campaigns had assumed the character of what moralists describe as " open conflict ... " leading to " mass and indiscriminate harm and destruction " to people of all races who lived in many parts of Central Europe .[15] The führer had launched a Blitzkrieg (lightning war) during which period most of West European countries were overrun . His troops went as far as North Africa in early 1941 . In June, the same year, Hitler had sent out his soldiers to the Soviet Union; captured Kiev and Kharkov in the Ukraine . Nazi " Total War " had far - reaching geographical implications . It was intended as politics of annexation which ushered in World War II . It included inter alia a programme of eugenic control and euthanasia carried out on millions of people otherwise described as racially harmful to the State .[16] Ideologically Hitler's war implied the destruction of everything that deviated from the political and racial Weltanschauung of the Third Reich . In this savage operation a large number of gypsies were forcibly sterilized or gassed to death .[17] The mentally disabled were despatched to death in many cities of Germany and beyond .

Hitler 's AKTIONS 14 F 13 responsible for the extermination of well over 20,000 persons knew no bounds . The Jews were in particular hunted down . Hitler 's Mein Kampf and Rosenberg 's Mythus des 20 - Jahrhundert and thoughtless speeches of Nazi sycophants contained attrocious anti - Jewish slogans and statements . Though during the Berlin Olympic Games of 1936 anti - Jewish activities were sort of mitigated, that was only to score political gains . As soon as the games were over, there flowed a steady barrade of anti - Jewish decrees . Some of the more obnoxious legislations prescribed that all male Jews should adopt the name " Israel " in their business ventures and all legal matters while the women were to use the name " Sarah " . Jewish street-names were replaced with the names of Aryans . The Mayor of Leipzig who resented this attitude had to resign his office when Nazi agents dismantled the statue of Mendelsohn, a Jew, which was one of the famous Merkmale of the city . Not only in business life, even on the social arena, Jews were segregated . They were denied acess to public parks, swimming pools, public transport and their children humiliated in state schools . In country villages, Nazi fanatics posted bills which read " Jews come here at their own risk . "

Indeed Hitler's total war was both socially and psychologically destructive . So far from facts before us, it can be argued that the war was a premeditated conflict by which the Nazis carried out unlimited pogrom on defenseless people . At this stage of the paper, one is prompted to ask some questions : what caused the Nazis to subject the Jews to such inhuman treatment? Were they jealous of Jewish success in business, learning and the arts? If non of the above, why were the Jews specially marked out to be butchered in thousands? These are issues I will presently address myself to in the next section of the paper .

The Reichskristallnacht and its Consequences

The episode leading to the horrors of the Holocaust cannot be properly understood without a consideration of the tragic violence associated with the Kristallnacht of November 9 - 10, 1938 . This was a night of anti - Jewish riot throughout Germany . The motive for this brutal event was anchored on a blood - libel trumped up against the Jews that they drank the blood of christian children in their rituals . In another allegation, they stated that a full - blooded Aryan German was murdered by a Jew living in France . Paul Joseph Goebbels (1897 - 1945), Hitler 's minister of Propaganda (1933 - 1945) took it upon himself to stir up public sentiments against the Jews . The Führer himself was said to be the author of a callous fiction which claimed that the Jews led a " capitalist - communist conspiracy " meant to ruin the Germans and their economy . Furthermore, Nazi Stormabteilung (stormtroopers) whipped up popular anti - Jewish feelings and invited the mob to undertake violent reprisals against the Jews as a " spontaneous re-action of the Aryan people " . Shops, business houses of well over 7,000 Jews were destroyed, synagogues were burned down and some 91 Jews were murdered in cold blood . Over 30,000 well - to - do Jews were arrested on the pretext that it was " for their own good," but, in fact, the intention was to force them to emigrate . The monstrosity of the events consequent upon the Kristallnacht offensive was the fine of one billion Deutschemarks imposed on Jewish community . Inspite of this burden, various socio - economic restrictions were imposed which resulted in mass poverty and suicides among peasant Jews . The economic power and business success enjoyed by the Jews was envied by the Germans . The Kristallnacht represented part of the culminations of German hatred of the Jewish race and their enterprise . In 1940, two anti - Semitic films appeared; namely Jud Süss by Veit Harlan and Der Ewige Jude by Fritz Heppler . These motion - pictures futher aggravated the desire for the persecution of the Jews throughout German - occupied territories . In a very recent contribution, G. Fleming informs us that the racial doctrine of Nazi Weltanschauung was based on a triple credo : (a) the fundamental inequality of mankind on the basis of genetic traits; (b) the existence of various human races; and (c) the existence of an irrevocably inferior race, the Jews .[18] This obnoxious doctrine was largely derived from Darwinian evolutionary theory which postulated the superior right of the stronger against the weak . It was in the light of this theory that Nazi agents maintained that the Aryan - Anglo Saxon races must be on the top with others like the Slavs and Jews at the bottom line . For this, the Nazis argued that over - alienation with the Jews posed the danger of extinction for the Aryans .[19] At one time,it was believed among Nazi agents that the non - human race such as the Jews would serve the Herrenvolk (the master race) . Later on, there developed the desire to exterminate the worthless races as they were nothing but vermins . As the economy was depressed, the Jews became a convenient scapegoat . And to find excuse for their murderous acts, the Nazis accused Jews of imperialist designs, of plotting against the German state and of unethical fiscal conducts . The Nazis approved of the disenfranchisement of the Jews and subjected them to special racial laws . To achieve a Judenrein Europa, the Jews were massively exterminated on grounds of their race .

The leader of the extermination squad was Martin Borman, one of the most cruel of Hitler's aides . From 1941 the pogrom was continued under the supervision of anti - Semitic vanguards. A special Schutzstaffel (SS) Commandos were set up to continue the systematic extirpation of the Jews . This programme saw the removal of Jews from the Netherlands, Belgium and Austria . By the middle of 1941, this vicious exercise had caused the death of over four million Jews in various concentration camps .[20] In Austria, there inhabited 185,246 Jews after the annexation . Two thirds of them were compelled to emigrate and 65,459 were ruthlessly exterminated. The measures were so cruel that some 200 Jews were hidden by neighbours and other citizens at the risk of their necks.[21]

This pathological hatred for the Jews by the Nazis did not only stop at just depriving them of some basic human rights and the danger of extermination but also it was expressed through compulsory mass deportation . Heinrich Himmler (1900 - 1945), head of the SS and the Gestapo (1936 - 1945) had proposed Africa as a place to re-settle the Jews . But in 1941 it was decided to evacuate Jews to Eastern Europe where they were settled in labour Camps . Those found unfit for hard labour were liquidated by gassing while the able - bodied were put in ghettos with the promise of potato peelings and cabbage leaves .[22] Later in 1942 at the Wannsee Conference of 20 January, Adolf Eichmann outlined his plan for " The Final Solution of the Jewish question ", otherwise known as the Endlösung . Here, the Nazis took the decision to embark upon the brutal mass murders of the Jews .[23]

In September 1943, Nazi troops stormed Rome . As soon as they occupied the city, they enacted severe measures against Roman Jews . Nazi occupying forces extorted 50 kilos of gold in less than 36 hours from the Jews and insisted that if they did not comply, 200 of them would face deportation . Inspite of the fact that some Jews had converted to christianity, what was argued was " he is a Jew who has Jewish blood flowing in his veins, no matter what his religion may be ". By mid October 1943, the Germans had seized the Jewish Synagogue in Rome, looted its treasury and burnt its precious archives . On October 16, they had combed the Jewish ghettos . About 1,127 Jews were deported; of these only 327 were men . They were brutally treated and later conveyed to the concentration camps in Eastern Europe . It is stated that only 14 men and one woman could survive the ordeal; the rest were murdered .

To sum up this section, I submit that all these cruel measures could not have been executed successfully by one man alone . Hitler had willing accomplices amongst the christians . The tyranny of the Third

Reich received wide fervour among many German christians, catholic as well as evangelical christians . Over 200 members of the catholic clergy and nuns functioned as agents of the Gestapo from 1936 - 1945 . Was the Church not aware of these activities of the clerics? The Church's silence can best be imagined when seen through the lens of Elie Wiesel's own words :

> The world knew and kept silence and their solitude then was matched only by God's . Mankind let them suffer and agonize and perish alone . And yet they did not die alone, for something in all of us died with them .24

The Attitude of Pope Pius XII

S. Friedlander has joined several historians to raise the controversial question : what was the attitude of Pius XII to the persecution of the Jews? Why did the Roman Pontiff not publically protest to the Nazis?[25] Arguments pro and contra have been advanced to respond to these questions . The crucial issue is to delineate to which extent the Pope can be said to have shared responsibility for Nazi elimination of millions of Jews . Many historians have addressed the subject such that opinions are still varied and sometimes inconclusive . As far as data before do allow, the Pope's attitude was not different from the silence of German Bishops and cardinals . Some catholic ecclesiastical historians tend to play down the issue by arguing that even if the Pope was aware of the persecutions of other ethnic groups in different parts of Europe, he was not aware of the enormous scale and the extent to which the Jews suffered. In recent times our knowledge of the true position is further advanced by findings of the East London Auschwitz Committee . I freely quote :

> And there can be no question about whether he (the Pope) was in possession of all the facts . Letters from a Papal Ambassador in Czechoslovakia show that he knew the fate of the Jews, and reported it in February 1942 : ' ... it was incorrect to believe that the Jews were being sent to Poland to work; in reality, they were being exterminated there '; and there is plenty of other evidence of this knowledge in the highest levels of the Catholic Church . The silence of Pius XII extended even to the deportation of Italian Jews and especially the Jews of Rome ' under his very windows '.[26]

Evidence such as these do support the fact that the Pope who had great moral authority even among non - Catholics could have protested against the crimes of Nazism . It was customary that he as leader of millions of catholic christians, in times of global crisis, and on important world events speak out in warning . But, if so, why then did Pope Pius XII fail to make any pronouncements? Is it right to conclude, as many authors tend to do, that his protest and condemnation of the regime would have changed nothing .[27] I am relunctant to identify with this opinion . European Catholicism had erred . Let this fact be acknowledged . A loud protest voiced out by the Roman Pontiff would have offered encouragement for the free world to join him in denouncing

German extermination policy . Those who conclude on the possibility for retaliation by the Nazis are quite in error . They do not seem to recognize the fact that the Pope's silence continued even when Hungarian Jews were deported in May 1944 by which time Rome was already under the protection of the Allied Forces .[28]

In his traditional Christmas broadcast (1942), Pope Pius XII directed his attention to totalitarianism . He stated that hundreds of thousands of people had been subjected to oppression and persecution on grounds of their race . The address was cowardly written . The Pope refrained from explicit mention of the persecution of any ethnic group . Many western diplomats in Berlin at that time, were of the opinion that the Pope's utterances were not emphatic enough . Most of them had felt that he should have stigmatized Nazi Germany and called it names for their genocidal acts against the Jews . It was agreed that on moral grounds, the Pope had right to make the world know what had happened . In an address to the College of Cardinals on June 5, 1945 where he outlined his view of the events of the time, it was plain to observers that there were many things about which the Pontiff said nothing. While it was true that he condemned the racial theory of the National Socialism, he never spoke against concrete deeds in a specific way . This is why a chief character in the play The Deputy was represented to act out such a role as thought of the Pope . The Nazis should have been dressed down accordingly but they were not.[29]

Conclusion

In this paper, I have revealed the socio - political setting from which National Scialism emerged as a political system in a Germany that was insensitive towards democracy, parliamentarism, capitalism and even the modernization process.[30] I have gone ahead to uncover the level of disunity that prevailed in the ranks of the German episcopate and how a Church beset with division proved herself ineffective in the face of rising totalitarianism . To the best of my ken, these two factors contributed immensely towards the creation of a climate in which the genocidal crimes of the Nazis materialized unchallenged . In order to respond objectively to the issue of proper apportionment of responsibility, it is my submission that most of the German prelates did not fully recognize the import of the totalitarian system that was thrust upon their nation by a few dictatorial personalities . A few of the Party jingoists had made Germany a victim of a nest of unscrupulous men who dominated and controlled the propaganda machine to tyrannize the whole of Europe . The tragedy of the Catholics in Germany at that time was their lack of foresight to have perceived the evolution of Germany from established constitutional state to a totalitarian ideology which manifested itself intolerant to any other worldview . What the Catholic Bishops failed to acknowledge was that the Third Reich was not moved by private and individual protests but by public disclosures and sanctions . The gruesome mass murders of the Jews could have been stopped if the Bishops had stirred up the populace and appealed to the conscience of the world . This was a great omission complemented, in my opinion, by Pope Pius XII 's silence on Nazi racial policies and his failure to challenge the Reich in his 1942 Christmas message and his omission of the Jewish problem in his address to the Cardinals in 1945 . These factors lend support to the view that the Catholic Church shared co - responsibility not only in the rise but also in the crimes of totalitarian Nazism because as the old adage goes : qui tacet consentiret . It would therefore appear and probably correct that the Church held on to an illusion that amounted to co-operation with the Nazis .

Apart, however, from these concluding remarks; I wish to propose, as part of the contributions of my paper to the Conference, the following concerns for our future :

(a) that the terrors of the Holocaust continue to stare the world in the face as irreconcilable events which constantly dampen the light of the Christian Religion which preaches peace and love as its cardinal doctrines to mankind .

(b) that the terrible horrors of the Nazi death camps continue to prick humanity 's conscience and to alert our generation of the monstrosity of genocide .

(c) that the lessons of the Holocaust continue to send shock waves to all peoples who tread on the gun-powder of religious intolerance, bigotry and fanaticism as well as racial discriminations in the contemporary world .

(d) that in countries where Christianity and Islam or any other world religion are no good bed - fellows, the Holocaust, this ghastly episode of modern history leaves a lingering memory which must constantly provide a caveat for our own time and future .

(e) And finally, for a continued fruitful Christian - Jewish relations and dialogues, Christianity must be prayed to admit ignorance; accept culpability and bear share of responsibility for Jewish sufferings .

I would like to terminate with Hegel 's piece of advice :

" History teaches man one thing : man never learns from history ".

Notes and References

1. Here see, F. R. Stern, The Politics of Cultural Despair : A Study in the Rise of Germanic Ideology, Berkeley, 1961; E. Eyck, A History of the Weimar Republic, Cambridge, Massachusetts, 1963 .
2. In the State elections of that year 7000 candidates contested under 37 different political parties .
3. This fact has been documented in Hitler's Mein Kampf (1925) .
4. In that year's presidential elections, Hitler polled 13 million votes as against 19 million for Hindenburg .

5. Cf. C. R. Morsey, Die Deutsche Zentrumpartei, Düsseldorf, 1960 who believes that the furtive plans for a coalition with the NSDAP was suggested by Eugenio Cardinal Pacelli, the papal Nuncio to Germany. Pacelli later became the Pope (Pius XII) of the Holocaust era .See also idem., " Hitlers Verhandlungen mit der Zentrumsführung am 31 Januar 1933," in Vierteljahrshefte für Zeitgeschichte 9(1961)182 - 194; J. Becker, " Zentrum und Errichtigungsgesetz 1933 " in ibid., pp. 195 - 212 .

6. Here see the memoires of F. Muckermann, Im Kampf zwischen zwei Epochen : Lebenserinnerungen, Mainz, 1973, pp. 524 - 651 .

7. Here see, J.A Bach, Franz von Papen in der Weimarer Republik, 1981 - 1932, Dusseldorf, 1977 .

8. To corroborate this assertion I cite the Denkschrift (20 August, 1935) of the German Bishops where Cardinal Faulhaber wote : We trust, sir, Chancellor, that you will put an end to the campaign against the Papacy . It was the Pope who first extended a hand to you in the Concordat. On March 13, 1933 the Pope highly praised you in the presence of other high officials, because you were the first to separate yourself from Bolshevism ". Notice that this statement had been supressed in the Osservatore Romano, March 13 - 14, 1933 and the Acta Apostolicis Sedis 25(1933)106 - 123. In both texts no mention is any longer made of the papal praise of Hitler. For further information see, L. Volk, " Papstliche Laudatio auf Hitler ", SdZ 173(1963 - 1964)221 - 229 .

9. For details of this Papal Encyclical see, Acta Apostolicis Sedis 22(1930)547ff.

10. See C. Bauer,"Erzbischof Gröber und des Reichskonkordat ", in Alemann. Jahrbuch, Baden, 1970, pp. 187 - 331 .

11. A. Bäumler, Alfred Rosenberg und der Mythus des 20 Jahrhundert, Munich, 1948; R. Cecil, The Myth of the Master Race: Alfred Rosenberg and Nazi Ideology, London, 1972 .

12. On the ideological formation given to the Hitlerjugend see,L. Walkery, Hitler Youth and Catholic Youth 1933 - 1936: A Study in Totalitarian Conquest, Washington, 1970; H.W. Koch, The Hitler Youth: Origins and Development 1922 - 1945, London, 1975 .

13. And so did he reject to publish a pastoral letter after the attrocious trials in April, 1937 .

14. For the severe measures taken by the Nazis against the Church in Austria during the occupation see, R.V. Luza,"Nazi Control of the Austrian Catholic Church 1939 - 1941," in Catholic Historical Review, October, 1977, pp. 537 - 572 .

15. Cf. J. A. Selling, " Total War, The Use of Force, and Proportionality," Louvain Studies 9(1986)22 - 30, p. 27 .

16. Here see, G. Sereny, Into that Darkness: From Mercy Killing to Mass Murder, New York, 1974; K. Nowak, " Euthanasie " und Sterilisierung im " Dritten Reich ," Halle, 1977 .

17. See D. Kenrick and G. Puxon, Destins gitans: Des origines a la " solution finale," Paris, 1974; J. Botvitch, " Enkele gegevens betreffende de uitroeing van de Zigeuners in België ", in his Bijdragen tot de geschiedenis van de Tweede Wereldoorlog, 1976, pp. 153 - 173 .

18. G. Fleming, Hitler and the Final Solution, Hamish Hamilton, London, 1985, p.8 .

19. K. D. Bracher, The Age of Ideologies, Weidenfield and Nicholson, London, 1980, p. 123 .

20. The actual number killed exceed six million.Cf. example, L. Poliakou, Breviaire de las haine: Le IIIe Reich et les Juifs, Paris, 1951;G. Reitlinger, The Final Solution, New York, 1953; I Arndt & W. Scheffler," Organisierter Massenmord an Juden in National - sozialistischen Vernichtungslagern ", in Vierteljahrhefte fur Zeitgeschichte 24(1976)105 - 135 .

21. See E. Weinzierl, Zu Wenig Gerechte: Oesterreicher und Judenverfolgung 1938 - 1945, Graz, 1969 .

22. Cf. N. A. Auschwitz - Yesterdays Racism: a pack of materials for teachers, East London Auschwitz Committee, London, 1979, p. 4 . 4 .

23. Cf. B. Tlhagale, " Nazism, Stalinist Russia and Apartheid - A Comparism," in B. Tlhagale & I. Mosala, (eds.) Hammering Swords into Ploughshares : Essays in Honour of Archbishop Mpilo Desmond Tutu, Michigan, Eerdmans, 1987, pp. 265 - 278 .

24. E. Wiesel et al, Dimensions of the Holocaust, Northwestern University, Evanston, Illinois, 1977, p. 7 .

25. Cf. S. Friedlander, Pie XII et le IIIe Reich . Documents, Paris, 1969 .

26. N. A., Auschwitz - Yesterday's Racism, p. 12.2 .

27. For other views on this debate, see R. Leiber,"Pius XII und die Juden in Rom 1943 - 1944," in SdZ 167(1960)428 - 436 .

28. On this issue and the debates involved, see J. Raddatz, Was it good for the Pope to keep silent, Hamburg, 1963; Fischer, Pius XII and the Jews, New York, 1963; J. Conway, " The Silence of Pope Pius XII," in Review of Politics, 1965, pp. 105 - 113 .

29. For a critical assessment of the situation, especially in response to this question, see, J. L. Graubart, " The Vatican and the Jews : Cynicism and Indiffence," in Judaism 24(1975)166 - 180; C. Klein, " The Vatican and the German - Italian Anti - semitism in the Nineteen Thirties," in Judaica 31(1975)125 - 135; P. Matheson, " The Christian Churches in the Third Reich," Judaica 27(1971)132 - 146 .

30. Tlhagale, " Nazism ..., p. 266 .

CHRISTIANS PORTRAYING JEWS: STEREOTYPES IN THE OBERAMMERGAU PASSION PLAY

GORDON R. MORK

Purdue University, West Lafayette, Indiana, USA

ABSTRACT

The traditional passion play in the Bavarian village of Oberammergau, performed regularly since 1634, puts Christians in the roles of biblical Jewish characters. Rather than providing a reconciling bridge between Christians and Jews, however, the play has perpetuated negative stereotypes of Jews, contributing to anti-Semitism. Only since 1970 have improvements been made, but the play remains controversial.

KEYWORDS

Oberammergau: Passion Play: Christians: Jews: Jesus: Nazi: Hitler: anti-Semitism: Catholic Church: Vatican II Council.

INTRODUCTION

In the village of Oberammergau in the Bavarian Alps, once each decade for more than 350 years, Christians have donned costumes and learned lines to give portrayals of some of the most famous Jews of history: the heroes, traditionally, have been Jesus of Nazareth, his loyal disciples, Mary his mother, and a handful of followers; the villains have been the high priests, Annas and Caiaphas and their ilk, Judas Iscariot, the temple traders, and the Jerusalem mob; Pilate and the other Romans are presented as neutral or even praiseworthy characters. This paper will illuminate Christian attitudes toward Jews just prior to the Holocaust and will show the varying responses to revivals of stereotypes after the Holocaust.

THE PLAY AND ITS HERITAGE

Ever since Rabbi Joseph Krauskopf's vigorous criticism of the Oberammergau Passion Play in 1908, (1) Americans and others in the English speaking world have had the information available that the religious pageant clearly showed negative stereotypes of the Jewish world. In the dramatization and costuming, as well as in the play text itself, the play portrayed Jesus and his followers as heroes and victims, while "the Jews" were malevolent plotters guilty of deicide. Prominently featured was the line from the book of Matthew blaming the Jews as a whole of the death of Jesus:

Chorus: Jerusalem!
The blood of His Son will yet avenge on you the Lord.
People: His Blood be on us, and on our children!
Chorus: Be it then upon you, and on your children! (2)

Nevertheless, the play grew in popularity with English speaking visitors, both Protestant and Catholic, growing from several hundred at the turn of the century to several hundred thousand in the 1980's.

When Adolf Hitler took power in 1933, the villagers were concerned that they would not be permitted to put on their traditional religious drama, and that the newly appointed Nazi mayor, Raimund Lang, would substitute a specially written version. Indeed, Lang did commission Dr. Leo Weismantel, a writer of popular folk dramas, to work up a manuscript.(3) Several of the leaders of the village, however, who played major roles in the play, were upset by the attempt to change their tradition. They could not directly challenge the Nazi mayor, but they had connections via the neighboring village of Unterammergau with Gauleiter Adolf Wagner in Munich. Wagner had a weekend cottage on the shoulder of a mountain overlooking the villages of the Ammergau, and saw himself as something of a protector of the local traditions. When he challenged the mayor's plan, Raimund Lang disingenuously denied that he was making any change. Yet he continued to work with Weismantel on a new text secretly. The local townsfolk protested to Wagner once more, citing the fact that Adolf Hitler himself had seen the play in its traditional form in 1930 and declared it a German national treasure. They also pointed out, correctly, that Weismantel was not Nazi. This time Wagner issued a vigorous order to Raimund Lang and the town council of Oberammergau that the traditional text should be used again in 1934 (4) and the local Nazis quickly fell into line.

Adolf Hitler visited a performance of the play again in 1934, to the cheers of the local crowd and the many visitors. Press reports indicated that the Führer once more expressed his delight at the play, and Mayor Lang and the other local leaders responded enthusiastically and awarded him a large album of pictures from the play and the village.(5)

In early 1938 the villagers began to lay plans for the 1940 version of the play.(6) In a lengthy article in _Der Fremdenverkehr: Reichsorgan für den deutschen Fremdenverkehr_, August 19, 1939, the play was highly touted. Mayor Lang was quoted as saying that the play is "not a religious matter, but rather a three hundred year old tradition bound to blood and soil." The article quotes an unnamed "leading personality of the NSDAP" as saying that "the Passion Play is the most anti-Semitic play of which we are aware." And Hitler's utterances of 12 August 1930 and 13 August 1934 were cited as further proof of the legitimacy of the play under the New Order. The _Voelkischer Beobachter_ of August 24, 1939, announced "Vorbereitungen für die Passionsspiele 1940: Oberammergau vor neuen grossen Aufgaben", "preparations for the Passion Play of 1940: Oberammergau stands before new and great tasks." Mayor Raimund Lang is quoted at the time that play would be performed according to the will of the Führer and that the Reich Propaganda Ministry had declared the play to be "important for the Reich."(7) Of course the 1940 play never took place; war intervened. Yet Hitler still recalled his impressions of the play and its portrayal of Christians playing Jews while chatting over dinner in 1942: "One of the most important tasks will be to save future generations from a similar political fate and to maintain for ever watchful in them a knowledge of the menace of Jewry. For this reason alone it is vital that the Passion Play be continued at Oberammergau; for never has the menace of Jewry been so convincingly portrayed as in this presentation of what happened in the times of the Romans. There one sees in Pontius Pilate a Roman racially and intellectually so superior, that he stands out like a firm clean rock in the middle of the whole muck and mire of Jewry."(8)

THE POST-HOLOCAUST EXPERIENCE

As Saul S. Friedman has pointed out(9), the townsfolk had to argue to the American occupation forces in the late 1940's that their play was not anti-Semitic and was merely a harmless Christian tradition, in order to gain permission to put on the play again in 1950. Yet the text of the play in that year (and indeed in 1960 as well) was the same which had been used in 1934 and in the pre-Nazi years. After the theological changes brought about by the Vatican II Council serious voices began to be raised in Oberammergau calling for reform of the anti-Semitic stereotypes. Both Germans and Americans, both Christians and Jews, called for a major overhaul of the text of the play.(10) A faction in the village attempted to mount a completely new production of the play, based on an eighteenth century text by Father Rosner, in 1977, but the majority of the townsfolk believed it to be too radical a departure from the traditions of the nineteenth and early twentieth centuries, and it was laid aside.(11) The 1980 and 1984 versions of the play excised the most offensive lines from the traditional version, and added to the Prologue lines of welcome to Jewish visitors intended to deal with criticism:

> Greetings to you, brothers and sisters, of the people
> Who brought forth the Redeemer,
> Let no one try to find the blame in others;
> Let each of us recognize
> His own guilt in these events.
> God has made us all full of disobedience.(12)

There may be some additional small changes for the 1990 version. But the villagers continue to maintain that the play is not anti-Semitic in any respect, and often react defensively when anyone suggests otherwise.

CONCLUSION

Christians portray Jews as part of their religious drama and pageantry and have done so for centuries. Much of this drama reflects popular culture rather than carefully considered theological positions, and thus much of it falls into oversimplified stereotyping. Too often Christians are simply the heroes and Jews are the villains. Such was the case at Oberammergau. The traditional (but now officially rejected) theology of deicide was reinforced by non-biblical myths like the "wandering Jew."

Most Christians who participate in such dramas, or who observe them, are blissfully unaware that they are perpetuating hatreds which--under certain conditions--can lead to persecution and to genocide. After World War II, inhabitants of Oberammergau brought before the American denazification tribunals evidence that townsfolk sheltered individual Jews secretly throughout the war years, in order to demonstrate that the town was not "anti-Semitic." They argued that the city fathers had "resisted the Nazis" by protesting against Raimund Lang's attempt to replace the traditional text with Weismantel's specially written one in 1934. They rebuilt bridges with Americans who had developed close links with the town before the war, and continued to expand those relationships.(13)

The Christians of Oberammergau, and the Christians who come from all over the world to see them portray Jews, are not engaging in some anti-Jewish ritual. Yet elements of the old prejudices remain even today, virtually unnoticed by all but the sensitive few. Judas Iscariot wears the black and yellow garb in which Julius Streicher clothed his version of the "wandering Jew" during the Nazi times. And a figure known as "the Rabbi," who never appears in the Bible, still schemes against Jesus and gloats at his death. Are these early warning signs of some future Holocaust, or just meaningless artifacts of past prejudices?(14)

NOTES

1 A Rabbi's Impressions of the Oberammergau Passion Play (Philadelphia, 1908).
2 Act XIII, Prologue.
3 Weismantel-Lang correspondence, Weismantel archive, Seeheim-Jugenheim. I wish to thank Dr. Gertrud Weismantel for her kindness and help in my research.
4 Wagner-Lang correspondence, Bavarian State Archives, Munich.
5 The album was captured by U.S. forces after World War II, and is listed in the catalog of the Library of Congress, but it has disappeared from the shelves without a trace.
6 Staatsarchiv Munich, LRA 61616, Oberammergau, den 30.Januar 1938.
7 Bayrische Hauptstaatsarchiv, Munich, MWi 2804.
8 Hitler's Secret Conversations: 1941-1944 (New York, 1953), p. 457.
9 The Oberammergau Passion Play: A Lance Against Civilization (Carbondale, IL, 1984).
10 See, in addition to Friedman, Leonard Swidler and Gerard S. Sloyan, The Oberammergau Passion Play 1984 (New York, 1980) for a detailed analysis of the text, as well as articles by Donald J. Dietrich, David L. Kissel, and myself in Face to Face: An Interreligious Bulletin, XII, 1985.
11 The attempt was very controversial at the time, but received a handsome commemoration in 1987 with a display of models in the town's civic center and the publication of a large format book with color illustrations, Das Rosner Spiel: Eine Dokumentation . . . (Oberammergau, 1987).
12 1984 text, page 20.
13 On visits to Oberammergau in 1981, 1984, and 1987 I was welcomed, though an outsider, and I interviewed several prominent persons in their homes, including Hans Meier, the play director for the 1980 and 1984 productions, and Melchior Breitsamter, who played Pilate in 1934 and was one of the persons to protest the attempted change of text.
14 I wish to thank the National Endowment for the Humanities and the Purdue University Jewish Studies Program for supporting the research on which this paper is based.

MARGARETE SOMMER, BERLIN CATHOLICS, AND GERMANY'S JEWS, 1939-1945

MICHAEL PHAYER

HISTORY DEPARTMENT, MARQUETTE UNIVERSITY, MILWAUKEE, WISCONSIN

During the desperate years when Germany's Jews faced emigration, deportation, and mass murder in eastern Europe, Margarete Sommer was in charge of a church office in Berlin whose sole purpose was to help them. In this capacity Sommer became acquainted with all aspects of the ordeal that Berlin and German Jews faced. As a result of this work and of her ability to obtain information on anti-Semitic actions by the National Socialist regime before these took place, Sommer became the principal advisor to the German eqiscopacy on Jewish affairs. A study of this remarkable woman offers keen insights into what Catholics and the Catholic church did and did not do on behalf of Jews during the years of their escalating persecution.

The work of Sommer and her Berlin circle on behalf of Jews ranged from quiet dissent to resistance. It is not always possible to discern the line of demarcation. For example, Sommer often dealt with religious questions such as the proper conduct of Catholics during church services at which Jewish converts were present, or the inviolability of a sacramental marriage in which one of the partners was Jewish. These areas of friction between the church and the Nazi regime led Sommer to urge the German bishops, and even the pope, to speak out against Hitler, and led directly to her efforts to stop the 'transportation' of Jews to the ghettoes of Eastern Europe. Although they probably should not be counted as outright resistance, other activities, such as obtaining visas and providing for elderly, impoverished Jews, were of questionable legality in National Socialist Germany. But the point is that Sommer's circle of Berlin Catholics was drawn closer and closer to resistance as the National Socialist persecution of the Jews grew ever more extreme, until in the end they hid Jews.

Sommer and other Berlin Catholics were inspired to form themselves into a support group for Jews by Canon Bernhard Lichtenberg. But Sommer was not an amateur volunteer; having taken her doctorate in social work in 1927 from the University of Berlin, she devoted her entire life in social work. When the Nazis came to power, Sommer was working for the Prussian state welfare office, but she was soon dismissed "under severe political pressure" (Sommer, "Uebersicht"). Sommer was employed by Catholic Social Services, Caritas, when the frightful events of November 30, 1938, that we call Kristallnacht, took place. Thereafter, the famous Berlin priest, Canon Lichtenberg, began concluding daily mass with prayers for Jews. For several years Lichtenberg had directed the work of a new office called Special Relief of the Diocese of Berlin (Hilfswerk beim Ordinariat Berlin) which had been created to help Berlin Jews. Sommer gravitated toward the Special Relief office. By 1939 she was devoting so much of her time to it that Lichtenberg, hounded by the Gestapo and frequently in prison, depended on her to run the office. When Lichtenberg became almost totally incapacitated in 1941, Sommer was officially appointed the director of Special Relief by Konrad Preysing, the bishop of Berlin.

Yet, Sommer's influence clearly extended beyond the City of Berlin. Her historical significance lies in the fact that she used her Berlin experiences to try to influence the conduct of the entire German church in matters pertaining to Jews. In many parts of the country Jews had become something of an abstraction for Germans either because they had lost their ethnic identity or because they constituted only a very negligible portion of the population (Kershaw, 1983). But this was hardly the case in the city of Berlin where there were 190,000 Jewish citizens in 1936 of whom about 40,000 were Christian (Reutter, 1969). Through her work with Catholic Jews, Sommer became sensitive to the burdens which National Socialism had placed on the entire Jewish population. "The difficulty of this work," Sommer wrote after several years experience, "lies in the fact that those affected [by National Socialist anti-Semitism] are psychologically deeply depressed because of the hopelessness of the efforts [to help them] (Sommer, "Taetigkeit"). In addition, Sommer noted, those Jews who had become Catholic felt that the church did not care enough about them in their plight. Having become aware of their problems, Sommer dedicated herself to helping Berlin Jews. It was clearly her personal involvement with them in Berlin and her sensitivity to their predicament that led her to try to raise the awareness of the entire church to the desperateness of the situation of all Jews.

We may think of Sommer's work as having three phases. From 1938 through 1941 she facilitated Jewish emigration; during 1942 and 1943 she urged the Catholic church to speak out about atrocities against Jews; and, finally, during the last years of the war, she looked after Jews who were being 'transported' to the East and hid other Jews. Although it is useful to proceed along these lines, the activities of the second and third phase were often simultaneous. But let us begin with Sommer's activities on the eve of World War II.

When the National Socialist regime began persecuting Jews, those who had converted to Catholicism turned to the St. Raphael Society for assistance in emigration (Sommer, "Kirchlich Arbeit"; van Schewick, 1980). This was natural because the Raphael Society had been assisting Catholic emigration for the past 50 years. The difference was that in the past the prospective emigrant had been a victim of a sluggish economy but in 1940 he or she was a victim of state persecution. Since nothing helped Jews more than a passport out of the country, Sommer's Special Relief office worked with the Raphael Society in this effort. Much of her energy and the office's funds were spent in obtaining emigration papers from the German government and visas from host countries in Europe (Sommer, "Kurzer Bericht"). Unfortunately, this usually meant France or Holland (Sommer, "Kirchliche Arbeit"). Those who emigrated to these countries found themselves trapped in the Nazi web a second time due to German successes during the first years of World War II. It fell then to Special Relief to try to resettle these people once again (usually in Brazil).

After 1938 parents, whose children were classified by the regime as _Mischlingen_ (part Jewish), often applied to Special Relief to find homes for their children outside Germany (Sommer, "Statistische Uebersicht"). In 1939 about one of every four of the approximately 1,000 applications for emigration facilitated by the Special Relief office was a child. Between 1934 and 1939 about 2,000 German Jews succeeded in getting emigration and visa papers through the Raphael Society. Roughly 20 percent of these Germans were Berliners. These figures may strike us as relatively low (although certainly not insignificant); they must be understood, however, in the context of the difficulties involved in securing passports and visas. The Raphael Society dealt with almost 100,000 applicants before placing only 2,000 people. The ratio in the Berlin Special Relief office would, of course, have been very similar.

Special Relief often worked with the Reich Association of Jews in Germany (_Reichvereinigung der Juden in Deutschland_), in emigration work. Emigration costs of families that were part 'Aryan' and part Jewish were shared (Sommer, "Kirchliche Arbeit"). In Jewish-Gentile marriages the Reich Association of Jews would pay emigration expenses for the Jewish party or parties. There seems to have been some disagreement between the two offices on this point, but by and large they cooperated. In 1940, for example, the Reich Association of Jews referred 84 applicants to the Special Relief office, not because of the expense involved but because it was thought that they stood a better chance of obtaining emigration papers if they were processed by a church office (Bukofzer). The case of Alfred Fabian illustrates Catholic-Jewish cooperation. Fabian was held in a detention camp in 1939, but was eligible for release if funds to travel to Shanghai, China, for which he held a visa, could be found. His expenses ended up being shared by the Jewish Community (840RM), the Raphael Society (200RM), and Special Relief (sum not known) (Sommer, "Kirchliche Arbeit").

Although Special Relief served as a branch office of the St. Raphael Society, its objectives were much broader. The Berlin office attempted to provide moral support and welfare assistance of every sort for Jews. Originally, this meant Catholic Jews, since the Reich Association provided this service for others. When Ursula Benningson converted to Catholicism in July, 1939, her parish priest wrote to Special Relief to say that she should be given assistance (meaning, evidently, that her conversion was sincere). As the situation of

Berlin Jews became more and more desperate, confessional preference lost importance. Almost half of the men who received assistance from Special Relief in 1939-1940 were non-Christian Jews. A study of Margarete Sommer's notebook shows that about 20 percent of those whose emigration she assisted were non-Christian Jews, and that an additional 20 percent were Jewish converts to Protestantism. This principle applied to other areas of assistance as well. The kind of help provided by the Special Relief office ranged from supporting elderly people (about 37 percent of all adult clients), the sick and the handicapped, to providing for those who were too indigent to provide for their basic housing and nutritional needs. Almost half of the men who received assistance from Special Relief in 1939-1940 were non-Christian Jews (Sommer, "Statistische Uebersicht").

After the war began to take its toll in terms of battle fatalities and Jews were deported from Berlin in increasing numbers to concentration camps, Special Relief was faced with a new problem: orphaned children. A *'Mischling'* child, whose father was killed on the front and whose mother was killed by the National Socialists, was helpless. Special Relief sought to care for these children until it could place them in homes outside of the country (Sommer, "Kurzer Bericht"). This work took place relatively late in the war, and details on the number of such tragic cases are not available.

The various kinds of welfare work which Special Relief carried on were costly. In a five month period between August of 1939 and February of 1940 the office spent about 5,000RM on welfare, which was 1,000RM more than it spent on emigration (Sommer Nachlass). During the years of maximum emigration the St. Raphael Society spent 560,000RM to assist those who were leaving. Arguing that the large concentration of Jews in Berlin constituted a special case, the bishop of Berlin, Konrad Preysing, appealed to other bishops to contribute regularly to his Special Relief effort, especially to offset the required emigration fee (Preysing). It is not clear how the office decided to distribute its limited funds. A decision to dedicate the entire budget to emigration work never seems to have occurred to Sommer.

Largely because Bishop Konrad Preysing supported efforts on behalf of Jews, Sommer's influence spread from the city of Berlin to the entire country (Sommer, "Uebersicht"). This first happened in the fall of 1941 when Jews were obliged to wear the Star of David in public. This meant, of course, that Catholics and Protestants would worship at services along side of converts wearing the star. This situation seems to have caused greater turmoil among Protestants than Catholics, but it was also a matter of concern to the latter, and especially to Margarete Sommer. Evidently, some Catholics refused to kneel next to a Jew to take the eucharist at the communion rail, and some priests began avoiding Jews after the September, 1941, Star of David decree (*Veroeffentlichungen der Kommission fuer Zeitgeschichte* [henceforth, VKZ], 34, 550). Because of her position within the diocese, Sommer could address this issue "officially." Thus, we find Sommer writing to the dean of the German Catholic episcopacy, Cardinal Bertram, offering advice on how the church should deal with this matter. She warned that any prejudicial action, such as instituting separate services for Catholic Jews would be an additional psychological burden for them at a time when they were already being tormented. Sommer did not exaggerate. The diary of Erma Becker-Cohen, utilized by Claudia Koonz, demonstrates how painfully Christianized Jews felt the betrayal of 'Aryan' Christians who rejected them after the Star decree (Koonz, 1987). Sommer advised that bishops should awaken the consciences of priests and lay people with regard to the Jewish predicament and urge them on to a truly catholic community which lives in the spirit of charity.

The response of the church was disappointing and, in part, disturbing. Priests were instructed to avoid any announcements that would be embarrassing for Jewish Catholics, such as declaring a portion of the communion rail off-limits for them. Special Sunday services for Jews were to be avoided but when and if Jewish Catholics inquired about this, they were to be advised to go to the earliest possible Mass. Parish priests were advised not to bring this matter up, unless there was unrest among the faithful, in which case they were to be admonished in the spirit of St. Paul to have charity toward all. Jews should only be advised to attend separate services in the event that Gentile Catholics, such as bureaucrats or members of the National Socialist party, made a scene by leaving the church during services to protest the presence of Jews (VKZ, 34, 555-557). Cardinal Bertram's letter to the country's Catholic bishops, in which these directives were spelled out, concluded with a reminder from St. Paul that in Christ there is neither Jew nor Greek. But there was clearly "Jew and National Socialist party member" and, if it should come down to it, the former would be sacrificed in the interests of the latter. As the issue turned out, Becker-Cohen's case proved to be atypical, but the reaction of the hierarchy to Sommer's advice was hardly encouraging.

During the war years Sommer played a key role in warding off another National Socialist attack on Jews--the dissolution by decree of all Jewish-Gentile marriages. There was nothing the church could do, of course, if an 'Aryan' Catholic wanted to be rid of his or her Jewish spouse. A person needed only to apply to a court, and a divorce was immediately granted. Thus, in February, 1940, Werner Borcher divorced Stella, who was raised a Catholic although both her parents were Jewish. Werner provided very little money for the support of his children, before dropping out of sight altogether in 1943. As a Jewess Stella found it difficult to find work that would pay enough to support her family. Having to wear the Star of David distressed Stella because of her fear that it would lead directly to deportation (Borcher). After a time, she ceased wearing it, but then had to fear the consequences from the Gestapo if she was found out. Factors such as these made it extremely difficult for women in Stella Borcher's position to provide for their children. Many turned to the Special Relief office for child support assistance. Thus, when Sommer learned of the plan to dissolve all Jewish-Gentile marriages, she was well aware of what the impact on individuals and families would be.

Working with bishop Preysing, Sommer acted quickly to ward off the declaration on divorce. In November she wrote a strong letter to Cardinal Bertram in which she emphasized the violation of church law and the human tragedy that would ensue. It appears that the decree was enacted prematurely in certain areas in the city of Berlin, because Sommer was able to provide Bertram with concrete examples of the distress the decree would cause. In one case, an entire family committed suicide. Sommer pointed out that there were thousands of cases of sacramental marriages in Germany between Catholic Gentiles and Jews and that the fate of children was also involved. The proposed decree, barbarously inhumane in its terms, provided that a child of such a marriage could declare loyalty to either parent--if for the Jew, the future meant deportation; if for the Gentile, life in Germany as a sterilized, publicly identified Mischling. Would the bishops allow the state to "put asunder what God had joined together?" Sommer went so far as to urge the bishops to ask Pope Pius XII to intervene by writing personally to Hitler (VKZ, 34, 938ff). Thus, the proposed decree gave Sommer an excellent emotional and doctrinal issue with which to urge the hierarchy to act. A protest from Cardinal Bertram, together with planned, simultaneous local protests on the part of both Protestant and Catholic churches, forestalled the divorce decree (Klausener, 1979).

Thwarted in this direct attack on Jewish-Gentile marriages, the National Socialist regime began dealing with the 'problem' through police action early in 1943. On the last Saturday of February the operation code named Aktion Fabrik took place in Berlin. Without warning 8,000 Jews were taken to temporary, make-shift detention facilities, and then within 24 to 48 hours evacuated to concentration camps or ghettoes in eastern Europe. Among those who were deported were many Christian Jews who had married Gentile Christians. Margarete Sommer, after having witnessed the great Berlin razzia, set off immediately for Breslau, where she reported the details of the deportation to Cardinal Bertram. On the second and third of March, Bertram dispatched a strong protest to top National Socialist administrators, including Frick, Lammers, and Goebbels (VKZ, 34, 19-24).

The events of late February established a pattern of action and reaction on the part of the regime and the church. By April the bishops had worked out a coordinated, nation-wide response should the divorce decree be proclaimed (VKZ, 34, Entwurf, 62-65). Probably because of this threat, the regime continued to violate the sacramentality of Jewish-Gentile marriages by simply deporting the 'nonAryan' party. It became Sommer's role to report to German bishops on Nazi actions against Jews. She could provide little hope for a change in conduct. Jews were being arrested and deported on the most frivolous pretexts (going to an 'Aryan' barbershop, for example). Temporary detention (before deportation) was under cruel conditions (large rooms divided by chicken-wire into tiny cells of one cot's length and two cots' breadth). Just 14 days after the deportation of these Jews their families received word of their deaths. One case involved the deportation of a woman just 6 weeks after she had given birth to twins. Sommer's information was based on reports from Hesse, Austria, Westphalia, and Berlin. "In this way," Sommer concluded, "the administration was dealing with the 'mixed' marriage problem in widespread areas of the country" (VKZ, 34, 218-220).

The bishops' frequent protests, based on Sommer's stream of information, had some temporary effect. Jews in detention centers in Frankfurt and Bielefeld were allowed to return home in the summer of 1943. But in other areas, such as Upper Silesia where Jewish Christians were deported to Auschwitz, there was no respite. In the long run, of course, the protests of the bishops did not deter the National Socialists from killing German Jews. Late in the war, it appears that the operation was even expanded. In November, 1944, the director of Caritas in Silesia reported that as the Russian front advanced, Mischlingen who were married to 'Aryans' were being transported (VKZ Archive I A 25 j12 Correspondence of Caritas--Breslau Director).

Sommer's work as a consultant to the Catholic bishops was just one aspect of her life during the war. The other was working directly for Jews in the city of Berlin. When National Socialist policy changed from driving Jews out of Germany to deporting them to ghettoes in eastern Europe, the work of the Special Relief office took on a new character. It sought to provide last minute assistance for Jews who were about to be 'transported,' and sought to look after their needs after they had been resettled. To accomplish this Special Relief formed parish support groups. At the same time, Special Relief continued to look after orphaned Mischling children and to provide welfare for Catholic Jews as in the past. But let us turn to the more recent work made necessary by the regime's new 'transportation' policy.

Although occasionally a terrifying razzia took place, such as Aktion Fabrik on February 27, 1943 in Berlin, deportations were frequently--perhaps, normally--individual rather than collective (Gross, 1982). A family was simply notified that the time of its 'transportation' had come. However long a person or family might have anticipated such notification, its arrival often caused unimaginable despair, hopelessness, and trauma. As a rule there was only a few hours between the time of notification and the moment of actual departure from home. Mentally paralyzed, many people simply could not function during these terrible hours of uncertainty. Frequently they were incapable of thinking about the immediate necessities that would be of some practical use during the forced journey that awaited them.

The Special Relief office sought to help people through the moment of crisis. A group of parish volunteers, presumably people who knew the unfortunate deportees, stood ready so that one or two could go to the individual's or family's home at a moment's notice. Once there they attempted to prepare the person, "who in his bewilderment had lost all sensible orientation," for the imminent ordeal of 'transportation' (Sommer, "Kurzer Bericht"). The visitors helped with packing and took care of last minute household details. Mostly, of course, they attempted to comfort the persons about to be caught up in National Socialism's ghettoization operation. At some point a coded telephone message was made to the parish priest, who came to spend the sacraments of penance and the eucharist.

The scene conjured up by these last minute visits may strike as more grotesque than humane. Just what does one say to a person facing permanent departure from home and life or death in a concentration camp? There were, however, several circumstances which threw a softer light on the mission and which may help us understand it better. First, it appears that one of the visitors was herself Jewish. All of the personnel of Special Relief with the single exception of Margarete Sommer were Catholic Jews (Reutter, 1969). This could have a double significance. Since the person whose 'transportation' was imminent was often Christian, he or she would be given solace by a woman whose religious background was similar or identical. More importantly, the person offering solace faced exactly the same destiny, deportation, as the person whose imminent departure had occasioned her visit. Their common destiny undoubtedly made the compassion of the farewell mission genuine, allowing comforter and victim to bond in mutual support. Secondly, the victim was assured continuing assistance on the part of a support group from his or her parish. To this end circular letters made the rounds of Berlin parishes so that Gentiles who knew or recognized the names of 'transported' Jews could provide continued support by contributing food or dry goods for their use. Packages were sent to Warsaw, Theresienstadt, and Lodz where most Berliners were ghettoized (Sommer, "Kurze Bericht"). More importantly, the support group gave assurance to victims that if they were able to survive whatever ordeal lay ahead, and return one day to Germany, they could go "home". In other words, those who remained behind promised to keep track of the property of the deported. Restitution was, in fact, the main work of the Special Relief office during the years immediately following the war.

Since relief was organized by the Berlin diocese and carried out through its parishes, it might appear that Catholics were involved only with Catholics. Such was not the case. Sommer was explicit on this point, saying in her brief post-war memoire that aid was extended to all Jews (Sommer, "Kurze Bericht"). It is clear from other records that the National Socialist persecution of the Jews created a common bond among them that cut through lines of religious preference. Whether Christian or non-Christian, Jews pondered the meaning of the experience which gripped them. Thus, Gertrud Jaffe, a convert to Catholicism, worked in the missions of the Special Relief office to help as many as she could irrespective of their religious preference, and then decided, with great inner resolve, to give herself up for deportation and certain death in order to identify, as a Christian, with the suffering of her people (Sommer, Nachlass). It worked the other way as well. Jews who were not Christian, like Dr. Martha Mosse, worked to help and save other Jews regardless of their religion.

Although Special Relief and parish support groups attempted to comfort Jews about to be 'transported,' there were few illusions as to what fate awaited them. By the beginning of 1942 Sommer had detailed information about life in the ghettoes to which Berlin Jews were being herded: 30 to 80 people inhabiting one room; no heating; no plumbing, and four small slices of bread for a day's rations (VKZ, 34, 675ff.). After the war, Sommer wrote that she knew "from secret sources of information" that most of the Jews who were deported died soon thereafter (Sommer, "Kurze Bericht". Bernhard Loesener, of Nuremberg Law fame, may have been a steady informant. Sommer and her bishop definitely made contact with the SS officer, Kurt Gerstein, after his return from the death camps; see Friedlaender, 1969, and Laqueur, 1981.) But it is difficult to say how early she knew this. She hints strongly at it in her report to the bishops on the great <u>razzia</u> in Berlin early in 1943 when 8,000 Jews were "very cruelly rounded up and literally driven" into trucks. Explaining that authorities would not allow the families of the detained Jews to bring them provisions for the imminent 'transportation,' Sommer concluded that "precisely this circumstance... changed our suspicion that they had no future into a certainty" (VKZ, 38, 19-21).

At some point, certainly no later than the end of 1942, the Special Relief office began hiding Jews. There are a number of explicit references in Sommer's papers that establish this activity, yet it is difficult to piece together the story of how this was accomplished. Because of constant Gestapo surveillance and the great risk involved, Sommer and the other personnel of Special Relief preferred not to deal by letter or even by telephone, but by personal contact. Obviously, no systematic records would have been kept. Furthermore, to protect themselves from divulging information under duress to the Gestapo, no one was told or wanted to know what she did not need to know. Not even Sommer knew how many Jews were being hidden by Special Relief personnel or by parish support groups working with them, because, as she says in her post war memoire, it was a secret (Sommer, "Kurze Bericht"). Still, Sommer knew some particulars. When one of her coworkers at the Special Relief office, Lieselotte Neumark, faced deportation, she went into hiding with a Gentile family. After four weeks Neumark contacted Sommer through a third party to arrange a meeting. Not wishing to endanger any longer the family with whom she was hiding, Neumark asked Sommer to help her sneak herself into the next <u>Transport</u> (<u>Fraeulein</u> Neumark did not survive the war; see Sommer, Nachlass; letter to Anneliese Triller, Berlin, 11 Sept., 1946). Sommer was also aware that yet another Special Relief employee, <u>Fraeulein</u> Joachim, helped ill Jews and hidden Jews "at great personal risk" throughout the period of National Socialist persecution. But Sommer knew nothing about the efforts of other small circles of women.

The war-time experience of Susanne Witte, who functioned independently from Sommer and Special Relief, offer another glimpse of clandestine resistance. Just before the National Socialist era, Witte graduated from the Catholic German Women's League school for social work in Berlin. At some point during the 1930s she became friends with a <u>Fraeulein</u> Kirschbaum, a Jewish social worker who had converted to Catholicism. When the 'transportation' of Berlin Jews began, Kirschbaum asked Witte to hide her mother who was not Catholic and who was opposed to her daughter's conversion. During the years of the elder Kirschbaum's concealment in Witte's apartment, a number of other people became involved at various levels of risk to themselves. Witte's friends took turns providing food since it was difficult for two to live off of just one ration card. Occasionally, when Witte had to be away on a trip, <u>Frau</u> Kirschbaum would stay with one of Witte's friends. The involvement of the latter became greater when a Berlin priest who was hiding Jews and who knew that Witte was also involved in this, asked her to take in another refugee. Witte felt that this would be too dangerous for her, but she was able to place the Jew with one of her friends. <u>Frau</u> Kirschbaum survived the war; <u>Fraeulein</u> Kirschbaum did not (Witte, 1985).

Sommer's own experiences led her to try to coax her church's bishops into open conflict with the Nazi regime by encouraging them to confront Germans with the truth about the fate of Jews. (It is the sense of the documents that Sommer tried to get the German episcopacy to protest National Socialist atrocities against Jews, but not everyone would agree; Schewick, 120, says Sommer did not urge the bishops to speak out, basing his assertion on a statement Sommer evidently made in 1960. The documents now available in VKZ make this extremely doubtful.) She was obviously in a position to do this, having become the episcopacy's consultant on Jewish affairs. Sommer had gained this position through the good offices of her ordinary, Konrad Preysing, whose confidant she had become by the early '40s. Along with a small circle of bishops which included Preysing, Sommer pressed for a protest statement. The point of departure, the group suggested, must concern Christian Jews and sacramental marriages involving Jews, but the statement "must go clearly beyond that to include the atrocities against Jews in general" (VKZ, 38, 99-100).

Sommer made it her business to make sure that Cardinal Bertram knew about the atrocities which National Socialism was perpetrating against Jews, including German Jews, in eastern Europe. Since the German bishops spoke with one voice, Bertram had to be won over if a strong statement of protest was to be forthcoming. Not all of Sommer's reports to Bertram appear to be extant, but, judging from those that are, we can say that she was both timely and accurate. About the Kovno massacre (Oct. 27, 1941), which included Jews from Berlin and elsewhere in the Reich, Sommer reported that

> ...the Jews must undress (it could have been 18 degrees below freezing), then climb into 'graves' previously dug by Russian prisoners of war. They were then shot with a machine gun; then grenades were tossed in. Without checking to see if all were dead, the Kommando ordered the grave filled in (VKZ, 24, 675-78).

Thus, just slightly more than three months elapsed since the Kovno massacre until Germany's Catholic bishops and their titular head, Cardinal Bertram, had an accurate account of this atrocity. In 1943 Sommer reported to Bertram personally on the Berlin razzia, Aktion Fabrik, which concluded that the deported Jews would not live long. In August she filed her lengthy report that dealt with the treatment of Jews from a number of regions in Germany and Austria; this was the report which said that the 'Aryan' families of those who had been deported received death notices on them 14 days thereafter. At the exact same time Bertram also received an extraordinary letter from a Polish Jew, which provided page after page of accounts of the murder of four million Jews by Germans, and which concluded with the indictment that "every German, yourself included, is guilty of these atrocities" (VKZ, 34, 210-215). The months that followed brought more reports from Sommer.

Instead of winning Bertram over, Sommer's reports and urgings had the effect of straining the relationship between him and the Berlin circle of Catholics. After Sommer's August, 1943, report the Berlin group drew up a draft letter in the name of Germany's bishops which they submitted to Cardinal Bertram. "We will stand guilty before God and man if we are silent" about the regime's persecution of Jews (referring both to Christian and non-Christian Jews) (VKZ, 38, 220-221). The draft went on to demand specific rights for the deported Jews, such as healthy living conditions, correspondence privileges, religious services, personal contact with an inspection committee, and so on. Bertram refused to endorse the draft on the grounds that there was insufficient proof of the conditions which it sought to redress.

The situation between Cardinal Bertram and the Berlin circle deteriorated further in 1944. Since August of the previous year Sommer's reports to Bertram on German atrocities against Jews evidently increased in number and in detail. These reports appear to have been made personally by Sommer rather than by mail, no doubt because of the Gestapo. Bertram responded to Sommer by questioning the reliability of her sources, and by insisting on proof. It was, of course, impossible for Sommer to provide proof without disclosing the identity of those in the regime and administration who leaked information to her. She therefore continued to bring as detailed information as she could to Bertram, invoking the authority of her bishop and confidant, Konrad Preysing, to authenticate her mission. This exasperated Bertram who grew weary of Sommer's persistence. Bertram finally notified Berlin that in the future Sommer's reports would have to be undersigned by bishop Preysing verifying their details and correctness. "Please make this clear to Frau Dr. Sommer" Bertram wrote, "since my warnings don't help. Otherwise I will not schedule anymore appointments with her" (VKZ, 38, 350).

The problem was not just that Bertram refused to accept on face value the detailed accounts of atrocities with which he was presented. Rather, there was a complete lack of communication at the highest levels of the hierarchy. In November, 1943, Bertram wrote the Vatican Secretary of State, Cardinal Maglione, asking what could be done to provide the last sacraments for those being condemned to death in Poland and summarily executed. (Evidently, then, Bertram did believe that Jews were being killed.) By this time all higher officials in the Vatican knew about the mass murders in eastern Europe; even lower Vatican bureaucrats knew (Blet, 1975). But instead of writing back that it would be impossible to get permission to provide the last sacraments for the victims because Germans were murdering them by the tens and hundreds of thousands, Maglione assured Bertram that the Vatican was doing everything it could through local church officials (in eastern Europe) to get permission to spend the sacraments (VKZ, 38, 269-272).

The effort of Sommer and the Berlin circle to spread resistance through the entire German church failed. Rather than protest, the bishops pleaded faintly. In November, 1942, Cardinal Bertram urged that "other races" be treated humanely, as did the 1943 Fulda Bishops' Letter. Lacking in these pronouncements is the sense of outrage that typified their attitude toward euthanasia. There is no statement from the bishops that addressed the excruciating situation of Jews in the ghettoes or of those machine gunned in open pits so poignantly described by Sommer.

What we may conclude is that there was a small nucleus of Catholic women who understood the implications of National Socialist racial teaching in the 1930s and who were willing to become directly involved in resistance once the war began and the regime's anti-Semitism went berserk. The number of these women is unknown but it is confined to members of certain groups: the Elizabeth Society, the Catholic German Women's League, or Caritas. All women who involved themselves in hiding Jews were members of one or more of these organizations. Within these circles of women, some--it is impossible to guess how many--shared another characteristic; they were Jewish. Secondly, a larger number of Catholic women surrounding this nucleus were willing to assist in the work on behalf of Jews, but they could not or would not become committed to it to the extent of providing a shelter. These would be the people who worked in the Berlin parish support circle of the Special Relief office or the circle of friends around Susanne Witte, and members of the Elizabeth Society who sent provisions to the ghettoes in eastern Europe. All of these women were ready for the challenge when National Socialism posed the ultimate moral question of death for the disadvantaged and for Jews during the 1940s.

To allow oneself to formulate judgments on National Socialist racial teachings and to elevate them to the moral sphere was of course enormously stressful for any German living in the Third Reich. Most Catholics were surely relieved that their bishops did not demand extraordinary courage of them by forcing the racial issue, in other words, by making it a point of public conflict with the government. This meant that women who were prepared to resist had to act on their own or within a localized church affiliation. How many more women would have been willing to be directly involved in resistance had the bishops chosen to break openly with National Socialism over the treatment of Jews as they had over the treatment of the disadvantaged in the euthanasia dispute? How many members of the church's massive organizations of women would have at least been willing to participate in parish support groups on behalf of Jews had not their church leaders acted pusillanimously?

The failure in leadership among Catholic bishops--not to speak of hypocrisy on the part of some of them--comes through clearly in their statements immediately after the end of the war. Many of the bishops, anxious to defend the innocence of the Catholic populace as the occupational forces tried to sift out the 'good' Germans from the 'bad' ones, asserted that the ordinary man-on-the-street had no idea of the terrible crimes which their government had perpetrated on Jews in the East. (Many of the bishops' statements are reproduced in VKZ, 38; it is interesting to compare that of bishop Preysing, who wanted the church to oppose the government's anti-Semitism publicly, to the statements of others who did not--archbishop Groeber's for example.) But if it is true that Catholics were unaware of the Holocaust, the fault lies with their church leaders, who did know about it or could have known about it, but failed to tell them. The excuse usually given for their action, or lack of it, is the experience of the Dutch church. In the summer of 1942 the archbishop of Utrecht protested the deportation of non-Christian Jews, whereupon the German occupation forces immediately deported Catholic Jews in reprisal (Schewick, 114). But this excuse no longer held any validity in Germany in 1944 when the National Socialists, as we have seen, began deporting Christian Jews along with all other Jews.

The shortcomings of the German episcopacy should not keep us from recognizing the accomplishments of Sommer and the Berlin Special Relief office. Under Sommer's direction this office saved many orphaned Jewish children (perhaps dozens), obtained passports for hundreds of other Jews, and saved many additional Jews (perhaps several hundred) by hiding them until the collapse of National Socialism. The lives of these survivors testify to the success of Margarete Sommer and the Berlin circle of Catholics. Precisely because the response of the church to the Holocaust was disappointing, it is important for us to know that these Catholics--among them both Jews and Gentiles--crossed over the line of civil disobedience. They resisted National Socialism. They hid Jews.

REFERENCES

Blet, Pierre, et.al. (1975). Actes et Documents du Saint Siège relatifs à la Seconde guerre mondiale: Vatican City. Vol. IX.
Borcher, Stella. See her Lebenslauf in Bistumsarchiv Berlin (henceforth, BAB), Sommer Nachlass.
Bukofzer, Ernst Israel. See his letter to Special Relief, Berlin, 30 July, 1940. Sommer Nachlass in BAB.
Friedlaender, Saul. (1969). Counterfeit Nazi: London. 158.
Gross, Leonard. (1982). The Last Jews in Berlin: Simon and Shuster.
Kershaw, Ian. (1983). The Nazi Dictatorship: Oxford University Press. 358ff.
Klausener, Erich. (1979). In: Miterbauer des Bistums Berlin: (ed. Wolfgang Knauft) Berlin. 175.
Koonz, Claudia. (1987). Mothers in the Fatherland: St. Martin's Press. 15-16.
Laqueur, Walter. (1981). The Terrible Secret: New York. 50.
Preysing, Konrad. See his letter to the bishop of Osnabrueck, Berlin, May, 1939. Sommer Nachlass in BAB.
Reutter, Lutz-Eugen. (1969). "Die Hilfstaetigkeit Katholischer Organisationen und kirchlicher Stellen fuer die im nationalsozialistischen Deutschland Verfolgten." Diss: Hamburg. 105.
van Schewick, Burkhard (1980). In: Die Katholiken und das Dritte Reich: (eds. K. Repgen and K. Gotto) Mainz. 101-122.
Sommer, Margarete. Nachlass in BAB. Budget statement of 7 Feb., 1940.
Sommer, Margarete. Nachlass in BAB. "Kirchliche Arbeit fuer die Auswanderung der Juden und Mischlinge katholischer Konfession."
Sommer, Margarete. Nachlass in BAB. "Kurzer Bericht ueber Entstehung und Entwicklung des Hilfswerks beim Bischoeflichen Ordinariat Berlin".
Sommer, Margarete. Nachlass in BAB. "Statistische Uebersicht, 1939-1940."
Sommer, Margarete. Nachlass in BAB. "Die Taetigkeit des Hilfsausschusses fuer den katholischen Nichtarier im Jahre 1938."
Sommer, Margarete. Nachlass in BAB. "Uebersicht ueber Meine Taetigkeit".
Veroeffentlichungen der Kommission fuer Zeitgeschichte, Reihe A, 24, 34, and 38.
Witte, Susanne. (1985) Interviewed by the author in Berlin, June, 1985.

A STUDY OF DIETRICH BONHOEFFER AND THE JEWS

JANUARY - APRIL 1933

EDWIN ROBERTSON

33 Briardale Gardens

London NW3 7PN

It was not until Eberhard Bethge published his definitive biography of Dietrich Bonhoeffer in 1967 that we knew how early Bonhoeffer had concentrated on the question of the Jews in Germany. Even Karl Barth, who knew Bonhoeffer well, expressed surprise when he read the 'Biography'. He wrote to Bethge in My 1967, after reading the book:

"It was new to me above all else that Bonhoeffer was the first, yes indeed almost the only theologian who in the years after 1933 concentrated energetically on the question of the Jews and dealt with it equally energetically. For a long time now I have considered myself guilty of not having raised it with equal emphasis during the church struggle (for example in the two Barmen Declarations I composed in 1934). But then such a text would not have been acceptable to either the Reformed or the General Synod, given the spiritual predisposition of even the 'Confessing Christians' in 1934. But this does not excuse the fact that I (my interest lay elsewhere) did not offer at least formal resistance in this matter at that time". (1)

That was Karl Barth, who was in protest against the tendencies of the Protestant churches in Germany to welcome the coming of the Nazis. Erik Peterson, writing to Harnack in 1928, says quite bluntly:

"Sociologically and in outlook the Protestant Church corresponds roughly with the mentality and sociological status of the German National People's Party". (2)

Far more than Dietrich's father, Karl Bonhoeffer, his neighbours with whom the family were closely associated - Hans Delbrück and Adolf von Harnack - involved themselves politically. They had both successfully resisted Stroeker's anti-semitic activities and checked his attempt to introduce the Jewish question to the Protestant Social Congress. During the twenties, they had watched with growing concern the attempts by the Protestant Church to revive the atmosphere of pre-1918 Germany, of royalism and anti-semitism. The Protestants wanted a new authoritarianism and they were shot through with anti-semitism. They had little desire to defend liberal values and listened with delight to tales of 'western decadence'. The publication of 'Action Group' by Hans Zehrer,Edgar Jung,and Ernst Jünger was welcomed. In opposition to this tendency Dietrich's brother Klaus and his brothers-in-law Gerhard Leibholz and Hand von Dohnanyi, increasingly identified themselves with the Weimar Republic. It was not surprising therefore that the young Renate (daughter of Dietrich's sister Ursula)

could remember even as a child the many political conversations in the Bonhoeffer household:
"The Jewish question was the dominant theme in family conversations and with it all other political questions were connected" (3)
This attention to the Jewish question at an early date was personalized because Gerhard Leibholz was of Jewish parentage, as was Franz Hildebrandt, Dietrich Bonhoeffer's closest friend.

This was his background, how could he fail to be disgusted by some of the extreme statements issuing from Protestant church leaders. In America, 1930-1931, his interest was aroused in the racial question of 'negroes'. His elder brother, Karl-Friedrich, wrote to him expressing his approval of this interest, which he thought was the problem in America. In fact, he confessed that he had refused a post in America because he could not bear to think of his children growing up with this heritage. The children were hypothetical, at the time, and the judgement was without any real understanding of the greater racial problem rapidly growing in Germany. The naivety of his comment in January 1931 shows how easily liberal-minded young Germans could be fooled:
"At all events, our Jewish question is a joke in comparison; there cannot be any people left who maintain they are oppressed here. At any rate, not in Frankfurt . . " (4)

Bonhoeffer had not noted the rise of the National Socialist Party while he was in America, but its strength was evident as soon as he returned to Berlin. The election of September 1930, when he was on his way to the USA, had raised the number of seats in the Reichstag from 12 to 107; after his return that number rose further so that on 31st July 1932, the Nazis had 230 seats. Dietrich Bonhoeffer responded, but the summer of 1932 was largely taken up with ecumenical conferences, where his main concern had been the Church. He was painfully aware that the Church in Germany was not matched to the hour. He tried to work out what the role of the Church should be in the developing situation in Germany. But first he must be clear about what the Church really is:
"We can only say what the Church 'is', if at once we say both what it is from the human side and what it is from the divine side . . The Church is a bit of the world, a lost godless world, under the curse, a complacent evil world. And the Church is the evil world to the highest degree, because in it the name of God is misused, because in it God is made a plaything, man's idol . . But the Church is also a bit of the qualified world,qualified by God's revealing, gracious Word, which completely surrendered and handed over to the world, secures the world for God and does not give it up. The Church is the presence of God in the world" (5)
He did not fail to apply this theology of the Church to the real situation in Germany and prepared his students for the time when they would be asked to ascribe near divine honours to Adolf Hitler.

The Führer Prinzip

No one had any doubt about the attitude of Adolf Hitler and the Nazis to the Jews. Many Protestant Christians agreed with him, even if they were not so extreme in their expression, nor totally approving of the violence. Rubenstein and Roth, in their book, "Approaches to Auschwitz' maintain that Hitler's treatment pf the Jews was inevitable given the succession from the Gospel account of Pilate's washing of his hands, through Martin Luther to the Führer, who claimed that he would complete the work of Luther. Many German Protestants, but not all. The Bonhoeffer family viewed Hitler's accession to power as disastrous from the beginning. Their first comment was, 'This means war' and, as Renate said, all political questions of this kind were tied up with the Jewish question.

Bonhoeffer's first public statement after Hitler came to power was not specifically about the treatment of the Jews, but was consciously connected. He attacked the whole principle of a Führer, who could command absolute obedience. He did this in a broadcast which went out two days after Hitler came to power. His theme was, 'The Younger Generation's Changed View of the Concept of Führer'. In the course of showing the developement of the 'leadership principle' in youth work, he made no secret of his contempt for what he called ' the unnatural narcissism of youth made vain by old fools'. His broadcast was a theological talk on the structures of authority and the dangers of a growing tendency to make idols of the leader (Führer). The danger lay, he said, in the temptation of the leader to succumb to the wishes of those he leads, who will always seek to turn him into an idol. Such a leader soon believes himself to be infallible, making himself and his office an idol, thus mocking God. The broadcast was interrupted at this point, but enough had been heard to recognize his reference. He had already had experience of young Germans in his confirmation class. He had shown them care and help to such an extent that they certainly idolized him. But he saw the temptation and was already aware that the wrong kind of leader could soon lead these young men in post-war Germany to do things they might well be ashamed to do on their own initiative.

The broadcast was cut, but Bonhoeffer circulated the script. When this broadcast script (6) is compared with Bonhoeffer's preaching in this early period of concern, we can see how near the Jewish question was to his thinking. When on the 3rd February, Bernhard Rust was appointed Prussian Minister of Cultural Affairs, Bonhoeffer feared for his brother-in-law Gerhard Leibholz. Rust's words were unequivocal:
"First thing on Monday, the cultural invasion of the Bolshevics will come to an end. . I shall ask the churches outright whether or not they intend to help us in our fight against Bolshevism".

In Nazi propaganda, Bolshevism was early linked to certain sections of the Jewish community. Karl Marx was of a German-Jewish family converted to Christianity. Jews were also accused of profiting from the collapsing currency and making money while the brave Germans died at the Front in the Great War. Jews were accused of debasing the pure German culture. The accusations were contradictory, but none the less, Rust's references to 'our fight against Bolshevism' had an ominous ring. It was natural that the whole Bonhoeffer family should be concerned about Gerhard Leibholz and their many Jewish friends.

The Gideon Sermon

For some wekks, Bonhoeffer's preaching had shown evidence that he was concerned with a growing fear of the future. On 6th November 1932, his Reformation Day sermon was against all forms of Protestant pride, accusing his Protestant Church of falling from its first love (Rev. 2.4-5) and he called upon it to repent and return to its first convictions: "Remember then from what you have fallen, repent, and do the works you did at first" (v.5).

A fragment of a sermon on 1st December 1932 took Daniel 10 as the text and recalls an experience with a mixed group of German and French youth and the power of that text upon them. It was a Frenchman who read the text and as he came to the words, 'courage' and 'peace be with you', then, says Bonhoeffer, they were all transformed, their gloom was dispelled and together they repeated the words of Daniel, "Now, speak Lord for you have strengthened us". That confidence in God and hope did not nullify his fear for the Church and he frequently repeated words that he had used in that November sermon as the clouds gathered:
"It is becoming clear that we are in the eleventh hour of our life as a Protestant Church, that there is not much time left before the decision is made whether it is all over with this Church, or whether a new day is to dawn. We should also know that you do not

comfort a dying man with fanfares or try to call him back to life. Fanfares belong in funeral processions, there where a cold silence is overcome by an even colder noise, there where wreaths and the dead march decorate the decay. Children frightened in the dark streets, whistling in the dark and stamping their feet to make a noise and give them courage" (7)

As that Protestant Church welcomed Hitler to power a few weeks later, the fanfares and the noise of the funeral could be heard. Bonhoeffer's first sermon after Hitler's accession to power was the Gideon sermon. It was preached to a university audience in Trinity Church in Berlin, at the end of the academic term, 26th February 1933 (8)
The text was from selected verses in Judges 6,7 and 8, and the theme was the word of the Lord to Gideon: "The people are too many" (Judges 7.2).
The story of Gideon's army could so easily be paralleled with the Protestant Church at that time. The bands of S.A. men who were now going to the churches promised something like a revival and many clergy welcomed their larger congregations. There was some unease about the fighting that went on in the streets after the services, but there was something of a euphoria. Hitler's words had pleased too many. In his proclamation to the German people on 1st February 1933, Hitler had promised to take Christianity under his 'firm protection' and had called it 'the basis of our whole morality'. Bonhoeffer in his sermon warned against the mistaking of popularity for revival. Gideon could not win his battle with too many soldiers!
"Do not desire to be strong, powerful, honoured and respected, but let God alone be your strength, your fame and your honour. . Gideon who achieved faith in fear and doubt, kneels with us here before the altar of the one and only God, and Gideon prays with us: 'Our Lord on the cross, be thou our one and only Lord. Amen" (9)

March 1933

February ended with the Reichstag fire. In England, we all assumed that this had been accomplished by Göring's henchmen to enable the Nazis to destroy their opponents. In Germany, it led to the 'Reich President's Edict for the Protection of People and State', signed by Hindenberg. That edict of the 28th February was followed by an election on 5th March which gave overwhelming victory to the National Socialists. The people had voted away their liberty for the sake of a so-called security. The terms were horrific: "Therefore restriction of personal freedom, of the right of free speech, including the freedom of the Press, of the right of association and of public assembly, intervention in the privacy of the post, telegraph and telephone, authorization of search warrants and the confiscation and restriction of property, beyond the hitherto legal limits, will be admissible" (10)
The edict was to remain in force until further notice - in fact until 8th May 1945!
For the time being, only the politicians were threatened. The churches and universities did not feel threatened and made no protest. The Bonhoeffers felt reasonably safe, except when some of Dietrich's international friends came to visit. Paul Lehmann reports that when he was visiting his friend from New York days, Klaus Bonhoeffer would get up from time to time to see if someone was listening at the door!
The Bonhoeffer family was much involved in the trial after the Reichstag fire. Dietrich's brother-in-law, Hans von Dohnanyi, temporarily seconded to the Supreme Court, had to attend all stages of the trial of van der Lubbe, who was accused of starting the fire. Dietrich's father, as the senior psychiatrist in Germany was called upon, with his colleague, Dr. J. Zutt, for expert psychiatric opinion. They saw van der Lubbe three times in March and for this whole month the family was much disturbed by their involvement in 'this emotionally complex and in many ways

enigmatic case'. The result of their investigations disappointed everybody. There was no mention of guilt or innocence, whether van der Lubbe could have been instigated by others or was administered drugs during his interrogation. The report which was eventually published in a professional journal showed some sympathy for van der Lubbe, but it would have been out of the question for Karl Bonhoeffer to have given an expert opinion on anything other than medical matters. None-the-less the family felt involved and to that extent guilty. Dietrich felt this most powerfully of all and he never quite lost this awareness of guilt shared.

Bethge also points out the irony of the fact that it was the 'Reichstag Fire Edict', bearing Hindenberg's signature that four and a half years later closed Bonhoeffer's seminary at Finkenwalde, and it was in one of the concentration camps set up by the edict that he was executed.
Bracher assesses this Edict as 'the fundamental emergency law upon which the National Socialist dictatorship . . was primarily based' (11)

Klaus Scholder describes its immediate effect upon the Jews and Marxists, both of whom Hitler had earlier threatened with extermination:
"After the 5th March election victory, a wave of terror broke over Germany which lasted throughout the summer and very quickly engulfed tens of thousands of Germans. The instrument of this wave of terror was Hitler's feared young revolutionary army, the S.A. Its victims were Communists, Jews and other real or supposed opponents of the regime" (12)
The young radio producer, Jochen Klepper, gives a vivid contemporary account in his diary, subsequently published as, "Under the Shadow of thy Wings: 1932-1942". He was a protestant recently married to a Jewish woman:
"8. March: What is already demanded of us in the way of antisemitism is terrible. Even Schnabel's Beethoven recitals had quite suddenly to be removed from the programme. . at the very time when Oxford University was conferring an honorary degree upon him for his 'unequalled interpretation of German art'. At the radio station we can understand one another's situation, but the mutual respect has gone. Tired thirty and forty-year-old compromisers, intimidated by the primitive struggles for existence: from whatever angle we look at it, that is what we are.
11. March: It is a dreadful uneasiness, a dreadful pressure, a dreadful isolation - a fearful weakness, a fearful anxiety about existence.
29. March: On the whole Jewish boycott affair I have only one thing to say: I grieve for the Protestant Church". (13)

There are those who excuse themselves from action during this critical time by saying that information was difficult to come by. Of course, what was happening in SA camps and cellars was not generally known, although suspected. There were individual cases and enough information to know about the concentration camps and the first actions against the Jews, but Klaus Scholder is probably right in his assessment so far as the church authorities were concerned:
"But the undoubted difficulty and danger of getting information was only one side of the matter. The other was that . . the central authorities of the Protestant church, the Kirchenbundesamt in Berlin, did not want to have any information". (14)
Many attempts were made to collect information. Hans von Dohnanyi was compiling material for an indictment of Hitler. Elizabeth Rotten of Dresden wrote to Siegmund-Schultze troubled by the passivity even of what she called 'the minority in Germany who think and have remained sober'. As a result, Siegmund-Schultze told the Kirchenbundesamt that he was collecting material for his magazine, Die Eiche, to publish in the July edition 'to give our foreign friends certain information about the German situation.

In it there were to be 'explicit references to the excesses'. The official church did not want this and as a result, on 8th April, it was reported that Siegmund-Schultze was'giving cause for concern with his enquiries'. He was then arrested on 21st June and deported from Germany 'on the charge of helping Jews in ninety three cases.' (15)

After the Gideon sermon, there is no text for any preaching by Dietrich Bonhoeffer until the Ascension Day sermon on 'There is no church without joy', which he preached for Gerhard Jacobi on 25 May 1933.
But Bonhoeffer was not idle. He voted on 5th March and went to the poll with his friend of Jewish origin, Franz Hildebrandt: Franz voted for the Christian People's Party: Dietrich for the Catholic Centre Party, because of its international ties. Potsdam Day, 21st March, was used by Hitler as a means of capturing the imagination of the people. The display of pomp and ceremony was to mark the end of 'the bloodless and legal revolution', The Protestant Church was expected to acclaim and Bishop Otto Dibelius complied. Bonhoeffer, invited to tea with the Bishop a few days earlier, had insisted that 'acclamation was not the church's only role'. But on Potsdam Day something more dangerous was happening. The Treachery Law was promulgated and this gave Bonhoeffer real problems because he was not prepared to identify his evident loyalty to Germany with acceptance of Hitler's administration.

As anti-semitic and anti-communist measures increased, a boycott of Jewish firms was ordered and the 'reconstruction of the professional Civil Service' gave Germany its first non-Aryan law. Bonhoeffer's grandmother, Paula von Hase, at the age of 91 calmly walked through the SA cordon to shop at the Kaufhaus des Westens. About the same time, his parents went to live with Gerhard Leibholz and Sabine (Bonhoeffer's twin sister) in Göttingen so as to help them in the event of demonstrations. Dietrich and Klaus Bonhoeffer stayed on in Berlin, where among other things they held conference with Paul Lehmann about the best ways of getting information about what was really happening in Germany to America. In this way they were already committing treason.

<u>Bonhoeffer's treatment of the Jewish Question</u>

On 7th April, the restructuring of the Civil Service led to the Aryan Clauses which debarred Jews from public office. It was clear to Bonhoeffer that this would have seriou consequences for the Church. He sat down at once to work out the theological implications. This action may, as Bethge suggests, have been prompted by the proposal made by a group of ministers who gathered round Jacobi, but the suggestion was resisted. It was that they should discuss the Jewish Question and ask Bonhoeffer to write a paper to stimulate discussion. Many clergy felt much the same as the General Superintendent did when he heard of this proposal and disapproved:
"To me it is fairly understandable (ie the mob violence against the Jews!) because of what Jewry by its control of the Press, finance, the theatre, etc., has done to us . . that justifiable collective anger, even when the people's frame of mind is not specifically anti-semitic, should for once vent itself in violence."
Bonhoeffer's paper is all the more impressive when we realise the general tone of the church and its leaders. It dealt specifically with the attitude of the Church to the Jews. As we read it we must recall that this young theologian was 27 and that he was a Lutheran. Later his views would modify and he would attack the German Christian support for the treatment of the Jews more directly and with more information. But already in April, 1933, he saw the evil of what was happening and attempted to appeal to the Protestant Church to change the direction in which it was heading. The paper is entitled <u>The Church and the Jewish Question</u> (16)

The 450th Anniversary of Luther's birth fell on 10 November 1933. The Nazis at first intended to use this to rally Luther to their side and their German Christian supporters were already preparing for a national demonstration of the role of Adolf Hitler as the Führer who would complete the Reformation, which Luther had begun. There were ample texts from Luther of an anti-semitic nature to use. And later they would be used. Meanwhile, the main emphasis was on Luther as völkish prophet of the German people. His reference in Latin to his destiny to serve the German people (Germanis meis natus sum, quibus et serviam) in a letter of 1521 was given as a warm expansion when translated as, "I was born for my beloved Germans; it is them I want to serve" (17). Historians worked hard to show the comparison between Hitler and Luther.

Bonhoeffer caught the atmosphere of the time when he began his paper with two quotations from Martin Luther. First is a late quotation from 1546, which argues that Jews should not be treated differently from Gentiles when they become Christians:
"We would still show them the Christian doctrine and ask them to turn and accept the Lord whom they should by rights have honoured before we did. . . Where they repent, leave their usury and accept Christ, we would gladly regard them as our brothers".
That was, even in Luther's day an argument for making no distinction between Jew and Gentile in the Church. But he went further back to an early quotation from 1523 and added:
"If the Apostles, who also were Jews, had dealt with us Gentiles as we Gentiles deal with the Jews, there would have been no Christians among the Gentiles. But seeing that they have acted in such a brotherly way towards us, we in turn should act in a brotherly way towards the Jews in case we might convert some. For we ourselves are still not yet fully their equals, much less their superiors. . . But now we use force against them. . . what good will we do them with that? Similarly, how will we benefit them by forbidding them to live and work and have other human fellowship with us, thus driving them to practise usury".
These two quotations may not please us very much today, but they need to be read in the light of what was happening in Germany in 1933 and, of course, in context in Luther's day. They were very cleverly chosen. After this Bonhoeffer begins his comments on the actions being taken in April 1933. He defines them as subjecting the Jews to special laws by the state 'solely because of the race to which they belong'. This raises two questions for the theologian:
(a) "What is the church's attitude to this action by the state?, and "What should the church do as a result of it?" - taken together as one question.
(b) "What attitude should the church take to its members who are baptized Jews?"
Both questions, according to Bonhoeffer can only be answered in the light of a true concept of the church.
Bonhoeffer freely recognizes, in dealing with the first of these two questions that church has no right to address the state politically. It is the state which makes history, not the church. The action of the state must remain free of church intervention. That is good Lutheran teaching. But when the state is failing in its duty which is to 'create law and order' by too much law and order or by too little law and order, there are three possible ways in which the church can act. First, it can ask the state whether its actions are legitimate and in accordance with its character as state, ie. it can throw the state back on its responsibilities. Secondly, it can aid the victims of state action. "The church has an unconditional obligation to the victims of any ordering of society, even if they do not belong to the Christian community". In these two ways, the free church serves the free state without illegitimate interference.

"The third possibility is not just to bandage the victims under the wheel, but to put a spoke in the wheel itself". Such political action may be required if the state fails in its function of creating law and order. He further defines 'too little law' as 'if any group of subjects were deprived of their rights'; 'too much law' as 'where the state intervened in the character of the church and its proclamation, eg. in the forced exclusion of baptized Jews from our Christians congregations'. He adds that the prohibition of missions to the Jews is another example, but the exclusion of Jews from Christian congregations was the issue in hand. His assessment of the situation in April 1933 was that the first two actions - asking the state whether its actions were legetimate, and caring for the victims - were the compelling demands of the hour. Later, political action against the state may be necessary.

In attempting to deal with the 'quite special context of the church', he writes an unfortunate paragraph based upon Luther's 'Table Talk'. He repeats the old medieval teaching of the 'curse' upon the Jews for crucifying Christ. This is indefensible as Rubenstein and Roth have shown in their book, 'Approaches to Auschwitz' (18). But it should not lead us to disregard this remarkable document of a Lutheran theologian helping the Protestant Church to find its way out of an impasse. His theology at this point is based upon Paul's vision of the 'grafting of the vinestock back into the vine from which it was broken off - and that is more important for him than the medieval 'curse'. (19) Jews may rightly be offended at Paul's and Bonhoeffer's theology of the conversation of the Jews, but few can doubt the sincerity of his vision and his deep respect for what he would call God's ancient people the Jews:
"From here the Christian church sees the history of the people of Israel with trembling as God's own, free, fearful way with his people. It knows that no nation of the world can be finished with this mysterious people, because God is not yet finished with it. Each new attempt to 'solve the Jewish problem' comes to nothing on the saving-historical significance of this people". The importance of that must not be nullified by the reintroduction of the 'curse' to explain the suffering of this people. For Bonhoeffer rejects cheap moralizing by the church, which, looking at this "rejected people, humbly recognizes itself as a church continually unfaithful to its Lord"

Given his theology, it is inevitable that his hope lies in the conversion of Israel and then he tackles the second of his questions:
What attitude should the church take to its members who are baptized Jews? His unequivocal answer is that 'The church cannot allow its action towards its members to be prescribed by the state'. On this issue he calls upon all Christians to say with great clarity:
"Jew and German stand together under the word of God; here is the proof whether the church is the church or not".

A few months later, Bonhoeffer was engaged in drafting a Declaration at Bethel near Bielefeld and sent it to Karl Barth. If Bonhoeffer's clear attitude had been maintained and his Bethel Draft used at Barmen in 1934, we would not now have the shame of saying, "Barmen was silent about the Jews".

Edwin Robertson

REFERENCES

1. Eberhard Bethge, "Bonhoeffer:Exile and Martyr", pp.65-66

2. Quoted by Eberhard Bethge in "Bonhoeffer:A Biography", p.91

3. Renate Bethge, "Bonhoeffers Familie und ihre Bedeutung für seine Theologie" (Beiträge zum Widerstand 1933-1945,No.30)p.7

4. Eberhard Bethge, "Dietrich Bonhoeffer:A biography" p.110

5. Dietrich Bonhoeffer, "No Rusty Swords", pp.149-153

6. " " " , pp.186-200

7. Quoted by Edwin Robertson, "The Shame and the Sacrifice", p.84

8. Dietrich Bonhoeffer, "Predigten, Auslegungen, Meditationem I pp.349-358

9. " " " " pp.357-8

10. K.D. Bacher, W. Sauer & G. Schulx,"Die Nationalsocialistische Machtergreifung", p.87

11. " " " p.82

12. Klaus Scholder, "The Churches and the Third Reich", p. 254

13. Jochen Klepper, "Unter dem Schatten deiner Flügel", pp.41-46

14. Klaus Scholder, "The Churches and the Third Reich", p.257

15. " " pp.257-8

16. Dietrich Bonhoeffer, "No Rusty Swords", pp.217-225

17. Klaus Scholder, "The Churches and the Third Reich", p.545

18. R.L.Rubenstein & J.K.Roth, "Approaches to Auschwitz", 1987

19. Romans 11.

THE ECUMENICAL REPERCUSSIONS OF THE GERMAN CHURCH STRUGGLE.

J.H. SCHJØRRING

Institute of Systematic Theology

Deparment of Theology

University of Aarhus, Danmark.

It is no exaggeration to characterize the German Church Struggle as a crucial event in modern Christianity. However, it is also true that it was a struggle with specific German features. It has, nonetheless, been established that the endeavours of the Confessing Church, and the experience won, can serve as a model of ecclesial identity in times of oppression. [This statement refers to the Protestant churches and the Catholic Church as well. In this paper, however, only the Protestant churches will be examined].

The churches of the 20th century have so often, and in so many places, adapted to a totalitarian ideology and/or aggressive antisemitism. Against all such weary signs of impotence the Confessing Church remains with its prophetic call for resistance. The Barmen Declaration was the first concistent doctrinal statement by a church-synod prepared to insist on an inalienable identity, even at the cost of oppression or suffering.

There are, however, elements of paradox, even of contradiction in the German Church struggle. This ambiguity becomes evident if we adopt a more international, ecumenical perspective and bring the role of antisemitism into focus. Then it will appear that the Confessing Church also contains marks of short-sightedness and failure. This has not only been established in hind-sight by modern historians; it was already noted by clear-sighted ecumenical leaders in the midst of the events. A few of these church leaders lived within the German borders; others were from abroad, e.g. England and the Scandinavian countries.

The German Church struggle hence stands as a prophetic warning and a call, and as a bitter experience of failure. Only if the critical part of that history is taken into consideration is it worth while examining the German Church struggle and its implications for the present dialogue.

I. EARLY REACTIONS FROM BRITISH-ANGLICAN AND SCANDINAVIAN-LUTHERAN THEOLOGIANS.

It would not be misjudging to maintain that the critical views, voiced by renowned theologians and Church leaders of many countries as early as March or April 1933, exerted a pressure which was impossible to ignore in the German Foreign Office as well as in the administrative offices of the Evangelical Church. Towards the end of 1933 a confrontation began to seem imminent between a German-Christian theology, promulgated under the aegis of the executive leadership of the national church, and a very heterogeneous opposition promoted by ministers, theologians and laity from all regional churches. The signs of this impending confrontation were carefully scrutinized abroad by a number of ecumenical observers. They tried continously to avoid the impression that they used the ecumenical community as a cover for their main concerns in international politics. They were well aware of Germany's widerspread indignation against foreign criticism and knew that such criticism had contributed to the resurgence of nationalism which fed the Nazi movement. Ever since the Treaty of Versailles this nationalist sentiment had created a barrier against all international endeavours to secure peace by means of international legal arrangements. The ecumenical leaders had themselves, at great cost, experienced the range of Germany's "extrovert" animosity, so manifest within the ranks of the German theologians and Church leaders. This phobia had created great difficulties for any open exchange of views with the nascent ecumenical movement. The ecumenical leaders, who were both well informed and sensitive, were aware of the need to proceed with circumspection in order to maintain contact with their German colleagues in the spirit of solidarity. Nevertheless, it is also true that these ecumenical leaders were somewhat sceptical of the emerging Church opposition in Germany. The main lines in this development may be found with exemplary clarity in the relationships between Dietrich Bonhoeffer (1906-1945), George Bell of Chichester, England (1883-1958), and Valdemar Ammundsen (1875-1936) of Haderslev, Denmark.

After Hitler had assumed power, Ammundsen immediately discovered that the Nazi ideology manifested itself in an aggressive nationalism in his own diocese, close to the German border. Groups within the German-oriented part of the population attempted to question the border which had been drawn up in 1920, and these "home-German" circles used an extremely potent language which led Ammundsen to recall the national egoism and militarism which had precipitated Europe into the First Wold War. Admittedly, matters did not develop into actual border incidents, because the government in Berlin dissociated itself from the nationalist agitators in Schlesvig. Nevertheless, Nazism had shown itself to be a force to be reckoned with, and this fact had consequences for the Church.

What shocked Ammundsen was not only the fact that even ecumenically-minded theologians in Germany simply sat idly by as such tendencies gained ground. It was also painful for him to discover that even churchmen and theologians in whom he generally had confidence, such as Otto Dibelius and Ludwig Ihmels, felt the allure of the propagandistic slogans of the new party ideology. Many members of the Church sympathized with the battle against "godlessness", and promoted a common cause between churchmen and the new Nazi "movement for national renewal". Many leaders of the German Church were lulled by the sirens around them, and relied upon Hitler's declaration of March 23, promising to respect the rights of the Church. Most Church leaders even approved of such antisemitic measures as the boycott of Jewish enterprises, and the national Aryan-legislation enacted on April 7,1933. 1)

The fact that most German Church leaders remained silent - a silence which was punctuated only by the objections of individuals e.g. Bonhoeffer - made at the outset any sincere discussion between the ecumenical Church leaders and their German colleagues more difficult. Ammundsen was therefore forced to restrain himself from expressing his personal convictions when addressing the Germans, although he expressed himself quite freely to non-Germans. For example, Ammundsen wrote to Lord Dickinson, the president of the World Alliance, March 30 and April 8 concerning the new radical nationalism; he also referred to the Jewish persecutions. In Ammundsen's opinion these persecutions were deliberately planned and enacted by the Nazi party leaders, and hence not easily dismissed as ephemera. Ammundsen wrote, "the leading men, who claim to control all others cannot control themselves. Their speeches have been so vehement that the natural consequence would be to expel all Jews. And now it seems quite a strange way of confuting rumours about antisemitical excesses by proclaiming an economic boycot against the Jews". 2)

Ammundsen realized that German theologians had allowed themselves to get carried away by the popular enthusiasm at this "national renewal", named "Gottesstunde" (God's visitation), to the effect that they were ignoring what was fundamentally objectionable in the nationalism and racialist fanaticism of the Nazis. Ammundsen wrote to H.-L. Henriod, "The situation of the German churches is very dangerous. They are likely to be ensnared in a fatal policy, because they appreciate the fight of the Government against Bolshevism and Atheism and are offered might and glory, if they will bow to Hitler. On the other hand, protesting may easily mean martyrdom. The <u>Deutsche Christen</u> already claim the removal of Burghart and Dibelius, <u>although these men have</u> gone far in defending the policy of the Government". 3)

A positive attitude towards the new government characterized many of the leading German theologians, some of whom in fact belonged to the church opposition against the Deutsche Christen. As mentioned above, this fact complicated the international discussion. Outsiders would ask how it was possible for German churchmen to protest the German-Christian theology and ecclesiastical policies, while at the same time remaining open to the new "national renewal movement". Such critical attitude sometimes led Germans to characterize remarks from abroad as international slander lacking either knowledge or will to understand the German situation. At most, they were prepared to admit that there were a number of transient difficulties which Hitler, however, would be able to conquer.

When all these difficulties were becoming only too apparent during the summer of 1933 Ammundsen realized that Bonhoeffer was one of the few who recognized the seriousness of the situation. At the World Alliance conference in Sofia in September (that is, shortly before Bonhoeffer served as pastor to the Germans in London, where he met Bell), Bonhoeffer made a convincing impression when he attacked the German-Christian Church policy and the efforts to gain approval for an ecclesiastical Aryan-paragraph. In a letter to Bell, Ammundsen offered the following description of Bonhoeffer's efforts:

> There (Sofia is compared with Novi Sad, where Bell recently had chaired a meeting) the atmosphere was quite different, because we had no official representatives of the new German Church Authorities. The German delegates were Prof. Richter and the young lectures at Berlin, Dr. Bonhoeffer. He is a splendid

> fellow, sincere, utterly earnest, determined not to compromise with antibiblical measures. He is on the left wing of the opposition. He had himself attended the Prussian Synod and in a private circle he gave a description of the proceedings of the 'synod of robbers'. Our friend Dr. Brown turned quite round, when he heard how tyrannical had been the behaviour of the majority. 4)

'Barmen' in the ecumenical perspective.

During the winter of 1933-34 Ammundsen saw no reason to abandon his accusations against the German Church opposition for stopping halfway. It was prepared to resist Reichsbischof Müller, but failed to protest Hitler's policies, and perhaps even supported them, and in any case it ignored the fact that Müller was Reichsbischof at Hitler's behest and on his conditions. During the spring of 1934, while preparations were made in Germany for the Barmen synod, Bell and Bonhoeffer, in Britain, discussed in detail ways of the battle against Nazism without selling out on any issue. Bell's "Ascension Day Address" in May 1934 was thus intended as an ecumenical declaration of support to the German ecclesiastical opposition. At the same time Bell wanted to stress that the German Church struggle was not only an internal German problem which people in England or elsewhere might ignore. He maintained that, on the contrary, the whole of Christendom must recognize its responsibility in the light of so flagrant a threat. Bonhoeffer immediately expressed his unconditional support for Bell's address, and made the following characteristic comment,

> In its conciseness it strikes at the chief points and leaves no escape for misinterpretation. I am absolutely sure that this letter of yours will have the greatest effect in Germany and will indebt the opposition very much to you. And what I think is most important, this letter will help the opposition to see that this whole conflict is not only within the Church, but strikes at the very roots of National-Socialism. 5)

Inspired by the Barmen synod, Bonhoeffer called in the summer months for an ecumenical declaration of solidarity with the Confessing Church, which in the meantime had become more solidly organized. Bell discussed Bonhoeffer's suggestion in his correspondence with Ammundsen. As a result, Präses Koch and a representative of the Confessing Church were invited to the Fanø conference as "guests and authoritative spokesmen in a very difficult situation". When Heckel learned of this, he protested sharply, but nothing came of it.

Ammundsen was fully aware of the implications of these measures. He refrained from condescending criticism of his struggling German brothers in the faith, and expressed, precisely, the excruciating aspect of their situation,

> We are faced with a very difficult situation. More and more it becomes clear that the position of the Emergency League People is untenable: to accept Hitler, but decline Müller. For Hitler and the whole Nazi ideology and regime means the support of Müller, indeed his only basis is not spiritual, but merely political. So our friends in Germany who will be loyal to the true principles of the Christian Church can hardly avoid being drawn into a political opposition, and what that means we know. We need much wisdom in order to say the truth and on the other hand not to precipitate events. 6)

Bonhoeffer, too, realized which way events were heading. He wanted to interpret Fanø as a kind of ecumenical international Barmen, which would adopt the same stances as the Confessing Church had taken inside Germany. He described his own position in a letter to Ammundsen,

> At the thought of Fanø I am more afraid of many of our own people than I am of the German Christians.

> On our side people want to be terribly careful not to appear to be unpatriotic, not so much out of fear, as out of sadly mistanken sense of honour.---It is necessary to speak quite honestly also in relation to our position with regard to the State, for the sake of Jesus Christ and the ecumenical cause. It must be clear, however terrible it is, that our time of decision is at hand: National Socialist <u>or</u> Christian; that we are forced to go one step forther now than we were a year ago (I know that you already said it then! 7)

On the 11th August 1934 Ammundsen had a secret meeting in Hamburg with six major members of the Confessing Church. On this occasion Ammundsen had the opportunity to speak of the inconsistency which he regarded as the fundamental liability of the Confessing Church, i.e. its protest against Müller while professing obedience to Hitler. Ammundsen maintained that when we are confronted with the absolutizing of the priviliges of the State, as was the case with National Socialism, exemplified by the Führer-principle, this consistitutes a situation of conflict for every Christian, since the absoluteness of the political claim entailed an infringement of the First Commandment. Referring to the oath which had been ordained a few days previously by the national synod of the Reichskirche, Ammundsen maintained that any such compulsory oath would necessarily precipitate conflict, since it contradicted every conception of Christian freedom. At the same time Ammundsen emphasized the courage which had been displayed by the pastors of the Confessing Church in protesting the compulsory oath from their pulpits. He emphatically condemned every tendecy of outsiders to speak with arrogance and condescension of the German situation. Such an attitude was extremely misplaced; moreover, it was unreasonable to establish a sort of judgment-tribunal outside of Germany, unless one simultaneously admitted that no Church could claim to be free of error. Ammundsen described in a report how precarious the situation was, and how much support and solidarity his German friends could expect with these concluding lines,

> These men have a terrible conflict against powers outside, but also inside themselves. They are put at a post with a tremendous responsibility, surrounded by dangers; our conversation for instance revealed the danger that the real spiritual issues could be buried under questions of law and tactics. But they are sincere Christians, willing even to suffer, and I admired their courageous and cheerful behaviour. They need our fellowship and prayer. 8)

Ammundsen was nevertheless unable to support Bonhoeffer's major goal at this time: to persuade the ecumenical movement to make a clean break with Heckel and his State-controlled activity. Bell and Ammundsen agreed that the situation within Germany was not sufficiently clear to German citizens as to permit the movement to impose such a rupture on their German brethren.

After the Fanø conference in August 1934 neither Bell nor Ammundsen could be shaken in their sympathy for the Confessing Church, but neither would contribute to the imposition of the new intra-ecclesiastical divisions, not even when the Confessing Church, in 1935-36, began to be affected by fragmentation. Their relationship to Bonhoeffer was severely tested when he, in his great articles in 1935 and 1936, drew even sharper consequences from his ecclesiology, while at the same time expressing his expectation of ecumenical understanding and assent. 9) In the end he was obviously disillusioned, because the ecumenical leaders had failed to draw the necessary consequences from Barmen and Fanø. However deep the disagreement between Bonhoeffer on the one hand and Ammundsen and Bell on the other hand went it was unable to ruin the cooperation they had established. Ammundsen did not live to experience the clarification of the ecumenical stance that followed the events of the autumn 1938, among them the "Kristallnacht", as he died in December 1936. Bonhoeffer, however, once again renewed the common understanding and the friendship which bound him to Bell, as he proved it at a meeting in Sweden 1942, when he revealed details of the conspiracy against Hitler. 10)

The sequence of his relationship points to a more principal problem concerning the significance for ecumenical discussion today, namely the dogmatic criterion for defining the nature of the Church. Both Bell and Ammundsen maintained that the Church by its very nature has to be open to culture and comprehensive. Contrary to such liberal 'cultural-Protestantism' the German theology which dominated the Barmen Synod saw precisely this broad church theology making the Church vulnerable to ideological infiltration, because liberal theology fails to insist on a strictly confessional definition of the Church's identity. Bell and Ammundsen were, however, by no means uninterested in the problem of the Church's self-identity. They too realized that the Church could not allow its identity to rest on presuppositions which were foreign to it. They were, however, rather more inclined to define the nature of the Church in the light of practical worship, that it, on the basis of the historical reality of the Church and its liturgy. This was an obvious point of departure both for Bell, an Anglican, and for Ammundsen, a Dane steeped in the tradition which on this point goes back to the important 19th century Danish theologian and churchman, N.F.S. Grundtvig. To Bell and Ammundsen ethics were rooted in sound judgment and common sense; but they had no consistent theory.

In a German context, however, such as the synod at Barmen, the theological identity of the Church was established on the basis of academic doctrines and the conclusion arrived by the synod.
How unconstructive and fruitless would it not be in the present situation to permit these attitudes to exclude each other? It is an urgent task for ecumenical theology to day to insist on a dialogue with the purpose of integrating the two patterns.

II. THE LUTHER-ACADEMY DURING THE THIRD REICH.

A similar complexity can be observed within the Lutheran Church. As a result of endeavours by leading representatives of the board of the Lutheran World Conference an international institute had been established. It aimed at common research and dialogue between scholars and churchmen from many national Lutheran Churches. The Prominent Luther-scholar Carl Stange (1870-1959) of Göttingen became the first director. In 1932 he founded the Luther-Academy which arranged annual conferences in Sondershausen/Thüringen. Two Scandinavian New Testament-scholars, Frederik Torm (1870-1954) of Copenhagen and Erling Eidem (1880-1972) of Uppsala were elected to the presidential board. In 1931 Eidem had been aprointed successor of N. Söderblom as Archbishop of Uppsala, and 1933 he became President of the board of the Luther-Academy.

These conferences were important for Lutheran dialogue across the frontiers, but - as it turned out - the atmosphere became increasingly affected by the divergent political judgment on the part of the German hosts and their guests. The contextuality of Lutheran confessional identity proved more influential than probably expected by any of the leading persons. The spread af antisemitc fanaticism within the Hitler-state appeared to be the stumbling-block for the sceptic visitors from outside, whereas Stange persistently denied the right of such criticism.

Archbishop Eidem criticised the development in Germany in two ways. On the one hand he regarded Germany as the mother-country of the reformation, and he admired the achievements of theological scholarship by German colleagues. On the other hand he was shocked by the power of nationalism and racist propaganda which became part of the official national attitude after Hitler's seize of power. Eidem hesitated to take over the chair as President of the board, mainly because he was concerned about the risk of letting his position as archbishop be abused as a legitimation of measures which he considered alien to traditional Lutheran heritage. After the first antisemitic excesses in late March 1933 he used his position as chairman of the Swedish Ecumenical Council and sent a protest to the central office of the Protestant church in Berlin. In a private letter to Torm he explained the decision expressing himself in much stronger language to his Danish friend, "The fruits of the new regime are truly bitter. Racism and national overestimation must be considered as most alarming utterances stemming from the essence of old Adam". 11)

Eidem had received very precise information concerning the Nazi ideology and church politics from the Swedish chaplain in Berlin, Birger Forell. Torm, too, was well informed. He read all sorts of journals and periodicals, including the extremely antisemitic journal "Der Stürmer", edited by J. Streicher. He was shocked by many statements by prominent church leaders in whom he had trusted, e.g. Ludwig Ihmels and Otto Dibelius. In March these men supported the national enthusiasm after Hitler had identified the new political system as the only possibility of overcoming the power of godlessness which had dominated during the Weimar Republic. With reference to such statements Torm wrote Eidem on April 3, "When somebody in that way subjects himself to National Socialism and the Swastika, where does then the cross remain?". 12)

It is true that Carl Stange, whose politics were rooted in the German Kaiserreich, never became a member of the Nazi partv; but his reaction differed from the line taken by his Scandinavian colleagues. He requested them urgently to understand the defeat of Marxism as a historical event which enabled such renewal of public life in Germany that no detailed criticism should be allowed to cast a shadow over the "national rebirth". Therefore he instructed the visitors of the summer conference 1933 to refrain from any criticism of the political system in Germany. A few months later he visited Sweden and Denmark and was confronted with critique from colleagues in the Swedish Church and at universities. Whatever he heard, he retained a national-apologetic optimism, persistently denying foreigners the right of statements of misgiving. He claimed that foreign sceptics had no ability to establish a thorough investigation. 13)

Torm also turned to Gerhard Kittel, with whom he had kept scholarly contacts for several years concerning biblical exegesis. Now Torm wanted to dissociate himself from Kittel's stance on the "Jewish question".

Kittel insisted, however, that he himself had not changed his view of Judaism, but regarded it "as a Christian duty to be honest to the perspective of the New Testament, which knows of a special position of the Jewish people after Calvary". Kittel requested Torm to avoid condemnation of German theologians, adding that most critics from outside were unable to understand the kind of change in German national life, achieved after "15 years of disastrous self-estrangement". 14)

Two important conclusions can be drawn from this exchange between Torm and Kittel. First: Kittel was so positive in his general appraisal of National Socialism generally and Hitler personally (he pointed to Hitler's "sense of justice"), that he - like Stange - turned his back to any criticism from outside Germany. Secondly: his notion of race had such impact on his theological thought that he regarded Jewish Christians as specific church-members not to be compaired with Christians of German origin.

As the Nazi ideology increasingly showed its true colours, the Lutheran heritage proved unable to keep the relations betweeen Carl Stange and the Scandinavian members of the board intact. Stange maintained that the church-struggle in Germany was on its way to be solved. His patriotism and his efforts to carry on the academy were so persistent that he turned a blind eye to totalitarian control and discipline in party and state, if he did not even approve of them. The political events in the autumn of 1938, not least the "Kristallnacht", brought the conflict to the point where common confessional identity could no longer keep the community going. In November 1938 Torm wrote to Stange that it was impossible to talk any Dane into accepting to lecture at the summer conference of 1939, "It was said that after all that has happened recently in the Jewish question and in church affairs it was imposible to overlook what might happen in the future, and therefore nobody in Denmark was willing to make appointment for the summer. At least it was quite impossible to find a preacher". 15)

Stange responded immediately with obvious indignation. He considered Torm's position as chairman of the Danish Council for Mission among Jews as a factor which might explain his judgment concerning the development "resulting from the Jewish murder in Paris". This statement proves that Stange totally overlooked the outrageous cruelties during the"Kristallnacht". In addition to such justification of persecutions against Jews he also complained of Torm's earlier frequent criticism which he regarded as a general political disapproval of Germany. Thus Stange insisted that he had kept trying to maintain a truly ecumenical character of the conferences, whereas Torm, in his opinion, had permitted himself to make critical references to internal aspects of German politics. 16) The cooperation could obviously not continue any longer, and it proved impossible to brigde the contradicting evaluations. Torm and Stange continued to correspond in brief, official letters, but the gap was not closed when Stange undertook an attempt to reestablish the Lutheran-academy after the war.

Torm, on the other hand, remained in close contact with Eidem. Referring to Stange's letter he pointed out to Eidem that it was not just a matter of his own personal bitterness towards Stange. What concerned him rather more was the fact that foreign guests in Germany were made objects of the propaganda from the Third Reich, at the same time being muzzled themselves. He mentioned a recent law in the church of Thüringen (where the conferences took place) which prohibited to baptize Jews and to serve Jewish Christians. Finally he asked Eidem whether it was possible to have any kind of official community with a church which by such attitude had itself left the Christian church. 17)

Without opening a discussion about Torm's possition as seen from an actual dogmatic point of view concerning Christian mission among Jews it must be mentioned, at least briefly in this context, that he did not limit his concern about the German struggle to this question. He became one of the leading Danish historiographs of the German church struggle, publishing three books and a large number of articles. Furthermore he was a leading member of a committee which was formed in the summer of 1936 upon the suggestion of the Archbishop of Canterbury in order to provide help to baptized Jewish refugees from Germany. 18) This committee had to resign officially after the German occupation of Denmark, but Torm went on with secret and illegal help to all groups of Jews in Denmark, culminating with his support to the successful rescue of most Danish Jews to Sweden in

October 1943.[19)]

CONCLUSION. During the last decades D. Bonhoeffer's reformulation of the protestant heritage has served as the starting point for a general self-criticism within the Lutheran tradition. Not least the imminent danger of antisemitism owing to consistent features within traditional Lutheran doctrine has been noted. At the same time the theory of "two reigns" has been considered as a most influential explanation of the general failure within Lutheran churches to take a responsible stance admidst the challenges in modern social and political life. The above-mentioned case-studies indicate the need of a balanced view in order to avoid a superficial application of such theories. At the same time the complicity of leading Lutheran scholars and church leaders in the disastrous disqualification of Jewish identity should by no means be forgotten or made inoffensive. This risk exists as soon as a balanced view of the "Wirkungsgeschichte" of modern Lutheranism is replaced by simplistic accusations lacking any analytic documentation. The demand for a precise criticism should not be taken as an attempt to exempt the Churches in Scandinavia from the critical evaluation of their own attitude during the Nazi period. Such Pharisaism would be an outrageous weakening of responsibily facing the necessity of viewing the German church struggle as an ecumenical experience. The representatives from the Scandinavian churches as mentioned above spoke to deaf ears in their own countries, a deficiency on the part of the church majority. This is even more tragic considering the fact that Scandinavians lived with unhindered access to free press-coverage, a fact which is equally true for Switzerland and Holland as well. This widespread passivity though bears no comparison with active complicity in the Genocide. Nonetheless the specific features of the German church struggle should not be accentuated with such effect that Churches outside Germany could escape critical examination.

1) For inctroduction to the early German Church Struggle see, Robert P. Ericksen, The Barmen Synod and its Declaration: A Brief Synopsis; John S. Conway, The German Church Struggle: Its Making and Meaning; both in, The Church confronts the Nazis. Barmen Then and Now. Ed. by Hubert G. Locke (New York and Toronto 1984). Klaus Scholder, The Churches and the Third Reich. Vol. One: Preliminary History and the Time of Illusions, 1918-1934. Richard Gutteridge, Open thy Mouth for the Dumb! The German Evangelical Church and the Jews 1879-1950. (Oxford 1976) John S. Conway, The Nazi Persecution of the Churches 1933-1945 (London 1968). Peter Matheson, The Third Reich and the Christian Churches. A Documentary Account of Christian Resistance and Complicity During the Nazi Era. (Edinburgh 1981).
2) Ammundsen to Lord Dickinson, March 30 and April 8 (concept), Ammundsen's Papers, Royal Library, Copenhagen, Ny Kgl. Saml. 2700, Vol. 8. As to Ammundsen generally see Frode Beyer, Valdemar Ammundsen. Liv og Tanker (Copenhagen 1954). Jens H. Schjørring, Oekumenische Perspektiven des deutschen Kirchenkampfes (Leiden 1985). As to the situation in Germany April 1933 see the titles in note 1 and further Armin Boyens, Kirchenkampf und Oekumene 1933-1939. (München 1969); Jonathan Wright, 'Above Parties'. The Political Attitudes of the German Protestant Church Leadership 1918-1933 (Oxford 1977).
3) V. Ammundsen to H.-L. Henriod, April 9, 1933. Archive of the WCC, Geneva. (284 43). Germany. The Church Situation 1933.
4) Ammundsen to George Bell, Oct. 5, 1933. George Bell' Papers. Lambeth Palace Library, London. Vol. 27. As to George Bell generally see Ronald C.D. Jasper, George Bell. Bishop of Chichester (London 1967). Kenneth Slack, George Bell (London 1971).
5) D. Bonhoeffer to George Bell, May 15, 1934, D. Bonhoeffer: Ges. Schriften I, p. 194.
6) V. Ammundsen to G. Bell, July 23, 1934, G. Bell's Papers, Vol. 1.
7) D. Bonhoeffer to V. Ammundsen, August 8, 1934. Ges. Schriften I, pp. 205ff.
8) Ammundsen's report was sent to G. Bell. See G. Bell's Papers, Lambeth Palace Library, Vol. 1. Copies in: WCC Library, Geneva. Life and Work. Executive Committee, Fanø, August 1934; and Ammundsen's Papers, Vol. 132. As to the Fanø meeting see further, Eberhard Bethge, Dietrich Bonhoeffer. Theologe. Christ. Zeitgenosse; Armin Boyens, Kirchenkampf und Ökumene 1933-1939. Nils Karlström, Kyrkan och nazismen. Ekumeniska aktioner mot nazismen 1933-1934 (Uppsala 1976); Jens H. Schjørring, Ökumenische Perspektiven des deutschen Kirchenkampfes (Leiden 1985).
See also: Andreas Lindt (Ed.) George Bell-Alphons Koechlin Briefwechsel 1933-1954. (Zürich 1954).
9) D. Bonhoeffer, Die Bekennende Kirche und die Ökumene. In: Ges. Schriften I, pp. 249ff; Zur Frage der Kirchengemeinschaft. In: Ges. Schriften II, pp. 217ff.
10) D. Bonhoeffer, Ges. Schriften I, pp. 372; An der Schwelle zum gespalten Europa. Der Briefwechsel zwischen George Bell und Gerhard Leibholz 1939-1951. Ed. by E. Bethge and Ronald C.D. Jasper, Stuttgart 1974, pp. 56ff. See also E. Bethge. Dietrich Bonhoeffer, pp. 850ff. and J. Glenthøj (Ed.). Dokumente zur Bonhoeffer-Forschung 1928-1945. Die Mündige Welt V, Munich 1969, pp. 260ff.
11) E. Eidem to F. Torm, April 6, 1933. Torm's Papers, 6448, Rigsarkivet, Copenhagen (trsl. by the present author). As to Eidem generally see E. Murtorinne, Erzbischof Eidem zum deutschen Kirchenkampf 1933-1934 (Helsinki 1968) Jens H. Schjørring, Ökumenischen Perspektiven des deutschen Kirchenkampfes; Nils Karlström, Kyrkan och nazismen, Ekumeniska aktioner mot nazismen 1933-1934. (Uppsala 1976).
12) F. Torm to E. Eidem, April 3, 1933. Eidem's Papers. Landsarkivet Uppsala C II 4.
13) C. Stange to Torm, July 7, 1933. Torm's Papers (note 11). As to Stange's visit in Sweden see Jens H. Schjørring, Theologische Gewissensethik und und politische Wirklichkeit. Das Beispiel Eduard Geismars und Emanuel Hirschs (Göttingen 1979).
14) G. Kittel to Torm, June 12 and August 31, 1933. Torm's Papers (note 11) As to Kittel generally see Leonore Siegele-Wenschkewitz, Neutestamentliche Wissenschaft vor der Judenfrage. Gerhard Kittels theologische Arbeit im

Wandel deutscher Geschichte (München 1980); Robert P. Ericksen,Theologians under Hitler. Gerhard Kittel, Paul Althaus and Emanuel Hirsch (New Haven 1985).
15) F. Torm, December 10, 1938. Torm's Papers (concept, trsl. by the author)
16) Ibid.
17) As to the situation in Thüringen 1939, see Kurt Meier, Die Deutschen Christen. (3. ed. Halle 1967).
18) The background of the Danish Committee is told in a declaration by J. Toftegaard. See J. Nørregaard's Papers. Rigsarkivet Copenhagen, 6073, Vol.7.
19) Aage Bertelsen, October' 43. (New York 1954); Lene Yahil, The Rescue of Danish Jewry. Test of a Democracy (Philadelphia 1969); Harold Flender, Rescue in Denmark. How occupied Denmark rose as a nation to save the Danish Jews from Nazi extermination (New York 1961); Jørgen Glenthøj, The Danish Rescue of Jews in October 1943. In: Human Responses to the Holocaust: Perpetrators and Victims, Bystanders and Resisters (Ed. by Michael D. Ryan New York and Toronto, 1981).

Christian attitudes and responses to the Jewish plight in Eastern Europe 1933–1945 and after

CHAIRPERSON **Professor Ronald Modras**

RAPPORTEUR **Dr David Kranzler**

POLAND, AFTER THE HOLOCAUST *

IWONA IRWIN-ZARECKA

Department of Sociology and Anthropology, Wilfrid Laurier University, Waterloo, Ontario N2L 3C5, Canada

* Paper prepared for the conference "Remembering for the Future", Oxford, July 1988

At the heart of emotionally charged debates about the Poles' attitudes to the "Final Solution" is the question of moral responsibility for the near annihilation of Polish Jewry. Also, at issue is the virtual absence of such a moral question on Poland's public agenda.

The refusal of most Poles to examine their country's record vis-à-vis the Jews has eventually become as significant as the record itself. As we have increasingly come to understand, no country, no people, no institution can claim a flawless record during the Holocaust. Still, that an ever-widening search for those responsible (however peripherally) is being undertaken in America or Canada or Switzerland or France testifies to the presence of conscience. Here too, especially in the case of France, debate and controversy abound. In France, the "memory battle" over the Holocaust is fought internally, not solely in response to Jewish challenges. In Poland, on the other hand, the few voices of conscience which have been raised - many only quite recently - represent so unpopular a position that they are overwhelmed by the noise of protest. And when the challenge to Poland's conscience comes from outside - as it did from Claude Lanzmann and his Shoah (seen in Poland in late 1985), the protest becomes even louder.

This Polish refusal to accept a measure of responsibility for the fate of Polish Jews has itself become subject to analysis. Both its implications for historiography (Gutman, 1986) and its roots in the collective self-definition of Poles as victims (Mendelsohn, 1986) have been raised. To an extent, my own work (Irwin-Zarecka, forthcoming) has been devoted to that issue, in analyzing the larger problem of Poland's neutralizing the memory of the morally difficult past[1]. By looking at the Poles' position towards the Holocaust within that context, I began to recognize that the concern with Polish-Jewish relations before and during the Holocaust is essentially incomplete, if not analytically misguided. Only when we - and the Poles - focus on the period immediately after the Holocaust may we understand that past more critically.

Poland, after the Holocaust, was a place many survivors wished to leave as quickly as possible (see, esp.: Bauer, 1970). For some Jews, living in the mass graveyard the country had become was simply too painful. Others believed their traditional ways would be impossible to maintain under the Communist rule. Most of all, though, Jews were fleeing the cold, at times violent, reception in their native towns and cities. An estimated 1,500 Jews lost their lives between the end of the war and the summer of 1947 - in random killings, in organized assasinations, in pogroms (Dobroszycki, 1973). The violence climaxed on July 4, 1946 in Kielce. An accusation of ritual murder led to a day-long frenzy in which thousands of city folk participated: 41 Jews died, many more were wounded. For safety, the wounded were moved to another town, the atmosphere in Kielce remaining laden with hostility (Hillel, 1985).

News of the pogrom spread fast. In its aftermath, some 100,000 Polish Jews left a country they could no longer consider their home (Gilbert, 1985). The Kielce pogrom, for all its shock, did not, however, spell the end to anti-Jewish actions. The trial of nine perpetrators, the only effort to punish those responsible, became a cause for wide-spread popular protest (Hillel, 1985). Even the delayed condemnation of the violence by Church authorities offered a clear warning to the Jews: since they were siding with the Communists, Poland's chief enemy, they should accept the consequences (see: Bauer, 1970; Smolar, 1986). And indeed, in what amounted to a civil war at the time, Jews and Communists (or simply Jews as Communists) remained choice targets.

Speaking "objectively", as some historians in Poland now do (see: Kersten, 1986), the conflict between Poles and Jews was a political one. Already during the war, Jews were perceived as disloyal to Poland for their sympathy for and cooperation with the Soviets (who occupied the east of Poland on September 17, 1939). At the end of the war, the Jews came back from the Soviet Union, high in the ranks of the Communist army and the security forces. And they were soon joined, if not in action, then in support, by the Jews who managed to survive in Poland itself. Thus, so many fewer than ever before, Jews would come to occupy a position of unprecedented power within Poland's ruling elites[2], at exactly the time that most Poles were struggling against what they considered another Soviet occupation.

The facts may support this view. When applied to the pogrom in Kielce, it translates into explaining the events as the result of Soviet (or at least Communist) provocation, aimed at distracting international attention from a referendum crucial to the new regime's credibility.[3] Some of my independent sources seem to confirm such an interpretation. Yet for all its plausibility, this political approach to the "Jewish question" in Poland after the Holocaust ignores the key consideration - simply that the anti-Jewish violence was taking place after the Holocaust. How could the mass extermination of the Jews, which Poles had witnessed from so close, not change the hostile definition of the Jew? How could a trauma of such magnitude not shake Poland's conscience?

Both morally and intellectually, pursuing these questions might sharpen our focus on the period of the Holocaust itself. On a moral plane, these are questions about Poles and Jews only, questions which cannot be answered by recourse to the "attenuating circumstances" of the Nazi terror or the sheer size of the Jewish community. On an analytical plane, the non-trauma of the Holocaust is important for understanding the basic premises of Polish-Jewish relations. It is also the key to an appreciation of the pain which almost inevitably surfaces when survivors speak of Poland. For most Poles, this pain is incomprehensible. And, it frequently comes to be interpreted as an "anti-Polish obsession".

Such pain cannot be easily disassociated from the pain of being a survivor. Yet we must also remember that more than one-half of Jews who were in Poland during the period in question (1944-1947) were not "survivors" in the usual sense. After fleeing the Nazis to the Soviet Union, those Jews faced hardships, deportations to the far east, hunger, and, often, death (see: Gross and Grudzińska-Gross, 1983); they were, however, beyond the reach of the "Final Solution". Their return to Poland was their first encounter with the enormity of destruction; theirs was the pain of loss and the pain of helplessness, not the numbing memory of the "univers concentrationnaire."

Another substantial group had survived by passing as "Aryans." We still know little about their experience, but what we do know (see: Borwicz, 1969; Tec, 1984; Grynberg, 1965, 1969), and what I gathered from conversations with people who "passed," feelings they carried into freedom were very mixed. Depending on individual memories of the five years (or four or two - the length of stay on the "Aryan" side varied considerably), there would be gratitude to those Poles, and those Germans, who helped one to stay alive, but there would also be recollections of the threat and the fear, of the extremely close calls, of the intense risk in the very act of living.

Jews who were coming out of hiding added to that mixture of light and dark their memories, memories of strangers who helped, of friends who betrayed, of human solidarity and of greed. And even those Jews who managed to survive on their own, often in the partisan units in the forests, were not without memories of acts of support, however small, from the local population.

In short, the experience of surviving was too varied (in its balance of acts of decency and acts of betrayal, and in its degree of connectedness with the actions and attitudes of Polish Christians) to allow for a singularly negative view of the Poles. Indeed, in the comments of survivors, it is impossible not to hear the full range of hope for and despair at the human condition (see, esp.: Gilbert, 1985).

Yet if being in Auschwitz and living among Poles under false identity, or hiding in the attic and fighting alongside the victorious Red Army, were all such different experiences, all these Jews did ultimately return. To most, the magnitude of destruction was a shock; though hope persisted during these first years, most survivors were now confronted with their specialness - their families, their communities, their world had disappeared. They were also confronted with the fulness of their exclusion from the Polish universe of concern. As Kazimierz Brandys, a Polish writer and a Jew, aptly expressed it, "Jews were not mourned" (1983:33). Indeed, they were often greeted with a mixture of surprise and disappointment, especially by the neighbours who now lived in their houses, ate from their plates and sat on their chairs. Jews were clearly not welcome.

Sensing exclusion was not new; for many Jews, it was a part of their experience during the Holocaust. But, as I have argued, the complexities of each individual's story of survival could and often did mute the feeling. Little could soften the impact of hostility on return (see also: Lewis, 1987:19). (This, incidentally, might help to explain why so many Jews who showed no previous sympathy for the Communists would come to support the new regime; the government did, in theory and in practice, call for a full integration of the Jews into Polish society.) Jews welcomed the voices of the Polish democratic opinion, raised in their defense, and the small acts of kindness and remembrance from ordinary people. But especially after Kielce and the Jews' failure to gather support from the Church, this most important of moral authorities, many recognized the impossibility of remaining in Poland (see: Bauer, 1970; Hillel, 1985; Gilbert, 1985:811-831).

It was the pain of seeing the death of one's people greeted with wide indifference and often satisfaction, which would be imprinted on the Jews' memory of Poles and Poland. During the deportations, some Jews had already heard words of gratitude to Hitler for "solving Poland's Jewish problem." At the time, though, noone could yet envision the completeness of the destruction. To hear those words after the Holocaust was to be denied even the comfort of hope that the Holocaust could become a lesson and a warning. To see Jews beaten up by the crowds was to realize the issue was not symbolic.

Why is that pain so rarely understood by Poles? Why does that pain not become a challenge to their conscience?

We have already touched on one aspect of the answer, and that is the politization of the "Jewish question." With Kielce in particular so heavily implicated in the political schemes of the times, it becomes fairly easy to interpret the violence as politically motivated. And with Jews so numerous in the ranks of the despised new authorities, it is also easy to claim that whatever the hostile reaction, it was not anti-Semitism, but justifiable anger at the people collaborating with Communists.

Discussing the post-war "Jewish problem" in political terms is a relatively recent development. The first article on the Kielce pogrom, by Kersten, which followed the first time the victims of the pogrom were honored by Poles, came only in 1981, at the initiative of the then legal Solidarity. Before, this pogrom, let alone other killings, had had no place on the public agenda. Even Jews would not readily discuss what happened after the war - even in private - they were, after all, staying in Poland. Most young Poles, even today, after both the regime and the Church joined in to commemorate Kielce (beginning in 1986), would not know the extent of anti-Jewish violence. The remembrance of Kielce, relegated to the category of a "shameful episode," does not include remembrance of the hundreds of other victims. For people born after the war, whose main source of conscience-troubling questions is Poland's collective memory, ignorance, more than any other factor, may be responsible for silence[4].

But what about the older generation, people with first-hand memories?

It is to the great credit of a young Polish researcher, Alina Cała, that we may answer this question somewhat empirically. In 1974, while conducting an ethnographic study of the stereotypes of the Jew among the rural population in southeastern Poland (a region once home to many Jews), Cała was struck by the numerous off-hand references to the post-war killings. Ten years later, she was able to follow up this theme, now with the help of student interviewers who, time after time, recorded tales of murder (1984, personal communication). More shocking than the events themselves was the matter-of-fact telling of them. To the witnesses, even in 1984, murdering Jews in 1946 seemed "natural," not calling for the kind of moral consideration one gives to killing innocent people.

Cała's findings very much confirm our general impression from survivors' testimonies - that after the Holocaust, Jews often felt they should have been dead. After years of round-ups, deportations, shootings, and the Jews' disappearance from community after community, it finally became possible for Poles to take the absence of Jews for granted.

In Poland, the lengthy Nazi occupation was responsible for profound demoralization. For a long five years, the moral codes of civil society applied only narrowly to the immediate community. Stealing, cheating, killing -- all acquired new moral definitions outside that community, as they do at times of war. The "numbing" effect of witnessing continuous terror against one's people helped split moral standards into the worlds of "us" and "them."

The question here is not whether attitudes to Jews were affected by this general demoralization - all attitudes likely were. The key question is where the Jews belonged in the moral war zones. Were they considered part of the family, with all the implicit rights and obligations? Were the Jews to stand outside the shared universe of concern? Or were they classified as enemies?

If the political interpretation of anti-Jewish violence following the Holocaust assigns the Jew to the role of real (or potential) enemy, the view offered by the peasants denies him even that much presence. After all, the rules of war in general and of civil war in particular may provide a moral justification for killing enemies. Killing non-persons, long since condemned, requires no such moral work; it also does not raise questions.

People who do remember those years have two means of morally neutralizing that memory. One, widely adopted by the opinion-makers, including those within the Church, is to treat anti-Jewish violence as a part of the politically violent landscape of post-war Poland. The other, as expressed by the peasant witnesses, is to exorcise the Jew from the sphere fo moral relevance.

To understand how the fate of Jews after the Holocaust could remain a non-issue for Polish conscience, we should focus on the politization of the questions. Among people capable of raising voices of conscience, not only was it a common explanation for what had happened, but it was also to gain strength. Indeed, it is only within the last few years that the view of "Jews as a political problem" has lost ground to that of "Jews as an interesting subject." With the prominent Jewish participation in the Stalinist apparatus of oppression, and with the forced involvement of the remaining Jews in the power struggles of 1968, the Jew as a political figure retained significance. Today, the Jews are likely to be identified (also by the regime) with the present political opposition, but they are no less likely to be associated with Communism in the past. The growing diversity among groups opposing the regime, which offers a growing exposure to the ideas inspired by the traditional nationalistic Right, almost guarantees the persistence of the image of "Jew = Communist."[5] In short, the historical distance from the period immediately following the Holocaust does not automatically de-politicize the "Jewish question" at the time.

Yet to understand the dynamics of neutralizing memory at source (in other words, the ways in which defining the Jew defines the realm of applicable morality), it is not enough to focus on the mythic grip of Jews-as-Communists. Here, the peasants' tales of murder, together with sources now available (see: Bauer, 1970; Dobroszycki, 1973; Gilbert, 1985; Hillel, 1985) point to a much more complex picture than the one provided by political historians. Some Jews were certainly killed as Communists; others, perhaps most, were killed as Jews. The ominous role of greed cannot be ignored; neither can the disappointment at the incompleteness of the "Final Solution". And, too, there was fear, the fear of revenge, an unarticulated testimony to the deeply-buried sense of having done something to elicit the Jews' revenge. (I am not using the term "guilt" here, for a fear of consequences is not the same as a sense of guilt.) All the old stories of "Christ killers" and all the new stories of "Soviet lackeys", the notion of blood-libel and the mere fact that a few Jews survived - the motives for the violence were varied. What was missing - and this is perhaps the hardest to understand from the perspective of Western reflection "after Auschwitz" - was the horrifying lesson of the Holocaust.

An inquiry into what happened immediately after the Holocaust cannot by itself explain why the Holocaust was not a trauma for most Poles. What it can do is encourage different questions about the period of the Holocaust, as well as focus attention on the years to follow, years which brought little, if any, change to the non-challenge of the "Final Solution".

One must be very careful, when speaking about Poland, not to cloud the issues with familiar terms. "After Auschwitz," for example, is not missing from the Poles cultural vocabulary after 1945. The meaning of "Auschwitz" for Poles, though, is very different from its meaning here.

Auschwitz (or rather Oświęcim, the Polish name by which the camp is usually known) is not, for Poles, a symbol of Jewish suffering. Rather, it is a general symbol of "man's inhumanity to man" and a symbol of the Polish tragedy at the hands of the Nazis. It is a powerful reminder of the evil of racism, and not a singular reminder of the deadliness of anti-Semitism. In the most literal sense of memories evoked on site, it is an "Auschwitz without Jews." [6]

The "Auschwitz without Jews" and, more generally, the memory of the Nazi occupation, possesses all the qualities of a trauma of victimization. Indeed, if there is any one subject that has been worked and re-worked in the last decades, it is that of the Polish experience during World War II. What critics and outsiders often perceive as the obsessive preoccupation of Polish writers and artists with the years 1939-1945 has helped both to remember that trauma and to heal the wounds.

To remember the victimization is not a moral challenge, however. If anything, the Poles' exemplary record of resistance to the Nazis offers considerable moral solace. But where does the memory of the Holocaust fit into this memory of the victim? The answer is that it fits only in so far as Jews too were victims of the Nazis. Indeed, the persistent commemoration of "six million Polish victims of genocide" - a figure which includes the three million Polish Jews - testifies to the ease of appropriating the Jewish dead as one's own.[7]

The figure of "six million Poles" does more than that. It also grants the dead Jew the status of a Pole, in a post-mortem acceptance of the Jews' membership in the Polish family. And this represents a reading of the past which renders that past unrecognizable. The Jew not only appears to be mourned on a par with others - which he was not - he also appears to have always belonged, which he did not. The destruction of the Jewish community, when reclaimed as the loss of Polish lives, acquires a sense of trauma which it did not have, at least for the majority. And the sharing in suffering, together with assigning all the blame to the Nazis, helps eliminate questions about the Poles' action and inaction towards the Jews.

This neutralization of memory, so well served by "Polonizing" and universalizing the Holocaust, could not work as well as it does were it not for its foundation in the Poles' experience during the Holocaust. The absence of moral challenge is not something that can be created utterly after the fact. At issue here is not the simple denial of responsibility. At issue, I believe, is the assignment of the Jew to a moral zone outside that shared by Poles, a zone where "responsibility" does not apply. In other words, identifying Jews as co-victims in the genocide of Poles does not silence the questions which have troubled Polish conscience. The questions were never there to begin with.

There were, as we know, many Poles for whom the fate of the Jews during the Holocaust did matter - the individual Gentiles who heroically saved Jews. There were also those in Żegota, an organization helping Jews after September 1942, and the members of the underground (most notably, the Home Army courier Jan Karski), who worked hard to awaken the world to the magnitude of the disaster (see: Lacqueur, 1980). There were artists who responded to the Jewish tragedy with great compassion and moral outrage; poems by Czesław Miłosz are those best known in the West, but there were others (see: Borwicz, 1947). And, survivors' testimonies mention countless "little" people who felt solidarity with the Jews (even if they did not act). But as a whole, the Polish society, as represented by its underground political organizations and the underground fighting units, granted the Jews the status of a separate group throughout the war. The Polish government-in-exile, while itself including Jewish representatives, steadfastly refused to extend such representation to Jews in Poland (Engel, 1987). The Home Army, the largest of resistance units, had some Jews in its ranks, some even as officers; they, however, were not known as Jews (see: Borwicz, 1980). In the very real sense of civic participation, the Jew, after 1939, lost his membership in the body social.

To this legal and practical exclusion, compounded by the Nazi policies of ghettoization gradually applied throughout the occupied territory, we must add an equally important symbolic factor - the continuous legitimacy of anti-Semitism (see also: Smolar, 1986). In Poland, opposition to the Nazis did not come to mean - as it would in Western Europe - opposition to their anti-Jewish measures. However, Polish anti-Semites, even at their most vicious, never advocated extermination as the solution for the "Jewish problem." Polish anti-Semites, unlike their Western counterparts, did not officially join in with the Nazis, however close they might have collaborated with them through their own anti-Jewish actions. The far Right of the Polish resistance movement was still a part of the Polish underground, while calling for - and engaging in - hunting the Jews. Those closer to the middle of the political spectrum discussed Poland's "Jewish problem" throughout the war (see: Gross, 1986). And it was one of the founders of Żegota who stressed that Poles should not forget that the Jew was their enemy (Kossak-Szczucka, cited in Smolar, 1986). In short, the Nazi anti-Jewish project, as abhorrent as its methods were to most Poles, was excluded from the continuing history of Polish-Jewish relations. It was as if, after an "intermission" forced by the war, Polish-Jewish affairs were to resume in the same form as before.

History proved this perception right. After the "Final Solution", Poland's "Jewish question" lost none of its urgency. Only its perception changed, from primarily an economic problem to a political one.

It is clear that this could not have happened without the continuing legitimacy of the local varieties of anti-Semitism. What remains hard to understand is that so much legitimacy could remain when the rest of the world, recognizing the horrors of the Holocaust, began to condemn anti-Semitism to silence. In North America, in France, and, with special urgency, of course, in Germany, expressions of anti-Jewish feelings were publicly unacceptable; appeals to people's anti-Semitic attitudes were no longer legitimate vote-gathering strategies. As we may now better appreciate, restricting the political usefulness and public prominence of anti-Semitism does not spell its end; restrictions may simply displace it, rename the Jew as a "Zionist", and themselves become the root of strong resentment (see: Finkielkraut, 1982, 1983; Lewis, 1987). Yet a condemnation of anti-Semitism, if not as effective as one might like it to be, does indicate that things have changed after the Holocaust. How is it that in the country where the "Final Solution" was witnessed daily, anti-Semitism retains, even now, a rather substantial legitimacy?

This question is both moral and political[8]. It is also a question about the dynamics of remembrance, especially when asked of the present efforts to recover Poland's Jewish heritage, efforts undertaken in the spirit of respect and reconciliation. The question acquires special poignancy when we recall that the persistent legitimacy of anti-Semitism co-exists with the virtual absence of Jews, or that the "target population" in this case consists of, at best, some 15,000 people (see: Kirshner, 1983).

It should be stressed that at issue here is not so much anti-Semitism as its legitimacy. At issue is not the fact, reported by a Polish researcher in a Catholic journal Znak, that negative stereotypes of the Jew remain popular among university students (Łukaszewicz, 1983), or that people with "Jewish looks" would be verbally abused when queing for food at the time of worst shortages in 1981. (If this were the issue, Poland would compare favourably indeed with places like France or the United States, where anti-Jewish incidents are not rare.)

At issue, rather, is the parish in Warsaw which, publicly and openly, distributes "Protocols of the Elders of Zion", and other equally vicious, if not so famous, anti-Semitic literature. At issue is the considerable appeal of the now resurrected ideas of Poland's openly anti-Semitic National Democratic party. At issue is also the prominence of the hard-line Communist attacks on "Zionists, Trotskyites and revisionists." Most of all, at issue is the persistence of the "objective" view of anti-Semitism as inevitable, given the presence of Jews and their position in society.

It is only now, the reasoning goes, when Jews are too few truly to matter, that Poland no longer has a "Jewish problem." It is only now that persuasion, education and appeals to decency can effectively dislodge the remnants of the past attitudes. Time, together with active efforts to present anti-Semitism as morally wrong may, perhaps within the next generation, make anti-Semitism disappear[9].

To declare anti-Semitism morally wrong is to deny it legitimacy. The problem lies, though, with defining what constitutes anti-Semitism and what does not.

The term itself, used and abused by critics and proponents of anti-Jewish sentiments, is problematic. Yet I suspect few Western analysts would agree with a Polish reviewer of a book on Father Maximilian Kolbe (Turian, 1983) who commented that Kolbe's pre-war attacks on the Jews' dominance of the economy were not anti-Semitism, but a legitimate and logical reaction to the situation. On the other side of the spectrum, for North Americans in particular, it seems rather striking that, in Poland, it is anti-Semitism to suspect someone of having Jewish origins.

The very labeling of such "suspicion" as suspicion, or the equating of Jewishness with a "dark secret," offers one of the better clues to the problem. With often the best of intentions, and with the legacy of deadly Nazi "reminders", there remains the basic definition of Jewishness as something best to ignore, to consider irrelevant, when dealing amicably with Jews[10].

I say "with the best of intentions" because the idea indeed belongs to a liberal, humanistic ethos of Poland's most respectable intellectuals. Its history dates to the nineteenth century, when progressive social philosophy saw the solution of the "Jewish question" in the Jews' Polonization. In today's Poland, where most Jews would best be described as "Poles of Jewish descent" (and where the memory of 1968 purges, directed at thousands of such people, is still fresh), to define anti-Semitism as naming someone a Jew makes a great deal of sense. It also well reflects the symbolic reality of the situation - the fact that in the Polish language both "Jew" and "Jewish" can be used as singularly negative epithets.

Yet if identifying anti-Semitism with pointing to a person's Jewishness certainly makes sense, it also perpetuates, however subtly, the view of the Jew as not-quite-humanly-on-a-par with the Pole. And when this is combined with condemnation of anti-Semitism, the reasoning seems irreproachable.

The assumption that, both individually and collectively, the Jewish presence must pose a problem removes a whole structural level from the phenomenon of "anti-Semitism" - precisely that of the exclusion of Jews from the shared moral universe. In specific historical terms, taking it for granted that Polish Jews, during the Holocaust, had to be outside the body social (see, e.g.: Lipski, 1983), makes it extremely difficult indeed to question that exclusion on moral grounds, or to see it as a form of anti-Semitism. The issue of responsibility for the ultimate fate of Polish Jews thus retains a very different moral relevance from that of responsibility for the fate of the Poles. With the Jews' exclusion as a given, indifference to their plight becomes "natural"[11].

Before the Holocaust, it might have been plausible to argue that the Jews' exclusion from the Poles' universe of moral concern sprang "naturally" from the Jews' insistence on remaining a separate national community. Such an argument loses its plausibility when applied to the period of the Nazi occupation, but is refortified by the realities of Nazi policies and propaganda, both aimed to divide Poles and Jews. The general inddifference to the plight of the Jews can then be understood as a direct result of the Nazi terror, and especially of Poland's unique death penalty for even the smallest acts of aid to the Jews. The small proportion of survivors, when it is not simply contested[12], becomes explainable through the logistic impossibilities of saving millions of Jewish Jews. And, in the history books (see: Drozdowski, Tygodnik Powszechny, May 17, 1987) as well as popular opinion (see: Prekerowa, Tygodnik Powszechny, March 19, 1987), the Jews' passivity in the face of death seals the argument.

For the exclusion of the Jews from the Polish family, from the common moral universe, to become an issue, Poles must look to the period immediately following the Holocaust. It was then, with the Jewish community nealy annihilated, with the Nazis gone, with the concerted efforts by the new government to integrate the Jews (at the time, collectively and individually) into Polish society, that the Jew became ever more alien, ever more of a problem, a "natural" target for murder. To see this as morally unproblematic is difficult indeed, even allowing for the rationalizations of identifying Jews with Communists.

The challenge here, emotionally and intellectually, lies in recognizing the non-traumatic quality of the Holocaust as it had entered the Poles' experience and their memory. For many years, the public silence on the subject of Polish-Jewish relations, together with the public prominence of the "Polonized" Jewish victims, worked to prevent any such recognition. Today, when Polish-Jewish relations are being discussed, and when the Holocaust is gradually regaining its Jewishness, as it were, a critical assessment of the post-war record becomes possible. That it remains only a possibility thus far is an issue which deserves careful consideration.

People troubled by the ever wider repertoire of forgetting, denying and banalizing the Holocaust, have expressed grave concern with Poland's memory of an "Auschwitz without Jews." The developments of recent years - the massive efforts to commemorate the Jewish victims, the wide exposure given to Poland's Jewish heritage, the calls for a dialogue with Jews and Judaism, and the calls for a re-assessment of Poland's record on the "Jewish question" - seem to some to signal a change for the better.

Having studied these new developments, I too see the emerging remembrance of the Jew as a positive contrast to his previous exclusion from Poland's memory. For the young generations in particular, the increasing availability of resources for exploring Jewish culture, Jewish history and Jewish philosophy - on primarily Jewish terms - offers an unprecedented opportunity to develop respect for and empathy with the Jew. Intellectual and emotional "normalization" of things Jewish can only be seen as positive in light of the previous identification of "Jewish" with "problem."

On a moral plane, however, the response to Poland's re-discovery of the Jew must be a cautious one, if not a warning about the comforts of remembrance. And nowhere is that warning more needed than in the new memory space accorded to the years following the Holocaust. What has happened over the last few years shows the potential for remembering to become a way of forgetting.

In very specific terms of facts and figures, the focusing of remembrance on the Kielce pogrom alone obliterates all the other victims of anti-Jewish violence. The politization of Kielce, however historically justifiable, silences the wider questions of moral responsibility. Even when such questions are raised, the political density of the current situation deprives them of much popular impact.

In 1987, a year after the regime and the Church joined in a very public commemoration of the pogrom and its victims, Jerzy Urban, the government spokesman and Poland's most prominent "court Jew," went on record as sharply criticizing the position taken by Catholic bishops after Kielce. The furious public reaction to Urban's statement resembled the protest to his earlier castigations of the then newly declared saint Father Maximilian Kolbe. Urban used Kolbe's record as a publisher of anti-Semitic literature to remind Catholic intellectuals that the Church has not always stood for just causes. His remarks were seen as so inflammatory that Church officials called for Urban's resignation

Flatly denying the grounds for Urban's criticism of the aftermath of Kielce, the Church re-confirmed the position it formulated in 1986 - that it has always been against anti-Jewish violence. In November 1987, Urban defended himself against the charges of slander by quoting from the official Church pronouncements after the pogrom. To the credit of the editors, Tygodnik Powszechny, an influential Catholic weekly, published Urban's "open letter", this being the first time that a Polish reader would have been confronted with the record of the Church[13]. Urban's letter stood alone, though; the subject was closed.

Apart from the fact that Urban is not a popular figure (to say the least), his statement in Tygodnik Powszechny also went directly against the journal's earlier position regarding the reaction to Kielce (Zbrodnia..., July 6, 1986). By selecting only the voices of conscience from its 1946 issues, Tygodnik Powszechny made it appear - just as the bishops have - that Catholic opinion at the time condemned the pogrom unequivocally. With the great gap between the authority of the Catholic hierarchy and lay Catholic intellectuals and that of a despised spokesman for the regime, it is indeed highly unlikely that the whole debated issue, with all its moral implications, made any difference in the popular view of the past. And, one should emphasize, the debate was still only about Kielce.

On a much less public scale, Cała's findings on the peasants' reaction to the killing of Jews, reported in a lecture in 1984, met with protest, disbelief, and, at most, comments about the "marginal nature" of the phenomenon. Her audience, I should add, consisted of interested and concerned participants in the annual "Week of Jewish Culture," organized by the Warsaw Club of Catholic Intellectuals, people often deeply troubled by Poland's record in Jewish affairs.

Commemorating the victims of Kielce is uncomfortable for the Poles; discussions which accompany this commemoration speak of the "dark chapter" in Poland's history, of the need to confront it, of the need to see the mob behind the provocateurs[14]. Ultimately, though, the memory of Kielce may offer comfort in its apparent episodic quality. Most importantly, the very fact that Kielce is remembered at all is irreproachable testimony to the presence of conscience.

Speaking now much more generally, today's remembering of the Jew carries the same potential for comforting the Poles. If, as I have argued here, it is the Jews' exclusion from the zone of moral relevance that presents the utmost challenge to Polish conscience, today's granting the Jew full membership in the Polish family, in all its new "naturalness", can cover the traces of the past. The warmth of nostalgia, the often very direct expressions of a deep sense of loss, the appeals for the obligation to remember the Jew - in effect, mourning the Jews after a forty-year delay - testifies to the Poles' goodwill and moral decency. The long years of silence, when explained at all, testify to the oppressiveness of the regime (especially censorship), or, more universally, to the psychological need for time to heal the wounds[15]. On both counts, the Holocaust emerges as a trauma that Poles could not confront earlier - in itself an infinitely more comfortable proposition than a realization of how the destruction of Polish Jewry had not been a trauma. And the very acts of remembrance can then appear as something natural indeed. The positive glow, emanating from the present kindness to the Jew, softens the impact of the past.

To be perfectly clear on this point: the current efforts to recover Poland's Jewish heritage have not been undertaken with the desire to forget. However cynical the regime's motivations for "being nice to the Jews" may be - witness the persistent idea of direct financial rewards - the reasoning is pragmatic, not spiritual. However varied the intentions among opposition and lay Catholic intellectuals, theirs is the - often hard - work of remembering. Even the Church, with its emphasis on improving Catholic-Jewish relations in the future, rather than examining its own past, cannot be accountable for more than its unwillingness to scrutinize its own record. In short, inviting the Jew into Poland's memory is not a deliberate strategy to disarm him. The effects of such an invitation, though, may ultimately neutralize the moral challenge of the past. Remembering the Jew today as if one had always been inclined to do so denies the pain of returning survivors; it reduces their memory, turns their voices into "anti-Polish prejudice." And until their voices are listened to, the past will remain comfortable.

I should point out, in conclusion, that the memory of return remains at a half-articulated stage, even in the West. If bearing witness to the Holocaust was eventually to prevail over the survivors' need for silence, bearing witness to what happened upon their return is still rare. Among Polish Jewish writers, for example, only Henryk Grynberg (who left Poland in 1967 for the United States) described his experience at liberation in a book, Zwycięstwo (1969), or "victory" - a sadly ironic title indeed. Nechama Tec, in her autobiographical account Dry Tears (1984), talks openly about the emotional difficulties of discussing the return. Lucjan Dobroszycki, a historian at YIVO, who published, in 1973, a study of 1944-1947 in Poland and who is working on extending the account of that period, finds this research extremely taxing (1988, personal communication). Together with Bauer's study of the "flight and rescue" (1970), the book by Hillel, issued in France in 1985 and a chapter in Gilbert's work on the Holocaust (1985:811-831), offer the most detail about the survivors' experience during those years; it is the closest we come to "Poland, after the Holocaust" literature.

Whether it is for the different quality of pain, or for the sense that an event of such magnitude as the Holocaust overshadows whatever happens afterwards, the events of 1944-1947 remain only partly known. Yet to ask that they be discussed in Poland is not to ask for more survivors to come forward and testify; theirs is a memory we hardly have a right to intrude upon. It is to ask that Poles, as they now celebrate their country's Jewish heritage, search and re-search Poland's record vis-à-vis the Jew for the moral lessons it carries for them. It is to reconfirm the general call of many younger Polish intellectuals[16] for a fully critical understanding of the past, while pointing to the specific area where such understanding is at once most needed and most lacking.

Time, more than anything else, works for the emergence of critical reflection, capable of confronting even the hardest of moral challenges. As the younger generations of Poles come to know the Jew as an interesting Stranger, but also, more and more, as their culture's essential Other, they need not automatically question their parents' and grandparents' attitudes and actions. But they are better prepared to ask questions, to listen to the Jew's voice and, ultimately, to understand his pain.

NOTES

1. As a cultural sociologist, I approach "collective memory" at its most publicly visible - popular publications, films, exhibitions, monuments, commemorative markers - in an effort to understand what resources are available for making sense of and remembering the past.

2. Because the Jews were highly placed in all of the newly established Communist regimes, there are grounds for suspecting that their selection was part of the Soviet strategy of domination (see: Lendvai, 1972).

3. Checinski (1982) argues this case most forcefully. Since he had himself been actively involved in the security forces, the objectivity of his account remains suspect, the merits of inside information notwithstanding.

4. As recent (February/March 1988) reports in the Polish press indicate, Witnesses, a new documentary on the reaction to the pogrom of inhabitants of Kielce, may become a turning point for the discussion. The film apparently shows just how deep was the indifference to the fate of the Jews at the time.

5. Even among Communist writers, especially after the 1968 protests, Jews became identified with the Stalinist excesses (see: Lendvai, 1972). Within Poland's political opposition, the most influential statement along the same lines comes in the collection of interviews with past Communist leaders (Torańska, 1985) - of the seven, five are Jewish.

6. The long debate surrounding the plans to have a retreat for Carmelite nuns in Auschwitz, resolved early in 1987 by the Church agreeing to establish an "information center" instead, shows most vividly the difference in the meaning of "Auschwitz" for Poles and Jews.

7. In this respect, there are few differences indeed between the regime, the Church and the opposition. The Pope's remarks in Auschwitz in 1983 (see: Grynberg, 1984) granted the figure of "six million Polish victims" particularly strong legitimacy.

8. On the political side, it is essential to distinguish theory and practice. Denouncing anti-Semitism (also in terms of legislation) may have been the official policy of the regime, but the regime's practice, since 1967 in particular, made it possible for the opposition to identify anti-Semitism with the state. The picture has become much more complex with the pro-Jewish turn-around by the regime in 1982/1983.

9. The view is shared across the political spectrum. The important exception is the work of Eisenbach (see: 1983) and that of his student, Cała (see: 1984).

10. In this respect, the presence of a small group of young "return Jews," who vocally and publicly discuss Jewish topics and who receive support and encouragement from within Catholic circles, suggests a general shift in attitudes to Jewishness (see: Irwin-Zarecka, forthcoming).

11. Bartoszewski (1986), a historian who was himself active in organized aid to the Jews, expresses this view in an especially irreproachable way: for him, only those who died when saving the Jews, had done "enough".

12. In Polish publications, the number of survivors varies from one hundred to four hundred thousand (these totals excluding the Jews who fled the country).

13. The émigré journal Aneks did publish, in 1986, a special issue on "Jews as a Polish problem," including a discussion by Smolar of Kielce and its aftermath. According to one of the contributors, Jan Gross, there was little public or private response to this important critical statement (in part due to the publication, shortly afterwards, of the discussion on Polish-Jewish relations during the Holocaust in Poland's influential Tygodnik Powszechny).

14. This is true of both the regime and the opposition publications. The difference lies in their identifying those behind the provocation; the regime, understandably enough, maintains that it was the work of the "fascist underground."

15. To see either or both of these factors as complete explanation is conveniently to forget that Poland's collective memory in general defended itself remarkably well against ideological manipulation, and that it worked with little delay to absorb the Poles' own trauma of the Nazi occupation (see also: Ash, in Krall, 1986).

16. The impetus here comes primarily from the growing discomfort with the resurrection of Polish nationalism, anti-Semitism included. Although, in practical terms, the persistence of anti-Semitism is judged as a marginal concern, in symbolic terms, it has acquired high priority for many opposition intellectuals.

REFERENCES

Ash, Timothy Garton
1986 "The life of death"
in: Aneks, no. 41/42
(also in: The New York Review of Books, Dec. 19, 1985)

Bartoszewski, Wladyslaw
1986 "Polish-Jewish relations in occupied Poland, 1939-1945"
in: The Jews in Poland, Abramsky et al (eds.)
Oxford: Basil Blackwell

Bauer, Yehuda
1970 Flight and Rescue: BRICHAH
New York: Random House

Borwicz, Michał
1947 Pieśń ujdzie cało...Antologia wierszy o Żydach pod okupacją niemiecką
Warszawa: Centralna Żydowska Komisja Historyczna w Polsce

1969 Vies interdites
Paris: Casterman

1980 Spod szubienicy w teren
Paris: Księgarnia Polska

Brandys, Kazimierz
1983 "Miesiące"
in: Kultura, no. 6/429 (19-41)

Cała, Alina
1984 Kwestia asymilacji Żydów w Królestwie Polskim (1864-1897). Pozycje, konflikty, stereotypy
Warszawa: Instytut Historii PAN (Ph.D. dissertation)

Checinski, Michael
1982 Poland: Communism, Nationalism, Anti-Semitism
(trans. in part by Tadeusz Szafar)
New York: Karz-Cohl Publishing

Dobroszycki, Lucjan
1973 "Restoring Jewish life in post-war Poland"
in: Soviet Jewish Affairs, no. 2 (58-72)

Drozdowski, Marian Marek
"Dzieje najnowsze w maturalnych klasach"
in: Tygodnik Powszechny, May 17, 1987

Eisenbach, Artur
1983 Z dziejów ludności żydowskiej w Polsce w XVIII i XIX wieku
Warszawa: Państwowy Instytut Wydawniczy

Engel, David
1987 In the Shadow of Auschwitz: The Polish Government-in-exile and the Jews
Chapel Hill: University of North Carolina Press

Finkielkraut, Alain
1982 L'avenir d'une négation. Réflexion sur la question du génocide
Paris: Seuil

1983 La réprobation d'Israël
Paris: Denoël/Gonthier

Gilbert, Martin
1985 The Holocaust. A History of the Jews of Europe during the Second World War
New York: Holt, Rinehart and Winston

Gross, Jan Tomasz
1986 "Ten jest z ojczyzny mojej...ale go nie lubię"
in: Aneks, no. 41/42 (13-36)

Gross, Jan Tomasz & Irena Grudzińska-Gross
1983 "W czterdziestym nas matko na Sybir zesłali..." Polska a Rosja 1939-1942
London: Aneks

Grynberg, Henryk
1965 Żydowska wojna
Warszawa: Czytelnik

1969 Zwycięstwo
Paris: Instytut Literacki

1984 Prawda nieartystyczna
West Berlin: Biblioteka Archipelagu

Gutman, Yisrael
1986 "Polish and Jewish historiography on the question of Polish-Jewish relations during World War II"
in: The Jews in Poland, Abramsky et all (eds.)
Oxford: Basil Blackwell

Hillel, Marc
1985 Le massacre des survivants. En Pologne après l'holocauste (1945-1947)
Paris: Plon

Irwin-Zarecka, Iwona
1988 Neutralizing Memory: The Jew in Contemporary Poland
New Brunswick, N.J.: Transaction Books
(forthcoming)

Kersten, Krystyna
"Kielce - 4 lipca 1946 roku"
in: Tygodnik Solidarność, Dec. 4, 1981

1986 Narodziny systemu władzy. Polska 1943-1948
Paris: Libella

Kirshner, Sheldon
1983 "Outlook for Jewish community of Poland bleak"
in: The Canadian Jewish News, June 16

Krall, Hanna
1986 Shielding the Flame. An Intimate Conversation with Dr. Marek Edelman, the Last Surviving Leader of the Warsaw Ghetto Uprising
(transl. from the Polish by Joanna Stasinska and Lawrence Weschler)
New York: Henry Holt and Company

Laqueur, Walter
1980 The Terrible Secret: An Investigation into the Suppression of Information about Hitler's "Final Solution"
London: Weidenfeld & Nicholson

Lendvai, Paul
1972 Anti-Semitism in Eastern Europe
London: Macdonald & Co.

Lewis, Bernard
1987 Semites and Anti-Semites. An Inquiry into Conflict and Prejudice
New York: W.W. Norton & Company

Lipski, Jan Józef
1983 "Polscy Żydzi"
in: *Kultura*, no. 6/429 (3-9)

Łukaszewicz, Łucja
1983 "Sterotyp Żyda u studentów"
in: *Znak*, no. 339-340 (2-3), Feb./March (453-463)

Mendelsohn, Ezra
1986 "Interwar Poland: good for the Jews or bad for the Jews?"
in: *The Jews in Poland*, Abramsky et al (eds.)
Oxford: Basil Blackwell

Prekerowa, Teresa
"Sprawiedliwi i 'bierni'"
in: *Tygodnik Powszechny*, March 29, 1987

Smolar, Aleksander
1986 "Tabu i niewinność"
in: *Aneks*, no. 41/42 (89-134)

Tec, Nechama
1984 Dry Tears. The Story of a Lost Childhood
New York: Oxford University Press

Torańska, Teresa
1985 Oni
London: Aneks

Turian
1983 "Zdaniem laika: Kolbe żywy"
in: *Więź*, no. 5(295), May (57-61)

Urban, Jerzy
"List rzecznika prasowego rządu"
in: *Tygodnik Powszechny*, Nov. 8, 1987

"Zbrodnia kielecka"
in: *Tygodnik Powszechny*, July 6, 1986

--*-*-*-*-*-*

THE SWISS PRESS CAMPAIGN THAT HALTED DEPORTATIONS TO AUSCHWITZ AND THE ROLE OF THE VATICAN, THE SWISS AND HUNGARIAN CHURCHES

Prof. David H. Kranzler
Queensborough Community College Holocaust Archives
Bayside, NY 11364

INTRODUCTION

One of the recurring myths in Holocaust literature maintains that nothing was, or really could have been done, to rescue Jews in substantial numbers from the Nazi genocide machine. Even recognized historians claim that all the efforts by sincere, courageous individuals in the free world, Jews and non-Jews alike, could accomplish very little in the face of bureaucratic indifference to moral values, the refusal of the Allied powers to believe what they regarded as "atrocity stories," and, of course, widespread anti-Semitism pure and simple.[1]

Such assumptions fail to take into account the complexity of human nature, which defies all efforts to label human beings solely in political, ideological, religious or even moral terms. One of the basic theses of Judaism is that no human being is completely good - or completely evil, for that matter. Much of the good or evil that he does depends on stimuli that are brought to bear upon him either by accident or by deliberately guided developments. Even individuals generally dismissed as hostile or at best indifferent to the values of justice and human dignity may be goaded into supporting them by an influence that brings out the best in them. This holds true also in the case of individuals - to varying degrees, anti-Semitic - who otherwise might have been insensitive to the plight of the Jews during the Nazi Holocaust.

One striking argument in support of this thesis is the success of the campaign inspired and orchestrated during the summer of 1944 in Switzerland by George Mandel-Mantello (better known as Mantello), the secretary-general of the El Salvadoran legation in Geneva. This press campaign, beginning with four brief cables sent to the world by a news agency in Zurich, brought to international attention the desperate plight of Hungarian Jewry and conditions in the Auschwitz death camp. The resulting outcry from diplomats, church leaders and ordinary citizens forced Admiral Nicholas Horthy, the regent of Hungary, to stop the deportation of the 150-200,000 Jews who were still in Budapest, and who represented all that was left of Hungary's prewar Jewish population of nearly a million.

George Mantello, the man who forced the hand of the "neutral" press of Switzerland, was a traditional Jew who, from his early youth, had been active in the Revisionist Zionist movement, an activist, right-wing force in world Zionism. Before the war Mantello and his brother, Joseph Mandel, owned a prosperous textile manufacturing business in partnership with several highly-placed non-Jewish Rumanian army officers.[2]

Mantello's business dealings took him through all of Central Europe. Thanks to his connections, he also served as an amateur diplomat, with the title of honorary consul for El Salvador to Czechoslovakia, Hungary and Yugoslavia. In 1939 he exchanged his Rumanian allegiance for El Salvadoran citizenship.

In the course of his travels through Central Europe he witnessed first hand the brutalities of Nazism when German troops marched into Vienna in 1938 and then into Prague in 1939. In 1941, Mantello himself miraculously escaped from a Nazi prison in Belgrade. With the help of his Rumanian connections - by that time Rumania had become an ally of Hitler's Germany - Mantello made his way to neutral Switzerland in August, 1942 and was appointed permanent secretary-general of El Salvador's legation in Geneva. His brother Joseph had already settled in

Switzerland a year earlier and established a textile business there.[3]

MANTELLO IN SWITZERLAND

Once safe in Switzerland, Mantello resolved to do everything in his power to rescue his fellow Jews in Nazi-occupied lands. He hoped to unite all the Jewish organizations and the representatives of international Jewish bodies in Switzerland in this cause. To his dismay, he learned that even the Nazi threat to the very survival of European Jewry was not sufficient to overcome the deep-seated ideological and internecine rivalries that divided the various Jewish organizations into antagonistic camps.[4]

However, thanks to his diplomatic status and the support of his consulate Mantello was able to make his own major contribution. Recha Sternbuch of Montreux and Israel Chaim Eis of Zurich, two independent Swiss rescue activists, had succeeded in protecing Jews under Nazi occupation who had Latin American diplomatic papers. For reasons of their own, the Nazis honored such papers held by Jews. Jewish individuals who possessed such documents were exempt from wearing the yellow Star of David and were not compelled to live in ghettos. Many of them were interned in special detention camps such as Vittel, Tittmoning and in a "privileged" sector of Bergen-Belsen, where they were held for eventual exchange and accorded relatively decent treatment.[5]

However, the cost of such documents was high, ranging from 400 to 3,000 Swiss francs. A thriving black market developed among some Latin American diplomats who sought to cash in on the misery of the Jews.

Mantello found a way of circumventing this obstacle. As soon as he was established in Switzerland, he purchased a building for the Salvadoran consulate which he eventually turned into a factory that mass produced Salvadoran citizenship papers to be issued free of charge to any Jew in Nazi-occupied Europe.

Notwithstanding the fact that exorbitant sums were still paid to disreputable sources, Mantello's operation depressed the market price for the precious Latin American papers.[6] Many of these papers were forged copies vital to Jews who later took refuge in the "protected homes" set up in Budapest by Sweden's Raoul Wallenberg and the Swiss and Spanish legations.

RESCUE IN BUDAPEST

But all this was a prelude to what was perhaps the greatest single rescue operation of the Holocaust era: the cessation of mass deportation of Jews from Budapest, the only ones still left in Hungary.

The story begins with the Nazi occupation of Hungary in March, 1944, and the escape from Auschwitz, one month later, of Rudolf Vrba (Walter Rosenberg) and Alfred Wetzler (Josef Lanik). The two men made their way to Slovakia, where their eyewitness testimony resulted in the drafting of the Auschwitz Protocol by the Slovak Jewish underground led by Rabbi Michel Ber Weissmandl and Mrs. Gisi Fleischmann. In the middle of May, 1944, when the deportation of Jews from Hungary began, Rabbi Weissmandl and his associates sent copies of this document to representatives of international Jewish organizations stationed in Switzerland and Turkey, together with Weissmandl's now-famous plea to the Allied powers to bomb the railroad lines leading to Auschwitz. These representatives in turn sent copies of the Protocol to the Jewish Agency in Jerusalem.[7] Unfortunately, Mantello did not receive a copy. Jewish leaders in Switzerland, though freely availing themselves of his "document manufacturing service," did not bother to inform him of this communication. Weissmandl and his associates, on the other hand, had no contact with Mantello for the simple reason that they had not yet heard of his operations.[8]

Meanwhile, Mantello organized two important "lobbies" in his efforts to rescue Hungarian Jews. One, the Association of Swiss Rabbis, was headed by Rabbi Dr. Zvi Taubes and the former chief rabbi of Holland, Rabbi Tobias Lewenstein. The other, the Swiss Committee for Assistance to Jews in Hungary, was popularly known as the "Banyai Committee," after its chairman, Mihaly Banyai.[9]

When a news blackout obscured events in Hungary, Mantello managed to obtain first-hand information about the situation. On May 22, 1944, a week after the deportation of Jews from Hungary to Auschwitz had begun, Mantello sent his friend, Dr. E. Florian Manoliu, the Rumanian commercial attache in Bern (a non-Jew), to Hungary with a dual mission: to obtain a first-hand report of conditions there and to distribute 1,000 signed Salvadoran papers to

Hungarian Jews, including Mantello's parents in the town of Beszterce Transylvania, which had been annexed by Hungary.[10]

Unfortunately, Manoliu could not save his friend's family, since by the time he reached Beszterce, all of the Jews had been deported to Auschwitz. He had lost more than a week in Vienna, where he was interrogated by Nazi authorities who knew of his reputation as an anti-Nazi. On June 19, Manoliu arrived in Budapest, where he immediately called on the Swiss consul, Charles Lutz. Lutz, in turn, took Manoliu to see Miklos (Moshe) Krausz, head of the Palestine Office, the agency charged with the task of issuing Palestine immigration certificates. With Hungary now under Nazi occupation, Krausz had taken refuge with Lutz. In exchange for the 1,000 Salvadoran papers sent by Mantello, Krausz gave Manoliu two crucial reports. The first was a copy of the Auschwitz Protocol, which described in detail the gassing of 1,765,000 Jews in Auschwitz up to April, 1944. The second recorded the ghettoization and deportation of over 335,000 Hungarian Jews during the period from May 16 until the middle of June, 1944, at the rate of 12,000 per day.[11]

Manoliu gave to Krausz the calling card of Krausz's friend and official counterpart in Geneva, Chaim Posner, on which Posner had written a note in Hebrew. Krausz wrote a letter for Manoliu to take to Posner, giving the bleak situation of the 150-200,000 Jews still in and around Budapest. "We only have a few days left ... Should the Christian world want to do something, there exists the possibility of rescuing several thousand people ... There remain but two options: suicide or else to accept the fate ordained for us..."

Instead of going on to Bucharest, as originally planned, Manoliu rushed back to Geneva, arriving in the evening of June 20, 1944. He met with Mantello, and gave him the reports on the deportations and the tragic news about his parents.[12]

Though grief-stricken, Mantello plunged into a frenzy of activity to save those that could still be saved. The days following Manoliu's return blended into nights as Mantello planned and attended one meeting after the other in an effort to convince incredulous church leaders, diplomats, intelligence men and government officials that the reports about Auschwitz and the fate planned by Adolf Eichmann for the Jews of Hungary were not "atrocity stories" but unadorned, naked truth.

Throughout the night of June 20, three girls worked at translating a combined version of the Auschwitz Protocol and the Krausz letter into English. By 6 o'clock in the morning of June 21, Mantello had somehow been able to obtain a duplicating machine enabling him to make 50-60 copies for an initial distribution.[13]

That evening he summoned the members of the Association of Swiss Rabbis and the Banyai Committee for an emergency meeting the next morning, at which he presented the Protocol and the Krausz letter.[14]

Next came a meeting with two prominent Swiss churchmen: Mantello's friend Pastor Paul Vogt, head of the Fluchtlingshilfe of Zurich, and Pastor Hans Schaffert, secretary of the Swiss Protestant Council. Once convinced that the reports from Auschwitz and Hungary were reliable, Vogt became a catalyst in enlisting the aid of other Swiss church dignitaries. But when Mantello suggested that he, Vogt, sign an accompanying letter that was to be sent out with copies of the reports, the pastor explained that his authority alone would be insufficient. He proposed that he sign the letter along with three other renowned theologians: Professors Karl Barth, Emil Brunner and Dr. Visser t'Hooft, head of the Swiss Ecumenical Council of Churches.[15]

It must be remembered that, fearful of Germany and Italy, Switzerland maintained strict censorship control not only of published material but even of telephone conversations. Swiss newspapers and individuals were therefore forbidden to disseminate reports of Nazi atrocities unless they had first been published in some other neutral country.[16]

Without waiting for official authorization from the three, Mantello put their names to the accompanying letter, which read:

> We are sending two reports from Hungary with an accompanying letter of June 19, 1944, which came via diplomatic channels to Switzerland from a highly reliable source. These reports have profoundly shaken us. Due to our deep sense of responsibility we feel obligated to make you aware of these two reports. We have no doubt that you will make the effort to read these reports and to spread

them among your circles. The proper authorities have already been fully apprised of these [reports].

Signed:
Karl Barth, Emil Brunner, Visser t'Hooft, Paul Vogt[17]

After Mantello had distributed the first copies, Karl Barth was questioned by the Swiss censorship police (who had listened in on Barth's conversations with Vogt). Asked whether he had authorized the use of his name, Barth snapped, "You see my name there, don't you?"

On June 24, Vogt called another meeting which was attended by Professor Koechlin, president of the Swiss Federation of Evangelical Churches, Pastor Hans Schaffert, and Karl Barth, along with Mantello, Rabbi Zvi Taubes, the latter's son Dr. Jacob Taubes, and Rabbi A. Kornfein. At this meeting, Vogt's oral telephone agreements with Barth, Brunner and t'Hooft were "officially" authorized.[18]

In this manner, a universally respected, authoritative church body lent its support in the effort to overcome censorship and make its allegiance clear to numerous officials, including some whose attitude toward the Jews in Nazi-occupied Europe was indifferent if not negative. Most important, however, such a prestigious roster of clergy would make it possible to establish international connections, especially in the Western world.[19]

Under Barth's direction, these thousands of copies were sent to university professors and intellectuals throughout Switzerland.[20]

On June 25, Mantello and Rabbi Taubes met with Barth and Koechlin who turned to the <u>Bundesrat</u> in Bern and the International Red Cross; the latter was specifically requested to provide protection for the Jews in Budapest.[21] On that same day, Dr. Visser t'Hooft and Pastor D. A. Freudenberg, executive secretary of the Swiss Ecumenical Council of Churches, cabled the following message to the Archbishop of Canterbury, Dr. William Temple, and Dr. Samuel Cavert, secretary of the American Protestant Union:

> TRUSTWORTHY REPORTS STATE TWELFETHOUSAND [sic] HUNGARIAN JEWS DEPORTED DAILY TO AUSCHWITZ UPPERSILESIA STOP TOTAL ESTIMATED ALREADY FOURHUNDREDFIFTYTHOUSAND STOP ... MANY DEAD ON ARRIVAL STOP [so] FAR NO PUBLIC REACTION HUNGARIAN CHURCHES STOP SUGGEST NEW RADIO APPEAL AND WARNING TO WHOLE HUNGARIAN NATION STOP OECUMENICAL REFUGEE COMMITTEE ALSO ISSUES APPEAL
>
> T'HOFFT, FREUDENBERG[22]

Four days later, t'Hooft and Freudenberg sought further help from Temple and Cavert, asking them to use immediate means, including radio broadcasts, to inform the people of Hungary about the monstrous crimes that were being committed by their leaders.[23]

While the dignitaries of the Catholic Church in Switzerland did not join as readily in the campaign as the Protestants, one must single out Dr. Johannes Duft, an influential member of the Swiss Catholic party and the Swiss <u>Nationalrat</u>, who worked closely with Mantello's brother Joseph Mandel and Rabbi Taubes in obtaining support among other members of the <u>Nationalrat</u>.[24]

Mantello and the Association of Swiss Rabbis had performed one of their most successful missions on June 22, when Dr. Zvi Taubes met with Monsignor Philippo Bernadini, the papal nuncio and dean of the diplomatic corps in Bern. Bernadini was another splendid humanitarian who throughout the war utilized his position and strategic location to work for the rescue of Jews. Bernadini immediately dispatched by courier to the Vatican a copy of the reports, the Krausz letter and the accompanying letter signed by the four Protestant theologians. A constructive response from the Vatican came quickly.[25]

The day before (June 21), Mihaly Banyai had attempted to arrange a meeting with Manoliu and Roswell McClelland, the American representative of the U.S. War Refugee Board sent to Switzerland in order to facilitate the rescue of the Jews. Banyai assumed that a personal first-hand account by a diplomat such as Manoliu, plus reports of the escapees from Auschwitz and a Jewish leader still trapped in Budapest, would move this powerful American official to take a more positive attitude. But according to Mantello's recollections, McClelland told Banyai, "I have no need to meet with that man [i.e., Manoliu]" and, indeed, he never did.[26]

By June 22, Banyai decided that McClelland should at least receive copies of the reports and the Krausz letter. Banyai also informed him how, during a brief encounter at the Rumanian-

Hungarian border with Wilhelm Filderman, a notable Rumanian Jewish communal leader, Manoliu had learned that Rumania was quietly permitting the entry of Jewish refugees from Hungary.[27]

Several days passed before McClelland even answered the communication.[28] Not until July 4, when the press campaign in the Swiss newspapers was in full swing, did Landreth M. Harrison, the American minister in Bern, send a one-page letter to the U.S. War Refugee Board regarding what he called, in quotes, a "reliable report." Obviously skeptical that Jews were being murdered en masse, he claimed that the report "may in part be based on a mistranslation of the words 'Ausrottung' [extermination] and 'Entjudung' [de-Judaization]." Harrison engaged in semantics with who had "planted" [sic] the report and who had insisted that the Hungarian policy of "Entjudung" of the Hungarian cities meant that the Jewish elements [sic] there were actually being put to death.[29]

Not until June 24, after Jaromir Kopecky, the minister in Bern representing the Czechoslovak government-in-exile, had given McClelland not only Mantello's version of the report but also an original copy of the Auschwitz Protocol sent via the Czech underground did McClelland even consider the possibility that the Jews of Hungary might be in danger. In a brief cable to Washington, he mentioned the Auschwitz Protocol, Weissmandl's plea to the Allies to bomb the railroad lines leading to Auschwitz, and the deportation of Jews from Hungary, but made no reference to Mantello, Manoliu or Banyai. Not even when he finally sent two different versions of the Protocol to Washington (one of them Weissmandl's) over four months later did he include the Hungarian report.[30]

Fortunately Mantello, who had come to know McClelland's attitude was far more resourceful. He had obtained the help of many sympathetic individuals for his rescue scheme. Banyai found that he got more support from the "Hungarian National Front," an anti-Fascist group in Switzerland, than he received from the representative of the U.S. War Refugee Board. The "National Front" distributed hundreds of copies of the reports to universities all over Switzerland.[31]

WALTER GARRETT

Mantello achieved his ultimate triumph on June 22, when, together with Dr. Max Kimche, a respected lawyer and Jewish communal leader, he went to Zurich to see Walter Garrett, director of the news agency Exchange Telegraph. Garrett eventually agreed to distribute the Mantello version of the Hungarian report and the Auschwitz Protocol to the Swiss and foreign press. A son-in-law of Britain's former Prime Minister Neville Chamberlain, Garrett had known and trusted Mantello. Nevertheless, Garrett initially hesitated to distribute the reports (the authentication provided by the Swiss theologians was yet to come). Mantello suggested that if Garrett was still not convinced he should telephone General "Freddie" West, the British military attache and highest intelligence officer in Switzerland. West told Garrett that he had complete confidence in Mantello. Both West and Allen Dulles, head of the OSS, had reason to be grateful to Mantello who had provided the use of the Salvadoran diplomatic pouch to send millions of dollars' worth of chronographs and other valuable instruments for military use out of Switzerland, through Axis-dominated territory.[32]

The next day Mantello paid a personal call on General West. In the meantime, Garrett, now assured that Mantello's report had come from unimpeachable sources, became the primary agent in disseminating world-wide the two reports.[33] He first went with Mantello to see Allen Dulles. Dulles had been privy to a great deal of information about Nazi atrocities against the Jews. Nevertheless, Garrett recalled that, after reading the two reports handed to him by Mantello, Dulles was "profoundly shocked. He was as disconcerted as I [Garrett] was and said, 'It has to be used immediately.'"[34]

In view of Dulles' access to vast amounts of classified information, the historian Walter Laqueur found it difficult to comprehend his reaction of shock and dismay.[35] Nevertheless, Mantello, decades later, clearly recalls what Dulles said after reading the report: "While I know a lot of the facts, I have never seen such a clinically detailed report about Auschwitz put together in this way."[36]

Dulles immediately sent to the State Department in Washington, to the attention of Secretary of State Cordell Hull, the four long cables into which Garrett had condensed the reports from Auschwitz and Hungary. The first of these cables opened with the words:

> NEUTRAL DIPLOMATS AND CATHOLIC CHURCH OF HUNGARY VOUCH ABSOLUTE TRUTH OF THE FOLLOWING REPORTS ...

The third cable began:

> FOLLOWING DRAMATIC ACCOUNT ONE DARKEST CHAPTERS MODERN HISTORY REVEALING HOW ONE MILLION 715 THOUSAND JEWS PUT TO DEATH ANNIHILATION CAMP AUSCHWITZ-BIRKENAU ...

The fourth cable concluded with the following important addendum for the benefit of skeptical editors and reporters:

> GARRETT ADDS ABSOLUTE EXACTNESS ABOVE REPORT UNQUESTIONABLE AND DIPLOMAT CATHOLIC FUNCTIONARIES WELLKNOWN VATIKAN [sic] DESIRE WIDEST DIFFUSION WORLD-WIDE AND EXCHANGE[37]

In order to comply with Swiss censorship rules forbidding the issuance of "Nazi atrocity tales" Garrett datelined the cables Ankara, Turkey. For added credibility, he attached the letter signed by the four Swiss theologians.[38]

On the night of June 23, Garrett cabled President Roosevelt, Prime Minister Churchill, British foreign minister Anthony Eden, the Archbishop of Canterbury, Queen Wilhelmina of Holland and Archbishop Francis Spellman. That same night he delivered copies of the report to the offices of major Swiss and foreign newspapers, bicycling his way through the blacked-out streets of Zurich.[39]

The first reaction came in the form of an open letter to Hungary's Regent Horthy from Pope Pius XII, dated June 25, 1944, in which which the Pontiff appealed to Horthy to "do everything in your power to save [as] many unfortunate people [as possible] from further pain and sorrow." By July 1, 1944, Horthy assured the Pope that "I shall do everything in my power to enforce the claims of Christian and humane principles."[40]

Meanwhile, on June 26, President Roosevelt, through Secretary of State Hull, sent the first of two strongly-worded warnings to Admiral Horthy.[41] Roosevelt demanded that Hungary put an end to the deportations and all other anti-Jewish measures. He said, "I rely not only on humanity but also upon the force of weapons," and threatened that "Hungary's fate will not be like that of any other civilized nation ... unless the deportations are stopped."[42] On July 2, 1944, Budapest was subjected to a heavy American air raid. Whether or not their assumption was justified, Horthy saw the bombing as a sign of American displeasure.[43]

Foreign Secretary Eden in the House of Commons in a press dispatch from London, dated July 5, said he'd received reports from reliable sources about the "barbarian deportations" of Jews from Hungary to Poland.[44]

Reports reaching Horthy from the Hungarian embassy in Switzerland along with the public statements from the Pope and the President of the United States prodded him to call a meeting of his Crown Council on June 26, 1944 at which he declared:

> I shall not tolerate this any further! I shall not permit the deportations to bring further shame on the Hungarians! Let the Government take measures for the removal of [Laszlo] Baky and [Laszlo] Endre! The deportations of the Jews of Budapest must cease! The Government must take the necessary steps![45]

But it took further pressures to move Horthy to action. The day after the Crown Council meeting, the Swedish minister in Budapest reported to the government that the Swedish Red Cross had expressed interest in helping the Hungarian Jews. Would the Hungarian authorities give their approval to such activities?[46]

As worldwide protests against Hungary mounted, Horthy's Prime Minister Dome Sztojay unsuccessfully attempted to refute them.[47] On June 28, 1944, reacting to the two reports he had received from Allen Dulles, Archbishop Spellman addressed an impassioned plea over the radio to Regent Horthy and the Hungarian nation, in which he said:

> This news has shocked all men and women who have a sense of justice and possess human sympathy ... The action of the [Hungarian] government is in flagrant contradiction with the Catholic faith professed by the great majority of the Hungarian people. It represents a negation of the most glorious pages of the Hungarian history and cultural traditions of the country.[48]

At last Cardinal Jusztinian Seredi of Hungary sent out a pastoral letter condemning the deportations. Though, as we shall see later, Seredi did not succeed in getting it distributed widely, the letter did not fail to make an impact on Hungary's ruling circles. The next day, on June 30, Sweden's 85-year-old King Gustav V sent his own appeal to Horthy asking him, "in the name of humanity" to "take steps in favor of those of this unfortunate race who still can be saved."[49]

Not until these responses from the West were received did a significant number of articles begin to appear in the Swiss press. As of June 30, only 20 articles had been published about Auschwitz and the plight of Hungarian Jewry. Finally, worldwide reaction set off the cycle of events that caught the Hungarian government off balance.[50] Even the Nazis in Germany and their Hungarian satellite could not resist such an avalanche of condemnations. On July 4, 1944, Horthy, under the impact of worldwide protest and the July 2nd Allied bombing of Budapest ordered the German minister, Edmund Veesenmayer, to stop the deportations. From then on, the Regent of Hungary found himself under increasing pressure from the Nazis, who were now determined to get rid of him.[51]

Meanwhile, on July 7, Max Huber, president of the International Red Cross (IRC), requested information about the Jews from the Hungarian government. Huber, for whom this was to be the first step in a long personal involvement on behalf of the Jews, said he needed this information in order to ease the concern of worldwide public opinion. He also sought permission for a representative of the Red Cross to visit some of the internment camps where Jews had been assembled for deportation, and to supply them with food and clothing.[52]

On that very day, Horthy learned that the ministers Laszlo Baky and Laszlo Endre, whose dismissal he had called for at the Crown Council meeting on June 26, were plotting a pro-Nazi _putsch_ to unseat him. Horthy sprang into action. He dismissed the two insurgents, and at the same time put a stop to the deportation of all Jews effective July 7, 1944. Though the Germans, under the direction of Adolf Eichmann, subsequently managed to spirit small transports of Jews out of the Hungarian internment camps to Auschwitz, Horthy on July 18 informed Hungarian diplomatic representatives throughout the world that the cessation of deportations had become official policy.[53]

Now the number of press articles grew rapidly. In July and August the cables Garrett had thrown into the mailboxes of Zurich's newspaper offices generated close to 400 articles in the Swiss press alone.[54] Thousands of copies of the reports on Auschwitz and Hungary _per se_, were added to thousands of copies of a book by Pastor Vogt on this theme, which created an uproar in a country normally known for its staidness and imperturbability. There were mass demonstrations in Basel and Schaffhausen, intercession and memorial services in Basel and Zurich. Churches, city councils, labor unions and organizations of all kinds published letters of protests, many of them addressed personally to Horthy.[55]

One particularly powerful letter was sent by the Federation of Swiss Women's Organizations, headed by Mrs. Clara Neff, to Horthy's wife, in which the women raised their voices "in the name of countless Swiss women to express our shock and pain at the inconceivable suffering that has befallen the Jews threatened by extermination in Hungary." By the next day, Mme. Horthy had answered that she would "do everything in her power to obtain recognition for the principles of humanity." On July 8, an article particularly critical of "Christian, noble and chivalrous" Hungary soon circulated in Budapest clandestinely and made a strong impact on Horthy.[56]

What exacerbated matters for both the Hungarians and the Germans was the fact that Mantello personally sent copies of all the protest articles in the Swiss press to the Hungarian and German embassies with his added warning, "You will have to pay for this!"[57] Naturally, the Germans sought to put an end to this flood of protests by putting pressure on the Swiss. But the latter replied that the "... voice of the press cannot be suppressed without running the danger that it will find even more dangerous means of expression." What was important, the Swiss added, was that, "we consider it essential to have a German denial of the rumors about the Auschwitz and Birkenau camps."[58]

On the other hand, there were in the Hungarian embassy in Bern a number of officials who, because of their concern for Hungary's deteriorating international image, cooperated with Mantello and his plans for the rescue of the Jews. Prominent among these men was Imre Tahy, the interim _charge d'affaires_. When Mantello bombarded the embassy with the newspaper articles, Tahy used the material to write reports to Horthy, pressuring the Regent to ease the situation of the Jews in Budapest as much as possible.[59]

THE SWISS PRESS GOES INTO ACTION

The worldwide response to the cabled texts about Auschwitz and Hungary triggered an unprecedented outcry in the normally sedate press of Switzerland. Swiss newspapers of all shades of political opinion carried screaming headlines that set off a reaction even in Nazi-occupied Europe.[60]

The articles represented churches, labor, farmers, professionals, intellectuals, students, officials, women's associations, and ordinary burghers throughout Switzerland. Their common denominator was their refusal to remain idle any longer in the face of an Auschwitz. A fair notion of the vehemence of the publications - and their readers - can be gleaned from a few sample headlines. Here are some of the headlines: "Inhumanity!", "Factories to Murder Human Beings", "New Documents on the Massacre of Jews", "Terrible Abominations", "Gassed and Burned", "The Extermination of Jews", "The Tragedy of Hungarian Jewry", "A Diary of Atrocities", "Murder of the Innocents", "Systematic Annihilation of Jews in Gas Chambers in Upper Silesia", "We Are All Guilty in the Outrageous Crimes Against Jews", "The True Face of Hungarian Regime", "By Our Silence We Have Helped Hitler", "Put An End to Deportations in Hungary", "Slaughter of Human Beings", "Monstrosities in Hungary", "Protests and Warnings" "We Cannot Remain Silent", "Protests Against Odious Persecutions", "The Protest of the Swiss People".[61]

Perhaps the following excerpts from only two articles in the two small newspapers will reflect the overall response of the Swiss to the revelations of the atrocities perpetuated by the Nazis upon the Jews:

> A profound upheaval . . . has seized the entire Swiss nation . . . leaving no doubt about [the reports'] accuracy, has given us an insight into the gruesome fate that has befallen Hungarian Jewry. The sensitivities of our generation have become dulled by the terrible events of the World War that has already been raging for five years . . . [But] when we realize that this is happening in the heart of Europe in whose culture we have taken such great pride, and in a country . . . especially proud of its Christianity and chivalry . . . then we can no longer practice the reserve of neutrals. . . But we are required to raise our voice not only as men and as Christians, but also as Swiss people. . . when hundreds of thousands of defenseless people . . . sent to their deaths. There is no "neutral" way of ignoring such behavior.[62]

The second, headed, "We Women," voiced the protests of a women's organization, which read in part:

> Protests are a platonic gesture. Yet there are events against which one must protest because if humanity is silent then the stones must cry out!... For five years we have heard news of mass deaths, bombardments, persecutions, deportations. We hear it, but somehow it doesn't enter our conscience ... Still what has been happening to the people like all others before G-d are also our brothers, we cannot turn away. We women, as well, because we are women, want to raise our voice in an emotional, passionate protest... the events which are far worse than the darkest Middle Ages.[63]

For purposes of comparison, one might glance at the July 3, 6 and November 26, 1944 issues of The New York Times. The first two were based on the Mantello version of the two reports.[64] The Times printed these in columns in 12 by 2 inches and 21 by 2 inches respectively, and placed them on pages 3 and 6, respectively. The third Times article, based solely on the full report of the original Protocol sent by McClelland, did make the front pages, because it featured a report from the U.S. War Refugee Board. Headed "US Board Bares Atrocity Details Told by Witnesses at Polish Camps," this article was given a double two-inch column at the bottom of page one and an additional 44 inches on page 24. Compare this American coverage with the 25 articles in the Nationalzeitung of Basel or the 18 in the Neue Zurcher Zeitung, Switzerland's top-circulation newspaper, and many others with two, five, ten and more issues, with front-page articles in three-inch columns, averaging 20-30 inches in length, but many 30-40 inches long. Some Swiss newspapers devoted to the Nazi atrocities the entire front page, or half on an inside page. And, as we have seen, they wrote in much more emotional terms than the New York Times.

The New York Times, of course, had its correspondent in Switzerland, as did other American newspapers, and those that did not, could have reprinted the information from the Times. But very few did. Only when foreign correspondents, and even Swiss correspondents, noted that Daniel Brigham, the Times reporter, had featured the Mantello version received from Walter Garrett and Paul Vogt, did they take the report seriously.[65]

One can only imagine the impact a press campaign in the U.S. and England, even though less emotional than that which developed in Switzerland, would have created. At the very least, such a campaign might well have generated sufficient pressure on the Allied governments to bomb the railroad lines to Auschwitz.[66]

So forcefully did the Swiss press focus on the horrors of Auschwitz that took even those Swiss papers less inclined to criticize Hitler found it difficult, if not impossible, to refute or ignore the reports of Hitler's systematic plan for the annihilation of European Jewry. As the press campaign in Switzerland reached fever pitch, it became increasingly difficult for any Swiss medium of communication to remain aloof.

Not even the Nazis wished to be publicly identified with Auschwitz. This is evident from a conference held for the foreign press by Helmut Sundermann, the Reich's press director and assistant to Minister of Propaganda Joseph Goebbels, as reported in the pro-Nazi Pester-Lloyd of July 21. The headline read, "The World Will Enjoy Peace Only After the Establishment of an International Quarantine for All Jewry."

Speaking openly before representatives of the foreign press, Sundermann characterized the outcry in the Swiss press as, ". . . intentional agitation and instigation, especially the statements disseminated by the enemy about the allegedly serious grievance in dealing with the Jewish residents in Europe." Sundermann sought to create the impression that the deported Jews were merely being quarantined for the benefit of mankind. Addressing himself specifically to the massive press campaign, he said, ". . . they [i.e., the Jews] are instigating newspapers and other organizations to spread false information throughout the world about the alleged mistreatments and grievances."

To counter the agitation of the press, the Nazis even produced a propaganda film which, in effect, showed the cruelty with which the Hungarian Arrow Cross guards had in reality treated the Hungarian Jews during the deportation process. This, supposedly in contrast to the gentle manner in which German nurses removed the Jews - by then more dead than alive - from the cattlecars at the Auschwitz station. Incensed, the Hungarians demanded that the film be removed from circulation. The Swiss and foreign journalists, reacted with skepticism toward the German portrayal of their "humane" nurses.[67]

While most of the Swiss press concentrated on the immediate consequences of Nazism and Auschwitz, there were some intellectuals, albeit a very small number, who looked at the long-range impact of Auschwitz. To this writer, the following appears to be the earliest such perspective written by a highly respected journalist. He writes, among other things:

> The attached reports were received by us from a quarter which leaves no doubt as to their veracity . . . Yet regardless of the undisputable proofs, something within us still refuses to believe them. Even more than by the annihilation of European Jewry, we are stung by the destruction and renunciation of humanity. . . this method of dealing with a conflict by the most ghastly, inhuman and disgusting means. These are things we somehow cannot accept as true, inasmuch as the consequences for the future of civilization will be immeasurable and eternal . . . here are complexes of guilt and horror, with consequences beyond imagination . . . Europe is sicker than we would like to admit . . .[68]

THE CHURCH IN SWITZERLAND

The role of the churches in Switzerland, Hungary and, of course, the part of the Holy See itself, were crucial in the campaign to save the remnants of Hungarian Jewry. The greatest protest, however, was by the Protestant churches, especially those in free Switzerland. In Nazi-occupied Hungary, on the other hand, the Protestants were nearly as indifferent as the Catholics. The Vatican was in a class by itself.

We have already pointed out the extraordinary role played by Pastor Vogt. A defender of refugees in Switzerland of every creed, Vogt, head of Fluchtlingshilfe, fought for them in the face of opposition by such "restrictionists" as Dr. Heinrich Rothmund, chief of the Swiss Alien Police. Rothmund delighted in enforcing the cruel laws of refoulement which most Jews, were subject to, and sent them back across the border to certain death at the hands of the

Nazis.[69]

As early as 1943, Vogt had publicized photos of Nazi atrocities and preached the doctrine of Christian love for all the oppressed, including Jews. His motto was, "A church that offers no haven to the suffering can never be a Church of Jesus Christ." He was a fearless spokesman for these victims of persecution by government authorities and private agencies. In the words of one Swiss author, Vogt "recognized and accepted the duty of being the voice of the silent, the emissary of the hunted."[70]

Yet, there is no doubt that Vogt's hour of glory came when he acted as a catalyst in the 1944 news breakthrough that saved the last surviving Jews of Budapest. While he lacked the prestige of Karl Barth and the other two theologians who signed the letter accompanying the two reports, he was the link enabliang them to act. He was responsible for the distribution of the reports to thousands of key church leaders and laymen. He persuaded hundreds of churches of the Zurich canton to preach on the subject of the reports.[71] He virtually stormed the Swiss Parliament, demanding help for the imperiled remnants of Hungarian Jewry.[72] It was Vogt's copy of the report that got into the hands of the New York Times correspondent and thus resulted in a fairly adequate article carried by the Times on July 6.[73]

By that time, even Dr. Rothmund began to urge that Jewish refugees be permitted to enter Switzerland. On July 12, the odious anti-Semitic regulations were changed to allow Jewish refugees into the country.[74]

Within weeks of the arrival of the reports from Auschwitz and Hungary, Vogt had compiled and published a small but widely disseminated book in a run of 7,000 copies, entitled, Soll Ich Meines Bruders Huter Sein? (Should I be My Brother's Keeper?) The book included a number of sermons he delivered against the persecution of the Jews, among them one that he preached on June 27 in the Leonhardskirche in Basel, in which he prayed:

> O Holy God, it is with profound shame and deep fear that we come before Thee today. Thou hast inquired of us regarding our brother the Jew ... we are not worthy to stand before Thee, because we Christians loved so little and had so little faith ... [with the result] that, in the midst of our Christiandom godlessness seeks to exterminate the entire Jewish people and we can no longer prevent it. . .

In addition to Karl Barth, Emil Brunner and Visser t'Hooft, other notable Protestant leaders were Pastor A. Freudenberg, Hans Schaffert, and Dr. A. Koechlin, whom we have already mentioned. These men actively promoted and preached not only sympathy for the Jews of Hungary but called for efforts to save them.[76]

All of these religious leaders helped influence lesser known church and laymen, editors, publishers and students, whose disgust at the Nazis and Hungarian atrocities was mirrored in the Swiss press.

A typical example of a Protestant protest was Dr. Erny of the Basellandschaftlichen Kirchendirektion, (Church Office of the Province of Basel) notified the Reformed Pastors to publicize Dr. Koechlin's report of June 29, which read:

> In recent days we have received horrible news concerning the extermination of Hungarian Jewry ... These events are so monstrous that our churches cannot remain silent. I also sent an urgent letter to the Bundesrat and the International Red Cross with an urgent request to do everything possible to rescue the surviving Jews of Hungary ...

He concluded with the announcement that, "The Board of Directors will meet on July 6 to see what further steps will be necessary."[77]

The Swiss Catholics, or at least the leaders of their church, were not so willing to support the protest. The one attempt by Dr. Joseph Meile, the bishop of St. Gallen, to arouse the Catholic Church into protesting to Horthy and appealing directly to the Hungarian Catholics ended in failure. And one must not ignore the attempts of Switzerland's six or seven larger Catholic newspapers for efforts to rescue the Jews. Similar help came from many small, local Catholic publications, whose grassroots support in the overall effect was crucial.[78]

LONG RANGE EFFECTS

In addition to the immediate success in halting the mass deportations to Auschwitz, there were a number of lesser, but nevertheless important long-range results of the press campaign that saved the lives of countless Jews during the last year of the war. Among these one must include the dispatch of the incomparable Raoul Wallenberg to Budapest by the King of Sweden, on June 30, following his letter to Horthy.[79] Both Sweden and Switzerland took on a much more active interest in the surviving Jews of Budapest. For example, by October 30, Switzerland announced its recognition of the various protective papers issued by the Vatican, the Spanish, the Latin American governments, especially El Salvador. Over 16,000 people in Budapest held Salvadoran papers, many forged copies of Mantello's originals. Other protective papers were issued ad hoc by both Wallenberg and Charles Lutz, the valiant Swiss consul in Budapest.[80]

The more favorable climate of opinion produced by the press had direct repercussions in Switzerland itself. Besides reversing the laws of refoulement which now permitted all endangered Jews to enter Switzerland, it now made it easier for the two trainloads with close to 3,000 refugees to enter, one from Budapest via Bergen-Belsen, the other from Theresienstadt.[81]

Spain, too, became involved indirectly in the rescue of Jews in Budapest, when it approved the entry of 1200 children to Tangier in Spanish Morocco. Though never meant to be anything more than protective devices, these entry papers provided the International Red Cross with the legal framework for its involvement with the rescue work in Hungary. Eventually the Spanish were to protect 3,000 Jews in the international ghetto set up by November 15, 1944.[82]

SUPPLEMENT - HUNGARIAN CHURCHES

In Hungary, unlike Switzerland, there was no difference between the Catholics, who comprised the vast majority of the country's population, and the Protestant minority when it came to condemnation of the Nazis. If either Church showed any concern about the fate of the Jews, the prime objects of their solicitude were those who had converted to Christianity or Christians whom the Nazis considered as non-Aryans because of a Jewish parent or grandparent.[83]

It would be too simplistic to explain this difference in attitude between the churches of Switzerland and Hungary by pointing out the obvious fact that while Switzerland was neutral throughout the war, Hungary was under actual German occupation. The Catholic clergy still maintained a powerful influence in Hungary, especially since the Horthy government "officially" retained its independence. In Denmark and Holland, both under Nazi occupation since 1940, Catholics and Protestants managed to unite in public opposition to Nazi policies. When Bishop Aron Marton of Transylvania launched an anti-Nazi protest couched in fearless, vigorous terms, the Hungarian authorities could do no more to him than banish him from the region.[84]

Undoubtedly, the hesitancy of Hungary's churches to make their voices heard on behalf of the Jews was influenced by a long tradition of anti-Semitism in Hungary. The upheavals experienced following World War One were attributed to Jews or Jewish connivance. The Jews were blamed first for the fall of the Hapsburg monarchy at the end of World War I, then for the rise of liberalism and socialism, which the Church hated and feared, and of course for the brief period during which Hungary was ruled by the Communists under Bela Kun, who was a Jew. Indeed, Horthy came to power in 1919 largely as a result of his bloody repression of Communism. During the 1930s anti-Semitic sentiment in Hungary was reinforced by Nazi propaganda from Germany and neighboring Austria.[85] Thus, Hungary became ripe for the anti-Jewish legislation that was enacted during the early part of World War II, and willing to cooperate in the deportation and extermination of the Jews after the German Wehrmacht had marched into Budapest in March, 1944. It is significant that, due to a shortage of SS personnel in Hungary, Adolf Eichmann could never have ghettoized and deported most of Hungarian Jews if he had not had the ready and active assistance of the Hungarian gendarmerie.[86]

While Swiss religious leaders championed the rights of Jews as human beings, whatever representations against the Nazis came from Hungary invariably emphasized the indignities inflicted on Jews who had converted to Christianity and on Christians of Jewish descent. The plight of Hungarian Jews as individuals entitled to certain personal and civil rights was never stressed.

Even the protests issued by Cardinal Seredi, the Primate of Hungary, first against the third anti-Jewish law of 1941, which introduced certain provisions of the Nuremberg racial legislation into Hungary's law books, and then (in April, 1944) against the order compelling Jews to wear the Yellow Star of David stressed the converts. The Hungarians did not emulate the valiant Danes or even the Dutch, who publicly rejected such manifestations of anti-Jewish discrimination.[87]

Only when he was requested by other more concerned religious leaders such as Bishop Baron Vilmos Apor of Gyoz to take a public stand did Seredi take action. Only after the Pope's message of June 25, 1944 did Seredi issue a pastoral letter to be read in all Catholic churches. But even that letter stressed concern for Jewish converts to Christianity.[88]

Even this attempt to influence Catholic churchgoers against Nazism was nipped in the bud when Minister of the Interior Istvan Antal stopped the circulation of Apor's letter and smoothed over the matter with Seredi. The Sztojay government, aware of Seredi's concern for Jewish converts to the church, made a few concessions. In return, Seredi, on July 7 (the day Horthy stopped the deportations of Jews) replaced his original letter with a substitute saying, in effect, that his letteraaad not been meant for general circulation but was intended only for the bishops, and that quiet negotiations were being conducted with the government about the status of the Jews "and especially the converts."[89]

Seredi then moved to appease the more humanitarian bishops under his jurisdiction who were calling for public action on behalf of the Jews. He wrote them confidential letters, indicating his long personal history of private intercession in favor of the Jews and claiming that secret negotiations had already yielded many concessions for Hungarian Jewry.[90]

As noted by Professor Randolph A. Braham, Hungary's Protestant church was also primarily concerned with the situation of the converts. In April, 1944, they approached Horthy, asking that the converts and the Christians of Jewish origin be spared the indignity of having to wear the Yellow Star.[91]

In May, 1944, Laszlo Ravasz, Senior Bishop of the Reformed Church, investigated rumors that Jews were being deported from certain localities. When these rumors were confirmed, he approached Cardinal Seredi, proposing that Hungary's Protestant and Catholic churches unite in a joint protest against the deportations of Jews. Seredi refused the invitation.[92] On June 23, 1944, a delegation from both of Hungary's Protestant denominations presented a memorandum of protest to the government. The protest was summarily rejected.[93]

Two days after the publication of the message from Pope Pius XII, Seredi refused a second request from the Protestants for a united stand on behalf of the Jews. Finally, Ravasz went ahead on his own and drew up a pastoral letter over his own signature, to be read in all Protestant churches. But this letter, too, was intercepted by the government and diluted with concessions to converts and vague promises to the Jews, much as had been done with the pastoral letter from the Catholic Bishop Apor.[94]

At the same time, Angelo Rotta, the papal nuncio in Budapest, ceaselessly prodded Seredi, to make a direct, public plea to the government to stop the deportations. On May 15, when the deportations first began, Rotta himself addressed a strongly-worded letter to the government, condemning its war against the Jews. This was the first official protest against Nazi policy by a representative of the Pope.[95]

The government responded with the standard bromides about the deportations, namely, that they were merely being "re-settled" for labor.[96]

On June 8, 1944, Rotta went directly to Seredi, demanding that the cardinal speak out in behalf of the Jews. Seredi's response was to shift the blame to the Vatican. It was "deceitful" for the Apostolic Holy See, the Cardinal said, "to maintain diplomatic relations with the German government which carries out the atrocities."[97]

THE VATICAN

In the end, of course, on June 25 the Vatican did depart from its traditional stance of at best sending private communications. It did so as a result of the publicity initiated by Mantello, four Protestant theologians and Walter Garrett.

Unlike many other quarters, the Vatican could not plead ignorance of Hitler's genocide plan.

It had many trustworthy sources of information, for instance, in two neutral countries, Turkey and Switzerland. In Ankara there was Archbishop Angelo G. Roncalli (later Pope John XXIII), who was highly sympathetic toward the Jews.[98]

In Bern there was the papal nuncio, Monsignor Philippo Bernadini, who obtained information on the situation of the Jews through Swiss representatives of various Jewish organizations.[99]

Nevertheless, the Vatican did not involve itself publicly in behalf of the Jews of Hungary until after the beginning of the Swiss publicity campaign. Pius XII did not even break his silence in October 1943, when the deportation of Jews from Rome confirmed earlier news concerning their fate.[100]

Only the pressures emanating from Switzerland, including the protests voiced by the four eminent Protestant theologians, could cause the Pope to speak out on June 25, 1944. Even then, the message was couched in discreet diplomatic language, in contrast to the stern warnings issued by Cordell Hull, for example. Nevertheless, the note from Pius XII to Regent Horthy served as a powerful weapon. Since Hungary was an overwhelmingly Catholic country, the Pope's words carried tremendous weight, even with Horthy, who was a Protestant. Consider, then, the effect that a stern, outspoken warning from the moral voice of conscience in Rome could have had on Hungary's policy toward the Jews.

CONCLUSION

A study of the articles published by the Swiss newspapers about Auschwitz and the danger to Hungarian Jewry in the summer of 1944 makes it clear that the vast majority of Switzerland's newspapers were (and still are) of a conservative bent. Of the 170 newspapers that carried protest articles during the years of World War II, 102 were small-town papers, roughly divided equally between Protestant and Catholics, leading one to believe that, except for a few socialist papers and one published by the Freemasons, the overwhelming majority of Switzerland's press reflected a climate of opinion that rejected liberalism and "progress." One would expect that if the readers of these papers were to be questioned as part of a public opinion poll, they would reply in a manner indicative of deep-seated prejudices, including anti-Semitism.

Yet we find that it was precisely these newspapers which, in response to the appeals of Mantello, Garrett and the four Swiss theologians, came out in fierce protest against what was being done to the Jews of Hungary. Their outrage was directed particularly against Auschwitz and what it symbolized, suggesting that it is not really possible to lock individual human beings into the constraints of ideological labels. It also suggests that if people, no matter how prejudiced they may appear, are confronted by evil incarnate they will feel duty-bound, at least publicly to reject it. Evidently, Mantello, Garrett and the four Swiss Protestant clerics understood how to reach deep into the souls of humankind, confronting them with the choice of rejecting or accepting Auschwitz, with which not even the Nazis cared to be publicly identified.

Horthy and Pius XII, too, publicly had to reject Auschwitz when the pressures of public opinion became too great. But history must record that the people of Hungary, not subjected to such pressures, nor taught to view Auschwitz in the perspectives the Swiss were made to see it, remained silent.

FOOTNOTES

1. See for example, Henry Feingold, The Politics of Rescue: the Roosevelt Administration and the Holocaust, 1938-1945 (New Brunswick, New Jersey, 1970); Richard Breitman and Alan M. Kraut, American Refugee Policy and European Jewry 1933-1945 (Bloomington, Indiana, 1987).
2. Besides the works of Jeno Levai and more recent books, much of the material on the press campaign is based upon examination of the hundreds of original newspaper clippings and documents obtained from Mr. Mantello. In addition, this writer conducted a dozen taped interviews with Mr. Mantello over the past several years. All "interviews" refer to Mantello, unless noted otherwise. 3. Interview. 4. Ibid. Cf. also Jeno Levai, Abscheu und Grauen vor dem Genocid in aller Welt [Levai, Abscheu] (New York, 1968), pp. 10-12. 5. See this author's, Thy Brother's Blood: the Orthodox Jewish Response During the Holocaust [Kranzler, Brother's] (New York, 1987), pp. 102-104. Among Mr. Mantello's private papers are numerous "original" and duplicates of Salvadoran papers. 6. Interview. Also taped interview of Mr. Herman Landau, executive secretary of HIJEFS, a rescue organization in Switzerland connected to Vaad Hatzalah, the New York-based Orthodox rabbis' rescue organization. 7. See for example, the papers of Roswell McClelland [McP] Boxes 56-60 in the collection of the War Refugee Board [WRB], FDR Library. This author found eleven copies of the Protocol in the archives of the Jewish Agency in the Zionist Archives in Jerusalem. 8. Interview.
9. Levai, Abscheu, pp. 24. Also interv. 10. Levai, Abscheu, p. 31. 11. Ibid., p.32.
12. Ibid., p. 33; Interv. 13. Interv. The girls made an error in transcription of the figures for each country, accidentally deleting the 50,000 deaths for Lithuania. This gave a total figure of 1,715,000 for the Protocol instead of the correct number of 1,765,000. This error enables the researcher to readily trace Mantello's version from the others. Cf. Levai, Abscheu, p. 34. See copy of both in McP, Box 56, WRB. 14. Interv. 15. Interv. This was the first of two meetinngs with Vogt. The second meeting took place on June 24 with the Rabbis Committee. Levai, Abscheu, pp. 39, 55-6. 16. See Alfred A. Hasler, The Lifeboat is Full: Switzerland and the Refugees [Lifeboat] (New York, 1969), pp. 122-123; Levai, Abscheu, pp. 157-160. 17. Copy of the July 4, 1944 German-language version in McP, Box 60, WRB.
18. Interv. It is important to take into consideration the very stringent Swiss attitude toward lying. 19. Levai, Abscheu, p. 39. 20. Ibid., p. 40. 21. Ibid., p. 39. Also interv. 22. Ibid., p. 40. 23. Ibid. 24. Ibid. 25. Ibid., p. 54. 26. Ibid., p. 25. Cf. also Carlo Falconi, The Silence of Pius XII (Boston, 1970), p. 61; John F. Morley, Vatican Diplomacy and the Jews During the Holocaust (New York, 1980), esp. pp. 67-68, 79-80. For more background see this author's, Heroine of Rescue (New York, 1984), Chap. 6. 27. For McClelland's remark see interv. See Banyai-McClelland corres. esp. June 21-July 4, McP, Box 60, WRB. 28. Ibid., 6/22/44. 29. Ibid., 7/7/44; Landreth M. Harrison-Mr. Huddle, 7/4/44. McP, Box 56, WRB. 30. See McClelland to John Pehle, 10/12/44. McP, Box 58, WRB.
31. Interv. 32. Ibid. Also Wesner Rings, Advokaten des Feindes [Advokaten] (Zurich, 1966), pp. 142-144. 33. Ibid. Also interv. 34. Advokaten, p. 144. 35. Walter Laqueur, The Terrible Secret [Secret] (Boston, 1980), pp. 98-99. 36. Interv. 37. See complete English-language texts in Jeno Levai, Zsidosors Europaban [Levai, Zsidosors] (Budapest, 1948), pp. 68-72. 38. Interv. 39. Advokates, p. 144-146. 40. Eugene [Jeno] Levai, Black Book on the Martyrdom of Hungarian Jewry [Black Book] (Zurich, 1948), p. 232. 41. Ibid., pp. 232-233. The second is reported by the Exchange Telegraph, 7/15/44. Levai, Abscheu, p. 179.
42. Ibid., p. 229. See also New York Times, 6/27/44; Braham, Politics, pp. 754, 756.
43. Ibid., p. 754; Black Book, p. 229. 44. Ibid., p. 230. 45. Ibid., p. 243. For the effect of the early press campaign and outcry see cable from the German Ambassador Edmund Veesenmayer to Joachim Ribbentrop, July 6, 1944. NG 5523, Document 187 in Randolph Braham, The Destruction of Hungarian Jewry: a Documentary Account [Braham, Documents] (New York, 1963), Vol. II, p. 426. 46. Black Book, p. 245. 47. Ibid., p. 228. Hungary would find it particularly difficult to refuse suggestion from Sweden, which had been protecting Hungary's interests throughout the war. Ibid., p. 245. 48. Levai, Abscheu, pp. 126-7. For complete English-language text see Harvey Rosenfeld, Raoul Wallenberg (Buffalo, 1982), p. 231.
49. Black Book, p. 231. 50. The count is based on an analysis of the list in Levai, Zsidorsos, which, though incomplete, is close enough for the generalizations. This author's collection includes a number of aritcles not found in Levai. For the effect of the campaign on Horthy, see n. 45. 51. Black Book, Chap. XII. See also Braham, Politics, pp. 754-762.
52. Ibid., pp. 1059-1061. 53. Black Book, Chap. XII and Braham, Politics, pp. 759-762, 767.
54. This author possesses this number. The largest proportion of articles appeared during the period of July 10-21, as many as 38-40 appearing on July 14-15. 55. Levai, Abscheu, pp. 75-76, 78, 81-82. 56. National-Zeitung, 7/23/44; Neue Zurcher Nachrichten, 7/25/44.
57. Interv. 58. Levai, Abscheu, pp. 233-234. 59. Ibid. Cf. also confidential report by Friedrich Born to the IRC, 10/23/44. McP, Box 57, WRB. 60. My thanks to Mr. Francois Burgy, archivist of the World Council of Churches, for his valuable help in identifying the ideological background of most Swiss newspapers. 61. These are in sequence:

Basellandschaftliche Zeitung, 7/8; Volksrecht, 7/17; La Sentinelle, 7/25; Volksrecht, 7/15; Samdschaftler, 7/12; Berner Tagwacht, 7/11; Der Bund, 7/11; Die Nation, 7/13; Appenzeller Anzeiger, 7/13; Courrier du-val de Travers, 7/12; Der Wehnthaler, 7/19; St. Gallen Tagblatt, 6/27; Volkstimme, 8/29; Basler Nachrichten, 7/26; Burgdorfer Tagblatt, 7/23; Volksrecht, 7/15; Nationalzeitung, 7/6; Besner Tagwacht, 7/7; Gazetta Ticinese, 7/14; Badener Tagblatt, 7/13. **62.** Der Badener Tagblatt, 7/12. **63.** Der Landbote, 7/29. **64.** Both contain the figure of 1,715,000. Also obviously the reports publicized by Vogt were given to him by Mantello. **65.** Cf. Harrison to Huddle, 7/4/44. Box 56, WRB. **66.** The newspapers covered the full ideological spectrum. **67.** Levai, Abscheu, pp. 222-223. **68.** Aktion Nationaler Wiederstand, nd. [ca. July '44]. **69.** See "Rothmund" in index of Lifeboat. **70.** Ibid., p. 297. **71.** Levai, Abscheu, pp. 41-48. See his book Bruder, for two such sermons. **72.** Lifeboat, p. 286. **73.** See Vogt's Bruder. **74.** Lifeboat, p. 329. **75.** Vogt, Bruder, p. 13. **76.** Levai, Abscheu, p. 43. Paul Vogt, Soll Ich Meines Bruders Huter Sein? (Zurich, 1944), pp. 36-37. **77.** Ibid., p. 45. **78.** Ibid., pp. 392-393. **79.** Black Book, p. 231. **80.** Braham, Politics, pp. 1080, 1087-1089. **81.** Ibid., p. 287; Kranzler, Brother's, pp. 109-115. **82.** Braham, Politics, pp. 1030-1031. Cf. Otto Winkelmann to Heinrich Himmler, 7/1/44 in Braham, Destruction, doc. 188, p. 430. **83.** Braham, Politics, p. 1041. This entire supplement is based essentially on Braham, Politics. His chapters 30-31 are excellent summaries of the church response to the deportations, although Levai's Black Book contains almost all the texts of the various memoranda on this theme. **84.** Ibid., p. 1047. **85.** Ibid., pp. 1027-1029. Braham does not note fact that Bela Kun was Jewish, a factor in the Hungarian anti-Semitism. **86.** Eichmann only had about 150 SS men in Budapest. **87.** Braham, Politics, p. 1042. **88.** Black Book, pp. 202-203, 206-207, esp. re text of the Bishop of Gyorz's appeal to Seredi. One must be aware of the fact that both the Catholic and Protestant organizations for Christians of Jewish origin were in the forefront of the protests to the government. Ibid., pp. 217-218. See also pp. 196-201 for the ongoing responses through June 30, when Nuncio Rotta begged even Veesenmeyer to help mitigate the harsh deportations. **89.** Braham, Politics, p. 1040. For "extras" added by the priests to the official letter, see Black Book, p. 216. **90.** Ibid., p. 211-212. For the July 20 letter by the Reform and Lutheran churches to Horthy, see Vogt, Bruder, pp. 88-90. **91.** Braham, Politics, p. 1042. **92.** Black Book, p. 218. **93.** Ibid., pp. 218-222. **94.** Ibid., pp. 222-224. **95.** Saul Friedlander, Pius XII and the Third Reich: A Documentation [Pius XII] (New York, 1966), p. 218. See also Black Book, pp. 197, 214. In the latter, the dissatisfied Bishop of Apor responded to Seredi and included a complaint re renewed deportations from Kistarcsa. **96.** Ibid., p. 220. **97.** Ibid., p. 202. Rotta responded that he had protested to Horthy which was also aired on BBC. **98.** See Carlo Falconi, The Silence of Pius XII (Boston, 1970), p. 61. See also Jacob Griffel, (unpublished typeset memoirs, n.d. [ca. 1955]), p. 16. Griffel was Agudah's representative in the Jewish Agency's rescue committee in Turkey. Copy of manuscript courtesy of Mr. Charles Miller. **99.** Kranzler, Heroine, Chap. 6; Pius XII, pp. 104-110. **100.** John F. Morley, Vatican Diplomacy and the Jews During the Holocaust 1939-1943 (New York, 1980), pp. 180-186.

ON THE RELATIONS BETWEEN THE BALTIC PEOPLES AND THEIR JEWISH NEIGHBORS BEFORE, DURING AND AFTER WORLD WAR II

DOV LEVIN

The Institute of Contemporary Jewry
The Hebrew University of Jerusalem

INTRODUCTION

Even though the 250,000 Jews living in the Baltic countries (Lithuania, Latvia and Estonia) comprise a relatively small part of the world Jewish population and of the six million Baltic nationals who themselves constitute a small minority of the European population, the topic we propose to discuss here is of particular significance, especially considering the following facts:

1. The percentage of Baltic Jews murdered in the Holocaust (about 95 percent) is among the largest for all of Europe.

2. A considerable number of Baltic Jews - if not the majority - were massacred by or with the active assistance of Lithanians, most of whom were Catholic, and Latvians and Estonians, most of whom were Lutheran.

3. A considerable number of these peoples served as volunteers in the Nazi militia or police, actively participating in the murder of Jews in neighboring Byelorussia and Poland.

4. Even after the Nazi occupation, Jewish Holocaust survivors were still harmed and even killed by their Christian neighbors.

In Jewish and non-Jewish historiography, presentation of these appalling facts has been accompanied on several occasions by the following statement which, on a superficial level, would seem controversial: Until the Holocaust the Jews lived among the Baltic peoples in relatively good conditions, with special provisions for autonomy which were looked upon with favor by the whole world. In this connection, there has also been reference to the fact that the first Jews to settle in the largest Baltic country, Lithuania, were ceremoniously invited by the Grand Duke Vytautas the Great. (It should be noted that the present year marks the 600th anniversary of that historic event, which took place on June 24, 1388.)

All of these facts considered together would elicit the following questions:

a. How did the relations between the Baltic peoples and the Jews deteriorate to the point of the terrible crisis that took place during the Holocaust period?;

b. What were the underlying reasons or factors that brought this about?

c. Did the above-mentioned facts constitute a tragic episode in the time-honored relations between the two parties under discussion, or are they irreconcilable, at least for the foreseeable future?

This paper, based on preliminary findings of research in progress at the Institute of Contemporary Jewry, will attempt to provide at least a partial answer to these questions, arguments and ensuing counter-arguments. Naturally, the survey and analysis of these issues will be presented in chronological order.

A. THE BALTIC PEOPLES AND THE JEWS: PRE-WORLD WAR II

The Czarist regime, which ruled the Baltic nations from the 18th century to World War I, oppressed the Jewish minority as well as the majority peoples, the Lithuanians, Latvians and Estonians. Given that situation, the Jews occasionally cooperated with the majority peoples on the political level in enterprises such as the uprising of 1905 and the elections to the "Duma" (the Russian parliament).[1]

At the end of World War I, the Baltic peoples succeeded in establishing their own independent states following a worldwide political struggle and relatively long wars against the military forces fighting for Germany on the one hand and Soviet Russia on the other. Several thousand local Jews, many of whom were volunteers, participated in those battles. Local Jewish personalities (who had gained a reputation abroad) attained influential positions in international institutions and solicited political and economic support among their correligionists in the West for the newly-established Baltic states, which had undertaken to grant broad autonomy to their minorities, including Jews. Even during that ideal period there were pogroms in several areas of Lithuania and Latvia, initiated by nationalist military forces in those countries. This painful issue was raised at the time by the American representative to the Paris Peace Conference.[8]

Internal economic and political factors combined with a feeling that, as it were, "the 'Moor' (Jew) has done his job and now he can go". This led to a continuous decline in the relations between the majority peoples and the Jews, which in turn brought considerable restriction of Jewish autonomy. The Estonians constituted a certain exception - but even among that small nation, whose population was about one million, the early 1930s saw the rise of nationalistic and antisemitic elements headed mainly by the Vabadusliitlased (Veterans of the War of Liberation), and the Noored Kotkad (Young Hawks). In Latvia, a similar role was fulfilled by the Perkonkrusts (Cross of Thunder); and in Lithuania the Gelezinis Vilkas (The Iron Wolk), also known as the supporters of A. Voldemaras, had secret contacts with elements in Nazi Germany in order to wage pogroms against the Jews in Lithuania.[3]

Along with these organizations, which perpetrated extreme antisemitism, other organizations dealing with economic concerns rapidly emerged. The largest of these in Lithuania was Verslas (profession), whose main slogan was "Lithuania for the Lithuanians". That organization, with several branches throughout the country, made public statements in its weekly magazine by the same name, on the radio, and elsewhere, demanding that the government limit the area where the Jews were permitted to engage in economic activity.[4]

Despite everything mentioned above, one cannot disregard the fact that relatively speaking the situation of the Jews in the Baltic nations was better than in other Eastern European countries such as Poland and Rumania.

B. THE CRISIS IN RELATIONS DURING WORLD WAR II - THE CRITICAL PERIOD

After the outbreak of World War II Lithuania, Latvia and Estonia were forced, with the enactment of the Ribbentrop-Molotov Treaty, to make the military bases in their territories available to the Soviets. This severely wounded the national pride of the Baltic peoples which, as mentioned, had just been liberated from that despised foreign entity twenty years earlier. Thus the Jews, who had known persecution in the past, once again became a scapegoat and were singled out for violent attacks. When Vilna was returned to the Lithuanians in October 1939, bloody riots ensued against the Jews resulting in about 200 casualties.[5] Similarly, there was an increasing number of attacks against Jews in the city streets. In several towns, windows of Jewish homes were smashed and some dwellings were even set on fire. Since these acts and others were committed in several locations at the same time, it can be assumed that the activity was organized and probably carried out by extreme Right wing groups associated with Nazi Germany.[6]

That was the situation in June 1940, when the Soviet troops occupied the three Baltic nations which became full Soviet republics within a short time. Thus it is no surprise that the entry of the Red Army came as a relief to a large sector of the Jewish population,[7] particularly when everyone agreed that the alternative would have been Nazi occupation and all that it entailed. The Lithuanians, Latvians and Estonians, however, were upset and bitter about the Russian occupation, since for them it meant losing the independence they had gained after over a hundred years of Russian rule. Local Communist groups and sympathizers, who did not respect the nationalist sentiments of the majority population, and staged enthusiastic demonstrations to welcome the infantry and armoured corps of the Red Army. Although there were various peoples, including Jews, among the crowds of demonstrators, it was the Jews that particularly aroused the anger of the nationalist elements.[8]

In the process of Sovietization, all of the restrictions that had been imposed on the Jews over the years were lifted. Some Jews, particularly those belonging to the Communist camp, which had been operating as an underground group until then, became prominent on various levels of the ruling establishment, including the military and internal-security forces. In addition, institutions of higher education were opened to Jewish youth. At the same time, however, many Jews were also harmed by developments that accompanied Sovietization, such as: the nationalization of commerce and industry; the obligation to work on the Sabbath and Jewish festivals; the abolition of the Jewish educational system; and dissolution of political institutions and closure of Yeshivot (Jewish religious schools) including the Slobodka and Telz yeshivot which were among the best known schools in the Jewish community. During that period, Zionist youth groups also engaged in underground activity.[9] Despite all of this, the majority peoples saw the Jews as the representatives of the disdained Soviet authority which which had been imposed on them through military force by the Red Army. Anti-Jewish sentiment escalated steadily and was sustained by the strong nationalist underground that operated in the Baltic countries with secret aid from Nazi Germany throughout the period of Soviet rule. About two weeks before the German invasion, on the evening of June 13, 1941, forces led by General Ivan Serov N.K.V.D. arrested almost 60,000 Baltic citizens, including 12,000 Jews who were singled out by the authorities as "enemies of the nation". They and their families were exiled to labor camps in Siberia and to other remote regions of Russia. Because of the sudden blow that befell the Baltic population, they either did not notice or refused to acknowledge that the number of Jews who suffered in those activities was at least twice that of the majority peoples.[10] In fact, because a few Jewish functionaries had been on the committees in charge of planning and carrying out the expulsions, the Jews as a whole were blamed for what had happened.

The national underground organization, the Lithuanian Activist Front (L.A.F.), whose operations were inspired and supported by the Nazi intelligence service as well as by a wide range of groups among the population, initiated the acts of subversion and agitation that were openly directed against the Jews in anticipation of the impending war between Russia and Germany. One of the proclamations issued by the L.A.F. in the Summer of 1941 read as follows: "Lithuanian brothers and sisters: The time has come to make a final accounting with the Jews... The ancient right of refuge for Jews in Lithuania granted in the time of Vytautas the Great is hereby abolished. Every Lithuanian Jew, with no exception whatsoever, is hereby warned to leave the soil of Lithuania immediately..."[11] In another proclamation, Lithuanian traitors were given an opportunity for amnesty "if they could prove that they have killed at least one Jew". The proclamation ends with a call to Lithuanians: "At the designated time seize their [the Jews'] property so that nothing will be lost".[12]

Realizing that these threats were serious, some Jews managed to escape to the internal regions of Russia. Indeed, just when war broke out between Germany and Russia (on June 22, 1941) prior to the entry of the Wehrmacht, there were serious attacks against Jews in at least 40 Lithuanian communities. In 25 communities women were raped; and in 36, rabbis were brutally tortured.[13] In Kovno a communique issued by J. Bobelis, a colonel in the Lithuanian army, was one of the factors that fomented the rioting. The communique, issued a day before the entry of the Germans, stated that for every German killed by a Jew, a hundred Jews would be killed in return. When the Germans entered the city, many Lithuanians were inspired to perpetrate blood baths in the well-known suburb of Slobodka and other locations. They did not stop at killing, but tortured people and engaged in terrible mass orgies.[14] Among those who actively participated in those murders - especially the instigators - were prominent leaders and public figures. In this connection, it is appropriate to quote a few passages from the diary of Helena Kutorgiene, a Lithuanian physician and Righteous Gentile,[15] who wrote an account of these atrocities: "With the exception of a few individuals, all the Lithuanians, and especially the intelligentsia who lost their positions during the Soviet regime, hate the Jews...the coarse Lithuanian mob, as opposed to the total apathy of the intelligentsia (who in all likelihood agree with them), acted with such beastly cruelty that by comparison, the Russian pogroms seemed like humanitarian deeds... I cannot believe my eyes and ears. I am totally shaken up by the force of blind hatred which they cultivate to satisfy the most base instincts."[16]

Unlike the classic pogroms perpetrated by various anonymous groups (such as the "black hundreds"), a large number of Jews in the Baltic countries, particularly those residing in small towns, were murdered by former neighbors, classmates, customers, and the like. Indeed, in a number of cases the victims would plead with their murderers, whom they had known as children, to shoot them straight in the heart and spare them a painful death.[17]

The victims' profound disenchantment and frustration with the murderers, who were devout Christians, was well expressed by Sheina Gertner, a teacher and writer who miraculously survived the massacre in the town of Valbalninkas:

> "I think and see our yard in my little town. I play with Lithuanian children from the neighborhood. My friend, Verute, prays to Jesus every time she loses a game. I ask why she is mentioning her God's name every minute. 'Jesus is the best,' she says. 'If you get a slap on one cheek, you must turn the other cheek. Jesus helps all the people who have faith in him, who pray for him. Jesus helps people not to commit crimes.' The last thought draws my attention. 'Jesus, why can you not cut the hands of the murderers? Why do you not help them to defeat their beastly instincts? The murderers go to church and bless your name. They have faith in you. They have promised you to be noble. On Sundays they go to church in their best clothes. Now, I see two neighbors who eagerly obey the command to kill. Where are you Jesus?"[18]

Be that as it may, by the end of 1941 there were only 50,000 Jews left in the Baltic countries. Most, if not all of them lived in ghettoes or labor camps.

There were unsuccessful attempts to appeal to Christian leaders and public personalities who were known as liberal intellectuals - and thus their true attitude came to light. For example, when Jewish mothers, who were worried that their children had been lost during the first days of the invasion appealed to the head of the Red Cross, the well known Dr. Zhilinskis, his response was: "He who rejoiced in the past - will now be the one to mourn."[19]

The Lithuanian Bishop V. Brizgys warmly received a delegation of Jews, but when he was asked to intervene with the German authorities he replied: "In so doing I could endanger the Catholic Church in Lithuania and I cannot assume such a responsibility."[20] When they suggested that he at least distribute a letter to his followers to prevent them from participating in the massacres, he replied: "The Church cannot help you. I personally can only weep and pray."[21]

Here it should be noted that a considerable number of Lithuanians, including prominent clergy, signed telegrams congratulating Hitler.[22] As far as we know only three people appealed to the authorities on behalf of the Jews[23], and even that was mainly after great majority had already been murdered.

There was even less intervention on behalf of the Jews by Estonians and Latvians. In the few Latvian sources dealing with this issue, it is mentioned that the Lutheran Archbishop Grinbergs tried unsuccessfully to intervene with the German authorities against the mass murder of Jews.[24] This evidence was countered by the historiographer M. Kaufmann, an authority on Latvian Jewry during the Holocaust period: "...from the Latvians, with whom we had co-existed for several hundred years, and with whom we had passed through good times as well as bad, we should have expected human rather than animal treatment.... The deans of the Lutheran and Catholic churches of Latvia...were certainly not blinded by the crimes committed by their fellow Latvians. Why did they not utilize their lofty and holy pulpits to preach against these mass slaughters, to which so many Latvians were party? Finally they, too, left Latvia together with thousands of Latvians who were involved in the crime of decimating Jews, and who escaped with possessions robbed from the victims."[25]

The losses sustained by the Germans in Stalingrad and on other fronts in 1943, and their refusal to let the Baltic peoples regain independence led to an intensified orientation towards the West. Consequently, and possibly also out of a sense of conscience, they began to help those Jews who remained and even became involved in rescuing them. The initiative for such activity was generally taken by the Jews, but in some cases Christians also encouraged them to escape from the ghetto, providing them with asylum and sustenance. One such Christian was the sailor Janis Lipke, who arranged and provided asylum in remote villages for about 40 Jews from Riga. Most of the people who helped the Jews had very limited financial resources: they were poor farmers, menial laborers, housekeepers who saved the children they had brought up, and the like. Some did this purely out of humanitarian motivations, without any financial or political gain. There were, however, some doctors and clergymen, including Rev. Br. Paukstys, among the rescuers. Whether Paukstys' motivations were missionary or humanitarian, he rescued quite a few Jewish children after baptizing them. Another Catholic personality, the monk Br. Gotautas, who did a lot to rescue Jews, explained the motivation for his dangerous activity as follows: "The world should know that there are decent people among the Lithuanians".[26] The librarian of Vilna University, Ona Shimaite, who had been involved in the Social Revolutionary (S.R.) movement in her younger years, not only rescued Jews but also hid books and manuscripts belonging to the cultural repositories of the Jewish community of Vilna. When caught by the Gestapo, she was brutally tortured but would not disclose the whereabouts of the Jews she was hiding. In addition, she established a committee for the rescue of Jews. Similar institutions were established for the same purpose by anti-Fascist (Communist and pro-Communist), Catholic Church and nationalist groups. However, beyond the symbolic and ethical significance of such activity, it not only came too late but was also too little - hence its effectiveness was very limited, both in absolute and relative terms.[27]

After the Germans, hastened by the approach of the Red Army, withdrew from Lithuania in the Summer and Fall of 1944, less than 1,000 Jews (at the most 0.4 percent of the Lithuanian Jewish population before the Nazi occupation), who had been rescued by Christians (Lithuanian, Polish and Russian), remained in that country. The situation in Latvia was even worse - only 200 Jews remained, 0.3 percent out of the 70,000 who had lived in that country before the Nazi occupation; and in Estonia - only 10 Jews(!), 0.1 percent out of over 1,000 who had lived there before the Nazi occupation.[28]

Following the German withdrawal, several thousand local Lithuanian, Latvian and Estonian collaborators, including some who had murdered Jews, left the Baltic countries. Most of them are now living in the United States, Canada, Australia, Sweden and West Germany. A few of the murderers who did not manage to escape remained in their native countries which came once again under Soviet rule.

* * * *

The facts mentioned above are at least partially relevant to the first question posed at the beginning of the paper: How did relations between the Baltic nations and the Jews deteriorate to the point of the terrible crisis that ensued during the Holocaust? From the material compiled thus far, four main factors can be discerned which may also provide a certain answer to the second question: "What were the underlying reasons or factors that led to the crisis and all it entailed?". These can be described follows.

<u>Economic Crisis</u> - This factor, which had not been encountered for several generations, became a pressing concern on the eve of World War II - although unlike in Poland, economic strife was not accompanied by violence in the Baltic countries. During the Soviet rule, economic crisis was mitigated but not eliminated. When several hundred Jewish clerks attained managerial positions which had previously been closed to them in major financial enterprises, the Baltic nationals considered this an indication of their own decline. Moreover, during the Nazi occupation Baltic citizens took over the property of Jews who had been murdered and imprisoned in ghettos and labor camps.

<u>The political factor</u> - When the Baltic peoples gained independence, the political support they had received over the years from Jews and the opinion of the world Jewish community became much less significant. Moreover, when these countries entered the German sphere of influence, such support was not only undesirable but even detrimental to their national interests. During the Soviet regime, the Baltic peoples and the Jews already had conflicting political orientations. During the Nazi occupation, the Baltic peoples' struggle for political independence was accompanied by intensive involvement in the murders. At the same time, however, thousands of Jewish refugees from Lithuania, Latvia and Estonia were conscripted into the Baltic division of the Red Army. Thus, the fact that so many Baltic Jews were in the ranks of the Red Army enabled the Soviets to claim that

the Baltic peoples were fighting side in side with the Soviet Union.

The emotional factor - Before the war, this had primarily been expressed by random eruptions of fanaticism, especially among the Gentile students and urban population, against the peculiar behavior, as it were, of their Jewish colleagues. However, under the Soviets it became a dominant factor affecting every facet of relations between Jews and non-Jews. The appointment of a young Jew as officer of the militia was perceived by the Baltic peoples as an act of ingratitude and treason - particularly when it was the job of the same officer to arrest and expel distinguished Baltic citizens who had been considered patriots.

The moral factor - Even though most of the Baltic peoples were religious Christian peasants, there were hardly any expressions of extreme religious fanaticism among them. However, between the two World Wars the relations between Christian and Jewish religious leaders usually did not go beyond formal meetings. In any event, the relations were good enough that the Jews were justified in expecting their support. Notwithstanding the fact that in general they did not live up to these expectations, many of the people who rescued Jews were religious Catholics whose motives were mostly ethical. The same went for the handful of the intellectuals who rescued Jews, although their activity was mainly directed towards their Jewish colleagues. Cooperation between Communists and Jews was inspired by political motivations rather than the desire to aid the Jews as victims.

Although the last factor had a relatively limited impact, the four together played a significant role during the period of Nazi occupation; the short period of Soviet rule from 1940-1941 hastened the onset of a credibility crisis. Undoubtedly, during the Soviet regime (before the Holocaust) the intense aggressiveness of the Baltic peoples, which was a product of their deep frustration, could only be restrained by force. Hence the pogroms and bloody riots incited by many Baltic nationals during and after the retreat of the Red Army in the summer of 1941 were, to a certain extent, a mass insurrection which the Nazis encouraged and utilized to their advantage. As research progresses we will obviously find additional factors and reasons that will shed further light on this complex question.

C. FROM THE END OF WORLD WAR II TO THE PRESENT

The third question, posed at the beginning of this paper, concerns the nature of the relations between the Jews and Baltic peoples from the end of World War II to the present and in the foreseeable future. This question is no less complex than the previous ones.

It should be noted that despite the political changes and the atrocities perpetrated in the Baltic countries during and after World War II, most of the Baltic people still live on their soil and in their own state, and their standard of living is among the highest in the entire Soviet Union. The small number of local Jews who survived the massacres and deportations have also succeeded economically. For a short time around the end of the war there were a few brutal attacks on Jews, mainly in small places.[29] However, there were various attempts by Jews to take revenge on those who had murdered their loved ones.[30] Subsequently the relations between the Jews and the Baltic peoples began to stabilize, eventually becoming almost normal. This can be attributed to the following factors: Hundreds of arrests and trials carried out by the Soviet authorities against those who had murdered Jews; public statements condemning persecution of Jews,[31] and public commemoration of the victims.[32] Be that as it may, many members of the younger generation in these countries are being educated with information and values that decry the atrocities of the Nazi regime and those who perpetrated them. In recent years there has even been evidence of a certain rapprochement between the few Jews who have remained in the Baltic countries and the majority population regarding the issue of the State of Israel. Among other reasons, this is probably because of the opposition to the Soviet government and policy that still exists among the Baltic nations. Those who immigrated to Israel from that region after the Six Day War described the jubilant reaction of the Baltic peoples after Israel crushed the Arabs, who receive massive support from the Soviets. At farewell parties for Jews emigrating to Israel some Baltic nationals still congratulate the Jewish people, implicitly expressing the hope that they themselves will gain independence in the near future. Indeed it is hard to determine to what extent such support for the Jews and their demand to immigrate to Israel comes from the heart or from political and utilitarian motives. As it is, every Jew emigrating from these countries today leaves behind an apartment, a job and other possessions that are passed on to the members of majority society. In contrast to the period immediately following the War, when Jews left without any hesitation,[33] those who emigrated later have had mixed feelings about what they are doing, as Sheina Gertner, the teacher quoted earlier, put it when she immigrated to Israel in the 1970s:

> The day comes to say goodbye to our neighbors. It is not easy. We have many good friends among the teachers. At the same time I cannot forget the great evil that some Lithuanian people had done. They helped the Nazis to kill. I cannot find an answer. What was the power of evil that converted normal people into beasts of the jungle? I cannot forgive. I cannot forget. All I can do is hope.[34]

A different, perhaps more optimistic view is expressed by the writer Icchokas Meras, who was rescued by a Christian Lithuanian in the town of Kelme:

> Kelme taught me to see the world through the eyes of a Lithuanian and not to forget that I am a Jew.
> Kelme is my Lithuania and my Jerusalem
> Probably, everything lies in this: my relations with the Jewish nation and Israel; my relations with the Lithuanian nation and Lithuania....
> And if every man truly has his own guardian angel, it must be that I was accompanied then, and perhaps am now, by two angels - one, in the name of Yahweh, and the other in the name of God who exists in three persons.
> Perhaps, that is why when I write about the Jew, I think of the Russian, the Latvian or the Czech; and when I write on the Jew and the Lithuanian, I think about man.[35]

* * * *

The relationship between Baltic nationals who have immigrated to the West and their Jewish counterparts who survived the Holocaust is another issue. During the first years after the War there were verbal and physical confrontations between each of these groups, most of whom had been in D.P. camps in post-War Germany. Now, however, the conflict has reached a point where the two sides are conducting a polemical debate in newspapers and magazines. In this continuing debate, Jewish survivors have made serious accusations against a large portion of the Baltic people, claiming that they murdered, tortured and robbed their Jewish neighbors and that the religious and political leadership failed to speak out as they should have.[36] Such accusations are refuted by the other side, and the following motifs are most frequently used in their counterargument: a. the idealization of the coexistence in the past (before World War I); b. minimalization of destructive activity in the Holocaust (murder and persecution); c. disproportionate maximalization (to the point of exaggeration) of positive involvement (rescue, aid, etc.); d. tenacious and consistent attempts to prove the similar fate during World War II that befell both the Jews and the peoples of Eastern Europe among whom they lived; and similar explanations. In other words, a continuous attempt is being made to project a <u>symmetrical formula</u> depicting the situation of the Jews and that of the non-Jews to prepare the basis for some form of mutual understanding.

It should be noted that one of the pressing problems of Baltic emigres, particularly the elderly among them, is the fact that they are far away from their homeland which, as they see it, is ruled by a foreign occupier. Even though 44 years have passed since they left their homes, the Summer and Fall of 1944 remain a gloomy period in their minds, marking the beginning of their exile and renewed domination of their states by the Russians. Thus, to this very day, they are truly enraged when Jewish survivors from the same countries justifiably recall the very same months as a "period of liberation" from the Nazi inferno, and the Red Army as a liberating force! To a certain extent this is quite similar to the controversial situation of Summer 1940 when the Jews, in contrast to the Baltic peoples, saw the entry of the Red Army as an act of salvation. To this very day, the Sovietization of the homeland remains a traumatic issue for Baltic emigres, and they still engage in intensive political activity on behalf of their brethren.[37] Hence many Baltic personalities, for political, tactical and other reasons, attempt to mark the beginning of the controversial period from June 22, 1941 (the Nazi occupation of the Baltic states) to June 15, 1940 (the Soviet occupation of the Baltic states), with the intention of <u>including</u> the years 1940-1941 - the first period of the Soviet regime. In this connection, a former member of the Latvian Parliament, J. Lejins, takes to task the editors and contributors of <u>The Jews of Latvia</u>, a volume which has appeared in Israel:

> The history of any minority cannot be considered separately from the history of a majority people. This applies to every country. However, some of the writers of history jump straight from 1939 to 1941 and in so doing break the continuity of

> events. The "forgotten" year is therefore of the utmost importance. Without it, it is impossible to comprehend the events that occurred later.[38]

From the examples of arguments of the Baltic emigres presented here, a symmetric pattern is almost self-evident and can be summarized as follows: a) Both sides (i.e., the Baltic peoples and the Jews who lived in their midst) suffered extremely heavy casualties during World War II; b) The Baltic peoples suffered mainly from the Soviet Communist elements, while the Jews suffered mainly at the hands of the German Nazis; c) On both sides there were cases of negative fringe elements - those who collaborated with the Communists in carrying out killings among the Baltic peoples, and those who collaborated with the Nazis in killing Jews. d) The results were thus equal.

According to the emigre press, this would lead to a further conclusion: as both sides had lived together peacefully for centuries and during the war both suffered heavy losses, why should they not seek a renewed dialogue in order to reinstate their pre-Holocaust relationship? Of course, this would require that we forget what happened between the two sides during the war and regard it as a lamentable, tragic episode. This is possible now, more than ever, because time has healed the wounds of the past - and especially because both sides living among the "free peoples" are still threatened by the joint enemy - Soviet totalitarianism "which has not yet been subdued."[39]

These are the main arguments espoused by the Baltic peoples in their debate with the Jews. There have been repercussions which have recently become evident in the course of the debate. We refer, first of all, to the negative attitude of many Baltic emigres towards the trials being held in Western countries, particularly in the United States, where former Baltic citizens are accused of perpetrating crimes against Jews and against others during the Nazi occupation. A campaign being waged by Baltic emigre activists in the United States against the Justice Department's Office of Special Investigations (O.S.I.) has been characterized by concealed antisemitic propaganda themes.[40] Following these trials, there has been a markedly aggressive tone in Baltic diaspora publications towards the Jewish establishment in general and Holocaust survivors in particular. It is claimed that such accusations are guided to a large extent by motives of vengeance characteristic of Jews ("an eye for an eye"), as compared to the humanitarian approach of the Christians which preaches mercy.[41] Therefore such publications demand that the Jews throughout the world call an immediate halt to the campaign of condemnation and slander against those peoples in whose midst they have lived. In reaction to this unwarranted campaign, antisemitic trends are increasing rapidly. Furthermore, these campaigns may only serve as confirmation of the opinions prevalent among the general public against Jewish aggressiveness as expressed by the State of Israel's behavior towards its Arab neighbors etc.

Rev. J. Prunskis of the Lithuanian American Council recently proposed this arrangement: The Association of Lithuanian Jews in Israel should come out with a public statement that only a few individuals participated in pogroms and murder of Jews and that the Lithuanian peoples in general were totally innocent; in exchange the Lithuanian American Council should refrain from publicizing information on involvement of Lithuanian Jewry in the deportations to Siberia that took place in 1941. This proposal, of course, was rejected outright.[42] In fact, the booklet published afterwards by the Reverend Prunskis includes a chapter entitled "During Soviet Occupation,"[43] in which there are some facts taken from publications that had appeared under the Nazi occupation.

* * * * *

Lately the Baltic emigres have begun to adopt a more rational and less traditional approach. The articles of M. Goberis, Dr. Br. Kaslas and Dr. St. Sereika, for example, express a desire to initiate serious dialogue between the two parties in question (Baltic emigres and Jews) - to dare to tell the truth which "can only be of considerable help to the Baltic people and consolation to the Jewish people."[44] In his latest book, the Lithuanian Bishop J. Brizgys, who resides in the United States, now exhibits greater understanding of Jewish behavior in the "critical years" (1940-1941) . In contrast to earlier statements, he writes:

> "Just as it is impossible to claim that the Lithuanians were to be blamed for all the crimes of the Bolsheviks, it cannot be claimed that the Jews were responsible for everything the Bolsheviks did. Both the Jews and the Lithuanians gave their support to the Communist Russians, but both were extremely few in number." [45]

The Latvian historian A. Ezergailis came to a similar conclusion:

> "There is no basis for believing, as Himmler's propaganda proclaimed, that Latvia during the communist occupation was run by Jews or Jewish Chekists. Soviet government of Latvia consisted of Latvians alone and the chief of the Cheka of Latvia, Novikov, was also a Latvian. We have no reason to think that the proportion of Jewish sympathizers with communism there was higher than that in the local population."[46]

Such statements, combined with the fact that the deportation of 12,000 Baltic Jews to Siberia in 1941 and similar acts are no longer ignored, may indicate a new trend. This particularly characterizes the younger generation of Baltic researchers and historians who were brought up and educated in the democratic, humanitarian environment of the West as, for example, Prof. A. Ezergailis, mentioned above, Prof. V.S. Vardys, Prof. R.J. Misiunas, Prof. T. Paerming and others. Furthermore, because commentary on the events of 1940-41, which was so distorted, served as an excuse for the murder of Jews during the Nazi occupation, the hope is that the new approach of the younger generation will effect a change in the attitudes of their predecessors and that the situation will be cast in its proper light. This will help clear the air between the two conflicting sides - and this may happen by the end of this century.

In this spirit, let us conclude this paper with an excerpt from an article written by a Jewish survivor, which appeared in a newspaper published by Lithuanian emigres in Canada. In the article, a differentiation is made between the older and younger generation of Baltic emigres:

> Many of the old generation have <u>not</u> learned the lesson of even the most terrible deeds carried out in their homeland by their compatriots. I am afraid to say that in this matter it is a hopeless case. In my opinion, it is impossible to argue or to make accounts with such prejudiced and fascist people.... In the final analysis, they, and even more so those they are protecting, will stand before the Court of Heaven, or the judgement of history, or both of them.... I intend to maintain two way contacts...with the <u>young generation</u> of Lithuanian immigrants in the Western world by scientific research, publications, and personal encounters. Not only are their hands clean, but their approach is generally substantive and correct. Furthermore, there are among them persons of intellectual honesty who seek the truth, come what may. With all my heart I hope that their numbers may increase! I am therefore optimistic as to the democratic approach of the <u>coming generations</u>.[47]

NOTES

1. For details see: Mendel Bobe, Perakim betoldot yehudey Latviya (Tel Aviv, 1965), pp. 166-172. (Hebrew); Uriyah Katsenelenbogen, "Litvakes", in: Lite, vol. I, M. Sudarski, et. al., eds. (New York, 1951), pp. 384-386. (Yiddish).

2. At the meeting of the Committee for Baltic Countries on July 7, 1919, Lieutenant Colonel Green stated: "The second danger is the antisemitic movement, which at the moment is gaining ground among the population." E.L. Woodward and R. Butler, Documents of British Foreign Policy, 1919-1939, First Series, vol. III (1919), p. 16.

3. A document of the German Foreign Ministry that fell into American hands after the War (marked NG-4041), indicates that at the end of the 1930s the Germans gave money to the supporters of Voldemaras to encourage pogroms in Lithuania, but refused to give them arms.

4. Verslas (Kaunas), February 10, 1940.

5. Information and documentation on these riots can be found in: Leiser Ran, Ashes from Jerusalem of Lithuania (New York, 1959), pp. 267-301. (Yiddish).

6. See footnote 3.

7. This feeling was duly expressed in an article by the leader of the Jewish community in Vilna, Dr. Jacov Wigodski entitled "We Feel Relieved", Vilner Togblat (July 4, 1940). (Yiddish).

8. A few memories from those times are recalled by the former President of the Latvian parliament J. Lejins in Latvian-Jewish Relations, published by the World Federation of Free Latvians in Canada, 1975, p. 14.

9. For more details on the tribulations of the Jews in all of these aspects see: Dov Levin, Between the Hammer and the Sickle - Baltic Jewry Under Soviet Rule During World War II: A Volume of Collected Articles (Jerusalem, 1983). (Hebrew).

10. See: Romuald J. Misiunas and Rein Taagepera, The Baltic States - Years of Dependence: 1940-1980 (New York, 1983), p. 61 (note 79).

11. The full contents of the Proclamation can be found in: Masines Zudynes Lietuvoje: 1941-1944 (Mass Murders in Lithuania: 1941-1944), vol. I (Vilnius, 1965), p. 50. (Lithuanian).

12. Ibid., p. 49.

13. These minimal data were calculated on the basis of evidence from over 100 Lithuanian communities, in: Lithuanian Jewry, vol. IV (Tel Aviv, 1984), pp. 237-373. (Hebrew).

14. A description of one such horrible event (in the Lietukis garage in Kovno) by Lithuanian witnesses see: Mass Murders in Lithuania op. cit., pp. 231-232; "Die Morder Werden noch gebraucht" ("The Murderers are Still Being Used"), Der Spiegel, 17 (April 23, 1984), pp. 123-126.

15. One of about 100 Lithuanians recognized by Yad Vashem as Righteous Among the Nations. About ten people from Latvia have received this recognition, and one from Estonia.

16. Quoted by Ona Shimaite in her article "Litviner un yidn be'et der nazi okupatsye" ("Lithuanians and Jews Under the Nazi Occupation"), Lite, vol. I (New York, 1951), p. 1666. (Yiddish).

17. One of these incidents occurred in the town Kursenai, in Northern Lithuania. "Right before he was to be executed, a young man named Tshernikhowski recognized a close acquaintance, a Lithuanian named Adulas. He said to Adulas: 'Aim well and kill me instantly so that I won't have to be tortured.' Tshernikhowski's 'friend' fulfilled his wish. See: Lithuanian Jewry, op. cit., p. 344.

18. Sheina Sachar-Gertner, The Trees Stood Still, Holocaust Survivors Publishing Co.,

Framingham, Mass., 1981), p. 28.

19. Eliezer Yerushalmi, Pinkas Shavli, a Diary from a Lithuanian Ghetto 1941-1944 (Jerusalem, 1958), p. 35. (Hebrew).

20. See the testimony of one of the members of the delegation: Leib Garfunkel, The Destruction of Kovno's Jewry (Jerusalem, 1959), p. 41.(Hebrew).

21. Quoted from the reminiscences of one of the members of the delegation: Jacov Goldberg, Note from the Jewish "Council of Elders" in Kovno Fun Lezten Churbn (From the Last Extermination) 7 (May 1948), p. 39. (Yiddish).

22. Among those who signed the telegram were: Archbishop J. Skriveckas; Bishop V. Brizgys; former President Dr. K. Grinius; former mayor of Kovno J. Vileisis, and others. See Mass Murders in Lithuania, op. cit., p. 53.

23. "What about the Jews of Lithuania? Of the 2,300 words contained in the memorandum, only eight(!) deal with the Jews, stating that the Lithuanian people does not look with approval upon the 'measures' being taken in relation in relation to the Jews of Lithuania - that is all..." L. Garfunkel, "Setting the Record Straight - True Facts About Lithuanian Attitudes Toward the Tragedy of Lithuanian Jewry", in Lithuanian Jewry, Vol. IV (Tel Aviv, 1984), p. 51. (Hebrew).
The memorandum was signed by: Reverend M. Krupavicius, Prof. J. Alekna, and former President Dr. K. Grinius (see footnote 22 above).

24. A. Spekke, History of Latvia (Stockholm, 1951), p. 402.

25. Max Kaufmann, "The War Years in Latvia Revisited", in: M. Bob et. al., eds. The Jews of Latvia, (Tel Aviv, 1971), p. 366.

26. Sofija Binkiene, "Be ginklo kariai", Soldiers Without Arms (Vilnius, 1966), p. 166. (Lithuanian).

27. The conclusion reached after a comprehensive study conducted by Sarah Neshamit. See the conclusion of her article "Rescue in Lithuania During the Nazi Occupation (June 1941-August 1944), in: Rescue Attempts During the Holocaust (Jerusalem, 1976), p. 329.

28. This estimate, which is on the high side, is based on analysis of a considerable number of books, articles and collections of documents including data on actual cases where Jews were rescued in Baltic countries during the Holocaust.

29. The head of the Gel family, for example, was murdered in this way in the town of Josvainiai. M. Karnovski, "Two Meetings", in: Keidan Memorial Book, ed. J. Chrust (Tel Aviv), 1977, p. 283. (Hebrew).

30. See the chapter "The Hour of Vengeance" in: Aba Gefen, The Unholy Alliance (Jerusalem, 1973), pp. 60-66.

31. The impassioned article by a Lithuanian professor, R. Mironas, in Tarybu Lietuva (February 15, 1945) made quite an impression . At the end of the article, he blames himself for failing to raise his voice publicly, and the last sentence reads: "At that time there were, unfortunately, so many scum and so few truly human beings."

32. Memorials were erected in several communities where Jews had been murdered, although some of them merely indicate that victims were Soviet citizens without specifying whether they were Jewish.

33. M. Karnovski wrote the following when he left Kedainiai, Lithuania: "I did not look back when I left you, the city of my birth. May your murderers be damned. I can be somewhat comforted knowing that you will have to live under occupation forever. Lithuania will never be independent again. The sickle of Russia has trampled on you. May it crush you, so help me God." M. Karnovski, op. cit., p. 285.

34. Sheina Sachar-Gertner, op. cit., p. 94.

35. From Icchokas Meras' speech on accepting the Lithuanian Writers' Asssociation Award

November 25, 1917, Lituanus, vol. 27, no. 3 (1981), pp. 8-9.

36. See the resolutions of the Conference of Jewish Survivors from Lithuania and the American Territory of Germany held in Munich on April 15, 1947, Unzer Veg 109 (July 22, 1947).

37. On the attitudes of the Baltic peoples after World War II, see: Dov Levin, "The Soviet Communist Motif and its Effect on the Subject of the Holocaust in the Historiography of the Baltic Diaspora", in: THe Historiography of the Holocaust Period (ed. Yisrael Gutman and Gideon Greif), Jerusalem 1988, pp. 209-234.

38. J. Lejins, Latvian Jewish Relations, published by the World Federation of Free Latvians in Canada, 1975, p. 14.

39. From the editorial "A Nation Accused", Teviskes Ziburiai (Light of Homeland) 29 (July 15, 1976). The reference is mainly to the article "Facts Accuse" by Dov Levin which appeared in the previous issue of the newspaper.

40. On Anti-Semitism in the anti-O.S.I campaign, see: An ADL Special Report: The Campaign Against the U.S. Justice Department's Prosecution of Suspected Nazi War Criminals (New York, 1985), pp. 24-36.

41. Such motifs can be found in an article by Rimkus, "Kodel tas nelemtas antisemitizmas" ("Why This Unexpected Antisemitism?) in: Teviskes Ziburiai (November, 1981). (Lithuanian).

42. The exchange of letters was published in Forum 37 (Spring 1980), pp. 111-116.

43. Dr. Juozas Prunskis, Lithuanian Jews and the Holocaust (Chicago, Ill., 1979), pp. 12-16.

44. On this sensitive subject see: Dr. St. Sereika, "Opiuoju", Teviskes Ziburiai (March 28, 1982). (Lithuanian).

45. See Vysk. Vicentas Brizgys, "Kataliku Baznycia Lietuvoje, 1940-1944" ("The Catholic Church in Lithuania in the Years 1940-1944"), (Chicago, Ill., 1977), p. 177. (Lithuanian).

46. Andrew Ezergailis, "Latvia, 1940-1941", entry in The Encyclopedia of the Holocaust (in press).

47. Dov Levin, Report from Jerusalem Concerning the Delicate Subject, Teviskes Ziburiai (February 4, 1982). (Lithuanian).

The Catholic Church in Poland and Antisemitism, 1933-1939: Responses to Violence at the Universities and in the Streets

Ronald Modras

Saint Louis University, 221 N. Grand Blvd., St. Louis, MO 63103

The Nazi-engineered pogrom known as Kristallnacht (November 9-10, 1938) evoked expressions of outrage from scores of religious leaders in Europe and the United States. Using as an excuse the assassination of a German diplomat by a young Jew, the Nazis incited riots throughout Germany and Austria. Jewish homes were set on fire, Jewish shops looted, a reported ninety-one Jews were killed, and 267 synagogues partially or completely destroyed. Mass arrests followed and some 30,000 Jewish men were sent to concentration camps.[1] Catholic dignitaries like the archbishops of London,, Paris, Baltimore, Boston, and San Francisco joined a wide spectrum of political and church leaders to condemn the persecution. Mass meetings were held and joint statements issued. Much was made of Pope Pius XI's prior condemnation of Nazi racial theories and his remarks earlier that year to a group of Belgium pilgrims declaring that "it is not possible for Christians to take part in anti-Semitism. We are Semites spiritually."[2] Yet, curiously and conspicuously, no response to Kristallnacht came from the Vatican. The magnitude of the violence and bloodshed were not deemed as warranting anything stronger than had already been said. The official Catholic response in Rome was silence. The same was true for Poland.

The church had developed a formidable Catholic press in Poland, ranging from popular weeklies and diocesan monthlies to scholarly journals. these, like the Polish bishops, uttered little or nothing in comment on Kristallnacht, let alone criticism. but the Polish church also boasted two daily newspapers, the Maly Dziennik (Little Daily) published by the Franciscan friars at Niepokolanow, and the Glos Narodu, located in Krakow. Established to present the news from a Catholic perspective, they reported the story of the German pogrom and editorialized in its wake in a manner at once consistent with their policies and indicatory of the Polish church's stance toward antisemitic violence.

From the time of its inception in 1935, the Maly Dziennik had been characterized by antisemitism. Its coverage of the Nazi pogrom proved to be no exception. The story of seventeen-year-old Hershel Grynszpan killing a third secretary of the German embassy in Paris, Ernst vom Rath, received detailed treatment. The headline announced that the murder was an act of revenge for the persecution of Jews in Germany.[3] Two days later the headlines announced not the pogrom but the death of vom Rath, followed by the subheading "Demented Jews not satisfied with the blood of a third rank official." The report goes on to say that the death of vom Rath, a "victim of Jewish brutality," unleased violent anti-Jewish manifestations in cities throughout Germany. With no further details or comment about the destruction, the report simply noted that "one can expect that now Chancellor Hitler will employ the so-called 'final' policy toward the Jews."

Rather than dwell on Jewish injuries, Maly Dziennik preferred to concentrate its attention on the Jewish press in Poland, which it described as tearing its garments over the tragedy of the Jewish community with "frantic raving," trying to defend the assassin. For the Catholic daily, Jewish references to Grynszpan as a lone eccentric were attempts to trivialize a vindictive crime, and Jewish despair a justified fear for its "hide." A

Jewish reference to vom Rath as a "third rank official" invited the retort: "Of course! World Jewry would prefer to transplant systems like that in bolshevik Russia, so that instead of third rank officials, they could shoot with impunity at first rank dignitaries. What a shame that the gentlemen [of the Jewish press in Poland] beside rending their garments of their fate in Germany, do not mention what their compatriots are doing in the blood-drenched Soviet states."[4] A week later the Catholic daily ran a story under the headline, "What to do with the Jews?" Nobody wants them.[5]

Glos Narodu, had formerly been a Christian Democratic daily, but in April, 1936, came under the control of the archdiocese of Krakow and its archbishop, Prince Adam Sapieha.[6] It too spared its readers the details of the destruction and focused its first report on the mass arrests. Two days later it published a lengthy editorial on the fact that the Germans were holding all Jews responsible for the crime of an individual. "The anger of the German nation, caused by Grynszpan's crime is understandable," it stated. "The murder was committed in cold blood and had the character of revenge. Revenge not on an individual but on the German nation. The murderer himself had said so. One cannot be surprised, therefore, at the outbreak of indignation in the Third Reich and at the demonstrations. . .The Third Reich is in the process of breaking the shackles that Jews have laid upon Germany's economic and cultural life. Still we cannot approve the methods of their actions, although we recognize their purpose: the liberation of Germans from Jewish servitude. Grynszpan's crime at such a moment necessarily calls forth a reaction from the German masses."

While the German masses could be excused, not so the German authorities. Their punishment of the entire Jewish community in Germany for the act of an individual "cannot be defended in the light of ethics." Glos Narodu questioned the morality of confiscating Jewish property and of the massive internment of Jews in concentration camps. But then with an eye obviously cast on what it deemed the Polish situation, the daily went on: "Every nation -- certainly Germany as well -- has the right to defend itself from subjection to so foreign a nationality as the Jews and their injurious influence on social life. . . .But always within the limits of ethics, i.e., the limits drawn by the universal Christian morality that views every human being as a neighbor." Public life is becoming barbarous and can be saved only by a return to Christian ethics.

After describing Hitler's policies as a "war of extermination" against the Jews, the editorial then criticized German Jews for remaining in Germany and world Jewry for "raising a fuss." Jews are "guests" in Germany as they are in Poland. If hospitality has been withdrawn, Jews have no alternative but to sell their businesses, "even if at a loss," and to emigrate. Some Jews have already done so, but not all. And why not? "Is it because they are still attached to a country that does not want them: In doing so, are they not themselves tempting their persecutors?" Instead of protesting, Jews should realize that it is necessary for them to emigrate from Europe as quickly as possible. The League of Nations and governments of Europe will help find them a place. And to those Jews who do not wish to consider any place other than Palestine, the editorial concludes with "nonsense." Not all Jews could fit there anyway.[7]

The editorial elicited outrage from Jews and gratitude from Catholics for presenting the "Christian position." The Nowy Dziennik, a Zionist paper, responded that up to now the world has been divided into those who admire Hitler's treatment of Jews and those who condemn him: Glos Narodu, however, constitutes a third camp: those who want to "understand" Hitler. Glos Narodu found the remark appropriate, appealing to the principle that revolutions should not be simply condemned but also understood. "What National Socialism is doing in Germany is a real revolution. It does not help us to close our eyes to this and condemn everything in it wholesale because of the cruelty it commits. Glos Narodu is possibly the Catholic publication in Poland which has fought against Nazism the most. No Catholic daily has informed [its readers] so exactly about what is happening in the Third Reich or fought so resolutely against neo-paganism and racism. But our position does not blur our vision. We see clearly that Nazism has had and does have its reasons for coming out resolutely against Jews. We do not praise its barbarous methods but we recognize the reason for its war as valid."

As an alternative to Nazi barbarity, Glos Narodu again advocated emigration, and since Palestine does not appear feasible at this time, then South America, Australia, or Africa. Jews have no right to refuse accepting any place other than Palestine. "Germany has withdrawn hospitality and so have the nations of Eastern Europe. The example of Germany may unfortunately prove to be contagious. Anyone who wants to save Jews from a fate such as the Third Reich is preparing from them ought to begin thinking now about a place for Poland's Jews too. This is not a threat but a simple deduction of objective consideration. Above all, it lies in the interest of Polish Jews themselves. And it is in their power. They have many influential friends in both Washington and London. Since it is so easy for them to obtain protests from these governments in favor of the Jewish cause, certainly they could support Warsaw's efforts to find colonies for the Jewish masses in Poland if only they would want to."[8]

Maly Dziennik and Glos Narodu could not and did not pretend to speak for the entire Catholic church in Poland. They did have immense influence, however, especially Maly Dziennik which enjoyed the largest circulation of any daily newspaper in the country. The editors of both newspapers were answerable to their respective bishops, who by the very definition of their office had the right and duty of supervision. That the foregoing articles and editorial opinions were not idiosyncratic but representative of the thinking of Catholic bishops and clergy as a whole can be seen by putting them in the context of the Catholic press as a whole as its response to antisemitic violence in Poland. Stories of university disturbances and street riots had appeared in their pages regularly in the 1930s. The attitude of the Catholic press to these events tells us much about the attitudes and opinions of the church's intellectual and clerical elite, those who claimed for themselves the moral authority to lead the laity and form its conscience.

VIOLENCE AT THE UNIVERSITIES

Violence in inter-war Poland, like elsewhere in Eastern Europe, began early at universities and comparable institutions of higher learning.[9] By the mid-1930s university riots in Poland had begun to take on the appearance of an unalterable fact of nature.[10] A cause for resentment and the reason most readily offered as an excuse was the disproportionate number of Jews in the professions. In 1931, 56% of Poland's medical doctors were Jewish; 33.5% of its lawyers; 43.3% of its educators; 24.1% of its pharmacists and laboratory workers.[11] The policy of numerus clausus, admitting only a limited number of Jewish applicants into the universities, had been introduced before the war in Czarist Russia, including its Polish territories. Poland continued the policy after the war so that, by the 1935/36 academic year, the number of Poles studying at universities and similar institutions was 77.8%. Jews constituted 13.1%, only somewhat more than the 10% which they represented in the population. Of the Jews who had passed entrance examinations but were not accepted into universities because of the numerus clauses, there were some instances of a few converting to Christianity for the sake of a higher education. More frequent were incidents of Jews studying and receiving degrees abroad, especially in the field of medicine (59 Jews in 1933; 93 in 1934; 52 in 1935). That made the number of Jews completing their studies and beginning medical practice closer to 30% of all new graduates.[12]

The numbers alone of Jewish students, however, did not account for antisemitism at the universities. In 1934, one year after Hitler took power, there arose the Oboz Narodowo-Radikalny (National Radical Camp) or Naras, as they were called, a Polish imitation of Germany's Nazi party. After only a few months the Polish government disbanded them for antisemitic violence. They broke up into several smaller groups, among them the Zwiazek Narodowy Polskiej Mlodziezy Radikalnej (National Association of Radical Polish Youth). This group of young Polish fascists was responsible for some of the more deliberately planned actions like the occupation of university buildings.[13] But as Glos Narodu itself admitted, the university disturbances were but one segment of the total antisemitic front in Poland, and it would be impossible to demand indifference to the Jewish question from students when "the whole society is thinking and talking about it."[14]

In their determination to identify Poland with Catholicism, several student organizations succeeded in getting a crucifix hung in the Auditorium Maximum of the University of Warsaw.[15] And reading the pages of a periodical entitled Mlodziez Katolicki, we encounter the thinking not of national radicals but of ordinary Catholic university students who have interiorized the attitudes and concerns of their Catholic elders and church leaders. We find, for example, so unlikely a student concern as Jewish ritual slaughter, decried as barbarous and a ploy to maintain a Jewish monopoly in the meat industry.[16] We find Jews blamed for demoralizing youngsters in public primary schools by introducing coeducation and diminishing the number of hours religion is taught.[17] The Jewish "psyche" and ethic is described as materialistic and cynical, irreconcilable with and posing a danger to the spiritual, idealistic psyche and ethic of Catholic Poland.[18] From a member of the Sodality, a Catholic student organization, we hear about the destructive influence of Jews on all Latin civilization, with an appeal to the authority of Austrian Bishop Gfoellener of Linz: "It is the duty of every good Christian to fight against the spirit of international Judaism, which has aligned itself with international masonry." Such an attitude, we are told, does not mean indulging in racist antisemitism, which has been condemned by the Holy See and whose barbarous methods contradict Christian charity. But it does mean taking measures to isolate Jews so as to protect the rest of society from their harmful influence.[19]

By mid-decade, isolating Jews had become a concern of more than a few Catholic students. It developed into a nation-wide campaign to segregate Jewish university students by compelling them to occupy so-called "ghetto benches." First at the Lwow Polytechnicum in 1935 and then at the University of Wilno, Jews were forced by the other students to take seats in a particular hall.[20] Catholic students saw the ghetto benches as their right and petitioned university and government officials to establish the separate seating by official regulation. Jewish and other sympathetic faculty members resisted the segregation, and the Minister of Education at first regarded the students' demands as unconstitutional. But by 1937, the rectors of the schools of higher learning in Warsaw, as elsewhere, gave in to the students and established the separate seating by official ordinance. The universities had been for some years already the scene of student disturbances. By 1937 shouting matches and scuffles during lectures and physical attacks against Jewish students had become commonplace. University officials justified the ordinance on the grounds that separate seating would be a means of avoiding further disruption and restoring order.[21] Jewish students saw it as an insult to their dignity. They protested with hunger strikes and boycotts, preferring to stand silently during the lectures rather than take the segregated seating.

Threatened with disciplinary action, including expulsion, the Jewish students continued to pressure university administrators for withdrawal of the ghetto benches. They Jewish students were joined in their efforts by sympathetic Polish students, described by the Maly Dziennik as socialists or as known for their radical ideas and leanings toward masonry.[22] As late as August, 1939, Jewish students met with sympathetic democratically inclined professors who promised to intercede with the authorities on their behalf.[23] Professor Michalowicz of Warsaw even declared his determination to resign his chair if the segregation was not discontinued.[24] The German invasion the following month precluded the necessity of any such action on his part.

With notable exceptions like Professor Michalowicz, Catholic leadership was either indifferent to or aggressively in favor of the ghetto benches. Michalowicz had earlier forbidden the segregated seating in his lectures as unconstitutional and contrary to his conscience as a faithful Christian.[25] The more typical reaction like that of Glos Narodu saw it as "natural and basically healthy" that Polish students were concerning themselves with the Jewish question. It was a "manifestation of patriotism" that student newspapers were bluntly calling for Poland's emancipation from a Jewish domination that constituted a virtual "fourth partition." The students have cause for alarm. Looking at the future, they have to fear that their studies will not lead them to employment in fields being filled with Jews, like law and medicine.[26]

The Jewish community and its organizations joined the students in their struggle against the ghetto benches, seeing them as only a first step in an attempt to segregate Jews and then eliminate them from the professions altogether. There was little reason to believe that the benches would lead to peace in the classroom when the leaders of student organizations in Warsaw issued a statement naming Jews as the "primary obstacle" to Poland achieving greatness. The Jewish question would only be resolved when the last Jew leaves Poland. In the meantime, the student representatives called for such measures as: removing Jews from the army, requiring them instead to pay a tax or do compulsory labor; removing Jews from all jobs in national and local government; withdrawing Polish citizenship from all Jews who obtained it after 1918; not allowing Jews of Masons to serve as professors or lecturers in universities; not recognizing the diplomas obtained by Jews abroad; not allowing Jews to change their names to Polish.[27]

Not satisfied with ghetto benches at the universities, the Maly Dziennik ran an article calling for their introduction into public high schools.[28] As part of a series on the "nationalizing of Polish life," it published letters from high school students echoing the sentiments of their Catholic parents and teachers: Don't buy anything from Jews. . . . England, France, and Denmark don't want them; why should Poland be the haven for the world's Jews? . . .Let them find a place in Madagascar, Cameroon, Tanzania, or Guiana.[29]

While it generally tolerated or even welcomed the students' antisemitic attitudes, the Catholic press was also at least mildly critical of violent manifestations of those attitudes. Glos Narodu, for example, saw no causal relationship between the two: "Despite our entire sympathy for the anti-Jewish reaction of society, we must say that in the academic sector this movement is at times taking on unethical and unchivalrous forms. There is no right to lynch anyone. No one may be beaten for being a Jew." The editors did not care to believe that students with Catholic convictions were perpetrating the violence, and then excused them as being carried away by passion without thinking of the consequences.[30] The Catholic daily took pride in the fact that antisemitic incidents in Krakow did not degenerate to excesses, or "at least very rarely." While critical of deliberate, systematic actions like student occupation of university buildings, Glos Narodu withheld indignation for accts committed in the heat of passion. Instead it blamed the heightened aggressiveness of the students on the "indifference of society," for not realizing the students' hopelessness. The older generation must replace their "platonic" support with one that is real and active. This will not encourage but prevent the excesses "that shock us" by making them unnecessary.[31]

A much more consistent position toward student violence was taken earlier by Father a. Szymanski in the pages of Prad, a publication of the more democratically inclined Catholic student organization Odrodzenie (Rebirth). Though he insisted that Poland must be a Catholic nation, he expressed a sympathetic understanding of the difficulties Jews face as a minority in a country where they are required to keep their stores closed on Sunday as well as their own Sabbath. He criticized student violence as social anarchy and against the commandments. Christ the Good Shepherd provides for sheep, not wolves. The priest especially decried the occasions when students used the Mass for nationalist demonstrations. They would leave church shouting antisemitic slogans and rampage in the Jewish quarter, where they would break windows and destroy property, eventually clash with the police and be arrested. It was a minority of students who acted this way, the priest admitted, but their behavior should not be trivialized. It is a profanation of religion.[32]

Exactly what percentage of Polish students engaged in violence is impossible to say. A memorandum of the American Jewish Congress cites a statement by Senator Malinowski (February 12, 1937), which gave the number of Polish students participating in riots as 1,500 out or 48,000.[33] That would make the numbers approximately three percent. More pertinent to our consideration is the relative silence of the Catholic hierarchy and clergy in the face of this student rioting. One hears no high level calls from chanceries or pulpits against the ghetto benches and but few condemnations of student violence. Professor Michalowicz's rejection of ghetto benches on the basis of his Catholic conscience received notice precisely because of its exceptional nature. And he did not go without rebuttal.

One of the most prominent clerical antisemites in interwar Poland was Monsignor Stanislaus Trzeciak. He responded to Michalowicz in the pages of Maly Dziennik by quoting the New Testament and identifying the Jews of their day with Jesus' adversaries. "You are of your father the devil, and you will is to do your father's desires." (Jn. 8,44). He accused Jews of "satanic" works in russia, Mexico, and Spain,, and of trying to demoralize and revolutionize Poland. "If your hand or your foot causes you to sin, cut it off and throw it from you" (Mt. 18,8). Revolutionary, anti-governmental activity spreads like gangrene in the Jewish community and must be isolated and amputated. Why should ghetto benches be unconstitutional, when the Jews themselves practice separate seating for women in the synagogue? Jews constitute an alien, hostile, and harmful force in Polish society and require isolation. Jews require not only ghetto benches at universities but "numerus nullus," no admission at all.[34]

Trzeciak was not the only Catholic to call for numerus nullus at universities. Writing in Pro Christo -- Wiara i Czyn (For Christ -- Faith and Action), Ignacy Zaleski warned against believing that the fall in numbers of Jewish university students would in time transform the structure of Poland's educated class. The Jewish community was too strong, wealthy, and organized, and Polish students too poor and encumbered by the indifference of the past. Jewish competition was a threat to Polish culture, a festering ulcer needing to be lanced. Half-measures were like band-aids; only depriving Jews of their political rights would do.

Depriving Jews of access to Polish universities was a first step in that direction.[35] Sentiments like these had their impact, and by 1938, in some university departments at least, numerus nullus was de facto if not de jure in effect. for the 1938/39 academic year, no new Jewish students were admitted into the departments of medicine and pharmacy at the University in Krakow. In Lwow no Jews were accepted into the Academy of Veterinary Medicine or the department of mechanics at the Polytechnic. In Warsaw no Jews were accepted into the department of veterinary medicine or pharmacy. In Poznan, for the second year in a row, no Jews were accepted into the university at all.[36]

A Pole who criticized the ghetto benches or university admission policies would be blatantly accused by the Maly Dziennik of "democratic liberalism," socialist or masonic tendencies, or of serving Jewish interests.[37] Much more sophisticated was the Przeglad Powszechny (Universal Review), a high-level journal edited by the Jesuits and arguably the premier vehicle of Polish Catholic scholarship. Here we find a thoughtful consideration of the "Nationality of christ and Ghetto Benches" by a priest who would become one of Poland's most prolific and respected theologian, Wincenty Granat. He confronts those who argue that ghetto benches must be condemned, that separation from Jews means separation from Christ. Granat rejected the racist theories of those who deny Jesus' Jewishness and claim he is an aryan. He admitted that ghetto benches would be morally evil if they would lead to hatred and prevent the conversion of Jews to the church. But if these extremes can be avoided, separation from Jews can not only be permitted but in some cases even required by Catholic teaching. Catholics are entitled to have their faith and Christian morals protected from spiritual disintegration. Jews constitute a high percentage of anarchists and atheists, and the declarations of popes and synods attest to their bad example. The recent Plenary Synod of Polish Bishops rejected the coeducation of Catholic children with Jews. Segregation may be seen as a means of self-defence. Moreover, love of country may require separating Jews from Polish society in order to defend it from being spiritually disarmed or lost altogether.

Ghetto benches, Granat argued, are not necessarily a symbol of racial hatred. A Polish nationalist may not uncritically adopt the racial theories of Nazi Germany, and a Catholic may not fight against a Jew as such. But every race has its virtues and vices, and Poles may fight against Jewish vices, so long as they do not embrace unchristian theories or unethical methods of warfare. Poland has not established ghettos. Polish Jews have free access to all spheres of cultural and economic life. The Jewish intelligentsia is free to disseminate its ideas about humanitarianism, free thought, sexual license, and "progress." It is free to fight against those they call "clericalists and anti-cultural hooligans of the nationalist camp." Professors of the old liberal stripe trivialize the ghetto benches as an inconsequential youthful prank. But college youth are a seismograph of ideological change. They cannot create their own ghetto, so they seek a symbol. In an age marked by nationalist symbols like the swastika, fasces, hammer and sickle, "Polish youth regard the ghetto benches as one of the symbols of national rebirth."[38]

VIOLENCE ON THE STREETS

The international economic crisis of the 1930s hit Poland with particular severity. Mid the anger and frustration of joblessness, the news from Nazi Germany struck a responsive chord among antisemitic National Radicals, National Democrats or "Endeks," and a wide spectrum of youth. Whether it was a handful of hoodlums assaulting Jewish pedestrians or a full-scale riot, the Polish Catholic press would invariably describe an act of anti-Jewish violence as an "incident" (zajscie). After the death of Marshall Pilsudski in 1935, the frequency of such "incidents" increased along with the death toll and destruction.

> The stabbing of a Pole by a Jew sparked a riot in Grodno (1935). National Democrats were held responsible for the riot, which left one person dead, at least six injured, and thousands of dollars of broken glass. The issue, wrote the Maly Dziennik, was "not separate sporadic excesses but the reaction of almost all informed Polish society which intends to shake off its dependency on Jews. . . .The Jewish question is agitating the whole society."[39]
>
> In Przytyk (1936), National Democrats attempted to impose a boycott of Jewish businesses by haranguing Polish customers away. When a fight led to a riot in which a Christian was killed, mob violence resulted in two more deaths and the virtual destruction of the Jewish quarter. The Nationalists were

> inciting anarchy, charged the Minister of the Interior, Premier Skladowski. He blamed them for three deaths and ninety-nine instances of Jews being beaten.[40]
>
> In Brest-Litovsk (1937) a riot was set off when a Jewish butcher killed a policemen. For sixteen hours the rioting raged as the police looked on and the governor did nothing to stop the violence. Three Jews were killed,, more than fifty injured, and the Jewish quarter laid waste. The following month, a similar incident in the pilgrimage city of Czestochowa led to a week of pillaging, until calls for peace from the local bishop and mayor finally restored calm. When Jewish newspapers described the rioters as robbing Jewish stores, Maly Dziennik cried "lies!" The mob did not rob, it threw the goods from the stores into the street.[41]

The church could hardly ignore the violence that was sweeping Poland. The head of the Evangelical Church in Poland, Dr. Boursche, denounced the antisemitism as "un-Christian." He declared that violence against Jews contradicted Christian ethics and that pastors under his jurisdiction would preach against antisemitism in their churches.[42] The Catholic press and clergy responded as well, but in a tone set by the bishops. Their criticism of the violence was much more nuanced and hardly denunciatory.

Certainly the most celebrated response was the 1936 statement of the Primate, Cardinal Hlond. In it he proclaimed that Nazi racial theories and violence against Jews are contrary to Christian ethics. It is "forbidden," he wrote, to "demolish a Jewish store, damage their merchandise, break windows, or throw things at their homes. . . .It is forbidden to assault, beat up, maim, or slander Jews." the context for these moral prescripts, however, was a statement by the Cardinal, identifying Jews with bolshevism, theism, usury, fraud, and prostitution. Jews, he charged, are corrupting morals and waging war on the church. While discouraging violence, he encouraged Catholic Poles to "prefer your own kind" when shopping. "One may love one's own country more, but one may not hate anyone. Not even Jews."[43]

Earlier in 1934, before the bloodier riots, a delegation of rabbis had visited Cardinal Alexander Kakowski in Warsaw. They pointed out the influences that Germany was having on "a certain faction, especially youth," bullying and beating Jews on the streets. The rabbis petitioned the Cardinal to issue a pastoral letter, to appeal for an end to the violence that was defaming Poland's good name. Kakowski's published response was to "condemn all violence and excesses, from whatever side they come from, whether Catholic or Jewish. Even the most complex questions and problems should be resolved in accord with the dictates of Christian ethics." But then the cardinal went on to point out that Jewish atheists are "fighting against the Christian religion, ridiculing its dogmas, and insulting its clergy." Jewish publishers were "inundating" Poland with pornography. While not all Jews are responsible for them, such actions "have helped to create antisemitic feelings in the Polish community and may have led to regrettable excesses."[44] If subsequent reporting of this meeting is any measure, it was not the Cardinal's criticism but explanation of antisemitism that made the most lasting impression on Catholic consciousness.

When the Jewish press accused the Catholic clergy of not speaking out against antisemitic violence, the Catholic Press Agency (KAP), semi-official organ of the Polish bishops, responded; "All excesses and brutal means of war are unworthy of the name Christian and ultimately do not attain their goal. The Catholic clergy certainly does not approve of any violence and does not neglect to remind the faithful that the highest commandment of Christian ethics is the command of love of God and love of neighbor without regard to race, nationality, or religion. . . .But Jews who complain about excesses ought to remember that they are not without fault in this regard." The statement then proceeded to advocate a "cultural separation of Poles from Jews" because of Jewish radicalism, bad example on Polish youth, and the "negative traits in the Jewish character which grate on Christians." The Jews themselves could help keep people calm by "overcoming the faults, which render mutual co-existence difficult."[45]

The tone set by the bishops and their press agency resonated in the rest of the clergy and Catholic press. Their ambivalence was exemplified by Glos Narodu: violence against Jews is unethical and "primitive." Breaking windows does not solve Poland's Jewish question. Leave the windows alone but empty the Jewish stores of Christian clients. That is the only effective method of ridding Poland of the Jews.[46] Primitivism was a typical and early criticism of Nazi Germany in the Polish Catholic press. Poles could understand and even sympathize with Germany's antisemitism but not when it employed violence and banditry. The Nazis were "hooligans" behaving like "wild animals," like the "Vandals and Huns of old."[47]

While the Catholic press used such disparaging language for the Nazis, when describing Poland's own antisemites, the rhetoric proved much more defensive. "It is permissable to defend yourself against an aggressor," wrote Fr. Paul Kuczka in Kultura. Jews are advocating divorce, free-love, and birth control. They encourage distrust in the Catholic clergy. "We stand before a life and death struggle with Judaism. The fate of the church and nation hangs in the balance." Unlike that of Germany, Poland's nationalism follows Christian principles. But Jews are fomenting revolutionary unrest. They are capitalists, communists, socialists, and masons. They have chosen certain Catholic countries for "subversive experiments." France has fallen as their first victim. "The ethical stand in our war with the Jews is clear. Christian ethics allows you to defend yourself against an aggressor, even if the aggressor should thereby lose his life."

War is evil, Fr. Kuczka admitted, but in defense of superior values, a "necessary evil." although you may elect to voluntarily suffer personal harm, you may not stand by passively when the life of a neighbor or of the nation is threatened. "Whatever the consequences for an aggressor that result from a war, he is responsible for them himself." If you had a guest who demoralized your children, took away their bread and ideals, would you hesitate to throw that guest out of your house just because he might thereby sprain an ankle? What would have happened to Poland at the Battle of Grunwald if its defenders had been afraid to use the sword? "We do not have to worry about the fate of the Jews. They are a hundred times richer and more powerful on this earth than we are and can manage without Polish bread, whereas we would perish without it."[48]

Justifiable self-defense was the appeal CAtholics made not only against Jewish revolutionaries. One had only to visit Warsaw's Jewish quarter, Nalewki, to experience the hostile, foreign atmosphere there. Nothing comparable could be found in Poland among Germans and Ukrainians. Polish antisemitism is a "healthy reaction against a foreign body" that requires expulsion.[49]

Economic self-defense was the excuse used to explain the violence at Przytyk. The polish peasant "has ceased to be a source of exploitation and experiment for others." In some areas of Poland, especially in the east, Polish farmers must deal exclusively with Jews who not only buy and sell but set the price. Sometimes the farmer does not see a single cent. Because of poverty, massive emigration from the farms to small cities has brought Polish peasants into economic competition with Jews for jobs in trade and commerce.[50]

Blaming the victims is a commonly observed reaction to violence, and the Polish Catholic press proved no exception. When innocent Jewish pedestrians were attacked by a gang in Wilno, the Maly Dziennik announced, "Incidents provoked by Jews." A Polish youth who had been shouting out support for Christian commerce had been manhandled by Jews earlier in the day.[51] The violence at Brest-Litovsk was the "harvest of hatred," wrote Maly Dziennik, not Polish hatred of Jews but "the incredible fanaticism of Jewish hatred." When the Jewish butcher killed the Polish policeman, there was a spontaneous, impulsive, uncontrollable reaction. Rather than railing with hatred against Poles, Jews should stop crying persecution and emigrate. "There is a lot of gunpowder lying round and every spark leads to an explosion." No appeals for peace and calm from the Polish side will do any good when Jews are making the sparks.[52]

In view of the Catholic press, antisemitism in Poland was caused by the Jews, not only the revolutionary atheists but the religious orthodox as well. In Poland as elsewhere in Catholic europe, there was a long-standing belief that the Talmud permitted Jews to practice a double-standard of ethics, one for Gentiles, another for one's fellow Jews. The Talmud, it was claimed, allowed cheating, theft, and false oaths.[53] Especially vicious in these accusations was the priest editor of Pro Christo, Fr. Marian Wisniewski. Because of their dishonest talmudic principles, he wrote, the Jews were most to blame for Poland's economic problems. Not for their race were Jews to be condemned but for their "diabolical" Talmud, in whose name they do battle with christ and the church and undermine Catholic faith and family.[54] Catholic authors had to make it quite clear that they were not expounding the racial antisemitism that had been condemned by the Vatican. Hence Pro Christo emphasized that it was not condemning Jews as such nor disparaging the Hebrew Scriptures. The Old Testament was divinely revealed, but not the Talmud with its superstitions and unethical principles. By embracing the Talmud, Jews had "betrayed" Moses and become "apostates" from the faith of Abraham and the bible. A work of human hatred and despair, hostile to Christianity and rife with blasphemies, the Talmud "may not be regarded as a religious book, which we are obliged to tolerate."[55]

All Poles did not respond to antisemitic violence in the same way. Some of the Polish intelligentsia attempted to counteract antisemitism in the pages of the Wiadomosci Literackie (Literary News) and in 1936 began planning for a congress in Lwow on the "Battle with Antisemitism." Maly Dziennik called into question the Polishness and patriotism of these critics, painting them as left-wing liberals associated with masonry and under the influence of Jews. It could not approve of violence against Jews, wrote the Catholic daily, but neither would it close its eyes to the violence which the "Polish-Jewish intelligentsia" was perpetrating. By combatting antisemitism, these Polish intellectuals were promoting the supremacy of Jews in all areas of Polish life. Such a Poland would be "communist-Jewish" and no longer Poland.[56]

The educated were not the only Poles to criticize the antisemitic wave of the 30s. When the clergy advocated the expulsion of Jews from the country, ordinary CAtholics would question if it were Christian to deprive people of a roof over their heads just because they were Jews. Then too there was the attitude that "all Jews are scoundrels, but the Jew I deal with is exceptionally decent." The Przewodnik Katolicki (Catholic Guide), a popularly written weekly, dealt with such scruples with a variety or arguments. there simply was not the room in Poland for all the "exceptionally decent Jews," since practically every Pole knows one. And where you find counterfeiting, pornography, and prostitution, there too you will find a Jew. The popular Catholic weekly described antisemitism as a badge of honor. It means you love your own nation more than you do strangers. The contrary means "you wear a Jewish coat and hundreds of Poles shiver from the cold for lack of work. You wear Jewish shoes and hundreds of your countrymen go barefoot, because Polish workplaces are not open. You give your wages to Jews, and thousands of your unemployed brethren go hungry." There is no need to abuse or persecute Jews. Just support your follow Catholics, your own kind.[57]

To justify if not violence at least their prejudice, Poland's Catholic antisemites had to answer the objection that they were not repudiating the gospel. Jesus had commanded love of neighbor, love even of enemies. How could antisemitism be reconciled with such clear Christian teaching? The Catholic answers to that question have already been insinuated, but it bears observing that both clerical and lay Catholics felt obliged to deal with it. Their rationalizations of antisemitism took a variety of turns.

One young writer, a student, distinguished between the obligations of individuals and those of societies. What is admirable and proper for an individual may be irresponsible for a society. The "Jewish Question" in Poland is not one of individuals but of a Catholic society defending itself and its culture from the destructive influence of Jewish culture. Positively, this means Catholics should imitate Jewish solidarity and expand their culture.[58]

Another student interpreted the commandment by distinguishing between spiritual and material interests. When it comes to purely material matters, you may put your neighbor before yourself, as was taught in the parable of the Good Samaritan. But in spiritual matters, as St. Thomas Aquinas teaches, there is a hierarchy of responsibility: first to care about your own soul, then those who belong to you, your family and nation, and finally total strangers. As Cardinal Kakowski indicated to the rabbis, Jews are demoralizing the country. The whole Christian world is being depraved by Jews with their movies, cabarets, and modern ways od dancing. It is precisely the love of neighbor that commands us to save ourselves and those near to us from moral downfall. Living together with Jews hinders our salvation. Like Jesus we must drive away Satan and those who aid him. Of course, Catholics will not use weapons except when necessary in self-defense. Economic measures and depriving Jews of all positions of influence will be enough to have them leave.[59]

Of all Catholic periodicals, Pro Christo was predictably among the most radical. We are bound to love our own more than we love strangers. When you hang a bandit or lock up a thief in defense of your fellow-citizens, you do injury to the aggressor but are demonstrating true love for your neighbor. Poland need not remain a second Palestine forever. Poles have a right to defend themselves from Jews without worrying about the injury they may inflict thereby. Jews are like ungrateful guests who have takes over the home of their host. Jews and their Judaized Polish allies are trying to blackmail Catholics by holding up the commandment to love your neighbor. But it is the church and its priests, not the rabbis, who give the true interpretation of the commandment. "The church has always taught that war and the vindication of one's just rights in no way contradicts the Christian religion or love of neighbor, and aryans ought not to scruple in this regard when defending themselves against Jews."[60]

An angry article on "Love and Hate" by one Fr. Charszewski was published in Pro Christo in response to a Christmas poem that had appeared in a secular daily paper. The poem had described Polish children taking pity on a Jew and a German, both refugees from the Nazis. A heavenly figure then appears and breaks the traditional Polish Christmas wafer with the German, the Jew, and the Polish children. This, wrote the priest, was no less than sacrilege, breaking the Christmas wafer with a non-believer and, if a German refugee from the Reich, then obviously a communist. Charszewski proceeded to criticize Polish sentimentality, "dulcis sanguis Polonorum." Toleration is a national failing of the Poles, and it is a falsified gospel that tries to justify it. The "accursed liberals" try to defend Jews in the name of progress and Christian love, but as there is no salvation, neither is there progress outside the church. And having real love requires having real hate. Real love demands hating cruelty and tyranny, and that means hating and fighting against not only communism but liberalism as well, for one leads to the other. As Pope Pius XI taught, the father of socialism is liberalism, and its heir will be communism. Liberals rejoice in the persecution of Catholics in Mexico and Spain. Quite properly Pope Pius IX called liberalism a "pestis perniciosissima," a most pernicious pestilence. Liberals claim to defend the oppressed, but their cold altruism and false humanitarianism is only an attempt to ape the Christian love of neighbor. Liberals accuse Christians of being animals for refusing to allow themselves to be devoured by them. Poland has been paradise for Jews but purgatory for its own people. There may be some exceptional and fine persons who are Jews but they all follow their leaders. The "synagogue of Satan" is in a struggle with the church, but they will not prevail so long as there is more true love and true hate.[61]

Finally, if antisemitism occasionally led to violence in Poland, the church could point to the fact that things were worse elsewhere. The Catholic press took offense at the fact that Jews were sending reports to foreign newspapers about persecution in Poland. How could one speak about persecution when every day hundreds of Jews were seeking asylum in Poland and escape from Austria, Germany, Czechoslovakia, and Hungary? One of the Jewish representatives to the Polish parliament, Grynbaum, after a trip abroad, was quoted as saying: "When you leave Poland and see what it is like, you then return gladly."[62]

In light of the foregoing, one can understand why there were no expressions of outrage at the Kristallnacht pogrom from the bishops and clergy of Poland. They were hardly in a position to condemn Germany and Austria, when they had not condemned antisemitic violence in Poland. To be sure, the Catholic leadership in Poland regularly described violence as unethical; but the tone of the criticism was too muted, and the criticism itself too hedged around with the elaboration of circumstances to warrant being called a condemnation. And rather than criticize, let alone condemn the anti-Jewish hostility that regularly generated the violence, the Polish Catholic press saw it as a "healthy" nationalism, properly committed to keeping Poland and Polish culture identified with Catholicism.

In their struggle against separation of church and state in Poland, Catholic leaders waged war against those most interested in effecting and maintaining that separation. Their hatred of liberalism as much as their fear of communism fueled the clergy's crusade to limit as much as possible the secularizing influences of liberal Jews and their non-Jewish allies. The ghetto benches were both a symbol and a fist step toward segregating Jews and circumscribing their impact on Polish society. The violence that erupted around the ghetto benches and economic boycott was regarded as an unfortunate but inevitable by product of a necessary struggle. Victims of antisemitic violence were unlucky but not altogether innocent casualties of war. With the analogy of a just war to define Catholic efforts to maintain a preferred status for the church, violence could be justified as self-defense. Hatred of those designated as enemies could be rationalized as love for family and neighbor. Indifference, or worse, Catholic criticism of antisemitism could be interpreted as aiding the aggressor. Traditional Polish tolerance, formerly a virtue, could be rebuked as a vice to be uprooted, or at least a virtue that could no longer be afforded.

Catholic leaders in Poland criticized the antisemitic brutality in Germany and Austria as barbarous and primitive. But self-interest prevented them from criticizing too loudly. When that brutality came to Poland in September of 1939, it was too late to inaugurate a massive change of public opinion. Mental habits and attitudes had become too ingrained, and when the German death machines began to operate on occupied Polish soil, the characters were already defined. Catholic orthodoxy had helped define them: the Poles were victims but Jews, if not enemies, were aliens. Certainly the numbers changed the nature of the crime, but the precedents has already been set. Antisemitic violence was always unethical, but it could be explained.

NOTES

1. Yehuda Bauer, A History of the Holocaust (New York: Franklin Watts, 1982), pp. 108-109. See also the standard reference works.

2. National Catholic Welfare Council News Service, 5 December 1938.

3. Maly Dziennik, 9 November 1938.

4. Ibid., 11 November 1938.

5. Ibid., 19 November 1938.

6. Wieclaw Myslek, Kosciol Katolicki w Polsce w Latach 1918-1939 (Warsaw: Ksiazka i Wiedza, 1966), p. 205.

7. Glos Narodu, 16 November 1938.

8. Ibid., 19 November 1938.

9. Ezra Mendelsohn, The Jews of East Central Europe Between the World Wars (Bloomington: Indiana University, 1983), pp. 73, 186-189.

10. Pro Christo, 13/5 (1937) p. 7.

11. Mendelsohn, Jews of East Central Europe, p. 27.

12. Pro Christo, 13/5 (1937) p. 8.

13. Glos Narodu, 29 November 1936.

14. Ibid., 29 October 1936.

15. Maly Dziennik, 23 January 1936.

16. Mlodziez Katolicki (1936) pp. 15-17.

17. Ibid., (1936) pp. 13-16.

18. Ibid., (1935) pp. 9-12.

19. Ibid., (1934) pp. 22-23.

20. Mendelsohn, Jews of East Central Europe, p. 73.

21. Maly Dziennik, 9 October 1937.

22. Ibid., 9 October 1937; 30 October 1937.

23. Ibid., 26 August 1939.

24. Ibid., 10 August 1939.

25. Ibid., 26 October 1937.

26. Glos Narodu, 29 October 1936; 27 November 1936.

27. Maly Dziennik, 8 June 1938.

28. Ibid., 14 September 1938.

29. Ibid., 23 March 1939.

30. Glos Narodu, 29 October 1936.

31. Ibid., 27 November 1936.

32. Prad (1932) pp. 239-245.

33. The American Hebrew, 23 July 1937, p. 13.

34. Maly Dziennik, 26 October 1938.

35. Pro Christo, 13/5 (1937) p. 15.

36. Maly Dziennik, 27 October 1938.

37. Ibid., 12 July 1937.

38. Przeglad Powszechny, 217 (1938) pp. 181-185.

39. Maly Dziennik, 23 November 1935; 4 February 1936.

40. Ibid., 16 January 1937.

41. Maly Dziennik, 25 June 1937.

42. The American Hebrew, 26 February 1937, p. 925.

43. August Cardinal Hlond, Na Strazy Sumienia Narodu (Ramsey, New Jersey: Don Bosco, 1951), pp. 38-52.

44. Wiadomosci Archidiecezalne Warszawskie (1934) pp. 248-249.

45. Prad (1936) pp. 81-82.

46. Glos Narodu, 5 July 1936.

47. Pro Christo, 9 (1933) pp. 501-503.

48. Paul Kuczka, Kultura, 8 November 1936.

49. Eugeniusz Januszkiewicz, Kultura, 29 August 1937.

50. Stanislaw Nowak, Kultura, 12 July 1936.

51. Maly Dziennik, 8 September 1938.

52. Ibid., 20 May 1937.

53. Nowak, Kultura, 12 July 1936.

54. Pro Christo, 10 (1934) pp. 246-248.

55. Ibid., 14/9 (1938) pp. 306-307.

56. Maly Dziennik, 14 June 1936.

57. Przewodnik Katolicki (1935) pp. 676-677; (1938) p. 28.

58. Mlodziez Katolicki (1934) pp. 24-25.

59. Ibid., (1935) pp. 12-14.

60. J. Dobrowolski, Pro Christo, 10 (1934) pp. 262-268.

61. X. Charszewski, ibid., pp. 331-360.

62. Przewodnik Katolicki (1939) p. 83.

METROPOLITAN ANDREI SHEPTYTS'KYI, UKRAINIANS AND JEWS DURING AND AFTER THE HOLOCAUST

S. REDLICH

History Department, Ben-Gurion University of the Negev,
Beer-Sheva, Israel

When we say "remembering" - what do we actually mean? Jewish collective memory? the non-Jews' reactions to the Holocaust? or perhaps - an attempt to reconstruct an "impartial" picture of "what actually happened"? The prevailing tendency among Jews has been to remember primarily and very often exclusively their pain and tragedy. It seems that traumatization prevents us from admitting those relatively few instances of compassion and assistance "from the outside." Is this the correct way to view the past and remember it for the future? Shouldn't we rather seek a more realistic, though by no means artificially balanced, approach?

Jewish attitudes towards Metropolitan Andrei Sheptyts'kyi (1865-1944), archbishop of L'viv and head of the Ukrainian Uniate [Greek Catholic] Church in Galicia, could serve as an example of a "selective" memory and conflicting interpretations. In order to do justice to truth and history Sheptyts'kyi should be examined within several contexts: the history of the Ukrainians and their relations with Russians/Soviets, Poles and Germans/Nazis; Ukrainian-Jewish relations; Sheptyts'kyi's attitude towards Ukrainian nationalism and his theological stand vs. Jews. There is no question that Sheptyts'kyi became throughout his lifetime and still remains today a controversial figure. Some consider him a saint and a saviour, while others accuse him of collaboration. The following would be an attempt to reconstruct a multidimensional Sheptyts'kyi, often motivated by conflicting interests and acting within changing and tragic realities.

For centuries, Ukrainians and Jews lived side by side in Eastern Europe and were usually part of a "triangle", whose base was the ruling element, either Poles or Russians, and whose sides were formed by Ukrainians and Jews. Only the proper understanding of this "triangular" relationship provides a true historical background.

Jews performed the role of economic middlemen between the Polish nobility and the Ukrainian peasantry. This, of course, caused hostile attitudes towards Jews. Ukrainians also tended to believe that the Jew had control over their churches, although historically this may be quite incorrect. The image of the Jew in Ukrainian folk-tradition assumed the form of somebody who controls both property and spirit. Moreover, anti-Semitism became in time a significant component within the evolving Ukrainian nationalism.

The Chmielnicki pogroms of the 17th century, a symbol and prototype of Jewish martyrdom, as well as the Haidamack atrocities of the 18th century had a traumatic effect on the collective memory of East European Jewry. Chmielnicki and the Cossacks, who represent to the Jews the very essence of cruelty, were and are perceived by the Ukrainians as symbols of national heroism. This diametrically opposed perception of historical personalities and events makes mutual understanding and compassion very difficult. The pogroms of the 1880s and the early 20th century, as well as anti-Jewish outbursts in the wake of the Bolshevik revolution, continued to reinforce the image of the Ukrainian as murderer and pogromchik. Attempts at Ukrainian-Jewish coexistence and cooperation within the framework of an independent Ukrainian state were short-lived.

Eastern Europe continued to form the major arena of Ukrainian-Jewish relations in the years between the two world wars, although considerable numbers of Jews and Ukrainians emigrated to the New World. Those who remained in Europe found themselves again close to each other in independent Poland and in Soviet Russia. There seemed to be a chance for improved relations on both sides of the border; but in spite of some efforts towards parliamentary cooperation in Poland during the 1920s, Ukrainians basically tended to view their Jewish neighbours as natural allies of the ruling Poles. The aggravation of the nationality problem in Poland in the 1930s and especially the growing oppression of the Ukrainian minority by the Poles, had a negative effect. This presented new opportunities for Fascist and Nazi influence in Ukrainian nationalist circles. Traditional anti-Semitism began to absorb the racist theories of Nazism.

As for the USSR, the new regime tried to eradicate anti-Semitism in the 1920s and some parallel national interests of both Jews and Ukrainians emerged in Soviet Ukraine. However, the onset of Stalinism in the 1930s caused a renewed inflammation of dormant antagonisms. The growing role of the security apparatus, the Stalinist terror and, above all, the horrors of collectivization - became linked in the Ukrainian mind with the image of Judeo-Bolshevism. This image grew even worse during the short but significant period of 1939-41, when Eastern Poland was ennexed by the Soviets. The Jew was again perceived by the local Ukrainian population as a collaborator with the hated Bolshevik regime. All this took place on the eve of the Nazi occupation of Eastern Poland, densely populated by both Jews and Ukrainians. This was also the immediate background to the Holocaust.

What were Sheptyts'kyi's attitudes toward and relations with Jews before the war?

Knowledge of Jews and Judaism was part and parcel of Sheptyts'kyi's intellectual and practical environment since his youth. We know that at the age of twenty, Sheptyts'kyi started his study of Hebrew, which he continued in his later life. This must have been the beginning of his interest in Semitic studies. Within a relatively short period of time he could both write and speak Hebrew. In August 1905, he travelled to the Holy Land with a group of Moravian pilgrims, and in September 1906 he returned there with a pilgrimage of about 500 Ukrainians, who visited various points of interest to Christians. Sheptyts'kyi apparently planned to found there a Greek-Catholic center for pilgrims.

Sheptyts'kyi's social and philanthropic activities formed one of his major concerns to which he devoted time and money. In the early 1920s, he travelled through western Europe and North America in order to collect funds for the victims of World War I in Galicia, especially for orphans. His charitable projects provide a useful precedent and point of reference, when considering his assistance to the Jews during World War II. Already during the early part of the century Sheptyts'kyi's philanthropic deeds extended at times to Jews. Among Sheptyts'kyi's Jewish-oriented philanthrophy was his regular contribution to the pre-Passover collection of funds for the poor of the Jewish communities in eastern Galicia.[1] Moreover, his major social project, the establishment in 1903 of the "Narodnia Lichnytsia" (The People's Clinic) in L'viv (expanded to a full-scale hospital in 1938) was in fact a non-sectarian clinic which served Jews as well as Ukrainians and Poles.[2]

A most indicative expression of Sheptyts'kyi's relations with Jews were his meetings with the elders of Jewish communities during his regular canonical visits. A report on one such visit states that "he was greeted by church processions, the clergy... and also by rabbis with a Torah. He thanked the rabbis and the Jewish delegation in their Hebrew language."[3] The Metropolitan's contacts with Jewish religious and communal leaders in Galicia were apparently welcome and appreciated in Jewish circles. Thus, in July 1935, the Jewish daily Chwila published a greeting by the L'viv Jewish community on the occasion of Sheptyts'kyi's seventieth birthday. The greeting dwelled upon the Metropolitan's high moral and ethical standards, and also mentioned the friendly feelings enjoyed by Sheptyts'kyi among the Jewish population.[4] On that same occasion Sheptyts'kyi was personally greeted by the Chief Rabbi of L'viv, Dr. Ezekiel Lewin.

There is no doubt that genuine feelings of humanitarianism and compassion motivated Sheptyts'kyi in his relations with Jews. However, there were also additional elements behind his Jewish-oriented activities. A pastoral letter entitled "My Hebrew Speeches," distributed by Sheptyts'kyi to Ukrainian Greek Catholic clergy in the early 1900s, may provide a clue to some of his religious and theological motivations.[5] Sheptyts'kyi apparently had been criticized for his "special" relationship with Jews. In his pastoral message, he informed that "antisemitic Viennese journals, having learned about such an event [Sheptyts'kyi's response in Hebrew to Jews greeting him with the Torah] accused me severely of Judaizing."[6]

It is also possible that criticism against his behaviour was voiced among Ukrainian clergy. Sheptyts'kyi decided to respond to these accusations by discussing explicitly his "Jewish encounters". Since his letter seems to be quite significant for our understanding of Sheptyts'kyi's motivations, it will be quoted here at some length.

> "... I believe that when a man who is granted by Christ the task of preaching the Holy Scripture faces nonbelievers, even for a single moment, he should not miss the opportunity to preach God's message to them. When I face assembled Jews, who are ready to listen to me, I cannot avoid considering them as fellow men exposed to eternal perdition. That is why I consider it my duty to take advantage of this opportunity to convey to them at least one word of the Lord's revelations. I accomplish this while talking to them. Indeed, I do it in their tongue and language, since this has been the custom of Christ's church for twenty centuries. The preachers of the Scriptures accomodate themselves to those to whom they preach. This is the only means to bring the represented truth closer to the listener's souls. If such a speech while being greeted with the Torah were made in the Russian or German language, it could not have been the preaching of the Bible but would have made an impression of a secular talk. In such a situation, the preacher must arouse the interest of his audience and touch that part of its soul in which he can find a religious response. This could not be attained even by speaking in the German-Jewish jargon (Yiddish), since that would become a discussion of financial matters. A speech in Hebrew fits this need. Though not everyone of the listeners fully understants this speech, all are more or less familiar with some Messianic texts of the Old Testament. And if in the soul of any amongst them there is a spark of religious sentiment, it might be kindled under the influence of the uttered words of the Holy Scripture. That is why I usually start with a Messianic holy text.
>
> It has often happened that the listeners were so familiar with the text, that they recited it one word ahead of me. To these texts, I add some commentaries in the Christian spirit or another text which leads to a Christian interpretation of the former text. Thus, I offer them as far as possible, the thought of expectation, love, and the search for the Messiah. I do not expect great results. I am satisfied if even one lost soul finds in my words a distant reflection of God's truth and even for a second ponders upon those prayers which are being repeated daily perhaps without any attention..."[7]

Sheptyts'kyi then went on to explain his motivation for financial aid to the Karaites: "For that same reason I contributed a donation to the Galician Karaites, for the poor of their community, and I am ready to talk to them at the first opportunity. I believe that every thread of Christian love for one's fellow man which links the faithful with non-believers may become by the Grace of God, an opportunity for bringing them nearer to Christ's teaching."[8] This explanation may apply as well to Sheptyts'kyi's donations to Jewish communities. Sheptyts'kyi had in mind, at some time, the establishment of Judeo-Christian communities modelled after similar groups in early Christianity. One such community is supposed to have existed in L'viv, but the overall results of this plan were negligible.[9]

The interwar period posed increasing problems and difficulties for Sheptyts'kyi. In the early 1920s, the hopes for Ukrainian independence were thwarted, as we know, by both Bolshevik Rusia and nationalist Poland. The 1930s brought new oppression and suffering to the Ukrainian population on both sides of the border. Forced collectivization, the famine in the Soviet Ukraine and the "pacification" campaign in Poland resulted in growing frustration among the Ukrainians, which in turn bred violence and terror. Sheptyts'kyi, close to the moderates in the Ukrainian political circles, consistently condemned acts of terror by Ukrainian extremists. His consistent pre-war denunciation of violence and terror was a signficant antecedent to his stand on this matter during World War II.

Sheptyts'kyi's attitude vis-a-vis Bolshevik Russia became more critical than in the past. The Bolsheviks loomed in his mind as the personification of a double evil. They were committed in his view against both God and the Ukrainian people. Sheptyts'kyi's outspoken anti-Bolshevik and anti-Communist stand in the interwar years had also some effect on his attitude towards those Jews whom he identified with the hated regime and ideology. Thus already in 1920, when an attempt was made to establish a Soviet republic in Galicia, Sheptyts'kyi criticized it severely and maintained that it was organized by a "Jew-dictator." A church publication close to Sheptyts'kyi wrote in 1936 about a "common front" supported by radicals, socialists, masons and - Jews.[10] It should also be remembered that if throughout the 1930s Sheptyts'kyi expressed time and again his unequivocal criticism and opposition to

Communism, to the Soviet Union, and to its supporters in the West, he did not show any similar critical sensitivity towards the expansion of Nazi totalitarianism.[11]

In the 1930s Ukrainian public opinion became increasingly influenced by the right wing nationalist organizations and press, which presented an utterly negative image of the Jew. The major elements in the press were: Judeo-Bolshevism; the threat of international Jewry; the Jew as an alien parasite and admiration for the fascist and Nazi models. Numerous anti-Jewish comments appeared in connection with the short-lived but ideologically and emotionally significant episode of Ukrainian Subcarpathian autonomy. Anti-Jewish sentiments were expressed not only in the contents but also via derogatory language and images, part and parcel of traditional Ukrainian antisemitic folklore. Though differenciation and diversification in respect to Jews and Jewish-related issued existed, explicit anti-Semitic views became increasingly visible. This must have contributed to the growing receptivity to anti-Semitic Nazi ideology and propaganda.[12]

We do not know what was the exact stand of the Uniate clergy on Jewish-related issues. We may assume that since many among them were nationalistically minded and since the extremization of Ukrainian nationalism was accompanied by antisemitic overtones, anti-Jewish moods probably increased. However, there were also other voices. Bishop Ivan Buchko, a close associate of Sheptyts'kyi and an enthusiast of the Metropolitan's "Hebrew encounters" with Jews, spoke publicly against anti-Semitism and condemned Hitler's neo-paganism. Buchko also openly supported the anti-Nazi criticism of Cardinals Faulhaber and Innitzer.[13]

The Soviet annexation of eastern Poland in September 1939 created additional tensions between the Jewish and Ukrainian population. In spite of the disruption and suffering inflicted by the Soviets upon Jews and Ukrainians alike, the image of the Jew as a sympathizer with the new regime became prevalent among the non-Jewish population of the annexed territories. There was indeed some Soviet-oriented enthusiasm among Jews. In order to understand this, one should remember the rapidly deteriorating condition of the Jews in pre-war Poland, their apprehensions of what might happen to them under Nazi rule, the atmosphere of lawlessness and violence during the disintegration of Polish authority after the German invasion, and Soviet propaganda concerning the solution of the Jewish problem in the Soviet Union.

Although Soviet condemnation of antisemitism in the annexed territories was far from comprehensive, some Ukrainians indeed were punished for antisemitic behaviour, a fact which might have contributed to further emotional reactions on the part of the Ukrainians.[14] Another factor which undoubtedly affected Ukrainian attitudes towards Jews was the influx of thousands of Jewish refugees fleeing from the German-occupied territories of western and central Poland into western Ukraine. The "visibility" of the Jews thus became increasingly pronounced and contributed to the growth of an anti-Jewish mood.

Such feelings were apparently expressed as well by some church officials in Galicia. One church report on the conditions in the Soviet-occupied section of Poland stated that the best treated group there were Jews. A local bishop in Przemysl complained in his letter to Rome that the diocesan chancery office building had been given to Jews.[15] Sheptyts'kyi himself, in a letter to Cardinal Tisserant, spoke of the "immigration of an enormous number of Jews" who "make life more difficult." Discussing the disruption and changes resulting from the Soviet annexation , the Metropolitan went on to remark that: "The Jews in prodigious numbers invaded the economic life... and gave the activities of the [Soviet] authorities a character of sordid avarice which one is accustomed to see only among Jewish petty merchants..."[16] As the spiritual Christian leader of the Ukrainians, Sheptyts'kyi was particularly saddened and angered by Soviet atheistic education and indoctrination of local Ukrainian youth. In another letter to the Vatican he reported "our greatest fear is for school children and for youth in general... Principals of these schools [under the Soviets] were often Jews or atheists..."[17]

Sheptyts'kyi's most vehement condemnation of Soviet rule was expressed in a letter written a number of weeks after those territories have been captured by the German army, in the summer of 1941.[18] An American authority on the subject commented that the nearly two years of Soviet rule in eastern Galicia "created a state of mind in which the Ukrainians of the area would at least initially welcome any force which opposed the Soviet Union."[19] It seems that in the eyes of many Ukrainians - and to some extent even in the mind of a man like Sheptyts'kyi - Jews were associated with the Ukrainian traumas resulting from their Soviet experience.

The situation changed drastically on June 22, 1941 with Hitler's attack on the Soviet Union. German armies entered L'viv a week later. A basic question relevant to Sheptyts'kyi's attitude towards Jews during the Holocaust is that of Ukrainian attitudes towards the Germans in general and Sheptyts'kyi's reaction to German rule in particular. Without going into the details of the various Ukrainian political and national groupings and their respective stands vis-a-vis Hitler's Germany, one may argue that the overall reaction of the Ukrainian population was one of relief from the Bolshevik regime and hopes for Ukrainian sovereignty to be implemented by Germany. German concessions to the Ukrainian population included the reopening of churches, whose existence had been curtailed during the preceding two years of Soviet rule. This, together with Ukrainian national expectations must have increased pro-German sympathies among Ukrainian clergy.

The occupation of eastern Galicia by German forces resulted in acts of vengeance by Ukrainians against suspected collaborators with the Soviets. Moreover, the prevailing confusion as to German intentions in respect to the Ukraine was used to proclaim Ukrainian statehood. Sheptyts'kyi's initial reaction to the rapidly unfolding events was positive and even enthusiastic. In a pastoral letter "to the Ukrainian people," the Metropolitan declared: "We greet the victorious German army as a deliverer from the enemy."[20] In a letter to the Vatican, written at the end of August 1941, Sheptyts'kyi stated in a similar vein: "We should support the German Army, which freed us from the Bolshevik regime." He also alluded to his hope that a German victory in the war would eliminate "atheistic militant Communism once and for all."[21] Sheptyts'kyi's national and religious interests and their impact on his initial attitude towards Germany, were clearly spelled out. In a letter sent to Hitler in February 1942, signed by Sheptyts'kyi and other Ukrainian personalities, a commitment to Ukrainian-German cooperation was repeated several times. The signatories expressed their hope and wish that Hitler's "New Order" in Europe should make possible the establishment of an independent Ukraine.[22]

Hitler's policies and intentions towards the Slavs were not yet fully apparent, and numerous Ukrainians, Sheptyts'kyi among them, assumed that the mutual Ukrainian-German hatred of Soviet Russia would suffice to cement an anti-Bolshevik alliance and ensure Germany's support for Ukrainian national objectives. At the very same time, the Nazi occupation of western Ukrainian lands portended the ever-growing suffering and ultimately the total annihilation of the Jews.

Immediately upon the arrival of the German army in L'viv, Einzatsgruppe C started to carry out violent acts, including killings of local Jews. Ukrainians participated in these pogrom-like activities. Such anti-Jewish acts were motivated by traditional folk anti-Semitism and by the more recent Jewish-Bolshevik association in the minds of the local Ukrainian population. It should be remembered that Nazi antisemitic propaganda, prior to the war, used extensively the "slogan" of Judeo-Bolshevism. An especially ominous Ukrainian allegation against the Jews was that they cooperated with Soviet security agencies in the arrest and murder of Ukrainians prior to the Soviet abandonment of the city.

Between June 30 and July 7, about 4,000 Jews were massacred in L'viv by German units with the assistance of the Ukrainian auxilliary police. On July 25-27 about 2,000 Jews were murdered in a progrom-like fashion under the slogan of "Petliura days," signifying Ukrainian revenge for the assassination of Semen Petliura by a Jew in 1926. All in all, some 30,000 Jews are estimated to have been murdered in this massive pogrom wave during the first few weeks of Nazi occupation of Eastern Poland. The Ukrainian militia assisted German police units during anti-Jewish "actions" which followed. Ukrainians were also used in German labor and extermination camps.[23] However, there were also Ukrainian moderate organizations which did not engage in anti-Jewish activities.[24] There were also, of course, instances of Ukrainian individuals aiding and saving Jews. According to one estimate hundreds of Ukrainians attempted to aid Jews and about 100 were executed as a result by Nazi authorities.[25] The Ukrainian nationalist underground was either indifferent or outright hostile to the Jews. Similar sentiments prevailed among Ukrainian clergy. This, then, was the general context within which Sheptyts'kyi's wartime attitudes and activities concerning Jews must be viewed.

The tragic and dramatic news of pogrom-like acts by Ukrainians and of the Nazi use of the Ukrainian militia in the rounding up and killing of Jews must have reached Metropolitan Sheptyts'kyi. Dr. Lewin, Chief Rabbi of L'viv and a personal friend of Sheptyts'kyi, asked him to intervene with the rioting mobs: "Sometime ago you told me that you consider yourself a friend of the Jews. I ask you now, in this hour of mortal danger, to give evidence of your friendship. I ask you to save thousands of human lives."[26] A young Ukrainian confessed to the Metropolitan, apparently at the same time, that he had himself "murdered seventy-five people in L'viv in one night."[27] However, it was only in early 1942 that Sheptyts'kyi expressed himself unequivocally on the matter of Ukrainian assistance to the Nazis in their crimes against the Jewish population.

It is possible that during the first few months after the German invasion the 76 year old and ailing Sheptyts'kyi was overwhelmed by the unexpected events and still believed in the establishment of a Ukrainian national entity under German auspices. However, the situation must have become clearer in his mind as time passed. The regular and continuous use of violence by the Germans, as well as the growing disappointment among the Ukrainians in respect to German assistance for their national aspirations, must have had an effect. What disturbed him most was apparently the demoralizing and dehumanizing impact of Nazi behaviour upon the local Ukrainian population, especially Ukrainian youth, many of whom adopted extreme stands already in the 1930s. Sheptyts'kyi expressed such concern on a number of occasions. In a letter to Heinrich Himmler, written in February 1942, the Metropolitan deplored German treatment of the local population, especially of the Jews, and protested against the use of the Ukrainian auxilliary militia in anti-Jewish activities.[28] Sheptyts'kyi considered this appeal of utmost importance. He spoke about it with Rabbi Kahana (one of the Jews assisted and saved by Sheptyts'kyi), and mentioned it in a letter to the Vatican.[29]

The summer of 1942 witnessed in L'viv as well as in Warsaw and other localities the intensification of the Final Solution in the form of mass deportations of Jews to the death camps. Whereas former German "actions" were carried out under various pretexts of "relocation" for labour purposes, the summer 1942 deportations were openly perceived as leading to annihilation. Massive deportations of Jews from the L'viv ghetto took place between August 20-23, the number of the deported reaching 50,000. The events of August 1942 were among the most shocking and cruel throughout the years of Nazi rule in L'viv. It is not surprising, therefore, that a highly dramatic condemnation of the Nazi regime by Sheptyts'kyi appeared in a letter to the Vatican, written in the wake of these events.

The letter actually summed up Sheptyts'kyi's disappointment with and accusations against the German rule. He wrote: "Liberated by the German army from the Bolshevik yoke, we felt a certain relief... [However], gradually the [German] government instituted a regime of truly unbelievable terror and corruption... now everybody agrees that the German regime is perhaps even more evil and diabolic than the Bolshevik [regime]. For more than a year not a day has passed without the most horrible crimes being committed... The Jews are the primary victims. The number of Jews killed in our region has certainly surpassed 200,000... "[30] The murderous and inhuman nature of the German treatment of Jews became increasingly exposed. "In time," according to Sheptyts'kyi, "they began to kill Jews openly in the streets, in full view of the public."[31]

Among the evils of the new way of life under German rule Sheptyts'kyi also mentioned "national chauvinism," alluding perhaps not only to its German aspect. The use of such expressions as "rabid wolves" and "monsters" in describing German rule revealed Sheptyts'kyi's moral judgment of the Hitlerite regime. What hurt Sheptyts'kyi most was the devastating influence of the Nazi-type frame of mind upon his fellow Ukrainians and Greek Catholics. In a letter to Cardinal Tisserant, written in September 1942, Sheptyts'kyi expressed once more his displeasure at the recruitment of Ukrainians into the auxilliary police and for using them by the Germans for "perverted purposes."[32]

Sheptyts'kyi's major attempt to influence the Ukrainian population and to counteract the immoral standards of Nazi rule was carried out through pastoral letters. Some were printed, some were spread by word of mouth. It is nearly impossible to estimate the actual impact of these appeals upon the Ukrainian population and the clergy. However, the very fact that the Metropolitan felt the need to repeat them time and again points to the tremendous difficulties involved.

To what extent were Sheptyts'kyi's pastoral messages meant to stop immoral deeds in respect to the Jewish population? The Jews were not mentioned explicitly in any of his public appeals known to us. One should keep in mind that terror was applied not only to Jews but also in Ukrainian-Polish relations and among the various Ukrainian factions. It is in this general context that the condemnation of crimes committed against Jews should be sought.

Sheptyts'kyi's most famous pastoral letter, issued in November 1942 under the symbolic title, "Thou Shalt Not Kill," deals with all forms of homicide.[33] Although political murder is mentioned as an example, it is sufficiently clear that the letter condemns all kinds of murder. Sheptyts'kyi seems to have been preoccupied with the fear of what he defined as "murder addiction," i.e., the acceptance of the killing of fellow-men as a common norm of behaviour. The fact that Sheptyts'kyi gave a copy of this letter to Rabbi Kahane in 1943, when the latter was hiding in the Metropolitan's quarters, indicates that Sheptyts'kyi himself considered it as a Jewish-related appeal.[34] Yet another indication for Sheptyts'kyi's concern about the massive killings of Jews was his discussion with Dr. Frederic, a French expert on eastern Europe who collaborated with the German Foreign Office and visited Sheptyts'kyi in September 1943. In their conversation, the Metropolitan expressed once more his opinion that "Germany is worse than Bolshevism," and accused the Germans of inhuman behaviour towards Jews.[35]

The two major existing testimonies on Sheptyts'kyi's attempts to rescue Jews during the German occupation are those by Rabbi David Kahana, who served during the 1930s as the Rabbi of the Szatnochy Street Synagogue in L'viv, and by Kurt Lewin, the son of Rabbi Dr. Ezekiel Lewin, Chief Rabbi of the L'viv reform Jewish community on the eve of the war. When Rabbi Lewin visited Sheptyts'kyi in his residence at St. George Hill on July 2, 1941, the Metropolitan urged him to remain there, but the latter decided to go back to his family and congregation. He was apprehended on the same day and murdered together with other Jews. It is perhaps symbolic of Ukrainian-Jewish relations at the time, that whereas the leading Ukrainian eccelsiastic personality offered his assistance to Rabbi Lewin, other Ukrainians took part in killing him.[36] After the Rabbi's death, contacts were maintained between Sheptyts'kyi and the Lewin family. On Sheptyts'kyi's recommendation, the Rabbi's two sons, Kurt (Isaac) and Nathan, stayed at various Greek Catholic monasteries and at St. George's Cathedral complex until the arrival of the Red Army in L'viv in the summer of 1944.

Rabbi Kahana was sheltered on Sheptyts'kyis recommendation starting in May 1943. Prior to that, during the major deportation "actions" in August 1942, Rabbi Kahana approached the Metropolitan with a request to help in the saving of Scrolls of Torah, to which Sheptyts'kyi readily consented. Most of the Jews rescued by Sheptyts'kyi and his assistants escaped from the L'viv ghetto and labor camp between August 1942 and May 1943. The ghetto was liquidated in June 1943 and the camp in the fall of the same year.

As for the organizational aspect of his assistance, it seems that the Metropolitan acted on behalf of the Jews through certain fully trusted personnel, such as his brother, Klementii, head of the Studite Order and Mother Josefa. Another central figure was the Reverend Marko Stek, who seemed to act as a "contact man" between St. George and the various monasteries within and outside L'viv. Usually it was easier to shelter women than men, and children more so than adults. Rescued children were given false baptismal certificates, Ukrainian sounding names, and they were delivered to monasteries, convents and orphanages. Some Jews were assisted by Studite monks to cross the borders into Romania and Hungary. It seems that a "network" of the most trusted, moral, and courageous among the ecclesiastic personnel were mobilized by Sheptyts'kyi to perform the complex and dangerous task of rescue. They were exposed not only to the external threat of the German authorities, but also to criticism and opposition from within.[37] The lower strata of the clergy were quite anti-Semitic and many among them must have been opposed to rescuing Jews. Rabbi Kahana, in a recent interview, confirmed this assumption. Clergymen of the Ukrainian Autocephalous Church (one of the three principal churches in the Ukraine, the other two being the Orthodox and the Uniate) were apparently the most anti-Semitic. A survivor's testimony quotes a priest's sermon in which he implored his flock: "Dear merciful people ... do not give a piece of bread to a Jew ... whoever knows about any hiding place of a Jew, look for him and inform the Germans."[38]

A discussion of Sheptyts'kyi's attitude towards Jews during World War II can never be complete without touching upon the issue of Christian theology and the stand of the Holy See. The traditional hostility of the Christian church towards Jews and anti-Jewish theological myths led, at least partially, to an atmosphere of indifference and animosity among the non-Jewish populations of the Nazi dominated countries. For a variety of reasons, such feelings ran particularly strong in East Central Europe. Some Christians perceived the Nazi-organized killings of the Jews as an unavoidable realization of the Christian call for the punishment and destruction of those who rejected Christ.[39] The debate concerning Pope Pius XII, including Rolf Hochhuth's <u>The Deputy</u> and John F. Morley's study of the Vatican's reactions to the Holocaust, seem to point to the moral failure of the Papacy during a period of extreme crisis and challenge.[40] Sheptyts'kyi's attitudes and behaviour during these difficult and crucial years must be placed also within this context.

In a letter to Rome describing Nazi atrocities towards Jews, written in August 1942, Sheptyts'kyi remarked: "The only consolation one can have in these terrible times is that nothing comes to us without the will of our Heavenly Father. I think that among the massacred Jews there are many souls who converted to God, because never through the centuries have they been placed in a situation as they are in the present, facing for months on end the possibility of a violent death."[41] A discussion that occured in September 1943 between the Metropolitan and Rabbi Kahana (as related by the latter in his memoirs) might shed additional light on Sheptyts'kyi's theological thought. According to Kahana, the Metropolitan told him: "Did you ever... ask yourself what the reason is for the hate and inhumane persecutions against the Jewish people from the early times up to the present? ... He asked me to locate chapter 27, phrase 25 in the Gospel according to Mathew, 'And all the people answered: His blood be on us and on our children.'"[42] Shortly after this discussion, Sheptyts'kyi apologized to Kahana: "In this grave situation, when the Jewish people is bleeding profusely and bearing the sacrifice of hundreds of thousands of innocent victims, I should not have mentioned this subject... please forgive me."[43]

As far as conversion and baptism of the rescued Jewish children are concerned, existing testimonies vary. Rabbi Kahana maintains that such tendencies were visible in Sheptyts'kyi's environment, especially on the part of his brother Klementii. However Yitshak Lewin and Zvi Barnea (Chameides) testified that no such attempts were made. The latter stated: "In 1944, after our liberation, the Metropolitan returned the Jewish children to the remnants of the Jewish community in L'viv as soon as foster families for them could be found."[44]

To conclude, an attempt will be made to answer two significant questions, i.e., why were Sheptyts'kyi's attitudes towards Jews complex and what determined this complexity, and how is he reflected in Jewish memory today.

Paul R. Magocsi, in his preface to a collection of essays on Sheptyts'kyi stated that a constant dilemma in the Metropolitan's life was "how to make Christian morality the basis of everyday reality."[45] Another student of Sheptyts'kyi's early career argued that he was "an important ally of the Ukrainian national movement, but only in so far as this was consistent with Christian principles."[46] The tension between his Christian worldview and the realities pertaining to Ukrainian nationalism were to mark Sheptyts'kyi's attitudes and acts in the years to come. Already in the interwar period, but much more during the war and the Holocaust, Ukrainian nationalism became increasingly extreme, violent and antisemitic. Sheptyts'kyi, as a leader of the Uniate Church and as a symbolic focus of Ukrainian national aspirations was forced into an impossible situation. He tried to preach Christian morality while not dissociating himself from the nationalist elements. He was torn between his moral and humanist values and his compassion for frustrated Ukrainian nationalism.

John S. Conway in an essay on Catholic attitudes towards Jews under Nazi rule correctly remarked that one should not exaggerate the potential influence of the Church in times of inflamed nationalism and pointed out its fear of exposing its ineffectiveness with the masses as a result of an unequivocal stand on the Jewish issue. The Church leaders were striving to preserve their influence in circumstances of rapid erosion.[47] Sheptyts'kyi should be viewed in precisely this context. His situation was even more difficult than that of his ecclesiastic contemporaries. His co-nationals, the Ukrainians, and particularly the young generation, were more extreme, violent and antisemitic than most other populations in Nazi occupied Eastern Europe. His deeds on behalf of the Jews should therefore be appreciated even more than those of other church leaders.

As for the Jews, his stand stemmed from various sources: his humanist approach, his lifelong relations with Jews, but nonetheless from traditional Christian theology. Sheptyts'kyi's relations with Jews during the Holocaust fit the preliminary findings of a conference held in Jerusalem several years ago. They "yielded a complex picture of diverse and often contradictory reactions"[48] and indicated that "even in Eastern Europe the relation between the churches and the Jews during the period of Nazi occupation was more multifaceted than hitherto had been assumed".[49] In Sheptyts'kyi's attitude to the Jews one finds, likewise, complexities, tensions and conflicts.

As far as the historical image and memory of Sheptyts'kyi are concerned, various and at times conflicting views prevail. The Jewish memory of the man and his deeds is seriously affected, not only by his stands vis a vis Ukrainian nationalists and Nazi Germany, but also by the traditionally negative Jewish view of Ukraine and the Ukrainians. The utterly hostile Soviet approach to Sheptyts'kyi may have also exerted its influence upon official Israeli decision makers. The fact remains that in spite of numerous appeals to Yad Vashem Rememberance Authority, the granting of the "Righteous Among the Nations"title to a man who initiated the survival of some 150 Jews and expressed his criticism of Nazi anti-Jewish policies - was denied. As this paper reveals, Sheptyts'kyi's attitudes towards Jews were marked by tensions, inconsistencies and conflicts. Yet, compared with the churches and populations in Nazi occupied Europe, Sheptyts'kyi's statements and deeds on behalf of Jews place him among that humane and courageous minority who during the time of trial believed that they were their brothers' keepers.

NOTES

1. David Kahana, Yoman geto levuv (Jerusalem, 1978), p. 157.
2. Ann Slusarchuk Sirka, "Sheptyts'kyi in Education and as a Philanthropist", to be published in Paul R. Magocsi, ed., Morality and Reality: The Life and Times of Andrei Sheptyts'kyi.
3. Berezhan'ska zemlia: istorychno-memuarnyi zbirnyk (New York, 1970), pp. 189-191.
4. Chwila, July 31, 1935. See also Dilo, August 1, 1935; and Yitshak Lewin, Aliti mi-spetsyah (Tel Aviv, 1946), p. 85.
5. Poslanie pastyrske Andreiia Sheptitskoho Mitropolita Galitskoho, Arkhiepiskopa L'vovskoho, Episkopa Kaments'a Podol'skoho do Dukhoven'stva soedinenykh eparkhii. O kanonichnoi vizitatsii (Zhovkva, 1902), pp. 16-19.
6. Poslanie pastyrs'ke, p. 16.
7. Ibid., p. 18.
8. Ibid., pp. 18-19. In another pastoral letter, written two years earlier, Sheptyts'kyi expressed his religious toleration toward non-Christians, including Jews, as long as they fulfill "the divine will to the best of their power and ability." Pravdyva Vira (1900), reprinted in: Tvory Sluhy Bozhoho Mytr. Andreia Sheptyts'koho, Vol. 1: "Pastyrs'ki Lysty,' (Toronto, 1965), p. 70.
9. Edward Prus, Wladyka Swietojurski: Rzecz o arcybiskupie Andrzeju Szeptyckim (1865-1944), (Warsaw, 1985), pp. 157-158.
10. Ibid., p. 71.
11. For a discussion of German-Ukrainian relations during this period see Ryszard Torzecki, Kwestia ukrainska w polityce III Rzeszy (1933-1945) (Warsaw, 1972).
12. Shimon Redlich, "Jewish Ukrainian Relations in Interwar Poland as Reflected in the Ukrainian Press." Paper delivered at the International Conference on the History and Culture of Polish Jews, Jerusalem, January 31-February 5, 1988. To be published in the Conference proceedings.
13. "Episkop I. Buchko proti antisemitizmu (Bishop I. Buchko Against Antisemitism), Dilo, September 18, 1936.
14. The Jewish Chronicle (London), December 29, 1939.
15. John F. Morley, Vatican Diplomacy and the Jews During the Holocaust, 1939-1943 (New York, 1980), p. 133.
16. Letter dated December 26, 1939, Actes et Documents du Saint Siege relatifs a la Seconde Guerre Mondiale, Vol. III: Le Saint Siege et la situation religieuse en Pologne et dans les Pays Baltes 1939-1945, Pt. I: 1939-1941 (The Vatican, 1967), Doc. 79, pp. 170-171.
17. Cyrille Korolevskij, Metropolite Andre Szeptyckyj, 1865-1944 (Rome, 1964), p. 362.
18. Letter dated August 30, 1941, Actes et Documents, Doc. 297, pp. 437-442.
19. John A. Armstrong, Ukrainian Nationalism, 1939-1945 (New York, 1955), p. 27.
20. Cited in Kost' Pan'kivs'kyi, Vid derzhavy do komitetu (New York and Toronto, 1957), p. 112.
21. Letter dated August 30, 1941, Actes et Documents, Doc. 297, p. 440.
22. Roman Ilnytzkyj, Deutschland und die Ukraine, 1939-1945, Vol. 2 (Munchen, 1958), pp. 276-279.
23. Ukrainian attitudes toward Jews during the Holocaust are discussed in: Philip Friedman, "Ukrainian-Jewish Relations During the Occupation," in his Roads to Extinction: Essays on the Holocaust (New York and Philadelphia, 1980), pp. 176-208), and his Their Brothers' Keepers (New York, 1978), pp. 130-136. See also Shmuel Spector, The Holocaust of Volhynian Jews, 1941-1944 (Jerusalem, 1986); Aharon Weiss, "Jewish-Ukrainian Relations in Western Ukraine during the Holocaust Period (1941-1944)." Paper delivered at the "McMaster Conference on Jewish-Ukrainian Relations in Historical Perspective", 19 October 1983, McMaster University, Hamilton, Ontario and Ukrainians and Jews: A Symposium (New York, 1966), pp. 123-147.
24. See Philip Friedman, "Ukrainian Jewish Relations", p. 187.
25. Interview with Aharon Weiss, Hotam, Al-Hamishmar, September 4, 1987, p. 20.
26. Cited in Kurt A. Lewin, "Andreas Count Sheptytsky, Archbishop of Lviv, Metropolitan of Halych, and the Jewish Community in Galicia During the Second World War," The Annals of the Ukrainian Academy of Sciences, Vol. 7, No. 1-2 (23-24), 1959, p. 1660. Sheptyts'kyi also urged Rabbi Kahana to tell him about the fate of the Jewish community in L'viv. See Kahana, Yoman geto lvuv, pp. 154-155.

27. As stated in the "Frederic Report", quoted in Raul Hilberg, The Destruction of the European Jews (New York, 1973), p. 330.
28. At least three persons testified to have seen Sheptyts'kyi's letter to Himmler, however neither the original nor a copy of the text of the letter is available. For details see Kost' Pan'kivs'kyi, Roky nimetskoi okupatsii (New York and Toronto, 1965), pp. 29-39; Lewin, 'Andreas Count Sheptytsky", p. 1661; and Kahana, Yoman geto levuv, p. 155.
29. Kahana, Yoman geto levuv, p. 155. The text of the letter to the Vatican dated August 29-31, 1942 is in Actes et Documents, Vol. III, pt. 2: 1942-1945 (The Vatican, 1967), Doc. 406, p. 628.
30. See letter, dated August 29-31, 1942, Ibid., p. 625.
31. Ibid., p. 625.
32. Eugene Tisserant, L'eglise militante (Paris 1950), p. 14.
33. Andrei Sheptyts'kyi, Pys'ma-poslannia Mytropolyta Andreia Sheptyts'koho ChSVV z chasiv nimets'koi okupatsii, Biblioteka Lohosu, vol. XXX, part 2 (Yorkton, 1969), pp. 222-231. It should also be mentioned that as early as July 1, 1941, in a pastoral letter discussing the newly established Ukrainian Stets'ko government, Sheptyts'kyi urged its members to ensure the safety and well being of all, regardless of religion, nationality, and social status. See Roman Ilnytzkyj, Deutschland und die Ukraine, p. 274.
34. Kahana, Yoman geto levuv, p. 155.
35. See note 27.
36. For additional details, see Yitshak Lewin, Aliti mi-spetsyah (Tel Aviv, 1947), pp. 27, 59, and a letter from Mr. Kurt Lewin to Mr. Roman Boytzun, December 6, 1984, with a copy to the author.
37. This summary of Sheptyts'kyi's rescue of Jews is based on Kahana, Yoman geto levuv; Y. Levin, Aliti mi-spetsyah; Kurt I. Lewin, "The Metropolitan Andrei Sheptyts'kyi in the years 1942-1944: Recollections of an Eyewitness." Paper delivered at the University of Toronto Conference," Andrei Sheptyts'kyi: His Life and Work", November 23, 1984; Kurt I. Lewin, "Andreas Count Sheptytsky" and an interview with Mr. Kurt I. Lewin in New York City, December 24, 1984. For a testimony on Sheptyts'kyi's rescue of the two sons of Rabbi Kalman Chameides, the former Rabbi of Katowice, see a letter by Zvi Barnea (Chameides) to the Editor, The Jerusalem Post, January 24, 1986 and a letter by Leon Chameides to the author, dated January 22, 1986. Both responded to my article "Sheptytsky and the Jews", The Jerusalem Post, December 13, 1985. See also Joachim Schoenfeld, Holocaust Memoirs: Jews in the Lvov Ghetto, the Janowski Concentration Camp, and as Deportees in Siberia (Hoboken, N.J., 1985), p. 46 and interview with Rabbi David Kahana in Zahala, October 19, 1987.
38. See: Shmuel Spector, The Holocaust of Volhynian Jews, p. 192.
39. Robert Michael, 'Christian Theology and the Holocaust", Midstream (New York), Vol. 30, No. 4, April 1984, pp. 6-9. Nazi Germany, the Churches and the Holocaust are discussed in Otto D. Kulka, Paul R. Mendes-Flohr eds., Judaism and Christianity Under the Impact of National Socialism (Jerusalem, 1987).
40. See Carlo Falconi, The Silence of Pius XII (Boston and Toronto, 1970); Saul Friedlander, Pius XII and the Third Reich: A Documentation (New York, 1966); and John F. Morley, Vatican Diplomacy and the Jews (New York, 1980). For a "revisionist" view see: Owen Chadwick, Britain and the Vatican During the Second World War (Cambridge, 1987).
41. Letter dated August 29-31, 1942, Actes et Documents, p. 628.
42. As related in Kahana, Yoman geto levuv, p. 157.
43. Ibid., p. 158 and interview with Rabbi Kahana, October 19, 1987.
44. Letter by Zvi Barnea (Chameides) to The Jerusalem Post, January 24, 1986. See also: Yitshak Levin, Aliti mi-spetsyah, p. 175, Kurt I. Lewin, "Andreas Count Sheptytsky", p. 1665 and interview with Rabbi Kahana, October 19, 1987.
45. Paul R. Magocsi, ed., Morality and Reality, preface (to be published in 1988).
46. John-Paul Himka, "Andrei Sheptytskyi and the Ukrainian National Movement before 1914", to be published in Morality and Reality.
47. John S. Conway, "Catholicism and the Jews during the Nazi Period and After", in Otto Dov Kulka and Paul R. Mendes-Flohr, eds., Judaism and Christianity under the Impact of National Socialism (Jerusalem, 1987), pp. 447-448.
48. "Introduction, Judaism and Christianity", p. 12.
49. Ibid., p. 16.

MARGIT SLACHTA'S ACTIVITIES IN SUPPORT OF SLOVAKIAN JEWRY 1942-43

Maria SCHMIDT

MTA - Soros Foundation,
Hungarian Academy of Sciences
Institute of History
Budapest, Úri u. 53. 1014 Hungary

This paper was written with the support of the MTA - Soros Foundation

"A lot of things are happening now in the name of Christianity which are contrary to its teachings" (1)

"...my starting point is the Christian tenet that love obliges us to respect the natural God-given rights which apply to everyone without exception and what cannot be abrogated. These are the rights to life, to make a living, to health, to freedom of conscience, to posses honestly-acquired property etc." (2) These words were written by Margit Slachta in her periodical "Word of the Soul" in January 1943 in an attempt to help Jews who were obliged to do labour service. Margit Slachta (born in Kassa in 1884, died in 1974 in Buffalo) was a prominent figure in the political life of Hungary between the wars. She was a conservative monarchist who was ahead of her time in organising support for women and families. She also initiated schemes to train social workers. She established the Catholic Women's Party in 1919 and was elected to Parliament as a member of this party. She was the first woman M.P. and held her seat from 1920 to 1922. In 1923 she founded the "Social Brotherhood" movement (3) which provided professional trained social workers in the fields of women, children and family care. As a Christian she fought against racial inequalities and all kinds of inhuman behaviour. (4)

In 1938 following the Anschluss, Hungary and Germany became neighbours and Hungary was unable to resist the spirit of Nazism emanating from Germany at this time. Hungary took the side of the apparently invincible force of Germany firstly because of its geo-political position and secondly because the Hungarian political leaders' primary aim was to regain the territory lost after the great war. (5) The rise of this German ideology led to restrictions in the rights of those Hungarian citizens who were considered to be Jewish. (6)

Margit Slachta immediately defended the persecuted Jews by attacking racial discrimination and giving practical support to those in need, regardless of her own safety. (7) She struggled against the rising tide of anti-Semitic propaganda and encouraged her religious superiors to condemn the persecutions and acts of cruelty which were taking place. In 1941 the Hungarian authorities without any pressure from Germany, implemented a drastic "clearing action" as a result of which nearly 20,000 Jews, who were unable to adequate establish their Hungarian citizenship, were deported to Kamenec-Podolsk. (They were later killed by German extermination squads.) Margit Slachta went to the Ministry of the Interior to state her outrage at these atrocities.

"We raise our voices in opposition to the fact that officially-sanctioned mass atrocities can take place in our country. We do this as members of the human race, as Christians and as Hungarians. As members of the human race all our human feelings and natural instincts rebel against these acts. As Christians, we see these acts as direct contraventions of the commandments of God and our religion. As Hungarians, we are unable to stand aside and watch the defilement of our Hungarian integrity embodied in these disgraceful acts. (8)

In the spring of 1942, representatives of Slovakian Jewry asked for Slachta's assistance. As a result of the redrawing of Hungary's borders after the Great War, a large number of Hungarian lived under Slovakian rule and a number of the persecuted Jews were also Hungarian. This however, was not the prime motivating factor in Slachta's decision to give help. She was a Catholic who believed in brotherly love and the universality of Christian teachings but she was also a politician. She realised that anti-Semitism and racial hatred are not confined by national frontiers just as the proclamation of Christian love does not respect borders. In protecting Slovakian Jews and spreading Christian principles she both defended her own Church and expressed her concern for her own country.

The laws passed in March 1939 by the Slovakian authorities conferred total civil rights only on those who were Slovaks. The civil rights of the Jews (who made up 4 % of the population) were restricted. Before the Munich Agreement, the Slovakian Jews played a considerable role in the economic and cultural life of the country and in the professions (for example 50 % of the doctors were Jewish). The majority of Slovakian Jews were middle-class and their culture and mother tongue was Hungarian. These factors provoked strong anti-Semitism among the Slovakian intelligentsia which saw them as rivals and as betrayers of the national cause.

The Codex Judaicum issued on the 10th September 1941, which was based on the Nuremburg Laws, removed the Slovakian Jews' legal rights. The measures taken against them: the wearing of a distinguishing mark, the confiscation of their possessions, their separation and ultimately their deportation, started at the beginning of 1942.

Slachta went to Pozsony (Bratislava) in the spring of 1942 to see for herself what was taking place. "The persecution of the unfortunate Jews began in the days leading up to Easter. It was officially announced that they would be taken to work, but there are reports that the girls will be forced to fall prey to soldiers in bars in the area behind the Eastern Front. These reports have been confirmed by extremely reliable sources. The assembly point in Bratislava was the local armaments factory. I will not here go into details of their treatment ... Slovakia pays Germany 500 marks, that is 6,000 Slovak crowns for every Jew dealt with. In these circumstances one could say that the picture the town presents is hellish. One aspect of this Hell is the fact that while thousands of Jews are being denied their legal rights, are defenceless and are in a pitiful situation, Christians flock to the churches but do not give shelter to the unfortunate victims. They eagerly absorb the poison of hatred which is injected into them by regular and well planned propaganda ... I came home with a churned -up soul. My conscience almost tells me I am an accomplice when I have not tried to do everything in my power to put an end to these acts... The purpose of my letter is not only to pass an information, I wish to beg you to vouchsafe to persuade the Hungarian bishops to take steps - as bishops - against this Satanism. Surely there are no political frontiers before God so I feel that we are not exempt from the responsibility of attempting to save our poor fellowmen. Is it impossible to consider that the Hungarian beishops could contact their Slovakian counterparts on this matter? ... Could they not be persuaded to excommunicate the weekly communicant, Bela Tuka, (9) the churchman Tiso, (10) and his fellow churchman and Lord Mayor Bela Kovács if they refuse to stop this trade in human beings, this killing and defilement?" (11)

Slachta also sent similar letters to other bishops, to all the respected members of the religious hierarchy as well as to well-known secular figures. She contacted anyone who she hoped would be able to help.

"As a result of my experiences in Austria and Czechoslovakia I now understand the mechanism of the hands which prepare people for these horrible acts and even what their appetite for them. This is now being expressed in our country ... So when I knock on every door begging for protection for our Jewish borthers against the cruelty of the pagans, I am also bearing in mind the interests of our country and our own interests ... I think that if there is no one to take risks, any cause will fail and the cause of the Church, its possessions and schools will be lost ... I think that if the bishops are prepared to take steps, they should take action against the Prime Minister and next to force the Minister of Interior to totally prohibit the poisoning of people's minds by hatred." (12)

The official view of the Church, (13) taking political considerations into account, made it impossible for the Hungarian bishops to undertake dissemination of Christian values in the way represented by Slachta. The representatives of the Catholic Church in Hungary along with the leaders of the other Christian Churches voted in support of the first Anti-Jewish Law in 1938 and the second in 1939. They turned a blind eye to the stiring up of hatred which took place in religious forums, and they were frequently unashamed of expressing anti-Semitic views in the name of "Christian morality". Very few people in the Catholic Church or in Hungary as a whole were attracted by Slachta's intransigent Christian viewpoint, her realisation of the constancy of values, or her understanding of the limitations of political power. Those in positions of power in the Church hierarchy failed to give clear, unambigous guidance to their flock. They failed to take concerted action both at this time and later, in the summer of 1944, when huge numbers of Hungarian Jews were being exterminated.

Between March 1942 and March of 1943, 58,000 Slovakian Jews were transported to extermination camps. The spring of 1943 saw the preparations for the deportation of the remainder, nearly 25,000 mostly Christians of Jewish origin. Again Slachta tried to help. This time she turned to Pope Pius XII. Slachta found out that Francis Spellman, archbishop of New York, whom she had met in the United States, planned to visit Rome in March. It was well known that Spellman was close to Pope Pius XII. Slachta managed to obtain a passport by using her connections in conservative and liberal political circles and with the support of Mrs Ilona Horthy, the wife of the Regent she flew to Rome. There Spellman received her and arranged an audience with the Pope.

"The invitation was for 11.45 on Friday for a personal interview ... (I was wearing a grey veil and no hat). I had never felt as I did then, my face was burning, my hands, usually dry, were clammy and tears were welling up in my eyes. This state of mind was only partly caused by the fact that we were waiting for the Holy Father, I was more deeply moved by the burden of the cause of 20,000 people. We had to wait for half an hour during which I calmed down... The Holy Father came in. We were left alone. He asked me to sit down but he himself remained standing. I started like this: I am here on behalf of 20,000 people under sentence of death. I mean the Slovakian deportees. This is only a name, in reality it means the execution of the people. He said yes - at that point... He listened to me all the way through. I gave him the details of these appalling acts and he expressed his shock... I can say the following: he listened to me but said very little. I will never forget the way he looked at me. It was deep, deadly serious and beneficent. I felt deeply moved that evening and even the next day." (14)

Slachta hoped for support from the U.S. President through Archbishop Spellman. She summarized her concrete and effective proposals under five headings. She hoped that these proposals, if accepted, would be of assistance to the persecuted Jews. In full awareness of Fascist methods, she asked for a pledge of immediate retribution on Germans in America if further deportations took place. She also proposed that neutral countries like Spain could represent the interests of the Slovakian Jews and take them temporarily as refugees. In order to gain the goodwill of the Slovak government she suggested monthly payments of 150,000 Swiss francs. (15) She drew up a questionnaire for her Slovakian sources (16) in order to ascertain how many of the victims were old, young, men, women, children or ill. Some of these suggestions were taken up in Budapest in the summer of 1944. The assistance given by neutral powers and their papers giving protection saved the lives of thens of thousands of Hungarian Jews.

Pope Pius XII, to some extent as a result of Slachta's requests, ordered the seven bishops of Slovakia to intercede with President Tiso, Prime Minister Tuka and Mach, the Minister of the Interior. They were asked to protest against deportation of the remainder of the Jews. He also ordered that a pastoral letter signed by all seven bishops be read out in every church in Slovakia. In this letter they explained why the deportation was not in accordance with Christian beliefs. (17)

The deportation planned for the spring of 1943 was cancelled. The Slovakian Jews gained time and Slachta's activities may have had some effect in gaining this reprieve. The changing situation at the front also played its part in that it promoted insecurity among the Slovak leaders.

It should also be noted that $ 50,000 "ransom" money was paid by the Bratislava Rescue Committee, (18) (the self-defence body of Slovakian Jewry) to the S.S. in the person of Dieter von Wisliczeny in order to obtain this suspension of the deportations. This sum, two dollars per head, came to Slovakia through international Jewish organisations. (19)

In spite of this respite, the remaining Jews met their fate in the autumn of 1944. On the 19th of August an uprising broke out in Slovakia and many of the partisans were Jewish. (20) After suppression of the revolt, the deportations resumed and in the course of these nearly 10,000 people were transported to Auschwitz or other death camps.

At this stage the unthinkable had occurred. In Budapest Slachta was again on hand to assist the victims. Refering to the experience of the German and Dutch bishops, she encouraged Cardinal Serédi the Archbishop of Hungary to take action. Members of the Social Brotherhood allowed their houses and official papers to be used by the victims and hid and saved the lives of more than 1,000 people.

Slachta, in her insistence on the following of Christian teaching, stood against the spirit of her age. "Even in these dark hours, she dared to remove ignorance, lack of love and hatred from her heart" (21) in oder to help her unfortunate fellow-men. (22)

REFERENCE

1) Letter from Margit Slachta to Ilona Horthy. (13.8.41) in Tamás Majsai "Documents from the history of the Jewish deportations from Kőrösmező (1941). The annual journal of the Raday collection IV-V volumes 1984-85 p. 217.
2) Slachta's "New Year Letter" which aroused considerable controversy. It was attacked in all the right-wing press.
3) The Social Brotherhood (1923-48). The religious head was Count János Mikes bishop. It's president was Margit Slachta. The Brotherhood was established in five countries and by the late 1930's had nearly 200 members. It was also active in the U.S.A.
4) Slachta spent a considerable period in the U.S. in the late 1920's. She was again elected to Parliament in the period 1945-48. She remained loyal to her conservative principles and determined politician and thus became increasingly isolated in the movement towards a one-party state. The establishment of a Communist regime in 1949 forced her to leave Hungary. She moved to the U.S. and involved herself in the work of Brotherhood.
5) Hungary was the principle loser in the Twenties which followed the Great War. The size of the country (excluding Croatia) was reduced from 283,000 km2 to 93,000 km2. The population from 18,2 million to 7,6 million. Of these 63,000 km2 went to Czechoslovakia with 3,5 million inhabitants, of which 1,072,000 were Hungarian.
6) Between 1938 and 1941 three "Anti Jewish Laws" were passed by the Hungarian parliament. The first, in 1938, was entitled "the more-efficient protection of the balance in economic and social life". The second, in 1939, "the limitation of the expansion of Jewish influence in public and economic life". The third, in 1941, contained measures about inter-racial marriage.
7) Margit Slachta was beaten up by Arrow Cross thugs in the autumn of 1944 because she had hidden Jews.
8) The reports on the circumstances of the deportation in Kamenec-Podolsk by Count György Apponyi, Margit Slachta, Dr. Imre Szabó and Countess Erzsébet Szapáry. Quoted in Majsai (op. cit) p. 219.

9) The then Prime Minister of Slovakia.
10) The then President of Slovakia.
11) Slachta's letter to the bishop of Kalocsa, Count Gyula Zichy, 27th April 1942 (in the possession of Ilona Móna), typed original.
12) Slachta's letter to Gyula Glattfelder, the bishop of Csanád. 29th April 1942 (in the possession of Ilona Móna) typed original.
13) The reply of Gyula Glattfelder, bishop of Csanád is a fair reflection of the official position of the Church, "Dear Sister Margit, ... without authorization, I can confidentially inform you that the bishops have already raised their voices against the atrocities and if this was not done openly this was only because we would have had to face unimaginable reprisals the consequences of which would have only damaged the unfortunate Jews or (which is, after all, more important for us) the Christians of Jewish ancestry ... To discuss the affairs of a foreign power in our forums and to ask for disciplinary measures to be taken in territory outside our borders has to be considered to be not only impossible but also dangerous. I do not feel that the bishops can undertake this task. What would Hungarian public opinions have to say if the German bishops were to interfere in Hungarian affairs? Hence I would not advise you to start a campaign against the alleged atrocities in Slovakia because this would only raise the stakes and would create even more bitterness. I know very well that we have to run the risk of going to a concentration camp but only in the line of duty. To bring this fate on ourselves would damage not only the individual but more importantly, the cause."
14) Slachta's own essay, typed original, 13th March 1943 in the possession of Ilona Móna.
15) Slachta's letter to Spellman from Rome (not dated), probably March/April 1943, in the possession of Ilona Móna. The complete text of the letter in Maria Schmidt "Action of Margit Slachta to rescue Slovakian Jews" in Danubian Historical Studies. Vol. I. no. I. Spring 1987. pp. 56-69.
16) Typed original (Ilona Móna).
17) Margit Slachta's report in the 123rd meeting of the National Assembly (16. 1.47.).
18) Scupina Pracovna.
19) Der Bericht des jüdischen Rettungskomitees aus Budapest. Vorgelegt von Rezső Kasztner.
20) Approximately 20 % of the partisans were Jewish (see Ladislav Lipscher: Die Juden im Slowakischen Staat 1939-45, Oldenbourg, 1980.)
21) "New Year Letter" January 1943 (c.f. 2.)
22) Margit Slachta has been recognised by the Yad Vashem of Jerusalem as a "Righteous gentile". She was also given the right to plant a tree in the Avenue of the Righteous. Two other members of the Brotherhood also received twis honour: Sister Sara Salkházi and teacher Vilma Bernovits. On the 27th of December 1944 both of them were executed by the Arrow Cross for hiding Jews.

Christian attitudes and responses to the Jewish plight in Southern and Western Europe and by the Vatican 1933–1945

CHAIRPERSON **Dr Asher Cohen**

RAPPORTEUR **Professor Eva Fleischner**

GREEK JEWS AND CHRISTIANS DURING WORLD WAR II

STEVEN BOWMAN

JUDAIC STUDIES PROGRAM, UNIVERSITY OF CINCINNATI,
CINCINNATI, OHIO 45221-0169, U.S.A.

According to the Greek census of 1928 - the last before WWII and one which reflected the politics of Greek nationalism after the recent exchange of population with Turkey - some 96% of the population of Greece was identified as orthodox Christian. The remainder consisted of Muslims, Jews, Catholics, and Armenian Christians divided among a host of ethnoi.

As the theme of this conference is Christian and Jewish attitudes and actions during the Holocaust, it may be of value to describe the relationship of the Greeks to their church and address also the question how this relationship affected their actions toward the Jews. First, however, it is necessary to delineate briefly the attitude of the Orthodox Church toward the Jews and later to examine how this attitude affected the subsequent actions of its clergy during the war years.

The Greek Orthodox Church is the oldest of the Christian churches and the most important, at least insofar as the Balkans and Eastern Europe are concerned. Its varied attitudes toward Jews and Judaism are a blend of politics and religion that reflect the east much more than the west. During the period that the Church was paramount throughout the Aegean hinterlands as the "Ministry of Religion for the Byzantine Empire", its attitude toward the Jews, the legacy of which is still evident in the modern Church, followed several contradictory patterns.

The first task of the Church was to Christianize the Greek-speaking peoples. This was an ongoing process which lasted over a millenium and which was only partially successful. Like its corollary Hellenism among the Semites, Greek Orthodoxy provided only a thin veneer to reorient the pagan Hellenes. The armies of Constantine and his successors encouraged the adoption of Christianity and then dealt with heretics as outlaws. The masses of Egypt, Palestina, Syria and Anatolia responded by turning to Islam after conquests by the latter in the 7th, 11th and 15th centuries: today only pockets remain of the eastern Christian religions many of which reflect the particular sectarian dissent adopted prior to the Arab and Turkic conquests.

To this Church, Jews and Judaism represented a foil, the challenge against which Christianity must forge its identity. This was difficult enough. On the one hand was the inertia of a moribund polytheistic world seeking ever new models of salvation. Yet the Hellenistic world was heir to the best of Greek civilization. On the other hand was Judaism which through the fourth century was still a strong attraction to upper class pagan women for conversion and their male counterparts for emulation. The problem of Christianity was to redefine its adherents as the True Jews - Verus Israel - and thus defeat Judaism while at the same time absorbing the political and cultural legacy of classical civilization and thus defeat Hellenism. Concurrently, it had to maintain its complicated New Testament (canonized only in 325 by the compromise of Nicaea) mission of salvation for Jew and Gentile alike. The dialectical pressures of this Damoclean mission would have driven a lesser ideal over the brink. As it was, it led to two conflicting attitudes within the Church.

In Greek Orthodoxy, Judaism is treated as a bête noir and Judaizing a crime. When the Church had power, individuals were prosecuted for the latter charge. Jews, on the other hand, were protected by the official Church due to certain theological precepts butressed by inherited legal constraints. These may be listed briefly as follows:

1) Salvation can be obtained only by a voluntary conversion and wish to be baptized. Therefore the Church refused to accept forced conversion by the state, a practise resorted to in the 7th, 8th, 9th, 10th and perhaps 13th century by a succession of Byzantine emperors for various political reasons. In the 8th century, for example, the long memory of the Church and the Jews was rewarded only after some 70 years by the recognition in 796 of the illegality of forced baptism under Leo the Isaurian in 724. This is not to say that zealous ecclesiastics, primarily monks, might not force the issue on their own initiative, thus emulating independently various ecclesiastical policies under the western church. But these rare actions were rejected by the official Church. Thus Baptism in the Orthodox Church was not the indelible sacrament it came to be in the Roman Catholic Church where it seems to have served both theologically and among the masses as a kind of feudal oath. The Orthodox Church was more sophisticated in this respect and hence condemned attempts at forced baptism.

2) Some Jews had to remain visible as Jews. One reason was to show the victory of Christianity over Judaism; the former with its wealth and power, the latter a *Judea Capta*. (This imagery is crudely caught in the facade of Notre Dame de Paris with its two maidens flanking the main portal and brazenly proclaiming the triumphalism of its twelfth-century iconography.) Or as put by the Church Fathers: the Christians represented Abel and Jacob, both blessed; while the Jews represented Cain and Esau, both rejected. Thus the reality of society should reflect the biblical symbolism. A second reason was to exhibit the historical link between the world of the Old Testament and that of the New - an idea concretized by the fourth-century Bishop of Caesarea, Eusebius, in his two important works *Praeparatio Evangelica* which recorded the Jewish-pagan confrontation and *Demonstratio Evangelica* which argued the Christian victory. This latter reason was as much a theological response to Paul's quip "A remnant will return" as it was an answer to the pagans who continually challenged the Christians for their bona fides and historical credentials.

3) A non-expressed reason was the Roman legal heritage which had declared Judaism a *religio licita* - a permitted religion - and thus entitled to survive within Roman society. Non licit religions were outlawed and destroyed by the army. As the upholder of the Roman state after Constantine had made Christianity first a *religio licita* and then favored its growth and development until his successors recognized it as *the* official religion of the empire and abolished every other religion *except* Judaism, Christianity could not successfully delegitimate its rival and progenitor despite attempts to do so indirectly from Theodosius II to Justinian. That Justinian was able to outlaw the Samaritans by removing them from their inclusion within a broad definition of Judaism and subsequently sent his armies to destroy their altar on Mount Gerizim along with their villages is an indication of what could have been done to Jews and Judaism had not Christianity been constrained by the previously listed reasons.

Thus Christianity found itself bound by theology and law to protect its rival whose sacred literature it was claiming to be its own. It is little wonder that Byzantine and subsequent Orthodox literature is replete with polemics and apologetics against Judaism.

While the above remarks have been of necessity superficial, what is of most interest for this essay is that Greek Christians, for the most part, have overcome the inherent schizophrenia of the complicated Orthodox attitudes toward the Jews. Not so the Slavs (and to some extent Latins and Germans) for whom the subtlety of Greek thought ever remained beyond the ken of all but a few intellectuals. Therefore the history of Greek Orthodoxy must be treated separately from the traditions of Greek Orthodox influence outside of Greece where the virulence of anti-Judaism and hostility to Jews has earned for those East-European societies the dubious sobriquet of antisemitic. (This diasporic Greek Orthodox legacy is also a major factor in a developing Palestinian anti-Zionism.)

A second observation may be offerred here which has a bearing on the subject of this paper. Greek Christianity as a religion is more within the female sphere than within that of the male. Its development of Mary as heir to Isis, of the Christ child as a rejection of the pagan father's prerogative of infanticide, of the panoply of saints to replace demigods and also to foster martyrdom, and the heady ritual of the liturgy: all point in this direction. The women's refuge is the ecclesia, the males' harbor the taverna. The Greek male with his penchant for social homosexuality and intellectual intercourse would rather argue theology than practise religion. The secularization of this predilection would see him replace theology with political ideology in the twentieth century and fight two generations of civil war over the question of a German king of the Hellenes rather than concern himself with a Semitic King of Kings. Thus during the period of the Holocaust, that is the dodecanal from 1932-1945 with its antecedent fears and post-war traumas, we should be aware of a division in Greek society between the church and the women on the one hand (with a few exceptions and these are by no means unimportant) and the complicated political arena within which the males functioned and performed. This observation is not to belittle the influence of the church over the male however. The structure of Greek society and especially of family relationship has become interwoven with church ritual and Christian influence. The pathos of the Passion, too, strongly affects the male population and incidentally makes the three-week period between Purim and Passover/Easter potentially the most explosive time in Greek Jewish and Christian relations.

A final point to be added on the Greek Christians is the question of hospitality which in the Greek world is as proverbial as it is in the Arab. In the case of the Greeks however, it is as ancient as that of the Jews. The earliest traditions of both peoples emphasize the religious obligation to protect the stranger at one's hearth. The conviviality of Greek society has secularized this ancestral obligation and made it the most prominent phenomenon of their culture, at least to foreigners. Greek peasants offerred hospitality during the war to British and Germans alike. While understandably the latter examples were more rare and should be dealt with separately from the welcome extended by urban and village collaborator, nonetheless it is recorded that even the enemy, whether Italian or German, was entitled to the sanctity of the ancestral tradition of hospitality once he had renounced by capture or defection the status of occupier and oppressor. With respect to Allied escapees, the Greek population's acceptance of the viciousness of the German reprisal policy rather than surrender the stranger/guest whom they swore to protect has become proverbial if little understood by western outsiders.

It remains to add a few preliminary remarks on the Jews. Greek Jews represent several different traditions. The largest group demographically was the huge semi-autonomous colony at Thessaloniki which for over 400 years had acted as a Jewish metropolis for Balkan Jewry. It was Spanish-speaking in the main and by the twentieth century had become an historical anachronism. Its history during the 1920s and 1930s would be a struggle against the forces of Venizelist nationalism. The Nazis would finish the process of helleniztion of that ir ve-em be-Yisrael. Sephardi colonies existed throughout Northern Macedonia and Thrace situated mostly along that ancient trade route from Durazzo to Istanbul called by the Romans the Via Egnatia. In western and southern Greece, including Crete and Chalkis, were the Greek-speaking communities, many descended from the mediaeval Romaniotes as in Ioannina while others had been assimilated in the course of time to the local culture. The third group of Jews was the Italian-speaking Jews of the Ionian- and Dodekanisi with their mother cities respectively in Corfu and Rhodes. With the exception of the older generation of Salonki Jews who were either monolingual or knew also Turkish or Bulgarian and the Italian spheres, the other Jews all knew some Greek or were in the case of the youth after 1936 Hellenophones. Under the rule of the Dictator Ioannis Metaxas (1936-1941), the increased pressure of hellenization in the schools succeeded in giving a great many Jewish youth the requisite tool to survive incognito among the Greek Christians.

One more important point should be made about the Jews which is really a general historical observation yet so pertinent to the tragedy in Greece as we shall see. The Jewish communities in Greece never effected a democratic revolution in terms of their relationships with the rest of the population. The Jewish communities were semi-autonomous bodies cut off by religious and economic factors (and in some cases, notably Thessaloniki, linguistic) from their Greek Christian neighbors. The heads of the Jewish communities however maintained more than cordial relations with Greek civil, ecclesiastical and military authorities. Except for individuals - and these mostly in business - Jews did not mix with the local Christian population but rather maintained a social and endogamous exclusiveness parallelling that of other ethnoi of Greece. (We might note in passing that the same sentiment applies even to Greek villages which viewed even other villagers as strangers.) The Jews were however more conspicuous by their urban profile. This visibility was exacerbated by the tensions inherited from Christian competition as noted above and from the nineteenth/twentieth-century upsurge of Greek nationalism which witnessed the ugly problem of the blood libel sweep across the Ottoman world in the second half of the nineteenth century and the vulgar aspects of demographic hellenization in the twentieth.

The Jewish community, a non militant urban commercial and artisan class, maintained an alliance with the ruling classes in Greece much as they had done during Ottoman and Byzantine times. Their politics thus ran counter to the major Greek political concerns. They stood outside the Venizelist-Monarchist dispute that rocked Greece from WWI to WWII. In Saloniki they bowed gratefully to Metaxas, a dictator, who put an end to Greek politics and its overt strife which had been primarily against them. The traditional friendliness of the Jews to the royal house was incidentally to bear results in the reciprocal friendliness of the latter toward individual Jews in hiding during the war years. Thus the Jews functioned on their own inertia, oblivious to the revolutionary rhythms of modern Greece and relied on their alliance with local and national powers. It was this traditional approach to survival as Jews (tried and tested over two millenia of diasporic existance) that ill prepared them for the totalitarian novelty of Nazism which was to destroy them.

The leadership of Greek Jewry was also old. There was little new blood among the community heads who had served since the first world war. These were in the main traditionalists, whether in their attitude toward assimilation (as much as necessary to preserve the continuity of the community), French influence (the mission française of the Alliance Israélite Universelle network), Zionism (expressed in the split between the older leadership and the "Young Turk" Revisionists who lacked community power). Thus they could not (as indeed only a few Cassandras worldwide could) recognize the revolutionary character of Nazism which masquaraded behind the Wehrmacht civility and Austrian Gemütlichkeit of the occupiers of Greek towns. To these leaders and the older generation in general, partisans were outlaws and socially unacceptable. They were youth in rebellion who challenged old ways and endangered the elders who remained at home and their traditional ways. As Ismail Kadare put it in his _Chronicle of Stone_ (London, 1987): "Young boys and girls are sitting together in the cellars to sing forbidden songs. They say they want to destroy the old world and rebuild a new one... They say that blood will have to be spilled for this new world to be built." How much more would bourgeois parents who looked backwards be abhorrent to their daughters joining partisan bands in the mountains and sleeping under the stars without chaperon. (Incidentally we should note that morality among the Greek partisans was extremely high.) This social conservatism cannot be ignored by the historian especially since it is one of the underlieing elements in the revolutionary atmosphere of the 1940s against which an undisciplined youth was rebelling.

To the average Greek whose memory is guided by historical myths and his own experience, the attitude toward Jews was basically positive. We should qualify this generalization by excluding the Anatolian Greeks who were settled in Thessaloniki by Venizelos as agents of his hellenizing goal: these were to be national, political, and economic competitors to the Jews there. Among the average 'old' Greek population, then, the Jews who spoke Greek and who had participated in the many wars of the twentieth century had won a reputation as loyal fellow citizens. This fact and generally accepted opinion was emphasized over and over by Greek political leaders from Eleutheros Venizelos himself to Emmanouil Tsouderos, the wartime Prime Minister of the Government-in-Exile in Cairo and his postwar successor Constantine Tsaldaris, and acknowledged by the average Greek Christian in the streets of occupied Greece. Ioannis Politis, a prominent Greek political figure during the 1930s and 1940s, estimated in 1944 that every Greek Jew who survived the war in Greece had been helped by at least one Greek. Postwar information suggests that this may be an understatement.

These preliminary remarks about the Greek Church, Greek society and Greek Jews are necessary to understand the categorization of attitudes and actions which now follows. Unfortunately space does not permit comparison with other Christian societies during the Holocaust period. Such comparison is fundamental to a clearer understanding of the vicissitudes of the Jews in the different arenas of their respective agonies. Nor can we explore here the efforts of the Greek governments in London and Cairo or the relations between Greeks and Jews in their many diasporas. Such detailed investigation will expose the mechanics and the motives for the impressive record of support and rescue of Jews in occupied Greece.

The Greek Orthodox Church actively supported the Jews of Greece during the period of occupation and deportation. How and why are the two corollary aspects of this impressive record. Archbishop Damaskinos of Athens issued an encyclical to his priests to succor Jews citing the New Testament - "There is neither Jew nor Gentile in Christ." He reminded his flock that Christ was himself a Jew and therefore Christians should assist Jews to escape the predators. Second, he authorized issuance of false baptismal certificates thus providing an ecclesiastical parallel to the police chief of Athens, Colonel Anghelos Evert (also in the Resistance), who issued false identification papers to numerous Jews. Third, he took a large number of Jewish children under his protection. Fourth, he protested against forced conscription of Jews (and also Christians) and later protested to both the Greek puppet government and to the German representatives against the deportation of Jews. The declaration to the former included as co-signatories a list of leading intellectuals and politicians of Athens and was unprecedented in occupied Europe. The latter protest (if not both) was done at the behest of a prominent Jewish figure Asher Moissis. Archbishop Damaskinos in Athens was parallelled by the concern of Gennadeios, Bishop of Thessaloniki, and even the Germanophile Prime Minister Rhalles., as well as the latter's predecessor. Both protested the deportations of the Jews repeatedly to the Germans in response to the pleas for help addressed to them by Rabbi Zvi Koretz of Thessaloniki. To the Greek Christians, the Jews were after all Greek citizens. Why deport them or treat them separately from the Greek Christian population? At the very worst, let them be interned within the borders of Greece, perhaps on one of the prison islands.

The attitude of the Church leadership filtered down to the local level where it found a welcome support. Various bishops encouraged their counterparts - the local chief rabbis - to flee to the mountains and arranged for their escape. Thus the aged Rabbi Pesach of Volos was warned and escaped to the mountains with the aid of the partisans and survived the war. The Bishop of Karditsa saved his French tutor who happened to be Jewish. When the Germans knocked on the door during their lesson, the bishop hung his great cross around the tutor's neck and after opening the door introduced him as his beadle. Shortly thereafter the tutor fled to Athens with his family and hid for the duration of the war. Local civil leaders too warned their Jewish counterparts - the presidents of the communities - to flee and aided them to escape, at least in the smaller towns such as Katerini. In Ioannina the mayor preserved the Torah scrolls until after the war, while those of Patras were also returned. In Rhodes it was the Turkish consul and the mufti who saved these artifacts. Thus the older alliance, forged over the generations and through the centuries, in the final analysis held true and bore fortunate results. It is unfortunate that for many reasons some Jews did not heed these warnings and in the case of Ioannina tragically rejected them. The latter result however detracts little from the intent.

The Catholic Church in Athens and Thessaloniki were not far behind their Orthodox cousins. Under the direction of the French ambassador, soup kitchens were set up to distribute food supplied through the Red Cross to the needy (including many Jews) in both cities. These also assisted in hiding Jews and in taking in Jewish children. One of the Greek tragedies is that there was no Jewish Brigade in Greece and too few survivors to redeem these orphans.

Those Jews who escaped to the mountains can be divided into two groups: 1)Those who hid and survived as a result of Greek hospitality (also practised by village Vlachs in Thessaly) which was extended to those who asked for it. (If one had gold, it was of course easier and less degrading but I have not heard of one case where anyone was turned away.) True, traitors turned in Jews, but they also turned in Greek Christians and Communists and anyone else wanted by the authorities; 2) and those Jews who joined the Resistance. About 900 of the latter were fighters, according to Joseph Matsas, the late Ioannina scholar of Greek Jewry and himself a veteran of the Resistance, while several thousand more assisted as nurses and doctors, liaison and logistics, interpreters, etc. In other words, wherever their education and skills best prepared and served them. This latter story is still untold, but information has been accumulating on the varied activities in the mountains. More interviewing and research is necessary before the full parameters of this story can be told. Perhaps one should note that most Jews remained incognito in the mountains. Why tempt fate? In many cases the village Greek was helping not a Jew but an urban Greek - perhaps who was just as alien. Whether or not he knew his religious affiliation was of little import to the host.

The Greek resistance was more ideological than religious, and its history is extremely complicated. Suffice it to say that most Jews lived in areas controlled by EAM-ELAS, a loose confederation of socialist and communist groups ultimately controlled by the Communist Party of Greece (KKE). Jews were welcomed along with anyone else who could be recruited. But for some reason ELAS, the military arm of EAM, and EAM itself was most hospitable to Jews. Spefic historical reasons for this have not yet been uncovered - there were no Jews among the leadership of EAM or the KKE - if indeed there were any beyond the various ones alluded to earlier.

In Thessaloniki where one might have expected overt sympathy, given the tensions of the 1920s and 1930s, to the persecutions of the Jews - and a misreading of sources could tend to support such an hypothesis, the situation was most complicated and therefore eschews generalizations. The population of Thessaloniki by 1941 was 75% Greek and 25% Jewish reflecting the massive influx of Anatolian refugees during the 1920s and the continued emigration of Jews since 1900 which had all but halved the Jewish population to circa 55,000. After Thrace was given to Bulgaria by Hitler following the Axis partition of Greece, the Bulgarians instituted a reign of terror aimed at the enforced Bulgarization of the new territories. Thousands of Greeks were slaughtered; tens of thousands fled west to German-occupied Thessaloniki. The Greek puppet governments in Athens tried desperately to alleviate their situation through various measures. The deportation of Saloniki Jewry in the Spring of 1943 provided much new housing for these latter refugees.

Since the late 1920s a fascist-type organization called EEE had emerged in Thessaloniki which drew its political support mainly from the young and unemployed Anatolian refugees. These actively challenged and fought with Jews until Metaxas clamped down on the group. Their newspaper, the Venizelist organ "Makedonia", was both viciously provocative and antisemitic. Its virulence was deemed responsible for the bloody Kambel riots in 1931 which ultimately led to a large-scale emigration of Jews from Thessaloniki to Palestine from 1932-1934. Already by 1933 the EEE was receiving funds and other support from the Nazis in Germany which financed their spread from Saloniki to other Greek cities. Yet there is little heard from or about the EEE after the German occupation of Thessaloniki in 1941 despite its reemergence from the obscurity of the Metaxas period. The bombing of its Thessaloniki headquarters by the Greek Resistance seems to have been the death blow to a moribund organization.

During the German occupation Christians and Jews suffered alike at first from the arrests of prominent intellectuals and political leaders (at least those who did not or chose not to escape) and the predatory treatment of the wealthy. Since a majority of the shopkeepers were Jewish, however, they felt the brunt of the German sack of the city. Jews particularly suffered from the great famine during the winter of 1941-1942 because they were primarily urban while the Christians had more access to the surrounding villages. The Jewish community was also poverty-stricken with an inordinately high percentage of poor. These indigents were a result of several factors: heavy emigration of the wealthy and middle classes since 1900; the fire of 1919 which destroyed the predominantly Jewish center of the city and left the majority of Jews homeless and without central institutions; economic competition by Anatolian Greek refugees; the hellenization policies of the Athens government some of which adversely affected the Jews commercially; ineffective local leadership that was in addition sharply divided over Zionist issues; the general poverty and political chaos in northern Greece. The community had been in precipitous decline throughout the interwar years: marginal survival among the poor became impossible after occupation and the death rate leaped astronomically during 1941 and 1942.

In addition to soup kitchens established by the Jewish community (with some help from EAM) and by the French Catholic community, the local Orthodox community also gave assistance as reported by George Exindaris (former Minister of Agriculture and Governor-General of Macedonia) who escaped from Thessaloniki to Cairo in mid 1943 where he rejoined the Greek government in exile. He related the failure of German attempts to stimulate antisemitism, the strong sympathy for the Jews among the public, and the appearance of an underground organization called EBE (Greeks, Help the Jews!) to give them moral and material support. This organization antedates the fighting resistance in Thessaloniki which by the summer of 1943 still numbered but a handful. By that date over 95% of Saloniki Jewry had been deported to Auschwitz.

True, Thessaloniki profitted from the deportation of the Jews. It received finally the valuable real estate of the extensive graveyard for which it had been negotiating nearly a decade. Also it now had homes to house the Thracian and other refugees: these would become a serious local problem after the war. Yet it was a Pyrrhic profit as Exindaris, a longtime friend of the Jewish community, suggests. The city actually lost more than it gained; some Christians realized it at the time and the city has acknowledged it in various ways since the war.

In other cities, primarily Athens, Jews were unstintingly aided by the local Christian population. Among these Christians were many Anatolian Greeks, a fact which points up the necessity to treat the complexity of Thessaloniki in a separate fashion. True, the Jewish percentage of the population was extremely small in Athens - about 3500-4000 with an additional 5000 refugees mainly from Thessaloniki amid some half a million - and had a legacy of goodwill that extended back over a generation. The level of assimilation among Athenian Jews was very high and enabled them to integrate more effectively with the Christian population. (This was also the general case among the Jews of central and southern Greece.) Also the German occupation of Athens came only after the surrender of Italy and its removal from the war in September 1943 and lasted until October 1944. Thus the Jews in Athens had only a year of fear and persecution while nearly all of Greece already knew of the deportations in the North and had been educated in German brutality by Hitler's reprisal policy which destroyed Greek villages wholesale and regularly executed men, women and children of the Resistance or as hostages.

Nearly all of the Saloniki refugees and their families found hiding places either together or as individuals. Most of Athens Jewry also went underground and successfully hid either in the city or in the mountain villages of Free Greece which harbored so many during the war. Both groups hid with business colleagues or school friends; the latter bonds are particularly strong in Greece. Jews from Central Greece filtered south to Athens leisurely during the occupation and hiding places for them were found by the Resistance, primarily EAM which had a number of Jews working within its varied organizations. A network was established which found temporary hiding places in the city and then passed Jews along to an 'underground' ferry service run by EPON (EAM's navy) and supported by the Palestinian Hagganah and the British SOE (although the latter apparently did not know of the predominantly Jewish nature of this ferry service) which brought them to neutral Turkey. No one except a traitor/collaborator (including several Jews) would turn over a Jew in hiding. Despite their own destitute situation, Greek Christians did not turn in any Jews for the reward offerred by the Germans. Many indeed were shot for harboring Jews and other wanted individuals against the law. In fact it was mainly those Jews who allowed themselves to be caught by having registered in conformance with Stroop's Athens edict of October 3, 1944 who were eventually sent to Auschwitz. These however constituted only a small percentage of those in hiding. perhaps less than 10%.

In retrospect, we should say that the Greek national character was primarily responsible for assistance to the Jews both in its official ecclesiastical status - the hierarchy and the laity of the Greek Orthodox Church - and in its secular hellenic tradition - hospitality to one in need and hatred of the German invader. The Jews were considered as Greek citizens, loyal and apolitical. (The post-liberation story would necessitate a qualification of this statement, but for the war years it will suffice.) Greece as a democratic state claimed to harbor no anti-Jewish tendencies despite Greek Orthodoxy being its official religion for 96% of the population. Greek politics thus succeeded in superseding the social and religious tensions inherent in its social structure, at least insofar as the Jews were concerned. Sources and memoirs suggest that this is an accurate assessment.

There was no official anti-Semitism in Greece (and very little social antisemitism) and neither could the Germans introduce it despite attempts to stimulate it or exaggerated interpretations by the Wehrmacht of random actions, in particular post-deportation looting. During the Metaxas dictatorship young Germanophile bureaucrats who had been influenced by the Nazi atmosphere of their university experience in Germany had been more rigorous in carrying out hellenization policies than their Greek-trained colleagues. Reports to the Alliance Israélite Universelle from their local directors do not indicate however any anti-Semitism in these actions. The universities of Thessaloniki and Athens, for their part, frankly rejected German anti-Semitism through manifest sympathies with their Jewish students. Nor did Greeks participate in the destruction of the various Greek Jewish communities, although the antagonisms in Thessaloniki exacerbated an already impossible situation there. In addition to the Anatolian Greek - Sephardi Jewish antagonisms, Thessaloniki was the seat of the German army in northern Greece: the Jewish fate there was sealed beyond reprieve. Only a few Saloniki Jews were spirited out by Christian friends and fellow students after the deportations began. Many of the remainder and especially among the young chose to share the fate of their families even when offerred the opportunity to escape. There are a number of stories of youth who escaped to the mountains through various underground networks, but who rejoined their families after the deportations began --- knowing full well that they would not return from their destination. Finally, survivor recollections from Corfu, Didymoteichon and other locales emphasize the sympathy expressed by the Christian population during the deportations, various attempts (some successful) at rescue of individuals, and supply of food and water during the tragic last journey. While certainly there was a psychological element of concern for a suffering victim, these reports reflect that special character of Greece - of which one aspect is "Freedom or Death" - that necessitates more detailed study.

REFERENCES

GREEK ORTHODOX - JEWISH CONSULTATION published in The Greek Orthodox Theological Review (1977) and in The Journal of Ecumenical Studies (1978).

Bowman, S.B., "Jews in War-Time Greece: Select Annotated Bibliography" in Greece in the 1940s: A Bibliographic Companion, ed. John O. Iatrides (Hanover, N.H., 1981), 83-94.

------------, "Jews in War-Time Greece," Jewish Social Studies, Winter 1986, 47-62.

------------, forthcoming entries in the Encyclopedia of the Holocaust: Greece, Athens, Salonica, Thrace, Corfu, Rhodes.

Kitroeff, Alexandros, "Documents: The Jews in Greece, 1941-1944 - Eyewitness Accounts," Journal of the Hellenic Diaspora, 1986, 5-32.

--------------------, "Greek Wartime Attitudes Towards the Jews in Athens," Forum, 60, Summer, 1987, 41-51.

Sevillas, Errikos. Athens-Auschwitz. Translated and Introduced by Nikos Stavroulakis. Athens, 1983.

Stavrianos, L.S., "The Jews of Greece," Journal of Central European Affairs, VIII, 1948.

Immigrant Jews, Christians and French Jews

Asher Cohen
University of Haifa

It is obvious that a title such as the above requires some clear definitions. None of them are easy nor self evident. For this study we view as Christians not only those who represented the Churches, but all who defined themselves as motivated by Christian considerations. We shall concentrate on those who held no anti-Jewish opinions. The French government in Vichy was surrounded and influenced by some important and well known Christians, both Catholics and Protestants, but these will not be discussed here.

The Jewish population in France, more than in any other European country, was clearly divided into two, or even three or four distinct components: the Jews who had been French for several generations; those who had immigrated into the country from the end of the nineteenth century and up to 1914, including their children; the immigrants mainly from Eastern Europe, who had come in the period between the two World Wars; and finally the Jewish refugees from Germany and Austria after 1933. For present purposes we shall make a less sophisticated distinction: identifying the first as French Israélites, and the latter two as immigrants. There are no reliable statistical data on the above mentioned population, and all quantitative evaluations are vague and tentative. The Jewish population of some 350,000 in France, in 1940, included 200,000 of foreign origin.

It should be kept in mind that from its very beginning the new French government in Vichy sought Christian support, mainly that of the Catholic Church. Coming after seventy years of anti-clerical republican regime, this was for the Catholic hierarchy and for many believers, an unexpected change of tremendous importance, and they judged the government on its educational policy, which was extremely favorable to the Church, rather than on its policy in the "Jewish question".

The first anti-Jewish legislation began shortly after the German occupation and the establishment of the government in Vichy. The first ordinances related only to the occupied parts, while the government legislated for the entire territory. The German occupying forces made no distinction between French and immigrant Jews; the anti-Jewish legislation of the French government did. The anti-Jewish laws were considered by most of the Christians, as by the majority of the French including the first resistants, as compliance to German dictates, though we know today that there was no factual basis for this belief. The objective of this paper is to show the development of Christian attitudes on this particular issue, and to demonstrate that they evolved parallel with the attitudes of the local French Jews.

In the minutes of the first Assembly of cardinals and archbishops of the "unoccupied" zone, in August, 1940, typical elements of the Church's attitude can already be found. On the one hand the participants acknowledged the existence of "an international Jewish community to which are attached the Jews of all nations" an expression that reminds us of the notions of the famous "Protocols", and on the other, that "a State cannot brutally drive away the Jews with no regard to their activities, to deny their natural, individual or familial rights."(1) The document was only lately published by François Delpech.

The first publicly known protest against the anti-Jewish legislation was a letter from the President of the French Protestant Church, Pastor Marc Boegner (March 26, 1941), to the Chief Rabbi of France, in which he criticized the law but also included statements declaring that:

> the State has been faced with a serious problem because of the massive immigration of a large number of foreigners, Jews or non-Jews, and because of the hasty and unjustified naturalizations, [...] a law which [...] strikes indiscriminately at the Israélites, who have been French for numerous generations, and often for centuries, and at those who were naturalized yesterday.(2)

Since this was an official document of the Protestant national council, it was carefully phrased. At that time, not only were some 40,000 immigrant Jews interned in French camps where they were being helped by Boegner and various Protestant organizations, but the naturalized Jews too had already been expelled from civil service and liberal professions, and extensive denaturalization was under way. But, would the pastor have written these grave words had he not been sure that they would not offend the Chief Rabbi? This letter was widely publicized, first by the Protestant pastors, then by the underground press and finally by the legal press in Paris, which depicted Boegner as a traitor to Pétain's regime. It also influenced a certain Christian public opinion. People who wrote to the Marshal, seeking to help Jews, often quoted from it, or even attached a copy to their own letters.

Another text was prepared in the Theology Faculty of Lyon to condemn the second anti-Jewish Statute. It contained not only the same ideas, but nearly the same expressions, such as: "hastily accorded naturalizations" and "one cannot deny that there is a Jewish question".(3) It was banned then by the ecclesiastical hierarchy for being too critical of the government. Statements to the effect that on the one hand, there was a Jewish question in France because of immigration though it should be resolved in a humane manner, and on the other, that legislation and policy should distinguish between French and immigrant Jews, characterized the pro-Jewish attitudes and were most common in appeals by Christians to help or to save Jews. In one of the letters written by a Christian woman to Petain we can distinguish the xenophobic motives widely used by the government in its propaganda, together with the deep concern for the "others", the French Jews.

> That one should take measures against foreigners and the naturalized, is all in justice for the good of the country, but don't you think, Monsieur le Maréchal, that the others have a right to their little spot in the sun, not have to tremble the way they have been doing for months, and even to help remake a strong France.(4)

During the same period, from late 1940 to early 1942, several protests were addressed to the government by French Jews. In all those known, they emphasized their centuries of contribution to the nation, mainly in the field of military performance, even if they were well known public figures.

> Israélites by religion, or descendants of Israélites [...] those who have had the honor to serve under your command in the armies, those whose sons and brothers have fallen for the salvation of all, those whose parents and ancestors have spilled their blood side by side with your parents and ancestors [...] French not by adoption, but forever [...](5)

In an unpublished text written by the well known historian, Louis Halphen, in

1941 or 1942, the idea was developed that the French Jews were of the same ethnic origin as the French Christians, and related to Jews of other countries only by common religion.(6) Another famous historian, Marc Bloch, wrote in his will, before going into the Resistance, that his sole allegiance was to the French nation and that if possible, his five citations should be read at his grave.(7)

At the same time that the text of the Theology Faculty of Lyon was prepared, the Consistoire protested in a letter addressed to Marshal Pétain. In previous statements the Consistoire had protested against the inhumane conditions of the foreign Jews in French concentration camps, but when the second Statut des Juifs proclaimed the government intention to intern "même les Français", the reaction was incomparably stronger: "the law knows and recognizes only a herd of Jews, where the nationality, even French, is only an accessory without value or scope."(8)

Obviously, the French Israélites, both on the individual and the collective organized level, emphasized that they expected to be considered French, and as such, privileged by the government. Common to all the texts we have mentioned, whether from Christian or Jewish source, is that they expected the government to act in a humane and civilized manner toward the immigrant Jews. They could not be excluded from the human race, and certainly no cruelty or atrocities were to be permitted. Nevertheless, a clear distinction was made between the generations-old French Jewry and the immigrant Jews, or even those who had been naturalized lately and were thus legally French. These attitudes were widely accepted and can be considered as accurate expression of both Christian and French-Jewish public opinion. Dr. Joseph Weil, himself of Alsatien stock, wrote on the attitudes concerning the interned immigrant Jews:

> The French Jews displaying their pedigree with pride, leisurely counting and recounting their five, six, seven generations of ancestors on French soil, participate in this burlesque comedy. They help their co-religionists with devotion and with all their might, but in the name of humanitarian sentiments much more than in solidarity in the face of an indignity and a common misfortune.(9)

Still, there were some exceptions and the most important among these was the Cahiers du Témoignage Chrétien, which first appeared in November, 1941. This was an underground paper of both Catholic and Protestant theologians, expressing the opinion that all racism is in flagrant contradiction to basic Christian values. No distinction was ever made between French and immigrant Jews. The April number (IV-V) was called "Les racistes par eux-mêmes" and contained an anthology of racist quotations, opposed to anti-racist theories. The Protestant theologian, Karl Bart, the condemnation by Pius XI and several other Dutch and German prelates were quoted. There was no mention of any French source or of the contemporary pope, Pius XII.(10) This was the expression of a very small dissident group, certainly not authorized by the Catholic hierarchy, even if we know that all the bishops of the "unoccupied" zone were sent a copy of the paper and no effective efforts were made to halt its publication.

In December, 1941, the great Catholic writer, Paul Claudel, sent a letter to the Chief Rabbi: "I am writing to tell you of the disgust, the horror, the indignation felt [...] by all good French and especially the Catholics."(11) This letter was published in full by the clandestine Combat.(12) This was the first time that an important Petainist Catholic personality took a stand against the anti-Jewish policies. It happened at the same time as the first appearance of the Témoignage, but completely independent of it and from a totally different section of Catholic public opinion.

During 1941 and the first months of 1942 the number of immigrant internees in the south decreased from the initial 40,000 to less than 10,000. On the other hand, from May to the end of 1941, more than 8,650 Jews were interned in the north, among them more than 2,000 prominent French Jews. The organized reaction to these arrests, most of them made by the French police in Paris, was hardly different from what had been expressed till then. Nevertheless,

French popular reaction, recorded in August by the police in Paris, expressed solidarity with the French Jews and there was no opposition to the rounding up of the immigrants, with some exception for veterans of the French army. The first important round-ups and deportations came in 1942. They started in Paris on July 16-17, continued at the beginning of August in the camps of the south, and at the end of the month from the towns and the villages of the "unoccupied" zone. They were all directed against immigrant Jews only.

Some protests, none of them published, were sent to Vichy following the round-ups in Paris. Mgr. Suhard, the archbishop of Paris, wrote in the name of all the bishops of the occupied zone of his "deep sorrow" for "so many mothers and children being arrested."(13) The Consistoire, in its protest worded this time with unprecedented strength, wrote very similarly of "great numbers of small children separated from their mothers with the most extreme violence."(14) The same elements, concerning mainly the arrests of children and women, is clearly reflected both in the reports of the prefects and even more in the great number of articles that appeared, for the first time since the occupation, in the underground press.

On August 17, after the southern camp inmates had been transferred to Drancy, but before the Jews of the towns were taken, Rabbi Jacob Kaplan, in the name of Chief Rabbi Schwartz and the Consistoire, had an audience with Cardinal Gerlier, archbishop of Lyon and First Primate of the Gauls, to ask his intervention. The rabbi's main argument was that "thousands of innocents have been sent to Germany, not to work there, but to be exterminated."(15) This was the first time that such an eventuality was brought up by an official personality in France. Effectively, two days later, the archbishop addressed a letter to Pétain, in which he wrote of "the nature of the treatment, or that foreseeable, for the physical organization of the convoy [...] that ignores the essential rights of all human beings and the fundamental principles of charity."(16)

In coordination with Gerlier, Pastor Boegner sent his letter of protest the next day. While Mgr. Gerlier completely ignored the information brought to him by Rabbi Kaplan, Boegner worded his letter in a much sharper style. He wrote, inter alia, that "the truth is that men and women who were refugees in France for religious or political motives were handed over to Germany, many knowing in advance the terrible fate awaiting them."(17) In fact, these men and women were not deported for any political reason but simply because of their "racial" origins. On September 9, Boegner went personally to see Pierre Laval in a last attempt to save at least the children from deportation, but the French Prime Minister remained unmovable; the children must go, too. The pastor concluded this dialogue with the deaf with the sad conclusion: "I spoke to him of massacre, he replied on gardening", since Laval persisted in repeating the German propaganda that Hitler was establishing Jewish settlements in the East.(18)

At this time, the strongest and the clearest protest was that of the Consistoire.

> The fact that the people handed over by the French Government were gathered without regard to their physical condition, among them sick people, old men, pregnant women and children, confirms that the deportees were not meant to be used as manpower by the German Government, as claimed, but for the well defined purpose of exterminating them ruthlessly and systematically.(19)

None of these protests was made public, but the Consistoire sent its text to a great number of personalities and it thus had a relatively large distribution. There was no mention of them in the underground papers.

While the arrests in the occupied territory and the deportation from the camps passed with relatively little reaction from Christian public opinion, the round-ups in the cities were immediately followed by a strong and unexpected popular reaction. A Frenchman in Nice wrote to the prefect on August 26, the day that the police started to collect the Jews. The letter was short and clear, very typical of the reaction we often find elsewhere and we reproduce it _in extenso_.

> I have just learned that the Jewish refugees are being given to Hitler for Poland - even old men, women and children. I do not like Hitler - but I am for collaboration. This is not collaboration, however, but slavery, it is inhuman! As a Frenchman of old stock, as a combatant, as a Catholic, I implore you to stop immediately!(20)

A large number of similar letters, reports on the south presented to the prefects, reports of the delegates of the _Commissariat aux Questions Juives_ and finally reports by the prefects to the government on September 1, all gave the same picture: French public opinion disagreed with the unselective arrest of the refugees and even more, with their extradition to the Germans. This last element reflected the hurt national pride and seems to have been a major element in these reactions. The Christian component of the reactions is everywhere dominant.(21) As some of the contemporary reporters remarked, this was the first case, since the summer of 1940, in which the Vichy government was widely criticized by popular opinion. Such was the situation in the southern towns and villages, on the eve of the first public declaration against the deportations.

As a matter of fact, the first bishop to react after the Jews were taken from the camps, was Mgr. Saliège, the archbishop of Toulouse. His pastoral letter was read in all the churches on August 23, despite the expressed interdiction of the prefect.

> In our diocese, touching scenes have taken place in the camps of Noe and Recebedou. The Jews are men, the Jewesses are women. The foreigners are men, the foreigners are women. Not everything is permitted against them, against these men, against these women, against these fathers and mothers. They are members of the human race; they are our brothers, like so many others. A Christian cannot forget this.(22)

On the 30th, on the morrow of the great round-ups in the south, it was Mgr. Théas, the bishop of Montauban, who issued his pastoral letter to be read "with no commentary, at mass in all the churches and chapels of the diocese."

> I want to voice the indignant protest of the Christian conscience and I proclaim that all men, Aryan or not, are brothers since they have been created by God; that all men, whatever their race and religion, are entitled to respect from individuals and from states. The present antisemitic measures are an affront to human dignity, a violation of the most sacred rights of an individual and of the family.(23)

Cardinal Gerlier prepared a message to be read on Sunday, August 6, "to which not a word should be added." Unlike the first two, he clearly retained the Pétainiste tone and reaffirmed his loyalty to the Marshal. Nevertheless, he was "openly asserting the imprescriptible rights of a human being, the sacred character of family ties, the inviolability of the right of sanctuary and the insistent demand for that fraternal charity which Christ made a distinctive badge of his disciples."(24)

On the same Sunday the pastoral letter of Mgr. Délay, the bishop of Marseille, was also read. Of all the texts, his was the one that expressed the most far reaching understanding of Vichy and even repeated the rather antisemitic accusation that the immigrant Jews caused "so much harm" to France. On the other hand, he was the one that dared to say that the Jews were "arrested en masse, only because they are Jews and foreigners, men, women and children, personally blameless, separated from their families and sent perhaps to their death."(25)

On September 22, the Reformed Church sent a circular letter to all the churches to be read by the pastors the following Sunday.

> [...] divine law does not concede that families desired by God should be broken up, that children should be separated from their mothers, that the right of sanctuary and its mercy should be disregarded, that the dignity of the human being should be violated, and defenseless

> individuals delivered to a tragic destiny. [...] The Gospel orders us to consider all men, without exception, as brothers for whom the Savior died on the cross. Besides, how could the Church ever forget that the Jews are children of the flesh of the very people from the Savior of the world was born?(26)

There was no other public protest from any of the other prelates of France. All four Catholic bishops, including two archbishops, came from the "unoccupied" zone, where there were 35 bishops, including seven archbishops. Undoubtedly this was a minority expression among the high clergy of the south. One cannot comment on those who chose to remain silent. Some of them were antisemites, like Mgr. Caillot, the bishop of Grenoble, but many of the others certainly were not. We still lack adequate local research for most of them and the fact that the ecclesiastical archives still remain inaccessible, does not encourage such research. Nevertheless, we do know that some of the silent bishops did have a positive attitude toward the Jews and even contributed immensely to their rescue. One of these was the bishop of Nice, Mgr. Rémond. For example, the report sent by the local representative of the Commissariat in Nice on his refusal to cooperate is significant.

> After such ostracism which by Mgr. Rémond's order strikes at our services, we estimate that the Jews will have all the facilities to procure false christening certificates. [...] We can assert that we are witnessing a sort of coalition for the defense of the Jews, whose position is being strengthened from day to day.(27)

A comparison of these texts with those of 1940-41 reveals great similarities, but there are basic differences from the attitude expressed by the Témoignage, which opposed any discrimination on religious or, even more on racial grounds. All the bishops and even the Consistoire emphasized the inhuman treatment in the same way as was done by the Assembly in 1940, by Boegner and the Theology Faculty of Lyon in 1941. The argument of the bishops was identical to the popular opinion expressed in many letters and reflected in most of the reports. It was the indignation in face of brutal violence and not a specific sympathy for the persecuted immigrants that made the French Christians react. Gerlier accepted that the government "has a problem to resolve" and Délay admitted that "the Jewish question poses difficult problems." The messages of Saliege and of Theas were less ambiguous. The French Israélites, through the Consistoire, reacted with less compromise, but the basic approach was not different. They did not argue, like the Témoignage, the basic incompatibility of discrimination with French tradition, but rather emphasized the inhumane treatment, and the inclusion of unemployable categories and veteran volunteers of the French army. This does not prove automatically that the French Jews were motivated by the same feelings as the Christians; nevertheless, it does suggest that they were reluctant to react outside the framework of a wide general consensus, or at least in harmony with a respectable part of non-Jewish public opinion.

The basic attitudes of most of the Christians, and of French Jews as well, remained to a great extent unchanged, although they constituted an unexpected element in the totally new situation of the implementation of the Final Solution. From the very first days of the debacle Christian public opinion had a pronounced nationalist tendency. The immigrants were alien and the Jews doubly so. Traditional antisemitism was not the main motive and there was hardly any sign of popular antisemitism at any time during the war. The differences perceived by Christian public opinion were cultural and not "racial". If this very public opinion, actively or passively supported racist legislation, it is an inherent contradiction and not a flaw in the research. Public opinion was nationalist and remained so even after August, 1942. It reacted to inhumane round-ups and the extradition, which was perceived as a national insult. It happened when Germany was still at the peak of its success and we can hardly assume that the development of the war decisively influenced the attitude toward the Jews. For the French, the Second World War was never a Jewish war.

The public declarations of the bishops did not create the public reactions; the two were born simultaneously. Nevertheless, the fact that some bishops did raise their voices encouraged both the lower clergy and the common believers to help rescue Jews. It certainly influenced government policy. Laval brought it up in his negotiations with SS Brigadenfuehrer Karl Oberg, pointing to Cardinal Gerlier as "the head of the anti-government opposition". The chief of the German police accepted this as an argument to slow down deportations. Perhaps he also had transportation problems and this provided an easy solution for him. A year later, in August 1943, when the problem of denaturalization of the immigrant Jews came up, Pétain asked the opinion of the representative of the episcopate in Vichy, Mgr. Chapoulie, who answered that it would lead to deportations, and "new deportations would provoke an amplified wave of emotions and sorrow among the Catholics, and it is probable that the bishops would feel compelled to make themselves heard once more."(28) Pétain refused to sign the act.

In the reports presented by the prefects or by the agents of the <u>Commissariat</u> for the Jewish Question, the assistance of Christians was, justly, always emphasized. Often, names were indicated of pastors and priests who had given false baptismal certificates or provided hiding places to Jews. The same was confirmed in numerous testimonies of survivors. Clearly, no distinction was made as to what kind of Jews. In a conclusive report of the <u>Commissariat</u> for the period right after the first deportations, from October 6, 1942, based on seven regional reports from the south, the conclusion was: "Headed by the high clergy, a large part of the French population rises against the measures taken at the end of August; the people of France understand nothing of the Jewish question."(29)

A gradual change in attitudes took place only from the end of 1942 and thereafter. Social assistance, both for those in French concentration camps and for refugees in the "unoccupied" zone and in Paris, had existed since 1940. This was partly organized by the immigrant organizations and partly by Christian and <u>Israélite</u> bodies. When the problem of the Jews became one not of discrimination but of survival, social help, especially in a legal framework could not give an adequate answer to deportation. That situation required opinions and attitudes which could be translated into actions. Those that could be effective were illegal.

During the last months of 1942 it still seemed that mainly the immigrants were in danger of deportation. Some people, including one or two Catholic priests, l'abbé Glasberg or le père Braun, for example, helped the Jews, often not in a strictly legal way, but this was rare and took care of only a few individual cases. It is not the aim of the present paper to present an exhaustive list of rescue activities. This has not yet been done and perhaps never will be. Nevertheless, it is valuable to adduce a small number of important examples to show the tendencies.

At the beginning of 1942, a group of intellectuals comprising Jews, some of them immigrants and Communists, Protestants and Catholics, founded an underground organization under the name of Mouvement National Contre le Racisme. The initial aim was to inform public opinion of the racist persecution. Two journals were published, one in each zone, J'accuse and Fraternité. From July this organization became one of the most efficient instruments to rescue children, especially in Paris, by using the very important assistance of Pastor Vergara, the director of the Protestant school, "La Clairière".(30) At the same time, Jewish children were also saved by various other Jewish-Christian organizations, in Paris.

During the deportation from Lyon, a group of 108 children was rescued from the camp of Vénissieux, in a combined action of Catholic priests, the OSE organization, some French <u>Israélites</u> and a Communist Jew.(31) Vital help was also provided by Cardinal Gerlier, who backed père Chaillet, his representative and the soul of the illegal hiding of the children from the prefect who sought to deport them. This first organized rescue of the children brought about the establishment of a network of an underground OSE, led by a Jew, Georges Garel, but most of the children were rescued through the intermediary of various ecclesiastical schools and organizations. The diocese of Toulouse, thanks to Mgr. Saliège and above all his auxiliary bishop, Mgr. Courrèges d'Ustou, was one of the most important centers of these activities.(32)

A similar organization, led by a Sepharadi Jew, Moussa Abadi, also specialized in rescuing children, and was directed by him from the bishopric of Nice under the personal protection of Mgr. Remond.(33) In Marseille, with important ramifications in various cities of the south, a small group led by "André" Bass came into existence to provide Jews with false papers and to indicate rescue possibilities. The group consisted of some Dominicans, Jesuits and père Marie-Benoît the Capucin, two pastors, several members of the Jewish scout movement and some "notables" of the traditional society of Marseille.(34)

Other chapters of the rescue movement were organized by the Protestants in the Cevennes. This is a rather poor region in the south of the Massif Central, a traditional hideout of persecuted Protestants. The village of Le Chambon-sur-Lignon and the school of Collège Cévenol became famous because of the number of Jews and other refugees rescued there. This was typical for the entire area, and all the Jewish rescue organizations knew that a person sent to any pastor of these villages would be well received.(35) The Protestant Youth organization, the CIMADE, transferred some of its members from legal social assistance to an illegal network of smugglers of persecuted persons to neutral Switzerland.(36) In a great number of cases, Jews were rescued by ecclesiastical institutions and monasteries as well as by gentile individuals motivated by humanistic and Christian convictions.

The differences between the immigrant Jews and the French <u>Israélites</u> tended to decrease to a large degree when after November, 1942, the persecutions became less and less selective. Many of the French Jews joined the Resistance on an individual basis, but many others adhered to specific Jewish organizations. In 1943 the Jewish Resistance organizations succeeded in creating a central coordinating body. This included the Communists and the Zionists and had a certain preponderance of immigrants. The main representative body of the <u>Israélites</u> remained the <u>Consistoire</u>. Clandestine negotiations to establish the joint representation were conducted above all in view of the approaching liberation. An agreement was reached in the last months of that year and the unification document was signed in January, 1944, to establish the <u>Conseil Représentatif des Juifs en France</u> (CRIF).(37) It was a long process, and while the new body was much less than a unified leadership, it was nevertheless, an institutionalized collaboration between the two Jewish entities. For the first time, since the large scale immigration in the 1920's, the immigrants, including the Communists and the Zionists, were accepted as an integral part of French Jewry. We could observe that the process was parallel to the changes in the Christian attitude to the same immigrant Jews.

By the time of the liberation, the immigrant community of the Jews in France had become a more or less accepted part of modern France. The process is reminiscent of the acceptance of the late nineteenth century immigration after the First World War. This time also it came about after a long period of suffering, partly in recognition of the persecutions the Jews had endured and largely due to the French government and administration, and partly for their participation in the Resistance.

NOTES

1. Parts of the minutes are quoted by François Delpech, "L'épiscopat et la persécution des Juifs", <u>Eglises et chrétiens dans la IIe guerre mondiale</u>, (Edited by Xavier de Montclos, Monique Luirard, François Delpech, Pierre Bolle), Presses Universitaires de Lyon, 1982, v. 2, p. 283.

2. Pastor Boegner's letter to the Chief Rabbi of France, Isaie Schwartz, March 26, 1941, <u>Quelques actions des Protestants en France en faveur des Juifs persecutés sous l'occupation allemande, 1940-1944</u>, ed. CIMADE, Paris 1946, p. 5. The same day he also sent a very similar letter to Admiral Darlan. Both letters are published by Pierre Bolle, in: <u>La France et la question juive</u>, (Edited by Georges Wellers, André Caspi, Serge Klarsfeld), ed. Sylvie Messinger, Paris 1981, pp. 192-3.

3. Eglises et chrétiens, v. 2, pp. 288-9, and the very important clarifications by Wladimir Rabi and François Delpech, ibid., v. 1, pp. 195-201.

4. Archives Nationales, Paris (AN), AJ38-67, letter from Canadel par Rayol (Var), May 16, 1942.

5. Letter of protest, April, 1941, signed by fifteen well known personalities, Centre de Documentation Juive Contemporaine (CDJC), CCDXIX-104, published by: Adam Rutkovski, La lutte des Juifs en France, pp. 49-50. Similar letters, ibid. pp. 44-46, Amouroux, Quarante millions de pétainistes, pp. 463-75. See also, Jacques Meyer, "Sur la politique de Vichy et les anciens combattants juifs (1940-41)", Le Monde Juif, n. 108, 1982, pp. 139-150. This protest was even quoted by France Libre, on June 12, 1942, Les voix de la liberté, Ici Londres, 1940-1944, (Edited by Jean-Louis Crémieux-Brilhac), La documentation française, Paris 1975, pp. 138-9.

6. Louis Halphen, Le Judaïsme en France, (manuscript), Bibliothèque de Documentation Internationale Contemporaine, Paris, Q pièce 195, Res/1-2.

7. Marc Bloch, L'étrange défaite, Paris 1946, pp. 193-4.

8. CDJC, LXXII-2, published by: Rutkovski, p. 53. The law, commonly called the second Statut des Juifs of June 2, 1941, Journal Officiel, June 14, 1941.

9. Joseph Weill, Contribution à l'histoire des camps d'internement, CDJC, Paris 1946, p. 19.

10. Renée Bédarida, Les armes de l'esprit; Témoignage Chrétien (1941-1944), ed. Ouvrière, Paris 1977, pp. 41-42, 111-137, 312-322; and also: "Les 'Cahiers du Témoignage Chrétien' et l'antisémitisme", in: La France et la question juive, pp. 211-230.

11. The letter dated December 24, 1941, published in: Cahiers Paul Claudel, n. 7, La figure d'Israël, Gallimard, Paris 1968, p. 324.

12. Combat, n. 2, February 1942.

13. Quoted by: Monseigneur Guerry, L'Eglise en France sous l'occupation, Flammarion, Paris 1947, pp. 19, 40; Jacques Duquesne, Les catholiques français sous l'occupation, Grasset, Paris 1965, p. 256; Serge Klarsfeld, Vichy-Auschwitz, Fayard, Paris 1983, v. 1, p. 280.

14. Quoted by: Klarsfeld, Vichy-Auschwitz, v. 1, p. 295.

15. Report of August 17, 1942, a copy of which was given to me by Chief Rabbi Kaplan, to whom I express my deep gratitude. See also, Jacob Kaplan, L'épreuve de la persécution, Minuit, Paris 1952, pp. 88-94.

16. Klarsfeld, Vichy-Auschwitz, v. 1, p. 342.

17. Quelques actions des Protestants en France, pp. 11-12; quoted also by: Klarsfeld, Vichy-Auschwitz, v. 1, pp. 344-345.

18. Quelques actions des Protestants en France, pp. 14-15.

19. A protocol of the meeting that prepared it and the protest, quoted by: Klarsfeld, Vichy-Auschwitz, v. 1, pp. 358-361.

20. Archives Départementales des Alpes-Maritimes (ADAM), 166.W.12.

21. Number of similar letters, AN, AJ38-6, -61, -244, -3596, -3598; Archives Děpartementales des Bouches-du-Rhône (ABDR), M.6.11058, M.6.11070, on these letters: A. Cohen, "Pour les Juifs", Pardès, n. 1, pp. 142-3.

22. The pastoral letters were published several times, see: Klarsfeld, Vichy-Auschwitz, v. 1, p. 355; the prefect's intervention, ibid. pp. 353-4. The only change made by Saliège was, that speaking of the events in the camps, he replaced "scènes épouvantables", by "émouvantes".

23. Ibid., p. 369.

24. Ibid., p. 405.

25. Ibid., pp. 412-413.

26. Quelques actions des Protestants en France, pp. 15-16.

27. AN, AJ38-244, and see also, -243.

28. Klarsfeld, Vichy-Auschwitz, v. 1, pp. 407-409, v. 2, pp. 330-331.

29. AN, AJ38-244.

30. Jacques Ravine, La résistance organisée de Juifs en France, Julliard, Paris 1973, pp.109-113;

31. Anny Latour, La résistance juive en France, Stock, Paris 1970, pp. 60-62; René Nodot, Les enfants ne partiront pas!, Lyon 1970; see also Glasberg on this, on Gerlier and the "autochtone" French Jews, Eglises et chrétiens, v. 1, pp. 203-205.

32. Testimonies of Georges Garel, Archives of Contemporary Jewry, Hebrew University, Jerusalem, 1/64, CDJC, CCXVIII-104-6; L'OSE sous l'occupation allemande, Geneva 1947, pp. 58-63; Latour, La Résistance juive en France, pp. 40-42, 62-68.

33. Testimony of Moussa Abadi, CDJC, CCXVII-7; Ralph Schor, Monseigneur Paul Rémond, un évêque dans le siècle, Serre, Nice 1984, pp. 117-122. Latour, La Résistance Juive en France, pp. 68-70.

34. Testimony of Joseph (Andre) Bass Archives of the Institut d'Histoire du Temps Présent, Paris, 72-AJ98, CDJC, CDXLVI-6-7; Poliakov, L'auberge des musiciens, pp. 92-94; Lucien Lazare, La Résistance Juive en France, Stock, Paris 1987, pp. 183-184.

35. Philip P. Hallie, Lest Innocent Blood be Shed, Harper & Row, New York 1978, pp. 120-142; Cévennes, Terre de refuge, 1940-1944, (Edited by Philippe Joutard, Jacques Poujol, Patrick Cabanel), Presses du Languedoc, Club Cévenol, 1987.

36. "Passages de frontières", souvenirs de Genèviève Pittet, Quelques actions de protestants de France, pp. 67-70. See also, Yad Vashem Archives, Jerusalem, M-31/316.

37. Adam Rayski, "La fondation du Conseil représentatif des Juifs de France", Le Monde Juif, n. 51 (1968), pp. 32-37; Lazare, La Résistance juive en France, pp. 293-296.

CAN THE FEW BECOME THE MANY? SOME CATHOLICS IN FRANCE WHO SAVED JEWS DURING THE HOLOCAUST*

Eva Fleischner

Montclair State College

ABSTRACT

This paper focuses on a study of French Catholics who saved Jews during the Holocaust. It analyzes come taped interviews with rescuers, and seeks to determine their motivations. Given the ancient anti-Jewish tradition in Christianity and the ambivalent relationship of the French Catholic bishops to the Vichy government, these "Righteous among the Nations" present us with questions: How did they overcome Christian antisemitism? In what ways were they different from other Catholics? What lessons can be learned from their actions that may help us to overcome Christian antisemitism in the future?

Let us at the outset define two limitations of this paper. First: We shall confine ourselves to the French Catholic Church.[1] Secondly: Our principal focus will be on the actions and motivations of some individual Catholics who were personally interviewed, rather than on the Church as institution. While interviews which are conducted forty or forty-five years after the event cannot give us infallible historical evidence, they represent a unique type of testimony, one which will no longer be available to us some years hence. In order to give the actions of these persons their proper setting, we must first briefly consider two historical factors: Christian antisemitism, and the attitude of the official Catholic Church toward Jews and Judaism during the Shoah.[2]

CHRISTIAN ANTISEMITISM, OR THE "TEACHING OF CONTEMPT"[3]

As a result in large part of the horror of the Shoah, the age-old existence of Christian antisemitism is today widely acknowledged; as is the view that it laid the foundation for much of western antisemitism. Many Christians, including some of the highest authorities in the Church, today admit the Teaching of Contempt.

Briefly summarized this teaching, found in liturgy, preaching, and theology, has for nearly two thousand years presented the Jewish people as spiritually dead, cursed, punished by God because they had rejected the Messiah. By the early second century the infamous deicide charge had been formulated. Jews came increasingly to be depicted as the enemies of God, allies and agents of the devil. As the Church became identified with the temporal power of the Roman Empire these attitudes were concretized in anti-Jewish legislation, and frequently led to discrimination, accusations of blasphemy and ritual murder, which in turn prompted persecution, expulsion, and mass slaughter.[4]

---

*The research discussed in this paper is part of a larger study begun in 1985, at the suggestion of Professor Yehuda Bauer. It was, and remains, our hope that the study of Christians who saved Jews during the Holocaust may provide some insights into How Christian antisemitism can be overcome. I am deeply indebted to Professor Bauer for his inspiration and support. A grant from the Vidal Sassoon International Center for the Study of Antisemitism enabled me to take a leave of absence from Montclair State College and to spend six months, first at Yad Vashem, then in France. The work begun in those months was continued during my return to France in the summers of 1986 and 1987.

It can be, and has been, cogently argued that the Teaching of Contempt, while not sufficient in itself to explain the Shoah, helped prepare the soil for Hitler's all-out "war against the Jews."[5] The schema proposed by Raoul Hilberg is well known: To the medieval Church's attempt to solve the "Jewish question" through converting Jews or -- that failing -- expelling them from their native countries the Nazis added a third step, annihilation.[6]

The pervasiveness of this teaching in Catholic tradition (and in Christian tradition in general) raises questions concerning Catholics who saved Jews during the war. Had these persons somehow "escaped" the Teaching of Contempt? If so, how? Had they acted in spite of it? What obstacles, in themselves and in their communities, did they have to overcome? Had they acted consciously as Christians? How did their Christianity differ from the Christianity of the majority? Can we discern the motivations that led them to rescue Jews? These are some of the questions that form the background of the present study.[7]

THE FRENCH CATHOLIC CHURCH DURING THE SHOAH[8]

We are concerned here with the official body of the Catholic Church in France, the Assembly of Cardinals and Bishops. Two major chronological phases can be discerned in the attitude which this Assembly took toward the persecution of Jews: from the beginning of the Vichy regime in June 1940 to the summer of 1942; and, the summer and fall of 1942.[9]

The long silence (June 1940 - summer 1942). This was a critical period, because the machinery for the persecution of Jews was now set in place: the first and second Jewish Statutes, of October 3, 1940 and June 2, 1941 respectively; and the establishment of the General Commisariat for Jewish Questions under Xavier Vallat on March 29, 1941.

The Church did not react publicly to these measures. It was reluctant to criticize Pétain, and eager to prove its loyalty to his government. In this it reflected French public opinion in general during the months following France's defeat. The country was shattered morally. The Vichy government represented for many the only hope of regaining some dignity and -- so they thought -- of maintaining some independence from Germany. This hope was focused largely on the person of Marshal Philippe Pétain, who enjoyed enormous prestige as the hero of Verdun in World War I. There were many in France, even among those who later joined the Resistance, who sincerely believed at first that any decision made by Pétain could not but be for the good of France. Only gradually did it become clear -- and to many it never became clear -- that Pétain had bartered away the honor and soul of France.

If the figure of Pétain had great appeal for the French in general, this appeal was heightened in the case of the Catholic Church. Pétain had never been a particularly "good" Catholic.[10] But when he assumed the reins of government in the moment of national crisis he used a language that found deep resonance among Catholics. He spoke of repentance, of the need for France to expiate its sins and to return to traditional moral values. The Church, which had not fared well under the Third Republic, felt itself rehabilitated.[11] This explains in part the loyalty to Vichy even on the part of those bishops who, in 1942, were to protest the inhumanity of Vichy's anti-Jewish measures.[12] It is the background for Cardinal Gerlier's famous words in Lyon in October 1940: "Pétain is France, France is Pétain."

The silence is broken (summer and fall 1942). The summer of 1942 was a turning point, both in the persecution of Jews and in the public's response to it. As the deportations gained momentum and the trains rolled throughout France, many who until now had been silent began to speak out. This was true also of the Catholic hierarchy; for a brief period it assumed a role of moral leadership. In less than one month five bishops issued official protests, two of them in a prophetic voice.[13] The Archbishop (later Cardinal) of Toulouse, Jules-Gerard Saliège, was the first to speak. On August 23, 1942 he ordered a letter to be read in the churches of his diocese in which he passionately decried the inhuman treatment of Jew:

> .... That children, women, men, fathers and mothers, should be treated like a vile herd of cattle, that members of the same family should be separated from each other and sent to an unknown destination -- it was reserved for our time to witness this tragic spectacle. Why does the right of asylum no longer exist in our churches?....[14]

Inspired by Saliège's example the bishop of the neighboring diocese of Montauban, Pierre-Marie Théas, in turn wrote a pastoral letter which was read the following Sunday, August 30.[15]

> .... I must make heard the indignant protest of the Christian conscience, and I proclaim that all men, aryan or non-aryan, are brothers, because they are created by the same God; that all, whatever their race or religion, are entitled to respect from individuals and the State.

> The current antisemitic measures are in contempt of human dignity, a violation of the most sacred rights of the individual and the family ....[16]

Three more declarations followed in September: from Cardinal Gerlier of Lyon, Bishop Delay of Marseille, and Bishop Mousseron of Albi. While deploring the inhuman treatment of Jews, both Gerlier and Delay mentioned "the problem" posed for France by the refugees, and asserted the government's right to "take all appropriate steps."[17]

Even though these declarations excused the Vichy government, their impact on French public opinion was considerable. This impact can perhaps best be gauged by Vichy's attempts to have Saliège's letter suppressed (without success). Police reports dealing with the Jewish question that were kept throughout France between the summer of 1942 and the fall of the Vichy regime in 1944 also express frequent concern about the influence of the bishops' declarations on the rank and file of French Catholics.[18] One can only speculate how different the course of history might have been, and how many lives might have been saved, if the bishops had spoken out earlier and with one voice, and had thrown the full weight of their considerable spiritual authority into the scales on behalf of the Jews. "What a tragedy, that this happened (only) in the fall of 1942. If all this had been said in 1941, when the deportations had as yet hardly begun!"[19]

SOME WHO COULD NOT BE SILENT

It is against this background that we shall now make the transition to the main focus of our research on individual Catholics who saved Jews. Let us begin with excerpts from an unpublished document, a war-time diary kept by a young French woman, Germaine Ribière.* At the time of the first entry she was twenty-two years old, a student at the Sorbonne.[20]

A Voice in the Wilderness [21]

May 14, 1941. This morning they began rounding up Jews. 7,000 Jews in the fourth arondissement [the Marais, ancient Jewish quarter of Paris]. Most of them are said to be Polish Jews, and the poorest ones at that. Has the great dance begun in France? My God, give me strength.

They had to be ready in an hour, and were told to take along food for one day. We don't know where they are going .... I ache for them in my whole being, I ache for my Jewish brothers and sisters .... My God, permit me to suffer with them. Accept their suffering, make it life-giving.

May 27, 1941. For the past two weeks the sky has become more and more overcast. The Church, the hierarchy, remain silent. They allow the truth to be profaned. Father Lallier [a priest in charge of the Catholic student movement in Paris] told me that there are more urgent things for us to worry about than the Jews. Last Saturday, when we told him that we wanted to write something about the Church and the temporal order, he urged us not to speak about racism [the reference here is to the Catholic Student Movement of which Germaine was an active member].

The tide is rising, rising. I am afraid that one of these days, when we wake up, it will be too late and we shall all have become Nazis. I am afraid, because people are asleep. Those who should keep watch are the ones who put others to sleep. We must shout the truth no matter what the cost. But who will do it? I know that there are Christians who are willing to accept martyrdom if necessary; but they do not know what is happening. They wait for a voice, and the voice does not speak. We must pray that it will speak.

France has betrayed her soul, and now Nazism is gaining the upper hand. All genuine values are dragged in the dust. We no longer have any honor. Petain has become the French Hitler. The great dance has begun and the world is blind. It is blind because it is afraid of death. The clergy remain passive. As in Austria, they accept what is happening ....

---

*I wish to express my gratitude to Germaine Ribière for giving me permission to publish excerpts from her diary.

June 1941. I am in Paris for a few days, we have to put the affairs [of the J.E.C., the Catholic Student Movement] in order. I have the impression that the earth is shaking, and I am shaking along with it .... Often I long to go away, all alone. But this would be running away. The world is our stage leading to God. We must not burn this stage, we must live it to the best of our ability.

August 31, 1941. Catholic Action is in total confusion. There is chaos everywhere, an immense confusion .... And in the midst of it all, a small number of people who see clearly .... But those who, with all their might, fight against a policy of collaboration with Germany because they know what is at stake, they are accused of mixing religion and politics, the throne and the altar!

March 24, 1942. Persecution of the Jews. Christ suffers in his body, and we Christians stand by and watch. I do not want to be a spectator.

This week I visited two camps.[22] Total contempt for the human being. At Récébédou the guard, a little drunk, grabbed a young Jewish boy by the throat, held him motionless for a few moments, then had his fun by brushing his face with the toilet broom -- and it was not clean. Many other similar scenes.

Yesterday I visited Rabbi Deutsch [of Limoges]. I told him to make use of me in any way he can. I am willing to do anything for them, with the help of God. I cannot run away.

March 25, 1942. There is no way out. Humanity is the body of Christ. One part of that humanity is being tortured, those who are Jews. And we look on in silence as the crime is being perpetrated. We are the accomplices of evil, and we are at peace.

It is the body of Christ himself that is being tortured. We say that we believe in Christ, that we love him, yet we allow him to be despised. No, I cannot tolerate this silence, I cannot lie. I shall go all the way, with the help of God.

April 24, 1942. Since my last entry this immense history of the Jewish people continues. Man sinks each day more deeply into the mire of sin. The camps continue to run, the world of Satan heaves beneath our feet. But Christ will conquer in the end.

June 1, 1942. For the past month much tension: visits to the internment camps, absence there of any Catholic witness.[23] Always the problem of the human being, torn by sin....

June 11, 1942. The problem of the Jews -- no, the mystery of the Jews. The mystery of the human being. I try to confront all this. Always alone, in solitude, alone with Christ.

November 14, 1942. The Germans crossed the demarcation line on November 11, armistice day. I am crushed by the misery all around me.

February 4, 1943. Every day the evil grows. Nazism increases its grip, the Catholics are asleep. Last Wednesday, January 27, the whole team of Amitié Chrétienne was arrested by the Gestapo.[24] Thursday evening I went to the archdiocese [Lyon] to ask what could be done about the children and the Amitié. The Cardinal's [Gerlier] private secretary told me: 'The Cardinal has enough stories like this one, he certainly won't go along.' Later I called the Cardinal. He cleverly referred me to G, dean of the law faculty at Lyon .... All of them, one after the other, are cracking under the pressure. I don't understand: We are told to bear witness to Christ. I am tired of this ridiculous prudence, of this fear of physical death!

n.d. 1943. I spoke about morality with Msgr. T. [a distinguished member of the Catholic University of Lille, in the north of France]. 'We must not try to put Christian morality everywhere,' he told me. And he went on to comment on St. Thomas .... It really is strange: Under the cloak of St. Thomas they slip in Maurras![25]
Why do we speak of Christian morality as if it were some sort of seasoning which

> one may or may not add to life, at certain moments? Why do we refuse to see Christ everywhere? As if all that is good, all at is just, all that is true were not Christ's? It is almost as if we were ashame f him. We no longer witness to him in public because, in our hearts, we do give him what is his. We speak of "discretion" when we should say "cowardice." Under the pretext of being discrete, we betray, we scandalize. And, by a clever juggling act, we keep our consciences pure .... what hypocrisy!

Let me briefly comment on these journal entries. The date of the first entry, May 1941, is significant. It is written more than a year before the first official Catholic protests against the persecution of the Jews were to be heard.[26] Nor had Témoignage Chrétien, which was to become one of the main organs of Christian spiritual resistance, been founded at this time; the first issue appeared six months later, in November 1941.[27]

Thus, Germaine Ribière was without any support from the official Church[28] -- a source of pain for the devout young Catholic woman. Several entries in her journal speak of her vain hope for a prophetic voice, a voice that could galvanize Catholics who might be willing to give their lives, if only they knew what was happening. "But the voice does not come."

Not only did she have no support, but she ran into explicit opposition and criticism from Church officials (cf. May 27, 1941, and February 4, 1943). In one of our conversations she referred to an incident in connection with one of her frequent visits to the internment camps. It was a Sunday, and upon leaving the camp she went in search of a Mass in a nearby village. The last Mass had been celebrated, so she asked the priest to give her communion, explaining why she was late. "You mean you went to see those people?" He refused to give her communion.[29]

No wonder that she feels alone and longs to get away from it all. But to escape would be to evade her responsibility, to go against her conscience; not to take seriously the demands of this world, which is "our way to God."

Given the focus of this paper let us ask: Is it possible to know what sustained this young woman in the midst of the indifference all around her, in the midst of her loneliness? Can we pinpoint the sources of that inner strength which shines through these pages? She herself provides part of the answer. Let me quote from one of our conversations (December 18, 1985):

> EF: You saw so clearly the passivity, the failure, of the Church. What sustained you in your faith? What kept you from giving up, from leaving the Church?
> GR: Christ. I come from a region of France where there are vineyards [she was born in the Limousin]. When I read in the gospel Jesus' parable of the vine and the branches I understood. I knew what a vine is, the analogy was perfect for me. Humanity is the body of Christ. I felt as if I were holding the vine and the branches in my hand.... How could I have denied this relationship?

It was this sense of the oneness of all humanity, which was grounded, for her, in Christ, that prompted her to tell Rabbi Deutsch of Limoges that she was willing to let herself be used in any way possible on behalf of her Jewish brothers and sisters (cf. above, March 24, 1942).

The atmosphere at home had also been decisive. "My mother raised us to have respect for life, to marvel at life, at all life, ... Our house was always open to everyone. Whenever someone was in trouble they would come to see my mother, even in the middle of the night." Among those in trouble were Dr. Gaston Lévy and his wife. Her mother gave them the papers of Germaine's sister and her husband, who were in North Africa. Dr. Lévy looked after her mother during her last illness, despite the open disapproval of neighbors, one of whom was overheard to say, at her mother's funeral: "Can you imagine what she [Germaine] did? She had a Jew look after her mother!"[30]

Germaine speaks of her mother's courage, and how "she shared everything with us, as we came and went. She never tried to hold me back with a single word. Even when she was sick, shortly before her death, she told me: 'Maine, you must leave again, I know. Don't worry about me. I know that you are needed, that you must go back to Lyon.' And so, I was away when she died, they called me home."[31]

Besides her deep faith and her mother's influence, another factor may have enabled her to keep going: she was never afraid. "I simply did what had to be done, I lived those days as if they were part of everyday life.. I think that is why I was able to sleep at night all through the Occupation."[32] What to others appeared heroic -- "We used to call her our Joan of Arc"[33] -- to her was the simple response to the need of the moment.

Although I had not realized it at the time, a small incident on the occasion of our first meeting was to provide me with an important clue into this woman's character and approach to life. We had arranged to meet, at her suggestion, for noon Mass and then to have lunch together. We were walking to the restaurant, engrossed in conversation, when she suddenly interrupted herself: "I am worried about this little girl, I wonder if she has lost her mother." I had noticed, vaguely, a little girl in front of us, about two years old, but had not really "seen" her. Germaine had seen, and worried. As it turned out the mother was close by, walking ahead of the child. As I came to know her in the months that followed, and to learn of the extraordinary things she had done during the war -- crisscrossing France, going back and forth to Poland, infiltrating the Gestapo -- I realized how much of a piece she is. She is Germaine Ribière because she notices a little girl who may be lost and in need of her help, in the middle of Paris in 1985, just as the Jews needed help during the war.[34]

A priest in Carcassonne

Let me next speak of Fr. Albert Gau, honored by Yad Vashem in September 1987. A priest of the diocese of Carcassonne and active in the Resistance from the very beginning, Fr. Gau saved the lives of many Jews. Several "covers" served him well. As chaplain of the local high school, and director of the charitable works of the diocese, he used the large building at his disposal as a convenient place to turn out false papers and store the necessary equipment. He had managed to steal official seals from the Gestapo files, "we were well equipped!" The building also doubled as his living quarters, and he often hid Jews there for a time. A restaurant he had opened, which was supposedly run by some women he knew, was another convenient front. And the Carmelite convent on the outskirts of town, of which he was the chaplain, cooperated gladly when ever he needed help. On one occasion the superior admitted into their cloister a Jew who was being pursued by the Gestapo, and disguised him as a Carmelite nun. [35]

Fr. Gau had the tacit support of his bishop, who asked to see the texts of his sermons at the cathedral ahead of time and approved them. Eventually, however, as protest against the anti-Vichy tone of his sermons mounted, the bishop asked him to stop his clandestine activities. "It is getting too dangerous, the Gestapo is after you, Father." That same day a woman rang his bell. She was Jewish, and pregnant. Fr. Gau invited her in, then he called the bishop. "I have a pregnant Jewish woman here. You told me to stop, so I'll send her over to your place, you have plenty of room." The bishop replied quickly: "Go ahead, do whatever you have to do, but keep her!" [36]

Despite his cordial relations with his bishop Fr. Gau is critical of the attitude of the French hierarchy during the war:

> What I reproach them is their obedience to the State, to Marshal Pétain. In my view, even if Pétain had been duly elected, we had to disobey him because he was a tool of the Germans .... But Vichy granted the Church certain privileges for its schools, it reinstituted processions, etc.[37] And so the bishops supported the government. Even the courageous Cardinal Saliège had too much respect for the State .... When the bishops told the people that they must obey and do forced labor in Germany, as a patriotic duty, I distributed circulars to all the young people of our region, saying: If a bishop tells you to go to the S.T.O. [obligatory labor service] he loses his authority, you need not obey him. I don't tell you to join the Resistance, but I do tell you to act according to your conscience .... As you can imagine, the bishops didn't like me. Until the Liberation -- then they were glad to be able to point to me ...." [38]

Fr. Gau was denounced several times and had three narrow escapes from the Gestapo. "Yes, of course it was dangerous, but it was the greatest period of my life.... And when you are young you are not so easily afraid." [39]

He had become a priest at the age of twenty-five. The local seminary had seemed too narrow to him and he had asked to be sent to Paris, to Saint Sulpice. "There I found an international atmosphere, freedom of thought, and great teachers." [40]

The rescue of Jews was not, according to his own words, a religious issue for him. "It wasn't really a question of religion for me, it simply had to be done. They were living in frightful conditions, hiding in cellars, hunted day and night.... They suffered so much." [41] Independence of character, love of the truth, courage, and compassion -- all these played their role in the help Fr. Gau gave to Jews.

The woman who hid Jules Isaac*

In August 1986 I spent three days in the home of Germaine and Jacques Bocquet, who had hidden Jules Isaac for more than a year during the war. What follows is based in part on our conversations, in part on an article written by Germaine Bocquet.[42] First, some historical background.

In November 1943 Jules Isaac's entire family, with the exception of his oldest son Daniel who was fighting with de Gaulle's forces in Algeria, was arrested in Vichy. They were later deported to Auschwitz, where his wife, daughter and son-in-law perished; the youngest son managed to escape from Auschwitz and survived. Isaac himself escaped arrest through one of those bizarre "accidents" in which the history of the Shoah abounds: he was out of the house getting a haircut when the police came. His initial reaction, upon finding them gone, was one of desperation. He presented himself at police headquarters, so that he could join his family in whatever lay ahead. It was 6 p.m. and the office was closing; he was told to come back the next morning. During the night friends convinced him that his arrest would not save his family; he had a work to do and must go into hiding. A week later he met Germaine Bocquet.

Germaine and her husband Jacques belonged to the Resistance network of Edmond Michelet in Brive.[43] By November 1943 the situation had become so dangerous that the members of the network decided to disperse. Germaine and Jacques had moved in with Jacques' mother -- who lived in an isolated corner of France. When contacted by another member of the Resistance and asked if they would be willing to hide someone who was being hunted by the police Germaine readily agreed (Jacques was away on a mission at the time). She was asked to meet the stranger in Clermont-Ferrand, and told him of the primitive conditions under which he would have to live with them -- no running water, gathering wood to heat the house, etc.; he did not mind. She did not want to know his name -- "It was too dangerous. And besides, the fact that he was a hunted man was all I needed to know." But he insisted on revealing his identity to her. So it was that Jules Isaac came to spend more than a year with the young couple. Twins were born to them while he was there, and a lifelong friendship developed between them and the one they call to this day "the uncle."

Few external events punctuated the isolated existence of that year. "He drew comfort and the will to live from his work, into which he plunged almost as soon as he came to us." The "work" was a first revision of the manuscript that was to become Jesus and Israel.[44] He needed all sorts of religious books for his research, all Germaine had was a Bible and daily missal. Thanks to a friend, Fr. Klein, a priest of the Sacred Heart at a village not far away, she was able to make regular trips to the library of the convent there, equipped each time with a list of books Jules Isaac needed.

> He began to tell me at length about the purpose of his book, the importance of which I did not at first understand. In my mind antisemitism was a by-product of Nazi racism, and I was quite unaware of its roots in Christian teaching. The religious education I had received [see below] had instilled in me respect for the Jewish people, and gratitude that they had given us the prophets, the Virgin Mary, Christ, and the apostles. Jews were for me the people of the Covenant, of God's promises. And Jesus, the Messiah, was a faithful son of the Law, which he had come to bring to perfection, not to abolish. I had never heard the Jews spoken of as Christ-killers; I had been taught that our sins had crucified Jesus. Later, during the Occupation, in the deeply Christian milieu of Edmond Michelet, I encountered nothing but sympathy for Jews and the desire to help them; not even the faintest trace of antisemitism.[45]

Her conversations with Jules Isaac, as he worked on his book, were the young woman's first encounter with Christian antisemitism.

> He made me read the texts he was collecting. Many were terrible in their virulent hatred of Jews. And they were the work of famous Christian theologians --Catholic, Protestant, and Orthodox! I was stunned to learn how many texts from scripture had been used to create a climate of misunderstanding, even of hatred, of Jews. I learned, with deep pain, of the responsibility of the Christian churches for what Jules Isaac was to call the Teaching of Contempt, a teaching which has contributed to the genocide of the Jewish people. From that day on I understood the urgency and importance of his mission....

---

*I wish to express my thanks to Claire Huchet Bishop for putting me in touch with Jules Isaac's son Daniel; and to M. and Mme. Daniel Isaac, who gave me the name and address of Mme. Germaine Bocquet, and told me much about Jules Isaac. Let me also take this occasion to thank Germaine and Jacques Bocquet for their warm, open-ended hospitality in their beautiful home in a hidden corner of southwest France.

> When spring came the two of us used to go for long walks in the countryside -- he was a tireless walker. He would speak to me of his life: of the passionate commitments he had lived with his friend Peguy; of the Dreyfus Affair; of the Great War, and of his work as historian. And always he would come back to the subject that preoccupied him more than any other: Christian teaching about Judaism. Often, our walks would end with his invitation to me to read a text from one of the Church fathers. Sometimes, after reading me aloud pages he had just edited, he would ask: 'Is this too painful for your Christian sensibility? Am I being too harsh?' He was, indeed, harsh at times. But can you water down the truth?[46]

It was in those months that Germaine discovered an aspect of the Christian tradition of which she had known nothing until then. Because of the focus of my research I was particularly interested to try and understand the reasons why, for so long, she had been ignorant of this aspect of Christianity. Several factors became clear as we talked.

Early childhood. Her mother had died when she was two years old. Her father, a brilliant, highly educated man, lover of the classics, friend of Léon Blum (they had been classmates at the Ecole Normale Supérieure), held an important post in Paris. He had become an atheist. Already his mother, who was born in 1958 and had been a public school teacher, had been strongly anti-clerical and an ardent supporter of the Second Republic. "We had every kind of newspaper and magazine at home, but religious publications were banned."[47] Germaine's early childhood was lived in a vibrant intellectual atmosphere, devoid of all religion. "Maybe I was fortunate. Had I grown up in a traditional Catholic milieu I might have encountered antisemitism."

When she was eight years old her father, despite his aversion to religion, decided to have her baptized, "for social reasons. He thought it would increase my chances of a good marriage later." With baptism came three years of obligatory religious instruction, to which he agreed as a matter of honor. Little did he anticipate the profound changes those three years were to bring into his daughter's life.

First encounter with Catholicism. The catechist who was in charge of the religion classes in Germaine's school in Versailles was a young woman, then in her early twenties, by the name of Françoise Derkenne, who was destined to become, after World War II, one of the leaders of the catechetical renewal in the French Church. Her influence on the children was profound, as was that of the school chaplain, a priest from the local parish. Between them catechist and priest instilled in the children a love of God, and, young though they were, the beginnings of a life of prayer. In the catechism classes the children were taught stories from the Bible. "The Jews were for me the people who gave us Jesus."

Those three years marked the child so deeply that when they came to an end and her father told her, "At last you are done with all that nonsense!" she replied: "Oh no, Papa. It has only begun!"[48] Behind his back she started going to daily Mass, and continued her religious education throughout high school.

The catechist. I wanted to know more about the woman who had exerted such a crucial influence in Germaine's life (I had met Françoise Derkenne twenty-five years earlier, but in an entirely different context in which the question of Judaism did not arise). One week after my visit with the Bocquets she graciously agreed to see me in her Paris apartment. She spoke of her early years as a young catechist. Biblical studies for lay Catholics, especially for women, were unknown in the 1920's. But she told her children of the great biblical figures as she prepared them for Christmas, beginning with Abraham. Had she known, I asked, what we today call the Teaching of Contempt? "No. I came from a deeply Christian family, there was no antisemitism at home. And my love of philosophy had always led me to approach my faith critically. I simply discarded elements that seemed distorted and harmful to me."[49] We can arrive at several conclusions from these two encounters:

The fact that Germaine did not know any antisemitism in her earliest years was due, according to her own analysis, to an enlightened, anti-religious, intellectual milieu.

When she did encounter Catholicism, at the age of eight, it was a Catholicism free of antisemitism; a Catholicism that instilled in the child the seeds of an abiding love for the Jewish people. This was due to the work of a remarkable teacher and a remarkable priest, both devout Catholics. Were they typical? Probably not; but this heightens, rather than lessens, their significance.

Françoise Derkenne's freedom from Christian antisemitism, forty years prior to Vatican II, was not due to any deliberate effort on her part, not to an avant-garde theology concerning Judaism, but to a Christian home untouched by antisemitism, to her own critical good sense and love of truth, and to her concern for the children in her care. She wanted to educate them in an authentic love of God and neighbor.[50]

GENERAL FINDINGS

Let us now go on to speak about the interviews in more general terms. Of the forty-six rescuers interviewed twelve were lay women, nine nuns, five were lay men, and twenty were priests or religious. Of these, ten have been honored by Yad Vashem as of December 31, 1987.* [51]

We shall first address the question of motivation. Beyond the conviction, shared by all, that Jews must be helped because they were victims, no single common motive emerged. The rescuers acted for a variety of reasons: compassion, patriotism, personal contact with Jews, love of Jews and Judaism, repentance for Christian antisemitism, obedience to authority, the demands of Christian faith, love of Christ, resistance against the hated Germans, a sense of Justice, the influence of a teacher. At times there is no "reason" at all, but simply a spontaneous impulse to help. [52]

The question of proselytism should be raised in this context: to what extent was it a motivating principle? Many instances are known where Catholics had Jewish children baptized, especially in convents. If I do not include it in the list of motivations, this is so because I found little evidence of it. This does not mean that the desire to convert the persons helped may not have been present. Our study here encounters two problems inherent in all oral history: How accurate is the memory of those interviewed, especially many years after the event? and, Are they, perhaps unconsciously, "reconstructing" reality? This second question is particularly pertinent in the case of Catholics, for whom much has changed with regard to Jews since Vatican II, including the issue of proselytism. Traditionally Jews have been an object of conversion for the Church, as they still were frequently during World War II. In recent years, officially since 1977, the Church has renounced proselytism of Jews. Since all my interviewees were aware of this change might they, consciously or unconsciously, have claimed not to have attempted to convert Jews, even if they had done so at the time? The question remains open.

If we cannot prove that the hope for baptism did not motivate some of the rescuers, there is evidence that some at least had no thought of, or even emphatically rejected, proselytizing. Let us give some examples:

Fr. Daniel Pézeril, then a young priest in Paris and today an old bishop, made out more than a thousand false baptismal certificates for Jews, most of whom he never met. [53] -- Rolande Birgy, who found homes for many Jewish children in the French Alps before sending them to Switzerland always made sure, first, that the families hiding them would respect the children's Jewish faith. She also arranged, on the weekly day when French children went to catechism classes, that priests would instruct the Jewish children in their own scriptures. [54] -- A nun who was director of a large boarding school in Paris during the war had hidden many Jewish children there, sending them across the demarcation line whenever possible. In response to my question whether she had thought of having these children baptized I received an emphatic No, and the following story:

> A woman who was a friend of the school came to see me one day; this is what had just happened to her: She had been walking in the street, when a policeman came out of the metro carrying a little Jewish boy in his arms. He looked around furtively and, seeing no one else in the street, came up to the woman. 'Madame, won't you please take him? I am supposed to take him away, they have already arrested his parents. I can't get myself to do it, please take him!' She did, and took him home with her. Then she came to see me.
>
> I asked her what she intended to do with the child -- he was perhaps three years old, very beautiful. 'I'll keep him and raise him as if he were my own son.' And she did. A year later she came to see me again and said: 'You know, Sister, I have been thinking that we really ought to have the boy baptized.' 'I don't agree,' I said, 'we don't have the right to do it, neither of us is his mother.' She did not understand, and we began to argue. 'You understand nothing,' she angrily told me. I told her, 'Madame, you are the one who doesn't understand. You are not the child's mother. He won't be adult for another fifteen years or so. Only then can he say, I am a Jew, I want to remain a Jew. Or, I don't.' She went away in anger, she did not understand.

---

*I wish to express my deep appreciation to Dr. Mordecai Paldiel, Director of the Department of the Righteous at Yad Vashem, where I began my research in the summer of 1985. He spared neither time nor effort to acquaint me with the work of his department, making available to me all the materials in the archieves. Dr. Paldiel shared with me his extensive knowledge of the efforts that have been made by Yad Vashem for more than thirty years, and that continue to be made, to honor those who saved Jews during the Shoah. The help I received at Yad Vashem greatly facilitated my work in France.

I am not suggesting that these cases, and others that could be given, were typical; only that the hope for baptism was not the single, universal motivating factor it is sometimes said to have been.[55]

Several other conclusions may be drawn from the interviews.

1. People's actions do not always coincide with their ideology. Not infrequently their deeds are better than their ideas (or theology). Some examples:

I was told by several people that they had encountered no antisemitism before the war, in their religious upbringing, religious communities, or among fellow seminarians and priests. "The Teaching of Contempt? No, never." Yet, some of the old Christian stereotypes were evident in our conversations, such as: "I feel sorry for them because they still don't see." "They don't have the full truth." "When Jesus came they didn't recognize him," etc. Such statements were usually made matter-of-factly, without hostility. All those who made them had saved Jews, had risked their lives. Some spoke with great fondness of the Jews they had known and helped.

The fact that these stereotypes were still alive in them, unrecognized, twenty years after Vatican II points to the tenacity of Catholic teaching. At the same time, their actions indicate that existential circumstances, such as a situation of great need, can play a more decisive role than catechism or theology in spurring one to action.

2. I found a further discrepancy at times between a person's attitude and actions, and family background and education. One of my initial assumptions had been that family had played a major role in shaping an individual's attitude toward Jews. This proved not always the case. Some had reacted against their family background. Circumstances, or a friend or teacher, had played a more decisive role than family. Again, some examples:

Father Michel Riquet, S.J. came from an <u>Action Francaise</u> milieu: his godfather had been a close associate of Charles Maurras. Yet, as a seminarian this man had developed a deep sympathy for Jews. He attributed this to two factors: to a philosophy teacher of his (Jacques Maritain), and to his friendship with two religious Jews he had met in thc Scout movement in the early 1930's.[56] -- A nun from an aristocratic family spoke of antisemitism at home [not unusual among "the Right" in France]. She had rejected it "because it is unChristian and unjust," she replied in answer to my question.[57] Such examples indicate that family background did not always play a decisive role. Some reacted against it, or overcame family prejudice as a result of other influences, or out of their own conviction.

3. In some cases theory and practice coincide. A person's actions and attitudes are rooted in their faith and background.

Germaine Ribiere (cf. pp. 3 above) is a striking example of such inner consistency and harmony. Rolande Birgy, already referred to in another context, also illustrates this point. She told me at the start of our conversation that "at home, we never read the New Testament without the Old. I remember how, as a little girl of eight, I used to marvel that the Jewish people still exist."[58] This is all the more remarkable because Rolande was born in the early 1900's, at a time when practically no Catholics read the Bible. Equally remarkable is the following story:

Roland spent much of the war in the French Alps, the <u>Haute Savoie</u>, hiding Jewish children and getting them into Switzerland. One day she was arrested by the French police. An official came to see her in jail, and the following conversation ensued between them:

he: Why on earth do you help those Jews?
she: because I am French, and Catholic!
he: but you surely know that the Jews killed Christ?
she: Monsieur, let me tell you something. Anyone who has had any catechism at all knows that it wasn't the Jews who killed Christ, but our sins!
he: (sheepishly) I guess you are right .....[59]

This is an example, incidentally, of both the Teaching of Contempt, and the overcoming of it.

While I found that people in whom family background, faith, and action coincided were the exception, they were -- perhaps for that very reason -- particularly impressive. They give one a sense of the potential power of a lived Christian faith when uncorrupted by prejudice.

4. French Catholicism at the time of the <u>Shoah</u> was not a uniform phenomenon.

There were those who, in their Catholic education, had received a positive image of Jews and Judaism. Others had encountered the Teaching of Contempt, but had reacted against it on the basis of their own Christian conviction and understanding of the Gospel. And there were those who had helped Jews in spite of having been influenced by the Teaching of Contempt.[60] None of this is surprising, given the varied faces of the Catholic Church in France in the 1930's.[61] I encountered in my interviews frequent references to Catholic movements, periodicals, and intellectuals, such as Le Sillon and Marc Sangnier, Esprit and Emmanuel Mounier, Temps Present and Stanislas Fumet, the Dominicans of Les Sept, Jacques Maritain and others.[62] Many of those interviewed spoke of the profound influence of these movements or individuals on their lives. They had acted as an effective and powerful antidote to the antisemitism of the Right, in particular of the heirs of the Action Française. The latter were deeply and inherently antisemitic, and provided a fertile seedbed for the often virulent antisemitism of the Vichy government.[63]

THREE PERSPECTIVES

Is it possible, out of this complex and at times contradictory evidence, to gain some insights that may shed a new light on the relationship of Jews and Catholics? Or, to reformulate the question: Does this research suggest ways by which the few can become the many? Three basic perspectives are suggested by this study.

1. Some Catholics were not only free of antisemitism and any influence of the Teaching of Contempt, but had received in their religious education or seminary training a positive image of Jews and Judaism. "Abraham is our father." "Spiritually we are Semities." "Jesus was a Jew." "The Jews are the people of God." "They are our roots," etc. This vision of Judaism was so powerful that, when they did encounter Christian antisemitism during the war (e.g., in the silence, or hostility, of some church officials), this failure of their Church spurred them on to greater efforts in combatting antisemitism. Their pain, unlike a sense of guilt which can either paralyze or lead to a new antisemitism,[64] proved productive and fruitful. There is no denial here of the Church's sins; these women and men see them more clearly than many other Catholics. Instead, the failure of their Church drives them to continued and consistent effort to eradicate antisemitism from Christianity; inspires them to a lifelong struggle to work for a new attitude vis a vis Judaism in the Catholic Church.

Jews and Judaism are here seen in a positive light, in accord with an authentically biblical Christian faith.

2. For many of the people interviewed the rescue of Jews played an important part in their struggle against racism and Hitler, in the battle for democracy and freedom. For a very few, however, the destiny of the Jews was, and remains, the key to the destiny of humanity; and the destruction of the Jewish people carries with it the potential destruction of humanity. Thus, for Germaine Ribiere the agony of the Jews is not only their agony, not only her agony, but the agony of all. Jewish identity and destiny are here seen from the perspective of the God of Abraham, Isaac, and Jacob, of Moses and of Jesus.

Jews and Judaism are interpreted in the light of the Hebrew scriptures, as paradigmatic for all humanity.

3. The one common motivation present in all is their compassion for Jews as victims. Many rescuers would have done -- and did do -- as much for any other human being in need. "We helped them because they were victims, period," because they were unjustly persecuted," "because they had nowhere to go," "because they were in deadly danger," etc. These Catholics saw in the Jewish victims fellow-human beings in need who must be helped. They lived, consciously or unconsciously, Jesus' parable of the Good Samaritan, recognizing in the hunted Jew their neighbor.

Any oppressed human being is my neighbor, therefore just as surely the Jew.

CONCLUSION

What possibilities do these perspectives hold for the overcoming of Christian antisemitism? What can we learn from the actions and beliefs of Catholics who saved Jews during the Shoah that will help build a new relationship between Jews and Christians? At least three challenges for Christian education are suggested by the lives and deeds of the men and women studied.

1. the need to instill in Catholics a positive view of Jews and Judaism, grounded in a Christian faith uncorrupted by antisemitism;

2. enabling Catholics to see Jewish history and destiny from within the revelation of the Hebrew scriptures, as paradigmatic of human destiny as such;

3. educating children and young people in such a way that they will recognize in the hunted and oppressed, whatever their creed, color, or race, their neighbor, their own "flesh and blood", and will, therefore, reach out to the downtrodden and oppressed of the earth whoever they may be and wherever they may cross their path.[65]

This love of neighbor is not exclusively Christian, although Christians can find in Jesus' life and teachings one of its finest expressions. Jesus was a Jew, a product of the Judaism of his time. The teaching of love of neighbor, which is found also in other world religions, thus has come to Christianity directly from Judaism. Christians, however, have frequently claimed a monopoly on this teaching, because they have claimed a monopoly on divine revelation, on love of God, and on God's love. In actual fact they have often, in the name of love of God and Christ, persecuted others, particularly the people from whom they received their own revelation. What is asked of Christians is not to love better than others, but simply not to pervert the teaching of Jesus and what is best in their own tradition.

NOTES

1. It should be emphasized, however, that the aid to Jews in France during the Shoah was frequently a genuinely ecumenical undertaking, and that Protestant leaders spoke out on behalf of Jews earlier than did members of the Catholic hierarchy. See Jean-Marie Mayeur, 'Les églises devant la persécution des Juifs en France,' La France et la Question Juive. 1940/1944. Centre de Documentation Juive Contemporaine (Paris: Sylvie Messinger, 1981). Also Pierre Bolle, 'Les protestants et leurs églises devant la persécution des Juifs en France,' ibid.

2. The term shoah, Hebrew for catastrophe or disaster, is gradually replacing the over-used term Holocaust.

3. The phrase was coined by the French historian Jules Isaac, in his book The Teaching of Contempt(New York: Holt, Rinehart and Winston, 1964; French edition 1959). It has since become a widely used synonym for Christian antisemitism.

4. The following are some of the best-known and most accessible works on the subject: Alan T. Davies, Anti-Semitism and the Christian Mind (New York: Herder and Herder, 1969). A Roy Eckardt, Elder and Younger Brothers (New York: Schocken Books, 1973); with Alice L. Eckardt, Long Night's Journey into Day (Detroit: Wayne State University Press, 1982). Edward Flannery, The Anguish of the Jews (New York: Paulist Press, 1985, rev. ed.). Franklin H. Littell, The Crucifixion of the Jews (New York: Harper & Row, 1975). James Parkes, The Conflict of the Church and the Synagogue (Cleveland: World Publishing Co., 1961). John T. Pawlikowski, Catechetics and Prejudice (New York: Paulist Press, 1973). Rosemary R. Ruether, Faith and Fratricide (New York: Seabury Press, 1974). Clark Williamson, Had God Rejected His People? (Nashville: Abingdon, 1982).

5. This phrase, which is also the title of Lucy Dawidowics' history of the Holocaust, reflects a view shared by a number of scholars: that the destruction of the Jews was Hitler's over-riding preoccupation, eventually assuming greater urgency in his mind than defeating the Allies.

6. Raoul Hilberg, The Destruction of the European Jews (New York: Quadrangle Books, 1967), p. 3.

7. In preparation for my research I constructed an instrument consisting of 169 questions, covering a broad spectrum of questions relevant to the subject. Its purpose was to guide me, rather than to be used as such. I wish to express my thanks to Joan Ringelheim and Alice and Roy Eckardt for the valuable help they gave me.

8. See the following works on this subject: Xavier de Montclos et al., ed., Eglises et Chrétiens dans la IIe Guerre Mondiale. La France (Lyon: Presses Universitaires, 1982). Centre de Documentation Juive Contemporaine, La France et la Question Juive. 1940/1944. Deuxième Partie: Les Eglises (Paris: Slyvie Messinger, 1981), pp. 143-260. Jacques Duquesne, Les Catholiques Français sous l'Occupation (Paris: Grasset, 1966; rev. ed. 1986). Michael R. Marrus and Robert O. Paxton, Vichy France and the Jews (New York: Schocken Books, 1983). Pierre Pierrard, Juifs et Catholiques Francais (Paris: Fayard, 1970).

9. See Mayeur, 'Les églises devant la persécution des Juifs en France,' pp. 148-160; François Delpech, 'L' éspiscopat et les Juifs d'après les procès-verbaux de l'Assemblée des cardinaux et archevêques documents,' in Eglises et Chrétiens, pp. 281 ff.

10. Duquesne, op. cit., pp. 22-27.

11. Ibid., pp. 41-60; Marrus and Paxton, op. cit., pp. 197-203.

12. See also Duquesne, op. cit., pp. 244-269; and Mayeur, op. cit.

13. The letters of Archbishop Saliège of Toulouse, and Bishop Théas of Montauban. The protests constitute a small minority -- five out of a total of eighty.

14. Msgr. Saliège, Un Evêque Français sous l'Occupation (Paris: les Editions Ouvrières, 1945), p. 81f.; transl. mine.

15. Bishop Théas asked a young social worker, Marie-Rose Gineste, to type and duplicate his letter. She then distributed it personally to every church in the diocese, except one whose pastor was known as a collaborator, covering more than a hundred kilometers a day on her bicycle.

16. In Duquesne, op. cit., p. 253; transl. mine.

17. Duquesne, op. cit., p. 253f.

18. George Wellers, in La France et la Question Juive, p. 257.

19. Ibid., p. 258.

20. Germaine Ribière was honored by Yad Vashem in 1067. I quote from the letter of Louis Domb, a survivor, who helped initiate the proceedings: "... between 1940 and 1945 she gave up her studies and left her family, in order to dedicate herself entirely, and with all the risks this involved, to saving Jewish children. A devout Catholic, well known to the Catholic hierarchy, she worked tirelessly with the team of Msgr. Saliège, Fr. Chaillet, Fr. Braun, etc..... I can personally testify to her intense activity and to the great risks she took to hide and save Jewish children... . As soon as the Allies liberated the concentration camps she rushed to Germany and worked there for several months, trying to save survivors...". Yad Vashem files, letter addressed to the Israeli ambassador in Paris, July 19, 1966; transl. mine.

21. This title refers to the silence of the official Church. At the level of individual, particularly intellectual, Catholics, a profound spiritual renewal between the two world wars now led to a movement of deliberate and methodical resistance to Nazism and Vichy. Among the leaders of this spiritual resistance were Stanislas Fumet, Henry Frenay, Emmanuel Mounier, François Mauriac, Edmond Michelet etc. See Duquesne, pp. 111ff., and Pierrard, pp. 307ff.

22. Internment camps in the south of France -- e.g., Gurs, Rivesaltes, Récébédou, Brens -- where Jews as well as non-Jews were interned under inhuman conditions.

23. While Protestant chaplains ministered to Protestant internees, there were, initially, no Catholic chaplains, because the bishops were reluctant to allocate funds for this work.

24. The Amitié Chrétienne had been founded late in 1940 by a group of Catholics, among them Jean-Marie Soutou, Germaine Ribière, Frs. Glasberg and Chaillet. It quickly received the support of Cardinal Gerlier and Pastor Marc Boegner. The idea of a clandestine publication, which was to become Témoignage Chrétien, grew out of these early beginnings in which Catholics, Protestants and Jews worked together to help Jewish refugees. See Duquesne, p. 150, and Pierrard, p. 323f.

25. Charles Maurras, leader of the Action Française, an influential, conservative, nationalistic movement. It enjoyed great prestige after World War I among French Catholics of the Right, to many of whom it appeared as the guarantor of patriotism and family values, a bulwark against democracy and liberalism. Its journal, by the same name, was the chief organ of an integrist, anti-modernist, antisemitic Catholicism. Condemned by Rome in 1926 the Action Française retained a strong hold on many, and left its imprint on the antisemitism of the Vichy government. See Marrus and Paxton, pp. 23-53; Landau, 58-70; Pierrard, 170ff., 232ff.

26. Msgr. Saliège's letter, read on August 23, 1942, cf. above, p. 2.

27. Les Cahiers du Témoignage Chrétien became one of the chief tools of Christian spiritual resistance. Founded in Lyon by the Jesuits of Fourvière the periodical was published clandestinely between November 1941 and July 1944, and diffused throughout France. The April-May, 1942 issue was devoted entirely to antisemitism. See Renée Bédarida, Témoignage Chrétien. Les Armes de l 'Esprit (Paris: Les Editions Ouvrières, 1977), and her two-volume fac simile collection of the periodical (13, rue Jacob, 75006 Paris). -- The journal which appears under the same name since the end of the war no longer represents the spirit of ecumenism and Christian concern with Judaism that were so typical of the war-time periodical.

28. For the growing opposition to Nazism and Vichy on the part of individual Catholics, cf. note 21 above; also Duquesne, op. cit., and Bédarida, Les Armes de l'Esprit.

29. Conversation with Eva Fleischner, December 18, 1985. Emmanuel Mounier, founder of Esprit, suffered a similar experience. During his second imprisonment the prison chaplain declared himself unable to give him communion, because Mounier refused obedience to the authority of Vichy. See Duquesne, p. 59.

30. Conversation with Eva Fleischner, December 18, 1985.

31. Ibid.

32. Ibid.

33. Cardinal Henri de Lubac, S.J., to Eva Fleischner, in conversation, Paris, October 1, 1985.

34. Her rescue activity on behalf of Jewish children continued after the war, when she brought the Finaly children back from their hiding place in Spain. Nor did this end her involvement with Judaism. She continues to edit Rencontre, a journal of Jewish-Christian dialogue which she helped found with Fr. Roger Braun, S.J. In November 1985 she brought the news of the Carmel at Auschwitz back from Poland, which galvanized the French Church into protests that ultimately contributed to having the convent moved. See Eva Fleischner, 'Contemplation and Controversy, "Commonweal (June 20, 1986, and March 27, 1987).

35. Conversation with Eva Fleischner, Carcassonne, November 4, 1985.

36. Ibid.

37. Ibid. The reference here is to the cult of Notre-Dame de Boulogne, which swept France from 1940 until the end of the war and drew huge crowds of pilgrims throughout the country. Vichy encouraged the devotion.

38. Ibid. This is a reference to the awkward situation in which the Catholic hierarchy found itself at the end of the war, when many of the bishops were accused of having collaborated with Vichy and the Germans. See Andre Latreille, De Gaulle, la Libération, et l 'Eglise Catholique (Paris: Les Editions du Cerf, 1978); and 'l 'épiscopat de France dans la guerre,' in Eglises et Chrétiens dans la IIe Guerre Mondiale, pp. 475ff.

39. Conversation with Eva Fleischner, November 4, 1985.

40. Ibid.

41. Ibid.

42. In Dans l'Amitié de Jules Isaac (Paris, 1981).

43. One of the first to recognize the perils of totalitarianism -- he issued a call to resist even before de Gaulle's appeal -- Edmond Michelet's home became a center of resistance already at the beginning of the war. Later deported to Dachau he survived the war to become minister in the French government. His home in Brive is now the Edmond Michelet Museum, supervised by his widow and children. The story of his imprisonment in Dachau is told by him in Rue de le Liberté.

44. Jesus and Israel (New York: Holt, Rinehart and Winston, 1971; original French ed. 1959).

45. Germaine Bocquet, Dans l'Amitié de Jules Isaac, 1981.

46. Ibid.

47. Conversation with Eva Fleischner, August 10, 1986.

48. Ibid.

49. Françoise Derkenne to Eva Fleischner in conversation, Paris, August 16, 1986.

50. Today in her eighties, Françoise Derkenne is engaged in work with the elderly. In 1987 she published a book, l 'Age de la Bienvieillance.

51. By this date Yad Vashem had honored a total of 460 French men and women. The numbers are constantly changing as new names are added to the honor roll. The process involved can be lengthy, since witnesses and solid evidence must first be found.

52. This is confirmed also by Nechama Tec's study, When Light Pierced the Darkness (New York, Oxford: Oxford University Press, 1985).

53. Conversation with Eva Fleischner, Paris, November 15, 1985. See also Duquesne, op. cit., p. 256.

54. Conversation with Eva Fleischner, Paris, August 28, 1986.

55. The fear on the part of Jews of losing their children through conversion is illustrated in the following instance: A Jewish delegation visited several Catholic and Protestant houses that hid Jewish children. Seeing only crucifixes on the wall, and no symbols that recalled their Jewish origin for the children, they concluded: "When all is said and done these works, however meritorious, are only a means to an end; the end is religious propaganda and proselytism." In Duquesne, op. cit., p. 262; transl. mine. While the accusation was unjust in some cases, it was warranted in others.

56. Fr. Michel Riquet, S.J., conversation with Eva Fleischner, Paris, September 9, 1985.

57. Sr. Francia de Linares, N.D.S., conversation with Eva Fleischner, Paris, September 10, 1985.

58. Rolande Birgy in conversation with Eva Fleischner, Paris, August 28, 1986.

59. Ibid.

60. The following story was told to me by M. Perre Michaux, who during the war was a student in Toulouse and distributed Témoignage Chrétien: "It occurred to me one day that I might need to have hiding places for Jews. So I decided to see whether some of my 'clients' would be willing to take in Jews. One of those I approached was a pastor. He looked at me for a few moments in silence, then he said: 'Monsieur, I really can't stand Jews. But I am a Christian. If you bring me a Jew, I'll give my life for him.'" "And he would have done it," my informant added. Conversation with Eva Fleischner, Paris, october 21, 1985.

61. See Lazare Landau, De l'Aversion à l 'Estime, pp. 203ff. and Pierre Pierrard, Juifs et Catholiques Francais, pp. 266ff.

62. Le Sillon, name of a journal as well as a movement, was founded by Marc Sangnier at the turn of the century. It had a profound impact on French Catholic youth, and was characterized by a liberal and democratic spirit. Condemned by Rome in 1910 as socialist and dangerous, many of its ideals have become part and parcel of the post-Vatican II Church. -- Emmanuel Mounier was the founder of Personalism. Together with his journal Esprit, which began publication in 1932, he became one of the spiritual guides for young French intellectuals committed to a Catholicism that affirmed human dignity. Initially in favor of a purely spiritual orientation, above political labels, Mounier was soon forced by the bitter attacks of the Right to take his stand on the Left which, "with all its imperfections, is the place of justice" (Emmanuel Mounier in Esprit, October 1932, p. 7f.) -- On the Dominicans and the journal Sept., see Alice Coutrot (Paris, Editions du Cerf, 1961).

63. Cf. Pierrard, op. cit., pp. 299ff.; Marrus and Paxton, op. cit., pp. 283ff.

64. See Yosef Hayim Yerushalmi's response to Rosemary Ruether, in Eva Fleischner, ed., Auschwitz: Beginning of a New Era? (New York: KTAV Publishing Co., 1977), p. 106.

65. At the time this article is being written the study by Professor Samuel Oliner on the Altruistic Personal has not yet been published.

THE UPPER ECHELONS OF THE CLERGY AND PUBLIC OPINION FORCE VICHY TO PUT AN END, IN SEPTEMBER 1942, TO ITS BROAD PARTICIPATION IN THE HUNT FOR JEWS

MR SERGE KLARSFELD

The round-up of August 26, and the continuing arrests mobilized large numbers of police throughout the Free Zone. As Chief Rabbi Hirschler indicated in his report of October 1:

> The Government wanted the operations as discreet as possible. It was no longer a question of a secret. The population had witnessed this man-hunt everywhere. Numerous doors had opened to give shelter to the fugitives.

Throughout the reports of the regional and departmental prefects, one finds an almost unanimous discontent on the part of the French confronted, in the Free Zone, by brutal anti-Jewish measures which the Government, however, dared not proclaim to undertake autonomously, nor explain publicly to a disagreeing population both because of the suffering caused to the Jewish families and because they violated France's tradition of asylum and hospitality. Loyal to its affirmation of the sovereignty of the Vichy regime, Laval did not, at any cost, admit that these measures were taken because he had decided, at the beginning of July, to reply favorably to the German request concerning the arrest, surrender and deportation of a certain number of stateless Jews.

Undoubtedly, the messages and reports of the prefects piled upon Laval's desk on September 1, must have convinced him that his decision was generally unpopular. In the light of the energetic reaction of the clergy against the Government's policy towards the Jews, it becomes understandable that from September 2 on, Laval, as we will see, hardened his attitude towards the heads of the SS, in the wake of the pressures of public opinion.

Between August 26 and September 2, having acted in an infamous manner, Vichy was confronted by the clearcut opposition of the majority of the French of the Free Zone, and was obliged to change considerably its behavior vis-à-vis the German authorities in the Jewish Question.

In the Limoges region, the local Prefecture noted that criticism was on "an emotional level", and that

> the measures taken regarding the foreign Jews were so impressive that the backlash in public order has not yet calmed down . . . One speaks of persecution. The clergy has become aroused and catholic circles indignant.

In the Creuse, "the population clearly disapproved of the measures taken." In the Indre, the first reflex was to rise up against what was termed "measures of persecution"; in the Haute-Vienne, "the measures implemented during the month of August concerning the Jews continue to agitate public opinion, particularly in catholic and protestant circles where it becomes a question of racism."

The Prefect of the Rhone related that "a large part of the public, especially in catholic circles, bears witness to a certain irritation." In the same region, the Prefect of the Ardeche reported that

> the Jewish Question, because of the arrest of foreign stateless Jews, caused a certain upheaval; due to the breadth of the harvest made in my department . . . a very large part of the population took pity on their fate.

In the Isère, "the very persons, who, the day before, regretted the presence in France of too great a number of Israelites intervened in favor of the good Jews." In the Haute-Savoie, "the Government's adversaries, exploiting the sentimentalism of the masses, of course, claimed that the measures taken had been dictated by the occupying authorities to a government too weak to oppose them, and that "the poor victims" were destined for certain death."

In the Saône-et-Loire, "the general population, among whom sentimental feelings had lost none of their vivacity, made known its fear of witnessing a pure and simple 'surrender' imposed by the heads of the Reich."

In the Toulouse region, the regional Prefect noted first that "numerous are those who tend to pity the fate destined for those concerned," and that the hospitality traditional to France, the inhumanity of the separation of families, the harshness with which the assemblies took place, were evoked; the discomfort of the surrounding material conditions of the transport, the precarious fate awaiting the families.

In the Gers, "the operations undertaken against foreign Jews . . . were naturally a convenient pretext for the Government's political adversaries." In the Ariège, "the measures provoked extensive commentary." In the Upper Garonne, the measures "provoked serious criticism motivated by the separation of family members and especially by their dispatch to the Occupied Zone, which would only be a step to their trip towards Germany." In the Lot-et-Garonne, "the measures taken against them were criticized by the great majority of the population." In the Lot, "the fate of the Israelites solicited among the population who judged them severely . . . It must be recognized that, although responsibility for the measures has been imputed to the German authorities, the Government has not been less severely blamed . . . The surrender to the Germans of foreign Israelites is considered by many as a national shame."

In the Alpes-Maritimes, "the measures have incontestably offended public opinion." In the Vaucluse, "the population has generally been compassionate."

Even in the Corse, where only a single Jew had been counted, the Prefect indicated that

> the echoes of the measures taken in the Free Zone have shaken public opinion and have become the object of hostile commentary . . . Corsican opinion does not understand that Israelites be surrendered to Germany, and sees in their extraction a sign of the subjection of the French Government.

Disapproval of the Free Zone population vis-à-vis measures striking out at stateless Jews was based on the reaction, often spontaneous, but it was also re-enforced and sometimes provoked by the particularly efficient role played by the high French clergy, moral guide to public opinion. Alone, without a spokesman, a sullen population would not have been able to counteract the plans of Laval and Bousquet; the same would have been the case for bishops preaching indignation in a void. On the other hand, the population and the clergy mutually buttressed each other in the salutary opposition which was not only in the final analysis a matter of honor but wrought immediate positive and durable results. Germans were to be grouped. During the evening, a counter-order from Vichy: the 84 children were to be placed on August 31 at 6 pm in a convoy of Jews from Nice passing through Lyons on their way to Drancy. On the same day, however, General de St. Vincent, Military Commander of the Lyons region, refused to give his soldiers to the Police Superintendent to supervise the embarkation of the Jews leaving for Drancy.

On Monday, the 31st, the 84 children were gathered by the Social Welfare Department for Foreigners, waiting to be taken to the station. At about 3.30 pm, Cardinal Gerlier called the Police Prefecture to protest the departure of the children stating that the "Amitiés Chrétiennes" (Christian Friendship League) was now responsible for them, as their parents had entrusted their guardianship to that organization before being sent to Drancy. Angeli informed Bousquet's services of the situation and Vichy postponed the children's departure, and Angeli learned that they had already been taken away at about 2 pm by the "Amitiés Chrétiennes." Father Chaillet was the force behind this umbrella organisation grouping Catholics and Protestants under Cardinal Gerlier's crosier, to come to the aid of foreign refugees. Convoked by Prefect Angeli, Father Chaillet refused to surrender the children of the "unfortunate Jews sent to exile and undoubtedly to death." The Lyons Police Superintendent then went to Cardinal Gerlier who confirmed and assured Father Chaillet's refusal. On the next day, at the Archbishopry, Angeli was confronted by Cardinal Gerlier who clearly and proudly proclaimed that:

> The gesture of the "Amitiés Chrétiennes" bore the significance of a protest by the Church against the surrender of foreign Israelites to the occupying authorities, that for him it was a moral imperative to protect them, having received the children from their parents' hands, but against the German Government. My protest, he added, by its very nature, re-enforces the Government in its relationship with the occupying authorities, as this shows to Germany the internal difficulties created in France by the surrender of Jews.

Angeli did not at all appreciate this judicious closing remark by Cardinal Gerlier, and placed R. P. Chaillet under home arrest.

At Vichy, on September 1, Cado, Bousquet's assistant, immediately informed the latter of the situation in order to make Laval aware of the events. The Head of the Government immediately warned Abetz, who cabled Berlin, transforming Chaillet's home arrest into total arrest. On September 2, Cardinal Gerlier diffused a communiqué to be read aloud in all the churches of the archdiocese on Sunday, September 6. This message would be all the more effective as the Cardinal did not reject Vichy's anti-Semitic politics as such:

> We will not forget that for the French authorities there is a problem to be resolved, and we realize the difficulties which the Government must confront.

But neither that nor "the great voice of Marshal Pétain" prevented the Cardinal from replying to the

> imperative and painful task of protesting from the depths of our conscience . . . the heart pains at the thought of the treatment suffered by thousands of human beings and even more, at the thought of what the future might hold . . .

The First Blow to Röthke's Plan

On that same September 2, a meeting was held in Paris between Oberg and Laval; on the next day, Hagen wrote his report. Laval explained to the Head of the SS and German Police in France

> that the demands which we have formulated for him concerning the Jewish Question have recently met with unequalled resistance on the part of the Church; the head of this anti-governmental opposition is, by the way, Cardinal Gerlier.

Laval adopted a new tone and mode of behavior in the presence of Himmler's representative in Paris, a change in attitude perfectly justifying the lucid reasoning of Cardinal Gerlier and his courageous decision to oppose Vichy's surrender of Jews, considered by many as ineluctable:

> In view of this clergical opposition, President Laval asks that, if possible, no new demands be made upon him in the Jewish Question. In particular, their number should not be an *a priori* imposition of quotas of Jews to be deported. For example, it had been demanded that 50,000 Jews be delivered for the 50 trains at our disposal. He begs us to believe in his total honesty when he promises to regulate the Jewish Question, but, he says, delivery of Jews is not like merchandise in a "Five and Ten" where one could take as much of any thing as one wishes, always at the same price . . .

Laval then recapitulated for Oberg and Hagen the commitments to which he would hold, and which, let us point out, were limited, in comparison to the stances taken by Dannecker and Röthke, who continued to affirm that on July 4, it had been a question between Laval and the heads of the SS, of an agreement concluded on the perspective of, in the final analysis, the deportation of all the French Jews. In this document, of which a copy was destined for Department IV–J, neither Oberg nor Hagen raised any objections against Laval's enumeration which ends with French Jews naturalized after 1933:

> He confirmed once again that, as stated in the agreements concluded, those Jews having lost their German, Austrian, Czech, Polish, and Hungarian nationality would be surrendered first. Then, as agreed, the Jews having acquired French nationality after 1933 would be surrendered. We gave a negative reply to the question by President Laval who wanted to know if the Head of the SS and the Police had still other demands to formulate in this matter. At that point, President Laval renewed his request that no special pressure be applied in this matter, in view of current difficulties.

Moreover, Laval confirmed to his interlocutors that the troublesome Darquier, whom he treated most sarcastically, "will not get from him what he asks for."

This conversation of September 2 was decisive for marking a change in the relationship between Laval and the German Police authorities in the Jewish Question; it was the first very clear psychological stop concerning the deportation measures in France envisaged during the last few days by the Department for Jewish Questions in Paris and in Berlin.

Actually, Röthke's plans were decided one week prior to this meeting, on the eve of the mass round-up in the Free Zone. Following the line of Dannecker who was preparing to leave France definitively, Röthke began the paper work preliminary to the deportation of all the Jews of France. Was this euphoria? Undoubtedly because after the difficult link of the beginning of August between the insufficient supply of Jews from the Occupied Zone, and the expected deliveries from the Free Zone, IV-J could see the arrival from the Free Zone of the contingents necessary for the August program: Some convoys were filled with no problem, and left regularly at a pace of 3 a week; moreover, Röthke expected to receive within a few days from the Free Zone, as promised by the French authorities, 11,000–14,500 Jews, but to a large extent his hopes would remain unfulfilled.

It is for this reason that, a meeting having been scheduled in Berlin for August 28 at Eichmann's IV-B4, Röthke sent one of his two aids, Horst Ahnert. On August 25, Röthke gave a handwritten note to Ahnert, requesting that he bring up in Berlin the following points, among which we will cite only the most important:

Can the October program be communicated rapidly, to enable the French Government sufficient time to arrest and deliver the necessary number of Jews? Let us remember that the September program foresaw 13 convoys, the same as for August.

As there were 260–280,000 Jews in both zones combined, according to Röthke, at the current pace of 13 convoys per month, it would take about 20 months to deport all the Jews of France. This was too long for Röthke, who asked Berlin to place at his disposal 20 trains per month instead of 13 for the evacuation.

For Röthke, due to exemptions from the wearing of the yellow badge by certain nationalities, on one hand, the French were led to believe that in the eyes of the Germans, the Jewish problem was a problem of nationality and not of race; on the other hand, certain consulates – on a lesser level, those of Switzerland, Spain and Portugal, but especially the Italian – behaved with "unbelievable insolence," refusing that the anti-Jewish measures applied to their nationals. Röthke wanted that as of September 1, the Jews of all European states at least be obliged to wear the yellow star and thus fall into the category of deportables, unless they were repatriated to their countries of origin.

Two days later, on August 27, in Röthke's absence, Heinrichson held a work session with Leguay and the head of his cabinet, Commander Sauts. The round-ups were under way in the Free Zone; the results were still not known, but according to Leguay, four trains comprising 1,000 Jews each, were expected from the Free Zone in the first days of September. Leguay promised to enforce respect of the dates of arrival for the convoys from the Free Zone. As concerned the October program, Leguay, who must already have been in possession of the mediocre results of the round-ups, asked first of all for a meeting with Röthke, and even thought it preferable that the meeting on this matter be held between Krochen and Bousquet. Leguay could not furnish exact details as to the law on the denaturalization of Jews who had got French nationality after 1933.

It was only by the note mentioned above by the head of the Gestapo of Vichy Geissler, on August 29, that Röthke learned that only 6,584 of the deliverable Jews were arrested by the French Police. It was too late to issue a counter-order to Ahnert to modify the maximalist requests of the IV-J for 20 trains per month from October 1. On the previous evening, the working session of the Department for Jewish Affairs of the RSHA in Berlin, took place under the direction of Eichmann. Röthke, who was guilty of over-optimism, had just placed himself in a most embarrassing situation, for his deputy, Ahnert, who related the proceedings of the meeting in a report dated September 1 had obtained even more than Röthke asked.

Eichmann, actually, had notified his representatives – in addition to Ahnert, probably those of Belgium and Holland – that the deportation of the stateless Jews of their territories be completed prior to September 30, 1942; the deportation programs were to be intensified until the end of October since rail transport would probably be deficient from November 1 to January 31.

For France, Röthke's request was more than granted by Eichmann:

> The RSHA is ready to have made available by the German Railways, one transport train per day for the month of October, and if necessary from mid-September on. It is necessary to communicate immediately to the RSHA the date at which this measure may be initiated.

Eichmann, moreover, confirmed to Ahnert that only the Jews whose nationality corresponded to those described by the category "stateless" could be deported. As for other foreign Jews, negotiations were in progress with the Minister for Foreign Affairs, but had not as yet come to a close. At the time, only the Bulgarian Jews could be added to the stateless Jews.

The Impossible September-October Program: 1942

Three days after that meeting in Berlin, that is to say, on September 1, Röthke visited the Delegation of the Secretary General of the Police for the Occupied Territories; Leguay being absent, he was received by the head of his cabinet, Sauts. Röthke was impatient to come to a final agreement concerning the schedule for the arrival of the trains from the Free Zone, aware of his promises to Eichmann, that is, 6 trains for the first half of September, and 45 trains for the second half of September and October, but did not know on what numbers to count from the Free Zone.

The figure of 6,584 arrests indicated to Röthke on August 29 by Geissler increased, but only slightly, to 7,100 according to Sauts, who admitted that "the number is clearly less than what Bousquet expected." The principal reason: there were leaks; the Jews were on their guard. Sauts hid behind Bousquet and Laval, then in Paris.

Disappointed and furious, Röthke without taking realities into account, exposed imperiously to Sauts the program to be implemented. He indicated to the recipients of the account of his meeting with Sauts, that is Knochen, Lischka, and Hagen, that this program was modified "on instructions from Berlin," while actually Berlin only furnished rail transport corresponding to Röthke's own needs: the deportation of 51,000 Jews, in all for September and October.

As arguments to justify this extravagant program, Röthke declared to Sauts that he knew that in the Free Zone, were tens of thousands of stateless Jews, which was highly exaggerated, as well as Belgian and Dutch Jews to be delivered along with the stateless Jews. Then Röthke proceeded to threats following Dannecker's style: what was in jeopardy was the Final Solution and the Führer's will, and moreover in the Occupied Zone, there were sufficient Jews to fulfill the program – the implication: sufficient French Jews. Immediately after Hitler's recollection, Röthke, to apply pressure on Knochen and Oberg, mentioned in passing in his report that they themselves must discuss the Jewish Question with Bousquet and Laval. Another piece of bad news for Röthke: Sauts informed him that the decree denaturalizing Jews who had become French after 1933 had not yet been published.

Röthke, in his conclusion, attempted with persistance to mobilize the energy of Oberg and Knochen: he reminded them that there would probably be no more convoys from November 15 on, and until January 30, he requested

> that the demands of Department IV-J be supported in their entirety and by all possible means . . . According to the conclusions regarding the Free Zone reached by SS-Hauptsturmführer Dannecker, the program may be fulfilled, if the French Government puts itself to the task with the necessary vigor. Since as of mid-September, it will be a question of the departure each day from Drancy of 1,000 Jews towards the East, we request that the necessary preliminary negotiations be undertaken with the representatives of the French Government, and that the demands formulated herein be presented to them.

Röthke added, still in order to pressure Oberg and Knochen, that at the time of the meeting of August 28 in Berlin, France's delay, in comparison to other countries, in the progress of the Final Solution: "There is a great deal to be caught up on before October 31, 1942."

Futile incitements and subtle threats by Röthke in the face of his SS superiors: on the next day, Laval added to the insufficient results of the round-ups in the Free Zone, the reticence of the Vichy Government in pursuing a confrontation with the militant resistance of the Church in favor of the Jews, incarnated by Cardinal Gerlier. But in view of the new demands, 50,000 Jews, Laval, as we have seen, retorted that he did not wish that *a priori* number of Jews to deport be imposed upon him, taking into account the recent difficulties.

Hagen who composed the account of that meeting of September 2, addended to it, on September 4, a note on "conversions of language regarding deportation to the East of Jews of the Non-Occupied Zone." Laval informed Oberg and Hagen that the foreign diplomats had asked him what the destination was of the deported Jews to date; he had replied that they were being deported to the South of Poland. "He now requests that he be informed of the way to answer to avoid divergences in the information we disperse." The accomplices consulted one another, embarrassed by the curiosity of the observers. What could the reply be, other than a weakly constructed unbelievable lie, when one thinks of the children and the elderly deported!

> It has been decided that President Laval would answer in reply to such questions, that the Jews transferred from the Non-Occupied Zone to the occupying authorities were transported to be employed at work in the General Government.

Auschwitz, in fact, was not part of the General Government, but of the territories annexed to the Reich . . .

On September 3, at 6 am, Ahnert transmitted to Hagen a note required by Oberg's right hand on the previous evening at 10 pm, because Oberg was to meet with Bousquet on the 3rd. It is a statistical note on the deportation previously implemented and on the possibilities for September-October taking up Röthke's arguments. On September 4, Hagen wrote the minutes of this meeting of Oberg and Knochen with Bousquet. The Secretary General of the Police accepted that Darquier place a representative of the CGQJ in each prefecture to control the implementation of the laws-decrees proposed by the CGQJ. Moving on to the anti-Jewish action, Bousquet declared that 7,000 Jews were captured, to be added to the 5,000 already interned, to make a total of 12,000 Jews in concentration camps. He stressed the opposition he met with due to the initiatives taken by the Church, especially by Cardinal Gerlier, and the ecclesiastics subordinate to him. The Government was facing actual insubordination by the clergy. Bousquet also recognized that public opinion protested in the wake of "the extreme, brutal and sometimes excessive" actions.

As did Laval, Bousquet asked that, in view of the difficulties created by the clergy, no figures be imposed *a priori* upon him, and he declared that it would prove, in all probability, impossible to fill daily, between September 15-30, a contingent of 1,000 Jews. For the moment, he is certain of "fulfilling as agreed the demands concerning the period to September 14."

The reactions of Knochen and Oberg in the face of the failure of the new ambitious plans of Röthke, supported by Eichmann:

> The Superior Head of the SS and the Police and the BDS have placed the stress on the fact that this was a well understood point of view and that measures in that direction would be taken.

In the face of a new situation in the Free Zone, in which Laval and Bousquet were confronted by a French population moved by the fate of the Jews, and a clergy which, especially its most eminent prelate, publicly took a stand in words and actions, against the anti-Jewish measures, Knochen, Oberg and Hagen, did not give priority to regulating the Jewish Question in the way Röthke and Eichmann wanted. They always considered as their priority the laborious docility of a France quietly active under the crook of Pétain and Laval for the strategic and economic interests of the Reich, as well as the security of the occupying troops guaranteed especially by the vigilance of a unified French Police under Bousquet's direction against the common enemies of the Reich and the Vichy régime.

In the meantime, on one hand Vichy's Police did not succeed in greatly augmenting the number of arrests of stateless Jews in the Free Zone; on the other hand, resistance to these anti-Jewish operations among the clergy and the public strengthened.

New Difficulties

On September 1, the Head of the Police noted that in Paris, Leguay was requesting the dispatch of fresh contingents from the Free Zone to feed the seven trains initially scheduled to leave from September 16-30. How were 7,000 Jews to be found when to date, out of 12,865 counted, only 5,876 had been arrested? Only 2,000 could be caught and this after new round-ups. To find another 5,000, it would be necessary to arrest the stateless Jews who entered France after September 1, 1931, when the "barometer" for the mass round-up had been January 1, 1936. But the author of this report addressed to Bousquet, did not hide the fact that:

> It is probable that such an operation would raise problems of a material as well as a moral nature, the latter due to the attitude of certain highly-placed personalities followed by a part of the public opinion.

On September 3, a new note from the same police headquarters evaluated at 20,000 the foreign Jews in the Free Zone apt to be directed towards Drancy; but this number would decrease by the 6,000 fugitive Jews, object of the round-up of August 26. As for the number of foreign Jews who had entered France between January 1, 1930, and December 31, 1935, their number must have reached 10,000; if they were to be arrested, a proportionately important part of them would inevitably benefit from exemptions.

In his ongoing quest for contingents to transfer to Drancy, on September 5, Bousquet ordered the regional prefects to proceed immediately to intern all the foreign Jews found having disobeyed the law. On September 8, Bousquet insisted once again, informing all the prefects of the Free Zone that:

> The Head of the Government requests you intensively search with view towards arresting stateless Jews in conformity with my instructions of August 30, 1942.

On that same day, Leguay counted a total of 9,872 Jews transferred from the Free Zone between August 7 and September 5, he expected no delivery before the one of about 500 Jews scheduled for September 14.

During those days, from September 1-8, difficulties for the Vichy regime continued to accumulate in the realm of its anti-Jewish actions, considerably limiting the number of arrests because of the clergy's and the French population's commitment, hostility to the arrests and surrender of the Jews to the Nazis for deportation.

Even in the Occupied Zone the police noticed on September 1 that "the population manifested its surprise at seeing the French Government place at the disposal of the occupying authorities" the Jews of the Free Zone. From every side surged towards the French authorities, Pétain, Laval and the prefects, protests emanating from the French elite circles reiterating to the governing authorities the indignity of their actions concerning the Jews, in similar and equally moving terms. They expressed a collective stance, especially of the catholic and protestant circles, those who would least be suspected of systematic opposition to the "National Revolution," those whose reactions might be most efficient, as it was influential, especially with the Marshal and his entourage, as well as the prefects who felt the Vichy regime being psychologically contested by his partisans.

For example, remonstrances such as those of September 1 by the Central Committee for Refugees and Expulsees from the North, Alsace and Lorraine, to the Prefect of the Lower-Pyrenees, can be found in numerous other letters of protest and touch the core of the problem:

> It seems to us that the honor of France, which for all time had given a fraternal hospitality to the persecuted people of other nations, demands this intervention in favor of small, innocent ones. We believe, on the other hand, that the upper echelon of the clergy is very actively involved in this question, which had greatly impressed it. It is a question of France's moral and spiritual honor.

The regional prefect of Toulouse reported to Bousquet, on September 3, that:

> The statement of the Archbishop of Toulouse concerning the Jews provoked strong feelings in all the departments of the Toulouse region, and continues to stimulate numerous conversations.

Monsignor Saliege's typewritten text circulated throughout the Free Zone, awakening consciences. In turn on September 4, following Monsignor Saliege, Monsignor Theas and Cardinal Gerlier, Monsignor Delay, Archbishop of Marseilles, diffused a pastoral letter which was read out on Sunday, September 6, the same day as the Communiqué of the Archbishop of Lyons, Monsignor Delay let

> the painful wail of the Christian Conscience ring out, upset by the measures recently decided upon and implemented these days, against men, women and children, guilty only of belonging to the Jewish race and being foreigners.

Certainly, the approach of the Archbishop of Marseilles was not altogether lacking in serious prejudices in the matter of the Jewish Question, and that he was undoubtedly not among those moved by the Vichy anti-Semitic legislation:

> We recognize that our country has the right to take all measures necessary to its defense against those who, especially in these last few years, have done it so much harm, and that it has the right to punish severely all those who abuse that hospitality which was so liberally accorded to them.

But this appreciation exactly follows the lines of Laval and Pétain, who urged an even greater intensification of the force of the protest by all those who shared his prejudices, among the public and within the Government:

> But the rights of the States have limits . . . To arrest en masse simply because they are Jewish and foreigners, men, women and children, who have committed no wrong, to separate family members and send them away, perhaps to death: is this not a violation of the sacred moral laws and the essential rights of men and the family, rights emanating from God?
>
> It is also often a lack of charity and simple humanity to execute such orders under absolutely inhuman conditions.

On October 19, when the French Central Consistory met, its president first chose to render

> homage to the admirable reaction of the French public and especially the Christian churches which multiplied expressions of sympathy, devotion and solidarity.

On September 9, in front of the Welfare Coordinating Committee, Chief Rabbi Hirschler very nobly expressed the recognition of French Jewry towards all those who had helped at the time

> of unjust and tragic measures implemented by the Government against certain Israelite foreigners for more than a month . . .
>
> In any case, in our sufferings, we have found sufficient active sympathy so as not to despair of humanity or of Free France.
>
> We have been responsive to the steps you have taken as far as the highest authorities in our country, to the unlimited devotion which you have not spared. We were equally moved by the messages and the bishops' letters – sometimes reckless – of your spiritual, catholic and protestant, leaders, as we were by their unceasing interventions.

The Advisor to Nunciature Pacini reported on September 8 that apparently, Laval had not been defeated by the high clergy's opposition, of which he complained, but he admitted that he would have wished to speak to the bishops of the Free Zone "and make them understand the difficult and delicate situation in which the Government presently found itself:" i.e. probably to explain to them discreetly that he was acting on a German request and not on his own initiative, as he unceasingly stated in public.

Laval could not ignore the press which, outside of France, generally exaggerated the number of Jews surrendered, reported these hostile reactions of the population and the clergy: On August 31, in the eyes of the Manchester Guardian:

> the deportations have provoked violent indignation . . . resistance to this racial persecution will be a new link between a great number of catholics who are represented by Maritain and the socialists and the trade unions who oppose Vichy's politics.

In "La Tribune de Genêve" on September 3, "the population reacted energetically against these measures." In Berne, the Ambassador to France confirmed on September 9 to Laval the emotion of the Swiss public-at-large. From August 29, the Swiss no longer turned back the hundreds of Jews from the Free Zone who crossed the border illegally. *The Times* of September 7 reported that "this anti-Jewish campaign created a violent appearance of discontent everywhere;" in the issue of September 9:

> the Catholic leaders parried with provocative refusal by Cardinal Gerlier's . . . Episcopal letters recommending to the French Catholics to render all possible assistance to the persecuted Jews were read out from all the pulpits of non-occupied France.

THE HOLOCAUST IN ITALY AND ITS REPRESENTATION IN ITALIAN POST-WAR LITERATURE

Professor Meir Michaelis

So far only two full-scale works on Italian Jewry under Fascism have appeared: Renzo De Felice's Storia degli ebrei italiani sotto il fascismo, first published in 1961 (3rd revised edition in 1972) and the undersigned's Mussolini and the Jews (1978, revised and enlarged Italian edition in 1982). Neither of these works concentrates on the "Final Solution to the Jewish question" on Italian soil. Ever since 1945, however, there has been a flood of memoirs, newspaper articles, papers in learned journals, polemical writings (books and pamphlets) and scholarly monographs dealing primarily or exclusively with the Holocaust in Mussolini's Fascist Social Republic. Some of the accounts by survivors have won fame throughout the Western world, most particularly Primo Levi's If This is a Man (1947, on the author's experiences at Auschwitz), Giorgio Bassani's The Garden of the Finzi-Continis (1962, on the persecution and deportation of a prominent family of Ferrarese Jews) and Silvano Arieti's The Parnas (1979, on the murder of Giuseppe Pardo Roques, the venerable President of the Jewish community at Pisa, by Himmler's myrmidons).

Of the problems that have emerged in this context and have given rise to controversy, four are particularly important: first and foremost, the respective roles of the Germans (SS, armed forces, and diplomats) and the Italians (Republican Fascists and career officials) in the liquidation of Italian Jewry between September 1943 and April 1945; second, the silence of Pope Pius XII and the attitude of the Catholic clergy; third, the attitude of the Italian people under German rule, with special reference to the partisans; fourth, the personal role of Mussolini as associate, ally and puppet of Hitler.

At the end of 1986 a new controversy was sparked off by a series of televised interviews conducted by an Italian journalist, Nicola Caracciolo, on aid to Jews during World War II, later published in book form, with a preface by Renzo De Felice and an introductory essay by Mario Toscano(1). Caracciolo's conclusion - that the Italian people had stood by the Jews in their hour of need - provoked sharp polemical reactions from various Italian Jews, including Tullia Zevi, President of the Union of Italian Jewish Communities.

Before discussing the above issues and controversies, we shall do well to deal briefly with the historical background.

Fascist racial policy, 1938-1943.

When Mussolini turned against the Jews in 1938, it was widely (and understandably) assumed that this about-face was forced on him by Hitler(2). After World War II, however, various students of Italian politics pointed out that this assumption was not confirmed by any documentary evidence(3). A first attempt at a scholarly examination of the problem (based on published sources only) was made in 1960 by the undersigned who arrived at the unexpected conclusion that the German dictator, far from trying to impose his anti-Jewish obsession on his Axis partner, had made a point of refraining from open interference in Italian domestic matters until the fall of Fascism in July 1943. The Duce's decision to break with the Jews was due, not to any irresistible foreign pressure, but to his recognition of Italy's changed alignment in Europe and more particularly to his desire to cement the German-Italian alliance by eliminating any strident contrast in the policy of the two Fascist Powers. These conclusions were subsequently confirmed by Renzo De Felice (who had access to the unpublished Italian records) and are now generally accepted(4). In 1985 Dino Grandi, Mussolini's Foreign Minister from 1929 to 1932 and his Ambassador in London from 1932 to 1939, claimed in his memoirs that in May 1938 his master had decided on the elimination of the Jews in response to an explicit request from Hitler(5). It is, however, clear from all the sources at our disposal that the anti-Semitic policy had been decided upon before Hitler's visit to Italy(6). On the other hand, recent research has thrown new light on the clandestine anti-Semitic activities of German agents in Italy and on the attempt to exploit the German-Italian cultural agreement of November 23, 1938, for anti-Jewish ends(7).

Mussolini's declaration of war on the Jews was hailed in Germany as a major ideological triumph; Hitler himself was greatly pleased and gave public expression to his gratification in a speech at the Nuremberg Party rally on September 6, 1938(8). During World War II, however, it became clear that the Duce's conversion to the racial gospel had failed to eliminate the divergence of views on the Jewish question: though side by side, the two Axis partners never marched in step, and this was reflected in systematic Italian resistance to Hitler's policy of genocide. While Jews were being rounded up and deported all over German-occupied Europe, those of Italian citizenship continued to enjoy complete immunity; what is more, the Italian-occupied territories in France, Yugoslavia, and Greece became havens of refuge for the Jews of those countries, at any rate until the Italian surrender to the Allied Powers. It remains to add that Jewish refugees from Germany and German-occupied countries continued to arrive in Italy throughout the period under review. In some cases Mussolini personally intervened in favour of Hitler's Jewish victims. When, shortly after the fall of Poland, the Polish-born wife of an Italian Jew requested his assistance on behalf of her aged parents, then trapped in German-occupied Warsaw, the Duce replied through the Chief of Police that he would order his diplomats to do their best. He was as good as his word(9).

Himmler's and Ribbentrop's Jewish affairs experts were extremely indignant at this open sabotage of the "Final Solution" and called for a swift and energetic reaction. Hitler, however, refused to share the indignation of his underlings; all that mattered now, he insisted, was Italian loyalty to the Axis - as long as Mussolini was firmly in the saddle, the Jews could do no harm. It was only after Marshal Badoglio's surrender (September 8, 1943) that the German dictator finally permitted the SS to extend the "Final Solution" of the Jewish question to the German-occupied part of the Italian peninsula.

The Holocaust in Italy, 1943-1945.

After the Italian capitulation to the Allies, King Victor Emmanuel III and Marshal Badoglio fled to Brindisi, Rome capitulated to Field-Marshal Kesselring's forces, Trieste was occupied by units of Field-Marshal Kesselring's Army Group B, and nearly all Italian troops in Yugoslavia, Greece, and the Aegean Islands surrendered to their former ally. On September 11, Kesselring declared all Italian territory, including Rome, to be a theatre of war under German military control; three days later Hitler signed blanket instructions for Albert Speer, his Minister of Armaments, concerning the "safeguarding" of the Italian war industry. As Mussolini had predicted in October 1941, Italy was now being "reduced from the position of a confederated province to the worse one of a colony", with fatal results for the Italian Jews(10).

In assessing the impact of the German occupation on the Jewish tragedy in Italy, we shall do well to bear in mind three basic facts. First, the geographical distribution of Italian Jewry: ever since the expulsions of 1492 and 1541 Italian Jewish life had been confined to the north of the peninsula, with the result that the area of Jewish settlement from Rome northwards, including the capital, remained under the complete control of the Germans until June 1944. Second, Hitler's decision (deplored by most of his advisers) to rescue his imprisoned brother dictator and restore him to power. If the setting-up of the ill-starred "Italian Social Republic" had enabled Mussolini to recover some measure of independence, it might have saved his Jewish subjects from a great tragedy, given the Duce's undoubted aversion to the German method of solving the Jewish problem; but since he was now virtually a prisoner of the Germans, his reinstatement had the effect of facilitating the implementation of the "Final Solution" in Italy. Third, Hitler's change of mind with regard to the projected occupation of the Vatican City. After the coup d'état of July 25, 1943, he announced his intention of going "right into the Vatican". Subsequently, however, under pressure from Ribbentrop and Goebbels, he agreed to spare the Holy See. Of all the decisions taken by Hitler after the Italian "betrayal", this was the only one which benefited the Jews, for it enabled the Church to save a not inconsiderable number of Jewish lives(11).

Even before the "liberation" of the Duce, Hitler had ordered the setting-up of a political and military system which would take effective control of the country and which would bring under its wing any future Fascist administration. Rudolf Rahn, the German Ambassador in Rome, had become plenipotentiary of the Greater German Reich; Obergruppenführer (SS Lieutenant-General) Karl Wolff, hitherto chief of Himmler's personal staff, had been appointed commander of the SS in Italy and "security adviser" to the projected Fascist puppet government. The two border provinces of Venezia Giulia and Alto Adige had been placed under two German Gauleiters, Friedrich Rainer at Trieste and Franz Hofer at Innsbruck. For the rest, Italy had been divided into two zones, operational and occupied, the former coming under Kesselring's Army Group South and the latter under Rommel's Army Group B(12).

Having lost his illusions about his erstwhile Italian mentor, Hitler was now determined to treat the part of Italy under his control as conquered as well as occupied territory. Hence, immediately after the Italian armistice, his henchmen began to extend his policy of genocide to Italy, without even waiting for the restoration of the Fascist regime. On September 12 Sturmbannführer (SS Major) Herbert Kappler, head of the Gestapo in Rome, was advised that Himmler wanted to proceed with a round-up and deportation of the Roman Jews; and on September 23 - the day the "Italian Social Republic" came into being - the Reich Main Security Office of the SS, headed by Himmler's chief lieutenant Kaltenbrunner, sent a circular to all its branches, specifying that "in agreement with the Foreign Ministry" Jews of Italian nationality could now be included in the racial measures. Meanwhile SS detachments carried out a pogrom in the summer resorts around Lago Maggiore - the first since the age of the Ghetto(13).

Although Kappler was a rabid Jew-hater, he was no more happy about the idea of deporting the Roman Jews than about the "liberation" of Mussolini (which he had vainly tried to prevent). He felt this new order was "yet another gross political stupidity"; the Jews of Rome, as far as he knew, were orderly and passive - perhaps the least dangerous element of the population. Hitler and Himmler, however, were determined to impose their anti-Jewish obsession on the German-occupied part of Italy, no matter what Kappler's views on the subject. On September 24 Himmler's office in Berlin dispatched a top secret message to Kappler, ordering him to arrest all Roman Jews, regardless of age, sex, citizenship, and state of health, and send them to the Reich "for liquidation". When Eichmann's attention was drawn to Kappler's objections, he reacted by calling in one of the ablest and most experienced of his aides, Hauptsturmführer (SS Captain) Theodor Dannecker, who had previously distinguished himself as Judenreferent in Paris and Judenberater in Sofia. At the beginning of October Dannekker arrived in Rome at the head of an execution team composed of forty-four armed SS men, including fourteen officers and NCOs. On October 16 - a Sabbath and the blackest day in the long history of Roman Jewry - the signal was given at 5.30 a.m. and the Judenrazzia began. Wherever Jews lived in Rome, they were brutally seized, regardless of age, sex, and state of health, and taken to the Collegio Militare (where Kappler was to be tried as a war criminal four years later); thence, after two daus, they were shipped off to the killing centre of Auschwitz. A Gentile Italian eye-witness subsequently recorded that it "all seemed like a scene out of hell": "The children were crying. Everywhere you could hear pleas for help and cries of distress...I could not understand why these innocent creatures should be considered a danger to Germany. I was terrified, but kept watching the scene, perhaps with an unconscious hope of somehow being able to help the victims. Suddenly a German NCO came up to me and told me to be off, accompanying his words with a persuasive push. There was nothing I could do but leave the place"(14).

The round-up was completed by 2 p.m., after which the Gestapo in Rome prepared a report, presumably written by Dannecker, signed by Kappler and addressed to Obergruppenführer Wolff, which throws light on the strained relations between Germans and Italians:

"Judenaktion according to plan worked out in this office exploiting all possibilities was to-day initiated and completed. Put into action were all available forces of the Security- and Order Police (Sicherheits- und Ordnungspolizei). Participation of the Italian Police in the affair was not possible, given their unreliability...Blocking off entire streets was not practicable considering the character of the Open City and also the insufficient aggregate of only 365 German police. Nevertheless...1,259 persons were arrested in Jewish homes and brought to a central collection point at a military college here. After the release of the half-breeds, the foreigners (incl. one citizen of the Vatican City), the members of mixed marriages (incl. the Jewish partners), the Aryan domestics and subtenants, there remained in custody 1,007 Jews...The behaviour of the Italian people was outright passive resistance which, in many cases amounted to active assistance...As the German police were breaking into some homes, attempts to hide Jews were observed, and it is believed that in many cases they were successful. The anti-Semitic section of the population was nowhere to be seen during the action, only a great mass of people who in some individual cases even tried to cut off the police from the Jews.. In no case was there any need to use fire-arms"(15).

Dannecker's Razzia horrified the Curia, the Catholic clergy, and the overwhelming majority of the Italian people, including even staunch Fascists. Himmler and his aides, on the other hand, were displeased to learn from Kappler that for every Roman Jew seized by the SS, eleven others had escaped. They were equally dissatisfied with Dannecker's subsequent operations all over Northern Italy which resulted in the deportation of another 2,000 Jews(16). At the beginning of December Kaltenbrunner's office notified Horst Wagner, head of Inland II (the internal affairs department of the German Foreign Ministry), that "the round-ups ordered by the Reichsführer SS have so far yielded no result worthy of mention (bisher zu keinem nennenswerten Ergebnis geführt)", Italian sabotage having enabled the overwhelming majority of the potential victims to go underground in time. But since the forces at Dannecker's disposal were quite insufficient for the remaining task, he would have no choice but to enlist the aid of the Republican Fascists, unreliable though they were(17).

So far the extension of the "Final Solution" to Italy had been treated as a private German affair in which the authorities of Mussolini's puppet regime had no business to interfere. When, the day after Dannecker's Judenrazzia, the President of the Italian Red Cross, General Giuseppe Boriani, called on the Gestapo in order to find out what was going on, he was told - apparently by Kappler himself - that it was "useless to concern oneself, useless to inquire: this was a matter which concerned only the Germans and no one else"(18). The Republican Fascists, for their part, launched an anti-Jewish policy of their own with the object of restoring a measure of Italian sovereignty. On November 14, 1943, the Fascist Party Congress at Verona endorsed a manifesto which defined "members of the Jewish race" as "foreigners" (stranieri), to be regarded as "enemy nationals" for the duration of the war. On November 30 the new Minister of the Interior, Guido Buffarini Guidi, ordered the arrest and internment of all Jews resident in the Italian Social Republic ("even if exempted and irrespective of citizenship") and the immediate confiscation of their property "for the benefit of the indigent refugees from enemy air attacks". On the following day this order was broadcast over the radio, with the result that thousands of Jews went into hiding or fled the country. (According to Eitel Friedrich Moellhausen, Rahn's second-in-command in Rome, this was precisely what the "Jew-lover" Buffarini had hoped to achieve). On December 10 Tullio Tamburini, erstwhile Fascist chieftain of Florence and now Chief of Police, instructed the heads of all provinces to exempt certain categories of Jews from internment, including the aged, the sick, the "Aryanized", and those with "Aryan" spouses. On January 4, 1944, a decree law was promulgated which, if applied literally, would have robbed the Jews of all their possessions and condemned them to starvation. The following are the most salient points of the law:

"Art. 7 - Real estate and its appurtenances, movable property, industrial and commercial enterprises and any other source of income within the territory of the State that are owned by Italian citizens of the Jewish race or considered as such by the provision of Law No. 1728 of November 17, 1938, even if those citizens have been granted exemption (discriminazione) by Article 14 of the said law, and by the law regarding the property of foreign persons of Jewish race, even if not residents of Italy, are confiscated in favour of the State and as-

signed to the Ente di Gestione e Liquidazione Immobilare - E.G.E.L.I (Bureau for the Administration and Liquidation of Real Estate).
Art. 8 - The confiscation decree is issued by the Chief of the Province (Prefect) involved, in charge of each property. The said decree will be in accordance with Article 475 of the Penal Code (C.P.P.C.) with the indication that it is to be enforced immediately and to be published in the Official Gazette of Italy...
Art. 10 - The Chief of the Province will be in charge of the opening of safe deposit boxes or closed accounts registered in the name of persons of Jewish race in banks or financial institutions..."(19).

E.G.E.L.I., the bureau in charge of the administration and sale of Jewish property, was established in 1939 for the purpose of managing "non-Aryan" property valued above a certain sum. The bureau survived the Badoglio interlude (July 25 - September 8, 1943); after the setting-up of the Fascist Republic, it moved its offices to San Pellegrino, where a staff of eighty-seven people - officials and employees headed by a commissioner, Leopoldo Pazzagli - carried out a dizzily accelerated job under the decree law of total confiscation. A memorandum to Mussolini from the Ministry of Finance, dated March 12, 1945, notes that in the course of one year (January 4 - December 31, 1944), the bureau received 5,768 confiscation orders: bank deposits amounted to lL 75,089,047.90; government stock to IL 36,396,831 (nominal value); industrial and other securities to IL 731,442,219; the value of land to IL 885,348,608, and of buildings to IL 198,300,003. The latter were calculated on capital levy and not on the building's commercial value at the time(20).

The systematic expropriation of Jewish wealth was undoubtedly dictated by the poor financial condition of the Italian Social Republic; but although sequestration was to yield a sum of well over two billion lire between December 1943 and March 1945, it did not even partially cover the heavy "occupation indemnities" demanded by the German occupiers(21).

The Germans, unable to implement the "Final Solution" with their own forces, now decided to exploit the Fascist racial measures for their own ends. Dannecker was recalled to Berlin where, on December 4, 1943, he took part in a conference on the Italian Jewish problem at the Foreign Ministry, the other participants being Sturmbannführer Friedrich Robert Bosshammer, Eichmann's expert on Italian affairs, and Eberhard von Thadden of Inland II. Bosshammer proposed that the Italians be congratulated on their decision to intern the Jews, adding that Berlin should press for the handing-over of the internees to the SS. Thadden approved of the first proposal but objected strongly to the second, arguing that a demand for the surrender of Italian Jews to Germans would probably give rise to a great deal of friction; Buffarini's order would be carried out with greater facility if internment in Italy were made to appear as the "final solution" and not as a prelude to deportation. In other words, the Jews and their Italian protectors should be lulled into a false sense of security, after which the SS would strike. Bosshammer and Dannecker agreed whereupon Inland II drafted a memorandum for Ribbentrop from which the following is worth quoting:

"With the forces at our disposal it is impossible to carry out a thorough search of all the...Italian communities. Since in the meantime the Italian Government has enacted a law providing for the segregation of all Jews in concentration camps, Group Inland II, in agreement with the Reich Main Security Office, proposes: that Ambassador Rahn be instructed to convey to the Fascist Government the satisfaction of the German Government with this law which is vitally necessary for security reasons; that (the Italians) be asked to speed up the implementation of this law and the setting-up of concentration camps in Northern Italy so as to enable us to remove unreliable elements from the operational zones ...and that they be informed of the German Government's readiness to supply them with experienced advisers for this purpose. In this way it would be possible for us to integrate (<u>einbauen</u>) what is now the execution team into the government agencies, to supervise the actual enforcement of this law and to harness the entire executive apparatus of the Fascist Government to the implementation of the anti-Jewish measures".

As for shipment to the East, Inland II was of the opinion that this subject had better not be raised with the philo-Semitic Italians for the time being: "The Reich Main Security Office has no objection to the tactical procedure proposed by Inland II"(22).

Five days later Ribbentrop expressed agreement with the above proposals. Dannecker had meanwhile returned to Italy, ostensibly in order to initiate the "requisite measures" in accordance with the decisions reached on December 4, in reality in order to extend the "Final Solution" to German-occupied Italy without delay. As early as December 10 the SS in Italy began to give orders to the local police which ran counter both to existing Fascist legislation and to the proposals approved by the Reich Foreign Minister. And on December 20 the head of the German Security Service (SD) at Bologna issued the following instructions to the Chief of the Bologna Police:

"With reference to our conversation of December 10, 1943, I request the handing over to me of the Jews arrested in accordance with the Italian decree (of November 30) in the following cases: 1) Pure Jews with Jewish spouses; in such cases the whole family is to be arrested and handed over to me, irrespective of age or state of health...2) Pure Jews who are nationals of Enemy States are likewise to be handed over to me...3) Under German law a Jew is defined as a person, at least three of whose grandparents were of pure Jewish stock or who, although born of mixed marriage, professes the Jewish religion; hence you are to arrest and hand over to me also those persons of the Jewish race who are exempt or are considered Aryans for the purposes of the Italian laws hitherto in force. I request that the Jews arrested in virtue of this directive be reported to me on the first and the fifteenth of each month. The evacuation of the arrested perwill be carried out by my office (<u>Dienststelle</u>), in agreement with the office of the commander of the Security Police and the SD in Italy"(23).

On the same day a similar letter was dispatched to the Police Chief of Modena, while in Milan the SS requested the Italian police to arrest and surrender to them all Jews under seventy years of age who had hitherto been exempt, including even "half-breeds" and invalids. Yielding to German pressure, Police Chief Tamburini dispatched the following cable to the heads of all provinces on January 22, 1944: "You should make suitable arrangements with the local German authorities to whom the dispositions made by order of the Duce have been explained... Consequently cause to be sent to the concentration camp all Jews even if hitherto exempted or privileged...Communicate arrangements reached"(24). Emboldened by Fascist subservience, the head of the SD in Milan went so far as to order the Police Chief of Varese to arrest even sick Jews over seventy and to hand them over to him within two days(25).

In January 1944 Bosshammer was appointed Judenreferent for Italy and charged with the task of directing "the fight against the Jews on Italian soil". On his arrival in Italy he installed himself in Verona; and in the ensuing weeks he established contact with the offices of the SD all over Republican Italy "in order to prepare the ground for the 'Final Solution'". Subsequently he called on Giovanni Preziosi, Mussolini's Inspector-General of the Race, in order to discuss the planned anti-Jewish measures. At Bosshammer's trial after the war it was revealed that Preziosi had stressed the need for respecting the Fascist race laws and that the German had expressed agreement, assuring his interlocutor that Jews with "Aryan" spouses would under no circumstances be deported to Germany or to the Eastern territories(26). Even before this meeting, however, it had become clear to all concerned that Bosshammer had no intention whatever of respecting Italian legislation designed to prevent him from making Italy <u>judenrein</u>; nor did he feel bound by the decisions reached at the Wilhelmstrasse on December 4. The Italians responded with vain attempts to restrain the overzealous Judenreferent. As early as January 20 Buffarini protested to the Germans against the "illegal" deportation of Italian Jews to the East, in addition to which he requested the commandants of concentration camps not to hand over Jewish internees to the SS; and on March 7 he issued a fresh decree on the racial issue which was immediately passed on to all German <u>Dienststellen</u> in the Fascist Republic and from which the following is worth quoting:

"In connexion with the relevant communication received from the Directorate-General of Demography and Race and with reference to the telegraphic circular of January 22, it is hereby reaffirmed that persons of <u>pure Jewish stock</u>, whether of Italian or foreign citizenship, are to be sent to concentration camps, <u>with the exception of old people over 70 years of age and invalids</u>. Jewish members of mixed families, including foreign Jews with Aryan wives...<u>will continue to be exempted from this measure</u>. Also exempt are all those who...are not considered members of the Jewish race for the purposes of the law of July 13, 1939-XVII, No. 1204 (sic), which is still in force"(27).

Bosshammer's reaction to this half-hearted challenge took the form of a countermand addressed to his subordinates which the latter duly passed on to the competent Italian authorities. As a result, the "Final Solution" was extended to all those Jews with "Aryan" spouses who had the misfortune to fall into the hands of the SS. The Italians, for their part, went on protesting against these violations of the Fascist race laws. On April 10, the Head of Verona Province pointed out to Bosshammer's superior, Brigadeführer (SS Brigadier) Wilhelm Harster, that the Jew Volterra should never have been interned at Fossoli, having an "Aryan" wife. Harster passed the letter on to Bosshammer who left it unanswered. On April 13 the Chief of the Modena Police informed the Italian commandant at Fossoli that another Jewish internee with a Gentile wife, Bassi, should be permitted to rejoin his family, "provided the German Dienststelle at the camp had no objection". The camp commandant replied on June 3 that the matter had been brought to Bosshammer's notice but that no reply had been received. On May 27 the same Police Chief drew the attention of the camp commandant to the case of the Jew Levi whose "Aryan" spouse had appealed to the Questura of Milan to secure his release; the latter replied on June 3 that Signora Levi's appeal had been duly passed on to Bosshammer's office but that no reply had been vouchsafed. On June 5 the Chief of the Modena Police advised the commandant that the Ministry of the Interior had ordered the release of the Jew Alces Piazza who was likewise married to a Gentile. The commandant replied on June 12 that he would gladly comply with the Ministry's order as soon as Bosshammer's consent had been obtained; but since all communications to him had so far remained unanswered, Piazza would have to stay at Fossoli until further notice. Finally, on July 24, even Preziosi felt compelled to enter a protest against Bosshammer's high-handed methods, informing the Head of Verona Province that the Jew Jenna (who had been arrested by the SS) should be set at liberty forthwith, being married to an "Aryan". However, the Jew-baiter Preziosi was as powerless to restrain Eichmann's emissary as the "Jew-lover" Buffarini(28).

It is clear from the above that the continued friction between Bosshammer and the Fascist authorities did not prevent the latter from loyally co-operating with him. And while it is true that over four-fifths of the Jews living in Italy succeeded in eluding the grasp of the SS and that most of these were saved by Italian "Aryans" of all classes, it is no less true that such successes as Bosshammer was able to achieve were largely due to (willing or unwilling) Italian collaborators. Thousands of Jews were arrested and interned by the Fascist police to be deported and killed by Himmler's myrmidons. Others were denounced by the local agents and spies of the Gestapo; yet others were tracked down by Fascist action squads, headed by notorious thugs who took advantage of the German occupation to do their worst. Not a few Jews had their hiding-places betrayed by Italian civilians who were actuated by greed for gain, the Germans having offered rewards for the denunciation of Jews.. In Rome Police Chief Pietro Caruso demonstrated his zeal by launching a Jew-hunt in February which resulted in the capture of several hundred persons. He even disregarded the sanctuary agreement between the Vatican and the Germans, permitting his men to raid the Basilica of Saint Paul where they seized six "non-Aryans"(29).

At the time of Badoglio's surrender there were some 44,500 Jews in Italy and Rhodes, about 12,500 of them foreigners. By the end of the war at least 7,682 of these had perished in the Holocaust. Given the insufficiency of the forces at the disposal of the SS and the difficulty of telling a Jew from a Gentile in a country like Italy, a large part of the "credit" for this result must go to Bosshammer's Fascist accomplices(30).

All students of the subject are agreed that, but for the establishment of the Fascist Republic, many more Italian Jews would have survived the Holocaust(31). Most experts would also agree with Eucardio Momigliano that the race laws enacted by Mussolini's puppet government are without parallel "in relations between nations"(32). The fact remains, however, that the Nazis regarded these laws as woefully inadequate. To the Fascists the Jews were "foreigners" and "enemy nationals for the duration of the war"; to the SS they were "subhumans" and permanent enemies of mankind. To the Fascists temporary internment was an adequate solution; the Nazis would not accept anything short of physical extermination. One noted scholar doubts whether Fascist legislation was designed to take wind out of the sails of the Germans, affirming that the Fascists were indifferent to the fate of the Jews. This thesis, however, fails to take account of the fact that the main objective of the Fascist leaders was the restoration of Italian sovereignty; since Hitler's policy of genocide constituted an infringement of that sovereignty, they were bound to resent it, whatever their feelings about the Jews. Moreover, even the Fascist anti-Semites - men like Roberto Farinacci and Giovanni Preziosi - never went so far as to call for the extermination of the Jews(33).

The silence of Pius XII and the Catholic clergy.

Ever since the appearance of Hochhuth's play Der Stellvertreter, the silence of Pius XII in the face of the Holocaust has been the subject of heated controversy. His critics have levelled four main charges against him. Gerald Reitlinger claims that his failure to protest against the massacres was motivated, not by Christian prudence, but by un-Christian cowardice (i.e., fear of arrest and deportation). Guenter Lewy and Renzo De Felice affirm that anti-Jewish prejudice prevented him from viewing the plight of the Jews with a real sense of moral outrage. Hochhuth and others contend that he could have saved numerous lives (if not put a stop to the mass murders), had he chosen to take a public stand on Hitler's "Final Solution". Cardinal Eugène Tisserant and other loyal Catholics reproached the Pontiff with failure to provide moral leadership for his flock. Tisserant, in a letter to the Archbishop of Paris, complained that "our superiors do not want to understand the real nature of this conflict", adding that he had vainly pleaded with the Pontiff to issue an encyclical on the duty of the individual to follow the dictates of his conscience rather than blindly execute all orders, no matter how criminal. Most recently an American priest, Father John F. Morley, has reached the conclusion that "Vatican diplomacy failed the Jews during the Holocaust by not doing all that it was possible for it to do on their behalf. It also failed itself because in neglecting the needs of the Jews, and pursuing a goal of reserve rather than humanitarian concern, it betrayed the ideals it had set for itself"(34).

The first of the above charges - that of "un-Christian cowardice - is obviously unfounded. As Count Ciano, Mussolini's Foreign Minister, noted in his diary, the Pope "is even ready to be deported to a concentration camp but will do nothing against his conscience"(35). The second charge - that of "anti-Jewish prejudice" - is mainly based on the fact that in 1941 the Holy See failed to object to the "Jewish statutes" introduced by the Vichy Government. But while it is true that the Vatican did not consider "defensive" measures against Jews in conflict with Catholic teaching, it is equally true that Pius XII was profoundly shocked by the German method of solving the "Jewish problem". In 1964 it was revealed by Pirro Scavizzi (a military chaplain with first-hand knowledge of the German-occupied East) that the Pontiff, on being informed of the mass murders, "cried like a child"(36). The third charge - that a forceful public stand by the Pope would have saved many lives - ignores the fact that Hitler toyed with the idea of occupying the Vatican City and deporting the Pontiff to Germany. The probability is that a public protest by Pius XII would not only have been unsuccessful in halting the machinery of destruction, but would have caused a great deal of additional damage - not least to the Jews hidden in the Vatican and the monasteries. The fourth charge - that the Pontiff failed to provide unequivocal moral guidance to his flock - has been raised by those within the Church who felt that, in the face of monstrous evil, it was wrong to be guided by "reasons of state".

In sum, Pius XII was a diplomat who thought it his duty to keep silent ad maiora mala vitanda. His critics may be right in affirming that, in failing to speak out, he missed an opportunity for regaining stature; but they are wrong in accusing him of "un-Christian cowardice" or indifference to human suffering. If he was guilty of an error of judgment, it does not follow that his silence was due to unworthy motives; nor is it likely that a public protest would have saved the life of a single Jew.

As for the Italian clergy, it is generally recognized that priests, monks, and nuns were in the forefront of those offering help to persecuted Jews, whatever their prejudices against the "Christ-killers": "Theirs was an altruism that lay-people may often expect as a matter of course from the religious, but that can never be taken for granted. In Italy, most men and women of the Church were a credit to their calling"(37).

The attitude of the Italian people.

The following extracts from the diary of Bernard Berenson, the celebrated Jewish humanist and art historian in Florence, throw light on the attitude of the Italian people towards the "Final Solution" on Italian soil:

"November 4th, 1943:...With the Nazi occupation, Jews naturally feared the worst and took to the macchia (bush). As many as ten or twelve are hiding in a villa near Siena. One great landed proprietor, brother and cousin of officers high in the army and navy, has been flitting from hole to hole, and at last has decided to take shelter in the small apartment of a friend in the heart of Florence...It was said that the Fascist prefect, the moment he was installed, warned Jews to leave their homes and go into hiding.
December 2nd:...It seems that the prefect is beside himself, threatens to resign if the execution (of Buffarini's order to arrest and intern Jews) is insisted on.
January 25th, 1944:...I am seeing friends who, unlike myself, have no drop of Jewish blood to taint their veins. They are at least as horrified over the treatment of Jews as I am, and can get it as little out of their minds...The other day a parish priest of this diocese was arrested for harbouring a Jew. The Cardinal of Florence intervened, declaring that he himself was the culprit and requesting to be jailed in place of the priest; which, of course, resulted in the liberation of the prisoner.
September 1945:...(The Italian people's) sympathies for suffering, whether physical or moral, are wide and warm...Nowhere else have I encountered like generosity and self-sacrifice. Marchese and Marchesa Serlupi Crescenzi were little more than acquaintances when they offered me shelter at serious risk to their peace of mind, and even their personal safety. They took me in, and treated me not as a refugee...but as if it made them happy to have me, to serve me, to see to my every comfort...Unforgettable proofs of friendship were given me by the German Consul, Gerhard Wolf, and by the assistant chief, now chief of police, Virgilio Soldani Benzi...Despite alarms and excursions, nobody in any situation gave me away. I learned afterwards that some friends deliberately avoided finding out where I was, not to run the risk of betraying it under torture"(38).

No Italian Jew would disagree with Berenson's tribute to the "generosity and self-sacrifice" of Italian Gentiles who saved Jewish lives during World War II. Quite a few, however, would deplore the fact that he singled out for praise a Fascist prefect, a Fascist police chief, and a German consul - all the more so because such praise was exploited by Fascist apologists for their own ends(39). Nor would they approve of facile generalizations about the Italian national character. The controversy over the "kindly Italians" and "Fascism with a human face" came to a head in 1986 after the publication of Nicola Caracciolo's abovementioned volume on Jewish survivors and Italian rescuers in which he extolled the resistance of the Italian civil and military authorities to Hitler's policy of genocide, adding that Mussolini himself had aided the Jews, albeit in an "ambiguous and contradictory manner"(40). In reply Rossella Fubini, an Italian Jewess, pointed out that anti-Semitism had been imposed on the Italians by Mussolini, not by Hitler, that until July 1943 Italian Jewry had been persecuted and humiliated by the Fascists, not by the Nazis, and that the opposition of the Italian people had been confined to murmured regrets and individual acts of kindness. When Hitler extended the "Final Solution" to Italy, numerous Italians, especially of the lower classes, had come to the aid of the victims; but there was another side to the picture which Caracciolo had chosen to ignore(41).

In the following year this other side was dealt with by Susan Zuccotti, an American Gentile, who affirmed that the focus on Jewish survivors and Gentile rescuers had distracted attention from other, equally important aspects of the issue: "Does the high number of rescuers in Italy imply that Italians generally are more compassionate and altruistic than other people? Certainly the answer is negative. On the contrary, despite their international reputation as warm and immensely humane people, Italians are not known for the civic virtues or dedication to charity sometimes associated with altruism". Most Italians rejected anti-Semitism, opposed the war, disliked Fascism and hated the Germans. But there were others who followed Mussolini and Hitler to the end: "How do we explain the effusively anti-Semitic Italian press (there was no other in occupied Italy), the informers, the prison guards whose cruelty to political prisoners was exceeded only by their cruelty to Jews? Or the politicians who decreed that Jews should be interned, even while they knew that internment would insure deportation?" The roots of the Holocaust "lay in the racial laws imposed upon a reluctant populace...It peaked only during the German occupation - a time that brought the worst elements of the society to the surface and intimidated all the others"(42).

Neither Fubini nor Zuccotti mentioned the partisans in this context. This is a regrettable omission, for it was they who wrote the most creditable chapter in the history of Italian opposition to the Holocaust. Jews who joined the Resistance found themselves once more accepted as "Italians among Italians"; even foreign Jews were welcomed with open arms, as can be seen from the memoirs of Marek Herman and Isacco Nahoum(43).

The role of Mussolini

What of Mussolini himself? According to Renzo De Felice, he did not become an anti-Semite until after his rapprochement with Hitler: "Until 1937 the idea of an official anti-Semitism was completely alien to him. The Jews of Italy enjoyed, under Fascism, neither more nor less of the same 'liberty' enjoyed by other Italians. Persecuted Jews from abroad found in him, if not a protector, at any rate a political leader who frequently rendered assistance and opened the doors of Italy to them, unlike - it should be honestly recognized - many heads of state of other countries". True, Mussolini had prejudices against Jews even before the rise of Hitler, but they had little effect on his official attitude(44).

Mussolini's own pronouncements on the subject were as contradictory as those on all other subjects; but it is possible to discern a guiding thread through the maze of inconsistencies. First, he never shared the prevailing view that Jews are simply "Italians"; he could like or dislike them, admire or revile them, overrate or underrate their power, defend or persecute them; but, unlike most of his compatriots, he never managed to take them for granted. Second, he rejected the German brand of racialism, an unfeigned conviction which he repeated to intimates even after the adoption of the race laws. Third, as long as he regarded Jewry as a force to be reckoned with, he did his best to court it, whatever his views about "English" Zionism or "Jewish" high finance; but when Hitler proved its utter powerlessness in the face of persecution, he was thereby freed from an "inhibiting factor". Fourth, after his jump from "philo-Semitism" to anti-Semitism, he was anxious to defend himself against the well-founded charge of mimicry; he therefore made an elaborate, if ultimately futile, effort to fabricate an indigenous brand of "spiritual" racialism, a counterblast to the "materialistic" doctrine of blood and soil. Fifth, he never aimed at the physical extermination of the Jews; all he wanted was to remove them from the mainstream of Italian life and, if possible, from Italy altogether. Finally, the Jewish question outside Italy served him as a means of asserting what little liberty of action from his Axis partner he was able to maintain. This eminently political consideration helps to explain why the Italian-occupied territories in France, Yugoslavia, and Greece became havens of refuge for the Jews of those countries. From an index of abject servility to Hitler in 1938 - all the more abject because unsolicited - Mussolini's attitude towards the Jews became a test of his remaining autonomy in the course of World War II(45).

After the Italiam armistice and the establishment of the Italian Social Republic, Mussolini lost control of the anti-Jewish policy he had initiated five years earlier. The writ of his Fascist puppet government did not run beyond the road-blocks of Gargnano, the hamlet on Lake Garda where the Duce set up his headquarters in October 1943; his attempts to remove the Jewish question from German hands were therefore doomed to failure from the start. His internment order, even if designed to protect the Jews, had the effect of facilitating the task of Eichmann's emissaries; so had his decision to denationalize his Jewish subjects and declare them to be "enemy nationals" for the duration of the war. And while it is true that Mussolini was too much of an Italian to approve of Hitler's "Final Solution", it is no less true that he and his henchmen helped to create the conditions in which the Holocaust became possible. In the words of Piero Caleffi, an Italian senator who was both a veteran anti-Fascist and a survivor of a German concentration camp: "Consciously or not, the Fascists had been the originators (<u>anticipatori</u>) of the extermination camps"(46).

Mussolini was certainly not a monster on Hitler's scale. Even so, we cannot but agree with Renzo De Felice that Fascist racial policy was in a sense more shameful and more criminal than its German model: for Hitler at least believed in the "guilt" of his Jewish victims whereas Mussolini was perfectly well aware of their innocence(47). Moreover, Hitler's anti-Jewish mania was directed against people who were undeniably his enemies, if only because he left them no choice; Mussolini's racial laws, on the other hand, were aimed, not against Jewish anti-Fascists (who were being eliminated anyhow), but against those "Jewish Italians" who had until then been among his most loyal supporters - Fascists of the first hour, families of Fascist "martyrs", and officers of the Fascist militia.

Long before the formation of the Rome-Berlin Axis there were acute observers who feared that Mussolini's totalitarian pretensions would bring him into conflict with the Jews, including Robert Michels, the famous sociologist, and Bolton King, a noted student of the Risorgimento(48). After World War II Renzo De Felice reached similar conclusions in his study of Italian Jewry under Fascism. The sporadic manifestations of Fascist anti-Semitism prior to the rise of Hitler, he argued, had little bearing on Mussolini's subsequent conversion to the racial gospel; what really prompted him to throw in his lot with Hitler and declare war on his Jewish subjects was Fascism's "lack of respect for the most elementary values of the human personality" and its "presumption to represent the whole truth". De Felice did not use the term "totalitarian" in this connection; but twenty years later, in the fifth volume of his biography of Mussolini, he became more explicit. After the African war, he now maintained, many Italians hoped for a relaxation of dictatorial rule; Mussolini, fearing that any relaxation would lead to the disintegration of Fascism, responded by unleashing a "process of totalitarization" which rendered both the Axis and the persecution of the Jews inevitable. De Felice's thesis received support from the undersigned and from an eminent Italian-Jewish historian, Leo Valiani(49).

Conclusion

While no agreement has been reached on any of the issues discussed above, a few conclusions have rarely been challenged. First, Mussolini broke with the Jews on his own initiative, without any open German pressure. Second, Italian co-operation was essential for the partial success of the "Final Solution" on Italian soil; but for this co-operation the Germans would have been very largely helpless. Third, the Italian clergy played a most creditable part in the fight against Hitler's policy of genocide, whatever the personal attitude of Pius XII; the priests, monk , and nuns who risked and sometimes lost their lives to save Jews demonstrated great courage and compassion. Finally, the vast majority of the Italian people was never converted to anti-Semitism, despite the ceaseless anti-Jewish propaganda campaign conducted by the Fascists since 1938.

Notes

1) N. Caracciolo, Gli ebrei e l'Italia durante la guerra 1940-45, Roma 1986.
2) See, e.g., E. Momigliano, Storia tragica e grottesca del razzismo fascista, Milan 1946, p.49.
3) See, e.g., M. Vaussard, Histoire de l'Italie contemporaine, Paris 1950, p.257.
4) M. Michaelis, "On the Jewish Question in Fascist Italy. The Attitude of the Fascist Regime to the Jews in Italy", Yad Vashem Studies IV, 1960, pp.24-41; R. De Felice, Storia degli ebrei italiani sotto il fascismo, 3rd ed. Turin 1972, pp.242-43.
5) D. Grandi, Il mio paese. Ricordi autobiografici, Bologna 1985, p.444.
6) R. De Felice, op. cit., p.256.
7) K. Voigt, Zuflucht auf Widerruf. Die Emigration aus den vom Nationalsozialismus beherrschten Ländern in Italien. I (unpublished manuscript).
8) Reden des Führers am Parteitag Grossdeutschland 1938, München 1938, p.26.
9) Testimony of Signora Fanny G. Minerbi (1960).
10) G. Ciano, Diario 1937-1943, ed. R. De Felice, Milan 1980, p.545.
11) M. Michaelis, Mussolini and the Jews. German-Italian Relations and the Jewish Question in Italy, 1922-1945, Oxford 1978, pp.345-47.
12) Ibid., p.347.
13) L. Picciotto Fargion, "The anti-Jewish Policy of the Italian Social Republic", Yad Vashem Studies XVII, 1986, pp.19-20.
14) M. Tagliacozzo, "La Comunità di Roma sotto l'incubo della svastica. La grande razzia del 16 ottobre 1943", Quaderni del Centro di Documentazione Ebraica Contemporanea III, p.23.
15) Institut für Zeitgeschichte/NO-2427.
16) On Fascist disapproval of the Razzia see A. Tamaro, Due anni di storia 1943-1945, Rome 1949, pp.239-40; on Himmler's disappointment Yad Vashem Archives/TR-10/754a/Anklageschrift in der Strafsache gegen Friedrich Bosshammer, p. 263.
17) Memorandum by Wagner, December 4, 1943 (Yad Vashem Archives/NG-5026).
18) M. Tagliacozzo, loc. cit., p.34.
19) L. Picciotto Fargion, loc. cit., pp.28-29.

20) Ibid., pp.29-30.
21) S. Bertoldi, Salò. Vita e morte della repubblica sociale italiana, Milano 1976, pp.310-12.
22) Yad Vashem Archives/ Anklageschrift, pp.265-7.
23) Ibid., pp.19-21.
24) Public Record Office/F.O.371/WR435/42843.
25) Yad Vashem Archives/TR-10/754b/Strafsache gegen Friedrich Bosshammer, p.22.
26) Ibid., pp.24-25.
27) Ibid., pp.26-27. For Law No. 1024 see M. Michaelis, Mussolini and the Jews, pp.254-55.
28) Ibid., pp.34-35.
29) M. Michaelis, op. cit., p.390.
30) G. Donati, "Persecuzione e deportazione degli Ebrei dall'Italia durante la dominazione nazifascista", Ebrei in Italia: deportazione, resistenza, ed. Centro di Documentazione Ebraica Contemporanea, Milan 1975, pp.31-33.
31) R. De Felice, Storia degli ebrei sotto il fascismo, pp.451-60; M. Michaelis, Mussolini and the Jews, p.389; L. Picciotto Fargon, loc. cit., p.49; S. Zuccotti, The Italians and the Holocaust. Persecution, Rescue, Survival, New York 1987, pp.166-69.
32) E. Momigliano, op. cit., p.119; V. Paolucci, La stampa periodica della Repubblica sociale, Urbino 1982, pp.28-30.
33) For details see M. Michaelis, "La persecuzione degli ebrei", in: La Repubblica sociale italiana (Atti del convegno Brescia 4-5 ottobre 1985), Annali della Fondazione Luigi Micheletti II, Brescia 1986, pp.373-75.
34) M. Michaelis, op. cit., pp.373-77; J. F. Morley, Vatican Diplomacy and the Jews during the Holocaust 1939-1943, New York 1980, p.209.
35) G. Ciano, Diario 1937-1943, p.430 (entry for May 14, 1940).
36) H. Stehle, Die Ostpolitik des Vatikans, München 1975, p.239.
37) R. De Felice, Storia degli ebrei italiani, pp.466-69; M. Michaelis, Mussolini and the Jews, p.388; S. Zuccotti, The Italians and the Holocaust, p.209.
38) B. Berenson, Rumor and Reflection, New York 1952, pp.143,163,218,443. On Consul Wolf's assistance to Jews cf. Wolf to Rahn, November 6, 1943 (Foreign Office Library/London/131/I/71042.
39) See, e.g., G. Pisanò, Mussolini e gli ebrei, Milan 1967 (Pisanò is currently a neo-Fascist Senator).
40) M. Caracciolo, Gli ebrei e l'Italia, p.18.
41) R. Fubini, "La giustizia e il pietismo: su una recente trasmissione televisiva", La Comunità XI, December 1986, p.5.
42) S. Zuccotti, The Italians and the Holocaust, pp.283-86.
43) M. Herman, Diario di un ragazzo ebreo nella seconda guerra mondiale (preface by Primo Levi), Cuneo 1984; Isacco Nahoum "Milan", Esperienze di un comandante patigiano, Milan 1981.
44) R. De Felice, Storia degli ebrei italiani, pp.235-36; for a similar but slightly more critical assessment see M. Michaelis, "La persecuzione degli ebrei", loc. cit., p.367.
45) D. Carpi, "The Rescue of Jews in the Italian Zone of Occupied Croatia", in: Rescue Attempts during the Holocaust. Proceedings of the Second Yad Vashem International Conference, ed. Y. Gutman, Jerusalem 1977, pp.465-525. While stressing the importance of the political aspect, Carpi rightly insists that the rescue of Jews in the Italian-occupied territories cannot be explained solely on the basis of diplomatic interests: "Soldiers and civilians on all levels participated in the rescue work and almost everyone regarded the issue first and foremost as a humanitarian problem, which had to be solved for reasons of conscience, which were beyond political considerations"(p.506). See also A. M. Canepa, "Half-hearted Cynicism. Mussolini's Racial Politics", Patterns of Prejudice XIII, November-December 1979, pp.25-26 and M. Shelach, Heshbon damim. Hatzalat yehudei Kroatia al yedei ha-Italkim 1941-1943, Tel Aviv 1986, passim.
46) P. Caleffi, Si fa presto a dire fame, Milan-Rome 1955, p.135.
47) R. De Felice, Storia degli ebrei italiani, p.450.
48) R. Michels, "Der Aufstieg des Faschismus", Neue Zürcher Zeitung, December 29, 1922; B. King, Fascism in Italy, London 1931, pp.48-49.
49) R. De Felice, Storia degli ebrei italiani, pp.450-51; id., Mussolini il duce. II: Lo Stato totalitario, Turin 1981, pp.3-155,488-89.

THE CATHOLIC CHURCH IN CROATIA, THE VATICAN AND THE MURDER OF THE CROATIAN JEWS

M. Shelah

University of Haifa, Haifa, Israel

Shortly after the end of World War II Archbishop Stepinac, head of the Catholic Church of Croatia, as well as a number of his aides were brought to trial before a Yugoslav court. They were convicted for collaboration with an aid to the government of the satellite "Independent Croatian State" (Nezavisna Drzava Hrvatska - N.D.H.) and sentenced to lengthy terms of imprisonment. Much evidence of their guilt was presented during the trial and in books published subsequently in Yugoslavia - in a serious attempt to show that the Catholic Church of Croatia, aided and abetted by the Vatican, not only knew of the crimes committed by the Pavelic* government, but actually supported the latter and frequently encouraged these activities. Furthermore, it was proven that many priests had taken part in murders and atrocities against Serbs, Jews and Gypsies.[1]

Some West European scholars added arguments of their own to this issue, basing them on Yugoslav documentation, as part of the rather stormy debate about Pius the 12th's attitude to the Nazis and the extermination of Jews and other national and ethnic groups.[2] In reply to its accusers, the Vatican tried to present its own position - publishing, in a rather unusual gesture, documentation of its activities during W.W.II.[3] There is no doubt that the large and varied body of evidence available today, enables us to discuss the Vatican during W.W.II and the position of the Catholic Church of Croatic more objectively.[4]

The Catholic Church of Croatia held a special position under the Pavelic regime - similar to that of the Church in Slovakia and to some extent, in Hungary. The Catholic character of the regime and the religious fervour of its leaders granted the Church strong influence upon the state. The deep-rooted piety of the Croatians and the involvement of Church representatives in all aspects of life in the state created an exceptionally advantageous position for Church leaders, with regard to information about current events and the ability to act according to their lights.

Thus review will not directly discuss Pius the 12th's attitude to Nazi Germany and the Jews. Its primary subject are the deeds and misdeeds of the Catholic Church in Croatia and the Vatican's attitude to the Jews there.

THE CATHOLIC CHURCH IN CROATIA BETWEEN TWO WORLD WARS

In order to understand the activities of the Catholic Church in Ustasa Croatia one has to examine, at least briefly, the status and influence Catholicism had in this country prior to the outbreak of W.W.II.

In Church documents dating from W.W.II., Croatia is sometimes mentioned as "the Bulwark of Catholicism" (Antimuralis Christianitatis). The term was generated by a concept that was to

---

*Ante Pavelic was the leader of the separatist Croatian terrorist movement, the "Ustasa", whom the Germans and the Italians appointed head of the Croatian state after the division of Yugoslavia in April 1941.

some extent grounded in history: Catholic Croatia is an advanced outpost against the encroachment of heresy - Orthodox from the East and Moslem from the South. According to this version, waves of anti-Catholic barbarism were for many generations repelled on the threshold of Croatia, which again and again became the saviour of Western Christian civilization.[5]

Real historical events generated a myth, which was then fostered and nurtured until it became an article of religious fanaticism: If the Croatian bulwark were breached, the Anti-Christ, whatever the shape he was going to assume, would defeat the adherents of the true religion. This myth was reinforced by the Russian revolution and the wave of irrational hysterics that spread in its wake and did not spare the Catholic Church. From here onwards Croatia (besides Hungary, Poland, etc.) seemed to be the last bulwark of Catholicism. According to this almost demonic view of the world, the Serbian Orthodox had struck an alliance with the Communists to defeat Catholicism. The fact that Yugoslav inter-war governments were perhaps even more anti-Communist than the Vatican did not matter at all; as usual with a myth, facts could not budge it.

This irrational world picture was reinforced by fears grounded in Yugoslav reality - the rivalry between the Croatian Catholic and the Serbian Orthodox Church. The Serbs, governing the country in an authoritarian manner, discriminated against Croatians; the Catholic Church, indentifying with the Croatians, feared that the Orthodox Church would utilize the situation to enroach upon its prerogatives and limit its activities.[6]

The Croatian clergy consistently and energeticaly supported the parties - primarily the large Peasant Party - that tried to gain as much autonomy as possible within the framework of the Yugoslav state. The reasons are understandable - autonomy would enhance the Church's freedom of action. While the top echelons of the Croatian Church and the Vatican tried to further their interests primarily by diplomatic means (as during the negotiations for a concordat with the Belgrad government in 1935), their cleric taught Croatian nationalism to the faithful, telling them that it was identical with Catholicism. The majority of Croatians were uneducated peasants, who looked for spiritual and political guidance primarily to the village priest - their supreme authority in current affairs as well as in religious matters. The priest, who at best was semi-educated, interpreted daily events in his Sunday sermons in a simplistic and vulgarized manner. The more the tension between the various nationalities in Yugoslavia rose, the greater the number of priests who were carried away by extremist moods. Not a few of them, including high-ranking officials, aided the Ustasa's conspiratory-terrorist activities; some were even members of the movement.[7]

The Vatican employed its habitual caution in advertising this attitude - in order not to damage its (more or less) correct relations with the Belgrad government.

The Yugoslav government itself, although fully aware of the state of affairs among Croatian Catholics, did not harass them and was too cautious to infringe upon clerical institutions. It tried to alleviate Catholic hostility by giving appointments in the Croatian Church hierarchy to individuals it considered moderate. The outstanding event in this context was the appointment of Archbishop Aloys Stepinac as head of the Croatian Church - passing over candidates of much greater seniority. The Yugoslav government assumed - mistakenly, as it were - that Stepinac, who had fought with the Serbian army at Salonika during W.W.I., was a supporter of the multi-national Yugoslav state. This assumption was soon proven false. The Archbishop's diary shows that he was suspicious of Belgrad already in the thirties, that he harboured hostility if not hate for the Orthodox Church and aspired to an autonomous, if not a separatist solution for Croatia.[8]

However, there was an additional element involved. The virulent anti-Communism of the Vatican turned among Croatican clergy into abysmal hatred. It is therefore not surprising that Croatian Catholics considered Hitler's ascent to power a blessing. In October 1940 the official Croatian Church organ, "Hrvatska Straza" published an article, stating that "Today's Germany knows that Croatia sympathizes with Germany's struggle for justice and renewal ... it is a known fact that Croatian nationalists supported National-Socialist Germany from the very beginning of her struggle."[9]

The attitude of the Croatian Church towards the Jews can be defined as "moderate antisemitism" - the classic Christian view of the Jews as the sect that had refused to accept Christ's gospel, had crucified him and was therefore condemned to eternal humiliation. In practice the Church did not oppose steps aimed at limiting the Jew's freedom, or legislation that discriminated between them and other citizens - while trying, at least in Croatia, to convert as many Jews as possible. In this sphere the Croatian Church gained considerable success;[9a]

not a few Croatian Jews, especially from among the wealthy, became Catholics. The initiator and executor of the 1940 "Numerus Clausus" law for schools was the Yugoslav Minister of Education, the Catholic priest Korosec. However, the ideological antisemitism of leading Church officials acquired "Stuermer" type virulence and savagery among the clerical rank and file. In addition to the murder of Christ, the Jews were accused of Bolshevism, of collaboration with the plutocracy and of what was at the time the ultimate crime in Croatia - support for the hated Serbian authorities. In spite of these trends, actual anti-Jewish acts were not severe and the Jews were not harassed or in particular discriminated against - be it because of their small numbers, or because of their modest economic and social position. Relations between top Church dignitaries and local Jewish community leaders were decent; in some cases there were personal connections, which no doubt came in useful during the critical years.

THE CHURCH BLESSES THE ESTABLISHMENT OF INDEPENDENT CROATIA - THE VATICAN RECOGNISES IT DE-FACTO

The Croatian Church as well as the Vatican rejoiced in the collapse of Yugoslavia in a April 1941. For both the establishment of an independent Croatian state held great promise.

The Ustasa leaders, headed by Ante Pavelic, were known for their piety; the "Ustasa Principles" stated explicitly that "being Croatian is identical with being Catholic, because this is the official state religion." It went on to emphasize that for the Croatian people the moral centre of gravity lay in orderly religious and family life.[10]

The support of the Church for the new regime was publicised the day after the establishment of the Croatian state. On April 11th, 1941 Archbishop Stepinac conveyed his feelings of joy to the senior Ustasa representative in Zagreb, Slavko Kvaternik. In his pastoral letter for Easter, of April 28, which was read out all over Croatia, Stepinac appealed to the clergy and the people to support the new regime with all their might; he promised that "on the basis of personal acquaintance with those who head the state today, I am convinced that our people will be granted understanding and assistance to the full. I believe and hope that in the newly revived Croatian state the Church will enjoy full freedom in the dissemination of the principles of truth and justice which cannot be refuted."

In order to translate these words into the language of prayer, Stepinac issued an order in the beginning of May - to perform a "Te Deum" for the well-being of the new state in all churches.[11]

The Vatican, notwithstanding its sympaty for the Pavelic government, chose to be prudent. The Holy See argued that it recognized states established in war-time only after the end of war. In mid-June 1941, in response to pressures exerted by Stepinac and other Catholic circles, the Vatican sent a representative with the rank of Visitator to Croatia - the Benedictine Father Ramiro Marcone. He had no diplomatic experience whatsoever, but was counted among the friends of the Vatican Secretary of State, Maglione, and enjoyed his patronage.[12]

For obvious reasons the Croatian government granted Marcone senior diplomatic status in spite of his semi-official position. He participated at all official events as doyen of the diplomatic corps and did not miss any opportunity to appear in public with the leaders of the regime.[13]

SOME REMARKS ON THE CROATIAN CLERGY

Before we set out to describe the Church's activities with regard to the Jewish question, it will be proper to devote a few words to some individuals among the Church officials involved in the affair.

First and foremost among those was Aloys Stepinac, Archbishop of Zagreb and head of the Croatian Church. It is worthwhile to stress once again that Stepinac's views were nationalist Croatian and that he greeted the establishment of an independent Croatian state with fervour. Like Church officials all over Europe and in line with the official Vatican position, he was extremely anti-Communist - believing that if the choice is to be between the U.S.S.R. and Germany, the latter was the lesser evil. It is not true that he supported the Nazi regime, as Yugoslav historians are trying to prove. We will see further on that the Germans quite rightly regarded him as a rival or perhaps even an enemy. On this subject he was of the same opinion as Pius the 12th - that Communist domination of Europe spelt ruin for the Catholic Church.

One may say that his policy was to wield influence upon the regime from within. This choice became his undoing - he lost on both counts. On one hand his success in the prevention of atrocities was modest, so that he had to face the world (and God) as a passive supporter of Pavelic and his gang of murderers. On the other hand he was ultimately forced to witness the final and complete collapse of his aspirations for Croatian independence and the fall of the state to the Communists. His failure, morally and in practice, was neither due to an evil mind nor to support of a murderous regime. It was primarily a consequence of his being the wrong person in the wrong place, at the wrong time.[14]

In contradistinction to Stepinac, a number of his bishops collaborated eagerly and often gladly with the regime. The worst among those was the Bishop of Sarajevo, Ivan Saric. On May 25, 1941, his paper published an article under the title "Why Are the Jews Persecuted ?". We read there that "the descendants of those who hated Jesus, persecuted him to death, crucified him and persecuted his disciples, are guilty of greater sins that their forbears. Jewish greed increases. The Jews have led Europe and the world towards disaster - moral and economic disaster. Their appetite grows till only domination of the whole world will satisfy it ... Satan aided them in the invention of Socialism and Communism. There is a limit to love. The movement of liberation of the world from the Jews is a movement for the renewal of human dignity. Omniscient and omnipotent God stands behind this movement."[15]

On June 15, 1941 the same paper wrote that "the time has come to abandon the stupid arguments attributed to Jesus' disciples, saying that the evil and the criminal should be fought fairly and nobly ... Gregorius the 7th already swept the Church of this filth with a hand of iron."[16] In addition to inciting against the Jews, Saric appropriated Jewish property for his own use.[17]

The Bishop of Djakovo, Aksamovic, behaved in a similar way. He published an article in his paper, saying that "today it is the sacred duty of every citizen to prove his Aryan origins."[18]

The outstanding figure in the sphere of ideology was Ivan Guberina, a professor of Theology. In a series of articles Guberina attacked Croatians who protested against Ustasa atrocities, calling them "spiritual dwarfs", and arguing that it were the Croatian state and people's natural right "to purge its organism of poisons."

"The Ustasa movement", Guberina writes, "rallied to this task. It needs the means like a physician performing a cure. Where necessary, one has to operate ... it is Croatia's right, also according to the rules of Christian morals ... to destroy its attackers by the sword ...". According to Guberina one must not wait for the enemy to attack; "against these opponents defense is permitted, and when necessary, pre-emptive defense. One must not wait for the attack."[19]

It should be noted that Stepinac did nothing to silence these voices. While the upper ranks of the Croatian Church were disseminating hostility to national minorities, eulogizing themselves and "appropriating" property, not a few among the rank and file clergy were busy with what Guberina called "purging the organism of poisons." Dozens, perhaps even hundreds of priests and monks shed their priestly apparel and donned Ustasa uniforms, in order to share in the "sacred work" of murder, rape and robbery. One of those, the priest Mate Mugos, urging his colleagues on, wrote in the "Novi List" paper: "So far we have served the Catholic faith by means of the prayer book and the cross. The time has come to do so by means of the rifle and the pistol."[20]

A number of names stand out among these murderous clerics: Filipovic Majstorovic, the "devil" of the Jasenovac and Stara-Gradiska concentration camp; Bozidar Bralo, of Bishop Saric's entourage, head of the Ustasa security police at Sarajevo - one of the initiators and executors of the expulsion of Jews from this town; Dyonisy Juricev, head of the Department for Religion at the Ministry of Renewal (the chief ministry for religious conversion and expulsions); Ilija Tomas, one of the chief murderers in Hercegovina - and a great many besides these.[21]

CONVERSION

When the Ustasa leaders seized power they proclaimed their intention to purge the state of "alien elements", i.e. primarily of Serbs and Jews. The Serbs were to be converted, expelled to Serbia or exterminated. The Church was not directly involved in expulsion or extermination, but its authority certainly covered the matter of conversion. There was no doubt that compulsive conversion contradicted basic principle of faith - and the Church could not ignore the fact that the majority of Serbs who accepted conversion did so to evade being massacred. If so, what was the right course for the Church ? Should it support compulsive conversion and thus, as the latter's advocates claimed, save the Serbs ? Or should it insist on the principle of inner conviction as the only basis for conversion ?

Church institutions in Croatia discussed the subject fairly often. The instructions issued stated somewhat half-heartedly that priest should not convert anyone who does not do so voluntarily - but in reality they shut both eyes in the face of compulsive mass conversions.[22] If the wish to save lives had been the sole motivation one could hardly blame the Church - but this is not the whole story. In letters written by many priests one finds the argument, that one should regard the affair of compulsive conversion as the work of God, who wishes to restore erring children to the bosom of the true Church.[23]

For our discussion the conversion of Jews is more important. As mentioned above, not a few Croatian Jews converted to Christianity between the wars. However, at the end of April 1941, with the proclamation of race-laws in Croatia, it became clear that Jews would not gain anything by becoming Christians. Moreover - even Jews who had converted to Christianity years earlier - they, or their parents - were not excempt from anti-Jewish measures. It was neverthless assumed that the Church, owing to its strong influence, would be able to persuade the Croatian government no to impose the new legislation on converted Jews. Many Jews therefore converted after the occupation of Croatia. Their exact number is not known, but one source states that the affair concerned 60% of the Jews in Zagreb.[24] The Catholic Church accepted converts for two reasons: **(a)** a number of these converts would remain Christians for life; **(b)** perhaps this was a way to save Jews from death. Emil Schwartz, secretary to Rabbi Freiberger of Zagreb, met in October or November 1942 with the secretary of the Vatican representative in Zagreb, Masucci. During their talk the latter said that he knew the majority of converted Jews would revert to Judaism after the war - but the Croatian Church, supported by the Vatican, had aggreed to baptise them as Christians in order to save their lives.[25] However, to the detriment of the Church, the race-laws did not allow for the protection of converted Jews. Stepinac tried to change this - already on May 22, 1941 he sent a letter to the Croatian Minister of the Interior, Artukovic, who was responsible for the implementation of these laws:

"... In my letter of April 23 (the letter was not published, but the remark proves that the Church knew about the race-laws before they were publicly announced at the end of that month. - M.S.) ... I had the honour to ask your Excellency to grand some consideration in (the formulation of) the race-laws to Christians of Jewish extraction. However, in the law that was proclaimed on the 30th of the same month this matter was not taken into account. The regulations announced in recent days strike equally at the guilty and the innocent. Today an ordinance was published, ordering Jews to wear a special badge, independent of gender, age or religious adherence. Senior officials claim ... that even in Germany this kind of legislation was not put into practice with such rigour. No one questions the means aimed at removing the economy (from Jewish hands) and delivering it into nationalist hands. This is to prevent the accumulation of capital by non-national elements ... but this does not mean one has to deny people belonging to other nationalities or races the very means of existence. To brand those with marks of disgrace is a moral and humane issue. These moral laws are not only valid with regard to individuals, but also with regard to state authorities.

We therefore appeal to you, sir, to issue regulations so that even in the framework of antisemitic legislation, and similar legislation concerning Serbs, the principles of their human dignity be preserved. (We appeal to you) to cancel the order that Jews have to wear this badge ... and especially we ask you to reconsider the question of Jewish converts ...

Finally, it is my duty to call your attention to an additional consideration ... the Holy See does not regard these laws with favour. Do you believe that just now, after the Holy Father received the Poglavnik (Pavelic) and his entourage in such a friendly manner, while efforts are being made to gain recognition for our state by the Holy See, it is advisable to create an atmosphere of controversy and opposition ? I hope sir, you will not consider it an offence that as a bishop have expressed my opinion frankly.

Yours, with due respect, Archbishop, head of the Church Synod."[26]

This letter already reveals Stepinac's tactics towards the Croatian government. We discern the following components: **(a)** In principle, consent to the removal of alien (Jews and Serbs) elements from the nation's social and economic life; **(b)** support for the measures implemented to this end, but qualified by the demand to preserve "human dignity" (a notion that in reality remained vague);

(c) opposition to measures motivated by racial arguments (therefore, opposition to the "yellow patch" to be worn by Jews); **(d)** the demand for special and different treatment of Jewish converts.

Stepinac did not limit himself to arguments of moral nature, in the spirit of Christianity, but based these on political considerations. His principal argument was that anti-Jewish legislation, in particular if implemented drastically, was liable to prevent the recognition of independent Croatia by the Vatican. On the face of it Stepinac's letter can be interpreted as tacit consent to the policy of discrimination and expulsion. One should, however, remember that at the time Stepinac sent his letter to Artukovic (May 1941) mass arrests of Jews had not yet begun.

EVENTS IN CROATIA - VATICAN REACTION TO USTASA MASSACRES

In the beginning of August 1941 news of the Ustasa's terrible deeds and massacres carried out against Serbs and Jews began reaching the Vatican. The Vatican representative in Zagreb reported on the situation with regard to Croatian Jews: "Croatian Jews are forced to wear a special badge ... with the letter Z in the centre (Zidov, i.e. Jew - M.S.). This badge arouses hatred (toward Jews) in Croatian hearts, causes economic damage and drives Jews to convert to Christianity. I do not consider it impossible that supernatural forces and divine providence are involved (the italics are mine - M.S.). Our priests consent to requests for conversion on the assumption that (at least) the children of converted Jews, who will attend Christian schoold, will (in future) become true Christians."[27]

The Vatican Secretary of State, Maglione, says in his reply that the Vatican representative should continue discreet activities in order to prevent the recurrence of what he calls "regrettable actions" (Fatti Lamentati) against the Serbian population. With regard to the Jews Maglione writes:

"If your Eminence (Marcone) can find a suitable occasion, he should recommend in a discreet manner that would not be interpreted as an official appeal, that moderation be employed with regard to Jews on Croatian territory. Your Eminence should see to it that activities of a political nature engaged in by the clergy should not cause friction between the parties, and that the impression of loyal cooperation with the civil authorities be always preserved."[28]

It appears that the Vatican employed extreme caution even with regard to what Maglione calls "regrettable actions" or, in straight language - mass murder of Serbs and Jews. The honourable Secretary of State urges his representative in Zagreb to avoid any action which could be interpreted as a confrontation, mild as it may be.

The same position was taken by Vatican dignitaries in their talks with Pavelic's special emmissary, the priest Kerubin Segvic, who came to Rome early in September 1941 and remained there till the end of the month.

At a meeting with the deputy Secretary of State, Monsignor Montini (the future Pope Paulus the 6th) Segvic discovered that "the slander has even reached the Vatican" and that he had to refute it. And indeed, Montini appeared to have been convinced and arranged an audience with the Pope for Segvic. During this audience the Pope did not utter a single word against Ustasa atrocities; according to Segvic "the Pope frankly revealed his joy when he saw that the Holy See could rest assured that Croatia always remain a Catholic country. He (the Pope) knew that Europe owed Croatia a great debt, for it had defended Catholicism and Catholic civilization."[29]

THE BISHOPS' SYNOD RECOMMENDS - STEPINAC SPEAKS OUT

The horrifying events in Croatia and the question of compulsive conversions finally drove Stepinac to convene the Bishop's Synod on November 17-20, 1941. For three days the questions of conversion and the Church's attitude to the persecution and murder of Jews and Serbs were discussed in the presence of the Vatican representative, Marcone. Stepinac reported the results of the Synod directly to Pius the 12th

"The Bishops' Synod discussed the affairs of those who suffer today and sent a letter to the head of the state, in which it demands that he treat the Jews in a humane manner as far as possible, considering the presence of the Germans. The case of those recently baptised and descendants of baptised Jews (of long ago) was in particular emphasized."[30]

The Bishops' letter to Pavelic said the following:

"The Catholic Episcopate of Croatia, at the Bishops' Synod on November 18, announces that it has been informed of cases in which (the authorities) treated converted Jews or the children of those who have been Catholics for a long time, and have been completely absorbed into the Croatian people, as if they were non-converted Jews. Their personal liberty was taken away and their property confiscated. We therefore turn to you, the state's Poglavnik, with the following request: Let personal and civil liberty and their property be returned to those Jews and their descendants, who after having been converted should not be regarded anymore as Jews. We also request the authorities not to impede the activity of Catholic priests who in the course of their duties wish to visit these converted Jews imprisoned in concentration camps, in order to attend to their spiritual needs."[31]

We see that the letter to Pavelic was in fact different from the impression created by Stepinac's report to the Pope. The Bishops' Synod intervened exclusively on behalf of converted Jews.

The Croatian authorities launched a widespread manhunt for Jews from July to December 1941. Two thirds of the Jews were caught and imprisoned in camps in Croatia. The mojority was murdered - a minority was imprisoned in a few centres, among which the most important one was the concentration camp at Jawenovac.[32]

THE CHURCH AND THE DEPORTATIONS OF AUGUST 1942

The first wave of arrests ended in the beginning of 1942 and till August of that year persecutions relatively subsided. Nevertheless, reports on negotiations concerning the Jews continued to come in during these months - namely, a plan to hand the Jews over to the Germans, to be deported to the East. In response to these reports, Stepinac sent a letter to Artukovic, the Croatian Minister of the Interior, on March 7, 1942, saying:

"Sir, rumours (have come to my knowledge) of impending mass arrests of Jews who are to be sent to concentration camps. If indeed such a course is being planned I take the liberty to appeal to you to prevent by virtue of you authority an unlawful attack on citizens who are not personally guilty of anything. I believe it will damage our good name if it becomes known that we have solved the Jewish question radically, i.e. in an extremely rough manner. The solution of the problem must refer only to crimes committed by Jews - meaning that innocent people must not be persecuted."[33]

Stepinac ultimately tried to protect all Jews. However, even in this letter the dominant note is still the wish to appease - when besides general moral arguments he recruits the feeble claim that the regime's prestige might suffer. It is hard to believe that Stepinac truly considered the persecutions to be the work of what he called "irresponsible people" - but it is possible that he wanted to leave an opening for the leaders of the regime to retreat without losing face.

The rumours that reached Stepinac also spread to the Vatican and the Croatian representative there began to fear for Croatia's status. At the end of April 1942 Stepinac went to Rome. On his arrival he sent the Pope a nine page long memorandum, claiming that Ustasa atrocities were anomalies, carried out without knowledge of the authorities. The only existing report on the visit comes from a Croatian source (the Vatican has not published anything yet), so that it is possible that this review does not contain the whole truth. Rusinovic, the Croatian representative at the Vatican, wrote to the Croatian Foreign Minister, Lorkovic:

"(Stepinac) informed me of the main points in the memorandum he sent to the Pope; I can assure you that it is very favourable for us in its attack on the Serbian Cetniks and the Communists, whom he regards as the cause of all ills ... In his (Stepinac's) opinion actions by whoever it is should be prevented and no one should be permitted to attack independent Croatia ... Stepinac was granted an hour long audience by the Pope."[34]

A week after his return from Rome, Stepinac once again launched a public attack on Ustasa atrocities in a sermon before thousands of Catholics. On May 24, 1942 he was very outspoken:

"All races and nations were created in the image of God ... therefore the Church criticized in the past and does so in the present all deeds of injustice or violence, perperated in the name of class, race or nationality. It is forbidden to exterminate Gypsies and Jews because they are said to belong to an inferior race ..."[35]

A week later, on May 31, he delivered another sermon on the same subject, saying:

"Those who are astonished or even ridicule our statement that peace will be achieved through love and those who claim that peace will be achieved by the sword, I remind of St. Augustinus words 'Peace is the continuation of the proper order. It demands that man recognise his own foibles and the supremacy of God' - (I say) that those who long for better days, for times of peace, must render unto God what belongs to God and be humble in his face. The continuation of the proper order demands the proper treatment of neighbours; i.e. to treat men as God's creatures just like ourselves, and not as wild beasts."[36]

Rumours of an already accomplished German-Croatian agreement spread about the same time. Representatives of the Jewish community in Zagreb, headed by their Chief Rabbi Freiberger, sought the help of the Church. It seems that Stepinac advised Rabbi Freiberger to send a personal letter to the Pope. On August 4th (eight days before mass expulsions began) the Rabbi of Zagreb wrote to Pius the 12th:

"I dare, with all due respect, to appear before your Holiness and to convey, as Chief Rabbi of Zagreb and spiritual leader of the Croatian Jews, my and my community's deep gratitude for the sympathetic attitude of the Holy See's representatives and the leaders of the Church towards my unfortunate brothers. The biblical command, 'thou shalt love thy neighbour as thyself', whatever his religion, is kept only by those who believe in an omnipotent God who is the father of humanity. In this crucial hour, when the fate of what is left of our community is going to be decided for better or for worse, we raise our eyes to you, your Holiness ... I am afraid that we, whose strength is increasingly ebbing away, will not live to see the day of deliverance without the generous aid of your Holiness. Believing that your words will receive God's blessing we are convinced of your success and pray to omnipotent God to grant us the strength to survive."[37]

In a reply to this letter sent on August 29th (near the end of the transports) the Vatican instructed its Zagreb representative to thank Rabbi Freiberger for his letter, but "prudently, tactfully, in accordance with circumstances."[38] It is hard to understand the aim of the instruction to act "prudently". Was the intention not to let the Chief Rabbi hope for too much ? Or not to cause a rift between the Vatican and the Croatian government ? At the end of September Marcone found the time to report to the Vatican on the August events. He wrote, in a letter of September 30th:

"... during recent weeks (i.e. the time of the transports - M.S.). I frequently met with the Chielf Rabbi of Zagreb, Freiberger ... he is full of gratitude on account of the Holy See's activities on behalf of the Jews. He found that also I and my secretary kept in constant with the head of the police. Unfortunately we were unable to change the course of events, but many requests we filed for the release of Jews from expulsion, were granted. All those of mixed families, Catholics and non-Catholics were saved."[39]

It is difficult to decide whether Marcone's report on partial success convinced the Vatican to persist in its "moderate policy" towards the Croatian government. In any case, Maglione continued to instruct Marcone. On October 6th he wrote: "The Holy See continues to receive news and letters concerning the sorrowful and alarming situation of Croatian Jews. (The letters) were accompanied by appeals to us to intervence on behalf of these unfortunate people ... I therefore request you Eminence, among other matters, to call the attention of the relevant authorities, with proper tact, (my italics - M.S.) to this affair."[40]

As mentioned above, Maglione recurrently stresses "proper tact". There is no indication that the Vatican considered more energetic or more public intervention. We should remember that by mid 1942 the Vatican was in possession of a great deal of information from authorized sources, not only from the Allies, about the total extermination of the Jews sent to the East.[41] The measure of the Vatican's sensitivity to these reports is expressed in an instruction issued by Montini, to prepare a memorandum, in which "it will be emphasized that the Holy See has received information about harsh treatment of Jews. It was impossible to verify all information received, on every possible occasion, in favour of the Jews."[42]

Marcone acted according to the instructions issued by the Secretary of State. In a letter of November 8th he wrote: "... I did best to relieve the sorry situation of the Croatian Jews. I discussed the matter again and again with the Poglavnik and the chief of police, who told me frankly that he cannot cancel the measures imposed upon these unhappy people, and that sooner or later all of them would be sent to Germany (my italics - M.S.)."[43]

Although criticism by the Church was uttered quietly and "tactfully", it caused anxiety among the Ustasa leadership. At the end of November they sent their close ally and staunch supporter, the military Vicar-General Cecelja to Stepinac. The meeting between the two appeared in a report by the German police attache in Zagreb, Helm, to his superiors: "The Croatian government has recently sent Dr. Cecelja, a Catholic priest loyal to them, to Archibishop Stepinac in order to mediate between them. Cecelja was instructed to tell Stepinac that the Croatian government was not satisfied with his attitude to the young Croatian state. He not only failed to praise the Ustasa's Catholic piety; they have been informed that he voices criticism (against them) privately and recently also at public meetings. The Archbishop replied (to Cecelja) that the Church obeys the laws of God. Cecelja may tell his government that the Church would continue to criticise terror acts against the population. The Croatian government will have to bear full responsibility for the growth of the Communist partisan movement ... because of severe and unlawful measures employed against Orthodox Serbs, Jews and Gypsies, in imitation of German methods."[44]

DIFFERENCES OF OPINION AT THE VATICAN

As we have seen, Vatican policy towards Croatia was tortuous and varied. A few rebukes and a few caresses; Praise on one hand and dissatisfaction on the other.

The outstanding representatives of this course were the staff at the Secretariat of State, Montini, Tardini and Maglione. In March 1942, during Montini's fist meeting with the Croatian representative, Rusinovic, the former said: "What is happening in Croatia ? Is it possible that so many crimes are committed here ? What is the truth about your harsh treatment of detainees ?"

Rusinovic managed to convince Montini that all these were lies spread by Croatia's enemies. Montini expressed his satisfaction and added that the Holy See regarded this information (about atrocities) with a measure of doubt.

Subsequently Montini praised the Croatians who, according to him, "have fulfilled their historical assignment to this day and will go on doing so also in future."[45]

Tardini, Montini's colleague at the Secretariat of State, behaved in a similar manner. At his first meeting with Rusinovic, in the beginning of April 1942, he spoke like a teacher admonishing an outstanding pupil who had gone off the rails: "Croatia is a young state," said Tardini, "youngsters often err because of their age. It is therefore not surprising that Croatia has also erred. It is only human, understandable and quite justified." Further on he explained that "a true Christian has to forgive his enemies, even if those have caused him much harm, and that such forgiveness is politically expedient."[46]

The Secretary of State, Maglione, the superior of these two, was an experienced, clever and prudent diplomat. During his meetings with Croatian representatives he chose to keep silent for most of the time - or, as the Croatians said "to listen attentively" - from time to time throwing out vague remarks that lent themselves to various interpretations.[47]

There is no doubt that the initiative for this course of policy rested with Pius the 12th. There is not even a hint to be found that he ever voiced or implied the Vatican's disapproval of Croatian brutalities in his meetings with Ustasa leaders. On the contrary - Pius took care to praise the Poglavnik's Catholicism again and again, and to glorify the Croatian state as the defender of Christianity against Communist heresy.[48]

The Pope used now and then to bless visiting groups of Ustasa; among those was a large group from the security police, headed by the super-murderer Dido Kvaternik.[49]

Not all Vatican dignitaries accepted Pius the 12th's position. The most outspoken among those was the French Cardinal Eugene Tisserant, head of the section for the Eastern Churches. At one of the meetings with the Croatian Vatican representative, Tisserant said: "In Croatia murder, arson, gangsterism and robbery are everyday occurences. I do not know the whole truth, but I know for certain that the Franciscans participate in all this ... how can civilized and educated people behave in such a way - in particular priests ?" Rusinovic tried to refute Tisserant's accusations, but the French Cardinal did not give in.[50]

EFFORTS BY THE CHURCH TO PREVENT THE 1943 TRANSPORTS

A period of respite came once again with the end of the August 1942 transports. Summer and autumn passed, the year of 1942 drew to its end. In the beginning of 1943 rumours spread among the Croatian public and among what was left of Croatian Jews, that transports to the East were to be renewed. As those concerned this time were mainly converted Jews or members of mixed families, the Church was quick to intervene. Activities aimed at the prevention of renewed transports reached their peak in March 1943. In the course of this month, on the 14th[51] and on the 28th[52], Stepinac delivered two sermons against racial discrimination. On March 6th he sent a sharp letter to Pavelic, defending his Jewish proteges:

"Poglavnik, a great deal of panic has broken out in Zagreb and in provincial towns following the ordinance to register every non-Aryan. People fear that even couples, married lawfully in church, will be separated ... I hereby proclaim that such proceedings are stark violence of which no good will come ... how can a rational man believe that thousands of (Catholics) belonging to mixed couples will remain silent, while their beloved are being violently exterminated and their children exposed to an unknown fate ? ... As representative of the Church I ask you once again to issue instructions - to preserve the civil rights of everyone who was converted. I also appeal to you in the name of humane feelings to prevent that harm be done to innocent citizens of our state ... I am convinced that these deeds were carried without your knowledge, by irresponsible people, motivated by passion and the lust for revenge. If indeed these measures were imposed by the intervention of a foreign power in internal affairs of our state, I will not hesitate and raise my voice even against this power. The Catholic Church is not afraid of any secular power, whatever it be, when it has to protect basic human values ...[53]

This is a trenchant letter that does not play around with vague terms and calls a spade a spade. And indeed, there is no doubt that the letter achieved what it was meant to achieve, at least with regard to mixed families. From this date onwards Jewish spouses or their children were neither arrested anymore nor were they sent to concentration camps. In isolated cases, where a mistake had been made or the Germans tried to act on their own, the regime came to the aid of these people and almost all were released. It is worthwhile to note that Stepinac threatened in his letter to speak out against the Germans, refering the responsibility to Pavelic. The fatherly advice of previous appeals was replaced by an explicit threat. Neither did Stepinac limit himself to the protection of converted Jews and mixed families. A paragraph in his letter speaks about every detainee in concentration camps - also in forceful language, though much less so that the first part of the letter. In retrospect we may say that the inclusion of all Jews in his forceful protest would not have done harm and would certainly have enhanced the honour of the Catholic Church.

The Vatican representative, Marcone, intervened with the authorities separately, but at the same time.[54] Articles about Croatian atrocities appeared in the Western press. The Vatican began to fear accusations of indifference in the face of Ustasa savagery. To prevent this Maglione requested in April 1943 that Marcone prepare a memorandum on his own and Stepinac's activities in aid of Serbs and Jews.

In reponse to this demand Marcone sent a letter on May 8th, in which he discussed compulsory conversion and the persecution of Serbs. He said that most of the accusations were slander spread by Serbian circles, who used to harass Catholics at the time of the Yugoslav state.[55]

Meanwhile the last great manhunt against Croatian Jews was launched on May 3rd. On this occasion outstanding proteges of the Church were sent to Auschwitz - headed by the President of the Jewish Community of Zagreb, Dr. Hugo Kohn, and the Chief Rabbi of Zagreb, Dr. Freiberger - a personal friend of Archbishop Stepinac. The intervention of Church officials on behalf of Jews failed completely - except members of mixed families the majority of Jews, including converts, were sent to Auschwitz.[56]

STEPINAC JUSTIFIES PERSECUTION OF JEWS "TO SOME EXTENT"

This time that Vatican was not satisfied with written reports and asked Stepinac to come to Rome. Before he set out he sent the Vatican a batch of documents, bearing evidence, according to the accompanying letter, of "1. ...What we did for the Serbs, in spite of the fact that they did us wrong throughout the twenty years of the Yugoslav state; 2. What we did for the Jews." Further on Stepinac wrote: "Contrary to Serbian propaganda against the Church in Croatia, the historical truth is that the Catholic Church of Croatia raised its voice also before senior state officials at a time, when such actions were liable to endanger other interests of the Church. This was confirmed and appreciated by Serbs who are not motivated by hatred but by truth and gratitude." Here Stepinac comes to his main point, listing the achievements of the Ustasa government: Christian education of Ustasa soldiers, obligatory religious instruction in schools, promotion of the network of Church schools, financing of colleges for the clergy, social welfare activities, repair work in churches etc. The first two paragraphs have a bearing on our discussion and read as following:

"The Croatian government fought vigorously against abortion, which not only threatened to ruin Croatia, but also the Church. There were said to be 20,000 abortions annually, but a loyal Catholic physician told me that there were up to 60,000. The Orthodox authorities in Belgrade did nothing to stop this evil, which had been initiated primarily by Jewish and Orthodox doctors (my italics - M.S.). The Croatian government banned pornographic publications, which were also primarily printed and distributed by Jews and Serbs (my italics - M.S.).[57]

This highly apologetic letter was accompanied by documents intended to reinforce Stepinac's claim.[58]

Stepinac arrived in Rome on May 24th and remained there till June 4th. At his meetings with Vatican dignitaries he suddenly became an enthusiastic advocate of the Ustasa state, heaping praise on it and trying to present it in a highly favourable light. The climax came at his meeting with the Pope. Lobkovic, the Croatian representative at the Vatican, reported on the Archbishop's visit.

"The Archbishop of Zagreb stayed in Rome from May 26th to June 3rd. I was in close contact with him for the whole time ... according to information from various sources and to what the Archbishop told me himself, he delivered a very favourable report on Croatia. He (Stepinac) told me that he concealed a few matter with which he disagreed (my italics - M.S.). In order to present Croatia in a favourable light he reminded (the Pope) of our laws against abortion, and this was received very well by the Vatican. Basing his argument on these laws, the Archbishop justified to some extent the measures emplyed against the Jews, who were the main supporters and perpetrators of these crimes in our country.[59]

The question how far this document can be trusted is of great importance. If Stepinac indeed concealed from Vatican officials "a few matters with which he disagreed", and if the did "justify to some extent the methods ... against the Jews", he thus supported, though indirectly, Ustasa crimes which at the time had reached horrific dimensions. I believe that Lobkovic's report is correct (although it is not a shorthand transcription of the talk between Stepinac and Pius the 12th), because the argument that the Jews supported abortion also appeared in Stepinac's letter of May, 24th (in addition to the matter of pornographic literature published by Jews). It is therefore clear that Lobkovic did not invent this. It should be noted that Stepinac met with the Pope a few days after the remnant of Croatian Jews had been sent to concentration camps. In practice his talks at the Vatican made no difference whatsoever, as the majority of Croatian Jews had already been murdered at the time - but their appear as an ugly moral stain.

The Archbishop of Zagreb did not persist in his enthusiastic endorsement of the regime for long. Less than six months later, on October 31, 1943, he published a pastoral letter that was read out in churches (a public reading that caused the arrest of a few dozens of priests), in which he said: "The Catholic Church cannot accept that races or nations, merely because they are big or strong, will do violence to weaker races or nations. A regime that executes hundreds of hostages for a crime whose perpetrator has not been caught, is a pagan regime. No good has ever come from such deeds, nor will any good come from them in future."[60]

Such proclamations made the Germans nervous. As we learn from a letter by the German Foreign Ministry to their embassy in Zagreb, they regarded Stepinac as a dangerous enemy:

"(Stepinac) intervened many times personally on behalf of persecuted Jews and Orthodox ... his influence with the Croatian people is enormous and his authority is unchallenged. This is apparently the reason why he continues to live in the Archbishop's palace in Zagreb."[61]

A later German document, of July 1944, sent by the German embassy in Zagreb, says:

"(Stepinac) shows a positive attitude to the Orthodox and the intelligentsia. He always had a weak spot for the Jews."[62]

There is no doubt that Stepinac was against the Germans and had voiced his opinion more than once - and it is therefore not surprising that they suspected and sought to oust him.

CONCLUSION

The easiest way to summarize this chapter would be to condemn the Church altogether - because it did not protest explicitly and in public against the muder of the Jewish people and the murder of Croatian Jewry. It is, after all, a religious institution claiming high moral standards for itself and proclaiming Jesus' gospel of compassion all over the world. Today it is clear that the argument, recurrently employed until a few years ago, that the Church either did not know or did not believe that the Jews were being exterminated, is spurious. Documents published by the Vatican leave no doubt that it received abundant information, concerning activities of the Germans and their allies, from numerous reliable sources, and that one had to blind or devoid of faith to doubt the truth. In mid-1942 at the latest the Holy See knew that Jews were being exterminated in camps in Poland and in Croatia.

However, Church circles maintain the Vatican leadership had come to the conclusion, that under prevailing circumstances public protests were useless and could even make matters worse for the Jews. The only way to save what could still be saved was in their view, quiet, behind-the-scenes activity; material aid and pressure exerted by Church dignitaries on governments and leaders who were in a position to prevent or to limit persecutions. In the view of these Church advocates, this non-heroic activity was the most effective under given conditions. And indeed, Vatican documents bear evidence of widespread activity by the Holy See in aid of the Jews.

However, the choice of unpublicised activity was not only dictated by considerations of what was best for the Jews. From a political point of view, the ideological position assumed by Pius the 12th and his entourage dictated a moderate attitude to Nazi Germany and even more so the satellite governments, like Croatia. The profound fear of Bolshevism generated the preference of Hitler over Stalin. Very few among the Vatican leadership were genuine Nazi supporters - but until the final years of the war many considered Hitler's Germany a bulwark against Communism. This attitude was even more pronounced with regard to satellite governments, whose pro-Catholic positions made them Vatican favourites. Again and again, and even in the face of the barbaric behaviour of Pavelic's followers, we find the argument that the leader of Croatia was a pious Catholic and that his followers were meticulous in the performance of their religious duties and rendered aid to the Church.

The Vatican and Church leadership in Croatia sought to avoid any activity liable to undermine the Ustasa regime. The deep-rooted hostility towards the Orthodox Serbs, who had allegedly harassed Catholics in pre-war Yugoslavia, prevented more energetic actions against the Zagreb government. Moreover: the Holocaust raging in front of their eyes did not uproot their traditional Christian antisemitism (to be distinguished from the Nazi version). This came to the force in utterances delivered on various occasions - reaching a climax in Stepinac's letter quoted above, in which he accused the Jews of promoting abortion and disseminating pornographic literature. It is therefore difficult to accept the claim that Church officials were exclusively motivated by considerations of what was good for the Jewish cause.

Furthermore - the Croatian Church headed by Stepinac kept silent in the face of murderous actions committed by local monks and priests. None of those was expelled from the Church or even admonished.

Nevertheless one has to say that the Church of Croatia and the Vatican were opposed to the murder of Jews. They supported the removal of Jews from economic, social and cultural life in the Croatian state, but they never supported murder. Behind the scenes Stepinac and Marcone acted energetically and often forcefull in order to prevent murders. They defended converted Jews and mixed families. Not a few Jews were saved by these activities - and the material aid they rendered to those who survived when the transports ended, was real and noteworthy.

NOTES

[1] See: Viktor Novak, Magnum Crimen, (Zagreb; 1948); Tajni Dokumenti o odnosima Vatikana i Ustaske N.D.H. (Zagreb: 1946); Sime Simic, Vatikan protiv Jugoslavije (Titograd: 1958); Dokumenti a protunarodnom radu i zlocinima jednog djela Katolickog klera, ed: Joza Horvat and Zdenko Sambuk (Zagreb: 1946); Ivan Cvitkovic, Ko je bio Alozije Stepinac ? (Sarajevo: Izdavacka Djelatnost, 1988).

[2] Edmond Paris, Genocide in Satellite Croatia (Chicago: The American Institute for Balkan Affairs, 1961); Henry Lauriere, Assasina au Nom de Dieu (Paris: 1951) Two controversial and non reliable books which nevertheless include important facts.

[3] E. Cavalli, Il processo Dell'Arcivescovo di Zagabria, (Vatican: La Civilitta Catolica, 1947); Richard Patee, The Case of Cardinal Aloysus Stepinac (Milwaukee: 1953). These books approved by the Vatican include numerous letters by Stepinac to the authorities. However the most important source are the Vatican documents refering to the refugee question: Actes et Documents du Saint Siege Relatifs a la Second Guerre Mondialle, ed: Blet et al., vol. VIII-IX, (Vatican: 1972, 1975).

[4] Carlo Falconi, The Silence of Pius XII, (London; Little Brown 1970). Falconi tries to be objective, but he does not utilize all available Vatican documentation.

[5] ibid., pp. 265-266. The Ustasa priest Ivan Guberina summarized the matter in his article "The Catholic Structure of Croatia" thus: "Croatia becomes the bulwark and the fortress of Catholicism ... in moments of most severe crisis." He goes on: "Croatian nationalism is one of the most important fortifications of Western civilization ... the meaning of Croatian nationalism is not just love ... for the homeland, (but) loyal service to the whole West."

[6] Anthony Rhodes, The Vatican in the Age of the Dictators, (New York; 1973) pp. 324-325. Rhodes claims that the Croatian Church received 32 million dinars assistance from the Yugoslav government, while the Orthodox Church receive 46 million. He thereby in fact refutes the complaint that Catholics had been discriminated against - because the number of Orthodox was greater. Actually the average of government assistance rendered to the various religious denominations was the following: Orthodox = 5.65 per capita, Catholics = 6.05, Moslems = 9.48, Jews = 16.5. Harriet Pass Freidenreich, The Jews of Yugoslavia, (Philadelphia: The Jewish Publication Society, 1979), p. 105.

[7] Falconi, op. cit., p. 271; Ferdlo Culinovic, Okupatorska Podjela Jugoslavije (Beograd: Vojnoizdavacki Zavod, 1970) p. 359 N. 360. After the establishment of the Croatian State, many priests announced proudly that they had been Ustasa members at the time of the Yugoslav state. The Bishop of Sarajevo, Saric, wrote that he had been an Ustasi since 1934.

[8] Stepinac wrote in his diary on 12.10.1939: "Everything bears evidence that we are going to have a great deal of trouble with Belgrad. Because of the Serbs' mendacity I will not be surprised if it ultimately comes to a confrontation between Croatians and Serbs." On 26.3.1941 he wrote: "Ultimately the Serbs and the Croatians belong to different worlds; two poles which will never draw nearer to each other ... the (Orthodox) schism is the greatest curse of Europe, perhaps even greater than the Protestant curse. It is devoid of moral (principles) and laws, it breeds no sense of justice and no decency." Tajni Dokumenti, op.cit., pp. 23-24.

[9] ibid. p. 26.

[9a] Friedenreich, op.cit., p. 110; In 1938 the number of converted Jews in Yugoslavia was 821, most of them in Croatia, whose Jewish population numbered 40,000.

10 Culinovic, op.cit., p. 185.

11 ibid; Falconi, op.cit., p. 270.

12 Yugoslav historiography reveals some strange contradictions with regard to Vatican recognition of Croatia. On one hand Yugoslav historians claim that there was no difference between de-jure and de-facto recognition. On the other hand they present dozens of documents, showing that the Croatian government exerted pressure to gain de-jure recognition. If there was no difference, why all these efforts ? For example, Fikreta Jelic-Butic, *Ustase i Nezavisna Drzava Hrvatska*, (Zagreb: Liber 1977), pp. 214-221.

13 ibid., pp. 324, 415-'L6.

14 An excellent analysis of Stepinac's character and his unsuitability for the role circumstances made him fulfill, appears in: Falconi, op.cit., p. 316; There are many photographs of Stepinac in the company of Ustasa leaders and Germans, Cvitkovic, op.cit. pp. 80-81, 224-225.

15 Katolicki Tjednik, 25.5.1941, (Sarajevo).

16 Tajni Dokumenti, op.cit., p. 120.

17 Falconi, op.cit., pp. 295-296.

18 F. Culinovic, p. 360.

19 Tajni Dokumenti, op.cit., pp. 89-90.

20 Novi List, 24.7.1941.

21 Culinovic, op.cit., pp. 260-261; the list of Franciscan monks who took part in massacres; Paris, op.cit., pp. 107-115.

22 Falconi, op.cit., chapter 4-6.

23 From the private collection of Dr. Yelinek of Ben-Gurion University, Beer Sheba, blue file No. 62. I am grateful for permission to use the collection.

24 Archives of the Association of Yugoslav Jews in Israel (Jerusalem) B-93/17, p. 5.

25 Central Zionist Archives (Jerusalem), S 26/1394, p. 5.

26 Cavalli, op.cit., pp. 253-256.

27 S. Seige, Vol. VIII, op.cit., p. 261, N.l.

28 ibid, pp. 261-262.

29 Tajni Dokumenti, op.cit., pp. 39-40.

30 S. Seige, Vol. VIII, op.cit., pp. 368-369.

31 Cavalli, op.cit., pp. 256-257.

32 Menachem Shelah, *The Murder of the Croatian Jews by the Germans and their Followers during World War II* (Hebrew) (Ph.D. thesis, Tel-Aviv University, 1980) pp. 149-153.

33 Cavalli, op.cit., p. 258.

34 Falconi, op.cit., pp. 314-315.

35 Cavalli, op.cit., pp. 56-57.

36 Wiener Library, 207N2/109B, (BBC Listening Service).

37 S. Siege, Vol VIII, op.cit., p. 611 (Photocopy of the original letter).

38 ibid., pp. 611-612, N.l.

39 ibid., p. 669.

40 ibid., p. 675.

41 ibid., p. 669.

42 ibid. ibid.

43 ibid. p. 710.

44 Rhodes, op.cit., pp. 330-331.

45 Falconi, op.cit., p. 335; Tajni Dokumenti, op.cit., pp. 62-63.

46 ibid., p. 66; ibid., pp. 337-338.

47 Falconi, op.cit., p. 340.

48 ibid., p. 348.

49 Additional visits with the Pope: a half-hour audience given to Pavelic in May 1941, a meeting with representatives of the Ustasa youth in February and December 1942, and with members of the Croatian colony in Rome in February 1942; a meeting with 400 Ustasa officers in September 1943 and a meeting with Ivan Verner, the mayor of Zagreb in April 1943. See Vladimir Dedijer, *Vatikan i Jasenovac*, Beograd: RAD 1987, pp.124, 137.

50 Falconi, op.cit., p. 388.

51 Patee, op.cit., pp. 271-276.

52 Cavalli, op.cit., pp. 259-262.

53 S. Seige, Vol. IX, op.cit., pp. 187-188.

54 ibid., pp. 218-219.

55 For reports on transports that reached the Vatican see: ibid., pp. 221-222, 287.

56 ibid., p. 223.

57 ibid., pp. 224-229; the appendix includes 34 documents, most of which already appeared in Patee and Cavalli's books.

58 Tajni Dokumenti, op.cit., pp. 127-128; Falconi, op.cit., pp. 315-316.

59 Rhodes, op.cit., pp. 331-332.

60 Politisches Archiv des Auswaertigen Amtes (Bonn) - Inland ID Kroatien Kirche 1501/43, p.2.

62 ibid. Kult 4-677/44, p. 2.

Christian attitudes and responses to the Jewish plight in English-speaking countries 1933–1945 and after

CHAIRPERSON **Dr Robert Everett**

RAPPORTEUR **Professor Richard Pierard**

GERMAN REFUGEE PHYSICIANS IN SCOTLAND 1933-1945

KENNETH E. COLLINS

Wellcome Unit for the History of Medicine, University of Glasgow, Glasgow G12 0TQ, Scotland

During the 1930's and 1940's some hundreds of refugee physicians from Central Europe, who were overwhelmingly of Jewish origin, were given the opportunity to obtain qualifications which could be registered in Britain by taking the examinations of the Scottish Triple Qualification Board.

Refugee physicians began arriving in Britain soon after the Nazi accession to power. The Nazis had moved quickly with their anti-Jewish measures and Jewish doctors were among their first targets. As early as 22nd April 1933 restrictions were placed on the numbers of doctors in National Health Insurance practices and these limits were gradually extended to other medical men (Sherman,1973).

Deprived of their professional livelihoods on racial grounds in Germany, the refugee physicians sought to enter medical practice in their countries of exile. This was not to be easy as many countries, such as Britain and the United States, had regulations which gave their own nationals certain privileges as far as medical practice was concerned.By the end of 1933 there had been 60,000 emigrants from Germany of whom about 80% were Jewish(Sherman,1973).

The pattern of German policy towards Jewish medical students completing their medical studies had not been definitively laid down by 1934. By March 1934 the admission of non-Aryan medical students was completely restricted (Stevens,1975). A Jewish medical student, who had completed his studies but had not yet taken his final examinations, had the alternative of trying to take examinations in a country like Italy, with which Britain had reciprocal medical qualification arrangements, or trying to graduate in a German university not yet under Nazi control. Thus, it was still possible for Jews to graduate in medicine in Hamburg in 1934 (Collins,1987). However, those students who had been excluded at an earlier stage of their undergraduate course would have required to start afresh their medical studies abroad and few managed to do this.

By 1936 about 1,800 physicians had left Germany and the largest group, numbering about 650, settled in Palestine. There were about 400 in the United States, where licensing procedures were being progressively tightened even in such 'liberal' states as New York, and about 300 in the United Kingdom,almost all of who were of Jewish origins (*Jewish Echo*,1936). The medical refugees began to arrive in Britain during 1933, although one German Jewish doctor requalified in 1928 after studying at Anderson's College,the extra-mural, or non-university,medical school beside the Western Infirmary in Glasgow (Jewish Echo,1928).

The arrival of some medical refugees in Britain during 1933 prompted the Secretary of the British Medical Association, Dr. George Cranston Anderson, to write to the deans of all the British medical schools to remind them that medical qualifications obtained in Britain would enable the doctor to practise in any of the British dominions and colonies (British Medical Journal,1933). This letter expressed the concern, communicated to the General Medical Council (GMC) from South Africa, as well as Australia and New Zealand, that it should not be easier, and quicker, to qualify in Britain and move on to these countries than it would have been to go there and qualify in the first place (General Medical Council Minutes ,1934). The reply of the General Medical Council had been that the licensing of medical practitioners was solely a matter for the licensing bodies while the GMC concerned itself with the maintenance and improvement of standards.

This reply had also been given to Dr. M. D. Eder, of the newly formed Jewish Medical Emergency Association, who had asked for some easing of the restrictions of the English Conjoint Board (General Medical Council Minutes,1933). These required foreign physicians to spend two years, instead of one year, from June 1933, in the process of taking British qualifications. This led to Scotland, and not England, becoming the chief destination of refugee physicians.

The same issue of the British Medical Journal which had contained Dr. G. C. Anderson's letter in September 1933, included a communication from the honorary secretary of the Medical Information Subcommittee of the Jewish Medical and Dental Emergency Association, which was acting in co-operation with the Jewish Refugee Committee. They were anxious to reply to the statement, which had been made at a BMA Council Meeting in July 1933, that over 800 applications had been received in Britain from German doctors. It was pointed out that only 180 foreign doctors had been registered with their committee and that only half of these were seeking British qualifications. A substantial proportion had already been placed in Edinburgh and Glasgow, with smaller numbers in other centres. This concern to allay medical fears over the scale of the immigration was to be a regular concern of both the Jewish bodies and the Home Office, who had to refute wild rumours which were circulating.

The number of refugee doctors entering Britain between 1933 and 1935 was small, and it was made clear to them that obtaining a British qualification gave no guarantee that the practitioner would be able to register for medical practice in Britain. Nevertheless, the spectre that the medical job market would be flooded by an alien influx was being constantly invoked both in sections of the press, such as Lord Beaverbrook's Daily Express, and in certain sections of the British medical profession itself (Hearst,1965).

It was predictable that there would be opposition to the arrival of foreign doctors from the Medical Practitioners' Union, whose General Secretary, Alfred Welply took a consistently anti-alien line. However, the entry of refugee doctors in any number was also opposed strenuously by Lord Dawson of Penn. Dawson, the Royal physician, was also President of the Royal College of Physicians of London, and had espoused progressive policies in regard to the provision of health care. He had been a leading member of the BMA committee set up to formulate plans for the establishment of a Ministry of Health and in 1918 had outlined plans for a comprehensive health service. He had served two terms as President of the British Medical Association (BMA) and had not been afraid to deal with such controversial issues as birth control and euthanasia (Brown,1965). Speaking at a meeting at the Royal College of Physicians in London in February 1932 Dawson told the members of the various medical licensing bodies present that British medical students should have some protection, and that it should not be unduly easy for foreign practitioners to qualify (Cooke,1972; Craig,1971). He said that the admission of foreign doctors would subject British homes to foreign influences and asked why the United Kingdom should be the only country to have such easy terms for the admission of foreign doctors (Sherman,1973).

At that meeting it was agreed by all the medical licensing bodies, with the sole exception of the Scottish Triple Qualification Board, to adopt uniform regulations. It would become necessary for the foreign doctor to take an examination in anatomy and physiology and to do two years of clinical work before presentation for the final examinations.

It was Lord Dawson's view, expressed to the Home Secretary, Sir John Gilmour, at a meeting in November 1933, that there might be room in the United Kingdom for a few refugee physicians of special distinction but the 'number that could usefully be absorbed could be counted on the fingers of one hand' (Home Office Records). At his meeting with the Home Secretary Lord Dawson said that the view he expressed on the subject of German Jewish doctors had the full and entire support of his Council who were 'alarmed' by the prospects of these refugee physicians entering the British register. He was sceptical about 'the habit of the Jews to settle in a new civilisation rather than in an old one'. He reiterated the view that people of an established reputation in Germany had 'nothing to teach us and could not be of any advantage to this country'.

Supporting Lord Dawson at the meeting was Sir Holburt Waring, President of the Royal College of Surgeons of England, who accompanied Dawson to the Home Office. Sir Holburt pointed out the numbers of American Jews who were studying medicine in Scotland and then returned to America 'much to the annoyance of the authorities there'. The Home Secretary replied that study and requalification did not automatically confer the right to practise and he noted that it would be impossible to refuse these refugees the opportunity to study and they could not be returned to Germany in view of the situation there. He suggested that the licensing bodies meet again as circumstances had changed since the meeting at the Royal College of Physicians in London in 1932.

In sharp contrast, the Scottish Board continued to allow foreign graduates to take the final examinations after only one year of clinical studies and there was no requirement to take anatomy and physiology examinations. In Scotland the foreign graduates would sit the materia medica and pathology examinations on arrival and take the final examinations one year later. It was little wonder that the overwhelming number of refugee physicians requalified in Scotland. Indeed, the Scottish regulations were well known in Germany and refugee doctors sometimes made only the briefest of stops in London, after their arrival in Britain, before making their way to Edinburgh for the examinations there.

After the meeting at the Home Office, Dawson wrote to the Home Secretary asking him to express the opinion that the Scottish Board was the only 'backslider' to the Secretary of State for Scotland who could then communicate this view to the Scottish colleges (Home Office Records). Dawson had thought that the Home Secretary had agreed with the English policy that foreign students should commence by taking anatomy and physiology examinations followed by two years of clinical training before the final examinations. In a marginal note to Dawson's letter the Home Secretary recorded that he had not agreed with Dawson's contention but had pointed out to him that the remedy lay with the medical profession. Subsequently, Waring expressed the view that the medical bodies felt they could achieve more by using their own machinery than by going through the Home Office. They intended to continue discussions with the Scottish

Board to try to persuade them to bring their regulations into line with those in England. The Scottish Secretary was informed by the Home Secretary about the discussions with the Presidents of the English Royal Colleges, but if any pressure was exerted by this channel, it was singularly ineffective.

Pressure was applied to the Scottish Board by the English medical bodies at a further meeting of the licensing bodies in London in January 1934. The English bodies agreed to tighten the regulations further by increasing the time required for requalification in medicine from two to three years. The Scottish representative present said that it would be useless for him to take a proposal about lengthening the study time back to his Board. It was their view that it was the purpose of the medical licensing bodies to protect the public and not the medical profession (Craig,1971). The Scottish Triple Qualification Board remained adamant that the undertakings that they had already given to refugee physicians about requalification regulations should be honoured. They were prepared to stand up to pressure applied on them to try to bring their regulations into line with those in force in England.

Lord Dawson had been expressing the anti-alien sentiments which had been widely current during the 1930's, but it is noteworthy in this context that, during a visit to Nazi Germany in 1936, he was able to sympathise with his German hosts, who included Hitler and von Ribbentropp, about 'Jewish excesses' although he disagreed with the methods then being employed in Germany to deal with the problem (Watson,1950).His views had carried some weight within the English medical bodies but he had been unable to influence his Scottish colleagues.

Many reasons can be adduced for the differing Scottish and English attitudes. There was a long Scottish tradition of attracting overseas doctors who would not be expected to practise there. In contrast there was an English expectation that the refugee practitioners would compete for employment with English graduates. It was not unusual for the Scottish medical student body to contain a substantial foreign component based on the twin characteristics of economic good sense allied to humanitarian sentiment (Collins,1987). It was thus expected that the refugee practitioners would form yet one more strand in Scotland's export of medical personnel.

The question of accepting some German Jewish medical men was discussed and agreed at a meeting of the Medical Committee of the Glasgow Royal Infirmary on 18th September 1933 (Glasgow Royal Infirmary Minutes,1933). It was decided to accept 24 refugee practitioners although reservations were expressed about the teaching together of graduates and undergraduates because their education needs differed. It was therefore agreed that the needs of local students should be satisfied before allocations for foreign students were made. The hospital Superintendent, Dr. Grant, took the initiative in this matter after conferring with Dr. John Orr, who was Dean of the Medical School of the Royal Colleges in Edinburgh (MSRCE) where most of the remaining Germans were being placed. While there were said to be no places available at the Western Infirmary in Glasgow, the Victoria Infirmary, situated in the south side of Glasgow, had some places for foreign students, and could allocate them once the needs of local students had been met.

This action by Grant and Orr gave hope and encouragement to the refugee physicians, some of whom were in considerable despair at the prospect of being unable to find a medical school which would enable them to continue in their profession. The favourable replies received from Glasgow and Edinburgh by doctors who had written upwards of thirty letters around the country were naturally greeted with great joy (Collins,1987). However, not all the refugee doctors were able to proceed immediately to take British qualifications. A number had been so traumatised by their experiences in Germany that they found the prospects of study and examinations an ordeal which would have to be postponed till their health improved (Collins,1987). Others worked in a variety of non-medical positions until their services were made available under the wartime medical emergency regulations

Following the initial acceptance of German Jewish doctors in Edinburgh and Glasgow in 1933-1934, further refugees were accepted for study in the following academic year (Collins,1987). In Edinburgh there had been 43 Germans, of whom all but three were medical graduates, at the MSRCE in 1933-1934. In June 1934 John Orr reported to a meeting of the Governing Board that he was dealing with applicants who had to receive Home Office permission to study in Britain and that the Germans were being registered as medical students. A meeting of the Glasgow Infirmaries Joint Consultative Committee was called in September 1933, to discuss the situation, the first time the committee had met for more than two years.(Glasgow Royal Infirmary:Minutes of Meetings and Managers). It was agreed that Germans arriving in Glasgow would be enrolled at St. Mungo's College, the extra-mural,or non-university, medical school of the Glasgow Royal Infirmary. St. Mungo's College had been in danger of closing during the 1920's because of the low level of student recruitment but with the influx of students from Germany and America the student roll increased, and the future of the College was secured.

As with the American students the position for German medical graduates trying to enter the universities was much more difficult. Unlike the situation in the extra-mural schools, where there was a surplus of teaching places, there was increasing competition for the available space in the medical faculties. In Glasgow, for example, the annual intake of medical students was reduced from 200 to 180 in 1935 as the smaller number was thought to be sufficient for the medical needs of the community, as well as being as much as the hospital teaching facilities could adequately support (Illingworth,1971). As in the discussions over the admission of Americans the priority for admissions was resolved in favour of the interests of local students.

As far as the Germans were concerned, they were seeking short-term clinical and examination facilities and had no interest in undertaking further lengthy undergraduate studies. In this respect the flexibility of the extra-mural colleges suited their needs. Financially too the arrangements at the extra-mural schools were advantageous to the usually impecunious refugees. The fees at most British medical schools ranged from £35 to £50 per annum while the examination fees due to the Scottish Triple Qualification Board for all the required subjects, including the Finals was £30 (Society for the Protection of Science and Learning (SPSL) Records).

This led to the further concentration of the overseas medical students in the extra-mural medical schools of Glasgow and Edinburgh. With the needs of the refugee practitioners being met in the extra-mural schools there seemed little need for the universities to allocate any of their scarce places to foreign candidates. By the mid-1930's all applications to the universities from students furth of Scotland were being rejected(Collins,1987).. In 1934 alone there were over 100 applications to the Medical Faculty of the University of Glasgow from German doctors (Glasgow University Senate and Medical Faculty Minutes).

The situation for German refugee physicians was similar in Edinburgh although one student did manage to enter Edinburgh University after leaving his studies in Austria after only one year and after having spent a few months as a research assistant in Cambridge. This student, whose mother was Jewish, was the son of a Professor of Law at Heidelberg and his entry to the Medical Faculty in 1934 was regarded by the Dean as Edinburgh's 'gift' to Heidelberg University on the occasion of its 400th anniversary! (Collins,1987).

This concentration of overseas students in the extra-mural medical schools created some friction between the universities and the extra-mural schools over the usage of shared facilities. The University of Glasgow expressed its concern over the number of alien students receiving tuition in the Pathology Department of the Glasgow Royal Infirmary, as the University had certain rights for its students under regulations dating back some twenty years. However, the managers of the Royal Infirmary rejected this criticism and insisted that the running of the Pathology Department should remain in their hands (St. Mungo's College Minutes).

Orr had little difficulty persuading his colleagues in the Edinburgh extra-mural college that he was not interpreting the regulations too widely both by the admission of significant numbers of refugee doctors and by giving them exemption from language testing on account of their relative fluency in the English language. He was given permission, with little dissension, to continue his liberal admission policy as he had been able to show that there was surplus teaching capacity at the Edinburgh Royal Infirmary (MSRCE Admission Committee Minutes,1933). His policy was endorsed at a subsequent meeting of the Governing Board where there was only one dissenting voice out of fifteen members.

Even though the Scottish regulations permitted successful candidates to complete their requalification in one year there were cases in which the progress was even more rapid. A former Professor of Internal Medicine at the University of Berlin, lived for a time in Edinburgh and Glasgow while he prepared to take the examinations of the Triple Qualification Board. He sat his finals after only nine months, after special permission, but failed the examinations! In his case the Home Office also agreed to make an exception in not requiring him to make an undertaking to leave the country after qualifying, as was required with some others (SPSL Records). While some of the examiners encountered by the refugees proved to be difficult, few of the refugee doctors reported problems with the actual conduct of written papers or oral examinations. Many of the examiners were extremely tolerant towards their highly qualified candidates, some of whom had international medical reputations, and orals were conducted in a friendly and social manner(Collins,1987; British Medical Journal,1986).

Orr must also have been very patient with the refugee doctors. One had arrived too late for enrolment but Orr was eventually convinced of the candidate's determination after the doctor had made repeated visits to his office. This doctor managed to solve his English language problems by reading the The Scotsman and by frequent visits to the Leith Repertory Theatre as well as by talking to as many people as possible (Collins,1987). The wife of one of the refugee doctors described the course her husband had taken as 'rather a farce'. The teachers in the Faculty, she recalled, could not help but recognise his superior knowledge and exempted him from lectures and classes (SPSL Records).

Some of the German refugees reported feeling that they were second-class citizens within the extra-mural colleges but this feeling, shared by some of the Americans, may have reflected the general status of these colleges within the medical framework of Edinburgh and Glasgow. In any case the classes were helpful for those making their first efforts to adapt to British medicine.

About half of those refugees taking the Triple Qualification had done so by 1936 and numbers fell gradually over the next few years, although they still made up more than 10% of the new licentiates of the Scottish colleges until 1941, when the wartime emergency regulations were introduced. (Table 1) This indicates that most of the German refugees who took the Scottish qualifications arrived in Britain in the early years of the Nazi persecution, and the numbers of those taking the examinations fell as the number of practitioners entering the country dropped both under pressure from the medical organisations and with the increasing difficulties in leaving Germany. However, even the total numbers of those becoming Scottish licentiates did not amount to 1% of the British medical profession.

Table 1

Refugee Doctors Obtaining Scottish Triple Qualification

	No. of Refugees	Total No. of Licentiates	% Refugees
1934	75	148	50.7
1935	83	203	40.9
1936	25	159	15.7
1937	43	199	21.6
1938	37	204	18.2
1939	31	237	13.1
1940	20	221	9.0
1941	16	138	11.6
1942	2	125	1.6
1943	6	103	5.8
1944	7	117	6.0
1945	4	132	3.0
TOTAL	352	1986	17.7

source : Matriculation Albums of the Scottish Triple Qualification Board

The flow of practitioners northwards to take their final medical examinations in Edinburgh continued. The numbers had been falling after 1937 as doctors postponed their chances of re-entering the medical profession and took up non-medical posts instead. However, it should still be remembered that many refugee doctors were continuing to sit for the Triple Qualification. Not all were studying in Scotland, as some other medical schools, such as in Manchester, were helping candidates prepare for the Scottish examinations. The large majority of refugees taking the Triple Qualification in 1934 and 1935 had studied in Scotland but from 1936 an increasing number were studying in London, Manchester, Birmingham and Cardiff. Nevertheless, the number studying in Glasgow and Edinburgh remained important and outnumbered any of the other British medical centres outside London. (Table 2)

Table 2

Place of Study of Refugees Obtaining the Triple Qualification

	Glasgow	Edinburgh	London	Others	Total
1934	18	37	13	7	75
1935	28	17	25	13	83
1936	4	5	14	2	25
1937	10	7	22	4	43
1938	7	10	16	4	37
1939	1	8	18	4	31
1940	3	3	12	2	20
1941	3	5	5	3	16
TOTAL	74	92	125	39	330

source : Matriculation Album of the Triple Qualification Board

While the numbers using the facilities of the extra-mural medical schools continued, the situation in Scottish universities was quite different. In June 1938 Edinburgh University Medical Faculty stated that they were in general sympathy with 'the many Austrian students whose racial origins or political sympathies had caused them to be placed in a most unfortunate position' but they were mindful of the current climate of opinion in Britain and felt that it would be unwise to provide special facilities for the admission of foreign students(Edinburgh University Medical Faculty Minutes). Later in the year, however, the University did agree to admit 3 Czech doctors on a request from Sir Robert Hutchison, Chairman of the Home Office Advisory Committee. In December 1938 they agreed to take one of the Austrians, with exemption from university fees, after receiving another letter from Sir Robert Hutchison, this time in his capacity as Chairman of the Refugee Selection Committee.

At the University of Glasgow the Medical Faculty also decided in June 1938 not to undertake the free education of one Austrian Jewish student(Glasgow University Medical Faculty Minutes). In fact the Glasgow University attitude at this time to the refugees appears to have been unfriendly. Sir Hector Hetherington, the Principal of the University of Glasgow, was unwilling to chair a fund-raising meeting or to sign a petition on behalf of the refugees because of his 'official position' (SPSL Records). Sir Hector had been actively campaigning for an end to the extra-mural medical schools which he felt were of benefit only to the freelance teachers who drew their income from the students and paid only a token charge for the facilities they enjoyed (Illingworth,1971). Sir Hector was concerned at the very considerable numbers of overseas students in the extra-mural schools, which he felt led to the exclusion of qualified British students from the available places. However, his reference to 'less eligible aliens in less reputable institutions' was intended only to imply criticism of the extra-mural colleges and not any antagonism to Jews *per se* as eligible local Jews continued to be admitted to the university (Illingworth,1986).

In Aberdeen, no German doctors or medical students were admitted in 1933 as priority was being given to local candidates (Aberdeen University Senate and Medical Faculty Minutes). However, Hans Kosterlitz was admitted as a research student in physiology in 1933 and permitted to take clinics to qualify for the Triple Qualification in 1938. Kosterlitz subsequently had a distinguished academic career in Aberdeen, becoming Professor of Pharmacology in 1968. In 1938 the Senate agreed to take an Austrian medical student without fees and in 1939 3 German doctors were admitted to research projects. Thus the portal of entry into British medicine for the refugees remained substantially through the Scottish Triple Qualification. Even Kosterlitz, a researcher in a university department found this the easiest route to a British qualification. The examinations of the Scottish Triple Qualification Board were being taken either after study in the extra-mural schools or at an approved hospital, usually in London but also at some other British centres.

Thus the traditional liberal voice of the Scottish universities was muted during the response to the influx of refugee physicians. The universities made a number of useful gestures but they could not compete with the practical facilities offered by the extra-mural schools. The universities were undoubtedly concerned about the needs of local students and they were aware that the needs of the foreign students were being met not just in the lecture theatres of the extra-mural schools but in the very hospital teaching facilities that the universities and colleges shared.

There was a definite antagonism between the universities and the extra-mural medical schools and the fact that the extra-mural schools could pursue an independent policy while dependent on many of the teaching facilities attached to the universities, increased their vulnerability. Thus the universities were able to use the very attraction of the foreign students to these schools as a prime reason for the need to abolish them.

The onset of war gave further scope for the utilisation of the skills of all those medical refugees who found themselves in Britain. To augment the specialist pool the newly formed Emergency Medical Services (EMS) could call on some 500 refugee practitioners (Hamilton,1982). Under Defence Regulation 32B the General Medical Council was empowered to give temporary registration to physicians who had qualified in such countries as Germany, Italy, Poland and Czechoslovakia. Regulations were clarified with an Order in Council in November 1941 which made clear that doctors from the various countries would be placed on the Register and would be eligible for civilian service (General Medical Council Minutes,1941).In addition to the 500 doctors who entered the EMS the remaining 800 refugee doctors, who had not yet obtained British qualifications, were also placed on the Register. Despite this a number of doctors still came to Edinburgh to take the Triple Qualification, possibly because they felt that the new war regulations might prove to be temporary. However, the doctors who were temporarily registered during the war were placed on the permanent Register following the passage of the Medical Practitioners and Pharmacists Act of 1947.

As the war progressed the number of refugee doctors in employment increased. In May 1941 less than 10% were in employment, the figure of 700 unemployed alien practitioners being given in April 1941. This number fell slowly during the rest of 1941 and by the beginning of 1942 the number in employment had risen to 64% (Hearst,1965). There was still some antipathy to the employment of alien doctors but by the end of the war their outstanding contribution to the British war effort was widely acknowledged.

The majority of the Germans had pleasant memories of their stay in Scotland, despite the problems with the language and the strain on older doctors of a return to medical studies. For some, however, the definite objective of the Scottish qualifications was a simpler goal than the struggle for a suitable job after leaving Glasgow or Edinburgh (Stevens,1975). The atmosphere was easier in 1933 and 1934 when there was considerable sympathy for the plight of the refugees. As war approached there was increase in 'spy fever' and all foreigners, no matter their sympathies. were treated with suspicion.

In 1933 it had been easier to enter Britain as no visa was required if evidence of financial support could be provided.

Although the Scottish universities had been unable or unwilling to accommodate many of the German or Austrian refugees the war years in Edinburgh saw the establishment of a Polish School of Medicine at the University of Edinburgh in February, 1941, with Polish lecturers and students (Rostowski, 1955). During the nine sessions there were 228 graduates from the Polish School of Medicine and some 19 obtained the postgraduate degree of M.D.

In fact there were many local initiatives being carried out on a local level which helped to keep alive the ideals of humanity in medicine. For example, with the increasing numbers of Jewish doctors coming out of Austria from 1938 there were particular problems facing the large numbers of psychiatrists and psychoanalysts entering Britain where the field was less developed than it had been in Vienna. Angus MacNiven, Medical Superintendent at the Gartnavel Royal

Hospital in Glasgow, made great efforts to find posts for refugee psychiatrists and the Garntnavel staff included many refugees in different forms of clinical attatchments. MacNiven used the talents of Karl Abenheimer, a former lawyer and judge in Mannheim who had trained in analytical techniques with Jung, at Gartnavel Royal and in the running of the Lansdowne Clinic, for nervous disorders (Collins, 1985).

At the Crichton Royal in Dumfries good use was made of refugee psychiatric expertise. Appointed Physician Superintendent in 1937 Peter McGowan sought to develop research and enhance the reputation of his hospital by bringing to Dumfries figures of distinction in psychiatry. Thus, Willy Mayer-Gross, formerly Associate Professor in Heidelberg, was appointed Director of Clinical Research and the conditions were created for a stream of young psychiatrists, including some refugees, to be attracted to Dumfries (Tait, 1971). In Edinburgh too, refugee psychiatrists were integrated into the hospital service and the staff of Sir David Henderson at the Royal Edinburgh Hospital included Erwin Stengel, later Senior Psychaitrist at Crichton Royal and Professor of Psychiatry in Sheffield. Another prominent refugee psychoanalyst was William Kraemer, the main colleague with Winifred Rushforth in the founding of the Davidson Clinic in Edinburgh, who was co-founder of the Marriage Guidance Council for Scotland.

Despite the activities of those who were hostile to the medical incomers the majority of the refugees had pleasant memories of their stay in Scotland, despite the language difficulties and the problems posed to the older doctors by the return to undergraduate medical studies. Refugee groups were formed in Edinburgh and Glasgow and some of the first refugees studying in Glasgow found comfort in the Zionist activities organised by Dr. Lewis Rifkind (Rifkind, 1937). After the war the refugee practitioners gradually dispersed all over Britain and many emigrated. By 1987 a little more than half of the survivors were in the London area with about 10% still in Scotland, mostly in Edinburgh and Glasgow. Many of the refugees found it difficult to enter their former speciality in Britain and the largest group entered general practice though with large groups in internal medicine, psychiatry and the surgical specialities. (Table 3)

Table 3
Careers of German Licentiates

	No.	%
General Practice	60	37,3
Internal Medicine	20	12,4
Psychiatry and Psychoanalysis	13	7,4
Surgery	12	7,4
Private Practice	11	6,9
Radiology	6	3,7
M.O.H.	6	3,7
Paediatrics	6	3,7
Obstetrics/Gynaecology	5	3,1
Bacteriology/Pathology	5	3,1
Dermatology	4	2,5
Others	10	6,2
TOTAL	162	100.0

Data obtained from Medical Directories for refugee physicians who obtained the Triple Qualification between 1934-1945.

The 352 doctors who had obtained the Scottish Triple Qualification had cause to be grateful to the Examination Board for their determination to maintain the existing regulations. In particular they were grateful to John Orr in Edinburgh and Dr. Grant at Glasgow Royal Infirmary who were equally determined that clinical teaching should be made available to the newcomers.

Scottish psychiatrists like Dr. Peter McGowan in Dumfries, Dr. Winifred Rushforth in Edinburgh and Dr. Angus MacNiven in Glasgow had given refugee psychiatry and psychoanalysis the chance to flourish, and in making use of the skills of William Meyer-Gross and Erwin Stengel they served their hospitals well.

The support for the refugee physicians by the Scottish extra-mural colleges can only be taken to display genuine humanitarian concern, although buttressed by solid financial support that the additional student body provided. While many of the refugees undoubtedly did hope to move on to other countries, it was likely that many would seek to practise in Britain, in competition with local graduates. They could not be compared to the American students whose aim was to return home to the States as quickly as possible, and in fact only a handful of Americans actually remained in Britain. In addition the Scottish colleges felt bound by an undertaking made to the refugees that their requalification regulations would continue to remain in force.

The Scottish universities did not respond in the manner of the extra-mural colleges constrained as they were by their primary concern of providing a medical education for increasing numbers of local students. They showed their concern in other ways such as in support of the projects of the SPSL, formerly known as the Academic Assistance Council, which provided assistance for academic refugees and in setting up the Polish School of Medicine. In any case they were certainly aware of the warm reception being offered to the refugee practitioners by the extra-mural colleges and by the various hospitals who were giving the refugee physicians their first opportunity to practise in Britain.

The Scottish colleges had to be sensitive to the views of their members and fellows and could not have consistently conducted a policy far out of line with the wishes of their membership. The senior members of the medical profession in Scotland, who formed the leadership in the Royal colleges and the hospitals, followed the Scottish pattern set in earlier years of enabling outsiders to obtain British qualifications not easily obtainable elsewhere.

CONCLUSION

For a few years Scotland was home to about 200 refugee practitioners preparing for their final examinations. For the others, who were able to find places elsewhere for their clinical training, it was only the prospect of the Scottish examinations which gave them the chance to find places to study, and often the will to continue in medicine. As we have seen some of the refugees studied in England but took the Scottish qualifications. However the essential feature of the period was that German medical graduates could take the final examinations of the Triple Qualification Board after only one year. This facility remained constant during the years of the refugee influx and contrasted with the more restrictive policy of the English colleges. In an age of intolerance the hand of friendship was gratefully received.

ACKNOWLEDGEMENTS

I would like to acnowledge the assistance of Dr. Derek Dow,Archivist to the Greater Glasgow Health Board;Liz Fraser,Secretary of the SPSL; Colin Harris,Principal Library Assistant,Bodleian Library,Oxford; Howard Davies,Search Department,Public Records Office,Kew,London; Lawrence Bebbington,Librarian,Royal College of Physicians and Surgeons of Glasgow; Dorothy Wardle,Librarian,Royal College of Surgeons,Edinburgh; Weiner Library,London; Colin MacLaren, Archivist,Aberdeen University Library; Dr. J.L. Potter, Exceutive Dean of the Faculty of Medicine,University of Edinburgh;Sir Charles Illingworth;the refugee physicians (who requested that they should not be individually identified).

References and Notes

Aberdeen University Senate and Medical Faculty Minutes.1933-1939

BMJ.(1986),i,4

BMJ Supplement.(1933),165

Brown, G.H.(ed),1955,Munk's Roll:Lives of the Fellows of the Royal College of Physicians of London.Royal College of Physicians,volume V,446-449

Collins, K.E.,(1987),Jewish Medical Students and Graduates in Scotland.1739-1945.,Ph.D.thesis,University of Glasgow,233-274

Collins, K.E.,(1985),Glasgow Medicine.5,18-19

Cooke, A.M.,(1972),A History of the Royal College of Physicians of London.Oxford University Press,volume 3,1069-1072

Craig, W.S. ,(1971),History of the Royal College of Physicians of Edinburgh.Blackwell,349-350

Edinburgh University Medical Faculty Minutes.1933-1939

General Medical Council Minutes for 1933.volume LXXX,130-131

General Medical Council Minutes for 1934.volume LXXXI,160-162

General Medical Council Minutes for 1941.volume LXXVII,82-83

General Medical Council Minutes for 1942, volume LXXVIII, 4-5, 50-51
Glasgow Royal Infirmary: Minutes of Meetings of Managers and Committee, (1933), 172, 191
Glasgow University Senate and Medical Faculty Minutes, 1933-1939
Hamilton, D., (1982), The Healers, Canongate Press, 225
Hearst, E., (1965), Weiner Library Bulletin, volume XIX, 27-28
Home Office Records, HO45/15882/666764, Public Records Office, Kew
Illingworth, C., (1971), Sir Hector Hetherington: University Statesman, George Outram & Company, 55
Illingworth, C., (1986), personal communication
Jewish Echo, (1936), Glasgow, 11 September, 12
Jewish Echo, (1928), Glasgow, 20 August, 6
MSRCE Admission Committee Minutes, (1933)
Rifkind, L., (1937), Lewis Rifkind, Lewis Rifkind Memorial Commmittee and Glasgow Poale Zion, 17-18
Rostowski, J., (1955), History of the Polish School of Medicine : University of Edinburgh, University of Edinburgh Press
Sherman, A.J., (1973), Island Refuge: Britain and the Refugees from the Third Reich, Paul Elek, 20-23, 48
SPSL Records, Bodleian Library, Oxford
St. Mungo's College Minute Book, 1914-1941, May, 1937
Stevens, A., (1975), The Dispossessed, Barrie and Jenkins, 123, 130
Tait, A.C., (1971), Review of Clinical Services at Crichton Royal, Dumfries and Galloway Health Board Archives
Watson, F., (1950), Dawson of Penn, Chatto and Windus, 286-293

CANADA AND THE HOLOCAUST

JOHN S. CONWAY

UNIVERSITY OF BRITISH COLUMBIA, VANCOUVER, B.C., CANADA

During the Holocaust, Canada maintained a position as by-stander par excellence - a fact that has been almost universally deplored by writers ever since. Especially severe criticism has been levelled at Canada's immigration policies during the 1930s and 1940s.[1] The insensitivity, even indifference, of the Canadian authorities towards the plight of the European Jews, which led to the refusal to provide safe havens for them in Canada, was matched by only limited support for these refugees from the Canadian public, including the churches. In the light of our current knowledge of the sufferings undergone by Nazi Germany's victims, the consequences of Canadian apathy cannot be denied. But these attitudes towards Jewish immigrants during the 1930s can only be understood if the particular socio-historial developments in Canada of the early twentieth century are taken into account.[2]

In the 1920s and 1930s Canadian politics were dominated by two developments: The Great Depression and a growing sense of nationalist self-awareness. The collapse of the stock market in 1929 and the subsequent restrictions on credit and trade dealt severe blows to the fragile industrial development in Canada's central region of Ontario and Quebec. The crash was immediately followed by the no less severe agricultural depression in the western provinces, largely due to natural causes and lasting for several years. Politically these catastrophes not only strengthened the fissiparous character of Canadian federalism and concentrated attention on Canada's domestic problems, but also revealed the inadequate resources, both institutionally and ideologically, of the government in Ottawa to deal effectively with such a situation. When in 1935 Mackenzie King returned to power, he adopted a policy of unremitting caution, particularly in those areas which might prove dangerous to national unity, such as foreign policy and immigration. As Prime Minister, Mackenzie King led from behind, and it is clear that he was not prepared to challenge the strong feelings of nativism and anti-alienism in the mind of the Canadian public, which were only nourished by the economic climate of those years.[3]

The second significant factor was the growth of Canadian national self-consciousness in both the English-speaking and the Francophone communities. Spurred on by the mythology of Canada's heroic efforts in the First World War, this search for a distinctive identity during the inter-war years saw the establishment of numerous new Canadian institutions, but at the same time led to a determination to cast off the remaining shackles of dependency as a British Dominion in such areas as foreign policy, and by implication the bonds of all external influences. In French Canada, a new determination to resist the encroachment of the Anglo-Canadian majority and to pursue the distinct aspirations of a Francophone cultural destiny brought to the front a more educated literate group of younger politicians, insistent on provincial rights and autonomy, and strong advocates of a separate development for French-Canadian society. As a nearly independent nation, Canada became increasingly reluctant to accept direction from Europe, thereby increasing her sense of geographical separation and isolationist tendencies.

In this situation, the rise of Hitler and his subsequent measures against the German Jewish population prompted only a limited response in Canada. If the violent war-time hatreds of Germany had moderated since 1918, there was still a widespread mistrust of European politics and a disinclination to become involved. On the other hand, some elements in the German Canadian immigrant population,[4] and some branches of the staunchly anti-communist Mennonite communities in the western provinces showed a more open sympathy for Nazism.[5] The largest ethnic German organization, the German Canadian Bund, was an early convert to Nazi ideals. And although its meetings never attracted more than a small following, its dynamic and aggressively conducted campaigns certainly had an impact on the German-speaking community, which was carefully monitored by both the Canadian Jewish Congress and the Canadian Communist Party. After 1933, five of the seven German language newspapers printed in Canada tended to be sympathetic to the Nazi cause. For example, both the newspapers serving the Mennonite communities, the Mennonitische Rundschau and Der Bote demonstrated strongly anti-communist and antisemitic tendencies. Praise for Nazi teachings and for Hitler's success in the "new" Germany found frequent mention.[6]

In Quebec, in 1934, a racist nationalist group calling itself the National Social Christian Party was established to propagate the views of the European dictators, calling for the overthrow of democracy, and, more infamously, for the regulation of "the Jewish question." Its leader, Adrien Arcand, openly based his appeal on antisemitic sentiments, though there is no evidence that he was directly subsidized by the Nazis.[7] On the other hand, this movement could claim considerable support from Quebec's Roman Catholics. In Alberta, in 1935, the election of the provincial Social Credit party was undoubtedly helped by implicit anti-semitic, though not pro-German propaganda, which, in view of the entrenched attitudes of the strongly Protestant population, was to leave a lasting legacy.

While such groups found little support from the mainstream of Anglophone Canadian society, their radical polemical agitation in favour of political extremism, and their confrontational style of operations, raised serious questions about the continuing validity of the prevailing Canadian ideology--that of the successful integration of all Canadians into a tolerant liberal democracy. Many of these movements appeared to be supported by the unassimilated members of immigrant groups--as was clearly the case with pro-Nazi Germans in western Canada, and, as was widely suspected, with pro-communist factions across the country.[8] Hence the argument gained strength that Canada should impede the importation of any further sources of inter-racial or inter-ethnic conflict. Immigration restriction seemed an expedient response to the restiveness of Canadian nativists and a chance to defuse the bigotry and violence which were implicit in the expression of their anti-alien sentiments.

Hitler's rise to power, and the subsequent change in Jewish fortunes, became an immediate concern for the Canadian Jewish community, then numbering some 150,000, of whom 60,000 were resident in Quebec. It was they who organized the first Canadian protests in April 1933 against the Nazi mistreatment of the Jews in Germany, such as a meeting in Montreal at which the Anglican bishop played a prominent role.[9] But the government in Ottawa was disinclined to act. Two weeks later, however, a counter-protest was also held in Montreal under the auspices of a populist and antisemitic group, Les Jeunes Canada, which openly questioned the reports about Nazi handling of the Jews, and insisted that Canadians should instead turn their attention to the menace of the Jewish presence in Canada.[10]

In these circumstances, it was hardly surprising that the Jewish community's fears were enhanced by the threat of German violence spreading to Canada. As one prominent speaker warned a Zionist audience in April 1933: "Unless something is done quickly the Jewish people may meet the same fate in Canada that Jews are meeting in Germany. The fire is dormant in Canada, it has not yet blazed up, but the spark is there. Germany is not the only place with prejudice. Look at Quebec."[11]

There can be no doubt that the antisemitism of many Canadians reinforced their antipathy towards Hitler's principal victims. In Quebec, (French, catholic and conservative), Jews, especially German Jews, were identified with Marxism, materialism, and atheism. In English-speaking Canada, social discrimination against Jews was openly practised. But such attitudes, including a belief in the unassimilatable character of non-British ethnic immigrant groups, were part of long established racial stereotyping, which had early on become fixed in the minds of Canadian nativists. The economic hardships of the depression years only reinforced such trends. The fear of competition for the few available jobs went hand in hand with the belief in the necessity of preserving the predominant British, or in Quebec, French, cultural patterns. The conviction that Canada's destiny was still linked with the exploitation of its vast untapped natural resources and farm lands in the North, coupled with the evident social disorders in the urban areas, were the principal reasons why Canada's immigration policies during the 1930s closed the doors to all except agricultural settlers. It was a climate profoundly unsympathetic to the mainly urban German Jewish refugees.

In 1938 Hitler's aggressive policies were made evident with the occupation of Austria in March, followed by immediate demands for the return to Germany of the Sudentenland districts of Czechoslovakia. Hundreds of thousands of additional refugees now sought sanctuary. President Roosevelt's response was to convene an international conference at Evian in France in July 1938, but the participation of Canada was only half-hearted. Mackenzie King was aware of strong opposition to any increased inflow of Jewish refugees, especially in Quebec, where for example the St. Jean Baptiste Society organised a petition signed by 128,000 members opposing "all immigration, and especially Jewish immigration."[12] Reassured by the Americans that the conference would not seek to alter existing immigration restrictions, the Canadian Prime Minister sought to adopt a loftier tone. The plight of the refugees was a sign of the increasing international instability. The real cause lay in the intolerant policies of the refugee-producing governments. Any Canadian willingness to accept large numbers of these victims would only lead such repressive regimes to "manufacture" more refugees. In King's view, "other governments with unwanted minorities must not be encouraged to think that harsh treatment at home is the key that will open the doors to immigration abroad."[13] Evian was therefore an attempt to mobilise international pressure to have these policies reversed, and in particular to persuade the German government to abandon its racist persecutions - a misreading of the situation undoubtedly strengthened by the highly favourable view of Hitler gained by Mackenzie King during a visit to Germany in 1937.

This illusion was shattered by the events of the Crystal Night of November 1938. A new wave of sympathy for the Nazis' Jewish victims sprang up in Canada. In a quite unprecedented manner, "Protestant churches prayed for them while community leaders denounced the Nazis for their 'bestial and shocking persecution of a helpless minority'."[14] The Canadian Jewish Congress successfully organised protest meetings in English-speaking Canada to mobilise the outpouring of support. Even Mackenzie King acknowledged privately that some more Jewish refugees would have to be admitted, since this was "right and just, and Christian."[15] But within a few days, even before a well-organized Jewish group could reach Ottawa to appeal for a relaxation of immigration controls, political caution once again prevailed. The Quebec cabinet ministers were solidly opposed to any change of policy, and the Prime Minister capitulated. "Nothing was to be gained," he noted in his diary, "by creating an internal problem in an effort to meet an international one."[16] Above all, dissension between one part of Canada and another had to be avoided.

This rebuff forced the Canadian Jewish Congress to change its strategy. Hitherto it had relied on private representations, and discouraged any Jewish publicity, out of fears of arousing an antisemitic backlash. Severe strains had already been experienced within the Canadian Jewish community. Many Jewish groups, especially those with relatives in Europe, were highly critical of the Congress's tactics, and indeed, because of their fractured relationships with the more established Jewish leaders in Montreal and Toronto, were openly hostile to allowing the Congress to claim that it represented the Jewish community in Canada.[17] But the government's negative response now obliged the Jewish community to look elsewhere for friends. With the warm encouragement of the Canadian League of Nations Society, a new organisation was founded in December 1938, the Canadian National Committee on Refugees and Victims of Political Persecution. It drew its support from the more internationalist anti-Nazi segments of English-speaking Canada, including some of the main-stream church leaders. But these were well-meaning and dedicated elitists without much of a popular following. As was the case for most of similar voluntary agencies, they were strong on ideas, but short of financial support.

Nevertheless, in the spring of 1939, a nation-wide educational campaign was launched. 9,000 copies of a pamphlet "Should Canada Admit Refugees" were circulated through local branches and women's organisations, such as church auxiliaries, chapters of the Business and Professional Women's Association and the YWCA. The humanitarian sentiments expressed were admirable, but the recipients, however sympathetic, carried little political weight. Inevitably, since there were so few refugees arriving to whom practical help could be offered, the meetings of the Committee were principally occupied with passing high-sounding resolutions, deploring the sluggishness of the government to respond to the international refugee crisis, and calling for the arousal of public sympathy. On the other hand, the Committee's supporters did not see themselves as mobilising forces against the Liberal government, which, on other grounds, most of them supported. Indeed the chairman of the Committee, Cairine Wilson, was herself a Senator, and believed that the effective strategy was to seek to persuade influential members of the government from within. The Committee was prepared to cooperate with the immigration authorities, in order to win them over to a new and more relevant vision of the contribution that Canada might make. Similar sentiments were voiced by numerous church bodies at this time. In September 1939, for example, the General Synod of the Church of England in Canada declared: "This meeting expresses the conviction that the Canadian government should continue to explore the possibility of the immigration of selected groups of Jews and non-Aryan Christians from Austria and Germany, so far as is possible and desirable, and thus assume a share in the responsibilities of finding a home for these unfortunate victims of political oppression."[18]

Some of the more politically aware members of the Committee saw that their influence would be of little avail unless supported by a large consensus of the whole population. Unable, or unwilling, to recognise that racist attitudes, especially towards orientals or French Canadians, still prevailed in most of English-speaking Canada, some Anglophones were not averse to seeking to lay the blame for the government's inactivity on the attitudes of Quebec. According to one prominent United Church minister in Toronto, Dr. E.M. House, "the most important factor in the immigration blockage is French Canada, and the almost complete subservience of the Ottawa government to its dictation. In the past few years, a narrow and vicious nationalism has gained complete ascendancy in Quebec. . . The plain fact is, as everyone who has dealt with Ottawa knows, when Quebec says no, the government sits down."[19] Others, however, were convinced that even these obstacles could be overcome if their appeals for Canadian generosity could be repeated often enough. Yet, despite all these efforts, the wall of public indifference remained unbreached. As Reverend Clarence Silcox, general secretary of the Social Service Council of Canada, and one of the founders of the Canadian National Committee for Refugees, noted in March 1939, Canada's failure to respond to the refugee crisis was due to the "moral and intellectual confusion" caused by the strength of Canadian nativism, the bad economic situation, xenophobia in Quebec, but above all to the existence of latent antisemitism. As Senator Wilson herself acknowledged: "It has been unexpectedly difficult to arouse public sympathy into meaningful action."[20]

In order to combat this trend, Silcox and others undertook a public education campaign urging Canadians to take a wider view of immigration possibilities, and pointing out the advantages for Canada to be gained by recruiting the services of the many talented refugees now clamouring to be admitted. But despite the general support of the press for less restrictive policies, the government remained unmoved. In July 1939, when the ill-fated liner "St. Louis," with 900 Jews aboard, sailed for North America, F.C. Blair, Director of Immigration in Ottawa, refused to consider admitting any of them to Canada."[21]

Evidence now indicates that Blair was personally racist in his attitudes, and took every opportunity to frame the restrictive regulations in place to exclude Jewish applicants from succeeding in reaching Canada. His standing in the Ottawa bureaucracy, and his resolute determination to defend his sphere of responsibilities, led to frustration amongst his colleagues,[22] and continual exasperation amongst the officials of the Jewish organisations whose petitions were so unfeelingly and repeatedly rejected. But Blair was conscious that his narrow view of the future of Canadian society was shared by the majority of the public, and supported by the members of the Liberal government. As for Mackenzie King, as Erich Koch has remarked, "while his intentions were honorable, he always managed to justify his inability to carry them out by telling himself to do so would endanger the delicate balance of forces in the country. No one was better equipped than F.C. Blair to prevent upsetting this balance."[22] Humanitarian concern for the casualties of a world increasingly in turmoil was not part of the mandate on which King's government had been elected. The majority of Canadians, not only those in Quebec, were motivated by a clear disinclination to become involved in a situation which was assumed to have little possible benefit to Canada.

In the light of Canada's post-war experience, her attitude towards the admission of refugees before 1939 presents a sorry picture of missed opportunities. Yet with storm clouds of war gathering over Europe, the government's prime concern was at all costs to preserve national unity. Its success did enable Canada to join the war effort in September 1939 as a united country, a development which soon remedied the economic dislocations of the previous decade. But even the general opposition to Nazi aggression did not lead to any widespread sympathy for its Jewish victims, or willingness to admit them in large numbers to Canada. The outbreak of war in fact only sharpened the restrictive tendencies of the Ottawa bureaucracy now fearful that "subversive" elements, in the pay of, or blackmailed by Nazi agents, might turn out to be the instruments of a future fifth column. In 1940, even transit visas for refugees en route to the U.S.A. or to Latin America were refused.[24] The anti-alien feelings of the country grew steadily as the news of the war grew worse. When the war scare reached the Pacific coast, this sentiment was to climax, under pressure from the vast majority of the established social, economic and political organisations in British Columbia, in the unabashedly racist persecutions of the thousands of Japanese Canadians in the province, who were forcibly evacuated from their homes, whose property was confiscated, and who were threatened with deportation unless they dispersed across Canada.[25] Only a few valiant churchmen opposed this outburst of racism, and gave support to the interned Japanese during their years of exile from their homes.

A particularly crass example of this xenophobia concerned the fate of the only sizeable group of Jewish refugees to arrive in Canada during the war years. In the spring of 1940, the British government invited Canada to provide internment facilities for German prisoners-of-war and others, whose presence in the U.K. might prove to be a serious security risk. In both countries, it was widely believed that the German successes of early 1940 were due to the underground activities of Nazis, subversives and spies. In fact more than a third of the 6,673 persons shipped to Canada in July 1940 were refugees from Nazi Germany, who had sought asylum in Britain and had been interned on the Isle of Man in the panic of the invasion scare. Seventy-five percent were of Jewish or half-Jewish origin. A third were boys, aged between 14 and 20. But the British authorities, in what can only be described as an unforgiveable war-time blunder and bureaucratic bungling, failed to inform the Canadians of these differences.[26] When the ships tied up in Quebec, heavily armed guards were on hand to receive these suspected 5th columnists. They were astonished when the first group to disembark consisted of a complete Yeshiva, and the second a cohort of Catholic priests. "My God," said one of the guards, "they have got into their disguise already." They were imprisoned in makeshift camps, many of them in remote forest areas. Only after vigorous protests were the Nazi prisoners and pro-Nazi German nationals placed in separate camps from the civilian refugees.

Since the Canadian authorities disclaimed all responsibility for these unwanted arrivals, whose presence in Canada was only for the duration of the war before eventual repatriation, the claims of the Jewish refugees for release in order to join in the anti-Nazi struggle, met with only incredulity and bureaucratic red-tape from the military officials in charge of Canadian internment operations. Even if they had been wrongfully deported to Canada, there could be no question of treating them as potential immigrants. As enemy aliens, young and of military age, many were still regarded as dangerous to Canadian security. The Canadian government therefore joined in a convenient "conspiracy of silence," and saw no reason to make amends for the British government's "indefensible injustice." It was not until late 1940 that the Canadian National Committee for Refugees and the Canadian Jewish Congress became aware of the true situation. When the matter was raised in the House of Commons in Ottawa, the minister responsible declared that it would not be in the public interest to release any information. As far as the Canadian authorities were concerned, it was solely a British responsibility.

For the inmates themselves, their frustration at being treated as prisoners-of-war, and subject to military discipline, was only compounded by the Canadian refusal to make any changes without authorisation from London. Nor did it take long for the Canadians to discover that the active leaders in protesting against these conditions had been members of the pre-war German Communist party. As Erich Koch recorded, "Invariably, the communists were in the forefront of those making demands, <u>for</u> recognition of the refugee status, <u>against</u> the use of prisoner of war stationery, <u>against</u> sites "unfit for human habitation," <u>against</u> mail delays, <u>for</u> receiving radios and newspapers, and so on. Communists were activists and trouble makers; the few Nazis in our camps behaved like lambs."[27] It was a situation guaranteed to arouse the deeply-rooted official dislike and actual fear of communist elements in the Canadian military and political establishments, and only reinforced the conviction that such men were quite unsuitable to be considered for release in Canada. In this attitude, it would appear, they were joined by most of the more established members of the Jewish community, whose sympathy for their co-religionists was mixed with a disinclination to be openly associated with these "enemy aliens." Any declaration of solidarity might be misconstrued by extremists as disloyalty in war-time. The limited amount of assistance offered to the internees was therefore tendered discreetly and on an individual basis.

The frustration of these internees was only made worse when the news percolated through that the British authorities had recognized the fallacy of their too-sweeping incarceration of all "enemy aliens," and were in the process of liberating many of the Jewish refugees still interned in Britain. Some of those who had enjoyed their short stay of hospitality in Britain now desired to return there; others were anxious to be free to join relatives in the United States; others had no connections and desired only to be safe from the possibility of being handed back to German control in some possible exchange of prisoners. In the meantime all had to work, usually in the woods, cutting trees for pit props, 6 hours a day for a daily wage of 20 cents. To be sure, for many of the younger internees, the camp schools were, as Professor Gregory Baum later noted, a wholly beneficial experience. Their teachers were drawn from the wide range of talents to be found in the camps, and the variety of dramatic and musical events which flourished showed a remarkable ingenuity. But these were a small substitute for the hope of release.

For its part the Canadian Jewish Congress was caught between those who wanted energetic steps made to secure the internees' freedom, and others who deplored any distraction from the still more urgent plight of Jews in Europe now facing imminent annihilation. In Ottawa, the reaction of the immigration officials was predictable. As Blair commented at the time: "No doubt there are numbers of these peope who are quite friendly to the British cause whose cases must appeal to our sympathy. I have wondered sometimes whether the "mistake" in sending them here was not intentional on the part of some person overseas. . . It would be impossible to justify before public opinion in Canada the release of these internees in Canada and it would also open again the matter of making Canada a waiting room for people who want to get into the United States." Since these refugees had been sent to Canada for "safekeeping" by the British authorities, and not by any deliberate choice of the Canadian government, their liberation could only cause difficulties for the immigration officials. There would be accusations of "queue-jumping," and insoluble difficulties would arise if they turned out to be unsuitable for resettlement in Canada. "The Government," Blair wrote to the Director of Internment Operations, "as we are both aware, does not want any wholesale delivery of these internees to Canada."[28]

By the end of 1940, the British government finally acknowledged its unfortunate error, and sent a senior official to Canada to arrange the return of the civilian refugees who so desired to the United Kingdom, on the condition that they voluntarily agreed to serve in the British forces or do other war-related work. The alternative was to remain in the internment camps in Canada until such time as the Canadian government allowed them to be released under the prevailing regulations. For those with no affiliations in Britain, or too young for military service, the prospects were hardly inviting. Only after many more months was the Canadian government prepared to accept the release of those with first-degree relatives in Canada, students, skilled or agricultural workers. Thanks to hard work by the Committee of Refugees, private sponsors were found, prepared to vouch for these "friendly aliens enjoying temporary liberty in Canada." At the end of 1943 an Order-in-Council was finally passed granting 952 refugees eligibility for eventual Canadian naturalization after the war. Many of them went on to have distinguished careers in their new homeland.

This small victory was, however, an isolated one. Canadian barriers to giving sanctuary to refugees remained firm, undoubtedly backed by the findings of a 1943 public opinion poll, when 80% of the respondents were opposed to any attempt to bring large numbers of immigrants to Canada. Anti-refugee and antisemitic sentiment remained particularly noticeable in Quebec, and was stirred up by the province's premier, Duplessis, for his own ends. Thus at the very moment when the Jews of Europe were being murdered daily in their thousands, Canadian opinion remained indifferent to their fate. This attitiude cannot be explained by ignorance. Canadians, like their American neighbours, were well enough informed, even though, as Deborah Lipstadt has shown, press reports of Nazi atrocities against the Jews were frequently relegated to the inside pages of the newspapers, or given scant attention by the editorial writers.[29] Since Canadians were almost wholly dependent for their news on British or American sources, there was little opportunity for developing a separate sense of the crisis. And like their counterparts in other western countries, the Canadian educated elite shared the widespread scepticism about tales of atrocities taking place in unverifiable circumstances in remote and unreachable countries. Canadians undoubtedly demonstrated the same failures of imagination as their allies. Above all, it has been suggested, the Canadians' sense of geographical remoteness from the battle fields, their inability to relate their own experience of hard times to the sufferings of the persecuted Jews, and the minimal contact they had with the outside world, were part of that "tyranny of distance," which resulted in Canada's being less responsive than her allies or than some other countries to the plight of the Jewish refugees.[30] In Ottawa, the government, increasingly conscious that Canada was very much a junior partner in the determination of Allied strategy, faithfully followed the line adopted by the U.S.A. and Britain that the best way to end the Jewish miseries in Europe was to defeat Nazism as quickly as possible. The rescue of refugees remained a minor concern compared to the larger issues of winning the war.

The groups most alert in Canada to the dimensions of the Holocaust were the relatives of Jews entrapped in Nazi-occupied lands. Their repeated representations for intervention on behalf of their families placed an almost impossible burdon on the leaders of the Canadian Jewish Congress, only too well aware of the obstructionism of the Canadian authorities. These expectations could almost never be fulfilled, yet, in the face of the mounting catastrophe, they could not be denied. The dilemma confronting such men as Saul Hayes, executive director of the Canadian Jewish Congress throughout the war years, was insoluble, and it was a tribute to his persistence that he maintained his campaign despite the discouraging lack of success. By the end of the war, the officials of the Canadian Jewish Congress were forced to recognise that their influence in the corridors of power was negligible. "The

Jewish community was not an important part of the domestic power equation. . . It had no leverage sufficient to combat successfully the anti-refugee and anti-Jewish sentiment abroad in the land."[31] Later criticisms of the Congress, or accusations that its officials were too concerned to preserve their image of respectability, vastly overestimate what the organisation could have achieved in the existing climate of Canadian opinion. The wishful thinking of post-war years cannot ignore the overwhelming contemporary evidence that, during the period of the Holocaust, Canada was, or thought itself to be, a by-stander.

In 1945, Canada emerged as one of the victor powers, and with a new sense of its independent identity. A fresh breed of younger more progressive civil servants began to play a significant role in Ottawa's decision making. Particularly in the Department of External Affairs, the influence of men like Lester Pearson gained ground. Profoundly affected by the revelations of the Nazi atrocities, and daily impressed by stories of individual suffering, they now began to plead for a more imaginative response on behalf of the survivors of the Holocaust. The Canadian Jewish Congress was also unremitting in its efforts to flood the immigration authorities with applications from relatives to have the surviving Jews rescued from the charnel house of Europe. In May 1946, the government announced that first-degree relatives would be permitted to resettle in Canada, though no promise was made of any immediate action, which would have to wait until the international situation was more stable, immigration offices opened again in Europe, and shipping became available. Priority was in any case to be given to those whose assimilation, it was presumed, would be easiest - British settlers, Polish veterans, even some of the thousands of expellees from the Baltic countries, many of whom had fought alongside the Germans, but who still retained their image as hard-working farmers. Refugees, especially Jewish refugees, now derogatively designated as D.P.s, were conspicuously low on the list of priorities. For those officials anxious for Canada to play a larger role in international affairs, this gap between the enormity of the refugee crisis and the meagre response of Canada became increasingly a source of concern. They were supported by a growing number of business men, anxious to maintain Canada's expanded production capacity. But public opinion lagged behind. In October 1946, a Gallup Poll, asking Canadians which potential immigrants should be kept out, not surprisingly found that Japanese were first on the list. The second most undesirable group was not German, but Jews.[32] This evidence of intolerant prejudice, even after the genocidal character of the Nazi persecution of the Jews was universally known, was only reinforced by the widespread belief that the solution to the problem of the D.P.s lay in their repatriation to their countries of original origin. Those Canadians who still maintained their restrictionist views about immigrants were vocal in their opposition to Canada's becoming the dumping ground of other nations' unwanted or surplus peoples.

But even those in favour of a more active immigration policy remained highly selective as to who and how many should be let in. As Canadian policy has shown subsequently, this sentiment has only been marginally mitigated. To this day, a strongly vocal anti-immigrant feeling remains, especially in times of economic dislocation. On the other hand, support for refugee concerns has grown largely due to the successful integration of several refugee groups in the 1950s and 1960s. The long-standing fixation on agricultural priorities was abandoned, and a willingness to provide more participation from the private sector was finally achieved in 1979, when private, especially church groups, were encouraged to sponsor refugees beyond any family connections, which proved highly beneficial for the "boat people" from Vietnam.

When, after 1948, Canadian economic self-interest prompted the admission of more immigrants, and Canada was finally prepared to offer a haven for the homeless Jews in Europe, it was to be an irony of history that a still more attractive destination should have become available. The re-creation of the State of Israel in May 1949, and its offer to receive all Jews, meant that in fact Canadian recruiters were frequently disappointed. To the relief of some of the old-style immigration officials, the prospect of being swamped by unmanageable numbers of Holocaust survivors was now allayed. Although many Jews in subsequent years did choose to resettle in Canada, their numbers have not been such as to lead to the divisive polemics of earlier decades.

One aspect of the new immigration policies was, however to have unfortunate consequences. Amongst the many thousands of European refugees admitted after 1948 were some who had successfully concealed their part in assisting the Nazi atrocities in eastern Europe. Unwittingly, Canada gave asylum to a few of the perpetrators, as well as the victims of the Holocaust. Alerted to this unwelcome prospect, the Canadian Jewish community was unable, after so many years of combatting immigration restrictions, to insist on their reimposition. As in the parallel cases of Australia and the United States, the harbouring of numerous criminals went overlooked in the large-scale European immigration after 1945, at a time when, in any case, the war-time destruction of personal files made the task of identifying those with Nazi records virtually impossible.[33]

In 1946, the defection of Igor Gouzenko, a Soviet embassy clerk in Ottawa, revealed to a shocked public that Soviet espionage had been practised on a large scale in Canada. Fear and suspicion of Communism began to replace antagonism against the now seemingly overthrown Nazism. In 1948, the British government told its Commonwealth partners that since the new political dangers from the Soviet Union required a revised stance towards Germany, it had therefore decided to suspend quietly any further persecution of war criminals. The Canadian government did not disagree. As a result, it possessed neither the necessary information, nor the political will, to track down the possible presence of Nazi or pro-Nazi criminal elements among the many new arrivals in Canada. Screening procedures were noticeably relaxed, in comparison to former years. Optimistically, the Canadian government believed that resettlement in Canada would erase the hatreds of war-time in an atmosphere of harmonious co-existence. Undoubtedly the government was bolstered by the evident public desire in the post-war years to put the past behind them. There was no widespread sentiment in favour of bringing to justice all those who had instigated or assisted in the horrors of the Holocaust.

It was therefore not until decades later that a few activists in the Jewish community decided to follow the example of a handful of crusaders in the United States to demand a more forceful pursuit of Nazi war criminals suspected of being in Canada. In 1982, despite evident misgivings in the Jewish community, several Holocaust survivors, led by Mrs. Sabina Citron of Montreal, established the Canadian Holocaust Remembrance Association, one of whose tasks was to urge the legal prosecution of any such suspects. But not until 1984, when sensational reports were circulated that the notorious Auschwitz doctor, Joseph Mengele, had attempted to seek refuge in Canada, was the government pressurised into action. It then appointed a Commission of Inquiry on War Criminals, under a Quebec judge, Mr. Justice Deschêsnes. His report, published at the end of 1986, found that there was no evidence that Mengele had ever entered Canada, but that there were indeed over 100 suspect residents in the country, far fewer than the numbers first suggested, but nevertheless warranting further investigaton. At the same time, he recommended that the Canadian Criminal Code be amended so that any resident of Canada could be charged with war crimes or crimes against humanity, without limitation of time or space.[34] In 1987, these changes were passed by Parliament, and in December 1987 the first individual, a former police officer from Hungary, accused of assisting the deportation of Jews to Auschwitz, was arrested in Ontario.

Encouraged by their inital success, the Canadian Holocaust Remembrance Association determined to pursue further legal challenges, in order to ensure that the Holocaust would not be forgotten - or even worse, denied. In 1985 Canada witnessed two spectacular trials, both dealing with the Holocaust - or rather, with its denial. In Ontario, a recent German immigrant, Ernst Zundel, was charged with knowingly publishing information likely to cause harm to social and/or racial tolerance - specifically by denying the events of the Holocaust. Immediately following, in Alberta, a former high-school teacher, and mayor of the small community of Eckville, Jim Keegstra, was accused of wilfully promoting hatred against an identifiable group, namely the Jews, having for several years taught his students a rabid antisemitism, including his opinion that the Jews had largely fabricated the "legend" of the Holocaust.

Zundel's trial took place in Toronto, the chief centre of Canadian Jewry, and therefore attracted wide attention. Since he made no secret of his energetic efforts to purvey Nazi propaganda, or of his admiration for the Nazi leaders, he quickly lost all public support. Nevertheless, the refusal of the judge to take 'judicial notice' of the events of the Holocaust enabled the defence to parade a number of internationally-known Holocaust-deniers, whose otherwise baseless opinions thus found a considerable hearing. Their attempts to cast doubts on the historical factuality of the Holocaust met with increasing sceptisism, especially from the numerous survivors who attended the court or gave evidence for the prosecution. Zundel's conviction and proposed deportation from Canada was however overthrown on a technicality, and a second trial has now been ordered.

In some ways, the trial of Jim Keegstra in Alberta was a more significant event. Keegstra is a native-born Canadian, had no connections with Germany, and was too young to have been in the second world war. His virulent antisemitism and his consequent denial of the Holocaust in fact represented the views of a considerable body of supporters in that part of Canada. The prevalence of conspiratorial theories about the dangers of international finance or Jewish bankers, heavily weighted with traditional Christian prejudices, showed that Jewish-Gentile attitudes since the Holocaust had hardly changed in this province. This may explain the reluctance of his fellow teachers, the local school authorities, the provincial government and even the Alberta churches, to denounce the outspoken indoctrination he was giving to his students, let alone to take action in the courts against him. His conviction and fine of $5,000 was unlikely, therefore, to avert the danger that such views would continue to be held.[35]

As is clear from the experience of other countries, such as the United States, France or Germany, such denials of the Holocaust are part of a new antisemitic sub-culture, aided and abetted by the so-called "revisionist historians," seeking to save the world from the sinister forces deriving from the "evil empire" of the Soviet Union, or the "illegitimate" State of Israel. Canada has not been immune to such ideas. Nevertheless, these trials not only gave rise to a significant debate about the tolerable limits to be imposed on those who seek to propagate deliberately distorted views of history, but also had a salutary effect on public consciousness in Canada about the Holocaust. Indeed, the results of these trials led to a heightened sympathy and awareness of the sufferings inflicted on the Jewish people during the years of Nazi oppression. Canadians were not persuaded to any greater extent to doubt the historical record of the Holocaust.[36]

By contemporary standards, the Canadian attitudes of fifty years ago, including those of the churches, towards the victims of Nazi persecution, especially the Jews, were heartless and apathetic. According to one authoritative source, Canada, in allowing only some 4,000 Jews to immigrate throughout the period of the Holocaust and beyond, "has, arguably, the worst record of any country of the western world."[37] The prevailing racism and introspective myopia which characterized the po itica attitudes of many Canadians, and frequently their government, in the 1930s must be acknowledged. In the intervening years, Canadian society has greatly changed, in part, it may be claimed, because this lesson of the Holocaust has been learnt. Canada is now officially committed to a policy of assisting refugees, and has often shown commendable sympathy to the victims of international violence. Tragically, however, the readiness of repressive governments to persecute, expel, or even exterminate their citizens for reasons of political or ideological expediency, has only increased, as more than 12 million refugees in today's world can testify. To combat such powerful forces, and to prevent the spread of international anarchy, will require greater efforts from the world community than has so far been mobilized. In this endeavour, it is to be hoped, Canada will play, in the future, a more courageous part.

REFERENCES

[1]See Irving Abella and Harold Troper, None is Too Many. Canada and the Jews of Europe 1933-1948, Toronto 1982.

[2]As Michael Marrus has recently remarked, many of the accounts of the policies of the bystanders apply "the standards, value systems, and vantage point of the present, rather than those of the period being discussed," being "more concerned to condemn rather than to explain": The Holocaust in History, Toronto 1987, p. 157.

[3]In the eyes of one distinguished Canadian historian, the Liberal government "represented the huddling together of frightened people uncertain of their way in a chaotic world": Arthur Lower, Colony to Nation, Toronto 1946, p. 519.

[4]See Jonathan F. Wagner, Brothers Beyond the Sea. National Socialism in Canada, Waterloo, Ontario 1981, pp. 64-117.

[5]Frank H. Epp, Mennonites in Canada, 1920-1940. A People's Struggle for Survival, Toronto 1982, pp. 548-54.

[6]Wagner, op. cit., p. 103-6.

[7]Lita-Rose Betcherman, The Swastika and the Maple Leaf. Fascist Movements in Canada in the Thirties, Toronto 1975, p. 38-43.

[8]Gerald E. Dirks, Canada's Refugee Policy. Indifference or Opportunism? Montreal 1977, p. 53.

[9]See David Rome, Clouds in the Thirties. On Antisemitism in Canada, 1929-1939, Section 4, Montreal 1978, p. 3A-6.

[10]Rome, op. cit., p. 21 ff.

[11]Toronto Star, April 24, 1933, quoted in Betcherman, op. cit., p. 52.

[12]Abella and Troper, op. cit., p. 18.

[13]ibid., p. 27.

[14]Betcherman, op. cit., p. 18.

[15]King Diary, November 12 and 15, 1938, quoted in Abella and Troper, op. cit., p. 39.

[16]King Diary, March 29, 1938, quoted in Abella and Troper, op. cit., p. 17.

[17]ibid., p. 14.

[18]Quoted in Dirks, op. cit., p. 68.

[19]Quoted in Dirks, op. cit., p. 69.

[20]Quoted in Dirks, op. cit., p. 71.

[21]Quoted Abella and Troper, op. cit., p. 64.

[22]See J. Gibson, quoted in Eric Koch, Deemed Suspect. A Wartime Blunder, Toronto 1980, p. 201.

[23]Koch, op. cit., p. 201-2.

[24]By contrast, the Canadian government took the initiative in proposing to bring over 4,500 British evacuated children to Canada. But a scheme to include 100 orphans of Continental origin was refused.

[25]W. Peter Ward, White Canada Forever. Popular Attitudes and Public Policy Towards Orientals in British Columbia, Montreal 1978, Chapter 8.

[26]See Koch, op. cit.; also Harry Seidler, Internment, Sydney 1986.

[27]See Koch, op. cit., p. 163.

[28]Ibid., p. 202-4.

[29]Deborah Lipstadt, Beyond Belief. The American Press and the Coming of the Holocaust, 1933-1945, New York 1986.

[30]See Canadian Forum, Vol. 62, No. 724, Dec.-Jan.1982/83, p. 237.

[31]Abella and Troper, op. cit., p. 283.

[32]Ibid., p. 232.

[33]For the striking parallels between Canadian and Australian attitudes during the Holocaust, see M. Blakeney, Australia and the Jewish Refugees 1933-1948, Sydney 1985; ed., W.D. Rubinstein, Jews in the Sixth Continent, Sydney 1987, chap. 11; "On Being a German-Jewish Refugee in Australia," The Australian Journal of Politics and History, Vol. 31, no. 1 (special issue) 1985; For the United States, see Alan A. Ryan, Quiet Nightmare: Prosecuting War Criminals in America, San Diego 1984; Rochell G. Saidel, The Outraged Conscience: Seekers of Justice for Nazi War Criminals in America, Albany, New York 1984.

[34]Commission of Inquiry on War Criminals. Report. Part I Public, Honourable Jules Deschênes, Commissioner, Ottawa, 1986.

[35]See the excellent account of this trial by David Bercuson and Douglas Wertheimer, A Trust Betrayed: The Keegstra Affair, Toronto 1985; also David R. Elliott, 'Antisemitism and the Social Credit Movement. The Intellectual Roots of the Keegstra Affair' in Canadian Ethnic Studies, Vol. XVII, no. 1 (1985), pp. 78 ff.

[36]See Gabriel Weimann and Conrad Winn, Hate on Trial. The Zundel Affair. The Media. Public Opinion in Canada, Oakville, Ontario 1986.

[37]Abella and Troper, op. cit., p. x.

A TALE OF TWO TRIALS:
Antisemitism in Canada 1985

Alan Davies

Victoria College, University of Toronto
Toronto, Ontario, Canada

In January, 1985, Ernst Zündel, a German landed immigrant in Canada, was brought to trial in Toronto, Ontario, under Section 177 of the Criminal Code of Canada for publishing and circulating (in forty-two countries) information that he knew was false and inimical to the public interest, i.e., that the holocaust was a Jewish fraud. A photo-retoucher by trade, Zündel operated a small printing press in the (fortified) basement of his Toronto house. In April, 1985, James Keegstra, an Alberta high school teacher, was brought to trial in Red Deer, Alberta, under Section 281.2 of the Criminal Code for promoting hatred against the Jewish people in his social studies classroom in the small town of Eckville (of which he was also mayor) between September 1978 and December 1982. Both men were defended by the same attorney, Douglas Christie, the ambitious founder of a small separatist political party in western Canada; both were convicted. Zündel received fifteen months in prison for his offense. However, upon appeal, his conviction was overturned on technical grounds (the judge was deemed to have acted improperly) and a new trial with a new judge is currently under way. Keegstra was fined $5000 for his offense; his appeal is still pending.

Zündel and Keegstra are both similar and different. Both, obviously, are ardent antisemites. Both, also, are highly exhibitionistic, and thoroughly enjoyed their respective hours in the sun. Zündel, a more intelligent man than Keegstra and a more accomplished actor, arrived for his sentencing with a blackened face (because whites cannot receive justice in Canada) carrying a cross like Jesus on his way to Calvary. The cross bore the inscription, "Freedom of Speech"; not only was Zündel, like Jesus, being crucified by an evil society, but freedom of speech was being crucified as well. Not content with this charade, the self-anointed victim also wore an industrial hard hat on his *via dolorosa*, ostensibly to protect himself from angry Jews, in reality to attract as much attention to himself as possible. The helmet-shaped hat was vaguely reminiscent of the Wehrmacht. Keegstra made no attempt to imitate this performance. At the opening of his trial, however, he sported a "Freedom of Speech" button, and his admirers regularly appeared in the courtroom with buttons inscribed "Truth -- the Final Solution"! Christie did his best in both trials to turn the two defendants into political martyrs by making the right of free speech the hinge of both cases. Subsequently, he published a small tract on the subject.

On a deeper level, both men share the conviction (real or feigned) that the former National Socialist regime in Germany has been utterly maligned, and that few, if any, Jews perished at Nazi hands. Arthur Butz's revisionist classic *The Hoax of the Twentieth Century* was discovered in Keegstra's private library, and Zündel's defense featured a parade of notorious revisionists, including Robert Faurisson and Ditlieb Felderer. Both men, therefore, subscribe to the hoary theory of Jewish conspiracy against the non-Jewish world. However, during the Keegstra trial, the alleged holocaust hoax was a secondary motif; during the Zündel trial, it was the issue *par excellence* (Zündel was actually indicted for distributing his own revisionist composition *Did Six Million Really Die*? together with another antisemitic tract *The West, the War and Islam.*). Yet, in both cases, the crown was faced with the enormously difficult task of demonstrating wilful intent to inflict harm on the Jews; the question of motive was of critical importance. If either defendant had managed to convince his jurors that no wilful harm had been intended, no conviction would have been possible. It is a tribute to the skill of the two crown prosecutors that neither Keegstra nor Zündel succeeded in establishing any real moral credibility in their respective testimonies. In fact, in the end, they convicted themselves largely out of their own mouths (Troper, 1985, p. 10).

Antisemitism is a disease with more than a single strain, and these two arch-antisemites, in spite of their affinities, are not the same. Keegstra is an extreme Protestant fundamentalist who has plucked his dark thoughts about Jews and Judaism out of the religious obsessions of the Christian ages; Zündel, whose religious views (if any) are not apparent, is an extreme German nationalist who wishes to rehabilitate the Third Reich and thereby save Germany's 'honour'. They represent traditional and modern variations on the same underlying theme: Jewish iniquity. I will examine Keegstra first, and at greater length.

KEEGSTRA

It was the French existentialist philosopher Jean-Paul Sartre who, in an inspired passage, once described antisemitism as a form of "Manichaeism", i.e., of radical dualism in which ultimate goodness and ultimate evil are engaged in mortal combat: "Knight-errant of the Good, the anti-Semite is a holy man" (Sartre, 1948, pp. 40-43). Subpeoned as an expert witness by the crown, I was reminded of these Sartrean lines as I listened to Keegstra inform the court about the powers of darkness scheming against Christian civilization. A devout and strict Christian with high moral ideals (smoking, drinking, dancing and playing cards are serious sins to Keegstra), he was certain that he could identify these powers, and no less certain that God, the God of the Bible, was on his side. The Word of God is clear and plain: one is either for Christ or against him, and, since the Jews are obviously against him, they must be for the devil, and to be for the devil must mean to favour the destruction of Christianity and its institutions. Judaism, therefore, is an evil religion, premised on a hatred of Christ, the Son of God, causing Jews who take it seriously to become evil themselves. The basic source of this evil is the *Talmud*, which, according to Keegstra, instills feelings of hatred for Christ and Christianity in Jewish hearts, teaching them to cheat and perhaps even murder Christians in the bargain. Not even the disclosure under cross-examination that he had never studied Jewish history, and knew nothing or next to nothing about rabbinic literature (except what he had read in blatantly antisemite sources) could shake Keegstra's convictions in this respect. He knew the truth, and the truth had made him free. Furthermore, good 'Christian' friends (later identified as members of a far-right organization in Canada called *The Canadian Intelligence Service*) had supplied him with reliable books that revealed the *real* truth about the *Talmud*, and, since he trusted his friends, he also trusted their books. Jewish books, on the other hand, can not be trusted, for, as everyone knows, Jews are liars, being the children of the devil who is the 'father of lies' (*John* 8:44). The *Talmud*, moreover, says terrible things about Christ and Christians: a fact that Keegstra's authorities and mentors never let him forget. One of his friends had even examined the English (Soncino) translation in a public library. In the mind of this knight-errant of the Good, the powers of darkness and their earthly allies were easy to name.

While the Jews are certainly the devil's mort important agents in the cosmic struggle, the father of lies, according to Keegstra, has other instruments as well. University professors, for example, also tell lies, especially historians who are fearful of losing their positions should they publish unpopular and unconventional views. Such persons, it seems, are secretly censured and controlled behind the scenes by their Jewish masters. As a university graduate himself (in industrial arts), Keegstra was in a good position to evaluate academics. Distrusting orthodox opinion, he insisted that students should learn to think for themselves, as he himself had always done. As a teacher, his main concern was to inculcate this principle in his Eckville classroom, so that no one fell victim to the conventional interpretations of Jewish-intimidated historians who were afraid to tell the truth about past and present events. It was his Christian responsibility to make certain that this young charges enjoyed a well-rounded education. It was his Christian responsibility to expose the deceitful professors and their mainstream publishers, together with the other liars of the age. It was his Christian responsibility to resist the powers of evil that are seeking through socialism, communism, international capitalism, etc. -- all of which are really extensions of Talmudic Judaism -- to gain domination over the world. Socialism, communism and international capitalism all speak of a radical new order, and, for Keegstra, this was a seditious Jewish utopia that could only be constructed on the ashes of Christendom. War and revolution, especially revolution, are the means through which this brave new world is to come to pass. As a young history student (in a survey course or two) at university, Keegstra soon realized that his instructors were not providing the 'real' reasons for the wars and revolutions of the last two hundred years. He would make good the deficiency.

Revolution was his forte, especially the French Revolution (1789). Here is an excerpt from a 1981 class assignment on this subject by one of his students.

> <u>The World Menace since 1776</u>
>
> . . . The best place to start will be with a ruthless cutthroat known to the world as Adam Weishaupt. He . . . was a jesuit but disliked the church so he broke away from it when he was 25-30 years old. In 1771 Adam Weishaupt disappeared mysteriously until May 1st 1776. (Incidently this date is said to be Satan's birthday). During these five years Adam Weishaupt had been writing a plan in which he was going to take over the world with. In order to get this plan he had sold his soal to Satan. This plan was based on deseption and was made up of five points . . . .
>
> (a) destruction of all Monarchy & legal government
> (b) destroy all religions -- especially Christianity
> (c) abolish marriage (children raised by the state)
> (d) abolish private property (land) and all inheritances
> (e) abolish all loyalty and allegiance
>
> . . . . Adam Weishaupt, after announcing his plan organized a secret society. This organization was called the "Illuminaty" (sic) which means the enlightenment. . . . It was the Illuminaty which was behind the French Revolution.
>
> In 1789 was the first revolution started by the Jews to set up this new world order under a one world government. . . . The entire revolution was conducted by a pack of Jewish leckies who went under the name of Jacobins. . . . The Jacobins would ride around in packs and bash in childrens heads, rape the women and then drown them. They would also cut open the stomaches of men and let them bleed to death. . . .
>
> This essay shows how the Jews are conspiring to take over the world. And when they do they will set up a New World order under a One world gov't. I have shown in this essay since 1776, with Adam Weishaupts five point plan, the Jews have been causing anarchy & chaos throughout the world. I have also shown that where ever the communist rule it was set up by Jews. In my opinion this must come to a dead halt. We must get rid of every jew in existence so we may live in peace & freedom.

I have suppressed the name of the youthful author. It does not matter in any case, since virtually every essay submitted to Keegstra repeated this extraordinary thesis. Indeed, as a few unsympathetic ex-students testified, *not* to explain the French Revolution in terms of the Faustian Adam Weishaupt, the sinister Illuminati and the evil Jews was to flirt with genuine academic danger; it meant that one was not thinking for oneself, but simply regurgitating misinformation from mainstream historians who were merely puppets controlled by Jewish puppeteers. But most of Keegstra's students apparently believed him. Those who did not, and their parents, finally instigated an inquiry that eventually led to his dismissal and subsequent indictment, although not without many difficulties (Bercuson & Wertheimer, 1985, pp. 65-84). Then, in a criminal court with a new audience, in fact, with half the nation as his audience, he had the opportunity to elaborate on the great conspiracy to his heart's content.

Keegstra, of course, had his mentors. One of them was Nesta Webster, a now-forgotten Englishwoman who specialized in conspiracy theories during the World War I era. A morbidly romantic woman with a clairvoyant turn-of-mind, Mrs. Webster apparently regarded herself as the reincarnation of a French countess during the 1789 revolution who could, so to speak, describe from an eyewitness perspective. Intensely antisemitic, she became, in later years, an ardent supporter of British fascism. Keegstra treasured her books, especially *Secret Societies and Subversive Movements* (1924), which, judging from his numerous marginal notations, was a favourite text. Its thesis certainly compells attention.

According to Mrs. Webster, a series of conspiracies that really constitute a single vast conspiracy account for the great political upheavals in history. In different ages it has assumed different forms -- ancient gnostics, Syrian assassins, Jewish cabbalists, mediaeval Knights Templar, Freemasons, Illuminati, etc. -- and its true leaders are both virtually unknown and endowed with superhuman powers. Ultimately, they represent an "occult power" in league with the powers of darkness; hence, they are both cosmic and demonic. Their constant aim is the destruction of the existing social order, especially Christianity and its realms, in order to found a totalitarian empire, wholly evil in character. The main historic roots of the conspiracy lie in the Jewish Cabbala, and, while Jews are not the sole conspirators, Mrs. Webster regarded them as the arch-conspirators. However, it is all such a mighty labyrinth of plots within plots and secret societies within secret societies that no one, not even Mrs. Webster, has ever fully understood the entire matter. Nevertheless, like Virgil guiding Dante through Hell, she was determined to explore as much of this dangerous terrain as possible. Not surprisingly, her allegations possess a fantastic quality, reflecting the peculiar mood of the war and post-war periods when spies, conspiracies, assassinations and revolutions saturated the news. Obviously, the author was obsessed with the fear of conspiracy against Britain; obviously also, she had imbibed the popular antisemitism of the era, especially in upper-class British society. In spite of her attack on occult powers, her analysis displays a romantic fascination with both the occult and the Orient whose "inscrutable character" is in her eyes the "cradle of secret societies". Behind the various historic forces can be detected the eternal (Manichaean) conflict of the powers of darkness and the powers of light.

Keegstra was impressed. He could detect nothing implausible in her thesis -- no errors or lacunae; he only knew that she had made sense out of things, and that was enough. The untutored eye would not recognize the disreputable character of most of Mrs. Webster's French and German sources, i.e., a host of anti-Masonic, anti-Jewish reactionary clerics and aristocrats who festered in constant resentment of the new political order in France and its seismic effects on other nations. Naturally, such writers railed against democracy, demonizing the French Revolution, all later revolutions and everyone deemed responsible for these nefarious events. Thus they fell on the Freemasons, The Bavarian Illuminati, the (French) Protestants and, of course, finally the Jews, thereby shifting responsibility for the 'devil-instigated' revolution from the old regime and the church. Mrs. Webster, for some reason, paid special attention to the short-lived Illuminati, and, as a result, Keegstra's students heard a great deal about Adam Weishaupt. Weishaupt was a somewhat enigmatic figure, but, in spite of his radical social ideas, scarcely the evil genius that his calumniators imagined. Most of these nineteenth-century writings mixed up racial and religious language -- good Christians (French, Aryans, Catholics) versus bad Jews (non-French, Semites, Talmud-believers) -- especially after 1870, when a defeated France (at Prussian hands) sank into a xenophobic mood and treason was in the air. Men such as August Barruel, Alphonse de Toussenel, Henri Gougenot des Mousseaux and E. N. Chabauty thought of themselves as pious and moral Christians at war with the devil and his agents. They believed in simple cosmologies that eliminated ambiguity from history, and wanted to turn the clock of European history back to pre-1789 time. No progress was permissible; everything had to be frozen as it was in the former age. Modernity signified change, and change was evil. Since the emancipated Jews were identified with modernity (democracy, capitalism, socialism, communism), they too were evil and had to be placed back into their mediaeval ghettos before they succeeded in contaminating the Christian world.

In order to hold modernity at bay, the French reactionaries incorporated nationalistic, racistic and antisemitic slogans into an anti-modern worldview in which the 'Christian' past was opposed to the 'anti-Christian' present. Typically, these men regarded themselves as the custodians of the nation's moral and spiritual legacy, and invested 'Christian' France with all of the virtues that had seemingly disappeared from the contemporary republic. As Stephen Wilson has pointed out (Wilson, 1982, chaps. XIV and XVI), rural society was exalted over urban society, or the pure Christian country over the corrupt Jewish city; pre-capitalist industry was exalted over industrial capitalism, or the peasant/artisan over the factory proletarian; order, hierarchy and authority were exalted over disorder, egalitarianism and relativism, or a system with firm moral boundaries over a system in which change and revolution were endemic. In short, the reactionaries turned to visions of a pre-modern Christian utopia -- a type of paradise lost -- and insisted that society conform to their static and rigid model with its authoritarian principles -- otherwise, the Anti-Christ would prevail.

Keegstra, although a Protestant fundamentalist in twentieth-century Canada, is cast in the same psychological mould. Like the writers whose sentiments he absorbed through Nesta Webster, he also revealed in his testimony a pathological fear of liberalism, rationalism and modernity, together with the same desire to turn the hands of the clock in a backward direction. As the nineteenth-century French reactionaries had sought to make France 'Christian' again, Keegstra clearly sought to make Canada 'Christian' again. A man with a political agenda, he was, and remains, an ardent member of the federal Social Credit Party, as well as a onetime candidate for its leadership.

Born in the 1930s as a rightwing Christian response to the crisis of the social order, Social Credit has always contained an antisemitic component. Its theory, as formulated by Major C.H. Douglas, its English founder, connected the ills of the Depression era with the claim that control over financial credit had fallen into the hands of international bankers who manipulated capitalism for private gain. By implication, these bankers were mostly Jews. To cure the ills of the age, the state had to regain control of the monetary system; this would be accomplished by issuing 'social credit' in the form of a dividend for every citizen, thereby restoring purchasing power. To prevent inflation, a mediaeval style 'just price' would be established for all products. In this fashion, both financial security and personal freedom would be enhanced without resorting to socialism or collectivism (the movement was fiercely anti-socialist and anti-communist). Moreover, the Social Credit way of life was deemed both moral and biblical; indeed, it was identified with the true Christian social order. For many years, the party held power in Alberta under the charismatic leadership of William (Bible Bill) Aberhart, a fundamentalist radio preacher and teacher, and his successor William Manning. Once in power, however, it lost its zeal for ideological orthodoxy, and simply became another conservative government. Neither Aberhart nor Manning were personally antisemitic.

Keegstra, however, is a purist, and, like Major Douglas himself, a firm believer in the authenticity of the *Protocols of the Elders of Zion* (Palmer, 1982, p. 153). Antisemitic myths, especially the notion of a mythological link between Jews and money, fit comfortably in the Social Credit worldview. In addition, the dreaded bankers were largely easterners with their head offices in Toronto and Montreal, cities with substantial Jewish communities. Furthermore, the Social Credit tendency to identify itself with Christian values and Christian civilization fit into a homogeneous view of society and a dislike of religious, cultural and ethnic pluralism. This, in turn, fits into a nativist pattern which, in spite of the large immigrant population, can still be found in small town and rural Canada. The antisemitic strain, always stronger in the federal than in the provincial party, frequently surfaced among federal M.P.s during the war and post-war periods, and, although Social Credit has now disappeared from the House of Commons, still endures.

During his trial, Keegstra said little about his political ambitions, posing as a peaceful citizen who abhorred violence and wished no harm to anyone. His only concern was to force people to think and, like Socrates, to direct them to the truth. But conspiracies are obviously dangerous; can one discover the truth and remain indifferent in its face? Can one have one's eyes opened to the 'real' nature of Judaism, and sit idle? Can one worship Christ and watch complacently while the body of Christ is devoured by its enemies? Can one expose the still extant Illuminati and their hidden masters and not wish to block their path? Keegstra was a man with a mission, and his mission had political dimensions; why, otherwise, would he have stood for parliament and for the leadership of his party? A call to arms was implied. Whatever the Eckville teacher intended or did not intend, at least one of his students drew the logical conclusion to the lesson of the day: "We must get rid of every jew in existence so that we may live in peace & freedom."

While not all the conspirators are Jews, and not all Jews are conspirators (about 8% according to Keegstra), it is a wise precaution to suspect the entire Jewish community nevertheless. The worst Jews, of course, are Talmudic Jews, but 'atheistical' Jews (such as Leon Trotsky) who in some way still possess a Talmudic mentality are also dangerous. The *Talmud*, according to Keegstra, teaches the Jews to tell lies; Zionism, consequently, is a Jewish fraud. Another Jewish fraud is the holocaust, as the revisionist historians have proved. Historical revisionism was not Keegstra's personal hobby, but he certainly found it congenial. Anti-Talmudism is an old anti-Jewish theme, with its roots in the Middle Ages (Cohen, 1982), and Keegstra was familiar with at least one modern antisemitic writing of this genre, *The Talmud Unmasked* by I.B. Pranaitis (1892). Not knowing anything about Judaism, Keegstra assumed that Jews read their sacred books as orthodox Christians usually read the Bible, i.e., in a wooden, literalistic and absolutistic fashion. Hence, the relatively few anti-Christian passages in rabbinic literature were given an exaggerated significance as if they constituted the foundation of Jewish faith. Their historical context during the age of Christian power and anti-Jewish hostility (the fourth century) was also ignored. Like all antisemites, Keegstra lacked understanding of the character of rabbinic reasoning and its dialectical temper; his only reaction was one of hysteria. The *Talmud* was evil, the rabbis were evil and their spiritual descendants are also evil -- this simple conclusion obsessed his mind. Thus, as Arthur Butz declares (Butz, 1976, pp. 246-247), the reason Jews invent monstrous lies about mass murders stems directly from their Talmudic roots. The holocaust is merely the latest Jewish fabrication.

Keegstra did not take kindly to the charge of antisemitism. Antisemitism, in his view, was still another Jewish fraud: a smear word invented by Jews to obscure their conspiratorial activities (he said this in court). It is not antisemitic to tell the truth -- Keegstra's truth. The holy man in the stand, his voice ringing with sincerity, seemed to be surrounded by his own cloud of witnesses; all the Jew-haters of the Christian ages were gathered in the shadows of the Red Deer courtroom. Yet I do not think that Keegstra's antisemitism was merely the reiteration of an old fanaticism. It had some modern components as well, notably a terrible fear of even the slightest alteration in familiar symbols and mores lest the entire scheme of things crumble into ruin. At all costs, time has to be arrested in its course, for the insecure psyche can stand only so many blows, and every day spawns new wars and rumours of wars. Keegstra, the son of immigrant (Dutch) parents, and the child of both insecurity and (I believe) poverty, born in the Depression era and raised in the World War II era, puzzled and tormented by the ravages and perils that encircled his life, haunted, like so many others, by the mystery of evil, was surely in search of some form of absolute reassurance. Tragically, he found it in an extremist ideology. A perfectly sane man -- we are not dealing here with mental aberration in the clinical sense --, he nevertheless lacked the self-knowledge, critical acumen and inner wisdom that a more intelligent assessment of both his internal feelings and the external world would have required. Like Adolf Eichmann in Hannah Arendt's famous description, Keegstra, the man who prided himself on his mental originality, could not think at all; instead, his mind ran only in clichés. "Clichés, stock phrases, adherence to conventional, standardized codes of expression and conduct have the socially recognized function of protecting us against reality, that is, against the claim on our thinking attention that all events and facts make by virtue of their existence". (Arendt, 1963, p. 55) Thus he was impervious to alternative explanations regarding scripture and history, and it was useless to instruct him. Unable to engage in genuine reflection, he could only interpret the struggle between good and evil dualistically, for dualism, the religion of immaturity rather than maturity, does not necessitate thought, only belief. It also leads naturally to the demonization of one's foes. In the end, Sartre's "Knight-errant of the Good" proved a pathetic figure: a nobody who wanted to be a somebody, and who chose a foolish path to fame. In spite of everything, it was difficult not to feel sorry for him as he fell from his pedestal.

ZÜNDEL

A curious incident, one of those strange coincidences of life, illuminates Ernst Zündel's character. In the early summer of 1985, I found myself in need of minor surgery. Having arranged an appointment with a Toronto surgeon, I was waiting in his office with a few other patients when suddenly a new patient arrived: a man with an industrial hard hat on his head whose features had appeared on television and in the press regularly for the past several months (the trial had concluded only recently). The newcomer pronounced his name to the receptionist in an unnecessarily loud voice and turned with a beaming smile to the other occupants of the room, hoping for public recognition. Obviously disappointed at the lack of response, he sat down adjacent to me to wait his turn with the surgeon. Apart from observing him on one occasion in the courtroom, this was my only encounter with Ernst Zündel. I did not, of course, speak to him, but, in those few few moments, I formed an indelible impression of an arch-exhibitionist, of a man who craves the limelight and who will seek it at any cost. Is his antisemitism a pretext as well as a predilection? Such a thing is not impossible.

At any rate, Zündel is certainly a man with a mission. A non-Canadian, he nevertheless speaks of "we Canadians" (in the preface to his tract *Did Six Million Really Die*?) and, in 1968, actually had the temerity to present himself as a candidate for the leadership of the federal Liberal Party. Like Keegstra, some kind of hunger for power seems indicated, although, unlike Keegstra, he did not choose a fringe party with antisemitic propensities as the instrument of his aspirations. No liberal in either the large or the small "l" sense, Zündel, in fact, merely seized the opportunity afforded by the 1968 Liberal leadership convention (which chose Pierre Trudeau) to attract attention to himself, exactly as he later seized the same opportunity in a surgeon's waiting room. His real political philosophy is revealed in his unbounded admiration for Adolf Hitler (he is apparently the author, under a pseudonym, of a work entitled *The Hitler We Loved and Why*) and in his determination, in his last sentence of his tract, to debunk that "vast imaginary slaughter" that Jews call the holocaust, thereby removing the mark of "eternal shame" from a "great European nation". Germany, not Canada, is the object of his passions, but not democratic post-war Germany and most definitely not the 'other Germany' that resisted National Socialism -- the Germany of Bernhard Lichtenberg and Dietrich Bonhoeffer, for example. A young German who really sought the rehabilitation of Germany's honour could have chosen to place these authentic German heroes on a pedestal; Zündel, however, selected Hitler as his personal hero, and Nazi Germany as the true Germany, rather than a criminal aberration. This choice reveals his essential character.

According to Stanley R. Barrett, Zündel's personal metamorphosis began in Montreal when the young German immigrant encountered the elderly Adrien Arcand, Canada's arch-fascist during the pre-war era and Quebec's would-be Führer (Barrett, 1987, p. 158). "In distant Canada he made a German out of me", Zündel declared. Although Canadians have largely forgotten the fact, antisemitic and fascist movements flourished in Canada in the 1930s, fed by popular fears of a Bolshevik revolution as well as by the acute suffering of the Depression. Like fundamentalist Protestant Alberta, traditionalist Catholic Quebec already contained the seeds of both religious anti-Judaism and political authoritarianism; it was not difficult to cause them to germinate when the entire western social order was in a state of crisis. Arcand was a journalist with propagandistic talents who established his notoriety by writing for the fringe nationalistic press. One thing led to another, and, in 1929, he helped to found the *Ordre Patriotique des Goglus*, a superpatriotic society dedicated to the preservation of Quebec's 'Latin character', social purification and the antisemitic *achat chez nous* (buy French) movement (Betcherman, 1975, p. 7). Later, in 1934, inspired by European fascist models, Arcand founded *Le Parti National Social Chrétien* with himself as leader in order to rescue the nation from the corruptions of democracy. Swastikas and blue uniforms distinguished its meetings, together with other paramilitary paraphernalia. Needless to say, antisemitism of the most virulent description was an essential ingredient in the new party, which, while it never attracted mass support, certainly made its presence felt in Quebec (and elsewhere in Canada) until the Second World War. This was the man from whom, in his retirement years, Zündel learned what it meant to be a German. One is almost reminded of the aged Houston Stewart Chamberlain bestowing his apostolic blessing on the young Adolf Hitler!

That Zündel's antisemitism (unlike Keegstra's) has modern nationalist and racist rather than pre-modern religious roots is clear from his willingness to invoke the Aryan myth. Not only does he converse in this vein (Barrett, 1987, pp. 158-159), but his tract *Did Six Million Really Die?* contains an introduction, replete with racist language, by the British antisemite Richard E. Harwood. Zündel describes this nonentity as a "specialist" in the diplomatic and political aspects of the Second World War. The Aryan myth, of course, is the great race of the white Europeans that arose during the nineteenth century after its popularization by Arthur de Gobineau in his monumental *Essai sur l' inégalité des races humaines* (1853-55) and by other writers. It posits the existence of a primordial white race in the Himalayas from which descended the founders of every significant civilization in world history, including the ancestors of the modern Germans. As Mircea Eliade once declared, the mythical Aryan was really a kind of Adamic figure, at once the ancestral father and noble hero of the vitiated children of modernity, in whom they found renewed strength and racial purity (Eliade, 1963, p. 183). As such, he saved them from the wasteland of the modern industrial age. Anyone alienated from the present could seek renewal in the past and energy for the future by turning to the Aryan myth and its national variants (e.g., Anglo-Saxondom); although a secular and scientific construction, it served a type of spiritual purpose. Widely believed at one time, this quasi-scientific quasi-historical account of white origins was shattered by the western revulsion against Nazi racism and its evil practices during the Second World War. Today, only extremist groups (such as the American so-called 'Church of the Aryan Nations') still foster Aryan language. During his trial, even Keegstra took pains to disassociate himself from these discredited ideas, declaring that all men were made by the same Creator with the same blood, but Zündel, on the other hand, did done nothing of the kind. For him, the myth is not a myth but scientific and historical fact.

The core of Zündel's antisemitism, however, lies in the art and science of historical revisionism, a necessarily post-holocaust and post-World War II enterprise that could never have been conceived before the birth of modern propaganda and its innumerable techniques for manipulating public opinion. As Jacques Ellul has pointed out, the goal of the propagandist is to create a sham universe in which the real world disappears into a "world of hallucinations" (Ellul, 1964, p. 372); thus he gains power in society. Cleverly, the revisionists have used the suspicion of official versions of the truth that has become endemic in western nations today in order to argue that the holocaust is merely another such world of hallucinations, and that the Jews are the arch-propagandists of history. Like Keegstra, who wanted to teach his students to think for themselves instead of believing the textbooks, Zündel, on his own account, merely sought to set the record straight in his tracts; truth, and truth alone, was his subject. Do not believe the official historians; they are obviously anti-German liars. Indeed, during his trial, according to many observers, highly respected holocaust historians such as Raul Hilberg and even actual Jewish survivors called as witnesses by the crown were "grilled and belittled" in a savage fashion by the defense attorney (Weimann & Winn, 1986, p. 29); not Zündel, but the holocaust itself was placed on trial, and even the press accorded as much respect in its daily reports to the bogus experts who testified for the defense as to the distinguished individuals who testified for the prosecution. Not to believe in the holocaust was portrayed as a perfectly reasonable position; if one side could speak of "revisionists", the other side could speak of "exterminationists". Both views, it was argued, are equally viable options. Although no one can be certain, it is quite possible that Zündel, in spite of his conviction, succeeded in sowing some seeds of doubt concerning the historicity of the holocaust among the public at large. This, after all, was his intended purpose.

The propagandist who knew how to turn the tables on his victims did not have to rely on his own so-called research alone. *Did Six Million Really Die?* was based largely on the pioneer work of the late Paul Rassinier, the French revisionist who helped to inaugurate this new school of thought. In fact, by the time Zündel's basement press (Samisdat Publishers) swung into operation, the holocaust denial movement was already well established. As a consequence, the catalogue of revisionist allegations and the twisted evidence cited in their support had been drawn up and made available for further improvisation. The quality of Zündel's argument can be illustrated by a single example. (a) The memoirs of Rudolf Höss, the Nazi *Kommandant* of Auschwitz, are a communist forgery; (b) their spurious character is demonstrated by the fact that Höss is made to say that Jehovah's Witnesses at Auschwitz approved of the murder of the Jews since the latter were the enemies of Christ; (c) the Soviets are known to have disliked the Jehovah's Witnesses and to have persecuted them; (d) hence the defamation of the Jehovah's Witnesses in the Höss memoirs proves their communist authorship.

So little reflection is require to see that this series of associations proves nothing of the kind that the reader is tempted to wonder if Zündel himself really believes his own syllogisms. Perhaps he does, perhaps he does not. Paradoxically, it is possible to believe and disbelieve something at the same time. Is it all an elaborate and deliberate exercise in that complex psychological process known as self-deception? In any case, the result is similar: a nefarious attempt to reverse the judgments of history at the expense of its most tragic victims in order to assuage the wounded feelings of a German nationalist who simply cannot come to terms with his country's crimes. As Stanley Barrett has concluded, it is not the conviction that the holocaust is a hoax that caused men such as Zündel to become antisemites; it is their initial antisemitism that led them to view the holocaust as a hoax (Barrett, 1987, p. 14). Except for the Jews, the world would still regard Germany as a great nation.

Zündel, I believe, was an antisemite before he became a revisionist; in that sense, he resembles Keegstra. Was it really Arcand who made a German out of him, or is that claim merely a fabrication? With such an actor-exhibitionist it is impossible to tell, nor does it really matter. Whether traditional or modern, whether religious or secular, whether Christian or anti-Christian, antisemites, in the final analysis, are much the same. Consequently, one can speak of them in the same breath. As Sartre also noticed, in dealing with antisemitism we are dealing with a passion, not an idea.

As I write these words, Zündel's second trial is in midstream, though with considerably less public attention than three years earlier. Its outcome remains uncertain. Whether convicted or acquitted, however the defendant's fate will not end the battle with historical revisionism and its peculiar mode of antisemitic discourse, since others of his ilk are certain to take up the torch. Already, in New Brunswick, another high school teacher, Malcolm Ross, had been accused (although not yet indicted) of similar offenses to Keegstra and Zündel. Should he be brought to trial, I have no doubt that Douglas Christie will make his services available for the defense. A new strain of antisemitism has appeared, and a new generation of antisemites has been born. It would be too sanguine to expect their early demise.

CONCLUSION

Neither Keegstra nor Zündel can be described as representative of the social, religious and political climate in Canada today; they are essentially fringe figures. Yet neither is a total anomaly in Canadian society, since antisemitism has older roots in both Anglo and French Canada, and both men have been helped by this fact. On the other hand, being immigrants themselves, they also seem to have drawn much of their support from European immigrant communities already predisposed to some antisemitism, notably farmers in rural Alberta and expatriot Germans in Toronto. This became apparent at their trials. Moreover, there are certain ideological as well as psychological parallels between the two men. Both long for former ages: Keegstra for a Christian world destroyed by modernity and revolution, and Zündel for the era of Germany's power and greatness. Both, in defiance of reality, insist on restructuring life according to their own preconceived blueprints. Both, it seems to me, are profound examples of the most extreme form of wilful self-deception. Nonentities though they are, their trials merit international attention because they demonstrate vividly that antisemitism, whether of the classical or modern variety, whether religious or racial, is still alive and well in certain corners of the west, and still a menace that requires constant vigilance.

NOTE

The material on Keegstra is a condensed version of my articles "Keegstra in Red Deer", *Touchstone* (January 1987) pp. 33-39 and "The Queen versus James Keegstra", *The American Journal of Theology and Philosophy* (forthcoming).

REFERENCES

Arendt, Hannah (1963). *Eichmann in Jerusalem: A Report on the Banality of Evil*, Viking Press.

Barrett, Stanley R. (1987). *Is God a Racist: The Right Wing in Canada*, University of Toronto Press.

Bercuson, David & Wertheimer, Douglas (1985). *A Trust Betrayed: The Keegstra Affair*, McClelland-Bantam.

Betcherman, Lita-Rose (1975). *The Swastika and the Maple Leaf: Fascist Movements in Canada in the Thirties*, Fitzhenry an& Whiteside.

Butz, Arthur R. (1976). *The Hoax of the Twentieth Century*, Historical Review Press.

Cohen, Jeremy (1982). *The Friars and the Jews: The Evolution of Mediaeval Anti-Judaism*, Cornell University Press.

Eliade, Mircea (1963). *Myth and Reality* (trans. Willard R. Trask), Harper & Row.

Ellul, Jacques (1964). *The Technological Society* (trans. John Wilkinson), Vintage Books.

Palmer, Howard (1982). *Patterns of Prejudice: A History of Nativism in Alberta*, McClelland & Stewart.

Sartre, Jean-Paul (1948). *Anti-Semite and Jew* (trans. George J. Becker), Schocken Books.

Troper, Harold (1985). "The Queen v. Zündel: Holocaust Trial in Toronto". In *Congress Monthly* (July-August). 10.

Wilson, Stephen (1982). *Ideology and Experience: Antisemitism in France at the Time of the Dreyfus Affair*, Fairleigh Dickinson University Press.

ANTISEMITISM IN THE UNITED STATES 1918-1945

Leonard Dinnerstein

University of Arizona, Department of History, Tucson, Arizona 85721, USA

The United States witnessed its worst period of hostility toward Jews between the ends of World Wars I and II. Antisemitism flourished during these years and many Jews wondered whether their lives might become as tenuous as those of coreligionists in Europe. It was from the 1920s through the early 1940s that sentiments which had been in the air for centuries, and which had been clearly observed in their developing stages, crystallized into a powerful antisemitic force. While we have numerous analyses of parts of this prejudice, as well as the reaction of Jews and others to it, there is no comprehensive study of American attitudes toward Jews from 1918 to 1945.[1] This paper, therefore, will be an attempt to put the antisemitism of American society during that period into a broader perspective.

Most Americans have never liked, but have almost always accepted--to a certain extent--Jews in their midst. The nation's traditions and laws preach tolerance while people in this country have often expressed the vilest attitudes toward foreigners and minorities. Immigrants have been welcomed, but until they shed their foreign heritage they have rarely been respected. Thus Europeans who espoused any one of a number of Protestant faiths have been more quickly absorbed than those of Catholic backgrounds. Jews, until the late nineteenth century, were too few in number to cause much comment or concern except during the crisis of the Civil War.

Many Americans, often optimistic about the future, thought that in time both Catholics and Jews would recognize the superiority of Christian Protestantism and move into the mainstream by accepting the nation's major values. When this did not happen quickly enough, centuries-old views of both of these groups flared into open and periodic episodes of both anti-Catholicism and antisemitism. In terms of American history the greatest and most persistent venom was directed toward the Catholics; by the end of the nineteenth century, though, enough examples of antisemitism appeared to question whether anti-Catholicism would continue as the major anti-white prejudice.

Both anti-Catholicism and antisemitism were directed against groups of people who in time might be absorbed into white America. The same cannot be said for racial prejudice. At no time did a majority in this country ever conceive of amalgamating with blacks, Indians, or Asians. These groups were of a different color, and consequently believed to be of a lower species. Such views were almost universally accepted and as a result discriminatory legislation against them was enacted as far back as the colonial period. Not until 1967 did the United States finally outlaw miscegenation statutes.[2] To be sure, there were some voting and occupational restrictions placed upon Catholics and Jews in colonial America but most were eliminated before the end of the eighteenth century; the last was taken off the books when New Hampshire allowed Jews to vote in 1877.

Thus, while Americans had a history of legislative discrimination against racial minorities, it had far more benign official policies toward groups with a different religion. In fact, the first amendment to the Constitution, adopted in 1791, specifically enunciated the fact that "Congress shall make no law respecting an establishment of religion, or prohibiting the free exercise thereof...."

As a result of this prohibition Jews in the United States have almost always enjoyed freedom and opportunities often unavailable to them in Europe. Even during the worst years of antisemitism in America, from the 1920s through the middle of the 1940s, conditions for Jews in the United States were vastly superior to those of most of their European brethren. But American Jews, aware of their advantages, also became apprehensive that times and circumstances were changing in the United States and they feared that the freedoms and opportunities which had heretofore existed might be so curtailed as to make them vulnerable to absorption into, and/or elimination from, American society. In retrospect such suspicions seem unwarranted but to those Jews who endured life in America between the end of the first and second World Wars, no apprehensions about their future were dismissed out of hand.

America came out of World War I extremely disillusioned, feeling weakened by a variety of European influences, and determined to keep America for the Americans. Both physically and intellectually WASP (white, Anglo-Saxon Protestant) Americans wanted to separate themselves from foreign influences. Not only did they develop a strong chauvinistic nationalism, which emphasized the cult of the Anglo-Saxon and 100 percent Americanism--which they equated with Protestantism--but they worried as well about maintaining cultural hegemony in a land where increasing hordes of foreigners continued to pour in from abroad. Not only were the immigrants "taking over" the cities of the nation, but they appeared as well to be the vanguard of political revolution.[3]

Of all these newcomers, the Jews were the most hated and despised. They had apparently dominated the Bolshevik Revolution in Russia, had elected a Socialist Congressman from New York City (Morris Hillquit), and were now allegedly spreading subversive ideas in this country. According to one writer, Burton Hendrick, "the Yiddish press of New York City is extremely socialistic. The great newspapers edited by Jews, published by Jews, read by Jews, are preaching political principles whose success means the destruction of the American system of government."[4]

Such views were so commonly accepted that the publication in Henry Ford's Dearborn Independent in May, 1920 of the fabricated "Protocols of the Elders of Zion," which purportedly documented Jewish plans to take over the world, met with widespread acceptance. Ford's attacks on the "international Jew," who had alledgedly caused the Bolshevik Revolution and who was now determined to undermine other nations' political systems, appealed mostly to rural Protestant fundamentalists in the West and the South-- people who had already learned that the Jews had killed Christ, rejected His teachings, and controlled the world's finances.[5]

Throughout subsequent issues of the Dearborn Independent readers were reminded that the national "genius" was "Christian in the broadest sense." Jews, on the other hand, were immoral and devious, and advanced themselves unfairly through "racial loyalty and solidarity" which was unlike the WASPs who believed in "individual initiative." Why Henry Ford began his campaign against the Jews has never been made clear but the fact that millions of Americans accepted his rantings reflects the temper of both the people and the times.[6]

More than 100 prominent Americans, including President Woodrow Wilson and former President William Howard Taft, issued a statement in 1921 denouncing unjust prejudice and Louis Marshall, President of the American Jewish Committee, eventually won an apology and a retraction from Ford for anything that might have been misinterpreted as antisemitic. After Ford's recantation in 1927 the Dearborn Independent ceased its campaign against the "international Jew".[7] But the retraction did not have the same impact on the public as the seven years of continual charges against Jews.

The fears of radicalism and foreigners overwhelming the country were seen not only among those considered extremists (and here we may include the Ku Klux Klan) but among the nation's most respected and prominent citizens. Many of the sons of turn-of-the-century Jewish immigrants were maturing and seeking educational, economic, and social advancement in the 1920s. Major elements in the dominant society, however, regarded their presence in institutions of higher learning as an "encroachment" that should be discouraged and curtailed.

President A. Lawrence Lowell of Harvard brought this issue to national attention when he suggested in 1922 that limits be placed on the number of Jews admitted to the university. A national debate ensued in elite and intellectual circles as to the wisdom of such a position but once enunciated the idea proved compelling, and many of the most prestigious schools in America quietly adopted a "selective" admissions policy.[8]

Once again fear of being intruded upon and undermined by Jews dictated the course of action. Too many Jews had apparently moved too quickly into colleges and universities and, once accepted, overwhelmed the less studious WASP students. The Jews seemed insatiable for knowledge, drove up academic standards, and were apparently turning men's finishing schools into intellectually challenging environments. Accused of being "greasy grinds" and "drudges," the Jewish students threatened to produce a "New Jerusalem" at Harvard and other Ivy League enclaves. Students and faculty alike found a few Jews in the classroom "tolerable" but as their numbers increased so too did expressions of antipathy. They were accused both of assimilating too quickly and not fitting in at all; of not being sufficiently fervent in their ardor for sports, of lacking college spirit, of setting too high an intellectual standard, of undermining the social prestige of a school, and of not drinking and smoking like their "cultured" and "civilized" Anglo-Saxon peers. In short, the Jew was different and not wanted. As one young man explained, "Harvard should be the natural segregating place of the Anglo-Saxon [for they] founded this country and this college. The Jews tend to overrun the college, to spoil it for the native-born Anglo Saxon young persons for whom it was built and whom it really wants."[9]

The restrictive policies on admission of Jews adopted by Harvard had already been inaugurated at Columbia and New York University and would soon be incorporated by other schools as well.[10] Moreover, the students' opinions were shared, if not influenced, by their elders, siblings, and peers in every walk of life. Not only were Jews not wanted in schools, they were not seen as desirable neighbors, friends, employees, colleagues, or associates or any kind. "Socially desirable" people, or more specifically WASPs,[11] were thought to be the only ones well-bred individuals should associate with; hence during the 1920s the barriers became even more firmly erected in housing, employment, clubs, and resorts.

The decade witnessed the birth of the "restrictive covenants" in housing where owners pledged not to sell their homes to Jews and other unacceptable groups[12] and newspapers freely accepted advertisements for rentals that read "Gentiles only."[13] An essayist in <u>The Atlantic Monthly</u>, however, did not consider such activities "antisemitic." "Many Americans resent with special bitterness the intrusion of Jews into circles where they are not wanted," he wrote. "But it cannot be said too often that social discrimination is not anti-Semitism. It is rather a form of social protection." It is only aimed at Jews who challenge it, he added.[14]

Employment agencies also found that Jews were unacceptable to most employers. By 1930 estimates ran as high as 90 percent of firms that would not employ Jewish white collar workers in New York City and similar discrimination existed throughout the country. Physicians, attorneys, librarians, engineers, and would-be academics found high barriers. They knew that only tokens would be hired--and those might often be flukes.[15] These policies were particularly apparent in the 1920s and worsened in the following decade. Rabbi Stephen S. Wise of New York City acknowledged, "the only profession I know of that does not bar Jews is the rabbinical profession."[16]

Logically, people who did not want to study, live, or work with Jews would surely not want to play or socialize with them either; hence they were barred from elite college organizations, fraternities, prestigious clubs, and prominent hotels and resorts. Occasionally individuals were admitted, and in some smaller communities there were too few Jews or their dues and contributions were necessary to keep a club going, so membership was less restrictive. But the general practice throughout the nation was to keep Jews out while at the same time refusing to articulate such attitudes publicly. "The first rule of most clubs, colleges, and societies that apply 'quotas' to restrict Jews," <u>Time</u> magazine later observed, "is to deny that they would do any such thing."[17]

In contrast to the caution of private clubs, public hotels and resorts did not hesitate to make their policies known. Advertisements in The New York Times and the New York Tribune often used terms like "Gentile patronage" or "Christian patronage." Later on these phrases were changed to euphemisms like "restricted clientele" and "Resort for Discriminating Families" but they had the same meaning. Such restrictions existed in every part of the country. Arizona's Camelback Inn was as discriminatory as a Pennsylvania mountain resort which described its location as "altitude one thousand feet; too high for Jews."[18]

Given such attitudes toward Jews and most other non-white Protestants as well, it is not surprising that in the 1920s the American Congress passed the nation's most restrictive immigration laws. First in 1921; and when that proved insufficient to stem the tide of undesirable newcomers, again in 1924. Almost all Asians were barred and a quota system for Europeans, favoring people from England, Germany, and Ireland was established. Jews thought that the new laws were particularly aimed at keeping their brethren out and they were correct. One commentator who praised the immigration law probably expressed the dominant theme of the decade when he wrote: "America can yet be saved for Americans."[19]

The supposed centers of Christian morality, the Protestant churches, could not, according to historian Martin Marty, "rally widespread Protestant opposition to immigration-exclusion laws. Anti-Semitism was common, also in some of the church press." During the 1930s in the United States attention would focus on some of the more extreme and reactionary Fundamentalist Protestant ministers like William Pelley, Gerald B. Winrod, and Gerald L.K. Smith as harbingers of fascism and antisemitism, but they often articulated--albeit in demagogic form--accepted Protestant teachings.[20] Adults did not like Jews; children's textbooks in church schools emphasized the failings of Jews, and religiously oriented periodicals, from the most fundamentalist through the more liberal, reiterated the alleged sins of the Jews.[21] Christian Century, a voice for liberal Protestants, carried on a crusade throughout the 1920s and 1930s to convert Jews to Christianity. In 1934 an editorial expressed the view that "it must be clear to both Jew and Gentile that a social or racial group which sets itself with impenetrable determination to resist the normal influences of culture transfusion, and confirms its isolation by religious sanctions, is doomed to disaster."[22]

The unrelenting onslaughts against Jews in the 1920s left them dazed and at a loss as to how to respond and how best to get Christians to be more sympathetic to, and less antagonistic towards, them. A variety of tactics were attempted but none achieved success. Carefully worded statements were made to political officials against the restrictive immigration bills and the American Jewish Committee even prepared a report "to demonstrate to Congress the desirability of Jews as immigrants."[23] Henry Ford was forced to apologize for his attacks against the Jews and the Ku Klux Klan was formally denounced. Quiet negotiations were attempted with university admissions officers suggesting that quotas restrict only the "unassimilable" Jews but not those of German-American background. In 1928 Jewish organizations strongly backed the formation of a National Conference of Christians and Jews which was designed to improve good will between the groups. And most Jews were admonished by coreligionists to recognize that their public behavior reflected upon everyone of the faith. Some Jews changed their names, converted to Christianity, or simply stopped practicing the faith in which they were reared. B'nai B'rith held a conference in New York City in November, 1930, seeking ways in which to deal with the existing employment discrimination, but little came of it. None of the American Jews, however, had any inkling of how much worse conditions would get in the 1930s, and how much more intense expressions of antisemitism would become in the United States.[24]

Before we move into the 1930s, it is important to note that one cannot overemphasize the cumulative effect of the attitudes that crystallized earlier. A New York Jewish socialite, Maud Nathan, complained in 1933 that "the prejudice against Jews, of which one was not conscious fifty years ago, has become so serious that today it is a burning question and is frankly spoken of as 'The Jewish Problem.'"[25] That same year the editors of The Christian Century acknowledged

> the Christian mind has never allowed itself to feel the same human concern for Jewish sufferings that it has felt for the cruelties visited upon Armenians, the Boers, the people of India, American slaves, or the Congo blacks under the Leopold imperialism. Christian indifference to Jewish suffering has for centuries been rationalized by the terrible belief that such sufferings were the judgment of God upon the Jewish people for their rejection of Jesus. If it is God's judgment, why should Christians interfere, and why should they sympathize?[26]

More than "God's judgment," the severe economic crisis of the depression decade made people angrier and more frustrated. In their desperation to lash out at some culprit responsible for their plight they turned toward a traditional villain--the Jews. Jews have always been an available and socially acceptable target for people's woes in Christian societies and horror stories about them abound. Therefore Jews have come to fear societal crises because they are always victimized by members of the dominant culture in stressful periods. Thus it is not surprising that the literary, social, and genteel antisemitism of the 1920s not only continued but turned uglier as well. Over 100 new and specifically antisemitic organizations formed in the United States in the 1930s, including the Silver Shirts, the Friends of Democracy, and the National Union for Social Justice, to name a few.[27] A journalist observing the nature of the developing changes commented, "to paraphrase Voltaire, if there were no Jews, it would be necessary to create them in order to have a scapegoat for the desire of the masses to vent an important rage against bad times."[28]

The depression that began in 1929 and the advent of Hitler to power in 1933 were the two major factors which contributed to the greatly increased degree of antisemitic feelings in the 1930s and 1940s. In addition, Catholic antagonism toward Jews, which had been muted despite its constant presence, was channeled and more dramatically articulated before the decade ended. Even the black people, whose voices few paid attention to but whose expressions toward Jews had heretofore been mixed with envy and identification, were particularly vitriolic in their comments--a sure sign that expressions of antisemitism were acceptable in Christian America.

But it was not only the "masses" that vented their spleens against the Jews. Both the economically deprived and the financially secure expressed similar thoughts, although not always in the same language. A Mount Vernon, New York, man wrote in 1933:

> before we see this Hitler flareup end, it would not surprise me to have it reach America and have the blessing of the very men who have been damning Hitler now. Because when the Jew finally reaches that point when he will be satisfied at nothing but complete control of money, business, society, and government, well, goodbye Jew. And it is only a question of time until the ever-recurring pogrom becomes necessary....[29]

A Pennsylvania legislator declared that the Jews have all the gold and money while the Gentiles have only "the little slips of paper."[30] In her autobiography, Laura Z. Hobson recalled being at a dinner party where the discussion turned toward Hitler and Germany. One of the guests remarked:

> "The chosen people ask for it, wherever they are."
> "Oh, come on," another man said. "Some of my best friends are Jews."
> "Some of mine are, too," I heard myself saying, slowly. "Including my mother and father."[31]

The types of people with whom Hobson dined also despised the nature of President Franklin D. Roosevelt's attempts to pull the nation out of the depression. They did not like the men and women that he brought into his administration nor did they approve of his New Deal programs. The President sought talent wherever he could find it, and for the first time in American history significant numbers of Jews appeared prominently in a large number of places in the government. Moreover, he relied heavily on the advice and ideas of Felix Frankfurter, Dean of the Harvard Law School, and Supreme Court Justice Louis D. Brandeis. Within his own circle, the President was extremely close with San Rosenman, his former chief assistant while he was Governor of New York. And at different periods during his stay in the White House Ben Cohen and David Niles were also quite important to the President. Some agencies, like the Securities and Exchange Commission, and the Departments of Agriculture, Labor and the Interior, had contingents of Jews in extremely responsible positions.[32] One embittered citizen told a magazine writer, "You can't find an official in that whole place [government] who hasn't got a damned Jew lawyer sitting by him at his desk."[33]

Many of the most affluent Americans accused Jews of controlling the President and of being responsible for the administration's "Jew Deal." Antisemitic verbiage "became an obsession among the members of the country-club establishment," and "upper-class political chatter mirrored the bigotry prevalent in upper-class clubs and organizations." A well-known Jew, Governor Herbert Lehman of New York, cautiously remarked that the presence of large numbers of Jews in the administration had been "noted, especially by people in Washington, and has caused much comment which is not by any means friendly."[34]

One did not have to be either affluent or in Washington to sense the increased animosity. As one moved from city to city the sentiments apparently remained the same. A Chicago businessman with "a reputation for liberalism" indicated "the Jews are the cause of all our troubles in this country and I wish that every one of them could be deported." Many Protestant Fundamentalists in Los Angeles believed that the Jews were responsible for the depression. A Catholic priest in Akron, Ohio, claimed almost the same thing when he said, "the Jews here are at the bottom of most of our troubles and will someday suffer for it." And in St. Louis anti-Semitic slogans appeared frequently. Some of the community parks and pools even displayed signs reading: "Restricted to members and Gentiles only."[35]

Evidence of increased antisemitism throughout the country had a devastating effect on American Jewry. The incidents and expressions in the 1920s were hard enough to handle, but "leading members of the Jewish community," Fortune magazine reported in February, 1936, "men who had previously looked to the future with complete confidence--have been shocked into fear. The apprehensiveness of American Jews has become one of the important influences in the social life of our time." Fortune's concern with the rumors and accusations led it to examine tales about Jewish power in the business world. Most American Jews were themselves poor or living on the margin of poverty in the 1930s but they had to endure accusations that they controlled the banks and monopolized economic opportunity in America. The journal's lengthy analysis of those charges led to the conclusion that there was absolutely "no basis whatsoever for the suggestion that Jews monopolize U.S. business and industry." Nonetheless, those who held such beliefs refused to relinquish them.[36]

Perhaps the most surprising source for the attacks on Jews came two months after publication of the Fortune article. The liberal Protestant journal, The Christian Century, which had begun analyzing "The Jewish Problem" in the late 1920s and continued doing so well into the 1930s, published a series of pieces practically demanding conversion of the Jews to Protestantism, blaming them for their sorry predicament in the United States, and warning them, in veiled terms, of dire consequences should they refuse to comply. While continually attacking antisemitism *per se*, The Christian Century reinforced the views of respectable bigots who thought of themselves as tolerant and right-thinking.

The first of the 1936 articles appeared on April 29 and proclaimed that in a dynamic society it was difficult for two religions to be tolerant of one another. A May 13 editorial continued the onslaught:

> The Jew will never command the respect of the non-Jewish culture in which he lives so long as he huddles by himself, nursing his own 'uniqueness,' cherishing his tradition as something which is precious to *him* but in the nature of things cannot be conveyed to others, nor participated in by others.

On June 9 another editorial proclaimed:

> The simple and naked fact is that Judaism rests upon an impossible basis. It is trying to pluck the fruits of democracy without yielding itself to the processes of democracy. In a dynamic society a national culture cannot help seeking the unity of all its component elements.

Then, on July 1, came the denouement. Again denying that it possessed any antisemitic feelings, the editors of Christian Century concluded that Jews "must be brought to repentance--with all tenderness, in view of their age-long affliction, but with austere realism, in view of their sinful share in their own tragedy."[37]

Such pronouncements from one of the nation's premier and responsible Christian journals carried a great deal of weight in the United States. The Christian Century was not a radical or rabble-rousing publication; it was run by intelligent--and often liberal--individuals. Some people even considered it the mouthpiece of liberal Protestantism. Its views could not be dismissed as the rantings of the lunatic or fundamentalist fringe. And while The Christian Century did not speak for America, it did reflect, to a considerable extent, what millions of ordinary middle class Protestants thought--and for that reason its expressions represented more than just the opinions of its editors.

At about the same time that Protestant misgivings concerning the role and position of Jews in this country received so much journalistic attention Catholic hostility also became more apparent. The depression did not bring on Catholic antisemitism but it, along with major world events, exacerbated existing prejudices and together they led to the most vituperative expressions of antipathy.

Catholics and Jews differed on a wide variety of issues both domestic and international. Catholics generally favored, and Jews opposed, state aid to parochial schools, religious instruction in public schools, censorship, and bans against divorce, birth control, and abortion.[38] In politics, Irish Catholics worked against, and Jews worked for, the election of Fiorello La Guardia as Mayor of New York City in 1933.[39] Nationally both groups backed the New Deal but as it turned to the left Catholics generally distanced themselves from Roosevelt while Jews embraced him. Catholics in general, and the church in particular, favored order, authority, and conservatism. Some of the more liberal Jews valued intellectual exploration, socialism, and even communism. Internationally American Catholics opposed the government's recognition of the Soviet Union[40] and the Catholic Church found little to criticize in Hitler's policies; many Jews, on the other hand, saw Hitler as the devil and thought that Stalin would lead the world to a socialist nirvana. Thus, the seeds of discord, animosity, and misunderstanding were well placed in a variety of areas. Combined with the garden variety of antisemitism derived from Christian teachings and economic myths, the potential for explosive incidents was never far beneath the surface. And then came the Spanish Civil War which one student proclaimed

> aroused more animosity between Catholics on the one hand and liberals and Jews on the other than did any other single issue. Pro-Franco Catholics and pro-Loyalist Jews tended to see the opposite cause as a basic threat to their own institutions and way of life, and to overlook the defects of those whom they supported.[41]

In July, 1936 a military coup, led by General Francisco Franco, attempted to overthrow the popularly elected, left-wing, Spanish government. The fracas turned into a civil war with the Soviet Union aiding the established government and the Catholic Church, along with Nazi Germany and fascist Italy, backing the rebels. The Spanish Civil War drew world-wide attention. To Catholics in the United States who supported Franco it seemed quite clear that the front ranks of the anti-Franco movement were "dominated by Jews."[42] Whether this was true or not is unclear but there can be no doubt that most American Jews, including those extremely visible among the anti-Franco forces, stood with the existing Popular Front government in Spain.

The war capitulated Catholic-Jewish animosities into the open with Catholic periodicals and priests most forceful in expressing their views. Two of the leading diocesan newspapers, The Boston Pilot and The Brooklyn Tablet "loaded the dice in advance...against every Catholic who opposed Hitler and Mussolini, queried the virtues of Franco or supported the New Deal." Catholics were advised to read only their own publications and shun those published or dominated by Jews. One critic also indicated that the handful of Catholic journals which tried to give some perspective to the Franco-Loyalist conflict "--the Commonweal, the New World, the Catholic Worker--were doomed to failure from the start. There is no parallel in all our history for the rabid abuse they brought down on themselves."[43]

By 1938, therefore, spokesmen for the Catholic hierarchy in the United States either articulated the party line or remained silent. One priest, Father Charles Coughlin, had already established a reputation as a national critic of malevolent and predatory economic forces. In 1935 he complained about "the Tugwells, the Frankfurters and the rest of the Jews who surrounded" the President, and in 1938 sharply turned his criticism against the Jews. The July, 1938, issue of his publication, Social Justice, reprinted the fraudulent "Protocols of the Elders of Zion." In a November radio address he then launched what historian David H. Bennett characterized as

> a slashing, full-scale, anti-Semitic crusade, accusing the Jews not only of devising Communism but also of imposing it on Russia, and excusing Nazism as an understandable effort to block the Jewish-Communist plan for subjugating Germany.[44]

Coughlin's speech came less than two weeks after the brutality of German assaults upon Jews on Kristallnacht shocked the civilized world. Nonetheless when Commonweal, a liberal Catholic journal, attacked Coughlin and criticized his attitudes, the Reverend Francis Borgia Steck, O.F.M., wrote to the magazine to point out that the views Coughlin uttered were

> no more anti-Semitic than what Archbishop Mitty told us over the radio on November 16 and what Monsignor Fulton Sheen said in his sermon at the recent Pan American Mass here in Washington. With these two dignitaries of the Church Father Coughlin is in mighty good company.[45]

Although the thoughts Coughlin and other Catholics expressed were not completely new, public reaction to them was explosive. Coughlin struck a responsive chord among those frustrated by the enduring depression and the failure of Roosevelt to really turn the economy around. In a number of American cities where Irish Catholics, the backbone of the Church, and Jews lived next to one another conflicts had often arisen in the past but they intensified after the radio priest began his antisemitic crusade.[46]

Not only were Catholics aroused by Coughlin but his remarks reinforced antisemitic beliefs throughout the United States. Time magazine, in May, 1939, ventured to say what most respectable voices preferred to avoid.

> That talk about anti-Semitism has grown like a weed in the U.S. during the last decade is a fact that no well-informed U.S. citizen can truthfully deny. Yet the U.S. press has for the most part studiously, purposefully, and almost universally ignored the subject. Though some segments of the press itself are not altogether free from anti-Semitic bias, its attitude in general has been a reflection of the belief of many influential Jews that to recognize anti-Semitism is to encourage it.[47]

In June that year historian Henry Pratt Fairchild observed that in the United States "some degree of hostility or dislike of Jews in general is very widespread, even among the most broad-minded and kindly disposed of his associates." The Catholic Interracial Review noted in July that "the rapid spread of anti-Semitism has caused well-justified concern." Diary entries of David Lilienthal, of the Tennessee Valley Authority, in July and again in December, 1939, indicated that antisemitism "is more in evidence now than for a long time." In November, a New England Episcopalian wrote that he had lived "over forty years in a country where 'something would have to be done about the Jews.' I've been surrounded by and part of a passive anti-Semitic multitude of Christians." But there had been "no concerted effort. No active desire to do something." But in 1939, he emphasized, there were leaders. There were active and organized efforts to do something about the Jews and it frightened him.[48]

As anguished as the New England minister was, it did not compare with the fears and anxieties of American Jews who desperately tried to reverse what appeared to be the continual and unrelenting growth of antisemitism in the United States. A 1940 Congress Bulletin article noted that "at no time in American history has anti-Semitism been as strong as it is today."[49] To be sure, American animosity did not compare in severity with what was happening to Jews in Europe but American Jews did not know what calamity might next occur in the United States. Community leaders admonished one another and fellow Jews to remain circumspect in their public behavior, to draw no attention to themselves as Jews, and to disassociate themselves from any group considered foreign to American society.[50] "Conservative Jews," a 1938 article in The Nation indicated

> faced with the insanity of anti-Semitism, are tempted to abandon rationality themselves and accept as their own criteria of behavior the prejudices that operate against them. A radical Jewish labor leader or public official is looked upon not merely as a wrong-headed fellow but as a menace to the race; a Jew who militantly espouses even the cause of free speech is considered a person of dubious judgment.[51]

Jewish defense agencies were formed in many American cities. The American Jewish Committee's executive committee seriously discussed how they might combat the widespread whispering campaign that there was a Jewish-communist plot to overthrow the government. Jews themselves, at a loss for appropriate explanations, attributed the source of antisemitism to the new Jewish immigrants coming into the country, they wished that the migration would cease.[52]

Public opinion polls came into vogue toward the end of the 1930s and their surveys also measured an increase in American antisemitism which continued rising during World War II. Whereas 36 percent of those polled in May, 1938, thought Jews had too much power in the United States, by 1945 58 percent held such beliefs. And when asked which groups menaced this country the most during World War II, Jews ranked third behind our official enemies, the Germans and the Japanese, in 1942, but first, well ahead of these other groups, by June 1944, almost a full year before the war ended in Europe. A poll taken in November, 1942, asked American high school students which of the following groups, if any, would be their last choice as a roommate. The percentages of their responses were:

Swedes	5%
Protestants	4%
Negroes	78%
Catholics	9%
Jews	45%

Irish	3%
Chinese	9%
Makes no difference	5%
Don't Know	3%

That same month Fortune asked factory workers: "Which of the following groups would you least like to see move into your neighborhood?" They answered:

Swedes	3%
Protestants	2%
Negroes	72%
Catholics	4%
Jews	42%
Irish	2%
Chinese	28%
Makes no difference	13%
Don't Know	5%[53]

Wartime criticism of Jews also questioned their patriotic fervor. As far back as the Civil War Jews were accused, in both north and south, of being unpatriotic slackers, draft-dodgers, and profiteers. Such charges reemerged during World War I and surfaced again in World War II.[54] While the United States was fighting the Nazis, a professor at New York's City College reportedly told a colleague, "The Battle Hymn of the Jews is 'Onward, Christian soldiers, we'll make the uniforms.'"[55] And throughout the country an oft-told anecdote had it that

> The first American soldier to kill a Jap was Michael Murphy.
> The first American bomber to sink a battleship was Captain Colin Kelly.
> The first American to prove the effectiveness of a torpedo was Captain John Bulkley.
> The first American flier to bag a Jap plane was John O'Hare.
> The first American Coast Guard to detect a German spy was Ensign John Cullen.
> The first American to be decorated by the President of the United States for bravery was Lieutenant Patrick Powers.
> The first American to get new tires was Abe Cohen.

The names of the individuals in the numerous versions of the ditty changed as did the specific attributes but the heroes were always called O'Shaugnessy or McGuire or Flannegan or something similarly Irish while the first one to get a set of new tires or a defense contract would always be a Finkelstien, Goldstein, Lipshitz, or some other obviously Jewish person.[56] Soldiers and others who consorted with the military also acknowledged this widespread animosity toward the Jews.[57] That such impressions prevailed among millions in the United States is attested to in a January 1945 Christian Century editorial:

> No single factor has done more to render insecure the position of the modern Jew than the charge that he is not completely, wholeheartedly, first, last, and all the time a citizen of the country in which he resides, but that he attempts to hold a dual citizenship which in actuality works out to be a divided loyalty, with his primary loyalty given to an allegiance other than the land in which he lives.[58]

It is not surprising, therefore, that American Jews, battered for more than a generation by escalating indications of hostility toward them, were psychologically downtrodden and forlorn. One of them wrote in January 1945:

> Anti-Semitism has not yet become a national menace to the United States. It is only at the stage where it is a personal tragedy that humiliates, frightens, and embitters individuals. It is obviously beyond the capabilities of the minority of Jews--the group against whom it is directed--to stop the progress of anti-Semitism here. They are too weak and too few. The greater part of the task of up-rooting anti-Semitism must be done--if at all--by the Gentile majority with the Jewish minority cooperating.[59]

In recent decades it has become fashionable to criticize President Franklin D. Roosevelt for what he did not do to help save the Jews of Europe from Hitler's ovens. Even Jewish leaders in the United States have been excoriated for not having exerted as much pressure as they might have to force American officials to take more vigorous action in regard to rescue. Some of those people who have reexamined American policies have concluded, as David Wyman has written, that "Roosevelt's indifference to so momentous an historical event as the systematic annihilation of European Jewry emerges as the worst failure of his Presidency." And a number of Jews of the United States, another individual pointed out, "were emotionally and ideologically so absorbed with their internecine struggles, rivalries, and efforts to achieve hegemony in the Jewish community that the perception of the urgency of the rescue was, if not ignored, at least generally diminished."[60]

Yet when one recalls the experiences of American Jews in the United States in the period between 1918 and 1945 the question must also be asked, "what could they have done?" No one has yet explained how even if that effort had been made, how one moves a hostile people to embrace a cause or force a powerful President to ignore overwhelming public sentiment in an attempt to save the lives of people about whom most of the nation was at best totally indifferent, and at worst, quite antagonistic. "The plain truth," historian David Wyman has written,

> is that many Americans were prejudiced against Jews and were unlikely to support measures to help them. Antisemitism had been a significant determinant of America's ungenerous response to the refugee plight before Pearl Harbor. During the war years, it became an important factor in the nation's reaction to the Holocaust.[61]

Unfortunately, many of those who have seen how effective American Jewry has been in articulating its concerns to politicians on every level since the end of World War II, and how successful Jews and Jewish organizations have been in influencing legislators and the courts during the past forty years, assume that Jews in this country have always been among the more important lobbyists. But that is simply untrue. Before 1945 there was almost no Jewish influence at any level of government, and Jews who did have the ear of important politicos were often loathe to discuss issues of Jewish concern. Ironically, during those years when Jews had the least influence, they were widely perceived to be enormously powerful, and in the period when they have had the greatest impact upon the course of national and international affairs, the general public has been almost oblivious to their activities.

American Jews did become politically influential after World War II and antisemitism subsided considerably after the war, and again in the 1960s. It has not disappeared, of course, but the most blatant kinds of bigotry are no longer publicly acceptable. Conditions for Jews in the United States are thus far better than they were during the interwar period. But a discussion of the changes requires still another article.[62]

SOURCES

1. One exception is Leo P. Ribuffo, The Old Christian Right: The Protestant Far Right From The Great Depression To The Cold War (Philadelphia: Temple University Press, 1983).
2. Loving v. Virginia, 388 U.S. 1 (1967).
3. Ribuffo, The Old Christian Right, pp. 5, 9, 12; John Higham, Strangers in the Land (New Brunswick: Rutgers University Press, 1955), p. 271; David O. Levine, The American College and the Culture of Aspiration, 1915-1940 (Ithaca: Cornell University Press, 1986), pp. 147-148; W. Gunther Plaut, The Jews In Minnesota (New York: American Jewish Historical Society, 1959), p. 279.
4. Higham, Strangers in the Land, p. 278; Max Vorspan and Lloyd P. Gartner, History of the Jews of Los Angeles (Philadelphia: The Jewish Publication Society of America, 1970), p. 144; "American Jews in The Bolshevik Oligarchy," Literary Digest, 60 (March 1, 1919), 32; Burton S. Hendrick, "The Jews in America," World's Work, 45 (1923), 594, 597.
5. Higham, Strangers in the Land, p. 285; Ribuffo, The Old Christian Right, p. 10; Ribuffo, "Henry Ford and The International Jew," American Jewish History, 69 (June, 1980), 437.
6. Ribuffo, "Henry Ford," pp. 453, 470; Johan J. Smertenko, "The Jew: A Problem for America," The Outlook, 152 (August 7, 1929), 599.
7. "Anti-Jewish Propaganda," The Outlook, 127 (January 26, 1921), 125; Heywood Broun and George Britt, Christians Only (New York: The Vanguard Press, 1931), p. 42.
8. Broun and Britt, Christians Only, pp. 89-90; Morton Rosenstock, "Are There Too Many Jews at Harvard?" in Leonard Dinnerstein, ed., Antisemitism In The United States (New York: Holt, Rinehart & Winston, 1971), pp. 102-108.
9. Laura Z. Hobson, Laura Z: A Life (New York: Arbor House, 1983), p. 357; William T. Ham, "Harvard Student Opinion on the Jewish Question," The Nation, 115 (September 6, 1922), 225; "The Jew in America: a Jewish University?" The Nation, 116 (May 16, 1923), 573; Harold A. Woodruff, "Jews Go To College," Harper's Magazine, 163 (September, 1930), 424-25; Levine, The American College, pp. 146, 150, 156.
10. Dan A. Oren, Joining The Club: A History of Jews and Yale (New Haven: Yale University Press, 1985), chapter 3; Higham, Strangers in the Land, p. 278; Marcia Graham Synnott, "Anti-Semitism and American Universities: Did Quotas Follow the Jews?" in David A.

Gerber, ed., Anti-Semitism in American History (Urbana: University of Illinois Press, 1986), 233 ff.; Harold S. Wechsler, The Qualified Student (New York: John Wiley and Sons, 1977), p. 35; Rebecca Grecht, "Anti-Semitism at Barnard," The Nation, 115 (October 4, 1922), 337; Broun and Britt, Christians Only, pp. 112-113; W.E.B. DuBois, "Opinion," The Crisis, 24 (August, 1922), 142; L.B. Rose, "Secret Life of Sarah Lawrence," Commentary, 75 (May, 1983), 54; American Jewish Committee, "Minutes of the Executive Commit tee," V, part 2, pp. 1608-1609, cited hereafter as AJC Minutes; Levine, The American College, p. 149.

11. Levine, The American College, p. 146.
12. Vorspan and Gartner, History of the Jews of Los Angeles, p. 205; Elaine H. Maas, "The Jews of Houston: An Ethnographic Study" (unpublished Ph.D., Department of Sociology, Rice University, 1973), p. 58; Robert Kotlowitz, "Baltimore Boy," Harper's Magazine, 231 (December, 1965), 62.
13. AJC Minutes, V (1929-1932) 1539-40; Vorspan and Gartner, History of the Jews of Los Angeles, p. 205; Allen duPont Breck, The Centennial History of the Jews of Colorado, 1859-1959 (Denver: The Hirschfield Press, 1960), p. 198; Kenneth L. Kusmer, A Ghetto Takes Shape: Black Cleveland, 1870-1930 (Urbana: University of Illinois Press, 1976), p. 170n.
14. Ralph P. Boas, "Jew-Baiting in America," Atlantic Monthly, CXXVII (May, 1921), 662.
15. Henry L. Feingold, Zion In America (New York: Twayne Publishers, Inc., 1974), 266; Broun and Britt, Christians Only, pp. 165, 232; Vorspan and Gartner, History of the Jews of Los Angeles, p. 206; Daniel J. Kevles, The Physicists (New York: Alfred A. Knopf, 1978), p. 211; L.S. Feuer, "Stages in the Social History of Jewish Professors in American Colleges and Universities," American Jewish History, 71 (June, 1982), 455, 460; Elinor Grumet, "Elliot Cohen: The Vocation of a Jewish Literary Mentor," in Studies in the American Jewish Experience, edited by Jacob R. Marcus and Abraham J. Peck (Cincinnati: American Jewish Archives, 1981), pp. 11-12; Sidney Hook, "Anti-Semitism in the Academy: Some Pages of the Past," Midstream, 25 (January, 1979), 49; Murray Friedman, Jewish Life in Philadelphia, 1830-1940 (Philadelphia: ISHI Publications, 1983), p. 18; Helga Eugenie Kaplan, "Century of Adjustment: A History of the Akron Jewish Community" (unpublished dissertation, Department of History, Kent State University, 1978), pp. 435-436; Samuel B. Hand, Counsel and Advise: A Political Biography of Samuel I. Rosenman (New York: Garland, 1979), p. 233; AJC Minutes, V (February 10, 1924), 1125-1126; Michael E. Parrish, Felix Frankfurter And His Times: The Reform Years (New York: The Free Press, 1982), p. 157; Lloyd P. Gartner, "Assimilation and American Jews," in Bela Vago, ed., Jewish Assimilation in Modern Times (Boulder, Colorado: Westview Press, 1981), p. 179; Michael Gerald Rapp, "An Historical Overview of Anti-Semitism In Minnesota, 1920-1960 -- With Particular Emphasis on Minneapolis and St. Paul" (unpublished doctoral dissertation, Department of History, University of Minnesota, 1977), p. 24; Jerold S. Auerbach, "From Rags to Robes: The Legal Profession, Social Mobility and the American Jewish Experience," American Jewish Historical Quarterly, 66 (December, 1966), 251; Jacob Rader Marcus, "Zionism and the American Jew," American Scholar, 2 (1933), 287.
16. Broun and Britt, Christians Only, p. 125.
17. E. Digby Baltzell, The Protestant Establishment (New York: Random House, 1964), pp. 237-238; Marc Lee Raphael, Jews and Judaism In A Midwestern Community: Columbus, Ohio, 1840-1975 (Columbus: Ohio Historical Society, 1979), p. 236; Judith E. Endelman, The Jewish Community of Indianapolis: 1849 to the Present (Bloomington: Indiana University Press, 1984), p. 172; Ida Libert Uchill, Pioneers, Peddlers, and Tsadikim (Denver: Sage Books, 1957), pp. 162-163; Rapp, "Anti-Semitism in Minnesota," p. 29; Amy Hill Siewers, "Judaism in the Heartland: The Jewish Community of Marietta, Ohio (1895-1940)," The Great Lakes Review, 5 (Winter, 1979), 31; Dwight W. Hoover, "To be a Jew in Middletown: A Muncie Oral History Project," Indiana Magazine of History, 81 (1985), 151; Vorspan and Gartner, History of the Jews of Los Angeles, pp. 144, 205; John Cooney, The Annenbergs (New York: Simon and Schuster, 1982), p. 185; Robert A. Rockaway, "Anti-Semitism in an American City: Detroit: 1850-1914," American Jewish Historical Quarterly, 64 (September, 1974), 50-51; "Sense or Nonsense?" Time, 46 (August 20, 1945), 92.
18. Jeffrey Gurock, "The 1913 New York State Civil Rights Act," AJS Review, 1 (1976), 111; Rapp, "Anti-semitism in Minnesota," p. 187; Blaine Peterson Lamb, "Jewish Pioneers In Arizona, 1850-1920" (unpublished dissertation, Department of History, Arizona State University, 1982), pp. 268-269; Broun and Britt, Christians Only, p. 251.
19. Hendrick, "The Jews in America," p. 377; Roy L. Garis, "How the New Immigration Law Works," Scribner's, 76 (August, 1924), 188.

20. Ribuffo, The Old Christian Right, pp. 104, 228; William G. McLoughlin, Jr., Modern Revivalism: Charles Grandison Finney to Billy Graham (New York: The Ronald Press, 1959), pp. 471-72.
21. "Jews and the Crucifixion," The Christian Century, 45 (February 2, 1928), 136; Philip Bernstein, letter to the editor, The Commonweal, 14 (June 17, 1931), 187-188.
22. "The Jewish Problem," The Christian Century, 51 (February 28, 1934), 281; see also "The Modern Jew and Christianity," The Christian Century, 44 (June 23, 1927), 780; Nicholos C. Polos, "Black Anti-Semitism in Twentieth Century America: Historical Myth or Reality?" American Jewish Archives, 27 (1975), 8-31; J. Theodore Hefley, "Freedom Upheld: The Civil Liberties Stance of The Christian Century Between the Wars," Church History, 37 (1968), 189; Philip S. Bernstein, "Unchristian Christianity and the Jew," Harper's Magazine, 162 (May, 1931), 660; Everett R. Clinchy, "The Borderland of Prejudice," The Christian Century, 47 (May 14, 1930), 623, 624; "Jews and Jesus," The Christian Century, 50 (May 3, 1933), 584; "The Tragedy In The Romance," The Christian Century, 50 (July 19, 1933), 924-925; Albert Levitan, "Leave The Jewish Problem," The Christian Century, 51 (April 25, 1934), 555; "The Jewish Problem," The Christian Century, 53 (June 10, 1936), 846; Ribuffo, The Old Christian Right, p. 275.
23. AJC Minutes, IV (December 12, 1920), 929.
24. AJC Minutes, IV, 929; V, 1626; Anson Phelps Stokes, Church and State in the United States (3 volumes; New York: Harper & Bros., 1950), II, 462; Endelman, The Jewish Community of Indianapolis, pp. 173 ff.; Levine, The American College, pp. 154 ff.
25. Maud Nathan, Once Upon A Times And Today (New York: G.P. Putnam's Sons, 1933), p. 275.
26. "Jews and Jesus," The Christian Century, 50 (May 3, 1933), 582.
27. Norton Belth, "Problems of Anti-Semitism in the United States," Contemporary Jewish Record, 2 (May-June, 1939), 9.
28. Johan J. Smertenko, "Hitlerism Comes to America," Harper's Magazine, 167 (November, 1933), 662.
29. Richard F. Nelson, "Nothing Will Save Us But A 'Pogrom!'" The Christian Century, 50 (June 28, 1933), 850.
30. AJC Minutes, VI, 178.
31. Hobson, Laura Z, p. 115.
32. W.M. Kiplinger, "The Facts About Jews in Washington," Reader's Digest, 41 (September, 1942), 3; The New Dealers by Unofficial Observer (New York: The Literary Guild, 1934), p. 322.
33. Albert Jay Nock, "The Jewish Problem in America, II," The Atlantic Monthly, 168 (July, 1941), 74; see also Auerbach, "From Rags to Robes," p. 266 and Leonard Dinnerstein, Uneasy At Home (New York: Columbia University Press, 1987), pp. 60 ff.
34. Myron Israel Scholnick, "The New Deal and Anti-Semitism In America" (unpublished dissertation, Department of History, University of Maryland, 1971), pp. 76-77; Zosa Szajkowski, "The Attitude of American Jews to Refugees from Germany in the 1930's," American Jewish Historical Quarterly, 61 (December, 1971), 106.
35. "Anti-Semitism Is Here," The Nation, 147 (August 25, 1938), 167; Vorspan and Gartner, History of the Jews of Los Angeles, p. 206; Alfred Winslow Jones, Life, Liberty, and Property (Philadelphia: J.B. Lippincott Co., 1941), p. 216; Burton Alan Boxerman, "Reaction of the St. Louis Jewish Community To Anti-Semitism, 1933-1945: (unpublished dissertation, Department of History, St. Louis University, 1967), pp. 257-258.
36. "Jews in America," Fortune Magazine, February, 1936, reprinted in Leonard Dinnerstein and Frederick Cople Jaher, eds., The Aliens (New York: Appleton-Century-Crofts, 1970), pp. 230, 234, 236.
37. "The Jewish Problem," The Christian Century, 53 (April 29, 1936), 625; "Jews, Christians and Democracy," ibid., 53 (May 13, 1936), 697; "Jews and Democracy," ibid., 54 (June 9, 1937), 734-736; "Tolerance Is Not Enough!" ibid., 53 (July 1, 1936), 928.
38. Lloyd P. Gartner, History of the Jews of Cleveland (Cleveland: Western Reserve Historical Society, 1978), p. 300; Edward C. McCarthy, "The Christian Front Movement in New York City, 1938-1940" (unpublished M.A. thesis, Department of History, Columbia University, 1965), p. 171.
39. McCarthy, "The Christian Front," p. 177; Ronald Bayor, Neighbors in Conflict (Baltimore: The Johns Hopkins Press, 1978), passim.
40. McCarthy, "The Christian Front," p. 161; Robert Dallek, Franklin D. Roosevelt and American Foreign Policy, 1932-1945 (New York: Oxford University Press, 1979), p. 79.
41. McCarthy, "The Christian Front," p. 161.
42. J. David Valaik, "In The Days Before Ecumenism," Journal of Church and State, 13 (Autumn, 1971), 473.
43. George N. Shuster, "The Conflict Among Catholics," American Scholar, 10 (Winter, 1940-1941), 11, 13; Valaik, "In The Days...," pp. 468, 470; Time, 31 (June 13, 1938), 55.

44. Michael R. Beschloss, Kennedy and Roosevelt (New York: W.W. Norton & Co., 1980), p. 120; David H. Bennett, Demagogues in the Depression (New Brunswick: Rutgers University Press, 1969), p. 279.
45. Rev. Francis Borgia Steck, O.F.M., "Father Coughlin and the Jews," The Commonweal, 29 (December 30, 1938), 269.
46. Dinnerstein, Uneasy At Home, pp. 149-177; The New Republic, 95 (May 25, 1938), 66-67; Frederick M. Thrasher, The Gang: A Study of 1,313 Gangs in Chicago (abridged edition; University of Chicago Press, 1963), pp. 149-150; McCarthy, "The Christian Front," p. 170; Judd P. Teller, Strangers and Natives (New York: Delacorte Press, 1968), p. 38; Samuel G. Friedman, "From Neil Simon: A New Film, a New Play," The New York Times, March 24, 1985, II, 31; Carolyn F. Ware, Greenwich Village, 1920-1930 (Boston: Houghton Mifflin Co., 1935), p. 140; Paul S. Holbo, "Wheat or What? Populism and American Fascism," Western Political Quarterly, 14 (September, 1961), 735; Wallace Stegner, "Who Persecutes Boston?" The Atlantic Monthly, 174 (July, 1944), 48 ff.
47. "Hush-Hush Ends," Time, 33 (May 8, 1939), 52.
48. Henry Pratt Fairchild, "New Burdens For America," The Forum, 101 (June, 1939), 317; "The American Pattern For Anti-Semitism," Interracial Review, July, 1939, p. 99; The Journals of David E. Lilienthal, The TVA Years, 1939-1945 (New York: Harper and Row, 1964), pp. 116, 148; "The Shadow of Anti-Semitism," The American Magazine, 128 (November, 1939), 92.
49. Quoted in David Brody, "American Jewry, The Refugees and Immigration Restriction (1932-1942)," in Abraham J. Karp, ed., The Jewish Experience in America (5 volumes; Waltham, MA: American Jewish Historical Society, 1969), V, 336.
50. Ibid., p. 344.
51. "Anti-Semitism Is Here," p. 168.
52. AJC Minutes, VII, 128; Brody, "American Jewry...," p. 339.
53. Charles C. Stember, Jews In The Mind of America (New York: Basic Books, 1966), pp. 121, 128; Michael R. Marrus, The Holocaust In History (Hanover, NH: University Press of New England, 1987), p. 162; Public Opinion, 1935-1946, under the editorial direction of Hadley Cantril (Princeton: Princeton University Press, 1951), p. 477.
54. Bertram W. Korn, American Jewry and the Civil War (Philadelphia: Jewish Publication Society of America, 1951); Gordon W. Allport and Leo Postman, The Psychology of Rumor (New York: Henry Holt & Co., 1947), p. 11; Harry W. Flannery, "The Secret Enemy at San Francisco," Free World, 10 (July, 1945), 56; Selden Menefee, Assignment: U.S.A. (New York: Reynal and Hitchcock, Inc., 1943), p. 14; "The New Wave of Anti-Semitism," New Currents (June, 1943), 3; Aaron Goldman, "The Resurgence of Antisemitism in Britain During World War II," Jewish Social Studies, 46 (Winter, 1984), 41.
55. Morris Freedman, "The Knickerbocker Case," Commentary, 8 (August, 1949), 122.
56. PM (New York City), June 17, 1945, p. 20; Selden C. Menefee, "What Americans Think," The Nation, 156 (May 5, 1943), 763; Menefee, Assignment U.S.A., p. 102.
57. Walter White, A Man Called White: The Autobiography of Walter White (New York: Viking Press, 1948), p. 246; Studs Terkell, "The Good War" (New York: Ballantine, 1985), p. 20; Flannery, "The Secret Enemy," p. 57; Friedman, "From Neil Simon," p. 31.
58. "Have Jews a Jewish Citizenship?" The Christian Century, 62 (January 3, 1945), 5.
59. David L. Cohn, "What Can The Jews Do?" Saturday Review of Literature, 28 (January 27, 1945), 9.
60. David S. Wyman, The Abandonment of the Jews (New York: Pantheon Books, 1984), p. xi; The New York Times, March 21, 1984, p. B4; Leonard Dinnerstein, "What Should American Jews Have Done to Rescue Their European Brethren?" in Simon Wiesenthal Center Annual, 3 (1986), 278-279.
61. Wyman, The Abandonment of the Jews, p. 9.
62. See Dinnerstein, Uneasy At Home, pp. 178-196.

JAMES PARKES: A MODEL FOR CHRISTIANS IN THE TIME AFTER THE HOLOCAUST

ROBERT ANDREW EVERETT

Chaplain, Fairleigh Dickinson University, Teaneck, New Jersey and Pastor, Emanuel United Church of Christ, Irvington, New Jersey, 2218 Stecher Avenue, Union, New Jersey 07083

James Parkes was born in Guernsey in 1896. Following his service in the British Army during World War I, he entered Hertford College, Oxford University, and studied theology under H.D.A. Major and Cyril Emmet, both noted theologians in the Modernist movement of the Anglican Church. The influence of the Modernist movement on Parkes is a key to understanding his work because it enabled him to approach Christianity with a critical eye, and it allowed him freely to question traditional teachings which did not account for historical facts. The Modernists stressed truth as a criterion for any theological statement, and when Parkes discovered that Judaism was not the dead, arid, legalistic religion about which he had been taught, even at Oxford, he had to respond with a plea for a new Christian theological position concerning Judaism.

After Oxford, Parkes was ordained in the Anglican Church, thanks to the help of William Temple, and he began to work in such ecumenical organizations as the Student Christian Movement, the World Christian Student Federation, and the International Student Service. In 1929, James Parkes was asked by the International Student Service to devote his time and energy to the Jewish Question. Antisemitic riots were taking place in many European universities and the Nazi party and other anti-Jewish organizations were growing in political strength in Germany, Austria, and Poland. In his work at the I.S.S., Parkes had already encountered the antisemitic sentiment on the university campus, and he arranged for a conference to take place in France on that very issue. He accepted the assignment to do research and writing on the question, and the result of his work was the publication of his book, The Jew and His Neighbour, in June of 1930. From that date on until his death in 1981, Parkes devoted a major part of his life to the study of antisemitism and the problem of Jewish-Christian relations.

Parkes was a pioneer in this field, and for many years his was often a lonely, prophetic voice. As he wrote in his autobiography, "I learned very early that to evolve a new attitude to Jewish-Christian relations was to be a lonely job". Today a growing number of Christians have begun to re-think Christianity's traditional position on Judiasm and the Jewish people, and most of them point to the Holocaust and the establishment of the State of Israel as important factors in their thinking. The pioneering aspects of Parkes' work can be shown by the fact that he was writing about the Christian roots of antisemitism and the roots of a Jewish State years before the Holocaust and the creation of the State of Israel. In addition, he saw the profound theological implications of changing Christian attitudes towards Jews, and he began to write about the need for a new theology which accepted the validity of both Christianity and Judaism. The subjects about which

Parkes wrote have not been of primary interest to most Christians, and his work has not received the kind of attention it deserves. But as more Christians involve themselves in the area of Jewish-Christian relations, Parkes' work will take on added significance.

As Christians become more conscious of the Holocaust, the roots of antisemitism in Christian teachings and the role it played in developing the historical context in which the Holocaust could take place have come under close scrutiny from Protestant and Catholic scholars. Difficult problems arise for the Christian who realizes that the Church must rethink some basic theological positions if there is to be any success in removing antisemitism from the Christian mind. The shrewd observers have seen that the Church cannot simply condemn antisemitism as an evil without also correcting those traditional teachings of the Church which have contributed to anti-Jewish thinking. It is easy to condemn something as evil as antisemitism, but it is much more difficult to admit complicity in the problem and to begin the process of eliminating antisemitism from one's own teachings. Failure to do otherwise, however, presents the Church with morally untenable situation of condemning something which it helps to perpetuate by its own teachings. It could also be charged that if the Church fails to correct those teachings which have contributed to antisemitism in the past it provides, in effect, a post-Holocaust justification for the murderers who systematically set about killing six million Jews between 1933 and 1945. Even if the Church does go about its proper task of correcting its anti-Jewish teachings, it still must face up to the charge that it helped to contribute to the fate of the Jews in the Holocaust. One Protestant spokesman who has taken a strong stance against antisemitism in the Church is A. Roy Eckardt, and he has asked, "Could there be a more damning judgment upon the Church of our century than this one--that not until after the day of Auschwitz did Christians see fit to fabricate a correction of the record?"[1]

To many Jews and Christians, Auschwitz, the symbol of the Holocaust, is an historical event which effects the way we read both the past and the future. Franklin Littel has called the Holocaust an "Alpine Event" in human history. The Canadian theologian Alan Davies has written that "For Christians, Auschwitz, geographically and symbolically located in the heart of Christian Europe, suggests the moral disorder of the 'Christian' civilization that permitted the Nazi philosophy to grow in its midst".[2] Eckardt has suggested that the Holocaust is such a turning point in human history that the dating of years whould now be marked as B.A. (Before Auschwitz) and A.A. (After Auschwitz). In the face of the events of the Holocaust, the Christian is confronted with the task of examining the role of the Church in developing the soil upon which the Death Camps were built. Understanding the historical and theological development of the anti-Jewish tradition in Christianity is essential to this task. The need to reinterpret the tradition is a necessay corollary to the task. The life's work of James Parkes was devoted to this task, and his pioneering effort serves as a guide for Christians finding their way through the antisemitism of the past to a new and better understanding of the relationship between Judaism and Christianity.

Parkes' in-depth study of the problem of Christian antisemitism began in 1931, when he started work on a doctorate at Exeter College, Oxford University under Professor Maurice Powicke. The subject of his work at Oxford was an inquiry into the origins of antisemitism. While pursuing his doctoral work, Parkes came to the horrifying conclusion of the total responsibility of the Christian Church for turning a normal xenophobia into the unique disease of antisemitism. He published his thesis in 1934 entitled, The Conflict of the Church and Synagogue: A Study in the Origins of Antisemitism, and it remains one of the most important studies on antisemitism to date.

It is Parkes' contention that the roots of modern antisemitism are to be found in the religious conflict between Christianity and Judaism. He rejects theories which base antisemitism on racial or economic ideas. The "main responsibility" , he writes, "must rest upon the theological picture created in patristic literature of the Jews as a being perpetually betraying God and ultimately abandoned by Him".[3] This picture was based on a certain way of reading Holy Scriptures which radically divided Christians and Jews between the good and the evil. This reading took no account of Jewish reality, but rather, created a caricature of Judaism and the Jewish people which was clearly abnormal and distinctly different from ordinary group conflict. He writes:

> The Christian theologian did not set out deliberately to blacken the character of his Jewish opponent, nor did he deliberately misrepresent his history. He cannot be said to have been actuated simply by hatred and contempt. His mistake was due to his belief in the verbal inspiration of the Scriptures which he read on the basis of two separate communities. This is apparent in the whole volume of the literature of the time, with its complete silence about contemporary Jewish life. It is always the historical picture of the Jews in the Old Testament which moves the eloquence of the writers, never the misdoings of their living Jewish neighbours.[4]

For Parkes, it was this distortion which provided the foundation of modern antisemitism, even when antisemitism took a decisively anti-Christian, anti-religious turn as it did in many of the racial theories of antisemitism.[5] He concluded his study in The Conflict of the Church and Synagogue with the following observation which is still relevant for today. Being that it was written in 1934, in the time before the Holocaust, it certainly has a prophetic ring to it.

> Fresh crimes were added to the historic crimes of the Old Testament. Ritual murder, the poisoning of wells, the profanation of the Host, all these are natural growths from the picture created by a Chrysostum or a Cyril. And the falsification of Jewish history itself persisted, and has persisted up to the present time in popular teaching. Scholars may know today of the beauty and profundity of the Jewish conception of life. They may know that 'some Jews' were responsible for the death of Jesus. But the Christian public as a whole, the great and overwhelming majority of the hundreds of millions of nominal Christians in the world, still believe that 'the Jews' killed Jesus, that they are a people rejected by their God, that all the beauty of their Bible belongs to the Christian Church and not to those by whom it was written; and if on this ground, so carefully prepared, modern antisemites have reared a structure of facial and economic propaganda, the final responsibility still rests with those who prepared the soil, created the deformation of the people, and so made these ineptitudes credible. [6]

It was on this argument that Parkes based his thesis that antisemitism's origins lie in Christian teachings not in the relations between Jews and Gentiles in the Greco-Roman world. Parkes is clearly on the side of those who see a direct connection between the anti-Jewish tradition in Christianity and the Holocaust. In Parkes' view there is "no break in the line" from the charge of deicide and divine punishment against the Jews to Hitler's death camps, and he says that "the line is still unbroken by any adequate recognition of the sin, by any corporate act of amendment or repentence" on the part of the Church.[7]

The work which Parkes did on the history of Christian antisemitism, coupled with his own discoveries about the history and nature of Judaism, forced him to reject the traditional teaching of the Church concerning the Jews. He held firmly to the position that "good theology cannot be built on bad history", although it does not follow that good history would necessarily create good theology. Yet, Parkes believed that it was essential that a new theology be created which would provide a new basis for Christianity's relationship with Judaism. In considering this new Christian task, he wrote about its moral necessity. Referring to the antisemitic tradition in the theology of the Church, Parkes stated:

> What of those Christians who cannot sincerely maintain such a position? Can they any longer escape their responsibility for doing something about a tradition, however ancient or revered,

> which has produced such results? Of what value is the freedom given to scholarship to search and declare what it believes to be true, if scholars assume no moral responsibility for the results of this research? And here the charge, which lies on all Christian congregations involved must be held to lie with especial responsibility on the shoulders of Christian scholarship. It has so far refused the responsibily, but history will not thereby hold it innocent.[8]

Parkes took this challenge seriously, and he attempted to provide the foundations for a new theological perspective. He proposed to change four basic elements of Christianity's traditional view of Judaism. Briefly outlined, they are:

1. The Church needs to accept that the New Testament is incorrect in its teachings about the Jews, and the Church should pay more attention to the historical facts about Judaism and the Jewish people.
2. The Church needs to qualify its claims to religious truth.
3. Christian theology should make a shift from christocentric to theocentric theology.
4. Christianity should relate to Judaism on the basis of equality.

The biblical question troubled Parkes a great deal because he realized how difficult it would be to convince most Christians of the problem. In spite of the progress made in freeing Biblical interpretation by the different school of Biblical criticism, little of that criticism seems to have filtered down to the question of the Jews and Judaism. The New Testament image of the Jews still seems to dominate most Christian ideas concerning the matter, particularly as concerns the Pharisees, the Jewish Law, and the deicide charge. It is here that we find Parkes' Modernist background having a decided influence on him. He insisted that the New Testament picture of Jews and Judaism be properly corrected in light of the historic facts about the Pharisees, the development of the Jewish Law, rabbinic Judaism's history, and so on. This would not mean that one concludes that there was no tension between Jesus and some of the Jewish leaders of his day, but it would mean that the image of Judaism would not be based on the one-sided picture found in the New Testament. The historical realities of the issues involved would also have to be taken into account. Parkes was critical of the idea that the New Testament supplies the Christian with all he/she needs to know. He wrote that "if, in fact, the apostolic age had been far purer and better than all subsequent Christian epochs, it would be a poor commentary on the intelligence of God".[9]

The touchstone for most Christian thinking on this problem has been Paul's view found in Romans 9-11. Parkes took exception to this dependency on Paul. This is not because Parkes rallied around the old liberal cry of "Back to Jesus", rather it is because Parkes did not believe that Paul really spoke to the modern problems confronting the two religions. He wrote that "it is no good to ask me how I reconcile my views with those found in the Epistle of Romans. I don't, and I long ago discovered that question irrelevant. In St. Paul's days, neither developed rabbinic Judaism nor Nicene Christianity existed. But it is with these we have to reckon with today".[10] He did admit that his initial impression from his university days was that Paul was right and nothing survived in Judaism but an arid and formal legalism once it had rejected and separated from Christianity. Parkes realized, that his initial reaction to the problem remained the usual Christian viewpoint, but, in the face of the antisemitic past of Christianity and the historical realities of Judaism, a new interpretation was required.

Parkes' willingness to subject Scripture to this type of critical analysis was crucial to his position. He believed the roots of Christian antisemitism could be traced back to the New Testament, therefore something had to be done to help people interpret the texts anew. This position would prove unacceptable to fundamentalists, and possibly even to most liberal or neo-orthodox Christians, but Parkes saw no other way of dealing with the

Biblical roots of antisemitism. He made the following suggestion.

> There remains the problem of the anti-Jewish passages in the New Testament. Here, also, the way forward must rest on positive understanding, not negative condemnation. For those who are complete fundamentalists in the most liberal sense, I confess that I have no solution to offer. But for the rest of us, whatever our Church, I believe that we can teach that the living Christ is, has been and always will be, the corrective of what at any time, and in any way, men have said or written about him.[11]

Parkes rejected the whole idea of Biblical infallibility, and held to a position of critical study concerning the Biblical texts. Concerning Biblical criticism, he said that "such an attitude to the Bible presents a far more compelling and attractive picture of the activity of God than those seven words 'the Bible is the Word of God' could ever do".[12] This was clearly the route Parkes believed Christians needed to go if antisemitism was ever to be eradicated from the Christian tradition. His Modernist background made this an easier decision for Parkes to make than it would have been otherwise.

A second point which Parkes considered important also had roots in his Modernist training. Parkes believed that the Church had been too liberal in stating how much religious truth its doctrines contained. He believed that a mistake made by most contemporary theology had been to take too seriously Bonhoeffer's claim that "man is an adult" and the idea of "religionless Christianity" which followed from it. As Parkes saw it, man is, at best, an "infant prodigy", who is guilty of youthful exaggeration concerning his knowledge and truth, and he also viewed the Church as having been guilty of making similar exaggerations. He wrote that "the claims of the church to the truth is one thing; the claim they so frequently make to complete or absolute truth at this extremely youthful stage of the world's existence is on <u>par</u> with all other claims to omniscience associated with extreme youth".[13]

Much of Parkes' concern over the sweeping claims to truth made by the Church rested on his own theological understanding of the nature of God and belief in God. Parkes believed that it was possible to do theology after the Holocaust because he believed that God will ultimately set right the evil which stemmed from the abuse of free-will. He rejected the terms "just" and "omnipotent" as descriptive of God's character, and, he argued for such terms as "benevolent", "intelligent", and, most of all, "responsible". The basis of all faith in God is the belief that God will put things right.[14] God is responsible for correcting evil, but not responsible for its existence. He also believed that proof of God's existence is not possible. He wrote:

> I believe God exists. I am intellectually aware that this belief is a hypothesis which I cannot prove. But, I am also intellectually aware that it is a reasonable hypothesis.[15]

"Theologians are foolish", he wrote, "to claim to know about God as he really and fully is".[16] He also thought that sceptics and atheists are valuable because they serve "to ensure that the good do not slumber over their partially won discoveries...."[17] Parkes demanded that the Church recognize that any claims to truth must be qualified, and this was especially true when speaking theologically. Certainly, he did not wish to imply that the Church can make no claims to God's truth, but he argued that these claims needed to be seen as being a corner <u>of</u> God's truth, not a corner <u>on</u> God's truth.

Although it would be easy to dwell on the negative aspects of antisemitism and Christian theology, Parkes made an honest effort to produce from his work on antisemitism a positive alternative to the Christian tradition. In a letter he wrote to me in 1972, Parkes outlined what he believed should be the underlying motivation for the quest for a theology without antisemitism. "What is worth doing", he wrote, " is the understanding of the positive problem of deepening, broadening, and developing the intellectual and spiritual understanding of the basic Jewish-Christian relationship in the purpose of God; and then the encouraging of the dialogue which should emerge from such an understanding." His efforts to produce a theology based on such premises led to what I call Parkes' "theology of equality".

In order for this theology of equality to work, Parkes believed that Christian theology needed to shift its emphasis from being christocentric to being theocentric. By theocentric theology, Parkes meant that Christian theology would define itself in light of God's many revelations, including Calvary, rather than the christocentric theology in which Christianity defines itself and everything else on the basis of Jesus Christ alone. Christocentric theology has been the predominate influence on Christianity, and contemporary theologians like Barth and Pannenburg have been essentially christocentric theologians. So too, however, were Christian neo-orthodox thinkers like Reinhold Niebuhr, with whom Parkes had great affinity on many other issues. Parkes was well aware of this, and he wrote:

> It was natural that in the first flush of excitement the early church thought the acceptance of Christ was all that mattered. But it was unfortanate that the attitude persisted and persists. The church is entirely christocentric.[18]

He faulted christocentric theology on three points.

1. It created a doctrine of Divine activity in which Christ occupies an exclusive position.
2. It has created a situation in which the church preached that Christ is the solution to every problem in human life, in spite of the evidence to the contrary.
3. It introduced the concept of "salvation in Christ" whose exclusive nature consigns the majority of humanity to Hell.[19]

Christocentric theology needed to be changed, according to Parkes, because it "has not only led the church into deplorable beliefs and activities, but has failed, of itself, to meet the whole of human need".[20] If theology remains christocentric, it would also mean that Jews would remain outside the boundaries of God's people, and Judaism would continue to be perceived as having no truth left in it. Conversion would be the only way Jews could once again share in God's truth. Parkes argues that a move back to theocentric theology would help avoid the problems christocentric theology presented to Jewish-Christian relations, and that it would also mean that the doctrine of the Trinity would be more faithfully represented in theology.

As Parkes saw it, christocentric theology tended to reduce the significance of the first and third person of the Trinity. In his opinion, this led to the Church being blinded to an active concept of a personal and immediate God. Parkes was quite critical of theologians like Barth whose chrisocentric theology makes God into the Wholly Other who has no contact with human history on a daily basis. He argued that christocentric theology made Christian theology too narrow in its concept of God, and thus, the Church is unable to see the activities of God as revealed in places other than Christianity. What Parkes proposes is a new Christian theology which is theocentric in nature, but which does not destroy Christian self-identity nor exclude Judaism as a valid source of divine revelation.

His ideas for this theology is based on his application of the Christian doctrine of the Trinity to explain the meaning of God's revelations and his own anthropology. Parkes argued for a new way to express the meaning of the Trinity. The term "person" is changed to "channel" because Parkes believed that this helped to avoid the metaphysical problems the term "person" introduces. He also believed that the term "channel" helped to make clearer how God acts.

In defining his anthropology, Parkes wrote that the individual experiences life in three ways: A. as social being, B. as person, C. as a seeker of truth. It is his contention that these three experiences of the individual are absolutely necessary to the whole person, but that none of the three are subjected to the other or the lesser of the three experiences. As in the Christian Trinity, there is one individual with three distinct modes of activity. Parkes then shifts from speaking about anthropology to speaking about theology. "So, I believe", he wrote, "it is with the three expressions of the experience of man in Judaism, Christianity, and Humanism. They are related to each other as are the three circles of the Trinity".[21]

Parkes believed that his move from christocentric to theocentric theology was a move which enabled him to broaden the dimensions of the Christian interpretation of God's revelatory activity, and which enabled Christianity to accomodate other revelations besides Calvary. Unlike christocentric theology, Parkes' theocentric theology accepts a doctrine of progressive revelation. This clearly had the marks of Modernist theology. Parkes argued that there were different revelations of God, and once a revelation occurs it is not to be superseded by a later one. "The stages of God's revelation once achieved are never lost", he wrote.[22] With this thesis, Parkes simply argued that Sinai, Calvary, and the Renaissance were all revelations of God which occurred in their proper time in history, and from which certain aspects of God and His power can still be ascertained and tapped. In reference to his own theological understanding and historical work, Parkes wrote that he was "forced into the apparently absurd proposition that both Christianity and Judaism are needed by man".[23]

In relating this theory of revelation back to his anthropology, Parkes understood the role of the three revelations of God as corresponding to the three expressions of the human experience. Sinai is the first revelation, and the channel through which flows the power of God as it relates to man as social being. Parkes argued that the central message of Sinai is that "God is active as ruler in the ordering of people in society, and it is with that activity that Judaism was constantly preoccupied".[24] Unlike traditional Christian interpretations of Sinai which have made it only a forerunner or an incomplete form of Christianity, Parkes argued that Sinai represents a source of divine power flowing into history which reveals God to man as social being, and that this power is still channeled through Sinai today, through Judaism. Parkes wrote that "the center of Judaism is a natural community. Its whole emphasis is on man as social being, related to other men through righteousness and justice. It insists on human responsibility, on definable and achievable objectives."[25] Continuing his attack upon the antisemitic tradition of Christianity, Parkes wrote that "the only right attitude is one which recognizes the equality of the Synagogue as the vehicle of a divine purpose of fulfillment, the recipient of a still valid divine revelation."[26]

Some Jewish critics of Parkes have felt that the image of Judaism in Parkes' system is incomplete and misleading. Parkes does not deny that Judaism is concerned about other experiences of life as well, but he is convinced that at its center is man as social being. In stating his case, Parkes wrote:

> It would be absurd to pretend that Judaism is unaware that man is person, and that the relationship of persons is through love, or that man is a seeker, and that what he seeks is truth. But, Judaism has not developed these possibilities with the same intensity and the emphasis on the way of life of a community does not lend itself naturally to that development.[27]

In addition, with Parkes' interpretation, the Law in Judaism takes on a meaning different from the usual negative connotations it has in the minds of most Christians because it is through the Law that the power of God is incorporated into the teachings of the people themselves.

According to his scheme, Christianity serves as the channel through which God reveals Himself in terms of man as person. Parkes accepted the Christian doctrine of the Incarnation as providing the explanation of the concept of God-in-human-life. It was through the life of Jesus of Nazareth that this power flowed into human history, power concerned with man as person. Parkes argues "that the Christian, recognizing Jesus' divinity as well as his humanity, believes that Jesus saw far more than death in the crucifixion is as true as that the Jews see more in the Torah than a law of commandments and ordinances".[28] The revelation at Sinai is not completed with the advent of Christianity. Christianity is but another revelation of God which has no superiority over any other revelation before or after Calvary, but its equal. As with Sinai, Parkes does not imply that man as person is the only concern of Christianity. Rather, he argued that while Christianity is aware of man as social being and seeker, "it has constantly tried to subordinate this to the personal aspects of life".[29] Whereas Judaism has emphasized the fulfillment of God's will in human history, Christianity has emphasized the future life of the individual.[30] Both religions are concerned about these problems, but their emphasis is different. They also have had different views about messianic expectations. Parkes believed that Judaism was being faithful to its own beliefs by not recognizing in Jesus the promised Messiah since the Christian Messiah fulfills so little of the Jewish expectations. According to Parkes, "as long as Christianity remains a living religion it will rest on the bold statement that God himself, of His own free will entered into human life and history", and thus its emphasis will remain on man as person.[31]

In addition, Parkes thinks that the concept of the "chosen people" is also a useful concept by which to distinguish the differences between Judaism and Christianity. This concept has, of course, been used by Christians to present a derogatory picture of Jews on the one hand, and to claim that Christians were themselves the "chosen people", not the Jews. Parkes believed that the concept operated in both religions, albeit in different ways. It was this discovery which he felt was very important in the development of his thought. He wrote:

> It was, therefore, of fundamental importance to the development of my theology that I gradually came to see that the main distinction between Judaism and Christianity was that the one was the Divine imperative to an <u>elect nation</u>, and the other a similar imperative to the <u>elect from every nation</u>. The natural community was the subject of Judaism, and all descriptions of Judaism as <u>a church</u> were completely false. On the other hand, Christianity was, from its very beginning, a body <u>called out</u>--which, after all is what <u>ecclesia</u> means--from the natural community of which each person happens to be a member.[32]

Parkes saw the differences between the two religions expressed clearly in their understanding of the nature of their call, but he also argued for their calling being of equal value to each other.

To complete his trinitarian model, Parkes argued that the Age of Truth, the Renaissance, marked the revelation of God as it concerned man as seeker of truth. "In the revelation of the Indwelling Spirit, God released the power to understand and to control the world he had devised, including man himself."[33] Humanism has been the channel through which this power has been sent, and the search for truth remains its one objective. Parkes saw this third revelation as caring less for the other two experiences of man, and said that "it tends to be the most intolerant, perhaps because it is the youngest of these revelations".[34] His opinions about the Renaissance show again the influence of his Modernist training. Rather than seeing it as an enemy of religion, Parkes saw the Renaissance as being an essential part of God's revelation and plan for His world. It is a bit unusual, but it is not out of character, given Parkes' theological position on other questions. It is with this revelation that Parkes' unique revelation trinity is complete.

It is on this theology of equality that Parkes would base a new Jewish-Christian relationship. This new relationship would be based on the premise that Judaism is a valid revelation of God, whose importance is equal to Christianity's importance. There is no idea of Judaism being a dead religion, or Jews being cursed by God for being a deicidal people. Parkes also rejects the idea that salvation could be found only in Jesus Christ. "There must be no suggestion that one nature or activity of God is more or less important than another. All are equally divine, and in contact with any we are in contact with God."[35] Parkes is not suggesting that both religions are the same or that the hope of the future is the denial of the particular nature of either Judaism or Christianity. What Parkes is saying is that God has revealed Himself differently at different times through different "channels", and that each channel, while important in the overall divine plan, is also able to stand alone as a particular source of divine power. One channel does not succeed another in the order of their appearance. What this theology of equality is trying to do is to make Christians more aware of their particular place in God's creation without feeling the need to deny God's activity elsewhere. There is certainly no motive on Parkes' part to convert Jews to Christianity because his theology of equality makes conversion unnecessary and undesirable. Judaiam is part of God's overall plan for creation, and as such, it is necessary for it to survive intact and to continue to provide a channel of God's power. They do not need to become Christians. He wrote:

> In this time and generation, not only do I not desire to see the conversion of all Jews to present forms of Christianity, but I do not seek the union of the two religions. That may happen in the future. But it can only happen when I can bring all that I value of the Christian tradition to the common pool and the Jew can equally openly bring all that he values of the Jewish tradition. And that day is certainly not yet, and in our present circumstance a religion made out of patches and compromises and superficial synthesis would be a monster lacking the very qualities which give each tradition its permanent value to humanity.[36]

Parkes did not want Judaism or Christianity to give up the necessary exercise of determining its own identity or belief system, but he did suggest that Christianity do this with an awareness of the dynamic and fluid relationship God has with his creation. His historical work made it necessary for Parkes to urge Christianity to recognize the contributions Judaism has made both as a religion and as a people, and also to recognize the sin of antisemitism being directly related to Christian teachings. "It is to proclaim", he wrote, "the legitimacy, indeed the necessity, of Jewish survival that I have so long paid so much attention to the theological aspect of Jewish-Christian relationship; and have insisted on the theological equality of the revelation of Sinai and the Incarnation."[37] In adding up the factors involved in creating a new Christian attitude toward Jews and the creation of a new theology, Parkes came to the conclusion that a recognition of the equal validity of the two religions <u>via</u> his theology of equality will provide the means by which Christianity can make a positive step forward in truly eliminating antisemitism from its theology.

In examining Parkes' work, one finds that he has provided Christian theology and the Church itself with many of the historical and theological correctives needed in order for the quest to create a theology free of antisemitism to succeed. Malcolm Diamond is correct when he writes that "as we survey the work of James Parkes it will soon be obvious that his understanding of Christian dogma and his singular view of the relation between Judaism and Christianity are not likely to be shared by many Christians. Yet, because of his penetrating insights into Judaism and his thoroughly documented and trenchantly expressed views on Christian responsibility for antisemitism, his work presents a challenge which no Christian can ignore."[38] Since Parkes was a pioneer in the field of Jewish-Christian relations, much of his work is seminal, particularly the theological writings. Like his earlier writings, there seems to be lacking a solid philosophical basis. But, we should not underestimate the importance of Parkes' work because of its seminal nature. He was one of the first Christians to deal with this problem of Christian antisemitism and its consequences, and his work has influenced many of the theologians now working on this problem. His work on the history of Christian antisemitism still remains the major contribution of a Christian to solving this problem. His theology of equality helped to point the way for other Christians to follow.

Parkes remains essential to any Christian quest for a theology without antisemitism. For while his seminal work may be in parts incomplete, his work provides a glimmer of hope for a future in which Christians theology will no longer either overtly or covertly justify antisemitism. Parkes' pioneering work in this field is now bearing fruit. People like Roy Eckardt, Franklin Littell, Clark Williamson, Eva Fleischner, Rosemary Ruether, Alan Davies, Paul Van Buren and John Pawlikowski among others are all continuing the work which Parkes began in the thirties and forties. Parkes helped to bring many people in the Church into the battle against antisemitism, a battle which he called "a battle for decency and fellowship in communal life."[39]

The Holocaust has been the turning point for many Christians to begin the battle against antisemitism. It should not be forgotten that Parkes saw the full demonic implications of the Christian antisemitic tradition before the Holocaust began. He saw early on the responsibility of the Church for creating and perpetuating antisemitism. Roy Eckardt has asked the question: "Does the affirmation that the task of the Christian Church is to bring the world into the Covenant through Jesus the Jew contribute in and through itself to the perpetuation of antisemitism? In the measure that the answer is yes, The Christian gospel can no longer be preached."[40] Eckardt's position may appear too radical for many. But isn't the time after the Holocaust a time for radical statements and change? In the face of this demand, James Parkes can provide guidance and direction for Christians dealing with the "bad conscience" of the Church over its treatment of the Jews. With the writings of James Parkes, one can get a good start on the quest for a Christian theology which in no way contributes to the evil of antisemitism.

FOOTNOTES

Books and articles by James Parkes are listed by title without repeating author's name. Where the term, "by John Hadham", is included refers to books written under Parkes' pen name.

1. A. Roy Eckardt, "Can There Be a Jewish-Christian Relationship?", The Journal of Bible and Religion (Vol. XXXIII/April 1965/no. 2), p. 124.
2. Alan Davies, Anti-Semitism and the Christian Mind: The Crisis of Conscience After Auschwitz (New York: Herder and Herder, 1969), p. 37.
3. The Conflict of the Church and Synagogue: a study in the origins of antisemitism (Cleveland, Ohio: The World Publishing Co.; Philadelphia: The Jewish Publication Society of America, 1961), p. 375.
4. Ibid., p. 374.
5. See Uriel Tal, Christians and Jews in Germany (Ithaca and London: Cornell University Press, 1975).
6. Conflict of Church and Synagogue, p. 376.
7. Anti-Semitism: A Concise World History (New York: Quadrangle Books, 1963), p. 5.
8. Judaism and Christianity (Chicago: The University of Chicago Press, 1948), p. 167.
9. God in Human Progress by John Hadham (Harmondsworth: Penguin Books, 1944), p. 15.
10. Prelude to Dialogue: Jewish-Christian Relationships (New York: Schocken Books, 1969), p. 188. See also my article, "Dealing Honestly with Judaism and Jewish History", Journal of Ecumenical Studies (23:1, Winter 1986).
11. Judaism and the Jewish People in their World Setting at the End of 1973 (The author, Iwernc Minster, Dorset, England, 1974), p. 12.
12. Prelude to Dialogue, p. 204.
13. Good God: sketches of his character and activities by John Hadham (Harmondsworth: Penguin Books, 1944), p. 36.

14. Transcript of Television Program aired on ABC-TV, January 25, 1975, p. 3.
15. Common Sense About Religion (London: Victor Gollancz, 1961), p. 75.
16. Good God, p. 5.
17. Ibid., p. 18.
18. Prelude to Dialogue, p. 208.
19. Ibid., p. 208.
20. Ibid., p. 210.
21. Ibid., p. 216.
22. Good God, p. 92.
23. A Reappraisal of the Christian Attitudes to Judaism (Church End Barley, Royston, Hertfordshire England, The Parkes Library, no. 3, reprinted 1962), pp. 20-21.
24. God at Work in science, politics, and human life (New York: Philosophical Library, 1952), p. 94.
25. Prelude to Dialogue, p. 217.
26. Judaism and Christianity, p. 174.
27. Prelude to Dialogue, p. 217.
28. The Foundations of Judaism and Christianity (London: Valentine, Mitchell, 1960), p. 164.
29. Prelude to Dialogue, p. 217.
30. The Concept of the Chosen People in Judaism and Christianity (New York: The Union of American Hebrew Congregations, 1954), p. 12.
31. God in Human Progress, p. 20.
32. Prelude to Dialogue, p. 193. The Concept of the Chosen People, p. 32.
33. God at Work, p. 149.
34. Prelude to Dialogue, p. 218.
35. God at Work, p. 63.
36. Judaism and Christianity, p. 12.
37. Jewry and Jesus of Nazareth (Barley: The Parkes Library, 1964), p. 19.
38. Malcolm Diamond, "Honesty in the Christian-Jewish Interchange." The Journal of Bible and Religion (Vol. XXXIII, April 1965, no. 2), p. 115.
39. Judaism and Christianity, p. 179.
40. A. Roy Eckardt, Your People, My People (New York: Quadrangle, 1974), p. 249.

THE ATTITUDE OF THE AMERICAN FRIENDS SERVICE COMMITTEE TO REFUGEES FROM NAZISM, 1933-1950

HAIM GENIZI

BAR ILAN UNIVERSITY, ISRAEL

The aim of this paper is to analyze the uniqueness of the services rendered by the American Quakers to refugees from Nazism in the U.S. and in Europe. In addition, this study compares AFSC's attitude toward victims of the Holocaust during the Hitler era and after the war.

The American Quakers, or the Society of Friends, numbered in 1933, 112,000 members[1]. Their belief that "there is in every human being something of the Divine", generated a respect for all men, nations, as well as individuals, and opposition to any kind of violence. Their deep interest in social matters derived from the notion that religious experience and social concern are strongly related[2].

The American Friends Service Committee (AFSC) was established in 1917 with the double purpose of providing Quakers an opening for relieving human need and a moral alternative to military service.[3] As its first project, the AFSC conducted a feeding program for German children. Up to 1924 the Quakers, with the financial support of American philanthropists, were instrumental in feeding up to 1,200,000 children a day in Germany.[4] These ties with the German people influenced the decision of the AFSC to direct its relief activities in post-World War II Germany on behalf of the German population. Even after the conclusion of the feeding project in Germany, the AFSC's staff remained in Europe to coordinate relief work. Through Quaker centers in Berlin, Vienna, Paris and Geneva the AFSC, along with Friends of different nationalities, were engaged in relief work, community development, educational programs and social action projects. Their intention was to spread the 'Quaker spirit' and to cultivate international understanding.[5]

The Nazi ascent to power and the suppression of non-Aryans in Germany provided an opportunity to respond again "to the cry of human suffering". As a matter ot fact, the Quakers were in a position that enabled them to intervene more efficiently on behalf of the persecuted than almost any other agency. Through their existing centers they could easily expand the type and scope of the services. Furthermore, as a result of their earlier operations in Germany, they had gained experience in mass feeding and first-hand knowledge of Germany and its people. They had won the Germans' appreciation and were known for their impartiality, devotion and political non-involvement. In most cases even the Nazis treated them respectfully. Quaker non-partisanship and dedication to human need, opened before them doors which neither governmental nor religious officals were allowed to enter.[6]

During the first years of Hitler's regime, the scope of the AFSC's activities on behalf of refugees was surprisingly small. This was probably the outcome of a dilemma caused by the anti-Jewish measures in Germany. Some Quakers feared that supporting Jewish cause would seriously compromise their reputation in Germany. Furthermore, close relationship with German Friends led to inaction, owing to the fear that open criticism would either offend, or do harm to the latter. Therefore, American Quakers were almost completely silent as far as public denunciation of Nazi anti-Jewish policy was concerned.[7]

The Quakers were not only reluctant to criticize publicly German policy, but also did not show much concern for the victims of persecution. In spite of a contribution by the American Jewish Joint Distribution Committee (JDC), the allocation of money for foreign service relief in 1934 dropped to $17.000 from $20.000 in the previous year.[8] Unlike the European Friends, American participation in the L'Entr'aide, a Quaker relief project in Paris, was minimal. American Quakers,in common with their compatriots, showed apathy toward the fate of refugees. James G.McDonald, High Commissioner for Refugees, tried to enlist the Quakers' support for the Paris L'Entr'aide, pleading politely at first and later more directly, but apparently in vain. "Mr. McDonald has not succeeded in getting much from the American Quakers," reported his secretary, in July 1934.[9] Norman Bentwich, the British Jewish leader and chief assistant of the High Commissioner, toured the United States in 1935, campaigning for Christian support of non-Jewish refugees. He came out frustrated from a meeting with a Quaker group in Philadelphia, who were "disappointingly passive." "Even with the Friends, the springs of charity seem to have dried up in this dry land," he lamented to McDonald.[10] "I must say that I was bitterly disappointed with the reception. I could not believe that there was such indifference to the human work which the Friends are doing in Europe for these victims of religious and racial persecution," he wrote to Clarence E. Pickett, AFSC's executive secretary. "I do feel so strongly that American Friends cannot stand aloof."[11] McDonald, after his own experience at Philadelphia, was not surprised. "I am not very optimistic about the Quakers here," he observed.[12] Up to August 1935, no funds has been collected by the AFSC for the Paris L'Entr'aid. Characteristically, the Friends Intelligencer and the American Friend,the two leading Quaker journals in America, rarely commented, editorially, about Jewish persecution, or about the refugee issue in general.[13] Thus, contrary to the general conception, the American Friends were reluctant to assume responsibility for Jewish and even Christian refugees. During the years 1933-1938 there was little to distinguish the American Quakers from the Christian community at large, as regards their apathy toward the victims of Nazi oppression.

The events in 1938 and especially the riots of Kristallnacht, on November 10,1938, roused the American Quakers to action. Up to that time the care of refugees was almost a one-man effort, that of Hertha Kraus, who personally rendered services to 150 refugees of all denominations in Germany, Latin America and the United States.[14] With the growing refugee cry for help, institutionalization of the relief services in the United States became the order of the day. The Foreign Service Section, which was chiefly responsible for overseas operations, was interested in forming a separate committee that would deal with those refugees who were already in the country. So, in December 1938 the Refugee Division was established, with headquarters in New York City.[15] Thus, institutionalized help of the Quakers for refugees in America made a belated appearance, years after several other sectarian agencies had first entered the field. The fact that other relief organizations had already been operating, was naturally an advantage for the Quakers. It enabled them to define independently their function and areas of activity. Since the AFSC was neither a fund- raising body, nor a relief organization proper, it limited its services to certain fields, generally services not provided through other committees. The Quakers were eager to get beyond relief, into reconstruction. They wanted to undertake projects only when they were able to promote a "better way", and to show that way into action.[16] "Orientation and hospitality" were the catchwords. They gave thought to social and intellectual absorption, and to the psychological crisis that enforced immigrants had to undergo. One of the chief purposes of the Refugee Division was to prepare newcomers to become not only American citizens,but also an integral part of the American society and its culture.[17]

Volunteer staff was characteristic of the Quaker help for refugees. A considerable part of the services, both in offices and in the field, was rendered by volunteers, both Friends and sympathizers. In August 1940, for example, 25 volunteers contributed 1.250 hours of work to the Refugee Division,(which became a Committee). That ensured lower overhead expenses than other committees were burdened with.[18]

From the outset it was decided to limit the case load to the handling capacity of the staff; to refrain from publicity and the attraction of refugees to the Committee. The intake policy was carefully examined. It was decided to undertake "only those (cases) for whom we, as Friends, felt a peculiar responsibility." Indeed, the Committee dealt only with Friends, or those recommended by them.[19] However, the group projects were open to the members of all religions, without discrimination.

Several orientation and training programs were offered, which may be considered the Quakers' unique contribution to the absorption of refugees. Hostels were one of the means used to help newcomers adjust themselves to the American scene. Commencing from the summer of 1939, the Sky Island hostel in West Park, New York, opened its gates to 35-40 refugee guests at a time. For a period of 3-4 weeks courses were given, in an informal way, in American history, U.S. politics, geography of the country, music and driving. Cooperative life with the American staff, along with personal tutoring in English, greatly improved the newcomers' ability to speak English. The volunteer staff aimed at giving a realistic understanding of the American way of life.[20] The success of the Sky Island project led to the establishment of two additional hostels, in Scattergood, near West Branch, Iowa, and in Quaker Hill, Richmond, Indiana. The places were carefully selected in friendly communities, with a view to the settlement there of most of the refugee visitors. While Sky Island was a summer hostel, in Scattergood refugees stayed for four months and sometimes more.The hostel idea won support among refugee organizations, like the National Refugee Service (NRS), that took care of Jewish refugees, and the American Committee for Christian Refugees, who worked for Protestants. These committees referred their clients to the AFSC hostels, covering their expenses.[21]

Another somewhat similar Quaker project was the Cooperative College Workshop. The Refugee Division, with its small budget, concentrated its services on a selected group of refugees, teachers and college professors. To overcome their painful process of adjustment to the American educational system, Hertha Kraus initiated the Pennsylvania College Workshop in Haverford, as an educational center. From 1940 a selected group of 20-25 teachers were given intensive instruction in orientation courses in many fields.[22] The American Seminar for refugee scholars, teachers and artists, in Wolfeboro, New Hampshire, was a parallel project to the Cooperative Workshop, with almost the same aims and very similar methods. It was a summer school, that provided a concentrated program of vocational counseling. Probably equally important was the psychological effect upon the participants of the seminar. "The consciousness of being a 'refugee', a victim of past circumstances, was offset by the possibility of becoming a contributor of the future," wrote one of the refugees.[23]

The Refugee Division offered a variety of services during 1940-1942 for scholars, teachers and students, such as securing teaching positions, scholarships, internships, hospitality, training opportunities and counseling. In 1941, 375 teachers and students were placed by the Committee.[24] In spite of the small number of teachers helped, in consideration of the difficulties confronted, and in comparison with the record of the Emergency Committee in Aid of Displaced Foreign Scholars, the Quakers may be credited for that achievement.[25]

One of the means employed by the Quakers for the Americanization of refugees was the organization of social and cultural activities. Newcomers were invited to Quaker homes, to monthly parties at the Friends Meeting Houses and to Powell House in New York, which was the Committee's hospitality center. In the latter, language courses, parties and trips were offered. English and Quakerism proved to be the most popular study courses. Altogether, since 1943, the Powell House entertained more than a thousand monthly refugee visitors. In Catholic circles such operations were criticized, the Friends being accused of aiming their activities at the conversion of refugees to Quakerism. In fact, not only Catholics, but also Orthodox Jews, complained of Quaker conversionism.[26]

To carry out even such small-scale projects, the Refugee Committee badly needed the practical support of large relief agencies as regards information, counsel and especially funds. Its relationship with the JDC was an example of wholesale interfaith cooperation on refugee matters. This precedent was established during World War I, when the American Friends and the JDC worked together in a German mass feeding program. A $5000 contribution in 1933 to the AFSC, proved to be one of the JDC's best 'investments', and initiated a long period of productive and trustworthy cooperation, eloquently expressed by Clarence E. Pickett: "We are already deeply indebted, as Christians, for the way in which Jews have helped us to carry on our work, but it is because of the common purpose to serve the needs of humanity, that many of us share, that we venture to offer this opportunity of cooperation."[27]

The Friends frequently reported to the JDC on refugee situation in Germany. Coming from an impartial source, these reports were very much appreciated by Jewish leaders, which they regarded as the best objective information on what was really going on in Germany. "I have no doubt that they render a type of service that no other organization is in a position to do," indicated Joseph C. Hyman, JDC's executive secretary.[28]

Cooperation with the American Jewish Committee (AJC) was also helpful. In 1939 the AJC launched an educational campaign to correct misconceptions concerning the number of refugees coming into America. Pickett agreed to give his name to a pamphlet, called <u>Refugee Facts</u>, which appeared under the imprint of the AFSC. The AJC prepared, printed and distributed a quarter of a million copies of the pamphlet, which received wide publicity.[29]

With the entry of the United States into the war, which was followed by a drastic reduction in immigration,the Friends, like other refugee agencies, were confronted with the need to adapt their services to changing conditions. The situation became so grave that the very existence of the Refugee Committee was put into question. Arthur Dunham, an American Quaker, submitted on March 3 1942 an exhaustive report, which recommended a drastic reduction of migration services, a staff reorganization, a cut in the budget, the transfer of cases to other agencies and the establishment of an advisory committee. The report created frustration among the Division's staff. Although the Division continued its services, the reduction of its budget, the changes in personnel and the demoralization of the staff, hampered the effectiveness of its work.[30] As a result, the Quaker activities on behalf of refugees in America were limited to orientation and Americanization. The hostels, the American seminars and the College Workshop were only pilot projects on a small scale, which signaled to the big relief agencies the "Quaker way" of treating refugees. Though Friends initiated and implemented these programs, a considerable part of the funds and most of the beneficiaries came from other agencies, including Jewish ones. Although AFSC representatives participated in almost every refugee conference, voicing their protest against immigration policy, against anti-alien and anti-Semitic prejudices, it seems that they were unable to change the hostile atmosphere. Even more significant was the Committee's failure to rouse the Quakers to favorable action in regard to that subject. Rufus M.Jones, Clarence Pickett, Hertha Kraus, along with several dozens of Friends, enthusiastically and wholeheartedly labored on behalf of victims of oppression. But the rank and file members of the Quaker communities contributed neither financially nor by absorbing refugee families. As James Vail, an active Quaker on behalf of refugees, complained as late as 1943:" We cannot have people in desperate need in Europe, finding one Friend who cares what happens to them, and then coming to this country to find no Friends who care." Therefore, it seems that as far as the activities on behalf of refugees in the United States were concerned, the Quakers probably received more credit than they deserved.[31]

In regard to AFSC's operations abroad, however, the picture was quite different. The whole organization was foreign-minded, concentrating on help of the needy overseas. Ever since its foundation the AFSC had been operating in Europe. On the Continent, Friends of different nationalities had already been working on behalf of refugees. Thus, by their living example they served in activating and deepening the involvement of the American Quakers in refugee affairs. AFSC staff in Europe worked in close cooperation with other agencies. As already mentioned, Jewish agencies, like the JDC and HICEM, benefited from Quaker intervention. In response to a JDC request, the Quakers sent a commission to Germany in 1939, headed by Rufus M. Jones, the Committee's chairman, to ascertain the exact situation of Jews and non-Aryan Christians, and to help if necessary. The JDC contributed $100.000 for relief distribution. After a meeting with Heydrich, head of the Gestapo, the commissioners reported that German officials had been "unfailing in their courtesy and friendly interest." They visited concentration camps, Quaker centers and relief agencies in the Reich and its neighboring countries.[32] The commissioners' visit had no direct results. Nazis did not change their emigration policy and certainly did not cease from their persecutions. However,Jewish groups benefited from cooperation with that prestigious and impartial body. While JDC provided financial support, as well as staff- members and local workers for Quaker projects in Europe, the AFSC made a valuable contribution. In November 1940, JDC agents turned to the AFSC to send a representative to Lisbon, because only a non-Jew was acceptable to negotiate with the Portuguese government. When in May 1941 the relationship between the JDC and the American consul in Lisbon deteriorated, AFSC was once again called upon for help. Because of the friendly relationship that existed between the Quakers and the American consul, the problem of the issuing of visas was satisfactorily resolved. In 1942 the AFSC man in Paris succeeded in persuading the German commander not to close the JDC canteen there. These were only a few examples of the services that the AFSC was able to render as a non-Jewish organization.[33]

The growing commitment of the Quakers to the refugee cause found its expression in their collaboration with American immigration authorities. When in 1939 Pickett learned, of a shortage of clerks at the American Consulates in Vienna, Berlin and Prague, he offered to recruit German-speaking Friends, whose salaries would be covered by private contributions. His offer, however, was turned down by the State Department[34]

One of the issues that had occupied the Quakers' relief mission to Europe was feeding and rescuing refugee children. Between November 1938 and August 1939, the Society of Friends in Vienna handled 1978 cases of children, 882 of whom it helped to emigrate. The AFSC cooperated with the New York-based German Jewish Children's Aid, shouldering the responsibility for the selection and examination of the youth.[35] The Quakers' commitment to the rescue of refugee children and to their reception into the United States was clearly demonstrated by their role in the Non-Sectarian Committee for German Refugee Children and its successor bodies. Pickett was the moving spirit and acting director of the Non-Sectarian

Committee. Furthermore, in several plans made for the rescue of children, the Quakers were assigned a major role, such as contact with governmental authorities, both in the United States and abroad, and the selection of children and their escort to America. The AFSC and the Committee for the Care of European Children had made strenuous efforts to evacuate refugee children from France. Between March 1941 and August 1942, 309 children were evacuated from France in five transports. Even that small achievement necessitated a great deal of work. It took eight months of struggle to overcome the bureaucratic red tape holding up the evacuation of one group of fifty children. The Friends' efforts in that direction is noteworthy, despite the limited success of these programs.[36] In France, the AFSC was also occupied with the distribution of food and vitamins. Although the Quakers' efforts to feed European children were "largely a story of frustration," as Pickett put it, they nevertheless succeeded in sending two ships in 1941 with supplies for French and Spanish children. Some 50.000 children were fed daily during a period of twelve weeks. In collaboration with the Unitarian Service Committee, the JDC and HICEM, the American Friends provided food in 1941 for 84.000 internee children in unoccupied France and vitamins for 100.000.[37]

In addition to France, AFSC teams provided services to refugees and internees in Portugal, Spain, North Africa and Cuba. In Madrid, since 1943, David Blickenstaff, an AFSC member, headed and energetically operated the Office of Representation in Spain of American Relief Organizations (ORSARO). This office, which coordinated relief activities in Spain, served as an "embassy to stateless persons", and took care of refugees. The AFSC, as a member of ORSARO, was responsible for selecting and escorting children on their way to America and tried to help evacuate people from Spain.

In the course of a decade, the scope of AFSC services was meaningfully expanded, from an expenditure of $17.000 in 1934, to $1.911.300 in 1944. Although the needs were always greater than the available funds, generally speaking the Quakers enjoyed a better financial situation than did other relief agencies. In 1940, for example, the income was nearly one million dollars and in 1944 it more than doubled.[38]

With the termination of the fighting, in the spring of 1945, millions of uprooted people were wandering through devastated areas, looking for food, shelter and medicine. The American Quakers, like other relief agencies, decided to continue their programs in France, Spain, Portugal and North Africa. However, since the Friends always operated on a supplementary basis, AFSC officials decided to transfer certain services, as well as clients, to other organizations. They stepped out of migration work, closed the AFSC office in Geneva, referred inquires for the location of people to the Central Location Index Agency, stopped to provide affidavits, and transferred clients to appropriate agencies.[39] While certain services were liquidated, the Quakers renewed others and even expanded them. In France, they had vocational and rehabilitation programs for Spanish Republicans, and established community centers for DPs and French citizens. In 1945, the AFSC expended in France the sum of $733.316. In 1947 the budget was $226.300.A Spanish Republican welfare program was conducted by a joint team of Friends, of whom 13 were Americans, 11 British and 66 were Spanish, French and other nationals. Quaker aid to France included help to 700.000 German POWs, interned in Southern France.[40] In Spain, AFSC expended in 1945, $95.477, and in the following year the sum was $75.000.[41] Gradually, the financial burden of the activities in Spain and Portugal was transferred to the Intergovernmental Committee on Refugees.[42] While in France, Spain and Portugal the Quaker involvement decreased after the war, in Italy the amount expended increased meaningfully. In 1945 the AFSC expended $37.000, in 1946 this sum almost doubled ($76.390).[43]

Thus, AFSC projects concerning Spanish Republicans, French nationals and Italian girls continued and even expanded after the war.What was the attitude of the American Quakers toward seven million Displaced Persons in Germany and Austria? How did the Friends face the problem of people who had suffered from Nazi persecution?

After the liberation of Europe, the Allied forces had to deal with the difficult problem of taking care of over seven million DPs, who were slave laborers, prisoners of war, survivors of concentration camps,people who voluntarily had come to Germany to help the Nazis, or who had fled from the advancing Soviet army. In a successful drive, during a remarkable short period, most of those people were repatriated. Nevertheless, approximately one million DPs, such as Balts, Ukrainians and Poles, remained in DP Assembly Centers, because they refused to return to Soviet- dominated territories, either for fear of standing trial for collaboration with the Nazis, or because of their anti-communist activities. There were also Jewish DPs, who fled East European countries, because of violent anti-Semitism. The difficult job of caring, feeding, clothing and housing a million people, rested on the shoulders of the Military. To be released from some of its duties, the Army transferred to the United Nations Relief and Rehabilitation Administration (UNRRA), the tasks of

administering DP camps and providing supplementary supplies, recreational facilities, health and welfare services, vocational guidance and self-help projects.[44]
The AFSC turned in June 1945 to the American military authorities and to UNRRA, expressing the desire to join the DP relief program in Germany. The Committee proposed to dispatch a team of experienced social workers "to be assigned as a unit" to administer a center of DP children, or adults, "who will need protected care of restoration to normal life."[45] The Committee also asked to consider the establishment of rest and recuperation centers for the rehabilitation of "depleted people of leadership caliber."[46] Thus, the American Friends proposed to work in Germany through two different channels: supplementary relief work for DPs, particularly children, and rehabilitation among German civilians. After some delay,on August 11,1945, the AFSC received permission to dispatch a team of six workers to Germany for relief work among DPs, under UNRRA auspices.[47] After six months' service (August 31 1945-March 1 1946), the Quaker UNRRA team was disbanded. In spite of repeated requests from AFSC circles to work with DPs, which found its expression in several plans suggested by the Committee, no independent undertaking took place among the DPs.[48]

Why did American Friends fail to provide relief for the DPs in Germany? What caused the AFSC to abandon an extraordinary opportunity to provide help to victims of the war, who were really in great need of every kind of assistance? Why did the expenditures for France or Spain surpas five or six times the money spent on the DPs in Germany in 1945?[49]

The work under military rule in Germany and Austria was a difficult experience for the pacifist Friends. Unlike relief work in Spain, Portugal, France or Switzerland, the AFSC had to adhere to orders, which they disagreed with,and to wear uniform, which in principle its members opposed. In spite of Quaker reluctance, they agreed "to comply with military law and to serve under the jurisdiction of the commander of the formation to which the members of the agency may be attached."[50] There were, however, Quakers, like David Hughes, who was a leading member of the British team in Germany, who declared that he "cannot conscientiously work with Military Government any longer."[51] William C. Edgerton, on the other hand, who was a member of the AFSC team to DP camps, found his relations with the Military, "considerably less of a problem" than he had expected. In the course of the months he served in Germany, he became strongly convinced "that the negative part of our pacifism, our refusal to take part in war, is meaningless and sterile by itself." He stressed the importance of "positive" pacifism, which he considered as a "unifying principle." The service in Germany brought him to "see the whole thing in a different perspective."[52]

The relations with UNRRA seriously impaired Quakers' efforts to work on behalf of DPs. The ambivalent attitude to UNRRA began in 1944, when AFSC considered the dispatch of Friends to UNRRA teams.The Quakers feared losing their identity in that huge organization. "It would not be acceptable ... to go in merely to take orders without freedom of action to shape the pattern of relief."[53] Apart from loss of identity, Pickett was apprehensive that the Quaker idea of fellowship to oppressed people might lose ground in mixed teams with UNRRA, which would be some kind of betrayal of confidence. While UNRRA was solely concerned with physical relief, the AFSC had a "special duty toward spiritual reconstruction," maintained Pickett.[54] After some hesitation, AFSC decided to cooperate with UNRRA. A representative was dispatched to the UNRRA directorate and eight or nine Quakers joined UNRRA personnel in Europe. Pickett later termed the relationship as "most cordial," and even defended the agency against its critics.[55] Not everyone in the Committee shared that view. After one year's experience, the Friends found that their early fears had been justified. In retrospect, they questioned the desirability of collaboration, because of their inability to contribute, as Quakers, to the cause.[56]

The six months' experience of the team of six American members in Germany,in 1945-46, clearly proved the truth of that reservation. UNRRA officials dispersed the Quakers, assigning each to a different job, most needed at that time. Accordingly, "individuals felt that they had not done a job as an organization, that they had not been doing an AFSC job", as Barclay Jones, the AFSC Commissioner to Europe, pointed out. E.N.Wright, concluding his team's service, demanded for the AFSC "greater independence of action and a more definite field or fields to work in, if it is to continue its cooperation with UNRRA." Thus,on March 1,1946, the first team to work with the DPs withdrew from the field.[57]

UNRRA officials, who "very much regretted" the withdrawal of the AFSC first team, considered the possibility of finding a special project which would satisfy the Quakers. After some deliberations, UNRRA Child Care Division suggested to the AFSC "to take over the direction of some of our children centers for unaccompanied children".[58] Nothing came out of several plans suggested, and the AFSC had no independent program in DP camps.

In contast to the American Quakers, the British Friends Relief Service (FRS), developed a remarkable active role in the DP camps in the British Zone of Germany. AFSC men,as individuals, went to England to complete a thorough training course, before they were ready to join FRS teams.[59]

Not everybody was happy with lack of AFSC operations for the DPs in Germany. Senior members of the Foreign Service Executive Committee criticized, time and again, the fact that American Quakers did not contribute "to the grave and immediate problem of DPs in the camps of Germany." In spite of "the concern of a number of people on the staff that we should be doing more for the DPs", as was reported in October 1949, no serious efforts had been made to correct that situation.[60] A natural conclusion of AFSC inactivity on behalf of DPs was its withdrawal from the U.S. Displaced Persons Commission as a recognized relief agency.[61] Thus, AFSC's insistence to provide relief only as a team, and to concentrate upon special projects in which the 'Quaker way' could be demonstrated, contributed to its failure to respond adequately to the cry of the suffering of DPs. Therefore, AFSC's slogan that it provides help to the most needy, is questionable.

In spite of a few voices of criticism, the failure to dedicate efforts to help DPs did not disturb most of the staff and did not create an atmosphere of embarrassment. This was, probably, due to the fact that American Quakers participated at that time in a huge undertaking of spiritual message and reconciliation, and distribution of supplies to the German and Austrian population.[62] Indeed, AFSC had special relationship with the German people, since the child-feeding operation in 1917. After World War Two, the Quakers were deeply moved by the miserable conditions of the German civilian population. In a remarkable letter to the Archbishop of Freiburg, Germany, the Quaker attitude to the German people found its eloquent expression:

> "At last the long awaited moment has come when it again becomes possible to grasp your hands and to tell you that we are the same, as of old unfailingly devoted to you in love.... We therefore come to you in the spirit of repentance and in the consciousness that our share of guilt obliges us to share your suffering and that only this sharing of suffering will enable us to help you."[64]

The Quakers saw in their work for the German people a "message of reconciliation". Spiritual, rather than material aid, which the AFSC helped to distribute, was the main purpose of Quaker activity. Since the end of the war, Quaker circles discussed the need of "spiritual and educational" rehabilitation of Europe,"not only as a message, but as a way of life."[65] As a letter of encouragement from Philadelphia headquarters to the AFSC staff in Germany indicated:

> "Our lasting contribution to Germany is not the food, which is quickly consumed, but the memory which people will have that we came in a non-partisan way, trying to bring some help to the hopeless and some message of the dignity and worth of every individual."[66]

These were the aims of the American Quakers in their mission to Germany. Here they were able to contribute as Quakers. The friendly attitude to the civilian population and the wish to mingle among them, led,partly, to the Quaker refusal to wear uniform, because they did not want "to be identified in the German mind with the occupying forces."[67]

The Quakers, like other voluntary agencies, were permitted to provide relief for German civilians in occupied Germany only through the Council of Relief Agencies Licensed for Operations in Germany (CRALOG), which was established on February 19 1946. To October 1,1947,CRALOG shipped to the three Western zones, 40.584.724 lbs. of food, clothing and medicine, whose estimated value was thirty million dollars.[68] The AFSC, as an authorized CRALOG agency, served as an intermediary for many local and national religious and German ethnic organizations to channel funds and supplies to Germany. There were great national bodies, like the American Relief for Central Europe and the American Relief for Germany (ARG), with branches in many cities, as well as small groups, like the New York Concert Committee, or the German Singing Society. Each of them appealed to its constituency for funds, medicine, clothing, shoes, blankets, toys, educational and religious supplies. AFSC's expenditures for Germany in 1946 reached the sum of $2.023.000 (out of the annual budget of $5.391.540). Eighty percent of the money for Germany came from the affiliated agencies. The joint Quaker team that operated in Germany included, in April 1947, 52 members: 22 British, 22 French and 8 Americans.[69] The Quakers supervised the distribution of supplementary meals to thousands of children in the three Western zones; participated in the management of summer camps for 5000 youth; were instrumental in sending clothing, shoes, blankets, powder milk and medicine to the homeless; provided mail and parcel post services to prisoners of war;and finally, assisted in sending C.A.R.E. packages and money transfers to Germany. AFSC expenditure in Germany leaped from $10.961, in 1945, to more than two million dollars, in 1946.[70]

One of the special contributions of the American Quakers was the establishment of community centers in badly destroyed cities. Barracks were bought in Sweden and Switzerland and were erected in Frankfurt, Darmstadt, Cologne, Berlin, Brunswick and Freiburg. These centers offered daily activities for children and a warm place for old people. There were rooms in the center for shoe repair, carpentry, clothing repair and laundry-all on a self-help basis. The centers also provided educational and recreational facilities. The Americans did not run the centers, but brought "a concrete evidence of our interest and concern and the personal touch and contuct from outside," as Hertha Kraus explained the project, which was her initiative.[71]

Although Germany was high in AFSC agenda, Austria also received close attention. In October 1945, the help to the Austrian population was seriously discussed. AFSC relief to Austria was established gradually in three phases: distribution of food and clothing, mainly for children, through local agencies; industrial rehabilitation, such as the glass industry; and the erection of community centers. In 1946, due to the serious shortage of food and clothes, the American team of 8 members, assisted by local workers, concentrated on the first item. The AFSC Austrian relief expanded from $28.026, in 1945, to $400.000 in the following year.[72] In adition to Austria, AFSC, in collaboration with the British FRS, operated in Poland and Finland, mainly in a child feeding program.[73]

Participating in such a cooperative organization as CRALOG, with inefficiency on the one hand, and where every agency was working for its own aims and constituency, on the other, obviously led to friction and anger in Quaker circles. Unlike the AFSC, that provided relief without discrimination, other CRALOG corresponding agencies were interested in bringing help to their people. The Catholics and Lutherans, for example, insisted on distributing of supplies through local church authorities, instead of distributing food according to the greatest need, i.e. orphans and children.[74] Since AFSC personnel in the field was scarce,8-13 members for the three zones of Germany,they were unable to superwise the distribution of supplies, while other agencies had native counterparts to do the job. So AFSC could not guarantee to the donors that their contribution reached those greatest in need. Sometimes the situation was so desperate that many agreed with Claude C. Shotts, AFSC representative to CRALOG, who wrote in November 1947, "I hope the AFSC is continuing to consider the possibility of withdrawing from CRALOG at the earlier possible date that it can be done without injuring the effectiveness of its own German program." As a matter of fact, that was the Quaker dilemma, how to withdraw, without impairing AFSC projects. Although since December 1946 Quaker grievances reached boiling-point, there were serious arguments against leaving CRALOG, as an AFSC memorandum summed them up:"The AFSC has the reputation with other agencies of going its own way and being rather uncooperative." Breaking with CRALOG would be a proof of that "reputation." Withdrawal from CRALOG would arouse "considerable questions about its functioning", among its affiliated German ethnic groups. Furthermore, such an act could badly injure, and even stop, the child-feeding program, as well as other AFSC projects. The inter-office memorandum concluded its deliberation, writing:"This may not be the time to withdraw, but I believe we should be looking carefully to an end of the present relationship and work toward it."[75]

AFSC's difficulties as a licensed CRALOG agency, had repercussions on the home front, as well. The affiliation with twelve German ethnic groups, with purposes and methods of operations that were "not compatible" with those of the AFSC, embarrassed Quaker circles. The connection with the American Relief for Germany (ARG), is a case in point. That organization, with offices in Milwaukee and Chicago, was blamed of "continuing the Nazi propaganda", through its close association with the Stauben Society, which was termed as "the clearing house of Nazi propaganda".The Anti-Nazi League, a non-sectarian committee, called on the Quakers to break off their relations with a body "whose primary aim is to spread the Nazi poison propaganda of hatred."[76] The Anti-Nazi League's public attack upon ARG, inevitably involved the AFSC and embarrassed its leaders. Sumner A. Mills, director of the AFSC central European relief program, responded that affiliation did not mean "endorsement of creed." The AFSC was working with many agencies on relief projects and it "does not and cannot be presumed to endorse the beliefs of any group."[77] Apparently,the Anti-Nazi League's exposure of the Stauben Society's strong influence upon ARG's board, impressed a number of Quakers, who questioned the AFSC relationship with the AGR. In addition to the Nazi link, the Quakers opposed the use of their name for political fund-raising, (particularly in beer parties). The AFSC was reluctant to work with an organization which it could not control. In spite of the opinion of staff members that "we should discontinue our relationships with ARG", a new memorandum of agreement was drafted, after long deliberations, in July 1947.[78]

To be sure, all of these activities in Germany, Austria and Italy, as well as in other countries, were not directed on behalf of Displaced Persons, but rather on behalf of the civilian population. Eager to demonstrate that Quakers did not disregard the DPs, several memoranda pointed to the AFSC activities in the United States. "This statement has been prepared in response to a number of recent inquiries as to just what the present functions of our DP Services... are," declared Kathleen H. Hanstein's memorandum of October 1949.[79] The AFSC participated in the Citizens Committee on Displaced Persons, which lobbied for an emergency DP act. Eventually, Congress passed two DP acts (in 1948 and 1950), which allowed the admission of DPs. Accordingly, to June 1952, 393.542 refugees settled in the United States.[80] To face the staggering problems of securing jobs and housing, sending assurances, selecting prospective immigrants, receiving them at the piers, offering them temporary shelter and resettling hundred of thousands of newcomers during a short period, new relief committees were established, such as the Lutheran Resettlement Service and the National Catholic Resettlement Council. Existing agencies,such as the United Service for New Americans, expanded their activities. What was the AFSC contribution to that almost unprecedented resettlement undertaking? The Individual Services Unit (ISU), which was reorganized in June 1947, had a two fold responsibility: it handled all requests for services to individuals, and was responsible "for all general activities on behalf of DPs." The Unit usually cared only for individuals who had been referred to by Quakers, or friends of Friends. Many of these individuals were not displaced persons.[81] Sevices offered by ISU included a very limited migration program. "We... continue to carry a minimum migration record, but this is gradually dwindling, and it is our policy to refer new immigration queries to other agencies," reported an ISU worker in June 1947.[82] However,on a small scale, ISU continued to provide services of general counseling, employment counseling, hospitality and location services. The AFSC turned over to appropriate relief agencies most services, including selecting and escorting immigrants.[83] On a limited scale the Unit continued, for a while, the placement services for academicians and teachers. Out of 366 men who applied for employment opening, to August 15,1947, the Unit successfully placed 54. After that date, all AFSC cases were transferred to the American Committee for Emigre Scholars, Writers and Artists.[84] The gradual withdrawal of Quaker relief activities in the U.S. was in a wide front. It did not ask for governmental license for offering corporate affidavits for refugees. In 1947, it embarked upon a campaign to stimulate Friends to work for Assurances for immigration of DPs, but with meager results.[85]

Characteristic of this attitude was the withdrawal from the DP Commission. In October 1948, the AFSC applied to the Commission to be permitted to act as a recognized agency. A year later, however, Clarence Pickett wrote to the Commission that "during the intervening months it became clear that we would not be in a position to undertake the kind of project we had envisioned." Therefore, he requested "that our name be removed."[86]
Quaker hostels, which were popular in the war period, continued to operate. Responding to the queries of Earl G. Harrison, of the Citizens' Committee, as to how Quakers intend to join the great resettlement project, Clarence Pickett answered:"It is our belief that our particular contribution to DP resettlement in this country would lie largely in the field of hostels."[87]

The American Quakers were more active in participating in public committees. AFSC representatives dutifully participated in every non- sectarian, private, governmental and international organization that labored for the DPs, such as liaison officer to the International Refugee Organization, member of the DP executive committee of the American Council of Voluntary Agencies for Foreign Services, member of the Central Location Index Agency, to name a few. The AFSC wholeheartedly supported the DP legislation. It was affiliated to the Citizens' Committee and testified on its behalf before the House sub-committee on Immigration and Naturalization.[88] While on behalf of German civilians AFSC funnelled in 1946, $2.023.000, for DP services in the U.S. it expended during the same period the sum of $42.000 only.[89] Not everybody on AFSC staff was happy with such limited operations, or rather, with such lack of activities on behalf of DPs in America. Criticism on this approach was voiced time and again at the executive board meetings of the Foreign Service Section. Apparently, it was ineffective, since the AFSC did not change its course.[90]

The American Friends Service Committee, with a budget of seven million dollars and two hundred workers operated in 1947, in Asia as well. Following the Biblical slogan "if thine enemy hunger-feed him," the Quakers began in 1946 to offer relief and rehabilitation to Japan. India and China also received massive aid.[91] Another area that the AFSC entered in 1948 was Arab refugee camps in the Gaza strip. A team of 50 Quakers from nine countries, provided food, medicine and other supplies to 200.000 Arab refugees, from January 1949 to April 1950.[92]

In conclusion, while the AFSC provided help during World War II for refugees from Nazism, Christians as well as Jews, in the post-war era it failed to integrate into the massive relief program for one million people, both in Europe and in the U.S. On the other hand, it dedicated its energy, personnel and funds to the German and Austrian civilian population. How can one explain this seeming deviation from the Quaker slogan that it always helps the most needy?

A close examination of AFSC's activities clearly shows that it embarked on a program only when it was able to operate as a unit, on a supplementary basis. Furthermore, the Friends always stressed the importance of concentrating upon special pilot projects, in which they would be able to demonstrate 'the Quaker way'. Quakers did not provide 'pure relief' without considering the pros and cons. Since in cooperation with UNRRA in the DP camps their help was badly needed, as individuals, but not as a Quaker unit, AFSC withdrew from the DP program. However, in helping German civilians, there were certain fields, like the child nutrition program, or neighborhood centers, where they could propagate Quaker teaching of responding "to the cry of human suffering". Thus, there was no real deviation in Quaker operations during the post-war era. The Friends constantly maintained their policy "to get beyond relief into the more far-reaching openings for reconstruction and rehabilitation", to use the words of Clarence E. Pickett, the executive secretary. Jack Hollister, a leading Quaker in relief to Germany, explained further the meaning of that spiritual mission: "to give them (the Germans) a sense of participation in a Wider Quaker Fellowship."[93]

In spite of this reservation, The American Friends Service Committee clearly demonstrated devotion and faith to help the oppressed. For this constant service during the war and afterwards, the AFSC, together with the British Friends Relief Service, received in 1947, the Nobel Peace Prize.

NOTES

1. See, William E. Nawyn, American Protestantism's Response to Germany's Jews and Refugees,1933-1941 (Ann Arbor, Michigan; UMI Research Press,1981),p.107.
2. Draft of a Foreign Service Policy, November 20,1944 (The archives of the AFSC, Philadelphia.The files of Foreign Service,1944, Policy. Hereinafter cited as AFSC,FS).
3. Charles Chatfield, For Peace and Justice: Pacifism in America,1914-1941 (Knoxville, University of Tennessee Press,1971),pp.7-8.
4. See, the Foreword of Rufus M. Jones and Clarence E.Pickett in AFSC, Refugee Facts (1939),p.3.
5. AFSC,Minutes, Sub-Committee of Foreign Service Executive Committee, Report of Study of Refugee Division, April 14,1942 (AFSC,Minutes File=MF).
6. AFSC, Refugee Facts,p.3; Report of the Quaker Commission to the Third Reich,July 1,1939 (JDC archives, New York City, the files of AFSC).
7. Emma Cadbury to Carl Heath, April 7,1933 (AFSC,General File=GF,Austria,1933); Hertha Kraus to Clarence Pickett,March 27,1933 (ibid. Germany).
8. AFSC,Minutes, Meeting of the Foreign Service Section, December 11,1933 (AFSC;MF); Grace E.Rhodes to James McDonald, April 10,1934 (The Papers of James G. McDonald, Columbia University, New York City. Hereinafter cited as MP;GC=General File, AFSC)
9. Olive Sawyer to Andre Wurfbain, July 17,1934 (MP; The files of High Commissioner=H); McDonald to Hugh W.Moore, March 18,1934 (MP:GF:AFSC).
10. Norman Bentwich to McDonald, May 7,1935 (MP:GC).
11. Bentwich to Pickett, May 14,1935 (MP:GC).
12. McDonald to Bentwich, June 21,1935 (MP:GC).
13. Nawyn, American Protestantism's Response,p.109.
14. Hertha Kraus to CEP (Clarence E. Pickett), n.d. (AFSC:GF:1938 ;FS;RS).
15. Margaret E.Jones, Albert and Anne H. Martin, Elizabeth B.and D.Robert Yarnall, to the AFSC, October 1938 (AFSC:GF:1938;FS).
16. Clarence E. Pickett, For More Than Bread (Boston: Little, Brown & Co. 1953),p.202; Robert O. Byrd, Quaker Ways in Foreign Policy (Toronto; Toronto University Press, 1960),pp.22-23,86-87.
17. Kathleen H.Hanstein to Carolyn Zelany, January 25,1946 (The papers of the National Refugee Service=NRS, folder 1315, YIVO, Institute for Jewish Affairs, New York City); Pickett, For More Than Bread,p.142..
18. Minutes of the Refugee Committee, AFSC, September 26,1940 (AFSC:MF); Confidential Study

Concerning the Cost of Raising Relief Funds of the Foreign Relief Appeals in the Churches, June 1941 (Moss papers,box 145, the Federal Council of Churches collection, the Archives of the Presbyterian Historical Society,Philadelphia.)

19. Report of Hertha Kraus, n.d. (AFSC:GF:1938:FS:RS); Minutes,Refugee Committee,AFSC, February 3,1939 AFSC:MF).

20. "Summary of two memoranda in re-projects of the AFSC",1939 (JDC archives, AFSC); John F.Rich, "Americanization Through Quaker Hostels", 5pp. ms. n.d.(NRS papers,1315, YIVO).

21. AFSC, Refugee Division, Report, January 1-May 31,1942 (NRS papers, 1315, YIVO); Joseph Hyman to Henry Ittleson, July 24,1939 (JDC archives, AFSC); AFSC, Refugee Section, Executive Committee, January 15,24,1940 (AFSC:MF).

22. AFSC,Minutes, Refugee Committee, September 26,1940 (AFSC:MF); AFSC, Haverford Cooperative Workshop, 1941 (AFSC:GF:1941:RS).

23. AFSC, "American Seminar for Refugee Scholars,Teachers and Artists, Summer 1942 (AFSC:GF:1942:FS:RS); Claudia Gardiner, "An Experiment in Cooperative Scholarship" (AFSC:GF:1940:RS).

24. AFSC, Minutes, Refugee Section, October 24,1940 (AFSC:MF); Services for Refugee Scholars, Teachers and Students, AFSC, _Annual Report, 1941_ (AFSC:GF:1941:FS).

25. Stephen Duggan and Betty Drury, _The Rescue of Science and Learning: the Story of the Emergency Committee in Aid of Displaced Foreign Scholars_ (New York: Macmillan,1948), pp.62,86-88.

26. AFSC, _The Powell House Crier_, September, November,1944 (HIAS-HICEM papers, VII:61, YIVO); Bruce M. Mohler to Charles D. Gorman, October 4,1935 (The Papers of the National Catholic Welfare Conference, box 23, at the Center for Migration Studies, Staten Island, New York); Mohler, Summarization of Correspondence, February 25,1941 (_ibid_.box 82); The author's conversation with Prof. Hyman, August 3,1978.

27. Clarence Pickett to James N.Rosenberg, April 1,1935 (JDC archives, AFSC).

28. Hyman to Rosenberg, April 11,1935; Pickett to Hyman, December 6,1934; Cyrus Adler to the JDC, November 7,1933; Hyman,Memorandum to the Board of JDC, November 2,1933 (JDC+ archives, AFSC).

29. Memorandum, FNT (Frank N. Trager) to SW,December 29,1938 (The archives of the American Jewish Committee, New York City, Refugees, 1938-1944. Hereinafter cited as AJC): Pickett to Trager, April 5,1939 AFSC:GF:1940:Committees and Organizations=C&O); Pickett, _For More Than Bread_,p.148; H.W.Levy to Trager, September 1939 (AJC, Refugees). 30.AFSC, "Brief Summary of Major Recommendations from Report of Study of Refugee Division", May 1942 (AFSC:GF:1942:FS:R.); AFSC,Minutes, Advisory Committee of the Refugee Division, February 23,1943 ; AFSC, _Annual Report, 1943_ (NRS papers, 1315,YIVO).

31. AFSC, Minutes, Advisory Committee, Refugee Division, February 23,1943 (AFSC:MF);The AFSC was on _The Nation_'s Honor Roll for 1939 "for its unostentatious non-olitical and enormously effective work of bringing physical relief to the innocent victims of war and aggression." _The Nation_, 150 (January 6,1940),p.6; In addition, the AFSC, jointly with the British Friends, received, in 1939, the Wateler Peace Prize awarded by the Carnegie Foundation in the Heague, for their activities on behalf of refugees. Nawyn, _American Protestantism's Response_,p.134.

32. Pickett to Hyman, January 4,1939; Rufus M.Jones and Clarence Pickett to Paul Baerwald, January 20,1939; Baerwald to Pickett, January 25,1939; Hyman to Pickett, January 3,1939; Pickett to Hyman, January 4,1939 (AFSC:GF:1939); "Report of Quaker Commissioners to the Third Reich," July 1,1939 (JDC archives, AFSC).

33. Schauffler to Staff, March 12,April,1941; Letter no.76 from Philip Conard, October 4,1941 (AFSC:GF:1941:RS); Margaret Frawley to Pickett, March 30,1942 (AFSC:GF:1942,C&O).

34. Pickett, _For More Than Bread_,pp.140-141; Pickett to James G. Vail, February 4,1939 (AFSC:GF:1939); AFSC,Minutes, Refugee Committee, April 28,1939 (AFSC:MF).

35. Society of Friends, Vienna, October 16,1939; Mary Rogers to Lotte Marcuse, February 15,1940; Marcuse to Greenleigh, February 20, 1940 (The papers of German Jewish Children's Aid=GJCA, box 151, YIVO).

36. See, "Proposed Plan for German Refugee Children", n.d. (GJCA, box 151, YIVO).

37. Pickett, _For More Than Bread_,pp.181-182,179; F.Van Den Arend to AFSC, May 27,1941 (AFSC:GF:1941:FS:R); Robert C. Dexter to Pickett,April 2,1942 (AFSC:GF:1942:C&O).

38. AFSC, _Annual Report_, 1943 (NRS papers,1315,YIVO; AFSC, Foreign Service Budget, January 1,1944-January 1,1945 (AFSC:FS:1944:Finance); AFSC, Minutes, Refugee Section, Executive Committee,March 22,1940 (AFSC:MF); AFSC, Statement of Available Cash, Relief Division, November 30,1944 (AFSC:FS:1944).

39. Marjorie P.Schauffler to Howard W.Wriggins and David Hartley,January 19,1945 (AFSC;DP;1945;Italy); Margaret Frawley to Margaret Jones,July 31,1945 (AFSC;1945; Switzerland); Kathleen H.Hanstein to Philip E.Ryan, August 16,1945 (AFSC;DP Services =DPS;C&O,American Red Cross,1945); K.H.Hanstein to Samuel Sequerra, August 26,1947 (AFSC;DPS;1947; Correspondence); H.W. (Howard Wriggins) to LKC (Lorraine K.Cleveland),

July 20,1945; K.Hanstein to David Hartley, April 19,1945 (AFSC;DPS; 1945;Correspondence, Overseas).

40.AFSC,Foreign Sevice Section-Relief and Refugee Divisions, Statement of Income and Expenditures, Year Ended December 31,1945; (Hereinafter cited as Expenditures, 1945);AFSC,FSS,Budget, Year Ending September 30,1947. (Hereinafter cited as Budget,1946).(AFSC,DPS;1945,1947, Finance); Marjorie Schauffler to Steve Cary, April 25,1947 (AFSC;DPS;GF;1947); AFSC, Foreign Service Staff Meeting,October 22,1945 (AFSC;DPS;1945, Correspondence Overseas).

41.AFSC, Expenditures,1945; Budget,1946; AFSC,FSS, Minutes, September 29,1945 (AFSC;DPS ; 1945; Correspondence).

42.M.W. Beckelman to Lawrence MacGregor, July 17,1945 (AFSC;DPS;1945;C&O;IGC).

43.AFSC,Budget,1946.

44.See, Leonard Dinnerstein, America and the Survivors of the Holocaust (New York: Columbia University Press,1982),pp. 9-12.

45.J.Barclay Jones to UNRRA and SHAEF, July 10,1945 (The archives of the United Nations=UN, New York City. The Files of UNRRA,PAG-4/3.0.11.0.1.6:8).

46.Undated one page ms.begins with the words "The AFSC has learned with great satisfaction that Mr. Earl G.Harrison is going to Germany." (UN archives,UNRRA,PAG-4/3.0.11.0.1.6:8)).

47.Robert Murphy to Barclay Jones, July 28,1945; JCT on AFSC,August 6,1945; M.Bradford to Major Jones, August 11,1945 (UN archives,UNRRA, PAG-4/3.0.11.0.1.6:8).

48.Paul S. Edwards to Lilli Kochler, April 24,1947 (UN archives,UNRRA, PAG-4/3.0.11.0.1.6:8).

49. AFSC, Expenditures,1945; Budget,1946.

50. Report of the Quaker Commissioners, February,1946 (AFSC;Germany;1946;Reports); Barclay Jones to UNRRA and SHAEF, July 10,1945 (UN archives,UNRRA,PAG-4/3.0.11.0.1.6:8).

51."Report on the FRS Retreat and Conference, held at Bielefeld, Germany,March 7-10,1947," March 28,1947 (AFSC;Germany;1947; Conferences).

52.William C.Adgerton to AFSC, January 23,1946 (AFSC;Germany; UNRRA Reports;1946).

53.AFSC, Minutes, Foreign Service Executive Committee, January 17,1944 (AFSC;MF).

54.AFSC, Minutes, Foreign Service Section, April 27,1944 (AFSC;MF).

55.Pickett, For More Than Bread,p.191.

56.Ilja Dijour to L.K.Cleveland, February 13,1945; Cleveland to Dijour, February 15,1945 (HIAS-HICEM papers, VII;63;YIVO);AFSC;Minutes, Foreign Service Section, May 5,1945 (AFSC;MF).

57.Report of Edward N.Wright to the AFSC, for the Month of September 1945; E.N.Wright to UNRRA US Zone Headquarters,February 21,1946 (UN archives, UNRRA,PAG-4/3.0.11.0.1.6:8).

58.William S.Boe to Assistant Director Relief Services, Division Child Welfare Officer, February 13,1946; Paul B.Edwards to Lilli Koehler, April 24,1947 (UN,archives, UNRRA, PAG-4/3.0.11.0.1.6:8).

59.A.J.B. "Report of Discussion on April 9,1946, at FRS Friends House, London. Subject:American Personnel for FRS";Unidentified to Julia Branson, April 27,1946 (AFSC, Germany,1946,Reports); On the relief activities of the British Friends Relief Services in Germany, see Roger C.Wilson,Quaker Relief: An Account of the Relief Work of the Society of Friends, 1940-1948. London:George Allen and Union, 1952.

60.Marjorie Schauffler to Steve Cary, April 25,1947; Memorandum: "Present Services of the AFSC for DPs",July 1,1947; Kathleen Hanstein to Clarence Pickett et al, October 25,1949 (AFSC; DPS; Germany;1947).

61.Clarence Pickett to Edward M.O'Connor, October 5,1949 (The National Archives, Washington D.C. The files of DP Commission, box 4).

62.The priority was in this order. See, AFSC, German Relief Conference, November 22-23,1946 (AFSC;Germany;1946).

63.Edward N.Wright,"There Are the People I Have Met", Report,n.d.(ca. August 1946),(AFSC; Germany;1946; Reports); See also, W.W."Living Off the Land," n.d. (ibid. 1947).

64. Gilbert MacMaster, A Page from Fastenhirtenbrief 1946 of the Archbishop of Freiburg, Germany, Circulated on the 22nd of February, 1946 (AFSC;Germany;1946).

65.Roswell McClelland to Clarence Pickett, May 11,1945 (AFSC; Switzerland; 1945).

66.Jack Hollister to Dear, April 22,1947 (AFSC;Germany;1947).

67.J.B.Jones to UNRRA and SHAEF, July 10,1945 (UN archives, UNRRA,PAG-4/3.0.11.0.1.6:8); Report of the Quaker Commissioners to Germany, February 1946 (AFSC;Germany; 1946;Reports).

68.See, Immediate Release, February 19,1946 (UN archives, UNRRA, PAG-4/3.0.11.0.1.6:12); CRALOG, Report, October 1,1947 (AFSC;Germany;1947;C&O).

69.AFSC,Budget,1946; Hollister to Dear, April 22,1947 (AFSC; Germany;1947).

70. AFSC, Foreign Service Section, "Services for Persons in Germany", January 1,1947; AFSC, "Quaker Work in Germany," December,1947 (AFSC; Germany;1947); AFSC, Expenditures, 1945; Budget, 1946.

71.AFSC,German Relief Conference, November 22-23,1946 (AFSC; Germany;1946); Jack Hollister to Arthur Joice, May 1, 1947(AFSC;Germany;1946;C&O); Clarence Pickett to Dear Friend, n.d. (AFSC;Germany;1947).

72. AFSC, Foreign Service Staff Meeting, October 22,1945 (AFSC;DPS;1945;Correspondence Overseas); George Mathias to R.A.R. Parminter, May 24,1946 (UN archives, UNRRA,PAG-4/4.2:24); AFSC,Expenditures, 1945; Budget, 1946.

73. B.M.Wellington to M.Creagh, July 20,1946 (UN archives, UNRRA,PAG-4/2.0.6.1:15).

74. Overseas News Agency, German Edition, Landrum Bolling, "CRALOG A Failure", September 14,1946; Sumner Mills to Joseph Simmons, September 16,1946; Claude Shotts to Jack Hollister, February 19,1947 (AFSC;Germany; 1946,1947; C&O).

75. Claude Shotts to Wesley Huss, November 10,1947; See also, Jack Hollister to Elmore Jackson, June 27,1947 (AFSC; Germany;1947;C&O); Memorandum from Julia E. Branson, December 20,1946 (ibid. 1946).

76. Herman Hoffman and James H.Sheldon to Rufus Jones, May 20, 1946 (AFSC;Germany;1946;C&O).

77. Mills to Anti-Nazi League, May 23,1946 (AFSC;Germany; 1946;C&O).

78. Memorandum, Giles L. Zimmerman, "American Relief for Germany and AFSC Relationships," July 17,1947; Joe Brown to Claude Shotts, July 21,1947, "Report on Relationships with ARG"; William K. Russell to Otto R. Hauser, September 16,1947; "Memorandum of Agreement Between AFSC and American Relief for Germany",July 23,1947 (AFSC;Germany; 1947;C&O).

79. Kathleen H.Hanstein to Clarence Pickett et al. October 25, 1949 (AFSC;DPS;1949;General); See also, Pickett to Earl Harrison, April 28,1947; "Present Services of AFSC for DPs", July 1,1947 (AFSC;DPS ;1947;C&O).

80. Dinnerstein, America and the Survivors of the Holocaust, p.286, Table A12. See in Dinnerstein a detailed discussion of U.S.DP Legislation.

81. AFSC,ISU,"Job Analysis, as of June 1,1947 (AFSC;DPS; 1947;General); Elizabeth F. Berth to Clara Brown, October 21,1947 (ibid., Branches).

82. Agnes Gallagher to Paul B.Johnson, June 3,1947 (AFSC;DPS; 1947; Branches).

83. AFSC, "Present Sevices of AFSC for DPs," July 1,1947 (AFSC; DPS;1947; General); K.H.Hanstein to Ingeberg Olsen, August 24,1945; "Planning Discussions Re: Migration Service," February 10,1945 (AFSC;DPS; 1945; C&O).

84. AFSC,ISU, "The Counselling and Placement Services for Refugees," November 20,1947 (AFSC;DPS;1947;General); A.B. Miller to Pickett, September 15,1947 (ibid.,C&O).

85. AFSC, Kathleen Hanstein to Pickett et al. October 25,1949 (AFSC;DPS;1949; General).

86. Clarence Pickett to Edward M. O'Connor, October 5,1949 (National Archives, DP Commission, box 4).

87. Pickett to Harrison, April 28,1947 (AFSC;DPS;1947;C&O).

88. K.Hanstein to Pickett et al. October 25,1949 (AFSC;DPS; 1949;General).

89. AFSC, Budget, 1946.

90. Marjorie Schauffler to Steve Cary, April 25,1947; Hanstein to Pickett et al. October 25,1949; ISU,"Job Analysis," July 1,1947; "Present Services of AFSC for DPs," July 1,1947 (AFSC;DPS; General; 1947,1949).

91. Pickett, For More Than Bread,p.194. Hoffman and Sheldon to Jones, May 20,1946 (AFSC;Germany;1946;C&O); AFSC, Budget,1946. See a detailed report on AFSC relief and rehabilitation activities in Asia, Pickett, For More Than Bread, chapter 7.

92. Pickett, For More Than Bread,pp.284-285,274-284; AFSC, Quaker Work Among Arab Refugees (Philadelphia, 1950).

93. Pickett, For More Than Bread,p.20; Jack Hollister to Dear, April 22,1947 (AFSC;Germany;1947)

SOME CHRISTIAN RESPONSES IN BRITAIN TO THE JEWISH CATASTROPHE. 1933 - 1945.

RICHARD GUTTERIDGE.

SELWYN COLLEGE, CAMBRIDGE, ENGLAND.

1933

The issue of the Jewish Chronicle on April 7, 1933 contained an appeal to the leaders of British Christendom to raise their voices loudly in widespread, unflinching protest at the blatant persecution of the Jews in Germany based upon "devilish doctrine and negation of all that the Churches preach and hold dear". Richard Downey, Roman Catholic Archbishop of Liverpool, had already a few days previously assured the Jewish Society of the local University that he would do all in his power to protest. True to his word, at an inter-denominational rally in the Central Hall he denounced the effects of narrow, grasping racial prejudice. "The friends of Germany, those who wish her well," he declared, "are anxiously watching her to see if they can discern any symptoms of a change of heart."[1] At a similar meeting in London on June 27, Dr Lang, the Archbishop of Canterbury, gave an assurance that it was not organised out of any kind of hostility to the German nation. He appealed to Hitler and his Government to restrain the vehemence of their followers. There was, he felt, a great hope that before long the German People would understand the real basis of national strength and self-respect. In the meantime it was necessary for those for whom justice was a part of their heritage to speak out if only to ease their own conscience. A speaker on behalf of the Free Churches professed indignation at evidence of the violation of civil and religious freedom, for which they themselves had had generation after generation to adopt a historic stand, but denied any desire to interfere in the internal life of such a great country as Germany. A Catholic layman, after expressing admiration for much that had been achieved by Hitler, advocated telling the Führer very respectfully but very firmly that acts of injustice to the Jews and others would cause the collapse of his regime.[2]

At the General Assembly of the Church of Scotland there was issued the first of an annual sequence of solemn statements denouncing anti-semitism and its incitement to persecution. In May, the General Purpose Committee of the Methodist Church publicly expressed its indignation at the persecution of the Jews as an expression of racial injustice and cruelty, tempered by appeal to both rulers and people in Germany to make a complete and speedy end to a policy which effectually alienated the sympathy with the German People which was coming to prevail throughout the world.[3] An Editorial in the Methodist Recorder pointed out that there were Christians in Germany who had "hitherto been almost unaware of the semitic strain in their blood" and were now beginning to realise the predicament of their likely catastrophic involvement.[4]

William Temple, the Archbishop of York, in May called for an understanding of the cause and character of Nazi Germany which, as he claimed, had "gained the support of a large number of the best citizens of the country". Whatever excuse, he added, might be made for deeds of violence committed in the course of a revolution, no condemnation could be too severe for the persecution and the organised terror which had undeniably ensued.[5] At another meeting he insisted that there had never been a revolution accompanied by so large a measure of systematic bullying, and this forbad silence at the infringement of civilised standards.[6]

The Bishop of Gloucester, Dr Arthur Headlam, performed a unique feat in the mid-summer issue of his diocesan gazette by simultaneously condemning the foolish and violent treatment of the Jews in Germany, and launching his own attack upon many of them as constituting an unpleasant and unhealthy alien element within German society with a measure of responsibility for the violence of Russian Communism and for using their free thinking Judaism as basis for attack upon the Christian Faith.[7]

The Catholic Times and The Catholic Herald both struck a discordant note in 1933. The former, which on March 17 emphasized that the extermination of the Jews was a main plank in the Nazi programme, a fortnight later condemned international Jewry for the present state of world distress,for propagating irreligion and immodesty and for being in sinister fashion behind the grievous world-wide persecution of Catholics. "If", as it was stated, "Jewry had cleaner hands, it would be easier to show sympathy, but it has only itself to blame for its present predicament in Germany". While not condoning the oppression of Jews as individuals, international Jewry had to be regarded as a "heinous thing, the stamping out of which would be beneficial".[8] The latter, when referring to anti-semitic discrimination and violence in Germany, usually made out that Catholics were experiencing worse suffering, if not in Germany, then in other parts of the world. "We do not", it was stated, "assail Fascist Italy and applaud Soviet Russia, as do some of our loud-voiced and hypocritical contemporaries, to whom wholesale murder and incendiarism in Spain are of no consequence - as they are anti-Catholic - while far lesser wrongs done in Germany are most infamous because done against Jews".[9]

Those in Britain involved in Christian missionary work among the Jews tended to regard the persecutions promoted by the Nazis as a moment of opportunity. At the Annual General Meeting of the Barbican Mission a speaker declared, "What a wonderful time for winning the Jews! Just at this time, when they are suffering sorely, when their hopes are crushed and hearts broken. Now is the time to proclaim the love of Him whom they crucified."[10] In the journal of the Church of England Mission to the Jews is to be found a similar tingle of excitement. "What a marvellous evangelising agency the Jews could become, scattered all over the world! Think of the possibility of the Jews being filled with the Love of Christ!"[11]

1935 - 1936

Immediately before the promulgation of the Nuremberg Laws on September 15, 1935 there appeared in The Catholic Times a paragraph stating that the Jewish problem would not be solved by harshness and injustice, it being a problem due to separate Jewish and national religious consciousness and accentuated through Nazi measures aimed at inculcating a sense of inferiority in Jewish minds. It was the view of the writer that it would be far better for the German authorities to attain to a proper understanding with the Jewish leaders that would allow for a charter of rights and duties, mutually agreed and binding on both sides. This should at least allow the two sides to live side by side without constraint, persecution and bad feeling.[12] That such a suggestion could have been seriously advanced can only be described by us today as an astounding failure to recognise that the cruel and inhumane treatment to which the Jews had already been patently subjected was part and parcel of the implementation of the official NSDAP programme.

The Nuremberg legislation had the effect of depriving the Jew of all rights of citizenship and grading him to the state of a pariah. After September 15, the term 'non-aryan' had acquired a legal and constitutional meaning, and German anti-semitism, as Andrew Sharf has expressed it, "was no longer some kind of tactics on the part of her leaders or an expression of enthusiasm on the part of her followers: it was procedure established by law and embodied in the constitution."[13] The Catholic Times in its next leader entitled 'The Jews' acknowledged that as a result of the decrees just published, the Jews had become practically an outlaw people, disinherited and segregated, and on racial not religious grounds such as would have been formerly the case. Branding race exaltation as the sheerest lunacy, with half of the present hostility resting upon mere suspicion, the writer complained of such modern propaganda against the Jews having reached British shores and been swallowed by some of his fellow-citizens, and he pleaded for fair play for the local victims.[14]

The British Weekly, the Free Church organ, commented only briefly on what had happened, by odd selection for particular stricture of the decree forbidding 'aryan' servants below a certain age accepting employment in Jewish households, and expressing the naïve hope that the Führer might be induced to reconsider so unmerciful an edict that would cause unemployment to thousands. A further lame observation was to the effect that so long as Hitler made himself responsible for what seemed to us cruel measures because of a certain admixture of blood, he would never secure from us unreserved friendship and good will.[15] The Tablet in similar fashion featured in its comment the comparatively minor decree forbidding Jews to fly the national flag, though permitted to display Jewish colours under State protection.[16]

The Church of England Guardian after deliberation took the matter really seriously. The goal was none other than the extinction of Jewish life in Germany in relentless, deadly and pitiless destruction, and to be carried out regardless of loss of sympathy, friendship and respect from much of the outside world. "Worst of all," the Editor concluded, "would be the loss of Germany's own soul. If the exercise proved successful, and there were no more Jews left to persecute, the evil spirit would seek other victims to devour, and turn to other forms of persecution. European Christians were looking on with shame and dread."[17]

On September 20, at the autumn session of the Church of England Assembly, the Bishop of Chichester was the proposer of a cautiously worded resolution expressing sympathy with the persecuted Jews in Germany and trusting that Christians in Britain and elsewhere would make it plain to the rulers in Germany that continuance of their repressive policy would arouse indignation and jeopardise confident relations. George Bell confessed his great reluctance in fulfilling this role, as he had a profound admiration for Germany and appreciated the real creative work being done by National Socialism in many aspects. Nevertheless, he felt compelled to undertake the task on both Christian and humanitarian grounds, because a wrong was being committed unworthy of a great civilised nation. What he sought to invoke was not wrathful invective but a friendly appeal to desist from the present course of action. It is difficult to believe that Bell, who was so well informed as to what was really afoot in Germany, could have hoped that the Führer and his entourage would respond to so soft a touch. What Bell presumably desired was a public expression of open concern from the Established Church in a form that was not calculated to worsen the plight of those needing succour.

Dr Parsons, Bishop of Southwark, who also spoke in controlled terms, emphasized the unreasonableness of the Nazis in making it impossible for the Jews to live in Germany and at the same time making it increasingly difficult for them to leave it except as paupers. His concluding remark was to the effect that for the future welfare of Germans and Jews alike, who had both contributed so much for humanity, the present rulers of Germany should be urged to come to a wiser, humaner and more truly noble mind.

Despite the extreme care shown by the two bishops, it was not altogether surprising that a dissenting lay voice was raised requesting that the motion should not be put. The issue under review was declared by him to be purely and simply a political one, and not a religious but a race question. It was, therefore, not the function of the Church to interfere politically, particularly as Englishmen with their dubious record should be the last in the world to dictate how another nation should handle a race question. Germany had the right to deal with their race problem in their own way. The Nuremberg legislation was actually a great victory for the moderate forces at work in Germany. A motion such as proposed could well strengthen the extremists among the Nazis.

This contribution caused Bishop Hensley Henson, of Durham, to rise to his feet, not equipped with a prepared speech, but for that very reason perhaps, all the more pungent and electrifying. Henson was famed for clear and incisive oratory. He had three points to make. Nazi Germany through its treatment of the Jews was in peril of excluding itself from the fellowship of civilised people. The nonsense about race, as if it were some particular poison in the ancestry of Judaism to be guarded against by all manner of restrictions, was sheer hallucination. It was preposterous that the 'children of Christendom' with such a basic obligation to the Jewish People should turn on the ancient People of God to whom they owed religiously, spiritually and morally, almost everything they valued. Most arresting of all, Henson declared that, on learning of one base device added to another to degrade, wound, injure and finally destroy the Jews, he felt a kind of blind rage within himself, that they could not draw the sword and go to the help of the low against the mighty.[18] Henson won the attention of the nazi Völkischer Beobachter, the London correspondent of which charged him of incitement to war, and suggested that the 'English High Church' would do well to concern itself with its own affairs, such as the shootings in Belfast, the plight of the miners and the squalor of London suburbs. The Bishop became a hero to the British community of Jews who recommended that his speech should be circulated in Germany in pamphlet form, where it was apparently read widely and with appreciation.[19]

On January 28, 1936 Henson learnt that British universities were being invited to take part in the celebration of the 550th anniversary of the foundation of Heidelberg University which had been obliged to expel its Jewish professors and refuse admission to Jewish students. He felt enraged at the thought that any British university should demean itself by presenting a congratulatory address to a learned institution that was so racially intolerant. George Bell in support said that a rocket in The Times was just what was wanted. This was duly fired on February 4, and contained the superb sentence, "It cannot be right that the universities of Great Britain, which we treasure as the very citadel of sound learning, because they are the vigilant guardians of intellectual freedom, should openly fraternise with the avowed and shameless enemies of both."[20]

George Bell had been since 1933 devoting himself with dogged persistence to the task of arousing interest in church circles in the predicament facing Christians in Germany of Jewish ancestry, but with discouraging results. Refugee relief was very largely conceived of in purely Jewish terms. An outcome of the passing of the Nuremberg decrees with the formalised and obligatory distinction between 'aryan' and 'non-aryan' highlighted the plight of Christian refugees.[21] The Archbishop of Canterbury issued on May 1, 1936 an appeal for £50,000 in support of 'non-aryan' Christian refugees, 2,500 of whom were reckoned to be in actual destitution. Nearly a fifth part of the money raised by the British Jewish community had been spent on Christians. This generous help could scarcely be anticipated in the case of new arrivals.

William Simpson, so well known and revered later as General Secretary of the Council for Christians and Jews, wrote to The Church Times drawing attention to the National Christian appeal for refugees from Germany. He described the parlous plight of Christian men and women of partial Jewish origin accepted on sufferance in Britain and other parts of the world whose future was without hope unless supported by other Christians. He quoted a Jewish refugee friend who said "We Jews know why we are being persecuted, and as a People are accustomed to it. These others do not understand. Why don't you Christians do something practical to help them?"[22]

1938 - 1939

Bishop Bell, whose aim was consistently not just to protest by word but to do something definite and practical, was disheartened at the paltry support given to the National Christian Appeal for Refugees, which was wound up in 1937 after having raised but £11,000 from Christian sources at home and abroad. He straightway formed a Church of England Committee for 'non-aryan' Christians which continued in being right up to the end of the War. At the Church Assembly in June 1938 he raised the issue of the sufferings in Germany and Austria,[23] avowing that he was not being political or out to attack "the leadership of the great German State". His object was to exhort the British Government to do everything possible to assist in the emigration of those in such great distress and to invite Christians everywhere to give evidence of their sympathetic fellowship. It would be wrong, in his opinion, to make a separation, and leave Jews to Jews and Christians to Christians. It was a matter of appeal to all humanity. Except for the wonderful contribution of the Quakers and of certain individuals,[24] the Christian response had been woefully small. The significance of the Master, whom they professed to serve, being a Jew was but dimly recognised. Four days later Bell made his maiden speech in the House of Lords, pleading for the Government to provide suitable training for younger refugees in Britain and scope for colonial settlement.[25] On the eve of what proved to be the dilatory and inconclusive Refugee Conference at Evian, he was signatory to an appeal to the British delegation to urge the Conference to act with speed and courage, if Christianity were to mean anything, civilised standards were to be preserved anywhere and the great democracies were to retain their ancient tradition of freedom and right of asylum.[26]

There was no doubt that there would be an outraged reaction from the Churches in Britain to the events of 'Crystal Night' and their aftermath. It was hard to come to terms with the sheer brutality of the whole operation but six months after the euphoric greeting that had been given to the Munich agreement. In a letter to The Times, Archbishop Lang claimed to speak for the Christian People of this country in the expression of indignation. Silence was impossible in face of the excesses of hatred and malice that had been revealed, though it was distasteful to have to write as he did, just when there was a general desire in Britian to be on friendly terms with the German nation.[27] Archbishop Downey censured the savage treatment of the Jews as a crime against humanity and in no wise, as Germany would claim, a matter of internal policy and just her own concern.[28] Dr James Black, the Moderator of the Church of Scotland, wrote to the Chief Rabbi deploring the cruelty which brought the so sorely afflicted Jewish People once more under the harrow, and praying that God would so stir the hearts of all decent men and all sane nations, so that the persecution should stop.[29]

The Baptist Union in deeply deploring and condemning the vindictive measures taken as being unworthy of a strong nation, was worried lest the prospect of improved relations between Britain and Germany should be seriously prejudiced. "We respectfully ask the Prime Minister to represent to the German Führer the disappointment and distress felt at recent happenings, and request parties to the Munich agreement to consult together with other Powers in order that the work of appeasement may be carried forward."[30] In The Guardian the nazi lust for cruelty was declared to be maniacal and, while sympathy was felt for the Prime Minister and his high-minded policy of appeasement, it was felt that the temper of the British People might rise to a point of demanding "no more touch with hands reeking with innocent blood".[31] The Church Times was pessimistic of the outside world's capability of stopping or mitigating such insensate racial rage. The crisis that 'Munich' had circumvented was still very much alive with civilisation in mortal danger. Further denunciation was valueless, but prompt rescue action on behalf of the victims, with room for settlement in America and the British Dominions, was of paramount importance.[32] The British Weekly struck a pious note, admitted shared guilt for what had happened, and recommended a Day of Humiliation, Penitence and Intercession throughout Christendom.[33] The contribution of The Catholic Times can only be described as weird. After having disavowed the issuing of protests as dangerously inflammatory and not in the interests of the afflicted Jews, the editorial unfolded an incredibly sinister plot, akin to the Protocols of Zion, with Germany in the role of victim of what was to be described as the "Money Power"; a plot largely Jewish in inspiration and out to strangulate the Third Reich. In the inevitable warfare the Jews in Germany had become the unfortunate hostages.[34]

A most effective Protest Meeting was held in the Albert Hall in London on December 1, with the Chief Rabbi, William Temple and the Cardinal Archbishop of Westminster together on the platform. It was Hinsley who stole the thunder on this occasion. In 1935 Hinsley was a surprising but inspired choice for Westminster, a sixty-nine year old Yorkshireman, who brought a much needed breath of fresh air into his native branch of the Catholic Church. He was of a blunt but warm and fatherly disposition and determined that English Roman Catholics should be patriotic, free of suspicion of fascist leanings and able to fulfil their role in national life. He himself could not comprehend how a true Christian could be a convinced Nazi, and employed a vigorous and uncompromising style of speech and unambiguous terminology in castigating unrighteousness and oppression. Hinsley began by declaring that "we meet on the ground of a common humanity". There was no intention of participating in a political demonstration. He was present to uphold the dignity and rights of human personality against tyranny and persecution upon whomsoever, and wheresoever committed. He proceeded to assert that "in the twentieth century we fondly dreamed that we had so far advanced in culture that the principle of practical toleration had become almost universal, at least among superior races. Now Nero who revelled in the persecution of Jews and Christians in incendiarism appears to some as a model of righteousness."[35]

Dr Goebbels' newspaper, Angriff, was swift to complain of such preaching of hatred, with the sneer that Hinsley was once a missionary to negroes, and that that must have accustomed him to adopt so remarkable a tone. Cardinals had been making the cause of the Jews theirs, and that could explain the entry into the lists of the Cardinal arm in arm with the heretical Archbishop of York and the Chief English Rabbi to challenge the twentieth century.[36]

As well as expressing shock and outrage at the Pogrom, it was accepted that the utmost needed to be done to encourage the sponsoring, admission and settlement of Jews and 'non-aryan' Christians who could manage to flee from their persecutors. Thousands of children, in particular, ought to be brought out without delay. Church congregations up and down the land should be making themselves responsible for the care of a certain number of refugees, with committees set up in towns and villages. People, it was believed, were anxious to help. It was up to clergy and ministers to give a lead.[37]

Bishop Bell presented to the Church Assembly on November 15 a motion welcoming the formation of the interdenominational Christian Council for Refugees from Germany, and desiring the Church of England to set an example of generous giving with the Central Board of Finance voting the sum of £5,000 for aid to refugee Christians of Jewish descent. Bell estimated that there were probably as many 'non-aryan' Christians as full Jews in dire distress. If money were forthcoming, the Government would not make any specific restrictions and action could be speedily taken. So far the total amount contributed by Christians had been mean in the extreme. To Bell's gratification the Assembly recommended the figure of £50,000 from central funds.[38] He himself set the magnificent example by personally guaranteeing, subject to Home Office permits being granted, support of twenty 'non-aryan' pastors and their families. A few weeks later his guests had arrived, some owing their release from concentration camp solely to his invitation, and were provided with initial accommodation within his diocese.[39]

On December 19, Cardinal Hinsley convened a representative gathering in order that Catholic work for refugees might be placed on an altogether broader basis in concern for all those in need.[40] The Secretary of the Catholic Committee for Refugees in his turn was able to report a willingness to provide help for others than fellow Catholics, and wrote, "We love the Jew because he is our fellow man. We love the Christian of whatever creed, because he shares our love for Christ."[41] In March 1939 the Hierarchy of England and Wales issued an appeal to the Faithful to join in relieving all those suffering persecution, irrespective of race or belief, describing such action as the privilege of following the example of the Good Samaritan.[42]

The Free Church leaders made known their support of the National Council for Refugees and Lord Baldwin's General Fund in a letter to The British Weekly in which they pledged money to the point of sacrifice, hospitality for children in need, and vigorous representation to Government and Members of Parliament, that Britain should vindicate her historical mission as friend and helper of the Oppressed.[43]

William Simpson, at a public meeting, expressed his deep sense of despondency at the failure of the Government to respond adequately to the refugee crisis. It had flung the already overwhelming problem upon the group of voluntary organisations which had been wrestling with it for the past four or five years. He could not take seriously governmental schemes for settlement in Tanganyika and British Guiana that were both unworthy and unrealistic.[44]

The English Quakers, as could be expected, were concerned with practical relief action rather than indignant protest. The work undertaken by their 'German Emergency Committee' since 1933 has been described as "often tiresome, never spectacular and without glory". The staff employed was increased to sixty in December 1938 in the attempt to cope with as many as 14,000 case files. The Committee changed its name in 1942 to 'The Friends' Committee for Refugees and Aliens', and the Quaker Office held the stories of 22,000 people who had asked for help.[45]

In the Church of Scotland, where service to the Jews was concerned, the evangelistic motive was undoubtedly decisive. The Mission to the Jews Committee reported annually to the Assembly as to activity both in the home field and on the continent of Europe and in Palestine. A wider concern can be detected after the Crystal Night Pogrom and throughout 1939. This is clear from perusal of the Church's magazine, Life and Work. The organising Secretary of the Committee appealed for assistance to be given to 'non-aryan' Christians who had been labelled as Jews. Christianity and humanity demanded that something definite should be done speedily for their rescue. Notice was given of a complete reorganisation of plans for coping with the hospitality so urgently required for both children and adults. In Edinburgh a meeting was held to further Jewish and Christian fellowship and better understanding, friendly discussion of points of difference and agreement and joint measures to encounter anti-semitism.[46]

Outstanding among the Scottish missionaries was Robert Smith who was appointed in 1935 for full-time service in Prague; an admirable choice of a young minister who had himself experienced out in Germany the early days of the nazi revolution and quickly became aware of the fragile situation of continental Jews and of their needs. Smith produced a yearly report. In 1936 he told of his efforts in presenting the relationship of Judaism and Christianity, and how he had developed a sympathetic message for young Jews not satisfied with barren materialism and prevailing scepticism. He reported on his work among a few of the multitude of men, women and children who were literally starving and so full of fear. In 1937 he dealt upon the dark and heart-rending refugee problem, remarking how hypocritical it could be to work in the traditional missionary style without being prepared to seek to alleviate distress. In 1938 he emphasized how much his usefulness as missioner depended upon the generosity of the Church at home in supplying funds in aid of refugee relief. Finally, in 1939 Robert Smith wrote of the struggle to avert spurious conversions among the multitude of Jewish refugees. A frank statement which he issued to all enquirers resulted in only ten per cent persevering in application for baptism, with six months of instruction obligatory.[47]

During 1939 there were some notable expressions of satisfaction at the prospects of a fertile harvest in missionary activity among Jews both at home and abroad in their present predicament. Such an attitude was manifest at the Annual General Meeting of the Church of England's Mission to the Jews. Dr Perowne, the Bishop of Worcester, in his presidential address declared that the Jews, having to suffer as never before, were turning to Christ. The Society's General Secretary, the Rev. C. H. Gill, emphasized the prime importance of bringing the Gospel message to refugees, for never, in his view, had there been such a spirit of enquiry. Bishop Tubbs, Dean of Chester, described the works of the Mission as being "the supreme act of reparation for the wrong of centuries". At another C.M.J. meeting a speaker insisted that the Jewish problem, so often treated as a humanitarian one, ought to be regarded as a fundamentally spiritual one, namely how Jesus Christ was to be presented as a reality to God's Ancient People. The Bishop of Fulham, responsible under the Bishop of London for the supervision of Anglican ministration in parts of Europe, appealed for further financial support for the work of C.M.J. on the grounds that, owing to political conditions, there was what might be described as a mass movement of Jews towards Christianity. Such was an opportunity that should be seized with thoughtful encouragement of true conversion of heart. At the Annual Meeting of the Barbican Mission to the Jews, the Director, the Rev. J. E. Davidson, described how on visits to Europe he had found Jews eager to listen to the Gospel, leading to confession by a considerable number of them, after very careful instruction, of faith in Christ. God, he felt, was indeed working out His purpose in a wonderful way. In contrast to such evangelistic fervour a sobering remark of James Parkes in a sermon delivered in Oxford in 1939 merits quotation. "We have failed to convert the Jews", he said, "and we shall always fail, because it is not the will of God that they shall become Gentile Christians; anti-semitism has failed to destroy the Jews, because it is not the will of God that essential parts of His Revelation should perish."[48]

1942 - 1944

As in the latter half of 1942 there was an increasing awareness of the sheer devilry of the calculated campaign of extermination, British Church leaders did not hesitate to raise their voices, with William Temple, who had been enthroned as Archbishop Canterbury in April, and Cardinal Hinsley pre-eminent. On June 10, Hinsley presided over a Czechoslovak Protest Meeting in London, and expressed condemnation of the mass murder of innocent human beings and the appalling atrocities committed against a whole population, and described the cruel persecution of Jews merely because of their Jewishness as an outstanding outrage against all sense of justice and humanitarian principles. Following reports of 700,000 Jews being massacred in Poland, both archbishops gave vent early in July to their feelings on the European Service of the BBC. Temple spoke of "so terrible a violation of human and divine law", while Hinsley in his typically forthright style decried the attitude of those who rejected offhand what did not directly concern themselves and saw fit to dismiss sneeringly the clearest of evidence as British propaganda. "But mighty is the Truth; murder will out", maintained the Cardinal. "Innocent blood cries to Heaven for vengeance, and the Lord will repay in good time".[49]

On October 15, George Bell, addressing his fellow bishops in Convocation, declared Hitler to be the arch-destroyer whose force was for killing, as exemplified by the ceaseless and systematic deportation of the Jews including the thousands of refugees from Vichy France, where they thought they were safe from the Oppressor.[50]

A packed meeting was held in the Albert Hall in London on October 29, convened to help in publicising the enormity of nazi bestiality, with an audience of ten thousand, many of whom were largely unaware of what was really happening. Dr Hertz, as The Church Times recorded, spoke with prophetic fire in the name of the six million upon whom sentence of death had been pronounced. William Temple declared that the purpose of the meeting was not to stir up hatred or the spirit of vengeance, but to utter the judgement of civilised men upon such an unparalleled reversion to barbarity, and to make a united pledge to effect such deliverance as could be wrought. "It is hard", he said, "to resist the conclusion that there is a settled purpose to exterminate the Jewish People, if it can be done".[51]

A fortnight later Temple took the opportunity in a speech in the House of Lords to draw attention to the "horror going on almost at our door", and to plead that aid should be given to the Swiss in their service to fugitives and provision made for a generous grant of visas to any who could reach the shores of Britain. What really mattered was to do all that was humanly possible, resisting being bound by categories in rendering help or calculations as to whether Britian's generosity exceeded that of other nations.[52]

Cyril Garbett, Temple's successor as Archbishop of York, was warmly cheered when he spoke in the House of Lords on December 9, urging the Government to state solemnly that, when the hour of deliverance came, retribution would be dealt, not only on the cold-blooded brutes who ordered the massacres, but also on the thousands of underlings who appeared to be joyfully carrying them out. The Archbishop's request found answer on December 17 in the publication of the "Solemn Statement" read in the House of Commons and simultaneously in Washington and Moscow.[53]

The Christmas Eve editorial of The Church Times did not mince words in referring to the Nazis possessing "minds like plague-ridden sewer rats, extirpating not merely a culture but a People for the sake of a perverted delusion", and expressed horror at the massacre being heightened by the sheer impotence of means to succour the victims. Similar sentiments were expressed at this time by the religious press of the country with the exception of The Catholic Herald. As was pointed out in The Jewish Chronicle, the Herald provided a grudging admission of the suffering of the Jews accompanied by warnings against swallowing wholesale certain atrocity reports which might prove to be but propaganda. In the Christmas number of the Herald, it was suggested that wartime accounts were apt to become embroidered in uncertain and dangerous transmission, while it should not be forgotten that the murder of thousands of Catholics in Russia, Mexico and Spain was passed over in silence by those leading the campaign in informing the world of anti-Jewish atrocities.[54]

William Temple was a tower of strength throughout 1943 and up to his sudden and tragic death in September 1944. The Jewish Chronicle described his frequent contributions as direct, downright, concise and clear. In 1942 it was his tact and patience that ensured the collaboration as Co-Presidents in the newly formed Council of Christians and Jews of both the Chief Rabbi and the Cardinal Archbishop who were apprehensive of overmuch religious fraternisation and possible embarrassing involvement.[55] In January 1943 he joined with his fellow Archbishops of York and Wales in publishing in the name of the whole episcopate a statement that plainly avowed the threatened extinction of six million Jews within Germany and German-occupied Europe, and appealed to all civilised nations, neutral and allied, to do their utmost to provide sanctuary wherever possible, and urged the United Kingdom Government to offer immediate refuge within the British Empire, thus setting an example to the rest of the world.[56] On March 23 the Archbishop spoke at length in the House of Lords, calling for the most generous scale of help and temporary asylum for any Jews able to quit hostile territory. He objected that by no means everything possible was being done. He recommended revision of the scheme for visas allowing entry into Britain and upbraided the Secretary of State for the Colonies for not yet having honoured his recent promise regarding the admission of Jews to Palestine. "What matters", he declared, "is that we should open our doors, so that all who can may come". Procrastination of all sorts was his chief target, and he deprecated talk of exploration as to what could be done rather than decision, when tens of thousands of Jews were being slaughtered on many days. He closed with the ringing words - "At this moment we have laid upon us a tremendous responsibility. We stand at the bar of history, humanity and God".[57] Addressing the Council of Christians and Jews shortly before Christmas, Temple emphasized the utmost importance of keeping alive the spirit of both indignation and compassion, and thereby testifying to the sacredness of human life for all persons and races and the equality of all mankind before God.[58] William Temple's final communication consisted of a message to Hungary on July 7, 1944, submitted through the BBC European Service. Following the reliable information that he had received of the wholesale round-up of Hungary's Jews with little chance of their survival, he felt impelled to inform the Christians of that country, if the facts were concealed from them, and to beg them to save such Jews as they could. His concluding words were, "I speak as a Christian who cannot help to Christians who can. For the honour of our common Christianity I implore you to do your utmost".[59]

Alongside this may be appropriately quoted an extract from Cardinal Hinsley's last public message. It was addressed on March 1, 1943 to the World Jewish Congress meeting in New York - "I denounce with utmost vigour the persecution of the Jews by the Nazi oppressors ... Words are weak and cold, deeds, and speedy deeds, are needed to put a stop to this brutal campaign for the extermination of a whole race. Justice must be done, and quickly. It is little use uttering tirades against anti-semitism. Jews and Christians are our fellow-men and brethren. If Christian mercy finds no place in the nazi breast, then the lesson of stern retribution must be given, in such wise that never again shall these hideous wrongs be possible ... To all who have the power to help or rescue, we appeal for appropriate reaction."[60]

In July 1943 the Bishop of Chichester, as indefatigable and well-primed as ever in championing the cause of would-be refugees, took part in a House of Lords debate. In his gentle but firm manner he proved highly critical of official policy and calculated delay. He detected a deterioration in determination in grappling with the problem. What was required was "action, no longer machinery". He expressed his disappointment at the vague and meagre results of the international conference held in Bermuda in April. An official pronouncement at its conclusion made no mention of the Jews or of the pressing need for temporary asylum for those who could escape. Convinced that ordinary Germans did not know the scale of the nazi extermination programme, increasing efforts should be made through publicity in their own tongue to bring home to them the awful guilt and the ghastly stain on the German character.[61]

Archbishop Garbett was so forthright in preaching retribution that he was criticised in some quarters for unchristian utterance. He remained impenitent. He judged that it was worthwhile stressing the coming retribution, if it could result in staying the hands of at any rate some of the criminals. In a speech in London in 1944 he declared that, while it was horrible to destroy great cities by bombing, it was far more horrible to think of torture and massacre of innocent men, women and children.[62]

It would be regrettable if the impression were to be given that bold and forceful utterance came almost exclusively from the very top. Notable contributions were readily forthcoming from less elevated, but still influential, levels. Canon Guy Rogers, Rector of Birmingham, who maintained a close fraternal relationship with the local Chief Rabbi, Dr Cohen, which included joint services of witness and intercession, gave vent at a public meeting to his indignation at the procrastination in high places in coming to the aid of the refugees in words that became quite well known: "If their trembling steps halt, we will scourge them with the flail of our tongue, we will embarrass them with questions, we will expose their malingering, till they act."[63] William Simpson in a well received broadcast address stressed what Christians owed to the Jews by remarking that "potentially they are our most important allies in our struggle to attain peace on earth and good will among men".[64] James Parkes remarked at a public gathering that, when we are told by the Government to be prudent lest we raise anti-semitism here, the right reply is insistence that all Jews on flight who can reach our shores should be welcomed, and that the future should be planned <u>with</u> rather than for them.[65] Sidney Dark, Editor of <u>The Church Times</u> during the period referred vividly to the Jewish tragedy in a volume of his reflections published during 1943. He wrote as follows:- "The torturing and the killing go on, and nothing of any practical value has yet been done to save more than a handful of the Nazi victims. This is a striking example of the fact that, without genuine moral leadership, there can be no effective action, and the reason is that, unless men are carried away by righteous anger or by noble aspirations, they will always hesitate, count the risks, and begin to wonder whether action will not result in more harm than good ... Because of the moral insensibility that made this country in some small degree an accomplice of Hitler in the early days of his power, it is the more obvious that this country should at all costs do all that is within its power to save as many as possible of the unfortunates from what may be, as one prays, the final outburst of Hitler's satanic fury."[66]

The recommendation was made in 1942 to call together a conference, such as had never taken place hitherto, between the Church of Scotland and the local Jewish community. This wider outlook did not, however, permit of the Kirk co-operating in the formation of the Council of Christians and Jews owing no doubt to suspicion that the new body might compromise on Christian principles, it being understood that there would be no place for conversionist activities or hopes. The proposed meeting did take place in January 1943 and with other Scottish Churches taking part. It was agreed on the Christian side that far more was required than an expression of pity for Jewish People in their calamity. Christians were seen as involved with them in a world catastrophe of the first magnitude that had brought humanity to the abyss of destruction. It was agreed to set up a Jewish-Christian Committee for study, mutual enlightenment and joint action without lowering the standards of Christianity or Judaism, and with each side true to the implications of its faith. Thereby weapons would be forged to help defeat the common enemy of anti-semitism.[67]

After assisting in 1939 a number of refugees from Czechoslovakia to find their way to Britain, Robert Smith was unable to return to Prague, as war was imminent. He was immediately appointed Secretary of the Scottish Christian Council for Refugees which became an admirable vehicle on an ecumenical Christian basis with amicable links with Jewish organisations. In due course, the Moderator of the General Assembly for the year became a Co-President of the Council of Christians and Jews, and Smith was later involved in the formation of a similar Scottish Council, which in 1943 welcomed the Church of Rome into membership.[68]

The traditional missionary impulse, while largely dormant, was far from extinguished as witnessed by the statement of the Moderator at the 1944 Assembly that the Jews needed not only sympathy but faith to give meaning to life again, faith to restore their souls, and by the Grace of God faith to see that to which they had been blind for so long.[69]

Under the heading 'Kirk and Jews' in the 1944 volume of <u>Life and Work</u>, it was reported that of the British staff in Budapest one missionary did not come home to Scotland. Her name was

Jane Haining, matron of the Girls' Home. She had elected to stand by her girls, and in May 1944, following the German occupation of Hungary, she was arrested, and despatched to Auschwitz. Recent information had told of her death there in hospital on July 17. "While so many among the stricken people of Israel were going down to death, she went down with them."[70]

REFERENCES

(Abbreviations: British Weekly - B.W.; Catholic Times - C.T.; Church Times - Ch.T.; Guardian - G.; Jewish Chronicle - J.C.; Life and Work - L.W.; Tablet - T.)

1. T. 15.4.33.
2. Johan M. Snoek - The Grey Book, Assen, Netherlands, 1968, pp 68-69. The Grey Book provides an indispensable Collection of Protests against Anti-Semitism and the Persecution of the Jews, issued by Non-Roman Catholic Churches and Church Leaders during Hitler's Rule.
3. Methodist Recorder 18.5.33.
4. Ibid. 2.12.33.
5. Snoek - pp 67-68.
6. Ch. T. 27.10.33.
7. J. C. 11.8.33. Richard Griffiths - Fellow-Travellers of the Right, London, 1980, p 76.
8. C. T. 28.4.33.
9. Catholic Herald 15.7.33. Andrew Sharf - The British Press and the Jews under Nazi Rule, Oxford, 1964, pp 18-19.
10. The Record 19.5.33.
11. Jewish Missionary Intelligence, March 1933.
12. C. T. 13.9.35.
13. Sharf - pp 43-44.
14. C. T. 20.9.35.
15. B. W. 19.9.35.
16. T. 3.9.35.
17. G. 15.11.35.
18. Church Assembly Proceedings, 1935, Vol. XVI, pp 467-479. Owen Chadwick - Hensley Henson, Oxford, 1983, pp 255-256.
19. J. C. 6.12.35.
20. Chadwick op. cit. pp 258-260.
21. Ronald Jasper - George Bell, Bishop of Chichester, Oxford, 1967, pp 135-137.
22. Ch. T. 26.6.36.
23. Church Assembly Proceedings - 1938, Vol. XIX, pp 389-395.
24. The Bishop of Chichester's remarks about 'certain individuals' provides a welcome opportunity of paying tribute to two dedicated Christians, who in the most practical fashion responded to the needs of the refugees in general. The one was a Methodist minister, Henry Carter, who was the indefatigable co-Chairman of the Board of Management at Bloomsbury House, which was the nerve centre for all refugee work, the other, Lord Gorell, an anglican layman, who in February 1938 became Chairman of the Refugee Children's Movement, and consequently in time the legal guardian of over nine thousand of them, and with the cordial approval of the Chief Rabbi and Cardinal Hinsley. Such compassionate and practical concern for all who were strangers or afflicted and so warm a desire to promote fruitful relations between Jews and Christians were the hallmark of the contribution of 'Bill' Simpson, who generously helped and so much inspired the present writer in his studies.
25. Jasper op. cit. p 143.
26. G. 8.7.38.
27. The Times 12.11.38.
28. T. 26.11.38.
29. B. W. 24.11.38.
30. B. W. 24.11.38.
31. G. 18.11.38.
32. Ch. T. 18.11.38.
33. B. W. 24.11.38.
34. C. T. 18.11.38.
35. T. 10.12.38. Thomas Moloney - Westminster, Whitehall and the Vatican. The Role of Cardinal Hinsley, Tunbridge Wells, 1985, pp 209-210. The whole of Chapter 11 of this work, entitled 'The Jewish Connection' is well worth studying.
36. T. 10.12.38.
37. G. 2.12.38.

38. Church Assembly Proceedings, 1938, pp 503-516.
39. Jasper op. cit. pp 143-145. Werner Simonson - The Last Judgement. An Autobiography., Gerrards Cross, 1969, pp 85-86.
40. Moloney op. cit. pp 215-216.
41. T. 7.1.39.
42. T. 4.3.39.
43. B. W. 2.12.38.
44. J. C. 2.12.38.
45. J. O. Greenwood - Quaker Encounter, Vol. 1, 'Friends and Relief', York, 1975, pp 266-269.
46. L. W. 1938, p 381, 1939, pp 46, 90, 342.
47. L. W. 1935, p 323, 1936, p 405, 1937, p 5, 1938, p 528, 1939, p 127.
48. The Record, 1939, pp 137, 138, 327, 505. James Parkes - Voyage of Discoveries, London, 1969, p 155.
49. Snoek - pp 235-240. Ernest Hearst - The British and the Slaughter of the Jews, Wiener Library Bulletin, Vol. XXI, No. 1, pp 32 ff. David Wyman - The Abandonment of the Jew. (Paper back ed.), New York, 1985, pp 23-24.
50. G. K. A. Bell - The Church and Humanity, London, 1946, p 80.
51. Ch. T. 6.11.42. Snoek, pp 238-239.
52. Snoek, p 240.
53. Snoek, p 241.
54. J. C. 2.10.42. Sharf - op. cit. pp 94, 136-137. Moloney - op. cit. pp 220-221.
55. See William W. Simpson - Jewish-Christian Relations since the Inception of the Council of Christians and Jews in Transactions of the Jewish Historical Society of England, Vol. XXVIII, pp 94-95.
56. Snoek, p 242.
57. Snoek, pp 245-248.
58. J. C. 10.12.43.
59. Snoek, p 256.
60. Quoted in full in John C Heenan - Cardinal Hinsley, London, 1944, pp 221-222.
61. G. K. A. Bell - op. cit. pp 123-128.
62. J. C. 3.3.44.
63. J. C. 29.1.43. Guy Rogers - A Rebel at Heart, London, 1956, pp 221-224.
64. J. C. 27.8.43.
65. J. C. 19.3.43. James Parkes, according to J. C. 24.12.43, declared on another occasion that the Christian has ten times as much to learn from Judaism as the Jews have to learn from Christianity.
66. Sidney Dark - I sit, and I think and I wonder, London, 1943, p 124.
67. L. W. 1943, pp 40 ff.
68. Information kindly supplied by the Rev. Robert Smith.
69. L. W. 1944, p 103.
70. L. W. 1944, p 153.

THE IMPACT OF HOLOCAUST SURVIVORS ON AMERICAN SOCIETY: A SOCIO-CULTURAL PORTRAIT.**

by William B. Helmreich
City College of N.Y. &
CUNY Graduate Center.

Introduction

"Their battered suitcases, rolled-up blankets, and other personal belongings, which they held on to during frightful years of captivity or semi-slavery, tell endless stories of human suffering....Reporters aboard the SS Marine Flasher tell us how these passengers, instead of breaking down as a result of their past tribulations, were very active and cheerful throughout the journey. Many volunteered to do odd jobs; a group of orphaned youths helped the short-handed kitchen staff. A barber clipped the hair of the officers."[1]

Thus begins one of the first accounts of the 173,000 Holocaust survivors who came to the United States and Canada in the years 1945 t0 1952.[2] There is an almost buoyant quality to some of these early descriptions. Indeed,the immigrants are sometimes described as "pioneers" emulating America's earlier arrivals,by proponents of immigration eager to garner sympathy for the refugees. On the other hand, the social work journals tell a somewhat different story. They write of immigrants who have difficulty adapting to the relatives and friends who welcomed them into their

**The author wishes to thank Iris Berlatzky and Leon Volovici of Yad Vashem Archives and Paul Ritterband of City University of New York for their generous advice and assistance.

homes, of the struggle to find adequate housing and decent jobs.[3] Similarly, the psychiatric literature presents cases of individuals who experienced anxiety,depression, and paranoia, often lumping their diagnosis under the now common term, "concentration camp survivor syndrome."[4]

What, in fact, really happened to the survivors in the last forty years ? How did they fare in their efforts to start over ? How did they do economically ? What about their family lives and, in particular, their children ? Did those who came in their youths begin new careers or attend universities in any appreciable numbers ? What were the contributions of the refugees to American life and to the Jewish communities in which they so often settled?

There has been very little written about these questions because until now the emphasis has been on the pathology of the survivors, their psychological problems and to a lesser but still considerable extent, their physical ailments.[5] This is due largely to the fact that it is those with the most serious problems who came to the attention of psychiatrists,psychologists, and social workers. The successful or unsuccessful treatment of these individuals was then written up and published in journals.

Unfortunately, we do not know how representative these cases are of the average survivor who did not request therapy and this constitutes the vast majority of survivors. No doubt there were many survivors who needed treatment and never received it, many who suffered nightmares for years and accepted it as part of the survivor's burden. Nevertheless, we cannot establish patterns from which generalizations can be drawn until we have truly random samples made up of non-clinical groups of survivors. In short, we need a "sociology of the survivor community" that will complement the already significant contributions made by the therapists. Only in this way will we able to understand the survivors as a community.[6] What follows in these pages is a beginning effort to answer the sociological question of what the survivors achieved as a group in the United States.

Arrival in America

In the years between 1945 and 1952, hundreds of ships traversed the route between Europe, usually Bremerhaven,Germany, and various U.S. ports, most often New York and Boston carrying thousands of refugees. Their fare was often advanced by either the Hebrew Immigrant Aid Society (HIAS) or the United Service for New Americans (USNA). The boats,with names like the Uruguay, Marine Perch, Marine Jumper, New Hellas, General McRae, General Muir, and the Marine Marlin, were actually U.S. Army transport ships that had been pressed into service after seeing extensive duty during the war. Between October 30,1948 and July 21,1952 308 ships (as well as 284 planes) arrived,bringing almost 400,000 Jews and Gentiles, to the U.S.[7]

The accomodations were scarcely luxurious. As Willie Herskovits, a passenger on the Ernie Pyle, currently living in Brooklyn, N.Y. described it:

> "The boat left from Bremerhaven. But for three months there was a strike. It took us thirteen days and cost $225.00 each for me and my wife. There were maybe 1,000 people on the boat and they were, I think, all Jewish. There were about 200 people to a room and three beds, one on top of the others.[8]"

There were no planned activities for the passengers. The small library was usually used as a meeting place where people discussed what they would do once they arrived in America, the occupations they would enter, the friends and relatives who would assist them. The majority suffered from seasickness and many recalled spending a good portion of the trip lying in bed.

Nevertheless, their discomfort was soon forgotten once the trip ended. Luba Bat, the niece of American labor leader Sidney Hillman, was one of those passengers. Looking out from the deck of the SS Uruguay in 1946 as it steamed into New York's harbor, she observed: "The sight of the grandiose skyscrapers fascinated me; in Poland we called them "cloud scratchers." Her aunt,

Bessie Hillman, asked Luba to smile for the photographers as she alighted from the ship "Why smile?," she asked. "Don't ask <u>kashes</u> (questions)," retorted Hillman, "Just smile; this is America."[9]

In most cases, the immigrants were met by a representative of HIAS, who guided them through customs. These individuals were generally fluent in several languages, including Yiddish, and were trained to deal with a variety of problems that could and did come up after the passengers disembarked. Among them might be having an ambulance at the dock for a man who required hospitalization because he had taken ill during the trip, serving as interpreter to immigration officials, cutting through red tape so that an immigrant would make the train bound for St. Louis where he would be met by anxious relatives, etc., etc.[10]

<u>Resettlement of the Immigrants</u>:

The majority of immigrants remained in the New York area, but sizeable numbers of refugees took up residence elsewhere. The following table indicates the distribution in the period 1945-1952:

<u>Table One</u>
<u>Postwar Jewish Immigration to the United States</u>

Dates	Total	To NYC Area	To Rest of Country
1945: May-December	4,000	2,800	1,200
1946	15,535	10,870	4,665
1947	25,885	18,116	7,769
1948	15,982	11,187	4,795
1949	37,700	20,571	17,129
1950	14,139	8,861	5,278
1951	16,973	8,416	8,557
1952	7,236	4,307	2,929
Totals 1945-52	137,450	85,128 (62%)	52,322 (38%)[11]

By the end of July 1949, arrivals under the 1948 DP Act had been settled in 334 communities in 43 states. HIAS had offices in Boston, Philadelphia, Washington D.C., Chicago, San Francisco, Seattle, and Baltimore. According to the Council of Jewish Federations, family agencies in Newark, St. Louis, Kansas City, Milwaukee, Minneapolis, Oakland, Portland, Oregon, and St. Paul, reported that in 1948, one-half or more of their caseloads were immigrants.[12]

These figures are important in terms of understanding the contributions of the survivors. What they mean is that the survivors came into contact with a broad cross-section of the American population. They did not settle in Jewish ghettos alone. Moreover, those who went elsewhere were forced to interact with others who knew little about their culture and experiences. Indeed, survivors who settled outside of the major Jewish population centers often prided themselves on having become more Americanized. One such individual , a resident of Minneapolis, recounted how she had little in common, after 40 years, with survivors who had remained in New York and still thought like "greeners."[13]

In many, perhaps the majority of instances, refugees settled outside the New York area at the urging of HIAS which frequently made the arrangements for their new communities while the refugees were still in the DP camps. In part this was motivated by a desire to dispel the stereotype that Jews were only capable of dwelling in urban ghettoes. There was also the feeling that the immigrants would assimilate faster in places with small Jewish populations.[14]

Quite a few (how many is not known) immigrants eventually drifted back to major Jewish communities because the adjustment was too difficult in outlying locales. Some, however, found that life in the hinterlands could be appealing. One couple decided that they would stay only one month in the small Texas community of McAllen, to which they had been sent by the resettlement agency. Much to their surprise they fell in love with the town and remained: "McAllen had, in short, captivated her, drawn her deeply into its small-town life and ways. The kindness of the people! The warmth they had shown so unstintingly."[15] Another immigrant explained her decision to move to Kansas City as follows:

> "I believe they were overcrowded, those states. So we just picked Kansas City. We took the map and we looked at it and we said, the President of the United States (Truman) comes from Missouri. From Independence, but that is close to Kansas City. We took the heart of America and came here." [16]

Among the arrivals were over 1,000 survivors who became farmers. They settled in places like Vineland, New Jersey, Petaluma, California and Danielson, Connecticut. In many cases the farmers were helped by the Jewish Colonization Association. For example, the Association placed nineteen families of DPs in the Niagra Peninsula of Ontario where they established fruit and dairy farms.[17] The Jewish Agricultural Society, which also assisted the immigrants, organized educational and cultural activities to aid the DPs such as talks on purchasing and marketing,poultry medicine, and related topics.[18] This was necessary because many of the refugees had no experience in farming. They had simply chosen this way of life because they wanted an environment away from the city with clean air and quiet. In fact, an occupational survey of Jews in European DP assembly centers found that only 2.8% could be classified as being in farm -related activities.[19]

Other survivors were sent to American universities under the sponsorship of the Bnai Brith Hillel Foundation. Many of them made good use of their educational opportunities and became successful professionals. Typical was Eugen Schoenfeld who studied at Washington University in St. Louis and later became Chairman of the Sociology Department at Georgia State University. Another survivor studied at the University of Washington in Seattle and became a successful painter.[20]

Working in America:

Knowing the type of work engaged in by the immigrants is of value in assessing the contributions they ultimately made. We can say at the onset that they were handicapped in several ways. First, their experiences during the war had tremendously weakened them in most cases and the majority were still recovering, both physically and psychologically,when they arrived in the U.S. Second, they spoke little or no English and were unfamiliar with American culture and ways. How unfamiliar can be discerned from the vignettes the respondents describe in various interviews. One survivor tells how how he arrived in Boston and was told to travel by train to Philadelphia where arrangements had been made for him to work and live. He protested to the agency official in charge that he had relatives in New York City. When told he could visit them on weekends, he asked how this could be arranged if he had no pass or special privilege allowing him to travel from Philadelphia to New York! He was both surprised and relieved when informed that in America no such permission was required.[21]

Most of the immigrants who came here were between the ages of fifteen and thirty five. It was this group that was most likely to have survived the rigors and hardships of the war. Many of them were therefore compelled to interrupt their education and training and this left them at a disadvantage when it came to starting over in a new land. In addition, the occupations for which they had been trained were not always in demand here and this made retraining necessary. In some professions such as law, their training was not considered valid or relevant. Added to this were the normal problems of adjustment that face all immigrants.

The evidence we have suggests that the refugees made strenuous, often heroic efforts to overcome these deficiencies. The resilience and survival skills they had demonstrated during the war were, it appears, often transferred to the American scene. Typical of such efforts was the case of Edward Goodman, a St.Paul, Minnesota resident:

> When I came here I tried to get a job in international trade---with what I was doing in Czechoslovakia. And so I went to all the big companies...who had an international department. Went to Minnesota Mining. to Cargill, General Mills, Pillsbury, Honeywell. Everybody was very nice...It's wonderful. Wonderful experience. We'll hire you...I worked with an agency downtown and they told me, "Ed, there isn't a single Jew working in these companies," and they say "You'll <u>never</u> get a job there. You might as well forget it." That

> was the end of my looking for an affluent career in the United States."[22]

But it was by no means the end for Goodman. It was only the beginning,for, as he recalls: "I was hungry and we had nothing to live on. And I looked for a job high and low. That was in 1948 and there was big unemployment in the United States." Finally, the Jewish Family service found a job for him---making sandwiches during the graveyard shift in a restaurant called Hasty Tasty. We see here not only the difficulties,but the perseverance that was required, perseverance that did not, as the following account indicates always pay off:

> "They asked me if I am a cook. In fact the only thing I knew how to cook is hot water. But I was making sandwiches and hamburgers and they promoted me the third night to make waffles, and that was my downfall. Was a very busy Friday night, and I forgot to take the waffle out----smoked up the place, lost their customers. They picked me up and they kicked me out so fast they says I should never come back."[23]

In her book, New Lives, Dorothy Rabinowitz asserts that "survivors in considerable numbers involved themselves in building and construction careers----immensely successful ones,as it turned out, for some of them."[24] As an example she mentions the Shapell brothers, who survived Auschwitz and became leading manufacturers in the nation,of prefabricated houses. Although more empirical research is needed, there seems to have been a trend among the survivors to enter occupations where they could be independent. One could speculate that their experiences had made them reluctant to put themselves in a position where others could determine their fate. The initiative required of someone who chooses to be an entrepreneur, the risks they took,were also rooted in their experiences. They were people who had often literally returned from the dead and they therefore felt that they had little to lose.

In an effort to determine these and other behavioral patterns, 236 oral histories on deposit at Yad Vashem were analyzed. The tapes were made by survivors who attended the 1981 World Gathering of Holocaust Survivors held in Jerusalem.[25] Based on a content analysis of these tapes it would appear that the survivors preferred to operate independently irrespective of their income level. The following instances typified the general views and experiences of the immigrants:

> "So we went to Hartford and there was a landsman who owned a fruit store that I met. And he was a son of a bitch; he used me up...He paid me $42.00 a week . I worked seven weeks. He was a very bad guy...Then I went to work for myself as a roofer and fours years later I got a house that I built for myself."[26]
>
> "So we came to Cleveland...where my sponsor lived. I got a job raking and cleaning on a golf course...Then, when the golf season ended I got a job as a plasterer. Then I worked as a cabinetmaker. Twelve years ago I went out on my own in draperies."[27]
>
> "When I came to America in Richmond in 1947 I decided to open up a service station. Since I saw America as a land on wheels I decided the future for service stations is good. Then I went into the auto parts business. Now I have two stores and 28 people working for me."[28]

In 1981 the Federation of Jewish Philanthropies/United Jewish Appeal under the direction of the sociologists, Paul Ritterband and Steven M. Cohen, conducted the largest ever survey of Diaspora Jewry. A sample was drawn from the population of the New York Metropolitan Area which included New York City, Nassau, Suffolk, and Westchester Counties, which had a combined Jewish population of 1.7 million persons. The low refusal rate and the large number of respondents, 4,505 heads of household, make it one of the most reliable surveys undertaken by scholars studying the Jewish community. Included in the sample were 112 Holocaust survivors plus about 100 respondents whose spouses were survivors, making it one of the only truly random, nonclinical samples of survivors. In the past, most samples have been made up either of hospitalized patients or individuals in therapy, or of restitution claimants. A preliminary analysis of the data has been done and more research is currently underway with these survivors. The material itself is available through the North American Jewish Data Bank (NAJDB) the City University of New York.

One question of interest is the income level of survivors. Survivors' income was compared with a control group of American Jews who are not Holocaust survivors (referred to in this article as "non-survivors"). Table Two presents the results of this comparison:

Table Two

Income	Survivors N=53	"Non-Survivors" N=1601[29]
less than $5,000	7.55%	7.68%
$5,000-$9,999	22.64	11.18
$10,000-$14,999	9.43	8.06
$15,000-$19,999	9.43	9.12
$20,000-$24,999	7.55	10.74
$25,000-$29,999	15.09	8.99
$30,999-$39,999	9.43	14.37
$40,000-$59,999	9.43	14.62
$60,000-$79,999	0.00	6.00
80,000-$99,999	5.60	3.06
$100,000 +	3.77	6.12

One of the popular stereotypes about survivors among both Jews and Gentiles is that they have done very well financially when compared to other Jews. Table Two suggests that this is not the case. It appears that the non-survivors' income level is, on the average, somewhat higher though the differences are not that great. On the other hand, as many survivors as non-survivors report earnings of $80,000 or more (the differences are minute.) When one considers the disadvantages which so many survivors had to overcome their income level assumes even greater significance. Let us turn now to the question of what they do with their income.

Giving in America:

A comparison of contributions to charity irrespective of its Jewish or non-Jewish nature,between survivors and non-survivors,revealed no significant differences among those who contribute less than $2,000 a year. However, among those who donated more than $2,000 annually survivors outnumbered non-survivors by better than two to one.

The differences between the two groups are even more interesting when one examines specific charities. Survivors are more likely to contribute to the Red Cross than non-survivors but less likely to give to other medical causes than non-survivors. Why this is so is a matter of speculation. Survivors are less likely than non-survivors to financially support the arts and other cultural activities. Perhaps this is because the survivors are less assimilated and hence less apt to give to non-Jewish activities. There is some support for this hypothesis when we evaluate their contributions to Jewish causes. Both groups contribute equally to the United Jewish Appeal but their patterns of giving diverge sharply when other Jewish causes are considered. Survivors are considerably more likely to give money to other Israel-related causes than non-survivors. They are also more than twice as likely to contribute to local Jewish schools. In part, this may be due to their overrepresentation among the Orthodox segment of the Jewish population. Still, this cannot be the only reason since the survivors give substantially more than non-survivors to Jewish causes of all types.[30]

The qualitative research on this question supports the figures given here. The oral histories on file at the American Jewish Committee[31] and the Yad Vashem tapes, contain many statements about the pride felt by the survivors regarding their financial support of Jewish causes and, in particular, Israel. Writing about the work of the immigrant organization in Vineland, New Jersey, known as the Jewish Poultry Farmer's Association, (JPFA) one observer noted:

> "Who would think of a UJA Drive or a JNF Drive without participation of the JPFA. They not only contributed their proportionate share of money in these drives, but banded manpower, leg work and officers to further the projects.[32]

<u>Involvement in Communal Life</u>

In an article that appeared in 1955 in <u>Commentary,</u> Nathan Glazer discussed at length the Jewish revival in America. The Holocaust and Zionism were, in his view, unimportant factors in this revival, especially when compared to Jewish migration to the suburbs.[33] There is evidence, however, that even in the 1950s Holocaust survivors were involved in Jewish affairs, especially with respect to Israel and the Holocaust. The involvement of survivors in fund-raising for Jewish charities in Baltimore, was widely praised by community leaders there who cited it as "an exemplary display of their integration into the community.... They have done honor unto Baltimore and honor unto themselves."[34]

The farming communities in which the survivors settled, because they were insular and cohesive enable us to more fully assess the contributions of the immigrants. In some of the South Jersey communities such as Vineland, the Jewish community had existed for some time. In others, such as Danielson, Connecticut, the survivors founded new communities. In both instances,the survivors brought with them a desire to preserve Jewish culture and in so doing they raised the level of Jewish consciousness to new heights. In some cases, the influx of refugees prevented these communities from dying out entirely. This was especially true in the California communities.[35] The following account provides insight into the breadth and scope of such involvement:

> "Here was a real Yiddish life transplanted from Eastern Europe to our shores. Many of our so-called "Native American Jews" had almost forgotten what a Yiddish word was, a Jewish play, a Yiddish concert. The group activities from the very beginning created actually a new Yiddish culture era in Vineland .....Some are actively engaged in the work of the Poale Zion,the general Zionist group, Mizrachi, and Hadassah....Their cultural activities in celebrating our Jewish holidays are something to talk about. It brings back that nostalgic feeling to many Jews who have never seen, witnessed or even forgotten the real side of Jewish life.[36]

There is a perception that interest in commemorating the Holocaust really began to grow after the Eichmann trial. Perhaps, but it is equally clear that the survivors themselves were memorializing the Holocaust almost from the time they arrived in the United States. In an article that appeared in Der Yiddishe Farmer, the writer speaks about the guilt feelings resulting from leading a happy, contented life while others are dead. Readers are reminded that the Holocaust martyrs had exhorted their fellow Jews: "Don't forget us! Tell the world! Take revenge."[37] In addition to services, communities often invited speakers, one of whom was the famous novelist, Chaim Grade. In his talk he urged listeners not to dwell on the past but to focus instead on the new State of Israel.[38]

The activities of these communities have been preserved through journals and books written about them. More research needs to be done on the survivor communities elsewhere. Still, there is no reason to believe survivors living in New York and in other parts of the country were any less vigilant in remembering the past. Interviews now being done suggest that it was through the landsmanschaeften that the Holocaust experiences were shared and recalled. All the major cities in the U.S. with substantial survivor populations had "Newcomer" organizations, in addition to the landsmanschaeften and these served as a bridge between the old culture and the new.[39] In 1955, for example, over 300 persons attended a Warsaw Ghetto memorial service at the YMHA Club in Newark, New Jersey. The city also was home to an organization known as the Association of European Refugees of New Jersey. Its goals included support for Israel, Jewish education, recreation activities, and charitable causes. The organization, which was founded on May 21,1955, also organized trips to the Farband Unser Camp in Highland Mills, New York where they went boating and swimming. Kosher food was served and theatrical performances were presented.[40] All this suggests a rich cultural life that undoubtedly had a profound effect on other members of the larger Jewish communities in which they lived.

Strong support for Israel is another characteristic that distinguishes the survivor community and this must be seen in the context of general Jewish support for Israel among American Jews.

Fifty percent of American Jews do not contribute money to Israel and at least three in five Jews have never visited Israel.[41] The following table,based on the 1981 survey of New York Jews, demonstrates conclusively that even in New York, where Jewish support for Israel has traditionally been quite strong, the involvement of survivors is greater than that of the average New York Jewish resident:

Table Three

	Survivors N=111	Non-Survivors N=2,771
have never visited Israel	29.73%	61.02%
have visited Israel once	20.72	23.13
have visited Israel twice or more	49.55	15.84

Survivors are clearly far more likely to have visited Israel than non-survivors. An equal number seem to have been to Israel once. One visit is not especially significant, it can be argued, because it does not represent a real commitment for the most part. A person may go to celebrate a child's bar or bat mitzvah. They may travel to Israel as part of an organization-sponsored activity. True commitment can more readily be judged when people visit the country more than once. Survivors are <u>more than three times as likely</u> to have visited Israel at least twice as non-survivors. This suggests a continuing and deeply felt involvement with the State. It can be safely assumed that such individuals are likely to be more involved with Israel-related activities in the U.S. and that they make contributions in varying ways toward enriching Jewish life as a result of such a commitment. Although the analysis is still incomplete, available data seem to to indicate that survivors are considerably more apt to belong to Jewish organizations of all sorts than are non-survivors.[42] If so, this would further substantiate the argument that survivors have had a major impact on Jewish life in America.

The Children of Survivors:

A community is often measured by what happens to its children. Do they identify with the culture ? How successful are they in their own lives? As in the case of survivor studies, much of the literature has focused on pathology.[43] The validity of these studies in terms of generalizations can be challenged on the grounds that the samples were small, were not random, and were drawn from clinical populations, namely those who had sought help. In any event, these researchers have rarely dealt with the question of achievement among children of survivors.

One exception to this pattern is the work of Helen Epstein. In her report prepared for the American Jewish Committee, she notes that 85 percent of the survivors who were interviewed were married, more than half of their children were students, and 23 percent had entered the professions.[44] Epstein estimates that there are about 500,000 children of survivors alive today and she describes them as largely middle-class and college-educated.[45]

Until more systematic research is conducted it will be impossible to fully evaluate the contributions of the survivors' children but it can be stated that simply by having children, the survivors contributed to the continuity of the Jewish community. They did not take the position that the world was too horrible a place in which to raise children. Commenting on this, Steven Riskin, a rabbi currently living in Israel, said: "What makes Jews remarkable is not that they believe in God after Auschwitz, but that they have children after Auschwitz; that they affirm life and the future."[46] Generally speaking, when survivors are asked what achievement they take the greatest pride in, they reply: "My children [and grandchildren.]"

The psychological literature discusses at great length the various problems that can and do afflict children of survivors. Included in these are anxiety, depression, hostility, and shame. Some children learn to cope with these feelings better than others. Regardless, the experiences of the parents affect almost all children in one way or another. In a recent novel, Barbara Finkelstein discusses the problem with great insight. She notes that there exists a paradox in that the survivors are frequently seen by their children as all-powerful, even indestructible people who "made it through hell", notwithstanding the nightmares and paranoia which they subsequently suffered from. What is important is that they made it. On the other hand, in their ill-fitting clothes, short physical stature, foreign accents, and discomfort as immigrants to a new culture, they seem frail and weak. 'How did these "schleppers" ever make it?', wonders the child of such a family. 'Were they once strong and self-confident?'[47] For a child searching for a role model, these are difficult matters to sort out. And yet, it is precisely because children of survivors must carry such burdens with them, that they have the opportunity, through heightened sensitivity and awareness, to make others understand such issues. It is hoped that future studies will more properly evaluate the processes and dynamics that are involved here. In the meantime, it is possible to say something about the effect that the survivors themselves have had on making the larger society aware of their own unique experiences.

A Moral Legacy:

Until now we have been speaking of the effect of the survivor on the Jewish community but with respect to the issue of morality and values, the survivors' impact extends to the Christian community too. Every time survivors speak to a class of students or participate in a community forum, they contribute to an awareness of the meaning of the Holocaust. No one has as yet counted the number of such events but there have surely been thousands of them. In one such instance a survivor from Commack, Long Island addresses a high school class and, expressing her belief in a world of justice, implores her audience to "Please, please never stop asking, 'Why?'" The students, visibly moved, rise and applaud and a girl puts her arms around the speaker and whispers: "We will remember. We will bear witness."[48] Every such encounter, every life touched, represents a contribution made by the survivors towards ensuring that a Holocaust will not happen again. It is both their duty and their opportunity to serve as the world's conscience as long as they are alive and to the degree that they succeed in this endeavor they affect the course of history.

Inasmuch as the survivors tend to see everything through the prism of their unique background, they influence society's thinking in other ways too. The analysis of the Yad Vashem tapes revealed a heightened concern for the rights of all minorities among the survivors. Said one:

> "We live in a small world. We cannot afford to let anyone suffer. When the air is destroyed we all breathe it....if the Jewish people or any other people are treated badly, we are all in for a bad time. If anything happens to one group of people, all the other minorities should stand up for them."[49]

Whether, this is true of survivors in general awaits further study. Still, wherever and whenever such views are expressed, they demonstrate an ability to extrapolate from one's experiences in a way that enhances the general good.

Other ways of thinking predicated on Holocaust experiences also emerged in the Yad Vashem tapes. One woman expressed her sympathy for both the hostages in Iran and returning Vietnam War veterans as follows: "I feel a lot for the Vietnam soldiers. When I came back from the war, nobody cared if I lived or died."[50] She, and several others expressed the deep fears that the Watergate trials aroused in them:

> "I watched Watergate. It's almost identical to Germany. Haldeman and Erlichman. They were of German descent. It's all loyalty. They say you have to lie. And the hush money. That was always going on in Germany. I didn't eat; I didn't sleep. I was sitting at the TV. And I used to sit and cry. Nixon brought back all the Germans to me.[51]

No studies have yet been done on political participation among survivors. There are two U.S. Congressmen who are survivors, Tom Lantos of California and Sam Gejdenson of Connecticut. What is clear, however,is that the survivors have a highly favorable attitude toward America. The above mentioned respondent asserted that, despite her apprehensions, the fact that Watergate burglars had been held accountable proved that America was a good country. Other researchers and writers have similarly commented on the appreciation that survivors have for the U.S. as a land that accepted them into its midst.[52] Interviews done so far by this researcher suggest that the majority of them vote in elections and that they do so because of an acute awareness of what it means to have such rights denied and abrogated.

****

Summing up, it is apparent that survivors have made contributions in a number of areas. By settling in many different communities they have made certain that their influence will be felt throughout the country. They have, as we have seen, entered a wide variety of occupations and professions, and despite the disadvantages of their circumstances, have managed to do quite well. A large proportion of them seem to have been self-employed. The survivors have also shown themselves to be quite generous in terms of charity, especially for Jewish causes,and their involvement with the State of Israel and in other Jewish activities has been uniformly high. Their children have also done well, although more research needs to be done on this question. Finally, the survivors have contributed in a tangible way to raising the level of moral consciousness in this country and, one can assume, everywhere else too.

How many of them have actually spoken about their experiences to others is not that important. What is significant is that because of what they represent when they do good, they can have an enormous effect on others, one totally out of proportion to their numbers. To the extent that they have succeeded in doing so, it can be said that theirs is a message of hope and renewal, a message that,even after one has experienced terrible trauma and suffering, it is still possible to remain human---and humane.

Notes:

1. Alfred Werner, "The New Refugees," Jewish Frontier, July 1946 :23.

2. Kurt Grossman Mss.. Leo Baeck Institute, New York City; folder "USNA Correspondence Misc. 1944-55" Box 148, Central Jewish Federation and Welfare Funds Mss., American Jewish Historical Society, Waltham, Mass.; Joseph Kage, "Canadian Immigrants....Facts, Figures and Trends," Rescue, Fall 1953 :5. The number of immigrants to the U.S. was about 137,500 while the number who entered Canada was approximately 36,500, including 2,000 who came in 1953.

3. See, for example,Beatrice Frankel and Ruth Michaels, "A Changing Focus in Work with Young, Unattached DPS," Journal of Jewish Communal Service, 27 (March 1951) :321-331; Fred Berl, "The Immigrant Situation as Focus of the Helping Process," Jewish Social Service Quarterly 26 (March 1950) :377-392; Sidney S. Eisenberg, "Phases in the Resettlement Process and their Significance for Casework with New Americans," Jewish Social Service Quarterly 27 (September 1950) :86-96.

4. See, for instance, William G. Niederland, "Clinical Observations on the Survivor Syndrome," International Journal of Psychoanalysis,49 (1968) :313-315; M.A. Berezin "The Aging Survivor of the Holocaust. Introduction," Journal of Geriatric Psychiatry 14, No. 2 (1981) :131-133; G. Bychowski, "Permanent Character Changes as an Aftereffect of Persecution," in H. Krystal Ed.) Massive Psychic Trauma. New York: International Universities Press, 1968 :75-86; Bruno Bettleheim. Surviving and Other Essays. New York: Knopf, 1979.

5. See P. Chodoff,"Effects of Extreme Coercive and Oppressive Forces: Brainwashing and Concentration Camps." in S. Arieti (ed.) American Handbook of Psychiatry. New York: Basic Books, 1959 :384-405; T.S. Nathan, L. Eitinger, and H.Z. Winnik, "A Psychiatric Study of Survivors of the Nazi Holocaust; A Study of Hospitalized Patients." Israel Annual of Psychiatry and Related Disciplines 2, No. 1 (1964) :47-80; Shamai Davidson, "The Clinical Effects of Massive Psychic Trauma in Families of Holocaust Survivors," Journal of Marriage and Family Therapy 6, No. 1 (1980) :11-21; V.M. Morosow, "Late Sequelae in Former Deportees and Concentration Camp Survivors," Journal of Neuropathology and Psychiatry, 58, No. 3 (1958) :373-380; H. Krystal (ed.), Massive Psychic Trauma. New York: International Universities Press, 1968.

6. An exception is Morton Weinfeld, John J. Sigal, William W. Eaton, "Long Term Effects of the Holocaust on Selected Social Attitudes and Behaviors of Survivors: A Cautionary Note. " Social Forces 60 (1981) :1-19. See also, Jack Nusan Porter, "Is there a Survivor

Syndrome?: Psychological and Sociopolitical Implications." Journal of Psychology and Judaism, 6, No.1 (1981) :33-52.

7. Memo to America. The DP Story: The Final Report of the U.S. Displaced Persons Commission. Washington, D.C.:U.S. Government Printing Office,1952.

8. Interview, December 30,1987.

9. Luba Bat, Phoenix, n.d., n.p., mimeograph. Yad Vashem Archives.

10. Jack Shafer, "HIAS Pier Representatives Welcome Immigrants Here." Rescue, January 1947 :4-5.

11. Kurt Grossman Mss. and USNA Correspondence.

12. Morris Zelditch, "Immigrant Aid," American Jewish Yearbook,1950, 51, Philadelphia: Jewish Publication Society, 1950 :195,198.

13. Interview, Hinda Kibort, February 25,1988.

14. Leonard Dinnerstein, America and the Survivors of the Holocaust, New York: Columbia University Press,1982 :203.

15. Dorothy Rabinowitz, New Lives: Survivors of the Holocaust Living in America, New York :Avon, 1976 :125.

16. Helen Epstein, A Study in American Pluralism Through Oral Histories of Holocaust Survivors. New York: William E. Wiener Oral History Library of the American Jewish Committee,1975 (Report.)

17. Theodore Norman. An Outstretched Hand : A History of the Jewish Colonization Association, London : Routledge and Kegan Paul,1985 :246.

18. Joseph Brandes, Immigrants to Freedom: Jewish Communities in Rural New Jersey Since 1882, Philadelphia : Jewish Publication Society, 1971 :329.

19. Dinnerstein, America and the Survivors :278.

20. Sylvia Rothchild (ed.), Voices from the Holocaust, New York: Meridian,1982 :314-321.

21. Interview, Willie Lieberman, January 6,1988.

22. Minnesota Oral History Archives, Jewish Community Relations Council, Minneapolis.

23. Ibid.

24. Rabinowitz, New Lives :19. This is actually the only book-length treatment of post-Holocaust survivors that does not focus exclusively on pathology. Well written and insightful it is, nonetheless, based on a small non-random group of survivors. It makes no claim to scientific validity but is instead written from a journalistic perspective.

25. For more on the attitudes of these people, see William B. Helmreich, "Research Report: Postwar Adaptation of Holocaust Survivors in the U.S.A.," Holocaust and Genocide Studies, 2, No. 2 :307-315.

26. Abraham Jacubowski, Yad Vashem Archives (YV), 26a.

27. Jacob Hennenberg, YV, 195a.

28. Israel Ipson, YV, 371.

29. The response regarding income is notoriously low on surveys.

30. A full assessment of the extent of survivors' contributions in relation to their income is currently underway.

31. Wiener Oral History Collection.

32. I. Harry Levin, "Vineland----A Haven for Refugees." The Jewish Poultry Farmers Association of South Jersey, 10th Anniversary Journal, 1962 :5.

33. Nathan Glazer, " The Jewish Revival in America: I," Commentary, 20 No. 6 (December 1955) :493-499.

34. "Baltimore Newcomers Group Participates in Campaign," Rescue, April-May 1951 :5.

35. For more information on this process, see Jacob M. Maze, "Petaluma---Oldest Jewish Farm Settlement in California," The Jewish Farmer, September 1957 :121; Benjamin Miller, "Jewish Farmers in Connecticut," The Jewish Farmer, May 1958 :77-81; Shlomo Zecktser, "Der Neier Yiddishe Yishuv in Danielson, Connecticut," ("The New Jewish Settlement in Danielson, Connecticut), Der Yiddisher Farmer, May 1958 :96 (Yiddish.); Shaul Yurista, "Erste Shritt." ("First Steps"), The Jewish Poultry Farmers Association of South Jersey, 10th Anniversary Journal, n.d. :47 (Yiddish.)

36. Levin, Vineland,1962

37. Breina Goldman, "Zum 14ter Yizkor Tog Nuch Unzere Kedoishim." ("On the 14th Remembrance Day of our Martyrs"), Der Yiddisher Farmer, June 1957 :90 (Yiddish.)

38. Breina Goldman, "Hazkoroh Nuch die 6 Million Kedoishim," ("Remembrance for the 6 Million Martyrs"), Der Yiddisher Farmer, May 1958 :97 (Yiddish.)

39. Interview with Willie Herskovits, December 30,1987; also, correspondence with Professor Hannah Kliger who is conducting research on landsman schaeften in the United States.

40. Josef Butterman, Jewish Displaced Persons in Germany and in the United States of America, 1945-1960; A Report. New York,1960 (available at Yad Vashem.)

41. William B. Helmreich, "Misguided Optimism," Midstream, January 1988 :31.

42. Based on preliminary results made available through the North American Jewish Data Bank, City University of New York.

43. S. Rustin, Guilt,Hostility and Jewish Identification Among Adolescent Children of Concentration Camp Survivors. Unpublished PhD. Diss., New York University,1971; Judith Kestenberg, "Psychoanalytic Contributions to the Problem of Children of Survivors from Nazi Persecution," Israel Annals of Psychiatry and Related Disciplines, 10, No. 4 (1972 :311-325; Hillel Klein, "Families of Survivors in the Kibbutz: Psychological Studies," in H. Krystal and W. Niederland (eds), Psychic Traumatization. Boston: Little Brown,1971;

44. Epstein, Study in American Pluralism :11-12.

45. Helen Epstein, Children of the Holocaust.New York: Bantam,1980 :178-179.

46. Address at Israel Center, Jerusalem, April 25,1987.

47. Barbara Finkelstein, Summer Long-a-coming. New York : Harper & Row, 1987 :247.

48. Ruth Minsky Sender, "A Survivor's Duty is Not to Forget," The New York Times, Sunday March 27,1988, Section 12 :29.

49. Sam Harris, YV, 10; Rabinowitz, New Lives :108.

50. Rose Murra, YV, 317.

51. Ibid.

52. See Doris Kirschmann and Sylvia Savin, "Refugee Adjustment---Five Years Later," Jewish Social Service Quarterly, 30 Winter 1953 :200; Rabinowitz, New Lives :139; Epstein, Study in American Pluralism :3; G.R. Leon, et al, "Survivors of the Holocaust and their Children: Current Status and Adjustment," Journal of Personality and Social Psychology.41 (1981) :503-516.

BAPTISTS AND THE HOLOCAUST

E. Earl Joiner

Stetson University
Campus Box 8353
DeLand, Florida 32720

Baptists are now the largest Protestant group in America, 27,377,422 (1985). These together with Baptists in other countries around the world total 32,483,408, making Baptists a rather significant force in the modern world (Southern Baptist Handbook, hereafter shall be referred to as SBH, 1987). The major growth which put them in this position has occurred after the Holocaust, but it began much earlier.

Baptists began as a small persecuted minority of dissenters in England in the 16th century. Though they had some kinship with one of the radical wing of the Reformation, the Anabaptists, modern Baptists trace their ancestry to the early English Baptists and American Baptists who were the offspring of the early British Baptists. During their early history, Baptists were often persecuted and sometimes imprisoned in England and in America. When England passed the Edict of Toleration in 1689, some of the persecution ceased, but since most of the early colonies had established church systems Baptists and other minorities were still victims of many pressures, including the necessity of paying taxes to support the clergy of the established churches. Thus they were tolerated, but not really free.

Before the American revolution, Roger Williams joined the small Baptist movement after being expelled from the Massachusetts Bay Colony and established Rhode Island, the first colony dedicated to religious freedom. When the revolution came, the few Baptists in the American colonies were reluctant to fight England because of their gratitude to England for their guarantee of religious toleration. They finally decided to join the revolutionaries hoping to gain complete religious freedom.

After the revolution, Baptists petitioned the first Continental Congress to include an article in the Constitution which guaranteed religious freedom for all. They did not succeed, but they continued to press their claims, and worked with others to bring into being the first amendment to the Constitution which states that "Congress shall make no law respecting an establishment of religion, or prohibiting the free exercise thereof."

During and after the revolution, the Baptist movement spread over the colonies on the eastern seaboard and grew in number, and were among the effective groups in relating to the pioneers in the great westward push.

By the time, Hitler came to power in 1933, Baptists in America had grown from 1,125 in 1683, to 9,188,508 in 1933, and in the world they numbered 11,136,612 strong By 1939 there were 4,949,174 Southern Baptists and 10,894,826 Baptists in the U.S., and in the world the number had reached 12,472,059 (SBH, 1940). In the early 1900s, moreover, Baptists in America particularly developed a strong sense of social responsibility. It is noteworthy that Walter Rauschenbusch, the well known prophet of the Social Gospel, who wrote during the early 1900s, was a Baptist. He gained wide fame with his publication of Christianity and the Social Crisis, in 1907. Despite the fact that Rauschenbusch adopted the critical study of the Bible associated with the names of German scholars like Schleiermacher, Ritschl and Harnack, he hated militarism, and with the rise of Germany before and during World War I, his popularity declined with the growing opposition to Germany in America.

Baptists however, continued to grow because Rauschenbusch, while he represented well the growing sense of social responsibility among Baptists, did not represent typical Baptist views in other ways (Robert T. Handy, ed., 1966).

The growth of Baptists from an important minority in the early colonial period to an influential and powerful group in the early years of the 20th century is reflected in the significant role they played in the prohibition movement. This movement lead to the 18th Amendment which became effective in 1920, and prohibited the manufacture and sale of alcohol as a beverage in the United States. Its repeal the same year Hitler came to power in 1933, may also reflect the decline in Baptists' sense of social responsibility. It also paralleled the decline of the social Gospel in America. It certainly reflected the widespread belief that prohibition was a failure. For Baptists as for other Protestants in America the passing of the prohibition amendment quite apart from the issue of alcohol, demonstrated the power that church groups could have when they reached consensus on an issue they considered important.

Baptists have shared with Jewish people three things which should have made them ready to identify with the Jewish people in their time of suffering during the rise of Naziism to the pinnacle of power, and during the Holocaust. First, they shared a common history of persecution, with the Jewish people suffering most in part because of their longer history. Second, they have shared with the Jewish community in taking the Hebrew Scriptures with great seriousness. Also they have shared with the Jewish people a sense of responsibility to obey God even at the risk of persecution. Third, they have shared a common commitment to religious freedom, and the separation of church and state. One would expect that these shared experiences and convictions along with Baptists' growing sense of social responsibility should have produced many expressions of sympathy for the sufferings of the Jews during the rise of Naziism and during the Holocaust itself.

The purpose of this paper is to examine the responses Baptists made to the plight of the Jews, and the contribution they made to the atmosphere in which much of the western world, including the Christian world, stood by and did little to prevent or stop the Holocaust.

THEIR AMBIVALENCE

The question we examine here is how important did Baptists consider the issue of growing anti-semitism in the rise of Naziism to be. The first answer appears to be that they were rather ambivalent. On the one hand, many Baptists,according to one study a majority of American Baptists,regarded the Jews as the chosen people of God. On the other hand, a significant minority of American Baptists have believed that the Jews were most responsible for the crucifixion of Jesus. The minority included 46% of American Baptists, 38% of Southern Baptists (Charles Glock et al, 1966).

This ambivalence made Baptists easily vulnerable to two extremes, tempted either to show favoritism to all Jews because they were Jews, or to show hostility to all Jews because of their perceived corporate guilt. It also produced a conditional attitude which distinguished between those Jews who were possible converts to Christianity and those who were not. Sometimes great kindness toward Jews is shown and commended to others that is calculated to lay the foundation for winning them to Christianity. In all fairness, however, it appears that in some cases the kindness was a genuine expression of caring and appreciation for others regardless of race or religion. On this positive note, for example Mrs. H. A. Hunt who published a column in the Florida Baptist Witness, on "The Jew," expressed keen appreciation in 1932 for Julius Rosenwald of Chicago, pointing out that he gave away four times as much as he left. She praised him for his self-denial and the good he did with his money. Further, she wrote: "Like the late Nathan Straus, his happiness lay in unselfishly serving others, and also like Mr. Straus, be belonged to the race that has given to American many other Philanthropists." (Florida Baptist Witness, hereafter shall be referred to as Witness, 1932). For several months in 1932 and 1934 Mrs. Hunt gave advice on proper Christian attitudes toward the Jews. She wrote that church officers should include in their prayers "a petition for the Jews and for Christians that they may manifest to the Jews a kind spirit and take a deeper interest in their spiritual welfare."(Witness, 1932). Further, she suggested that "A Christian friend of the Jews, when unfair remarks are made about them in his presence, uses the opportunity to defend them and give interesting information about them." (Witness, 1932). Mrs. Hunt also expressed keen interest in the growing support in some circles of American government for the cause of Zionism. (Witness, 1933). Moreover, she expressed deep concern over the recent news of starving Jews in Poland.

However, the generous attitude of Mrs. Hunt toward the Jewish people seems not to be typical of Baptists in the 1930s, if we judge by their published writings. For example, Rev. and Mrs. Russell wrote in the Witness also in 1932 that ". . . the Jew still hates Christ and all who represent Him." (Witness, 1932). Such a strong negative statement of course may in part reflect the frustrations these missionaries were facing in Palestine at the time. Even so, the anti-semitism seems obvious.

In some cases the ambivalence did not involve direct prejudice against the Jews, but rather gave support to the notion that some races were superior and other inferior. Such notions could not only be transferred from one race to another. At times racist and anti-racist views could be held by persons quite unconscious of the contradiction. A classic example is my professor of preaching, Dr. J. B. Weatherspoon, who wrote a review of Applied Eugenics, published by Popenoe and Johnson in 1918, and revised in 1934, and recommended the work as a thorough and dependable treatment of the subject. The book argues that some races are inferior to others (Review and Expositer, hereafter shall be referred to as Review, 1934). Ironically, a few years later, Dr. Weatherspoon, who served on the Social Service Commission for many years, played a significant role in getting forward looking reports passed by the Southern Baptist Convention which condemned racism (SBC, 1941, 1943). Did he change his views about racism, or did he believe that one could believe in the racial superiority of one race over another without being racist? In his case the answer is likely that he did not see any necessary connection between the ideas of racial superiority and discrimination. He was in fact opposed to all forms of racial discrimination. Even so, in the context of the academic world of the 1930s we cannot avoid the conclusion that he was among many who did not recognize the interrelatedness of belief in racial superiority and racism in the 1930s. By the 1940s, however, he and other Baptists learned the dangers of such racism from Hitler (SBC, 1944).

This ambivalence moreover, was widespread among Baptists, in Europe and in America, and though it was expressed in different ways it created a schism in the very soul of Baptists and also produced a number of other responses to the rise of Nazism that also contributed to the atmosphere which was partly responsible for the Holocaust.

FEAR

The rise of Hitler struck fear in the hearts of many informed Baptists in Germany, Europe, and America. In 1934 in the year after Hitler came to power, the Baptist World Alliance met in Berlin, at the same time the Baptists in Germany were celebrating their 100th anniversary of the beginning of Baptist work in Germany. Baptists outside Germany were well aware of the political unrest there and some suggested that the leaders of the Baptist World Alliance change the meeting place to London. Having received assurance from the Germans of their safety and desiring to affirm strong support for German Baptists, the leaders decided to stick with the plan of meeting in Berlin. Even so, apprehension over the political situation in Germany kept many from attending. Despite that fact, the meeting in Berlin drew the largest attendance in the history of the Baptist World Alliance (Review, 1934). Even so, some who attended were fearful of their own safety and concerned for the freedom and well being of the German Baptists. These Baptist leaders had heard talk also of the creation of one national church in Germany to which all denominations would be related. When they expressed their anxieties to the German authorities, Archbishop Ludwig Meuller invited a small group of leaders to his home and assured them that the free churches would continue to be free (Review, 1934).

These reassurances helped reduce the apprehensions of many of the delegates, but not all. Despite their claims to the contrary, John R. Sampey, President of Southern Baptist Seminary claimed he saw fear and apprehension in the eyes of the German Baptists who attended the Alliance meeting. (Western Recorder, 1934). Moreover, the discussion of the Report of the Commission on Nationalism by Paul Schmidt, a German Baptist, seems to this writer to betray his own fear that his approval of the report might get him in trouble with the German authorities, since the report warned of the dangers of nationalism. He claimed that the church could do nothing but condemn decadent nationalism, which he did not define, and teach healthy patriotism (Baptist World Alliance, hereafter shall be referred to as BWA, 1934). Similarly, when German Baptist F. Fullbrandt, argued that if the churches are to be effective and useful they must cooperate, we wonder if that statement betrayed fear also (BWA, 1934).

PROTEST

The third response of Baptists to the rise of Naziism and the maltreatment of the Jews in Germany was protest. The awareness of Baptist leaders in 1934 of racial discrimination in Germany and other places in the world was expressed in a resolution protesting religious oppression and racial discrimination against Jews and others (BWA, 1934). Narrow, unselfish nationalism was also condemned in the report of the Commission on Nationalism chaired my N. J. Nordstrom of Stockholm, Sweden. In condemning nationalism however, while he listed its dangers, including the threat to missions and to the peace and freedom of the church, he made no mention of the danger to the Jews (BWA, 1934).

In 1933, the Northern Baptist Convention adopted a mild resolution which deplored race hatred and discrimination in both the United States and germany (BWA, 1934). In 1938, the General Council of the Northern Baptist Convention adopted a rare specific resolution which expressed deep concern for the suffering of many minorities, including the Jews of Germany. The resolution also requested President Roosevelt to call an international conference to deal with the refugee problem, and urged the government to preserve the tradition of the United States as a haven for the oppressed (Nawn, 1980).

Agencies and individuals related to the Southern Baptist Convention responded with some strong statements also. In 1938 the Alabama, Georgia, and North Carolina Annual Conventions passed resolutions strongly condemning Germany's anti-Jewish measures. North Carolina Baptists called for changing immigration laws to make possible the admission of more refugees (Nawn, 1980). Some of the Baptist journalistic responses to news about "Krystallnacht" in the South were equally strong. The editor of The Biblical Recorder, a North Carolina Baptist newspaper, registered a strong protest, warning Germany of God's judgment, and lamented the refusal of Cuban and America to admit 900 refugees on the St. Louis, A German vessel. This editor of the Biblical Recorder was the most outspoken among Southern Baptist journalists. Most Southern Baptist journals condemned German cruelty to the Jews, but showed little understanding of what was happening.

Baptist individuals and organizations also responded by protesting in various ways. Baptist Harry Emerson Fosdick, pastor of Riverside Church in New York, protested often. Edwin McNeill Poteat, pastor of the Pullen Memorial Church in Raleigh, North Carolina, during the early 1930s, did so often, but according to Nawn, he was not a typical Southern Baptist pastor (Nawn, 1980). In fact, public protest of Nazi racial policies and sympathy for the Jews were rare in the Southern Baptist Convention. Some of the expressions of sympathy for the plight of the Jews among Southern Baptists were related to their prime interest in doing mission work among them (Nawn, 1980).

When the American Christian Committee for German Refugees was organized in 1934 as an interdenominational effort to deal with the refugee problem created by Nazi racial policies, it sought to parallel supplement Jewish efforts. The organization came to include people from Protestant, Catholic and Jewish faiths. Northern Baptists' efforts were a part of this group. In fact the group created a film featuring an address by a well known minister, Harry Emerson Fosdick, in Riverside Church to publicize the cause. When the film was shown at Riverside, it attracted 2,000 people. It attracted such wide publicity that the Nazis attacked the film, describing it as Jewish propaganda and an unfair attack on national socialism. Unfortunately, the film was not very successful. In fact, the expenses of the committee sometimes consumed as much as 70% of the money raised. For example, in 1939, when a goal was set for $600,000, only $200,000 was raised. The committee therefore was always in financial difficulty, although it did receive a great boost in 1940 with a $100,000 gift from the United Jewish Appeal (Nawn, 1980).

When the Baptist World Alliance met in Atlanta, Georgia in 1939, it turned out to be the largest Baptist gathering in history with 12,445 registered. In his presidential address George W. Truett stated that Baptists insist on religious liberty for all, including Jews, but he made no mention of their special plight at the time (BWA, 1939). In contrast to the fear and relief which dominated the minds of many Baptists assembling in Berlin five years earlier, and where the element of protest was very mild, by 1939 the growth of concern among Baptist leaders from around the world was strongly expressed by more statements of protest that came from several leaders. Again, however, some ambivalence was obvious. In his report of the five years between Berlin and Atlanta, J. H. Rushbrooke, General Secretary of the Baptist World Alliance, reviewed the work of the Alliance in defending religious freedom and protesting religious repression in various countries, including Russia and Rumania, but he made no mention of the special plight of the Jews. He did take note of the fact that not all that the Baptists said in Berlin had been freely published, and that 18 months after 1934, German authorities suppressed further circulation of reports (BWA, 1939).

M. E. Aubrey of London, in an address entitled, "Christianity and the Totalitarian State," condemned the recent imprisonment of Martin Niemoeller, the removal of 100 German pastors from office, and the forbidding of 40 ministers to preach, but he too failed to mention the terrible plight of the Jews (BWA, 1939). German Baptist Paul Schmidt, responded strongly to Aubrey in his address entitled, "Liberalism, Collectivism and the Baptists." He began by reporting that one Baptist speaker cannot speak for all. Otherwise he would have to take exception to the previous speaker's (Aubrey) remarks. He went on to say that many lacked a proper understanding of what the real situation was in Germany, decried the meddling in political affairs by the church, and argued that some kind of collectivism may be justified for a nation to be strong and progressive. He argued, moreover, that to disobey men in authority is all right only when "the witness of Christ as personal Lord is at stake." (BWA, 1939).

William A. Mueller, a native German Baptist who was then teaching in the United States, apparently took Schmidt's remarks as suggesting that as long as German ministers confined their work to witnessing to Jesus Christ as personal Lord, they were completely free. Mueller had recently traveled in his own native land again, however, and took issue with Schmidt. Mueller's recent visits in Germany convinced him that the earlier Baptist passion had declined, and that the German Baptists had easily accepted the view of the distinction between the kingdom of God and the kingdom of the world that blinded them to the fact that this world is still God's world. Thus, he protested the lack of a clear word from the Baptist people of Germany concerning the burning issue in their land -- the issue of anti-semitism. While they claimed to be free, he reported seeing in Stettin that summer an ordinance on the bulletin board of a Baptist church, forbidding the distribution of religious pamphlets in nearly 50 strategic streets and public squares in that city (BWA, 1939).

PRAISE AND SUPPORT FOR HITLER

The most surprising Baptist response to the rise of Naziism and the widespread anti-semitism that went with it to this writer was the praise and support Hitler received and the hostility directed toward the Jews. The praise and support Hitler received and written expressions of hostility to the Jews were not always expressed together. Some gave verbal support and praise for Hitler without expressing anti-semitism. Others gave expression to strong anti-semitic statements without expressing support for Hitler. In some instances support and praise for Hitler was largely unrelated to the Jewish question, but was rather grounded in other factors. Examples will illustrate these varieties.

Mild expressions of support and appreciation were expressed by leaders of the Baptist World Alliance in 1934 when their initial fears were replaced by relief after being assured of their safety by the Nazi leaders. During the few days they were in Berlin, the delegates felt secure, and expressed confidence that the Baptists' of Germany would continue to enjoy their freedom (BWA, 1934). No one at this meeting could fail to note the strong support to Hitler and German National Socialism given by the German Baptist leaders who spoke at the meeting. Paul Schmidt, editor of Warheitzeuge, affirmed support for his government, and suggested that the reshaping of the nation was the task of the government, not the church (BWA, 1934).

German Baptist F. Fullbrandt was high in his praise of Hitler and National Socialism. He said that no one has opposed the flood of unbelief that was threatening the well being of Europe and the whole western world like Hitler and the National Socialists (BWA, 1934). He went on to say that Hitler had put the churches to shame in dealing with Bolshevism, and that Hitler was doing what the churches should have done long ago (BWA, 1934). What he thought that the churches should have done is not clear, but it is clear that he believed the Baptist churches of Germany should support Hitler.

After reflecting on their experiences in Berlin in 1934, at least two prominent American

Baptist ministers made strong statements of admiration and support for Hitler. One was M. E. Dodd, president of the Southern Baptist Convention. In expressing support and praise for Hitler, Dodd explained that many sources he had consulted convinced him that the recent movements in Germany were not religious or racial, but political and economic. He wrote that since World War I, 200,000 Jews from Russia and other places had come to Germany, and that most of them were communist agitators against the government. Moreover, he reported that when the Germans discovered the Jews occupied positions of influence in government, education, and business, all out of proportion to their size, and used them to injure the German people and advance their own interests, the action taken by Hitler to change things was appropriate. He reported that over 50% of the lawyers and teachers in Berlin were Jewish, and that though the Jews represented only 1% of the influential positions. Apparently, Dodd had read of the political rhetoric Hitler used to justify his actions and took them at face value. The lack of critical judgment in his statements of course may reflect some ignorance of the facts. It may also, however, reflect anti-semitism (M. E. Dodd, 1934).

Similarly, John W. Bradbury, a Baptist pastor in Boston, Massachusetts, (U.S.A.) after returning from the 1934 session of the Baptist World Congress, wrote that it was great to be in a land where sex literature could not be sold, and where no gangster films filled with violence could be shown. With obvious satisfaction, he wrote that:

> The new Germany has burned masses of corrupting magazines and books along with its <u>bonfires of Jewish and communistic</u> libraries . . The New Germany is serious minded. It would be well for other nations to take it seriously too. Ninety percent of the people are in back of Hitler . . . I traveled through many cities and never heard a single strain of jazz music (John W. Bradbury, 1934).

It appears that in the 1930s support and praise for Hitler and the new Germany were related to three factors which are hard to separate. One was the element of anti-semitism among Baptists which we have noted earlier. The other was the fear of communism with which the Jewish element in Europe in general and in Germany in particular was associated, at least in their minds. It is incredible in retrospect, that they accepted Hitler's simplistic justification of his actions so easily. A factor in their naivete is that anti-semitism, widespread in Europe and America, in secular and religious minds, together with a growing fear of communism blinded their insight. Another factor in the Baptist support for Hitler was the conservative sound of Hitler's stress on individual morality which was shared by many Baptists. The growth of conservative personal morality was accelerated by a conservative theology and ethics which was expressed in their revolt against theological liberalism and the social gospel. The social gospel which stressed changing society through political and economic means, prominent in American Christianity, was never taken seriously by most conservative Baptists, and lost ground in American Protestantism following World War I and the depression of 1929. The fear of communism however, increased, and Hitler was viewed in the early years by Baptists and others as a bulwark against communism (Charles F. Leek, 1934).

By 1939, when the Baptist World Alliance met in Atlanta, Georgia, the perception of Hitler by Baptists outside Germany was changing. German Baptists still defended Hitler and National Socialism, but in England and in America Baptist support for Hitler began to decline. Even so the most common reason for the change appears not to be a growing concern for the plight of the Jews, but the fear of the loss of freedom for the clergy in Germany. As we have noted, an exception here was William A. Mueller, who criticized his fellow Baptists in his native Germany for their blind support of Hitler and their blindness to the racial problem that was reaching serious proportions in Germany and in America. As we shall see, however, the voice of Mueller and the few others who spoke out in 1939 were lonely voices. They were in sharp contrast to the views of Charles F. Leek, who wrote in the <u>Alabama Baptist</u> that while he did not approve of Hitler's Jewish measures, the German Jews were not only responsible for their plight, but that the American Jews could expect similar treatment unless they change (Nawn, 1980).

SILENCE

The most common Baptist response to Hitler's Germany and his repressive measures against the Jews, especially between the years 1933 and the early 1940s, was somewhere between the extremes of praise and protest. The most accurate word to describe this median seems to be silence. Their silence is especially surprising since in their early history they too were persecuted and harassed. Close examination of the situation of Baptist life in various countries, however, reveals a number of factors which make their silence at least partially understandable though hardly excusable. The first factor is particularly characteristic of the Baptists in Germany. Their first real freedom came with the rise of Naziism. Baptists in Germany were part of a free church group receiving no state support, stressing individual piety and avoiding political involvement. From their beginning in Germany in 1834, they were harassed, persecuted, ostracized, fined and imprisoned periodically until the rise of Naziism. Like the Baptists of the early Puritan era in America who were reluctant to join the fight for the revolution because of their gratitude to England for the edict of toleration, German Baptists were reluctant to criticize the Nazis who gave them the first freedom they had known (Robert D. Linder, 1971; David T. Priestly, 1971).

A second reason for the silence of German Baptists was that even though they fought in the courts and in legislature for recognition, they still respected the government because they believed it was God. Despite persecution by Lutherans, they were still influenced by Luther's doctrine of two kingdoms, which distinguished between the work of God through the church and through the state. Their radical understanding of the separation of church and state made German Baptists even less inclined to get involved in criticism than the Lutherans (David T. Priestly, 1971).

Third, and closely related because of their non-involvement in political affairs, German Baptists were politically uneducated. Also because of their non-involvement position, they never took a position either of loyalty or opposition to the Nazi state (David T. Priestly, 1971).

Fourth, many Baptists in Germany and elsewhere were simply preoccupied with other things. Because of their small size and their silence, German Baptists were largely ignored by the government, and went about their business of evangelism. In fact, when Germany annexed other countries, the Baptists of Germany instead of criticizing the state authorities, view these events as providing them with new opportunities for evangelism. Contacts were therefore made with other Baptists in these countries. However, the German authorities soon restricted the activity of all church groups to Germany, and the continuation of the war soon brought all such activities to a halt (David T. Priestly, 1971).

Fifth, while only four German Baptist pastors belonged to the Nazi party, many lay persons and youth were active in party organizations. Near the end of the war, however, the German Baptists became increasingly aware of the danger of losing their freedom even in Germany. Some pastors attracted the attention of the police by praying for peace rather than a German victory. Such prayers were regarded as too political and the pastors were warned. A few spoke out in protest, but only three Baptist pastors went to prison. Because of their silence in Germany there were no Baptist martyrs. Because of their silence also the Baptists of Germany were never really tested. From their silence, it appears that they accepted the German government's explanation for its measures against the Jews (David T. Priestly, 1971).

Outside Germany, the most conspicuous examples of silence among Baptist were from the Southern Baptist Convention of the United States. In the Southern Baptist Convention, representing the largest group of American Baptists, the Convention itself offered no resolutions of protest concerning the treatment of the Jews in Germany from 1933 to 1941. Whether or not this silence was due to ignorance or indifference one may debate. Certainly information on the plight of the Jews was not only available, it was reported in the 1940 edition of the Southern Baptist Handbook, published by the Southern Baptist Convention. Here the Convention reprinted information from the Watchman and Examiner, reporting the number of Jews in Germany and Austria who had committed suicide (30,000), how many were in prisons or concentration camps (30,000), how many emigrated (330,000), how many had been murdered (13,000). The reasons for their silence are somewhat similar to those of the German Baptists. For one thing, their focus on social ethics was so narrow, particularly in the period paralleling the rise of Hitler, that it ignored major issues of state morality, stressing instead such issues as smoking, drinking, gangster movies, and women wearing red lipstick. Another reason for their silence was their stress on evangelism. Southern Baptists stressed evangelism in such a way as to play down social issues. The criticism by F. M. McConnell, editor of The Baptist Standard, of the amount of attention given to social, economic, and political issues in the 1934 meeting of the Baptist World Alliance was typical of many Southern Baptists in attendance (William L. Allen, 1982). The silence of many Southern Baptists during the rise of Hitler and during the Holocaust may also have been due to the racism that has a long history among Southern Baptists. The racism of many Southern Baptists is well documented by Spain and Eighmy (Rufus Spain, 1961; John Lee Eighmy, 1972). Another factor in the silence of Baptists outside Germany was their belief that Hitler's measures were justified by his efforts to oppose Communism. A factor in the silence of American Baptists generally may be their preoccupation with the suffering of Baptists in other places. An address by Ed. A. Bell, representative in Europe of the American Baptist Foreign Mission Society, illustrates this point. He noted at the 1947 meeting of the Baptist World Alliance that he had recently traveled extensively in Europe and note the extensive suffering of Baptists and others, but did not mention the suffering of the Jews (BWA, 1947). Similarly, according to Nawn, the Southern Baptist Convention was totally silent on the plight of the Jews from 1933 to 1941. However, the Convention called on the government to intercede with the Rumanian government on behalf of the Baptists being persecuted in that country (Report From the Capitol (1979; 1983). My own research supports the observation of Nawn.

In fact, the issue of anti-semitism which is central to the tragedy of the Holocaust was largely ignored by many Southern Baptist writers until after the Eichmann trial in 1961. It was apparently easy for most Baptists to forget about the Holocaust for even after the Eichmann trial which attracted world wide attention, the Holocaust was still ignored in most Baptist publications. After the Eichmann trial there was a significant increase in the number of Baptist published articles about the Jews, which seemed to reflect a rethinking of attitudes toward the Jews at least among some Baptist writers. From 1961 to 1983, however, I did not find a single article among Southern Baptist journals and news periodicals with the term Holocaust in the title.

In addition to the facts already mentioned, it is possible that many Baptists did not know what was happening until it was too late to engage in any effective efforts. It also seems possible that some were confused by German propaganda and influenced by patriotism and the fear of Communism. Since America was attacked by the Japanese and ended up fighting in Africa, Europe, and the Far East many of its people including Baptists and political leaders, were so taken up with the war effort as a whole, that they simply overlooked the special plight of the Jews.

CONFESSION OF FAILURE

After many years of silence the Southern Baptist Convention, now the largest Protestant denomination in the United States, passed a resolution on prejudice, in which they disavowed anti-semitism as erroneously inherent in Christianity (SBC, 1971). In 1972, the Convention passed a stronger resolution offered by B. Elmo Seoggin, which mentioned the Holocaust directly, confessed the failure of Southern Baptists to take a sufficiently vigorous stand against Hitler's measures against the Jews, and calling for an end to anti-semitism. The resolution also cited the fact that Baptists and Jews share a common heritage of persecution and suffering for conscience sake (SBC, 1972.) Similarly, after agonizing for many years over their own silence during the Holocaust, the Evangelical Free Church Congregations in Germany drew up a statement at the Congress of the European Baptist Federation held in Hamburg on August 2, 1984. In the statement they expressed shame and grief and the desire for divine forgiveness. They reported that some among them saw the truth about the Nazi regime, warned against it and protested the injustice, but lamented that the Baptists of Germany as a group did not ally themselves with the efforts of others in opposing Naziism. The statement ended with the expressed hope that Baptists might learn from this chapter in their history (Christian Jewish Relations, 1984). For reasons indicated in this paper, all Baptists need to confess their failures also and to join all Christians and Jews in learning from our mistakes and working together to prevent such a catastrophe as the Holocaust from recurring.

GROWTH OF CONCERN

Two agencies related to the Southern Baptist Convention have expressed concern for the sufferings of Jews in recent years, however. One of these agencies was the Home Mission Board whose earlier expressions of concern for the Jews was related primarily to their interest in converting the Jews to Christianity. In the last few years, there appear to have been a shift of focus in which departments of the Home Mission Board worked closely with a number of Jewish agencies to increase mutual understanding and work together to reduce anti-semitism.

The other Baptist agency that has expressed concern for the sufferings of the Jews was the Baptist Joint Committee of Public Affairs, organized in 1950 and supported by nine different Baptist groups in the United States. This organization is dedicated to the preservation of religious liberty and the separation of church and state. The committee published the first article with the word Holocaust appearing in its title in 1983. (Of course one must remember that the term "Holocaust" as the descriptive term for the destruction of 6 million Jews became widely known only in recent years.) However, the Joint Committee had expressed concern for the Jewish victim of persecution from its earliest days (Report From the Capitol, 1963, 1979). In 1979, James E. Wood, Jr., who served as Executive Director from 1972 until 1980, received the Isaiah Award from Rabbi Matthew Simon of the American Jewish Committee, in appreciation for the many expressions of concern for the Jewish victims of persecution in Europe (Report From the Capitol, 1979).

LEARNING SOME LESSONS

In the last 20 years (1960-1980) Baptists have undergone a self-evaluation in their attitudes toward Judaism and have given increasing attention to the dangers of anti-semitism and the need for better understanding between Christians and Jews. Perhaps this is one of the lessons we have learned. There are several others. A second lesson is that our own history of suffering from persecution and lack of religious freedom requires us to be particularly sensitive to preserving the need to preserve the freedom and rights of others. Otherwise we will break faith with our own history. We must take advantage of all opportunities to learn what is happening in our world and be ready to witness and act to prevent or stop injustices against any religious or ethnic groups.

Third, we need to learn that theological statements can have consequences we do not intend, and that we need to consider the ways our theological statements can affect others. Baptists and other Christians need to review their literature and to become acutely aware of the danger of broad generalizations about "the Jews," particularly in the interpretations of the crucifixion of Jesus. All language and terms that might encourage or perpetuate anti-semitism attitudes or actions should be carefully avoided.

Fourth, we need to be very wary of the relation of the church to the "powers that be," which may or may not be ordained of God. To be too closely identified with the state involves the risk of being used and/or losing the power of protest. To be too distant from the actions of the state can result in losing all influence. Either extreme can result in religious groups being used or abused.

Baptists, other Christians, and Jews should recognize the mutual right to live freely and witness to their faith without fear of unfair criticism or repressive actions. Baptists and Jews should work with other religious groups to free the world from all racial and religious repression, and thus prevent another Holocaust.

REFERENCES

Allen, William L. (1982). Christian Century, 890ff.

Baptist World Alliance (1934). Minutes, 65, 13, 17, 24; (1939), 37, 159, 198, 203, 207-208.

Bradbury John W. (1934). Watchman Examiner, 996.

Christian Jewish Relations 17 (1984).

Dodd, M. E. (1934). Florida Baptist Witness, 4, 13.

Eighmy, John Lee. (1932). Churches in Cultural Captivity, Chs I, II.

Florida Baptist Witness (1932), (1933), 9.

Glock, Charles and Stark, Rodney (1966). Christian Beliefs and Anti-semitism, 196.

Handy, Robert T., ed. (1966). The Social Gospel in America, 1870-1920, 258-259.

Leek, Charles F. (1934). Alabama Baptist,

Linder, Robert D. ed. (1971). God and Caesar: Case Studies in the Relationship Between Christianity and the State, 102-103.

Nawn, William E. (1980). Unpublished doctoral dissertation, 94, 97, 123, 155, 172-181, 182ff, 491-492.

Priestly, David T. (1971). Conference On Faith and History, 102-117.

Report From the Capitol (1979; 1983).

Review and Expositor (1934), 476-477.

Southern Baptist Convention Annual (1941), 126-127; (1943), 107; (1971), 79; (1972), 75.

Southern Baptist Handbook (1940) (1987).

Spain, Rufus (1961). As Ease in Zion: A Special History of Southern Baptists, 1865-1900, 71.

Western Recorder (1934).

Wood, James E. (1983). Report From the Capitol, 2.

HERZOG, DE VALERA AND IRISH POLICY TOWARDS JEWISH REFUGEES IN THE 1930S AND 1940S

DR DERMOT KEOGH MA Ph.D.

University College, Cork, Ireland

INTRODUCTION

On 3 May 1945, the Taoiseach (Prime Minister), Eamon de Valera, accompanied by the Secretary of the Department of External Affairs, Joseph Walshe, visited the German Legation in Dublin to express condolences on the death of Adolf Hitler. The following day, Michael McDunphy, the Secretary to President Douglas Hyde, paid a similar visit. The Irish government had decided - against the advice of leading diplomats - to adhere strictly to the dictates of the protocol to be observed following the death of a head of government with which the country had formal relations. This was perhaps the most controversial decision of de Valera's political career; it was certainly an action for which he was condemned internationally and de Valera's reputation never recovered in the eyes of many who were outraged by the apparent insensitivity of the Irish leader.[1]

Some months later, the Department of Justice produced a memorandum on refugee policy. Under Section C, headed JEWS, Irish policy was reviewed:

> The immigration of Jews is generally discouraged. The wealth and influence of the Jewish community in this country appear to have increased considerably in recent years and there is some danger of exciting opposition and controversy if this tendency continues. As Jews do not become assimilated with the native population, like other immigrants, any big increase in their number might create a social problem.[2]

Both the visit by de Valera to the German Legation on the death of Hitler and the above section from the Department of Justice memorandum, taken together, might incline a reader to the conclusion that de Valera was pro-German and that Irish refugee policy during the Second World War was prejudiced against the Jews. In reality, de Valera was strongly pro-Allied and the Irish policy of neutrality was heavily weighted in favour of Anglo-America.[3] The Irish policy towards Jewish refugees is quite difficult to explain. It must be set in the context of Irish refugee policy in general. De Valera was not anti-semitic but there is evidence of anti-Jewish prejudices among some senior members of the Irish civil service. A modified version of Bernard Wasserstein's conclusion on British policy between 1939 and 1945 could be applied with caution to Ireland:

> There is little to celebrate in this account of British policy towards the Jews of Europe between 1949 and 1945. A few flashes of humanity by individuals lighten the general darkness. Churchill's attitude towards the Jews was one of sympathy and compassion. But the good effectiveness of his interventions in favour of the Jews was repeatedly blunted by the actions of his subordinates. The generous impulses of a small number of officials and politicians stand out from the documents mainly by virtue of their isolation amidst an ocean of bureaucratic indifference and lack of concern. The overall record leaves a profoundly saddening impression.[4]

As will be demonstrated, the Irish experience - although similar to that of the British -

differed in a number of important respects. De Valera occupied a position of far less influence in the international arena than did Churchill. De Valera was not approached as often as Churchill throughout the war to take a more positive stance on the Jewish refugee question. Although Irish refugee policy in general was very restrictive, de Valera invariably made exceptions when appeals were made to him directly from Jewish leaders and organisations. The intermediary role played by his friend, the Chief Rabbi of Palestine, Isaac Herzog, is of great importance in this regard. De Valera usually swept the opposition of his officials to one side when confronted by an urgent request. Available evidence does not reveal a single case of an appeal to admit a group of Jewish refugees during the war being flatly turned down by de Valera. However, while it is possible to detect what Dr Wasserstein has termed 'the generous impulses of a small number of officials' there was something more in the Irish civil service than a mere 'ocean of bureaucratic indifference and lack of concern'; There was - in one case at least - irrefutable evidence of anti-Semitism and strong anti-Jewish prejudice in the case of some others.

HISTORICAL BACKGROUND

In 1881, there were 394 Jews in Ireland. By 1911, the number had risen to 3805. There were 3749 in 1936 and 3907 ten years later. The Jewish population, according to census returns, had only increased by 158 during the war.[5] (Of course, that does not reflect accurately the number of Jewish refugees admitted to the country between 1939 and 1945.) In Ireland, the Jewish community constituted a very small minority in a country that was overwhelmingly Roman Catholic:

POPULATION 1926

Denominations		Saorstat E. (Twenty-six Cos.)	Northern I. (Six Cos.)	Totals
Catholics		2,751,269	420,428	3,171,697
Other Religions:				
Episp.	164,215		338,724	502,939
Presb.	32,429		393,274	425,703
Method.	10,663		49,554	60,217
Jews	3,686			
Baptists	717			
Others	9,013		54,841	63,854
	220,723	220,723	836,133	1,056,856
TOTALS		2,971,992	1,256,561	4,228,553

Dated 3 April 1937 in de Valera Papers, 1995/1A; another sheet, dated 3 June 1937, contained the following information:

> 'Including 9,031 "Others" with 3,686 Jews, making a total of 12,717 non-Christians, the Christian population of the Free State is over 99.5 per cent.
>
> Jews are not recorded for Northern Ireland, but if "Others" are regarded as non-Christian the total population of Northern Ireland includes over 95.6 per cent. Christians.' 6

In a country where the Jewish community constituted such a tiny minority, there was a record of good relations between Jews and the dominant religious grouping. There was one serious episode of inter-religious conflict fomented, in the city of Limerick in 1904, by a Redemptorist priest John Creagh. Some elements of the Catholic community subjected that small community to intimidation, commercial boycotts and physical attacks.[7] There were no fatalities but it was a very serious episode which revealed attitudes of deep-seated prejudice in the Catholic community. Although the Limerick attacks were not repeated in other parts of the country - there were over 3000 living in Dublin in 1911 - there is evidence of strong anti-Jewish prejudice at different social levels in the catholic community. In the socialist trade unionist, James Larkin's newspaper - the Irish Worker - the cartoon reproduced below from a 1903 edition portrays the crudest anti-Semitic stereotypes:

GENTLEMEN OF THE JEWRY

[We have no objection to any man, Jew or Gentile, on account of his Nationality or Creed. What we do object to is the practice, which is becoming all too common, of Foreigners masquerading under Irish Names.—Ed.]

The closed nature of Irish Catholicism is revealed in strong prejudices against the Jews. Popular Catholic literature, The Cross, Irish Rosary, Irish Mind and Catholic Bulletin, emphasised the alleged triangular relationship between the Jews, Freemasonry and international communism. Fr Denis Fahey - a Holy Ghost priest - and the Jesuit, Edward Cahill were two of the most important Catholic polemicists of the 1930s. Isaac Herzog, who had first come to Belfast in 1918 to minister to the Jewish community, became Chief Rabbi of the Irish Free State in the 1920s. He had to voice his opposition to the growing prejudice against the Jewish community in Catholic journals and expressed by minor public figures in the 1930s. He had to go into print to challenge the attacks on the Jews in the columns of the Cross. A further illustration of anti-Jewish feeling was expressed by an A.W. Rollins who complained about the butchering of meat for use by the Jewish community.

> Why should privileges be given to foreigners in this country? It might be said that this was a religious matter, but if cannibals come to this country should they be allowed to eat the people because it was their religion.[9]

These remarks were part of a general attack led by Paddy Belton on the Jews. This was again reported by Herzog to the archbishop: 'The trouble really is that Mr Belton is preaching his Jew-hatred and his insulting attitudes towards the Jewish religion under the colours of Christianity'. The Chief Rabbi feared 'lest, God Forbid, popular passions become inflamed and serious disturbances result as a consequence'.[10] Alive to the dangers from such prejudiced quarters, de Valera made explicit reference to 'Jewish Congregations' in the religious article of the new Irish constitution adopted in a plebiscite on 1 July 1937.[11] When Herzog left Ireland later that year for Palestine he took with him a deep respect for Eamon de Valera.

Shortly before Herzog left for Palestine, the Jewish community in Dublin had cause to become aware of one Charles Bewley, Irish Minister Plenipotentiary and Envoy Extraordinary to Berlin. In an interview in Uhr Blatt, Bewley had been quoted as saying: 'That your Reich and its leaders has many admirers among our youth is a well-known fact.'[12] Bewley was reprimanded for his diplomatic gaffe by his superiors but it did not stop him sending the most prejudiced reports to Dublin on the treatment of the Jews in Germany. For example, Bewley reported on 9 December 1938 in a fashion which showed him to have moved very close to a Nationalist Socialist line in his attitude towards Jews. His thesis was that Jewish communities, in Germany and other European countries, were a disruptive influence because

> even when settled in a particular country for centuries, (they) do not become assimilated to the people of that country, but, when the interests of the country of their birth come into conflict with their own personal or racial interests, invariably sacrifice the interests of the country of their birth to Jewish interests.

He was to repeat the mischievous argument of 'dual loyalty' in other reports. Bewley writes of 'the whole press, theatre, cinema, stock exchange the banks' being 'completely under Jewish control' before Hitler came to power. Space does not allow the detailed repetition of Bewley's prejudiced reporting from Berlin. In the same report, Bewley rationalised the special treatment meted out to Jews in various countries suggesting that 'it is of course necessary to be aware of the particular circumstances prevailing in each country before it is possible to judge whether the measures adopted are necessary or not'. Bewley argued that that naturally did not apply to cases of deliberate cruelty on the part of the government 'but I am not aware of any such towards Jews on the part of the German Government'. He believed that there had not been an episode in connection with Jews in Germany which 'could even remotely be compared with the atrocities of the Communists in Spain or Russia or the English in Palestine'.[13] By coincidence, George Clare, who belonged to a Jewish family from Vienna, was kept waiting for a visa to Ireland and had to undergo the experience of the *Kristallnacht* in Berlin. Both he and his mother received their visas for Ireland the following day.[14] In 1939, Bewley parted company with the Irish diplomatic service. But for a small country, his failure to report objectively on the situation in Germany throughout the 1930s is difficult to estimate at the policy level. Bewley's positive influence on Irish foreign policy was negligible. His influence on refugee policy is more difficult to assess.[15] However, Bewley was quite unrepresentative of the Irish diplomatic service but his ideas - albeit in a more diluted form - may have found some favour with a number of senior administrators who had been educated in a Catholic tradition as influenced by priests like Denis Fahey and Edward Cahill. For other civil servants, the words of *Irish Times* editorial were more representative of their views:

> Here in Ireland the Jews are not a separate people; they are a part of the nation to whose welfare they have contributed in large measure. They have done fine service to our industry, our commerce and our art, and, if we have tolerated them - to use an objectionable phrase - we have been more than repaid by their presence in our midst....'[16]

IRISH REFUGEE POLICY DURING THE SECOND WORLD WAR

The Secretary of the Department of External Affairs, Joseph Walshe, wrote to a diplomat in 1939 soon after the outbreak of war: 'Small nations like Ireland do not and cannot assume role of defenders of just causes except their own'. That note of harsh realism pervaded Irish refugee policy in the 1930s and 1940s. The Department of Justice, under Minister Gerry Boland, proved very intransigent. His Secretary, S.A. Roche and Assistant Secretary, Dan Costigan, remained stoutly opposed to any efforts to liberalise the refugee policy. The Minister of Industry and Commerce, Seán Lemass, and his departmental officials were vigorously averse to allowing large numbers of refugees into the country. The Department of External Affairs, as represented by Walshe, was very conservative in its views and deeply opposed to allowing refugees into Ireland particularly those with a left wing background. However, his second in command, Frederick H. Boland, was more open-minded and his liberal views in this area were shared by the Secretary of the Department of the Taoiseach, Maurice Moynihan. (De Valera retained the portfolio of External Affairs from 1932 to 1948.)

Ireland had participated in the inter-governmental conference at Evians in July, 1938. Dublin was in full sympathy with the objectives for which the conference was convened but as long as the country remained a country of emigration it was felt by the Department of Justice that she could not make a contribution to the resettlement of European refugees. A month later, the Department of Justice had demonstrated its intransigence by refusing to grant University College Dublin permission to bring twelve Austrian students, displaced by the political turmoil in their country, to Ireland to do degrees on scholarship. In a draft letter to the President of University College Dublin, Denis J. Coffey, the Department explained its position further. It was stated that the country was over-crowded at the professional level. The Minister could not raise objections to the granting of visas if an undertaking could be given that the students would not remain in Ireland after graduation. But as that was not possible, it was the decision of the Minister not to grant visas.

The draft letter was sent to the Taoiseach's office and after further exchanges between the two departments, Professor Coffey was told on 10 September 1938 that the required number of visas would be granted. (It is unclear whether the full number of visas granted was ever taken up.) There was at least one medical student who transferred to Dublin from Vienna.

In November 1938, de Valera favoured the setting up of an Irish Co-ordinating Committee for Refugees. Another University College Dublin Professor, J.W.T. Dillon was involved. With the support of de Valera and the Ceann Comhairle (speaker of the Dail), Frank Fahy, Dillon was in a position to write to the Taoiseach on 10 November 1938: 'I think I may say that, thanks to the good offices of Mr Fahy and the generous support you gave us, we have now established friendly working relations with Departments concerned.'[17] A Department of Justice memorandum, dated four days later, set out rather modest objectives for the committee. There was agreement to admit fifty people who had already some training in agriculture with the Kagram group near Vienna. Once trained, they were to enter either Australia or South America. Two private houses had been put at the disposal of the group and the Department of Agriculture was prepared to cooperate. Justice were ready to give visas. There was also agreement about the admission of twenty adult refugees who would be maintained by wealthy people abroad. There was further ministerial agreement to bring in twenty children who would be given temporary residence in the country. But that was as far as the Minister for Justice was prepared to go.[18] The memorandum further pointed out:

> These proposals relate only to Christians with Jewish blood. The Co-Ordinating Committee are of opinion that this country should confine its efforts to such persons as there are adequate funds subscribed by the Jewish Communities in other countries to deal with the cases of professing Jews.

Such a judgement is very difficult to defend in the context of the actual situation regarding the Jewish Community in Europe in the autumn of 1938.

Sean Lemass,in the Department of Industry and Commerce,supported that policy. He was resolutely opposed to admitting foreign doctors to practice in Ireland and 'in the absence of very special circumstances' the Minister for Justice agreed with him. Not even the intervention of the Papal Nuncio, Paschal Robinson, supported by the Vatican, could persuade the Irish government to change its mind on that question.[19] Unless a refugee had a particular professional skill not to be found in Ireland, there was no chance of their being accepted as a rule.

Irish policy tended to discriminate against Jews. A relevant action from a 1945 Department of Justice memorandum has already been quoted in the introduction. S.A. Roche, Secretary of the Department of Justice, cast further light on his interpretation of policy when he wrote to Maurice Moynihan on 25 October 1946:

> Our practice has been to discourage any substantial increase in the Jewish population. They do not assimilate with our own people but remain a sort of colony of a world-wide Jewish community. This makes them a potential irritant in the body politic and has led to disastrous results from time to time in other countries.[20]

A further Department of Justice memorandum, prepared for Government on 28 February 1953, argued that it had been policy to apply the alien laws 'less liberally' in the case of Jews. The official in question, Peter Berry, wrote under the heading 'Position of Jews' -

> In the administration of the alien laws it has always been recognised in the Departments of Justice, Industry and Commerce and External Affairs that the question of the admission of aliens of Jewish blood presents a special problem and the alien laws have been administered less liberally in their case. Although the Jewish community in Ireland is only 3,907, according to the 1946 census, there is a fairly strong anti-Semitic feeling throughout the country, based, perhaps, on historical reasons, the fact that the Jews have remained a separate community within the community and have not permitted themselves to be assimilated, and that for their numbers they appear to have disproportionate wealth and influence.[21]

The head of military intelligence (G2), Dan Bryan, had supported a very restrictive policy toward the entry of 'aliens' during the war and he saw no reason to revise his position in 1945: 'I see no reason to depart from the general principle adopted since the start of the Emergency that aliens should not normally be allowed to come here.'[22]

Colonel Bryan addressed the Jewish refugee question specifically and wrote:

> Writing with full recognition that the Jewish problem is a very thorny and contentious one and that accusations of anti-Semitism are easily aroused, I wish to state that the extent to which Dublin has become what may be described as Jew conscious is frequently coming to the notice of this branch. It is a problem which has only a limited security aspect but I am quite satisfied that any relaxation of the control on aliens entering this country will lead to an influx of continental Jews here, in addition to those Jews who enter here as British subjects.

From this evidence it must be argued that it was the disposition of the Departments of

Justice and Industry and Commerce to operate the Aliens laws less liberally in the case of Jews. An application in 1939 to give a certain quota of the total percentage of refugees being admitted into the country was refused and opposed by Justice whenever it reappeared.[23]

These memoranda paint a rather bleak picture of Irish policy towards Jewish refugees during the war. The situation can be made to appear even gloomier when reference is made to the action of the Archbishop of Dublin, John Charles McQuaid, in breaking up the Pillar of Fire Society which had been set up by lay people of both faiths to foster Christian-Jewish dialogue. There were also the speeches of Oliver J. Flanagan in the Dáil which were most prejudiced and very anti-Jewish. Furthermore, there were the efforts by the Italian Minister in Dublin, Vincenzo Berardis, to spread the doctrine of anti-Semitism through the legation's propaganda sheets. The Department of External Affairs had to step in to warn Berardis to desist. When 'calling him in' did not get the desired result, a formal complaint was made directly to Rome against the Italian envoy.

Despite the restrictiveness of the policy, de Valera did make major concessions, when approached, by the Jewish community. In 1939, the Taoiseach instructed the Irish envoy to the Vatican, W.J.B. Macaulay to assist Rabbi Herzog in his efforts to get an audience with the Pope or the Cardinal Secretary of State. Cardinal MacRory of Armagh had also written to the Pope on Herzog's behalf, stating that 'before going to Palestine he spent many years as a Rabbi here in Ireland and he and I were good friends'. The outcome of Herzog's intervention at the Vatican is not known from Irish sources.

In 1943, de Valera gave permission for the admission of 500 Jewish children followin an intervention by President Roosevelt on behalf of the American Jewish Advisory Committee.

In 1943 and 1944, the Irish envoy at the Vatican, T.J. Kiernan, was instructed to intervene with the Pope directly on behalf of the plight of the Jews of Central Europe and of Hungary in particular. Kiernan was vigorous in the execution of his diplomatic instructions. He became very friendly with leading members of the Jewish community in Rome and was held in high esteem by them.[24] Those who were aware of de Valera's efforts on behalf of Central European Jews were not critical of the Taoiseach. In Ireland, the Jewish Representative Council had an opportunity in 1944 to express its reaction to a series of articles in a New York journal, PM, alleging anti-Semitism in Ireland:

> The Jewish Representative Council of Éire repudiates as false, irresponsible and mischievous any suggestion that the government of this country is anti-Semitic or that there is any organised anti-Semitic movement in Éire. The Jewish Community live and have always lived on terms of closest friendship with their fellow Irish citizens. Freedom to practise their religion is specifically guaranteed in the Irish Constitution. No Irish Government has ever discriminated between Jew and non-Jew.

A Jewish member of the Dáil, Fianna Fáil TD, Robert Briscoe, also came to the defence of the government stating that 'the Jewish Community in Éire are taking their full share in the Auxiliary Defence Forces of the country and that they wholeheartedly support the government's policy of neutrality.'[25]

The fact that some of the most prominent Jewish communities in Ireland were prepared to refute allegations of anti-Semitism so forcefully in the country does not prove that the same people were entirely satisfied with government policy on Jewish refugees. All had to have been aware of the restrictiveness of the policy towards any group. But Dublin was a very small community and among the professional elites there were few political secrets. The fact that de Valera had been prepared to respond to requests for help from Herzog would have been well known. The Irish government remained more willing throughout the war to help lobby on behalf of the persecuted Jews of Europe than to open the frontiers to receive them as permanent residents: 'Small nations like Ireland do not and cannot assume role of defenders of just causes except their own'. That line of Joseph Walshe's remained a guiding principle of Irish foreign policy. Such a self-preservative instinct was not uncommon in Europe during the Second World War.

WAR AND ITS AFTERMATH

It is difficult - on the basis of available evidence - to estimate accurately how many Jewish refugees came to Ireland during and after the war. An official of the Department of Justice explained in a memorandum on 28 February 1953 that there were no records of the number of aliens, displaced persons or naturalised Irish citizens who were of Jewish blood 'as official records are not kept on the basis of race or religion' but observation from time to time seemed to indicate that there were quite a number of Jews. There were about 1000 refugee children - including 500 Germans, over 200 Poles and over 200 Austrians - admitted for temporary care in selected centres or in the homes of suitable people. That group included 100 Jewish children. Many of those children had left but a small number had been informally adopted.[26]

The same document estimated that there were in all about 2,700 aliens registered as permanently living in Ireland. That number did not include British subjects who were exempt from the application of the aliens laws, alien children under 16 years of age, aliens who were wives or widows of Irish citizens and aliens in the country for less than a three month period. The corresponding figure in 1948 had been 1,466.

Of the 2,700 registered approximately 620 were refugees and stateless persons and of the 620 about 170 were students at university who had guaranteed admission to their own countries or elsewhere on completion of their studies. In addition to the 2,700, there were about 800 people (exclusive of about 300 of British origin) who had become Irish citizens by naturalization and of these 800 naturalized Irish citizens over 300 were formerly refugees or stateless persons. Since the war it was estimated that about 1,000 refugees had found a permanent home in Ireland. The memorandum further stated that 'the question of the admission of aliens of Jewish blood presents a special problem and the alien laws have been administered less liberally in their case.' However, even such a modest refugee policy record was achieved against the stiffest of opposition from the Departments of Justice and Industry and Commerce.

The Department of Industry and Commerce remained opposed to the adoption of a liberal refugee policy. Seán Lemass was opposed to such a policy on the grounds that by the end of 1945 there were 62,000 men and 8,000 women unemployed. Moreover, since 1940, the government had issued 133,584 travel permits for men seeking employment outside the state and 58,776 for women. Lemass expected many of these to return from England. Army demobilisation in both countries was expected to add to the numbers seeking work.[27] The Department of Justice was prepared by the end of November to go some way towards accepting the Department of External Affair's proposal to admit about 250 refugees within twelve months. Iveagh House felt that Ireland had to make a contribution towards the relief of displaced persons in Europe 'by offering temporary refuge to a limited number'. The government discussed the issue on 14 December 1945. The exchanges were harsh but the minute of the meeting read: 'Generally, it was felt that a liberal attitude should be adopted.' The Minister for Industry and Commerce was minuted as saying that he would be in favour of a liberal policy on a highly selective basis.'[28] The Taoiseach agreed to meet with the Minister for Justice and relevant senior civil servants to work out policy guidelines. In the discussions which followed, de Valera argued that 'he would be prepared to contemplate the admission, ultimately, of at least 10,000 aliens.'[29] The Taoiseach had pushed the debate from discussions on the admission of 250 refugees to an acceptance of as many as 10,000.

The question of Jewish refugees remained more problematical. Irish policy was tested in 1946 when an application was made for permission for 100 orphaned Jewish children from Poland to be admitted to Ireland. An English Jewish Society had acquired Clonyn Castle, in Delvin, Co. Westmeath together with 100 acres in which they proposed to house the children. The London-based organisation that made the application proposed to make arrangements for their emigration after a specific period. The Minister of Justice, Gerry Boland, refused approval: in August 1946:

> It has always been the policy of the Minister for Justice to restrict the admission of Jewish aliens, for the reason that any substantial increase in our Jewish population might give rise to an anti-Semitic problem.[30]

In September 1946, Herzog (spelled Hertzog (sic) in Department of Justice documents) visited Dublin and called on the Taoiseach, and on the Minister for Justice. According to Maurice Moynihan, who replied to a stiff letter from S.A. Roche, the Secretary of the Department of Justice, de Valera had been 'non-commital' in his answer to Herzog but the Taoiseach's view was that permission 'should not be withheld'. De Valera would not press for an official guarantee that they (the children) will in due course be allowed into another state. Justice gave permission in November 1946 for the admission of the children. But they refused an application for the admission of a limited number of adults to look after the children. Such was the level of political and administrative hostility that de Valera had to face when making positive recommendations for the admission of Jewish refugees. The Department of Justice was far more willing to admit prominent pro-Axis political refugees such as Leon Degrelle. This bias reflected an obvious political pre-disposition of some senior official in that department.

De Valera was out of office from 1948 until 1951. But refugee policy had not changed significantly upon his return. Ten Jewish families (20 adults and 20 children) applied for temporary two-year admission to the country in 1953. Briscoe, who was a member of de Valera's party, brought members of the Joint Distribution Committee to see Boland. The application was being made on behalf of the ten families of orthodox Jews who had escaped from Communist Europe into Austria. The refugees would be supported while in Ireland by the Joint Distribution Committee. Justice opposed the application. Peter Berry, the official entrusted to making the case for the Department, opposed the selection of refugees on racial or religious grounds. He argued against groups that wanted to 'jump the queue'. On 13 March 1953, Moynihan wrote to the Department of Justice that the government had decided that five of the Jewish families were to be admitted for a minimum period of two years.[31] De Valera had compromised but he had refused to accept the harsh line of the Department of Justice. That was his style. But the Irish refugee policy - particularly in relation to European Jews - was as ungenerous as it was representative of the time.

FOOTNOTES

1. Dermot Keogh, Ireland and Europe 1919-1948 (Gill and Macmillan, Dublin 1988), see Chapter VI.

2. Department of Justice memorandum, 24 September 1945 S11007A, State Paper Office (SPO) Dublin Castle, Dublin.

3. **Keogh**. Ireland and Europe, see Chapter IV, V and VI.

4. Bernard Wasserstein, Britain and the Jews of Europe 1939-1945 (Clarendon Press, Oxford 1979).

5. Census of Ireland, 1961.

6. Ibid., 1926.

7. Pat Feeley, 'Rabbi Levin of Colooney Street, The Old Limerick Journal, March 1980, and by the same author 'Aspects of the 1904 Pogrom', The Old Limerick Journal Summer 1982.

8. The Cross, 1 May 1934; Besides writing a reply to the editor, Herzog complained to the Roman Catholic Archbishop of Dublin, Edward Byrne; the prelate supported Herzog against the Cross.

9. see Irish Press and Independent, 29-31 December 1936.

10. Herzog to Byrne, 1 January 1937 (Edward Byrne Papers, Dublin Archdiocesan Archives, Clonliffe College, Dublin).

11. Dermot Keogh, The Vatican, the Bishops and Irish Politics, 1919-1939 (Cambridge University Press, Cambridge, 1976), see Chapter VII and Dermot Keogh, 'The Irish Constitutional Revolution', Administration, January 1988.

12. Irish Times, 6 April 1937.

13. Charles Bewley to Secretary of External Affairs, 9 December 1938, Department of Foreign Affairs (D/FA), Confidential Report Series, Public Record Office, Dublin.

14. George Clare, Last Waltz in Vienna - the destruction of a family, (Macmillan, London 1980), pp. 204-212 and 228-229.

15. Interviews with retired diplomats.

16. Irish Times, 10 April 1937; see also interesting pamphlet with refuted crude arguments against the Jews, Dr Moody 'Why are the Jews Persecuted' (Catholic Truth Society, Dublin 1938).

17. Dillon to de Valera, 10 November 1938, S11007, SPO Dublin.

18. Department of Justice Memorandum, 14 November 1938, S11007, SPO Dublin.

19. Actes et Documents du Saint Siege relatifs a la Seconde Guerre Modiale Le Saint Siege et les Victimes de la Guerre, Vol. 6, March 1939 - December 1940 (Libreria Editrice Vaticana, 1972), pp. 306-397.

20. S.A. Roche to Maurice Moynihan, 25 October 1946, S11007 B/1, SPO Dublin.

21. Peter Barry, Department of Justice memorandum 1953, S11007 B/2, SPO Dublin.

22. Dan Bryan, 6 January 1946 (Confidential source).

23. Berry to Coyne, 16 February 1953 and memorandum 28 February 1953, S11007 B/2, SPO Dublin.

24. D/FA P4/2 (Irish Embassy to the Vatican, Villa Spada, Rome).

25. D/FA P40 Department of Foreign Affairs, Iveagh House, Dublin.

26. Department of Justice memorandum, 28 February 1953, S11007 B/2, SPO Dublin.

27. Department of Industry and Commerce memorandum, 12 December 1945 - submission to government. S11007A, SPO Dublin.

28. Moynihan minute, 15 December 1945, S11007A, SPO Dublin and CAB 14 December 1945 G.C. 4/127 item 4, SPO Dublin.

29. Maurice Moynihan memorandum, 21 December 1945, S11007A, SPO Dublin.

30. Department of Justice memorandum, 28 April 1948 S1100& B/1 SPO Dublin.

31. S11007 B/2 SPO Dublin.

AMBIVALENCE OR ANTISEMITISM? CHRISTIAN ATTITUDES AND RESPONSES IN BRITAIN TO THE CRISIS OF EUROPEAN JEWRY DURING THE SECOND WORLD WAR

Dr Tony Kushner

Department of History, University of Southampton, Southampton
S09 5NH

An understanding of the holocaust, it has been suggested, remains 'the unconquered Everest of our time'. This does not, of course, mean that no attempt should be made to study the events that led to the destruction of six million Jews. Yehuda Bauer, Claude Lanzmann and others have indeed stressed the importance of 'demystifying' the holocaust; the need to spend more time studying 'how' and less on 'why' the catastrophe could have occurred.[1] Recently part of this historical process of freeing the holocaust from possible mythology has been to study the responses to the persecution of the Jews from the public as well as the state in Nazi Europe. Genocide was, after all, attempted by flesh and blood humans and not demons. Moreover a global perspective has been adopted, with the reaction of the free world to the crisis of European Jewry coming under particular scrutiny. This essay will contribute to these historiographical developments. It will focus on Christian attitudes and responses in Britain to the holocaust, and will lay particular stress on popular reactions.[2]

Christians reacted to the news of the persecution and extermination of European Jewry in a very complex manner. Responses in Britain varied from a degree of support, through total disbelief to utter horror. Whilst it is true that personal psychology played a role, it will be suggested that none of these responses can be fully understood without reference to past Christian discourse on the Jews. Indeed it will be argued that properly to comprehend the British response in the Second World War, we need to consider Christian attitudes that drew inspiration from as far back as the early modern era and even the middle ages.

It is clear that by 1939 the position of Jews in British scoiety had changed beyond all recognition from that in the medieval period. The point is illustrated by the comments of a senior Home Office official during the war itself. Sir Alexander Maxwell, referring to a scheme whereby the government made financial arrangements for the maintenance of Jewish refugees in Britain, stated that it would 'reverse the historic practice by which governments have borrowed money from the Jews and will introduce a new procedure by which the Government will lend some money to the Jews!'. By the twentieth century Anglo-Jewry was free of any legal restraints and in the war the British government did its utmost to meet the specific religious needs of its Jewish population such as Kosher food and religious facilities.[3] Nevertheless, it is important to realise that the Jewish stereotype, in Britain as elsewhere, possesses a 'massive durability'. As Norman Cohn has indicated with regard to the Jews 'myths do not necessarily disappear with the circumstances that first produced them. They sometimes acquire an autonomy, a vitality of their own, that carries them across the continents and down the centuries'. Before we examine the specific response during the Second World War, it is thus vital to examine the legacy of earlier Christian thinking about Jews.[4]

In the modern period it has often been assumed by historians of antisemitism that Britain is 'different'. Recently this view has been challenged and scholars have pointed to various traditions of intolerance towards Jews in British society. Their work, however, has been by no means totally accepted. In the medieval period, there is no such doubting of the virulence and impact of English antisemitism. Indeed in many ways, England was at the forefront of the persecution of the Jews. Ritual murder and blood libel accusations originated in England which was the first country to undertake the widespread expulsion of the Jews in 1290. Nowhere was the Christian image of the Jew as usurer, demonic Christ-killer and perpetual alien stronger. All three aspects of this religious-sponsored antisemitism intensified in the thirteenth century. With the hostility of the populace and the removal of the state's protection, life for England's Jews simply became untenable. Yet it would be misleading to suggest that the response to the Jews in this period consisted only of straightforward rejection. Even in the middle ages this Christian response contained both ambivalent and contradictory elements. On the one hand, and increasingly so in the last century of settlement in England, Jews were seen - most clearly in the frequent blood libels accusations - as dehumanised devil figures. On the other, Jews could be accepted if they rejected their religion and embraced Christianity. Indeed some Jews were allowed to remain in Britain after the expulsion on the condition that they practised the Christian faith. It was the relative weight of these two responses - first total rejection of the Jew because of his origins, but second acceptance of him as a potential Christian - that was to determine the reaction to Jews in Britain well beyond the Middle Ages.[5]

Christian ambiguity towards Jews was further complicated by reactions to the Bible. Dorothy Sayers, the novelist, summarised the essential ambivalence of Christians on this matter in 1946. She remarked that for many people Jews underwent a transformation 'in the blank pages between the Testaments: in the Old, they were 'good' people; in the New, they were 'bad' people - it seemed doubtful whether they were really the same people'. Even in the medieval period in England there was an element of respect for the Jews of the Old Testament. By the mid seventeenth century this strand of religious philosemitism, powerful amongst the Puritans, partly enabled the return of the Jews in 1656. But even these philosemites did not accept the Jews as real people. To the former, as Todd Endelman has suggested, ''the Jews' were little more than the personification of some abstract religious idea or feeling'. Moreover the millenarianist philosemites wanted the Jews to be allowed to settle in England, not for Judaism to flourish, but for it to disappear. It was hoped that by treating the Jews humanely, the Jews would be drawn to Christianity. They believed that the conversion of the Jews would then herald the Messianic age.[6]

Religious arguments, therefore, from open hostility to sympathy, but mainly characterised by a fundamental ambivalence, were vital in determining the response to the Jews in England up to the seventeenth century. But how far had this changed by the modern period? It will be suggested here that although the discourse of the nineteenth and twentieth centuries had altered profoundly, it was still influenced by earlier religious viewpoints despite its new secular form. The emancipation of the Jews in Britain, finally completed in 1858, illustrates this point. Emancipation was granted on the unwritten understanding that Jews move closer to British society. Acceptance, if found at all by the Anglo-Jewish élite, depended on total assimilation, often including conversion. If antisemitism persisted after emancipation, then this was the fault of the Jews for their failure to remove their differences.[7] This had a close parallel in the Christian belief that Jews were responsible for antisemitism. The Jews had crucified Christ and had subsequently refused to accept him as the Messiah, hence they were responsible for their own persecution. Furthermore the medieval church imagery of the Jew as an alien, usurer and demon persisted in the twentieth century in a modernised and secularised form. The 'Wandering Jew' was transformed into the alien Jewish immigrant, the usurer through Shylock into the international financier and finally the devil-figure into the omnipotent world Jew, most infamously in The Protocols of the Learned Elders of Zion.[8]

It is also important to emphasize that although organised religion no longer played a central role in the lives of the British people by the twentieth century, Christianity was still highly important in shaping attitudes to Jews. Part of Jewish childhood in the inter-war years consisted of being held personally responsible for the death of Christ. Taunts such as 'who killed Christ with a butcher's knife?' were part of a Gentile attitude instilled by the influence of family, school and church. On a more organised level, although some hostility to Jews was based on racial or ethnic grounds, as with the British Union of Fascists, religious influences were also present. The names of some of the most virulent antisemitic and pro-Nazi groups active in Britain in the Second World War illustrate this point - The Militant Christian Patriots, The British Protestant League and the British Council for Christian Settlement in Europe.[9] On the positive side, religious philosemitism also survived in twentieth century Britain. Blanche Dugdale, a Christian Zionist and campaigner on behalf of Jewish refugees, wrote, after her first visit to a synagogue, 'these are indeed The People of the Book...two thousand years seemed but as yesterday'. Eleanor Rathbone, another great fighter for the refugees, identified with the Jewish people because of 'the romance of the prophets'. Whether the events in the war changed Christian attitudes to Jews will be dealt with later. Now, having set the complex background, we must analyse Christian responses to the plight of European Jewry in the Second World War.[10]

Throughout the 1930s and the war itself, there was no shortage of condemnation by Church leaders of all denominations of the Nazi persecution of Jews. Successive Archbishops of Canterbury, Bishops of Westminster and major non-conformists were all deeply moved by the plight of European Jewry. Moreover the Church, and particularly groups such as the Methodists, Quakers and Christadelphians were prominent in offering asylum to Jewish refugees from Nazi oppression.[11] On the surface, therefore, with regard to the Jews of Europe, there are reasonable grounds for referring to the 'by and large...good record of the Churches in England during the Hitler period'.[12] A more critical analysis will, however, reveal the strengths and limitations of the Christian response. This will allow an assessment to be made of whether Britain, as a Christian nation, could have done more to help the Jews of Europe.

Total support for the extermination of the Jews was exceptional and rarely, if at all, openly admitted in Britain. Sometimes such support was simply the result of a general Jew-hatred on the part of the individual, and thus genocidal antisemitism 'one of the few things that I agree with Hitler about'. Others used Christianity as a basis for their arguments. A Mass-Observer in 1939 suggested that as Jews had persecuted Christ, they had 'no right to squeal now... In fact the more Jews liquidated the better'.[13] Such apparent pleasure in the brutal treatment of the Jews was, it must be emphasised, comparatively unusual. Nevertheless the sentiment that the Jews were responsible for their own downfall was common amongst many Christians in the 1930s. Jewish refugees found it hard to convince their Christian hosts that it was the actions of the Nazis and not themselves that had forced them to seek refuge. They were often asked 'what have you really done that you had to leave your country?'. To many Christians in Britain, the answer was simple: 'The Jews crucified Christ. They are now suffering for their actions'.[14]

In the war itself, the sheer scale of Nazi antisemitic brutality forced some to reconsider their attitudes. But such a process was not easy. The very strength of past beliefs, particularly that the Jews, by rejecting Christianity had 'earned' their persecution, made them difficult to shake off. A Scottish novelist, despite being ashamed of her own antisemitism had 'a tendency to think serve them right before one can catch oneself up' when she heard press reports on the extermination of the Jews in 1943. In a similar vein, an article in The Christian News-Letter in May 1941 suggested that it was Jewish profiteers' 'irresponsible and conspicuous behaviour' that had allowed Hitler to take control in Germany. Here not only were the Jews being blamed for their own misfortune, but they were also seen as a malevolent influence on society. Again such views revealed a much deeper Christian attitude towards Jewry. As a rail clerk from Golders Green put it: 'it seems to me that the crucifixion of Christ shows the underlying beastliness of the Jewish race'.[15]

It was fear of the satanic nature of the Jew, and of Jewish power in society that led some Christians to doubt the stories of the persecution of the Jews in the war. If the Jew was seen as a threat to the Christian world, a dangerous force and a perverter of morality, then it became difficult to accept that he was also a victim. Whilst caution is necessary when generalizations are made in this area, it must be suggested that elements in the Catholic community in Britain were particularly prone to fears of Jewish power. The Catholic Chesterbelloc circle and The Britons were important in spreading Jewish conspiracy theories in British society after 1918 and such anxieties about Jews persisted into the war. Jews were seen as the persecutors rather than the persecuted. Medieval Catholic perceptions of Jews were simply updated. Jews were widely blamed for the development and spreading of Bolshevism, the modern weapon of the anti-Christ. From there, Jewish Bolshevism was responsible for the persecution of Catholics in Russia, Spain and Mexico, or more locally for spreading communism and 'oriental' sexual morality in the East End of London.[16]

Such fears were voiced strongly in the Catholic Herald and it was this paper in particular that questioned the accuracy of the reports of the atrocities against the Jews. In September 1942 the plight of the Jews in France became clear in Britain. Nevertheless, the Catholic Herald warned its readers 'to avoid swallowing wholesale the current reports of the anti-Jewish persecution'. This doubt continued after Anthony Eden's declaration in Parliament in December 1942 which outlined how millions of Jews had already perished. The Herald remained unconvinced stating that 'for the exact truth we must wait until the war is over'. Even as late as 1944, when the destruction of Hungarian Jewry was taking place the Herald would not accept the accuracy of the reports. Indeed in the last year of the war, it ignored reports of the liberation of the concentration camps and the confirmation of the holocaust. Instead it ran a six month correspondence on whether or not there was a world Jewish conspiracy.[17]

It might be suggested that the Catholic Herald was in a category of its own. Whilst it is true that the paper was often an embarrassment to the leaders of the Catholic community in

Britain, it was not unique in its fear of Jewish power or its refusal to believe the news of the Jewish catastrophe. The Catholic Times in December 1942 suggested that it was 'no secret that the recent wave of propaganda about German atrocities against the Jews was Russian inspired' - a view with which the Catholic Review was in full agreement. Nevertheless a sense of balance is required. At the same point, the Bishop of Westminster, Cardinal Hinsley, condemned 'the brutal persecution of the Jews' and The Tablet believed that 'nothing like the horrors now going on in Eastern Europe has been seen before'.[18] Moreover, although Catholics were prominent in these early attempts at the denial of the holocaust, they were by no means alone. The militant Scottish Protestant, Alexander Ratcliffe suggested in 1943 that the atrocity stories were all Jewish invention and that there 'was not a single authenticated case on record of a single Jew having been massacred...under the Hitler regime'. Non-Catholic Christian pacifists such as the Duke of Bedford, Ethel Mannin and John Middleton Murry all attacked the alleged role of Jews in international finance and went on to disbelieve the atrocity reports during the war. In these cases, a Christian distrust and fear of Jews thus led to an actual denial of the news of the destruction of European Jewry.[19]

It is important to stress that such blatant denial of the reality of Jewish persecution was not the dominant reaction of Christians in Britain during the war. Nevertheless even in the philosemitic world, such as in the Council of Christians and Jews, doubts about the accuracy of the reports existed, as will be shown shortly. The basic reason for this response relates to the essential ambivalence of the Christian community towards the Jews. Whilst therefore the news of the Jewish tragedy most commonly led to a reaction of sympathy it was rarely accompanied by total support of the Jews themselves. Such ambivalence was classically stated by the statesman Harold Nicolson in 1945: 'Although I loathe antisemitism, I do dislike Jews'.[20] As Dorothy Sayers indicated, Christians in Britain possessed a bi-furcated image of the Jews. The ambiguity this created, as will now be illustrated, determined the parameters of the sympathetic Christian response to the Jewish crisis in the war.

In October 1939 the British government published a White Paper on German atrocities, including those against Jews. The government believed, however, that the White Paper was a failure because the public regarded its contents as mere war propaganda.[21] Such an analysis, it must be suggested, was pessimistic. A Mass-Observation survey in 1940 revealed that the public was still greatly aware of the dire plight of European Jewry. The most common comment was that 'I would like not to believe the stories about the persecution of the Jews...but I think there is too much evidence not to believe'. Nevertheless belief was not necessarily a sufficient factor to guarantee action. As another observer wrote when asked about the persecution of the Jews: 'Must you? One had almost forgotten them'. In the case of others, however, '(Jewish) sufferings under the Third Reich are quite sufficient indictment against the Hitlerian regime. Their deliverance is one of our chief war aims'. Yet this Christian humanitarian sympathy towards European Jewry was of an unorganised nature, and would remain so for the first years of the war.[22]

The most likely forum for such sentiment to be expressed were through existing Christian-Jewish organisations in Britain. The Society of Jews and Christians, a small group of progressive Christians and Liberal Jews, had met violent opposition from both communities since its formation in 1927. Nevertheless by the 1930s close contacts had been established between Christian and Jewish refugee organisations. Indeed, Bloomsbury House, the refugee organisations' headquarters was to be the springboard for future Christian-Jewish co-operation. As the late W.W. Simpson has suggested, 'it was...out of the close, friendly and fruitful cooperation that had developed in the Bloomsbury House experience that the Council of Christians and Jews was born'.[23]

The Council of Christians and Jews (CCJ) was created in March 1942 and officially launched in October of that year. Over forty years later the CCJ is a well-established and respected organisation. Its birth, however, was anything but easy and its early years full of controversy. Informal links between the Board of Deputies of British Jews, Christians active in the struggle against antisemitism such as James Parkes, W.W. Simpson and Henry Carter and prominent Churchmen such as the Archbishops of Canterbury and York and the Bishop of Westminster had existed since the late 1930s.[24] Nevertheless attempts made at the start of the war by Parkes, the Board and the Dean of St. Paul's 'to consider a permanent Council of Jews and Christians to study the problems arising in Jewish-Christian relations and to formulate and carry out plans for developing those relations toward complete friendliness' made little progress. Indeed Simpson, secretary of the Christian Council for Refugees, wrote to Parkes as late as July 1941 stating that 'when one thinks of Hitler's anti-Jewish acts... the sum total of all that everybody has tried to do in this country so far seems very small indeed'. A few months later a member of the International Hebrew Christian Alliance wrote to the Bishop of Chichester warning that unless Jewish Christian cooperation was achieved soon 'the real question is, will there be any Jews left in Europe to concern oneself about?'.[25] Only by the end of 1941, with a slow Christian awareness of this fact and a realisation that antisemitism in Britain was also a problem were the demands for a more powerful Christian-Jewish umbrella organisation put into action. On the Jewish side there was a desire to gain the support of influential Christians against antisemitism, on the Christian a genuine revulsion against Nazi antisemitism, coupled with a belief that the latter was 'part of a general and comprehensive attack on Christianity...and on the ethical principles common to both religions'.[26]

With a few notable exceptions, such as the Bishop of Gloucester, Arthur Headlam, the leading church figures of the 1930s and Second World War made unqualified attacks on Nazi antisemitism.[27] Eventually, by 1942, their concern at the plight of European Jewry allowed qualms about Jewish-Christian cooperation to be put aside, enabling the creation of the CCJ. In turn, the CCJ provided a forum for Christians to express their horror at the persecution of the Jews. At the second executive meeting of the CCJ in April 1942 a model resolution was written for Church groups 'to place on record (their) increasing concern at the Nazi treatment of the Christian Church and the Jewish community in Germany and German-occupied territories'. That there was a demand for such a resolution is clearly indicated from governmental records. Letters and petitions with hundreds of names from Christian groups were frequently sent to the Foreign Office. They demanded that the government do its utmost to rescue the Jews of Europe and offered their homes and rations if such action succeeded.[28]

The British government was unwilling to consider any such measures. It knew that the chances of rescue were remote, but also believed that any influx of Jewish refugees would lead to a dangerous rise in the level of antisemitism in Britain. Were its fears justified and could the Christian community have done more to change government policy?[29]

The government was aware that the response in Britain to the Jewish plight was not straightforward. In October 1942 Herbert Morrison, the Home Secretary, told a Christian-Jewish deputation that although 'the general body of public opinion in this country was humanitarian and deeply sympathetic of the plight of the refugees...there was also a body of opinion which was potentially antisemitic' and that it was important 'not to ignore the existence of this feeling'. Morrison was correct to point out that antisemitism existed in war-time Britain. Indeed the stresses of the war led to an intensification of earlier hostility towards Jews. Jews were widely blamed for black marketeering, avoiding military service and many other 'unpatriotic' war activities. Yet was Morrison pessimistic when he suggested that 'any substantial increase in the number of Jewish refugees (would lead to) serious trouble'?[30] It will be suggested here that Morrison, by failing to understand the full complexity of Christian attitudes to Jews, overestimated the significance of antisemitism in Britain. Nevertheless weaknesses in the Christian response enabled Morrison's negative policy to succeed.

The ambivalence of Christians towards Jews became more obvious during the war. A survey carried out in Britain during 1940 suggested that nearly half the sample believed that Jews were an oppressed people. Paradoxically, however, only 18% felt that Jews were deserving of sympathy, and Jews were still widely seen as a threat in society. This dichotomy in attitudes becomes clearer as the news of the full horror of the destruction of Jewry in 1942 and 1943 increased. The government's Home Intelligence reports indicate widespread indignation, anger and disgust at the Germans' anti-Jewish atrocities in Poland. Home Intelligence nevertheless indicated that 'much of the feeling about the atrocities (was) on the lines of 'I don't care much for the Jews, but this is terrible''.[31] One individual who stated that he had 'nothing but sympathy (for) the Jews abroad' but 'did not like the Jews as a race' was typical.[32]

This indicates that sympathy was rarely for the Jew <u>as a Jew</u>, but was simply directed at the Jew as a victim. The barbarism of the Nazi treatment of the Jewish people undoubtedly shocked the Christian conscience in Britain. This did not necessarily lead to a reassessment of the place of the Jew in a Christian society. Sympathy did not extend to the Jew at home who could still be seen as a problem or an irritant. Thus Home Intelligence discovered in early 1943 that although German anti-Jewish atrocities 'continue to be regarded with horror...as a result of the publicity, people are more conscious of the Jews they do not like here'. There were limits to this Christian antipathy, however, and it did not necessarily extend to rescuing Jewish refugees. The individual who 'did not like the Jews as a race' nevertheless saw 'no reason why we should not welcome (Jews abroad) and offer them asylum as long as they need it'.[33]

Antisemitism did put some restraint upon public responses to this issue. In February 1943 a poll on whether the British government should help any Jewish refugees who could get away found that 78% were in favour. Only 13% were totally against, often giving antisemitic reasons for their opposition. However, the poll also revealed that only 55% wanted 'as many as can come' to be let in. Fewer than 10% wanted those arriving to be received indefinitely. The poll therefore showed strong public sympathy to the Jewish plight, but also limitations on the amount of hospitality that should be given to them.[34] These limitations were partly the result of antipathy to Jews in general. As the war progressed such antipathy made it hard for pro-refugee groups to maintain public interest in the plight of the Jews. George Orwell recognised this point at the end of the war when he wrote that antisemitism in Britain had 'the effect of making people callous to the sufferings of Jews in other countries'.[35]

Could groups such as the CCJ have changed government policy to the Jews of Europe given the public's ambivalence and the state's reluctance to take action? The difficulties of the CCJ in this matter should not be minimised. Whilst the government was sensitive to any antisemitic sentiment in the war it paid little attention to indications of pro-Jewish sympathy. The reaction of the Foreign Office to a church petition from Birmingham demanding government aid to the Jews illustrates this point. One Foreign Office official minuted 'it seems hardly necessary to enter this resolution. We get any amount of the same thing and generally just cross them off'. Another was even more curt: 'It is a waste of paper'.[36] This, however, was in 1944. From December 1942, when the Allied governments issued their declaration condemning the extermination of the Jews, until mid 1943 the British government was concerned about public opinion in this matter. It was particularly worried about pressure coming, in the words of a senior official, 'from an alliance of Jewish organisations and Archbishops'.[37] In December 1942 the Foreign Office believed that this pressure could 'only be met by a new policy'. Yet later it believed 'that the situation (could) be held', and no meaningful action be taken. Was this the fault of the Christian-Jewish organisations?[38]

The response of the CCJ in this period reveals some of the limitations of Christian sympathy for the Jews - even in this most philosemitic of institutions. It was not until the major revelations about the atrocities against Jews in late 1942 that the CCJ was stung into action over this issue. It decided in December, despite some doubts on the part of the Executive Committee, to send a deputation to the Foreign Office. Remarkably, some of its misgivings were due to a reluctance to accept the stories of Jewish persecution. It was thus proposed to ask the Foreign Office to establish 'the authenticity of the reports which had been received from various sources as to the treatment meted out to Jews in Eastern Europe'. A CCJ delegate told the Foreign Office that 'there was a tendency even amongst the clergy to discount general statements about these atrocities'. Indeed at this point Selig Brodetsky, President of the Board of Deputies, wrote that with the notable exception of the Archbishop of Canterbury he found a general spirit of disbelief in the CCJ itself.[39]

It is thus not surprising given the CCJ's reserved attitude that the deputation was easily deflected by the Foreign Office. After their first meeting, Richard Law, the Foreign Office official who met the CCJ minuted that 'in spite of the fact that the deputation expressed great appreciation of my alleged sympathetic attitude, I don't think that I gave anything away'. Christian-Jewish umbrella groups such as the CCJ and Bloomsbury House did not actually want to embarrass the government on this issue. By March 1943 there were even suggestions within the CCJ that it was spending too much time protesting against Jewish persecution abroad. Thereafter until the end of the war the CCJ concentrated on examining domestic antisemitism.[40]

In April 1943 representatives of the Allied governments met at Bermuda to discuss the Jewish refugee problem. In fact the Bermuda Conference was designed simply to satisfy the pro-refugee lobby that something was being done. There was no real intention of taking meaningful action. It was an indication of the failure of humanitarian sentiment in the free world to assert itself in terms of policy. Furthermore, in any statements made with regard to Bermuda the British Cabinet decided 'to avoid implying that refugees were necessarily Jewish and refer to refugees by nationality rather than by race'. At the same time as Bermuda, Bloomsbury House launched a fund-raising exercise for all refugees, in order, according to Lewis Namier, 'to cover up the Jewish...character of the appeal'. In both cases there was a reluctance to officially acknowledge that Jews were particularly suffering under the Nazi regime. It was a reluctance that had its roots in a Christian inhibition for accepting the Jews on their own terms, and thus, as with the CCJ, a failure to come fully to grips with the Jewish catastrophe.[41] At home the implications of this response can be seen in the Christian treatment of Jewish refugee children in the war.

The response to the refugee children highlighted Christian sympathy to the victims of Nazi oppression. Apart from the British Union of Fascists, there was very little opposition to the 10,000 children who came to Britain in the twelve months before the war. This was in stark contrast to the considerable concern voiced about the admittance of adult refugees. There are two reasons for this. Firstly children had an added emotional appeal and secondly they were not an immediate economic threat in terms of jobs. But did this sympathy extend to the children's religion, the vast majority of whom were Jewish?[42]

In some cases the answer was yes. Chaim Bermant who as a child refugee was evacuated in the war to Annan recalls that he 'must have been the first Jew (his hosts) had encountered outside of the Bible and they regarded me with something like awe, as if I was a close relative of Jesus Christ'. This was a classic religious philosemitic response. The child refugees of the Jewish Secondary School evacuated to Shefford in Bedfordshire met a similar response. The village foster parents took a pride in the religious observance of their ultra-orthodox evacuees to the extent of chastising them if they failed to follow all the Jewish rituals. Shefford, thanks to the close supervision of its teachers, became a 'Noah's Ark' where the Jewish refugee children were 'shelved, stored and remembered like a treasure'. Thus at one extreme there were some fervent Christians who, in the words of the Board of Deputies, 'held dear Jews on account of their religion' and were, as in the case of Chaim Bermant 'grimly determined to keep (him) Jewish'.[43] Nevertheless, great friction developed between the Bloomsbury House based Refugee Children's Movement (RCM) and the orthodox authorities in Britain over the issue of the spiritual well-being of the young Jewish refugees during the war.

The RCM's main concern was to find decent homes for the 9,534 boys and girls under its care. Nearly 90% were Jewish and according to the RCM 'the basic principle of the Movement with regard to the religious welfare of these children is that each child should receive instruction in the faith in which it was brought up, and that no child should be allowed to change its religion without every possible effort being made to ascertain the views of the parents or some near relative'. In practice, according to supporters of the Chief Rabbi's Emergency Council on Jewish education (CREC), the RCM acted as a 'Child-Estranging Movement'. Was this a fair analysis?[44]

Several problems faced the RCM. Firstly although 90% of the children were classified as Jewish, many came from assimilated backgrounds and their religious identity was often unclear. Secondly the initial confusion caused by the sudden arrival of 10,000 children was intensified by the outbreak of war and the following evacuation. In many cases the RCM simply lost control of its charges. The spiritual well-being of the Jewish refugee children came to depend on local committees and more often on individual Christian hosts.[45] Whilst in theory on a national level the RCM opposed any attempts at proselytization, locally the situation was less secure. More than anything, the refugee children wanted to be accepted. To this end they were willing to compromise all of their cultural background. As one girl remembers 'I learned very quickly to omit any reference to my nationality when being introduced to people, and I adopted the same attitude to my religion'. On the Christian side there were hosts 'who claimed the price of conversion in return for their generous hospitality'. In some cases such pressure was blatant and the children forced to attend Church and Sunday school. More common, however, was the subtle and effective method of offering kind treatment in the hope that this would attract the children to Christianity. Lore Segal, a child refugee from Vienna remembers a row between two members of the local Church Refugee Committee because one had shouted at her. The other argued 'that's never the way to make a Christian out of her'. One of her friends was divided between a desire to please her hosts by converting to Christianity and to honour her parents by joining them in Palestine. Eventually she committed suicide. Such incidents were rare, but the pressure, either direct or indirect, for the children to adopt a new religion was immense. As the CREC feared, many lost their Jewish faith.[46]

In the Christian response to the Jewish refugee children certain clear themes emerge. A small but significant number of young refugees were fully accepted by their Christian hosts as Jews and every effort was made to preserve their religion. Another small element were forced to practise Christianity as the price of acceptance. The most common treatment, however, was offering the Christian way of life to the children in the hope that they would abandon Judaism. This resulted in many children slowly and untraumatically becoming Christians.[47] Nevertheless, in such circumstances the refugee children, desperate for psychological security, had, in reality, little choice but to adopt the religion of their hosts. Overall, therefore, with some significant exceptions, the Christian response was one of immense sympathy which was translated into practical hospitality. This stopped short, however, of respect for the children's original religion.

The strengths, but also the limitations, of both popular and organised Christian responses to the Jewish plight at home and abroad have now been illustrated. One final important question needs to be addressed. Did knowledge of the Nazi atrocities remove religious based hostility to Jews in Britain? An indication of the strength of such antisemitism is provided by the response to Jewish evacuees in the war. Many hosts refused to believe that their evacuees were Jewish because they had no horns! A Jewish East Ender remembers that when she was evacuated to the country 'the old stories of ritual slaughter were still very prevalent indeed'.[48] The survival in the twentieth century of medieval Church imagery of Jews as agents of the devil reveals the strength of Britain's antisemitic traditions. Indeed the early history of the CCJ indicates the barriers that still existed between Church and Synagogue. As W.W. Simpson, its first secretary, commented 'the period of (the Council's) gestation had been long and not without its anxieties'.[49]

Although there was a consensus that antisemitism was essentially evil, both Jews and Christians were reluctant to join an organisation that might be used for inter-religious debate. Cardinal Hinsley joined the CCJ only after a year of negotiations in which assurances were made to him that it would not be used forthis purpose. In May 1942 the Chief Rabbi briefly resigned because he saw the CCJ as a 'Society for the Promotion of Spiritual Inter-Marriage between Jews and Christians'. Here was an indication of the religious tensions that still persisted even in an organisation which had purposely avoided any reference to Christian-Jewish dialogue.[50]

One of the early tasks of the CCJ was to try to remove the hostile image of the Jew in Christian teaching. It was not an easy task. Even in the war Jews were still blamed for the Crucifixion. A reader of Tribune was shocked to hear a five year old tell a Jewish friend 'you are a naughty girl - why did you kill our Jesus?' Moreover, this was not a monopoly of the immature. In 1941 W.W. Simpson broadcasted on the B.B.C. warning his listeners about the evils of antisemitism at home and abroad. He received many letters of protest from Christians reminding him of the Jewish responsibility for Christ's death.[51] Indeed Dorothy Sayers' Man Born to be King and other religious broad casts on the B.B.C. during the war tended to negate the work of the CCJ in trying to reevaluate the role of the Jews in the crucifixion. Easter remained a difficult and sometimes dangerous time for Jewish children.[52]

Despite the Nazis barbaric and irrational destruction of European Jewry, there was still widespread religious belief that Jews were ultimately responsible for antisemitism. Jews had both killed Jesus and subsequently refused to recognise him as the Messiah. Instead they clung to the belief that they were the Chosen People. Only when they recognised that Christians had taken on the Jews' historic role would antisemitism end. As James Walsh, editor of the Catholic Times put it, it was Jewish pride in being the Chosen People 'that brought persecution on the Jews'. Antisemitism was thus not the Christian's fault 'for the most part of the solution lies with the Jews'.[53] H.G. Wells remained totally unmoved by the destruction of European Jewry. To him it was the inevitable reaction to Jewish religious exclusivity. Christians such as James Parkes who suggested that antisemitism actually had its roots in Christianity rather than in Judaism were in a small minority and generally ignored. Only in a post-holocaust generation of Christians would Parkes' views gain any respect.[54]

Any attempt to draw up a league table measuring hostility to Jews in all the Christian sects in Britain is fraught with danger. Nevertheless, as has been shown with the issue of disbelieving anti-Jewish atrocities, the Catholic world remained particularly hostile to Jews. There were major exceptions such as Bishop Matthew and Cardinal Hinsley, but widespread antipathy to the 'perfidious Jews' persisted in the war. Dr. Heenan, later to become Bishop of Westminster, revealed the nature of this Catholic concern in 1940. He attacked Jews for their Communism, the old Catholic bogey, but said that only lapsed Jews in Britain engaged in such activities. Indeed he differentiated 'the better kind of Jew (who) is drifting very rapidly towards the Catholic Church'.[55] At the other end of the religious scale, non-Conformists were more aware of the debt Christians owed to the Jewish religion. One Jewish soldier was surprised to find that his bed had been made by a Welsh Methodist 'because Jesus was a Jew'![56]

Yet hostility to Jews (as well as sympathy) existed in every part of the Church. The strength of such Christian antisemitism is well illustrated by the activities of James Parkes and W.W. Simpson in the war. Both were prominent members of the CCJ and at the very forefront of the Christian attack on antisemitism. Without their initiatives it is doubtful whether the CCJ could have been created. Even so they were still capable of attacks on alleged Jewish malpractice in Britain. Simpson was actually asked by the B.B.C. to remove his comments 'about the behaviour of certain types of Jews today' from a broadcast in 1943. Similar sentiments expressed by James Parkes at the end of the war brought forth accusations of 'sugar coated antisemitism' from irate Jewish readers. In both cases Parkes and Simpson attempted to appease the hostility of their Christian audience who for much of the war were more concerned about the Jewish irritant at home than the Jewish tragedy abroad.[57]

The events in Nazi Europe led some to re-examine their attitude to the Jews. The CCJ was one result of this reassessment. From 1942 until the end of the war of the most exciting features of its activities was the spontaneous development of local branches right across the country. Yet although events in the war prompted this revising of Christian thinking, the process was a slow one. W.W. Simpson, who, as secretary of the CCJ, was most in touch with responses to the new organisation, was aware that it was well ahead of its time in being sympathetic to the Jewish religion.[58] This was not always the case even within the CCJ. Blatant conversionists such as William Paton of the International Missionary Council and Church Mission to Jews were excluded. Nevertheless William Temple, Archbishop of Canterbury and chairman of the CCJ could write to James Parkes that 'I do not think I could interpret my interest in promoting Christian-Jewish friendship as in any way precluding an equal interest in attempting to convert Jews'. If he had to choose, conversion 'would take precedence of the other'. Despite this view Temple held together the CCJ in its early turbulent days and was the most prominent Churchman in demanding aid for the Jews of Europe.[59]

George Orwell, writing at the end of the war, doubted whether modern antisemitism could possibly be religious in origin. He believed that twentieth century Europe did not care enough about religion to attack people if they were not Christian.[60] This study has indicated that Orwell was mistaken, for although some attitudes had become modernised and secularized, the basic response to Jews in Britain was determined by a Christian discourse. The complexities of the latter, a result of a process of over a thousand years of thinking on the subject, defined both the strengths and weaknesses of the Christian response to the crisis of European Jewry. Pure religious hatred - or love - for the Jew was rare and thus few either supported the destruction of the Jews or would have welcomed a mass influx of Jewish refugees into Britain. The most dominant reaction was one of ambivalence. It was marked by a sympathy to the Jewish plight yet an antagonism to the survival of the Jewish religion; by opposition to Nazi antisemitism but antipathy to the Jews at home. It is true that the British response to the destruction of European Jewry has to be put in perspective. As a Foreign Office memorandum stated after the war 'His Majesty's Government were not responsible for countless Jewish deaths and suffering. The Nazis were responsible'.[61] Yet the British government whilst appalled by this Nazi barbarity were unwilling to consider any major rescue attempt. For this failure Christians in Britain were partly responsible. Unable to accept the Jews for their religion, few Christians were able to understand the full enormity of the Jewish catastrophe. As James Parkes was aware, Christian protests tended to be superficial and to 'enter the field somewhat late'. Like the Puritans of the seventeenth century, Christians in Britain during the Second World War wanted 'Hebrew without tears, philo-semitism without Jews'. In short it was a response that was inadequate to the crisis of European Jewry.[62]

FOOTNOTES

1. L. Langer, The Holocaust and the Literary Imagination (New Haven, 1975), p7; Y. Bauer, The Holocaust in Historical Perspective (London, 1978) Chapter 2 and C. Lanzmann, 'Shoah as Counter-Myth' The Jewish Quarterly (1986), pp11-12.

2. For public responses see S. Gordon, Hitler, Germans and the 'Jewish Question' (Princeton, 1984). R. Breitman, 'The Allied War Effort and the Jews, 1942-1943' Journal of Contemporary History (1985), pp135-156 covers recent literature on the subject.

3. Maxwell note to Herbert Morrison, 11 July 1941 in P.R.O. HO 213/298. For the British government supplying Kosher meat in the war see P.R.O. MAF 88/140.

4. E. Rosenberg, From Shylock to Svengali (London, 1961), pp13-14; N. Cohn, Warrant for Genocide (London, 1967), p254.

5. See C. Holmes, Anti-Semitism in British Society: 1876-1939 (London, 1979) for claims of a strong tradition of intolerance, and John Vincent's review of this book in The Times Higher Education Supplement, 16 November 1979 for an opposing view. T. Kushner and C. Holmes, 'The Charge is Ritual Murder' Jewish Chronicle, 29 March 1985 deal with medieval antisemitism in England. See also S. Menache, 'Faith, Myth, and Politics - The Stereotype of the Jews and Their Expulsion from England and France' Jewish Quarterly Review (1985), pp351-74.

6. D. Sayers, A Vote of Thanks to Cyrus (London, 1946), p24; T. Endelman, The Jews of Georgian England 1714-1830 (Philadelphia, 1971), p56 and D. Katz, Philo-Semitism and the Readmission of the Jews to England 1603-1655 (Oxford, 1982) passim.

7. See B. Williams, 'The Anti-Semitism of Tolerance' in A. Kidd and K. Roberts (ed) City, Class and Culture (Manchester, 1985), pp74-102 and T. Endelman, 'Communal Solidarity Among the Jewish Elite of Victorian London' Victorian Studies (1985), pp491-526 for an examination of the impact of the emancipation 'contract'.

8. For the persistence and transformation of such imagery see Holmes, op.cit.; pp107-115.

9. For experiences of childhood antisemitism see Manchester Jewish Museum, tape J24 and B. Kops, The World is a Wedding (London, 1963), p35. The extremist groups are covered in A. Kushner, 'British Antisemitism During the Second World War' (Ph.D., Sheffield University, 1986) chapter 2.

10. N. Rose (ed), Baffy: The Diaries of Blanche Dugdale 1936-1947 (London, 1973), pxv; M. Stocks, Eleanor Rathbone (London, 1949), p323.

11. See F. Iremonger, William Temple (Oxford, 1948), pp566-7; R. Jasper, George Bell (London, 1967), p137; J. Heenan, Cardinal Hinsley (London, 1944), p221 for attacks on Nazi persecution of Jews by prominent Christians. M. Berghahn, German-Jewish Refugees in England (London, 1984), p115 refers to the role of non-conformists in the refugee movement.

12. R. Gutteridge, 'The Churches and the Jews in England, 1933-1945' in O. Kulka and P. Mendes-Flohr (ed), Judaism and Christianity under the Impact of National Socialism, 1919-1945 (Jerusalem, 1987), p353.

13. For support for Hitler's extermination of the Jews see Mass-Observation Archive (M-O A) DR2588 October 1940 and E. Allen, It Shall Not Happen Here (London, 1943), p1; M-O A: DR1230 June 1939.

14. Imperial War Museum, refugee tape no 4494; M-O A DR1182 June 1939.

15. M-O A: DR1534 March 1943 for the novelist; 'The Nazi Creed' The Christian News-Letter, 7 May 1941; M-OA: DR2078 June 1939 for the clerk.

16. For the Chesterbelloc circle and The Britons see Holmes, op.cit.; chapters 6 and 9 and G. Lebzelter 'H. Beamish and The Britons' in K. Lunn and R. Thurlow (ed), British Fascism (London, 1980), p51; Catholic Herald, 25 October 1940 and 24 December 1942 for 'Jewish' Bolshevism. See A. Sharf, The British Press and Jews Under Nazi Rule (London, 1964), p18 and Thomas Moloney, Westminster, Whitehall and the Vatican (Tunbridge Wells, 1985) chapter 11 for discussion of Catholic attitudes to the Jews.

17. Catholic Herald, 18 September and 24 December 1942, 14 July 1944.

18. See Moloney, op.cit.; pp220-1 on the Herald; Catholic Times, 24 December 1942; The Tablet, 26 December 1942; Catholic Review, 1 January 1943.

19. A. Ratcliffe, Truth About the Jews (Glasgow, 1943), pp15-16; for Bedford see his correspondence with the Board of Deputies in the Board of Deputies archive (BD) C6/9/3/2, 14 November 1941; Mannin in Peace News, 14 August 1942; F. Lea, John Middleton Murry (London, 1959), p312.

20. N. Nicolson (ed), Harold Nicolson: Diaries and Letters 1939-1945 (London, 1967), p469.

21. For the White Paper see P.R.O. FO 371/23105 C16788 and Sargent minute, 5 February 1940 in FO 371/24422 C2026 on its alleged lack of impact.

22. The quotes are from M-O A: DR 2486, 1206 and 2669 October 1940 respectively.

23. W.W. Simpson 'History of the International Council of Christians and Jews' (unpublished ms., chap 3 p17, Southampton University Archive, Simpson papers). See also his 'Jewish-Christian Relations Since the Inception of the Council of Christians and Jews' Transactions of the Jewish Historical Society of England (1981-2), p91.

24. For early links see BD C15/3/17 memo 'Jewish-Christian Relations' (1939).

25. Dean of St. Pauls, proposal on Jewish-Christian cooperation in BD B5/4/3; Simpson to Parkes, 15 July 1941 in Parkes papers, University of Southampton, 16/715; Lewison to Bishop Bell, 3 November 1941 in Parkes papers 16/51.

26. See James Parkes to Selig Brodetsky, 16 June 1942 in BD C15/3/21 F2 and 'Aims of the Council', 20 March 1942 in CCJ archive, University of Southampton.

27. For Headlam see R. Griffiths, Fellow Travellers of the Right (Oxford, 1983), pp76, 176-7 and the Archbishop of Canterbury's comments in Hansard HL vol 126 col 812-9, 23 March 1943 for a total attack on all forms of antisemitism.

28. CCJ Executive minutes, 13 April 1942, University of Southampton. For petitions see P.R.O. FO 371/36659 and FO 371/36663.

29. See B. Wasserstein, Britain and the Jews of Europe 1939-45 (Oxford, 1979), pp130-2 and Kushner, op.cit.; pp492-499.

30. Morrison, 28 October 1942 in P.R.O. FO 371/32681 W14673. For war-time antisemitism see Kushner, op.cit.; passim; Morrison, 31 December 1942 P.R.O. CAB95/15 JR (43).

31. M-O A: FR 523B October 1940; P.R.O. INF 1/292 no115-118 (8 December 1942 - 5 January 1943).

32. Quoted by M-O A: FR 1648 March 1943.

33. P.R.O. INF 1/292 no118 (29 December 1942 - 5 January 1943); M-O A: FR 1648 March 1943.

34. The poll was commissioned by the National Committee for Rescue from Nazi Terror. See its minutes, 9 March 1943 in the Parkes papers, University of Southampton 15/057. The report was published in News Chronicle, 26 March 1943.

35. For difficulty in maintaining interest see the National Committee for Rescue from Nazi Terror minutes, 7 April 1943; George Orwell, 'Antisemitism in Britain' Contemporary Jewish Record, April 1945.

36. Cheetham and Randall minutes, 4 May 1944 in P.R.O. FO 371/42751 W6988.

37. Law minute, 7 May 1943 in P.R.O. FO 371/36731 W6933.

38. Randall to the Cabinet Committee on Refugee Problems, 29 December 1942 in P.R.O. FO 371/36651 W2069 and minute, 29 January 1943 in FO 371/36694 W416.

39. CCJ Executive minutes, 3 December 1942, University of Southampton; report of meeting with Foreign Office in P.R.O. FO 371/32682 W17401; Brodetsky to Greenberg, 8 December 1942 in

Greenberg papers, Anglo-Jewish Archive 110/4.

40. Law minute, 16 December 1942 in P.R.O. FO 371/32682 W17401; CCJ Executive minutes, 4 March 1943. The 19th meeting of the Executive Committee was devoted to a discussion of domestic antisemitism and thereafter the plight of European Jewry was rarely mentioned.

41. For Bermuda see David Wyman, The Abandonment of the Jews: America and the Holocaust 1941-1945 (New York, 1984), chapter 6 and P.R.O. FO 371/36725 W6785; P.R.O. CAB 65/34 Wm (43) 10 May 1943; Namier to Crozier, 15 April 1943 Manchester Guardian Archive, John Rylands Library B/N8A/209. For the failure to comprehend the 'Jewish' aspect of the tragedy, see Wasserstein, op.cit.; pp132-3.

42. See Action, 7 January 1939 for fascist opposition to the child refugees. E.J. Baumel, 'The Jewish Refugee Children in Great Britain 1938-1945' (M.A., Bar Ilan University, 1981), pp11-12 comments on the different responses to refugee children and refugee adults.

43. C. Bermant, Coming Home (London, 1976), p66; J. Grunfeld, Shefford (Tiptree, 1980), p90; Board of Deputies report 'Internal Causes of Antisemitism' (1942) in BD C6/9/1/3 F5.

44. Refugee Children's Movement, Second Annual Report 1940 (London, 1941); Union of Orthodox Hebrew Congregations, The Child-Estranging Movement (London, 1944).

45. See J. Baumel, 'Twice a Refugee: The Jewish Refugee Children in Great Britain During Evacuation' Jewish Social Studies (1985), pp175-184.

46. K. Gershon (ed), We Came as Children: A Collective Autobiography of Refugees (London, 1966), p89; Baumel, 'The Jewish Refugee Children', pp136-7; L. Segal, Other People's Houses (London, 1965), pp147, 157-168.

47. See Gershon, op.cit.; passim for this slow process.

48. For Jews and horns see Grunfeld, op.cit.; p3; Spitalfield Books, Where's Your Horns? (London, 1979), p22; B. Kops, op.cit.; p132. The Jewish Women in London Group's exhibition 'Daughters of the Pale' Tower Hamlets Library (1986) quotes Ena Abrahams on ritual murder accusations.

49. W. Simpson, 'Jewish-Christian Relations', p95.

50. For Hinsley see CCJ Executive minutes, 8 September 1942; Chief Rabbi to Brodetsky, 26 May 1942 in BD C15/3/21 F2.

51. Tribune, 22 January 1943; Jewish Chronicle, 17 October 1941 on the response to Simpson's broadcast.

52. For complaints about Sayers' play see the Jewish Chronicle, 16 April 1943 and CCJ archive, Southampton University 10/7. Naomi Grunfeld remembers being bullied at Easter during the war by fellow pupils because 'you killed our Lord'. Interview with the author, 17 July 1984.

53. Walsh in C. Newman (ed), Gentile and Jew (London, 1945), pp287-8. A Mass-Observation survey carried out in April 1943, 'Public Opinion on Means of Overcoming Antisemitism' found that Walsh's analysis was commonly held and that most suggestions amounted 'to a statement that it was up to the Jews themselves to combat antisemitism'. See M-O A: FR 1669 L.

54. For Wells see 'Messenger from Poland' Channel 4, 25 May 1987; Parkes in Newman, op.cit.; p215.

55. BD B4/CAR 11 and CAR 14 contain correspondence between Jews and Catholics relating to tension between the two communities. See Catholic Herald, 26 March 1943 for a defence of the term 'perfidious Jew'; Heenan in Jewish Chronicle, 27 December 1940 and Catholic Herald, 29 November 1940 and 3 January 1940 and later comments in his Not the Whole Truth (London, 1971) pp248-51.

56. Quoted by B. Henriques, Fratres (London, 1951), p143.

57. Simpson to Parkes on the B.B.C., 7 September 1943 in Parkes papers 16/715; Parkes memorandum on his own Enemy of the People, 1945, correspondence with Penguin Publishers in Parkes papers, University of Southampton.

58. W.W. Simpson, interview with author, 9 September 1984.

59. E. Jackson, Red Tape and the Gospel: A Study of William Paton (Birmingham, 1980), pp283-4; Temple to Parkes, 19 April 1942 in Parkes papers 17/10/2.

60. Orwell in the Observer, 30 January 1944.

61. November 1945 memorandum in P.R.O. FO 371/45383 E8450.

62. Parkes to Bishop Bell, 14 July 1938 in Parkes papers 16/51; D. Katz, op.cit.; p244.

PROBLEMS AMERICAN CATHOLICS HAVE IN DEALING WITH THE HOLOCAUST

Rev. Michael B. McGarry, C.S.P.
Rector, St. Paul's College
3015 Fourth Street, NE
Washington, D.C., 20017-1199
U.S.A.

> Was not the Holocaust a terrible test--which the Church failed?...It may be...that the question whether Christianity is to remember the Holocaust or dismiss it is a question of the ability and the right of Christianity to survive in a form in any way conformable to the Scripture.[1]

Thus Professor Elwyn Smith proposes that the very right or even possibility for Christianity to survive depends on the its ability to remember, and it is my conviction that he is correct. Boldly and paradoxically our conveners have titled our coming together "Remembering for the Future." Thus, Dr. Smith, the Conveners, and I feel that _remembering_ is critically important for our various communities, be they American, Christian, or Jewish. Even Roman Catholic official statements suggest that fundamental Christian education (catechesis) must include reflection on this sad moment in our common history:

> Catechesis should...help in understanding the meaning for the Jews of the extermination during the years 1939-1945, and its consequences.... [Catholic] education and catechesis should concern themselves with the problem of racism, still active in different forms of anti-Semitism.[2]

But how and why a community of tradition appropriates a particular moment in history as important for its self-understanding is a profound problem. Both Professor Smith and I (and many others) think that it is in the self interest of Christianity to remember the Holocaust. Indeed, Christianity must somehow figure out why its own resources, far from stopping the the Nazi onslaught, were even enlisted as part of Hitler's propaganda machine. No, it is for the health of Christianity itself, to say nothing of its newly positive, but fragile relationship with Judaism, that we must remember the Holocaust if we are to have a future. As Irving Greenberg wisely noted,

> It is clear that Christianity will not be able to overcome its legacy of guilt for the Holocuast without a major purging of its sources of Jew hatred...The capacity for major development can come only from recognition that the Holocaust is an orienting event in Christian history.[3]

It is critical to note, however, that abstractions do not remember, only persons do. "Christianity" cannot remember anything; only Christians can remember. As one born three years after the liberation of the camps and in the year of Israel's independence (1948), I cannot speak of "remembering" the Holocaust. For the present generation of Christians, most of whom were not alive during the Holocaust, the problem of the Holocaust is not one of remembering but of learning. In my own country, the expression "remember the Alamo" once exerted considerable power over the American psyche; it does not inspire much patriotism today. Sadly, but realistically, the commandment to "remember the Holocaust" may inspire as little response today for a certain generation, even though the Holocaust occurred only fifty years ago. Thus the issue confronting us today, I believe, is not so much remembering as it is a matter of _learning_.

The purpose of my paper today, then, is to admit the critical requirement that Christians remember the Holocaust by identifying and addressing the peculiar hurdles which _one_ group of Christians (namely, American Catholics) have in learning about, and appropriating, the Holocaust as a critical _moment in Catholic Christian history_.

As I have already asserted, religious traditions do not remember, only _members_ of tradition remember through their historiography and theologies. Not necessarily with conspiratorial or evil intent, they recognize (and thereby establish) some memories as precious and essential, other memories as marginal if curious, and still others as dangerous and to be put on "the Index of forbidden reading." For the most part, I think it can be said that the self-understanding of modern Christians has not been formed by a full history of Christian anti-Judaism and antisemitism. Indeed, one could make a case for just the opposite claim, as Edward Flannery has asserted in his oft-quoted remark, "Those pages of history Jews have committed to memory are the very ones that have been torn from Christian (and secular) history books."[4]

If the memory of the Holocaust is critical to Christian survival and development, and if learning about this tragic moment in Christian history is to fill in this Christian lacuna, the following problems must be admitted and addressed. The problems are _general_ _human_ problems as well as distinctively _American_ and _Christian_, although I ask the readers to question which problems apply to their situation, _mutatis mutandis_.

I. THE PROBLEMS: IN GENERAL

A. _The Holocaust is Missing from Our History Books_. My upbringing was marked by twelve years of Catholic primary and secondary education in California. Never, in my recollection, did we address the Holocaust as a _memorable_ moment in history, let alone in "sacred history." This observation is not strictly anecdotal but rather typical as recent studies indicate.[5] American elementary history books did not devote (and to this day do not devote) attention to the special plight of the Jews during World War II. Either one finds the Nazi attempt to exterminate the Jewish people as a sidelight of World War II or one finds it ignored altogether. While one should be careful not to immediately impute conspiratorial motives for this absence (indeed, one may search long and hard for a reference to the Turkish massacre of Armenians of the earlier part of this century or to Stalin's efforts at starving the Ukrainians), the peculiar dimensions of the Holocaust require that its nature, history, and consequences be forthrightly and carefully included in American history textbooks. These peculiar dimensions include the fact that it was in the midst of a modern, Western, civilized, scientifically-advanced, and Christian country that this onslaught occurred.

From a Christian perspective, there are additional hallmarks to note. The Holocaust was not a half-hearted effort to exterminate a few unnecessary or troublesome people, but rather a single-minded, technologically sophisticated attempt to annihilate the Chosen People, the original people of God. This is quite unique, this is quite frightening, and this makes the Christian requirement absolute. True it is that genocide, wherever it occurs, is a horrendous crime that Christians must denounce unequivocally and immediately. The fact, however, that Christianity formed the cultural and historical matrix for the atheistic Nazi ideology requires that Christians seek out the possible constellation of ideas and native atmosphere which could not stop the Nazi onslaught, and, sadly, might even have fueled it.

As Gerd Korman has noted, "For most historians in America World War II cast so narrow a shadow that they almost missed the destruction of European Jewry."[6] To some degree, this is true also of Jewish historians. Sustained reflection on the Holocaust in Jewish writings did not emerge until sometime after the early 1960s. There are many reasons for this which will take us too far afield. Suffice it to say that only relatively recently has the catastrophe of the Jews taken center stage in the recounting of World War II.

As one studies the Holocaust itself, whether one dates it from 1940 or 1938 or 1933 or the end of World War I, one finds a broader history--that of antisemitism[7]--forming the foreboding cloud of what happened in our century. If the Holocaust is missing from our history books, equally absent is the history of Jewish-Christian relations and, coterminus with it, the history of antisemitism. The consequences of ignoring the Holocaust and antisemitism in Christianity are dire; indeed, avoiding those consequences is the very purpose of this conference. Fr. Flannery is correct, then: remembering, through historical studies, the Holocaust and what led up to it may have the salutary effects of both removing some of the internal grounds for antisemitism and leading us to a new self-understanding of Christian identity vis-a-vis our Jewish brothers and sisters. In the end, ignoring the Holocaust and its historical antecedents may turn out to be "an important contributor to the extraordinary durability of this longest hatred of human history."[8]

Recently Dominican Sister Rose Thering, professor of education at Seton Hall University, New Jersey, studied to what degree contemporary Church documents have affected Catholic educational institutions in the United States in their portrayal of Jews and Judaism and in their education about the Holocaust. The results of her study indicate that the sort of truncated history which I received in Catholic schools is today not typical of Catholic schools. Today close to 65% of all high schools teach the lessons of the Holocaust (for an additional 33%, the Holocaust is included in the Church History course) as opposed to only 14% in 1970. Her longitudinal study reveals that

> It is evident that the Colleges/Universities and High Schools who responded in this research are definitely aware of the 'teaching of contempt' that was partially responsible for the Holocaust. These institutions today have corrected this negative teaching are are offering courses in Judaism, noting its enduring Covenant to the present time. These institutions teach in a positive way about Jews and Judaism.[9]

B. The Holocaust is Beyond Understanding. For many, history's usual task of making something understandable is precisely what renders the Holocaust unreachable. They counter that the Holocaust is unique, beyond history, beyond relevance. Lucy Dawidowicz and others have outlined in grisly detail the massive scale of the Nazi enterprise to eliminate a whole people simply because they were that people.[10] How does one understand the totally irrational? One studies for years to accumulate the tools, which are manipulated by native intelligence and sharpened by practice, critique, and review. For those who see the Holocaust as totally irrational, what tools does one employ to dissect it?[11]

Remedying the Holocaust's absence from history textbooks requires a more nuanced, thought-through response than just to include it in the curriculum, however essential that may be. The Holocaust requires understanding, insight, and reverence; it presents a special challenge to encompass and to fathom. Dangerous it is, however, to label or (ironically) to determine that the Holocaust is not understandable. Dangerous is it because it takes away from us the resources, and worse, the responsibility to prevent its happening again. Therefore, the task must begin with the assumption that the Holocaust's uniqueness does not render it totally unreachable. At the same time, one must not flatten it out such that winds up simply as one of a series of this century's human tragedies. Description must precede analysis. Unique dimensions need to be balanced with comparisons with other genocides and catastrophes. To teach the Holocaust requires that we ask, methodically and painstakingly, What actually happened? How did it happen? The analysis must ask questions like, What factors created an atmosphere within which the National Socialist doctrine could survive and even thrive? What were the ideological forerunners to this enterprise? What about technology and the wherewithal for such a complete project? What was the place of the university and its professors, the medical professions? The difficulty of the task is surpassed only by its urgency.[12]

II. THE PROBLEMS: AMERICAN

A. We Americans Do Not Like History or Geography. We Americans have a particular problem with learning any historical period. Some have observed that Americans do not study history, they "make history." We often bring to our study of history regional biases which make it particularly difficult to see events far away or from another perspective. We may not be as allergic to history as Henry Ford was when he asserted "History is bunk"; but we have amazingly dramatic historical and geographical blindspots.

To give but one example of geographical bias, in my own California upbringing, we learned that the beginnings of our country included the arrival of the Spanish missionaries and conquistedors. However, while living in Boston, I got the distinct impression that the story of our country began in New England and moved West, with hardly a mention given to Native Americans, the French in southern Canada, or the Spanish in Florida, Texas, and California.

Another example illustrates Americans' difficulty in taking history very seriously. During President Waldheim's 1987 visit to Pope John Paul II, it was not unusual or infrequent to hear Americans utter the equivalent to, "Why do the Jews have such a problem with the Pope meeting with Waldheim? After all, the Holocaust was more than forty years ago. Can't they let bygones be bygones? Surely Austria and Germany have moved beyond the terrible days of World War II." Or one might have heard, "When are the Jews ever going to get off the Holocaust? Can't they let go of it?" Americans of a certain age remember when Japan was our mortal enemy and the Soviet Union was our ally. "If we can grow, why can't the Jews," they complain.

B. We Americans Suffer From Compassion Fatigue and Numbness. Furthermore--and this is another problem--Americans may be victims of "compassion fatigue." We are painfully aware of famines this year in Bangla Desh, Sudan, Ethiopia; human rights violations in Central America, Poland, the Philippines, the People's Republic of China, Lebanon, and East Timor. We have Live Aid, Farm Aid, and AIDS Aid; we walk for hunger, dance marathons for "Jerry's Kids." We have Easter Seals, Christmas Seals, and Save the Seals. We work for the end of nuclear weapons and a replenishing of the ozone layer.

Beyond "compassion fatigue," there is what might be called "psychic numbing." "Psychic numbing" describes the dulling of the moral and emotional sensors to any kind of suffering or death. When we hear that "the Jews" wish us now to go back more than forty years, have compassion, and seek to attend to something unpleasant yet far away, our moral circuits say "Enough. I can't take it any more..." In a culture permeated with death--violence, famine, nuclear threat, and little hope for a future--a quite understandable response is such psychic numbing.[13]

C. We Americans Often Wonder, What is so Unique About the Holocaust, Anyway? Another problem which affects many Americans is the concern about uniqueness. "After all," many people say, "millions of non-Jews--cripples, Gypsies, Catholic priests, homosexuals, Poles, and others--died in Auschwitz. What makes the Jews so special that we should attend their pain, more than forty years old now, and not so unique after all?"

D. We Americans are Quite Individualistic in our Approach to Social Issues. Perhaps it was the French social philosopher Alexis de Tocqueville who, in his Democracy in America, first noted the American characteristic of "individualism." A complex constellation of factors has shaped the American character; among these must be included the fact that the United States was founded in revolution over against its "mother-country" and therefore always since in contradistinction to it. It strives to be on its own with no dependence on the "Old World." Furthermore, the frontier mentality of a country with almost limitless possibilities offered by simply "going West" put a premium on hopes for the future with little value paid to links with the past or relations to our forebears. The frontier mentality fostered mythic characters of the pioneer and the cowboy as people who sought their fortune and their future divorced from commitments to community. In our system of law and self-understanding, the rights of the individual are paramount but what is often missing is a commitment to the "common good." These rights for the individual guarantee freedom, which is

> perhaps the most resonant, deeply held American value...Yet freedom turns out to mean [for Americans] being left alone by others, not having other people's values, ideas, or style of life forced upon one, being free of arbitrary authority in work, family and political life. What it is that one might do with that freedom is much more difficult for Americans to define.[14]

Rugged individualists have a particularly hard time seeing the connections between us and the victims, between us and the victimizers, and between us and the bystander. "Whatever happened in Germany" during those years is part of "the Old World," after all, and did not we Americans finally liberate the camps? Why come back to us now insisting that we "learn the lessons of the Holocaust"?

Social theorist and theologian John Coleman thinks that Catholicism may have at its disposal the resources to counter this American tendency. As he hopefully points out,

> [T]he greatest possible strength of Catholicism in social ethics consists in its potential for generating primordial loyalties to a community which transcends the nation, to weave into Catholic life a texture of deep symbols which could evoke for Catholics a sense that they are citizens and members of a community of worldwide dimensions.[15]

III. THE PROBLEMS: CATHOLIC AND CHRISTIAN

A. We Christians Tend to Avoid our Bad Moments or We Compartmentalize Them. For many years, Catholic history was written in service of describing the glory of the Church and its triumph in the world. Episodes which besmirched or called into question that interpretation of history were often absent from textbooks. Hence, the Inquisition, bad Popes, critical histories of the Reformation, and polemics against the Jews among the early Church Fathers often did not find their way into books written for popular consumption. Only with the advent of modern, historical critical writing, combined with academic freedom, have some Church authorities been able to distinguish (a.) the legitimate requirement of the historian to write about, and interpret, all the evidence and (b.) the historian's own loyalty to the Church.

Another tendency of Christian apologists and historians has been to compartmentalize secular and "religious" history. Many Christians considering the Holocaust possess a vague feeling that atheists, anti-religionists, and other non-Christians were the only ones responsible for the National Socialist regime. Thus, inquiries about Christian complicity in the Holocaust provoke quick dismissal: "Certainly, the Holocaust is not a part of Christian history! It is impossible for a Christian to have been a Nazi!"[16] The truth of the matter is sadder; as Allan Brockway has noted,

> The Christian religion, bereft of faith, fell easy victim to the Nazi religion, for especially when it came to the Jewish people, there was little difference between them at the level of belief. The principal difference was that whereas the church remained the bearer of Christian faith despite itself, there was no vestige of such affirmation of the human individual within Nazism.[17]

B. Guilt, or "I'm Not Guilty." Related to the issues of age ("I didn't live then") and geography ("I never lived in Europe, let alone in Germany") is the aversion to what some Christians see as a laying on of unmerited guilt. The push to study the Holocaust, many of them construe, is a Jewish ploy to do a "guilt trip" on Christians for something which the vast majority are not directly responsible for...and they resent it. Many Christians advise that Jews abide by a certain "let bygones be bygones" approach. That is, "I was not there, why are they trying to make me guilty for something I had no control over? Why can't they just forgive and forget?" One heard such expressions often during President Reagan's visit to Bitburg and during President Kurt Waldheim's visit to Pope John Paul II in 1987.

C. The Quick and Facile Solution: "Christians Were Not 'Christian' Enough." Many Christians claim that the key to understanding Christian complicity in the Holocaust is that Christians simply were not "Christian enough." That is, if they--Catholic or Lutheran--had simply followed the teachings of Jesus, they would not have thwarted the Holocaust. The relation between one's faith and trying to turn around the Nazi death machine is difficult to measure. More limited in scope might be the relation between religious faith and saving Jews during World War II.

The relation between robust and true Christian faith and rescuing Jews is a new fascinating research area. Nechama Tec, in her very important When Light Pierced the Darkness,[18] indicates that there is a quite ambiguous relation between Christian faith and Christian rescue of Jews. For instance, some very good (i.e., religious practicing) Catholics were very antisemitic, yet saved many Jews. As one Polish observer noted,

> Suddenly it occurred to them [Polish Catholic rescuers] that through their anti-Semitism they might have participated in something which was at odds with their basic religious precepts...Their reasoning was as follows: 'I have participated in something evil. I must erase what I did. The only way in which I can hope to erase it is by helping Jews.'[19]

On the other hand, many of those who cooperated with the Nazi project cited religious motives. For instance,

> [A Polish inmate in Birkenau:] You Jews have crucified

> Christ and that is why a curse is upon you, an eternal curse. [Another:] If God takes no pity on your people, how can you expect pity from a human being? [Still another:] It was not Hitler who killed the Jews. It was God's will and Hitler was his tool. How could I stand by and be against the will of God?[20]

In sum, then, the relation between religious practice and courage still needs to be investigated. At very least, what is clear is that being a "good Christian" did not guarantee that one would have the courage to save Jews, and, conversely, the absence of strong faith and confessing atheism were not predictors that one would not save Jews in Poland.[21] Hence, the quick dismissal of the Holocaust for further Christian reflection based on the bromide that "Christians were simply not Christian enough," begs the question. But it may well be the case that the appeal to this facile solution is the very protection Christians seek from a more frightening prospect: that investigating the Holocaust and its relation of Christianity to its causes might be devastating to Christian faith.

C. <u>The Painful and Fearful Prospect: There is Something Within Our Very Christian Tradition which Provided a Positive Atmosphere for Nazism.</u> "How can you, in the light of what happened, remain Christians?" Thus a Jewish student challenged Eva Fleischner and other students in a course on the Holocaust in 1973.[22] The prospect that our beautiful Christian heritage--with its images of Madonna and Child, healings of lepers, and resurrection from the dead--might also have an underside which dismisses the Jewish people because they are that people is abhorrent at first, and usually dismissed as quickly. But the words of Aarne Siirala need to be seriously thought through in the context of remembering the Holocaust for the future:

> It has been one of the basic weaknesses of the Western theological tradition--a weakness it shares with most of Western philosophy--to ignore the connection between ideologies and violence. It is not surprising, therefore, that the Holocaust has been considered predominantly as irrational outbursts of subhuman violence.[23]

Many Christians may well feel the terrible weight of that question as they venture into the dark Holocaust world and all that preceded and caused it. Indeed, when Christians and Christianity were put to the test in Nazi Germany, they failed. The conclusion, perhaps too quickly, presents itself: Maybe Christianity does not have the mettle to sustain such examination? As Christians plunge more deeply into the Holocaust world, they look for the precursors, the clues, the pollutants in the atmosphere which allowed, supported it in happening.[24] And they are confronted by the long history of antisemitism which has its roots in the New Testament itself.[25]

Furthermore, beyond the New Testament is the history of Christian dogma. Since many theologians have begun to make an "ideological critique" of Christian affirmations, a number of traditional areas and propositions have come under siege since, and because of, the Holocaust. These include supersessionist notion of the Church as the sole heir of messianic promises and "true peoplehood of God"[26]; the undifferentiated mandate to convert all to Christianity[27]; and the unnuanced proclamation that the Messiah <u>has</u> arrived and has fulfilled all prophecies from the Hebrew Scriptures.[28]

Just as troubling as the doctrines and propositions which may have fueled the Nazi fire are the postures and spiritualities which may have given aid and comfort to the Christian bystander during the Holocaust. Elie Wiesel has often been quoted that we will truly understand the Holocaust only when we understand it from the viewpoint not only of the victim and the perpetrator but also of the bystander. This raises for Christians the question of what kind of spirituality do they foster and what kind of spirituality provides the courage to cease being a bystander. (Obviously, this is closely related to characteristically American individualism, so it is no wonder that much of popular American religiosity finds its center of gravity in a personal, individual relation with Christ: "Jesus is my personal Lord and Savior.) In the wake of the Holocaust, any spirituality which poses that one is most Christian by a primarily individualistic relationship with God, with a concomitant disdain for the world or even a sharp dichotomy from the world must be avoided. As David Tracy has pointed out,

> Insofar as one kind of Catholic [or Christian] spirituality is spiritualizing (or unworldly) and privatizing (or non-public) and insofar as that spirituality aided individual Christians to avoid their historical responsibilities in the situation of the Holocaust, contemporary Catholic theological reflection on salvation and spirituality needs to become more suspicious of all nonworldly, nonpolitical forms of spirituality.[29]

No wonder, then, that many Christians fear entering the Holocaust world. They rightly suspect that such a journey will take them farther back than 1920 and deeper than simply a change in behavior. They will find therein antisemitism's roots in their Sacred Books, they may discover virulent words and deeds of antisemitism in their history, they will wonder that their own Church was powerless to counteract the Nazi onslaught and that their own religious doctrines could be abused, or even used, to sustain an atmosphere within which the Nazi ideology could thrive. And they find an urgent requirement that long held doctrines, hitherto immune to an ideological critique from the Christian-Jewish encounter, need profound alteration. Such a demand, such a change can be terrifying. And perhaps most frighteningly and profoundly, we Christians, confronted by the Holocaust, may find ourselves aligned with some of our Jewish colleagues, having to raise the very question of God:

> [T]he Holocaust releases a suspicion upon...any easy (and easily sentimentalized) notions of God as a God of love and, through that suspicion, releases as well a recognition of the need for theologians to reconsider the possibility of retrieving often-overlooked resources.[30]

In other words, after the Holocaust, what kind of God can we believe in? If we come up with an impassioned God threatening fear and punishment, who got punished, for instance in the *Shoah*, and for what? If we believe in a marvelously unbounded love-God, where was S/He? Who, in the *Shoah*, was loved by this God? Christians may fear that a sentimental notion of God was shattered by the Holocaust, but what God is left?

Dietrich Bonhoeffer claimed that "only a suffering God can help us now." Jews find the foreshadowing of an aching God in the Talmud (*Exodus Rabbah II*,5), where it is said, in commenting on Exodus 3:4 ("God called to him out of the thornbush"),

> The Holy One, praised be He, said to Moses: 'Do you not feel that I am in pain just as Israel is in pain? Understand this from the place out of which I am speaking to you: the thorns! If one could possible say so, I am sharing Israel's sufferings.'
>
> That is the reason why it is said in Isaiah 63:9: 'In all their afflictions He was afflicted.'[31]

IV. CONCLUSIONS

Whether "only a suffering God can save us now" is the topic for another place and time. In this essay, we have sought merely to outline many of the problems which American Catholics have in dealing with the Holocaust. Because of space limitations make those recommendations sketchy at best. Some are much easier to overcome than others. We have elaborated on some possible solutions, while with others we have merely described their contours, while still others we have simply mentioned. Not all are equally difficult, nor are all equally solvable.

We are left with the question, though, if Adolph Hitler had been successful in annihilating the Jews, would Christians--Americans or Europeans--have "had a problem dealing with the Holocaust"? We do not have this as a real question, thank goodness, because the Jews have survived and their endurance as a vibrant people must mean something. I would assert that the survival of the Jews and their thriving need to be seen as part of solution to all the problems--historically, sociological, and theological. If, against the technologically single-minded project to slaughter them, they have survived, then can we say they did so because God wants it? And, if God wants it, what is our responsibility? And so, perhaps the greatest challenge in a post-Holocaust world is to fathom the meaning of the God-willed survival of the Jews in a positive light. And this not only for the sake of the Jews, but for the sake of the Church itself.

While I have outlined some of the peculiar problems which Americans may have in dealing with the Holocaust, I do not want to omit the special gift which we may have for the world. That is, with the largest Jewish population in the world, we Americans have the enviable opportunity to be in dialogue with our Jewish brothers and sisters to forge new understandings. Again, some Christians may fear facing the positive meaning of Jewish survival, but I think that such meaning would have to include the following:

1) The survival of the Jews certainly puts to rest the theological notion that the Jews are cursed to wander the earth.

2) The survival of the Jews beckons Christians to hear how the Jews understand and define themselves;

3) The survival of the Jews challenges Christians to understand the place of land, and hence Israel, in Jewish self-understanding;

4) If the survival of the Jews can in some way be seen as the expression of God's will, then Christians need to honor God's will by not seeking the end of the Jewish people through conversion. It is not out of guilt but out of conviction that Christians must reevaluate their notions of conversion.

"Remembering for the Future" in for the post-Holocaust Christian means that we reexamine our own need for conversion. As Gregory Baum has noted,

> After Auschwitz the Christian churches no longer wish to convert the Jews. While they may not be sure of the theological grounds that dispense them from this mission, the churches have become aware that asking the Jews to become Christians is a spiritual way of blotting them out of existence and thus only reinforces the effects of the Holocaust. The churches, moreover, realize the deadly irony implicit in a Christian plea for the conversion of the Jews; for after Auschwitz and the participation of the nations, it is the Christian world that is in need of conversion.[32]

Because they passionately believe in a Jew whose death brought forth life, Christians must give themselves to a similar task: that of taking from the near death of their own tradition in the Holocaust the opportunity for new life...which will come only if they remember, only if they learn.

* * * * * * * * * * * * *

V. ENDNOTES

[1]Elwyn Smith, "The Christian Meaning of the Holocaust," in Journal of Ecumenical Studies 6(1969):419-422, p. 421f.

[2]Commission for Religious Relations with the Jews. "Notes on the Correct Way to Present the Jews and Judaism in Preaching and Catechesis in the Roman Catholic Church, 1985." In Helga Croner (compiler and editor), in More Stepping Stones to Jewish-Christian Relations (New York: Paulist Press, 1985), pp. 220-232, p. 231.

[3]Irving Greenberg, "Religious Values After the Holocaust: A Jewish View," in Abraham Peck, ed., Jews and Christians After the Holocaust (Philadelphia: Fortress Press, 1982), pp. 63-86, p. 85.

[4]Edward H. Flannery, The Anguish of the Jews: Twenty-Three Centuries of Antisemitism. Revised & Updated. (New York: Paulist Press, 1985), p. 1.

[5]See Gerd Korman, Yad Vashem Studies VII (1970) and "The Holocaust in American Historical Writing," Societas 2(1972):3:251-270; Lucy S. Dawidowicz, The Holocaust and the Historians (Cambridge: Harvard University Press, 1981).

[6]Gerd Korman, Yad Vashem Studies VII (1970), p. 262.

[7]Following James Parkes: "'Antisemitism'...is not a scientific word, entitling it to a hyphen, nor has it anything to do with something called 'Semitism,' entitling it to the capitals. It is a political term meaning 'Jew-hatred.'" From James Parkes, "Judaism and the Jewish People in Their World Setting at the End of 1973," pamphlet distributed by the Canadian Council of Christians and Jews (Toronto, 1974).

[8]Flannery, op. cit., p. 2

[9]Rose Thering, O.P., Ph.D., Jews, Judaism, and Catholic Education. (South Orange, New Jersey: Seton Hall University, and New York: Anti-Defamation League of B'nai B'rith, 1986), p 71. Cf. also Eugene J. Fisher, Seminary Education and Christian-Jewish Relations: A Curriculum and Resource Handbook. (Washington, D.C.: National Catholic Education Association [NCEA], 1983).

[10]Lucy S. Dawidowicz, The War Against the Jews, 1933-1945. (New York: Holt, Rinehart, and Winston, 1975).

[11]For a helpful and brief survey, see Gregory Baum, "Theology After Auschwitz," in The Social Imperative: Essays on the Critical Issues that Confront Christian Churches (New York: Paulist Press, 1979), pp. 39-69.

[12]Cf. Mark Weitzman, "Coming to Grips with Teaching the Holocaust," Momentum (publication of NCEA) 24(1988):55-57, among others, for a good short outline. See also the curriculum entitled "Teaching History and Ourselves" (Brookline, Massachusetts) for a particularly fine example of what I am describing.

[13]Cf. Robert Jay Lifton and Richard Falk, INDEFENSIBLE WEAPONS: The Political and Psychological Case Against Nuclearism (New York: Basic Books,

1982), pp. 105f, for further description of "psychic numbing." See also Robert Jay Lifton, The Nazi Doctors: Medical Killing and the Psychology of Genocide (New York: Basic Books, 1986), pp. 418-465.

[14]See Robert N. Bellah, et. al., Habits of the Heart: Individualism and Commitment in American Life (Berkeley: University of California Press, 1985), p. 23

[15]John A. Coleman, An American Strategic Theology (New York: Paulist Press, 1982), p. 236.

[16]"Once, in a Jerusalem lecture, I employed the term 'Nazi Christian.' Afterward a visiting Christian stormed forward to protest that 'Nazi-Christian' is a contradiction in terms. I could only agree--and add that, at least for twelve years, the conceptually impossible had been empirically factual." Emil L. Fackenheim, TO MEND THE WORLD: Foundations of Future Jewish Thought (New York: Schocken Books, 1982), p. 281.

[17]Allan R. Brockway, "Religious Values After the Holocaust: A Protestant View," in Abraham J. Peck, op. cit., pp. 53-62, p. 58.

[18]New York: Oxford University Press, 1986.

[19]Ibid., pp. 104f.

[20]Ibid., p. 137.

[21]See ibid., p. 148, for the range of possible reactions which Catholic beliefs had on Jewish rescue in Poland.

[22]See Eva Fleischner, "The Crucial Importance of the Holocaust for Christians," in Harry James Cargas, ed., When God and Man Failed: Non-Jewish Views of the Holocaust (New York: MacMillan Co., 1981), pp. 23-36, p. 29.

[23]Aarne Siirala, "Reflections from a Lutheran Perspective," in Eva Fleischner, ed., Beginning of a New Era? Reflections on the Holocaust (New York:KTAV, 1974), pp. 135-148, p. 139.

[24]See Elisabeth Schussler-Fiorenza and David Tracy, eds., The Holocaust as Interruption (Concilium, Vol. 175), (Edinburgh: T. & T. Clark Ltd., 1984).

[25]See Edward H. Flannery, op. cit., and Malcolm Hay, The Roots of Christian Anti-Semitism. [Current Edition (New York:Freedom Library Press, 1981)].

[26]On supersessionism, see Clemens Thoma, A Christian Theology of Judaism (New York:Paulist Press, 1980); Michael B. McGarry, Christology After Auschwitz (New York: Paulist Press, 1977), pp. 5f; John Pawlikowski Christ in the Light of the Christian-Jewish Dialogue (New York: Paulist Press, 1982).

[27]See Michael McGarry, "Contemporary Roman Catholic Understandings of Mission," in Martin A. Cohen and Helga Croner, eds., Christian Mission/ Jewish Mission (New York: Paulist Press, 1982), pp. 119-146; Tommaso Federici, "Mission and Witness of the Church," Origins 8(September 19, 1978):273-283.

[28]See Rosemary Radford Ruether, "An Invitation to Jewish-Christian Dialogue: In What Sense Can We Say that Jesus was 'the Christ'?" The Ecumenist 10(1972):1-10; idem, Faith and Fratricide: The Theological Roots of Anti-Semitism (New York: Seabury Press, 1974); John T. Pawlikowski, op. cit.; and Eugene B. Borowitz, Contemporary Christologies: A Jewish Response (New York: Paulist Press, 1980).

[29]David Tracy, "Religious Values After the Holocaust: A Catholic View," in Abraham J. Peck, op. cit., pp. 87-108, p. 96.

[30]Ibid., pp. 105f.

[31]Quoted from Jakob J. Petuchowski, ed. and trans., Our Masters Taught: Rabbinic Stories and Sayings (New York: Crossroad, 1982), p. 4.

[32]Gregory Baum, "Rethinking the Church's Mission after Auschwitz," in Fleischner, op. cit., pp.113-128, p. 113.

* * * * * * * * * * *

Rev. Michael B. McGarry, C.S.P., is rector of St. Paul's College, the Paulist Fathers' Seminary in Washington, D.C. He serves on the Advisory Board to the Secretariat of Catholic-Jewish Relations for the National Conference of Catholic Bishops. He is the author of Christology After Auschwitz and numerous articles on Christian-Jewish relations.

THE CRY THAT SILENCE HEAVES

M.F. NEFSKY

Department of Religious Studies, University of Lethbridge
University Drive, Lethbridge, Alberta T1K 3M4

ABSTRACT

The paper examines the attitudes and actions of the Protestant Churches in Canada during the Nazi era, 1933-45, in regard to the National Socialist revolution, Jewish persecution and its culmination in the Holocaust, and the refugee crisis. Consideration is given to whether the Churches functioned as the voice of cultural religion or as a prophetic voice in Canadian society during this critical period.

INTRODUCTION

During the Nazi era the English-language Churches in Canada assumed the role of harbinger of bad tidings. From a period early in the era they warned their Canadian constituency of the dangers of totaliterianism in general, of the Nazi dictator more specifically and of imminent war if the armament trade did not cease to flourish. In regard to the Canadian Protestant Churches the following discussion considers three interrelated issues: the Churches' response to the National Socialist revolution; the degree of their awareness and concern with Nazi persecution and its culmination in the Holocaust; and their attitudes towards immigration and the refugees crisis. The socio-economic conditions that brought Hitler to power were not without their Canadian counterparts. In order to understand the Churches' attitudes and responses adequately, it is necessary to consider briefly the Churches' response to the Canadian scene and the degree to which this response affected their attitudes toward events in Nazi Germany. These attitudes were by no means consistent throughout all the Canadian Churches or within the same Church over time. There were, however, certain issues that all the Protestant Churches chose to address, although in some instances the treatments of the issues varied widely.

The discussion in this paper is based on archival research on the mainline Protestant churches in Canada during the Nazi era: the United Church of Canada, the largest of the Protestant denominations, the Church of England in Canada, now called the Anglican Church of Canada, the Presbyterian Church in Canada and the Baptist Convention of Ontario and Quebec, the predominant Baptist Church in Canada at the time. According to <u>The Canada Yearbook 1943-44</u> the members of these Protestant denominations constituted over half of the total Christian population (52.5%) and ninety percent of the total Protestant population. Although this analysis is not definitive, it is certainly indicative of the concerns expressed by the Canadian Churches at the time.[1]

The Churches' attitudes regarding Nazi Germany and the critical events of the period were published in various forms by the Church press. The regular Church periodical was not only the largest and most obvious source of information for understanding the Churches' attitude but it was the form most accessible to the reader constituency. These periodicals contained articles regarding church matters, stories of general interest and items of information concerning major events worldwide. It is these latter items that serve as the source of information regarding the Churches' response to the Nazi era. Although they dealt with so-called secular issues, these items were often expressed in theological terms in the form of sermons, addresses or editorial articles. The writers of these articles were often renown and highly reputed by the Church communities. They were frequently members of the ministry who chose the Church periodical as the vehicle through which to address the evils they perceived. Their opinions, therefore, had much to do with shaping the attitude of the Church proper. Often the most significant articles were reprints of sermons, addresses, speeches and commentaries delivered outside of Canada or by non-Canadians. Since they were published by the Canadian Church press, it is fair to assume that these articles either represented the opinions of the Church communion or were intended as "food for thought."

There is no way of determining how the Christian reading public responded to these articles and items of information, nor is there any way of knowing the extent to which the Church newspaper actually influenced readers' opinions or indeed the extent to which the Church press was actually ready by its constituency. Although every Church periodical included a section for letters to the editor, these letters were always in accordance with the editorial perspective. Critical letters, however, served less to confirm or contradict than simply to be provocative. In effect, then, this discussion concerns the attitudes of both the average Protestant who read the church periodical and the Church press which addressed issues of concern by articulating them in terms of Church doctrine and dogma. The determination of the Churches' attitudes must be viewed in light of the fact that, in a way, the Church structured contemporary events by virtue of their selection and inclusion within the Church press. The criteria by which these events were selected and retold offers insight into the attitudinal stance of the Church. The accounts relate not how it was but how it seemed to be to the Church press,[2] and it is primarily these views which will be examined here.

The time period treated in this discussion ranges from 1933, the year the Aryan laws restricted and excluded Jews and other non-Aryans from professional and public life, to the end of 1945 when post-war rehabilitation of a defeated Nazi Germany was the issue at hand. In order to understand more fully the Churches' response during this period, the time-frame has been subdivided into three units. The first stems from January 1933, when Hitler became Chancellor of Germany to September 1939, with the declaration of war. These were the prewar years, a time when, despite the evidence of Nazi brutality, Canada was not yet personally touched nor Germany, as yet the official enemy. The second unit ranges from the onset of World War II to the end of 1942. Once Canada entered the war, Canadians could no longer remain aloof. They were now personally involved and formally committed to the Nazi defeat. The news of military campaigns related one Nazi victory after another. In 1940 Denmark, Norway, Holland, Belgium, Luxembourg and France fell to Nazi invasion. During 1941 and 1942 Hitler committed a tremendous expenditure of men and resources to the Russian campaign.[3] Aside from the belief that good prevails over evil there were few, if any, signs that the Allied command would defeat Hitler's forces. To Canadians who lived through this period, they were the "black years" of World War II. The last unit ranges from early 1943 to the end of 1945. Early in 1943 the Nazi campaign in Russia became a costly fiasco. By the end of 1944 an Allied victory was almost certain, and in May 1945 Nazi Germany surrendered unconditionally, bringing about "the final destruction of Nazi tyranny."[4]

THE CHURCH PRESS: 1933-1939

As early as 1933 the Canadian Churches were responding to the events within Nazi Germany. In February of that year The New Outlook, the United Church organ, commented that Hitler's appointment as the new Chancellor of Germany had come "with a good deal of surprise to the world...Many friends of Germany are frankly alarmed by the situation." The article concluded that "Hitler is a petty prophet, proclaiming a Messianic hope, and inflaming the youth of Germany with the spirit of militaristic nationalism."[5] Not all references to Nazi Germany and Hitler were of this nature; in some instances the Church press succumbed to rationalization. A 1935 address, "Hitler's Germany," suggested that irrespective of Hitler's methods, "it can at least be said that he has saved Germany from a disaster worse than any which he has inflicted," and to his credit, has created "an ordered society from which abuses of various kinds have been cleared away"(!)[6] The Rev. J. Gordon Jones commended the Germans for being quite prepared "to do anything to change present conditions."[7] At least the Germans were doing something about their difficulties, which was more than Canadian Christians were doing.

Carrying this admiration still further the zealous Germanophile the Rev. H.B. Hendershot argued that if a "few injustices" were being committed, Canadians ought to realize that, whatever his faults, Hitler was merely trying to put the nation's house in order.[8] As late as February, 1939, the Rev. J.E. Ward wrote approvingly that "from a defeated and starving people, the Germans have been brought to a position of tremendous power and fitness." That this had been forced upon them did not change the picture.[9] Dr. Watson Kirkconnell, in a presidential address, maintained that National Socialism had given the German people a new meaning in life; "it has restored their pride in their country, their race and themselves; it has given them a thrilling sense of direction and destiny."[10] Germanophilic remarks in the Church press did not pass without rebuttal. The Rev. Claris E. Silcox, for example, described the Hendershot variety of Germanophilia as a "German Psychosis" while the Rev. J.C. Carlile reproved a German Baptist's account of "freedom of religion" in Germany.[11]

Others, less ebullient about the new regime, wondered why the most respectable people of Germany supported Hitler. "It may be that [the German] people are so weary of the unending struggle," one author wrote, "that they will tamely acquiesce in whatever is done by the Nazi chief."[12] Millions of people were unemployed and millions more paid below subsistence wage, the German people were suffering and Hitler offered them hope. For some Church members Hitler was sincere in his expressed desire for peace. It was not Hitler but his underlings who were "responsible for the acts of terrorism."[13] Hitler was regarded "as a modern Messiah, who has arisen to redeem his people from the intolerable shackles- the spiritual and physical- imposed by the Allies in 1919."[14] Still, it was incredible to the Rev. D.V. Warner that Hitler would offer paganism as a solution to a nation with a thousand years of Christian civilization and culture. How long would the German people endure such a travesty of government?[15]

Early in the prewar period some Church members maintained that the Allies were ultimately to blame for the events in Germany. The Treaty of Versailles, conceived in bitterness and hatred, had given birth to a grieving and anguished nation. In a full-page article entitled "The Challenge of Germany" Maude Royden argued that "We have created conditions in which no nation could remain sane."[16] Even Dr. Richard Roberts, hardly a Germanophile, maintained that the present situation in Germany was not wholly due to "the perversity of the German people." Rather he saw Hitlerism as the last resort of a desperate people, for whom we were all in part responsible.[17] Even after evidence of Nazi cruelties hit the religious press, some Church members continued to blame the Treaty of Versailles for events within Nazi Germany. In 1936 the Very Rev. W.R. Inge, Dean of St. Paul's in London, indicated that through the Versailles Treaty we had done everything in our power to insult and humiliate the German people.[18] Although many Church members were sympathetic to Germany suffering, the belief that the Allies were ultimately responsible was by no means universal. To some, it had "been evident for a long time that the Germans were flouting the Versailles Treaty," violating every pledge they had made in 1918.[19] Although the culpability of the Treaty of Versailles was a significant issue in the Church press, on the whole, more coverage was allotted to the violence and brutality of the Hitler regime.

Almost as swiftly as the Nazi boycotts against the Jews were instituted in April 1933, the Church press responded. For the Church "the bigoted and savage attacks upon Jews in Germany... called forth bitter condemnation."[20] Following the implementation of the Aryan laws, the Church press reported on "the wild programme of persecution organized by the Nazis against the Jews...more inhuman and atrocious than any that has occurred since the Middle Ages."[21] The Baptist Church condemned these activities as being neither decent nor Christian and expressed the hope that the entire Christian Church would concert their efforts in protest against these outrages.[22] The Church press continued to report the "ruthless persecution of the Jews" throughout the subsequent years. Several Church leaders remarked that it was high time to arouse public opinion over the plight of the Jews.[23]

In 1936 The Presbyterian Record published a series of articles dealing with Nazi Germany. One of these articles, discussing the nature of the Jewish persecution, considered the information revealed by the former League of Nations High Commissioner for German Refugees, James G. McDonald in his letter of resignation, which he tendered in order to make the world see "the horror and tragedy of it all." He had argued that the Nazi regulations, designed to persecute and destroy the Jewish population, were not only an outrage to Jewish feelings but robbed Jews of their human rights. Describing the situation as "a problem of serious international concern," McDonald pleaded that "world opinion move to overt the existing and impending tragedies."[24] Two years later The New Outlook referred to these tragedies as "an organized, cold-blooded terrorism."[25] In February 1939 Dr. Conrad Hoffman, Secretary of the Committee on the Christian Approach to the Jew (from the International Missionary Council), prophesied the future of Germany Jewry: "Hitler...is determined to 'cleanse' Germany of all Jewishness which means [he] resorts to a slow process of annihilation."[26]

While Church press reports ranged from phlegmatic to emotive, they did at least occasionally relate the Jewish persecution in the prewar period. In the early years it was difficult to believe that these reports were true, despite the increasing evidence for their authenticity. Notwithstanding, some in the Church press found it "quite understandable" for Germany to have such a "deep distrust and hatred of the Jews."[27] H.B. Hendershot accused the Jews of having "unfairly pushed themselves to too great prominence during a period of dislocation and unrest," and therefore the present situation was a rather natural reaction.[28] In other words, as the Right Rev. A.C. Headlam, Bishop of Gloucester, claimed, many of the victims of the Nazi injustices thoroughly deserved their blows. As aliens in Germany, the Jews had been neither wise nor grateful to their host country.[29]

Other articles concurred with this attitude. In 1936 Dr. C.H. Kerr suggested that "the Germans are now treating the Jews exactly as the Jews once treated other peoples they thought might contaminate them...they set out to exterminate them."[30] The report of the Baptist World Alliance Congress, which had met in Berlin in 1934, suggested that although "excesses occurred and irresponsible persons committed some atrocious deeds...at the worst it was not one-tenth as bad as we have been <u>made</u> to believe."[31] Although significant and salient for the times, these views did not predominate in the Church press. For the most part, when the Church press discussed Nazi persecution in the prewar years, it expressed a considerable measure of sympathy for the Jewish plight and the refugees crisis. From 1938 the press condemnation included all nations treating Jews "as if they were plague carriers."[32] The Rev. Morris Zeidman of the Presbyterian Church described the Jews as "the most hunted, the most persecuted and the most helpless creature in the whole of Central Europe."[33] Subsequent to <u>Kristallnacht</u> (November 9-11, 1938) articles continued to treat the brutality of the Nazi attacks upon the Jews. The Rev. D.M. MacMillan wrote that Christians should take to heart the fact that "hundreds of thousands of human beings have been ruthlessly persecuted for no other reason than they have been born Jews."[34]

Despite the reports of Jewish persecution and the expressions of sympathy, the Church press offered few practical solutions to the problem. From 1935 on prominent Church leaders made conscious attempts to inform the Church membership of the plight of Jewish refugees. By 1936 the refugee crisis began to dawn on the Church at large. Fifty representatives of the major Protestant churches drew up a manifesto in response to James McDonald's letter of resignation and distributed it to all members of Parliament and throughout Canada. This manifesto not only protested against the Nazi treatment of the Jews and other non-Aryans but also declared the Canadian Church could no longer remain silent on this issue. The manifesto continued that "...should the flow of exiles from Germany not cease, we feel that Canada should share with other countries the responsibility of providing a haven for at least a reasonable number of selected refugees."[35] Clearly "a <u>reasonable</u> number of <u>selected</u>" refugees does not suggest a call for all-out rescue; nevertheless, the manifesto indicated an increasing sensitivity to the Jewish plight and a willingness on the part of Church leaders to use public opinion to apply pressure to the Canadian government. Still, the manifesto did not precipate any action. As Dr. Conrad Hoffman argued in the same year, "Christian agencies have so far done little in the way of relief - they have contented themselves with protests."[36]

By 1938 the Canadian Churches initiated some active programmes of relief. The United Church press, emphasizing the need for relief for both Jewish and Christian refugees, appealed to Canadian Churches on behalf of the International Council of the World Alliance for International Friendship to make every effort to assist and relieve the refugees.[37] In the September prior to <u>Kristallnacht</u> the Anglican Church Council for Social Services passed a resolution, urging the Canadian government to "continue to explore the possibilities for the Immigration *[sic]* of selected groups of Jewish people and non-Aryan Christians from Austria and Germany, so far as is possible and desirable, and...*[to]* assume a share of the responsibility of finding a home for these unfortunate victims of political aggression."[38] In the aftermath of <u>Kristallnacht</u> the Baptist Church passed a resolution, suggesting that instead of wasting "our energies in condemnation of the persecutors," the Church offer refuge "for those persecuted people" on the grounds that such persecution was "entirely opposed to those principles of Christianity, democracy and freedom which are dear to the hearts of Canadians."[39]

When it appeared that these resolutions and exhortations were falling short of action, the Church leaders intensified their efforts. An editorial in January 1939 in <u>The Presbyterian Record</u> quoted a plea issued on behalf of the Archbishop of Canterbury. Moderator of the Church of Scotland, Moderator of the Federal Council of Evangelical Free Churches and other non-Canadian religious leaders, that "in the name both of our Christian faith and of common humanity...*[Dominion governments]* open their doors generously to refugees before it is too late..."[40] In March of the same year W.M. Rochester, the editor of <u>The Presbyterian Record</u> referred to the indescribable misery of the Nazi victims seeking asylum. Denouncing the government's closed-door policy, Rochester argued that as a Christian nation Canada should not be daunted by material considerations: "Help is needed. Let us give it and at once."[41]

By this time the Canadian Churches were expressing little confidence in the government; "there is every sign that the Canadian Government, if it acts at all, will act with discreditable hesitation." Excluding refugees from a country so large and sparsely-settled, they argued, was as unconscionable as the crude immoralism of the Nazis.[42] Still incredulous of the machiavellian conduct of the federal government, the United Church argued plaintively: "Surely, the government cannot forever remain indifferent to this appeal."[43] When humanitarian appeals seemed ineffectual, the Church press attempted to overcome Canadian xenophobia by appealing to material considerations, assuring its readership that history could demonstrate the unanticipated benefits to a country offering a haven to refugees. Still, the press affirmed that since a truly Christian nation has the moral obligation to help the needy, self-interest ought not to be the sole motivation.[44]

Shortly before the onset of World War II representatives of the Protestant Churches and other Canadian-wide groups joined together under the auspices of the League of Nations Society in Canada to face the problem.[45] Various presbyteries and synods passed resolutions to urge that "a wise and well-controlled immigration policy be adopted by the Dominion Government."[46] The Canadian Baptist Convention, convinced that immigration would provide the sorely needed impetus to the still sluggish Canadian economy, supported an open-door refugee policy on both ethical and economic grounds.[47] One Anglican member, however, severely criticized the half-hearted resolutions passed by most Churches. With the emphasis on "selected refugees" and on the benefits accruing to Canada from these refugees, "we seem to be far more interested in what we can get from the refugees than what we can give them."[48] Canon W.W. Judd, General Secretary of the General Council for Social Service, concurred with the sentiments expressed but suggested that to demand the present government to open the door to refugees widely "would in the end help to seal it fast." If the government could be persuaded to open the door even a few inches at least, Judd argued, some of the Nazi victims would be saved.[49]

Dr. Kirkconnell in a radio lecture, addressing the refugee crisis, argued prophetically that "whether their despairing screams will be heard in time" would depend on the Christian nations of the world. If Canada as a Christian nation coldly allowed the refugees to perish on the doorstep of the world, she would be just as guilty as the Nazis for their persecution and suffering.[50] Recognizing the indescribable brutality of the Nazi regime towards the Jews in particular, Dr. Kirkconnell insisted that fewer than fifty percent of the victims of the Third Reich were in fact Jews. In order to succeed in their appeal for refugee aid, the Church press had to convince its readership that the majority of the German victims were, in fact, not Jews.[51] The press, in the main, could not deny the hostility, prejudice or sheer indifference of a large section of Canadian Christendom to the refugee crisis. The fact that the victims might have been Jews was reason enough to raise barriers not only in the minds of government ministers but in that of the Church at large. This was epitomized in the poignant lack of public outcry at the government's refusal to allow the desperate Jewish refugees on the oceanliner St. Louis - the "Voyage of the Damned" - to land on Canadian soil in June 1939. Reporting the plight of these refugees, the press exclaimed that "in the meantime the cry of Israel is heard in the whole world."[52] Later that year the Canadian Quaker G. Raymond Booth encapsulated the attitude of much of the Canadian Church toward the refugees: "Between Nazism which drives them forth and a certain kind of Canadianism which seeks to bar their coming, there isn't much to choose from morally."[53]

The Canadian Churches were uniform in expressing their dread of another world war. Commenting on Britain's conciliation policy, a 1938 issue of The New Outlook stated that there were clearly only two alternatives in dealing with Hitler: appeasement or war.[54] Appeasement was a controversial issue. In treating the recently published Germany Unmasked the reviewer argued that neither concessions nor compromise should be made with Hitler for it would only serve to whet his ravenous appetite.[55] In 1939 the Church press came to the conclusion that irrespective of appeasement Hitler would continue to pursue his perverted Nietzschean dream.[56] It is to the pursuit of this dream that we now turn.

THE CHURCH PRESS: 1939 - 1942

Convinced by 1939 that there was little good about Nazism, the Church press justified Canada's engagement in the war. Ernest Bogard, in a review of Hitler's Speeches and the United States, argued that "the Nazis were not in the least interested in equality, justice or peace."[57] The year 1940 brought news of successive Nazi victories. Before long the Church press reported that Nazi forces were sweeping across Europe like a cyclon, crushing all opposition. It was becoming evident that Nazi Germany was considered less a foe than evil incarnate. "After the last conflict the world had thought it knew the infamy and cruelty of the Germans; it was mistaken, for the present struggle has revealed depths of iniquity hitherto unsuspected."[58] Appalled by the cruelties perpetrated by the German rulers, the Church press argued that the

"Church must not hesitate to condemn Nazi rule as intrinsically evil."[59] What the press found still more horrific was "that what we believe to be evil, Germany believes to be good...a direct repudiation of the basic Christian dogma."[60] An article by the Archbishop of York confirmed this view: "The terrifying thing about the Nazis is that they believe that they are right. The trouble with them is not the telling of lies; it is what Plato called the lie in the soul."[61]

As the war clouds grew blacker, the sense of the Nazi evil grew more overwhelming. In 1941 Dr. Reinhold Niebuhr, a famous American theologian, argued that a Nazi triumph would not mean a return to the barbarism of the Dark Ages but the creation of something new and altogether worse than the world has ever seen."[62] It was becoming evident that the evil might of Nazi Germany had to be crushed. No longer were most Church members laying the blame for Nazi Germany on the Treaty of Versailles. Rather than denying its culpability, some writers defended its intent. Roman Collar implied that the Treaty had become the "bêtes noir of world conditions" primarily as a result of successful German propaganda,[63] but there were still others who insisted that the Allies made mistakes at Versailles.[64] Most authors, however, supported Roman Collar's view. Admitting that the Treaty had no spirit of forgiveness, the Rev. T.N. Tattersall argued that neither had the Germans any spirit of repentence, and "forgiveness without repentence is unknown in any moral order."[65] Pursuing this line of thought, the "Philadelphian" commented that the "Germans have escaped very lightly indeed in their sufferings, compared with those they inflicted on others in the past."[66] In a self-reproving analysis the Archbishop of York, Cyril Garbett, commented in 1942 that we were too slow to act because we could not believe that such perversion of civilization was possible: "We thought Hitler was deplorable rather than damnable, and that is our condemnation."[67]

The one notion, expressed uniformly throughout the Church press, was the ultimacy of the need to defeat Nazi Germany. By this time peace alone was not the ultimate goal: "the peace we can have today is Hitler's peace. We want God's peace..."[68] Yet, defeating Hitler would not in itself save the world: "the enemy lies deeper."[69] There was more in Hitler than Hitler himself; Hitler embodied "all the malaise of the pre-war world: loss of direction, loss of soul, sense of impotence, man-worship, elements of devil worship."[70] As the Archbishop of York explained, saving civilization from Hitlerism required destroying the very roots from which it had sprung.[71] Hitler and Hitlerism sprang from "a soil of despair, resentment and wounded pride." Promised peace, happiness, work and wages, the German people turned to Hitler as their saviour and blindly followed his lead.[72] Elevating himself to the position of God, Hitler claimed "control over the bodies, minds and souls of the German people."[73] The Protestant Church came to recognize Nazism not merely as a pagan faith antithetical to Christianity but as a crusade, "the greatest crusade the world has ever seen."[74] It sought to replace "the tortured pain-torn figure of the crucified Christ" with a more appropriate Teutonic symbol.[75] Already the Germans had proven themselves "to be realistically and fanatically committed...to that kind of faith."[76]

Nazism was perceived as an evil religious crusade that could be stopped only by engaging the spiritual as well as the military. In 1942 the Archbishop of York maintained that they could preserve justice, freedom and truth "only by a faith in God which controls our political philosophy as well as our political actions."[77] This political application of faith was expressed in a conscious discrimination between Nazi Germany and the German people. Contending against the indiscriminate bombing of Berlin, the editor of The United Church Observer remarked that it is "not the German people who decide Hitler's strategy."[78] This expressed compassion for the German people was not universal. Sir Robert Vansittart argued that "there have been and are Germans who may not have liked executing the programmes of their leaders; [but]...the fact remains that the programmes of their leaders always have been executed."[79] Still, an element of compassion prevailed. Quoting John Foster Dulles, The Canadian Churchman described the German people in 1941 as generally apathetic; they were loyal, disciplined, and would fight, but "what they want is peace."[80]

The Church press was generally horrified at the news reports coming from Europe, but as to the persecution of the Jews specifically references dwindled significantly. Expressing the recurring sentiment that the Jews were merely the 'scapegoat' for Germany's ills, The Canadian Baptist argued that the treatment of the Jews should have come as no surprise; Mein Kampf showed a remarkable continuity of purpose: "the extirpation of the Jews and the enlargement of the Third Reich."[81] In a 1940 address Dr. Adolf Keller, the Secretary of the Central Bureau for the Relief of Evangelical Churches, presented the refugee problem boldly: "there is no end...From destitution to despair they go homeless, foresaken "only because" a demonic power decrees to these people who are like ourselves: 'Die! There is no place for you among mankind!'"[82] Attempting to explain the pacifist turned militant, the Baptist press listed a series of appalling assaults by Germany on "the Poles, the Jews and other races and religions."[83]

Despite the decline in the number of reports on Nazi persecution, the dispatches from Europe were sufficient to lead the press to comment that "too surely...we are in the throes of the cruelest, fiercest and most titanic combat this world has ever experienced."[84] The more numerous the reports and the greater the destruction, the more inconceivable the horror. As the Archbishop of York warned, "the cruelties and atrocities" in Poland were "so ghastly", they defied comprehension.[85] In December of 1942 the press published the speech of the Archbishop of Canterbury in which he argued that the Nazi fury was so concentrated on the Jews, it was difficult not to believe "that there was a settled purpose to exterminate them."[86] It was so difficult to believe, that many of the reports treated the victims of the Nazi fury in general.

The Archbishop of York stated that the overwhelming evidence attested not only to the ghastly cruelties and atrocities but to the fact that they were "committed not by a small handful of sadists, but by thousands of Germans and as far as we know not a protest has been raised either by those who are ordered to commit them or by the people of Germany who must have some knowledge of what is done in their name."[87] Perhaps the most prophetic statement was printed in the 1942 Christmas issue of The Canadian Churchman. "It is unlikely that more than a remnant of the Jewish population will survive."[88] In other words, by the middle of 1942 the Churches were informed about and reporting to their readership not only military events but also - though certainly less so - the mass persecution of the Jews. For many of the Church leaders it was not until this time that the real significance of the Jewish persecution began to dawn. Given the information the Church possessed, what solutions did the press offer to its readers during this period?

Dr. Adolf Keller argued in his 1940 address that "no one of us is responsible for this ruin [of the Jews] but...unless we raise our voices for justice and extend our hands for mercy" the refugee will not live to see it.[89] The executive committee of the Council for Social Service of the Anglican Church deplored the public indifference to the refugee crisis.[90] In 1940 the Baptist Convention of Ontario and Quebec passed a more extensive resolution to urge the Canadian Government to receive "the victims of Nazi persecution [as] part of Canada's war effort."[91] Anxious to move Christian conscience regarding the nature of the Jewish plight, the Rev. C.J. Lamb implored "not only...the Church but...every decent-minded citizen in Canada" to accept responsibility for the refugees and demand their admission to Canada *en masse*.[92] Yet, despite the Church resolutions and motions to urge the Canadian government to participate in refugee relief, "the streams of Christian sympathy and love" were more like rivulets, hardly able to dent the "barriers of Canadian national selfishness."[93] Once again, G. Raymond Booth indicted the Church: Canada was "second on the list of civilized countries in the world giving the least offer of help and assistance to the refugees of Nazism."[94] First on the list was Soviet Russia, a non-Christian nation. Did Canadians take pride in this? Concluding his article, Booth asked the readership: "Is it up to us to do something to help or is it just none of our business?"

In addition to the resolutions appealing to the Canadian government, the Churches turned for a solution to a higher authority; they offered prayer. The Baptist Church expressed the hope that their prayers would ascend with those of the Jews "that these wanderers [the Jews] may be attracted to Him."[95] In the fall of 1939 the Churches arranged for a special day of prayer for refugees on the North American Continent. Toward the end of 1942, when the Holocaust was more or less public knowledge, The Canadian Baptist continued to offer prayers in their "Daily Bible Readings" for, among others, the "suffering Refugees".[96]

In 1941 Hitler gave the German people his first promise for a complete victory within the year. Hitler knew that he had to win final, complete and decisive victory or he was lost. By the end of 1942 victory had escaped his grasp but he would leave his mark on the European populace.

THE CHURCH PRESS: 1943 - 1945

At the end of 1942 eleven governments released a joint declaration confirming the reports of the Nazi atrocities. Throughout this period the Church press reported further atrocity stories, often with caution and restraint. On the whole, the Churches continued to equate Nazi Germany with evil incarnate. After discussing the brutalities and outrages perpetrated against various peoples in Europe, the Bishop of Chichester concluded: "I regard Hitlerism as the arch-enemy, as the focus point of evil things."[97] The readership was frequently reminded that their fight was not against Nazism alone but also for religious liberty and freedom. Although force of arms could overthrow the Nazi tyranny, there was yet a greater tyranny to defeat: the Nazi idolatry rooted in men's minds.[98] By this time it was evident that Nazism was more than a political movement; it was "an *ersatz*-religion" with a firm core of pagan worship and a belief in its own racial superiority. No wonder that Nazis could "deny other peoples the right of existence,...and...treat them with ferocious savagery."[99]

Whether to blame the German people equally for the Nazi evil remained an issue. One view regarded Hitler as solely responsible, "excusing the average German citizen as a dupe of a master mind."[100] Should one "identify the Nazi wolves with the German sheep?" asked the Rev. C.J. St. Clair Jeans.[101] On the other hand, it was argued that the German nation must face the consequence of its guilt, having itself "conducted a struggle against God."[102] Another contributor commented that those who wrote "in impassioned terms about the sufferings of Germans in the bombed cities forget the prolonged and awful sufferings of the Poles, the Czechs and the Jews of all nations."[103]

Despite the intensity of European activity during this period, the Church press presented only a few reports on Nazi persecution and terror. These reports, however, were significant. Recognizing the apparent boundlessness of Hitler's hatred and persecution of the Jews, The Canadian Churchman repeated the British Archbishops' public condemnation of "barbarous and inhuman" Nazi policy of "cold-blood extermination."[104] W.M. Rochester directed the readers' attention to the atrocities of the war: "when you think of the treatment of the Poles, the Jews and others, at the hands of the Nazis, you stand aghast...The savagery of it all afrights us."[105] By the middle of 1943 graphic details of "life" in the concentration camps found their way into the Church press. A reprinted address by the Archbishop of York vividly portrayed the unique horror of the Jewish persecution, depicting the "starvation; exportation in 'trains of death'; wholesale massacre by shooting and poison gas." In the Archbishop's words, it was a "bloodbath on a gigantic scale, to which no parallel can be found."[106] Toward the end of 1944 the United Church press admitted—perhaps on behalf of all the Protestant Churches—that "for some time we were reluctant to accept at face value the accounts which occasionally leaked out of the atrocities perpetuated by the Nazis against the conquered people." However, eye-witness accounts of reputable American correspondents*[!]* verified the reports, depicting "the scientifically brutal way in which men, woman and little children were destroyed in mass murder gas chambers."[107] Given that the Churches expressed concern for the Jewish plight in this last period, what sort of solutions did they offer then?

In 1943 a motion was passed in the General Synod meeting of the Anglican Church to urge the Canadian government "to welcome victims of political persecution...regardless of race or creed."[108] Asserting that "millions of human beings are being tortured to death in Nazi-occupied lands," one United Church member implored the nation to save these victims before they were destroyed.[109] The Presbyterian Church, as its counterparts had earlier, suggested urging the Canadian Government "to open the doors of our Dominion to a fair share of the refugees as opportunity presents itself, and to provide as far as possible for the immediate necessities of such refugees..."[110] However, eight months later an article appeared in The Presbyterian Record, suggesting that such Christian charity was not universal within the Canadian Church. Despite agreement among Canadian Church leaders (Moderator Dr. Ketchen, Primate Owen, Archbishop McGuigan and Moderator Dr. J.R.P. Sclater) to support the admission of refugees, the Presbyterian Board considered the issue "a knotty point."[111] The fact that "considerable discussion *[over this]* knotty point" was required before the board concurred with the Church leaders is very significant.

Later in the same year an article entitled "Unlock Our Door To Refugees" referred to the thousands of people, especially Jews, who "are packed into cattle cars and taken to Poland to be shot." The article argued that "a moral obligation lies heavily upon all who can take steps to prevent such slaughter."[112] The following year a correspondent challenged the integrity and morality of Canadian Christendom: "Are we on the road to become so callous that the fate of three million people fails to stir us to lend our influence toward some solution to this problem?"[113] Toward the end of 1944 the Churches made representations to the Secretary of State for Foreign Affairs regarding, among other things, measures to rescue Jewish victims of Nazi persecution.[114] By this time the Churches were reflecting the Allied confidence in the imminent defeat of Nazi Germany. Consequently, issues of concern in the Church press shifted from military campaigns and Nazi atrocities to the salvation of the German body and soul.

The Church press was divided in regard to the expression of this concern. Whatever the extent of German guilt, there were those who called for compassion for "a people dumb, dull, apathetic, living still, but not alive; and yet dead, but bare of aims and hopes, and therefore only 'moving corpes'."[115] "Out of the Ashes - What?" insisted that there were surely "countless numbers who were innocently hurtled along by a demoniac and dynamic mass movement..."[116] On the other hand, there were those who insisted that there must be no delusions about the dimensions to which evil could grow. In his book The Church Looks Forward the Archbishop of Canterbury had maintained that "the trouble with the Nazis is not that they do not practise what they preach; it is that they do preach what they practise."[117]

It was universally accepted in the Church press that Germany be regarded with a Christian attitude, but to treat the Germans with Christian fellowship would be no mean task. It required taking steps to "assuage passions of hatred and revenge and remove fears of recurrence of war."[118] Restrictions and controls would naturally be necessary but the German people had to be given the opportunity to recover not only materially but spiritually, for the German guns might have been silenced "but the spiritual battle is not yet won."[119] The Baptist press was more cautious than that of the other Churches in anticipating hasty protests and criticisms of the Allied postwar measures. Whereas the United Church press insisted that "the German people must not be sentenced collectively for the atrocities of the Hitler state,"[120] the Baptist press maintained that the suffering which Germany brought upon herself would be alleviated only gradually, and that "this generation of Germans will bear some of the economic, political and cultural marks of it to their dying day."[121]

The Canadian Church, on the whole, did not solely blame Germany for the European fiasco. Hitler could never have succeeded "in wielding such deadly power had we not provided the tools - those fears and antipathies - which he so cunningly used to divide and immobilize us."[122] The Baptist press, however, was less self-incriminating in its evaluation of Nazi Germany. "Thanks Be To God!" argued that from the very beginning the German people were "drunk with the wine of conquest" but that at last "we have been delivered...from the brutalities of a brutal race which would have happily annihilated all peoples but her own."[123] The Baptist was the most vociferous of the Church presses in its refusal to diminish the responsibility of German Christians for the success of National Socialism. Acknowledging that there were European Catholics, Protestants and Orthodox who were determined adversaries of Nazism, it admitted that there were "many - perhaps a majority of Protestant Christians - (who) yielded to the totalitarian pressure and sought deviously to rationalize their faith in conformity with the Nazi ideology,..."[124] Whatever their defence, they allowed Nazism to grow and flourish; "their sin is that they were morally incapable of facing up to its monstrous desecration of national ideology while it was still formative and capable of control."[125]

DISCUSSION

The Nazi era was not a period of particularly penetrating religious or moral insight for the Church in Canada. In the 1930s the Protestant Church tended to reflect the escapism and reactionary attitudes of the Canadian public at large. Most of the Church, like most Canadians, was overcome with inertia.[126] Although recognizing the ontologically threatening nature of Nazism, the Protestant Church was slow to grasp the ultimate significance of the Nazi foe. The German soil which brought forth Hitler and Nazism had also given birth to the Protestant Reformation, great theologians and philosophers, great artists and musicians. Canadian Protestantism, especially its liberal Churches which were for the most part the voice of the Protestant press, could never truly comprehend that such total evil as Nazism could spring forth from such creatively fertile soil. In <u>None Is Too Many</u> Irving Abella and Harold Troper argue that "in the midst of the suffering and tragedy of the Holocaust the Canadian Church remained silent.[127] How could this be?

We have seen that early in 1933 the Church press acknowledged Hitler's ascension to power with apprehensiveness. From the beginning of the Nazi era the Church press was under less of an illusion than the Canadian public regarding Hitler's intentions. By the time war was declared, it became evident in the Church press that Nazism had the power to touch the soul of the German people far more effectively than the Protestant Church had touched the hearts of its own constituency. Nazi Germany had to be defeated not because it was stretching its grasp over the whole of Europe, nor because it denied the most fundamental human rights, nor even because of its cruel and barbaric persecution of the Jews[128] but because everything it did and said was totally anti-Christian.[129] By 1943 when Hitler had failed to achieve his victory, the most pressing question in the Church press was the future treatment of a defeated Germany. In this regard the press took upon itself the role of conscience. Only action directed by a faith in God would suffice to bring about total defeat; indeed, the Church "must recognize this evil and deal with it...still acting as Christians toward Germany."[130]

The major events of the Nazi persecution of the Jews were also reported in the Church press, although once war was declared this reporting was superseded by accounts of the European campaign. The press portrayed more or less vividly the Jewish persecution resulting from the Aryan laws, its increased intensity after the Nuremberg laws, the wide-spread pogrom of

Kristallnacht, the almost European-wide mass deportation and massacres of Jews and other non-Aryans (Einsatzgruppen) and finally the planned extermination of the Jews. Throughout the Nazi era the Church press published protests against the Nazi treatment of the Jews and printed Church resolutions urging an open-door policy for Jews and other victims of Nazi persecution.

How can the Canadian Church be charged with silence? The Church was not silent! At least the Church press, the principal organ for mass communication, was not silent. What do Abella and Troper mean by the term "silent"? The poem "The Three Silences of Molinos" by Longfellow suggests that there are three silences, first of speech, the second of desire and the third of thought.[131] That is, before one speaks, one must have the desire to speak, and before the desire they must have the thought, the knowledge. Silence, then, may be based simply on ignorance. Are Abella and Troper saying that the Church was silent because it did not know? With the many reports of mounting persecution and the later accounts of mass murder, one can assume that those who read the Church press were more or less informed. The silence of the Church was not a silence of ignorance or lack of information. There is, however, a difference between what the Church members had read and what they chose to believe.

There is also the ignorance of disbelief. Perhaps this is the meaning of the silence of the Church. Prevailing wartime conditions brought about a problem of press credibility. During this period news was carefully censored; confirming evidence from governments was not forthcoming. Reports were disseminated on all sides for propaganda purposes. Many of the press accounts were inconsistent in numbers and details. Since the Nazi government functioned in a context of secrecy, using euphemisms to relate relevant information, suspicion arose regarding reporter reliability.[132] Given the fabricated atrocity stories circulated during World War I, the reports of Jewish persecution were greeted with scepticism. Church members, believing that civilized people could not act so uncivilized, assumed that the reports were at least somewhat exaggerated. In the words of the Archbishop of York, it was incredible "to believe that such a perversion of civilization was possible."[133]

The silence of the Protestant Church, then, was not the silence of thought. The Church knew but could not believe; it failed to grasp the full significance of National Socialism, Jewish persecution and the refugee crisis. Perhaps, the silence of the Church refers also to the silence of speech. A few prominent ministers and church members did express their views in the Church press; in fact most of the critically significant articles treating these issues were written by a small group of caring and conscientious Christian leaders and spokespersons. The Church as a whole, however, in terms of the number and kinds of contributions to the Church press, was not particularly concerned. As Alice and Roy Eckardt lamented, "the voices that were raised merely helped to make the general stillness louder."[134] The Church proper was, for the most part, silent but it was silent for several reasons, many of which were rooted in the socio-economic conditions of the Depression.

The 1930s was one of the most devastating decades Canada ever faced. In the early years of the decade the Canadian industrial machine was grinding to a halt. Almost 20 percent of the Canadian labour force was jobless; economic recovery was slow and uneven.[135] Though the downswing ended in 1933, a severe recession in 1937-38 retarded recovery, which was still far from complete when the war broke out in 1939.[136] Contributing to the economic decline was a decade of natural disasters. Drought, swarms of grasshoppers and rust spores laid waste vegetation and soil; farming was impossible. Many Canadians attempted to wait out the drought, others looked elsewhere for subsistence. The Church was profoundly concerned with the social, economic and political problems of this period. The problems in the West continued almost unabated but for the provisions supplied by the Church in the East.[137]

Even without an economic crisis the 1930s would have been "a period of controversy and confrontation." Despite the insoluble nature of the Depression, Canadians demanded political action.[138] The Bennett and King governments' ineptitude in dealing with the social, political and economic problems, however, diminished the promise of the social order. Mistrust in the democratic process was intensified by the apparent corruption of the Liberal government in Quebec and the government's suppression of the press in Alberta.[139] The prewar period was a time of great suffering; it produced psychological as well as physical depression. Psychologically, the 1930s brought about loss of faith in the notions of personal security and the democratic process: "a generation learned that the independence and security they gained from work was largely illusory."[140] Many Canadians looked more or less seriously to other political systems for succour and solace. The resultant loss of faith in the democratic process was particularly disturbing to the Church, which considered the concept of political democracy indigenous to its heritage. It was an exceedingly cautious and xenophobic mind-set that developed as a result of these conditions.

Anglo-Saxon nativism, which prevailed in Canada, grew more intense during this period. Despite the fact that little more than half the population was British in origin, British institutions were revered and British standards constituted the ideal norm for Canadian aspirations. "Canadian identity was somehow linked with the British connection."[141] Canadian Protestantism was, more than Canada as a whole, committed to the British connection. British ideas and institutions were considered the spiritual as well as racial heritage of Canada. There were also strong emotional ties with Britain, especially for some of Canada's social, economic and political policy makers. This Anglo-Saxon nativism acerbated the cultural divisions within Canadian society, by rallying against so-called foreign elements: the European immigrants, French-Canadian Catholics and Canadian Jews. These strong anti-alien attitudes played a significant role in keeping immigration and refugee numbers exceedingly low.[142]

Another issue relevant to the silence of the Church was the problem of regional disparity. The regional cleavage in Canada was particularly evident between French and English Canada. Industrialization exacerbated the cultural division between English and French Canadians by bringing rural, Catholic Quebec out of its isolation and into contact with the new, alien ideas of urban, Protestant Canada. Unionization by industry contributed to the growing cleavage, since management tended to be English Canadian and labour, French. Threatened with the loss of their social identity and cultural integrity, French Canadians began to accentuate their language, religion and provincial autonomy, broadening the cleavage still further.[143]

In response to the conditions of the Depression, some Canadians flirted with fascism and socialism and had a rather exaggerated fear of Communism. When Pope Pius XI condemned Communism for destroying the family and economy, the French-Canadian antipathy toward Communism grew still stronger, and fascism became their bulwark.[144] In Quebec the Parti National Social Chrétien began to flourish. It combined Italian and German fascism and ran on a platform not unlike its early European counterparts. Uncritical of Nazi Germany, French Canada at times even condoned the persecution of the Jews. French Canadians feared, possibly rightly so given the current government, that an open-door refugee policy would mean an increased Anglo-Saxon Protestant population, thereby reducing French Canada - largely Catholic - to a smaller minority. They also feared that Jewish refugees would take over the business and wealth of the province, leaving French Canadians unemployed and impoverished. Largely for these reasons French Canada adamantly opposed opening the door to refugees, especially Jews.[145] In view of the evidence of Liberal party corruption in Quebec, Prime Minister King, whose Liberal government was less than favoured in Quebec, considered the French Canadian vote critical to his political future. Since the rest of Canada remained relatively silent on the issue of Jewish persecution and the refugee crisis, King—as he was inclined to do—adopted the line of French Canada and kept the doors tightly shut.[146]

In the prewar period Canadians generally perceived Nazism as just another foreign nationalistic movement. Although never exceedingly interested in international affairs or in participating in international diplomacy, during the 1930s Canadians had become increasingly introverted. Against the catastrophic events occurring in their daily lives, European events seemed very remote; like earthquakes or famines, "they made the headlines but...were soon forgotten."[147] During the prewar period the Protestant Church was silent partly in fear that criticism of Germany would lead the Nazis to escalate their persecution. Of still greater concern was the fear that criticism would lead Canada closer to the impending war most Canadians dreaded.[148] As the war clouds grew thicker, the Church hoped beyond hope that Nazi Germany would be satisfied with the return of her former colonies and with the right to deal with her internal matters freely.[149] This, of course, included her treatment of the "Jewish problem." Despite the protests regarding the treatment of the Jews and resolutions urging an open-door refugee policy in the Church press, the Church membership was generally more preoccupied with surviving under the difficult living conditions of the 1930s and avoiding war. They gave neither the persecution of the Jews nor the refugee crisis priority in their expressed concerns.[150]

The Protestant Church was silent not because it did not know nor totally because it did not believe. The silence of the Church was the silence of desire, stemming from either indifference to or tacit approval of Nazi activities. There is evidence in the press of some Church leaders and ministers who were avidly anti-Semitic; for example, the Anglican Bishop Headlam, the Rev. Hendershot of the United Church, Dr. C.H. Kerr of the Presbyterian Church. They did not, however, speak for the Church as a whole. Almost as soon as their anti-Semitic remarks appeared in the press, prominent Church leaders - the same persons who argued on behalf of the refugees - refuted them in the form of editorials, disputations and letters to the editor. It would hardly be accurate to suggest that the silence of the Church stemmed from tacit approval of the persecution of the Jews. The Church was not totally silent in this regard. Its silence resulted, in large part, from apathy; "most of the Canadian Church seemed indifferent to the suffering of German Jews and hostile to their admission to Canada."[151]

The most important reason for this indifference, according to the Rev. Claris E. Silcox, was "the existence throughout Canada...of a latent anti-Semitism."[152] To be fair there were many respectable Christians in Canada who would not personally have mistreated a Jew. They would not have supported violence against Jews but neither would they have opposed it. Beneath the surface of their Christianity "were uncrystallized but negative feelings about Jews" in general.[153] Normally, this latent anti-Semitism would have had little effect but during the Holocaust crisis it meant that a large body of otherwise decent and considerate people were predisposed to indifference. The Church press was aware of the problem of anti-Semitism in their midst. As early as 1936 Dr. Conrad Hoffman remarked that "one would almost think sometimes that there was some peculiar inhibition that tended to prevent Christian people in general from making their religion really practical."[154] The saddest lament of all was one writer's regret for the Church's contribution to the persecution of the Jews, and for the fact that many of those who did not contribute to it did not protest against it.[155] Protesting for an open-door policy for refugees two months before the war, one politically astute author argued that the government would follow an open-door policy only if public opinion favoured such a policy and made itself felt.[156] Public opinion was not favourable. It would come as no surprise when Hitler ridiculed the world for a "concern in refugees which led to no concrete action."[157]

The Church press did not desist from publishing the occasional self-recriminating article after the onset of war. In 1943 the Rev. Claris Silcox admitted that between 1936-39 only a few Christian leaders showed any great concern for Jewish refugees. The greater tragedy still was that some professed Christians "shouted out against allowing any Jews to find sanctuary among us."[158] Describing the indifference more graphically, another writer grieved: "If they had been cattle, they would have been welcomed anywhere. As human beings [as Jews] they were wanted nowhere!"[159] Perhaps a quotation from Reinhold Niebuhr, quoted in the Church press, best articulated the Canadian attitude towards an open-door refugee policy: "We hate the horrors the Nazis perpetrated against the Jews...but we still don't want too many of them coming to America because we feel it would increase the anti-Semitism feeling too strong already."[160] In other words, charging the Church with silence has less to do with the silence of speech than with the silence of desire. In Canada during the Nazi era there was an absence of strong desire to rescue the Jews. Without the desire, notwithstanding the thought or knowledge, there would naturally be silence of speech, for one speaks out only when there is desire to do so.

In So It Was True! Robert Ross discussed various implications of the silence of the Church. Despite the fact that the Church press provided the information of the Jewish persecution and extermination, the articles failed to persuade effectively enough to bring about significant action by the government or large, influential groups. This is epitomized by the response of the American and British forces who, upon liberating German concentration camps in the spring of 1945, were utterly incapable of articulating what they saw. Yet, what they saw had been portrayed in the religious and secular press for some time. The press had simply failed to persuade them.[161] The Churches had also failed in concerting their effort. This failure is indicative in a statement published in the Acts and Proceedings of the Presbyterian Church as late as June 1943. Acknowledging the persecution and torture of the "Jewish Race", the Saskatoon Presbytery went on record "as being sympathetic to that race, and anxious to be of help to them," concluding that as far as they were aware no Church in Canada had taken a like stand.[162] The lack of awareness evident in this statement stands out glaringly. Yet, with concerted effort the Church could have utilized the full weight of Christian resources to arouse the public out of its indifference and, thereby, more effectively demand the Canadian government to fulfill its responsibility.[163]

The actions taken by the Canadian Church - rallies, protests, resolutions - were all modest enough to have little success in changing public opinion or the government's attitude toward the Jewish plight and the refugee question. Despite its potentially significant voice in Canada, the Church did not effect a massive outcry; there was no moral outrage, no moral indignation.[164] This failure led Dr. J.H. Oldham to accuse the Church of not only "complicity for failure to act" but more directly "complicity through apathy" - a silence rooted in "callous indifference."[165] As the Archbishop of York bemoaned near the end of the war: "When the anguished call came...we would not take heed...these acts of aggression in far-away lands were no concern of ours."[166]

At this point one must ask what the Church could have done during this period. In a full-page article the Archbishop of Canterbury maintained: "It would be mere blindness to realities to suppose that the heart of the present rulers of Germany could have been changed by any

Christian plea, or that non-resistance to their acts could have changed it."[167] But is this truly the case? Had the Church press effectively influenced their constituencies, had the potentially significant voice of the Protestant Church been realized, the Church might have succeeded in demanding effective action from the government. If the Canadian government had conveyed to Nazi Germany that it opposed the persecution of the Jews and others enough to offer them santuary, perhaps other nations would have followed suit. Then perhaps the Nazis would not have attempted to solve their 'Jewish problem' with such confidence and determination.[168] With due regard to the war effort, the Church had a moral imperative to demand of the government everything that could possibly have been done to save the victims of Nazi persecution. If these demands had been made, if only a few or even no lives had been saved, the moral imperative would have been fulfilled,[169] and silence would not have been the Church's present indictment.[170] However, this will never be known for the moral imperative was left wanting, and as with Molinos, one reads Canadian Church history and is left distraught...with dreams and visions that should have been.

REFERENCES

[1]According to the 1941 Canadian Census, the United Church constituted 19.2%, the Church of England 15.2%, the Presbyterian Church 7.2%, the Baptist Church 4.2% of the Canadian population. The Canada Year Book 1943-44 (Ottawa: Dominion Bureau of Statistics, 1944) p. 108. These four Churches constitute 90% of the total Protestant population.

[2]Philip Abrams, Historical Sociology (Ithaca: Cornell University Press, 1982), p. 193; Max Weber, The Method of the Social Sciences (New York: Free Press, 1949), p. 169-70. See also A.R. Louch, Explanation and Human Action (Berkeley: University of California Press, 1969).

[3]Marcel Duncan, (ed.), Larousse Encyclopedia of Modern History (London: Paul Hamlyn, 1964), p. 381; George C. Kohn, Dictionary of Wars (New York: Facts on File Publications, 1986), p. 514; James Trager, The People's Chronology (New York: Holt, Rinehart and Winston, 1979), **pp. 953-83.**

[4]Duncan, Larousse Encyclopedia p. 381; Kohn, Dictionary of Wars, p. 515.

[5]'The German Venture', The New Outlook (8 February 1933), p. 123; 'When Liberty Dies, Death Stalks', The Canadian Baptist (12 July 1934), p. 2.

[6]'Hitler's Germany', The New Outlook (29 May 1935), p. 560.

[7]Rev. J. Gordon Jones, 'What Can We Do About It?' The Canadian Baptist (7 December 1933), p. 14. He added that if Canadian Christians were half as devoted to the principles of Christ as the Nazis were to those of Hitler, "there would be a sincere change in our attitude toward the present conditions and we would be that much nearer to realizing the Kingdom of God."

[8]'The German Point of View', The New Outlook (9 August 1933), p. 84.

[9]'Democracy, The Canadian Churchman (9 February 1939), p. 84.

[10]Dr. Watson Kirkconnell, 'The Price of Christian Liberty', The Canadian Baptist (17-24 August 1939), p. 5.

[11]C.E. Silcox, 'German Psychosis' The New Outlook (16 August 1933), p. 598; J.C. Carlile, 'Freedom of Religion in Germany - A Reply', The Canadian Baptist (15 September 1938), p. 5.

[12]'Is Hitler Master of Germany?' The New Outlook (15 March 1933), p. 235; 'The German Peril' Ibid (22 March 1933), p. 251.

[13]'London Letter', The Canadian Churchman (30 November 1933), p. 726.

[14]'Hitler's Germany', The New Outlook (29 May 1935), p. 560.

[15]'The World Crisis', The Montreal Churchman (May 1937), p. 18.

[16]'The Challenge of Germany', The New Outlook (22 November 1933), p. 825; 'The German Bombshell' Ibid (25 October 1933), p. 725.

[17]'If Jesus Went to Germany', The New Outlook (15 November 1933), p. 805; cf. 'If Jesus Went To Germany', The Canadian Baptist (1 February 1934), p. 4.

[18]'Nazism', The Canadian Churchman (7 May 1936), p. 292; 'Hitler's Germany', The New Outlook (29 May 1935), p. 544. See 'Letter to the Editor' by Fair Play, Ibid (5 February 1936), p. 130; 'With the German Baptists', The Canadian Baptist (19-26 August 1937), p. 4; Ibid (9 February 1939), p. 14.

[19]'I See in the Papers', The Canadian Baptist (11 April 1935), p. 2; 'I See in the Papers', Ibid (17 September 1936), p. 2; 'Never Forget', The New Outlook (12 July 1933), p. 519.

[20]'Anti-Jewish Bigotry' The New Outlook (29 March 1933), p. 267; 'Germany and the Jews', The Canadian Baptist (6 April 1933), p. 3.

[21]The New Outlook (12 April 1933), p. 299; Ibid (17 May 1933), p. 387; 'The Jews and the World Crisis' The Montreal Churchman (December 1941), p. 20; 'Ill Treatment of the Jews', The Canadian Baptist (27 April 1933), p. 5.

[22]'The Cleansing of Berlin - And How!' The Canadian Churchman (28 September 1933), p. 584.

[23]See, for example, 'A Chat With The Editor' Ibid (23 January 1936), p. 50.

[24]'Germany and the Jews' The Presbyterian Record (May 1936), p. 132.

[25]'Overshadowed Austria' The New Outlook (27 May 1938), p. 507; 'The Challenge of Germany' Ibid (22 November 1933), p. 825; cf. 'When Liberty Dies, Death Stalks', The Canadian Baptist

(12 July 1934), p. 2.

26 'The German Refugees' The Canadian Baptist (2 February 1939), p. 7.

27 'Editorial in Brief' The New Outlook (12 April 1933), p. 301.

28 H.B. Hendershot, 'The German Point of View' Ibid (9 August 1933), p. 584.

29 'Holy Church Throughout The World' The Canadian Churchman (19 October 1933), p. 631. See also M.K. O'Meara, 'In Germany This Summer' Ibid (5 October 1933), p. 60 which, likewise, questions the validity of the persecution stories, having seen 'Jews dressed as well as anyone else, with perhaps more fondness for jewelry.'

30 Dr. C.H. Kerr, 'The Light of the World' The Presbyterian Record (December 1936), p. 367.

31 'Berlin, 1934' The Canadian Baptist (6 September 1934), p. 3; italics added. This attitude tended to be more representative of German Baptist reporting than of the Canadian Baptist press in general. See, for example, 'Freedom of Religion in Germany' by Dr. Hans Luckey of Hamburg, Ibid (15 September 1938), p. 5.

32 'Baptists and Religious Liberty', Ibid (10 March 1938), p. 5.

33 Rev. M. Zeidman, 'The Jews', The Presbyterian Record (February 1938); also 'The Jews', Ibid (September 1938), pp. 273-74.

34 'The Sovereignity of God' Ibid (July 1939), pp. 217-19; cf. 'Germany and the Jews', Ibid (January 1939), pp. 4-5. See also 'Healthy Instincts', The New Outlook (18 November 1938), p. 1095.

35 'Canadian Churches and German Refugees' Social Welfare (March 1936), p. 25-26; 'The Manifesto on German Refugees' Ibid September 1936, p. 93.

36 'Practical Christianity' The New Outlook (11 March 1936), p. 236.

37 Ibid (16 September 1938), p. 875; also 'The World of Religion' Ibid (7 October 1938), p. 958 and 'The Cry of Man's Anguish', Ibid (16 December 1938), pp. 1224-25.

38 'Anglican Action on the Refugees' Social Welfare (Winter 1939), p. 64. See also the resolution passed by the International Council of the World Alliance for International Friendship Through the Churches which sought to do all they could to awaken public opinion to 'the great evils involved in the systematic ostracism and persecution of the Jewish race and thousands of Christians who have kinship with the Jews', Ibid (September 1939), p. 32.

39 'Moose Jaw and the Jews', The Canadian Baptist (1 December 1938), p. 12.

40 W.M. Rochester, 'Germany and the Jews' The Presbyterian Record (January 1939), pp. 4-5. The editorial ended with the critique that 'Canada as a nation must not be wanting at this time in such a grave crisis...'

41 W.M. Rochester, 'Without a Country' Ibid (March 1939), pp. 67-68.

42 'Is It Nothing To You"' The New Outlook (10 February 1939), p. 120; cf. "Is It Nothing To You?' in The Canadian Churchman (2 March 1939), p. 130.

43 'The Refugees', The New Outlook (15 March 1939), p. 4.

44 'A Chat With The Editor-Political Refugees' The Canadian Churchman (2 February 1939), pp. 66.

45 Twenty-Fourth Annual Report The Council for Social Services of the Church of England in Canada (1939), pp. 18-19. See note 147.

46 W.M. Rochester, 'Without a Country' The Presbyterian Record (March 1939), pp. 67-68. The significant word here is 'wise', for Abella and Troper testify that the immigration policy of the Canadian government was in fact well controlled but hardly wise. See also 'Refugees', The New Outlook (1 July 1939), p. 10; 'Let The Church Be The Church' Fourteenth Annual Report, Board of Evangelism and Social Service, The Anglican Church of Canada (1938), p. 52. See also 'The Convention Resolutions', The Canadian Baptist (29 June 1939), p. 11.

47 'The Convention Resolutions', The Canadian Baptist (29 June 1939), p. 11.

48 J.E. Barrett, 'The Open Door For Refugees' The Canadian Churchman (16 February 1939), p. 100.

49 'The Open Door For Refugees' Ibid (23 February 1939), p. 121.

50 'Canada and the Refugees' Ibid (23 February 1939), p. 121.

51 For example, 'Editorial in Brief', The New Outlook (20 May 1936), p. 469; 'Human Dumping', Ibid (15 July 1938), p. 674; W.M. Rochester, 'Germany and the Jews' The Presbyterian Record (January 1939), pp. 4-5; 'A Chat With The Editor-Political Refugees' The Canadian Churchman (2 February 1939), p. 66; 'Is It Nothing To You?' Ibid (2 March 1939), p. 130.

52 'Have We The Courage?' The Canadian Churchman (27 July 1939), p. 442; W.F. Ambrose, 'The Wandering Jews' Ibid (15 June 1939), p. 378. 'The Plight of the Jewish Refugees', The Canadian Baptist (15 June 1939), p. 3.

53 G. Raymond Booth, 'The Holy Innocents, 1939' The Canadian Churchman (21 December 1939), p. 734.

54 'Terms of Friendship', The New Outlook (22 April 1938), p. 384. The Canadian Baptist press was less inclined to entertain the alternative of an appeasement policy regarding Nazi Germany.

55 'Supermen on the Rampage', Social Welfare (September 1936), pp. 119-20; 'The Confusion of British Public Opinion', The New Outlook (3 June 1936), pp. 532-33.

56 This refers to Nietzsche's doctrines of the Ubermensch (Superman) and the 'will to power'. It was evident in Mein Kampf that Hitler had a dream of subjugating all 'weaker peoples' of the world. As the Baptist press argued, it was 'impossible for Hitler to think any

peaceful thoughts. He is ever ready to feed the hatreds and the fears of the German people", 'I See In The Papers', The Canadian Baptist(23 February 1939) p.3.

57 'America in a World of War', The Canadian Churchman (12 February 1942), p.111; cf. 'The Baptist Youth', The Canadian Baptist (15 February 1940),p.11: Germany "has lied, broken her word repeatedly, stolen other's property and killed mercilessly." Even before the war the Baptist press argued: "You cannot deal with mad war dogs", 'Munich and After', The Canadian Baptist (25 May 1939), p.13.

58 'Our Empire in Fateful Fight', The Canadian Baptist (15 June 1940),p.3.

59 'Columbia', The Canadian Churchman (7 March 1940), p.157; 'Round About', Ibid,p.228. "Never was it more certain that we who oppose Nazi Germany are standing, a living barrier between the incarnate spirit of evil and all that is God-begotten and God-honoring in the life of man", 'The Allies See It Through', The Canadian Baptist (15 June 1940),p.10. See Rev. John Pitts, 'Is Hitler Anti-Christ?' The Presbyterian Record (September 1940),pp.265-66.

60 'Ministry of Information-Religions Division', The Canadian Churchman (6 June 1940),p.358. Dorothy Sayers, who made this comment, was a famous novelist and playwright of the time.

61 'Freedom, Justice and Truth', Ibid (5 February 1941),p.84; 'Freedom, Justice and Truth', The United Church Observer (15 February 1942), p.27.

62 'We Must Believe in Divine Providence, Says Reinhold Niebuhr', The United Church Observer (15 June 1941),p.1; 'God in Our Time', Ibid (15 September 1941),p.2; 'God in Our Time', The Canadian Churchman (4 September 1941),p.483; 'The Powers Behind Hitler', The Canadian Baptist (1 October 1940),p.4.

63 'As I See It', The United Church Observer (15 February 1940),p.14.

64 'Christmas While Cannons Roar Across the Battle Fields', The Canadian Baptist (15 December 1939),p.3; 'German Mentality', Ibid (15 April 1940),p.14; 'The Treaty of Versailles-Another Point of View', The United Church Observer (1 July 1940),p.17.

65 'War and God's Judgment', The Canadian Baptist (1 February 1940),p.7.

66 'Thinking It Over', The United Church Observer (15 May 1940),p.43; 'Agrees With Roman Collar' Ibid (15 June 1940),p.17.

67 Ibid (1 March 1942),pp.3,30.

68 'God's Peace Not Hitler's', The Canadian Baptist (1 June 1940),p.3; 'The Peace Terms', Ibid (1 March 1941),p.3.

69 'We Are Enemies of Dictatorship', Ibid (15 October 1940),p.9.

70 'Round About', The Canadian Churchman (30 November1940),p.661.

71 'Freedom, Justice and Truth', Ibid (5 February 1942),p.84; 'Freedom, Justice and Truth', The United Church Observer (15 February 1942),pp.3,27.

72 'The Moral Equivalent of the Devotion of the Nazi Youth', The United Church Observer (15 January 1941),p.10; 'Reviews of New Books', Ibid (15 December 1941),p.19.

73 'Is Hitler Anti-Christ?' The Presbyterian Record (September 1940),p.266; 'The Nazi Faith and the Christian', The Canadian Baptist (1 October 1942),p.1.

74 'What Has the Church Done?' The United Church Observer (1 September 1940),p.10. This passage continues, "Its philosophy, its ideas, its professed teachings, are the most anti-Christian that have appeared on this earth since our Lord was crucified." See also 'Agrees With Roman Collar', Ibid (15 June 1940), p.17; cf. 'Back to Orthodoxy' The Canadian Baptist (1 October 1942),p.9.

75 'The Swastika to Replace Cross', The Canadian Baptist (15 January 1942),p.5; 'God-Or the Feuhrer!' Ibid (1 April 1942),p.8. Mein Kampf was to supersede the Bible as the greatest written work, maintaining the highest ideals and code of ethics for the German people.

76 'Dreams of Christian Humanity', Ibid (1 April 1942),p.3.

77 'Justice and Freedom in God', The United Church Observer (1 March 1942),p.30. See also 'Opinion of British Christians Unanimous Against Reprisals', Ibid (15 November 1940),pp.1,26; 'German Defeat Will Be Due to Lack of Spiritual Resources', The Canadian Baptist (15 October 1940),p.2.

78 'Opinion of British Christians Unanimous Against Reprisals', The United Church Observer (15 November 1940),pp.1,26; 'Days That Shook The World In Flanders Field', Ibid (15 June 1940), p.5.

79 'Germany's Black Record', The Presbyterian Record (March 1942),p.71; 'War's Dilemma', The Canadian Baptist (1 January 1941), regarding the British blockade against the German people, 'for the war is their responsibility as well as Hitler's" (p.3).

80 'Ecumenical Mission of the Church Today', The Canadian Churchman (12 June 1941), p.377.

81 Review of 'The Moral Issues of War', The Canadian Baptist (1 May 1940), p.2; 'The Powers Behind Hitler', Ibid (1 October 1940), p.4. See also 'Hitler Tells the World', The New Outlook (3 February 1939), p.99; 'Canadian Post-Mortem on Refugees', Social Welfare (Spring 1939),p.83. See 'Liberty', The Canadian Churchman (23 January 1940), which referred to the treatment of the Jews as "the refinement of cruelty. It reduced them to lower than slaves, even than beasts" (p.82). Also 'War May Days', The United Church Observer (1 June 1940), p.5.

82 'Central Bureau for Relief of Evangelical Churches in Europe, Foreign Affairs Bulletin', The Presbyterian Record (March 1940), p.85.

83 'Life by Battle or Death by Human Slavery', The Canadian Baptist (1 March 1941), p.12.
84 'Sufficiency of Christ for a Suffering World', Ibid (15 June 1942), p.1.
85 'From Over and Across', The Canadian Churchman (10 September 1942), p.509.
86 'Too Horrible To Think About', Ibid (24 December 1942), p.754.
87 'From Over and Across', Ibid (10 September 1942), p.509.
88 'The Church Overseas-The Church in Poland', Ibid (31 December 1942), p.771.
89 'Central Bureau for Relief', The Presbyterian Record (March 1940), p.85. The United Church Observer discussed the same address but without reference to the Jewish question (1 February 1940), p.3.
90 'Canada and the Refugees' The Canadian Churchman (7 September 1939), p.489.
91 'Resolutions at Ottawa', The Canadian Baptist (1 July 1940), p.2.
92 'How Long, O Lord!' The Canadian Churchman (17 April 1941), p.249.
93 Diocese of Toronto Synod Journal, Eighty-eighth Session (4 May 1940), p.183, Appendix A.
94 'Toronto' The Canadian Churchman (30 May 1940), p.350.
95 The Canadian Baptist (15 February 1940), p.4; Ibid (1 January 1941), p.5; cf. 'Let Us Pray', the front cover of The Canadian Churchman (23 February 1939).
96 For example, 'The Family Altar', The Canadian Baptist (1 November 1942), p.5.
97 'Church Unity in the United Nations', Ibid (1 February 1943), p.1.
98 'God Loves, God Cares', The Canadian Churchman (21 December 1944), p.732; 'Hitler Couldn't Scare Pigeons', Ibid (30 November 1944), p.684; 'Men and Affairs-Nazism and Religion', The Canadian Baptist (15 May 1943), p.2.
99 Review 'Hitler Attacks Norway', The Canadian Churchman (14 October 1943), p.578; 'The Shorter Catechism', The Presbyterian Record (June 1943),pp.163-64; 'The Freedom to Worship', The Canadian Baptist (1 April 1943),pp.4,11.
100 'Hitler Not Entirely To Blame', The Canadian Churchman (6 May 1943), p.287.
101 'What Shall We Do With Germany?' The Presbyterian Record (April 1945), p.100.
102 'The Germans Must Be Punished', The Canadian Churchman (12 October 1944), p.564; 'Nazi War Monuments" The Canadian Baptist (1 August 1945), p.12; cf. 'Passionate Believers', Ibid (15 June 1944), where it stated that the Germans "believed in their Fuhrer as an incarnation of God. They believed in blood and soil and saw a world prostrate at the Teuton's foot.... Because they believed, they conquered" (p.1).
103 'Bombing Policy', Ibid (16 August 1943), p.11.
104 'From Over and Across', The Canadian Churchman(14 January 1943), p.25; 'The Empire as Refuge from Massacre', Ibid (25 February 1943), p.121.
105 'The Shorter Catechism', The Presbyterian Record (June 1943),pp.163-64.
106 'The Persecution of the Jews', The Canadian Churchman (15 April 1943), p.230; 'Conference on Post War Role of Religion', The United Church Observer (1 May 1943), p.26.
107 'Atrocities', The United Church Observer (15 September 1944), p.4. The article continued with a story of Lublin's concentration camp in Poland which "is too brutal and horrifying beyond description."
108 'What Happened at the General Synod Golden Jubilee-Day by Day', The Canadian Churchman (23 September 1943), p.527.
109 'Conference on Post War Role of Religion', The United Church Observer (1 May 1943), p.26.
110 'On Behalf of the Jewish Race', The Presbyterian Record (June 1943), p.147. The article also encouraged the membership to denounce anti-Semitism wherever it is found and to remember at all times that"'The Author and Finisher of Our Faith' was born of Mary, a Jewish maid."
111 'On the Rampart-Open Canada to Refugees', The Presbyterian Record (February 1944), p.41.
112 'Unlock Our Door To Refugees', The United Church Observer (1 October 1943), p.11.
113 'A Challenge to Christians', Ibid (15 March 1944), p.11.
114 Ibid (15 August 1944), p.1.
115 'The Spiritual Outlook in Germany', Ibid (15 July 1945), p.5; 'The Spiritual Outlook in Germany', Ibid (1 August 1945), p.21.
116 'Out of the Ashes-What?' The Canadian Baptist (15 June 1945), p.3.
117 'These War Thoughts' Ibid (1 May 1945), p.8; cf. 'Dr. Oldham Warns of Wrong Approach to Germany', The United Church Observer (1 December 1944), p.1.
118 'Sir Stafford Cripps on Treatment of Germany'. The Canadian Churchman (5 July 1945), p.386.
119 'Religion in Colleges', The Canadian Baptist (15 September 1945), p.3.
120 The United Church Observer (5 July 1945), p.5.
121 "Attitudes of Christians to Germany Today', The Canadian Baptist (1 September 1945), p.8.
122 'Am I My Brother's Keeper?' The United Church Observer (1 February 1944), p.11; 'What Shall We Do With Germany?' The Presbyterian Record (April 1945), p.100.
123 'Thanks Be To God', The Canadian Baptist (15 May 1945), p.3; cf. 'Transitory and Abiding', Ibid (15 June 1945), which discussed the Nazi obsession with the belief in their racial superiority, an obsession which created "strong animals without conscience, pity or imagination" (p.3).
124 'European Church and German Nazism', Ibid (1 October 1945), p.8; 'Germany's Regeneration', Ibid (15 October 1945), p.8.

125 'Out of the Ashes-What?' Ibid (15 June 1945), p.3.
126 A.T. Davies and M.F. Nefsky, 'The United Church and the Jewish Plight During the Nazi Era, 1933-1945', Canadian Jewish Historical Journal 8/2 (Fall 1983) 57; Keith Clifford, 'Religion in the Thirties: Some Aspects of the Canadian Experience', The Dirty Thirties in Prairies Canada (eds) D. Francis and H. Ganzevoort (Vancouver: Tantalus Research Ltd, 1980),pp.128-32.
127 Irving Abella and Harold Troper, None Is Too Many (Toronto: Lester and Orpen Dennys, 1983) p.284.
128 Robert W. Ross, So It Was True! (Minneapolis: University of Minnesota Press, 1980) described the failure of World War II to intervene on behalf of the Jews. The war was fought to defeat Nazism. There were no side endeavours to free or save the Jews or even to inform them that they had not been forgotten (p.289). For reasons why no rescue attempts were made see David S. Wyman, The Abandonment of the Jews (New York: Pantheon Books, 1984), pp.335-8.
129 'The Church and Political Problems of Our Day', The United Church Observer (1 June 1940), p.8; 'The Foundations of Morals', Ibid (15 September 1942), pp.11,27. See 'Niemöller's Warning', The Canadian Churchman (16 November 1944), p.643: " I approved when Hitler attacked the Jews for I thought that they were detrimental to German culture. I likewise approved when Hitler liquidated the trade unions for I thought they were detrimental to our economic life. It was only when the Nazis attacked the Churches, and my own Church in particular, that I realized what Nazism really was."
130 'Dr. Oldham Warns of Wrong Approach to Germany', The United Church Observer (1 December 1944), p.1.
131 'The Three Silences of Molinos'

'Three silences there are: the first of speech,
The second of desire, the third of thought;
This is the lore a Spanish monk, distraught
With dreams and visions, was the first to teach.'

132 Wyman, The Abandonment of the Jews, pp.322-23; Ross, So It Was True! pp.265-66,278.
133 'Justice and Faith in God', The United Church Observer (1 March 1942), p.3.
134 Alice L. and Roy Eckardt, 'Again, Silence in the Churches' The Christian Century (26 July-2 August, 1967), p.970.
135 'Justice and Faith in God', The United Church Observer (1 March 1942), p.3. H. Blair Neatby, The Politics of Chaos (Toronto: Macmillan, 1972), p.46; Lita-Rose Betcherman, The Swastika and the Maple Leaf (Toronto: Fitzhenry and Whiteside, 1975), p.2; Michel Horn, The Great Depression of the 1930s in Canada (Ottawa: Canadian Historical Association, 1984) no.39, p.3. See also Barry Broadfoot, Ten Lost Years (Toronto: Doubleday, 1973).
136 Horn, The Great Depression, p.20. See also Donald G. Creighton, Dominion of the North: A History of Canada (Boston: Houghton Mifflin, 1944).
137 The Canadian Churchman (2 March 1933), p.137; 'Rax Me That Bible', The Presbyterian Record (March 1937), p.87.
138 Neatby, The Politics of Chaos, pp.30-1,34-5,49.
139 Betcherman, The Swastika and the Maple Leaf, p.2; The New Outlook (20 September1936),p.910. Prime Minister King's insensitivity to the Canadian suffering is illustrated in his remark that 'what is needed is not so much a changed social or economic system as a changed heart" (The New Outlook, 15 March 1933, p.238).
140 Horn, The Great Depression, p.20; Neatby, The Politics of Chaos, p.22.
141 Neatby, The Politics of Chaos, p.166; cf. Robert Bothwell, Ian Drummond and John English, Canada 1900-1945 (Toronto: University of Toronto Press, 1987),pp.299,312-13.
142 Betcherman, The Swastika and the Maple Leaf, pp.45-7; Wyman, The Abandonment of the Jews, p.7. See also Howard Palmer, Patterns of Justice (Toronto: McClelland and Stewart, 1982).
143 Neatby, The Politics of Chaos, pp.41-7.
144 Davies and Nefsky, "The United Church and the Jewish Plight During the Nazi Era, 1933-1945", pp.56-7; Betcherman, The Swastika and the Maple Leaf, pp.2,81-7. See also The New Outlook (22 April 1938), p.388; The United Church Observer (1 July 1939), pp.15,32; The Canadian Churchman (5 May 1938),p.291.
145 Quebec papers such as La Nation, L'Action Catholique, L'Action Nationale frequently published vicious anti-Semitic statements. See, for example, Victor Teboul, 'Antisémitisme: Mythe et Images du Juif au Québec', Voix et Images du Pays 9 (1975) 107-8; Richard Jones, L'Idéologie de L'Action Catholique (Québec: Les Presses de L'Université Laval, 1974), pp.69-72. On 6 December 1938 the Canadian League of Nations Society sponsored a national conference in Ottawa. Both Jewish and non-Jewish organizations were represented, including such notables as the United Church Rev. Claris E. Silcox and the Anglican Canon W.W. Judd. No French Canadian organization was represented. See Abella and Troper, None Is Too Many, pp.18,45.
146 "The astute Mackenzie King knew that there were no votes to be gained in admitting Jews; there were, however, many to be lost" (Abella and Troper, None Is Too Many, pp.281-82);'Unlock Our Door To the Refugees', The United Church Observer (1 October 1943), pp.11,26.
147 Neatby, The Politics of Chaos, pp.163-64.
148 'Canadian Christians and German Refugees' Social Welfare (March 1935), pp.25-6.

149 Neatby, The Politics of Chaos, pp.173-74; Betcherman, The Swastika and the Maple Leaf, p.101.

150 This is evident in the greater number of Church press articles addressing their more immediate concerns and in the apparently apathetic response to those articles treating the persecution and refugee crisis. Very few letters to the editors, for example, sought to address these latter issues in greater depth or indeed to address them at all.

151 Abella and Troper, None Is Too Many, p.51.

152 See 'Canadian Post-Mortem on Refugees' Toronto (21 March 1939), United Church Archives, Claris E. Silcox Papers, Speeches; published in Social Welfare (September 1939).

153 Wyman, The Abandonment of the Jews, pp.12,13.

154 'Practical Christianity', The New Outlook (11 March 1936), p.236.

155 'Good Friday and Missions to the Jews', The Montreal Churchman (April 1938), p.8.

156 'Refugees', The United Church Observer (1 July 1939), p.10.

157 'Hitler Tells the World', The New Outlook (3 February 1939), p.99.

158 Rev. Claris E. Silcox, 'Let My People Go!' The United Church Observer (15 April 1943), p.11.

159 'Jesus - A Refugee!' The United Church Observer (15 January 1944), pp.11,26.

160 'Niebuhr Demands Christians Face Problem "Practically"' The Canadian Churchman (28 September 1944), p.539.

161 Wyman, The Abandonment of the Jews, pp.324-25.

162 'On Behalf of the Jewish Race' Acts and Proceedings, no.22 (June 1943), p.147.

163 Ross, So It Was True!, pp.286-87.

164 Ibid, pp.287-88,291.

165 'Sees Lack of Moral Passion Helping Growth of Barbarism' The Living Church (20 May 1945), cited in Ross, So It Was True!, pp.291-92. See also 'The Sin of Doing Nothing' in The Canadian Baptist: "One can sin as greatly by doing nothing as by aggressive participation in some wrong" (2 June 1938), p.3.

166 'Am I My Brother's Keeper?' The United Church Observer (1 February 1944), p.11.

167 'A Call to Repentance and Trust' The Canadian Churchman (26 October 1939), p.599.

168 Wyman, The Abandonment of the Jews, p.334; Abella and Troper, None Is Too Many, pp.32,280.

169 Wyman, The Abandonment of the Jews, p.335.

170 "Could a cultured people descend to such depths of evil without us also being culpable?" asked the Archbishop of York, in 'Justice and Faith in God', The United Church Observer (1 March 1942), p.3.

VARIETIES OF ANTISEMITIC RESPONSES TO THE HOLOCAUST WITHIN AMERICAN CONSERVATIVE PROTESTANTISM

Richard V. Pierard
Professor of History
Indiana State University
Terre Haute, IN 47809 U.S.A.

INTRODUCTION

The response of the conservative Protestant community in the United States to the existence of the Jews in general and their plight in World War 2 in particular has been confused and inconsistent. On the one hand, the literature and sermons of its spokespeople reveal a deep reservoir of sympathy for Jews and identification with the Jewish heritage, but on the other hand, traditional antisemitic ideas and stereotypes repeatedly appear, sometimes in the least expected places. This is a situation which sensitive conservatives recognize has to be confronted and dealt with.

DEFINITIONS

What is meant by antisemitism? The very term itself has been a matter of vigorous debate among scholars and popular writers alike, but in order to enable an intelligent assessment of its prevalence in conservative Protestant ranks, a working definition is necessary. In this study antisemitism will be viewed as the unreasonable, unprovoked, irrational reaction of dislike, distaste, or revulsion for any Jew or anything Jewish, whether this be in word or deed. Antisemitic or, more accurately, anti-Jewish expression runs a wide gamut from the bigoted outpourings of Jew-haters to the more sedate kinds of stereotyping that are not overtly malicious in their intent and the great variety of insensitive comments about Jews and Judaism that flow from ignorance.

The rubric "conservative Protestant" covers individuals who are generally referred to as "evangelicals" or "fundamentalists." Three features distingush them. First, they are committed to the "infallibility" or even "inerrancy" of the Bible, and they regard it as the central source of authority in spiritual matters. Second, they emphasize the necessity for a personal relationship with God through faith in Jesus Christ. This may be a crisis ("born-again") experience or something which developed over a long period of time, but it is more than merely church membership or assent to a creed. Finally, they feel an obligation to share their faith with others, a practice which they may label "witnessing," "evangelism," or "preaching the gospel."

The problem of defining conservative Protestantism is greatly complicated by the differences that exist in evangelical ranks. To the outsider these appear to be trivial but to conservatives they are of enormous consequence. There is considerable debate as to what parts of the Bible should be taken literally and what parts figuratively. Some fundamentalists stress separation from all other Christians who deviate even the slightest from them in doctrine or lifestyle. Arminians and Calvinists argue over whether Christ's atonement is restricted to an "elect" or salvation is open to all. Charismatics and Pentecostals express an experiential faith that many other theological conservatives regard as excessively emotional. Dispensational premillennialists construct an elaborate prophetic system in which Jews have a significant position and glorious future. They believe Jesus Christ will come again to establish his reign over earth, and then the Jews will recognize him as their Messiah and become an integral part of his kingdom.

However, Anglo- or British-Israel prophetic thinkers and the amillennialists who do not anticipate a special "kingdom age" at Christ's return both deny any future role to the Jews and make the church the beneficiary of the Old Testament promises. Adherents to theonomy or dominion theology agree that the church superseded Israel in God's plan, but they go on to say that the church has the task of establishing the kingdom on earth and bringing all people into submission to divine law and then Christ will come. On the fringe of conservative Protestantism are the racialist "Identity" churches which freely use evangelical terminology but are repudiated by almost all evangelicals and fundamentalists because of their highly unorthodox doctrine of Christ and interpretations of Scripture as well as their commitment to violence. It is clear that generalizations about conservative Protestants must be made with care, and one will find exceptions to almost any statement made about them.

DOES ANTISEMITISM EXIST AMONG CONSERVATIVE PROTESTANTS?

In American religious history, conservative Protestantism can best be understood as a twentieth century phenomenon. It is a response to the challenge of liberal Protestantism to the earlier evangelical orthodoxy and to the growth of religious pluralism in general. Most evangelicals and fundamentalists today regard themselves as "pro-Jewish" and look upon antisemitism with revulsion. Nevertheless, there are a number of preachers and writers within their ranks who from time to time have said or written things that are clearly antisemitic in nature.

This goes beyond the common stereotyping that has prevailed for so long in discussions of Jews, such as "they always look after their own," "they have funny-shaped noses," "they have an uncanny ability to make money," "they control the banks and the mass media," "they don't like Christians," and so on. Because of an intense hatred of communism which set in after World War I and a tendency to identify with the social and economic status quo which dates back to the Gilded Age, evangelicals were susceptible to much more dangerous kinds of stereotyping, such as the belief that the international Jewish "conspiracy" was responsible for communism, Jews "polluted the blood" of the white or "Aryan" peoples, and the "Christ-killers" were out to drive Christianity from the face of the earth.

In the following pages a number of these will be identified which impinge on our understanding of the Holocaust, although space limitations preclude an in-depth exploration of them and the citations must of necessity be seen as representative of a significantly larger body of opinion. To be sure, they are at best a minority opinion among conservatives, but they do poison the spiritual well of evangelicalism and, worse still, there is always the possibility that if political and economic conditions in the United States deteriorate in the 1990s, people may begin to blame "the Jews" for their troubles and these ideas would then become attractive and convincing. The lesson of the Holocaust is that this must never be allowed to happen.

DIVINE JUDGMENT FOR UNBELIEF

Some preachers maintain that the Holocaust is part of the divine judgment upon Jews for their unbelief. The argument goes like this. Because the people of Israel turned away from the Lord and were disobedient to his commands, the curses spelled out in Deuteronomy 28 and by various of the prophets, especially Jeremiah, have fallen upon them. They were driven from the land, scattered throughout the world and subjected to continual sufferings. As radio preacher Dale Crowley put it: "His covenant people FAILED him. There was not a statute they did not violate, and not an ordinance they did not desecrate." Yet, God was rich in mercy to his people and sent prophets and chastisement, but they did not repent. "The dark history of Israel's failure to hearken to God's word finally reached a sad climax in their rejection of God's Son, their Messiah." Instead of welcoming him who had been foreseen in scores of Old Testament prophecies, the Jews rejected, despised, and crucified him. "They were the fig tree on which, when the Master came by, he found no fruit, and therefore pronounced the curse upon it."[1] The result was that the Romans "exactly fulfilled" the predicted judgment in the brutal conquest of Palestine.

Still, through the centuries the Jews continued lo live in unbelief. As fundamentalist leader Gerald B. Winrod wrote in 1935, this "disobedient and rebellious people" from the very beginning mounted an "assault" on Christianity. Wherever they went in the dispersion that followed the destruction of Jerusalem, they "carried burning hatred in their hearts for the saints because they were constantly reminded that Christ had predicted their downfall." But, he went to say, "it is not a safe thing for non-Christians to persecute Christ's saints. God will not permanently excuse or condone such crimes. History is replete with judgments being visited fast and furiously upon individuals and nations who have made this mistake."[2]

Their evil system was best revealed in the Talmud, whose contents have been "exposed" in various antisemitic tracts, the most famous of which are I. B. Pranaitis, The Talmud Unmasked: The Secret Rabbinical Teachings Concerning Christians (published in Latin in 1892 and issued in an English translation during the 1930s by the notorious American antisemite E. N. Sanctuary), and Elizabeth Dilling, The Plot Against Christianity (c. 1964). These are still being distributed by right-wing book sellers, and their contents have been recycled by innumerable pamphleteers.[3] As one of these, Glen Berry, put it, Christians are God's people, the "true Jews," while the Pharisee Jews mentioned in the New Testament are "Talmudists," who follow the "traditions" which Jesus condemned and "are the devil's people." These Talmudists "have no hope and are without God in the world." They "are the pagans, the heathen, the children of this world who live after the lusts of the flesh, the destroyers of the earth."[4]

With such an attitude toward Jews, it was easy to justify the Holocaust as simply one more judgment upon them. Thus, shortly after the war the Jewish-Christian itinerant evangelist, Hyman J. Appelman, ascribed the extermination of the European Jews to the premise that they had forsaken Christ.[5] Three decades later, Baptist evangelist John L. Bray insisted that "all the past sins and guilt of Jewish people which led to their dispersions from the land years back was as nothing compared to their guilt in their rejection and death of the Lord Jesus Christ." They could not escape their responsibility for "the actual murder of the Son of God." In so doing, "the nation of Israel settled forever their fate as an earthly race." All the prophecies concerning the tribulation they would suffer for rejecting Christ were fulfilled from the siege and destruction of Jerusalem in C.E. 70 through Bar-Kochba's rebellion in 132-35 and their captivity in many nations and "the holocaust of tremendous numbers of them killed in Europe in our own lifetime."[6]

The insensitivity inherent in this position was vividly revealed to me a few years ago through an encounter I had in Poland. As I stood before the Warsaw Ghetto monument and tried to comprehend the tremendum of the human tragedy which this stark piece of stone represented, I expressed to another American beside me the profound sense of dismay which I as a Christian felt there. The person, who was a prominent Baptist preacher, responded almost flippantly: "There is no problem understanding what happened. They had said: 'His blood be on us, and on our children.'" In other words, the phrase recorded in Matthew 27:25 that was shouted by a small but angry mob demanding the crucifixion of Jesus justified the fate of an entire people!

DENIAL OF JEWISH IDENTITY

One of the strategies of Christian antisemites which has the practical effect of downgrading the role of Jews in the world, the uniqueness of their travail in World War II, and especially their right to a separate national existence is to declare that modern-day Jews are not really the descendents of Abraham, Isaac, and Jacob. Instead, they are either of "Asiatic" origin or are so "mongrelized" through intermarriage with other racial stocks that the claim to any sort of separate identity is an absurdity.

There are a number of variations in the argument, but essentially it is this. God made unconditional promises to Abraham and his progeny. Abraham would be the father of a great nation, God would bless those who blessed him and curse those who cursed him, and in him all the peoples of the earth would be blessed. Abraham accepted this by faith and that was counted to him as righteousness (Gen. 12:1-3; 15:5-6). Then he made a conditional "law covenant" with the Children of Israel at Sinai in which they would be a kingdom of priests and a holy nation if they collectively and nationally obeyed the law of the Lord. However, Israel failed to keep its vow and the "old covenant" became void. This was succeeded by a "new covenant" of grace which was open to all people through faith in Jesus Christ who died for the redemption of all humankind.

Because they neglected to obey God, the children of Israel were scattered from the land. The ten northern tribes (clans) were taken captive by Assyria in 720 B.C.E. and the two southern ones were carried off by Babylon a little over a century later. A remnant from the tribe of Judah returned after the seventy years in exile and reestablished the temple worship. The area in which they lived came to be known as Judea and the inhabitants as Jews. After the Maccabean revolt in the second century a Jewish monarchy was established. A century later the Romans moved in and set up a protectorate. The Jews developed an elaborate civil-religious system, but so many foreign racial elements had entered into the population that few racially pure Israelites remained.

To this people came Jesus Christ, who because of the virgin birth did not actually have Jewish blood in his veins. Yet, his putative father (and perhaps his mother Mary as well) could trace their lineage to David, and Jesus came as the son of David to found a new type of kingdom. As Baptist Bible teacher William D. Herrstrom explained, the genealogies in Matthew and Luke were of Joseph and were just for "identification." Jesus was placed in the womb of Mary by the Holy Spirit which meant he was not a Jew and did not possess the blood of fallen humans. Thus, "Christ did not have in His veins the Jewish blood of Abraham the adulterer, of Jacob the schemer and bigamist, of David the adulterer and murderer, of Solomon--sex-fiend of the ages with seven hundred wives plus a harem of 300 concubines to satisfy his lust; or of a Tamar who became a mother through incestuous intercourse with her father-in-law; or Rahab the harlot; or Bathsheba the adulteress."[7]

The Jewish religious leaders were jealous of his following among the masses, and they conspired to have the Roman authorities execute him as a revolutionary. Because they rejected the gospel message that Jesus preached, God rejected the Jews once and for all, and soon afterwards the Romans snuffed out the semi-autonomous Jewish state, slew most of the people, and carried off the survivors into slavery. The remnant practiced a "Talmudic" faith and retained a sense of religious identity through the synagogue worship, but they had been cut off as God's chosen people. Christians became the heirs to the covenant of Abraham, and as the outspoken racialist conservative preacher Gerald L. K. Smith declared, the curse of God was upon the "apostate" Jews.[8]

At this point appears a sort of inverted supersessionism. The covenant with Abraham had never been abrogated because it was unconditional. The promises to Israel that line the pages of the prophetic books were still valid, but not for that unbelieving people called the Jews. They had been cut off forever due to their rejection of their Savior and King. However, God preserved his people who had been taken in the first captivity by Assyria, even though they had "forgotten" their true origins, and through the centuries they wandered westward across Europe until they reached the sanctuary foretold in 2 Samuel 7:10, the place which Yahweh appointed for his people Israel where they would no longer be afflicted by "the children of wickedness." This new home was the Atlantic littoral and British Isles, and thus "the Celto-Anglo-Saxon and kindred peoples and nations are literally modern Israel." The United States is the "great people" prophesied by Jacob during his last days which would arise from Joseph's elder son Mannasseh and the British Commonwealth is the "multitude of nations" that would come from the younger son Ephraim (Gen. 48:19).[9]

The "Joseph-people" were prepared by God to receive Christianity and had the destiny to be a light to the nations. The Christian faith struck its deepest roots in the Anglo-Saxon peoples and they were the center of the world-wide missionary movement. Moreover, being Israelites themselves, they had a "propensity for theocracy," and as evangelical writer Pat Brooks recently put it, "no other nation but America has had its beginnings so rooted in a covenant relationship with God, except ancient Israel." She goes on to say:

> The nation born at Sinai has been reborn here. That is why attempts to turn it into a humanistic, socialist state are so serious. A certain confrontation lies ahead, as the Joseph-people awaken to their identity and their destiny, as children of the King of kings and citizens of His kingdom. The powers of darkness simply cannot stake a permanent claim to this land, Joseph's land.[10]

Anglo-Israel preacher Clyde Edminster adds that the United States literally is a "Bible People" and a "Bible Nation." God promises that if America conforms its ways to his commandments, he will bless the nation with peace and prosperity. If Americans disregard his law and walk in their own way, they will undergo trials and tribulations and bring needless suffering, strife, and death upon themselves.[11]

Most Anglo-Israel writers feel that God is finished with the Jews and that the people who call themselves such are not really true descendents of Israel. The position expressed by Gerald L. K. Smith may be regarded as typical. Those who lived in Judea at the time of Jesus were "aliens, Canaanites, and people with strange blood" who corrupted and usurped the authority over the true Israel. These "apostates" who called themselves Jews were referred to by Jesus as the "synagogue of Satan." They posed as the seed of Abraham but were not, and Jesus identified them by saying, "Ye are of your father, the devil" who was a murderer and liar from the beginning (John 8:40-44). These "interlopers" and "imitation Israelites" framed Jesus and secured his execution because they feared that he jeopardized their authority over the people. Jesus distinguished between the devout and the apostates by referring to them as sheep and goats, and a "selection" [!] was made between those who constituted the true and the false Israel at the first Pentecost following the resurrection. The sheep were those who repented and became Christians.

The goats--the synagogue of Satan--continued to perpetuate their false doctrines by representing themselves as Abraham's seed. They launched a "world-wide progaganda campaign" to convince people that they were "God's chosen people," when in fact "there is nothing in the Scripture to establish the theory that Christ's worst enemies are God's chosen people." They "have stolen for themselves a name that belongs only to the Cross of Christ--the name Israel." The devout Israelites gathered from the face of the earth lost their identity in the blood of Christ and have been "circumcised by faith." The great covenant made with Abraham was fulfilled "in the obedience of mankind to the will of His Gospel."[12]

One variation on the continuing existence of the Jews found in this literature is that there are virtually no genuine Jews per se. The Maccabees allegedly forced Samaritans and Edomites to become Jews, and they constituted a subversive element that mingled with true Hebrews and watered down the racial stock. Yet more important is the contention that most European Jews are descended from the Khazars, a Turkic people that lived in the region of southern Russia north of the Black Sea. A ruler of the Khazars converted to Judaism and brought in Talmudic scholars to train his people in the new faith which was established in the kingdom. Two centuries later the territory was conquered by the Varangians, and those Khazars who still adhered to Judaism wandered toward the west. They became the ancestors of the Ashkenazic or east European Jews, who thus were not even Jews at all. Those who were expelled from the land by the Romans after the conquest in 70 C.E. were the progenitors of the Sephardic or Mediterranean Jews, and most of them were not pure Israelites. If there are no Jews as such, then they have no right to claim for themselves a homeland.[13]

The implications of this for modern day Jews are ominous. The Holocaust was something they brought upon themselves, because they refused to accept Christ and always functioned as a foreign element among the peoples where they lived. They refused to be assimilated and clung to the fiction that they were God's chosen people and needed to return to the land from which they had come.

Some of the most vicious antisemitic and especially anti-Zionist assertions have flowed from these premises. For instance, Alfred E. Forte, leader of "The Sect of the Lord Jesus Christ," a fundamentalist group headquartered in Pennsylvania that stresses the equality of Jesus Christ and the Father and importance of the second coming of Christ, declared in an open letter peppered with Bible references that the Jews "established a 'do your own thing religion' that the Jealous God hated and rejected." They "desecrated the temple through unbelief." As for the doctrine that the Jews are God's chosen people, it "is a lie embraced by organized religion, exploited by the Zionists, oppressors of the helpless, shedders of innocent blood, for a land that is scripturally not theirs." The Jews accepted responsibility for the death of Christ, and Israel chose to "become a nation of bastards, children that do not know their father." Satan "paid off their descendants by having the false prophets deceive the rulers of the Gentiles into supporting the Zionist lie and displacing over six million Palestinians...to establish a republic of Anti-Christ called the state of Israel, organized religion's Golden Calf."[14]

Another example is an essay by a prominent Pentecostal preacher in California, Dr. Max A. X. Clark, which discussed the ongoing Arab-Israeli conflict. The writer called Israel "a synthetic state" that "covets more territory," and the harsh treatment of the Palestinian Arabs bore witness to the "great injustice" that was being done there. "Zionist manipulators" caused the U. S. to ignore every friendly Arab gesture, and the actions of the "gangster nation" Israel was making the situation steadily worse. If the Jews initiated a war, "they would be committing their greatest blunder since their rejection of Christ the Messiah--and the resultant destruction of Jerusalem a generation later." The Israelis were "usurpers" who had no historic roots in the Holy Land, and the worst thing Americans could do would be to continue to back Israel's policies.

Clark then explained why "this Christian" did not support the Jewish state:

> If the King of the Asiatic Khazars in the seventh century had not established as the state religion of the Khazar kingdom a religious belief founded upon the pseudodox [<u>sic</u>] teaching of the Babylonian Talmud there would have been no Zionist invasion of Palestine in the 20th century, and no Zionist revolution in Palestine in 1948. The hideous and horrible consequences of Zionist aggression in the Holy Land are the result of the unbridled fanaticism of followers of the Talmud! The pseudo-religious flavor of Zionist aggression in Palestine was, of course, a form of deception calculated to enlist Christian cooperation.

He concluded by chiding his fellow believers for assigning prophetic significance to Zionism and failing "to rightly identify the true Israel in the world today" which is the Christian church. The "Ashkenazum descendants of the Khazars" who called themselves Jews could never claim ancestry with Abraham, Isaac, and Jacob because their forefathers never even saw the Holy Land. The "Chosen People" were the "righteous nation which keepeth the Truth" and recognized Jesus Christ only as the way, the truth, and the life.[15]

The extreme racialists among the Identity adherents teach that there were two groups in the world. One is the children of Yahweh, the true Israelites, who are the "seed of the woman," the white people of the world and Jesus is of this line. The other is the progeny of Lucifer, the "seed of the serpent," descended through Cain. They are the parasites who destroy culture and tremble at the thought of Jesus. The Jews belong to this line and and are thus Satan's seed. They must be thwarted and their power broken.[16] The moderates, however, who still hold to a traditional understanding of evangelical Christianity, believe that Jews can still receive Christ by faith and be saved, but of course they must abandon all their Jewishness. Nevertheless, there is no place in either program for a separate Jewish consciousness.

ANTICOMMUNISM

One of the canards most frequently found in antisemitic literature is the accusation that Jews are responsible for communism. Conservative Protestants have manifested an implacable and almost irrational hatred of communism from the Bolshevik revolution to the present, and fundamentalists in particular regard communism as the greatest and most unmitigated evil in all of history. Their rhetoric reached its greatest excesses in the 1930s and again in the Cold War years, but a revulsion to communism and marxism and anything remotely associated with these, such as liberation theology, democratic socialism, and the welfare state is evident even in much current evangelical preaching. The association of Jews with communism has been a stock-in-trade of secular antisemites throughout the twentieth century, and their ideas all too easily filtered into the preaching of evangelical conservatives who, with their penchant to condemn the moral evils of the day and to blame these on satanic conspiracies, all too frequently succumbed to the temptation to cast aspersion at "unbelieving Jews." This had the net effect of dulling their sensitivity to the kind of hatred that made the Holocaust possible.

Post-World War I fundamentalists were intrigued by the notorious _Protocols of the Meetings of the Learned Elders of Zion_, the Tsarist Russian forgery that was translated into English soon after the war. Two of the leading preachers of the interwar years, Gerald B. Winrod and Arno C. Gaebelein, touted the _Protocols_ as the work which explained the controlling influence which Jews had on the Bolshevik movement and the spread of international communism. The conspiratorial origins of communism were explained in the document--the sinister Illuminati, Karl Marx, the Jewish assault on religion, the enormous power exercised by money, utilization of the "ends justify the means" principle, promotion of civil disorder, and international cooperation by Jewish elites to achieve world domination. The fundamentalists added their own gloss on the text and maintained that anywhere from 75 to 83 percent of the Bolshevik leaders were Jews and that Jewish banking interests financed the revolution.[17]

No Cold War era figure was more bitter in his hatred of communism than W. D. Herrstrom. In an editorial in his _Bible News Flashes_ in 1955 he declared that communism was based on the teachings of the Talmud, the continuation of the traditions of the elders, which would be the system of the future antichrist. Since "86 percent" of those who set up the Bolshevik regime were Jews, it was easy to see that the antichrist himself would be a Jew. The communists formed and controlled the U.N. which aimed at world government. When this was accomplished, the antichrist would destroy the sovereignty of all nations, set himself up as the supreme dictator, and outlaw Christianity. All Christians would be regarded as "anti-Semites" and sentenced to death for refusing to worship the Jew. "The spirit of Jew-worship which stalks the world today in the political and religious world is the spirit of antichrist and is helping to set the stage for the coming and coronation of the...Jewish False Messiah."

The question facing his readers was: "Are you anti-Semitic and pro-Christian, or are you pro-Semitic and anti-Christian?" They could not be both. The "stooges of communism" had brainwashed the American public in preparation for worshipping the coming Jewish antichrist. "If you say you are not anti-Semitic, it is tantamount to saying you are not a Christian or that your profession of Christianity is not genuine." Such a person was "a Judas Iscariot playing both sides to retain prestige and popularity."[18]

Similar comments linking Jews with communism appeared with regularity in the extremist publications. An editorial in an Anglo-Israel oriented magazine, _The Answer_, affirmed without flinching:

> Any patriotic Anti-Communist Crusader who is really and honestly for America, can't help but expose the Jew as the international villain behind Communism and the great conspiracy. And if they don't expose the Jew but cleverly seek to conceal him in a maise [sic] of confusion and propaganda, they must themselves be one of the devil's crowd or a dupe.[19]

The hard rightist Christian Vanguard maintained that Hitler's persecution of the East European white peoples was the ultimate cause of his defeat. These whites wanted to join with him and forever rid the earth of the Jews, but he considered them as inferiors. Thus, the communist Jews used this division within the white race to destroy both Hitler and the anticommunist East European whites.[20]

Pat Brooks discovered that modern socialism and its off-shoot, communism, had its origins in the ancient mystical Cabala (Kabbalah) which she said was an "occult" work. She traced it through a number of medieval mystical cults, the Illuminati and Freemasons, and finally to Karl Marx. Jewish Marxists dominated the socialist movements, the Bolshevik revolution, and the Communist International. The Jewish Rothschild banking family financed the Bolsheviks even as they were backing Zionism. The Protocols described "in detail the very situation on earth today: an ominous control by an antichrist elite seeking a socialist world government." She concluded: "Possibly one of the best kept secrets in the West today is that Communism is overwhelmingly a Jewish movement."[21]

Theodore Winston Pike, who calls himself an "evangelical writer and researcher," avers that there was a "saturation level involvement of Jews in socialism during the last hundred years" and that "the great majority of Jews today are liberals" and Jewish-controlled organizations "have a vested interest in promoting and protecting liberalism." Furthermore, Jews played the leading role in the Russian revolution and the majority of all young Soviet Jews were communists. The New Deal was tolerant of communists and home and abroad, and the result was that Jewish communists penetrated the nuclear weapons program and provided Russia with the "near-entirety" of atomic and hydrogen bomb technology. The majority of the leadership of the postwar American Communist party were Jews. All the radical movements which emerged in the mid-sixties and early seventies as well as "such enduring fountains of mischief as the ACLU" contained a disproportionate number of Jews.

Pike finds that in contrast to the usual image of the "persecuted Jew" who historically has been the victim of persecution, the "evidence suggests that in fomenting international revolution, the Jews have made possible a degree of slaughter, persecution, slave-labor, and imprisonment which almost make their own sufferings pale in comparison." Why, then, do they devote themselves so single-mindedly to this "monstrous experiment" and continue to provide the leadership and zeal for such a movement? It is because Israel in her "apostate" condition intends to create the agency that will make the antichrist possible.[22]

This obsession with the allegedly Jewish origins of communism obscures the reality of hardship and persecution that is an every-day fact of life for Jews living in the Soviet Union and Eastern Europe. On the other hand, the excessive promotion of anticommunism can lead to a trivialization of the Jewish experience during World War II and play into the hands of those who downplay or deny the Holocaust.

THE DENIAL OF THE HOLOCAUST

The nation was shocked by the revelations of the Nazi death camps at the end of World War II, and for a generation Americans accepted without question the fact that as many as six million Jews perished at the hands of SS death squads operating on Soviet soil, in gas chambers in Poland, and in brutal concentration camps throughout Hitler's far-flung empire. Thus, the movement for Holocaust "revision" that began in the late 1960s, gained momentum in the 1970s, and peaked shortly after 1980 was a profoundly unsettling development.[23] Still, it is clear that extreme antisemites from the early 1950s had been working to debunk or at least downplay the extent of the German action against the European Jews, and some of this spilled over into conservative Protestant writings as well.

One of the most widely read books on the far right in the early 1950s was John Beaty's The Iron Curtain Over America. Although it was primarily a Cold War tract, it promoted the Khazar myth and the supposed Jewish role in the Bolshevik revolution. Beaty also took a pro-German stance, insisting that the "powerful Eastern European element" that dominated the Democratic party favored the killing of the "world-ruling and Khazar-hated race of 'Aryans.'" The result was the unconditional surrender policy which unnecessarily prolonged the war and led to the slaughter of many more Germans than would normally had happened. Moreover, vast numbers of aliens fleeing "Hitler's persecution" entered the United States during the war years and many more refugees afterwards. This alien-dominated government fought the war for the annihilation of Germany, which was "the historic bulwark of Christian Europe." Curiously, Beaty said nothing about Germany's Jewish victims but rather bemoaned the fate the country was suffering at the hands of such American Jews as Henry Morgenthau, Jr. This set the stage for a reassessment of Germany as the victim of crimes at the hands of Jews and communists.[24]

This and a pamphlet by Kenneth Goff, Hitler--The 20th Century Hoax (1954) were praised by W. D. Herrstrom in 1955 as truthful accounts of what happened during the war. Drawing upon the ideas in these, the Baptist preacher claimed that Hitler was a Kremlin stooge who was picked and trained by the communists to destroy Germany. The Fuehrer was also a Jew, his program was financed by Jews, and he had Jewish advisers. His "so-called anti-Semitism" was designed to fool the German people and to drag America into a war so it would shell out all its wealth, war equipment, and military know-how to the Russian Bolsheviks and thereby enable them to conquer the world. As for the millions of Jews that Hitler was supposed to have murdered, they "were smuggled into the United States illegally, many of them across the Mexican border."

Herrstrom contended that "a few of us who had done extensive research and were blessed with that rare gift of 'discernment'" knew all along that Hitler was a communist and not an anti-Semite and did not believe the newspaper reports about the terrible persecution of Jews in Germany. On the contrary:

> The communist "big lie" about anti-Semitism in Germany was calculated to stampede Americans into defending, financing, protecting, and building up the Russian Bolsheviks to a place of world power. What anti-Semitism there was in Germany was calculated, not to kill the Jews, but to move them out of Germany and into the United States.

They were first "steeped in Marxism" and then ejected and scattered to the ends of the earth in order to "leaven" the whole world with Marxist ideologies and prepare the way for the Reds to take over. Those fundamentalists who believed the communist-controlled press were only deceived by Hitler. They believed the "big lie" that he was an anti-Semite, turned aside from preaching the gospel of Christ, and wasted millions of words denouncing Hitler, "only to find they themselves were the greatest anti-Semites because they were denouncing the Jew, Hitler." If their interpretation of Genesis 12:1-3 were correct, that is, those who criticized a Jew came under God's "curse," then every member of the "faction of Fundamentalism is under a curse for not approving of Hitler."[25]

Herrstrom and others like him saw the Jews as the force behind both Hitler and Soviet communism. A variation on this theme was the spurious "Speech of Rabbi Emanuel Rabinovich Before a Special Meeting of the Emergency Council of European Rabbis in Budapest, Hungary, on January 12, 1952." This secret address "revealed" that the Jews intended to precipitate World War III within five years in order to achieve their goal of world domination. It was noted that during the 1930s "our propaganda campaign" aroused anti-American passions in Germany while at the same time it stirred anti-German feelings in America. Now the same thing was being done throughout the world. "A war fever is being worked up in Russia by an incessant anti-American barrage, while a nation wide anti-Communist scare is sweeping America." The campaign was forcing the smaller nations to ally with one or the other of these, and it would be necessary to stage anti-Semitic outbreaks in the United States to weld the people into a devoted anti-Russian unit. Also, "we may have to repeat the grim days of World War II when we were forced to let the Hitlerite bandits sacrifice some of our people" in order to provide the documentation that would "justify our trial and execution of the leaders of America and Russia as war criminals....The death of a few thousand Jews in exchange for world leadership is indeed a small price to pay."

The Rabbi Rabinovich speech has been repeatedly recycled in antisemitic literature, and in fact it turned up again only last year in a leaflet produced by Mark Margoian, a lone wolf Christian anticommunist racist in Waukegan, Illinois, who calls himself, "God's True Prophet for the End of the World." But, this is simply a document that was manufactured in 1952 by one of the leading American antisemites, Eustace Mullins. Not a shred of evidence exists to show that such a meeting ever took place or this addresses was given.[26]

Another twist is to declare that Hitler was justified in taking action against the German Jews. In the 1950s Herrstrom said Hitler tried "to outlaw Jewish prejudice against Gentiles," but he failed. It was this "whining attitude" of complaining about Gentile prejudice that "caused the Jews to wear out their welcome among all the nations of the earth." Three decades later, retired U. S. Army Colonel Gordon "Jack" Mohr, who according to his brochure "is a well-known fundamental Baptist lay evangelist," asserted that Jews were driven from every country where they took refuge, not because of their religion but their practices. The Jew's primary allegiance was always to Jewry, and thus he never could be trusted. Mohr then stated that Jews were a "parasitic people" that lived off the host nation, sucked its economic lifeblood, and controlled its media and government. The Jews in Germany were not hated

> because they were "non-Aryans," as we have been told by the Jewish controlled press, but because when the financial collapse of Germany occurred following World War I, the Jews descended on this unhappy country, buying up German property for a few cents on the dollar and making the lives of the German people a nightmare.[27]

Stan Rittenhouse, a stockbroker and political lobbyist who also claims to be a graduate of Bob Jones University and "a deacon in a fundamental Bible-believing Baptist church," reported that "more and more historians are now recognizing that the reason Hitler rose to power in the early 1930's was due to the way the Jewish community was exploiting Germany and her people." The defeat in World War I brought about devastating economic destruction and the Jews took advantage of the situation. The resulting exploitation contributed to the later rise of antisemitism. They were like the "carpetbaggers" who arrived in the South after the Civil War.

As is the case in any country where this happens, when the Jewish community got the upper hand in Germany, they abused their power and demonstrated "intolerance" for the non-Jewish community. As the contempt, ill will, and arrogance resulting from the notion of Jewish superiority over non-Jews surfaced, the reaction on the part of those being taken advantage of was antisemitism. It was essentially a defense mechanism. "So, in reality, the Jews become their worse [sic] enemy. They are the cause of their opposition; the effects are their victims responding in defense." The same is now true in America, where the "Zionists" have "increased power and influence" and are promoting anti-Christianity. When the Jews rejected Christ, they rejected tolerance of othere, and their intolerance is bringing a reaction.

Getting back to Germany, Rittenhouse cited Reader's Digest to support his contention that "a grave Jewish problem" existed there. The Polish Jews were pushing in on the country and already had obtained "an unduly large share of good professional positions" in Berlin and Hamburg. In Berlin, half the lawyers and medical doctors were Jews, the largest and most important newspapers were under Jewish control, and they had made great inroads on the educational system. "Starting from the undoubted facts that a Jewish minority had secured an overlarge measure of professinal success, and that in some cases the preferment was due to racial influence, Hitler reached the position that 'there can be no good Jew.'" From this the writer concluded: "Among other negative factors in pre-Hitler Germany, the Jews were Jewish racists, pomoting each other while, at the same, denying opportunity to the non-Jew. More than likely, this added to the growing ill will toward the Jewish community."[28]

Like their secular counterparts, the conservative Protestant antisemites move from blaming Jews for Germany's action to denying the Holocaust ever happened or at least trivializing it and scaling it down to where it was only one of many examples of man's inhumanity to man in the twentieth century. Rousas John Rushdoony, the godfather of the "theonomist" faction in evangelicalism, attacked the prevailing accounts of the Holocaust in one of his books: "Did the Nazis actually execute many thousands, tens, or hundred thousands of Jews? Men to whom such murders were nothing had to blow up the figure to millions."[29] Rittenhouse reported that historians have begun to review the Holocaust "in a more calm and objective manner." Jewish statistics revealed that in 1933 there were only 550,000 Jews in Germany and the exodus had already begun. "This is a long way from six million." There were only 3.1 million in Poland as well. "Consequently, the figure of 6 million is beginning to appear a bit high."[30]

A Canadian Christian warrior against the Jews, Malcolm Ross, insisted that a policy of extermination was not in effect, and the piles of corpses seen in the pictures were not gassed victims but those who died of starvation, disease, and Allied air attacks. "Knowing the connection between Communism and Judaism, it might arouse interest to know that ALL the 'extermination' camps are located in what is now Communist-controlled territory." He added that some Germans who confessed to thse crimes at Nuremberg did so under tortore. (His source for this is Senator Joseph McCarthy!) Also, there were no blueprints in existence outlining gas chambers or any orders from them. The International Red Cross report in 1947 found no evidence of genocide. "Because Christians are now learning to count, there is tremendous pressure to keep this information from getting out."[31]

On the other hand, there were other holocausts. In 1981 Pat Brooks declared that there was "a red flow of blood wherever Illuminist or Marxist ideas have taken root--145 million lives since 1917." That figure represented "_only_ the victims of Communism" and none of the war casualties from both World Wars. "_There_ is a holocaust, like no other! Yet we continue to hear about a holocaust of six million Jews dying under Hitler, although this figure has been grossly exaggerated." (She mentioned books by two notorious far right authors, James Combs and Arthur R. Butz, as her authority for scaling down the number.)

She complained that she had long been irritated by the whole "holocaust hassle." To be sure, any murdered by others oppressing them were too many, whether six or six million. What amazed her was "that we _constantly_ hear about the Nazi atrocity, while we hear _nothing_ of the 145 million plus who have died and are dying daily under Communism!" Four years later, she had upped the ante by 10 percent. "Oddly enough, Hitler's atrocities against the alleged six million Jews are widely regarded as a 'holocaust,' but Red murders of _161 million_ since 1917 are not! _Why?_"[32]

From north of the border came a query from Malcolm Ross: "What about the Ukrainean holocaust of the early 1930's, instigated by Communism, which is reported to have killed over 7 million Ukrainians? Or what about the Cambodian holocaust, or even the brutal Beirut slaughter following the Israeli invasion? And what about the Abortion Holocaust which is taking place daily in our Christian lands?"[33]

Of all the forms of antisemitism, the endeavor to debunk the Holocaust is the most reprehensible. Fortunately, in spite of the exceptions just cited, most conservatives who were critical of Jews were not prepared to buy into this absurd obfuscation of reality. Nevertheless, the tendency of some to trivialize the Holocaust or to scale down the proportions of the Nazi action to where it was just a by-product of a vast war effort must be viewed with concern.

"FOR FEAR OF THE JEWS"

Why do "Bible-believing" Christians not stand up more firmly against the Jews and counter their pernicious influence in the world? The antisemites customarily respond by referring to a biblical passage, John 19:20, which described a meeting of Jesus' disciples shortly after his resurrection where he appeared to them. They had gathered in a room behind locked doors "for fear of the Jews." (The phrase also appears three other times in John--7:13, 9:22, and 19:38.)

In other words, these people see Jewish power as all-pervasive. They claim that various forms of pressure are brought to to bear on Christians to silence their criticism. Those who dare to question even the "terrorist acts of the Zionists" (namely, in Palestine) are labeled as "cursed of God" because of Genesis 12:3. One evangelical said that "Satan" has succeeded in making the epithet "anti-Semitic" into "a weapon of terror far more frightening to Christians than the scriptural 'anti<u>christ</u>' term!" The bankers who hold the bonds on or have loaned money to evangelical churches will foreclose on them if they should venture to speak against the Jews. And, because of the key places in government which they occupy, they are in a position to persecute Christians. As Rittenhouse puts it:

> If the Jews had the absolute power in the United States like they do in Israel, there would be persecution and prosecution of the Christians by this "alien elite" like America has never seen in its history. Should the Jewish community continue to gain influence in the American government, especially the bureaucracy and <u>courts</u>, the American Christians will get a taste of the persecution coming by those who oppose Christ. Toward the end of the Church Age, the largest, most effective force against Christianity will come from the Jewish community worldwide and Israel in particular.[34]

Although this sounds like nothing more than the rantings of a paranoid bigot, it is the perception and belief of many in the evangelical and fundamentalist churches. It is something that will not easily be countered, even though one unrelentingly perseveres in giving people the facts about Jewish culture and beliefs and the history of Jewish-Christian relations through the ages.

To conclude, those in the conservative Protestant churches who are concerned about reconciliation between Christians and Jews are faced by a real challenge. They have their work cut out for them.

ACKNOWLEDGEMENTS

The author expresses his appreciation to the The Vidal Sassoon International Center for the Study of Antisemitism at the Hebrew University of Jerusalem and to the Research Committee of Indiana State University for financial assistance in the preparation of this essay.

REFERENCES

1. <u>Capital Voice</u> 16 (Aug. 1, 1967): 2.

2. Gerald B. Winrod, <u>The Jewish Assault on Christianity</u> (Wichita, KS: The Defenders, 1935), 9. 33. 39. This work has been reprinted and is for sale on many of the far right book lists.

3. Glen Berry, <u>Freemasonry: Antichrist Upon Us</u> (N.p., N.d.), 51-53.

4. For a concise analysis and refutation of such falsifications of the Talmud, see Morris Kominsky, <u>The Hoaxers: Plain Liars, Fancy Liars, and Damned Liars</u> (Boston: Branden Press, 1970), 166-80.

5. Quoted in Arnold Forster, Anti-Semitism in the United States in 1947 (New York: Anti-Defamation League, 1948), 20.

6. John L. Bray, Israel in Bible Prophecy (Lakeland, FL: The Author, 1983), 59-60, 75.

7. W. D. Herrstrom, "Why Christ Couldn't Have Nationality," Bible News Flashes (Galva, IL) 16 (Feb. 1955): 4-5.

8. Gerald L. K. Smith, Is It Unscriptural to Criticize the Jews? (Los Angeles: Christian Nationalist Crusade, n.d.), leaflet.

9. The Answer (Tacoma, WA) 2 (June 1969): 3-4.

10. Gerald L. K. Smith, Who Are God's Chosen People? Certainly Not the Jews! (As We Now Know Jews). This undated brochure is currently distributed by the Sons of Liberty in Metairie, Louisiana, a mail order book service which features extremist and racist materials.

11. The Answer 2 (June 1969): 3.

12. The Khazar legend is part of the stock-in-trade of antisemites. Just when it first appeared is a matter of debate. The British racialist Nesta Webster mentioned it in the 1920s, while some utilize the apostate American Jew Benjamin H. Freedman as their source, and his pamphlets on this are frequently quoted. Others credit the novelist Arthur Koestler, whose book The Thirteenth Tribe (New York: Random House, 1976) popularizes the story. Pat Brooks, for one, gives credit to both Freedman and Koestler. Hear, O Israel, 54-62, and A Call to War (Fletcher, NC: New Puritan Library, 1985), 52, 55-56.

13. Open letter, Oct. 24, 1985, copy in the author's possession. The biblical citations are omitted.

14. Max A. X. Clark, "Hell over the Holy Land," National Christian Journal (Oakland, CA) 10 (1956): 4-7.

15. Noteworthy works that treat various aspects of the Identity movement are James Coates, Armed and Dangerous: The Rise of the Survivalist Right (New York: Hill and Wang, 1987; Philip Finch, God, Guts and Guns: A Close Look at the Radical Right (New York: Putnam, 1983); "The 'Identity Churches': A Theology of Hate," ADL Facts 28 (Spring 1983): 5-16; and Anti-Defamation League of B'nai B'rith, Extremism on the Right: A Handbook (New York: ADL, 1983).

16. See Gerald B. Winrod, The Truth about the Protocols (Wichita, KS: The Defenders, 1935); and Arno C. Gaebelein, The Conflict of the Ages (New York: Our Hope, 1933), 95-103. Both books as well as the 1934 edition of the Protocols have been reprinted by extreme rightist groups and may be purchased from mail order booksellers. The Kansas-based Winrod was clearly the leading Jew-baiter among the fundamentalists, but by the late 1930s he had begun to lose much of his following. He was one of the defendants in the 1944 sedition trial of American "fascists." His career is traced in Leo P. Ribuffo, The Old Christian Right: The Protestant Far Right from the Great Depression to the Cold War (Philadelphia: Temple University Press, 1983). Holocaust scholar David A. Rausch points out that Gaebelein personally had a deep love for Jews and despised antisemitism, but he was quite attracted by conspiracy theories. Thus, he saw the Bolshevik leaders as "apostate" Jews who sacrificed their faith for the communist movement, and the Protocols seemed to him at the time to be an accurate account of what unbelieving Jews intended to do. He later repudiated this view and dropped the passage from subsequent editions of his book. Rausch, Arno C. Gaebelein, 1861-1945: Irenic Fundamentalist and Scholar (Lewiston, NY: Edwin Mellen Press, 1983), 131-46.

17. Bible News Flashes 16 (May 1955): 6-7.

18. The Answer 5 (Dec. 1972): 25.

19. Christian Vanguard, no. 2 (June-July 1971): 3.

20. Theodore Winston Pike, Israel: Our Duty...Our Dilemma (Oregon City, OR: Big Sky Press, 1984), 125-40.

21. Pat Brooks, The Return of the Puritans (Fletcher, NC: New Puritan Library, 1983), 59-78; Hear, O Israel, 60, 71, 101-4; A Call to War, 30, 59-60.

22. For an introduction to the controversy and its chief players, see Frank P. Mintz, The Liberty Lobby and the American Right: Race, Conspiracy, and Culture (Westwood, CT: Greenwood Press, 1985), 107-26.

23. John Beaty, The Iron Curtain Over America (Dallas: Wilkinson Publishing Co., 1951), 74-78. It has also been reprinted by a right wing bookseller.

24. Bible News Flashes 16 (Jan. 1955): 8-9.

25. Kominsky, The Hoaxers, 127-29; Margoian leaflet dated July 4, 1987 in possession of the author.

26. Bible News Flashes 15 (June 1954): 12, 14; Jack Mohr, Hell Hath No Fury Like! (Bay St. Louis, MS: The Author, n.d.), 3.

27. Stan Rittenhouse, "For Fear of The Jews" (Vienna, VA: The Exhorters, 1982), 208-9. The identifying quote is on the book's dust jacket.

28. Rushdoony, The Institutes of Biblical Law, quoted in the Long Island Newsday, May 30, 1982, p. 17.

29. Rittenhouse, "For Fear of THe Jews", 129-30.

30. Malcolm Ross, Christianity Vs Judeo-Christianity (Moncton, N.B.: Stronghold Publishing Co., 1984), pp. 19-20, 29.

31. Brooks, Hear, O Israel, 106; A Call to War, 37.

32. Ross, Christianity Vs Judeo-Christianity, 19.

33. Gordon "Jack" Mohr, Woe Unto Ye Fundamentalists! (Bay St. Louis, MS: The Author, n.d.), 3-4; Brooks, A Call to War, 31-32; Rittenhouse, "For Fear of the Jews", 126-27.

"HAVE YE REMEMBERED THE JEWS, MINE ANCIENT COVENANT PEOPLES?": THE JEWS, THE MORMONS AND THE HOLOCAUST

Douglas F. Tobler

Brigham Young University
403 KMB, Provo, UT 84602

In the Book of Mormon, an ancient document revered as scripture by members of the Church of Jesus Christ of Latter-day Saints (Mormons), there is this passage of chastisement and warning from an ancient prophet:

> And what thank they [the Gentiles] the Jews for the Bible which they receive from them? Yea, what do the Gentiles mean? Do they remember the travails, and the labors, and the pains of the Jews, and their diligence unto me, in bringing forth salvation unto the Gentiles?
>
> O ye Gentiles, have ye remembered the Jews, mine ancient covenant people? Nay; but ye have cursed them, and have hated them, and have not sought to recover them. But behold, I will return all these things upon your own heads; for I the Lord have not forgotten my people. (Book of Mormon, 1982)

This scripture captures something of the unique positive relationship which Mormons have had throughout their century and half's existence with Jews, but it also may be understood as a prophetic for the way Gentiles--Mormons included--have treated Jews. Unlike much of traditional Christianity, Mormons have no history of anti-Semitism; on the contrary, while they too blamed the Jews for the crucifixion of Jesus and viewed later persecutions as God's punishment, at the same time they believed the covenant with Abraham was still in force, identified themselves as the Josephite part of Israel,--even if by adoption--thus shared with Jews in both the blessings and responsibilities of that Abrahamic Covenant. In spite of their sins and backsliding, so Mormons believe, God has not forgotten his covenant people, the Jews; He will yet gather them back to Palestine and Jerusalem, will help them fight their mortal battles after their return, and finally will bring about their redemption as they recognize Jesus as Messiah (McConkie, 1958). One Mormon scholar has called this Mormon view of the Jews, with its emphasis upon the Jewish return to Palestine, a kind of "religious Zionism".

> The Jewish return is neither a recent innovation nor a passing fancy in LDS [Mormon] dogma but rather a quite fundamental teaching advanced for a century and a half by nearly every possible level of ecclesiastical authority. Latter-day Saint scripture is saturated with the idea. . .For nearly a century and a half, the idea of the Jewish return has been as sacred to Mormons as it has been to Jews. From 1820 until 1967, hundreds of speeches, prayers, pamphlets and books demonstrated the breadth and depth of the Latter-day Saints' belief regarding this aspect of their gospel plan. According to them, the Lord has chosen the family of Israel to effect his purposes on earth, and the two most important clans in this family are currently the Jews and the Mormons (Green, 1967).

Mormon philosemitism has not been just theological, but practical as well. The first Mormon prophet, Joseph Smith, studied Hebrew under a Jewish scholar in the Mormon city of Nauvoo, Illinois. In 1840 he sent an Apostle, Orson Hyde, to dedicate the land of Palestine to the return of the Jews. Later in the 19th Century, a small but vigorous Jewish community grew up in the Mormon Kingdom of Utah. One Jewish scion and historian, Leon Watters, has described the harmony between the two groups as "a strange phenomenon which made the contact of present-day [1952] Jews with the Mormon people in Utah unique in the annals of history" (Watters, 1952). Nineteenth Century Mormons also viewed themselves--in light of their own unique half-century of persecution in American society--as "co-sufferers" with the European Jews, whose fate they followed closely in the press (Van Orden). Mormons also became outspoken supporters of Zionism already in the 19th Century, considered the Balfour Declaration a major step toward the realization of the Jewish return and therefore a highly visible fulfillment of prophecy, both ancient and modern, and worked in the United States after 1945 for the establishment of the State of Israel.

Nevertheless, in spite of this unique record, Mormons were, like most of the rest of Christendom, ominously silent during the years 1933-45, when European Jews rapidly moved from crisis to catastrophe could have used any and all, even Mormon influence and moral support. Mormons thus became part of the mass of Christian and American bystanders who failed to recognize in time that what was happening to Jews was not merely an internal German political matter, that became swallowed up and to outside observers partially lost in the war, but a universal moral attack by the incarnation of evil. Christians ought to have demanded action in defense of endangered fellowmen, in keeping with the great commandment of both Judaism and Christianity to love neighbor as self. In this way, Mormons, too, failed to "remember [God's] ancient covenant peoples."

The Mormon Church came to this unfortunate position, however, <u>not</u> from the background of any kind of theological or institutional anti-Semitism, although it would appear that isolated individual members, both in America and in Germany, may have contracted a form of the disease from their contemporary surroundings. Mormon indifference stemmed primarily from an over-emphasis on the transcendent nature of the message; they were more interested in assuring eternal life than in dealing fully with the human problems in the here-and-now. Their silence also derived from the traditional New Testament Church-State doctrine which they shared with other Christians, from their own unique historical-political experiences, from their American vantage point, and from their concern not to endanger the lives of their co-religionists in Germany by criticizing the Hitler regime. Mormons were also small and powerless; having had no ties with other Christian Churches, they saw themselves unable to make a difference. At the same time, Mormon leadership vigorously condemned the war--and all war--as an evil and undoubtedly saw the Holocaust as another element of the war, deriving from the same evil source.

I.

Given Mormon-Jewish history, one might have expected something different. The most visible expression of Mormon "religious Zionism," the Palestine Mission of Orson Hyde, came early in the church's history. "Let the land become abundantly fruitful when possessed by its rightful heirs," Hyde had prayed in 1844. "Incline them [the Jews] to gather in upon this land according to thy word. . . . Inspire the hearts of Kings and the powers of the earth to look with a friendly eye toward this place." Before 1930 four additional official visits by Church leaders were made to reinforce the commitment; each time on their return to Utah they brought the Mormon community up-to-date on what was taking place there (Barron, 1979).

During the same years when Mormon periodicals and newspapers not only turned out a steady stream of news, about the Jewish settlements in Palestine and the progress of the Zionist Movement, they also chronicled and bemoaned the miseries befalling European Jews, especially the rise of modern anti-Semitism in Europe (Barron, 1979).

Closer to home, the relationship between Jews and Mormons in Utah had continued to be good even into the years following World War I. Writing in 1981 after over a half-century of life among the Mormons, Professor Louis Zucker, an English scholar at the University of Utah, reflected on the earlier Jewish Mormon experience in "Zion":

> The Church [Mormon] has done the Jews deeds of kindness: in the early days, the gift of the Jews' original cemetery incorporated now in the larger B'nai Israel cemetery, and the loan of church buildings in Temple Square for High Holyday worship before there was a synagogue--Brigham Young, the benefactor in both ways; [and there was] the brotherly hand extended in gratitude with a nice check to Congregation Montefiore, seventy-five years ago [in 1906]. (Zucker, 1981)

Earlier, Utah had shocked the nation and caused a stir in 1916 by electing a native German-Jew, Simon Bamberger, its first non-Mormon governor. Jews had rarely achieved such political recognition in states with much larger Jewish populations. Bamberger had been nominated on the Democratic ticket by one of the Mormon Church's hierarchy and a distinguished intellectual, B.H. Roberts, who told his audience, "When our ancestors were back in early Europe drinking vodka or its equivalent from the skulls of their enemies, the ancestors of my candidate were in Syria and Palestine contributing to literature, the arts and commerce." (Salt Lake Tribune, 1916) Bamberger was supported by numerous other prominent church leaders, although his Republican opponent, Nephi Morris was a well-known and respected Mormon. (Morn, 1966)

Five years later, while speaking in New Zealand as part of a year-long, round-the-world trip in 1921, Mormon Apostle David O. McKay, a former educator and later a member of the Church's First Presidency during the Holocaust years waxed almost euphoric over the significance of the Balfour Declaration. His views are typical of numerous expressions about Jews by Mormons from 1917 until well into the 1920s:

> Christmas, 1917, ought to have been, as it undoubtedly was in many hearts, one of the most glorious celebrations of our Lord for over 1600 years. What did it mean? It meant the door was open for the return of the Jews to their own land. Isn't it a significant thing that the Prime Minister of England said that the Holy Land should now be set apart for the stricken Jew? (Taylor, 1921).

He then offered a prophecy:

> In a few months my companion [Hugh J. Cannon] and I will stand on that same spot [where Apostle Orson Hyde had stood in Palestine in the 1841] not many years, comparatively speaking of the past, since 1843-[sic]-now 1921. It may be our privilege, and yours if you go there, to go into a Jewish nation presided over by a Jew, a President of the Jewish Republic, the first to preside over a Jewish nation since the Savior. (Taylor, 1921)

That same year, 1921, apparently during an outbreak of anti-Semitism, the Mormon Church President Heber J. Grant, who, like his predecessors, was revered as a prophet, made the following official declaration in the Church's World Conference, April 5. This statement constitutes the official Church position on this matter from 1921 to the present, and there is reason to believe that it represented -- and still represents -- the conviction and sentiment of the overwhelming majority of Church members:

> Some of you may be familiar with the agitation that is going on at the present time, in the publications, against the Jewish people. There should be no ill-will, and I am sure there is none, in the heart of any true Latter-day Saint, toward the Jewish people. . . .And let no Latter-day Saint be guilty of taking any part in any crusade against these people. I believe in no other part of the world is there as good a feeling in the hearts of mankind towards the Jewish people as among the Latter-day Saints. (Grant, 1921)

This same evaluation was made six decades later by Louis Zucker, who had arrived in Salt Lake City in 1928. Zucker was an informed observer during the whole era before, during and after the Holocaust. Few if any people, Jews or Mormons, understood the relationship as well. He provides clear insight into Mormon attitudes toward Jews. On the subject of anti-Semitism among the Mormons, Zucker wrote:

> I know that anti-Semitism festers in varying degrees in some Mormons as in other Gentiles and that anti-Semitic publications have been widely distributed from places in Utah. . . . So far as I am aware, I have not personally suffered from anti-Semitism. . . . I have perceived no signs of anti-Semitism in any office, school or government, where I was known, or known to be a Jew . . . . Perhaps others have seen and heard anti-Semitic attitudes and remarks among Mormons beyond my awareness. This [emphasis in original] may safely be said: there is probably no Christian-Gentile culture which is less disposed to anti-Semitism than the Mormon culture here in Zion. (Zucker, 1981)

Zucker also recalled some specifics; for example, at the time of Hitler's coming to power in 1933, his fellow professors -- mostly Mormon -- at the University of Utah thought him the best person to "present a paper attempting to explain why the Nazis were oppressing the

Jews." At about the same time, he was invited by the editor of the Church-owned Deseret News to write an editorial informing its readers about an upcoming World Zionist Congress (Zucker, 1981).

Zucker and his wife were not lukewarm, unbelieving Jews. Nor was he one to gloss over differences. As a convinced Zionist, none could misunderstand his allegiance and commitment:

> Mind you, my wife and I were not assimilated Jews. Our lifestyle and theirs [the Mormons] diverged. We had our own Sabbath, our own holy days and historical commemorations. I did not eat certain prohibited foods, the synagogue was our church, we had our own symbols, we had interests and concerns as son and daughter of the Jewish people, we had substantial knowledge about Jewish matters that they did not have. . . .Could it be there would not have been so much rapport between them and us had we been assimilated Jews? (Zucker, 1981).

Indeed, Zucker maintained in retrospect, it would have been "difficult for us, if not impossible, to stay in Salt Lake City any longer than we had to" if there had not been a vibrant Jewish community there. (Zucker, 1981)

As a faithful, believing Jew Zucker bridled at the tendency of Mormons to "magnify similarities" and "etherealize differences" between themselves and Jews, a habit Mormons still indulge in. Then, as now, Mormons tended to be long on sympathy and short on knowledge and understanding of what Jews were and what they believe. He rightly contrasted such examples the "Christ idea, which seems to me to be heart-central in Mormonism" and the "Talmud, which, these two thousand years, almost, has been central to Judaism, its heart and soul." "There is" he concluded, "simply no meeting ground between the Mormon line of argument and the Pharisaic or Rabbinic development of Scripture into the Talmud." And, then, presciently, for its impact during the Holocaust years, the "one [Mormonism] speaks of Salvation in the next world; the other speaks of Halachah, the way, ethical conduct in human relations." (Zucker, 1981)

Thus, on the eve of the Jewish crisis in Germany here was a case where Jews, an incredible minority, living in the only place in the world where they were considered Gentiles, had developed with a Christian religious faith a happy relationship which was basically satisfying to both. Mormons may have even had a better relationship with Jews than with other Christian Churches that had persecuted them so vigorously. Still, Mormons were inclined, as Arnold Green has pointed out, to see their concern for the Jewish destiny as more a confirmation of their own prophecies and less for recognizing Jews as fellow human beings and children of the same God.

II.

When Hitler and the Nazis came to power in 1933, the Mormon church had an estimated 700,000 members, mostly clustered in the American Mountain West. The dominant governing power of the Church rested in the First Presidency, a triumvirate dominated by the president and prophet--God's mouthpiece on earth--Heber J. Grant, a man with strong pro-Jewish sentiments. He had been Church president since 1917. His counselors, J. Reuben Clark Jr., and David O. McKay, were also men of broad education and experience. Clark had already made a reputation as a respected international lawyer and diplomat; he had served as Undersecretary of State and recently, as American ambassador to Mexico. He had had the most political experience of the three and his voice played a considerable role where political decisions were concerned.

Ironically, though having had the most international experience, he had strong isolationist and even pacifist tendencies. Unlike Grant and McKay, Clark was less enthusiastic about Jews, having had some unhappy experiences while living in the Eastern United States. Still, it is difficult to see him as being anti-Semitic (Clark, 1988). Both Grant and Clark had ties with the larger American business and political communities, but they were hardly major players. By contrast, McKay was an educator, whose perspective was more internationalist, undoubtedly enhanced by his trip around the world in 1921. But for all three, political matters were considerably less significant than fulfilling the mission of the church, which was to bring the message of the restoration of the original Christian Church to the entire world and to gain as many converts as possible. This, they and all Mormons believed, was the best--and, in the end, only--way to bring peace in the world and individual salvation in the world to come. Grant articulated it succinctly, as he had done many times before, in a radio address entitled "A Message to the World," broadcast by sixty-eight stations in the U.S. and Canada on May 12, 1935, and later published in Der Stern, the official voice for German-speaking Mormons. The message was "to preach faith in God and Jesus Christ, to reaffirm the eternal nature of life and man, and to tell the world that Mormonism was original Christianity restored with all its truths, authority and ordinances" (Grant, 1935). All else was secondary to Mormons.

The Church's policy toward governments reflected the traditional New Testament separation of power between this world and the one beyond in a formulation by Joseph Smith known as Article 12 of a kind of Church creed called The Articles of Faith. It states: "We believe in being subject to Kings, president, rulers, and magistrates, and in obeying, honoring and sustaining the law." Virtually every Mormon wherever he or she lived in the world, knew this statement and considered it the official position on the matter.

A fuller explication of the Mormon canonical views on the relationship of church and state is found in another book of modern scripture, the Doctrine and Covenants, divine revelations given to Joseph Smith and his successors. Section 134 states:

> We believe that governments were instituted of God for the benefit of man, and that he holds men accountable for their acts in relation to them, both in making laws and administering them, for the good and safety of the society.
>
> We believe that no government can exist in peace, except such laws are framed and held inviolate as will secure to each individual the free exercise of conscience, the right and control of property, and the protection of life.
>
> We believe that all men are bound to sustain and uphold the respective governments in which they reside, while protected in their inherent and inalienable rights by the laws of such governments; and that sedition and rebellion are unbecoming every citizen thus protected, and should be punished accordingly; and that all governments have a right to enact such laws as in their own judgments are best calculated to secure the public interest; at the same time, however, holding sacred the freedom of conscience.
>
> We do not believe it just to mingle religious influence with civil government, whereby one religious society is fostered and another proscribed in its spiritual privileges, and the individual rights of its members, as citizens, denied. (Doctrine and Covenants, Sec. 134)

While the thrust of these declarations is clearly to admonish Mormons to support civil governments, the command is not absolute. Mormons are to "sustain and uphold the respective government . . . while protected in their inherent and inalienable rights." Governments are also no longer worthy of support if they do not "hold sacred the freedom of conscience" of their citizens. In other revelations, Joseph Smith was told that "That law of the land which is constitutional, supporting that principle of freedom in maintaining rights and privileges belongs to all mankind" and that "I, the Lord God, make you free, therefore you are free indeed; and the law also maketh you free." (Doctrine and Covenants, Sec. 98) Mormon doctrine had also justified the American Revolution and the establishment of the American Constitution:

> Therefore, it is not right that any man should be in bondage one to another.
>
> And for this purpose have I established the Constitution of this land [USA], by the hands of wise men whom I raised up unto this very purpose, and redeemed the land by the shedding of blood. (Doctrine & Covenants 101)

Mormons were under obligation to support legal governments -- but not any price.

The tension between Church and State had been heightened by more than a half-century of confrontation with the American federal and state governments before 1900, as well as with virtually all European governments in countries where Mormons had proselyted. The policy of confrontation gave way to one of accommodation as Utah was granted statehood in 1896 and Mormons began to find their place in American society. With the exception of polygamy, no beliefs had been surrendered. Mormons were to be "in" the world, but not "of" it. In the process the Church had grown in numbers and influence; it could in this way better achieve its primary transcendent mission following in an ever secularizing world, but also a world of increasing religious diversity and toleration.

These conditions also caused the Church to begin to change its policy of "gathering new European converts to the U.S. and Utah. Throughout most of the 19th century, Europeans who joined the Mormon Church were vigorously counseled to emigrate to "Zion" in order to strengthen the fledgling kingdom in the American West. But by 1900, they were asked to remain. The Church had gained enough strength to survive, and there were fewer economic opportunities in Utah than before. European converts were not punished if they continued to emigrate--and many German Mormons did in the Weimar days after the turmoil and privation of World War I--but the Church policy was clear. At the same time, the Church would also be strengthened by building second and third generation Mormon families in other countries besides the U.S. and Canada. This sizing up of economic conditions in America, and especially the Mountain West, together with the reversal of the policy of gathering, may have later been one factor in Mormon leaders' not speaking out in support of the policy of rescue for German and European Jews, although Utah Senator Elbert D. Thomas, an active Mormon, was one of the few in Congress in the sad days of the Holocaust to work for the Jewish rescue effort (Wyman, 1984). But, all these developments emphasized the Mormon desire to "get along" with a widening variety of governments, except the Communists, in order to achieve their spiritual objectives. This did not mean that Mormons were not concerned about the here-and-now, as later unique welfare achievements in the age of the Depression would demonstrate; but they would accept "some political limitations" as long as the message of salvation could be preached and members protected in the practice of their faith.

III.

It is against this background that the Mormons confronted Hitler's Third Reich, both in Germany and in the United States. Mormons had been proselyting in Germany since 1850, but had had relatively little success until after World War I. In the years immediately after the war, Mormon conversions in Germany skyrocketed to between 1100 and 1800 each year until 1924. By 1930, Germany had more Mormons than any other country in the world--12,000--except the United States (Scharffs, 1970). In both countries there was great optimism for the Mormon future in Germany.

There was, notwithstanding the prejudices of World War I, a strong corresponding pro-German sentiment among Mormons in Utah. Joseph Smith had admired the German language and the Luther translation of the Bible. There was, in addition, by 1933, a sizable, active and respected first and second generation German community as well as literally thousands of former German missionaries who had lived in that country among the people for at least three years, had learned the language, and had come to love the people who had fed, sheltered and supported them. Mormons felt a strong identification with the country and people, admired many of their national character traits, and viewed the culture as one of the greatest in the world. Even the most prominent Jews in the community, both those like Alexander Neibauer and Moritz Rosenbaum, who had converted, as well as Zucker, Bamberger and the Auerbachs, who had not, were German Jews who took pride in their heritage. In the Mormon community as elsewhere, before 1933, there was an unusual compatibility between being pro-German and pro-Jewish.

Mormon leaders were also sympathetic. J. Reuben Clark believed, with John Maynard Keynes and others, that Germans had not received a fair deal by the Allies in the Versailles Treaty, and because of this, he thought he could understand why Germans, in their desire for recognition and restoration of their injured national pride, had turned to Hitler (Clark, 1987). But, if there was support for things German, there is no evidence that Mormon leaders or members generally ever believed in or sympathized with National Socialist doctrine, although they could support some ideas like the restoration of national pride, the opposition to Communism and the desire to overcome the moral decadence of the Weimar era.

At the same time, Mormons never disavowed any of their pro-Jewish doctrines and attitudes; they lamented the behavior of the Nazis toward the Jews, but did not understand the central role of the Nazi anti-Jewish hatred in Third Reich policies.

From the beginning the Mormon policy was to "get along" with the Hitler regime, although in 1933 and 1934 some Mormons in Germany were quite convinced that the government would send the American missionaries packing (Ralph Kelly). Probably the main reason that the Mormon Church were not dissolved, as happened to some "comparable" sects, was not, as one recent historian has written (King, 1982), because of a "conjunction of Weltanschaungen" between Nazis and

Mormons, but the fact that the dominant transcendent objectives and political accommodation of the Mormons did not challenge the regime. The major interests of the two did not meet. Moreover, the 15,000 or so Mormons in the country hardly posed a threat to the increasingly powerful Nazi juggernaut, especially after the Party had consolidated its power in 1934. Although the power of the Mormons in the U.S. had also been growing, it was still hardly a serious force, although Ambassador William Dodd thought the Mormons in Germany might have gotten some special consideration from the Nazis because of their influence in Washington (Dodd, 1941).

Although Mormons were an American-based sect like the Jehovah's Witnesses and the Christian Scientists, they did not, as we have seen, deny support to legitimate government or refuse to bear arms. At the same time, while they believed in the gifts of healing, which the Nazi's objected to, this practice did not exclude seeking competent medical attention. Mormons were thus in these matters more in the mainstream of Christianity, though they held a different attitude toward Jews.

The First Presidency of the Church had given considerably authority to the two mission presidents on the scene. Thus, when, on September 8, 1933, a Gestapo investigation team visited Dr. Oliver H. Budge, the Mormon mission president in Berlin who presided over some 6500 German Mormon and 90 American missionaries, he was asked what is "our [Mormon] position so far as the present National Socialist government is concerned," Budge's reply, as he reported it later to the First Presidency, was conciliatory:

> We have our own Church and our own convictions concerning what it advocates, and we expect to carry our convictions through for the sake of our eternal salvation, so long as we do not come in conflict with the fixed laws of the government. (German-Austrian Mission History, 1934)

Clearly there were principles--belief in God and Jesus Christ and in the belief in truthfulness of the restored Christianity, the concept of being part of the House of Israel, as well as loyalty to Church leaders--which no true Mormon would disavow, even if confronted with death. But it was also true, Budge told his interlocutors, that Mormons

> are also taught, especially, to be able to class themselves with the best citizens of the country, and to support, in the fullest sense of the word, the ordinances and laws of the town, the state, and the country in which they live. The authorities of our church have no advice to give regarding party politics, leaving the members free to identify themselves with whatever party they choose; but, in any event, we teach that the present party in power, and the laws governing the country, be supported by the church. (German-Austrian Mission, 1934)

Earlier, Budge had written a letter to his missionaries in March, 1933 which set down the policy they were to follow and also let German Mormons know the Church's official unpolitical position:

> By this country's officials and citizens we have been and are still being treated with respect. You are hereby notified to refrain from discussing or giving your opinion concerning the political situation, either in private or in public. You are also warned against writing anything whatsoever concerning politics or concerning the present situation in any of your local or foreign correspondence, including letters to your parents and friends. Anyone of you who fails to take this advice *will* have occasion to *regret it*. [Italics in original].
>
> There is no immediate occasion for uneasiness on your part. Just be wise and humbly go about your business. Anything concerning our missionaries will be handled from this office, if occasion requires. (Budge, 1933)

Thus, throughout the years of the Third Reich, the Mormon position vis-a-vis the Hitler regime was rigorously unpolitical. The leadership in Salt Lake City, to whom all Mormons looked for guidance, considered the Hitler regime legitimate, if "detestable"; it appeared to have the support of the German people, a powerful factor because of their reverence for democracy. Moreover, what the German government did was to them more an internal political matter than an international moral one. Their primary objective was to keep the Church in Germany intact, not unlike the Catholic position, to continue to try to gain converts among the Germans and to avoid giving the government cause either to dissolve the Church or persecute its members. This policy was fully supported by Mormons in the United States and by the mission presidents and missionaries in Germany. It did not keep some missionaries from developing animosities toward the regime, but it was also true that some were positively impressed by the regime's early achievements.

German Mormons were generally as they had always been, more Mormon than German. They were also overwhelmingly from the lowest social classes and thoroughly unpolitical. They supported the Church's position, although a small minority was nevertheless drawn to National Socialism and another minority quietly opposed to Hitler from the beginning. Only gradually and very belatedly did Mormons both in and out of Germany come to recognize National Socialism for what it really was, a competing Weltanschauung which made total claims on human beings. First, the Nazis would destroy the Jews; then Christians, including the Mormons, would be next.

During the years before the outbreak of World War II, Mormons were well aware of what the Nazi regime was doing to the Jews. Missionaries and German Mormons saw the persecutions virtually every day, but none of them ever dreamed that these would culminate in the Final Solution.

Roy Welker, an American educator replaced Oliver Budge as the Mormon mission president in Berlin in 1934. He remained until 1937. His experience in Leipzig in September 1934, as he noted in his journal, is typical of the experiences of the other six who served at one time or another between 1933-39. The missionaries stationed in the city introduced him and his wife to a Jewish women, a Frau Kammerling, who had often rented rooms to missionaries in the past. "She told us many stories of the government's persecution of the Jews which revealed another side of things to us. We were surprised and shocked at her stories" (Welker, 1934).

Through a questionnaire sent to former missionaries, I was able to get an idea of the missionaries experiences with Jews before the Holocaust. One missionary, Wilfried Fluit, recounted how they learned from their Jewish landlady that her son, a doctor who had served valiantly in World War I, found it difficult to understand why after 1933 he was "despised and hated." Later, Fluit remembered seeing a large crowd gather in Braunschweig to see the Jewish editor of the _Braunschweiger Beobachter_ pursued by Storm Troopers to the roof of the newspaper's building. "When they were almost close enough to grab him, he jumped to his death." Stanley Rees also lived with a Jewish family who "were always cautious and careful. They knew they were in constant jeopardy."

Missionaries also found opportunities to help some Jews they encountered. John Skola recalled going to "a Jewish doctor for my eye and I was the only patient he had." Rolland Rose knew a German Jew who owned a dye factory. "His factory had no work or employees. He talked to us because we were Americans; we would walk to a park to talk." Later he joined with other missionaries to give a Jewish Mormon money to leave the country.

Another account, by Byron Belnap, who told about a Herr Goldberg, also a Jewish Mormon in Wuppertal-Elberfeld. Because he was married to a Christian, Goldberg received no help from the Jewish community and none from any other source.

> At night he was often picked up by the police and sent to the border. The next day the other nations would send him back, and this continued to repeat itself. To my knowledge the only help he ever got was what we missionaries could do for him. At this time we were rationed to 1/4 pound of butter a week, which we often gave to him.

Virtually every missionary in Germany observed the events of _Kristallnacht_. When Donald Petty and Rolland Rose reported the burning of the synagogue in Bad Homburg to the Mission Office in Frankfurt Main, they were told "the same situation had occurred in all parts of Germany and that we were just to keep a low profile on these things and not criticize anything that had happened" (Petty, 1986).

If missionaries saw much and were able to do only a little in pre-war Germany, the record of German Mormons is more mixed. While a large majority followed the code laid down by Heber J. Grant in 1921, there were some exceptions. Some were undoubtedly the product of fear of the police, but others may well have represented anti-Jewish prejudice. One local Mormon official in Hamburg put up a sign on the meetinghouse door that Jews were no longer welcome there. Harvey Hatch remembered how local Mormon leaders in Nuremburg refused to baptize a young woman who wished to become a Mormon, because her father was a Jew. Another missionary,

Hyrum J. Smith, was astounded at the overt anti-Semitism in the congregation where he was serving. Some time in 1936-37 he invited a Jewish family to Mormon services. The father brought his young son, but did not remain himself. The boy was snubbed by the members. "They told me that no Jew boy was going to take the sacrament [eucharist] and that Jews were not welcome in the meetings."

German Mormons usually found their services visited by the police. Consequently, references to Israel and Jews, long an integral part of the services, became less frequent in hymns and sermons. That some Nazis knew very well the historic attachment of Mormons to Jews and were unhappy about it was brought home in an early article entitled "Jews and Mormons" in the Aryan Rundschau of June 18, 1933. The article upbraided Mormons for their doctrinal and personal sympathies with Jews and for having elected a Jew governor of their state. Mormons even call themselves "sons of Israel," the journal continued, "and have always been very friendly with Jews" (Aryan Rundschau, 1933). In 1935 an exhibit set up in Chemnitz, where there was one of the largest Mormon congregations, to tell about the Book of Mormon incurred the wrath of a city councilor. Missionaries reported his comment that "Mormons must be Jews since [they] used the Israel [sic] and Hebrew languages" (German-Austrian Mission History, 1935).

But neither in Germany nor in Salt Lake city in the pre-war era did Mormon leaders speak out in support of the Jews. The Deseret News carried a series of reports on the Nazi boycott of Jews and the flight of German Jews in 1933, but also reported the Nuremberg Laws of 1935, this time without comment (Deseret News, 1933 and 1935). It also carried extensive coverage of the Kristallnacht and its aftermath and commented that the "bitter hatred toward the Jews" of the Germans was "appalling" (Deseret News, 1938). In 1937, the Mormon President Heber J. Grant, then an elderly man, had made a visit to Germany. The purpose of the visit was to calm the fears of German Mormons and American missionaries. Later, his counselor, J. Reuben Clark Jr., made two visits, one in 1938 and one in 1939. At a meeting of the First Presidency in 1939, Clark mentioned the possibility that missionaries could be "thrown into concentration camps, with all the horrors that entails" (Quinn, 1983), so he was conscious of the realities of German life.

In spite of all this information, it appears that Mormon Church leaders in Salt Lake City continued to view the situation as a political issue, and this in spite of the fears of Thomas E. McKay, who in 1939, while serving his third mission in Germany, wrote to his brother David O. McKay that conditions in Germany were getting worse, and it might not be long until the Mormons, as well as all other Christian Churches, will be squeezed out (McKay 1939). Clark felt very strongly that people from one nation should not meddle in the affairs of another, a widely-held attitude by many, which Hitler exploited. Undoubtedly, another major reason was precisely so as not to endanger the lives of the exposed German Mormons and missionaries and also possibly to destroy the Mormon community there.

Other Mormon leaders--but only a few--at home took contradictory positions. An apostle, Melvin J. Ballard, in a conference address in April, 1938 returned to an earlier Mormon theme that recognized the Jews as being in "another peril," but claimed to see the hand of God in it. "Even Hitler is used as an instrument in the hands of God, of driving them where the Lord wants them" (Ballard, 44). But Levi Edgar Young, a prominent Mormon and a professor of history at the University of Utah, described the Nazi persecutions as being the "most terrible blotch on world history" (Salt Lake Telegram, 1938).

IV.

Just days before World War II broke out, all the American Mormon missionaries and most of their leaders were immediately recalled. After May 1940, German Mormons were left on their own, cut off from contact with church authorities in America. Most German Mormons with whom I have spoken had seen many examples of the brutal treatment meted out to the Jews in the pre-war era, but they did not know about the Holocaust. Walter Speidel described how his Jewish schoolmates in Stuttgart disappears (Speidel, 1986) Even the young Helmut Hubener, who composed and printed handbills against the regime in late 1941 and January of 1942 and paid for it with his life in October, 1942, apparently did not know about the Jews (Keele and Tobler, 1984). Erich Bernhardt, a Mormon in Herne, explained that most Mormons he knew thought the Jews were being taken to concentration camps and would later be sent to Palestine. For this reason some of the more politically naive thought Hitler might, in the long run, be helping the Jews. Bernhardt knew it was worse, but he did not know how bad!

> My father told me that they were treated badly, not that they were killed I didn't know about this [the annihilation] during the war and we thought it was propaganda. The extent of what really happened was not known to the masses (Bernhardt, 1985).

Friedrich Gassner's experience was different; he knew. He had been drafted in June of 1942 and sent to Russia. While waiting for a train, he saw women and children working on the railroad. He asked a German guard, "Where do these people come from?" He was told they were "from home."

> "These are Jews. They work here and their numbers shrink every day. They get less to eat every day and have to work hard and those who don't die come into a different train.'
>
> At this time a train came into the station. 'These are going to Bialystok and there they are to be gassed.' And this [was] the very first time that I had heard that Jews were gassed. . . .But the broad masses in Germany didn't know about it (Gassner, 1985).

One Mormon family in Hanover and another young man in Homburg did try to make a difference. Max Reschke, a shop steward in a pharmaceutical factory in Hannover, was so overcome with grief at what was happening to the Jews on the Kristallnacht that he wept. But he did more. He rescued his Jewish friends, the Scheuerenbergs, from a column being driven up the streets by armed guards and eventually got them over the Swiss border whence they eventually made their way to Shanghai. They lived to tell the story.

Reschke had less success in helping Kurt and Kaete Lazarus. For hiding Kurt in his home, Max was sent to prison for a few weeks in Ahlen; Lazarus perished in a maximum security prison in Hameln. After trying to care for Kaete Lazarus, Reschke was forced to see her deported eastward in 1941 with the remaining members of the Hanover Jewish Community. The full story of Reschke's heroism has yet to be told. Part of Reschke's motivation, he said, derived from his Mormon conviction that Jews were still God's chosen people. The young man was Walter Schmidt, then living in Hamburg. When Solomon Schwarz, a member of the same congregation as H bener, was excluded from their services, he was invited to another congregation, presided over by Walter's father, Alfred, who refused to be intimidated by the Gestapo. But Schwarz became a pariah and was first put in jail for refusing to wear the Jewish star; later he was confined to an all-Jewish home. Walter Schmidt made Schwarz's welfare his concern. While repeatedly threatened with detainment in a concentration camp, Schmidt visited, cared for and comforted Schwarz until the latter was sent to a concentration camp. He was never heard from again (Schwarz, 1978).

While these events were going on in Germany, Mormon leaders in Salt Lake City were silent on the Holocaust then in full progress. One scholar, Michael Quinn, has found no mention of the Holocaust in J. Reuben Clark's papers and David Lawrence McKay said he knew of no references to it in his father's. People in Salt Lake City were, however, hearing some of the awful news coming to America, but it always was linked to the war. A July 3, 1942 Deseret News editorial began: "One of the most pitiful of all the stories to come out of the war in Europe is that concerning the hapless Jews. . . .It has been a consistent policy of the Nazis to obliterate the Jews wherever they have gone" (Deseret News, 1942).

Later that year, on November 25, 1942, the Deseret News carried an extensive Associated Press report, together with a photo of Dr. Stephen Wise revealing Wise's information--confirmed by the State Department--that more than two million Jews had already been slaughtered (Deseret News, 1942). Nevertheless, Mormons and their leaders seemed either not to have understood what these reports meant or found them all "beyond belief" (Lipstadt, 1986). And this in spite of their earlier direct experiences with the Nazi regime. In any event, no Mormon voices were raised in protest until 1944 when David O. McKay indirectly gave expression to his awareness by describing Hitler as the "world's most notoriously brutal gangster" (McKay, 1944).

After World War II, a German Mormon, Hans Guertler, meditated on his country's recent somber past as he wrote a history of the Hamburg Mormon congregation. His lamentation might have applied to Mormons everywhere:

On the horizon it is getting black!
Only missing is the wind,
Then the disaster takes its course,
But we are blind, are blind.

(Am Horizont zieht's schwarz herauf!
Nur fehlt nur noch der Wind,
Dann nimmt das Ungl ck seinen Lauf,
Doch wir sind blind, sind blind.) (1957)

After the war, Mormon leaders and German Mormons learned with the rest of the world the extent of the catastrophe that had befallen the European Jews. One soldier and former German missionary, Alvin Schoenhals, who had openly criticized the Hitler regime while a missionary, was among the first to visit Bergen-Belsen and see the final results of the Final Solution. He was staggered by the experience. Perhaps as an expression of their sense of tragedy, Mormons vigorously supported the Zionists in their drive to establish the State of Israel and rejoiced when the dream became a reality (Zucker, 1981). One has the feeling that the rejoicing was no longer primarily an expression of fulfilled Mormon prophecy but of genuine concern for the Jewish people.

V.

There are important lessons for Mormons to learn from the Holocaust. One is that even if they had no tradition of anti-Semitism and did not hate Jews, it was still possible to be a moral bystander. Mormons lacked the power to prevent the Holocaust or to rescue the Jews, even if they had recognized what was going on and had acted. But they were also blind, blind to a larger evil perhaps because they were focusing too narrowly on their own and did not recognize a need for broader concern and to make a moral statement in behalf of the Jews, whom they professed to consider as brothers. Their vision was yet too parochial when God's other children, even His other covenant people, were daily perishing in the flames. Being a serious Christian can never be compatible with moral indifference and apathy.

But perhaps we should not be too harsh. It was a difficult dilemma. How could one living in the security of the American mountains make statements that might jeopardize the life and liberty of fellow German Saints. On the other hand, is not Abraham Lincoln's counsel still accurate that "what is morally wrong can never be politically right."

The Christian message is both a message of transcendence and immanence. To gain eternal life with God remains the supreme goal of Christians in this life, but the concerns of human beings--God's children--in the here-and-now form a seamless web with the infinite. Mormons believe that what we do in the here-and-now will determine the nature of our eternal relationship with God. It was Jesus who told all that "inasmuch as ye have done it unto the least of these my brethren, ye have done it unto me." The failure to act when our fellow men face a catastrophe, as the Holocaust posed for the Jews, may, in fact, constitute a violation of the second great commandment, to love neighbor as self, and by implication also the first. Mormons have also been taught that a religion that cannot save man in the here-and-now will not be able to save in eternity. Parochialism and overemphasis on preaching the transcendent message may have darkened the Mormon vision of their broader Christian duty toward Jews.

The Church of Jesus Christ of Latter-day Saints numbered less than a million in 1933; it was a unique, if inconspicuous American sect. In the 1980's it has grown to over six million and has been recognized by some non-Mormon scholars (Stark, 1984; Shipps, 1985) as the newest "world" religion. Recognizing earlier myopia and indifference toward the Jewish branch of Israel can become the basis of a new world-wide view where not only Jews, but Arabs, Black Africans and all of humanity can find in Mormons caring fellow brothers and sisters in the family of man. If so, remembering the past can lead to a blessing for the future.

References

"Actions of Nazis Declared Most Terrible Blotch on World History," Salt Lake Telegram, November 23, 1938.
"Juden und Mormonen," Aryan Rundschau, June 18, 1933.
Ballard, Melvin J. (1938) Conference Report. Salt Lake City.
Barron, Howard H. (1979) Judah: Past and Future. (Horizon) 83, passim.
Bernhardt, Erich. (1985) Oral Interview. LDS Church Archives
Book of Mormon. (1982) Salt Lake City. "2 Nephi 29:5-6."
Clark, J. Reuben III. (1988) Oral Interview. March 12.
Deseret News (1933) April 1, 4; (1935) September 16; (1938) November 10, 12, 16; (1942) September 12, November 25.
Doctrine & Covenants. Sections 134; 98:5-7; 101:79-80.
Dodd, William E., Jr. and Martha Dodd, (eds.) (1941) Ambassador Dodd's Diary, 1933-1938. (New York) 125.
Gassner, Friedrich. (1985) Oral Interview. LDS Church Archives
German-Austrian Mission History. (1934) LDS Church Archives
Grant, Heber J. (1935) Der Stern, 67 (June 15, 1935) 177-181.
Grant, Heber J. (1921) "Attitude of the Latter-day Saints Towards the Jews," The Improvement Era, Vol. 24 (June) 747.
Green, Arnold H. (1967) A Survey of Latter-day Saint Proselyting Efforts to the Jewish People. Masters Thesis, Brigham Young University, 15-17, 137.
Guertler, Hans. (1957) Hamburger Gemeinde Geschichte. In author's possession.
Keele, Alan F. and Douglas F. Tobler. (1980) Sunstone 5 (November-December), 20-29.
Kelly, Ralph. (1934) Journal
King, Christine Elizabeth. (1982) The Nazi State and the New Religions: Five Case Studies. (New York: Edwin Mellen Press), 59-87.
Lipstadt, Deborah E. (1986) Beyond Belief. (New York: The Free Press),
McConkie, Bruce R. (1958) Mormon Doctrine. (Salt Lake City: Bookcraft),356, 357, 359.
McKay, David O. (1944) The Improvement Era 47 (November) 657.
McKay, Thomas E. (1939) Diary, 1939. Brigham Young University Library.
Morn, Frank Thomas. (1966) Simon Bamberger: A Jew in a Mormon Commonwealth. (Masters Thesis, Brigham Young University), 117-120.
Petty, Donald. (1986) Oral Interview. LDS Church Archives.
Quinn, D. Michael. (1983) J. Reuben Clark: The Church Years, 81.
Reschke, Stephen. (1987) "The Holocaust. . . Conscience and Compassion." Unpublished Paper, Brigham Young University.
Salt Lake Tribune, (1916) August 19.
Scharffs, Gilbert W. (1970) Mormonism in Germany. xiv, 60.
Schwarz, Annamarie. (1978) Letter to Rudolf Wobbe. August 23. In author's possession.
Speidel, Walter. (1975) Oral Interview. LDS Church Archives.
Shipps, Jan. (1985) The Story of a New Religious Tradition.
Stark, Rodney. (1984) Review of Religious Research, Vol. 26 (September), 18-27.
Taylor, George S. (1921) Report of Sermons of Elder David O.McKay. . . , Huntly, New Zealand. April 23-25, 1921. LDS Church Archives.
Van Orden, Bruce A. (1986) "Mormons and Jews: Persecuted Israel." Unpublished paper in possession of author.
Watters, Leon L. (1952) The Pioneer Jews of Utah. (New York, American Jewish Historical Society), 8.
Wyman, David S. (1984) The Abandonment of the Jews: America and the Holocaust, 1941-1945. (New York: Pantheon Books),153, 194.
Zucker, Louis C. (1981) Sunstone, Vol. 6, No. 5. (Sept. Oct.), 35-44.

Helpers and rescuers: Ethical, psychological and religious factors

CHAIRPERSON **Mr Douglas Huneke**

RAPPORTEUR **Dr Mordecai Paldiel**

WHAT LIGHT DOES THE JEWISH EXPERIENCE SHED ON THE IDEA OF A MULTI-CULTURAL BRITAIN?

PETER D BISHOP

Centre for Multi-Cultural Studies,
Brighton Polytechnic, Falmer, Brighton, BN1 9PH.

The history of Jews in Europe is largely a story of people who suffered from a variety of prejudices which were based upon religion and culture as well as economics and politics. The suffering of Jewish people in Christian Europe (Muslim Spain provides an obvious exception to the rule that in Europe Jews were usually at best second-class citizens) occupied a whole spectrum of experience, from discrimination in employment, through the forcible herding of people into ghettoes, to the extreme point of the holocaust.

It is the intention of this paper to suggest:

1) that the persecution of Jews in Christian Europe has been directly related to deeply rooted religious and cultural prejudices;

2) that it has also reflected a related but different set of prejudices commonly expressed in Britain (and no doubt elsewhere as well) against newcomers;

3) that there are close parallels between the experience of, for example, late nineteenth century Jewish immigrants in Britain and post-1945 immigrants from the New Commonwealth; and that

4) the Jewish experience therefore suggests certain lessons which should be applied by Christians as the major religious community, but also by Jews, secularists and others, to questions that arise in present-day plural and multi-cultural Britain.

In a Christian context any question relating to 'the Jewish experience' must take account of the long history of anti-Jewish attitudes in Christian writing and practice. Hostility to Jewish people is a regrettable but persistent feature of Christian history. The facts that Jesus and his first followers were all Jewish, that they adhered in some degree to Jewish religious and social customs, and that the leaders among the early Christian community continued to worship at the temple in Jerusalem have been submerged beneath assumptions that tend to distort or disregard the history of Christianity's Jewish roots. A trivial illustration of that is that whilst the fact that the first apostles were all men is often used as an argument against the ordination of women in Christian churches, the equally if not more obvious fact that they were all Jewish has never to my knowledge been used to support the view that only people of Jewish extraction should be admitted to ordination.

The Christian interpretation of Judaism which survived and flourished after 70CE was prefigured in the earlier New Testament writings of Paul, the leading apostle to the Gentiles. In Paul's letters we find unequivocal expression of the idea that the Christian Church is the new Israel, to be established in place of the old Israel whose people were 'made blind to the truth' and who will be admitted to salvation only when the Gentiles have been fully gathered into God's kingdom: 'When that has happened the whole of Israel will be saved'. The ultimate destiny of the Jews is good, Paul argued, but for the foreseeable future they are a rejected people: 'In the spreading of the Gospel they are treated as God's enemies for your sake; but God's choice stands, and they are his friends for the sake of the patriarchs' (Romans 11.28).

The intention of Paul's theology clearly was to emphasize the grace of God, and to give vigorous expression to the conviction that people's relationships with God do not depend upon the keeping of narrow rules but upon God's acceptance of them, freely offered. Paul's doctrine of grace has enthused and fired the Church on many occasions in its history. But as Paul presented his ideas in the New Testament, in the context of his own rivalry with the Jerusalem Church and his desire to break completely with Judaism to form a Gentile Church, a negative side of the doctrine of grace was stated. Grace and freedom were associated with the Christian Gospel; law, formalism and disobedience were associated with Judaism: '... those who relay on obedience to the law are under a curse ... Christ bought us freedom from the curse of law by becoming for our sake an accursed thing.' (Galatians 3.13).

This particular piece of religious and cultural stereotyping has had profound consequences. Even today it is probable that only the most sensitive of Christian preachers avoid implying, on the basis of the New Testament, that legalism is forever associated with Judaism and grace with Christianity. But as we know, in the centuries which saw the initial growth of Christianity and its establishment as a major religion, the picture of the Jews was often drawn even more harshly than this, by attributing to Jewish people corporately and for all time blame for the death of Jesus. 'His blood be on us and our own children' was taken literally as an invitation to abuse and persecute Jews in the name of Jesus.

The preaching of some of the great figures of the early Church provides dramatic evidence of the extremes to which criticism of the Jews was taken. Hippolytus, who lived from about 170 to 236CE, was one of the theologians of early Christianity who preached sermons against the Jews. Like many preachers since, he seems to have been fond of rhetorical questions. The answer his own questions eventually evoked, however, was damning:

> 'Why was the temple made desolate? Was it on account of the ancient fabrication of the calf? Or was it on account of the idolatry of the people? Was it for the blood of the prophets? Was it for the adultery and fornication of Israel? By no means, for in all these transgressions they always found pardon open to them. But it was because they killed the son of their Benefactor, for He is co-eternal with the Father.'

The great fourth century doctor of the Church to whom was attributed the name Chrysostom, or golden-tongued, in deference to his power as a preacher, explicity accused the Jews of deicide, a charge which was to be repeated on many occasions:

> 'If someone had killed your son, could you stand the sight of him or the sound of his greeting? Wouldn't you try to get away from him as if he were an evil demon, as if he were the devil himself? The Jews killed the Son of your Master ... Will you so dishonour Him as to respect and cultivate His murderers, the men who crucified Him?'

It is hardly surprising that these bitter criticisms of Jewish people issued in legislation when the Roman Empire became predominantly Christian. By the late fourth century Jews were excluded from holding civil and military rank, and were then gradually banished from all kinds of public office, and from acting as lawyers and judges. In 423 Jews were forbidden to build new synagogues or to repair old ones. Two years later they were ordered to observe Christian times of fasts and festivals, and in the fifth century were also forced to listen to sermons which criticized Judaism and attempted to convert Jews to Christianity.

Anti-Jewish attitudes and practices increased dramatically during the crusading period, and the Christian councils enforced the isolation and identification of Jews living in Christian society. Officially expelled from England in 1290, and not permitted to return until the time of Cromwell, Jews in Christian Europe continued to suffer theological denigration as well as other kinds of opposition.

The persecution which drove Jews westwards across Europe in the last quarter of the nineteenth century was the result of many factors, political and economic as well as religious. But constantly in the background of European anti-Semitism was the religious bigotry which was firmly rooted in centuries of Christian practice and theology. Rosemary Ruether (1974) was not exaggerating when she wrote:

> 'We begin to realize that what Nazism revived was not a long-dead set of attitudes and practices, but a world only recently dissolved in the West, still maintained in the East, whose myths were still live, glowing embers easily fanned into new flames.'

Nor has Christian anti-Semitism been simply the result of conscious anti-Jewish polemic or feeling. So strongly has it been bound up with Christian roots that it has grown imperceptibly in the most unlikely soil. Charlotte Klein, in Anti-Judaism in Christian Theology (1978) showed how closely connected are the most ordinary and apparently innocent exercises of Christian theology and anti-Jewish attitudes. Having examined the writings of some of the most influential continental theologians and biblical scholars she concluded that much of them implied strongly anti-Jewish sentiments, and that this implicit element in their writings about the New Testament or early Christianity continued to exercise a profound influence on theological students, clergy, and other serious students of Christianity. She cited a large number of German and French theologians and biblical scholars who write confidently and in the most damning terms of the scribes and Pharisees on the basis of the New Testament accounts of them. Dibelius, Grundmann, Lagrange, Jeremias, Schurer, Meyer and others were shown in their writings to be taking at face value a presentation of the Pharisees which is not based upon historical material but simply upon the Gospel records. In so doing they have disseminated among their many readers the notion that the New Testament portrayal of the scribes and Pharisees is an accurate one. Klein's bleak view of the influence of Christian scholars on perceptions of Judaism among Christians was mitigated to some extent by her survey of some Anglo-American authors. This suggested that widely-read New Testament commentators such as Nineham and Fenton have been much more objective in their treatment of the Jews than many of their continental counterparts. But Charlotte Klein's research indicated that, whether in continental Europe, the UK, or the USA, those who follow the biblical texts without the aid of form or redaction criticism are likely to absorb and reproduce the stock prejudices.

Such a gloomy picture needs to be balanced by reference to some of the much more positive things that have happened in Christian-Jewish understanding since the holocaust. For example, many Christians have attempted to take seriously the 'Ten Points of Seelisberg', which among other things advised Christians:

> to remember that Jesus was born of a Jewish mother of the seed of David and the people of Israel, and that his everlasting love and forgiveness embraces his own people and the whole world;
>
> to remember that the first disciples, the apostles and the first martyrs were Jews;
>
> to avoid distorting or misrepresenting biblical or post-biblical Judaism with the object of extolling Christianity;
>
> to avoid presenting the Passion in such a way as to bring the odium of the killing of Jesus upon all Jews or upon Jews alone.
>
> (The Council of Christians and Jews, 1974)

In the wake of the holocaust more official responses were made by the major Christian churches. In October 1965 the Second Vatican Council promulgated its declaration on The Relationship of the Church to Non-Christian Religions including a section on attitudes to Judaism which repudiated, perhaps in rather grudging terms, the doctrine that held all Jews responsible for the death of Christ. The Declaration did not, as some had hoped, acknowledge a measure of Christian responsibility for the persecution of Jews, neither did it address itself to continuing theological difficulties in the way of genuine Christian-Jewish understanding. But it did represent a measure of real progress at the time in removing the possibility of grounding opposition to Judaism or the Jewish people in the official teaching of the Church (Abbott 1967).

Protestant churches, through the World Council of Churches, made bolder declarations on this issue in a number of statements and publications which began at the time of the formation of the WCC in 1948. The first Assembly of the WCC, Amsterdam, called upon all churches represented there to denounce anti-Semitism as irreconcilable with the practice of the Christian faith and a sin against God and man. Following the establishment of the Consultation between the Church and the Jewish People by the WCC in 1965, further statements on Christian-Jewish relationships were made in 1968 and in 1977, when Christians were urged to scrutinize carefully those New Testament passages which have encouraged anti-Jewish sentiment to avoid traditional stereotypes (von Hammerstein 1978).

The major Christian churches, then, are well aware of the need to challenge anti-Jewish elements in Christian theology and teaching, and to foster friendly relationships between Christians and Jews. However, that awareness is itself an indication of how directly the persecution of Jews in Europe has related to deeply-rooted religious and cultural prejudices. In looking at questions that have to do with cross-cultural and inter-religious understanding and tolerance in present day Britain it will be necessary to bear in mind, and take to heart, the lessons that can be learned from centuries of Christian anti-Jewishness as well as from the holocaust itself.

Another set of issues that need to be explored if we are to understand the nature of attitudes to Jews in modern Britain has to do with the Jewish experience of immigration. The years between 1881 and 1905 are particularly instructive both because they encompass the period of major Jewish immigration from a culturally very different context in Eastern Europe and because they provide illuminating comparisons with the experience of later groups of newcomers to Britain.

During the nineteenth century emancipation had won for the Jews, as for Catholics, Nonconformists and others in British society, equality before the law and in matters of civil rights. But the arrival at the end of the century of Jewish refugees, who were clearly not part of the middle-class world inhabited with such marked success by the largely Sephardic Anglo-Jewish community which benefitted from emancipation, evoked fresh prejudices. There was exaggeration of the numbers of those who were coming, compounded by fears about threats to employment, cultural and religious differences, and political opportunism.

It is now clear that at the end of the nineteenth century estimates of the numbers of Jewish refugees arriving in Britain were grossly exaggerated. Whitaker's Almanac of 1892 suggested that 140,000 Jews were arriving in Britain every year. By contrast the Board of Trade estimated that some 7,000 Jewish immigrants settled in Britain in 1891, 3,000 in 1892 and less than 3,000 in 1893. The numbers were then thought to have remained fairly steady at around 2,500 a year for the rest of the eighteen-nineties. Some popular estimates claimed that there were seven million Jews in Britain by 1910, against a more realistic figure of about 300,000. The 1911 census recorded 106,082 people who were born in Russia and Poland, and most of those can be assumed to have been Jewish refugees and to have represented the greater part of primary immigration of Jews since 1881. Concentration of newcomers in particular areas, such as Stepney and Mile End, encouraged the inflated views that were abroad of the total number of Jews arriving in the country and provided a convenient lever for politically inspired opposition to 'alien immigration' (Gartner 1960).

There was also much local resentment of the cultural differences of the immigrants, an experience which was to be repeated in respect of New Commonwealth immigrants sixty or seventy years later. The east European Jews dressed differently from English people. They were accustomed to wearing distinctively Jewish dress, and the men retained their beards and long hair. There were difficulties with the language, for of course the newcomers spoke Yiddish, together with Russian or Polish, and whilst the men quickly acquired English through necessity, the women who lived more encapsulated lives were slower to learn the new language. There were surprising local objections to the Jewish observance of the Sabbath and to Jews working on Sundays; surprising because the level of churchgoing in the East End of London was low even at that time, and the objections are likely to have been based not upon deeply held religious convictions but upon a sense of the inappropriateness or threatening nature of cultural differences.

Another cause of resentment was the claim that the influx of Jewish immigrants was displacing British workers in the employment market. It was suggested that Jews were prepared to work and live at levels Englishmen would not (although the charge was levelled even more frequently against Irishmen), and that they were therefore taking jobs that otherwise would have belonged to native-born Englishmen. In fact, Jewish immigrants were often successful in establishing their own businesses and often preferred to work in enclosed Jewish communities rather than attempt to find work with Gentile employers. The great example of this was the tailoring trade, in which Jewish entrepreneurs were responsible for the development of a market in new clothes for poor people. Far from competing with Gentiles for work, they established themselves in an area of work that had hardly existed previously (Gainer 1972).

Political opportunism also took advantage of, and helped to create, feelings against the Jewish newcomers. Political opposition to immigration policy was expressed by the British Brothers' League, which was formed in February 1901 and held its first meeting on May 9th of the same year. The League expressed widely felt popular sentiment. In its first year of existence its membership reached 45,000, and the League's popularity was evident from its first meeting which attracted an audience of some 4,000 and the attendance of most East London Members of Parliament (Bermant 1975). The influence of the League appears to have been most marked among working-class people in areas where there were high concentrations of immigrants, and those attending public meetings heard a reiteration of the familiar charges that Jewish aliens were taking jobs from local people, causing overcrowding and insanitary conditions in housing, and contributing to the destruction of the English Sunday. The British Brothers'

League caused excitement and, for the Jews, unpleasantness, in the East End, but it had only limited political influence. More significant in its impact on policy-making was the Immigration Reform Association, formed in February 1903 with more limited objectives than the League's blanket condemnation of 'alien immigration', and with more carefully established links with parliamentarians, especially in the Conservative Party. The Immigration Reform Association limited its opposition to the immigration of 'bad characters', those likely to become a charge on charity, those with 'any loathsome or contagious disease', and any who were 'defective in mind and body'. Pamphlets were produced by the Association on such subjects as Destitute Aliens, Criminality among Aliens, and Aliens and Overcrowding, and the presentation of these issues was calculated to arouse opposition to the continued immigration of Jewish aliens, even though, for example, the level of criminality among such people was low and the diminution of housing stocks in East London was the result of many factors besides immigration.

Political pressure then led to the setting up of the Royal Commission on alien immigration in January 1902. When the Commission reported in August 1903, it rejected most of the allegations that had been made against the Jewish immigrants. There was found to be no substance in suggestions that the immigrants brought infectious diseases into the country, that they caused wages of British workers to fall by undercutting, or that they contributed to substantial increases in the number of paupers. The hearings before the Commission served to dispel a number of damaging myths that had grown up around the Jewish immigrants. How instructive for later anti-immigration policies to note that, with two dissentiants, the Commission bowed to political and public pressure and proposed that legislation should be introduced to control immigration.

As a result of that proposal the first piece of legislation in modern times to restrict immigration into Britain was enacted, in the form of the Aliens Act of 1905 - an Act specifically designed to inhibit further immigration of Jewish refugees from Eastern Europe. The aims of the Act were not stated quite so baldly, of course. It was 'undesirable and destitute aliens' who were to be prohibited entry; and 'aliens' were defined as those travelling as steerage passengers in groups of twelve or more per ship (modified by the new Liberal Government of 1906 to twenty per ship). And there were clauses exempting from the provisions of the Act those who could claim to be refugees from political or religious persecution. Nevertheless, the 1905 Aliens Act can be seen as a model of sorts for later, post Second World War, immigration legislation, carefully framed as it was to avoid charges of sectarian, religious, or cultural bias, and yet calculated to exclude a certain group of people belonging to a particular cultural and religious background.

In the experience of Jewish immigration between 1881 and 1905 we see many of the attitudes that were to emerge later in response to immigration from the New Commonwealth. The opposition to immigrants was strongest in the main areas of settlement. It focused upon many of the obvious and external characteristics of the immigrants: they looked different, spoke a different language, professed a different religion, had different customs, married within their own community, and therefore it was thought they would not assimilate. In addition, said the critics of Jewish immigration, these people do not understand our customs, their standards of hygiene are not the same, they are dirty, they are lazy or too hardworking, they threaten our jobs, our culture and our environment. Politicians recognised that there was political capital to be made out of the immigration issue, and so finally legislation was passed which did little to address the problems of the newcomers' adjustment to a strange society, or that society's understanding of them, but which could be seen as a kind of political achievement.

During the eighty-three years since the Aliens Act was passed things have changed considerably for the Jewish community. In spite of the problems generated by the rise of Fascism in England in the nineteen twenties and thirties, the Jews have come to be regarded as a model of successful accommodation to British society. Members of more recently arrived groups have been advised by their leaders to 'emulate the Jews', and have often seen the Jews as examples of how to preserve a distinctive religion and culture whilst being successful in British society. Muhammad Anwar (1979), in his study of Pakistani Muslims in Rochdale, commented:

> 'It is interesting to note that while there is a lot of covert hostility by Muslims towards Jews their success in preserving their religion and culture is held up as an example by many Muslims in this country.' (p.159)

Now a Chief Rabbi has joined the senior Anglican bishops in the House of Lords, and surely there can be few more eloquent testimonies to the way in which Jews, despite religious and cultural differences, have been embraced by the British establishment.

Does the history of the Jewish experience in Britain over the past one hundred years or so have any relevance, then, to the problems and opportunities of present-day pluralist Britain? Does the story of gradual Jewish accommodation to British society have any light to shed on attitudes that should now be adopted by Christians as representatives of the majority religio-cultural group in Britain, and by Jews as models of successful accommodation, towards new minority groups in Britain, and towards the creation of a multi-cultural society?

Before attempting to answer these questions, it might be helpful to examine some of the parallels between the experience of late nineteenth century Jewish immigrants in Britain and that of post-1945 immigrants from the 'New Commonwealth'.

We have seen how numbers were grossly exaggerated when people in the East End of London commented on the Jewish immigration after 1881. The exaggeration of numbers, sometimes clearly deliberate and sometimes perhaps just the result of ignorance, has been part of the British response to New Commonwealth immigration in a number of ways. Just as the initial concentration of the Jewish immigrants in particular areas led to inflated ideas of the total numbers entering the country, so that patterns of settlement of Afro-Caribbean and Asian newcomers encouraged the idea that the country was being 'flooded' with New Commonwealth immigrants. Colin Brown, in The Third Policy Studies Institute Survey of Black and White Britain (1984) wrote:

> A large proportion of the black population lives in a small number of local authority areas, and within these areas the black residents tend to be concentrated in a small number of electoral wards. This uneven distribution means that black people, although a tiny proportion of the national population, have been seen to be relatively numerous in some localities, and this has often contributed to very innaccurate perceptions of the total size of the black community ... and to some wild ideas about the national figures. (p.18)

But it was not only the uneven distribution of the newcomers that misled people about their numbers. Politicians and the media encouraged the tendency to use the word 'immigrant' as a synonym for black and Asian residents of Britain, and this has led to a number of popular misconceptions. One is that British people by and large appear to be remarkably unaware of the fact that most immigrants into Britain since the Second World War have been white. The 1961 census, just one year before the first major anti-immigration legislation began to close the door on primary immigration from the New Commonwealth, showed that the country of origin of the largest group of immigrants was Ireland. At that stage what the census called the 'coloured Commonwealth' had provided only 20% of those born outside the United Kingdom, compared with 38% from Ireland, 33% 'foreign', and 9% 'other Commonwealth'. The 1971 census again revealed that by far the largest number of foreign-born residents in the United Kingdom had come from Ireland (more than the total of those born in India and the West Indies put together), and that the total for Ireland, Germany, America and Poland exceeded the total for India, Pakistan, the West Indies, Cyprus and Africa (Allen 1971, Rose 1969, CRE 1978). Yet in this period the word 'immigrant' had commonly come to be used, often perjoratively, for black or coloured residents in Britain rather than simply as a descriptive term for those who had in fact immigrated. Increasingly that usage has been applied even to the children of original immigrants. Exaggeration of the numbers of people from the Caribbean or the Indian sub-continent has been compounded by the invidious practice of attaching the label 'immigrant' to whole communities, even to those who are British-born, and avoiding its use for genuine immigrants who happen to be white. When the occasional call for the repatriation of immigrants has been heard it is clear that the word has been used in this tendentious and inaccurate way, and that advocates of such a policy have not apparently had in mind the possibility of sending Irish people back to the Republic or one or two distinguished members of the Royal Family back to their place of origin. The consequences of attaching such a label to second or even third generations of Britons whose parents were born in the Caribbean or in Asia could be extremely serious and very damaging.

Jewish refugees were accused of stealing jobs from British workers. Such accusations have been made against immigrants from the New Commonwealth, in spite of the fact that many of them were invited by public or private employers to come and fill gaps in the labour market in Britain in the post-war years, especially in jobs that involved shift-work or that were for other reasons unpopular with British workers. As unemployment has risen in recent years the disadvantage of blacks and Asians has increased dramatically. The PSI survey commented:

> 'Undoubtedly the most important change has been the rise of unemployment rates among Asian and West Indian men and women to very high levels. The faster growth of unemployment among blacks than among whites has opened up an area of massive racial disadvantage

that was absent in 1974.'

The survey shows that, compared with a 1974 figure of about 4% unemployment for blacks and whites, the 1982 position was:

	men	women	
white unemployment	13%	10%	
West Indian origin unemployment	25%	16%	
Asian origin "	20%	20%	(Brown 1984, p.174).

Particularly disturbing is the fact that far fewer young people of Asian and West Indian origin have jobs than do their white contemporaries. The charge of stealing other people's jobs in these more recent cases has been exacerbated by patterns of disadvantage and discrimination which have excluded many of the minority communities from the labour market. For younger people in the black and Asian communities, many of them not themselves immigrants, discrimination in employment is a particularly offensive practice. A study of white and black school leavers in Lewisham in 1977 showed that even then black school leavers were three times as likely to be unemployed as white; and that those who were in employment had taken longer to find work, had made more applications, and had been to a greater number of interviews than white school leavers.

A study conducted between June and November 1976 in the London north DHSS region revealed that of 317 applications for clerical grade jobs, one third had been from black candidates and two thirds from white candidates. From these applicants, only ten blacks were offered jobs in comparison with seventy-eight whites. Yet of those rejected, more of the blacks than of the whites possessed minimum educational qualifications (Olerearnshaw 1983). The very poor prospects for young black people in Britain are mirrored by the exceptional disadvantage of black and Asian women. Commenting on the current situation in the city of Sheffield, Swasti Mitter (1987) has pointed out that 'young black women are three times as likely to be unemployed than young white women, whilst black women employed by the local authority are most concentrated in those areas most at risk from the effects of compulsory tendering and privatisation (in cleaning and catering). ... some sections of the Asian community where appropriate employment prospects are few and far between have no alternative but to take work in the home'.

Elsewhere, Swasti Mitter (1986) points to the low pay and exploitation of women, and especially black women, which has been an increasing feature of the clothing industry, the main trade of those early Jewish immigrants:

> '... between 1978 and 1983 in the fashionwear sector of the clothing industry alone, the loss of jobs in the official sector resulting from a transference of work from the open to the hidden economy has been five times as great as that resulting from import penetrations.'

The suspicion that black and Asian newcomers, like the Jews before them, displace other workers is not well founded. On the contrary such newcomers - and their children - face serious and continuing disadvantage in employment in Britain in a way that is compounded by high rates of unemployment generally.

Political opportunism of the kind that helped to create feelings against Jewish newcomers in the late nineteenth and early twentieth centuries has been exhibited even more clearly in relation to New Commonwealth immigrants and their descendants. Perhaps the first clear demonstration of the use of the 'race' issue in recent times occurred in the 1964 General Election at Smethwick, where the Conservative candidate, Peter Griffiths, defeated Patrick Gordon-Walker, the prospective Labour Foreign Secretary, in a campaign in which race and immigration issues were highlighted by means of such unpleasant slogans as, 'If you want a nigger as a neighbour, vote Labour'. In 1968 Enoch Powell 'espoused in apocalyptic language sentiments about "total bans" on black immigration and "repatriation" that were being expressed until then only by fringe right-wing forces' (Ben-Tovim and Gabriel 1982). The incorporation of race and colour issues into political discourse and campaigning was greatly helped by Powell's articulate presentation of a theme which included little examined notions of cultural and racial difference, fed on fear and resentment, and was encouraged by the assumption that Britain would soon be swamped by alien groups. In a speech at Southall in 1971 Powell suggested that:

> 'It is ... truly when he looks into the eyes of Asia that the Englishman comes face to

> face with those who would dispute with him the possession of his native land.' (Quoted Gilroy 1987)

The same theme was expounded more viciously in the same period by the National Front, whose members linked opposition to New Commonwealth immigrants with anti-Jewish sentiments. Barry Troyna (1982) has commented:

> 'The racist premises of NF ideology are underpinned by a much broader conspiratorial interpretation of Jewish plans to dominate the world. According to this view, Jewish domination will be achieved by encouraging miscegenation - thereby destroying the purity of all other races - whilst forbidding Jews to marry outside their own religious group.'

As one leading National Front member, put it, '... if Britain were Jew-clean she would have no nigger neighbours to worry about.' (Tynedale 1965). Both Conservative and Labour Governments responded to often deliberately heightened fears of black immigrants in a series of legislative measures designed to limit immigration into Britain from the New Commonwealth.

In the days of the British Empire all those who were subjects of the British sovereign were deemed to be British citizens. When the Empire dissolved into the Commonwealth the legacy of that constitutional provision lingered on. But gradually, in response to pressures in Britain which encouraged the view that there is a peculiar danger in accepting immigrants who are not white-skinned, the preferential status of immigrants from what used to be called euphemistically the 'New Commonwealth' was eroded. Between 1962 and 1982 a series of legislative measures were designed to restrict the entry into Britain of black and coloured people. The first of these measures was the 1962 Commonwealth Immigrants Act, which introduced a system of employment vouchers for Commonwealth immigrants. Vouchers for unskilled and semi-skilled people were progressively phased out, and those for people with specific jobs to come to drastically reduced, from 30,130 in 1963 to 2,290 in 1972. Part of this process was achieved through the 1965 White Paper, which reduced the number of work vouchers and ended the issue of such vouchers to unskilled workers (Rees 1982).

In 1968 another Commonwealth Immigrants Act, partly designed to limit the immigration of Asians - but not whites - from East Africa, introduced the principle of the 'patrial' clause. Under this provision holders of UK passports issued outside the British Isles were made subject to the immigration control of the voucher system unless one of their parents or grandparents had been born, naturalized or adopted in the UK or in a Commonwealth country which had been self-governing before 1948. The distinction between New and Old Commonwealth, or in broad terms between black and white Commonwealth, was made explicit in this measure. The 1968 legislation also introduced into immigration policy the possibility of barring from entry into Britain British passport holders who had no other nationality. In apparent contradiction of international law, some holders of British passports were rendered Stateless by this Act.

The patrial principle was carried further by the 1971 Immigration Act, which extended the distinction between patrial and non-patrial from Colonial passport holders to the world at large. (As we now know, special legislation was to become necessary in 1983 to restore to non-patrial Falkland Islanders rights of entry to Britain which legislation had denied them but which the new jingoism of the post-Falklands era insisted they should have.) Britain's entry into the EEC in 1972 further emphasised the disadvantages of non-patrial Commonwealth citizens by creating in effect a new definition of British nationality and declaring that for the purpose of movement within the EEC patrials are British citizens but non-patrials are not. Additionally, nationals of EEC countries were - and are - allowed to enter the UK freely to work and seek work, as are Irish citizens. Ann Dummett (1976), in her clear summary of this complicated legislation, makes the point that the distinction between patrial and non-patrial is very complicated, so much so that 'it is possible for brothers and sisters in the same family to be some patrial and some non-patrial'.

It is difficult to resist the impression that legislation on immigration since 1962 has not been designed simply to control immigration or to regulate the numbers of people who might work or settle in Britain, but that it has been intended to discriminate against black people and to enshrine an element of racial prejudice in legislation. As John Rex and Sally Tomlinson (1979) have written,

> '... the status of a black or brown immigrant from the Commonwealth, if not of all black and brown men in Britain, has already been declared to be different from, and inferior to, that of the native-born British citizen.'

The British Nationality Act of 1982 finally defined and divided British nationality by creating three types of citizenship to replace citizenship of the United Kingdom and Colonies. Under this Act British Citizenship is restricted chiefly to people born in the UK with a father or mother who is a British citizen or who is settled in the UK, or to people born outside the UK to existing UK citizens. Two other categories of citizenship have been created, however, to provide a legal, if not an actual, home for those many citizens of the ex-Empire who have retained a link with Britain but who do not fit into the 'patrial' category. These two new kinds of partial British are Citizens of the British Dependent Territories, for the few remaining legacies of empire, and British Overseas Citizenship for ex-empire citizens who find themselves clinging to the British connection in countries now independent of Britain (H.M.S.O. 1981).

Recent legislation on immigration is profuse and complicated, and much more difficult to comprehend than the 1905 Aliens' Act. The point of summarizing some of the main provisions of this legislation, however, is to emphasize the fact that had such provisions been applied in the late nineteenth century, few of the Jewish immigrants of the 1880s and 1890s would have been admitted to the UK.

A feature of British reactions to Jewish immigration between 1881 and 1905 was a resentment of cultural differences as expressed in language, dress, religion and social customs. A similar, if not stronger, reaction has been an obvious part of the response to post-1945 immigrants, although in this more recent case perceptions of cultural differences are clearly connected with racial antagonism. Part of the strategy of the political right has been to suggest that there are essential differences between immigrants from European backgrounds and those from Asia or the Caribbean; hence the now common use of the word 'immigrant' for British-born people whose parents came from the 'New' Commonwealth, and the avoidance of the word not only for second generations with origins in the 'white' world but also for white immigrants who have been settled for some time in this country. A view has been propagated that people who share to some degree in the cultural traditions of Asia are so essentially different from the majority of the British population that they can never be accommodated; if they adhere to religions that do not have a long history in this country, then so much the worse. Such an attitude runs through much of the rhetoric of Enoch Powell, with his vision of 'unassimilated and unassimilable populations ... alien wedges in the heartland of the state.' (Quoted in Gilroy 1987). It is echoed by such lesser exponents as the MP who last year questioned the wisdom of encouraging young men from ethnic minority communities to join the British army. In time of war, he claimed, we would not know where their allegiance might lie (The Guardian 11/3/1987). Such attitudes appear to flourish in spite of the long but still comparatively recent history of a multi-cultural empire in which soldiers of many different religious and cultural backgrounds frequently fought for the empire not only in local wars but also in the two World Wars.

The 'alien wedges', however, are the result not simply of a perception of irreconcilably different cultures but also of a racial antagonism which we might see as the equivalent in today's situation of the 'theological denigration' that for so long militated against Jewish people in Christian Europe. Early Afro-Caribbean immigrants whose language was English, who were practising Christians, and who had been brought up to look upon Britain as the mother-country were to be regarded as much 'alien wedges' as, say, Urdu or Punjabi-speaking Muslims from Mirpur or Bengali-speaking Sylhetis. And their children are likely to be thought of as more alien than first-generation immigrants from southern Italy, or Poland, or Spain. The prospect of an accommodation along the lines of that achieved by the earlier Jewish immigrants does not seem bright.

This brings us, then, to the question of what lessons from the Jewish experience can be applied, by Christians as the major religious community in Britain, but also by Jews, humanists and others, to issues that arise in present-day plural and multi-cultural Britain.

There is first the question of racism. Clearly differences of attitude towards certain kinds of newcomers are based upon prejudices that derive from largely spurious ideas of 'race' and from differences in colour. The origins of such prejudice among the British can be related to a certain kind of experience of empire, to pseudo-scientific ideas of race that fitted well with imperial expansion, to political opportunism, and to more general theories of prejudice formation. Historically, however, racism has not been confined to a kind of colour prejudice nor to imperial experience. The most pernicious effects of a certain kind of racism were seen in the holocaust. The Fascist ideology of the Third Reich was wedded to a curious, misguided, but powerful myth of 'Aryan' supremacy which in fact was a belief in the supremacy of a group of Nordic people. As we know, the Aryan myth of the Nazis served to heighten prejudices against black people, but in its European context was especially effective in stimulating suspicion and hatred of the Jews. In the light of Hitler's misunderstanding of who the Aryans were, it seems to be an unpleasant irony of history that people whose distant ancestors may have included genuine Aryans, or Indo-Europeans, of northern Indian are today the victims of racial prejudice and discrimination in Britain. The holocaust has shown us extreme and terrible consequences that can result from racism. It therefore should encourage us to be particularly diligent in combatting racism wherever it occurs in our own communities or in present-day society. Reflection upon the experience of the holocaust surely will encourage Christians and Jews to be in the forefront of efforts to end discrimination against black and Asian people in employment, legislation, education and other public fields.

Related to this is a kind of 'theological denigration' which has sometimes been used to bolster arguments against black and Asian immigrants and their descendants in Britain. Of course, it takes a different form from the Christian anti-Semitism surveyed above. But it has about it chillingly familiar echoes of the same kind of sentiments. There is an assumption in some quarters that people who have brought with them to Britain the traditions of Asian cultures cannot be expected to accommodate successfully to life in Britain, and that those previously settled in Britain cannot be expected to accept <u>them</u>, because the cultural differences are so great that they ensure that Asians will remain permanently at odds with the rest of British society. Why should this be? Not, presumably, because Asian cultures include different kinds of music and dance, of food and dress, from those of western Europe. Major differences of taste in food, dress, music and dance exist in Europe quite independently of Asian cultures, as most families made up of middle-aged parents and teenage children could testify. The argument about threateningly different cultures surely rests on other grounds. So far as one can understand it, it seems in part to depend upon an inherited view (which might itself be a legacy of several centuries of imperial success) which regards the cultures of Asia and Africa as morally and spiritually inferior to those of the West. Put in such bald terms, the notion sounds absurd. But is there not still a lingering dream among many British people that the world outside Europe and north America is essentially chaotic and ill-formed? At the time when Jewish refugees were migrating into Britain Kipling could write dismissively:

Ship me somewhere East of Suez
Where the best is like the worst
Where there ain't no ten commandments
And a man can raise a thirst.

Morality might be expected to be different - and undoubtedly inferior - beyond Europe. And even the best-intentioned of nineteenth century missionaries could not avoid the sense of spiritual, as well as moral and technological, superiority which was inextricably bound up with ambitions of sacrificial service towards those who were perceived to be the especially needy people of the world. So Reginald Heber's famous hymn, written before his own departure to become Bishop of Calcutta, included the lines:

Can we, whose souls are lighted
With wisdom from on high,
Can we, to men benighted,
The lamp of truth deny?

The firm conviction that the British or European had the truth, whilst the people of Asia were benighted, was perhaps less crudely antagonistic than early Christian claims that the Jews had rejected the truth when it was offered and had killed the Son of God, but it contained none the less a degree of religious and moral denigration which persists in some common religious attitudes to adherents of non-Christian faiths. In the light of the holocaust we need to ask again whether Christians - and Jews also? - are too easily prone to stereotypes of Muslims, Sikhs and Hindus in Britain that may in their own ways be as unfair and potentially damaging as Christian caricatures of Judaism.

The 'theological denigration' of Judaism that goes back to Christian beginnings has done immense damage to Jews and to Christian-Jewish relationships. In the current situation in the UK we need to beware of the danger that a similar kind of denigration could imperil relationships between Christians on the one hand and Muslims, Sikhs and Hindus on the other. Religious exclusivism has been reassessed by some Christians in recent years, and has led to more sympathetic understandings of other people's faiths. It is now more common than once it was to hear or read Christians asserting that people of other faiths may have their own ways to salvation; that it may no longer be legitimate to repeat the traditional formularies of <u>extra ecclesiam nulla salus</u>, or even of 'outside Christ, no salvation'. In so far as this happens it may be regarded as a parallel to the post-1945 reassessment of Christian-Jewish questions and the willingness of some Christian scholars to re-examine, for example, the Gospel accounts of the Trial of Jesus, or of the Jewish roots of Christianity generally, in the light of

Jewish scholarship and susceptibilities.

However, it would be naive to assume that openness to other faiths has become a hallmark of the Christian churches today. So far as the UK and North America is concerned one of the unmistakable features of modern Christianity is the growth of more exclusivist forms of Christianity at a time when churches in the 'mainstream' of the Christian traditions are declining in numbers. The popular religious appeal of narrow views presented as certainties, reinforced by highly-charged emotional experience, and encouraging an exclusivism towards other kinds of Christians, let alone towards people of other faiths, should not be underestimated. The relationship of such religious attitudes to uncompromising political views which totally reject those outside the circle of 'true believers' is seen clearly in Northern Ireland and in the alliance of right-wing politics and religion in the USA. It is not a pretty sight, but it would be foolish to ignore its popular appeal.

In the face of these phenomena more liberally-minded Christians must continue to struggle to overcome stereotypes of Muslims, Sikhs and Hindus by serious study of their religious traditions and by personal meetings in order to develop a richer and more sympathetic understanding of other faiths and those who embrace them, and also by that curious reflexive process which such encounters often engender, of the essentials of Christian faith also.

It may well be that Jews can help Christians in this particular pilgrimage. As some Jews and Christians have begun to try to understand one another better after the holocaust, so they *both* have to try to understand people of other faiths better. There is a significant contribution to be made to multi-cultural Britain by Christians and Jews together.

REFERENCES

Abbott, W.M. (ed) (1967). *The Documents of Vatican II*, Geoffrey Chapman. 665-667.

Allen, S. (1971). *New Minorities, Old Conflicts: Asian and West Indian Migrants in Britain*, Random House. 46.

Anwar, M. (1979). *The Myth of Return*, Heinemann Educational. 159.

Ben-Tovim, G. and Gabriel, J. (1982). 'The Politics of Race in Britain' in Husband, C. (ed) (1982). 148-150.

Bermant, C. (1975). *A Point of Arrival*, Eyre-Methuen. 140.

Brown, C. (1984). *Black and White Britain. The Third PSI Survey*, rptd. (1985), Gower.

Chrysostom. 'Eight Orations Against the Jews', 1.7, quoted in Ruether. (1974). 130.

Commission for Racial Equality. (1978). Fact Paper 2, immigration - numbers and dispersal.

Council of Christians and Jews, The. (1974). *Facing Realities: Aspects of Christian-Jewish Understanding*. 4-5.

Dummett, A. (1976). *Citizenship and Nationality*, Runnymede Trust.

Gainer, B. (1972). *The Alien Invasion. The Origins of the Aliens Act of 1905*. Heinemann. 3.

Gartner, L.P. (1960) *The Jewish Immigrant in England 1870-1914*, Simon Publications. 43-49.

Gilroy, P. (1987) *There Ain't No Black in the Union Jack*, Hutchinson. 45.

Hammerstein, F. von. (1978). *Christian-Jewish Relations in Ecumenical Perspective*, WCC, Geneva. 6,7.

Hippolytus. 'Expository Treatises Against the Jews', 7, quoted in Ruether. (1974). 128.

H.M.S.O. (1981). *British Nationality Bill*, and *Immigration into Britain: Notes on Regulations and Procedures*

Husband, C. (ed) (1982). *'Race in Britain. Continuity and Change'*, Hutchinson.

Klein, C. (1978). *Anti-Judaism in Christian Theology*, SPCK.

Mitter, S. (1986). *Common Fate Common Bond. Women in the Global Economy*, Pluto. 131.

Mitter, S. (1987). 'Black Women and Unemployment', paper presented at the Centre for Multi-Cultural Studies, Brighton Polytechnic.

Olerearnshaw, S. (1983). 'The Promotion of Employment Equality in Britain', in Glazer and Young (eds), *Ethnic Pluralism and Public Policy*, Lexington/Heinemann.

Rees, T. (1982). 'Immigration Policies in the United Kingdom', in Husband, C. (ed) (1982). 83.

Rex, J. and Tomlinson, S. (1979). *Colonial Immigrants in a British City*, Routledge and Kegan Paul. 47.

Rose, C.J.B. (1969). *Colour and Citizenship*, Oxford University Press. 72.

Ruether, R. (1974). *Faith and Fratricide: the Theological Roots of Anti-Semitism*, Seabury Press. 215.

Troyna, B. (1982). 'Reporting the National Front', in Husband, C. (ed) (1982).

Tynedale, J. (1965). Spearhead. Quoted in Troyna (1966). 266.

GLIMPSES OF LIGHT IN A VAST DARKNESS: A STUDY OF THE MORAL AND SPIRITUAL DEVELOPMENT OF NAZI ERA RESCUERS

DOUGLAS K. HUNEKE

WESTMINSTER PRESBYTERIAN CHURCH
240 TIBURON BOULEVARD, TIBURON, CALIFORNIA 94920 (U.S.A.)

ABSTRACT

The Nazi destruction of European Jewry has given the human community an exceptionally anamorphic self-perception. Informed by the evil, indifference, and torpidity of the Nazi era, this study, begun in 1979, identifies significant, stable, and reproducible characteristics in the moral and spiritual development of Christians who rescued Jews and other endangered persons between 1933 and 1945. A two part typology of rescue is presented and a summary of the means of intervention used by the rescuers in Central and Eastern Europe. A brief narrative describes some of the rescues to identify and illustrate a constellation of commonly shared characteristics that enabled rescuers to act. In response to the lessons and implications of the rescuers' actions a brief report is included on a moral development curriculum that is based on the research findings, employing the rescuers as models of compassion. The testimony of Nazi era rescuers serves two additional, important purposes. The impartial and disinterested witness of rescuers complements the testimony of survivors, directly challenging and successfully refuting revisionists and others who deny the reality of the Holocaust. Finally, the rescuers are unique moral role models for those who seek to be altruistic and as such serve to restore a measure of hope and dignity in what was otherwise a tragic and evil era.

INTRODUCTION

The names that are synonymous with murderous evil and unspeakable crimes against humanity are well known. Nearly everyone can identify Adolf Hitler, Klaus Barbie, Josef Mengele, and Adolf Eichmann. Why do so few people know the names of Andre and Magda Trocme, Aristides de Sousa Mendes, John Widner, Herman Graebe, Gertrude Luckner, or Stefka Job? Their names should be well known because they are synonymous with compassion, selfless courage, and the protection of human life. The Christians who rescued Jews during the Nazi era were a distinct minority, a faithful remnant among the millions of people living in all of Central and Eastern Europe. Fewer than 6,000 people defied laws, customs, dangers, and societal pressures in order to act altruistically on behalf of Jews, peasants, dissidents, and others who had become the targets of the National Socialists.

Most of the rescuers were unlikely characters who did not stand out in their religious, social, vocational, or political settings. Little distinguished them from their neighbors and co-nationalists. For the most part, they were simple people who performed their daily routines until some act of brutality or the arrival of a frightened stranger, a survivor, galvanized their compassionate spirits and propelled them into activities that most others were unwilling or unable to consider. In spite of almost insurmountable odds, they managed to act honorably in an evil era. Only in the past ten years have governments and scholars turned their attention to the men, women, and children whose actions earned them the honored title, "Righteous Among the Nations."

What enabled these people to take such risks on behalf of strangers? What values, skills, world-views, and religious faith exposed their compassion, allowing them to stand with the victims against the flood tide of murderers and bystanders? Beginning in 1980, with a Faculty Research Grant from the Oregon Committee for the Humanities and an award from the Memorial Foundation for Jewish Culture, I was able to interview both rescuers and the rescued and study in the archives of the Department of the Righteous at Yad Vashem. What follows is a summary of my finding.

THE MEANS OF RESCUE

Most of the Jews who were saved from the Nazis benefited from random, unpredictable interventions on their behalf. The majority of interventions were single, serial rescues; that is, one uninvolved person hid one endangered person at a time. When one rescue was accomplished and that Jewish person went elsewhere, and usually after a recuperative period for the rescuer, another Jewish refugee was given protection.

In spite of the risks, many family units hid Jews. This second means of rescue was a significant alternative to single, serial rescues. When families offered protection they planned their intervention carefully and proactively and routinely involved everyone in the decision, implementation, and security. The risk that a family member might betray the mission of the others accidentally was great -- most families feared that a child might innocently mention that refugees were at the family home. For this reason some of the adult rescuers were secretive about the identities of their "guests" in order not to put the children or other family members in a compromising position and further endanger their guests.

A third means of rescue involved work-related relocations. Altruistic persons who held positions of authority succeeded in sequestering Jews by claiming a war-related priority for their service in labor columns. Though their methodologies and motives were different, the German industrialist, Oskar Schindler, and the German railroad engineer and manager, Herman Graebe, are models of this style of intervention. For example, Graebe would requisition Jewish workers for a column using falsified work contracts and then relocate the workers in an area away from the mobile killing units (Einsatzgruppen). Both men skillfully bluffed and bullied the German regional commanders into accepting their priorities.

A fourth means of rescue involved entire communities of persons who intentionally decided to save the lives of refugees. Building from a common ethic the leaders of a community guided the people or members to hide and protect Jewish refugees. There were few large scale communal rescues reported. The two most prominent accounts are of the French Huguenots in the village of Le Chambon, led by Pastor Andre Trocme and of the priests of Assisi, led by Father Rufino Niccacci.

A fifth means of rescue involved the establishment of elaborate underground rescue networks reminiscent of similar structures developed to protect fleeing slaves during the American Civil War. Jewish refugees would be received at one location and moved to other areas, away from Nazi or collaborationist activities. The leaders in the railroad network were well known to each other and had multiple connections that allowed them to act like the hub of a wheel, sending refugees out to rescuers through the spokes of their network. Seventh Day Adventist John Widner used connections with his fellow Adventists. Widner, a student in France at the time when the Petain government began cooperating with the Nazis, took more than 800 Jews and 100 Allied aviators over the mountains, delivering them to the safekeeping of his colleagues.

There was also a national rescue effort that involved the cooperation of an entire state. Most notable in this category were the Danes. In this rare case, government leaders and civilians engaged in resistance-through-rescue. The record of this amazing achievement is well documented. Employing a different strategy, the Swedish government enabled its diplomat, Raoul Wallenberg, to dispense passports and identity cards and to establish safe houses for the Jews of Budapest through the Swedish legation in that city.

There were many people who, for various reasons, believed that they could not participate in direct interventions, but who willingly used their professional skills to benefit those who were involved in rescue. These people procured food, papers, lodging, transportation, and clothing.

Except for some subversive rescues described below, most rescuers avoided any physical confrontation with the Nazis and collaborators, because they believed that it was morally inconsistent to use violence to combat violence, or because they had no comparable means of matching the fire power of the Nazis.

A TYPOLOGY OF RESCUE

During my research, I discerned five clusters of rescue types that I subdivided under two major categories. There was some overlapping of typologies, but generally the accounts fall naturally into the categories (Table 1).

Table 1

Category of Rescuers
Rescues as a Means to an End
Subversive
Conditional
Rescues as an End in Themselves
Ideological
Communal
Friendship

In the first category, "rescue as a means to an end," the rescue interventions were effected in order to have impact on a Nazi system or structure, not for the purposes of altruism. There are two subdivisons of this category. The first, "subversive rescues," had as its primary goals the intentional subversion or inconveniencing of Nazi operations. For the rescuers in this subdivision, the victims were of secondary significance in a contest between themselves and the military forces. Many of these rescues involvcd violence against the Nazis. Those that were non-violent provided excellent opportunities to achieve both humanitarian and strategic ends. The second subdivision is that of "conditional rescues." Rescues that were performed for reward or personal gain or some quid pro quo failed to meet the generally accepted standards of altruistic behavior and were not considered in this study. In numerous situations, however, rescuers required that certain conditions be met before a rescue was accomplished. These conditions did not in any manner benefit the rescuer. One person informed rescue organizers that he wanted to be certain Germany was near defeat before he would cooperate. Another rescuer, a German, stated emphatically that he would only harbor highly educated Jews because they would be essential for the re-building of Europe after the defeat of the National Socialists. He indeed rescued a number of well-educated persons using this primitive version of "life boat ethics."

In the second general category, "rescues as an end in themselves," there are three subdivisions. Rescues in this category had no other purpose than direct relief of the victims. The first subdivision is "ideological rescues." The rescuers in these instances reported that they were simply doing their human duty. This report was nearly always substantiated by follow-up interviews with those who were rescued. The rescuers point to religious or humanitarian motivations as the root of their behavior. There is clear evidence of a strong commitment to a consistent and coherent value structure that linked the values to the intervention behavior. Overwhelmingly, these values were based on religious teachings (such as the biblical parable of the "good Samaritan" or the kingdom teachings in Matthew 25), moral role models, and institutional affiliations.

The second subdivision, "communal rescues," has been introduced previously. These rescues were carried out by groups of people who shared the following characteristics: (1) they lived in close geographical proximity (same village, city, convent, or parish); (2) shared common, long-established values; (3) had a unifying force other than rescue that existed prior to 1933 (belief, creed, or an institutional structure); (4) association was intentional and voluntary; and (5) had established an intentional plan and network to accomplish their interventions. Rescues by partisan or underground groups were not considered in the study because they fit more clearly in the subversive, means-to-an-end category and because they routinely used violence to accomplish their ends. The communal rescues suggest the value of an organized ethic, ensuring effectiveness and security. The absence of many, large-scale church sponsored rescues challenges the effectiveness of the institution's ability to actualize its justice and compassion teachings prior to and during the period of the Holocaust.

The final subdivision, "friendship rescues," offers proof of the importance of pre-catastrophe relationships between victims and rescuers. In each instance the rescuer was either a friend of the victims or, in some lesser way, acquainted with them. In more than two thirds of the cases studied, there was some degree of familiarity or relationship established between the parties. In all of the cases the rescuers reported that they had some meaningful knowledge of Judaism or a degree of familiarity with Jewish lifestyles. Two researchers, Bibb Latane and John Darley, point out that "A particular bystander might feel especially responsible for a certain victim when a relationship already exists between them ... and he [the rescuer] may be led to help a mere acquaintance, even if there is no friendship involved." (1) Other researchers (Coopersmith and London) confirm that once rescuers begin to help a known person, they tend to generalize their compassion to others in similar situations.

TRAITS OF NAZI ERA RESCUERS

A major purpose of my study was to identify common factors that might have predisposed the rescuers to their altruistic interventions. A pioneer in this research was Perry London. (2) In his initial studies he identified three dominant qualities in the rescuers. My research confirms and expands his findings (Table 2).

Table 2

Traits of Rescuers

Traits of Rescuers
Spirit of Adventurousness
Parental Model of Moral Conduct
Socially Marginal (Religiously Inspired Non-Conformity)
Empathic Imaginations
Theatrical Skills
Spirit of Hospitality
Personal Experience with Suffering
Containment of Prejudice
Group Intervention (Communal)

London's first conclusion was that the rescuers had a discernible spirit of adventurousness. These people were risk-takers in multiple areas of their lives (vocationally, socially, politically, and recreationally). I would qualify London's description of this trait by noting that while rescuers showed a marked proclivity for adventure, they were not reckless or impulsive. They calculated their actions carefully before engaging in them. Numerous rescuers reported that they engaged in elaborate planning procedures in order to maximize security and reduce the risk to the people they were helping. A Dutch rescuer who was an accomplished and award-winning skier, regularly waited for nightfall and then traversed the route he would take the next morning with the refugees. He did this to be certain that military snow patrols had not moved into the area he would be traveling.

London also identified the fact that the rescuers had an intense identification with a parental model of moral conduct. Virtually all of the rescuers in my study reported a close, significant tie with one or both parents who acted morally, who made use of a decidedly moral vocabulary, and who actively practiced their values. In most cases only one parent was reported to have been the moral parental role model; this should be an encouragement to contemporary single parents who question their ability to effectively communicate altruistic values and skills to their children. In the cases when both parents had articulated the same values, rescuers reported that this values agreement gave them confidence later in life. When they became Nazi era rescuers they experienced no ambiguity in their decision to break the laws and deviate from the accepted behavior against Jews.

The rescuers recall that their parents based their moral teachings on religious concepts or quotations. There also seemed to be a useful and practical folk-wisdom or common sense quality about the moralizing. The Dutch rescuers in my study reported that frequently the Bible lessons had to do with kindly behavior or how to get along with people and life. One Dutch man indicated that his father connected the feeding of strangers and the care of widows and orphans with the biblical mandates for such behavior. These teachings were recalled as he undertook his rescues. It must also be noted that there was no gender specificity -- males and females seemed to play equal roles as moral parental models.

Finally, London asserted that the majority of rescuers were socially marginal. In my interviews I took great pains to confirm this difficult to measure, but significant finding. Marginality took many forms. There was a 14-year-old Baptist rescuer in Poland whose marginality is noted by her age and by the fact that she lived in a predominantly Roman Catholic country. There was a Catholic nun who led a rescue effort in southern Holland -- a predominantly Protestant region; and a Reformed tradition minister who went to a predominantly Roman Catholic region to start a rescue network. There were cases where Christians were married to Jews or had significant social and vocational contact with Jews. This was most unusual at that time and would have contributed to an identification of social marginality.

The concept of social marginality suffers from definitional deficiencies and also presents certain quantitative difficulties for many social scientists. Traditionally, the concept ignores the significant factor of religiously inspired non-conformity that is regularly linked with biblical directives to compassionately care for those who are vulnerable, disenfranchised, and who suffer oppression and injustice. One Dutch rescuer summed up the matter of religiously inspired non-conformity when she quoted St. Paul's admonition in Romans 12:2, "Be not conformed to this world, but be transformed to a completely new way of thinking so as to know what is the good and acceptable and perfect will of God." She went on to say that, "For me to kill or betray Jews would have been to conform to evil. I had no choice but to follow God's will and save Jews from the Nazis."

Rescuers whose altruism was substantiated by biblical teachings that valued non-conformity to ill-willed authorities, found further encouragement and support in biblical social ethics. These rescuers reported being directly influenced by such teachings as Matthew 25:31-46, in which Jesus taught that Christians who gave food to the hungry, water to the thirsty, welcomed strangers (sojourners), shared clothing with the needy, and visited the sick and prisoners, did those acts to Jesus himself. The rescuers also referred to Jesus' summary of the Ten Commandments and the teachings of the prophets, in Matthew 7:12 (commonly referred to as "the golden rule"), "Always treat others as you would like them to treat you." They also quoted or paraphrased the portion of Matthew 22:34-40 that directs Christians, "You must love your neighbor as yourself." The moral admonition of the parable of "the good Samaritan" (Luke 10:29-42), "Go thou and do likewise," was commonly paraphrased and used to explain an intervention.

Religiously inspired non-conformity coupled with the social ethics of the Christian Scripture became intellectual mandates to intervene on behalf of desperately endangered people. A German rescuer noted that the Nazi era interventions, which he justified using biblical passages, afforded him an important and comforting sense that there was consistency between his religious beliefs and how he lived his life.

I have identified six additional qualities or traits that the rescuers share in common and that distinguish them from the general population. First, the rescuers had sophisticated "empathic imaginations." The essence of the empathic imagination is the ability to place oneself in the actual situation or role of another person and actively visualize the effect and the long-term consequences of the situation or role on that person. The German rescuer, Herman Graebe, had one of the most effective empathic imaginations of all the rescuers I interviewed. He developed it with his moral parental model, Louise Graebe, who routinely asked her son, "Fritz, what would you do?" This was never an idle or rhetorical question and it was always asked in a situation of moral choice or personal relationships. Mrs. Graebe would help her son develop an answer and at the same time guide him with her values.

The extent to which Graebe's empathic imagination grew and developed was evidenced at the edge of a mass grave in Dubno, the Ukraine. There he watched his contemporary, an anonymous, naked Jewish man, point to the sky and speak to his young son moments before the two descended to a ledge in the mass grave and were murdered. In Graebe's empathic imagination he and his own young son became the two Jews standing before the pit. Forty years later, Graebe vividly remembered thinking at the time what he would say to his son if they had been the ones waiting to be murdered, "I, too, would point to heaven and assure him that where we were going there would be no more mass graves and no SS." As he walked from the scene, heartsick, his mother's question crossed into his consciousness: "And Fritz, what would you do?" Graebe went on from this encounter to establish a successful rescue network in the Ukraine.

Closely related to the above trait is the rescuers' ability to present themselves and control a critical situation. This is a theatrical skill common among a significant number of the rescuers who had participated in a stage play, developed acting skills, or frequented the stage theatre. A number of rescuers related how they practiced breathing, posture management, and planned their wardrobes and locations. One rescuer reported how he "rehearsed scenes and outcomes" in order to have a response for any possible situation. These theatrical skills greatly contribute to the development of the traits of social marginality and empathic imagination.

Next, the rescuers were quite adept at hospitality. The skills related to hospitality are learned at home from moral parental models. The rescuers removed endangered people from intensely hostile environments, offering them a respite from the forces that sought their destruction. They gave the refugees food, drink, warmth, rest, protection, and other creaturely comforts. They welcomed friends and strangers alike and provided whatever was necessary and available to them. Hospitality is the specific training ground of altruism. Henri J.M. Nouwen, a Roman Catholic theologian, has written the following description of this quality:

> "In a world full of strangers, estranged from their own past, culture, and country, from their neighbors, friends, and family, from their deepest self and their God, we witness a painful search for a hospitable place where life can be lived without fear ... That is our vocation, to convert the hostis into a hospes, the enemy into a guest and to create the free and fearless space where brotherhood and sisterhood can be formed and fully expressed." (3)

Another common trait shows that most rescuers had significant personal experience with suffering and death prior to the onset of the war. They might have seen badly injured people returning from wars or watched members of their families suffer debilitating and often fatal illnesses, and die at home. The end result of these experiences was that the rescuers felt neither fear nor revulsion in the face of another's suffering. It did not morbidly attract them nor weaken their resolve to combat it. On the contrary, most of the rescuers came to see imposed suffering and death as unnecessary, inappropriate, and inhumane. Most of the rescuers reported that the traumatic impact of a particular incident was shared within the family and given perspective by parents. Their experiences with suffering enhanced their empathic imaginations and contributed to their careful planning during wartime.

Another important trait is that the rescuers had all learned to confront and manage their prejudices. Entrenched and culturally validated stereotypes of specific individuals or groups often determine political, social, and legal actions that may result in dehumanizing attitudes toward, and injury to, the individuals or groups. When these stereotypes are challenged or set aside in deference to a greater consideration of human decency or a more egalitarian world view, the effects of prejudice and brutality can be avoided. All of the rescuers had developed a certain world view that enabled them to interpret the persecution of Jews and others as morally repugnant. Obviously, friendships, working associations, or even vague, general acquaintances facilitated this quality. Moral parental role models also contributed to the skills related to containment of prejudice. It is important to note that Perry London contends that many of the rescuers were anti-Semitic in regards to certain limited religious and cultural outlooks and yet they had an umbrella value system that prevented them from translating their anti-Semitism into genocidal behavior. One rescuer commented at length about her belief that the Jews had brought on the suffering of the Holocaust because they had failed to follow the Ten Commandments and because they crucified the Christ and refused to leave Judaism for Christianity. She was shocked when asked if her perspective could be understood as a theological restatement and justification of the National Socialist decision to eliminate the Jewish population. Upon reconsideration she concurred, offering the umbrella caveat, "But the Jews are human beings. No one has the right to kill people because of what they believe."

The last trait (or factor) was not as common to the larger population of rescuers, but has tremendous implications for the historical interpretation of the Holocaust and the prevention of future acts of inhumanity. The most successful rescues, in terms of numbers saved and shared risks, were the communal rescues. Rescuers involved in single, serial interventions are quick to relate the profound, nearly disabling fear that gripped them whenever they acted. Many of the rescuers required sabbaticals lasting several weeks or months before they regained courage for the next rescue. To their credit most of these altruists persisted in their efforts.

In those instances where groups of people or whole communities engaged in rescue work, many more endangered people benefited. The risks of infiltration and detection were enormously high, but the results were equally great. Communal rescues were orchestrated by religiously based groups with credible and inspiring leaders. If a leader was taken away, as happened with Pastor Trocme in Le Chambon, others were able to step in and continue the work. More importantly, a supportive community of coworkers offers the nurturance of a commonly held compassionate vision, affirmation of shared values, a broad base of mutual responsibility, a diversity of skills, and a system or structure that guaranteed or, at least increased, the likelihood of effectiveness and security. Compassionate interventions leading to the well-being of victims will be most successful when there is a community of like-minded persons with an organized ethic that supports such interventions. Institutional Christianity reaps a justifiable condemnation when it fails to prepare people to act in a pro-human manner or fails to build both an ethic and a structure that protects human life and ensures the dignity of persons.

There is one final notation about the rescuers that has to do with the consistency of their behavior. The following two examples speak to the qualities of a majority of the rescuers. I interviewed a Polish farm woman who spent three years hiding Jewish refugees in various places on her farm. When the course of the war turned against Germany and straggling young German infantrymen were in danger of being killed by the populace, she began hiding them in the same places where she had hidden the Jews. At Yad Vashem I spent several days interviewing a Dutch woman who had saved forty Jews. As the interview went on during the second day she began looking at her wrist watch. Several times I inquired about her fatigue or other commitments that she might have. Finally, this eighty-year-old woman said, "I have truly enjoyed my time here, the reunions with those I loved, but I am anxious to return home. I am the coordinator of refugee resettlement for my church and tomorrow we are welcoming two families who have lived on the South China Sea for months. I think I need to be there even though I am scheduled to remain here for another week." The skills, traits, and predispositions are an ingrained, consistent pattern in the lives of the vast majority of rescuers. They continue to be caring and helpful people.

I have incorporated the findings and implications from the study of Nazi era rescuers into a moral development curriculum. The rescuers and the accounts of their activities serve as models in the design. The curriculum encourages the establishment of family-based norms, articulated by the resident parent(s), and joined with a foundation of theological, ethical, philosophical, humanitarian, or metaphysical teachings. The program is adaptable for use in public, private, and parochial schools. Strategies for caring and helping behavior (altruism) derive from examples provided by the participants. Empathic imagination is encouraged in this process and through impact brainstorming and preview, role rehearsal, and a variety of practiced theatrical skills relating to self-presentation. Social marginality (non-conformity) is presented and discussed using the examples of Nazi era rescuers and relevant biblical, literary, or theological materials. Following an altruistic intervention a family or school group conducts an impact review, further brainstorming, and concludes with an appropriate, ritualized observance of the intervention. This curriculum was incorporated with the pro active pro social design of Dr. Susan Gilmore and her associates at the University of Oregon (Eugene, Oregon, U.S.A.). It has been field tested in public schools, church education programs, and with a group of university students.

The testimony and study of Nazi era rescuers serves at least two more significant and invaluable purposes. The impartial and disinterested witness of Christians and other non-Jews who rescued Jews and additional endangered persons during the Nazi era complements the testimony of survivors. Together, they directly challenge and successfully refute those who erroneously and with suspect motivation contradict or seek to revise the historical reality of the Holocaust.

It is my hope that the world will pay ever greater attention to those men, women, and children who acted with compassion and courage. I hope that the world will learn their names and celebrate their lives. The rescuers of the Nazi era restore a healing vision of humanity; they lift up the cause of kindness and dignity; they redeem our weakened hope for the future. Albert Camus, when he accepted the Nobel Prize, said of those who lived and worked for the betterment of the world after the Fascist and Nazi eras,

> "We had to fashion ourselves an art of living in times of catastrophe in order to be reborn before fighting openly against the death instinct at work in our history." (4)

We who live in the nuclear age must come to understand the concerns and the works of the Nazi era rescuers as an antidote for the tremendous death instinct at work in our times. The compassionate acts of the Nazi era rescuers did not develop *ex nihilo*, but rather were rehearsed and affirmed in ways that ensured their continued refining and practice. We dare not do anything less than that in our schools, colleges, universities, churches, and synagogues.

FOOTNOTES

1. Bibb Latane and J.M. Darley, *The Unresponsive Bystander: Why Doesn't He Help?"* New York: Appleton-Century-Crofts, 1970, p. 34.

2. Perry London, "The Rescuers: Motivational Hypotheses About Christians Who Saved Jews From The Nazis," in J. Macaulay and L. Berkowitz, Altruism and Helping Behavior, New York: Academic Press, 1970, p. 244.
3. Henri J.M. Nouwen. Reaching Out: Three Movements of the Spiritual Life, New York: Doubleday and Company, 1975, pp. 46-47.
4. Albert Camus. "Camus at Stockholm, The Acceptance of the Nobel Prize," translated by Justin O'Brien. Atlantic Monthly. May, 1958, p. 34.

BIBLIOGRAPHY

Hallie, Phillip. Lest Innocent Blood Be Shed: The Story of the Village of Le Chambon and How Goodness Happened There. New York: Harper and Row, 1979.

Huneke, Douglas. The Moses of Rovno. New York: Dodd, Mead, 1985.

Keneally, Thomas. Schindler's List. New York: Simon and Schuster, 1982.

Oliner, Samuel and Oliner, Pearl. The Altruistic Personality: Rescuers of Jews in Nazi Europe. New York: Free Press, 1988.

Ramati, Alexander. The Assisi Underground: The Priests Who Rescued Jews. New York: Stein and Day, 1978.

Rittner, Carol and Meyer, Sandra. The Courage To Care: Rescuers of Jews During the Holocaust. New York: New York University Press, 1986.

Yahil, Leni. The Rescue of Danish Jewry. Philadelphia: Jewish Publication Society, 1969.

Barriers to Gratitude

Sarah Moskovitz Ph.D.

Professor Human Development and Counseling
Director of the Child Survivor Archive
California State University at Northridge, CA 91330

ABSTRACT

The question of gratitude toward their Christian hiders on the part of Jews who were children in their care during the Holocaust is explored. Using a questionnaire that reveals facts and feelings a number of relevant factors are identified.

* * *

We lived in gloomy valleys between forbidden peaks,
sad, silent specters of holocaustal terrors
our constant companions.
Deep inside our memory boxes - Cerberus guarding Pandora's box
securely fastened, never opened, acid etched
with hideous demons.
Hidden inside:
the tears we could not cry,
the words we could not speak
the memories we dared not face.
the dreams we dared not dream.

First verse of Memory Boxes
by R.Gabriele Silten,1988

* * *

INTRODUCTION

This paper examines the question, sometimes accusation, addressed to Jews who were hidden with Christians during the Holocaust: "Why aren't they more grateful?" "Why aren't they now taking care of those Christians who are now elderly?" These questions are asked not only among Christians but among Jews. At least three foundations have recently been started in the U.S.A. to care for the hiders, two have been initiated by former hidden children Sam Oliner, and Pierre Sauvage, the third by Rabbi Harold Shulweiss and Eva Fogelman, neither of whom were hidden.

The primary instrument of this research is a questionnaire mailed to the membership of the Child Survivor Association in Los Angeles. Since I do not know how many on the mailing list were in camps, wandering or in hiding, I am unable to determine what percentage of those in hiding returned the questionairre. I did not expect a large return because of previous work I did with Child Survivors who had been in hiding, from therapeutic work with those who had been hidden as children and from experience with Dr. Flo Kinsler co-leading time-limited (8 weeks) therapeutic discussion groups at Jewish Family Service, West L.A. Office under the direction of Ethel Schy.

I had gained a knowledge of the depth of the pain surrounding the hiding period as well as how pervasive the taboo is for many against speaking of it, a taboo which amounted to coming out of hiding at the end of the war only to go back in to a second kind of hiding about that experience. One result of that experience is a life-long barrier to looking back.

Thirty responses were recieved in time to be included and this paper consists of an analysis of twenty seven of these. (Three were excluded because the respondents were over sixteen at the end of the war, too old to be considered Child Survivors.) The questionnaire is included in entirety as Appendix One.

The questionnaire sought to recall memories and feelings experienced during the time of hiding. I assumed that fuller knowledge of these memories and feelings would provide some of the necessary data with which to illuminate the gratitude issue. The present paper is based on information gained from part of the questionnaire:

Questions one through eight, deal with age, time in hiding, location, whether the child was alone or with parents or siblings, knowledge of whether hiders recieved money and whether there was contact with parents or other protectors during hiding. These answers constitute PART ONE: BACKGROUND DATA.

Questions nine, eleven a-h, and twelve constitute PART TWO: FEELING DATA.

This information will be presented and discussed followed by PART THREE: CONCLUSIONS .

Before going further, it is important for the readers to examine their own assumptions or fantasies about the hiding experience because the issue of gratitude and the nature of expectations for gratitude are intimately bound with one's assumptions of what the experience of hiding was like for children. Do these include representations of loving havens among heroic, kindly strangers acting as foster parents? Or relative comfort with one's own family in an attic like Anne Frank? Or safety in convents where self-sacrificing nuns took care of childrens needs?

The major purpose of this paper then is to examine the actual experience of hiding as it is remembered by the people who lived it as children and to make this remembered reality more widely known . The question of gratitude may then be seen in relation to that reality.

* * *

PART ONE:BACKGROUND DATA

Realities of the outer world of Time, Places, Persons and Money

Question 1. Age when you went into hiding:

Age 0 through 3 : 6 people
Age 4 through 7 :11 people
Age 8 through 11 : 7 people
Age 12 through 14 : 3 people

With three exceptions these people were age ten and under and the majority, a total of seventeen people were age seven or under when they went into hiding. A young group developmentally. By subtracting the age when they went into hiding from age when the war ended (question 2) we obtain the number of years in hiding, which is as follows:

One year : 2 people
Two years : 4 people
Two and one-half years : 1 person
Three years :12 people
Four years : 3 people
Four and one half years : 1 person
Five years : 4 people

Thus twenty of the twenty seven people spent three to five years of their chidhoods hidden.

With whom were you hidden, or were you alone? is the point of Question 3.

With both parents all the time	:4 persons
With both parents part of the time	:2 persons
With one parent all of the time	:1 person
With one parent part of the time	:2 persons
With a brother or sister (no parent)	:4 persons
All alone part of the time	:4 persons
All alone all of the time	:10 persons

Only four people were fortunate to have both parents with them all the time; as did Anne Frank. The majority, seventeen, of these hidden people were alone either part or all of the time. Assuming that the younger the child, the more need for tender care, this is a very vulnerable group of children. For in addition to their young age and intense need for warmth and attention from the caretakers, they often were separated from their parents continuous care in abrupt even brutal ways and circumstances.

Upon reflecting on the good fortune of those who had parents with them, one must consider the unique stresses even for this group. For example one child who was ten years old, hidden with both parents reflects on her constant concern for her mother's deteriorating health while in hiding. Another reports pleading with his ever more despairing father not to commit suicide while they were hidden. That boy was then around six years old.

Question 4 deals with the child's security centered on the stability of location and caretakers. Being moved from place to place after loss of parents would add the hardship of further disruption of attachments to people and familiar environments.

Furthermore,lest we think of places as homes, attics, cellars only let's remember that pig-sties, barns, under garbage dumps, in fields and ditches are also mentioned.

In how many places were you hidden? is Question 4:

One place	: 7 people
Two places	: 3 people
Three places	: 7 people
Four places	: 4 people
Five places	: 2 person
Six places	: 1 person
Seven places	: 0
Eight places	: 1
Nine places	: 2 people

It appears that during the time they were hidden more than one half (seventeen persons) of this group of children had three or more different caretaking environments to which to adapt after loss of their own familiar surroundings with their normal expectable caretaking. Even those who were with parents during this time could not be said to have had caretaking that was normal in the sense that it was on the parents own turf, without parental fears of being exposed pervading the atmosphere.

A closer analysis of the people who were hidden Alone and the average number of places they were in reveals that of the ten people who were All Alone the whole time of hiding:

5 places were experienced by 2 people
4 places were experienced by 0
3 places were experienced by 4 people
2 places were experienced by 2 people .
1 place only was experienced by 2 people.

On average then, children who were all alone were hidden for approximately three years and were moved more than twice (2.8) times. This means two to three additional serious losses of caretakers occured after the initial most serious loss of parents. From the responses to Question 5 we learn that:

8 children were hidden in France
6 in Poland
5 in Belgium
3 in the Netherlands
3 in Italy/Yugoslavia
1 in Hungary
1 in Ukraine

The question of payment for hiding is answered in Question 6.

14 persons out of 25 answered Yes, their hiders were paid.
5 persons answered that they Didn't Know.
8 persons answered No, their hiders were not paid.
Of the 8 who answered No, 2 reported that money was paid after the war in gratitude.

Questions 7 and 8 deal with whether the hidden child had contact with parents or an underground representative during the war. In response to question 7, of the nineteen children who never had parent with them (but may have had a brother or sister) only five had memory for someone who came around to see them. Two said they realized this person paid their hiders. Another said she recalled a lady who came around once a month and was shot by the Germans. One recalls a priest who came to see him. And one was visited in her convent by two "Jewish young ladies passing as Christians". At around the age of twelve she had been moved around from a private home where she had been severly abused and eventually settled at the convent. She feared her mother would never find her and was heartened by the three visits of the Jewish young ladies because she felt they would be able to let her mother know where to find her after the war. (Sadly, her mother and father did not ever return from Auschwitz.)

Was there contact with parents? If such contact were possible hope and attachment for parents could be kept alive. Unfortunately, of the twenty people who were alone at some time during the war, only four had any repeated contact with a parent. One said "my parents took a big chance and came to see me." (One survivor from Belgium that I worked with in a therapeutic discussion group, blames herself to this day for her parents death. Her parents came out of their own hiding place to visit her. She stood at a window and watched them being arrested.)

Another recalls her parents coming with food and clothes several times. One of the little girls hidden in a convent between the ages of six and nine had a mother in that convent who worked there, passing as a nun. But because they had to pretend they were not related in order to stay safe (nun's do not have children...) the child experienced her mother as avoidant, always keeping her at a distance. The proximity therefore was not a source of comfort, but of severe confusion and stress.

Another who was between the ages of twelve and fourteen in hiding in Belgium reports that letters through a third person kept her in occaisional contact with her mother. And lastly one person recalls that in the four years of his hiding, his father came twice, and an uncle came once to tell him father had been killed.

Given the paucity of contact as seen above with people to whom the child had been bonded prior to hiding we would suspect that strong feelings of loneliness and isolation, of not mattering to anyone could be prevalent...

* * *

PART TWO: DATA ABOUT FEELINGS
Realities of the inner world

What feelings do people recall as predominant as they think about hiding? These are elicited by Question 9.

Before continuing this report, it is necessary to state that for a person who was in hiding to confront this part of the questionnaire may, in many cases, be an act of courage. Some people have so many painful recollections of how they felt at this time in their lives that even in extensive psychotherapy with psychoanalysts (four to five times a week) they do not talk about this part of their lives for a long time if ever.

Three persons who were hidden between the ages birth to three, three to six, and three to seven all say they have NO Memory at all of that period. (Memory loss for periods in which there was loss of important attachments may be a primitive way of coping with the loss by blotting out the pain of it. Amnesia in this case, one could say is a radical detachment.)

I have arranged the adjectives that people used to answer Question 9 which asks for recall of predominant feelings during hiding on an approximate continuum of having had feelings of happiness and safety though physical discomfort to varying aspects of intense psychological discomfort. Some people identified several feelings: 51 feeling were reported by 25 people.

The term Loyalty Conflict, below was first pointed out by Hans Keilson (1978) in describing hidden children. It is used here as a summary term for the feelings expressed, e.g. "My Jewish upbringing, though not orthodox was in constant conflict with the day to day teachings of the very Christian Reformed Calvinist family I lived with." This man reports trying to remember Sabbath songs on Friday night under the covers of his bed, singing softly to himself. He was then between ten and thirteen years old. Still in touch with his hiders today, the conflict continues as the mother of the family that hid him still urges him to become Christian - "it's not too late." she says.

FEELING (Positive)	Number of times mentioned	
Safe with parents "despite bad moments"	1	
Happy (on farm which was fifth hiding place)*	1	
Sense of Adventure	1	
SUM of FEELINGS	3	POSITIVE

* * *

FEELING (Negative)	Number of times mentioned	
Just to survive	1	
Physical discomfort: cold, hunger, confinement	10	
No control, confused, lost	7	
Loyalty conflict	3	
Sadness-loss-longing abandonment	11	
Anger, resentment	4	
Fear, anxiety	15	
Amnesia-no memory for entire period	3	
SUM OF FEELINGS	57	54 NEGATIVE

Only three of the fifty-seven adjectives used to recall predominant feeling are positive. The great majority of feelings,fifty-four reflect both physical and psychic pain. The difficulty of thinking, talking, integrating this period of life may now be better understood in terms of avoidance of pain. Therefore when adults post-war said to children "Forget about what happened, don't talk about it" because the adults could not bear to hear it we can understand why children co-operated. But in the pacts of silence between them there were created the forbidden Memory Boxes in R.G. Silten's poem, the NO Tresspassing areas deep within discontinuous interrupted selves.These lacunae and feelings about them have direct bearing on the issue of gratitude, for gratitude requires the ability to freely think about and evaluate what has happened and remember it with good feeling.

Why is amnesia placed in the negative end? Because my experience with people who suffer this indicates that they have a gnawing fear of memory breaking through, that when it does it will reveal something unbearable. They fear their own thoughts which can cause distress, feelings of incompleteness and self doubt.

*This person omits any feelings about the previous 4 hiding places ,focussing only on the last happy one,which may be evidence of a survivor adaptive mode of "focussing on the good".

Question 11, which asks people to assess how they feel they were treated by their hiders is central to an understanding of the question of gratitude, for obviously one could assume more chance of feelings of gratitude toward places where one felt warmly treated. Conversely one could expect less in situations where cold indifference or even abuse predominated.

11. TREATED WITH WARM AFFECTION, KINDNESS, LOVE

a. all of the time		7 places
b. some of the time		6 places
c. COOL INDIFFERENCE, NO WARMTH		10 places
d. THREATS TO BE TURNED IN:		13 places
Occaisionally	4	
Frequently	7	
All the time	2	
e. HARSH CRITICISM REJECTION		13 places
Occaisionally	1	
Frequently	10	
All the time	1	
f. HIT, BEATEN		4 places
Occasionally	3	
All the time	1	
g. SEXUALLY MOLESTED		6 places
Occaisionally	3	
All the time	2	

In thirteen places people felt warmly treated even loved all or some of the time.

Cool indifference was the form of treatment chosen ten times to describe their experience in hiding. Three of these places were convents where the girls were between seven and eleven years old while in hiding there. While we can presume that coolness from their caretakers, hardship, hunger and cold were the lot in general of all the non-Jewish girls as well, it must be remembered that Jewish children were aware of being in far greater danger; they were separated from parents,not knowing where they were, feeling worry and longing. They felt acutely deprived when the Gentile children recieved packages containing jars of jam and extra rations which were then portioned out while the Jewish children recieved nothing and watched the others eat (personal communication Kaplan, A., 1985; Wortman, J.,1986; Schwartz, M. 1987). In many institutions and convents, Gentile children were allowed to go home for Christmas and other holidays. Jewish children had no homes to go to. Under these circumstances, having no one to turn to for support, being treated with cool indifference is not as neutral as it may sound and puts the child in stress of emotional deprivation.

The hardships for the hiders maintaining discipline with uprooted, troubled children can well be imagined. Cruel or frightened hiders in thirteen hiding places maintained discipline through use of threats to turn the child over to the Nazis. These must have resulted in creating further problems of insecurity for the child and of the child's behavior (bedwetting etc for the hider.) One person wrote that these "threats occurred in four different families over a period of 2 years" (frequently).

When taken together, harsh criticism rejection and threats of denouncement, (not just being turned out, but turned over to dangerous enemies who would kill you), could be considered a pwerfully destructive combination constituting severe emotional abuse occuring as they did over a period of years. Seven places used all of the above plus physical and or sexual abuse. Children in these places lived in Hell.

Sexual abuse occured in six different places:

Two girls occaisionally, over a period of 3 years (age 4-7) and (age 6-9). The second child (age 6-9) was one of the people who responded that she felt she was loved, treated with warm affection and kindness, yet also reports being occaisionally treated with harsh criticizm and rejection, occaisionally beaten and occaisionally sexually abused. Her ability to juxtapose all of the above illustrates how confused a child could become in such circumstances and how that confusion lingers til today.

The third child, abused ages 10-12 comments as follows:

"The people that hid my sister and I were regarded as good Catholics in the community and had an excellent reputation! I found them to be hypocrites who pretended to be good. They exploited my sister and I and would at the least provocation remind us that we were putting them in danger. The husband and his brother molested me when they drank."

Two more people reported sexual abuse <u>all of the time</u>. One of the two was abused between ages seven and ten and writes:

"I don't remember any reactions at all from the Belgian family, except from the husband. He started by taking me on his lap at twilight, and with the whole family around us fondled me. I thought it felt so good. After that feeling of caring I had I realized that sometimes when he approached my bed I should keep quiet if it hurt and then when I cringed at other times when he approached, he promised not to hurt. He would also tell me to get coal during the day in the cellar, or some preserves and then he would come down there too. I always obeyed wondering though if it was going to hurt or not."

The second person who reports being abused all of the time was between nine and eleven and was abused by an older boy who stayed with the hiders: she was beaten and starved by her hider and this boy offered her bread and butter and attention. She suffers guilt over having given in to him.

The only male to report sexual molestation writes: "in the church, the priest attempted several times to 'play' with children."

The last part of <u>Question 11 asks for any happy experiences that can be recalled from the time of hiding.</u>

Most people left this blank. One wrote "you are joking". Another wrote "happy does not apply".

Ten people were able to recall something. Five recalled memories related to their parents; three people recalled the occaisions when they saw their parents; the fourth recalls the closeness with her mother while they were in hiding together and the beauty of the countryside they were in. The fifth recalls closeness with her father and how he helped pass the time by telling wonderful stories as they watched rows of ants.

An additional three recall friendships with other children; two report that these friendships still exist forty five years later. Two people recall Christmas surprises: one recieved doll clothes for her doll made by the older convent girls and the other reports a special room with many presents that she had not been allowed in for weeks by the kind and wealthy woman who hid her.

As a whole we see that if we divide the continuum a through g and total the number of positive responses in a and b (treated with warm affection, loved most or some of the time) we find a total of thirteen responses on the positive side, and forty-six on the negative; i.e for every one place remembered positively there are four remembered negatively.

One can speculate why negative treatment was so high. Surely the hiders as well as other children were living in stressful wartime conditions. The stress of taking risks to hide people, especially a child who might blurt out something to create suspicion can certainly be seen as possibly adding more tension. We know (from the child abuse literature) that high stress in adult caretakers increases the risk for becoming abusive.

The last question is: <u>Question 12, Were you able to express your feelings to anyone while you were in hiding?</u>

Given the intense distress that children were experiencing we search here for the possible relief and comfort that being able to express feelings to someone might have offered. However the answers to that question for the most part do not show that relief to have been available. We cannot even take for granted that those who were hidden with parents were able to confide their feelings freely to them. For as one person responds "We lied to each other, that it was O.K. that everything was fine." Another whose brother died of a childhood desease while in hiding because no doctor could be called, reports "I could not tell them how I felt and cause them more pain. We never spoke of our feelings." This is a person who has come to a series of Child Survivor Discussion groups saying she has never cried about her experience and feels bottled up. She has come to be able to cry...

The results from this question are tabulated as follows:

With whom hidden	Feelings expressed to whom	Yes	No
1. Alone	Children,adults in convent	1	
2. Parents	No one		1
3. Alone	No one		1
4. Alone	Friends (age13-16)	1	
5. Parents and alone	No one		1
6. Parents	No memory (0-5)		
7. Parents	No one		1
8. Parents, Aunt	Aunt	1	
9. Alone	Peers (12-14)	1	
10. Alone, mother	No one		1
11. Alone	No one		1
12. Alone	No one		1
13. Parents/15 people	No one		1
14. Alone	No one		1
15 Brother	Brother	1	
16. Mother	Mother	1	
17. Parents	Parents	1	
18. Alone	No one		1
19. Alone	No one		1
20. Sister	Sister	1	
21. Alone	No one		1
22. Sister	No one		1
23. Alone	No one		1
24. Sister	No one		1
25 Alone	No one		1
26. Alone/Aunt	No one		1
27. Parents	No one		1
	SUM	8	19

One third of the children were able to express feelings to someone. But what is especially interesting is that the someone may have been a relative or a peer but in no case was it the people with whom they were hidden.

* * *

PART THREE: CONCLUSIONS

We now begin to see the complexity of the gratitude issue; that it is not simply a question of children whose lives were saved by being hidden being grateful for that. We see a number of important factors profoundly suffusing the memory of having been hidden. At least some of these factors are:

1) The number of places hidden which indicates the number of disruptions of chances to make stable relationships;

2) The emotional tone of the experience which is remembered as a predominant feeling which was intensely laden with fear, anxiety, isolation and sometimes with guilty feelings of disoyalty to parents and Judaism

3) The quality of relationship with the caretakers, how kindly indifferently or abusively one was treated.

4) How open the hiders were to hearing the child's feelings. This last point has special relevance to the expectations for gratitude now being discussed.

It is unrealistic to expect that people, even that relatively small group that was well treated, who have learned in childhood that their lives depended on being a hidden person that it is best not to express your feelings, to ignore them and not trouble others with them, that their feelings are not considered import- -it is unrealistic to expect these same people to suddenly become expansively expressive of feelings and of gratitude for a time in their lives dominated by fear,silence,and loss. It is so unrealistic an expectation that it borders on preposterous.

But it's more than 40 years later! Some might ask: hasn't that been enough time for the hidden children to deal with their memories and be free of the pain? And the answer appears to be No! For I know of no person who lost parents while they were hidden to be free of pain. In fact some who have been unable to remember and deal with memory are just now in their 50's beginning to be able to think feel and talk or write about their experience, having themselves been in hiding, cut off from their fearful past, that forbidden part of themselves.(See for example Friedlander,S. 1979: and Tec,N. 1984). Robert Krell, the eminent Canadian psychiatrist who was a child in hiding sums it up when he says "During the war we learned fear and silence. After the war there was more fear and silence." (1988).

But shouldn't the fact that their lives were saved make them eternally grateful to their hiders even if the treatment was bad, one might ask? And again the answer cannot be simple, for many Child Survivors who lost forever their parents, families, homes, towns, homelands and stable continuity with their earlier selves while they were in hiding are not as grateful for their lives as some might presume. The many abandonments, uprootings that they have experienced have left many with heavy burdens of loss carried life long; it is not at all unusual for a child survivor to express the feeling that "I should have gone with my mother and died with her".

Three additional sources of complexity bear on the gratitude question. The first is that some of the children knew that the hiders were paid by their parents or other responsible adults. A second is that for many Child Survivors the memory blocks, taboos about talking about this period and fear of thinking about it would have created an avoidance for that period and dealing with anything related to it. Third and last, those child suvivors treated warmly by their hiders who would expectably be the people most likely to want to express gratitude to them as adults might paradoxically find it most difficult to do so because it is that group of survivors who would have the most intense loyalty conflict as relates to their own parents, even if the latter had died. This conflict would be revived by contact with their warm hiders and would therefore in some cases be avoided.

We see that gratitude cannot be assumed as a moral imperative for people who were hidden as children without knowledge of the true experience of hiding, how it really was for them. Furthermore I believe we must overcome the recent tendency toward overidealization of <u>all</u> of the hiders, perhaps arising as counterweight to years of neglect of the hiders by the public. We must not negate their courage in circumstances so virulent that even today they keep secret from their neighbors (in Poland for instance) that they were hiders.

Furthermore we must continue to ask ourselves honestly if we ourselves could in similar circumstances become hiders. But we must not overidealize. For to do so is to presume certain benign perfection on the part of all hiders and pay no attention to the realities of how the children were treated. To ignore this does a great disservice to the Child Survivors who are further burdened by blame derived from a false assumption that all of their experience in hiding was warmly protective and good, and that they are somehow meanly ungrateful.

* * *

ACKNOWLEDGEMENTS

(This writer owes special thanks to four people who were in hiding as children; Mirijam Wheeler and Charles Kessler who first opened the door (Moskovitz,1983) Roger Kaufman whose reaction to a paper accusing Jews of ingratitude toward their Christian hiders triggered this work and Maya Schwartz,nee Mandel-Finkel whose suggestions for the questionnaire were invaluable.)

REFERENCES

Friedlander,Saul. (1979).When Memory Comes, Farrar, Strauss and Giroux, N.Y.

Kaplan,Augusta. (1988). Personal Communication, Los Angeles

Keilson,Hans. (1979). Sequentielle Traumatisierung Bei Kindern. (Sequential Traumatization in Children) Forum der Pschiatrie. Stuttgart:Ferdinand Enke Ferlag

Krell, Robert. (January 28, 1988). Lecture to the Second Generation Conference at U.C.L.A.

Moskovitz, S.(1983).Love Despite Hate; Child Survivors of the Holocaust and Their Adult Lives Schocken Books, New York.

Schwartz, Maya. (1988). Personal Communication Los Angeles.

Tec, Nehama. (1984). Dry Tears, Oxford University Press, New York.

Wortman, Joan. (1988). Personal Communication, Los Angeles, 1987.

APPENDIX 1.

page one of questionnaire

(Reader of this paper please NOTE:
LARGE BLANKS SPACES FOR ANSWERS HAVE BEEN OMITTED TO SAVE SPACE IN THIS APPENDIX)

If you need more space to answer any question or feel you have more to say please use back of pages.

1. How old were you (approximately if you dont know) when you went into hiding?

2. How old were you (again approximately if necessary) when the war ended?

3. Were you with a parent? both parents? brother, sister,? or were you alone?

4. Were you hidden in more than one place? If so how many?

5. Were you in the countryside?
In a city with a Christian family?
In a convent or monastery?
Can you state where in what country, city or region this was?

6. Do you know if the people who hid you were paid to keep you?
Paid by your parents or by an underground organization?

7. Did anyone from one of these organizations come to visit you?
If so, what was that like for you?

8. If you were hidden by yourself, without parents, did you hear from them or about them at any time during hiding ?

9. What feelings were predominant for you while in hiding?

10. What activities, work or play do you recall?

11. Circle the number of the phrase or phrases that best describe how you feel you were treated by those responsible for you while you were hidden:

a. I feel I was treated with warm affection and kindness.I felt loved.

b. Some of the time with warm affection and some of the time not

c. With cool indifference. I was there and they fed me etc. but there was no warmth. I was a burden to them

d. With threats to be turned in if I did not behave:
Occaisionally Frequently All the time

e. With harsh criticism, and rejection:
Occaisionally Frequently All the time

f. With being hit, or beaten:
Occaisionally Frequently All the time

g. I was sexually molested by someone in the family that hid me.
Occaisionally Frequently All the time

Please give more detail on the back of this page if you are able about any of the above that you have circled as true.

page two of Questionnaire

h. Can you recall any happy experiences while in hiding. If yes please describe on the back of this page.

12. Were you able to express your feelings to anyone while in hiding? If yes, to whom?

13. Did you have any awareness of what was going on in the war? What did you understand or know in your own child's way?________________________

14. Did you experience any bombing? ____

Did the persons who hid you try to make you feel safe? ________________________

If yes, how?____

15. Did you have any favorite hopes or fantasies while in hiding? Please tell what they were.

16. Did you have any recurring dreams or nightmares? If so what were these?

17. What was the most difficult thing for you during that time?

18. When you were most miserable what kept you going or comforted you?

19. Is there anything more you wish to add that this questionnaire has so far not given you the opportunity to say?

20. If you had the opportunity to ask a question of others who were in hiding, what would it be?

Thank you again for your thoughtful replies.
With appreciation for you and your experience,

Sarah Moskovitz

RESCUERS OF JEWS DURING THE HOLOCAUST: JUSTICE, CARE AND RELIGION

P. M. OLINER and S. P. OLINER

Humboldt State University, Arcata, California

ABSTRACT

What meaning did helping Jews have for rescuers? Did rescuers' values differ from those of nonrescuers? What part did religion play in the rescue decision? To answer these questions, 700 rescuers, nonrescuers and rescued survivors were interviewed in Poland, France, Germany and the Netherlands primarily, but also including some from Italy, Belgium, Denmark and Norway.

INTRODUCTION

In the midst of Holocaust, somewhere between 50,000 to a million non-Jews risked their lives and sometimes those of their families to help Jews survive.[1] While constituting but a fraction of the total population under Nazi occupation, their significance transcends their numbers. If the perpetrators of genocide remind us of the human potential for evil, those who rescued Jews remind us of its potential for goodness. As participants and passive spectators of genocide represent the tragedy of the human experience, rescuers exemplify its hope. If we are to create a future without Holocausts, we need to understand not only the determinants of genocide but also what enables people to actively intervene on behalf of its victims.

General conditions relating to national traditions of civic equality and tolerance, Jewish assimilation, type of Nazi control and SS presence, geography and terrain as well as the responses of elites help explain why and where rescue occurred (Fein, 1979; Baron, 1988). But some forms of rescue behavior occurred in all countries under Nazi occupation. While broad social conditions facilitated or inhibited rescue, they do not fully explain why only a small percentage participated in rescue even in those countries presumably representing optimal conditions, and why rescue behavior occurred in those countries presumably representing the least conducive conditions. What this suggests is that rescue was also a matter of individual choice. If we are to understand the determinants of rescue behavior, we need to probe it at the individual level as well as the broad social and institutional level.

In search of such understanding, the Altruistic Personality Project (Oliner & Oliner, 1988) interviewed some 700 individuals who lived through that horrendous time, most of them in Poland, Germany, the Netherlands and France but also including some from Italy, Belgium, Denmark and Norway. The interview, which took from two to eight hours, was based on a questionnaire (including more than 400 items) developed specifically for the purpose of the Project. Four hundred and six of the interviewees were certified Yad Vashem rescuers; evidence provided primarily by their rescued survivors had established that they had acted out of humanitarian considerations alone, risked their own lives, and received no remuneration of any kind for the rescue act. One hundred and twenty six were nonrescuers; individuals living in the same countries as rescuers but not identified by Yad Vashem as rescuers. They served as a comparison or control group; that is, external circumstances or personal attributes assumed to contribute to rescue behavior were compared statistically with this group. Our interviewees also included 150 rescued survivors also used for statistical comparisons.

Our study led us to conclude that character was a powerful explanation for rescuer behavior.

Clustered around a generalized attribute we call extensivity, it enabled rescuers to perceive or take advantage of opportunities where others did not or to actively seek opportunities where others did not.

Broadly defined, extensivity means the tendency to assume commitments and responsibilities toward diverse groups of people. It includes two elements: the propensity to attach oneself to others generally and the propensity to do so inclusively. The many factors which comprise this attribute emerged from varied and complex analyses and are elaborated in the Oliners' study of rescuers (1988). For our purposes here, we focus on two themes which suggest some of the details of this characteristic: (1) the meaning rescuers attributed to their behavior, and (2) learned attitudes and values which might have prepared them to act on such meaning with particular emphasis on religion.

THE MEANING OF RESCUE

Meaning generally refers to the intention or purpose one wishes to convey by a given expression or behavior. Identical acts may have different meanings for the actors; not infrequently, a single act may have several meanings to the same actor. Rescue behavior was no exception; it had different meanings for different rescuers, and it frequently had more than one meaning for a given rescuer.

To assess the meaning of helping Jews, we asked rescuers the following question: "Can you summarize for me the main reasons you became involved?" A single rescuer frequently gave several reasons; in general they included five major categories.

Helping Jews was a way to please some external authority for approximately 3 percent of rescuers; a parent, a religious or resistance group representative (e.g., "I did it only because it was my mother's wish," "the minister asked me" "I was ordered by my [resistance] group to do it"). For approximately 8 percent, it was an act of patriotism, usually emerging in the context of military cooperation with Jewish fighting units. Approximately a sixth of rescuers (17 percent) perceived rescuing Jews as a way of showing their hatred for Nazis; any act of defiance was a form of manifesting such hatred. But for the overwhelming majority (87 percent), helping Jews had an ethical meaning even when other meanings were also attributed to the behavior (Table 1).

What constitutes ethical meaning? There are at least two distinct conceptions of ethics in western philosophy with counterparts in psychological analyses. The dominant orientation, exemplified in the work of philosophers Immanuel Kant (1963, 1964), John Rawls (1971), D. A. J. Richards (1971) and psychologist Lawrence Kohlberg (1969, 1974), is variously labeled the Kantian tradition, rational morality, the morality of the "right" and the morality of justice. We call it the ethics of equity. It is based on fundamental conceptions of fairness; fair exchange, fair allocation of resources, fair rewards, fair punishment and fair procedures. Fairness requires rationality (choices based on reason rather than emotions) and universality (without attention to special interests including one's own).

For a minority of rescuers (20 percent), helping Jews was a way of demonstrating equity, fairness for all people. The language of equity was essentially this: Justice requires that only guilty people be punished; Jews were innocent victims. All people are equally entitled by right to considerations of justice and Jews were no exception. Representative comments in this category included "It was unfair that I was safe simply because I was born a Protestant," "These people were innocent, I had ascertained that," "These people just had the right to live like other people; not just Christian people."

The other orientation is an emerging point of view which has not yet penetrated mainstream considerations. Reflected in the works of philosophers Iris Murdoch (1970), Lawrence Blum (1980) and Nel Noddings (1984) and psychologist Carol Gilligan (1982), it might be called "the morality of the good," "the morality of connectedness," or the morality of "direct altruism".[2] We call it the ethic of care. This orientation emerges out of a direct connection with the welfare of another person without mediation by notions of fairness. Whereas equity is based on reciprocity, care endorses a willingness to give more than is received. Whereas equity emphasizes fair procedures, care insists on benevolence and kindness. Equity asks that we do our duty in accordance with reason, rectitude, righteousness; care insists that we act of concern and interest of the other alone. Because care asks that the interests of the actor be abandoned in favor of those of another, it goes beyond what can reasonably and fairly be expected of individuals in a society, approaching the unreasonable and the unfair.[3]

The language of care was dominant among rescuers (76 percent) (Table 1). The language of care

Table 1: Reasons Given for Activity[a]
(Can you summarize for me the main reasons you became involved?)

a. Rescuers vs. Rescued Survivors	Rescuers (n=222) (%)	Rescued Survivors (n=93) (%)
Self-centered motives (money, desire to convert to Christianity, exploitation)	0.0	5.4
Patriotism	8.1	1.1
Hatred of Nazis	16.7	10.8
External approval	2.7	0.0
Religion	15.3	25.8
Ethical	86.5	82.8
Equity	19.4	25.8
Care	76.1	66.7
Friends, lovers, relations	15.8	28.0
Jews	3.6	2.2
Universal ethical	49.5	29.1
Universal equity	14.9	6.5
Universal care	38 3	23.7

b. Rescuers vs. Actives	Rescuers (n=222) (%)	Actives (n=43) (%)	Significance (chi-square)
Patriotism	8.1	44.2	.0000
Hatred of Nazis	16.7	37.2	.004
External approval	2.7	0.0	NS
Religion	15.3	0.0	.01
Ethical	86.5	34.9	.0000
Equity	19.4	14.0	NS
Care	76.1	23.3	.0000
Friend	15.8	0.0	.01
Jews	3.6	0.0	NS
Universal ethical	49.5	20.9	.001
Universal equity	14.9	7.0	NS
Universal care	38.3	14.0	.003

a. Respondents frequently gave more than one reason for their activities. Each reason received one tally in the appropriate category. If the respondent repeated the same type of reason more than once, it was recorded as one tally in the appropriate category for that respondent.

concentrated on compassion, concern and affection for others and the need to relieve their suffering ("I felt sorry for them" "I did it out of sympathy for them," "My husband told me that unless we helped, they would be killed; I could not stand that thought"). The need to relieve the suffering for special individuals--lovers and friends--was expressed by approximately 16 percent of rescuers (e.g., "They were good friends; I liked them very much," "Nobody was going to touch those children; I would have killed for them"). But the obligation to relieve suffering was frequently also expressed as applying universally (e.g., "Any kind of suffering must be alleviated," "When you see a need you have to help," "You need to turn to those who suffer and are in pain").

The above were the meanings rescuers themselves attributed to their behavior. Since it is not uncommon for individuals to attribute lofty motives to their behaviors--a tendency called the augmentation principle--testimony from those they helped is instructive on this point. The overwhelming majority (83 percent) of rescued survivors in our sample also perceived at least one of the people who helped them as acting out of ethical considerations. And while approximately a fourth (26 percent) saw it as a statement of equity, the majority (67 percent) saw it as a statement communicating care (Table 1).

It might be surmised that any act of resistance toward Nazis had a similar meaning. We have some hint in our data that this was not the case. Among our group of nonrescuers, was a subgroup of 53 individuals we called "actives." Actives were primarily people who claimed to have participated in general resistance but also some who claimed to have helped Jews (sometimes both), but for whom we had no external corroborating evidence. We asked them the same questions we asked rescuers: "Can you tell me the reasons you became involved?" Their responses were significantly different from those of rescuers; 44 percent said "hatred of Nazis," 37 percent said "patriotism" and only 35 percent identified an ethical reason (Table 1).

In sum, what the above suggests is that whereas acts of resistance meant many things, helping Jews was perceived above all as an ethical challenge. (As one rescuer involved in general resistance explained it, "When it came to the Jews, that was a moral question.") While ethical considerations included notions of equity, rescuers primarily invoked the ethics of care. However, whether in relation to equity or care, most rescuers perceived their ethical obligations as broadly inclusive in character, extending to all human beings.

LEARNED ATTITUDES AND VALUES

Was there something in rescuers' backgrounds which allowed them not only to perceive helping Jews as an ethical issue, but also which prepared them to act on this perception? Our data suggest there was, and it emerged from comparisons between rescuers and nonrescuers in relation to experiences in their families of origin and personality factors. Learned values were an integral part of the total picture.

We askeu rescuers and nonrescuers alike to name the most important things they learned about life from their mother, father or other most influential person in their growing up years. We also asked them additional questions relating to their sense of patriotism and religiosity in their growing up years, immediately before and during the war as well as today. Learned values distributions largely paralleled reasons.

Rescuers did not differ significantly from nonrescuers with respect to having learned patriotic values. Only a small percentage of rescuers and nonrescuers (8 percent and 4 percent respectively) claimed to have learned this value in their parental homes. But they did apparently learn it elsewhere for the majority of rescuers and nonrescuers alike said they were very patriotic in their youth (65 and 68 percent respectively).

Nor did rescuers differ from nonrescuers with respect to having learned the importance of conventional values--such as propriety or dependability--in their parental home. In similar distributions, rescuers and nonrescuers highlighted learning to value being good mothers and fathers, manners, avoidance of alcohol and obscene language, and punctuality. In similar distributions, too, they claimed to have learned the value of independence and self-sufficiency.

But rescuers differed from nonrescuers with respect to other values, evidenced either by parental omission or commission. Only one percent of rescuers, said they had learned to be obedient as compared to 9 percent of nonrescuers; 19 percent of rescuers emphasized learning values relating to economic competence--such as hard work, vocational skills and thrift--as compared to 29 percent of nonrescuers. Obedience is an attribute which Alice Miller (1984) among others has highlighted as preparing the way for subservience to tyranny; emphasis on economic competence is alleged to be inversely related to spiritual or "impractical" concerns.[4]

And in fact, rescuers in statistically higher percentages emphasized learning ethical values in their parental homes (70 percent as compared with 56 percent). However, such differences were not evident in relation to equitable values, but rather in relation to caring values (Table 2).

Almost identical percentages of rescuers and nonrescuers (44 and 46 percent respectively) said they had learned to value truth, honesty and respect. Such virtues are fundamental to considerations of fairness, whether in respect to commercial transactions or personal relationships. Both rescuers and nonrescuers thus appeared to subscribe to the ethics of fairness similarly. In significantly higher percentages, however, rescuers emphasized learning to help others, care for them and love them (44 percent as compared with 25 percent

Table 2: Values: Most Influential Parent/Role Model[a]

	Rescuers (n=219) (%)	Nonrescuers (n=118) (%)	Significance (chi-square)
Patriotism	8.2	4.2	NS
Religion	15.5	16.9	NS
Values relating to self	24.2	34.7	.05
Economic competence	19.2	28.8	.05
Independence	6.4	8.5	NS
Conventional	35.2	41.5	NS
Propriety	21.0	27.1	NS
Dependability	16.0	13.6	NS
Obedience	1.4	8.5	.003
Ethical	70.3	55.9	.01
Equity	43.8	45.8	NS
Care	43.8	24.6	.0007
Universal ethical	39.3	15.3	.0000
Universal equity	14.2	7.6	NS
Universal care	28.3	8.5	.0000

a. Respondents characteristically noted multiple values. Each value noted was recorded as one tally in the appropriate category. If the respondent repeated the same value more than once, it was recorded as a single tally in the appropriate category for that respondent.

of nonrescuers). As several noted, this meant going out of your way to help, regardless of what others did; a value which they said their parents not only preached, but modeled through their own behavior. Additionally, significantly more rescuers made a point of saying that their parents had emphasized ethical obligations--equity or care--as universal in character (39 percent as compared with 15 percent of nonrescuers) (Table 2). Characteristic comments in this category included: "They taught me to respect all human beings," "My father taught me to love my neighbor and consider him my equal whatever his nationality or religion," "He taught me to respect all human beings."

In short, values rescuers emphasized learning in their parental homes largely paralleled in distribution the reasons they gave for helping Jews. Rescuers thus credited their parents with having taught them the values which were strongly implicated in the meaning which they conferred on helping Jews. It was in the context of parental day to day expressions of ethical obligations that rescuers apparently learned their values. Helping Jews in the extraordinary events of the Holocaust was thus but an extension of routine behavior. As many rescuers themselves expressed it, "it was just an ordinary thing to do." Among significantly larger percentages of nonrescuers, it was simply not ordinary.

Of course, we cannot be certain that respondents' claims about values emphasized in their parental homes are accurate. It may be the case that the rescue act itself transformed rescuers' views in particular about their pasts. We attempted to deal with this potential source of bias by asking questions about learned values at the very beginning of the interview whereas the questions about reasons were asked towards its end, thus trying to minimize a particular "mind-set" in which responses to one set of questions shape responses to subsequent ones. It should be noted, too, that our questions about values learned from parents were open-ended; we did not suggest desirable answers by presenting respondents with a list of values which they were to rank or with which they were to indicate agreement. Respondents thus shaped their own language and thoughts. Of course, such precautions do not necessarily preclude biased responses, but they do add plausibility to the argument that values learned from parents did indeed influence the rescue decision with respect to many rescuers.

THE RELIGIOUS ELEMENT

Because it is of particular interest to this conference, we single out the religious element for special consideration.

The Holocaust signified the failure of Christianity for it occurred in the heart of Christian culture, but it did not necessarily signify the failure of particular Christian individuals or groups. The Huguenot congregation in Le Chambon, for example, led by their pacifist pastor Andre Trocme and his wife, are exemplary representatives of the positive impact of religion; this extraordinary community provided a safe haven for some five thousand Jews (Hallie, 1979; Sauvage, 1985/86). But since perpetrators and bystanders also included Christians, this leads to the question of whether there was something special about rescuers' Christianity. Our data suggest there was, but it was not to be found in religious affiliation per se nor in the intensity of religious commitments.

For some 15 percent of rescuers in our sample, helping Jews had a religious meaning (Table 1). Some simply saw it as a way of pleasing God; "I knew God would approve," "I knew God wanted me to do it." Others, particularly members of the Dutch Reformed Church, said that they had learned from their religion that "Jews were God's special people."[5] Yet a larger percentage (25 percent) of rescued survivors said their rescuers were motivated by religion. Hence, religion was an important factor for some rescuers, albeit a minority of them. (That religion had a special place in rescue not shared by those who participated in general resistance is suggested by the fact that no actives conferred religious meaning on their behavior.) (Table 1).

The above appears to imply that rescuers may have been raised in a more religious household, may have taken their religion more seriously or at least been more religious than nonrescuers. This however, did not turn out to be the case.

In general, respondents who were more religious before the war, were also more likely to have been religious while growing up and today, were more likely to have had more religious parents and were more likely to marry someone religious (Table 3). But there was no difference between rescuers and nonrescuers with respect to the religious factor (Table 4).

Table 3: Religiosity Factor

Item	Loadings[a]
Before the war, were you very religious, somewhat religious, not very religious, or not at all religious	.86471
How religious were you when you were growing up? Were you very religious, somewhat religious, not very religious, or not religious at all?	.73862
(Today), do you consider yourself very religious, somewhat religious, not very religious, or not at all religious?	.71841
Was your father very religious, somewhat religious, not very religious, or not religious at all?	.62447
Was your mother very religious, somewhat religious, not very religious, or not at all religious?	.57187
Before the war, was your husband/wife very religious, somewhat religious, not very religious or not religious at all?	.37594

a. Loadings show that these six items were highly intercorrelated.

Rescuers did not differ from nonrescuers with respect to early affiliation with a religious institution; approximately 90 percent in both groups were so affiliated (62 percent of rescuers and 72 percent of nonrescuers were Catholics; 32 percent of rescuers and 23 percent of nonrescuers were Protestants; the remainder considered themselves non-sectarians or were affiliated with a different group). Approximately 45 percent in both groups had attended a parochial elementary school.

Religiosity in their home environments were also statistically similar; 49 percent of rescuers

Table 4: ANOVA: Religiosity Factor[a]

	Rescuers vs. Nonrescuers				
Means[b]					
Total population			.00		
Cell means, rescuers			.08		
Cell means, nonrescuers			-.08		
Source of Variation	Sum of Squares	df	Mean Square	F	Significance of F
Covariates	.847	2	.423	.655	
Sex[c]	.150	1	.150	.232	.630
Age[d]	.610	1	.610	.943	.332
Main Effects[e]	1.195	1	1.195	1.849	.175

a. The religiosity factor consists of six intercorrelated items indicating the extent to which respondents had lived in a religious environment and perceived themselves to be religious.
b. The higher the score, the more religious the life of the respondent has been.
c. Covariates indicate that sex is not significantly related to religiosity.
d. Covariates indicate that age is not significantly related to religiosity.
e. The main effects show that rescuers did not differ from nonrescuers with respect to religiosity.

said their mothers were very religious and 43 percent of nonrescuers made this claim; approximately 5 percent in both groups said their mothers were not at all religious. Approximately 33 percent of rescuers said their father was very religious and 22 percent of nonrescuers made this claim; somewhat more than 10 percent in both groups said their fathers were not at all religious. Approximately 15 percent in both groups said that religion was one of the most important things they had learned from their most influential parent or role model. Nor did rescuers differ from nonrescuers with respect to their own religiosity while growing up or before the war. Approximately 73 percent of rescuers said they were either very or somewhat religious growing up; 72 percent of nonrescuers made this claim. Somewhat less than 70 percent in both groups said they were either strongly or somewhat religious before the war. (Table 5).

What this imples is that religious affiliation, the religiosity of the home environment and individual religiosity are not helpful in explaining rescue. Since several rescuers and rescued survivors do point to religion as influencing them, however, something else appeared to be operating within the religious understanding of rescuers as compared with nonrescuers; something which influenced their interpretation of religious obligations.

Our data are suggestive on this point. Rescuers who saw religious meaning in the rescue act frequently went on to elaborate what that meaning was; most commonly it was interpreted as an ethical obligation which extended universally. As one Pole expressed it:

> I have always considered all people regardless of their nationality, ethnic origins or race, religion, and so on, as members of one great family: mankind. This feeling has deep roots in Polish tradition, history, Christian teaching, and the attitudes of my parents and their predecessors. They (my parents) taught me about God and respect for human beings, to respect others.

Even among those who said they had learned from their religion to see Jews as God's special people, several went on to explain that this really meant all people:

> My background is Christian Reformed; Israel has a special meaning for me. We have warm feelings for Israel--but that means the whole human race. That is the main principal point.

The above suggests that it was the ethical content of religious commitments rather than

Table 5: Religiosity

	Very (%)	Some-what (%)	Not very (%)	Not at all (%)	Signif-icance (Chi square)
a. Parents					
Mother					
Rescuers (n=164)	49.4	36.0	9.8	4.9	
Nonrescuers (n=111)	43.2	43.2	9.0	4.5	NS
Father					
Rescuers (n=140)	32.9	31.4	25.0	10.7	
Nonrescuers (n=106)	21.7	40.6	24.5	13.2	NS
b. Self					
Growing up					
Rescuers (n=210)	38.6	34.8	18.6	8.1	
Nonrescuers (n=120)	25.0	46.7	19.2	9.2	NS
Before war					
Rescuers (n=119)	31.1	37.8	19.3	11.8	
Nonrescuers (n=120)	21.7	42.5	24.2	11.7	NS
Today					
Rescuers (n=206)	40.3	32.5	11.7	15.5	
Nonrescuers (n=103)	25.2	45.6	18.4	10.7	.01

religiosity itself which made the difference. Religious commitment did not assure a commitment to ethical values; a finding which has been corroborated in several studies besides our own. As Adorno and his associates (1950) found almost forty years ago, identification with a religious body does not ensure endorsement of values of tolerance and brotherhood. Several studies suggest an inverse relationship: more intense religiosity is frequently associated with greater prejudice.[6] Rescuers who conferred religious meaning on rescue, tended to perceive religious and ethical meaning as inseparable.

What was the origin of this perception? Again, our data suggest the importance of the parental home. We were able to identify four basic "types" of rescuers; one of them was characterized by very solid family relationships. The dominant characteristic of this group was feelings of great closeness to their families of origin; mothers, fathers, and their families as a whole. They were the only type which also was frequently associated with a high degree of religiosity; self, parents and spouse. Parental discussion about Jews occurred frequently among this group. Since this was not necessarily the result of personal contacts with Jews--some knew Jews while others did not--it suggests that Jewish visibility may have often arisen in a religious context, as indeed it did for Reformed Church members in particular who commonly engaged in Bible readings in their homes. Yet to presume that parental discussion of Jews in such households was necessarily positive is not warranted by our data, for they indicate that this type was just as likely to have been exposed to ethnocentric views as not. Also commonly associated with this type was parental emphasis on values of care and dependability which continue to be manifest today; respondents in this group are involved in a high degree of community helping currently (Table 6). What this suggests is that parental caring values, internalized because of solid family relationships, were more influential even among religious rescuers than religion per se. When religious experiences confirmed caring values and further conferred a special favored place for Jews,

Table 6: Strong Family Attachment Factor: Summary Factor Analysis

Item	Loadings[a]
Family closeness[b]	.66626
Parents talked about Jews[c]	.45430
Close friends[d]	.37855
Community helping today[e]	.34737
Personal potency[f]	.34151
Religiosity[g]	.33616
Social responsibility[h]	.30494
Ethnocentrism[i]	.16976
Jews at school[j]	-.10200
Jewish coworkers[k]	.07144
Jewish friends[l]	-.05848
Jews in neighborhood[m]	-.05113

a. Underlined loadings indicate strong intercorrelations. Nonunderlined loadings indicate no intercorrelations.
b. This is a summation of four items measuring closeness of family members, closeness to significant other role model, to mother and to father when growing up.
c. This is an item summation of whether mother, father, or significant other ever discussed Jews.
d. This is a single item measuring the extent to which respondents had close friends while growing up.
e. This is one of two factors which emerged in relation to postwar helping behaviors.
f. This is one of two factors which emerged from self-attributed personal qualities when respondents grew up, including able to make decisions, independent, adventurous, willing to take chances, able to take responsibility and self-confident.
g. This is a factor relating to religiosity of self, parents and spouse.
h. This is a summation of the variables of values of care, dependability and independence which were derived from values passed on to the respondents by most influential role model.
i. This variable is an item summation based on classification of what respondents were told about Jews by pooled responses from mother, father, and significant others. It includes measures relating to stereotypes and differentiated status of Jews.
j. This variable is a summation of three items indicating whether Jews had attended the elementary school, gymnasium or university of respondents.
k. This variable is a summation of two items relating to whether respondents or their spouses worked with Jews before the war.
l. This variable is a summation of four items indicating whether respondents had close Jewish friends while growing up, knew any Jews while growing up, whether respondent's spouse had Jewish friends before the war or whether the respondent had Jewish friends before the war.
m. This is a single item relating to whether Jews lived in the neighborhood of respondents before the war.

the propensity to help was heightened. However, even when parental environments were not particularly favorably oriented toward Jews, respondents were apparently able to transcend their ethnocentricity because of parental caring values internalized as a result of solid family relationships.

In short, as Sauvage (1985/86) has suggested, there _was_ something special about the Christianity of religious Christian rescuers;[7] they were more likely to have internalized ethical standards as a result of good and loving parents, who themselves subscribed to such standards and reinforced them in a religious context. Parental culture appeared thus to be a most important determinant of rescue behavior. Religion in this context is less an element apart from other conditions of living and relating, but is rather embedded in the whole of living in which trust and mutuality, nurtured in the warmth of parental caring, is reenacted in religious expressions.[8]

What conclusions can we draw from the above? Our findings do not point to a single value which all rescuers shared in common nor to a single value which was exclusive to them; there were many areas of convergence between rescuers and nonrescuers. There are however at least two points of importance which appear to be warranted on the basis of the above.

The first concerns the nature of responses to victims of genocide generally. That genocide is above all an ethical challenge is certainly nothing startling--our study lends empirical support for what others have recognized through different means. What our study emphasizes, however, is something which perhaps has not been so clear. People who assume responsibility towards its victims may be primarily propelled by an ethic of care--by their sense of compassion and their acceptance of personal responsibility to relieve suffering--rather than considerations of equity. Rational considerations of justice can of course inspire passionate commitments. But it is possible that those who are most responsive to genocidal victims are particularly committed to relieving suffering. If that is the case, then it has different implications for socialization and education.

The second concerns the nature of morality generally. As Iris Murdoch (1970) has observed, the moral life is not something which emerges suddenly in the context of traumas. Rather it arises piecemeal in the routine business of living. It begins with parents who emphasize broadly inclusive ethical values--including caring and social responsibility--which they teach in the context of caring family relationships. Assuming caring roles appears to require pre-rehearsed scripts and previously learned skills acquired in ordinary activities. If we seriously want to cultivate those characteristics associated with rescuers, then we cannot leave the job to parents alone. Other social institutions, including religious and educational institutions, will need to seriously reconsider their roles, responsibilities and routine behaviors. Until social institutions accept the responsibility to nurture inclusive ethical commitments in the context of caring environments, it is likely that no more than a fragment of the population can be counted on to prevent future holocausts.

REFERENCES

Adorno, T. W., Frenkel-Brunswik, E., Levinson, D. J. and Sanford, R. N. (1950). The Authoritarian Personality: W. W. Norton.

Baron, L. (1988). In: The Altruistic Personality: Rescuers of Jews in Nazi Europe: (S. P. Oliner and P. M. Oliner) The Free Press, 13-48.

Bettelheim, B. (1971). The Informed Heart: Autonomy in a Mass Age: Avon.

Blum, L. A. (1980). Friendship, Altruism and Morality: Routledge & Kegan Paul.

Fein, H. (1979). Accounting for Genocide: National Responses and Jewish Victimization During the Holocaust: Holocaust Library.

Friedman, P. (1978). Their Brothers Keepers: Holocaust Library.

Gilligan, C. (1982). In a Different Voice: Psychological Theory and Women's Development: Harvard University Press.

Glock, C. and Stark, R. (1966). Christian Beliefs and Anti-Semitism: Harper & Row.

Hallie, P. (1979). Lest Innocent Blood Be Shed: The Story of Le Chambon and How Goodness Happened There: Harper & Row.

Kant, I. (1959). Foundations of the Metaphysics of Morals (Trans. L. W. Beck): Bobbs-Merrill.

Kant, I. (1963). Lectures on Ethics (Trans. L. Infield): Harper & Row.

Kant, I. (1964). The Doctrine of Virtue (Trans. M. Gregor):Harper & Row.

Kohlberg, L. (1976). In: Moral Development and Behavior (ed. T. Lickona): Holt, Rinehart & Winston.

Kohlberg, L. (1969). In: Handbook of Socialization Theory and Research (ed. D. A. Goslin): Rand McNally.

Miller, A. (1984). For Your Own Good: Hidden Cruelty in Child Rearing and the Roots of Violence: Farrar, Straus & Giroux.

Murdoch, I. (1970). The Sovereignty of Good: Routledge & Kegan Paul.

Noddings, N. (1984). Caring: A Feminine Approach to Ethics and Moral Education: University of California Press.

Oliner, S. P. and Oliner, P. M. (1988). The Altruistic Personality: Rescuers of Jews in Nazi Europe: The Free Press.

Rawls, J. (1971). A Theory of Justice: Harvard University Press.

Richards, D. A. J. (1971). A Theory of Reasons for Action, Oxford University Press.

Rokeach, M. (1970). Psychology Today: 33-58.
Sauvage, P. (1985/86). Humboldt Journal of Social Relations 13, 252-259.
Wright, J. E. (1982). Erikson: Identity and Religion: The Seabury Press.

NOTES

1. Numbers of rescuers are at best estimates. Philip Friedman (1978) estimates that of the approximately two million Jews who survived, one million received some active assistance from the Christian population; allowing for the fact that some people engaged in multiple rescues and that a single rescue in some cases involved multiple people suggests an average of one non-Jewish helper for each Jew helped. On the other hand, Mordecai Paldiel, Executive Director of Yad Vashem, estimates 50,000 (personal interview). Since Yad Vashem recognition requires more than occasional acts of active helping, the lower figure may be more accurate if the more rigorous criteria are applied.
2. This is Blum's (1980) term.
3. Because it also frequently singles out particular people or groups for special concern, it is commonly considered unfair and unreasonable. As Blum (1980) argues, however, singling out particular persons or groups for unreasonable concern is not of itself unfair if it does not simultaneously deny the rights of others.
4. As B. Bettelheim (1971) observed, "The more man is geared toward achieving 'practical' results, the more he may view the making of inner decisions that lead to no practical end as a waste of energy" (69).
5. Members of Dutch Reformed Churches, who comprised but 8 percent of the population, accounted for an estimated 25 percent of rescues in Holland (Baron, 1988).
6. Glock and Stark (1966) explain this as a result of Christian particularism, "a disposition to see Christian truth as the only religious truth" (208). If their efforts to convert others are unsuccessful, particularists express their latent hostility overtly. Rokeach (1970) attributes it to a self-centered preoccupation with personal salvation which results in an indifference toward worldly concerns, including social inequality and injustice.
7. Noting that Le Chambon shared a similar view of Jews as the People of God, Sauvage (1985/86) raises the provocative question whether "...righteous Christians were, in particular, Christians who were comfortable with the Jewish roots of their faith, indeed with the Jewishness of Jesus? Were they Christians for whom Christianity was, perhaps, more the religion of Jesus than the religion about Jesus?" (254). If Sauvage means by this greater concern with the ethics of Jesus rather than the particularism of Christianity, our data suggest an affirmative answer.
8. In an elaboration of the religious dimension in Erikson's work, Wright (1977) observes that the trust engendered by the loving relationship of mother and child is fundamental to its transcendant ethical expression in religious life. "For Erikson", he writes, "religion is inextricably bound up in the mutuality of trust. Religion is an institution which restores that trust, in part, through meaningful ritual...As a dimension of life, religion is interrelated with all of life" (150). Our data tend to support this association of ethical religiosity with caring, loving parents in which trust is an important component.

THE ALTRUISM OF THE RIGHTEOUS GENTILES

Mordecai Paldiel

YAD VASHEM
Jerusalem, Israel

The deeds of non-Jews who, in Nazi-occupied Europe, risked their lives to save Jews from destruction have confounded many students of altruistic behaviour. It is suggested in this paper that altruism in its variant forms is an innate human predisposition which modern society has caused to be restricted to insignificance but which the Righteous Gentiles have desmonstrated can be aroused to assume dominance over our behaviour for short spells of time. Furthermore, that its manifestation does not show it to be restricted to a select talented few but is a quality shared by all; hence, capable of flourishing within a great range of human experiences.

- - - - - - - - - - -

In the history of religious thought, the idea of two opposing spirits contending for man's soul comes generally under the heading of "dualism." In Jewish thinking, these take the form of the good vs. the bad inclination (<u>yetzer hatov</u> and <u>yetzer harah</u>). Rabbinic teaching professes the necessity of the presence of these two opposing inclinations in the reality of a God-ordained world. The bad inclination, accordingly, is not necessarily evil. It is responsible for man's drive, competitiveness and sexual impulse, whereas the good one -- encompased and rooted in the Torah, the divinely ordained ritual and ethical religious ethos -- is the former's counterpart; an indispensable element to dampen the effects of an inclination which unrestrained and left to itself would negate life's ultimate purpose and undo God's creation. Thus understood, the bad inclination only turns evil when not counterposed by the good inclination. When balanced by the other spirit, it serves a constructive role. As in the following rabbinic saying: "If not for the <u>yetzer harah</u>, no man would establish a household, marry a woman and beget children, nor be enterprising" (Genesis Rabbah 9). However, left unchecked to its own wiles, the bad inclination becomes a destructive force. Hence, the rabbinic approach was to call for a proper balancing of these two God-given impulses in man's soul and behaviour.

The tension between these two somewhat irrational and irreconcilable drives is also a theme preoccupying the minds of many thinkers. In early Christianity, Paul in his Epistle to the Romans gives voice, almost in desperation, at the torment in his soul caused by these two incompatible spirits: "I do not understand my own actions. For I do not do what I want, but I do the very thing I hate... So then it is no longer I that do it, but sin which dwells within me... I can will what is right, but I cannot do it. For I do not do the good I want, but the evil I do not want is what I do. Now if I do what I do not want, it is no longer I that do it, but sin which dwells within me." (Romans 7:15ff.)

This tension, which many thinkers understood to be the result of a dichotomy in the cosmic world, and by consequence in the structure of man's soul, led some religions to advocate a struggle against the evil spirit in order to allow man to subsist as an ethical being, undisturbed by sinful thoughts. One need but mention the teachings of Ohrmazd and Ahriman in Zoroastrianism and of the Spirit of Light vs. the Spirit of Darkness in Manichaeism, or the various Gnostic philosophies which proliferated at the dawn of Christianity, as so many testimonies of the effort of religious thinkers to grapple with this predicament. Christianity elected to accept the reality of evil and posit its institutions and sacraments as a remedy against its harmful effects in day-to-day life. This teaching was to have a long-lasting effect for close to two millenia in the shaping of religious and eventually secular thinking -- the theory of man's fallen state and depravity as a result of Original Sin and Adam's Fall.

According to Augustine, the earliest most dominant thinker of the Fall theory, Adam's disobedience, in primeval times, caused his descendents, seminally present in Adam and Eve, to be born for all times and generations in a state of sin and depravity, appearing in the form of the unbridled and inordinate tyranny of sexuality over the other of man's faculties. The very act of begetting children inevitably stains the offspring with original sin; hence, all mankind is literally born into sin. So oppressive and overwhelming is the affliction of man's fallen state, that he cannot even begin to raise himself out of the mire of sinfulness without the help of God's prevenient grace -- through the Church and its sacraments (Augustine, The City of God, Bk. XIII, 14).

The effect of this teaching of man's fundamentally depravity, so cogently argued by Augustine in the 3rd century C.E.,left its mark -- with different variations -- in the Church's theology and was adopted with a vengeance by Reformation thinkers such as Luther and Calvin. That man remains in a state of sin as a result of Adam's disobedience in primordial times and that the Church is the primary agency through which man may seek rectification through the intercession of the Son and Holy Spirit -- to cleanse and retore him, if only momentarily, to his pristine state -- has remained a cardinal tenet of most churches. This emphasis on man's depravity has also influenced the philosophies of many secular thinkers.

Thomas Hobbes, in the 17th century, professed that man was an incorrigible aggressive creature. "If one plant, sow, build, or possess a convenient seat, others may probably be expected to come prepared with forces united, to dispossess and deprive him, not only of the fruit of his labour, but also of his life, or liberty," Hobbes magisterially argued (Leviathan, ch. 13, pt. 1, p. 81). And, where it not for strong authoritarian governments, able to curtail and control man's inherent aggressiveness, life on earth would be nothing but "solitary, poor, nasty, brutish, and short " (ch. 13, pt. 1, p. 82).

Man's aggressiveness is an important theme even in the teaching of a decidedly non-religious thinker such as Sigmund Freud. This inherent hostility, according to Freud, constantly tempts man to subdue and subjugate his neighbours: "to use him sexually without his consent, to seize his possessions, to humiliate him, to cause him pain, to torture and to kill him. _Homo homini lupus_ (man is a wolf to man) (Civilization and its Discontents, 111). Man is but "a savage beast to whom consideration towards his own kind is something alien" (112). In restraining and containing man's inherent hostility and uncontrolled sexuality and their sublimation to socially creative acts, civilization and society try to harness the fundamentally self-destructive predispositions and inclinations in man to socially beneficial acts. Following this logic, society is but the product of a defensive need; to contain an aggressiveness which left to itself would go berserk and, by the force of its suicidal nature (_thanatos_) lead to man's undoing and the end of civilization. Man, as a social being, is allotted a life of controlled neuroticism, without the hope of ever transcending the inherent aggressiveness in his nature.

Man's inherent aggressiveness has also become a popular idea with some social scientists, the scientific validity of their theories having been questioned by others. It has been demonstrated that the philosophy of _ei omnia inimica sunt_ (all are his enemy) has developed into a handy tool and an expedient explanation to legitimize a type of society where the individual person is driven to excel, not in moral behaviour but in his self-fulfillment and self-aggrandizement, in a competitive struggle to maximize one's economic and social position at the expense of the other and weaker party -- and for the country as whole, an aggressive and expansive foreign policy meant to add to the economic, political and military strength of the home country (A. Montagu, Man & Aggression).

The theory of aggressiveness as the predominantly constituent element in human behaviour (kept in check by society's laws) has assumed near-dogmatic stature in the modern era,with many people failing to detect the pseudo-scientific origin of this supposedly rational explanation -- the theory of man's depravity as a result of Original Sin and Adam's Fall. This theory, of man as an egotistic being, bent on his self-gratification, even in the vulgar meaning of the term, with everything else subsumed to the fulfillment of his egoistic impulses, even of acts of charity and kindheartedness, became a hallmark of modern secular thought in certain circles. For many, the idea of common may as capable of acts of charity, with no other ulterior motive in mind save the well-being of the beneficiary of his gratuitous charitable deeds, seemed a far-fetched, inconceivable and naive idea. Man's aggressiveness was held to be the bedrock reality upon which the whole social superstructure was founded. The atrocities of two World Wars, capped by the unspeakable crimes of the Nazis and the senseless slaughter of millions of Jews, only seemd to strengthen and confirm this negative premise on man's basic constitution. Then, from the ashes of the Holocaust, emerged the deeds of the Righteous Among the Nations and showed that the last word had not yet been spoken on man's ultimate nature.

In speaking of the Righteous Gentiles of World War Two, we have in mind the thousands of non-Jews who, in Nazi-occupied Europe, risked their lives to save Jews from persecution and death; asking nothing in return, no monetary compensation nor other tangible benefits, save the friendship of those under their benevolent care. Help given to Jews, in many cases total strangers to the rescuer non-Jew, came in many ways, but mostly took the following forms:

1) Sheltering a Jew in one's own home -- in a small unused backroom, an upstairs stuffy attic, a narrow double wall, a cold dark cellar, a specially constructed shelter beneath the living quarters with only room to lie down and hardly any fresh air to breathe; a farmsteader's barn or pigsty; a distant shed or cave or a hole in a far-away field. Shelter could also be found in various lay and religious institutions: orphanages, nursing homes, homes for the mentally retarded or in monasteries and convents -- in all these instances, out of sight from the outside world and hidden from public view throughout the period of hiding.

2) For those prepared to weather the risk of detection by circulating openly as non-Jews, a whole array of new false identities had to be acquired and improvised, and these were furnished by various underground organizations, as well as churches and clergymen who issued false baptismal certificates as a means of obtaining bone fida new identities.

3) Transferring Jews to safer places, in isolated regions, off-the-beaten track, such as the Le Chambon area in the mountaineous Massif Central in France, or across borders where refuge could be found under safer skies. This involved accompanying adults and children on surreptitious journeys through great distances inside occupied territories to the border, then meticulously planning a safe crossing at specific points and hope not to be apprehended by overzealous border patrols of both countries occupying the frontier. Failure could spell imprisonment or in the best of cases being driven back across the border, into Nazi-held territory, as the Swiss border guards were wont to do for years.

Precise statistics of the number of Jews saved from the Nazi and collaborationist henchmen through the help of individual non-Jews are not available although the number runs into the tens of thousands -- not enough to stem the tide of the Holocaust but sufficient to help recreate many new lives and give the world a fresh look and reassessment at the positive side of human nature which theologians, sociologists and psychologists have for years laboured to mask, villify and malign, or simply dismiss as insignificant.

Let it be pointed out that many of these rescuers were apprehended and carted off to Nazi concentration camps, where they either perished or suffered permanent physical damage to their health. One thinks of Joop Westerweel of Holland, who led groups of Jewish youth across occupied Belgium and France to the Spanish border. He was arrested and executed by the Germans. Or of the Russian Orthodox nun, Mère Marie, who sheltered Jews in the Church's compound in Paris, and was eventually to be arrested and consumed by the crematorium flames of the Ravensbrück women's concentration camp. Or of Anna Bogdanowicz, who sheltered a single Jewish girl in Kielce, Poland, in spite of warnings from her own husband, and was taken to Auschwitz where she died from typhus. Not to mention the many other lesser known persons, victims of Nazi brutality.

This novel phenomenon in the annals of altruism has led some to speculate on the possible motivations of these rescuers of human lives. A number of theories have been advanced which we shall presently outline and which shall occupy our attention for the rest of this article.

Perry London, is the earliest of a group of sociologists to offer explanations on the Righteous conduct, based on interviews of rescuers who had left their native homelands and resettled in the U.S.A., as well as on interviews with survivours who benefitted from the rescuer's help. In a 1970 study, he listed three main characteristics which he found among these rescuers:

1) a spirit of adventureness and an affinity with exciting activities;

2) an intense identification with a parent of a very strong moral character -- not necessarily religious, but holding very firm opinions on moral issues and serving as a model of moral conduct;

3) a sense of being socially marginal, such as a Seventh Day Adventist minister in the largely Calvinist or Catholic Netherlands (London 245 ff.).

To these must be added the observations of Douglas Huneke, in a more recent study:

4) skill, stamina, cleverness and competence which he found among a large group of Righteous Gentiles. One rescuer, for instance, was an accomplished skier and wilderness expert; others knew how to create false situations and live a life that was deceptive, if need be, or were in physical good shape and could therefore stand up to the rigors of stress and want (Hunneke 16-18).

Eva Fogelman, in a 1985 study, found that rescuers fall into two groups: those motivated by moral values and others whose motivation was chiefly emotional and based on personal links with the victim.

Nechama Tec, a sociologist , in a recent comprehensive study of the motivations of Polish rescuers, found that rescuers from Poland fit a behaviour which she labels as "autonomous altruism." She defines this as a sense of individuality, self-reliance and personal commitment for the helpless and needy; a non-heroic, matter-of-fact perception of one's rescue deeds; an unpremeditated and unplanned beginning of rescue activity; and an "universalistic" perception of Jews defined as helpless beings and totally dependent on the protection of others (Tec 188).

These theories, while uncovering certain behavioural traits and frames of mind among certain rescuers, helpful to our understanding of the diversity of human responsiveness, are generally insufficient explanations for the behaviour exhibited by these all too-common men and women during the Holocaust, for the following reasons:

1) Rescuers displayed all, a few or none of the ideas propounded. Some did exhibit an independent frame of mind; others allowed themselves to passively become involved in circumstances beyond their control and wound up risking their lives to help Jews in ways unimaginable to them at the outset -- hence, with the exception of a handful, not the product of the rescuer's initiative, assertion, or determination.

2) For each of the examples advanced to suggest one or all of the theories, similar numbers of examples can be illustrated to demonstrate the opposite case; i.e., the lack of strong parental identification; of belonging to a non-marginal group; the absence of a spirit of adventureness and of not being especially adept in a particular skill or exhibiting stamina and competence in a particular field. The following will, for instance, illustrate the weakness of the marginal case theory.

(a) In France, it is true that the marginal Protestants produced a high rate of rescuers, but so were Catholics prominent in the rescue of Jews. Granted that even it if were to be established that French Protestants on the average helped slightly more than their Catholic counterparts, one should bear in mind that a large number of these became involved in rescue activities at the behest of their pastors and church elders -- to a greater extent than Catholic persons, as the Le Chambon case clearly demonstrates. This has to be measured against the decision of individual Catholic clergymen to risk their security and welfare to help Jews without clear guidance from their church hierarchy.

(b) French Protestants, as well as Dutch Calvinists, Ukrainian Baptists and Hungarian Methodists saw the Jews as God's chosen people and, consequently, to be protected and saved. Hence, the motivation could be religious/theological rather than their being a marginal group.

(c) On the whole, the overwhelming majority of rescuers originated within the dominant ethnic religious group of each country. This is true for French, Belgian and Polish Catholics as it is for Dutch Protestants and Greek Orthodox believers.

3) The explanations advanced are exceedingly comprehensive and all-encompassing; too vast to properly register and analytically portray the Righteous phenomenon. If all, or most, of those displaying the characteristics of the theories heretofore enumerated had volunteered to help Jews escape the Nazi dragnet, we should be counting their numbers in their hundreds

of thousands, if not millions, not as is the case, in their thousands -- perhaps several tens of thousands, in a continent with a population of several hundred million inhabitants. Quite evidently these attributes were not sufficient to coerce people to stake their lives for the sake of others.

4) The element of risk and fear is not properly taken into account. The Nazi terror machine was one of the most brutal in history. Retribution was swift and terrifyingly inhuman, without regard to the rights of the individual person. Fear gripped the masses of the conquered peoples of Europe at the thought of loss to one's life and those of one's loved ones, as a result of apprehension for the slight infraction of Nazi laws, without recourse to normal judicial channels and procedures. Help extended to Jews was known to be a major infraction, as the conquered peoples of Europe were constantly alerted on the dire punishment awaiting them for violating Nazi anti-Jewish measures. It seems, therefore, that if one were to accept all the theories advanced for the behaviour of rescuers of Jews, they could be valid and legitimate for circumstances other than the Nazi world where the fear of losing one's life was not an immediate day-to-day reality for extended periods of time.

5) A derivative of the previous observation would be that the altruistic characteristics previously mentioned are confined to socially sanctioned deeds; to acts which society looks at with favor; of helping others in need where the helper perhaps suffers some loss to his time, money and convenience, and is prepared to sacrifice greater and lesser amounts of these socially sanctified self-seeking goals—never his life and the life of his family. The moulding of an altruistic model for Righteous acts under Nazi-type conditions, one would have to base on different premises and presuppositions.

6) Some of the explanations proferred tend to elevate the rescuers to a stature not in common with ordinary men and women, transforming them into persons who stand out from their society in many respects, not only in the domain of rescue of Jews. The image created is of singularly gifted individuals, psychologically sane and mature, with a high degree of self-confidence in their abilities, and of elevated moral standing. If so, they are certainly not the average person one meets in day to day encounters, but of a different breed. The truth, as the record amply demonstrates, is quite otherwise; that the overwhelming majority of the Righteous Gentiles of the Holocaust period did not particularly stand out from their surrounding society and could not easily be discernable as unique individuals in day to day encounters with them. Moreover, one cannot in all fairness describe them as especially ethical persons in their general behaviour or more heroic in their deeds than their next door neighbours or of society at large, save in one respect: at a particular and specific moment in their largely uneventful lives they decided to commit themselves to an exceedingly heroic, dangerous and highly moral course (one which, incidentally, they themselves do not view as anything but a normal response to the suffering of others) -- the saving of Jewish lives threatened with death -- by sheltering them at the risk of their own lives. Before and after that dramatic episode in their lives, their behaviour shows very little of being different from others in their midst -- of those who, unlike the rescuers, did not gird their loins to help alleviate the suffering of the Jews among them and wrest them from the hands of the Nazis.

This, indeed, is the crux of the Rigtheous phenomenon. What makes ordinary men and women, exhibiting the same characteristics as their contemporary fellow citizens, follow a radical altruistic course, at odds with prevailing norms and inviting the prospect of retribution on their person and their families by an adversary who would stop at nothing to impose his will on the conquered peoples of Europe? Those who did challenge the Nazis in this regard, it is as though they were momentarily snatched out from the reality of their regular existence, of their customary habits and mores, and propelled into a different realm and reality and to a type of behaviour the reasons for which have remained unclear to them to this day and continues to puzzle students and laymen researching these charitable deeds forty years after the event. The Nazi storm over, they returned to their normal routine and practice and are not distinguishable from their neighbours in their behaviour patterns or moral attributes; of prejudices, like or dislikes. The theories so far advanced fall short of satisfactorily explaining this phenomenon.

7) This leads me to the final observation. The previously enumerated theories seem to imply a decision by the rescuer, rationally arrived at; the person having clearly reasoned and measured out the ethical and moral implications of his behaviour and the consequences to his own safety, then made a conscious decision to stake all dear to him in order to uphold these cherished values. But this would be misleading and not representative of the true state of mind of the majority of rescuers.

The evidence on hand seems to indicate that the decision to stake one's life and welfare to help Jews in distress was anything but rationally arrived at. One is tempted to think that precisely because very little of clear-sighted conscious thinking was involved in the interplay of objective and subjective factors, the momentous decision to help, in spite of all the dangers attending such a decision, was able to be taken. Had it been otherwise, it is doubtful whether more than a handful of persons would have been prepared to confront what their rational minds told them about their own personal security, and overcome the clear dictates of their self-preservation in order to venture out on the dangerous undertaking of helping Jews over an indefinite period of time. As most of the previously enunciated theories seem to imply a high degree of rational decision-making they cannot, in the face of the evidence to the contrary, be adduced as legitimate explanations for the behaviour of the Righteous Gentiles of the Holocaust period.

Where then does the answer reside? What other dimension of human behaviour have we overlooked; one which could possibly offer a legitimate and valid explanation for this extraordinary behaviour by largely ordinary men and women?

Before venturing on a new course of rendering a possible explanation to the Righteous conduct of these singular men and women, let us for a moment retrace our steps and first ponder what meaning lies embodied in the term "altruism."

This term was coined by the French philosopher Comte in the 18th century to underline acts of goodness by individual persons of a pro-social disposition, for the greater good of the common weal and involving a certain but only minimum measure of self-sacrifice and discomfort on the part of the doer. This was the response of Comte and his followers in France and England to those who like Hobbes a century earlier had suggested man's egoism and aggressiveness as the main motors of individual behaviour. Altruism was introduced as an antithesis to egotism. This observation on the meaning of altruism, coupled with our previous rejoinder to the several interpretations on the altruistic behaviour of the rescuers of Jews during World War Two, leads us to the following preliminary conclusions:

1) The altruism heretofore alluded is related to socially conditioned norms having the good of society and its values as its principle object and is generally not one which involves great risks or makes self-sacrifical demands upon the altruistic doer. Although it alludes to a certain frame of mind and, hence, helpful in leading us in a certain direction it is not a handy tool for a realistic appraisal of the altruism of the Righteous Gentiles of the Holocaust period where the loss of one's life, security and property was a constant potentially terrifying reality to the rescuers of Jews. As Perry London, in his pioneer study of the Righteous motivations, has correctly underlined, the Righteous Gentiles acted under great pressure, against a background of social isolation, and under circumstances of repressive fears. He terms their conduct "the most extreme form of heroic behavior which we expect to encounter" (P. London, 1963).

2) The Righteous themselves, the heroes in question, are surprised at the attention showered on them. As Nechama Tec has observed, most rescuers see themselves as non-heroes and interpret their deeds matter-of-factly. Their responses to queries on their motivations are, moreover, frankly puzzling -- not what one would legitimately term as rational explanations. In fact, most have difficulties in articulating clearly enunciated and sensible responses and prefer not being asked about it. This is a far cry from the 18th century rationalist explanations of altruism and their modern interpreters, which imply a mental disposition not **inhibiting the flow of sensible responses.**

3) This leads us to the conclusion that the rescuers of Jews of World War Two do not quite match the altruistic explanations heretofore mentioned. These definitions seem to address themselves to more socially-sanctioned altruistic types of behaviour, not to ones where helping Jews was in many countries an offense against age old enshrined social prejudices, let alone a social desiderata.

We are led to seek an explanation for the altruism of the Righteous Gentiles in a totally different direction -- a different realm, and yet very close to the essence of human nature; as novel as it is paradoxically self-evident; mysterious in its origin and yet very convincing in its simplicity, so as to make us wonder why we have not noticed it earlier as it stood at our threshold. I propose to define it as follows: altruism is none but an innate human attribute present in all persons in various degrees, hence natural to our being and constitution. Its manifestation ought therefore not be the cause of our astonishment and predicament.

Carl G. Jung's theory of archetypes may serve a handy tool to help us evaluate this new thinking. Archetypes are, according to Jung, universal and primordial images and symbols, not the fruit of individual experience,which guide our lives and day to day behaviour. Whether we are aware of their presence or not, they are the centers of our psychic energy and have a "numinous" life-like quality. They are likely to be manifested in critical circumstances, either through an exterior event or because of the release of some inner charge. Finally, archetypes are manifested in conjunction with events in one's innermost life (C.G. Jung, Collected Works, Vol. 9).

Borrowing this idea from Jung, we submit that altruism as such, including its extreme variations, such as gratuitous love -- what in rabbinic teaching appears under the formula of hesed and in Christianity as "grace," is an archetypal reality and parent to a numinous power capable of momentarily wresting us from our conditioned behaviour and summoning us to be at its behest; this, in spite of the other socially-conditioned behavioral patterns militating against its manifestation -- what Jung termed the "persona" (the sum total of the conventional attitudes that an individual adopts because he belongs to certain groups, and manifests itself in racial, social and national prejudices).

To repeat, we submit that altruism is a sui generis human archetype, thus natural to our being; the origin of which may remain a mystery to us, but the presence of which cannot be disputed. Why, then, one may legitimately rejoin, does it remain dormant in most of us? The answer to this is that it does not. Altruism, as such, is a permanent facet of our psychic life. However, its manifestation has all but been limited to a tolerable minimum so as not to threaten a social fabric based on ego-seeking norms and patterns, to which we are all subtly conditioned. Altruism, on the other hand, in its attempts of seeking greater outlets for its manifestation, is propelled by its numinous power to cause man, at times, to be unwittingly captured by its energy;who, without quite fully aware of the sudden transformation within him, is lead to the performance of meritorious charitable acts. When under the full sway of this archetypal attribute, man acts without consideration of the other behavioral variables and the mostly rational and objective evaluations tending to thwart him from a course frought with danger and not looked at with favour by society at large. These conflicting norms have temporarily been stilled. In such rare instances, the hesed archetype causes one to momentarily ward off and overcome socially conditioned mores and patterns of behaviour, which if fully present would have prevented him from risking his life and well being for the sake of others, especially for a socially despised minority, and for indefinite periods of time.

The altruistic archetype may or may not produce a permanent alteration in one's behaviour. It rather does not, for its full manifestation is, as stated, of momentary nature. The deed accomplished, it recedes in the background and to its original inferior position vis-a-vis the other more dominant and powerful socially shaped modes of behaviour (of our prejudices, likes and dislikes) who reassert themselves and reestablish their mastery over our lives. However, when under its sway -- on rare occasions -- the agent of good deeds does not comprehend his behaviour as anything untoward and unnatural, and he is hence surprised and at a loss when explanations are solicited from him many years after the event. Answers such as: "It was the most natural thing to do," or "it was something that had to be done", is common among the Righteous Gentiles of the Holocaust period. It is one of those acts which the rabbis have imparted eternal value and which immortalizes its doer. Thus the statement: "A person may acquire immortality in a single deed."

We furthermore submit that this archetypal attribute, present at all times in reduced and insignificant quantities, manifests itself strongly in order to uphold the principle of the sanctity of life. When injuries threaten to sensibly damage and demolish this sacrosanct life principle, the hesed archetype takes shape, assumes form and manifests itself forcefully in some persons, defying all rational considerations to the contrary. It seizes the individual person and tilts him in its direction, then recedes in the background once the deed accomplished and the damage to the life principle repaired.

To sum up, the hesed archetype is as inherently human as is the equally legitimate and potent aggressive archetype, itself too of non-rational origins, but is not fully part of our behavioural pattern because of its repression by society which does not tolerate the interplay, let alone imposition, of another mode of behaviour threatening the pursuit of one's ego (of one's self-aggrandizement at the expense of others),and only allows minimal flows of altruistic input as long as it is not brought about at the expense of the doer's convenience, let alone his welfare, property and life. Society, by sanctioning a greater reliance on the self-seeking pleasure principle with an aggressive competitiveness as its concomittant complement, has successfuly restrained the altruistic archetype from any long-lasting influence in our lives and prevented it from sharing a constructive and equalyzing influence in the affairs of mankind. A too greater emphasis on competitiveness leads to Western type societies, which have produced technological wonders, changing forever the face of civilization and opening new vistas of explorations and advances in the many fields of the natural sciences, but at a heavy price -- of total wars and genocidal atrocities, with the Holocaust no doubt one of its extreme and hideous concretizations.

This then is the thesis of this paper: that the goodness displayed by the overwhelming majority of these Righteous Gentiles is not a mystifying phenomenon, requiring an arduous exercise into the intricacies of their social, psychological, ethnic, religious and economic backgrounds, in order to create like-minded models of select groups of extreme altruistic persons, but a basic human trait which needs to be aroused from its enforced slumber and cultivated -- by tolerating its soothing presence in our lives, instead of repressing it. Helping others in need at great discomforts to oneself ought not be viewed as a praiseworthy but unnatural type of human responsiveness but a natural and necessary predisposition as are the other legitimate intuitive drives such as competitiveness, honour, wealth and lust. Thus, what is needed is to redress the balance upset by an overzealous reliance on man's so-called depravity; to not only quote and seek support in the Genesis statement on man's evil inclination since birth, but on the equally forceful Psalms statement of man a being but a step lower than the angels.

Phrased in Jungian terminology, what is required is the dethronement of the persona's stifling dominance over our lives in order to allow a **better** "individuation" through **a greater assimilation of the hesed** archetype's input; to a process that leads to the unification of one's personality and results in making the "self" (the invisible, unconscious, and innermost center of personality in which the light and shadows have equal stabilizing roles) the most central of all archetypes.

The Holocaust may not necessarily be a vindication of the Fall theory and of man's depravity, as so many are inclined to pessimistically and hopelessly concur, but the result of an over-reliance and subtle justification of the aggressiveness in us over all other as yet unexplored subconscious modes of behaviour; of the dominance of the yetzer harah at the expense of the yetzer hatov. Man's task is not necessarily the fulfillment of the pleasure principle with as little neurotic fallback as possible, as Freud would want us to believe but, as the Righteous Gentiles of the Holocaust have demonstrated, also to abide by the much greater command concerning the well-being of humanity as a whole. The cardinal rule of "love thy neighbour as thyself," ridiculed by Freud as a naive and hypocritical teaching, ought not be an ethic relegated to the few idealistic persons, removed from the mainstream of social interaction (the medieval saint, or lamed-vovnik of Jewish lore) but a daily guide to social behaviour and responsiveness, shared by all; a necessary and salutary complement to our inborn competitiveness -- for the greater good of humanity.

The task is not so much to meticulously search out and select the few Righteous persons, so as to be able to praise, honour and salute them ... from a distance, but the rather no-less arduous charge of looking into our own souls in order to widen the channels through which the altruistic archetype, buried in the deep recesses of our fathomless mind, may flow unimpeded; to permit it to rise and manifest itself, so as to assume an elevated position and proper role in our lives and behaviour.

REFERENCES

Freud, S. "Civilization and its Discontents", in: Collected Works, Vol. 21. London: Hogarth, 1973.

Fogelman E. & Lewis-Wiener, V. "The Few, the Brave, the Noble," in: Psychology Today, August 1985, 61-65.

Hall, C.S. & Nordby, V.J. A Primer of Jungian Psychology. N.Y.: Mentor, 1973.

Hobbes, T. Leviathan. Oxford, Basil Blackwell, 1946; chapter 13.

Huneke, D.K. In the Darkness... Glimpses of Light, 1980 (unpublished).

--- The Moses of Rovno. N.Y.: Dodd, Mead & Co., 1985; 177-187.

Jung, C.G. "The Archetype and the Collective Unconscious," in: Collected Works, Vol. 9. Princeton, N.J.: Princeton University.

Kaufmann, H. Aggression & Altruism. N.Y.: Holt, Rinehart & Winston, 1970.

London, P. "The Rescuers: Motivational Hypotheses About Christians Who Saved Jews from the Nazis," in: Macaulay J. & Berkowitz, L. Altruism & Helping Behavior. N.Y.: Academic, 1970; 241-250.

London, P. Research Prospects, 1983 (unpublished).
--- The Empirical Study of Righteousness, 1963 (unpublished).
Montagu, A. (ed). Man & Aggression. N.Y.: Oxford University, 1973.
Rushton, J.P. & Sorrentino R.M. (eds). Altruism & Helping Behavior. Hillsdale, N.J.: Lawrence Erlbaum Assoc., 1981.
Tec, N. When Light Pierced the Darkness. N.Y.: Oxford University, 1986.

LEARNING HOPE FROM THE HOLOCAUST

by Pierre Sauvage

Friends of Le Chambon
8033 Sunset Boulevard #784
Los Angeles, CA 90046
U.S.A.

Tel.: (213) 650-1774

I am a 44 year-old European-born Jew.

That means that around the time of my birth, much of my family was humiliated, tortured and murdered--while the world watched.

I am a descendant of the persecuted, the heir to bitter memories.

I am the father of two young children.

It is in these capacities that I presume to participate in this important conference, and I will not adopt the dispassionate tone of scholarly discourse; the Holocaust and its legacy are not subjects which I wish to address as if I had nothing personally at stake.

As Elie Wiesel has asked, "What does one *do* with such memories of fire--with so many fragments of despair?"

One can never be the same after groping with the realization that it is possible for man to hate that much, for man to love that little. What one *does* with that knowledge, what lessons one derives from that recent past, has the power to shape how we live, perhaps to determine our very ability to live.

Are we good? Are we evil? Are we strong? Are we weak? Is it natural to care about others? Is it natural to be indifferent? Is trust realistic? Is hope possible? Is God relevant?

For a Jew today, the questions, the implications, take on a special urgency.

Was the Holocaust nothing more than a candid, exacerbated expression of the world's true feelings about the Jews?

Is there is no real point in genuinely cultivating non-Jewish friends and allies since you need only scratch a *goy* to find an antisemite?

Is antisemitism, mild or pestilential, an irreversible aspect of the Jewish destiny, even a necessary part of our present self-definition?

Must survival itself, under these circumstances, become the main Jewish objective--even if there is no ostensible point beyond physical survival, even if what survives is not rooted in the Jewish spiritual heritage, even if what survives is virtually unrecognizable?

Whether one derives these lessons from the Holocaust or less defeatist ones, it is not a matter of choosing to derive lessons from the Event or declining to do so, and that is true even for those who display no interest in probing the nature or impact of that human tragedy, those who wish to "move on."

Lessons are automatically learned from any experience, let alone a traumatizing one. What we must do is strive to make those lessons explicit, while pondering the facts that explain them--or challenge them.

As psychologist Carl Rogers said, "The facts are friendly."

And so we must, indeed, learn and acknowledge the facts. We must, indeed, remember for the present and for the future.

But merely repeating that we must remember does not help us to do so. It is not easy to let in something on such a scale, something that challenges our very faith in ourselves.

Remembering cannot be merely an act of blind will. Remembering has to be a creative act.

We must find *ways* of remembering. We must have incentives to remember. We must challenge ourselves as to what we choose to remember, and why.

Referring to George Santayana's famous dictum that "Those who do not remember the past are condemned to relive it," Rabbi Harold Schulweis has pointed out that if memory is not used with wisdom, it too can boomerang; that to remember one part of the past so powerfully that it eclipses all else is also to condemn oneself to its recurrence.

"The problem of our generation," Elie Wiesel has said, "was that if we looked too intently in the direction of the dead, we ran the risk of being tempted to join them."

So we must be careful as to how and what we remember. We must remember that remembering is only a tool, an indispensable key to life--but not an end in itself.

We Jews, of course, are experts at remembering, experts at interpreting our tragedies and making those interpretations serve us for our future.

Every year, for instance, shortly before *Yom Hashoah*, the Day of Remembrance of the *Shoah*, we celebrate Passover, still remembering and working out that bondage that scarred us and traumatized us so long ago.

During the timeless ritual of our seder, our Passover dinner, we symbolically dip the bitter into the sweet. And we end by opening the door to the spirit of Elijah, prophet of good tidings, asking him to bring us that message of hope, to reinforce our faith in the goodness of man.

The ritual for Yom Hashoah is still in its infancy. But must we not, once again, figure out how to brush the bitter against the sweet? Must we not, then, look for the sweet? Not remain for generations stuck in the bitter?

"It takes moral courage to grieve," wrote Kierkegaard. "It takes religious courage to rejoice."

In his book "Optimism: The Biology of Hope," anthropologist Lionel Tiger asserts that optimism is "a biological phenomenon," rooted in the genetic make-up of our species.

Can we confront the Holocaust and remain true to our optimistic natures? Can we rejoice in the presence of murder, of indifference to murder?

We know that there was some good too amidst the bottomless evil, but we also know that there was not enough of it.

What's there to get excited about? Why should we care?

Rabbi Schulweis, who has been for so long a prophetic voice about the Holocaust's necessary lessons of hope, tells a story about the Baal Shem Tov, the founder of Chassidism.

The Baal Shem Tov had a dream. He dreamt that right in front of him was a heart, a heart that embodied in it all the evil in the world.

The Baal Shem Tov began pounding and pummeling that heart, striving to destroy it utterly.

Until he heard a sound coming from deep inside the heart.

It was the cry of a baby.

And the Baal Shem Tov stopped pounding.

Innocence and guilt, good and evil are as inextricably bound together as night and day. They define each other, they need each other, they become meaningless on their own.

Every act of evil and apathy, every moment of hate and inhumanity, every individual and collective failure of will, of intellect, of character, of spirit, can best be confronted, illuminated, accepted, if we remain attuned to their opposites, if our ear does not become deadened to the soft sound of innocence, if we continue to remember that at each and every level of moral decay there was the potential for human solidarity, that this potential was demonstrated time and again sometimes in the most astonishing ways and in a wide range of situations, and that it is essentially the gap between our *proven* human potential and our dreadful human frailty that we must learn about, probe, remember.

How can we measure that gap if we pass on only the failure? How are we to see, how are we to assess, how are we to remember the moral landscape of the Holocaust if we must peer at it only through the pitch-black night of Auschwitz?

Philip Hallie, an eloquent student of evil and good, has written of the need for "realistic hope."

If we merely give lip service to hope, if we perceive it deep down as an unjustified, unrealistic response to the past, we create a tragic, self-fulfilling prophecy, and hope turns into an inappropriate response to the future.

The moral landscape during the Nazi era was not flat. There are fragments of hope to be discovered in the rubble.

Why then do we know so little, why have we cared to know so little about the *chassidei umot ha'olam*, for instance, the righteous Gentiles of all nations, who, according to Jewish beliefs, will have a share in the world to come.

They were, for the most part, seemingly ordinary men and women. But it was given to these people to save lives. It was given to the Christians among them to practice their faith.

"They were so few," we are always told--again and again and again.

Is that really the only important thing we need to know about them? Does moral or spiritual significance bear some relation to numbers? For that matter, what criteria do we have by which to decide what is few and what is many in the midst of such an unprecedented hell?

And in any event do we not believe, we Jews most especially, that even tiny minorities may possess important, even divine truths?

Let me be clear. My point is not at all that those times were "better" than we've acknowledged thus far. Indeed, I suspect that in many respects they

were far worse, the nightmare greater and more debasing.

Death camp survivors will sometimes say that they haven't told us all, that they hold back for our sanity and theirs. I will never forget hearing Wiesel tell a group of students in 1984, seemingly out of the blue, that "We haven't even begun to tell the tale," and that when they do, "the world will tremble."

I for one have come to believe that such statements are not mere hyperbole.

There are more facts to be learned, more pain to be endured. "It is impossible for the physician to heal," said a Chassidic master, "if he does not open up the wound and lay bare its evil."

And thus Irving Greenberg has reminded us not to make any statements regarding the Holocaust that wouldn't remain credible in the presence of burning children.

I have an eight year-old son and a one year-old daughter. I take such an admonition seriously.

My children will know all about the burning children. They will know about the evil of which men are capable.

But they will also know, I hope, that while it is possible to succumb to evil and apathy, it is also possible to recognize and overcome evil and apathy; that the world is ours to make; that there is strength to be derived from being oneself; that there is joy and peace and happiness to be gained from caring about other people.

"To love one's self in the right way and to love one's neighbor are absolutely analogous concepts," wrote Kierkegaard, "are at bottom one and the same."

Those too are potential lessons from the Holocaust. Are they not as necessary for grown-ups as they are for children?

Do we not need something to hold on to as we strive to absorb our capacity for evil, our capacity for apathy?

For my part, I am especially interested in the latter, in passive bystanders, in indifference to evil which, according to Elie Wiesel "is worse than evil for it is sterile as well."

Living in America, I am stunned, for instance, at how much smug comfort we take in the fact that the Holocaust didn't happen there, that the murders were plotted and committed elsewhere.

But it wasn't, of course, just "them" and "there"; the Holocaust occurred on America's watch.

To be a bystander to a murder is to be changed by it. To be a bystander to the Holocaust is to be changed by it for many generations to come.

Nor is it just a matter of the government or of leadership. Ordinary citizens too knew more than we've let on and perhaps avoided knowing even more.

Moreover, the war effort and the flag-waving patriotic hoopla have obscured the powerful, dark forces that continued to permeate American life long after Pearl Harbor, as George Seldes had told us all along and as Charles Higham has recently underscored in his startling books "Trading With the Enemy," which bluntly details corporate America's amoral collaboration with the Nazis, and "American Swastika," which underscores how easily the American ethos accomodated itself to antisemitic and pro-fascist sentiments and activities.

Even a swashbuckling Hollywood hero could be an active Nazi supporter off-screen and get away it, as Higham revealed in his earlier biography of Errol Flynn.

France has had its "*Sorrow and the Pity*," that pioneering documentary about French attitudes during the Occupation. Is it not time for an American "*Sorrow and the Pity*"?

By the same token, is it not time to learn more about the Americans who cared?

Rev. Howard Brooks, for instance, spent the summer of 1941 in France as a representative of the Unitarian Service Committee, primarily administering medical services in the squalid internment camps set up by the Vichy regime.

Upon his return he wrote a book, "Prisoners of Hope: Report on a Mission," which was published in 1942, and in which he says the following:

> **It is a curious sensation to see children in a camp for the first time. There is something unreal about it; you find it hard to believe. . . . Seeing these child internees, I felt for the first time the whole inhumanity, the appalling cruelty, of the situation. I realized in a new way how merciless the world had become. If there were anything worse than this imprisonment of children, I thought while there, it was the indifference of the world, the fact that the world was not revolted.**

In December 1942, anyone browsing through a well-stocked newsstand might have noticed the cover of The New Republic magazine, which listed as its lead offering, in strong bold letters, an article entitled "The Massacre of the Jews."

The article's author was Varian Fry, whose extraordinary tale of rescue and derring-do in Marseille, France in 1940-41 will sooner or later be romanticized and made famous by the movies or television--possibly by me.

After being kicked out of France with the complicity of the U.S. Department of State, Fry continued to stay informed about what was going on in Europe and sought to break through to his apathetic countrymen.

He begins his article as follows:

> **There are some things so horrible that decent men and women find them impossible to believe, so monstrous that the civilized world recoils incredulous before them. The recent reports of the systematic extermination of the Jews in Nazi Europe are of this order.**

Fry goes on to outline the massacre, stating that "Letters, reports, cables all fit together" and "add up to the most appalling picture of mass murder in all human history."

After listing a few concrete proposals for help, Fry quotes a letter from a correspondent in France asking whether the U.S. will, at least, take in more refugees than Switzerland.

"This is a challenge which we cannot, must not, ignore," he concludes.

And that is what it was possible for an American to read and ponder during Christmas of 1942.

I have a fascination for such contemporaneous records of what it was possible to know, what it was possible to feel, what it was possible to do.

Such testimony of word and deed is as valuable to us, I contend, as any testimony we have on that virulent time in our history.

It allows us to see evil through the eyes of the good.

It spares us nothing of the truth, but it contains within itself, because of its source, because of when it was given, because of its very existence, a legitimate, necessary, helpful element of consolation--the proof that it was possible to care.

There is one other contemporaneous record I would like to cite and it is perhaps the most startling of all--certainly the most provocative.

The words were written by Labor Zionist leader Hayim Greenberg, a European-born American Jew. They were published in February 12, 1943 on the front page of *Der Yiddisher Kemfer* ("The Jewish Militant") under the title "Bankrupt!"

I will quote the first paragraph, as published in English in 1964:

> The time has come, perhaps, when the few Jewish communities remaining in the world which are still free to make their voices heard and to pray in public should proclaim a day of fasting and prayer for American Jews. No--this is not a misprint. I mean specifically that a day of prayer and of fasting should be proclaimed for the five million Jews now living in the United States. They live under the protection of a mighty republic governed by democratic laws. They move about freely through the length and breadth of the land. The vast majority of them have enough food to eat, clothes to wear and roofs over their heads. And if any wrong is committed against them, they are free to protest and to demand their rights. Nevertheless, they deserve to be prayed for. They are not even aware what a misfortune has befallen them, and if they were to look at themselves with seeing eyes they would realize with shock how intolerable this misfortune is. This misfortune consists of the vacuity, the hardness and the dullness that has come over them. It consists in a kind of epidemic inability to suffer or to feel compassion that has seized upon the vast majority of American Jews and of their institutions; in pathological fear of pain; in terrifying lack of imagination--a horny shell seems to have formed over the soul of American Jewry to protect and defend it against pain and pity. At a time when the American Jewish community is the largest and most influential in the world, at a time when the eyes of millions of Jews in Europe who are daily threatened with the most terrible and degrading forms of physical extermination are primarily turned to American Jewry, this American Jewish community has fallen lower than perhaps any other in recent times, and displays an unbelievable amount of highly suspect clinical "health" and "evenness of temper." If moral bankruptcy deserves pity, and if this pity is seven-fold for one who is not even aware how shocking his bankruptcy is, then no Jewish community in the world today (not even the Jews who are now in the claws of the Nazi devourer) deserves more compassion from Heaven than does American Jewry.

As Greenberg goes on, he becomes more specific in his "indictment," as he puts it, targeting prominent Jewish organizations. He ends, however, with the poignant admission that for all his indignation, he does not know if it is still "objectively possible" to do anything, or who should do it, or how it should be done.

Greenberg's wartime colleague Marie Syrkin views things more charitably: "That American Jews achieved pitifully little is their sorrow, not their shame."

To be sure, the American Jewish community of the war years did not have the social, political, and economic confidence it has now, and as I mentioned earlier, there is still much to be learned about what the United States then was really like, and about the difficulties American Jews faced in pressuring the government to save the Jews of Europe.

But how is it that in his nostalgic 1987 film "*Radio Days*," set during the Holocaust, Woody Allen could casually portray American Jews as seemingly indifferent to, or ignorant of, the plight of their European brethren--and do so without one single critic, one single letter to the editor, one single Jewish publication (to the best of my knowledge), bringing up with dismay, surprise or disapproval this aspect of the film!

Do we really take it for granted that this was a typical or an acceptable response?

Does this indifference to the indifference not suggest that there remains much unfinished business with regard to this chapter of our history?

Commenting about the lack of resistance among ordinary Germans under the Nazis, Bruno Bettelheim points out that "the more energy it took to manage anxiety, the less inner energy remained for the courage to act." Similarly, in the context of Hiroshima and the continuing nuclear threat, Robert Jay Lifton has charted the process of "psychic numbing" in which we commonly engage as victims or potential victims of disaster.

Does the American experience of the Holocaust, Jewish and non-Jewish, not cry out for further exploration of that no man's land between knowing and not knowing, further probing of the nature and consequences of anxiety and psychic numbing, further consideration of what it takes to perceive the truth and act upon it, further awareness of the possible consequences of having failed to do so?

However, if I thought that all I would learn was what terrible and deficient people we were and are, if I found myself merely hammering yet another nail in our psychological and spiritual coffin, if I wasn't convinced that at virtually every stage and virtually every level I would find exceptions to the rule, if I didn't have Rev. Brooks and Varian Fry and Hayim Greenberg as companions in this research, I do not believe I could pursue this interest effectively and I am not sure I would wish to pursue it at all.

In December 1940, an American writer wrote the following: "Our only hope will lie in the frail web of understanding of one person for the pain of another."

The historian David Wyman, a Christian, uses that quote from John Dos Passos to convey the moral framework for his sensitive study of the Roosevelt administration's "Abandonment of the Jews."

Our only hope still lies in the frail web of understanding of one person for the pain of another.

To those of us who must look at ourselves through the smoke and night of Auschwitz such a web is hard to see or even to believe in.

The world turned away even from the cries of burning children. America, sweet land of liberty, turned away.

But is that all we must understand about those times, about ourselves?

Must we not begin to care that there *were* parts of that frail web that somehow held on? If we are to strengthen that web, can we afford *not* to care, not to ask: Who? Why?

In his book "Of Blood and Hope," Samuel Pisar, my first cousin (my mother's nephew) and the only member of the family to survive the death camps, asks whether those who have experienced only "normal life" can understand that "the sacrifices required to cope with some of the world's problems are much less than they suppose," while the dangers involved in ignoring those problems "are infinitely greater than they imagine."

In this age that plays with Mutual Assured Destruction, that threatens to turn the planet into a gigantic gas chamber, has it not become imperative that we locate within ourselves untapped emotional, psychological, and spiritual resources if we are to rescue our future?

"Man if afraid of things that cannot harm him," said the Chassidic master Rabbi Nahman of Bratzlav, "and he knows it, and he craves things that cannot be of help to him, and he knows it; but in truth the one thing man is afraid of is within himself, and the one thing he craves is within himself."

"The greatest evil that can befall man," said Goethe, "is that he should come to think ill of himself."

To be sure, I have personal, biographical reasons for caring about lessons of hope and for people who embody them.

The existence of these people was woven into the very fabric of my life, since I myself was born and sheltered during the Holocaust in a haven of peace known as Le Chambon-sur-Lignon.

There, the day after France surrendered to the Nazis, the pastors of this mountain village in south-central France proclaimed the need to resist violence "through the weapons of the spirit."

There, the peasant and villagers of the area, mostly the proud descendants of Huguenots, defied the Nazis and the collaborationist Vichy regime and turned their tiny community into occupied Europe's most determined, most persistent haven of refuge for the oppressed.

There, some five thousand Jews *were* saved--by some five thousand Christians.

I have told the story of Le Chambon, as I have come to understand it, in a feature documentary film, "*Weapons of the Spirit*."

What I do not say in the film, however, is that I did not grow up with stories about Le Chambon or with stories about the Holocaust. Indeed, I grew up in an intensely secular home that was conceived as a total break with the past, with the Holocaust, with being Jewish, with memory.

Thus Le Chambon affected my life twice, and I'm no longer certain which of the two times is the most important.

To the Jewish baby, Le Chambon provided physical security and survival, a place to be born, a place to be welcomed into this world.

To the traumatized Jewish adult who returned there after a long absence, Le Chambon offered keys to psychological and spiritual survival and growth, a new way of looking at myself and at others.

"Are a few flashes of light enough to illuminate the darkness?" Elie Wiesel has asked.

Since that is all there was, dear Elie Wiesel, does not the answer have to be yes?

To be sure, the challenge of goodness is an especially daunting one for scholarship.

"He who would do good to another," wrote Blake, "must do it in minute particulars."

Who records, who passes on such minute particulars?

Moreover, good may be inherently hard to analyze, hard even to remember; what comes naturally is harder to notice, harder to describe than what is twisted and aberrant.

The very process that develops mastery in thought, in articulation, in scholarliness, may become a stumbling block when it comes to an appreciation of the nature of good deeds, just as it has not proven to be the most effective tool for moral progress--as the Holocaust devastatingly demonstrated.

Indeed, "It takes a great deal of elevation of thought," Emerson observed, "to produce a very little elevation of life."

The righteous didn't think about what they were doing; they did it. I think about what they did, and I don't do it. Yet only in my life, not in academic papers, can I compellingly demonstrate that I take their message seriously.

Eva Héritier, daughter of rescuers of Jews during the Holocaust, holding Jewish infant Pierre Sauvage in 1944. Her parents play an important role in *"Weapons of the Spirit,"* Sauvage's feature documentary about the wartime Christian oasis of Le Chambon, France.

"We feel in one world," said Proust, "we think and name in another. Between the two we can set up a system of references, but we cannot bridge the gap."

Encounters with evil deaden feeling, while encounters with good revitalize it.

Why then have we so stubbornly avoided these encounters? Why have we relegated the good and the strong to the footnotes of history? Why have we so persistently turned away from the light?

Are we perhaps simply afraid of that light, afraid of what it may illuminate, afraid of its challenge?

Do we not sometimes wallow in guilt and failure less as a result of some past defeat than as an excuse not to have to try again?

Could it be that the overbearing emphasis on human ineffectiveness during the Holocaust also serves as the ultimate and crafty excuse we seek for not facing the facts of our own continuing, individual accountability?

Could it be because next to evil, we tend to come out looking good?

Could it be because next to good, we may be forced to ask ourselves questions we would prefer to avoid?

But can we afford not to learn these facts about our history and about human nature?

Do we Jews not need to know that the whole world did *not* stand idly by while we were slaughtered? Do we not need to know who our friends were then--and who they may be today, and tomorrow?

Do Christians not need to know that even then, there *were* Christians, there was at least one Christian village?

Does everyone not need to know that it is possible to act well even under the most trying circumstances?

Do we not need the memory of the just in order to improve and enrich our human spirit, that is to say, our connections with ourselves, that is to say, our connections with others?

Do we not need it to challenge the gnawing, widespread cynicism about our species?

Do we not need it to rebuild trust?

An Israeli Holocaust survivor, writing in Los Angeles' B'nai B'rith Messenger, recently stated that he had learned his lesson from the *Shoah*: "It is that Jews must never trust anyone but themselves to ensure their survival."

That one must depend on oneself for survival is, of course, true.

That one must never trust *anyone but oneself* is, in my view, utterly wrong, and the statement takes on a tragic resonance in the light of Israel's current policy for survival.

Erik Erikson has written that "If you have forgotten how to trust, you may be driven to cultivate active mistrust and insist defiantly that everybody is against you."

Trust, on the other hand, is merely hope in the other's sense of human solidarity and personal responsibility.

Whatever the tragedies in one's past, whatever the challenges in one's present, to rule out that hope is to live alone; to rule out that hope is simply to give up.

A person who cannot trust is untrustworthy. A Jew who will not trust is not tapping into the spiritual momentum of Judaism.

"To be a Jew after Auschwitz," Emil Fackenheim has written, "is to have wrested hope--for the Jew and for the world--from the abyss of total despair."

Times are changing. It took forty years.

Until recently, the historical consensus was that there were only three major protagonists in the drama of the Holocaust--the murderers, the victims, and the bystanders--but there is no longer any Holocaust conference where the matter of righteous Gentiles doesn't come up.

Jewish organizations are beginning to tie themselves in to the issue. The name Raoul Wallenberg has become famous, and Le Chambon too is no doubt on its way to a celebrity status it fears greatly.

I am sure both the upcoming United States Holocaust Museum in Washington and the Simon Wiesenthal Center's future Beit Hashoah/Museum of Tolerance in Los Angeles will include prominent references to this or that act of rescue.

Jerusalem's Yad Vashem, which holds high the Jewish flame by honoring righteous Gentiles along the Avenue of the Righteous, may eventually acknowledge their existence in their museum displays as well.

For some, this is an ominous development.

For some Holocaust survivors, there is the desire that the world feel guilty--and the fear that the world will use the righteous to feel less guilty, to let itself off the hook.

But the actual guilty ones are dying just as the survivors are dying, and even Eichmann's grandchildren are not, in fact, guilty of anything (although it can fairly be expected of them that they manifest a heightened sense of responsibility).

Moreover, to let itself off the hook all the world needs to do is to ignore the Holocaust, to act and talk as if it had no real relevance to us today.

But is there nevertheless a risk that we will indeed "take the edge off the Holocaust," falsify the record by sweetening it, dilute the haunting truth of our moral dereliction?

As Michael Berenbaum has asked, are we beginning to "Americanize" the Holocaust by bringing to it an American proclivity to focus on the silver lining rather than the cloud? Are we looking for "*cheap grace*," for "easy sources of consolation"?

I think that view underestimates the righteous, underestimates the contagious power of good.

Authentic moral witness discourages evasion in others. Indeed, far from exploiting or distorting such witness, those who wish to continue evading challenging facts have the sense to steer clear of such testimony.

The Roman Catholic Church, for instance, for all its vague, occasional references to instances of Catholic rescue, sadly continues to display very little real interest in playing up and confronting the actual deeds and beliefs of its righteous Catholics, even those who became martyrs to their faith in the process of helping the Jews.

Until Philip Hallie published "Lest Innocent Blood Be Shed" in 1979, virtually nobody had ever heard of Le Chambon, and it took a Jew to write the story.

To play up true Christian witness is to face the magnitude of Christian apostasy.

The existence of authentic righteous Christians cannot be used to whitewash Christianity because these were Christians who believed that their faith had to express itself in deeds, and they know--and we know--that religion all too easily let's itself get away with mere words.

Try to use a righteous Gentile to whitewash the world and you'll find that it simply doesn't work. That they were a distinct and small minority is inherent in their very stories, in their very witness.

We learn by example.

That is the way it begins. That is the way it continues.

Examples of authentic righteousness breed righteousness; they cannot have the opposite effect of creating self-righteousness and falsehood.

However, I see a different sort of risk in the growing celebrity status of rescuers during the Holocaust. It is that we will use another ploy in our human grab bag of avoidance tricks and shunt them aside as super-heroes, as saints, as icons.

All of us who have focused special efforts on righteous Gentiles know how wasteful, how inaccurate that would be.

People who act well, even people who risk their lives to help others, are normal people like you and me.

What they do is not beyond our reach.

Let's learn from them rather than celebrate them. Let's not put them on pedestals so we can tip our hats and ignore them. Let us learn to view them as people with a solid, productive grasp on life, not as incarnations of the sort of fairy-tale virtues we tend to preach and ignore.

"There are no great men," said Winston Churchill, "only ordinary men facing a great challenge."

To be sure, we're going to feel increasingly guilty about how little we've cared about them, how little we've thanked them, how little we've worried about their own well-being after the war and still today. To be sure, they deserve our gratitude.

But they know, as Emerson put it, that "The reward of a thing well done is to have done it."

So let us be careful with our praise, with our award-giving, with our monument-building, and of course with our movies. Let us preserve the essential simplicity and naturalness of these people, of such conduct.

Let us not duck the essential message of the rescuers which is identical, as I see it, to the most fundamental message of the Holocaust: we are responsible for what we do on earth.

Richard Rubenstein and John Roth begin their recent book "Approaches to Auschwitz" with the apt words of Hannah Arendt: "Comprehension . . . means . . . examining and bearing consciously the burden which our century has placed on us--neither denying its existence nor submitting meekly to its weight."

We are responsible for not letting history beat us down--when it is occurring or as we remember it later on.

André Trocmé, the late pastor of Le Chambon, was a man who lived his whole, eloquent, pacifist's life in furtherance of his Christian ideals.

Yet he confided to his unpublished memoirs that his faith was, ultimately, a faith in the possibility of good on earth, "without which," he added, "the

theoretical existence of God doesn't interest me."

Yes, "The Holocaust is primarily about defeat not about victory, about tragedy and not triumph, about failure not success," as Michael Berenbaum has found it necessary to underscore. Yes, it suggests, "the failure of the human spirit."

***And yet*, must we not also rediscover, stress, and prove--even while addressing the Holocaust, especially while addressing the Holocaust--that the ultimate triumph of the human spirit remains within our grasp?**

As human beings, as parents, as descendants and ancestors, we have fundamental responsibilities here, and we were long ago admonished to take them on:

"I have set before you life and death, blessing and curse. Therefore choose life, that both thou and thy seed may live."

Henri and Emma Héritier, here posing in 1944 outside their farm in the village of Le Chambon, France, were among the rescuers of the area who sheltered 5,000 Jews during the Nazi occupation, as told in "Weapons of the Spirit," Pierre Sauvage's new feature documentary.

REFERENCES

Berenbaum, Michael (1987). "The Nativization of the Holocaust," Judaism.

Berenbaum, Michael (n.d.). Unpublished paper for the United States Holocaust Memorial Council.

Berenbaum, Michael (1987). Unpublished paper presented at the Association of Holocaust Organizations (U.S.) in Dallas, June 17, 1987.

Bettelheim, Bruno (1960). The Informed Heart: Autonomy in a Mass Age. New York: Macmillan, p. 274

Bible. Deuteronomy 30:19.

Blake, William (1804). Jerusalem.

Brooks, Howard L. (1942). Prisoners of Hope: Report on a Mission. New York: L. B. Fischer Co., pp. 31-32.

Cohen, Brigitte-Fanny (1987). Elie Wiesel: Qui Etes-Vous?. Paris: La Manufacture, p. 42. Translated by Pierre Sauvage.

Dos Passos, John (1940) as quoted in Wyman, David S. (1984), The Abandonment of the Jews: America and the Holocaust, 1941-1945. New York: Pantheon, p. v

Emerson, Ralph Waldo (1844). "New England Reformers" in Essays: Second Series.

Erikson, Erik H. (1959). Insight and Responsibility. New York: Norton, p. 89.

Fackenheim, Emil L. (1978). The Jewish Return Into History: Reflections in the Age of Auschwitz and a New Jerusalem. New York: Schocken, p. 31.

Fry, Varian (1942). "The Massacre of the Jews," The New Republic, December 21, 1942.

Goethe, Johann Wolfgang von, as quoted by Nathaniel Branden (1983), Honoring the Self: Personal Integrity and the Heroic Potentials of Human Nature. Boston: Houghton Mifflin, p. 11.

Greenberg, Hayim (1964). The Inner Eye: Selected Essays, vol. 2, edited by Shlomo Katz. New York: Jewish Frontier Association, pp. 193-194.

Greenberg, Irving (1977). "Cloud of Smoke, Pillar of Fire: Judaism, Christianity, and Modernity After the Holocaust," in Auschwitz: Beginning of a New Era?--Reflections on the Holocaust, edited by Eva Fleischner. New York: KTAV, p. 23.

Hallie, Philip (1979). Lest Innocent Blood Be Shed: The Story of the Village of Le Chambon and How Goodness Happened There. New York: Harper and Row, p. 8.

Higham, Charles (1983). Trading With the Enemy. New York: Delacorte Press.

Higham, Charles (1985). American Swastika. New York: Doubleday.

Higham, Charles (1980). Errol Flynn: The Untold Story. New York: Doubleday.

Kierkegaard, Søren (1848). The Journals of Soren Kierkegaard: A Selection, edited and translated by Alexander Dru (1938). Oxford University Press.

Kierkegaard, Søren (1847). Works of Love. Translated by Lillian Marvin Swenson (1946). Princeton University Press.

Lifton, Robert Jay (1967). Death in Life: Survivors of Hiroshima. New York: Random House.

Lifton, Robert Jay and Falk, Richard (1982). Indefensible Weapons: The Political and Psychological Case Against Nuclearism. New York: Basic Books.

Mass, Haim (1988). "Shamir Visit: Fifty Year After," B'nai B'rith Messenger, March 11, 1988.

Nachman, Rabbi in The Tales of Rabbi Nachman by Martin Buber (1956). Translated from the German by Maurice Friedman. New York: Horizon Press, p. 37.

Pisar, Samuel (1980). Of Blood and Hope. Boston and Toronto: Little, Brown & Co., p. 23.

Rogers, Carl (1961). On Becoming a Person. Boston: Houghton Mifflin Co., p. 75.

Rubenstein, Richard L. and Roth, John K. (1987). Approaches to Auschwitz; The Holocaust and its Legacy. Atlanta: John Knox Press. Quoting Hannah Arendt (1950), The Origins of Totalitarianism.

Santayana, George (1905-1906). The Life of Reason.

Schulweis, Rabbi Harold M. (1976). "The Holocaust Dybbuk," Moment, Feb. 1976.

Schulweis, Rabbi Harold M. (1981). "Anger, History and Love," Moment.

Schulweis, Rabbi Harold M. (1987). "A Theology of Goodness," unpublished paper presented at Second Generation conference, Los Angeles, Dec. 27,

1987.
Syrkin, Marie (1987). "Did Zionists Abandon European Jews?" Reconstructionist, May-June 1987, p. 31
Theis, Edouard and Trocmé, André. "Message des deux pasteurs du Chambon à leur paroisse," unpublished, June 22, 1940. Translated by Pierre Sauvage.
Tiger, Lionel (1979). Optimism: The Biology of Hope. New York: Simon and Schuster, p. 40.
Trocmé, André. "Autobiographie," unpublished. Translated by Pierre Sauvage.
Yosef, Rabbi Yaakov, Ben Porat Yosef, as quoted by Samuel H. Dresner (1960), The Zaddik: The Doctrine of the Zaddik According to the Writings of Rabbi Yaakov Yosef of Polnoy. New York: Schocken, p. 84.
Wiesel, Elie (1984). Question-and-answer session at Claremont-McKenna College, Feb. 21, 1984.
Wiesel, Elie (1979). "A Prologue: Why Should People Care?" in Roth, John K., A Consuming Fire: Encounters With Elie Wiesel and the Holocaust. Atlanta: John Knox Press.
Wiesel, Elie (1985). "The Brave Christians Who Saved Jews from the Nazis," TV Guide, April 6, 1985.

Pierre Sauvage, director of "*Weapons of the Spirit*," in the ruins of the farmhouse in Le Chambon, France, where he was born during the Nazi occupation. Sauvage and his parents were among the 5,000 Jews sheltered in this unique Christian oasis during the Holocaust.

Jewish and Christian youth at play during the winter of 1944 in Nazi-occupied France, as shown in "*Weapons of the Spirit*," Pierre Sauvage's feature documentary about the unique, wartime Christian oasis of Le Chambon, France.

ALTRUISM DURING WORLD WAR II

NECHAMA TEC

University of Connecticut, Stamford Campus, Scofieldtown Road,
Stamford, Connecticut 06903 U.S.A.

Those who during World War II selflessly risked their lives to save Jews are often referred to as "righteous Christians."[1]

What did such rescue mean? What kind of characteristics and motivations do these rescuers share?

Though the definition of righteous Christian applies to all those who selflessly risked their lives for Jews, efforts required for such rescue varied with time and place. These variations in turn can be traced to a series of interrelated conditions that functioned as special obstacles and barriers.

Foremost among these was the fact that the Nazis applied different kinds of policies and controls to different European countries. In part these policies and controls depended on racial evaluations. Thus, the Nazis defined all Slavs and those who lived in the Baltic countries as subhuman, as only slightly above the racial value of Jews. In contrast, the highest racial rank was reserved for the Scandinavians, while the rest of Europeans fell somewhere between these two extremes. The Germans, however, were not always consistent in applying their racial evaluations. Moreover, a particular kind of policy and control, in a particular locality, could and did change with time.

Another condition affecting the possibilities of rescue was the level of anti-Semitism in a given country. No doubt within an anti-Semitic environment denounciations of Jews and their Christian protectors were more common. Besides, in a society hostile to the Jews, their rescue was likely to invite disapproval, if not outright censure from other countrymen. Finally, too, with pervasive anti-Semitism, even the helpers themselves might have been influenced by anti-Jewish images and values. When saving Jews, therefore, they too might have had to overcome their own negative attitudes and ideas about Jews.

Aside from these cultural patterns, the sheer number of Jews and the degree to which they were assimilated must have also affected their chances of rescue. It is easier to hide and protect fewer people. Also, the easier it was for the Jews to blend within their milieu, the less dangerous was it for others to shield them. Finally, too, for prospective rescuers it would have been easier to identify with those with whom they had more in common. For a variety of reasons then one can assume that the less differentiated the Jews were from the rest of the population the less dangerous it was to protect them.

Out of all European countries the Germans had selected Poland as the center for Jewish destruction. Most European Jews were sent to Poland to die. For this decision the Nazis left no records. What they left were records of unprecedented devastation. In fact, the Holocaust drama was played out in the most gruesome ways in Poland. As an extreme case and as a center of Jewish annihilation, Poland may serve as a key to an understanding of other less extreme cases.

Concentrating on Poland, this paper relies on empirical research of Christian Poles who risked their lives to save Jews and Polish Jews who survived the war because of such help.[2]

When the Germans took over Poland in 1939, the Nazi party and the SS were in full control. From the beginning, all Polish citizens were deprived of political liberties. Partly because the Nazis defined Poles as subhuman, they felt unconstrained in their application of destructive policies. When it came to the persecution of the Poles, the Germans were selective, concentrating on the elites: church leaders, academics, prominent artists, and professionals. Some of them were murdered without delay, while others were sent to concentration camps where many of them died. Moves against the Polish elites came together with the persecution of Jews.[3] While the persecution against Poles was selective, the destructive policy against Jews, the so-called "Final Solution," was aimed at every Jew. As such, the Nazi process of Jewish annihilation happened in stages.

To Poland, these stages were introduced early and with a high degree of ruthlessness. Starting with identification of Jews, the next step was expropriation and removal from gainful employment, followed by isolation from the rest of the population. By 1941, practically all Polish Jews were placed into ghettoes. These were located in the most delapidated areas of urban centers where overcrowding, filth, epidemics, and starvation were the order of the day. It is estimated that in the ghettoes alone 20% of the population perished.[4] The next and final stage in Jewish destruction was either outright mass executions or deportations to concentration camps.

To further reduce Jewish options of survival, on October 15, 1941, the Nazis passed a law that made any unauthorized move outside the ghetto a crime punishable by death. The same punishment applied to Poles who helped Jews move to or stay in the forbidden Christian world, the so-called "Aryan" side. This law was both widely publicized and strongly enforced.[5] Executions of Jews and Christians followed. These, too, were widely publicized and names of the executed Poles and Jews were posted in public places.[6]

The Nazis also offered special rewards to those who would help them find illegal Jews and their protectors. This created a virtual Jew hunt. Denouncement and blackmail was a constant companion of the runaway Jews and their rescuers. Still, as the Nazi abuses multiplied so did the efforts to escape from them. Grave dangers did not prevent some Jews from moving to the Christian side and some Poles from helping them`to do so.

In addition to the ruthlessness with which the Nazis punished Poles for interfering with their policies of destruction, those who saved Jews had to cope with the traditionally strong Polish anti-Semitism. In prewar Poland, in particular, Jews were subjected to an array of discriminatory practices. They were barred from certain kinds of employment, their businesses were subjected to boycotts, and their participation at universities was severely curtailed. These anti-Jewish measures were sometimes associated with physical abuse.[7] Also, in a parliamentary speech, in 1937, the Polish foreign minister Jozef Beck insisted that Poland had space only for half a million Jews.[8] The rest the government had considered resettling in Madagascar, a plan that was also studied by Nazi Germany.[9]

Indeed, in prewar Poland, anti-Semitism had penetrated into all aspects of society. Derogatory remarks about Jews were taken for granted and automatically accepted.[10] Such pervasive anti-Semitism no doubt functioned as an additional, powerful barrier to Jewish rescue.

Interference with Jewish rescue might be traced yet to another source. Poland had the highest concentration of European Jews, 3.5 million. They were also least assimilated. For centuries, Poles and Jews lived in separate worlds. The Jews dressed, looked and behaved differently. According to the last prewar census, in 1931, only 12% of the Jews identified Polish as their native language, 79% mentioned Yiddish, and the rest Hebrew.[11] In prewar Poland, 50% of the Jewish children attended Jewish schools.[12] According to some estimates, less than 10% of Polish Jews could be described as assimilated.[13]

In view of these conditions, Poles who wanted to protect Jews had to overcome formidable barriers. Foremost among them were the Nazi prohibitions and their rigid enforcement. Next came the traditionally strong Polish anti-Semitism. For Poles who were helping Jews knew that they were acting in opposition to the existing anti-Semitic values and were thereby inviting their countrymen's censure and disapproval. On a more subtle level, because of the pervasiveness and acceptance of anti-Semitic images and values, most Poles had a hard time escaping from their influence. By no means overt anti-Semites, on the unconscious level some Polish rescuers were influenced by these pervasive anti-Semitic patterns. In a sense, therefore, when saving Jews, some of them were acting in opposition to their own anti-Jewish images and values.[14]

What kind of a person could withstand all the pressures, and despite all the threats and dangers, stood up for the persecuted Jews? What prompted these people to risk their lives in an undertaking that showed little promise of community support?

I view these rescuers as a special category of altruists.[15] By-passing the many definitions of altruism, I rely on one that sees altruism as behavior "carried out to benefit another without anticipation of rewards from external sources."[16] When dealing with the rescue of Jews, a distinction between two types of altruism seems appropriate: normative and autonomous.

Normative altruism refers to helping behavior demanded, supported, and rewarded by society. In contrast, autonomous altruism refers to selfless help, that is, neither expected nor rewarded by society. Indeed, autonomous altruism may be opposed by society and at times may involve grave risks to the helper.

Thus, society demands that a mother should donate a kidney to her child, that a child should aid an ailing parent. However, society does not ask of its members to sacrifice their lives for strangers, particularly not for those whom society despises. Indeed, saving Jews was an act beyond and above the call of duty, in that it put the actor in conflict with his society's expected values. In this sense, then, those who without regard for external rewards risked their lives to protect Jews fit the definition of autonomous altruists.[17]

Guided by the concept of altruism, for preliminary clues, I considered some scattered cases of rescuers from different countries. Already this step yielded some intriguing though tentative conclusions.

Without exception and regardless of the country they came from, helpers insisted that, for them, saving Jews was a natural duty. In the overwhelming majority of cases, their protection of Jews fit into an already established pattern of helping the needy. These people took their help for granted, finding it hard to explain. One of their typical answers was: "Of course I helped them, but I cannot tell you why."[18]

Additional evidence shows an inability to blend into their environment, a condition identified by London as marginality.[19] With it came repeated denials that their protection of Jews was extraordinary or heroic.

To illustrate, Jeffrey Jaffre, a Christian helper, had a Swiss father and a Latvian mother and, later on, a Jewish stepfather. He seemed to have been suspended not only between different cultures, but also between different countries and religions. As a young student, he had acquired a reputation as one who would defend the persecuted and the helpless. In 1940, he helped save fifty Jews and many others. Yet he categorically denied that his actions were heroic or special.[20]

An incident from Belgium offers a glimpse of another similar case. A Belgian Jew recalled his search for someone who would take in his young son. He approached a number of upright, decent citizens whom he knew well. None was willing to take the child. He met with continual refusals. Time was running out. On the verge of desperation, the father made one final attempt and asked a French woman, whom he barely knew. She was unmarried, and for years had an open affair with a married doctor. This took place in a small town. She had a reputation of a rebel and had associated mainly with Bohemians. Unlike the conformist and law-abiding citizens, who refused the father's pleas, in a matter-of-fact way she agreed to take the boy and saved him.[21]

One finds the same pattern in a Huguenot community in France, known for its heroic protection of Jews. In Catholic France, the Huguenots are a minority and thus religiously differ from the rest of the population. Andre Trocme, a pastor who was responsible for offering massive protection to Jews, was particularly different. Half German, half French, he was atypical within this atypical community. Those who helped him save Jews were also special and their aid to Jews was a continuation of past acts of charity.

As a rule, these villagers perceived their protection of Jews as natural and denied that their actions were extraordinary or heroic. They also insisted that it was immaterial whether those they helped were Jewish or not. What mattered was that those on the receiving end were suffering and helpless.[22]

At once very similar and different is the case of the Dutch underground figure Joop Westerweel.[23] Joop was a Christian anarchist, a pacifist, a teacher, and a fighter for social causes. As a young man, he emigrated to the Dutch West Indies where he incurred the displeasure of the authorities because he spoke out against the exploitation of the natives.

After six years, Joop returned to Holland. At that point, he established a school that relied on the Montessori principles.[24] During the war, Westerweel's behavior was also special. He and his wife, Will, placed their small children in foster homes, gave up all previous employment, and joined the underground where they became totally absorbed in fighting the injustices committed against Jews. The couple organized a network of hideouts and smuggled Jews across the border into Spain. After a year, Will Westerweel was arrested, tortured, and sent to jail and then to a concentration camp where she survived fifteen months of confinement. Her husband was not as fortunate.

Aware that the Gestapo knew about him and were looking for him, Joop kept changing documents. In the end, the Nazis caught up with him. He was arrested in the summer of 1944 as he tried to smuggle two Jewish girls out of the Edinhofen camp. A false identity card failed to protect him. The Nazis soon discovered who their prisoner was. They sent him to the camp of Vught. Five months of torture followed. The underground's continuous efforts to free him were frustrated. Only after five months, with the help of a Dutch camp physician, did they conceive of a definite rescue plan. But this, too, failed. The doctor was caught with the plans of Joop's escape and paid with his life.

When he was being tortured, Joop Westerweel worried about others. A message smuggled out to his friends read: "You know I shall never betray you. . . . I am a very ordinary person, so please don't idealize me. . . . I have just to pass these difficult days. If my fate is doomed, I shall go as a man." True to his words, he never revealed names. Instead, as Joop Westerweel was lead to his death, he recited a freedom song he loved.[25]

What shared characteristics did the rescuers in my study have? In terms of conventional categories such as class, religion, political involvement, friendship with Jews, and, to some extent, involvement with anti-Semitism, they represent a very heterogenous group. While some of these variables show different kinds of associations to rescue, none could serve as a predictor for this selfless help. Only when I examined such rescuers at close range did I find a cluster of shared characteristics and conditions similar to those found among the scattered cases from different European countries. They are: (1) An inability to blend within their environment, a characteristic that resembles closely London's concept of marginality. But because marginality has a negative connotation, I have chosen instead to use the term "individuality" or "separateness" to describe this characteristic. (2) A high level of independence and self-reliance that causes these individuals to pursue personal goals regardless of how these goals are viewed by others. (3) An enduring, strong commitment to help the needy that began before the war and that included a wide range of activities. (4) A matter-of-fact attitude toward rescue that sees it as a mere duty, which explains the repeated denials of rescuers that their protection of Jews was extraordinary or heroic. (5) An unplanned beginning to rescue efforts. (6) Universalistic perceptions of the needy; the ability to disregard and set aside all attributes of the needy except their dependence and helplessness.

Cutting across conventional ways of classifying people, such as class, religion, politics, friendship, and, in part, even anti-Semitism, the characteristics they do share point to a set of interdependent hypotheses.

Space limitations demand that I exclude from this presentation the vivid but lengthy qualitative data.[26] What follows, therefore, is only a partial illustration of my findings and hypotheses.

Overall evidence shows that these courageous Poles were, at best, only loosely integrated into their communities. Their individuality or separateness appears under different guises. Moreover, its effectiveness and impact upon rescue depends on and is related to other shared attributes and motivations.

To begin with, what does being an individualist entail, and what else does it suggest?

Being on a periphery of a community means being less affected by the existing social controls. With individuality, then, comes fewer social constraints and more freedom. In turn, more freedom means more independence. A high level of independence has other important implications. For freedom from social constraints and a high level of independence offer an opportunity to act in accordance with personal values and moral precepts, even if these are in opposition to societal expectations. If rescuers are less controlled by their environment and more independent, they are more likely guided by their own moral imperatives, whether or not these imperatives conform to societal demands.

Of the rescuers I interviewed directly, none had trouble talking about their self-reliance and their need to follow personal inclinations and values. In addition, nearly all of the 189 helpers (98%) saw themselves as independent. All of the Jewish survivors I spoke to also described their rescuers as independent and as being motivated by special personal values. In addition, a quality often mentioned in the testimonies and memoirs of survivors and one that comes close to independence, is the rescuers' courage. Of the 308 Jewish survivors, the overwhelming majority (85%) described their helpers as courageous.

Not necessarily aware of their individuality, practically all of these rescuers were aware of their independence. Connected to their consciousness about independence was also an awareness that they were propelled by moral standards and values not necessarily shared by others, standards that did not depend on the support and approval by others but rather on their self-approval. Again and again, they repeated that they had to be at peace with themselves and with their own idea of what was right or wrong.

Closely related to the rescuers' moral convictions and values was their long-lasting commitment to stand up for the needy. This commitment was expressed in a wide range of charitable acts that extended over a long time. Support for such a long-lasting commitment to help comes also from the entire sample of rescuers. Sixty percent of them had a past history of charitable deeds. For the remaining 40%, this kind of information is unavailable. Here the survivors became a more reliable source of information. Invariably they presented a glowing picture of their protectors by almost unanimously defining them as "good natured" and by describing their efforts on behalf of the needy as limitless and enduring.

What do such repetitive and enduring actions mean?

As a rule, we take our repetitive ideas and actions for granted. What we take for granted, we usually accept. Further, what we take for granted and accept, we rarely analyze or wonder about. In fact, the more firmly established patterns are, the less likely we are to examine them and think about them. In a very real sense, therefore, the constant pressure of, or familiarity with, ideas and actions does not mean that we know or understand them. On the contrary, to the extent that customary patterns are accepted and taken for granted, this in itself may impede rather than promote understanding. Closely related to this tendency is another one. Thus, that which we are accustomed to and tend to repeat doing, we have a hard time seeing as extraordinary, no matter how otherwise exceptional it may be. In a real sense, therefore, immunity to seeing the special and extraordinary leads to missed opportunities.

There seems to be a continuity between the rescuers' past history of charitable actions and their protection of Jews. That is, risking their lives for Jews fits into a system of values and behaviors that included helping the weak and the dependent. This analogy, however, has serious limitations. Most disinterested actions on behalf of others may involve inconvenience, even extreme inconvenience. Only rarely do such acts suggest that the giver may have to make the ultimate sacrifice of his or her own life. For these Poles, then, only during the war was there a convergence between historical events demanding ultimate selflessness and the already established predisposition to help.

What special effects, then, did this past history of aiding the poor have on the rescuing of Jews?

This past history of helping the weak might have been responsible for the rescuers' modest appraisal of their life-threatening actions. Such modest appraisal was expressed in a variety of ways. Thus, most rescuers (66%) perceived their protection of Jews as a natural reaction to human suffering, while others, almost a third (31%), insisted that to save lives was nothing exceptional. In contrast, only 3% described the saving of Jews as extraordinary.

Refusal to perceive the drama of these life-threatening and risky actions was expressed in other ways. Thus, some Poles omitted from their accounts events that attested to particularly noble and courageous aspects of their rescue. This tendency is apparent from a comparison of information collected from matched pairs of rescuers and rescued.

Indeed, whereas the Jews were glad, even eager, to praise their protectors, the rescuers were reluctant to talk about their aid. Even those who did spoke only in timid and restrained ways. As a rule, I had to prod and probe before any of them mentioned those aspects of help that put them in a particularly favorable light. Instead, they consistently underplayed the risks and sacrifices inherent in this kind of aid.

More freedom and more direct expressions of this need to minimize the exceptional qualities of rescue relate to comments about heroism. Not only did most helpers deny that aid to Jews was heroic, they became embarrassed when this possibility was suggested to them. Furthermore, to underplay the heroism of their actions, they pointed to their fears while rescuing. Half of the rescuers mention such fears, while for the other half information about fears is lacking. In contrast, hardly any of the survivors describe their protectors as fearful.

In short, the rescuers tried to remove their aid from the exceptional and extraordinary. Some did it by describing it as merely a duty. Some pushed the dangers into the background; some emphasized that they followed the value of saving a life; some tried to diminish the danger of their actions by seeing it as simply another part of a threatening environment.

Given the matter-of-fact perceptions of rescue, it is not surprising that this aid often began in a spontaneous, unpremeditated way. In fact, unplanned and unanticipated, this participation would start either gradually or suddenly.

Such an unplanned and sometimes sudden way of extending help only underscores the rescuers' need to stand up for the poor and helpless. In fact, so strong was this need to help, so much was it a part of their makeup, that it overshadowed all other considerations.

Asked why they had saved Jews, the Poles emphasized over and over again that they had responded to the persecution and suffering of victims and not to their Jewishness. What compelled them to act was the persecution, the unjust treatment, and the people's need for help and protection.

This ability to disregard all attributes of the needy, except their helplessness and dependence, I refer to as universalistic perceptions. Evidence for the presence of such universalistic perceptions of the needy comes from a variety of sources.

Indirect motivational data on rescue show that 95% of these helpers feel that they were prompted by Jewish needs for help. This is in sharp contrast to the 26% who helped because it was a Christian duty or to the 52% who did so as a protest against the Nazi occupation. Clearly, however, more than one kind of motivation was involved. Of the Jewish survivors, 81% said that it was their suffering that made these Christians offer them protection. These universalistic perceptions of the needy are further expressed by the fact that only 9% of those rescuers limited their aid to friends. The rest offered help to all kinds of people, including many strangers. When the sample of Jewish survivors is consulted, 51% of them say that they were protected by strangers, 19% say that they received aid from friends.

The compelling moral force behind the rescuing of Jews as well as the universal insistence that what mattered was the victims' position of dependence and unjust persecution combined to make such actions universalistic. In a sense, it was this moral force that motivated the rescuers independently of personal likes and dislikes. Some of those I spoke to were indeed aware that to help the needy, in general, and the Jews, in particular, one did not necessarily have to like them. Liking and helping, they knew, did not necessarily go hand in hand.

I believe that the findings and the theoretical interpretations presented in this paper deserve further study. Persecution, discrimination, and prejudice are a part of our everyday life. More often than not, those who are victims of such evil forces cannot effectively fight back. Knowing who would stand up for the persecuted and the helpless, knowing what factors are involved in the protection of the poor, the dependent, and the downtrodden, is of utmost theoretical and practical importance.

NOTES

*This is a revised version of a paper, "Rescue and Rescuers During World War II," presented at the 22nd Annual Meeting of the Canadian Association of Sociology and Anthropology, Canada, June, 1987.

[1]Bejski, Moshe, "The Righteous Among The Nations and Their Part in the Rescue of Jews," in Gutman, Y. and Rothkirchen, L., eds., The Catastrophe of European Jews (Jerusalem: Yad Vashem, 1976), pp. 582-607.

[2]Evidence about these two groups comes from the following sources: (a) unpublished testimonies of the rescuers and the rescued that are a part of different archival collections; (b) published diaries written by Jews who survived by living illegally in the forbidden Christian world and diaries written by Polish rescuers who helped them survive; and (c) in-depth interviews conducted with each of these groups, the rescuers and the rescued. Information was collected from 189 rescuers and 308 Jewish survivors. In addition, the Jewish sample offers information about 565 rescuers.

[3]Bartoszewski, Wladyslaw, The Blood Shed Unites Us (Warsaw: Interpress, 1970), pp. 227-228; Bartoszewski, Wladyslaw, "Egzekucje Publiczne W Warszawie W Latach, 1943-1944" ("Public Executions in Warsaw, 1943-1944"), Biuletyn Zbrodni Niemieckiej W Polsce (1946), No. 6, pp. 211-224; Friedman, Filip, "Zaglada Zydow Polskich W Latach, 1939-1945" ("Jewish Extermination in Poland, 1939-1945"), Biuletyn Glownej Komisij Badania Zbrodni Niemieckiej W Polsce (1946), No. 6, pp. 165-208.

[4]Hilberg, Raul, The Destruction of The European Jewry (New York: New Viewpoints, 1973), p. 174.

[5]Dawidowicz, Lucy S., ed., A Holocaust Reader (New York: Behrman House, Inc., 1976), pp. 67-68.

[6]Berenstein, Tatiana and Rutkowski, Adam, Assistance to the Jews in Poland (Warsaw: Polonia Publishing House, 1963); Datner, Szymon, Las Sprawiedliwych (Righteous Christians) (Warszawa: Ksazka I Wiedza, 1968); Ringelblum, Emmanuel, Notes From The Warsaw Ghetto (New York: Shocken Books, 1975); Wronski, Stanislaw and Zwolakowa, Maria, Polacy I Zydzi, 1939-1945 (Poles and Jews, 1939-1945) (Warszawa: Ksiazka I Wiedza, 1971).

[7]For evidence supporting these assertions, see: Heller, Celia S., On the Edge of Destruction (New York: Columbia University Press, 1977), p. 69; Korzec, Pawel, "Anti-Semitism in Poland as An Intellectual, Social and Political Movement," in Fishman, Joshua A., ed., Studies On Polish Jewry (New York: YIVO Institute for Jewish Research, 1974); Lestchinsky, Jacob, "The Jews in the City of The Republic of Poland," YIVO Annual of Jewish Social Science (1946), Vol. 1, pp. 156-159; Lestchinsky, Jacob, "The Industrial & Social Structure of the Jewish Population of Interbellum Poland," YIVO Annual of Jewish Social Science (1956-1957), Vol. II, p. 246; Lifschutz, L., "Selected Documents Pertaining to Jewish

Life in Poland, 1919-1938," in Fishman, Joshua A., ed., Studies on Polish Jewry (New York: YIVO Institute for Jewish Research, 1974), p. 280; Wynot, Edward D., Jr., "A Necessary Cruelty: The Emergence of Official Anti-Semitism in Poland, 1936-1939," The American Historical Review (October 1971), Vol. 76, No. 4, pp. 1035-1058.

[8]Korzec, "Anti-Semitism in Poland," op. cit., p. 91 (p. 13).

[9]For a historical account of this plan, see: Friedman, Philip, "The Lublin Reservation and the Madagascar Policy," YIVO Annual of Social Science (1958), Vol. 8, pp. 151-177.

[10]Tec, Nechama, "Polish Anti-Semitism and Christian Protectors," East European Quarterly (1986), Vol. XX, No. 3, pp. 299-315.

[11]Polonsky, Anthony, Politics in Independent Poland, 1921-1939 (Oxford: The Calderon Press, 1972), p. 40.

[12]Lifschutz, "Selected Documents," op. cit., p. 280.

[13]Heller, Celia, "Poles of Jewish Background -- The Case of Assimilation Without Integration in Prewar Poland," in Fishman, Joshua, ed., Studies on Polish Jewry (New York: YIVO Institute for Jewish Research, 1974), pp. 242-276.

[14]For a discussion of these issues, see: Tec, Nechama, "Righteous Christians in Poland," International Social Science Review (Winter, 1983), pp. 12-19; Tec, Nechama, When Light Pierced the Darkness, Christian Rescue of Jews in Nazi Occupied Poland (New York: Oxford University Press, 1986).

[15]London, Perry, "The Rescuers: Motivational Hypotheses About Christians Who Saved Jews From the Nazis," in Macaulay, Jacqueline R. and Berkowitz, Leonard, eds., Altruism and Helping Behavior (New York: Academic Press, 1970), pp. 241-250. As far as I know, London was the first to apply the concept of altruism to the study of Christian rescuers of Jews.

[16]Macaulay, Jacqueline R. and Berkowitz, Leonard, "Overview," in Macaulay and Berkowitz, eds., Altruism and Helping Behavior, op. cit., pp. 1-9. I leaned on their definition of altruism.

[17]This theoretical distinction has been suggested by David L. Rosenhan, "The Natural Socialization of Altruistic Autonomy," in Macaulay and Berkowitz, eds., Altruism and Helping Behavior, op. cit., pp. 251-268.

[18]Flender, Harold, Rescue in Denmark (New York: Simon and Schuster, 1963), p. 181.

[19]London defined marginality as a rescuer's inability to blend into his or her environment, op. cit.

[20]Jaffre, Jeffrey, Stepson of a People (Montreal: Admiral Printing, 1968).

[21]Hellman, Peter, Avenue of the Righteous (New York: Atheneum Publishers, 1980), pp. 3-58.

[22]Hallie, Philip, Lest Innocent Blood Be Shed (New York: Harper and Row, 1979).

[23]This is the common spelling of his name. One exception is Philip Friedman, who spells it as Westerville. See: Your Brothers' Keepers (New York: Holocaust Library, 1978), p. 66.

[24]Levin, Nora, The Holocaust, 1933-1945 (New York: Schocken Books, 1973), p. 418.

[25]Hausner, Gideon, Justice in Jerusalem (New York: Holocaust Library, 1968), p. 260.

[26]Such extensive qualitative analysis makes up a large part of my book, especially Chapter 10. See: When Light Pierced the Darkness, Christian Rescue of Jews in Nazi Occupied Poland, op. cit.

The challenge to the Christian and Jewish communities: Faith, theology and life after the Holocaust (Christian-Jewish relations)

CHAIRPERSON **Dr Beverly Asbury**

RAPPORTEUR **Dr Franz von Hammerstein**

THE CHALLENGE TO THE CHRISTIAN COMMUNITY IN GERMANY: FAITH, THEOLOGY AND PRACTICE AFTER THE "HOLOCAUST"

Paul Gerhard Aring, Dr.theol.habil.

Melanchthon-Akademie, Kartäuserwall 24b, 5ooo Köln 1
Universität/Gesamthochschule, Lotharstr.85, 41oo Duisburg

This is the summary of some historical and theological researchs. Such researchs and their consequences for our present time force us to pay attention to an old rule of the theological science: demonstrable facts are less important or deciding than interpretations of these facts. Thus the history of the Christianity and of the Christian Churches is the history of their exegesis and interpretation of the book which is called "The Bible".

With regard to our theme this statement gets an oppressing acuteness.

The longer the more it became absolute impossible to affirm that any kind of interpretation of the "Holocaust" could be more important than all the details of cruel events and facts 50 years ago. With or without "Bible": the so called "Holocaust" in Germany - the country of the lutheran reformation - burst all human imagination. More than ever we are feeling it as the deciding turning-point for the whole Christian theology at least in Germany, for the traditional Christian doctrine, preaching, teaching, faith, confessing, thinking and feeling about Jesus Christ. Not the rabbi of Nazareth will come in question. We begin to realize: the Christian associate with this rabbi Jesus, thus the Christian "christology" was the original and actual precondition for the "Holocaust".

I have to substantiate this statement.

What had happened twothousand years ago in the history of Christianity? Some days after the public execution according to martial law a few women and fellows of this rabbi Jesus experienced in an inexplicable manner that the crucified arose from death. 50 days later - at "Pentecost" - they have been overwhelmed by a new experience of faith: the "living crucified" began an historical epoch which his fellows at Jerusalem signified as the beginning of God's world-wide eternal kingdom. "Christianity" started. Only its spreading by mission is demonstrable, not its origin. Only the appearances of religious experiences like the so named "Easter" (1.Cor.15 a.o.) are demonstrable, not the deeper roots of them. Although the Christianity forgot this simple principle very soon, it will remain as an historical burden which will weigh very very heavy, because the influence of the Christian message was and is going on through the centuries. This influence was and is stamping thoughts and emotions and the behaviour of numberless individuals and societies.

In my opinion these preliminary remarks are necessary because of some fundamental considerations. In course of the occidental history the Christian churches and their theology (anywhere, but especially in Germany) misused their religious experience, their message and tradition about Jesus Christ, their conviction and self-consciousness, their power-by-authority and their basic-doctrine about Christ's "divine imperial omnipotence" to persecute all those people who didn't follow them in confessing the messianity and divinity of Jesus Christ and his Church. Because of the common theological interpretation of the majestic title "Christos", not because of any personal experience and feeling about the Jesus of Nazareth it happened that many many million of human-being have been killed - each of them a singular person, created and beloved by the "Almighty" and therefore unique and "God's image". Never this German Christian theology minded: "...he that toucheth you toucheth the apple of God's eye" (Zechariah 2,8).

Once again: these million and million individuals - under them numberless Jewish women, children and men - have been killed by Christians everywhere not because of the Rabbi of Nazareth but because of the later following christological interpretations of him and of his "resurrection".

Today we speak about the "Easter-experience" on ground of the New Testament. With other words: we find the literary sediment about this undiscutable-religious-experience of "Easter" in all the texts of the so named "New Testament". The basic experience of the "resurrection of Christ" is the deciding key to our understanding and interpretation of this New Testament. We have to read and to interprete its texts as personal-concrete testimonies of faith and conviction, not as historical reports. Let me insert only one example for this consideration: in a very concrete situation of oppression, persecution, danger of life and personal temptation in the early Christian time Jesus should have said to certain individuals - so Matthew (10,32f.) - something about confessing or denying of him. Surely this statement was valid for one of the concrete situations at that time. But today we realize that a Christian doctrine resp. a "christology" of the first centuries with all its special interpretations generalized and forgot this concrete context of this and of each statement in the New Testament. So it could happen that the dangerous and unrealistic ideology of a "doctrine of verbal inspiration" arose and impressed the theology of the church.

On this way the Christian conviction of a "world-supremacy of Christ" came into being and therefore the doctrine and conviction of a Christian world-supremacy with all its power-politics and claims for an absolute authority of the Church and its clergy. Church and clergy got political power in spite of all what the Rabbi of Nazareth taught. Their influence became immense in public, state and society. For a common feeling "the almighty Christ" and "the almighty Church" became identical. People who opposed because of their different religious insight became marplots and dangerous intruders of the society. At last they became enemies of God and Christ and the Church. So arose all what we remember in the history of the Christian Church: heterodoxy, heresy, persecution and trials of heretics, sects, sectarianism, fanaticism, indoctrination, "Index Librorum Prohibitorum", inquisition, denomination, denominationalism, "anathema", excommunication, schism, wars of religion, crusades and crusaders with all their incredible crimes, missionary rivalry till in our modern times, oppression of the freedom of conscience also in the present Church, anxiety about heterodoxy or false doctrines, dissension and separation of churches throughout the centuries, clerical struggles for power, clerical intrigues and so on - the history of Church and Christianity is like a irritating mirror of all human imperfection and madness.

People who had to trace and to suffer from this untrustworthy Christianity were especially the Jews. They were suffering from the growing Christian thinking in terms of "victory", absolutism, exclusivity. They were suffering from the rapidly expanded influence of the churches in their concrete society. They were suffering from the fact that it was impossible for them to accept the Rabbi of Nazareth as their "Messiah" because of the behaviour of his Christians and the common situation of mankind and world. Nothing changed there although Christianity proclaimed the new "messianic" age. The expanding Christianity must become more and more a strange unbiblical religion for the Jews - not in any accordance with their own biblical religious traditions.

It is senseless to conceal that the roots of the "Holocaust" are reaching very deep in the history of the Christian Church and its theology. This insight will remain as a burden and guilt on the shoulders of Christianity as long as the Christians "after Auschwitz" continue to preach and to teach and to pursue their "mission" as usually in the past "before Auschwitz". After more than 30 years of service in my German Church and theology I have the burdening impression that this general situation did not change essentially yet. I am feeling alarmed considering that the Christian "Before-Auschwitz-Theology" (thus the traditional Christian interpretation of the belief in the resurrected Christ and his "world-supremacy") is found in sermons, in teaching, religious instruction, new and old hymn-books, normal worships and their liturgies, common prayers, in Christian art and literature and sacred music, in church-law and church-constitutions and church-discipline, in daily parochial-politics, in newspapers of the churches and so on - till today! A few exceptions confirm the rule. Many examples which I collected in the 30 years could be cited to show a continuous "christology of the separation from Israel and the Jews" which nowadays is leaving its marks upon ecclesiastical thinking, feeling, emotions and practice!

And I try to see further on. The extent of such a "bypassing of Israel and the Jews" and the fervour with which it has been exported by the Christian mission from the West and has become inherent in the thinking and emotions of Christian churches around the world, would merit a special investigation. I experienced it in my time in an Asian church, later on in my personal engagement within the ecumenical movement of our time. I think it is horrible to meet ancient Christian prejudices in the theological literature, in education-schemes, in church-constitutions and therefore in a general feeling of church-members in Asian or African churches. We can only think in fear and trembling how fervently our churches have preached the "superiority of Christianity" and therefore the consequent disqualification and demonizing of the Jews and therefore (theologically!) the destruction of the unique dignity of Israel and the claim to set up strong barriers against Israel and the Jews like against enemies of God and His kingdom and His Church

This deep-rooted idea and behaviour ultimately made possible what we presently name "Shoa" or "Holocaust".

The vote of the Protestant Rhenish General-Synod of January 1980 and its resolution "On the Renewal of the Christian-Jewish Relationship" pointed out this fact quite unequivocally. We have to declare and to explain: Theologically it is neither honest nor responsible to consider and to proclaim the belief in Jesus Christ and its christological interpretations as if that Christian barrier of thought against Israel and its appalling culmination in the "Holocaust" never had happened.

On this background we have to state that in spite of all what happened in the past the ancient thinking about a "Christian mission-duty" towards the Jewish people wherever they are found is living continually. I could demonstrate it with a fullness of statements, interviews, articles, sermons and other observations in the daily life of the German churches. The with it connected problem becomes nearly unbearable when I consider: also today ("after Auschwitz") convinced Christian individuals and groups, churches and missionary societies are regarding it as a vital task to reach out to the Jewish people with the message of Christ. I have to avoid misunderstandings: I am deeply impressed by all the personal inset and engagement which we find in the long history of this Christian mission to the Jews (1). This history is an accumulation of individual stories! The burden, members of the mission to the Jews had to take because of their love to Jews for Christ's sake, is admirable and exceedingly worth of appreciation. They performed their service in personal honesty and integrity. But they did it (and they continue to do it) without the necessary critical question about our general Christian attitude towards Israel. that means our attitude to the traditional Christian message and belief of "Jesus Christ". Here - if on the whole! - we will meet the key to a new relationship between Church and Synagogue.

The already mentioned Protestant Rhenish Church in Germany declared in the resolution about "Renewal of the Relationship between Christians and Jews" in January 1980, that Christians as well Jews are both witnesses of God in their common world. "Therefore the Church cannot claim a special mission-charge concerning the Jews like possibly such a charge concerning the other people; the permanent-valid appeal of Israel as God's people and the special commission of Israel towards the nations forbid it" (2). Other churches in Germany including the Roman Catholic Church said it with other, but similar words.

I like to suggest that at present we experience an important development in this question of Christian-Jewish relationsship. I can only refer to small but remarkable steps on this toilsome way! Let me describe it in terms of the traditional theology (Christian and Jewish)!

We Christians are discovering by degrees in our dialogue with Jewish friends the continuity of the both "biblical testaments" and their fundamental axiom: God's never denounced covenant with Israel. That means in such theological terms: God has turned towards His Israel and promised that through His people all the world will discover that He's "the Lord". In this covenant with God, Israel despite all what it had to experience in the long way of its history never experienced God's revocation of the covenant. This eternal covenant endures, remains valid and incontestable and topical with all its implications. We do not have the authorization to limit such implications, for instance by excluding the present state of Israel or by restriction this principle (in a typical Christian habit) on Jews who are "believers". We Christians have to accept: Also Jews who may be indifferent are members of God's people and therefore of God's covenant with His Israel.

This "biblical" message of God's covenant and its significance for the whole mankind are a new invitation to the Christians to spell again their fundamental basis of confession and belief: "Jesus the Christ" and his significance. May be it will become troublesome and vaxatious, because all our theological and pious and personal traditions are rooted too deeply. But we should begin it as soon as possible if we like to gain a new credibility for our Christian "confession of faith". Let me summarize:

In the covenant between God and Israel the man of the small Galileen town Nazareth plays a vital role for us, the "gojim", the "gentiles" thus all the nations outside of Israel. This is so. and this will remain so!

Through Jesus and those who are bound to him in the fellowship of his disciples (because through him they discovered God anew, totally anew) it is told to us that all the world (Jews and Gentiles, Israel and the Nations) are summoned and incorporated into the communion of God's covenant. Now all the nations (we!) have the right to take place in the covenant with God in which Israel already is at home, irrevocable, for ever. To repeat it: in the person of this Jesus we - the gentiles - have discovered that we too belong to the family of God's covenant!

Therefore (overwhelmed by this experience of "salvation") we hail and praise "our" Jesus as our "Christ", as our "Son of God", as our "Kyrios" (against all the claims of the Roman Emperor!), as the "Messiah out of Israel" who has opened the door of his fathers house for us and for all human-beings around the world. In usual theological terms it menas: for us - the "gentiles" - he is "the way, the truth and the life" (vide John 14); he guided us to the place where Israel already dwells: into the communion of God. Now we out of the gentiles, we Non-Jews. we Christians or Non-Christians - all we human-beings are invited and called-up to start like Abraham, like Israel in its whole history on the prepared way of God's "thora" (his directive, his fatherly assistance, his way of life) and to get out of our "country" into a land that He will show us (vide Genesis 12): into His future, His eternity, His "shalom". This future of God (and therefore this our future) is finally prepared by Him who loves His Israel and His Gentiles (and us today).

We, the "Christians", the nations outside of Israel, received this promise of God's "salvation" by the Jew Jeschua (Jesus) whom we confess as our "Christ(os) of God" or "Messiah".

"Our" Jesus - son of his people Israel - bound us together with God's people Israel which had to suffer the indescribable "Holocaust".

We Christians in Germany, involved in the present Christian-Jewish Dialogue, begin to have a presentiment of its deepest significance for us all. In opposition to many traditional Christian doctrines in our German Churches and theology we are seeing another centre of gravity in our spiritual presence:

In Jesus of Nazareth (so we are feeling it in terms of faith resp. Christian ideology) God started His final work of "creation". We experience and believe and confess it in theological terms of "resurrection from the dead". Jesus "resurrected from the dead". We believe and confess it. And we believe and confess that "we are new creatures in Jesus Christ"; "old things are passed, all things are become new" (2.Corinthians 5,17). This all happened by the grace of the Almighty, the God of Israel. Deepestly ashamed we realize: Jewish fellow-creatures descry their suffering throughout the "Christian" centuries in terms of the "passion" of Jesus and the rebirth of their State of Israel behind all Christian traditions of "resurrection" and "new life". So it becomes recognizable: the Rabbi of Nazareth Jesus doesn't separate the Jews and the Christians - he is joining them "for time and eternity".

That means theologically: Jews and Christians are awaiting together the Messianic consummation of the world. This waiting is dynamically active: it gives the assurance that the both are living together in the communion of the covenant with God the father. While waiting together the Jews don't need the Christian missionary testimony - they are already there (since a very long time!) where Christians like to transport them! - but they start anew to pay attention to Christian expressions of faith! We begin to understand that it is not indispensable to formulate a special Christian identity by setting up polemical barriers against Israel and Judaism. In terms of the New Testament: When for instance Jews repudiate Jesus as the "Messiah/Christos of the gentiles", it is to be interpreted according to the apostle Paul (Romans 11) that they would prefer to remain faithful and obedient to the will of God as revealed to them from their special religious experience. Israel is till today - so the apostle Paul - God's witness in front of the whole world. Nothing can change it. Neither in the past nor in the presence nor in future. Who attacks Israel, he attacks God. The living God. The eternal God...

And we continue: Together with Israel we (Christians from among the Gentiles) are summoned along the path to the "Kingdom of God" - by the Jew Jesus whom we believe to be "the Messiah" (the "Christ"). On this way of our "pious remembering" it becomes a hitherto unrecognized theological significance. We Christians (especially in the "Christian" Germany!) should consider anew the biography of the Jew Jesus!

He lived as a member of his contemporary Jewish society in which he cannot be represented as an "outsider". He was descended from a Jewish community in Galilee. He had family ties in Bethlehem and also in Jerusalem. As a sign of God's covenant with Abraham and his seed, he was circumcised and presented in the Temple as the firstborn of his mother Mirjam - prescribed by the Holy Writ. In accordance with all traditions of his Israel, the boy Jesus was roused and instructed according to the belief in God the Creator and Father and Redeemer. He called upon God in praise, intercession and lamentation. He studied the Thora and lived by the daily experience of "exodus", of all what happened after "Sinai" and the "exile" and the return to Zion and the prophetic preaching, in the general longing for the "Messiah" and the common expectation of God's final time. Guide-lines of his daily life were the commandments and God's dual precept of love. Both directed him to a life for those who "travail and are heavy laden" (Matthew 11). So when he turned towards his fellow-men, he lived and taught obedience to the will of God. He showed himself consistently to be a son of his people in the belief that God had chosen it to be the light unto the nations, to all mankind. With many of his contemporaries, Jesus longed fervently for the kingdom of God to dawn in his lifetime. When, in trying to attain recognition of the will of God, like the prophets of Israel before him and other Jewish groups of his age, he came in conflict with certain attitudes among his people, this happened in his zeal for the holiness of God. While numerous instances of such internal Jewish disputes can be gleaned from the New Testament, they should never be levelled as generalizations against the Jewish people as a whole, against its belief and tradition. They originated in concrete situations which cannot claim to have any universal and eternal validity. God's choice of Israel to be the people of the covenant was never questioned by Jesus.

The teaching of Jesus as identified in the texts of the New Testament is an interpretation of the Thora, both in agreement with and in contradiction to some other interpretations of the pharisaical and rabbinical Judaism of the time. In his parables, Jesus described the dominion of God as it should manifest itself in the life of man. Like others, he opposed the misuse of the Temple in Jerusalem and the notorious opportunism of the ruling castes. He wished to see God's commandments put into the daily practice of his people - nothing more. Together with his Israel, Jesus suffered under the power and despotism of the foreign Roman rule, and it was under this Roman foreign (Non-Jewish) law that he finally met his end, crucified according to martial law.

In theological terms: Together with the whole Jewish tradition we say, that with this execution of Jesus, an image of God ("imago Dei") was destroyed. When Christians, on the strength of their religious tradition say, that it is precisely t h i s "imago Dei" which has been resurrected and re-established , they voice a conviction which Jews cannot share with them. The Jewish view of the "God of life", of the "conquest of suffering", of "guilt and death", is very different from that held by "those from among the Gentiles".

These again point out the J e w s were the first to participate in that religious experience of "Easter" which they accepted as God's revelation of Himself and passed on to the gentiles by the "kerygma", thus the new Christian message of "salvation". Till today in each generation anew there are Jews who are convinced to find their way to God's "salvation" by the way of Jesus, of his gospel and his church, whereas till today in each generation anew there are Non-Jews who are convinced to find their way to God's "salvation" by the way of Israel and the Thora. God's spirit "bloweth where it listest, and thou...canst not tell whence it cometh, and whither it goeth..." (John 3,8). These facts cannot contest this general view.

With other words: In Israel's experience of God and faith, it is G o d who is at work, who creates life, who judges and saves, who reconciles and perfects. This acting of God, made known by the history and the presence of Israel, can be paraphrased, in theological terms, as "the spirit of God" or as "God in action". In the nations experience of God and faith, it is, God in Christ, God acting through Jesus Christ, God as "the spirit of God" or "the Holy Spirit" or as God in action" resp. "Christ in action" as the creator of life, as the judge and saviour, redeeming and perfecting, to whom the history and the presence of Christianity bear witness...

Thus: it is God who - throughout the world, for Jews and Gentiles, for Synagogue and Church - is the beginning and the end, the future and the eternal hope, the only and the same God to whom Jews like Non-Jews are calling their prayers, their yearning for "schalom", their confession of guilt and their thanksgiving for redemption and liberation. They all do it in human words, very imperfectly, often stammering like children, again and again bound to any concrete times resp. places resp. situations in which "the word becomes flesh" (John 1). Words or terms are only ciphers or codes or images and pictures for a deeper reality behind them.

We Christians have to learn from the Jews and their tradition that a religious belief, such as our belief in Christ and our "christology", therefore can neither be canonized nor dogmatized. Considering this we Christians come very close to the biblical, essentially dogma-free, Jewish thinking and openly approach the state of mind where nothing of topical relevance is lost. On the contrary, many aspects of the spiritual and religious situation between Christians and Jews could show us by this way a new impush for our relationship!

Concrete, unforeseeable situations in our life, tend to produce that personal experience which the "Old Testament" records in its "language of revelation and covenant" and the "New Testament" in its "language of resurrection and Pentecost". That means: God permits man to experience His reality, His presence, His power to change. This concrete experience was given concrete expression in the same way both in biblical and postbiblical times, even until our time: in the "martyria" of any "status confessionis", in the language of prayer, in personal testimonies, in meetings of the community, in the celebration of worship, in the commemoration of the Passover-meal and of Maundy Thursday, in the daily way of life, in service to others, in the patience and certainty of each day's new beginning, in the "imitatio Jesu" and its effect upon others, just as in the obedience to the teaching of the Thora. Each of these expressions symbolize what is meant both by the Jewish "schema Jisrael" and the Christian "I believe in Christ". God's people, the Jews, and God's people, the Gentiles, are by the common history of the covenant, joined together as the one people of God. "Christology" is the experiment to explain the significance of the Jew Jesus as the "Messiah for the nations". This "Messiah from Israel" opened for us the gate into the communion of God's eternal covenant, in which Israel already since a long time dwelt.

On this background we ask our Jewish friends in the Christian-Jewish dialogue: please accept the boundaries of the covenant as being open to all nations! And we ask our Christian friends in this dialogue and through them the Churches and their theologians: do what you can do to spread such a new view upon the very ancient biblical basic-experience of God's covenant with Israel and through Israel with all mankind. Together we all must start to learn anew that God's "schalom" is at last beyond all human understanding, but more realistic and further reaching and all-embracing than our claims to exclusiveness or sole authority could ever grasp.

R e m a r k s :

1) Compare the following books and their detailed informations about literature:

Paul Gerhard Aring
Christliche Judenmission. Ihre Geschichte und Problematik dargestellt und untersucht am Beispiel des evangelischen Rheinlandes
Neukirchen 198o
ISBN 3-7887-0617-1

Paul Gerhard Aring
Christen und Juden heute - und die "Judenmission"? Geschichte und Theologie protestantischer Judenmission in Deutschland, dargestellt und untersucht am Beispiel des Protestantismus im mittleren Deutschland
Frankfurt/Main 1987
ISBN 3-89228-037-1

2) Handreichung Nr. 39 für Mitglieder der Landessynode "Zur Erneuerung des Verhältnisses von Christen und Juden"
Mülheim/Ruhr 1980, p. 28

FOUR THEOLOGIANS: REVISION OF CHRISTIAN THOUGHT AFTER AUSCHWITZ

B. A. Asbury
University Chaplain-Director of Religious Affairs

Vanderbilt University
Nashville, Tennessee

Abstract - The Holocaust has forced a reexamination of Christian belief and its relationship to the Jewish people. As a result, theological revision is well under way. Some Christian theologians, such as A. Roy Eckardt, Alice L. Eckardt, and Paul Van Buren, significantly revise Chrisitan doctrine to accommodate it to the historical reality of the Holocaust. Other thinkers such as John T. Pawlikowski, O.S.M., and David Rausch, seem to seek to accommodate the Holocaust and Christian doctrine in such a way as to avoid radical revisions of orthodox Christian tenets.

INTRODUCTION

This paper represents a coming together of personal, existential concerns and scholarly interests. The motivation behind writing it is personal and intellectual and led to the pursuit of the subject. That is, the paper is a matter related to a deep caring; it is not, in a pejorative sense, "academic".

I am a white American male, a Southerner, a Protestant Christian, an ordained minister of the Gospel, and an heir of a tradition that has been anti-Judaic to the core. I am within a year of being sixty years old, aware of the Shoah (the Holocaust) since I was a teenager, deeply struck by it all my adult life. Much of the work that I have done over at least the past twenty years has had to do with accommodating my Christian beliefs and traditions to the historical reality of the Holocaust. The more that I have become a "student" of the Holocaust, the greater has become my sense of urgency for finding an appropriate and meaningful revision of Christian theology that is sufficient to the reality. Along with the urgency has gone a deep dissatisfaction, beyond impatience, both with theologians who seemingly have never encountered the Holocaust or who, having done so, attempt to accommodate its reality to traditional orthodox theology, thereby acknowledging the Holocaust but somehow insistent on not revising Christian belief in its light.

The surge of scholarship relating to the Holocaust in the past decade or so has finally produced major revisions which I continue to read and examine existentially as well as intellectually. That is, for Christian theology today to satisfy my soul and mind, it must face the reality of the Holocaust and then revise Christian doctrine and practice in such a way as to open a clearing so that believers may see in a new way.

Given my personal commitments, it is natural that I have a "point of view", a perspective from which I read the works of others. In this paper, I have selected the works of five writers. Four of them are trained as theologians, A. Roy and Alice L. Eckardt, John Pawlikowski, and Paul Van Buren. The other, David Rausch, is trained as an historian, but he writes without question as a committed evangelical Protestant and often in a theological vein.

THE ECKARDTS

The Eckardts offer a natural starting point. The work of A. Roy Eckardt has pioneered in this area of study. The subject is of vital importance to both him and Alice L. Eckardt. They write both together and separately, and if I tend to treat them frequently as one, it is not meant to blur the distinguishing characteristics of each author so much as it is to acknowledge the convergence of their thought. In many ways, they provide the benchmark or the plumbline by which to judge all other Christian theological revisions in the light of the Holocaust. Both go to the heart of the issue: *whether, when confronted with the history of Christian-inspired evil and violence, one can now find Christianity morally credible.*

> "A consequence of the Christian condition.............is that every affirmation of faith and every moral judgment and hope become existentially problematic. So shattering an event as the Holocaust has opened a crisis within every facet of Christian, Jewish, and other thinking.....And through the culpable actions of many men, the history of God.....The Holocaust is a crisis for man and God alike. For both, it is much more of a danger, but it need not be less than an opportunity."[1]

The Eckardts seize the opportunity, knowing that "the persisting presence of Christian antisemitism demands a wholehearted rethinking of the church's teachings."[2] And they see the ultimate test to be the Resurrection, because, on the one hand, the consummated resurrection of Jesus is central to the faith of most Christians. And, on the other hand, it is only by dealing with this doctrine, which Jews deny, that Christians may overcome their anti-Judaic prejudices and be able to reaffirm Jewishness. The Eckardts put it bluntly: "The Resurrection is the relentless force behind every other Christian derogation of Jewry". [3] It is the root of Christian destructiveness, because Jewish people do not believe in the risen Christ. Christians reason that in the Resurrection, God has shown the Christian cause to be right and true; the Jews are, therefore, wrong. Consequently, to address the Resurrection is far more than a matter of merely debating and changing doctrine. It is a matter of life-and-death, a matter of Christian credibility, of whether Christianity can live its ethic of love as a first priority among human beings.

> "If faith must be transformed by history, and everything potentially genocidal challenged, I must raise the question: can one affirm the Resurrection without at the same time continuing the displacement theology of the church? Perhaps at one time it was possible; perhaps at some future time it will be again; but now it is so overlaid with Christian triumphalism that it is hard to see how it can be done. The Resurrection was seen to prove that Jesus was the Messiah not just a human messiah....; not just a person with great faith in the imminent coming of the Kingdom of Heaven.....Instead the Resurrection experience transformed him into a divine-human figure; the very incarnation of the Holy One --- the exact opposite of everything Jews believed about God who was a totally Transcendent Being of absolute awe."[4]

There can be no doubt that the Eckardts make a radical theological response to the Holocaust. They are courageous, daring, and untiring in their rethinking and reassessment of theology. And they are no fools. They see clearly why "any demythologizing of the Resurrection of Jesus comprises a logical and substantive impossibility."[5] They see the point of Christian Fundamentalism and its literal teaching of bodily resurrection in opposing interpretations of the Resurrection as "symbol" or "myth". From a Fundamentalist perspective, such interpretations "spin intellectual spider webs and become the victim of a vague esotericism."[6] In their Biblical literalism, Fundamentalists are often at one with Jews in unflagging opposition to all things abstract. But the Fundamentalists pay a fearful price in order to keep "body and soul together." In the Eckardts' view, they "escape heresy only by violating historicalness, surrendering existential responsibleness, and falling into superstition."[7] In other words, Fundamentalists, along with many other Christians, obliterate the distinction between hopefulness and consummated event. They take the Resurrection to be an accomplished fact and thereby fail to "comprehend the nature and meaning of historical fact". The Eckardts assert: " In the name of the rational truth of Jewishness and of historicalness, Christian Fundamentalism has to be rejected. . . . the error of the literalist notion of the somatic Resurrection of Jesus is its prematurity."[8] That is, Jesus has not yet been raised from the dead, and since he has not been, then Christianity may be able to rid itself of its doctrine of replacement, of supersessionism, of triumphalism and of its continuing crimes against the Jews. "Thus does the Christian revolutionary work, at the very heart of traditional Christian affirmation, to sever the link between the Church's teaching and the convictions that led to the Holocaust."[9]

The thought of the Eckardts is more complex, sophisticated, and wide-ranging than can be shown in a brief exposition, but this gives an example of why they establish the benchmark of accomodating Christian theology to the historical reality of the Holocaust. However, there is one other matter that must be covered, because to leave it out would be to distort their thought. That is the matter of the State of Israel. A. Roy Eckardt has put it like this:

> "The existential challenge to the Christian community. . . . is whether there is a historical word from God that at once saves the Christian church from forlornness and saves it from unabated victimizing of the Jews. Is there a special historical event that judges and redeems the victimizing Resurrection? Is there an event of God that in the very moment that Christians are undergoing the dreadful trauma of necessarily rejecting the Resurrection in its victimizing aspects will nevertheless bring assurance, an event that will say 'I accept you'? Such an event may be the State of Israel . . . . The one allowable and fitting gift for Christians is the State of Israel as a sign and a witness that God continues to accept human beings totally apart from the Resurrection of Jesus Christ."[10]

Writing in the same vein, Alice Eckardt develops a "commandment", that "Christianity must stop exalting suffering and sacrifice".[11] She writes that Jewish martyrdom must be both rejected and forbidden, and seen as a profanation of the Divine Name. Pain and suffering do not elevate but diminish the human person and the image of God in that person. The role of victim is a dehumanizing one that dehumanizes the victimizer as well.

> "If God is a God of liberation, then God must be the God of the oppressed, and the God of those who seek to liberate either themselves or others. And that must include the State of Israel which seeks to end the helpless condition of Jews in the world after the Holocaust. Helplessness is not hopeful in a world where power predominates. The courage of Jews is to be found, for that matter, in their daring to embody the hopes of two thousand years in the fragile and vulnerable vessel of a state (especially a state in one of the most exposed and unstable areas of the world). It is a Christian obligation not only to support Israel in its times of trial and danger, but to underwrite the very principle of power and sovereignty as a valid means of protecting the community, preserving the Covenant, and combating evil. [12]

The Eckardts make these assertions at the very time that many Christians shy away from support of Israel. They suggest that this diminishing of support may be tied to Christian notions of suffering and sacrifice. That is, perhaps Christians could only support Israel as long as it was weak and a victim. In any event, Christians today may well fail to see that it is through the State and its power that Jews may be saved from another Holocaust. Alice Eckardt calls for Christians to re-enter history in a new way, turning away from "assuming God-like powers or unassailable claims to truth."

> "Christians will rediscover the sense of being God's partners in completing the Creation, which will require overcoming all forms of alienation without negating diversity, which will seek to preserve and enhance instead of destroying and diminishing....In such a world, Holocaust and genocide will not be repeated, at least not with Christian complicity.[13]

VAN BUREN

Paul Van Buren's way of accommodating Christian theology is very different than that of the Eckhardts but certainly no less a major revision. The difference seems to lie within Van Buren's commitment to the historicity and validity of the Christian Tradition. He will revise it according to the Sources, within the Tradition, using every appropriate scholarly and methodological tool. And he has been brought to see the need for doing this by the same two realities, the Holocaust and the State of Israel, that have motivated the Eckardts. But where the Eckardts' thinking leads them to move in revolutionary, radical thought outside or beyond the Tradition and its sources, Van Buren stays within it. It is as if he knows that the Christian community can never be brought to accept the Eckardts' perspective on Resurrection. He both anticipates and understands the objections of such ecclesiastical scholars as Pawlikowski. Van Buren continues to hope that the churches can and will come to accept a reinterpretation in and of the Tradition that will free it forever of its anti-Judaic bias. While Van Buren turns in a different direction from the Eckardts, he is no less committed to ending the crime that goes on to this day.

> "....our historic contempt of the Jews helped us to quietly look the other way when a full third of God's people were slaughtered. To worry about a possible incoherence in our idea of God when we have this larger matter before us would be like someone worrying about an untuned piano aboard the Titanic or about whether or not Adolph Eichmann underfed his cat. By all means let us aim for coherence and clarity...for the world may overhear us and we have no wish to mislead or confuse; let us only not consider this our most serious problem."[14]

Van Buren asserts that it is a Christian responsibility, after the Holocaust, to take special care not to weaken the Jewish people. Such care means forgoing attempts to convert Jews. It means cooperative efforts and dialogue. But even there, Van Buren cautions against the taking of Jewish customs and traditions into the Church. Christians presume too much when we take Jewish traditions as ours on our own "honorary" terms. In other words, Christianity has its own Tradition, and it needs major revisions to overcome its anti-Jewish bias. Given our dissatisfaction after Auschwitz with the conduct of the Church, Van Buren holds that it would be immoral and intolerable for the Church not to learn from its errors and to make a new response to its living Lord. However, Van Buren knows full well that the purpose of revision is not to create a "Judaism for Gentiles". God has given a Way to the Jews and a Way to the Gentiles, and the Gentiles must come to understand,respect, and accept the Way of the Jews and the Reality behind it. Because, after all is said and done, that Reality is the Lord, Israel's God, the One whom Christians also adore. Judaism, is, therefore, essential to the Church's understanding of Christ.

In Van Buren's view, Christians have been called to follow Jesus the Jew, but that call has come by way of the further calling of the Apostle Paul. The calling has come to Gentiles *qua* Gentiles to follow Jesus, and the followers are to be called "Church", not "Israel". God has called Israel to follow Torah, and God has called the Church to follow Jesus Christ. But the Covenant is one, not two; not "old" and "new". There is "one eternal covenant between God and the Jewish people" and Jesus is seen in Christian scripture as standing within the Covenant.

In *Christ in Context,* Van Buren explores the implications of his views in a chapter on "The Novelty of Jesus Christ". He wants to make absolutely clear that he stands "squarely in the mainstream of Christian Tradition". He has put his concern even more straightforwardly.

> "Some of my fellow Christians are uneasy about whether I am making clear the novelty of Christ in my theology. They seem to think that Jesus represented something absolutely new and unique in the world and that I am qualifying that newness and uniqueness. I in turn am uneasy about some of my fellow Christians, who seem to take so for granted their own existence as Gentiles who have come to know the love of the God of Israel that they don't see the miracle in it. They don't seem to see that what God has done with them is what is radically new in the history of God's relationship with this world, so they want to put all the novelty onto Christ. Well, yes, they are in part right. That was and is an utterly novel role which God has assigned that Jew to play, but the assignment lies within the context and is itself a part of God's covenantal self-determination. The novelty is only novel because it lies within that community, and this, I am coming to see, is what lies at the heart of the classical Christological discussions and formulations. Novelty, yes, but also continuity: what led to the formulations of Nicaea amd Chalcedon was the fact that both sides are there in the apostolic witness to Christ, and that in turn is because both sides are there in the Scriptural witness to God and the covenant."[15]

Auschwitz motivates Van Buren, then, to make a radical reformulation of Christian doctrine. He does not call for Gentiles to become Jews or to hold to those features of Torah that mark Jews as Jews. God's capacity for novelty is affirmed and with it the doctrine of the Triune God as fundamental for the Church's understanding of God's covenantal actions.

Such a development of thought was bound to make Van Buren skeptical of the Eckardts' view of Resurrection. There can be Jewish faith without Easter but no Christian faith without it. Where the Eckardts see Resurrection as the root of all Christian anti-Judaism, Van Buren sees the root to be "the transformation of the original witness to Jesus as a Jew committed to the renewal of his people in their covenant with God into a witness to an anti-Judaic Jesus in deepest conflict with his people".[16] Ressurection to Van Buren, if preached "in accordance with the Scriptures" (I Cor. 15:3-4), can undercut anti-Judaism because it underscores the continuity of the risen Jesus with the Jew from Nazareth.

Jesus is seen as having no cause of his own, as living solely for God, as concerned entirely for the reign of God on earth. The Resurrection attests to the continuity of Jesus with the God of the Covenant and, properly understood, cannot give rise to the triumphalist theology in the manner deplored by the Eckardts.

Actually, there are points of great convergence between the Eckardts and Van Buren. All three see Resurrection in non-eschatological and non-triumphalist terms, and Van Buren acknowledges in a note less of a disagreement than he had earlier perceived.[17] A careful reading of their works shows little disagreement on the interpretation of the Easter-event. One must conclude, therefore, that it is a matter of a differing emphasis in locating the wellspring of anti-Judaism so that it can be adequately addressed in the light of the Holocaust. The emphasis with Van Buren lies in the crucifixion, and in his chapter on "The Crucified One" in *Christ in Context,* he treats the Holocaust more directly and explicitly than anywhere else in his work.

> Where the cross has been taken to be central, it has been seen to be so both as the remedy for corruption, variously conceived, and as a revelation of God. . . .Today, however, we are invited if not compelled to reconsider all past reflections on the passion of Jesus at Gentile hands---consisting (according to all accounts) of a night and one morning's humiliation, and death following three hours of torture---in the light of the passion nineteen centuries later of six million more Jews at Gentile hands, consisting in innumerable cases of months or years of humiliation, starvation, beatings, and torture, before being shot to fall into mass graves, or gassed and burned to ashes in crematoriums.[18]

Van Buren sees that Christians must change not only their behavior but also their faith. Auschwitz has consequences for what we believe and requires a radically new reformulation. Van Buren reminds us that as Jesus is unique for the Gentile Church, so every one of the six million was one of the elect of God, each one unique and distinctive.

> Surely no word about the death of Jesus will be credible, even to ourselves, if it is unmindful of the deaths of six million of his people after nineteen centuries of preaching redemption, and practicing contempt, in his name.[19]

Auschwitz raises the most fundamental questions about Christian assertions of the victory of the cross over death. After the Holocaust, can Christians still say that death is swallowed up in victory? Auschwitz confronts the Church with unavoidable questions and suggests "that we should be more circumspect in speaking of God's intention in connection with the cross". In the light of Auschwitz, we must now question the formulation that the Cross was "once for all". Such a conclusion has for Van Buren lost its logical force.

> ...Auschwitz may teach us what we should have learned from Golgotha: that God's omnipotence as such is that God can and does enter into the pain and suffering of his children.[20]

Van Buren articulates two rules. The first will govern our language so that we shall not speak of the death of Jesus in such a way as to lessen the death of anyone else, especially those Jews killed in the Holocaust. The second bears on our understanding of God and tells us that as the death of Jesus hurt God, so the death of six million of God's children hurt God even more.

Van Buren goes on to explore the problem of "where God was", a problem he addresses frequently in his "Theology for the Jewish-Christian Reality". In all that he writes, he concludes that "God requires that the Church take unqualified responsibility before Him with His history with us."[21] In other words, it may well be that we should come to see that God offers us a model of covenantal love that surrenders to God's covenant partners the lead in restoring what is corrupt in God's creation. In which case, the consolation for the victims may be their trust that they do not suffer alone, and their act of trust in God in such circumstances may be to weep as much for God's pain as for that of themselves and their fellow human victims.[22]

Such a view of God places responsibility on the human partners to the Covenant for the future of God's cause. *We* shall have to take responsibility for how it works out. Such a view of God also shows one who will not evade pain and suffering when God's human partners misuse their responsibility and commit such atrocities as Auschwitz. God will suffer with God's people, and God's power can only be understood in the light of winning human cooperation in siding with God's cause of justice and peace. God's cause still has a future. The story is not finished. Human beings have been called to engage for God's cause.[23]

PAWLIKOWSKI

Van Buren's work, like that of the Eckardts, is strikingly original and deeply radical. As we turn from them to John T. Pawlikowski, we find a work which is more derivative in nature. Pawlikowski's writings present good and accurate summaries of the thought of a great many Jewish and Christian theologians. His primary concern is "dialogue" between Christians and Jews. He focuses on the relations between Judaism and Christianity, and his work, therefore, is of a different order than what we have considered so far. It is a synthetic undertaking, akin to this paper, and valuable as such.

Pawlikowski has an obvious and stated concern with the Holocaust's challenge for Christian theology. His monograph of 1978 makes it clear that the Holocaust impels "an ecumenical and inter-religious dialogue."[24] Pawlikowski surely is not oblivious to an equally imperative need of theological revision; he quotes revisionist theologians at great length. But the revisions which seem most to motivate him are those that will produce attitudes that will permit dialogue.

In Pawlikowski's view, the Holocaust was due primarily to "modern secularism". He acknowledges that its practitioners drew moral support from the anti-Jewish, anti-Judaic biases of Christianity. Pawlikowski does not seek to exonerate the church, but he seeks to place the primary blame elsewhere.

> ".....the springboard for the Holocaust came from Western liberalism's distorted attempt to create the universal person..."[25]

The Roman Catholic antipathy toward Western liberalism, articulated and criticized so compellingly over thirty years ago by John Courtney Murray, S.J., still holds sway, even after Vatican II. By holding it to be the central cause of the Holocaust, however qualified by assertions of the "long tradition of anti-Semitism in Christian theology and preaching," one can quickly infer that the thrust of Pawlikowski's work will be quite different than that of the Eckardts and Van Buren. His writings bear out the inference.

That does not mean that it is a simple matter. Pawlikowski's work cannot be fitted to a scheme of simply accommodating the Holocaust to Christian theology by dismissing or minimizing the problems Christians face. He faults the Church at numbers of points and calls for the creation of a new ecclesiology.

> "As we begin to penetrate the veil of silence that has covered the Holocaust in Catholic circles, we can begin to see more clearly some of the theological postures which at least made indirect complicity with the Nazis a possible option for Roman Catholicism." [26]

The words "indirect complicity" give another important clue to how Pawlikowski's work differs significantly from that of the Eckardts and Van Buren.

At root, he wants somehow to be able to maintain the Catholic tradition; chastened, purified, but left largely intact. His work sidesteps the problems faced by revisionists who question and reformulate the Tradition. Pawlikowski confines himself more closely to the concerns of ecclesiology even as he seeks the same outcomes as the Eckardts and Van Buren.

> "In short, what is called for in the light of the Holocaust is a vision of church as immersed in history, recognizing that it is only within history that its still incomplete nature can still be realized. One must understand that the salvation process is directly inhibited by regimes such as Nazi Germany and that the church can never reach its ultimate goals while non-Catholics suffer punishment and death. Only such an ecclesiology can have legitimacy after Auschwitz."[27]

The compexities are obvious here. What are the "ultimate goals" of the church? To whom does the "salvation process" belong? Over and again, just as one comes to accept that Pawlikowski really intends to accommodate Christian theology to the Holocaust, something appears that raises the suspicion that the "old agenda" of triumphalist Christianity remains in a more hidden form. At the very points where it seems that Pawlikowski might readily embrace Van Buren's revisionist theology, he attacks it as "Judaism for Gentiles" that does not respect the "uniqueness" of Christianity.

The fact that Pawlikowski makes such a charge over and over again despite the care Van Buren uses to dispell it has led me to wonder exactly what the problem with Pawlikowski is. He is certainly scholarly and accurate in presenting his views, and a reviewer wants and needs to be fair, to respect his well-meaning, well-documented, highly respective dialogic undertaking. Still, there is the question about why he misrepresents the thrust of Van Buren's work.

The basic problem, I think, can be found in the very approach of "dialogue". Pawlikowski seems to assume that the problem is one of "religion", a problem between "Judaism" and "Christianity", a problem to be worked out by dialogue, for understanding, for greater respect for each other's religion.

The Eckardts see the problem as the "Christian crime" against the Jews. Therefore, Christian theology must be accommodated to the reality of that crime. It must be revolutionized, revised, in whatever ways necessary.

Van Buren sees the problem in terms of the "Jewish-Christian Reality". The Reality is One. The Ways to the Reality have developed differently. But the Covenant is One and the Christian Way must be accommodated to the Reality. The Holocaust demands no less, for without accommodation, Christians will continue in an unrevised, uncorrected Tradition that has led to the Crime against the Jews.

Pawlikowski also wants to move beyond the Crime, and he embraces theological revision. But, generally, when he treats the Eckardts and Van Buren, he pulls back. There is a stopping point, short of theirs. Pawlikowski wants to affirm and keep what he holds to be Christianity's "uniqueness". While he asserts that this "uniqueness" does not imply that the Christological vision of human salvation is automatically superior to the Jewish vision (or other religious visions)", he does not make plain why such a claim to "uniqueness" is free and clear of such an assumption.[28]

It is a central concern of Pawlikowski's that revisionist theology will produce "Judaism for Gentiles." He seems not to assess the motivation of theologians such as the Eckardts and Van Buren. He is concerned about the implications of their conslusions, and he is clearly concerned to preserve the Roman Catholic Tradition, the Western Christian Tradition, in pretty much its present doctrinal form. In regard to Van Buren, he writes,The centrality of Pawlikowski's concern that revisionist theology, regardless of motivation, will produce "Judaism for Gentiles" leads one to suspect him of the pragmatic religious concern of preserving the Western Christian Tradition in pretty much its present form. In regard to Van Buren, he writes,

> "If the only difference betwen the Messianic vision of Christianity and Judaism respectively is that the Gentiles now understand the plan of human salvation, then why bother with a separate faith community? Why not simply incorporate the Church into the Synagogue, at least on the level of theological theory?[29]

And with respect to the Eckardts' view of the Resurrection there is this:

> Eckardt's insistence on the theological significance is a point well made, *though I do not feel* (emphasis added) it rules out the category of resurrection as he argues it must." [30]

Where the Eckardts and Van Buren engage in careful analysis and exposition, Pawlikowski seems to appeal more to a deep *a priori* commitment and to "feelings". It seems evident that he has a "felt need" to keep Christianity unique and separate. He would appear to prefer a two-covenant theology to Van Buren's signle covenant one. To be sure, the writings of Pawlikowski being examined here were written before Van Buren's *Christ in Context* appeared, and had he been able to avail himself of Van Buren's views on the Incarnation, Pawlikowski might have been less inclined to use the term "Judaism for Gentiles".

The very term might well be taken to imply the inferiority of Judaism although Pawlikowski does not want to mean that. Still, why use the term when there is virtually nothing in their works to warrant it? Regardless of intention, the term is pejorative and dismissive. One can believe that the Eckardts and Van Buren have gone "too far" without resorting to such epithets or caricatures. Indeed, Pawlikowski would probably find that most Christians, Protestants, Orthodox, and Catholics alike, agree with his assessment that their revisions will never be accepted in the Church.

And yet another problem remains, and it is how to purge the Church of its triumphalist, supercessionist theology without such radical revisions. Pawlikowski holds that it can be done by adhering to an Incarnational theology, cleansed of the "tragic aberrations" in the development of the Christian Tradition. Van Buren is no less incarnational in his theology. Incarnation is not the difference between them. It finally comes down to a differing assessment of how integral anti-Judaism is to Christian faith and behavior and what is required to cleanse "Christology of those aberrations." The contrast between Pawlikowski, on one hand, and the Eckardts and Van Buren, on the other, is a contrast between minimalist and maximalist responses to the Holocaust in revising Christian theology. The Eckardts and Van Buren are open to acknowledging that the Christian way and the Jewish way are not the only possible avenues to salvation or the good life. In contrast, Pawlikowski writes

> "The old goal of achieving universalism through the baptism of all races and nations is no longer a possibility. The only realistic path to universality now is through dialogue with people of other faiths and ideologies."[31]

Nothing could make clearer the distinction between the maximalist and minimalist perceptions and the resulting work of revision. With Pawlikowski, it comes down to this, that

> "in the final analysis and after much soul-searching I stand ready to claim that the Holocaust has not undercut the deepest meaning of Christology. . . .especially when that Christology is placed, as it must be, with*in* its Jewish setting.[32]

For Pawlikowski, certain conventional Christological claims are now suspect, and the Eckardts and Van Buren must be taken seriously. However, the core, "the deepest meaning of Christology", is intact and ready to be engaged in dialogue with Judaism. The dialogue itself is a "monumental and difficult task" that, given the reality of Auschwitz, can no longer be postponed.

Appreciative as I am of Pawlikowski's writings, I find his views far less persuasive. Yet, I have little reason to doubt that most of the Church is far more open to dialogue than to a radically reformulated faith. Pawlikowski continues to make an invaluable contribution to dialogue, but my mind and soul find the Eckardts' and Van Buren's more revolutionary approach closer to what the Holocaust demands of the Church.

RAUSCH

This appraisal of theological revision in the light of the Holocaust was intended to include the perspective of an American Evangelical Christian. The Evangelical movement, after all, has demonstrated great strength in American religious life, and in recent years it has led the growth curve among American churches. The book that imediately called attention to itself was *A Legacy of Hatred* by David A. Rausch, a historian at Ashland College Theological Seminary in Ohio. The reviews of his book have been good, and such scholars as Dr. Karl Hermann Voss have spoken glowingly of Dr. Rausch. Therefore, I turned to the book with high expectations.

What I found in *A Legacy of Hatred* is very different from what I found in the works by the Eckardts, Van Buren, and Pawlikowski. *A Legacy* is not a book of theological revision, and in a very real sense it does not belong in a theological survey and appraisal at all. However, in the absence of other writings by Evangelical Christians addressing the issues of theological revision in the light of the Holocaust, it is important to examine why it fails to speak to the issues addressed by the other authors examined here.

A Legacy seems to presuppose an audience which has not been exposed to the history of Nazi Germany and the events of the Holocaust. The book, therefore, is really a short history of the Holocaust with a few brief chapters at the outset and the conclusion which attempt to put that history in a context of past and future. It begins and ends without encountering the concerns addressed by the studies by the Eckardts and many others which show anti-Judaism to be at the very heart of Christian tradition. Rausch seems to see the Holocaust as "a case study" about "the structure of evil, the dangers of civil religion, and moral responsibility in an immoral environment."[33] Even as Rausch asserts that "Hitler drew upon centuries of anti-Semitism", he fails to recognize or explore the solid connection anti-Judaism has with Christian faith and practice.

So warned, what one should expect from Rausch's book are object lessons about evil, warnings about false (civil) religions, and moral exhortations about human and Christian responsibilities. That is exactly what we get, and one is not inclined to argue with such an agenda, regardless of reservations about its analytic adequacy or political effectiveness. What we do not get is any sense of urgency about reconsidering the Christian enterprise itself and its missionary efforts to the rest of the world.

It is, therefore, almost inevitable that Rausch will see Christian anti-Judaizers as not being "real Christians" and that he will portray Christians who rescued Jews as the "real Christians," the normative believers who acted according to the requirements of the Gospel. Why those "real Christians" were the rare exception he does not really address. Where the Eckardts see a direct line between such dogma as resurrection and triumphalism, victimization, and violence, Rausch sees only a gospel distorted by racists who "disdain the rights and privileges of human beings and seeks to dehumanize any but the approved group."[34] The Eckardts demonstrate a direct connection between Christian tradition and racist theories and practices; Rausch's brief history of Christian anti-Judaism concludes with a sense of dualism, a "racial anti-Semitism that will be coupled to religious anti-Semitism in the nineteenth century." In his chapter on "The Christian Resistance Movement", the same bifurcation is present.

> "(The resisters) strove to be Christian in their attitude toward other religions and races, seeking to unlearn the prejudice bolstered and sustained by the community around them."[35]

Prejudice is a "learned behavior", and clearly not learned from Christianity. Rausch never explores why most Christians were and are so susceptible to such "learned behavior" or why "the large majority of (German) Christians accepted the status quo, supporting the war effort with patriotic fervor."[36]

The failure to arrive at the opposite conclusions shared by the Eckardts, Van Buren and Pawlikowski, explain why Rausch does not proceed to engage in revision of Christian theology. Were he to reach those conclusions and proceed to revise theology accordingly, the trauma to Evangelical Christianity would be very great indeed, given its literal approach to Scripture and its conservative posture toward orthodox Christian doctrine. Therefore, it is not surprising to find Rausch concluding that "the Bible nowhere advocates racism."[37] Racism is a sin; something Christians oppose. Christians are really the good people, those resisters to the Nazis who acted heroically, who did the hard thing, who rescued Jews in spite of prevailing hatred. Rausch warns us that we live in a time "when even religious words can be twisted into rationalizations for genocide" by propaganda and prejudices. He calls for "real Christians" to resist these outside pressures and to reclaim the title *Christian*, saying "he or she must strive to approach the *balance* of Jesus' life in the area of prejudice and racism---or be honest and refrain from using the name or claiming to imitate his life."(*emphasis mine*) Bigotry and prejudice are outside and evil forces, "antithetical to God's will".[38]

CONCLUSION

Where Pawlikowski goes a long way toward confronting anti-Semitism in the Christian tradition, drawing up only at the line of Christian uniqueness, Rausch shows no indication of how Christianity itself has produced racism, victimization, and violence. Even as he proclaims that prejudice and hatred are a part of our legacy, he calls for us to shed them as extraneous accretions. He concludes, therefore, with moralism and not with revisionism. His work illustrates how far many Christians have to go in even encountering the reality of the Holocaust. His real value lies in introducing the problem to those who still know it not nearly fifty years after the Holocaust. Rausch's work makes clear to me that what satisfies my soul and mind will not speak to the souls and minds of many, many Christians. Those Christians may discover and learn from Pawlikowski generations before they discover and ponder the writings of the Eckardts and Van Buren. The latter may be writing largely for the generations to come, and their works will give witness in the future that, at the very least, the questions were known and some radical answers were posed in the last decades of the 20th Century. If I hope that their writings are discovered sooner, it is because of how much is at stake. What is finally at stake in pursuing such radical revision of Christian thought is the future relationship between Christian and Jew. Unless Christians come boldly to believe that Jews can and do know the full truth of God without ever becoming Christians; unless Christians and Jews can negotiate a new and liberal Christian theology on the terms of which both can agree; unless Christians can freely abandon their claims to religious primacy and accord equal status and respect to other religions; unless and until these changes come to pass, the most that we can hope for is pragmatic cooperation in shared causes. And even with the realization of such a hope, we shall have to continue to fear a renewed cycle of victimization and violence. The Eckardts and Van Buren show us a better way.

REFERENCES

Eckardt, Alice L. and A. Roy, *Long Night's Journey into Day* -"Life and Faith After the Holocaust", (Detroit: Wayne State University Press, 1982).

"Post-Holocaust Theology: A Journey Out of the Kingdom of Night", *Holocaust and Genocide Studies,* Vol. 1, No. 2, 1986, pp. 229-240.

Eckardt, A. Roy, "Is There a Way Out of the Christian Crime? The Philosophic Question of the Holocaust", *Holocaust and Genocide Studies*, Vol. 1, No. 1, 1986, pp.121-126.

Jews and Christians: The Contemporary Meeting, (Bloomington: Indiana University Press, 1986).

Pawlikowski, John T., O.S.M., *The Challenge of the Holocaust for Christian Theology* (New York: The Center for Studies on the Holocaust, 1978).

What Are They Saying About Christian-Jewish Relations?, (New York: Paulist Press, 1980).

Christ in the Light of the Christian-Jewish Dialogue, (New York: Paulist, 1982).

"Jews and Christians: The Contemporary Dialogue", *Quarterly Review,* Vol. 4, No. 4, Winter 1984, pp.23-36.

Rausch, David A., *A Legacy of Hatred:Why Christians Must Not Forget the Holocaust*, Chicago: Moody Press, 1984.

Van Buren, Paul, *A Christian Theology of the People Israel*--A Theology of the Jewish-Christian Reality, Vol. 2 (New York: Seabury Press, 1983).

Christ in Context---A Theology of the Jewish-Christian Reality, Vol. 3 (San Francisco: Harper &Row, 1988).

Discerning the Way--A Theology of the Jewish-Christian Reality, Vol. 1, (New York: Seabury Press, 1980).

"Theology of the Jewish-Christian Reality", *Religion and Intellectual Life*, Vol.3, No. 4, Summer 1986.

NOTES

1 Eckardts, *Long Night's Journey*, p.55.
2 *Ibid.*,p.128.
3 *Ibid.* p.130.
4 Alice Eckardt, "Post Holocaust Theology", p.237
5 Eckardts, *Long Night's Journey,* p.131.
6 *Ibid.*, p.131.
7 *Ibid.*, p.132.
8 *Ibid.*, p.132
9 *Ibid.*, p.133.
10 A. Roy Eckardt, "Is There a Way Out?", p.126.
11 Alice Eckardt, "Post-Holocaust Theology", p.238.
12 *Ibid.*, p.238.
13 *Ibid,* p.239.
14 Van Buren, *Discerning the Way*, p.51.
15 Van Buren, *Religion & Intellectual Life*, Fall 1987, Vol. V No. 1, p.99.
16 Van Buren, *Christ in Context*, p.110.
17 *Ibid.*, p.110.
18 *Ibid.*, pp.158-9.
19 *Ibid.*, p.160.

20 *Ibid.*, p.165.
21 Van Buren, *Discerning the Way*, p.181.
22 Van Buren, *Christ in Context*, p.166.
23 *Ibid.*, p.182.
24 Pawlikowski, *The Challenge of the Holocaust.*, p.17.
25 *Ibid.*, p.21.
26 *Ibid.*, p.24.
27 *Ibid.*, p.31.
28 Pawlikowski, *Christ in the Light*, pp. 14ff.
29 *Ibid.*, pp. 18-9.
30 *Ibid.*, pp.18-9.
31 *Ibid.*, p.127.
32 *Ibid.*, p.147.
33 Rausch, *A Legacy of Hatred*, p.2.
34 *Ibid.*, p.14.
35 *Ibid.*, p.153.
36 *Ibid.*, p.166.
37 *Ibid.*, p.204.
38 *Ibid.*, p.168.

FORGIVENESS AND REPENTANCE: SOME CONTEMPORARY CONSIDERATIONS AND QUESTIONS

ALICE L. ECKARDT

Lehigh University, Department of Religion Studies, Bethlehem, Pennsylvania 18036, U.S.A.

ABSTRACT

The very remembrance of the Shoah has all too often led to mutual recrimination, with many Christians telling the Jewish community to "forgive and forget" and Jews wondering how different their Christian neighbors' lack of sympathy and understanding is from the indifference of the world during the Holocaust. Trials of war criminals and other political events create further dissensions. This paper will explore and reconsider the fundamentals of the concepts of repentance and forgiveness, their theological and biblical bases, and popular usage in order to try to discern the source of these disparate perspectives that hinder understanding as well as sources that may provide help.

Repentance and forgiveness are themes central to both Judaism and Christianity. The acts of repenting, asking for forgiveness, (in some cases doing penance), and being forgiven are intended to end a state of alienation and hostility between individuals, and between humans and God, (1) and to reconcile the parties. Yet ironically, the question of forgiveness with reference to the Holocaust is a source of continuing misunderstanding, hurt, and recrimination. Many Christians are annoyed or even angered by the Jewish people's insistence on remembering the Shoah and its victims, and their continuing concern about bringing the perpetrators to justice. The more restrained of these Christians tell Jews to "forgive and forget." Others issue subtle threats in the form of concerned warnings such as "by declining to forgive, I fear that [Jews] unwittingly invite [a recurrence of the Holocaust they are trying to prevent]." The more vehement say that Jews are uncharitable and even vengeful in their attitudes.(2) Most Jews are disturbed and worried by such attitudes. They cannot help but wonder how different their Christian neighbors' lack of understanding and sympathy today is from the indifference of the world during the Holocaust. If six million deaths are to be forgotten so quickly, is a lower value placed on Jewish life? Do these attitudes indicate that the Christian world does not wish or intend to learn any lessons from the Shoah, nor to face any of its own culpability?

The conflicts and worries have been exacerbated and brought into the public domain by three recent events that occurred in the political realm and yet which had religious aspects and fall-out: President Reagan's visit with Chancellor Kohl to the military cememtery at Bitburg in the Federal German Republic where a number of SS men are buried (June 1985); the election of Waldheim as president of Austria after disclosures of his military activities and responsibilities during World War II (1986); and Pope John Paul II's reception of Waldheim at the Vatican where he greeted him as "a man of peace" (1987).

* * *

Superficially the issue seems absurdly simple. If a person has done something harmful to another person (3) and expresses regret or remorse, we tend to presume that forgiveness will and should be given to him by the person harmed. But that presumption ignores many questions: What is the nature and severity of the harm done? Is the person who was harmed alive to be asked forgiveness? Can someone else give it on behalf of such a person, especially if that person is dead as a result of the other individual's acts? How sincere is the repentance, and how can that sincerity be judged? Must there be something more tangible than words of remorse? Is the person who has been harmed -- or her/his relatives -- required to extend forgiveness if it is asked for? Suppose the perpetrator of the hurtful act does not regret what s/he did; must forgiveness be given anyway? What function would that have? What is the relationship of forgiveness to the legal process of judgment and punishment for one's deeds?

A basic question in the present context, as well as in many others, involves time and memory. Should the lapse of a certain number of years require that the person or persons wrongfully treated act as if the hurt was never perpetrated? Or rather, is it incumbent on them to forgive the act because of the passage of time, and then proceed to put it all behind them? Is it in their self-interest to do so? (4) On the other hand, if there has been no indication of repentance on the part of the perpetrator, or no punishment imposed by the state's legal system, the victim (or the surviving relatives) may well feel as if the evil deed had only just been committed. No healing has been possible and the wound remains open. In such a case, to expect the victim to forget, no less to forgive, may be demanding the impossible, or at least the saintly.

So far I have been speaking only about individual behavior; what about collective responses? Can a social group, especially a national society, repent of its actions, or of the actions of a preceding generation? If so, how does it demonstrate that repentance, that turning around? If it does not do so in some way, what are the consequences? These questions introduce the issue of collective versus individual guilt, the nature of social responsibility, and the influence of the past on the future.

* * *

Both Christianity and Judaism recognize that there are sins that are a matter between humans and God, and others that are intrahuman transgressions. (5) Even so, both acknowledge that any harm done to a person is also an act God. Or as David Daiches puts it, "a true moral crime is an offense against the divine order of the universe." (6) Within the intrahuman category, an act may involve only two people, and be of a non-litigious nature. Or it may be of concern to an entire community and may also call for legal action in the cause of justice. While the two spheres -- the personal and the social -- are not identical, they often overlap.

Within Judaism repentance (teshuvah) must represent a turning around in one's behavior and intention, a return to God and God's Teaching (II Chron. 7:14; Jer. 3:12; 31:32). That is all God desires, and the divine compassion and mercy ensure a readiness to pardon the repentant sinner even when repentance is made just before death. But repentance should be more than saying, "I'm sorry"; it must be genuine and deep-seated. It is made abundantly clear (for example, in various parts of the Talmud, and in Maimonides' numerous chapters on teshuvah) that a momentary penitence that lacks the intention to persevere in refraining from repeating the evil act is useless; it will not secure forgiveness. Similarly, merely relying on Yom Kippur (Day of Atonement) to secure expiation will not avail.

Moreover, though repentance and Yom Kippur may elicit divine pardon for sins the person has perpetrated against God, they will not be sufficient for transgressions against another person. In this case appropriate compensation to the injured party must be made directly: "God does not clear the guilty in matters relating to humans unless reparation precedes all else (Yoma 8:8). The wrongdoer must first win pardon from the person wronged." (7)

What then is the obligation of the injured party? If the offender has done everything possible to compensate for the har , and shows genuine repentance, s/he should be forgiven wholeheartedly. Medieval rabbis especially taught that to forgive is the most beautiful thing a person can do. (8) Since humans depend on God's mercy, they should be ready to extend mercy to others. (9)

Not surprisingly, given Christianity's origins in Judaism of the first century, many of these precepts are repeated in the Christian Writings of the New Testament. When John the Baptizer, Jesus, and the apostles called for people to repent so that their sins might be forgiven (Mt. 3:2; Mt. 4:17; Mk. 1:14, 15; Acts 3:19), they intended that people should turn away from their sinful way of life and turn back to God and the life for which he had provided instructions. Within the community sinners were to be rebuked and if they repented, were to be forgiven (Lu. 17:3). A strong note of leniency in the interpersonal sphere is expressed in Luke's gospel when Jesus admonishes his followers to forgive a person even if he sins seven times in one day and yet each time says "I repent" (Lu. 17:4).

The need for direct conciliation between individuals is repeated in Jesus' teaching that one should not approach the altar with a gift for God until he has first gone to the brother who has something against him and been reconciled with that brother (Mt. 5:23). A person should be forgiving and merciful to others because God is merciful and forgiving. In fact, s/he should not expect divine forgiveness if s/he has been unforgiving and hardhearted to another person (Mt. 6:14; 18:23-35; Mk. 11:25; Lu. 6:35-37; James 2:13). (10)

Some differences began to appear as the synagogue and church parted company and the church struggled to establish itself independently. During the first four centuries of the Common Era the church required public penance from a member who had strayed from the morals and strictures of the community and then wished to be reaccepted. By the fifth century recurrent confession and private penance replaced public penance. In the twelfth and thirteenth centuries two theologians (Peter Lombard and Thomas Aquinas) first defined penance as a sacrament, and this definition was formally adopted by the Council of Florence in 1439(11) Luther and subsequent Protestant reformers objected to the Roman Catholic system of penance with the priest playing the central role in dispensing absolution from eternal punishment. Luther insisted that this was a matter between the person and God, and that God only required contrition and obedience -- "sorrow for sin and turning to God in trust and obedience." True penitence meets with God's complete forgiveness. (12) Evangelical Christianity came to emphasize apostolic and Pauline teaching that repentance is not merely a single act but a full experience in which abhorrence is felt for the sin now abjured and one experiences a "constant disposition toward complete amendment of life." (13)

Both the Catholic emphasis on confession and penance as a sacrament, and the Protestant emphasis on justification by faith alone tended to focus on the human-divine aspect of repentance and forgiveness, and to relegate the need for person-to-person acts of repentance and forgiveness to lesser significance.

In addition to Christian emphasis on repentance as a private and personal matter between the individual and God (even if a priest acted as the intermediary), some of Jesus' sayings appear to go beyond the teachings of Tanakh and thus they have created difficulties in achieving a common understanding of forgiveness. While scholars are well aware that we should not compare or contrast the Christian Writings ("New Testament") with the Tanakh ("Old Testament") but rather with rabbinic writings of the time since both are additions to and interpretations of Tanakh, most Christians do not share this awareness. Nor do they know the rabbinic writings, which reveal the changes that had occurred within Judaism itself by the first and second centuries. As a result the differences appear to be more significant (sometimes startling) than they actually are. For example, within the gospel of Matthew passages present Jesus as saying, "You have heard it said . . ., but I say . . ." (Mt. 5:22, 38, 43). In each case the contrast presents Jesus (hence Christianity) as advocating a superior morality to that of Judaism. In fact, the contrasts are either unfair (even untrue) or invalid with regard to the Judaism of that time. In addition to the false impressions created by contrasting the two sets of sacred writings, the early Christian writers and churchmen deliberately sought to emphasize the distinctiveness of Christianity, and thereby to demonstrate Christianity's moral and spiritual superiority. Thus the claim to be the "new Israel" replacing the "old Israel" could be sustained. In this way it became generally accepted within the Christian community over centuries that Christianity taught its members to be merciful and forgiving whereas Judaism taugh its adherents to be hardhearted and vengeful. With such a fundamental attitude established and repeatedly taught it is hardly surprising that few Christians today are prepared to consider any differing Jewish views pertaining to forgiveness as anything but a demonstration of an inferior ethic.

Additional difficulties are caused by some of the absolute precepts that Jesus is reported to have taught, such as:

> Do not resist evil.
> If someone hits your right cheek, offer him your other cheek.
> If someone takes your cloak, let him have your coat also.
> If someone forces you to go one mile, go with him two miles.
> Love your enemies and do good to those who hate you; bless those who curse you and pray for those who persecute/abuse you. (14)

One of the difficulties is internal to the Christian community as it considers whether these precepts are to be understood as absolute requirements for all believers or whether they are ideal standards against which we are to measure, and thus improve, our standards and behavior. (15) Obviously Christians as a whole and Christendom as a civilization have not lived by these teachings (though some individuals and sectarian groups have chosen pacifism as their way of trying to fulfill one precept). Nor is there any evidence that Christians are, in fact, more forgiving or less concerned with protecting themselves or their property than Jews. (16)

The other difficulty is again one of making comparative and judgmental evaluations, with either side seeing its own ethical standards as better than the other's. The incomprehensibility felt by many Jews toward such unqualified commands is expressed by Alex Byron: ". . . when I feel that my people are being abused, I find that I am unable to 'turn the other cheek' for, as a result of the massacre of one-half of the Jewish nation, I have but one cheek left." (17) In contrast to the Christian claim that Jesus' teachings and the church's ideals are superior to those of the rabbis and synagogue, the Jewish counterclaim is that such precepts as Jesus' represent an impossible ethic of perfection, which neither can nor ought to be applied in a world of imperfection. To do so would be irresponsible. (18) By contrast, the counterclaim goes, Judaism seeks to create an ethical system that, while reflecting heavenly goals, is operative on earth. For this reason it does not command you to love your enemy, but it does advise that if two people ask for your help and one is your enemy, help him first. (19) Moreover, the Jewish ethical system is designed to be operative for the collectivity as well as the individual. (20) Instead of commanding "resist not evil," it admonishes "eradicate evil from your midst"; "Hate evil! Love the good! . . . establish justice in the gate!" (Amos 5:15); do not stand idly by the blood of your fellow humans. (21)

* * *

In the discussions and sometimes acrimonious exchanges that occur between Jews and Christians (22) regarding the Holocaust and forgiveness the distinction between what is possible or responsible for an individual to do and what is possible and responsible for a society to do is often not taken into account. If an individual chooses to forgive a person who harmed him in some way, perhaps no one else will be injured by such selfless generosity, and perhaps the act will help to redeem the wrongdoer. We must say "perhaps" because it also possible that someone else will suffer subsequently, and it is also possible that the wrongdoer will simply be confirmed in his destructive behavior and psychological makeup. But if a people that has been decimated many times over by others acting out their bigotry and hatred were to offer to overlook these deadly assaults by generously forgiving, it would only encourage other assailants. And if a government decided to pardon all criminals, what would happen to that society? Would such a decision be a responsible one? (I realize that a legal pardon is different from saying "I/We forgive you" but at the state level nothing but a legal pardon would be meaningul.) Pope John Paul II visited Mahmet Ali Agca in prison. He forgave the man who had shot and wounded him. Was this an admirable action? Many -- probably most -- Christians find it so. But Herbert Marcuse recalls how shocked he was to learn that Walther Rathenau's mother had visited her son's assassin and forgiven him. He believes that "easy forgiving [of crimes of torture, assassination, and murder] perpetuates the very evil it wants to alleviate." (23) It should be noted, however, that the Pope did not ask that the prisoner be released. He recognized that Agca must bear the social consequences of his wrongdoing, (24) quite apart from the victim's willingness to extend a personal pardon, (25) and that reconciliation was never meant to diminish the practice of human justice. He was aware that society's claim for protection against a would-be killer cannot be set aside.

Although this claim is normally asserted with considerable vehemence by a community when a vicious rapist or serial murderer is at issue, we find a strange reluctance, and even opposition, on the part of many local and national communities to insist on it when it comes to Holocaust murderers. Again and again we find that sympathy is extended to the wanted murderer, SS guard, or other involved person, and resentment or anger is directed against the surviving victim(s) who wish to see these individuals brought to court. How are we to understand such unsual attitudes and behavior? Why is it the victimized who are expected to ignore their sufferings, and, in fact, perhaps reexperience them in some way?

Let us consider some alternative hypothetical situations. Suppose one had been a neighbor of a person who was then arrested for a particularly gruesome series of murders some years earlier. Would one oppose that person's being arrested and brought to trial because s/he had been a decent neighbor? Would one tell the relatives of the victims that they ought to forgive the person and not prosecute the case? (26) Or suppose one were the spouse, parent, or child of a person cruelly assaulted and murdered. Would one then be so ready to advise forgiving and forgetting?

The need that relatives of victims feel for the discovery and punishment of the perpetrator is more than a desire for revenge, although that is how outsiders often perceive it. Rather, these people, who have also been victimized by the crime, are more keenly aware -- no matter how subconsciously -- that murder is an attack on the very foundation of society. "The death of an innocent victim is a loss to the whole society as a communion of persons." (27) Judaism and Christianity both speak of God's "righteous anger" (as well the divine mercy). If we are made in the divine image, righteous anger must be one of the attributes with which we are endowed. If so, we must be expected to use it when it is appropriate, as in seeking to see justice done. (28) As the Talmud expressed it centuries ago, murder is "bad for everyone . . . and no one should profit . . from someone's death at all." (29) Immanuel Kant pointed to the crucial difference between murder and other crimes (an observation that while profound does not require an advanced education): "There is no likeness or proportion between life, however, painful, and death. . . ."; (30) the victim can never be restored to life and the community. Hence, social outrage in such cases is an expression of moral outrage. When social outrage is absent, one should be concerned about the morality of the community.

All of the foregoing should apply six million-fold to the perpetrators of the Final Solution. Yet here is where we find social outrage most curiously missing. Is it simply a matter of geographical distance in the case of people in Brtain, the United States, Canada, etc.? Or is it simply a matter of chronological distance? (Again, however, we need to think of our hypothetical cases to evaluate parallel responses.) Is there something in the sheer numbers of victims that somehow deadens moral sensitivities? Is it because an entire nation and its allies were involved in the killing? (But doesn't that call for greater concern, especially since it established a precedent that needs to be annulled?) Or is there something more worrisome and perhaps even sinister? Is it a result of not wanting to acknowledge the ideological roots of the antisemitism that culminated in the mobile killing squads and death camps? Is it a way to avoid facing up to the widespread support of and indifference to the Holocaust even on the part of one's own faith community or nation? Are people afraid of their own propensity for evil? Does it represent a certain affinity with the intention to rid the world of Jews?

During the 1970s on two different occasions a number of church groups and Christian individuals appealed to the Dutch government to pardon three German Nazis who were imprisoned in The Netherlands after having been found guilty of war crimes. The basis of the appeals was that these men were elderly and could no longer do any harm, and that Christian charity ought to allow them to live their last years in their own homes. Yet survivors of the camps, both Jewish and non-Jewish, immediately began to manifest varying degrees of trauma at the mere thought of these men being free again. Only the testimony of leading psychiatrists, along with public protests, prevented an "act of clemency" that would have seriously harmed some of the very people who had already suffered under these three criminals. To whom should clemency and sympathy be directed first? Is the failure to consider those who have already endured loss, pain, and injustice, and instead fixating sympathy on the perpetrators a case of unthinking adherence to a theological ethic without other aspects of that ethic?

In 1985, following President Reagan's visit to the Bitburg cemetery, the director of the Frankfurt's Kammerspiel theater undertook to produce a play by Rainier Fassbinder, a play that had already caused much controversy. The main character in the play, unnamed and identified simply as "A Rich Jew," was made to fit the crude stereotype of the Jew as usurer, exploiter, lecher, and Svengali. (31) Moreover, the play contains Jew-haters who mouth such sentiments as how unfortunate it was that someone had forgotten to gas the Rich Jew. Once again agitation for and against the production erupted, with bad feelings developing on all sides, and strange alliances being formed. (Those Germans who wish to bury the past did not want to see the play produced any more than Jews who do want the past remembered -- especially in Germany.) Proponents of the play's production argued for "a return to normalcy," for doing away at last with "'exaggerated' moral inhibitions concerning the past." and the need for the theater to be uncensored. The archbishop of Cologne declared, "We should not, again, and again, exhume past guilt and mutually [sic] committed injustices, in constant self-torment." Moreover the Jews were told that "they should not only tolerate the play but welcome it as an educational piece about the undesirability of taboos." As Johann N. Schmidt comments, they were to be "forced into a reconciliation whose terms were to be defined by those who would be forgiven. Former prisoners of extermination camps were told 'to give up their well-functioning symmetrical moralism that discerns between culprit and victim, confession of guilt and moral self-complacency.'" (32)

The Jewish residents of Frankfurt refused to accede to such arguments and they occupied the stage of the theater when the curtain went up, and the production was finally cancelled. However, a great deal of bitterness and recrimination had been generated, and many of the few thousand Jews were made to experience a great deal of fear and anguish. Nor is that the end of the matter. Directors in other German cities have expressed interest in mounting a production, despite the Frankfurt affair, and an actual attempt has been made to do so in Rotterdam. Since many literary critics find the play to be poor drama, what is behind all the interest in putting it on the stage? Schmidt finds that "Fassbinder's play uses antisemitism as a mere stereotype to provoke a cheap aesthetic thrill." (33) Is that also the motivation of the theater people? Or, again, is there a hidden desire to strike out against the Jews in a way that can seem acceptable? Is that why the victims of antisemitism and Nazism are being made to suffer again in an entirely unnecessary way?

I suspect that many Christians and gentiles who oppose Jewish efforts to make memory of the Jewish victims a public memory, and who advise Jews to forgive the victimizers and then put the past behind them want to ignore the issue of antisemitism (including the Christian variety) and go on as if there were no problem about which they themselves should do something. (34) Or at least if that is not their [conscious] motive, suppressing the memory of the _Shoah_ would make things more comfortable.

On Sunday, 30 June 1985 BBC-1's "Choices" program had an audience-participation program on the subject of forgiveness, chaired by Msgr. Bruce Kent. It was an appalling example of the superficial, restricted, and sentimental response that one generally hears to this issue that involves very profound and complex moral and social issues.(35) Of all the people who spoke, only one indicated some awareness that the first step ought to be taken by the wrongdoer; that s/he should repent for what s/he had done and seek to make some kind of amends. Most of the comments were to the effect that one ought to forgive, that one damages oneself by not doing so. No imagination was exercised to consider other positive ways by which one could cope with the "harmful" grievance one feels as a result of injustice against oneself, one's loved ones, or one's community. Would not determining never to harm any innocent person, or working to bring about the necessary changes in the instruments and institutions of social injustice, or giving compassionate care to another victim be as effective a way of developing and expressing one's moral concern as forgiving the offender(s) who had harmed you? For that matter, is not the effort to bring a known murderer to justice a moral action that benefits the community and at the same time demonstrates the value that one has for human life?

Despite Christianity's traditional theological emphasis on the human propensity to be and do evil, this predominantly Christian audience gave no consideration to the presence and effective working of evil that was represented by the situations and actions that were said to require forgiveness, even though the slaughter of six million Jews in Europe was referred to by the program host and one survivor in the audience. The participants in this program confirmed my conviction, based on much reading and discussion, that today, Jews, who traditionally have been more optimistic about human nature than Christians both theologically and in their day to day lives, are more keenly aware of radical evil than Christians who, at least in the first world countries, are comfortable and unafflicted. This significant difference in Jewish and Christian experiences no doubt accounts for much of the disparity in perspectives and conflict over whether forgiveness can be given easily to those who have committed evil beyond measure. (36) By contrast, Christians of South Africa, living with the evil of apartheid, are well aware of the reality of evil and its socially-supported structures. The Kairos Document: A Challenge to the Church, issued first in September 1985 and then revised and reissued in 1986 by thousands of South African Christians including theologians and church leaders, bluntly states that "it is totally unChristian to plead for reconciliation and peace" between "a fully armed and violent oppressor" and a people who are defenseless and oppressed. "It is asking us to become accomplices in our own oppression, to become servants of the devil . . . ." There can be "no reconciliation, no forgiveness and no negotiations . . . without repentance." (37)

We need to consider whether individuals with more theological sophistication than the BBC program participants, persons who have had more intensive exposure to or relations with people of other faiths would respond in a significantly different way to the question of when, how, and if forgiveness should be given. In The Sunflower Simon Wiesenthal has conveniently provided us with a sample of this kind. Thirty-two thoughtful, informed individuals eminent in various fields of endeavor, with varied national and religious backgrounds were asked to read Wiesenthal's account of an unusual encounter of a Jewish concentration camp inmate with a repentant, dying SS man who desperately wanted a Jew's forgiveness for an atrocity against a village of Jews in which he had participated. (38) The thirty-two people were then asked to consider what they would have done in that situation.

What do we find?

Of the total group nine respondants wrote that the Jewish prisoner (Simon) should have granted forgiveness to the penitent SS man (Karl). Eight of these nine are identifiably Christian and the ninth is a non-Jew. Father Edward Flannery makes one of the most categorical of the affirmations: "I find it impossible to defend" Simon's "refusal" to grant Karl's plea for forgiveness. "To refuse pardon after repentance is a form of hate, however disguised." The issue of whether Simon had the right to forgive Karl in the name of all Jews "appears to me irrelevant." (39) Gustav Heinemann, Federal Minister of Justice and then President of the Federal German Republic (1969-1974), gives as the basis for his affirmative answer: "The conflict between Justice (in the form of Law) and Forgiveness is the thread that runs through [the] story. Justice and Law, however essential they are, cannot exist without Forgiveness.

That is the quality that Jesus Christ added to Justice and with which he gave it life." (40) Christopher Hollis, British journalist, former MP, and well known Catholic, argues that for Christians and Jews alike "the law of God is the law of love. We are created in order to love one another . . . . We are under obligation to forgive our neighbor" no matter how often he offends us in order to reforge the bonds of love. Hollis grants that under other circumstances it would have been reasonable to demand that the SS man do some service for Jews to give evidence of his sincerity. He admits that he is stating what for him is "the absolute moral law": Christ's prayer for the forgiveness of his own murderers while hanging on the cross. (41) Léopold Senghor, Senegalese politician and writer, attributes Simon's refusal to forgive on the ground of the "Old Law." However, since there is the "New Law" of Christ, he believes, as a Christian, that Simon should have forgiven Karl.(42) Msgr. John Oesterreicher observes that "to no other creature but man, made in God's image, has it been granted to forgive. Faculties are given in order to be used." He celebrates the grandeur of "man's power to pardon" as proclaimed in both Jewish and Christian Scriptures. (43) Gabriel Marcel and Jacques Maritain of France are more restrained in their conclusions that "it would have been better" had Simon chosen to forgive. They do not fault Simon for not having done so, however, and they acknowledge Simon's cruel situation and his inability to forgive atrocities committed against others. (44)

Curiously enough, Christ is referred to by two non-Christian respondants -- a Jew and an agnostic -- in their arguments against forgiveness. After quoting at length from Jesus' Sermon on the Mount, Hermann Kesten observes that "Christ nowhere says that one should forgive mass-murderers. . . [nor] does he say that one must forgive the murderers of one's children" -- to which he adds, "if he had said so, I for one would have disagreed with him." (45) It is the Irish author Constantine FitzGibbon who compels one's attention especially. He writes that thinking of his own son, today I think "I would have reacted with Christian brutality . . . I would remember Christ's remark that it would be better that a millstone be put about [a person's] neck and he were cast into the sea than that he should harm one of these little ones. . . ."(46)

Of the twenty-one who declare against Simon's forgiving (including the two just mentioned), four can be identified as Christian: Friedrich Heer and Kurt von Schuschnigg of Austria, Poul Georg Lindhardt of Denmark, and Martin Marty of the United States. Schuschnigg, who was Chancellor of Austria before the Third Reich absorbed that nation, and then was a prisoner of the Nazis from March 1938 until May 1945, argues that "one can only pardon an offence which has been directly inflicted upon oneself"; and not even one's own family could come under this heading. "No one can forgive what others have suffered. The Creator alone, and nobody else, can forgive blood guilt and inhuman conduct." (47) Heer and Lindhardt agree: "No person has authority to forgive mortal sins which another has committed against other people" (Heer). Lindhardt quotes, in agreement, from one of the Jewish camp inmates: "What has been done to you personally, you can, if you like, forgive and forget. . . . But . . . it would have been a great sin to take other people's sufferings on your conscience." Schuschnigg adds that only religious absolution gives any real meaning to forgiveness. (48)

Martin Marty, American Protestant theologian, writer, and educator, is the most outspoken about what a Christian should advise a Jew in this situation: he must keep silent. "Non-Jews and perhaps especially Christians should not give advice about the Holocaust experience to its heirs for the next two thousand years. . . Cheap instant advice from a Christian would trivialize the lives and deaths of millions." Moreover he worries that "crimes against a people will be taken less seriously if individual persons start forgiving in their name, [and we may then] soon forget to tell the story." Despite all the foregoing, Marty concludes with a hope that he might have been "free" enough to be able to mediate grace even in this situation. (49) Poul Lindhardt, Protestant minister and dean of a divinity faculty, is particularly concerned about the way in which, after the war, demands were made by Christians that "all should be forgiven and forgotten." He quotes from an unnamed Christian foundation which issued the following: "Today's world <u>demands</u> that we should forgive even those who still provoke us by their attitude. It demands that we draw a line under the whole business, <u>just as if nothing of consequence had ever</u>

happened" (italics added). (50) Heer also is angered by "a pseudo-humanism and a superficial, verbose Christianity" that seeks to end the trials of criminals by claiming that "'the poor devils . . . have atoned enough'. . . . Such false, lying appeasers want to besmirch man's true dignity [which] consists of persistence to the end in the effort to solve the great human problems again and again . . . ." (51)

Constrast these demands on Jews with the following: "Anyone, who after the Second World War, demands that we should forgive and forget everything is expecting us to be as barbaric as the murderers, who have forgiven themselves everything and forgotten all their inhuman deeds" (Kesten). And: When evildoers forget without repentance and confession, "their forgetting is nothing more than a continuation of their crime" (Manès Sperber). (52)

A number of other writers also deal with the negative effect on society that forgiving and forgetting will have. David Daiches, university professor in Britain and noted literary critic, observes that unless individuals and society make moral judgment "there simply can be no pattern of civilised behaviour underlying a culture. . . ." And if individuals can attribute their sadistic and destructive impulses to psychological, sociological, or physiological factors, there will be no incentive for them to suppress those inclinations. Hermann Kesten adds, "A State that forgives mass-murderers is on the way out." And Hans Habe holds that "amnesty granted to an unpunished murderer is a form of complicity in the crime. It does not foster forgiveness, it precludes it." (53) The French author Roger Ikor goes even further when he writes that "some crimes are so atrocious that [any] justice becomes ineffectual in dealing with them, turning thereby into injustice." He believes there is a case to be made under certain circumstances for "raw revenge." (54)

But these respondants are also concerned for the victims who can never rejoin the human community. Roger Ikor quotes a man who had been tortured by the SS: "The millions of innocent people who were tortured or slaughtered would have to come back to life before I could forgive." Ikor himself believes that to forgive the murderers is "to condemn the dead a second time." Kesten asks, "Is there any Jew or Christian or [Muslim] or atheist who has the right to forgive the slaughter of a million Jewish children?" Cynthia Ozick sums it up: Forgiveness "is pitiless. It forgets the victim. It negates the right of the victim to his own life. It blurs over suffering and death. It drowns the past. It cultivates sensitiveness toward the murderer at the price of insensitiveness to the victim." (55)

One contribution to The Sunflower still needs to be mentioned, that of Milton Konvitz, who most successfully consider many of the questions along with the Jewish tradition. He suggests that Simon should have explained to Karl that he could not speak for Karl's victims, for the Jewish people, or for God. But as a Jew, he had been taught to act with compassion. And that he had been taught that God, the Compassionate One, is always ready to accept the repentant sinner. He might then have concluded, "insofar as you reach out to me, and insofar as I can separate myself from my fellow Jews, . . . my broken heart pleads for your broken heart." (56)

Is there yet another alternative that has not been suggested by any of the discussants, and that perhaps takes repentance into account more fully? I suggest there is, and one that may by analogy be helpful in the broader consideration of our topic. If Karl (the SS man) truly repented of his gruesome deed and wanted to make amends in whatever limited way that was available to him, he should have asked the nurse to bring into his room one or more of his SS colleagues and told them his story and of his change of heart and mind. He should have done everything he could to persuade them of the evil of the Nazi program of mass murder, and urged them to try to save however many Jews they could in whatever situation they found themselves. (Since Karl knew he was dying and was already in constant agony, he did not have to worry about more pain or death.)

Since the injured parties in this case were all dead, and there was no possibility of Karl being able to locate, no less contact, any surviving relatives, or even neighbors, the closest ones to whom some form of restitution could have been made were other Jews threatened with similar cold-blooded murder. By attempting to convert some of the SS killers to his conviction, he would have been fulfilling the requirements of repentance: turning away from evil in as total a way as possible, and turning toward good. He would have been engaging in a deed concerned with perpetuation of life -- the best penance possible for having participated in taking life. Had Karl acted in this way perhaps he would then have been entitled to turn to a Jew for further consolation, had he still felt the need, for then his penitence would have been given substance and could have been perceived as a true teshuvah -- return. But he would still not have been entitled to ask a victim for forgiveness. As Emil Fackenheim has expressed it (though not in relation to Wiesenthal's book), "the authentic repentant ex-SS man must live bravely without the assurance of forgiveness; indeed he will sternly insist that, in this case, grace would be cheap." (57)

* * *

Mark Goulden advises that we need to ask ourselves "in whose hands lies the privilege of granting forgiveness?" One reply is that of the poet Dryden: "Forgiveness, to the injured doth belong." But since six million of the "injured" are dead, they are unable to give any response. Goulden adds, "if the dead can't forgive, neither can the living." (58)

On 3 April 1985 the lead editorial in The Times (London), entitled "In Holy Week III," gave an intriguing reply to Goulden's query. "If Jesus in the Godhead can forgive even unlimited evil, as Christians . . . believe, then it is well to remember that it is as a Jew that he does so, a Jew forgiving Christians for their sins against his holy race. Only a Jew has that right. The problem of evil . . . is not to be solved by some intellectual analysis which makes evil intelligible. . . . The real problem of evil is how it is to be forgiven, and by whom?"

Another answer to the provocatively worded question "in whose hands lies the privilege of granting forgiveness?" is an obvious one: God. But can even God forgive such slaughter? Emil Fackenheim finds that it is dubious theology to answer yes. (59) He is joined in such wondering by a number of others, among them Elie Wiesel, Alexander Donat, Leon Wells (all three, survivors of the death camps). But must not anyone who has even vicariously looked into that Kingdom of Night be compelled to wonder what measure of divine forgiveness or even compassion could compensate for or alleviate the terrible losses and anguish that unnumbered persons have endured -- and not endured? Is it not at last time for God to do the asking -- to plead with his people for their forgiveness? For the Covenant, which was meant to sustain life, seems to have been death-bearing instead. Would not the Creator have foreseen this consequence? Should not the Compassionate One have made the task of bringing the Torah to the world less fearsome? Perhaps God needs and wishes for our forgiveness as much as we desire hers. When the compassion of God stands in judgment on the divine demand, and when God, forgiving us, is also forgivable and forgiven, then the Covenant is both transcended and fulfilled. (60)

* * *

I have not tried to give definitive answers to the perplexing and many-sided problems associated with the concept of forgiveness. (Repentance is, I believe, a less difficult issue, though we are often reminded by Jews that a continuous stance of mea culpa is so uncomfortable that it may very well produce a backlash of resentment and renewed hatred. Perhaps penitence in action is less likely to produce this effect.) However, I think that there are several key factors for any acceptable resolution of the disputes. The most important one is time. There is a time to ask for forgiveness, and there is a time to wait to ask. The victims and the Jewish people as a whole need time to absorb the enormous pain and loss they have sustained in this century. They need to be able to feel safe for an indeterminate period of time (which they have not yet experienced) before they should be called on to assist others with their problems of guilt and remorse.

The second factor is memory. World-shaking and world-shaping events can only have their impact by becoming a part of the future they are to influence. History is focused and directed by remembrance of those events and their immediate and long-range consequences. The Shoah should be one of those events.

Yet "there is evidence that the world has conspired to forget the monstrous atrocities that shamed mankind and made a mockery of religion and humanity, even though they occured within living memory." (61) Obviously the Final Solution has had its physical and demographic impact. But can it be the beginning of a turning in our world history? a turning away from the evils it so totally represented, and a turning toward a better appreciation of all lives and all cultures -- a teshuvah? The only possibility (faint as it may be) lies in remembering; and building that memory into our civic, religious, and educational traditions.

The third factor is compassion, combined with understanding. We need to cultivate these virtues and practice them in place of fault finding and sanctimoniousness. We are able to ask for compassion and understanding for ourselves much more easily and with greater chance of success if we have demonstrated it ourselves, not merely once or twice but on a regular basis. Compassion involves having empathy as well as sympathy: comprehending what it is like to walk in another's shoes. And who knows where those shoes will take one. Perhaps we should give up the word forgiveness and settle for compassion -- it is more understandable and less ambiguous.

But if we are to stay on the topic with which this paper began, let us consider a prayer-poem, unsigned, that was first published in a French weekly in 1962.

"The Prayer of a Jew, Under Torture in a Concentration Camp"

"Peace be to men of bad will, and an end to all revenge, and to
all words of pain and punishment,
The horrors are beyond measure, they pass the limits of the
understanding of man;
So many have borne witness with their blood!
O God, do not put their suffering upon the scales of Thy justice,
Lest it be counted to the hangman, lest he be brought to answer
for his atrocities.
But to all hangmen and informers, to all traitors and evil ones,
do grant the benefit of the courage and fortitude shown by
those others, who were their victims;
. . . The benefit of their resignation and great dignity; the
benefit of their silent sorrow and unflinching spirit and
that brave smile which dried their very tears.
Grant the benefit of the burning love and sacrifice in those
harrowed, tortured hearts, which remained strong and stead-
fast in the face of death and unto their weakest hour.
All this, O Lord, may it count in Thine eyes, so that their sin
be forgiven.
May this be the ransom that restores justice.
And all that is good, let it be counted, and all that is evil, let
it be wiped out.
Grant, O God, to our enemies that they no longer think of us as
victims, with pangs of anguish and ghostly terror.
Nay, let us help them to forgo their frantic rage.
And that is all we ask of them, and when all this is over and gone,
may we be permitted to live like men amongst men.
May peace come once more upon this earth, peace to men of good
will; and may it descend upon the others also.
Amen" (62)

NOTES

1.Repentance and a consequent change of behavior can also be directed toward nature even though no direct response is possible

2.A.C. J. Phillips, The Times (London), 8 June 1985, on the occasion of President Reagan's visit to the Bitburg cemetery; Alvin Rosenfeld, "The Holocaust in Jewish Memory and Public Memory," Dimensions 2,3 (Fall 1986): 12.

3.Many bodies of law recognize that harm extends to verbal insult, defamation of character, false accusations, etc. According to rabbinic law shaming a person in public is equivalent to shedding blood (Berakhoth 43b, cited in

Philip Birnbaum, A Book of Jewish Concepts, rev. ed. (New York: Hebrew Publishing Co., 1964, 1975), p. 75.

4. That may be the small grain of insight in the saying "Forgive and forget."

5. I am omitting the sins against the Creation/environment since we have a sufficiently complex situation as it is.

6. Daiches in Simon Wiesenthal, The Sunflower (New York: Schocken Books, 1976), p. 108.

7. Birnbaum, p. 670. Cf. Ex. 34:7, and Nu. 14:18.

8. Birnbaum, p. 487.

9. Birnbaum, p. 569.

10. The most well known expression of this is found in the prayer Jesus taught his disciples which includes the petition (variously worded), "Forgive us our debts/trespasses as we forgive our debtors/those who trespass against us" (Mt. 6:12; Lu. 11:4).

11. Vergilius Ferm, An Encyclopedia of Religion (New York: Philosophical Library, 1945), p. 571.

12. Luther regularly attacked the Roman Church for succumbing to Jewish error and his criticism of penance was no exception. He denounced acts of penance with Judaism's avowed "works righteousness" and legalism.

13. Ferm, p. 657. Cf. II Cor. 7:9, 10; Acts 26:20.

14. See Mt. 5:44; Lu. 6:27, 35.

15. If the first alternative is true, must we not conclude that Jesus introduced a new and more demanding "law"? And since, for Paul, the law must be kept in its entirety or the person living under it is "cursed" (Gal. 3:10; cf. Rom. 2:17-18, 21-23; 3:20; 4:15), Christians would find themselves in the same untenable position as Jews who failed the one hundred percent test.

16. It should be noted that Shylock in The Merchant of Venice is a far more merciful person than his Christian adversaries, though this is seldom noticed.

17. Alex Byron in Martyrdom and Resistance 14, 1 (Sept.-Oct. 1987): 12.

18. Maurice Lamm, "After the War -- Another Look at Pacifism and SCO," Judaism 20, 4 (Fall 1971): 421.

19. Birnbaum, p. 487. A prominent rabbinic teaching is that he "who turns an enemy into a friend is the bravest hero."

20. Lamm, p. 422.

21. Lamm, p. 423.

22. I am using the term Christians here fairly loosely, insofar as it is usually not possible to determine how faithful a church-goer or supporter a person is, or whatever criteria one would use. I am going by what references a person makes as the basis for her opinion or in the course of his remarks.

23. Marcuse in Wiesenthal, p. 170.

24. Eva Fleischner, Sister Mary Jo Leddy, Sister Carol Rittner, "The Appearance of Forgiveness, the Reality of Justice," October 1987.

25. There is still the question of whether the Pope's act of forgiving his assailant affected reconciliation, since the Catholic sacrament of reconciliation requires an admission of guilt and repentance (cf. Fleischner, Leddy, and Rittner). Did Agca meet these conditions?

26. Even if the relatives followed this advice, the state would not be exonerated from carrying out its duty to protect society.

27. David Novak, Violence in Our Society: Some Jewish Insights (New York: The American Jewish Committee, 1983), p. 23.

28. Hans Habe argues in a similar way but sutstitutes the words forgiveness and punishment for mercy and righteous anger as imitations of God (in Wiesenthal, p. 124).

29. Novak, p. 23, and citing TB San. 3b, Tos., s.v. "mokee."

30. Cited by Novak, p. 19.

31. Lothar Kahn comments that "a case can be built for the Rich Jew being the most decent and honest of the characters in the play" ("The Fassbinder Affair," Midstream XXXII, 2 [February 1986]: 52). Such subtleties, as in the case of Shylock, seldom reach the audience to overcome the negative effects of the stereotype.

32. Johann N. Schmidt, "'Those Unfortunate Years': Nazism in the Public Debate of Post-War Germany," lecture delivered at Indiana University, 15 Oct. 1986 and published by The Jewish Studies Program (1987), p. 10.

33. Schmidt, p. 6.

34. Cf. A. Roy Eckardt, "The Christian World Goes to Bitburg," in Geoffrey Hartman, ed., Bitburg in Moral and Political Perspective (Bloomington: Indiana University Press, 1986), p. 85.

35. Even Bill Moyers' television program "Understanding Evil," which was made up of lengthy excerpts from a conference attempting to deal seriously with another (though related) subject, also failed, on the whole, to come to grips with radical evil. Even Raul Hilberg's presentation about all the levels of German society that knowingly and willingly participated in cold-blooded mass murder failed to move the conference into appropriate comprehension of how radical evil can pass for normality, which makes it that much more evil.
36. Still, empathy is another human attribute, and one does not have to experience tragedy or injustice in order to be affected by it. European Christians who lived under German Nazi occupation tend to have somewhat more awareness of what such unlimited power reveals about the depths of human depravity and the relative ease by which individuals can be corrupted.
37. John A. Coleman, "The Kairos Document," The Ecumenist 24 (1986): 33. The original statement was written and issued by 150 South African theologians and church leaders; the second edition involved thousands of church people.
38. The story concerns a young German who had been converted from being an altar boy in his Catholic Church to becoming (in time) a member of the SS. He eagerly went to fight for his Führer and country in Eastern Europe. His illusions began to fray as he began to discover what was being done to the Jewish people in those countries, especially when he was ordered to participate in a roundup of Jewish villagers after which they were incarcerated in a building which was then doused with gasoline and set ablaze. Haunted by the scene for weeks after, the young soldier ceased to exercise proper battle caution and was mortally wounded. Swathed in bandages, wracked by his conscience, remorseful over his own role in that terrible event, and dying a slow, agonizing death in a military hospital, he secretly asked a nurse to bring one of the Jewish prisoner-laborers to him. The Jew (Simon), most of whose family and friends had already perished under the Nazis and who expected his own death daily and momentarily, had to listen to the SS man's story and then decide whether he could give the forgiveness that the soldier so desperately sought (though did not directly request). Discussions among his fellow Jewish inmates and later with a prisoner who had been a Catholic seminarian produced many opinions but no agreement, and the question about his own decision continued to plague Simon even while he struggled to survive the Nazis' "Final Solution."
39. Flannery in Wiesenthal, pp. 113, 114.
40. Heinemann in Wiesenthal, pp. 129-30.
41. Hollis in Wiesenthal, pp. 133, 134.
42. Senghor in Wiesenthal, p. 203.
43. Oesterreicher in Wiesenthal, p. 179.
44. Marcel and Maritain in Wiesenthal, pp. 169, 170-71.
45. Kesten in Wiesenthal, pp. 152-53.
46. FitzGibbon in Wiesenthal, p. 111.
47. Schuschnigg in Wiesenthal, p. 202.
48. Heer, Lindhardt, and Schuschnigg, pp. 128, 164, 202.
49. Marty in Wiesenthal, pp. 173, 174, 175-76.
50. Lindhardt, pp. 164-65.
51. Heer, p. 126.
52. Kesten and Sperber in Wiesenthal, pp. 149, 205.
53. Daiches, Kesten, Habe in Wiesenthal, pp. 107, 151, 123.
54. Ikor in Wiesenthal, p. 142.
55. Cited by Ikor, p. 140; Kesten, p. 151; Ozick in Wiesenthal, p. 187.
56. Konvitz in Wiesenthal, p. 160.
57. Fackenheim, "Concerning Authentic and Inauthentic Responses to the Holocaust," unpublished paper prepared for the International Conference on the Holocaust, New York, N.Y., 1975.
58. Goulden in Wiesenthal, p. 119.
59. Fackenheim, ibid.
60. Alice L. Eckardt and A. Roy Eckardt, Long Night's Journey Into Day: A Revised Retrospective on the Holocaust (Detroit: Wayne State University Press and Oxford: Pergamon Press, 1988), p. 95.
61. Goulden in Wiesenthal, p. 116.
62. Reprinted in Katharine Hargrove, ed., The Star and the Cross (Milwaukee: The Bruce Publishing Co., 1966), p. 279.

HOLOCAUST THEOLOGY AND LATIN AMERICAN LIBERATION THEOLOGY: SUFFERING AND SOLIDARITY

by

Marc H. Ellis
Maryknoll School of Theology
Maryknoll, NY 10545

With the decisive victory of Israel in the June 1967 Six Day War, certain trends in Jewish theological understanding crystallized. It might be said that the war itself posed both sides of a dialectic present in Jewish life since the discovery of the death camps in 1942, and the emergence of the State of Israel in 1948: the dialectic of Holocaust and empowerment. Because of the perpetual diaspora situation of post-70 Judaism and the difficulty of humanly absorbing the Nazi attempt to impose a "final solution" to the Jewish question, theological responses to this new dialectic were naturally slow in coming. A revolution in theological thought was needed to match the revolutionary change in the Jewish condition, i.e., the loss of European Jewry, the shift of diaspora Jewish power to North America, and the reality of a Jewish state. After the Six Day War, that philosophical transformation was solidified and articulated by Holocaust theologians who, in despair and courage, chartered a theology which is now normative for the Jewish community throughout the world.[1]

In its beginnings, Holocaust theology, as pioneered by Elie Wiesel, Emil Fackenheim, Richard Rubenstein and Irving Greenberg, was radical, incisive and controversial. It spoke about and named the collective trauma the Jewish people had experienced as a, or often as <u>the</u> formative event of Jewish history. Holocaust theologians juxtaposed the Holocaust with the biblical origins of the Jewish community to pose the question of God's fidelity to a covenanted people. They challenged the Rabbinic tradition both in its theological analysis of the diaspora condition and the type of leadership, or lack thereof, it provided in the moment of great adversity. At the same time Holocaust theologians critically analyzed the dark side of modernity with its landscape of mass dislocation and mass death.[2]

While the formative event of Holocaust encouraged retrospective probing of traditional Jewish understandings in the theological and political realms, it demanded even more urgently the development of a framework for sustaining Jewish survival in the present. For if the Holocaust theologians understood anything with great clarity it was that the Holocaust was the most disorienting event in Jewish history. Thus in the midst of broken lives and shattered faiths, Holocaust theologians needed to articulate a future for the Jewish people.[3]

The genius of the Holocaust theologians was that they understood the prospective search needed to be as radical as their retrospective probings. And that somehow within the radical questioning of past and future, the Jewish people would need a sustaining faith, one no longer overtly theological, in the present. Hence, in order to survive in the face of a disorienting event, a redefinition of what it meant to be Jewish was the task before this emerging theology. A practising Jew as one who engaged in study, ritual and observance of the law was no longer an adequate definition, and Holocaust theologians knew it. They also understood that religious affiliation or nonaffiliation would be insufficient a test for fidelity to the Jewish people. What they offered instead was a framework to integrate diverse experiences and outlooks into a strong solidarity with the future of the Jewish people. No longer would the primary commitment to synagogue, to liberal/radical politics or to an assimilationist indifference suffice. What was needed was a broad and energetic commitment to the commands of the Holocaust experience: memory, survival and empowerment, especially as embodied in the State of Israel. It was these commands which allowed for the continuation of the people so that at some point in history there would be a context for the resolution of the questions posed by the Holocaust event. In a sense, Holocaust theologians gathered the people together for the only kind of Sinai experience possible after the Holocaust.[4]

The task of charting the future of the Jewish people was even more complex than its internal community components. The new Sinai, in gathering Jews of different persuasions into a transformed covenant, demanded a radical probing of the diverse worlds Jews lived within, including the world of Christianity and modernity. Indictment of historical Christianity was simple enough, at least in its overt institutional capacity; apathy toward, complicity in and solidarity with the murderers was the order of the day. The "righteous gentiles" were clearly a minority to be mentioned, though often in passing and surely as exceptions. The collapse of European culture and values, the need to emphasize the dark side of the ideology of progress, the failure of the democracies to respond to massive Jewish refugee populations -- these were more difficult issues to face. Modernity, as a promise to the world of human betterment and freedom, and especially emancipation for the Jewish people, needed a radical analysis as well. Thus Holocaust theologians confronted a dual crisis of massive proportions involving the shattering of the Jewish people and modernity.

Just as they responded to the crisis of Jewish life by creating a framework for solidarity among the Jewish people, Holocaust theologians responded to the crisis of modernity by envisioning a solidarity for those consigned to the other side of a century of progress. Richard Rubenstein and Irving Greenberg have crystallized this struggle to articulate a theological thesis for our time: "The passing of time has made it increasingly evident that a hitherto unbreachable moral and political barrier in the history of Western Civilization was successfully overcome by the Nazis in World War II and that henceforth the systematic, bureaucratically administered extermination of millions of citizens or subject peoples will forever be one of the capacities and temptations of government."; "The victims ask us, above all, not to allow the creation of another matrix of values that might sustain another attempt at genocide." The terrible tragedy of the Holocaust thus lay in the future as much as in the past.[5]

THE LIMITATIONS OF HOLOCAUST THEOLOGY

By 1975, just eight years after the conclusion of the Six Day War, Holocaust theologians had addressed the crisis of the Jewish people and modernity, proposed a framework for solidarity among the Jewish people and others suffering around the world, and thus had outlined the essential dimensions of Holocaust theology as we inherit it today. Holocaust theologians had succeeded in the task that faces all theology: to nurture the questions that allow us to understand the history we are participating in and creating. Yet it was at this moment, the time when Holocaust theology became normative for the Jewish people, that its critical edge became elusive. Holocaust theology was succumbing to that which all theologies inevitable succumb: it no longer could address the questions critical to the history the Jewish people were creating. The reasons for this failure are complex and beyond the scope of this essay. Suffice it to say here that Holocaust theology emerged out of a situation of powerlessness that demanded a mobilization of psychic energy and material activity toward empowerment; the dialectic of Holocaust and empowerment acted as a counterbalance and a critique of weakness and empire. However it did not have within it a way of analyzing power once achieved. Because of the experience of Holocaust, the theology lacked objectivity regarding power in Jewish hands. It could not address the cost of our empowerment.[6]

In fact as the situation in Israel changed over time, with expanded borders, two decades of occupation, the invasion of Lebanon and an increasing role in global arms sales and foreign policy intrigue, Holocaust theology's dialectic remained as it crystallized at the moment of the 1967 triumph. What did change was its emphasis on empowerment and the diminishing critical role of the Holocaust event. We might say that in this process the Holocaust became the servant of power, called upon to legitimate activity that hitherto was seen as unethical, even immoral. Jews in the United States were in the most difficult situation of all diaspora communities: maintaining a highly visible support of Israel and creating the climate for an expanded U.S. role in support of that state as necessary for its survival, while being relatively powerless to affect Israeli domestic and foreign policy even when in profound disagreement.[7]

As Holocaust theology lost its ability to enter critically into the contemporary situation of the Jewish people, its reliance on empowerment became more and more obvious. A strange paradox ensued which continues today: a theology which poses the most radical religious and ethical questions functions politically in a neo-conservative manner. Not only are the four most articulate Holocaust theologians neo-conservative in their political stances, they help to legitimate the shift of Jewish intellectuals from the left to the center and right of center on the political spectrum. Even Holocaust theologians with liberal credentials bear analysis: by the 1980s Irving Greenberg, who wrote so eloquently about the prophetic call of the victims of the Holocaust in the 1970s, is supporting the reemergence of American power under Ronald Reagan, specifically the stationing of medium-range missiles in Europe, the Strategic Defense Initiative, the expansion of rebel forces in Angola, support of the Contras in Nicaragua, and withdrawal from UNESCO. At the same time, he warns against the misuse of the prophetic to undermine the security of the State of Israel: "There is a danger that those who have not grasped the full significance of the shift in the Jewish condition will judge Israel by the ideal standards of the state of powerlessness, thereby not only misjudging but unintentionally collaborating with attempted genocide." The subliminal if not overt message is clear: those who dissent carry a heavy burden even to the point of creating the context for another holocaust.[8]

From the beginning and more exaggerated today, a sense of isolation and abandonment underlay Holocaust theology. Warnings about the prophetic within the Jewish community should be seen in this light: an underlying strain in Holocaust theology sees the world as hostile to Jewish interests and survival. Therefore any public criticism of Jewish empowerment endangers the survival of the Jewish people. In fact, from the perspective of Holocaust theology, a new anti-Semitism has arisen in the world since the advent of Jewish empowerment exemplified by the United Nations, Third Worldism, and radical movements on the left. These institutions and movements threaten Jewish survival because of their critical attitude toward the United States, Western cultural economic and military imperialism and Israeli domestic and foreign policy. Yet these are precisely the arenas of struggle which Jews have often gravitated toward, as an expression of the prophetic impulse. Holocaust theology is more and more isolated from these movements and there is an intense feeling that they have abandoned the Jewish community. Isolated and abandoned by the left, Holocaust theology comes into alliances with those in the center and the right, some of whom have traditionally been anti-Semitic but now support Israel for religious and political reasons. For groups on the Christian evangelical right, for example, the support of Israel is a portent of the last days of creation and a symbol of a state who, existing in a sea of Arab peoples, knows how to defend itself and is unafraid to exercise its power. For others in the center, Israel is a staunch ally and essential bulwark of democracy in an unfriendly, strategically important and tumultuous sector of the world.[9]

Increasingly the consensus surrounding Holocaust theology is being challenged by movements of Jewish renewal, sometimes in theological language, though most often in non-theological terms. A neo-orthodox form of renewal in the United States led by Arthur Waskow is one example, attempting to revive rabbinic Judaism in a modern setting and emphasizing those religious sensibilities which promote justice. New Jewish Agenda is another example, gathering secular and religious Jews to counter the neo-conservative drift of the Jewish community. Among other things, Agenda proposes a renewed emphasis on the ethical tradition within Judaism, supporting the continuing civil rights struggles for Blacks and women, calling for an end to United States interventionism, asking for a reasoned discussion of the Middle East which includes Israeli security and a Palestinian state. The recently formed journal _Tikkun_, seeks to counterbalance the conservative journal _Commentary_ and provide a voice for justice concerns and progressive political, cultural and religious ideas. In Israel similar movements are diverse and increasingly energetic, spanning the spectrum from center to left including Peace Now, Oz veShalom and the Committee to Confront the Iron Fist.[10]

Thus both in the United States and Israel movements of dissent have appeared to challenge political and religious sensibilities which underlie Holocaust theology. Though few address the theology directly, they all operate within the environment Holocaust theologians have helped to create and in may ways legitimate. The movements listed have other things in common: while recognizing the dialectic of Holocaust and empowerment as important, they experience a need for a new dimension of theological and political activity, namely a renewed exploration of the ethical dimension of Jewish life in a time of empowerment; a sense that isolation and abandonment can only be overcome by renewing bonds of solidarity with those struggling for justice around the world, including the Palestinian people; a feeling that the future of the Jewish community is at stake and that the time to move forward is now. Finally they have in common their place on the periphery of Jewish life, addressing a normative theology which is pervasive with powerful institutional backing.

It is becoming increasingly clear that while new theological perspectives are necessary within the Jewish community, and that internal Jewish resources are critical to this task, the power of the status quo consensus and the limitation of resources at hand render the hope of renewal problematic, if not impossible. In fact the crucial variables may lie in the feelings of abandonment and isolation which increase daily. The renewal of Jewish theology and politics, then, may need a bridge to other communities outside of the Jewish world in order to gain perspective on Jewish suffering and the cost of Jewish empowerment. Perhaps the great paradox of Jewish history is that one of those communities which may be of assistance in Jewish renewal is its age old persecutor, Christianity, or more specifically, those parts of the Christian world undergoing their own renewal.

SUFFERING AND SOLIDARITY

At the same time that Holocaust theology was coming to the fore in the Jewish community, the struggle for justice in Latin America was developing a theological voice. Latin American liberation theology emerged in the 1960s as a response to at least four levels of crisis: political, economic, cultural, and religious. At the Second General Conference of Latin American Bishops at Medellin, Colombia, in August-September 1968, the situation of Latin America was described as one of injustice and despair that "cried to the heavens." In analyzing injustice, the political, cultural, and religious were linked together.

> Just as Israel of old, the first People (of God), felt the saving presence of God when He delivered them from the oppression of Egypt by the passage through the sea and led them to the promised land, so we also, the new People of God, cannot cease to feel his saving passage in view of true development, which is the passage for each and all, from conditions of life that are less human, to those that are more human. Less human: the material needs of those who are deprived of the minimum living conditions, and the moral needs of those who are mutilated by selfishness. Less human: the oppressive structures that come from the abuse of ownership and of power and from exploitation of workers or from unjust transactions. More human: overcoming misery by the possession of necessities; victory over social calamities; broadening of knowledge; the acquisition of cultural advantages. More human also: an increase in respect for the dignity of others; orientation toward the spirit of poverty; cooperation for the common good; the will for peace. More human still: acknowledgement, on man's part, of the supreme values and of God who is their source and term. More human, finally, and especially, faith, the gift of God, accepted by men of good will and unity in the charity of Christ, who calls us all to participation, as sons, in the life of the living God who is the father of all men.[11]

In 1971, just three years after the bishops' statement at Medellin, an extended discussion of the problems facing Latin America and a theology which addressed them was published by Gustavo Gutierrez, a Peruvian priest, under the title Teologia de la liberacion, perspectivas. Translated into English in 1973 with the title A Theology of Liberation: History, Politics and Salvation, this book and its author articulated an important shift in the vision of politics and theology for people living on the underside of Western history, as well as for those within Western society becoming aware of the nightside of their Western inheritance. It is not too much to claim that this book ignited a worldwide revolution in the way Christians understand theology and its relation to social change.[12]

Though diverse and nuanced in its original argument and further developed in later works, especially in La fuerza historica de los pobres (1979: in English translation, The Power of the Poor in History, 1983) and Hablar de Dios desde el sufrimiento del inocente (1985: in English translation, On Job: God-Talk and the Suffering of the Innocent, 1987), several themes are of critical importance from the first: the movement from a model of developmentalism to liberation in the social and political fields; the movement from a Christendom model, albeit updated and modernized, to a liberationist understanding of the Christian message. Involved here is the understanding of sin as individual and social and the eschatological promise of Christ as touching the spiritual and political, fused but not absorbed: a tension calling a people forward into the struggle for liberation in this world.[13]

Far from distancing himself from the Western world, Gutierrez argues his political and theological agenda from within the Western framework. Indeed, it is the political and theological failure of this framework, at least in Latin America, which occasions the theology of liberation. For Gutierrez, the developmentalist approach and the ideology of modernization are confronted by the increasing impoverishment and division within Latin American societies; the churches' inability to address the social order from a radical faith perspective is on the verge of leaving it as irrelevant and even harmful to those who struggle for justice. The critique is strong and unsparing: Latin Americans are experiencing in their lives the inability of the Western economic and religious system to deliver the goods it promised.[14]

The dialogue Gutierrez encourages with political and religious models of change is also distinctly Western. To begin with, he emphasizes the need to use the social sciences to analyze the structures of society, including, and especially, the structures of injustice. Citing the call of the Second Vatican Council to search out the signs of the times, Gutierrez utilizes the social sciences to help Christians discern those signs. Along with other methods of analysis, Marxism is cited as providing a "fruitful confrontation" with contemporary theology. For Gutierrez, it is to a large extent due to Marxism's influence that theological thought, "searching for its own sources, has begun to reflect on the meaning of the transformation of this world and the action of man in history." Thus Marxism's importance as a tool of analysis is superseded by the introspection demanded of the church to rediscover its own radical message of transformation. Still, Marxism is only one of the many Western schools of analysis Gutierrez cites; the philosophical and psychological ideas of Descartes, Hegel, Kant, Freud and Marcuse are also used to show the development in Western thought of the social and personal elements of liberation which, according to Gutierrez, liberation theology brings together in a new configuration.[15]

Gutierrez also explores the history of Roman Catholic theology to provide the backdrop for the changes needed in the Latin American situation. In fact, his book, A Theology of Liberation, begins with an analysis of the two classical forms of theology -- theology as wisdom, found in the early centuries of the church, and theology as rational knowledge, a concept initiated in the twelfth century. According to Gutierrez, theology as wisdom was above all monastic, promoting a spiritual life "removed from worldly concerns"; it used Platonic and Neoplatonic categories, stressing a dualistic understanding of the world with, as time went on, the consequent devaluation of earthly life. Theology as rational knowledge established itself as a science, an "intellectual discipline, born of the meeting of faith and reason." Unfortunately, from the thirteenth century on, there was a degradation of this understanding of theology. The demands of rational knowledge, for example, were reduced to systematization and exposition and finally to an ancillary discipline of the magisterium of the church. Gutierrez sees the task of the contemporary Latin American church to realize the strength within these theologies by dispensing with the aberrant transformations they have suffered through history.[16]

Theology as Critical Reflection on Praxis is the model of theology which Gutierrez feels emphasizes the spiritual and rational dimensions of previous theology and responds to the new philosophical and political emphasis on people as masters of their own destiny developed in the West since the Enlightenment. For Gutierrez faith in a God who loves us and calls us to the gift of full communion with God and each other is not foreign to the transformation of the world; rather, it leads necessarily to the facilitation up of that brotherhood and sisterhood in history. Hence the emerging understanding of orthopraxis, which is not meant to deny the meaning of orthodoxy understood as a proclamation of and reflection on statements considered to be true. As Gutierrez sees it, the goal is to "balance and even to reject the primacy and almost exclusiveness which doctrine has enjoyed in Christian life and above all to modify the emphasis, often obsessive, upon the attainment of an orthodoxy which is often nothing more than fidelity to an obsolete tradition or a debatable interpretation. In a more positive vein, the intention is to recognize the work and importance of concrete behavior, of deeds, of action, of praxis in the Christian life." Thus Gutierrez's definition of theological reflection is a criticism of society and the church insofar as they are called and addressed by the Word of God, and is a "critical theory, worked out in the light of the Word accepted in faith and inspired by a practical purpose -- and therefore indissolubly linked to historical praxis."[17]

At the same time that Gutierrez investigates the Western political and theological tradition, including the political and theological crises engendered by it, he also places Latin America and its indigenous peoples in a critical relationship with the West. This is in fact where Gutierrez develops the distinctive Latin American flavor of his political and theological outlook. For if Latin America has benefited from Western political and religious thought, it has also been an object of Western domination. Remarkably, it has also retained its own distinctive history, especially among those banished to the underside of history -- the "nonpersons" of this world. These nonpersons are the objective reality of the historical crisis in the West, the ones who prompt the challenge to regain the particularity of the Latin American experience.[18]

For Gutierrez nonpersons are the ones on the margins, the exploited, the unseen; collectively, they are those absent from history. They are the exploited classes, marginalized ethnic groups, and despised cultures, the ones who are dying before their time. The last years have seen an irruption of these poor in history in Latin America and around the world. The result is a new and difficult language for affluent Westerners to understand. According to Gutierrez, nonpersons are learning to speak without interpreters; they are rediscovering themselves and making the system feel their disquieting presence. At the same time, they are becoming less and less objects of manipulation and social work mentality and more and more the agents of their own destiny -- forgers of a radically different society. Nonpersons are creating a history that no longer originates within the dominant classes but with those on the underside of history. Thus history is seen from a different perspective: the movement for liberty among the middle classes in the West, for example, seen from beneath has meant new and more refined forms of exploitation of the very poorest in Latin America. For the wretched of the earth "the attainment of freedom can only be a result of a process of liberation from the spoilation and oppression being carried on in the name of 'modern liberties and democracy.'"[19]

Of course, the irruption of the poor has occurred throughout history though it is reaching a more profound level today. At certain times the poor have had spokespersons on their behalf. Gutierrez cites Bartolome de las Casas, a sixteenth century Spanish missionary to Latin America, because he inverted the question of heathen and saved. He pointed out that the Spaniards were placing their own salvation in jeopardy by degrading, exploiting and murdering the indigenous people of Latin America. Las Casas also had the "prophetic depth" to see the Indians as poor people rather than as heathens. In a letter to the Spanish ruler, Las Casas wrote that if the Indians' conversion to Christianity could not take place without their death and destruction, it would be better "for them never to become Christians." More recently, Gutierrez sees revolutionary ferment in Mexico, Bolivia and Guatemala in the 1950s, the socialist revolution in Cuba, and the figures of Camilo Torres and Che Guevara as "symbolizing so many others -- anonymous, committed, setting an indelible seal on the Latin American process, raising questions and exerting definitive influence in Christian circles." For Gutierrez, however, the gathering momentum is seen more and more as the active participation of the poor themselves in becoming aware and articulate about their own world, giving rise to a new person and believer, to a new way of living and theologizing the Christian faith. The process is radicalized and revolutionary because of this participation and Christian articulation rather than in spite of it. As Gutierrez points out, the irruption of the poor has political and religious significance: "To participate in the process of liberation is already, in a certain sense, a salvific work."[20]

What then is the power of the poor in history? According to Gutierrez, they reverse our perceptions of political, economic and cultural history. They remind us of the other side of power and affluence. But more, the irruption of the poor seeks a remaking of history -- subverting history, turning it around, making it flow backward, not from above but from below. From this viewpoint, the great wrong is to become, or to continue to be, "a 'super-versive,' a bulwark and support of the prevailing domination, someone whose orientation of history begins with the great ones of this world." Subversive history is the "locus of a new faith experience, a new spirituality, and a new proclamation of the gospel." Thus the power of the poor in history and in Latin America today is to continue the ancient prophetic tradition of Judeo-Christianity in light of contemporary anguish and possibility: it is to announce the reality of a God who struggles with the poor against domination and oppression.

> What had been a dominated, repressed theology, an underground spring working its own way to the surface, today has burst into the sunlight in uncappable geysers. Rivulets have formed, then streams, and now, in the rivers of this theology, we recognize not only the tributaries of the present situation , but waters flowing from the living wellsprings of a historical, concrete past as well. These torrents are thundering straight for the windows of the great ones of this world. They in turn peer out and see all this, only too well. The waters are mounting for them. Their time is up. The ill humor, the thinly-veiled contempt -- even the occasional condemnations that these movements provoke -- are not long for this world. The

poor of the earth, in their struggles for liberation, in their faith and hope in the Father, are coming to the realization that, to put it in the words of Arguedas, "the God of the masters is not the same." Their God is not the God of the poor. For ultimately the dominator is one who does not really believe in the God of the Bible.[21]

A COALITION OF MESSIANIC TRUST

The reactions of the Jewish community to the emergence of liberation theology have been diverse, from ignorance to curiosity to critique and dismissal. To the curious, liberation theology represents the possibility of a politically active force for uplifting poor and oppressed people, though for the curious, their knowledge of Christianity (and of Judaism too) is often limited, and thus they observe from a distance. For Jewish theologians and institutional leaders, the rise of liberation theology can be more difficult. aome see this revival as an ancient form of Christian triumphalism returning in a new guise. At the same time, for many Jews liberation theology's call for social transformation presages chaos; they fear such restructuring can lead only to totalitarian Marxist regimes.[22]

There is another element here as well. In most liberation theologies, the Jewish Exodus is used as a paradigm of revolution, but contemporary Jews are nowhere to be found in the writings of the theologians. This continues an age-old Christian tradition of seeing the Jewish people as bequeathing the "Old Testament" and Jesus and then disappearing from history, their mission accomplished. The use of the Jewish story is coupled with our historical invisibility. Thus, liberation theologians often miss an element crucial to the Exodus story itself: that it has a history of interpretation by the people who lived the story and who live today.[23]

The movement to place Jesus within the history of the Jewish people--which is at the same time the rescuing of Jesus from the other wilderness of various Christian traditions--also opens once again the horrible landscape of the crucifixion. For Jews, of course, the accusation of responsibility for Jesus' crucifixion is an indelible mark of the last 1900 years--years which culminated in the death camps of the Nazi period. And since that time, ecumenical relations have been predicated on the removal of that stigma, which to some extent has been accomplished since Vatican II. But some liberation theologians in their description of the historical Jesus come dangerously close to posing this problem again. This, combined with a militant Christian social movement, understandably arouses Jewish concern. The sign of the cross as a banner for social reform is greeted with both skepticism and fear.[24]

Moreover, the ecumenical movement over the last thirty years has primarily taken place among educated white middle-and upper middle-class Christians and Jews who have vested interests in continuing the political status quo. The rise of liberation theology questions the religious integrity of those Christians who base their faith on cultural symbols and ritual assent rather than on socio-political transformation. Have Jews been talking with people whose Christianity is now being challenged? The ironic twist is that despite the Holocaust, many Jews are now quite comfortable with the institutional Church. Moreover, they are extremely uneasy with grass-roots Christian movements. This comfort is bound up with preferring known religious affirmations to the unknown, but also with the institutional protection sometimes afforded the Jewish community by Catholic and Protestant institutions that have moral and political leverage in Western societies. That some unfamiliar configuration of Christianity and Christian institutions might emerge raises the level of Jewish anxiety.

The most frightening aspect for parts of the Jewish community, however, is the Third World character of liberation theology and its emerging cross-cultural solidarity. Charges of imperialism and neo-colonialism are part and parcel of these movements, and the United States is a frequent target in their critique. At the same time, Israel is heavily involved on the side of the government in some of the areas where liberation struggles are the strongest and most symbolic, as noted earlier. Thus the fear that movements of liberation will not only be critical of America but also of Israel leads some to accuse these movements of anti-Semitism.

In a more significant way, the reflections of the Jewish community after the Holocaust do not resonate with triumphal language in the theological realm. On the one hand, the Exodus--God who rescues the people from bondage--is contradicted by the Holocaust event; on the other hand, the need for empowerment renders prophetic voices naive and even dangerous. If Christians have appropriated the Jewish Exodus and the prophets without reference to the contemporary heirs of the Hebrew Scriptures, it is also true that the Jewish community, because of our history, has been reluctant to claim its own heritage.

It is clear, then, that the impasse between the Christian theologies of liberation and the Jewish community is multifaceted and complex, with many strains and tensions that will exist into the future. The question, it seems, is not how to go beyond the tension but how to move constructively within it. The choice to be with and for the empire in this struggle seems, on the face of it, to be safer and less complex: to choose to move with those who seek community is to promote a configuration that may change both the Christian and the Jewish perception of the world. By placing ourselves in the struggle for justice, we of the Jewish community may discover the other side of our own history.

At the outset it seems that the theological task of dialogue between the post-Holocaust Jewish community and the emerging theologies of liberation is framed in confrontation: a God unable to rescue the people within the Holocaust versus a God leading the people to freedom and justice. Or, if Israel is a redemptive sign somehow connected to God, the connection remains hidden while the Christian theologians of liberation boldly announce that building of God's kingdom. And yet, when analyzed more closely, the triumphal strain in liberation theology is increasingly countered by strains of doubt in religious language. For the liberation of the oppressed, like the experience of the concentration camps, is not a superficial testimony to religious certainty. Rather it is a test of God's fidelity and of human struggle characterized by abandonment and death.

To those who struggle for liberation, theological language is increasingly tested. This has prompted Gustavo Gutierrez to write a commentary on the Book of Job. With Job, Gutierrez asks how one can speak about God in the face of the suffering of the innoncent: "How are we to talk about a God who is revealed as love in a situation characterized by poverty and oppression? How are we to proclaim the God of life to men and women who die prematurely and unjustly?" For Gutierrez, this cry cannot be muted. Those who suffer are right to protest because, like Job, their bewilderment is understandable and, in a sense, an expression of their faith. Theology in Latin America cannot be done without taking the suffering of the innocent into account and thus at some point the theologian "must cry out, as Jesus did, 'My God, my God, why has thou forsaken me?"[25]

As with Job, the suffering in Latin America today chastens religious language while promoting human solidarity. Gutierrez writes that "God is a presence that leads amid darkness and pain" and quotes Luis Espinal, a priest martyred in Bolivia: "Train us, Lord, to fling ourselves upon the impossible, for behind the impossible is your grace and your presence; we cannot fall into emptiness. The future is an enigma, our road is covered by mist, but we want to go on giving ourselves, because you continue hoping amid the night and weeping tears through a thousand human eyes." For Gutierrez, this is what Job did: "He flung himself upon the impossible and into an enigmatic future. And in this effort he met the Lord."[26]

At the conclusion of his study of Job, Gutierrez writes of the Jewish Holocaust as an "inescapable challenge to Christian conscience and an inexcusable reproach to the silence of many Christians in the face of that dreadful event." The question of human suffering and God's presence is an essential one, but for Latin Americans the question is now "How are we to do theology after Auschwitz?"

> The reason is that in Latin America we are still experiencing every day the violation of human rights, murder, and the torture we find so blameworthy in the Jewish Holocaust of World War II. Our task here is to find the words with which to talk about God in the midst of the starvation of millions, the humiliation of races regarded as inferior, discrimination against women, especially women who are poor, systematic, social injustice, a persistent high rate of infant mortality, those who simply "disappear" or are deprived of their freedom, the sufferings of peoples who are struggling for their right to live, the exiles and the refugees, terrorism of every kind, and the corpse-filled common graves of Ayacucho. What we must deal with is not the past but, unfortunately, a cruel present and a dark tunnel with no apparent end.[27]

Rather the question asked in Latin America is "How are we to do theology while Ayacucho lasts? How are to speak of the God of life when cruel murder on a massive scale goes on in "the corner of the dead"?[28]

Even more radical a questioning of religious language and certainty is made by Joan Casanas, a Spaniard and long-time resident of Chile, who describes the gap between injustice, political activity and theological language in a fascinating essay, "The Task of Making God Exist." Casanas begins with the question "Activist, What Do You See in the Night?" and cites a conversation with Christian activists after the overthrow of Salvador Allende's government in 1973, shortly before the massacre of the Chilean people began.

> We were discussing the importance of the religious language and expressions of Christian faith that Chileans were incorporating into the struggle underway in their homeland. We reached this conclusion: there is no need to tell the people that God is with them, that God will help them to overcome the right-wing plot; that God is their friend and will save them. For the more a people becomes organized and fights for socialism, the more it realizes that no one outside its world, not even God is doing anything on behalf of the people's liberation other than what the people itself is doing. It would be better for us to be silent about what God is and what God can do."[29]

The problem is that most theologians, even liberation theologians, want to mold the experience of those who struggle for justice into theological categories to which the people themselves no longer relate. But activists want to know "what we are living through and seeing, and what has been given to us in the present; not what we have been 'taught' as being 'good,' and what we have 'assented to' with 'religious' fidelity."• For Casaßas, a concrete example of this is the prayer of petition.[30]

> Many individuals and groups do not feel comfortable...with a prayer that consists in asking for things from God, even though those things may be justice or the strength to fight for it. A little old woman from the Christian community in my neighborhood, a working woman who had been exploited all her life remarked at a community faith celebration, "Yes, we have asked God often to let justice come and let Somoza go, but God does not listen at all." I think this checks, or even checkmates, the most brilliant pages of theology, as far as talk about God and God's treatment of us is concerned. Hers was not the sarcasm of the rationalist spinning theories about God, but the disappointment of the poor exploited person who has nothing against God, but who senses that God should be something other than what has generally been thought and taught.[31]

At the same time that Casanas rejects talk of God's omnipotence, he also rejects the more recent theories of the crucified God who refuses to act with force and instead suffers with the people until liberation. The reason for the rejection of this theological category is similar to the prayer of petition: revolutionary activists do not see this kind of God in the night.[32]

For Casanas, direct knowledge of God is impossible, especially in an unjust society. Those who affirm God's presence in an unjust society often see God as legitimator of that injustice--but can that conception of God be accepted? Theism becomes a form of idolatry, a worship of false gods. In this case a certain atheism is necessary, a refusal to believe in a God who sanctions oppression. Still, the theologians who recognize most theism as idolatrous continue to place limitations on those who explore God through revolutionary activity.

> When those who fight and die today for real, concrete justice--the justice that capitalism impedes--do not speak of God and, for example, do not experience God as Father, it is thought and said, even in the most "advanced" theology or pastoral writing, that something is lacking in them. It is said that they must be "evangelized," that we have a "message" to give them, that we know something about God that they do not know... If many of those fighting and dying selflessly for the people's liberation have not discovered that "God exists" and is "Father," is it not possible that this "message" that "God exists" and is "Father" may not be as profound, at least in its formulation, as it has generally seemed to us? Has what many activists have not discovered by giving their lives for the oppressed been discovered by a Videla, a Pinochet, a Somoza, or the bishops who honor them? Has some "apostle" told it to them, and they believed it with all their mind and heart? Is it so easy to know something about God in a world where injustice is so rampant?[33]

What Casanas is describing is a new understanding of fidelity, a broadening of language and conceptualization in the struggle for justice. Under such conditions the certainty of God falls away, though the absolute refusal of God is also questioned. For some, religious tradition does nothing but hinder the revolutionary struggle; others admire its continuity among the people as a source of strength in adversity; still others see tradition as providing clues to a possible reconstruction. Casanas' point is that those who struggle in the present proceed with the insights that are bequeathed within the moment, and that entering the depths of history is the way of fidelity.[34]

As Casanas moves from a triumphal Christianity to one which is open to the insights which come from struggle and death, the Jewish experience of the Holocaust comes into view. Though faith did not disappear in the Holocaust, certainty did and the Exodus and prophetic traditions are confronted with a horror which shatters ancient precepts and beliefs. If Casanas starts with the question "Activist, what do you see in the night?", the Holocaust raises a similar question for the Jewish victims: "What did you see in the night?" Is it possible that by recounting the night vision of the Holocaust victims Jews might be able to provide the basis for a dialogue with those who today are peering into the darkness with fear and trepidation? Could it be that Jews are not alone in the night but are joined by sisters and brothers in a new continuity of struggle and affirmation, a retrospective solidarity across religious and geographic boundaries which might portend a flesh and blood solidarity for the future? As we probe the night together, perhaps we can begin to imagine a broader tradition of faith and struggle which is confessional for past atrocities, is bold in allowing the experiences of peoples to speak, unfettered by religious or political constraints, in short, one that allows the reality of night to speak.[35]

As with the night of which Casanas speaks, the night of Holocaust is ever present. The darkness contains many peoples. They are different--each with their own history and voice; they are also similar--rooted in oppression and resistance, abandonment and affirmation, prayer and negation. But in the night, if just for a moment, they are one.

Consider the reality of death and abandonment first from a Jewish mother of Eastern Europe, then from the eyes of a pastoral worker in Guatemala.

> I had my daughter in my arms and ran after the truck. There were mothers who had two or three children and held them in their arms running after the truck. We ran all the way. There were those who fell--we were not allowed to help them rise. They were shot right there wherever they fell. . . . When we all reached the destination, the people from the truck were already down and they were undressed--all lined up. All my family was there--undressed, lined up. The people from the truck, those who arrived before us. . . . When it came to our turn, our father was beaten. We prayed, we begged with my father to undress, but he would not undress, he wanted to keep his underclothes. He did not want to stand naked. Then they tore off the clothing of the old man and he was shot. I saw it with my own eyes. And then they took my mother, and she said, let us go before her; but they caught mother and shot her too; and then there was my grandfather, my father's mother standing there; she was eighty years old and she had two children in her arms. And then there was my father's sister. She also had children in her arms and she was shot on the spot with the babies in her arms. . . .[36]

> All day long we were fleeing. We ran seeking the the ravines. We brought all the injured from the other villages; there were many. The largest number were women and little children. We hid in the mountains, but the women wore clothes of many colors, and from the helicopters they could see us very well. We saw the helicopters begin to fly in circles, surrounding us all. They began to machine-gun the people. The only way of saving ourselves was to run to the ravine and throw ourselves into it, which was quite steep. We began to run and run to the mountain, falling and falling. The small children ran alone. They were being left behind, getting lost among so many people; and all shouted, "Mama, Mama." One woman cried; she cried a lot, talking in the language of Quiche. I didn't understand well what she said. Someone said to me, "She's crying because her child was killed." I had seen the little child. She had been born 15 days earlier. The woman had carried the child on her back. She felt when she was running, and she fell on the child and it was killed. She said, "God is going to punish me. I have a great sin on me because I have killed my child." A woman said, "God is not with us, God has abandoned us. If we haven't done anything bad, if we haven't asked for so much, why does God abandon us now?"[37]

Commonality can be found in resistance as well. During the Somoza dictatorship two

Nicaraguan peasants discuss their movement toward armed resistance, as does a Warsaw ghetto fighter.

> ALEJANDRO: "One sentence here is very clear: 'Therefore do not fear the people.' The fear you have is that they're going to do you some harm. And when are they going to do you harm? When you're against certain systems, certain injustices. That is, we're absolutely forbidden to be afraid of telling the truth, of being against anything that will endanger us, even our lives. It's clear that for the sake of justice we have to risk even our bodies. They can kill the body but they can't kill the cause for which we fight.
>
> Another boy said: "I think like you, Alejandro, that here, the government we have in Nicaragua, it does whatever it wants with us, with the people, and because we're afraid we don't fight against these injustices. According to what it says here we shouldn't be afraid of that, because if they're doing an injustice to the people we should fight. And all right, let's die, the body isn't worth anything and they can destroy our bodies but not our souls. It seems to me then that we ought to fight and not submit."[38]

The Warsaw ghetto fighter writes:

> The number of our losses, that is, the victims killed by shooting and by the fires, in which men, women and children have been consumed, is immense. Our last days are approaching. But so long as we have arms in our hands we will continue to fight and resist. We have rejected the German ultimatum demanding our capitulation. Aware that our day is at hand, we demand from you to remember how we were betrayed. What we have experienced cannot be described in words. We are aware of one thing only: what has happened has exceeded all our dreams. The Germans twice ran from the ghetto. Keep well, my dear. Perhaps we shall meet again. But what really matters is that the dream of my life has come true. Jewish self-defense in the Warsaw Ghetto has become a fact. Jewish armed resistance and retaliation have become a reality. I have been the witness of the magnificent heroic struggle of our Jewish fighters.[39]

Prayer becomes an act of affirmation, a prelude to martyrdom. As told by an eyewitness, Shlomo Zlichovsky, a Polish Jew and a teacher, prepared for his death in much the same way as did Salvadoran Archbishop Oscar Romero.

> Then, as the last preparations were being made for the hanging, I, too, looked into the face of Shlomo Zlichovsky. It was smiling with joy. I stood in the crowded place, in the midst of many humiliated Jews. But suddenly a spirit of encouragement passed over all of us. The gallows were standing in a row, under each of them a chair in readiness. The Germans were in no hurry. A pity to waste a single moment of the "entertainment." But Shlomo Zlichovsky, still singing, urged them on: "Nu! (come on already), and jumped on the chair in order to put his head into the hanging loop. Some moments passed. We all held our breadth. Deathly silence came over the market place, . . .a silence that found its redemption as Shlomo Zlichovsky's mighty voice was shattering it in his triumphant _Shema Yisra'el_. We were all elevated; we were exalted. We shouted . . . without a voice; cried . . . without tears; straightened up . . . without a movement; and called, called altogether in the innermost recesses of our souls: _Shema Yisra'el_. ("Here, O Israel: The Lord your God, the Lord is One").[40]

Romero writes:

> My life has been threatened many times. I have to confess that, as a Christian, I don't believe in death without resurrection. If they kill me, I will rise again in the Salvadoran people. . . . If they should go so far as to carry out their threats, I want you to know that I now offer my blood to God for justice and the resurrection of El Salvador. . . . A bishop will die, but the church of God, which is the people, will never perish.[41]

The commonality found in the night does not mitigate the unique quality of historical events, nor does it encourage a superficial universalism. It may, however, create a bond of solidarity where the feelings of isolation and abandonment, experienced by Jews and Christians in different historical situations, once held sway. In short, when solidarity retrospectively and in the present is affirmed, a transformation of both communities is possible. The Holocaust is an event where Christians can see their complicity and in the night their own suffering; Ayacucho is the event where Jews can see their own lives in a different light and as a call to activity on behalf of justice in the present. Jews can alos begin to see their own complicity in Ayacucho today. Both events raise, in a serious way, the question of God's presence and human solidarity.

Thus the commonality found in the night calls Jews and Christians into a dialogue which may preface an embrace, though not without facing serious and difficult questions. Johann Baptist Metz, a German Catholic theologian, sees the Christian response to the Holocaust in this light: "We Christians can never again go back behind Auschwitz: to go beyond Auschwitz, if we see clearly, is impossible for us of ourselves. It is possible only together with the victims of Auschwitz." Will Jews be able to see the challenge as boldly? That challenge may be stated paraphrasing Metz: "We Jews can never go back behind empowerment: to go beyond empowerment, if we see clearly, is impossible for us of ourselves. It is possiblle only together with the victims of our empowerment." Though the history is complex, with many twists and turns, ultimately we can only move forward with the Palestinian people and all peoples who are struggling for liberation. Metz cautiously suggests that Jews and Christians could one day arrive at a "coalition of messianic trust ... in opposition to the apotheosis of banality and hatred present in our world." This coalition would be of immense benefit to both communities and to the world.

If Holocaust theology placed the essential question of Christian life before the Christian community, that is, what does it mean to be a Christian after Auschwitz, Christian liberation theology placed the essential question of Jewish life before the Jewish community, that is, what does it mean to be Jewish after Auschwitz and within empowerment? To answer the questions posed by Holocaust theologians, Christian liberation theologians realized that a new theology was needed. Similarly, to answer the questions posed by liberation theologians, a new Jewish theology is needed. Building on the insights of Holocaust theology but responding to the changed situation of the Jewish people, this theology seeks the rebirth of the ethical and the prophetic within the mandate of empowerment. Christian theologians wrestle with the suffering of the people, seemingly helpless before the task of empowerment; Jewish theologians must now distinguish the paths within empowerment, to search out those which are consonant with the deepest impulses of the Jewish people. Do the paths of empowerment chosen today move us closer to a human and fulfilling liberation or do they begin to emulate that which we so desperately sought to escape? How do we discern the difference between empowerment and liberation? This is the future task of Jewish theology, a task that can only be imagined in the present in its initial articulation.

ENDNOTES

1. For an extended analysis of the themes in Holocaust theology see Marc H. Ellis, Toward a Jewish Theology of Liberation (Maryknoll, NY: Orbis, 1987), pp. 7-24.

2. For an early, radical and controversial analysis of these themes see Richard L. Rubenstein, After Auschwitz: Radical Theology and Contemporary Judaism (New York: Bobbs-Merrill, 1966) and ibid., The Cunning of History: Mass Death and the American Future (New York: Harper and Row, 1975).

3. Of course, the first priority was to survive as a people so that a future was possible to imagine. This question of survival was posed by Emil Fackenheim as the commanding voice of Auschwitz. See Emil Fackenheim, God's Presence in History: Jewish Affirmation and Philosophical Reflections (New York: New York University Press, 1970).

4. For an interesting exploration of this new framework see Irving Greenberg "Cloud of Smoke, Pillar of Fire: Judaism, Christianity and Modernity After the Holocaust," in Auschwitz: Beginning of a New Era? ed. Eva Fleishner (New York: KTAV, 1977), pp. 7-55, and ibid., "On the Third Era of Jewish History: Power and Politics" Perspectives (New York: National Jewish Resource Center, 1980).

5. Rubenstein, Cunning of History, p. 28; Greenberg "Cloud of Smoke," p. 29.

6. For an extended discussion of Holocaust theology's inability to analyze the case of empowerment see Ellis, Jewish Theology of Liberation, pp. 25-37.

7. In effect, a new pragmatism is stressed which allows the "occasional use ofimmoral strategies to achieve moral ends." With this understanding, the memory of the Holocaust enables Israel to be a "responsible and restrained conqueror." See Irving Greenberg, "The Third Great Cycle in Jewish History," Perspectives (New York: National Jewish Resource Center, 1981), pp. 25, 26. The recent uprising in the occupied territories and the response of Israeli authorities exemplify the difficult position diaspora Jews are in relative to Israel.

8. Ibid., p. 25. Also see ibid., "Third Era," p. 6 and ibid., "Power and Peace", Perspectives 1 (December 1985): 3, 5.

9. For an extended discussion of this view of anti-semitism see Nathan Perlmutter and Ruth Ann Perlmutter, The Real Anti-Semitism in America (New York: Arbor House, 1982).

10. Regarding Waskow, Agenda and OZ veShalom see Ellis, Jewish Theology ofLiberation, pp. 49-58. My view of Waskow and OZ veShalom is more critical now than it was when I wrote the book. Tikkun shows some promise though certain limitations are becoming evident: The Committee to Confront the Iron Fist, a group of Jewish Israelis and Palestinians, is more important than its numbers.

11. Second General Conference of Latin American Bishops, The Church in the Present-Day Transformation of Latin America in Light of the Council (Washington, D.C.: National Conference of Bishops, 1979), p. 28.

12. See Gustavo Gutierrez, A Theology of Liberation: History, Politics and Salvation, trans. and ed. Caridad Inda and John Eagleson (Maryknoll, NY: Orbis, 1973).

13. Gutierrez, Theology of Liberation, pp. IX-XI. For further developments of Gutierrez's thoughts see ibid., The Power of the Poor in History, trans. Robert Barr (Maryknoll, NY: Orbis, 1983) and ibid., On Job: God-Talk and the Suffering of the Innocent, trans. Matthew O'Connell (Maryknoll, NY: Orbis, 1987).

14. Ibid., pp. 24-28, 256.

15. Ibid., pp. 9, 27-32.

16. Ibid., pp. 3-15.

17. Ibid., p. 10.

18. Though, as yet, not fully developed in his writings, Gutierrez sees Latin America as Western and non-Western. See ibid., Power of the Poor, p. 113-117.

19. Gutierrez, Power of the Poor, pp. 193, 190, 186. That Latin American liberation theology begins with the nonperson is the essential difference between it and progressive theology in Europe and North America. Gutierrez writes: "Progressive theology seeks to answer the questions of the nonbeliever; liberation theology confronts the challenge of the nonperson" (ibid., p. 92).

20. Ibid., pp. 195, 190, 72. The Ecumenical Association of Third World Theologians meeting in New Delhi, India in 1981 defined irruption as the dramatic movement of the "exploited classes, marginalized cultures and humiliated roles. They are bursting from the underside of history into the world long dominated by the West. It is an irruption expressed in revolutionary struggles, political uprisings, and liberation movements." See Irruption of the Third World: Challenge to Theology, ed. Virginia Fabella and Sergio Torres (Maryknoll, NY: Orbis, 1983) p. XII.

21. Ibid., p. 204.

22. For a typical and unfortunately superficial response to Christian liberation theology see Leon Klenicki, "The Theology of Liberation: A Latin American Jewish Exploration," American Jewish Archives 35 (April 1983): 27-39.

23. This absence of a contemporary Jewish people is noticeable in all the liberation theologies cited above. Typical is Gutierrez's discussion of the Exodus in his A Theology of Liberation, pp. 153-167.

24. For an example of an emphasis on the death of Jesus see Jon Sobrino, Christology at the Crossroads: A Latin American Approach, trans. John Drury (Maryknoll, N.Y.: Orbis, 1978). For an overall discussion of contemporary Christian and Jewish perspectives on the trial and death of Jesus see John T. Pawlikowski, "The Trial and Death of Jesus: Reflections in Light of a New Understanding of Judaism," Chicago Studies 25 (April 1986): 79-94.

25. Gutierrez, On Job, pp. XIV, 97.

26. Ibid., pp. 91, 92.

27. Ibid., p. 102.

28. Ibid. Gutierrez continues: "Job shows us a way with his vigorous protest, his discovery of concrete commitment to the poor and all who suffer unjustly, his facing up to God, and his acknowledgment of the gratuitousness that characterizes God's plan for human history. It is for us to find our own route amid the present sufferings and hopes of the poor in Latin America, to analyze its course with the requisite historical effectiveness, and, above all, to compare it anew with the word of God. This is what has been done by those, for example, who have in recent years been murdered for their witness of faith and solidarity with the poorest and most helpless, those now known as "the Latin American martyrs" (p.102).

29. Joan Casanas, "The Task of making God Exist," in The Idols of Death and the God of Life: A Theology, ed. Pablo Richard et al., trans. Barbara E. Campbell and Bonnie Shepard (Maryknoll, N.Y.: Orbis, 1983), p. 113.

30. Ibid., p. 114.

31. Ibid., p. 115.

32. Ibid., pp. 115, 116. Casanas writes, "I do not believe that the Omnipotent who,because he so chooses, shelves his omnipotence and allows himself to be oppressed and massacred with the people for the alleged reason that it is love that must conquer has proven to be the type of God whom the most altruistic and heroic activists experience as an ultimate dimension and horizon of their struggle" (p. 116).

33. Ibid., p. 121.

34. Ibid., pp. 133, 134.

35. For my own struggle with this question see Marc H. Ellis, "Towards a Contemporary Understanding of Exile," in Israel, the Church and the World Religions Face the Future (Tantur, Jerusalem: Ecumenical Institute for Theological Research Yearbook, 1983-1984), pp. 113-128.

36. In the District Court of Jerusalem, criminal case No. 40/61, the Attorney-General of the government of Israel v. Adolph Eichmann, Minutes of Session No. 30, pp. L1, M1, M2, N1.

37. Joyce Holiday, "The Battle for Central America," Sojourners 11 (April 1982): 17.

38. Ernesto Cardenal, The Gospel in Solentiname, vol. 1, trans. Donald D. Walsh (Maryknoll, N.Y.: Orbis, 1982), pp. 255-256.

39. Quoted in Reuben Ainsztein, Jewish Resistance in Nazi-Occupied Eastern Europe (London: Paul Elek, 1974), pp. 643-644.

40. Eyewitness account quoted in Eliezer Berkovitz, With God in Hell: Judaism in the Ghettos and Deathcamps (New York: Sanhedrin Press, 1979), pp. 21, 22.

41. Quoted in Placido Erdozain, Archbishop Romero: Martyr of Salvador, trans. John McFadden and Ruth Warner (Maryknoll, N.Y.: Orbis, 1981), pp. 75-76.

FAITH AND ETHICS AFTER THE HOLOCAUST:

What Christians Can Learn from Jews

by

Darrell J. Fasching
University of South Florida,
Cooper Hall 317, Tampa Fl 33620 USA

Two Types of Faith and Morality

Different models of faith have different moral consequences. That is the hypothesis I wish to explore in the aftermath of the Holocaust. How is it possible that, in spite of more than 2000 years of oppression and persecution, Jews remained faithful to their tradition? And why is it that Christians, who in the beginning were also persecuted, became a persecuting religion and abandoned the central Gospel injunction of loving one's neighbor, even one's enemy, as oneself? Life and history are more complex than the simple answer I wish to propose hear. But I propose it simply and starkly, in order to highlight what I do take to be an important factor in any more complex accounting of moral courage and moral failure during the Holocaust. My hypothesis is that the dominant model of faith in Judaism is more complex than that which achieved dominance in Christianity. That complexity has been a training ground in the courage of moral resistance to evil, and its absence in Christianity accounts, in large part, for the Christian propensity to compromise and accommodate Christian morality to political/social orders whose own inherent ethic runs directly counter to the love of neighbor and enemy. Simply put, Judaism is grounded in an understanding of faith as a dialectic of *trust and questioning*, even to the point of calling God into question, whereas in Christianity the element of *questioning* was largely lost and the dialectic of faith collapsed into an ethic of trust as *total and unquestioning obedience*.

Both traditions allow that trust and obedience play a central role in the life of faith and both appeal to Abraham as a model of this trusting faith. But in Judaism Abraham is remembered not only as the one who exemplifies the obedience of the Akeda (the binding of Isaac to be sacrificed, Genesis 18:16-33) but also as the one who questions and challenges God to be just (e.g., the story of Sodom & Gomorrah, Genesis 22). For Biblical, Talmudic and Hasidic Judaism, faith is an ongoing dialogue and debate with God which serves as a training ground for moral autonomy, rooted in a strong sense of human dignity as a reflection of being created in the image of a God who is without image. The reduction of faith, in the Christian case, to unquestioning trust and obedience, by contrast, has taught quite another moral lesson; namely, the subjugation of moral autonomy to finite moral authorities, religious and/or secular-political, who pretend to speak for (or as) God, even when the obedience demanded runs counter to the Gospel message of love of neighbor and one's enemy. The result has been the persistent and repeated tendency of Christians, Protestant and Catholic alike, to accommodate their faith and moral vision to dehumanizing ideologies of the status quo, and so become a *negative witness* to the very transcendence they proclaim.

My task in this paper is to show how the Jewish model of faith has enabled Jews to continue to stand in continuity with their tradition, even after the Holocaust, whereas the Christian model leads to a dead end; namely, the death camps of the Holocaust. Christian faith and ethics after the Holocaust therefore face a far more serious problem of discontinuity than does Jewish faith and ethics. Faced with this impasse, Christians, would do well to learn from Jews and recover the dialectical fullness of the Biblical meaning of faith as the basis of a post-Holocaust social ethic - an ethic which Jews and Christians might come to share in a common struggle against the demonic and dehumanizing forms of power which continue to threaten our world.

Faith After Auschwitz: The Problem of Continuity

The problem of faith after Auschwitz is a different problem for Jews than it is for Christians. For Jews the question is: *How could God have allowed this evil to happen?* Pressed still further, the question becomes: *Can we still believe in the God of the Covenant, the God of History, after Auschwitz?* For Christians, it is not only that the Holocaust represents incomprehensible evil in the world, but that they themselves did so much to pave the path that leads to it and then did so little to prevent it. When the story of Western history is told and confronted honestly, it turns out that Christians, those who claim to be followers of the *Messiah* who brings peace and justice, did much to forge the path that leads to Auschwitz with teachings of supersession and contempt and a history of forced baptisms and/or expulsions, synagogue burnings, pogroms, etc. No wonder Hitler could tell two Catholic bishops, who protested his treatment of the Jews, that he was just finishing what the church started.[1]

For the Jew, it is God's credibility that is in question after the Holocaust. For Christians, it is their own credibility that is in question. How could those who claim to be followers of the Messiah be the bearers of so much hatred and destruction? How could they who were taught by Jesus to love their neighbor, and indeed even their enemy, stand by so passively while Jews were slaughtered? How could they who were called to be *in* the world but not *of* it be so completely conformed to the demonic and destructive world of Hitler's Germany?

For both the Jew and the Christian, the Holocaust represents a rupture, a dividing line. Whoever confronts the Holocuast in its incomprehensible magnitude knows it is no longer possible to be either a Jew or a Christian in the traditional ways of one's ancestors. Both Jews and Christians, for different reasons, are forced to rethink the meaning of their faith and ethics after Auschwitz. For Jews the Holocaust represents a challenge to the continuity of their faith. For Christians the Holocaust presents a moral problem which in turn forces a rethinking of the meaning of their faith. Once the Christian faces the historical links between Christian anti-Judaism and the Holocaust it becomes a moral imperative not to repeat the sins of one's ancestors. Moral integrity demands that the Christian rethink and reshape the Gospel message so as to eradicate the teachings of contempt and supersession. The need for reshaping the Gospel message is now widely recognized and being dealt with by theologians. In a previous paper I attempted to suggest how the Holocaust functions as a hermeneutic criterion for all future Christian theology.[2] In this present paper I wish to address the question of Christian ethics in the light of the Holocaust and suggest that quite apart from the obvious need to root out the teachings of supersession and contempt and to rethink the messianic/Christological claims of Christianity, there is a fundamental weakness in the Christian understanding of faith which accounts for the moral weakness of Christians in their failure to stand with their Jewish brothers and sisters during the Holocaust. Unlike the Jewish understanding of faith, the Christian understanding encourages not the moral courage to witness to a transcendence which calls this world into question but rather a conformity to the world which reduces the God of transcendence to an ideological legitimation of the status quo and the powers of death.

When Christianity broke off from Judaism there seems to have occurred a diminishment of the idea of faith as found in the Biblical tradition and continued in Rabbinic and Hasidic Judaism. The covenantal understanding of faith as a dialogue in which the Jew was expected not only to trust and obey God but also was allowed to question, and even call into question, the behavior of God seems to have disappeared in Christianity. The complex dialectic of faith as *trust* **and** *questioning* came to be reduced in Christianity to an very different understanding of faith as *unquestioning trust and obedience.* It is this dialectic of trust and questioning which seems to be providing post-Holocaust Judaism with the thread of continuity which enables it to go on, even as the absence of this dialectic helps to explain the moral failure of the ethical traditions of Christianity during the Holocaust - a failure which leaves Christian faith and ethics standing at a dead end and in need of a fundamental reformulation.

Chutzpa - Faith as Wrestling with God: The Thread of Continuity in Post-Holocaust Jewish Faith

Chutzpa/Wrestling with God in Pre-Holocaust Judaism

There is in the Jewish tradition, says Beldon Lane,

> "an audacious faith, almost bordering on insolence that stalks the high country of belief and disbelief. It seems especially prevalent in the rarefied air above Mt. Sinai. Rooted deeply in the human experience of adversity and anguish, it opens onto a landscape where God and human beings walk as friends. 'Chutzpa k'lapei shamaya' it is called in the Jewish tradition - a boldness with regard to heaven. From Moses, the Psalmist, and Jeremiah to such rabbinical figures as Honi the Circle Drawer in the first century B.C.E. - from Levi-Yitzhaq of Berditchev in the hasidic world of Eastern Europe to the pain-soaked novels of Elie Wiesel - it echoes through the Jewish past with a stubborn insistence.[3]

There is in Judaism, an understanding of *covenant* as a personal - communal relationship which essentially a two way street. It is a dialogue between God and his people grounded in a set of mutual expectations. The formula "I will be your God and you will be my people" is understood as a moral contract of love and commitment obligating **both** parties. Jews are obligated to live by the commandments but God also has obligations, to be with his people, to guide them and protect them.

Abraham, as the patriarch of Judaism, is held up as a model of faith who exemplifies both the dimension of trust and obedience to the will of God and at the same time a model of one who has the audacity or chutzpa to remind God that he also has obligations.

Abraham represents the model of trust and obedience in the story of the *Akedah*, the binding of Isaac (Genesis 22), where he unquestioningly obeys God's command to sacrifice his only son Isaac. At the last minute of course, God, satisfied that Abraham is truly trusting and obedient, intervenes and provides an alternative animal sacrifice. Ronald Green has pointed out that contrary to the typical Christian/Kierkegaardian interpretation; namely, that God can give commands which contravene morality, "Jewish thinkers refused to relinquish a moral conception of God."[4] The Jewish midrashic tradition has interpreted the story, for instance, as implying Isaac's willing cooperation, giving up his life and "not an enjoined violation of the ethical."[5]

Contrary to the Kierkegaardian reading of Abraham (and in support of Green's position), the Judaic model of Abraham as a man of faith balances the Abraham of trust and obedience with the Abraham who has the chutzpa to call God into question. The incident of course is the confrontation with God over the fate of Sodom and Gomorrah (Genesis 18:16-33). Here Abraham learns of God's intention to destroy all the inhabitants of both cities because of the preponderance of decadence in these cities. Abraham presumes to bargain with God and eventually gets him to agree to spare both cities if he can find ten just men. For our purposes the core of this dialogical encounter occurs when Abraham has the chutzpa to protest the potential taking of innocent lives by reminding God: "Shall not the judge of all, himself, be just? (18:25)" Abraham presumes to call God into question and remind God of his responsibilities.

Faith, in Judaism, as exemplified in the stories of Abraham, is seen as a dialogical and dialectical tension of trust and questioning. Trust is not seen as precluding the challenging and questioning of God, trust is not a Kierkegaardian unquestioning obedience, but rather a confidence that the two-way street of the covenant relationship both permits and demands this kind of honesty between God and the person of faith. The element of chutzpa in this dialogical covenant relationship seems to be most prominent precisely when the tragedies of life seem to call into question the very justice of God.

Probably no other book in the Tanak illustrates this more profoundly than the Book of Job and probably no other book speaks as eloquently to the post-Holocaust situation of Jews. The story of Job of course is the story of a man who was a model of piety and goodness and whose faith seems arbitrarily tested by having family, health and property taken away from him. His wife and his friends all come to *comfort* him by trying to convince him that he must be guilty and therefore deserve all these punishments. But Job knows better. He is innocent and unwilling to look bad and suffer just so God can look good. Unlike the pious Job of the ancient folk tale contained in the framing story (chps. 1&2 and 42:7-17), the Job who is introduced in chapter 3 is angry and defiant. In the framing story God and the Satan put Job on trial but now the Job who speaks in the rest of the book has the chutzpa to reverse the roles and put God on trial. Job demands a hearing before this God but says before hand that even if he got such a hearing it would not be a fair one, for "how can a man be acquitted before God?... If I summoned and he answered, I do not believe he would heed me. He would crush me with a tempest" (9:2 and 9:15-18). Nevertheless, he issues his challenge: "Let Shaddai answer me" (31:35)

When God finally does respond to Job's challenge, it turns out just as Job predicted, he is crushed by the power and might of God in a whirlwind as "with a tempest." Job is intimidated into recanting and repenting by the shear power of God. But just when it seems the dust has settled and the point of the story has been made, a paradoxical twist is added to the narrative which turns everything upside down. For in the final chapter, God turns to the comforters and says to the first, Eliphaz: "My anger burns against you and your two friends; for you have not spoken truth of me, as did Job, my servant. So now ... make a burnt offering for yourselves, and Job, my servant, will pray for you, for I will accept him, so that I may not do anything rash to you, for you have not told the truth of me, as did Job, my servant" (42:7-8). Job's chutzpa, it seems has prevailed. He has wrestled with God and man and prevailed. God, it seems, impugns his own behavior in order to defend the dignity of Job against the false piety of his friends who would make Job guilty in order to make God appear just. The book of Job offers no final answer for the coexistence of God and evil/injustice, but it does affirm that God is on the side of human dignity, even if God has to be against God in order to be for the human person.

The Biblical narrative that best sums up this understanding of faith as chutzpa is of course the story of Jacob wrestling with a stranger (Genesis 32:22-30). Jacob, on his way to reconciliation with his brother Esau, camps alone by the river Jabbok at night. There he is accosted by a stranger who wrestles with him until daybreak. Jacob demands that the stranger identify himself but he will not. Instead he requires Jacob to do so and then blesses Jacob and promptly changes his name to *Israel*, meaning - "wrestler with God, since you have wrestled with God and man, and have been the victor" (Genesis 32:28). And as the sun rises and the stranger flees, Jacob walks away limping, resolving to call the place *Peniel* meaning "I have seen God face to face and yet my life has been spared" (32:31).

Faith in the tradition of Abraham and Job, faith as a dialectic of trust and chutzpa, is the faith of Israel. The naming story of Israel as a people defines the community of faith as those who wrestle with God and man and prevail. It is this communal, dialogical and dialectical tradition which was preserved in post-biblical Talmudic and Hasidic Judaism and largely lost to the history of Christianity. Where the Christian tradition tended to focus on answers formulated as doctrine, the Talmudic tradition focuses on questions and the vigorous debate over, and with, God's word.

The Talmudic tradition, says Jacob Neusner, sanctifies the capacity to doubt and to criticize. "The wonder of the Talmud is its tough-minded claims on behalf of the intellect, not in search, but in the service, of God."[6] God is found in the "thrust and parry of argument." Talmudic debate is in fact a ritual for experiencing God. And yet, although the Talmudic scholar is vigorous and bold in his questions, his questioning cannot be divorced from the mythic context in which it takes place. The Talmud is constructed on a dialectic of trust and questioning which is foundational to faith as an expression of chutzpa. According to one Talmudic story Rabbi Eliezer ben Hyrcanos began to prove his interpretations of the Talmud by working miracles. But other scholars challenged and chided him for such tactics and invited him instead to "wrestle with us over the text." Finally Rabbi Eliezer called on heaven to vindicate his interpretation and a heavenly voice responded: "What do you want already with Rabbi Eliezer? The Halakha is always as he says." However Rabbi Yoshua stood up and cried out "You, Yourself God, told us on Mt. Sinai to follow the community of those who agree on the truth." After this God was silent. Later the prophet Elijah was asked to interpret that silence and "he smiled ... and said, 'My children have defeated me. My children have defeated me!'"[7] The Talmudic way is the art of wrestling with God and man and prevailing.

This same understanding of faith as Chutzpa is embodied in the mystical-Hasidic traditions of Judaism as well. The Hasidic master Rabbi Levi-Yitzhaq of Berditchev, it is said, one day asked a poor tailor to speak of the argument he had had with God that day in his prayers. The tailor responded:

> I told the Master of the Universe, ... today is the Day of Judgment. One must repent. But I didn't sin much. I took a little left-over cloth from the rich. I once drank a glass of brandy and ate some bread without washing my hands. These are all my transgressions. But *You*, Master of the Universe, how many are *Your* transgressions? You have taken away small children who had not sinned. From others you have taken away the mothers of such children. But, Master of the Universe, I shall forgive You Your transgressions, and may You forgive mine, and let us drink *L'Hayyim* [to life]!" That year Reb Levi-Yitzhaq proclaimed that it was this tailor with his argument who had saved the Jews. "Ah," he added, "but if *I* had been in his place, I would not have forgiven the Master of the World such great sins in return for a little leftover cloth. While I had Him, I would have asked that He send us His Messiah to redeem the World![8]

Enough has been cited here to suggest that the understanding of faith as Chutzpa has a long and continuous history in Judaism prior to the Holocaust. What is important to note is the power this tradition seems to have to make being a Jew possible even after the Holocaust. In the post-Holocaust era, this tradition seems to offer to Jews not only a powerful understanding of faith, but one which binds their past and future into a unity. Moreover, it is also extremely suggestive for a post-Holocaust ethic.

Chutzpa/Wrestling with God in Post-Holocaust Jewish Theology

If Judaism's faith was a faith grounded in answers, the Holocaust might well have meant the end of Judaism. But the faith of Jews, it seems, is not grounded in answers to metaphysical questions but in a covenant relationship of ongoing dialogue and debate, a continuous wrestling with God. More than any other factor, it seems to me, it is this which is providing the foundation for post-Holocaust Jewish theology. Let me briefly suggest evidence for this from three leading Jewish authors who are struggling to find a path for Jews after Auschwitz: Emil Fackenheim, Elie Wiesel and Irving Greenberg.

Emil Fackenheim, like other post-Holocaust Jewish theologians, has raised the fundamental question: Where was God at Auschwitz? Like, virtually all other Jewish authors on this subject, he rejects the pious traditions of the past which accounted for misfortune by suggesting that it is punishment for sins, for failure to keep the covenant. That will not work in this case, he tells us, for the Jews who died in the death camps were overwhelmingly Jews from the most pious and observant communities in Europe.[9] God cannot be let off that easily. But then where was God? And how can one continue to be Jewish in the face of God's seeming abandonment of his people in the death camps? In response to these questions, Fackenheim says:

> There is a kind of faith which will accept all things and renounce every protest. There is also a kind of protest which has despaired of faith. In Judaism there has always been protest which stays *within* the sphere of faith. Abraham remonstrates with God. So do Jeremiah and Job. So does, in modern times, the Hasidic Rabbi Levi Yitzhak of Berdiczev. He once interrupted the sacred Yom Kippur service in order to protest that, whereas kings of flesh and blood protected their peoples, Israel was unprotected by her King in heaven. Yet having made his protest he recited the Kaddish, which begins with these words: "Extolled and hallowed be the name of God throughout the world...". Can Jewish protest today remain within the sphere of faith? .... In faithfulness to the victims we must refuse comfort; and in faithfulness to Judaism we must refuse to disconnect God from the holocaust. Thus in our case, protest threatens to escalate into a totally destructive conflict between the faith of the past and faithfulness to the present.[10]

In spite of this, the Jewish theologian does not have to invent an answer to the question: "How is faith possible after the Holocaust?" It is more a matter of observing that an answer has emerged in Jewish experience.

Neither religious or secular responses to the Holocaust have proven satisfactory. After Auschwitz, there is no haven for a Jew in either the sacred or the secular. Jews were rounded up and taken to the death camps whether they thought of themselves as religious or not. Assimilation into the secular world proved to be no more protection than the affirmation of religiousness. What has spontaneously emerged however is a movement beyond the distinction of sacred and secular to a **Jewish** response to the Holocaust. It is, it would seem, a product of the chutzpa which defies both the sacred and the secular powers in a refusal to abandon one's Jewishness. It is as if today, whether a Jew thinks of himself as religious or not, he or she refuses to grant a posthumous victory to Hitler by abandoning his or her Jewishness. Even the secularist Jew proudly and defiantly continues to affirm Jewish identity." Today the distinction between religious and secularist Jews is superseded by that between unauthentic Jews who flee from their Jewishness and authentic Jews who affirm it. This latter group includes religious and secularist Jews. These are united by a commanding Voice which speaks from Auschwitz." [11] This is a voice which Jews, almost without realizing it, have heard and responded to. One which forbids them to despair of either God or humanity, although they have every right to do so. Instinctively Jews have responded with chutzpa, wrestling with God and humanity, and they continue to prevail. And they continue to ask, "Where was God?" and "Where was humanity?" But at the same time, they refuse to complete Hitler's work and grant him his final victory - they affirm their Jewishness and resist the "forces of Auschwitz" which still menace the world.

Like Emil Fackenheim, Elie Wiesel also seeks to discover a path for post-Holocaust Judaism. As a voice out of the Holocaust itself, Elie Wiesel speaks with a unique authority. More than any other author, Wiesel deserves to be seen as the bearer of the tradition of chutzpa in our post-Holocaust world. Wiesel tells us: "I remember my Master ... telling me, 'Only the Jew knows that he may oppose God as long as he does so in defense of His creation"[12] To be a Jew "means to serve God by espousing man's cause, to plead for man while recognizing his need of God."[13] Or again, "Judaism teaches man to overcome despair. What is Jewish history if not an endless quarrel with God?" Many times God has had reason to give up on human beings and has not. But also

> "There were many periods in our past when we had every right in the world to turn to God and say, 'Enough. Since you seem to approve of all these persecutions, all these outrages, have it Your way: let Your world go on without Jews. Either You are our partner in history, or You are not. If you are, do your share; if You are not, we consider ourselves free of past commitments. Since you choose to break the covenant, so be it. And yet, and yet ... We went on believing, hoping, invoking His name. In the endless engagement with God, we proved to Him that we were more patient than He, more compassionate, too. In other words, we did not give up on Him either. For this is the essence of being Jewish; never to give up - never to yield to despair."[14]

Wiesel has assumed the role of a kind of *Job* in the post-Holocaust world. Standing, like Job, in the dialectical and dialogical tradition of chutzpa, he chooses to put God on trial and call him to account. This is a persistent theme throughout his writings which culminates in his play *The Trial of God*.[15] The play is set on the eve of Purim in 1649, in a small town which has just been decimated by a pogrom. Only the innkeeper Berish and his daughter Hanna survive. Then a small band of minstrels join them in the inn where Berish filled with anger both against the Christian mobs and against God for permitting such atrocities, proposes that they put God on trial. Outside events are building toward another pogrom and a priest appears periodically throughout the trial to warn them to flee. Berish initiates the trial in the role of the prosecuting attorney. But who will defend God in this trial? The question is barely asked when a stranger named Sam appears and volunteers to take the role.

And so the trial begins. Berish levels the charges: "I - Berish, Jewish innkeeper at Shamgorod - accuse Him of hostility, cruelty and indifference. Either He dislikes His chosen people or He doesn't care about them - period! But then, why has He chosen us....? Either he knows what's happening to us, or He doesn't wish to know! In both cases He is ... He is ... guilty! Yes, guilty!" Sam, however, is a skillful defense attorney. Job's comforters should have had him on their side. God, he argues, is kind, compassionate and loving. Who can presume to speak for the suffering of the dead? "The dead belong to the dead, and together they form an immense community reposing in God and loving Him the way you [Berish] have never loved and never will. (*To the court*) He is asking , Why murder - why death? Pertinent questions. but we have some more: Why evil - why ugliness? If God chooses not to answer, he must have his reasons. God is God, and His will is independent from ours - as is His reasoning."[16] Or again, Sam argues, "Faith in God must be as boundless as God Himself. If it exists at the expense of man, too bad. God is eternal, man is not."[17] But before the trial can be brought to conclusion it is interrupted by the impending second pogrom. The priest urges them to flee, or if they wish, convert. But Berish responds, "My sons and my fathers perished without betraying their faith; I can do no less."[18] And yet, though he is prepared to die for his faith he is not ready to forgive God and bring the trial to an end. "The trial will go on.... [says Berish,] I lived as a Jew, and it is as a Jew that I shall die - and it is as a Jew that, with my last breath, I shall shout my protest to God! And because the end is near, I shall shout louder. Because the end is near, I'll tell him that he's more guilty than ever!" The play ends with **Sam laughing** because those around Berish take Sam for a holy and just man, a tzaddik, who sought to defend God. The final stage directions for the play confirm hints contained earlier in the play: "**Satan** is laughing. He lifts his arm as if to give a signal. At that precise moment the last candle goes out, and the door opens, accompanied by deafening and murderous roars."[19]

The Trial of God embodies the paradox of Jewish faith, the paradox of trust and chutzpa. But it is more than a work of the imagination. It is based, Wiesel tells us, on an experience he had in the death camps, where he witnessed three rabbis who "decided one winter evening to indict God for allowing his children to be massacred."[20] And when the trial was over and God was found guilty, the rabbis realized it was time for prayers and so they bowed their heads to pray.[21] The dialectical and dialogical faith of trust and chutzpa is not the fictive invention of post-Holocaust theologians, it is a lived faith, a tradition of faith reaffirmed in the very bowels of the death camps.

When we turn to our third theologian, Irving Greenberg, we find this same appeal to tradition of chutzpa. What is most valuable about Greenberg's response is the ethical implications which emerge from his treatment of this theme. Greenberg takes issue with the response of Richard Rubenstein, another of the prominent post-Holocaust Jewish theologians, for Rubenstein believes that God died at Auschwitz. The God of the Covenant and History proved himself to be a fiction - nowhere to be found. He quotes Rubenstein's declaration that "Jewish history has written the *final chapter* in the terrible story of the God of History.... the world will *forever* remain a place of pain ... and *ultimate defeat*."[22] Greenberg's response to this is direct: "After the Holocaust, there should be no final solutions, not even theological ones."[23] What Greenberg finds unsatisfactory in Rubenstein's response to Holocaust is his "definitiveness." Rubenstein has broken with the paradoxical dialectic of Jewish existence - the dialectic of trust and chutzpa. Rubenstein has abandoned the Talmudic-Hasidic path of *questioning existence* and settled for a definitive answer. He refuses to wrestle with the un-named God.

Greenberg however chooses to wrestle with this God and so spells out his own understanding of Jewish existence after the Holocaust. Like Fackenheim and Wiesel, but in his own way, he suggests that the line between believer and unbeliever, religious and secular has been eliminated. After Auschwitz faith for the Jew is a dialectical faith of *moments*. There are moments when one has faith and moments when faith is overwhelmed by the immensity of the Holocaust. If the Holocaust sometimes overwhelms the faith of a Jew and leads him or her to ask "where was God?", it also at times overwhelms a Jew and leads to the question where was humanity; secular, enlightened and scientifically sophisticated humanity. The Holocaust has relativized and demythologized our confidence in both the sacred and the secular. One can have no absolute hope in either. If God seems to have abandoned the Jew then so has science, technology, history and all other categories of secular hope.

The ethical implications of this dialectical and momentary faith, which is tossed to an fro between the sacred and the secular, is that one should be skeptical of all movements, religious or secular, whether of the left or the right. **"Nothing dare evoke our absolute, unquestioning loyalty, not even our God, for this leads to possibilities of SS loyalties."**[24] At this point, Greenberg appeals to the writings of Elie Wiesel and the tradition of chutzpa. God needs to be accused for his betrayal of the Covenant and this too is part of the dialectic of momentary faith. "Wiesel teaches us that in the very anger and controversy itself is the first stage of a new relationship perhaps the only kind of relationship possible with God at this point in history."[25]

If the line between sacred and secular and between belief and unbelief has blurred, there is in fact a new line that separates faith from unfaith - the deed. After Auschwitz, actions speak louder than words. An ethic of chutzpa challenges all appeals to God and religion which simply serve to denigrate human dignity and violate the image of God in which we are created. The ethic of chutzpa appeals to God against God in the name of God's creation. An ethic of chutzpa is the proof of authentic faith. It shows itself in those actions which refuse to accept the Nazi strategy which sought legitimation for genocide by classifying Jews and others as less than human, as animals. It insists that all definitions of the human violate the transcendence of the human as created in the image of a God without image. Genocide begins by defining the human so as to exclude its victims from the privileged circle. Authentic faith, after Auschwitz reveals itself in those actions which deny this option and protect human dignity and equality against every form of defined dehumanization. It is action not words which tells us who has experienced the reality of God. Thus Greenberg argues that during the 1967 war against Israel, it was Sartre who spoke out against a potential genocide and Pope Paul VI who was silent. After Auschwitz, Greenberg concludes, we must say that it is Sartre, not the Pope, who has shown himself to be a man of faith, one who has experienced the reality of God and God's image in every human being.[26] Or again, he argues that in Israel today, it is the secular Israelis who represent authentic faith and not the Orthodox Jews. For it is the secular Israelis who insist on the admission of all Jews to Israel and not orthodox Jews, who even after the Holocaust, would turn their backs on some Jews who do not meet their "religious" standards. Here the final paradox of the tradition of chutzpa reveals itself. The tradition that calls God into question is the tradition that calls human beings into question as well - in the name of the image of God in all creatures. It is the paradox of appealing to God against God and human beings on behalf of God's creation. Wherever human freedom, dignity and equality are championed, there the reality of God is affirmed.[27]

The Apostasy of the Christian Witness During the Holocaust

What Went Wrong?

What went wrong with Christianity during the Holocaust. Why did the majority of Christians, and especially clergy, either actively or passively support Hitler and his "final solution to the Jewish problem?." As Franklin Littell sums it up: "The truth is that the Church Struggle was fought out within the institutions themselves, not between "insiders" and "outsiders," that most church constituents apostatized and only a small percentage remained faithful...".[28] For the most part the Church Struggle focused on the question of the institutional autonomy of the Church and the Jewish question was largely ignored, except in cases of baptized Jewish converts, who of course "belonged to the Church" and therefore were an issue of Church autonomy. Even the famous Barmen declaration of the Confessing Church did not raise the issue of the treatment of the Jews. The leading figure in the formulation of that declaration, Karl Barth, later after the War, upon learning of Dietrich Bonhoeffer's insistence, already in 1933, that the central question to be faced is the "Jewish question," indicated that "I have long felt guilty that I did not make this problem central, in any case not in public, for instance in the two Barmen declarations of 1934 which I had composed.... There is no excuse that I did not fight properly for this cause...".[29] The sad truth however, is that even Bonhoeffer, one of the few to face this issue and struggle on behalf of Jews was a better person than Christian theologian, for he continued to hold that "the church of Christ has never lost sight of the thought that the 'chosen people', who nailed the redeemer of the world to the cross, must bear the curse for its action through a long history of suffering.... The conversion of Israel, that is to be the end of the people's suffering."[30]

There are those who suggest the Church was powerless to do anything under the totalitarian rule of Hitler. But there is strong evidence to indicate otherwise. In a comprehensive study, *Accounting for Genocide,* Helen Fein does a country by country analysis, which tries to understand who did and did not resist Hitler and aid the Jews, and why. She observes that "German instigation and organization of extermination usually succeeded because of the lack of counterauthorities resisting their plans, not because of their repression of such resistance.... Accommodation to authority in the absence of counterauthorities offering models for resistance leads to victimization of the socially designated target."[31]

The failure of the Church during the Holocaust was primarily a failure of leadership. Among those who did resist the Nazis and aid Jews, the preponderance were ordinary laymen, acting on their own.[32] What was lacking was the leadership of "counterauthorities". Fein's data suggest that the Church could have made a decisive difference, as indeed it did on a few occasions:

> Where both state and church refused to sanction discrimination as in Denmark - internal resistance was highest. Where the state or native administrative bureaucracy began to cooperate, church resistance was critical in inhibiting obedience to authority, legitimating subversion and/or checking collaboration directly. Church protest proved to be the single element present in every instance in which state collaboration was arrested - as in Bulgaria, France, and Rumania. Church protest was absent in virtually all cases in which state cooperation was not arrested. Church protest was also the intervening variable most highly related to the immediacy of social defense movements that enabled Jews successfully to evade deportation. The majority of Jews avoided deportation in every state occupied by or allied with Germany in which the head of the dominant church spoke out *publicly* against deportation before or as soon as it began.... The greater the church resistance, the fewer Jews became victims.... By contrast, states in the colonial zone with high Jewish victimization are states in which the dominant church was actively antagonistic toward Jews....[33]

Organizationally, Fein argues, the Church was the ideal institution to lead such a resistance because its membership spanned all social classes, its leaders were spread throughout the state, it had access to ruling elites, resources for hiding Jews and the prestige to significantly legitimate or delegitimate state policies.[34] Fein also points out that many of Hitler's orders "were averted, subverted, or countermanded - extermination of tubercular Poles, mass deportation of the Dutch, catching the Jews of Denmark, burning of Paris, destruction of Germany. The order to exterminate the Jews was not checked because it was already taken for granted that getting rid of the Jews was a legitimate objective."[35] Also, "outside the SS zone, no German sanctions have been reported against clergy for protest alone. No churches protested in the SS zone."[36]

The burden of the failure of the Church during the Holocaust falls squarely on the leadership in both the Catholic and Protestant traditions. As Fein's study indicates, had they taken greater initiative the history of the Holocaust might well have been very different. At the very least the Church would now be able to look back with pride rather than shame. That of course is not now possible. As Sarah Gordon, in her study *Hitler, Germans and the Jewish Question* indicates, "although very few Catholic leaders preached against racial persecution, even fewer Protestants did."[37] Franklin Littell puts the number of Protestant Pastors who remained faithful to the Confessing Church at approximately 20 % and only a minority of these directly addressed the issue of the treatment of Jews.[38] "The most ironic statistic of the Third Reich ... was that more Catholic priests and Protestant ministers died in the German army than were put into concentration camps: from an actuarial point of view it was safer to oppose Hitler than to support him."[39] Gordon's research suggests that Catholics generally offered the Nazi's less support than did Protestants, although we are talking of small minorities in both churches. On the other hand, Fein suggests that Catholic "high prelates" were less likely to speak out publicly against the deportation of Jews.[40] But the greatest shame of the Church was "the tendency for all church-going Catholics and Protestants to be more anti-Semitic than were those who no longer attended services regularly. Certainly religion, per se, was no antidote to anti-Semitism."[41]

On reviewing the history of the Church during the Holocaust we must sadly conclude that the Church was tested and found wanting. The Church was not a leaven in the world speaking and acting on behalf of the human dignity all persons, and most especially Jews. The Church did not witness to the truth of the sanctity of the life of all persons created in the image of God. The Church did not strive to transform the world but rather became obediently conformed to the Nazi world. One should not take anything away from the exceptional heroes of the rank and file in the Church who did act courageously, but it is sad that they had to do so with so little encouragement and almost in spite of the Church leadership. What went wrong? Undoubtedly a full answer to that question would be very complex, but I would suggest that an important element in an answer to that question is a fundamental flaw in the dominant model of faith and ethics found within Christianity. The simple answer would be to say that the Church substituted the state for Christ as her Lord. But it is more complicated than that. **Christian faith came to be defined as requiring (in**

varying degrees) obedience to the state as an aspect of obedience to Christ. Therein, I believe, lies the heart of the problem.

Faith as Unquestioning Obedience

Somewhere along the way, as Christianity separated itself from its roots in Judaism, the dialectical and dialogical understanding of faith as a paradoxical unity of trust and chutzpa was lost. In the Gospel tradition, the life of Jesus is primarily portrayed as a model of unquestioning and trusting obedience. Even in the Garden of Gethsemani, on the night before his crucifixion, when Jesus is depicted in the Gospels as directing some questions to God as to whether his suffering and death is necessary, he concludes with "not my will, but yours be done" (Luke 22:42). And Christians are enjoined to follow Jesus, emulating his obedience even unto death on the Cross (Philippians 2:1-8).

Now faith as a fierce and unquestioning loyalty to the will of God revealed in Christ could be an ethically powerful force for good in the world, were the will of God confined to the message of love of neighbor, and even one's enemies, as oneself. But when the message of God in Christ is taken to included the theme of supersession, the myth that gentile Christians replace Jews as God's chosen, and when it is thought to include the requirement of obedience to the state, the implications become ominous.

While the ethical implications of the supersession myth are receiving and should receive primary attention, the focus of our concern here is the second theme - faith as unquestioning obedience to God and the state. Even if the Nazi's had invented anti-Semitism instead of simply adapting the Church's traditions of anti-Judaism, the Church would probably still have gone along with the Nazi's, based on its teaching of faith as unquestioning obedience, especially in its Lutheran form.

The Gospel tradition, of course, has elements in it that put it in sharp opposition to the state. The book of Revelation is ample evidence of that and many would say that the Sermon on the Mount would qualify also. But there is another strand embodied in the teachings of Hellenistic diaspora Jewish followers of Jesus, like Paul of Tarsus, himself proudly a Roman citizen. Such missionaries were anxious to establish good relations between the Christian community and the ruling order of gentiles, becoming all things to all people, in order to convert some of them. As the post-biblical period set in and the apologetic movement of the gentile Christian Logos theologians was set in motion, there was an even greater anxiousness to show that Christianity was no threat to Rome and that Christians could be good citizens.

When Christianity went from being a minority and sometimes persecuted religion to being first the favored religion under the Roman emperor Constantine (313 C.E.) and finally the only legal religion of the empire under the emperor Theodosius (381 C.E.), churchmen of the 4th century were extremely impressed by this reversal of fortunes. Men such Eusebius of Caesarea, author of the first history of the Church, and later Augustine, perhaps the most influential theologian in the shaping of Western Christianity, took this amazing victory of the Church over the empire as a sign of God's will and God's favor. The emergence of the Roman empire came to be seen as the will of God for the establishment of a universal order of peace to facilitate the spread of the Gospel. It was a mutually beneficial interpretation. The empire gained stability from a new legitimating religion and Catholic Christianity gained a favored and protected ascendency over its Christian and non-Christian rivals. At least since the time of the Reformation the alignment of the Church and State, which began with Constantine, has been seen by the Anabaptist traditions and their late Medieval precursors (and since then by outside sympathizers) to be the greatest fundamental mistake of the Church in its entire history. But the Anabaptist tradition itself was a persecuted minority within the Church precisely because of this position. On the other hand, to varying degrees both the Catholic and the main strands of the Protestant Reformation (Lutheran and Calvinist) in varying degrees accepted this alliance as proper and necessary. With the acceptance of the linkage between Church and State as providential came the implication that unquestioning obedience to Christ requires obedience to the state. To be sure there were various qualifications on this obedience. Both Aquinas and later Calvin, for instance, allow for revolt against unjust rulers under very specific conditions. Luther, however, took the most extreme position, suggesting that in fact under no conditions is revolt permissible. That extreme ethic of obedience goes a long way toward explaining both the passive and active cooperation of the churches with the Nazis. But even in its less extreme Catholic and Calvinist forms the presumption is still on the side of obedience to the state.[42]

The key scripture which seems to have promoted this occurs in Paul's letter to the Romans:

> Let everyone obey the authorities that are over him, for there is no authority except from God, and all authority that exists is established by God. As a consequence, the man who opposes authority rebels against the ordinance of God; those who resist thus shall draw condemnation down upon themselves. Rulers cause no fear when a man does what is right but only when his conduct is evil. Do you wish to be free from the fear of authority? Do what is right and you will gain its approval, for the ruler is God's servant to work for your good. Only if you do wrong ought you to be afraid. It is not without purpose that the ruler carries the sword; he is God's servant, to inflict his avenging wrath upon the wrongdoer. You must obey, then, not only to escape punishment but also for conscience' sake. You pay taxes for the same reason, magistrates being God's ministers who devote themselves to his service with unremitting care. Pay each one his due: taxes to whom taxes are due; toll to whom toll is due; respect and honor to everyone who deserves them (Romans 13:1-7).

Such as statement, carrying the weight of scriptural status, especially from one as prominent in the Christian tradition as Paul, naturally promoted an identification between obedience to God in Christ and obedience to Caesar, that is, the state. And it is this statement that Luther appeals to in formulating his extreme position in response to the peasant revolts of his time. The peasants it seems responded favorably to Luther's message of the freedom, equality and dignity they had in Christ. They felt encouraged by it to revolt against the nobility whom they believed abused and ignored their freedom, equality and dignity. Luther was then forced to clarify his position on the two kingdoms through which God rules the world: the spiritual inner kingdom of God ruled through the Church and the outer physical kingdoms of the world ruled through his established rulers. Through the first God rules with the *right hand of love and compassion* and through the second God rules with the *left hand of justice and wrath*. The freedom of the Gospel, it seems, is only and inner spiritual freedom. The equality of all in Christ is only to be realized in the next life. Here in this world there can never be equality, God acts through the state to establish order and everyone one must learn to accept there assigned place in the social order. Only God can establish rulers and only God can remove rulers. It is not permissible for human beings to revolt, even against a vicious and unjust ruler.

Luther did express some sympathy for the plight of the peasants and considered the German Princes to be corrupt. In *Admonition to Peace* addressed to the German Bishops and Princes he declares "in your temporal government, you do nothing but flay and rob your subjects, in order that you may lead a life of splendor."[43] And yet he did not think it permissible for the peasants to seek to overthrow these authorities established by God. When the revolt began he issued another pamphlet, *Against the Robbing and Murdering Hordes of Peasants,* which reminded the German Princes that they were to be the instruments of God's wrath and so he counseled them that "any man against whom sedition can be proved is outside the law of God and the Empire, so that the first who can slay him is doing right and well... For rebellion ... makes widows and orphans, and turns everything upside down.... Therefore let everyone who can, smite, slay, and stab, secretly or openly, remembering that nothing can be more poisonous, hurtful, or devilish than a rebel. It is just when one must kill a mad dog; if you do not strike him he will strike you, and a whole land with you...".[44] This infamous event confirms the underlying conservatism of Luther's Gospel which set the tone of church - state relations in the history of Germany. The model of faith as obedience to God and the rulers of this world which emerges here sets the Church on a dead-end path, a path in which Christian faith and ethics self-destructs in the death camps.

A full account of the propensity to affirm the duty and obligation of obedience to the state in Germany would have to include more than an appeal to this tradition of interpretation of Christian faith and ethics. One would have to deal with the history of Germany and the European conspiracy to keep Germany divided and weak since the time the Protestant - Catholic wars in the aftermath of the Reformation. And then there is the psychological repercussions from the Napoleanic conquest and ignominious defeat in World War I and the burgeoning nationalism that was emerging in the 19th century as Germany belatedly struggled for the status of a nation-state with an almost obsessive need to compensate for its previous history of humiliation, etc. I do not want to suggest a one factor explanation of history, least of all of this specific slice of history. But I do want to isolate an important factor in that history - the role of religion. And I do want to know why the Church failed. And I want to learn what the Church needs to do differently.

In addition to the factors of the myth of supersession and the teachings of contempt, and in addition to the reduction of faith to unquestioning obedience, there is a least one other component to the religious dimension of Christian apostasy during the Holocaust. Christian faith has not only been an unquestioning faith but it has assumed that it somehow has exclusive rights to God. It is as if the doctrine of the Incarnation, i.e., of the Word of God become flesh in the person of Jesus, somehow gave exclusive ownership of God to Christians. In this claim Christians have shown themselves to be, in some important and fundamental respects, one with their pagan forbearers in the history of anti-Semitism.

It is common to divide anti-Semitism into two types: sociological and religious. The first is thought to be due to the clash of cultures in which Judaism insists on retaining its distinctive culture and traditions which the larger culture takes as an offense to its assumptions of "superiority". This is supposed to typify pagan, especially Hellenistic, anti-Semitism. The second, religious anti-Semitism, is said to be due to the specific Christological religious claims of Christianity and tied to myth of supersession. In fact, I believe that while there are important differences between them, the anti-Judaism or anti-Semitism of pre-Christian pagans, that of Christians and of neo-pagan/neo-Christian Nazis are all fundamentally religious, and as such exhibit similar sociological characteristics. All three types exhibit a fundamental rage at the sheer existence of the Jew as one who is "other," or "alien" or a "stranger" who does not conform to their world.

In the pre-modern world Jews refused to assimilate and be conformed to the world around them. The refusal of the Jew to assimilate lead pagan and Christian alike to a violent rage against the Jew, because the "otherness" of the Jew reminded them that what is truly sacred, or holy or transcendent cannot be owned by them. God cannot be domesticated. The existence of the Jew has reminded the pagan and Christian alike that God's ways are not the same as their ways. The existence of the Jew reminded the Hellenist or the Christian or the Nazi that perhaps their truth, their values, their way of life was not final, true and ultimate. The very existence of the Jew called their values and way of life into question and hinted at a God who might very well call them into question. In the world of the Holocaust, the existence of the Jew was a burdening reminder of "faithfulness" to the Christian conscience of those who preached the value of not being conformed to the world but practiced conformity to the world of Nazi values,- a reminder Christians were only to happy to have out of site and out of mind.

In the Nazi period this rage against the Jewish witness to transcendence escalated to a point of no return. The religious rage masked itself in the myth of race which made assimilation as a "final solution" an impossible option. Hence the Nazis turned to genocide. But make no mistake about it, the rage against the Jew (whether pagan, Christian or Nazi) is a scarcely disguised rage against the God of transcendence, the God who cannot be used to legitimate Christian hegemony or Nazi hegemony, the God who cannot be owned or used for the political and ideological purposes of the will to power. The God who is the limit of all conformity to this world. **The attempted genocide of the Jews is a thinly disguised attempt at the deicide of God, in which the perpetrators have all too typically projected their own motives onto the victims as a justification for their own actions.**

Christians need not have been so deeply implicated in the Nazi program of genocide against the Jews. Christians should not have been so deeply implicated in the "final solution." Christians should have stood firmly against Hitler and with the Jews. But given that Christians were in fact deeply implicated, the question to be addressed is - What needs to be changed in Christianity so as to prevent that kind of complicity with evil from occurring again. My analysis of the history of two kinds of faith and ethics embodied in the histories of Judaism and Christianity is meant to suggest where the problem lies in the Christian tradition and why. And having established that, to suggest what Christians might learn from Jews about faith and ethics, so as to reconstruct Christian faith and ethics in order to better live up to its own best ideals. In a post-Holocaust world there is a need for a chastened Christianity to link arms with a determined Jewish people in a common strategy to defeat the powers of darkness which threaten to bring down a final and permanent holocaust upon us all.

Starting Over: Christian Faith and Ethics After Auschwitz

"This day I set before you life or death, blessing or curse. Choose life, so that you and your descendants may live, in the love of the Lord your God, obeying his voice, clinging to him; for in this your life consists..." (Deuteronomy 30:19&20).

The Need for a New Beginning

Hitler has been defeated, but like the beast in the book of Revelation which seemed to be slain and was not and so reappeared, new Hitler's could appear once more. We live in a world in which new Hitler's are possible. Still the defeat of Hitler is a reprieve and Christians have been given a chance to repent of their past, a chance to make a new beginning. Once more Christians are offered the choice - life or death and encouraged to choose life.

But unlike Jews, who have found a strand of continuity with their past through the traditions of chutzpa, which gives them life and enables them to go on, I do not think we Christians have fully faced up to the moral problem of continuity with pre-Holocaust Christianity. Pre-Holocaust Christianity is an obscenity. Full continuity with that tradition is fundamentally immoral. The only excuse for continuing that tradition of "faith as unquestioning obedience," linked to the myth of supersession might be ignorance. But in our world ignorance is inexcusable and fatal.

Any form of Christianity, as I have argued elsewhere,[45] which is to survive Auschwitz must pass through the fires of Auschwitz which stand in judgment of pre-Holocaust Christianity. As Irving Greenberg has succinctly put it, after Auschwitz: **"No statement, theological or otherwise, should be made that would not be credible in the presence of the burning children."**[46] Minimally, what this means is that all traces of the supersession myth must be removed from Christian teaching and preaching and the authenticity of the ongoing covenant of the Jews must be affirmed. To accept the authenticity of the Jewish/Mosaic covenant means that Christians will have to accept that there are others who belong to God in their own right - that Christians have no monopoly on God through Jesus. Finally the understanding of Christian faith and ethics grounded in *unquestioning obedience* must be reexamined and reformulated in the light of the lessons of history. Christian's too ought to hear a commanding voice from Auschwitz, a voice of judgment demanding a *metanoia*, that is, a change of heart or a turning around (conversion).

In this paper I have chosen to tackle one strand of the reconstruction that needs to take place - the reconstruction of the understanding of faith and its ethical implications. In the light of the Christian apostasy at the time of the Holocaust, I do not see any way to go back to the Christian understanding of faith as unquestioning trust and obedience. That option has proven itself spiritually and morally bankrupt. From faith as obedience came an ethic of obedience to Caesar as if to God. And from that came a loss of transcendence. The Christian church was no longer *in but not of* the world. Instead it came to be conformed to the world and a *negative witness* to the transcendence of God. The irony is that the very church which developed the theory that Jews were, by their homeless wandering, a *negative witness* to the truth of Christianity turns out to have grasped the truth in reverse. It is the Jews who have been faithful, *in but not of* the world, and Christians who have become the embodiment of the *negative witness*.

What is required is a little humility on the part of Christians. Christians must be willing to learn from their Jewish brothers and sisters, - to learn the full meaning of faith in the biblical tradition, faith as a living covenant, a dialectical and dialogical covenant characterized by the paradoxical tension of trust and chutzpa. After Auschwitz, Irving Greenberg suggests, there is no refuge to be found in either the sacred or the secular. Rather, as in the tradition of chutzpa, both God and man must be called into question for the sake of God's creation, especially in order to protect the human dignity of every person as created in the image of God. The test of authentic faith after Auschwitz lies in the deed. God's witnesses are those who act to protect the human dignity and equality of every person. I am convinced that, had the understanding of faith among Christians been that of chutzpa, the apostasizing Christians during the Holocaust would have been a minority rather than a majority. Christians who have, historically, all too often taken faith to be an unquestioning trust in and obedience to both the sacred (God) and the secular (state) would have been prepared to question both. And they would have been prepared to act on behalf of God's creation and against Hitler and the god of the Deutsch Christians.

The world can no longer afford the luxury of unquestioning faith. Unquestioning faith is pagan faith. Unquestioning faith is a nearly universal characteristic of religion throughout the world. Virtually all forms of religion have asked followers to sacrifice their will and surrender themselves to a higher reality. And all faith that asks for a total surrender of will is finally, not only pagan but demonic, even if it is faith in Jesus or the God of Jesus. For all such faith is a training ground in fanaticism which blurs the distinction between God and the state and leads to the dehumanization of the *chosen* victims of the state. The only authentic faith is a questioning faith, a faith prepared to call even God into question. The difference between God and the idol is that idols will brook no dissent. The test of authentic faith is the possibility of dissent against **all authority** in the name of a human dignity which reflects the image of God.

Starting Over

The way back to authentic faith, for Christians, is a difficult one, because it is not morally possible to embrace so much of the pre-Holocaust traditions of Christianity. If it is the case, for example, that the Gospel itself teaches a faith of unquestioning obedience, how can Christians legitimately embrace an understanding of faith as chutzpa without abandoning their identity as Christians?

The answer to that question is threefold.

First, the Christian who would seek to preserve his or her identity will lose it, whereas the Christian who is prepared to lose his or her identity, for Christ's sake, shall find it (Matthew 16:25) .

Second, in the Gospel stories of Jesus we still have an echo of the tradition of chutzpa, even though, for the most part, it seems to have been suppressed as Christianity left the Jewish and entered the gentile world. There are two parables in Luke's Gospel which suggest that chutzpa was part of the tradition on the teachings of Jesus. In Luke 11:1-13, Jesus tells a parable about a man who knocks on a friends door in the middle of the night and asks for a loaf of bread and refuses to leave until he gets it. The lesson of this parable, we are told is that one should pray to God with unrelenting persistence, demanding that God listen. If one is demanding enough, God will hear and respond. In a similar parable in chapter 18:1-8, Jesus tells of a widow who took her case before an uncaring judge and won by wearing the judge down with persistence, for the judge reasoned "I am going to settle in her favor or she will end by doing me violence." The lesson Jesus draws from this is: "Will not God then do justice to his chosen who call out to him day and night?" One could also turn to the dying words of Jesus on the cross. Usually Christians prefer to think of the last words in Luke's Gospel "Into your hands I commend my spirit" (Luke 23:46) or John's final words "It is finished" (John 19:30) where the tone is much more in accord with the image of a Jesus as trusting and obedient even unto death on the cross. But in the earlier Gospels of Mark and Matthew the final words are - "My God, My God why have you forsaken me" (Mttw 27:46 and Mark 15:34). If one remembers that these were believed to be the very last words of Jesus by the early Christian communities that gave rise to these Gospels their impact can be rather startling. This is not a submissive Jesus but a Jesus who challenges God and calls God into question with his dying breath. Nevertheless, the tradition of chutzpa in the Gospel is such a slender thread that I doubt it can bear the whole weight of what is required.

Third, the appropriation of the tradition of faith as chutzpa can only succeed as long as Christians continue to reject the paganizing and gnostic teachings of Marcion who, in the early Church, tried to reject the teachings of the Tanak (Old Testament) and base Christianity on edited selections from Luke and Paul. The Gnostic tradition sought to oppose the savior God of the gentile Christians to the creator God of the Jews, suggesting that the latter was the source of evil while the former was the source of good. Early Christianity rejected those teachings as heresy and insisted that the creator God and the savior God are one and the same, that the God of Abraham and the God of Jesus are the same. The tradition of faith as chutzpa is available to Christians because they share a common heritage with the Jews. It was the Deutsch Christians who wanted to reject that common heritage in favor of an Aryan Jesus. A post-Holocaust Christian faith will see the glaring error of that strategy and will learn to reaffirm the unity of tradition between Jews and Christians, but with the humility, this time, to allow that perhaps Jews have a better understanding of that common tradition since it is theirs first. An exclusively New Testament faith is not a Christian faith but a gnostic and neo-Nazi paganizing faith. As Krister Stendahl puts it, the Tanak or "Old Testament" is a book for the "long haul."[47] Without it, the faith of the New Testament becomes truncated and short sighted. A New Testament faith is in inadequate, only a Biblical faith will do. And if that is the case, then Jews do indeed have something to teach Christians about the paradoxical complexity of faith as a dialectic and dialogue of trust and chutzpa.

Whether Jews feel they have any reason to teach Christians the meaning of faith is another question, one a Christian cannot answer. But one can hope they might be persuaded, for historically the kind of Christian faith that has been most hazardous to the health and well being of Jews has been precisely the gnosticizing kind, the kind which was prepared to cut all ties to the Jewish tradition.

Chutzpa as the Foundation of Post-Holocaust Social Ethics: Problems and Prospects

While the theme of wrestling with God has not been predominant in the Christian understanding of faith, it has not been entirely absent either. However the way it has been used typically tends to subvert rather than utilize the ethical potential of this theme. Simply appealing to this understanding of faith does not guarantee that it will result in an ethic of chutzpa. In fact, one should take it as an axiom of Christian ethics that if an ethical norm can be subverted it will be. Thus in order to suggest the appropriate application of this norm, I will first point out two abuses of it and then suggest what I believe to be an authentic use of chutzpa, a mean between these extremes. These typical forms of abuse are :1) psychological individualism and 2) political collectivism.

Authentic wrestling with God occurs within the context of a community and tradition which promotes individuality and moral autonomy. Such a community stands in tension with the wider society, yet is committed to the dignity of all human beings, within and beyond that community, so much so that it is prepared to call God into question in the name of God's creation and the image of God in all persons, especially the stranger. The abuse of the *wrestling* theme occurs when the tense link (i.e., being *in but not of* this society) between the community and the larger world is replaced by a conjunction between *individualism* and *collectivism* which makes the collective norms of society final and ultimate. It is these contrasting options which need to be explored in this concluding section.

Wrestling with God: Luther's Psychological Individualism

Probably the most common use of the theme of wrestling with God in Christianity is in the literature on spirituality and the inner life. Here wrestling with God is typically reduced to a psychological inner struggle between God and the inner self or soul almost to the exclusion of concern for and commitment to the well being of the whole of creation beyond the self. It is appropriate to our subject matter to use Martin Luther as an example here. Luther's thought and experience have had a profound impact of the Western philosophical-psychological tradition, both religious and secular. He stands in a venerable tradition which can be traced from Plato through Augustine to Luther and beyond, culminating in the work of Kierkegaard and Nietzsche. In this tradition God is seen, from Augustine's *Confessions* onward, as seeking out the individual and acting upon him or her inwardly through the emotions. Augustine interprets the inner struggle of his life as a kind of wrestling and quarreling with God. He feels torn between God and the world, in which he is drawn first toward one and then the other. The struggle is finally over when he surrenders his will to God and is turned around (*conversio*), away from the world and toward God. Conversion occurs at the moment of surrender of self **when God is the victor.**[48] Luther stands in this Augustinian tradition, in which God wounds in order heal and slays in order to give life.[49] God can appear as the enemy who attacks the self but only for the purpose of bringing about a conversion, a transformation, a surrender of will - at which point God the enemy reveals himself as God the redeemer. In Luther these two sides of the *God experience* almost split in two. At times Luther's volatile psychological experience of God borders on a Gnosticism which splits God into two Gods - one of wrath and the other of love. I say almost, because I think Luther does hold these two sides together, but barely so. For Luther faith is a paradox that begins with the paradox of the two sides of God. According to Luther:

> Faith has to do with things which are not seen [Heb. 11:1]. Thus that there may be room for faith, everything which is believed must be concealed; but it cannot be more deeply concealed than under the contrary appearance, sensation and experience. Thus when God brings to life, he does it by killing; when he justifies, he does it by making guilty; when he exalts to heaven, he does it by leading to hell... Thus he conceals his eternal goodness and mercy under eternal anger, his righteousness under unrighteousness.... The outward appearance of grace is as though it were pure anger, so deeply is it

> concealed .... Thus even to ourselves it always seems as though God wishes to abandon us and not keep his word, and that he is beginning to be a liar in our hearts. And finally, God cannot be God unless he first becomes a devil and we cannot go to heaven unless we first go into hell, and cannot become the children of God, unless we first become the Devil's children... But the world's lies in their turn cannot become lies unless they first become the truth, and the godless do not go down into hell, unless they have first been to heaven, and do not become the Devil's children unless they have first been the children of God. And finally the Devil becomes and is no Devil, unless he has first been God... We have spoken in extreme terms of this, and we must understand what is just as startling, that God's grace and truth, or his goodness and faithfulness, rule over us and demand our obedience... For a little while I must accord divinity to the Devil, and consider our God to be the Devil. But this does not mean that the evening lasts for the whole day. Ultimately, his steadfast love and faithfulness are over us [Ps. 117:2].[50]

This is a very powerful statement of religious experience. But when it is placed in the context of the total structure of Luther's theology it is clear that this kind of wrestling with God is a form of psychological individualism, whose purpose, as in Augustine, is to finally bring the individual into submission to the will of God. In this wrestling match it is God who is the victor, God who prevails, and the individual person who comes to surrender his or her will to the one who "rule[s] over us and demand[s] our obedience". When this psychological experience is placed within the context of Luther's two kingdoms theology, which forbids the individual to intervene in the social order, even when rulers are unjust, it is clear that this kind of wrestling with God will not give rise to chutzpa, to the questioning of authority; sacred or secular. Its final outcome will be submission to the will of the God who rules over the world with his left-handed wrathful side and over the Church with his right-handed compassionate and forgiving side. God's will must finally be respected and obeyed as it is expressed through both "hands" - through both the church and the state. In this model *wrestling with God* has been reduced to psychological individualism. Wrestling with God does not lead to championing the world, against God if necessary - on the contrary, one can safely ignore the world and concentrate on one's individual relationship to God and one's individual salvation. The ethic implied in this model of faith leads to quietism and conservatism in the social realm, and to an ethic of duty as unquestioning obedience to the responsibilities of one's station in life.

Wrestling with God: Emmanuel Hirsch's Political Collectivism

Individualism and Collectivism are two sides of the same coin. A nation of individuals, having no intermediate mediating communities with distinctive traditions and values, between the individual and the state, is a collectivist society in which the criterion of dignity and equality is *sameness*. In such societies the primary crime will be *differentness* - the differentness of a community with an alternative scale of values which refuses to be assimilated. Such communities function as a limit on the authority of the state and represent a threat to the security of the collectivist identity. As a result collectivist societies will always try to control, suppress and, if possible, eliminate such communities. Psychological individualism and political collectivism are mutually reinforcing identity structures which relate in the manner of Descarte's two worlds of unextended and extended substances or Kant's noumenal and phenomenal worlds, or in the manner described by Luther's *two-kingdoms* theology. That is, they function as two correlated but mutually unobstructive worlds. As Luther once put it, it is possible for a Christian to be both a hangman, expressing God's judging wrath in society by executing its criminals, and at the same time a loving, forgiving and compassionate Christian in one's personal life.[51] These two realms are structured in such a way as to guarantee that they will not interfere with each other and in such a way as to mutually reinforce each other. They break apart and enervate the tense *unity in diversity* of life which is held together by an ethic of chutzpa rooted in compassion for the created world and the image of God in all persons. In a collectivist society, those who are not *the same* (e.g, Aryan, in Nazi collectivist society) are not considered human but less than human (e.g., *tiermensch* or *animalpersons* as the Nazis called Jews). And all who are defined as outside the human community are therefore outside the community of moral obligation. In such a world it is possible to spend your days fulfilling your obligation to society in an unquestioning ethic of duty, gassing Jews and other *aliens* who are *different* and return home to be a loving father or mother to ones children, and a concerned neighbor and citizen among those who are the *same*.

Thus the theology of Emmanuel Hirsch *(1888-1972)*, a leading theologian of the Nazi sympathizing Deutsch *Christians*, with its Aryan collectivist tendencies, fits very well into the Lutheran ethos of Nazi Germany and with the private psychological angst of Luther's subjectivist piety. For the characterization of Hirsch's theology, I am indebted to the recent fine study of *Theologians Under Hitler* by Robert P. Erickson[52] In 1933 "Hitler named Chaplain Ludwig Müller (1883-1945) as his special 'Plenipotentiary for questions on the Protestant Churches.' Hirsch immediately became a major backer and advisor to Müller and remained so through the struggles of the months ahead."[53] He became a leading spokesman for the Deutsch Christian movement and against the Confessing Church in which Karl Barth was a major figure and his chief opponent. In 1937 he became an official member of the Nazi Party. For six years, during Nazi rule, he was Dean of the theological faculty at the University of Göttingen. After the war, at age 57 in 1945, he was forced into retirement because of his associations with the Nazi party. During his years of teaching he was considered the leading scholar on Kierkegaard, producing a classic work on his thought in 1933.

As Hirsch develops his theology from the onset of WWI through his forced retirement in 1945, the concept of Volk played an important and integrating role. He distrusts all ecumenical internationalism as artificial and finds the German Volk to be the natural and proper vehicle for the Church and the Gospel. The Gospel and belief in God, he said, "sharpens in our conscience the law and the duty to do and to suffer everything for our own *Volk* and our own state, without regard for our own person."[54] In good Lutheran (and Catholic) fashion he argues that the church provides the moral order which the state needs and the state provides the political order needed for the spread of the Gospel. The Jews, on the other hand, are a foreign race with a foreign history who tried to disguise their *differences* and infiltrate the German Volk. Judaism is a legalistic religion of an alien people. Only Christianity is a religion founded upon a free, personal and individual relationship to God. Indeed since Jesus came from Galilee "according to all the rules of scientific probability, Jesus was of non-Jewish blood"[55] and his teachings were not Jewish teachings. All this fits well with Hirsch's insistence that the ethic of obedience in Christianity fits naturally with the hierarchical ethos of the German Volk (Hirsch distrusts the artificial equality that democratic regimes try to create) and the natural destiny of the white or Aryan races to rule history. Hirsch sees Hitler's coming to power as a fateful and providential moment in this history. And he is grateful to the Nazis for bringing to an end the never ending questions and debate that plagued modern Enlightenment culture. In response to Freiderich Gogarten, who insisted that "'the final word in religion is the question,' Hirsch insists that his theology and concept of ethics and conscience are based upon *knowledge.*"[56] Faith, it seems, is an affirmation in the "absoluteness" of God beyond all questions and questioning, for "where the invisible is grasped by conscience, there grows an obedience which is ready courageously and unselfishly to wander the long toilsome path of suffering resistance, which alone can lead our Volk again up the heights."[57]

All of this is what we might expect from a Nazi and a Deutsch Christian. But what has it to do with our theme of wrestling with God and the ethics of chutzpa? The answer is, that as early as 1914, Hirsch did allow that there was one kind of questioning that was permissible. In the early days of WWI, Hirsch preached a sermon on Genesis 32:22-32, Jacob wrestling with the stranger. In this sermon war is depicted as an unavoidable part of history used by God for his purposes. And "all the sacrifices of possessions and blood are nothing but the attempt to force from God a decision in our favor; [if] we do not leave him alone, then he will bless us."[58] Indeed, "where great things are at stake, where it involves what role a Volk shall play in world history in the future ... there it would be immoral, unfaithful, and cowardly to give in.... War is a judgment of God, but a Volk has the right to demand this judgment of God only if it is ready, if necessary, to bleed to death in this war."[59]

Six years later, Hirsch returned to this theme in his book *Deutschlands Schicksal,* where he describes war as a "question to God." The "God of history ... blesses only those ... who set all their power and will on their freedom and their life goals. He does not listen to a Volk which questions only half-heartedly, which does not struggle for its life seriously and to the ultimate degree."[60] Moreover "If war truly is a question to God, yes, a struggle with God, which strikes investigatively at the main pillars of the national being, then it is an inconceivably hazardous undertaking. On can only justify it if one carries it through to the end, if one does not leave God alone until he gives his blessing. Fighting a lukewarm war, without the will to do and sacrifice everything, seems to me to be also a religious crime."[61]

Here we have it. The other end of the spectrum of the Christian use of the them of wrestling and chutzpa. If Luther subjectivized it, Hirsch objectivizes it and turns it into a political/collectivist parable for the legitimation of war on the part of nation-states in general and the destiny of the Volkish state in particular. Unlike Luther's wrestling with God, Hirsch's wrestling does issue in an ethic of chutzpa, but it is a counterfeit ethic. It is not an ethic which arises out of compassion for the suffering of God's creation to challenge God in the name of God. It is not an ethic which defends the image of God in every person. It is rather a collectivist ethic for the justification of the ascendency of the Aryan Volk over and against all others, but especially over and against the Jews. This ethic is not a demand for justice but a thinly veiled disguise for the will to power. Hirsch's definition of faith as *wrestling with God* is counterfeit because he is not wrestling with the God who is the limit to every state but rather with a god who has been domesticated for the purposes of legitimating the German Volk. Hirsch's God is not the God of transcendence but a ***negative*** *witness* to transcendence.

Beyond Individualism and Collectivism:
Chutzpa/Wrestling with God as the Foundation for Post-Holocaust Social Ethics

Both the psychological-individualist and the political-collectivist interpretations deviate from the authentic use of chutzpa because they fail to hold individuality and community in a tense paradoxical unity. What holds the individual in unity with the community is compassion for God's creation. This compassion is rooted in a recognition of the image of God in all persons and is prepared to call into question all authority, sacred (i.e., God) or secular (i.e., the state) which would abuse that transcendent dignity.

In the case of Luther, wrestling with God is reduced to a personal drama cut off from the social dimension of compassion. As a result it ends not in an ethic of chutzpa but an ethic of obedient submission. In the case of Hirsch wrestling with God has a social dimension and does terminate in an ethic of chutzpa, but it is a *counterfeit chutzpa*, because it is not the expression of a compassion rooted in a recognition of the image of God in every person but in the arrogance which demands special privileges - namely the right of the white Aryan race to rule over others. Just as Luther's wrestling with God has no place for the community, Hirsch's collectivism cannot deal with the value of individuals. For Hirsch individuals are expendable. The ethic of obedience makes noble the sacrificing of one's self, not for other persons but for *the race*, *the Volk*. Only the Volk or Aryan race has value. Individuals have value only by virtue of *sameness* (i.e., being Aryan) as opposed to difference. Those who are different must be expelled or eliminated. Unlike the ethic of Judaism, there is no room in Hirsch's ethic for welcoming the stranger or the alien.

An authentic ethic of chutzpa is rooted in the experience of community as the context for the promotion and sustaining of unique individuality which comes to expression in the compassion for the other, the alien or the stranger. When Christianity separated itself from Judaism and became a gentile religion it seems to have lost its capacity to accept the alien or the stranger as *different*. The stranger could only be welcomed as a potential convert to *sameness*. The stranger who remained a stranger within Christendom was like a nagging reminder, an implicit question, as to whether one could really have a monopoly on God. The stranger, if one really accepted him or her as an image of God, would require one to affirm that God really was transcendent and did not really belong to one's Volk. The stranger is a reminder that God cannot be domesticated. The ascendancy of Christianity over the Roman empire from Constantine (313 C.E.) to Theodosius (381 C.E.) was marked by a movement from tolerance to intolerance of the stranger. From the time of Theodosius Christianity became the only legal religion of the empire. All others were legally suppressed. Henceforth there were to be no strangers in the land. The audacity of Jewish people was twofold. First they refused to disappear or assimilate as did the pagans. And then to add insult to injury, the Jews insisted on the continuing validity of their own election and covenant as prior to and apart from the gentile covenant through Jesus. Jews insisted on remaining a witness to the transcendence of God by being *in but not of* the Christian world. But Christians insisted on an unconditional surrender of will to Christ **and** the empire. They insisted that faith was conformity to the world, once "Christianized." Intolerant of the transcendence of God (for after all God was now Emmanuel , that is, "God with us" gentiles), Christians accused the Jews of the very thought they were harboring in their breast - deicide. In the moment when the Jew was excluded from membership in Christendom, the path was opened which leads from deicide to genocide. And once Nietzsche, that favorite philosopher of the Nazis, had pronounced the death of God as official it was not long before the the attempted genocide of the Jew, the last reminder of God's transcendence, followed.

There can be no ethic of chutzpa in pre-holocaust Christianity because that kind of Christianity could only be a *negative witness* to the transcendence of God. The whole of Deutsch Christianity and of the Nazi program of the Holocaust is a such *negative witness*, a witness to the bestiality of human beings who are incapable of chutzpa because they are incapable of recognizing the image of God in anyone, others or themselves, and hence are incapable of the compassion and moral outrage necessary for an ethic of chutzpa. When human beings no longer live in awe of their being created in the image of the God who is without image, they resort to defining the indefinable. Instead of awe and questions before the wonder of the human, the Nazis and the Deutsch Christians knew what the human was and clearly defined it - the human is *the same as* Aryan. And they knew that those who were not Aryan, those who were *different*, were not human and therefore beyond the realm of moral obligation. And they knew who God was also, he was "god with us" - the Aryan Jesus. As Hirsch's theology suggests, the Nazi Deutsch Christians preferred a theology of answers to a faith rooted in transcendence and questioning. They preferred a theology of unquestioning obedience and a surrender of will to the Aryan Christ and his messianic precursor, Hitler. What is most sad is that even the confessing Church who stood in opposition to Deutsch Christians had more in common with them than they should have. The whole history of Christianity has too much in common with the Deutsch Christians. Pre-Holocaust Christianity is an obscenity. Not enough of Marcion's Gnostic heresy was rejected and far too much was retained.

The burning question that now remains is, can Christianity be de-paganized. Can it abandon the religiosity of unquestioning obedience and surrender of will? Can it return to its roots in Judaism to relearn the meaning of faith as *trust and chutzpa*, of faith as an affirmation of transcendence? Christians will know they have recovered that faith when, in their teaching and preaching, and especially in their actions, they are able to joyfully affirm the continuing presence of their Jewish brothers and sisters as "other" than themselves and a true sign of God's transcending presence. Christian ethics will have earned the right to the practice of chutzpa when the stranger and the alien is finally welcomed as a neighbor to be loved as ones' self. For it is out of that compassion that the ethic of chutzpa will emerge as a common ethic of Jews and Christians, and other strangers and aliens, against the dark forces that would lure humanity into yet another and even more engulfing Holocaust.

NOTES

[1] Rosemary Ruether cites this story from Hitler's *Tabletalk* in her book *Faith and Fratracide* (New York: Seabury Press, 1979), pp. 223 & 224.
[2] Darrell Fasching "Can Christian Faith Survive Auschwitz" *Horizons* Vol. 12 #1, Spring 1985.
[3] "Hutzpa K'lapei Shamaya: A Christian Response to the Jewish Tradition of Arguing with God," by Belden C. Lane in *The Journal of Ecumenical Studies*, Vol.23 #4, Fall 1986, p. 567 & 568. Throughout this paper I have standardized the spelling of *chutzpa* with a *ch* and modified quotations from Lane accordingly. Another source which is extremely helpful on the subject chutzpa is Mordechai Rotenberg's *Dialogue with Deviance: The Hasidic Ethic and the Theory of Social Contraction*. (Philadelphia: Institute for the Study of Human Issues, 1983). Although this work is not directly quoted in this paper, it was very helpful to me in thinking through the implications of this theme.
[4] Ibid., p. 17.
[5] "Abraham, Isaac and the Jewish Tradition: An Ethical Reappraisal," in *The Journal of Religious Ethics,* Vol. 10 #1, Spring 1982, p. 9.
[6] Jacob Neusner, *Invitation to the Talmud* (New York: Harper & Row, 1973), p. xviii.
[7] From the Babylonian Talmud, tract Baba Metzia, IV, 59b cited by Raphael Patai in *Gates to the Old City* (New York: Avon Books, 1980), pp. 244-245 and quoted in "Hutzpa K'Lapei Shamaya: A Christian Response to the Jewish Tradition of Arguing with God" by Belden Lane in *The Journal of Ecumenical Studies*, Vol. 23 #4, Fall 1986.
[8]. Patai, *Gates of the City* cited in "Hutzpa K'Lapei Shamaya" by Lane, p. 581.
[9] Emil Fackenheim *God's Presence in History* (New York: Harper & Row, 1970), p. 73.
[10] Ibid., p. 76.
[11] Fackenheim, p. 84.
[12] Elie Wiesel, *A Jew Today* (New York: Random House, 1978), p. 6.
[13] Ibid.
[14] Ibid., pp. 146 & 147.
[15] Elie Wiesel *The Trial of God* (New York: Schocken Books, 1979).
[16] Ibid., p. 131 & 132.
[17] Ibid. p. 157.
[18] Ibid., p. 154.
[19] Ibid., p. 161.
[20] Ibid., From the introduction entitled *The Scene*.
[21] Robert McAfee Brown *Elie Wiesel: Messenger to All Humanity* (Notre Dame: University of Notre Dame Press, 1983), p. 154.
[22] Richard Rubenstein "Homeland and Holocaust," in *The Religious Situation 1968* (Boston: Beacon Press, 1969), pp. 39-111 quoted in: Irving Greenberg "Cloud of Smoke, Pillar of Fire: Judaism, Christianity, and Modernity after the Holocaust" in *Auschwitz: Beginning of a New Era?* edited by Eva Fleischner (1977: KTAV Publishing House, 1977).
[23] Greenberg, p. 26.
[24] Greenberg, p. 38.
[25] Greenberg, p. 40.
[26] Greenberg, p. 47.
[27] Greenberg, p. 49ff.
[28] Franklin Littell *The Crucifixion of the Jews* (New York: Harper & Row, 1975), p. 44.
[29] Littell, 46.
[30] Littell, p. 51, quoting Bonhoeffer *No Rusty Swords*, p. 226.
[31] Helen Fein, *Accounting for Genocide* (Chicago: University of Chicago Press, 1979), p. 90.

32 Sarah Gordon's *Hitler, Germans and the Jewish Question* (Princeton: Princeton University Press, 1984) also confirms this. See especially chapter eight, *The Attitudes of the Churches.*
33 Fein, p. 67.
34 Fein, p. 71.
35 Fein, p. 92.
36 Fein, p. 94 & 95.
37 Gordon, p. 255.
38 Littell, p. 50.
39 "Objective and Subjective Inhibitants in the German Resistance to Hitler" by William Sheridan Allen in *The German Church Struggle and the Holocaust* (Detroit: Wayne State University Press, 1974), p. 122.
40 Fein, p. 94.
41 Gordon, p. 260.
42 This correlation cannot be the whole explanation, I admit. Other variables can hinder or promote this correlation. Fein's study indicates that resistance to Hitler was greatest in those states which had been in existence the longest and in which Church and state worked together against Hitler. On the other hand, those states most recently created and where the Church had a history of open anti-Semitism, most readily cooperated with Hitler. Undoubtedly there are complex variables to be to be accounted for in each specific situation. Nevertheless, the total level of Church resistance was so low and the total complicity so high that I believe the Christian ethic of obedience must be seen as a major variable.
43 Cited by Will Durant in *The Reformation* (New York: Simon and Schuster, 1957), p. 386.
44 Ibid., p. 390.
45 Darrell J. Fasching, "Can Christian Faith Survive Auschwitz?" in *Horizons* Vol. 12 #1, Spring 1985.
46 Greenberg, p. 23.
47 Krister Stendahl "The Jewish People in Christian Preaching: A Protestant Perspective" in *The Jewish People in Christian Preaching* edited by Darrell J. Fasching (New York and Toronto: Edwin Mellen Press, 1984), p. 73.
48 See my article, "Mythic Story and the Formation of Personal Identity in Augustine's Confessions" in *The Florida Speech Communication Journal* Vol 15, #1, 1987.
49 Augustine, *Confessions* Book II, chapter 2, translated by Rex Werner (New York: Mentor - Omega Books, 1963), p.42.
50 Quotations from Luther's collected works cited by Gerhard Ebeling in his book, *Luther: An introduction to his thought (Philadelphia*: Fortress Press, 1979), pp. 236 & 237.
51 See Paul Althaus *The Ethics of Martin Luther* (Philadelphia: Fortress Press, 1972), especially chapter four, "The Two Kingdoms and the Two Governments". The example of the hangman is found on p. 74.
52 Robert P. Erickson *Theologians Under Hitler* (New Have: Yale University Press, 1985). Chapter four is devoted to a discussion of Hirsch's life and thought.
53 Erickson, p. 147.
54 Emmanuel Hirsch *Deutschlands Schicksal,* 2nd ed. (Gottingen, 1922), p. 153 quoted in Erickson, p. 139.
55 Emmanuel Hirsch *Das Wesen des Christentums* (Weimar, 1939), p. 158 quoted by Erickson p. 164.
56 Erickson quoting Hirsch, p. 140.
57 Hirsch, *Deutschlands Schicksal,* p. 166 quoted in Erickson, p. 141.
58 Erickson, p. 125; quoting Hirsch's sermon, from Jens Hoger Schjorring's *Theologische Gewissenethik und politische Wirklichkeit: Das Beispiel Eduard Geismars und Emanuel Hirschs* (Gottingen, 1979), p. 58
59 Ibid., p. 125 quoting pp. 57 & 58.
60 Erickson, p. 135: quoting Hirsch, *Deutschlands Schicksal,* p. 108.
61 Erickson, pp. 135 & 136; quoting Hirsch, *Deutschlands Schicksal*, p. 109.

THE HOLOCAUST AND THE SUFFERING OF GOD

ROBERT SEITZ FREY, M.A. (Hons.)

P.O. Box 850
Columbia, MD 21044-0850
U.S.A.

ABSTRACT

Theological issues deriving from the Holocaust event are discussed with specific focus upon the challenge of those issues for Christian theology and Christian thinking. Reasons why the Holocaust is significant for all bodies and denominations of the contemporary Christian Church are delineated and examples of sensitive Christian responses to HaShoah are noted. Justification for viewing the Endloesung as one of the most dis-orienting experiences for the Christian churches in twenty centuries is presented.

The theodicean issues raised by the Auschwitz experience are discussed with emphasis given to the eschatological implications of the Holocaust. Human suffering, human freedom, moral evil, and Divine restraint are examined with reference to such scholars as Charles Hartshorne, Frederick Sontag, Kenneth Surin, Warren McWilliams, S. Paul Schilling, and John Hick. The suffering God motif as espoused by Abraham Joshua Heschel, A. Roy Eckardt, and Kazoh Kitamori is introduced along with the theological notion of providence.

The applicability of the suffering God idea to the reality of the Holocaust is weighed in the presence of philosophical arguments on theism and evil. The thought of David Hume and Fyodor Dostoyevsky serves as counterpoise to the suffering motif.

Bases for positing non-orthodox theodicean frameworks are demonstrated in Psalms, Ecclesiastes, Job, and Jeremiah. Weaknesses in the universal application of the suffering God idea to both moral and physical evil are noted.

KEYWORDS

Theodicy: dysteleological suffering: moral evil: suffering God motif: omnipotence: benevolence

DISCUSSION

Human beings now live in a world in which Auschwitz-Birkenau, Treblinka, and Babi Yar have already happened. The possibility yet exists for other more extreme state-sponsored and culturally sanctioned products of human imagination, engineering, and freedom in the near and distant future. Deity witnessed the rationally planned murders of thousands of children and adults day after day for nearly six years with no apparent response or succor. But the factories, gas vans, and ravines of terror and death were in fact moral evil writ large. Moral evil exists due to human choices and behavior. Physical evil, however, challenges the traditionally accepted nature of Deity more so than moral evil. For instance, the death of an infant for no known diagnostic reason is profound physical evil. This calls God's power, goodness, and love more into question than does the most horrific murder. The responsibility for murder is one removed directly from Deity because of the human agent involved. Yet the concrete results of both physical and moral evil are devastating for victim and survivor alike.

It was ordinary men and women who made the National Socialist extermination program work effectively on a daily basis. Human intelligence developed and marketed the Zyklon B and applied it to people instead of rodents. Human politico-scientific ideology and culturally applied theology designated certain peoples as Untermenschen, fit for the Endloesung. Bureaucratically, scientifically, rationally, culturally, and ideologically--the Holocaust was human evil. And moreover, horror is not to be found solely in the domain of the primitive, but also issues from the intellectually and technologically advanced. Perhaps there are really no God-related questions apropos to HaShoah at all. If, in theological terms, the Holocaust resulted from human freedom of will, what then did God have to do with it, other than that Deity created human beings and gave them the freedom to make choices? Such freedom requires that each person must bear full responsibility for and consequences of his decisions. It also allows for the maximum risk, which can result in lethal actions. Yet to search critically for God among the ashes of the Vistula or the heaving, bloated earth of the Ukraine is a challenging, even faith-shattering task. Long-cherished and heartfelt notions of Deity succumb as do established paradigms of sacred and profane history and images of human beings. The Divine dimension constitutes at least one basis of the Holocaust's unrealized transformational potential.[1] In the intervening 43 years, there has been no appreciable change in collective human behavior or thinking.

The image of the "suffering God" seems to be the only one that speaks with any compassion and moral validity after the Holocaust. "Suffering God" is not employed here to connote a Deity who becomes incarnate in a finite historical Being and event, as Jesus of Nazareth and his anguish in Gethsemane and on Golgotha. Rather, "suffering God" must be envisioned in a broader, more enduring sense.[2] What did it mean for God to suffer with the victims, both dead and living, of the Nazi Kingdom of Death? Deity's suffering, if indeed it did occur, was certainly not apparent. And yet if one can still believe in an all-good and loving Supreme Being after 1945, suffering with humankind would be one essential attribute. For the human conception of God not to devolve into the teratological, Deity's suffering during the Holocaust years is a necessary construct in the Divine definition. Once this premise is accepted as valid, the inscrutability of God can then be invoked, for we simply do not know what real difference God's suffering made. Perhaps in some intimate, personal, and profound way Deity's suffering did touch the being of a young mother as she shielded her infant by the open pit at Babi Yar. Or maybe a child was soothed a bit as his feet stood frozen to the ground outside the chambers at Treblinka during the winter of 1942. However, if we apply the inscrutability apologetic too soon, if we say God's ways are essentially unknown to humankind prior to genuinely confronting the issue before us, we have short-circuited the theological quandary of HaShoah. And to continue to maintain God's total omnipotence, impassibility, and immutability in light of Auschwitz is at best to render God meaningless and at worst to create a tyrannical monster of the Divine.

It has been suggested that the suffering God motif had its origins in the Exodus from Egypt and subsequent reflections on that biblically normative event.[3] God's response to and internal relation with His people's sufferings are also noted in the books of Judges and Psalms, and in the writings of the literary prophets[4] of the period after the Assyrian destruction of the Northern Kingdom. Yet suffering has also been interpreted to be an evil, an intrinsic frustration, and time-linked, and thus not part of Divine experience. A long and deeply rooted tradition categorically rejects the notion of suffering in God as completely contradictory to the Divine nature. For the most part, orthodox Christian doctrine after the Council of Nicaea limited Christ's capacity to suffer to His human nature. In contrast, the Patripassians of the second and third centuries held that Christ's redemptive suffering was the Father's suffering as well. For this and other theological reasons the Patripassians were denounced as heretical. The writings of Gregory of Nyssa,

Augustine, and Cyril of Alexandria link God's incapacity to suffer with His unchanging nature. The doctrine of divine impassibility remained dominant throughout the medieval period, the Protestant Reformation of the fifteenth century, and beyond. Thomas Aquinas and John Calvin held Deity to be incapable of passion in the form of sadness or anger. The long-standing tradition of excluding suffering from God's nature draws upon very strong Jewish and Christian affirmations of Divine transcendence as well as Aristotelian and Platonic notions of the eternal God as immutable and unswayed by feeling.[5]

The assertion has been made that the theodicy question--the justification of God in a world filled with evil--lies at the root of the theistic Weltanshauung.[6] The term theodicy, probably coined by Gottfried Leibnitz in his work Essais de Theodicee, derives from two Greek roots meaning "god" and "justice." Reconciling evil with the traditional understanding of the nature of God is not confined to the Holocaust event. Examples of presenting and wrestling with theodicean issues include the book of Job, writings of Church fathers Augustine and Irenaeus, Maimonides' Guide of the Perplexed, and medieval Jewish historian Levi ben Gershom's Wars of the Lord. On a note both positive and ironic, Frederick Sontag has suggested that "pursuing the problem of evil may reveal more of what God is like than the decent gods of religious optimism."[7] The voice of the existentialist is of great value too: "We heard whole blocks screaming and we understood that Evil, fruit of a free and sovereign will, is, like Good, absolute. ... Therefore, in spite of ourselves, we came to this conclusion, which will seem shocking to lofty souls: Evil cannot be redeemed."[8] Theistic religion must respond, not from the challenge of Evil's gauntlet, but to salvage and then nurture a new beginning. And not a new beginning of faith in God's existence only, but also of trust in Deity's steadfast relationship with a world filled with both silent and piercing screams. Finally, too, Christians and Jews must cultivate a willingness to live with alternative and evolving views of the nature of God. Evil has produced too many theological orphans not to respond.

As concepts, evil and theodicy both have developed and interacted within a concrete historical and ideological matrix. In antiquity, the problem of evil was given expression by the Greek thinker Epicurus and the Roman philosopher Anicius Boethius. Seventeenth-century Scottish philosopher David Hume phrased the issue like this: "Is he [God] willing to prevent evil, but not able? then he is impotent. Is he able, but not willing? then is he malevolent? Is he both able and willing? whence then is evil?"[9] Over the years, philosophers from G. W. Leibnitz to Immanuel Kant to Georg Hegel pondered the justification of God as have theologians from St. Aquinas to Alvin Plantinga and Hans Küng. Time has drastically changed the frames of reference of the issue at hand. The very delineation between philosophy and theology has been altered from the medieval subordination of philosophy to religion. During the Middle Ages, religion provided the matrix of understanding and relating to all of reality. Religion has now been largely replaced by scientific-rationalism and popular culture. Contemporary scholars point to the European Enlightenment as the great watershed in changing the conceptions of God, theodicy, and mankind. The Enlightenment shifted intellectual horizons so that in many ways theodicy has been transformed into "anthropodicy."[10] Many theologians no longer try to explain evil in the context of God, but accept as their premise that evil stems solely from the human condition. "The thinkers of the Enlightenment and their successors, having eschewed the principle of cosmic order (and thus the notion of a divine Cosmic Orderer), had in this way shifted the burden of the problem of evil from God to man himself."[11] The Aufklärer of the Enlightenment may have also operated to make theodicy a more critical issue by discrediting "the notion that nature possessed an immanent teleology," thus making "it less easy for theologians and philosophers to explain occurrences of evil and suffering in terms of a divinely ordained creative process inherent in nature."[12]

In its most straight-forward theodicean formula, the Holocaust presents the formidable challenge of reconciling excessive or dysteleological human suffering with a deeply entrenched theological tradition of an all-good and all-powerful Deity. Certainly it must be affirmed that the evil of l'holocauste was skewed disproportionately towards Jewish and Slavic populations and was in no way a means to a greater good. The Holocaust simply does not support the theological construct of Jewish and Christian tradition that all things will be justified at the End of Days, the eschaton. From the Christian perspective, A. Roy Eckardt posits that the terror of the Holocaust cannot be redeemed by any past event (including the Crucifixion and the Resurrection), no matter how holy or divine.[13] Instead, Eckardt looks to a future event as the only possible source of redemption for HaShoah. Likewise, it has been suggested that Christology reinterpret the Christ-event from past and present salvation to a future victory.[14] Yet how can one place the immeasurable terror and suffering of burning Jewish children within the schema and trajectory of a forward-looking eschatological theodicy? Postulation of a future event to set all things right sacrifices the meaning and pain in current temporal history as well as human free will to the arguable need for ultimate theological neatness. Why does rectification have to wait until the eschaton if indeed it was ordained to occur? Fyodor Dostoyevsky's character Ivan speaks these profound words to his brother Aloysha:

> But then there are the children, and what am I to do with them?...Listen: if all have to suffer so as to buy eternal harmony by their suffering, what have the children have to do with it--tell me, please? It is entirely incomprehensible why they, too, should have to suffer and why they should have to buy harmony by their sufferings. Why should they, too, be used as dung for someone's future harmony?[15]

Theodicist John Hick has identified the major and minor paradigms of explanation for human nature and suffering within the Christian tradition.[16] The dominant schema is associated with St. Augustine and sees man as a finite, perfect creation who falls disastrously away from the course of Divine intent. The Augustinian principle of viewing the world as "sub ratione peccati" (under sin)[17] has dominated Roman Catholic and Protestant theology well into the modern era. This negative image of the world has been perceived to be the source of fatalism within the Christian tradition and also the reason for the general withdraw of the Church from temporal history.[18] Church historian and theologian Franklin Littell reflects a similar point of view when he discusses the churches' "flight from history." The minority school associated with St. Ireneaus and other early Hellenistic Fathers of the Church in the two centuries prior to Augustine saw mankind as still engaged in the process of creation. This motif is therefore developmental and teleological.[19] Teilhard de Chardin's justification and fulfillment of the temporal process pivots upon life's eventual arrival at a positive Omega Point. His theory stands squarely within the alternative viewpoint attributed to Ireneaus. John Hick's eschatological "soul-making" theodicy also lies within this spectrum. Justification of the entire temporal process is to be found in "the magnitude of good to which it leads."[20] Though he does not see the extermination of six million Jews as God's will, Hick does believe that the victims of Nazi aggression "will have their place in the final fulfillment of God's creation."[21] Yet its has been argued that life points as much toward an abyss as toward Chardin's Omega Point[22] and the fulfillment of Hick's soul-making odyssey.

Both Christian and Jewish canonical corpora affirm that God is known by His actions within the temporal sphere. There is certainly ample justification for subjecting faith to the judgment of history. The Creation, the Exodus event, the Sinaitic covenental experience, and the <u>galut</u> in Babylon as well as the Crucifixion, the Resurrection, and the destruction of the Temple by Titus and his legions are interpreted as direct actions of Deity in the context of human history. From such Divine-human encounters, the nature of God was unfolded, though to be sure the Jewish and Christian faith communities accepted differing attributes of the Divine. If one grants that there exists adequate theological precedent for human understanding of God to follow from concrete historical events, contemporary believers are faced with an awesome reassessment of Deity in light of twentieth-century occurrences. And the <u>Judenvernichtung</u> constitutes one of the most devastating and dis-orienting experiences for Occidental culture and historico-theological interpretation in the twentieth century.

The traditional Christian historical world model conceives of the Resurrection of Jesus and his Second Advent as two towering peaks which stand far above the plane of tellurian experience.[23] These meta-normal events have provided the measure of all of history for nearly 2,000 years. When viewed strictly within this historical schema, the Holocaust is part of the plateau of human events--"another one of the multitude of human tragedies that will be transposed into goodness and glory at the terminus of time."[24] One directive out of the Holocaust for Christianity is to regard temporal history as having meaning independent of sacred history. The concrete reality of Auschwitz-Birkenau cannot be relegated to the status of a minor setback in the vector of forward gain[25] towards paradise. Likewise, as Lester Dean has noted, Christian-Jewish dialogue must move to a new level that recognizes the history of the Jewish people outside the frame of Christian sacred history. HaShoah should reveal that the Jewish people is a concrete, specific historical reality whose members bleed.

Theological consideration of an ongoing, ever-present Divine-human encounter, in effect, revelation, should be placed on the Christian agenda. Some Christian scholars, however, take exception to any revelation born of distortions of human nature, under the rubric of which they place the Holocaust event. It was Christian interpretation of events which said that Divine revelation did not cease at Mount Sinai, as Orthodox Jews would maintain; therefore, contemporary Christians cannot legitimately conclude that all revelation ceased with the Christ event. According to a theme set forth in Robert McAfee Brown's book, <u>The Pseudonyms of God</u>, Deity reveals Itself in a multitude of ways. It would appear to be an anthropomorphic limiting of God if we humans were to maintain that the unfolding of His nature reached its ultimate zenith in Jesus of Nazareth. Let us instead hope for the continued outpouring of God's revelation and support for humankind. By acting upon its affirmation that God operates in the confines of particular time and place, Christianity will be open to theological learning, christological redefinition, and"the wounding contingencies of time and space."[26]

The legitimacy of ongoing revelation meshes with Charles Hartshorne's postulate which, in contradistinction to twenty centuries of theological and philosophical discourse, states that God can indeed change and surpass Himself. Deity is not immutable or static, and change is not indicative of Divine weakness.[27] As bases for this construct of the Divine, Hartshorne drew upon a modification of St. Anselm's concept of God and David Hume's discussion of "mind" in <u>Dialogues Concerning Natural Religion</u>.

If one accepts the Holocaust to be of profound human and Divine significance and one is also open to the redirection provided by twentieth-century revelation (a term which by definition implies the possibility of change within Deity, or at least a greater sharing of It's nature with human beings) then the suffering of God is a legitimate theological postulate. And this despite the traditions of Christianity, Judaism, and Hellenistic antiquity. But far beyond an abstract postulate, this notion can also be a genuine source of solace and mature religious rootedness. The pulse of Divine suffering and responsibility for evil beats throughout biblical and rabbinic tradition, though to be sure the dominant theme of Orthodox Jewish theology from the Chronicler down to the end of the Old Testament period was that God will reward the righteous with good things and punish the wicked.[28]

Deutero-Isaiah (45:7) writes: I [the Lord] form light and darkness. I make weal and create woe [evil], I am the Lord, who do all these things. And in Lamentations (3:37-38) one finds: Who has commanded and it came to pass, unless the Lord has ordained it? Is it not from the mouth of the Most High that good and evil come? The <u>Mekhilta</u> on Exodus 20:23 says that: If I bring happiness upon you give thanks, and when I bring sufferings give thanks also.[29] Finally, the Deuteronomic account in 32:39 reads: See now that I, even I, am He, And there is no god with Me; I kill and I make alive; I have wounded, and I heal. Though God brings evil to pass, He is seen in anguish at the destruction of the Temple in the Midrash on Psalms 20:1.[30] Abraham Joshua Heschel has written of the pathos of God in the Prophets. For Heschel, <u>pathos</u> "is not a passion, an unreasoned emotion, but an act with intention, rooted in decision and determination;...signifying God as involved in history, as intimately affected by events in history, as living care."[31]

A responsive theology of Auschwitz includes the concept of God as "one who is not only _with_ the sufferer, but who suffers as well."[32] "The God that suffers offers us the comfort of His presence and points quietly toward the idea that He cannot change the situation, whatever this may do to one's theology!"[33] Indeed, the affirmation of Divine suffering seems to speak more profoundly to faith communities than does the denial of this perspective.

Warren McWilliams has critically examined the suffering God motif as developed by six post-World War II Protestant theologians. Discussed in his work _The Passion of God_ are a German Lutheran (Jürgen Moltmann), an American black Methodist (James Cone), an American Presbyterian (Geddes MacGregor), a Japanese Lutheran (Kazoh Kitamori), an American Congregationalist (Daniel Day Williams), and a Korean Methodist (Jung Young Lee). The passion of God is a crucial theme in each theology. "Moltmann describes a crucified God who participates in the human struggle for freedom and justice. Cone speaks of the God who identifies with the oppressed of the world. MacGregor's kenotic God suffers along with the world because of his loving self-limitation. Kitamori identifies the pain of God as the struggle he experiences between his love and his wrath. Williams discusses a dipolar God who is both vulnerable to the world's misery and invulnerable to final defeat. Lee develops a view of divine passibility based on God's _agape_ nature and his divine empathy."[34] According to Warren McWilliams' assessment, each of these theologians would agree "that unless God is capable of suffering, he is unable to be a God of love."[35] And "the only credible theodicy for Auschwitz is one that makes God an inmate of the place, one that acknowledges the possibility that he too hung on the gallows."[36] Unlimited companionship even during extreme human suffering occasioned by moral evil is a much neglected aspect of the Divine definition.[37]

Professor Charles Hartshorne believed that denying the omnipotence of God is too crude an attempt to genuinely come to terms with moral evil. Perhaps the need to deny God's omnipotence comes from invoking an overly mechanistic definition of the nature of power, Hartshorne thought. Defining power as the ability to control or structure events in the most beneficial way for humans is to limit God's decision-making capacity. One dominant theological definition of God's power includes His being able to manipulate temporal events in nearly _ex machina_ fashion. It is not a question of the amount of power that Deity wields but an understanding of that power which would eliminate the need to deny Divine omnipotence.

Other theologians have posited a self-limited Deity, one who is all-good and benevolent but who chooses to restrict Its power to preserve human freedom. The strength and mightiness of God are to be found not in what He can do--that is a given--but rather in what He chooses not to do. And unfortunately the Divine choice to act is not evident at the peaks of human pain and despair. According to Gregory Baum, "God is omnipotent (only) in the sense that there is ... no situation, however destructive, in which an inner strength is not offered to man, allowing him to assume greater possession of his humanity."[38] Furthermore, the traditional theological notion of providence as found in Christianity, Judaism, and Islam--that is, God provides for the individual in accordance with his piousness--is seriously challenged by the Holocaust event. And profoundly, John Pawlikowski remarks that "[t]he post-Auschwitz God-human relationship will have to be one in which we clearly acknowledge God's utter and inescapable dependence upon man as a partner in bringing about the ultimate salvation of the world."[39]

Let us consider a paradigm that attempts to integrate God's actions in the world with a post-Holocaust worldview. The experience of Noah as related in the book of Genesis involved God's efforts to intervene directly in the temporal historical process. The rainbow after the Flood was God's promise to humankind that He would no longer solve human moral problems in such a direct and overt manner. There would never again be cessation of life through Water. The experience of Moses on Mount Sinai which is recounted in the book of Exodus shows a fundamental shift in the God-human encounter. God's efforts now involve His working with humankind in a covenant relationship to achieve the fulfillment of His creation. A greater part of the burden is now with mankind. God provides the way of life, the _mitzvot_ of the Torah, and mankind must observe them. Morality was being shaped through the covenant experience.

Through the Auschwitz event, God may be showing human beings that the world is fundamentally under human direction. Human decision making and values do matter; humans are ultimately responsible for what they think, do, and believe. Auschwitz demonstrates the importance of individual and collective actions upon the moral fabric of society. It should not, however, point us in a direction of purely human solutions for peaceful, meaningful living. We cannot rely upon a Flood, or perhaps even upon the special nature of a covenant relationship for our well-being. Yet we must recognize the validity and necessity of God-centered values even after the specter of the Holocaust.

By means of direct response to HaShoah, all denominations and bodies of the contemporary Christian Church must recognize this event as significant. **Why** this has to be so is not at all obvious to many people who profess the Christian faith and, therefore, must be demonstrated. It is not the intent here to convey the idea that there has been no sensitive Christian response to the Holocaust. There have been notable beginnings made by such Christian scholars and theologians as Franklin Littell, John Pawlikowski, A. Roy Eckardt, Alice Eckardt, and Eva Fleischner as well as Rosemary Ruether, Paul Van Buren, Robert McAfee Brown, and Harry James Cargas. There have also been recent official Church statements as to the kinship of Judaism and Christianity and on the moral wrong of anti-Semitism, examples of which were Article Four of the "Declaration on the Relation of the Church to Non-Christian Religions" issued by the Second Vatican Council of the Roman Catholic church and the 1985 Vatican Notes for the proper presentation of Judaism in Catholic Preaching and Catechesis. Father Michael McGarry's work entitled <u>Christology After Auschwitz</u> is an excellent resource for official ecclesiastical issuances on Jewish-Christian relationships, anti-Semitism, and related themes.

Despite these efforts, the impact of the Holocaust as an event posing problems for Christian theology and Christian people has not begun to reach the laity level in any significant way, and remains much lacking among the pastorate as well. One is confronted with developing reasons for isolating the <u>Endloesung</u> as one of the most **dis-orienting** experiences for the Christian Church in nearly 2,000 years. What is it about the Holocaust that should cause Christians to extract it from all of the other human suffering which has occurred over the centuries, and invest this event with intrinsic and especial meaning? Why should Jewish suffering initiate Christian theological and moral issues?

There are several salient points which participate in providing substance to the above questions. First, there was **direct** involvement of practicing Christians in the National Socialist extermination program. Ernst Biberstein, the commander of Einsatzgruppen C, one of the mobile killing units which operated in the western Soviet Union early in the war, had been ordained a Protestant pastor in 1924. In addition, the thousands of civil servants and bureaucrats who made the extermination process work on a daily basis were often ordinary Christian men and women.

It is essential at this juncture to affirm that there were indeed Christians in Europe who, at great risk to their own lives, worked in a host of ways to save Jewish lives. The Huguenot village of La Chambon and its pastor Andre Trocme constitute a striking, positive example of Christian heroism on behalf of Jews. Yad Vashem's Avenue of the Just in Jerusalem bears concrete witness to the righteous Gentiles. Yet Eugene Fisher of the National Conference of Catholic Bishops has noted that "no church or nation can validly point to the numerically few rescuers as a balance to the basic truth that six million Jews were coldly murdered in the heart of Christian Europe."

To consider the Holocaust as an event requiring special Christian emphasis solely because of Christianity's direct complicity presents difficulty, as Robert Willis suggests, in light of Christian involvement in the enslavement of blacks in the Americas and in the destruction of Native American cultures. These events, however, stand in sharp contrast against the enduring and complex tradition of Christian theological and ecclesiastical anti-Judaicism. Centuries of anti-Judaic teaching and practice helped to provide for public acceptance of, and indifference to, Nazi anti-Jewish ideology and practice.

The longstanding tradition of negative Christian policy and outlook vis-a-vis Jews and Judaism is traceable from the patristic literature of the second to fifth centuries of the common era, including the writings of John Chrysostrom (Bishop of Antioch) and Augustine (Bishop of Hippo in North Africa). Themes of the Jews being a deicide people, and the exhausted value of Judaism as a religious system, were advanced. During the medieval period, official Roman Church policy towards the Jews was a dual one of social degradation and limitation (including the Jew badge and forced ghettoization) combined with theologically-premised protection. This double-edged policy was concretized through the decisions of the Third and Fourth Lateran Councils in 1179 and 1215; the Church-sponsored Trials of the Talmud in Paris, Barcelona, and Tortossa; and four major Church-inspired Talmud burnings. Further example is provided by the bull issued Pope Paul the Fourth in 1555 which enforced ghettoization in Rome and reinstituted the yellow headgear for Jews. It should also be noted that anti-Semitism deriving primarily from Christian imagery was supplemented, beginning in the late nineteenth century, by racial anti-Semitism as propounded by such people as German philosopher and economist Karl Eugen Duehring, and Wilhelm Marr.

The deep-seated attitudes which developed from such anti-Judaic policies and teachings contributed to, though certainly were not the sole cause of, Christian complicity in, silence to, and moral indifference towards the murder of Jewish men, women, and children in the 1940s. Christianity and its folk expression provided an extensive fund of negative images of the Jew, as detailed by Joshua Trachtenberg in his work The Devil and the Jews. In large part, the power of these images derived and continue to derive from religious sanction along with pervasive misunderstanding and misinformation about Jews and Judaism on the part of Christian laypersons and clergy.

The most profound basis upon which the contemporary Christian Church might continue in its beginning movement towards response to the Holocaust is the knowledge that Christianity is linked to the heritage of no other people as it is to that of the Jews. Christianity cannot establish an identity that does not include a rich and **living** relationship with the Jewish people. Therefore, Christian involvement in and silence to the mass murder of Jews, the very people from whom is derived theological perspective and spiritual sustenance, strikes at a basic level--as son to father.

Three images of the Holocaust have been recurrent over the years for me. They are of fingernail marks, ashes, and a young girl.

The fingernail marks refer to those indelibly clawed into the walls and ceilings of the gas chambers at Auschwitz-Birkenau. In a futile attempt to find air, people climbed on top of one another only to meet with the concrete barrier of the ceiling. The Zyklon B crystals used to kill at Auschwitz produced a cyanide gas that rose from the floor upwards. Fingernail marks in the concrete record the last agony-filled seconds of nameless thousands of people.

Ashes. Ashes by the truckload were dumped into the Vistula River during the peak operation of Auschwitz during the summer of 1944 when the Jews of Hungary were being liquidated. The ashes of parents and children; loved ones and strangers; rebbes and pupils. Ashes commingled into anonymity; the river washed away the memory.

And finally, a young girl. Hanged at Auschwitz, her last words to the inmates as they filed past her were, "Remember me." In a world filled with the glorification of killing, this girl, in pathetic defiance, asked to be remembered.

The watchword of the Jewish community after the Holocaust is also "Remember," that the Awe-ful will never happen again. Remembering, however, is simply not enough. If our memories do not produce response and positive change within ourselves and the collective human community, then the memory of the Holocaust, and of that young girl in particular, are rendered meaningless and in time will slip away. The change within ourselves must extend to allowing the God of Jewish and Christian tradition to be a silent partner in and with our human suffering.

ENDNOTES

1. Cf. Alan Rosenberg, "The Philosophical Implications of the Holocaust," in Perspectives on the Holocaust, ed. Randolph L. Braham (Boston: Kluwer-Nijhoff, 1983), pp. 2-3.

2. Hans Jonas, "The Concept of God after Auschwitz: A Jewish Voice," Journal of Religion 67 (1987): 6.

3. See Exod. 2:23-25 and 3:7-8.

4. See Judges 2:18 and Psalms 91:15, 23:4, and 16:8.
Terence E. Fretheim, The Suffering of God: An Old Testament Perspective (Philadelphia: Fortress Press, 1984, 1987), pp. 127,129.

5. S. Paul Schilling, God and Human Anguish (Nashville: Abingdon, 1977), pp. 249-51.

6. Jürgen Moltmann, The Future of Hope: Theology as Eschatology, ed. Frederick Herzog (New York: Herder and Herder, 1970), pp. 3-4.

7. Frederick Sontag, "Anthopodicy and the Return of God," in Encountering Evil: Live Options in Theodicy, ed. Stephen T. Davis (Edinburgh: T & T Clark, 1981), p. 143.

8. Jean-Paul Sartre, What Is Literature?, trans. Bernard Frechtman (New York: Philosophical Library, 1949), p. 219.

9. Nelson Pike, ed. Hume: Dialogues Concerning Natural Religion (New York: Bobbs-Merrill, 1970) Part X, p. 88.

10. Sontag, "Anthropodicy and the Return of God," p. 138.

11. Kenneth Surin, "Theodicy?," Harvard Theological Review 76 (1983): 228.

12. Surin, "Theodicy?," p. 229.

13. A. Roy Eckardt, "Christians and Jews: Along a Theological Frontier," Encounter 40 (1979): 125.

14. This interpretation of Professor Ruether was borrowed from Thomas A. Idinopulos and Roy Bowen Ward, "Is Christology Inherently Anti-Semitic?: A Critical Review of Rosemary Ruether's Faith and Fratricide." Journal of the American Academy of Religion 45 (1977): 205.
See Rosemary Radford Ruether, Faith and Fratricide: The Theological Roots of Anti-Semitism (New York: Seabury Press, 1974).

15. Fyodor Dostoyevsky, The Brothers Karamazov, trans. David Magarshack (New York: Penguin Books, 1978), p. 286.

16. John H. Hick, Evil and the God of Love (New York: Harper & Row, 1966), pp. 509-10, 515.

17. John T. Pawlikowski, "The Holocaust as Rational Event," Reconstructionist 40 (1974): 12.

18. Friedrich Heer, God's First Love: Christians and Jews Over 2000 Years (New York: Weybright and Talley, 1970), p. 406.

19. Hick, pp. 515, 517.

20. Hick, p. 521.

21. Hick, p. 398.

22. Sontag, "Anthopodicy and the Return of God," p. 146.

23. See Eckardt, "Christians and Jews," 90-92, 96 and Alan T. Davies, "Response to Irving Greenberg," in Auschwitz: Beginning of a New Era?: Reflections on the Holocaust ed. Eva Marie Fleischner (New York: KTAV, 1977), pp. 61-62.

24. Robert Seitz Frey and Nancy Thompson-Frey, The Imperative of Response: The Holocaust in Human Context (Lanham, Md.: University Press of America, 1985), p. 21.

25. Metaphor borrowed from George Steiner, In Bluebeard's Castle: Some Notes Towards the Redefinition of Culture (New Haven: Yale University Press, 1971).

26. Eckardt, "Christians and Jews," p. 92.

27. Charles Hartshorne, A Natural Theology for Our Time (LaSalle, Ill.: Open Court, 1967), pp. 127-28.

28. John Bright, A History of Israel, 3rd ed. (Philadelphia: Westminster Press, 1981), p. 449.

Koheleth in Ecclesiastes 9:2 went outside the orthodox tradition, however: All things come alike to all; there is one event to the righteous and the wicked. Even Jeremiah (12:1) asked: Wherefore doth the way of the wicked prosper? See also Robert Alan Hammer, "The God of Suffering," Conservative Judaism 31 (1976-77): 34-41.

29. As cited in Elliot N. Dorff, "God and the Holocaust," Judaism 26 (1977): 31.

30. As cited in John Fischer, "God After the Holocaust: An Attempted Reconciliation." Judaism 32 (1983): 317.

31. Abraham Joshua Heschel, The Prophets Part II (New York: Harper & Row, 1975), p. 11.

32. Hammer, "The Suffering of God," p. 34.

33. Hammer, "The Suffering of God," p. 35.

34. Warren McWilliams, The Passion of God: Divine Suffering in Contemporary Theology (Macon, Ga.: Mercer University Press, 1985), p. 191.

35. Warren McWilliams, "Divine Suffering in Contemporary Theology," Scottish Journal of Theology 33 (1980): 53.

36. Kenneth Surin, "The Impassibility of God and the Problem of Evil," Scottish Journal of Theology 35 (1982): 105.

37. Charles Hartshorne, Man's Vision of God and the Logic of Theism (Hamden, Conn.: Archon Books, 1964), p. xvi.

38. Gregory Baum, Man Becoming: God in Secular Experience (New York: Herder and Herder, 1970), p. 244.

39. Pawlikowski, "The Holocaust as Rational Event," p. 16.

JEWISH CHRISTIAN RELATIONSHIPS AS SEEN THROUGH THE EYES OF CHILDREN, BEFORE, DURING AND AFTER THE HOLOCAUST

Judith S. Kestenberg, Flora Hogman, Milton Kestenberg, and Eva Fogelman

From the Jerome Riker International Study of Organized Persecution of Children, Sands Point, NY

Relationships between Christians and Jews, adults and children vary from one historical epoch to another and from one geographical area to another. Intolerance rises with poor economic conditions and tolerance is on the upswing in times of affluence. This is true for individual and group development. A benign, loving atmosphere is a fertile ground for the acceptance of others. Deprivation, rejection and abandonment by parents and/or society cause bitterness and a desire for revenge. Loving or hostile attitudes are transmitted from generations to generations. Rooted in our biological heritage is a universal conflict between wanting to save children and promote one's biological future and wanting to kill children to reduce the burdens they place on their caretakers (Kestenberg, Kestenberg, and Amighi, 1988). To love children, one has to overcome the agelong wish to destroy them. In some cultures, during times of stress, parents and the community may accept severe deprivation to help their children survive. They have resolved the conflict in favor of rescuing children. In other cultures under stress, adults may sacrifice their children for the so-called good of society. They regressively accept the idea of a murderous God or an aggrandized community that survives at the cost of the lives of its children. In still others, the conflict between child killing and child saving is resolved by substituting a sacrificial lamb or scapegoat in the place of the child (Kestenberg and Kestenberg, 1986). In such cultures, both the parents and the children benefit from the selection of scapegoats which deflect the murderous tendencies of parents onto alien children.

Within these three broad categories, considerable variation may occur. Not every family necessarily follows the tradition of the community in which they live. In the midst of a child-loving culture, some families mistreat their children. Likewise, in the midst of a child-hating (Kinderfeindlich) culture, some families and subcultures take good care of their children. Where scapegoating is prevalent, and children are taught to hate outsiders, such as Jews, Gypsies or Blacks, we still find islands of acceptance and a feeling of responsibility to help the oppressed.

In this paper, we explore how children form images of religious faiths different than their own, and how they relate to each other in the midst of adult genocidal tendencies and actions. In section I, Judith Kestenberg documents the thesis that tolerance stems from a child's feeling threatened and unwanted and tolerance derives from a feeling of love and security. In section II, Flora Hogman highlights the Jewish childrens' perception of themselves and of Christian children before, during and after the war. In section III, Milton Kestenberg discusses the Christian childrens' perception of themselves and of Jews in East European nations, such as Poland, and in Germany. In section IV, Eva Fogelman brings into focus the relationship between the rescued Jewish child and the rescuer's children. Our data are collected from the literature and from numerous interviews conducted with child survivors and rescuers. We are grateful to them for sharing their biographies with us. We are also indebted to the many participants in this study in the United States, Canada, Israel, Poland, Czechoslovakia, Hungary, Sweden and Yugoslavia.

I. SOURCES OF TOLERANCE AND INTOLERANCE By Judith S. Kestenberg, M.D.

BRIEF SURVEY OF DEVELOPMENT. In the first year, as he conquers space and the objects in it, the baby becomes accustomed to the world around him. In the process of accomplishing this, he feels omnipotent; the whole world belongs to him. Satiated and warm, coddled and loved, he becomes generous and helpful, feeding his mother and bringing things to her. He goes through a phase of stranger anxiety which is overcome more easily in an atmosphere of trust within the family and the community. We expect him to grow up to be an altruistic individual who knows how to share. In contrast, a hungry and cold baby, brought up in a hostile environment, restricted in space, his feelings of omnipotence squelshed in the bud, may grow up to be distrustful and envious, craving for more space and riches.

In the second year, the child becomes aware of his own weight, his importance and his strength. He develops a new kind of omnipotence. He feels and behaves as if he were the king of the universe who can always have his own way. In his new grandeur, he will hit, push, and throw when people do not fulfill his expectations. However, if his caretaker does not engage in a power struggle, does not regress with him to hit and push, he ends up identifying with the tolerant attitude of the adults and is able to handle frustrations. In this benign atmosphere, he becomes clean instead of dirty, orderly instead of disorderly, helpful instead of hostile. If the caretaker fights with him, breaks his spirit, subdues him and behaves like him, the child feels threatened and degraded; he dreams of the time when he can take revenge and become more powerful and cleaner than the adult. When he grows up, he may retain an ambivalence, which makes it impossible for him to love without hate. It becomes difficult to evoke compassion in him and he looks upon the suffering of others with indifference.

In the third year of life, the child develops a new kind of omnipotence. He conquers time and wants to make all decisions himself. An understanding parent will let the toddler make some decisions in his own time without allowing him to put the whole household in disarray. At the end of this phase there is then reconciliation between parent and child, as they begin to cooperate in getting things done in an orderly sequence and on time. In contrast, the child who has been forced to always follow his parents schedule, does not learn to gauge time properly. He may wet himself before reaching the toilet and feel humiliated. The more he is afraid of feeling ashamed, the more he will need to shame and humiliate others, and the more he will impose his private schedule on them reducing them to the status of slaves.

The three-year-old leaves his babyhood behind him and emulates his caretaker, taking over some of his responsibilities himself. He identifies with his caretaker's maternality and wants to be a mother. He feeds his dolls and stuffed animals, puts them to sleep, cleans them and gives them things. All in all, he treats them the way he has been treated. If he has been beaten, he beats them; if he had been pushed or denigrated, he will do the same. In a benign environment, he will act like a good mother, love his "babies" and grow up to be a good parent. In a hostile environment, he becomes a tyrant and a nagger and may retain these traits in his adulthood. At odds with his parents and afraid of them, he worries that they will die and he will be abandoned and/or annihilated. The more he identifies with the child-hating attitudes of his caretakers, the more he will want to kill babies himself and will be tempted to do so when he grows up. The more he has been loved and protected, the more love and protection he will expend on others in his care.

The four-year-old gains a new feeling of grandiosity. He thinks that he is stronger than his father, who then has to be afraid of him. The five-year old becomes a rival of his father or mother and he wants to be the only one who is loved.

By the age of six or seven, the child is less dependent on his parents, as the school environment offers him the protection of the group and their leader. A teacher may reinforce the home environment or may create a conflict between principles taught at home and values of a public authority. To bridge this conflict, the child may develop a split in his ego. Within a hostile group setting, he may not agree to cruelty, but may be swept into it by contagion or by a fear of becoming a victim himself. A few are courageous enough to stand up for victims and protect them openly, others may do it secretly.

Children of school age form strong friendships, often creating cliques and excluding others. This may culminate in the formation of gangs in adolescence. If not discouraged by parents and educators, such behavior can lead to a cruel discrimination against outcasts. Through a split in the superego, the child may eagerly participate in cruelty in a group situation, while, as an individual he may be compassionate and gentle. In another type of split a child may be cruel to outcasts, but loving towards people in his own family or group. Lifton (1986) refers to this attitude in Nazi doctors as "doubling." Cruel to Jews, they were loving and tender to Germans.

The inconsistency in childrens' behavior can reflect mixed messages, conveyed by their parents. In contrast to overt expressions of hostility to children, many predominantly loving parents use subtle ways to communicate their feelings of animosity. It is not uncommon for a mother or father to tell their infant, "You are so sweet; you are good enough to eat." Quite a few mothers, when provoked, tell their children, "I will kill you." It is evident to the youngest child that it is parental rage which prompts this threat. Infants can react with depression and panic to the distorted features and tone of voice of an enraged parent. The traditional reading of fairy stories in which witches cook children and parents send them away to "seek their fortunes," incites the older toddler to distrust adults. The more afraid children are of their parents and educators, the more they need to deny their perception of ill wishes from the only people whom they regard as their protectors, the parents, and the more they are willing to accept such scapegoats as monsters, dragons, ghosts, witches, or Jews. No doubt, types of prejudice depend on what children hear from parents, teachers, clergy and friends. However, proud parents can transmit to their children that they are superior to others, an attitude which arouses anger and envy in those considered to be inferior. This can lead to a form of intolerance which denigrates Jews, but does not harm them. When conveyed to Jewish children, it can become the basis of anti-Gentilism which belittles Christians (Stein, 1977).

DISCRIMINATION. Little has been written about the development of tolerance, but quite a few authors have tried to explore the origin of discrimination against Jews. Grunberger (1964) describes the anti-Semite's immature ego "as though split and menaced with disintegration" (p. 380). He goes on to say that the anti-Semite's superego is an incomplete structure and the projections of his own wishes upon Jews betray their pregenital origin. Bass (1987) found that the fear of annihilation motivates the anti-Semite to annihilate Jews.

Fears of being eaten by Jews (as in blood libel) are based on fantasies which can be traced to feelings experienced in the first year of life. The common view that Jews are dirty has its origin in the time when the toddler became concerned with cleanliness. The idea that Jews are shameful can be traced to the toddler's preoccupation with accidents which caused him shame. However, anti-Semitism draws not only on pregenital sources but also on fears and fantasies from later developmental phases. Underlying the fear that Jews want to do Christians in, may be the three-year-old's fear of annihilation-death (Kestenberg, 1968). The image of the Jew as deformed and crooked may be based on the child's castration complex. Fears that the Jews despoil their women and want to take power away from Christians are often due to unresolved Oedipal wishes. According to Grunberger (1964) anti-Semites are recruited from the weak, shiftless, immature victims of narcissistic deprivation and of feelings of inferiority. Narcissism feeds on omnipotence and grandiosity which are used to 'heal' narcissistic wounds.

The more frustrating the environment the more prone is the older child and adult to a regression towards earlier, infantile outlets, and the more he wishes to undo the wounds suffered not only early in life, but also in the present. In Germany, the conditions after the defeat in World War II and especially in the pre-World War II depression were conducive to such a regression (Wangh, 1964, Kestenberg, 1988). Children, badly treated by their desperate and embittered parents, grew up ripe to be indoctrinated by ideas of German superiority. This grandiose myth could not be easily maintained in the face of increasing hardship and impending defeat. It had to be continuously reinforced by the contrasting image of the evil and denigrated Jew, depicted in Nazi textbooks, in media and other forms of propaganda (Franck and Asmus, 1983). With mounting anti-Semitism, Jewish children grew up, expecting to be victimized and persecuted. Gentiles were feared and oftentimes shied away from.

SHALL THE SON LIVE OR DIE? Grunberger (1964) writes that "...Judaism presents itself as the worship of the father..," who preaches morals to Gentiles and reproaches them for their sins (pp 382-83). Because they represent an external conscience for Gentiles, Jews are particularly feared and hated. The first and the most dramatic example of the Jewish challenge to other people's morality was their categorical rejection of infanticide in biblical times. Abraham's triumph over his wish to sacrifice Isaac constituted the birth of moral Judaism, based as it was on a reconciliation between father and son. The God who sent an angel to redeem Isaac, transformed himself from a godhead who demanded child sacrifice, into a divine, invisible protector of children (Kestenberg, Kestenberg, and Amighi, 1988).

In Christianity, the son Jesus, is sacrificed for the good of the people and his death is glorified. However, Christianity partially undoes the consequences of this sacrifice through Jesus' resurrection. In Jewish tradition, survival is emphasized rather than sacrifice (Rudavsky, 1987). Jewish children are taught that Jews are chosen from all nations to be bearers of truth, learning and justice. Jewish religion prohibits murder and admonishes parents to treat children lovingly and protect them so that they propagate God's law. Christian children are taught to look upon death as an entrance to heaven. Their spirit lives on after death. Catholic children often look upon their Jewish friends as deprived of salvation and needing to convert in order to be saved from hell. However, empathy and forgiveness may motivate them to help Jews and accept their differences. Perhaps, one of the basic differences between Judaism and Christianity can be condensed into one question: Shall the son live or die? This doctrinal difference subtly pervades many aspects of Jewish and Christian lives, respectively.

Independently, from other researchers (Matzner-Bekerman, 1984, Kanerfogel, 1985, Kestenberg, Kestenberg and Amighi, 1988), Schultz, a German theologian, found that throughout history, Jewish parents treated their children with greater kindness than Christian parents and early statistics indicate that infant mortality used to be lowest among the Jews (1986). Schultz suggests that the Jews, with their long history of expulsion and emigrations, learned not to expect protection for their children from authorities, but rather assumed the role of child protectors themselves. As a threatened minority, each child was their key to survival and and each child was treated with importance. These children grew up with the responsibility not to sacrifice themselves, but to live in order to tell the miraculous story of having been close to death and having survived. The children whose parents told them, "You must live," felt an obligation to survive the physical and mental hardships of the Holocaust. Many of these could endure the unendurable in order to stay alive. That does not mean that all Jews are loving parents and Christians are not. The differences stressed here are that traditionally Jewish parents value the lives of their children above all, while Christian parents, because of their belief in sacrifice and salvation, may risk their childrens' lives for a worthy cause.

The Jews have been repeatedly accused of the murder of Christ. This is often taken personally by Christian children who label individual Jewish children as "Christ-killers." Jews have also been periodically accused of using the blood of Christian children for making the Passover Matzoh. Schultz (1986) recognized that this accusation stems from the projection of the wish to kill one's own children and drink their blood, which for Jews would be a double sin. If the Jew is accused of sins which call for severe punishment, he can no longer act as an accuser and protector of humanity. His high moral stance which indirectly or directly stands as an accusation of others, is destroyed.

The Nazis' treatment of Jews reflects the desire to destroy Jews, not only physically, but morally. The Nazis took special pride in forcing Jews to go against their own laws and values. They forced pious Jews to desecrate the Holy book and made parents watch their own childrens' deaths. They were, however, not only anti-Jewish, but also anti-Christian. They condemned Christian teachings of compassion for the downtrodden. Where Christianity was devoutely observed, families not only took good care of their children, but also helped the persecuted people (see section IV). Nazis taught their adherents to be tough and they punished the altruists who risked their lives for others (see section III). Jewish children, threatened by the Nazis, often felt protected by Christians and by their religion (see section II). Even when conversion was not expected from them, sometimes they themselves wanted to convert and would refuse to go back to their Jewish parents after the War (see section II). Nazis robbed Jewish parents of their prerogative to protect their children. Christian families, priests and convents offered shelter and security to substitute for Jewish parents. In such cases the ethics of the Jewish-Christian culture prevailed and became a threat to Nazism.

By desecrating Jewish laws, killing Jews and combatting Christianity, the Nazis hoped to get rid of their accusers and to deflect their filicidal wishes from their own children to the Jews whom they reduced to the helplessness of children. This 'Mission' failed; they ended up sacrificing their own young sons as cannon fodder for their grandiose aspirations. Hitler who 'loved' youth and replaced their cruel fathers, abandoned them at the end and let the enemy kill them by the thousands.

II. JEWISH CHILDREN'S PERCEPTION OF THEMSELVES AND OF CHRISTIANS BEFORE, DURING AND AFTER THE HOLOCAUST By Flora Hogman, Ph.D.

This report and its conclusions are based on 26 interviews with child survivors aged one month to 13 years in 1939. They were originally from all over Europe.

BEFORE THE WAR AND ITS ONSET

For Jewish Children, Catholic maids represented the primary contacts with Christianity. A few Jewish children attended public or Catholic schools. Many had encounters with Christians on the streets, some lived among Christians. Children's perceptions had little to do with the concept of religion per se. Instead, they reflected their egocentric mode of thinking (Piaget, 1954). These perceptions were based on discrete, concrete events such as: having a Christmas tree; experiencing a wonderful relationship to a Christian maid; not being allowed to go to church; having children throw stones at them; realizing that Catholics did not get off for Jewish holidays. The parents' Jewish identity, their attitudes and coping styles generally contributed to the children's reactions to the Christian world. The children's relationships to their parents also influenced the way they reacted to Christians.

CHILDRENS' REACTIONS IN THE ABSENCE OF ANTI-SEMITISM. Survivors reported normal relationships with Christians. Some were friends with Christians while others were simply curious about Christianity and still others were not even aware of religious differences. In assimilated families little thought was given to Christianity or Judaism. For example, one girl was brought up in Vienna in a neighborhood where Jews and Christians of similar socio-economic status lived near one another. She never felt different from her Viennese playmates. A young boy who played in the fields with peasant Catholic boys in Czechoslovakia had little idea of the difference between a Jew and a Christian. Orthodox survivors of this study who as children enjoyed the customs and rituals of their upbringing described feeling good, special, different, better than others, and 'nurtured' by their religion. They also remember a happy home life. Children living in difficult home situations had more complicated feelings. Orthodox children had no wish to be like Christians, no jealousy, just curiosity and at times friendship with Christians. For example, before the war, Martha had a beloved Catholic maid and thoroughly enjoyed the Christian songs she taught her. These songs became a part of their wonderful relationship. Martha's parents were orthodox Jews, proud of their traditions and of their culture. She felt special as a Jew. Esther now feels that her orthodox mother was smart in allowing her to go to church with the Christian maid because her curiosity was satisfied. Jules, brought up in Belgium, was taught to respect the 'other' religion. He called the Christian neighbors 'aunt and uncle.' He was awed by priests and impressed by funerals. Dina, brought up in a Jewish neighborhood of Warsaw in a progressive, politically active Jewish family, recalls with great fondness her Christian maid, with whom she went to church. The maid was almost a mother to her since her own mother, a school principal, was often absent from home. In summary, in the absence of anti-Semitism, Jewish children had good relationships with Christians. Parents' attitudes towards Christians and their intimacy with their children had also an influence on their children's attitudes towards Christianity.

<u>CHILDREN'S REACTIONS TO ANTI-SEMITIC EXPERIENCES</u>. Anti-Semitism took the form of overt hostility (insult, throwing stones). Sometimes, even without direct attacks, the child felt unaccepted and uneasy about being different. Child survivors recount a wide range of reactions to anti-Semitism: from fighting back when possible and silent courage, to resignation; from anger to feeling left out and being envious. Children's perceptions of parental attitudes and reactions came to play an important role; for example, some parents fought back, others were afraid and resigned. The nature of the children's relationship with their parents, their self-esteem and positive Jewish identity also became increasingly important variables which determined children's reactions to anti-Semitism.

<u>Attitudes of Parents and Reactions of Children</u>. The example set by parents facilitated children's ability to stand up for themselves, thereby reaffirming their sense of worth and for the most part their Jewish identity. When parents were resigned, children often became angry at them, developed negative feelings about Judaism and became attracted to Christianity, especially in non-religious families. In time they developed loyalty conflicts and felt badly about themselves.

<u>Fighting Back</u>. Two girls whose families had emigrated from Poland to Belgium and France both fought back in school when they were called "dirty Jews." In one family the parents were Bundist, in the other, they were assimilated Jews. However, their values were similar, "one had to stand up for one's rights." A Roumanian boy, who had good relationships with Catholic children before the war, later courageously held on to his orthodox faith, as did his parents.

<u>Resignation</u>. Claire, a girl from an assimilated family in Poland, had learned resignation from her parents. She described how before the war she had a very traumatic interaction with Christians in a school where she was the only Jew. She was to sit through the religious instruction where the teacher, tears in her eyes, described how the Jews killed Christ. Claire felt ostracized by many of the children. She reacted by ignoring them and never told her parents about these incidents. She was 'stoic and proud.' She recalls how her father responded to a question why Jews are not liked, "That is the way it is." She resented her father for that, "My father failed me." Had he not been so resigned himself, Claire might have found better ways of defending herself. She might have felt good about being a Jew instead of feeling it was an inescapable calamity. She ended up hating Poles for their sadism and Jews for their cowardice. Two men from established families in Belgium and Germany respectively remember how angry they were at the outset of the war when their parents ignored the insults of Christians. At the time one of them came to admire Christians, the other admired Germans. Both were impressed with their power.

Two women, Blanche and Frida, describe the tense atmosphere in their refugee families in Paris. Their parents belittled Christians, advising the children not to trust them, and that their religion was nonsense. Their parents also complained a lot how difficult it was to be Jewish in Paris. Rita felt that her parents' fears and mistrust carried over from their native Poland to Alsace. These three girls whose parents were minimally religious could find little positive about being Jewish, and there was a chronic undertone of danger in the families. As a result, even though the children had little personal experiences with anti-Semitism, they wished to be like everybody else and yearned to belong to the 'other,' more attractive and safer environment. They felt ashamed of their parents' accents and manner which made them more visibly different. Both Blanche and Frida pretended to be French and Catholic in school. Rita had a wish to be French and to have a mother who wore pretty dresses like French ladies. She was ashamed of her parents' accents and envied the children who had a Christmas tree and were allowed to go to church. She often felt excluded. When asked what they thought about

Christianity, these three women remembered feeling, with a child's egocentric thinking, "Nobody accepted us." Thereby they expressed indirectly their own anger and frustration at the French world. However, their anger was mostly focused on their parents. One might speculate that they were afraid to show anger at the 'conqueror' directly. It might have been safer instead to deflect and release all negative feelings towards their parents of whom they were not afraid. At the same time these children thought that their parents' fearfulness (of which they were ashamed) resulted from their non-acceptance of Judaism. They were angry at their parents because they did not provide a stable and secure identity.

Relationship to Parents. The lack of pride in Jewish identity was at times difficult to separate from the children's relationships with their parents. The children loved Jewish life when they were happy at home. They also retained a greater sense of self-esteem and a deeper bond to their parents in the face of anti-Semitism. When children were not happy at home their interest in Christianity had a rebellious quality. For example, before the war one boy raised in a German Orthodox home would have preferred to have been a Christian because his maid was warm and more affectionate than his mother. He said, "I felt bad but I liked them (Christians)." An Austrian boy who was not close to his parents, resented that the other children didn't have to learn Hebrew or go to synagogue. He viewed Judaism according to what concerned his own life. For instance, he was resentful that he could not join the Hitler youth. Blanche, Frida and Rita, wanted to be French partly because the conflicts with their families made the outside world more appealing. However, their ambivalent feelings were difficult to handle.

Ambivalence. Generally, children did not have the knowledge or the capability to integrate their contradictory feelings and experiences. Frida who pretended to be French and Catholic, and ignored her mother in school, felt Jewish and safe at home, even though she fought a lot with her mother. She says these were two irreconcilable worlds. When the war started, Claire had to recognize that outside of school some Polish Christians were nice, even courageous. She states that this was overwhelmingly confusing to her. The images of good and bad parents and good and bad Christians existed side by side and evoked intense, incompatible thoughts and feelings. This conflict prevented the development of a cohesive perception of Jews and Christians. Several children developed feelings of inferiority and envy towards Christians, for which they compensated by feelings of superiority. They lost the feeling of being equal but different and that of being special no matter what. In summary, the children's ambivalence towards Judaism created many uncomfortable feelings which fuelled more negative feelings about themselves and eventually about their Jewish identity.

DURING THE WAR

RELATIONSHIP TO THE CHURCH. During the war many children were separated from their parents and often entrusted to Christian families or hidden in convents. (Some of these cases are described more fully in a forthcoming article to appear in the Psychoanalytic Review). At that time the church took on a prominent role as a source of hope and as a protector. The younger children especially projected onto the divine figures human qualities and created relationships with God, Jesus and Mary who became receptacles for their needs.

The Church as Family. Many ascribed the recovery of the sense of protection and safety they had lost after being separated from their parents to their mere presence in the church or in a convent. The sense of belonging to a family was furthered by the familial labels given to divine figures, "God the Father, Mary our Mother in Heaven." Children regained a way of feeling special through fantasies about those heavenly beings. A girl wanted to be Jesus' favorite in order to be special somewhere. Another girl created a personal God, "I asked for specific things, I felt special because God loved me. Go was at my disposal" (Hogman, 1985). After a sudden traumatic separation from his family a boy who was left alone, saw Jesus as pathetic and prayed for Him: he felt better for it.

The Church as Beautiful and Good. All the children were impressed by the rituals and the magic of the ambiance. The beauty of the place, the priest, the boys and the altar and the singing enabled them to feel a part of something good. The aesthetic quality made a profound impression on them. They seemed to equate beauty with goodness and with feelings of love. Beauty was at times contrasted with the dark, ugly, scary synagogue and with the feelings of ugliness they had as traumatized Jews.

The Church as Omnipotent Protector. The Christian God provided a figure all-knowing and omnipotent which frightened children were looking for. The presence of God gave reassurance and the belief that someone in the world had the power to reverse the terrifying reality.

Prayer. To have someone as powerful as God to pray to, provided a crucially active experience for children who felt totally helpless and passive, as illustrated in the following quotes. "I hoped prayer would achieve something. I was doing something for myself;" "I sang the Magnificat as loud a possible. It was my way of communicating with God. He had to hear me."

The Church as Fulfilling Dependency Needs. Feelings of love and dependency developed towards those divine figures who seemed to offer safety and hope. The child did not feel alone any more with this new attachment. This feeling often led to critical comparisons. Andre wanted to pray to the Madonna and did not want to go home. He denied being Jewish because Jews were bad. Rita was fascinated by the Virgin Mary. She was sophisticated and powerful, the opposite of her experience with a Jewish woman's role in her family. Sometimes the Jewish mother was seen as less warm and less pretty than a Catholic woman, especially in instances where the Jewish mother was a professional.

IDENTITY CONFUSION. Identity confusion describes the situation when children became ambivalent about being Jewish, critical of their parents and started to absorb the Christian culture they were exposed to. Children were most vulnerable when they confused being persecuted with being bad which eroded any positive feelings towards Judaism. Dina was so severely traumatized that she questioned whether the Jews were innocent, "They must have done something horrible," she said. Occasionally suffering and guilt in the Christian context became a way to explain and atone for the events of the war. Claire says, "To suffer will bring salvation." Frida stated, "Prayer and sacrifice will bring merit and faith and atone for the guilt of being Jewish" (Weinstein, 1986). Their dependency on the church in time created guilt feelings towards their own families and eventually anger at those who had caused loyalty conflicts.

Self-Esteem and Identity. Neither being hidden in Christian homes or convents nor being persecuted necessarily created deep-seated conflicts about being Jewish. One girl who felt special at home thought she must be special as herself, because she was saved. One Ukrainian boy also felt special as a Jew because, after hiding in the woods, he came out of the war alive. Jules who was hidden in a Catholic boarding school was awed by the beauty of the mass and grateful for the friendlship of Christian boys, but he held on solidly to his orthodox faith. What these child survivors seemed to have had in common was a deep-seated faith in themselves and for some of them, in their Jewish origins.

AFTER THE WAR

Children felt a resentment towards any adults who suddenly resumed their prerogatives as authorities. Some children, although resentful because they felt that their rescuers had abandoned them, secretly or openly practiced Christianity. While most of these survivors eventually returned to Judaism, a deep skepticism and a despair about losses often remained. It was difficult to reconcile all the suffering with any religious beliefs. Many saw charity as a Christian value and regarded Jews as selfish. Such feelings reinforced their negative Jewish identity developed through persecution and tended to see the church as seductive. Some struggled all their lives to transcend their negative Jewish identity and to develop a positive Jewish identity. For others, whose Jewish identity remained unshaken, the relationship has remained a mixture of mistrust, anger and gratitude. Having been saved by some Christians and denounced by others, they could not easily reconcile these contradictory experiences

CONCLUSION

In the absence of anti-Semitism Jews and Christians had good relationships. Children who felt strongly Jewish were less threatened in their identity by anti-Semitism than those who didn't feel intensely Jewish. Parental attitudes to anti-Semitism were as important as were their relationships to their children in determining children's self-esteem and the degree of their ambivalence towards Judaism. Well into their adult lives many survivors continued to integrate their split identities which resulted from living in two different worlds and feeling they belonged to neither. This was especially true for children who were hidden in convents or Christian homes.

III. CHRISTIAN CHILDRENS' PERCEPTION OF THEMSELVES AND OF JEWS BEFORE, DURING AND AFTER THE HOLOCAUST By Milton Kestenberg, Esq.

This report is based on 1) numerous interviews with Jewish child-survivors who recalled the attitudes of Christians in Eastern Europe and in Germany before, during and after the war. 2) interviews with Christians who were contemporaries of Jewish child-survivors, and 3) literature comprising childhood reminiscences of Jewish child-survivors and Germans.

Gentile children learned about Jews from their personal experiences, from their parents, friends, teachers and priests. Some children and families befriended Jews, others joined the ranks of anti-Semites and still others were indifferent. In most European countries anti-Semitism was centuries old but underwent periodic changes. It would become non-existent or latent over long periods of time only to flare up again during times of popular discontent when rulers needed a scapegoat. However, even during times of relative tolerance for Jews, anti-Semitism has maintained its presence in the form of anti-Jewish folktales, derived from politically motivated libels, and handed over from generation to generation.

Folklore Stories About Jews. Fantastic stories about Jews became part of indigenous folklore in many European countries. This can be best illustrated by the Blood Libel, a 2,000 year old myth that is still alive in some parts of Eastern Europe (Gilat, 1972). The following excerpts from interviews conducted in 1987 illustrates how such a tale can influence the behavior of a friendly and tolerant Polish child in modern times.

When sister Beata, who now resides in a Polish convent in southern Poland, was young there were many Jews in her town and her best friends were Jewish. When Jewish families were deported by the Nazis, Beata and her family cried. Although Beata had played with Jewish children on a daily basis, she never entered their homes. She explained her attitude by saying, "Oh, no, they would have taken my blood for matzos." The interviewer (M.K.) told her that the Old Testament forbade the consumption of blood. Beata knew the reference by heart and assured M.K. that the Bible was a holy book and everything written there was true. Thus she concluded the story about Jews using Christian childrens' blood for passover must be false. The Holy See had even condemned blood libel as recently as 1963, but most nuns in the convent still believed it. In a discussion with the Mother Superior, the latter conceded that the belief must be unfounded but she added, "Only one Jewish sect does it."

In Catholic countries, the image of Jews developed on the basis of religious precepts and prejudices. In the following case, children friendly to a Jewish girl and guided by a tolerant teacher, believed that she was personally responsible for Christ's death because she was Jewish. Anna Weiss never felt excluded in her Austrian school even though she was the only Jewish child among Catholics. However, one day when she came to school late, she heard the girls sing, "Die Weiss hat den Jesus Christus ermordet" (Weiss murdered Jesus Christ). Since this happened before the advent of the Nazis, Anna's father dared to complain to the teacher, who explained to the class that the Romans, not the Jews, killed Christ. At any rate, this had happened 1,900 years ago and Weiss did not live then. Furthermore, she told the children that Jesus wanted people to love each other instead of hating. One wonders whether this well-meaning explanation could remove the deep-seated prejudice, taught as truth by many teachers of religion, then a compulsory subject in Europe.

VARIETIES OF TOLERANCE AND ANTI-SEMITISM IN DIFFERENT COUNTRIES. We have no reports of pre-war anti-Semitism in such Eastern-European countries as Czechoslovakia and Yugoslavia; even during German occupation there were only certain ethnic groups who were anti-Semitic. In pre-war communist Russia, religious differences were disregarded. For instance, Ilya, a Jewish child, born in a small town in the Soviet Ukraine, reported that as a child before the war, he did not feel different than other children. His parents were non-believers as were the parents of his playmates. When the Germans invaded the territory, non-Jewish neighbors hid him and his mother. However, the Russian people forgot that Jews fought and died in the war, as did Ilya's father. Anti-Semitism was sanctioned by Stalin, and Russian children learned from their elders to despise Jews. Listening to this report, one wonders whether despite their defeat, the Nazis indoctrinated their enemies and thus provoked a regression to anti-Semitic Czarist times.

On the border of Czechoslovakia ajoining Hungary, child survivors report such well-known excesses as the stoning of Jewish children by Christian children even before the war. Hassidic youngsters were especially persecuted, their side locks cut off for the fun of it. Edelstein (1985) recalls that relations between Jews and Christians in Szatmar (Hungary) were normal except at certain holiday times. "Normal" included being teased and beaten. During the time of the Easter procession, Jewish shops, houses and windows had to be closed. If a Jewish child appeared on the street, he was severely beaten. After the procession, "normal" relations with Jews were restored.

Reports from Poland. After Pilsudski's death and the non-aggression pact with Germany in 1935, Polish anti-Semitism increased considerably. As in several other countries, hostilities of Christian children frequently took the form of gang warfare, whereby several boys would attack one Jewish child, call him names, beat him or throw stones at him. Girls were attacked too, but mostly chased and teased. Christian girls would taunt Jewish children, but would rarely beat them. The object of all these attacks was to humiliate Jewish children and make them feel ridiculous and weak. The image of the Jew as funny-looking, weak, cowardly, impractical and bookish could be only altered when personal experiences served to convince gentile children that Jews could be different. Many Polish children who did not do well in school were angry and envious when a teacher praised Jewish children. Yet, Jews were admired for being smart, for being rich and for having nice parents. Maids and nannies, employed by Jews, would confirm this view by spreading the word how kind and generous Jews were to them. They also became attached to the Jewish children they cared for and frequently volunteered to hide them during the Nazi occupation.

Polish teachers were allowed to hit children, but no excesses like those described by German teachers in Nazi schools have been reported to us. However, anti-Semitic remarks by teachers would incite Christian children to beat up their Jewish classmates. For instance, Jacob's elementary school teacher addressed the two Jewish children in the class, not by calling their names but by calling out, "Jew, stand up." The gentile children would then demean their Jewish classmates by calling them names and beating them up.

In Poland as well as in other countries, Nazi propaganda and the local excesses of their sympathizers increased the lust of children to hurt others cruelly. During occupation, Polish children became the scourge of Jews who wanted to hide or pass as Christians. Proud that they could recognize Jews, they betrayed them to their own enemies, the Nazi occupiers. However, despite the hate propaganda conducted by the Nazis and threats that any Pole harboring a Jew would be killed together with his family, many righteous Poles saved Jews from Nazi persecutors. Children participated with their parents in their rescue work and used their ingenuity to make the life of Jewish children, living with them, easier (see section IV). Only when the rescuing parents concealed from their children, that the "new cousins" were Jewish, did the children of rescuers show hostility to the newcomers or even betray their parents to the Nazis. For instance, when Hanna was praised by her Polish mother, as soon as the mother left the house, Hanna's Polish 'sister' pushed her out of the door. Nevertheless, these children formed a lasting friendship (Krall, 1983). Sometimes, children who suffered from Nazi atrocities, directed against "inferior slavs", developed a kinship to Jews as fellow sufferers. Several children, who were incarcerated in the Polen-Jugend-Verwahrungslager (Polish Youth Detention Camp) reported that they did not know any Jews until they came to this camp which adjoined the Lodz ghetto. One did not like Jews without ever having met one. However, all came to admire the Jewish craftsmen from the ghetto who came to supervise the young camp inmates and all became attached to their Jewish physician. A segment of the Polish population identified with Jews since their childhood. A unique example is that of Franciszek, whom we met in a synagogue in Poland. When we spoke to him we discovered that he was a Catholic, married to a Catholic and father of a Catholic. Yet, he attended synagogue every Friday evening and Saturday. He had been brought up in a Jewish neighborhood. During and after the occupation he witnessed pogroms, the burning of a synagogue and discrimination against his Jewish friends. All along, he felt that he belonged to them. In his adulthood he hypothesized that his ancestors were Jews and cited as proof the fact that his mother did not mix meat with milk and kept other customs which belonged to Jews.

After liberation, anti-Semitism did not cease in Polish schools. Jewish children were often discriminated against and Polish children sometimes refused to sit next to them. This was partly due to the persistence of Nazi propaganda and partly due to the Polish adults' increased anti-Semitism, now rooted in their disapproval of Jewish involvement in the hated Communist government. However, in recent years, Polish young people, especially the Catholic intelligentsia, are turning back to Jews, welcoming them and studying their history.

Reports from Germany. Prior to the rise of Nazism, Jewish children did not experience much anti-Semitism in Germany. However, the groundwork for anti-Semitism was laid. The rise of nationalism and volkish feelings since the nineteenth century, prepared German children to look upon themselves as superior to all other people. A narcissistic pride developed which counteracted feelings of inferiority and contempt children had for their defeated, yet cruel fathers. As discussed in section I, cruelty of parents instilled German children with hate and fear which was easily re-directed from their fathers to Jews.

Stangl, the notorious commandant of Treblinka, in interviews with Gitta Sereny (1974), recalled that his father had been a night watchman and that he often talked about his days in the Dragoons, an Austro-Hungarian elite regiment in World War I. Asked whether his father was kind to him, he "laughed without mirth" and said, "He was a Dragoon. Our lives were run on regimental lines. I was scared to death of him" (p. 25). He recounted the many times he had been beaten for transgressions. He described how his father "...put me on his knee and leathered me... he thrashed me so hard, his cut (a recent injury) opened and blood poured out." Stangl heard his mother scream, "Stop it. You are splashing blood all over clean walls" (p. 26). Alfons Heck (1985) reported that his uncle beat his son black and blue because he was kicked out of high school and could not attend university. Heck's own grandmother who was very attached to him "...habitually used to slap me silly."

Not only parents but German teachers also were empowered to beat children and many of them did it to an excess. They also tried to engage the children in their sadistic activity. Lucia K. (Franck and Asmus, 1983) recalled that when her schoolmate was punished by whippings, it was Lucia's duty to hold her during the beating sessions. Sometime the teacher would run through the whole class and beat the children without rhyme or reason. Heck (1985) states, "In pre-war Germany, teachers were expected to thrash their elementary school pupils. None of us could expect sympathy at home for having been whipped in school. On the contrary, any such complaint would usually invite a second, parental beating" (p. 12). He further states that Jewish children were beaten more severely and singled out for special treatment. The teacher made Jewish pupils sit in a corner designated "Israel." He wanted the Gentile children to despise Jews.

During the height of the Nazi indoctrination, strength and beauty were the highest Germanic ideals. It was preached that intellect weakens one because the thinking man cannot blindly follow rules (Klose, 1982, p. 153). Jews were seen as "...devious and cunning overachievers, especially in their aim of polluting our pure Aryan race, whatever that meant" (Heck, 1982, p. 3). Believers in national socialism were good people, all others were "dirty birds" (Schmutzfinke). Germans had a biological right to rule over others (Franck and Asmus, 1983). In schools and in youth groups, the right of the stronger was upheld and it was practically forbidden to help a weaker comrade (p. 121). Christian values, such as compassion and love were despised. Priests who opposed Nazis were taken to concentration camps and a new "German church" (Deutsche Kirche), perverted Christianity in the service of Nazism. Hitler Youth was encouraged to give up their church affiliation. Thus, the pre-war conscience, conveyed by good parents, was systematically undermined. The resulting excessive cruelty was not only directed towards the handicapped and the 'inferior races,' but also affected the relationships between German children. At certain times a school mate was singled out as a scapegoat. A group of children would throw water at the victim, claiming that he stinks, is dirty and needs washing (Franck and Asmus, 1983). German children's conscience was weakened by the contradictory messages they received. They had all the power themselves and had to obey unconditionally. They were taught that they should be daring and brave and sacrifice their lives for the good of Germany. They were afraid of dying, never of death. As they sang songs anticipating and glorifying their own death, Jewish children were dying instead of them. For those who could not cope with the direct responsibility for genocide, the Nazis offered the excuse of ignorance. They tried to keep their murderous activities secret and trained their children to ignore the disappearance of unwanted teachers and classmates. In this they were helped by parents who did not explain where the Jewish neighbors and friends had gone.

By looking away and not understanding, even religious German youth could also ignore the fact that they were acting in contradiction to their religion. Even though they believed that God was with them, they acted against Christian tenets. Excerpts from a poem by Julie Heifetz (1985) portray the postwar insights of a German who could be Catholic and Nazi at the same time.

> I was born a Catholic and a German...
> I wish I could give you a story
> that I was against the Nazis
> that I was a hero, a Righteous Gentile...
> Jews were freaks
> dogs who'd hurt you, cheat you,...
> I believed the principal, my teachers... (p. 35)

In another paradoxical split young national socialists befriended Jews. Deutschkron (1985), who spent the entire Nazi reign hiding in Germany, wrote about one of her classmates, "a member of the German girls' club (BDM) who took leave of me, she greeted me with her arm raised and 'Heil Hitler.'" Some German children felt compassion for Jews, but encouraged by adults to be tough, they neither protested nor doubted the Nazi cause. The split between feeling badly for the oppressed and the enjoyment of mass destruction was vividly described by Leonie Ossowski, a Nazi youth leader (Fritz, 1986). She and her classmates screamed, 'Hau Ruck, Hau Ruck' as they eagerly watched a synagogue burning and the SS men pulling the Jewish star down with a rope. When Leonie joined a little Jewish girl and cried with her, while the other children still yelled 'Hau Ruck,' the teacher told her a German girl must be tough. Nazi propaganda and activities completely undermined long-term relationships between German and Jewish children. Heck (1985) used to visit his Jewish friend, Heinz, in his home, eat his mother's cookies and enjoy the companionship of his relatives who were more tolerant and child oriented than his own family. Yet, after Heinz was expelled from school and Heck joined the Hitler youth group at the age of ten, Heinz soon became only a "fleeting memory."

In post-war Germany, anti-Semitism was legally forbidden. German teachers and students did not dare to show it openly. Some children were shocked to discover their elders' Nazi atrocities. The long period of denial, of being tough and blissfully ignorant was coming to an end. However, despite the best intentions, anti-Semitic remarks crept into the language, hurting Jewish children, but unnoticed by teachers and German students. For instance, a teacher would reprimand the class for being disorderly by calling their behavior "Juedische Wirtschaft" (Jewish mess). At first, the history of the Holocaust was not taught in German schools. Many children did not know about it until they saw such movies as "Justice in Nueremberg." Once they discovered the truth, they turned against their parents, who had concealed these facts from them and who had perhaps been themselves cruel oppressors and murderers. The children became afraid of their parents and in self-defense, they attacked them angrily. The fight between the children and, especially, their fathers, increased until children grew up and realized that they will get more information about the past if they are less belligerent (von Westernhagen, 1987). They now frequetly identify with Jews (Hardtman, 1982) and sometimes say that they would rather be victims than persecutors. Through their allegiance to the persecuted Jews they defend themselves against what they unconsciously perceive as a grand attack of their parents on themselves. Still, quite a few Germans are left whose Nazi indoctrination has not ceased operating. They still idolize Hitler and minimize Nazi atrocities.

Ulrich, interviewed forty years after the war ended, still believed that Hitler was a good leader. According to him, the only mistake Hitler made was that he treated the Ukrainians badly instead of eliciting more of their cooperation in their fight with the Russians. At the age of seventeen, Ulrich, who had just lost his father at the Russian front, enlisted in the German army, even though as the only son of a widow he could have been exempted from service. Ulrich became upset when the interviewer (M.K.) asked him, how it felt when his mother did not object to his endangering his life. It was difficult for him to accept that he felt rejected by his mother and that he still yearned for the parental love he missed, a love which he had hoped to get from Hitler, provided he sacrificed his life for him.

Judith and Milton Kestenberg are indebted to Dr. Janet Amighi for her constructive criticism and suggestions.

IV. THE RELATIONSHIP BETWEEN THE RESCUED JEWISH CHILD AND THEIR RESCUER'S CHILDREN By Eva Fogelman, Ph.D.

The psychodynamics of rescuing families during the Holocaust is a relatively uncharted territory. To recreate a clear vision of Jewish-Christian relations within the rescuing family it is therefore necessary to explore the wartime experience from three interrelated points of view, that of: the Jewish child survivor whom the rescuer family sheltered; that of the rescuer's children; and that of the rescuers themselves. This paper is based on in-depth interviews with Dutch, French, and Polish rescuers, their children, and the child survivors whom they harbored.

PRE-WAR SOCIALIZATION OF ADULT RESCUERS AND THEIR CHILDREN. Social-psychological study of rescuers reveals a warm, loving family environment (Grossman, 1984). An overwhelming majority of rescuers married for love and thus viewed marriage as an equal partnership in which husband and wife possessed shared ideals and struggled together to achieve shared goals (Fogelman, 1987). Rescuer couples usually came from similar socio-economic backgrounds and were raised in caring homes where at least one parent or significant other served as an altruistic role model (Fogelman, 1987); Tec, 1986). Male and female rescuers thus often performed altruistic acts as children, accompanying a parent or other close adult on visits to the needy. The rescuer's parents consistently instilled the values of tolerance for people who were different and gave their youngsters a feeling of independence and competence (Fogelman, 1987).

Those rescuers who had been religious in childhood generally raised their children religiously, and all family members attended church regularly and participated in family prayer. Christian teachings and Bible stories such as "The Good Samaritan" were part of the moral fabric of the home and the benevolent image of a self-sacrificing Jesus was vivid and alive in the imagination of rescuer children. Those rescuers who were non-religious tended to create a freethinking, intellectual environment where their children were encouraged to participate in adult discussions of art, music, literature, and current events. Anti-Nazi rescuers—whether religious or non-religious—also discussed politics openly and gave their children a sense that they too, as adults would actively participate in transforming society.

The Rescuing Family in Wartime. It is difficult to imagine just how radically rescuers' lives and domestic environments changed to accommodate their high-risk rescue activity during the war. Homes that modestly sufficed for the rescuers and their families were suddenly transformed into secret lodgings in which one to fifteen or more sometimes transient, but often long-term victims of Nazi persecution were hidden, fed and cared for. Rescuers started their activities in various ways (Fogelman, 1987): (a) young and old who were anti-Nazi joined an underground network which put them in constant contact with individuals who needed refuge; (b) non-Jews who prior to the war had close relationships with Jews either initiated help or were asked for a hiding place; (c) individuals who became aware of the imminent death of Jews either responded to a plea for help or felt an inner calling to offer help; (d) people such as nurses and psychologists helped as concerned, detached professionals; and (e) child rescuers responded to their parents' request to do certain tasks. During the war, Jews as a group became more visible to non-Jewish children when they saw them being marked with Stars of David on their outerwear; watched them being beaten, deported, killed on the streets; when classmates sat in back of the room and later disappeared. At the onset of rescue the children of rescuers did not necessarily know that a Jewish child was hiding in their home. The Jewish children often had a Christian name and knew not to undress (if male) in front of everyone. It was not until the parents warned them to keep a secret lest they all be killed that a new awareness set in.

The following case studies, based on interviews with children of rescuers, rescuer parents, and the child survivors they harbored, illustrate how the family environment influenced relations between rescuer children of varying ages and their adoptive Jewish siblings in Holland, France, and Poland.

Holland. Cornelia K. was ten years old when the Germans invaded Holland. She lived in a rural village outside of Amsterdam and was raised by religious parents who were members of the Protestant anti-Revolutionary Church Party. As a child she and he elder siblings attended Protestant Dutch Reform Church and fundamentalist Bible study where they learned that "Jesus was a Jew..." and that "Jews were special people: God's chosen ones. We were impressed by the Old Testament Bible stories of Moses, Abraham, Esther, and Noah, and in our hearts were very close to the Jewish people who we felt were our ancestors." Cornelia often went on "neighbor duty" with her mother, attending to new mothers and the sick and elderly of the community. Because there was no local synagogue, Cornelia did not have any direct exposure to Jews until the war broke out and at the request of her elder brother, her parents took in two Jewish adolescents. Cornelias brother who was a policeman refused to arrest Jews and became a "quisling" (collaborator). Though he was later sent to a cencentration camp, he was for some time a member of the Dutch resistance, and it was during this time that he realized that the "lives of Jewish children were threatened." He arranged to transport two Jewish teenagers, a boy and a girl, to his hometown where they were to be protected by his family.

Cornelia's first impression of the boy they harbored for two years was that "he was very brave," and "hardened" by his terrible experience of losing his family. Cornelia felt very "motherly" and protective toward him, and the whole family demonstrated a great deal of affection in an effort to "cuddle him, to make him feel loved." Though he did not look very Jewish, it was difficult for him to go out much because "even if he passed as a Christian he could have been sent like other Dutch boys to forced labor camp in Germany." Still, he bravely acted as a courier for the underground network of which Cornelia's family were members, as did Cornelia and her younger sister. The family's other charge, Sarah, was a fourteen-year old Jewish girl whom Cornelia adored, who was "so lovely and good-natured that you had to respond." For the two and a half years they lived together, Cornelia and the Jewish girl were "extremely close, like sisters." Cornelia and her family were especially impressed by the girl's spiritual discipline:

> She was so highly religious and observed all her fasts and holidays and sabbaths. She was so young and so far away from her family and we had a great admiration for her faith to her religion. We Christians are not always so faithful to our laws, but she was boldly Jewish, true to her ancestors. Even when there was very little food she would never eat pork or break kosher laws.

The family never tried to convert their Jewish charges, though lively discussions did take place between the youngsters about the differences in their religions, especially concerning Jesus, the Second Coming, and the Messiah. One of Cornelia's strongest memories is of a day that her Jewish "sister" Sarah lent her a coat:

> We didn't have many clothes during the war and I had to journey in the cold. Sarah said, "Please, take my coat," because she could not go out of hiding. Though we had removed the Jewish star, a yellow stain remained, and I remember how frightened I was. Boarding the train I finally realized as I had never before what it meant to be marked as a Jew, and I was very sad and terribly afraid.

The experience deepened Cornelia's emphatic engagement; she remembered trying to comfort Sarah who would often cry when she thought about her mother and father. In these moments of closeness the two girls, who looked "very much alike" transformed their pain into anger against "our common enemy: the Nazis." Early on, Cornelia and her own younger sister "learned to keep secrets. Under no circumstances were we to reveal anything to the Germans." During a neighborhood raid, German Soldiers burst into the house with guns and conducted a violent search which left the house destroyed. Sarah and the Jewish boy were hidden in a secret closet, and though held at gunpoint, Cornelia did not give them away:

> After the war a friend of my mother said, "You were a very brave child." I didn't understand what she meant and then she said, "You were afraid, and yet you never said to the German 'The Jews are in the closet.'" The thought would have never occurred to me.

In retrospect Cornelia explained that:

> When you are young, you love a challenge. I thought of myself as a little hero against the big Nazis. The best antidote to fear is action, and we did not become brave all at once. Little things added up. We brought this paper there for the underground... we took in these children... we made false passports... our involvement got deeper and deeper... but we were not all at once brave. The times forced us to give in and be a quisling (collaborator) or to fight back, and we would have rather died than cooperate with the Nazis.

After the war, Cornelia kept in contact with Sarah, her Jewish "sister." To this day she retains a strong feeling for the Jewish people and often speaks in synagogues about her wartime experience as part of a rescuing family. Although the positive religious imagery Cornelia learned in childhood is unique to specific Protestant fundamentalist sects, the themes of "sisterly" love and empathetic identification with the "adopted" Jewish children cropped up again and again in these interviews. These close sibling bonds generally lasted into adulthood. In Cornelia's case, her "sister" Sarah even looked like her ("We were both dark and had curvaceous figures") and this feeling of likeness, combined with Cornelia's capacity for empathy, may have strengthened their sibling bond, or may have facilitated her initial, warm acceptance of Sarah.

Henry DeVries and his family lived on the border between Belgium and Holland during the war. A non-religious Protestant, Mr. DeVries had an independent nature and was, according to Schlomo, one of the Jewish children he rescued, "Very anti-Nazi and extremely humanitarian."

In 1942, Schlomo and Eva's father was incarcerated in Westerbork. Their socialist and religious Jewish mother went underground. The children were separated and sent to different families by the underground. Schlomo, who was four-and-a-half years old at the time, remembers how a man took him on a bicycle, hid him in the bushes, and told him to wait until another man would pick him up. He waited, terrified, and after a while, Mr. DeVries came along. He was immediately warm and loving, but when the frightened Schlomo arrived safely to the DeVries home, he "cried and cried and then they put me to bed." Night after night, Schlomo cried until finally he was able to communicate his sadness to Mr. DeVries and his wife, "I told them that I wanted Eva who they finally understood was my sister." Mr. DeVries immediately said, 'If I can take in one child, I can take in two. Don't worry.'" Mr. DeVries alerted the network and asked that the little Eva, only three years old, be put in his charge. Not long after, Eva arrived. She recalls, "I was only three but I remember seeing their big, nice dog and how happy I was to finally see my brother!" Henry's own daughter, Greta, recalls, "I was twelve at the time they reunited. They were so happy to be together again that it really broke your heart..." Greta was very fond of the children:

> They were like a brother and sister. The little boy had asthma, and when he cried, it made me so sad that I cried, too. I didn't know if they would like me at first; they were so small. But I felt sorry for them, and helped my mother to tend to them and I read them lots of stories. The children in the neighborhood asked questions but we knew enough to keep quiet. We trained Eva and Schlomo to say they were orphans who were bombed out of Rotterdam and they played their roles well.

In an interview Henry DeVries disclosed that his own teenaged son was quite "spoiled" and "jealous" of his foster siblings. Greta, DeVries' daughter agreed, "he didn't have the same feeling for the Jews." But Eva and Schlomo, the child survivors, both said they "never noticed" any jealousy on his part, and Eva even perceived him as "a big brother; very protective." Eva went to to say that <u>she</u> was the one who felt "babied and spoiled. I was loved and cared for... I played happily on the street with the big dog. In fact, when the war was over, I didn't want to leave the DeVries family." Neither did Schlomo. But the children were returned to their mother, who in 1948 became very ill with cancer. Hearing the news, Greta, then seventeen years old, moved to Amsterdam so that he "brother and sister" would not be put into a foster home. When the children's mother died in 1948, Henry attempted to legally adopt them, but their mother had left notarized instructions that the children were to be sent to Palestine. Henry was furious, and could not understand how he'd been considered "A good enough parent in wartime, but not good enough now." Despite the DeVries' protests, Eva and Schlomo were sent on a children's transport to Palestine where they lived on a kibbutz. They eventually reestablished contact with the DeVrieses. When he visited Israel to plant a tree on the Avenue of the Righteous, Mr. DeVries saw how fulfilled the children were in their surroundings and he finally understood why the children's mother had wanted them to grow up in Israel. They are happily married. The DeVries family, with the exception of their son, is still in very close contact with both Schlomo and Eva, whom they call, with pride, "our Jewish children."

<u>France</u>. Beginning in 1940, the village of Le Chambon-Sur Lignon in South Central France led by its Protestant pacifist minister, André Trocmé, harbored and aided an estimated 5,000 Jews. (Hallie, 1979, Sauvage, 1987) Filmmaker Pierre Sauvage, Jewish child survivor who was born in Le Chambon, writes:

> ...in that little village, during World War II, the climate of the heart was warm, for it was in Le Chambon that people fleeing from the Nazis were welcomed and found a place of refuge. Adults as well as children were cared for by people in the village and by peasants from the surrounding countryside. Jewish children taken from internment camps like Gurs and Rivesaltes, were hidden and helped by these good people. There Jewish children went to school and had their lessons together with non-Jewish children from the area. They played tug-of-war and other games. They had a pig named Adolf.

Nelly Trocmé, Pastor Trocmé's daughter, was thirteen when the Germans occupied France. She dosn't remember Jewish children in her public school prior to the war, though one Jewish family lived in the village. Le Chambon was very Protestant, and Nelly was aware that some of her Catholic schoolmates were in the minority but their feeling of shared French nationality and language gave the children a sense that they were "all the same."

> The children joined us in school and I was very close to two Jewish girls who lived in our house. When you are thrown together the bonds are very strong. Remember, we shared the same room, went to school together, were part of the same scout group. Because I did not have a sister, these girls became my sisters. We shared the trauma of adolescence and became extremely close.

Politics and strategy were discussed freely in the Trocme home:

> We knew the importance of doing what was right, and learned to listen to our own conscience. We saw our parents disobey the law and were taught that a system that persecutes must be disobeyed.

While Nelly admits it was difficult because every decision "put us in danger," and because "no one could predict who would act in what way," she feels deeply fortunate to have been part of this rescuing family and community. Nelly's story points up the theme of difference and how it is perceived in adolescence. For her, the refugees did not seem initially strange or different because of their Jewishness, but because they spoke a different languange.

> In school, it was an unspoken assumption that one was not to ask where or how these (foreign) children came into our midst. Despite the language barrier we understood that they had suffered and that we should not add to their suffering by asking what could be embarrassing questions. We tried to make them feel welcome.

Jewish children in Le Chambon were integrated into the community; rescuing families in hostile or potentially hostile communities and neighborhoods had to live clandestine lives, and the Jewish children whom they protected were frequently completely isolated from the outside world. However, they were totally accepted by the "French families." Nelly, for instance, formed a sisterly relationship with the Jewish girls who were hidden in her home.

Poland. Alexander Roslan had a son and a daughter of his own when he decided to enter the Warsaw ghetto in order to smuggle out two Jewish brothers, while the third, hidden in a country village, joined the Roslans the following month. The youngest, David, had spent three of his first five years in the Warsaw ghetto. He remembers feeling terrified during the time he was separated from his brothers, "because I had been told not to let anyone see me naked. I couldn't sleep and I would not let anyone touch me, especially to change my clothes. All I ever wondered was "What did I do wrong?" David was an extremely cute little boy, and once reunited with his brother charmed the Roslan family and became Mr. Roslan's favorite. David calls Mr. Roslan's preferential treatment of him a kind of "affirmative action" on his part, because "he knew how unhappy I had been away from my brothers and my parents." Roslan's daughter, who was seven at the time, freely admits that "the rest of us were jealous of the extra fruit and vitamins that father gave to David." David, on the other hand, felt jealous that the Roslan children were allowed to "go out and play freely." "But we were all one family," Roslan's daughter recalls, "Sure there were jealousis, but they were normal, petty, family fights, no different from when my brother and I would argue before David and Jacob even arrived." Roslan's daughter had lots of Jewish playmates before the occupation and "never knew there was a difference between us."

She recalls the boys would joke about their circumcision and were told to be careful not to pee outside on walks, "but I didn't really know or understand why or what made them different." Both David and Jacob corroborated much of what Roslan and his daughter recalled. All felt that the tensions and rivalries in the family were a "normal part of kids living together," and all felt extremely close sibling bonds. Although her father, by his own admission, put his own children at extreme risk to save the Jewish boys, and though her own brother was killed by the Germans, the only resentment Roslan's surviving daughter could recall was that she was no longer allowed to bring other children into the house to play. "Still," she adds, "we all had fun at home... we played together, they were like my brothers." The Roslan family is still in close contact with their Jewish charges who now live in Israel.

CONCLUSION

The sibling bonds that developed between rescuer children and the Jewish children who were hidden into their families during the Holocaust were marked and have consistently endured in the forty year period since the war. The loving family atmosphere created by the rescuer parents fostered normal relations between the children. The rescuer children were made to feel part of the meaningful and humane act of rescue. Their active participation in protecting their "Jewish siblings" was an experience which "shaped their lives," and enhanced their self-esteem. Because rescuer children were taught tolerance long before the Holocaust and were not deprived of love once the family expanded, they could love and accept their "Jewish siblings." When the rescuers' children played an active role in the rescue activity they did not develop a high degree of jealousy or envy. Some identified with their new siblings, others developed maternal feelings towards them. Again and again, the Jewish children—no matter how different in age and background—were described by rescuer children as being similar to them, so similar that it was easy for them to form a brotherly or sisterly bond with them. In cases where differences were noted, the rescuer children developed a strong emphatic relationship with the Jewish children, as evidenced by descriptions of motherly, nurturing, and protective feelings.

REFERENCES

Bass, H. (1987). Unpublished Ph.D. Dissertation, Union Graduate School.
Deutschkron, I. (1985). Ich trug den gelben Stern, DTV.
Edelstein, D.B. (1985). Worlds Torn Asunder. KTAV Publishing House, Inc.
Fogelman, E. (1987). Unpublished Ph.D. Dissertation, City University New York.
Franck, N. and Asmus, G. (ed) (1983). Heil Hitler, Herr Lehrer. Rowohlt.
Gilat, Y. (1972). Encyclopedia Judaica. Vol. 4, 1120-1131.
Grossman, F. (1984). In: Toward the Understanding of Holocaust and Prevention of Genocide. Westview Press, 202-216.
Grunberger, B. (1964). J. Int. Psychoanal. 45/2-3, 380-385.
Hallie, P. (1979). Lest Innocent Blood be Shed, Harper and Row.
Hardtmann, G. (1987). Personal Communication.
Hardtmann, G. (1982). In: Generations of the Holocaust, pp. 230-245. Basic Books.
Heck, A. (1985) A Child of Hitler. Renaissance House.
Heifetz, J. (1985). Oral History and Holocaust. Pergamon Press.
Hogman, F. (1985). Journal of the American Academy of Child Psychiatry, 24/4, 390-396.
Kanerfogel, E. (1985) In: D. Blumenthal, ed., Approaches to Judaism in Medieval Times, 2, 1-34, Scholars Press.
Kestenberg, J., Kestenberg, M. and Amighi, J. (1988). The Psychological Perspectives of the Holocaust and of its Aftermath. Social Sciences Monograph and the Institute of Holocaust Studies, in press.
Kestenberg, J. (1968). J. Amer. Psychoanal. Assoc. 16, 457-519.
Kestenberg, J. and Kestenberg, M. (1986). Slaying Mankind's Most Pernicious Dragon Basic Human Aggression., Human Sciences Press, Inc.
Kestenberg, J. (1987). Issues in Ego Psychology. 10/2, 22-34.
Klose, W. (1982). Generation im Gleichschritt. Stalling.
Krall, H. (1983). Pismo II, 5/12, 61-77.
Matzner-Bekerman (1984). The Jewish Child,Halakhic Perspectives, KTAV Publishing House, Inc.
Piaget, J. (1954). The Construction of Reality in the Child. Basic Books.
Rudavsky, J. (1989). To Live with Hope, to Die with Dignity. University Press of America.
Sauvage, P. (1986). In: The Courage to Care, (eds. Rittner, C. and Myers, S.), New York University Press, p. 99.
Schultz, M. (1986). J. Psychohistory, 14/1, 1-24.
Sereny, G. (1974). Into That Darkness, Vintage Books.
Stein, H.F. (1977). Psychoanal. Quart. 46/4, 650-683.
Tech, N. (1986). When Light Pierced the Darkness: Righteous Christians and the Jewish Poles, Oxford University Press.
Von Fritz, H. (1986). Eine Jugend in Deutschland (1) Leonie Ossowski erinnert sich. Hessischer Rundfunk, Frankfurt am Main.
Von Westernhagen, D. (1987). Die Kinder der Taeter, Koesel.
Wangh, M. (1964). J. Int. Psychoanal. 45/2-3, 386-395.
Weinstein, F. (1986). A Hidden Childhood. Farrar, Giroux & Strauss.

CHOOSING LIFE BETWEEN THE FIRES: TOWARD AN INTENTIONALIST VOICE OF FAITH

Henry F. Knight

Baldwin-Wallace College, Berea, Ohio, U.S.A.

We are the generation
That stands between the fires.
Behind us is the flame and smoke
That rose from Auschwitz and from Hiroshima.
Before us is the nightmare of a Flood of Fire;
A thermonuclear holocaust
That could make every human city
A crematorium without a chimney.
It is our task to make from fire
Not an all-consuming blaze
But the light in which we see each other;
All of us different,
All of us made in the image of God.
We light this fire to see more clearly
That the earth, the human race, is not for burning.
We light this fire to see more clearly
The rainbow in our many-colored faces (Waskow, 1984, 14).

INTRODUCTION

Like Arthur Waskow, I "stand between the fires." My world is marked by two unique events of the past generation, Auschwitz and Hiroshima, linked together by the threat they now signify to the future. Unlike Waskow, I am a Christian, not a Jew, so I do not stand there as he does. Yet, I am profoundly affected by his particular stance as well as that of many of his brother and sister Jews. Like many of them, he confronts the unthinkable reality of Auschwitz and the unimaginable power of Hiroshima within the context of his covenantal faith story.

Without diminishing the threat to life that these events signal our generation, Waskow sets before us the choice Moses put before his people in the wilderness:

> "I have set before you life and death, blessing and curse.
> Therefore, choose life." (Deut. 30:19, RSV).

Moreover, he links this admonition with the divine intention of creation and God's covenantal bond with it. In a very clear and distinctive Jewish voice, Waskow speaks life to death and challenges God's people to take up and transform the memory of fire which has circumscribed our time into an occasion for choosing life.

Specifically, the **haggadah**, which Waskow's poem/prayer introduces, expresses a particular way of remembering the past for the future. It portrays liberation and exodus in a way that is meant to embrace and transform the despair of our situation (Waskow, 1984).

Waskow's particular invitation is not unique to him. Yet, the very way Waskow puts the challenge evokes the question of how one can voice such faithfulness and commitment in our time. Is not the faith that this poem/prayer expresses the foundation which is radically altered by the very reality it seeks to contain? Indeed, what happens to the voice of faith when it dares speak not just to but also from life "between the fires?"

It is this question that I try to engage in this essay. Though similar, my task is different than that of my Jewish brothers and sisters, however much I draw on their witness and faith. They seek **tikkun**, a mending of their world--a Jewish one. I seek a similar healing for my Christian world which is likewise ruptured. However, I also struggle to find a voice to express my world which not only addresses what happened to my Jewish brothers and sisters, but which also incorporates and challenges the role that traditional Christian beliefs and attitudes played in supporting the Nazi logic of destruction. Moreover, for this to be a truly constructive voice, it must also be capable of leading any who adopt it into a responsible exercise of power, as well as faith, in a nuclear age.

At the outset, I acknowledge the uniqueness of what happened in the event we can only approach with names like Auschwitz, **Shoah, Holocaust**. I begin, as well, with the sad knowledge of my faith world's long and sustained contribution to what happened. Like others, I am indebted to the critiques of Jules Isaac, James Parkes, Rosemary Reuther, Paul van Buren, Clark Williamson, Roy Eckhart, **et al**. However, I do not wish to debate the scope of responsibility for what happened (which they view in different degrees), since that would lead me astray from the task of this essay and the existential burden I feel as a participant in this problematic legacy. Instead, I wish to begin by acknowledging their important work and pursue a consequent, existential question: how may I speak of a loving God of creation and, as well, of the centrality of the Jesus story as a witness to that belief after Auschwitz? How can I give voice to my Christian faith in a responsible encounter with a world in which Auschwitz can happen (and happen again) as well as a world with such power in human hands that all creation is threatened by the capacity for genocide that was revealed a generation ago?

Clark Williamson concludes his incisive survey, Has God Rejected His People?, with a boldly put version of this same question:

> We [Christians] must be able to ask whether Christianity has survived Auschwitz and be ready to wonder: after all this, is it still morally possible to be a Christian, and if so, how?...If we do not all reexamine our theology in the light of the fires of Maidanek, can we avoid repeating the theology that made possible the final solution? (Williamson, 1982, 137).

BETWEEN THE FIRES

With Auschwitz, the unthinkable happened in history. A state bureaucracy devised and deployed a technology of death to fulfill what their official terminology designated as "the final solution to the Jewish question." Seemingly ordinary people, even educated people, participated in an extraordinary campaign to exterminate a whole population, a single people. They planned for, even sacrificed for, the total elimination of another group of human beings simply because of who they were: Jews. Even the dead, their memory and witness, were targeted for annihilation. Unthinkable--until it happened.

With Hiroshima, my own nation developed a technology to tap a new kind of power: atomic power, the energy source of the stars. Never before was there this kind of power in human hands. With it, we constructed a weapon that could destroy a single city. It happened not just once, but twice.

Each event was unique. With Auschwitz, humanity crossed a threshold it can never uncross. Never again dare anyone forget what human beings are capable of doing to others, even when they are educated and rational, not to mention obedient and orderly. At Auschwitz, sanity and rationality, madness and irrationality were reversed.

With Hiroshima, human technology pushed beyond ordinary limits of power and destruction. Boundaries of discrimination and proportion were erased. Now some forty years after, the entire planet can be destroyed in the span of thirty minutes. Together, the bureaucratic and so called "civilized" capacity for evil, along with the technological capabilities for destruction (including planetary annihilation) make ours a time of unparalleled concern.

Incomparable, yet nonetheless linked, the two unthinkables of Auschwitz (what human beings will do to others because they have) and Hiroshima (what human beings can do to the whole world because they have the technology) introduce a radically new situation which begs for theological guidance. And yet, many faithful people are no longer able to speak, even figuratively, about God's interventions in history, or about divine providence and covenant fidelity, nor, as well, about God's transcendence, without seriously questioning the adequacy of their faith language to confront what happened a generation ago.

Existentially as well as historically we live "between the fires." The basic trustworthiness of our faith worlds, even history, has been torn asunder. A God who can act in history and who does not has led some to formulate complex explanations of how God's actions are expressed through the ontological and historical structures of creation and human freedom. A God who chooses to be bound to a people in covenant fidelity and yet who is silent in their need has led some to develop subtle descriptions of divine solidarity and providence as well as others to hope for future actions of divine salvation and deliverance. However, the unique character of what has happened in our century, especially to the children, leads many, like myself, to declare that our fundamental faith worlds are torn and in need of repair (Fackenheim, 1982, 250-313).

With what existential and theological compass, then, shall we find our way? On what hermeneutic may we rely to fulfill our dual obligations to honor God as soverign of all life and to exercise the stewardship vocation we share for all creation (provided of course, that we can still commit to that)?

Some of us, no doubt, are guided by Irving Greenberg's well known criterion: "No statement, theological or otherwise, should be made that would not be credible in the presence of burning children" (Greenberg, 1977, 23). Indeed, my theological protest is rooted here. Yet, we still must ask: on what do we rely when we accept the transformative task of faith put forward by Waskow to make of fire a symbol not of death but of covenant life?

To live faithfully "between the fires" requires more than acknowledging the task before us. It requires nothing less than wrestling with the kind of faith perspective which can articulate such a faith commitment. Otherwise, it is an inauthentic voice, unable to confront the fires which threaten our world, our faith, and our children.

A VOICE IN THE WILDERNESS

If we truly live in a wilderness circumscribed by fire, then it is imperative that we find a voice which can speak in and to our situation. While honoring Greenberg's criterion, it must also link human beings to each other, themselves, as well as with God. Moreover, to be authentic in our time, it must do this on the other side of innocence. Consequently, what we seek is a voice of faith fit for our twentieth century wilderness, in what Paul Ricoeur calls a post-critical voice of second naiveté (Ricoeur, 1967, 1974).

Perhaps no one has articulated these concerns more eloquently than Elie Wiesel. Through his many novels, essays, hasidic tales, and of course, his autobiographical testimony, *Night*, he has guided countless individuals in their encounters with what happened to his people. In addition, Wiesel has spoken forthrightly of the threat of nuclear conflagration--yet without collapsing the distinctions between Hiroshima and Auschwitz. Moreover, he has eloquently linked these concerns with his passion for covenant life in spite of the untrustworthy character of the world we inhabit.

His essay on the **akedah** ("The Sacrifice of Isaac: A Survivor's Tale") in *The Messengers of God* is particularly instructive in this regard. In it, he leads his reader through a critical, analytical review of the midrashic commentary showing how the tradition of midrash wrestles with this story of divine providence and covenant faithfulness and how midrash even holds the **akedah** accountable to God's commitment to life.

Specifically, Wiesel's own midrash contends that a God who can intervene in the binding of Abraham's children and does not, no matter what the reason, must be challenged and resisted for faith, in faith, in the name of faith, and even in spite of faith. He argues that Kierkegaard is wrong in his well-known reading of this story. Abraham does not resign himself, as Kierkegaard asserts, in a teleological suspension of the ethical, and thereby suspend the covenant framework of the relationship. On the contrary, Wiesel maintains that God is covenantally bound to **Torah** and to life. Furthermore, Wiesel posits that Abraham resists and puts God on trial with his faithful obedience, reversing many traditional readings of the story (Wiesel, 1976, 90ff.). In effect, Abraham, in binding Isaac, says to God: "Choose life. Honor Your **Torah**."

To be sure, Wiesel's voice is not his own alone. It is profoundly Jewish, however specific it is to him personally. As well, it is post-critical. He speaks from the other side of innocence as one who has endured a long night's assault on his world and emerged as a witness to faith and to life. Nonetheless, he articulates a richly personal and passionate commitment to covenant life which links the critical and pre-critical aspects of his Jewish world which were torn apart by the Nazi campaign of extermination.

More specifically, his voice is post-critically midrashic. He wrestles with his faith tradition, pushing it, asking it the hard questions of historic Jewish experience. He takes his "night" to Jacob's night and Jacob's night to his, as he contends with this pivotal chapter in the story of Jacob's father. In fact, Wiesel's cumulative work chronicles his journey from pre-critical faithfulness, through critical tearing, to a post-critical recovery of faith.

To many, his witness has been a voice in the wilderness, which, however fragmentary, has brought a measure of healing, and even hope. In as much as Wiesel is able to choose and honor covenant life in even its most extreme violation, he articulates a post-critical voice of faith which cannot be dismissed as unreal or unspeakable. Having endured "the night" and transformed his memory into an offering for life, Wiesel bears witness to others that a similar voice of faith is authentically possible for them.

As Fackenheim points out in To Mend the World, a single act of healing (**tikkun**) grounds the possibility of **tikkun** for others (Fackenheim, 1982, 248-308 passim). For Wiesel, the act of healing is midrashic and self-critically incomplete--respectful of the mystery, evil as well as good, which has marked his life. Importantly, Wiesel's work is an interpretive response, not an explanation, though it puts the event within the Jewish covenantal story of faith. It is clearly open and vulnerable to the realities of Auschwitz. Even so, it clarifies where and how what happened was unique and radical, tearing the covenantal framework of Jewish life.

How, then, is Wiesel's post-critical, midrashic voice instructive for Christians? Is it adoptable, even adaptable? And if so, can it lead someone like myself to an authentic expression of his or her Christian faith? Is there an appropriate faith response as a Christian that is open and vulnerable to the memory of Auschwitz as well as to the role that Christian faith claims played in what happened there?

A HERMENEUTICAL PAUSE

Since we are limited by the finite boundaries of language to express God's relationship to history, we use that language figuratively. The logic of Wiesel's midrash presumes that the language used to articulate the divine intention for life should guide and even correct the metaphors we use to talk about God's relationship with history. In other words, Wiesel's post-critical voice seeks to articulate the divine intention for covenant life even as he wrestles with the language and the story of the **akedah**.

In the biblical story, God responded and provided a ram. Life was chosen. Isaac was spared and the **Torah** was honored. However, a generation ago the story was tragically distorted. This time, a demagogue selected Abraham's children--neither to test nor challenge their faith, but to destroy it and all Jewish life. The altar was history, fashioned not in faith by Abraham, but in the rejection of faith by a state bureaucracy. For the victims and their families (six million Isaacs), God did not provide. Yet, as Wiesel points out, the story did not end there. Other Isaacs, also intended for Hitler's sacrificial altar, were set free. They survived. The annihilation of Abraham's children did not happen. Hitler did not finally win. But the cost?!...That question, writes Wiesel, lingers and haunts, even as he concludes that the **akedah**, in this manner only, can be a story of covenant fidelity for the survivor (Wiesel, 1976, 73).

In the unbinding of Isaac, the **akedah** portrays the mutual binding of Abraham and God (Wiesel, 1976, 75, 90f.). God will provide for Abraham's offspring--not just Isaac. What happened a generation ago distorted and reversed the story--six million times. Even Abraham became the object of annihilation. The story either shatters under the weight of a contradictory history, or it has to be rethought and stretched in midrashic fashion. Rethinking or abandonment must follow; it cannot be left as it is. Wiesel concluded that the **akedah** could only be told as a survivor's tale (Wiesel, 1976, 96f.). It cannot be the tale which describes the fate of the victims who were murdered. That would be blasphemy.

In other words, it can be grasped and embraced with faith as a way of naming and proclaiming the intention of God in history for life as survivors convert their horror and suffering to prayers and offerings for the sake of their faith and that of their children. It cannot, however, be used without questioning its logic of intervention without also impugning the very One it seeks to honor as sovereign of life, the intention it originally sought to proclaim.

The interpretive categories employed by Roman Catholic theologian John Shea are helpful in understanding what is at stake in this hermeneutical distinction. According to Shea there are fundamentally two perspectives with which one embraces the narratives of God's involvement in history: an interventionist one and an intentional one (Shea, 1978). Either can be simplistic or sublimely complex. Nevertheless, they are rooted in and express different understandings of transcendence and power.

In the interventionist view, God, as Creator, intervenes in creation to establish a covenant people, deliver them from slavery, establish their nation, judge, sustain, and redeem them. Divine intervention can be conceived in extrinsic or intrinsic modalities, or a combination of modalities built on the analogy of a parent's care for a growing child who progresses to an autonomous adult in an independent relationship with his or her parent. Regardless, divine transcendence is understood as God's ability to intervene or not intervene in the specific history of the covenant people.

In the intentional perspective, God, as Creator, intends creation in a particular way. Life is to bear the qualities of peace, justice, righteousness. Creation serves life and life abundantly brought forth, abundantly lived, abundantly shared--with human beings intended as stewards of this divine purpose. In freedom, they may participate in God's unfolding intention for life; and so they are called, in the image of God to care for this gift they have received.

In this perspective, divine transcendence is understood as God's intention for the abundant life of peace, of justice, which is known convenantally. It is known in deliverance. It is known and embodied when the least of peoples becomes a people, a light to the nations, a people of significance and witness. God's faithfulness is to the divine intention and does not waiver. Human beings, in freedom, may participate and share in that. In faith, people are called to participate in it. Likewise, they may fall away from it--or, even, be driven from it and prevented by others from participating in it. Importantly, it is an intention known only in deeds. It is not an abstract universal but a concrete one--a universally significant aspect of covenant life that links life abundantly across generations, among people (friends and strangers), and with God.

Both metaphoric families of intention and intervention are present in scripture. They co-exist in dynamic tension with each other, stretching and sometimes correcting each other. Interestingly, they are both employed in the creation story of Genesis. In Genesis 1, the logic of intention, through the metaphors of speech (language, word), is used to tell of God's sovereign activity of creation. In Genesis 2, the logic of intervention is employed to describe God fashioning life out of the earth and giving it life by breathing into it. Together, they tell one story, even though there are remnants of two in its fabric.

However, Wiesel's midrashic voice is not simply a critical, analytical pause which recognizes the dynamic interaction of different perspectives in scripture. It is not enough to step back from the intentional and interventionist points of view in sacred scripture in order to move back into them with more understanding. Indeed, what happened at Auschwitz qualifies any re-entry, like Greenberg's criterion qualifies any theological statement. Wiesel's post-critical move is self-consciously from the side of the intentional perspective, with the divine intention for life providing hermeneutical guidance.

AN INTENTIONALIST VOICE

Auschwitz breaks down our language. Indeed, we are in the realm of figure and metaphor; however, as Wiesel's midrash illustrates, simply a self-critical awareness of this limit is not enough. In the shadow of Auschwitz, the logic of intervention and its metaphors must be questioned, and brought into an appropriate relationship with those of divine intention.

It may not be necessary to replace or reject them. However, the reality of what happened, as well as what did not happen, demands that the limits of the metaphors of intervention be articulated and challenged for the sake of using those metaphors in a different way, moving them from a position of primacy to a position of support and extension.

When covenant language leads to a conflict over the intending of suffering versus the intending of life, the divine intention for life provides the critical vantage point. The critique directed toward the logic of intervention is that this logic is not commensurate with the logic inherent in the metaphors of intention and creation which we use to express God's will and way with life. In other words, the metaphors of intention and creation are primary. Those of intervention are secondary and are faithfully used when they express the character of that divine intention in a manner that is not contradictory to it. Shea's categories, with some revision, give us a constructive way to describe this shift. Because of the importance of the critical, interpretive move which qualifies what Shea calls the intentional perspective, I have chosen to designate this as an "intentionalist voice" of faith. Although it may seem like an unnecessary grammatical complication to use the term _intentionalist_, the self-critical dimension of this interpretive move is essential. It builds on the critical appropriation of the intentional framework of scripture and its interpretive traditions.

As the discussion on Wiesel's midrashic voice illustrates, an additional interpretive move directed toward the intentional logic of scripture is required. People can be purposive without being self-critical regarding how they are intentional. Hence, the modifier is directed toward the adjective _intentional_ not the noun _intention_. That is, we must learn to cultivate a self-critical voice of faith which is able to articulate the intentional logic of scripture as primary. Moreover, we are dealing with a voice of faith, not a system of faith: a voice which enables us to tell the stories of faith on the other side of innocence--"between the fires." To be sure, it is a voice which can find expression in a variety of systems, so long as they remain self-critically aware of the limitations of their faith claims.

The concern for a self-critical voice of faith is not primarily methodological, although there are serious methodological implications. Rather, its overarching concern is how to reconcile the inconsistencies between its own faith commitments and the language of intervention which it uses to convey purpose, direction and, ultimately, trust.

ARTICULATING THE DIVINE INTENTION

The divine intention is the formal criterion for guiding the interpretation of this voice of faith; however, it may vary with regard to how it is expressed. Nevertheless, any articulation of the divine intention, regardless of its plural expression, would be true to itself only when it is concretely linked to real, lived faith.

The verb, to articulate, partakes of this very point. At its root, to articulate means to join together with a joint. An articulation is a jointed connection. It is a connecting place or device (_The Compact Edition of the OED_, 1971, s.v. "articulate"). We often use the word _articulate_ when we refer to making an interpretational connection visible and accessible for public discourse.

In the articulation of the divine intention, then, we speak of a specifically identifiable place or moment where linkage occurs--a deed, or action which embodies in a particular place and time the intention for covenant life. Still, the phrase, "the divine intention," is rather general and requires further commentary, lest it fail to serve the particular needs and obligations of covenant life.

Divine intention receives scriptural specificity in a number of ways. In each case, however, that specificity is relative to the point of view of the persons involved and the situation in which they seek to serve God's will. In the Hebrew scriptures, for example, God's intent for life may be referred to as peace, justice, or righteousness, depending on the context. Nevertheless, the divine intention, regardless of how it is conceptualized, will require concrete embodiment or articulation. (See Berkovits, 1969, for a thorough discussion of how these terms relate to one another in their Hebraic context.) Together, they serve the halakhic particularities of Torah life (van Buren, 1983, 62-64, 297f.).

In the scriptures of the Christian New Testament, one is more apt to encounter the identification of the divine intention with Jesus' parables about the Realm of God. Even so, his parabolic vignettes all point, not to a general and unembodied attitude about life, but to specific manifestations of obedient discipleship. As Crossan develops in _The Dark Interval_, Jesus' parables work to break open the stories of his faith world to provide creative space for them to speak to the concrete needs of the present. Using the language of intervention, they push metaphorically beyond the logic of intervention to the narrative's deeper meaning which is its heart, but never at the expense of the particularity of the situation in which he tells the parable (Crossan, 1975)--an intentionalist voice of **mitzvot**, if you will.

Regardless of the biblical concepts employed to express it, any authentic articulation of the divine intention is a specific act of "choosing life." Whether it is as routine as a noontime meal or a loaf of bread shared in hospitality with a stranger, or whether it occurs in the crisis of an individual's or a people's life, it is an act which participates in the very life that it chooses. Conversely, where the divine intention for life is not concretely embodied in real, everyday acts of justice, compassion, devotion, mercy, humility, then the divine intention is absent and not honored.

God's faithfulness is to covenant life--not just any kind of life. The spirit or ongoing dynamic of the divine intention is empowering, life giving and expanding. It calls forth the very life it intends. As God's intention holds for the life of all, it likewise holds for the life of the least. Therefore, it follows that insofar as it is absent in any one aspect, the intention for the whole is not fulfilled. Hence the emphasis falls on the particularities of history in the light of the divine intention for life.

In affirming God's singular loyalty to the divine intention, however it is expressed, we express trust in God's inclusive commitment to life to be gracious enough to call and draw any number of peoples to it--yet always through the particularities of history. It need not depend on divine intervention but on human responsiveness and responsibility to the One who intends peace, justice, righteousness. We can affirm, then, that there is one intention which we know convenantally, in a variety of circumstances. We do not need to ask how many covenants there are nor how God can honor two (or more!) without abrogating others. In other words, as we face the reality of Auschwitz, we discover the limits of the metaphors of intervention--leading us to rethink how we speak of God's transcendence and power, even covenant. If we speak of God choosing not to intervene in the name of covenantal faithfulness and respect, we challenge the intention of creation which we claim the covenant serves: creation's ongoing commitment to life and its liberation and loyalty. In the long run, using the logic of intervention in this way goes counter to the divine intention which covenant language seeks to honor.

An illustration, using the metaphor of a parent's care for a growing child: As a child grows in the care of his or her parents, the parents generally tend to intervene less and less in the decisions and actions of the child through life. A young child knows parental intervention as a frequent occurrence. A teenager experiences much less direct intervention. A single, young adult even less, and so on. In other words, as the child matures, the need for and mode of parental guidance changes. Divine providence can be and is often compared to such dynamics. Paul van Buren follows this line of thinking as he attends to similar issues regarding God's involvement in history.

Adopting the imagery of Isaac Luria, van Buren speaks of creation and its resulting governance as an act of divine self-limitation. God withdraws to make room for creation, freedom, decision, human action. In this manner, God binds God's own self to human being in covenant. Pointing out that a parent's non-interference with a maturing child need not be an act of indifference, van Buren explains that it requires active involvement, self-discipline, and deep, other intending love--a participation in absence. By analogy, God's apparent powerlessness, then, would be a reality chosen for the freedom and dignity of humanity (van Buren, 1983, 62-64, 297f.).

Surely it is one thing for a parent to withdraw influence and power in order for a child to grow into responsible adulthood. It is quite another, in the name of freedom, or even covenant loyalty, to posit that a loving parent would let his or her children be destroyed for the sake of their freedom. And not just killed--degraded and defiled! With regard to "the six million," such language must be qualified and delimited by the divine intention for life; otherwise, it imputes to God a culpability for needless, innocent suffering that is unjustifiable even if it were God's choice.

THE PASSION STORY IN INTENTIONALIST VOICE

While Jews and Christians might be able to share common cause as stewards of God's intention for life, they part company at the cross of Jesus. It has been a stumbling block to interfaith understanding through the centuries. Indeed, it has been a source of historic pain--fueling the fires of antisemitism, hatred, persecution, and eventually genocide, with its theology of contempt and accompanying charge of deicide. Even Luther was caught up in this distorted view of the Jew and covenant life in his interpretation of the cross's significance for the faith life of Christians (Rubenstein and Roth, 1987, 52-60). His and subsequent emphases on the cross have functioned as critiques of false triumphalism within the confines of their own faith worlds; however, they have failed in this regard outside their confessional universe. In the shadow of Auschwitz, this must change.

Then what do we do with traditional Christian language about Jesus' intention for life and the role of the cross in that? Can an intentionalist or midrashic encounter with the passion of Jesus faithfully honor this central affirmation of the Christian faith and at the same time honor the critique required by Auschwitz?

At the heart of the problem is the notion that Jesus' suffering is intrinsically salvific. It is illustrated in the way Jurgen Moltmann, who in attempting to deal with Jewish suffering and the role of Christian theology in that, misreads an oft quoted scene from Night. Assembled to view an execution of three of their comrades who were accused of trying to blow up a power station in the camp at Buna, Wiesel and his fellow inmates watched the final agony of a young boy hanging on the gallows, suspended between life and death unable, even, to die. Hearing someone behind him ask, "Where is God now?," Wiesel silently responded that God was hanging before them on the gallows (Wiesel, 1960, 76). Moltmann interpreted this as a witness to God's presence in the midst of suffering (Moltmann, 1974, 273).

While one can understand why Moltmann might project this interpretation on the scene, this is not Wiesel's intent and does not fit with the testimony he shares in Night, and, as well, in other writings. It is not an affirmation of meaning and divine solidarity in suffering, but a lament. Wiesel's next sentence expresses his despair without compromise: "that night the soup tasted of corpses" (Wiesel, 1960, 76). This is not an epiphany of divine solidarity with those who suffer. Other scenes from Night, such as one in which a young man named Meir kills his father for a piece of bread, are tragic reminders of what has been lost (Weisel, 1960, 113). In The Accident, Wiesel's protagonist, commenting on just this kind of suffering, explains:

> Suffering brings out the lowest, the most cowardly in man. There is a phase of suffering you reach beyond which you become a brute: beyond it you sell your soul--and worse, the souls of your friends for a piece of bread, for some warmth, or a moment of oblivion, of sleep (Wiesel, 1962, 53).

Such a theological affirmation as that made by Moltmann in The Crucified God shatters under the weight of the kind of suffering which Wiesel describes.

A **theologia crucis** which makes of suffering an intrinsically meaningful moment of solidarity with God is problematic for a faithful Jew. In the context of Auschwitz, it becomes problematic for a faithful Christian as well. Moreover, it would appear to be problematic for Jesus when he is allowed to be the faithful Jew that he was (van Buren, 1986, 1987 and Williamson, 1982).

Although it would be inappropriate to posit the actual motivation of Jesus with regard to his suffering and death (as distinct from the canonical interpretation), we can infer from Jesus' teachings and actions that he understood **Torah** to be life directed and serving life, not restricting it. With some measure of confidence we can assert that Jesus sought in his everyday acts, in his teachings, in his final days, especially, to honor Moses' admonition to "choose life" (Deut 30). It is, therefore, not inappropriate to characterize the Gospel portraits of Jesus as portraying him to be one who was continually finding ways and places in which he could invite a concrete, embodied choice for the renewal of covenant life (van Buren, 1983 and 1986).

Instead of saying there is life in the cross, we may more accurately point to Jesus' choice and actions for life in the face of the cross, countering the denial, betrayal, and rejection which he faced. That is, Jesus chose relationship with Peter, Judas, and the others in such a way that he included denial, rejection, and betrayal--thereby transforming them. Relationship chosen in the face of its violation means that relationship cannot be broken by that violation.

The traditional Christian expression that Jesus "had to die" can yield an alternative interpretation: it was inevitable that one so committed to life must face its radical denial in a final affirmation which, in embracing death, gives witness to life. In other words, neither God nor Jesus calls his followers to suffer, but to choose life in the most vulnerable of ways and places, even in the face of seemingly absolute evil. Suffering is risked, while life is chosen! Sacrificial life is seen as a style of choosing life which embraces the risk that goes with and courageously confronts suffering. This is what "to suffer with Christ" means in an intentionalist voice--to join in Jesus' passion for and vulnerability to covenant life.

Likewise, forgiveness is recast as a fruit of the covenant life embodied by Jesus. It need not be the consequence of appeasing a God ready to intervene in judgment--propitiation. Forgiveness can be conceived as a gift of his fervent embodiment of covenant life, even in the face of betrayal, denial, and crucifixion--an act of resistance in behalf of covenant relationship. Forgiveness is thereby proffered by the violated one and unearned.

In this way, Jesus' choices and actions for life confront their very denial. The relationship of Jesus with his disciples, fellow Jews, and God are stronger than any imperfection they encounter. Jesus, by choosing and honoring covenant life in its most extreme violation, overcomes the rupture in his covenant world. Healing is initiated from Jesus' side at the point of violation: betrayal, abandonment, humiliation, and degradation.

This is an important point. The cross, in itself, is not an epiphany. It is that place, **in extremis**, where, existentially as well as narratively, covenant loyalty is shattered. Therefore, Jesus' choice for fidelity and life is healing and life giving because it is embodied in precisely that place where it is violated. Moreover, the power of covenant life is confirmed, in faith, as reaching beyond death, transcending its violation as well as the one violated.

Covenant loyalty prevails in the story because of how Jesus enters and honors the covenant--**in extremis**. However, the passion narrative becomes a vulnerable paradigm in an intentionalist voice for it opens Jesus' passion to an arena of human suffering that it must embrace if his story is to have integrity in our time. In other words, his passion needs the voices of those like the **hasidim** of Buchenwald and Lublin who fervently chose life in the degrading universe of the death camps no less than the possibility of **tikkun** for Jews needs them. More importantly, the passion story needs their witness as confirmation (not the other way around) in full recognition of the power of their choice for life in the uniquely cruel situation of what happened to them (Fackenheim, 1982, 224f.). Their ability to sanctify life (**kiddush ha-hayyim**) in the face of the Nazi logic of destruction is essential for the passion story's insistence that, even in the face of evil and suffering, life may still be chosen and the divine intention for life served. As Fackenheim makes clear, "the Nazi logic of destruction was meant to drive the Jewish people into self-loathing and suicide...[It] was an assault on the Jewish people without precedent in history" (Fackenheim, 1982, 223).

In this manner, **theologia crucis** yields to a **theologia fervoris** (a theology of passion), yet without moving away from the crucial point of violation that is symbolized for Christians by the cross. Even so, to tell this paradigmatic story in intentionalist voice will be a bold step for the followers of Jesus. Nevertheless, it will be in line with the vulnerability embodied in his fervent commitment to covenant life, however much it might be resisted by his followers. How Christians name this final chapter in the life of Jesus affects how they live with that story and with others who may not. Moreover, it leads them into a different kind of engagement with suffering, with others, and with God's intention for creation.

FURTHER IMPLICATIONS

I have tried to distinguish, as Fackenheim says we must, between suffering having intrinsic meaning and the meaning which a religious response to suffering gives (Fackenheim, 1968, 18ff.). Wiesel's response to Auschwitz reminds us that even degradation can be transformed by remembering it so that life can be chosen and served, not death. This, it seems to me, is the meaning of the gift which Jews give to the world as their transforming act of memory. It is not, as a prominent Christian leader once misstated, that the Holocaust, itself, is the gift. This point is essential.

The life-giving power of naming one's world is disclosed in the shadow of Auschwitz. Wiesel, in a spirit similar to what I have described as a postcritical, midrashic voice, named what happened to his people **holocaust**. Utilizing the Greek form of the name for burnt offering in the **akedah**, he made of his memory of fire an offering of faith <u>in spite of</u> what happened there, for the sake of other Isaacs (Wiesel, 1976). In naming this faith shattering event in such a way, he found a way to speak life in the face of death, to affirm the faith story of his people in the face of covenant silence. It is a way of saying "we shall make of this unthinkable act an offering of faith. Its intention of death shall not triumph! The last word shall be life, not death." This is the power disclosed in the post-critical naming of what happened: the power of naming life in faith.

It is no longer necessary for power to be considered in primarily interventionist categories. Likewise, transcendence can be relocated as the divine intention for life which seeks particular embodiment in everyday actions. In this manner, Jesus can be seen as a distinct embodiment of the unique intention of God. For Christians, Jesus fully and distinctively participates in the divine intention for creation, and so gives it full incarnation; but he does not exhaust it. The intention is for all of life, not just one life, however much it may be embodied in one life, and even necessary that it be embodied in the extreme tests of life.

As I hope I have shown, interventionist categories of transcendence and power may not be simply problematic. They may, indeed, be dangerous and perpetuate the imperialistic tendencies that linger in displacement theological positions. For example, in an uncritical adoption of interventionist logic, even when that logic is used in a non-literal, figurative voice, history can become functionally constant, with God, however much claimed to be otherwise, a functional variable. Then, as God intervenes (in deliverance, salvation, judgment), choosing a people or person in history, history is thereby sanctified and emerges, in broad compass, as the object of God's faithfulness. In such fashion, history is guaranteed. It can, then, be invested with a monolithic, imperialistic status because it is the object of God's loyalty.

An editorial by popular author William H. Willimon illustrates this move. Arguing that peace can be as idolatrous as a nation's trust in nuclear weaponry, he sought to caution against investing final hope in ministries of peacemaking. He concluded, "It is not our task to make history come out right....History has already come out right, for the lordship of Christ has been established" (Willimon, 1987, 454). In the process, however, fear for the planet and for the meaningfulness of history was dismissed as idolatrous because history has already been guaranteed its final meaning in Jesus Christ.

Why is this important in this context? In addition to the imperialistic overtones in his conclusion, and the displacement theology it implies, the finitude and vulnerability of history are dismissed even as he argues that faith in God's sovereignty relativizes our most serious work. As a result, the frightening specter of nuclear conflagration is rendered impotent without being fully confronted as the unique threat it is.

Similarly, several years ago a major U.S. church leader, in an attempt to ground the vocation of peacemaking in a theology of creation, avoided the uniqueness of the nuclear threat to the planet by describing creation to be like a three act play with the first and last acts already written; the second act was simply being improvised by those who were dealing with the perilous realities of the late twentieth century (Brouwer, 1983).

I, too, seek to honor the relativizing primacy of divine sovereignty, and so, for that reason, speak of, and in, an intentionalist rather than intentional voice. But, after Auschwitz, no theological stance dare regard any tragedy as impossible or unthinkable. The unthinkable happened! That reality must be part of any realistic appraisal of the situation that haunts modern life. Therefore, faith "between the fires" calls each of us to take with equal seriousness both fires, past and future.

To link Auschwitz with Hiroshima is to recognize that history cannot ultimately be trusted; nor can the future! It is life that must be trusted and risked in history and for the sake of the future--covenant life, given by and reflecting the image of its creator.

SUMMARY

The unthinkable reality of nuclear annihilation is indeed possible. Creation is threatened, as well as history. The existential as well as the historical demand, therefore, is to learn to live in the present and care for the future, knowing the untrustworthiness of history.

An intentionalist voice offers a way of articulating faith which does not place its final trust in history. It does, however, require that it be risked in history for the sake of choosing and serving covenant life. To be sure, it is not an easy voice to speak, because it grows out of a tragic confrontation with history's possibility for evil--and my own as well. It must even face the possibility that human beings have the capacity for destroying history as well as the planet earth. Nonetheless, it is still a voice rooted in trust. **In extremis**, life was chosen, passionately and lovingly. This is the memory which the passion story must preserve and honor after Auschwitz. It is also the memory which echoes in the voices of the **hasidim** of Lublin and Buchenwald, and the witness of Elie Wiesel.

How, then, may I speak in this wilderness "between the fires?" In the stutter of an intentionalist voice. With Greenberg's criterion haunting every word of this paper, I realize that no statements have integrity in the presence of burning children. Silence is the only response. And yet, I cannot not speak. That is the double bind we all must confront and take into our speech. And so, I propose an intentionalist voice of faith with the hope that it is able to incorporate that silence into its speaking.

It will not be an easy voice to speak. Like the subtle attention given by a master organ builder who must "voice" his or her finished instrument in the place where it will be played, so must I, or anyone who speaks with me, do the subtle, nuanced work of voicing our faith claims so that our language and our related actions might express the divine intention of the One who has given us life to cherish, honor, and responsibly share.

REFERENCES

Berkovits, E. (1969). Man and God: Studies in Biblical Theology. Detroit: Wayne State University Press. 238-252, 326-348.

Brouwer, A. (1983). Speaking to participants in "Toward A Theology of Peacemaking in The Nuclear Age" sponsored by the Churches Center for Theology and Public Policy, Washington, D.C.

The Compact Edition of the Oxford English Dictionary (1971). Oxford: Oxford University Press.

Crossan, J.D. (1975). The Dark Interval: Towards a Theology of Story. Niles, IL: Argus Communications. 47-122.

Fackenheim, E. (1968). Quest for Past and Future: Essays in Jewish Theology. Bloomington: Indiana University Press.

Fackenheim, E. (1982). To Mend the World: Foundations of Future Jewish Thought. New York: Schocken Books.

Greenberg, I. (1977). Auschwitz: Beginning of a New Era?: Reflections on the Holocaust. (ed. E. Fleischner) New York: KTAV. 7-55.

Moltmann, J. (1974). The Crucified God: The Cross of Christ as the Foundation and Criticism of Christian Theology. New York: Harper and Row.

Ricoeur, P. (1967). The Symbolism of Evil (trans. E. Buchanan) Boston: Beacon Press. 3-24, 347-357, esp. 355ff.

Ricoeur, P. (1974). The Conflict of Interpretations (ed. D. Ihde) Evanston: Northwestern University Press. 289-293, 440-467.

Rubenstein, R.L. and Roth, J.K. (1987). Approaches to Auschwitz: The Holocaust and Its Legacy. Atlanta: John Knox Press.

Shea, J. (1978). Stories of God: An Unauthorized Biography. Chicago: The Thomas More Press. 89-116.

Van Buren, P.M. (1983). A Christian Theology of the People Israel, Part II of A theology of the Jewish-Christian Reality. New York: Seabury.

Van Buren, P.M. (1986). Religion and Intellectual Life, Vol. III, No. 4, 31-50.

Van Buren, P.M. (1987). Religion and Intellectual Life, Vol. V, No. 1, 81-116.

Waskow, A. (1984). The Shalom Seders: Three Haggadahs Compiled by the New Jewish Agenda. New York: Adama Books. 14-34.

Wiesel, E. (1960). Night. (trans. S. Rodway) New York: Avon Books.

Wiesel, E. (1962). The Accident. (trans. A. Borchardt) New York: Avon Books.

Wiesel, E. (1976). Messengers of God: Biblical Portraits and Legends. New York: Random House. 69-97.

Williamson, C. (1982). Has God Rejected His People?: Anti-Judaism in the Christian Church. Nashville: Abingdon.

Willimon, W. (May 6, 1987). The Christian Century, May 6, Vol. 104, No. 15, 453f.

SACRIFICE AND ATONEMENT :

An Investigation into the attitude of Jesus of Nazareth towards cultic sacrifice .

by

J.A. McGUCKIN

Department of Theology ,
LSU College of Higher Education,
The Avenue, Southampton SO9 5HB.

INTRODUCTION .

This paper is offered as preliminary material for a consideration of the use to which the concept 'sacrifice' has been applied in Jewish & Christian theology. This will have special relevance in any theological discussion of the challenge to providential theodicy raised by the Holocaust. The very use of a sacrificial term to describe the apalling genocide testifies to the continuance of themes in rabbinic theology which applied the notion of atoning sacrifice to innocent suffering.1 Early Christianity fastened on the term as a major vehicle for interpreting the death of Jesus. Some have argued that Christianity's subsequent employment of the symbols of sacrifice and victim led to a dangerous typology which could be perverted too easily into an ideology of oppression and cruelty. Three areas are of the utmost importance in what is clearly a central issue of our discussions . The first is an understanding of the essential differences between Jewish and early Christian understandings of sacrifice, and the attitudes of 1st century Hellenism and the subsequent attitudes of Christians who no longer had any essential understanding of the inner spirit of what biblical sacrifice signified. It is a crude line to draw, but in a sense it can be symbolised in the differences between Jewish and Hellenistic theologies of sacrifice, and illuminated by Judaism's definitive rejection of the lugubrious apotropaeic rites of the Hellenistic 'holocaust'. This area has already been extensively studied and will be presupposed here (2). The second area is Jesus of Nazareth's own attitude to the theology of sacrifice. This is the central concern of the present paper. The third area amounts to the political and psychological implications of the form which Jewish and Christian theology assumed in relation to these areas - an investigation of the suitability, for example, of the use of the term 'olah (burnt-offering, holocaust) which originally conveyed the sense of joyful surrender and willing gift to the God of the covenant to cover the wicked annihilation of six million . This final area of discussion is merely hinted at in the second conclusion to this study. This paper, therefore, is a preliminary and preparatory historical study in an area of central importance . Its methodology is to approach the New Testament text by means of modern Redaction Criticism. The main axioms of this method must be presupposed here (3) but the non-specialist reader should be aware that in modern critical study a clear distinction is drawn between the editorial alterations and additions of the evangelists, and the actual historical form of the sayings of Jesus. In other words some sayings are attributed to him later, and many others are significantly changed in the course of the decades of oral transmission of his words. A last word of introduction might be that the topic is so immense that I have been particularly aware of the pressing limitations of space. I have thus chosen to engage directly with the texts themselves rather than the secondary literature about them , although this does not reveal the full extent of scholarly controversy over many of the issues discussed. Limitations of space have also made complex and nuanced literary judgements perhaps appear as apodeictic utterances. Nonetheless the following discussion may at least serve to introduce some of the necessary considerations to approach a key theological area of our debate .

The substance of the argument that follows is that Jesus of Nazareth adapted the prophetic criticism of the cult that called for its purification by ethical involvement, and its transcendence in spiritual interiority (4). Was the older doctrine of 'spiritualisation' (if such it was) given in an attempt to reform the cult or to attack it ? Certainly the attitude is common in rabbinic theology after the fall of the Second Temple and also in Christian theology, all of which speak of a re-application of cultic sacrificial concepts in new domains. But if the prophets, the rabbis, and the early christians follow this approach (which we may describe as basically affirmatory of the value of the cult - precisely because it was a Torah observance for all time) then Jesus of Nazareth himself does not seem to . The prophetic doctrine, of which he was aware, was seemingly sharpened for him in a radical way by what he saw to be the implications of the End-Time . He preached the imminent advent of the Kingdom of God, and at the heart of his Kingdom theology stood a doctrine of reconciliation. This reconciliation he evoked without any recourse to the notion of cultic sacrifice , and he appears to conceive it as being prodigally bestowed on his people by a God who had returned not to destroy or avenge but to renew and purify his covenantal dealings with mankind. This universal reconciliation which Jesus preached was the unexpected 'wedding gift' attendant on the return of the Bridegroom, the God of Israel , and it formed the core of the eschatological ethic which Jesus used as his 'higher authority' in contemporary rabbinic argument, and to which he subordinated all other aspects of the Torah - included here were the Law's prescriptions relating to forgiveness, purification, and expiation by means of the ordained sacrifices. The eschatological force of the reconciliation he preached circumvented the whole system of sacrifice , for in his conception it was imminent, immediate, and prodigally accessible . This eschatological attitude led Jesus to take a radically different attitude to the abiding relevance of the Torah in all its prescriptions from that of the rabbis, and from that of many of his later disciples who attempted to systematise the implications of Jesus' doctrine while at the same time de-structuring the eschatology which lay behind it. In short, Jesus had no place for the cult in his theological schema. It belonged to the Age of This World and his eyes were filled with a vision of the Next Age Of The Kingdom . His doctrine of universal reconciliation is synonymous with the proclamation of the end of the Age, and it effectively rendered the sacrificial cult superfluous for him. It is, therefore , a matter of some interest to see that his own disciples , so shortly after his own death, re-apply that very image of sacrifice and offer it as a synopsis of his work and theological significance.

THE TRADITION OF THE JESUS - LOGIA.

It is our premiss here that Jesus himself said or did nothing to suggest that his death should be seen as a sacrifice in any cultic sense at all, and nothing to encourage the use of sacrificial concepts to illuminate the relationship of God to Israel. The use of sacrificial theology , of course, was used so early in the history of Christianity that it has since become, for all christians, the classic architecture of the way the life and death of Jesus are interpreted. Much is vested dogmatically in this area, and it is also clear from the literature that generations of scholars have not been free from defending interested presuppositions in their analysis of the matter. What follows is not intended to argue the non-applicability of this concept in Christian dogmatics. If used in accordance with classical Hebraic sacrifice notions, and in the light of what the New Testament actually says about the death of Jesus as sacrificial 'Type', then the term may indeed offer profound illumination. On the other hand , in the hybrid understanding of expiation sacrifices that grew up in Christianity once it had totally lost its Jewish matrix, from the third century CE onwards, the use of sacrifice could and did lead to lamentable results. The forensic obsession of an Anselm of Canterbury is but one example (5). In terms of the historical Jesus let us look at what the evidence suggests.

There is next to no mention of sacrifice within the recorded tradition of Jesus' words. This lack of material, in itself, may be non-significant , if it were really a case of **argumentum e silentio** but the few references that do exist (and it is most revealing to recall in the light of this paucity of material that the words of Jesus were gathered by disciples who saw this category as a major theological vehicle and thus had every reason to favour it and extend its application where they could) tend to sharpen our interest when they emerge neither as apologetic against the 'institutions' of Israel, nor generally interested in the concept at all, and at some times even disparaging. We can record here eight notable instances of the word or correlated context in the actual Jesus-tradition.

I. Mk.12.33. This first text to consider is not a logion of Jesus but spoken by a 'scribe' whom Jesus commends for his insight : 'To love Him with all your heart, with all your understanding and strength, and to love your neighbour as yourself, this is far more important than any holocaust or sacrifice. Jesus, seeing how wisely he had spoken, said : You are not far from the Kingdom of God.' There are no synoptic parallels for this , but it is clearly a reflection based on Hoseah 6.6 and it encapsulates the whole post-exilic tradition of cultic criticism to which Jesus seems to give unequivocal assent, from the new motivation of his Kingdom of God theology. The approach of the End Time makes the need for repentance so critical in Jesus' estimation that the prophetic doctrine becomes all the more urgent. Despite showing something of the evangelist Mark's interest in a gentile apologetic against the relevance of the 'Law', this affirmation of the scribe by Jesus has a solid place within the authentic 'Kingdom sayings'. At Mt.9.13 another citation of the same text of Hoseah 6.6. is used :'Go and learn the meaning of the phrase, What I want is mercy not sacrifice.' This time Matthew records Jesus as speaking, although we note that the logion is actually a biblical quotation. Matthew introduces the Hosean reference into a Gospel context of controversy with the scribes (a controversy we witness in Mark at this point) but he also introduces the self-same text, with Jesus speaking, later at Mt. 12.7. Both textual instances are Matthaean **propria**, unattested elsewhere in the tradition. He has used the Hoseah text to justify Jesus' 'apparent' breaking of the Law by an appeal to a higher aspect of the Law's demands. This is a classic rabbinism, and it is also typical of Matthew's Christology where he presents Jesus as a scrupulous observer of the Torah. The creation of a Jesus logion by biblical citation, together with the theological argument that is going on internally in Matthew's text make his usage here not such strong evidence for Jesus' real attitude as was given in the Markan text. Both Matthaean instances seem to be redactions, but they come round in the end to the same basic point in relation to sacrifice as that raised in the Markan text.

II. There is a logion of Jesus concerning the disciples as the salt of the earth, and needing to take care in case the salt should become savourless and be rejected. It is found in its fuller form in Mt. 18.9 and Lk.14.34-35. This clearly relates to the sense of salt as a symbol of purification and zeal. The image hinges on the sharpness of salt **per se** and has nothing at all to do with the phrase , attested only by Mark , 'Everything shall be salted with fire', which he uses at Mk.9.49 to introduce his own much abbreviated version of the salt-logion. Mark's phrase does have sacrificial connotations. In his Gospel context a series of Jesus logia are presented from Mk. 9.33 onwards, about the nature of discipleship . The latter part of this series shows pre-Markan literary characteristics of catch-word arrangement as the underlying principle behind the logia collection. The phrase of Mk.9.49: 'Everything shall be salted with fire', serves to relate a series of logia bound together by the catchword 'fire' to a series bound by the word 'salt'. In Mark's text the phrase stands as a warning of judgement on a disciple, and it does so precisely because it looks back to the logion about Gehenna's fire, as well as forward to the salt logion that follows. The logia of Jesus ,however, were assembled out of their historical context by the artificial device of word-association, and in consequence the very textual neatness of Mk. 9.49 brands it as a literary motif, not a spoken logion from the historical Jesus. In any case the supposed logion , if taken on its own terms, without reference to abutting sayings, is meaningless. If more indication were needed that what we have in 9.49 is Mark, not Jesus , then we need only note that the words are a conflated misquotation of Lev.2.13 (cf. Ezek.43.24) and are also Markan **propria.** All these things seriously call into question the authenticity of this 'salting with fire' phrase . In context, the phrase seems to bear a meaning for Mark that the sufferings of the righteous might be seen as sacrificial offerings. This is close to the tradition found in the Maccabean literature which grows into the rabbinic doctrine of the atoning merit of the sufferings of the righteous martyrs (6) and must have had special relevance to Mark given that his Gospel is clearly offered to a congregation undergoing persecution, a context which was certainly not applicable to the audience the historical Jesus addressed. The apparent Levitical allusion at 9.49, therefore, has nothing to do with Jesus , but comes from Mark and witnesses his own Paulinistic, sacrificial, theology of suffering, which shall be noted later.

III. Another enigmatic reference to sacrifice appears in the Lukan **proprium** of Lk.13.1, referring to two historical incidents of which no other historical source is cognisant - the Galileans killed by Pilate, and the collapse of a tower in the Siloam area of Jerusalem killing eighteen people. The text reads :'It was about this time that some people arrived and told him about the Galileans whose blood Pilate had mingled with that of their sacrifices. At this he said to them : Do you suppose that these Galileans who suffered this way were greater sinners than any other Galileans ? They were not I tell you.' The logion, although only attested by Luke is unquestionably authentic. It expresses a clear challenge to the older 'classic' form of providence theology which tried to draw a direct correlation between suffering and punishment - a view in several other instances rejected by Jesus. It is also clear, however, that the detail of the 'blood mingled with that of their sacrifices' is a detail which has impressed itself vividly on the evangelist rather than Jesus, for it forms part of the redactor's introduction to the logion-response. Jesus himself makes his point about providence and judgement, and allies this example of the death of the Galileans with that of the deaths in the collapsing tower block. The point at issue is clearly violent and premature death as such, and has nothing to do with the fact of sacrifice. It is entirely incidental to Jesus' point. The location of the incident mentioned is Jerusalem, and the implication is given that the Galileans were not priests, and this makes it likely that the occasion of the two events was the Passover celebrations, an occasion when nationalist hopes always ran high, and so many incidents occurred that Pilate brought the Caesarean garrison to supplement the Antonia forces for the whole of the festivities. Luke implies that Jesus was still on his journey to the capital and some unknown people brought him these two pieces of news. The more likely scenario is that the news was relevant to the hour because Jesus was at that moment engaged in preaching in Jerusalem itself. In this case the Passover in question could well have been the Passover week during which he was arrested. The mention of the term sacrifice, therefore, although incidental to the point Jesus is making about providence still has a bearing on our argument ,if the implications of his providence theology are applied. Luke's use of the detail of the mingled blood expresses his own, and doubtless that of the first reporters of the calamities, sense of shock and theological scandal. This 'scandal' emerges from the fact that these Galileans had so recently been worshipping God in the Temple (we ought not to think of a literal mingling of blood as if Pilate had ordered the troops to assassinate worshippers within the Court Of Israelites - for this is inconceivable) and therefore should have been 'at rights' with God, the ruler of all destinies . If Jesus decidedly takes the line that there is no direct correlation between 'being at rights with God' and suffering, then not only has he denied the major premiss of the post-exilic prophetic theodicy , but he has also negated the major reason for the continuance of the sacrificial system. It was in the aftermath of the exile that the final impetus was given to the formation of the Levitical code, and again the exile experience which determined Israel to purify the cult so that sacrifices might be continually offered to keep the Lord and His people in close covenant bonds. In other words the entire rationale of the sacrifices was to evoke a destiny of peace from God. If Jesus rebuffs such a providence theology, this unquestionably has ramifications in relation to the whole system of cultic worship. Admittedly the concept of sacrifice is incidental to the particular logion about the death of the Galileans , but it may be none the less revealing for that.

IV. The Boanerges incident is another oblique reference to a similar thing. The sons of Zebedee in Lk.9.54 ask Jesus if they should call down fire from heaven to consume a Samaritan village which would not receive them since he had 'set his face to go to Jerusalem'. The incident is not a logion (despite a logion being added as a gloss in some later textual traditions) and is only attested by Luke. He locates it in his 'Travel Section' ,a section of his narrative which abounds with many of his own theological motifs - including the 'setting of the face' to the holy city. In addition, the incident is not so much about Jesus as about the fiery characters of the Sons of Zebedee. All these things so far suggest later developments, redactive influences. And yet there is no substantial reason to dismiss the episode as unhistoric , and therefore the apparent connection of 'calling down fire from heaven' with sacrificial imagery ought to be investigated. The disciples are clearly evoking II Kings 1.10,12 where Elijah destroys the soldiers of Ahaziah to prove to all Israel that he is a man of God. The notion of fire falling from heaven to consume sacrificial offerings is another biblical symbol of special approbation by God (7). Two things must be noted in relation to Lk. 9.54 , however. In the first place the image is based on none of the texts which form the tradition of fire as 'special approbation' but quite clearly on II Kings 1.10, which although it grows out of that former tradition, is no longer part of it but has already adapted with the help of such ideas as found in Ps.18.7-8, or Gen.19.24, towards taking heavenly fire as a symbol of the wrath of God striking the wicked at the behest of the righteous. This is no longer 'sacrificial' . Secondly, the request is made by the disciples and 'rebuked' by Jesus. If the Boanerges express such a view of God's intervention in the world (a theological issue related to the Galilean/Siloam story discussed earlier) then they are wrong , and consequently told as much.

V. A most interesting phrase to consider is Mk.10.45 ; Mt. 20.28. This is the text :'The Son of Man came not to be served but to serve and to give his life as a ransom for many.' It is prefaced by the logion :'Anyone who wants to be first among you must be servant to all.' The life-ransom phrase quite clearly belongs to Mark's redactive comment on the logion of Jesus which was originally as listed in Lk.22.24f (cf. Jn.13.4-15). Even Mark himself gives the logion about humble service in its original context earlier in his text at Mk.9.35. When he repeats the same logion at 10.44 it is in order to introduce his phrase about the Son of Man's death as a ransom - a phrase taken from Paul (Rom. 3.24) and another indication, among many, of Pauline influence on the text of Mark's Gospel. As an evangelistic comment on what the Son of Man meant Mark's editorial intrusion is comparable to a similar comment in Mk.2.28 which again should not be taken as part of the original logion of 2.27. Matthew has followed Mark's usage in his text at Mt. 20.28, and thus also adopts the 'ransom' meditation. Luke, however, has followed his own tradition independently and cauterised the Markan addition at this point. The ransom phrase, like the phrase 'for many' (which appears significantly in the Markan/Matthaean accounts of the words of Jesus over the cup : Mk.14.24 ; Mt.26.28) with which it is associated is, therefore, not a Jesus logion but a Paulinism (8). When Luke comes , in turn, to the account of the eucharistic words over the chalice he similarly follows his independent source and once again removes the Paulinism 'for many' (Lk. 22.20) (9).

VI. Mt. 5.23 advises the hearer to leave an offering even in the very face of the altar if there is a matter of reconciliation that has to be attended to between the would-be sacrificer and his brother. This is not found in Mark,nor does Luke parallel it, although he does parallel the logion Matthew associates with it ,at Lk. 12.58-59. The sense of the logion in Matthew is clearly that the demands of reconciliation take precedence over the action of sacrifice. This must have been a particularly shocking statement for the hearers of Jesus because it reverses an established and accepted primacy of order - that God should be honoured above all else, and that men should be honoured as part of the divine honour, not apart from it. The 'rider' in Matthew :'then go back and make your offering' seems very limp indeed. It is clearly designed to soften the impact of the saying and all that it implies - and it seems to be redolent of Matthew's general principle that Jesus only broke a Torah prescript when it was a matter of fulfilling a higher one. This , however, does not represent the case, for Jesus' motivation in the face of the Law's obligations was not 'rabbinic' but eschatological . Even the postlude : 'then go back' ,does not soften the boldness of the logion's intent in any real way. I take it to be an evangelist's redaction added in the light of his principle stated just beforehand in Mt. 5.17-19. This passage clearly elaborates Matthew's own theology of the teachings of Jesus in terms which are so evidently anti-Pauline that they seem to date from a time when Paul's reputation had been more than enhanced by his martyr's death , and this puts us, at the very earliest,in the late 60's of the first century CE, far removed from the time of Jesus himself. Our conclusion is, then, that the logion of Jesus clearly taught that that duties of reconciliation in the light of the Kingdom rendered such apparently weighty matters as Temple sacrifice itself completely secondary. The force and rigour of this saying were subsequently softened by Matthew as part of his overall Christological concerns. He himself added the phrase : 'then go back and make your offering', which was not part of Jesus' intent at all, but even in adding this rather lame qualification he still does not destroy the vigour of what is essentially a dismissal of one of the most sacred images of II Temple-Judaism -the Israelite engaged in the very act of sacrifice. The demands of the Kingdom of God, for Jesus, carry all else away before their primacy of import.

VII. This next area of the tradition, like the one that follows ,is more complex than the isolated instances that we have looked at before. It amounts to Jesus' attitude to the Temple itself. Here, there are six relevant references to the Temple to consider :

(a) Mk. 2.23-28 ; Mt.12.1-8; Lk.6.1-5. A controversy in the fields.
(b) Mt. 23.16. The issue of swearing by the Temple.
(c) Mt.23.35 ; Lk.11.51 . The killing of Zechariah in the Temple.
(d) Mk.13.1-2 ; Mt.24.1-2 ; Lk.21.5-6. The ruin of the Temple and city.
(e) Mk.14.58 ; Mk.15.29 ; Mt.26.61; Mt.27.40; Jn.2.19-21. A misunderstanding to the effect that Jesus threatened to destroy the Temple.
(f) Mk. 11.15-19; Mt.21.10-17; Lk.19.45-48; Jn.2.13-17. Jesus causes a Fracas in the Temple.

VII (a). The controversy here hinges on the issue of the authority of the Son of Man within the context of the Law. Being accused of not following the ordinances, the point of the David analogy which forms the substance of Mk.2.23-28 is that the Law's strict prescripts may be circumvented by appeal to higher principle. In the one instance David's charismatic relationship with God legitimised or 'covered' his unlawful act in taking the Loaves of Offering for his soldiers. In Jesus' case the argument seems to say that again the special relationship with God enjoyed by the leader of these men takes greater precedence than complaints against his disciples' lax behaviour. The point originally seems not to have been an implied 'Davidic' comparison in any messianic sense, but rather an insistence on the authority he has from God, realised in these disciples who are the nucleus so far of his Kingdom preaching, and which cannot be gainsaid by any other authority (in so far as it comes from God himself) not even the ostensible authority of appealing to the prescripts of the Law. This episode I take to be another example of the certainty of Jesus that the implications of the advent of the Kingdom were henceforth the only absolute standard of reference. This important theology of the Kingdom has been mutated by Mark, from gentile christian interest, into an apologetic about the sabbath. The sabbath logion of 2.27 (not to mention the evangelist's own comment at 2.28) is ,however, attached to the controversy story in a most artificial manner which makes the redactional elements easy to identify.As Mark maintains it , the whole unit is still more to do with the 'authority' of Jesus than his personal status. In other words it is still ostensibly more of a 'Kingdom' pericope than a Christology. The Christological development is more evident in Matthew as one would normally expect. Matthew introduces an entirely new element into the story which is not supported by either Mark or Luke, and so from the outset raises our suspicions as to its historical authenticity. He makes Jesus say :'I tell you, there is one greater than the Temple here,' and he appends to this Hoseah 6.6. In the undoubted original sense of the story the purpose of the appeal to David is to evoke David's 'special' relationship with God. The site of his unorthodox behaviour, that is the Tabernacle, is incidental and peripheral. Matthew has made it central at the cost of disrupting the internal logic of the argument. The Christological argument Matthew is making is an internal echo of his own text at Mt.12.42. He frequently makes such internal associations as part of his particular style. From the Lukan parallel with that latter text (Lk.11.31) it is clear that this was the archetypal form . In its primary archetype,then, it has nothing to do with the 'Temple' at all. In addition, Matthew's supportive device of using Hos. 6.6. to emphasise his Temple reference in Mt. 12.6, is a repetition of his own earlier argument at Mt. 9.13. All of these literary indications show obvious signs of redactive alteration and make it clear that that phrase :'One greater than the Temple is here', is a personal theologisation of Matthew's, not an original Jesus logion.

VII (b). In Mt. 23.13-32 we find a sevenfold 'woe' pronounced on the pharisees. Examples of their teaching on selected points are singled out for criticism. The third of the woes (v.16-22) turns on two examples of 'sacrificial' practice , that is the value of swearing by the Temple, and by the altar of sacrifice. Luke parallels some of the woes of controversy but not this third one, and there are enough instances in Mark (10) to suggest that an early part of the Jesus logion tradition must have been a collection of his rabbinic controversies over points of Law interpretation (especially since his eschatological ethic must have given rise to so many). Most of the Law controversies have been diminished and reduced by the more overtly gentile interests of Mark and Luke. These clearly abbreviate much more than Matthew. But Matthew's text witnesses, in turn, far more than a simple desire to preserve such halachic controversies, because in many instances it adds to and extends them. In the case of swearing by the Temple this part of Matthew's text stands in close relation to Mt. 5.33 where Jesus is presented as forbidding any oaths to be taken at all. The theological point in 23.16-22 is in the main that the presence of the Holy One should not be profaned at all, but certainly not unnecessarily as in such oaths using holy places. I am not at all convinced that 23.16-22 represents the authentic Jesus of history but there are no absolutely strong grounds to reject this text short of saying that in the end it does not square with the general line emerging from the other evidence. This is to beg the question , of course. Smaller indications might come from the fact that the saying in Mt.23.16-22 does not sit happily with Mt. 5.34 in its view of the merit of oaths; also that the saying on 'the gold of the Temple' seems to speak about it with some reverence, which is certainly not the case in the definitely original logion about the widow's mite (Mk. 12.41-44, Lk.21.1-4) which reverts to a familiar pattern that the generosity of the poor woman is the richest thing in the Treasury; and also we might add that the substance of the story in Mt.17.24-27 had a similar unimpressed attitude to the Temple-Tax, an attitude which survives despite the legendary accretions (if the mention of the fish is not a contemporary joke relating to the peculiarities of the Kinneret 'St.Peter Fish'). If we were to take Mt.23.16-22 as an authentic part of the Jesus tradition we might note that the argument gains its force as it stands from a double comparison : (i) The Temple is holy as a symbol of the One who dwells in it, far holier than the Temple gold , and (ii) The altar is holy for it symbolises God's graceful dealings with mankind, far holier than the sacrificial victim which is sanctified by it. This is in essence a doctrine of the 'Presence' not a doctrine about cult, and in the end concerned with reverence for God using the Temple and altar as incidental symbols, not as central concerns.

VII (c) The logion concerning the death of Zechariah (Mt. 23.35; Lk. 11.51) is doubly attested. It has a firm place within the authentic logia and relates to the tradition of the last murdered prophet (NT. Zechariah son of Barachiah; II Chron.24.20-22 - son of Jehoiada) who was sacrilegiously stoned in the Court of the Temple by order of King Joash (BCE 853-796). The theological point Jesus seems to be making here is a 'prophetic' justification of his own ministry. The opposition which he has encountered to his claims about the End Time he interprets as a sign that he stands in the line of many other 'righteous ones' who were persecuted and oppressed because of maintaining the truth. Historically the saying can be located to Jerusalem, where it is entirely apposite, and it has a close relationship to other ironic remarks Jesus made about the fine architectural state of the 'Tombs of the Prophets' in the Kidron valley. The Jerusalem location and the caustic nature of the comments he makes on the murderous extent of the opposition he senses might also suggest that this saying comes from the final stages of his life, as seemed to be the case with the Galilean/Siloam pericope mentioned earlier. Once again, however, we note that the mention of the Temple is largely incidental. If one were to push some of the implications, they could be said to be the same as in VII (b) above : the Temple is not holy in itself only because of the presence of the Holy One in it. If his ways are not discerned , as with Joash and Zechariah, then it can become a place of bitter opposition to God. Even a prophet can be murdered in the Temple. If this logion does indeed come from the last week in Jerusalem it possibly post-dates the fracas he has himself caused in the Temple, and might express his own recollection of that clash, where he (rightly as events turned out) sensed that his actions there had involved him in considerable danger.

VII (d) There is a triple attestation of Jesus' words relating to the ruination of the Temple: Mk.13.1-2; Mt.24.1-2 ; Lk.21.5-6. In this case it seems to be Mark who has been the common source for the two others who, independently from one another, go on to follow Mark's lead in using this logion as a suitable prelude to collected logia about the tribulation of Jerusalem and the end of the world. Mark's text, therefore, is the key, but Luke earlier in his account adds a significant detail in related material which he has gained from another source : Lk.19.41-44. This is Luke's own prelude to the expulsion of the Temple traders, and in the episode Jesus sits on the Mount of Olives before he enters the holy city for the passover, and he weeps, foreseeing the destruction of Jerusalem. If this Lukan detail gives us the correct context then the most natural reading for the prophecies of destruction would be to locate them as expressions of Jesus' anxiety over the fate of the holy city - not a dispassionate prophecy of doom as is the case in Mark. In this context the remarks on the wonderful stonework of the Temple being pulled down until ' not one single stone is left upon another' would signify a lament for the fall of God's house. Luke takes the words to mean just that - but a fall of God's house at the hands of pagan armies , whereas Jesus probably meant the fall of God's house on earth in the terrible cataclysms of the End Time. Those eschatological woes could not be avoided , hence his lament; but they demanded an attitude of repentance, and this he was not sure of evoking any more successfully than his mission in Galilee had done there, and hence his anxiety for the fate of his hearers. This eschatological context we might evoke with the support of a possible parallel with Lk. 10.8-16, his remarks summarising the Northern ministry. The failure of that preaching tour had profound bearing on what was to happen immediately after they committed themselves to enter the gates of Jerusalem. It is clear, however, that Jesus' words of lament identify 'Temple' with Jerusalem. The two are interchangeable symbols and designate not only a city with a set number of inhabitants in a given sociological period, but far more than that - the whole complex of God's covenant presence to his people. In brief, the saying again does not relate to the Temple in any cultic sense **qua tale.** Jesus words were, of course, given greater force by the disciples in the light of the events of 70 CE, and the whole tradition of this prophecy was developed in the hands of subsequent christian generations as relating to a divine punishment on the nation for the rejection of Jesus. It is this later Christological tradition, which has already identified the crucifixion as an appeasement sacrifice and the Jewish nation as the unrighteous sacrificers, which goes on in its internal logic to speak of the disasters of 70 CE as the punishments intimated in Mt.23.35 (Lk.11.5) where the blood of Zechariah was spilled and cried out for vengeance. Such a theological accumulation of texts and proof-texts to create a web of correlated logia for another historical or theological situation is typical of rabbinic and early christian exegetical practice, but in this case the doctrinal result could not be further removed from Jesus' original meaning and intent. Filled with the intimation of God's calling in of the End-Time, and recently come from a failed mission in the Northern lake towns which he had devoted to the doctrine of eschatological reconciliation, he laments anxiously before the gates of Jerusalem in case his prophetic message to his people may be rejected again, and the 'Day Of The Lord' find them unprepared and unrepentant.

VII (e) Closely related to the above tradition of the fall of the Temple is a complex series of texts concerning Jesus' supposed remarks on 'destroying the Temple' himself : Mk. 14.58 ; Mk.15.29 ; Mt. 26.61; 27.40 ; Jn.2.19-21. The Matthaean parallels very much follow Mark's chosen direction. Mark himself is much concerned to show the 'miscomprehension' of Jesus enemies. This is done not from a motive of defending Jesus against the impiety of such a threat to destroy the Holy Place - and so there is no apologetic of defence at play here. The motive of miscomprehension is an **idée maitresse** in both the Gospels of Mark and John, and in both texts this particular episode of the Temple saying is used to highlight a Christological argument. John's version does not have the threat to destroy remaining with Jesus, but after demonstrating the misunderstanding at the root of this, the evangelist removes responsibility for the destructive threat (now applied to Jesus' body as the Temple) to the enemies who wish him dead (Jn. 2.19b). In Mark's case the evangelist clearly implies to his readers that those who made this charge were not only 'false witnesses', but had foolishly misheard the logion which had been openly set out at Mk.13.2 (q.v. Mk. 14.58). At Mk. 15.29 the evangelist returns to the same theme, and here he is basing his narrative of Jesus' sufferings on the text of Wisdom 2.12-20 which recounts the sufferings of the righteous man. Within this overall midrashic context we also note that the repetition of the Temple charge at Mk.15.29 is part of a definite redactive pattern in Mark, one of a triad of mockeries (14.65, mocked as a prophet; 15.16-20, mocked as a king ; 15.29-30 mocked in his priestly pretensions) which obviously have a Christological basis. In historical terms it is relatively easy to see how an apocalyptic lament that the Temple was to fall, followed by the same preacher giving a violent sign of his message by causing a fracas in the Temple (see VII (f) following) here becomes one & the same tradition heard and repeated by those who did not accept either his right to do such a thing or the content of his message. In spite of much theological elaboration on the part of the evangelists Mark and John who have developed this into a Christology which portrays Jesus as the priest-victim who brings the whole sacrificial system to its end and its fulfilment, at root the reported logion is not historically distinct from VII (d). In Mark's text the evangelist's whole motive emerges in that great moment of drama in his passion story : the centurion's awed proclamation while the Temple curtain tears from top to bottom (Mk.15.37-39). The action here is symbolic, it is entirely redactive, and textually gains its force by looking back to the opening episode of his Gospel story when similarly the veil of the heavens was torn apart in the great epiphany of the Baptism (Mk.1.10 ; cf. Is. 64.1-2)

VII (f) The tradition of the fracas in the Temple is more difficult to interpret (Mk.11.15-19; Mt. 21.10-17; Lk.19.45-48; Jn.2.13-17). It should not be called the 'cleansing of the Temple',however, because this nomenclature presupposes a controverted interpretation. If we again take Mark's account as the paradigmatic version, then Luke is seen to abbreviate so much that Jesus' 'anger' is clearly and solely directed at those who are buying and selling, thus turning the holy place into a place of commerce (as in John 2.16). This does not trouble itself with the historical fact that if the exchange of ritually certificated animals did not take place in the Temple, then the entire sacrificial cult as laid down in the Torah, would grind to a halt. Any mention of the 'selling of doves', essential to the sacrifices, is omitted by Luke, and he has emphasised a lead he took from Mark to the effect that Jesus' act sprang entirely from righteous anger at the way secular commerce had invaded the holy shrine . This interpretation of a spiritual protest against secularism is very much a gentile, outsider's view of the realities of the cultic system, and although it has become in some ways a 'standard reading ' of the episode, so that one speaks now of the 'cleansing of the Temple', it is more to do with Mark and Luke than with the Jesus of history. Matthew follows Mark's version closely at this point, and retains the Markan reference to the dove sellers. John expands the detail even more graphically - here Jesus drives out in a stampede not only the dove sellers and the money changers but the sacrificial animals as well , cattle and sheep. In the case of John, however, he has definite theological purpose behind his narrative. He has relocated the incident from its true historical setting in the last week of Jesus' life, and placed it at the head of his Gospel narrative, one of the opening gambits of the public ministry. The overall Johannine theme that Jesus' self is the true Temple warns us of his heavy redactive involvement. Nonetheless his extra detail about the scattering of animals cannot have been too far from the truth when we consider that the incident took place in the Hanuyot, possibly the lower halls which would have been filled with animals and people. While many have interpreted the fracas, deliberately caused, in the 'spiritual purification' manner mentioned above, others have read it as a provocative attack on the corruption of the Sadducean priesthood (11) but there is little other corroborative evidence to suggest this was an issue with Jesus in any particular sense . Mark records Jesus clashing with the Sadducees only over the question of resurrection theology(Mk.12.18f). It is the Markan detail, proper to his text, that Jesus :'Would not allow any man to carry anything through the Temple', that has been seen by some to confirm the motive of the fracas as a 'spiritual cleansing'. But this reading of the detail is again highly 'interpretative', not value free. If we ask what was the historical incident which leads the evangelist to tell it in such a way we are left, presumably, with some incident of knocking over somebody's load that they happened to be carrying at the time of the general mayhem - quite possibly a load of hay feed. If one imagines Jesus policing the upper colonnades and the Temple mount to ensure that no-one in the court of gentiles was carrying anything -then certainly he emerges as one zealous for the law to a minute degree, and fanatically guarding the holiness of the cult. But this picture of Jesus has no support from the general line of other logia. If one locates the whole incident in the lower subterranean terraces of the Hanuyot, however, then all comes together as one act, in one place; a sharp and deliberate causing of mayhem. Such is the history, but what is the motive for that mayhem ? Mark has clearly begun the long tradition that sees it as a 'purification' (which incidentally is an implicit validation of the Temple, not a rejection of it). Such an interpretation he has arrived at by means of an elaborate architecture of biblical proof-texts,a normal sign of redactive work apart from and around a logion tradition. The evangelist sees Jesus's advent to the Temple in the manner of a Zechariah-type Messiah (Zech.9.9; Mk.11.2f + plls.). The text of Zechariah has also supplied the detail ,for Matthew, of the thirty pieces of silver for which Jesus is sold (Zech.11.13; Mt.26.16). In Mark, the key issue to the present matter which he takes as his master theme of interpretation, thus influencing both Luke and Matthew considerably, is :'There shall be no more traders in the Temple of the Lord God of Hosts when that day comes.' And this is a direct borrowing from Zechariah 14.21 (q.v.) which speaks of a universal opening out of the cult to all the nations to such an extent that the notion of holy sacrifice will itself disappear within the profound sanctification of all aspects of the renewed life. The other key biblical texts used in the Gospel narrative are :'My house will be a house of prayer for all nations' (Is.56.7), and :'Do you take this Temple which bears my name for a robber's den ?' (Jer.7.11) . All of this theme of the opening out of Judaism to gentiles is a major interest of Mark's. More to the point, however, the entire substance of Jesus' words during the Temple incident has been supplied by the evangelist by proof texts in a midrash that synthesises wholly unrelated passages. What connection can there be between this violent gesture in the Hanuyot and an intention to signal gentile rights of access, outside the mind of the evangelist? It is evident that what was a definite historical incident, a violent gesture rather than a logion , happened in the Temple and Mark attempts to interpret this as part of his theology of gentile access to election through Jesus. This leaves us to ask what else could have been the significance of the act if 'spiritual purification' and 'renewal' emerge as secondary. The answer might be given more readily if we were to see the events simply as a noisy fracas, a deliberate causing of mayhem. To interpret this as something more than a mere friction between traders and disciples, to see it as a definite 'sign' and teaching device of Jesus we can fruitfully go to the explicit logia which have immediately preceded the event : the lament over the fate of the holy city and Temple, and we propose, therefore, that this fracas he causes is an acted-out form of the same message. What he appears to say by the mayhem is that the 'End-Time is upon us, there is no time left for all these things, or to be so involved in such matters as to be deaf to the message.' It is still a good thing to remember not to preach in a market place - it is bad for business. It is possibly in this localised conflict in the Hanuyot that Jesus reacts strongly to his apocalyptic message being challenged and turns over the tables to demonstrate vividly the reality of his vision. The root of the whole meaning lies in his apocalyptic sense of an impending crisis. To turn over a few tables is not the same thing as to 'destroy the Temple' in symbolic form. There is little connection between the smallness of the one act and the immensity of the other. The fracas in the Temple, then, is another example that Jesus was not 'against the Temple' as such. It simply, like all other things, passed out of significance in the light of the impending apocalypse. And this analysis with which we summarise VII (f) can rightly stand as an apt summation of all the other five instances of 'Temple' logia which we have treated above. The Temple and the sacrificial cult do not feature in his theological scheme which is totally dominated by the sense of God's approach, and entirely concerned with the proclamation of repentance and reconciliation.

VIII. The last of the eight instances of sacrificial references we set out to examine is the Jesus logion at the institution of the eucharist : Mk.14.22-25 ; Mt..26.26-29 ; Lk.22.19-20 ; I Cor. 11.24-25 . It turns on Jesus' explicit reference to the cup of wine as 'the blood of the new and everlasting covenant'. It is only if one accepts that Jesus was dominated throughout the Last Supper by sacrificial motifs that one can read the phrase :'Do this in remembrance of me' (Lk.22.19),as having 'sacrificial' import also (12). The term 'memorial' does feature in the sacrificial cult, but in the context of the Last Supper its use is more simply given in terms of the remembering of dead persons in a general , non cultic, sense. The command to take the cup and drink is to be understood in the light of the asseveration of Mk.14.25 ; Lk.22.15. In the eucharistic account Luke represents an important alternative tradition to Mark and is not simply following his steps. Jesus introduces his gift of the cup with a highly unusual oath of abstinence, designed to 'hasten' the advent of the Kingdom which he senses to be so imminent. The unusual departures from ritual are readily explicable if we somewhat distance our quest for the meaning of the meal from the Passover context, rather than presuming from the outset that the meal simply was the Pesach sacrifice, and then proceeding to abstract conclusions from that - which somewhat begs the question. There has long been controversy on this point. The argument proposed here is that the Passover typology (and sacrificial concepts attached to it) are historically secondary to other concerns which they themselves have overlaid. We ought, then, to establish a wider historical context of interpretation. Christian tradition, following Jesus' memorial instruction, centred on this meal as the heart of its proper liturgy, and into this tradition from the earliest times (as evidenced in the venerability of the custom already by the time Paul speaks of it in I Cor.11.17f) there came the sacrificial typology of the blood of the Paschal victim (Ex.12.21-28) and the blood-sprinkling of the covenant ratification (Ex.24.8). It is by no means easy to make clear historical judgements on the actual nature of Jesus' words in this instance, despite the classic and magisterial study by Jeremias (13) but it is our thesis here that the sacrificial theologisation so apparent in the phrase ' blood of the covenant ' is a **post-eventum** development, and that Jeremias' presumption that the phrase 'This is my body' means simply that :'Jesus speaks of himself as a sacrifice' (14) is not so straightforward as he suggests. In his study of the sacrifice issue Jeremias passes from a first position :'It can be assumed with a high degree of probability that Jesus had prepared the way for this comparison of himself with the sacrifice, earlier, in the passover meditation' , to an overall position :'It is inconceivable that Jesus should not have thought of the atoning power of his death' (15). These statements are curious presumptions. There is no evidence at all offered for the first, and for the second, which has hardened from an assumption into a certainty, the evidence given for the statement is that there exists later rabbinic evidence to suggest that such an attitude to atoning death was possible in the metaphysic of late second-Temple Judaism (16). Leaving the question for a moment whether the Last Supper was in fact the Passover celebration at all, we can note that the argument that Jesus must have seen his death as an atonement because this was a contemporary possibility - is no argument at all.
To interpret Jesus' breaking of bread in sacrificial terms derived from the Passover ritual is to neglect three very important aspects of that rite : (i) that the only sacrificial victim is the lamb itself , not the bread. Although the mazzoth is an 'offering' to the Lord it is nonsense to speak of violence being done to the bread in this ritual context ; (ii) that the expiating significance of the Passover is not highly marked in the celebration in the 1st century CE. Even christian theology which elaborates the Last Supper in an expiatory passover sense related to the cross can only do so by turning at frequent junctures in the argument away from passover typology to the more tractable areas of sin-offerings and blood purifications ; and (iii) that the death of the victim lamb **qua tale** is wholly superfluous in the meaning of the Passover celebrations. All three aspects make the drawing of parallels between the passover rite and the historical Jesus event not immediately obvious at all except in the light of an elaborated theology of sacrificial death - a theology which can only happen after the actual death of Jesus to give it coherence, and which thus is marked more by the hands of disciples than by any consistent logion tradition attributable to Jesus.

We spoke earlier of setting a wider context for our interpretation of the Last Supper, and despite the constraining limits of this present paper which demand an abbreviated argument, let us begin with an indisputable part of Jesus' actual words at the meal : his oath of abstinence (Mk.14.25; Lk.22.15; Mt.26.29) . As Jeremias has demonstrated (17) this is not merely a pledge to refrain from wine, but from food as well, and spoken not at the end of the meal, but at the beginning. It does not seem to be simply a passing ascetical gesture, and indeed has little to do with 'fasting' as such, a practice Jesus has significantly disavowed throughout his ministry as unfitting to the time of wedding celebrations he saw as implied in his sense of the advent of the Bridegroom to Israel. This argument, and its relevance to Jesus' doctrine of meals I have more fully elaborated elsewhere (18) . The refusal to eat is instead a radical asseveration expressing his faith in the imminence of God's saving act - the establishment of the Kingdom. By it, in a graphic way, Jesus suggests that he will not need to eat before the kingdom breaks in. I take this in an extended rather than a literal sense - a hyperbolic way of encouraging his disciples with the pressing closeness of the Kingdom. This is at least the second time we have such a firm commitment to the imminence of God's intervention. The first occasion of this (Mt.10.23) (19) was the asseveration that launched the missionary endeavours in the northern towns. Here at the Last Supper we have a similar context - Jesus' encouragement of his disciples as they are marshalled for a preaching assault on the city. The fact that this preaching assault was devastated by the death of Jesus does not alter the intended context, and we shall see subsequently that events within the meal that made it clear to him that the preaching programme might never materialise, turned his thoughts away from heady encouragement towards an anxious and disturbed re-evaluation of how matters stood. The asseverance that encouraged the first missionary tour of Galilee came home to him, and his disciples, in the aftermath of that tour, as an optimism for the work of reconciliation perhaps not matched by the realities of their encounters. The whole mission seems to have met with only qualified success at best (Lk.11.16-24). After this tour a period of wintering in Capernaum seems to have preceded this final movement in the Spring, for a ministry based in Jerusalem , culminating in the Passover during which he died. There are indications that the internal cohesion and loyalty of the disciples might have been weakened by the poor results of the first tour, and already starting to fray even before the arrival of the group in Jerusalem (20). Their enthusiasm for another round of apocalyptic preaching might have been accordingly qualified.At least one of them has had enough of it after he witnesses Jesus' behaviour in the Temple. The asseveration during the Last Supper is hard to rationalise if we take the meal as a Passover feast. How could Jesus arrange the pesach and then announce his intention to fast throughout it ? (21) Jeremias interprets Luke's phrase to have had the original meaning :'I earnestly wanted to eat the passover (lamb) with you, but now I shall not eat it until all is fulfilled in the Kingdom.' Likewise we ought to understand the passing round of the cup, in which Jesus does not participate either (22). If this is the case then this is not Jesus' 'Last Supper' at all because he has abstained throughout, and it certainly makes it all the more difficult to take such a clear distancing from the celebration, hand in hand with the suggestion that (a) this was the actual passover meal, and (b) Jesus self-identified with it to such an extent he drew the analogy between himself and the sacrificial lamb. None of this holds together. F C Burkitt and A E Brooke (23) took the phrase as conclusive evidence that this meal was not the Passover - in other words Jesus was still hoping at the beginning of the Last Supper to hold the Passover with them all at the end of the week.By the end of the meal, however, it had become clear to him that this would not be possible. The asseveration points us in another theological direction from Passover, and it is reminiscent of a consistent theological attitude throughout the ministry (still discernible in the prominence that the sign of feasting has in Jesus' praxis as well as his surviving parables, despite the great fragmentation that has occurred in the tradition of both) which uses the symbolism of the common meal as a vehicle for proclaiming the reconciliation Jesus felt to have been effected between God and Israel in the immediate prelude to the Kingdom. The staging of common meals during the Galilean tour seems to have been one of the preaching devices proper to Jesus, and these meals were undoubtedly the setting for many of the parables, as well as being important encapsulations of his entire theological message. The meals, in short, were his 'prophetic sign' on the advent of the Kingdom of God, using the symbol of the wedding feast to illuminate the active covenant between God and Israel, his restored bride. If the Kingdom's advent essentially means the active renewal of God's saving acts for his people , then the coming of the Kingdom is fittingly expressed in a doctrine that calls for an end to the fast and the commencement of the feast. In marked contrast to other notions of the eschatological feast, however, a notable feature of Jesus' common meals was the presence of the unpurified and unrighteous. This unique behaviour, which caused controversy at the time (24), so unlike other occasions of communal meals such as the Essene gatherings, or the early christian agapés which presupposed cultic purity, can be explained on the presupposition that it was peculiar to Jesus' understanding of the advent of the Kingdom that when God returned to Israel's living experience and reactivated his covenant presence for his people (who until then had to lament his distance by fasting, and pray for speedy deliverance) then the wedding gift he brought for the renewed betrothal was the reconciliation of his people. It seems to be Jesus' sense of the universal offer of this reconciliation that lay at the heart of his belief in the nearness of the Kingdom, and which formed the substance of his preaching. It is a concept of forgiveness so far-reaching and of such eschatological significance that it leaves the former methods of purification and atonement far behind, outmoded. The sacrificial system of purification and expiation belonged to the 'former age'. What Jesus anticipated was the restoration of the 'next age'. Whenever he speaks of justification and forgiveness it is quite decidedly in this sense of a direct, immediate, and prodigal grace which circumvents the sacrificial system in its all-inclusiveness (26). Central to the doctrine of the prodigal mercifulness of God, and consequent on it, is the demand in the Jesus-preaching for a prodigally merciful attitude to one's fellows (27), and this is why the meals he arranged and attended in the course of his northern preaching tour involved the unexpected mixing together of righteous and unrighteous, law-abiders and law-breakers.

We can designate these events as 'meals of reconciliation' and deduce that they must have been familiar to the disciples who in some instances must have had the task of arranging them. They were, then, designed to act out in table fellowship the implications of reconciliation and either admit his hearers into the experience of reconciliation he preached, or at least demonstrate to them their need of it.

The synoptic Gospels, Mark especially, still bear a sense of the strange circumstances attendant on the arrangement of the Last Supper (Mk.14.12-16 + plls.) Jesus seems to have made special preparations , without the advance knowledge of his disciples, for this meal. This, together with the signs noticed earlier that the cohesion of his disciples might have been clearly weakening at the prospect of a Jerusalem mission, may provide sufficient indication to see the Last Supper as a meal of reconciliation aimed no longer at northern villagers but at the disciples themselves, to bring home to them in one great effort, the demands of the doctrine of reconciliation they were to preach, and their own need of reconciliation with one another. When it became apparent to him that this reconciliation meal had not worked, and Judas' departure from the early stages of the feast dramatically signalled this, all hopes of a united ministry in Jerusalem are shattered, and his own thoughts seem to turn to the danger of death to which he has been exposed. It is at this point that the bread and wine cease to have for him their intended archetypal symbolism of fellowship and reconciliation and turn instead into ominous signs - broken bread, poured out cup; the bitterness of a failed initiative, the foreboding raised by a party where the guests refuse the invitation.

The tradition of Gethsemane where Jesus posts his disciples to keep watch while he prays in anxiety should be taken to mean that the disciples were not originally asked to keep watch with him in prayer, but to keep watch for him, on the approaches from the city gates across the Kidron valley. The place of his prayer is exactly on the ancient cross-road on route for an eastward escape from Jerusalem, either to the North avoiding the Via Maris , to the East into the trackless hiding places of the wilderness, or to the North-East in the free territories of the Decapolis. In the event , because of the failure of his watchmen, Jesus' agonising reevaluation of his planned ministry in Jerusalem is abruptly pre-empted. It is he alone who seems to hear the approach of the arrest party. These come with torches and lanterns and noise, because they do not expect to find Jesus anywhere near the place. The essence of Judas' betrayal was probably the site of their lodging, in Bethany, and an early morning raid would have entrapped the entire movement. The unexpected delay of Jesus by the cross-road at Gethsemane put the Temple-guards' otherwise excellent timing quite out of joint - and Temple guards we must take them to be despite some subsequent confusion over the matter since all agree that Jesus was brought immediately into the custody of the priests. Hearing their undisguised approach Jesus appears to have gone out to meet and pre-empt them, allowing those disciples who had remained with him to profit from the confusion and take to flight. If such a recreated scenario is right, then the possibility and danger of death which has struck him in the upper room does not become an unavoidable destiny until the garden of Gethsemane when his disciples' carelessness has effectively closed all his options. It is clearly understandable why the disciples, with poignant hindsight, should emphasise the prophetic and tragic nature of what in the end turned out to be his last words , and in the light of his subsequent execution should read a sacrificial intent into the whole meal, with the help of Passover symbolism, since in later years the distinction of what the meal actually was faded before the kerygmatic synopsis that 'Jesus died at Passover'. But if the meal was indeed intended as a reconciliation feast, as I have here suggested, then there is no reason at all to see why this should be invested with 'sacrificial' meaning from the outset, especially given the other evidence relating to Jesus' attitude to the cult. No reason at all, unless one is governed from the outset by dogmatic constricts. In short, the discussion of this last and most complex saying of Jesus about the 'blood of the covenant', if taken from a wider historical context suggests a very different conclusion indeed to that of Jeremias who figuratively attributes to Jesus the intention at the Last Supper of proclaiming :'I go to death as the true passover sacrifice'. Our conclusion here is that the original words referred with sadness to the bread and wine which had ceased to be symbols of joy and reconciliation and had turned in the light of the failure of the meal into symbols of his own life's danger.

This can be summarised as follows : (i) the historical context of the Last Supper was not the Pesach but the reconciliation meal that had characterised the northern ministry; (ii) the line of argument that equates broken bread with passover victim is singularly naive in losing sight somewhere of a lamb; (iii) the asseveration saying begins a process of testing and evaluation, clarified by Judas' betrayal, which continues on into his remarks about the bread and the cup as tragic signs, and leads us thereafter to the agonised hours in Gethsemane, where the evaluation is cut short by the subsequent carelessness of the remaining followers. This process of re-evaluation is begun by Jesus but pre-empted by the arrival of his enemies. In retrospect these historical events are accepted in faith by the survivers as no accidents of history, but the revelation of the hand of God, the destiny to which Jesus was moving urgently in his last week of life. Thereafter it is an easy step to recast the entire story of the meal in terms drawn from the theology of sacrifice and immolation which was familiar to them, and which seemed to them to be suitable for the explication of the mysterious and tragic events of that passover week in which the last meal featured largely.

CONCLUSIONS 1.

This paper has examined points of the original Jesus tradition which relate to the cultic notion of sacrifice. Our concern has been to enquire what was the attitude of Jesus himself to the usefulness of the concept of 'sacrifice' in expressing God's relationship with his people in the workings of his providential grace. To investigate Jesus' attitude in this regard calls for an exercise in disengagement for it is abundantly clear that from earliest times the notion of sacrifice has been used as a major vehicle for the interpretation of Jesus' death, and it has borne the weight of almost the entire christian theology of 'atonement'.

By briefly sketched redactive analyses this paper has been able to review only the attitude of Jesus himself,in selected key passages, but the conclusions have consistently accumulated, and the point to which they run is unequivocal. We may summarise as follows :

(1). The Jesus tradition (as distinct from that of subsequent Pharisaic disciples such as Paul, the evangelist Matthew, or the author of **Hebrews** , and those who are influenced by them) suggests that he himself did not use either sacrifice or Temple as important elements of his theological message. These parts of the Torah prescriptions, along with all the other aspects of the Law, Jesus seems to have subsumed under the all embracing vision of the demands of the End-Time, the Kingdom of God. The requirements of the New Age, repentance and acceptance of God's gift of reconciliation, were for Jesus so paramount that they took precedence over all other things, and all else was put in the shade by the towering urgency he attributed to the Kingdom and the duty he had received to preach it.

(2). On the rare occasions when Temple or sacrifice becomes centre stage in an argument or discussion Jesus radically subordinates these concerns to the demands of the Kingdom. Two clear symbols of this can be seen in the logion advising the would-be sacrificer to leave his offering at the altar and go home, if he is not at rights with his brother; and in the sign of the violent fracas he deliberately stirred up in the Hanuyot. This was interpreted in his own life-time by outsiders to his movement (and with some justification in terms of contemporary rabbinic theology) as tantamount to a radical breaking of Torah ordinances and a heretical deviation from the right path.

(3). The points of the christian tradition which attribute sacrificial categories to Jesus, particularly the Last Supper words of institution, do so with **post-eventum** hindsight, and often by means of inserting biblical proof-texts from the scriptures onto the lips of Jesus in the cause of creating a logion. This the later tradition does as part of a developing process of the interpretation of the shocking events of Jesus' abrupt arrest and execution in the Spring of 29 CE. The employment of sacrificial motifs is part of the tidying-up process, chronological, political, and theological, which constitutes the assembling of the charismatic life and teachings of Jesus into the form of the early church's kerygmatic proclamation.

(4). The unavoidable uncertainties of a redactive method seeking to illuminate 'original' events behind subsequent layers of ancient interpretation may lead to several instances of individual argumentation which can be controverted. Nonetheless the results of this redactive enquiry, applied to individual sayings , which reaches such a conclusion that sacrifice was not one of the operative categories of Jesus, can be supported by appeal to 'external' arguments, or wider aspects of the tradition. In this paper the wider context of Jesus' theology of reconciliation, the implications of his eschatological ethic, and the uncertainty he had regarding his fate until the very last moments at the Gethsemane crossroad, have all been pressed into service to corroborate the basic rightness of the historical deduction that Jesus of Nazareth did not employ the concept of sacrifice at all. His disciples attributed to him in the aftermath of his death.

CONCLUSIONS II.

The 'classical' form of sacrifice theology as laid forth in the Levitical prescriptions can be summed up as a theology of gift and grace (28). Here are none of the lugubrious rites of aversion known in the Hellenistic world ; stuffing victims into holes in the earth in fearful apotropaeic rituals, none of the grim associations of the brooding rite of the Hellenistic holocaust to the dark forces of the world. Israel's ritual of sacrifice expresses the joy of covenantal dedication. It is entirely, in the period of the II Temple, in the domain of what the Greek sacrificial theology called the Olympian rites of Therapeia. Even the sin-offerings, whatever their anthropological connotations in the distant past, are, in the classic form of II Temple practice,basically rites celebrating the gracious **Hesed** of God. There is no hint that the blood of the victims cleanses the Israelite by any mysterious power that it has independently of the sacrifice ; the purifying power of the blood flows, on the contrary, from God's gracious acceptance of the sacrifice. No stress, in the classical biblical doctrine of sacrifice is laid on the death of the animal victim as such - it is entirely incidental - expressive merely of the free and obedient gift of the worshipper. No significance is ever attached to transference of sins in some primitive, quasi-magical way within the classic understanding of the action of the **chattath** or the **asham** . These offerings are partly eaten by the priests 'as most holy things' (Lev.6) - they can hardly be envisaged as laden with the weight of sin. The only rite of transference is the ritual of the scape-goat, and precisely because this is seen to be laden with the weight of sin it is driven out, not fit for sacrifice to the God of holiness.

When the earliest christian theologians after Jesus began to use the notion of sacrifice with reference to his death, it was from the basis of close familiarity with the meaning and practice of the Torah prescriptions. The first applications of the idea by Paul are in the form of useful analogies (29), rather than systematic doctrinal elaborations. They represent very well his sense of how , in a mysterious manner, the death of Jesus was not a futile ending of a misguided hope, but central to Jesus' own faith in God's work of reconciliation, caused by that very faith, and somehow the paradoxical sign through which divine mercy was indeed given for his followers. In the course of time, however, the precise meanings of the classic sacrifice theology, which can still be presumed in the pharisaism of Paul writing in the mid first century CE, give way to a host of other influences and intrusions. The sacrificial analogies harden into the force of absolute dogma, and tend to overlay other more subtle indications within the tradition, that Jesus and his significance exceeded the ability of the notion of sacrifice to encapsulate. Within this narrowing of perspective many of the lugubrious influences of the Hellenistic understanding of rites of aversion crept back into the picture. Jesus was seen as a tragic victim, sacrificed unlawfully by the High Priest, bringing blood-guilt onto the whole Jewish nation, and sacrificed to appease an angry God. These gentile deviations misrepresented the original point of Paul, and the authors of **Hebrews, Revelation**, and the **1st.Johannine Letter** , but seeds of trouble were sown as early as the first Gospel accounts which were beginning to be composed in the context of a full-scale apologetic between Judaism and nascent gentile Christianity. This later use of sacrifice typology in christian thought not only sets the scene for the bitter attitude of the daughter to the mother which characterises so much of subsequent Christian - Jewish relations, but it involves Christianity in a constricted view of the glory of God, and binds it to an atonement theology that can speak of the necessary appeasement of an angry God, which is an affront to the entire thrust of the life and teachings of Jesus of Nazareth.

The events of the terrible genocide whose 50th anniversary we remember on this occasion were not a joyful burnt-offering to the Lord. It was no **'olah** or **Zevach** He received there , but the parody of true sacrifice by cruel and evil people who knew nothing of the ways of the covenant of **Hesed.** The innocent victims of that genocide form one of the greatest challenges of this century to the providence theology of Judaism and Christianity ;and the tradition common to both religions that innocent suffering is expiatory is a profound analogy to apply in discussing that challenge but on its own it is not enough, in this matter, to stand as an all-embracing theological answer, just as it is not enough simply to explain the works of the perpetrators of genocide as evil deeds. Here the theology of sacrifice falters.

The typology of sacrifice is profound and illuminating if one always recalls how it should be used to connote joyful and wholehearted dedication to the service of God and his given destiny. It is also a most dangerous typology to let loose if it becomes degenerated. These are important theological issues, and it is as a preliminary contribution to their discussion that the present paper relating to Jesus of Nazareth's attitudes to sacrifice is offered.

------- ooo0ooo -------

Notes to the text.

1. cf. C G Montefiore & H Loewe. **A Rabbinic Anthology.** London 1938. pp. 226,543,545; **Is.53.4f.**
2. R K Yerkes. **Sacrifice in Gk & Roman Religions & Early Judaism.** London 1953.
   F Young. **The Use Of Sacrificial Ideas in Gk. Christian Writers From the NT to John Chrysostom.** Philadelphia 1979. R Daley. **The origins of the Christian doctrine of sacrifice.** London,'79.
   E O James. **Origins of Sacrifice.** London 1933.
3. cf. I H Marshall (Ed) **New Testament Interpretation.** Exeter 1979 for a brief introduction to the principles of Redaction Criticism.
4. 1 Sam.15.22; Is.1.11-17; Jer.14.12; Hos.6.6; Amos.5.22; Mic. 6.6-8.
5. e.g. in the **Cur Deus Homo ?**
6. II Macc. 6.12-17; 7.30-38. IV Macc. (pre 70 or II century CE ?) 17.20-22; 6.28-29.
   F Young, op. cit. pp.66-68. R Daley, op. cit. pp.33-34.
7. Gen. 15.17 ; Lev. 9.24; Judg.13.19-20; II Chron.7.1; I K. 18.38.
8. cf. I Cor. 11.25; 6.20; 7.23; II Cor. 3.4-6; Rom.3.24; 8.3-4; Gal.3.13,15-20; 4.5,24.
9. q.v. critical apparatus to Gk. text of Lk.22.20.

Notes Continued :

10. cf. Mk. 7.1-13; 8.16;11.27-33; 12.13-36.
11. e.g. V Epstein. **The Historicity of The Gospel Account of the Cleansing of the Temple.** ZNW,55,1965,42-45. See also E Sanders, **Jesus and Judaism.** London 1985, ch.1.
12. cf. Joachim Jeremias. **The Eucharistic Words of Jesus.** London 1966. pp.237-255
13. Ibid. pp.237-255; Note also the relevance of Zech.9.11 as 'proof-text' in this instance.
14. Jeremias, op. cit. p.222.
15. Ibid. p.231.
16. Ibid. p.230, fns. 8,9,11.
17. Ibid. pp. 204-205, 217-218.
18. J McGuckin, **The Sign of the Prophet. Jesus' Doctrine of Meals.** Scripture Bulletin, 16, 2, Summer 1986, pp.35-40.
19. although see also Mk. 9.1 for which see also : J.McGuckin, **The Transfiguration of Christ In Scripture and Tradition.** New York 1986, chs. 1-2.
20. cf. Mk. 10.32; Mt.17.23 ; Jn.2.23-25; 6.59-62; 11.8,16,56-57. Also note the import of the parables of the growing seeds as in Mk.4 which seemingly connote an insistence on the arrival of the Kingdom despite all present appearances of failure.
21. Jeremias, op. cit. p.208.
22. Ibid. p.209, fn.1.
23. **St. Lk. 22.15-16. What is the general meaning ?** JTS,9,1907-1908, 569-572; ibid.17, p.295.
24. Mk.2.15-17; 7.5.
26. cf. Mk. 5.21; 11.25; 12.33-34; Lk.7.36-50; 18.13.
27. Mk.4.24; 12.29-31; Mt.6.12,14-15; 7.1-2; 18.32-35; Lk.17.4
28. cf R K Yerkes, op. cit. chs. 10-12.
29. see fn. 8 above.

Covenant and Holocaust <1>

Richard L. Rubenstein
Department of Religion
The Florida State University
Tallahassee, Florida 32312

Few, if any, of biblical religion's affirmations have been rendered as problematic by the Holocaust as the covenant between God and Israel. Nevertheless, if we reflect upon the original achievement of the Sinai covenant, namely, the uniting of diverse kinship groups lacking common roots or common faith into a religiously-legitimated community of moral obligation, the Holocaust becomes an object lesson in the consequences of the absence of a binding covenant between peoples.

Let us consider first, the problematic aspect of the idea of covenant. Although the Holocaust has been characterized as "the most radical counter-testimony to religious faith, both Jewish and Christian," some of the Jewish community's most faithful and observant religious leaders have offered a contrary opinion.<2> Following the prophets and earlier rabbis, they saw their faith in God confirmed by the catastrophe. According to Gershon Greenberg, the views of Rabbi Elchonon Wassermann of Baranovitch (1875-1941) are representative of Orthodox Jewish thought in the Holocaust years. <3> Writing between Kristallnacht and the beginning of the war, Wassermann interprets the Nazi onslaught as due to three Jewish "evils," secular nationalism, assimilation, especially through Reform Judaism, and the contempt for the Torah allegedly present in the scientific study of Judaism. For Wassermann, the Holocaust is but God's appropriate response against those who have proven unfaithful to his Torah. Wassermann also sees the promise of redemption as well as the element of punishment in the misfortunes. Indeed, Wassermann argues that the more intense the suffering of the people, the closer the advent of the Messiah. <4>

---

2 The phrase is from Irving Greenberg, "Cloud of Smoke, Pillar of Fire: Judaism, Christianity, and Modernity After the Holocaust" in Eva Fleischner, ed., Auschwitz: Beginning of A New Era? (New York: Ktav, 1977), p. 9-13.
3 Elchonon Wassermann, Ma'amar Ikvossoh Demeshicho Vema'mamar Al Ha'emunah (Treatise on the Footsteps of the Messiah and on Faith)(New York: 1939) [Yiddish], cited by Gershon Greenberg, "Orthodox Theological Responses to Kristallnacht: Chayyim Ozer Grodzensky ("Achiezer") and Elchonon Wassermann," paper presented at the Eighteenth Annual Scholars Conference On the Church Struggle and the Holocaust, Washington, D.C., 1988. I am indebted to Professor Greenberg for having made available to me this paper, as well as several others dealing with Orthodox responses to the Holocaust.
4 Wassermann, op. cit., par. 40, p. 40, cited and translated by Gershon Greenberg, op. cit.

Wassermann's life was fully consistent with his faith. When taken by four Latvian murderers to be killed in July, 1941, he spoke of his own death, as well as the deaths of others like him, as a sacrificial offering (korban) for the Jewish people:

> Let us go with raised heads. God forbid, that any thought should enter the mind of anybody to make the sacrifice (korban) unfit. We now carry out the greatest Mitzvah, Kiddush Hashem (sanctification of God's name). The fire which will burn our bodies is the fire which will resurrect the Jewish people. <5>

Wassermann's response to the Holocaust was typical of that of the Orthodox rabbinate of the period. Far from being a "counter-testimony," the events were seen as the fulfillment of God's plan.

Rabbi Joseph Isaac Schneersohn, the late Lubavitcher Rebbe, is yet another example of the same tendency. According to Schneersohn, Hitler is but God's instrument for chastising the Jews who have abandoned the ways of Torah; Nazism is divine punishment visited upon the Jews for rejecting the Torah and assimilation. <6>

Nor is the theme of the Holocaust as confirmation of Jewish faith restricted to Orthodox Jewish leaders. We find the same theme in the thought of Dr. Ignaz Maybaum, a Reform rabbi who served in England for many years. Maybaum argues that the Holocaust demonstrates the continung validity of God's covenant with Israel. <7> He affirms the classical Reform Jewish belief in the "mission of Israel" to bring knowledge of the true God and his Law to the nations of the world. Maybaum insists that God intervenes in history, especially the history of his Chosen People, and that the Holocaust was one of his most important interventions.

Nevertheless, unlike the Orthodox rabbis, Maybaum rejects the idea that the Holocaust was divine punishment. Instead, he regards the victims of the Holocaust as innocent, divinely-chosen sacrificial offerings. Using the crucifixion as his model for interpreting the Holocaust, Maybaum argues that God's purposes can only be understood by the nations of the world when God addresses them in language they are capable of understanding, namely, the language of death and destruction. The crucifixion speaks of God's activity to the Christian world in the language of death and destruction.

According to Maybaum, precisely because of the covenant between God and Israel, 6,000,000 Jews were fated to become sacrificial victims so that God's purposes for the modern world might be fulfilled: "The Golgotha of modern mankind is Auschwitz. The cross, the Roman gallows, was replaced by the gas chamber." <8>
Maybaum characterizes the Holocaust as the Third Churban, that is, an utterly destructive divine intervention in history which is world-historical in scope and significance. Such as event has as its purpose a decisive alteration of the course of history. For Maybaum, this divinely-crafted destructiveness also has a creative element. A Churban signals the end of one era and the beginning of a new and better one. However, the new era can only come into being if the old is destroyed. According to Maybaum, the earlier destructions of Jerusalem in 586 B.C.E. and 70 C.E. were the first and second Churbanot respectively. Both are seen by Maybaum as progressive. The first Churban enabled the Jews to bring knowledge of the true God and his Law to the pagan

---

5 Efraim Oshry, Churban Litta (New York: 1951), pp. 48-50, [Yiddish], cited and translated by Gershon Greenberg.

6 Joseph Isaac Schneersohn, "Redemption Now," Netzach Yisroel III (1948) 6-7 [Hebrew], cited by Gershon Greenberg, "Reflections Upon the Holocaust Within American Orthodoxy, 1945-1948," to be published in Ramaz Jubillee Volume, 1988.

7 Ignaz Maybaum, The Face of God After Auschwitz, Amsterdam: Polak and Van Gennep, 1965.

8 Maybaum, The Face of God After Auschwitz, p. 36.

nations beyond Judea's borders. If Israel had not endured the first exile, knowledge of God's word might have remained confined to one small community. The Roman destruction of Jerusalem, the second *Churban,* is seen as similarly progressive, enabling the synagogue to become the predominant Jewish religious institution. The destruction of the Temple's allegedly primitive religious life with its animal sacrifices led to the flowering of a "higher," more "spiritual" religious life involving prayer, worship and study. Maybaum also regards the loss of Jewish political independence as a progressive expression of divine purpose. The diaspora fulfilled the "mission of Israel" by enabling the Jews to spread the knowledge of God throughout the Roman empire.

For Maybaum the Holocaust is a further example of God's use of the Jewish people as sacrificial victims. In Maybaum's view God brought about the Holocaust in order to accomplish the final overcoming of the Middle Ages and the full transition of the peoples of the world into the modern world. Humanity's "sin," for which the Jews had to perish, was the retention by Europe of the old remnants of the medieval feudal world in an age in which they were no longer appropriate. After World War I the West could, according to Maybaum, have brought "freedom, land reform and the blessings of the industrial revolution to the East European countries." <9> Instead, they did nothing. As a result, World War I was in vain and Hitler was sent by God to bring about at an infinitely greater cost in human suffering what "the progressives" had failed to do.

The Holocaust was thus God's terrible means of bringing the world wholly into the modern age, a transformation that could not have occurred without the destruction of all that was medieval in Europe. According to Maybaum, the vast majority of the Jews who perished in the Holocaust were Eastern European Jews who still lived in a medieval, feudal way more or less as their ancestors had, ritually and culturally isolated from their neighbors. In spite of the fact that it took a Hitler and the ovens of Treblinka, Sobibor, Chelmno, Belzek and Auschwitz to destroy this "outmoded" way of life, Maybaum interprets the extermination of Eastern European Jews as yet another act of divine creative destruction. Maybaum further argues that with the passing of the communities in the East which had been the most faithful to the traditions of rabbinic Judaism, the world's Jews are concentrated in countries such as the United States, Western Europe, Russia and Israel in which they are free to participate fully in an era of progress, rationality, Enlightenment and modernity.

Nor does Maybaum flinch from carrying his theological argument to its bitter, logical conclusion. When Nebuchadnezzar sought to destroy Jerusalem, the prophet Jeremiah, acting as God's voice, referred to the king as "my servant Nebuchadnezzar King of Babylon." (Jer. 27.6) Jeremiah had no doubt that Nebuchadnezzar was only the instrument of the sovereign Lord of history. In a deliberate allusion to Jeremiah, Maybaum depicts God as declaring "Hitler, My Servant!" <10> Insisting that, like the Babylonian king, Hitler was God's instrument, Maybaum continues: "God used this instrument to cleanse, to purify, to punish a sinful world; the six million Jews, they died an innocent death; they died because of the sins of others." <11>

There are obviously enormous difficulties with Maybaum's theological interpretation of the Holocaust. One wonders, for example, how the destruction of Europe's Jews was a punishment for "a sinful world" which was either indifferent to or saw benefit in the disappearance of Europe's Jews. In any event, few, if any, serious students of the Holocaust are likely to find his interpretation of that terrible event credible. Nevertheless, like the Orthodox rabbis discussed above, Maybaum's views have a fundamental theological authenticity, integrity and consistency. Maybaum's way of viewing human events is distinctly biblical and is at least as old as the prophets.

---

9 Maybaum, *The Face of God After Auschwitz,* p. 67.
10 Maybaum, *The Face of God After Auschwitz*, p. 67.
11 Maybaum, *loc. cit.*

In the aftermath of the most monstrous assault on the physical and religious integrity of the community of Israel, it is hardly surprising that responsible spokesmen of both Orthodox and Liberal Judaism sought to defend their tradition with traditional arguments. Moreover, men like Grodzensky, Wassermann, Schneersohn and Maybaum understood exactly what required unambiguous intellectual and theological defense. Their problem was not the relatively painless task of reconciling faith in an omnipotent and omnibenevolent Deity with the existence of radical evil. Theirs was the infinitely more painful task of justifying the ways of God as the ultimate perpetrator of that evil.

How often have we heard that the God of Abraham, Isaac and Jacob is not the God of the philosophers? Scripture's God is the Lord who stipulates the conditions of his relationship to Israel in the covenant at Sinai. Hence, the fundamental question for the religious thinker is not _whether_ the existence of God can be reconciled with monumental historical catastrophe, but _how such an event can be understood in the light of God's covenant with Israel_. We have seen how Jeremiah, Grodzensky, Wassermann, Schneersohn answered that question. They were engaged in a fundamental activity of the religious thinker, that of providing their community with a credible theodicy, that is, the explanation of anomic phenomena in terms of religious legitimations. <12> In the case of biblical religion, vindication of divine justice must begin, as does biblical religion itself, with the covenant. That is precisely what Maybaum does.

It should be noted that none of these thinkers appeals to the phenomenon of human freedom to defend the justice of God's ways. It is sometimes argued that God is not responsible for radical evil because he has, so to speak, made a place for human freedom and responsibility. <13> This argument rejects the idea that the omnipotent Creator could be the ultimate perpetrator of radical evil. By contrast, both the Orthodox rabbis and Maybaum assume that Holocaust must somehow be God's handiwork. Their task is somehow to vindicate the justice of what God has wrought.

Moreover, whereas the unmerited suffering of even one innocent victim is sufficient to raise the philosophical problem of the contradiction between the omnipotence and the omnibenevolence of Divinity, in a religious tradition based upon covenant at Sinai the problem arises most insistently only when the fate of the entire community hangs in the balance. That is why Maybaum refers to three _Churbanot_ in the history of Israel and Emil L. Fackenheim refers to the same times of travail as "epoch-making events" which tested such "root experiences" of Israel as the Exodus from Egypt and the covenant at Sinai. <14> Although the Book of Job raises the question of the innocent individual sufferer, Scripture does not depict God as promising that the innocent _individual_ will be exempt from suffering in this world. Scripture does depict God as (a) electing a particular community as the object of his special concern; (b) promising to protect that community on the strict condition that they are faithful to his Law and (c) warning of dire _communal misfortune_ to be visited upon the community should it prove faithless.

Nor is the rejection of the Holocaust as "radical counter-testimony" limited to Jewish thinkers. I have often referred to my unforgetable encounter with the anti-Nazi Protestant leader, Dean Heinrich Gruber in Berlin four days after the erection of the Berlin Wall. During the interview Gruber declared it was God's will to send Adolf Hitler to punish the Jews and

---

12 Peter Berger, _The Sacred Canopy_ (Garden City: Anchor Books, 1966), p. 53.

13 See for example, Paul van Buren, _A Christian Theology of the People Israel_, Part II of _A Theology of Jewish Christian Reality_ (New York: Seabury Press, 1983), pp. 62-63. See also the response of Richard L. Rubenstein and John K. Roth, _Approaches to Auschwitz: The Holocaust and Its Legacy_ (Atlanta: John Knox Press, 1987), pp. 296-300.

14 Emil L. Fackenheim, _God's Presence in History: Jewish Affirmations and Philosophical Reflections_ (New York: Harper and Row, 1972), pp. 11-13.

likened Hitler to Nebuchadnezzar as one of the "rods of God's wrath." <15> The idea that the Holocaust was God's punishment for crucifying Jesus Christ enjoys wide currency among fundamentalist Christians.

Although I can in no sense agree with those who somehow see the justice of God in the Holocaust, I respect the theological integrity of those who hold that position. They take their faith in the God of the covenant with the utmost seriousness. They do not attempt to evade or gloss over the very explicit logical consequences of their biblical faith. They are not embarassed by the terrible curses set forth in Deuteronomy 28:15-68 as the penalty of infidelity to the covenant.

Most religious thinkers tend to gloss over the harsher admonitions of Scripture as well as the strictly logical entailments involved in affirming the existence of the God of the covenant in the face of Auschwitz. At least in the United States, they want a God with whom their clientele, the optimistic, liberal middle class, can feel at home. Unfortunately, the Holocaust, and much else in the twentieth century, belies such optimism. If nothing else, we can learn from Dean Gruber, the Orthodox rabbis and Maybaum the kind of affirmations which are consistent with the biblical image of God in the light of the Holocaust. Moreover, one ought not to denigrate these men as "literalists" or "obscurantists." All were intelligent men who understood what is required for a serious defense of their respective comunities' faith commitments. Nothing less than the truth of their community's teachings could have compelled them to take the infinitely painful positions they did.

At the same time, one can have a measure of sympathy for those who feel compelled to gloss over the problem of reconciling the God of the covenant with the Holocaust. Far more is at stake in religion than a coherent intellectual system. In no other institution are the existential crises of birth, growth, death, joy, sorrow, pain and mutual support more meaningfully shared. <16> For most persons, the functional benefits of religion rest on social and psychological needs as much as the quest for cosmic legitimation. Even the religious intellectual brackets his or her quest for theological clarity, when the crisis moments of personal and family life, such as the birth of a child, the uniting in matrimony, or the loss of a parent, demand a shared context of celebration or commemoration.

In the aftermath of so radical an event as the Holocaust, I could not accept a liberal theological position. I took the traditional view of the God of the covenant with the utmost seriousness, but could not accept it because of its implied imputation of guilt to the victims of the Holocaust and its tendency somehow to regard Hitler as an agent, albeit unintentional, of God's plan. <17> I was compelled to reject the idea of a covenant between God and Israel.

When I wrote After Auschwitz, I stressed both the punitive and exclusivist aspects of the doctrine of covenant and election. Over the years I have come to appreciate the other side of the picture: humanity's profound need for something like the covenant or its functional equivalent. At this point I turn to that issue. Thanks to modern biblical research, we now have reason to believe that the covenant at Sinai was originally a religio-political institution which served to create a new community of moral obligation for groups that previously shared neither kinship nor inherited religious traditions. Before the Exodus the name "Hebrew" referred to a number of peoples who in Egypt shared a common condition and and social location, that of slaves, prisoners or hostages, but were of diverse origins.

---

15 See, for example, Richard L. Rubenstein, After Auschwitz: Radical Theology and Contemporary Judaism (Indianapolis: Bobbs-Merrill, 1966), pp. 47-60.

16 This point was already made in Rubenstein, After Auschwitz, pp. 227-241.

17 See, for example, Rubenstein, After Auschwitz, p. 153.

<18> After fleeing, the escaped slaves and other fugitives, who together constituted the "Hebrews," required a compelling basis for community if they were to survive the natural and human hazards of the wilderness. Having shared the indignities of Egypt and the yearning for liberation, the Exodus constituted yet another shared experience.

In the ancient Near East, religion and community were co-terminous. Hence, the escapees could only become a united community if they were united in religion. Lacking organic relation to each other rooted in kinship, the diverse peoples could not unite under common ancestral gods or under the god or gods of a particular location. They could only unite under a God who was the author of their shared experience, that is, a God of History. The new basis for unifying the ethnically diverse band was enunciated in the prologue to the Decalogue: I am the Lord your God who brought you out of the Land Egypt out of the land of slavery. You shall have no other gods to set against me...for I am the Lord, your God, a jealous God." (Exod. 20:2-5

Yahweh's insistence on exclusive worship, the origin of our monotheistic exclusivism, had both religious and political consequences. It made the relationship between Israel and its God conditional and artificial rather than natural and organic. As in the Near Eastern suzereignty treaties which the covenant at Sinai resembles, God stipulates the conditions under which his protection will be given or withheld from those who swear fealty to him. <19> Thus, the blessings and curses in Deuteronomy 28 are but an elaboration of the conditional character of the Sinai covenant itself. Sinai also united those into a new community those who accepted Jahweh's worship and barred their return to the disuniting worship of their ancestral gods. After the Hebrews had become united, it was natural to claim that they had been kin all along and retrospectively to read back elements of continuity from their new God to their ancestral gods. The God of Abraham, the God of Isaac and the God of Jacob were taken to be identical with the God of Sinai. <20>

A primary social function of religions originating in a radical break with the past is to create a community for those who have none or whose inherited community has lost its relevance for their life situation. <21> The religion of the Sinai covenant is an example of this phenomenon. So too are early Christianity and Islam. In the case of Christianity, Jesus Christ became the basis of unity for peoples dwelling in close proximity to each other in the cities of the Roman empire who had hitherto been strangers. This has been given expression in the letters of Paul: "There is no such thing as Jew and Greek, slave and freeman, male and female; for you are all one person in Christ Jesus." (Gal. 3:28)

Before the development of covenantal treaties, kinship had been the primary principle of community organization. Today, racism, a contemporary expression of kinship, remains the defining principle. Covenant and racism are diametrically opposed ways of organizing communities. Covenant can unite diverse peoples under a common God or a shared body of law. Racism proclaims shared roots and kinship as the only viable basis for community. Merciless exclusion of the stranger is intrinsic to its very nature. A covenant relationship serves little purpose among members of a closed kinship group such as the Japanese, who constitute one of the most self-consciously homogenous nations in the world today. That may be one of the reasons why the Japanese are so resistant to biblical religion. In no other country have so many Christian missionaries labored with so litle success as in Japan. Less than one per cent of the population is Christian and the numbers are declining. <22> By contrast, a covenantal basis tends to be necessary

---

18 See George Mendenhall, The Tenth Generation: The Origins of the Biblical Tradition(Baltimore: Johns Hopkins University Press, 1973), pp. 19 ff.

19 See Mendenhall, The Tenth Generation, pp. 14-16.

20 See Gerhard von Rad, Old Testament Theology, trans. D.M.G. Stalker (London: SCM Press, 1975), Vol. I, pp. 3-14, 165-175.

21 See Montgomery Watt, Muhammed at Mecca (Oxford: 1953), pp. 151-53.

22 See Bernard Wysocki, Jr., "Christian Missions Convert Few in Japan," in Asian Wall Street Journal, July 16, 1986.

wherever diverse religious and ethnic groups must live together in a common community. The American Constitution can be seen as a secularized covenant which is peculiarly suited to an "invented" country like the United States with its biblical religious heritage and its pluralistic population. In the United States, the religious roots of American civilization are normally identified as "Judaeo-Christian" rather than simply Christian. This identification serves to include rather than exclude Jews from the American covenant. <23> Given the realities of modern communication, transportation, trade and world-wide migration patterns, most of the world desperately needs ways to define community that transcend older boundaries of obligation. Undoubtedly, the need has been felt in ever-widening circles from ancient times. When tribal groups and villages had little contact with each other, natural forms of religio-political affiliation sufficed. As humanity increased in number and as members of diverse groups were united in larger political entities such as the kingdoms of the ancient Near East and the Roman empire, kinship could no longer suffice as a basis for community.

In ancient times, and, as we shall see, still today, where no covenant existed between conflicting collectivities, there were no moral impediments to wars of enslavement and extermination. Thucydides describes the fate of the defeated Melians during the Peloponnesian War. The Melians had rejected the Athenian demand that they surrender and become tributary to Athens. In their dialogue with the Melians, the Athenians observed that "...the strong do what they can and the weak suffer what they must." When Melos finally collapsed under siege, the fate of the Melians was sealed. Thucydides tells the terrible story:

> ...the Melians surrendered unconditionally to the Athenians, who put to death all the men of military age whom they took, and sold the women and children for slaves. <24>

The treatment of the Melians had its parallel in the injunctions concerning the vanquished enemy in Deuteronomy:

> When you approach a city to make war on it, you shall offer it peace....if it does not make peace with you, but wages war against you, then you shall besiege it, and Yahweh your God will deliver it into your hands. You shall kill all the males with the sword. But the women and the children...you shall sieze for yourself. You may consume the spoils of your enemies which the Lord your God gives you. (Deut. 20:15) <25>

Want of a covenant or its functional equivalent has been a moral precondition for genocide in both ancient and modern times. Long before Hitler the Jews were regarded as largely outside of the German universe of moral obligation. By defining the Jews as collectively and for all generations murderers of God, the Christian Church had already prepared the way. By identifying the Jews as polluting vermin and bacilli, the National Socialists completed the work. We need not recall in detail the almost total indifference to the fate of the victims on the part of the predominant religious and political institutions of the Christian West before and during World War II. For our purposes, it is sufficient to note that the ascription of a deicidal and/or polluting identity to the Jews legitimated any act of violence and destruction, no matter how obscene, against them.

---

23 See Robert N. Bellah, The Broken Covenant: American Civil Religion in Time of Trial (New York: Seabury Press, 1975), pp. 87-112.

24 Thucydides, The Peloponnesian War, trans. Rex Warner (Harmondsworth: Penguin Books, 1980), p. 408.

25 There is debate concerning the degree to which the inhabitants of Canaanite cities were actually put to death. There were, apparently, some instances in which the injunction was put into practice in defense of Israel's religio-cultural world. See Johannes Pedersen, Israel: Its Life and Culture (London: Geoffrey Cumberlege, 1940), Vol. III, p. 24-25.

Where there was rescue and resistance, there one found some binding sense of moral obligation. Nor were the Jews the only group cast out of any shared universe of moral obligation by the Germans. By identifying the Slavs as Untermenschen and fighting a racial war of enslavement and extermination against them, the Germans made it abundantly clear that they regarded their eastern neighbors as without the slightest moral claim. In the past, even war did not completely cancel out a sense of moral obligation between combatants. Between the nations of Christendom, there used to be religiously legitimated sanctions against wars of extermination. Moreover, the warring powers understood that, in spite of the killing, peace would some day come and former enemies would once again have to live with each other. There was a consensus concerning the treatment of prisoners of war and conquered populations. During World War II Germany more or less fought the older kind of war in the West. It was never Hitler's intention to fight a traditional war in the East.

The Jews were not the only people characterized as vermin during World War II. In one of its confidential reports on the political and social mood in the United States, the staff of the Brtitish Embassy took note of widespread exterminationist sentiment against the Japanese and the popular view that the Japanese were "a nameless mass of vermin." <26> In March 1945, Leatherneck, the U.S. Marine monthly, carried a cartoon depicting the "Louseous Japanicas." The cure for the plague of vermin was described as the annihilation of "the origin of the plague, the breeding grounds around the Tokyo area, must be completely annihilated." <27> In his book, War Without Mercy, John Dower graphically describes the prevalence of exterminationist sentiment toward the enemy in both Japan and the United States during the war in the Pacific. <28> Between 1941 and 1945 the United States and Japan fought a racial war with no quarter given or mercy extended. Admiral William D. Leahy, President Roosevelt's Chief of Staff, described Japan as "our Carthage" and advocated a Carthaginian peace in a conversation with Vice President Henry Wallace in September 1942. <29> Lacking even the memory of a shared religious past, the United States and Japan were without even a minimal basis for a common morality. Calculations of power alone determined their relations. Unfortunately, that sorry condition continues to beset US-Japanese relations.

The Japanese have been described as a "people with an isolationist soul and an internationalist economy, an insular clannishness and a worldwide impact." <30> The contradiction may yet prove explosive for the world. To this day Japanese society is based upon the belief that the Japanese are one extended family founded thousands of years ago and radically different from the rest of the world. Isaiah ben Dassan, a Japanese nationalist intellectual who wrote a book entitled The Japanese and the Jews under an Israeli pseudonym, argues that the real religion of Japan is "Japonism." Ben Dassan points out that there is an unbroken, organic relationship between Japan's archaic religious and cultural roots and its contemporary religion. Ben Dassan contrasts biblical religion with "Japonism." A natural, organic relationship is said to exist between the Japanese and their gods. The gods of Japan are like natural parents who set no conditions for their loved. By contrast, the God of Israel is depicted as an adoptive parent who strictly stipulates the conditions under which he will bestow protection on Israel, his adopted child. Citing Deuteronomy 28 and other biblical texts, Ben Dassan notes the conditional character of God's covenental relationship to Israel.

---

26 H. G. Nichols, ed., Washington Dispatches, 1941-1945: Weekly Political Reports from the British Embassy (Chicago: University of Chicago Press, 1981), p. 558. Most of the dispatches were written by Sir Isaiah Berlin.
27 This cartoon is reproduced in Dower, War Without Mercy, p. 185.
28 John W. Dower, War Without Mercy: Race and Power in the Pacific War (New York: Pantheon Books, 1986), pp. 29, 36-37, 52-57, 70-73, 81-83, 90-92, 184-185, 196-197, 232-33, 247-49.
29 Dower, War Without Mercy, p. 54.
30 Jared Taylor, Shadows of the Rising Sun: A Critical View of the Japanese Miracle (New York: William Morrow, 1983), 91.

According to Ben Dassan, such a relationship is absolutely unthinkable to the Japanese. <31>

There is, however, an important reason why biblical religion is both conditional and non-organic. There is absolutely no way that a non-Japanese person can be embraced within Japan's sanctified community of moral obligation. To this day, the term *gaijin* or foreigner has the negative overtones of enemy as well as alien. A very large percentage of Japanese regard all *gaijin* as belonging to other, inferior species, if not less than human altogether. <32> The sense of the foreigner's otherness is so strong that Japanese executives and students sent abroad are suspected of having been contaminated by alien contact when they return home. The non-reciprocal character of Japanese trade relations is but the tip of the iceberg and the problems involved in Japan's sense of uniqueness are bound to grow as Japan's position in the international economy becomes ever more powerful.

The tragic encounter between Israelis and Palestinians is yet another example of the absence of a covenant. The refusal of the Arab states, save for Egypt, to recognize the State of Israel and their persistent threats, muted in western languages but explicit in Arabic, ultimately to push the Israelis into the sea have convinced most Israelis that they are confronted by an uncompromising, mortal foe. After the Holocaust, the promise of extermination is not one which Jews take lightly.

Since the Six Day War of 1967 critics of the State of Israel have complained of its failure to grant full political rights to its Arab citzens and its refusal to grant the right of self-determination to Palestinians in the occupied territories. Under Israeli rule no Arab can entirely escape being a political pariah. <33> Regretably, such criticisms fail to consider the fundamental reason for this condition: Citizenship is more than the abstract right to participate in elections or to claim equality of opportunity. Citizenship rests upon the unconditional obligation of the citizen risk his or her life in defense of the community. This is especially true of a small state in which a single defeat in war could easily spell the end of the community. Israeli Arabs cannot be faulted for their unwillingness to make a commitment to defend the State of Israel, but neither can the State be faulted for viewing Arabs as a potential security threat. Nor is there anything the Israelis could do to alter the texture of loyalties rooted in kinship and culture which bind the Palestinians to their fellow Arabs.

The real danger is that the conflict between the Israelis and the Palestinians will descend into a merciless, uncompromising war to the death. The fundamental problem between the Palestinians and the Israelis is whether a self-governing Palestinian community can coexist peacefully with an independent Israel. If the warring parties can find no solution to that problem, they will eventually be compelled to seek to drive the other side out of the land each claims as its historic inheritence. Already young Arabs taunt Israeli soldiers with the challenge, "Kill us all or get out!" And, they do not mean out of the occupied territories. If the conflict intensifies, more and more Israelis, perceiving a threat to their very existence, are likely to find reasonable Rabbi Meir Kahane's radical demand that all Arabs be removed from the occupied territories. It would take only one more Arab-Israeli war in which the Israelis emerge victorious for that policy to become official.

To this scenario we must add the stark reality of Israel's nuclear arsenal, whose magnitude has recently been confirmed by the Mordecai Vanunu affair. The fact that Israel may possess as many as two hundred hydrogen bombs cannot be separated from the experience of the Holocaust and Israel's perception that she is surrounded by mortal enemies. Having been taught by

31 Isaiah ben-Dassan, *The Japanese and the Jews*, trans. Richard L. Gage (Tokyo: Weatherhill, 1985), pp. 134ff.
32 See Jared Taylor, *Shadows of the Rising Sun*, pp. 28-39.
33 See for example, Anton Shammas, "A Stone's Throw," *New York Review of Books*, March 31, 1988.

the Holocaust of the value of international guarantees, it is hardly surprising that the Israelis have stockpiled an enormous number of nuclear weapons. The capacity grievously to damage or wholly to destroy an adversary is, at present Israel's most credible guarantee of survival. Nor is it likely that, faced with defeat in a war of extermination, the Israelis would go quietly into the dust.

Obviously, no person with any concern for humanity can rest content with such scenarios. What is needed today is an institution similar to that which enabled the Hebrews to unite under God at Sinai, a binding basis for community between men and women who share little but mutual distrust and fear. Unfortunately, it is easier to point to the need than to meet it. In the past the need was partly met in three different historical eras by the rise of Judaism, Christianity and Islam. With the globalization of world civilization and the perfection of long-range weapons of extermination, the need has returned with greater urgency than ever before.

At this point, we have reached the limits of analysis. If the past is any guide, the need for a new and broader basis for community is likely to be met, if at all, by religiously inspired men and women who have yet to be identified. Nor can we know whether a more inclusive covenant would avert or follow upon a large-scale, humanly-produced demographic catastrophe. Nevertheless, we need to place the problematic theological aspects of the biblical covenant in the broader context of the perennial human needs the older covenants were able to meet. The negative aspects of the biblical covenant are far less important than the example it offered of a way out of unremitting mistrust and destructiveness.

CAN CHRISTIANS BREAK THE SILENCE? A BRITISH RESPONSE TO THE HOLOCAUST

ISABEL WOLLASTON

DEPARTMENT OF THEOLOGY, ABBEY HOUSE, PALACE GREEN, DURHAM, DH1 3RS

ABSTRACT

The British philosopher of religion, Stewart R. Sutherland has developed a provisional theoretical framework in response to the problem of evil. His approach is heavily influenced by the concept of "moral rebellion", as it is expressed by Fydor Dostoyevsky and Albert Camus. As a consequence, Sutherland lays great emphasis on the insoluble nature of the problems of evil, and the importance of giving priority to the voices of victims. These concerns are also two of the major themes in the work of the Holocaust survivor, Elie Wiesel. This similarity in ideas justifies the use of Sutherland's theoretical framework as the basis of a Christian responses to the Holocaust.

INTRODUCTION

There have been a variety of Christian responses to the Holocaust in both Germany and the United States; the majority of which reflect the influence of the Holocaust survivor and writer, Elie Wiesel. In these two countries, the nature of the relationship between the Holocaust and Christianity (and the subsequent need to articulate a Christian response) has been a major theological concern. In Germany, notable - and indeed dominant - Christian responses include Johann Baptist Metz (among Catholics) and Jürgen Moltmann (among Protestants). The Holocaust - and its relation to Christianity - has also been a prominent theme in American religious thinking. Seminal contributions to this debate include Rosemary Radford Reuther's analysis of Christian anti-Semitism, and Robert McAfee Brown's response to the work of Elie Wiesel [1]. However, in the United Kingdom there have been singularly few theological or philosophical treatments of the Holocaust [2]. Instead, the dominant parallel concern has been with the more general question of theodicy. Stewart Sutherland is representative of those who have recently felt compelled to challenge the direction and ethical validity of this discussion [3]. The relevance of Sutherland's work to a debate concerning the Holocaust is twofold. First, as a continuation of the tradition of moral outrage in the face of innocent suffering; a tradition which is given classical expression in the work of Fydor Dostoyevsky and Albert Camus. Secondly, the significance of Sutherland's work becomes apparent through a consideration of the surprising, yet striking similarities between his ideas and those of Elie Wiesel. This similarities are surprising in view of Sutherland and Wiesel's complete independence from one another. I suggest that both of these factors justify the use of Sutherland's ideas as a framework for potential Christian response to the Holocaust.

It is necessary to view Sutherland's work within the context of British theological and philosophical discussion of the problem of evil. In the United Kingdom, only Ulrich Simon's A Theology of Auschwitz has received attention as a response to the Holocaust within the spectrum of 'professional' theologising. Simon is a Jewish convert to Christianity, who lived in Germany prior to his escape to England in 1933. His response to the Holocaust is therefore deeply personal, being significantly prompted by his national and religious background [4]. There have been recent tentative signs of increased interest in formulating a Christian response to the Holocaust, notably in the work of Richard Bauckham [5]. Despite these sporadic responses to the Holocaust, the dominant theological concern has remained the more general issue of theodicy and discussion has fallen into two main categories. The first promotes and defends traditional theodicy, and is illustrated in the work of John Hick, Basil Mitchell and Richard Swinburne. The second challenges the logical and philosophical coherence of theodicy and is classically expressed by the British analytic philosopher, Antony Flew [6]. Sutherland stands amongst those who are deeply dissatisfied with this state of affairs. He is critical both of those who defend theodicy and those who demolish it. In Sutherland's view, theodicy is an inadequate vehicle for responding to the problem of evil. He argues that any valid theology or philosophy must be rooted in the a priori belief that there are no "answers" or "solutions" to the problem of evil. In making this assertion his starting point, Sutherland aligns himself with the "moral rebellion" of an Ivan Karamazov or an Albert Camus.

ATHEISM'S RESPONSE TO THE PROBLEM OF EVIL: MORAL REBELLION

Although Dostoyevsky wrote <u>The Brothers Karamazov</u> prior to the Holocaust, the novel constitutes a response to smaller-scale horrors. Camus, of course, was writing in the immediate aftermath of Nazism. Both Dostoyevsky and Camus share a belief in the need to listen to the voices of the victims of suffering. The challenge posed by such voices to belief is given classical expression in the discussion between the atheistic Ivan Karamazov and his novitiate brother Alyosha. Ivan rejects theodicy because it fails to pay heed to the voices of the innocent victims of suffering. Camus moves beyond Dostoyevsky, in that he recognises both the power of Ivan's critique and its limitations. Camus argues that Ivan's critique is ultimately inadequate because it eventually lapses into nihilism. Dostoyevsky also recognised this weakness, hence his attempts to provide an effective counterbalance to Ivan's nihilism in the characters of Father Zossima, Alyosha; and Prince Myshkin in <u>the Idiot</u>. However, Dostoyevsky failed to discover an effective alternative to Ivan's nihilism. Camus suggests that the necessary counter-balance can be found in his concept of "metaphysical rebellion". [7]

Arguably, both Sutherland and Wiesel are following Camus in attempting to provide "a basis for Ivan's protest against innocent suffering, whether as theodicy or anthropodicy" [8]. Both agree, against Camus, that this "basis" preferably lies within the context of religious belief. Sutherland and Wiesel both explicitly acknowledge their engagement with the moral rebellion of Ivan Karamazov and Albert Camus. Sutherland is aware of Dostoyevsky's tentative attempts to respond to Ivan's challenge, and of Camus' interpretation. Of his two major books to date, the first considers the inadequacy of theodicy in relation to <u>The Brothers Karamazov</u>; while the second incorporates an analysis of the role of Prince Myshkin in <u>The Idiot</u>. [9]. The influence of Dostoyevsky and Camus on Wiesel is equally well-illustrated, particularly in <u>The Town Beyond the Wall.</u> [10]

The influence exerted by Dostoyevsky and Camus on Sutherland and Wiesel is hardly surprising. All four thinkers share the same sense of moral outrage in the face of innocent suffering. This similarity suggests that where reaction to the problem of evil is concerned, the difference between the believer and the non-believer (and between the Jew and the Christian) can become minimal. A shared sense or moral outrage serves to overcome momentarily ideological and religious difficulties. Sutherland suggests that this is because the problem of evil belongs to the "borderlands" between belief and non-belief, and therefore necessarily inspires a high degree of agnosticism or doubt in believers. He suggests that those atheists engaged in dialogue with belief (e.g. Camus) and those believers aware that faith incorporates a high degree of "ambiguity" (e.g. Kierkegaard) can come very close to one another. Wiesel presents a similar argument, repeatedly emphasising the role of moral protest and contention with God within belief. He cites both religious protesters (Job, Abraham, the Hasidic Masters) and more secular, "borderland" figures (Camus, Kafka). Indeed, in view of their ambivalent relationship with traditional orthodoxy, both Sutherland and Wiesel could themselves be dubbed "borderland" figures. The ambivalent nature of their relationship with traditional orthodoxy becomes apparent through a more detailed consideration and comparison of the ideas of Sutherland and Wiesel.

A CHRISTIAN RESPONSE TO THE PROBLEM OF EVIL: "STARTING ALL OVER AGAIN"

Stewart Sutherland grounds his whole philosophical approach in two basic, interdependent principles. Any discussion concerning either God or religious belief is only valid if it is rooted in these principles. The first asserts:

> <u>A religious belief which runs counter to our moral beliefs is to that extent unacceptable</u> [11].

The second principle demands that the basis of any attempt to speak theologically or philosophically must lie in the reality of human suffering:

> My intention is to begin ... with the plain fact of suffering, and to see what can be said theologically and religiously that is compatible with such a beginning. [12].

In Sutherland's view, theodicy is unacceptable because it requires the acceptance of assertions that run counter to our moral beliefs; demanding that the perspective of the victim be subordinated to that of a comprehensive divine purpose. From the viewpoint of theodicy, human suffering is the regrettable, but inevitable "price" to be paid for a higher good-namely human free will. Suffering is therefore regarded as meaningful within the context of a greater whole. Sutherland rejects this approach on two counts. First, he rejects any approach which sifts the focus away from the perspective of the victim. Second, Sutherland challenges the ascription of "meaning" to innocent suffering, and rejects any "solutions" to the problem of evil. Only the victim can ascribe meaning to his suffering, and even then only to <u>his</u> suffering. By revising his account of religious belief to incorporate the rejection of theodicy, Sutherland succeeds in containing the moral outrage of an Ivan Karamazov or a Camus within a religious framework. The rejection of theodicy is therefore the cornerstone of Sutherland's revisionary account of Christian belief:

> my present concern is most definitely not theodicy, for I do not believe that theodicy - the justification of the ways of God to man is possible. [13]

Sutherland proceeds to develop his argument by stressing that theodicy reflects a different understanding of reality to that expressed by the moral rebellion of Ivan Karamazov. To Karamazov, theodicy is at best irrelevant and at worst morally offensive. It is significant that Ivan never criticises the logic of theodicy. He does not dispute the conclusions reached, rather he refuses to accept them on moral grounds. Ivan's (and Sutherland's) rejection of theodicy is therefore not to be confused with the local objections of an Antony Flew. For Ivan, the question of whether theodicy is right or wrong is irrelevant:

> I don't want harmony. I don't want it, out of the love I bear to mankind. I want to remain with my suffering unavenged and my indignation unappeased, <u>even if I were wrong. [14].</u>

Ivan's outburst serves to illustrate the gulf separating Sutherland from those either attacking or defending theodicy. Ivan's objection to theodicy is primarily moral, rather than logical or philosophical. Similarly, Sutherland is defending and giving priority to a moral outrage which rejects all "answers" to the problem of evil - and indeed rejects any argument which suggests even the possibility that there might be "answers". The moral outrage expressed so eloquently by Ivan Karamazov belongs in a different dimension to theodicy. The theodicist and the moral rebel are speaking two different languages. Even if the theodicist could find an "intellectual solution" to the problem of evil, this would still be unacceptable to the moral rebel:

> Suppose we were to find a 'morally sufficient reason' for God's permission of the realities of evil and suffering as we know them would that be the end of it? Would be we satisfied? [15].

Sutherland develops his thesis concerning the different priorities of the theodicist and the moral rebel by considering their attitudes to data. He suggests that the effectiveness of theodicy depends upon viewing suffering in abstract terms - as the negative component in the equation of God's purpose in creation. The negative evidence of suffering is balanced against the positive value of humanity attaining salvation through the exercise of free will - the latter both necessitates and justifies the former [16]. Sutherland argues that the success of this equation depends upon viewing suffering in abstract terms. The equation collapses when confronted with the "human face" of the victim:

> Morally sufficient reasons for the permission of evil and suffering may seem convincing in the abstract. The human face of the victim belongs to a different dimension [17].

Camus and Dostoyevsky give expression to this "different dimension", and Sutherland provides a theoretical framework which enables such voices to be heard.

Any framework which pays serious attention to such voices necessarily differs from more orthodox, traditional approaches to belief-hence Sutherland's reference to "starting all over again". By starting with the "plain fact of suffering", Sutherland inverts the more traditional "order" of theology. Rather than viewing human suffering within a wider predetermined doctrinal setting, religious and theological statements are tested against the "plain fact of suffering". Those statements deemed morally objectionable are to be rejected [18]. This process inevitably results in the limitation of our religious affirmations. An increasing caution comes to permeate religious language:

> A theology which starts from the realities of suffering and evil in the world cannot avoid a high degree of agnosticism in its affirmations about God [19].

The fact that this acknowledgement forms part of the conclusion to God, Jesus & Belief reflects Sutherland's conviction that theology is necessarily provisional in nature. He suggests that religious belief be seen as analogous to a pilgrimage: is it "provisional and exploratory in character". Religious thinking ideally "includes the possibility of thinking again". [20] The "plain fact of suffering" serves to provide a constant reminder of both the provisionality and the limitations of religious language.

A JEWISH RESPONSE TO THE PROBLEM OF EVIL: CONTENTION WITH GOD

The work of the Holocaust survivor, Elie Wiesel, is also dominated by an adamant refusal to minimise the challenge of innocent suffering, and the problem this poses for theodicy. Wiesel rejects the traditional Jewish theodicy, "for our sins are we punished", as unacceptable [21]. Any suggestion that suffering may be interpreted positively within a wider providential framework is dismissed:

> Suffering is evil. Man is not created in order to suffer. If this were so, God could not be holy. God does not want man to suffer; man suffers against God.

Wiesel pre-empts Sutherland's demand that priority be given to the voices of victims when he insists that the sufferer is the only person entitled to ascribe meaning to his suffering, or to see it as a reflection of God's will. An outsider cannot do this - precisely because of his detachment. Yet the individual sufferer is also unable to "resolve" the problem of evil - because of his subjective involvement. The problem of evil is therefore essentially insoluble:

> Either you suffer too and in that case you cannot ask the question and dissociate yourself from it or you don't suffer and then you have no questions - or you have no right to ask questions. [23]

Wiesel therefore shares Sutherland's view that the answers proffered by theodicies bear little or no relation to the questions being asked.

Wiesel's rejection of answers to the problem of evil - other than on a purely personal level - lies behind his ambivalent attitude towards both the miraculous and the messianic. He is emphatic that no future reparation can cancel out the fact that innocent suffering exists. The injustice of innocent suffering, once perpetrated, can never be eradicated. Wiesel does not deny the parallel existence of good, nor does he dismiss the possible relationship existing between good and evil. His point is that good can never cancel out evil, or vice versa [24].

> Victory does not prevent suffering from having existed, nor death from having taken its toll ... Of course the mystery of good is no less disturbing than the mystery of evil. But one does not cancel out the other. [25]

The impossibility of providing "answers" to the problem of evil becomes all the more apparent when one moves to a consideration of the specific, i.e. the Holocaust. The innocent suffering inherent in the Holocaust, symbolised for Wiesel by the death of one million Jewish children, shatters any attempt at theodicy. There can be no appeal to the miraculous in order to "soften" the impact of the event. Nothing can change the past, nor diminish the injustice which that past contains:

> God himself cannot change the past; even he cannot negate the fact that the killer has killed six million times. How could he redeem himself? I don't know. I suppose that he cannot. [26]

The problem of evil must remain as on open question; one that cannot even be resolved by an appeal to the messianic future. Wiesel again pre-empts Sutherland in his adamant refusal to "ascribe" meaning to innocent suffering:

> The Holocaust makes no sense to me at all - on any level. I do not accept any explanation of the Holocaust in messianic terms. It would be blasphemy ... I do not accept any religious answer. I do not have any answer ... To me it is still a question, an awesome question. [27]

In Wiesel's view, theodicy represents the easier of two options as it suggests the possibility of open-ended questions concerning innocent suffering being resolved. The harder more challenging option is to insist that such questions remain unresolved. If the second option is adopted, it becomes necessary to acknowledge the limitations of our religious affirmations. While Wiesel would no doubt be unhappy with Sutherland's phrase, "a high degree of agnosticism", he appears to be sympathetic to the general thesis. By virtue of belonging to a different religious tradition, Wiesel prefers to use the more Jewish image of contention with God. He frequently asserts that part of Judaisim's strength lies in the fact that it allows, and indeed encourages, contention with God - on behalf of man. [28] Wiesel defines Judaism as "an endless quarrel with God" [29] Indeed, after the Holocaust contention with God is arguably the only authentic form of belief that remains:

> As far as belief in God is concerned, I would simply suggest to question Him and go on questioning Him <u>through</u> such belief. In doing so one remains within certain limits and within a certain tradition, namely the Jewish tradition.[30]

However, contention with God must be pushed to its limits if it is to retain its integrity. Wiesel suggests that the result of pushing contention to its limits is that faith becomes an intensely personal affair; a fact illustrated by his frequent refusal to speak of his own beliefs. [31] Wiesel prefers to talk of the despair or belief of others. His approach to the subject of belief is oblique; his attention being "to tell of others while telling of others". [32] Publicly, Wiessel either challenges God - as in <u>Night</u> or portrays the spiritual journey of others. [33] He argues that belief and contention can and should coexist; belief because it provides continuity with the past, and contention because it reflects the moral autonomy and authority of the individual sufferer.

Wiesel's work therefore emphasises the role of the victim and man's sense of moral outrage in the face of innocent suffering. Without doubt, such an emphasis comes more naturally to Judaism than to Christianity, as is illustrated by the tradition of contention with God in Jewish history. Both Sutherland and Wiesel agree that the emphasis should be on human concerns and possible achievements, rather than on God. Questions concerning theodicy are deemed irrelevant. Sutherland's response is to define theology as the "articulation of the possible". Wiesel's response complements this, in that he insists that there is no purpose in debating God's role in the Holocaust beyond a certain point. The debate must remain on the level of a series of unanswered and unanswerable questions. Yet, it is precisely because these questions are unanswerable that they possess the power to transform human attitudes - a message that Wiesel sees as encapsulated in the Book of Job: "it is given to man to transform divine injustice into human justice and compassion." [34] By striving to alleviate another's suffering, it becomes possible to find meaning in one's own. It is for this reason that the protagonists of <u>The Town Beyond the Wall</u>; <u>The Gates of the Forest</u>; <u>A Beggar in Jerusalem</u>; and <u>The Oath</u>, all ultimately elect to affirm life over death, and hope over - or out of - despair. [35] The absence of reassuring "answers" to the problem of evil serves to emphasise the role of human solidarity and the importance of belonging to a community. Wiesel's argument is effectively encapsulated in his repeated citation of the Hasidic master, Rebbe Barukh of Medzebozh:

> I know there are questions that have no answers; there is a suffering that has no name; there is injustice in God's creation - and there are reasons enough for man to explode with rage. I know there are reasons for you to be angry. Good. Let us be angry. Together. [36]

Wiesel therefore echoes both Dostoyevsky and Camus in rejecting Ivan Karamazov's "rebellion" as inadequate. "Rebellion" marks a necessary beginning, but requires further development. It must be grounded in a concern for human solidarity - a concern which Ivan rejects.[37] For Wiesel, "rebellion" must also preferably be grounded in a reformulated, traditional Jewish faith. This reformulation of faith necessarily begins on a personal and inter-personal level; only then can it subsequently begin to influence man's relationship with God:

> A new attempt must be made to define man's relation to God and man's relation to other men; in doing so he would change his relation to God. And a change in our relations to man would involve all our other relationships as well.[38]

CONCLUSION

A comparison of Sutherland and Wiesel serves to highlight a number of ground-rules for any potential response to the Holocaust. The most significant of these ground-rules is the central position given to the voices of victims in any valid response to the problem of evil. It is in this context that the value of using Sutherland as the model for a Christian response to the Holocaust becomes apparent. He is essentially a theorist, whose purpose is to construct a framework which enables the voices of victims to be heard. However, Sutherland is also aware that such voices will generally be the voices of others. In this respect, he differs from Wiesel who - as both theorist and victim - is defending and justifying his <u>own</u> right to speak. As a result, in Wiesel's work, the objective and subjective inevitably (and in all probability, intentionally) become blurred. In this sense, Sutherland and Wiesel illustrate the gulf separating the Christian and the Jew where the Holocaust is concerned. In the context of the Holocaust, the Christian necessarily speaks as an outsider - however well-intentioned. By contrast, the Jew is discussing what did happen - or what could have happened - to him. Sutherland's approach therefore illustrates the only direction a Christian response to the Holocaust should take. Although Sutherland never explicitly considers the Holocaust, the event represents the supreme example of the "plain fact of suffering". Consequently, applying Sutherland's two criteria, it is necessary for Christianity to reconsider its religious language in the light of the Holocaust. Those statements which now appear to "run counter to our moral beliefs" are to be rejected. Whether such a revision of Christian belief takes the shape of a modified form of the existing tradition, [39] or demands a break with this tradition [40] remains to be seen. Using Sutherland's ideas as the structure for a Christian response to the Holocaust would ensure the presence of a built-in reminder of the limitations of Christianity's "right to speak". In view of Christians' status as non-victims, the essential purpose of a response to the Holocaust is to ensure that Christianity listens - to the voices of the victims.

FOOTNOTES

1 Robert McAfee Brown is taken as representative of the many American responses to the work of Elie Wiesel, both Jewish and Christian, including: Michael Berenbaum, Ted Estess, John K Roth, Byron Sherwin.

2 There are a wide variety of reasons for this lack of interest in the Holocaust in the United Kingdom. The more obvious include Britain's historical isolation from the impact of Nazi anti-Jewish policies; both geographically, and in terms of the limited size of Britain's Jewish community.

3 D Z Phillips has made many similar comments on the subject. However, as Phillips' treatment of theodicy is much less systematic, priority has been given to Sutherland's ideas within the confines of this paper.

4 It is significant that Sutherland is a member of the Faculty of Theology and Religious Studies at King's College, London, of which Simon was formerly a member. Both Sutherland and Simon share a passionate interest in literature, and a belief in its capacity to enlarge perception and imagination.

5 See Richard Bauckham, Modern Theology, 83-97.

6 Antony Flew in Mitchell ed., A Philosophy of Religion, 13-5, 20-22.

7 Albert Camus, The Rebel, 50-6; see also 19-31, 243-57, 266-70.

8 Bauckham, 86.

9 S R Sutherland, Faith and Ambiguity , 1-27; Sutherland, Atheism and the Rejection of God; Sutherland, God, Jesus & Belief, 151-162.

10 The Town Beyond the Wall begins by citing The Idiot as a motto, and is permeated by reference to, and echoes of Camus. Bauckham suggests that Night is profoundly influenced by Camus' interpretation of Ivan Karamazov, 87-8. R.C.Lamont discusses Camus's influence on Wiessel in Rosenfeld and Greenberg eds., Confronting the Holocaust. Wiessel frequently cites both Camus and Dostoyevsky among the authors he admires and has been influenced by.

11 Sutherland, God, Jesus & Belief, 16.

12 Ibid., 21.

13 Ibid.

14 Dostoyevsky, The Brothers Karamazov, 287.

15 Sutherland, God, Jesus & Belief, 23.

16 In very general terms, this is the argument governing both John Hick's "soul-making" theodicy and Richard Swinburn's theory of a "half-finished" universe.

17 Sutherland, God, Jesus & Belief, 24.

18 Sutherland is making much the same point as Irving Greenberg when he claimed:

"No statement, theological or otherwise, should be made that would not be credible in the presence of burning children."

In Fleischner ed., Auschwitz: Beginning of a New Era?, 23.

19 Sutherland, God, Jesus & Belief, 199.

20 Sutherland, Faith and Ambiguity, 107.

21 For a discussion of Wiesel's views on theodicy see Michael Berenbaum, The Vision of the Void, 6-45.

22 H J Cargas, Harry James Cargas In Conversation with Elie Wiesel, 10.

23 Ibid., 20.

24 A point reflected in Wiesel's views on the relationship between the Holocaust and the establishment of the State of Israel: the two events are undeniably connected, but the latter does not "justify" or "cancel out" the former.

25 Wiesel, A Beggar in Jerusalem, 210.

26 Wiesel, Christian Century, 611-2.

27 Abrahamson ed., Against Silence, Vol. III, 313.

28 The idea of contention with God on behalf of man is a recurrent theme in Wiesel's writing, e.g. Souls On Fire, 90.

29 Wiesel, A Jew Today, 163.

30 Abrahamson ed., Against Silence, Vol. I, 144.

31 See Koppel and Kaufmann, Elie Wiesel: A Small Measure of Victory, 18.

32 Wiesel, Souls on Fire, 196-7.

33 This portrayal of the spiritual journey of others in particularlyu apparent in Wiesel's treatment of biblical figures, e.g. Messengers Of God; and the Hasidim, e.g. Souls On Fire.

34 Wiesel, Messengers of God, 235.

35 See in particular the discussion between the Rebbe and Gregor in The Gates Of the Forest, 189-203.

36 Wiesel, Four Hasidic Masters, 60; Somewhere A Master, 272.

37 Dostoyevsky, The Brothers Karamazov, 276-7; Bauckham, 85-6.

38 Abrahamson ed., Against Silence, Vol. III, 309.

39 The work of Jürgen Moltmann represents one attempt to modify the Christian tradition in response to the problem of evil in general, and to the Holocaust in particular. Moltmann's main modification to the Christian tradition is to reject the notion of divine impassibility, in order to develop his concept of the "Crucified God".

40 Sutherland agrees with Moltmann that the key to any revision of Christianity lies with christology. However, he feels that christology must be revised to such an extent that it, arguably, breaks with tradition. See God, Jesus & Belief, 129-94.

REFERENCES

Abrahamson, I, ed. (1985). Against Silence, 3 Vols., Holocaust Library.
Bauckham, R (1987). In: Modern Theology 4:1, 83-97.
Berenbaum, M (1979). The Vision of the Void, Wesleyan University Press.
Camus, A (1974). The Rebel, Penguin.
Cargas, H J (1976). Harry James Cargas In Conversation With Elie Wiesel, Paulist Press.
Dostoyevsky, F (1982). The Brothers Karamazov, Penguin.
Flew, A. In Mitchell, B Ed. (1971). The Philosophy of Philosophy, Oxford University Press, 13-15, 20-2.
Greenberg, I. In: Fleischner, E ed. (1977). Auschwitz: Beginning of a New Era? KTAV, 7-55.
Koppel, G and Kaufmann, H (1974). Elie Wiesel: A Small Measure of Victory, University of Arizona.
Lamont, R. In: Rosenfeld, A and Greenberg, I eds. (1978). Confronting the Holocaust, Indiana University Press, 80-98.
Simon, U (1978). A Theology of Auschwitz, SPCK.
Sutherland, S R (1977). Atheism and the Rejection of God, Basil Blackwell.
(1984). God, Jesus & Belief, Basil Blackwell.
(1984). Faith and Ambiguity, SCM.
Wiesel, E (1970). A Beggar in Jerusalem, Random House.
(1975). The Town Beyond the Wall, Robson Books.
(1976). Messengers of God, Random House.
(1978). Four Hasidic Masters, Notre Dame Press.
(1978). A Jew Today, Random House.
(1982). Gates of the Forest, Schocken Books.
(1982). Souls on Fire and Somewhere a Master, Penguin.
(1981). In Christian Century 98, 609-12.

The challenge to the Christian community with emphasis on theology and ethics

CHAIRPERSON **Professor John T. Pawlikowski**

RAPPORTEUR **Professor Larry Axel**

THE HOLOCAUST AND THE PROBLEM OF HUMANISM

LARRY E. AXEL

Department of Philosophy, Purdue University,
West Lafayette, Indiana 47907, U.S.A.

Andre Schwarz-Bart begins his extraordinary novel, The Last of the Just, a haunting treatise on suffering and the problem of evil, with the following words: "Our eyes register the light of dead stars" (p. 3). When we look back on a number of the events in our current century, especially at the noteworthy events of a period (1933-45) that most of us would call this century's most significant, we may conclude that our situation, religiously, has become radically different in a post-Holocaust world. When we gaze at the sky of religious possibilities, we look into the light of dead stars. When we consider the possibilities left to us after 1945, we realize that the situation--theoretically, existentially, theologically--has changed markedly. The older theisms and humanisms must now grow dim. Virtually every traditional presupposition is put into question.

Irving Greenberg and others have insisted, quite rightly, that no theological utterance should be affirmed today that is not credible in the presence of the burning children of Auschwitz. Much has been made, quite rightly, of the "silence of God" during this period, 1933-45, and of many other periods in history as well. Brought face to face with the presence of evil and the knowledge of suffering on a mass scale, theologians and philosophers have noted the paradigm of the Holocaust for the Problem of Evil. Much has been made, quite rightly, of the negative implications for traditional, humanocentric theism of this event. It has been recognized that the Problem of Evil, put in this form, poses a real dilemma--perhaps an insurmountable dilemma--for the traditional theist.

Unfortunately, however, we have long traded in convenient dualisms. It has been assumed, in too many circles, that where traditional theism is rejected because of the negative evidence of the Holocaust, then humanism is the logical remaining alternative. But does not the Holocaust (obviously) present a similar dilemma--indeed, even a more decisive dilemma--for humanism? Must not anyone who has encountered the facts of Auschwitz and Dachau conclude that it would be blasphemous to put humankind on any kind of pedestal, to place the human at the center of any religious system? Must we not extend Irving Greenberg's injunction demanding of humanistic claims the same requirement as that of theistic ones? No humanistic claim should be affirmed today that is not credible in the presence of the burning children of Auschwitz. The celebration of humanity, or any idealizing of the human structure, could scarcely be made in the face of such evidence. It is time for all of us to realize, theologically, the negative implications in the twentieth century of the Problem of Evil for humanism as well as for theism.

In critiquing the dualistic mentality of traditional theism and humanism, I seek radically to repudiate some of the fundamental assumptions on which much of Western religious thinking has been based for centuries. Unfortunately, in too many quarters we have not exercised sufficient vision and adventurousness, and we have become entrapped or encased in outworn models and ideological structures. It is a thesis of my project that for too long, in too many quarters in the West, students of theology and practitioners of religion have assumed that, broadly speaking, there are only two options available: theism and humanism. It is one of my aims to call into question the validity and vitality of both of these two options as we close this century, to challenge an accepted notion that there are--broadly conceived--only two options, and to suggest at least the beginnings of my concept of a third possibility, labelled (tentatively, at this stage of my reflections) "religious creaturalism." My new notion of religiousness, this innovative way of "doing theology," may challenge directly the styles and modes of approach of various important groups: theists, humanists, philosophers, systematic theologians, and defenders of the patriarchy.

Let us look back at 1945, especially at two specific dates: January 24 and April 29. On January 24, the Red Army occupied Auschwitz and found several tons of human hair, thousands of baby shoes, and the stench of corpse-fumed smoke from the crematoria. Earlier, in 1942, Heinrich Himmler had bragged to Rudolf Hess that Auschwitz would become "the largest human slaughter house that history had ever known" (Roth, 1980, p. 77). The killing center at Auschwitz--constructed for one purpose, to process live human beings into dead material--has become one of the main monuments of our current century and has even added a new term to our vocabulary. The camp provides a witness to twentieth-century humankind's barbarity, organizational ability, efficiency, cruelty, and madness. Three months later, on April 29, the Allies liberated the camp at Dachau, the oldest of the Nazi concentration camps. Since 1933 Dachau had served as holding center for some, the end of the world for others, as desolate work camp for many, a place of horrible medical experimentation for some, killing center for others. The world still seeks to "bring to justice" some of the perpetrators.

And so, we are brought face to face with the facts of suffering on an incredibly mass scale, with issues raised concerning the absence of divine intervention or the inadequacies of divine power or benevolence; and we are led eventually to what theologians and philosophers have called the Problem of Evil or the issue of theodicy. For theists, terrible dilemmas are raised. Much has been made--quite rightly, I believe--of the negative implications which these kinds of events raise for traditional theism. Anyone who wants to posit a traditional, humanocentric theism and who wishes to take evidence and experience seriously, to be "empirical," must recognize in evil (both so-called moral evil and so-called natural evil) a substantive threat to traditional forms of theism that posit a God of omnipotence, omniscience, omnibenevolence and control. Thus, various theorists have advocated forms of theism in new modes, be they "process" ones, "historicist" alternatives, or something else. And many of us who have wanted to follow an empirical method, who wish to take evidence seriously, have found persuasive the work of David Hume and that of a long line of his successors in seeing neither _a priori_ nor _a posteriori_ evidence for Design or a Designer or for the absolute benevolence or limitless power of any creator that might be posited. Not only have many people concluded that there is an absence of substantive evidence for traditional theism, but also that there may be evidence--in the widespread presence of natural and moral evil in the world--_against_ theism. Anyone who is seeking honestly to take account of the full range of our experience must reckon at least with the widespread sufferings and privations resulting from the machinations of both natural and human structures. There are certain things that cannot be ignored or eradicated by a theological vocabulary. Thus, it is definitely legitimate to ask the question: "Is it blasphemous for anyone to pray prayers of thanksgiving after the Holocaust?" "Is it obscene to proclaim the Psalms after Auschwitz?" People of good will have significantly different ways of answering this; these questions are by no means trivial. Should anyone who wishes to take experience seriously and who does not seek refuge in some kind of dualistic fideism, assert a theistic position after Auschwitz?

So, it _has_ been recognized that the Problem of Evil and the events of these years pose a real dilemma for the theist. To be sure, in many educated circles, traditional theism has now been repudiated in the light of disasters, suffering inflicted in a systematic manner, and the extermination camps of the Holocaust. In large part I agree with this repudiation. But I question the alternative that is advanced, in some quarters, as the _only_ alternative. In most circles where traditional _theism_ has been rejected in the light of the Enlightenment and in the shadow of our century's extermination camps and city-destroying bombs, _humanism_ flourishes. Indeed, humanism is seen by many observers as the logical alternative, the one remaining alternative, to traditional theism. And it is a humanism that, true to its etymology, often places the human at the very center of the universe or at the top of a pyramid of valuation, presenting the human being as virtually a legitimate object of worship.

Many forms of humanism, including certain traditions of religious humanism with a distinguished history, highlight the human structure as the most advanced of the many structures to emerge on this planet, or even, indeed, in the universe itself. In this way a form of anthropocentrism, or even anthropos-inflation, replaces the earlier monotheism. This revision can hardly be characterized as a very radical change. For if this kind of humanism simply moves into the vacuum created by the removal of the old theisms, if the older, hierarchichally-ordered theism is simply replaced by an hierarchically-ordered humanism in which humankind is placed at the top, then--structurally considered--it can hardly be announced that a very radical change has occurred. The patriarchy has simply been revised--not dismantled. One potentate, as it were, has simply been replaced by another. This kind of humanism, as the second option, often becomes, then, a form of anthropos-inflation, celebrating the achievements and status of the human.

In point of fact, the place reserved for God in the earlier religions is given now to humankind. Humankind is now proclaimed to sit at the top of creation's ladder, or at the apex of some pyramidal structure of worth and value, or at the very center of the universe itself. Humanity's rationality and achievements are celebrated, its creativity and ability are lauded, and its development toward greater future goods is confidently announced. The human structure is separated out and set apart from that of the other creatures and from other natural forms. Ignoring Copernicus and his successors in many other fields, the human places himself (yes, <u>himself</u> is most appropriate here) at the center of worth and significance, ignoring or discounting or denigrating the web of the universe. Perhaps because of the arrogance of the human species-ego, with the eclipse of traditional theism, a certain kind of humanism asserts itself and comes to the fore.

But let us remember, again, the Holocaust.

It has been recognized, as we have noted, that the specific events mentioned above pose a real dilemma for the theist. We do know that there has followed a repudiation of traditional theism in some educated circles. But should that lead us necessarily to humanism, at least the kind of humanism described above? To be sure, Auschwitz poses serious, perhaps even decisive, problems for the theist. But does not Auschwitz pose also a serious, perhaps decisive, problem for the humanist, at least for the person proclaiming the kind of species-arrogant humanism described above? Must not anyone who has encountered the intentional suffering and mass destructions of Auschwitz and Dachau (and hundreds of similar episodes in human history) conclude that it would also be blasphemous to put humankind on any kind of pedestal, let alone even to worship humanity? An empiricist, one who takes account of the evidence of experience, cannot easily or trivially engage in an idealizing of the human structure; and, of course, one should hardly engage in making a deity of that structure. The achievements of humankind can scarcely serve as adequate material for a religion; the activities of contemporary twentieth-century humanity would hardly warrant unqualified praise in contrast to those activities of pre-literate peoples or other creatures. We could not even unqualifiedly praise humanity as, without doubt, the best creature on this planet, or the most beneficent resident of this planet, let alone of the universe itself. The absurdity of that kind of talk must be recognized. We must call for an end to the human arrogance that would lead to these kinds of claims. And the student of theology must be especially vigilant for, and stridently critical of, any religious or non-religious option that encourages such arrogance. It is certainly nonhistorical, nonempirical, and ignorant--if not blasphemous--to laud humanity as the crowning glory of the universe.

If there were to be a conversation in the Auschwitz camp between a traditional theist (as described above) and a religious humanist (as presented here), each could fling damaging accusations at the other's position. It could legitimately be pointed out that, from 1933 to 1945, God should be seen as a <u>bystander</u> while humanity was a <u>perpetrator</u>. Obviously, neither God nor humankind would seem to warrant much praise. As we attempt to think (and live) our way through these matters, it is essential that we avoid the trap of confining ourselves to the time-worn dualism of theism and humanism. Are theism and humanism all we have? As we head into the twenty-first century, are there really only two religious possibilities available to us: the worship and adulation of God and the worship and adulation of humanity? For any of us who want to take the evidence of our experience seriously, and who wish to look beyond a humanly provincial perspective, these two religious perspectives--theism and humanism, as we have known them up to this point--hardly seem adequate or appropriate for tomorrow.

Can we move beyond the exclusivist dualism of theism and humanism? Just as we are trying to move beyond other dualisms (a project aided immensely by the work of women and men of feminist consciousness), e.g., the dualism of mind over body, will over passion, intellect over feeling, competition over communion, dominance over nurture, we must move beyond a dualism which sets the human apart from other creatures and structures, just as God was set radically apart in the older theisms. Can we find a humanism or a theism or a religious creaturalism which is not hierarchically modelled? Can we free ourselves from perspectives of domination as we try to do theology, as we live and think and have our being in a collaborative, relational way with nature, with one another, and with other creatures?

It is here, I maintain, that we may be able to forge a "religious creaturalism," a position that is neither "theistic" nor "humanistic," traditionally conceived. For this religious creaturalism, I draw on the tradition of liberal American theology as embodied in the "Chicago School" of the early twentieth century. While that tradition is often associated with the development of the so-called "socio-historical" method, and later with "process theology," it is the incorporation of William James' "radical empiricism" and Bernard Meland's "elementalism" that may be of utmost value. For an accurate portrayal of these contributions, much more would need to be said than can be developed here. But we can note that it was James' notion of radical empiricism that helped the Chicagoans (most notably Meland later on) to develop a non-dualistic theology and to call for a philosophy of relationality. A cornerstone of James' radical empiricism was his postulation that "the relations between things, conjunctive as well as disjunctive, are just as much matters of direct particular experience, neither more so nor less so, than the things themselves" (James, 1909, p. vii). Or, put another way by James, "The parts of experience hold together from next to next by relations that are themselves parts of experience. The directly apprehended universe needs, in short, no extraneous trans-empirical connective support, but possesses in its own right a concatenated or continuous structure" (James, 1909, pp. vii-viii).

Now, in everyday language, the theologians of the "Chicago School" saw this radical empiricism as a way of avoiding dualism and, instead, concentrating on the richnesses within perceptual experience itself. James, therefore, opposed any form of atomism and maintained that experience includes transitions and tendencies, conjunctive relations, and "next-to-nexts." The theologians expanded this and claimed that with a naturalistic method, they could locate ultimacy right in the flux of immediacy. The lived experience was regarded as rich with depth; the perceptual flux was seen as holding special fullness. As Meland was to say: "ultimacies and immediacies traffic together." Consequently, theology was regarded as oriented not primarily to a supernatural realm or to dualistic categories. The Chicagoans took James' words about philosophy to heart for theological method as well. James had maintained that philosophy must lie flat on its belly in the middle of experience, in the very thick of its sand and gravel. Too often, James commented, philosophy had instead maintained "the vision of things from above" (McDermott, 1967, p. 292). The theologians of the "Chicago School" wanted to see theology do the same, viewing religion in immanentalist, relational, and process terms. Static categories were jettisoned in favor of language that took seriously the fluid and relational nature of the world, its processes, and its interconnections. Here we find a rejection of dualism and atomism in favor of an organicism and relationism in human experience and in religious thought. Development, not stasis, was the byword. Relationality, instead of hierarchy, provided the model. Interconnectednesses, not things, ruled the day.

Bernard Meland (see, e.g., _Faith and Culture_, _The Realities of Faith_, and _Fallible Forms and Symbols_), as heir to this tradition, also sought to break free of the theism-humanism dichotomy. He makes no reference to transcendence in any supernatural sense. On the other hand, he has no interest in defending any form of humanism that tends to separate out the human from the web of the cosmos, or that leads to an inappropriate adulation of the human structure. Thus, he is insistent in criticizing the exaltation of humankind found in certain versions of humanism, "believing in the long run, such adulation will tend toward a spiritual decandence in man, that it will evoke in him a kind of arrogance and self-sufficiency which can only eventuate in ego-inflation" (Meland, 1935, p. 72). Meland seeks always a view that does not separate out the human. He aims to avoid a thin individualism that is not in keeping with the facts of our experience. Instead, he advances a philosophy of organism and an attentiveness to the matrix.

His is a view that at once wants to jar us out of our dualistic theisms and also to expand our perspective beyond the narrowness of an overly rationalistic or moralistic individuated ego-consciousness. Meland's work seeks to convince us that we live more deeply than we can think. He believes that in looking at notions like "depth," "ultimacy," "grace," etc., we can come to realize that these are elements present within the immediacies of experience as lived, though frequently unperceived. This kind of approach contrasts sharply with a supernaturalism that bifurcates the world into a dualism of the "natural" and the "supernatural." And, it is critical of a humanism that truncates the range of experience and reality and that too frequently identifies "reality" merely within the confines of human rationality.

There is an intriguing contemporaneity to James' and Meland's proposals. If we want to develop a new "religious creaturalism," we do not want to follow the normal pattern of hierarchical ideology and language in religious thought, which almost always trades in "what is above" statements, positing either God as divine potentate (as in theism) or humanity as creatural potentate (as in humanism) "at the top." Instead, we seek to reformulate this project toward relational and textured talk, showing the human as a connected and connectional creature within the ambiguous web of nature and of life. We humans have no privileged place above this web or outside this web from which to do our theologizing--or our living. So, this "creatural stance" involves getting back to an elemental openness to raw experience, to an awareness of the total datum of the lived body, to an appreciation of our creature-connectedness with other beings of this earth and with nature as a whole, freed from the restrictiveness of both an hierarchical viewpoint and a focused rational structure.

If we move toward a richer awareness of the nourishing aspects of the trans-cerebral matrix in which we live and move and have our being, we may gain a renewed sense of ourselves as contextualized creatures of the earth in the web of life. We can note the presence and power and nourishment of the ambiguous, the unmanageable, the spontaneous, the tragic, and the depth dimension of experience. Since we do live more deeply than we think, this approach will lure us to the concrete and the passionate, and to the unmanageable and the tragic that nourish us in mysterious ways. Theology too often seeks to resolve the ambiguities, to move from the concrete to the abstract. Theology must finally learn that a move from the concrete to the abstract is a move from more to less. Then we can finally come to regard ourselves as part of the web, rather than as set off from it, as a creature among creatures, a natural part of the cosmic matrix, integrally nourished and patterned by the rhythmed whole of which we are a part. We can come to regard the natural world not with the eyes of a separated, observant naturalist, but rather with the heart of a participating native.

Feminists, both women and men, teach us to move beyond various patriarchal dualisms--mind over body, will over passion, intellect over feeling, competition over communion, domination over mutual nurture, unilateral power over enabling activitiy, humans over other creatures. Most forms of theism and humanism participate in such a dualism, based on hierarchical thinking according to which we rank order certain structures in terms of ultimate worth. Both of these systems are usually couched in anthropos-species-arrogant forms. In humanism, humankind is set at the top. And in theism, humankind is usually presumed to be at the center of divine concern, divine consciousness and activity. This is audacious, arrogant, and pretentious, indeed. I hope that we can move beyond a dualism that persists in setting the human apart from all other creatures and structures, either as the center of worth itself or as the center of divine attention. If we could develop a sense of religious creaturalism in which we were not cut off from collaborative being, but rather were living in a relational way with nature, with one another, and with other creatures, our theological agenda would look very different, indeed. It would be different in at least four important ways.

Number one: we could repudiate the activity of what we have called in the past "systematic theology," in fact realizing that the term itself is oxymoronic. "Religious creaturalism" seeks the intensification rather than merely the explanation of experience-as-lived: the depths and ultimacies that attend our experience and its matrix of living and dying, of joy and pathos, of triumph and tragedy, of renewal and deterioration. This means that we must fully recognize, incorporate, and employ our whole experience as creatures in doing our theology, so that the resources of the passionate, the emotive, and the ambiguous, relational, and contextual are authenticated. Because these resources are concretely actual in our experience, not transcendent to it, theology ought to assist in this immersion in life, in the intensification of experience. As earth-creatures we do not live in straight lines; we truly do exist in a web, a network, a maze. For it must be seen that concrete experience, actuality, is always clothed in ambiguity. We must deconstruct any of our theologies that claim to name ultimacies exactly, that seek a "systematic" rendering of God, that honor abstraction at the price of intensity and creatural fullness.

Number two, I believe, follows directly: it is time for theologians and philosophers to stop constructing traditional theodicies ("justifications of the ways of God to humankind"). It should be seen as the height of religious arrogance, indeed, for humans to presume that instances of human suffering and disaster (while unfortunate, even in some cases devastating, for us) call into question the existence of God. There are events that cause horrible human suffering and lead to ruinous regression for us. But it is presumptous to assume that our welfare, the welfare of homo sapiens on this little planet, is at the center of divine activity and concern, or that human welfare and advancement are always more important than that of other creatures or other structures or other activities of the natural order. That view leads us to turn legitimate--but parochial--concerns into the theological "Problem of Evil." The jump is not warranted. If we adopt a stance of religious creaturalism, less self-centered and selfish, in which we realize that we are part of a web of life, where our particular activity is not the center of the cosmos and where nothing is guaranteed, then we need not "explain away" or attempt to find some cosmic explanation for what we have called "evil." Such a stance assigns to us a place in the universe and a role to which we are not entitled. And this approach has also seduced us at times to truncate our experience, marginalizing or denying those elements that bring genuine intensification. Too often, older theodicies have suggested that fullness of life has meant absense of tragedy and sorrow. It is time for us to put that aside.

Number three: I would like also to see our eschatological reflection (that is, reflection concerning doctrines of the last things and immortality) become less parochial, less individualistic, and less selfish. It is partriarchal and phallic of us to be so often primarily concerned with the fate of our individuated selves penetrating into the future. It is time for us to bring less linearity and more relationality to our eschatological thinking. We can embody more awareness of our status as evolved earth-creatures, of our affinities and interconnectednesses with the rest of nature, with the matter-energy matrix that has given us birth and of which, in some form, we shall always be a part. To the extent that we can move beyond egoism toward emphasis on a relationality in community and in the universe, we can attend to the "great matrix of being," "the cosmoc matrix of matter/energy," the "fabric of being" that is "everlasting" (Ruether, 1983, p. 257). A stance of religious creaturalism, aware of our nature connectedness, might lead us to more empathy with the matrix itself. We could realize that the death of our individuated self constitutes in a way our permission for other combinations within the matrix to go on. In some sense, each of us might see that what we may call "eternality" (or "life") is expressed briefly through this society of matter-energy that is called the "self," and then it moves on.

And to close, number four: I hope our agenda includes a move--drawing on a true understanding of "religious creaturalism"--beyond hierarchical thinking in our religious life. This revolution will be difficult, for this ideology has been in place institutionally and theologically for centuries. We have sought to climb Jacob's ladder rather than dance in Sarah's circle. Socially, we have established various apartheid systems, rank-ordering people so that we have human hierarchies rather than human communities, placing--in some ultimate sense of worth--men over women, whites over people of color, presidents over professors. And more to the point theologically, most traditional forms of theism and humanism have rank-ordered the worth of various things in the universe, so that a detachable god is posited above nature, or a certain species is praised to the exclusion of the other creatures. We need to move to a point at which we shall praise something by saying of it that it is "supremely natural" rather than missing this and always looking for the "supernatural" or that which is "above the natural."

Such a theology, a religious creaturalism, will progress beyond stasis to process, beyond individualism to contextualism, beyond hierarchy to community, beyond linearity to relationality, finally renouncing the truly damaging elements of patriarchy in our religion. This is our question now: can we build and sustain a religious ideology adequate to our experience without recourse to the hierarchical distinctions that have governed religious options in the past? Can we sustain a religious creaturalism that is both meaningful and non-hierarchically, relationally modelled? But we must persist in our dismantling of a self-serving, unrealistic, hierarchical humanism. We must regain a sense of ourselves as one creatural structure among many of the earth, as limited, as participating ambiguously in the pathos, majesty and creaturehood of the universe as a whole. To be sure, this is only a beginning, but it is a beginning which may hasten the day toward an end to human arrogance and creatural separation. This is no small step, indeed.

REFERENCES

James, William (1909). The Meaning of Truth (New York: Longmans, Green & Co.).

McDermott, John J., ed. (1967). The Writings of William James (New York: Random House).

Meland, Bernard E. (1935). "Mystical Naturalism and Religious Humanism," The New Humanist 8:72-74.

Roth, John K. (1980). "Holocaust Business: Some Reflections on Arbeit Macht Frei," Annals, AAPSS 450: 68-82.

Ruether, Rosemary Radford (1983). Sexism and God-Talk: Toward a Feminist Theology (Boston: Beacon Press).

Schwarz-Bart, Andre (1960). The Last of the Just (New York: Atheneum House).

CHRISTOLOGY AND THE FIRST COMMANDMENT

Eberhard Bethge

This topic represents a heavy burden. Over the centuries its weight has lamed or crushed most of those who sought to take it up. For this reason, the dialog between Jews and Christians has till now by and large avoided the issue of God. Michael Wyschogrod has thus observed: "The question of the one and only God in Judaism and the one but trinitarian God in Christentum is the last and most difficult question for the Jewish-Christian dialog". (1) The problem lies not only in the incredibly complex gnoseological history of the tracts on God and on Christ. More important is the way in which the two notions of God have been ghettoized as the banners of two rival intellectual and religious camps. On the banner of the Christian ghetto is the image of the allmighty God- Christus, in whose name the Jews have for centuries been banished into their own intellectual, religious and ultimately social ghetto. To remedy this situation, the higher mathematics of monotheistic or trinitarian speculation is of little use. Nevertheless, we cannot simply fold our hands in resignation and wait for a solution out of the blue As Christians we are challenged by this encounter with the Jews to return once again to the original foundations of our faith.

This paper is addressed therefore not to the Jewish partner in dialog but rather to my fellow Christians. Nonetheless I must confess that my thinking here owes its inception to the direct personal schock which I unexpectedly experienced in the course of my encounter with Jews after the Shoa, the Holocaust. Thus I would insist that we Christians need to listen to our Jewish partners particularly in this most delicate issue. Above all we need to listen when they point out to us, where they claim we have till now failed to listen. Only when we listen in this way can we avoid simply cementing time-old errors. It will not do, to speak of and about God in continued isolation. I am convinced that as Christians we can no longer give expression to our faith without attending to the objections of our Jewish partners.

I. Christological Credo after Auschwitz

1.) A Trial-version of a christological Confession

---

1 Wyschogrod, M. in Das Reden von einem Gott bei Juden und Christen, C. Thoma and M. Wyschogrod (ed.), Bern, 1984, p.13.

Protestant theologians are inclined to formulate their belief in their own words and, as pastors, they seldom hesitate to impose such confessions on their congregations. Often they are inspired by the appeal of modernity; in particular they are critical of the absence of the ethical element in the classical confessions: Bonhoeffer used to cite a confessional statement of Luther which concludes: "This then is the Christian faith, take heed of what you have to do and of what has been done for you". (2) I wish to begin therefore with a credal formula, which has taken form in my thinking over the last ten years in the wake of my being confronted with the reality of the Holocaust and in consequence of the discussions which accompanied and followed my awakening.

In an attempt to formulate the relationship between Christian profession of faith and political resistence to injustice, I arrived at the following formula:

> "I confess my allegiance to the Christ, who brings us God and life, who turns our thoughts and hearts <u>against</u> false gods and <u>toward</u> those who are their victims." (3)

To my surprise, a close acquaintance of mine, Martin Hinz of Magdeburg, siezed upon this statement as a "simple but luminous formula" (4) for all those who, in consequence of their encounter with Jews after the Holocaust, have sought to express their faith in Jesus the Christ in a new way, a way no longer expressing antijewish belief.

Behind this "formula" lies a multilevel history of personal experience, in particular my encounter with Jews in the wake of the Holocaust. It took shape in the context of my biographical and theological work on Dietrich Bonhoeffer. Admittedly this expression of a continued and intentional allegiance to Christ is by no means "simple"; it requires interpretation in a variety of directions. But first a warning! The christological dogma-complex forms a massive, labyrintian structure which is the product of centuries of construction and destruction, reconstruction and renovation, remodeling and rearranging. Anyone attempting to try to identify the central structural lines which order and support this complex from its foundations up to the pinacle of the cupola, is quite likely to be charged with reductionism, als though his intention were to pull down a cathedral and replace it with a primitive barracks. When, however, the encounter with the survivors of the Holocaust shall not be merely a transient episode but rather the beginning of a new epoch of Christian history and confession of faith, then we can no longer put off this kind of searching. Listen to the words of David Flusser, who puts his finger on the fateful development which transformed the disciples of Jesus from cooperating agents in the messianic drama of salvation into passive onlookers and worshipers. We can learn how the definition of our relationship to Christ has led us, by and large, to regard the <u>God-figure</u> Jesus Christ as being someone other than the <u>God of</u> Jesus Christ. In this way the figure of Christ has slipped inadvertently into a role of pagan idol-worship: as I would say in German, a "Götze" has assumed the place of "Gott". The divinized Jesus has been cut off from his Jewish biblico-historical roots and transformed into a greco-roman, mythical, imperialist, Germanic or American God-figure fitted to our socio-cultural needs. Christian theology and preaching have lost the ability "to think through and to formulate their confession of Christ within the framework of Judaic belief in God."Upon the "linguistic aliena-

---

2 <u>W.A.</u> 30 I 94

3 Bethge, <u>Bekennen und Widerstehen</u>, München, 1984, p.155.

4 Hinz, Chr., Brief vom 14.9.1984.

tion" followed the "religious and social isolation". (5) Christ was turned into a God, in whose name non-Christians, the Jews in particular, were to be banished into the social isolation of the ghetto and in the end, without our protesting, were delivered up to annihilation justified at least in part by elements of our christology.

2) Confession of Christ as a Christian "Sh'ma" in Response to the First Commandment?

This statement attempts to formulate belief in Christ in the context of the First Commandment. This is not the place to delve into the history of the different usages of the First Commandment in the various Jewish and Christian traditions. As my point of departure I have taken Luther's explanation in the Small Catechism: there he connects the abbreviated covenant formula - the God who promises himself to his people - with the command: no other gods! My formula recalls the situation of the original recipients of the covenant promises: their response was the daily prayerful recitation of the Sh'ma Jisrael: "Hear, O Israel, the LORD Our God is one LORD!" (Dt. 6:4). And this response they repeated all the more emphatically when they were being sacrificed to the gods of their oppressors. My formula took rise in my listening attentively to the critical appeal of the Jews in their unflagging repetition of the Sh'ma Jisrael: their emphatic confession of the one and only Lord and God, their allegience to his commandments and their unbroken trust in his universal future promises. That is to say, as Christians we have to listen to this Jewish confession, we have to formulate our allegience to Christ in the context of this First Commandment so that we do not set up any new god alongside the One God of the Covenent. In this context we must ask, does not our confession of Christ constitute our equivalent answer to God's merciful call to the covenent of life, is it not our Christian equivalent of the Sh'ma-formula, a confession of our submission to the First Commandment and of our thankfulness for inclusion in its promise.

3.) Confession of Faith and the Sh'ma in Opposition to other Gods and in Support of their Victims

The route which led me to this formula began with my work on Bonhoeffer's struggle for the faith. His was a two-pronged battle: on the one side the fight against the Gleichschaltung: the subordination of religion to the state (the Kirchenkampf), on the other, the struggle for and solidarity with the Jewish victims of the Gleichschaltung, a struggle which climaxed in his participation in the plot against Hitler's life. This topic became the central theme of my theological studies. At first, however, the question of correct or incorrect christology played little role in my reflection; instead my attention concentrated on the Act of Faith and its meaning for us today. I sought to grasp the consequences of our allegience to the band of Jesus' disciples: what does it mean when we express our belonging to Him, the Jew from Nazareth, the Revealer, for us Christians, of the God of the Covenant, the one and only Lord, the faithful one? I sought to interpret this reality, keeping in mind that the Jews once again were speaking to us inspite of our share in the Holocaust.

Along the way with my Jewish conversation-partners there came a turning-point, which offered me a wealth of new insights but at the same time brought me into a theatening conflict with deep-seated tabus of belief and piety. The stages along the route of this development were as follows.

5 Wiederkehr, D. in Das Reden von einem Gott ..., loc. cit.,p.141

At first, prior to my entering into direct dialog with the Jews, I enjoyed a certain degree of self-satisfaction: What with the Christian engagement in the struggle of the Confessing Church and its rediscovery of the meaning of the Bible and the Creed and with the participation, however marginal, in the political Resistance to the Nazi-Regime, I felt that we Christians did not cut all that bad a figure.

Then began a period of profound unsettlement, as I experienced how the Jews were opening up ever deeper dimensions of the Holocaust. These dimensions reached back beyond the perception of the inhuman suffering of Auschwitz to the beginnings of church history, indeed to the New Testament itself, where in consequence of the painful separation of the Church from Israel hostility against the Jews began to raise its ugly head. The reception of this revelation entailed a new perception of contemporary Jews and the meaning of their prayerful confession of the Sh'ma. I thus entered into a much more conscious encounter with living Jews and their faith.

There followed a breakthrough, revealing to me the implications of the fact that we Christians profess faith in one and the same Covenant as the Jews (6) And I began to grasp the fatality of a development which had led to the splitting of this one covenent into two temporally discontinuous covenants, the one, our Covenant, adorned with the trappings of eternal youth, the other tagged with appelations of antiquatedness and so delivered over in one form or another to destruction. The realization, that we Christians are incorporated into the one and only covenent of the Jews, led to an intensive rereading of the ancient Christian texts of the Bible and the Creed. Thus began for me a phase of breathtaking advance from insight to insight.

One of the first consequences of this development was the realization, that there is no place for what is traditionally called the "mission to the Jews". It is not the business of us Christians to bring to the Jews the God of covenant fidelity and his Tora, be it as "gospel", be it as "law".

A further consequence inaugerated the next and latest phase of development, as I overcame my reluctance and began to discuss christology with Jewish partners in dialog.

4.) The Relevance of the Jews for Christology

We have thus come to the point at which a brand new question forces itself upon us Christians: what is the service the Jews render us, when they refuse to include Jesus as the Son of God in their confession of faith. As far as I am concerned, it is irrelevant, whether their refusal is willful or not; what is important is the practical service they thereby render to us by their tenaciously holding fast to the unchanged formula of the Sh'ma Jisrael over centuries of brutal oppression and suffering in obedience to the First Commandment.

For my part, I can almost name the day, on which I learned to see our painful separation in the light of this service and so to begin to try and test in dialog the various formulations which might present themselves as an initial answer to this question.

5.) Two sources of inspiration: Bonhoeffer and Stöhr

The first date in my odessey of discovery was the day on which suddenly a passage in Bonhoeffer's Ethics, which I had

6 Der ungekündigte Bund, D. Goldschmidt and H. J. Kraus, (ed.), 2nd ed., 1963.

read hundreds of times over the decades, suddenly caught my eye and seized my attention, schooled now by the experience with a theology after the Holocaust. Bonhoeffer's statement reads: "The Jews hold open the question of the Christ." (7)

The point of this statement is precisely that in Christian circles the question of the Christ is regarded as closed once and for all and as having been answered finally and decisively for all times; from this position it follows that the question of ecclesiology is equally closed and decisively answered. Against this background, Bonhoeffer's statement asserts that there exists someone who holds the question open and who remains unimpressed by those who self-confidently assert the matter to be closed once and for all and who regard their answer as the ultimate and decisive weapon in the century-old conflict.

Bonhoeffer recognized, that the question of the Christ has remained inaccessible to the Jews, and that this is paradoxical, because this question originally belongs to the sphere of Jewish faith and so should be a Jewish possession. He wrote this sentence at a time, when his own allegiance to Christ was in jeopardy and could only be maintained untarnished by the total commitment of his person.

Thus the thought arises, do not the Jews have a decisive role to play in the answer given by Christians to the question of the Christ? Must not the "in-fidel" and critical refusal of the Jews be repeated time and again for us Christians, in order to spur us on to be better Christians? Can it be that we need the negation of the Jews, in order that in our enclosed garden of theological reflection, where christology is carefully tended and brought to ever new and imposing blossom, the poisonous shoots giving honor to a false god bearing the name of Christ be kept in check? Do we not have need of the witness of the Jews to protect us from a false worship of Christ cut off from the First Commandment given us by the one and only God of Sinai? Must we not take seriously the statement of Michael Wyschogrod, who says of verse 6:4 of Deuteronomy, the <u>Sh'ma Jisrael</u>: "For the self-understanding of the Jewish people and presumably for rabbinic Judaism this verse is the most important verse of the whole Bible"?. (8)

The statement of Bonhoeffer concerning the Jews who hold open the christological question stands squarely in the context of the faith which he formulated and practiced in an indisputable Christocentrism. My own expansion and variation of his observation is not to be found in the text of the <u>Ethics</u>. It is thus possible that I have read more into the statement than originally intended by the author. Perhaps I have only worked out the implications of what Bonhoeffer himself was not yet able to grasp. Be that as it may, the critical gene is there, the substance is present though only in nucleus. Should it be forbidden to build further upon the foundation he laid or to expand the clearing that he himself began?

The next critical date for the evolution of my thinking was a conversation some years ago at Arnoldshain. We were speaking of our separate yet common cause with the Jews, when suddenly Martin Stör introduced the key word "First Commandment" into the discussion, pointing out that together we confess it daily, we Christians in our recitation of the Catechism, the Jews in their recitation of the <u>Sh'ma Jisrael</u>.

---

7 Bonhoeffer, D., <u>Ethik</u>, 1963, p.95.

8 <u>Das Reden von einem Gott</u>..., loc. cit., p.30.

From that moment on, I have time and again returned to reflect upon that confessional statement impressed upon us from childhood on, its meaning remaining oft nebulous - where does one find these days "other gods beside Him"? - or depressing - "how does one love Him above all else? In the epoch of National Socialism we experienced once again something of the real meaning of the First Commandment, as for instance when the quasi-religious claims of the day were made explicit in the November 9th celebrations in the Feldherrnhalle.

Nevertheless I must confess that, in conjunction with my study of christology in the Twenties, I have no recollection of being confronted with a a treatment of a connection between the monotheism of the First Commandment and its practical realization in the development of christology. Of course it is possible that I failed to grasp the import of what was being said.

What would be the consequences, when the contemporary encounter with the Jews should help us to rediscover the connection between the First Commandment and the confession of Christ? What would follow from the attempt to interpret, to formulate and to confess our allegiance to Christ within, rather than without, the context of Jewish monotheism? Dietrich Wiederkehr, professor of fundamental theology in Lucerne, has described the fatal consequences of the trend of thinking that transformed the original christological highness-attributions into (neoplatonic) assertions about the hidden divine nature, forgetting their original meaning as predications of origin in and of relationship to the God of the Covenent and the inaugeration of His promised reign. (9)

The consequence is that christology and the trinitarian doctrine have to be confronted with the critical question. whether and how do they help us to understand and interpret the First Commandment better and to hold fast to the grace and the demand which it incorporates. When christologies do not serve this purpose, then they become ends in themselves, either as arbitrary expressions of meanings dictated by the contemporary zeitgeist in the service of a system of domination or as venerable museum-pieces, which have lost all ability to liberate in the spirit of the Covenant. The purpose of christological statements is to express in the language of the day, how Jesus of Nazareth is the Christ, the bringer of God's reign as the fulfillment of the covenent in which the First Commandment is the norm. Whether and how this fulfillment is already achieved is the legitimate point of controversy between Christians and Jews. Both sides in this controversy have to turn away from false gods. What the Sh'ma Jisrael is for the Jews, so must the confession of Christ be for us Christians, namely the critical test for the identification and repudiation of every form of idol-worship, be it ancient or modern, blatant or most subtle.

Christoph Hinz has called my attention to an observation of Gerhard von Rad: "that is what isolated Israel in the religious world: Israel knew what idols were and what constituted idol worship." (10) Hinz went on to say how unforgetable was von Rad's portrayal of the purifying fire which the First Commandment put to Christian theology and faith, for he went on to observe, "there is no utterance of faith which cannot be misused as an instrument of idol-worship!"

6.) "Messiah Israel's"? the Bad-Neuenahr-Statement of 1980

---

9 ibid, p.142.

10 Rad, G. von, "Die Wirklichkeit Gottes". in Wirklichkeit heute Referate und Arbeitsberichte vom Kirchenkongreß in Hamburg, 1958, p.95

In the light of the fact that christology should not entail a departure from the First Commandment but rather is ordered to be the expression and formulation precisely of the connection between Christ and the Commandment, I have come to grasp the meaning and importance of that controversial statement about the "Messiah Israel's" formulated by the Neuenahr-Declaration, a statement which has met with so much criticism, misunderstanding and outright rejection. Aware of the numerous christological formulas with their fatal idol-worshiping consequences, I understand the genitive case here as the inescapable assertion that Jesus is the Messias of Israel and not the neoplatonic Christ of the Greeks, who reduced the manifold New Testament christologies to a single abstract universal essence (Allwesen) or conflated them into a universal ruler (pantocrator) epitomizing ecclesiastical triumphalism and rationalizing Antijudaism - one way or the other this meant setting aside the First Commandment and cutting off Christ from the context of His living relationships.

By the same token, Christ is not the Teutonic Messias - a false idol shaped in particular in the 19th Century and brought to completion in the present century by people like Wilhelm Stapel its ugly fruit being the Nürnberg Laws, the so-called "Kristallnacht" and the Wannsee-Conference. Neither is He the American Messias preached by Jerry Falwell and his promoter Jessie Helms in Washington. Their "Jesus first" christology is but an instrument for the realization of American dreams. No! Jesus Christ must remain the Messiah Israel's: as the Messiah from the midst of Israel and for the sake of Israel, He remains inseparably bound to Israel. Only when we see him as the Messiah Israel's, will we avoid reducing his universal significance to our own particularistic universes. Jesus never denied his own Jewish particularity, never spoke of a kingdom other than that of the God of Sinai, the God of the Covenant with its commandments to protect His people from the cruelty of other gods. Neither in life nor in death did He distance himself even for a moment from the prayerful recitation of the Sh'ma Jisrael. In his personal engagement for the cast-outs and in his suffering and death for the reign of this God he obtained justification through His being raised from the dead

Thus the oft criticized and rejected genitiv in the Neuenahr-Declaration dare not be set aside. The First Commandment of the God of Israel who is as well the God of the Christians, demands this formula, in order that strange gods do not usurp His place and in order that the interpretation of Jesus of Nazareth not fall back into the antijewish and antisemetic patterns of the past.

Whenever christological thinking threatens to loosen the connection with the First Commandment, whenever it starts to obscure its meaning as God's judgment and liberation of those in bondage, then it becomes de facto a seduction into idol-worship and loses its hermeneutic function.

II. Bonhoeffer als a Trinitarian Man of Prayer

1. Christological Definition and Christological Act of Faith

Inasmuch as this paper is intended as a challenge to test christological confessions of faith in terms of their authenticity and integrity with respect to their relationship to the First Commandment and its Jewish expression in the Sh'ma Jisrael, it is useful to distinguish between the act of faith as act and the dogmatic formulae, which over the long course of history have been proposed, contested and then ultimately accepted or rejected. Both the act and the formulae have their individual historical contexts, their kairos and so also their legitimate and illegitimate functions. They are not everywhere and at the same time acceptable or reprehensible, and this holds not the least for their relationship to the First Commandment. What counts is whether they are used to stake out our own positions over against Jews and members of other Christian denominations or used to praise and magnify the God of the First Commandment. who suffers with us all and who liberates us from our suffering.

It is not that defined doctrine on the one side and the act of confessing the faith with praise or resistence to evil on the other have nothing to do with one another. Doctrinal reflection and definition have a legitimate function to protect the act of praise from enthusiastic self-deception. They train one in keeping critical discernment and distance. They formulate in objective form, what is and what is not: they force us back in retreat or push us forward into action. Their danger, however, lies therein, that they can seduce one into formulating ontic "Is-Statements"; in this way they can give rise to a closed system of tradition as a private possession, so to speak; they can instigate a struggle for positions and can thus become completely absorbed in their divisive role.

The act of christological prayer, of hymn and confession is not located in the sphere of possessive rights. It is not paramountly an act of setting things right but rather an act of professing loyalty or illoyalty. Admittedly, the doctrinal struggle can, under appropriate circumstances, itself become an existential act of faith, an expression of authentic loyalty to the God of the First Commandment.

Christine Ruth Müller has made an interesting observation in connection with Bonhoeffer's christology of the summer of 1933: the christological heresy of docetism he condemns in the sharpest terms, "but he makes no mention of the anathema against the ebionite heresy." (11) The ebionite teaching at least maintains the unicity of the God of Sinai; the docetic teaching on the contrary opened the way for the neoplatonic and imperialistic idolizing of Christ. The ebionite position is rooted in the Jewish Sh'ma, the docetic position allows "God's metamorphosis", making possible the appearance in 1933 of a Germanic Christ. Whereas the ebionite position is rooted in the Old Testament and "in the God of Abraham, Isaac and Jacob", docetism has its origin in pagan idealist thinking.

2) Trinitarian Prayer?

In the face of the rapidly expanding misuse of Christ as a false god in 1933, one can see how Bonhoeffer, inspired by biblical theology, moved in the direction of doctrinal definition in terms of the First Commandment. But what of his practical expression of faith? Until his death he held fast to the trinitarian forms of prayer and confession of faith. Emphatically he addressed his prayers to the Father, the Son and the Holy Spirit in all sorts of variations. Is this to be seen as a departure from the First Commandment in practice or is it rather the necessary consequence of his understanding of the First Commandment.

I recall the prayers, which he wrote for his fellow prisoners in Tegel at Christmas 1943. (12) They are among the deepest expressions of his piety. They are not spontaneous effusions but rather the fruit of prolonged meditation and disciplined working and reworking, stylistically reflecting his long years of training in the school of the psalms. Admittedly they are directed in this

11 Müller, Chr. R., unpublished Ms. 1984, p.19
12 Bonhoeffer, D., Widerstand und Ergebung, ed. by E. Bethge, new ed., 1970, p.158 ff.

concrete situation to the isolation of the prisoners in their cells and so reflect little on the situation of God's people and his endangered Covenent, but they are unthinkable without this implicit background.

The first of these prayers, for example, we would hardly recommend for use in a Jewish - Christian assembly. The barrier raised by the trinitarian form of address and the prayer to Jesus Christ is far too exalted. But for myself and in prayer with fellow Christians I can recite it and meditate upon it, not excluding the following passage in in second part of his text:

"Lord Jesus Christ,
You were poor
and miserable, imprisoned and abandoned like myself.
You know all our suffering;
You remain by me,
when no other human being supports me.
You do not forget me: instead You search me out.
You will, that I acknowledge You and that I
turn to You.
O Lord, I hear Your call and follow:
Help me!" (13)

The complete prayer begins with the address: "God, to You I call early in the morning, help me to pray"; it ends: "Your Name be praised, Amen." Over the above cited middle part with its address "Jesus Christ" I do not stumble, unless I know someone to be present, for whom Christian practice and Christian tradition serve as a barrier to understanding such a form of prayer.

Normally then I am not bothered by the thought, that with this portion of the prayer I might depart from the orientation to the one God of the Covenent, who is opposed to all other gods. On the contrary, I can thus better understand the fidelity of Him, who allowed His faithful servant to bear the consequences of that fidelity: the poverty, misery, imprisonment and abandonment of those who reject other gods. In the faithfulness of Jesus Christ I come nearer to experiencing the profanation of God's Name in the world. I find myself less tempted by the rich and attractive offers of other, ever newer gods. "...to You I turn...I hear Your call and follow!" Whither do I follow? To the one God of faithfulness, to Him who is opposed to all other gods, to the abused creatures of the One God, to the riches of His presence in His admonitions.

When that be the case, then profound differences become evident between two forms of prayer to Christ. On the one hand, a prayer to Christ, worshipping an idol as the Christ, giving sanction to foreign lords and their ideologies outside the community of the Sh'ma Jisrael - there where the court theologians are reduced to the role of being "hairdressers for the theological wig of the emperor"- (14); on the other hand, a prayer to Christ, which takes up the cross of remaining faithful to the one God and which, analogous to the Jewish fidelity to the Sh'ma Jisrael, time and again renews its commitment to discipleship in the spirit of the First Commandment.

Seen in this way, Bonhoeffer's devotion to the Christ should not be seen as a departure either from the First Commandment or from the Covenant formula with its demands on our practice

13 ibid., p.158.
14 Das Reden von einem Gott..., loc. cit., p.205.

of faith. On the contrary, Bonhoeffer's prayers are an affirmation of his firm commitment to both. Were that not the case, the confession of Jesus Christ and the prayers addressed to Him would in fact lead us away from the Christian trinitarian relationship to the one God of the First Commandment to a false tritheism foreign to authentic trinitarian teaching. Just as the Talmud describes the recitation of the Sh'ma Jisrael as "the taking upon oneself of the yoke of the Kingdom of Heaven" (15), so also can Bonhoeffer's practice of the discipleship of Christ in prayer be understood in the same fashion. Bonhoeffer's devotion to Christ can stand up to the test-question: how is it related to the First Commandment. He strictly opposed every form of devotion to Christ which opened the door sooner or later to powerful false gods. He recognized their seductive presence everywhere where the Christ of Israel is paganized or associated with heathen gods in syncretistic fashion. Around the corner he recognized the Christ-syncretists, who religiously sacrifice social victims to Christ-idols of Baal-like character, instead of offering themselves instead of and for the sake of such victims. One thinks of Bonhoeffer's famous inversion of the sentential structures of religion and faith - "Human beings turn to God in His state of need ... Christians stand by God in His suffering" instead of "Human beings turn to God in their state of need." (16) Do not such statements mean a consistent turning to the First Commandment and to those who pray the Sh'ma Jisrael? (this prayer was written in Tegel in 1944, when Bonhoeffer was quite well aware of the horrid path the people of the Sh'ma were being forced to tread.

Over ten years ago Rabbi Aschkenasy said to us, he did not want to make Jews of us but rather better Christians, when he called our attention to Israel's roots in the First Commandment and to our sins against this commandment and their consequences. Naturally he understood as we do, that an understanding between us in impossible regarding the confessional statement "Jesus Christ, true God and true man." For him this sentence is unacceptable, for us it is inseparable. Nevertheless he could reckon with the fact that for us Christians the fundamental dogma of the two natures is not simply a pre-given postulate to answered with yes or no. He saw that therein the practice of our relationship to Christ may also be implied, a practice which is existentially related to the One God. And with his "become better Christians" he clearly expected us to be answerable to the First Commandment and to be in a position to recognize the consequences of a departure from it. Did he not also trust us to be able to interpret this foundational dogma in the light of the First Commandment rather than in contradiction to it? A discussion in this direction would certainly be something quite distinct from the practice of making this fundamental conviction into a criterion of damnation for those, who on the last day still and again recite the Sh'ma.

III. Possible Allies in opposition to Other Gods?

The astonishing awakening of the Jewish-Christian dialog as a consequence of the realization of what the Holocaust means has carried us up to a lofty threshhold, from which each partner looks over to the other side, perceiving the perplexing image of the other, a vision which at once attracts and repells. Our perplexity is now all the greater, as we now have reached the critical question of the Christ. We had already enough to do, as we began to realize the consequences of the "unbroken single Covenant". The christological question we kept shut up in the closet of the mind.

15 Citation in Wyshogrod, loc. cit., p.4.
16 Bonhoeffer, Widerstand ..., loc. cit., p.382.

Now, however, we can no longer exclude this topic from discussion, if we want relly to know, where we stand for each other and what we mean to each other, after having for so long lived only in opposition to each other, and that under quite unequal living conditions.

Could it be that on this lofty threshold we have reached the point of sterile stand-still? Must we close again the doors so recently opened? I do not, and cannot believe this to be the case! For us Christians it would be fatal, were the Jews to cease to confront us with the question of the paganising of the churches and the idolizing of Christ. With this service to us they help us to keep the christological question open; they force us to uphold the relationship between the First Commandment and the confession of Christ. What such a stalemate for the Jews would mean, is not in my providence to say. But are we not together confronted with a demand for a common reflection and and effort to find a mutually shared form of expression? With pleasure and hope, I would like to cite here the description of our situation which Dietrich Wiederkehr gave in the context of a Jewish-Christian seminar in Lucerne in 1982/83:

"All in all it has become clear that the only place where we can reach an intelligent common understanding lies in the history of revelation. This was the ground from which the Jewish theological reflection moved forward to appreciate the suspenseful openness of God who transcends the categories of our thinking; from the same ground, however, the Christians originally developed their trinitarian doctrine. As Christian thinking more and more shut itself up into a fatal speculation about the internal relations in God it lost touch with this common ground originally shared with the Jews. It is imperative, therefore, to return to this common place, where _a common linguistic and symbolic tradition_ is to be found - the tradition in which the Jews continue to speak of the unity and unicity of God. In this tradition, in the Jewish reflection upon the form of God's presence in human history, the Christian symbols and concepts of the Trinity took their origin: Wisdom = Logos, Shekina = Doxa, Ruach = Pneuma. This is more than simply a fact of religious and theological history: to the extent that we concern ourselves with its implication we are led back to a common realm of experience." (17)

This only recently begun effort to find a common conceptual ground and a shared way of speaking must not, however, confine itself simply to the past: the contemporary false gods and their activized and passivized victims must equally be taken into account. In this shared "realm of experience" and dialog new lines of division come to the fore, lines of division which do not so much divide Christians and Jews in regard to diverse formulations of christology and the First Commandment but rather Christians from other Christians, Jews from other Jews. And so it can happen that Christians and Jews together come to stand on the one side and other Christians and Jews on the opposite side. Together those on the one side understand, those on the other fail to understand how the confession of Christ and the First Commandment fit together in the response of the _Sh'ma Jisrael_ and how the relationship between them is to be translated into word and deed. But both sides live and think and act in the spirit of the original act of fidelity, the act of God's fidelity to his people and the human response of trusting faith, which lies at the root of our relationship to him. Thus despite division, both sides concur with their acts of belief and prayer in that vast stream glorifying the One God and in the grace which that God lets stream into his troubled creation.

The encounter between Jews and Christians is not something

---

17 Ibid. p.225.

which occurs once and for all; neither is it something which produces a final peacemaking harmony. Were that to occur, the most likely result would be the absurdity that, along with the false gods and those who produce the ghettos, the God of Life would be extinguished.

That means, however, in addition, that the dialogical encounter does not necessarily mean that for the Christian his former ways of thinking and forms of piety must be extinguished.

Perhaps nothing of this sort must be feared. Those of us who experienced the theological renewal and the reawakening of faith produced by the work of Barth, Iwand, Bonhoeffer and - the Confessing Church will hardly be tempted or inclined to follow the liberal approach to revelation and christology and abandon the classical forms of the confession of Christ and christological thinking as did the salient theologians of the 19th Century, thus contributing to the 20th Century outburst of Antisemitism in the Church. Neverthless, the theologian in the tradition of the Confessing Church will have to acknowledge the service of the Jews for our Christian reappraisal of the relationships involved in christology and the First Commandment. For he must recognize that he has a duty to help in the task of building and rebuilding the ever threatened barriers against the false gods and their ghettos.

As to my own position, it has clearly been determined by the traditions in which I was raised; it is founded upon the ancient, more or less clearly formulated christologies of tradition; it is determined further by my professional responsibility for the protection of Christian teaching and the defence against its perversions; it is formed by the communal internalization of expressions and forms of the hymnal and the liturgy. As to my ethical-political socialization, this has been effected in a geographical, historical and "Christian" framework which I cannot escape. Given this enclosure I can only hope, that time and again there will be someone there - be this Jew or Gentile - who will warn me against the dangers not only for the faith but also for the persons I oversee, when Christ is transformed into an idol. The same holds for the Church at large. Those who confess belief in Christ need to have at their side, as close as possible, those who daily pray the Sh'ma Jisrael.

THE SUFFERING OF GOD

New perspectives in the Christian understanding of God since the Holocaust

Marcus Braybrooke

Brookwalk, 2 The Bassetts, Box, Corsham, Wilts. SN14 9ER

Does my belief in a God of love make sense in the shadow of the Holocaust? As Dr. Johann-Baptist Metz has written

'There is no truth for me which I could defend with my back turned towards Auschwitz
There is no sense for me which I could preserve with my back turned towards Auschwitz
And for me there is no God to whom I could pray with my back turned towards Auschwitz' (1)

The appalling horror of the Holocaust demands that I scrutinize my Christian inheritance and recognise the anti-Judaism by which it is stained and seek as honestly as possible not to perpetuate it. It means that any approach to Judaism and Jewish friends must be as a humble penitent, which makes me hesitate to speak about so profound an evil. But speak I must to discover the continuing possibility of faith and hope. For the Shoah exposes the depths of bestiality to which human nature - my human nature is capable. It shatters also any glib faith so that agnosticism seems more godly than traditional platitudes. Talk of a God who intervenes in history has lost credibility but faith in self-giving love as the only power strong enough to change the heart of men and women remains my deep conviction. Yet what is the 'power of self-giving love' and 'the strength of suffering'? Does it help to talk of a suffering God or do I speak in this way because I cannot cope with our human nakedness?

"Never shall I forget the faces of the children whose bodies I saw turned into wreaths of smoke beneath a silent blue sky.

Never shall I forget those flames which consumed my faith forever.

Never shall I forget the nocturnal silence which deprived me, for all eternity, of the desire to live.

Never shall I forget those moments which murdered my God and my soul and turned my dreams to dust.

Never shall I forget these things, even if I am condemned to live as long as God himself, Never". (2)

Elie Wiesel' words are echoed by Richard Rubenstein "we learned in the crisis that we were totally and nakedly alone, that we could expect neither support nor succor from God nor from our fellow creatures. Therefore the world will forever remain a place of pain, suffering, alienation and ultimate defeat." (3)

In one sense those who say the Holocaust raises no new issues for theodicy are right. The bewilderment of personal anguish or the cruel and needless death of one child raises the same question. In Dostoievsky's novel The Brothers Karamazov, Ivan quotes the suffering of innocent little children in order to show his Christian brother, Alyosha, that there is no God who can redeem such suffering. Ivan says that even if at the end of the world some great reconciliation takes place, he will never be able to forget the story of the little child who was turned out naked on the open steppe by a mad Russian General and torn to pieces in front of his own mother by the general's hunting dogs. Ivan says that no amount of reconciliation can ever justify the terrified suffering of that child and his mother and that he, Ivan, can never forget it. So he says to God, "I must respectfully return to you my entrance ticket to your heaven." Traditional answers are affirmed by many writers, but others no longer find helpful the picture of a God who intervenes in history, which is how God is pictured in the Bible. "We no longer believe in the God who has the power to annul the tragic necessities of existence" (4) says Richard Rubenstein and elsewhere he speaks of the "death of the God who acts in history." (5)

Other writers emphasise the real freedom of human beings and indeed of the natural order. God could not intervene to stop the Holocaust writes Paul van Buren(6) "without ceasing to be the God of love and freedom who has conferred responsibility and free creative power on His creatures." If God was able to intervene and stop the Holocaust and did not do so, then his character as love is questionable. To say that he gives his creation total freedom, eases his responsibility, but he must still accept responsibility for making the world with such freedom that the evil deeds of the Nazis were possible.

God shares our suffering

A number of writers speak of God as sharing human suffering and himself suffering. "All that we can suffer of physical or mental anguish is within the divine experience" wrote William Temple, "He has known it all himself. He does not leave this world to suffer while he remains at ease apart; all the suffering of the world is His."(7) Jurgen Möltmann similarly says "God not only participates in our suffering, but also makes our suffering into his own." (8) "It is necessary to remember the martyrs, so as not to become abstract. Of them and of dumb sacrifices, it is true in a real, transferred sense, that God himself hung on the gallows as Elie Wiesel was able to say. If that is taken seriously, it must also be said that like the cross of Christ, even Auschwitz is in God Himself. Even Auschwitz is taken up into the grief of the Father, the surrender of the Son and the power of the Spirit" (9) Interpreting so Jewish a tragedy in Christian terms may cause misunderstanding, but for Möltmann it is essentially a trinitarian interpretation, as is William Temple's, who says that "God remains outside the process, though it originates with Him and He guides." (10) God does indeed identify with human suffering and suffers with men and women: but his ultimate freedom is preserved - it is a voluntary sharing and identification.

Some writers see the cross as an historical expression of the eternal character of God. God does not just identify with human suffering, He is eternally suffering love. C.A. Dinsmore wrote early in this century, "there was a cross in the heart of God before there was one planted on the green hill outside of Jerusalem. And now that the cross of wood has been taken down, the one in the heart of God abides, and it will remain so long as there is one sinful soul for whom to suffer." (11) Canon Vernon Storr in The Problem of the Cross (12) wrote "The cross of Christ was no after-thought on the part of God, but was the expression at a definite historical period of something which represents an eternal actuality in the divine life."

Studdert-Kennedy

Such writing may have influenced Studdert-Kennedy, whose experience of the First World War made him reject 'stained-glass window' pictures of God.

"God, I hate this splendid vision - all its splendour is a lie ...
God, the God I love and worship reigns in sorrow on the tree,
Broken, bleeding, but unconquered, very God of God to me." (13)

Just as the war he said, sounded the doom of absolute monarchy upon earth, so we must abandon the idea of such power as vested in God. "We can no longer interpret ultimate reality in the terms of absolute monarchy if we are to reach the hearts of men." (14) "I don't know or love the Almighty Potentate, my only real God is the suffering Father revealed in the sorrow of Christ." (15) As Creator, God was no omnipotent monarch, but He "was forced to limit Himself .... He had to bind himself with nails, and take upon Himself the travail pangs of creation. The universe was made as it is because it is the only way it could be made, and this way lays upon God the burden of many failures and of eternal strain - the sorrow of God the Father which Christ revealed (16) "God is everywhere in history, but nowhere is He Almighty. Ever and always we see Him suffering, striving, crucified, but conquering ... all real progress is caused by the working of suffering love in the world." (17) Prayer is seen essentially as identification with God's way of suffering love.

C.E. Rolt

Similar ideas were more systematically developed earlier in a book written by C.E. Rolt just before the outbreak of the First World War. His underlying conviction was that the only omnipotence which God possesses is that of love. God's only power in the face of evil, he said, is the power of patient love, and in this love, through suffering, lies the only way to the conquest of evil. The world was never, from the first, a perfect world, it always contained evil, which in all its forms is hateful to God. "The whole earth groans aloud in anguish and degradation. And inwards, at the very centre of the world, these cries strike upon the ear of God, who hears them with an infinite grief: for at the inmost core of all things, there is no mere creative mind or vital force, there is a Human Heart, and that heart is broken."(18)"God, by the very nature of His omnipotence, is bound and tied hand and foot in the midst of this evil world, and is obliged to bear, not only the physical sufferings of the whole creation, but also of the far more bitter pain of human motive and sin."(19)Yet such suffering is the way to victory on earth and in the Godhead it is overcome and transmutted into glory. Yet "eternity is not independent of Time, it is time's crown and goal. God must, therefore, pass through time to attain to His own eternal Being. And in this passage, He must experience the pain as untransmuted pain.

Only thus can he transmute it and by it, attain to His own perfection." (20)

In the suggestion that God only attains to His own perfection at the climax of history, C.E. Rolt anticipated some of the writings of the Process Theologians, He recognised the real freedom of the creative process - that it is not foreknown by God, but that the future is genuinely open. The suggestion, however, that God's only power is the power of suffering love was only taken up by one or two writers for example B.H. Streeter, and interest in discussion of God's impassibility faded in the years after the First World War.

W.H. Vanstone

Recently it has been raised again by Canon W.H. Vanstone who starts with a discussion of the phenomenology love. He begins by looking at behaviour which shows love to be inauthentic. First he writes "the falsity of love is exposed wherever any limit is set by the will of him who professes to love: wherever by his will something is withheld. Therefore the authenticity of love must imply a totality of giving - that which we call the giving of self or self-giving." (21) Secondly, the authenticity of love is denied by the mark of control. "Love is activity for the sake of an <u>other</u> : and where the object of love is wholly under the control of the one who loves, that object is no longer an other." (22) Vanstone illustrates this by a parent's care for a child and from the field of artistic creation. In the case of a child, "each step of love is a step of risk : each step taken generates the need for another and equally precarious step." (23) Again if an artist works within the limit of what he knows himself able to do, he is not creative. "As the artist exceeds his known powers his work is precariously poised between success and failure, between triumph and tragedy : it may be that the work of art is marred beyond redemption, or it may be that powers hitherto unknown will prove adequate to the completion and triumph of his work," (24) There is therefore a risk or precariousness in love. For the lover or the artist the precariousness of love's endeavour is "lack of final control over the situation which it has itself created." (25)

Thirdly, the inauthenticity of love is shown by detachment. Some detachment, Vanstone recognises may be for the good of the person loved, but where love is authentic, "the lover gives to the object of his love a certain power over himself" (26) - "a power to make angry or to make glad; to cause grief or joy; to frustrate or to fulfil; to determine tragedy or triumph. It is the 'power of meaning' - the power of having meaning to, or value for, the one who loves. It is the power of affecting the one who loves. It creates a new vulnerability in the one who loves" (27).

From the three ways in which the falsity of love is exposed, Vanstone determines three characteristics of authentic love as "limitless, as precarious and as vulnerable." (28) Vanstone then reflects upon the love of God in the light of this description of authentic love. The activity of God in creation is limitless creativity. There is no interior limit to its own self-giving. There are no "unexpended reserves of divine power or potentiality" (29). The universe is the totality of being for which God gives Himself in love. It is therefore seriously misleading when popular devotion speaks of this power of God "as an immeasurable reserve which is held back from, not imparted to the totality of the creation ... The imagery of popular devotion suggests a divine supremacy over the universe ... and tends to reduce religion to the prudent recognition of divine supremacy". (30)

The activity of God in creation is also precarious. Creation's shape therefore, is not predetermined, nor its triumph foreknown. Every step contains the potential for tragedy and the existence of evil is the consequence of the precariousness of the divine creativity. "Evil is the moment of control jeopardised and lost; and the redemption of evil is inseparable from the process of creation." (31) Taking the death of the children who died at Aberfan as an example, Vanstone rejects the view that God willed their deaths as a means to some greater good, "we believe that, at the moment when the mountain of Aberfan slipped, 'something went wrong'; the step of creative risk was the step of disaster"(32) but faith believes God does not rest until the evil is redeemed. Vanstone rejects popular ideas of God's foreknowledge. "If the purpose of God in creation is foreknown and foreordained to fulfilment, then the creation itself is vanity. Within it nothing decisive happens and nothing new, it is merely the unwinding and display of a film already made. On the other hand to interpret the creation as the work of love is to interpret it as the new, as the coming-to-be of the hitherto unknown." (33)

Thirdly, the activity of God in creation must be vulnerable. This means that the issue of his love or tragedy or triumph depends upon His creation. Referring to Trinitarian theology, Vanstone makes clear that God's love for creation is not born of emptiness. God is complete in Himself; but love's self-giving or 'Kenosis' means that for being of the universe, the being of God is totally expended. "We may say that Christ the Incarnate Lord, discloses to us, at the climax of this life, that word it was that God spoke when 'He commanded and they were created'. It was no light or idle word but the Lord of love,in which for the sake of an other, all is expended, all jeopardised and all surrendered. The Cross of Christ discloses to us the poignancy of the creation itself - the tragic possibility that, when all is given in love, all may be given in vain." (34)

"The conventional representation of God", Vanstone summarises his argument, "is of one by whom, in the creation, nothing is expended and nothing jeopardised. Who presides serene over the assured unfolding of a predetermined purpose, whose triumph is assured before the activity begins, and who, in the appearance of giving, is ever maintaining, intact and unimpaired, His own supremacy. We see in this representation more of benevolence, of condescension, of manipulation and even of possessiveness than of authentic love." (35) God genuinely does not known the outcome of the creative process. He waits upon the response of his creation. He has no reserve powers - only in unfailing self-giving love he ever seeks to redeem the tragic." Where the issue is tragedy there remains only the unbelievable power of art or love to discover within itself through the challenge of the tragic, the power which was not there before - the power of yet further endeavour to win back and redeem that which was going astray. Where the issue is triumph, there remains only the will of love to surrender triumphant self-sufficiency in yet larger, more distant, more generous endeavour." (36) Vanstone therefore recognises the real freedom of the created universe where total freedom is the necessary consequence of God's love. The issue may be tragedy as well as triumph. God's only power is that of self-giving authentic love. This cannot prevent the horrors of history whether caused by natural disaster or human cruelty. Yet it ever seeks to redeem and to restore. Of the Aberfan disaster, Vanstone writes, "our faith is in a creator who does not abandon even this, nor those who suffered, wept and died in it, but He so gives Himself that He finds, for the redeeming of this, yet more to give, and knows no respite until the slag-heap has become a fair hillside, and the hearts of the parents have been enlarged by sorrow, and the children themselves understand and are glad to have so feared and wept and died." (37) Vanstone certainly does not minimise the reality of evil, but it is difficult to accept the reality of his hope. The fact of real evil does not invalidate the meaning of love, but the hurt cannot be done away and love carries an abiding scar, just as the Risen Christ bears the imprint of the nails.

Hans Jonas

It is interesting to compare Vanstone's writing with a lecture by Professor Hans Jonas on 'The Concept of God After Auschwitz'. He begins with a myth (38) "In the beginning for unknowable reasons, the ground of being, or the divine, chose to give itself over to the chance and risk and endless variety of becoming. And wholly so: entering into the adventure of space and time, the deity held back nothing of itself: no uncommitted or unimpaired part remained to direct, correct, and ultimately guarantee the devious working-out of its destiny in creation. On this unconditional immanence the modern temper insists. It is its courage or despair, in any case its bitter honesty, to take our being-in-the-world seriously: to view the world as left to itself, its laws as brooking no interference, and the rigour of our belonging to it as not softened by extramundane providence, The same our myth postulates for God's being in the world .... In order that the world might be, and be for itself, God renounced His own being, divesting Himself of His deity - to receive it back from the Odyssey of time weighted with the chance harvest of unforeseeable temporal experience: transfigured or possibly even disfigured by it. In such self-forfeiture of divine integrity for the sake of un-prejudiced becoming, no other foreknowledge can be admitted than that of possibilities which cosmic being offers in its own terms: to these, God committed His cause in effacing Himself for the world." He elaborates the myth by describing the emergence of life, which leads eventually to the appearance of man. "The advent of man means the advent of knowledge and freedom and with this supremely double-edged gift the innocence of the mere subject of self-fulfilling life has given way to the charge of responsibility under the disjunction of good and evil. To the promise and risk of this agency the divine cause, revealed at last henceforth finds itself committed: and its issue trembles in the balance. The image of God ... passes ... into man's precarious trust,to be completed, saved, or spoiled by what he will do to himself and the world." (39)

From the myth that he sketches, Hans Jonas tries to draw out a theological or conceptual translation. He speaks, he says, of a "suffering God". He distinguises this from the Christian conception by which he understands that the deity at one particular time entered into a situation of suffering. Rather he speaks of suffering on the part of God from the moment of creation, and certainly from the creation of man.

His myth speaks also of a becoming God. God is affected and made different by what happens in the world. "The Eternal progressively becomes different through the actualisation of the world process." (40)

Thirdly God is a caring God - "not remote and detached and self-contained but involved with what He cares for ... He has left something for other agents to do and thereby made His care dependent upon them. He is therefore also an endangered God, a God who risks something (41) "This", Hans Jonas continues, "is not an omnipotent God ... we cannot uphold the time-honoured (medieval) doctrine of absolute unlimited divine power" (42)

Hans Jonas rejects the concept of omnipotent power partly on logical and ontological grounds, but mainly on theological - as open to genuine religious objection. "We can have divine omnipotence together with divine goodness only at the price of complete divine inscrutability. Seeing the existence of evil in the world, we must sacrifice intelligibility in God to the combination of the other two attributes. Only a completely unintelligible God can be said to be absolutely good and absolutely powerful, and yet tolerate the world as it is. Now which of the three attributes at stake, the conjunction of any two of which excludes the third, are truly integral to our concept of God, and which, being of lesser force, must give way to their superior claim? Surely, goodness is inalienable from the concept of God and not open to qualification. Intelligibility, related to both God's nature and man's limitation, is on the latter count indeed subject to qualification, but on no account to complete elimination. The Deus absconditus, the hidden God, is a profoundly un-Jewish conception. Our teaching holds that we can understand God, not completely, to be sure, but something of Him - of His will, intentions, and even nature, because He has told us. There has been revelation, we have His commandments and His law, and He has directly communicated with some. Thus, a completely hidden God is not an acceptable concept by Jewish norms. But he would have to be precisely that if together with being good He were conceived as all-powerful. After Auschwitz, we can assert with greater force than ever before that an omnipotent deity would have to be either not good or totally unintelligible. But if God is to be intelligible in some manner and to some extent (and to this we must hold), then His goodness must be compatible with the existence of evil, and this it is only if He is not all-powerful. Only then can we uphold that He is intelligible and good, and there is yet evil in the world. And since we have found the concept of omnipotence to be doubtful anyway, it is this which has togive way." (43)

Hans Jonas goes further picturing God as divesting Himself of any power to interfere with the physical course of things and He responds to the impact on His being of worldly events - not beyad chazakah uzeroah netuyah, but with the mutely insistent appeal of His unfulfilled aim. Hans Jonas does not elaborate his ideas, but believes that creation from nothing holds together the oneness of the divine principle with the self-limitation which permits the existence and autonomy of the world. His myth, he says, pushes further the old Jewish idea of tzimtzum, the contraction of divine being, as the condition for the being of the world.

He draws certain ethical conclusions from his myth and its explanation. "The first is the transcendent importance of our deeds, of how we live our lives. If man, as our tale has it, was created "for" the image of God, rather than "in" His image, if our lives become lives in the divine countenance - then our responsibility is not defined in mundane terms alone ... Our impact on eternity is for good and for evil." (44) Secondly, "Having given Himself whole to the becoming world, God has no more to give, it is man's now to give to Him" (45)

Finally, Hans Jonas speaks of the gassed and burnt children of Auschwitz and the de-faced, de-humanised phantoms of the camp. "Another chance is not given them and eternity has no compensation for what has been missed in time ... I like to believe that there was weeping in the heights at the waste and despoilment of humanity ... Should we not believe that the immense chorus of such cries that has risen up in our lifetime now hangs over our world as a dark, powerful and accusing cloud? That eternity looks down upon us with a frown, wounded itself and peturbed in its depth? And might we not even feel it? ... But even if not their shadow, certainly the shadow of the Bomb is there to remind us that the image of God is in danger as never before ... We literally hold in our faltering hands the future of the divine adventure and must not fail Him, even if we would fail ourselves." (46)

Choan Seng Song

The Asian Christian Dr. Choan Seng Song recognises also the weight of responsibility that rests on us.

The suffering of the innocent may, God willing, move subsequent generations to repentance and reform, but this possible good does not mitigate the horror of the evil. Choan Seng Song, describes vividly the sufferings of the Vietnamese people especially the refugee Boat People. (47)

"The immense suffering of the peoples in Indochina is in fact the crisis of humanity - not just the part of humanity living in south east Asia, but the whole of humanity inhabiting the earth. The destruction of human lives in Indochina is the destruction of human lives in the other parts of the world. The contempt for human values in south east Asia amounts to contempt for human values in the rest of the world.

This destruction and this contempt have stretched the fragile moral fabric of humanity to a breaking point. When that breaking point is reached and the moral texture of humanity is torn to pieces, any vestige of humanity will disappear. All of humankind will find itself at the mercy of its own insatiable greed, bestial power, and uncontrollable insanity. The boat people are humanity on trial. The Cambodian holocaust is humankind before the judgement seat of the cosmic moral order.

But if humanity has been frantically working toward its own destruction, God seems also working frantically toward redeeming that humanity. In the refugees' faces distorted with agony, someone must have perceived the fact of God distorted with pain. In the disfigured bodies of the children fallen victim to hunger and bullets, someone must have seen God disfigured with horror. And in this whole senseless suffering of the Indochinese peoples, someone must have realised the meaning of God's suffering on the cross."

Choan Seng Song is perhaps rather optimistic in the evidence he cites that humankind is responding to the appeal of God in the Indochinese people. I agree that their appeal is an appeal to the conscience of the nations and that the only hope for the future is for that appeal to be heeded - but this must not appear to mitigate the evil of their sufferings. Perhaps we also have to commit ourselves to the way of suffering love because we believe it to be right without the assurance that it might be triumphant. Faith is as much a risk as the risk God took in creation.

Conclusion

Belief in a God of love cannot make sense of the horrors of the Holocaust. We live with the awareness of evil for which there is no compensation. Pictures of God which attribute to Him power which he did not use are morally unacceptable. We have to let go traditional concepts of omnipotence and impassibility and see that the suffering God speaks only through self-giving love ever appealing to us to make such love our own. Faith is the confidence that such love can not in the end be defeated and the commitment to make such self-giving love one's own. There can be no certainty that it will triumph. For faith is always risky, as risky as the creative process to which God unreservedly commits himself.

NOTES

1. Metz Johann-Baptist. Faith in History and Society: Toward a Practical Fundamental Theology New York 1980
2. Wiesel E. Night. New York, Hill and Wang 1960 pp 43-4, quoted in Auschwitz: Beginning of A New Era? Ed Fleischner, Eva. New York. 1977. Ktav.
3. Rubenstein, Richard. After Auschwitz. Indianapolis Bobbs-Merrill, 1968. pp 128-9, quoted Auschwitz op cit.
4. Ibid pp 153-4, quoted in Approaches to Auschwitz. Rubenstein and Roth. London SCM 1987.
5. Rubenstein Richard. Morality and Eros New York, McGraw-Hill 1970 pp 185-6, quoted in Approaches to Auschwitz op cit p 315.
6. Van Buren Paul Discerning the Way New York Seabury 1980 p 119.
7. Temple William Christus Veritas. London 1924 p.270
8. Moltmann Jurgen The Experiment Hope Philadelphia, Fortress Press 1975.
9. Temple op cit.
10. Dinsmore C.A. Atonement in Literature and Life pp 229-23. Cp Baillie Donald God was in Christ London Faber 1961 p.193.
12. Storr Vernon The Problem of the Cross London 1919. p 124. Quoted by Mozley J.K. The Impassability of God. Cambridge 1926 University Press p.153.
13. Studdert-Kennedy G The Unutterable Beauty London 1927 Hodder and Stoughton p 35 - 37 Cp House Francis in Theology LXXXIII Nov 1980 p 409.
14. Studdert-Kennedy G The Hardest Part p.99 quoted by Mozley op cit p 159.
15. Ibid p.10.
16. Ibid p.26
17. Ibid p.41-4
18. Rolt C.E. The World's Redemption 1913 p.127 Quoted by Mozley op cit pp.154-6
19. Ibid p 185
20. Ibid p.228
21. Vanstone W.H. Love's Endeavour, Love's Expense. London 1977. Darton Longman and Todd p.45.
22. Ibid
23. Ibid p.46
24. Ibid p.47
25. Ibid p.48
26. Ibid p.51
27. Ibid p.52
28. Ibid p.53
29. Ibid p.59
30. Ibid p.61
31. Ibid p.63
32. Ibid p.63
33. Ibid p.66
34. Ibid p.70
35. Ibid p.74
36. Ibid p.75
37. Ibid p.65
38. Jonas Hans The Concept of God After Auschwitz. pp 465-6. Reprinted from the Harvard Theological Review Vol 55 (1962) pp 1 - 20 in Out of the Whirlwind Ed Friedlander Albert, New York 1976 Schochen Books p 465-476. Also included in Jonas Hans The Phenomenon of Life: Toward a Philosophical Biology New York 1966 Harper and Row.
39. Ibid p.467
40. Ibid p.469
41. Ibid p.470
42. Ibid p.470
43. Ibid p.471
44. Ibid p.474
45. Ibid p.474
46. Ibid p.475
47. Choan-Sen Song The Compassionate God London 1982 p.249

THE BROKEN MIRROR: CHRISTIAN THEOLOGY AFTER THE HOLOCAUST

Dr. GAVIN D'COSTA

West London Institute of Higher Education,
Borough Road, Isleworth, Middlesex TW7 5DU,
United Kingdom.

INTRODUCTION

Kristallnacht, the "night of broken glass", like a shattered mirror reflects many views. Foremost is the night, the darkness that engulfed world Jewry; the night of which Elie Wiesel speaks of in his book of that name. (Wiesel 1981). It is a darkness in which even the word tragedy seems too feeble. "The year 1938 marks the high point of the Jewish ordeal prior to the extermination program." (Flannery 1985, 214). Another shard of broken glass reflects light; the light of the flames that engulfed six hundred synagogues reducing to ashes the Torah scrolls and the religious heritage upon which the western world was built. It is a light by which to see the darkness, by which to see, in the Nazi's words, a night of "popular demonstrations". On that day Dr Arthur Flehinger was ordered to read passages from Mein Kampf to his fellow Jews in Baden-Baden; a book which contains Hitler's cynical comment: "I believe that I am today acting in accordance with the will of the Almighty Creator: by defending myself against the Jew I am fighting for the work of the Lord." (Hitler 1974, 60). Flehinger read from this book while being repeatedly hit in the neck. He continues: "Those who had to read other passages after me were treated in the same manner. After these 'readings' there was a pause. Those Jews who wanted to relieve themselves were forced to do so against the synagogue walls, not in the toilets, and they were physically abused while doing so." (in Gilbert 1986, 71).

Nearly four hundred years prior to this incident, the great Christian reformer, Martin Luther had written of the Jews: "First, their synagogues should be set on fire, and whatever does not burn up should be covered or spread over with dirt so that no one may ever be able to see a cinder or stone of it." (Luther 1543). A little more than a thousand years before Luther, a canonized doctor of the Church, St. John Chrysostom, had written in his Homilies Against the Jews: "Flee, then, their assemblies, flee their houses, and far from venerating the Synagogue because of the books it contains hold it in hatred and aversion." (Chrysostom, 1:5).

The fragmented glass is also a shattered mirror by which Christianity must view itself after the Holocaust. The quotations above, accompanied by a fluctuating history of violent anti-Judaism and a near constant history of theological anti-Judaism rightly imply that the reflections from the shattered mirror reach far back into the past - during and before the Holocaust. In short, the Christian tradition of anti-Judaism cannot be absolved from partial responsibility for Kristallnacht and what followed. The night of broken glass is also a night in Christian history, a night in which the ashes of Torah scrolls are also the ashes of the holy books of Christianity. Freud was not without insight in writing that "in its depths anti-Judaism is anti-Christianity." (Freud 1955, 116-17).

The conference announcement correctly states that "The past has not been adequately confronted, the real problems have not been adequately faced. Christianity may not yet have fully recognized its role in the creation of a climate of opinion that made the Holocaust possible." It continues, "The lessons of the Holocaust must be used to emphasise the need to understand and respect all faiths and all people." It is perhaps still too early to draw lessons from that history - but in what follows I wish to reflect on that history primarily as a Christian theologian and as a member of the Roman Catholic communion - truly a communion of saints and sinners!

CHRISTIAN THEOLOGICAL REFLECTION AFTER THE HOLOCAUST

An all too small group of Christian (and Jewish) scholars have begun to investigate many areas of Christian theology and history related to anti-Judaism. These explorations have excavated the possible anti-Judaism in the New Testament itself (Baum 1965; Maccoby 1986), and in pre-Christian culture (Gager 1983). This has been accompanied by an examination of the Adversus Judaeo tradition in the early period of Church history (Isaac 1964; Williams 1935; Simon 1986), up to the present day (Flannery 1985). New Testament theology in this century and the last, has been critically reviewed for its assessment of Judaism and the Jewish people (Klein 1978; Sanders 1977), as has the doctrinal and liturgical aspects of contemporary theology (Pawlikowski 1982). There have also been numerous studies of the church's involvement with Nazi Germany during the war (eds. Littell & Locke 1974) and ecclesiastical documents after the war (ed. Croner 1977, 1985). All of this research has not resulted in consensus on fine details of the overall landscape, but concurs on the acknowledgement of varying degrees of anti-Judaism throughout Christian history. Sadly this is still not a commonly accepted fact among Christians - and one hopes that this conference will help redress this balance.

I do not wish to offer a survey of the various debates and topics. This task has been well executed by Pawlikowski (1980, 1982) and others. In this paper I wish to concentrate on one detail of this landscape: the claim that "Jesus is the Messiah" and its implications for Christian attitudes towards Judaism. Some theologians isolate this issue as central in understanding Christian anti-Judaism.

CHRISTIAN ANTI-JUDAISM AND THE MESSIAH

The problem can be summarised as follows: for nearly two thousand years Christianity has defined itself as the fulfilment of Judaism. The "new covenant" and "new Israel" were formed with the coming of the Messiah Jesus, and the Church that he established. Israel's history reached its fulfilment in these messianic events. Judaism should have flowered into Christianity - but (and here there are some variations) through ignorance or hard-heartedness the Jews rejected their true destiny. Hence, for most of Christian history Judaism has been seen as an anachronism. Some argue that this theology of fulfilment led to the theological extinction of Judaism and the subsequent attempts at historically liquidating the Jews was an inevitable corollary. (Ruether 1974).

Some theologians have therefore argued for what is called a "dual covenant" position. Christianity should view the Jewish and Christian traditions as two distinct yet complementary covenants. Jews, in remaining Jews rather than becoming Christians, are being faithful to their covenant with God - the same God who forged a further complementary covenant into which the gentiles were grafted. Neither negates the other. The fulfilment model should be abandoned as should mission towards the Jewish people. Both are anachronistic and theologically unjustified. (Ruether 1974; Parkes 1960; Rylaarsdam 1972). Some theologians extend the principles of this particular case to the world religions. Colonialist imperialism bears analogy to the anti-Judiasm fostered by theological supersessionism. Blindness to the many revelations in the world religions bears analogy to the theological obliteration of post Second Temple Judaism. (Ruether 1974; Baum 1977).

If the dual covenanters are correct, one must indeed review Christianity's attitude to Judaism (and its attitude to the world religions). In the light of the Holocaust this is an unavoidable task. I will examine some of the arguments concerning the claim of Jesus as Messiah and its relation to fulfilment theology and supersessionism. In what follows I shall try to begin to sketch an alternative to the dual covenanters.

JESUS AS MESSIAH AND FULFILMENT THEOLOGY

Christian supersessionism is rooted in its messianic claim. A number of theologian argue that Jesus cannot be proclaimed as the Jewish Messiah for a number of reasons. First, the messianic claim implicitly negates Judaism after the period of the formation of the Church and leads to a destructive fulfilment theology. Such a theology implies the theological negation of Judaism and eventually (and possibly inevitably) the historical liquidation of

Jewry. This argument has a theological and socio-political aspect to it. The theological negation of Judaism entails the denial of God's covenant and therefore fidelity with and to his people. This is un-Christian as it contradicts the fidelity of God affirmed in Christianity. (Mussner 1984, 16-34). Furthermore, if this fulfilment model is intrinsically related to the socio-political negation of the Jews, it is clearly unacceptable as it amounts to genocide! (Ruether 1974, 214-15).

The upshot of this is that mission is now inappropriate to the Jewish people. Some theologians further argue that Christian attitudes to Judaism should catalystically reorient Christianity's attitude to other religions, so that the Christian "message of hope does not imply that people are called to become Christians out of the great world religions. The church's claim to be the unique source of saving truth is a judgement on the systems of the world, not on the great world religions." (Baum 1977, 113). This is distinguished from those who argue that while there is no legitimate place for mission to the Jews, mission is valid to the other world religions as these religions are not analogous to Judaism. (Kung 1981, 132-50).

A second and related argument is that Jesus is not the Jewish Messiah because he has clearly not inaugurated the reign of God - as is expected of the Jewish Messiah. Hence: "For Judaism, Jesus cannot have been the Messiah, because the times remain unredeemed and neither he nor anything that came from him has yet altered that fact. In short, Judaism, in rejecting Jesus' messianic status, is simply reaffirming the integrity of its own tradition about what the word Messiah means." (Ruether 1974, 245; Lapide in Lapide & Luz 1979, 51-3). If this is the case, Christians can dismantle the claim that has been primarily responsible for supersessionism: "Jesus is the Messiah."

A third and related argument is that there are biblical grounds for suggesting that Jesus did not in fact claim to be the Messiah and it is only in later Hellenistic Christianity that the title became popular. Why did this happen? "Retaining the Messianic idea is chiefly due, it seems, to its psychological and polemic value in the Jewish-Christian debate. (Vermes 1983, 155). It was a deep embarrassment to the early Christians in their mission to the gentiles that their gospel, rooted in the life and teaching of their Galilean master, had failed to move the Jewish people en bloc. "Their obstinacy in rejecting the Messiah, the greatest of God's promises to Israel, was explained as the culmination of age-old wickedness and as the principle reason for the irrevocable transference of their privileges to the Gentiles." (Vermes 1983, 155).

Some theologians are not willing to embark on such a large scale revisionist exercise, but defer to the weight of tradition and argue that the title be kept but understood as signifying the Church's Messiah and not the Jewish Messiah. (Van Buren 1983, 350ff).

While I share the concerns of the writers above, and agree with them on certain points, I want to question their overall thesis which I have sketched above. I want to question it while still affirming the conference's aims: that "Christianity may not yet have fully recognized its role in the creation of a climate of opinion that made the Holocaust possible" and to this end, Christianity requires to explore the extent of anti-Judaism within itself. I also wish to affirm that: "The lessons of the Holocaust must be used to emphasise the need to understand and respect all faiths and all people." In keeping with this latter aim, I have also tried to relate the thesis above not only to the Jewish people, but with reference to its implications for people of "all faiths".

THEOLOGICAL AND SOCIO-HISTORICAL LIQUIDATION

If the theological notion of fulfilment leads to the socio-political negation of Judaism, then one must abandon such a theological position without qualification. The Holocaust must never be repeated. However, I think it is problematic to show an intrinsic link between theological fulfilment and socio-historical liquidation. My contention is not meant to deny that there is, and should be, justified Christian guilt about the Holocaust. Christian complicity and responsibility for anti-Judaism throughout history is undeniable. No theological or historical argument can eradicate this fact - or should try to. My point is a logical one. In the light of Christian anti-Judaism, has Christianity the resources to make universal theological claims about its normativity while preserving the integrity and rights to exist of those from other religions - and especially Judaism? In the light of Christian history, one must also ask, if we do find such resources for positive affirmation, do these resources also impose the duty of socially and politically implementing such affirmations. Pope Paul VI addressed this problem: "How can we reconcile the respect of persons and civilizations and sincere dialogue with them...with the universalism of the mission Christ entrusted to the Church?" (Pope Paul VI 1974).

One may tentatively point towards a reconciliation of this tension between universal claims and the integrity and rights to exist of those from other religions. Among the Second Vatican Council documents, so important in defining modern Roman Catholicism, is the Declaration on Religious Liberty (1965). This document is important for a number of reasons. It stands alongside the Decree on the Church's Missionary Activity (1965) which affirms the universal mission of the Church. Based on Christian revelation, the document on religious liberty affirms "that the human person has a right to religious freedom" so "that all men should be immune from coercion on the part of individuals, social groups and every human power, so that, within due limits, nobody is forced to act against his convictions in religious matters". Significantly, it continues: "The Council further declares that the right to religious freedom is based on the very dignity of the human person as known through the revealed word of God and by reason itself." (para 2). From this it follows that any form of mission that violates the rights of an individual or community (para 4) to practice their own religion is against the teachings of the gospel. It also follows that any social or political attempt to limit and curtail the freedom to practice one's religion, within due limits, is against the gospel. To the extent that Zionism is related to the freedom of the practice of the Jewish religion, then Christians should support these aims. In general, Christians are bound to strive to maintain the freedoms and rights of all religious communities and its own history regarding this matter must be judged by these teachings. The document (too timidly) acknowledges that Christians throughout history have fallen short of this requirement (para 12).

Regarding Judaism specifically, these statements should also be read in conjunction with those in the Declaration on the Relation of the Church to Non-Christian Religions (1965) where there is a solemn condemnation of "all hatred, persecutions and displays of antisemitism leveled at any time or from any source against the Jews." (para 4). It should also be noted in the context of this conference that this Declaration on the world religions was in its genesis a document on the Church's relationship to the Jewish people! The story of its metamorphosis into the document on the world religions, treating Judaism in the fourth section only, has been recounted elsewhere (Oesterreicher 1986, 103-298). It is one of the tragic ironies of Christian history that the beneficial aspects of this transformation away from a document solely on the Jewish people resulted in a momentous document in the history of the Church. In Cardinal Bea's words: "About these (world religions) it is, as far as I know, the first time in the history of the Church that a Council has laid down principles in such a solemn way." (in Cyriac 1982, 111 - my emphasis). The tragic irony is that the cost of such a document lay in the lack of focus on the depths of anti-Judaism within Christian history.

Regarding the Vatican documents, my logical point is this: Christianity has within its theological resources the ability to affirm the fundamental rights for the existence and practice of Judaism (or any other religion), while at the same time affirming its universal mission and normative claims. The thesis that theological fulfilment is intrinsically related to socio-historical negation is theologically unjustified. Historically there are many complex factors relevant to the way in which the principle of religious freedom has been subordinated to other concerns. Regarding the Jewish people, Christian anti-Judaism has been highly significant, but is also nuanced in its historical causality. (Yerushamli 1977, 96-106).

However, regarding mission to the Jewish people in the light of the Vatican documents examined above, I would like to develop a further point which is not explored in the Conciliar documents. Rabbi Abraham Heschel reminds us how history, and especially the Holocaust history, shapes Jewish perception of Christian mission: "to the Jews such an attempt to 'convert him' appears as an attack on the very existence of the Jews, a call to self-extinction." (in Da Silva 1985, 113). As long as such perceptions validly exist, it would be crass insensitivity to proselytise among the Jewish people. This is not a pragmatic restraint on mission, but one founded on theological grounds. If mission, even unintentionally, violates the "psychological freedom" of an individual and suggest "external coercion" then theologically it is unjustified. (Vatican II, Declaration on Religious Liberty para 2). All Jews may not agree with Heschel's perception but as long as there is even one voice of protest, Christians in the light of the Holocaust must seriously reconsider the appropriateness of mission to the Jews. I shall return to this point below.

But what of the argument that a supersessionist position negates the fidelity of God's covenant with the Jews and the Christian understanding of God requires and ensures such fidelity? First, there is no ambiguity in mainstream Christianity about the valid covenant made with Israel. The 'Old' Testament's inclusion in the Christian bible testifies to God's saving and revelatory covenant with the Jewish people. Second, if God develops and seals this covenant through Jesus then it does not necessarily follow that those who remain Jews after this time have actually rejected the development of the covenant in Jesus and his Church. This can be posited on historical and theological grounds. During Jesus' time and the subsequent few centuries there were many Jews who would have never heard of the sect of the Nazarenes or their preaching. It is absurd to say that for these Jewish people, their commitment to the covenant was wanting or dishonest. They rightly believed that they were keeping faithful to a valid covenant relationship.

Employing a distinction between the historical and existential confrontation of the gospel we can pursue the matter further. By historical I mean the explicit social and historical encounter with the preaching of the gospel - which many have never experienced: eg. the group outlined above. By existential I mean the inner and personal confrontation with the gospel which should accompany the successful historical preaching but is not necessarily concomitant. For instance, could the Jews of Germany in 1938 have been existentially confronted with the gospel? Historically, there is no doubt that many would have heard about the Christian message, but given the circumstances, it is highly questionable whether the gospel would have been heard existentially. I do not want to multiply such examples and every case must be considered in its socio-political, psychological and existential complexity. My point is that for a number of legitimate reasons it cannot always be assumed that when the gospel is preached the person is truly and existentially confronted by the truth proclaimed in Christ. (Congar 1961, 121-27).

It is clear that there were and are many Jews who have never been historically or/and existentially confronted with the Christian gospel and in this context, the continuing legitimacy of Judaism as a faithful covenanting relationship with God cannot be denied or minimized.

This is especially significant as Christians must consider themselves to be confronted in Judaism by a religious tradition which fosters and cherishes the roots of its own valid covenant with God. In this respect, Christians have much to learn about the ways of God through their Jewish partners. They do not confront a purely "man made" religion, but a tradition founded on a valid covenantal relationship. Hence, to this extent, the analogy of Judaism with the other world religions breaks down. Historically and theologically, Judaism has a unique relationship with Christianity. Such a relationship is recalled in the Vatican declaration on non-Christian religions in the following words: "The Church of Christ acknowledges that in God's plan of salvation the beginning of her faith and election is to be found in the patriachs, Moses and the prophets." It continues in the same paragraph: "On this account the Church cannot forget that she received the revelation of the Old Testament by way of that people with whom God in his inexpressible mercy established the ancient covenant." (para. 4). The world religions do not share this unique link, although this does not exclude them from the possibility of valid revelation.

Finally, the fulfilment view has often erroneously assumed a fait accompli regarding its professed fulfilment of Judaism. Fulfilment is seen as a task completed rather than historically enacted and thereby ongoing and incomplete. In an arrogant fashion for most of Christian history the Church has often assumed that it has everything to give and nothing to receive or to learn. If, as we have argued above, Judaism is to be viewed as a continuing relationship with God, then clearly Christians have much to learn about the ways of God from their Jewish partners. This learning process is part of Christianity's fulfilment. For instance, the value of the complementary and dialectical poles cited by Parkes and Rylaarsdam (1960 and 1972 respectively) lies in highlighting the way in which Christianity really has to fulfil itself in enacting and incorporating all such polarities within its own theological and pastoral life. (See Camps 1983; D'Costa 1986, 117-39). Only in this way can the Church be truly Catholic.

At this point it will be useful to refer to a sometimes controversial movement - the "Messianic Jews" and "Hebrew Christians" so as to explore some of the implications of the above remarks. These labels are loose umbrella terms for movements which claim to be the revival and continuation of an ancient and venerated movement - the first Jewish disciples of Jesus, many of whom were strict Torah faithful Jews! There is little documentation about such groups in the modern world but, as far as I am aware, there is considerable diversity among followers (Schonfield 1936; Jocz 1939; Juster 1986; Pruter 1987). The diversity ranges from Jewish followers of Jesus who regard Jesus as having abolished the Law, to those who appropriate and incorporate strict observance of the Law, and those who also accept the

Rabbinical authorities that developed after the fall of Jerusalem (64-70CE). There is also considerable diversity in attitudes to mainline Christian churches. This ranges from an intellectual and cultural alienation from an over-Hellenized Church where there is no wish to perputuate such Hellenization of Jewish messianic faith - to, a recognition of different charisms and ministries unique to messianic Jews compared to non-Jewish Christians which the groups themselves and some Churches wish to perpetuate and utilize (Lausanne 1980, 11). The significance of these remarks are not to endorse the sometimes questionable methods of proselytising or the political and financial support that some of these groups receive, but to highlight certain theological issues related to my remarks about fulfilment.

The first is that the Messianic Jews are a salutary reminder to Christians of the extent of their own dislocation and disjunction from their roots. Paul, in Romans, reminds a proud Hellenized church that they are a "wild olive shoot" depending for life on the "richness [or 'the rich root'] of the olive tree" (11:18-19). For Christians, the Holocaust in psychological terms is a terrible reminder of the effects of self-hatred and dislocation. Recovering the traditions and heritage which the Messianic Jews are so desirous of preserving is an important task in fulfilling the Church's catholicity. Not only can Christians deepen their own spirituality and practice by discovering their Jewish heritage, but in the process they can discover, respect, appreciate and learn from Jewish spirituality in the context of its appropriation through the channels of Rabbinical Judaism.

This has already begun to happen to a limited extent. For example, non-Jewish Christians who participate in the Passover meal have often found that they consequently have a deeper understanding of the "Lord's Supper" and have also been able to respect and learn from this profound Jewish practice. Another example, here drawing from the later Jewish tradition, is the attempt by Paul Levertoff to reflect on the doctrine of the Trinity in terms of the Zohar, the classical work of the Kabbalah. These exercises in indigenization are fraught with difficulties such as the dangers of a new type of religious imperialism, the suspicion of prosleytising by deception and the question of the limits of orthodoxy. It is argued that the strategy is: if one cannot convert the Jewish people then one can at least plunder their spiritual heritage. This is a new form of religious colonialism. Similarly, it is argued that if at first one cannot convert the Jewish person, then you dress up Christianity to look more like Judaism so that converts may be won. It is significant that these questions are generated in relation to indigenization in India, in regard to Hinduism and Indian Christians, and in Thailand and Sri Lanka, in regard to Buddhism and local Christians, because a similar principle is involved. Nevertheless, the tensions and controversy regarding these practices viz. Judaism have a unique and poignant aspect in the light of the Holocaust. However, similar developments in scholarship have been more quickly welcomed. The advances in scholarly research in understanding Christian origins through the study of first century Judaism, for example, have been enormous. (Flusser 1969; Sanders 1977; Rowlands 1985; Hilton & Marshall 1988). It is surely a legitimate hope that in exploring the riches of the roots of the olive tree, Christianity may be led to revalue its own shoots and branches, but also branches other that its own. That it may have taken the darkness of the Holocaust to cause many Christians to come to this recognition is a sad and regrettable fact. But these lessons have important wider ramifications in forcing Christians to review and incorporate the many spiritual practices (artistically, intellectually, pastorally, liturgically, etc.) in the world religions at large. It is again worth recalling that while the analogy of the olive tree and its roots cannot be uncritically applied to those outside the Judaeo-Christian tradition, there are other arguments related to the world religions which should cause us to rethink Christian attitudes. (D'Costa 1986; 1987).

While it is inevitable and necessary that most Roman Catholic Christians will utilize a Christocentric, Trinitarian and ecclesiocentric criteria for truth in the process of indigenization, it should be stressed that these are normative criteria rather than completed and closed criteria. They are open, as opposed to closed, to continuing depths of reflection and disclosure - as has been maintained in the notion of the development of doctrine (Newman 1906). And in this respect they are incomplete criteria as various facets are brought to light in the context of new and difficult challenges. The Holy Spirit will move wherever it wills and not be guided by any sectarian monopolising group. It is important to recognize that indigenization should be more of an imperative, as should dialogue, with the theological conviction that God is at work in Judaism - and, as I have argued elsewhere, that God is also at work in the world religions. (D'Costa 1986, 1987). Here there is a lesson to be learnt from the Noachide covenant, which Michael Rosenak of the Hebrew University has interpreted to extend to certain religions of the world (rather than to individuals alone). He concludes his study: "As such, the believing community knows that the whole truth is more than it experiences at any given moment, more even than what is in the circumference of its historical experience, even though God's whole truth for mankind is in the Torah, which is still to be learned, and, in the context of future knowledge and experience, still to be interpreted." (Rosenak 1987, 19). Rosenak has much in common with Newman!

The discussion immediately above has, I hope, demonstrated how a universal religion like Christianity can legitimate and maintain religious plurality without compromising its own beliefs. If this situation is established, I have also tried to show how the notion of fulfilment works both ways, so that Christians have every reason to enter into non-prosleytising dialogue with Jewish people. I have also tried to indicate the limited implications of these reflections upon Christian inter-religious dialogue in general. In conclusion, it cannot be stated that a fulfilment view negates the fidelity of God's covenant with the Jewish people. Rather it affirms it within certain parameters and does not exclude the notion of normativity of the revelation of God in Christ. Having tentatively suggested that there is not an intrinsic link between a (modified) view of fulfilment theology and theological and socio-historical anti-Judaism, I now wish to turn to a crucial supposition imputed as the cause of the danger in the fulfilment view - the messianic claim itself. Was Jesus the Messiah or not?

THE MESSIAH?

The term Messiah derives from the Hebrew noun Masiach meaning "anointed one" which relates to the Greek verb chrio meaning to "rub or put on". Christos , in the New Testament is used both as a surname (egs: Romans 5:6, 8; I Corinthians 1:12, 17; Hebrews 3:6/9:11) and as a functional titular description. There is considerable scholarly disagreement (not solely related to the context of Jewish-Christian relations) over: a) whether Jesus regarded himself as Messiah; b) in what manner the New Testament writers viewed Jesus as Messiah; and c) whether the answers to (a) and (b) result in a fulfilment view. It is interesting to note that Mussner positively answers (a) and has a high view regarding (b) while rejecting a fulfilment view! (Mussner 1984). The issues are indeed complex.

Furthermore, there is the supplementary argument that a rejection of Jesus as Messiah was and is perfectly legitimate on Jewish grounds for God's reign did not accompany Jesus and has not accompanied his followers - evil, suffering and injustice still prevail. There has been much recent research on Jewish messianic expectations. The fruits of that research indicate a single point of agreement - that there was no singly agreed notion of the Messiah prevailing in Jesus' time. (Scholem 1971; Rowlands 1985; Mowinckel 1956, others). Contrary to Ruether, there was no period of Judaism in which there was an "integrity of its own tradition about what the word Messiah" meant - and consequently, there can be no easy dismissal of a possibly genuine messianic claim. It is important to counter simplistic reductions of a complex issue. In what follows I can only suggest some possible paths for further exploration.

I would follow Mussner and others in arguing that Jesus regarded himself in messianic terms, while being well aware of nationalist and political messianic expectations of which he had no view to fulfil. (See for example: John 6:14-16/ 18:36-38; Acts 1:8ff; 1 Peter 2:13). (See also Moule 1977, 31-5; Dunn 1977, 41-5; Manson 1961; Cullman 1963, 111-36). There is a strong exegetical tradition which interprets the Messiah in terms of the servant songs of Isaiah. Such a reading would concede a certain polemical utilization of the term Messiah in the writers of the New Testament (as is argued by Vermes), but can clearly not restrict all such usage to this function alone. Such a reading can also allow for the fact that in Hellenized hands the Jewish servant figure recedes into the background - and as in the case of certain Hellenized Pauline communities it seems to signify a surname without any functional significance. That this latter point is the case, may support the view of the importance of this term for the earliest Jewish Christians, so much so that even as early as the time of Paul, it had evolved into something of a titular surname.

Scholem is also partly right in discerning an interiorization and individualization of the messianic idea in Christianity. However, through his social preaching and ministry, Jesus did proclaim the imminent reign of God (see for example: Mark 1:15/ 1:2-8; Luke 7:22 - and Kung 1981, B1, 1-2; Moltmann 1977, 133-96) and, through his resurrection and the pentecost events, Christians have properly come to view the beginnings of the eschatological reign - which is to be fulfilled and completed in the second coming. Where I agree with the dual covenanters (and perhaps this will justify my all too brief treatment of the issues above) is that the reign of God is not yet complete. Jesus' messianic ministry has been inaugurated, but is not yet fulfiled. Where I disagree, is in regard to the significance of this recognition. I would therefore wish to propose the following.

First, one cannot simply say that Jesus was not the awaited Jewish Messiah if there is a possibility that Jesus understood himself thus, but more importantly - his Jewish disciples used this term of him. Van Buren acknowledges a once legitimate messianic affirmation while the first followers of Jesus remained Jews. It is only when the Church became predominantly gentile that the Jewish character of the term was misused against the separated bretheren. (Van Buren 1983, 276-77). However, it is difficult to imagine that this Jewish sect who preached the Messiah's arrival were not already proclaiming a distinctive element - which caused them to be fervent missionaries among their own Jewish community. Proclaiming the Messiah was part of a complex and multi-faceted perception that in some way the longings of Israel had taken a decisive turn. (Moule 1977, 127-35).

Secondly, while Christians have every right to argue that their particular interpretation of the Messiah is definitive regarding this common history, they must nevertheless acknowledge the plurality of beliefs and expectations held by Jews in good faith concerning the Messiah. It is notable that Christian theologians who argue that Jesus did not make this claim are accepted without question within the Christian fold - without persecution or suspicion of bad faith. (The legitimacy of plurality within the Christian tradition is relevant in considering religious plurality in general). The Jewish scholar, Lapide remarks that "If the Messiah comes and then turns out to be Jesus of Nazareth, I would say that I do not know of any Jew in the world who would have anything against it." (Lapide & Kung 1977, 43). More candidly, Monachim Begin in commenting on the fundamentalist Christian support for Israel remarks: "That's fine, let them support us. When the Messiah comes, we can always ask him if he's been here before." (Begin 1987). In terms of demonstrating their interpretation, Christians can only point to the Church's messianic ministry and the awaited second coming. Upon this latter event Christians can only hope. There is no clear cut evidence.

Regarding the Church's messianic ministry, it is often difficult to identify the reign of God through the Church's life! And in the light of Christian particpation in the Holocaust, Christians require deep self-inspection and cleansing before they can have any confidence in pointing to the messianic minsitry entrusted to the Church. Hence, it is difficult to unambigiously maintain that Jewish people, past or present, have rejected their Messiah. Van Buren's suggestion that Christians proclaim the Church's Messiah rather than a Jewish Messiah cannot make theological sense. If Christianity's Jewish history and life source is to be acknowledged, any messianic claim must be particular (Jewish) and universal (gentile) - although, be it noted, not fully realized.

Thus, my third point is that Christianity's messianic claim should be understood in a self-critical fashion. Primarily it is a mirror for Christianity to critically purify itself so that is may truly take the messianic form and shape so determined by its founder. Historically it is guilty of constantly falling short of this goal. Rather than abandoning its messianic self-understanding, this very element may lead it out of its anti-Judaic history and into one of true service and solidarity with those who suffer, are oppressed and downtrodden. (Moltmann 1977).

Many will not agree with my reading of the biblical texts regarding the messianic claim and it is therefore important, in concluding this section, to partially divorce the messianic claim from fulfilment theology. Hence, even if my biblical interpretation is not accepted, the fulfilment view would not thereby be discredited. To some extent, those who focus on the Messiahship of Jesus as the cause of anti-Judaism are only partially correct. They are correct in so much as there is a historical and theological link with the usage of messianic claims and anti-Judaism. They are incorrect, so I have argued, in saying that this is inevitable or intrinsic. They are also incorrect in so much as fulfilment theology is not solely dependant on messianic claims. Nicaea and Chalcedon and the various doctrines concerning the divinity of Christ are also crucial in upholding and perpetuating a fulfilment theology. It is quite possible to argue that Jesus did not claim to be the Messiah and his disciples used the title in a purely polemic fashion and still argue, from the divinity of Jesus, that all religions (including Christianity) are both fulfiled and judged in the light of Jesus.

CONCLUSION

In this paper I have tried to suggest a tentative alternative to the dual covenant theologies. I have tried to suggest that Christianity, in the light of Kristallnacht and what followed, must re-examine and purge itself of its painful and shameful history of anti-Judaism. Only in doing so, can it rethink, restate or modify its central convictions.

Christian theology is impoverished and lacks credibility if it fails to consider the implications of the Holocaust, an event that rightly shattered its self-image. The night of broken glass also belongs to Christian history, while not wishing to detract from its seminal place in Jewish history.

I have suggested that Christians may still continue to proclaim that Jesus is Messiah and that the Christian community must fashion itself in the image of the suffering servant rather than imperialist victor. Furthermore, this claim cannot be used in a prosleytising polemic against the Jewish people who can be regarded as maintaining a genuine covenant relationship with God. In this respect Christians have much to learn from their Jewish brothers and sisters. This respectful listening and learning process does not inevitably lead to the denial of Christianity's universal relevance or mission, and I have tried to argue that Christianity has within its theological resources the ability to maintain its normativity while affirming and defending religious plurality. Furthermore, in the light of the Holocaust, Christian mission to the Jewish people must be questioned for good theological reasons - and not simply for pragmatic and diplomatic reasons.

The relationship of Christianity to Judaism is unique. However, these reflections while focused on Christianity's relationship to Judaism, also have far reaching implications for people from other faiths. It is indeed the case, and an important legacy of this conference, in stating the univeral (and not only unique) aspect of the significance of the Holocaust: "The lessons of the Holocaust must be used to emphasise the need to understand and respect all faiths and all people."

BIBLIOGRAPHY

Baum.G, Is the New Testament Anti-Semitic, Paulist Press, New York, 1965

Baum.G, "Rethinking the Church's Mission After Auschwitz", in ed. E.Fleischner 1977

Begin.M, The Times, April 7, 1987

Camps.A, Partners in Dialogue: Christianity and Other World Religions, Orbis Books, New York, 1983

Chrysostom. St.John, Homilies Against the Jews, (PG:48:843-942)

Congar.Y, The Wide World my Parish, Darton, Longmann & Todd, London, 1961

Croner.H ed., Stepping Stones to Further Jewish-Christian Relations, Paulist Press, New York, 1977

Croner.H ed., More Stepping Stones to Jewish-Christian Relations, Paulist Press, New York, 1985

Cullmann.O, The Christology of the New Testament, SCM, London, 1963

Cyriac.M, Meeting of Religions, Dialogue Series 3, Madras, 1982

Da Silva.A, Is There a New Imbalance in the Jewish-Christian Relationship?, Uppsala University, Uppsala, 1985

D'Costa.G, Theology and Religious Pluralism, Basil Blackwell, Oxford, 1986

D'Costa.G, John Hick's Theology of Religions. A Critical Evaluation, University Press of America, Lanham/London, 1987

Dunn.J, Unity and Diversity in the New Testament, SCM, London, 1977

Fleischner.E ed., Auschwitz: Beginning of a New Era?, KTAV, New York, 1977

Flannery.E, The Anguish of the Jews. Twenty Three Centuries of Antisemitism, Paulist Press, New York, 1985

Flusser.D, Jesus, Herder & Herder, New York, 1969

Freud.S, Moses and Monotheism, Vantage Books, New York, 1955

Gager.J, The Origins of Anti-Semitism. Attitudes towards Judaism in Pagan and Christian Antiquity, Oxford University Press, Oxford, 1983

Gilbert.M, The Holocaust. The Jewish Tragedy, Collins, London, 1986

Hitler.A, Mein Kampf, Hutchinson, London, 1974

Hilton.M & Marshall.G, The Gospel and Rabbinic Judaism, SCM, London, 1988 (forthcoming)

Isaac.J, The Teaching of Contempt, Holt, Rinehart & Winston, New York, 1964

Jocz.J, Jewish People and Jesus Christ, Baker Book House, Michigan, 1979

Juster.D, Jewish Roots. A Foundation of Biblical Theology for Messianic Judaism, DAVAR, Rockville, 1986

Klein.C, Anti-Judaism in Christian Theology, Fortress Press, Philadelphia, 1978

Kung.H, The Church, Search Press, 1981

Lapide.P & Kung.H, Brother or Lord? A Jew and Christian Talk about Jesus, Collins, London, 1977

Lapide.P & U.Luz, Jesus in Two Perspectives. A Jewish-Christian Dialog, Augsburg, Minneapolis, 1979

Lausanne Papers, Christian Witness to the Jewish People, Lausanne Committee for World Evangelization, Illinois, 1980

Littel.F & Locke.H eds., The German Church Struggle and the Holocaust, Wayne State University Press, Detroit, 1974

Luther.M, Von den Juden und ihren Lugen (On the Jews and their Lies), Wittenburg, 1543

Manson.T, The Servant Messiah, Cambridge University Press, Cambridge, 1961

Maccoby.H, The Mythmaker. Paul and the Invention of Christianity, Weidenfeld & Nicholson, London, 1986

Moltmann.J, The Church in the Power of the Spirit, SCM, London, 1977

Moule.C, The Origin of Christology, Cambridge University Press, Cambridge, 1977

Mowinckel.S, He That Cometh, Basil Blackwell, Oxford, 1956

Mussner.F, Tractate on the Jews, SPCK, London, 1984

Newman,J, An Essay on the Development of Christian Doctrine, Longman, Green & Co., London, 1906

Oesterreicher.J, The New Encounter Between Christians and Jews, Philosophical Library, New York, 1986

Parkes.J, The Theological Foundations of Judaism and Christianity, Vallentine-Mitchell, London, 1960

Pawlikowski.J, What are they Saying about Jewish-Christian Relations, Paulist Press, New York, 1980

Pawlikowski.J, Christ in the Light of the Christian-Jewish Dialogue, Paulist Press, New York, 1982

Pope Paul VI, "Discourse to the Synod of Bishops", Rome, September 19, 1974

Pruter.K, Jewish Christians in the United States. A Bibliography, Garland, New York, 1987

Rosenak.M, "The Religious Person and Religious Pluralism", in eds. Borckway.A & Halperin.J, The Meanings and Limits of Religious Pluralism, IJCIC/WCC, 1987

Rowlands.C, Christian Origins, SPCK, London, 1985

Ruether.R, Faith and Fratricide. The Theological Roots of Anti-Semitism, Seabury Press, New York, 1974

Rylaarsdam.J, "Jewish-Christian Relationship: The Two Covenants and the Dilemmas of Christology", Journal of Ecumenical Studies, 9, 1972, 249-70

Sanders.E, Paul and Palestinian Judaism, SCM, London, 1977

Scholem.G, The Messianic Idea in Judaism, George, Allen & Unwin, London, 1971

Schonfield.H, The History of Jewish Christianity, Duckworth, London, 1936

Simon.M, Versus Israel. A Study of the Relationship between Christians and Jews in the Roman Empire (135-425), Oxford University Press, Oxford, 1986

Van Buren.P, A Christian Theology of the People of Israel, Vol. 2, Seabury Press, New York, 1983

Vatican Documents: Flannery.A ed., The Conciliar and Post-Conciliar Documents, Fowler Wright, Leominster, 1975

Vermes.G, Jesus the Jew, SCM, London, 1983

Yerushalmi.Y, "Response to Ruether", in ed. E. Fleischner 1977

Wiesel.E, Night, Penguin, Harmondsworth, 1981

Williams.A, Adversus Judaeos: a Bird's Eye View of Christian Apologiae until the Renaissance, Cambridge University Press, Cambridge, 1935

NOTE

All diacritical marks have been omitted from the text.

THE PERSISTENCE OF <u>THEOLOGIA GLORIAE</u> IN MODERN ANTISEMITISM: VOLTAIRE, WAGNER, HITLER

ROBERT MICHAEL/PROFESSOR OF EUROPEAN HISTORY

HISTORY DEPARTMENT, SOUTHEASTERN MASSACHUSETTS UNIVERSITY
DARTMOUTH, MASSACHUSETTS 02790
U.S.A.

The essential First Cause of antisemitism is the distaste for, or hatred of, what has made Jews Jewish, i.e., Judaism.[1] In order for Christianity to establish its own sense of self, its legitimacy, its sanctity, it had to crush the theological dominence of Judaism.[2] As St. John Chrysostom had so eloquently put it, "Don't you realize, if the Jewish rites are holy and venerable, our way of life must be false."[3] Jews remained as "an indispensable reference group, enabling Christians to know themselves as Christians and to incarnate good by contrast with [Jewish] evil."[4] And so Jews, as Jews, had to be punished, preferably converted, oftentimes killed, for their loyalty to their own beliefs was seen as an "affront and a threat to the Christian image of itself."5 The Christian dilemma was that without Judaism, Christianity had no independent meaning. Judaism therefore had to be preserved, but as a corpse in suspended animation.

Christian theology—a powerful, pervasive[6] and anti-Jewish ideology—has dominated the perception of Jews in Christian nations for nearly 2,000 years.[7] The Churches' predominant, normative[8] theological position in regard to the Jews has been called <u>theologia gloriae</u>—an "inbred religious paranoia [that] has been a perversion of everything Jesus meant."[9] This antisemitic theology of glory generally holds that: l.The Christian Church, the new Israel—"ordained and sanctioned by God himself"—has triumphantly succeeded the cursed and rejected old Israel morally, historically, and metaphysically. 2.Jews denied the true Messiah, the Christ, and murdered him, for which all Jews are forever collectively guilty. 3.The Jews were paradigmatic evil-doers even before[10] their atrocious act of deicide. In the words of Hilary of Poitiers, Judaism was "ever . . . mighty in wickedness; . . . when it cursed Moses; when it hated God; when it vowed its sons to demons; when it killed the prophets, and finally when it betrayed to the Praetor and crucified our God Himself and Lord . . .. And so glorying through all its existence in iniquity . . .."[11] 4.Jews were not to be totally exterminated[12] since they adhered to the Law and gave Christianity the history that it needs to legitimize itself. They were "Witness People" who must live and suffer as examples of those who reject the truth of Christian faith.[13]

Christian theologians have turned the values of Judaism on their head (value-inversion) by means of a unique anti-Jewish Denkform. It attacked the traits most identified as Jewish (Covenant, monotheism, synagogue, kosher rules, circumcision, Chosenness, Promised Land, Jerusalem, Temple) by reinterpreting, modifying, and adopting them to fit the requirements of the Christian self-image. Through anti-Jewish theological myths and defamations, the Jews were pictured no longer as the Chosen, heros of holiness and moral living; they were instead "the earthly representatives of the power of Darkness."[14]

There was a minority position that required Christians to follow the moral teachings of Jesus "even" in regard to the Jews. Since those who held this position of theologia crucis[15] seldom if ever stated it in writing, we must assume their existence from the fact that theologians of glory continually complained about Christians who grew close to Jews or treated them as human beings rather than theological types, i.e., models for evil. Yet antagonism to the Jews has been nearly uniform among Christian theologians and prelates, with understandable impact on the faithful. How could Christians have learned to love the Jewish people when positive religious ideas about Jews "were lost in the blood of Calvary."[16] Among the Church Fathers, Gregory, the 4th-century Bishop of Nyssa, was typical. After comparing the Jews with Judas Iscariot, as did Jerome, he called them "Murderers of the Lord, killers of the prophets, enemies and slanderers of God; violators of the law, adversaries of grace, aliens to the faith of their fathers, advocates of the devil, progeny of poison snakes, . . . whose minds are held in darkness, filled with the anger of the Pharisees, a sanhedrin of satans. Criminals, degenerates, . . . enemies of all that is decent and beautiful. They are guilty of shouting: Away with him, away with him. Crucify him. He who was God in the flesh!"[17] In the same period, the greatest of the Church Fathers followed in lock step: Jerome created the identification of all Jews with the immoral use of money and with Judas Iscariot, and Augustine identified Jews with Cain.[18] In a stunning passage, John Chrysostom went so far as to assert that because Jews rejected Christ, they therefore deserved to be murdered. Like other obstinate animals, he stated, the Jews "are fit for killing. And this is what happened to the Jews: while they were making themselves unfit for work, they grew fit for slaughter."[19]

Chrysostom, like Isidore of Seville,[20] even approached racialist thinking.[21] Chrysostom argued that the crimes and sins of all earlier Jews were also those of contemporary Jews; he doubted that they could ever be authentically converted. Augustine had approached this kind of thinking as well, when he argued that no Jew could ever lose the stigma of his forebears' having rejected and murdered Christ.[22] The evil of the Jews, he wrote, "in their parents, led to death."[23] In the Middle Ages, the most important Catholic theologian, Thomas Aquinas,[24] had also come close to racism when he taught that the Jews were an inherently cruel people. "The Lord, in order to stir to compassion the Jewish people, naturally inclined to cruelty, wished to exercise them in pity even to animals, by forbidding certain practices savouring of cruelty to them."[25]

Following the tradition of theologia gloriae, Aquinas also pictured Jews as blasphemers and sinners, "slaves" and "enemies."[26] He advocated discrimination by prohibiting Jews from public office and limiting their ability to enter higher education and the liberal professions.[27] He even quoted Chrysostom: "Those who blasphemed against the Son of Man . . . had no excuse, no diminution of their punishment . . . in this world through the Romans, and in the life to come in the pains of Hell."[28]

Theologia gloriae was also the ideological basis for the papal Jewish policy of degradation.[29] From at least the I3th century until the I9th, the papacy made Jews virtual pariahs. They were seen as capable of any crime, "a frightful mixture of Cain and Judas."[30] This attitude toward Jews was forced on secular Christian authorities as well.[31] The vaunted papal protection was meant only for those Jews who did not subvert the Christian faith.[32] Yet Jews who openly and joyously practiced their Judaism were sometimes seen as subverting Christian faith by making their Jewish religion attractive. Inquisitors,[33] Crusaders, and other Christians involved in the mass murder of Jews knew that papal language was the language of theologia gloriae, often extremely hostile to Jews, and they sensed that the papal policy of protection was vague and inconsistent. The murder of Jews was not officially condoned,[34] but it was widely accepted throughout the Church, from top to bottom.

The power of theologia gloriae has continued into the modern period.[35] Virtually everyone living in the West identifies himself with some Christian faith or group, "whether or not they actually belong to a church or accept the precepts of their faith."[36] Antisemitic defamations, taught by religious education and textbooks, sermons and liturgy, have maintained their hold on the conscious and unconscious Christian mind. This has been shown by researchers at Pro Deo University at Rome, the Catholic University of Louvain,[37] and the University of California.[38]

Theologia gloriae has prepared most of the faithful to feel comfortable in accepting the anti-Jewish expression of secular ideas.[39] Anti-modernist, racist, and nationalist ideas and movements would not have necessarily become anti-Jewish had theological antisemitism not been so inculcated into so many Christians.[40] Religion has been the decisive factor in antisemitism both as an independent basis of Judenhass and the foundation upon which anti-Jewish secular ideologies have been built.[41]

While still acknowledging the existence and growing numbers of Christians who followed the path of theologia crucis, let us delineate three types of modern Christian antisemites who are products of Christian culture, family, training, and milieu, and whose antisemitism is essentially rooted in the predominant theology of glory: 1. Faithful Christians.[42] 2. Indifferent Christians, atheists, and agnostics. 3. Anti-Christian and anti-ecclesiastical Christians.[43] This paper will deal with three major figures in modern intellectual history— Voltaire, Wagner, and Hitler—who have usually been considered exclusively secular in their hostile attitudes toward Jews; yet they seem to reside in this third category.

As Arthur Hertzberg has noted, concerning Voltaire, "the earliest education of even the most secularized of modern antisemites was, without exception, in some of the nastier forms of religious Jew-hatred."[44] Voltaire grew up surrounded by religious antisemitism in his culture, his family, and his education. All French priests in their seminary training and after were taught that Judaism had no value.[45] Just as in the Patristic Period, most pre-Enlightenment literature pictured the Jews as paradigmaticly[46] hardhearted and diabolic apostates.[47] These attitudes of _theologia gloriae_ were expounded in every theological text, every catechism, and in every author who wrote about the Jews, including many of the best intentioned.[48]

"Like a pious Christian, [Voltaire] remained faithful to the collective animosities that he inherited from his early Christian upbringing and from which he was never prompted to free himself."[49] Voltaire's father was a Jansenist.[50] His mother's friend, the Abbe de Chateauneuf, Voltaire's godfather and "spiritual father,"[51] made the boy recite the long antisemitic poem, _Moisade_, which he already knew by heart.[52] From ages 10 to 17, his education was Jesuit, which had an indelible impact on his mind and morals.[53]

Voltaire has been seen as the great link between pagan and "secular" modern antisemitism,[54] "the man who _skipped over the Christian centuries_ and provided a new, international, secular anti-Jewish rhetoric in the name of European culture rather than religion."[55] Yet aside from his lack of emphasis on the deicide charge, Voltaire's antisemitism was typically Christian in nature. His was a classic case of a man who hated Christianity yet loved Christian antisemitism. As Jacob Katz has written, "Voltaire accepted . . . Christian accusations and incorporated them in his rationalistic indictment. . . . Voltaire's image of the Jews was that harbored by the Christian mind for generations."[56] Although on a rational plane he distanced himself from the Christian myth of Jewish host profanation, for example, there was still something about this defamation that fascinated him.[57]

Moreover, in the most systematic expression of his opinions, the _Philosophical Dictionary_, Voltaire seemed obsessed with an assault on the Jews.[58] He agreed with Jerome that the Jewish Holy Land was "the rubbish heap of nature."[59] In one article he asked, "why shouldn't the Jews have been cannibals? It was the only thing that was needed to make the people of God the most abominable on earth."[60] In the article, "Jew," the longest in the book, Voltaire followed the traditional religious attack on the Jews.[61] Sounding like the Church Fathers and Aquinas, he maintained that the Jews' "character was at all times to be cruel; and their fate to be punished. . .

. They are still vagabonds upon the earth, and abhorred by men, yet affirming that heaven and earth and all mankind were created for them. . . . In short, we find in them only an ignorant and barbarous people, who have long united the most sordid avarice with the most detestable superstition and the most invincible hatred for every people by whom they are tolerated and enriched."[62] It is difficult to determine whether Voltaire's conclusion to the article was sarcastic or serious: "Still, we ought not to burn them."[63]

A contemporary Jewish admirer of Voltaire's work, Isaac de Pinto, pointed out the dangers of his antisemitism rather keenly when he wrote to him in July 1762 that the chapter on the Jews further endangered a vulnerable minority. De Pinto pointed out that the Jews were no more ignorant, barbarous, or superstitious than any other people, and Voltaire should correct his anti-Jewish prejudice.[64] Voltaire replied 10 days later admitting the injustice of his bigotry.[65] Yet for the rest of his life he continued to attack Jews and Judaism more massively and bitterly than before.

In addition, his letter to de Pinto ended with the following words: "Voltaire, chretien, gentilhomme ordinaire de la chambre du Roi Tres Chretien."[66] Having purchased this title in 1746, he flaunted it until the end of his life.[67] Like so many others who appeared to reject the Christianity of their fathers, Voltaire seemed to flaunt the fact that he was a Christian on this occasion when he had to deal with a Jew who confronted him. And so when sides had to be chosen, Voltaire's "rational" attack on the Jews seemed to be reduced to "we Christians against you Jews." In an appendix to the Philosophical Dictionary written 25 years later, Voltaire continued to identify himself with Christianity.[68] In recounting all the abominations that Christians had perpetrated against the Jews, he repeated a half-dozen times "we" Christians have done such and such to "you" Jews; he also contrasted "our [Christian] priests" with "your [Jewish] priests."[69]

In the "Messiah" article, he wrote of "le Christ, fils de Dieu, enfin Dieu lui-meme" and that it was an indisputable fact that Jesus concealed "that he was the son of God, begotten from eternity, consubstantial with God."[70] This may have been pure sarcasm.[71] Nevertheless, in other ways Voltaire seemed to have had great respect and admiration for Jesus,[72] apparently sometimes coming close to accepting Jesus as the Christ. He cited, e.g., "the sacred authors, and Our Lord Jesus himself . . .."[73] He argued that Jesus best exemplified the valuable Christian virtues of "simplicity, humanity, and charity."[74] He called him "un homme juste" and compared him to the martyred hero of philosophy, Socrates.[75]

It was when Voltaire came to criticizing the Jews that he seemed closest to accepting Jesus' divinity. He argued that "the Jews, slaves to the letter, have never penetrated the meaning of Scriptures as we have." He wrote against the Jews, "ancient and modern," for denying "the divine nature of the annointed, of the Lord."[76] He observed that "when the Savior appeared, Jewish prejudices rose up against him. So as not to arouse their blind spirits, Jesus Christ himself appears extremely reserved on the score of his divinity." He called the Jews "rebels against the divinity of Jesus Christ."[77] And he accused them of slandering "our Savior" because of "their implacable hatred against the Christians and against the Gospels."[78] He even cited John Chrysostom! A recent scholar of Voltaire's religious attitudes is forced to concede that Voltaire had "succumbed in some measure to the antisemitism rooted in Christianity."[79]

Like Voltaire and so many other thinkers of the modern period,[80] Wagner and Hitler may have been anti-ecclesiastics, but were Christian enough to remain attached to anti-Jewish Christian concepts and symbols that they had absorbed in their youth. As in French-Catholic culture,[81] German-Christian society of the early 19th century was, by and large, repelled by ideas of equality and humane treatment for Jews who would maintain their Jewishness.[82] Even liberal German Christians essentially told Jews "to reform, conform, or to depart."[83] Typical of Conservatives was Fichte, who stirred a hate campaign against the Jews based in great part on religious differences: "They ought to have human rights . . .. But I see only one way to give them civil rights: to cut off all their heads in one night and put others on them in which there is not so much as a single Jewish idea. . . . Jewry . . . is cut off . . . from any fellowship with us by the most binding element that mankind has, his religion."[84] It is the last, crucial, sentence of this Fichtean statement that is usually omitted.

This anti-Jewish campaign resulted in the HEP (Hierosolyma est perdita) pogroms of 1819, which were also religiously oriented. In Würzburg, e.g., university students shouted down any defender of the Jews and read the following proclamation: "Brothers in Christ, . . . arm yourselves with courage and strength against the enemies of our religion; it is time to repress the killers of Christ. . . . Down with them, before they crucify our priests, profane our sanctuaries, and destroy our temples. . . . Up, all who are baptized; the holy cause is at stake."[85]

A half-century later, Richard Wagner was regarded as a freethinker and an atheist. He may have sometimes been hostile to the Church, but at the same time he considered himself an authentic Christian. He stated in 1851 that "if I have been a Christian in my desire to extricate myself from the worthlessness of the modern world, then I was a more honorable Christian than all those who, with impertinent piety accuse me of apostasy from Christianity."[86] Publicly and privately, Wagner believed in Christ and practiced the Christian sacraments of baptism, confession, and communion. To a friend he noted, "'You belong through baptism to Christ, now unite yourself once more with him through Holy Communion.' Christening and Communion are indispensable. . . . Christ is our intermediary . . .."[87] On the day before Christmas in 1877, he greeted Cosima as "Welcome, dear Christ!" and observed that Christ brought both "salvation" and "joy."[88]

Indeed, Wagner often erupted in support of the Christian point of view opposed to that of race. "One thing is certain: races are done for, and all that can now make an impact is—as I have ventured to express it—the blood of Christ."[89] "The blood of the Savior flowing from his head, from his wounds on the cross—who wishes to commit the outrage of asking whether it belonged to the white, or whichever other race?"[90]

According to George Windell, Wagner was "almost obsessed with Christ as the source of morality," and it was Christ's essence that he attempted to propagate through his art."[91] In fact, Wagner's greatest masterworks demonstrate the triumph of Christianity over paganism. In Tannhaeuser and Lohengrin he identified the Teutonic god Wotan with Christ, the Christian God the Son. Wagner stated that "The abstract highest god of the Germans, Wotan, really did not need to yield place to the God of the Christians; rather could he be completely identified with him. [In Wotan] was found the striking likeness to Christ himself, the Son of God, that he too died, was mourned and avenged—as we still avenge Christ on the Jews of today."[92]

Admirers of Wagner claimed that Parsifal had been inspired by the Holy Spirit and captured the essence of the Last Supper.[93] Wagner himself called it my "German-Christian sacred theatrical work." Its theme revolved around redemption through blood. Wagner saw the decline of Western culture cured through "divine purification . . . the partaking of the blood of Jesus, as symbolized in the only genuine sacrament of the Christian religion."[94] Wagner seemed enraptured by "the Gospel account of the day before [Christ's] death" and the mystical transformation of blood to wine and wine to blood.[95] And he wanted to communicate in his art the meaning of Christ and his sacrifice to Christians through his music.[96] According to Windell, Parsifal was a "profound statement of the Christian message," a manifestation of "the strongly Christian trend in Wagner's thought. . . ."[97]

Wagner's antisemitism was little different from that of the average German Christian, who perceived the Jews as profoundly evil beings, responsible for Germany's troubles and the world's ills. Wagner's beliefs about the Jews were primarily motivated by "deep religious conviction,"[98] i.e., theological antisemitism. Although early on he denied it,[99] his antisemitism was based essentially on the Christian theological conception of the Jews' nature.[100] Moreover, like many other Europeans, he did not consciously connect the theological antisemitism he had absorbed as a youth with his distaste for Jews.[101] As Wagner became more conscious of his Christian ties, his anti-Jewishness increased.[102] He regarded Jewish ritual murder one of "the curious practices of the Jews." Leon Poliakov argues that what takes place in Parsifal is actually a ritual murder reminiscent of the traditional Christian defamation against the Jews. Wagner himself had approvingly read Father Rohling's The Jew of the Talmud, which had gone into considerable detail about ritual murder.[103] Like so many Christian antisemites,[104] he wanted Christianity to be "de-Judaized" and rejected any link between "our Savior" and the God of the Jews.[105] For Wagner, the Jews were those "un-Germans" who stood as the evil force in Germany.[106] He wrote of "a repulsive otherness in the Jewish character." The Jews were under a "curse," and their only redemption was the "solution of Ahasver—destruction."[107] What precisely he meant by this, we do not know. He may have been referring to conversion of the Jews to Christianity. But we do know that in response to the report of hundreds of Jewish deaths at a theater fire in Vienna, Wagner admitted his lack of sympathy. He observed that "the most useless people frequented such an opera house . . . people too wicked for one to be much affected when they perish in masses." He then "made a drastic joke to the effect that all Jews should be burned at a performance of Nathan."[108]

Granted that the Nazi Ideenreich contained racist, along with nationalistic and anti-modernist, elements, yet race seemed almost an afterthought[109] necessary to explain or justify antisemitism to those Nazis who saw themselves as anti-Christian. It was theologia gloriae that supplied the basic foundation and formulation of Hitler's anti-Jewish ideology.[110] Like their theological predecessors, National Socialists believed that the Jews were forever evil and rejected by God. The Jew was not made in "an image of God," according to Hitler, but instead in "an image of the devil," that is, Jews are "the men of Satan."[111] Like the triumphant Church, Nazis regarded the Jews as their hated rival for men's souls; as scapegoats to account for a historical reality that violated their world view; as stateless beings.[112] For both, the degradation of the Jews was a means to establish their own identity and justification for being. They both felt that victory over the Jews was a form of metaphysical power over "evil" and political power over life.

The key figure involved in the Nazi outrages against the Jews during the Holocaust period was Adolf Hitler. Like the triumphal Church, Hitler seemed to believe that his assault on the Jews was consonant with "God's will."[113] He seemed convinced that he and the Churches were to fight Judaism along side each other.[114] At his famous 26 April 1933 meeting with two Catholic fellow-travelers,[115] Bishop Berning of Osnabrueck and Berlin Vicar-General Johannes Steinmann,[116] Hitler claimed that he was doing to the Jews what the Church had been doing to them for 15 centuries. The Church had regarded the Jews as dangerous and so pushed them into ghettos, recalled Hitler. "Perhaps I am doing Christianity a great service."[117]

Hitler, like Himmler and Streicher, had come from a strong Catholic[118] background that teemed with theological antisemitism. In addition to the influences on the young Hitler by the religious prejudices of his family and friends,[119] the masses and sermons he heard at the local church, etc., he had also been an altarboy and choirboy for two years at the Benedictine monastery at Lambach. It was here that he first developed the goal of perhaps becoming a priest himself. As he wrote in Mein Kampf, "I had an excellent opportunity to intoxicate myself with the solemn splendor of the brilliant church festivals. As was only natural, the abbot seemed to me, as the village priest had once seemed to my father, the highest and most desirable ideal."[120] If the abbot that Hitler admired and was instructed by, and who served as Hitler's role model, was typical of the time and place, he was an adherent of theologia gloriae. Later, at the Staatsrealschule in Steyr, Hitler took religion classes, where his grades ranged from adequate to satisfactory.[121] He was obviously familiar with the New Testament since, as we shall see, in both public and private, he several times quoted passages from the Gospels.[122] He received Communion in the Catholic Church at least until the 1920s,[123] when in his conversations with Dietrich Eckart,[124] he affirmed that he was still a Catholic.[125] In fact, until the very end, he allowed the state to withdraw a tithe for the Catholic church from his salary,[126] without ever publicly indicating that he was a man without belief in the Catholic faith.

Moreover, in Mein Kampf, Hitler confirmed that he was conscious of the Jews as a different religion. "I saw no distinguishing feature but [their] strange religion."[127] By 1909, Hitler had arrived in Vienna and was able to study the Christian antisemitism of its mayor, Karl Lueger, whom Hitler admired greatly.[128] Lueger headed the Christian-Socialist Party, a Catholic[129] political party, which had the widest support among the faithful and the priesthood.[130] This most powerful of Austrian parties had also republished several antisemitic articles taken from the Jesuit Civilta Cattolica.[131] Lueger himself had evaluated theologia gloriae: "Only Christian antisemitism is national and effective; it measures up to every standard of culture and humanity and proceeds naturally from the 1800 years of Christian life and teaching . . . ."[132]

Hitler likewise expressed his admiration for the anti-Jewish ideas of the 11th century Pope Gregory VII,[133] John Chrysostom, "and all genuine Christians of outstanding calibre."[134] He quoted Aquinas and Luther against the Jews.[135] He observed that Luther, whom he called "one of the greatest Germans," "the mighty opponent of the Jews," "a great man, a giant," had found himself in his anti-Jewish writings.[136] "He saw the Jew as we are only now beginning to see him today. But unfortunately too late, and not where he did the most harm—within Christianty itself. Ah, if he had seen the Jew at work there, seen him in his youth! Then he would not have attacked Catholicism, but the Jew behind it. Instead of totally rejecting the Church, he would have thrown his whole passionate weight against the real culprits."[137]

In his postwar political career, Hitler expressed Christian anti-Jewish theology several times in the words of the Christian Gospels: "My feeling as a Christian points me to my Lord and Savior as a fighter. It points me to the man who . . . recognized these Jews for what they were and sumoned men to fight against them . . .. In boundless love, as a Christian and a human being, I read through the passage which tells us how the Lord rose at last in His might and seized the scourge to drive out of the Temple the brood of vipers and adders. How terrific was His fight against the Jewish poison. Today, after two thousand years, with deepest emotion I realize more profoundly than ever before the fact that it was for this that He had to shed His blood upon the Cross."[138] On 12 April 1922 in Munich he had declared that "I would be no Christian . . . if I did not, as did our Lord 2,000 years ago, turn against those by whom today this poor people is plundered and exploited."[139] Later, in 1938 in a conversation with Hans Frank, his Minister of Justice, Hitler noted that "In the Gospel, when Pilate refuses to crucify Jesus, the Jews call out to him: 'His blood be upon us and upon our children's children.' Perhaps I shall have to put this curse into effect."[140]

Talmud and Torah, synagogues and beards—all items associated with Jewish belief—were the objects of a special assault by the Hitler regime.[141] If the Jews were considered simply racial vermin, "why," asks Emil Fackenheim, "the ceaseless, limitless efforts to degrade both Jews and Judaism?"[142] Without denying the obvious racist elements of Hitler's ideology, and noting that only a minority of theologians of glory called for extermination of Jews, it is evident that until 1941[143] Hitler publicly espoused the basic elements of theologia gloriae—and few objections were heard among the "faithful," the vast majority of Germans.[144] They responded favorably to Hitler's words and ideas in regard to discrimination, expropriation, and expulsion of the Jews. Up to the issue of mass murder, both he and his audience were caught in the toils of traditional Christian antisemitism. They spoke the same language of libel, the same vocabulary of violence against the Jews. They inhabited the same theological universe.

NOTES.

1 See Denis Prager and Joseph Telushkin, Why the Jews? (New York 1983), 22.

2 See John Gager, Origins of Anti-Semitism (NY 1983), 22-3, 114-5, 134-5.

3 Adversus Judaeos, 1.6.

4 Leon Poliakov, The History of Antisemitism (New York 1975), vol. 3, 28.

5 Benzion Bokser, Judaism and the Christian Predicament (New York 1967), 34-5.

6 See Robert Michael, "Theological Myth, German Antisemitism, and the Holocaust," Holocaust and Genocide Studies, vol. 2 (1987), 105-22 .

7 See Jacob Katz, "Was the Holocaust Predictable?" in Yehuda Bauer and Nathan Rotenstreich, eds. The Holocaust as Historical Experience (New York 1981), 36, 41; Arthur Hertzberg, Antisemitism and Jewish Uniqueness (Rudolph Lectures, 1973), 16. See also Pierre Pierrard, Juifs et Catholiques Francais (Paris 1970), 18.

8 See Gager, 269.
9 "Antisemitism and Theological Arrogance," Continuum (Autumn 1966), 413.
10 See Marcel Simon, Verus Israel (Paris 1948), 255.
11 Quoted by James Parkes, The Conflict of the Church and the Synagogue (NY 1979), 161.
12 Many adherents of theologia gloriae questioned the Jews' right to exist at all. See Joshua Trachtenberg, The Devil and the Jews; Jeremy Cohen, The Friars and the Jews (Ithaca, New York 1982); James Parkes, The Jew in the Medieval Community; Haim Ben-Sasson, "Popular Pressure Against the Status of Jews"; Edward Flannery, The Anguish of the Jews (New York 1985); Werner Keller, Diaspora (New York 1966); Poliakov; Yitzhak Baer, A History of the Jews in Christian Spain (Philadelphia 1978); Paul Grosser and Edwin Halperin, Antisemitism (Secaucus 1976); Heinrich Graetz, History of the Jews (Philadelphia 1940), vol. 4.
13 Augustine, in J.-P. Migne, ed., Patrologiae. Cursus Completus. Series Latina (Paris 1841, 1845), vol. 36-7, 705.
14 Hyam Maccoby, "Christianity's Break with Judaism," Commentary (August 1984).
15 See Douglas John Hall, "Rethinking Christ," in Alan Davies, ed., Antisemitism and the Foundations of Christianity (New York 1979), 177-84.
16 Pierrard, p. 298.
17 Gregory of Nyssa, "In Christi Resurrectionem," quoted by J.-P. Migne, Patrologiae . . .Graeca (Paris 1863), 685-6.
18 Jerome, The Homilies of Saint Jerome (Washington, D.C., 1964), vol. I; Migne, Patrologiae . . . Latina (Paris 1884), 26:1224; Augustine, "Reply to Faustus, the Manichaean," quoted by F. E. Talmage, ed., Disputation and Dialogue (New York 1975), 31. The vast majority of Eastern theologians held the same. See Jaroslav Pelikan, The Spirit of Eastern Christendom (Chicago 1974), 201, 212; Parkes, 305-374.
19 Discourse I, I, 5-6(My italics.) He also quoted Luke 19:27, "As for these enemies of mine who did not want me to reign over them, bring them here and slay them before me." Quoted by Ruether, 142. (My italics.)
20 Isidore of Seville had declared that the Jew's evil character never changes. He cited Jeremiah 13:23, "Can the Ethiopian change his color or the leopard his spots?" Quoted by Ruether, 130.
21 Europe's first institutionalized racism was likewise Christian. It occurred after Spanish theologians had held that Jewish beliefs had soiled all Jews. They concluded that rejection of Christ had corrupted the Jewish conversos biologically. Leon Poliakov, The Aryan Myth (New York 1974), 12-13.
22 Gerhart Ladner, "Aspects of Patristic Anti-Judaism," Viator2(1971), 362.
23 Augustine, Adversus Judaeos 7. 10, 8.11.
24 Aquinas' theological work was later declared the official position of the Catholic Church. By Pope Leo XIII on 4 August 1879.
25 Summa Theologiae (New York 1969), Ia 2ae, 102, 6.8. Later, in Germany and in Spain Christian theologians were involved in setting up racialist standards against

Jews. See Martin Luther, "On the Jews and Their Lies," Luther's Works, ed. Franklin Sherman (Philadelphia 1971), vol. 47, 138.

26 Aquinas, De Regimine Principum et de regimine Judaeorum (Turin 1924), 117; Opuscula Omnia, vol. I, 488.

27 Aquinas, Opuscula Omnia (Paris 1927), vol. I, 490, 494; Summa Theologiae, 2a 2ae, 9-12, 10. This same policy was put into effect by the Vichy regime during the Holocaust, with Aquinas specifically cited as justification. Jacques Nobecourt, "Le Vicaire" et l'Histoire (Paris 1964), 358, 360.

28 Summa Theologiae, 2a 2ae, 14, 3.

29 Solomon Grayzel, The Church and the Jews in the XIIIth Century (New York 1966),

30 Jules Isaac, Genese de l'Antisemitisme, (Paris 1956), 292-94.

31 Grayzel, 49.

32 Edward Synan, The Popes and the Jews in the Middle Ages (New York1965), 101.

33 Synan, 118, 137-9.

34 Parkes, The Jew in the Medieval Community, 85-6; Hans Liebeschutz, "The Crusading Movement in Its Bearing on the Christian Attitude Towards Jewry," Journal of Jewish Studies 10 (1959), 97-111.

35 All the traditional elements of the Catholic theologia gloriae, and worse, can be found in Martin Luther and the majority of Protestant reformers. See Heiko Oberman, The Roots of Antisemitism (Philadelphia 1984) and Robert Michael, "Luther, Luther Scholars, and Antisemitism," Encounter 46 (Autumn 1985), 339-70.

36 Claire Huchet Bishop, How Catholics Look at Jews (New York 1974), 28.

37 Bishop, 30-6.

38 Charles Glock and Rodney Stark, Christian Beliefs and Antisemitism (New York 1966).

39 See Jacob Katz, From Prejudice to Destruction (Cambridge, MA 1980), 320.

40 Terrence Anderson, "An Ethical Critique: Antisemitism and the Shape of Christian Repentance," in Alan Davies, ed., Antisemitism and the Foundations of Christianity, 213.

41 See Moshe Zimmermann, Wilhelm Marr (Oxford 1986), 112; Pawlikowski, 9; Glock and Stark, xvi.

42 See Pierrard, 27.

43 See Jacob Katz, From Prejudice to Destruction, 318-19.

44 Arthur Hertzberg, "The Anguish of the Jews," Continuum (Autumn 1966), 432.

45 Jewish citizenship was granted at the start of the Great French Revolution in a relatively close vote of the National Assembly when most of the clerical representatives were absent. Until the first years of World War II, the French Catholic Church actively supported every antisemitic movement that arose in France. Richard Rubenstein and John Roth, Approaches to Auschwitz (Atlanta 1987), p. 69.

46 Arnold Ages, The Image of Jews and Judaism in the Prelude of the French Enlightenment (Sherbrooke 1986), 114, 142, 153.

47 A vision that pushed these religious writers into "quasi-racist propaganda." Ages, 16-7, 124, 143.
48 Francois Delpech, "La Revolution et l'Empire," in Bernhard Blumenkranz, ed., Histoire des Juifs en France (Toulouse 1972), 268.
49 Katz, From Prejudice to Destruction, 43-4; see also Besterman, Voltaire, 86.
50 Poliakov, 92.
51 Theodore Besterman, Voltaire (New York 1969), 28, 31.
52 Abbe Duvernet, La Vie de Voltaire (Geneva 1786), cited by Poliakov, 494.
53 College Louis le Grand in Paris. Loyola and his Order generally followed the path of theological antisemitism. See James Reites, S. J., "St. Ignatius of Loyola and the Jews," Studies in the Spirituality of Jesuits (Sept. 1981); Letter of Voltaire, 1 April 1746, quoted by Besterman, 43.
54 Arthur Hertzberg, The French Enlightenment and the Jews (New York 1968), 10.
55 Hertzberg, The French Enlightenment, 313. (My italics.)
56 Katz, From Prejudice to Destruction, pp. 43-4.
57 Poliakov, 93.
58 Of its 118 articles, more than 30 attack the Jews.
59 Voltaire, in Peter Gay, ed., Philosophical Dictionary (New York 1962), 2:340.
60 Voltaire, in Gay, 1:88.
61 See David Levy, Voltaire et son exegese du Pentateuque (Banbury 1975), in Theodore Besterman, ed., Studies on Voltaire and the 18th Century, vol. 130, 253.
62 Voltaire, Philosophical Dictionary, William Fleming, tr., The Works of Voltaire (New York 1927), 3:266, 268, 277-9, 281, 284.
63 See Poliakov, 88; and Delpech, "La Revolution et l'Empire," 270.
64 Levy, 282.
65 Levy, 284.
66 Levy, 285.
67 J. Donvez, De quoi vivait Voltaire (Paris 1949), p. 126, cited by Poliakov, 493-4, n. 49. Voltaire "again became 'Christian'" in 1776 when he argued against six Jews. Poliakov, 90.
68 When he "haranges imaginary Jews in the name of Christianity." Poliakov, 88.
69 Voltaire, Philosophical Dictionary, William Fleming, tr., vol. 3, 313. (My italics.)
70 Voltaire, in Gay, , 1:173, 187.
71 It may be a triple sarcasm. William Trapwell, Christ and His "Associates" in Voltairian Polemic: An Assault on the Trinity and the Two Natures (Saratoga, CA 1982) [Stanford French and Italian Studies, vol. 26], 180.
72 Trapwell, 233. Trapwell argues that by the time he died in 1778, he had become very critical of the historical Jesus. Trapwell, 242.
73 Voltaire, in Gay, 2: 382-3, 387.
74 Voltaire, Letters on England (New York 1980), 121.
75 "Le Socrate de la Galilee." Trapwell, 187, 216.

76 Voltaire, in Gay, 2:384.

77 Voltaire, in Gay, 2:384-5.

78 Voltaire, in Gay, 2:386.

79 Trapwell, 245.

80 See Arthur Schopenhauer, Parega and Paralipomena: Short Philosophical Essays (Oxford 1974), vol. 2, 261, 264; Goethe, Goethe's Werke (Weimer 1887-1918), vol. 25: 210, vol. 37: 59-60, vol. 52: 267-7; Katz, From Prejudice to Destruction, 66-73; Alfred Low, Jews in the Eyes of the Germans (Philadelphia 1979), 70, 71, 323, 325; Werner Keller, Diaspora (NY 1969), 366, 367.

81 Many of the friends of the Jews, like Mirabeau and Gregoire, still did not respect Jews as Jews. See Barzilay, "The Jew in the Literature of the Enlightenment," 252-3.

82 Low, 31-4.

83 H. D. Schmidt, "Terms of Emancipation," Leo Baeck Institute Yearbook I (1956), 36.

84 Quoted by Keller, 390. (My italics.)

85 Quoted by Keller, 392-3.

86 Richard Wagner, Mitteilung an meine Freude, in Samtliche Schriften, vol. 4, 304.

87 Cosima Wagner, Diaries, 1878-1883 (New York 1980), 1:707-8.

88 Cosima Wagner, 1:1008.

89 Cosima Wagner, 2:771.

90 Gesammelte Schriften und Dichtungen (Leipzig 1883), 10:358

91 George Windell, "Hitler, National Socialism, and Richard Wagner," 223-4. In 1869 he wrtote the synopsis of a drama, entitled "Jesus von Nazareth." Cosima Wagner, 1:1015.

92 Quoted by Poliakov, 435 (my italics).

93 Poliakov, 456.

94 Quoted by Poliakov, 443, 450.

95 Cosima Wagner, 1:984.

96 He went to great lengths in vain to get his conductor, the Jew Hermann Levi, to be baptized so that he could conduct Parsifal as a Christian. Cosima Wagner, Die Tagebucher (Munich 1976), vol. I, 526.

97 Windell, "Hitler, National Socialism, and Richard Wagner," 234, n. 29.

98 George Windell, "Hitler, National Socialism, and Richard Wagner," in John Louis De Gaetani, ed., Penetrating Wagner's Ring (London 1978), 223-4.

99 In Judaism in Music.

100 See Katz, From Prejudice to Destruction, 191.

101 See Katz, The Darker Side of Genius (Hanover N.H. 1986), 42.

102 See Katz, The Darker Side of Genius, 100.

103 Poliakov, 456.

104 Uriel Tal, Christians and Jews in Germany (Ithaca 1975).

105 Gesammelte Schriften und Dichtungen, vol. 10: 118, quoted by Katz, The Darker Side of Genius, p. 109.

106 Frank Josserand, "Richard Wagner and German Nationalism," in Di Gaetani, ed., Penetrating Wagner's Ring, 207.

107 Richard Wagner, "Über des Judentum in der Musik," in Gesammelte Schriften und Dichtung, vol. 3:67, quoted by David Large, "Wagner's Bayreuth Disciples," in David Large and William Weber, eds., Wagnerism in European Culture and Politics (Ithaca 1984), 80, 312-3, n. 25.

108 Cosima Wagner, 2:766-773.

109 See the attacks on Rosenberg's neo-paganism by Hitler, Goering, Goebbels, and others. Hitler himself commented, on 11 April 1942, that "I must insist that Rosenberg's 'The Myth of the 20th Century' is not to be regarded as an expression of the official doctrine of the party. . . . It gives me considerable pleasure to realize that the book has been closely studied only by our opponents. Like most of the Gauleiters, I have myself merely glanced cursorily at it." Adolf Hitler, Hitler's Secret Conversations, 1941-1944 (New York 1953), 400. He mentioned his rejection of Rosenberg to Von Papen and Bishop Berning. Franz von Papen, Memoirs (London 1952), 261; Friedrich Heer, God's First Love (New York 1967), 477, n. 291. Goering reportedly called Rosenberg's Mythus "junk," and Goebbels described it as "weltanschauliches Gerülpse," "philosophical belching." "The Story of Rosenberg's 'Mythus,'" in Wiener Library Bulletin, vol. 7 (1953), 33. G. M. Gilbert, the psychologist who examined the Nuremberg defendents reports that none of them had ever read Rosenberg. Nuremberg Diary (New York 1961), 321.

110 See Alan Davies, Antisemitism and the Christian Mind (New York 1969), 59.

111 Hitler's speech of August 1923. See Wistrich, Hitler's Apocalypse (New York 1985), 31, 36.

112 There had been no legitimate place for the Jews in the societas Christiana, the mystical corpus Christi of the Church. See Cohen, The Friars and the Jews and Raul Hilberg, The Destruction of the European Jews (Chicago 1961), 3-4.

113 Adolf Hitler, Mein Kampf (Boston 1943), 65.

114 Klaus Scholder, "Judentum und Christentum in der Ideologie und Politik des Nationalsozialismus, 1919-1945," in Judaism and Christianity Under the Impact of National Socialism, 1919-1945 (Jerusalem 1982), 190.

115 Heer, 309; Pinchas Lapide, Three Popes and the Jews (New York), 239. We must be reminded that there were also Christian opponents of the Hitler Regime and all it stood for. The Jesuit Friedrich Muckermann, editor of the Catholic weekly Der Deutsche Weg, for example.

116 Also clerical consultant to the German Embassy to the Vatican and a papal privy chamberlain.

117 Quoted by Lapide, 90.

118 For the relationship between German Protestant antisemitism and National Socialism, see Michael, "Theological Myth, German Antisemitism, and the Holocaust."

119 See Paul Johnson, A History of the Jews (New York 1987), 472.

120 Hitler, Mein Kampf, 6.

121 Konrad Heiden, Der Fuehrer (Boston 1944, 1969), 49.

122 Robert Waite, *The Psychpathic God* (New York 1977), 35-6.

123 Walter Langer, *The Mind of Adolf Hitler* (New York 1972), 44.

124 Recorded in *Der Bolschewismus von Moses bis Lenin* (Munich 1924).

125 Cited by Heer, 284.

126 Michael Schwartz, "Are Christians Responsible?" *National Review* (1980), 956-7.

127 Hitler, *Mein Kampf*, 52.

128 Hitler, *Mein Kampf*, 121.

129 Lueger and his Christian Socialists had received a papal blessing and commendation from Leo XIII in February 1895. Henry Cohn, "Theodore Herzl's Conversion to Zionism," *Jewish Social Studies*, vol. 32 (April 1970), 101-10.

130 Victor Conzemius, "L'Antisemitisme autrichien au XIXieme et au XXieme siecles," in V. Nikiprowetzky, ed., *De l'antijudaisme antique a l'antisemitisme contemporain* (Lille 1979), 197.aaaa

131 Lapide, 81-2.

132 Quoted by Hermann Glaser, *The Cultural Roots of National Socialism* Austin 1964), 227.

133 He had forbidden "the synagogue of Satan" and "the enemies of Christ" from having any power over Christians. See Malcolm Hay, *Thy Brother's Blood* (New York 1977), 35.

134 Heer, 130.

135 Heer, 284

136 Quoted by Heer, 285-6.

137 Quoted by Heer, 286. (My italics.)

138 Adolf Hitler, *My New Order*, ed. by Raoul de Roussy de Sales (New York 1973), 26.

139 Norman Baynes, ed., *The Speeches of Adolf Hitler* (London 1943), vol. 1, 20.

140 Quoted by George Bailey, *Germans* (New York 1974), 196.

141 Yehuda Bauer, *The History of the Holocaust* (New York 1982), 156.

142 "Concerning Authentic and Unauthentic Responses to the Holocaust," *Holocaust and Genocide Studies* 1 (1986), 103.

143 When the policy of expulsion was clearly replaced by the extermination policy of the "Final Solution."

144 94 per cent of whom as late as 1944 still belonged to the Protestant or Catholic Churches. Peter Matheson, ed., *The Third Reich and the Christian Churches* (Grand Rapids 1981), pp. 99-101; Ernst Helm-reich, *The German Churches Under Hitler* (Detroit 1979), p. 40; Richard Gutteridge, *Open Thy Mouth for the Dumb* (Oxford 1976), p. 261, n. 36

THE SHOAH: ITS CHALLENGES FOR RELIGIOUS AND SECULAR ETHICS

John T. Pawlikowski, O.S.M., Ph.D

Catholic Theological Union
5401 South Cornell Avenue
Chicago, IL 60615-5698
USA

Extensive research into the ideological roots of the Shoah over the past several decades has surfaced some major challenges for Western social ethics, both religious and secular. In the ensuing discussion it will prove possible to highlight only a few of the especially significant ones. Before undertaking that effort, however, it would be important to set a basic context for understanding the Shoah.

As with any precedent-shattering event in human history attempts to uncover its genesis and significance have moved in varied directions. Having sifted through and reflected at length over these diverse interpretations for a decade or more the following perspective seems to integrate the available information better than others. It is a perspective that views the Shoah as inaugurating a significantly new era in human self-understanding, an era in which the extermination of human life in a guiltless fashion becomes thinkable and technologically feasible. The Shoah opened the door to an age in which dispassionate torture and the murder of millions have become acts not merely of a crazed, power-starved despot, not merely an irrational expression of xenophobic fear, not just a quest for national security, but a calculated effort to reshape humanity supported by ideological argumentation framed by some of the best and the brightest minds of the period. The Shoah was parented by some of the most sophisticated philosophers and scientists Western society has yet produced. Here lies its most sinister aspects, its fundamental challenge. While the attempt to annihilate the Jewish People had everything to do with the legacy of Christian antisemitism which provided an indispensable seedbed for Nazism, the Holocaust was not aimed solely at the Jews. Others such as Poles, Gypsies, and Gays were also to be exterminated or at least subjugated as part of the purification process in society. And, as Uriel Tal has argued, though the Nazis often sought to enlist the help of the Christian churches to achieve short-term goals, their ultimate objective was the destruction of Christianity as well. (Tal, 1987,66)

It certainly would constitute an unconscionable evasion of moral responsibility for Christians to ignore the active collaboration of many believing members of the church in the Shoah as well as the indirect, but real, participation of so many other baptized faithful as bystanders. But in the end we must see the Shoah as caused by something more than Christian failure. As Tal maintains, the Shoah was meant to respond to a universal crisis of the human person. (Tal, 1973-74.) But Tal nonetheless underscores the pivotal contribution of the Christian tradition to the genesis of the "Final Solution":

> The anti-Christian elements of racial anti-Semitism were interpreted in such a way that the traditional theological concepts of Christianity were not completely rejected; only their meanings were changed by using a pseudoscientific jargon and applied to the historical realities of that day, without the salutary correction of Christian discipline and belief.

> Racial anti-Semitism and the subsequent Nazi movement were not the result of mass hysteria or the work of single propagandists. The racial anti-Semites, despite their antagonism toward traditional Christianity, learned much from it, and succeeded in producing a well-prepared, systematic ideology with a logic of its own that reached its culmination in the Third Reich. (Tal, 1975, 305)

In the end Christianity cannot escape the question a fellow inmate posed to Alexandre Donat, author of THE HOLOCAUST KINGDOM: "How can Christianity survive the discovery that after a thousand years of its being Europe's official religion, Europe remains pagan at heart?" (Donat, 1965, 230-231.)

The focus on more generic ethical issues in this essay in no way implies therefore that questions directly involved with the Christian response to the Shoah are of secondary importance. They remain absolutely critical. It would be presumptuous for any Christian to delve into the overarching moral issues without first having grappled with Christian culpability during the Shoah itself. Having tried to be faithful to this responsibility in other writings, I would like to concentrate in this presentation on the more generalized and pervasive moral issues.

Basic to the Shoah's moral challenge is its embodiment of significantly altered perception of the relationship between God and Humanity. It was an attempt, Emil Fackenheim has written, to wipe out the "divine image" in history. "The murder camp," he insists, "was not an accidental by-product of the Nazi empire. It was its essence." (Fackenheim, 1978, 246.) What emerges as a central reality from the study of the Shoah is the Nazi desire to create the "super-person," to develop a truly liberated humanity in which only the Aryan race would share.

The new humanity the Nazis hoped to bring to realization would be free of the moral restraints imposed by previous religious beliefs and would be capable of exerting virtually unlimited power in the shaping of the world and its inhabitants. That is why the death camps were central. They were supremely the place where the Nazi exercised total, arbitrary control over who would live and who would die. The message was loud and clear. God was dead as an effective force in governing the universe. To attain their objective the Nazis were convinced that the "dregs of humanity" had to be eliminated or at least their influence on culture and biological development greatly curtailed. The Jews fell into this category first and foremost. They were classified as "vermin." But the Poles (particularly in their national collectivity), the Rom people, Gays and the mentally/ physically incapacitated were looked upon as pollutors of humanity, as obstacles to growth of human consciousness to a new level of insight and power. Their extermination under the rubric of humankind's purification assumes a theological significance intimately related to the Jewish question. Regretably the non-Jewish side of the Holocaust has not entered the theological reflections of either Christian or Jewish theologians up till now.

The primal issue for ethics posed by the Holocaust is how we are to respond to the sense of human liberation that was central to the Nazi worldview. As much as this may be painful to say, the Nazis were correct in at least one respect. They rightly perceived that some basic changes were underway in human consciousness. The impact of the new science and technology, with its underlying philosophy of freedom, was beginning to provide humankind on a mass scale with a Promethean-type experience of escape from prior bonds. People were beginning to reach an awareness of a level of human dignity and autonomy far greater than most of Western Christian theology had previously conceded. Traditional theological notions that were pivotal in determining moral behavior were gradually losing the tight grip they had exercised over people since biblical times. Much of Christian theology had tended to accentuate the omnipotence of God which in turn intensified the impotence of the human person and his/her inconsequential role in the governance of the earth. The Nazis were saying "no" to this traditional relationship and the moral code that was integral to it.

The Protestant theologians Michael D. Ryan has emphasized this direction of Nazism in his theological analysis of MEIN KAMPF. What is striking with respect to Hitler's "salvation history", as he calls it, is its absolute self-confinement to the limits of time:

> It amounted to a resignation to the conditions of finitude, while at the same time asserting total power for itself within those conditions. This is what makes the logic of MEIN KAMPF theological. By asserting total control within the limits of finitude, Hitler deified himself and made himself into the Savior of the German people. (Ryan, 1974, 160-161)

Uriel Tal moves in much the same direction as Ryan with regard to Hitler's deification. Throughout its lifespan, and not only in its formative years as some claims, major Nazi leaders tried to impart "a redemptive character both to the Fuhrer and to the Reich." Hitler simultaneously assumed the role of an "eschatological savior" as well as a modern political leader both during Nazism's pre-power days and throughout the length of the Third Reich. As Michael Ryan has insisted regarding the ultimate nature of Hitler's worldview, it involved "the deliberate decision on the part of mass man to live within the limits of finitude without either the moral restraints or the hopes of traditional religion...." (Ryan, 1974, 161)

The task for religious ethics after the Holocaust will be to search for ways whereby the new sense of human freedom that is a permanent fixture of modern consciousness can be affirmed but channelled towards constructive rather than humanly destructive purposes. Fundamental to this search will be major restatement of the God-human person relationship as the basis of moral norms. For secular social ethics the minimum requirement is a profound grappling with the necessity of maintaining some "transcendent" referent in human life as a way of guarding against the emergence in public life of what Franklin Littell has termed a "new coercive orthodoxy" or Clyde Manschreck has called "naked state sovereignty", both speaking out of their reflections on the Shoah experience. For religious ethicists the intensified sense of power and human elevation that the Nazis recognized as a novum of our age needs to be recognized as a crucial and inescapable part of the process of human salvation. That is why the mere repetition of biblical precepts, of the biblical view of God's relationship with creation, will not provide an adequate foundation for an appropriate ethical response to the Holocaust. Contemporary humanity experiences a greater sense of autonomy, a need for far more mutuality in the God-human person relationship, than was the case for the biblical world even in its latter phases. People today perceive dimensions to the Genesis notion of co-creatorship which has rightly assumed a new prominence in social ethics which far exceed the consciousness present in biblical times.

The challenge before ethicists is whether in the post-Shoah period they can formulate an understanding of the God-humanity relationship that will prevent the newly recognized creative power of humanity from being transformed into the destructive force that reared its ugly head during the Nazi era. Can we successfully frame this relationship in a way that new moral grounding will be provided for humanity's greatly enhanced power to shape itself and the creation it has inherited? Most ethicists have avoided facing this basic issue till now.

Several Jewish theologians have tried to confront this challenge to fundamental perceptions of the God-humanity relationship over the past several years. The first radical attempt came from Richard Rubenstein AFTER AUSCHWITZ, though Rubenstein has moved somewhat away from this question in more recent writings towards sociological interpretations of the Shoah and its implications for the morality of power. But AFTER AUSCHWITZ put the question on the table in a dramatic way. Classical categories of evil could not encompass and integrate the immensity of the Shoah.

Even those scholars such as Steven Katz who harbor serious reservations about Rubenstein's personal solution to this new reality consider him "absolutely correct in this judgment" about classical categories of evil. (Katz, 1983, 176.) Rubenstein himself suggested the necessity for humanity now to adopt a fundamentally "paganistic" outlook which involved finding "once again one's roots as a child of earth and to see one's own existence as wholly and totally an earthly existence." (Rubenstein, 1973, 267.)

While no ethicist has picked up on Rubenstein's radical call for a return to "paganism" as the basis for post-Shoah personal identity and morality he must be credited with highlighting the need to recapture our earthly roots as an antidote to the rational, technological culture that has become commonplace in Western society. The Nazis showed us, in their success with naturalist rituals, that these roots had been deeply repressed with

Christian theology bearing at least partial responsibility. Without doubt the "high gods of the sky", as he calls them, have lost their moral authority in the light of the Shoah. The old interventionist God of the theologians is dead as well, buried in the ashes of the Holocaust. The cry of the believer in our era may indeed become that of D.H. Lawrence, "God of Justice, when wilt Thou teach them to save themselves? " But I cannot agree fully with Rubenstein that a transcendent referent for morality has become obsolete after the Shoah. Several other Jewish religious scholars have tried to restore an understanding of God which will acknowledge a much greater role for human responsibility in the cessation of events such as the Holocaust. For them we must start the post-Shoah search for an image of God that can undergird human action with the premise that human freedom and human power have increased immeasurably in light of the Holocaust experience. It is to their reflections that we now briefly turn.

Emil Fackenheim argues for an image of God that bespeaks of curtailed power in comparison with previous divine images. For Fackenheim the prime responsibility for restoring this divine image in which omnipotence is no longer a quality falls upon the Holocaust survivors who resisted the attempt by the Nazis to totally eradicate the presence of God in human affairs. (Fackenheim, 1978, 251.)

Irving Greenberg's language is somewhat less blunt about curtailing divine power, but he shares with Fackenheim a conviction that a major readjustment is demanded in how we understand the force of covenantal moral obligations after the Holocaust. As Greenberg sees it, the Shoah forces upon us a thorough reconsideration of the nature of moral obligation, first and foremost for the Jew, but also secondarily for Christians and Muslims who in some way regard the Sinai covenant as foundational for their faith expression. In the Shoah, says Greenberg, God "opened the Jews to a murderous fury from which there was no escape. Yet the Divine could not or would not save them from this fate." (Greenberg, 1982, 15.) As a consequence, it is no longer possible morally speaking to maintain divine claims upon humanity by reason of the covenant. Put another way, the experience of the Shoah marks the disappearance God must undertake repentance, do <u>teshuvah</u>, "for having given his chosen people a task that was unbearably cruel and dangerous without having provided for their protection." (Greenberg, 1982, 15.)

These reflections on covenantal obligation in light of the Shoah experience lead Greenberg to proclaim the disappearance of any "commanded" dimension from the God-humanity relationship. "Covenantally speaking, one cannot <u>order</u> another to step forward to die." Any authentic understanding of covenantal obligation must now be voluntary:

> One cannot <u>order</u> another to go on a suicide mission. Out of shared values, one can only ask for volunteers. Similarly, God can no longer enforce or educate for the covenant by punishment. The most horrifying of the curses and punishments threatened in the Torah for failing to live up to the covenant pale by comparison with what was done in the Holocaust.....No divine punishment can enforce the covenant, for there is no risked punishment so terrible that it can match the punishment risked by continuing faithfulness to the covenant. If the Jews keep the covenant after the Holocaust, then it can no longer be for the reason that it is commanded or because it is enforced by reward or punishment. (Greenberg, 1982, 16.)

The voluntary nature of the post-Holocaust covenantal relationship unquestionably heightens human responsibility in the eyes of Greenberg:

> If after the Temple's destruction, Israel moved from junior participant to true partner in the covenant, then after the Holocaust, the Jewish people is called upon to become the senior partner in action. In effect, God was saying to humans: you stop the Holocaust. You bring the redemption. You act to ensure that it will never again occur. I will be with you totally in whatever you do, wherever you go, whatever happens, but you must do it. (Greenberg, 1982, 17-18.)

Not all Jews have taken kindly to Greenberg's proclamation of the voluntary covenant after the Holocaust, even some with a long record of social activism. Social critic

Rabbi Arnold Wolf has called this proclamation "the novel heresy of the twentieth century" that may breed unwanted chauvinism within the Jewish community. He considers Greenberg's rejection of an inherent "command" dimension to covenantal obligation a bold denial of a central Jewish view as well as potentially debilitating for Jewish morality in our time. He writes:

> We are the center of the covenant. We have the primary task of self-protection....We are the makers and unmakers of the mitzvot, since our existence is already a fulfillment of them all. We define the terms on which we are willing to survive. We do what we choose, not what God chooses.... (Wolf, 1983, 105-106.)

There is a kernel of truth in Wolf's critique even though I am convinced that Greenberg has basically articulated the post-Shoah moral condition of humanity in an accurate and responsible fashion. I will return to Wolf's critique subsequently.

Turning to a third major Jewish interpreter of the Holocaust, Arthur Cohen, we find a similar call for a major reworking of our notions of how God and the human community interact after the Holocaust, a process with deep implications for ethical foundations. Cohen's principal work THE TREMENDUM: A THEOLOGICAL INTERPRETATION OF THE HOLOCAUST has its roots in Gershom Scholem's writings on Lurianic Kabbalism and in the theodicy model of the "mysterium tremendum" proposed by Rudolph Otto in his book THE IDEA OF THE HOLY. Writing in response to Richard Rubenstein, Cohen argues that the Holocaust forces us to acknowledge two *tremenda* in this world. To ignore either is to distort reality:

> If the Holocaust of this century is an immensity, an event that alters our reading of the irrational eruptions of human society into upheavals of grotesque evil and compels us to assert of human action a capacity for systemic, radical evil, something new has occurred. To speak of human evil in this century as a human *tremendum*, a countervalence to the divine *tremendum*, is to propose not merely a literary device, but a categoric assertion about the implication of unbounded freedom, of freedom infinitized. That freedom yields the abyss of the *tremendum*, a force as power as the divine transcendence that appears to us out of the whirlwind of God's own *mysterium tremendum*. (Cohen, 1984, 64.)

Cohen's response to the reality of the two *tremenda* is to assert the absolute necessity for the *divine tremendum* to counter the destructive potential of human evil. But for this to happen we cannot approach God in totally traditional fashion. "God's entanglement in our history is deeper and more subtle than familiar and coventional theology construes it, (Cohen, 1984, 64.) he tells us in the same response to Rubenstein. Gone are the days when we could confortably picture God as the strategist of human history. The Shoah has destroyed any such perceptions of divine-human interaction. The post-Shoah God can legitimately be perceived (and must be so perceived if radical evil is to be kept in check) as

> the mystery of our futurity, always our *posse*, never our acts. If we can begin to see God less as an interferer whose insertion is welcome (when it accords with our needs) and more as the immensity whose reality is our prefiguration, whose speech and silence are metaphors for our language and distortion, whose plenitude and unfolding are the hope of our futurity, we shall have won a sense of God we may love and honor, but whom we no longer fear and from whom we no longer demand. (Cohen, 1981, 97.)

My basic response to the post-Shoah reflections of Fackenheim, Greenberg and Cohen on the God-moral responsibility linkage is that, despite some reservations, they provide the basic context in which I as a Christian ethicist must work today. For one, the role of the human community in keeping history free of further eruptions of radical evil akin to Nazism is strongly enhanced, as all three have insisted. In exercising this new responsibility humanity will be helping to restore the divine image as Fackenheim has suggested. The human role in the process of salvation has been substantially upgraded.

Humanity finds itself after the Shoah facing the realization that "future" is no longer something God will automatically and unconditionally guarantee, Survival, whether for the People Israel or humanity at large, is now more than ever a human proposition. In their differing ways Fackenheim, Greenberg and Cohen have made this fact abundantly clear. And we need to be profoundly grateful for that.

But despite my gratitude I must demur a bit from their approach. Here is where Wolf's criticism, though overdrawn, strikes a sympathetic chord with me. Has Greenberg, have Fackenheim and Cohen, left us too much on our own? Does God have any significant role after the Holocaust experience in the development of a moral ethos within humanity that can keep radical evil in check? I do not believe any of these Jewish writers have dealt squarely with this question. The role they now assign to God is not potent enough in my judgment.

The post-Holocaust ethical vision must be one that recognizes both the new creative possibilities inherent in the human condition as well as the utter necessity that this creative potential be influenced by a genuine encounter with the living and judging God. Only such an encounter will direct the use of this creative potential away from the destruction represented by Nazism. We must find a way of articulating a notion of a transcendent God which can counterbalance the potential for evil that remains very much a live possibility in the contemporary human situation. In other words we shall have to recover a fresh sense of transcendence to accompany our heightened sense of human responsibility after the Shoah. This is something I do not find Greenberg, Fackenheim and Cohen addressing in a persuasive way. Men and women will once more need to experience contact with a personal power beyond themselves, a power that heals the destructive tendencies still lurking within humanity. The newly liberated person, to be able to work consistently for the creation of a just and sustainable society, must begin to sense that there exists a judgment upon human endeavors that goes beyond mere human judgment. Such a sense of judgment is missing in Fackenheim's emphasis on human restoration of the divine image, in Greenberg's notion of the voluntary covenant and in Cohen's language about God as our "posse," "as insightful as each notion may be in its own right".

The old sense of judgment rooted in a notion of divine punishment will no longer suffice as the basis of religious ethics. The modern experience of the human community is that the worst atrocities can be perpetrated with apparent impunity. The only norm that can finally curb such atrocities is one rooted in an experience of love and unity beyond the narrow dimensions of this earth combined with the concomitant realization that actions such as those that shaped the Holocaust ultimately block the attainment of such love and unity.

The Holocaust has shattered all simplistic notions of a "commanding God." On this point I go full way with Greenberg, Cohen and Fackenheim. Such a "commanding" God can no longer be the touchstone of ethical behavior. But the Shoah has also exposed humanity's desperate need to restore a relationship with a "compelling" God, compelling because we have experienced through symbolic encounter with this God a healing, a strengthening, an affirming that buries any need to assert our humanity through the destructive, even deadly, use of human power. This sense of a compelling Parent God who has gifted humanity, whose vulnerability for the Christian has been shown in the Cross, is the meaningful foundation for an adequate moral ethos after the Holocaust. Hence I part company to a significant degree with Greenberg, Fackenheim and Cohen in positing this "compelling" God. I believe their approach leaves God's role too indirect. Talk of a purely voluntary covenant, of human restoration of the divine image or of God as simply the "posse" of the human future may in the final analysis leave us with a dangerously emaciated God.

At this point let me add that I am convinced that the kind of post-Shoah divine-human relationship for which I am calling will be discovered primarily through worship experiences. I have developed this thesis much more fully in an essay originally presented to a meeting of the North American Academy of Liturgy. (Pawlikowski, 1984, 315-329.) For our purposes here it is sufficient to assert that unless we can begin to create worship situations that expose participants to genuine encounters with a compelling God together with a consciousness of such realities as sin, freedom, dependence, solidarity, vulnerability and oppression, we stand little chance of influencing human decision-making in a significant way. And the absence of such influence will increasingly relegate the human condition to a condition in which there exist fewer and fewer moral constraints on the use of human power which technology is enhancing day by day.

The focus on the primacy of the encounter with the compelling God through worship leads right into another dimension of the effort to create a post-Holocaust moral ethos in society. It is the need to recognize the significance of what Reinhold Neibuhr called the vitalistic side of the human person. The regeneration of the vitalistic side of humanity, albeit in highly destructive directions, stood at the heart of the Nazi enterprise. The Nazis became aware of the tremendous power of this vitalistic dimension, for good or for ill. This was something the West, especially in its approach to morality, had blotted out from its sphere of vision. And I am convinced that the moral honing of this vitalistic dimension can effectively take place only in the context of symbolic actions. For the religious believer this means principally the worship experience. For the general society other avenues will need to be found. And everyone will need to give greater attention to the role that societal symbols (especially cultural ones) play in shaping the ethical tenor of a nation.

The failure of Enlightment-based liberalism to provide an effective moral counterweight to the Nazi manipulation of human vitalism shows the inadequacy of any exclusively rational-based morality after the Shoah. Irving Greenberg makes this point quite strongly. I basically side with him.

> How naive the nineteenth-century polemic with religion appears to be in retrospect; how simple Feuerbach, Nietzsche, and many others. The entire structure of autonomous logic and sovereign human reason now takes on a sinister character. ...For Germany was one of the most 'advanced' Western countries--at the heart of the academic, scientific, and technological enterprise. All the talk about 'atavism' cannot obscure the way in which such behavior is the outgrowth of democratic and modern values, as well as pagan gods. (Greenberg, 1977, 17.)

In light of the Holocaust we can no longer afford to give scant attention to the vitalistic dimension of humanity, to reduce it simply to the realm of play and recreation. The development of moral reasoning remains crucial, but it is no substitute for the healing of the destructive tendencies in humanity's vitalistic side which require symbolic encounter with a loving God.

Another result of the reflections on the Shoah experience is the enhanced appreciation for the significance of history. David Tracy has written of late how much such reflection has personally convinced him of the need to take history seriously and consequently of the necessity to alter his own theological stance:

> We Christian theologians have honestly come to terms with historical consciousness and historicity; we have developed a theological hermeneutics where the subject matter--the event itself-is once again allowed to rule in theological hermeneutic; we have recognized the Sach-Kritik that the religious event itself demands. But we have not returned to history--the real, concrete thing where events like the Holocaust have happened, where events like the state of Israel does exist. (Tracy, 1984, 16-17.)

Tracy then goes on to praise liberation theologians for being one of the few groups of Christian theologians who have indeed begun to treat history with the seriousness it deserves, though he faults them for not relating their thought to the Holocaust experience. He likewish identifies with Greenberg's and Fackenheim's call for a return to history.

A similar note has been sounded by Rebecca Chopp. She lays special stress on the profound connection between the literature emerging from the Shoah experience and liberation theology, a relationship she terms unique among Western religious writings. Both in her judgment create new theological space which in turn forces upon Christianity a fundamental reconceptualization of its theology. These are her actual words:

> Holocaust literature and liberation theology both agree on one foundational assumption; that the challenge to contemporary thought and action is the challenge of massive suffering. Christianity and Christian theology can no longer be content with addressing suffering on an individual level from Christian texts, symbols and traditions but must now criticize, interrupt

> and transform both action and reflection in light of past, prevailing and potential events of massive suffering. Liberation theology and Holocaust literature intererupt and disrupt Christianity and Christian theology with the question and the quest "who is this human subject that suffers history?" (Chopp, 1984, 23.)

She goes on to add that both liberation theology and Holocaust literature force upon us an understanding of history as not merely abstract notions of evolution or process but primarily in terms of the suffering realities of that history caused by various forms of human exploitation. The history that now must be the basis of theological reflection is not abstract history, but the history of human victims. And the voices and the memory of the tortured, the forgotten, and the dead must become primary resources for Christian anthropology.

Chopp's position has certain clear links with the contention of Tracy and feminist theologians Elisabeth Schussler-Fiorenza and Rosemary Ruether that biblical and patristic degradation of the Jewish People has broad implications. It set the stage not only for Christian acceptance of the Shoah, but also for similar cooperation with the forces behind the exploitation of women, colonialism and imperialism.

A further dimension of the history theme emerging from the Shoah experience has been raised by Johannes Baptist Metz. While his thought remains somewhat embryonic in this regard he has argued that any statement about God today, any attempt to express meaning, must be considered "blasphemy" if it does not meet the test of this event. For Metz Christians now need to interpret salvation primarily as alliance with Jews within history. The Shoah demands a genuine ethic of solidarity. He writes:

> But this means that we Christians for our own sakes are from now on assigned to the victims of Auschwitz--assigned, in fact, in an alliance belonging to the heart of saving history, provided the word "history" in this Christian expression is to have a definite meaning and not just serve as a screen for a triumphalist metaphysic of salvation which never learns from catastrophes nor finds in them a cause for conversation.... (Metz, 1981, 19-20.)

The argument being advanced by Tracy, Metz and Chopp about the significance of human history and ethics in all religious statement after the Shoah was actually surfaced in a preliminary form some years earlier by the Austrian Catholic philosopher Friedrich Heer. He insisted that the church's failure to challenge the Nazis in any effective way is symptomatic of how the church has dealt with other manifestations of evil, in particular war and the possibility of a nuclear holocaust. For him, the main problem springs from the church's withdrawal from history:

> The withdrawal of the church from history has created that specifically Christian and ecclesiastical irresponsibility towards the world, the Jew, the other person, even the Christian himself, considered as a human being--which was the ultimate cause of past catastrophes and may be the cause of a final catastrophe in the future. (Heer, 1970, 406.)

As Heer sees it, antisemitism is the product of a long-standing and deep-seated cancer within Christianity that began to grow in its classical period. The disregard on the part of Christians for the well-being of the Jewish people throughout history, especially between 1918 and 1945, can only be understood as part of a general disregard for humanity and the world. He attributes this attitude to the dominance in Christian theological thinking of what he calls the "Augustinian principle." This attitude views the world under the aspect of sin and ultimately leads to a sense of fatalism and despair about the world. Heer remains convinced that this fatalistic tendency constitutes every bit as much a danger today as it did in the period of the incubation of Nazism. In fact, he argues that millions of contemporary Christians share the responsibility for preparing the suicide of the church and of humankind in a new holocaust which may be brought about by nuclear warfare while the churches remain silent bystanders:

> There is a straight line from the church's failure to notice Hitler's attempt at a "Final Solution" of the Jewish problem to her failure to notice today's and tomorrow's endeavors to bring about a "Final Solution" to the human problem. The murder of millions of Jews during the Hitler era

> anticipated the murder of millions and perhaps hundreds of millions of human beings who would die if the great war returned--a war that could only end in mass murder and genocide. (Heer, 1971, 29.)

The only cure for this centuries-long pattern in Christianity, accroding to Heer, is to abandon the "Augustinian principle" and replace it with a return to the Hebrew Bible's roots of Christ's own piety and to even older roots--namely, to the original faith of Israel in which people felt themselves to be both God's creatures and responsible partners in the development of the earth.

I applaud the hermeneutical conversion in the writings of these post-Shoah Christian thinkers. What it means from my perspective as an ethicist is that ethics must now stand at the center of any authentic systematic theology. Ethics is not merely a practical discipline. "The central theological question today," Tracy maintains with the Holocaust uppermost in his mind, "is not the question of the non-believer but the question of the non-person-- those forgotten ones, living and dead, whose struggle and memory is our history." (Tracy, 1984, 17.) This is what the liberation theologians have clearly brought to the forefront of Christian theological consciousness. After the Holocaust the ethical implications of all systematic theological statements must be clearly articulated, for this event truly confronted us with a systematic, repeatable attempt to designate entire categories of people as non-persons.

There is one reservation I do have in connection with this call for the return to history after the Shoah. This return to history must be accompanied by new explorations into human consciousness, especially the extent to which consciousness harbors the roots of power and evil. There is not yet an adequate link established by any of the Christian or Jewish thinkers we have considered between history and human consciousness. We cannot ignore the Freud/Jung revolution in our reflections on the Shoah experience. An adequate ethic after the Holocaust will require a new appreciation of the profound connection between history and human consciousness with respect to both human and divine activity.

Connected to the "return to history" motif is the issue of power. Neither the Christians nor the Jews with whom we have interacted in this essay have as yet satisfactorily handled this difficult question. Irving Greenberg has undoubtedly been the most direct in positing the relationship between power and the Shoah although it has increasingly entered Richard Rubenstein writings as well. For Greenberg it would be immoral to abandon the quest for power. "Power inescapably corrupts," he writes, "but its assumption is inescapable" after the Holocaust.

The only option in the post-Holocaust world, if we are to avoid repetitions of the human degradation and evil of the Nazi period, is to combine the assumption of power with what Greenberg terms the creation of "better mechanisms of self-criticism, correction and repentance." Only in this way can we utilize power "without being the unwitting slaves of bloodshed or an explotative status quo." (Greenberg, 1981, 24-25.)

I share Greenberg's conviction that a central implication of the return to history demanded by the Holocaust is the willingness to use power. Thus, for me, a meaningful Christian ethic cannot simply reject the use of power in principle, though it certainly may decide that certain configurations of power (e.g. nuclear weaponery) are totally immoral even when the threat of human survival looms large. Here I would take issue with prominent Christian ethicist Stanley Hauerwas who argues for humility as the primary moral response to the Shoah. "What we require is not a god that underwrites our pretensions, but is capable of calling us from our false notions of power and control," according to Hauerwas. (Hauerwas, 1981, 34.) Though I share in Hauerwas' call for the inclusion of humility in post-Shoah ethics, I am unwilling to grant it the pre-eminence that it enjoys in his approach. Hauerwas fails to take seriously enough the human cocreational role after the Holocaust. This failure could prove negatively decisive, inhibiting humanity from assuming the governance of human affairs that is demanded now more than ever. His emphasis on humility without enhanced responsibility could result in people of faith becoming bystanders rather than central actors in human history.

The most recent attempt to think through the Shoah-power equation has come from Marc Ellis in a chapter entitled "The Cost of Empowerment" in his volume TOWARD A JEWISH THEOLOGY OF LIBERATION and an essay called "Learning to Live with Power" prepared for a symposium to be published soon in CHRISTIAN JEWISH RELATIONS. Ellis is quite critical of Irving

Greenberg's viewpoint in particular, though extends the critique to other key Holocaust thinkers as well, including Emil Fackenheim, Ellie Wiesel and Richard Rubenstein:

> The dynamic balance between Holocaust and empowerment found within their analyses of the Holocaust is lost when they enter the realities of the post-Holocaust world. Empowerment, almost without restraint, becomes the watchword. Greenberg's analysis of the State of Israel as the answer to the Holocaust, as the sign of deliverance, as the redemption out of nothingness, destroys the balance. The Jewish people recently liberated from the hell of Nazi Germany can become, in some minds, reluctant heroic warriors charting the historic course of redemption in a hostile world. Though the forms of oppression vary, the world remains essentially the same--hostile to Jewish interest and survival. (Ellis, 1987, 37.)

In my judgment Ellis is somewhat unfair to Greenberg in this critique. He completely ignores Greenberg's insistence on the need to develop better mechanism for the use of power. Be that as it may, I would join with Ellis in emphasizing the overall limitations of Greenberg's perspectives on power as a Shoah response. In my own exchanges with Greenberg I have often drawn upon the prophetic warning issued by the Catholic philosopher Romano Guradini in the light of his experiences in World War II. In a volume entitled POWER AND RESPONSIBILITY Guardini argues that the critical problem facing humankind in the post Nazi, Horoshima era will not be to increase power--though power will surely increase--but to curb power. "The core of the new epoch's intellectual task," in his view, "will be to integrate power into life in such a way that man can employ power without forfeiting his humanity, or to surrender his humanity to power and perish." (Guardin 1, 1961, XIII.)

I can generally join Ellis in asserting that ultimately the viewpoint associated with liberation theological ultimately represents a far more holistic, life--insuring ethical response to the Shoah than the mere power model championed by Greenberg. In the end, the Greenberg-Ellis disagreement comes down to this: shall we develop post-Holocaust ethics on the basis of personal survival alone (as legitimate as this might be up to a point) or must ethics now be grounded in the stress on solidarity with those who have been marginalized by the oppressive political forces of our time? While Ellis' position may require further refinement, I believe it is the better context in which to reflect on post-Shoah ethics.

Such then are some of the major issues I as a Christian ethicist see arising out of the Holocaust experience. The questions I have considered by no means exhaust the possibilities that might arise, but they remain central questions that cannot be avoided. They require ongoing dialogue between Christian and Jewish thinkers. Such dialogue, reflecting the salvific alliance, the alliance of Messianic hope, for which Johannes Metz has called, needs to continue in the future for the sustained moral health of both Christianity and Judaism.

REFERENCES

Chopp, R. (1984). In: The Holocaust as Interruption: (eds E. Schussler-Fiorenza and D. Tracy) Concilium 175, 19-25.
Cohen, A. (1981). The Tremendum, Crossroad.
Cohen, A. (1984). Journal of Reform Judaism 31, 61-68
Donat, A. (1965). The Holocaust Kingdom, Holt, Reinhart and Winston.
Ellis, M. (1987). Toward a Jewish Theology of Liberation, Orbis.
Fackenheim, E. (1978). The Jewish Return into History, Schocken.
Greenberg, I. (1977). In: Auschwitz: Beginning of a New Era?: (ed. E. Fleischer), Katv, 7-55.
Greenberg, I. (1981). Perspectives, 1981, 17-28.
Greenberg, I. (1982). Perspectives, 1982, 10-18.
Guardini, R. (1961). Power and Responsibility, Henry Regnery.
Hauerwas, S. (1981). Cross Currents, 31, 27-38.
Herr, F. (1970). God's First Love, Weybright and Talley.
Herr, F. (1971). Midstream 17, 22-35.
Katz, S. (1983). Post-Holocaust Dialogues, New York University Press.
Lawrence, D.H. (1967). Selected Poems, Penguin.
Littell, F. (1977). Journal of Ecumenical Studies 14:4, 4-17.
Manschreck, C. (1976). In: Church-State Relations-A Question of Sovereignty: (ed. B. Brown Zikmund), Exploration, 1-12.
Metz, J. (1981). The Emergent Church, Crossroad.
Pawlikowski, J.T. (1982). The Challenge of the Holocaust for Christian Theology, Anti-Defamation League.

Pawlikowski, J.T. (1983) In: Critical Issues of the Holocaust:(eds. A. Grobman and Daniel Landes), Rossel, 288-297; 410-418.

Pawlikowski, J.T. (1983) Worship, 58:4, 315-329.

Rubenstein, R. (1966). After Auschwitz, Bobbs-Merrill.

Rubenstein, R. (1973). In: The German Church Struggle and the Holocaust: (eds. F.H. Littell and H.G. Locke), Wayne State University Press, 256-268.

Ryan, M. In: The German Church Struggle and the Holocaust: (eds. F.H. Littell and H.G. Locke), Wayne State University Press,148-164.

Tal, U. (1973-74). Immanuel 3, 62-73.

Tal, U. (1975). Christians and Jews in Germany, Cornell University Press.

Tal, U. (1987). In: Judaism and Christianity under the Impact of National Socialism: (eds. O. Dov Kulka and P.R. Mendes-Flohr), 63-95, Historical Society of Israel.

Tracy, D. (1984). The Interpretation of Theological Texts, Indiana University (unpublished address).

Wolf, A.J. (1983). Sh'ma, 254, 102-105.

Christianity and Covenant in the Post-Holocaust Era

R.L. Platzner

Humanities Department
CSU Sacramento
Sacramento, CA 95819
U.S.A.

As Emil Fackenheim has often and eloquently observed, the Holocaust is the one datum of modern history that no serious theologian can afford to ignore. It has certainly become the point of philosophical departure for much of post-war Jewish theology, but what impact has the Holocaust had on the Christian community?[1] Has the Church begun to assess its own relation to, or role in, the Age of Auschwitz? Has it evolved a "holocaust theology," or at least a body of theological *responsa* equal in depth to the magnitude of spiritual challenge which the crime of genocide poses for the Christian conscience? And finally, has Christendom at last found within some of its most cherished traditions the true source of that "triumphalism" whose dogmatic expression is the doctrine of Israel's rejection by God, and whose secular ideological expression is the Final Solution?

I believe the answer to virtually all of these questions is affirmative: contemporary Christian theology has, at last, begun to examine not only the immediate historical question of the Church's contribution to the culture of hatred upon which Nazism so obviously fed, but also the larger theological issue of the real peril to Christian faith of continuing to maintain, without retraction or qualification, a doctrine of "supersession" that invalidates Judaism as a living faith by delegitimizing Israel's enduring commitment to its covenant with God. Institutionally, both the Catholic Church and the major Protestant denominations have proclaimed, repeatedly, their disavowal of antisemitism as a valid corollary of Christian teaching,[2] but individual Christian scholars have gone farther still--toward a theological "revision" (and ultimately a repudiation) of the exegetical logic upon which the doctrine of supersession relies, and it is to the latter issue that I first propose to turn my attention.

At the heart of the Christian claim (whether ancient or modern) to have dispossessed Israel as the chosen agent of human redemption in the world--the chief salvific role assigned to Israel in the Prophetic tradition--lie some of the most problematical texts of the New Testament: the Pauline letters to the Romans and the Galatians, and the "letter" to Hebrews. Of the three, Hebrews is perhaps the least ambiguous, consisting largely of an extended Neoplatonic *midrash* on the theme of Jesus as both ultimate sacrifice and eternal priest (a double displacement thesis). Thus, reasoning from the "lower," literal understanding of the earthly sanctuary to a "higher" typological exegesis of Exodus 25-6, the author of Hebrews asserts the superiority of Christ to Moses and Aaron, and the spiritual nature of the Covenant Christ has sealed with his blood, in in contrast to the transient, material Covenant established with Israel:

> . . .the ministry which has fallen to Jesus is as far superior to theirs [i.e. the Jews] as the covenant he mediates and the promises upon which it is secured (Hebrews 8:6).

The earthly sanctuary, therefore, is but a copy of "heavenly things," in Neoplatonic terminology a "shadow" or "false image," like the law itself, and who (except, perhaps, someone still imprisoned in Plato's cave) would prefer the carnal imitation of divine grace to the spiritual reality? As for the "old" Covenant, it has been superseded by the divine "oath" under which Christ assumed his mediatorial function, and with disarmingly circular logic the author of Hebrews asks whether a "New" Covenant would have been granted to humankind at all had the old Covenant not failed to achieve the redemption of Israel and the world. Seen from this perspective the old Covenant must appear obsolescent, at best; at worst, it can only seem an inferior rival on the brink of extinction.

Romans and Galatians offer a far more complex scenario and rationale for the displacement of the Obsolete Testament, if only because Paul seems determined to assign at least a pragmatic (and therefore temporal) function to the Law, or Torah as it would be described in a normative Jewish context. In Galatians 3:19, for example, Paul portrays the Law as a "temporary measure," intended essentially as an instrument of collective inculpation. According to this view, the Law cannot save, it can only indict, or at best, raise to the level of full consciousness the hopelessness of ever attaining "justification" through moral effort alone. Indeed, without the "promise" of redemption from sin made possible by the intercessory sacrifice of Christ, the Law comes to be perceived as both a "curse" and a form of "bondage," since neither righteousness nor spiritual freedom can be achieved, Paul insists, apart from or outside of the New Covenant of those who have become incorporate in Christ. Neither the Law nor the Covenant with Israel were ever intended, then, to accomplish what Christ alone can achieve, and while the Law and the Old Covenant are not in themselves a source of evil, they cannot (and have not) overcome the evil which grace alone can subdue.

Paul is even more explicit on this latter point in Romans 8:3, where the contrast between pistis (Faith) and nomos (Law) is related directly to the redemptive role of Christ:

> What the law could never do, because our lower nature robbed it of all potency, God has done: by sending his own Son in a form like that of our own sinful nature, and as a sacrifice for sin, he has passed judgment against sin within that very nature. . .

The Law may very well be "holy," in and of itself, as Paul elsewhere insists, but is is unavailing or ineffectual for those who live outside the Law (because they are Gentiles by birth) or for those who, though living under the Law, continually violate its precepts. Neither Greek nor Jew, therefore enjoys any spiritual "advantage" in the quest for salvation since neither possesses sufficient power to overcome man's "lower nature." And while Jews may rightly take pride in their historical covenant with God and in the "splendour of the divine presence" (Romans 9:4) made manifest on Sinai, only the "children born through God's promise" (reaffirmed through Christ's sacrifice) can legitimately describe themselves as Abraham's "true" descendants (Romans 9:8). On the basis of this equation, the early Church could (and did) claim to have displaced Israel in the line of Scriptural succession, and by virtue of having attained a "higher" righteousness through faith in the very Son of God apostate Israel had rejected.[3]

However, Paul (in contrast to many patristic writers) was apparently unwilling to renounce, altogether, the hope that "the men of [his] own race," might, out of "emulation" (Romans 11:14) of the Christian Gentiles, seek admittance to the community of those who had found in Christ the *telos* of the Law. And whether the word *telos*, in this context, is taken to mean either "end" or "fulfillment," or both, Paul's perception of contemporary Judaism emerges as essentially (if not consistently) *eschatological* in nature. It is on *that* basis that Paul can argue, paradoxically, that Israel's rejection of Christ was both necessary (for the salvation of the Gentiles) and an act of "blindness" whose cure (i.e. Israel's conversion) would accompany the fulfillment of precisely those messianic promises--and Paul specifically cites the resurrection of the dead--which Christ's first coming had left unfulfilled.[4]

By the second century, both the diminution of eschatological fervor and the virtual disappearance of any form of Jewish Christianity insured that the now pervasively Gentile Church would take a far less sympathetic and dialectical view of Jewish "obduracy" than had Paul, and with predictable theological consequences. As the *Adversus Judaeos* tradition in patristic literature makes clear, the forfeiture of Paul's visionary wish to unite Gentile and Jew in the service of the one God left the field of Christian polemic open to those who, like Cyprian, saw nothing in Judaism but the creed of a spiritually degenerate community whose rejection of the New Covenant, and subsequent rejection by God, the prophets of Israel had clearly foretold.[5] From that premise and a hose of Biblical *testimonia*, Chrysostom could draw the radical conclusion that Judaism was really a clever form of atheism ("No Jew worships God"), the synagogue a brothel or the lair of demons, and the Jews a race of deicides.[6] It is at this point, theologically if not historically, that the logic of supersession and the mania of genocide begin to converge.[7]

For those post-war Christian theologians who are engaged in examining or re-thinking the Christological and covenantal bases of Christian thought, the Holocaust stands as something more and other than just another tragic event of modern history--it stands, for them, as a *paradigmatic* event of Christian self-betrayal and self-recognition. For Franklin Littell the connecting links between the displacement theology I have just outlined and a post-Christian ideology of "racial" annihilation are direct and unambiguous. "The genocidal note," Littell insists, was "already present in the superseding or displacement myths," and thus the Final Solution can be seen as a "logical extension" of the patristic claim that "God was finished with the Jewish people" (Littell 30). "Theological antisemitism," Littell concludes, is therefore a perversion of Christianity, whatever its pedigree may be, and a betrayal of Christianity's proper role in history, which Littell defines as that of a theological "counter-culture" (Littel 4). For Christianity to play that role successfully, he argues, it *must* maintain some "living interaction with the people of the Torah" (Littell5).

An equally decisive "revisionist" posture toward traditional Christology--and the anti-Judaic doctrines it has spawned--has been adopted by Rosemary Ruether, whose Faith and Fratricide advances the thesis that displacement theology represents a "pathological" denial of the unredeemed character of history after Christ's sacrifice and the establishment of the Christian ecclesia (245). For the Church, she argues, Judaism preserves a living (and daunting) memory of the condition of covenant faith before Jesus' birth and in spite of his entry into human time, thus offering to the world a model of collective loyalty to a redemptive vision that Christianity cannot entirely absorb or preempt. And precisely because Judaism preserves a more ancient memory of covenant promises yet to be accomplished, it offers to Christianity a corrected sense of historical perspective. Divorced from its Judaic origins, Ruether warns, Christian faith can easily degenerate into a variety of millenialist delusions, or merge with some form of pagan ideology (220-25).

Even somewhat more conservative theologians like James Parkes and A. Roy Eckardt incline toward Ruether's view that the Church's refusal to acknowledge Judaism's living witness to God constitutes a "critical theological error in the heart of the Christian gospel" (Ruether 245). To correct that error, Parkes offers his own version of the doctrine of continuous revelation, in which Sinai and Calvary are perceived as paired focal events in an ongoing history of "incarnational" encounters with the divine:

> I believe that the relationship between man and God is continuous, that the spirit of God dwells in man, and that man finds his ultimate satisfaction only in communion with God. But on these two occasions there was, as it were, a spark between the terminals of "I" and "Thou" which made possible unique developments in space and time of this permanent communion with the Creator (Parkes, Judaism 28).

By emphasizing the "unique" character of each event, Parkes bypasses entirely the anti-Judaic invidium that often accompanies any evocation of the concept of progressive religious development. Indeed, Parkes is particularly emphatic on the foolishness of attempting any invidious comparison between Judaism and Christianity, and precisely because he perceives the two faiths as complementary rather than competitive forms of covenantal spirituality:

> The distinction between the two revelations lies not in the sphere of a purer or a less pure monotheism, nor, in spite of a good deal of Christian teaching, in the distinction between an affirmative and a negative attitude to this world. It lies in the complementary, not contradictory, sphere of the individual. That highest purpose of God which Sinai reveals to men in community, Calvary reveals to man as an end in himself. The difference between the two events, both of which from the metaphysical standpoint are identical as expressions of the infinite in the finite...lies in the fact that the first could not be fulfilled by a brief demonstration of a divine community in action; but the second could not be fulfilled except by a life lived under human conditions from birth to death (Parkes, Judaism 30).

The separation of Judaism and Christianity is an undeniable historical reality, Parkes concedes, but not necessarily an expression of the "divine intention" (Parkes, Judaism 31). Neither revelation, therefore, can be seen as complete or expendable, and though Parkes can neither formulate nor foresee the means by which a synthesis of belief systems might be accomplished, he is clearly not content with any form of "two-covenant" theology that precludes, by its very structure, any possible reunification of Christ to Israel. A distinct (albeit muted) note of eschatological expectation enters into Parkes' thinking at this point, and something very like the Pauline vision of a partly-hidden, partly perceived congruence of seemingly diverted paths, both leading to the same divine goal, begins to emerge. This vision affects, ultimately, Parkes' understanding of the Trinity as well, for in the latter he finds a mysterious, ontological basis for a third "way," which neither creed can truthfully claim to embody--an as-yet-unforeseen manifestation of God's presence to mankind, to which Sinai and Calvary will figure as dialectical anticipations (Parkes, Prelude 216-21).

Writing in a more confessional vein, A. Roy Eckardt attempts to mediate between what he has termed theologies of "continuity" and "discontinuity"--that is, Christian theologies which either accept or reject Israel's continuing role in that divine economy of salvation in which Christ is also a part--while recognizing that the ultimate and most appalling form of discontinuity is that which manifests itself in the neo-Marcionism of the "German Christian" movement that flourished during the Third Reich (Eckardt 81). Attempting to transcend this antinomy, and at the same time offer his own "dialectical" variation upon earlier theologies of continuity, Eckardt proposes a critical/extrapolative reading of Romans 9-11 (and of the entire supersessionist tradition) that places in harmonious perspective the necessarily tensive relationship between Jewish and Christian covenantalism. By aligning the theological role of Judaism with the historical role of the Protestant church, Eckardt finds in the Jewish witness of faith in the Father (and, correlatively, its witness of disbelief in the Son) a "protestant" affirmation of belief in a divine order and spiritual discipline outside of and beyond the dogmatic perspective of the Church. "The witness of Israel," Eckardt declares, "chastens the church" by opposing those "idols" (like unbridled and suicidal nationalism) which Christian cultures cannot seem to resist on their own (Eckardt 150). By virtue of its enduring "exile" within Christian civilization, Jewish faith in divine justice and in the "irrevocability" of divine election stands as a perpetual challenge to Christian complacency and other otherworldliness. And by adopting Franz Rosenzweig's vision of a bipolar covenant, in which each faith bears witness to God in its historically singular way, Eckardt can affirm Judaism's "enduring task"--which can be fulfilled, he insists, only by an adherence to Torah and to a postponed eschatology of a Messiah-to-come--while expressing gratitude that through Christ the one, abiding Covenant with Israel has now become "open" to the world (Eckardt 159-60).

At the core of Eckardt's theology of Judaism lies a conviction that is, for him, inseparable from a "true" Christian understanding of Providence and of the incarnate will of God in history: the realization that the "inner meaning of Israel" is to be understood only and finally as a "divine mystery," and explicable only in relation to the even greater enigma of the divine nature and its unfolding in time (Eckardt 43). The unity of that nature defies and transcends the divisions of culture, and in their transhistorical commitment to the one God, the "siblings" of the one Covenant cannot create a hierarchy of relationship that denies the will of the Father who has elected both to serve Him.

III

Viewed analytically, the post-Holocaust theological statements I have paraphrased above all reflect the dual agenda of post-war Christian ecumenism. At the very least, these recantations and refutations of displacement theology represent what the German Catholic scholar Franz Mussner has called "theological reparations:" that is, an expressed need, motivated by horror and contrition, to distance the Church from the culture of genocide, and more specifically from the pseudo-Christian ideology advanced by Nazi apologetics.[8] By denying that any scripturally legitimate doctrine of supersession can be derived from the New testament, revisionist Christian scholarship destroys the chief dogmatic prop on which all "theologies" of antisemitism once relied. Without scriptural sanction, anti-Judaic teachings, whether within or outside the institutional literature of the Christian churches, could then be more easily isolated and repudiated, thus (hopefully) laying to rest such classics of anti-Judaic preachment as Chrysostom's Antioch sermons or Luther's "Concerning the Jews and their Lies." Such cleansing of the extended canon of Christian thought was long overdue, and well before the Holocaust; after it, it has become inescapable.

The other and more problematic goal of post-Holocaust Christian theology--what Mussner has termed the "hermeneutic function" of the Holocaust itself (Mussner 4)--demands a commitment to philosophical reciprocity that exceeds the limits of institutional diplomacy. The fashionable term for such discourse of reconciliation is "dialogue," but from the Christian point of view what is often at stake is not just a deeper understanding of Judaism or a better grasp of the history of doctrinal evolutions within the church, but something more elusive: a sharpened sense of the complex dynamic that still governs the relationship between Judaism and Christianity. The singular complexity of that relationship best reveals itself in the recent revival of the so-called "witness-people" theory, thought in a dogmatic setting vastly different from that of Augustine and his contemporaries. In its ancient form the witness-people theory explained the "anomaly" of Jewish existence (and persistence in disbelief) as a sign of God's continuing anger toward Israel and as a consequence of His wish to use them as an _exemplum horrendum_ to the nations, a continuous warning of the consequences of collective apostasy (Flannery 52-3). Any attempt to preserve this teaching in its traditional, however, would have the unacceptable result of placing the Church on the side of the Third Reich, regarding the latter as a suitable instrument of divine judgment against the Jews, and few if any post-war Christian thinkers have even attempted to defend this thesis.[9]

Nevertheless, the witness-people concept has, though in a very different guise, begun to resurface, only this time in a manifestly revisionist context and as an expression of new ideas at work in contemporary soteriology. Roy Eckardt's argument, cited earlier, that Israel witnesses not only _to_ its own covenanted loyalty but also _against_ Christian idolatries, is one rather obvious illustration of this tendency of thought, but one that carries with it certain unanticipated theological consequences. Thus, when Eckardt declares that Israel's ultimate act of covenant-witness is its rejection of any creed (sacred or secular) that advances the claim of final and total redemption, he is, in effect, assigning to Judaism a corrective role once reserved exclusively for the Church, and by that stroke achieves nothing less than a complete inversion of traditional soteriological perspective. In fact, to argue, as he does, that Judaism is called by God to protest continually against the "unredeemedness of the world" (Eckardt 106) is to promote the corollary that, in Christ, the eschaton has not been fully "realized," that the work of world-redemption exceeds the capabilities of the Church, and that the plurality of covenanted relationships is a divine paradox and not mere human error. That Eckardt refuses to reject any or all of these possibilities reveals just how open, and even precarious, the process of theological reasoning has become for those Christians who find themselves summoned to evolve what one scholar has described as a "theology of mutual recognition."[10]

It would be foolish, or perhaps simply premature, to predict just how far beyond "mutual recognition" the Jewish-Christian dialogue may go, or to what extent the mere renewal of dialogue may already have altered the historical disposition of each faith-community toward the other. In the peroration of his ecumenical masterpiece, Two Types of Faith, Martin Buber speaks movingly of things "unsaid" (174) between Christian and Jew, and it is at least arguable that, from this moment on, the contentious rhetoric of displacement and duality may yield to a gentler, wiser discourse. One thing does seem presently clear, however, and that is, for an increasing number of reflective, spiritually awakened Christians living in the shadow of the ultimate denial of both God and humanity, it is no longer possible to withdraw from history into a delusive theology of self-aggrandizement and supersession.

Notes

[1]Emil Fackenheim and Steven Katz, among other Jewish philosophical writers, have actively promoted this view. For Fackenheim, the Holocaust approaches, in its momentousness and spiritual impact, those "root experiences" (like Sinai) through which a "commanding" presence is manifested to Israel (67-98). For Katz, the Holocaust is the inescapable starting point of all theodicidical reasoning (268-83). On the Christian side, Alan Davies, whose essay "Response to Irving Greenberg" appears in Fleischner (57-64), sees in the Holocaust (as in the Crucivixion) one more traumatic reminder of the "scandalous" nature of all human history seen from the Providential point of view. Similarly, Father John Pawlikowski, in his study of contemporary Christologies, observes in the work of German theologians like Kung and Moltmann a profound consciousness of the Holocaust as a primary challenge to Christian understanding of the Covenant and the Cross (47-8, 136-47).

[2]Rabbi Ben-Zion Bokser surveys the principal ecumenical pronouncements of Christian churches up to the mid-sixties (358-77) and finds both sincere contrition and continuing ambivalence. David Cairns, whose essay "Towards a New Relationship Between Christians and Jews" appear in Rousseau (197-206), makes similar observations with respect to the German Evangelical Church. Franz Mussner focuses mainly on Nostra Aetate, No.4 (1-4, 251-3), in which he finds an irreversible refutation of the doctrines of supersession and collective guilt--a view not widely shared by Jewish scholars.

[3]Clark Williamson, in his essay "Christ Against the Jews: A Review of John Sobrino's Christology" in Rousseau (145-53) outlines the fuller development of this argument in the writings of Tertullian, and points to its latter-day reincarnation in the "liberation theologies" of the later 20th century.

[4]John Gager places particular stress on the "apocalyptic orientation" of Paul's teaching (263-4) and on his dialectical view of Israel and of Christ, arguing that Paul never categorically rejected either the Law or Israel's Covenant. Instead, Gager suggests, Paul's chief concern was to demonstrate to his Gentile audience that Christ had become for them what Torah was for Israel.

[5]Father Edward Flannery provides a succinct summation of the adversus judaeos tradition within patristic writings (40-65), while Gager summarizes the testimonia employed by Cyprian to demonstrate, scripturally, the irrevocable rejection of Judaism and the Church's displacement of Israel (155-6). The Epistle of Barnabas, a non-canonical, early second century Christian exegesis of Exodus, provides a similar, typologically proof of the "smashing" (by God, not Moses) of the Sinai Covenant to make way for the New Covenant of Christ.

[6]Chrysostom is the principal (though by no means the only) source for this accusation (Meeks and Wilken 90-3), and he has no difficulty demonstrating to his audience that the synagogue is a meeting-place of demons.

[7]Littell (60-80) and Katz (292-5) argue forcefully for a causal link between the "diabolization of the Jew," through Christian doctrine and folklore, and the "secularization" of this demonic image in Nazi myth.

[8]Mussner's phrase--"theological reparation"--which he affixes to the fifth chapter of his Tractate on the Jews, has a very special historical resonance for his German audience. With that in mind, one can better understand the enormous weight that he attaches to the exegetical tradition from which theological antisemitism draws its appearance of respectability. For an understanding of the doctrinal roots and character of the "German Christian" movement, see Arthur C. Cochrane's essay, "The Message of Barmen for Contemporary Church History" in Littell and Locke (185-202).

[9]The one glaring exception to this general observation can be found in remarks attributed to Dean Heinrich Gruber by Richard Ruberstein (47-58). Whether or not Ruberstein actually related, with complete accuracy, the whole of his dialogue with Gruber is irrelevant to our purposes; his delineation of a traditionalist "theodicy of genocide" demonstrates the inherent absurdity of this entire line of reasoning.

[10]After surveying various attempts to re-write the terms of Jewish-Christian dialogue, Harold H. Ditmanson ["Judaism and Christianity: A Theology of Co-Existence," in Rousseau, 183-195] proposes a new understanding of Paul's covenantal theology to allow for both Jewish "identity" and "autonomy." John Pawlikowski and Paul van Buren attempt to carry this agenda one step further by suggesting specific terms of theological rapprochement. For Pawlikowski, supersessionist thinking, after the Holocaust, is not only a "moral obscenity" but more fundamentally an impoverishment of the Christian sense of Jesus' relation to his own history and culture. For van Buren, the parallel paths of Jewish and Christian faith lead directly to the Lord of history who remains, unalterably, the God of Israel. Christ's "new way" therefore opens the Covenant to the Gentiles without closing it to those who remain faithful to the "way of Torah."

Works Cited

Bokser, Ben-Zion. _Judaism and the Christian Predicament._ New York: Alfred A. Knopf, 1967.

Buber, Martin. _Two Types of Faith._ New York: Macmillan Publishing Company, 1951.

Eckardt, A. Roy. _Elder and Younger Brothers: The Encounter of Jews and Christians._ New York: Charles Scribners Sons, 1967.

Fackenheim, Emil L. _God's Presence in History._ New York: Harper Torchbooks, 1972.

Flannery, Edward H. _The Anguish of the Jews: Twenty-Three Centuries of Anti-Semitism._ New York: Paulist Press, 1985.

Fleischner, Eva, ed. _Auschwitz: Beginning of a New Era?_ Reflections on the Holocaust. New York: Ktav, 1977.

Gager, John G. _The Origins of Anti-Semitism: Attitudes Toward Judaism in Pagan and Christian Antiquity._ New York: Oxford University Press, 1983.

Katz, Steven T. _Post-Holocaust Dialogues: Critical Studies in Modern Jewish Thought._ New York: New York University Press, 1985.

Littell, Franklin H. _The Crucifixion of the Jews._ New York: Harper and Row, 1975.

___, and Hubert G. Locke, eds. _The German Church Struggle and the Holocaust._ Detroit: Wayne State University Press, 1974.

Meeks, Wayne A., and Robert L. Wilken. _Jews and Christians in Antioch: In the First Four Centuries of the Common Era._ Missoula: Scholars Press, 1978.

Mussner, Franz. _Tractate on the Jews: The Significance of Judaism for Christian Faith._ Trans. Leonard Swidler. Philadelphia: Fortress Press, 1984.

Parkes, James. Judaism and Christianity. Chicago: University of Chicago Press, 1948.

____. Prelude to Dialogue: Jewish-Christian Relationships. New York: Schocken Books, 1969.

Pawlikowski, John T. Christ in the Light of Jewish-Christian Dialogue. New York: Paulist Press, 1982.

Rousseau, Richard W., ed. Christianity and Judaism: the Deepening Dialogue. Scranton: Ridge Row Press, 1983.

Rubenstein, Richard. After Auschwitz. Indianapolis: Bobbs-Merrill, 1966.

Ruether, Rosemary. Faith and Fratricide: the Theological Roots of Anti-Semitism. New York: The Seabury Press, 1974.

Van Buren, Paul. Discerning the Way: A Theology of Jewish-Christian Reality. New York: The Seabury Press, 1980.

ON THE IMPOSSIBILITY AND NECESSITY OF BEING A CHRISTIAN: POST-HOLOCAUST REFLECTIONS BASED ON THE THOUGHT OF JEAN AMÉRY AND EMIL FACKENHEIM

JOHN K. ROTH

Claremont McKenna College, Claremont, California 91711, U.S.A.

ABSTRACT

Jean Améry's At the Mind's Limits: Contemplations by a Survivor on Auschwitz and Its Realities contains a chapter "On the Necessity and Impossibility of Being a Jew." In To Mend the World: Foundations of Future Jewish Thought, Emil Fackenheim asserts that "Christianity is ruptured by the Holocaust." Based on those perspectives, this essay reflects on the impossibility and necessity of being a Christian in a post-Holocaust world.

INTRODUCTION

Jean Améry's life took him from his native Austria to Belgium and then to captivity in Auschwitz. Liberated from Bergen-Belsen in April 1945, this philosopher waited twenty years before breaking his silence about Hitler's death camps. Among his autobiographical essays in At the Mind's Limits, which was originally published in 1966, is one entitled "On the Necessity and Impossibility of Being a Jew." There Améry describes a conversion that overtook him in his early twenties.

Highly assimilated, the only child of a Catholic mother and a Jewish father, Améry studied a newspaper in a Viennese coffeehouse. It was autumn, 1935. The Nuremberg Laws had just been promulgated in Nazi Germany. Améry's reading made him see--unmistakably, fatefully--that he was indeed Jewish. Henceforth he would struggle with the necessity and impossibility of that fact. The battle ended on 17 October 1978 with his suicide.

Summing up his dilemma, it seemed to Améry that the impossibility of his being Jewish hinged on the recognition that, "Everyone must be who he was in the first years of his life, even if later these were buried under. No one can become what he cannot find in his memories" (Améry, 1986, p. 84).[1] Améry's memories lacked the authority to define social reality in the mid-1930s. Increasingly, however, the Nazi state did possess such power. Its definitions made Améry Jewish even if his own memory did not. As he confronted that reality, the unavoidability of his being Jewish took on another dimension. By identifying him as a Jew, Nazi power made him "a dead man on leave, someone to be murdered, who only by chance was not yet where he properly belonged" (p. 86). Améry's response was to make an imposed necessity his: Accepting the Nazi judgment, "with the decision to overcome it through revolt , . . . I took it upon myself to be a Jew" (p. 90).

AN EXISTENTIAL POINT OF REFERENCE

Améry believed that "the Holocaust is truly the existential reference point for all Jews" (p. 93). We Christians would do well to contemplate how a related point pertains to us. The Holocaust must be an existential reference point for us just because that event focuses fundamental issues about the impossibility and necessity of being a Christian. No one has identified those issues more pointedly than the Jewish philosopher, Emil Fackenheim. Particularly in his 1982 book, To Mend the World: Foundations of Future Jewish Thought, he writes "Concerning Post-Holocaust Christianity" and asserts that "Christianity is ruptured by the Holocaust" (p. 278). That claim is tragic, because the rupture reveals both the historic failure of Christian practice during the Holocaust, whose roots are deep in centuries of religious antisemitism, and the problematic character of contemporary Christian belief.

If we Christians confront the rupture, Fackenheim believes, that encounter will involve "the 'destructive recovery' of the whole Christian 'tradition'--an enterprise whose outcome and consequences are unforeseeable" (p. 282). Fackenheim does not say so directly, but one of those consequences may be the impossibility of being a Christian. This sense of impossibility would not arise, as Amery's did, from the lack of memory, but it is nonetheless related to his experience. A post-Holocaust sense of the impossibility of being a Christian would derive primarily from recognition of the past. For some Christians that outcome is likely to produce outright rejection of Christianity, but significantly Fackenheim encourages a more dialectically nuanced result.

Fackenheim reminds us that social reality decisively includes Christianity. Despite the historical record, he is convinced the world's mending requires not that tradition's elimination but its reconstruction. Christians, Fackenheim implies, should take a stance akin to Jean Améry's. A post-Holocaust sense that it is no longer possible to be a Christian in a world that has been defined irrevocably and often so tragically by Christian theory and practice should be met by a spirit of repentant resistance that underwrites the necessity of overcoming the impossibility. The Christian reconstruction needed to help mend the world and Jewish-Christian relationships in particular depends on deeds. Hence as we Christians recover our past, we need to re-examine the possibilities it once contained and how we might build in a healing way on what was done with them. Realistically and hopefully at once, what follows here seeks to make a contribution in that direction.

APOSTASY NOT PERSECUTION

Cain quizzed God: "'Am I my brother's keeper?'" According to the biblical story (Genesis 4:1-16), this first-born of Adam and Eve did so in reply to God's inquiry concerning the whereabouts of Abel. Despite the ignorance implied by Cain's response, Abel's location was well known to them both. His blood crying to God from the ground, Abel was dead, murdered by his brother out of envy because he found favor not granted to Cain. The story says that God cursed Cain: "'When you till the ground, it shall no longer yield to you its strength; you shall be a fugitive and a wanderer on the earth'" (v. 12). Then God marked Cain for life so no one would kill him, and Cain departed to the east of Eden. Jewish and Christian histories have repeated that sibling rivalry, typically inverting the relation of elder to younger brother so that most often Christian Cains have slaughtered Jewish Abels. Thus it was during the Holocaust when Cain's question tested every Christian. Its indelible mark remains.

"If we claim to be Christians there is no room for expediency. Hitler is the Anti-Christ. Therefore we must go on with our work and eliminate him whether he is successful or not."[2] Implicated in the July 1944 plot against Hitler, the author of those words, long a dissenter against National Socialism, was hanged by the SS at Flossenburg on 9 April 1945 only days before Germany surrendered. Dietrich Bonhoeffer is frequently named to show that within Germany there was Christian resistance to the Third Reich. That resistance was not only individual but also institutional, for Bonhoeffer helped to lead the Confessing Church (Bekennende Kirche) that battled the Nazis and the accomodation of German Christianity to their policies. Among its membership, and in other segments of the German population as well, courageous men and women made strenuous efforts to stem the tide of antisemitism, to save Jewish families, and to strive for amicable relations between Gentiles and Jews, even if such efforts cost their lives. Once entrenched, however, Nazi totalitarianism was extremely hard to dislodge from within. It was easier to "go along." Most Germans did.

The German people were not uniformly rabid Jew-haters. Nor did Hitler come to power primarily because he advocated making Germany Judenrein--least of all by using gas chambers and crematoria. Hitler and his cohorts, obsessed with racial hatred and a murderous historical mission, nevertheless found the support they needed to assume dictatorial control of the German state and its population. Auschwitz eventually followed. It did so partly because most Germans were normal people. Unfortunately, normal people are not particularly heroic. Imperfect, they usually worry about themselves and their families first and about others--especially if the others seem alien--later, if at all. The compliance of normal Germans therefore helped Hitler target and dispatch defenseless persons by the millions. By contrast, opposition to Nazism by Bonhoeffer and other Germans was indeed heroic, all the more so as one recognizes that theirs was a minority example.

As a Christian, Bonhoeffer did not stand alone. In Germany a chorus of Christian dissent could be heard. Yet it was comparatively small, its timing off, its voice on "the Jewish question" erratic or faint if existent at all. As Hitler rose to power, an overwhelming majority of Germans could be called baptized Christians. Not all were practicing believers, let alone authentic followers of Jesus, but Germany was at the heart of Christian civilization. Only a small percentage of Germans would have denied a Christian identity. Indeed, despite Protestant-Catholic tensions, that identity did much to foster senses of German community. Far from opposing Hitler, early on most German Christians welcomed and trusted him. Their allegiance, moreover, was not offered in spite of his Jew-hatred but at times even because of it. Probably because they thought the claim incredibly exaggerated, their fidelity to the Reich was not shaken when leading Nazis such as Martin Bormann, Hitler's closest associate, paraded openly what Hitler believed but prudently downplayed, namely, that "national Socialism and Christianity are irreconciliable."[3]

Christian resistance to the Reich was excised by Nazi persecution. That generalization is valid, but more accurate, claims one Christian scholar, is the acknowledgment that "apostasy not persecution is the key word" (Littell, 1974, p. 16) in assessing why German Christians did not resist Hitler more effectively. Religiously equivalent to treason, apostasy occurs when people forsake their "loyalty to a community and its beliefs" (Littell, 1975, p. 75). That definition admits that not all baptized Christians are necessarily authentic Christians. To say or do some things and not to say or do others is to renounce a religious identity even if one still claims to possess it. Such distinctions, however, depend on norms that legitimize differentiations between genuine believers and apostates. Rarely are those standards simply agreed upon or easily enforced. Certainly they were much disputed within Hitler's Germany. Yet today the consensus is that apostasy was rife among baptized Christians in Germany and elsewhere during the Nazi era. For example, anti-Jewish legislation, Kristallnacht, and the methodical Einsatzgruppen, not to mention Treblinka and Auschwitz, demonstrated that in Germany Christian obedience to the state usually transcended loyalty to God, faith in Hitler commonly superseded dedication to Jesus, and true worship typically lost out to unrepentant idolatry as masses turned to the false gods of pure blood, race, and culture. Not only in Germany, elsewhere also millions of Christians did too little to thwart and too much to support a regime that would have sent Peter, Paul, Mary, and even Jesus to the gas chambers. Whether through failure to take Christian identity seriously, zealous commitment to a religion identified as Christian but fundamentally antithetical to Jesus' teaching, or some disposition in between, apostasy abounded in Christian civilization from 1933 to 1945.

THE BOUNDARIES OF OBLIGATION

As Jews were "defined, labeled, stripped, isolated, stored, and shipped" (Fein, 1979, p. 33), they were increasingly excluded--intentionally by the Nazis and their collaborators and at least functionally by most other communities--from circles in which people honor reciprocal responsibilities to protect each other. As far as Germany's churches were concerned, such an exclusion was driven home by the fact that Christians did protest Nazi encroachments when Christian lives were at stake, though imperfectly even then, but threats to Jews tended to be observed silently. Determination to care for one's own and to ignore or even to harm others in the process is natural, but other forces work within human existence, too. Among them are questions about the boundaries of obligation. "Am I my brother's keeper?" is one of those questions. And "Who is my neighbor?" is another.

According to the New Testament, Jesus explained that his Jewish way had two essential elements: to love God and to love one's neighbor as oneself (Matthew 22:37-40). For anyone who claims to be a Christian, a follower of Jesus, loving one's neighbor as oneself defines the boundaries of obligation. Hence it is critical to know how to answer the question, who is one's neighbor? Jesus deftly turned that question back on its asker with a parable about a Good Samaritan who cared for a defenseless victim who had been robbed, beaten, ignored by religious leaders, and left to die. Jesus' implication was that the Good Samaritan "'proved neighbor to the man who fell among the robbers'" because he let need--not race, nationality, class, or creed--define his universe of obligation. A Christian is to emulate the Good Samaritan's compassionate service. True Christians will never say they do so completely. They confess shortcomings, even willful failures, which is why they ask God to strengthen their resolve to keep trying. So it bears repeating: not all Christians are Christian. Authentic ones try persistently to be the Good Samaritan. Many others call themselves Christian, but that identification is inauthentic to the extent that they ignore the expanded boundaries of obligation suggested by Jesus. Of such narrowness, apostasy is made.

It is fantasy to presume that fully authentic Christians and churches could have prevented Auschwitz. Their numbers have always been too few. Numerous, however, were the less than authentic Christians who made possible the establishment of a powerful Christian culture hostile to Jews. They could have prevented the Holocaust, for in reality they were indispensable in bringing it about.

Sociology confirms these suspicions.[4] Both in percentages and in gross numbers, the degree of Jewish victimization in various European states correlates directly with the prevalence of prewar antisemitism in those places. Where antisemitism was intense, public cooperation in targeting Jews was easier, help for Jews scarcer, and Jewish evasion more difficult than in states with lower levels of anti-Jewish feeling. Yet there are problems in assuming that those correlations imply cause and effect. In virtually every case it is equally clear that whenever the Nazis chose to maximize their efforts, the Jewish death rate was staggering. Consider Poland: of its 3.3 million Jews, ninety percent perished. Add in Germany and Austria, the Ukraine and other Russian territories where the _Einsatzgruppen_ roamed at will, Hungary after the Nazi occupation in 1944: there are more than another 1.5 million Jewish deaths. Whatever inferences one draws about the levels of antisemitism in those areas, the Nazis had vast power to enforce boundaries of obligation that excluded Jews totally. That authority crumbled only as military might intervened from the outside. In only a few European countries did more than fifty percent of the Jewish population escape.

Antisemitism abounded, and where it did not, Nazi violence impeded public opposition by the major churches. Nevertheless, some correlations still hold. Where the churches resisted there were fewer Jewish victims. Where Christian officials spoke out against Nazi policies, Jews had more success in evading their enemies. Where significant Christian protest was found, state collaboration with the Nazis was checked. Likewise, when Christian protests were minimal or absent, such collaboration went unarrested. When both church and state maintained solidarity with Jews, the yield of victims was lowest of all. Had these correlations been more widespread, Nazi success would have been far less. Realistically, however, there is not much reason to think that the churches and people involved were likely to act very differently than they did.

CLOSER TO HOME

This analysis of Christian history related to the Holocaust has focused thus far on Europe. What was the reaction in the United States? Typical accounts of American reaction acknowledge that silence prevailed. Then they go on to explain that trustworthy information was lacking and that the geographical regions involved were sufficiently remote to situate Holocaust rumors far from the center of American consciousness. Auschwitz, after all, was an out-of-the-way place in eastern Europe, obscured by global combat that took heavy American casualties in the Pacific as well as in western Europe.

Recent scholarship does little to change the view that silence prevailed in the United States, but it also makes clear that one loophole, a simple appeal to ignorance, must be closed. That judgment holds not only for the American government but also for American Christianity. Important studies done by Robert W. Ross and David S. Wyman use the activity of the Protestant press as a point of reference. Their findings disagree. Ross contends that "'the whole story" of the Holocaust appeared "extensively, continuously, and often comprehensively in the American Protestant press" (1980, p. 258).[5] Challenging Ross's handling of the data, Wyman argues that the coverage was "hardly extensive." A more apt judgment, he believes, is that "the bulk of the Protestant press was silent, or nearly so" (1984, pp. 318, 413). The collision of these analyses, however, gives little comfort to those who would simply plead ignorance where the Holocaust was concerned. Degrees of awareness no doubt varied considerably, and ignorance may have been a legitimate claim in many individual cases, but in general American Protestants--especially those in leadership positions--were not uninformed. Although not always on the front pages, reports about Nazi treatment of the Jews had been carried in the American press from the beginning of the Third Reich. By November 1942 and regularly thereafter authenticated information about the Nazi extermination of the Jews was made public in the United States. One way or another, silence prevailed in spite of knowledge, a proposition valid for American Catholics as well.

If silence and accompanying inaction, but not sheer ignorance, were the norms for American Protestants where the Holocaust was concerned, it is also true that some Protestant leaders and groups, frequently sustained by support from American Jewish agencies, worked hard to arouse a meaningful response. Their achievements, however, make it possible to list shortcomings that warrant consideration, for each failure debunks the ease with which one can speak of "massive actions or interventions" (Ross, 1980, p. 287) to obstruct the Final Solution and punctuates the difficulty of actually launching them.

What Ross regards as a failure to persuade is at the heart of the matter. It involved the issue of getting Christians who knew what was happening to give the Jewish plight priority in their concerns. Usually their priorities fell elsewhere: early on to the persecution of the churches and later on to the war effort overall. In themselves, Hitler's constant anti-Jewish pressure and his annihilation of the Jews never became even a third or fourth order of business for American Protestants generally. The extent to which one interprets that outcome as a "failure," however, depends on several variables. They include an appraisal of what people, Christian or not, are most likely to do; an assessment of what they ought to do; and particularly in this case a reaction to the Christian understanding that sin is commonplace. Uncontestably, even when people believe that God's will enjoins them to love their neighbors as themselves, precious few do so persistently; and even when they do, their neighbors rarely seem to be among those they are prejudiced against. That such circumstances ought not to exist is a truth matched only by the fact that what is and what should be are usually far apart. There was a failure to persuade when American Protestant leaders confronted their fellow Christians with the Holocaust. To hold that such failure differed from what could reasonably be expected is to entertain a view of human nature and of Christian anthropology far more optimistic than any reading of history, politics, or of the Bible's unstinting exhortations against sin can sustain.

The point is not to condone a performance that could have been better than it was. It is to say that moral judgment demands historical perspective. For only if we understand how natural it was for Christians to forsake Jews during the Holocaust can we grasp the magnitude of the gap that needs to be closed between them and the enormity of the indifference that always underwrites powers that will harm defenseless persons. So it is important to add that a failure to persuade spawned a failure of concerted effort. Such as they were, Protestant responses were less than coordinated. Their organizers were diverse, the motives and aims of the groups varied, even the church communities that protested most did not speak with one voice. That outcome was nothing new. American Protestants have rarely been characterized by unified efforts on social issues. More distinctive have been their multiple and even conflicting responses, a quality ensured by the pluralism in their forms of governance, their teachings, their insistence on local autonomy, and their suspicion of hierarchical authority. Certainly they have never spoken with a single, harmonious voice concerning Jews--before, during or after Auschwitz. To speak of a failure of concerted effort to save Jews under Hitler is to speak of a real failure. To do so meaningfully also requires one to comprehend the odds that any greater success would have had to surmount.

Failures to persuade and to organize concerted action were compounded by the failure of even modest action. Relief funds were raised and aid dispersed. Rallies were held, petitions signed, statements issued, and committees formed, some bringing Christians and Jews together. Additional ways of protesting the Nazis' anti-Jewish measures included sending representatives to Hitler and to other Reich officials during the 1930s, and then after the onset of war, directing delegates to President Roosevelt and other governmental officials in the United States. That more could have been done in these areas is unquestionable. Imagination may have failed to envision other potent measures, too, but realistically to conceive of American Protestantism's doing anything that would decisively have blocked Hitler's genocidal plans for the Jews is wishful thinking. In theory the dispositions, the groundwork, and the power to muster such a campaign might have been available, but not in practice.

American Protestants did concur with the U.S. government that the only way to stop Hitler and to close the death camps was to crush his Reich militarily. But here, too, a failure shadowed the eventual Allied victory. It can be said, for instance, that "leaflets, broadcasts, and bombings of rail lines, the barracks of the SS, even the camps themselves would have been a welcome sign that the Allies knew what was going on and that they cared" (Ross, 1980, p. 290). Such morale-raising and life-saving acts were not carried out for the Jews, but they might have been, and perhaps Protestant influence could have encouraged those missions.

A fifth failure is alleged, one of moral passion and confession after the full reality of Majdanek and Treblinka became known. In contrast to the vigorous reaction of the American Protestant press to the atomic bombing of Hiroshima and Nagasaki, the Holocaust's greater devastation elicited little more than stunned silence. To bring an indictment of failure in this instance, however, may seem inconsequential if not misguided and hypocritical. Americans did annihilate Japanese cities; they did not create Nazi death camps. Nor can moral outrage reverse the clock. Even confession for things done or undone, whatever its healing effect, will not resurrect the Holocaust's victims. Stunned silence has greater integrity than the silence of indifference or forgetfulness, and yet there is a need for moral passion and confession after Auschwitz. Christians--Protestant and Catholic, American and European--could have prevented Hitler's destruction of the Jews. No one individual or group could have done it singlehandedly, but if there had been more effort by Christians and churches, the acts of resistance could have multiplied. An accumulative effect might have taken hold far in advance of 1945. Such points must be underscored emphatically after all the forceful reasons have been analyzed to show why it was natural for Christians to fail as they did. What happened never had to be. To say otherwise encourages indifference and forgetfulness toward Hitler's victims. It also dishonors those Christians who did work to save the Jews, some at the risk of their own lives.

THE AVENUE OF THE RIGHTEOUS

When documentation shows that they saved Jewish life for unselfish reasons, non-Jews are honored at the Avenue of the Righteous of Nations, which is part of the Israeli Holocaust Memorial, Yad Vashem, in Jerusalem. Although most of these "Righteous Gentiles" were baptized Christians, not all were practicing believers. Fewer were church leaders. Authentic Christians, however, are visible at Yad Vashem, and their numbers grow. The Avenue of the Righteous is formed by commemorative trees, the first ones planted in the 1950s.[6] They stand in double rows along the walk that slopes upward to the memorial buildings. Too numerous to be placed along the original route, recent additions make a grove on a scenic knoll nearby. One wishes for forests of trees and for countless avenues, but at least some Christians made a start.

One-third of Europe's Jews were not killed by the Nazis. Jewish endurance, ingenuity, and resistance alone account for much of that fact. Yet it is not uncommon for survivors to stress that they would not have lived unless non-Jews helped them. For example, a Lithuanian librarian, Anna Simaite, delivered dozens of Jewish children from the Vilna ghetto. The Swedish diplomat, Raoul Wallenberg, used his political authority, plus financial support from the American War Refugee Board, to shelter thousands of Hungarian Jews before disappearing inside the Soviet Union.[7] Beyond the publicized cases are many other courageous acts of mercy and resistance. No isolated person could do very much to save Jewish lives during the Holocaust. Rescue depended not only on individuals but on groups of people working together. Networks of assistance, which involved communities and institutions at least to some extent, were critical. It is vital to remember those facts in assessing the performance of Christians. Some Christian communities and institutions, as well as individuals, served better than others. If the admirable cases originated more at the local level than through the energy of national or international ecclesiastical bureaucracies, that result suggests what might have been accomplished if maximum Christian power had benefited the Jews.

Magda Trocmé was invited to plant a tree at Yad Vashem in 1972. Dedicated to her late husband, André, it branches out to remember more than a solitary Protestant minister. Along with a more recent tree in her honor, its roots and foliage represent their children, the members of their church, and nearly all the citizens of Le Chambon-sur-Lignon.[8] It was late September 1934 when the Trocmés began their work in the small Protestant church at that unremarkable village in the Cévennes mountains of southeastern France. Descendants of a Huguenot religious minority, violently persecuted in earlier French history, the congregation responded to the new pastor and his wife as their helpfulness and practical version of Christianity enlivened its conventional if sturdy faith.

During World War I, André Trocmé had lived in a part of France occupied by the Germans. As he saw the devastation of war, Andre also made friends with one of the enemy, a German medic. He was a Christian who believed that a follower of Jesus ought not to kill. Permanently influenced by the German's example, Trocmé gradually forged a theology that stressed nonviolent resistance to evil. Evil he interpreted rather simply as harm-doing to human life, and André's emphasis was on resistance to it as much as on nonviolence. The negative injunction--"Do not kill"--was insufficient. It had to be supplemented by positive action to relieve suffering and to stop harm-doing. The Christian's responsibility was to be vigilant for ways to move against destructiveness. Such was André Trocmé's interpretation of Jesus' commandments to love God and one's neighbor as oneself. Remarkably well, the Chambonnais would practice what their Protestant preacher taught them.

Life's quality in Le Chambon had been rejuvenated by the Cévenol School, a private academy envisioned by Trocme and administered by Édouard Theis, who doubled as André's assistant, plus Roger Darcissac, another close friend. Along with Magda Trocmé, they led Le Chambon to seize the special opportunities to resist which came that way after France fell to Hitler on 22 June 1940. Geography placed Le Chambon in Vichy, that unoccupied region south of the Loire River which the Nazis permitted their puppet, Marshal Philippe Pétain, to govern. Within four months, the Vichy regime enacted major anti-Jewish legislation and authorized the internment of foreign Jews. Measures in the occupied zone were even more punitive and swiftly applied. On 28 March 1942, the first deportations for Auschwitz left the Drancy transit camp. In Paris that July, another roundup netted thirteen thousand non-French Jews. Awaiting deportation, nine thousand of these victims were hideously imprisoned in a sports stadium, the Velodrome d'Hiver. Half were children under sixteen. None of them survived. Pétain's government prepared to follow suit. Fifteen thousand foreign Jews were handed over to the Nazis for deportation in August 1942, and three months later, when the Germans occuped Vichy, there were few havens of any kind for Jews on French soil. Le Chambon remained one of them.

During the winter of 1940-41, Magda Trocmé had answered an evening knock at her door. There stood a frightened woman who identified herself as a German Jew. In northern France she had heard that there might be help in Le Chambon. Could she come in? Magda Trocmé's answer was, "Naturally." That single word says a lot. From then on Jewish refugees arrived almost daily. None were turned away. They were fed, hidden, and whenever possible spirited across the Swiss border by cooperating Chambonnais, some devout Christians and some not, who were convinced that it is simply wrong to leave anyone in harm's way. Why these acts did not bring full Nazi retribution to Le Chambon has not been fully explained, for the activities there were less than completely secret. But one crucial explanation has been identified: Major Julius Schmäling, a Nazi who had governmental responsibilities for two years when the Germans occupied this region of France. He knew what the people of Le Chambon were doing and let it happen. Likewise, André Trocmé and his followers knew that they had some protection, and they did not let their opportunity slip away.[9]

Aiding endangered Jews was not something the unpretentious Chambonnais Christians regarded as heroic or unusually good. It was only the natural fulfillment of their commitment. Not that they overlooked the danger or the need for care. Organization, trust, and planning were essential to their success, just as it had been indispensable for a groundwork of teaching and learning to be laid for them to root their commitment. The Chambonnais did not save everyone. They were not, after all, professional rescue specialists but only ordinary folk who had to improvise their resistance against trained killers.

Ninety thousand Jews in France lost their lives to those professionals. The amateur lifeguards of Le Chambon rescued only a few hundred. If that contrast does not overwhelm their achievement and drive it toward triviality, then one might point out that their relative isolation in an inconsequential town may have kept them out of the spotlight because the French police and the Gestapo had more important prey to nab. The Chambonnais had the luxury of room to maneuver, moreover, because they lived in Vichy France, and later during the Nazi occupation they got help from Major Schmäling. Or if those mitigating circumstances are insufficient to place Le Chambon in a context that diminishes its brilliance, it can be argued that nonviolent resistence could hardly provide a model for bringing down the Third Reich, not to mention the fact that the Chambonnais' conduct was, above all, imprudent. On the latter count, for instance, note what happened to André Trocmé's young cousin, Daniel.

A slender teacher with a heart ailment, Daniel Trocmé had accepted Andre's invitation to come to Le Chambon to help coordinate rescue efforts on behalf of refugee children. If the police raided Le Chambon looking for Jews--and they did so with increasing frequency as the war went on--warnings usually came in time to enable the refugees to hide in the surrounding countryside. Once the warning came too late; the Gestapo caught Daniel and his children. Though he could have found a way to save himself, Trocme refused to leave the young deportees. He never returned to Le Chambon. It was learned later that he died at Majdanek. Confirmed, too, was the fact that even after his death the Gestapo kept trying to verify what Daniel Trocmé's compassion for Jews mistakenly led them to suspect, namely, that he himself was Jewish. If Daniel Trocmé was imprudent to get involved, it is also true that a tree in his honor lives today at Yad Vashem. It questions prudence, especially from a Christian point of view, just as it also warns that no life is trivial, no circumstance inconsequential, and no model of resistance without cost.

How goodness happened at Le Chambon suggests why it did not happen in too many other communities of baptized Christians. Le Chambon had leaders who self-critically evaluated what it means to follow Jesus. They took the parable of the Good Samaritan as normative, which meant that their universe of obligation broke the boundaries of racism, nationalism, and antisemitism. This leadership prepared its followers to look for opportunities to resist harm-doing. The preparation included awareness that it is critical to act in time. The Chambonnais were receptive. Without that disposition, André Trocmé would have been a forgotten voice in the wilderness, and he would have no tree along the Avenue of the Righteous. Perhaps those French men and women were responsive because they were the inheritors of a minority status that had brought suffering to their ancestors. Outside the establishment, perhaps they were more naturally inclined to help others in similar positions. Or perhaps because they encountered refugees not en masse but as individuals, the Chambonnais could recognize human hurt in ways that touched their better natures and did not overwhelm them with the hopelessness of meeting a need so vast that nothing one could do would make much difference. It would be wrong to discount such possibilities. It would also be wrong to overlook that these people chose to help when needy Jews stood before them.

The Chambonnais could have done otherwise, just as those who failed to do nearly as much could have acted differently. Yet in the case of the latter's failure, the factors that saved Le Chambon from apostasy were largely missing, which is to say that the links of Christian responsibility form a chain reaching far back in time. Those who were in a position to give a better account of themselves as Christians stand guilty of making less than a fully authentic Christian witness. The factors that led them to those fateful choices included the lack of self-critical leadership with an awareness akin to André Trocmé's, the absence of preparation that would have purged the antisemitism in Christianity, and too little stress on the significance of acting in time to prevent harm-doing. Instead of working to make their followers receptive to messages of that kind, Christian leadership itself took familiar lessons to heart, ones that their followers could accept more comfortably. Hence nationalism, racism, antisemitism, prudence that disarmed protest, and caution that urged too few to start resisting--those cultural teachings were baptized as Christian. Nothing new had happened, however, for such is the stuff that has typically entrenched the nominal but culturally dominant forms of Christianity. Sadly, the Holocaust demonstrates how much harder it is to convert baptized Christians into authentic Christians than to make them antisemitic killers, accomplices to murder, and indifferent bystanders. "Am I my brother's keeper?" Cain's natural way is crowded. The rugged Avenue of the Righteous is not. Unless Christians join those who took the road not taken, they betray the one they claim to follow and crucify the ones they should embrace.

THE MENDING OF TRUST

Although Jean Améry was not among those who found refuge in Le Chambon, he did survive Auschwitz. Decades after his release from Bergen-Belsen, he observed that "the expectation of help, the certainty of help, is indeed one of the fundamental experiences of human beings" (Améry, 1986, p. 28). But the gravest loss produced by the Holocaust, he went on to suggest, was that it radically undermined that "element of trust in the world, . . . the certainty that by reason of written or unwritten social contracts the other person will spare me--more precisely stated, that he will respect my physical, and with it also my metaphysical, being" (p. 28). Hoping to revive at least some of the trust that Améry lost, there are social scientists who are trying to clarify why people such as the Chambonnais helped the defenseless while so many others did not.[10] Just as it is clear that very few of the rescuers regard themselves as moral heroes, it may be that an "altruistic personality" will emerge from these Holocaust studies. Whatever we can learn on that score is important, especially for post-Holocaust Christians. As another Jewish survivor, Pierre Sauvage, aptly puts the point:

> If we do not learn how it is possible to act well even under the most trying circumstances, we will increasingly doubt our ability to act well even under less trying ones. If we remember solely the horror of the Holocaust, we will pass on no perspective from which meaningfully to confront and learn from that very horror. If we remember solely the horror of the Holocaust, it is we who will bear the responsibility for having created the most dangerous alibi of all: that it was beyond man's capacity to know and care. If Jews do not learn that the whole world did not stand idly by while we were slaughtered, we will

> undermine our ability to develop the friendships and alliances that we need and deserve. If Christians do not learn that even then there were practicing Christians, they will be deprived of inspiring and essential examples of the nature and requirements of their faith.
> If the hard and fast evidence of the possibility of good on earth is allowed to slip through our fingers and turn into dust, then future generations will have only dust to build on. If hope is allowed to seem an unrealistic response to the world, if we do not work towards developing confidence in our spiritual resources, we will be responsible for producing in due time a world devoid of humanity--literally.[11]

Can we Christians face up to the Holocaust scars that deface humankind and especially our own tradition? Will we seriously affirm that Jews in particular are essential members of our universe of obligation? Will we replicate the example of those exceptional Christians who acted well on behalf of Jews during the Holocaust? In sum, can we grasp how necessary it is for us to reckon with the impossibility of being a Christian? To the extent that we put into practice affirmative answers to those questions, we will have more dust to build on. Such approaches to the mending of trust, especially Jewish-Christian trust, depend on determination to resist the wasting of life with undeceived lucidity.

NOTES

1. Born in Austria as Hans Maier in 1912, Améry fled Nazism by going to Belgium in 1938. There he later joined the Resistance. Captured by the Nazis in 1943, he was tortured and sent to a series of concentration camps. See also Améry (1986). Levi (1988, pp. 25, 127-148) provides additional insight on Améry. For futher elaboration on numerous issues raised by this present essay, see Rubensein and Roth (1987). Portions of the latter work have been adapted for use here.

2. Cited by Littell (1974, p. 15).

3. Bormann's "Circular on the Relationship of National Socialism and Christianity," from which the quotation is taken, is reproduced in Conway (1968, pp. 383-386).

4. See Fein (1979, pp. 50-120).

5. The following discussion, including the outline of the five failures by American Protestants, draws upon Ross (1980). For further discussion about the reporting of the Holocaust in the American press, see Lipstadt (1986) and Wyman (1984).

6. The Bible likens a righteous person to "a tree planted by streams of water, that yields its fruit in its season, and its leaf does not wither" (Psalms 1:3). At Yad Vashem, which means "place and name" (see Isaiah 56:5), evergreen carob trees honor the "Righteous Gentiles." Durable in Israel's climate, this tree is also a Christian symbol. Tradition holds that John the Baptist came from a spring-fed valley nearby; the bean pods produced by the carob tree are probably the "locusts" that sustained him in the wilderness (see Mark 1:6).

7. For more on non-Jews who risked their lives to save Jews during the Holocaust, see Rittner and Myers, eds. (1986).

8. The following account is indebted to Hallie (1979).

9. At the time of this writing, Hallie is completing a book about Major Schmäling, an intriguing Nazi whom Hallie has described as "a good man in an evil cause."

10. Perhaps the most ambitious and promising work of this kind is the Study of the Altruistic Personality Project, which is headed by Samuel P. Oliner. This sociologist is a Holocaust survivor who was hidden by Polish Catholics during World War II. His important autobiography tells that story (Oliner, 1986). Oliner and his team have interviewed hundreds of rescuers and survivors to clarify the factors and motivations that led people to save Jewish lives during the Nazi era. Although exceptions to them exist, among Oliner's more important discoveries are the following: (1) Rescuers, women and men alike, came from different social classes and diverse occupations. (2) They had learned and deeply internalized values such as helpfulness,

responsibility, fairness, justice, compassion, and friendship. (3) They had friends in groups outside of their own family circles or immediate communities. (4) They had high levels of self-confidence and self-esteem and were not afraid to take calculated risks. (5) They knew what was happening around them, and, in addition, benefited from a supportive emotional network--their rescue efforts met with approval from family members or others who could be trusted. Oliner believes that, if he were in trouble and could identify persons with these qualities, his chances of receiving assistance would be excellent. Oliner and Oliner (1988) contains a report on his findings.

11. Pierre Sauvage was born during the Holocaust in Le Chambon. A distinguished filmmaker, he has produced Weapons of the Spirit, a prize-winning documentary about that place. He also heads The Friends of Le Chambon, an organization that honors those who saved Jews during the Holocaust. His words are quoted by permission.

REFERENCES

Améry J. (1984). Radical Humanism: Selected Essays. Edited and translated by S. Rosenfeld and S.P. Rosenfeld. Bloomington: Indiana University Press.

_____. (1986). At the Mind's Limits: Contemplations by a Survivor on Auschwitz and Its Realities. Translated by S. Rosenfeld and S.P. Rosenfeld. New York: Schocken Books.

Conway, J. (1968). The Nazi Persecution of the Churches: 1933-1945. New York: Basic Books.

Fackenheim, E.L. (1982). To Mend the World: Foundations of Future Jewish Thought. New York: Schocken Books.

Fein, H. (1979). Accounting for Genocide: National Responses and Jewish Victimization during the Holocaust. New York: The Free Press.

Hallie, P.P. (1979). Lest Innocent Blood Be Shed: The Story of the Village of Le Chambon and How Goodness Happened There. New York: Harper & Row.

Levi, P. (1988). The Drowned and the Saved. Translated by Raymond Rosenthal. New York: Summit Books.

Lipstadt, D.E. (1986). Beyond Belief: The American Press and the Coming of the Holocaust. New York: The Free Press.

Littell, F.H. (1974). "Church Struggle and the Holocaust." The German Church Struggle and the Holocaust. Edited by F.H. Littell and H.G. Locke. Detroit: Wayne Street University Press.

_____. 1975. The Crucifixion of the Jews. New York: Harper & Row.

Oliner, S. (1986). Restless Memories: Reflections of the Holocaust Years. Berkeley, Calif.: Judah P. Magnes Museum

Oliner, S.P. and Oliner, P.M. (1988). The Altruistic Personality: Rescuers of Jews in Nazi Europe. New York: The Free Press.

Rittner, C. and Myers, S., eds. (1986). The Courage to Care: Rescuers of Jews during the Holocaust. New York: New York University Press.

Ross, R.W. (1980). So It Was True: The American Protestant Press and the Nazi Persecution of the Jews. Minneapolis: University of Minnesota Press.

Rubenstein, R.L. and Roth, J.K. (1987). Approaches to Auschwitz: The Holocaust and Its Legacy. Atlanta: John Knox Press.

Wyman, D.S. (1984). The Abandonment of the Jews: America and the Holocaust, 1941-1945. New York: Pantheon Books.

RACISM AND THE HOLOCAUST: A CHALLENGE TO AFRICAN CONCEPTS OF CHRISTIAN MORALITY

M. A. UMEAGUDOSU

Department of Religion
University of Nigeria, Nsukka
Anambra State, Nigeria
West Africa.

ABSTRACT

The barbarous nature of the Nazi holocaust and genocide on the Jews in Germany between 1939 and 1945 can be viewed as a dehumanization of God's own creatures; and infact, as something unique in quantitative terms. This paper contends that in the African Christian perspective, there is no moral scrupples in holocaust, because, it is a great violation of the whole gamut of the Fundamental Human Rights as stipulated by the Vatican II and Human Rights under International law. As such, we are arguing that there is need to respect all faiths, races, and human life. Moreover, Nations should try to accommodate people from other nations to ensure a better future for all humankind. In South Africa, for example, there has been cases of holocaust by the racist regime against the countries of Namibia, Angola, Mozambique, Zimbabwe and Guinea-Bissau, but the Nazi holocaust seem to be the peak of all. In Uganda also, Idi Amin spear-headed the holocaust against fellow Ugandians, same is true of Macias Nguema against his people of the Equatorial Guinea. Back home in Nigeria, there was a great pogrom against those from the East which resulted to the civil war of 1967 to 1970. Therefore, what this paper attempts to accomplish is to highlight some recurring incidents of holocaust and at the same time to highlight the African Christian revulsion on the Nazi holocaust from the Biblical perspective. Given the political, economic social and religious atmospheres of Nazi-Germany at the time in question, there was no way the Jews constituted a potential danger to the whole Nazi population. In the same vein, the black population in South Africa do not pose a threat to the white race, and as such, the issue could be located in the spheres of racial segregation, superiority and anti-semitism. This paper concludes that any doctrine of superiority based on racial discrimination is morally condemnable, socially unjust and dangerous to future well-being of nations. Therefore, efforts should be made at international levels to curb such inhumane treatment in order to revitalize the ideals of all human society.

INTRODUCTION

The recurring incidents of holocaust the world over, and the Nazi holocaust of the Jews in particular, coupled with the presence of floating groups of oppressed and homeless people present the Christian World and the international bodies of our time with one of their greatest challenges. There has been cases of forced movements and some migrants accommodated by other members of another community, but the plight of the Jews in Nazi Germany between 1939 and 1945 was a sharp contrast of this World-wide hospitality. The nature of that holocaust can only be imagined than expressed. Their main purpose was to wipe out the Jewish race simply because they were Jews. Thus, G.M Kren and L. Rappoport (1980) cited how Hans Frank, the Nazi governor of Poland categorically said "We ask nothing of the Jews, except that they should disappear". This very statement, and the subsequent treatment meted to the Jews was the high water-mark of anti-semitism and racial intolerance. The fact that the Nazi government in Germany killed millions of the Jews is no exaggeration. Their systematic killings and the crude methods employed in the execution can be said to be unique in quantitative terms.

It is no gainsaying that anti-semitism was rampant in almost all European countries at that time, but there was no European nation that had not got her own quota of the Jews. Thus, it becomes very difficult to grasp immediately why the Nazis engaged in the massive killings of the Jews. The fact cannot be ruled out that from time to time tension could surface between the Jews and the Nazi people, but the crux of the matter is the use of "gas chamber" to easy off their killing and after that, to the crematoria. Thus, B.C. Crum (1947) pointed out that "in 1945, with the Allied forces becoming triumphant, the Nazis packed several hundred Jewish inmates of the camp into freight cars, and the journey to the crematoria began". He only gave us the incident of the Dachau camp, however, other camps by implication automatically suffered the same fate. It was a long planned act because the Germans had earlier created death camps exclusively for the Jews, but never for other aliens in the same country. One definitely will wonder - why only the Jews?

The causes of the Nazi holocaust on the Jews.

"There is no fire without smoke". Some occurrences, experiences, massacres and their types are bound to have their causes - both remote and immediate. Historically, it was not the Nazis who first persecuted the Jews, but why the Nazi holocaust rang much bell was because of their intentions, the magnitude of the number and the method adopted in the act. Thus, the remote causes of the holocaust could be seen as follows:- firstly, Norman Cohn (1967) sportlighted the fact that "over very large areas of the earth, Jews have traditionally been seen as mysterious beings endowed with uncanny, sinister powers". This wrong image has affected their total relationship with other people. We can also recollect the time when the Jews (Synagogue) and the Christians (Church) were competing for converts in the Hellenistic World, the Christians accused the Jews of being full of evil spirits, committing all kinds of atrocities. Moreover, from the time of the first crusade onwards, the Jews were accused of combating Christianity and harming Christians. Christians saw them as possessing limitless powers for evils. At that time, the Clergy indulged in spreading ill-founded rumours against the Jews which sort of affected their socio-religious images almost all over the World. The animosity became so acute that in the eyes of most Christians they were seen as demons in human form; and this false demonology has affected the image of the Jews in every aspect of human endeavour, with the result that other people began to look at the Jews with great suspicion. Secondly, during the Middle Ages, Jews were almost wholly without legal rights and were frequently murdered by the mob (Ibid., 1967). Naturally, these experiences in turn influenced and encouraged the Jewish tendency to exclusiveness. Cohn went on to say that during the long centuries of persecution, Jews became a wholly alien people, compulsorily restricted to the most sordid trades, regarding the Gentile World with bitterness. Economically, the Jews were seen as capitalists who were always exploiting other nations. One would be tempted to ask if other nations would like to appreciate and accommodate the Jews if they idle away their time without trading to earn some living? This should be seen as social injustice because people should be given the freedom to choose a trade and live by it. In those days there was acute, resentment at the power of Jewish bankers especially by the left-wing antisemitism - notably France and Germany. (Ibid., 1967). Thirdly, there was the "myth of the Jewish World-conspiracy" which could be traced back to the demonology that was woven around the Jews for centuries past. According to this myth, (Ibid., 1980) "there exists a secret Jewish government which, through a world-wide network of camouflaged agencies and organizations, controls political parties and governments, the press and the public opinion, banks and economic developments". This "myth" is self-explanatory, for it was alleged that the Jews were planning to over-power and dominate the whole World economically and otherwise. With this new social tension, almost all the nations began to dread the Jews especially when it comes to economic transactions. However, in the eyes of some people the Jews still had a highly symbolic significance - being portrayed as the symbolic of the modern world because they were very energetic and enterprising. Fouthly, anti-semitism had been a European tradition, a kind of neurotic "racial" hatred, but it was the Nazis who began to elevate antisemitism to an article of political and cultural faith. In this vein, Colin Holmes (1979) noted that the "hostility towards the Jews is usually directed toward their status, power and influence in society: in short, in Freudian terminology it is a form of ego-hostility". He went on to say that anti-semitism was a "perfectly natural" tendency that arose from the exclusiveness of the Jews. One can admit that their exclussiveness stemmed from some of the unwarranted mob actions against them especially during the Middle Ages. As such, their separatist nature, though repulsive to other people, could be a way to run away from unwanted death. Fiftly, the immediate existence of the Jews in Nazi was perceived as a threat to the designs of those wanting them out of the way. This is evidenced in the statement of Hans Frank, the Nazi Governor of Poland - "that the Jews should disappear" (G.M. Kren, 1980). This "wish" was not without reason, for, Holmes (1979) pointed out that "it was the economic role of certain Jewish middlemen, coupled with the alien visibility of the Jews at a time of socio-economic unrest which resulted in attention being directed toward the Jewish community". In this issue, one could see the economic basis to hostility. The German people had been nursing this economic exploitation over the years and looking forward to a possible onslaught. But the inner logic of the issue is that the Jews never caused the World economic depression that was experienced after the First World War, as to make them scape-goats who will be earmarked for total annihilation. Moreover, they never imposed their religion on the Nazis, and as such, the cause cannot be placed in the context of religion. Could it then be political? But, it is gathered that politically the Jews posed no physical challenge to Nazi authority, they claimed no territory nor posed a threat to prevailing religious or cultural orthodoxies"; they simply lived in ghettos. On the whole, it can be basically seen that it was the traditional German anti-semitism prevalent at the time which sparked the holocaust. This situation persisted prior to Adolf Hitler's regime, but, there was no time the total extermination of the Jewish race was made a State policy than the era of Adolf Hitler.

Judging from the remote causes of the holocaust outlined above, one will be forced to place the immediate causes on the "head" of Adolf Hitler. There is no gainsaying that the major force behind the holocaust was Adolf Hitler; for, it was he who spear-headed the creation of death camps, gave "orders" and saw that the orders were scrupplously carried out. Thus, Kren (1980) asserted that "under the direction of its political leadership and with the support of its military, industrial, and human resources, Germany created the holocaust ... Hitler was the major force behind it". David Irving (1977) came out with a contrary view that Hitler was not even aware that extermination of the Jews was taking place, that the blame was laid on Heinrich Himmler. However, his thesis has been unconditionally rejected by many historians on the grounds of distorted information. It was universally accepted that Hitler was the brain behind the holocaust, for he was able to generate mass enthusiasm of the people who had already seen the Jews as "inferior race corrupting humanity" and "essentially inward-looking (Colin Holmes, 1979). As such, he manipulated highly influential people in all parts of Germany and succeeded in carrying out his brutal act. There was no concrete evidence of the atrocities committed by the Jews in the land of Germany as to see the act as a way for vengeance. However, some have seen the act as the explicit high-level political policy of Adolf Hitler; in the sense that some records reveal how the Jews helped the Germans in all their war efforts by supplying manual and skilled labour. Moreover, they rendered other help to the soceity for its upkeep. Therefore, it could be that the social image of the Jews was highly repulsive to the German nature, so much that they decided to exterminate them. Given the fact that historically the Jews were subject to Assyria, Babylon, Persia, Greece and Rome at one time or the other, and could hardly enjoy some forms of freedom and independence, could they have been so utterly exterminated as to suffer extinction? Whether the Nazis were out to make the Jews 'a political failure' is a matter for conjecture.

Resistance by the Jews

Resistance is natural to human beings, in short, to all living creatures. As human beings, it will be a language of mystery if the Jews were unable to exert some forms of resistance to their ugly situations. Behind this background, G. Kren (1980) is of the opinion that various writers tend to agree that resistance efforts depend upon three considerations:- namely "the probability of success, the intensity of oppression and the presence of an alternative authority system". The issue is whether the Jews could meet up with these criteria. For a success to be achieved, the Jews ought to present a common front; but, on the contrary there was divided loyalty religiously and politically. There was the conservative, semi-mystical religious sects who tend to withdraw into themselves to await a heavenly judgement on the enemy. There was the Zionist group, the largest so far, who, because of one reason or the other were highly divided into different competing factions. There were also the bourgeois group - the socialists who rejected Zionism outright as a solution to the Jewish problem. Their policy was a recognition of Jewish national-cultural autonomy based on the Yiddish language. On the political side, these types of divisions were prominent, with the result that there was no united front. There were also mixed ideals of various Jewish fighting groups ranging from personal revenge to left and right-wing Zionism and socialism. One could see that some acts of sabotage were true perils constraining resistance; coupled with the fact that, as aliens in Germany, there was a total absence of any unitary alternative authority system. What is more, the Jews had no government in exile and no form of encouragement from any of the Allied powers. In effect, there was no strong nationalistic tradition to serve as the basis for a coherent resistance program.

They lacked some form of socio-political authority system, and as such, could not leap beyond the already existing system in Germany. Also, they could neither resist nor revolt because the authority system in Germany could not easily be challenged. The foregoing reasons created some kind of "a line of least or no resistence" to the strong German army and their Government which had a powerfully established authority system coupled with the fact that there was no serious distractions or disturbances from any external body as to divert their attention. But G. Kren (1980) pointed out that the Jews could fight in ghettos, forests and camps, only that they lacked an effective consensus and a morally authoritative leadership that could issue the call to arms." As long as the Jews lacked some kind of unity politically and otherwise, the probability of any resistant success became very remote. Kren only pointed out that organized Jewish resistance only occurred in Poland and Soviet Union; and their reactions were eventually quelled. But in Germany, "ignorance" coupled with the Nazi strategy gave no room for resistance or revolt. We gathered that the Nazis craftly lured the Jews into the train with the assurance of being transfered to another camp. Probably, the unhealthy conditions of their camps motivated an easy acceptance to change. Those who were not willing to go were forced out by the Schutz Staffeln (S.S.) "protective guards". However, the foregoing has portrayed the fact that the Jews never revolted in Germany nor were a party to any form of revolution. Many factors contributed to their inability to resist at that crucial momment.

Reactions of the Great World Powers and the Church at the period of the holocaust.

Given the fact that the Jews offered little or no resistance, either because of ignorance or whatever, could it be possible that other European nations were not aware of the plight of the Jews in Germany as a whole? Did the "gas-chamber" operation and cremation happen just one day? The Jewish social image, as seen by the Europeans, notwithstanding, at least one should expect other European nations, especially, the Great World powers like Britain, America and Russia to intervene, and denounce the holocaust so as ro minimize bloodshed. However, B.C. Crum (1947) has summarized the reactions of the two powers - Britain and America as follows:-

> The British Information Service was ready to help. So was the Zionist Organization of America, so were the United States Army, the Institute for Arab American Affairs, the American Christian Palestine Committee, the American Jewish Committee, the Arab Office, the American Refugee Services and the American Red Cross".

These bodies contributed immensely to the resettlement and rehabilitation of the survivors from Germany, Poland and Austria, to the only available place - Palestine. This had portrayed the humanitarian outlook of the British and American Governments. The Nazi holocaust was seen as the peak of racial intolerance; and acute neurotic racial hatred on the Jews. These Great World Powers, in their efforts to curb the type of massacres the Jews suffered in Germany spearheaded the enactment of the Fundamental Human Rights. Thus, at the San Francisco Conference which drafted the Charter of the United Nations, a proposal to embody an international bill of rights in the Charter was put forward. A Commission was set on Human Rights in 1946; and by December 10, 1948, the Universal Declaration of Human Rights was adopted (United Nations and Human Rights, New York, 1968). With this Charter, the Jews, and people all over the World were able to assert their rights in certain situations.

As these powers were trying their best to resettle and rehabilitate the survivors, it is germane to know the extent to which the Christian Church had endeavoured to intervene on the issue. From all indications, the Church delayed in action. If the Church had taken prompt action, at least the Nazi holocaust on the Jews could have taken a different turn. Given the fact that Italy (the Papal See) had cordial relationship with the Nazi Government and would not want to spoil it, at least they could have instilled sanity into the minds of the Nazis. Nevertheless, whatever help the Church rendered after the holocaust had been completed could be appreciated, but our argument is, at that particular time of the massacre, how far did the Church intervene to curb further spilling of blood? It is worthy of note that the moral duty of the Church is to protect human life, as such, it falls within the obligations of the Christian Church to at least do something to alleviate the sufferings of people, see to their needs, resettlement and rehabilitation. Whether the Christian Churches of the time of the holocaust met with any of the above duties is a matter for conjecture. However, it is necessary to highlight the African Christian challenge to holocaust.

The African Christian Challenge to holocaust.

In the New Testament Scripture, Jesus enjoins us to love God and love our neighbours as we love ourselves. He buttressed this fact with the story of the Good Samaritan who showed love to a stranger. In the same light, Hans Hung (1979) explained that "my neighbour can also be a stranger, a complete stranger, any one who turns up at this particular juncture", thus, showing the urgency of love required at any give situation. Therefore, Christ expects us to share our love with the sufferers, refugees, the handicapped, war victims and even our enemies. For Fletcher, (1966) "only one thing is intrinsically good, namely love: The ultimate norm of Christian decisions is love: nothing else". Thus, the African Christian has that urge for the love of the human person acruing from the African cosmology.

Africans conceive of the space as essentially made up of three parts - namely:- the sky, the Earth and the Spirit World. Of the three, man is placed at the centre inhabiting the Earth and being surrounded by all kinds of spiritual forces. On account of these, man should be given maximum protection for his dear life religiously and physically. Africans imbibed Christian tradition; and the moral traditions associated with the Jewish and Christian religious are compatible with that of the African traditional society, but, in contradistinction with that of the Nazis, given the holocaust incidence. One may ask the morality of that act, that is, the generally accepted conduct of an act. If we take the bulk of the Ten commandments as "written in the hearts of every human being", we can assert that the Nazis have misused their conscience in their extermination of the Jews. Their conscience were dead. Alan Donagan (1977) is of the opinion that for Judaism and Christianity morality is seen as a theory of system of laws binding upon rational creatures, as such, the content of which is ascertainable by human reason. Jews and Christians identify this code of conduct as binding on themselves by virtue of religious truth. Therefore, their morality is one of reflective observance of moral rules. In terms of morality one learns how to act well; how different persons and cultures should find happiness in different ways of life. Morality is thus the only common condition of seeking happiness. Hence, it is morally wrong to undertake an unjust war - a war without any right intention. The Nazi holocaust on the Jews is a perfect example of unjust war. Suffice it to say that those who carried out the execution were simply "obeying orders" - a devotion "to duty for duty's sake", (Ibid, 1977), but their conscience were too weak to indulge in such inhumane act. There are no human feelings in their blood; for that massacre was a unique" act in itself in the history of man. Morality requires us to act as human rational beings, capable of weighing a situation before acting. Adolf Hitler had clerverly lured the Nazis into committing an atrocity which has gone into the world directory as essentially brutal, barbarous and heartless, all in the name of "power". The words of the Bible are held by many as the only source of peace and justice; that is why all peace movements have their grounds upon the Bible. With this good and valuable works human beings are responsible to improve human life, protect it as strongly as possible, but never to destroy. It becomes pertinent that we challenge the root of the Nazi holocaust and its injustice in the perversion of personality and ethics. The Nazi action was a clear structural injustice against the Jewish race.

For the African Christian, "individual life has a purpose guided by the morals of society" (Kola Oyedepo, 1986) and that is why people try to maximize goodness. Good is essential for personal relationships and the Christians always endeavour to adhere to the tenets of fellowship. These tenets have provided some religious sanctions and the motivations for moral action. For instance, if the Nazis had decided to eject the Jews out of their country, just as Idi Amin did to the Asians in Uganda, that could not have attracted much of World condemnation, at least, their plight could have been recognized as an international problem and its solution in turn could have assumed an international character. In fact, it is highly difficult to examine the motivations of some of the aggressive acts like killings and other forms of physical violence that transgress the accepted social norms. In this light, Tedeschi Smith and Brown (1974) have argued persuasively that an act is considered specifically aggressive and inappropriate if it is seen as intentionally detrimental to the victim, unprovoked, offensive and antinormative. Generally, people admit the sanctity of human life and the Bible has directed that human beings are created in God's own image. As such, we are morally bound to respect the life of the human person. Thus, the moral principle which prohibits the killing of human beings "Thou shalt not kill" is meant to protect the value of human life. The moral law is the expression of God's will for humans, indicating the way God wants us as rational beings to believe. Hence, St. Paul asserted that moral law is that law written by God in the hearts of all human beings. Therefore, there is no excuse to transgress the moral law since everyone's conscience is witnessing the fact that God has already written it in everyone's heart. As rational beings we are obliged by the moral law to know that killing is bad and must be avoided. Joseph Omoregbe (1979) has pointed out that man is by a moral being and as such should be morally responsible for his actions. He summarized his thesis by saying "You must live a moral life because you are a social being, a member of a society and a rational being". This by implication means that to live in a society one has to observe certain moral rules as demanded by the society. This opinion has been expressed by men like Thomas Hobes, Hegel and Henri Bergson because, human society is basically built on the principles of morality and its violation is abhored by the members of the society. Therefore, from the moral view point, human actions should be an instrument employed for the attainment of certain desirable objectives. In short, it must have a good focus of intention. Although the American moralist Joseph Fletcher (1967) has warned never to pass moral judgment on any action without taking into account the intention, the circumstances and the consequences of the action; for these are the factors that can make an action morally good or bad. Judging from these factors there was no moral scrupples in the Nazi holocaust of the Jews in Germany because, their main intention was to eliminate the Jews from the earth, simply because they were Jews. There was no concrete evidences of the wrong done as to cause consequences of utter destruction or extermination. Therefore, the command that the "Jews should disappear" is a morally bad statement and the subsequent action of massacre are highly condemnable. For, it is intrinsically wrong to kill human life irrespective of the intention and the circumstances, for no consequence can make them good(Immanuel Kant.)

Generally, the ethics of African Traditional Philosophy is a transcendental ethics. This by implication means that moral values are not the creation or the invention of the society nor of the individual. Moral rules are the expressions of the transcentental moral order which is beyond man and to which both human beings and the society must conform. (Omoregbe, 1979) Thus, the African Christian endeavours to exhibit goodness of character by avoiding immoral actions that could be detrimental to human life. Philip Curtain (1964) avers that while "most Britons assumed that African culture and African race were somehow interdependent, the accepted social theories still gave priority to man's moral rather than his physical nature". This is in line with African cosmology, because, the Africans abhore anything that will cause disorder, and disrupt the efficient functioning of the Universe, or incure the punishment of the ancestors. As such, Edmund Ilogu (1974) opined that "the African society in its pursuit of 'the good' (life) had looked upon suffering as real calamity that can hamper life". Christian ethics generally grew out of the Bible, both as a guide for individual life, as well as for living as a believer in Christ, in the fellowship of the Church and of the community in the world. The ethical teaching of Our Lord Jesus Christ can be summarized as - Love of God and love of one's neighbour (Mk. 12:29-31). This 'neighbour-love' principle is enshrined in the African Christian philosophy. Ilogu (1974) saw African morality as "communalistic". Infact, Africans are very hospitable, and by Christ's injunction their "brothers' keepers". This traditional feature of the African way of life is supported by contemporary African thinkers like "Kwame Nkurumah, Julius Nyerere, and Leopold Senghor" (Omoregbe, 1979).

Peter Singer (1980) is of the opinion that "in every society known to us there has been some prohibitions on the taking of life. Presumably no society can survive if it allows its members to kill one another without restriction". This implies that each society tries to instill some kind of moral obligation to its members. Moreover, moral duties do spring from positions of trust and roles of a social group, for instance, being a neighbour. For the African Christain, it becomes our moral duty to preserve the lives of our fellow human beings and not to kill them with impunity as the Nazis did to the Jews. Thus, Joseph Fletcher (In Peter Singer 1980) gave the list of what he calls "indicators of Humanhood include self-awareness, self-control, a sense of the future, to relate to others, concern for others, communication and curiosity". One can say that if the Nazis possessed these features, they really made nonsense of them; because Fletcher regarded them as truly human qualities. According to Immanuel Kant (Singer, 1980) "respect for autonomy is a basic moral principle". For him, the autonomy of an individual is the most Fundamental choice of that person, and one of the most Fundamental Human Right is the 'Right to life'. Thus, the gravest violation of the person's autonomy is to kill or destroy the life of that person whose "choice" was to live. This summarizes the African Christian revulsion to holocaust. Ernest Sandeen (1982) is of the opinion that "church diplomats who had worked for post war peace faced the threat of nuclear war and a breakdown of international order". His information stems from the fact of the Churches' revulsion to bloodshed by the use of a sophisticated nuclear weapon. But the Nazi 'gas chamber" method was the peak of all. He went on to narrate that the First Assembly of the World Council of Churches (W.C.C.) at Amsterdam in 1948 declared that "war is contrary to the Will of God". That the Christian Church has a responsibility to improve human life, to expose, denounce and challenge the roots of any war, war itself and all forms of social injustice. War is condemned as a structural injustice against God's creatures. That is why Christians stress the idea of living a morally good life so as to be at peace with one another. Hence, Kola Oyedepo

(1986) asserted that "moral life is essentially an endeavour to maximize goodness; rightness on the other hand is the capacity to produce good". Thus, the moral tradition associated with the Jewish and Christian religious according to Alan Donagan (1977) is highly compatible with the African Christian concepts of morality in the sense that it has to do with the generally accepted norms of the individual conduct. Moreover, African Christian morality is in accordance with the nature of human beings and the working of the Universe. The African is always afraid of the Universe and as such will not spill blood so as not incure any punishment from the ancestors. Thus, morality is conceived as virtue because common morality is upheld by God and so has a religious sanction. Therefore, the violation of this virtue implies the violation of human rationality. Human beings have conscience, as such, it becomes natural for them to act morally. According to Christian ethics, it is morally wrong to serve in unjust war. In short, war of any type is morally bad. Common morality has to do with human actions; and human agents are always held responsible for the outcome of an action, as such, both Adolf Hitler, the "SS" guards and all Nazi community are held responsible for the loss of millions of lives of the Jewish race. However, our discussion on Nazi holocaust will be incomplete if we do not highlight some recurring incidents of holocaust or genocide in the African continent to know how far they tally or differ.

Cases of Massive killings in the African Continent:

It is germane at this juncture to highlight some cases of genocide in Africa to see how far they are related or differed from what happened to the Jews in Nazi Germany between 1939 and 1945. However, this is by no means a detailed account of the wars in Africa, but, what will be of interest is to know the causes, the way the massacres were carried out and their aftermath. Moreover, the plight of the Refugees will be given some attention. Given the adage that "No man is an Island", implies that individuals belong to one particular race or the other. The right to life should prevail in every human society for a peaceful co-existence of the members. This is the more reason why we should concern ourselves so deeply and wholeheartedly with the cases of holocaust anywhere in the World. Thus, racial discrimination by way of colour and ethnic groups should be curbed in our human societies the world over. It concerns us as human beings to delve into the critical and deplorable conditions of others to know how for we can help to prevent such occurrences in the future. The issue that concerns us here is the indiscriminate massacres that has been experienced in the continent of Africa, and the protracted apartheid regime in South Africa which has claimed millions of lives of the African people.

Society is dynamic. The aspects of human society is continually changing and as people become more and more civilized, they also become more aware of their rights politically, economically, culturally and religiously in their various societies. Generally, the causes of wars and massacres can be located in the following dormains:- race, colonialism, geographical boundary, suppression, religion, ethnicity, bad government, economic exploitation, denial of fundamental rights, to mention but a few. Apart from tribal skirmishes, the wars that have claimed so many lives are the ones between the African countries and their colonial masters. In harsh conditions, angry people rebel, this is natural to human beings. Hardships had been the immediate, ultimate and direct spur to collective violence against the colonial regime. This is because, when people experience an intolerable gap between their value expectations and capabilities they make demands to alleviate their hardships. If their demands were not met it always resulted to wars; the Sudan issue is a case in point.

Mohamed Omar Beshir (1974) highlighted the Sudan revolution of 1924 by the armed men against the British. The revolt probably was caused by some denial of their rights, economic exploitation and suppression. Eventually, British troops crushed the rebellion because the natives sabotaged the Sudan troops. Moreover, there was a lot of opposition to the revolt hence, lack of support by the masses and some religious leaders. There was also a lot of divided loyalty on the part of the natives. The fact that the religious leaders did not support the revolt stems from the African Christian revulsion on bloodshed. This is because people or moralists have seen war as intrinsically bad. The aftermath of the revolution was one crisis following another in Sudan until in 1969, May 25, when Colonel Gaafar Nimeiri took over power. There is no revolution that is devoid of bloodshed, but in this one those who revolted were conscious of what they wanted. They were in their land but virtually not free to do as they wanted nor had the freedom to make a choice. The Colonial master was not planning to exterminate them to extinction but it was an effort to quell the revolt and listen to their requests. That was not so with the Jews in Germany who enjoyed no freedom but were forced to "disappear" simply because they were aliens in that land.

In Mozambique also, the Portuguese indulged in indiscriminate bombing and killing of civilians men, women and minors, this is against the International Law with regard to wars. The massacre was so enormous that the bombing of 24th of July, 1965 has been known as "Black Saturday" (John Paul, 1975). Many of them were mercilessly machine-gunned inside a lake, and many of their houses burnt. Evidences abound of bombed lakeshore villages possibly with Napalm bomb. One would ask, the morality of using these nuclear weapons to destroy life. This type of massacre is one of the gravest effects of colonialism in the continent of Africa because, it is always a merciless one because of lack of kinship ties. The natives were not given enough freedom to express their grievances with the result that revolt was thought as the last resort. Economic exploitation is to rampant in Africa, and when this tension is aggravated with social and political instabilities, the resultant effect is war. However, reasons for revolt or war vary from country to country.

The situation in Equatorial Guinea was a fairly different one. The political and economic exploitation of the Spaniards notwithstanding, it was Macias Nguema, according to Max Liniger-Goumaz (1979), who spearheaded the massacre of his fellow country men in his craze for power. It was he who in January, 1969 inaugurated a long list of political assassinations after killing Ondo Edu, who returned from exile in Gabon. That after violent speech against the Spaniards in his January, 1969 trip to Rio Muni, and the violent intervention of Spanish armed forces, he proclaimed a state of emergency. It is on record that from 1969 to 1976 the President - Nguema had liquidated more than six-hundred men of high-ranking order, women and some minors; while some thousands fled for their lives and went on voluntary exile. To crown it all, on the National Day, October, 12 1978, Nguema was said to have ordered thirty-two new executions. This is an African killing fellow countrymen in cold blood. That was a morally bad incident, for he only wanted to eliminate strong people before he was able to rule. One wonders the morality of exterminating fellow countrymen. From this ugly act, he had denied many people the "right to life" as stipulated in the Human Rights Act. His mischievous acts could be related to what the Jews suffered in the land of Germany, but the difference is that the Jews were in another country and were massacred by the host country.

The South African Situation.

There has been a long standing war between the indigenes of South Africa and the White race that arrived there around 1652. So, in narrating the story J.L. Boshoff (1980) said that they came in contact with the Hottentots, the indigenous nomadic people who lived in the area. After a few years a "war" broke out of which the White settlers were victorious in virtue of their sophisticated weapons. Peace treaty was negotiated on the proclamation of a boundary or a fence which ultimately found expression in the policy of segregation. Consequently, the boundary procalamation did not work and as such endless number of clashes, and war ensued. These wars were in the bid to acquire more lands for expansion. The White settlers became victorious in view of their modern war weapons and as such, they started giving orders. Contrary to popular opinion, Boshoff categorically asserted that the relationship between White and black was not solely the invention of white man of South Africa. He rather sees the issue by way of incompatibility of the two cultures. Already a certain pattern of living had emerged from a vastly different ways of life, social system, custom, dress and behavior patterns and as such, there was problem of accommodation. He went on to saying that the situation became worse after the second world war, and with the discovery of gold and diamond the black man was almost exclusively the servant of the white in South Africa. In the same issue, Alex La Guma (1972) decried that it was the discovery of "gold" and "diamond" which made South Africa the hunting ground of International capitalism and eventually laid the foundation for racial discrimination particularly in industries. He narrated how the pioneer imperialist, Cecil John Rhodes categorically said "I have made up my mind that there must be class (race) legislation ... The Native is to be treated as a child and denied the franchise. We must adopt the system of despotism such as worked well in India in our relation with the barbarians of South Africa ... These are my politics and these are the politics of South Africa". The foregoing statements have provided a good focus on the genesis of suppression, exploitation, class distinction and finally racial discrimination prevalent in South Africa. All these acted as barriers to private investiments by the blacks. Their backwardness stemmed from the fact that they were forcefully pushed to the rural areas as evidenced by the Urban Areas Act of 1945. Thus, Patrick Wilmot (1983) quoted from the Act that "No African shall remain for more than seventy-two hours in any urban, semi-urban, mining, or any other "prescribed" area unless he produced proof that (a) he has since birth resided continuously in such an area. This Act has portrayed the magnitude of social injustice and segregation, economic deprivation as well as the right to any land tenure in one's own country. This is the highest water-mark of apartheid and deprivation of freedom of movement.

The protracted war in South Africa has left a bitter taste in many months. The root causes of the war could be located in the domains of "race", "colour bar" and "class distinction". The degree of separation is so high that market, church Institutions, social gatherings are simply - white for the whites while, black for the blacks. In that situation the blacks only enjoy a much lower average standard of material well-being than the whites who are highly placed. It was the affluence of the whites that resulted to class barriers. Therefore the problem is compounded. Hence, W.H. Hutt (1964) asserted that "if the evident backwardness of the masses is caused by deliberate policy rather than by unrestrained population growth and a paucity of natural resources, there is certainly cause for complaints of class injustice but not of colour". This has created social inferiority and psychologically had affected the social image of the blacks. Thus, the character of the apartheid in South Africa is an acute "separate development". This separate development profoundly influenced subsequent history and one can add that it was the introduction and practice of that separate existence that had spread the cancer of apartheid in the whole of South Africa. This in turn has kept the black inhabitants in a perpetual agony of social inferiority, economic exploitation, political maladjustment and social injustice. By all indications, the blacks lived in the arbitrary will of the whites. They had from time suffered from an inferiority, and irreparable harsh conditions. But one has to understand that it was the sophisticated arms of the whites which made them victorious, and as such, they continued their routinized terror against the blacks. Naturally, the blacks would endeavour to break out of this routine, and in the attempt to do so war ensued. The gravity of the bloodshed experienced in South Africa has been likened to the Nazi holocaust of the Jews in Germany as expressed by Alex La Guma (1972) "No doubt people could have expressed similar incredulity about Nazi Germany when told that soap had been manufactured from the fat of victims of the concentration camps". The South African holocaust, although likened to the Nazi's is a little bit different when we consider their locations. In South Africa the owner of the land is denied that ownership and were being oppressed by foreign people in the land; while in Nazi, the Jews were foreigners and were being massacred by the native Nazis. In Germany the Jews lived in Ghettos but were marketing together with the Germans, but in South Africa everything was done in a separate mood; the market is "colour-blind". The survivors of the Nazi holocaust were faced with the decision of fleeing to another country or going back home wards to Palestine. The degree of holocaust in South Africa has rendered many homeless with the result that some flee to other neighbouring countries in search of shelter. These refugees face the problems of re-adjustment, accommodation, health, family disintegration, subordination, malnutrition, insecurity, freedom, subservience and many other deprivations. The degree of separatism in South Africa is so much that the whites used to call the blacks "black stinking dogs", in short, "a good for nothing". Racial discrimination has automatically a negative connotation culminating to structural violence. It has also harmful and revolutionary consequences. Internally, it sparks direct violence from those discriminated against as a result of stress, hardship, anxiety, frustration, inequality, injustice and diverse deprivations. Thus, the white regime in South Africa has spread its sword to the countries of Angola, Namibia, Botswana, Zimbabwe, Mozambique, Zambia etc. As they continue to bomb and destroy civilians they make a mockery of the principles of the United Nations and all the international, cultural, political, economic and religious concepts of human rights, equality and dignity. However, numerous decisions have been taken by the United Nations, Afro-Asian solidarity, tricontinental movements and others to impose all forms of sanctions against the racist regime.

On National levels, there has been recurring incidents of genocide of tribes against tribes due to ethnic rivalries; or a "one-man" coup, in the bid to rule. This paper endeavours to highlight issues of massacres in Uganda, Zaire, Nigeria and Rwanda-Burundi. In Uganda the issue was not that of revolt by either the peasants or the army than of "a-one-man" craze for power - Idi Amin. Thus, Iain Grahame (1980) commented that "Idi Amin chose a course that was to take his country back down the dark tunnel to an era of barbarism and internecine slaughter". Although Idi Amin's coup d'etat of 1971 was remarkably bloodless, the type of massacres metted out to fellow Ugandans during his rule could only be imagined than expressed. Amin exercised unlimited powers of arrests, detention, torture and kill of thousands of civilians, who, for one reason or another have been suspected of opposition to his regime. He divided his Nubian henchmen into "striker units" whose task was to round up such "unwanted" persons. Evidences abound of the killing of thousands of citizens many from Acholi and Lango tribes of Northern Uganda from which the ousted President Obote had drawn much of his support (Robert Fraser, 1975). The massacre was so much that Amin's Foreign

Minister, Wanume Kibedi, who was serving at Musoga estimated the number as nearing one hundred thousand citizens. He categorically said that "General Amin's personal involvement in the liquidation of thousands of innocent Ugandans was beyond dispute or contradiction" (Ibid., 1975). In the same vein, Henry Kyemba, who served in Amin's Ministerial capacity until 1977, who also revealed to the public. "The shocking brutal story of the Hitler of our Time"; gave the number retrieved by boatmen from Owen Falls at forty-thousand deed bodies, plus, ten-thousand eaten by crocodiles ..." (Grahame, 1980). He even unveiled the fact that Owen Falls was one out of the other three dumping areas.

It was also noted that early in 1972 that some of the worst killings took place at Mutukula, a small village close to the Tanzanian border. Hundreds of pro-Obote officers and other ranks had been herded into cells, and a large number were savagely murdered in cold blood. The casualties were over five-hundred people. What is more, at the "Yoweri Triangle" in Uganda, the massacre was so much that the number estimated at ten-thousand was even said to be a conservative estimate. Under Idi Amin, Uganda invaded Tanzania in November, 1978, the number massacred was very enormous that Idi Amin boasted "My bulldozer were kept busy burying the dead", with all these untold massacres under Idi Amin, the press nicknamed him "A blood-thirsty tyrant" and "the Hitler of our time; thus, matching his genocide with the Nazi holocaust of the Jews in Germany under Adolf Hitler. But while Hitler used "gas-chamber" for his operation and burning of their dead bodies, Idi Amin dumped some dead bodies into the Owen Falls to ease off the problem of burying. Therefore, the genocide carried out by the orders of Idi Amin of Uganda has been seen as the peak of it all; and as being "unique" in the history of the African continent.

Holocausts in different nations in Africa were noted for their uniqueness; the Zairian issue is a case in point. The chaotic period in Congo (Zaire) was put between 1960 and 1965. Ghislain Kabwit (1979) has noted that Mobutu has ruled Zaire with "an iron fist" since he came to power in 1965. He had an 'iron-grip' control over the notoriously, undisciplined and brutal national army called Les Forces armees Zaioises (F.A.Z.). That Mobutu's government was universally known for massive violation of human rights along with military exactions perpetrated on civilians. It was reported that in 1969 hundreds of students at the University of Lovanium were massacred in cold blood by soldiers who panicked when they attempted to demonstrate against the Government because of unpaid scholarships, shortage of food, and general lack of educational facilities. This brutal act of killing the students is the highest holocaust on the "holy innocents", incredible to the eye of a Christian, and worthy of condemnation. It was also narrated how in late January 1978, as many as seven hundred civilians to two thousand, according to emigre groups in Brussels were reportedly killed by the brutal suppression of a rebellion in Bandundu Province, about five hundred miles from Kinshasa - (Kabwit, 1979). Moreover, the refugees who fleed to Zambia from Kolwez have asserted that the Zairian army has killed hundreds of Lunda tribesmen, the entire village were being razed and burned by soldiers in retaliation for their alleged support of the Katangan exiles. The reason for this massacre does not hold water. It clearly shows that those who gave orders for the massacre were devoid of godly spirit and had no atom of moral standing.

The Nigerian case:

Many scholars have written about the remote and immediate causes of the Nigerian civil war of 1967 to 1970; which was a war between the Igbo tribe and the other tribes in Nigeria. Like the Poet who described "Ibadan" as being "scattered on the seven hills, like a broken China in the sun"; so can be likened the natural, geographical make-up of the country amalgamated to be called "Nigeria". Geographically, Nigeria is heterogenous; made up of different native groups with diverse cultures, and by implication thousand and one different dialects. As was difference in cultures so were their outlook, attitude to life, religion and even rate of development. Moreover, the distances between one ethnic group to the other is so far away that Sir Hugh Clifford, who governed the country from 1920 to 1931 decried

> "Nigeria is made up of a collection of independent Native States, separated from one another ... by great distances, by differences of history and traditions, and by ethnological, racial, tribal, political, social and religious barriers" (Kirk-Greene, 1967).

In the same vein, Alexander Madiebo (1980) pointed out the heterogenous make-up of the country which has made void any form of unity. This heterogenous portrait of Nigeria is evidenced by three strong ethnic-oriented parties prominent before the war. These were the North Peoples Congress (NPC) for the North, Action Group (AG) for the West; and National

Convention for Nigerian Citizens (NCNC) for the East - each struggling for supremacy. Thus, ethnic consciousness was the order of the day - which precipitated a long untold disunity, animosity and feeling of suppression and exploitation. Paul Anber (1967) buttressed these facts when he argued that "like the Jews, to whom the Igbo have frequently been likened, they progressed, despite being a minority in the country, filling the ranks of the Nation's educated, prosperous upper classes". Naturally, animosity, hatred and the like could be metted to such a group and all forms of discrimination could follow. However, General Olusegun Obasanjo (1980) summarized the causes of the war as follows:- "The war itself was the culmination of an uneasy peace and stability that had plagued Nigeria from Independence. That uneasy peace and stability had their genesis in the geography, history and demography of Nigeria". Considering the foregoing remote causes of that civil war, there should be a more careful and incisive analysis of the causes, because, the grudges started long ago, while revolution sparked one day.

There is no gainsaying that it was the Military coup of January 15, 1966 and the partiality in the assassination of the corrupt old civilian leaders, which gave impetus to the civil war. It was a chain reaction. When major General J.T.U. Aguiyi Ironsi, an Igbo man, took over power, there was a kind of obsession for Igbo supremacy especially among the Igbo people living in the Northern parts of Nigeria. This eventually sparked off some kind of misunderstanding resulting to massive civil riot in the North in May, 1966. The Igbo people who were living in the places called "strangers' quarters" were easily located and massacred in large numbers estimated to three thousand. Thus, anti-Igbo sentiment erupted strongly in the North, that on July 29, 1966, the Northerners struck back killing Aguiyi Ironsi and many Igbo high ranking officers. It can be noted that it was this very counter coup that struck the highest death toll in the civilian Igbo population in the North. The pogrom was so much that even the estimate given at fifty thousand was said to be a conservative one. Then, the civil war which followed was estimated to have claimed about three million lives on the whole. Thus, Nkembirim Bernard (1977) commented that "in Nigeria - Biafran war, the tribes lost their grip and engaged in the most brutal and extreme savagery, the cause of which cannot be confined to inter-tribal, nor limit it to the wealth that could accrue from the oil". Eventually, the war was called off when the heart of Igboland - Owerri and Orlu were reached.

One can see that, as the Jews lived in ghettos in a foreign land (Germany) so did the Igbo people lived in "strangers' quarters", but, in their own fatherland. The Jews did not wage war against the Germans but in Nigerian case, there were riots, coups and finally civil war. Although the war was shortlived, when compared with what is now happening in South Africa, the massacre was enormous. The crux of the matter is the measures to be taken by all and sundry, to avoid history repeating itself. There should be religious tolerance. As there are diverse tribes so are diverse religious groups; and as such, efforts should be made for one group to tolerate the other. For instance, sometime in the North, there was religious disturbances from the maitesine group which claimed the lives of innocent citizens. However, efforts are now being made by different church leaders towards Religious Dialogue and ecumenism. The Federal Military Government are trying their best to ensure equal political and economic opportunities for all citizens by adopting different policies and carrying out Programmes such as: (SFEM) Second Tier Foreign Exchange Market; (SAP) Structural Adjustment Programme; (DIRFRI) Directorate of Roads, Food, and Rural Infrastructures; and (MAMSER) Mass Mobilization for Economic Recovery, Self Reliance and Social justice; Rural Development Programmes and Educate Women for Development are geared towards togetherness, sense of belonging and hard work. All these help to ensure better life for the citizens and those yet unborn.

Rwanda - Burundi issue

The two territories of Rwanda and Burundi were entrusted to Belgium as a League of Nations Mandate after the First World War; but as a United Nations Trust Territory after the Second World War. In Rwanda, there has been long existing grudges by the Hutu peasants against the Tutsi monarch. It was alleged that they were being denied of their political rights, being suppressed and highly exploited. Rene Lemarch and (1970) noted that the Hutu peasants revolted in November 1959. That upheaval was a kind of social and political revolution directed against both Tutsi hegemony and monarchical rule. It was a long and painful enterprise which may not have succeeded without the auxillary support extended by the Belgian administration to the insurgents. Race issue lay at the core of the debate when a group of Tutsi elders, at the Mwami's Court issued some nasty statements that "their ancestors came to the throne by reducing the indigenous Hutu tribe to a state of servitude, and as such, there could be no basis for brotherhood between Hutu and Tutsi". (Ibid, 1970). The Hutus saw this as an afront to their own persons, and promptly challenged the historical symbols of Tutsi supremacy - and permanent Hutu inferiority. Thus, Tutsi monarchy caused such deep revulsion among the Hutu elites that they launched an attack against it. They forcefully ejected the traditional ruling elites and eventually abolished Tutsi monarchy. By November 10, 1959, Rwanda had become a country torn by violence, with thousands of people massacred and about twenty-two thousand fled to other places like Burundi, Bimba, Gisenyi and Astida. It was said that by 1960 the refugees who sought asylum abroad grew rapidly to about one hundred and thirty-thousand (Report on Ruanda-Urundi, 1960). The mass exodus of the Tutsi was possible because many of their houses were burnt and crops devasted, so they were faced with double tragedy. With this peasant revolt, the Hutus, with the help of the Belgians were able to install their chiefs and subchiefs. On the whole, the refugees had an unanimous conviction that they owed their fate to a deliberate racial bias on the part of the administration of the Belgians. This allegation was unfounded because, it was the arrogancy of the Tusi elders that sparked the revolt which claimed the lives of many people and created acute refugee problems in some countries around.

Holocaust and Refugee Problems

From all indications war can see that genocide or holocaust is a key factor of mass exodus of people from their countries of origin to another. Other factors generating refugees include civil wars, colonialism, oppressive governments, persistent apartheid politics as we have in South Africa and at times natural disaster. From these factors, it has been recognized that Africa has the greatest volume of refugees in the world. Internal strifes notwithstanding, the swelling tide of thousands of men, women, and children fleeing colonial and racist reppression in South Africa are enough to make the volume of refugees very enormous. Thus, the issue of political revolutions accruing from liberation efforts from colonial domination has sort of affected the political image and stability of the African continent. Refugee issue arises mainly after any war; the first and second world wars are typical examples. It was during the Second Warld War that large movement of refugees were experienced in Europe. Those who were worstly hit were the Jews fleeing from the Nazi Germany. Those who delayed their going were mercilessly massacred through the "gas chamber". Most of the Jews at the time in question chose to go back to Palestine. They were helped by the International Refugee Organisation (IRO) created by the United Nations Organisation for this purpose. In the same vein, there is no doubt that help came from the American Refugee Services; the American Red Cross, British Information Service, American Jewish Committee and American Christian Palestinian Committee. All these helped in the rehabilitation and resettlement of the Jews. The outcome of the plight of the Jewish refugees made the United Nations General Assembly in 1946, decide on how best to assist genuine refugees and displaced persons. They saw it as an International problem; which must be tackled promptly by "all and sundry".

Refugee situation should be seen as an acute human suffering and it has its effects on both the country of origin or the country of refuge. The tragic positions of refugees have unveiled the economic, social, humanitarian, legal and political problems. Morever, the bad effects of population shift and and population decrease cannot be over-emphasized. Most of these problems have their peculiar characters and it falls within the portfolio of different governments, voluntary organisations, United Nations International bodies and Organization of African Unity, to work out modalities of restoring refugee to a legitimate right for a normal and dignified existence. These modalities should relate to the return and rehabilitation of all refugees in their countries of origin or in acute cases, in their resettlement areas. From the United Nations document on Human Rights, (1978) we gathered that in "1951 the Convention on status of refugees revising and consolidating previous international agreements on the subject and extending their scope, was adopted by the United Nations Convention of Plenipotentiaries on the status of Refugees and stateless persons". It was also gathered that the International Refugee Organization ended its work in 1952 and was replaced by the United Nations High Commission for Refugees (UNHCR). This very body provides material help to refugees and in this respect, the legal assistance provided to indigent refugees to enable them retain lawyers in legal proceedings is commendable. In addition, it provides international protection, under the auspices of the United Nations. The above has shown that since the inception of the United Nations Organization, much efforts have been made to protect refugees the world over. There are about thirteen African countries who are covered by the activities of the United Nations High Commission for Refugees.

The African Continent must be commended by their unqualified reception of genuine refugees despite the great numbers involved. By all indications refugees in Africa have been received in a true brotherly spirit. Besides food, shelter and shared governmental services, free land for cultivation has always been made available to them. According to Osita Eze, (1984) the Organization of the African Unity (O.A.U.) provides that members shall co-operate with the office of the United Nations High Commission for Refugees (Art. VIII (1). It is also accepted that the efficiency of the measures recommended by the Organization of the African Unity Convention to solve the problem of refugees in Africa necessitates close and continuous collaboration between the Organization for African Unity and the United Nations High Commission for Refugees. Maduagu Michael, (1987) quoting from Africa Today, (1986) pointed out that "according to a 1985 survey, Ethiopia, generating 1,286,500 refugees topped the list of source countries of refugees in Africa, followed by Angola (358,000), and Uganda (282,100). On the other hand, the chief asylum countries were Sudan (1,094,000) followed by Somalia (550,000), Zaire (238,100 and Tanzania (179,000); The refugee population in Africa has grown so much that it is difficult to know the exact number and the conditions in which they live. However, in as much as some Organizations give material support in cash and kind, different African governments should endeavour to make life somehow bearable. This they did by making land available to them to make them economically viable, become self-reliant in respect of self-grown food and also to earn some cash in order to afford some daily expenses. All these notwithstanding, the Governments of refugees should bring the new communities to a stage of social viability providing health and educational facilities to ensure adequate communication and social integration. These are vital because, these refugees are people whose Fundamental Human Rights had been adversely violated - either through internal conflict, revolutionary struggle or racial segregation as in the case of Nazi against the Jews and the white race regime in South Africa.

It can be noted that the Nazi holocaust on the Jews between 1939 to 1945 was so awful in the eyes of the World that "The Universal Declaration of Human Rights was adopted on December 1948 in the form of a resolution of the General Assembly. All the fifty-eight member States voted for its approval. (United Nations, 1968). Article I of that Declaration proclaims that: "all human beings are born free and equal in dignity and rights". It strikes us here that in South Africa, the blacks are looked down upon by the Whites. The blacks are reduced to a subservience level and as such they do not enjoy equal rights with the Whites. Article 2 denounces segregation by way of race, sex, language, colour, religious political or other opinions etc. The violations of these Rights have been the bone of contention in South Africa and in Nazi Germany. Those massacred were denied that Right to life. It is no surprise that in the first part of his great document, Pope John XXIII gave a bill of the fundamental rights of man which, 'are universal and inviolable and therefore altogether inalienable" (1961). It is on these rights that the right order among men must be based. The First Article is "The right to Life (Physical and personal security)". God has stamped some sacredness in the human life and as such, it is worth preserving as long as God designs to sustain it. Life is made for the service of God and man's neighbour in the community, and must not be destroyed with impunity. Therefore, all authorities have that definite moral obligation to protect every innocent person from any direct violation of his right to life. In a bid to protect human life many world bodies have demonstrated this in their own different ways. For instance, the "Freedom Charter of South Africa" was unanimously adopted at a "Congress of the People" held in Kliptown, near Johannesburg on 25 and 26 June (1955). This Charter is all embracive and it is on that platform that the "Freedom fighters" are winning some sympathy. Also, the "Asian Regional Conference for Action against Apartheid was held in Manila, Republic of the Philippines, from 24 - 26 May, (1982) under the sponsorship of the United Nations Special Committee against Apartheid in co-operation with the Government of the Philipines. Above all there is now what we call "International Day of Peace" for the whole human race. The United Nations Organization has set off a day, every third Tuesday of September each year, to be observed as the "World's International Day of Peace". They have seen that millions of people around the world still live with the scourge of war, and war of genocide holocaust and the like had claimed so many lives that efforts should be made for a peaceful international co-existence. There is no moral scrupples in spilling blood and as soon as the root cause (war) is attacked, people will enjoy some air of dignity, liberty and oneness in the World.

SUMMARY AND CONCLUSION

From all indications, the Nazi holocaust on the Jews sparked off some kind of concern in the moral obligations of the World Bodies and threw a big challenge to the Christian Church. Given the fact that antisemitism was in vogue in "the Europe of the time", it was Adolf Hitler who made the wiping out of the Jewish race in Germany a state policy. The strategy adopted by Hitler and his men were so barbarous that other Nations kicked against it. We are talking about it now because it is seen as being "unique" in quantitative terms. Inshort, for the whole of Europe it was a "shocking unbelievability". It evoked some feelings in the hearts of the people especially from the testimony of the survivors. For the Jews today, that holocaust has come to serve as both the Political and moral foundation for the State of Israel. It must always be remembered lest the Jews again become vulnerable to destruction. Something tragic had happened to the Jewish race and our stand should be that history "does not repeat itself."

The Nazi, holocaust on the Jews called into question the morality of that nation. The act alone has thrown much challenge to the other World Powers and more importly to the Christian Church of the time. The holocaust stands as a moral crisis, for neither law nor religion could comprehend the massive killings than the "neurotic hatred the Nazis had on the Jews". Psychologically the profound impact the holocaust had on the people was so great that people were stripped of moral authority and security and one wonders why modern European civilization could not provide some form of moral security to its inhabitants. If the holocaust was seen as an internal matter one wonders what will become of the future survival of humankind. If it was on a moral-ethical basis that other states could not interfer in the act, was that also bound on the Church? One cannot make out a concrete reason why the Christian Church intervened very late. This is because, it is the Church's moral obligation to see to the well-being of human beings as Gods own creatures, or could it be seen that the Holy See was dancing to the tune of German Government? However, the humanitarian characters of Britain and America were portrayed on the type of help they rendered to the Jewish refugees from Germany by way of repatriating them to Palestine and their rehabilitation. They also took the lead in rallying round other nations to establish the International Refugee Organization under the auspicies of the United Nations Organization to look into the affairs of the refugees. This body was later replaced by the United Nations High Commission for Refugees whose duty was to see to the material needs both in cash and kind, rehabilitation and negotiation of safety repatriation of the refugees to their places of origin or to another area of settlement.

The Jews and the Christians see morality as a theory of system of laws binding upon rational creatures, and they see this code of conduct as binding on themselves by virture of their religious truth. In view of this, the African Christian revulsion on the holocaust stems from the fact that the Nazis misused their conscience in their extermination of the Jews. "Holocaust" with all its horrors should be treated by appealing to the Biblical injunction - "Thou shalt not kill". In the final analysis we are saying that there is no morality in spilling innocent blood. The Nazi holocaust should be condemned for all its injustice in the perversion of personality and ethics. For the African Christian, individual life has a purpose guided by the morals of society, for that reason people try to maximize goodness. In this light we are morally bound to respect the life of the human person as stipulated in the International law of the Fundamental Human Rights.

The Nazis had actually done a "new" thing against the whole human race - that is, killing people by burning. There had been recurrent massive killings in many countries in Africa, as earlier pointed out, but none can be compared with what Hitler did not even Idi Amin of Uganda, popularly known as "The Hitler of our time". Moreover, most of the genocidal acts that had happened in Africa were more of Inter-tribal wars; but that of Nazi was the extermination of a particular race who were living in their midst, all in the name of racial hatred; and this racial segregation is what has made life unbearable in the Southern Part of Africa. Thus, the aftermath of genocide or holocaust can be seen to be refugee migration, insecurity, economic and political instability. However, the UNO, OAU and their Organs have in no small measure proved to the World that they are capable of handling the refugee issues. It is germane to delve into the root cause of refugees, and attack it squarely. This, can be achieved if their are love, racial tolerance, and peaceful co-existence. Hospitality should be the main goal of all nations.

On the whole, peace is being sought on international levels with the result that the third Tuesday of September each year is set apart as the "World International Year of Peace". One would admit that if the Nazis were living peacefully with the Jews at that time there would be no room for the massive killing of the Jews. Efforts should be made at international levels to curb such inhumane treatment in order to revitalize the ideals of all human society. Moreover, all Christendom should recognize their role in creating a climate of peaceful co-existence among peoples by virtue of what Christianity professes and what people expect from the Christian tenets and ideals.

REFERENCES

Anber P., (1967) In: The Journal of Modern African Studies, Vol.V, No.2, 163 - 179.
Beshir, M.O. (1974) London, Rex Collings 81-102.
Boshoff, J.L., (1980), In: RACE AND ETHNICITY: South Africa, and International Perspective, Cape, David Philip Publishers Ltd., 72-78.
Chatfield, C. (1982) In: The Bible and Social Reform, Pennsylvenia, Fortress Press 105-131.
Cohn, N. (1967) London, Eyre and Spottiswoode, 194-215
Crum B.C. (1947), New York, Simon and Schuster Publishers 93-107
Curtain P.D. (1964), Wisconsin, the University of Wisconsin Press 234-280.
Donagan, A. (1977) U.S.A. The University of Chicago Press 1-47.
Eze, O. (1984), Nigeria, Macmillan Publishers Ltd., 163-211
Fletcher, J. (1967), London, S C M Press Ltd., 231-241.
Fletcher J., (1980) In. Ethics in a Permissive Society, Great Britain, William Collins Sons & Co. Ltd., 69-91.
Guma A.L. (1972), London, Lawrence and Wishort Press Ltd., 1-32.
Holmes, C. (1979), New York, Holmes and Meier Publishers, 36-119.
Hutt, W.H. (1964), Great Britain, Andre Deutsch Ltd., 9-31
Iain G., (1980), London, Granada 81-93.
Ilogu, E. (1974), Enugu, Nok Publishers Ltd., 118-169.
Irving D. (1977) In: The Holocaust and the Crisis of Human Bheaviour; New York Holmes and Meier Publishers 18.
Iwe, N.S.S. (1986) quoting Article I of The Pontificate of Pope John XXIII 137-153.
Kabwit, G.C. (1979) In. The Journal of Modern African Studies, Vol.17, 381-407.
Kirk-Greene, A.H.M. (1980) In: My Command, Ibadan, Heinemann, 1-13.
Krausnick, H. (1968), In: The Holocaust and the Crisis of Human Bheaviour: New York, Holmes and Meier Publishers 1 - 15.
Kung, H., (1979), New York, Doubleday and Company Inc., 143-156.
Liniger-Goumaz, M. (1979), London, The Scarecrow Press Inc., 92-95.
Madiebo A.A., (1980) Enugu, Fouth Dimension Publishers, 1-10.
Maduagwu, M. (1987) Africa Today Vol.32, No.4, 72.
Nkembirim, B.A. (1977) In: The Journal of Modern African Studies, Vol.5, Nos.1-4, 84-89.
Obasanjo, O. (1980), Ibadan, Heinemann, i-xi, 1 - 13.
Omoregbe, J. (1979), England, Global Educational Services, 1-100.
Oyedepo, K. (1986) In: Religion and Ethics in Nigeria, Nigeria, Daystar Press, 14-27.
Paul, J. (1975) Great Britain, Penguin Book Ltd., 119-124.
Singer, P. (1980), Cambridge, Cambridge University Press, 72-92
Tedeschi, J.T. Smith and Brown R.C. (1974) In: The Journal of Personality and Social Psychology, No.51 Vol.2 540-562.
Wilmot, P.F. (1983) Nigeria, University of Ife Press Ltd., 1 - 31.
The Freedom Charter of South Africa, (1979), New York, 1-7
International Day of Peace, (1982) New York, United Nations.

The challenge to the Christian community with emphasis on early Christianity and overall historical considerations

CHAIRPERSON **Professor Frederick Schweitzer**

RAPPORTEUR **Dr Jacobus Schoneveld**

AUSCHWITZ AS SYMBOL

Robert P. Carroll

Dept of Biblical Studies
University of Glasgow
Glasgow G12 8QQ
Scotland, UK.

Es ist niemals ein Dokument der Kultur, ohne zugleich ein solches der Barbarei zu sein.
- Walter Benjamin.

The twentieth century resonates with the names of places and events which beggar description as moments of appalling terror and destruction - the Kaiser war of 1914-18 with its trench warfare and the casualties of the Somme and other now famous places; the Serbo-Croatian and Armenian massacres of the earlier part of the century; the Soviet Gulag and the murdered millions of Stalin's Russia; the Hitler war of 1939-45 and the concentration camps of the Third Reich; Hiroshima and Nagasaki; the tens of millions murdered in Mao's China; the terrible slaughters throughout Africa, especially in the Congo and Burundi and those associated with Idi Amin and Obote in Uganda; the Vietnam war and the subsequent reign of terror presided over by Pol Pot; South American dictatorships; the Russians in Afghanistan and the Iran-Iraq war. To many Europeans outstanding in that, by no means exhaustive, list are the place names of the death camps of Nazi Germany. It is neither wise nor necessary to provide league tables of destruction and evil for this century, but the _frisson_ still felt when the roll-call of Nazi camps is heard indicates the permanence of the horror associated in the European psyche with those awful places.

To speak once more and to go on repeating the story of these camps, where so much brutality and murder took place within living memory, is always difficult but never uncalled for. Even for those who are neither survivors of nor party to what happened during the German Reich of 1933-45, the task of contemplating these places remains on the agenda of the living. For can those who come after the events or who had no part whatsover in them escape the recollection of them or even dare to be silent about the eclipse and death of civilization in this century? To be silent in the presence of such destruction and so many deaths is appropriate as a human response to the death of the tribe. But to remain silent after the gestures of mourning and sadness have been completed is to betray the dead by forgetfulness, concealment or the refusal to speak out on behalf of the violated. For those who had no connections with the events the task of thinking of and speaking about them, even the recollection in pain of what happened, cannot be avoided because if only those who were there and survived are entitled to speak who shall speak when these survivors are themselves dead? The memory of those places in the living will die someday and then it will be too late for remembrance if others have not taken up the story already.

But how is the matter to be voiced by those who were not there? How can the outsider speak of things beyond knowledge and experience? How is one who is neither German nor Jewish, Christian nor survivor to speak of something which happened in the heartland and _heimat_ of European culture? With what words can those who come after speak of what has gone before? A Raul Hilberg may dispassionately dissect the anatomy of bureaucratic murder whereby a people were rendered invisible throughout Europe and effectively destroyed from off the face of that continent. A Peter Weiss may indict a generation by naming the murdered ones name by name. But these evocations of the murderous past have been created already without exhausting the possibilities of remembrance or definitively describing that past. The recital of the facts associated with the geography of death and the German alphabet of terror (eg Auschwitz, Belsen, Chelmno, Dachau...) will remain as a permanent and a perennial response to the need to remember what happened during the Nazi apocalypse, but other means of trying to understand what happened and its significance will be developed also. It remains incredibly difficult to speak of these places in language precise and appropriate to what happened there. The poetic minimalism of a Paul Celan and the baroque prose of a George Steiner are different responses to the matter which illustrate the kinds of language which may capture aspects of the camps but not exhaust the need for a manifold linguistic representation of the events of 1933-45. The novels of Elie Wiesel or Primo Levi illustrate a more oblique approach to the quest for understanding and the innumerable studies of the camps indicate the vast quantities of factual information available on the subject.

For me, who is not a Jew or a Christian and who was born during the Hitler war in a neutral country (Dublin 1941), the problems of speaking of these things are almost insuperable. That may be sufficient condition for attempting to speak of them! To ignore them and to behave as if they had never happened would be worse than to speak inarticulately about them. It would be as if an astronomer were to ignore a black hole detected in space just because he happened to be working on some other aspect of astronomy at the time. In our moral universe the camps are the equivalent of a black hole, absorbing all discourse of meaning and morality and presaging an anti-universe wherein all elements of civilization and culture are annihilated. In order to speak about these places in this paper I shall approach the problem obliquely and speak of the Shoah indirectly. Indirectly as the pious use circumlocutions of the divine name and obliquely because to rehearse once more the stark details of what went on in those camps would be to freeze the mind yet again and never pass beyond the introductory details of the ghettoes, resettlement trains, and the physical features of the camp sites. All values and judgments are transvalued and even transmogrified by what happened in those camps and to deal obliquely with them is the only way I know how to keep the task of remembrance without finding it impossible to speak at all. To keep alive the memory of what once happened to millions of people in our time by trying to grasp the causes and implications of the camps is all I can offer here. In the words of Paul Celan ('Shibboleth'):

> Set your flag at half-mast,
> memory.
> At half-mast
> today and for ever.

I

AUSCHWITZ AS SYMBOL

The number of camps created by the Third Reich between 1933 and 1944 are too many and variable to permit a short comprehensive account of the camps and anything less than a multi-volumed book would be an inadequate depiction of them. In view therefore of the space at my disposal I have decided to focus on Auschwitz as a symbol standing for all the many camps which were used by Germany to impose its will on others. The creation of Auschwitz in 1940-2 transformed an obscure Polish town, Oswiecim, in Upper Silesia (restored to the Reich after the conquest of Poland) into a complex of camps (Auschwitz-Birkenau, Monowitz) which made its Germanized name into a byword for the Endlösung 'the final solution'. It was chosen because it afforded easy access by rail and had great potential for expansion under optimum isolation conditions, even though the area itself was hardly promising for human habitation - Hilberg describes the camp as being 'encircled by stagnant fish ponds which permeated the compound with dampness, mist, and mud' (1961, 563). It is not possible to provide accurate statistics of the numbers murdered by various means, including being worked or starved to death as slaves of the Reich, at Auschwitz; different accounts give different numbers from 1.5 million to 4.5 million dead! Whatever the precise figures may be, they are a staggering testimony to the murderous policies of the Reich and make Auschwitz a name synonymous with death. As such the name may stand as a symbol for all the concentration camps.

In treating Auschwitz as a symbol it is not my intention to concentrate on the minutiae of daily life in that godforsaken place or to describe yet again the horrors and atrocities perpetrated in the camps. They are too well known to require repetition here or are more than adequately documented by Hilberg and Lucy Dawidowicz (usefully summarized in Rubenstein & Roth, 126-58 as an alternative to these magisterial authorities). My concern is not with the phenomenology of the death camps nor with the concrete details of how the enemies of the Reich were dehumanized before being murdered and their bodies disposed of by whatever technological means available. My purpose here is to allow Auschwitz to stand as shorthand for all the many camps and to symbolize the processes whereby the Reich was able to unleash its murderous hatred of other people. The stages whereby labour camps became annihilation camps and the constantly changing policies of the Reich towards the Jews will have to be subsumed under the notion of Auschwitz as symbol. There are simply too many features connected with the extermination of the Jews and the destruction of the enemies of the Reich (whether ethnic, political or homosexual) to allow for a responsible historical account of the story of how the camps came into existence as a preface to my real interest in this paper. I wish only to concentrate on what I see as a number of important matters which arise out of the notion of Auschwitz as symbol. Even these selected items are only a small part of the much larger story of the camps of 1933-45 and it is inevitable that distortions will be introduced into an account so selective in its concerns. Such distortions are part of the problem of speaking of Auschwitz in the first place!

II

A CLUSTER OF SYMBOLS

When Auschwitz is scrutinized as a symbol it quickly becomes apparent that there are a cluster of symbols involved in the study and every aspect of the place can serve a symbolic purpose. If the names of each person who died there are tracked down then there develops a matrix of family connections and history which would sustain a large-scale account of much of the social history of Europe and Russia in the nineteenth and twentieth century. Thus for example Milena Jasenska and the two sisters of Franz Kafka died in Auschwitz and immediately the world of Czech-German letters and Kafka's contribution to world literature are conjured up. Such interconnections can be multiplied a millionfold for Auschwitz and beyond for the other camps and a huge peopled history annihilated by the Reich comes tantalizingly into focus. Whatever other symbols Auschwitz may be made to stand for it primarily represents the killing times in Europe when so many people were wiped out along with their families and their personal histories. The loss is both catastrophic and unimaginible - before it the rational mind seizes up and cannot function properly. It is therefore easier to consider Auschwitz as a symbol of the end point of many facets of European culture and civilization and to concentrate on this cluster of symbols as a way of speaking about the unspeakable.

Walter Benjamin's perceptive observation in his essay 'Über den Begriff der Geschichte' ('On the concept of history') VII that 'there is never a document of culture which is not at the same time one of barbarism' is a truth of which Auschwitz stands as a preeminent symbol. Whatever may be said about other atrocities and the murder of millions elsewhere in the world of the twentieth century, the death camps of the Third Reich brought to a conclusion the long history of European civilization. The optimist may wish to regard the camps as a caesura in European culture and civilization, but realism here demands that Auschwitz be taken seriously as a full stop. With its roots in the demise of the old Roman empire and its glories in the Renaissance, the scientific revolution and the Enlightenment, European culture ran its course and in the twentieth century created two world wars and everything that Auschwitz symbolizes. Alongside the achievements of da Vinci and Michelangelo, Rembrandt and Rubens, Shakespeare and Goethe, Bach and Mozart, Newton and Einstein, Kant and Hegel, Pascal and Kierkegaard, Spinoza and Faraday must also be set the story of this century with its many millions massacred in the wars of nationalism and the camps of such ideologies as Nazi Germany and Soviet Russia. The old Hebrew myth of paradise which possessed the tree of life in its midst also knew another tree which it called 'the tree of the knowledge of <u>good and evil</u>'. European culture is well symbolized by that second tree! Good and evil are so intertwined in European civilization that it is now unreasonable to attempt to separate the two and to the credits of art, literature, philosophy, and science must be added the debits of the camps. Of this moral bookkeeping Auschwitz is a symbol.

At the same time it must be recognized that often accounts of European culture avoid any mention of Auschwitz or are silent about the events of which Auschwitz is only the most prominent example. The barbaric document which is also European civilization's story is a long tale of oppression and invasion, war and torture, over the centuries until in this our century the statistics and technologies of murder reach peaks unimaginable in previous ages. By and large the two stories (the double helix of culture!), though intertwined, are not the work of the same people, so there is no question of a Mozart or a Beethoven being held responsible for the evil deeds perpetrated in their time. Rather the connection between culture and barbarism is more complex and less easily made than Benjamin's <u>aperçu</u> would suggest, though to be fair to him he is only making a general point. However the connections between the two are to be teased out (eg culture is only skin-deep!), it is remarkable how many people fail to make any connections whatsoever between them. It is still possible to read books on philosophy and theology, history and art without finding any awareness of the barbarism practised in this century. Historical works about the distant past may be exempted from this requirement to acknowledge the barbarity of our day, but no work about how we live now or how we should live can or should avoid a serious scrutiny of Auschwitz.

The centuries of European culture flowed into Auschwitz and there civilization was stripped of its skin-deep veneer. Every facet of daily life among people who had inherited the great cultural achievements of those centuries was tainted by the Nazi ideology and exposed as incapable of resisting that ideology. German culture could not resist the Nazis nor could any of the cultures which were overrun by it. The unmasking and exposure of civilization by the events of 1933-45 are among the most painful features of that time for us who live after that period. No longer can we regard ourselves as cultured and civilized because in our time these things were done at Auschwitz. What protection against barbarism did our civilization afford? It would be wrong to single out European culture as the only victim of barbarism, as if only westerners were vulnerable to ideology. We must guard against this kind of ideological slippage which identifies the problem with fascism when fascism is only the form European barbarism took. In Soviet Russia and Mao's China the camps were even more successful in annihilating millions of people, so marxist ideology proved to be at least as barbarous as fascism. However, for those of us who are European Auschwitz is a symbol of grave moral degeneration which puts a question mark against the value and depth of our cultural history.

Auschwitz primarily symbolizes what may be done by one nation to any number of other nations. Given the prerequisites of ideology and culture, technology and power, any nation may develop along the lines of modern Germany and under the peculiar circumstances of post-1918 society fall into the hands of a powerful ideology wedded to a bureaucratic-enabling technology which will develop into a death camp mentality. The development of the state and its concomitant nationalism in the eighteenth and nineteenth century helped to give rise to the genocidal movements so characteristic of the twentieth century. Of all this Auschwitz is undoubtedly a symbol. The Gulag is the symbol under slightly different conditions! Attempting to compare the relative merits of dying in Auschwitz or in the Gulag is an unwise academic exercise, though it is worth noting the following comment from Joseph Brodsky's autobiographical essay 'In a Room and a Half' in which he discusses with his father precisely that issue:

> ...I found myself asking him which concentration camps in his view were worse: the Nazis' or ours. "As for myself," came the reply, "I'd rather be burned at the stake at once than die a slow death and discover a meaning in the process." (Brodsky, 501).

Brodsky himself is a fine example of what the different ideological concentration camps had in common: a profound antisemitism. Socialisms of every hue in the twentieth century have been distinctly antisemitic in outlook and practice, though more recent forms have tended to disguise this central feature by making spurious distinctions between being a Jew and being a Zionist. What Auschwitz also symbolizes is the final arrival point of a very long history of European antisemitism. Since the fourth century when the Christian churches began to hold councils that antisemitism was built into the warp and woof of European society. In nineteenth century political movements and ideologies antisemitism had a strong place, especially in the writings of Karl Marx and in German society. Auschwitz is where that long history blossomed into its final and fullest flowering and therefore Auschwitz is the permanent symbol of antisemitism. This is where antisemitism leads!

Among the cluster of symbols constituted by Auschwitz we may note the roles of technology and science. Auschwitz symbolizes how these features of European culture since the scientific revolution of the seventeenth century could be used by a political ideology to make the death camps much more effective and even possible in the first place. The great spread of camps all over the greater Reich was facilitated by the superb railway systems of nineteenth and twentieth century Europe. Locations were chosen in relation to these systems and much of the resettlement programme of the Nazis was dependent on the efficient running of the trains. Claude Lanzmann's Shoah underlines that feature of the Reich's policy with particular reference to Treblinka and one of the most famous images of Auschwitz, apart from that infamous gate bearing the legend 'Arbeit macht frei', is that of the railway tracks running into the camp. Tadeusz Borowski's story 'This Way for the Gas, Ladies and Gentlemen' captures the role of the trains in the transportation of so many people to their deaths in a way that only the gifted writer seems to be able to freeze-frame moments of the awful history of those killing times. The railways, the flowering of nineteenth century technology, played a fundamental part in the efficient transportation of millions of people to their deaths, just as the great slave-carrying ocean-going ships had transported from Africa to America the victims of the African slave-trade of previous centuries and just as international air travel in the 1970s and 1980s has facilitated the spread of AIDS. Technology may appear to be a neutral feature of any culture, but it can be used by ideologies or can play unforeseen parts in the general development of a particular culture. The role of technology in Auschwitz may also be seen in the extermination processes used to kill Jews and others as vermin by means of Zyklon B gas (cf. Hilberg, 561-72). Here technology and the industrial complex combined because the SS did not themselves manufacture Zyklon and therefore had to make use of private firms which were part of the chemical industry. Zyklon was a poison gas used for *Schädlingsbekämpfung* 'combating of vermin' and its use to gas the Jews in Auschwitz brought together scientific technology and cultural antisemitism in a most macabre way.

The role of medical science in the Reich is too well-known to bear much repetition here, but the way medical experimentation was carried out on the hapless victims of Nazi ideology makes of Auschwitz a symbol of perverted science. Given the nature of concentration camps as *Arbeitslager* 'work camp', the role of doctors in their running was fundamentally important. They had to determine who was fit for work and who was not. This selection process decided the speed with which inmates died in the camps. The doctors were also involved in making sure that the *Desinfektoren* who adminsistered the Zyklon B in the gas chambers were themselves protected from exposure to the gas (cf. Lifton, 161). Apart from the various forms of medical killings such as injections of phenol in the euthanasia programme, the doctors of Auschwitz are most notorious for their experimentations on the inmates. Josef Mengele was the most infamous of all the doctors there and was noted for his 'flamboyant detachment...and efficiency' (Lifton, 347). Auschwitz was famous for the experimental impulse of its doctors who specialized in sterilization and castration (Lifton, 267-302). Here the social roles of medicine were combined with medical science in order to run the camps with greater efficiency and, at the same time, contribute to (pseudo)science. As a symbol of this amoral science Auschwitz is a permanent reminder of how technology and science may be used in the service of an ideology to destroy life systematically. It is not a service confined to the camps or the Reich, but remains a constant possibility of all scientific enterprises. The contemporary concern with pollution, the thermonuclear threat, and the military-industrial complex are all further examples of how science and technology can be used to create widespread death in a culture. Auschwitz as symbol of this unholy marriage of heaven and hell is a dire warning about the need to recognize the dangers of assuming endless good may come of the neutral sciences. Science, technology, medicine are all part of an overall culture and cannot be practised independently of the prevailing ideologies in a society, so they need to be scrutinized continually by humane and moral values lest they facilitate the kinds of outrages practised in Auschwitz and the other camps. The honoured professions of science and medicine are nothing like as value-free as is often thought to be the case and the need for social responsibility in these professions as well as the critical scrutiny of them from the outside remain prime *desiderata* in any civilized community.

In isolating the various features of culture which were exposed at Auschwitz and which therefore allow Auschwitz to be a symbol of them I can only produce a limited number here. Much longer and far more sophisticated lists could be produced by others and also under other circumstances. One element in my selected cluster must be a religious one. Although I shall devote a section to certain religious issues involved in the camps I want to stress one dominant religious belief of which Auschwitz is a symbol in this section in order to underline the terrible exposure of cultural baggage brought about by Auschwitz. Auschwitz is a primary symbol of the impotence of the traditional Jewish-Christian belief in an intervening and miracle-working deity. The belief that there is a god who is all-powerful and all-good and who regularly (or continuously) intervenes to save his (or hers: radical degenderizing of the deity cannot save the doctrine of divine protection) pious followers or to protect the innocent cannot survive Auschwitz. The systematic murder of men, women and children which Auschwitz best typifies exposes that belief as hollow. Of course that belief did not fail because of Auschwitz; Auschwitz was simply the last and greatest example of the falseness of the belief. Auschwitz is a symbol of its falseness. The infinite impotence of the traditional deity has long been known in religious circles and much of the finest writing in the Hebrew Bible centres on the problems raised by experience for the conviction that the god Yhwh protects and saves Israel. The books of Job and Qoheleth underline the point and the lament psalms illustrate the existential problems caused by the collapse of the belief. Various Assyrian, Babylonian and Roman emperors repeatedly devastated the city of Jerusalem with its sacred temples of Yhwh and demonstrated the falseness of the belief that Jerusalem was Yhwh's city and therefore inviolable. The prophetic traditions may be read as desperate attempts to protect the belief by arguing just causes for the various destructions, with an underlying conviction that ultimately the city would be safe. These tensions between belief and experience are features of much Jewish writing after the fall of Jerusalem in 70 CE and the stories told about Elisha ben Abuya illustrate the argument perfectly. I doubt if Auschwitz could add to Elisha's arguments, but it should effectively terminate any surviving vestiges of the belief in a national myth of divine protection. Dostoyevsky's Ivan Karamazov argued in The Brothers Karamazov that he had to return his ticket to God because of the sufferings of one child; what would he have said of Auschwitz? Ivan was right of course! The suffering of one innocent person is sufficient to wreck the theological claim about a righteous deity who works good in the earth. How much more do the murdered millions of Auschwitz reinforce that argument! There may be authentic religious responses to Auschwitz which can incorporate that godless place into a theology of suffering and divine presence (cf. Cohen; Surin), but Auschwitz itself is a permanent symbol of the falseness of the belief in a protective deity. It also stands as a symbol of the need of human communities to rid themselves of the myth, be it national or personal, of divine protection. At Auschwitz neither god nor man could save nor would save and the ideologies associated with such religion and society are themselves rendered useless by their inabilities to prevent or oppose Auschwitz.

If all the cultural streams of civilization and religion which flow into Auschwitz are demonstrated to be incapable of resisting that place of death, can nothing positive be said about the experience of the death camps? As a symbol Auschwitz will always stand for the place where millions were murdered under conditions which still do not bear thinking about. Nothing can change that fact. No matter how the story is told Auschwitz is a black hole in our universe of moral discourse. There may be modal logics in which the name Oswiecim will not necessarily indicate a town associated with death, but in this world in which we live and have our being Auschwitz will always symbolize the death camps of the Reich and stand for the millions who died in those camps. That is an unchangeable fact of our history. Individuals may be able to point to virtue and noble acts in these terrible places, but the overwhelming achievement symbolized by Auschwitz is the outrageous death of millions. If it is necessary to attempt to formulate a positive symbol of which Auschwitz may be the concealed bearer let it be stated in Jewish terms. Auschwitz is the symbol of the absolute need of the Jews to have their own homeland. The history of antisemitism having reached its logical goal in Auschwitz with the annihilation of two-thirds of European and Russian Jews, there can be no future for Jews in Europe. Today the empty spaces in German cities, where once stood the ancient synagogues of European civilization, testify silently but graphically to the success of Hitler's Judenrein policy. A history of pogroms begun in Germany during the first Crusade ended in 1945 with the destruction of the European Jews. So Jews must live somewhere else in order to live at all! They must have a state of their own, a homeland which will afford them all the protection they are likely to get anywhere in the world. It seems to me that Auschwitz is also a symbol of this need for a homeland. Not that the need was created by the camps, far from it. But Auschwitz does underwrite the reality of that need because it is arguable that had the Jews of Europe lived elsewhere in their own land before the rise of the Third Reich the modern history of the Jews would have been greatly different from what it is now. The matter may be more complicated than this statement of it, but my only concern here is the suggestion that Auschwitz be seen as a symbol of the need for a Jewish homeland.

This cluster of symbols is but a selection of certain features of European culture thrown into relief by the death camps of the Third Reich. The argument needs much more space to be given the sophistication it requires to have an explanatory value, but even its brevity and lack of sophistication may serve to make some connections between European culture and the camps. If we are to remember the past and to avoid repeating it, it may be necessary to see how the camps arose out of cultural beliefs and practices which did not have their origins in this century. The camps did not spring miraculously from the wicked thoughts of the Nazi leaders without any historical precedents, but were the theory and practice of hell (to use a phrase of Eugen Kogon's) - a hell only too long and well gestated in the matrix of European culture. Of this Auschwitz is a primary symbol and it is as such a symbol that I am concerned with what happened between the years 1933-45. I have nothing else that I can contribute to the discussion but this insistence that Auschwitz was no freak occurrence, a cultural singularity, in European history. The sum total of all the things which were practised in all the camps, of which Auschwitz may be taken as shorthand for a terrible story, had its origins many centuries before this century. If Auschwitz has anything to teach us yet it must be this fact that the congeries of movements which came together in the triple camps of Auschwitz had been a long time developing. It is as a symbol of this phenomenon that Auschwitz becomes an abstract of a very long and complex history of religious, political, and cultural forces and movements. To one of the most important features of this history I now turn.

III

IN THE KINGDOM OF THE CROSS

When the power of the Roman empire eventually was channelled through the Christian churches the fate of the Jews was sealed. Before that period Jews and Christians had had to live together within the Roman empire on terms which varied from friendly to combative, but after the formation of Christendom the relationship between them was radically transformed. Fourth century Judaism may have been 'born from the womb of Christianity' (Neusner, 176), but in the kingdom of the cross it was a hated child! From this period onwards Jews would have to live under the sign of the cross and suffer the fluctuating fortunes of a pariah people among its enemies. The cruel irony of Jewish life among the Christians is one of the permanent stains on the reputation of Christian civilization and the Jewish experience of the cross as a symbol of life mocks that symbol. What had started as the transformation of a Roman instrument of torture and public execution (inherited and developed from the Assyrian mode of impaling enemies of the state on stakes) into a symbol of life quickly became a symbol of persecution, degradation, and death for the Jews. In this century the Nazi transformation of a Buddhist symbol of life into the swastika (Hakenkreuz) completed the crucifixion of the Jews at Auschwitz and all the other camps. Between these two crosses the long history of the Jews in Christian culture and civilization takes its course until in Auschwitz the ultimate crucifixion of the Jewish people wipes out the Jews of Europe. It is a profoundly depressing history and Auschwitz is its stark symbol!

This is a conference for Jews and Christians on the impact of the Shoah and genocide in general, so it is appropriate that we should focus on the experience of the Jews living in the kingdoms of the cross (Christian and Nazi). Generalizations of this kind are perhaps not very helpful for discussion, but it is important that at the very outset of this type of conference we should be very clear about certain fundamental issues. It is an indubitable fact that Christian antisemitism, with its roots in the New Testament, is the determinative factor in the Christian treatment of the Jews throughout the golden ages of Christianity. With the break up of Christendom during the Renaissance and the Reformation there may have developed more sentimental and political attitudes to the Jews (eg Cromwell's readmission of the Jews to England for chiliastic reasons), but these also would lead (via Martin Luther) inexorably to the Endlösung. There may have been individual Christians who were not antisemitic and even occasional groups of Christian churches for whom Jews were irrelevant because they did not share the same territory, but the overwhelming experience of Jews among Christians throughout Christendom has been one of living under Christian hegemony and therefore of being particularly vulnerable to outbursts of Christian devotion to mocking and murdering Jews. We may modify that picture with numerous counter-examples of good relations between Christians and Jews, but the framework of Jewish existence in the kingdom of the cross has been a constant of antisemitic bullying, persecution, and periodic pogroms.

On page one of the first edition of his magisterial work on the destruction of the European Jews Raul Hilberg rightly starts his story with a brief analysis of Church policy as carried out by the state against the Jews. In order to understand what happened at Auschwitz it is necessary to start in the fourth century when the churches gained the political power which permitted them to enforce their religious ideology on Jews. From that point on the Jews' card was marked and they were forcibly converted or barred from openly practising their religion or discriminated against by laws, practices and attitudes. Hilberg defines three major anti-Jewish policies: conversion, expulsion, and annihilation. What is most frightening about his analysis is the comparative table he makes of 'Canonical and Nazi Anti-Jewish Measures' (1961, 5-6) in which he shows the parallels between the attitudes and practices of the churches to the Jews and those of the Nazis. Right from the Synod of Elvira in 306 to the Council of Basel in 1434 (Sessio XIX), that is over a period of eleven hundred years, the official Christian treatment of Jews was one of increasing discrimination against them. The Nazis needed to invent little, only adapt and develop the Christian principles of antisemitism in conjunction with a killing ideology and the Endlösung was made possible. At the same time, the rulings of the synods and councils had created a culture of antisemitism so that by the time the German state had come under Hitler's power the social constraints against the Jews had been democratized completely. Auschwitz began in the Synod of Elvira in 306! Nothing happened or was done by the churches throughout all those centuries which could undo the cumulative force of the antisemitic rulings and the great massacre of Jews associated with the crusades and the Easter pogroms were just punctuation marks in the syntax of Christian attitudes to the Jews. Auschwitz is the end of that story.

In the context of this particular conference I would submit that Auschwitz is primarily a symbol of the age-old treatment of the Jews by the churches. I am not saying that Auschwitz was enacted by Christians or that the churches officially set up Auschwitz. By 1940 it did not matter what the churches said or thought in Nazi Germany. By then it was centuries too late to do anything about antisemitism because it had become ingrained as an attitude and a way of life. The Nazis were able to depend on the popular hatred of Jews, whether in Germany, Austria, Poland, or wherever, to facilitate their programmes against the Jews. They could rely on the local populace to smash up synagogues and beat up individual Jews because the people were already deeply antisemitic in outlook. Kristallnacht underlines the effectiveness of the long centuries of Christian hatred of and propaganda against the Jews. There may have been individual Christians who were not particularly antisemitic, but even the theologians tended to think in terms of antisemitic ideology. Those who today idolize (idealize?) Dietrich Bonhoeffer as the radical theologian for our times may be surprised to find in his writings evidence of this antisemitic theology, but it was so endemic among Christians that the best theologians were not necessarily free of it (for Bonhoeffer the Jews were under the curse for crucifying Jesus, a curse which was evidenced by their long history of suffering). This kind of slack thinking is inevitably the product of a climate of opinion which determines how people think and the words with which they think! As Rubenstein and Roth say in their discussion of this factor among theologians '...few of them saw that the critical line ought to be drawn over Nazi treatment of Jews. Not enough in their Christian heritage or individual thinking equipped them to make that judgment.' (207-8). For most Christians the Jews were non-persons long before Nazi ideology existed, so that when Hitler came to power it was not difficult for the belief that Jews were vermin to become the practice of annihilating such vermin. Christians had no obligations to Jews to treat them with respect or to extend to them the normal courtesies of being human. 'In a word, most German Christians at the time felt no sense of apostasy because Jews were not considered as existing within the Christian universe of moral obligation. On the contrary, as alien outsiders of a special kind, Jews were not really the "neighbours" Christians ought to love.' (Rubenstein & Roth, 207). The logic of all this means that the Christian churches helped over the centuries to construct the ideologies which gave rise to the concentration camps. Auschwitz has its roots in the New Testament and the councils of the churches, its fruits in the long history of antisemitic persecution of the Jews, and its final harvest in the redevelopment of the Polish town Oswiecim into the labour and death camps which we loosely call Auschwitz.

Behind the social ideology of Christian antisemitism lies a more profound disjuncture between Jews and Christians. At the heart of the deadly quarrel between two religions which share, to some extent, common roots is the survival of the Jews. According to some early dominant beliefs and domain assumptions of the Christian churches Jesus of Nazareth represented the ultimate in divine revelation and the worshipping communities which grew up around beliefs about him were the sole recipients of divine grace. The Jews who crucified Jesus were cursed by that action and cast off from divine favour. Failure to believe in Jesus as the ultimate revelation became a sign of eternal damnation and the churches strove to persuade people to convert to such beliefs. Jews refused to accept as true what the churches believed, failed to be converted and gave every sign of being content with their own religious beliefs and practices. If what Christians believed was true how could the evident dissonance of such continuing Jewish communities be explained? Conversion is always a good dissonance resolving response, but many Jews refused to be converted. They just went on being loyal to the Mosaic Torah, practising circumcision and following halakhic ways of life. They were therefore a mystery and an outrage to the truth of the Christian gospel. If they persisted in their way of life then clearly Jesus had not fulfilled and abrogated the Torah rendering Jewish belief obsolete. The Jewish covenant persisted and undermined Christian ideology because there could hardly be two covenants and two households of faith. The Jew became the anti-Christ because the existence of the Jews argued the mistakenness of the Christian belief that the gospel had replaced Jewish beliefs! So everything had to be done to wipe out the ideological scandal constituted by the Jews. They must be made to believe the gospel and if they would not believe then they must pay severe penalties for their lack of faith. Hence the council rulings against Jews and the restrictions put on Jews who persisted in remaining Jews. With the passage of time the two ways of life became utterly different, antagonistic and mutually exclusive and the Jew became the bad conscience of the churches. Christian claims to be the exclusive recipients of divine grace via sacraments and beliefs could not tolerate an alternative view which recognized the Jews as equally favoured by the divine. If the Jewish covenant still functioned then what price the new covenant of the Christians? How could there be two radically different covenants governing the affairs of humans and the deity? So at every point the persistence of Jewish communities posed serious ideological problems for Christian ideology. Those problems remain to this day!

That is a rather simplistic analysis of the ideological disjuncture between Jews and Christians, but a short paper is neither the place for sophistication nor for a comprehensive account of complex social causation theories. Put in very simple theological terms the central problem is this: if the new covenant of the Christian gospel has cancelled the old covenant of Moses, then what is it that prevents Jews from being converted to Jesus? If, on the other hand, the Mosaic covenant is still operative, as the continuing practice of the Jews demonstrate it is, then what can be the status of the new covenant? Is it necessary or just optional? Should it be regarded as a kind of Judaism for the Gentiles or is it universal truth? Given the direction many of the churches were heading in under the influence of gnostic beliefs and Greek philosophy, not to mention the power structures of the declining Roman empire, Jewish and Christian beliefs and practices were rapidly becoming comprehensively different from each other. Few of the proto-Jewish roots of the gospel survived in the development of the Christian ideology which helped to form Christendom, but the notion of Jesus as the messiah tended to distort even the few remaining connections with Jewish thought. If Jesus had been the (Jewish) messiah why had the Jews not accepted that fact? This is not the place to go into the complexities of the messianisms of Judaisms (as Jacob Neusner has taught us to think in terms of!), except to say that we should not imagine that what the New Testament says about Jesus as the messiah bears much resemblance to messianic thought of that period! However, the rejection of Jesus as the messiah by the Jews became a central feature of the Christian belief that the Jews were peculiarly perverted as a people and wilfully intent on denying the obvious truth of the gospel. Thus they became fair game for persecution because they had known the truth and had deliberately rejected that truth in spite of being fully aware of the significance of what they were doing. The gospels are written from that standpoint, especially the gospel of John which singles out the Jews for particular obloquy. Perhaps sophisticated neutestamentlers may be able to modify the viciousness of New Testament antisemitism by various hermeneutical devices and beautifully balanced accounts of precisely just what is going on in the period when the gospels were written. But to those who came after the generations which wrote the New Testament sophisticated exegesis was neither here nor there. They read these stories and took them at face value. They therefore branded all Jews in subsequent ages as 'Christ-killers' and treated them accordingly. Auschwitz is striking testimony to the effectiveness of the gospel writers in stirring up hatred of the Jews. Unfortunately, the two millennia which separate Auschwitz from the gospels are bridged by a profound, even a pathological, hatred of the Jews and in the twentieth century the only true symbol of crucifixion remains, not the figure of Jesus on a Roman gibbet, but the Jew hanging on the barbed wire of a concentration camp!

I have eschewed sophistication of analysis because I think it is fundamentally important that we face reality here and recognize that there is an integral connection between the long history of the Christian treatment of the Jews and what happened at Auschwitz. That connection is not simply with the social practices of Christians against Jews down the centuries. It goes much deeper than that. It is at the very heart of Christian belief itself. In some sense the rise of the early churches was parasitic on Jewish beliefs and practices which shaped the forms Christian worship and behaviour took. Sharing the struggle for position and power in the Roman empire Jews and Christians lived together for centuries without any decisive deteriorations in the relations between them, though there were many fluctuations in the fortunes of the different communities (cf. Gager). Once the shift in power within the empire began to favour the Christians and their ideology the writing on the wall appeared for the Jews. It was not a case that bad Christians persecuted the Jews while good Christians stood idly or helplessly by. It was much more a matter of the ideology developed by various churches, once empowered by state control in the period after Constantine, became the instrument of the destruction of the Jews. The persecution and proscribing of the Jews was the outworking of that ideology and the Christian faith itself the beneficiary of the spoliation of the Jews!

I have emphasized this unpleasant aspect of Christian practice because it is far too late in the day for us to continue to refuse to recognize the unacceptable face of Christianity in its dealings with other people throughout its history. We cannot go on making excuses for Christian antisemitism as if it were just a case of bad table manners! It was always a serious matter and always completely unacceptable as a way of living in the world, but today we know that such behaviour, intolerable in its own time, once tolerated can over the centuries become the prologue to genocide. Perhaps it was never the declared intention of the churches to annihilate the Jews. Perhaps they only wanted to convert them! But what happens when a people refuse to be converted? What then? What do you do when the Christian mission to the Jews does not result in the mass conversion of the Jews? Well, you confiscate their property, you make them wear distinctive badges of identity, you harass and punish them, you forcibly convert them and murder them if they convert back to their former religion, you burn their sacred books, you disbar them from public office, you herd them into ghettoes, and periodically you allow the good Christians of the parish to run riot during Easter by massacring the Jews. In short, you rehearse for Auschwitz! You may not know that that is what you are doing. It may not be your intention to go as far as Auschwitz. But pray tell me this: what in all the long history of the Christian treatment of the Jews could be seriously described as a refusal of Auschwitz? Hindsight may now inform us, without mercy, of where all this antisemitism will end - but, in the name of whatever god you worship and believe you serve, when did antisemitism not end in Auschwitz? Antisemitism is neither wrong nor vicious because of what happened at Auschwitz, that was just the practice perfected by modern technology in the service of ideology. When the first Christian council began the long warfare against the Jews and initiated the first acts of cruelty against the Jews, then it was wrong and vicious. All Auschwitz did was to take up those Christian principles and put them into practice in a more thorough-going comprehensive way. Of course it did more than that because it also murdered many non-Jews, but there is only a quantitative and not a qualitative difference between the murder of Jews by Christians and their murder by the Nazis in Auschwitz.

What I am trying to articulate here is the notion that behind any Christian mission <u>to</u> the Jews lies the road to Auschwitz. The refusal of Jews to be converted leaves Christians <u>with</u> the difficult task of convincing themselves that the mission should go on in spite of the obduracy of their mission-fodder. In the age of Christendom that refusal to be converted gave rise to profoundly antisemitic legislation, persecution and the long sorry road to Auschwitz. The modern Christian missioner cannot now take that road ever again, yet the mission goes on in many Christian circles! I am not talking about dialogue between Jews and Christians, should there be any Jews after Auschwitz who feel that such a platonic activity has any point. Jews and Christians talking to one another are not in the business of mission; they are not trying to sell each other something. But for many Christians that dialogue can be mistaken for mission or can be a way into mission. Even after Auschwitz there are still Christians head-hunting Jews! In other words, Auschwitz has become a symbol of the fact that nothing has been learned by some Christians. How widespread this belief among Christians that Jews must be converted to Christianity is I do not know. I do know that it is more popular than it ought to be. Examples could be multiplied from many sources, but for the sake of brevity I shall just refer to one recent publication: David W. Torrance's pamphlet of 1986 <u>The Mission of Christians and Jews</u> (Handsel Press, Edinburgh). Torrance is a parish minister of <u>the Church of Scotland</u> and ought to know better because he works with representatives of the Jewish community in Scotland. But by page eight of an eleven page document the mission <u>of</u> has become mission <u>to</u> the Jews and he is openly talking about evangelizing the Jews as well as the Gentiles. For him the Jews must come to see Jesus as their Messiah and be saved. Christians who do not seek to influence Jews for or against Christ are behaving 'contrary to the whole spirit and teaching of the New Testament'! Here is a writer who clearly knows the history of antisemitism through the ages and is explicitly aware of the Holocaust, but is equally able to bypass all that history in order to read the New Testament, with reference to a sentimental image of the Jew which he has, as if nothing had happened to the Jews at the hands of the Christian churches between the time of Jesus and Auschwitz. In other words, not even Auschwitz can penetrate the sensibilities of some Christians where the Jews are concerned. This may not be Christian antisemitism, but I suspect that it is something equally as bad. Let then Auschwitz also stand as a symbol for this example of bad faith, with its sentimental notions of what Jews are and its sunday school naiveté of belief untouched by historical reality at any point.

How the Christian churches are to come to terms with their long history of persecuting the Jews I do not know. What I do know is this: until there is a general recognition of just what has been done to the Jews in the name of Christ for nearly two millennia now and an equally general repentance of the whole sordid history of trying to convert the Jew there can be little hope that Christians will ever understand Jews. Until the connections between that history and Auschwitz are seen and understood and the sorry business of molesting the Jews by way of mission desisted from there can be no mature adult relations between the two religions. Legend has it that when in 1440 at the trial of Gilles de Rais, for appalling crimes against children, before the details of each atrocity were read out the prosecutor walked across to the crucifix hanging from the wall and covered it up. It was felt that some things were too awful for that figure to hear. What contemporary gesture could the Christian churches make as a response appropriate to the horror felt as the details of what went on in Auschwitz are read out? I suspect that the horrors of Auschwitz beggar the imagination and short circuit the brain so as to leave us without appropriate ritual or gesture that would be commensurate with the events of that evil place. Certainly no Christian gesture could redeem the antisemitic past of the churches or pacify the pain of Auschwitz, but might there be any way in which the churches could now say 'let us recollect the memory of all these dead by silence and gesture, remembering that our sins also helped to make this place'? Perhaps only the dead of Auschwitz could answer this question and for them it is too late to hold conversation with the living. Auschwitz stands as the symbol of their everlasting silence!

IV

AUSCHWITZ ABUSED

It is hardly possible to write as an outsider about Auschwitz without running the risk of abusing the subject. By abuse here I mean using for purposes other than remembering and describing it. It is so easy to incorporate the concentration camps into points scoring in arguments. A good example of that technique appeared in The Times for 9 May 1987 when Sir Immanual Jakobovits, the Chief Rabbi of Orthodox synagogues and congregations in Great Britain, wrote in his article 'Chernobyl, a smitten god' the following paragraphs:

> Jewish gods, too, have taken terrible punishment. Some have exploded quite a while ago. The nineteenth century German founders of Reform Judaism believed with absolute faith that the process of Emancipation leading to full equality for Jews would be completed if only they would give up being different - praying in the same language as other Germans did, eating the same food, observing the Day of Rest as Christians observed their Sunday, and altogether giving up everything that made Jews and Judaism distinctive.
>
> This idol of individual assimilation which was trying to bring salvation exploded in the very country in which it was invented, to be eventually melted down and incinerated in the crematoria of Auschwitz.

This is just Jewish Orthodoxy berating Reform Judaism and using Auschwitz to score a very cheap and despicable point in a poor argument. What was melted down and incinerated in the crematoria of Auschwitz was not simply assimilationist Jews or Reform Jews, but Jews of every kind and distinction! Good and bad Jews, observers of the commandments and atheistical Jews, Hasidic Jews and Jewish converts to Christianity - all of these were consumed by Auschwitz which made no distinctions among Jews as to their orthodoxy or otherwise. If Auschwitz had destroyed only the assimilationists there might be point to the Chief Rabbi's cheap gibe, but it does not even have the virtue of being truthful. It is very much an abuse of Auschwitz in order to impale opponents in an argument. That is what I mean by abusing Auschwitz and it is very easy to fall into the practice.

I am therefore conscious of the dilemma of speaking of Auschwitz at all without abusing it. In order to understand it and to articulate that understanding of it it is necessary to speak of it. Yet it is also possible to turn Auschwitz into a commodity and trade with it in arguments and debates. Jewish sceptics say 'there's no business like shoah business' when they want to make the point that certain Jewish political schemes use the terrible events symbolized by Auschwitz to advance their own political causes. It is always tempting to turn such tragedies into moral stock which will serve polemical purposes no matter how cautiously one approaches the subject of the camps. It is natural to turn moral outrage into arguments, even if the content of such arguments is the annihilation of millions of people. The dead easily serve the living. Perhaps we should be morally more sensitive, but exactitude of response to Auschwitz is such a difficult thing to judge that silence might be a more appropriate response - if only silence did not collude with forgetfulness.

I speak here as a complete outsider, yet I would make a few observations about the abuse of Auschwitz which I think are germane to any discussion about the camps. At the moment the acceptable word to describe what happened to the Jews in the camps is Shoah 'destruction'. It is a fair description of what happened there and avoids the connotations inherent in other words such as 'Holocaust' or Hurban. However, it does tend to make the camps a purely Jewish matter. This is a fair description of the camps from a Jewish perspective. But many other groups of people were murdered in these camps and talk of Shoah can marginalize or even render them invisible! It may not be the intention of those who use the word Shoah to ignore the others who were murdered alongside the Jews. It may just be the case that the numbers of Jews killed were so great that a Hebrew word best describes the camps. If it is possible to ask for sensitivity towards the others who also were destroyed there without denying the centrality of the annihilation of the Jews I think abuse of Auschwitz may be avoided. The first concentration camp opened was Dachau in March 1933 and it was designed for enemies of the Reich, especially German dissidents. At this stage the Jews were not the intended inhabitants of the camps. When Auschwitz was first mooted it was designed for Polish and Russian prisoners of war and only with its development did it become a death camp for the Jews. The Nazi ideology also had as its targeted victims gypsies and homosexuals. No doubt there was a deeply pathological hatred of Jews which, as the war progressed and went against Germany, transcended all other priorities and made the destruction of the Jews an absolute obsession of the Nazis. But it would be an abuse of Auschwitz if we did not recognize and remember that millions of non-Jews were done to death by the camps in the name of the Nazi ideology. The number of pink triangles (the homosexual indicator) was nothing like as great as the number of yellow stars (the Jewish indicator), but the intensity of persecution and the finality of death was shared by both groups. I have no wish to offend sensibilities with this point, but no account of the camps will be a true one if we do not recognize that many different groups of people were murdered there. To make the camps solely a Jewish matter is to abuse Auschwitz.

The point being made here develops the argument of section III in terms of general prejudices in society. Within the Christian economy of Christendom homosexuals suffered greatly for reasons too complex to examine here. The German Reich under Hitler continued this persecution by more systematic means and also set about the annihilation of many different minority groups. I do not wish to give the impression that Jews were the only people hated by the Christian churches or that the Hitler regime only tried to destroy the Jews. The fate of the homosexuals in Christian history and under Hitler remains as an indictment of our past and also as a terrible warning about our immediate future!

Part of the uneasiness I feel about the Jewish description of the concentration camps as the Shoah is the chauvinism of this partial naming of the terror. Of course from a Jewish viewpoint it was the ultimate shoah of the Jewish people in Europe and it is only reasonable that Jews should describe it as such. But it was so much more than that! The millions of non-Jews who were murdered in the camps also must be remembered. Perhaps not necessarily by Jews should they be remembered. But can we really talk about the camps seriously and ignore those others who also were degraded, tortured, and done to death? Jews may speak for Jews but who shall speak for the others? Who now speaks in remembrance of all the murdered gypsies and the slaughtered homosexuals? Can they really be consigned to silence because they did not belong to identifiable peoples as did the Jews? Surely not! If Auschwitz is made a purely Jewish affair then it is not only betrayed but abused. Such things can hardly be said without giving unintended offence or sounding insensitive, but insensitivity is as far from my mind as possible. I just want to articulate what I see as a danger of chauvinistic treatments of Auschwitz. From a Jewish perspective it is perfectly justifiable to have created in Yad Vashem a tree-lined avenue known as 'the forest of the Righteous Gentiles' where trees are planted to commemorate the deeds of non-Jews on behalf of Jews during the killing times. I do however worry about such a definition of righteousness as 'doing good to Jews'. I feel that this is a dimunition of Micah's counsel from 'to do justice and to love ḥesed' to a modified 'to do justice to Jews...'! Understandable in the circumstances perhaps, but does it not tend to suggest a certain proprietary view of justice and an annexation of the camps? Goodness knows, the Jews of Europe encountered very little human kindness from non-Jews in their odyssey to the camps and it is very appropriate that where they did encounter it it should be celebrated now in Eretz Yisrael. The existence of the state of Israel gives the destruction of the Jews in the camps a perspective and a setting which no other group of similarly destroyed people are likely to match. This then tends in the popular imagination to make Auschwitz seem to be purely a Jewish matter and 'the Righteous Gentiles' concept confirms this perception. It is not a particularly important point, but it is symptomatic of a tendency to abuse Auschwitz (even if unintentionally!).

Death on the scale which the camps produced makes Auschwitz a very difficult subject for rational discussion. The mind is ill-equipped to deal with such terror and destruction. Also it always seems to verge on the edge of impiety and sacrilege to analyze critically the events of 1933-45 from the perspective of the many victims of the slaughter. Hannah Arendt's controversial journalism on the Eichmann trial in Jerusalem in 1961 caused such anger and outrage when it was first published in 1963. Much of that outrage was no doubt justified because Arendt could be profoundly insensitive in her judgments and had a completely intellectualized approach to such sensitive matters as the systematic murder of so many millions. But she did raise important issues in her treatment of the Eichmann case which cannot be ignored just because of her tendency to take a patrician view of things. Leaving her strange notions of 'the banality of evil' aside, her indictment of the Jewish leaders of the various Jewish communities for complicity in facilitating the Nazi destruction of the Jews gave most offence. The role the Jewish Councils (Judenräte) played in the organization and pacification of the ghettoes and as go-betweens for conveying the instructions of the Nazis to their people is now too well known to require repeating here. The recent attempt to produce Jim Allen's play Perdition at the Royal Court Theatre Upstairs in London in 1987 caused such a furore that the production had to be cancelled before it could be staged. It is difficult to judge whether Allen's play was just one more example of antisemitism posing as anti-Zionism (a standard intellectual sleight of hand in British political debate whereby anti-Israeli sentiments are promulgated) or was a more substantive discussion of a very real problem in the background of Auschwitz. Anybody who has read Chaim Kaplan's diary of the Warsaw Ghetto will know just how critical of their leaders some Jews were. Kaplan certainly writes more harshly of them than either Arendt or Allen does. Indeed, he is so scathing of various named individuals for their collaboration with the Nazis that I have great difficulty understanding why Allen's play should have been forced off the stage. Most plays that deal with historical subjects are hopelessly inaccurate - Shakespeare being the most notorious example - as to historical detail, but the issues they raise are what matter and the writings of Kaplan, Arendt, and Allen do raise a minor issue of some importance in any discussion of Auschwitz. I suspect that here we may well have what I can only call an abuse of Auschwitz. Auschwitz is abused, I think, when the awfulness of what was perpetrated there is also allowed to blur or conceal other features of the 1933-45 period.

This is a very difficult and sensitive area for discussion and I only raise it under the heading 'Auschwitz Abused' because I think it also should be on the agenda for remembrance. We do the dead of Auschwitz no service by pretending things elsewhere were otherwise. It is not for those who were not there to stand in judgment or condemnation of those who in that period did what they thought was best or collaborated with the enemy for reasons best known to themselves. They are all dead now and many suffered the same fate as those they imagined they were protecting from such a fate. The luxury of moral judgment is always available to those who are not party to the struggle and it should be avoided here in the most absolute way. Yet why should anybody be surprised or outraged at the suggestion that some of the leaders of the Jewish communities were less than perfect in the face of appalling pressures and threats? Since the days of the Hebrew prophets the leadership of the community has been the target of accusation and abuse. Why should things be different even in the shadow of Auschwitz? It will do us no harm to remember that the Jews of Europe were no better and no worse than most people - the Nazi ideologues excepted - in most places and at most times. They were murdered because they were Jews, not because they were good or bad human beings! To read the diaries of a Kaplan or a Czerniakow is to be reminded of the ordinariness of the Jews in the Ghetto and of the foibles and fallibilities of their leaders. Auschwitz and other places removed these ordinary people from the face of the earth forever. Perhaps respect for the dead demands that we be silent about their faults and the weaknesses of the *Judenräte*. On the other hand, perhaps glossing over such matters is to abuse Auschwitz in some hard to define way. Fault-finding is the least of our prerogatives when discussing what Auschwitz stands for, but idealizing its victims may also be a fault in us!

IN CONCLUSION

At the end of his lecture published as 'The Concept of God after Auschwitz: A Jewish Voice' Hans Jonas, *the* scholar of gnosticism and exiled victim of the Nazis, says 'All this, let it be said at *the* end, is but stammering. Even the words of the great seers and adorers - the prophets and the psalmists - which stand beyond comparison, were stammers before the eternal mystery.' (p.13). Having attempted to speak of Auschwitz in relation to God in terms of Kant, Plato, and finally the Lurianic Kabbalah with its notions of *En-Sof* and *tzimtzum* he concludes with that confession of just stammering. Beside his lecture *this piece of mine* is but dust and ashes. After Auschwitz mind, heart, and mouth are stopped by the enormity of what it stands for. The human imagination cannot encompass what went on there and human syntax can only describe the outer edges of its facticity. Torn between the silence, awestruck in its intensity, which is appropriate to the horror of the place and the absolute need to speak of the place, for here silence would be collusion, mind and heart are paralyzed. Auschwitz symbolizes the beyond of human experience, understanding, and ratiocination, yet in itself it is what has actually happened in our time. It is no phantom of surrealistic imagination but a set of historical facts now embedded in our consciousness and demanding of us our attention - 'attention must be paid!' Attending to Auschwitz is, however, a most painful experience. The pain of recollection is heart-searing and inexpressibly beyond words. But in a conference such as this we must use words when we speak to each other! So the subject eludes our careful definitions and our over-cautious qualifications of everything we say. Human beings ought never to have to contemplate something as awful as Auschwitz because they do not have the means, linguistic or emotional, of dealing with it. Countermanding that pious wish is the dreadful fact that Auschwitz happened and therefore is now a part of our agenda of thought. It has to be contemplated. It will be spoken of. How will always remain the dilemma. How can the unspeakable be spoken and how can the unthinkable be thought? More than forty years after the dismantling of the camps the dilemma remains, even though many words and more thoughts have been expended in order to speak responsibly of Auschwitz. Genocide remains a political problem in today's world and ideology still constructs prison camps and mass slaughter. Auschwitz may have brought an end to that kind of ideology in Europe, it has not meant an end to it elsewhere. Auschwitz remains a symbol of our century.

In this paper I have tried to say a few things about what Auschwitz as a symbol means. I am deeply conscious of the fact that nothing said here touches the real Auschwitz, but my concern is more with talk about Auschwitz than with the place itself and its many deaths. I am more aware of the problem of abusing Auschwitz with certain kinds of talk about it because talk can have a cheapening effect. Just as the early Christian preaching of the cross (the so-called kerygma) cheapened the death of its Jewish victim and made him part of somebody else's ideology - an ideology which contributed so much in the long run to the creation of Auschwitz - so Auschwitz may easily be turned into somebody else's kerygmatic sermon and made to function as a hostage to ideology. Auschwitz as unusable horror and absolute terror remains after all our talk of it is over and refuses our ideological attempts to control it. The dead of Auschwitz have the last word and it is absolute silence.

REFERENCES

Allen, J., Perdition, Ithaca Press, 1987.

Arendt, H., Eichmann in Jerusalem: A Report on the Banality of Evil, Penguin, rev.ed. 1977.

Benjamin, W., Gesammelte Schriften I.2 (eds R. Tiedemann & H. Schweppenhäuser), Suhrkamp Verlag, 1974.

Borowski, T., This Way for the Gas, Ladies and Gentlemen, Penguin, 1976.

Brodsky, J., Less Than One: Selected Essays, Penguin, 1987.

Celan, P., Selected Poems, Penguin, 1972.

Cohen, A., The Tremendum: A Theological Interpretation of the Holocaust, Crossroads, 1981.

Dawidowicz, L., The War against the Jews 1933-45, Pelican, 1977.

Gager, J.C., The Origins of Anti-Semitism: Attitudes in Pagan and Christian Antiquity, OUP,1983.

Hilberg,R., The Destruction of the European Jews, Quadrangle Books, 1961.

Jonas, H., Journal of Religion 67/1, 1987, 1-13.

Kaplan, C.A., Scroll of Agony: The Warsaw Diary of Chaim A. Kaplan (ed A.I. Katsh), Hamish Hamilton, 1966.

Lifton, R.J., The Nazi Doctors: Medical Killing and the Psychology of Genocide, Macmillan, 1987

Neusner, J., Vanquished Nation, Broken Spirit: The Virtues of the Heart in Formative Judaism, CUP, 1987.

Rubenstein, R.L. & Roth, J.K., Approaches to Auschwitz: The Legacy of the Holocaust, SCM Press, 1987.

Surin, K., Theology and the Problem of Evil, Basil Blackwell, 1987.

THE GOD OF HISTORY: BIBLICAL REALISM AND THE LECTIONARY

Fredrick C. Holmgren

North Park Theological Seminary
3225 West Foster Avenue
Chicago, IL 60625-4987, U. S. A.

ABSTRACT

The Hebrew Bible and the New Testament witness to God's activity in history. Frequently, however, at preaching and teaching levels within the Christian tradition, God's involvement in history is viewed as God in control of the events of history; in them he is thought to be continually working out his purpose for humankind. It is an unprobed, triumphal interpretation of life; God's purpose is seen to be at work in every event of life -- even in the Shoah. This view of history glorifies God but it does so at the expense of confronting times of "interruption" when the world returns to Tohuwavohu. Further, it urges a passive response to life in a world which demands that people assume their role as responsible partners of God. The contemporary Common Lectionary, together with other earlier lectionaries, underscores heavily this understanding of history by the texts that it includes and excludes. The following article argues that the Lectionary is out-of-balance and suggests the inclusion of other texts that would reflect more accurately the realistic thinking of the Hebrew Bible -- texts that would help us approach the Shoah.

THE GOD WHO ACTS IN HISTORY

The Biblical Theology Movement of the 1950s (primarily a Christian movement) made popular the phrase "the God who acts" in history. [1] This expression itself, however, did not introduce something brand new to Jewish and Christian thought because the roots of this emphasis are deeply embedded in the soil of Scripture. Further, for both the Jewish and Christian communities today, the question of God's presence in history is a continuing topic of discussion. [2]

"COMMON TENDENCY" IN CHURCH: HANDS-ON CONTROL

Within academic circles, the discussion is carried on at a technical theological-philosophical level, but, as Charles Wood observes: "Theological understanding of the notion of an act of God has been notoriously complicated by a common tendency to think of acts of God as extraordinary events." [3] This "common tendency," which finds strong representation within lay and ministerial circles (the focus of my paper), assumes also, I think, a divine "hands-on" control of the universe; it represents a confidence that God is assertively and continuously working out his purpose within history. This view is succinctly summarized by William Loper: [4]

> One of the unique things about Christianity is the belief that God controls history. . . .the central belief of Christianity is that God entered the stream of human history to change its course permanently. This is why the calendar centers on the birth of Jesus, dividing history into B.C. and A.D. We believe that God became man and entered human life and the world has never been the same since.

Or further:

> It is central to our Christian convictions that God is now, always has been, and always will be the Lord of history. He created the universe and the world in which we live, he directs its course, and he controls its ultimate destiny.

Dr. Loper is correct, still today, when he observes that "most Christians will nod their heads in agreement" with this statement of faith. We may not, it is admitted, understand or perceive always this divine activity in history because to human eyes God's presence may be hidden. Nevertheless, on the basis of many biblical texts, the proclamation of God's assertive presence in historical events stands at the center of Christian witness.

THE NEW TESTAMENT: GOD'S PURPOSE FOR HUMANKIND

New Testament texts are generally supportive of this view of God and his relationship to the world. These texts are shaped by the figure of Jesus through whom God, according to Christian theology, worked out his greatest mighty act. Jesus is the dramatic affirmation that God is actively working out his will -- his plan -- in history:

> But when the time had fully come, God sent forth his Son . . . . (Gal 4:4)

> For he has made known to us in all wisdom and insight the mystery of his will, according to his purpose which he set forth in Christ as a plan for the fulness of time, to unite all things in him, things in heaven and things on earth. (Eph 1:9-10)

> This was according to the eternal purpose which he has realized in Christ Jesus our Lord . . . (Eph 3:11)

JESUS: TRUSTING AND OBEDIENT

Jesus is represented as one who waits trustingly upon God to act. He does not seek his own will, rather as he said: "My food is to do the will of him who sent me, and to accomplish his work" (John 4:34). He is the willing victim -- the willing sacrifice on the cross. All four gospels give considerable space to the description of his suffering and death: without complaint, without violence, without attempt to escape God's purpose for him, he goes to his death. People meant it for evil but God meant it for good (cf. Gen 50:20).

JESUS' TRUST OF GOD'S PLAN: MODEL FOR CHRISTIANS

New Testament preaching validates the wisdom of Jesus' trust; although he died on the cross this death was but a necessary step that led to victory which is symbolized by the resurrection (see e.g., Phil 2:5-11). This ultimate victory which Jesus won has made a monumental impress not only on the New Testament literature but on later Christian preaching as well. Jesus, the obedient, trusting son whose trust led him to and through the cross to resurrection, becomes the model for Christians as they face the evil of this world. God's act in Jesus guarantees the rightness of trusting God, of not resisting, of not striking back, of praying for enemies, of giving what the enemy demands, of being willing to die (see Matt 5:11, 38-44, 24:9-14; 1 Cor 4:10-13; 2 Cor 4:10-12). Many passages in the New Testament, including those listed above, call people who follow after Christ to be sacrifices offered to God. While calling for an active faith in God, they urge a passive response to history.

THE LECTIONARY AND THE GOD OF HISTORY

This emphasis on God's assertive control of history is heavily underscored by the texts selected for inclusion in the contemporary Common Lectionary which is widely used by churches in the United States. In fact this Lectionary outdoes the Bible itself in emphasizing God's controlling hand on history; it excludes several New Testament passages -- and numerous Old Testament texts -- which call attention to the assertive defense of oneself, the use of common sense, quick thinking, or shrewdness in responding to threatening situations. [5] The following New Testament passages, for example, are not included in the Lectionary:

Matt 10:16 Jesus gives advice to the Twelve saying that they should "be wise as serpents and innocent as doves." This admonition occurs in the context of opposition to the mission of the disciples and seems to call forth a "practical wisdom" which would guide them in responding to those who oppose them. [6]

Matt 2:16 The text declares: "Then Herod, when he saw that he had been _tricked_ by the wise men, was in a furious rage . . . ." The Lectionary does include the observation that the wise men "warned in a dream not to return to Herod, . . . departed to their own country by another way." (Matt 2:12) This latter passage, however, emphasizes God's care for the Magi and does not stress the cleverness of the wise men as does Matt 2:16.

Joh 8:59 When his opponents begin throwing stones at him, Jesus "hid himself, and went out of the temple."

Joh 10:39 The enemies of Jesus "tried to arrest him but he escaped from their hands."

Joh 12:36 In response to hostile questioning, Jesus "departed and hid himself from them."

LECTIONARY: NO HINT OF JESUS ACTING TO PROTECT SELF

Are the above three passages that speak of Jesus hiding himself an embarassment to those deciding on the Lectionary texts? These texts appear to depict Jesus as a human being who takes a common-sense action to save himself in a time of danger. Observe by the way that, according to Matt 10:23 (also not in the Lectionary), _Jesus himself_ instructed his disciples to flee from any town in which they were ill-treated. Was it feared that these passages would present a picture of a Jesus who was weak of faith -- a Jesus who was not fully trusting in God? It seems clear that this kind of text had no appeal to the creators of the Lectionary. This is borne out not only because the above passages are excluded but because other passages _are included_ in which the themes of escape and hiding occur (e.g., Luke 13:31 and Luke 4:30).

LECTIONARY: JESUS DOES NOT HIDE FROM HIS ENEMIES

In the above texts from Luke, Jesus is presented as a strong and trusting servant of God. In Luke 13:31 it is recorded that some pharisees warned Jesus: "Get away from here, for Herod wants to kill you." Jesus refuses to heed the warning; instead he is defiant and tells the pharisees to inform Herod that he intends to continue what he is doing. At another time, Jesus is surrounded by a menacing crowd. Jesus escapes them -- not by hiding -- but by "passing through the midst of them" (Luke 4:30). One has the image of the commanding figure of Jesus striding through the enemy crowd; trusting in God's plan for his life, he is not intimidated by them. This same kind of emphasis may be seen in another passage (included in the Lectionary) that has the theme of escape (Matt 26:51-53); it occurs in the context of the betrayal of Judas and the seizure of Jesus:

> Then they came up and laid hands on Jesus and seized him. And behold, one of those who were with Jesus stretched out his hand and drew his sword, and struck the slave of the high priest, and cut off his ear. Then Jesus said to him "Put your sword back into its place; for all who take the sword will perish by the sword. Do you think that I cannot appeal to my Father, and he will at once send me more than twelve legions of angels?"

JESUS: GOD VALIDATES JESUS' TRUST IN HIM

The message of this dramatic passage is the basic witness of the New Testament concerning Jesus: Jesus is not a pitiable victim who is sent to his death, rather he is one who sees that the way of suffering and death is God's way of achieving victory in this world. He could have escaped if he wanted to but he would not do so because he trusted that even in betrayal and death God was working out his will in him. Jesus is the willing and triumphant sacrifice. As we observed above, this obedient, self-sacrificing Jesus, who does not lift a hand to protect himself, who remains silent before his accusers (because he is confident that God will care for him), stands as the model response of the Christian to the world.

The Lectionary heavily underscores this emphasis by failing to include in the recommended texts for preaching, passages (such as those listed above) that speak of resourceful action by Jesus and others that led to survival. Notice, by the way, that the narrative about Paul's escape from his enemies in Damascus by means of secretive action in the night and help from friends (see Acts 9:25; cf. 2 Cor 11:33) is not in the Lectionary. Another passage, however, which tells of the escape of the apostles from prison due to intervention by "an angel of the Lord" (v. 19) *is* included, namely Acts 5:17-26. The Lectionary sends a clear message: God is in charge; he protects his own and when it accords with his purpose he confounds his enemies.

THE LECTIONARY AND THE HEBREW BIBLE

The New Testament emphasis on God's activity in history is a major theme in the Hebrew Bible also. However, in the larger literature of the Old Testament there is another theme which gives needed balance, that is, the need of people to be wise, resourceful, and assertive regarding the saving of oneself and others. Unfortunately, the Lectionary does not include many of these latter passages among those texts recommended for preaching. In the Old Testament, as in the New, the Lectionary celebrates -- to excess -- the God who "controls" and intervenes in the history of Israel. Numerous passages from the Pentateuch, the Psalms, and the Prophets emphasize strongly the mighty acts which God has done and will do for Israel.

THE LECTIONARY: THE NEED FOR BALANCE

The purpose of this paper is not to deny that God is active in history; it seeks rather to call attention to an imbalance in emphasis within the Lectionary. This imbalance has serious implications for the Church's response to the world in which Christians live. As it now stands, the Lectionary texts appear to urge a passive, waiting, and trusting attitude on the part of Christians. This passive stance toward life not only expresses one's willingness to endure personal suffering and oppression, it suppresses the desire to take action for others. Influenced by the view that God is controlling the events of history (surely all that comes our way must represent *in some way* God's purpose!), we allow ourselves and others to be run over by history (i.e., by this God-of-History who has been created by popular theologians and preachers).

Evidence of this imbalance in the Lectionary may be seen, for example, by observing that texts which call attention to human resourcefulness, assertiveness, and survival-shrewdness (i.e., lying, scheming, secretiveness, and seduction) are missing from the lectionary texts. Unlike the Lectionary, the Bible itself is not embarrassed by these texts; they reflect the realism of Israelite faith -- its ability to appreciate assertive human action that confronts chaotic events relating to the community. The following texts (and texts of a similar kind elsewhere) are left out of lectionary selections:

Exod 1:15-21 The mid-wives lie to protect the lives of male babies. God rewards them for this act.

Exod 2:11-22 Moses intercedes to rescue a Hebrew slave and protects the daughters of Jethro from bullying shepherds.

Exod 3:18 God instructs Moses to lie (to be evasive? not to tell the whole truth? be ambiguous?) to Pharaoh so that the Hebrews may escape from Egypt (cf. Exod 5:1,3).

Josh 2:1-21 The spies from Joshua's army are saved by the lie of Rahab (vv. 4-6). See also James 2:25 (not in the Lectionary) where it is said that Rahab was justified by works in that "she received the messengers and sent them out another way."

Judg 4:17-21 Jael pretends to offer safety to the fleeing Sisera but, when opportunity presented itself, she killed him. Her deed is celebrated in the Song of Deborah (Judg 5:24-27).

Jer 38:24-28 Jeremiah lies to the princes of Judah in order to protect King Zedekiah and himself.

1 Sam 19:11-17 Michal deceives the servants of Saul in order to save David.

1 Sam 20:1-7 David asks Jonathan to lie to his father and to note his response so that David may discover Saul's intention toward him.

1 Kgs 1:1-40 Nathan and Bathsheba scheme to have David appoint Solomon as his sucessor.

Ruth 3:1-18 Ruth agrees to follow Naomi's suggestion which gives promise of security for them (i.e., that she visit Boaz in the field after a night of drinking and seductively lure him toward marriage).

Neh 2:11-16 Nehemiah makes a secret inspection of the wall about Jerusalem to avoid precipitous confrontation with his opponents.

Esth 4--7 Mordecai and Esther scheme to overthrow Haman's plan to kill the Jews.

THE LECTIONARY: UNEASY WITH A SURVIVAL ETHIC

The above passages which record the use of deceptive words and acts as well as violence in order to preserve life and/or to guarantee future, are often viewed as negative aspects which may undercut the central ethic of the Bible. In early and pre-modern Christian exegesis, for example, there was considerable uneasiness concerning the crafty response of the mid-wives to Pharoah (Exod 1:15-21). Among those condemning the lying of the midwives, and all lying, were Augustine, Gregory, and John Calvin. [7]

Today, a good number of scholars would agree with Martin Luther, who defended the lie of the mid-wives because it was told in the midst of persecution. [8] But even among contemporary authors there are those who hold that the midwives may have been telling the truth (!) and, if not, then to observe: "Even if they lied, it is not for their deceit that they are commended, but for their refusal to take infant lives, God's gift." [9] One does not wish to disagree with this statement, but, why is this kind of comment necessary? The comment arises because within the Christian tradition there is a mistaken identification of lying with "false witness" against the neighbor (cf. e.g., Exod 20:16) and therefore it is believed that lying is always wrong, that one should never tell a lie. It is assumed to be a basic principle established by God and if one is to be obedient to God then one should not tell lies -- ever. This is not, however, what the Bible teaches. The Bible does not call us to obey abstract principles; it summons us to relationship and humaneness. H. L. Ellison's remark is to the point: [10]

> There is in fact far less condemnation of lying in the Old Testament than we find in the Church today. That is because of its deep understanding of the plight of the small man brought face to face with those who have thrown aside all mercy and morality. To be killed for the sake of the truth is a noble ideal, but all too often the skilled interrogator knows how to frame his questions so that silence can betray and condemn others to death.

In this and other areas Israelite faith is more concerned about relationships than principles; in times of threat to self and community it offers realistic counsel for survival.

THE LECTIONARY: BY GRACE AND NOT BY WORKS

In the Christian tradition, Paul's epistles are of commanding importance; Christian theology, by and large, has been Pauline theology. The apostle lays heavy emphasis on the sinfulness of humankind and the necessity of reliance on God, who has revealed himself in Christ. Many interpreters have presented his message as an unambiguous one: We are saved by grace (God's initiative and power) and not by our works.

Under the influence of Pauline theology, the Christian tradition has tended to emphasize what God has done and will do and, correspondingly, has often had low expectations of people and their ability to do the good. It would appear, therefore, that the above Old Testament passages are missing from the Lectionary not only because they represent a shadowed ethic but, further, because they stress too much the resourcefulness of people.

PASSAGES EXCLUDED FROM LECTIONARY CHALLENGE PASSIVITY

What holds all of the above passages together is the rejection of a passive stance before the events of history -- the refusal to accept what is happening as something caused by or allowed to occur by God. These passages contest the idea that in everything we are to see the hand of God; they rebuke the religious person who, "adjusting himself to his captivity" in an oppressive situation, says, "it is the will of God." [11] Here in these narratives is a call to action that puts the welfare of people (even one's own welfare!) above some principles of teaching that relate to "normal" life and community. They challenge the "triumphal" presentation of history that speaks of life as a continous flow under the guidance of God.

THE EXCLUDED PASSAGES KNOW HISTORY AS "INTERRUPTION"

The acts of violence, lying, shrewdness, and seduction recorded in the above texts are a recognition that there are periods in life that disrupt history; they are "interruptions." [12] In these situations life goes wild, the world returns to the Tohuwavohu. The excluded texts help us to see that in such times one may be forced to do what one would not do in normal times.

These texts express kinship with people in all ages who suffer persecution; they prepare us for the "interruptions" of life that threaten personal safety and the survival of community. The midwives, Moses, Jael, and Esther provide dark wisdom for people caught in nightmare, people who, like Wallenberg and Jews trapped by the Nazis, must lie, scheme, bribe, and double-talk in order to survive or maintain life for others. [13]

THE EXTRA-LECTIONARY TEXTS HELP US APPROACH THE SHOAH

The "shaded" acts recorded in the texts excluded from the Lectionary challenge the view that: 1. Everything in life is under divine control; 2. God, by himself, is working out his plan which will in the end be fulfilled; 3. One must wait patiently for the end when God steps out of the mystery of the present and proves himself to be the victor. These passages challenge the abstract concept of the continuity of history; they are a necessary critique of the God-who-acts-in-history formula. In these texts we have a reminder that day-by-day historical events (especially in life's wild times) do not fit well into the triumphal "salvation history" which the Church proclaims. Further, these passages "hear" the complaint of lay-persons who often lament that religious teaching lacks realism. Finally, these texts which are usually excluded from church lectionaries, can help us to better approach the Shoah, this Event which refuses to be enclosed in a traditional God-of-History interpretation.

THE SHOAH: RUPTURE OF LANGUAGE, INTERRUPTION OF HISTORY

Susan Shapiro speaks of the "rupture" that has taken place in language because of the Shoah: [14]

> It is not only the meaning of particular words in particular languages that have been corrupted and, thus, broken by the event. It is the very coherence and meaning of language in general and of God-language in particular that was negated. This rupture within language is the radical negation of our assumptions and conceptions of the human subject that ground the very coherence of language. Furthermore, this rupture within discourse cannot be mended simply by appealing to an undisrupted, ever-available God-language, for our basic conceptions of a Just and Merciful God are themselves thrown into question by the event. Both discourse in general and God-language in particular are thus ruptured, their coherence shattered, their meaningfulness broken.

One cannot approach the Shoah (or the monumental amount of cruelty and suffering on which the Shoah casts its black light) simply "from above" -- from the point of view of God or some fully-formed interpretation about God and his relationship to the world. No! It must be seen also "from below" through the eyes of people who experience the Interruptions of history, who know well the rupture of life. [15]

> Liberation theology and the Holocaust literature demand that history be received in its full interruptive character. History is not to be understood in terms of process or evolution but in terms of rupture, fragmentation, suffering, totalitarianism, oppression, etc. In this interruption that is history, human subjects must be taken not as abstract subjects but as real victims, and the voices of the tortured, the forgotten, the dead, and the living must be listened to and interpreted in a truly Christian anthropology.

JOB'S FRIENDS AND THE LECTIONARY

The book of Job speaks to the issues of "rupture" of religious language and history as "interruption." In the face of Job's suffering the Friends continue a traditional God-language and insist that God is in charge. For them there are no inconsistences, no disruptions; they are committed to the continuity of history. If experience stands over against their interpretation of life, so much the worse for experience; their "truth" will stand! They cannot see, for example, what is obvious to anyone who has removed his "theologian-glasses," that the wicked are not always punished (see the words of Bildad in Job 18). Job struggles unsuccessfully with his Friends; they will not change their "truth" even though it contradicts reality. God, however, gives a more serious hearing to Job's words (Job 42:7-9).

Unfortunately, the Lectionary gives us a poor representation of texts from Job. In addition to Job 19:23-27 which is chosen because of its supposed affirmation of life beyond the grave and Job 7:1-7 which offers no hope of future life, the Lectionary gives us Job 38:1-11, a text which could have been suggested by Job's Friends! The pericope in Job 38 appears to share the point of view of Eliphaz (Job 15:1-13): it reproaches Job for thinking that he can challenge God. The Lectionary ignores the ending of the book that clearly favors Job's stance over against that of the Friends. No doubt the Lectionary regarded Job's questioning words (and the affirmation of Job in 42:7-9) as too dangerous for church congregations; it was viewed as a threat to the accepted and safe God-acting-in-history interpretation. <u>In the Lectionary -- but not in the Bible -- the Friends have won!</u>

RUN OVER BY THE THEOLOGIANS' "GOD-OF-HISTORY"

It is all too easy to accept the Friends' interpretation of history, because it is uncomplicated and seemingly a comforting proclamation, but, if the book of Job is to be believed (and if life's experiences have any weight at all), such a proclamation honors a false God; it denies reality and encourages a passive stance toward life. To believe too much and too simply that God controls history is to risk the danger of being run over by history, or, more accurately, to be run over by the abstract created by theology, the God-of-History. This view involves us in denial of times of "interruption"; when life goes wrong we attribute it to God's mysterious purpose and in so doing often allow others to suffer the hurt of history.

> One of the great escapes from confronting human evils is to put the blame for everything on God. Egged on by religious traditions that purport to find the "finger of God" behind every event in human history, some people now seek to find "God's purpose for the Holocaust" or for other historical disasters. [16]

The God-of-History doctrine forces us to find a divine purpose in every event of life; as Job's Friends we make life conform to our view of what life should be. It encourages people to stand back -- in spectator fashion -- and watch God work out his will in the world. An extreme expression of this interpreta- tion of life may be seen in the following statement which comes from a Sunday School magazine addressed to adults. It is a response to the 1967 war which threatened the existence of the state of Israel: [17]

> As this is written in September 1967 it appears that Israel is well able to defend herself and to survive nationally. By the time you read these lines it is entirely possible though not at all likely that the Israelis may have been annihilated. If so, we shall simply know that God's time has not yet come for the fulfillment of his promises to the Jews. Whether we are now witnessing the final regathering of the ancient people of God or whether more defeats are in store for Israel before she gains permanent possession of Palestine, we may depend implicitly upon the promises of the Book.

Here sits the spectator watching God at work in our world. Convinced that life moves along under God's control, he patiently waits for God to act; God has his own time and his own way. Admittedly the above comment is an extreme

example of what belief in the God-of-History can mean, yet we should not overlook the fact that even today there are many conservative-evangelical Christians "watching" the Middle East for some hint of God's plan for that region, for Jews, and the world.
Further, within the wider Church there are large numbers of Christians who adopt a passive attitude toward the events of life. When painful events take place in society, the response of many Christians today is that of Dietrich Bonhoeffer in 1937. During this period of Nazi rule, he declared: "Above all let us learn that faced with the enemies of God and his church all we can do is pray." [18] However, Bonhoeffer and others who lived during this time of "interruption" changed their view as the inhumanity of that period continued to assault them.

Waiting for God to take action often allows -- and encourages -- an oppressor to continue his cruelty. Naturally not every one who believes that God is acting in history carries this view to the extreme of believing that he controls every event that takes place or that there is no room left for human initiative. Nevertheless, the church's emphasis on God's activity in history, which finds an unusually strong expression in the Lectionary, tends to create Christian communities that pull back from difficult problems in society and leave them in the hands of God. We need to give a listening ear to the words of Walter Brueggemann: [19]

> We have been so afraid of works-righteousness and legalism that we have not developed a theology of responsibility. . . We are held responsible for our decisions. We do have choices to make which cannot be regarded as trivial. The future is very much the result of the kind of choices we make. No one will make our choices for us. We cannot turn it over to God. We cannot abdicate. Our hesitation in stressing responsibility as a primary theological datum has helped to produce the social indifference and irresponsibility which is all about us in American culture.

These words were written in 1972 but in 1988 they still have point. Hundreds of years of cruelty and destruction have not disauded us from trusting the God-of-History who works in and controls the events of life. Even the Shoah, before whose terror words fail, has been unable to dislodge this doctrine so deeply set within Church proclamation. As Job's Friends, we continue to hold to an interpretation of life that is vigorously contested by experience.

No doubt we, with the Friends, affirm this interpretation of God in history because any other view would seem to denigrate him. However, the "reality thinking" of the texts from the Hebrew Bible (those excluded from the Lectionary) indicate that we do not need to be passive to life nor in denial of experience in order to give honor to God. These texts tells us that God by himself does not protect babies from the planned murder of a ruler, a Hebrew slave from the beating fists of an Egyptian, women from bullies, or a whole community from mass murder. To attempt to discover divine purpose in the violence of oppression is to deepen the pain because it denies reality; to leave such things in the hands of God is to escape responsibility -- to reject our partnership with God.

BRINGING BALANCE TO THE LECTIONARY

Among the many issues under deliberation in the church today (e.g., in the areas of theology and worship), the discussion of the Lectionary deserves rank one priority. It represents Christian theology to people who after worship leave the church to be a people of God in the world. The Lectionary needs to speak to all the experiences of life in that world, including the times of "interruption" when life becomes Tohuwavohu. It needs balance! Lectionary texts must speak about God but they should give attention also to what people have done and can do to survive periods of Interruption.

The light reflected from the Shoah's fire, has enabled us to see the black holes of history. Our time demands a Lectionary that does not encourage us to deny what our eyes see; we need a Lectionary that represents the eyes-open realism of the Bible. Some texts to be considered are those Old Testament passages cited already in this paper (i.e., those excluded from the Lectionary). They address people who are living in a world in which the symbols of faith are absent -- a world in which the One to whom these symbols point is distant and hidden. These texts speak to those who are walking on the edge of life (or death); they reveal understanding of those times when people survive only through quick, clever, decisive speech and action. Further, the stories of the midwives, Moses, and Esther are stories the whole church -- living in "normal" times -- needs to hear. Such stories keep us in touch with the dark realities of life and they restrain us from making simple, triumphal, but hurtful witness (to people who have endured suffering) about the God who controls history and expresses his purpose in the events of history. Without the balance of these kinds of texts, the Lectionary caricatures the Bible and reality.

ACKNOWLEDGMENT

I am grateful to Leanne L. Torgerson, Tutor in the Hebrew Bible, North Park Theological Seminary, for invaluable assistance in the preparation of this paper.

REFERENCES

1. G. E. Wright, The God Who Acts. Chicago: Allenson, 1952, 11-13.

2. M. Lerner, "God and History," Tikkun 2/2 (1987) 9-10 and 2/3 (1987) 64-65 in dialogue with A. Waskow; L. Gilkey, "Scripture, History, and the Quest for Meaning." In: History and Historical Understanding. Eds. C. T. McIntire and R. A. Wells (Grand Rapids: Eerdmans, 1984) 3-16.

3. C. M. Wood, "The Events in which God Acts," The Heythrop Journal 16 (1975) 278.

4. W. C. Loper, The Lord of History. Philadelphia: Westminster, 65, 9.

5. Other earlier lectionaries consulted also reveal an avoidance of these kinds of passages. With few exceptions, texts that are excluded from the Common Lectionary (see our listing of passages on the following pages) are also missig from these pericopes. Some of the lectionaries examined were: the Rhine-Prussian (1838); the Saxon (1842); the Hamburg (1843); the Wurtenburg (1843); the Thomasius-Bavarian (1865); the Eisenach (1896); the Lutheran (Sweden, 1921). Unfortunately, the author and the title of the book in which this information was presented are unknown to me. An analysis of these lectionaries indicates that the Common Lectionary, which has been in use in the U.S.A. since the early 1980s, represents well a long tradition in the Christian Church, that is, the dismissal of texts that emphasize the "resourcefulness" of people in difficult times.

6. C. Porter, "Wise as Serpents: Innocent as Doves. How Shall We Live," Encounter 48 (1987) 22-24.

7. B. Childs, The Book of Exodus. Philadelphia: Westminster, 1974, 23-24.

8. B. Childs, Exodus, 231.

9. A. Cole, Exodus. Downers Grove, Ilinois: Intervarsity, 1973, 55.

10. H. Ellison, Exodus. Philadelphia: Westminster, 1982, 8.

11. R. Alves, A Theology of Human Hope. New York: Corpus Books, 1969, 94.

12. For a development of the idea of "interruption" in history, see the various essays in Holocaust as Interruption. Eds. E. S. Fiorenza and D. Tracy (Edinburgh: T. & T. Clark, 1984).

13. See H. Rosenfeld, Raoul Wallenberg, Angel of Rescue. Buffalo, N. Y.: Prometheus Books, 1982, 82, 94 and D. Kranzler, Thy Brother's Blood: The Orthodox Jewish Response During the Holocaust. New York: Mesorah, 1987.

14. S. Shapiro, "Hearing the Testimony of Radical Negation," In: Holocaust as Interruption, 3.

15. R. Choop, "The Interruption of the Forgotten." In: Holocaust as Interruption, 20.

16. M. Lerner, "God and History," Tikkun, 2/2 (1987) 9.

17. Cited by G. S. Strober in Portrait of the Elder Brother: Jews and Judaism in Protestant Teaching Materials. New York: American Jewish Committee, 1972, 41.

18. See F. B. Nelson and D. Bloesch, "A Bonhoeffer Sermon," Theology Today, 38 (1981/82) 469.

19. W. Brueggemann, In Man We Trust: The Neglected Side of Biblical Faith. Richmond: John Knox, 1972, 61.

Following are the biblical texts listed in the following tables and the pages on which they are to be found.

Table 1

EX1 = Exodus 1:15-21	p 5	EX3 = Exodus 3:18	p 5
JOS = Joshua 2:11-22	p 5	JUD = Judges 4:17-21	p 5
RUT = Ruth 3:1-18	p 5	S19 = 1 Samuel 19:11-17	p 5
S20 = 1 Samuel 20:1-7	p 5	IKG = 1 Kings 1:1-40	p 5
NEH = Nehemiah 2:11-16	p 5	EST = Esther 4--7	p 5

Table 2

M2 = Matthew 2:16	p 3	M16 = Matthew 10:16	p 3
M23 = Matthew 10:23	p 3	J8 = John 8:59	p 3
J10 = John 10:39	p 3	J12 = John 12:36	p 3
ACT = Acts 9:25	p 4	2CO = 2 Corinthians 11:33	p 4

TABLE 1

DATE	TITLE	EX1	EX3	JOS	JUD	RUT	S19	S20	IKG	NEH	EST
900	Traditional	0	0	0	0	0	0	0	0	0	0
1838	Rhine-Prussian Selections	N	A	0	0	0	N	N	N	0	0
1842	Saxon Pericopes	N	N	0	0	N	A	N	N	N	0
1843	Hamburg Pericopes	0	0	0	0	0	0	0	0	0	0
1843	Wurtemburg Selections	0	0	0	0	0	0	0	0	0	0
1860	Hanover Pericopes	N	N	N	0	0	N	N	N	0	0
1865	Thomasius Selections	N	N	0	0	0	N	N	N	N	0
1896	Eisenach Selections	N	N	0	0	0	0	0	0	0	0
1921	Swedish Selections	0	0	0	0	0	0	0	0	0	0
1971	Roman Catholic Sunday Lec	N	A	N	0	0	N	N	N	N	0
1974	COCU Lectionary	N	A	N	0	0	N	N	N	N	0
1983	Inclusive-Lang. Lect., A	N	N	0	0	0	N	N	N	N	0
1984	Common Lectionary	Y	Y	N	0	N	N	N	N	N	0
1984	Inclusive-Lang. Lect., B	N	N	0	N	0	N	N	N	0	0
1985	Inclusive-Lang. Lect., C	N	N	N	0	0	N	N	N	N	0
1986	Inclusive-Lang Lect, Rev.	Y	Y	0	0	N	0	0	0	0	0

Key to the tables: Y = text is included in lectionary; N = text is not included in lectionary; 0 = book of the Bible is not included in the lectionary; A = lectionary selection ends before text or begins after text in same pericope; S = lectionary selection skips text (i.e., includes passages on either side of text).

TABLE 2

DATE	TITLE	M2	M16	M23	J8	J10	J12	ACT	2CO
900	Traditional	Y	N	N	Y	N	Y	N	Y
1838	Rhine-Prussian Selections	N	A	N	Y	N	N	N	N
1842	Saxon Pericopes	N	N	N	N	N	N	Y	N
1843	Hamburg Pericopes	N	Y	Y	N	N	A	N	N
1843	Wurtemburg Selections	A	Y	A	N	N	A	N	N
1860	Hanover Pericopes	N	Y	Y	N	N	Y	N	N
1865	Thomasius Selections	N	N	N	N	N	N	N	N
1896	Eisenach Selections	A	N	A	N	N	N	N	N
1921	Swedish Selections	A	N	A	N	N	N	N	N
1971	Roman Catholic Sunday Lec	S	A	A	N	A	A	A	N
1974	COCU Lectionary	A	N	A	N	N	N	N	N
1983	Inclusive-Lang. Lect., A	S	Y	Y	N	N	N	N	N
1984	Common Lectionary	S	A	A	N	Y	A	A	N
1984	Inclusive-Lang. Lect., B	N	N	N	N	N	N	N	N
1985	Inclusive-Lang. Lect., C	N	N	N	N	N	Y	N	N
1986	Inclusive-Lang Lect, Rev.	A	N	A	N	N	Y	N	N

Key to the tables: Y = text is included in lectionary; N = text is not included in lectionary; 0 = book of the Bible is not included in the lectionary; A = lectionary selection ends before text or begins after text in same pericope; S = lectionary selection skips text (i.e., includes passages on either side of text).

JESUS THE JEW AND THE GOSPEL OF MATTHEW

Alastair G. Hunter

Department of Biblical Studies,
University of Glasgow,
Glasgow G12 8QQ,
Scotland.

INTRODUCTION

The horrific events of the Holocaust have cast a long shadow over the world, and the study of scripture within the Christian community has (thankfully) not escaped that shadow. The study of the Hebrew Scriptures and the New Testament is conducted now with a much sharper awareness of their Jewish origins. In particular the character of the first followers of Jesus as part of the wide spectrum of Judaism has begun to be taken seriously as a presupposition of the study of the Gospels and the life of Jesus. Jesus was a Jew, his disciples were Jews, and the roots of their teaching and understanding of Jesus are firmly set in the faith of Judaism as it emerged in the early and middle first century CE. Thus Jewish Christians, later labelled as heretics and given the pejorative name of Ebionites, have a good claim to be closest in time and spirit to what Jesus himself represented.

Although the Christian scriptures of the New Testament may appear to be detached from recent world history to the point almost of irrelevance, there are deep wells of tradition, ultimately traceable to the Gospels' attitude to the Jews, which provide hidden nourishment for antisemitism and which played no small part in making the Holocaust possible. The double charge of having rejected the Messiah and of having crucified God is implicit in the gospel traditions and was explicitly developed as a justification for regular pogroms against the Jews from the earliest times in Christian Europe. And while the charge of deicide is less frequently heard today, it still occurs in disguised form in those modern dismissals of Judaism which focus on a supposed Jewish 'failure' to recognise the divinity of Jesus. What was in essence originally a matter of faithfulness to the *shema* - rejection of the unthinkable claim that a human being, a Jew at that, was God incarnate - has thus ironically become for Christians evidence of the *un*faithfulness of the Jews! And although Hitler's regime could hardly be described as Christian the ease with which his insane and vicious plans were carried out in Europe was due in no small measure to a readiness on the part of many Christians, infected by cultural anti-Jewish sentiment, to pretend ignorance of, when not actually enabling, the apparatus of the 'final solution'.

Since a primary difference between Jews and Christians lies in their different perceptions of the nature of Jesus, it is clearly of the essence of any Jewish-Christian dialogue that this matter be addressed. Certainly such an approach is not going to lead to a single composite faith, nor would that be a welcome outcome; it is one of the real advances of the twentieth century that the *givenness* of the multiplicity of faiths is now broadly accepted as a positive thing. But accepting the need for a plurality of religious insights is to be strictly separated from any acceptance of the idea that these insights must be in permanent conflict of a destructive kind. This is why a new 'quest for the historical Jesus' is appropriate: not that we might disinvent Christianity, but that we might open up possibilities for Christianity in relation to Judaism which build upon our common origins. (In this regard it is worth mentioning the considerable burgeoning of 'intertestamental' studies in the universities, and the growth of comparative work on the common first century matrix of both religions. In the University of Glasgow, for example, I share with a New Testament colleague the teaching of a course entitled

'Jewish and Christian Beginnings' whose purpose is to elucidate precisely the kind of issues we have been outlining.)

SYNOPSIS

In the preface to perhaps his most famous work, Jesus the Jew (1976, p.10), Geza Vermes indicated that he intended to take the discussion further. 'Jesus the Jew is the first part of a trilogy: it sets the scene of Jesus' activity and determines what kind of Jew he was. A second enquiry, The Gospel of Jesus the Jew, will be devoted to a reconstruction of his authentic message. Lastly, in a work still without a title, I intend to investigate the transformation of the man, Jesus of Nazareth, into the divine Christ of the Christian faith in the works of Paul, John and other New Testament writers.' The second of these three projects found limited expression in three lectures published under the title The Gospel of Jesus the Jew (1981); the third is yet to come, though others have not neglected the matter in the meantime: see for example the work of E.P. Sanders (1977,1980,1981), and the most recent of Hyam Maccoby's books, The Mythmaker (1986).

In a recent study of the Temptation narrative in Matthew's Gospel (Hunter, 1986), I argued that the primary function of that passage - an original creation by the Jewish Christian 'School of Matthew' in Antioch - was to demonstrate that the title 'Son of God' had the primary meaning of a faithful son of the Torah. It served, therefore, not as a definition of divinity, but 'to portray Jesus as an orthodox, observant Jew of his time' (p.20). A conclusion of this kind raises more general questions about the status of the doctrine of the divinity of Jesus, and the possibility that it emerged predominantly within the Greek churches, developing certain trends in Hellenistic Judaism (thus Hunter, 1985, pp.40-58; Maccoby, 1986). There is a danger of circularity here, of assuming the primacy of a Jewish understanding of Jesus in the early decades of the Church, applying that to a reading of Matthew, and then using that reading to support the original claim! Fortunately we have some degree of control in the form of external witnesses to the situation which gives us access to the community from which Matthew's Gospel emerged, its tensions and self-understanding.

Using these controls, and coupling them with a further investigation of specific features of the Gospel, I hope to suggest that there exists within the present form of the Gospel, and recoverable without too much difficulty, that very 'Gospel of Jesus the Jew' of which Vermes has spoken and written. Any such approach must come to terms with the clear indication of strong tensions in the communities at Antioch: the strength of the Matthaean attack on 'the scribes and the Pharisees', and the sharp distinctions between 'saved' and 'damned' which are implied in chapters 24 and 25, culminating in the self-condemnatory gloss of the Barabbas legend, 27:25, 'And all the people answered, "His blood be on us and on our children!"' - a text which, more than any other, has served as a pretext for that oppression of the Jews which has so tragically marred the Christian centuries. Accordingly, I will first consider the question of the situation in which Matthew's Gospel was written, and to which it is presumably addressed. This will lead in turn to an examination of Matthew 23, a passage whose virulence and unfairness is a continuing hindrance to Jewish-Christian understanding. Finally, and on a more positive note, I will offer a preliminary approach to the problem of finding that 'Gospel of Jesus the Jew' which I believe to be embedded in Matthew, and which is revealed by the characteristic way that Matthew develops the Markan traditions in his opening chapters.

1. MATTHEW'S TIME AND PLACE

There is a fair consensus concerning the likely dating of Matthew, pace John Robinson's attempt to relocate everything in the New Testament in the period prior to 70 CE (Robinson, 1976) and proposals to revive the Griesbach hypothesis of Matthaean priority over Mark (Farmer, 1976). The structural complexity of the gospel indicates that it comes from a community of some standing and with access to learning and an extensive literature (Stendahl, 1967), which has reflected on the issues over a considerable period of time. And allusions to the destruction of Jerusalem in 70 CE without that being a central theme (Mt 23:37-39) suggest a date of composition in the last quarter of the century. At the other limit, it seems clear that Ignatius of Antioch knew and made use of Matthew (Fenton, 1963, p.11; Brown & Meier, 1983, p.25). Since he was dead by 117 CE, perhaps martyred as early as 107, and is traditionally given as bishop of Antioch from 69 CE, a date at the latest near the beginning of the second century seems indicated. The problem of place is perhaps not so readily resolved. But while admittedly no definitive answer can be given, the claims of Antioch seem very strong indeed. Eduard Schweizer, for example, favours Syria (1976, pp.15-17), and Brown & Meier (1983, pp.22-27) present very convincingly the evidence for a specific locus in Antioch.

This is not a trivial point. The likelihood that we can place Matthew in Antioch in the last quarter of the first century is of importance in delineating the tensions and assumptions which inform the gospel. The city of Antioch was founded in 300 BCE by Seleucus Nicator following the defeat of Antigonus in the struggles for power which erupted on the death of Alexander. Situated near the river Orontes, it soon became an important metropolis, and by the first century CE was one of the largest Hellenistic cities in the Roman Empire. There were Jews in Antioch from the time of its first foundation, and by the mid second century BCE they had established the right to observe their own customs and to govern themselves (Josephus, War, 7.3.3). They survived, relatively unscathed, the change-over to Roman rule and even the events of 66-73 CE, so that 'the Christian church at Antioch had a constant and largely undisturbed matrix out of which to grow and against which to define itself' (Brown & Meier, 1983, p.32). Josephus claims that many Greeks were attracted to the Jewish faith, and this is confirmed by other evidence of the significance of proselytism in the Graeco-Roman world (Schürer/Vermes, 1986, pp.150-176). There is no doubt that the diaspora developed its own characteristics marking it off from Palestinian Judaism, Philo Judaeus being perhaps the most dramatic example, and perhaps Paul if we follow Maccoby (1986). But the central importance of Jerusalem and its cultus was scarcely in question - a fact confirmed both by the Book of Acts and by Jewish sources. Paul's ambiguous relationship with the leadership in Jerusalem points this up clearly. He is at pains to show that his conversion was not through Jerusalem, and that he neither visited the city nor discussed the matter with anyone there (Galatians 1:15-17). The significance of this, in view of his expression of bitter disappointment about having been pre-empted by the 'Jerusalem' party in Antioch (Galatians 2, especially vv.11-14), is obvious: Jerusalem had considerable power over Antioch, and Paul wished, in the interests of a Hellenising version of the new faith, to distance himself both from Jerusalem and from the Jewish party in Antioch. Yet the same traditions reveal that even Paul was aware that he could not dismiss the authority of Jerusalem. His participation in the so-called 'Council of Jerusalem' (Acts 15) shows that he needed the approval of the mother church, just as his attack on Peter in Galatians reveals that he felt betrayed by that same church. That all of this is a mirror of the relationship between Jerusalem and the Jewish diaspora in Antioch is hardly in question: it is doubtful if James and the other leaders in Jerusalem thought of themselves as anything other than Jewish.

The first notice we have of a mission to Antioch by followers of Jesus is in the aftermath of the persecution following Stephen's death (Acts 11:19-26). The dispersal at that time may well have been specifically of 'hellenists', the party from whom the seven deacons were chosen (Acts 6:1-6), one of whom was in fact 'a proselyte of Antioch'. It would be natural for them to address themselves also to those Gentiles who were already attracted to Judaism, and we can readily understand how in such a situation there would arise the crucial question of the extent to which observance of Jewish rites was mandatory. In fact the account in Acts specifically notes that although some spoke only to the Jews, others from Cyprus and Cyrene spoke also to 'Greeks'. The text is uncertain here - the reference may be to Greeks proper, or to 'Hellenists'. In either case, a new situation had arisen requiring new tactics. Jerusalem was not slow to respond, and sent a delegation under the leadership of Barnabas, whom the traditions present as a modest and conciliatory figure. It is not without significance that to assist him in his task of moderating affairs in Antioch Barnabas sent for Saul - the man whom he had endorsed as a new Jewish convert to Jesus, and whose first experiences after his conversion were of another Syrian city, Damascus. In many ways, this must have seemed an ideal situation in which to allow the new apostle to 'cut his teeth' - a hellenistic city with a sizeable Jewish population, not unlike Saul's own native Tarsus. We are so accustomed to think of Barnabas as the junior partner in the famous missionary team that we forget that in the beginning Saul was Barnabas's protege, and Antioch his first real test. As we shall see, later events suggest that Saul failed that test or, at least, that the turn of events in Antioch left him isolated and with a sense of having been rejected by the Christian community there.

It was apparently in Antioch that the crucial questions were most sharply raised regarding the future of 'Christianity', 'Judaism' and the relationship between the two. Could one be a Christian without also being a Jew? Which of the characteristically Jewish beliefs and practices were essential, which optional? Is the issue one of clear alternatives, or are we dealing with a spectrum of opinion all the way from strict orthodox rabbinic followers of Jesus to thoroughly hellenised former proselytes and Gentiles for whom the teachings and practices of Judaism were of little ultimate moment? The very use of terms like 'Christianity' and 'Judaism' is of course a peculiarly Antiochene phenomenon, which itself may be evidence for the central role of that city in the contest which led ultimately to the separation of Hellenistic Christianity from Rabbinic Judaism. It is well known that the term christianoi was first used of the disciples there (Acts 11:26) - Meeks & Wilken (1978, p.16) suggest that it was because it was there 'that they first stood out from Judaism as a distinct sect'. Ignatius is the only Apostolic Father to use the expression christianismos (Christianity), and to use it in contrast with ioudaismos (Judaism) in Philadelphians 6:1. The distribution of ioudaismos in early Christian sources is noteworthy: in the New Testament, only in Galatians 1:13,14 and 2:14, where the context is that of the debate between Paul and Jerusalem over the situation in Antioch, and in Ignatius (Magnesians 8:1, 10:3, and Philadelphians 6:1). Further, the verb 'to Judaise' (ioudaizein) is a hapax legomenon in the New Testament in Galatians 2:14 and occurs also in Ignatius, Magnesians 10:3.

The decision to allow certain converts to remain uncircumcised must have been a controversial one, and Acts 15:1 makes it clear that it did not pass unopposed. The meeting in Jerusalem between Paul and Barnabas on the one hand, and 'the party of the Pharisees' on the other (a description which will be important for our reading of Matthew 23) was moderated by the leaders of the Jerusalem church. Of the latter, we find James and Peter in particular named (together with the more shadowy John) as opponents of Paul in Galatians 2:9 and lumped by association with the 'false brethren' of v.4. James, the brother of Jesus, was a major figure in the early Church, head of the Jerusalem community and hence arguably in a position of some authority, given the status of that city. Peter's position is less clear. 1 Corinthians 1:12 implies that he had a party of supporters, and his role in the Antioch affair suggests that he was seen as an important mediating figure, a role also indicated in the famous Cornelius story in Acts 10-11. Peter's standing in Matthew's Gospel is well known (thus 16:17-20: he appears there as 'the chief Rabbi of the universal church, with power to make "halakic" decisions ... in the light of the teaching of Jesus,' and he is presented 'as the human authority for the church as a whole' (Brown & Meier, 1983, p.67). The implication of the account in Acts of the 'Council of Jerusalem' seems to be that those who were described (ironically?) by Paul as 'the pillars of the church' (Galatians 2:9) at first adopted a mediating position between Paul and the Judaisers. This proved impossible to maintain: a polarisation took place, and we later find 'the party of James' associated not with the via media but with the extremists (Galatians 2:12).

The Council, faced with irreconcilable opposites, came down on the side of a modus vivendi which tried to balance all shades of moderate opinion: the mission was to be decided between Peter (to the Jews, Galatians 2:7-8) and Paul (to the Gentiles); the concept of two gospels was introduced (circumcision and uncircumcision); in recognition of the importance of Jerusalem, the gentile churches were to collect for 'the poor' in Jerusalem. But, like all such compromises, some things were left unresolved (Paul's status; dietary laws - cf Acts 15:20,29; 21:25, and Paul's comments on the subject in his letters), and new problems were introduced. The effective unity of the church, if it had ever existed, was now gone, and the faction of extreme Judaisers was excluded, and so still remained a problem. The compromise on diet is interesting. It suggests, if historical, a willingness on the part of gentile Christians in Antioch to preserve unity if at all possible. And since the issue at the centre of the argument reported in Galatians is precisely that of diet - of who may eat what and with whom - we are presented with a plausible reconstruction: an agreement was reached to maintain the outward observations of Jewishness; despite this, and under the influence of the developing gentile Christian community in Antioch, both Peter and Barnabas, characteristically eager to bring a reconciling influence to bear, associated with this party; however, when reminded of their remit by a delegation from Jerusalem, they (quite properly) withdrew. After all, if Peter were known to have eaten with Gentiles he would no longer be acceptable as an apostle to the Jews. It was this which led to the disagreement which so vexed Paul: but reading between the lines, we might propose that it was Paul, not the others, who was unwilling to accept what had been decided. What gave the matter a bitter personal twist was the 'defection' of Barnabas. We should not assume that Paul's erstwhile companion and mentor was a vacillating character; the fact that Barnabas decided as he did shows just how tricky was the situation at Antioch. That Paul had not been a calming influence is suggested by Barnabas's decision, when the next mission was planned, not to accompany Paul. I suspect that the story about Paul's reservations on account of Mark (Acts 15:36-41) is an attempt to save face: in reality, Barnabas chose Mark in preference to Paul. The end of the matter sees Paul defeated and in some disarray. He is reported in Acts 18:22 as having paid one more visit to Antioch, but only the bare fact is recorded. He does not (as in Caesarea in the same verse) 'greet the church', neither does he (as in Galatia and Phrygia in v.23) 'strengthen all the disciples'. All that is said as a rather sad footnote to the scene of his earliest mission, is that he 'spent some time there'. No more.

The clear implication of our analysis of the records pertaining to Antioch is that the church there was at the heart of a long-standing dispute about the place of Torah regulations in the Christian church. Meier (Brown & Meier, 1983, pp.2-8) argues that from the very beginning there were at least four kinds of Christian mission in that city: (1) a Jewish mission of ultra-conservative character which insisted on circumcision and was antagonist to Paul (though it is certainly not without interest that Pharisees and zealous adherents of Judaism could still regard themselves as followers of Jesus); (2) a moderately conservative group which insisted on the observance of some customs; (3) Jewish Christians and Gentile converts who did not insist on complete Torah observance (represented by Paul, who has more time for the law than some of his extreme statements suggest); (4) and a radical group which saw no abiding significance in Jewish cult and feasts. This range of opinion is hardly surprising: it merely reflects the variety of ways in which adherents, God-fearers and proselytes might associate with the long-established Jewish community.

There is a wide gulf between the 'defeat' of Paul thus described and the clear dominance of Paul in the writings of Ignatius of Antioch. The latter is clearly anti-Jewish, though Meeks & Wilken (1978, p.19-20) see his main attack as directed to Judaeo-Christians. The Jewish community in Antioch continued in relative freedom throughout the second and third centuries, occasioning regular attacks from Christian writers. These, however, may have been coded criticisms of Judaising groups within the church. 'Christian writers at large applied the term "Jew" to any Christian who was thought to have denigrated the divine status of Jesus.' And 'a further cause of sensitivity towards Judaism may be found in the fact that the Antiochene church itself was seen by the rest of the Christian church as lying too close to Judaism for comfort.' (Wallace-Hadrill, 1982, p.20). Apparently, then, the special circumstances of Antioch which lie behind the events of Paul's career were no passing phenomenon, but a permanent matrix. Little wonder, then, that it should have been from Antioch that a gospel emerged which was thoroughly Jewish in concept and execution (Hunter, 1986, pp.10f), yet which presented the claims of a Christian church with a messianic understanding of Jesus. That gospel belongs, most probably, to the last quarter of the first century, and therefore might help us to understand how the defeat of Paul in Galatians was transformed into the triumph of Pauline Christianity in Ignatius. We approach Matthew, therefore, as a window into the mind of the early Jewish-Christian church in Antioch as it struggles to reach an understanding of the nature of Jesus and his significance for the world.

2. MATTHEW 23

No one whos reads the twenty-third chapter of Matthew's gospel with genuine awareness can fail to be impressed by the passion of its language and the strength and bitterness of the invective hurled therein at the misfortunate 'scribes and Pharisees'. Not surprisingly, the passage has produced a number of memorable images and maxims: 'practise what you preach', 'blind guides', 'to strain out a gnat and swallow a camel', 'whited sepulchres', 'whoever exalts himself will be humbled, and whoever humbles himself will be exalted'. If that were the extent of its influence, the chapter would be innocent enough. But there is a much more serious issue involved - no less a question, indeed, than the comprehensive damning of the collective reputation of an entire people. In sermon after sermon and book upon book the trite and disturbing slander is repeated: 'The Jews are the kind of people described in Matthew 23; it was people like that who opposed Jesus, who rejected him, who killed him.' What makes the matter worse is that this ludicrous distortion is perpetrated not just by the simple-minded whose major crime is ignorance, but by apparently sophisticated, intelligent church leaders and scholars who continue to take Matthew 23 at face value, as though it were an eye-witness, objective, historical account. Scholars who in other areas of their intellectual life exercise finely honed critical faculties may be found naively using the gospels in general and this passage in particular as sources of value-free information on the practices and beliefs of the Jews and their religious leaders in the time of Jesus, with little or no recognition of the thoroughly prejudiced nature of their sources.

The lack of rigour implied by this process is easily demonstrated in the present case. Thus, for example, the accusation that Pharisees travel over land and sea to make converts (v.15) - which is of course only reprehensible on the basis of a rejection of the Pharisaic faith - is hardly substantiated by much evidence. As far as we know, Rabbinic Judaism was more concerned with putting its own house in order than with the planning and execution of missionary campaigns. The kind of proselytism described in Schürer/Vermes (1986, pp.150-176) is not what is implied by this verse, and when Filson (1960) claims that there is abundant evidence for the practice indicated by Matthew he is engaged in a perfectly circular argument. For the one fragment of evidence quoted when the subject of evangelism by Palestinian Judaism is raised is invariably Matthew 23:15! Thus Schürer/Vermes (p.160): 'even the Pharisees in Palestine can be portrayed as eager to find converts: "you traverse sea and land to make a single proselyte" (Mt. 23:15)', and Schweizer (1976, p.440): 'Verse 15 is evidence of intensive Jewish missionary activity, a possibility usually ignored (sic!).' Given the obvious bias of chapter 23, sober judgment would surely reject such an unsupported witness. The only Pharisees of the time that spring to mind as having 'travelled over land and sea' are Josephus and Paul. We only have their word for it that they were Pharisees, the former was hardly a missionary, and it is difficult to imagine that the latter would not have been utterly repudiated by orthodox Rabbinic circles!

A second example which in itself is of little substance, but none the less diagnostic of the problem, concerns the 'seat of Moses' referred to in v.2. The metaphorical nature of the figure used here cannot be doubted; but such is the zeal for 'historical' accuracy that both Albright & Mann (1971) and Fenton (1963) interpret it to mean that there was in the synagogue a seat so named. Fenton compounds the felony by adducing Luke 4:20ff in support, as if the mere fact that Jesus sat down in the synagogue proved anything - we may assume that the existence of seats or benches of some kind would not be of special significance. (Just to confuse the matter further, Howard Kee is currently arguing that there were no synagogue buildings as such prior to the second century CE, leaving us with a metaphorical seat in a non-existent building!).

Much of chapter 23 is, of course, sheer rhetoric, and would have been immediately recognised as such in any secular text. It is only the canonical nature of the Gospel which has protected it from the application of critical common sense. Comments like: 'They impose burdens on others and do nothing themselves' (v.4), 'They love places of honour at feasts' (v.6), 'They shut the kingdom of heaven against men; they neither enter themselves nor let anyone else in' (v.13), 'They are like whitewashed tombs - righteous on the outside, full of hypocrisy and iniquity within' (v.27f), are perfectly obviously rhetorical. It passes belief that any of them should ever have been entertained for a moment as an objective account of the religious sect of the Pharisees in the time of Jesus. That they were - and still continue to be - so regarded is a tribute to the triumph of religious bigotry over intelligence. It hardly requires the heavy artillery of biblical criticism to dispose of such nonsense! No doubt some of the issues raised in Matthew 23 were genuine current controversies - the dimensions of phylacteries and fringes, the use of titles, the style of oaths. But the second and third of these concerned the church as much as the synagogue, and there is sufficient evidence that the problems were debated in rabbinic circles in similar terms, expressing the same concerns, though probably not as early as the time of Jesus.

Vigorous rejection of the accuracy and historicity of Matthew 23 is only part of the story. It is important also to recognise its pronounced literary character. Stendahl (1967) goes a long way towards demonstrating that Matthew's gospel comes out of a lengthy Jewish-Christian scribal tradition in his church. Matthew's use of 'prophets and wise men and scribes' (23:24, compare vv.7-10 and 13:1-2; contrast Luke 11:49, 'prophets and apostles') seems to indicate this special character of the church in Antioch (Goulder, 1974, p.150). The emphasis on 'wise men and scribes', peculiar to Matthew, sheds a revealing light on the concerns and priorities of the Matthaean church and gives it a remarkably rabbinic tone. Garland (1979, pp.18-32) emphasises that the chapter is very markedly a Matthaean composition and is integral to the longer context of chapters 21-25 which itself displays a clear structure. Goulder (p.429) claims that 180 out of the 646 words it contains are characteristic of Matthew. The first twelve verses form a statement of the central thesis (vv.2-3) which is then commented on and culminates in a sub-theme (vv.11-12), the two forming an inclusio. If J.D.M. Derrett is right (1981), this first section is still more complex, containing a rabbinic-style midrash on Isaiah 54:13 and Jeremiah 31:33f. The remainder of the chapter moves through a series of seven woes (the number is no doubt significant) which Goulder (p.421f) has proposed matching with the blessings in 5:3-12, and culminates in the famous prophecy ex eventu concerning Jerusalem which points up the shift in power from temple to synagogue, and from synagogue to church. That a transfer of influence is intended is suggested by the saying in v.33 which probably marks the end of the series of woes: 'You serpents, you brood of vipers, how are you to escape being sentenced to hell.' This repeats the charge brought against the Pharisees and the Sadducees by John in 3:7ff, where they are rejected as children of Abraham. We thus have a second inclusio: John's condemnation of his opponents in the context of the authority of Abraham at the beginning of the mission of Jesus, Jesus's condemnation of his opponents in the context of the authority of Moses at the end of his mission (all that remains after chapter 23, before the passion narrative, is a long passage of private explanation to the disciples in chapters 24 and 25). As we will see in the next section, the connection and contrast between Jesus and John is essential to the structure and meaning of the gospel, so that v.33 is revealed as no casual echo of 3:7, but a deliberate balanced motif.

What emerges from our discussion so far is that, far from being the hot-headed outburst of a moment's passion, Matthew 23 is a carefully shaped rhetorical diatribe against a group who are perceived by the writer as dangerous enemies. They are described as 'scribes and Pharisees', though they can scarcely have been (as the material superficially indicates) the historical opponents of Jesus during his lifetime. Whether the Jewish community in Antioch presented a genuine threat to the Christians in the last part of the first century may be questioned: the Jews had their own problems to look to, and the slow process of defining rabbinic Judaism was occupying the full attention of the new leadership in Yavneh. Moreover, it seems somewhat strange that if Matthew's prime target was Pharisaic Judaism he did not make more positive use of the catastrophe of the destruction of the Temple in the failed revolt of 66-70 CE. The somewhat elliptic nature of the reference might perhaps be understood as evidence that his prime target was _not_ the Jews _simpliciter_. The conclusion of our consideration of the emerging Christian church in Antioch was that it faced a potentially destructive internal conflict about the degree to which observation of Jewish customs was necessary or desirable - a debate which was by no means settled by Ignatius's time, and which clearly rumbled on into the third and fourth centuries. What all of this seems to suggest is that it does not make much sense to interpret Matthew 23 as a Christian-Jewish polemic. According to Garland (p.215), in the context of Matthew's community polemic against the Jews is not important. Matthew's intention is twofold: to elucidate the problem of God's rejection of the Jews and their rejection of Jesus, and to warn the church against going the same way. This seems to me still to be too weak as an explanation. The intensity with which Matthew 23 makes its case goes far beyond the explication of a historical lesson or analogy. We are aware, reading this chapter, that there really is an enemy out there, a tangible opponent against whom this invective is directed. We know from the history of religions that the bitterest disputes are between those who, to an outside observer, scarcely seem to differ at all. The deepest hatred of protestant bigots is reserved, not for catholics, but for protestants who are deemed to have compromised the true faith. Might this not be the most appropriate model for our reading of Matthew?

There are, I believe, several clues to the solution of the puzzle.

(1) The reference in Acts 15:5 to 'some believers who belonged to the party of the Pharisees'.

(2) Paul's own claim to be a Pharisee - indeed, to be a more observant Pharisee than any of his opponents (Acts 23:6; 26:5; Philippians 3:4-6).

(3) The use of 'Jewish' and 'judaising' amongst Christian writers at Antioch.

(4) The opening words of Matthew 23: 'Then said Jesus to the crowds and to his disciples, "The scribes and the Pharisees sit on Moses' seat; so practise and observe whatever they tell you".'

That Paul, for all his animosity to the judaisers, can be reported as a strict Pharisee; that one of the church parties involved in the debate in Acts 15 was Pharisaic: that the very focus of our discussion should begin by asserting, of all things, the validity of Pharisaic authority derived from Moses - that, in short, to be a 'Pharisee' was a perfectly respectable position within the early church, must point strongly in the direction of a reading of Matthew 23 as an _inner-Christian_ debate. This fits very well indeed with the known context of Antioch. Moreover, the dating of Matthew to (probably) 80-90 CE suggests that we have in the sharp dispute which chapter 23 reveals evidence of an intermediate stage between that revealed by Acts and that presupposed in Ignatius. A distinction is being drawn between 'ideal Pharisaism' and the burdensome and pedantic imposition of narrow-minded legalism, a distinction which has reached the stage of rendering the actual title 'Pharisee' unusable. Interestingly, a very similar development is found in rabbinic sources, in which the word _perushim_ (Pharisees) gradually acquires the meaning of 'those who are unacceptably extreme _in their_ observance of the law', even attracting on occasion the very adjective which is so pointedly used by Matthew: 'hypocrite' (Bowker, _passim_, 1973). What we find in Matthew 23, then, is a church responding from within its _broadly Jewish_ context to the threat of those who would abort the process of discovery and freedom which was then under way by insisting on an inappropriate level of ritual observance. But it must be stressed that the context is _Jewish_-Christian: Moses is supreme, and Jesus the prophet, the messiah, the faithful son of the _Torah_ (Hunter, 1986) whose _halakhah_ is the true interpretation of the law (Matthew 5-7). The fault of the 'Pharisees' is _not that_ they are Jews who have rejected Jesus, but that they are judaisers within the church who, like Paul, have refused to accept the terms of the Council of Jerusalem. Paul ultimately turned his back on the whole Jewish experience, and helped to open the door to the hellenistic reinterpretation of Jesus as the God-man within the trinity which definitively divided the church from its Jewish roots. The 'Pharisees', by insisting on the total subordination of Jesus and his followers to their extreme interpretation of the law, effectively widened the gap by stressing the differences rather than those things which were common, thus ensuring in the end that Jewish Christianity would be condemned to the status of heresy and its insights lost to the world. Matthew, in its first form, stands as a testament to that insight, a last attempt to explain Jesus the Jew and present him as the faithful son of God, obedient to Torah, the expected Messiah in whom would be fulfilled the law. The injustice done the Jewish Christians by this cruel twist of history has begun to be redressed in the twentieth century - see, for example, the treatment by Georg Strecker in the 1964 reprint of Orthodoxy and Heresy in Earliest Christianity (Bauer, 1972, pp.241-285). In my final section I will make some tentative proposals towards the recovery of that 'Gospel of Jesus the Jew' which I have suggested might be found within the Gospel of Matthew.

3. 'THE GOSPEL OF JESUS THE JEW'

In my earlier article, 'Rite of Passage' (Hunter, 1986), I argued for an interpretation of Matthew 4:1-11 which took seriously the rabbinic character of the piece and gave due place to the scriptural themes which informed it. From this perspective there emerged a strikingly Jewish understanding of Jesus's sonship in relation to a firm adherence to the central tenets of the faith in Deuteronomy 6:4-5. As a corollary I noted that whatever we take the title 'son of God' to mean, it can hardly, in the original context of 4:1-11, have been a definition of divinity.

It seems improbable, given that the style of the temptation narrative is very much in keeping with the rest of the Matthaean material, that these emphases should be unique. It is likely that having identified them in one place we might note them elsewhere. However in the light of our discussion in the first two sections, a more general question might appropriately be addressed: are there redactional-critical criteria which might point to, or give us access to an earlier form of the gospel in which the Jewish messianic 'reading' of Jesus was predominant, and which was subsequently elaborated in the interests of the hellenistic group? We have seen how the general situation in Antioch, and the likely victims of the attack in Matthew 23, match the thesis of a Jewish-Christian community under simultaneous attack from both Hellenists and extreme Judaisers, and we have proposed a niche for Matthew at an intermediate stage between Acts/Galatians and Ignatius. If a further refinement of the Gospel as it now stands is possible. we may be able to reconstruct a theology of the Jewish Christians of Antioch in the mid to late first century.

It has often been claimed that structurally Matthew's Gospel is a kind of imitation of the Pentateuch, with Jesus as a second Moses called out of Egypt and revealing a new law on the mountain (or a new interpretation of the old law). The allegory cannot be pressed too far, for the emphasis of the gospel is obviously on the messiahship of Jesus and this can hardly be regarded as a characteristic of Moses. Thus, although I have argued (1986, p.17) that Moses is one appropriate role-model for Jesus in the temptation narrative (4:1-11), other pericope clearly present him as Messiah. He is the one for whom John/Elijah is the forerunner (3:1-7), he is publicly recognised by Peter (16:13-16) - a recognition confirmed by the transfiguration episode which pointedly, and only in Matthew, repeats verbatim God's words of commendation at his baptism (17:5 = 3:17) - and it can hardly be doubted that the eschatological material concerning the 'son of man' in chapters 24 and 25 has a messianic emphasis. Nevertheless, there are clearly visible fivefold structures in the gospel which could well have been deliberately intended to echo the Torah (Stendahl, 1967, pp.24-26; Fenton, 1963, pp.14-16). The most commonly quoted is the existence of five 'concluding formulae' in 7:28, 11:1, 13:53, 19:1 and 26:1, each coming at the end of a major section of discourse. This structure readily produces a five-book 'torah', with the birth and passion narratives standing outside as a sacred biography of the Messiah. A less well-known pattern concerns the place of the Baptist in relation to Jesus which is indicated five times, in chapters 3, 11, 14, 17 and 21. In addition to these we find two ten-fold patterns: the ten formal announcements of the fulfilment of prophecy (1:22; 2:15,17,23; 4:14; 8:17; 12:17; 13:35; 21:4; 27:9) and ten passages dealing with the sonship of Jesus (3:17; 4:1-11; 8:29; 11:25-27; 14:33; 16:16; 17:5; 26:63; 27:43: 27:54).Granted the general synoptic hypothesis that Matthew is a reworking of the Gospel of Mark plus other sources, and the thesis of Stendahl concerning the formation of Matthew, it seems most unlikely that such patterns are random or accidental. They are not, however, chronologically equivalent, for they intersect each other in a manner which suggests some development in time. I will endeavour by means of a more detailed examination of this phenomenon to uncover that earlier stratum which has been the goal of our enquiry.

(a) The Prophecies

The ten 'fulfilled prophecies' in Matthew are striking in three respects: they all follow a nearly identical introductory formula; they are unique to Matthew; and they differ noticeably from other quotations from scripture in the gospel, even when these are taken themselves as a fulfilment of scripture. Alongside this observation we note the further significant fact that all but two of the non-formulaic references to fulfilled prophecy are quotations from or obvious developments of the Markan original (3:3; 11:10; 13:14; 15:7; 21:13; 21:42; 22:43; 26:31; 26:54,56). The two exceptions are, firstly, the words given to the wise men in 2:5 ('They told him, "In Bethlehem of Judea; for so it is written by the prophet ..."'), and 21:16, a quotation from Psalm 8:2. A further significance in respect of the formula quotations is the fact that the greatest density of them occurs in the birth narratives in chapters 1 and 2, where they are integral to the stories which are recounted. Stendahl (1967, p.204) is worth quoting in this connection. He writes that 'the formula quotations ... are of two kinds: (a) The quotations in the Nativity Story, where the whole context seems to be constructed with the quotation as its nucleus - and as its germ from the point of view of growth. (b) The quotations added to Marcan material, of which he further observes that they 'do not give the impression of having been picked up from a source which happened to contain a suitable quotation; ... the Marcan text was the starting-point of the quotation.' Now given the striking difference between the two sets of fulfilled prophecies, one of which is almost wholly Markan in origin, the other unique to Matthew, and given the integral connection between the formula set and the birth narratives, a rather attractive hypothesis presents itself. Might we not conclude that the earlier edition of Matthew lacked the story of the virgin birth and the flight to Egypt, and the associated collection of ten formula quotations? If this were so, one of the two non-Markan, non-formula quotations (that in 2:5) would also disappear, leaving us with a set of ten fulfilments of prophecy only one of which was not rooted in the Gospel of Mark from which Matthew constructed his story. The introduction of the extra fulfilment may then be easily explained as a necessary addition to complete the ten.

(b) The Baptism of Jesus

We can treat this hypothesis in relation to the text which we have before us.
We note first that the Gospel begins with a genealogy proving the descent of Jesus from Abraham (the reference to Mary in 1:16 presumably belongs to the secondary birth narrative). This list is carefully enumerated as three sets of fourteen generations - a concern for number and structure which we already know to be inherent in Matthew. The genealogy forms a prologue to the main story, which begins with the appearance of John in 3:1. The abruptness of John's emergence on the scene is remarked upon by many commentators, and may be contrasted with Luke's account where the gap (presumably of several decades) between the birth of Jesus and the coming of John is filled by a bridging narrative. This implies that the infancy stories are more integral to Luke. By contrast Matthew's narrative when shorn of the later nativity story follows the form of Mark rather closely, launching straight into the events which started off the ministry of Jesus and within which are to be found its significance. This close juxtaposing of John with the prologue reveals immediately the significance of the denunciation of the Pharisees and Sadducees as false children of Abraham (3:7-10): we already know that Jesus is the true son of Abraham. We noted above the existence of a significant inclusio between Jesus, Abraham and the 'brood of vipers' in chapter 3 on the one hand, and Jesus, Moses and 'you serpents, you brood of vipers' in chapter 23. This is now seen to be part of the essential structure of the Gospel. The connection with Abraham has a further important part to play. I have elsewhere (Hunter, 1986:2, pp.17f) argued for the theological centrality of Genesis 15:6 in the Abraham traditions - a significance which was certainly picked up by Paul in Romans 4 and Galatians 3. (It might not be unreasonable to suggest that it is significant that such a discussion should be found in Galatians, given the importance of Chapter 2 of that letter in our opening section.) The key term in this confession is 'righteousness', a Hebrew concept which is regularly rendered by the Greek word dikaiosune. While not explicitly used in Matthew 4:1-11, it is clear that the testing of Jesus is designed to prove him a 'righteous' son of God. The term is important in Jesus's first great discourse (5:6,10,20; 6:33) where the terms of the 'new Torah' are discussed, and it forms a keynote of the final discourse, both in the harangue against the Pharisees (23:28,29, 35) and in the picture of the final judgment in 25:31-46, especially vv.37,46. These observations enable us to make sense of the brief dialogue between John and Jesus in 3:14-15, which many commentators find singularly (and needlessly) obscure. It is there emphatically not to cover any hypothetical embarrassment Matthew felt at John's having baptised his superior, the (sinless) Messiah. (If it were a matter of embarrassment, why would Matthew have significantly strengthened the form of the verb in v.13, altering Mark's 'came ... and was baptised' to the emphatic 'came ... to be baptised'?) Rather it is a precursor of the temptations in 4.1-11. John, like Satan, tries to deflect Jesus from his proper course, and

with a very similar argument: 'You are much too important to be subject to the normal laws of God; you are above such controls'. It is Jesus's answer which reveals the purpose of the conversation: his response to John is to insist on being baptised immediately. The Greek, aphes arti, conveys a sense of urgency (not, as is often implied, the idea of postponing a valid objection for the sake of outward formality) and should probably be read 'let me go [to baptism] now' in preference to 'let it be so now' (compare the use of the same verb a few words later: tote aphiesin auton, 'then he let him'). And the reason for Jesus's desire for baptism is that through it he will be seen to have fulfilled the demands of precisely that righteousness, that dikaiosune, which the son of Abraham must possess. It is in consequence of this decision that the son of Abraham is then acknowledged by God as his son, and the stage is set for the Gospel of Jesus the Messiah, the son who by his absolute faithfulness to Torah and his complete love of his fellow human beings satisfies exactly the conditions which were expected of the Messiah, and is therefore rightly to be seen as the harbinger of the kingdom of heaven which is to replace the failed kingdoms of the world. It is this gospel which Matthew presents, and in which we can glimpse that Jesus who was later obscured by the Graeco-Roman deity we now know as 'Christ'. That very title, though formally merely the Greek translation of the Hebrew title 'Messiah', is symptomatic of the change of essence which occurred with the hellenisation of Christianity. To call Jesus 'Christ' is to imply his divinity. To speak of him as 'Messiah' keeps the door open to a more human conception of the teacher whose story we repeat.

(c) The 'John' Structure

If the Gospel of Matthew can be understood in terms of a presentation of the story of Jesus as rooted in the event of John, we can go further and identify a structure built round this starting point. As part of this structure we will show how the theme of the son of God continues to be discussed, and how an earlier collection of discourses on the theme of the kingdom has been absorbed into it. This section is admittedly somewhat sketchy; it consists essentially of a proposal for reconstructing the hidden 'gospel of Jesus the Jew' which was spoken of at the beginning of this essay.

The person of John the Baptist recurs or is referred to four times in Matthew after the opening chapters: in 11:1-9, 14:1-12, 17:1-13 (the last verse in parlticular), and in 21:18-32. Including chapter 3, the specific topics dealt with are, respectively, John's Baptism, his identity as Elijah, his death and rumoured resurrection, his identity as Elijah, and his Baptism - a clearly chiastic structure which is typical of the Gospel (Fenton, 1963, pp.15f). The five 'movements' of the drama of Jesus which are thus defined can be broadly presented as having a mirror-significance in relation to John; thus:

I 3:1-10:42 BAPTISM

Jesus's mission is begun as a result of his commissioning through John's baptism (3:1-17).
The disciples are commissioned by Jesus (10:1-42).

II 11:1-13:58 ELIJAH

John is clearly revealed as the reincarnation of Elijah (11:1-19).
Jesus the prophet is rejected by his own people (cf Elijah after the contest on Mount Carmel) (13:53-58).

III 14:1-16:28 DEATH & RESURRECTION

The resurrection of the dead John is falsely rumoured (14:1-12).
The death of Jesus (which will lead to his resurrection) is announced (16:21-28).

IV 17:1-21:17 ELIJAH

Elijah (=John) and Moses revealed with Jesus (17:1-13).
The prophet Jesus, rejected in Nazareth, is welcomed in Jerusalem, acclaimed by the crowds (21:1-17).

V 21:18-27:54 BAPTISM

John's authority to baptise used in debate with the temple authorities (21:18-32).
Jesus's baptism of death reveals his authority (27:51-54).

The more familiar fivefold structure of the discourse is subsumed within this pattern. The indications are that it was separate and earlier, since the formulae which mark the end of each discourse are not significantly distributed in the 'John' structure. The first two of these discourses are in our section I, the others in II, IV and V. What seems likely is that these five represent a set of church/synagogue teachings under the general heading of 'The Torah of the Kingdom of Heaven'. They are, specifically: The Law of the Kingdom (5-7); The Proclamation of the Kingdom (10); The Nature of the Kingdom (13); The Heirs to the Kingdom (18); and The Coming of the Kingdom (24-25). That they come from the 'Matthew school' is certain - they have limited sources in Mark, but have been greatly elaborated by Matthew, and we might guess that at one stage the community in Antioch used them along with the earlier Gospel. That they are all primarily addressed to the disciples is not without significance, if we follow Stendahl's suggestion that the 'School of Matthew' was above all concerned to produce 'a handbook and a storehouse for teaching, preaching and church government' (1967, p.206).

(d) The 'Son of God' Theme

It cannot be denied that the idea of Jesus as 'son of God' is a key to the early Christian understanding of his mission. What I have argued already indicates my position on how that title was to be interpreted in the earliest stages, and indeed down to the time when the first real Gospel of Matthew was published (presumably in the late first century). There are ten passages in which the subject is dealt with in Matthew, and it is noteworthy that they are distributed in a manner which correlates very precisely with the five-fold 'John' structure. The first three, in Section I, and the last three, in Section V, are closely connected:

> 3:17, the first acknowledgement by God, and 27:54, the final recognition by the centurion and the guards at the cross.
>
> The devil's provocative use of the title in 4:3,6 is repeated in the high priest's challenge in 26:63.
>
> The madmen's mockery in 8:29 anticipates the mockery of the chief priests and elders in 27:43.

In Section II we find a brief meditation on the fact that recognising the relationship between Jesus and God is a matter of revelation (11:25-27), and in Section IV this is repeated in dramatic terms in the transfiguration (17:1-8). This latter passage by quoting exactly the words of God to Jesus in 3:17 with the addition of 'listen to him' advances the idea of the faithful son with which the gospel began by reminding us that Jesus, as the supreme representative of the new Torah, is the true successor of Moses whose teaching and life both demand our acceptance (unlike the 'Pharisees' of 23:2-3). Finally in Section III, the pivotal section of the Gospel in which the messiahship of Jesus is openly acknowledged, there is an echo of the centurion's words in 14:33, when Peter's lack of trust leads to a recognition by others of Jesus's significance (the English translation 'worshipped' for prosekunesan is question-begging, depending on an unspoken assumption about the significance of the 'son of God' title: it may well refer simply to that act of recognition which is indicated by bending the knee). This prepares us for the mirror passage in which Peter finally does himself take the step of faith which leads to his being confirmed as the rock of the church (16:16).

CONCLUSION

What this analysis shows is that throughout Matthew's gospel there is a double concern to demonstrate the true sonship of Jesus and to reject any exaggerated claim which that title might lead to: to aver that Jesus is the true Messiah, and to deny that he claimed equality with God; to assert his uniqueness and his authority for the church, but to deny that he in any way had broken or rejected the foundation of Torah on which that church, just as much as the synagogue, was built; to present, in short, the Gospel of Jesus the Jew, the Messiah of Israel. Not all Jews accepted that claim. But at least it was a claim that they could understand, and it is a context for dialogue which perhaps opens the door a little. And if our corollary that the reason for the writing of Matthew's Gospel lay in the tense situation of the Christian community in Antioch is granted, we may further clear the ground by acknowledging that we who are Christian have grievously erred in too readily taking Matthew's rhetoric literally. Undoubtedly we are left with a cruel paradox: that the gospel which has most to offer by way of a genuinely Jewish perception of the man Jesus is at the same time the one which has most grievously damaged the Jews. We cannot rewrite these ancient texts, but if we can together understand them better we may perhaps be able to understand each other better too, and learn not to defend our modern prejudice on the ground of ancient error. For if Matthew was guilty of misjudgment in using the leading figures of a certain kind of Judaism as a code for his real targets, Christian Europe has compounded that error incalculably by fastening upon it as an excuse for the inexcusible. If our present discussion helps to discredit the excuse, and teaches us to look at our own faults rather than those of our supposed enemies, it will not be entirely worthless.

BIBLIOGRAPHY

W.F. Albright & C.S. Mann — Matthew (Anchor Bible) [NY: Doubleday, 1971]

W. Bauer — Orthodoxy and Heresy in Earliest Christianity (ET) [London: SCM, 1972]

J. Bowker — Jesus and the Pharisees [Cambridge Univ. Press, 1973]

R.E. Brown & J.P. Meier — Antioch and Rome [London, Geoffrey Chapman, 1983]

J.D.M. Derrett — 'Matthew 23:8-10 a Midrash on Isaiah 54:13 and Jeremiah 31:33-34' Biblica 62 (1981) pp.372-86

W.R. Farmer — The Synoptic Problem [Western North Carolina Press, 1976]

J.C. Fenton — St Matthew (Pelican New Testament Commentaries) [Harmondsworth, Middlesex, 1963]

F.V. Filson — Commentary on the Gospel According to Matthew [London: A & C Black, 1960]

D.E. Garland — The Intention of Matthew 23 [Leiden: Brill, 1979]

M.D. Goulder — Midrash and Lection in Matthew [London: SPCK, 1974]

A.G. Hunter — Christianity and Other Faiths in Britain [London: SCM, 1985]

'Rite of Passage', Christian Jewish Relations 19 (1986) pp.7-22

(2) 'Father Abraham', Journal for the Study of the Old Testament 35 (1986) pp.3-27

H. Maccoby — The Mythmaker: Paul and the Invention of Christianity, [London: Weidenfeld & Nicolson, 1986]

W.A. Meeks & R.L. Wilken — Jews and Christians in Antioch, [Chico, California: Scholars Press, 1978]

J.A.T. Robinson — Redating the New Testament [London: SCM 1976]

E.P. Sanders — Paul and Palestinian Judaism [London: SCM, 1977]

(ed) — Jewish and Christian Self-definition (2 volumes) [London: SCM, 1980, 1981]

Emil Schürer — The History of the Jewish People in the Age of Jesus Christ (Revised and Edited by G. Vermes et al). [Edinburgh: T & T Clark, 1986]

E. Schweizer — The Good News ACcording to Matthew (ET) [London: SPCK, 1976]

K. Stendahl — The School of St. Matthew [Lund: C.W.K. Gleerup, 1967[2]]

Geza Vermes — Jesus the Jew [London: Collins/ Fontana, 1976]

The Gospel of Jesus the Jew [Riddell Memorial Lectures, University of Newcastle Upon Tyne, 1981]

D.S. Wallace-Hadrill — Christian Antioch [Cambridge Univ. Press, 1982]

ANTI-SEMITISM IN THE GRECO-ROMAN PAGAN WORLD

Robert J. Littman

University of Hawaii

The long history of anti-semitism in the west, the consistent persecution of Jews throughout Europe during the middle ages, and the anti-semitism of modern times resulted in the attempted genocide of the Jews by Hitler and the German people during the Second World War. Consequently, the study of anti-semitism has become a topic of vital importance, not just on an academic level of morality and history, but also on the very issue of survival of Israel and the Jewish people. We have the belief that if we can understand the nature of anti-semitism and its causes, then perhaps we can do something to combat it, and to mitigate its effects. To understand any phenomenon, we must understand its origins. Modern anti-semitism is a product of a Christian Roman Empire, and to understand why the Christian Roman Empire was anti-semitic, we must investigate two areas: first, anti-semitism in the pagan Greco-Roman world; and second, anti-semitism in the early Christian religion, both before it became the official religion of Rome and after. This paper confines its scope to the first part of that question, the nature of pagan anti-semitism,[1] and leaves it to other papers in this conference to deal with early Christian anti-semitism.

Our western world is a direct descendant of the Greco-Roman civilization. By the second century C.E. the Roman empire extended politically as far as England in the west, in the north into German to the Danube, to the south to North Africa and Egypt, and in the east as far as Arabia, Syria and Babylon. The Romans in the western part of the Empire imposed the Latin language and culture, and in the east the Greek language as well. Our modern western world is the heir to the classical tradition. All our genres of literature derive from the Greeks and Romans, our medical theory until the 19th century was based on Hippocrates and Galen, our western philosophical systems based on Plato and Aristotle. The Latin language remained the lingua franca of Europe until the 18th century. Our art and science directly descend from the Greeks and Romans. The dominant religion of the west, Christianity, was the official religion of the Roman Empire after the fourth century. Western civilization can be said to be a Greco-Roman civilization.

The second major influence on our heritage is the Near Eastern tradition. Two lines of influence are present. One is the early and direct influence of Egyptian, Mesopotamian and other near eastern traditions on Greek culture, which include the origin of literature, the alphabet, coinage, beginnings of astronomy and technology. The other is the Judeo-Christian tradition. By the fourth century C.E. Christianity had moved from a position of a persecuted religion to toleration by the Edict of Milan in 313 C.E. With the conversion of Constantine, Christianity shortly was to become the official religion of Rome.

Anti-semitism existed in both the Greek and Roman world. Salo Baron commented, "Almost every note in the cacaphony of medieval and modern anti-Semitism was sounded by the chorus of ancient writers."[2] A major cause of that anti-semitism was the nature of the social structure of those societies. Greek city states were autonomous political institutions composed of citizens, foreign residents, and slaves. Unlike our modern society, citizenship could be achieved only through birth from two, or in some cases, one citizen parent. Jews and other foreigners were consided resident aliens. Consequently, Jews remained non-citizens in the Greek cities where they dwelt. Furthermore, even had they been offered the opportunity to gain citizenship, they would not have accepted, for citizenship meant the acceptance and worship of the gods of the city, which was anathema to the Jews. In the early Roman empire, the Jew had similar problems, though citizenship was less restricted in that society.

Christian anti-semitism adopted the anti-semitism of the Greco-Roman world, but it had two additional important motivating factors. The first was the rivalry with Judaism as a competing religion. The second, inextricably linked with the first, was a theological anti-semitism, begun by Paul.

Greco-Roman anti-semitism had as its basic cause xenophobia toward the Jews. A general xenophobia existed in the society, but attitudes toward the Jews were more extreme because of the Jewish refusal to assimilate to Greek and Roman cultures. This manifested itself in the Jews' adamant refusal to worship the tutelary gods of the city or state because of their monotheistic beliefs. Each city had its tutelary gods, and rulers, particularly in the Near East, were worshipped as divine. The entire Hellenistic society viewed Jews with suspicion because of this refusal. In Rome they fared slightly better, but as the Empire adopted the divine ruler status for past emperors, their refusal to join in these rites, fostered increasing hostility and suspicion.

The Jewish dietary laws and circumcision increased the wall of separation. Other groups in the Greek city states and Roman empire did not resist and were gradually absorbed.

The dislike of Jews and Jewish practices were vastly increased in the first century C.E. for several reasons:
(1) Throughout the first century C.E. the unruly and rebellious province of Judea was a constant source of irritation to Rome. This disaffection of the province culminated in the Jewish revolt 66-70 C.E.
(2) The spread of the diaspora in the first century C.E. through voluntary emigration from Israel, the dumping of Jewish slaves on the slave market after the revolt in Judea, and through extensive proselytism, increased the exposure of the Romans to Jews and thereby increased anti-semitism as Jews continued to refuse to assimilate. Proselytism increased dramatically in the first century C.E. and was a further source of resentment. Further, in the first century C.E. Rome was successful in absorbing many foreign elements culturally and politically into its empire, and the failure to absorb Jews was therefore all the more obvious.

Before we look at anti-semitism in the Greco-Roman world, a brief survey of the Jews and the Jewish diaspora is necessary, though anti-semitism is not always linked to an existing Jewish population. For example, England was without Jews from the expulsion by King Edward I in 1290 C.E. to the restoration of the Jews under Cromwell in the 17th century, and yet anti-semitism was pervasive in English literature and thought during this period.

The Jewish people settled as an independent people in Palestine, with their capital in Jerusalem, in the last part of the second millennium B.C.E. They formed a monarchy, which lasted until the middle of the first millennium, though at times they came under foreign control. Judea continued as a quasi-independent kingdom until it became a Roman province in 6 C.E. Its real power came to an end, however, in 70 C.E. when the Roman general Titus destroyed Jerusalem to end the Jewish revolt from Rome. While the early monarchy was independent, after the capture of Jerusalem in 597/8 B.C.E. by the Babylonians, Judea came under increasing foreign domination. The Persians succeeded the Babylonians in the sixth century and politically dominated the region until they in turn were dispaced by Alexander the Great and his Macedonian Greeks in 333 B.C.E. After the death of Alexander in 323 B.C.E., control of the region fell to his generals, with Ptolemy controlling Egypt and Judea, while Seleucus grabbed the eastern part of the empire. Judea became a battleground for the Ptolemaic and Seleucid rulers, until in 168 B.C.E. a revolt by the Maccabees set up an independent kingdom, called the Hasmonean dynasty. In the late second century B.C.E. Rome extended her dominion into Asia Minor and Syria, and Judea became an independent kingdom under Roman protection. In 6 C.E. Rome annexed Judea as a Roman province under a procurator; this arrangement lasted until the Jewish revolt of 66-70 C.E. Thereafter legates governed the province and a legion was stationed there. Finally, a second revolt in 132 C.E. to 135 C.E. under Bar Kochba, was crushed. Jews were then forbidden to settle in Jerusalem; the city was rebuilt and renamed Aelia Capitolina.

By the time of the Jewish revolt in the first century C.E. the diaspora extended throughout the Mediterranean. It was so extensive at this time that there were perhaps 50,000 Jews settled in Rome itself, with 11 synagogues in the city, one named for Augustus.[3] Perhaps 10% of the whole Roman empire was Jewish, with perhaps 20% of the eastern half.[4]

The diaspora had begun in 586 B.C.E. when Nebuchadnessar conquered Jerusalem and transported many of the upper classes and nobility to Babylon. Though under Zerubbabel some returned in 528 B.C.E., after Babylon fell to the Persian Cyrus, many remained, and the the Jewish community there had flourished until the third century C.E. In the fifth and fourth century B.C.E. Jewish mercenaries settled at Elephantine in Egypt. After the conquest of Persia by Alexander, Jews settled throughout Alexander's empire, and were particularly attracted to Antioch, Rhodes, and to the new city of Alexandria in Egypt, where they were invited by the Ptolemies to settle.[5] The flourishing community at Rome was established in the middle of the second century B.C.E. The first century C.E. Jewish writer Philo[6] describes the diaspora, "Egypt, Phoenicia and Syria, Pamphylis, Cilicia, most of Asia as far as Bithynia, and remote corners of Pontus; and similarly in Europe, Thessaly, Boeotia, Macedonia, Aetolia, Attica, Argos, Corinth, and most of the Peloponnese. Islands also contain colonies, e.g. Euboea, Cyprus, Crete. I say nothing about the regions beyond the Euphrates." He fails to mention the Jewish settlements in southern France and Rome. Philo[7] comments on the widespread impact of the Jews, that while Romans reject foreign influence, "this is not so with ours. They attract and win the attention of all, of barbarians, of Greeks, of dwellers on the mainland and islands, of nations of the east and west, of Europe and Asia, of the whole inhabited world from end to end. For who has not shown his high respect for that sacred seventh day....That the sanctity of our legislation has been a source of wonder not only to the Jews but also to all other nations is clear both from the facts already mentioned and those which I proceed to state."[8] Josephus remarked "the masses have long since shown a keen desire to adopt our religious observances, and there is not one city, Greek or barbarian, nor a single nation, to which our custom of abstaining from work on the seventh day has not spread, and where the fasts and the lighting of lamps and many of our prophibitions in the matter of food are not observed."[9] This influence of Judaism is another indication of size and importance of the Jewish diaspora in the Roman Empire.

ATTITUDE OF GREEKS TO JEWS

While trade existed between Greece and ancient Palestine during the Minoan period, there appeared little Greek contact with Jews until Alexander the Great conquered the Persian empire. The earliest literary reference to Jews appears in the Athenian historian Herodotus in the fifth century B.C.E. He does not refer to the Jews by name, but rather to the Syrians of Palestine who practice circumcision.[10] The Hellenistic writers of the third and second centuries B.C.E., such as Theophrastus and Hermippus, viewed the Jews as a people of philosophers.[11]

The first major armed conflict between Jew and Greek was the Jewish revolt from the Seleucid Antiochus IV Epiphanes in 168 B.C.E. While the traditional view is that Antiochus enacted anti-semitic measures, such as a ban on the observation of the Torah and on circumcision, recent scholars[12] have argued that Antiochus was promulgating his measures at the behest of Hellenized Jews as a political move to attack the Hasidim who were leading the revolt. The Greco-Roman attitude to the Jewish practice of circumcision is evident in Antiochus' decrees. The prohibition of circumcision became a favorite way to strike out against Jews, as seen in the edicts of Hadrian after the Bar Kochba rebellion.[13] The Greeks and Romans believed that the body was the temple of the soul, and as such should not be mutilated. Circumcision was considered an extreme form of mutilation. In the Hellenistic period Jews who wished to assimilate, at times would undergo an operation to remove the marks of circumcision. Another indication of the hostility of the Greco-Roman world to circumcision was Paul's decision not to require circumcision for Christian proselytes, but that only a circumcision of the heart was required. Paul recognized that the Greco-Roman hostility to circumcision was hampering the spread of Christianity. Often around Jewish synagogues there grew up a group of "fellow travelers" who were not circumcized because of their reluctance to undergo the procedure, and thus they did not become full converts. The Jews of the Hellenistic period came into contact with Hellenism and under its influence adapted much of the Greek culture, and even in many places adopted Greek as their first language. In Alexandria this resulted in the translation of the Hebrew bible into Greek, known as the Septuagint. Even in the Jewish catacombs in Rome, we find Greek often the favored language of inscriptions. While Jews came to constitute a large portion of the city of Alexandria, as non-Greeks they remained non-citizens, although they had control of their own affairs as a self-governing organization called a <u>politeuma</u>.

In general, during the Hellenistic period anti-semitism was minimal, although Jews were always regarded as outsiders, and some resentment existed toward them because of their practice of circumcision and their monotheism, which prevented them from joining in the worship of the gods of the city and the acceptance of the divine status of the secular kings, so common in the Near East. Despite some universalist tendencies of Hellenism, Jews remained outsiders wherever they settled in the diaspora, neither permitted nor willing to assimilate completely into the culture of which they were a part. They were consequently regarded in the same way as any outside group, of which there were many--that is they were treated with a certain distance and a certain hostility.

With the emergence of Rome on the scene, the picture became more complicated. While Greek city states tended to expand like amoeba, dividing and forming new entities until they were spread throughout the Mediterranean--as Plato says, "like frogs sitting on the edge of a pond,"--the Romans from their earliest origins were expansionistic, but also assimilated all they came into contact with. Their pattern was similar throughout their history. They first would conquer a neighboring people, then make them a subject people, then give partial citizenship cives sine suffragio and finally give full citizenship. We can see this progression with the Romans' extending full citizenship first to the neighboring tribes they conquered near Rome, then to all Italy in the first century B.C.E. and finally to all the empire in the Edict of Caracalla in 212 C.E. Rome expanded into southern Italy and Sicily in the third century B.C.E. and into Greece and the Near East in the second century. With this expansion Rome encountered a greater variety of peoples than she had previously known, and their absorption and assimilation proved more difficult. We can see this even with the domination of the Latin language. In the European portion of the Empire, Latin was the dominant language, while in Greece and Asia Minor it never replaced Greek as the major language of the area.

The Romans were successful in absorbing many religions and peoples, from Mithraism and Christianity to the peoples of Egypt. But Jews withstood this absorption. Jews refused to assimilate because they would not give up their monotheism, their dietary laws and circumcision. A major factor in anti-semitism was the unwillingness to assimilate, which was linked to what the Romans considered an arrogance. The Jews considered their religion and customs unique and superior to that of their neighbors.

The first and second centuries C.E. were the most crucial for attitudes toward Jews for several reasons. In this period we find the spread of the diaspora and its growth through emigrations from Palestine, reproduction and proselytism. Rome consolidated its position in Judea with annexation in 6 C.E. The crushing of the Jewish revolt, which lasted from 66-70 C.E., with the destruction of the Temple at Jerusalem, devastated the political and military power of the Jews of Palestine, and cemented Roman control. The unsuccessful Bar Kochba revolt in the second century was the final blow to Jewish influence in Palestine until the 20th century. The emergence of Christianity in this period became another factor.

Let us turn to the Jews of Alexandria in the first century C.E. and to the anti-semitic writings of Apion. While the anti-semitic outbursts at Alexandria during the first century C.E. were not typical of the Roman empire, the writing of Apion and the anti-semitic attitudes of Alexandria probably influenced the early Church one of whose centers was in Egypt.

The Jews at Alexandria, as was the case in most Hellenistic Greek cities, formed their own politeuma. In 38 C.E. anti-semitic rioting broke out in Alexandria. According to Philo (Against Flaccus) the anti-semites persuaded the Roman governor Flaccus to attack the civil position of Jews. Synagogues were seized. Jews were declared aliens and strangers and were resettled into one section of the city. Paralleling these civil actions, anti-semitic political clubs, possibly with Flaccus' support, attacked Jews and Jewish property with pillaging, torture and murder. After several months of rioting, Flaccus was arrested and taken to Rome for trial. The Jews and Greeks of Alexandria both sent delegates. Before the issue could be resolved, the emperor Caligula was deposed and killed and Claudius succeeded him. In a famous letter that survives[14], he ordered the Alexandrians to behave gently and kindly toward the Jews and not to dishonor any of their customs in the worship of Jewish privileges granted by Augustus, but refused them citizenship. He warned the Jews not to look for anything further, and not to invite to Alexandria other Jews from Syria and Egypt.

The rioting was caused by a combination of political reasons and hostility of Greeks against Jews. It was symptomatic of anti-semitism that continued in Alexandria into the second century C.E. In 66 C.E. there were anti-semitic outbreaks of violence, probably prompted by Jewish revolt in Palestine, not only in Alexandria but also in Antioch, Damascus and in Syria. In 115 C.E. matters came to head when the Jews of Cyrenaica in Egypt attacked Greeks and Romans in the city. This violence spread to rebellion against Rome in Alexandria and in most of Egypt and Cyprus. This revolt was suppressed by 118 C.E. and the Jews excluded from Cyprus. Their influence and power were also broken in Cyrenaica and Alexandria.

In an important anti-semitic work from this period, the Acts of the Alexandrian Martyrs, Isodorus[15]--an anti-Jewish, anti-Roman Greek--argued that Jews should not be given citizenship. The tenor of the Acts is anti-semitic as well as anti-Roman. The fact that the Acts were still copied in the third century C.E. indicates the persistence of these attitudes, even with a greatly diminished Jewish presence in Alexandria.

Josephus[16] added more information about the hatred of the Alexandrian Greeks toward Jews. In reference to 66 C.E. after the Roman troops pulled back on orders from their general, "but the Alexandrian populace in the intensity of their hate, were not easily called off and were with difficulty torn from the corpses."

The most prominent calumniator of the Jews at Alexandria was Apion, who lived in the first half of the first century C.E.[17] Apion was a Greek writer from Egypt and was well-known as a Homeric scholar and author of a history of Egypt. He lived and wrote in Rome and travelled throughout Greece. A naturalized citizen of Alexandria, he represented the Greeks of Alexandria in their embassy to Rome in 38 C.E., while the Jew Philo represented the Jews.[18] Apion is reputed to have written a work "Against the Jews."[19] Apion apparently was an influential figure, possibly the head of the Library of Alexandria, and a popular writer; because of this status he became a target for Josephus. Josephus countered Apion's arguments on the civic status of Jews in Alexandria and his slanders about Jewish religious practices and the role of Jews in Egypt. Apion attacked Jewish practices of circumcision and refusal to eat pork. This became a favorite theme by many future writers. Apion also repeated the the tale of a golden head of an ass in the Holy of Holies at the temple in Jerusalem. Most outrageous was his account[20] that "They (Jews) would kidnap a Greek foreigner, fatten him up for a year, slay him, sacrifice his body with their customary ritual, partake of his flesh.... The remains of their victim were then thrown into a pit." Apion's slander seems to prefigure the medieval accusation of Jews taking the blood of Christian babies for the Passover.

Apion was an important figure in the anti-semitic attitudes of the Roman empire because his influence extended beyond Alexandria. As a well-known scholar, the pupil of Didymus and successor to Theon as the head of the Alexandrian school, his influence was enormous.

Roman authors of the first century B.C.E. and the first century C.E. best illustrate the attitudes and position of the Jews at this time.[21] The Roman orator, politician, and philosopher Cicero (106-43 B.C.E.) was very disparaging towards Jews in his two speeches, Pro Flacco and De Provinciis. In both works his motives for attacking Jews are to aid his case. He exposes other groups, the Mysians, Phrygians, Carians and Lydians to similar vituperations. Apparently Jews of Rome at this time (59 B.C.E.) were enlisted on the side of Cicero's enemies.[22] Cicero[23] remarks, "Each state, Laelius, has its own religious scruple, we have ours. Even while Jerusalem was standing and the Jews were at peace with us, the practice of their sacred rites was at variance with the glory of our empire, the dignity of our name, the customs of our ancestors. But now it is even more so, when that nation by its armed resistance has shown what it thinks of our rule; how dear it was to the immortal gods is shown by the fact that it has been conquered, let out for taxes, made a slave." While Stern[24] explains away these remarks of Cicero as politically motivated rather than as any real anti-semitic attitude, the issue is not what the inner feelings of any individual are, but rather public statements, writings and action that may influence public opinion and behavior.

Judea was indeed a rebellious province, difficult to govern. The various factions and sects, the Sadduccees, Pharisees, Idumeans, Samaritans and other groups were so contentious that even during the siege of Jerusalem by Rome, they were slaughtering one another. One means of attacking these rebellious Jews was to strike at the practices that differentiated them, and that they held so dear, such as circumcision. The attitudes toward the stiff-necked Jews of Judea were transferred to Jews of the diaspora. Roman writers and Greek writers of the Roman Empire tended to ridicule the Jews and look upon them with disfavor. One only has to look at the remarks of Rome's leading poets Horace, Juvenal and Martial. Jews in the Roman Empire fared well from legal standpoint, with equality of rights, self-government, and protection of the law, though they were not admitted to citizenship. While the practice of Judaism by Jews was permitted, proselytism was disapproved, and was a source of friction with the authorities. The Jews of Rome were expelled from the city in 139 B.C.E. and in 19 C.E. and in the reign of Claudius (41-54 C.E.) Domitian persecuted Jewish and Christian converts, and Antoninus Pius' ban on circumcision of gentiles was probably aimed at proselytes. Septimius Severus went one step further and banned conversion altogether.

Cicero called Judaism a barbara superstitio--"a barbaric superstition." Certain religious practices of Jews were held up to ridicule, especially circumcision, which became synonymous with Jew itself in such writers as Horace[25] and Persius,[26] Petronius[27], Juvenal and Martial.[28] Martial, for example talks of "lecheries of circumcised Jews,"[29] while Petronius remarks "He has only two faults.... He is circumcized and he snores."

The Roman satirists also ridiculed the sabbath, as well as abstention from pork. According to Philo[30] Caligula demanded to know of the Jewish delegation from Alexandria why they abstained from pork. While many scholars have asserted, based, on these satirists, that the Romans were anti-semitic, Gager[31] argues that since eccentricities such as these would be a target for satirists, it is a serious mistake to infer from these texts that individual authors or Roman literary circles harbored negative feelings about Judaism. Gager might be correct if the anti-semitic utterances were confined to these satirists. But if we look at all the material from the first century B.C.E. to the first C.E. we find that the remarks of the satirists form part of a general pattern of anti-semitic attitudes of the Romans toward Jews. Attitudes, however, were not generally transformed into anti-semitic actions, except at Alexandria and with the anti-Jewish riots in various diaspora cities, which were largely motivated by a fear and hostility to the Jewish revolt from Rome in 66 C.E.

To see a representive view of Jews in the first century C.E., we have only to look at the works of the Roman historian Tacitus, who was writing at the end of the first century C.E. and the beginning of the second. Tacitus prided himself on his objectivity. He says in the preface to his Annals that he is writing sine ira et studio, "without anger and partiality." Hence, when we come to his account of the Jews in Book 5 of his Histories, which is a preface to his treatment of the Jewish War, we can surmise that his attitudes reflected current Roman attitudes. Tacitus saw the Jews as a "strange religion, very different from the rest of mankind," and that "Among the Jews all things are profane that we hold sacred; on the other hand, they regard as permissible what seems to us immoral." Tacitus did not want to prohibit Jews from practicing their religion, but saw Jews as wicked, inclined to lust, who separated themselves from others by circumcision, and whose proselytes despised Roman gods and lost their feelings of patriotism to Rome--in short Jews were a <u>sceleratissima gens</u>--"a most wicked race."[32]

Another factor in anti-semitic attitudes was the rise of Jewish proselytism in the first century C.E. As we have noted, Jews were expelled from Rome for proselytism during the reign of Claudius. The remarks and attitude of Seneca--the Roman philosopher and tutor to Nero--dating to the middle of the first century, are of particular importance. Seneca's political position as advisor to Nero during the early part of his reign made the philosopher one of the most powerful men in the Empire. It would not be unreasonable to assume that his anti-Jewish attitudes influenced Nero and may have spilled over into anti-Christian prejudice that contributed to Nero's persecution of the Christians during his reign. Seneca, in general, was hostile to oriental religions. In the fragments of <u>De Superstitione</u>, probably written in the 60's C.E at the height of the Jewish proselytizing movement, he labeled Jewish practices as superstitions and attacked the observance of the sabbath and the lighting of sabbath lights. Seneca's position was discussed by St. Augustine: "Along with other superstitions of the civil theology Seneca also censures the sacred institutions of the Jews, especially the sabbath. He declares that their practice is inexpedient, because by introducing one day of rest in every seven they lose in idleness almost a seventh of their life, and by failing to act in times of urgency they often suffer loss....But when speaking of the Jews he says: Meanwhile the customs of this accursed race have gained such influence that they are now received throughout all the world. The vanquished have given laws to their victors."[33] Seneca's opinion on the sabbath lights are preserved:[34] "Precepts are commonly given as to how the gods should be worshipped. But let us forbid lamps to be lighted on the Sabbath, since the gods do not need light, neither do men take pleasure in soot." Seneca's writing on Jews and attitudes indicated both the size and importance of Judaism in the Empire, and reflected a general hostile attitude on the part of the Roman aristocracy and imperial household. Juvenal in Satire 14 talked of the son of a Roman citizen becoming a full convert to Judaism in language that suggested conversion was common.[35]

Thus in the first century attitudes were mixed. Jews comprised perhaps as much as 10% of the population of the Empire, with half the Jewish population in Palestine and the other half in the diaspora. Some of the Roman aristocracy was sympathetic, but the majority was hostile. Jews had a decent legal status, as good as any until the 20th century. Greco-Roman anti-semitism in the first century C.E. rose from many causes:
(1) the view of Jews as outsiders who refused to assimilate, and who practiced monotheism, which prevented them from worshipping the gods of the state. Their dietary laws and circumcision both separated themselves and offended the Romans as barbarous practices:
(2) the Jewish revolt in Judea and the difficulty of governing the factions in Judea, which fueled the general anti-semitism of the Romans;
(3) social and cultural hostility to Jewish practices and attitudes; and
(4) proselytism by the Jews.

The anti-semitic attitude of the Roman empire was a social-cultural anti-semitism rather than a religious one. Christianity was to adopt this social cultural anti-semitism and add a religious one to form Christian anti-semitism, which persists to this day.

Because of Paul, Christianity--which began as a sect of Judaism--rejected the dietary laws and circumcision of mainstream Judaism. This rejection may have contributed to their ability to win out over Judaism in the contest for proselytes. Christianity thus was more easily assimilated by Rome than Judaism, and managed to become the official religion of the Empire. As a sect that had diverged from Judaism and as a competitor to Judaism for proselytes, it was an enemy to Judaism. With this competition, it developed a theological anti-semitism--the Jews were denyers and killers of Christ. Christians took over the anti-semitic arguments of pagan Rome, and attacked circumcision and the dietary laws as a barbara superstitio. They combined these attacks into the full blown anti-semitism of the late Empire and Middle Ages. Jews henceforth suffered not just from anti-semitic attitudes, but also from a severe reduction of their legal and political rights. Thus Christian anti-semitism can be said to spring from two sources--the pagan anti-semitism of the Greco-Roman world, and the theological anti-semitism begun by Paul.

FOOTNOTES

1. Much has been written on ancient anti-semitism. The following are the most important works on the subject. For the primary sources the encyclopedic work of M. Stern, Greek and Latin Authors on Jews and Judaism (Jerusalem 1974-1984) 3 vols, contains most of the ancient texts on the subject in Greek and Latin with English translation and short commentary. The complete works of Josephus and Philo should also be consulted for primary material. For the papyrological material see V. Tcherikover, A. Fuks and M. Stern, Corpus Papyrorum Judaicarum 3 vols. (Cambridge, Masss 1957, 1960, and 1964) (hereafter CJP). For secondary material see several fine articles by Louis H. Feldman, "Anti-Semitism in the Ancient World," in History and Hate (ed. D. Berger) New York 1986, pp. 37-65; "Philosemitism among Ancient Intellectuals," Tradition 1 (1958-59) 27-39. Also, J.L.Daniel, "Anti-Semitism in the Hellenistic-Roman Period," Journal of Biblical Literature 98 (1979) 45-65; S. Davis, Race-Relations in Ancient Egypt: Greek, Egyptian, Hebrew, Roman (New York 1952); J.G. Gager, Moses in Greco-Roman Paganism (Nashville 1972) and The Origins of Anti-Semitism: Attitudes Toward Judaism in Pagan and Christian Antiquity (New York 1983). See also the monumental work of Jean Juster, Les Juifs dans l'Empire romain 2 vols (Paris 1913); J.N. Sevenster, The Roots of Pagan Anti-Semitism in the Ancient World (Leiden 1975); R.L.Wilken, "Judaism in Roman and Christian Society," Journal of Religion 47 (1967) 313-330; S.Zeitlin, "Anti-Semitism," Crozer Quarterly 22 (1945) 134-159. See the important work of M. Simon, Verus Israel. Etude sur les relations entre chrétiens et juifs dan l'empire romain (Paris 1964). See also V.Tcherikover, Hellenistic Civilization and the Jews (Philadelphia 1959).

2. S.W. Baron, A Social and Religious History of the Jews (New York 1952) I 194.

3. For the Jews of Rome in general see H.J.Leon, The Jews of Ancient Rome (Philadelphia 1960).

4. Baron (note 1 above) I 370-372.

5. Josephus Contra Apion i 22.

6. Legatio ad Gaium 281-2.

7. <u>Vita Moises</u> ii 20-25.

8. Philo <u>Vita Moises</u> ii 20-25.

9. <u>Contra Apion</u> ii 282.

10. Herodotus <u>Histories</u> II 104.3

11. See M. Hengel, <u>Hellenism and Judaism</u> (Philadelphia 1974) 255 ff. for the Hellenistic Greek writers see Stern (above note 1) ad loc.

12. V. Tcherikover, <u>Hellenistic Civilization and the Jews</u> (Philadelphia 1961) 175-203; E. Bickermann, <u>From Ezra to the Last of the Maccabees</u> (New York 1962) 93 ff.

13. It is uncertain whether Hadrian's ban on circumcision predated or post-dated the revolt. His edict forbidding castration certainly pre-dated it. Whether this was the legal basis for banning circumcison, or there was another decree is uncertain. The <u>Historia Augusta</u> (Aelius Spartianus <u>Hadrian</u> xiv 2) says Jews were not permitted to practice circumcision (quod vetabuntur mutilare genitalia).

14. <u>CPJ</u> n. 153.

15. <u>CPJ</u> II 156c pp. 78 ff.

16. <u>Jewish War</u> 2. 498.

17. Stern (above note 1) I, 389-415.

18. Josephus <u>Antiquities</u> 18.257ff.

19. Clement of Alexandria <u>Stromata</u> I, xxi 101.3. Stern I 389 suggests this is not a separate work but a portion of Apion's <u>History of Egypt</u>, either the 3rd or 4th book.

20. <u>Aegyptiaca</u> apud Josephus <u>Contra Apion</u> II 93-85.

21. Feldman, "Anti-Semitism in the Ancient World" (above note 1) p. 30, went through all the comments of ancient authors catalogued in Stern and found 18% were favorable, 59% neutral and 23% unfavorable. Since the survival of material from antiquity is uneven, these types of statistics are of little use. What is evident is that the major writers of Rome, when they mention Jews, do so unfavorably. Moreover, it is these major writers, like Cicero, who are read by medieval Europe, and therefore have the greatest influence.

22. See Stern (above note 1) I 193-195 and Leon (above note 2) 5 ff.

23. _Pro Flacco_ 28.69.

24. Stern (above note 1) I 194.

25. _Satires_ I 9.30.

26. _Satires_ i.5.184

27. Fr. 37.

28. see Stern (above note 1) I ad loc.

29. Martial 7.30.

30. _Embassy to Gaius_ 361.

31. Gager _The Origin of Antisemitism_ (above note 1) p. 57.

32. Tacitus _Histories_ 5.1-13.

33. _De Superstitione_ apud Augustinus _De Civitate Dei_ VI 11.

34. _Epistulae Morales_ xcv 47.

35. See Gager _The Origin of Antisemitism_ (above note 1), 59-62 for other examples.

ANTISEMITISM AND THE CHRISTIAN MYTH

Hyam Maccoby

Leo Baeck College
Sternberg Centre for Judaism,
Manor House,
80 East End Road,
London N3 2SY

INTRODUCTION

A distinction needs to be made between Christian theology and the Christian myth. Topics which appear not very important in the theology may be very important in the myth. The Christian creeds are expressions of theology, and they make little reference to the Jews, or to the figure of Judas Iscariot. But in the myth, the Jews (often typified as Judas Iscariot) are very important _dramatis personae_, acting the role of antagonists to Jesus, his betrayers, rejecters of his divinity, and unconscious performers of the divine sacrifice which brings salvation. Thus it is the narrative rather than the theological elements in Christianity that are responsible for the 'teaching of contempt'. These narrative elements are especially powerful for children, who, by contact with the basic Christian story, become deeply impressed with a negative and frightening image of the Jews.

Changes made in abstract formulations of theology, in relation to the Jews, are likely to be ineffective as long as the basic story continues to be impressed on the imaginations of children. When adults are told that the story has to be interpreted theologically in a sophisticated way in order to obviate hatred of the Jews (e.g. by regarding the Jews in the Gospels as symbolic representatives of human evil rather than as a guilty nation), such interpretation, in most cases, comes too late. In any case, such interpretation does not exonerate the Jews but only excuses them, and leaves them as paradigms of evil, rather than as a valid religious and cultural tradition. Thus theology which tries to act as a corrective to the narrative drive of a myth is always inadequate. The only real corrective is fundamental change in the myth itself.

Jewish-Christian dialogue must direct itself to this problem rather than to questions of theology. This is very difficult, as it involves what may be felt as an attack on basic Christian doctrine, rather than on misunderstanding of it. But without such an approach, the essence of the problem remains untouched, and Jewish-Christian dialogue is merely cosmetic.

THE MYTHIC ROLE OF THE JEWS IN CHRISTIANITY

If the Jewish rejection of Jesus were alone the key to Christian antisemitism (as some have argued), there would be no difference in quality between Christian and Muslim hostility to the Jews, since the Jews also rejected Muhammad. In fact, however, there is a great difference, in that Christian antisemitism has a mythic dimension lacking in the Muslim attitude to the Jews. Muslim hostility to the Jews has been, on the whole, until recent times, on the same level as

Muslim hostility to Christians. Though this has often led to violence and persecution, there has been no diabolization of the Jews in traditional Islamic thinking. In very recent times, to be sure, diabolization of the Jews has occurred in Islam for political reasons, but, significantly, with material drawn from Christian sources such as the blood-libel and the Protocols of the Elders of Zion, since Islamic tradition contains no such materials.

The diabolization of the Jews in Christendom arises not from Jewish rejection of Jesus but from the Jewish mythic role as the murderers, or rather deicides, of Jesus. Murder alone would not have produced this diabolization, for the judicial murder of Socrates by the Athenians, for example, had no such outcome; but the alleged judicial murder of Jesus by the Jews was combined with the deification of Jesus, so producing the mythic crime of deicide. Even this would not have produced the depth of loathing and metaphysical fear involved in antisemitism, were it not the death of Jesus was mythologised as a cosmic sacrifice, so that the Jews figure in the myth as the sacrificers of God. Though they do not intend his death as a sacrifice, but rather act from motives of malice, they bring about the necessary death that functions as salvific for members of the Christian Church.

The Jews thus figure in the central Christian myth of salvation in a role that can be paralleled elsewhere in mythology. A god who brings salvation by his death is often coupled with an evil power or god who brings about the necessary death: thus Osiris is killed by Set, Baal by Mot, Baldur by Loki. The figure of Judas, in the Gospels, has just this quality of fated evil; but Judas is the eponymous representative of the Jewish people, and has been so understood throughout the history of Christian antisemitism. Judas betrays Jesus because Satan 'enters' him (John 13:27), and Satan is the evil deity who strictly corresponds to Set, Mot or Loki. The Jews are his earthly acolytes, and are regarded as Satanic. The role of Satan as engineer of the death of the divine Sacrifice has no analogy in Judaism, and therefore the Christian Satan is a new creation of Christian mythology, with analogies only in pagan sacrificial myths.

Mythology often has its roots in ritual, and we may ask: What was the ritual in which myths of the slaying of a good god by an evil god were grounded? The answer is to be found in rituals of human sacrifice. Where a human sacrifice is performed at times of great stress (especially at the foundation or threatened destruction of a city or tribe), the guilt of the deed of blood was often shifted to the figure of an Executioner, who was cursed and driven into the desert, but who retained some sanctity as the performer of the deed that saved the tribe. The story of Cain is a remnant of such a ritual. The Hebrew Bible, with its abhorrence of human sacrifice, has changed the sacrifice of Abel into plain murder; yet the immunity of Cain, together with other details, preserves the outline of the original story. When the Church Fathers identified the Jews with Cain and Jesus with Abel (Tertullian, Chrysostom, Aphrahat, Augustine), they sensed the sacrificial overtones of the Cain and Abel story.

The Jews perform the role of Sacred Executioner for Christian society, and this accounts for the strange mixture of loathing and awe that characterizes antisemitism. When the Executioner of the divine sacrifice is cursed and driven into the desert, the tribe washes its hands - like Pilate - of the responsibility for the murderous deed that has brought their salvation. Since the tribe depends utterly on the death of the victim for its salvation, it wants him to die. But this desire inspires great guilt, which is projected as hatred onto the person deputed to perform the sacrifice. The more the executioner is hated and cursed, the more the tribe feels absolved for the murder which, in reality, they have themselves arranged.

THE AFFINITIES OF THE CHRISTIAN MYTH: GNOSTICISM AND MYSTERY RELIGION

There is a strong drive in Christianity to derive all its doctrines from Judaism. In recent years this drive has manifested itself in attempts to prove the essential kinship between Christianity and the intertestamental literature, especially the Qumran writings and the Pseudepigrapha. These attempts have strangely by-passed the central element of violence in the Christian myth: no-one has even attempted to show that the Pseudepigrapha or Qumran writings contain the idea of the salvific death of a divine being. It has been argued that Christian dualism need not be traced to an immediate Hellenistic source, since the Jewish intertestamental writings (themselves affected by Hellenism) contain a similar dualism. But the basic narrative elements which go to make the Christian myth are nowhere present in the Jewish literature. Striking parallels to them, however, can be found in non-Jewish Hellenistic myth and literature. These parallels are to be found especially in Gnosticism and in the mystery cults. In the present paper, it is not necessary to go into the vexed question of the historical connections between Christianity and these Hellenistic forms of religion. The pendulum seems to have swung once more in the direction of affirming a pre-Christian date for the origins of Gnosticism (Quispel), and recent archaeological discoveries appear to confirm a pre-Christian concept of salvific death and resurrection in the cult of Attis and other mystery gods (Vermaaseren). Here it is not necessary to take sides on the question of historical origins, but rather to point to the essential affinity between mythological themes in Christianity and in Hellenism not shared by Judaism. Whether Christianity influenced these Hellenistic groups or the other way round is less important than to identify the narrative elements which they have in common, by which they share a religious identity different from that of Judaism.

Gnosticism In certain forms of Gnosticism, the Jews were regarded as the agents of a cosmic force for evil. Gnostic antisemitism may be seen, for example, in the document The Apocalypse of Adam. The characteristic myth of Gnostic antisemitism is that the world was created by an evil God, the Demiurge, who in giving the Torah to the Jews, made them his chosen people. Nevertheless, the true high God has transmitted the true gnosis through a line of initiates beginning with Seth. Characteristically, Gnostic antisemitism selects from the Hebrew Bible non-Jewish personalities, such as Seth, Enoch, Melchizedek, as the guardians and transmitters of a tradition of knowledge, or gnosis, which rivals and surpasses the Torah, and relegates the Jews to an inferior position as the acolytes of a false or inadequate God. Because of its Jewish content, drawn from the Hebrew Bible, Gnosticism is now regarded by many scholars as Jewish in origin. A better understanding may be that Gnostic antisemitism arose among groups on the fringes of Judaism, comprising prospective or lapsed converts to Judaism. These groups were fascinated by the Hebrew Bible and the claims of the Jews to chosenness, but reacted by turning the Jewish material on its head, so producing an antisemitic myth. A cultural rivalry and envy provide the motivation: an ambivalent love-hate relationship to Judaism led to a myth expressing the desire to supplant and usurp the Jewish position as the favourites of God, but coopted Jewish literature to create such a myth. Once fashioned, the myth acts as a vehicle for aggressive feelings towards the Jews and as a powerful agent of antisemitic propaganda, which without the myth's broad imaginative appeal would remain on an abstract level.

The Christian antisemitic myth shows many points of contact with that of Gnosticism. The Torah is not described as evil, but as limited. It was not given by an evil God, but by limited supernatural beings, angels (Galatians 3: 19-20, Acts 7:53), an idea totally opposed to Jewish tradition despite the efforts of some scholars to find it there. The world was not created by an evil God, but it has fallen under the rule of one, Satan, 'the prince of this world' (John 12:31). The Jews, by continuing to revere the Torah after its validity has ceased, have become the minions of Satan. Thus Christianity presents a moderate form of the dualism of the Gnostic myth, somewhat watered down, but still retaining the antisemitic picture, constructed out of biblical materials, of the Jews as the acolytes of a false God and a false gnosis.

In pursuing its programme of appropriating biblical materials to its own purposes, Gnosticism provided a rival or alternative tradition to that of Judaism; instead of the Jewish succession of prophets, an alternative was posited, a succession of lone voices, bearers of gnosis pointing to an other-worldly solution to the ills of this world. Christianity carried out this work of appropriation in a more thorough-going fashion. It took over the Jewish prophets themselves, as Christians or proto-Christians, aware in advance of the whole Christian sacrificial myth of salvation. Islam later carried out a similar usurpation of both Judaism and Christianity, representing the leading figures of the Jewish and Christian stories as having been proto-Muslims. This element of usurpation is a powerful source of antisemitism, as argued particularly by Rosemary Ruether, but it is not in itself an ingredient in the myth, but rather an outcome of the fact that the myth is constructed out of Jewish materials. That this new construction is alien to the Jewish understanding of their own materials leads to its rejection by the Jews, who are thus put into the position of renegades and sinners against the light, instead of being the heroes of the story.

Yet the Gnostic supersessionary method of the alternative tradition is not entirely lacking in Christianity. The use of Melchizedek in the Epistle to the Hebrews, for example, is very reminiscent of the Gnostic method: Melchizedek is instanced in order to prove that there has always been an order of priesthood apart from, and superior to, the Jewish Aaronic priesthood. Paul even uses Abraham in the same way: i.e. not as an example of an Israelite hero who was a proto-Christian, but as a pre-Israelite who demonstrated the way of faith which would eventually supersede the era of the Torah (Galatians 3:6-9).

Mystery religion In the Gnostic myth, a succession of redeemer figures is pictured as descending into the world and sometimes suffering persecution at the hands of the Jews; but this is not a central feature, and the main aim of the redeemer is to impart gnosis, not to suffer a sacrificial death. Christianity, however, has given a central position to the element of violence. The redeemer figure of Gnosticism has been amalgamated with the redeemer figure of the mystery-cults, in which a dying-and-resurrected god brings immortality to his worshippers by his sacrificial death. This element introduces into Christianity a type of antisemitism that is even more virulent than that of the Gnostic sects.

The mystery-cults themselves were not antisemitic, since the figure of the Sacred Executioner in them was that of a rival god, and no human group was identified as his acolytes. The antisemitism of the Gnostic sects did identify the Jews, a recognizable human group, as the enemies of gnosis, but it was left to Christianity to deepen the guilt of the Jews by turning the redeemer into a unique sacrificial figure rather than one of a succession of bringers of gnosis. The uniqueness of Christianity lies precisely in this amalgamation of Gnosticism with mystery-religion to form an antisemitic myth of unparalleled potency.

The mystery-cults were not imbued with the cosmic dualism of gnosticism. There was no sense of despair about the evil of this world in the mystery-cults, which offered immortality not as an escape from damnation, but as a kind of bonus for those privileged to take part in the mysteries (though the Orphic mysteries should probably be regarded as an exception in containing an element of world-weariness). Moreover, the mystery-cults were local in their reference, each cult being indigenous to a particular area, Attis to Asia Minor, Adonis to Syria, Osiris to Egypt. Gnosticism, on the other hand, was a universal belief, providing a way of salvation and escape for all mankind, and speaking to the human condition itself. This universality (which necessarily lacked the historical dimension found in Jewish messianic universalism) gave the Jews an evil universality, as representatives of cosmic evil and enemies of the the universal solution to the human problem. This universality was taken into Christian antisemitism, with the extra dimension given by the concept of a unique redeemer who saved mankind not through gnosis but by his sacrificial death brought about by the powers of evil through the instrumentality of the Jews.

THE DEVELOPMENT OF THE CHRISTIAN ANTISEMITIC MYTH

By what steps was the Christian antisemitic myth established? Jesus himself and his earliest followers in the Jerusalem Church had no notion of it. They were practising Jews who were looking forward to a messianic age, or kingdom of God, in which the Jews would be the honoured priest-nation of the world, not cosmic villains. Jesus' death was not regarded either by him or his Jewish followers as a divine sacrifice to atone for the sins of the world.

The earliest appearance of the Christian myth is in the writings of Paul. Here we find the deification of Jesus, combined with the concept of his death as a cosmic sacrifice in which the powers of evil sought to overwhelm the power of good, but, against their will, only succeeded in bringing about a salvific event (I Corinthians 2:8). We find already in the writings of Paul the concept of the Jews as the unwitting agents of salvation, whose malice in bringing about the death of Jesus is turned to good because this the very thing needed for the salvation of sinful mankind. He says that the Jews 'are treated as God's enemies for your sake' (Romans 11:28), a phrase that sums up the role of the Jews in the Christian myth as the Black Christ who assumes the burden of guilt for the bloody deed without which there would be no salvation. True, Paul also says that at the end of time the Jews would be relieved of the burden of this role, and this has been taken to show a friendly attitude to the Jews incompatible with antisemitism; but far more practically important is that Paul marks out the Jews for the foreseeable future as a nation bearing the displeasure of God.

Paul describes the Jews as both malicious (I Thessalonians 2:15-16) and blind (Romans 11:8). The combination of malice and blindness is the exact analogue of the myth of Balder, in Norse mythology, in which malice is personified by the wicked god Loki and blindness by the blind god Hother, and both together bring about the salvific death which alone guarantees a good crop and salvation from death by famine.

Paul took the cosmic drama of good and evil from Gnosticism, and so took over also the dramatization of the Jews as the representatives of cosmic evil. But by combining the myth of Gnosticism with the myth of the mystery cults, he sharpened and intensified the antisemitism already present in Gnosticism. The Jews became not just the opponents of the figure descended from the world of light, but the performers of the cosmic sacrifice by which the heavenly visitant brings salvation. The Jews thus become identified as the dark figure which in myths of the deaths of gods causes the saving death - Set, Mot Loki; and the stage is set for the long career of the Jews in the Christian imagination as the people of the Devil. The elements which Paul took over from Judaism to embellish his non-Jewish myth - the religio-historical element which set the death of Jesus in a panorama of world history - gave his vision a grandeur far beyond the parochialism of other mystery-cults. At the same time, this only intensified the antisemitism, because there was now an aspect of usurpation, and an interest in blackening the Jewish record in order to justify the Christian take-over of Jewish sacred history.

The myth adumbrated by Paul was then brought into full imaginative life in the Gospels, written for the use of the Pauline Christian Church. A fully-rounded narrative of mythological dimensions is now elaborated on the basis of historical materials, which are adapted to provide a melodrama of good and evil. The powerful image of Judas Iscariot is created: a person fated and even designated by his victim, Jesus, to perform the evil deed, possessed by Satan and carrying out his evil role by compulsion, yet suffering the fate of the accursed - a perfect embodiment of the role of the Sacred Executioner, deputed to perform the deed of blood, yet execrated and loathed for performing it. While Judas performs the role on the personal level, the Jewish people performs it on the communal level: actuated by blindness and malice in alternation, callingfor Jesus' crucifixion in the climactic Barabbas scene and accepting responsibility for the sacrifice by saying, 'His blood be on us and on our children!' (Matthew 27:25). What in Paul's letters was just the outline of a myth has become definite and replete with narrative quality, an instrument for cultural indoctrination and the conveyor of indelible impressions to children and the unlearned. At the same time, certain incompatible features of the historical reality are deleted. Responsibility is removed from the Romans; their cruel, rapacious rule of Judaea is softened into a benevolent paternalism, their chief representative, Pontius Pilate, actually a bloodthirsty money-grubber, is represented as well-meaning and mild. The political aspects of Jesus' claim to messiahship are obliterated, and thus the sole responsibility for his death is laid at the door of the Jewish religious leaders. To this end fictitious religious conflict between Jesus and the Pharisees is introduced, and his conflict with the High Priest, which was actually political, is represented as religious. Jesus, by being made into an atoning sacrifice in a cosmic war between good and evil, has been removed from all political realities and from the actual circumstances of his death as a Jewish messiah-figure. The whole story, by being removed to the mythological level, has mythologised the Jews too.

In the subsequent history of the Church, the mythological role of the Jews as deicides and sacrificers of the incarnate God is elaborated and the Jews are further demonized. This process took several centuries to accomplish fully, for ordinary Christians tended at first to treat Jews as ordinary human beings with whom they could have normal social relations. Several councils of the Church forbade such social relations, and great Christian preachers such as St. John Chrysostom denounced all friendliness towards the Jews and built up the picture of the Jews as an accursed nation with whom no Christian should fraternise. Yet the Jews as they were placed more and more in the role of a pariah class in Christendom fulfilled a societalrole, just as they filled a necessary role in Christian mythology. This role was similar to that played in Hindu society by the Untouchables, except that the latter do the physical dirty work of society, while the Jews, in the Christian economy, do the moral dirty work, which is regarded as necessary, but unfit for Christians; it is therefore fortunate that there is a class of damned persons which is available to do this work. Thus the Jews were pushed into the activity of 'usury', forbidden by the Church, but actually essential to the economy. In many regions, the Jews were forced to provide the public executioner of condemned criminals; who better than the Jews, the performers of the necessary murder or execution of Jesus, to perform the official bloodshed of Christian society?

The performance of a necessary function, however hated and despised, was a kind of protection to the Jews. By being always present as the suffering culprits, paying endlessly for their murder of Jesus, they lifted the guilt of that murder from Christians, who by venting their moral indignation on the Jews could feel themselves to be accepted by Christ. Moreover the prophecy of Paul (Romans 11:25-6) gave rise to the belief that the Second Coming of Christ could occur only when the Jews became converted to Christianity; this belief saved groups of Jews from annihilation at times. At the time of the Second Coming, however, it was believed that the Jews would disappear, either by being absorbed into the Church as converts (a hope embodied in the Christian legend of the Wandering Jew), or (a more sinister alternative) by being annihilated in the wars of the Antichrist against the army of the returned Christ. The latter alternative was held by millenarian sects, and had respectable backing in Christian authoritative literature, but was frowned on by the official Church, on the whole, as it led to populist outbreaks that could turn against the Church itself and its temporal leaders.

At the time of the Second Coming, the Jews would no longer be necessary, because the sacrifice of Jesus would no longer be necessary. Christ Triumphant appears when the problem of human sin (which gave rise to the need for a divine sacrifice in the first place) has been finally conquered. When the suffering Jesus on the Cross is no longer needed, a demonic people acting as his accursed executioners is also no longer needed; they can disappear, either by conversion or by annihilation. At times of millenarian excitement, the method of annihilation was indeed tried; this was the aim of the mobs who carried out huge massacres of Jews at the time of the Crusades. Millenarian movements often contained the scenario that the Antichrist would be a Jew who would be hailed by the Jews as their Messiah, and would actually set up a Jewish Empire based on a rebuilt Temple in Jerusalem, but would be defeated by the armies of Christ, when the Jews would be annihilated to the last man. This scenario lies behind the secular, post-Christian movement of Hitler, in which Hitler himself took the role of Christ Triumphant, and in which many of the slogans of Christian millenarianism - including the expression 'the thousand-year Reich' - were employed. Post-Christian antisemitism can be thus be more dangerous to the Jews than Christian antisemitism itself, for in post-Christian antisemitism, the moral restraints of Christianity have disappeared, and the naked myth of the demonized Jew remains, in an atmosphere of populist millenarianism where the possibility of a pure, _Judenrein_ Utopia is envisaged.

Post-Christian antisemitism, whether of the right or of the left, derives its mythological themes and scenario from the Christian myth, even though the rationale for the demonization of the Jews has shifted to considerations of racialist or Marxist theory.

POPULAR AND OFFICIAL CHRISTIANITY

The distinction made in this paper between Christian theology and Christian mythology might be otherwise expressed as a distinction between 'official' and 'popular' Christianity. 'Official' Christianity, it may be argued, does not regard the Jews as cosmic villains, but as fallible human beings who reacted to Jesus in a humanly natural way, as any other people might have done in their place. Moreover, the extent to which the death of Jesus was a sacrificial one is subject to much discussion and debate in Christian theology. It would be conceded by most people, on the other hand, that 'popular' Christianity has interpreted the Gospel story in the way described above: as the story of the sacrificial atoning death of a divine figure done to death by evil forces of which the Jews were the human agents who thereby incurred a curse. 'Popular' Christianity, it might be conceded further, received far too much encouragement from official sources, in the mistaken belief that simple piety was thereby promoted: thus the Church encouraged Passion plays and ecclesiastical art which portrayed the Jews in a demonic light. The remedy does not lie in any radical revision of Christian doctrine or myth, but in the abandonment of the policy of toleration of 'popular' Christianity, and the inculcation of more sophisticated interpretations of the Gospel story.

This, however, is a facile solution that arises from a failure to understand the gravity of the problem. The alleged huge gap between 'official' and 'popular' Christianity requires explanation: how did it come about that the Gospel story has consistently produced a deep loathing of the Jews issuing in acts of violence and massacre? A story which has consistently produced such results needs to be assessed in the light of Jesus' saying, 'Ye shall know them by their fruits.' Moreover, the alleged gulf between 'official' and 'popular' Christianity is impossible to sustain in the light of historical facts. Many of the most fervent upholders of 'popular' Christianity have been canonised saints of the Church. Their view of the Jews as an accursed people did not prevent their canonisation and was not even taken into consideration as a negative factor.

It has to be recognised that a given story has its own narrative drive which resists attempts at re-interpretation. 'Do not trust the teller, trust the tale,' is an old principle of exegesis. The meaning of a story may be a matter of disagreement between different exegetists, but the experience of century after century during which a story has consistently produced the same impact must surely be regarded as decisive.

THE DEIFICATION OF JESUS

The factor that lifts the story of Jesus from history into myth is the deification of Jesus. The death of a human being may be a tragedy, but the death of a divine being can only be a cosmic mystery which can be interpreted only in terms of atonement and sacrifice. In _The Myth of God Incarnate_, a number of Christian theologians drew attention to the moral disadvantages of the deification of Jesus and called for the reversal of this as a disastrous error. Unfortunately, they failed to include the issue of antisemitism in their discussion. Antisemitism is in fact an outcome of the deification of Jesus. The opponents and killers of a god must themselves be given mythological status as devil-figures.

In the past, all versions of Christianity which denied or modified the divine status of Jesus (Ebionism, Pelagianism, Arianism, Socinianism, Unitarianism) led to the diminution or elimination of antisemitism. Those tendencies in present-day Christianity which stress the role of Jesus as a human teacher or prophet, rather than as a divine sacrifice, are the most hopeful for the elimination of Christian antisemitism. The more stress is laid on Jesus' life rather than on his death, the more the Jews will cease to be regarded as mystical figures of evil.

The study of the historical Jesus is most important in this context. Since the deification of Jesus lifted him out of the realm of politics, his messianic claim was divested of its political connotations and his conflict with the power of Rome was transformed into a conflict with Jewish religion. The affinity of Jesus' teaching to that of the Pharisees is now increasingly recognised, and the Jewishness of Jesus, established by comparison with the rabbinic writings, destroys the Gospel picture of conflict between Jesus and his Jewish religious contemporaries. At the same time, the hostility to Jesus shown by the High Priest, who was a political appointee of the Romans, can be understood in its historical context, without any demonising effect on the Jews as a whole.

The dismantling of the Christian antisemitic myth will also have a profound effect on post-Christian antisemitism. Post-Christians of every kind, whether of the left or of the right, or middle-of-the-road liberal agnosticism, are all more affected than they think by the Christian myth as it relates to the Jews, whom they have not yet succeeded as seeing as normal human beings, rather than as actors in a nightmare mythological drama.

Under the influence of Rudolf Bultmann, many Christians and post-Christians think of the Christian myth as having a reality and beauty transcending all historical enquiry. This attitude tends to put myth beyond the reach of criticism, and reinstitutes a kind of fundamentalism on the symbolic level. But myth is still subject to moral criticism; it is always imperative to ask, 'What are the moral effects of this particular myth?' Judged in this manner, the Christian myth, despite, or because of, its imaginative power as a drama of good and evil, cannot be adjudged a force for good, in that it has been directly responsible for the antisemitism that culminated in the Holocaust. The cry, 'Who killed Christ?' was heard at the time of Hitler's Holocaust and at every other massacre of Jews in Christendom: this is the reason that Hitler's massacre of the Jews met with silent acquiescence from the vast majority of his subjects.

BIBLIOGRAPHY AND REFERENCES

Bousset, Wilhelm, 'Antichrist'. In: Encyclopaedia of Religion and Ethics, John Hastings, ed., Edinburgh, 1908, vol.1, pp. 578-81.

Cohn, Norman, The Pursuit of the Millennium. London, 1957.

Davies, Alan T., ed., Antisemitism and the Foundations of Christianity. New York, 1979.

Gager, John C., The Origins of Anti-Semitism. New York, 1983.

Hick, John, ed., The Myth of God Incarnate. London, 1978.

Maccoby, Hyam, The Sacred Executioner. London, 1982.

Maccoby, Hyam, The Mythmaker. London, New York, 1986.

Quispel, G., 'Gnosticism'. In: Encyclopaedia of Religion, Mircea Eliade, ed., New York, 1987.

Ruether, Rosemary, Faith and Fratricide. New York, 1974.

Stroumsa, G., Another Seed: Studies in Sethian Gnosticism. Leiden, 1984.

Trachtenberg, Joshua, The Devil and the Jews. New York, 1966.

Vermaseren, M.J., Cybele and Attis: the Myth and the Cult. London, 1977.

THE HOLOCAUST AND CHRISTIAN THEOLOGY: A SPECTRUM OF VIEWS ON THE CRUCIFIXION AND THE RESURRECTION IN LIGHT OF THE HOLOCAUST

James F. Moore, Assistant Professor of Theology

Valparaiso University
Valparaiso, IN, USA

INTRODUCTION: DIALOGUE AND CHRISTOLOGY

The Holocaust is a deeply disturbing historical event. It is also a shattering theological challenge. Few serious Christian thinkers would challenge these two claims. Difference of opinion arises only on how extensive the disturbance is and how thorough the shattering. Following Irving Greenberg's lead, John Pawlikowski has argued that the Holocaust is an "orienting event" for theology.[1] That is to say, the Holocaust and whatever and all that it means becomes a standard by which all theological statements are to be judged. Of course, this means that Christology, the heart of Christian theology, must also be judged by the standard of the Holocaust.

This truism creates a series of related problems for the Christian theologian. First, in order to bring the Holocaust to bear on any theological statement implies that we can understand the implications of the Holocaust well enough to use the event as a standard. Claims to understanding are dubious especially given the view of Elie Wiesel recorded just 10 years ago that he had failed to communicate the message he aimed to bring.[2] Surely if the eye-witness can claim nothing but failure how can Christian theologians so deftly use the Holocaust as a measuring stick of their theological claims? Still we may be able to isolate certain key implications of the Holocaust as working standards of judgments at least on the authority of those who have long worked to study this event:

1. The Holocaust is a radically negative event meaning that this event reveals for us the nature of radical evil
2. The Holocaust is an indictment of naively optimistic views of human possibility
3. The Holocaust is an indictment of Christian anti-Judaism in all aspects that it appears

A second serious problem confronts the post-Holocaust Christian theologian, a problem that has plagued theology since at least the 18th century. There is a radical pluralism within Christianity that makes determination of precisely what Christology is difficult at best. When that pluralism is coupled with the negative standards of the Holocaust, the Christian theologian is confronted with a broken theological language that is only with difficulty used to supply a working view of "orthodox" Christology. To speak, then, already means that the theologian risks distortion, debate, and misunderstanding.

This second problem leads to a third that is crucial to this discussion. Christology is the central standard of Christian theology for most Christians. How does the theologian bring the radically negative standard of the Holocaust to bear on the radically positive claims of Christology? This third problem is, of course, the most crucial for Christian theology since in the balance lies the possibility not only of doing authentic Christian theology after Auschwitz but also whether there can be an authentic Christianity after Auschwitz. Of course, this is the most radical way that this challenge can be posed, but it is also the way that the centrality of this issue can be clearly shown.

This paper will address these three central problems by both reviewing the work already done by theologians who have given us a full spectrum of possible responses and by developing a constructive view of Christology sensitive to the problems as have been stated above. The focus of this investigation and proposal will be a theological interpretation of the Crucifixion and Resurrection of Jesus. Central to this effort, however, is the developing Jewish-Christian dialogue that not only has provided the necessary context for Christian theology after Auschwitz but has been fruitful in giving direction for a discussion, like ours, on Christology.

THE DIALOGUE AND ITS DEVELOPMENT

Jewish-Christian dialogue since the end of the second world war has achieved much in moving toward a relationship of mutual respect and benefit. Surely this achievement comes because of the efforts of a few in the early stages (especially in contexts like that of Seelisberg) of conversation. We can also claim that dialogue was enhanced immeasurably with the decree Nostre Aetate issued at the second Vatican Council in the mid-sixties. These events have opened the doors to a conversation both academic and general that signals a new era in Jewish-Christian relations. Still, it has only been within the last fifteen years that serious consideration of Christian theologies of redemption and christologies have become a focus for these dialogues.

A gathering of a number of important thinkers from both sides in New York in 1974 under the heading, "Auschwitz: Beginning of a New Era," marked the occasion for both Irving Greenberg and Elie Wiesel to issue their challenges for a new effort in examining issues. It was also the opportunity for Rosemary Ruether to offer her stunning thesis that anti-semitism is the left hand of christology.[3] Ruether's point was not just that theological statements through the centuries had fostered the cultural anti-semitism in the West but that the Christian scriptures particularly in their portrayal of the narratives of and about Jesus (the crucifixion and resurrection being central) are the source for western cultural anti-semitism. In fact, christology in its present form, by Ruether's thesis, could not help but be anti-semitic.

Ruether subsequently made these claims more thoroughly and forcefully in her book, Faith and Fratricide.[4] This radical critique of the heart of Christianity meant simply that any post-Holocaust christology would be markedly altered or it would continue to be anti-semitic. The challenge was obvious. Christians serious about dialogue must take up a quest of re-shaping christology if their authenticity as dialogue partners was to be upheld. Christology had to become a topic for dialogue at least from the perspective of Christians. Our task, then, is to examine what the options have been for such a re-shaping of christology. Four thinkers give us useful insight into that project -- A. Roy Eckardt, Juergen Moltmann, Rosemary Ruether, Paul van Buren.

THE ISSUE OF CHRISTOLOGY AS CENTRAL

No one has addressed these matters with more earnestness than A. Roy Eckardt. Eckardt's 1982 book Long Night's Journey into Day is an effort to do what he says others have found difficult, pose the difficult questions to the heart of Christian theology.[5] There can be little doubt, Eckardt argues, that the crucifixion and the resurrection have been the primary catapult toward anti-semitism in Christianity, the resurrection more than the crucifixion. Even more, later thinkers built on the foundation already there to create a christology that was fundamentally anti-Judaic. Christology is the central issue for Christians as we respond to the Holocaust.

Of course, christology is the central issue not only because Christians have for long formed anti-Judaic views built right out of Biblical teaching but also because the Holocaust challenges the very notions that Christians have for long associated with christology - messianic hope, transformation of life, intervention of God in history, the fundamental value of human life, the primacy of forgiveness, the truth of the revelation of God in Christ. Christians cannot respond adequately to the Holocaust without responding to Rosemary Ruether's claim that only a new christology can now work or to Irving Greenberg's argument that Christian claims are now forever tainted.[6] Christology is the central issue.

Finally, christology must be the central issue for Christians since christology is at the heart of Christian claims. John Pawlikowski argues that the one unique aspect of Christian witness is the claim of the incarnation.[7] If this is even nearly true, then to take away christology would be to take away Christianity. To make a "Christian" response, therefore, demands that christology be central despite the problems we will encounter which are detailed above.

A SPECTRUM OF VIEWS

Even if we focus attention on one area of Christian thought and then on one corner of that area (the crucifixion and the resurrection), we are still faced with a broad plurality of views that call themselves Christian. These views might all be sympathetic to the necessity of a response to the Holocaust and new Jewish-Christian relations and still differ quite widely on both the matter of what is christology and what adjustments must be made to respond to the Holocaust. Thus, only a spectrum of views can adequately portray the Christian response to the Holocaust.[8] This spectrum is also limited but can provide a basis for seeing possible new resolutions of old problems. Four major traditions of response can be highlighted: (1) the one who preserves the use of traditional language and traditional theological categories, (2) the one who focuses attention on preserving a Christian tradition that is adjusted to make room for Judaism in the theological arena, (3) the one who finds traditional language inadequate but is reluctant to suggest new theologies and new theological language, and (4) the one who offers radical changes in tradition in order to respond to the Holocaust.

Preserving Tradition

The Christian theologian who aims to preserve tradition as a response to the Holocaust sees traditional language as a resource for building new relations between Jews and Christians. Dorothy Soelle, for example, uses the traditional theology of the cross as a way of addressing the broad question of suffering and the form of suffering encountered in the Holocaust.[9] For Soelle, the cross must remain a redemptive symbol for Christians. Eckardt, for all of his arguments otherwise, stakes claim to a fairly traditional affirmation of the resurrection as the only hope we can affirm.[10] All this comes on the heels of his claim that the resurrection is a particularly problematic feature of Christian confession because of the long history of Christian anti-semitism growing out of resurrection theologies. Still, the important theological work of Juergen Moltmann remains the most obvious example of the theologian preserving tradition as a means for making response to the Holocaust.

Moltmann's major contribution to christology, <u>The Crucified God</u>,[11] represents not only the prime work of a major scholar but also a specific effort to take, with all seriousness, the Holocaust. Even such a harsh critic as Roy Eckardt allows that this work is an important contribution to the Christian response to the Holocaust. The work that Moltmann does is intentionally aware that the Holocaust must be a central consideration for any serious contemporary theologian.

The major structure of the work, however, remains thoroughly traditional in its language. Jesus is viewed as a unique figure to be understood as opposed by the ruling religious elite. The main opposition centered around the distinction between Jesus' gospel and "the Law". Jesus was an innocent victim of suspicious even egocentric leaders. All of these points are maintained as a necessary Christian reading of the Christ narrative. Moltmann's point is that God reveals himself most fully as the suffering God who persists in mercy even as he is rejected by his people. The problem with this structure is that Moltmann despite his claims to take seriously the Holocaust has fully disregarded the role that traditional Christian theology played in producing anti-semitism in the West. Each of the points of the Christ narrative described above is identifiable as specific (at least implicit) representation of what Jules Isaac called a "Teaching of Contempt."[12]

The issue at stake is whether traditional Christian language can provide a workable language (let alone a useful language) for post-Holocaust theology. If that traditional language simply repeats the same teaching that fed anti-semitism in the past, then the language becomes an abomination not only to Jews but also to Christians. Moltmann is concerned but his very stature makes his naivete about language all the more problematic. Many liberation theologians who have followed much of the lead of Moltmann have reproduced the teaching of contempt even in spite of the specific intent to form a theology for the oppressed.[13]

The problem extends in another direction. Even if Jesus could be seen as a representative of the oppressed (can we or do we want to say that?), then who is the oppressor? That very question creates a central ambiguity in Christian claims. If Jesus' death was redemptive (and Christians must contend that it was), then who is the enemy that Jesus' death gives salvation from? Certainly Moltmann's claim that in Jesus we meet the crucified God means that his theology places blame on the Jews primarily (even if we mean by that the Jewish leaders) who must be viewed as necessarily in opposition to God. Doesn't this simply repeat the charge of deicide?

But, of course, to the Jew this view opens the door to an ambiguity about the suffering of Jews in Auschwitz and elsewhere. Is God now on the side of the Jews? Is the Law now a valued part of God's plan? If so, what way does Jesus and his gospel give redemption to these who are oppressed? Moltmann is sensitive to be sure but he has created a christology that is unacceptable to the post Holocaust Jewish-Christian dialogue. Eckardt, on that matter, is correct.[14]

Though there may be some other ground by which traditional language can overcome this taint of the Teaching of Contempt, most of those who attempt a christology woven together with traditional language fall prey to the same difficulty, that traditional christological language places the Jews outside of the theological circle of redemption with only the possibility of being once again included if Christians can give them a place. The language is inherently a teaching of contempt which finally is broken on the idiocy of the Holocaust.

The Jews with a Given Place in God's Plan

Another approach to a Christian theology of Judaism is particularly represented by Paul van Buren.[15]Van Buren has created a general theology which begins with the premise that Jews have an integral place in God's plan that was in no way changed with the Christ event. While van Buren will use traditional christological language, he must, therefore, challenge some of that language which inherently excludes Jews from God's gracious activity after the resurrection. To do that requires a major re-ordering of the language of christology. The claim for the ultimacy of crucifixion as revelatory event must be tempered. God was not only in Christ but also in the covenant with Israel.

Such a theological position must conclude that there is no ultimate opposition between Jews and Christians, law and gospel. Each have a place in God's wider plan which simply expanded to include the Gentiles with the Christ event. Christianity is Judaism for the gentiles. Of course, Christianity is clearly not Judaism for anyone in the post-Pauline world, so even that claim must be modified to give Jews a unique place, their rightful place, in God's plan.

Van Buren's position is an effort to make Christianity theologically inclusive of the Jews and of course christology is a central part of that task. The gentile participation in Jewish hope for the future is completely dependent upon the Jew Jesus. Our way to hope is linked not only with Jesus but also his Jewishness. Therefore, the Christ event, far from ending the era of Judaism in favor of a new age, must necessarily continue that era in the way that Judaism continued to hope through the centuries. The link between Judaism and gentiles is a link of knowledge, awareness.

Van Buren's view holds much promise (as with others who have proposed this two-covenant position), but suffers from a basic problem. Christianity is not historically Judaism for the gentiles. Whatever might be said idealistically about what Christianity ought to be is tempered by what has been. If Jesus intended to bring Judaism to the gentiles - lead them to know the hope that Jews hope - then we must conclude that the experiment has been an abysmal failure. The gentile world has been with Christian assistance thoroughly anti-Judaic (a few scholars and saints excluded).

Of course, the failure might be seen as that of the followers of Jesus (God as always dependent on the observance of his people). Van Buren after all proposes a fresh start built on a claim about what is essential to Christian witness. But if Jesus had been successful, then in what way is Jesus different than the others who sought to bring Judaism back to its roots and others to recognize that hope. Christianity is not unique, only the historical moment is unique (with the charismatic character of Jesus). The crucifixion is not redemptive both in fact and in theology, only the intent of Jesus' teaching and Christian witness. The resurrection becomes mere symbol of hope. In short, we do not have Christianity or christology.

Van Buren's work is remarkable but the end result seems no more adequate to a Christian response to the Holocaust than that of Moltmann. Above all, Van Buren's approach seems to be ahistorical; he cannot thereby give an adequate theological account for the development of both Judaism and Christianity and, with that, the living nature of each religious confession. History may have said too much to allow us to recover the pristine past so easily.

A Language Left in Ambiguity

There are a number of theologians who would be less sanguine about the meaning of theological language post-Holocaust than either Moltmann or van Buren. Indeed, David Tracy argues in his recent book that all theological language is plagued by ambiguity as a condition of our post-modern world.[16] Even more, Tracy argues that the radical negativity of the Shoah leaves all claims to truth ambiguous, bearing divided, divergent even contradictory implications.

A. Roy Eckardt has shaped a theological response to the Holocaust that takes this claim seriously.[17] Even though, as we have already noted, Eckardt continues to use traditional language, he does so with unmistakable irony. The resurrection for Eckardt is an event that has become entirely anticipatory and, therefore, unfulfilled -- even the Jew Jesus sleeps with his brothers and sisters awaiting the future resurrection.[18] Eckardt's position suggests the view of many who would see theology operating after Auschwitz only on the unsure ground of "as if" -- we continue as if what we claim were true. This is a theology with little to be sure about but much to hope for. The abiding strength of this position is both the full realization of the negativity of the Holocaust but also the necessity of a re-affirmation of hope.

This position of ambiguity is profoundly unsettling to most who find living with ambiguity religiously threatening, but we may be faced with a generation that must endure such unsettling. Since this position has seemed to me to be the most adequate approach to a post-Holocaust theology, I will be seeking a means for translating ambiguity into a working Christian response to the Holocaust, especially in shaping a theology of the crucifixion and the resurrection.

RE-STRUCTURING THE TRADITION

Before suggesting a constructive position, however, we must take up those theologians who have suggested a radical re-structuring of the tradition as a way to respond to the Holocaust, most especially Rosemary Radford Ruether.[19] This type of response can take two forms -- a radical rejection of scripture that is anti-semitic and a rejection of basic theological tenets that would prevent rapprochement between Christianity and Judaism. The narratives recounting the crucifixion and resurrection of Jesus seem logical candidates for such radical re-thinking since much of the tradition behind the "teaching of contempt" stems from portions of those narratives from the gospels. And traditional theologies of the cross and resurrection would be rejected out of hand.

Ruether's position has always been more implicit than explicit regarding the second strategy but quite clear about the rejection of scripture that is anti-semitic. No scripture that teaches contempt of the Jews could hold authority for her theologically. Thus, Ruether's explicit rejection of all absolutist claims as a reification of history seems to imply a rejection of traditional resurrection theologies of a new age of the kingdom of God. Ruether has always argued rather that theology must take a position of proleptic hope and not of accomplished fulfillment. There could be no new age of the kingdom yet ushered in by Jesus' resurrection.

In like manner, Ruether has rejected the universal claim for Jesus' crucifixion as the saving event opting instead for only the paradigmatic nature of Jesus' life and death for his followers. The crucifixion not only need not but perhaps cannot in some occasions be the paradigm for salvation. Ruether would, thus, reject positions like that of Dorothy Soelle or Juergen Moltmann that hold to the universal salvific character of the crucifixion.

Though enticing, Ruether's view always seems like a road too easily adopted, too easily avoiding the history of the teaching of contempt as part of the Christian story now. We may finally be faced with a full re-structuring of our Christian theology; however we are too close to the event of the Shoah now to move so quickly to eradicate its causes or effects even if we could accurately name them.

A CONSTRUCTIVE POSITION

If I am not yet ready to follow Ruether's lead fully, I am thrust back to the unsettling position of ambiguity. Tracy has argued, however, that such acceptance of ambiguity into our theological language may provide a profoundly positive way to proceed.[20] Ambiguity introduces the character of the unknown and the uncertain back into our theologizing that may in the end be the best guard against theological fanaticism and absolutism. The recognition of obvious ambiguity also reduces us to a theological humility that may allow for the presence of competing claims, life styles, and religious ways of being and doing that need not be resolved into a single truth.

How would such a position be reflected in a Christian view of the crucifixion and resurrection? First, we could step back from the universal claim that knows God too well and makes God too easily accepting of suffering as salvific. There is great ambiguity in the crucifixion that bears as much of a negative claim as a positive claim. Rather than tragedy (the hero is not fatally flawed), this is irony - the one who would seek peace receives violence, the one who stands for God is a prime target for destruction. The claim is ambiguous though. Not all the righteous suffer, we cannot give such easy meaning to our experience. However, the recognition of this dimension of the crucifixion narrative introduces once again the negativity of our experience into our theology, we cannot continue to be so certain that there is salvation for the righteous, only a continuing hope for redemption.[21]

This image of the tragic hero is precisely that which cannot be sustained in any post-Holocaust christology. The tragic hero in this case cannot theologically fit the stereotypical Greek model of the character with a fatal flaw for tradition has it that Jesus is perfect. Thus, the passion narrative has always carried a transferrance of flaw. The tragedy is not so much in the hero but in the long history of Christian reading of the narrative that finds the flaw not in Christ but in "those who crucify him." Only a fresh reading of this narrative can provide a genuine post- Holocaust christology.

The most damning passage which illustrates clearly this problem is Matthew 27:24-25:

> "So when Pilate saw that he was gaining nothing, but rather that a riot was beginning, he took water and washed his hands before the crowd, saying, 'I am innocent of this man's blood; see to it yourselves.' And all the people answered, 'His blood be on us and on our children!'" (RSV)

Others have skillfully exposed the historical inaccuracies in this text.[22] My concern is to uncover the theological inadequacies of this text and the tradition that has used it. The text is located in a critical place in Matthew's Gospel since the thrust of the gospel is to lead the reader through a series of events that have left Jesus quite helpless having been abandoned by disciples and, ultimately, by God. Thus, Pilate's response has clearly focussed our attention upon the question of who crucified Jesus. The text is filled with irony, but the interpretive tradition has seldom taken that irony seriously. Pilate may be weak but he is not viewed as responsible for the crucifixion. Only one group assumes responsibility, the people, the Jewish people. That transferral of guilt is damning enough in itself, but the tradition does more. Given the thrust of the gospel as read by many, this text represents the ultimate choice of rejection by the Jews (especially Jewish leadership) of Jesus' ministry, his messiahship. The final nail is, of course, the bold statement "His blood be on us and on our children." According to tradition, the guilt is accepted without remorse and passed on to future generations.

Naturally, Christian tradition has read this narrative as tragedy - the tragic story of Jewish condemnation. Chrisitans have for centuries hoped to undo the tragedy through Christian mission to the Jews. This sense of tragedy has often led Christians, especially leaders, to protect Jews from ultimate annihilation (the Nazi genocide is not a direct result of this longstanding teaching of contempt). Nevertheless, the point is clear. Despite continuous efforts to spiritualize this narrative and universalize the guilt, the message is that the Jews are ultimately responsible for the death of Jesus.

We might hope that we are beyond this tradition. The real tragedy of Jewish history, the tragic treatment of the Jews by Christians over the centuries and the twentieth century twisting of Christian anti-semitism into the horror of Auschwitz certainly ought to cast away this theology of guilt from our reading of the crucifixion narrative. But, that is not the case. Too often these texts are read without comment or with continuing reaffirmation of the traditional theology of the text in worship services in Christian congregations throughout the world. We have not yet escaped this pattern of transferring the guilt to the Jews. They are still, often implicitly and subtly, the scapegoat for us. [23]

There is little wonder, then, that Eckardt takes both Moltmann and Wolfhart Pannenberg to task for their christologies.[24] The argument that Jesus is the servant who suffers innocently at the hands of the Jewish leaders, the prophet who in his teaching announces the kingdom of God in fullness serves to sustain this history of contempt. Despite Moltmann's efforts to identify the Christ with the innocent sufferer of each generation, the oppressed, he still sustains the claim that Jesus' main target is the oppression of the Jewish leadership of his day.[25] Such a position can only reaffirm the claim that "all the people" according to Matthew's gospel were guilty of crucifying Jesus and in their rejection turned away from God. However we might read the claim of the divinity of Jesus, Moltmann's image of the crucified God must ultimately mean that "the people" rejected God in Christ, they crucified God.

Ellis Rivkin's arguments are persuasive to me in his claim that the question must become not who but what crucified Jesus.[26] Historically speaking, the Romans must be held accountable for their role (particularly Pilate, despite the Matthean narrative). And if they are at the center of the action, then Jesus must have been crucified for his perceived political threat as much as for his prophetic teaching. If taken seriously, as it should be, Rivkin's argument would make enormous difference to any theological rendering of this text.

In fact, this re-thinking of the narrative once again drives us to recognize the irony of this text. In Christian interpretation, the blood of Jesus is blood of atonement. Surely Matthew accepted this view even as he recorded this text we are considering. If Jesus blood is an essential part of God's redemptive plan, then Pilate's actions are indeed ironic. He washes his hands to proclaim his innocence, but in so doing he rejects the blood of Jesus. Pilate is by no means innocent.

Of course, the same irony plays into the words of "the people". Indeed, the text reads as though the people bear the guilt, but if Jesus' blood is the blood of atonement, then their very actions bind the people to Jesus in this act of sacrifice. The ritual scene seems almost to recreate the image of the temple sacrifices - his blood be upon us. The tradition suggests that the people are guilty while the image suggests that the people are made clean, they are innocent.

Thus, the scene is read as a farce as it surely was. It is a ritual enactment of the actual fact, that Pilate was responsible for the death of Jesus and the people were innocent because Jesus death was fundamentally the death of a politically dangerous figure. In all of this metaphor is imbedded what must be assumed both historically and theologically -- that Jesus **chose** to be crucified!!! Jesus had a choice. His death was not that of an oppressed person but that of a person able to choose his fate. If Jesus is to be seen as servant of God (and I think that this image is the most fitting), then he chooses to be that servant in the face of the political power of the Roman Procurate and with the full awareness of the consequences of that power.

If these claims are the foundation out of which we can and should build our theology of the cross, then we now have tools with which we can make response to the Holocaust. First, any claim that Jesus in his suffering is the oppressed servant and, thus, identifies with the oppressed at Auschwitz is inauthentic and obscene. Jesus had a choice which he fully made knowing the consequences. Those who died at Auschwitz had no choice! They could do nothing to reverse their sentence. Thus, any theology of the cross is filled with irony in the face of the Holocaust, a fact that Eckardt argues with complete persuasiveness.[27] Jesus as servant can make sense in response to the Holocaust only if his death is transcended by the tragedy of Auschwitz for the crucified Lord can only identify with the victims at Auschwitz if he should choose to identify himself and his God with these Jews. Even then we do not know what such a choice means. Even if we say that Jesus must be identified with the victim we do not know what hope lay in such a claim since these people, nearly all these people, died. Their blood is upon us and upon our Lord.

And can we round off the negativity of the crucifixion with the victory of resurrection since that event is also ambiguous in its message? The resurrection of one merely emphasizes more strongly the unfinished nature of our hope. And our hope does not diminish our pain. In fact, the resurrection of Jesus as a theological claim, now post-Holocaust, is both a confession of hope and of despair, for the resurrected one must be eternally identified with the continuing pain of the world he chose to love. Jesus cannot escape that fate since death no longer brings completion.[28] The resurrection is filled with the same irony as the crucifixion - hope guardedly affirmed in spite of the pain of our world.

If ambiguity even concerning the resurrection is to be a controlling factor in our post-Holocaust theologies, then we must be explicit about how that ambiguity affects our theology. Surely, one effect is that certain theologies cannot work anymore. Thus, Eckardt's critique of both Pannenberg and van Buren is more than illustration of a theological debate but rather the strong claim that the way that Pannenberg and van Buren treat the resurrection cannot be genuine in a post-Holocaust christology.[29]

Pannenberg's position is now well known.[30] Pannenberg holds that the resurrection is an historical event as a prolepsis of the future kingdom of God. In that way, this is not the resurrection of a single person but a breaking into history of the eschatological future. Pannenberg's efforts to explicate this view have never been fully satisfactory, however the view has had enormous impact on other thinkers. Eckardt's critique is two-fold. First, the view is fundamentally an affirmation of the longstanding claim of fulfillment theology, even if proleptic. It is an ontological claim that the resurrection transcends and in that transforms ontic history. Indeed, the claim is difficult to sustain with any analysis of ordinary history but crumbles in the face of Christian complicity in the Holocaust. At the very least, we are left with ambiguity, any kind of understanding of what this transformation of history means is beyond us in the face of history so recent in our memory.

Eckardt's second critique is more far-reaching. Pannenberg's theory of the resurrection is ultimately tied to his view of the crucifixion. The resurrection is, for Pannenberg, the affirmation of the truth of Jesus over-against the oppressive forces in Judaism of the time. In other words, the resurrection is a tool which serves to sustain the teaching of contempt we have just fully dismissed. I am not sure that Pannenberg's view of the resurrection can be maintained apart from his view of the crucifixion since implicit in the resurrection, in this view, is this theology of conflict and of supercession.

Van Buren's view is no more acceptable for Eckardt. Van Buren's position on the relation between Christianity and Judaism leads directly to his treatment of the resurrection for van Buren focusses attention of the way of discernment. Jesus is that figure through whom the gentiles are invited onto the way of God. The resurrection is then the advent of this mission to the gentiles. Now, van Buren is certainly to be commended for his effort to challenge us to restore the Jewish roots of Christian faith and theology, but the view makes the resurrection little more than a trumpet call to mission.

The problem with this view, and van Buren is certainly not the only one to espouse the view, is that it fully ignores the way that the resurrection has been at the heart of Christian anti-Judaism throughout history. Indeed, the earliest impact of the resurrection was not to found a mission to the gentiles but rather to the Jews. Even if the ultimate effect of the resurrection has been to create a fully gentile church; the flip-side of that mission has always been a claim of antipathy toward the Jews who have obstinantly refused to join the mission. It seems more than idealistic to me that we can write off history by saying that genuine Christianity is and always has been Judaism for the gentiles.

No matter how we devise this theology we are ultimately left with the fact that Christianity is in no way Judaism for anyone. The two are separate traditions, faiths, ways of life. It is this factor more than any other that enables us to bring the necessary ambiguity to bear upon our theologizing. If Christianity is not Judaism, then the resurrection serves to emphasize not our relation with Jesus but the gulf between our gentile world and the Jew, Jesus. Surely any theology of mission can make sense only when we can speak of mission with the Jews, when we are led to dialogue and mutual respect.

This point can be illustrated by a brief analysis of another passage in the gospel of Matthew, Matthew 28:16-20:

"Now the eleven disciples went to Galilee, to the mountain to which Jesus had directed them. And when they saw him they worshiped him; but some doubted. And Jesus came and said to them, All authority in heaven and on earth has been given to me. Go therefore and make disciples of all nations, baptizing them in the name of the Father and of the Son and of the Holy Spirit, teaching them to observe all that I have commanded you; and lo, I am with you always, to the close of the age." (RSV)

This passage is filled with twists that would require much more space than we can make available to unravel. Thus, I will focus on a couple of critical matters. First, this is a record of a resurrection appearance. It is the only appearance to the eleven recorded in Matthew's gospel; thus this passage has the duel purpose of describing the impact of the resurrection on the disciples and the intent of the resurrected Lord. In the context of the first matter, we are confronted by the strange counterposing of two responses -- some worshiped him but some doubted. We are not told either what led to the act of worship and what that means or why some doubted or even what they doubted. The first point seems odd given the Jewish setting of this encounter (the disciples and Jesus) and especially the matter of worship as it was treated earlier in Matthew's gospel at the point of the temptations of Jesus (4:10, "You shall worship the Lord your God and Him only shall you serve.") This odd counterposing is further enhanced by the way Jesus is said to respond. He acknowledges neither response as if to say that neither is an acceptable response to the resurrection. Now that leaves us with an ambiguity that the text only partially resolves -- how then shall we respond?

In fact, the ambiguity that is displayed in this text gives reason to argue that the resurrection of Jesus is not an event that has meaning in and of itself. The resurrection has meaning only in the words that Jesus shares (which we cannot be certain are Jesus' words). Jesus first calls the disciples to mission (to go and make disciples in every nation). The baptism to be performed is the baptism of discipleship. Whatever else Christians have made baptism to mean, Matthew fully intends to connect baptism with discipleship. The disciples are to observe all that Jesus has commanded (which in Matthew is the whole Law and the prophets). Observance is the appropriate response to the resurrection.

But to say this is as much to say that the resurrection changes nothing. Would the disciples not have taught observance anyway? Indeed, the resurrection seems to be an affirmation of one thing alone -- the lifestyle of faithful obedience to Torah. If there is no word of completion, no indication of victory or vindication, then this faithful obedience becomes the center of our response. The last words of the text serve to reinforce this claim - Jesus remains with the disciples until the end of time. **The resurrection is not the consummation of history.** There is no full kingdom of God, no ultimate victory over evil. If our response must be faithful obedience regardless, then our attention is naturally directed away from the risen Jesus to God, to the end of time.

This text has, of course, been used to verify the new Christian mission that separates Christian from Jew. Even the command to go into every nation has been used to prove the foundation for the mission to the gentiles. Indeed, we are the fruit of that mission, we are those gentiles. But can we say that the mission has been fulfilled if we are not prepared to observe all that Jesus commanded? Surely now is the time to recognize that we can no longer spiritualize this text or play games like gospel and law in our interpretations. Now, post-Holocaust, we are commanded by this very same Lord to at the very least honor those who have observed, those who strive to be faithful. Now is the time to make of the resurrection a potential link between Christian and Jew forever breaking the back of fulfillment theologies that would make the resurrection a triumphalism that is always a slap at the Jew.

But also, post-Holocaust, the language of resurrection is brought into question. What possible hope is there in one man's resurrection even if ordained by God over against the lives of all those children whose names are even forgotten by most, some not even known. The language of resurrection is now broken as the heart of the resurrected

Lord must certainly be. Even using the term leaves us empty when we walk through the gates of Auschwitz as I have. What hope dare we speak there? Eckardt's view that only a future hope can possibly be genuine is a bold attempt to liven the word "resurrection" again.[31] But future hope is ambiguous, full of waiting and anticipation. Never certain. Even Jesus waits with us. Our question is, "Can we gentiles possibly learn to use the word in this way?" We must try.

We can also see the final critique of van Buren's view rise out of this analysis. If Christianity is Judaism for the gentiles, and there is no indication that the disciples mission is simply that, then that mission is a Jewish mission. That is to say, it is a mission to the world to heal the world, to call the world to observance, to teach the world faithful obedience and loving kindness. Perhaps as Christians learn to listen to their Jewish partners in dialogue, they will again learn the meaning of this resurrection narrative that is so vital to our faith.

The kind of theological response that emphasizes ambiguity means not so much rejection of theological claims as the full recognition of the uncertainty that all Christian claims bear, most especially the central narratives of the crucifixion and the resurrection. Such an uncertainty drives us to listen more fully with openness to our Jewish brothers and sisters who not only teach us about our theological heritage but also represent for us a continuing symbol of our own need for theological redemption. A fully open Jewish-Christian dialogue given this sort of theological response to the Holocaust would provide the optimum context for maintaining the necessary ambiguity in our theologizing.[32]

A RETURN TO ECKARDT

The position I have outlined above is sketchy and requires a more thorough treatment of the Biblical narratives as well as the history of Christian theological thinking in order to shape a more complete post-Holocaust theology of the crucifixion and resurrection. Nevertheless, these rudimentary sketches do provide a framework for projecting an adequate theological response to the Holocaust and its victims. In that way, we would produce an adequate theology for the post-Holocaust dialogues between Christians and Jews.

The unsettling claim of uncertainty merged with hope is, however, forcefully and brilliantly developed by A. Roy Eckardt as noted above. While his position differs from mine in some particulars, Eckardt does represent how such a theology of ambiguity might look more fully developed. His position is volatile as might be expected verging on full denial of central Christian confessions on the one hand and retreating back into fragments of traditional Christian language on the other.[33] Eckardt holds those extremes together through a continuing mode of irony that sharply emphasizes the brokeness of our theological language. Thus, Eckardt stands alone as one who leads, beckoning others to follow with insight and further challenges.

Eckardt's use of the term "resurrection" as the way to point to future hope may still be troubling to many. Despite the fact that we, Jews and Christians, both can claim this term as our own, there is little doubt that the word has been too completely Christian in the past for it to be a term easily used by us both. While we do not mean that the hope is simply the Christian hope for resurrection to which Jews must assent, just the use of the term creates that impression. I wonder if there is an alternative.

There is a far greater concern, however, in the use of this term. I am constantly confronted with the challenge that Irving Greenberg long ago gave us,[34] that we must not say anything that could not be said in the presence of the one million children who died. Can we speak of resurrection in front of these children? Perhaps Eckardt is correct, that we are at that point when we must speak of resurrection. I am not sure. We are still not yet a full generation beyond this horror. Are we too impatient? Indeed, we might also take heed of Elie Wiesel wondering what meaning such hope has in the face of what we have now experienced. We cannot know God's mind, but we can know that there will always be some emptiness in our talk of hope, even future hope.

We can overcome this dilemma only through dialogue. Christians cannot be confident judges about this matter. I suspect that we must speak of hope and do so with as much confidence as we can muster. We must do so not to allow the voice of darkness to be heard so loudly. Over against the "Kingdom of the Night" we must proclaim at least a dawn. But we do so with the ambiguity as with all of our talk now. We do not know hope as future hope. We know hope as the child in one of the marvelous tales related by Yaffa Eliach, in our mother's arms, the safest place in the world.[35] Can we know with the kind of certainty that makes us persevere that a future hope can suffice? We do find in those who are faithful, those who are loving, those who are courageous, faithfulness, love and courage. Perhaps we will also find hope in and through those who are hopeful. Or even more, perhaps we will find hope in those things and through those people who give reason for hope, who heal, who are noble, who are gracious. Such victory is won ever so slowly and with little assurance. But in these things, we will learn how to use our language once again.

Eckardt does not stand alone in terms of the desire to find a language that adequately serves the post-Holocaust dialogue. Others, even those holding such differing views as Moltmann, van Buren and Ruether, are also shaping and re-shaping theologies that can give ground for both full recognition of the evil of Auschwitz as well as the reality of a new openness between Christians and Jews. There is hope in that fact alone that progress can be made to a new world of inter-faith respect, particularly if that concern lays open the possibility for Christians to re-think, even re-shape, their theologies of the crucifixion and resurrection.

EPILOGUE

What I have written thus far is, as it were, a message for my Christian colleagues in terms of a reminder of what we have said and a suggestion about what might be otherwise said in response to the Holocaust. I have always had in mind our partners in dialogue as I have written these reflections, but there is little in these words that reflect the voice of our Jewish partners. I cannot as proxy speak for them but I must add one more important word from the prominent Jewish scholar, Emil Fackenheim, as a necessary element in our post-Holocaust reflections on the crucifixion and the resurrection. Fackenheim argues, in God's Presence in History, that one command must be heard by all Jews after Auschwitz. "In ancient times, the unthinkable Jewish sin was idolatry. Today, it is to respond to Hitler by doing his work."[36] Indeed, we Christians must hear that word. We too cannot respond to Hitler by doing his work. If Hitler's work was to annihilate Judaism as well as all Jews, then we cannot promote a Christianity that in any way aims to do away with Judaism. We cannot ask Jews to turn from their Judaism.

Now, even if we have long ago put away Christian exclusivism and triumphalism often associated with the crucifixion and the resurrection narratives (as I have shown in this essay), we might still be subtly expecting that Jews will see in the Christian story the source of hope that combats Auschwitz. The position I have argued for, the position of ambiguity, aims to put to rest this kind of theologizing. And we must ask whether the naive hope of the resurrection can even be a satisfactory Christian hope after Auschwitz. That is to say, the spectrum of views presented in this essay represent views put forth by scholars seriously concerned about the progress of dialogue. We must ask whether some of these views must be rejected as inadequate responses to the Holocaust even if they are presented in good faith. We must act to announce this so that those who do teach and preach in the name of Christ are, at least, challenged to hear the commanding voice of Auschwitz. Our task is certainly not finished with theological debate but continues in an effort to resolve the matter of how Christianity is going to be presented by teachers and preachers today and in the future. That is our present task.[37]

NOTES

1. John Pawlikowski, Christ in the Light of the Christian-Jewish Dialogue, (New York: Paulist Press, 1982), p. 5.
   cf., also Johann Baptist Metz, The Emergent Church, (New York: Crossroad, 1986), pp. 18ff. and
   Irving Greenberg, "Cloud of Smoke, Pillar of Fire..." in Auschwitz: Beginning of a New Era? Eva Fleischner, ed., (New York: KTAV, 1977), pp. 20-52.

2. Elie Wiesel, "Art and Culture After the Holocaust" in Auschwitz: Beginning of a New Era? Eva Fleischner, ed., (New York: KTAV, 1977), p. 405.

3. Rosemary Ruether, "Anti-Semitism and Christian Theology", in Auschwitz: Beginning of a New Era? Eva Fleischner, ed., (New York: KTAV, 1977), p. 79.

4. Rosemary Ruether, Faith and Fratricide, (New York: Seabury Press, 1974).

5. A. Roy Eckardt and Alice Eckardt, Long Night's Journey into Day, (Detroit: Wayne State University Press, 1982).

6. Rosemary Ruether, "Christology and Jewish-Christian Relations", Jews and Christians After the Holocaust, Abraham Peck, ed., (Philadelphia: Fortress Press, 1982), pp. 37-38.
   and
   Ibid. Greenberg, pp. 11-13

7. e.g., ibid., Pawlikowski, pp. 134-135.

8. I have already argued this point for Christian theology as a whole many times but especially in the forthcoming:
   James Moore, "A Spectrum of Views: Traditional Christian Responses to the Holocaust", Journal of Ecumenical Studies, Winter 1988.

9. Dorothy Soelle, Suffering, (Philadelphia: Fortress Press, 1975), p. 146.

10. Ibid., Eckardt, p. 150.

11. Juergen Moltmann, The Crucified God, (New York: Harper and Row, 1974).

12. Jules Isaac, The Teaching of Contempt: Christian Roots of Anti-Semitism, (New York: Holt, Rinehart and Winston, 1964).

13. This critique, unfortunately, holds for even the best and otherwise notable volumes such as:
    Leonardo Boff, Jesus Christ Liberator, (Maryknoll, N.Y.: Orbis Books, 1978), or
    Jon Sobrino, Christology at the Crossroads, (Maryknoll, N.Y.: Orbis Books, 1978).

14. Ibid., Eckardt, pp. 108-110.

NOTES

15. Paul Van Buren, Discerning the Way, (New York: Seabury Press, 1980).

16. David Tracy, Plurality and Ambiguity, (New York: Harper and Row, 1987), pp. 82ff.

17. Ibid., Eckardt, pp. 140ff.

18. Ibid., Eckardt, p. 150.

19. Ibid., Ruether, "Christology and Jewish-Christian Relations", pp. 37-38.

20. Earlier in his reflections, Tracy argued for the necessity of ambiguity in religious language:
David Tracy, "Religious Values after the Holocaust: a Catholic View", Jews and Christians After the Holocaust, Abraham Peck ed., (Philadelphia: Fortress Press, 1982), pp. 92ff.
But more recently of the value of ambiguity:
David Tracy, Plurality and Ambiguity, (New York: Harper and Row, 1987), pp. 66ff.

21. This statement is only a teaser of course demanding a more thorough scriptural study that could give foundation to the arguments only briefly hinted here.

22. cf., Ellis Rivkin, What Crucified Jesus? (Nashville, TN: Abingdon Press, 1984), pp. 16-36.

23. Among many potential illustrations we are particularly struck by the scene in Claude Lanzmann´s film, "Shoah", in which some Polish Catholics talk of the local Rabbi quoting this passage from "Matthew" as a judgment explaining the horror of the Nazi persecution and genocide.

24. Ibid., Eckardt, pp. 87-110 (on Moltmann), pp. 129-130 (on Pannenberg).

25. Ibid., Moltmann, pp. 126ff.

26. Ibid., Rivkin, What Crucified Jesus?

27. Ibid., Eckardt.

28. Again, this statement is only a beginning sketch that aims to suggest the direction of a more detailed theological and hermeneutical exploration. I am reminded, though, of the striking passage from Elie Wiesel´s Night (New York: Bantam, 1960), p. 32: "...even if I am condemned to live as long as God Himself." Surely death unto life is a hope that remains ambiguous for us until the end of time.

29. Ibid., Eckardt, pp. 129-133.

NOTES

30. Wolfhart Pannenberg, Jesus -- God and Man, (Philadelphia: Westminster Press, 1968).

31. Ibid., Eckardt, pp. 149-150.

32. And, thus, I suggest the obvious that my observations are only at the beginning of a process of re-examination in dialogue of basic theological principles. What emerges now will be a theology reft with ambiguity but also with promise.

33. One of the most striking examples of this approach can be found on Eckardt's concluding page (already referenced above) on which Eckardt both denies the traditional Christian view of resurrection but affirms the ultimate power of that word as a source of hope.
Ibid., Eckardt, p. 150.

34. Irving Greenberg, "Cloud of Smoke, Pillar of Fire: Judaism, Christianity and Modernity after the Holocaust," Auschwitz: Beginning of a New Era? Eva Fleischner, ed., (New York: KTAV, 1977), p. 23.

35. Yaffa Eliach, Hasidic Tales of the Holocaust, (New York: Avon Books, 1982), pp. 31-32.

36. Emil Fackenheim, God's Presence in History, (New York: Harper and Row, 1970), p. 84.

37. I am continually impressed by the work of John Pawlikowski in this matter. As I praise him, though, I am compelled to respond to the question, why have I said so little about his work on Christology? I have done so little with Pawlikowski for two reasons. First, John admits that a theology of the cross as the focus of a post-Holocaust christology is inadequate, and while he does much to raise critique of Moltmann, Sherman and Hall, et.al., he forms his christology around a reconstructed view of the incarnation. Second, I am unconvinced that such a move resolves our problems since I cannot understand how the incarnation can be maintained as unique unless it is ontologically constitutive. If it is so, then such an argument seems especially vulnerable to the sad history of the teaching of contempt and the obvious fact that a transformation of creation has not even in the slightest taken place through the event of the incarnation. In fact, just the opposite seems to be the case. I need to hear more from John to resolve these problems for me. Naturally, I find his book to be an important contribution to dialogue on christology:

John Pawlikowski, Christ in the Light of the Christian-Jewish Dialogue, (New York: Paulist Press, 1982).

REREADING CHRISTIAN SCRIPTURES AFTER THE HOLOCAUST

FREDERICK A. NIEDNER, JR.

Valparaiso University, Valparaiso, Indiana, 46383, U.S.A.

INTRODUCTION

Few things affect how individuals or communities see the world around them or how they live within that world more than certain kinds of stories which they hear with some frequency. Particularly potent are the narratives by which religious communities provide individuals with a sense of identity and a grasp of the meaning and purpose of life. The community stories which individuals hear repeatedly, beginning in childhood, and which they experience for themselves in the community's rhythm of ritual, provide a basic, permanent structure from within which all other experience is interpreted and into which all other knowledge and understanding is integrated.

For all the generations since the exodus from bondage in Egypt, Jewish people have proclaimed the story of that event from the Torah and commemorated it in the Passover seder. With each retelling it has shaped within its community of hearers a consciousness of being chosen and beloved of God. It has given not only a way to live but a purpose for living in that way, and it has shown the community to whom that story belongs how its members relate to all the other peoples of the earth. This story answers life's greatest questions. The questions might at first seem simple. For example, why is this night different from all other nights? The answers are finally much larger: Because this people is different from all other peoples.

At various points in the history of ancient Israel, the need arose to read their story in new ways. Particularly when Israel suffered devastation such as that which came at the hands of Babylon, and the covenant with God seemed broken, the story required re-telling and re-reading so that it would enliven the community once more and give _yeshua_, a meaningful place and way of being in the world. The story now retold also created a new picture of Israel's place among the nations and how the people of God related to all those others.

Christians have also told a story so as to shape both community and individual identities and to offer a sense of purpose and meaning. The story of Jesus of Nazareth, whose friends and followers believed they had found in him the _messiah_ of Israel, is told and retold among Christians as "gospel," that is, "good news." Christians, too, regularly rehearse the seder of Passover, but they do it not so much to remember the exodus itself as to recall a particular retelling of the exodus story, the one which was told on the night when Jesus celebrated Passover for the last time with his disciples. Thus, when Christians have gathered over the centuries to remember the story most central to their communal sense of identity and purpose, they relive it as "the night when he was betrayed."

The Christians' story does not end with betrayal. It concludes with the proclamation that the one betrayed and crucified was taken from the grave to be with God, while his spirit remains with those who had trusted him. Thus, the Christian community story intends also to be a story of liberation and freedom. Nevertheless, rehearsing the Passover portion of that story in the way Christians do makes it shape the consciousness of the remembering community differently than it had done before. The story which had first been told so as to identify hearers among those released from bondage and set free, now in the Christian rehearsal serves first of all to place the community among victims betrayed in the dark of night. Different tellings of the same story do indeed create different worlds for hearers to inhabit.

It is in many ways a misfortune, perhaps even a tragedy, that for various reasons the canon of Christian scriptures was not allowed to grow long enough to include works written after Christianity was no longer a besieged and oftimes persecuted minority. Virtually every document in the Christian canon came out of circumstances involving controversy and persecution in which Christians were a distinct and disadvantaged minority, and as a result, the official, authorized tellings of the story of Jesus construct a radically polarized world in which everyone outside the Christian community is a threat at worst and at best they are poor, benighted children of darkness. Obviously, much within the Jewish canon, too, invites one to identify with a tiny minority, a faithful remnant whose very existence is threatened by hostile outsiders. However, the Hebrew scriptures also contain material from periods when the greatest need was to live faithfully in a world where "we" had real power. Among the many salvific effects of retaining the Hebrew scriptures as Christian canon is that at least the Christians have stories about kings like David and Solomon and the collected oracles of prophets who chided kings and tried to instruct them concerning the godly use of power. Mostly, though, Christians have continued to live, despite their power and majority status in many places since Constantine's time, in a world created by apocalyptic tellings of the community's story. That apocalyptically formed world is filled with enemies, traitors, and the willfully blind, all of them under the control of the vast powers of evil.

Who are these enemies, traitors, and willfully blind folks whom the Christian canon has for so many centuries taught its hearers to fear and distrust? Rome, to be sure, is specifically named as the new Babylon and an enemy of both God and the community, but Rome has switched sides, as it were, and is no longer a threat. Who is the traitor? Judas, Judah in Hebrew, is his name. And who simply could not see in Jesus the messiah of Israel, despite all the urging of his followers? The Jewish people. The Pharisees. The chief priests, scribes, and elders of the Jewish people. These now are the specifically named agents of evil in the world which the Christian canon creates.

For two millennia the story of Jesus has been told and retold, and long after Christianity had become a thoroughly hellenized Gentile movement and a political power whose struggles and difficulties no longer had anything much to do with Jews and Judaism, the Jews have remained those named specifically as the enemies and traitors in the Christian community story.

Liturgical reenactments of the Christian story in various ages have incorporated that feature in ways too numerous to survey here. A 12th-century liturgical drama entitled "Visitatio Sepulchri" may be typical of how Christians learned to tell their story. As the three women approached Jesus' tomb, the third one sings, "Heu! Nequam gens Judaica, Quam dira frendet vesania! Plebs execranda!" ("Alas! Evil frenzied Jewish race! What madness rul'd this deed so base? Past all amending!" Smoldon, 1967).

Little wonder that Christians have helped to instigate pogroms, thinking they were doing God a favor. Little wonder that even when Christians have not been the instigators or even participants in oppression of Jewish people, for the most part they did nothing to stop it. Little wonder that in the dark hours we know today as the Holocaust, as Jews were led away to the camps the Christians of the world, with few exceptions, appeared only in the role Elie Wiesel has named "the face in the window" (1982). The Christians' community story had placed them in a world where the Jews were an accursed race of traitors, enemies of God who were somehow getting what they deserved. Some Christians, mostly in Germany and elsewhere in Europe, risked and even gave their lives intervening on behalf of Jewish people in those years, but for the most part the world's Christian community stood by and watched.

Obviously, many things within the human soul cause people to shrink in the face of great, institutionalized, bloodthirsty evil run amok. No community, religious or otherwise, is immune from the paralysis of fear and the great temptation to stand by and watch while others are victimized. For Judaism and Christianity, however, that temptation is more perversely dangerous than for most, since near the heart of both faiths is the command to care for the poor, the homeless, the orphan, the widow, the stranger, whoever it might be and no matter how the other came to be in that condition. Indeed, Jesus taught his followers that they were to love their enemies (Matt. 5:44). Christians, therefore, have placed themselves and their integrity as Christians in grave jeopardy by shaping their view of the world with a story that puts another people under judgment and in a place outside the bounds of care.

Christian communities have never fully faced up to the dangers inherent in their use of a largely apocalyptic, polarizing canon. There may be many reasons for that failure, among which is the likelihood that the danger was never perceived or recognized as such. After all, serious examination of and reflection upon the great power of narrative discourse is a relatively recent development. People have long known that stories had power and many have known how to use that power, but that is not yet to understand why stories do what they do to human perception nor to take responsibility for what one's story might cause or create.

The Nazi Holocaust, by virtue of its unimaginable immensity, has brought Christians closer to looking at what their story says and does. So many, many people died in the Holocaust, and so many lives were shattered. Broken forever, too, were many of the old constructs for understanding God, human nature, and and the relationship of both to evil. Gone, too, is a time when Christians can ignore the potential their canon contains for perpetuating old hatreds and for giving life to new ones. Specifically, the Holocaust presents a demand that Christians do whatever it takes to keep their sacred story from either empowering or allowing the hatred of Jews and Judaism which the Holocaust epitomized. Christians owe the victims of the Holocaust at least that much by way of a remembrance. Acting responsibly with their canon is also a moral issue for Christians, for it is surely no less immoral to run about naively with a story that has the capacity to cause or facilitate killing than it is to be careless with nuclear devices which can do the same thing. Irresponsible handling of potentially deadly things can no longer be tolerated.

How shall Christian communities respond to such a demand? Should Christendom throw out its canon, or at least all the parts tinged with polarizing, apocalyptic, and anti-Jewish thought and expression? Or might they let stand but disavow and systematically ignore all such parts of Christian scripture? Perhaps one could neutralize such stuff by means of an editing process similar to what is being done to rid scriptures of sexist language. Could today's Christians produce and agree upon a new canon, or part of one? Any such responses are fraught with obvious and probably insurmountable difficulties. After some 17 centuries of using the same canon, and given the fractured nature of Christendom, it is hardly likely that there could ever be agreement on any significant alteration of the canon's scope or contents. Careful, sensitive editing so as to avoid certain anti-Judaic language might help some, and that work is already going on in some circles. Ignoring, or even disavowing, the polarizing, anti-Jewish portions of the canon would be an irresponsible and dangerous solution, so long as those portions are kept within the canon. First, there would be no way to prohibit their use, or misuse, so long as they remained. In addition, such a solution would be like leaving dangerous weapons or stores of toxic chemicals lying about but pretending they do not exist. Sooner or later someone will push the button or loose the flood of poison.

There is another possibility. If Christians have learned anything at all from their Jewish heritage, as embodied in part in the Hebrew scriptures, they should recognize that the present moment in history lies in the shadow of a great devastation which requires a genuine re-telling or re-reading of its most cherished community story. Christianity must find a way to do with its gospel story what the Isaianic prophet of the Babylonian captivity did with the exodus story. That is, the story must be retold or reread in such a way that its true heart and its salvific power, if it has such, is rediscovered and empowered.

What follows in this essay is a proposal for how Christians might learn to re-read the Gospel of Matthew. Because Matthew is written from a thoroughly Jewish perspective but at the same time contains statements which can be read as radically anti-Jewish, this piece of Christian scripture serves as an excellent challenge to and test case for the possibilities of salutary re-reading.

THE GOSPEL OF MATTHEW: AN OLD READING

Any summary of how an ancient document has been read and understood over many centuries will surely risk oversimplification and will flirt with misrepresention of certain traditional perspectives. Nevertheless, something of a consensus concerning Matthew's message, specifically as it relates to questions concerning the relationship between Jewish people in general on the one hand and followers of Jesus on the other, and the attitude God takes toward both groups, does exist and can be summarized.

According to Matthew, when Jesus was born in fulfillment of the scriptures and by the power of the Holy Spirit, gentile astrologers came to adore him as a king, but all Jerusalem was troubled. Indeed, the Jewish king slaughtered many Jewish babies in an attempt to kill the child, thinking he might become a rival. The child was saved by means of an escape to Egypt. This event represents something of a reversal of the exodus story and as such it is a sign that the Jewish people, by their response to Jesus, have forfeited the election by God which is associated with the exodus event (Matt. 2).

As John baptizes Jesus, a voice from the heavens proclaims publicly that Jesus is the son of God (3:13-17), and then Jesus proceeds with a career of teaching and healing which demonstrate unmistakably that Jesus is the messiah of Israel whose actions fulfill the scriptures, and that he is also the new and greater Moses whose teachings supersede those of Moses. Matthew divides Jesus' teachings up into five major blocks of material, the first of which is the so-called "Sermon on the Mount," so as to depict Jesus as the new Moses. Frequently during this period of his career, Jesus had unpleasant encounters with Jewish teachers, usually named as Pharisees, who were opposed to everything Jesus did and said. Most often the controversies centered on how to observe the Sabbath (e.g., 12:1-8), and the Pharisees play the role of heartless legalists while Jesus is the champion of compassion.

In the final stages of the story, Jesus triumphantly enters Jerusalem, which is stirred up as it had been at news of his birth, and he instigates a major confrontation with the officials of the temple (21:1-9). The temple officials and "elders of the people" subsequently plot to destroy Jesus (26:1-5), which they do with the help of a traitor, Judas, on the evening and morning of Passover. The Roman governor, Pilate, would have prevented all this, but the people of Jerusalem were to the point of rioting so as to have their way, and "all the people" of Jerusalem finally shout, "His blood be on us and on our children!" (27:21-25) As Jesus died, the great temple curtain was torn in two (27:51), and the gentile soldiers proclaim that Jesus was "the son of God. " (27:54).

On the first day of the week, women from from the group of Jesus' followers found his tomb empty, an angel explains he has been raised from the dead, and soon the women see and speak with Jesus himself (28:1-10). Meanwhile, the temple officials and Pharisees have bribed the soldiers who guarded the tomb and have begun rumors that the story of Jesus' resurrection was a hoax perpetrated by his disciples (27:62-66). Finally, on a mountain in Galilee, Jesus commissions his disciples to go out to "all the nations" with his message (28:16-20).

In this telling of the story, Jesus is unmistakably the long-expected messiah of Israel and the son of God, and his disciples are clearly the kindly and faithful good guys, while the Pharisees, the temple officials, and finally all the people of Jerusalem, are willfully blind to Jesus' true identity. They are murderous plotters, and they ultimately bring an eternal curse upon themselves as they bring about the death of the messiah. Jesus is then vindicated by the resurrection, and the Jews, or at least their leaders, are proved to be liars and accursed murderers. Moreover, because of the Jew's rejection of Jesus, the election of God has now been lost to them and has been given over to the gentiles instead.

Another feature of the predominant, traditional, Christian reading of Matthew which needs to be accounted for at this point is the thoroughly hellenistic frame of reference out of which the story was told once the Christian community and the Jewish community no longer overlapped. To hellenized gentiles, the term "son of God" quickly came to mean something like a "divine being," and so Jesus was understood to have been a divine being who had come to earth from somewhere else, taken on flesh and blood, and after dying and rising had returned to where he had come from. Moreover, the term messiah lost its Jewish character and simply became a titular equivalent of "son of God" as understood in hellenistic fashion. Thus, the Jews were guilty not only of murdering Jesus, but of "deicide" as well.

This, then, is the powerful and potentially dangerous story which Christians tell their children and by which they shape, perhaps more thoroughly than they realize, their children's world, attitudes, and behaviors. Can the story be defused and safely kept? If so, what would it take to remove its explosive or toxic characteristics? How could it be re-read in such a way that it was still true to the best characteristics of Christianity but did not make enemies of anyone, Jews or otherwise?

THE GOSPEL OF MATTHEW: POSSIBILITIES FOR RE-READING

Several primary features of Matthew's gospel not only allow room for a new reading, but they cry out for a reading of the story different from the traditional one described above. First, and most significantly, the author was a Jew who, while apparently writing in Greek (though that is debated), thought in Aramaic and had an overall agenda which would have been virtually unintelligible outside Judaism in the first century C.E. The arguments between characters in Matthew all center around debates only Jews would have understood or cared about, and in all probability, most, if not all, of the people Matthew anticipated would be reading his work were Jewish. This point alone ought to give readers pause if they think that Matthew in any way intended to have his account become a legitimating agent for the general oppression or slaughter of Jewish people simply because of their being Jewish.

The second feature is closely related to the first. If Matthew was interpreting Jesus' life and teachings from a Jewish perspective, it is virtually inconceivable that he would have thought of Jesus in a hellenistic way, that is, as a divine redeemer who came from somewhere else to take on flesh and blood. Beliefs among Jews concerning messengers ("angels") of God or the expected, eventual return of the prophet Elijah attest to Jewish thinking on the possibility of someone coming from God, or being sent by God for some godly purpose. However, the monotheistic thrust of Judaism would hardly have found room for, much less have generated, notions of Jesus as a divine being in the way that Christians later came to describe him.

The debate among Jews in Matthew's day concerning Jesus would therefore not have been about the possibility of his divinity, but about whether or not he had come from God. That is, were his message, behavior, and apparent intentions godly and legitimate? Matthew said yes, others said no, and one of the burdens of Matthew's gospel was to prove somehow to his opponents in this debate that Jesus' teachings had indeed been godly and were legitimate expressions of faithfulness to God within the general framework of Judaism. The issues involved mostly had to do with the way (halakah) to live in accordance with torah. Sabbath laws, distinctions between clean and unclean, the operation of the temple, and the relationship of Jews to gentiles were among the most hotly contested topics, which was nothing new with the appearance of Jesus. These had been issues for a long time, and they would remain so. In any case, Jesus' apparent intent was to teach a way of faithfulness to torah which Matthew believed was good and godly, one which did not diminish life but gave and preserved life, and one which was surely sanctioned by God.

Matthew offers several kinds of arguments on behalf of his position in this argument. First, he uses the story of the virgin birth to say that Jesus had come from God, not to say that God had physically impregnated Jesus' mother and thus Jesus was somehow ontologically divine. Second, he describes the baptism as an event at which Jesus is anointed (messiah) by the spirit of God for the purpose of doing the godly work for which he had been dispatched or called, and he is named "son of God," again, not so as to describe him ontologically, but as a claim meant to legitimate Jesus' message. This one, Matthew argued, spoke what God wanted spoken. Third, Matthew portrays Jesus as one who had come in the spirit of Moses, even as he describes John the Baptist as having come in the spirit of Elijah (17:9-13). The similarities Matthew develops between Jesus and Moses, such as certain allusions in the story of Jesus' birth to Exodus accounts and Jewish legends concerning Moses' birth, the five "books" of teachings, or the concluding scene atop a mountain, do not require an understanding of Jesus as being somehow greater than Moses. In fact, in Matthew's account, Jesus intends to teach nothing new and nothing contrary to Moses. Rather, Jesus offers a way to live faithfully within torah (cf. especially Matt. 5-7). Finally, Matthew seeks to legitimate Jesus by citing scripture which was "fulfilled" in Jesus activity. Despite the great complexities involved in this particular technique of Matthew, the overall point is simple: Jesus' picture of God's rule in the world and the faithful response that rule seeks from God's people was consistent with what God has always been doing and asking, as can be seen in the scriptures. In sum, the real issue surrounding the life of Jesus, as Matthew understood it, was not the question of whether or not he was a divine being, but whether or not Jesus' way of obedience to torah was legitimate, godly, and within the bounds of authentic Judaism.

The third major point which leads toward a salutary re-reading is the reminder that Jesus' teachings, his message or "gospel," was not about himself but about God. Hence, Matthew's story, though it is the story of Jesus, is also ultimately a story whose purpose is to promote a specific understanding of and obedience to God. If Matthew sought to engender faith in Jesus, it would have been faith that what Jesus had invited his hearers to think and believe concerning God was indeed legitimate and truthful. Evidently, Matthew's opponents assessed Jesus' message as blasphemous and judged him an untruthful, illegitimate witness to God's desires and intentions (22:62-65). Once more, however, the point is that neither Matthew nor Jesus sought to begin a new religion or a loyalty to any God besides the God with whom Israel had been wrestling for many centuries, and thus, Matthew's frustration with his contemporaries was not on the grounds that they rejected Jesus as a new and better God and Lord, or even as a new a better Moses, but on the same grounds that many in Israel's history, like Amos, Hosea, or Jeremiah had been frustrated with their contemporaries. At issue were such things as faithful obedience to God's wishes and the place of the temple in Israel's worship of God.

Matthew's anger, which grew out of that frustration, is obvious and undeniable. No other gospel writer went to the lengths Matthew did in order to discredit his opponents. The Sermon on the Mount's critique of hypocrisy (5:17-20; 6:1-18), the vitriolic denouncing of the scribes' and Pharisees' alleged hypocrisy in Matt. 23, and the not so subtle allegory concerning the faithless vineyard tenants in 21:33-46, all attest to the bitterness of the dispute in which Matthew and his opponents were engaged. It is important to note here, too, however, that the issue is not over abandoning Judaism for something else, but over what is the way to be faithful to God and torah.

Matthew also issued thinly veiled threats against his opponents. In his telling of the parable of the marriage feast (22:1-14), and in his telling alone (cf. Luke 14:16-24), the king sends troops to attack and destroy the guests who make excuses and choose not to join in the celebration. Judgment is swift and certain, according to Matthew. Jesus does not wait a day as in Mark to enter the temple and reorganize it, nor does it take a whole day in Matthew as in Mark for the fig tree which was unprepared for Jesus' arrival to wither under his curse (cf. Matt. 21:10-19 and Mark 11:11-21). It has often been suggested that Matthew, who is usually understood to have written after the destruction of Jerusalem in 70 C.E., saw the sack of Jerusalem as God's judgment on the people of Jerusalem for their rejection of Jesus' message. Even if that is the case, and the argument is strong that it is, Matthew has still not said anything outside the mainstream of traditional Judaism. If the heart of Matthew's message is a perspective on God and a way of faithfulness to torah, then Matthew is really only doing the same thing as Amos or Jeremiah, both of whom threatened a future destruction or interpreted a present destruction as God's judgment upon hypocrisy. It is not rejection of Jesus which warrants destruction as punishment, but rejection of God's wishes, though surely in Matthew's case those wishes are understood as Jesus described them (12:31-32). The distinction may seem slight, but it is significant in the attempt to find a re-reading because a crucial element of that re-reading must be precision about Matthew's motives. Matthew did not mean to suggest abandonment of Judaism or diminishing of the importance of faithfulness to torah. The dispute was about the practice of Judaism, not the validity of it.

Even if Matthew did threaten his opponents with judgment, and even if he thought he could see the hand of God in the events of 70 C.E. much as Jeremiah and Ezekiel did at the time of the destruction of 586 B.C.E., Matthew did not see those events as God's last word on Jerusalem or Judaism. Evidence to support this assertion may be seen in the so-called "formula quotations" in Matthew and in the study of forgiveness Matthew has woven into the story of Jesus. Both of these are unique Matthean developments.

Matthew's gospel is filled with quotations and allusions from the Hebrew scriptures, and his use of scripture has been examined frequently in recent decades. Among the more significant topics in this larger discussion is the group of eleven quotations Matthew introduces with a formula such as, "All this took place to fulfill what was spoken by the prophet. . ." Each of the citations is unique to Matthew among the Christian gospels. Once (2:6) the formula occurs on the lips of the Jerusalem priests who cite Micah 5:2 to the gentile astrologers. In all other cases, Matthew as narrator explains that events took place in such a way as to fulfill something in the scriptures.

A brief look at any one of the citations makes it quite clear that Matthew meant for his readers to take the context of the citation he quotes, not merely the citation alone, as somehow explanatory of the events in the life of Jesus he is describing in his own narrative. Perhaps the most readily illustrative example is the Matthew 2:15 citation of Hosea 11:1, "Out of Egypt have I called my son." The context in Matthew is the so-called "flight to Egypt" of Jesus' family so as to escape Herod's attempt to murder the child. Hosea 11:1 begins a lament spoken by God concerning Israel's unfaithful involvement with the Baal cult, and God goes on to threaten a return to Egypt and bondage, or what might be termed a reversal of the saving exodus event. It is easy enough to understand Matthew as invoking that same kind of threat against his own contemporaries. As noted above, that has been a predominant interpretation of Matthew's motives for citing Hosea 11:1. The most striking feature of Hosea 11, however, is that though God threatens this reversal of the great saving event, even considering for a moment a repeat of the destruction inflicted on Sodom and Gomorrah (cf. Hos. 11:8 and Deut. 21:18-21), God decides not to do that because Israel is too precious. The pain of that thought is too much for God.

Obviously, Matthew meant for the reader to consider the context of Hosea 11:1, not merely the quoted portion, as interpretive of this early part of the story of Jesus. Precisely how much of the context Matthew meant to invoke is now impossible to determine. Matthew is not present to explain. However, an examination of the contexts of all these formulaic quotations Matthew cites from scripture reveals that the context of every single citation contains a promise of one kind or another that God's ultimate intention is the rescue or salvation of Israel, Judah, or Jerusalem. It is difficult to imagine that could be a mere coincidence.

A brief survey of several of these citations is instructive, though not all are discussed here because some cannot be treated briefly. At 1:22-23 Matthew cites Isaiah 7:14, which promises the birth of a child called "Emmanuel" who will be a sign for king Ahaz. The whole point of Isaiah 7 is that God can be trusted to save Jerusalem from its enemies. Micah 5:2, which the Jerusalem priests use to locate the birthplace of a messiah as Bethlehem in Matt. 2:6-7, stands in a context which explains that despite a siege laid by the Assyrians, God will save Israel and "the rest of his brethren shall return." The recall of Rachel's devastation over the Babylonian slaughter in Jeremiah 31:15 (cf. Matt. 2:17-18) invokes from the context of the cited text the message that though Rachel weeps now, God hears the weeping and will restore Judah. "There is hope for your future, says the Lord." Matthew's intentions for referring to Isaiah 11:1 in connection with Jesus' family settling in Nazareth (Matt. 2:23) are not altogether clear, but the context of the Isaiah reference is such that the primary promise of God is to see to the rescue of Israel. As Jesus begins his preaching, Matthew (4:14-15) cites Isaiah 9:1-2, which stands in a context which claims that salvation is coming for those in anguish, including both Israelite tribes as well as "Galilee of the nations." As Jesus begins to heal people, Matthew (8:17) refers to the servant poem of Isaiah 53, which eventually promises the healing and vindication of God's beaten down servant, Israel. As Jesus enters Jerusalem, Matthew (21:4-5) fashions a new prophecy from parts of Isaiah 62:11 and Zechariah 9:9 and says that the prophecy was fulfilled. The intent is most likely to have the reader consider the context of both citations as instructive at that point in Matthew story. Isaiah 62 promises that Zion will not be forsaken, and Zechariah 9:9 stands in a context which promises that God will end warfare so as to save Zion/Jerusalem and bring peace to the nations. Finally, the curious combination of Zechariah 11:12-13 and Jeremiah 18:2-3, cited in the story of Judas' demise (Matt. 27:9) in such a way as to contain also an allusion to Jeremiah 32:6-15, would seem to suggest that although God will judge harshly the "worthless shepherds" of his people, there is surely hope for Judah and Jerusalem.

Matthew's point would seem to be twofold. First, the life and career of Jesus, as Matthew understood it, was quite in line with what the scriptures say God has been doing and working toward ever since becoming involved with Israel, namely, saving and keeping covenant faithfulness with Israel. Matthew did not understand Jesus as having sought to do anything different from or opposed to God's longstanding, permanent agenda. Furthermore, Matthew seems to have thought, in line with much of the tradition represented in the scriptures, that Israel was preserved not only for its own sake, but for the sake of "all the families of the earth" (Genesis 12:1-3) or so as to be a "light to the nations" (Isaiah 49:1-7). Presumed in this tradition is the assumption that God not only will, but ultimately must, preserve Israel and Jerusalem. That is the sign of God's faithfulness. Matthew does not give up the belief which saturates the scriptures that God and Israel are inextricably bound together, and neither can give up the other and still retain integrity. Matthew's use of Hosea 11, where this idea is stated quite plainly, as well as the whole string of texts Matthew cites, each of which recalls God's consistent promise, are sufficient warrant for concluding that despite Matthew's own frustration over the inability to convince his contemporaries about the significance of Jesus' life and teachings, he did not believe God would ever abandon Israel or Jerusalem. Whatever the devastation of 70 C.E. meant, it did not mean that God had turned his back on his covenant or his people.

God, for Matthew, remained the God of Israel. Faithfulness to that God was Matthew's goal, and the same may be said of Jesus as Matthew understood his message and tells his story. The fact that both Jesus and Matthew had opponents among their fellow Jews is evidence that there were different ideas and beliefs about how that faithfulness was to be lived out, or about how God's purpose of making Israel a light to the nations was to be served. Neither Matthew nor Matthew's Jesus, however, found the means to those ends somehow outside the pale of Judaism's central beliefs and traditions.

Matthew's preoccupation with the dynamics of how sins are forgiven is a second major theme in Matthew which would suggest that Matthew could not have understood destruction or punishment to be God's final word about any or all of God's people. At several junctures, narrative material unique to Matthew discusses the topic of forgiveness of sins. Matthew introduces the theme with the note that Jesus' name was to be a sign that "he will save his people from their sins" (1:21). The theme climaxes in the events leading up to Jesus' death and finally in the death itself. The critical scene is that in which Pilate offers to free a prisoner and proceeds to give the people a choice between Jesus and Barabbas. Although there are complex textual difficulties involved, it seems that in the original Matthean text, Barabbas' full name was "Jesus Barabbas," and thus Pilate's question was, "Whom do you want released, Jesus Barabbas or Jesus who is called Christ?" (27:17). The choice is for Jesus Barabbas, and Jesus who is called Christ is soon crucified. Though many questions might be raised by such a reading, the significance of the name Jesus in Matthew's scene is unmistakable. If that is the name associated with forgiveness, and in the final moments there were not one, but two men so named, it is very possible that Matthew means to be describing a scene like that in the atonement ritual described in Leviticus 16. The directives there specify that the priest shall present two identical goats before the Lord, and one, determined by casting lots, is to be released and sent off into the wilderness, while the other is to be killed to make atonement for the people. The blood of the second is said to cleanse and hallow the people of Israel (Lev. 19:19). Juxtaposing the two pictures, the pair of goats and the pair named Jesus, makes of Jesus of Nazareth in Matthew's understanding a sacrifice which works atonement.

To substitute people for animals in an atonement ritual setting may seem to Jewish readers a rather odd, untraditional explanation on Matthew's part. However, it is a literary device by which to attempt an explanation of the significance of Jesus' death which only Jewish people who knew the atonement ritual would even begin to understand. As such, it is yet more evidence that Matthew understood everything about Jesus and the significance of Jesus in a thoroughly Jewish way.

Awareness of the atonement ritual's importance in Matthew's picture of the death scene helps to explain in a salutary way the people's cry to Pilate at the end of the Barabbas scene: "His blood be on us and on our children!" (27:25) That statement, which has so consistently been understood not only as the people taking responsibility for Jesus' death, but also as some sort of eternal curse which they invoked upon themselves, can be seen in a whole new light. In the context of an atonement ritual, the blood of the goat which is killed cleanses and hallows the people of Israel, and if Matthew was consciously using the atonement ritual in order to interpret Jesus' death, then surely he understood the promised effect of the blood of the sacrificed one. This, too, might seem odd or even offensive in a certain way to Jewish readers either in Matthew's time or today. It assumes that there was something in these events for which the people needed to be forgiven, and that, obviously, would likely not have been a common viewpoint in Matthew's day nor is it at present. What is important and significant, however, is that Matthew believed that Jesus' death had effected the forgiveness of the people--all the people--and that would surely call into question the legitimacy of a reading of Matthew which renders the people of Jerusalem or Jewish people in general as accursed outsiders who have forfeited their place as God's chosen ones.

Between the naming of Jesus and the atonement scene, Matthew probes the extent of God's forgiveness and the dynamics of forgiveness within a community. A full discussion of this theme is neither possible nor necessary here, but certain features of it bear upon the topic of re-reading Matthew in a salutary way. First, Matthew understands forgiveness in such a way that a person's inability to forgive others keeps him or her from being forgiven by God. Matthew appends a note to that effect at the conclusion of the Our Father prayer (6:14-15) and makes a much larger point of it in the parable of the wicked servant who, though forgiven his great debt, would not forgive another a trifling debt (18:23-35).

Second, Matthew apparently believed there were no limits to what could be forgiven or how often it could be forgiven. Jesus tells Peter he must forgive the same offence as many as "70 times 70," that is, as often as it happens or as often as it takes (18:21-22). The magnitude of forgiveness is also a theme in the story of Judas' relationship with Jesus in Matthew. In Matthew's last supper scene (26:20-29), Jesus identifies Judas as the traitor, but then proceeds to offer to him along with the others the cup which Jesus says, only in Matthew, contains "blood . . . which is for the forgiveness of sins." In the betrayal scene, Jesus, only in Matthew, calls Judas "friend" (26:50). Even in that moment, Judas is still considered friend. Finally, in the scene describing Judas' death (27:3-10), a scene which is juxtaposed to Peter's denial (26:69-75), the reader is shown two possible results from two different responses to the fracture of a relationship. Both could have returned and been welcomed. Peter eventually did, but Judas gave up on himself.

Third, Matthew understands forgiveness to have a fundamentally relational character, not merely a transactional nature. The explanation in 18:10-20 concerning how a sin within a community is to be handled is the primary text here. First, God is described as one who would stop at nothing in order to have every last sheep in the flock returned to him should it become lost. Next come the directives for handling sin among community members. Though many issues of translation and authorial intention are involved, here, the point is that community members must proceed as God does, allowing absolutely nothing to break up the community. Even if a person insists on making himself or herself an outsider ("tax collector or a gentile," 18:17), and Matthew's model for treatment of such folks is Jesus, the community will not tolerate such a fracture but will expand its circle so that no one is ever outside the bounds of care.

All this is to say that the spirit of Matthew's gospel is such that the use of Matthew for the purpose of excluding, cursing, or in any way justifying harm done to anyone, Jewish or gentile, is utterly unwarranted. Matthew's understanding of forgiveness is such that an unforgiving spirit cannot itself share in forgiveness, and forgiveness has no limits. Evidently Matthew was able to forgive his opponents even if his later readers could not.

CONCLUSIONS

Christians have always claimed that their story was "good news," and thus they have always implicitly taken upon themselves the task of making sure that their story gave birth to love, joy, peace, patience, kindness, goodness, faithfulness, gentleness, and self-control. The Holocaust has shown in a dramatic way that the story can be told in such a way as to promote or justify both idolatry and base inhumanity. Hence, Christians must face anew the challenges inherent in a salutary reading and telling of their gospel. The challenge is ultimately a moral one, in response to which Christians must learn to live up to their own identity claims as those are made and granted in their community story.

First, a morally responsible reading of a work such as Matthew requires that the reader understand how much Matthew loved Judaism and sought to be faithful to torah. For those who would take Matthew as their own community story, or at least one version of it, responsible reading and telling of that story today requires learning to love Judaism and torah. A salutary reading of Matthew requires that Christians not see Jewish people as enemies or outsiders, but learn instead to identify with them as fellow-wrestlers with the one God, creator of heaven and earth.

Second, if Matthew is a measure of Christian integrity, then Christians must play the role of restless reconcilers in the world, especially in relationship to those who have been family but who are now separated or alienated by some fracture. Christians are not authorized or commissioned by Matthew to be conquerors, but only to take the commandments, as Jesus had taught them, to the nations and to work without ceasing at forgiving sins, that is, at letting go of those things which divide and poison relationships.

Third, Christians, like Jews, must learn anew in every age how faithfulness to the one creator of heaven and earth takes shape and is lived out. The most serious challenge to Christians in this attempt result from the adoption of hellenistic thought forms used for explaining the identity of Jesus and Jesus' relationship to God. Historically, hellenistic christological formulations have made way for a kind of worship of Jesus which makes Jesus a divinity separate from the God of Abraham, Isaac, and Jacob, and hence Christians have found permission in that christology for divorcing themselves from Judaism, and perhaps even from the God who created heaven and earth.

Finally, Christians must learn to be constantly sensitive to the toxic, polarizing potential which their canon holds by virtue of the circumstances out of which its documents grew. Simply ignoring the problem courts future disasters and in the shadow of the Holocaust is an intolerable negligence. There is likely no one way to re-read Matthew, or any other telling of the Christian community story, which will meet these challenges simply and efficiently, but these challenges as well as the warrants for a salutary re-reading make such work a primary moral responsibility for all Christians, especially those who lead Christian communities or who teach children what it means to be a Christian.

REFERENCES

Smoldon, W. L. (1967). Visitatio Sepulchri, A Twelfth-Century Easter Music-Drama: Oxford University Press.

Wiesel, Elie (1982). The Town Beyond the Wall: Schocken Books.

TORAH IN THE FLESH

A NEW READING OF THE PROLOGUE OF THE GOSPEL OF JOHN AS A CONTRIBUTION TO A CHRISTOLOGY WITHOUT ANTI-JUDAISM

JACOBUS SCHONEVELD

International Council of Christians and Jews, Martin-Buber-Haus, Werléstraße 2, 6148 Heppenheim, Federal Republic of Germany

Christian theology, in particular the doctrine on Christ, has for many centuries been infested with anti-Judaism. After Auschwitz, Christians are challenged to develop a Christology without anti-Judaism: a doctrine on Christ that does not deny but affirm the integrity and the worth of the Jewish people and the Jewish faith. At the heart of Christology lies the doctrine of the incarnation, and at the source of this doctrine lies the Prologue of the Gospel of John, in particular, the short sentence: "And the word became flesh", or in the Greek original: "kai ho logos sarx egeneto" (John 1:14). A new look at this central statement of Christian faith is therefore necessary.

LOGOS EQUALS TORAH

Obviously the first question to be asked is: what is meant by "Logos"? In this paper the hypothesis is advanced that in the Prologue of John Logos is to be equated with Torah. First, reasons for this hypothesis are given and then some thoughts are offered on the theological consequences of this hypothesis, especially with regard to the relation of the Church to the Jewish People.

The equation of Torah with divine Wisdom is well documented. According to E.E. Urbach 1), the remnants of the Wisdom myth referring to Wisdom's pre-existence and its presence at the creation of the world were transferred to the Torah. In Proverbs 8:22 ff Wisdom says:

> "The Lord created me as the beginning of his way, the first of his acts of old... When he established the heavens, I was there... When he assigned to the sea its limit, so that the waters might not transgress his command, when he marked out the foundations of the earth, then I was beside him, like a master workman (another reading is: as a little child), and I was daily his delight, rejoicing before him always, rejoicing in his inhabited world, and delighting in the sons of men".

This divine Wisdom through which God has created the world and sustains and rules it is equated in Jesus Sirach (24:23 (cf. vs 9) with the "Book of the covenant of God Most High, the law which Moses has prescribed for us as the heritage for the community of Jacob". In Baruch 3:9-4:4, Wisdom by whose means God laid the foundation of the world, inhabited it with animals, and guided the stars, is equated with the Torah. Speaking about God the text says:

> "This is our God; there is none to compare with him. The whole way of knowledge he found out and gave to Jacob his servant and to Israel, whom he loved. Thereupon Wisdom

> appeared on earth and lived among men. She is the book of the commandments of God, the law that stands forever" (Baruch 3:35-4:1).

In the same sense the Rabbis spoke of the Torah as an instrument with which the world was created (Sifre Deut. 48; Avot 3:18).

In Philo, Wisdom (sophia) is identified with Logos which he describes as cosmological principle in De Opificio Mundi 16-19,24. There he compares God with an architect building a city, who makes first an outline in his mind and, as if in wax, models a city of the mind" and after this model builds a city in the reality.

> "In like manner we must think of God. When he designed to found the Great City (i.e. the world), He first conceived its types, and from them composed a world of the Mind (kosmos noetos) and then using it as a model completed the world of the senses... The world of the mind (kosmos noetos) is nothing else than the word (Logos) of God in the act of creating a world" 2).

But we also find in Philo the identification of the Logos with the Torah with its positive and negative commandments:

> "The Law (<u>nomos</u>) is nothing else but the divine <u>Logos</u> prescribing <u>what</u> one should do and prohibiting <u>what</u> one should not do" (De emigratione Abrahami, 130).

There is a remarkable parallel between the midrash attributed to Rabbi Hosha'yah (c. 225 CE) (Bereshi Rabba 1:1) and Philo's passage in "De Opificio Mundi" on the Logos as cosmological principle, but in the Midrash this is the Torah. The midrashic statement expounds Proverbs 8:22 ff as follows:

> "The Torah says: 'I was the instrument of the Holy One, blessed be He'. As a rule, when a human king builds a palace, he does not build it by himself, but calls in an architect, and the architect does not plan the building in his head, but he makes use of rolls and tablets to know how to make the rooms and wickets. Even so the Holy One, blessed be He, looked in the Torah and created the world. And the Torah declares: 'with <u>re'shit</u> (be-re'shit, in the beginning, is here understood as: <u>with</u> the beginning) God created', and <u>re'shit</u> means none other than Torah, as it is said: 'The <u>Lord</u> made me <u>re'shit</u> (as the beginning) of His way'" 3).

That Philo's conception of Logos has real and profound analogy with the rabbinical understanding of Torah is recognised by Martin Hengel who agrees in this regard with Kurt Schubert. While Schubert allows for the possibility of a direct dependence of the midrashic statement on Philo, Hengel is of the opinion that Philo and the Midrash draw on an early common tradition 4). Daniel E. Gershenson summarizes the usage of the concept of Logos as follows:

> The Word of God (devar Adonai) appears in the Bible as divine teaching, i.e. medium of revelation and guidance, ... the instrument of creation... and the instrument that controls nature. The Word of the Lord is identified directly with Torah in Psalm 119 (passim), and the attributes of the Word or Torah (Psalm 89; 119) are ascribed to Wisdom in the first nine chapters of Proverbs. Indeed, Torah and Wisdom are identified in the apocryphal books Ben Sira (24:1-21, 22 ff) and Wisdom of Solomon (6:18 ff) in all the same aspects... Philo applies the term Logos, or the holy logos, to Scripture itself, i.e. the Law (IV Quaestiones et Solutiones in Genesis 140 ; I Som. 229)... It is sometimes the same as wisdom (I L.A. 65, etc), because it is the most inclusive expression of the thoughts and ideas of God, which in turn are identified with the Law, or the Torah,

> with the pattern of all creation and with the law that directs and maintains all things. Philo's identification of logos with Wisdom and Torah parallels the identification of Torah and Wisdom and the Word of God in rabbinic literature, and conforms to the roles assigned to each in Scripture and rabbinic sources" 5).

C.H. Dodd recognises that it would be legitimate to identify Logos with Torah 6) and Gerhard Kittel also sees a close connection between Logos and Torah in the Prologue of John. Quoting Otto Proksch he considers both terms as interchangeable 7). Raymond E. Brown stresses what he calls the "Semitic Background" of the Prologue's use of "the Word" and mentions in this connection i.a. the "Personified Wisdom" and the "Jewish speculation on the Law (Torah)" 8). (Dodd, Kittel and Brown come, however, to different conclusions from those outlined below).

If it is generally recognised that Wisdom equals Torah and Wisdom equals Logos, it seems on the grounds stated above, very well possible to close the triangle and to conclude that Logos equals Torah. If a Jew hears about "The Word", "Ho Logos", in such an absolute use, he cannot but think of the Torah. In John 10:35 "graphe" (scripture), i.e. the Torah, is placed in parallel with "nomos" and "logos", in John 5:38,39 "ton logos" is paralleled with "tas graphas", and in John 15:25 we find the same combination of logos, nomos and scripture (ho logos ho en toy nomoy auton gegrammenos). These verses from the Gospel of John itself provide support for the equation of Logos and Torah. Further support is found in the combination of the verb "tereo" (= to observe) with "logos", as "tereo" is frequently used in connection with words for commandments, or prescribed festivals. See John 8:51,52,55; 14:23f; 15:20; 17:7, 1 John 2:5.

A TRANSLATION OF THE PROLOGUE

In the following a translation of the Prologue of John is proposed, based on the understanding of Logos as Torah in the broad meaning indicated in the above quotation from Gershenson, namely the Torah revealed to Moses on Sinai which is at the same time the means, or the instrument, with which the world has been created and is maintained. An important key word is "egeneto" (or derivatives from the same stem). It means "came into being", "became", "came to pass". For the sake of using the same word throughout the translation, it is translated as "emerged". In order to put the equation of Logos and Torah into relief, "Logos" is translated as "Torah".

(1) In the beginning was the Torah
and the Torah was towards God
and Godlike was the Torah 9)
(2) It was this which was in the beginning towards God.
(3) All things emerged through it
and apart from it not one thing emerged.
(4) What has emerged in (or: through) it, was life.
And the life was the light of the human beings.
(5) And the light shines in the darkness,
and the darkness did not take it away.
(6) There emerged a human being sent forth from God,
his name was John.
(7) It was he who came to witness
in order that he witnessed about the light in order that
through him all would be faithful.
(8) Not he was the light, but (he was there)
in order that he witnessed about the light.
(9) (The Torah 10)) was the true light that enlightens
each human being coming into the world.
(10) In the world it was,
and the world emerged through it,
and the world did not recognize it.
(11) To that which was its own it came
and those who were its own, did not take it up.
(12) But whoever took it, to those it gave power
to emerge as children of God,
to those who were being faithful to His Name:

(13) not from blood, nor from the desire of flesh, nor from the
desire of man, but from God they have been caused to emerge.
(14) And the Torah emerged as flesh
and tabernacled among us
- and we beheld the glory of it,
glory as of an only one from Father -
(it - the Torah - was) full of grace and truth.
(15) John witnesses about it and has shouted saying:
It was this of which I said:
"The one who is coming after me, has emerged before me,
because my principal he was",
(16) because out of its fullness we all took
even grace upon grace,
(17) because the law was given through Moses.
The-grace-and-the-truth emerged through Jesus Christ.
(18) God - nobody has ever seen Him.
As an only son 11), ever at the Father's bosom,
it was he who showed the way.

JESUS CHRIST: TORAH IN THE FLESH

The Prologue is a poem with a forward movement building up its tension towards a climax at the end: "The-grace-and-truth emerged through Jesus Christ". The poem starts with "en arche", "be-re'shit" (in the beginning) and recalls the already quoted midrashic statement on Proverbs 8:22 ff (The Lord created me at the beginning of his way") in Bereshit Rabba 1:1: "The Torah says`'I was the instrument of the Holy One, blessed be He'... He looked in the Torah and created the world". Then the poem continues in the style of the Wisdom literature to speak about the life-and-light-giving qualities of the Logos, the Wisdom or the Torah.

Then, suddenly, there is a break in the flow of the poem which in effect heightens the tension: there appears a person with the name of John, who plays the role of a messenger, who witnesses to the divine light calling people to be faithful to the Torah. Then the movement continues and - in the style of the Wisdom literature - dwells on how God's Logos, Wisdom or Torah was received by the world. This part recalls Jesus Sirach 24:4 ff where Wisdom is described as wandering through the world looking for a place where it can dwell, until it finds a foothold among the people of Israel, or Barukh 3:20 ff which describes how even the rulers of the world and the great artists did not grasp the true wisdom, which was only revealed by God to the people of Israel and was then accepted by them. Also the tradition preserved in b. Avoda Zarah 2b comes to mind, which says that God "offered the Torah to every nation and every tongue, but non accepted it until He came to Israel who received it":

The children of God who according to vs 12 take up the Torah and are faithful to God's name are to be understood as the Israelites who have received God's Torah and are loyal to it. The Israelites are called children of God in Deut. 14:1, which is cited in Avot 3:18: "Beloved are Israel, for they were called children of the all-present... Beloved are Israel, for unto them was given the desirable instrument... through which the world was created, for 'I give you good doctrine, forsake ye not my Torah' (Proverbs 4:2)". Here appears again the cosmological significance of the Torah. The Israelites are also called children of God in Deut. 32:5f, 20, Wisdom of Solomon 2:13, 16, 18 and elsewhere. Allegiance to the Torah transcends racial descent, as those who are obedient to the Torah are God's children: "from God they have been caused to emerge" (vs 13). This verse may reflect the spreading of the Torah of Israel among the peoples around the Mediterranean sea, transcending racial and political boundaries. Josephus writes about the spread fo the Torah in "Against Apion" (2.282): "As God permeates the universe, so the Law has found its way among all mankind" 12).

The poem continues its movement: a new development is announced in enigmatic terms: "And the Torah emerged as flesh and tabernacled among us full of grace and truth". There is in this connection also reference to the "glory", the kavod. But before the veil of the secret is lifted, the flow is again interrupted by another reference to John who is portrayed as God's messenger witnessing about the Torah and its life and light. The Torah is then connected with someone whose name is not yet mentioned but in an enigmatic way only hinted at: someone who is coming after

John, but has emerged before him and whom he recognised as his "protos", his "first", his principal. The poem leaves no doubt that the Torah was prior to John: because, since the Law was given through Moses on Sinai, not only John, but "we all" have received grace upon grace out of the fulness of the Torah. Then suddenly, without any connecting conjunction, the veil is lifted, the secret is made known, and the person who until now was only enigmatically hinted at, is openly called by his name:

"The-grace-and-the-truth emerged through Jesus Christ".

We must pay attention to the fact that the verb following "the-grace-and-the-truth" is in the singular, not in the plural, which means that grace-and-truth is seen as a hendiadys, as one single concept. For the first time the expression appears in vs. 14 in connection with the word glory (in vs 14) and its second appearance in vs 17 is followed by the statement that nobody has ever seen God (vs 18). This suggests that "grace-and-truth" must be understood in the context of the story of the revelation of God's glory to Moses after the restoration of the Tabels of the Torah (Exodus 33 and 34). Moses asks God to show his glory, but God answers him: "you cannot see my face; for man shall not see me and live". Then God lets pass his glory before Moses and Moses sees God's back, not his face, and among the words spoken by God is the expression: "rav hesed we-emet" which is picked up in John 1:14: "pleres charitos kai aletheias", "full of grace and truth". The invisibility of God, the appearance of God's glory after the restoration of the Tables of the Torah, and the words "full of grace-and-truth", they all suggest a conscious reference to the theophany of Exodus 33 and 34.

Against this background the verses 14 to 17 are to be understood as follows: The glory of the Torah was seen when the Torah emerged as flesh, as a human person in Jesus Christ. Through him emerged the grace-and-truth which is inherent in the Torah, as Psalm 25 says: all the paths of the Lord (on which he leads people through his Torah) are "hesed we-emet". What happened in Jesus Christ is of the same rank as the passing of the glory of God 'rav hesed we-emet' before Moses after the restoration of the Tables of the Torah. The Torah emerging as flesh, as a human being in Jesus Christ is analogous to what Moses experienced when God let pass his glory before him.

Verse 17 has almost always been understood as presenting the contrast between law and grace: 'the law was given through Moses, but the grace and truth came through Jesus Christ'. In the Greek text there is no word that can justify a translation with "but". No contrast is implied. Rather should this verse be read in connection with the preceding verse: "out of its fullness we all took even grace upon grace"("charin anti charitos"). God gives one grace after the other: first out of the fullness of the Torah we could receive the Mosaic legislation, and then we could receive out of the Torah's fullness its glory, its grace-and-truth as revealed in the person of Jesus Christ. This revelation of the glory of the Torah as grace-and-truth in Jesus Christ is of the same order as the revelation of God's glory at Sinai. This glory of God also filled the tabernacle with the Ark of the Covenant containing the Torah. What then happened, happens now again in the person of Jesus Christ. This seems to be the sense of: "and the Torah tabernacled among us". Bultmann, who follows in his commentary the common view that verse 17 presents the contrast between law and grace, admits that this contrast is otherwise foreign to John and that in no way verse 14 and 16 lead us to expect such contrast. He assumes that this verse comes from the Pauline school. But it is entirely unnecessary to construe such a contrast. In another part of the gospel, in John 10:35, it is stated: "kai ou dunatai luthenai he graphe": "The scripture cannot be unbound", cannot be deprived of its binding character. This reminds us of Matthew, 5:17: "Think not that I have come to unbind the law and the prophets; I have not come to unbind, but to implement".

Returning to vs 14: "Kai ho logos sarx egeneto", the following translation is proposed: The Torah emerged as flesh, as a human person, as a person of flesh and blood (basar wa-dam). The Torah was embodied, personified in Jesus Christ. Jesus Christ was the Torah in the flesh, the Torah in person. That such a notion is not far-fetched can be shown from a passage in Philo. At the end of the Book on Abraham (de Abrahamo, 276) he writes to sum up what he had written about the patriarch:

> "This life of the first and founder of the nation is, as some would say, agreeable ... to the law, but as my discourse has shown, it is Law itself and an unwritten code".

The Law (the Torah) is embodied in Abraham.

There are also parallels to such a notion in the rabbinical literature, e.g. when Eliezer ben Hyrkanos was gravely ill, his disciples said that a scroll of the Torah lay in distress (b. Sanhedrin 101a). Eliezer was so to speak a living Torah scroll, he embodied Torah.

Jesus is the Torah in the flesh and as such he shows the way (exegesato). The common translation: "The only son... has made him known" is not likely, because no object follows the verb. It is more likely that the verb must be taken in its simple, original meaning: to show the way, as a leader, a "hegemon" does (see: Liddel-Scott, s.v.) Josephus uses the word in the sense of expounding the law (Bellum, 1:694, 2:162; Antiquities 18:81 13)), so that it may have a halakhic connotation: showing the right way according to the Torah.

The expression "doxan hos monogenous para patros", "glory as an only one from Father" is a further echo of notions that come to expression in the Wisdom literature, e.g. in the Wisdom of Solomon, 7:22, where it is said that there is a spirit in Wisdom which is "monogenes", alone in its kind, and - in vs 25 - that Wisdom is an emanation clear as sunlight from the glory of the Almighty ("aporroia tes tou pantokratoros doxes eilikrines").

After the poem has revealed the name of Jesus Christ as the one through whom the grace and the truth inherent in the Torah have emerged, it presents Jesus as the Teacher of Torah in the Book of Proverbs, because the words in John 1:18: "as an only son ('monogenes'), ever at the Father's bosom, it was he who showed the way" seem to reflect Proverbs 4:2,3: "Do not forsake my Torah; when I was a son with my father, the only one in the sight of my mother, he taught me" (The Hebrew word "yahid" (the only one) is in the Greek versions of Aquila and Symmachus rendered as "monogenes", whereas the Septuagint has "agapomenos", the beloved one). As the embodiment of the Torah Jesus is in the Prologue of John - and in the whole gospel - the authoritative Teacher of Torah and its ultimate interpreter.

In vs 14 Torah, or Wisdom, seems to be referred to as a "monogenes", whereas in vs 18 it seems to be the Teacher of Torah that is so called. Since the Torah is embodied in Jesus Christ as its authoritative Teacher, monogenes can signify both the Torah and the Teacher by whom it is personified. The Johannine Jesus is indeed first and foremost the great Teacher. He is often called "Rabbi" in the Gospel of John, e.g. in John 3:2, where Nicodemus addresses Jesus with the words: "Rabbi, we know that you are a teacher come from God".

ON THE AUTHORITATIVE INTERPRETATION OF THE TORAH

What fruit does this interpretation yield in terms of a christology without anti-Judaism? At first sight very little, because it seems that also this interpretation of the Prologue the Gospel of John fits into the frame of reference of a replacement christology, in which Jesus appears as the new and the better Torah replacing the Torah given to Israel. Many traditional designations of the Torah are in the Gospel of John applied to Jesus. The best known text is: "I am the Way, the Truth and the Life; one one comes to the Father but by me". Way, Truth and Life are common descriptions of the Torah. Here Jesus seems to claim to be Torah, indeed the Torah in person, Torah in the flesh. Eternal life, in Judaism mediated through the Torah, is in John mediated through Jesus. According to John, Moses wrote about Jesus, and if the Jews would understand their own scriptures, they would have to admit that the claims of the Johannine Jesus are true (John 5:39-47). Many more quotations can be given to support the assumption that Jesus came to replace the Torah. As these have been rehearsed for many centuries, there is no point in doing this again.

But at a closer look some facts deserve attention. Nowhere says the Gospel of John that the Mosaic Torah has been abolished: John 10:35 was already quoted: Scripture cannot be unbound, cannot lose its binding character. Concerning the observance of the Sabbath, Jesus gets involved in a halakhic dispute that only makes sense on the basis of his acceptance of the binding character of the Sabbath commandment. Although in John 5:18 Jesus' opponents push the argument that Jesus abolished the Sabbath because he allowed a man whom he had healed on Sabbath to carry his pallet, and on this ground they wanted to kill him, in John 7:22, 23, it becomes clear that Jesus and the "Ioudaioi" (whoever they may be) differ on what one is allowed to do on Sabbath. Jesus argues that it is permissible to heal a person on Sabbath with a reasoning of the category of "qal wa-homer" (literally:light and heavy", here: the inference a minori ad majus): If the Torah permits circumcision on Sabbath, involving only a part of the body, then a fortiori it is permitted to heal the whole person on Sabbath. This argument is in fact put forward by Rabbis who lived in the same period as in which the Gospel was written, as Dodd points out by quoting similar statements by Rabbi Eliezer ben Hyrkanos and Eleazar ben Azariah, Tannaites of the Second Generation (c. 80-120 CE) 14).

Another example of the affirmation of the Mosaic Torah is found in the story of the Samaritan woman (John 4). Here the controversy surfaces between the adherents of the Samaritan Torah and the Jewish Torah: Jesus who in this story is identified by the Samaritan woman as a Jew says to her: "You (Samaritans) worship what you don't know, we (Jews) worship what we know, because the salavation is from the Jews". In this context Jesus seems to say that meesianic salvation is based on the Jewish Torah, but will include a manner of worship "in spirit and truth". This probably reflects a situation after the destruction of the temple. As a matter of fact, the synagogue worship in rabbinical Judaism could legitimately be defined as a worship in spirit and truth. But in view of the whole polemic trend of the Gospel of John towards the Pharisees, it is not very likely that this is meant. These words seem to refer to the worship practised in the Johannine community. There may be some connection with the criticism of the Temple as voiced by the Qumran community. Raymond Brown is of the opinion that John 4 reflects a stage in the development of the Johannine community, when a Samaritan group who were critical of the Temple joined it.

Dealing with the question whether the Christian doctrine of the incarnation has anti-Jewish implications one cannot ignore the horrible passages in John 8 directed against the "Ioudaioi", whoever they may have been, nor Chapter 9 in which a lengthy dispute with the Ioudaioi is recorded. Both chapters seem to reflect a bitter conflict in which the majority of a Jewish community had excommunicated (the expression 'aposunagogos genetai', 9:22, is used) those from its midst, probably the Johannine community or its prominent leaders, who professed Jesus to be the Messiah. Thus the venomous words about the Jews in Chapter 8 must be understood as the strong reaction of members of the Johannine community against their expulsion from the synagogue. so that we have here to do with a sharp inner-Jewish dispute, not unlike the dispute between the Qumran community and the Jewish leadership in Jerusalem.

From John 9:28, 29, we get a clue about the issues at stake in the conflict between the Johannine community and the Ioudaioi. They say: "We are disciples of Moses, but we don't know where this one (Jesus) comes from". The issue under debate concerned apparently the source of authority with regard to binding interpretation of the Torah. In rabbinic Judaism which seems to be represented by the Ioudaioi, the authority to lay down halakhic rulings was put into the hands of those who had been authorised to do so by their teachers in a line of succession of teachers going back to Moses. This is expressed in the first chapter of the tractate "Avot". (1:1):

> "Moses received Torah from Sinai and delivered it to Joshua, and Joshua to the Elders, and the elders to the Prophets, and the Prophets delivered it to the Men of the Great Synagogue. These said three things: Be deliberate in judging, and raise up many disciples, and make a hedge for the Torah".

The expression: "we are disciples of Moses" reminds us of this opening verse of Avot. The Johannine community apparently did not submit to the authority of these "disciples" of Moses who claimed to lay down halakhic rulings or to "judge" (Hebr.: "din"), as the technical term for such ruling is. It maintained that Jesus had been authorised directly by God to lay down such rulings, as is stated in

John 5:27: "God has given him (Jesus) the authority (exousia) to make judgement", to lay down halakhic ruling and to give binding interpretations of the Torah (cf. the use of the word "to judge" after the halakhic argument on the question of the permissibility of healing on Sabbath: "don't judge by appearances, but judge with right judgment", John 7:24). This authority is also expressed in John 3:34-36):

> "For he whom God has sent, utters the words of God, for it is not by measure that he gives the spirit. The Father loves the Son, and has given all things into his hands. Who is faithful to the son has eternal life. Who is obedient to the Son shall not see life but God's wrath remains on him".

"Giving all things into the hands" of the son probably means laying into his hands the power to make authoritative decisions regarding the interpretation of the Torah. In rabbinical Judaism this power lay in the hands of the rabbis who formed a leadership that was sanctioned by tradition to decide on matters of halakhah by majority decision. According to the Johannine community this power was directly bestowed on Jesus, so that "the disciples of Moses, probably the rabbis, were bypassed. Expressed in general terms, the conflict between the Johannine community and the Ioudaioi was apparently a conflict between charismatic leadership directly derived from God and tradition-oriented leadership based on majority decisions of the authorised scholars of Torah.

Here the famous conflict between the two rabbis comes to mind who were almost contemporaries to the Johannine community, Rabbi Eliezer ben Hyrkanos and Rabbi Joshua ben Hananyah, on the question how halakhah, i.e. binding law, is to be determined on a certain matter (b. Bava Metzua 59 a). The conclusion is that even a bat-kol, a heavenly voice, is not admissible for the determination of halakhah, but only the majority devision of the duly authorised sages. It seems that the Johannine faction within the Jewish community based itself, so to speak, on a bat-kol in the form of Jesus' "uttering the words of God" (John 3:34). This must have been unacceptable to the majority of the Jewish community and have led to the excommunication of the Johannine group, just as Rabbi Eliezer was excommunicated when he refused to submit to the majority decision. After Jesus' glorification it was the Holy Spirit who took his place: "He will teach you all things and bring to your remembrance all that I have said to you" (John 14:26) and "he will guide you into all the truth" (John 16:13).

If thus, according to this understanding of the Gospel of John, the Torah is embodied in Jesus and he is the Torah in the flesh, and thus its authoritative interpreter, then there is no reason to assume that in the view of the Johannine community, Jesus did away with the Torah. On the contrary, he even appeals to Moses in his conflict with his opponents saying that they are unfaithful to the Torah. The Johannine community thus puts Jesus's interpretation of the Torah and his halakhic ruling in opposition to the Ioudaioi, who probably represent Rabbinic Judaism.

JESUS'S ORAL THORA

What does this mean in respect to the attempt, to develop a doctrine of the incarnation which is not a denial of, nor even a treat to, the integrity and validity of Jewish faith? Although the Torah is held in high esteem by the Gospel of John, this gospel seems of no great help to this attempt. because it is clearly impossible on the basis of this gospel to develop a christology or a doctrine of the incarnation that recognises the legitimacy of rabbinic Judaism. There is a strong exclusivist tone in John: "No one comes to the Father but through me"; "Who is disobedient to the Son shall not see life, but God's wrath remains on him".

Or is this too quick a conclusion? One should look at the whole picture: In Pharisaic and rabbinical Judaism, the Written Torah is applied, interpreted and, in exceptional cases, even overruled by the Oral Torah, the living tradition of the authoritative reception of the Torah by the community. This Oral Torah has such a high rank that it is given equal honour as the Written Torah, and is presumed to also have been given to Moses on Sinai. In the Gospel of John, Jesus - and after his glorification the Holy Spirit (the Paraclete) - provides the Oral Torah. Jesus is therefore given the same rank as the Torah itself, and thus can be called the

Torah in the flesh, the incarnated Word of God. The issue between the Ioudaioi and Jesus is then: Which Oral Torah is the valid one and is to be adhered to. The Pharisaic Oral Torah is rejected by the Johannine community in favour of the Oral Torah given by Jesus. They say: "Lord, to whom shall we go? You have the words of eternal life" (6:68).

But what is the content of Jesus's Oral Torah, of the Torah embodied in Jesus? Jesus speaks many times in the Gospel of John about his commandments. This very fact is an important support for the hypothesis that the Logos in the prologue of John is to be understood as Torah. But with regard to the specific content of his commandments, only rather general statements on loving one another are given, but virtually no concrete injunctions. It is as if one reads from the Book of Deuteronomy only the first eleven chapters containing the background and the conditions connected with the giving of the Torah, but stops before chapter 12 which begins with: "These are the statutes and ordinances which you shall be careful to do in the Land which the Lord, the God of your Fathers, has given you to possess".

If Jesus so much emphasizes his commandments, what are they, what is their content? If it is true that "scripture cannot be unbound", then these commandments can be no other than those contained in the Torah, but they receive, according to John, their true and authoritative interpretation through Jesus. Yet, when one looks for specifics of this interpretation one remains in the dark. The only exception, as far as John's account is concerned, is Jesus's interpretation of the Sabbath commandment mentioned above. It is, however, interesting to note that this interpretation with regard to the permissibility of healing on Sabbath is in agreement with the rabbinic halakhah which is based on the same reasoning as given by Jesus 15).

Jesus speaks about a new commandment that he gives:

> "A new commandment I give to you, that you love one another, even as I have loved you, that you also love one another" (John 3:34)

This is further elaborated in John 15:12:

> "This is my commandment that you love one another as I loved you. Greater love has nobody than this, that one lays down one's life for one's friends".

But what is new about this commandment in comparison with e.g. Leviticus 19:18: "Love your neighbour as yourself"? Although the novelty of Jesus's teaching is often seen to lie in the saying: "Love your enemies", here in the Gospel of John only love for one's own circle of friends is mentioned. There is reason to presume that giving one's life for one's friends is the new element. Looking for more specifics of Jesus's Oral Torah we may turn to the other gospels, especially the gospel of Matthew. But also there the content of Jesus's Oral Torah does not seem to be so radically different as to justify the anti-Jewish polemic of the gospels. The reasons for this hostile sentiment seem to lie elsewhere.

If Jesus is the embodiment of the Torah, the Torah in the flesh, can then the "imitatio Christi" bring people closer to the Oral Torah of Jesus? The notion of the imitation of Christ contains a mystical component, which may be present in John 6:53 ff:

> "Truly, truly, I say to you, unless you eat the flesh of the son of man and drink his blood, you have no life in you..."

If Jesus is the Torah in the flesh, if in him the Torah emerges as "basar wa-dam", as flesh and blood (i.e. as a human person), then "eating his flesh" and "drinking his blood" may indicate the communion with Christ through which a person is imbued with the Torah and is brought to living a life in accordance with the way the Torah was embodied in Jesus.

But it is important to keep in mind that there are in the gospel of John - or in the other gospels - no specific contents of Jesus's Oral Torah that clearly contradict the rabbinic Oral Torah. It may well be that the gospels provide an incomplete picture of tensions and controversies between the early, mainly Christian-Jewish communities and those sections in Judaism that accepted the Pharisaic Oral Torah and rabbinical authority. The Gospel of John seems to be a very Jewish gospel, written by and addressed to Jews who held Jesus for the embodiment of the Torah. The gospel gives only slight hints concerning the inclusion of Gentiles in the church, e.g. when Jesus says that he has "other sheep that are not of this fold" (10:16) and when there is mention of "some Greeks" (12:20). The gospel reflects a fierce and rather ugly debate between groups within a Jewish community over the true interpretation and application of the Torah. It is quite possible in the light of Jesus's repeated reference to his commandments that the Johannine community as a community of Jews committed to the Torah, had on the basis of Jesus's Oral Torah developed a halakhah that was opposed by the Pharisaic community.

THE BODY OF CHRIST, THE TORAH IN THE FLESH

What theological and christological consequences are to be drawn from all this for the church in the present? Only a very brief outline can be given here. Today the church is very different from the Johannine community with its Jewish membership and its particular halakhah which was not determined by Pharisaic, or rabbinic, tradition but by him who was proclaimed as the Torah in the flesh, the one through whom the grace and the truth inherent in the Torah had appeared and the authoritative interpretation of the Torah was given. This appearance was of the same order as the appearance of the divine glory to Moses after the Tablets of the Torah, and thus the covenant, were restored. This Johannine community felt that it had been given the final and definitive interpretation of the Torah in the words of eternal life (John 6:68) spoken by Jesus.

With regard to consequence for the present it is essential to notice that this community of Jews has ceased to exist. In the opinion of Raymond E. Brown 16) it was soon innerly divided in various factions which fought each other tooth and nail, and gradually disappeared from history as a separate identity. About the year 90 it began to admit Gentiles. The faction whose views have been preserved in the Letters of John subsequently merged with the Apostolic Church which had a very large Gentile membership. Another faction moved to the heretic communities of Docetists, Gnostics and Montanists.

As the Johannine Community does not exist any more, the issues that were at stake in its conflict with the Ioudaioi, representatives of what became rabbinic Judaism, are no longer relevant, and also the sharp controversy which is reflected in the Gospel of John has become obsolete and does not need to burden anymore our relations with the Jewish people in the present.

Where does this leave the church, overwhelmingly consisting of Gentiles, which, on the one hand, has gradually eliminated all Christian forms of Judaism from its midst but, on the other, has preserved the Gospel of John as part of its canon? What are thus the christological implications of this interpretation of the Prologue of John? If Christ is the embodiment of the Torah, the Christians as members of the Body of Christ are intimately associated with the Torah. There is, however, one important distinction that must be kept in mind: the Torah was given to Israel in order to be implemented to its full extent in the Land of Israel. Gentile Christians are, however, not members of the people of Israel, nor are they linked to the Land of Israel. They belong to other nations and live in other lands. Paul had made the decision that the Torah was not meant for Gentile Christians, but that there was for them access to the God of Israel apart from the framework of the Torah, since the biblical promise that Abraham would become the father of many nations, had been fulfilled in Christ. He used the argument that God's promise to Abraham was unrelated to the Torah revealed to Moses and was even prior to the commandment of circumcision. There, Paul taught that the Gentile Christians had not to be concerned about the questions how to relate to the Torah. As Paul lived in the conviction that the old world was on the verge of disappearing, he did not see the need of an elaborated guidance for their lives in the light of the Torah.

But the old world order has not disappeared and the gospel of John is in the canon of the Church. Against the Marcionites who draw the consequences of one line in Paul's thinking to the extreme, the church made the conscious decision to keep the Torah in its canon and to declare that it was also meant for Gentile Christians. The general tendency, however was to deal with the Torah, now called Old Testament, as a text which was in an allegorical or typological way made to say what the Church confessed about Christ, and to use this text to legitimize the Church's status and to support its claim to be the true heir of the Covenant of Israel, to the exclusion of the Jewish people.

THE TORAH AS PARADIGM FOR THE GENTILE CHURCH

If Gentile Christians take seriously that their Lord Jesus Christ is the embodiment of the Torah and his Spirit is also today with them to guide them into all truth, they must find a different access to the Torah, indeed outside the frame of reference of Rabbinic Judaism and develop an attitude and an approach to the Torah in accordance with their situation as non-Jews, who don't belong to the people of Israel and for whom the Land of Israel is not the Land of Promise. In terms of the midrash which states that God offered the Torah to all nations, but that only Israel had accepted it, one may say that in the creation of the Church out of the Gentiles, the Torah was again offered to the nations of the world and accepted by those from among them who confessed Jesus as the Christ, as the Torah in the flesh. One may further embroider on this midrashic theme: According to the midrash in the Mekhilta of R. Ishmael, Bahodesh § 5 (ed Lauterbach II, 234) God had offered the Torah to the Nation telling them what its main content was, namely the commandments: You shall not kill, you shall not commit adultery, you shall not steal. As they refused the Torah he turned to Israel and Israel said: "na'aseh we-nishma'" (we will do and we will listen) and only then he gave the Torah in all its details and established his covenant with Israel. The Torah was then shaped according to the specific situation of the Jewish people and, in later ages, interpreted - and in exceptional cases even changed - according to their needs in different situations.

In Jesus Christ the Torah given to Israel through Moses is shining full of its grace-and-truth, because the Torah is embodied in him. With their incorporation in Christ through baptism, Gentile Christians receive the Torah in that specific form in which it was given to Israel. The Christian "Old Testament" is the Jewish "Tanach" (or a translation of it). Yet since they are not Israel, but belong to other nations and since they are not linked to the Land of Israel, where God's covenant with Israel is to be lived, they cannot receive the Torah as Jews. They must under the guidance of the Holy Spirit work out the details of their own national, social, economic, political, cultural and individual life in the light of and in analogy with the Torah given to Israel, or to be more precise: in analogy with the way the Torah was concretely worked out in its details and specifics, when it was given to Israel and applied to its situation. This means that they must not read the Torah in an allegorical nor in a typological, but in an "analogical sense" and interpret and apply its commandments in relation to the specific needs and challenges arising from the many different situations in which they as non-Jews from many different backgrounds live. In this manner the Torah given to Israel and interpreted by Israel, serves as a paradigm for them, and thus one can say that it has to be read in a "paradigmatic sense". In this task of receiving the Torah in their Gentile way by reading it in an analogical or paradigmatical sense, they may be helped by the rich experience the people of Israel has gathered during more than two thousand years in working out the details and the specifics of their life in the covenant under the Torah in different times and different situations. There is much to be learned from Israel in this respect, also from its conflicts about the right interpretation of the Torah, such as the conflict with the Johannine community, and many other conflicts in later centuries.

The Church is more than ever in need of a halakhah, a discipline of life derived from the Torah which God has graciously offered first to Israel, and then in Jesus Christ as the embodiment, or the incarnation, of the Torah, to others. Here the first contours of a new Christian doctrine of the incarnation may emerge. In such doctrine there is no place for theories of replacement or substitution of the Jewish people by the church. But the Jews incorporated in the People Israel, and the Christians incorporated in the Body of Christ, are called to be faithful to God who has given both of them His Torah full of grace and truth.

NOTES

1. Urbach, E.E., The Sages, Their Concepts and Beliefs, Jerusalem (The Magnes Press, The Hebrew University), 1979, p. 287.
2. Cf. Dodd, C.H., The Interpretation of the Fourth Gospel, Cambridge (the University Press), 1954, p. 67
3. Cf. Translation by Urbach, o.c. p. 199
4. Hengel, M., Judentum und Hellenismus, Tübingen (JCB Mohr/Paul Siebeck), 1979. S. 311; Schubert, K., Die Religion des nachbiblischen Judentums, Freiburg-Wien (Herder), 1955, S. 19.
5. Encyclopaedia Judaica, Volume 11, Jerusalem (Keter Publishing House), 1972, p. 461 f.
6. Dodd, o.c. p. 273, see also 85 ff
7. Kittel, G., (Hrsg.) Theologisches Wörterbuch zum Neuen Testament, Band IV, S. 138 f. also S. 100
8. Brown, R.E., The Gospel according to John, Volume I (i-xii), London (Geoffrey Chapman), 1971, reprinted 1982, p. 420 ff (American original edition: 1966)
9. The word order makes the traditional translation "and the word was God" unlikely. In that case we would have expected "kai ho logos en ho theos". Raymond E. Brown remarks in his commentary (see note 8) on this verse that the grammatical rule that predicate nouns are generally anathrous, cannot be invoked here to prove that an identity of logos and theos is meant, since the "I am" formulae (John 11:25, 14:6 etc.) that imply identity and to which "the Word was..." in the Prologue is akin, have the article. Philo makes a clear distinction between ho theos (with article) and theos (without article). Ho theos is God Himself, the source of divinity; the logos is never identified by Philo with "ho theos", but can be indicated by "theos", to be understood as the divine energy working in the world. Therefore, I have chosen for the translation: "Godlike". I admit that this translation is also not entirely satisfactory. The New English Bible paraphrases: "What God was, the Word was".
10. This translation follows Rudolf Bultmann in: Das Evangelium des Johannes, 16. Auflage, Göttingen (Vandenhoek & Ruprecht), 1959, S. 31 f. who considers vs 9 as the direct continuation of vs 5 so that the subject of the sentence is the Logos and "to phos" is predicate.
11. Here the reading: "monogenes huyos" has been chosen. If one chooses the reading "monogenes theos", one might translate: "As a unique divine being, ever at the Father's bosom, it was he who showed the way".
12. Quoted by Gager, J., The Origins of Anti-Semitism: Attitudes Toward Judaism in Pagan and Christian Antiquity, New York-Oxford (Oxford University Press), 1983, p.61.
13. Kittel, Theol. Wb. zum N.T. Band 2 (s.v.)
14. Dodd, o.c. p. 79
15. See the quotations from Tos. Shab. 15, 16 (edition M.S. Zukkermandel, p. 134) and of Rabbi Eleazar ben Auariah in b. Joma 85 a-b, (two contemporaries of the Johannine community) given by Dodd, o.c. p. 79
16. Brown, R.E., The Community of the Beloved Disciple. The Life, Loves and Hates of an Individual Church in New Testament Times, New York/Ramsey, Toronto (Paulist Press), 1979, p. 145 ff.

THE TAP-ROOT OF ANTI-SEMITISM: THE DEMONIZATION OF THE JEWS

Frederick M. Schweitzer

History Department
Manhattan College
Manhattan College Parkway
Bronx, New York 10471
USA

Those who set themselves to combat anti-Semitism will soon find that they are contending with something infinitely more formidable than xenophobia or religious prejudice. What makes anti-Semitism a hydra is the devil theory of the Jews. That demonization is so deeply rooted in Christian tradition and the Western civilization of which it is an intrinsic part as to be, seemingly, inseparable from them.

The beginnings of that most literal-minded, simplistic species of dehumanization is a passage in the Gospel according to St. John (8:43-7). There Jesus is reported as arguing with "the Jews," and tells them that neither God nor Abraham but the devil is their father. "Why do you not understand my words? because you cannot hear the truth. You are of your father the devil, and the lusts of your father you will do. He was a murderer from the beginning and kept not within the truth because there is no truth in him. When he speaks a lie, he speaks naturally, for he is a liar and the father of lies. But because I speak truth, you do not believe me. He who is of God hears God's word; you do not listen to the word of God because you are not of God." Thus it fell out that the Jews came to be depicted as children of the devil, lies and deception, and Judaism itself can be seen by devout Christians - what higher sanction than sacred Scripture - as a lie and deception, the Jews persisting in it because they are partisans of the devil and the lie.

In the New Testament and in the Christian middle ages and well into the early modern period, certainly during the Reformation, the devil is a very real personage, fearsome, and not the near-abstraction that is Satan in the Old Testament. In Hebrew Scripture little is said of Satan and nothing about a conspiracy of Satan and/or demons in league with human beings against the divine governance of the world. As set out in David Langton's history of the idea of the devil, Satan, A Portrait, in the older biblical books the diety is a tribal god and the source of good, the source of evil being the other tribes' gods; the univeral deity revealed to us by Isaiah (45:7) is the source of both: "I form the light and create darkness, I make peace and create evil - I the Lord do all these things." In time the threatening aspects or functions of God are detached and embodied in the persona of Satan. The Book of Job is part of the transition: in one segment (older) Yahweh is the source of Job's troubles, whereas in the prologue (later) it is Satan; so too David's temptation to conduct his famous census: in II Samuel 24 the King is tempted by God, in I Chronicles 21 by Satan.

When we come to the Dead Sea Scrolls and then the New Testament, we find that Satan has developed into a formidable antagonist of God. The world is divided in a prodigious struggle between the Kingdom of God and the Kingdom of the Devil. Satan and his legion of demons are the relentless enemies of Jesus (whom the devil tries to tempt in a famous passage of the Gospels) and of his followers whom they scheme to ruin in body and soul; consistent with this manichean world-view, many of Jesus' miracles are cures of people possessed by demons - Satan's agents; so also the passage quoted above, John 8:43-7.

St. John Chrysostom's Eight Orations against the Jews is a vivid rendering of the devil theology. One of the formative influences on the Church and greatest of the Greek Fathers, he is the complete anti-Semite, for only the racial variety appears to be absent. Of what are the Jews guilty? he asks. "Of rapine, cupidity, deception of the poor, thievery, and huckstering. A whole day would not suffice to tell their crimes." St. John will try, however: "How can Christians dare have the slightest converse with the Jews who are lustful, rapacious, greedy, perfidious bandits." Here we have the Jew in two of his stereotyped roles: Shylock and lecher. "They are the most miserable of men, inveterate murders, destroyers, men possessed by the Devil"; "...those God-fighting Jews ... they are fighting against the commands of God and dancing with the Devil." Their affinity with the animal kingdom is another familiar motif. "Debauchery and drunkeness have given them the manners of the pig and the lusty goat. They know only one thing, to satisfy their gullets, get drunk, and kill and maim one another. Indeed they surpass the ferocity of wild beasts..." - such verbal assault has the dangerous effect of depriving the Jews of their common humanity and invites the attacker, or his followers, to inflict almost anything on the victims, like the rioting students I once saw hurling acid at the police, but only after they had anesthetized their consciences by shouting "fascist pigs" at them. As for the Synagogue, St. John takes his cue from the Book of Revelation on "Satan's Synagogue." It is "a theatre and a house of prostitution, a pirates' cave, the lair of wild beasts, a place of shame and ridicule; it is the domicile of the Devil, their rituals are criminal and impure, their religion is a disease," "plague," etc. Always the devil intrudes. Logically then, Christians must, "Turn away from the Jews as from a plague, flee their assemblies, their homes, their synagogues," for they are the "pest" of the universe. This leads, in the middle ages and long after, to segregating them in ghettos, where they will not pollute their Christian neighbors. He does not urge his listeners to proselytize, but says ominously that the Jews are like an old plough horse that can work no longer and so is "marked for slaughter." The Resurrection makes Judaism obsolete, "ready for slaughter." Such passages as these and perhaps the most extraordinary of them all, "The souls of the Jews and the places where they congregate are inhabited by demons," became evermore memorable as the medieval obsession with Satan and demons grew. By one calculation there were 2,665,866,746,664 demons populating the medieval air, each one of which according to the 1398 definition of the Paris Theological Faculty, and cited approvingly two centuries later by Jean Bodin in his De magorum daemonomania, "is considered the persistent and implacable adversary of God and man."

In other media and at all social levels we find the same images of the Jews. In painting and sculpture, particularly in the middle ages, Jews are depicted with the physical characteristics that identify them with the devil, such as the horns with which Michelangelo equipped his celebrated Moses. The significance of such anatomical embellishments was strikingly rendered for visitors in the fall, 1982 exhibit at the New York Jewish Museum, "The Jews in the Age of Rembrandt." As the catalogue specifies, "Michelangelo's Moses has horns; Rembrandt's does not. With this minor act of iconographic surgery, the image of the Jew was translated from the realm of monsters to the realm of men."

The pointed hat (widely required of Jews as a means of identification) was twisted to give it the appearance of horns; a horn-shaped piece was attached to the badge (the point of identifying Jews by crimson hats or yellow badges being that they were dangerous and so had to be made known to the public). Often the medieval artist graphically provides the Jew with a tail, whether of devil or goat; par excellence, the goat is the devil's creature and is a frequently used symbol in art. (A vivid instance is Goya's painting in the Prado, Madrid, "Witchcraft," with witches adoring the devil in the form of a goat.) Supposedly disguised as a goat, Satan roamed about the world seeking the ruin of souls; goats were also the steed of sorcerers, witches and Jews, who usually are seen ludicrously sitting on it backwards - as it is shown in illustrations for Joshua Trachtenberg, _The Devil and the Jews_. The goat is also symbolic of lechery, reminding one of St. John Chrysostom's "lustful" and "carnal Jews" who have "the manners of the pig and lusty goat." There follows from this devil - and animaldom - connection the "Jewish stench," _faetor judaicus_; with the waters of baptism, according to many a medieval tale, the _faetor judaicus_ is instantly dispelled by a heavenly fragrance of sweetness and truth, but it returns to overwhelm the apostate if he relapses.

The devil-Jew equation is also to be seen in the red wig identifying Satan in dramas and miracle plays. Jewish characters frequently wore a red wig, identifying them as automatically as a Roman collar did a priest or a wimple a nun. The arch-traitor Judas Iscariot was usually depicted as having red hair, and anyone with red hair was "suspect," the color of the sly foxes it was characteristically note. An echo of these fixations is Fagin's red hair in Dickens' _Oliver Twist_.

As "children of the devil," Jews, it was firmly believed, were endowed with supernatural power and were conspiring the ruin of souls, the destruction of innocence and virtue, of the Church, Christendom, and so forth. It is all in behalf and by command of their lord and master, His Satanic Majesty, whose pledged vassals they are. That pledge of allegiance (paralleling or parodying the oath of homage between kings and their feudal chieftans) fired the imagination of many an artist; sometimes the Jews are assembled in Parliament encircling H.S.M. or, as in a woodcut c.1620, nefariously debasing the currency.

Such myths were nourished also by the medieval cluster of ideas centering on the coming of the Anti-Christ. The Anti-Christ was often equated with the Messiah Jews prayed for. As a Christian commonplace had it, "If Jesus was the Messiah, the only person for whom the Jews could be waiting, by their own method of arguing also, is the Anti-Christ." Variously the Anti-Christ was said to be a Jew, the Wandering Jew, Satan, a bastard, the son of a Jewish prostitute, etc. This last appears to have been an unwitting inversion of the Gospel story, according to which Jesus is born of a Jewish virgin and enters upon a public ministry of three and a half years; at the end of time the Anti-Christ, born of a Jewish prostitute, reigns for three and a half years of catastrophe and tribulation, which are followed by Jesus' Second Coming. The alliance of Jews and the Anti-Christ (as one of the numerous medieval Anti-Christ plays puts it) was to "raise up Judaism again." The Jews will become powerful and would destroy Christendom, or, as one Professor Heinrich Langenstein of Vienna calculated in the sixteenth century, the Anti-Christ, "with the help of Jewish money, would conquer the world in two and a half years." (It all begins to sound like _The Protocols of the Elders of Zion_!)

The Anti-Christ is often a figure of great learning and erudition, demonic erudition one should say, since the origin of all his cunning knowledge was the devil. Interestingly, an early version of the Faust legend portrays him as a Jew who signs the pact in blood with the devil to attain power, omniscience, and sexual virility. On the one hand, most Jews, including women, were educated in response to a religious commandment, and Jewish tradition valued education as the jewel beyond price (a system of mandatory elementary education can be traced as early as the last century before the Christian era); on the other hand, Christian tradition held learning suspect (e.g., St. Paul in Romans 1:21-2 on "speculating to no purpose" and I Corinthians 1:18-22 dismissing Greek wisdom) and condemned Faust to hell; one should note that the great majority of medieval Christians, including some kings, were illiterate ("Rex illiteratus, asinus coronatus" was a common expression, possibly first uttered by the future Henry I of his father William the Conqueror), and until the onset of universities in the thirteenth century, schools were few and small, confined essentially to the monasteries, and devoted to the spiritual life.

Assimilated in considerable measure to the theme of the Anti-Christ, as one of his followers and an enemy of Christianity, was "Ahasuerus," the Wandering or Eternal Jew. Purportedly, he had been a party to the Crucifixion and was often equated with the Gospels' "Malchus." He came to symbolize the Jewish people as the guilty authors of the Crucifixion, condemned to eternal suffering, and in his endless wanderings rendering testimony to the truth of Christianity. Less incriminating than demonization, seemingly, but still ominous is his equation with Cain, making Cain, "the sign of Cain," "circumcision the sign of Cain," etc., emblems of the Jewish people in contrast to Abel as a prefiguration of Jesus and Christianity. Lacking any compelling sanction in the New Testament, the conception of the Wandering Jew nevertheless caught the Christian imagination of many an author of Anti-Christ and passion plays - he was reported to have been seen and accosted as late as c.1720 - as well as of Romantic poets such as Goethe and Shelley.

Another dimension of this satanophany is the part ascribed to Jews as magicians, especially as sorcerers and necromancers, and not excluding, in that superstitious age, physicans and apothecaries, astrologers and alchemists. Magic would seem to have been a Jewish monopoly and principal enterprise! Jewish success in all these devilish callings was attributed -in the most literal way - to the devil. Books of magic, incantations, etc., employed many Hebrew names, words and formulations, and, indeed, the authors of books of magic (beginning with Moses and King Solomon, it was said) were presumed to be Jews. It was assumed also that Hebrew was <u>the</u> language of magic - thus Benvenuto Cellini's friend, a Sicilian priest and necromancer, "began to utter the most terrible invocations, and to call by their names many of the princes of the demonic legions, speaking the while in Hebrew words, also in Greek and Latin ... so that soon the whole Coliseum was full of them." It seems also that those who spoke Hebrew were feared as magicians, sorcerers, or whatever.

One sovereign reason for burning the Talmud (committed to the flames so often that only one manuscript survived from medieval Europe) was the belief that it was a massive arsenal of magical weapons, and therefore a source of power to the eternally plotting Jews and of enormous danger to Christians. Slightly less implausibly, the mystical Kabbalah was attacked as a great corpus of the magician's arts and was studied as such in the Renaissance by the humanists, Pico della Mirandola and Johann Reuchlin. Pope Saint Pius V condemned such studies; in 1569 he expelled the Jews from the Papal States, except for Rome and Ancona, and explained in his decree that "The worst of it is that they [the Jews] seduce a great many imprudent and weak persons with their satanic illusions, their fortune-telling, their charms and magic tricks and witcheries, and make them believe that the future can be foretold, that stolen goods can be recovered and much else can be revealed." By then and for another century or more, the characteristic justification offered for massacres, despoilment, or expulsion of Jews was accusations of sorcery, whereas in earlier centuries it had been the blood libel.

Burning the Talmud acquired another powerful, but related, motive in the thirteenth century, when, in 1239, it was declared by Gregory IX to be "heretical." The line of reasoning here was that talmudic Judaism, fashioned by the rabbis, was a "new" religion and represented the abandonment of biblical Judaism. As ever, the devil was the author of this heresy: "The devil undoubtedly misled them [the rabbis] and deprived them of a sense of understanding the truth," explained one of the great Judaeophobic friars of the age, Raymond Martini, "so that they are less intelligent than asses as regards divine scriptures." What followed ineluctably from this drastic shift in the Christian assessment of Judaism was that Jews, devotees of "the cult of the devil," - as it was now designated - forfeited the legally- and theologically-based toleration (going back to St. Augustine and Pope Gregory I), and were to be treated like any other heretics or pagans. There began a cycle – that carried to

the end of the middle ages -of persecution, expulsion, and forcible conversion. It is also from the thirteenth century on that demonization and the idea of the Jews as Satan's agents took hold of the Christian mind, clerics and laity alike.
The creation of rabbinic-talmudic Judaism, destructive of scripturally-based Judaism, was seen as a plot. And it is from the thirteenth century onwards that the notion of the Jews plotting in ever more-encompassing circles of conspiracy - Protocols style - began to take its familiar form. Pope Innocent III had already explained that his re-issue of the traditional charter affording Jews certain rights and immunities, Sicut Judeis, was limited "only [to] those who have not presumed to plot against the Christian faith." Christendom's most formidable danger, the Mongols, were perceived as allies of the Jews, who were reported to have hailed the khan as "the son of David"; according to the chronicler Matthew of Paris there was in 1241 a great international conference of Jews from all over Europe, who had decided to aid the Mongol cause by smuggling thirty barrels of weapons under the ruse of sending them thirty barrels of poisoned wine. Already in the twelfth century the Norwich blood accusation incident was attributed to the decisions of an international assembly of Jews at Narbonne.

In retrospect, the papacy's condemnation of the Talmud as "heretical" and its declaration of war on talmudic Judaism - conforming to the analyses and prescriptions of the Dominican and Franciscan friars, many of whom were inquisitors - was the pivotal event of Jewish history in the middle ages. The dual tradition by which, as it were, Jews had been humiliated and sometimes persecuted with one hand, but, with the other, tolerated and sometimes protected, came to an end. Thereafter, a ramified ideology of demonization, a phobia over global conspiracies, and a theologically-buttressed contempt inspired policies of condemnation, expulsion, and forcible conversion. After something of a lull in the period of the Renaissance, the Counter-Reformation papacy, particularly Paul IV, resumed the condemnations, expulsions, and "mission to the Jews" on much the same basis as the thirteenth-century friars had promulgated.

Sorcery and magic were the quintessential explanation for the success of Jewish physicians, in an age when medicine, drugs, poisons, etc., were all closely affiliated with those superstitious modes of understanding natural phenomena - even the merchants who dealt in medicinal herbs, many of them Jews in this enterprise as in many others, especially those importing the rarest ones from afar - were feared as magicians. By the sorcerer-doctor's infernal arts, many a Christian patient was supposed to have been poisoned. In 1610 the professors of medicine at Vienna solemnly declared that Jewish physicians were required by their religious law to kill one-tenth of their Christian patients by plying them with poisoned drugs; a tradition still current in eighteenth-century Spain had it that the proportion was one-fifth. And as one can see in Martin Luther's diatribe, not only Jewish doctors and apothecaries, but all Jews were implicated as masters of the fine art of poisoning: "If they [the Jews] could kill us all, they would gladly do so, aye and often do it, especially those who profess to be physicians. They know all that is known about medicine in Germany; they can give poison to a man of which he will die in an hour, or in ten or twenty years; they thoroughly understand this art." Even more succinctly he explained Jewish success in medicine: "The Devil can do much." In the later sixteenth-early seventeenth century not less than nine English plays - of which Marlowe's Jew of Malta is the best known -feature the Jew as poisoner. He had become a stock character at a time, incidentally, when there were no Jews in England and had been none in the three centuries since their expulsion in 1290.

Perhaps related to this Jewish penchant for poisoning was the idea of the Jews as bearers of plague and infection, as the fomentors of epidemics. They were perpetually accused of poisoning the water supply, of having "imported the plague from India," and so on through many permutations. The devastating Black Plague of 1348 and after, which carried off three-quarters of the population in some parts of Europe, was imputed to the Jews as part of that world conspiracy "to kill and destroy the entire Christian faith"; for "seven years" had they been making their arrangements to poison the wells from Toulouse to Calabria, etc. Not only blamed, Jews were punished, usually after torture trials and forced confessions, in the usual lynch-mob way. The fact that owing to ritual hygiene requirements, e.g. to bathe and put on clean clothes for the Sabbath, Jews sometimes suffered fewer casualties was taken as proof of their culpability, despite the fact, as Jews pleaded, that they had greatly to augment their cemetaries to bury Jewish victims. After all St. John Chrysostom, who abounds in pathological metaphors, saw in the Jews "the pest of the universe." In the sixteenth century the epidemic spread of syphilis to North Africa, Egypt, and the Ottoman empire was likewise blamed on the Jews - particularly on those expelled or fleeing Spain and Portugal.

It was for purposes of magic that Jews purloined the sacred Host of Christian Communion, and in a general way Jews were understood to be "accustomed together with their prince the devil to profane the sacraments." "Host desecration," of what for Jews could not possibly be "the body of the Lord" but simply an unleavened piece of bread, was the sufficient cause for numerous persecutions; even more bizarre was "the bleeding Host" (probably caused by a scarlet microbe that can form on bread held in dank places) whose "suffering" was blamed on Jews who had "stabbed" it. Although there were probably more accusations against Christians, for Jews the charge was almost inevitably fatal. Initially, it was normally only the culprit who came to grief, but before long large numbers of Jews were accused as accomplices and whole communities were decimated, expelled, and so on. In contrast to their handling of the blood accusation, the popes' interventions and condemnations of Host desecration charges were rarely effective or determined; in the centuries following the proclamation of the Feast of Corpus Christi in 1264, the papacy was relatively indifferent to the issue - perhaps in the Reformation under the impress of intense Protestant attack on the dogma -until the Feast became a notorious Jew-baiting occasion in Rome and was the subject of a poem by Robert Browning.

The infamous blood accusation and ritual murder charge were part and parcel of all this superstition. Jews were thought to require the blood of an innocent Christian child for a variety of ritual, magical and medicinal purposes - by the sixteenth century it had long been proverbial that, vampire-like, "Jews cannot exist or live without Christian blood." The most common form was the offering of sacrifice to Satan at Passover, notwithstanding that sacrifice in Jewish ritual had ceased with the destruction of the Temple in the first century, and that any notion of blood offering or consumption is repugnant as barbaric and violates the laws of kashrut. The Christian text that inspired these blood-dripping phantasmogoria is the famous verse in the Gospel according to St. Matthew (27:25), "His blood be upon us and upon our children" - it is one of the foundation stones of anti-Semitism and stands among the texts most frequently cited down the centuries by anti-Semites. Accordingly, Jews were believed to endure endless hemorrhages, male and female alike menstruated, young and old were plagued by a cycle of bloody sores, etc., for which the only relief was to bathe in the blood of an innocent Christian child, kidnapped and "sacrificed" for the occasion. Some of the supposed victims became the center of cults, like "Little St. Hugh of Lincoln" in the thirteenth century and Simon of Trent in the fifteenth. The grotesque perversity of the beliefs and rituals imputed to the Jews, which were so widespread in the early modern period, can be seen in the following account: on his death bed a Jew's face is smeared with Christian blood and someone whispers to him, "If Jesus, in whom the Christians believe and upon whom they set their hopes is the true Messiah, then may this blood of an innocent child who died with faith in his Redeemer help you to eternal life." By Christian blood the Jews will save themselves, for, as we saw earlier, Judaism is a lie and a snare, and therefore inefficacious. There was a ritual murder accusation in Massena, New York in the 1920's.

The Jew as financier - "usurer" - made him a partner and abettor of Satan also. Usury was the devil's invention, according to popular plays and folk wisdom. Shakespeare's Shylock, pursuing his pound of Christian flesh in the Merchant of Venice, 1590's, is dubbed a "fiend"; "Certainly the Jew is the very devil incarnal." By the twelfth century Church theologians and canonists had classified usury as a crime, placing it in the same category as arson, homicide, sacrilege, and sorcery. In the thirteenth century, probably before and certainly after, Jew was as readily equated in the Christian lexicon with usurer or merchant as he was with sorcerer or magician. We find an example in King St. Louis IX's decree of 1254: "The Jews must desist from usury, blaspheming, magic, and necromancy." A Jewish prominence, then as now, as jewel merchants corroborated the myth: gems were valued not merely for adornment or investment, but as talismans for warding off harm and disease, or breaking evil spells. Portentous was the action of Pope Alexander IV, 1257, declaring "usury" to be "heresy," the origin of heresy being, of course, the devil; in 1311 Clement V made that equation more official and legally binding, thus placing usury under the jurisdiction of the Inquisition.

That would seem to complete the circle of Jewish complicity and culpability. They are the devil's instrument in all evil things, that is to say in whatever Christians in medieval-early modern times feared. The awesome, threatening Jew stands forth in many guises: sorcerer and magician; physician-poisoner, bearer of plagues; seducer-lecher; Host desecrator, ritual murderer, kidnapper; usurer-capitalist-exploiter-Shylock, and in the gangster version, Fagin; their longed-for Messiah is the Anti-Christ we await in fear; they are too learned and smart, whereas the Christian tradition was suspicious of learning, trusting more in the promptings of the guileless, uninstructed heart; they are stalking us relentlessly in a world conspiracy.

In Martin Luther's writings on the Jews we have in the most perfervid language a precis of almost all of this. He is replete with references to Jews as animals, parasites, etc. as well as demons, agents of Satan, etc. They are capitalist exploiters, arch-criminals, subverters of Christianity, "a plague, pestilence, pure misfortune." "Luther would very probably sit in the dock today," the notorious Julius Streicher pleaded at Nuremberg in 1946, "if his book had been taken into account by the Prosecution. He said in this book on the Jews and their Lies that the Jews are a serpents brood and one should burn down their synagogues and destroy them." It is indeed the paradoxical truth that Luther, the greatest revolutionary against the Church, papacy, and the Catholic tradition in theology, nevertheless gathered up the Church's anti-Semitic heritage and - imparting nothing original with the exception of the flaming language -gave it a new lease on life. This is particularly evident with regard to the theme of demonization, and it is notable that Luther cites the most critical text, John 8:43-7, early on in his treatise. Thereupon the Judaeophobic assertions cascade relentlessly before the reader: The Jews are not "God's people. And if they are not God's people, then they are the devil's people.... the wicked Jews cannot be God's people.... The devil with all his fallen angels has taken possession of this people.... God often wanted to exterminate them, but Moses interceded for them.... They are like the devil, who knows very well that God's word is the truth and yet with deliberate malice contradicts and blasphemes it.... When you see a Jew, cross yourself and say 'There goes a devil incarnate'.... They alone want to have the Messiah and be masters of the world." In his shorter but equally vitriolic Schem Hamephoras, Luther outdid even himself, purporting to believe that the Jews "have transformed God into the Devil, or rather into a servant of the Devil, accomplishing all the evil the Devil desires, corrupting unhappy souls, and raging against himself. In short, the Jews are worse than the devils." What then is to be done? Like St. John Chrysostom, Luther was skeptical of converting the Jews - it was "impossible," the same as trying to "convert the Devil.... [for they are] condemned to the flames of hell." Therefore, burn their synagogues and houses - "toss in hellfire" - and bury with dirt whatever will not burn; burn or remove from them their prayer books, talmudic works, and "also the entire Bible"; on pain of death let their rabbis be barred from teaching; let all Jews be outlawed and thus endangered on the public highways; and let none of them pray or teach or even give thanks to the Lord in public -

such is their "sevenfold guilt." In 1938 the Lutheran bishop of Thuringia, Martin Sasse, was inspired to celebrate Kristalnacht by issuing excerpts from Luther's diatribe. He rejoiced in the fact that that pogrom - when "the synagogues of Germany are aflame" - coincided with his hero's birthday, and "thus is capped the blessed struggle of our Fuehrer for the liberation of our people." To Bishop Sasse at least, the spirit of Luther was perfectly attuned to the events of the day. "In this hour the voice must be heard of the man, who, as the German Prophet of the sixteenth century, ... became the greatest anti-Semite of his time, the warner of his people against the Jews."

It is the thesis of Joshua Trachtenberg's The Devil and the Jews and Norman Cohn's Warrant for Genocide that the Nazi ideology of the Jew as menace and archconspirator, armed with superhuman powers, plotting for world dominion and the enslavement of the human race, etc., etc., has its origin in and is simply the secularized version of the demonization of the Jews. Only the devil is taken out, the Jews looming all the larger as menace and enemy. Though hardly the sole repository of the secularized version, the most notorious is The Protocols of the Elders of Zion, a principle buttress of Adolf Hitler's Judaeophobia. In conversations with Herman Rauschning that are recorded in The Voice of Destruction, Hitler spoke in decidedly medieval accents. The Jew represents the very principle of evil, evil incarnate, he pronounced. "I have read The Protocols," which he acknowledged were forgeries, but if historically false, they were, like classical drama, "intrinsically correct." The Protocols "simply appalled me, the stealthiness of the enemy and his ubiquity." "It is impossible to exaggeratge the formidable quality of the Jew as an enemy." To Rauschning's interjection as to what the real issue is, Hitler replied, "The struggle for world domination will be fought between us, between Germans and Jews.... There cannot be two Chosen People. We are God's people.... It's the sheer simple undiluted truth. Two worlds face one another - the men of God and the men of Satan!" In the same screed and equally atavistic, "The Jews, of course, invented capitalism. Let us make no mistake about it - capitalism is an invention of genius, of the Devil's own ingenuity."

The fact that at Treblinka (and probably other death camps) Jews were compelled to dress up as devils was not simply for the amusement of the camp guards and the gentile prisoners, but a macabre echo of the demonization of the Jews. Hitler and the Nazis were afraid of the Jews as, in Joachim Fest's apt phrase, "negative supermen," and the fewer the Jews the more dangerous they were, the most dangerous being "the intellectual Jew." From another perspective, at his pretrial interrogation at Nuremberg, 1 April 1946, Rudolf Hoess, the commandant of Auschwitz, recalled that Himmler had explained to him that "the reason" was that "if the extermination of Jewry did not take place at this time the German people would be eliminated by the Jews." Why was it necessary to kill the children? "Because they were dangerous to the German people?" "A child of three or four years old was dangerous to the German people?" "The German people could not rise at all because of the four-year old Jewish children[?]" "Yes" was the answer of the designer of Auschwitz to all these questions. "The leitmotiv of fear, of German cruelty as a result of that fear, had become the principal keynote of my entire war experience," the Italian war correspondent Curzio Malaparte concluded in his memoirs, Kaputt; "Poland [was] where the morbid ... quality of its nature was revealed to me in its full complexity. That which drives the Germans to cruelty, to deeds most coldly, methodically and scientifically cruel is fear. Fear of the oppressed, the defenseless, the weak, the sick; fear of women and of children, fear of the Jews."

It was because the Jews were a "menace" that the Germans sought to annihilate them to the last man, woman, and child, that they shipped them by the millions on the railroads from the ends of Europe to the death camps even though at enormous cost to the war effort, and that they persisted in genocide to the last hour of the war. Whereas other peoples, such as the Poles, were not "dangerous," never having undergone a two-millenia process of demonization, and so could be enslaved by the millions and exploited in the most ferocious manner for the benefit of the German war effort: "Our guiding principle must be that these people have but one justification for existence," Hitler himself explained of the Slavs in 1942, "to be of use to us economically," the point being that in the Third Reich Slavic peoples and others did have, Jews did not have a "justification for existence." It was an astounding revelation for some Germans that the phobias and obsessions about Jews were entirely baseless. At a war-crimes trial in 1947-48, S.S. General Erich Bach-Zelewski testified, "I am the only living witness but I must say the truth. Contrary to the belief of the National Socialists that the Jews were a highly organized group, the appalling fact was that they had no organization whatsoever.... It gives the lie to the old slogan that the Jews were conspiring to dominate the world and that they were so highly organized.... If they had had some sort of organization, these people would have been saved by the millions but instead they were taken completely by surprise."

That lesson has not been universally and unequivocally learned. Obviously, the devil theory of the Jews did not die with Hitler and the Third Reich. "There undeniably exists a mystical fear of the Jews," Nicolas Berdayev lamented in his Christianity and Anti-Semitism. This paranoia (unfortunate term but appropriate, alas) I find childish and embarrassing, humiliating and scandalous. It thwarts attempts at Christian-Jewish dialogue, most of all when it lingers in the air in ghostly fashion. One bumps up against it the way a blind person groping for a doorway runs into a wall of stone. My exposition will, I hope, faciliate dialogue, by showing what one is up against, rather than hampering it, by demonstrating how intrinsic to Christianity this complex of fear and hate has been. As Professor Baron remarked, anti-Jewish polemic "became permeated with magical ingredients which deeply colored the emotional reactions of medieval Christians, and [these] have ever since seriously handicapped understanding among the two faiths." Those of us who are Catholics must be undeterrably frank and relentlessly honest in sifting out our heritage. Much marvelous work is being done, by Father John Palikowski, to mention only one. Yet several generations are needed to effect the Second Vatican Council's imperative - as now understood - to purify the Church's teaching of Judaeophobia and set the historical record straight. I take my stand with Rabbi Tarfon's remarks in the Talmud, "You are not required to complete the work, but neither are you at liberty to abstain from it," and with Pope St. Gregory the Great, "Though scandal be taken at truth, it is better to permit the scandal than to abandon the truth."

II

An excursus on the theme of Japanese anti-Semitism in World War II will confirm the view that the demonization of the Jews, and the consequent fear of them as a "menace" and so forth, was the most fatal ideological antecedent of the Shoah.

Until 1931 and the invasion of Manchuria, the Japanese show very little consiousness of the Jews. This generalization needs to be qualified in that Japanese Christians and missionaries since the 1850's were aware of Jews and Judaism. It was widely known that the New York banker Jacob Schiff of Kuhn, Loeb, & Co. - incensed by the tsar's Black Hundreds and the Kishniev pogrom of 1903 - had extended a loan crucial for the navy during the Russo-Japanese war and had been instrumental in floating a second (Warburg of Hamburg) and third loan (Cassel of London). A Japanese Christian, Juji Nokada, reflected widespread attitudes when he wrote in 1934: "The Jewish people is generally said to be a matchless race in wealth, brains, talent and technique. We perceive how wonderful a race it is, judging from the fact that almost every number one figure in every sphere and era comes out of this race. This is surely the most Western of Asiatic people. And the Easternmost Asiatic people is also the number one courageous nation in the world and famous for winning every battle in which it has engaged. This is the Japanese race.... It was ... Jacob Schiff who helped Japan.... there are also Jewish people who are at present extending Japanese foreign markets.... they are buying Japanese goods and planning an anti-German boycott. The Japanese are not the kind of people to forget kindness to them."

Japanese anti-Semitism was a by-product of Japan's Siberian incursion, 1918-22, during the Russian civil war. Japanese forces operated closely with Russian White armies, such as that under Gregorii Semonov, who is remembered for having issued each of his troops a rifle, canteen, and copy of The Protocols of the Elders of Zion. Younger Japanese officers, many later to be army leaders, were very susceptible to the anti-Semitic poison; several of them became full-fledged anti-Semites and "experts" on the Jews; in the 20's and 30's they wrote many anti-Semitic tracts and pamphlets, translating, plagiarizing, adopting the Protocols and much else as they thought appropriate to Japan and the Far East. One of these, who had been posted to Semonov's headquarters and rivaled Goebbels and Streicher in such concoctions as Jewish Control of the World, was Colonel Yasue: "The Bolshevik Revolution is part of the Jewish plot; Zionism seems to be the goal of the Jews, but they actually want to control the world's economy, politics and diplomacy. Unless the Japanese realize this danger Japan will be left behind in the struggle for world supremacy; The League [of Nations], Freemasons, May Day Celebrations are under Jewish Control. The Jews are revolutionaries and they are encroaching on the Manchuria economy, and the Japanese should guard their interests in both Japan and Manchuria against the Jews. I dwell on the Jewish problem ... [for] besides such powers as Great Britain, the U.S., France ... there is a nation with no statehood and settled in those countries and have an influence there surpassing that of the native people so [that they] have a good control of the states. Furthermore, they are maintaining close contact among themselves and are boldly fighting to get the world at their mercy and achieve their ultimate ideal.... almost every state is a double state, a compound of two opposing nations.... The U.S. Government on the surface, [but] internally a Jewish U.S. Government [functions]." An equally redoubtable anti-Semitic fulminator was Yasue's naval colleague, Captain Inuzuka: "The League of Nations is a tool of Jewish financiers ... They intend to drive the Japanese out of China.... The Sassoon [banker centered in Shanghai] is in control of the Chekiang financiers through his close relations with the Chinese National Government which in turn controls the Central Bank of China. The anti-Japanese activities in England are all instigated by Jewish freemasons.... They are responsible for the immorality of the Japanese youth by showing of their [Jewish] films.... the Jews control the American press and thereby public opinion, turning it against Japan." The Jews are "the source of evil thoughts, I warn you that there is a by far greater national peril than the danger of an armed conflict and that a gang of 'Masonic' Jews have incessantly been master-minding international intrigues against Japan behind the scene in Britain, the United States, China and Russia ... "

From this volcanic flow of anti-Semitism was drawn, however, not the conclusion that the Jews as enemy and danger had to be destroyed, rather that Japan should ally itself and "use" the Jews' power, wealth, and influence to attain Japan's imperial ambitions. ("Utilization of the Jews" was a characteristic phrase.) To Inuzuka, the reality of the Jews, "namely the immeasurable golden power of control over the financial, political and industrial worlds and their characteristic that they do not have a country for peaceful living and military force, are absolutely favorable to our country. There is a strong probability of success [for our policy to enlist them in our cause]." Plans and proposals were put forward to settle, variously, 18,000 to 900,000 European Jews in China, Manchuria, Korea, the Shanghai area, and elsewhere - "it shall be in the form of a Jewish autonomous territory like Biro-Bidzhan, and shall be under the protection of Japan," "Manchurian Israel," etc. Would those Jews "take over"? Minister of Commerce and Finance Ikeda was all confidence: "Of course Japan can control the Jews! No matter where we settle them, we will maintain control.... Their self-government will be only on a local level. After all, are we not as able as the Chinese? Hundreds of years ago, China permitted thousands of Jews to settle in the Kaifeng region. Did they take over? By no means! In time, China, having benefited from their cleverness and industry, calmly swallowed them up until today there is no such thing as a 'Chinese Jew'. Surely we Japanese ... can do as well. And dangerous or not, we need the Jews.... their settlements will encourage others to release the capital we can't get any other way. By simply welcoming these beleaguered Europeans, we will gain the affection of the American Jews who control the press, the broadcast media, the film industry ... and possibly President Roosevelt himself. We cannot afford to alienate the Jews. If Japan imitates Germany's severe control of the Jews, discrimination will develop in connection with our foreign trade. On the other hand, if Japan goes in the opposite direction and befriends the Jews, entirely new economic possibilities will open up before us."

Little of these grandiose schemes were implemented or came to much. Japan's Jewish policy shifted a good deal: down to 1935 it was neutral and indifferent; thereafter to 1941 it was pro-Jewish and enthusiastic for the "alliance"; from 1942 to war's end and more directly subject to German influence, it shifted back to varying degrees of indifference and anti-Semitic hostility. But there were no massacres or persecutions, and one will not find in the 160 volumes of The International Military Tribunal for the Trial of War Criminals: Far East any reference to Jews as victims. In fact, approximately 60,000 European Jews survived in Japanese domains, some 18,000 in Shanghai; the Mir Academy of Lithuania after many viccissitudes found its way to Brooklyn and to Israel.

Why then the difference between the Japanese policy of "alliance" and German genocide? The Japanese had imported and swallowed every kind of anti-Semitism, and in its vilest form, such as Henry Ford's International Jew, which was of particular significance to them. But for all the fantasy and rabid rhetoric, Japanese anti-Semitism never ceased to regard the Jews as human beings. They were neither demoted to the animal world of goats, swine, vermin, bacilli, etc., which will justify any kind of inhumanity; nor were they demonized as a superhuman enemy, negative supermen, etc. Thus Japanese policy could be rational and pragmatic if also farfetched, rather than irrational and paranoid. Captain Inuzuka came close to putting his analytical finger on the point in a memorandum of 1940: "Is a Jewish problem fearful as alleged by the anti-Jewists? No; there is nothing to be afraid of unless we oppress, persecute and discriminate them without reason.... [The danger appears] only in [the] society of Western individualism where a strong religious prejudice exists but ... in Japan does not exist. In Japan ... we treat the Jews without any racial or religious prejudice ..."

Thus there was no "mystical fear" of the Jews in Japan, therefore no "warrant for genocide." Shoah is inconceivable in Hitler's Europe without centuries of Christian tradition, according to which the Jew was identified with Satan, Anti-Christ, the eternally wandering and plotting Jew, and so forth. The Christian image and myth of the Jew are not transferable to non-Christian societies and civilizations, since their Weltanschauungen are so radically different. A notable exception to the rule is, however, Islam, where, e.g., the Protocols, blood accusation, and much more of the same tenor flourish as nowhere else. No doubt the source of that susceptibility is Islam's Judaeo-Christian heritage as well as the conduit afforded by the Christian Arabs. Thus Moshe Perlmann has concluded that "to a very great, decisive measure, Islamic polemic directed against Jews and Judaism originated from and was fed by Christian sources."

CONCLUSION

Certain lines for future inquiry suggest themselves. What factors, e.g., in the Lutheran Scandinavian countries, nullified the image of the Jew as a demonized predator and menace? What is the precise relationship of words to deeds: how do verbal and other forms of defamation translate into violence and persecution? Is fear, as in Malaparte's exposition, a principal motive spring of aggression? As far as I know Freud and the psychologists say little about fear as a source of human aggression. How significant for the Shoah was the (unique?) double de-humanization of the Jews - as sub-human animals and as superhuman demons? If racial hatred was the most lethal factor in causing the Holocaust, to what degree had Jewish demonization been a decisive element in shaping the racial ideology and making the racial antipathy for Jews more extreme than that for other peoples?

REFERENCES

Baron, Salo W., A Social and Religious History of the Jews, 18 vols., (New York, Columbia U.P., 1952-83).

Berdyaev, Nicolas, Christianity and Anti-Semitism, (New York, Philosophical Library, 1954).

Cohen, Jeremy, The Friars and the Jews: The Evolution of Medieval Anti-Judaism, (Ithaca, Cornell U.P., 1982).

Cohn, Norman, The Pursuit of the Millenium: Revolutionary Millenarians and Mystical Anarchists of the Middle Ages, 3rd ed., (New York, Oxford U.P., 1970).

Cohn, Norman, Warrant for Genocide: The Myth of the Jewish World Conspiracy and the Protocols of the Elders of Zion, (New York, Harper & Row, 1967).

Dicker, Herman, Wanderers and Settlers in the Far East: A Century of Jewish Life in China and Japan, (New York, Twayne Publishers, 1962).

Edwards Jr., Mark U., Luther's Last Battles, (Ithaca, Cornell U.P., 1982).

Fest, Joachim C., Hitler, tr. fr. Ger. by R.& C. Winston, (New York, Random House: Vintage, 1975).

Hilberg, Raul, The Destruction of the European Jews, rev., 3 vols.,(New York, Holmes & Meier, 1985).

Kranzler, David, Japanese, Nazis & Jews: The Jewish Refugee Community of Shanghai, 1938-1945, (New York, Yeshiva U.P., 1976).

Lewis, Bernard, The Jews of Islam, (Princeton, Princeton U.P.,1984).

Luther, Martin, The Jews and their Lies, tr. fr. Ger. by Martin H. Bertram, in vol. 47 of "Luther's Works," (Philadelphia, Fortress Pr., 1977).

Mendelsohn, John, ed., The Holocaust: Selected Documents in Eighteen Volumes, (New York, Garland, 1982).

Malaparte, Curzio [Suckert], Kaputt, tr. fr. It. by Cesare Foligno, (New York, Dutton, 1946).

Moore, R.I., The Formation of a Persecuting Society, (Oxford, Blackwell, 1987).

Poliakov, Leon, The History of Anti-Semitism, tr. fr. Fr. by Richard Howard, vol. I, (New York, Vanguard Pr., 1965).

Rauschning, Hermann, Voice of Destruction, (New York, Putnam's, 1940).

Tokayer, Marvin and Swartz, Mary, The Fugu Plan: The Untold Story of the Japanese and the Jews during World War II., (London, Paddington Pr., 1979).

Stow, Kenneth R., Catholic Thought and Papal Jewry Policy, 1555-1593, (New York, Jewish Publication Society of America, 1976).

Trachtenberg, Joshua, The Devil and the Jews: The Medieval Conception of the Jew and its Relation to Modern Anti-Semitism, (New Haven, Yale U.P., 1943).

THE WITNESS OF GOD'S PEOPLE TO THE WORLD AFTER THE HOLOCAUST

H. EBERHARD von WALDOW

Pittsburgh Theological Seminary, 606 North Highland Avenue
Pittsburgh, PA 15206, U.S.A.

The Holocaust has opened up a new chapter in the relations between Christianity and Judaism. In spite of the traditional differences, both sides have become aware of the common basis which should be strong enough to sustain the strain of deep disagreements. This paper is trying to draw some consequences from this new situation. Jewish-Christian dialogues are the basis for any new development, but they are no end in themselves. What must follow is a new understanding of belonging together which can be expressed through the development of a theology of the People of God including Jews and Christians alike. In order to do so, Christian theology must first overcome its long tradition to understand the term People of God exclusively as the Church of Jesus Christ. In addition, the mission of the People of God must be redefined as giving a witness, and there must be a clear understanding regarding the addresses. Who are the ones God's people are sent to and what is the witness which they are in need to hear? The discussion of these questions begins with a brief historical survey of the Christian understanding of the concept of the People of God, of the recipients of their witness and of its content.

THE CONCEPT OF THE PEOPLE OF GOD IN THE CHRISTIAN TRADITION

It is common knowledge that Christianity started within Judaism as a Jewish sect (Ben-Chorin, 58ff). The first Christians were Jews. They prayed in the temple of Jerusalem, Acts 2:46, worshiped in synagogues, Acts 6:9; 9:2, and adhered to the commandments of the Torah. The Roman authorities did not differentiate between Jews and Christians and considered the beginning struggle of these two religious groups as an inner Jewish affair. As a result, Christianity began under the umbrella of the Jewish religion with all the privileges of a *religio licita*.

There were two major points of controversy between traditional Judaism and the new Christian group in its midst. The first centered around the person of Jesus from Nazareth. Christians believed him to be the fulfillment of the messianic expectations of the Old Testament and, therefore, applied to him all the honorific titles of the Old Testament and of contemporary Judaism which were understood as messianic titles such as Son of God, Son of David, *Kyrios*, Son of Man, etc. Consequently, the Jesus group understood itself as the eschatological People of God of the end of the days under Jesus Christ and they expected his imminent return (Ruether in Peck/Wiesel). As such they called themselves "the elect" or "the saints."

The new self-understanding of this small Christ community within traditional Judaism is expressed very clearly by their confession formulae (Cullmann). The oldest is probably the brief, one-membered liturgical formula "I believe that Jesus Christ is the Son of God" (Acts 8:37, Western texts only; I John 2:22; 4:15; Heb. 4:14). Another example is Phil. 2:6-11 with its climatic statement "Jesus Christ is Lord."

Closely related to this christological issue was the interpretation of Christ's death and resurrection. Christians charged that "Jesus of Nazareth, a man attested to by God with mighty works and wonders ---, this Jesus, delivered up according to the definite plan and foreknowledge of God, you crucified and killed by the hands of lawless men. But God raised him up ---" (Acts 2:23f; 3:14f; 4:10; 10:39f). This death was understood to have taken place "for our sins" (I Cor. 15:3; I Pet. 3:18; I Tim. 2:6), as the writer of Ephesians states in his programmitic introduction: "Through (the shedding of) his blood we possess freedom in him, forgiveness for our lapses" (Eph. 1:7).

The other major point of controversy was the understanding of the Torah which goes back to the preaching of Jesus (Klein, 39ff). Contemporary Judaism believed the will of God was revealed in the written Torah and interpreted and applied to all possible situations in daily life by the scribes, theologians and teachers. Obedience which God demands is a matter of faithfully and accurately fulfilling the letter of God's law and the details of its interpretations. Contrary to this, Jesus taught an obedience of the heart guided by understanding of God's will and intentions, which leads to affirmation from within. Such new radical obedience, on the one hand, frees from the letter of the Torah, and on the other includes the whole will of man, their thoughts, desires and intentions. This freedom from the letter meant also freedom to revise the letter where it had become obsolete, meaningless or insufficient.

Another aspect is inseparably connected with the teachings of the Apostle Paul. First, as the learned Pharisee Saul, he saw the new Christians as an insult to the God of Mt. Sinai who had revealed his Torah to his chosen people as his will and as the way of truth, or as his definition of right and wrong or good and evil. Following traditional beliefs, this Torah must be taught as a light to those who are in darkness and as a guide to the blind (Rom. 2:18f). But, later, having become a Christian himself, he discovered that the crucified and risen Jesus Christ is the <u>telos</u> (= goal) of the law (Rom. 10:4). Salvation comes without the Torah through faith in Jesus Christ (Rom. 3:21). With the development of this revolutionary message Paul opened the doors for the gentiles to become Christians, without the need to join Judaism first. With this message, on the one hand, Paul infuriated his fellow Jews who accused him of teaching to forsake Moses, telling them not to circumcise their children or observe the customs (Acts 21:21, 28; 23:29). On the other hand, for the Jewish Christians the questions were: how much and what of the Torah was binding for them?

Both issues in dispute, Jesus Christ and the interpretation and binding character of the Torah could not be resolved by way of a compromise between the Synagogue, the gentile Christians and the Jewish Christians in the middle. The riot scenes in the book of Acts (Acts 4:1-3; 5:17, 26; 6:11f; 8:3; 12:1-3; 21:27ff;; 22:22f; 23:12f) show clearly that religious emotions went high and overzealousness made a reasonable discussion, that might have led to a compromise, impossible. So the Christians split off from the synagogue and formed their own congregations with their own meeting places. This was a development of enormous consequences for both Judaism and Christianity. At the time of the primitive church this split was probably unavoidable and necessary, but at the same time it was tragic.

The split was necessary because it sharpened the issues and defined the dividing line between Jews and Christians. Christ was considered the separating factor because of the understanding of the person of Jesus Christ, his teaching and the meaning of his death and resurrection (Klein, 92ff). So, Judaism became the antagonist who was used by the Church to define her identity: the people who accept Christ over against those who reject him (Lapide/Moltman, 9ff). With this, the early Christian confession "Jesus Christ is the Son of God" took on an anti-Jewish edge. An immediate practical consequence of this split was the unimpeded admission of gentiles to the Christian congregations. This led to the eventual transformation of the Church into a gentile Church.

On the other hand, this split was the great tragedy right at the beginning of the history of the Church of Jesus Christ. The prevailing climate of hostility between the old and new religion overshadowed the inseparable bonds between Christians and Jews. Christianity is unthinkable without its Jewish roots. To begin with the obvious, both groups worship the same God and besides him "there is no saviour" (Isa. 43:11). Christians simply added to the traditional Old Testament epithets or characterizations of God - such as Creator, the God of Abraham, Isaac and Jacob, the God who brought Israel out of Egypt, the God of Sinai - another one, the Father of Jesus Christ. The sacred scriptures of the people of Israel became the Bible of the primitive church. Jesus, believed to be the Son of God, was a Jew and the honorific titles applied to him came from the Jewish tradition. Jesus' teaching was deeply rooted in Judaism (Ben-Chorin, pp. 63ff). Even his new interpretation of the Torah develops ideas already present in the tradition. What he says about total obedience that goes beyond the letter of the law continues the <u>paraneses</u> of the deuteronomic preachers with their appeal to gratitude, to inner disposition of the heart "You shall love the Lord your

God with all your heart, and with all your soul, and with all your might." Also the prophetic tradition must be mentioned in this context (Zimmerli, 98ff). All this means, Jesus Christ not only separates Christians from Jews, he also binds them together. The entire Old Testament shows that Israel lives from promise to fulfillment, towards God's actions in the future with the coming of the Messiah at the end of the days. So does the Church of Jesus Christ, waiting for the parousia, the return of Christ in glory.

Not even the epistles of the Apostle Paul are so anti-Jewish as they appear to be. In recent decades, the study of Paul has shifted away from the emphasis of influences from the Hellenistic world. Instead the focus is now more on his roots in Jewish-rabbinic and apocalyptic traditions, and even the Old Testament itself is more and more discovered as a key for the understanding of Paul's theology (Barth).

The hostile climate during the period of the primitive church did not allow these common points to play the role which they should have played. Instead the anti-Jewish attitude of the primitive church was carried over into the following centuries. With this the history of the Christian Church, which had superseded Judaism as the People of God, began.

Since its separation from Judaism, the Christian Church fought on two fronts, against Judaism and against the world of paganism. In the 2nd century, the fight against Judaism was continued. The struggle over the validity and binding character of the Jewish Torah may have come to an end, but it was a regrettable fact, that the early church was unable to give up or even to soften its anti-Jewish attitude in order to take seriously its bonds with the descendants of Old Testament Israel. At the beginning of this period, the Epistle of Barnabas goes so far as to explain that the Old Testament was not even intended for the Jews. In all its parts and details it must be read allegorically as Christ prophecies. This anti-Jewish attitude is continued from the early Apostolic Fathers to the writings of the Church Fathers (Hruby; Ruether, 117ff) and in its clearest form it found its expression in a special literary genre that has been called the Adversus Judaeos literature. The reasons for this continued hostility may not be quite clear, but it shows that Christianity was still understanding its identity in contrast to the Jews.

At the same time, this new religion had to confront the world of Hellenism and paganism. This confrontation took place on both the political as well as the intellectual scene. With their rejection of the caesar cult, Christians found themselves in direct confrontation with the Roman authorities. In this context, their confession Kyrios Christos assumed a political edge. Christ is Kyrios and not Caesar (E.g. Phil. 2:11; Rom. 10:9; I Cor. 12:3; Cullmann). This led to persecutions and martydom. The intellectual struggle was carried out by the Apologists. Christianity had become a religion to be reckoned with in the pagan world and Hellenistic philosophers begun to attack Christianity. The Christian mission was at stake and the Apologists, well trained in Hellenistic philosophies, fought back. They took on the task to demonstrate - if not to prove - that Christianity is based on revealed truth and as such superior to all pagan religions as well as philosophies. Here Christianity was established as the norm which must be used to discover the foolishness of the other religions or to measure the degree of truth of philosophy.

In the medieval world the situation of the Christian Church had completely changed. The eschatological People of God at the beginning of Christianity had become the one institutionalized and centralized, authoritative, universal Church, and the pagan Roman Empire had given way to a universal Christian state under a Christian emperor.

After completion of the Christianization of the peoples north of the Alps in the 8th century, there was no serious outside challenge to the papal church anymore. The 8th century saw the confrontation with the new Islamic religion in Spain, in South France and later, during the period of the crusades, in the Middle East. There was the ongoing missionary activity along the Eastern frontier. But both events did not generate a significant theological discussion. Basically, there was no outside challenge to the Church anymore. There was no need for a Christian witness beyond the church walls. This was a period for an extensive monologue of the Church with itself.

The development of the Christian doctrine was concluded. Theology in the early medieval period was largely preoccupied with interpretation of dogmas and their developments into the categories of believing and knowing. The task of the previous centuries to formulate doctrine had given way to the task to demonstrate the necessity of such doctrine and to articulate their truth in a comprehensible and reasonable manner. The concepts of the one universal Church and the universal state in a unified world under God were brought together in the unity of an impressive edifice of Christian doctrines based on the unity of philosophical and theological thinking. In this world, Jews were considered an undesirable relic of the past. The pendulum swang between unfriendly toleration and outright persecution.

The period of the Reformation followed with a different kind of preoccupation of the Church with itself. Spurred by the spirit of the Renaissance where human interest shifted from the world of God to the world of man and people began to question the all-powerful and divinely ordained orders, the Reformation set in as a protest against the institutionalization of the gospel and the resulting belief in good works as the way to heaven and controlled by the Church. Now, with the rediscovery of God's mercy, quite naturally, Jesus Christ, christology and soteriology became again the center piece of Christian theology. The emphasis on faith over against good works led to the rediscovery of the Church as the People of God and communio of the believers. From now on Christian theology is again Christ-centered, and this in all its dogmatic loci. This theological reorientation did not extend over Israel and Judaism. According to Luther, the meaning of the Old Testament was to prefigure Jesus Christ. Christians are the spiritual Israel, Jews were accused of idolatrous partiality and self-righteousness. However, Luther saw his time as the eschatological end time and therefore - like the first Christians - he expected the Jews prompted by the discovery of the true gospel to turn to Christ. But since Luther's efforts to convert Jews proved unsuccessful, he became very hostile and returned to the traditional anti-Judaism of his time (Gritsch/Tanenbaum). This situation regarding the Jewish question during the time of the Reformation is reminiscent of the Middle Ages. The Church was preoccupied with itself, and whenever this is the case, the Jews are an annoying alien element. On the other hand, with its emphasis on christology, the Reformation resembles the ancient Church. Whenever christology is emphatically moved into the center of Christian thinking, the attitude towards Jews turns hostile. With this attitude towards Jews and Judaism the Christian Church moved into the modern age.

During the centuries following the Reformation, the situation of the Church was ambiguous. On the one hand, Christian theology continued to be preoccupied with itself. The period immediately following the Reformation has been called the period of confessionalism. Lutherans and Calvinists were busy to define themselves, to dissociate themselves from each other and to transform the content of the Bible into a textbook of revealed truths with absolute tenets and final formulae. On the other side of the spectrum, the Catholic Church tried to regain its strength and to recuperate from the shock of the Reformation. This led to the counter-reformation with the focus on topics such as faith and works or scripture and tradition. In this context neither one of these confessions felt any need for dealing theologically with the Jewish question. The old baggage was simply kept in the closet.

On the other hand, Christianity or Christian theology was confronted with a new intellectual world with the new enlightened human mind as the determinative factor. The traditional understanding of the world with its orders based on religious foundations was coming to an end. The supernatural, once the basis for understanding reality had become the problem of the limits of human reason. Man, once understood as God's creation destined to live within divine orders, now understands himself as a natural being who must rely on his own reason and his own senses. These changes that have their roots in the Renaissance led to the beginning of the new age of secularism with this new attitude of the human mind penetrating all areas of life and reality. Religion had become a private affair. The reaction of the Church to this new challenge was slow. There could be protest in form of a retreat into orthodoxy, into piety and spirituality, or plain reduction of religion to morality or an appendix to philosophy. A positive outcome of this confrontation was the emergence of historical-critical theology which led to a critical review of all aspects of Christian teaching with the new tools of historical-scientific research.

Whatever the reaction of the Church to these fundamental changes was, the most important effect was that a principle borderline between Church and world had developed. The secularized world under the control of the all-powerful human mind emerged as the new partner of the Church to talk to. The issues were the relationship between the word of God and the world, or the situation of man before God and the role of the People of God in the world. With all this the Church found itself in a position similar to the one after the apostolic age. At that early time, the Church was talking to the world of Hellenism and paganism. Now a new genuine partner had appeared on the scene, the world of secularism with its various manifestations during the time following the Enlightenment.

In principle, this is still the situation today, the Church of Jesus Christ, understanding itself as the People of God on earth, facing a secularized world. However, the boundary is not quite clear, rather it is blurred and fluid. The Church which is not of this world, but in this world, has become in many regards part of this world. In many instances, the teaching of the Church or Christian life has made adjustments to the world, or in turn, the secular world has adopted some aspects of Christianity (Judeo-Christian Heritage), while ignoring others that are running counter to certain cultural traditions or trends. Nevertheless, in principle the constellation is clear, the Church proclaiming Christ as Lord, over against the world in which man poses as Lord.

This began with the Renaissance and it fully took effect with the Enlightenment. There are, however, differences between this past and our present. The man of the Enlightenment was optimistic, full of self-confidence, and fully aware of his newly found freedom he set out to conquer the world. Today's situation is different. This optimism is gone. The secularized man of today is insecure, confused, helpless and full of fear in a world with more and greater problems than he is able to handle.

Facing this situation, the People of God is called today to confront this world with the word of God which the believers know, but which the world does not. Or, in other words, the People of God is called by God as his witness to give testimony that God is Lord and not man. In the light of this, two questions must be asked:

1. Who is the witness?
2. What is his testimony?

GOD'S PEOPLE AS HIS WITNESSES:

Who is the People of God? According to the tradition of the Christian Church which was briefly outlined above, this is of course the Church of Jesus Christ, the new People of God in the new covenant. However, after the Holocaust, the Church cannot speak this way anymore. This is exclusive language which implicitly would allow the old replacement theology to continue: the old covenant is revoked, the Church of Jesus Christ has replaced Old Testament Israel, and quite automatically, unfaithful Israel becomes part of the godless world. Consequently, mission to the Jews is a special task within the general Christian witness to the world.

When Christians want to take the Holocaust seriously, it is not enough to show shock and horror over the killing of six million Jews. It is also not enough to join those who exclaim "remember" or "never again," or to focus on the reasons that made these atrocities possible. First of all, Christians must recognize the Jews as human beings, and discovering them as their fellow human beings they must ask "who are they?" Once this question is raised, they remember the Old Testament which takes up two-thirds of their Bible and which they believe to be or to contain the word of God. Here they discover that part of the basis of their faith is a presentation of the history of the People of Israel, or God's history with this people. Here God gives the answer to their question.

The Bible tells us, the People of Israel, the Jewish people, our fellow human beings are made in the image of God like Christians believe they are. Now the monstrosity of the Holocaust begins to emerge. Human beings made in the image of God killed six million other human beings made in the same image. What a terrible insult to God the Creator! At this point other, in one way or another, similar genocides come to mind. This demonstrates what humans without God, left to their own devices in a sinful world, can do. But the biblical story does not end with Genesis 11. It continues with the election of Abraham, God's covenant with him, and leads after a long roundabout way to Mt. Sinai. Here God makes a covenant with Israel. The result is a unique relationship between God and this people. Yahweh becomes Israel's God and Israel God's people. Inseparably connected with this covenant concept is the Torah (Ben-Chorin, 165ff). God gives it to Israel and his people must live by it. The purpose of this covenant if for the first time stated in Genesis 12:2: Israel shall be a blessing to all the nations out of which she was elected for the covenant. Later, in the prophetic tradition this is stated differently. Hosea is using the old priestly formula "knowledge of God/Yahweh," which means knowing who God is and knowing God's Torah as God's order for people to live peacefully together. According the Dtjes. Israel is Yahweh's witness to all the nations whom he has chosen to testify that he is God and no one else (Isa. 43:10, 12; 44:8). In the paranesis of Deut. the nations who see Israel's wisdom and understanding coming from the Torah, state full of envy and admiration: "Surely, this great nation is a wise and understanding people" (Deut. 4:6). In Isa. 2:2-3 the prophet expects the nations of their own accord to come to Jerusalem in order to learn this Torah. It is Israel's task as Yahweh's covenant people to bring the knowledge of the one and true God and his Torah to all the nations of the world.

This covenant is an eternal covenant (Gen. 17:7, 13, 19; Exod. 31:16; Lev. 24:8). Israel may break it by not lving up to her covenant obligation, but God cannot and will not revoke it. Even during the darkest hours of Israel's history, after the catastrophy of 587, when Israel had ample reason to doubt the validity of the covenant, Isa. 40:27, it was reaffirmed that "the word of our God will stand forever," Isa. 40:8.

In the light of all this, the answer to the question, "who is the People of God?" must be the People of Israel of the Old Testament and their descendents, the Jewish people today. This means, Christians, when they believe to be the People of God through Jesus Christ, they do not replace the Old Testament Israel, rather they are an addition. What they believe to be the new covenant is not a substitute for the old one, rather it is the old Sinai covenant in a revised and new edition. So, we ask again: who is the People of God today? The answer is: Jews and Christians together constitute the People of God and they together are charged to bring the knowledge of God to the godless world.

Once again we must return to the primitive church and its separation from Judaism. At that time, the separation was a tragic necessity because Jesus Christ had to be established as the basis and center of Christian beliefs. The Jewish community rejected Jesus as the Christ and refused to recognize their traditional God as the father of Jesus Christ. However, this separation was too radical. "A great chasm had been fixed" which the Church has been unable to cross throughout its history. At that time the focus was exclusively on the problem of Christology so that the strong historical and theological ties, beginning with the fact, that Jesus Christ himself was a Jew, were overlooked. The God of the Old Testament Israel has many characteristics. He is not only the Father of Jesus Christ. He is also God the Creator, the God of Abraham, Isaac and Jacob, the God who brought Israel out of Egypt, and the God of Sinai. With the adoption of the Jewish holy scriptures as Christian Bible, these characteristics of the God of Israel became part of the developing Christian belief system and, therefore, Christianity will always be connected with Judaism. This the primitive Church failed to see. As a result, it was not understood that Israel's God as the God of history continues the history with his people beyond and after the cross of Jesus Christ alongside the Christian Church, and overshadowed by the polemic of the Apostle Paul against the Torah as a tool for salvation, the full and lasting meaning of the Torah was not fully appreciated. The root of this development was that in the early Church God, the father of Jesus Christ, had absorbed all the other traditional characteristics of the God of the Old Testament. The Christ-centrism of Christian theology had become a Christ-monism and whenever this happens, there is no room for appreciation of Judaism.

This development could have been prevented had the primitive church fully understood the implication of their accusation "this Jesus, delivered up according to the definite plan and foreknowledge of God, you crucified--" (Acts 2:23; 3:17f; 4:27f). According to this, the Jewish people were used by God to carry out his plan, but if this is so, the participation of the Jews in the crucification cannot be explained in terms of guilt.

Christianity after the Holocaust has to reestablish the fact that the People of God in a secular godless world is constituted by Judaism and Christianity together. They are the ones who know God, the godless world does not.

Recognition of this fact must lead to a reorientation of Christian theology which will deeply affect the traditional doctrine of the Church. As long as the Church defines itself as the "assembly of all believers among whom the gospel is preached--" (Augsburg Confession VII) or as the body of Christ, there seems to be no problem. But when the Church continues with the claim to be the People of God in the new covenant called by God to bring the witness of Christ to the world, the problems begin. This self-understanding was developed when theologians saw no need to take Judaism seriously or when Christian anti-Judaism was not recognized as a danger. Today such statements cannot be repeated anymore. A Church that defines itself as the People of God implies that the Jews are not part of it. When the task of the Church is exclusively seen as the Christian witness to the world, Judaism becomes part of the world and the Christian witness is also directed to the Jews. Of course, Christian ecclesiology is Christ-centered. There cannot be a Christian Church without Jesus Christ. The entity "Church" cannot be separated from Jesus Christ, but the entity "People of God" can. Christians cannot claim that they constitute God's people on earth alone. Based on the Bible, they can only claim that they are part of God's people. Only this leaves room for the Jews. They are the other part. This means, the traditional Christian doctrine of the Church must be preceded by a doctrine of the People of God. This People of God is the larger body encompassing Christians and Jews, and since the Church of Jesus Christ exists only as part of it, Christian ecclesiology can only follow the doctrine of the People of God. A theology of the People of God must include several elements:

1. There will be a Jewish way to talk about the People of God and there will be a Christian way. Both are based on the Old Testament, but in the Jewish tradition this basis leads to the midrashic and talmudic tradition, whereas in Christianity it leads to the New Testament. Both groups will probably speak a different language reflecting different histories. However, both groups will speak about the same issue but each leaving room for the legitimacy of the other.

2. The Christian way of speaking about the People of God must begin with Jesus Christ, because Christians believe that Jesus the Jew extended the original Sinai convenant to include gentiles. Jesus Christ, of course, is the regrettable cause for the division into two groups within the People of God. This division led to the separation in the primitive Church. After the Holocaust, however, this separation must be reduced to an internal affair within God's people. This division should never be allowed again to destroy the appearance of the one People of God as a unity before the secular world.

3. A Christian theology of the People of God is largely based on the Old Testament, the part of the Bible which Jews and Christians have together. Here, Christian study of the Old Testament will have to make a major contribution. The Old Testament as part of the Christian canon has been a perennial problem. The question was, what is the Christian interpretation of the Old Testament, or, what is the message of the Old Testament for Christians? There was never a fully satisfactory answer. Allegorical or typological exegesis denied the Old Testament its own message. Contrastation with the New Testament - in terms of prophecy and fulfillment or law and gospel - did not do justice to the Old Testament, and the historical approach where the religion of Israel is the historical precursor of Christianity could not solve the problem (Gunneweg). It is quite understandable that in the 19th century, influenced by the new historical-critical approach which had undermined the traditional understanding of the Old Testament eminent theologians such as F. D. Schleiermacher at the beginning of the century and Adolf Harnack at the end levelled harsh attacks against the Old Testament. Schleiermacher was willing to tolerate the Old Testament in the canon as an appendix to the New Testament (Kraus, 173) whereas Harnack went so far as to call for its abolishment as the major order of the day (Kraus, 386).

Against this background, the Old Testament gains new importance as basis for a theology of the People of God. In the writings of the Old Testament the covenant people give testimony of their belief in God the Creator of world and mankind, in the God of Abraham, Isaac and Jacob, in the God who brought Israel out of Egypt, in the God of the Sinai covenant who gave the Torah, and in the God who gave the promised land. This, however, is not just the testimony of a past age, or a voice from a preliminary state of Christianity. This testimony comes to us from a past age, but it is still the testimony of contemporary Judaism, God's people in the old convenant side by side with Christianity. As such, this testimony of the Old Testament is still valid today. For Jews today the God of the Old Testament is still the Creator, the God of the promises to the patriarchs, of the covenant and the Torah, or the Lord of history. When in Christianity this God has become the father of Jesus Christ, these Old Testament beliefs and images are still valid and relevant. Without them the Christian God would be incomplete. This is the living God of his people today, Jews and Christian together.

4. Development of a theology of the People of God is not just a matter of self-understanding or identity. A theology of the People of God leads to an imperative. This is the calling of the Old Testament covenant people, to be a "light to the nations," or to bring to them the knowledge of God. In the post-Holocause era it is indeed a great step forward that a Jewish-Christian dialogue has developed almost everywhere. This was overdue after centuries of hostility or indifference in order to get to know and to learn to respect each other. However, once it is rediscovered that Jews and Christians are bound together by more than just the need for a dialogue, this dialogue becomes the basis for a "christian theology of the people of Israel" (van Buren) which leads to the discovery that a "Christian theology of the people of Israel" is actually a theology of the People of God. The next step is the witness of the People of God, Jews and Christians together, to a godless and secular world. The question is not, can there be such a common witness in the light of the differences between Christians and Jews? The question can only be: what is this common witness? Without taking this step and pushing for this question, the Christian dialogue with Jews, even if conducted with the best intentions, or well meant and enlightened statements about the one and eternal covenant, will remain empty rhetoric. What is this common witness? Or in terms of content: What can Jews and Christians say together to a world that seems to be in dire need for a credible and relevant witness from God's people.

THE CONTENT OF THE TESTIMONY

What the People of God can say as a testimony to the world, as a light to the nations, will to a large degree depend on the answers to two basic questions: Based on their common Biblical foundation, where are areas of agreement where Jews and Christians can speak together? What does the world of today need to hear as the testimony of the ones who believe that God is in charge?

The search for answers here is confronted with two hurdles, one posed by the disagreement between Judaism and Christianity, and the other by tradition. A credible witness of Christians and Jews must show that both are basically making the same points. The witness of the one part of the People of God must not invalidate or neutralize the witness of the other. Unless both parts testify to the same facts in basic agreement, the testimony will be ineffective. Each side will speak its own language, reflecting its own traditions. This is regrettable and at the same time in the light of our past unavoidable, but the content must basically be the same.

When Christians want to speak in unison with Jews, they have to avoid the points of controversy between them, such as: Jewish monotheism and the Christian doctrine of the Holy Trinity, the Jewish concept of the transcendence of God and the Christian doctrine of incarnation, messianic expectation in Judaism and Christology, and the understanding of the Torah in the Jewish and of <u>nomos</u> in the Christian tradition. The difficulty begins with the traditional Christian terminology. Christians like to talk of the Christian witness to the world, or they want to spread the gospel of Jesus Christ. In shorthand, they want to evangelize. The problem is that this rhetoric is exclusive. There is no room for the other partner in God's covenant. He is either not taken into account, or he too is the object of evangelizing. In this terminology, the traditional Christ centrism has become Christ monism, which means Christian theology cannot say anything without pointing to Jesus Christ. Within a theology of the People of God, a deliberate attempt must be made to open up the Christ centrism so that the differences between Judaism and Christianity are transcended to one basic joint testimony.

The other hurdle is the tradition. In Protestantism content and language of the witness were shaped during the Reformation. As was pointed out above, this was a struggle within the Church, between late medieval catholicism and the reformers. At that time, the Church was struggling to rediscover its very essence. The redemptive work of Jesus Christ was the focal point and consequently salvation, mercy, justification and sanctification became major topics. In addition, in the new philosophical context of Renaissance and humanism that led to a new understanding of man, the Reformation helped the Church to free itself from medieval balast and to become a modern Church in a modern world. The Reformation could become such a powerful movement only because the issues of the day were addressed in a relevant and credible manner. The language of the Reformation shaped Protestant theology, it characterized the message of the protestant churches, and even today's protestant teaching and preaching to a large degree still reflects the issues and the language of the Reformation.

However, the time has changed, man has changed and the situation today is completely different. The Renaissance man and the humanist of the beginning of the 16th century who with his newly discovered freedom of the mind and intellectual self-confidence set out to conquer the world around him, has given way to the man of the end of the 20th century. He thinks he is in charge to run the affairs of his world and has immense power at his disposal to do so. But more and more is he discovering that he cannot. He is insecure and full of fear, there is no common denominator anymore in his pluralistic world, and traditional values and principles are crumbling away. The pace of life in the modern world has become so fast that there is no time for reflection and intellectual catching up. In view of this situation, the traditional language of the Reformation explaining the gospel of Jesus Christ has become irrelevant. The secular man in the godless world of today cannot be addressed like the man of the 16th century who was about to liberate himself from the legacy of the Middle Ages. The good news of the gospel which he needs does not derive so much from the second article of the apostolic creed rather much more from the first and the Old Testament, and this is an area where Christians and Jews can to a large degree speak in unison.

Based on the theology of the cross the Christian witness has always emphasized salvation. However, the traditional "you are saved, you are forgiven through God's mercy" which still reflects the setting of the Reformation lacks relevance in the situation of the people of today and should be interpreted differently. In today's world the good news is not that man is in charge to run this world, rather the God of the Bible is. Humans do not have to worry about how to do it, and humanity may know that the future of this world does not depend on questionable human decisions. Man's dominion of the world is a dominion under God's authority. This God is God the creator, and his creation means that he created order out of chaos (Westermann, 150ff). With this act he has established himself as the one and only God and as the Lord of the world. A world created by God means a world of order. There is order in the universe, in all aspects of nature and in time and history. This order needs to be recognized. There is no need for man to search for an order or to establish his own. There is no need for him to make up his own scale of values or principles. Rather, when man accepts God's order he stays within it, protects it and maintains it.

This new interpretation of the Gospel means to shift the Christian emphasis from salvation to the Torah. It was God's mercy that he gave (sola gratia) his Torah to man to live by, and it is God's continued mercy that he makes his Torah known even in a fallen and sinful world. This is an area where Christianity has a lot to learn from Judaism.

In order to understand the Torah fully Protestants will have to revise their traditional understanding of this important term. In the context of soteriology and through the polemic of the Apostle Paul Torah = nomos is in bad repute. However, the Jewish tradition is more helpful in this context. The Septuagint rendition of Torah with nomos is too narrow and legalistic (Ben-Chorin, 165ff). Martin Buber preferred the German "Weisung," in English "instruction, directive." The Torah is the center piece of the Jewish religion and as such it is based on the concept of order. God's order is not only established in the world of nature but also in the world of man. Here the Torah regulates how people live with one another and under God's authority within this order. As such the Torah marks the way to shalom with all the different elements which this loaded term encompasses, such as peace, welfare, wellbeing, harmony, prosperity, wholeness, etc.

The Torah of course covers all aspects of human life. However, one aspect deserves special attention. Today, this is the area of war, peace and justice which has gained particular importance ever since, thanks to modern technology, wars have deteriorated to indiscriminate mass killings and humanity lives under the constant threat of nuclear destruction. This issue overlaps with the issue of justice. In order to build up and to maintain the nuclear arsenals immense amounts of money and human resources are spent which otherwise could be used to improve the quality of life and to meet human needs. In this situation, it is the special responsibility of the People of God to turn to the basis of their knowledge of God and to look for guidance. Under the impact of the new problems posed by the nuclear age, an Old Testament train of thought will come to light that has been neglected throughout the centuries as a result of accommodation of Judaism and Christianity to common secular thinking and customs. At the end of this paper, there is no room for details (von Waldow), only a general summary can be given here. Based on the Old Testament as a whole the message is: in God's creation and within the order which he has created, there is no room for war. Among humanity which is created as a unity in God's image the idea that one human being kills another is an abomination. Before God, war is sin. This is the bottom line which must not be watered down by human concepts trying to justify at least some kinds of war. Peace cannot be based on military power (Deut. 17:14ff; Isa. 30:15f (7:9); 31:1-3; Ps. 20:7f; 33:16-18; 44:4-8; 46:9-11; 147:10f), it is the result of justice and righteous in human society, according to the prophets, "but let justice roll down like waters and righteousness like an ever flowing stream" (Amos 5:24; cp. also Mich. 6:8).

This issue receives special emphasis through a striking historic coincidence. In 1945, the news about the full extent of the Holocaust broke. The civilized world learned that for the first time in history the institutions and organizations of a society were used for reasons of ideology to systematically destroy with the tools of modern technology a certain group of people. At the same time, the first atomic bombs were dropped destroying entire cities with their people. This sequence of events demonstrates what humans who do not respect any limitations imposed upon them by God's order in which they were placed to live can do with the power of technology which they have created. The gas chambers of the concentration camps demonstrate where the world was in 1945, but the atomic bombs ushered in a new age. What happened to European Jewry becomes now a warning. Humans are now able to multiply this destruction in the nuclear age unless they learn restraint which can only come from the word of God.

Here lies the particular relevance of the witness of the People of God today. Coming from the experience of the Holocaust and in view of what has become a possibility in the nuclear age, their testimony with regard to God's order in this world has become the order of the day, and the question before Jews and Christians alike is: can they do that together as the People of God confronting a godless world?

Justice, in particular social justice or in more general terms, the individual in the society, is another topic that needs to be addressed by the Jewish-Christian testimony. Here we are dealing with a long tradition that goes back all the way to the Enlightenment. This was the time when enlightened philosophers developed a comprehensive view of man and human society, and from here they derived the idea that each person is born with the moral claim on some basic rights which ought not to be denied by any government. These "natural rights" such as "liberte, egalite and fraternite" were decreed in the French Revolution, or as "life, liberty and the pursuit of happiness" were written into the American Declaration of Independence.

These ideas were developed in opposition to the absolute state. At that time, the state represented the ultimate power over humans and the intention was to limit its power in order to protect the individual. On the other hand it must be noted that the idea of some basic natural and unalienable rights of the individual was not developed in the context of Christian theology. At that time, as was pointed out above, theology had its own and different agenda with other issues. The Church failed to respond to contemporary questions or to participate in the discussion of the day.

Without doubt, the Church with its special interest in humanity and human dignity could have made a major contribution. However, to a large degree Christian theology still understood the empirical state as a God given order. This made it impossible to develop new concepts that would have been more appropriate for a modern age. As a result, the development of the new ideas regarding human rights was left to secular philosophies.

The traditional formulation of the "droits de l'homme" took place at a time prior to the industrialization and the technological age (Mueller, 107ff). 200 years ago the major threat to human dignity came from the states and their governments. Today the situation is different. Besides the state a new and not less powerful entity has emerged which again is threatening human dignity. This is the economy with its various manifestations such as banks, corporations or financial institutions. Even states are subjected to it. No one seems to be in full control of it, but clear is that the economy poses new threats to human dignity so that the traditional human rights of the 18th century do not suffice anymore. All modern societies are involved in this development. States depend on the world economy and individual members of a society on the economy of their respective country. Many decisions made in the board rooms of the economic power centers affect the lives of the people more immediately than actions of governments. Here the livelihood of people, their jobs, their standard of living and the quality of life are at stake. In view of this new phenomenon new human rights need to be formulated; not to replace the traditional ones. They are unalienable, but to supplement them. To the basic human rights of the 18th century must be added today as not less basic the right to make a living, the right to work, the right to basic health care, the right to a minimum education or the right to a pension for old age. All this can be understood as today's development of the right "to life and pursuit of happiness" in the American Declaration of Independence.

There are very strong Biblical foundations for all this. The two creation stories, when placed into our present day context, abound with allusions and references offering themselves as basis for a theological/ethical discussion of these issues. Following the statement about the imago Dei Gen. 1 speaks of man's dominion over the earth. According to Gen. 2, life is a gift of God, and work is assigned to man as part of his dignity. This work is meaningful work, tilling and keeping the garden. All this calls for the development of a theology of human dignity, and this can be done by Jews and Christians together. In the 18th century the Christian Church failed to respond to the questions of its time so that secular answers were given. Today the situation is similar and God's people is challenged again. The question is: can Jews and Christians as the People of God pull themselves together and this time formulate basic human rights that protect human life and the quality of life and reflect God's order in this world?

There is one more issue that offers itself for a common witness: God is the Lord of history. For today's ears this may sound very abstract, but it is as relevant as the topics discussed before. As the Lord of history God started world history with day one, and He continues to manage the course of events, and He is going to bring it to a conclusion "at the end of the days." Historical deeds of God such as leading Israel out of Egypt and bringing her into the promised land, or using the Pharao for His pruposes and assigning to the leaders of the ancient superpowers, Nebuchadnezzar or Cryros of Persia, the role of his agents to carry out His plans, did not stop with the end of the Old Testament. God's history with His people in the world continues, and what the Old Testament says about God as the Lord of world history is as valid today as it was at the time of the Old Testament prophets. In this context the words of the prophets concerning foreign nations become very relevant (Amos 1-2; Isa. 13-23; Jer. 46-51; Ezek. 25-32). However, in the life of the Church today they play no role whatsoever. What does the message of the God of the Bible as Lord of history mean in our world today? (van Buren, 184ff) What does this mean in a world that has lost its hope that a better future can come from man? What does this mean in a world that saw the horrors of the Holocaust? What does this mean in a world where man is constantly frightened because of the capability to blow up the entire planet? These questions certainly put the belief that God is the Lord of history to the test.

The answer must be found in the context of the belief that Jews and Christians together are on their way to "the end of the days" when God will complete his work of creation and redemption, and when all nations of the world will come to serve the one God. But what does this mean after the Holocaust? (Katz, 141ff) Jews and Christians must test their belief in God as the Lord of history in the light of this event and try to formulate something that can be offered as a help to a world that does not have the benefit of the word of God and therefore is more confused than God's people.

These are just some issues that should and could be addressed in a testimony of the People of God to the world of today. There are certainly others. However, going into more details would exceed the scope of this paper. Here the intention was only to point to the necessity to move beyond Jewish-Christian dialogues by establishing Jews and Christians together as the People of God which is sent by God to be the light of the nations.

This is a new challenge for Jews and Christians alike in the post-Holocaust age. However, somehow this challenge reminds us of the situation in the 1st century. At that time the People of God faced their first historic challenge, the proper reaction to Jesus of Nazareth. At the beginning of their history as the People of God Jews and Christians failed this test and appeared before the world as "a kingdom divided against itself." The Holocaust is the threshold to a new age with another historic challenge and the question is again: can Jews and Christians respond together as a common witness in this world?

REFERENCES

Barth, M. (1967). Theologische Studien 19, 3-82.
Ben-Chorin, Sch. (1982). Theologia Judaica.
van Buren, P. M. (1983). A Christian Theology of the People Israel.
Cullmann, O. (1944). The Earliest Christian Confessions.
Gritsch, E. W. and Tanenbaum, M. H. (1983). Lutheran Council in the U.S.A. Luther and the Jews.
Gunneweg, A. H. J. (1978). Understanding the Old Testament.
Hruby, K. (1971). Schriften zur Judentumskunde 2.
Katz, St. (1983). Post-Holocaust Dialogues.
Klein, Ch. (1978). Anti-Judaism in Christian Theology.
Kraus, H. J. (1969). Geschichte der historisch-kritischen Erforschung des Alten Testaments.
Lapide, P. and Moltmann, J. (1980). Israel und die Kirche: ein gemeinsamer Weg?
Müller, G. (1978). Israel hat dennoch Gott zum Trost. Festschrift für Schalom Ben-Chorin.
Peck, A. J. and Wiesel, E. (1982). Jews and Christians after the Holocaust.
von Rad, G. (1965). Old Testament Theology, Vol. II.
Ruether, R. R. (1974). Faith and Fratricide.
von Waldow, H. E. (1984). Horizons in Biblical Theology 6, 27-48.
Westermann, C. (1974). Genesis I/1.
Zimmerli, W. (1978). Old Testament Theology in Outline.

The challenge to the Jewish community: Religion, life and the state of Israel

CHAIRPERSON **Rabbi Albert Friedlander**

RAPPORTEUR **Dr Dina Porat**

TOWARDS A NEW PSALTER

EVELYN ADUNKA

Marktgasse 8-10/41, 1090 Vienna, Austria

ABSTRACT

The concept of a "New Psalter", which is described by the Austrian author Friedrich Heer, and consists of the remained texts of the Shoah, will be analyzed in this paper to survey inasmuch the expression and the idea of a "New Psalter" can be justified in all it claims to be.

KEYWORDS

Friedrich Heer: A "New Psalter." Jizchak Katzenelson. Margarete Susman. Chaim A.Kaplan. Eliezer Berkovits: "Holy Scriptures." Emil L.Fackenheim: "614th Commandment." Adi Ophir: "The Sanctification of the Holocaust." Nelly Sachs, Paul Celan and other Jewish poets of our century.

INTRODUCTION

The starting point for the following considerations is a sentence of Friedrich Heer, the distinguished Austrian Catholic writer and historian, which he wrote in his monumental work: "God's First Love", published in Germany in 1967 and in London by Weidenfeld in 1970:
The immeasurable, inconceivable Jewish catastrophe of the twentieth century has found its expression - as far as that is humanly possible - not in a theology or philosophy or in an epic work, but in a body of Jewish songs and poems which form in its unresolved, uncompleted inherent wholeness a New Psalter." (p.572/573) The claim of this sentence means the application of a Biblical, literary category to the events of the Shoah in a very explicit and definite way.

Comparable ideas can be found in many texts, which I will analyze in this paper. About these texts I want to examine firstly the so-called metaphysical dimension of the Shoah; secondly their allegory and comparability with the Holy Scriptures; thirdly their convergence with and the use of explicit Biblical categories, and fourthly the possibility or impossibility of maintaining this tremendous claim.

DISCUSSION

Heer himself mentioned three examples for his "New Psalter", which I also will interpret: Jizchak Katzenelson, Nelly Sachs and Paul Celan. (p.574, 578)

It was often said that Jizchak Katzenelson, who perished in 1944, was truly the Jeremiah of the Shoah. David Shimoni even said about him: "Here, incarnate in the one human being, was Abraham binding his son to the altar, Isaac, the human sacrifice, Job and Jeremiah. Is there another being on earth that could contain all this excruciating anguish? That could endure this unspeakable horror?" (p.39)

In his great poem "The Song of the Murdered Jewish People" Katzenelson addreses the prophet Ezekiel of whom he says, that in the present situation even he cannot beseech the exterminated with as much faith as he once had. He could not say one single word: "Could your words still awake the bones? What remained, Prophet, of my exterminated people? Not one piece of bone." (p.18)
For Katzenelson this means that the persecutions and hostilities were so immensely strong and destructive that they have burst even the Biblical imaginations and dimensions. For traditional Jewish thinkers this is almost inconceivable, because for them the Biblical standards were entirely unsurpassable.

Also the hostilities against one's own faith became stronger. The victory of the Nazis could go so much further that mankind would come to regard the Jewish people as a mere invention or fiction. As Katzenelson wrote: "My people was only invented. An illusion. Jews lived whom I invented. They never existed. Never again will they exist on earth." (p.18)

Once again he formulates his outcry to Jeremiah and Ezechiel and is asking himself doubtfully: "Ezechiel, does he see us? Does Jeremiah know, what is happening? Who still needs them? Should I still wait for them, hesitate before I write my last song?" (p.20)
But then he says to Isaiah, whose experience was as nothing compared with what Katzenelson must see and suffer: "Isaiah, never did you form a more tremensous word! Isaiah, never were you as small as he was! (A Jewish child whom Katzenelson is describing). Isaiah! Never were you as great as he was. Never so good. Never so truthful. Never, Isaiah, was your faith more sincere than his!" (p.43)

Katzenelson feels that the Germans were filled with some kind of metaphysical hatred against his people. A people whose children for him had "the humility of Moses, the man of God; they were poor and tortured like Job, beautiful like the righteous Joseph in a strange land - in exile - in Egypt." (diary, p.53)
But the Germans do not hate this people like all other human beings. No. They demonize them: "The Germans hate God. And they are spitting in his face. Each unknown human being died as the image of God." (p.54, 24)
And if in that way they want to destroy His image, His Holy people, then they are really evoking a metaphysical decline: "Has God's power fallen? God's sun does not shine any more." (p.56)

Katzenelson's despair is becoming greater and greater. Deep in his heart he starts a revolt against God who has permitted this catastrophe. He has a reckoning with the "seven heavens" of which he says: "You I have loved like I love only my wife, o Heavens! You have deceived my old people...Prophets trembled before you. How loyal they were to you. Do you still remember Moses? Do you still remember Joshua, Heavens, who has called you? Also Jeremiah cried: Heavens, listen! Who should hear, if not you? Are you emptied, emptied of love?...Heavens, are you fast asleep?" (p.59/60)
Katzenelson knows only too well <u>which</u> people is exposed to extermination: Don't you recognize us any more? We are the people that has spread God's word, a people, who is God's witness, and our fathers were saints. And we are even better. If ever my people has been a chosen one, because it suffered for others, it is now...In each child there was a Gaon's searching soul. Children give light to the night. Consecrated to you was each child through God's covenant of blood...My people has helped to enoble the world." (p.60/61, 95)

With these last verses a new development starts. A convergence with the Biblical examples and events, but already their surpassing. The events of the Shoah are much more cruel and brutal, comparable and describable only basically. And they concern almost a whole people, millions of human beings.
Katzenelson is already asking a single devastated town: "Are you God's battlefield?" (p.41) In facing that he can say of himself: "I am a prophet." And for his people goes the same: "Out of each jew cries, terrified, a Jeremiah." (p. 60) Although he later takes back this claim and says of himself: "No prophet am I. But I struggle, full of pain, about the word.." (p.89)
Therefore it could have said about him:"...he may have felt a certain psycho-

logical kinship to his ancestors, the prophets. Like them he was summoned to carry out a task which was beyond his ability, beyond the ability of any human being...No prophet or Biblical hero was ever called upon to such an incredible undertaking. Jeremiah and Ezekiel saw the destruction of their land; Katzenelson saw the annihilation of his people. Job was bereft of his children and afflicted with pain, yet even the celestial Satan was admonished to 'save his life'. Katzenelson lost everything and everybody and the German satan was now about to take his life too. The voice commanding the poet is not the voice of the omnipotent and omniscient God of the prophets in whose wisdom and justice they believed. The poet's skies are blind and empty...(p.121)

Finally Katzenelson comes to the point: "No God, o Heavens, lives in you." (p. 62) But he is torn by doubts and states full of bitterness a few pages later: "God lives. God smiles. God's people is perishing." (p.78)
If God, the Eternal, dies, then everything is destroyed. If all will be destroyed, then also He, God himself, has to die. For Katzenelson, even God himself cannot stand up to <u>this</u> destruction: "God himself trembles. And flees." (p.95) For that all has become senseless; the destruction cannot be restricted. To the heavens, which have become accomplies of the murderers, he cries: "Rejoice, Heavens, with the German...burn the earth. And rise the flame of the earth, which shall burn you!" (p.62)

In one of the most impressive passages Katzenelson describes how the end of the Jewish people on earth would also mean the end of the divine word, law and salvation, which would die with this people. He knows that "the Bible of Israel and its moral laws are at the root of all that is good in the nations."(diary, p.81)
In the "Song of the Murdered Jewish People" he writes: "Tonight the last Jew burns...For ever they will be silent, like Jeremiah and Isaiah and Ezekiel in the yellowed page of the Bible...in God's book of fairy-tales. The word of salvation, that was written by God's hands, lies with the dead of my people who are lost without trace. Empty are the houses of devout learning, the places of worship...And the wisdom of an old people is no more alive, and with the old people perished an old people's spirit...Their death soon will be forgotten. And no Jew will stand up any more in the fight for human rights, never sacrificing his happiness for the happiness of all. And never again will a Jew relieve someone else's pain...Once there has been a people. It has been. But it was not allowed to live. Finished. Smashed. An old fairy-tale, sad. The Bible tells of its beginning, filled with agony, for many millenia. Earth, do not avenge my people! The nations themselves, whose hatred is defeating us, are preparing their destruction." (p.97/98)

What Katzenelson could not know: The history of the Jewish people continued, in a glorious new dawn, even though overshadowed by the smoke of the crematoria. Without the creation of the State of Israel, Katzenelson's horror vision would have become reality. But this fact does not make his words less valid. On the contrary, we still have not become sufficiently aware of their reality, and therefore I have quoted them here despite of their length. But they are, thank God, only a part of the historic reality of our time.
As Eliezer Berkovits said to me: "What is important is, that it happened when it was absolutely necessary to happen. I maintain that after the Holocaust if we had nothing else just the Holocaust, we would have been in a situation of complete despair and we would hardly have been able to continue. But that it came at <u>this</u> moment, that we maintained this nonsensical faith we might say and we still had enough strength to do it, and that it came in a moment when it was most needed in the history of the Jewish people, this combination makes it one of the greatest miracles in history."

A comparable convergence with the Biblical example can be observed in the texts of Margarete Susman and Chaim A.Kaplan.
In her most important work, "The Book of Job and the Fate of the Jewish People" the great humanist Susman interprets the fate of Israel with the help and the example of the Biblical book of Job. She writes that "just like the fate of Job reflects the fate of the Jewish people and at the same time the depth of human destiny in general, so is circumscribed in the people of Israel at the same time the innermost circle of humanity, and it is in itself humanity's symbol and representative...As the representative of all the humiliated and insulted of

the earth, it is just like Job singled out to represent humanity in general for the constantly renewed asking of the ultimate human questions. (p.50, 214) With this interpretation of a contemporary event through "the great unified Biblical truths and events" (p.12) she soon goes far beyond the horizon she set herself. She is not only feeling a distance "which separates today's man, who is influenced by entirely different powers and realities, from the people of the Biblical Israel",(p.78) but she also sees that with the present event a universal destruction overtook mankind as never before in its history. "The Jewish people is precisely the point on which this dark power has put its finger to achieve by the dissolution of this tiny core the dissolution of all peoples and of everything human." (p.48)

Like Katzenelson and Kaplan, Susman sees that the Shoah - for which they did not yet have a special word - surpasses Israel's suffering in the Bible: "Meanwhile the storm broke, and the fate of the Jewish people took forms which reached the fate of Biblical Israel and even surpassed it." (p.79)
For Susman this extermination was in the end methaphysically intended. This view could be proved with many examples and events: The atrocities and hatred of the Nazis, evoked especially by religious Jews. (See also the "Hasidic Tales of the Holocaust" by Yaffa Eliach).Susman writes:
"With its variety of reasons and in spite of the amalgamation with barest practical considerations and utilizations, it was in its real depth a metaphysical hatred...It was the demon of the coldest and most furious hatred for life, which has ever appeared on earth." (p.119)
One of the obvious conclusions of this, which is till today immensely relevant, is, that herefore "the problem of the Jewish people can never be on the same level with the other nations", (p.66)as often has been attempted.

But if the world has not changed after <u>this</u> extermination - here Susman touches directly on Elie Wiesel - then definetely something has collapsed, then its dehumanization was not temporary, but was expanded and deepened, although not as clear and visible as during Nazism: "This fate, these atrocities did not shake the world in its depth. But if this more than satanic evil is not recognized and if the responsibility for that is not accepted with a burning conscience, then something has collapsed in our world, which yesterday still was standing." (p.118)

The subject of Susman's book, which was concluded after the creation of the State of Israel which she favoured, is the failure of the Biblical truth, which could not radiate to the outside and could not change and influence especially the Germans, with whom the Jewish people has lived so intensively together. Susman does not come to the same conclusion as Katzenelson, that the heavens are emptied and apparently the God of the Jewish people isnot the God in whom he always has believed, but also for her God's name and fate is affected by this universal destruction: "For not only the image of the Jewish man, but also of man in general is lost for us; today the name of man is for us not more readable than the name of God." (p.151)

Chaim A.Kaplan, who wrote his diary, in which we possess one of the most important and authentic primary sources of the Shoah, under the worst conditions in the Warsaw Ghetto, has no doubt about the total uniqueness of this extermination of his people. (And this should be pointed out to all who today start to deny this fact again): "The gigantic catastrophe which came over polish Jewry, has no parallel, not even in the darkest period of Jewish history. This concerns especially the depth of the hatred." (p.155)

At least one of Kaplan's worried questions can be answered today affirmatively: "Who will ever write about our poverty and make it immortal? Where is the poet of the people of polish Jewry who will tell the whole tragedy and keep it for ever in the reliquary of his tears? Poet of the people, where are you?" (p.94)
But especially Kaplan knew that finally he demanded something impossible: "Only someone who gets to feel the rule of the Nazi tyranny in all his 248 organs and 345 tendons, only such a writer...could give a true description of the pathological phenomena which is called Nazism." (p.137) Only a little part of the authors which are interpreted here can necessarily comply with this condition - thank God for that! - But we must never forget that at any time only

a tiny part of the full horrifying reality of Nazism can be described. Really understand it can only someone who went through it. But in the deepest human context not only he.
Kaplan also felt that innermost strength which kept and sustained the Jewish people even in this deepest abyss: "It is a wonderful excessive strength, which is granted only to that part of our people which is deeply rooted...even those who deny the miracles will admit that there works in us a certain elemental strength which sustains and supports us." (p.157,282)

For Kaplan too the atrocities which he must witness surpass the Biblical events: "The rumours which we hear from the provincial towns, are worse than the messages of Job." He feels this so strongly, that he even says: "Only a pen inspired by God can put these impressions on paper", and he laments the terrible events which have overwhelmed, terrified and deadened him, "so that I have not the strength, neither physically nor spiritually, to analyze these events and to immortalize them with the pen of a learned scribe." (p.346, 248, 384)
In another passage Kaplan is calling himself a grandson of the prophet Isaiah. Therefore Abraham I.Katsch can say correctly of Kaplan: "There are moments where the diary expresses the blazing rage of an old-time prophet who evokes the wrath of Heaven on the enemies of his people." (p.12/13)

In a passage where he writes about the council of the Jews (Judenrat), Kaplan quotes a famous saying from Holy Scriptures about the infinity and greatness of the Lord, which is describable as little as the monstrosity and outrageness of the deeds of the Nazis. The universe stands satanically on its head; the laws of God and the laws of evil became reversed. This holy saying was later recalled by Manès Sperber, who wanted there to express the same idea as Kaplan. He formulated is so brilliantly that I want to quote it here: (p.329)
"'Even if all the firmament were made of parchment, all the trees were pens, all the seas ink, and even if all the inhabitants of the earth were scribes, and they wrote day and night - they would never succeed in describing the grandeur and the splendour of the Creator of the universe.'Fifty years separate me from the child who learned to recite these opening lines of a long Aramaic poem that had been transmitted, with an unalterable oral commentary accompanying it, from generation to generation. I come back to the resonance of these phrases whenever I bring myself, once again, to the realization that we will never succeed in making the <u>hurban</u> - the Jewish catastrophe of our time - understood to those who will live after us. The innumerable documents that we owe to the indefatigable bureaucracy of the exterminators, the many narratives by witnesses who miraculously escaped, the diaries, chronicles and records - all these millions of words remind me that 'even if all the firmament...' (Fackenheim, God's...,p.72)

Even more than Margarete Susman, Chaim A.Kaplan was filled with the feeling, that only an author, who would have got the power of expression, lucidity and divine inspiration of the Bible, could adequately describe those events which surpass and eclipse the Biblical world. If then the standard of the Bible is burst, that in the least would mean that many scriptures of the Shoah are so sacred that they are comparable to the Holy Scriptures of the Bible.

Eliezer Berkovits was the only one until today - as far as I know - who came to this conclusion, with the one exception of the Cristian author Friedrich Heer, as quoted above. Berkovits literally writes in his "Faith after the Holocaust": "When one day the last written messages from the ghettos and the death camps will be assembled in an edition worthy of the depth of their truth and inspiration, mankind will possess in them a new collection of holy scriptures...The ghettos and concentration camps that saw so much demoralisation and human degration, were also the holy of holies on this earth...It was the Holy of Holies on earth, sharing in the very majesty of Sinai, when God descending upon it, proclaimed His 'Thou shalt not kill!' Who knows whether that wretched little attic was not wrapt in even greater majesty than Sinai! At Sinai God proclaimed, in the ghetto a hunted human being, at the risk of her own life, enacted God's commandment." (p.78,77)

What Berkovits is saying with that, means, that the sanctification and holiness of the Thora was nowhere greater than under the worst possible conditions in the concentration camps and ghettos, when the Germans tried everything that was possible to stop the Jewish people from fulfilling God's own law on the Holy Thora. Therefore the reports and evidences about these events can be called sacred, and even can be regarded as parts of the Holy Scriptures of the Jewish people. They belong inseparable to them and to the history of their influence and effect on humanity.

I have asked Eliezer Berkovits, an orthodox rabbi, in Jerusalem, what he has meant by the expression "Holy Scriptures". In his reply he told me also another important detail: "What is really the essence of the psalms? Essentially, it was human creation. A man was all his personal experience turning to God. I can imagine that these poems...if one bears in mind under what condition they were created I would say they were innocent more than the original psalms, in the point of view of their holiness...We were in an innocence more that the psalms we have got. Because very often the tillim are based on a personal experience of an individual. For instance in the psalter you got a very moving chapter: Out of the depth that I call you. That is one person who calls from its own personal depth. But when a person in the ghetto calls from its depth he is calling from a comprehensive, almost universal depth of human failure."

So for Berkovits as for other rabbis it is self-evident, that a "New Psalter" should be possible, and even that one day it will be written. In my conversation with him I explicitly used the expression "New Psalter". Again we find the motif in Berkovits' words, that he events of the Shoah surpass the Biblical world. He explained this to me, as quoted above, with a very concrete and for the "New Psalter" very important example.

The Psalter consists of praise and thanksgiving of God, but also of lamentations, questions, doubts and outcries to and against Him. Just as this complete scale of human passions and qualities individually reach from deepest despair to the highest development of human greatness, just like that was it collectively suffered and experienced by the Jewish people during the Shoah. This, too, Berkovits has expressed brilliantly: "At Auschwitz and Treblinka, in the camps and in the ghettos, man sank to his lowest level yet, but there too he was exalted to his highest dignity...Confronting Auschwitz one faces ultimate evil, but also the ultimate of goodness. The vaster the degradation and the misery, the more miraculous the manifestation of man's faith in the values and meanings he cherises." (p.76, 84)

But the praise and thanksgiving of the Psalms found their greatest parallel in an historic event of this century. Because for Berkovits the State of Israel and the Six-Day-War meant a "messianic moment" in history. (p.156) And he is asking himself: "Did we really experience one of those rare occasions, when God - almost as in biblical times - made his presence manifest as the Redeemer of Israel?...What was not granted to any other generation was awarded to the people in Zion - an encounter with all Jewish history, a very real communion with all the generations. It was as if they were conversing with the patriarchs, walking with king David, listening to the voice of the prophets, comforting the martyrs." (p.144/45, 155)

To speak of Holy Scriptures like Berkovits means not in the least to believe in some sort of a new revelation. I mention this, because that expression can be found in literature twice. Firstly it was Elie Wiesel, who, in the words of Emil L.Fackenheim, "has dared to compare Auschwitz with Sinai in its revelatory significance - and he has added that we are not listening." (p.53)
And Irving Greenberg speculates with the idea and possibility of a new revelation through Auschwitz. (Brocke, p.136-77)
This view was strongly criticized by Michael Wyschogrod, and, as I believe, not totally wrongly. To see in the Holocaust an act of revelation for him is the most serious theological error, because "in the revelation God tells man a message, of which he wants to that man should possess it...acts of revelation are acts of salvation." (Brocke, p.189, 190) "Should the Holocaust finish to be a marginal event for the faith of Israel, should it come into the inner sanctum and become there the ruling voice, to which Israel listens, then Israel would listen to a demonic voice...If there is still hope after the Holocaust, then only because for those who believe, the voices of the Prophets speak louder than the voices of Hitler..." (Pfisterer p. 186)

I believe that in the category of revelation, no comparison or repetition is possible. The absoluteness of the Law, the Thora, which stands in the center of the Jewish faith, contradicts such an idea. On Mount Sinai God revealed the universal, eternal - also ethical - laws of the Thora. In Auschwitz man tried to destroy this law together with its followers and representatives with utmost cruelty and hatred. Seen like this, Auschwitz, which, according to many authors, was metaphysically intended, would mean a rebellion against the decalogue, an Anti-Sinai. It could, if we were sufficiently aware of this, shake us up, and bring us back to the truth of Sinai. This is the only possible connection between Auschwitz and Sinai. The act of revelation of the Holy Thora and the act of the destruction of its representatives, the divine act and the human act, are not comparable. They cannot, and should not, be put on the same level.

With the Psalter it would be different. The Psalms are not the Law itself. They are scriptures about this law and were written after the revelation. They are prayers, praise and thanksgiving, outcries, lamentations and questions to God. They are, as Philipp Birnbaum in the "Encyclopedia of Jewish Concepts" expresses: "The keynote of the Psalms is simplicity of heart, faith in God, and good conduct. In the Psalms we find the human heart in all its moods and emotions - in penitence, in danger, in desolation, and in triumph." (p.623) The psalmist struggles with the reality of this world and with the reality of the Law and its enemies; he struggles for his faith and for God, because he is tested so strongly by his suffering, individually, as later in Auschwitz collectively almost the whole jewish people.

Because the Psalter has not got the same absoluteness in Jewish tradition as the Thora, it is possible even for orthodox rabbis to speak of a "New Psalter" and of new "Holy Scriptures". Only to speak of a New revelation would overthrow the foundations of judaism.
A "New Psalter" would therefore mean nothing else than a continuation of the eternal dialogue between man and his creator. In the course of history men have written again and again texts, poems and songs like and comparable with the Psalms. The more extreme the conditions and hostilities, under which they were written, have been, the nearer they come to the depth, spirituality and holiness of the Biblical Psalter. Therefore it can be easily understood that the concept of a "New Psalter" was developed with the texts of the Shoah and of this particular time.

Therefore Rabbi Louis Jacobs could answer my question whether in his opinion a "New Psalter" would be possible, affirmatively: "Why not. I don't see anyone would have any objection to that. This kind of material is liturgically already used in many congregations. So maybe if it lasts long enough, it might even be canonized - just like the Talmud was."

Later in this paper we will see an example for that in the context of Nelly Sachs. Just like one of her poems I also found parts of the diary of Anne Frank quoted in a "memorial service for the six million."
And Rabbi Abraham Rosenfeld has composed an Elegy "in memory of the martyrs of the Holocaust" (p.XXV) for the liturgy for the Day of Tishah B'Av. There he writes: "Our flesh and our hearts fail at the destruction of our portion,/All of us raise lamentation for the destruction of half of our nation,/For the (European) holocaust ranks equal to the destruction of/our Temple." (p.174) That means that for him the greatest catastrophe in the history of the Jewish people, the destruction of the Temple, is on the same level as the Shoah. But after the destruction of the Temple Judaism was changed radically and could therefore survive. And it is no accident that today in Judaism we can observe many comparable changes.
Many of the Kinot for Tishah B'Av, which are not referring to the Shaoh, remind us in spite of that of the cruelties of the Shoah in their own descriptions of the atrocities of their time.

That reminds me of Dov Potkin, an ultra-orthodox hassidic writer of Thora scrolls in Mea Shearim, who agreed with me in a much more restricted way: "These texts could be turned in liturgy, sure. They could be put into praying. But to call them a "New Psalter" is a poetic exaggeration. The Book of Psalms, written by King David, could not be matched. Nothing could this contain.

I don't think anyone could come very close to King David. To say this is like a poetical nicety, but I don't think a reality. It could be used in prayers, but it could never be called a new book of Psalms. But new things were added to Jewish prayerbooks all the time, especially in time of sufferings. So I don't think he should do to much of it...To say, that one could call these texts Holy Scriptures, the simple meaning of that I would take is, that you will have statements, which will be like the ones said in the Bible. If I would have been in a concentration camp and I was writing things about G-d and everything, these texts would have been full of the same thoughts that are in the Bible. This is nothing extraordinary. These thoughts the people wrote down in the camps and ghettos, these thoughts were holy thoughts - but there will be nothing new about them."

His point of view is clear. In order to understand him it is necessary to know that for him, as he said to me, the Shoah was not worse than the slavery in Egypt and the expulsion of Spain. He lives completely integrated in Jewish history and Jewish law. Not only that, but the lack of understanding about the Shoah and National-Socialism of the people of Mea Shearim in general is shared by him too. To give only one example: They publicly and explicitly compare Teddy Kollek and the zionist police with the deeds of the Nazis.

Emil L.Fackenheim also writes in his book "God's Presence in History" something in connection with the already quoted passage of Manès Sperber, which is comparable with the ideas of Greenberg: "As we have seen, even the ancient rabbis were forced to suspend the Biblical 'for our sins are we punished...' We too may at most only suspend the Biblical doctrine, if only because we, no more than the rabbis, dare either to deny our own sinfulness or to disconnect it from history. Yet, suspend it we must. For however we twist and turn this doctrine in response to Auschwitz, it becomes a religious absurdity and even a sacrilege." (p.73)

That means contrary to Greenberg, not to add something to the revelation, but to suspend something from revelation - in the widest sense of the word. In spite of this difference both views imply a claim of absoluteness just like or at least no less than the Biblical one.

Fackenheim's "614th commandment" and his considerations about a "Midrashic Existence after the Holocaust" in connection with Elie Wiesel are also dealing with Biblical or rabbinical categories. To speak like that would mean no less than trying or claiming to rewrite the oral Thora in the face of the experiences of this century. Fackenheim himself says about this question: "Surely we must cherish their memory, study as we would Holy Writ the diaries, books, records written in blood for our sake, relieve their lives in songs of sorrow and joy." (1978, p.253/54)

Although it does not concern specifically our subject, I want to mention another very beautiful example for the adoption and using of the word "midrash" in the interpretation of modern literature. In an essay about Erich Fromm's book "The Art of Loving" Rabbi Jakob J.Petuchowski called this book a "20th century midrash on love." In writing that he is "fully aware of what the function of midrash has always been..." (p.543) And he calls it a "profoundly Jewish book." (p.546)

From an entirely different not theological point of view Adi Ophir criticizes "The Sanctification of the Holocaust". (But he does not see that already the expression "Holocaust" implies in some way a "sanctification", what many authors stated). Ophir is afraid that a "religious consciousness built around the Holocaust may become the central aspect of a new religion...Perhaps from that Holocaust altar...a mighty belief will spring forth, seven times greater for its absurdity than the belief of Abraham...The Holocaust is God...The new religion is already taking form today." (p.61/62) For this "new religion" he is even formulating four commandments and he sees that "already a central altar has arisen which will gradually turn into our Temple..." (p.63)

Ophir's criticism on "sanctifying the Holocaust" has nothing to do with the possible holiness of texts which we have discussed above. He is only afraid that a Holocaust myth would blur the humanness of the Holocaust and that it "makes it difficult to understand...as a product of a human, material and ideological system." (p.63)

But I have mentioned his criticism here because he speaks there about possible dangers which should not be overseen and which especially in the context of Greenberg I have already discussed. Another dangerous element for modern Jewish, secular identity after Auschwitz can possibly be noticed, if one sees in anti-semitism and the Shoah, that means to say not in genuine Judaism itself, which cannot be cut off its religious roots, the primary elements for the formation of Jewish identity. For this heteronomy, which Ophir has expressed exaggeratedly, I remind only of Sartre's famous sentence: "The Jew is a man, whom the others regard as such", which unfortunately was partly correct.

Anyhow even Elie Wiesel regards the Holocaust "as a sacred subject." (Berger, p.166) "One should take off one's shoes, when entering its domain, one should tremble each time one pronounces the word. (p.167) Wiesel later laments "that the Holocaust has become a desanctified theme",(p.171) although it must be noticed that of course he did not mean it in the cynical and insensitive sense of Adi Ophir.

André Neher sees in his book "The Exile of the World" in Elie Wiesel's "Night" "from end to end a rewriting of the Akedah in the obscure light of the Night of Auschwitz." (p.216) Just like Neher speaks with that from a rewriting and continuing of the Bible, thus comparable with that Wiesel says about himself: Every survivor of the holocaust could have written' the Book of JOb," and Neher added to that: "it is indeed for that reason that, more than the Akedah, the Book of Job is the breviary of revolt for the man of Auschwitz." (p.219) Neher expressed also the Six-Day-War in Biblical categories. As in the psalms we notice again besides the depth of despair the richness of redemption. Therefore I want to quote this passage: "If the biblical promise of the Land permits and perhaps even obliges us to recognize the strides of history in Jerusalem as footsteps of the Messiah, if the historic gathering of the dispersed and dead of the Exile around the Western Wall from June 1967 can only be regarded as a resurgence of the biblical Word, breaking the silence of millenia, has the end, then, found its embodiment, has history reached its goal, and has silence been completely vanquished?" (p.227)

It was already mentioned that in our century a lot of poems were written which are comparable with the psalms, before, during and after the Shoah by Jewish and non Jewish poets. Friedrich Heer especially emphasized two names: "In this new Psalter, pressed of Israel's carrying of the cross and suffering to death, in this new Psalter of a new religiousity and spirituality of the one mankind, the songs of Nelly Sachs and Paul Celan...will receive a special place."(p.578)

Nelly Sachs, whose unique poems incorporate the immensity of the catastrophe of the Shoah and its utmost cruelty, and also the spiritual survival of the Jewish people, was a poetess who lived completely in the Biblical world. She took this as her basis and starting point. Therefore Kurt Pinthus could call her "the conclusion in the german language of that three thousand old ancestral line which began with the psalmists and the prophets." (1966, p.49/50) Erwin Leiser went even further and said about her: "She is a sister of the prophetic characters in the history of Judaism..." (p.186) For Olof Lagercrantz Nelly Sachs has in her poetry "something in herself from that strength of prophecy which characterizes Biblical ecstatics." (p.100)
She herself was more modest and wrote in a letter: "Someone like Dante and Shakespeare would be necessary in order to show mankind this abyss - but thus a weak woman must do it." (p.53) The writings of hassidism influenced and helped her enormously, because there she read "that each one is allowed to do it, also the peddler...and therefore it sings in there in the very old rhythm, where the prayers of the patriarchs resound, and the many fountains from which Israel drank, can be heard." (p.43)

In one of her most famous poems, Nelly Sachs writes: "O these chimneys, they are ways of freedom for the dust of Jeremiah and Job..." By this, she says, that the spirit of the Jewish people survived, that it could not be imprisoned and exterminated by the Nazis. Isaiahs arrow which he hid in the quiver is explicitly her message which "the prophets and poets carry through the centuries." (Lagercrantz, p.60)
In one poem, the greatness of which really gets close to Biblical texts, she is asking herself, what would happen, if the prophets stood up again in our world of today. This poem was incorporated in a conservative Mahzor for the

musaf prayer in the liturgy of the Yom Kippur service - and in our context this fact is very relevant: "If the prophets stood up/in the night of mankind/like lovers who seek the heart of the beloved/night of mankind/would you have a heart to offer?...if the voices of prophets/blew/on flutes made of martyred children's bones/and exalted airs burnt with/martyrs' cries-/if they built a bridge of old men's dying/goans-/ear of mankind/occupied with small sounds/would you hear?"

In another of her poems, Nelly Sachs writes: "Land of Israel/now where your people/comes home tear-stained from the corners of the world/in order to write anew the Psalms of David in your sand..." With that she comes already very close to the concept of a "New Psalter". Of King David she said, that he has built "the Psalms' refuge of the night for the wounds of the way." Lagercrantz adds that Nelly Sachs' own poems are these refuges on the way to God. (p.106) But most important is, that she herself has written in her mystery play Eli: "The new Pentateuch, I say to you, the new Pentateuch/is written with the mould of fear/on the walls of the cellars of death." (1977, p.133)
We will never know what she felt when she wrote these lines. But they remind remind me also of rabbi Leo Adler, who according to W.Weber has asked the question,"if the Jewish people once will have the strength to bear witness like Moses did in order to break through the accumulated demon of the world like once in the Exodus of Egypt." (Sachs, 1966, p.36)

Nelly Sachs' poem "If the prophets stood up" also recalls a poem by Paul Celan. For him this problem is even greater and the doubts which gnaw at his faith, strengthened. He is not asking whether a prophet could still be heard, but whether his Biblical language could still do justice to the events of this time: "Would come,/would come a man,/would come a man to the world, today, with/the light beard of the/patriarchs: he were allowed/would he speak of this time, he/were allowed/only to babble and babble/ever and ever..." (p.27)

If for Celan with this poem the Biblical word has lost its validity and its meaningfulness, then it became void, a nothingness like its creator, who would have become with that a nobody. This was the obvious conclusion to which Celan came in one of his most famous poems: "Nobody kneads us again from earth and clay/nobody speaks to our dust./Nobody/Praised be you/Nobody./For your sake we want to/blossom./toward/You./Nothing/we were, we are, we will/remain blossoming:/the rose of Nothing/of Nobody./With/the style/light like the soul,/the filament desolate like the sky,/of the red crown/from the purple word that we sang/over, o over the thorn." (p.26)
The structure of communication between God and man is not destroyed in this poem, and even if Celan cannot believe any more the one whom he adresses, he is speaking to him despite that. The paradoxical hope against hopelessness, which is typical for Judaism, has found in this poem one of its most perfect expressions.

George Steiner recently wrote about this poem, which is headed by the word "psalm", the following formulations: "Celan has written a psalm to Auschwitz, which is at the same time an 'anti-psalm', such as matter at the same time anti-matter postulates and refutes. The Jew in the Shoah speaks to and against the non-speaking God and not speaking of God. As long as the Jew turns to God, God must listen. It could be, that in the world of Auschwitz, this forced listening became that fragile thread - the filament - at which God's existence hangs, the survival of God in a sky, a cosmos which became desolated. But it also could be that the compulsion to articulation in Judaism, that the law of the dialogue even with, even against a dumb God, will insistently be continued." (p.210/11)
In this text George Steiner comes to a conclusion, which exactly corresponds to the precondition of this work: "Only with a theological-metaphysical scale of values, only with a sharpened watchfulness with regard to the vitality of theological-metaphysical imagery and symbolism in the collective consciousness of the West one can hope to come to more lucidity in regard to the aetiology, the causal dynamics of the hatred of the Jews and the experience of Auschwitz." (p.207)

It does not surprise any more, that Nelly Sachs, who stood with Paul Celan in an intensive lyrical dialogue, called his book "Sprachgitter" in a letter

his "Zohar". (p.233) This means that she compares it with that mystical book of Judaism, which not only has influenced Nelly Sachs enormously but from which was said that it came to a virtually canonical reputation and that it became - after the Thora and the Talmud - the most influential book in Jewish tradition. (Birnbaum, p.189)
Peter Mayer notices about Celan's poem "Psalm", for which he chose this liturgical form, that the poet took from the psalms the pecularities of the form and of the melody, "the change, which is important for the psalms and especially for the lamentations, from loud complaint to the immediate following praise of the Lord." (p.36)

In 1978 Paul Konrad Kurz edited a book with the title: "Psalms from Expressionism till the Present Time." In this anthology consisting of 325 pages 64 poems have the word "Psalm" in their title. In this book there are Jewish and non-Jewish poets, divided in the following sections: "Difficulties of the singers of Psalms today; trust in the Psalms of the Expressionists; Psalms of Jewish poets; Psalms of non-Jewish poets; anti-Psalms, parodies, satire; marginal Psalms and motives of Psalms; Psalms of nature; political Psalms; Psalms about Psalms; Psalms of Christian poets today; Psalms of Christian poets yesterday; Psalms in dialect." (p.5-11)

Kurz writes in his book that Jewish authors have "a specific relationship to the genre "Psalm": "They continue to speak the very old genre of Hebrew poetry in the third millenium", but "with the death of Nelly Sachs and Paul Celan the Jewish speaking of the Psalms in German became silent." Kurz examines "important material and thematical starting points in the Hebrew Psalms" and finds that only the Psalms of History are written no more. For him Psalms are a forgotten genre, which today is ignored. "In the course of philosophical enlightenment in the 18th century the genre Psalm in German literature died." (p.298-300)

The renaissance of the writing of Psalms is probably connected with the fact that the poets feel more strongly than ever before in history that in this engangered century it became much more necessary to try to come into a dialogue with God, to get an answer from him and in any case to stay in touch with him. Kurz tried a similar defintion of the Psalm: "A Psalm is a religious poem, which contains an invocation of God", and he goes further and asks the question, that, if the old singer of the Psalms has participated in prophetic speaking: "Would it be conceivable that poetic texts of today have prophetic strength? Should also writers participate as revivalists and awakened and listeners of the truth of the word in the millenia-old stream of the prophetic?" (p.314)

But it also must be said here that in this anthology the Shoah almost never or only marginal occurs, and that the selection of the poems was not always really successful. Not everyone of the texts in this book can be called really a Psalm or be like a Psalm.
On the contrary I believe that the invocation and struggling with God and for an answer from him today can be found much more in texts which were published in other anthologies and which were written by Jewish poets during and in the time of the Shoah.
Despite that fact the relevance of Kurz's book as the most impressing example for todays poetical feeling about and writing of "Psalms" cannot be denied.

Before I will interpret these Jewish poems I want to mention three modern examples of todays writing of "New Psalms".
First ofall there is Arnold Schönberg, the great Jewish composer, with his fragmentary work "Modern Psalms". Schönberg originally thought, according to Karl H.Wörner, to continue the 150 Biblical Psalms and "to the first one he wanted to give the number 151." (p.148) But Schönberg's Psalms, of which he could complete only 15, cannot be called particularly Jewish. They are basically religious and worldly meditations without great poetic power of expression. Therefore their value especially lies in their character as the late personal confessions of Arnold Schönberg. (Kurz, p.77-80)

In 1984 Leonhard Cohen published his "Book of Mercy", which is called a "sequence of modern Psalms." In 50 sections very profane passages change with memories of the Thora, the peace of the sabbat and even of a minjan. And there can be found genuine texts of prayer, of which I only want to quote one short example: ""Holy is your name, holy is your work, holy are the days that return to you. Holy are the years that you uncover. Holy are the hands that are raised to you, and the weeping that is wept to you...Holy, and shining with a great light, is every living thing, established in this world and covered with time, until your name is praised forever." (p.122)

Finally should here be mentioned Ernesto Cardenal with his "Latin-american Psalms", the original title of which was: "Salmos". There we learn to remember, as Kurz writes, that the very subject of the Psalms of the Old Testament were the poor. (p.301) - It is particularly remarkable that no other Christian or Jewish poet of our century comes so close to the power of expression and meaningfulness of the Biblical Psalms. I want to illustrate that on one example, where Ernesto Cardenal, the Christian poet, considers the fate of Israel in this century.
He writes to the Psalms 43, 44: "Now we are the exiled,/the refugees without an identity card,/the exiled in the concentration camps,/the condemned to forced labor,/the burned in the crematoria-/and our ashes were scattered./We are your people of Auschwitz/of Buchenwald/of Belsen and/of Dachau./From our sort they made lampshades,/from our fat soap./Like lambs to the slaughter/you let us be pushed into the gaschambers./You let it be, that one displaces us./You offered us for sale on the junk market,/and it was found no purchaser..." (p.124) When Cardenal wrote these texts, he really must have felt,that the events of this century, especially the Shoah, can be described only be "New Psalms". For him more than for other authors the Biblical form of expression and thinking remains, but the events have changed radically.

In the Jewish poems I want to interpret now at last, many motives which I have mentioned and discovered before, will encounter us here again.
Many poets have felt that with the Shoah a world has collapsed.(And this feeling was right - there has collapsed a world!) Else Lasker-Schüler already had a premonition in her poem "End of the World": "There is a weeping in the world/ As if God would have died..." (Kurz, p.55)
And much later Rose Ausländer wrote: "They come/with sharp flags and pistols/ they have shot all the stars and the moon/for that remains no more light/there we have dug the sun/It was an endless eclipse." (p.100)
And Alfred Gong formulated in his poem: "Israel's last Psalm": "It is the last Psalm,/and our voice is trembling./there is a great fear among us. We sing/ to shatter the faith of the fair knights of death." (Seydel p.307)
But most simple and deepest, so comprehensible and endlessly sad, the fourteen year old David Rubinowicz probably has said it his diary: "Such a little girl like a flower, that she could be shot, that is surely the end of the world." (Glaser, p.109)

In this time, when that could happen a million times, Nachmann Rapp was asking the poets for new prophets: "Poets of my time, scattered on the seven seas,/ the head covered with ashes, scattered in agony and suffering-/o would you hear the fiery outcry of dying mothers,/which prepares us for life in mortal anguishes./There is no limit for pain and sorrow and mourning,/the burning lamentation streams from our eyes like blood./So be prophets and stand on the battlements/prepare for our coming people their day." (Witt, p.205/6)

That means that the very old task of the prophets of Israel to show the people the right way of life, is said here about the poets.
Jakub Sonschein asked a similar question: "Who will write the great book of the end and/the struggle of Polish Jewry/A man will come and will write on white parchment in red letters/no hand will extinguish it/no axe will hack it off." (Witt, p.270)
For an indestructible legacy for the time to come also longs Dowid Sfard: "When I leave the earth/who will express for the hatred of the murderers/in Jiddish words all the triumphs and agonies?...Who will with a Jewish song/ mould the golden chain/that it will reach in the time to come...?"
About his own word Sfard composes the touching lines: "...I have mounted it in my heart/want to nurture it with my blood/if the night darkens the sky/it shall preserve its light." (Witt, p.187-88)

Berthold Viertel too finds that only a word which is divinely inspired as the word of the Bible, here in the sense of the New Testament, can correspond to these events of the Shoah: "Unless it be with the tongues of angels/would help us any other singing?" (Hakel, p.156)
Hermann Broch, even more pessimistic, feels that only an entirely new language could express that infinite horror: "Those who pale in the cold sweat of the execution/daily, nightly/who have a fever as in hell/today would have the right to sing/and if they would do it/they would do it in a terribly new language/where no word would resemble another word." (Schlösser, p.129)

By three specially beautiful examples I want to show the corporative closeness of the Jewish people with its whole history and all its generations - and therefore also their life in and with the Biblical word, which constantly is reflected in Jewish poetry.
Dowid Einhorn writes in his poem "My People": "O how I feel your blood crying inside me/100 generations remind me and accuse me/sanctified in God on the world's scaffold/when the flames torture you." (Witt,p.44/45)
And Ilse Blumenthal-Weiss formulates in "Departure for the Transport": "I have seen men/massed together like lumps/They all were many thousands of years old." (Kaznelson , p.361)

Or Hermann Hakel in his poem: "Jewish Child 1945": "...And suddenly picked up/ when I cried for help/I stand all of a sudden above/on the mountain of Sinai." (Kaznelson , p.371)
Hakel, who lived in Vienna until his death in 1987, once said to me: "When I read the Bible for the first time, I always had the feeling: That is I! I then always wanted to write like the Bible: So clear, so simple and naive as one tells a tale. But I didn't succeed. When I told this to Canetti, he replied: 'Nobody can do this'". (Adunka, p.19)
Hakel also wrote a poem which he entitled "Psalm". When I asked him about it, he gave me a reply, which most certainly is valid for many other poets, including Celan: "Just as one still says the word 'God' and does not really always believe in him, one still uses the word 'Psalm'".

Comparable with Blumenthal-Weiss, as quoted above, Friedrich Heer, who was very close to Judaism, said to me a few days before he died, that he feels as if he were 2067 years old. (He was 67 at that time).
Again comparable with him, Lucie Begov, a Viennese and a survivor of Auschwitz, who described her experiences in a book, wrote: "From my assimilation in Austria, i returned to my Jewish faith, and between 1938 and 1945 I rushed through the history of my people until the time of Moses. Within seven years, I somehow became 3700 years old." (p.30)

The ineffectiveness of the Biblical word, and also the interpretation of Nazism as a rebellion against the Decalogue, is expressed by Eliahu Rajsman: "Where did you throw the tablets of the Law/when blood burned in the fire?" (Witt, p.207)
Even more clearly and more drastically it is seen by Moshe Schulstein: "There he hangs in my view, the hangman smeared with blood/is it he to whom the way of the Pentateuch is leading?/Man, whom God created in his image, created to treacherous murder and violence./Has God carved in him his traces, his signs/ formed him each limb, shaped and carved/is he the man - man in God's image?" (Witt, p.247)

The conviction that the spirit of the murdered Jewish people could not be extinguished and destroyed by the Nazis is one of the strongest and most important motives in this kind of poetry. In a poem by Henry Sternberg entitled "The Unforgotten", which is dedicated to the dead of Theresienstadt, he says: "But the love that you have sown/will remain in eternity just as today." (Kaznelson p.356)

Most beautifully and most humanly - here I would say even most sacredly - it is expressed by Ilse Blumenthal-Weiss, a survivor of Theresienstadt:
"I cannot hate/They beat me. They kick me with their boots/I cannot hate/I only can atone/For you and for me/I cannot hate/They strangle me. They hurl stones at me/I cannot hate. I can only weep/Bitterly." (Schlösser, p.110)
And even more in her poem "Confession": "Revile me, defile me/I bear the curse

and the mockery/Push me, hurl me/I stand before God/torment me, oppress me: I serve the law/Take hold of me, bind me/I pray to God/kick me, drive me/to the gallows and scaffold/hound me, mock me/I believe in God." (Kaznelson p.132)
This faithfulness of the Jewish people to its covenant with God, as expressed in these two poems, this faithfulness really surpasses even God's loyalty itself. This is the Jewish people which was exterminated in the Shoah - of which we still today are not aware enough - because till that day we, and especially the Germans, abstract from the victims of the Shoah.

The need to rebuild and renew the world after this great destruction of our civilisation was felt by many poets. Frank Zwillinger sees this break even in Biblical dimensions: "Just as before the Flood we go through the gates/in an ever strange part of the world, without thanks/and only one purpose in our gestures/to become a foundation stone for a new world." (Schlösser, p.285)
Even more intensely it was felt by Awrom Suzkewer: "Should I start from the beginning/Should I, who is not an Abraham, because of brotherhood, shatter all idols...?" (Witt, p.266)
After this destruction the strength of the individual must become much stronger than ever before. Just as Suzkewer Pessach Binezki feels that too: "We who remained after that time/we want to build renewed our reality/let's lay the foundations newly/deeper and longer lasting and one for three." (Witt, p. 256)

This persistence still does not find its limits. It goes further to our last motif, which we hardly noticed until now: The feeling, shared by many poets, that God too was affected, that He himself is suffering, and even that He now needs man more than ever before in history.
Dowid Einhorn wrote already in 1912: "I bear the sins of all men/the pain of the perpetrators and of the victims/From where should I take all the strength/ to get to the fire and from there to bless God?" (Witt, p.43)
But Rachel H.Korn found the most impressive and moving formulation in this context: "I became already so mature through pain and suffering/Even God Himself/can entrust into my hand/so that I guide Him safely/into that land... Tell me, why do you hesitate, my God?/This night I have repaired all the ways/ and have repaired each bridge/up to the silent house/are you afraid, perhaps, o God/to go back to this world?" (Witt, p.121/22)

If even God himself is horrified by the world of the Shoah, He must be guided back despite that, because only He can give the saving blessing to fallen man. Leonard Bernstein must have felt this when he wrote his Third Symphony, called "Kaddish", which had its first performance in Tel Aviv in 1963. (I want to remember also the great poems "Kaddish" by Friedrich Torberg in 1943, and by Masha Kaleko in 1945, which I only can mention here).
In his great dialogue with God Bernstein says: "My sorrowful Father/If I could comfort you,/hold you against me,/Rock you and rock you into/sleep... Rest my Father. Sleep, dream./Let me invent your dream,/dream it/With you, as gently as I can./And perhaps in dreaming, I can/help you/Recreate your image, and love/him again."

CONCLUSION

A "New Psalter" according to Jewish tradition is possible, and I am sure that one day it will be written. But it must be totally removed from any idea of a "new revelation" or of a "sanctification of the Holocaust."
The reasons and criteria for a "New Psalter" would be firstly the metaphysical implications of the Shoah; secondly that the Shoah far surpasses all Biblical scales in its size, its cruelty and its horror; and thirdly, that therefore many poets feel that only Biblical - that means divinely inspired - language - could deal with this event.
I have found many texts to which these categories can be applied, and I presented them in this paper in a small selection. They are so impressive that they speak for themselves and that is was not always necessary to interpret them in great detail. I only have tried to read them in a different light than normally we are used to.
With the concept of a "New Psalter" the Shoah will become an integrated part of the collective memory of the Jewish people, exactly as became the Biblical events - in order to prevent its dangers in future times.

Friedrich Heer with his formulation has intuitively pointed the way to a concept which has a significance for the future of the Jewish people that today is still beyond all estimation.

ACKNOWLEDGEMENT

The author would like to thank Edwin Roth for help with the translation.

REFERENCES

Adunka Evelyn: Hermann Hakel. Illustrierte Neue Welt. January 1988. p.19.
Ausländer Rose: Gesammelte Gedichte. Köln 1977.
Begov Lucie: Das verkannte Volk. Vienna 1969.
Berger Alan L.: In: Judaism. Spring 1982. p.167-176.
Berkovits Eliezer: Faith after the Holocaust. New York 1973.
Bernstein Leonard: Journey for Peace. Vienna 1985.
Birnbaum Philip: Encyclopedia of Jewish Concepts.New York 1969.
Brocke Michael (ed.): Wolkensäule und Feuerschein. München 1982.
Cardenal Ernesto: Das Buch von der Liebe. Gütersloh 1981.
Celan Paul: Die Niemandsrose. Frankfurt am Main 1980.
Cohen Leonard: Wem sonst als Dir. München 1987.
Eliach Yaffa: Hasidic Tales of the Holocaust. New York 1982.
Fackenheim Emil L.: God's Presence in History. New York 1970.
Fackenheim Emil L.: The Jewish Return into History. New York 1978.
Glaser Hermann (ed.): wohnungen des todes. Bamberg 1961.
Hakel Hermann: (ed.): Die Bibel im deutschen Gedicht. München 1959.
Heer Friedrich: Gottes erste Liebe. München 1981.
Kaplan Chaim A.: Buch der Agonie. Frankfurt am Main 1967.
Katzenelson Jizchak: Lied vom letzten Juden. Zürich 1951.
Katzenelson Jizchak: Song of the Murdered Jewish People. Ghetto Fighters 1980.
Katzenelson Jizchak: Vittel Diary. Ghetto Fighters 1972.
Kaznelson Siegmund: Jüdisches Schicksal in deutschen Gedichten. Berlin 1959.
Kurz Paul K.: Psalmen vom Expressionismus bis zur Gegenwart. Freiburg 1978.
Mayer Peter: In: Evang. Akademie Hofgeismar, Protokoll Nr.97. Kassel 1973.
Lagercrantz Olof: Versuch über die Lyrik der Nelly Sachs. Frankfurt 1967.
Neher Andre: The Exile of the World. Phila. 1980.
Ophir Adi: In: Tikkun. Volume 2, Nr.1. p. 61-66.
Petuchowski Jakob J.: In: Commentary. Volume XXII. 1956. p.543-549.
Pfisterer Rudolf: Von A bis Z. Neukirchen-Vluyn 1985.
Rosenfeld Abraham: Tisha B'Av Compendium. New york 1983.
Nelly Sachs: das Buch der N.S. (ed) Bengt Holmqvist. Frankfurt 1977.
Nelly Sachs zu Ehren. Frankfurt 1966.
Schlösser Manfred: An den Wind geschrieben. Berlin 1982.
Seydel Heinz (ed.):Welch Wort in die Kälte gerufen. Berlin 1968.
Steiner George: In: Akzente. Heft 3. 1987. p.194-212.
Susman Margarete: Das Buch Hiob und das Schicksal des jüd.Volkes. Zürich 1948.
Witt Hubert: (ed): Der Fiedler vom Getto. Leipzig 1968.
Wörner Karl H.: In: Neue Zeitschrift für Musik. Heft 3, 1957. p.147-151.

RESCUE EFFORTS AS REFLECTED IN AMERICAN RABBINIC JOURNALS

JUDITH BLEICH

Touro College, 30 West 44 St.,
New York, New York, U.S.A.

Much has been written regarding the response -- or better, lack of response -- of Jews who resided in the United States to the plight of European Jewry during the course of World War II. It has been charged that American Jewry failed to exert influence upon the American government for a variety of reasons, primarily because they could not speak to the administration with one voice and because they dissipated their resources in internal bickering over trivial matters. In face of catastrophe, American Jewry became paralyzed by hopeless organizational deadlock.[1]

A singularly noteworthy exception to the generaly pallid reaction of American Jews to the raging Holocaust were the almost frenzied activities of a small group of Orthodox rabbis and scholars who headed newly founded yeshivot (talmudic academies) and sponsored rabbinic publications in the United States at that time.

As a small and dedicated group they worked within both the public and private sectors and were prepared to employ the most unconventional methods in order to alleviate the suffering of even individual Nazi victims. The very informal nature of their activities and the fact that they were not viewed as official establishment spokesmen may have given their representatives a greater measure of freedom and flexibility. Added urgency was lent to the activities of this segment of the community by the fact they numbered among their ranks many who were themselves refugees and whose immediate families were yet in Europe.

The rescue efforts of these individuals have not received the attention they merit.[2] A chronicle of those efforts is recorded in the pages of two rabbinic periodicals with limited circulations, Ha-Pardes and Hamsilo. Examination of issues of these two journals during the period 1939-1942 reveals frantic activity directed to alleviating the plight of European Jewry in general and the European yeshiva community in particular.

The twelve volumes of the rabbinic periodical, Hamsilo, were published in New York from February 1936 to February-March 1947. Although originally designed as a monthly, in later years there were numerous combined issues with the result that, at times, the journal appeared only three or four times a year even less frequently and in the last two years. The periodical was edited by Rabbi Nisan Telushkin as the organ of the Rabbinical Board, Association of Orthodox Rabbis of the City of New York (Va'ad Ha-Rabbanim de-New York Rabbati).[3] While the major portion of the journal was published in Hebrew, with the feature articles devoted almost exclusively to rabbinic and talmudic scholarship, there was also a Yiddish section containing articles and news items designed to appeal to a somewhat broader-based readership not entirely limited to rabbis and scholars. Hamsilo constitutes a rich repository of rabbinic scholarship of the time. However, it also serves as a valuable historical source for religious life in the United States in the over a decade which its publication spans, reflecting diverse facets of communal life and highlighting the issues and problems that agitated the leaders of the Orthodox community.

The prestigious, independent Hebrew rabbinic monthly Ha-Pardes has a much longer and more varied background. Founded in Poland in 1913 under the editorship of Rabbi Samuel Aaron Ha-Levi Pardes, it has appeared with regularity in the United States since 1927 where it was published in Chicago until 1950 and thereafter in New York. Until the advent of Hamsilo, as the only rabbinic journal published in the United States, Ha-Pardes exerted considerable influence and was widely read by many rabbis and learned laymen. As a consequence of the high calibre of its scholarship the journal enjoyed an international reputation. Indeed, it has served as a scholarly forum for publication of original talmudic novellae and halakhic responsa and, over the years, has been graced by contributions of the foremost European and American contemporary rabbinic writers. Several pages in each issue are devoted to editorials, news items and announcements regarding religious and educational matters. Thus the interests and concerns of the Orthodox community are reflected in the pages of this journal. Of the two journals, Ha-Pardes constitutes a far richer source of historical information. However, the articles in Hamsilo, although fewer in number, are significant and serve as a further independent source corroborating the extent of the involvement of the Orthodox community in rescue efforts.

The multifaceted rescue activities reflect in these journals merits detailed study and will be analyzed here in terms of (1) goals and agenda (2) accomplishments (3) political activism (4) dissemination of information and (5) leadership.

I. Goals and Agenda

The mobilization and galvanization of the Orthodox community was spurred by concern for the future of institutions of Torah learning and the rescue of leading Torah scholars. The spiritual and cultural leadership of Orthodoxy was centered in Europe in the rabbinical academies and yeshivot of Poland and Lithuania and was faced with imminent extinction. The American Orthodox community in a very real and immediate manner sensed that its destiny was linked to, indeed contingent upon, the fate of the educational and religious elite of Eastern European Jewry. It was to the preservation of these scholarly and rabbinic personalities and the institutions of learning with which they were intimately associated that the immigrant Orthodox rabbis directed their greatest efforts.

The concentration of yeshiva students in the city of Vilna and Rabbi Chaim Ozer Grodzinsky's yeoman efforts on their behalf were the proximate causes prompting the formation in November 1939 of the Emergency Committee for War-Torn Yeshivoth, Vaad Hatzalah, as a formal rescue organization sponsored by the Union of Orthodox Rabbis of the United States and Canada under the presidency of Rabbi Eliezer Silver of Cincinnati.[4] Ha-Pardes served as the major publicity organ for the Vaad Hatzalah and, from the organization's inception, not a single issue of Ha-Pardes failed to include material pertaining to Vaad Hatzalah activities.

United States Jews looked upon themselves, and were perceived by their European coreligionists, as placed in a uniquely providential role. As a writer in Hamsilo commented:

> Providence has placed a great responsibility on us American Jews who are the only ones who are able to help . . . . as free citizens of our blessed country, we dare not forget millions of our miserable brethren . . . Providence brought us to our blessed land of America in order that we might be a saving angel . . . in this catastrophic time.[5]

History had conveyed upon them the privileges of freedom and prosperity and the concommitant awesome responsibility to use those blessings on behalf of their fellow Jews. Both American and European rabbis cited the midrashic statement, a kindness has the Almighty done for us that he has dispersed us among the nations." Dispersion proved to be a blessing in disguise for the relatively young, but secure, American Jewish community could provide a haven for beleaguered fellow

Jews.[6] "Virtually the only source [of support] lies in the land of America and the very survival of yeshivot in Israel and the Diaspora depends upon it," wrote Rabbi Chaim Ozer Grodzinsky in a similar vein.[7]

The Joint Distribution Committee was hailed by the Orthodox community as a valued and effective rescue and relief agency whose record was formidable. Understandably, however, the Joint directed its activities to the entire spectrum of relief needs of all Jews in countries of oppression.[8] By contradistinction, the focus of Vaad Hatzalah was primarily upon the needs of the rabbis, sages, scholars and students of Torah. While, subsequently, Vaad Hatzalah proudly proclaimed that their office had not turned away any individual Jew who approached it on behalf of European refugees, it did not ever deny the priority accorded Torah scholars.[9] Accordingly, with all due regard for the importance of supporting the work of the Joint, the leaders of Vaad Hatzalah in their appeals for funds emphasized the uniqueness of their own contribution. Upon encountering difficulties with local federations who urged them to subordinate their own appeals to general community-wide fundraising efforts, they staunchly affirmed their determination to conduct a separate campaign.[10]

The leaders of Vaad Hatzalah recognized full well that they were engaged in an effort upon which their own fate depended. In the balance was the future of Torah scholarship in the entire world. The European yeshivot were the life-blood of the Jewish people, the repository of the oral law tradition and of the accumulated wisdom of centuries. The learning they represented could not be reproduced by parthenogensis.[11] Rabbi Jacob Levinson of the Vaad Hatzalah presidium wrote:

> The pipeline of influence stretches across the ocean from Europe to American Jews. All genuine rabbinic leadership that we possess in this country came to us from there. With all our efforts we still have not reared great scholars of Torah. If the sages and leaders of the people overseas do not find secure refuge in the United States then, heaven forfend, . . . our future is endangered.[12]

The general level of learning and religious observance in America was abysmally low. European yeshivot constituted a reservoir of scholarship. If brought to these shares, European rabbis and scholars would enrich and ultimately transform the American Jewish scene:

> Therefore, when we save a sage or a scholar . . . and when we bring from the lands of danger yeshiva students who have absorbed the spirit of Torah . . . new blood, life-blood, are we injecting into the body of American Jewry. We are not extending help to individuals but to the nation.[13]

The conviction that the survival of the yeshivot would determine the quality of the religious life of the community was thus a determinant factor in all Vaad Hatzalah policy decisions. The rescue activities were deemed to be self-serving rather than altruistic. "Saving the yeshivot constitutes self-preservation because in saving the yeshivot we save ourselves," declared Rabbi Abraham Kalmanowitz.[14] A prominent lay leader voicing the same sentiment added, "It is only fitting that our efforts are under the auspices of the Vaad Hatzalah (rescue committee). But it is not the yeshivot we are engaged in rescuing. We are rescuing ourselves."[15]

The extent to which the Vaad Hatzalah succeeded in this objective and to which their hopeful predictions were realized may be traced in these rabbinic periodicals. In the course of time, the journals welcomed the arrival in America of an array of outstanding rabbinic scholars, including Rabbi Michal Feinstein, Rabbi Aaron Kotler, Rabbi Mendel Zaks, Rabbi Rueven Grozovsky, Rabbi Abraham Jofen, Rabbi Israel Chaim Kaplan, Rabbi Eliyahu Meir Bloch, Rabbi David Lifschitz and Rabbi Moshe Shatzkes.[16] Many of these individuals joined the faculties of existing United States yeshivot or talmudical academies, including the Rabbi Isaac Elchanon Theological Seminary, Yeshiva Rabbi Jacob Joseph, Mesivta Tifereth Jerusalem, Mesivta Torah Vodaath and Ner Israel, enhancing their standing, or founded new yeshivot and centers of Torah study destined to play an important role on the American Jewish scene such as Telz in Cleveland, Yeshivat Chachmei Lublin in Detroit, Mir, Bet Yosef and Tomchei Temimim Lubavitch in New York.[17] Indeed, the years following the World War witnessed a radical change in the texture of American Orthodoxy. This transformation was not a haphazard development, but on the contrary, may to a large extent be attributed to the directed immigration and rescue policy of the founders of Vaad Hatzalah and to their concerted effort to transpose the European yeshiva tradition to American shores.

II. Accomplishments

From the founding of the Vaad Hatzalah through the end of 1942, its major activities may be traced in the following sequential order: 1) the gathering of Yeshiva students in Vilna; 2) the move of numerous scholars to Japan; 3) their relocation to Shanghai; and 4) the assistance rendered to scholars stranded in Siberia.

A felicitous series of events brought about what has often been described as "the miracle of Vilna."[18] Following Soviet occupation of eastern Poland in the fall of 1939, a large number of *yeshivot*, with their student bodies and faculties fled Poland for Lithuania upon hearing the report that the Soviets had returned Vilna to the rule of the then independent and neutral state of Lithuania. Most of these *yeshivot* relocated in Vilna itself or clustered in the small towns and villages surrounding Vilna. At the advice of Rabbi Chaim Ozer Grodzinsky, renowned scholar and leading rabbinic figure in Vilna, each yeshiva-in-exile maintained its separate and independent identity. Rabbi Grodzinsky, addressing his letters to Rabbi Eliezer Silver, appealed to the United States Orthodox rabbinate to provide material support for the continued existence of these exiled *yeshivot* and to organize a large-scale rescue effort on their behalf.

As foreign nationals, the legal status of these students who found themselves in Vilna was precarious. Nevertheless, following the intercession of the yeshiva deans and rabbis, the Lithuanian authorities, granted the yeshiva students permission to remain in the country as foreign refugees provided there be an assurance that provision be made for their material support and that they would produce documents demonstrating a destination to which it would be possible for them to migrate.[19] Toward the end of Rabbi Grodzinsky's life, it was known that a Soviet takeover of Lithuania was imminent. Accordingly, Vaad Hatzalah strove to send funds for the maintenance of the exiled *yeshivot* in Vilna, while endeavoring to find ways to transplant the *yeshivot* to the Holy Land and to America.[20] At one point, Rabbi Silver discussed the projected transfer of one of the major *yeshivot* to America, where it would function under the name "Golus Yeshiva."[21] In order to obtain a full report regarding the nuances of the situation in Vilna, the Vaad Hatzalah undertook the sending of an envoy to Lithuania.[22] The envoy, Doctor Samuel Smith of Cincinnati, returned with a full report regarding the status of the exiled *yeshivot* and the pressing need to obtain transit visas for the scholars.[23]

By December 1940, the urgency of the plight of the *yeshivot* was perceived more keenly than ever by the Vaad Hatzalah. A proclamation of the Union of Orthodox Rabbis on behalf of the *yeshivot* declared: "The destruction is great! Millions of our Jewish brothers flutter between life and death . . . Who can describe the great destruction . . . of the institutions from which we drew the illumination of Torah . . . Now we are in a position in which actions are expected of us, to stretch out a helping hand to . . . hundreds of leaders of Is-ael . . . who call out to us, 'Save us.'"[24]

Hamsilo devoted an entire issue to the theme of the perilous fate of the *yeshivot* which had found a temporary refugee in Lithuania and to a description of ten of the most prominent of the *yeshivot* exiled to Lithuania: Baranowitz, Grodno, Volozhin, Lomza, Mir, Novardok, Slonim, Kamenitz, Kletzk and Radin. According to reports in *Hamsilo*, twenty-four hundred students from twenty-one institutions of learning had found a haven in Lithuania. *Hamsilo* urged support of Vaad Hatzalah's campaign goal of one-half a million dollars on behalf of the exiled *yeshivot*.[25]

In its January 1941 issue, *Ha-Pardes* began to report the progress of the second stage of the yeshiva rescue campaign, i.e., the hegira of yeshiva students from Vilna to Japan. Haste was urged in sending funds to cover the cost of transit visas and travel expenses to Japan and ultimately for transportation costs for those hopefully destined for the United States or Palestine.[26] To emphasize the immediacy of the situation, Ha-Pardes now began to publicize the texts of telegrams containing urgent messages, e.g., a request from Joseph Shub for ten thousand dollars on behalf of the Vilna scholars, a six thousand dollar request from the Jewish Agency in Istanbul for transit visas for refugees who had obtained entry permits to Palestine and a list of the names of rabbis and students whose names were not yet included in official lists and were therefore not receiving aid from Hias or the Joint.[27]

Ha-Pardes reported that Rabbi Herzog had obtained entry permits to Palestine on behalf of two hundred rabbis and fifteen hundred students. A contingent of scholars had already arrived in Japan. The need for funds was urgent and immediate and rabbis were urged to travel around the country on behalf of this cause. While the sum of $140,000 had already been collected to date, the rhetoric of the campaign advertisements reflected an awareness that the possibility to obtain transit visas might vanish and hence it was imperative to hasten the remittance of funds for the purchase of tickets.[28] The April 1941 Ha-Pardes continued the narration of the dangers and difficulties encountered by refugees in transit to Japan and their urgent need for financial assistance. It also reported the arrival in Palestine of two prominent Torah scholars, Rabbi Eliezer Yehudah Finkel and Rabbi Yitzhack Ze'ev Soloveichik, through the efforts of Vaad Hatzalah.[29]

Of all the yeshivot there was one that was saved in its entirety and that continued to function throughout the war as a vibrant center of learning. The saga of the rescue of the Mirrer Yeshiva constitutes a special chapter in the history of the Vaad Hatzalah and the pages of Ha-Pardes are replete with its account. An article in Ha-Pardes by Rabbi Kalmanowitz entitled "And He Fled and Lived," describes the fate of this historic yeshiva founded in 1917. After the flight of several hundred students to Lithuania, Rabbi Kalmanowitz had been sent as an emissary to the United States where he raised funds and secured visas to facilitate the move to Japan of over 305 individuals. When the Russians first occupied Lithuania, various consulates in Kovno briefly continued to function. At that time, the Dutch Consulate had furnished many yeshiva students with entry visas to Curacao. On the strength of those visas the Japanese Consul issues transit visas to Japan. Without such documents, it would have been dangerous for the students to undertake the journey through Siberia. At the propitious moment when permission to leave was given, they were able to flee from Vilna since they did have the visas in their possession. However, funds to cover expenses and transportation were urgently required. Rabbi Kalmanowitz was able to collect the funds in record time in order to enable the refugees to reach a haven in Japan. The account concludes with a list of names of those who had been saved and had reached Palestine or the United States.[30] Subsequent issues of Ha-Pardes presented the list of students who had escaped to Japan.[31]

The further move of the Mirrer Yeshiva from Kobe, Japan to Shanghai, China was recorded in Ha-Pardes of September 1941. For the first time, an English account was added, describing the dramatic tale of the yeshiva's rescue and the subsequent deportation from Japan to China. This singular departure from the journal's usual format highlights its commitment to publicize the plight of the imperiled yeshiva students and the concerted efforts to raise the necessary funds. The text of telegrams, also in English, describing the arrival of the yeshiva community in China were included.[32]

With the United States entry into the war on December 7, 1941, the situation of the yeshiva students in Shanghai became more precarious and the methods of sending assistance more complex. Thus the January 1942 issue of Ha-Pardes published several telegram messages from Shanghai (transmitted via Stockholm and Buenos Aires) regarding the welfare of the yeshiva and noted that Rabbi Kalmanowitz was endeavoring to find legal means to continue sending assistance to the yeshiva in Shanghai via neutral countries.[33] News bulletins in Ha-Pardes throughout the course of 1942 reported on the continued functioning of the yeshiva. Telegrams were published indicating that study was continuing but financial assistance was necessary.[34] In order to continue its academic program the yeshiva had arranged for the printing in Shanghai of necessary rabbinic texts.[35] Lists of students were published together with a full budgetary report of funds expended on behalf of the Mirrer Yeshiva.[36] In the Ha-Pardes of November 1941 one finds a description of a group of 25 students and three rabbis who had received visas to Canada. These individuals arrived in Montreal from Shanghai, subsequent to having received Canadian visas and United States transit permits through the efforts of Vaad Hatzalah and the assistance of the Polish government in London.[37]

While hundreds of yeshiva students who had reached Japan later relocated to Shanghai, numerous others of those who had fled the Vilna region remained perforce in Siberia. Throughout 1942, apart from the reports regarding Shanghai, Ha-Pardes news of Vaad Hatzalah activities focused increasingly upon the needs of those Jewish scholars in the Asian provinces of Russia. As early as February 1941 a detailed eyewitness account of the tribulations and privations of the refugees in transit written by an individual who had reached Japan noted that many hundreds were stranded in Siberia.[38] In the next months, telegrams from Siberia to Rabbi Kotler[39] and Rabbi Zaks[40] reported on the hardships experienced there by students from Kletzk and Yeshiva Chafetz Chaim and urged readers to respond to an appeal to send packages of food and clothes. Thereafter, almost monthly, news bulletins in Ha-Pardes stressed the terrible hunger and cold described in communications from Siberia and pleaded for generous and speedy assistance.[41]

Apparently, skeptics challenged whether it was indeed possible for funds and provisions to reach Siberia. For this reason Ha-Pardes articles repeatedly emphasized that the office of the Vaad Hatzalah was open and readers might come to the office to examine the telegrams of appeal and receipts for packages and thereby ascertain for themselves the necessity and feasibility of sending assistance to the Siberian refugees.[42] Moreover, Ha-Pardes stressed that, while the assistance of the Joint extended to Jews in most parts of the world, the Joint did not conduct relief activities in territory subject to Soviet rule because they had no representatives in those areas.[43] While it was indeed possible to transmit funds to Siberia, exchange rates were inordinately high, and therefore, transmission of packages of food and clothing, facilitated by means of Vaad Hatzalah contacts with the Red Cross was a more practical and preferable means of sending help. The Vaad Hatzalah was negotiating with neutral countries in the Far East to establish a route for sending tangible aid to the refugees but cautioned that, if successful, this method would also involve considerable financial outlay. The realities of the situation were underscored by a telegram from Siberia published in the May 1942 Ha-Pardes giving lists of names of students of yeshivot Kletzk, Telz, Kamenitz, Grodno, Bialystok and Lomza.[44] Vaad Hatzalah efforts had already accounted for over $25,000 in monetary assistance and packages. However, there appeared to be some 3,000 scholars and students in the region of Samarkand, Turkistan and Siberia whose situation remained precarious.[45]

The possibility of rescuing and transporting some of these scholars to Palestine remained a paramount objective. One news article reported on sixty visas that had been obtained and the need for funds to cover the transportation expenses.[46] Another item recounted efforts of the Union of Orthodox Rabbis to persuade authorities in Washington to exert pressure on Great Britain to open the gates of Palestine to those Jews in Siberia fortunate enough to have received permission from the Soviet government to leave.[47] In the interim, Ha-Pardes articles dramatized the situation by repeatedly including lists of scholars in Siberia.[48] The general press was implored to publicize the urgent need for financial assistance to ameliorate the plight of the refugees in Siberia.[49]

One of the most concrete Orthodox relief activities reflected in the pages of both journals was the campaign for procurement of affidavits. A steady stream of news articles and editorials emphasized that executing affidavits constituted a great mitzvah. Rabbis and synagogue presidents were instructed to exhort their congregants weekly, and especially on the high Holy Days, regarding this holy obligation.[50] A moving letter from the Viennese rabbinate addresed "in the name of thousands" to the rabbis of America, published in both Hamsilo and Ha-Pardes, implored them "to alert members of synagogues to send affidavits on behalf of their European brothers. If individuals alone are unable to do so, they should join [to sponsor an affidavit] as a group . . . Do not delay the hour. We are awaiting your help with yearning."[51] With distress, one writer commented on the failure of many synagogue leaders to respond to the request for affidavits and formal letters of invitation even though this did not involve a monetary expense on their part and emphasized that the pressing need for affidavits must be publicized far more widely in the press.[52]

Apart from Vaad Hatzalah, there existed only one major Orthodox institution whose sole raison d'être was relief, viz., Ezrat Torah, an organization founded during World War I for the collection of charitable funds, particularly on behalf of indigent rabbis and scholars. Every single issue of Ha-Pardes carried at least one announcement urging support of Ezrat Torah, usually prominently displayed on page one. Ezrat Torah officials stressed that its support was geared toward individual scholars and their families, not to institutions, and therein lay its distinction from the Vaad Hatzalah.[53] A characteristic feature of Ezrat Torah's concern was care of refugee families following their relocation in the United States or the Holy Land and a consequent serious endeavor to find suitable job placement for the refugee rabbis.[54] It should be noted that, from time to time, beneath the appeal for Ezrat Torah, Ha-Pardes carried brief notes urging support of both the Joint and of the United Jewish Appeal,[55] as well as, on occasion, advertisements for the purchase of U.S. war bonds.[56]

In addition to the regular coverage in Ha-Pardes of the activities of Vaad Hatzalah and Ezrat Torah, the journal also reported on a number of other specialized rescue and relief organizations sponsored by the Orthodox community. Particularly extensive coverage was given, in numerous issues, to the rescue activities and projects of both Lubavitch and Agudath Israel. With the arrival in the United States of the Lubavitcher Rebbe, Rabbi Joseph Isaac Schneersohn[57] whose stated aim was rescue of students of Lubavitch yeshivot stranded in Europe, a special ransom fund was inaugurated and Ha-Pardes faithfully recorded its campaign announcements. At a later date several news articles recounted successful attempts to secure visas and depicted the odyssey and eventual arrival in the United States from Siberia via Japan of close to 40 Lubavitch students and scholars.[58] In addition to standard rescue activities, Agudath Israel sponsored clothes drives and campaigns to supply beleagured Jews with matzot and religious articles such as lulavim and etrogim. Reports on Agudath Israel conferences reflect the priority on their agenda of rescue and relief activities, their energetic efforts to secure affidavits and outline their ongoing diplomatic negotiations in Washington. Ha-Pardes, June 1941, includes a comprehensive itemized budget and report of expenditures incurred by Agudath Israel in these rescue activities.[59] Beginning in 1940, one finds a number of reports pertaining to the relief activities of the Council of Hungarian Yeshivoth.[60] Finally, there are occasional reports of the Bobover Relief Society[61] and of the rescue activity and projects of the Mizrachi.[62]

A January 1943 summary in Ha-Pardes gave figures for the number of individuals assisted throughout 1940 and 1941, those enabled to reach Palestine or Canada, those assisted in Shanghai and help rendered to individual refugees in Morocco, Spain, Portugal, Switzerland, and San Domingo.[63]

Taking into account the relatively small size of the Orthodox community, the variety of relief organizations it promoted and their considerable record of achievement stands in stark contrast of that of the Jewish establishment. By February 1942 this group could already point to an impressive list of achievements. At no point did they waver in their conviction that they were engaged in the most significant venture imaginable and that they had "written a golden page in the history of American Jewry . . . thanks to a closely-knit group of Jews devoted to Torah and tradition . . . we have succeeded in rescuing from the lands of bloodshed the greatest scholars of Torah Judaism in Europe, those spiritual giants who connected the chain [of tradition] for generations and who sustain the survival of our Torah people."[64] But they were aware that a gargantuan task lay ahead, and that sacrificial responses were called for, not complacency. There lingered a sense of inadequacy voiced much earlier by Rabbi Silver, "Indeed, we can say we are guilty. For if we had money we could save thousands."[65] Ultimately, the response to relief efforts would serve as a measure of the calibre of the American Jewish community:

> Only when every conscious Jew in our country will correctly evaluate his obligation to this holy rescue work will it be possible to say of the Jewish settlement in America that at the time of the greatest

> crisis in Jewish history it answered the cry for help of our brethren who are in distress and captivity . . . They helped not only rescue Jewish souls but . . . preserve the continued existence of the Torah.[66]

III. Political Activism

Traditionally the Orthodox community tended to maintain a low profile in political matters and was reluctant in pressing its interests before the general public. Both Ha-Pardes and Hamsilo included feature articles as well as editorials opposing boycotts and public protests against Germany.[67] The rabbis feared that such action might lead to repercussions against Jews under the Nazi regime. This was a matter regarding which Rabbi Y. E. Henkin, the highly regarded executive director of Ezrat Torah, had strong feelings and several articles bearing his name in both journals focused on this theme. He extolled the sagacity of maintaining a posture of humility in diplomatic negotiations with the nations of the world and urged concentration of Jewish resources upon charitable efforts and rescue endeavors rather than upon public political confrontation.[68] At a later date, one finds Rabbi Henkin inveighing, for similar reasons, against the concept of a Jewish brigade or a Jewish army.[69]

It is well known that American Jewish protests were muted as a result of the unfounded sense of trust placed by American Jews in Franklin D. Roosevelt and their feeling that Roosevelt must be supported, not challenged.[70] The journals are replete with expressions of the adulation and awe with which the Jewish community regarded Roosevelt. Following the United States initiative in conjunction with the Evian Refugee Conference, glowing telegrams of thanks were dispatched to the President by the major Orthodox organizations.[71] Ha-Pardes praised his name which

> will be inscribed as an everlasting memorial in Jewish history and will be written in letters of gold in the chronicles of Israel . . . It is proper that in all synagogues blessings be pronounced for President Roosevelt . . . . Blessed be forever, Franklin Delano Roosevelt, President of the land of freedom and liberty . . . a man elevated above the populace, his peer is not to be found in the entire enlightened world.[72]

At the same time Hamsilo editorialized

> Blessed is President Franklin Delano Roosevelt to the God of Israel and His people . . . the Jewish people will not forget . . . fathers will tell sons of the star that shone for them from the land of justice and liberty, of the giant of the spirit, President Franklin Delano Roosevelt, who appeared for Israel in its hour of distress.[73]

Throughout the months and years that followed, the extravagant praise continued unabated. Roosevelt was perceived as a "saviour angel, a great man of spirit whose humanitarian love will remain as a memorial to a latter generation,"[74] "our enlightened President, lover of righteousness and justice,"[75] and "an enlightened President, hero of the World War."[76] In contrast to the political leaders of other countries, Roosevelt was believed to be a singular champion of Jewish rights, "the only one in a dark world whose heart is awake to every downtrodden and despondent person."[77] "We do not have today in the entire world a government like ours with an individual . . . with all the attributes of a noble man such as is Franklin Delano Roosevelt who intercedes on our behalf."[78] Even after it might have been evident to others that significant assistance was not forthcoming from Roosevelt, rabbinic leaders yet referred to him as a "man of gigantic stature, cultivated and noble of spirit, praised and blessed in his deeds"[79] and as "our great President, giant of righteousness and uprightness."[80] They were convinced that Roosevelt himself wished to do far more for the Jewish cause, but that he was restrained by powerful members of the Senate.[81]

Only as fear of impending doom motivated the Vaad Hatzalah to redoubled efforts, does one sense a growing frustration and disenchantment with agencies of the American government and an unprecedented militancy and activism on the part of the rabbinic leadership. One of the most vigorous expressions of the new approach was an article entitled "Go Out And Protest" that appeared in Ha-Pardes of May 1941, bearing the byline of Rabbi Eliezer Silver:

> The time has come to protest in our capital, in Washington, the capital of the United States. It is time to knock on the doors of the White House regarding the injustice done to us on the part of agents of the United States outside the country. Not long ago we were privileged to be greeted warmly by the government. It promised us to look favorably on bringing great Talmudic scholars and yeshiva students here from the lands of bloodshed, to save them from annihilation and oblivion.
>
> . . . . The representatives of the United States in the lands of bloodshed have hardened their hearts. They place stumbling blocks in the way of our rabbis and great scholars. Instead of a blessing they have brought a curse because [the rabbis] have left their residences and remain on the road in places of danger. No one perceives the pain and shame. How we have become ashamed!
>
> Let us shout. Let us protest in the streets of Washington. Let us cry out regarding the injustice done to us. Behold our President, praised in the mouths of all, does only good to every country and to downtrodden people, supports all who fall down. How can he harden his heart to the scholars and sages of Israel who wander from city to city, and who are endangered? Let us travel together to Washington, to shout and to protest.[82]

In 1942 following news reports of the destruction of Polish Jewry, the tone of disappointment and chagrin is ever more noticeable. "And what are we doing for them [the Jews of Poland]? Nothing!" exclaimed one editorial. Disillusionment with the Jewish establishment is evident in the query: "Where are those Jews who are close to the government?"[83] Repeatedly the conviction is expressed that were protests but to be heard in Washington a favorable response might yet be elicited. Jews should protest, picket the White House in sackcloth and ashes, implore that boatloads of food be sent to Jews in the Polish ghettos.[84] A resolution of the Union of Orthodox Rabbis urged that pleas for food to be sent to the Polish ghettos should be addresed to Roosevelt, "whose heart is gracious and merciful." The Allies had permitted food to be sent to Axis-occupied Greece because the population was starving. Moreover, the rabbis argued, Jews in the ghettos were incarcerated and hence their status was similar to that of prisoners of war to whom food was permitted to be sent even during wartime.[85] A January 1943 report in Ha-Pardes summarizing Vaad Hatzalah political activism throughout 1942 focused on continuing diplomatic efforts, including persistent lobbying in Washington for visas, pressuring Great Britain for entry permits to the Holy Land and efforts to obtain legal means to render assistance to refugees through negotiations with neutral countries in the Far East for that purpose.[86]

IV. Dissemination of Information

It has been well established that even if American Jews themselves did not believe the reports of Nazi atrocities, American Jewish leaders certainly did: "Should not this problem of credibility have elicited from them a strong public relations effort to convey the truth to the largest number?" . . . the leaders of American Jewry should have made it impossible for their followers to ignore the awful truth." [87] The charge that they had failed to make their constituencies aware of the bitter reality could assuredly not be addressed to the sector of the community represented by Ha-Pardes and Hamsilo. Whatever the verdict may be regarding their rescue efforts, the indictment of equanimity and dispassion that falls squarely on the American press in general[88] has no applicability whatsoever to these rabbinic writers.

The rabbinic journals served as a reliable source of news and information regarding the fate of the Jews, and in particular the Torah scholars, in Europe. Unlike reports in the general press there was little occasion for a credibility gap to develop. The information in the rabbinic journals was presented in as concrete a manner as as possible: (1) The entire text of telegrams from Jews in Vilna, Warsaw, Shanghai and Siberia was published. (2) The veracity of these reports was further attested by eyewitness accounts of refugees who had reached the United States. Incalculably significant in this respect were the reports of key rabbinic figures who had escaped the European holocaust in whose truthfulness the Orthodox community had full confidence. (3) In publicizing the work of the Vaad Hatzalah, the journals played a key role in presenting, on the one hand, concrete reports of accomplishments in a series of reports detailing exact budgetary information, and lists of the names of individuals assisted, as well as, on the other hand, presenting detailed progress reports of the campaign for funds in the various cities and regions of the United States.

With the move of the scholars to Japan, the Vaad Hatzalah campaign entered a phase of escalated activity. "And You Are Silent?" was the caption of a stark, full-page block letter appeal in Ha-Pardes signed by the presidium of the Vaad Hatzalah which read as follows:

> Where are you American rabbis? Where are you synagogue leaders, young and old? . . . Is it the time to be silent?
>
> Thank God we have the means, permits from the government to bring [the refugees] here . . . over three thousand souls call out to us from their bitter oppression: "Save us!"
>
> Day and night we are occupied with rescue activity . . . We have loaned tens of thousands of dollars. Who can enumerate the telegrams we receive daily with dreadful cries and pleas? . . . But we are lacking money for tickets and expenses . . . our hand is unable to help because of a lack of means, and you are silent?
>
> Where is the zeal to rescue the souls of the great scholars of our people? . . . Delay the reading of the Torah in the synagogues! . . . Protest by day! Protest by night! . . . Open hearts! Storm! Scream! Go out in alleyways and streets and call out for the ransom of captives. Rabbis of America, can you be silent? When our Scrolls of the Law, our sages, are in the dung heaps? Can you stand idly by their spilled blood? Will you be able to be tranquil when our holy and great ones will be exiled to the depths of Siberia?[89]

The June 1941 Ha-Pardes continued to note that time was essential in raising funds for visas and tickets. The realities of the situation were brought home to readers by publication of the lists of names of those families already settled in Kobe, Japan. At this time, a sense of desperation enters these appeals as the leadership of Vaad Hatzalah is faced with the knowledge that more could be done but sufficient funds are not forthcoming. Filled with a feeling of accomplishment at the number and stature of scholars who had reached the United States and Palestine, they were nonetheless overwrought with concern for the great numbers yet in peril en route. Vaad Hatzalah's appeals conveyed the sense of urgency and frustration:

> If we had the financial means, we could save the majority. . . . The gates of rescue get narrower from day to day and it is our obligation to be zealous. Do not stand idly by the blood of your brother. Stretch out your hands. Help us . . . Many ways are yet open at this time but, if not now, heaven forfend, the gates of rescue may yet close . . . Wake up brothers. We call you to action! Send money! Send affidavits! . . . Save while it is not too late. The Union of Orthodox Rabbis turns to you in a plea that you be inscribed in its army of rescue.[90]

Editorials in Hamsilo bemoaned the fact that the awesome fate of European Jewry had not moved the American Jewish community sufficiently to impel its various factions to strive for a united rescue effort that would transcend rivaling petty organizational interests. In the past, notes one editorial, at least the enemies of the Jewish people prompted Jews to unite in face of a common danger. However, even before the threat of a present-day Haman, American Jewry remains splintered in congresses, conferences, committees and orders.[91] Two years later, a writer noted that there could be no question that members of the community at large were simply indifferent and insensitive to the peril and pain of their European coreligionists. Were they alert to the cries of anguish, factionalism and partisanship would assuredly not be so prevalent: "Not only are the strata of our people divided, followers of the Jewish Congress, the Jewish Conference, American Jewish Committee, Zionist and non-Zionist 'Emergency Councils,' but even we, Orthodox Jews, have found these times most propitious for widening and deepening the splits within our ranks."[92]

Ha-Pardes, on the other hand, while bemoaning the factionalism prevalent in the secular community,[93] was far more sanguine about the situation among the Orthodox and claimed with pride that

> We can note with gratification the ability and capacity for unity manifest these days on behalf of the appeal for rescue of the refugee rabbis, scholars and yeshiva students. For authentic rabbis here and the heads of all the various Orthodox parties have united as one man, as friends and true comrades. The heads of Agudath Israel and its president, the heads of the Mizrachi and the various associations have joined with fiery enthusiasm in cooperative activities for the rescue of the scholars, with no differentiation as to whether they belong to this or the other party, sitting at one table in love and brotherhood.[94]

Moreover, a brief news item in Ha-Pardes reported on initial meetings of a projected united council of Orthodox organizations with representatives of Mizrachi, Agudath Israel, Young Israel, the Union of Orthodox Jewish Congregations, and the Union of Orthodox Rabbis.[95] Yet later, there followed an account of the formal decision of the two major Orthodox rabbinical organizations, the Rabbinical Council and the Union of Orthodox Rabbis to cooperate in support of the Vaad Hatzalah.[96]

Particularly vivid are descriptions in both Hamsilo and Ha-Pardes of communal fast days called for by the Orthodox rabbinate in response to the desperate situation in Europe. A world-wide communal fast-day was called for August 12, 1942. The day of fasting and prayer was proclaimed by the Chief Rabbi and Bet Din of Great Britain, the Chief Rabbinate of Palestine, the Jewish community in South America and the European neutral countries of Switzerland and Sweden. A telegram from Tashkent signed by the head of the Moscow Jewish community related that Russian Jews would also join in the appointed day of fasting and prayer. The American Orthodox rabbinate hailed the message as signifying the first occasion on which Russian Jewry had officially joined their coreligionists throughout the world in a religious matter since the Revolution.[97]

As the situation in Europe became graver, increasingly, the journals gave voice to a sense of disappointment at the complacency of American Jews. How were they able to sit contentedly at their own seder tables knowing of the anguish and privation of fellow Jews?[98] Assuredly, if they could pursue their normal lifestyle, they must have become insensitive, frigid individuals:

> If we were not frozen, when we hear of the terrible fate of the Jews of Poland our hearts would break. How could we eat?
>
> If, indeed, the sighs of our afflicted brethren penetrated deeply into our hearts we would not be able to sit a moment in peace in our homes; our terrible pain would not permit us to sleep in peace . . . In our thousands and tens of thousands we would storm and protest, day and night, raising our voices . . . stirring up the inhabitants of this free land, so that anyone with a spark of humanity would join our protest and the voice of afflicted Israel would be heard from one end of the land to the other. The general press would no longer be able to pass over in silence the oceans of tears and rivers of flowing blood . . . .
>
> The boiling blood of our brothers must melt the ice in our own blood . . . We are not permitted to be silent . . . Let us not be guilty. Let the individual wake up. Let the community wake up. Let

> us split the heaven and earth. Because our brothers, our beloved brothers, . . . wallow in their blood. And how can we be silent?[99]

How could American Jews continue the normal pursuits of their tranquil lives while the slaughter progressed in Europe, queried another writer in Hamsilo? How were they able to continue to attend the theater, to go to parties and banquets, to plan summer vacations? Did they think that one communal fast day was sufficient to assuage their guilt? Rather, the entire community should take an oath forswearing dances, banquets, and parties, to fast weekly on Mondays and Thursdays and to abjure meat and wine.[100]

Indeed, it appeared to some that American Jews were simply failing to meet the historic challenge. An editorial in Ha-Pardes bearing the caption in large block letters "But We Are Guilty" excoriated American Jewish leadership for turning a deaf ear to the pleas of their brethren: "Be embarrassed and ashamed, rabbis of America and Orthodox Jews. There are large cities that have not yet responded." If enough money could but be raised, the means could be found to save more lives and transport Jews to the United States or elsewhere. Why was American Jewish leadership so shamefully remiss? "American rabbis, rise up as one man!"[101]

V. Leadership

One of the most striking findings that emerges from study and analysis of the account of the rescue efforts reflected in these journals is the pivotal role played by four rabbinic figures: Rabbis Chaim Ozer Grodzinsky, Abraham Kalmanowitz, Aaron Kotler and Eliezer Silver.

The Vaad Hatzalah came into being as a result of Rabbi Grodzinsky's overriding concern for the future of the endangered yeshivot that had found a haven in the Vilna region. The organization was founded at a time when Rabbi Grodzinsky was in the last months of his life and suffering from the ravages of a terminal illness. Nonetheless, even from overseas, and from a sick bed, he remained the motivating spirit behind Vaad Hatzalah activities. He was in constant and direct contact with Rabbi Silver. It was as if Vilna and Cincinnati were one city, Rabbi Silver later reminisced.[102] Rabbi Grodzinsky incessantly pleaded on behalf of the yeshivot and their students. Vaad Hatzalah funds were sent directly to him for distribution and he served as the advisor and guide to the various yeshivot in exile. The last letter received by Rabbi Silver from Rabbi Grodzinsky was written but four days before Rabbi Grodzinsky's demise.[103] An anonymous biographical sketch published in Ha-Pardes relates that Rabbi Grodzinsky wrote his last letters in his own hand despite his weakened condition. When asked to allow others to write on his behalf and merely affix his own signature, he replied that if Rabbi Silver in Cincinnati and Rabbi Abramsky in London would see that he had written the letters himself they would extend themselves even more for the benefit of the yeshivot.[104]

Rabbi Eliezer Silver's charismatic personality was the powerful energizer of the organization in the United States. Reports of Rabbi Silver's travels, crisscrossing the country on fundraising and lobbying missions, his peripatetic pursuit of Vaad Hatzalah objectives and the impassioned prose of his signed appeals combine to grip the reader and hold him spellbound.

Finally, the record of rabbinic meetings in these journals reflects the imposing presence of both Rabbi Abraham Kalmanowitz and Rabbi Aaron Kotler. As refugees themselves, the very presence of these scholars exemplified the immediacy and urgency of the cause. Rabbi Kalmanowitz's superhuman efforts on behalf of the Mirrer Yeshiva have become legendary. His earliest travels across the country to raise funds and his regular commuting to Washington, D.C. in an attempt to secure visas for his students are recorded in the pages of Ha-Pardes. The successful rescue of virtually the entire faculty and students of the Mirrer yeshiva may be attributed in great part to his persistence and tenacity.[105]

The arrival of the prominent Torah scholar, Rabbi Aaron Kotler, whose immigration to the United States had been facilitated through the agency of Vaad Hatzalah, was hailed in the May 1941 issue of Ha-Pardes. The presence and zeal of Rabbi Kotler was to become a prime motivating force in the work of Vaad Hatzalah. Ha-Pardes reported on Rabbi Kotler's first formal address to members of the New York rabbinate in which he sated that his primary objective was to spearhead enhanced efforts of Vaad Hatzalah for the rescue of the yeshiva students: "Behold I am a father to children who are in the ocean and my goal is to save them . . . . I speak to you in the name of those whose voices you wish to hear but, at this time they are far from here."[106] Rabbi Kotler reported on the diligence and tenacity of the yeshiva students who continued the avid pursuit of their studies notwithstanding the dire straits in which they found themselves. "The soul strengthens itself miraculously."[107]

News regarding the persecution of the Jews was received, in general, with a great measure of skepticism. To many the stories of Nazi atrocities were almost too fantastic to believe.[108] The constant presence of these highly respected refugee rabbis at Vaad Hatzalah functions, their endorsement of Vaad Hatzalah policies and their eyewitness reports served to eradicate lingering doubts regarding the trustworthiness of the terrible news accounts and to force their colleagues to close the chasm between information and belief.

It is instructive to contrast these profiles with Frederick A. Lazin's analysis of the commitment of American Jewish Committee Leadership to rescue endeavors. Lazin notes that poor health and old age restricted the activities of the president, Dr. Cyrus Adler, and the chairman of the Executive Committee, Sol. M. Stroock. In general, the officers and leaders of the Committee chose to pursue other interests and responsibilites. For example, in May 1939, additional meetings scheduled for Sundays were a failure because too many members continued to go to the country for weekends. As a result, insofar as the Committee was concerned, a variety of personal and professional concerns took precedence over efforts on behalf of endangered brethren. Rescue of European Jewry was simply not a priority.[109]

The failure of both Jews and non-Jews to react in an effective and concerted manner during this period of catastrophe defies comprehension. In stark contrast stand the efforts of the individuals and organizations whose deeds are recorded in these journals. Their response to the challenge of the times stands out as an oasis of sanity in the wasteland of man's inhumanity to man.

NOTES

1. Henry L. Feingold, Review essay on No Haven for the Oppressed: United States Policy Toward Jewish Refugees, 1938-1945, by Saul S. Friedman, American Jewish Historical Quarterly, LVIII (September, 1968), 151.
2. Aspects of their contribution have been analyzed in essays such as Isaac Lewin "Attempts at Rescuing European Jews with the Help of Polish Diplomatic Missions During World War II, The Polish Review, XXII: 4, pp. 3-23 and Efraim Zuroff, "Rescue Priority and fund Raising as Issues During the Holocaust: A Case study of the Relations Between the Vaad Hatzala and the Joint," American Jewish History, LXVIII:3 (March, 1979), pp. 305-26 and various popular works, notably David Kranzler, Thy Brother's Blood: The Orthodox Jewish Response During the Holocaust (New York, 1987). However, a comprehensive study remains a desideratum.
3. Although his name does not appear on the masthead, Telushkin was the editor throughout. See Index for the Rabbinical Periodical "Hamsilo"; arranged by Yehudah Rubinstein (New York, 1977), p. 8, note and p. 17.
4. Ha-Pardes (hereafter P), XIII:9 (Dec., 1939), pp. 4-9 and XIV:11 (Feb., 41), pp. 15-16.
5. V: 4-5 (May-June, 1940), p. 3.
6. P, XIII:6 (Sept., 1939), p. 6 and XIII:7 (Oct., 1939), p. 4.
7. P, XIII:6 (Sept., 1939), p. 6.
8. P, XIII:10 (Jan., 1940), pp. 4 and 26-27 and XIII:11 (Feb., 1940), pp. 10-11. Cf., Zuroff, 305-26.
9. See, e.g., P, XV:6 (Sept., 1941), p. 1 and XVI:9 (Dec., 1942), p. 4.
10. P, XIII:11 (Feb., 1940), pp. 10-11.
11. P, XIII:10 (Jan., 1940), pp. 2-4; XIV:9 (Dec., 1940), pp. 2-3 and XIV:11 (Feb., 1941), p. 17; and Hamsilo (hereafter M), IV:11-12 (Dec., 1939-Jan., 1940), p. 14.
12. P, XIV:11 (Feb., 1941), p. 11.
13. Loc. cit.

14. M, V:4-5 (May-June, 1940), p. 8.
15. P, XV:11 (Feb., 1942), p. 7.
16. M, VI:4-5 (May-June, 1941), p. 2 and P, XV:6 (Sept., 1941), p. 7.
17. P, XV:8 (Nov., 1941), p. 4; XV:9 (Dec., 1941), pp. 4,5,7 and 9; and XV:12 (March, 1942), pp. 4-7.
18. P, XIII:8 (Nov., 1939), pp. 2-3 and M, V:4-5 (May-June, 1940), pp. 1-2 and 17.
19. M, V:4-5 (May-June, 1940), pp. 17-18.
20. P, XIII:9 (Dec., 1939), p. 6.
21. P, XIII:10 (Jan., 1940), pp. 26-27.
22. P, XIII:10 (Jan., 1940), pp. 4 and 27 and XIV:1 (April, 1940), p. 5.
23. P, XIV:4 (July, 1940), p. 3.
24. P, XIV:9, p. 3.
25. V:4-5 (May-June, 1940), pp. 1-20.
26. XIV:10, p. 11.
27. XIV:11 (Feb., 1941), pp. 1 and 3-4.
28. XIV:11 (Feb., 1941), pp. 15-16.
29. Pp. 3-4 and 19-20.
30. XV:4 (July, 1941), pp. 6-9.
31. XV:5 (Aug., 1941), p. 18 and XV:6 (Sept., 1941), pp. 45-47.
32. XV:6, pp. 2-5.
33. XV:10, p. 7.
34. XVI:4 (July, 1942), p. 28; XVI:7 (Oct., 1942), p. 2 and XVI:10 (Jan., 1943), pp. 9 and 18-23.
35. XVI:9 (Dec., 1942), p. 5. and XVI:12 (March, 1943), p. 8.
36. XVI:10 (Jan., 1943), pp. 19-22.
37. XV:8, pp. 3-4.
38. XIV:11, pp. 25-26.
39. XV:6 (Sept., 1941), p. 2.
40. VX:8 (Nov., 1941), pp. 2-3.
41. See especially XV:9 (Dec., 1941), p. 2 and XV:11 (Feb., 1942), p. 5.
42. XVI:2 (May, 1942), p. 4; XVI:3 (June, 1943), pp. 3-4; XVI:4 (July, 1942), p. 7; and XVI:5 (Aug., 1942), p. 2.
43. XVI:3 (June, 1942), p. 4.
44. XVI:2, pp. 4 and 13.
45. XVI:3 (June, 1942), p. 2 and XVI:10 (Jan., 1943), p. 9.
46. P, XVI:4 (July, 1942), p. 4.
47. P, XVI:5 (Aug., 1942), p. 8.
48. XVI:3 (June, 1942), pp. 7-9; XVI:7 (Oct., 1942), p. 2; and XVI:8 (Nov., 1942), p. 2.
49. XVI:5 (May, 1942), p. 2.
50. See, e.g., P, XII:11 (Feb., 1939), p. 2 and M, VII:10-11 (Oct.-Nov., 1938), pp. 16-17.
51. Cited in P, XII:10 (June, 1939), p. 5 and M, III:12-13 (Dec., 1938-Jan., 1939), pp. 21-22.
52. P, XIII:1 (April, 1939), p. 6.
53. P, XIII:11 (Feb., 1940), pp. 12-13. Cf., M, IX:4-9 (May, 1944-Sept., 1944), pp. 14-17.
54. P, XIII:3 (June, 1939), p. 27.
55. See also P, XIV:10 (Jan., 1941), p. 29 and M, V:3 (April, 1940), p. 4.
56. P, XVI:5 (Aug., 1942), p. 9 and XVI:7 (Oct., 1942), p. 2.
57. XIII:12 (March, 1940), pp. 4-5.
58. XV:1 (April, 1941), pp. 22-24 and XV:3 (June, 1941), pp. 26-27.
59. XV:3, pp. 28-29.
60. XIV:6 (Sept., 1940), pp. 39-41; XIV:8 (Nov., 1940), p. 9; XIV:9 (Dec., 1940), p. 33; XV:6 (Sept., 1941), p. 18; XV:9 (Dec., 1941), p. 7; and XVI:5 (Aug., 1942), pp. 19-23.
61. XII:12 (March, 1939), pp. 2-3; XIV:9 (Dec., 1940), p. 16; and XIV:10 (Jan., 1941), p. 32.
62. XIV:1 (April, 1941), pp. 5-6 and XIV:3 (June, 1941), pp. 31-32.
63. XVI:10, pp. 10-11.
64. P, XV:11 (Feb., 1942), p. 3.

65. *P*, XV:3 (June, 1941), p. 8.
66. *P*, XV:11 (Feb., 1942), p. 4.
67. *M*, III:3 (March, 1938), pp. 1-2; III:5 (May, 1938), pp. 14-17; III:8-9 (Aug.-Sept., 1938), pp. 18-19; and *P*, XII:8 (Nov., 1938), pp. 2-3.
68. *P*, XI:10 (Jan., 1938), pp. 20-21; XII:7 (Oct., 1938), pp. 4-5; and *M*, V:6-7-8 (July-Aug.-Sept., 1940), pp. 3-5.
69. *P*, XVI:3 (June, 1942), pp. 40-42.
70. Haskel Lookstein, *Were We Our Brothers' Keepers? The Public Response of American Jews to the Holocaust* 1938-1944 (New York and Bridgeport, 1985), pp. 210-212.
71. *P*, XII:1 (April, 1938), p. 26 and XII:3 (June, 1938), p. 16.
72. XII:1 (April, 1938), p. 3.
73. III:4 (April, 1938), p. 2.
74. *P*, XIII:2 (May, 1939), p. 5.
75. *M*, VI:6-7-8 (July-Aug.-Sept., 1941), p. 9.
76. *M*, IX:4-9 (May-Sept., 1944), p. 1.
77. *M*, IV:2 (March, 1939), p. 2.
78. *P*, XIII:3 (June, 1939), p. 5.
79. *P*, XV:6 (Sept., 1941), p. 9.
80. *M*, VII:7-8 (July-Aug., 1942), p. 1.
81. *M*, IV:1 (Feb., 1939), p. 5. Cf., III:10-11 (Oct.-Nov., 1938), pp. 16-17.
82. XV:2, p. 5.
83. *P*, XV:12 (March, 1942), p. 2.
84. *P*, XVI:1 (April, 1942), p. 2.
85. *P*, XVI:5 (Aug., 1942), p. 10.
86. XVI:10, pp. 10-11.
87. Lookstein, p. 210.
88. Deborah E. Lipstadt, *Beyond Belief: The American Press and the Coming of the Holocaust 1939-1945* (New York and London, 1986), pp. 274-276.
89. XIV:11 (Feb., 1941), p. 2.
90. XV:3, p. 3.
91. VI:2 (March, 1941), pp. 1-2.
92. VIII:10-11-12 (Nov.-Dec.,1943-Jan.,1944), p. 12.
93. XIV:10 (Jan., 1941), pp. 2 and 11.
94. XIV:10 (Jan., 1941), p. 13. Cf., Zuroff, p. 310.
95. XV:4 (July, 1941), p. 31.
96. XVI:12 (March, 1943), p. 17.
97. *P*, XVI:6 (Sept., 1942), p. 3 and XVI:9 (Dec., 1942), pp. 2-3.
98. *M*, IV:3 (April, 1939), p. 5.
99. *M*, IV:11-12 (Dec., 1939-Jan., 1940), pp. 2-3.
100. *M*, VIII:1 (Jan.-Feb., 1943), pp. 1-2 and 16-17. Cf., *M*, VIII:7-8-9 (Aug.-Sept.-Oct., 1943), pp. 10-11.
101. XV:5 (Aug., 1941), p. 2.
102. *P*, XV:11 (Feb., 1942), p. 3.
103. *P*, XIV:6 (Sept., 1940), p. 12.
104. XIV:12 (March, 1941), p. 4.
105. See especially *P*, XV:4 (July, 1941), pp. 6-9; XVI:9 (Dec., 1942), p. 5 and *M*, V:4-5 (May-June, 1940), pp. 17-18.
106. XV:3 (June, 1941), p. 8.
107. *Loc. cit.*
108. Lipstadt, pp. 240-274.
109. "The Response of the American Jewish Committee to the Crisis of German Jewry, 1933-1939, *American Jewish History*, LXVIII:3 (March, 1979), pp. 302-304.

SOLVING THE PASSOVER PROBLEM

Barry Ferst, Ph.D.

Carroll College, Helena, Montana 59625, USA

ABSTRACT

In order to find meaning in The Holocaust many theologians compare The Holocaust to the Hebrews' Egyptian bondage and deliverance. Nevertheless, this comparison does not yield a completely satisfactory meaning. I suggest that "The Passover Problem"--the finding of additional meaning to supplement the notion of bondage and deliverance--depends not on what is similar between Egypt and Germany, but on something God has learned and is attempting to pass on to us.

The Holocaust, the murder of millions during the regime of Adolph Hitler, has caused a great deal of soul-searching among people of good will. In a supposedly civilized world supposedly watched over by an almighty God, how could such a thing have happened, and since it did happen what could it mean?

If we conclude at the outset that The Holocaust was simply meaningless barbarity, then we are saying that it was merely a chance event occurring in an unfathomable Universe. This view probably is not an option for most of us, for it signals a surrender to irrationality.

However, if we assume that something can be salvaged from such barbarity, it might be what we might learn about how the world can be improved. I think that if we cannot find that message, then we have failed humanity and God.

Given that human rationality and a Supreme Being of the sort supposed by Jews and Christians exist, then it is necessary for us to find a meaning in The Holocaust and explain in rational terms how such an event could have occurred. We are obliged to provide an explanation that is human just in so far as it satisfied our need for a rational explanation, and divine just in so far as it would make sense that the Universe of a Judeo-Christian God would contain such a dreadful event.

In their search for The Holocaust's meaning, both Jewish and Christian theologians have compared European Jewry to the ancient Hebrews in Egypt. The comparison seems a good one: slavery in Egypt 3500 years ago and slavery in Nazi concentration camps; the flight from Egypt across the Red Sea and the flight from Europe across the Mediterranean; and the founding of a small Hebrew empire and the founding of the State of Israel. Here is the second book of the Pentateuch and the title of Leon Uris's novel. And as Jews for many centuries have celebrated deliverance at Passover, now they celebrate a post-Holocaust deliverance and the security of a national homeland.

The significance of The Holocaust, therefore, might be found in the idea of bondage and deliverance. But why bondage in the first place? To this some theologians have responded with an answer that has been traditionally employed to make sense of the Egyptian bondage, the

Babylonian bondage, the Spanish Inquisition, the ghetto and the shtetl. What they say is that God is punishing communal sin in order to correct, purify, and strengthen His people. As Richard L. Rubenstein in After Auschwitz: Radical Theology and Contemporary Judaism notes: "He [a post-war German religious leader] drew a parallel between Hitler and Nebuchadnezzar and asserted that, while both conquerors had acted with malice and in pursuit of their own selfish ends, they nevertheless were unknowingly also acting as the rods of God's wrath in punishing his sinful people...." (Rubenstein 65-66)

Punishment is administered through a strong dose of pain and sorrow; correction is achieved by prophetic calls for a return to holy ways; and purification and strengthening occur as elders die and as the evil ones are killed. All this is accomplished through the social bondage of the ghetto, the economic bondage of slave labor, and the total bondage of the concentration camp. After punishment and purification come deliverance.

Thus, The Holocaust is a punishment for turning away from God and righteousness. Yet, God has His chosen people and no matter how merciless the punishment, in the end He will provide deliverance--in this case a national homeland. This explanation seems to be humankind's stock defense of God's most indefensible actions.

I suspect that the meaning that this comparison of The Holocaust to the Pentateuch story provides has much going for it; it certainly is well-suited to a long tradition of prophetic and rabbinic thinking. Though this comparison is illuminating, it does not do enough, and it is the finding of additional meaning to supplement the traditional view of Jewish history in regard to sin, bondage, and deliverance that I have chosen to call "The Passover Problem." Specifically, there are two points where the idea of bondage and deliverance fall short.

First, if part of the purpose of bondage is to purify the community, then Adolph Hitler alone, or God forbid, God working through Hitler, failed. A community may be purified by the death of the tainted or wicked, but Hitler failed to destroy the old generation of Jews, and so his atrocities did not serve the same purpose as the Hebrews' wandering in the desert for forty years, which did do away with the old generation, including Moses. Nor did Hitler murder only the morally unfit, or provide a trial-by-fire for the Jewish people wherein only the most moral and religious would survive.

Rather, Hitler killed indiscriminately, the good with the bad, the strong with the weak. As Emil Fackenheim points out at the very opening of his new book, What is Judaism?: "The wicked ones [Nazis and those militarily opposed to Israel] did not single out pious or learned or committed Jews for defamation, persecution, and eventual murder: To be born a Jew was enough." (Fackenheim 9) In fact some sociologists make a good case for the position that the immoral and the more brutish had a better chance for survival than the physically weak and the altruistic. Actually, from what I know of such situations, I would guess that those who appear either weak or terribly defiant are the first to go. Hence, it was probably the average fellow who had the best chance of surviving.

Second, if God were attempting to strengthen faith through bondage and deliverance, we must wonder about many of those who survived the concentration camp and remain Jews but not Jews who have much respect for or belief in a God who allows the massacre of innocents. One of the great stumbling blocks to a strong Jewish faith today is the troubling questions raised by the events which took place in Europe from 1930 to 1945. Must not we conclude that God failed in His plan to strengthen Judaism?

In light of these two objections to the explanation and meaning that many theologians have suggested for The Holocaust, it is reasonable to claim that we still require more if we are to understand The Holocaust.

Therefore, I would like to propose something that I believe is both humanly comprehendible and divinely thinkable, though initially it might sound a bit strange. I would propose that the solution to The Passover Problem--the finding of additional meaning to supplement the traditional explanation of sin, bondage, and deliverance--depends not on what is similar between ancient Egypt and modern Germany, but on what God has learned since 1500 BCE and is attempting to pass on to us. I think that what God has learned is that evil people freely choose to do evil, and so it is divinely important that good people do good. The first time around, back in Mitzrayim, God did not understand this.

What I am suggesting is that one thing God has learned is that you cannot really convert truly evil people. He tried that the first time when He visited ten plagues upon the heads of the ancient Egyptians to turn them around so that they could see the evil of their ways. Well, the Egyptians did let "my people go" as the spiritual says, but we cannot forget that at the last minute the Egyptians rode after the fleeing Hebrews to get them back. And what did God do when the plan went astray--He could only drown the whole Egyptian army in the Red Sea!

It took forty centuries, but God finally realized that you cannot do much with really evil people. I mean how many plagues would have been necessary to turn around the author of Mein Kampf? Ten? Twenty? Thirty?--there still is an American Nazi party. The point is that God did not plague either the autocrats or bureaucrats who officiated at The Holocaust: they were exercising their God-given free will. But The Holocaust did plague the thinking of good men and women so that their moral consciences would move them to moral action--and this is the exercise of free will by good people.

But does this present us with a God who created, permitted, or at least did nothing to lessen The Holocaust's horror? This is the point made by B. C. Johnson in The Atheist Debater's Handbook when he contends the "moral urgency" and "virtue building" are absurd justifications for God's creating or permitting evil. A Supreme Being that creates or permits pain, disaster, and evil, so that humans may have opportunities for character building, is not the sort of Being most people would wish to worship, obey, admire, or place faith in. As Johnson wryly concludes: "A very large disaster could have been avoided simply by [God's] producing in Hitler a miraculous heart attack...." (Burr and Goldinger 135)

What meaningful response could be made to this very important philosophical argument? We must respond that God did not create The Holocaust; that was the product of many cultural and historical forces coming to fruition in a Hitler. Nor did God permit The Holocaust; it was permitted by quite a large number of human beings. And whether or not God did anything to lessen the pain of The Holocaust, I do not know; Johnson must and would grant me that. But is it too harsh a commentary on humankind, not God, to say that as history has shown, it takes a holocaust to give humans enough humanity, courage, and physical strength to make a State of Israel?

I do not think God worked for thousands of years to make The Holocaust a reality; rather I think God spent that time learning something about what He did make, human beings. And what God has learned is that you cannot change the heart of a Pharaoh, an Inquisitor General, a Cossack, or a Nazi no matter how many vermin, lice, and frogs you rain down and no matter how many first born you kill; but by plagues of conscience the conscience of good people is turned toward good actions, thereby making really good people really good.

I realize that the suggestion that God has learned something about a human's capacity for evil and goodness might cause some theologians difficulties. Concerning the issue of evil, if the suggestion that evil people can be incurably bad is bothersome, maybe it is just a matter of finally realizing with God that people do have free will, and some people are going to choose to do rotten things come hell or high water. This is not meant to imply that people are either essentially or incorrigibly evil, nor imply any other doctrine of original sin. Rather what I am suggesting is that some people, consciously and freely, by whatever criterion for "consciously" and "freely" is selected, choose to do what is heinous.

In regard to my contention that God learns, I suppose this would disturb people who believe that God is omniscient. However, there are three good reasons why the assumption that a supreme being can learn does not lessen the supremacy of this being. First, 3500 years has to be a mere wink to that which is eternal, and even less to that which is out-of-time, a characteristic sometimes ascribed to eternality. So, though God learns, we can still say, with all due solemnity, that learning occurs very fast, almost instantaneously.

Second, wisdom is a far greater attribute than knowledge, and there is no harm in supposing a god who is supremely wise but does not know everything. The wisdom of Solomon is not lessened by the fact that any college student today knows more facts than the King. Therefore, removing omniscience from a list of God's properties does not lessen His wisdom, a supremely more important feature. And there is an added benefit in doing this. By granting wisdom and denying complete knowledge, we steer clear of the puzzling contradictions raised by the theological imputation of human free will and Divine fore-knowledge.

Third, the notion that God knows all things fits well with a theology which pictures the Universe as a finished construction. Divine knowledge amounts to the last word in encyclopedias, and human knowledge is just a matter of uncovering about this Universe all the things God has placed in it. However, I would suggest that the picture that the Universe is a completed, closed system is outmoded. Contemporary physics, chemistry and biology not only discover what is there already, but often produce radically new items. A more modern metaphysics would picture a Universe which is open-ended and frequently infused with the fundamentally new. Unless God learns, He will be at a disadvantage when He converses with a molecular chemist or a physicist at Heaven's gate.

CONCLUSION

Now we have what God has come to understand about human behavior, but what of His attempt to pass this on to us? In a 1948 sermon on the evils of racial segregation, Rabbi Jacob M. Rothschild of Atlanta, Georgia, noted, "It becomes increasingly obvious that unless decent people take up the burden, the [US] South faces a return to the most primitive kind of bigotry and race hatred." (St. John 299) I suppose that once this lesson is learned the chore is to get decent people to do what they ought to be doing to make things a bit more humane. And it is just this fact and this chore that I see as the sad rationale and the hope-giving signification for The Holocaust. Some of God's Chosen People got some of His other Chosen People to change the world, or at least a little bit of it. God is trying to tell us that Chosen People act against the Hitlers who murder the spirit given half the chance and the rest of us without a second thought.

Getting good people to do good in situations we would much rather ignore because they would require superhuman power to correct, takes a superhuman effort--that this must be done is obvious to rational beings. I would like to suggest that the answer to The Passover Problem--the finding of a meaning in this latest holocaust--is that good people must do good if the world is to be a better place. What The Holocaust reveals is what God has learned.

REFERENCES

Fackenheim, Emil L. What is Judaism? New York: Summit Books, 1987.
Johnson, B. C. (pseudonym). God and the Problem of Evil, in Philosophy and Contemporary Issues, fifth edition. New York: Macmillan Publishing Company, 1988.
Rubenstein, Richard L. After Auschwitz: Radical Theology and Contemporary Judaism. New York: The Bobbs-Merrill Company, Inc., 1966.
St. John, Robert. Jews, Justice and Judaism. Garden City, NY: Doubleday, 1969.

SIDDUR, MACHSOR, AND THE SHOAH:
Contemporary Responses to the Catastrophe

by Albert H. Friedlander
Dean, Leo Baeck College
Rabbi, Westminster Synagogue
London

Liturgy is frozen theology. Beliefs which have risen out of life experiences have been patterned into an ordered arrangement--a siddur--in which their daily repetition enforces and re-enforces the teachings of the past. They become an experience of their professors, who make the formula of the past a description of the present. Yet each generation encounters new events which fight their way into the liturgy and bring with them new thoughts about the relationship between humanity and God. The new thought demands inclusion into the authoritative texts in which this dialogue between the finite and the Infinite takes place. For that reason, Siddur and Machsor--the liturgies for regular and festive services--continue to grow in contrast to the fixed canon of the Bible. Piyyutim (medieval poetic insertions) and time-bound prayers and meditations have found their way into the text. Some, the Kol Nidre for example, maintain themselves against the opposition of the rabbis; others fade away.

The Shoah should have changed all liturgies within the Jewish tradition; but this did not happen. Why? Some of the reasons behind the resistance to Shoah liturgies are discussed by the leading theologians of our time who place this query within their contemplation regarding the nature of God and of humanity **after** Auschwitz and who also want to define the nature of the event: Was it Churban? Shoah? Holocaust? Tremendum?[1] Was it unique? Much depends upon that last question. Lord Jakobovits, Chief Rabbi of Great Britain and the Commonwealth, recently wrote a preface to a new liturgical text for the Shoah created by Elie Wiesel and Albert H. Friedlander: The Six Days of Destructions: Meditations towards Hope. He hails it as

> "a distinguished and welcome contribution to the ever-growing religious literature responding to the Holocaust.."[2]

but wants it seen within the parameters of an approach which stresses that

> "..we must beware against breeding a Holocaust mentality of morose dependency among our people... We must shift the current emphasis on the survival of Jews to the survival of Judaism. For, without Judaism, Jewish survival is both questionable and meaningless.
> To me, the meaning of being a Jew has not changed with Auschwitz..."[3]

But in that case, as he points out elsewhere[4], there is no need for new liturgies, and the old texts suffice. And he cites current Israeli authorities who clearly indicate that new costoms, ceremonies and prayers dealing with the Holocaust should be rejected.[4] He is joined here by most traditional theologians who will refuse to see the Shoah as a unique event demanding new prayers. Tisha B'Av, mourning the destruction of Jerusalem and of the Temple, is the proper date, in their view, for expressing grief for all the suffering of the Jewish people throughout the centuries. The immediate problem which arises here is that these liturgies stress the suffering as the direct result of the sins of the Jewish people. Again, the Chief Rabbi notes:

> "The object of their mourning was not to recall and denounce the evil of the Romans; rather did their lamentations draw attention to their own failings and shortcomings, so that the lesson of the past would not be lost on the future."[5]

Can and should the survivors of the Shoah use this formula in order to understand their role in the world after Auschwitz? A number of religious leaders do say this in various ways--and it does not enter the liturgies precisely because the old lamentations are deemed not only adequate but also the proper response. This follows the pattern set by the great 11th century elegy of Kalonymus ben Judah of Mainz written for the victims of the Second Crusade:

> "Take this to your hearts, and prepare a sad funeral oration; put on mourning and roll in the dust, for their massacre weighs no less than the burning of the House of God...; and since we may not add an extra fixed season for the destruction and conflagration...therefore will I cause my cry of woe to rise this day (i.e., Tisha B'Av), and I will wail, howl and weep in bitterness of soul (Kinot, ed. A. Rosenfeld, p.134)" [6]

The matter cannot be settled by an appeal to tradition--one can always find opposing views. For example, after the 1648 Chmelnicki massacres, the Jews of Poland decreed a special fast day.[7] It did not endure. In our own time, the State of Israel decreed in the Knesset that the 27th of Nisan would be observed as a Yom Ha-Shoah, a Remembrance Day. Most calendars (including many Jewish publications) do not list that date. Yet in the last few years observance of that Memorial Day has grown, partially because of a new awareness of the Holocaust which has institutionalized itself, but also for more positive reasons. Many liturgies have been written for that day, mainly by Reform, Liberal, Conservative, and Reconstructionist communities, by chavurot, and by university students conducting their own services. The anguish and its challenge to the mind and heart of the Jew living in a world with its burnt out areas of Jewish life and with its memories cannot be ignored. Liturgies matter. Those who stand outside the community of worship can examine these texts for the questions that are asked. Often, they will discover that in contrast to their expectations these prayers do not contain glib answers or, indeed, any answers. When we turn to the liturgies of the non-Orthodox communities we do of course discover that the texts rise out of the theological premises of this section of contemporary Jewry. A proper study should compare them with the vast liturgical texts of all of Jewish life today. This would take us too far afield. What one can do in the context of this Oxford Conference of 1988 is to note the existence of prayers which mention the Shoah, ask whether or not these are aberrations or the expression of a growing tendency to confront the darkness after a period of silence, and speculate upon their efficency--if not efficacy.

I.

One of the early references within the regular liturgy which employed the word 'Auschwitz' is found in Service of the Heart (1967) used by the British Liberal movement:

> "Auschwitz and Hiroshima are among the dread and tragic symbols of our age. With far-seeing instruments the mind of man uncovers..secrets..but we have not learned to understand the hidden places of our hearts." [8]

The note at the back of the Siddur indicates that this new prayer by Chaim Stern develops the themes of the Yotzer and Ahavah Rabbah[9] The theme of Auschwitz is not developed, and is in fact absorbed by the questions asked of Hiroshima. At the time, just the word did send a shiver through the worshippers; but the fuller development of the theme came in that section of the liturgy which established special sections as meditations, including one "In Remembrance of Israel's Suffering." The note in the back of the text clarifies the approach used by the editors (John Rayner and Chaim Stern):

> "The martyrdom of European Jewry under the Nazis has given a renewed impetus to the commemoration of Israel's suffering generally, and of this, the culminating tragedy, in particular. There is, however, as yet no universally accepted date for such a commemoration. Some communities have chosen an already established Jewish fast day, such as the 9th of Av or the 10th of Tevet; others favour the 27th of Nisan, which is the anniversary of the Warsaw Ghetto Rising." [10]

The opening prayer in that section is as follows:

> "Our hearts go out to all who have suffered from the cruelty of their fellow men. But on this day we remember especially the pain and humiliation suffered by the house of Israel: exile and oppression, expulsions and ghettos, pogroms and death camps..we are tempted to say..with the poet.."To me the whole world is

one gallows." We ask anew with the Psalmist: "Why have You forgotten me?..

The agony of our people numbs the mind and turns the heart to stone. We can only wonder at the fortitude and courage of our forefathers..who said..:"Though You slay me, yet will I trust in You." And we can only prayer that we may be blessed with a measure of the faith which enabled them to remain loyal to God and to His Torah, even when he seemed remote from them and indifferent to their woe."[11]

The Biblical texts which follow are a mixture of lamentation and hope; and the religious problem is stated within a structure of universalism and reason which does not penetrate too deeply into the anguish and contradictions of a religious faith trying to come to terms with Auschwitz--only a small touch of God who 'seemed remote ..and indifferent'. Also, the problem as to whether the Shoah would be considered a 'unique event' is not asked. Rather, the death camps are subsumed under the general categories of Jewish sufferings...'exile and oppression, expulsions, ghettos, pogroms and death camps'. Traditional thinking is not challenged here, except in the sense that all of the Liberal liturgy is part of an opposing pattern of Judaism.

Six years later, in 1973, the High Holy Day Machsor of the British Liberal movement (the ULPS) was published. During that span of time, Holocaust theology had become almost a discipline, much of this due to the challenging writings of Richard Rubienstein (After Auschwitz (1966)[12] who could sometimes be ostracized but could not be ignored. The rabbis in Great Britain who prepared the text, again under the co-chairmanship of John Rayner and Chaim Stern, argued about many of the theological issues raised earlier here; but the liturgy did not change much from the pattern established in the Siddur of 1967. Only the 'martyrology', part of the additional service on Yom Kippur, opened itself to those problems. Since the acknowledgments in the back of the book list my work in that section, I must declare my special interest (but would also point out that many of the original prayers and selections from Holocaust authors came as the result of suggestions from my colleagues.)

The martyrology commenced with the 'Suffering Servant' passages from Isaiah 53, a text much used by Christians and in this instance reclaimed in what was already a theological statement for our time: the Jew as the 'Suffering Servant':

"We have felt the joy of being God's servant, but we have also felt the pain. This we now remember. We remember that we have been God's Suffering Servant."[13]

The prayers tried to remain within a universalistic framework:

"..we honour those of every race and continent who have been innocent victims of cruelty..we mourn them..."[14]

but goes on to 'we remember especially the suffering of our own people'. A selection from Karl Shapiro's "Travelogue for Exiles" ("Look and remember...")[15] remains as a note of universal mourning from a non-Jewish Jewish poet before the liturgy enters the established Hebrew lamentations of the Eleh Ezkerah of the traditional Musaf liturgy of Yom Kippur which commemorates the Asarah Harugey Malchut, ten rabbis killed by the Romans in the 2nd century. There was some resistance among the Liberal rabbis who felt that strange names like 'Chutzpit the Interpreter' would break the intensity of the moment, but this was overcome. A long historical review of the Ten Martyrs, followed by remembrances of the Rhineland massacres during the Crusades, and the creation of the Aleynu prayer, leads inexorably towards the Shoah.[15]

Modern poetry became the liturgical vehicle for these Shoah commemorations: Shlonsky's "Neder", Nelly Sachs's chorus of the orphans ('Chorus from those who were saved'); and the poetic prose of Katzetnik (Yechiel De-Nur, a survivor now living in Israel) gave a new depth to these prayers which did seem to fill a need of the worshippers.[16] A prose meditation on Leo Baeck in the concentration camp might have been expected within a Liberal community; but this was also the first time in Progressive liturgy that Yiddish was used at some length ('The Song of the Partisans': zog nit keinmol as du geist dem letzn weg..')[17] One major poem which the editors thought ".. might have been too difficult or too disturbing" was put into the notes: Palu Celan's 'Death Fugue'.[18] And the end of the Holocaust Liturgy blended into a celebration of the birth of the State of Israel (once again, a shift in the religious thought of the Liberal community which at one point was cool towards the State within the context of its rational and universalist tradition).

It is important to remember here that these prayers do not constitute an observance of Yom Ha-Shoah which still struggles for recognition. These prayers are part of the Yom Kippur liturgy where the majority of worshippers are in synagogue. In

1988, there is far more discussion of the Holocaust then there was 20 years ago. It is still doubtful that Yom Ha-Shoah and the new liturgies coming into being will find full acceptance. However, the Liberal movement in Great Britain is in the process of revising its liturgy again; and the discussions show more commitments to statements regarding the tragedy of our time, and more of an awareness of the theological problems facing a religious community which still seeks an answer to Job's question.

II.

American Reform Jewish liturgies came to the problems of the Shoah far later than the progressive Jewish communities of Europe. The old Union Prayer Book--still greatly beloved in some of the Reform temples--had its majestic universal vision which demanded prayer and concern for all those who suffer in the world, without special pleading for the Jewish people. When demands for a new prayer book became pressing, the vastness of an American Progressive movement compassing more than a million Jews made it more difficult to achieve unanimity. Committees were convened to examine countless texts submitted. In the end, the community was fortunate to enlist the services of Chaim Stern, the main liturgist of the Liberal prayer book in London; and the American text follows the British text quite closely. Before then, Herbert Bronstein had edited A Passover Haggadah (1974) illustrated by Leonard Baskin.[19] The very nature of the Passover Seder makes it possible to enlarge the text, to embellish it, and to link it with contemporary experiences. The logical place for inserts was after the prayer "hee sh'omdah la-avotenu" the prayer speaking of God's redemption and expressing confidence in Divine retribution. The Diary of Ann Frank, Shlonsky's Neder, and the poets Samuel Halkin and Anthony Hecht served as sources for Holocaust meditations which lead directly to the "Ten Plagues."[20] (Elie Wiesel and Albert Einstein are included in the ritual of the 'Four Sons' earlier in the text.[21]) The Haggadah continues to grow with insertions for the refusniks and Prisoners of Zion; and there is a whole development within its art and liturgy which is outside our scope, although proper tribute should be paid to Arthur Waskow's "Freedom Haggadah" and to the liturgies of the Reconstructionist movement. The chavurot, in particular, have made their prayers open expressions of concern for contemporary issues.

Shaarei Tefillah: Gates of Prayer was published in 1975. It is a genuine expression of American Reform Judaism, and the various committees did adapt and change the British model. In terms of the Holocaust, the prayers are virtually the same. However, it is worthwhile noting a recent addition to the liturgical publications of American Reform: Gates of the Seasons: A Guide to the Jewish Year (1983) points out that the section on Israel's Suffering (almost identical to the collection in Service of the Heart (see note 10) should now be used for a Yom Ha-Shoah observance. The book is a manual of instruction for a thousand Reform congregations, and it is worthwhile quoting the text in full:

"YOM HASHO-AH (HOLOCAUST DAY)

The twenty-seventh of the Hebrew month of Nisan, called Yom HaSho-ah, was in 1951 set aside as a day of mourning for the victims of the Holocaust by the Knesset (the Israeli Parliament). The Central Conference of American Rabbis in June 1977 called for the annual commemoration of Yom HaSho-ah on this date.

Anti-Seminitism and Nazism did not die with the end of World War II. The Sho-ah is a constant reminder of the potential for evil which lies below the veneer of civilization. The seeds of the Holocaust must not be allowed to find fertile soil again.

It is a mitzvah to remember the six million Jews who were murdered in the Sho-ah by attending special memorial services. With them we should also remember Chasidei Umot Ha-olam, the righteous non-Jews who gave their lives in attempts to save members of the Jewish people.

In order to fulfill the mitzvah of remembrance, it is suggested that a memorial candle be lit and passages found in Gates of Prayer be read (pp.407-411). Either as preparation or as part of the observance, one should spent time reviewing the events which lead to the Sho-ah and discussing ways of preventing its recurrence.

In keeping with the spirit of Yom HaSho-ah as a day of mourning, weddings should not be scheduled. It is further suggested that one eat a very simple meal on the eve of Yom HaShoeah as an act of identification and solidarity with those who were in the concentration camps and slowly starved to death.

Particularly important is providing for a permanent memorial to the Kedoshim, the holy ones who perished. Therefore, our Tzedakah on Yom HaSho-ah should be directed to institutions which preserve their memory."[22]

The particular stance of the Reform pattern manifests itself clearly. Since Yom Ha-Shoah takes place during the Omer season, traditional communities would not schedule weddings in any case. Also, the suggestion of 'a very simple meal' is not totally linked to fasting as a sign of mourning. Rather, it seems to arise out of a particular approach within American pedagogics--the 'simulation technique' of identifying oneself with the suffering in the camps. In this instance, it seems demeaning and diminuating as a practice, although the motives are undoubtedly decent. There exists a study of starvation in the Warsaw Ghetto, carried out by the doctors who starved to death,which is profoundly moving. Reminding oneself of this through 'a simple meal' does not seem to be the right way. At the same time, one must give credit to the Reform community which took the lead in the task of Holocaust remembering, and which has just published the new intra- and inter-faith liturgy for Yom Ha-Shoah and other occasions of remembrance. (Initially, that text was intended as a sixth scroll in a recent CCAR publication The Five Scrolls, where the Scroll of Lamentations had already been linked with memories of Auschwitz).[23]

The Machsor of the American Reform movement, Gates of Repentance, appeared in 1978, and is basically an American edition of the British Gate of Repentance. But there is an expansion and development in the Memorial Service. The British text has a short and clear text:

"Moreover, we are all bereaved. We are a people schooled in sorrow and acquainted with grief. Especially do we recall the precious millions who perished in the Holocaust: men and women, young and old, who suffered so innocently and were done to death so brutally. They lie in nameless graves in far-off forests and deserted fields. But they shall not be forgotten. We take them into our hearts and give them a place beside the cherished memories of our near and dear ones."[24]

The act of the remembrancer (George Steiner's term) comes to the fore here. We say kaddish for our own, weep for them, and do not expect the outside world to take this task from us.

In the American Machsor, the text expands and changes:

"... Heartbreaking have been the times that have fallen to our lot, O God. We have lived through years of tyranny and destruction; we are schooled in sorrow and acquainted with grief. We have seen the just defeated, the innocent driven from their homes, and the righteous suffer a martyrdom as merciless as any ages have witnessed.

At this hour of memorial we recall with grief all Your children who have perished through the cruelty of the oppressor, victims of demonic hate: the aged and the young, the learned and unlettered--all driven in multitudes along the road of pain and pitiless death. Their very presence on earth was begrudged them, for they brought Your covenant of mercy and justice to the recollection of Your enemies; they perished because they were a symbol of Your eternal law; their death has brought darkness to the human soul.

They lie in nameless graves, in far-off forests and lonely fields. And the substance of many was scattered by the winds to the earth's four corners. Yet they shall not be forgotten. We take them into our hearts and give them a place beside the cherished memories of our own loved ones. They now are ours.

We pray to You, O Source of mercy, that Your Torah, to which these Your children bore witness in life and in death, may come to glow with a renewed light in the human soul; that, remembering them, we may sanctify Your name in all the world. Thus will their memory become an enduring blessing to all Your children...."[25]

The Yizkor (Memorial Prayer) in Hebrew and English also speak of those who died al kiddush ha-shem: who gave their lives for the Sanctification of the Divine Name. The American text is thus greatly expanded. Some of the changes relate to differences of language, and to a more open response of a praying community accustomed to a richer rather than sparse text. But there is also the image of the 'death marches' and the ashes caught up by the winds moving across the chimneys of the crematoria. Even these images are absorbed in the concept of 'kiddush ha-shem, the sanctification of God's name which makes them 'k'doshim': martyrs rather than victims. They are assumed to be good and pure, shining lights. It is a claim that cannot be challenged: not for the innocent children, not for the Torah scholars, not for the righteous who lived outside the synagogue nor for those who had no chance to develop the innate goodness which harsh circumstances had suppressed. Yet the great and decent men and women who were caught in the net because they had Jewish grandparents--or the flawed human beings judged not for any sins but for their blood--these fit uneasily into such prayers. The wicked also had a right to life. When the liturgy views the victims as saints, it removes them from that existential reality in which we encountered them, loved them, fought with them.

But it might well be argued that there have not been prayers for them, and that our liturgies will not have prayers for them.

American Reform liturgies often abandon the traditional structure of the siddur in order to add contemporary poetry and prose. Congregations can and do publish their own prayerbooks. Representative of such liturgies is a San Francisco Machsor entitled Hear Our Prayer: Shma Kolenu by Herbert Morris subtitled: "Original Prayers, Meditations and Explanations". 26 It is particularly sensitive to the questions posed by the Shoah, and utilizes texts such as Zvi Kolitz's "Yossel Rakover's Appeal to God" (to be discussed below), and poetry of the Terezin children ("I never saw another Butterfly"). The theme keeps re-appearing in the prayers themselves:

> "Within our own generation, millions of our people were slaughtered. Men, women, children and infants perished. Their cry for help went unheeded, unheard. Forgive us, O Lord, when we turn aside from Your Presence for we remember with sorrow and with shame the brutality and the callousness of men and nations. The brotherhood of man is a dream yet to be fulfilled. May it come speedily in our day.." 27

and

> "To be a Jew after Auschwitz is to confront the demons of Auschwitz and to bear witness against them in all their guises. It is to believe that they will not prevail and to stake on that belief one's life and those of one's children's children (Emil Fackenheim)." 28

That text is preceded by a full page entitled "Hashoah (Holocaust) Remembrance" and is printed upon a photograph of clouds and sky.

III.

The liturgy of the Reform Jewish community in Great Britain (RSGB) is filled with references to the Shoah. In an article about to appear in European Judaism, Jonathan Magonet, Principal of the Leo Baeck College, writes:

> "As part of a major revision of the High Holyday prayerbook of the Reform Synagogues of Great Britain, Rabbi Lionel Blue and I were faced with creating a "martyrology" within the framework of the Additional Service for Yom Kippur.... (my) reservations..centred around the possibility of doing justice to such a task. By what right does anyone who was not personally involved in the Holocaust attempt to say something about it?" 29

Rabbi Magonet was influenced by the writings of Eliezer Berkovits who defines Jews today as 'Job's brothers' who have to believe as Job believed, and must question as did Job, a Job who often could not believe anymore. On that basis, Rabbi Magonet set up certain ground rules for writing a liturgy dealing with the Shoah. The first rule, based upon the writings of the author Peter Weiss, stated that

> "all that the artist could legitimately do was to assemble and present the stark documents themselves, the eyewitness statements and the accumulated evidence..a minimal intrusion by the artist, here liturgical composer, into the materials..(but) shaping and organizing..would intrude.." 30

Immediately, a problem arose regarding the including of material written after the event. Some of the fictional writing has come to be viewed as a true historical text, as other liturgists have discovered. At many American universities, students' High Holyday Services include "Yossel Rackover's Appeal to God". It was first written in Yiddish by Zvi Kolitz, and then Hebrew, English, and German plus other language translations appeared. I discussed the text and its problems (the authenticity of fiction) with Zvi Kolitz when he spoke for me at Columbia University in the sixties. Even now, when I refer to the text as fiction, I get violent letters from those who know it to be true, who have friends who met Yossel, who attack Kolitz for claiming to be the author. Rabbi Magonet also encountered this problem, both with that text and with a letter purportedly written by ninetey-three Jewish girls from Warsaw placed into a brothel but took their lives by poison after smuggling out their letter with its outcry of anguish and of faith. Rabbi Magonet writes:

> "I found a little book in Jerusalem, published by the Association for the Rehabilitation of Jewish Holocaust Orphans together with the Ministry of Religious Affairs, which contains the text of the actual letter...and we decided to use it..in the martyrology... When a colleague then raised a question about the authenticity of the document I wrote to Professor Lucy Dawidowicz who confirmed that the letter was a pious fraud. That particular event did not take place." 31

There were other problems met in that liturgy: some texts are too powerful and overwhelm the worshipper with horror, so that the context of a prayer service is broken and meaning is lost. Then, there is the actual message within the writings of survivors, which often raise deep anxieties and responses of guilt among Jews. There is even the guilt of survival, which can either lead to a fight against evil —or to a flight from reality. The whole problem of hating evil-doers rather than evil emerges and, again, the relationship between the worshipper and God is put to the question. Somehow, the text must not destroy the worshipper.

Rabbi Magonet and his colleague Rabbi Lionel Blue had edited the British Reform Siddur (1977) which had included a "Memorial Service for the Six Million". It is a brief, well organized liturgy which begins with a prayer:

> "We remember our six million dead, who died when madness ruled the world and evil dwelt on earth. We remember those we know, and those whose very name is lost.
> We mourn for all that died with them; their goodness and their wisdom, which could have saved the world and healed so many souls...
> We stand in gratitude for their example of decency and goodness. They are like candles which shine out from the darkness of those years...
> We salute those men and women who were not Jews and who had the courage to stand outside the mob and suffer with us...
> Because of our people's suffering, may such times never come again..." 32

Passages for study follow, including the last Musar talk by the head of the Slobodka Yeshiva in Kovno (Rabbi Nachum Yanchiker); a passage from Anne Frank's Diary, and an El Mole with the words "l'nishmot shisha milyon Acheynu v'achyotenu" which brings the contemporary awareness of feminine theology into the text. There are many variants of El Mole and Kaddish within current Holocaust prayers, with the names of the camps interposed between the words of the Kaddish (but not in the RSGB text). And there is a Study Anthology at the back of the Siddur where the theme of the Shoah occasionally emerges:

> "One of the causes of Auschwitz was—technology...
> The death of an infant moves us; the death of six million people simply stuns our senses.
> We are Eichmann's sons, removed from the consequences of our actions...
> Auschwitz—remembered within the community of human fellowship—can then (when shared suffering becomes a bridge between ourselves and others) become a question addressed to God. Then. But not until then." 33

The Siddur is thus enlarged; but it can and should be argued that the basic pattern of Jewish worship remains unchanged.

Returning to the Machsor of the RSGB, we can again follow Rabbi Magonet's own analysis of this work which wanted to find passages which comfort and affirm faith...

> "despite being painfully aware..that this may be a betrayal of all those whose faith was destroyed.
> Our solution was to select passages that reflected a variety of experiences and responses. We created five sections..the first "God in Light" recorded the words of those who found some meaning even in the suffering...A second section "God in Darkness" records those whose existence or words gave others hope:..an article from Der Morgen..a personal memoir by Rabbi Hugo Gryn.

The third section "The Faithful Witness" of those who recorded...Chaim Kaplan ...Dr. Israel Milejkowski, collecting the scientific work of doctors who documented..the effects of starvation..upon themselves. The fourth section, "The Honest Question" records the attempts of two "survivors" to evaluate the effects of returning to "normal" life, Natalia Ginzberg and Vera Elyashiv. The final section "The Reality of Faith" includes anonymous expressions of hope and generosity of spirit, from Ravensbruck and from a cellar wall in Cologne."[34]

The closing selections of this text were passages from Leo Baeck and from a poem by Hanna Senesh; and a summarizing prayer in which we can see the approach and the intention of the liturgists and their Reform colleagues:

"This is our legacy and this is our heritage, to make of it what we can.
May the tragedy of our history not embitter our lives.
May it not crush us in despair, nor twist and distort our vision.
For then those who died a martyr's death will have died in vain.
And those who died as senseless victims will have no redemption.
May these sacrifices mean that such terror and pain will vanish from the earth.
May these martyrs give us hope of the life that knows no death:
(the Hannah Senesh poem follows--'there are stars..')"[35]

There is a bridging passage going back to the general liturgy (the <u>Avinu Malkenu</u>) which ends with the Franz Rosenzweig call: 'Where do the wings of the gate open? Do you not knwo? INTO LIFE.'

The text falters occasionally (surely, they did not want to say 'senseless victims' but something like 'those who died a senseless death as victims'); but one can learn much from this honest grappling with the problems of the Shoah as they enter the liturgy. .....

When we ponder upon this admittedly small selections of non-Orthodox prayers which confront the Shoah, it becomes clear that most of the differences between the non-traditional response to the Shoah and the traditional prayers affirm the same basic insights: trust in God; viewing the Six Million basically as <u>k'doshim</u>, as holy martyrs; expressions of hope for the future; accepting the task of being 'kaddish-sayers' and lighting <u>Yahrzeit</u> candles. Reconstructionist approaches to a non-personal power making for goodness or a limited deity have no place in these liturgies. In the Progressive liturgies we explored faith that faltered but did not break. A Prayer given in the Hebrew Union College chapel on Yom Hashoah by a survivor thinks its way through the hard questions--'not as a non-believer--how could a non-believer feel the urgent need of reasoning with God?' but notes:

"This week we read from your Tora: <u>kedoshim tiheyu</u>. Have we perhaps misunderstood these words all along? Could it be that you never intended them to mean "you shall be holy" but rather "you shall be martyrs," usffering the extreme Passion for the sanctification of Your name. Yet the verse continues: <u>ki kadosh ani adonai elochechem</u> "for I, the Lord your God am..." not a "martyr", of course, but "holy." And the homiletic interpretation points out that Your <u>kedushah</u>, unlike ours, appears in full spelling, which means that it is unattainable and incomprehensible to our defective <u>kedushah</u>--Could it still mean "martyr", also with regard to You? Could You, too, be suffering in a way incomprehensible to us? Could it be that the <u>Shechinah</u> hid her face and wept bitterly, every time the door of the gas chamber was slammed shut?"[36]

Some answers begin to emerge for the questions we asked at the beginning. Was the Catastrophe unique? Most of the liturgists indicate that it was incomprehensible; some say that it can only be understand as a <u>tremendum</u>, a unique event standing well outside human comprehension. What is the nature of the human being? Most come to recognize both <u>yetzer tov</u> and <u>yetzer ha-ra</u>, with a stress towards evil rather than good. Yet all affirm the goodness of the victim; and some stress the possibility of goodness in the by-standers. Some of the Reform rabbis stress that the old prayers: <u>mipne chatta-enu and yissurim shel ahavah</u>-- the Holocaust as punishment for sins and as part of God's loving instruction and testing of His righteous ones--that these prayers can no longer be said. Yet some of the most liberal prayers hint towards the same understanding of a God who instructs us through our sufferings.

Rabbi Norman Solomon rejects the criticism of the traditional teachings:

"The reason that the non-Orthodox Holocaust historians reject "traditional" answers may be something quite other than the intrinsic inadequacy of those answers.. The traditional interpretation of suffering depend heavily for such cogency as they may have on the belief in life after death and/or the transmigration of souls. Equally, they depend upon a belief in the inerrancy of Scripture and in the authenticity of its rabbinic interpreation. Those beliefs have been under attack in modern times for reasons which have nothing to do with the Shoah."[37]

Rabbi Solomon does not feel that the Shoah was theologically unique, but does accept that uniqueness in a historical sense. In a way, he feels little need for new questions since all the questions on the nature of evil have been with from the beginning.

Perhaps the answer is silence. Some of the liturgies do refer to the silence of God, to the silence of humans. Those who confront the Shoah as a tremendum outside the mind of humanity recognize the power of silence. Yet somehow, in an imperfect world of imperfect persons, words are needed to keep us from drifting into apathy. Prayers are needed to link our concern with that of the Mitmensch. And religious services are needed to bring group expression before the altar, to assert our experience as a people, and to re-encounter God who is not only found in silence but also in speech.

The liturgies we examined are a beginning.
In the beginning was God.

.....

Albert H. Friedlander
Dean, Leo Baeck College
Rabbi, Westminster Synagogue
London, England

April 1, 1988

NOTES

1. Churban is the traditional theological term, with the "First Churban" and the "Second Churban" describing the destruction of Jerusalem and the Temple in 586 BCE and 70 CE (although Ignaz Maybaum, in "The Face of God After Auschwitz (1965) uses it within Reform theology.) Holocaust came into general usage through Elie Wiesel but, as has been pointed out by him and Bruno Bettelheim among others, it has uncomfortable connotations. Tremendum, brilliantly expounded in Arthur A. Cohen's The Tremendum, N.Y. 1981 may be the best term in theological discussion, but falters in general discourse. All these terms are used in the text, depending upon the context, authors discussed, etc. But there is no word we can use.

2. Lord Jakobovits, in letter to author, to be used as preface for The Six Days of Destruction, Meditations towards Hope by Elie Wiesel and Albert Friedlander, Pergamon Press, Oxford, June 1988.

3. ibid.

4. "Religious Responses to the Holocaust: Retrospect and Prospect" by Sir Immanuel Jakobovits (The B'nai Brith International Lecture Delivered in Jerusalem on 25 November, 1987.) Printed by Office of the Chief Rabbi, London, 1988. This is a distinguished and careful account of traditional thought and the Holocaust.

5. op.cit., (Letter to author for preface, p. 3).

6. op. cit., (Jakobovits "Retrospect and Prospect", p. 6.

7. Friedrich Thieberger Juedisches Fest, Juedischer Brauch, Berlin 1936, p. 401: "a public fast (taanit zibbur) was set, so that even today the 20th of Sivan is observed by the Jews of Poland in memory of the persecutions under Chmelnicki in 1648." These prayers ceased shortly after this text was published; initially, Yom Tov Lipmann Heller used medieval kinot to express the grief of the Chmelnicki pogrom: 'they are all one.'

8. Service of the Heart, ULPS, London, 1967, p. 160.

9. ibid., p. 488.

10. ibid., p. 503.

11. ibid., p. 287.

12. The work of Richard Rubenstein has certainly not received enough appreciation: vicious attacks and notoriety are no acknowledgment of the seminal influence he has had on Jewish and Christian Holocaust theology and history. Ultimately, his historical works The Cunning of History (1976) and Triage (1986) will receive full acknowledgment.

13. Gate of Repentance, ULPS, London 1973, p. 287.

14. ibid., p. 290.

15. ibid.

16. ibid., pp. 296-300.

17. ibid., p. 304. It was felt necessary to give an English transliteration (p.481).

18. At the time, the use of this poem (translation by Albert H. Friedlander) was bitterly contested. Celan, with whom I discussed the matter, felt that the poem was getting too much exposure. Here, one had to fight for its recognition.

19. A Passover Haggadah, (ed.) Herbert Bronstein, CCAR, New York, 1974.

20. ibid., p. 48.

21. ibid., p. 46.

22. Gates of the Season: A Guide to the Jewish Year (ed. Peter Knobel), CCAR, New York, 1983, pp. 102-103.

23. The Five Scrolls (eds. Albert H. Friedlander and Herbert Bronstein), New York 1984.

24. Gate of Repentance, (eds. John Rayner and Chaim Stern), ULPS,); London, 1978. p. 375 (the Memorial Service).

25. Gates of Repentance, (ed. Chaim Stern), CCAR, New York 1978. pp. 489-490.

26. Hear Our Prayer: Shma Kolenu (ed. Herbert Morris, San Francisco, 1982,pc

27. ibid., p. 73.

28, ibid., pp. 298-299.

29. "Creating a Holocaust Liturgy" by Jonathan Magonet; ms. for European Judaism for Summer 1988, p. 1.

30. ibid., p. 3.

31. ibid., p. 4.

32. Forms of Prayer for Jewish Worship (eds. Lionel Blue and Jonathan Magonet) RSGB London, 1977, p. 256.

33. ibid., p. 391.

34. op. cit., "Creating a Holocaust Liturgy", pp. 7-8.

35. Forms of Prayer: Days of Awe (eds. Blue and Magonet) RSGB, London, 1985, p. 517.

36. "An Uvechein and a Dayeinu Concerning Bergen-Belsen, by Werner Weinberg YOM HASHOAH April 30, 1981, HUC-JIR Chapel, Cincinnati, mimeographed; p. 3.

37. "Jewish Responses to the Holocaust" by Norman Solomon (pre-print for April 1988 Cracow Conference); Studies in Jewish/Christian Relations No. 4; Birmingham, U.K. (1988), p. 22. A thorough and scholarly presentation from a deeply traditional point of view fully aware of the radical position but unwilling to accept it to any extent.

A TRANSNATURAL THEOLOGY OF THE HOLOCAUST

RICHARD L. LIBOWITZ

Anne Frank Institute of Philadelphia, Post Office Box 40119,
Philadelphia, Pennsylvania 19106, USA

In an earlier age, humans sought to bring meaning to the world in which they lived by attributing events to the acts of beings with powers superior to their own. These deities -- the greater gods and the lesser spirits -- were to be found everywhere, each facet of nature a unique force demanding recognition and requiring appeasement. The sun and the moon were gods, so too the rivers and the mountains, from whom favor could be obtained through sacrifices and offerings. The world had been created by the coupling of the supreme male and female forces and its continuation was contingent upon proper duplication of the primeval event. Mankind played no significant creative role in the universe but was responsible for these ritual reenactments. This cycle of ritual renewal has become familiar to the readers of Mircea Eliade.

Three thousand years ago, one Mediterranean people was different. The authors of the Hebrew Bible, men and women of ancient Israel, looked beyond visible phenomena in their search for wisdom. They saw in the sunrise no god driving his fiery team across the sky but one aspect of their single God's creative acts. Nature was not a myriad of potentially hostile deities but evidence of the hand of God, who caused "the wind to blow and the rain to fall." They looked out at a universe that was of God, but knew it was not God. This differentiation between God and His works separated Israel's worship from that of the surrounding nations; confusion, leading to adoption of non-Israelite religious practices, could lead to the worst sort of heresy. Thus the rabbis explained that the Golden Calf had been intended as both a divine throne and a reminder of the invisible God who had delivered Israel from slavery. When the people confused symbol with reality and began to worship the Calf as their redeemer, they were punished severely.

The God of Israel may have been unseen, but evidence of the divine existence abounded within human history as well as nature. Israel further distinguished its God from the surrounding deities through the claim that He was also the God of History, taking an active interest and role in human events. Understanding history to be both linear and purposeful, life events were perceived as neither random nor accidental. God as Lord of History had enacted a covenant with the people Israel as part of His special plan; reward and punishment were meted out in accord with Israel's faithfulness to God's covenant.

Throughout its recorded history, the Jewish people has known more than its share of oppressions, persecutions and plain hard times. In other eras, priests, prophets and rabbis were wont to explain particular hardships in terms of God's collective punishment of Israel for sins caused by lapses in obedience to the dictates of the covenant. Losses in war, destruction of both Temples and the Dispersion of the nation were comprehended in this manner, an interpretation which managed to provide a ray of hope amidst the despair. "Because of our sins, we were exiled from our land," reads the statement included within the Musaf *Amidah*, with a tacit suggestion that repentance and a return to proper observance of the *mitzvot* will eventuate in an ingathering of the exiles to their ancient homeland.

Strict adherence to this traditional criterion for interpreting suffering could lead to an understanding of the Holocaust as the ultimate punishment for a collective sin of enormous magnitude. If such was the case, then the Holocaust must be understood as a representation of God's will. If the Holocaust was God's will, the Nazis -- Hitler in particular -- cannot be regarded simply as mass murderers but rather as agents of the deity, 6,000,000 slaughtered Children of Abraham notwithstanding. Some Orthodox Jews have attempted to justify the Holocaust along these lines and specifically in terms of divine retribution, punishment for the abandonment of a life based upon the *mitzvot.* The most recalcitrantly traditional continue to argue this premise, despite the fact that millions among the victims were either observant Jews who had never veered from the path of *Halakhah* or children, not yet at the age of responsibility for their actions. Among Christian students of the Holocaust, there are some who have offered a parallel explanation of the Holocaust as divine punishment, claiming that the road to Auschwitz began at Calvary, when Israel committed the act of deicide. For most, however, these rationales are too abhorrent to be acceptable. We seek other answers.

The most widely read Jewish voice emerging from the Holocaust belongs to Elie Wiesel. For tens of thousands of readers, in a variety of languages, his memoir Night was the initial literary exposure to the Kingdom of Night and remains the most vivid. Wiesel allows his readers to see questions of tremendous pain and significance, but he provides no answers, only empathy for their struggles. He is a survivor, an Orthodox Jew who describes himself as a witness and a story teller, and his self-definition is most accurate. Unlike more radical authors, he may raise questions about God's actions, but he never doubts the facticity of God Himself. Wiesel's witness cries out in anguish, but his pain does not arise from angry disbelief; his is the agony of one who continues to believe, in spite of all he has witnessed.

When pursuing an examination of post-Holocaust Jewish theology (or, post-Holocaust Jewish religious thought, for those who do not find the materials sufficiently systematic), it is not uncommon for one to begin with a reading of works by Richard Rubenstein, followed by those of Emil Fackenheim. Polar extremes in their backgrounds and attitudes, each man views the havoc wreaked in the name of a Final Solution and seeks to uncover a direction for future Jewish life.

Both Rubenstein, an American teenager during World War Two, and Fackenheim, grown to manhood in Europe, a concentration camp inmate and refugee, present insights into the God of Israel and His works using terms and concepts at sharp variance with the views of the prophets, medieval rabbis and Hasidic masters. Traditional understandings of the universe had always been based upon a faith in biblical revelation and a supernatural creator-God who works through (and occasionally enters) human history, particularly the history of Israel. Within their cosmology, men and women are required to assume responsibility for their particular actions, although ultimate authority abides within God who is the foundation of all.

Any questioning of God's role during the Holocaust is shaped by a primary conception of the deity. Maintenance of faith in a supernatural ruler of the universe, both anthropomorphic and anthroposensate yet ultimately transcendent, the perfect creator of an imperfect world who punishes His creations for their imperfections while rejecting responsibility for them, has become difficult for many in an age marked by ever greater reliance upon science and empirical investigation. How much more has that traditional God/faith suffered by the fact of the Holocaust, the light of Israel hidden by crematoria smoke. The Ancient One of Days may not have been destroyed; Israel's traditional ways survive unchallenged within many. But for those who can no longer proclaim a perfect faith, new answers are demanded.

Richard Rubenstein presents the most radical departure from traditional understandings of God and history of any Jewish theologian. Branded by some the Jewish "death of God" author when his collection After Auschwitz appeared in the 1960s, Rubenstein has rejected all attributions of the Holocaust to Jewish guilt and/or divine punishment. Speaking at Wayne State University in 1970, during the first of what became the Annual Scholars' Conference on the Holocaust and Church Struggle, he made his dramatic statement that he would give up Israel's God before he would accept the notion of Israel being guilty of any transgression which would legitimate such destruction. Rubenstein saw the crematoria of Auschwitz as symbols not only of millions of Jewish deaths but also the annihilation of the traditonal Jewish ideas of God which might be drawn upon to explain the killings. Israel's faith had helped the people withstand oppression and endure centuries of dispersion, but only at a cost of reducing much of Jewry to a state of passivity which included an apparent inability to recognize the dangers of the Third Reich despite many unmistakable signs.

As a result, Rubenstein has demanded that Israel make a fresh start. Declaring nothing salvageable within the ruins of the ancient beliefs, he has insisted a new Jewish *raison d'être* be established in which faith is replaced with force. He finds the potential source for his new rationales in Zionism and practical politics. "Zionism's real significance lies in the fact that twenty centuries of self-distortion, self-estrangement, and self-blame have ended for a people which is now free to live its own life at every level of emotional and cultural experience." (Rubenstein, 1966) Pragmatic actions, political influence and military might must provide the new bases for survival.

Despite his radical label, in some sense, Rubenstein did not go far enough. While removing Judaism's ancient superstructure by blasting at its base, he does not develop a clear blueprint for reconstruction of a system which may be spiritually viable in the age of Auschwitz; instead, he appears to minimize (if not negate) the spiritual factor within a survival system. His conclusion that traditional God concepts fail to explain the Holocaust and cannot provide all Jews with a rationale for maintaining Jewish life has proven itself acceptable, as has his defense of Israel against charges of some grave offense meriting punishment. The problem is in the totality of Rubenstein's accusation, that traditional Jewish values are both erroneous and harmful, "punishing man for being what he was created to be" (Rubenstein, 1966), which places a peculiar onus upon both survivors and others who continue to feel spiritually secure within traditional Judaism. At the same time, his replacement system and pragmatic values offer little uplift or inspiration.

Emil Fackenheim is frequently studied in contrast with Rubenstein, as the most vociferous opponent of the latter's religious nihilism. For Fackenheim, the surrender of German forces in May, 1945, changed only the nature of the war against the Jews, it did not bring about its conclusion. Hitler's goal had been the disappearance of the Jewish people, its faith and practices, from the earth (an effort which Rubenstein, for one, has contended was at least partially successful, as demonstrated by the heart of the Reich, Germany and Austria, having become and remaining functionally *Judenrein*). Armies may no longer clash, but Fackenheim sees the struggle against genocide continuing, the concentration camps, gas chambers and crematoria replaced by death through assimilation and spiritual despair. Every Jew who fails to identify as a Jew, who does not engender a positive Jewish identity within his or her children, pushes the Jewish people closer to the precipice of that cultural and physical oblivion intended by the Third Reich. Jewish survival is a *sine qua non*, its manifest need enunciated by that which Fackenheim describes as the "Commanding Voice" of Auschwitz, and which provides both warning and direction in a new "614th" commandment; "Jews are forbidden to hand Hitler posthumous victories" (Fackenheim, 1972). To underscore the necessity of continuing the battle, he assures his readers, "Jewish survival after Auschwitz is not one relative ideal among others but rather an imperative which brooks no compromise" (Fackenheim, 1972).

Fackenheim addresses his call for Jewish survival to the disaffected as well as those who have maintained Jewish religious practices. Placing nation above individual, he insists that secularist Jews are equally obligated to find those means whereby they can foster a positive identification with their Judaism. When they do, "even the most secularist of Jews bears witness, by the mere affirmation of his Jewishness, against the devil" (Fackenheim, 1972).

More optimistic than Rubenstein, Fackenheim has nevertheless been accused of a central negativity within his theories. His 614th commandment fails to offer a positive rationale for Jewish life, insisting only that Hitler be denied victory. While Fackenheim calls for Jews to bear witness of their faith to the world, he admits that Jews who do so must face a road "of pain and mourning, of humiliation, guilt and despair" (Fackenheim, 1972), but insists we are "forbidden to despair." Moreover, suggestions as to the identity of the Commanding Voice of Auschwitz further cloud some evaluations of Fackenheim's response. To some, the Voice is God, to others, it is either the death camp itself or those responsible for its existence. Thus the Voice's pronouncement may be either a warning or a challenge. If Auschwitz, a Nazi death creation, is the source of the Commanding Voice and since the 614th commandment focuses less upon the Jewish people than it does upon Adolf Hitler, one must wonder whether Fackenheim's ideas may be interpreted in such a manner as to justify the Holocaust as God's will and Hitler as the agent of God. Although Fackenheim specifically refutes any allowance of Hitler "to dictate the terms of our religious life," the possibilities for interpretation remain open.

With strengths and weaknesses to be found within each response, the problem which continues to be raised by many Jews is how one may -- like Rubenstein -- reject belief in the traditional Jewish understanding of God, yet retain a positive value system which does not eliminate the transcendent and -- like Fackenheim -- will include within it both "religious" and "secularists". Liberal religious movements of the late nineteenth century such as Ethical Culture advocated a universal moral code, similar to that of the biblical prophets, but provided their followers with no undergirding support system beyond rational sensibility. Such systems, posited upon strictly natural, non-dogmatic bases, offered little succor to their adherents within the concentration camps and have not provided a satisfactory alternative to supernaturalism in regard to fundamental questions of good and evil. The *Realpolitik* of Richard Rubenstein is based upon a logic at least as sound as the optimism of the Ethical Culturists, and offers far more substantial supporting historical evidence, which current world events seem to underscore.

It was in search for that alternative to the supernaturalism of Orthodox Judaism and the spiritual vaguery of Ethical Culture that Mordecai M. Kaplan (1881-1983) began to develop the theories which eventually coalesced as Reconstructionist Judaism. Drawing upon both traditional Jewish sources and the findings of turn-of-the-century sociologists, anthropologists and social philosophers, Kaplan proposed a definition of Judaism as the "evolving religious civilization" of the Jewish people. Judaism was a *civilization,* possessing all of the accoutrements of any national group, including a land (although the particular territory was not, at the time of Kaplan's writing, under the political control of the Jewish nation), language, legal system, cultural matrix and social institutions. Judaism was a *religious* civilization because the human relationship to and with the divine, as expressed in the concept of covenant, was central to the civilization. Finally, Judaism was an *evolving* religious civilization because it had passed through a series of major and minor transformations through the millenia of its history, a process which was continuing in the contemporary period (Kaplan, 1981; Libowitz, 1983).

In reducing religion to a factor --albeit central -- to the civilization rather than coterminous with it, Kaplan was drawing upon the researches of Emile Durkheim, who had asserted that religion was a product of those shared experiences which a group or society came to consider of ultimate significance (Durkheim, 1968). In underscoring this claim, Kaplan moved the central focus of the God-Torah-Israel triad from the deity to the Jewish nation itself. The civilization was a result of the national experience, affected by the nation's contemporary needs even as it helped shape responses to those needs and other life demands. Traditional understandings of Judaism were, according to Kaplan, no longer appropriate, although they were not to be labelled as wrong. The Orthodox conception of the universe and its mandated responses to particular situations were not to be compared with mathematical problems having a single "right" answer and an infinite amount of "wrong" responses; to Kaplan, the traditions of Judaism represented the collective wisdom of the ages, the best efforts to explain the universe which earlier generations could develop, based upon the informational resources at their disposal. The twentieth century, with its advances in scientific knowledge and its greater appreciation of human psychology, had come to different conclusions, consonant with its new understandings, perceptions and perspective. For those whom tradition continued to serve in a satisfactory manner, no change was advocated; Jewish civilization offered a sufficiently broad spectrum to permit diverse opinions to coexist in peace. The past was always to be respected but, when established customs no longer met the legitimate needs of the Jewish people, change was necessary. In seeking solutions to those needs, Kaplan not only advocated change but endorsed looking beyond ***Halakhah*** in order to draw upon any available resource, no matter its origin. He defended this break with tradition by arguing that the Jewish civilization -- like any national civilization -- has no need to justify its existence and must take any actions necessary for protection of its corporate existence.

Kaplan's radical redefinitions and justifications extended from sociology into theology, to the very definition of God. Drawing upon the writings of British poet, essayist and philo-semite Matthew Arnold (particularly Arnold's text Literature and Dogma), Kaplan developed the theological system which he called "transnatural." This system begins with the replacing of traditionally anthropomorphic God concepts with an understanding of university deity. God is the "power that makes for salvation," a force or pneuma which is transcendent in that it is beyond the individual human, yet immanent because a portion of it is possessed by every living creature (Kaplan, 1962). Descriptive concepts such as "God is love" are unhelpful, because they remove paradigmatic attitudes from the human realm. In their place, Kaplan substituted assertions such as whenever one acts in a loving manner, one demonstrates an aspect of divinity. Within this perspective, God becomes identified with (critics may say "reduced to") conscience, the internalized agency by which we make value judgements and moral decisions. The internalization of divinity does not eliminate the psychological need for ritual behavior, public worship or, most of all, prayer, but it does transform it. With God located in the human conscience, prayer, the traditional liturgical formulae that address God, will be introspective, rather than outer-directed. This is most appropriate, however. The greatest source for human transformation and salvation rests within the human psyche itself, making this type of self-centering prayer far more significant than critics of religious ritual would have it.

Kaplan never addressed directly the theological issues raised by the Holocaust, at least in part because he could rationalize those events in a manner that did not threaten his theology.

In this way, Kaplan's responses paralleled those of the extreme Orthodox from whom he was generally so far removed. As it has become a fourth movement within Judaism, Reconstructionism has directed its attention to the more visible needs of modern Jewry (self-definition, role of women, educational developments, etc.); yet the too often neglected transnatural theology offers perhaps the true middle ground for understanding God issues, particularly in relation to the Holocaust, bridging the chasm between total (supernatural) belief and complete (natural) rejection.

In relating the story of the trial of God, Elie Wiesel explains how a *din Torah* was gathered to hear the accusations and testimonies, then withdrew to consider the charges, the evidence and the talmudic case precedents. When it reassembled, the court declared God to have been guilty of violating His covenant and deserting His people. The guilty verdict required that a punishment be assigned, but what punishment could men apply to their Creator? The non-believer might denounce and reject the God of Israel, but that was not their way. The sentence was summarized by the rabbi who served as head of the court; "Now, it is time for our evening prayers." Rather than blaspheme or abandon the Name of God, Jews would continue to revere the Name and ahere to the covenant. God's punishment lay in the knowledge of His people's continued fidelity.

In a less formal manner, Richard Rubenstein placed God -- or, at least, the traditional understanding of God -- on trial and also found the defendant guilty. For Rubenstein, however, continued observance was neither punishment nor answer; faithfulness to a misguided and false conception had been a contributing factor to massacre. Although he held an affinity for many Reconstructionist ideas, a transformational theology would not suffice for the crisis at hand. Rubenstein's sentence was intended to obliterate traditional faith (some critics have declared this would continue Hitler's work, on a theological level). For himself, the answer lay in a newly rediscovered paganism, which he defended not as ancient idolatry but the means "to find once again...roots as a child of Earth and to see one's own existence as wholly and totally an earthly existence" (Rubenstein, 1974).

Emil Fackenheim did not approach this trial motif. If he had done so, he might have declared any trial of God to be in recess, the final verdict to be rendered by the future actions (and existence) of the Jewish people. His "charge to the jury," i.e., specific recommendations about the Jewish future, is of lesser significance than his insistence that "religious" and "secular" Jews share responsibility for that future.

Transnatural theology leads beyond Fackenheim and Rubenstein by rejecting supernaturalism without abandoning either the sacred nor the transcendent. God is understood as universal process, upon which it is impossible to assign responsibility for the Holocaust. Auschwitz represents a series of human actions; it remains a supreme example of the destructive capacity within free will. Judaism holds free will to have been a gift of God, but misuse of a gift is not necessarily the fault of the giver. We are informed of our powers of life and death, good and evil, in Deuteronomy and, although we are encouraged "therefore choose life", choice of direction remains ours. Transnatural theology refuses to permit the escape from human responsibility by blaming God. It forces us to accept in potentia and reality the capacity for evil inherent within us, while reminding also of the positive, divine aspects we may also display. It forces us to place divinity in a human context while viewing our actions on a universal stage. At the same time, it offers a means to continue in one's faith, transformed but still Jewish, troubled but not surrendering to despair.

REFERENCES

Arnold, M. (1970). Literature and Dogma. AMS Press.
Durkheim, E. (1968). The Elementary Forms of the Religious Life. Allen & Unwin Ltd.
Eliade, M. (1959). Cosmos and History. Collier Books.
Fackenheim, E.L. (1972). God's Presence in History. Harper & Row. 67-104.
Kaplan, M.M. (1981). Judaism As A Civilization. Jewish Publication Society.
Kaplan, M.M. (1962). The Meaning of God in Modern Jewish Civilization. Reconstructionist Press.
Libowitz, R.L. (1983). Mordecai M. Kaplan and the Development of Reconstructionism. Edwin Mellen Press.
Rubenstein, R.L. (1966). After Auschwitz. Bobbs-Merrill.
Rubenstein, R.L. (1974). In: The German Church Struggle and Holocaust: (eds. F.H. Littell and H.G. Locke) Wayne State University Press. 256-268.
Wiesel, E. (1969). Night. Avon Books.

HOLOCAUST AS PROGRESS
Reflections on the Thought of Ignaz Maybaum

Rabbi Dow Marmur

Holy Blossom Temple
1950 Bathurst Street
Toronto, Ontario
Canada
M5P 3K9

I

A Hasidic story(1) tells of a king who owned a precious diamond which sustained a scratch. No diamond cutter, however gifted, seemed to be able to repair the damage. But one day a jeweller came who not only restored the stone but even enhanced its value: he engraved a rosebud around the imperfection and used the scratch to make the stem.

Will God ever find a craftsman who could turn the deep scratch we call the Holocaust into a rosebud and transform the seemingly irreparable damage to the Jewish people into a work of art? Is it ever possible to look at the Holocaust as a prelude to progress?

Past calamities in Jewish history have been viewed in this way. The Biblical Prophets saw the mighty nations that afflicted Israel as God's tools in the ultimate interest of Israel. Later on, even the worst tragedies were regarded as intimations of impending Messianic times. Can the same ever be said about the destruction of six million Jews and countless millions of others between 1933 and 1945?

Contemporary Jewish thinkers have largely recoiled from a theology that sees the Holocaust as a positive force. They have at best pointed to some possible consolation for the tragedy, and often identified the creation of the State of Israel as a source of comfort to the bereaved Jewish people. But they have not said more than that, except for one Holocaust theologian: Ignaz Maybaum. The reflections that follow, based on his writings, are cautious and tentative, but brought here in the conviction that Maybaum's contribution to modern Jewish theology should not be ignored, if for no other reason than it is so traditional and so revolutionary at the same time.

II

Despite his ten books in English, several pamphlets, numerous articles and essays, Ignaz Maybaum is virtually unknown, even in the country where he lived during the second half of his life, England. The only scholar to pay serious attention to him is Steven T. Katz in his _Post -Holocaust Dialogues_ (2) and he is less than complimentary. It is not difficult to understand the reason: Maybaum put forward a theory which, on the face of it, is open to being misunderstood as offensive to the martyrs of the Holocaust and perjorative to East European Jewry which paid the heaviest price in the tragedy. Who was this man?

Ignaz Maybaum, born in 1897 in Vienna, was ordained by the _Hochschule fuer die Wissenschaft des Judentums_, the Liberal Rabbinic Seminary in Berlin, where his uncle Sigmund Maybaum was a celebrated preacher. After serving small congregations in provincial German towns, he returned to the capital and stayed there until 1939. During his six years under the Nazis, which included a spell in a concentration camp, he worked tirelessly for the welfare of the congregants he served.

He continued his pastoral activities and his writing after arriving in England shortly before the outbreak of World World II. First he gave guidance and comfort to the Jewish refugees from Germany to which his first book in English, Man and Catastrophe,(3)is a moving testimony. Later he addressed himself to a larger British public, both Jewish and Christian.

These later works reflect something of a shift in Maybaum's religious orientation. Reared in the more traditional milieu of German-Jewish liberalism, he found its English counterpart even more difficult to take than Orthodoxy. To start with - e.g. in his The Jewish Home (4) - he was critical of British Reform but subsequently, when he was called to serve one of its congregations, which he built up to become one of the largestin the country, he not only appreciated what Reform stood for but emerged as one of its most ardent exponents. He was among the founders of the Leo Baeck College in London, which in many ways saw itself as the heir of the Berlin Hochschule, and taught at that Rabbinic School until his death in 1976.

Here is not the place to offer a comprehensive survey of Maybaum's writings. The biographic thumbnail sketch is only intended as background to his startling assertion that the Holocaust is a gateway to progress.

For Maybaum, the liberal rabbi, Judaism was primarily faith in God, not an affirmation of Jewish identity. Steeped in the teachings of the Bible, he refused to consider the possibility that Jewish history was devoid of meaning. His starting point, therefore, was the conviction that even the tragedy he witnessed must lead to some higher purpose.

In an interview he gave on the occasion of his 70th birthday, (5) he said: "Auschwitz is the great trial. The Jew is tried, tested, like Abraham at Moriah. Those after Auschwitz who still believe in God, His justice and His mercy, are the right Jews, the remnant. Those who break down shall not belong to the remnant. The remnant is that part of the Jewish people which, like, Job, remains faithful to God though He slay them." This is a succinct summary of much that is contained in Maybaum's The Face of God After Auschwitz (6) and strewn across many other books: an affirmatin of faith in God as the greatest challenge for the contemporary Jew; Jewish "ethnic" survival will take care of itself, for God's assurance of a saving remnant cannot be in doubt. Even the horrible experience of the Holocaust does not change things but brings each of us survivors nearer to a decision whether we are willing to remain Jews or not.

Once Maybaum was ready to affirm Reform Judaism in practice, he was also prepared to take the theological consequences of his stance and openly attack Orthodoxy. His later writings contain passionate outbursts against modern manifestations of East European religiosity, be it in its Hasidic or in its legalistic forms. He did not bewail the decline of Jewish Orthodoxy, which he associated with the Holocaust. Perhaps its decline would be the beginning of a renewed Judaism, the faith of the remnant.

He refused to speak of the Holocaust as sho'a, the current Hebrew term meaning "destruction", and instead used the equivalent churban, because Jewish tradition has used the latter word to describe the destruction of both Temples in Jerusalem, events that epitomized cataclysmic national calamities which nevertheless resulted in progress. The Hitler epoch constitutes the third churban and thus contains the same potential for growth, even though we are not yet able to discern it.

In the same interview Maybaum said: "The first churban, with which we associate the Babylonian exile, made us into a people without a State but with a mission. The second churban, after the destruction of the Maccabean Commonwealth, established the Synagogue. For the first time mankind saw worship without animal sacrifice based entirely on the spoken word. The Holocaust is the third churban and it, too, will lead to progress."

When pressed to be more specific, Maybaum grew somewhat impatient with the interviewer, the author if this essay: "Don't tempt me. Don't force me to give you a philosophy of history. Hope is not calculation. You must never force me to specify my hopes." But he relented and added: "Were I to succumb to the temptation, I could point to the fact that after a thousand years of German oppression, the Slavs are now free. The Oder-Neisse line denotes progress. I could also say that the Ashkenazi, European, diaspora has become a world diaspora. That too is progress."

His faith in God forced Maybaum into a less admirable faith in progress and resulted in considerable political naivety as well as excessive disdain for Orthodoxy. But then, the Biblical Prophets may also have seemed naive to their contemporaries and they were known to exaggarate in order to make a point.

An aspect of Maybaum's naivety is his basic lack of appreciation of Jewish sovereignty as reflected in the existence of the State of Israel. Whereas Jewish nationalists have occasionally been tempted to equate post-Holocaust progress with the establishment of the State of Israel, Maybaum sees that progress despite Jewish nationalism, not through it. His Judaism is God-centered not land-centered. His interest in Israel arises out of the fact that millions of Jews live there, not because of the political and cultural implications of statehood. The Viennese Jew Ignaz Maybaum was greatly impressed by his only visit to the Jewish State, but the liberal rabbi Ignaz Maybaum was also greatly disturbed by the two poles of secularism and Orthodoxy which he identified with the old pre-Holocaust order of things. Somehow, Israel did not quite fit into his notion of _churban_ that leads to progress whereas the Diaspora did.

The last sermon in his collection _The Faith of the Jewish Diaspora_, sums up his attitude: "The State of Israel is one of the various settlements of the Jewish World Diaspora. We see today that the Jewish people remains what it was for two thousand years: a people of the Diaspora, a people denied the unity which political and national cohesion gives to the gentiles. God wills it, and say you all: 'So be it.'" (7) In line with his exaltation of the Jewish home as the center of Jewish life, Maybaum was cautious about the state, any state, including The Jewish State. He called his last book, published posthumously, _Happiness outside the State_. (8)

What for Emil Fackenheim, and many with him, is a new departure - the Holocaust as something _sui generis_ in Jewish history; Jewish statehood as a manifestation of radical change in the Jewish condition - is for Maybaum merely a confirmation "that the Jewish people remains what it was for two thousand years," still confined to the trust of Abraham - the _Akeda_, the binding of the Biblical Isaac by his father, is a central theme in Maybaum's writings - and the patience of Job. Jewish history, shaped by trust and patience, is the history of progress towards a Messianic future. Triumph and tragedy alike are tools in God's hands; the Holocaust is no exception.

III

Steven T. Katz is almost outraged by the implications of the idea that the Holocaust can be viewed as a sign of progress. He writes that "if the Holocaust is the price of freedom, or in this case progress and expiation, then better to do without such evolution and reconciliation - the price is just too high. It is morally and theologically unacceptable. To insist on it is to turn God, _kivyachol_ ('as if one could say this'), into a moral monster." (9)

Katz's critique must be taken seriously: "An impossible irony also discloses itself as a corrollary of Maybaum's suggestion that God used Hitler for His purposes. If the _Sho'ah_ is God's Will, if Hitler is "My servant,' then to resist Hitler is to resist God; to fight the Nazis is to fight the Lord. As such the Warsaw Ghetto resistors, the inmates who rebelled at Treblinka, the 'righteous of the nations' who risked death, and more often than not died, to save Jewish lives, all these were rebels against the Almighty." (10)

Katz describes Maybaum as "a victim of his inheritance; that is, of those earlier modernizing attempts which sought to evaluate and interpret Judaism primarily through alien standards and for largely apologetic purposes." (11) He sees too close a connection between Maybaum's _churban_ and the Crucifixtion and assumes that it comes "from Maybaum's great mentor Franz Rosenzweig." This, however, "does not make it true; it merely makes it an error with a pedigree." (12)

The establishment of the State of Israel is seen by Katz as "the antithesis of the Crucifixtion mentality." He understands the Jewish State to be the mouthpiece of Jews who "have now declared (seemingly with God's permission): we have suffered enough, died enough, been put upon enough; we wish to reject forever our state of powerlessness." (13)

IV

The view that the State of Israel is a sign that the Jewish people has emerged from powerlessness is nowadays commonly held by Jewish historians and theologians alike. On the face of it, it stands as a refutation, perhaps even a condemnation, of Maybaum's position. Had he been a Zionist, he could have used Jewish statehood as "evidence" for his theory; now, however, he has to reject it in favour of a worldwide Diaspora. Yet, it seems that some contemporary Jewish thinkers are not too far removed from Maybaum's position although their language and frame of reference are very different. There is a sense of renewal after the Holocaust without the rejection of Orthodoxy or Israel, and without a naive affirmation of Western culture and Western Diaspora Jewry.

Irving Greenberg is a case in point. Although he shares the view that the Holocaust and the State of Israel are signs that Jewish history has entered a new, third, epoch, his description of the two earlier ones shows similarities with Maybaum's understanding of churban. In an important essay Greenberg sees the first epoch as the Biblical Age, "the event... of great redemption, the Exodus," and the second as the Rabbinic Age, "an event of great tragedy, the Destruction of the Temple." He sees the new, third, epoch, as a synthesis, "beginning under the sign of a great event of destruction, the Holocaust, and a great event of redemption, the rebirth of the State of Israel." (14)

Greenberg hails this new era as something positive and refuses to make a break between what has been - two thousand years of powerless Diaspora existence - and what is now: less than four decades of Jewish sovereignty: "Exercise of power must be accompanied by strong models and constant evocation of the memory of historic Jewish suffering and powerlessness. It is so easy to forget slavery's lessons once one is given power, but such forgetfulness leads to the unfeeling affliction of pain on others... Memory is the key to morality." (15)

Echoes of Maybaum's stance are also discernable in Greenberg's understanding of revelation in this new epoch of Jewish history. Daringly Greenberg suggests that the Holocaust could be understood as a sign that God has abrogated the Covenant with Israel - a thought, incidentally, which Christian missionaries might be tempted, for no good reason, to use for their own purposes. In another essay Greenberg asserts that, despite God's action, Jews continue to keep the Covenant: "But the overwhelming majority of survivors, far from yielding to despair, rebuilt Jewish life and took part in the assumption of power by the Jewish people... Was there ever faith like this faith?" (16) The faith of the saving remnant?

"What then happened to the Covenant?", asks Greenberg and offers this answer: "I submit that its authority was broken but the Jewish people, released from its obligations, chose voluntarily to take it on again. We are living in the age of the renewal of the Covenant. God was no longer in a position to command, but the Jewish people were so in love with the dream of redemption that it volunteered to carry on its mission." In this way the Covenant has remained "a commitment, out of faith, to achieve a final perfection of being." (17) Is the new, voluntary, Covenant consistent with the traditional Orthodox position as reflected in the codes of Jewish law, or was Maybaum right after all?

V

Maybaum died without ever reading Irving Greenberg. It is, therefore, impossible to speculate whether he would have seen any points of contact between the views of this Orthodox non-conformist and his own "error with a pedigree." But we are entitled to think of Maybaum as we marvel at the way in which the Jewish people has "picked up the pieces" after the destruction, even to the extent of tempting some of its enemies to assert, despite incontrovertible evidence to the contrary, that the Holocaust never happened. We are entitled to reflect, albeit very tentatively - with all of Katz's strictures in mind - whether the tragedy of the Holocaust has not opened up new possibilities for the Jewish people by asserting both the continuity with earlier history and the departure from it, which it may one day be legitimate to describe as progress. What Maybaum surmised, Jewish history may vindicate.

Whether that progress will come through Western civilization, in which Maybaum had all too few doubts, or in some other way is not for us to say. But to assert our faith in continued growth of Judaism after the Holocaust appears to be legitimate.

REFERENCES

1) Quoted in Forms of Prayer for Jewish Worship, Daily and Sabbath Prayerbook of the Reform Synagogues of Great Britain, London 1977.
2) New York University Press, New York and London, 1983
3) Allenson & Co. Ltd. London 1941
4) James Clarke & Co. Ltd., 1945
5) Living Judaism (A quarterly journal of the Reform Synagogues of Great Britain), Spring 1967 p.72ff.
6) Polak & Van Gennep Ltd., Amsterdam 1965
7) Vision Press, London 1962, p219f.
8) Oriel Press, London 1980.
9) op. cit p.253
10) ibid p.254
11) ibid p.250
12) ibid p.252
13) ibid p.260
14) Irving Greenberg, The Third Great Cycle in Jewish History, National Jewish Resource Center, 1981 p.3
15) ibid p.25
16) Irving Greenberg, Voluntary Covenant, National Jewish Resource Center, 1982 p.16
17) ibid p.17

THE HOLOCAUST AND THE TRANSFORMATION OF CONSERVATIVE JUDAISM IN AMERICA

Pamela S. Nadell*

The American University, Washington, D.C. 20016

The crisis emanating from a Europe dominated by Hitler paralleled an era of striking change in American Jewish life. The "midpassage of American Jewry"--to borrow Lloyd Gartner's apt phrase for the years 1929 to 1945--brought the waning of the dominance of the East European Jewish immigrant experience as the majority of Jews living in America became American-born. Facing economic insecurity and rising anti-Semitism at home, which threatened to shatter their hopes for the American dream, American Jews began casting off the old leaders and established patterns of the past to craft new, more indigenously American forms of Jewish religious, cultural, and organizational life.[1] Nowhere was this transformation more evident than in the institutions, structures, and membership of the various branches of American Judaism. Conservative Judaism was no exception. Before World War II a small and struggling movement constantly in search of a constituency and support; after, it emerged as a powerful third force, the fastest growing and most dynamic form of American Jewish religious life.[2]

Conservatism's postwar appeal resulted largely from changes in American Jewish social life. By the 1920s Conservative Judaism was firmly established as a small, primarily East Coast based branch of American Judaism. Its parent institution, New York's Jewish Theological Seminary of America, founded in 1886, had weathered near bankruptcy and undergone a successful reorganization that brought Cambridge University scholar Solomon Schechter to its helm in 1902. It had, under Schechter's successor, Cyrus Adler, dedicated a new campus and by 1930 boasted of having graduated some 200 rabbis.[3] These men were members of the Rabbinical Assembly of the Jewish Theological Seminary of America (later simply the Rabbinical Assembly), Conservatism's professional association, founded in 1901. And the majority of these rabbis served in the 220 congregations that had joined the United Synagogue of America, the movement's congregational union, since its founding in 1913.[4]

The onset of the Depression, however, both halted Conservatism's promising growth and, as the crisis deepened, took a serious toll. Conservatism's national institutions faced grave financial problems. Mounting budget deficits seriously depleted the Seminary's endowment funds. The United Synagogue was almost bankrupted as member congregations failed to pay their dues. The Rabbinical Assembly, operating on a shoestring budget, had no resources whatsoever. Meanwhile, some financially strapped Conservative congregations demanded that their rabbis take voluntary salary reductions; others failed to meet their payrolls entirely.[5]

In 1930, with unemployment looming on the horizon, some members of the Rabbinical Assembly suggested limiting the number of new Seminary graduates, a step that would in effect halt the spread of Conservative Judaism at its source. But Louis Finkelstein, then Rabbinical Assembly president and later president and chancellor of the Seminary, envisioned that the solution to the problem of too few pulpits for Seminary rabbis was the creation of new positions, not the training of fewer rabbis. Even if America's Jews did not recognize it, American Jewry had too few spiritual leaders, not too many.[6] Finkelstein's vision, even in the dark years of the Depression, for expanding, not restricting Conservative Judaism, presaged the rapid postwar growth that a renewed and vigorous Conservative Judaism would make under his leadership.

In 1940 Finkelstein inherited the mantle of Conservative leadership following the death of Seminary president, Cyrus Adler. Adler, the pre-eminent American-born Jewish leader of his day, was a man of exceptional administrative talent. Dedicated to enriching American Jewish life, he was a tireless worker, simultaneously holding the presidency of five Jewish organizations and institutions, including the American Jewish Committee (1929-40) and Dropsie College (1908-40). His leadership of the Conservative movement was no exception. Adler had been associated with the national institutions of Conservative Judaism since their inception. Invited by the Seminary's first president, his former tutor, Sabato Morais, he taught there in its early years. In 1913 he helped found and later became president of the United Synagogue of America. When the Seminary's second president, Solomon Schechter, died in 1915, Adler, the only native-born candidate for the post, succeeded him, first as acting president (1916-24) and then as president (1924-40). Nevertheless, throughout his life he avoided the term Conservative Judaism; it never even appears in his autobiography. Rather he understood Conservative Judaism to be "a general term . . . applied to those congregations which have departed somewhat in practice from the Orthodox, but not in any great extent in theory."[7]

In April 1940 Adler died. One month later Louis Finkelstein became the Seminary's fourth president (president 1940-51, chancellor 1951-72). Born in Cincinnati in 1895 and raised for much of his youth in the Brownsville section of Brooklyn, where his father, Simon Finkelstein, was rabbi of the Orthodox Congregation Oheb Shalom, Finkelstein was ordained at the Seminary in 1919, a year after completing his Ph.D. at Columbia University. In 1923 he became the first graduate of the Seminary awarded <u>hatarat horaah</u>, classical rabbinical ordination, from Seminary Professor Louis Ginzberg. In the 1920s he was both a pulpit rabbi and a part-time lecturer at the Seminary. Only in 1931, after Ginzberg insisted that if Finkelstein were not hired full-time he would encourage his former student to quit the Seminary, did the future president become a full member of the faculty.[8]

In the 1930s as registrar, assistant to the president, and then as provost, Finkelstein began to lay the groundwork for the future development of Conservative Judaism. Convinced that the logical place to seek a sustaining constituency for Conservatism's national institutions was among Conservative Jewry, he guided the Seminary in establishing, in 1939, a permanent fund-raising division, the Department of Field Service and Activities, later more aptly named the Department of Development. He then persuaded his old friend, Scranton, Pennsylvania, rabbi Max Arzt to head it. Leaving Scranton, Arzt become a rabbi without a pulpit, traveling across North America to convince Conservative Jews of the Seminary's vital role in shaping American--more precisely, Conservative--Judaism and of their obligation to sustain it in its work.

Arzt's appeal for funds to sustain the Seminary hit home at a time when American Jews came to recognize that they needed religious leaders more than ever--to help congregations mobilize for the war effort, to console mothers and fathers whose sons were sacrificed to the war, and to lead American Jewry in mourning the growing mass destruction of its brethren in Europe. His success in the dark years of the war was soon evident. Annual contributions to the Seminary had raised a bare $23,000 in 1937; at the most 2,000 donors sustained the school. But Arzt's appeals led to a dramatic rise in annual contributions to $70,000 in 1939-40, $97,000 in 1940-41, $117,000 in 1941-42, $206,000 in 1942-43, $307,000 in 1943-44, and $517,000 in 1944-45. Of equal importance, the number of contributors jumped to 43,000 by 1946.[9]

These Seminary campaigns had major repercussions for the development of Conservative Judaism. Because the Seminary controlled both the fund-raising and the allocation of these monies, channeling relatively small percentages to the Rabbinical Assembly and the United Synagogue, the campaigns succeeded in making the Seminary dominant in Conservatism's fiscal affairs, setting the stage for the paramount role it would play in expanding and reshaping the movement in the postwar years.

The growing response to Conservative Judaism's appeal at home paralleled a chord Conservative rabbis struck out in the battlefields of Europe and the Pacific. In 1940, with America yet isolated from the conflict in Europe, the Rabbinical Assembly was still trying to deal with the problems of rabbinic placement brought on by the Depression. But just as the events of December 7, 1941 mobilized American men and women for the war effort, so too it called upon the men of the Rabbinical Assembly, opening extraordinary opportunities for the Conservative rabbinate. Following America's entry into World War II, Conservative leaders, like other religious leaders, adopted plans for expediting the procurement of chaplains for the armed forces. In 1942 three Conservative rabbis served as chaplains in the armed forces. By 1944 fully one-third of its men were armed forces chaplains.[10]

This call to the chaplaincy raised manifold opportunities for the rabbinate. Within the first year of war work, chaplains were discovering what would soon become a widespread feeling among the men of the Rabbinical Assembly--the army provided a rich field for winning men back to the synagogue and to Judaism. As they counselled the homesick and disheartened, led services, and sadly arranged military funerals, the chaplains became convinced that through their close contacts with young soldiers far from home, they were laying the groundwork for Jewish religious life in postwar America.[11] At the same time Conservative rabbis sensed that war-weary Jewish soldiers and civilians welcomed, in particular, Conservatism's philosophy of "historic continuity" with the past.[12] If the chaplains were right--that when Jewish servicemen returned home, they would turn to the synagogue, especially to the Conservative synagogue -- the Conservative movement would face a severe manpower shortage in the coming years. Already, there were not enough rabbis to cope with the wartime emergency. But if these chaplains succeeded in winning soldiers back to Judaism, when these men built their own homes and synagogues, they promised significant growth for Conservative Judaism.

The rapid postwar increase in Conservative synagogue affiliations confirmed its wartime leaders projection In effect, the rising numbers of new Conservative synagogues were both a reaction to the wartime experiences of American Jewish soldiers and an indication of the maturation of American Jewry. True to "Hansen's Law" of the immigrant experience, that the third generation was not unwilling to "remember" what the second generation had striven to forget, postwar American Jews--as Will Herberg demonstrated in his classic Protestant-Catholic-Jew-- affirmed their ethnicity by affiliating with the synagogue.[13] As Jewish soldiers returned home from the war, married, began their families and joined the suburban exodus, they and their wives founded new synagogues, more often than not Conservative ones, in their new neighborhoods. Although by 1945 United Synagogue member congregations had declined to 190, by 1954 they had jumped to 448 members, a 135 per cent increase in the ten year period.[14]

The chaplains' optimism for the future development of Conservative Judaism had been shared by Seminary President Finkelstein. But Finkelstein's vision for the future of Conservative Judaism went beyond an expansion of synagogue pulpits. Finkelstein recognized that Hitler's campaign against Jewish learning had destroyed the traditional foundations of Jewish religious life. The obliteration of the leading rabbinical seminaries of Central and Eastern Europe meant an end to the flow of the rabbis, scholars, and students, who in the past had largely sustained American Judaism. As the extent of the Nazi persecution of the Jews unfolded, it became evident that the massacre of 6,000,000 European Jews left American Jewry, by default, the central Jewish community in the world. Finkelstein laid bold plans for this Jewry's response to what he called the "spiritual crisis of world Judaism."[15] To guide American Jewry to rise to the challenges of its new position, he undertook a transformation of the central institution of Conservative Judaism, the Seminary.

For Finkelstein the essential commandment of Judaism was that only through study would all Jews, not just the scholars, achieve the understanding necessary to apply the norms of Torah to life in a world constantly in flux. Because the primacy of study lay at the heart of his vision of Judaism, the center of Conservatism had to be a school, namely the Seminary. He believed that the Conservative movement could only be as strong as the Seminary, asserting to his colleagues in the Rabbinical Assembly, "Don't deceive yourself . . . Your congregations are no stronger than the Seminary."[16] By virtue of its control over the movement's purse strings, and because of Finkelstein's influential personality and the prestige of the faculty, the Seminary, led by Finkelstein, triumphed as the sovereign power in the Conservative movement and reasserted--after the stasis of the Depression--its status as the fountainhead of Conservative Judaism.

Securing the Seminary's finances allowed for its transformation from a tiny school for the training of rabbis and teachers into a major multidimensional institution, nationally and even internationally prominent in Jewish and interfaith affairs. In a special conference held in 1946 Finkelstein publicly outlined the postwar plans forged in his early years as president. First, as Conservatism's chaplains had forseen, the Seminary would have to produce large numbers of rabbis for American and even for world Judaism to organize and staff the hundreds of new congregations expected to spring up in the coming years. It would also have to train large numbers of educators. The Seminary's Teachers Institute, established in 1909 under the direction of the rabbinical school's most controversial graduate, the founder of the Reconstructionist movement, Mordecai M. Kaplan, had been greatly weakened by the Depression and then by the diversion of young men and women to the war effort. It graduated only two students in 1946. But Finkelstein knew that new Conservative synagogues and their schools would need 2,000 new teachers. Educating large numbers meant the Seminary would have to expand its faculty, add to its library, which had suffered during the Depression, and fund more scholarships. Furthermore, it should educate not only rabbis and teachers but also cantors, scholars, and Jewish social workers. Because the New York school could not possibly do this job alone, the Conservative movement would have to establish new Seminary colleges throughout North America. In the postwar world the Seminary must also enter fields of service normally outside the purview of a theological school. It must reach out to Jewish laity by enriching their adult education programs, hosting summer retreats, expanding its museum, and producing radio shows. It must engage in interfaith dialogue and assert its moral leadership in ethical affairs to teach a world that had once gone mad never to do so again.[17] What is most remarkable is not the scope of Finkelstein's vision but the fact that he accomplished so much of what he set out to do.

During the war, Conservative rabbis and administrators had come to realize that they were going to have to nurture future leaders of the movement from within its own ranks. Until the war most Seminary students had been raised outside Conservative congregations; many were born in Eastern Europe. But the tragedy taking place there meant that the movement could no longer rely upon others to fill its ranks, nor should it. Consequently, in the early postwar period Conservative leaders created new programs designed to recruit their future leaders from within. Working closely with rabbis and their congregations, the Teachers Institute, led by Moshe Davis, who became dean (1946-50) following Kaplan's resignation from that post in 1946, turned its attention to high school education. It established the Leadership Training Fellowship (1946), a national Conservative high school that had been Kaplan's idea; the network of Ramah Camps (1947); and the Prozdor High School (1951). In each, faculty, rabbis, and teachers worked with select groups of teens, encouraging the best and the brightest to enter the Seminary, where they would embark upon careers as rabbis, teachers, and leaders of American, and especially of Conservative, Jewry.[18]

So that these students would continue their intensive Jewish education in college, the Seminary College of Jewish Studies established a joint program with Columbia University in 1953. Now students could simultaneously earn two degrees, a Bachelor of Religious Education and a Bachelor of Arts.

As anticipated, the composition of the Seminary student body changed in these years. By the late 1950's rabbinical students were by and large American born and increasingly came from Conservative homes. These students had good secular educations but were not as Jewishly well prepared as their predecessors, who had often been trained in European and American yeshivot. Since the core of the curriculum remained the texts of Jewish tradition--with Talmud assigned more hours per week than any other subject--the period of rabbinic training gradually increased from four to five and even six years.[19] Transforming young men, fresh out of college, into rabbis remained the raison d'etre of the school. Between 1940 and 1972, Finkelstein presided over the ordination of 662 men, half of all the Conservative rabbis ordained in the Seminary's first century.[20]

At the student and faculty breakfasts that opened each academic year, Finkelstein told the future rabbis, "If anyone asks you why you came to the Seminary, your answer should be that you 'came to be in the presence of great men.'"[21] The great men of the faculty that Finkelstein assembled included Talmud Professor Saul Lieberman (1940-83), also dean of the Rabbinical School and rector and, following Louis Ginzberg's death in 1953, Conservatism's reigning halachic expert; and Abraham Joshua Heschel, a charismatic professor of Jewish ethics and mysticism (1945-72), philosopher and social activist. These men, in essence, were the last of the generation of European-born scholars, educated in the academies of Jewish tradition (as well as the European university), to reach America's shores.

Consequently, because American Jewry could no longer turn to Europe for its scholasticism, Finkelstein determined to make the Seminary a center for the graduate training of Judaic scholars. Since its early days the Seminary had trained men to be scholars, for after all that was what a rabbi was. Some Seminary graduates -- like Charles Eliezer Hillel Kauvar at the University of Denver and Herman Hailperin at the University of Pittsburgh and Duquesne University -- had even introduced Jewish studies courses to the university classroom. In fact, since the nineteenth century the introduction of Jewish studies into the university curriculum had been one of the goals of Wissenschaft des Judentums, the movement for the Scientific Study of Judaism, and the Seminary claimed to be the American heir to that tradition. Yet by 1940, there were only two full-time faculty teaching Jewish studies in American universities. Still Finkelstein recognized that the time was ripe for the development of Jewish studies in the secular university, and he set out to make the Seminary the chief institution training the first generation of American professors of Judaica. Actively recruiting gifted undergraduates in the late 1950's and 1960's, he promised them curricula to allow those intending to be academicians, not rabbis, to specialize in Bible, Talmud, or Jewish history.[22] The Seminary thus played a major role in training the first generation of American-born, university Judaic scholars. Its graduates included the prolific author Jacob Neusner, Brown University Professor of Religious and Judaic Studies, and the future chancellors of the Seminary, the historians Gerson Cohen and Ismar Schorsch. Through their writings and their teaching these men--and women--enhanced the prestige of the Seminary and carried forth Conservatism's--and Finkelstein's--message of the primacy of study and scholarship in Jewish life to tens of thousands whom they might otherwise never have reached.

Now the Seminary's professional education of Jewish leaders extended to training cantors. The Seminary's charter had allowed for the awarding of the diploma of hazzan, certifying men as cantors. Yet only three graduates of the early school and but one between 1918 and 1939 had been awarded that diploma. With the destruction of the Jewish communities of Europe, the informal settings in which most American cantors had prepared for their careers no longer existed. At the same time American cantors required more formal education as their role in synagogue evolved from that of performer to integral member of the staff in charge of all music and many educational programs of the congregation. In 1947 Conservative cantors organized the Cantors Assembly. Aware that the Reform movement's Hebrew Union College planned to establish a professional cantorial school, these men encouraged the Seminary to create its own setting for the training of Conservative hazzanim, the Cantors Institute-Seminary College of Jewish Music (1952).[23]

But Finkelstein believed that the Seminary must educate more than Jewish leaders and professionals; it was also responsible for the education of Conservative laity. Proclaiming that lifelong learning is an integral part of what it means to be a Jew, the Seminary sponsored a host of adult education ventures, including the National Academy for Adult Jewish Studies (1941), and expanded its Museum of Jewish Ceremonial Objects into the Jewish Museum when, in 1947, it moved out of the Seminary to its spacious new home in what had been the Warburg Mansion on Fifth Avenue. To reach even wider audiences, Finkelstein, working with representatives of the Reform and Orthodox movements, launched the NBC-radio program the Eternal Light (1944) and the NBC-television program Frontiers of Faith (1951). Utilizing a dramatic rather than a documentary format, both series depicted the richness of Jewish tradition.[24]

The Seminary's mission extended even further. Not only must it educate Jews, it must also gather together scholars and clergy of all faiths to explore the moral, ethical, social, and technological issues confronting moderns. To encourage dialogue, Finkelstein established several institutes and conferences, including the Institute for Religious and Social Studies (1938); the Conference on Science, Philosophy, and Religion in the Relation to the Democratic Way of Life (1940), which published several volumes of its proceedings;

the World Brotherhood Movement (1955); and the Herbert H. Lehman Institute of Ethics (1958). While these conferences reflected the conviction that the horrors of the Holocaust and the responsibilities of living in the nuclear age held lessons for all, they also reflected one of the cardinal tenets of Conservative Judaism: its celebration of the American democratic tradition which had made the United States into a haven for American Jewry and a home for Conservative Judaism.

The expansion of the Seminary endeavors led to a concomitant expansion beyond New York. In 1947 the Los Angeles branch of the Seminary, the University of Judaism was established as the center for Conservative Jewish life in the West. Next Seminary leaders guided their graduate Rabbi Marshall Meyer in founding the Seminario Rabinico Latino-Americano in Argentina, a preparatory school for training Spanish-speaking rabbis who would conclude their studies in New York.[25]

Then the Seminary enhanced its presence in Israel. The school had had a close association with Zionism since its early days. Schechter's public support of Zionism had merely affirmed this stance. Since then Conservative rabbis and their congregations had put the movement on the map as staunchly Zionist. In the 1930's the United Synagogue built the Yeshurun Synagogue in Jerusalem. Although Finkelstein resisted Israeli Prime Minister Ben Gurion's call to transplant the school to the new state, the Seminary did build the American Student Center at Neve Schechter in Jerusalem. Completed in 1962, this eventually became the home for a year for all rabbinical students.[26]

The extraordinary expansion in Seminary activities, scope, size, and ambitions forced an administrative reorganization which made Finkelstein the chancellor of the Seminary in 1951. His centralization of the forces of Conservatism, at the same time that synagogue affiliations made it the largest denomination of American Judaism, made him more powerful than any single individual in the movement since Solomon Schechter. In the era when American religious society was divided into Protestant, Catholic, and Jew, Finkelstein, featured in 1951 on the cover of Time magazine, became one of the most widely known Jewish religious leaders of his day.

In the wake of the Holocaust and the return to religion evidenced in postwar America, American Judaism underwent a transformation. The influx of more traditional refugees revitalized American Orthodoxy. The suburban exodus of the postwar years and the subsequent boom in synagogue founding and building strengthened an already well-established Reform movement and dramatically reshaped American Conservatism into a significant third force in what was then the triumverate of American Jewish religious life. At the same time, as the institutions of higher Jewish learning in Europe lay in ruins, the Jewish Theological Seminary of America, under the vigorous leadership of Louis Finkelstein, rose to meet the challenges of postwar Jewish life. True to its motto, "and the bush was not consumed," Seminary leaders acted to ensure that the fires of Jewish learning had not been consumed by the Holocaust. Although Jewish learning had been extinguished in Europe, the postwar transformation of the Seminary guaranteed that its torch blazed bright in America, lighting the way for Conservative rabbis and congregants, students and scholars, and the world.

NOTES

This paper is based on my forthcoming book, Conservative Judaism in America: A Biographical Dictionary and Sourcebook, to be published by Greenwood Press (Westport, Conn.) in August 1988.

1 Lloyd P. Gartner, "The Midpassage of American Jewry," in The American Jewish Experience, ed. Jonathan D. Sarna (New York, 1986), pp. 224-33.

2 The major works on the development of Conservative Judaism are the following: Cyrus Adler, ed., Jewish Theological Seminary of America: Semi-Centennial Volume (New York, 1939); Marshall Sklare, Conservative Judaism: An American Religious Movement (1955; 2nd ed., Glencoe, Ill., 1972); Herbert Parzen, Architects of Conservative Judaism (New York, 1964); Moshe Davis, The Emergence of Conservative Judaism: The Historical School in Nineteenth-Century America (Philadelphia, 1965); Herbert Rosenblum, Conservative Judaism: A Contemporary History (New York, 1983); Marc Lee Raphael, Profiles in American Judaism: The Reform, Conservative, Orthodox, and Reconstructionist Traditions in Historical

Perspective (San Francisco, 1984); Abraham J. Karp, "A Century of Conservative Judaism in the United States," American Jewish Year Book vol. 86 (New York, 1986).

3 Jewish Theological Seminary, Rabbinical Department Lists.

4 United Synagogue Recorder 7, 3 (July 1927), p. 7.

5 On the impact of the Depression on synagogues, see e.g. Marc Lee Raphael, Jews and Judaism in a Midwestern Community: Columbus, Ohio, 1840-1975 (Columbus, Ohio, 1979), pp. 266-67; William Toll, The Making of an Ethnic Middle Class: Portland Jewry over Four Generations (Albany, New York, 1982), pp. 177-80; The Anshe Emet Synagogue, 1873-1973 (Chicago, n.d.), p. 16; on dues, see Proceedings of the Rabbinical Assembly 1955 (hereafter PRA), vol. 19, pp. 200-03. Lucy Dawidowicz describes how the Jackson Heights Jewish Center paid a token twenty-five dollars annual dues to the United Synagogue, rather than the $250 assessed; "Middle-Class Judaism," in her The Jewish Presence: Essays in Identity and History (New York, 1977), p. 79.

6 Louis Finkelstein, "Presidential Address: The Present and Future of Traditional Judaism in America," PRA 1930 vol. 4, pp. 9-19, esp. pp. 14-15.

7 Cyrus Adler, Lectures, Selected Papers, Addresses (Philadelphia, 1933), p. 251. On Adler, see his memoirs, I Have Considered the Days (Philadelphia, 1941); Selected Letters of Cyrus Adler, ed. Ira Robinson (Philadelphia, 1985); Abraham A. Neuman, Cyrus Adler: A Biographical Sketch (Philadelphia, 1942).

8 Eli Ginzberg, Keeper of the Law: Louis Ginzberg (Philadelphia, 1966), p. 139. On Finkelstein, see the biographical entry in Pamela S. Nadell, Conservative Judaism.

9 Max Arzt, "Conservative Judaism Comes of Age," PRA 1975 vol. 37, pp. 329-30; "Symposium: The Seminary Expansion Program," PRA 1944 vol. 8, pp. 302-22; Figures, Max D. Klein, "Seminary Campaign Committee," PRA 1945 vol. 9, pp. 17-18; PRA 1946 vol. 10, p. 207.

10 PRA 1942 vol. 8, pp. 56-60; PRA 1943 vol. 8, p. 164; PRA 1944 vol. 8, p. 282.

11 Harry Nelson, "A Chaplain's Pulpit," PRA 1943, vol. 8, pp. 200-06; Isaac Klein, The Anguish and the Ecstasy of a Jewish Chaplain (New York, 1974), esp. pp. 40-48.

12 Klein, p. 43; Louis Levitsky, "Spiritual Leadership in the Postwar World," PRA 1944 vol. 8, pp. 281-97, esp. pp. 285-87.

13 Hansen discussed in Will Herberg, Protestant-Catholic-Jew: An Essay in American Religious Sociology (1955; rev. ed., Garden City, New York, 1960), pp. 186-89.

14 On the number of congregations, see PRA 1955 vol. 19, pp. 200-03. I am indebted to Professor Norman Mirsky for drawing my attention to contemporary developments with the Reform movement's Union of American Hebrew Congregations. In 1950 under its president, Rabbi Maurice Eisendrath, the UAHC relocated its headquarters to New York City. The move reflected a decisive shift in the development of the UAHC which determined to reach out to the children of the East European immigrants forming new congregations in the postwar era to see if they would affiliate with Reform Judaism. This activity brought the UAHC into direct competition with the United Synagogue for synagogue affiliates. In 1947 the UAHC counted 364 members; in 1955, 520, a net increase of 156 compared to a net increase of 258 in the Conservative movement for roughly the same period; figures, Raphael, Profiles, p. 197.

15 Louis Finkelstein, "The Spiritual Crisis of World Judaism," News of the United Synagogue of America 2, 3 (April 1946), p. 4.

16 "Our Expansion Program -- A Revaluation," PRA 1946 vol. 10, pp. 205-35, p. 234.

17 Finkelstein, "Spiritual Crisis;" Teacher's Institute figures, Shuly Rubin Schwartz, "Ramah -- The Early Years, 1947-52," (M.A. thesis, Jewish Theological Seminary of America, 1976), p. 5.

18 On the changing backgrounds of Conservative rabbis, see Arthur Hertzberg, "The Conservative Rabbinate: A Sociological Study," in Essays in Jewish Life and Thought: Presented in Honor of Salo Wittmayer Baron, ed. Joseph Blau et al. (New York: 1959), pp. 309-32; on the impact of the recruitment programs, see Sylvia Ettenberg, "The Rabbi -- A Force in a Program for Recruiting Teachers," PRA 1956 vol. 20, pp. 223-28.

19 Eli Ginzberg, "Manpower for Conservative Judaism," PRA 1960 vol. 24, pp. 19-31; New York Times 4 Dec. 1958, p. 34.

20 Seminary, Rabbinical Department Lists; "Reports of the Membership Committee," PRA 1959-73 vols. 23-35.

21 Finkelstein, cited by Bernard Mandelbaum, "Letter to the Editor," Conservative Judaism, 39, 2 (Winter 1986-87), pp. 114-15.

22 PRA 1960 vol. 24, pp. 61-62.

23 Marjorie Wyler, "Cantors Institute: The First Twenty-five years," United Synagogue Review 32, 1 (Fall 1979), p. 6.

24 On adult education in the Conservative movement, see Simon Noveck and Lily Edelman,

"The Laymen's Institutes: An Adventure in Jewish Living," in Roads to Jewish Survival, ed. Milton Berger et al. (New York, 1967), pp. 270-71; Marjorie G. Wyler, "The Eternal Light: Judaism on the Airwaves," Conservative Judaism, 39, 2 (Winter 1986-87), pp. 18-22.

25 On the University of Judaism, see its publication Direction.

26 Louis Finkelstein, "The Achievement of the Rabbinical Assembly," PRA 1975 vol. 37, p. 325.

27 Time, 15 October 1951.

THE IMPACT OF THE HOLOCAUST ON ISRAELI SOCIETY AND ISRAELI EDUCATION(1)

Chaim SCHATZKER

Haifa University

ABSTRACT

For almost twenty years following the Second World War, educational literature in Israel did not deal with the problem of teaching the Holocaust. It was only just before and during the Eichmann trial that we were witness to a wave of publications dealing with the Holocaust as a didactic-educational problem. There was also a marked rise in publications following the Six Day War and the Yom Kippur War. Four trends characterized the approach to the Holocaust during the first period: (a) The demonization of the Holocaust operation and its executors (b) A process of psychological repression. (c) Wounded national pride. (d) An overcompensation in the form of sacral, ritual, and symbolic expressions. As a reaction to the educational shortcomings of those trends, a following second period adapted the "instrumental function" in teaching the Holocaust, which thereby tried to achieve educational, civic, democratic, moral, historical, national and general humanistic-universal aims. Influenced by the political events of the last years, a new "existential" approach seems to be gaining ground, which characterizes the feelings of certain parts of Israeli society.

KEYWORDS

Demonization, repression, apologetics, symbolic expression, "instrumental function", "existential approach".

For almost twenty years following the Holocaust, educational literature in Israel did not deal with the problem of its teaching. These were the years in which the extent and consequences of the Holocaust were revealed - thousands of books, witness reports, trial protocols and sources of all kinds were published. These years also witnessed the immigration to Israel of Holocaust survivors and their absorption within the country. They were also years of war and struggle for independence and the existence of the new State. Yet, the topic of the Holocaust was hardly broached in educational discussions and was almost not at all integrated as a unique and clearly defined component in the school system and its curricula.

Historical treatment of what has become known as the "Holocaust" has been greatly influenced by the fact that the Yishuv (Jewish community in Eretz Israel) upon hearing the news of the Holocaust, which began to reach the public at large at the end of World War II and which, until then, had either not been known about or did not seem to have penetrated public consciousness, suffered a traumatic experience which rocked the very core of its being. People failed to grasp the situation from a rational point of view. For this reason, the Holocaust has always been perceived as a "catastrophe" and not as a *continuous historical process* lending itself to research through historical, rational and causative reasoning. This has had weighty implications with regard to both our lives and attitudes to the Holocaust - implications which have determined four trends among Israeli society in its approach to and in the treatment of the subject in Education. These trends are:

a) The *demonization* of the Holocaust operation and its executors, similar to the Middle Ages conception of Satan, as the source and essence of all evil - an entity which man fears, rejects, hates, despises and constantly fights, but which remains beyond his comprehension and perception.

b) The *incomprehensibility* of the Holocaust, the vain efforts of some survivors to transfer the dimensions of that "other planet" to those who have not physically experienced it, their desperate drive to establish the Holocaust as a new cornerstone and criterion of mankind and the human condition (to the same extent understandable as impossible) have all led to a lack of communication between the lonely, forlorn community of survivors and their own children and the new generation. That indefinable and incomprehensible element which causes anxiety and negates the very essence of self-existence, has, despite its continuous existential presence, not been included as an inherent part of Israeli life - or its school curriculum - but had undergone a process of psychological repression.

c) The blow to the national and human pride of the Jewish nation, inflicted by the murder of one third of its people, hardened the survivors against any logical and rational argumentation on the subject of the Holocaust. The nagging problem of *wounded national pride* has, more than any other factor, constituted the focal point of interest and determined the problems of text books, professional and didactic literature and the instruction given in the classroom over a long period of time. Since the very essence of the Holocaust has not penetrated the national consciousness as a sequence of events related to causes conditioned by circumstances, the problem of Jewish resistance during the Holocaust has not been relayed as a realistic reaction to the situation but as a stereotype form of behavior which involved national disgrace and dishonor and and has given rise to such questions as: "Why didn't they emigrate?", "Why didn't they defend themselves?", and "Why did they go like sheep to the slaughter?". A generation of teachers and educators has been unsuccessfully struggling with these questions since the answers, convincing as they might be, were regarded by the students as apologies.

d) The repressed events of the Holocaust which were banished from daily life found compensation and even *overcompensation* in the deep emotional and spiritual reaction of Israeli society, which was conveyed on sacral-ritual memorial days and ceremonies and in symbolic expressions of mourning and solidarity with the victims. For many years, Israeli society gave expression to the Holocaust in memorial ceremonies and symbols rather than in instruction, in the perpetuation of the memory of the victims rather than in education, and in institutions such as Yad Vaschem, Kibbutz Yad Mordechai and Kibbutz Lochame Hagetta'ot rather than in University faculties and the school curriculum.

These four trends - each one understandable on its own - constituted an obstacle to any organized learning process aspiring to achieve rational ends through controlled means, guided by considerations relating to professional didactics and educational psychology. The need thereof, however, was demonstrated in all its severity by the dramatic turning point of the Eichmann trial in 1961. It was only just before and during that trial that we were witness to a wave of publications dealing with the Holocaust as a didactic-educational problem (2). Educators suddenly found themselves sharing in common the surprising discovery that the Israeli educational system had not fulfilled its duty in teaching the Holocaust, thus leaving the

Israeli students unprepared for the confrontation with the problems and revelations raised by the trial.

Since the Eichmann trial, educational literature has been constantly dealing with the topic (3), with a marked rise in publications following the Six Day War and the Yom Kippur War (4). Among the latest wave of publications are a considerable number of tested and fully articulated study programmes and teachers' extension courses which greatly surpass those of former years in both scope and frequency of appearance, as well as in other factors.

All these newer publications and curricula were based on two components: (a) the contemporary discoveries and conclusions of Holocaust research and (b) the various ideologies and world views within Israeli society, as well as changes in the society brought about by the passage of time. These publications were also influenced by innovations in the field of curriculum research and planning which has developed considerably during the last decade.

Above all, curriculum planners were determined to overcome the educational shortcomings resulting from the four, above mentioned, irrational trends within Israeli society in its approach to the Holocaust:

a) The demonizing trend, stemming from conceptual helplessness in the face of the grimness of the Nazi phenomenon, is not only at odds with scientific research and scientific attitude, but poses an obstacle to our deriving any possible lessons or conclusions from the events of the period. Since one cannot draw an analogy between Satan and man, any demonization is in the nature of a fixation on evil in an external object instead of a search for it in the soul of man. One must understand the *origin* of evil, its *structures* and *mechanism* and the atmosphere in which it thrives and acts, so as to frustrate any such phenomenon in the future, through a system of education which derives its orientation, in part, from past mistakes and blunders. If any lesson is to be learned from the Holocaust, there is no sense in blaming its execution on demonic monsters. For then it becomes both impossible and irrelevant to underline a *common human approach* to their actions. Placing Nazis out of the common human condition is precisely the obverse side of the Nazi's attitude towards Jews.

b) It lies in the nature of the process of psychological repression that what is repressed is condemned to return in a less controlled and therefore more dangerous way in times of crisis, weakness and shaken self-assurance, especially if it is applied to foreign policy and political life. It seems that new traumatic experiences, arising in times of stress and danger like the Eichmann trial, the days of tension which anticipated the outbreak of the Six Day War, the trauma of the Yom Kippur War as well as increasing economic and political difficulties, reversed the repression process, causing the repressed material to suddenly resurface. Thus the Holocaust changes from a symbol to a factor of reality, influencing consciousness and reactions in times of crisis, perplexity and desolation.

c) Questions like "Why did they go like sheep to the slaughter?" resulting from wounded national pride, have often become the primary center of any discussion on subjects connected with instruction concerning the Holocaust, shifting the focus from other, far more important issues. It seems that the addition of the word "Gevura" (heroism) to "Schoa" (Holocaust) has not contributed a great deal to Holocaust education. It focuses the schoolroom discussions even more upon Jewish Resistance during the Holocaust, with the teachers being pushed into a tight corner by students who assume the dual role of prosecutor and judge in matters which are totally beyond their emphatic judgment and with which they cannot possibly identify. Such discussions usually result in each side emerging with renewed belief in his own argument. Very rarely does a change in position and attitude occur as a result of another's relevant or practical arguments. This complication has long constituted the most widespread motif in the didactic literature dealing with the subject. Only the perplexity and shaken self-assurance which were inflicted on Israel in recent years brought about a mental readiness and a greater emphatic ability on the part of students to delve into the problematics of Jewish resistance and to put the term "resistance" into a broader, more spiritual context.

d) Without detracting from the importance of memorial ceremonies and symbols, their value should also be considered in terms of the psychology of learning. The various components of the learning process, such as cognition, perception, analysis, causality connections, conceptualization, generalization and deduction, differ from the psychological mechanism rooted in memorial days and ceremonies. By their very nature, the latter are not analytical processes. Their purpose is rather to induce a sense of sublimation amid the pain and the grief, thus raising the pain and the mourning to a metaphysical experience, beyond time and place, to enable man to come to terms with fate, often inexplicable and uncompromising, over which he has no control, yet which he must face and live with, aware of and wondering at the helplessness of his mere mortality. Both teaching processes and memorial ceremonies play essential parts in the life of men, societies and nations, but they are not identical. To confuse these two trends would be to harm them both; one cannot be substituted for the other. For a long time, however, the Israeli school system has done just this. The conception of sober teaching methods aiming at and expecting the awakening of emotions, feelings and attitudes as a concomitant effect and as a result of an internalized process taking place within the students was rejected, perhaps because of the dissatisfaction born of impatience with awaiting the emotional response to the relevant study process. Also perhaps, *it could not have been expected from a generation of teachers who have been personally involved in many cases* and who were being dragged at each and every step of teaching the Holocaust into the depth of bitter and dark memories, accusations and judgements. Instead, a dubious concept of "*emotional study*" was adopted, which perceived emotion as the cornerstone, aim, motivation, content and method of teaching the Holocaust. The further we moved away from the end of World War II, the more the ineffectiveness of this concept became obvious, both in the learning process as well as in the emotional responses it was supposed to engender - especially when applied to a generation of students which does not know what it is supposed to remember and with what it is supposed to identify emotionally.

The reaction to those educational and didactical shortcomings characterized the second period of Israeli education in grappling with the Holocaust.

The student rather than the survivors and their unpenetrable and untransferrable world of memories, the future rather than the past, instructing rather than commemorating, sober teaching methods rather than the former sacral-ritual ceremonies, universal and not only Jewish elements stood now as the focus of Israeli education in grappling with the Holocaust. These were characteristics of the time in which the first hopeful steps of the new state of Israel toward a full integration in the international community, as an equal and normal member, seemed to have been unexpectedly successful. Despite all difficulties, new avenues of Jewish history in harmony with other nations seemed to lie open.

What most of the relevant publications, curricula and educational efforts in the second period had in common was labelled the "instrumental function" of teaching the Holocaust.

Since one does not teach the events of the Holocaust just to tell the story, or to commemorate it in a sacral-ritual way, but rather to achieve educational, civic, democratic, moral, historical, national and general humanistic aims, the function of the teaching turned accordingly from an end in itself into a means or an instrument for education. By studying the Holocaust, the students should be made aware of and sensitive to those implicit structures and mechanisms, and thereby change their attitudes, reactions and personality and be better prepared to face the future. It seems that this approach too, by being stretched to its utmost limits, was brought in many cases to a point of absurdity. The danger exists that by being used by the various disciplines for their own ends, the Holocaust would lose its substance and unique definition. The result, in educational experience, has been in many cases a highly abstracted teaching of the subject, sometimes teaching it without Jews, sometimes teaching it without the Holocaust. The facts were often neglected in order to achieve some trivial educational objectives which could have been achieved just as well - and in cases like moral education certainly better - by another, less tremendous event or pattern of human or social behaviour.

By trying to make the Holocaust understandable, to shape it in accordance with our own and our student's capabilities in order to explain it and to derive educational lessons, values and orientations therefrom, there is a danger that it will be dwarfed, diminished and will lose its unique significance. Thus, "Holocaust" and what it stands for would be simply explained away; instead of making students sensitive to the abnormalities of the Holocaust, they would get used to it and learn to regard it as *one other possible way of human and social behaviour*.

It was perhaps due to the shortcomings of the "instrumental approach" to the Holocaust, that we are witness to some new directions in its treatment in Israeli education in recent years. None of the curricula which have been elaborated - all of them instrumental in some way or another (5) - has been entirely adopted by the Ministry of Education. The committee appointed by the Ministry to elaborate outlines for an agreed curriculum, which became necessary after the teaching of the Holocaust had been made compulsory in all secondary schools, could not reach any consensus and dispersed after a few sessions without accomplishing its task. A third trend, which might be called the *"existential approach"*, still unarticulated, but significant and characteristic for contemporary Israeli society, seems to have gained ground in influencing the teaching of the Holocaust.

This "existential" approach criticised the former "instrumental" approach as being too one sided, disciplinary, abstract, universal and sophisticated, thus missing the very core of the Holocaust, i.e. the *existential struggle of Jews caught up in an inhuman, dehumanizing situation, facing persecution, the conditions of the Ghetto and the machinery of death*.

By using interdisciplinary methods, including literature and, above all, testimonies of survivors who have not talked for years and seem to have now found more willing listeners, this approach intends to confront the student with the *horror*, to evoke in him a direct identification with the traumatic experience of the reality of Holocaust, and the Jewish world which was destroyed and lost (6).

It is hard to say what this approach hopes to achieve through such direct identification with the horror and what its motives are. Is it due to a certain affinity between the present situation of Israel, its political and economic problems and its existential uncertainty? Or is it the rapid growth of a violent international neo-nazi, antisemitic and antizionist movement, that we feel that we again are experiencing that inherent ancient historical law, that "all are always against us", and are therefore looking for our existential roots in the Holocaust?

Is it perhaps the hidden hope of political and religious extremists to strengthen their arguments through identification with the Holocaust? Or is it just one more revelation of a world wide phenomenon, i.e. turning the Holocaust into a symbol of the "condition humaine" of our time, characterized by the Vietnam War, Biafra, Cambodia, the energy crisis, unsolved economic and social problems, uncertainly and growing anxiety regarding the future, a phenomenon which was illustrated by the world-wide interest and reactions to the TV series on the Holocaust?

Since the present and its unsettled problems motivated this new interest in the Holocaust, there seems to be no other topic so saturated with unresolved emotions and spiritual conflicts, with self-accusation, accusation of others and the necessity for defensiveness and apologetics that demands a willingness to either cope with or repress the Holocaust.

NOTES

1. Other publications of the author on this subject are:

Chaim Schatzker (1977). "Das Schicksal des europaischen Judentums in Dritten Reich als didaktisches Problem in der israelischen Schule", in *Neue Sammlung, Zeitschrift fur Erziehung und Gesellschaft*, 17, Jan/Feb. Heft 1 Gottingen.

Chaim Schatzker (1980). "Formation vs. information, trends in Holocaust education in Israel, in *Forum on Jewish People, Zionism and Israel*.

Chaim Schatzker (1980). "The teaching of the Holocaust, dilemmas and Considerations, in *The Annals of the American Academy of Political and Social Science*, 450, July.

2. A selection from the many publications:

The Ministry of Education and Culture 1961, *Hora'at Haschoa B'beit Sefer, Diyunim Veiyyunim*, Arieh Bauminger 1961. "Haschoa V'hameri B'eney Haroar Hajisraeli", in Hachinuch.

Jisrael Gutmann (1961). Haschoa V'hameri, Nosse Limudi, Hakibbutz Haartzi, Haschomer Hazair.

Michael Hendel (1962). "L'horaat Haschoa V'hameri," in *Urim*.

Eliezer Jeruschalmi (1962). "Al Tochnit Haschoa," in *Maalot*.

Fredka Mazja (1961). "Ba'ayot Hahora'a schel T'kufat Haschoa," in *Alon Hachonchut*.

Sara Nischmit (1961). *L'toldot Haschoa V'hameri*, Hakibbutz Hameuchad.

Sara Nischmit (1962). "Limud Korot Haschoa, Ma V'kezad," in *Urim*.

Chaim Schatzker (1961). "Ba'ayot Didaktiyot B'horaat Haschoa," in *Yedion L'more L'historia*.

S.N. Herman, Y. Peres and E. Yuchtmann (1965). "Reactions to the Eichmann trial in Israel - A study in high involvement" in *Scripta Hierosolymitae*.

3. The following should be noted:

Gideon Hausner (1963). *Haschoa B'chinuch Hanoar*. S. Cohen (1964). "Arachim Chinuchiyim B'limud Nosse Haschoa," in Urim.

Fredka Mazja (1968). "L'bayat Hora'at T'kufat Haschoa V'likcha," in *Hachinuch*.

Arye Menscher (1965). "L'hora'at Hashoa V'hagewura," in *Hed Hachinuch*.

Chaim Schatzker (1968). Bayot Didaktiyot B'hora'at Haschoa, *Hachewra L'chinuch*.

Yad Vaschem (1969). *Hora'at Haschoa B'bet Hassefer Halichon*.

The Ministry of Education and Culture (1966). *Yom Haschoa V'hagewura*.

4. See for example:

Zvi Bachrach (1976). "Haschoa K'baya Historit," in *Ma'alot*.

H. Schadmi (1975). "Implikatiot Chinuchiot B'hora'at Haschoa, in *Hachinuch*.

5. See: Chaim Schatzker, Project Director, *Antisemitism and Holocaust*, 1979, Arye Carmon, Hashoa 1980.

6. Indication for this approach might be found in a still unpublished project which was carried out by a number of teachers in Jerusalem, 1979/80 under the auspices of some circles within the Ministry of Education and Culture and some circles within Yad-Vaschem.

Further also in the teaching methods of special centers for teaching the Holocaust, which have been established in "Massuah" and in "Beith Lochame Hagetaoth", in the visiting program of Israeli younsters in Auschwitz and in many programs of the Israeli Television.

CONCEPTS OF SUFFERING

DEBORAH SCHECHTERMAN

Oxford Centre for Postgraduate Hebrew Studies, Yarnton Manor, Yarnton, Oxford OX5 1PY

DEDICATION

In memory of my mother-in-law

Sarah bat Pinhas leveit Shuchman

the sole survivor of her family which was swept away in the Holocaust

According to a report, published in 1968, of an international conference which took place in "Yad Vashem" in Jerusalem, one of the scholars said, casually, that the Jewish faith received a severe blow in the Holocaust.(1) A similar event happened at a more recent meeting on the Holocaust that took place in Tel-Aviv in 1987.(2)

I was disturbed. Knowing neither of any publication of systematic research on faith and the Holocaust, nor about any other attempt to examine this subject, I wondered: why should various scholars, expert in their own scientific fields, express such definite ideas on a subject which has never gained proper scholarly attention? In fact, it is in an attempt to clarify the bases of those views that this study will analyse questions within the field called philosophy of religion by examining the concepts of suffering that emerged from the very occurrence of the Holocaust.(3)

This specific study, devoted to the concepts of suffering, will focus here on one of the manuscripts from the Archive of Photography of Beit Lohamei Ha-Geta'ot, the sigla of which is ד׳ 11711 Bergen-Belsen.(4) It is an undated document, written in Hebrew, which contains nine lines. Its first line reads: "Lifnei akhilat hamez yomar be-khavanat ha-lev". The author is not named, nor is the copyist, which may well be the author himself. However, perusal of the manuscript itself clearly indicates that it is a prayer composed for Pessah, Passover, in the light of the special circumstances in the Nazi camps, when even the basic food for day-by-day use was not available. When it came to Pessah, in order to survive, it was impossible to avoid eating hamez, leavened food. Thus it is a prayer one should say before eating hamez while it is Pessah, and it is entitled, therefore, Tefilah lifnei akhilat hamez. (5) From a codicological point of view it is a square type of script, copied by a copyist of Scripture, and from a morphological point of view it is similar to the square type which is to be found in the traditional medieval Hebrew manuscripts.

Attempts to trace the author of the prayer did not bring very satisfactory results. There were no further details about the document in Beit Lohamei Ha-Geta'ot, not even any record of the way it had arrived in the Archive. On the other hand, inquiries in the orthodox world indicated that the prayer seemed to be attributed to The Bluzhever Rebbe.(6) The Bluzhever Rebbe is a Holocaust survivor, one among only fourteen known survivors who passed through the Lublin Ghetto.• He became a hasidic figure with a remarkable number of stories by and about him. They are tales of spiritual strength, courage, faith, resistance and self-sacrifice. He himself has many memories from the nearly five years that he suffered in a succession of labour, concentration and death camps. His memories are devoted to describing the people whose great wish was that they would not lose their inner strength and that they would not be forgotten. Therefore, he is, indeed, a natural figure to attribute the prayer to, especially as it seems to fit in with the rest of the saga. Nevetheless, all the searching in the Holocaust libraries and archives in Israel and in the Wiener Library in London and all the studying of the contemporary Rabbinic literature were in vain. To sum up, it can be said that although it seems to be quite clear why the prayer would be attributed to him, I could not find any evidence that could confirm the fact that The Bluzhever Rebbe was indeed the author of the text.(7)

At this stage of my inquiries, I decided not to postpone publication any more and to leave this question, as many others related to the Holocaust, unanswered. But, strange as it might seem, I changed my mind and went to re-check my notes. It was, therefore, at the Library of the Jews' College London, when I had just realised that the last examination - re-checking a Rabbinic source - confirmed the previous one, that Ezra Kahn, who is the Librarian, came up to me and asked if he had noticed correctly what <u>tefilah</u> was lying on the desk in front of me. Thus I discovered that he had found this very same <u>tefilah</u> on a piece of paper inside an old book. One can, certainly, imagine our excitement, his at the manuscript of Beit Lohamei Ha-Geta'ot and I at his, but the important fact is that his version includes the name of the author. He is Abraham Solomon Levisson, a Dutch Rabbi, who died on the 25th of April 1945. And although it is quite obvious that there still needs to be a further careful examination, and that the identification is still, therefore, open to doubt, I choose, nevertheless, to bring this information before the reader, for it emerged from the attempts to solve the enigma of the author.(8)

Examining the <u>tefilah,</u> in the Beit Lohamei Ha-geta'ot manuscript version, by bringing the subject of suffering into focus, means tracing the roots of its concepts of and its approach to suffering, in the light of the problems that arose from the strong desire of the Jewish people for <u>Matzzot,</u> unleavened bread, and their deeply felt need to avoid <u>hamez.</u> It can be said, therefore, that the <u>tefilah</u> reveals a microscopic unit of the comprehensive spiritual effort that was made by them in order to overcome very specific suffering, both physical and moral. Yet before indicating the various considerations and their philosophical connections, it will be useful to explain the methodology of this study.

One of the foundation stones of this methodology is to look at the <u>tefilah</u> - a document of the Holocaust - using the same method which is employed by a researcher when he tries to look at a document from the viewpoint of Jewish thought. It is based, therefore, on three dimensions which are related to both the Holocaust and philosophy. The first is a panoramic one which, with regard to the background mentioned above, can be entitled, Faith and the Holocaust. For suffering is the essential part of the scepticism aroused by the very existence of the Holocaust. In fact, it is its heart, because as a philosophical problem it is connected directly with the problem of evil, its existence and its place in the universe, as well as with the concepts of God and His image.

The second dimension is the more established one, and is based on the paraphernalia within the field named philosophy of religion. The analysis will be carried out according to this same method, which means that one must understand that this present inquiry is not an organic study of theology. It should be emphasised, therefore, that although the study will analyse orthodox conceptions, it should not be undertaken from a religious standpoint at all. In other words, from this second dimension, the study bears upon the concepts of suffering, the propositions of theology and the reasoning of theologians, as well as the prior phenomena of religious experience and activities of worship upon which theology ultimately rests and out of which it has arisen.

The third dimension is the most fundamental one, examining those thousands of years of discussion of the quality of suffering, and the way in which it was brought into question by the victims themselves.

Needless to say, not only the third, but both of the other elements within the methodology which underlies this study, requires further explanation and elucidation - which I intend to carry out in another essay. Nevertheless, the fact that it is now at least stated enables us to turn to the detailed examination.

To begin with, what first of all becomes apparent is the question that the author and those who pray did not ask: "why?".

There is a complete absence of the complex elements of the "why", which had developed against the philosophical background of either scepticism or some kind of theodicy, when suffering as a feature of life had to be reconciled with the sorrow of the innocent which was deeper than could have been calculated, and when it came to children it seemed to be even worse. Therefore, such a complete absence alone can, perhaps, indicate that there was a most singular development in their approach, which seems to be entirely different from what one would expect when one follows both the process of the traditional discussions on suffering, and still more its arguments which involve all the complex elements of the "why" in the sense in which I am using the phrase. Against this absence stands "ve-hai ba-hem", he shall live in them. It is unequivocally the most essential motive of the tefilah, and I think that from a philosophical point of view it is not only a case of a different key motive, but is in some sense a motive which contradicts the complex of the "why", and it is, therefore, that or the other. Hence, there is no way of separating those two considerations - what is there and what is not - for only by understanding both the absence of the "why" and the dominant presence of "ve-hai ba-hem" is there the possibility of attaining a deeper understanding of the philosophical meaning of its conception.

The text of the _tefilah_ says: _"hinenu mukhanim le-qayem mizevatekha ve-hai ba-hem,"_ we are ready to perform Thy command, literally, "and he shall live in them", meaning that he shall live through them, and "them" alludes here to the ordinance and the judgments of God.

Although this idea of _"ve-hai ba-hem"_ - not exactly with this same nuance of the _tefilah_ but as _"vu-vaharta ba-hayim",_ "choose life", as a leading one in the Jewish faith which was used often enough by thinkers and Rabbanim throughout this awful period - was quite a well known fact by scholars of the Holocaust, it was not fully understood. Rubinson, for instance, in his "Concluding Remarks" speaks about one of the Rabbanim who permitted the neglect of the Jewish commands, saying that we need _"le-kadesh et ha-hayim",_ to sanctify the life, and not _"le-qadesh et ha-shem",_ to sanctify the Divine Name, by _"ye-hareq ve-al ya'avor",_ being killed and not trangressing.(9) And Robert Everett in his article "The Impact of the Holocaust on Christian Theology", while discussing the traditional idea that Jews were chosen by God to be His Suffering Servant, says that the Jewish people have learned well the "Rabbinic injunction - Choose life".(10) Yet "choose life" is not a Rabbinic injunction but a Biblical one, ñor is _"ye-hareq ve-al ya'avor etc."_ a Rabbinic saying from the _Sho'ah;_ it is a Talmudic source the terms of which were, indeed, seriously confused by Rubinson, and will now be explained.

The Book of Deuteronomy, chapter XXX, verse 19 reads: _"ha-idoti va-khem hayom et ha-shamyim ve-et ha-arez ha-hayim ve-hamavet na-tatti le-fanekha ha-verakhah ve-ha-qelalah u-vaharta ba-hayim le-ma'an tihye ata ve-zar'akha"_ - I call the heaven and earth as witnessess this day against you, that I have set before you the life and the death, the blessing and the curse: therefore choose the life, that both thou and thy seed may live. Hence the philosophical implication of the verse is the issue of free will, for in the literal sense it says that life and death are set before you in order that you may choose the portion of life. It is quite clear that in such a case there will be a hilkhatic implication as well, which emerges directly from the verse that alludes to God's counsel given to Israel to choose life.

And, indeed, the roots of the text of the _tefilah_ are both a Biblical source and a Talmudic one. _Ve-hai ba-hem_ is from The Book of Leviticus, chapter XVIII, verse 5: _"u-shemartem et huqotai ve-et mishepatai asher ya'ase otam ha-adam ve-hai ba-hem"_ - Ye shall therefore keep my ordinances and my judgments, which if a man do he shall live in them. In the _tefilah_ text, _"ve-hai ba-hem"_ is followed by _"ve-lo she-yamut ba-hem"_, and not die in them. It seems, therefore, that under the surface of the _tefilah_ lies not only the Biblical verse but the Babylonian Talmud, Tract Sanhedrin 74a, which discussess _yehareq ve-al ya'avor._ It says that if one is compelled, under threat of being killed, to commit any one of the crimes which are mentioned in the Torah, one might commit it and not be killed except in the case of idolatry, adultery or bloodshed. R. Ishma'el asked: whence do we know that if one were told under threat of being killed to worship an idol, he should rather worship than be killed? For it is written _"ve-hai ba-hem, ve-lo she-yamut ba-hem"_, "He shall live in them; which means not die in them." As this is almost the exact text of the _tefilah_ it is quite obvious that it is this concept that the _tefilah_ wanted to refer to. At this point, it ought also to be mentioned that those _halakhot_ of the Rabbi from the _Sho'ah_ which were described by Rubinson, such as eating non-kosher food or working on _shabat_, are very clearly those which are not in the category named _"ye-hareq ve-al ya'avor"_. Actually, there are special instructions of this kind even today in the Israeli Army, directed to the Jewish religious soldier, for instance, with regard to the necessity of working on _shabat._

Thus, by using this specific style based on Hebrew sources, and still more the actual words prescribed in the Talmud, this short _tefilah_ suggest a wealth of hilkhatic-philosophical combinations concerning this Holocaust case on _hamez_ during _pesah_, as well as the philosophical issue of suffering and free will, i.e. choosing between suffering or self-denial.

Aside from this suffering, which is the main issue of the _tefilah_, stands the more notable suffering when there is nothing one can do to escape suffering. Actually, almost all writings dealing with the philosophy of religion have discussions of this more notable topic with records of various kinds of sorrow and suffering, beginning with the Bible, the Christian scripture and the Rabbinic literature, and coming right up to medieval and modern philosophy and theology.(11) In traditional Christian theology, however, those various aspects of suffering were connected directly to the _Habitus corruptionis_ or the _Vitium_ - a general corruption of human nature - which was one of the fundamental elements in the development of the doctrine of _peccatum originale_, original sin.(12) And in Judaism it was symbolised by the great suffering of Job.

The essential question of Job in his agony was "why", and the chief sources in the Babylonian and Jerusalem Talmuds, and quite a number of the various philosophical interpretations which had discussions about the cause of suffering in the world, even with regard to the Holocaust, used Job as a symbol when they had discussed the complex of the "why".(13) In fact, we find this even in Maimonides, who attributed Job's defiant questioning "why" to his defective knowledge of God. He said: "she-ilu haya hakham lo haya mesupaq alav inyano", which means that if he were wise he would not have any doubt about the cause of his suffering.(14) Nevertheless, expressions of the limitation of human intellect when attempting to face the problem of suffering in the universe are to be found even in the discussions relating to Moses, who according to the Maimonidean philosophy differed completely from all other human beings. For Moses, according to Maimonides, is distiguished both from the philosopher because he was a prophet, and from the prophet because he received the shefa, overflow or emanation, from the Active Intellect directly onto his pure intellect, while the prophet received it onto his intellect through his imagination.(15) One cannot unquestionably assert whether, according to Maimonides, the prophet's intellect is above the philosopher's, and whether Moses had arrived at that intellectual knowledge of understanding the problem of suffering in particular. For when Maimonides referred to metaphysical theories, he was not willing to discuss them fully because they are within the field called ma'ase merkavah, and he applied, therefore, this sort of information on the Divine attributes in an esoteric method. Hence, what is important to us is that either Moses alone or no human being including Moses was able to reach the knowledge of understanding the problem of suffering.(16) Nonetheless, Maimonides explained this issue also with regard to the complex of the "why", interpreting Exodus, chapter 33, verse 13 "hodi'eni na et derakhekha", "Show me thy way", to mean that Moses prayed to God to grant him knowledge of His attributes. By this he referred to the Rabbinic literature that interpreted Moses asking for understanding of the problem of suffering in the universe.(17) The roots of the discussion are to be found in the Talmud. R. Yohanan in the name of of R. Yosei said that all Moses' requests were granted, which is in opposition to the saying of R. Meir. For R. Meir said that one request was not granted to him, i.e. the request about the suffering of the innocent.(18)

Hence suffering for one's beliefs is beyond the mere "why" expression. In fact, such expressions are to be found both in Judaism and Christianity. In Christian scripture, it seems to reach its climax in the crucifixion of Jesus, who accepted his suffering voluntarily out of love.(19) In Judaism the examples seem to be endless; however, it may be that the climax is to be found in a piyut for Yom Kipur, a liturgical hymn for the Day of Atonement, about aseret ha-rugei malkhut, the matryrdom of the Ten - in particular, those phrases which are to be found in R. Akiva, who accepted his suffering out of love as well. Yet throughout Jewish history in the diaspora, which overflowed with terror and bloodshed, if a Jew chose to suffer for the sake of his faith he would not ask "why", since he had already reached the level where, for him, there was the pure truthful belief in God and His Torah. He would know the limitations of the commandments as well as the acceptance of the act of kiddush ha-Shem, sacrifice God's name - that is martyrdom, and the essential fact that if he chose to remain a Jew he would suffer for his Jewishness.(20)

Speaking on the Jews and the Holocaust, the freedom to choose was rare, but it did exist, and we can find it here, in our tefilah. (21) What attracts the attention, and balances the concepts of the tefilah, is that it has been challenged in some recent philosophical discussion of this issue to develop a thesis which involved those same elements of free will and suffering. Those are discussions about Divine omnipotence and human freedom. In these discussions evil is not to be ascribed to God at all, but to the independent action of human beings, supposed to have been endowed by God with freedom of the will. In this solution the pain or the suffering may be justified as a logical necessity, together with cruelty which is not justified, but is also ascribed to human beings so that God cannot be held responsible for it. To explain why a wholly good God gave men free will although it would lead to some ultimate suffering, it must be argued that it is better on the whole that men should act freely, and sometimes err, than that they should be innocent automata, acting rightly in a wholly determined way. Critical comments on these arguments were offered in anther recent discussion.(22) Yet it is not the general aspects of each of the philosophical systems which concern us here, but rather the tefilah view, which seems, in spite of everything, to have emerged directly from traditional Rabbinic literature. Under the surface of this, there is, nonetheless, the fundamental view of the internal limited intellect against the Eternal Divine Intellect.

There is so much more involved in the concepts set forth in the tefilah because, aside from struggling and resolving the practical religious problem, there emerged a redoubtable dimension which is the suffering of the soul. For the implication of this practical solution of altering the commands of pesah for the command of ve-hai ba-hem was enormous suffering of the soul. It clearly speaks: "akh al zot da'avah libenu" - only on this our heart languished. And in the same style which has been demonstrated here in detail, it refers to what has been found to be the best to express those mixed and antagonised feelings of "keeping the soul" - meaning keeping it alive - against their will not to estrange their faith. Such is, for instance, the Book of Deuternomy, chapter IV, verse 9: "raq hishamer lekha u-shemor nafshekha me'od" - "only take heed to thyself and keep thy soul diligently". So taking the expressions and the reference to the Hebrew sources together, this one document evokes a tremendous affliction full of sorrow, misery and suffering of the soul.

*

I would not dare to explain the Divine attributes, nor dare I evaluate the concepts of the victims themselves. Nevertheless, I insist upon studying, examining and trying to clarify their attitudes, their approach and their concepts.

I have focused here on only one manuscript, so many more questions remain for the future. How many documents of this sort are there? Where are they? Will they reveal whether the victims used a philosophical background in order to face the suffering? What are the implications of their concepts for us?

NOTES

(1) Rubinson J., "Concluding Remarks" (Hebrew: "Divrei Sikum be-Kinus Binle'umi") Yad Vashem, Qovez Mehqarim , 7, p.189: "ulai hakhi traqi haya mazava shel ha-ortodoksya... ein safeq shederekh ha-hayim ha-ortodoksit savela maka nizahat." English trans. vol. V (1968) p. 202.

(2) A study day entitled "Dat ve'Emuna ba-Sho'a u-le-ahareha" Tel-Aviv 12.5.1987. It was just during a break, when one of the colleagues expressed, incidentally, the very same idea. Cf. Fackenheim L. E., From Bergen-Belsen to Jerusalem, Contemporary Implications of the Holocaust, Jerusalem 1975, p. 7. Fackenheim speaks on the fact that in a symposium on Jewish belief (1961) no question was asked about the Holocaust. In a Congress of the Departments of Philosophy named "Be'ayat ha-ra be-Mahshevet Israel" - The problem of evil in Jewish Thought - in April 1986 at Bar-Ilan University in Israel, no one had submitted a paper on this issue, myself included.

(3) On the field of philosophy of religion in general, see: Hick J.H., Philosophy of Religion, New Jersey, first published 1963.

(4) Thanks are due to Mrs. Hayah Levinson from the Archive of Beit Lohamei Ha-Geta'ot, Ghetto Fighter House, for her kind help during my research.

(5) It seems that this document was first published by H. Zaidman and was entitled there also *Tefilah lifnei akhilat hamez* . See: Eliav M. (ed.), *Ani Ma'amin; eduyot al hayehem u-motam shel anshei emunah bi-tequfat ha-Sho'a* , Jerusalem [1967]. I was not able to find a copy of the first edition, but in the second edition [1968] the *tefilah* is on p. 221. In spite of the fact that it is published in a non-scientific style, which means that it is with additional marks that were not indicated in the original, and it is also without notes or any kind of explanation, it became a source for several more anthologies. There is also a photograph of the *tefilah* in: Paibelovitz P., *Mipi Ud Muzal; Pirqai zikhronot min ha-tofet ha-Nazi* , Haifa 1970. Although the sigla is not mentiond in both of them, it is quite clear that they both refer to the same manuscript, 'T 11711 Bergen-Belsen, as they do say that it is from the Collection of Beit Lohamei Ha-Geta'ot which, as far as is known, has no other version of the *tefilah* .

(6) The Bluzhever Rebbe is Rabbi Yisroel Spira, the hasidic Rebbe of Bluzher. His wife, their only daughter, her husband and their children were exterminated in the Holocaust. On The Bluzhever Rebbe see: *A Path Through the Ashes, Penetrating Analyses and Inquiring Stories of the Holocaust from a Torah Perspective,* ArtScroll Judaiscope Series, first published 1986, pp. 152-162; Weinstock M.D., *Light in the Darkness,* London 1959, pp. 72-84.

(7) See also: H. Zaidman, *Tefilah lifnei akhilat hamez,* in: Eliav M. (ed.), *Ani Ma'amin; eduyot al hayehem u-motam shel anshei emunah bi-tequfat ha-Shoa* . It seems as if he thought that it was a collective creation, because he wrote that it was composed by Rabbanim.

(8) I intend to publish soon a detailed study of the author and the document of the *tefilah* itself. The latter will be based on all the versions known to us.

(9) Rubinson J., "Concluding Remarks" (Hebrew: *"Divrei Sikum be-Kinus Binle'umi"*) *Yad Vashem, Qovez Mehqarim* , 7, p.189.

(10) Everett A., "The Impact of the Holocaust on Christian Theology", *Christian Jewish Relations,* 15 No.4 (81) (December 1982), p. 5. In this article (pp. 3-11) he actually expresses his beliefs on the "many lies" which are to be found in the New Testament itself, and he also says that the theological antisemitism of the Church helped to prepare the foundation of the Holocaust.

(11) On systems of explanation and bibliographical list before the Holocaust see: Kilpatrick T. B., "Suffering", *Encyclopaedia of Religion and Ethics* , 12 (1920) pp. 1-10. On philosophical explanations and bibliography after the Holocaust see: Schwarzchild S. S., "Suffering", *Ency. Judiaca* 15, pp. 485-486; Sutcliffe E. F., *Providance and Suffering in the Old and New Testaments,* London 1953; Sandres J. A., *Suffering As Divine Discipline in the Old Testament and Post-Biblical Judaism,* New York 1955.

(12) On this subject see: Schechterman D., "The Doctrine of Original Sin in Jewish Philosophy of the Thirteenth and Fourteenth Centuries", *Daat* 20 (1988), pp. 65-90. Bibliographical lists: op. cit. pp.65-66 notes 1-2.

(13) The chief sources of interpretation on Job in the Babylonian and Jerusalem Talmuds are: The Babylonian Talmud, Tract Bava Batra 14b-16b; Jerusalem Talmud, Tract Sotah 5:8 20c-9.
On the complex of the "why" as the main problem of Job cf. Fohrer G., *Commentaries on the Book of Job,* Ger. 1963. According to Georg Fohrere's interpretation, the essential question the book sets out to answer is: what is the proper conduct of suffering man? So, he interpreted the whole book in the light of Job who wanted to understand the cause of suffering. See also: Glatzer N. (ed.), *The Dimensions of Job,* 1969. On this subject with regard to the Holocaust see: Zusman M., *"Iyov ve-goral ha-am ha-yehudi",* *Prozdor* (1962) pp. 2-4.

(14) Moshe ben Maimon, *Moreh Nevukhim,* Vol. III, Chapter 22.

(15) Maimonides' terms are those of Aristotelian philosophy. In accordance with this doctrine, Maimonides explained the various effects that the impulses descending from the Active Intellect produced on human intellect and his imagination. For the meaning of the terms in Maimonides and in Jewish Philosophy see: Efros I., *Munahim filosofiyim be-moreh nevukhim,* in *Mediaeval Jewish Philosophy,* Tel-Aviv 1969, vol. II, pp. 9-112; Klazkin Y., *Ozar ha-munahim ha-filosofiyim,* Berlin 1927. The terms are: *sekhel po'el* - Active Intellect; *shefa* - overflow or emanation; *dimyon* - imagination. On this issue see also: Reines A., *Maimonides and Abrabanel on Prophecy,* Cincinnati 1970.

(16) Moshe ben Maimon, Moreh Nevukhim, Vol. I, Chapter 54.

(17) Maimonides sayes that Moses asked two things, and the Talmud says: "three things did Moses aske..." See: Moshe ben Maimon, Moreh Nevukhim, Vol. I, Chapter 54; The Babylonian Talmud, Tract Berakhot 7a.

(18) The Babylonian Talmud, Tract Berakhot 7a.

(19) On the fundamental distinction in the matter of suffering between Judaism and Christianity see: Brod M., Heidentum, Christentum, Judentum 1921. According to Schwarzschild in his entry on suffering in the Ency. Judaica, he considers the attitude toward suffering the major distinguishing factor between Judaism and Christianity. See also: Sutcliffe E. F., Providence and Suffering in the Old and New Testaments, London 1953. He says that in Christianity it is among the conditions ordained and willed by God for the attainment of "our eternal destiny" (p. 2) and it is "put before us Christians to encourage us in faithful endurance" (p. 166). See also: Sandres J. A., Suffering As Divine Discipline in the Old Testament and Post-Biblical Judaism, New York 1955; Hick J. H., Philosophy of Religion, New Jersey 1963, p. 36-38; Bukovsky J., "Suffering", New Catholic Encyclopedia, vol. 3, pp. 775-776; Riga A., "Suffering - Christian Attitude", New Catholic Encyclopedia vol. XIII, pp.776-777; Schwarzchild S. S., Suffering, Ency. Judaica 15, pp. 485-486.

(20) On this issue see: Scharf F. R., "Saints or madmen? A meditation on Ephraim Oshry's Responsa from the Holocaust" The Jewish Quarterly 34 No. 4 (128) (1987), pp. 28-30; Fackenheim L.E., "On the Akedah, or Sacrifice and Martyrdom", Encounters Between Judaism and Modern Philosophy; A preface to Future Jewish Thought, Philadelphia 1973, pp. 53-77; Gutman Y., "Kiddush ha-Shem and Kiddush ha-Hayim", Simon Wiesenthal Center Annual I (New York 1984), pp. 185-202.

(21) Fackenheim had already explained in detail this radical and fundamental difference. See: Fackenheim L. E., From Bergen-Belsen to Jerusalem, Contemporary Implications of the Holocaust, Jerusalem 1975, p. 14: "Prior to the Holocaust Jews died for their faith... The more than one million Jewish children murdered by the Nazis died, not because of their faith... but rather on account of the Jewish faith of their grandparents..."

(22) Mackei J. L., "Evil and Omnipotence", Mind n.s. 64 (1955), pp. 200-212; Flew A., "Divine Omnipotence and Human Freedom, New Essays in Philosophical Theology, London 1963 (first published 1955), pp. 144-169; ibid, "Are Ninian Smart's Temptations Irresistible?", Philosophy 37 (1962), pp. 57-60; ibid, "Freedom is Slavery: a Slogan for our New Philosopher Kings", Philosophy 15 (1983), pp. 45-59; Smart N., "Omnipotence, Evil and Supremen" Philosophy 36 (1961), pp. 188-195; ibid, "Probably", Philosophy 37 (1962), p. 60; Oppenheim F. E., Dimensions of Freedom, New York 1961; Farrer A., The Freedom of the Will, London 1958; Benn S. I., "Freedom and Persuasion", Australasian Journal of Philosophy 45 (1967), pp. 259-275; Benn S. I. and Weinstein W. L., "Being Free to Act, and Being a Free Man", Mind LXXX (1971), pp. 194-211; ibid, "Freedom as the Non-Restriction of Options: A Rejoinder", Mind 83 (1974), pp.435-438; Watkins J., "Three Views Concerning Human Freedom", Philosophy 8 (1975), pp. 200-228; Cassinelli C. W., Free Activities and Interpersonal Relations, The Hague 1966; Gibbs B., "Taking Liberties with Freedom: a Reply to Professor Flew", Philosophy 15 (1983), pp.61-72.

REFERENCES

A Path Through the Ashes, Penetrating Analyses and Inquiring Stories of the Holocaust from a Torah Perspective (1986). 152-162.

Benn S. I. (1967). Australasian Journal of Philosophy 45, 259-275.

Benn S. I. and Weinstein W. L. (1971). Mind LXXX, 194-211; (1974). Mind 83, 435-438.

Brod M. (1921). Heidentum, Christentum, Judentum .

Cassinelli C. W. (1966). Free Activities and Interpersonal Relations .

Efros I. (1969). Mediaeval Jewish Philosophy, II.

Eliav M. (ed.), [1967]. Ani Ma'amin; eduyot al hayehem u-motam shel anshei emunah bi-tequfat ha-Shoa .

Everett A. (1982). Christian Jewish Relations, 15 No.4 (81), 3-11.

Fackenheim L.E. (1973). In: Encounters Between Judaism and Modern Philosophy; A preface to Future Jewish Thought, 53-77.

Fackenheim L. E. (1975). From Bergen-Belsen to Jerusalem, Contemporary Implications of the Holocaust .

Farrer A. (1958). The Freedom of the Will .

Flew A. (1963). New Essays in Philosophical Theology, 144-169; (1962). Philosophy 37, 57-60; (1983). Philosophy 15, 45-59.

Gibbs B. (1983). Philosophy 15, 61-72.
Glatzer N. (ed.), (1969). The Dimensions of Job .
Gutman Y. (1984). Simon Wiesenthal Center Annual I, 185-202.
Hick J.H. (1963). Philosophy of Religion, .
Kilpatrick T. B. (1920). Encyclopaedia of Religion and Ethics, 12, 1-10.
Klazkin Y. (1927). Ozar ha-munahim ha-filosofiyim .
Mackei J. L. (1955). Mind n.s. 64, 200-212.
Oppenheim F. E. (1961). Dimensions of Freedom .
Paibelovitz P. (1970). Mipi Ud Muzal; Pirqai zikhronot min ha-tofet ha-Nazi .
Rubinson J. Yad Vashem, Qovez Mehqarim , 7, 189-202.
Sandres J. A. (1955). Suffering As Divine Discipline in the Old Testament and Post-Biblical Judaism .
Scharf F. R. (1987). The Jewish Quarterly 34 No. 4 (128), 28-30.
Schechterman D. (1988). Daat 20, 65-90.
Schwarzchild S. S., Ency. Judiaca 15, 485-486.
Smart N. (1961). Philosophy 36, 188-195; (1962). Philosophy 37, 60.
Sutcliffe E. F. (1953). Provídence and Suffering in the Old and New Testaments .
Watkins J. (1975). Philosophy 8, 200-228.
Weinstock M.D. (1959). Light in the Darkness, , 72-84.
Zusman M. (1962). Prozdor , 2-4.

The challenge to the Jewish community: Religion, life and the State of Israel

CHAIRPERSON **Dr Normon Solomon**

RAPPORTEUR **Professor Edward Alexander**

THE ROLE OF THE HOLOCAUST IN ISRAELI ANTISEMITISM

Edward Alexander

Department of English
Tel-Aviv University
69978 Tel-Aviv, Israel

> When I saw the depths of crazy self-hatred to which some of my leftist friends had sunk, I started thinking. . . . I'm afraid of this self-hatred, because I know that it can be exploited. When Englishmen or Frenchmen hate themselves—and some do—it doesn't put their countries at risk. They're in their countries unconditionally. Whereas here, self-hatred is always connected to something else. . . .
>
> A.B. Yehoshua

That Jews may themselves be antisemitic long ago ceased to be an occasion for surprise, except to those completely ignorant of the history of Jews in Europe. Self-hating Jews have made such large contributions to the ideology and politics of antisemitism that it may fairly be called a product of the "Judeo-Christian" tradition. Examples are plentiful. Before Pope Gregory IX ordered the Talmud to be seized, examined, and publicly burnt in Paris and Rome, he was presented in 1239 with a detailed analysis of the manifold evils of the Jews' religious books by the Dominican brother Nicholas Donin, a Jewish convert. In the sixteenth century Martin Luther's seemingly innovative program of burning synagogues, destroying Jewish homes, confiscating the Talmud and all other Hebrew books, was in fact derived from the proposals of Johannes (formerly Josef) Pfefferkorn, the Jewish convert who had years earlier exhorted his German countrymen to "drive the old Jews out like dirty dogs and baptize the young children" and "take their goods and give them to those to whom they belong." Christians appear to have invented, all by themselves, the belief in Jewish male menstruation, but doubters among them received reassurance from Jewish converts such as Franco da Piacenza, who in 1630 revealed to the world the shameful secret that Jewish males of the lost tribe of Simeon menstruated four days a year.

When we "advance" from the old era of religious Jew-hatred to the modern one of political antisemitism, we still find Jews doing very well in competition with their gentile neighbors in the production of antisemitic fantasies, slanders, and lunacies. Karl Marx, converted to Lutheranism at age six, imputed to Jews other than himself false language, bad manners, sexual aggressiveness. Of the "Jewish nigger" Ferdinand Lassalle (himself a Jewish antisemite of formidable derangement) Marx wrote: "Always this constant babble with the falsely excited voice, the unaesthetic, demonstrative gestures . . . and also the uncultivated eating and the horny lust of this 'idealist.' . . . As his skull shape and hair prove, he is a descendant of those

Blacks who accompanied Moses on the exodus from Egypt . . . Now this combination of Jewishness and Germanness upon the Black basic substance must bring forth a strange product. The pushiness of this fellow is also nigger-like."[1] (Are these, one wonders, the sentiments for which Marx is today revered in the third world and the Israeli Labor Party?) Even today, when the whole world has known for almost half a century that antisemitism visited upon the Jews, including antisemitic Jews, evils greater than anyone had imagined possible, the tradition of Jewish antisemitism continues unabated, although it has taken on new, highly imaginative names, if not entirely new forms. In place of the Börnes and Krauses and Marxes we now have the Chomskys and Kreiskys and Navaskys.

Zionism, in the nineteenth century, proposed to establish for Jews a refuge from antisemitism. In the first instance, this would be a political refuge. Even so surly an anti-Zionist as Hannah Arendt was forced to admit that the Zionist movement was the only political answer Jews had ever found to antisemitism. But Zionism also aspired to cure the antisemitism of the Jews themselves, sometimes referred to as Jewish self-hatred (an awkward term because it so frequently identifies those very Jews inordinately consumed by self-love). Once liberated from the constant burden of peril that came from living as a feared and despised minority within an alien Christian culture, the more timorous Jews would no longer be driven to desperate stratagems for diverting gentile hatred of Jews in general onto certain segments of Jewry: ostjuden or Oriental Jews or Yiddish-speaking Jews, or Jews who were slow to shorten their jackets and beards and memories.

The Zionists also sought to "normalize" Jewish existence. Once Jews had the power and the responsibility of managing their affairs in a state of their own, they would surely repudiate the superstitious belief that suffering and powerlessness confer virtue. The protagonist of Haim Hazaz' famous story "The Sermon," when he is in his Zionist mood, declares that "Everything is rotten around suffering . . . history, life itself, all action, customs, the group, the individual, literature, culture, folk songs . . . everything! . . . Sorrow is prized higher than joy, pain easier to understand than happiness." Gershom Sholem thought that Hermann Cohen's description of them as "those people who want to be happy" was the wisest criticism ever made of Zionists. It was, of course, recognized by Zionists that normalization would bring with it many things less intrinsically desirable than happiness and national independence: Jewish prostitutes, Jewish thieves, Jewish political parties and their attendant insanities. Few Zionist theorists, however, anticipated that the normalization of Jewish existence would bring with it, along with the other vices, crimes, and historic hatreds of European societies, antisemitism.

It might be argued that some element of antisemitic feeling was already latent in Zionist ideology insofar as it repudiated the life of the European shtetl and ghetto as stunted, abnormal, and demeaning to Jews, a travesty of a great nation whose history was recounted in the Bible. Many a Zionist writer reacted as did the English poet Samuel Taylor Coleridge to modern Jewish decadence viewed against the background of a noble past. "The two images farthest removed from each other which can be comprehended under one term, are, I think, Isaiah--'Hear, O heavens, and give ear, O earth!'--and Levi of Holywell Street--'Old Clothes!'--both of them Jews, you'll observe."[2] Hazaz's protagonist gave classic utterance to the Zionist revulsion from Jewish life in the Diaspora: "Jewish history . . . has no glory or action, no heroes and conquerors, no rulers and masters of their fate, just a collection of wounded, hunted, groaning, and wailing wretches, always begging for mercy . . . I would simply forbid teaching our children Jewish history. Why the devil teach them about their ancestors' shame? I would just say to them:

'Boys, from the day we were driven out from our land we've been a people without a history. Class dismissed. Go out and play football.'" Many an Israeli work of fiction turns upon a generational conflict over the choice of names for children. The old folks, still tied to Diaspora memories, favor "Jewish" names like Mendele or Moishele or Zeitl, whereas the young, native Israelis want Hebrew or at least biblical names, such as Osnat and Ehud. Ben-Gurion himself was a prodigious redesigner of immigrant names that had the exilic taint on them.

One group of Israeli thinkers, called the Canaanites, carried these anti-Diaspora tendencies to the point where they sought to sever all connections between the state of Israel and the Jewish people. They believed that a new national identity was being formed in Palestine and later the state of Israel that was not Jewish at all. They argued that it was the anachronistic notion of Israel's Jewish identity that kept any sense of unity and shared history from developing among the various peoples in the Middle East: Maronites, Druze, Alawis, Kurds, Bedouins. For the Canaanites, Israel was rightly a nation of Hebrew-speaking gentiles. The Canaanites may have begun with certain ideas latent within Zionism, but they carried these to such extreme and radical form that they were recognized, and correctly, by the Zionist leadership as anti-Zionist in their aims and outlook, and were repudiated. One does not require a specially refined taste to recognize the antisemitic flavor of Canaanite ideology. Here is a sample from Yonatan Ratosh's 1944 manifesto called <u>Discourse</u>: "Here in the Hebrew land the Jew has removed the furry tails (<u>shtreimel</u>) from his head, cut off his side-locks, learned to mouth the Hebrew language and to utter slogans about a homeland and nationalism . . . But let us look with open eyes. He is the same Jew, the eternal Jew of the eternal Diaspora. In France he pretends to be a Frenchman, in Germany a German. Here he plays his game in Hebrew . . . He is the enemy who eats up all the best parts. He is the one who tramples on the best of our children with his obseqious pleading and fund-raising . . . "[3] The Canaanites failed as a movement, but the ideas of some of their leaders still make themselves felt today among certain segments of Israeli society, especially the militantly secularist left.

Nevertheless, it would be simplistic to allege that antisemitic feeling in Zion today derives primarily or even substantially (if indirectly) from Zionism itself. If Zionism repudiated the Jewish life that existed in the ghetto and shtetl, it did so in order to perpetuate Jewish life and not extinguish it. The Zionists acted from the conviction that distinctions could be made between those beliefs, customs, and attitudes that were peculiar to life in exile and those that were permanently, intrinsically, and universally Jewish. Along with other Jewish enlighteners, the Zionists believed that traditional, religious Jewish culture could be secularized in such a way that, as Hillel Halkin has written, it would remain genuinely and identifiably Jewish in all its aspects "while at the same time serving as the basis for a modern society whose members will share a common cultural identity that draws on what each of them has brought to it."[4] Whether Zionism will succeed in this ambition remains to be seen. Most Israelis are still pre-occupied with the more pressing question of whether their country will be able to survive forty more years of unremitting hostility from its neighbors; and some believe that the very sacrifices they have made in order to survive as a free and independent state have forged Jewish roots: "Spilt blood," writes the Israeli poet Yehuda Amichai, "isn't roots of trees,/But it's the closest to them/That man has."

But perhaps I have put the cart before the horse in speculating about the roots or antecedents of Israeli antisemitism before having given evidence that such a thing even exists. Indeed, I am more than a bit squeamish about providing anti-Zionists (as antisemites now call themselves) with yet another stick with which to beat the Jews, but I am afraid that the secret is already out. Awareness of it crops up in all kinds of places, sometimes in humorous form. The American novelist Philip Roth in his recent book _The Counterlife_ introduces a character who explains why she, notoriously stingy, contributes money to Israel. "'You know why I give to Israel?' . . . 'Why?' Grossman said. 'Because in Israel you hear the best anti-semitic jokes.'" The Israeli humorist and cartoonist Dosh, in a column of May 22, 1987 in _Ma'ariv_, drew a picture of a shopper in a supermarket specializing in antisemitic merchandise reaching for the top shelf carrying the most expensive package, which is adorned by a Stuermer-like caricature of a Jew and prominently labelled "Made in Israel." The article that this cartoon illustrated spoke of Israel's need to increase exports by embellishing products available elsewhere in the world with unique local characteristics. Israel had done this with certain fruits and vegetables in the past, and now she was doing it with defamations of Israel, produced _in_ Israel. Market research had shown a strong demand for documentary material to justify hostile attitudes to the Jewish state; but it also showed that customers were becoming more selective, and no longer willing to make do with grade B merchandise produced by British leftists or German neo-Nazis. No, these discriminating buyers wanted authentic material, from local sources; and Israeli artists, playwrights, intellectuals, aware of the tremendous opportunities for exporting antisemitism from Zion itself, were responding with alacrity to the opportunity.

But if Roth and Dosh are joking about antisemitism in Israel, it may well be that, as the French say, they laugh in order not to cry. Contemplate the following incidents and ask yourself whether they would have provoked jokes or outrage if they had occurred in any country except Israel. In 1984 a minor Israeli poet named Yitzhak Laor published a series of seven poems in a literary journal supported by the Arts Council of Israel, that is to say, by government funds. They dealt with the war in Lebanon from a leftist point of view, but with a virulence that went beyond garden-variety leftist effusions toward something distinctly reminiscent of the propaganda of Nazi Germany. Rafael Eitan was called "a lead nose-ring in the snout of the State," and Menachem Begin was described as a "greedy, grunting blood-sucker," but the most inflammatory epithets were reserved for religious young men in the army who had studied in the _hesder yeshivot_ of the Gush Emunim movement. In a poem entitled "A Hymn to the Gush," Laor puts the following speech into the mouths of the Jews: "They scorned us, but we shall celebrate this festival of our freedom, this feast of unleavened bread, with pious shakings, and holiness and with devotion, and in our _matzot_ these will be the blood of Palestinian youth, for just the same it's all a heathen slander." In spring of 1987, a much better-known Israeli figure, the left-wing Member of the Knesset, Dedi Zucker, followed Laor's lead. A few days after a Jewish woman named Ofra Moses was burned to death by a fire-bomb thrown into her car by Arab terrorists and the other passengers were badly burned (the Moses son died of his wounds some weeks later), Zucker, who first gained prominence in Israel a a leader of "Peace Now," and is much beloved of Western television reporters seeking Israeli-accented condemnation of Israel, took it upon himself to interpret the religious significance of the event. In a speech to those he called his "Palestinian brothers," delivered on the fourth day of Passover, Zucker said: "The Jewish settlers need Ofra Moses' blood. They are drinking it."[5] Thus did Zucker, whose previous excursions into the realm of theology had generally been on the level of Bob Dylan, his "culture hero"[6] perform a public service by supplying the one element of a traditional, "normal" European Passover that had been sorely lacking in Israel during the first thirty-nine years of its existence: the blood libel.

Both the poetical and the political blood libeller, it should be noted, defamed the religious Jews of Israel with impunity. A few people had the temerity to ask whether Laor's ejaculations ought to be subsidized by public funds, but they were shouted down with the usual cries of censorship. Zucker was not even criticized publicly, even though it is difficult to think of a democratic parliament anywhere in the world that would not have censured him or expelled him from elected office for thus indulging his baser impulses.

In the last two or three years several grisly incidents redolent of European antisemitism have shocked the Israeli public, or at least some segments of the Israeli public. In June of 1986, following a series of disputes between religious and secular Jews over the opening of movie houes on Friday nights and the destruction of Jerusalem bus-kiosks displaying half-nude women in suggestive poses, a synagogue in Tel-Aviv was vandalized, swastikas were painted on its walls, and many of its holy books burned. In December of the same year some soldiers, during their swearing-in ceremony at the Western Wall, flung the copies of the Hebrew Bible with which they had been presented, to the ground. In August of 1987 an eleven-year old boy wearing the long curls (payot) of the orthodox, was set upon in a Jerusalem street on the sabbath and shorn of his locks.[7]

But these sporadic outbursts of secularist zealotry are less important in the current burgeoning of antisemitic feeling in Israel than a weirdly refracted, nightmarishly distorted memory of the Holocaust. Many desperate Israelis, too lazy to think through the implications of the Holocaust for the Jewish state or too craven to acknowledge them[8], have decided that in this as in so many other things they will, like the ape in Kafka's story, "Report to an Academy," imitate the average European. We all remember how this clever ape, in order to find a way out of his cage, in which he can neither stand nor lie nor sit, imitates the ways of his captors, however disgusting they may appear to him: if they spit, he will spit, if they smoke foul cigars, so will he, and if they drink schnapps, he will drink schnapps. The half-educated Israeli intellectual or politician, descended from this ape, if he wants to evade the terrifying fact that Israel has for forty years been a beleaguered nation surrounded by enemies eager to reduce her to sandy wastes, will imitate the half-educated intellectuals and politicans of Europe by identifying some or all of his countrymen with Nazis.

The equation of Jews with Nazis antedates the Holocaust and the establishment of the State of Israel. It appears to have been a British invention, which Conor Cruise O'Brien has traced back to British official circles, which in 1941 were using the epithet "Jewish Nazi state" to refer to Jewish Palestine.[9] By now it is a mere wave on the dead sea of commonplace in the parlance of Israel-haters. The same Conor O'Brien, fresh from many conversations with Britons in 1982, proposed making this vilification a kind of litmus paper for the detection of antisemitism: "If your interlocutor can't keep Hitler out of the conversation, . . . feverishly turning Jews into Nazis and Arabs into Jews---why then, I think, you may well be talking to an anti-Jewist."[10]

The first step in transforming Jews into Nazis and Arabs into Jews is, of course, to "universalize" the Holocaust by concealing the specific identity of both the killers and their victims. Few historical "revisionists" have done this with the gross blatancy of Israel's most aggressive anti-religious politician, Shulamit Aloni. Describing the Demjanjuk trial as "more a vendetta than a punishment," she alleged that Holocaust education in Israel had failed because it taught youngsters that "the Nazis did this to the Jews instead of the message that people did this to people."[11] Once you have changed the

Holocaust from a crime of terrifying clarity committed by Nazis against Jews into a blurred, amorphous agony, an indiscriminate part of man's inhumanity to man, you have opened the door wide to those whose political purposes are served by making Arabs into Jews and Jews into Nazis.

Israelis of the far left, it goes without saying, have been heavily involved in this sordid enterprise for many years. Such desperadoes as Israel Shahak, Felicia Langer, and Lea Tsemel have for over a decade adorned virtually every one of their statements to the press on the Arab-Israeli conflict with references to Israel as a Nazi state, and to Palestinian Arabs as Jews. Shahak, in a book of 1975 called Le Racisme de l'Etat d'Israel, went a step beyond his competitors in slanderous bombast by stating that "The Jews of Israel, along with most of the Jews of the world, are at present undergoing a process of nazification."[12] But in recent years figures much closer to the center of Israeli political and intellectual life have also taken the plunge into the filth of antisemitism. In April of 1982 the journalist Amos Elon concocted a story, which turned out to be a tissue of lies, about books allegedly banned by the Israeli military government in Judea and Samaria. When questioned closely by Melvin Lasky of Encounter about what appeared to be gross misinterpretation of the facts, Elon replied: "It's all part of the preparations for a fascist regime! Soon we'll have it all, concentration camps as well as the burning of the books."[13]

During the war in Lebanon a host of Israelis, ranging from publishers of pornographic newspapers to university professors, whom nobody outside of Israel had heard of before became instant celebrities in Europe and America by characterizing the Israeli government, in the words of Professor Yeshayahu Leibowitz, as "Judeo-Nazi." Since 1982 Israelis of the most modest intellectual endowments discovered that the licentious equation of their country with Nazi Germany provided a short, ready, and often lucrative path to radio and television appearances and to the lecture circuit. They could also be enshrined as prophets in books about Israel that fall into the category known as Israel bashers. David Shipler's best-selling Arab and Jew, for example, relies heavily upon testimony from Israelis that their country is the one true inheritor of the regime that perpetrated the Holocaust. Shipler showed special diligence in ferreting out Israelis ready to malign their country according to formula. Dov Yermiya, who has made a profession of speechifying around the world about Israel's similarity to Nazi Germany, assured Shipler that he and his friends had predicted, way back in 1945, that the Holocaust would "affect . . . Jews in Israel for the bad," that the former victims would become "more or less similar" to the victimizers.[14] Another Israeli, a young publisher, told Shipler that when his army unit told the people of Nabatiyeh to come out of their houses and separate according to sex, he instantly saw in his mind's eye "the trains in the '40s in Germany, one side children and women, one side men." Ran Cohen, the leftist Knesset member, revealed to Shipler (not very reluctantly, we may be sure) his feeling that searching the Palestinian population for members of the PLO was just like the Nazis "making a selection from the Jewish people." Hillel Goldberg, a Hebrew University expert on ethics, praised by Shipler for his "precision . . . of reasoning," demonstrated his surgical exactness by saying that "What happened out there [in Sabra and Shatila] was somehow of a kind with what happened in the Holocaust." After all these examples, one is ready to believe the Arab writer who explains to a surprised Shipler how he came to use Treblinka as a metaphor for the "West Bank": "An Israeli friend of mine told me about this." Shipler himself at first "boils and rages" over the Arab equation between Ansar detention camp and Auschwitz, but he is helped to overcome his indignation by the radical Israeli journalist Cordelia Edvardson, herself a

Holocaust survivor. She explains to Shipler (as she was later to explain to readers of the Washington Post in October 1983) tht the Arabs' use of the slogan "Ansar is Auschwitz" was nothing more than the imprisoned terrorists' search for a Palestinian history.[15] But not even she was sufficiently prodigious an explainer to show why this search can take place only amidst the mournful coattails of the Jewish experience of discrimination, oppression, and murder.

In the arts too, the Holocaust has been exploited by certain Israelis for the purpose of besmirching their countrymen in general or their political opponents or religious fellow-citizens in particular as Nazis. It might be argued, as Norma Rosen has done in an important essay called "The Second Life of Holocaust Imagery,"[16] that the associative habit of artistic metaphor, which discovers likenesses in things apparently unlike, can serve to extend awareness and understanding of the Jewish tragedy during World War II. More often than not, however, making Jews into metaphors is a licentious habit serving pernicious ends. In Israel as elsewhere it reveals not merely the intellectual vulgarity and lack of distinction that pervade modern culture but the will to deceive through outrageous hyperbole. In 1985 a show by the Haifa Painters and Sculptors Association entitled "Israeli and Palestinian Artists Against Occupation and for Freedom of Expression" advertised itself in the stridently gaudy red, white, and black of the Nazi flag. How better to épater les Juifs in the Jewish state, especially in a building located on Zionism Avenue? The Nazi-style posters were more suitable than their designers had imagined, for the scandalous center of attraction of the show was a painting by one Harold Rubin depicting a Nazi thug with "Jewish" features and a Star of David on his hat, twisted (in the unsubtle style of Arab and Russian cartoons that appeared after the Six-Day War) into a swastika. The hoodlum's hand is raised in the Nazi salute, and the painting is labelled "Judenjugend," i.e., the Israeli Hitlerjugend.[17] One had only to look at this painting and a few others like it to understand why the exhibit's organizers had chosen for it so ungainly a title: anyone who voiced a protest about the antisemitic incitement in such works as Rubin's could be derided as an enemy of free expression. Israeli antisemites have derived at least one benefit from the Enlightenment: they know how to advocate, when it suits them, a tolerance so capacious that it tolerates fanatical intolerance itself.

At least one major Israeli cultural institution has virtually based itself upon the unrelenting pursuit of the Israeli-Nazi equation. In the article mentioned earlier, the Israeli humorist Dosh singled out the Haifa Municipal Theatre as the most consistently successful exporter of Israeli antisemitism to a world eager for something better than the shoddy goods turned out by Europeans, who had greater experience in antisemitic production but few fresh ideas and little sense of immediacy to their subject, Jews now being in short supply in Europe. The productions of the Haifa Company have been received with acclaim in Berlin, in Chicago, in Washington, in Edinburgh, despite the fact that no serious literary critic would place the company's playwrights on a level with Israel's many distinguished poets and novelists; and few critics would rank them above mediocrity. Whence, then, derives their astonishing success in the theatrical capitals of the world? The answer is that the Haifa Municipal Theatre specializes in Israeli-produced antisemitism--and also, an added attraction of a curious kind--government-supported antisemitism, since the theatre receives large public support from the Cultural Division of the Ministry of Culture and Education, support so generous that the company puts on productions, as one critic wrote, "overlavish even by Western standards."[18] When the Jewish community of Frankfurt protested in 1985 the Fassbinder play titled Trash, the City and Death, one of the protesters held aloft a poster reading "subsidized antisemitism." He might well have offered it to his co-religionists in Düsseldorf who have twice had occasion to protest against Haifa Theatre productions staged in that city as antisemitic, or encouragements to antisemitism.

The reasons why these Israeli theatrical productions find favor with foreign audiences eager for new lethal ammunition to fire at Israel are not far to seek. Yehoshua Sobol's _The Soul of a Jew_ recounted the career of the half-deranged Otto Weininger, an Austrian Jewish antisemite. The play offended many Israelis when it was first performed in October 1982, but was far more warmly received at the Edinburgh Festival, where it supplied the opening program in summer 1983. Sobol had already indicated his curiosity about Weininger in _Night of the Twentieth_ (1976), a play about young Jews who (in the third Aliyah) leave their homes in Europe for the purpose of driving the Arabs out of _their_ homes in Palestine, a play that ends with a degenerate Jew about to open fire on an Arab village. But this psychotic Viennese-Jewish antisemite seemed the very thing for the Haifa Company to produce in 1982 when the Lebanese War was raging and most of Europe was raging, as it does with some frequency, against the evil inclinations of the Zionists.

In the course of _Soul of a Jew_, Weininger insists frequently on the incompatibility of Judaism and Zionism, with special emphasis on the loathesomeness of the former. "'You have to understand,'" he tells a Zionist character named Clara, "'that Judaism is an abyss in the Jewish soul. It is bound to devour what we try to build upon it.'" Some of his anti-Jewish reflections are less "philosophical": "'From time immemorial Jews have never done a thing that does not pay off in hard cash.'" But mainly it is the contradiction between Zionism and Judaism that he insists on, as in his final speech before shooting himself: "'Zionism aspires to goals totally opposed to the spirit of Judaism. It needs to oppose and conquer Judaism from within, rid itself of Judaism once and for all . . . .'" At one point Weininger even goes so far as to say something favorable about Zionism, calling it "'the last remnant of nobleness left in Judaism.'" But this line appears only in the original Hebrew and had mysteriously disappeared when the play reached Scotland.

The familiar techniques of literary apologetics have been followed by Sobol's defenders among the journalists and assistant professors. Weininger is a literary invention, and why suppose that the author would put his own ideas in the mouth of a lunatic, any more than Swift put his ideas in the mouth of the narrator of _A Modest Proposal_ or _Tale of a Tub_? Unfortunately, Sobol himself has endorsed Weininger's definition of Judaism, for it seems to him a potent weapon in his struggle against the religious Jews of Israel. "I think Judaism is taking over Zionism," he said in commenting about the play. Referring to the (to him) deplorable elements of both Diaspora Jewry and Israeli religious nationalists, he continued: "Weininger, just as Zionism was beginning, saw where things would lead. If, 35 years after the establishment of the state, there isn't massive immigration, then Weininger's claim is pertinent." All of this authorial "interpretation," like many of Weininger's speeches, might be used to buttress the claim that Sobol is really defending Zionism in its pristine form against the incursions of religious obscurantism. But Sobol himself has made this a difficult task for even his nimblest apologists. What, asked an interviewer, was his underlying purpose in recreating the world of fin-de-siécle Viennese Jewish antisemitism? "We're used to seeing Zionism as a healthy thing. I want to show that Zionism is a sick flower which grows in sick soil." Since the title of his play in Hebrew--_nefesh yehudi_--implies a generalization--i.e., the soul of any Jew, the Haifa Rabbinate might have been forgiven for seeing Sobol's portrait of his misogynist, antisemitic, sexually perverted protagonist as a celebration of "blasphemy and deformity, depravity and Jewish self-hatred."

In the same tumultuous year, 1982, a theatre in Tel Aviv, not wishing to be outdone by Haifa in shocking the Jews, staged Hanoch Levin's The Patriot. This play is about a man eager to flee Israel's endless wars and ruinous inflation, who invests in land in Israel's administered territories, hoping to make a profit if a settlement should be built there, and a still greater profit if the government should dismantle the settlement and pay compensation. The play is replete with the orthodoxies characteristic of the herd of independent thinkers who comprise Israel's theatrical establishment: religious Jews are hypocrites, perverts, and sadists; Israeli parents are sending their children to war in order to make financial profit; and---this above all---Jews have become Nazis. Hanoch Levin's The Patriot became the first play ever to have been banned in its entirety by the Israeli Film and Theatre Censorship Board. The scene which caused Levin most trouble with the censors was the one in which the patriot must kick an Arab shoe-shine boy to maintain the standards of Jewish settlers in Judea and Samaria. The scene ends with the boy cowering in fear before the patriot's gun, a scene choreographed to refer to the famous picture of a Jewish boy in Europe cowering before the Nazis.[19] Coming a close second in its power to offend was a scene in which Jewish sabbath candles are used as instruments to torture Arabs.

The newspaper Ha'aretz conceded that The Patriot "may indeed seriously harm the basic values of the nation, the state and Judaism," but opposed censorship in accord with standard liberal dogma. People unacquainted with Israeli life need perhaps to be apprised of the curious fact that Israeli liberals go well beyond John Stuart Mill in their readiness to accommodate libel and sedition. Mill wrote that in every permanent political society there must be "in the constitution of the State something which is settled, something permanent, and not to be called in question: something which, by general agreement, has a right to be where it is, and to be secure against disturbance."[20] In a Jewish state established three years after the end of World War II that "something" might be thought to include the conviction that a Jew is not a Nazi, that Zionism is not racism, and that the victims of the Holocaust were Jews and not Arabs. But so far Israeli liberals have decided otherwise, with what consequences we may one day see.

In April 1984, the Haifa players gained more of the peculiar success that comes with scandal from Yehoshua Sobol's play Ghetto, first performed in Haifa. The English text of this Holocaust musical is introduced by an Israel critic named Uri Rapp who declares---appropriately enough, given what follows---that "historical accuracy is unimportant in a work of art." The play's hero is an anti-Zionist Jew named Herman Kruk who belongs to the socialist Bund party. Its chief Nazi, Kittel, turns out to be not just a great admirer of Jews (Gershwin is his favorite composer), but a Talmudic scholar whose mind was formed not in Tubingen or Heidelberg but in the Hebrew University of Jerusalem. He is also, needless to say, a devotee of Zionism, particularly of the Revisionist Zionism of Jabotinsky.[21] The Jews of the Vilna Ghetto are shown as eager to develop a commercial enterprise out of mending German uniforms, and to carry out round-ups (Aktionen) and selections. Jacob Gens, the Nazi-appointed Jewish chief of the ghetto, offers the following apologia for his conduct: "In order to spare some Jews their clear conscience I had no choice but to plunge into the filth, leaving my own conscience behind." For the Bundist librarian Kruk, the clear sign that Gens is the dutiful puppet of the Nazis' evil intentions is his "Zionist" speech requiring Hebraization of the ghetto. Any such encouragement of Jewish national feeling demonstrates that the Nazis have "succeeded," since "Nationalism breeds nationalism."

Sobol's Holocaust musical was soon exported to Germany and performed at the Freie Volksbühne of Berlin in June 1984. It was nominated by the German Critics Poll of "Theatre Heute" as best foreign play of the year in 1985, and Peter Zadek's German production was chosen as best show in Germany for 1985. Many German reviewers spoke gleefully of how the play depicted Jews as "accessories to the Holocaust," and one wrote that "Ghetto depicts how incredibly easily the Jews allowed themselves to be pushed into the role of victims, sometimes to the point of virtually obscene collaboration with the perpetrators."[22] At the party celebrating the premiere of Ghetto in Germany, the hosts showed an unerring instinct for the level of taste displayed by Sobol himself: they served cupcakes in the form of the yellow star. At another reception for Sobol during his company's 1985 tour of Germany, the director of a leading German theatre thanked his Israeli guests for having appeared there: "The works of Yehoshua Sobol," he asserted, "will help us to better forget Auschwitz." But then, caught by the embarrassment of unintended candor in words too true to be good, he corrected himself: "better understand the meaning of Auschwitz."

Having done so much to assure Europeans, especially Germans, that the Jews of Europe cooperated actively in their own destruction and were not morally distinguishable from the Nazis, who were themselves crypto-Zionists, the Haifa Theatre had now to demonstrate that the evil spirit of Nazism found its continuator not in Europe at all but in the very state that had given lodging to those who survived the Holocaust, the state of the Jews themselves. The Palestinian (1987) deals with a favorite cliché of contemporary Israeli writing, a love affair between an Arab and a Jew that is doomed to sterility and failure because of the prejudices and hostility of that convenient culprit "society," but especially of the Jews in that society. The Jews in the play are depicted as, for the most part, ugly, bigoted, brutal, "fascistic." The Palestinian Arab girl in the title role has been so attrociously treated by these Jews that, when asked for her address in one scene, she replies, "Nüremburg Avenue, corner of Auschwitz." The incipient Nazi tendencies of the Jews in his earlier play's concentration camp have now reached their full flowering in Israeli "Nazism." When invited by morbidly curious journalists to interpret his own play, Sobol, with characteristic intellectual delicacy, said that he was warning of the "danger of fascist tendencies in Israeli society" and, in a rhetorical question meant to implicate everyone but himself, asked "How much anti-Semitism do we carry within ourselves?" If we were to generalize from the example of Sobol, the answer would have to be: plenty.

In Germany, once again, many critics interpreted the play in the spirit of the Zionism-Racism resolution passed by the UN when Kurt Waldheim directed that august body; and they drew from it the lessons that Sobol intended. One praised it for showing "the existing reality of Zionism" and the way in which "the Israelis behave as a master race . . . towards the Palestinians." Another praised Sobol for having boosted German morale by "knocking the Jews from their pedestal of being taboo" and "showing them without their halo." Sobol had courageously displayed the "ugly" Israeli and had been unabashed about having this nasty specimen "express his fascist attitudes." Henryk Broder, to whose excellent discussion of the play's reception in Germany I am indebted, described how, at the play's premiere in the newly renovated Bonn theatre, the audience burst into frenzied, frantic ovations for the play and "showered Sobol with cries of bravo." Were they in ecstasy over the dramatic or lyric power of a play that the more sophisticated and reserved German critics variously described as "artistically and politically mindless, even embarrassing," "sentimental and trivializing," and "spewing kitsch"?[23] Or were they expressing their gratitude for being released at last from whatever burden of guilt they might have felt over their country's role in the greatest crime in history, released, moreover, by an Israeli Jew who assures them that the spirit of Nazism has moved to the Middle East and taken up residence among the Jews themselves? Some Germans, to be sure, were less grateful for a play that presented Jews in something like the way they had once been depicted in Nazi propaganda: all-powerful, aggressive, greedy, brutal. These ungrateful Germans were, of course, the Jews. The Jewish community of Düsseldorf, which had already protested vociferously in 1985 against the antisemitic flavor of Ghetto, now appealed to the Haifa Municipal Theatre not to perform The Palestinian there. Antisemitism, they argued, was already doing very well in Germany, and there was no need to carry coals to Newcastle. The theatre's board of directors, after endless wrangling, finally acceded to the Düsseldorf Jewish community's request in May of 1987. While the Düsseldorf Jews were wondering whether it was for such things as the Haifa Municipal Theatre that we needed a Jewish state the play was being performed elsewhere in Germany as well as in Holland and Belgium.

In February of this year the PLO's Madison Avenue branch contrived a scheme to send to Israel a ship intended "to echo the voyage of the Exodus." The event was laden with a great force of symbolic revelation, but what it revealed was not what its designers intended. The real Exodus, as some may still recall, was in 1947 carrying 4550 Jewish survivors of Nazi death camps, and was turned away from Palestine by the British who then ruled there. This year's Arab imitation of the Exodus carried 135 terrorists deported over the years from Israeli-administered territories, the sweepings from the gaming tables in Monte Carlo, the cafes in Paris and Rome, the lecture platforms of countless left-wing groups; they were accompanied by 300 journalists and 200 assorted well-wishers, among them Israeli Jews.

What moved each of the groups on this ship of knaves and fools to participate in the charade, the symbolic effort to recreate Palestinian Arabs as Jews? For what the New York Times (February 16) referred to as the "scores of minor Western dignitaries and journalists" the equation of Arabs with Jews and, in consequence, of Israelis with Nazis, affords a welcome escape from any lingering feelings, however faint, of responsibility for what their countries did, or allowed to be done, to European Jewry. As for the Palestinian Arabs, they have long been consumed by resentment that the Jews should be allowed to monopolize all that beautiful Holocaust suffering which they would very much like, *ex post facto*, to share. Freud spoke of a sickness he called "penis-envy"; Palestinian Arabs suffer from what might be called "Holocaust envy," a feeling so strong that it prevents them from seeing that their compulsive desire to appropriate a history that is not their own is itself powerful proof of just how contrived and artificial is the Palestinian sense of national identity. A movement that can conceive of itself only as a mirror image of its Jewish enemy is an anti-nation that derives its whole purpose and meaning from the desire to destroy a living nation.

But what moved the Israelis who wanted to participate in this PLo publicity stunt? What does it say about *their* sense of identity as Jews that they can confirm or discover it only by allying themselves with Arabs who are pretending to be Jews and who are constantly accusing the Jewish state of being essentially Nazi? Many plausible if not wholly convincing motives for antisemitism among Israelis may be named. I have already referred to the inducements of fame and fortune available to Israelis willing to denounce their country and countrymen as Nazis. I have also alluded to the desperate search for an explanation of the unrelenting hostility, for over four decades, of Israel's neighbors. It is an old law of Jewish history that external aggression, if maintained long enough, will exacerbate the tendency of the more timorous Jews to blame other Jews for the general misfortune of the community. Thus Yehoshua Sobol explains Arab unwillingness to accept the Jewish state by charging that Judaism is essentially "barbaric" and therefore by its nature a provocation: the Jews always, he says, "bring destruction on themselves by provoking great powers."[24]

The rabid secularism of Israelis who resort to antisemitism as a means of explaining the world may not exactly confirm the warning often given by characters in Isaac Bashevis Singer's novels that a Jew who rejects the Torah becomes a Nazi, but it does suggest the failure of dogmatically secular Zionism to provide Israeli Jews with a culture and an inner world of their own. For surely no Israelis so endowed would have resorted to their enemies' travesty of the Holocaust as a means of understanding their own past. In fact, if secular Zionism had succeeded in its intellectual and spiritual aims, its offspring would not have had to resort, as so many Diaspora Jews do, to the Holocaust as their only past. Jewish tradition holds that 600,000 Israelites witnessed the giving of the Law at Sinai; and historians record that in 1948 657,000 Israelites witnessed and participated in the birth of the State. Was not the birth of the state of Israel, a birth that took place only a few years after the greatest dying in the history of the Jewish people, a miracle? Was not the absorption, within just two years, of another 600,000 people--and this in the midst of severe economic hardship and in the wake of a war that had destroyed one percent of the population--a miracle? Were not the revival of Hebrew and the ingathering of the exiles miracles? The age of miracles is not past, but if you teach your children for two or three generations that God is incredible and revelation impossible, some of them will eventually fail to see miracles that take place before their very eyes, miracles in which they themselves have participated. Light is a quality of matter, but blind people don't see it. If young Israelis are torn asunder from their Jewish roots and their own history, taught, as Shulamit Aloni would like them to be taught, that the Holocaust was not perpetrated by Nazis against Jews, but by "people" against "people," some of them will grope toward potent forms of darkness in place of the light of which they have been bereft.

NOTES

1. All of these examples of Jewish antisemitism are discussed in Sander L. Gilman, Jewish Self-Hatred (Baltimore: Johns Hopkins University Press, 1986).
2. Table Talk, August 14, 1833.
3. Quoted in Arnold Ages, "Jewish Nativism," Congress Monthly, LV, (January 1988), 22, a review of James S. Diamond, Homeland or Holy Land? The "Canaanite" Critique of Israel. See also Rael Jean Isaac, Israel Divided (Baltimore: Johns Hopkins University Press, 1976).
4. Hillel Halkin, Letters to an American Jewish Friend (Philadelphia: Jewish Publication Society, 1977), p. 180.
5. Jerusalem Post, April 19, p. 2.
6. Ma'ariv International Edition, 21 August 1987 (Magazine).
7. Ma'ariv International Edition, 21 August 1987.
8. These "implications" are defined cogently, if grossly, by a character in the above-mentioned novel by Philip Roth: "'I am in Norway on business for my product and written on a wall I read: 'Down with Israel!' I think, 'What did Israel ever do to Norway?' I know Israel is a terrible country, but after all, there are countries even more terrible . . . Why don't you read on Norwegian walls, 'Down with Russia,' 'Down with Chile,' 'Down with Libya'? Because Hitler didn't murder six million Libyans? I am walking in Norway and I am thinking, 'If only he had.' Because then they would write on Norwegian walls, 'Down with Libya,' and leave Israel alone."

9. Conor Cruise O'Brien, The Siege (New York: Simon and Schuster, 1986), p. 258.
10. Jerusalem Post, 6 July 1982.
11. Counterpoint, September 1987, p. 7.
12. Le Racisme de l'Etat d'Israel (Paris, 1975), p. 267.
13. Jerusalem Post, 2 May 1982.
14. In Seattle, Yermiya petulantly attacked Jews who consider the Holocaust "a private asset . . . which must not be mentioned in the same breath as their own actions." --University of Washington Daily, 2 May 1981.
15. David K. Shipler, Arab and Jew (New York: Times Books, 1986), pp. 348, 340.
16. Norma Rosen, "The Second Life of Holocaust Imagery," Midstream, XXXIII (April 1987), 56-59.
17. See Ya'acov Friedler, "Jewish anti-Semitism," Jerusalem Post, 27 March 1985.
18. Harold Fisch, "Art and Statism: The Question of Funding the Arts," lecture delivered at first international conference of Institute for Advanced Strategic and Political Studies, Jerusalem, 1985.
19. See Marsha Pomerantz, "Storm Over Play," Jerusalem Post, 6 November 1982.
20. "Coleridge," essay published March 1840.
21. Ever since Hannah Arendt's spiteful and ill-considered remarks about Eichmann's "Zionism" in her book on his Jerusalem trial, it has been a commonplace among anti-Zionist propagandists that, in the words of that journalistic thug Alexander Cockburn: "the Nazis approved of Zionism." But the typical Nazi estimate of Zionism was expressed by a Nazi named Adolf Hitler in Mein Kampf: "While the Zionists try to make the rest of the world believe that the national consciousness of the Jew finds its satisfaction in the creation of a Palestinian state, the Jews again slyly dupe the dumb Goyim. It doesn't even enter their heads to build up a Jewish state in Palestine for the purpose of living there; all they want is a central organization for their international world swindle . . . "
22. Henryk M. Broder, "Sobol: Making a Scene," Jerusalem Post Magazine, 6 February 1987.
23. Ibid.
24. Jerusalem Post Magazine, 8 May 1987.

THE REACTION OF THE LABOUR MOVEMENT SCHOOL SYSTEM IN PALESTINE TO THE HOLOCAUST - THE AGGRAVATION AND MODIFICATION OF EDUCATIONAL DILEMMAS IN THE YEARS 1943-1948

Y. DROR

Haifa University, The School of Education of the Kibbutz Movement, Oranim,
Tivon 38910, ISRAEL.

INTRODUCTION

The socialist Labour Movement School System - the "Workers Stream" which was associated with the "General Labour Federation" (Histadrut) was one of the three main streams in the educational system of the Jewish community in Palestine during the British Mandate. The "General Stream" (which had a liberal- centralist outlook), and the national religious "Mizrahi" were also active. Jewish education enjoyed a high degree of autonomy in the period of the British Mandate (1918-1948). The supervision of the Mandatorial Department for Education was only administrative. Each stream took care of teaching and educational programs which were authorized by the Educational Department of the Zionist Labour Organization (and, from 1932, by the National Committee of the Jewish Community).
This system of "streams" also worked in Jewish education in the first years of statehood until its cancellation by the "Governmental Law for Education" from 1953 (Bentoitz, 1960, chapters 2, 4).
The Workers Stream founded in 1921, was for more than 30 years, the educational instrument of the Jewish Labour Movement which tried to combine international socialism with Jewish nationalism in towns and in villages. Until 1939, several "educational experiments" (which were expanded in a partly institutionalized educational movement) took place within this framework. The thirties were the transitional years of the "stream" from an "educational movement" into an "educational system": In 1931 a "Committee for Educational Institutions" was founded which, from 1934 became the "Centre for Education," charged with the administration of the "stream" in the General Labour Federation. From 1939, when it was officialy included in the National Department for Education, the "Stream" became an institutionalized educational system in every respect (Reshef, 1980). In extensive research by the author about the "Labour Stream School System" in the decade before the establishment of the State and the absorption of waves of mass-immigration (1939-1948); Dror, in preparation) the case under discussion was also investigated: How did the "Stream" react to the Holocaust in the years 1943-1948?
The case has an educational and public interest beyond the mere historical investigation. The Labour Movement and its educational system to a great extent represented the whole Jewish community, being at the peak of their political power. This also expressed itself in the central position of the "Stream" in the education of that time.[1] The whole Jewish educational system in the years under discussion concerned itself with the Holocaust, but inside the socialist "Workers Stream" the dilemma between the national and the international had more meaning. The horror of the Holocaust became known in the Jewish community in Palestine in November 1942 (Porat, 1986, p. 62); the State of Israel was established in May 1948 during the war for her independence. The educational reaction between the "Holocaust and the Revival of the Jewish State", between two wars, has a significance beyond the time and the place under discussion. Very important is also the comparison between the educational reaction immediately after the shock of the Holocaust and that after a couple of years. For all these reasons, the issue under discussion is presented here although it may seem of small scope.

A survey of sources and events, their periods and their significance.

The sources surveyed for this research are very extensive and they are an expression of the educational leadership and of the teachers in the field as well - in spite of the fact that only few of them occupied themselves with the Holocaust and the ensuing educational reaction in the years under discussion: all the protocols from different Labour School System institutions[2]: "Urim" - its periodical, "Hed HaGan" from the Kindergarten Teachers Federation, which had a considerable representation in the "Kindergarten Teachers from the Centre for Education", and the educational writings from the kibbutz and moshav movements belonging to the "Stream"; the registration of lectures and reactions on all study-days and all kinds of educational conferences organized by the "Stream" - including offprints and booklets prepared for this reason; the statements of "Stream" philosophers and leaders which were published in the aforesaid sources and also separately. The Labour School System consisted of schools in the towns and villages and also in the moshav movement and the three kibbutz movements of that time: "HaKibbutz HaMeuhad", "HaKibbutz HaArtzi", and "Hever HaKvutzot". In the moshav movement and the "Hever", parts, and special issues of the general publication were dedicated to educational topics; the two other movements had separate educational organs. All those were surveyed, emphasizing the part of the authors who were also included in the general "stream" organs: it is not our intention in this paper to present the specific reaction to the Holocaust from secondary movements in the "Stream", but to include what they have in common as part of the Jewish Labour Movement of those years.[3]

The survey of the sources teaches about the "there is" and the "there isn't" from the aspect of timing and the extent of facing up educationally to the Holocaust. The Jews in Palestine received first information "about the situation of the Jews in Europe" in September 1942, but the extent and the methods of the Holocaust became known only in the middle of November the same year (Porat, 1986, Chapter 1). In November a forceful article by Tabenkin, one of the leaders of the workers movement was published in "Tzror Mikhtavim", the educational organ of "HaKibbutz HaMeuhad", about "The School and the War". Together with it appeared the opinions of all the participants in the "Kibbutz Teachers and Children's Nurses Conference" who debated the subject. In the moshav movement organ "Tlamim" of March-April 1943, there were many reactions to the Holocaust and to Tabenkin's standpoint, by some of the most outstanding educators in the Labour Movement and the "Stream" (like Avigal and Halprin). "Hed HaGan" of the same time refers in a number of articles to the absorption of the Teheran children.

Only on 7.5.43 on the initiative of Avigal, one of the philosophers of the "Stream", the pedagogic committee of the "Stream" debated "that the time has come to call for a conference to discuss the questions concerning a state of emergency and war"; and in its resume it was decided that "it is possible and desirable to dedicate... a bi-annual conference...to the situation of emergency in education... which was extraordinary (in the days of the vacation)... (and will be dedicated) to the problem of education at this terrible hour."[4] In the summer of 1943 Avigal published again an extensive educational article concerning the Holocaust in "Urim" - "LeOr HaMoked" ("In the Light of the Fire") with his main thesis, which afterwards appeared to be in accord with the standpoint of most of the "Stream" educators.[5]

In the summer of 1943, in the organ "Ofakim", Tzvi Zohar, one of the leading educators in "HaKibbutz HaArtzi, wrote about the influence of the war in general - and especially on education in the diaspora without any outspoken comment on the Holocaust.

A year went by after the horrors of the Holocaust became known to the Jews of Palestine and a half year after the discussions in the pedagogic committee. In the autumn of 1944, finally, two general conferences of the "Stream" concerning the Holocaust took place. Before and after them, written material was given out to be used by the educators. The "Management Council", representing all the educational institutions in the "Stream", at its meeting in Hadera on 16-17 November 1943 heared Avigal's lecture and reacted to it. In December 1943, a general pedagogic conference was held in Tel Aviv and there also, with some additions, Avigal's lecture was read, as well as other lectures (including Tabenkin, who went beyond his initial thesis, and Shmuel Golan, educational leader of "HaKibbutz HaArtzi" which discussed "Education - Towards the Future" and the direct consequences of the Holocaust. His article under this name was published in "Ofakim" only at the beginning of 1944. Avigal's centrality at those conferences and in the resumes of the pedagogic committee was in contrast to the fears of the other leaders of the "Stream" to merely talk about the subject. In April 1944 the kindergarten-teachers held a conference initiated by their active pedagogic committee, which was called "The Holocaust of the Days in our Work". Prior and pursuant to this conference very useful and extensive material was issued. At this conference, it was openly discussed that some of the female speakers wanted to conceal the Holocaust from the children.[6] In the course of 1944 additional educational articles on the Holocaust were published in "Urim".[7]

In the other sources of the "Stream" - all surveyed from the end of 1942 until 1948 - almost no mention is made of the Holocaust and any educational reaction is only by way of duty or perfunctory, a tiny bit here and a tiny bit there, in the introductions of articles, debates and decisions. So, for example, "Hever Hakvutzot" whose activity in the movement and in education was very limited, contented itself with general reactions in its organs "Igeret" and "Igeret LaChinuch". In 1945 the centre for education published the collection "And a Stone Will Cry Out From the Wall (about the Holocaust in the diaspora)", containing poetry and prose from the Holocaust itself and its comparison with the expulsion from Spain.[8] In 1947-48, with the outbreak of the War of Independence and prior to the establishment of the State, the consequences of the Holocaust were linked to "the educational problems of the moment", discussed at several conferences where the dilemmas linked to it were discussed again. Consequently, a survey of the sources shows (a) the general tendency in the "Stream" to be slow in its educational reaction to the Holocaust for over a year from the day the magnitude of the disaster became known - including the wish to conceal the subject from the children, (b) the limited reaction, and (c) the concentration mainly on general conferences and written material in 1944 - and the late and much more limited dealing with the Holocaust in 1947-48.

Educational activities expressing the link with the diaspora and the Holocaust.

During the years of the war, the institutions of the "Stream" undertook several activities to underline the link with the diaspora and the Holocaust. Already at the beginning of the war meetings were held in the kindergartens and the schools to absorb diaspora children who emigrated to Israel, and the pupils sent letters and presents to the Jewish soldiers who went to fight at the front, and even planted trees in their names. When the Holocaust and the absorption of the "Teheran children" became known in 1943 and after the soldiers started to rescue the survivors of the Holocaust, those activities helped to make for living contacts with the diaspora and were emphasized at conferences and in several educational organs. Some of the educational institutions commemorated the Holocaust at the end of 1942 with ceremonies, strikes, petitions and even days of mourning. At the end of 1942 the "Rescue Operation" was organized. In all the educational institutions a fund-drive was held for the diaspora and the children also worked for it. "A program for the sake of the diaspora in the whole life of the schools," Yakov Halprin, one of the leaders of the "Stream" called it, and used the example of the Jewish National Fund.

In addition to these special activities, kindergartens emphasized drawings, talks, tales of heroism and creative games by the children concerning the diaspora and the Holocaust - and in the schools "knowledge of the diaspora" in literature and in history, its economy, art, communities and institutions. The basis of these activities was the contact with the diaspora and not a discussion of the Holocaust. The higher classes also emphasized physical preparation, gymnastics and trips, as part of the "Expanded Physical Training."[9]

The aggravation of the ideological dilemmas in the "Stream" as an indirect reaction to the Holocaust.

The "Workers Stream" even before the Holocaust had to face a number of basic ideological dilemmas linked with the relationship to Judaism and the diaspora. Has the emphasis to be on Judaism and Zionism - or on Socialism? On Jewish history or on general history? Were they to present Zionism as the real contemporary Judaism, isolated from the diaspora and denying it - or the chain of generations, the continuity of Jewish fate including the diaspora? Would they emphasize the socialistic exclusiveness of the "Workers Stream" with all its components - or the unity of the working class, the Jews of Palestine and the whole people? The reaction after the Holocaust sharpened the dilemmas in the national direction - based on force, sometimes, and accompanied by some leftist reservations. It did not include dealing with the direct dilemmas the Holocaust aroused, like for example the revolt as against "going as sheep to the slaughter" - as immediately after the horror people could only debate the indirect and known dilemmas.

In his talking about "the proportion between Judaism and Europeanism" Avigal remarked, in his speech in the "Management Council" and at the pedagogic conference in 1944, that "Judaism is much more humane than this European humanism... It is our duty to fortify from the inside the wall of Judaism in the hearts of our children before we decorate it with the beauties from Japhet. That's how our fathers acted again and again in crucial turning-point times... Such a radical turning-point from international universality towards a national fortification we find in the great Russian people, when the terrible Holocaust of the world war began to approach it... Maybe we are permitted to use this idea of "Special People" in the education of this generation for the sake of strengthening the feeling of self-esteem, which is also the strengthening of steadfastness in an hour of national emergency".[10] Minah Hefetz reacted and emphasized the superiority of Judaism over Socialism: "We have breached the walls to foreign influence, we have distanced ourselves too much from our heritage... until there is no socialistic regime, humanistic education will have no value - through Judaism talking about everything" - and Polani said that "We have to abolish the inferiority feelings of our children in respect to foreign culture," and "Its's desirable that someone should define exactly the relation between class and nationality."

The turning-point in the study of Jewish history and Judaism in general was underlined in the speech (and later the article) dedicated to the Jewish diaspora historian Dinburg (Dinur), who was also a guest of honour at the pedagogic conference and promised there to complete the publication of the sources for the history of the people of Israel. Moshe Talmi from Kfar Yehezke'el who welcomed him in the name of the conference, suggested "to intensity Jewish studies" - bible, legends (agadah), the daily prayer book and festival prayer book. The pedagogic committee debated much about this subject after the conference, and also heard and published in "Urim" Dr. M. Soloveitchik's proposal. Dr. Soloveitchik was the director of the education department in the National Committee and one of the leaders of the radical faction in the Zionist Labour Federation together with Goldman and Greenboim. The end of the process, which was influenced also by these people from outside the "Stream", came with the acceptance of the proposals to intensity Jewish studies in 1946.[11]

The emphasis on nationalism was accompanied in the years 1942-1944 by references to heroism, power, Jewish superiority and the need for education towards war. Tabenkin opened the public discussion in the "Stream" and in the labour movement in general about "Education towards War" in his article "The School and the War" of November 1942: "The education (for militarization of the Jewish community and of every person belonging to it) has to start from the kindergarten and not only from school, and even from the baby-house." "The oppressed people can be stronger than the evil one" - and Soviet Russia is an example of it. The images of Saul and David, the biblical images - educate towards ability in war, heroism and its evaluation, and comradeship in battle." Haim Shifroni and Yakov Salant, educators, and also from Ein-Harod, supported his ideas[12]. David Barash from Kfar Yehoshua supported, in his movement's organ "Tlamim", the "Education to struggle with all physical and spiritual forces for Jewish independence, economic and spiritual, and for a life of justice in the Jewish domain"; he also intended that "Massada (and not Yavneh) turn into an experience for our youngsters, (and) the blood of Massada is first of all our blood."[13]

Yakov Halprin (Niv), one of the leaders of the "Stream", underlined in "Tlamim" and on other occasions the need for balance: "The spring from which our students will draw their Jewish-national spirit will supply them their origial food in two ways - 'love your brother as yourself' on the one hand and 'an eye for an eye, a tooth for a tooth' on the other...[14] On the side of work and peace appears the slogan 'and for defence - defence at all costs'"; "In all generations they tried to exterminate us - our forefathers knew how to defend themselves... and we are ordered to lengthen this chapter of our history - in order to prove to our children that the basis of dedication to our honour and self-sacrifice for our defence was an inheritance of our forefathers from generation to generation."[15]

The booklet "The History of Defence in Israel" by Yakov Kna'ani was published in 1940 by The Centre for Education. Only four years later was it reviewed in "Urim" with the emphasis on "the events in which the Jews fought with arms in their hands," on the subject of "the defence of our people in the diaspora" illuminated by a "reference of sanctity" and on what is lacking - "the heroism of the Israelite Tribes in Arabia."[16]

Avigal, who opened and guided the public conference held in 1944, commented often on these: "One has to be strong" - he emphasized three times... "Consequently one has to know how to fight and to do everything connected with war and its ways." To "the high ideas of education" one has to add a goal required for achieving all the other goals - "education towards heroism... for self-defence and for the war of constructing a new world," the Jewish-Hebrew one. "We have to be ready physically and be able to use weapons and war-strategies."[17]

Bendori, from the activist B-faction in Mapai, supported him in the Councel in Hadera in 1943: "I don't know what is education for peace and what is education for war... We have to educate our children towards a struggle first of all for a homeland and also for a world-homeland."[18] At the conference at the end of the same year, there were more supporters: Tabenkin repeated his opinions, foreseeing the future: "Can Jewry educate its children in a period of wars between people... towards an inability to defend themselves in those wars?... Is self-defence immoral?... In this period the dream of pacifism has been destroyed... The dream that the government will renounce the sources of its rule... I don't suggest that our schools will teach the use of arms, but we have to educate in our schools that man fights for himself not only by talking and not only by expression, but also by means of his body and his spirit." Polani said: "We must glorify the heroism of struggling, whether it means martyrdom or self-defence; these values can strengthen our children in this time of emergency"; Leah Talmi said that "we don't have to cover up Joshua's conquest, the opposite - we have to show all the heroism in the bible" - and Rodnitzky added "we have to discover the hidden sources of light in Judaism, to show the children that we are exalted above other peoples."[19]

The booklet published for the National Conference of Kindergarten- teachers in the spring of 1944 included the opinions of Tabenkin and Avigal and of the kindergarten-teachers themselves: repeated comparisons between the Maccabees and the Jewish soldiers; emphasis on contact with the Jewish soldiers and their heroism in songs, stories and letters; an extensive description of war-games and children's heroism" - and a final observation on the games and the discussions as well: "We shouldn't let the children have a feeling of helplessness... We have to educate a generation to know and feel from childhood that miracles will not happen and that we cannot expect help from outside or from heaven. The solution to our hardships is inside us, in our will-power, spiritual readiness and the belief that when we will - we can."[20] In addition, the protocol of the lectures and discussions at the conference is full of quotations about Tabenkin's standpoint and other expressions of heroism; for example in the "theses" of the lectures ("We will sow in the hearts of our children love and honour for our heroes... respect for women, for the heroic mother..."; "...place the image of the hero at a distance... describe his superhuman qualities..."; "stories that educate towards devotion and love for the homeland and forge the character... towards love for the people and national pride"). There were also the slogans of the conference, like "from the Maccabees until the unknown soldier of our time the chain continues," "let the heroism of our defenders be an example for the life of your children," "let's sow in the hearts of our children admiration for the unknown hero like that for the Maccabeans," and "let the heroism of the diaspora live in our hearts for ever."[21]
The representatives of the left were opposed to this nationalistic line - and what is more, these were also the days of the split in faction B of Mapai and its getting closer, with "HaKibbutz HaMeuhad", to the left of the Labour Federation. Hanovitz from Heftzi-Bah from "HaKibbutz HaMeuhad" claimed that "it is my duty to give my children at school everything that's good, also from Europe." Tabenkin opted for an international world, in which nothing human is strange. Golan, form "HaKibbutz HaArtzi" and from the left, spoke against "national and cultural isolationism", and in his reaction asked Avigal: "Is it really possible to deny socialist teaching because it hasn't yet been realised"; and like him, Gerson who proclaimed that "the time to abstain from European culture hasn't yet arrived."[22] In contrast with them, some of the people from the moshavin spoke out openly against Tabenkin and his supporters in "Education towards War", and had more Gordonistic conceptions: "We are obliged, to our regret, to teach our children to hit the target with a stone... But in the meantime we can hit the brain of our student with a ritual of hitting" (Yakov Uri); "He calls for education towards war at a time of war and I call for education towards peace at a time of war" (Yoseph Shapira); "Education in times of emergency... its task is so to educate that we don't bring the times of emergency upon ourselves!" (Nathan Hofshi); Education towards war essentially turns into education towards hate" (Yitschak Belenki); "The road marked by comrade Tabenkin is a dangerous one" (Yakov Kna'ani).[23] But these were a minority against the nationalistic line.
All the speakers and writers about the Holocaust from an educational point of view supported the giving of prominence to the diaspora together with immigration and absorption, after the "denial of the diaspora" had been an educational principle for many years to glorify the pioneering in Eretz Israel: "We were occupied with our work, and our children were impressed that a noble and creating tribe grew here - and in the diaspora, a world of speculation and shopkeepers. We were content with this, because we turned it into a mighty creative lever, but we exaggerated in our inhuman attitude towards the diaspora - and we must normalize this... to unroll also the curtain of the mighty creation of the diaspora." Thus spoke Talmi from Kfar Yehezke'el in the Management Council in 1944; like him, many others changed their attitude towards the diaspora. Golan, from "HaKibbutz HaArtzi" explained the "deep contradiction between our renewed life in the Land and... the images of the way of life in Exile" - nevertheless we must now draw nearer to us "the strange diaspora that has been denied to the child." Avigal and Halprin talked about the knowledge of the "diaspora" as against "the Land" and even its love - including "martyrdom in its many variations" especially in the ghettos. The pedagogic committee appointed on 5.11.43 some of the senior educators in the "Stream" - Ehrlich, Zislah, Zvigel and Pinnels - for preparatory lectures in the branches about "Diaspora Jewry in our Education," before the conferences of 1944. Tabenkin, in his speech at the end of 1944 about the future, reminded them of "the Gathering of the Exiles," the absorption of orphans and other exiles by the tens of thousands "in a colonization-process." At the conference of the kindergarten-teacher, immigration and diaspora were tied together in the different educational activities, in order to modify the denial of the latter: "To the idea of the diaspora and immigration - the creation of a correct attitude towards diaspora and immigration - we linked the slogans "Open the hearts of your children to the Jewish survivors"... and "children will return to their Land." The textbook "A Stone Shall Cry Forth from the Wall" explained in detail the destroyed creation of the diaspora in the works of Hebrew authors who immigrated to Israel.[24]

The need for unity of class and people was strengthened after the Holocaust and was generally agreed upon: "It's our duty now..." Avigal remarked in his speeches, "to emphasize and to stress... in the education of our children the feeling of solidarity and mutual responsibility and the unity of destiny of all parts of the nation with its many classes and streams. We don't want uniform education... we want a unified nation." He demanded "a real peace-covenant between the factions in Mapai, an armistice - if not a union - between Mapai and 'HaShomer HaTzair', and also the unification of all the youth-movements in the Labour Federation." The approval of other speakers of these demands, and the understandable reservations of the leftists who clung to their ideological and political exclusiveness did not do much good to Avigal's call. National unity remained only a proclamation.[25]

<u>The exacerbation of the didactic curricular dilemmas in the "Stream" as a result of the exacerbation of the ideological dilemmas - an additional indirect reaction to the Holocaust.</u>
On the subject of didactics and curricula, the "Stream" had its doubts even before the Holocaust over the balance between the sciences (study preparing for livelihood) and the humanities (broad general education). Inside the humanities, there were several dilemmas: between the study of the material for the sake of study alone, in an objective manner - or selected parts of it, in order to bring out the actual moral benefits; between ideological contents and social techniques as forms of ideological education; between a clear ideological line and public-educational doubt; between formal education at school and the emphasis on the youth-movement. All those dilemmas were sharpened, following the Holocaust, in a topical ideological-humanistic direction, acknowledging the doubts about values and the importance of tightening the contact between the schools and the youth-movement. This exacerbation was a result of the ideological dilemmas; it was also a kind of indirect reaction to the Holocaust, because the time was not yet ripe to deal directly with its dilemmas. It was Avigal who led the public discussion about this issue, and his colleagues from the leadership of the "Workers Stream" and educators from the ranks mostly agreed with his proposals.
About "The proportion between science studies and humanities in our education" said Avigal at the conferences in 1944: "I believe we will return again to the original Jewish conception which places humanism - and mainly Jewish humanism - at the basis of education and turns the sciences into its slave, serving its exalted moral goals." As a result of emphasizing Judaism, Avigal assumed that objections should be made against the priority of the sciences, which is the pedagogic starting- point of the gentiles, and to return to Jewish humanities. He didn't object to the necessity of the sciences, but he assumed that changes should be made because of the emergency of the Holocaust because "can the school continue its normal working-program, laid down years ago, at a time that life is stormy and changing from one end to the other all the time?"
Inside the humanities Avigal sided with choosing selected parts, mainly historical, for the sake of actual moral consequences; "Aren't we obliged to choose from history, for every period and social situation, the fitting chapters, to serve as an example for our days in their actuality?... And the same for economic and political geography, the bible and literature." Avigal argued against the "stable, static, sanctified and frozen" study-program and emphasized also the quality of the acquired knowledge and not its quantity, for the sake of "moral improvement," "the ascent of the soul," and "the development of spiritual forces and an opinion based on moral principles."
The centrality of Jewish-humanistic concepts led Avigal to an epicuristic opinion about "social education" and the new dynamic didactic systems, which were among the main educational conceptions of the "Stream": "So we must pay less attention to the framework and more to the contents; less to the form of social organization and more to the essence of social life... In recent years we were too bogged down in didactic and methodical rules. I don't want to annul them... But nevertheless, I think they are not the most important. They are the tools and not the wine itself." This opinion of Avigal was given against the background of transferring many of the didactic systems from the "Stream" to the "General System" - and inevitably led to the conclusion that in the essence of the program the exclusiveness and the difference were being drained.
The national-moralistic emphasis and the Russian examples he gave did not bring Avigal to the one-way determination of how to transfer these values. Just because he thought that spiritual values are most important, he stood for "the activation of the soul," for "co- operation of the feelings and the wishes of the soul" during study, for the connection with world-encompassing issues following the Holocaust "between the heart of the educator and the heart of the student." The explicitly Jewish-humanistic idiological education had to be given to the students in the form of personal reference which is not indoctrination, but a kind of "Values Clarification."
This approach of the youth-movement was acceptable for the "Workers Stream" and therefore also Avigal's call for a combined spiritual influence of school and youth-movement was understood: "We must not only preach and demand but also stand up and do... In school and

youth-movement... To find ways to influence youth and act without delay for the unification of all youth-movements in the Labour Federation... We must... strengthen the contacts between the youth-movements and the schools."[26]

Some were against the humanistic, the actual and selective emphasis in Avigal's opinion - mostly among the leftists, and some who assumed, like Tabenkin, that the sciences are necessary to prepare the students for a life of pioneering, for the training of "worker and farmer, craftsman, sailor and miner." Most of the speakers and writers agreed with him, quibbled about hair-splitting definitions concerning priorities. Halprin wrote about the "vitality of the intensified humanistic education in these days." Shifroni - a man of scientific subjects - demanded changes in the curriculum with its Jewish- humanistic tendencies which brings "from the new Yiddish literature reflecting the life of the Jewish masses in all its aspects, from the revolutionary and pioneer-literature and from the literature of the Jewish resistance and its heroes." The textbook "A Stone Shall Cry Forth from the Wall" made a comparison between the Holocaust and the expulsion from Spain, and also other historical comparisons, with the Maccabeans and other heroes, are found by the dozens in all sources that have been surveyed.[27] As could be expected, there was almost no agreement to diminish the status of social education and the new-open methods also by those who agreed with Avigal's Jewish humanistic values - and assumed there is a completion and not a contradiction; on the other hand everyone agreed, even the leftists, to the importance of ideological thought and discussions and the combining of school and youth-movements.[28]

More balance in the presentation of the educational dilemmas following the Holocaust and prior to the War of Independence. At the end of 1947 and the beginning of 1948, before and at the beginning of the War of Independence, a number of educational conferences were held, dedicated to education at this time of emergency. The Holocaust was mentioned, by Avigal and other speakers. The educational dilemmas that arose after the Holocaust also returned before the new war; they were still indirect, and did not touch the Holocaust itself - but, from a distance of a few years, they were presented in a more balanced way and with more moderation.

At the educational council of the Labour Federation (the successor of the "Management Council") in the summer of 1947 Avigal lectured about "Our education - quo vadis?" The talk was about the negative educational factors existing as an aftergrowth of the Holocaust - "Nazism and Fascism in the world... the impotence of socialism... (and) our internal fascism." "The intensifying of Jewish studies" was presented as a way to a solution; but this time a more general definition was suggested: "Seeing mankind and the world in a Jewish mirror, from the original Hebrew civilization... To unify general humanities in a way that the evaluation of things will be from our specific point of view." Avigal still stood for "diminishing the gentile European humanities" - as he pointed out at a pedagogic conference held in the summer of the same year - but wanted more balance between the Jewish, the general and the socialistic: "We will give the culture of the world also to our children, but... through our channels... All the facts and the truths the school will teach him will join together into a system of ideas and experiences that will shape the face of the new Jewish-Israeli-Zionist- Socialist".

For all that, it was Avigal who resumed, in 1947, as part of "the contents of education in these days," a widening and strengthening of education for agriculture and technology, the necessary materialistic tools to realize the prophecy of building the land and the renewed Israeli society... The intensified physical training will be - together with agriculture and technology - an organic and integral part of the secondary education of youth."

Avigal's colleagues, already in 1944, did not agree with the diminishing of the importance of didactics and social education; and so, at the conferences in 1947 the need arose to combine both of them as educational tools of equal value. Halprin, before the debate in the Council about "The basis of our educational enterprise" emphasized "the eternal values of Judaism" side by side with "the new scientific pedagogics" and "the executive institutions of the children's community." Yehudah Ehrlich emphasized in "Bases of our Education" the "discovery of the light of Judaism and "a principle... we don't pay enough attention to: the organized social life of the children based on mutual assistance and esteem for others." In the resume of the symposium in which Ehrlich spoke in March 1948 - "Educational Problems in This Time" - the didactic activities and the students' communities were recalled as assisting proposals for "the search for a correct pedagogic way in the labyrinth of our days."

A part of the balanced tendencies discovered in the immediate reaction after the Holocaust were reinforced later, and things were written, discussed and summed up prior to, during and after the conferences of 1947-48: Zionism as the continuation of the diaspora and the chain of Jewish generations; national and class-unification; the desirable interaction between the youth-movements and the schools and the legitimacy of the reflections about ideological dilemmas.[29]

CONCLUSION

The reaction of the "Workers Stream" to the Holocaust as an example of the exacerbation and modification of indirect educational dilemmas following a severe national crises.

The reaction of the "Workers Stream" to the Holocaust in the years 1943-48, between the "Holocaust and the revival" forms an example for the aggravation and modification of existing and indirect educational dilemmas following a severe national crises.

The special and routine educational activities, were occuped more with the diaspora itself rather than with the Holocaust. The reaction came late and was minor; it was concentrated in an emotional outburst that lasted for about a year and then there was a prolonged silence; the desire to conceal the Holocaust from small children - all these were not pointed out as a judgement of wisdom after the event - but to illustrate the difficult educational problems, the "repression" when referring to the national trauma. In addition the exacerbation of the ideological dilemmas, with their tendencies towards power and nationalism is hard to criticize, because you "don't judge people until you have been in their place" - and these things apply to Judaism immediately after the Holocaus and to a community that was preparing to fight for its life in its "Massada" on the Carmel against the Germans who invaded Egypt. The exacerbation of the didactical dilemmas was a result of the Jewish-humanistic ideological emphasis - and when the contents were modificated after a couple of years and had passed, this tendency also applied to the educational systems. In both the domains, the educators did not touch the dilemmas of the Holocuast - not among themselves and not between them and the students - but only indirect dilemmas, that had existed anyway in the "Workers Stream". From the exacerbation of the indirect dilemmas and the modification later on, we can also learn about the pattern of educational reaction - also a kind of national "defence-mechanism" - for severe crises.

Delay; minority; concentration; silence; a desire to conceal; a tendency towards power and nationalism; exacerbation and modification; only indirect dilemmas - that's how the initial educational reaction of the Jewish Labour Movement in Palestine to the Holocaust is documented; let us remember and learn from it, from a distance of years, for the sake of the future.

NOTES

[1] About 25% of Jewish education belonged, towards the end of the period under discussion, to the "Workers Stream" according to a "general counting of the institutions belonging to the Department of Education of the National Committee, in the years 1944-45" (Labour Archives, 215 IV/979, p. 24) and Bentoitz, 1960, p. 72. Many of his educational principles - "The system of subjects," "The children's society," and its integration in physical work, training for agriculture etc. - were transferred also to other schools.

[2] All the protocols from the different institutions in the "Workers Stream", during all the years of its activity, are kept in the collection "The Centre for Education" in the Labour Archives; included in it and surveyed in the years under discussion are the institutions of the "Centre for Education (secretariat, management, plenum, council, special conferences), the institutions of the "Workers' Organization of the Centre for Education" (secretariat, central committee, congress/general conferences) - and the combined institutions of the "Stream" and the workers-representation - the Pedagogic Committee and the periodical "Urim" and its Publishing House.

[3] A debate about the specific educational reaction in the kibbutz Movement to the Holocaust will need, for example, a separate treatment of the issue of vanguard youth-movements in the diaspora and their contacts with the kibbutz in Israel - and these matters are too extensive for the scope and objectives of this article. Therefore we only surveyed the educational organs of the second-in-rank movements in the Labour Union and its "Workers Stream", and in particular the quotations in the general writings of the "Stream", and we did not examine the protocols of the different movements.

[4] A debate about the activity of the Pedagogic Committee in the summer, 7.5.43, the protocol of the Committee, Labour Archives, 215 IV/1192.

[5] M. Avigal, "In the Light of the Fire," Urim 8 (summer 1943), and also "At the Turning-point", pp. 228-234.

[6] The different conferences, detailed in the Labour archives in the "Archival Sources," and also, separately, in the booklets of "The Cenre for Education" / "Urim" Publishing House, "The National Conference of Kindergarten-teachers" and "The Holocaust of the Days in the Education of Our Children" (this booklet was not found in the archival sources and libraries - but was included in the bibliography, because it was named several times in lists of publications from "The Centre for Education" and "Urim" - for example in "A List of Booklets and Books," Urim, 3, (20) (October 1945), p. 85). For Tabenkin's words of December 1943 see the archives of HaKibbutz HaMeuhad. The resume "After the Conference" in December 1943 was held at the session of the Pedagogic Committee from 28.1.44 (The protocol of the Committee Labour archives 215 IV/1192). The different speakers at the sessions of the Pedagogic Committee expressed their fears of dealing with the Holocaust in different ways: "There is a

danger in the conference; it is a double-edged sword; we do not have to make alterations with every change" (Halprin); "We have method in our work; no alteration but profundity" (Uri Blum), and others. Avigal's opinion has been detailed in the work of Moran (1983), chapter 15. The desire to conceal the Holocaust from the children in the kindergartens was expressed explicitly and quoted in Urim 14 (November-December 1944), p. 10, 18, 58, for example.

[7] Y. Zidman and Ben-Yehudah, "The History of Defence in Israel" by Yakov Kna'ani, with an introduction by Y. Halprin (published by the Centre for Education, Tel Aviv), Urim 9 (September 1943), pp. 64-66; Y. Kna'ani, "Education Towards a New Conception of the World," Urim, 17 (January 1944), pp. 34-37; Y. Halprin, "The Problem of the Exile in the Education of Our Children"; S.Y. Pnueli (Pinels), "Our Hearts to the Diaspora", H. Shifroni, "The Teacher Towards the Future"; P. Wilder, "Arieh - Our Soldier", Urim, 11 (April 1944), pp. 3-11, 18-21, 60-64.

[8] Examples of small reminders here and there: "We assemble now in the days of the destruction of the afflicted Jewish Exile, in a fateful time for our people and a year of enlargment and prosperity for our educational institutions," declared "the Central Committee of the Organization of Educational Workers in the Workers Stream in view of the 17th congress of the organization," and the rest of the circular talks about the current activities (Urim, 15 (January 1945), pp. 94-95) - and so also in the decisions of the 17th congress, in the general introduction "Facing The Holocaust of Israel": "In face of the Holocaust in the House of Israel, it is the duty of the educators in Israel to educate the next generation in the spirit of the crucial tasks imposed on the Jewish community to absorb masses of children and youth" - and mostly deals with "the idea and enterprise" and "the organization" (Urim, 16-17 (March-May 1945), pp. 145-148).
"A Stone shall Cry Forth from the Wall" - see B. Mordechai and Y. Hannani, 1944-1945.

[9] "Arieh - Our Soldier" (See note 7); "Hed HaGan, year 8, booklets 3-4, 1943-1944, pp. 34-44; "The National Conference for Kindergarten Teachers: The Holocaust of the Days in Our Work," and the protocol of the Conference in Urim, 14 (November-December 1944), pp. 1-61; the report of Y. Budenik to the Centre for Education in Tel-Aviv about the month of mourning in the House of Communal Education of the Jordan Valley in Deganiah Aleph, 25.12.42, and again about "The Issues of the Rescue Operation," December 1942, Labour Archives, 215 IV/971; Y. Halprin, "The Problem of the Diaspora in the Educaiton of Our Children" (see note 7); a speech of Tabenkin, 24.12.1943, the Archives of HaKibbutz HaMeuhad, ibid, p. 8.

[10] M. Avigal, "The Problems of Our Education on Holocaust Days", Urim, 10 (January 1944), pp. 7-10 and also "In Days of Holocaust", pp. 242-245.

[11] Minah Hefetz in "The Management Council, 1943" and Polani, Talmi and Dinburg in "The Pedagogic Conference, 1943-1944" - see Labour Archives, archival sources. For the proposals of Talmi, Soloveitchik, Ehrlich and others for "The Intensification of Jewish Studies", see, for example, Urim, 15 (January 1945), pp. 38-41, and Urim, 20 (November-December 1945), pp. 4-13, and also the sessions of the Pedagogic Committee on the subject under discussion, in the Labour Archives IV 215: 3.5.44 and 23.1.46 (file 1185), including different circular in file 1392.

[12] Y. Tabenkin, H. Shifroni and Y. Salant, "Education in times of emergency," Tzror Michtavim, 7 (November 1942), pp. 1-15, 17-18, 24-25.

[13] D. Barash, "Education for Struggle," Tlamim, 34 (69) (March-April 1943) pp. 27-30.

[14] Y. Halprin, "To the Question of Education in Our Day," Tlamim, Ibid, pp. 32-36.

[15] Y. Niv (Halprin), "At Moments of Shock", Ibid, p. 89.

[16] See Y. Zidman and Ben-Yehudah, note 7.

[17] See M. Avigal, "The Problems of our Education on Holocaust Days," (note 10), pp. 2-4.

[18] Bendori in the "Management Council, 1943" - see Labour Archives, archival sources.

[19] Leah Talmi and Rodnitzky in "The Pedagogic Conference, 1943-1944" - Labour Archives. Tabenkin at the same conference - the archives of HaKibbutz HaMeuhad, pp. 7, 7A, 8.

[20] The booklet "The National Conference of Kindergarten Teachers - The Holocaust of the Days in Our Work", ibid, and resuming note on page 52.

[21] The protocol of the National Conference of Kindergarten Teachers, 1944-1945, Urim (see note 9).

[22] The pronouncements of Hanovitz and Gerson in the "Management Council 1943", and the pronouncements of Tabenkin and Golan at the "Pedagogic Conference, 1944-1945" see Labour Archives and the archives of HaKibbutz HaMeuhad, archival sources; Golan's speech at the Conference, about Education Towards the Future," was published in Ofakin, Volume 2 (winter 1944) pp. 2-11. About the standpoint of the left - see also A. Kafkafi, Ibid., 1988.

[23] Y. Uri, Y. Shapira, N. Hofshi and Y. Belenki published their reaction in the organ of their movement - Tlamim, pp. 15-19, 19-23, 23-27, 30-32. Y. Kna'ani wrote about "Education Towards a New Conception of the World", Urim, 10 (January 1944), pp. 34-37.

[24] The pronouncements of Talmi in the "Management Council, 1943" - Labour Archives, Ibid. The pronouncements of Golan are taken from his speech at the Pedagogic Conference, published in "Ofakim" (see note 22), p. 3. The pronouncements of Avigal - from "The Problems of Our Education on Holocaust Days" (see note 10), p. 6. Halprin (Y. Niv) in "The Problem of the Exile" in Urim, 11 (April 1944), pp. 3-11, and also in "In Moments of Shock", on p. 89 for example. The session of the Pedagogic Committee from 5.11.43 is included in the Labour Archives, 215 IV/1192. Tabenkin's quotations are from the archives of HaKibbutz HaMeuhad, p. 6, 15. The slogans of "The Conference of Kindergarten Teachers" were detailed in its protocol in Urim (see note 9), pp. 60-61. "A Stone Shall Cry Forth From the Wall", B. Mordechai and Y. Hannani, Ibid.

[25] M. Avigal, "In Days of Holocaust", Ibid. See also concerning youth-movements and their long-awaited and not realized unification: Dror, 1988 (in printing).

[26] M. Avigal, "In Days of Holocaust" - collected from his various writings.

[27] The opposition against and the approval of Avigal's standpoint are included in conferences and sessions named in the archival sources in the Labour Archives and the archives of HaKibbutz HaMeuhad; the pronouncements of Halprin - in "The Problem of Education in Our Day," Tlamim, Ibid., p. 35; Shefroni's proposal - in "The Teacher Towards the Future," Urim, 11 (April 1944), p. 21. "A Stone Shall Cry Forth From the Wall", B. Mordechai and Y. Hannani, Ibid.

[28] Here also are included the references to Avigal's proposals in the sources in the Labour Archives and in the archives of HaKibbutz HaMeuhad (see note 27). The background for the desired co-operation between the schools and the labour Federation youth-movements is detailed by Dror, 1988 (in printing).

[29] M. Avigal, "In Darkness and in Great Light," Ibid. His lecture on the Pedagogic Conference in Tel-Aviv in the summer of 1947 - "About the Contents of Education in These Days", printed also in "Hed HaHinuch" of August, the same year. His pronouncements in the Pedagogic Committee of the Labour Union about "Our Education - Quo Vadis?" were also published in: Urim, 32 (December 1947), pp. 3-13, and Halprin's pronouncements towards the debate in the Council - "The Order and the Deed" - were also included there, on pages 13-26. The symposium "About the Problems of Education in this Time," where Golan and Yehudah Ehrlich made speeches, was held on 18.3.1948 and was published completely in: Urim, 3 (34) (March 1948), pp. 231-252; its original registration is included in the archive for Jewish Education (see archival sources). The pronouncements of Avigal, Halprin and Ehrlich, the resumes and modified tendencies were collected from the afore mentioned and were edited in order to show the changes on the eve of the War of Independence.

BIBLIOGRAPHY

Archival Sources

Labour Archives / Lavon Institute, Tel-Aviv, The Collection "The Centre for Education" (215 IV).

The General Council of the "Management Council", Hadera, 16-17 November 1943, file 1068.

"The Pedagogic Conference, December 1944", file 1188.

The National Conference for Kindergarten Teachers: "The Holocaust of the Days in Our Work": The Borochov Suburb, April 1944, file 1702 (rough draft, also published in a separate booklet).

Protocols of the pedagogic committee for the years 1943-1944, files 1192, 1059.

Circulars, decisions and resumes from the different institutions of the "Stream" - in several files.

The Archives for Jewish Education in Israel and the Diaspora (named after Aviezer Yalin), The School of Education of the University of Tel-Aviv, a personal collection of Uri Blum, file 5.63/2604: "A Symposium about Educational Problems in this Time," Tel Aviv, March 1948.

The Archives of "HaKibbutz HaMeuhad", the Tabenkin-Memorial, Efal, 25A, a collection of Tabenkin's public speeches, A-16, "A Conference of Educators in Tel Aviv on the Subject: 'The Objective of Our Education in the Light of the Universal and Socialist Realities, 24.12.1943" (The Centre for Education, December 1943).

Periodicals (in the years 1942-1948)

Ofakim for Education and Culture, Workers Library, published by "HaKibbutz HaArtzi HaShomer HaTzair."

Urim, an anthology of questions about education and teaching, the General Labour Federation of Hebrew Workers in Israel, The Centre for Education and the Workers' Organization of the Centre for Education.

Igeret (Hever HaKvutzot),and lgeret LeInianei Chinuch (A letter for educational affairs.

Hed HaGan, The Centre of the Kindergarten Teacher's Association, Tel Aviv.

Tzror Michtavim (A Collection of Letters on Communal Education), Ein Harod: HaKibbutz Hameuhad, Educational Committee.

Tlamim, the Moshav Movement.

Research, Books and Articles

Avigal, M. "In Darkness and in Great Light," (People, About the Essence of Education in these Days; Our Education; Quo Vadis?) Education and Work - Articles on Problems in Education, Tel-Aviv: Urim, 1957, pp. 47-80.

Avigal, M. "In the Days of the Holocaust," (About Education in this Time; In the Light of the Fire; The Problems of Our Education in the Days of the Holocaust) At the Turning-point - Articles on Problems of Education and Teaching, The writings of M. Avigal, Vol. II, Tel-Aviv: Urim, 1945, pp. 213-260.

Bentoitz, Y. Education in the State of Israel, Tel-Aviv: Yehoshua Tchitchik Ltd., 1960.

Dror, Y. The 'Workers Stream' in Education 1939-1948, (in preparation).

Dror, Y. "The Contact Between the Youth-movements and the School in the Period of the Mandate - History and Tendencies." In Youth-movements - 1920 - 1960. Ed. M. Naor. Jerusalem: Edan, the Ben-Tzvi Memorial, 1988 (in printing).

National Conference for Kindergarten Teachers: The Holocaust of the Days in our Work, the Centre for Education the Borochov Suburb, April 1944.

Kafkafi, A. The Annulment of the Workers Stream in Education (1953). Tel-Aviv: HaKibbutz HaMeuhad, 1988 (in printing).

Moran, D. M. Avigal - An Educator and His Era, a thesis towards an M.A. in Humanities of the Tel-Aviv University, December 1983.

Mordechai, B. and Y. Hannani, A Stone Shall Cry Forth From the Wall (about the Holocaust in the Diaspora), School and Youth from Our new Literature, I. Tel-Aviv: Centre for Education, 1945-1946.

Niv, Y. (Halprin). "In Moments of Shock," For Us and For Our Children - Social and Family Problems in the Education of the Child, Tel-Aviv: Am Oved/Yalkut in cooperation with the Council of the Workers of Haifa, Cultural Committee, 1956/1957, pp. 87-94.

Porat, D. Leadership Trapped, Tel-Aviv: Am Oved/Ofakim, 1986.

Reshef, S. The Workers Stream in Education - The Sources and the History of the Educational Movement in the Years 1921-1939, Tel-Aviv: Tel-Aviv University and HaKibbutz HaMeuhad, 1980.

The Holocaust of the Days in the Education of Our Children - by Our Children, The Centre for Education, The National Pedagogic Conference, December 1943.

Orthodox Jewish Theology, 1945-1948:
Responses to the Holocaust

Gershon Greenberg
The American University
Washington, D.C. 20016

PREFACE

Orthodox Jewish theological reflections about the Hurban begin with Elchonon Wassermann of Baranowitch, Hayyim Ozer Grodzensky of Vilna and Kalonymous Kalman Spira in Warsaw in 1939 and persevere through the catastrophe with Issachar Teichtal in Budapest, Yitzchak Menachem Mendel Danziger in Treblinka, and Zvi Hirsch Meisels in Auschwitz. The reflections continue in the period following liberation, known as Shearith Hapleitah. Here we will explore the communities around Munich in 1947-1948, New York 1945-1948 and in Shanghai in 1947. Our explorations of the period are only a first step. The conclusions about the universality of response are tentative. Research needs to be done next on the 1945-1947 period in Germany, and the communities in Jerusalem, Buenos Aires and Lodz 1945-1948.

MUNICH: UPON THE EVE OF THE JEWISH STATE

THEOLOGICAL MOTIFS

The rabbis gathered around the Munich area in 1948 bring forth the observation that Jewish history is unique. Ben Tziyyon Firer, Resh Mesivtah of Yeshivah Etz Chaim in Ulm, points out that other minorities are able to surmount their problems through assimilation, but not German Jews. Jewish history is outside political rationale: How could the Nazi possibly profit from a war against the Jews? How could a Jewish State arise, especially at such dizzying speed, just after the Hurban and in a world split into billigerent camps?1 Chananiah Lippa Goldmann, Av Beth Din in Wasserburg and Neu-Pesth, points out that when other nations leave their native habitat and enter other national contexts they die off. Israel endures, and even though hardly loved by the nations into which she enters.2 Y.I. Thorn, Av Beth Din of Frankfort, points to the mass graves and dried bones of millions of Jews as tragic evidence of distinctiveness. Judaism is also uniquely able to resurrect itself after disaster. Moabite King Mesha and the Romans declare Israel lost, but history leaves them and not Judaism behind. Abraham's "coin," the Sages say, depicts old Abraham and Sarah on one side and young Isaac and Rebecca on the other (Baba Kamma 97b). Judaism is together old and young. Jerusalem is destroyed, while the Temple's stones are strewn around the Jewish diaspora to be used to rebuild Jerusalem. Now there are crematoria but also the emerging Jewish State.3 Moshe Halpern of Betar identifies Judaism, in the manner of Nachman Krochmal, with an absolute spirit which enables it to recover from all its declines. Other nations develop, flower and atrophy while Judaism does not.4 Yitzchak Zemba, president of Agudas Israel in Germany, avers that while other nations place natural existence and self-interest (Kiyyum) at their center, Judaism places spiritual ideals and self-transcendence (Hemshech). For example, the na'asseh ve'nishmah assertion (Exodus 24/7) means acceptance of obligations in Emunah, and rooting in an ideal referent.5

Y.L. Thorn explains that this uniqueness is anchored in a transcendental realm, and traceable to a divine force which shatters temporal limits. It is possible to continue to believe -- despite satan's current bloody reign and world-defiance to the Jewish value of rewarding the righteous -- because the dilemmas of the catastrophe are within the relative human context and its causal nexus. There is an absolute/objective dimension where divine determination is active. It directs empirical/human history in a way beyond human ken.6

The midrashic mind provides access to this dimension. Firer speaks of re-evaluating Judaism's declarations of faith, the Ani Ma'amim's. He explains that Hurban is the Chevlay Layda, mythic birth pains with colossal pouring forth of blood, which end with the birth of the child of the new Jewish State.7 Netzach Israel editor Naftali Baruch describes the Hurban as the Chevlay Moshiach (pangs of the messiah) preceding Asschalta Degeulah (onset of redemption). While the immediate postwar generation cannot apprehened the light of redemption because it is part of the transition, it can glimpse the messiah "behind the partition." It must dedicate itself to Torah and prayer to assure that Israel continues on the path to redemption.8 Mordechai Perlov, a Lubavitcher rabbi who comes from Russia to Schwebisch-Halle, brings forth the interpretation of the Akedah in Pirke de Rabbi Eliezer 31.9 The sacrifice experience leaves a legacy of confident trust in God, of self-sacrifice to the point of Kiddush Hashem, and a path to messianic redemption. The ashes of the ram are the Messirath Nefesh of Abraham, which make him capable of sacrificing Isaac. The veins are the strings of the harp which David plays with equanimity, based on confidence in divine providence in the face of enemy threats. The leather skin is the girding of Israel, in the faith that Elijah will come and proclaim the messiah. The horns caught in the thicket are the perseverance on the part of Abraham's progeny. The smaller horn on the left is sounded on Mt. Sinai, symbolizing the strength offered by Torah to help survive exile. The larger one on the right is sounded upon the ingathering of exiles. This entire legacy remains in Israel. Like a gold coin buried in snow until it is uncovered in spring, the legacy survives in the soul no matter the persecutions of Amalek from the outside. The soul can explode the ground in which it is buried and can help bring Judaism into its messianic "spring" through the Shema declaration, Torah and Mitzvoth.10 Chananiah Lippa Goldmann explains that Israel's survival is obviously not because it has land. It is due to the fact that Israel replaces geographical body with a soul afire with the spirit of God. Thus, while other nations die when they leave their lands, Israel can journey with God's teaching (Midrash Lamentations 1/5-6) and so endure. When there is Torah to replace land, Israel survives; without it, Israel hasn't the strength. The response to persecution, accordingly, is education. Thus when Hamann conspires to eliminate Israel, Mordechai teaches the children (Midrash Esther Rabbah 8/6, 10/6) and Hamann relents. Jehudah Meir Shapiro of Lublin (d. 1934) explains:

> At any place and time that tyrants arise, it is incumbent upon the rabbis to stand by the doorposts of education and develop the [minds and spirit of the] children . . . . The Gedolim of Israel did this in every generation. Now it is proper to do so even more intensely. The pouring of the blood of the pious is taking place in a horrible degree . . . We must gather the orphaned sheep, so they may [continue in the Sinai covenant] and not become part of a covenant of terrible exile (Shapiro, commentary on the concluding statement to Tractate Niddah).

Now the blood of the victims cries out from inside the ground. The burning bodies beg for the water of Torah to quench the thirst of their children. The parents who perished, "sanctified by (mimkudash) Auschwitz and Maidanek," expended their last breath in the hope that their children would be educated.11

ENACTMENT

The theological motifs of the Orthodox rabbis are enacted by Mitzvah, which in turn reinforces the theology -- in a sort of dialectical dynamic between myth and ritual. Beginning immediately after liberation, religious observance takes priority. On August 24, 1945 the rabbis of Landsberg who were liberated from Terezin pride themselves in conducting proper Kiddushin and Chuppah, their kosher kitchen, house of worship, Mikveh, Chevra Kaddisha to bury those killed by Hitler, and classes in Talmud and Shulchan Aruch. They plead for Machzorim, Siddurim, Tallitoth, Tefilin, Ethrogim, Hadassim and Lulavim.12 A cable of Sept. 1, 1945 reports the tremendous disappointment among the Displaced Persons in Germany over the failure of the Va'ad Hatzalah to provide ritual articles, especially in anticipation of the High Holidays.13 On August 30, 1945 Shlomo Baumgarten reports that during his visit to the German D.P. camps his own Tefillin were used from morning till evening by the residents. Hundreds assembled at his office all week long for a piece of Sabbath candle -- and some had to leave empty handed. The lives of some, he reports, depended upon receiving ritual articles:

> Many could possibly be saved if it were possible to satisfy these needs. Everything is lost if they cannot be satisfied. They cry: Save us! [This is a matter of] rescuing souls in the full sense of the word.14

Baumgarten reports that Bergen-Belsen children ask for Mezuzoth and Magen David symbols. "It is so little, yet so much." Each person wants a Siddur, even the non-religious.15 Yiddishe Shtimme editor Y.Y. Bistritzer reports that by April 1948 intense religious observance is widespread. Survivors, filled with gratitude for being saved, are committed to "replacing" the victims with Mitzvah. Former Musulmaenner hunt for Sifre Torah which may have survived. Synagogues of every type are founded. In some camps Kashruth is total. Marriage ceremonies -- people are desparate to marry and have children -- are Kehalachah. Ninety-nine percent of the male children are circumcised, including older ones. Educational institutions are established. Everyone in the camps lights candles on Erev Shabbat.16 Aaron Potashnik observes that in response to Hitler many radical and secular Jews are returning to Judaism.17 Firer observes that the heretics have become heretical about their heresy. For example, Yaackov Zerubavel:

> For decades I fought against Frimkeit because it made politics and business out of religion. [Then] in Poland I grasped for the first time the enormous strength of common Jewish faith, [which is] able to rise up to Kiddush Hashem and Messirath Nefesh. . . The simple folk and rabbis who went "singing and dancing to their deaths" had a belief which transcended time and entered eternity. . . This is no passive heroism. It is [the active] nourishing by generations of Jewish history to create a heavenly foundation for our nimble existence. A thought lit up inside me. If not for the [tradition of] Kiddush Hashem, the "passive" heroism of our parents, there would be no "active" heroism [now] with weapons. The ghetto uprising has the same source, only in worldly and contemporary form: deep, ebullient, unshakable belief in national revival, communal resurrection and universal redemption. In the tragic moments of individual death, this [source for] continuity of the whole [people] can be felt and seen. An eternal stream runs through the generations. [Even] if the possiblity of saving physical individual existence is extinguished, let the glory and dignity of the [spiritual] whole survive. It will surely remain alive.18

The theology is also enacted in connection with the emerging of the Jewish State. The Landsberg rabbis conclude their letter with "We await Aliyyah to our Holy Land." Bistritzer reports how religious parties are working on transplanting authentic religious life to the land of the fathers. The new State must be based absolutely upon Torah.19 Moshe Bernstein, Chairman of Brith Yeshurun (religious Revisionists) of Germany, explains that Judaism retains its essence despite unparallelled homelessness, sacrifice and persecution, because of its basis in eternal Torah and the kingdom of God (Malchuth Shamayyim). Just as Torah gives life to Judaism in exile, it must provide the life of the new State, which should serve to mend the world (letakken eth Haolam).20 Aviezer Burstein stresses that the same powers supporting Jews in exile must be drawn upon for support in the

State. As Jews leave Emek Habocho for the land of Israel, they must take Torah and Mitzvoth with them to establish the state.21 According to Yitzchak Zemba, Eretz Israel is solely a means to protect laws and keep Torah. The land is primarily for Hemshech, secondarily for Kiyyum.22

The Torah-based state is the only real hope for Judaism. The first regional conference of the German Brith Yeshurun in Foehrenwald in June 1947 takes place in the auditorium called "Bamidbar" (the camp newspaper bears the same name) -- the "desert" between exodus and promised land. The conference's motto is "through the Torah of Israel to the sovereignty of Israel for the unity of Israel." Its flag's inscription reads:

> Strictly Orthodox Jews everywhere! Our nation is a nation only through our Torah. Remember what Amalek-Nazis, may their name be erased, did to you. Religious Jews unite! Remember the Sabbath day to keep it holy. The goal of Brith Yeshurun is to establish the sovereignty of Israel within its Biblical boundaries and in accordance with the law of our holy Torah.

Y.L. Thorn of Frankfort declares that those now fighting in the Holy Land bear the torch which disperses the darkness of two-thousand years and carries God's word across the earth. While the world wants to convince Jews by force that they are holy in spirit but not in body, Jewish history tells of many fighters out to demonstrate that Jewish blood can storm the towers of the land and struggle for independence. An unnamed speaker, possibly Moshe Halpern of Betar, describes Galuth as a train travelling from place to place through catastrophes. The destruction of Eastern European Jewry -- the source of Judaism's biological, spiritual and cultural vitality and specifically of both American Jewish community and Aliyyah to Eretz Israel -- is destroying the "locomotive." Instead of fleeing to such places as America and Norway, Jews should realize that the train can be rescued only in Eretz Israel. Galuth must be fought like an enemy, with every last drop of energy. It is foolhardy to think that the Jewish minority has any place in Europe. Jews must seize control of their destiny, concentrate on the possibility of concentrating Jewish strength in Eretz Israel and creating national values there. Ze'ev Jabotinsky once said:

> When a sailing ship is caught in a hurricane, it could try to manipulate between the turbulent waves. But the power of the storm could also be used to one's advantage, to steer the ship to reach dry land.

If properly directed, the "ship" of diaspora could reach dry land -- the Holy Land. "Let us gird ourselve with faith in our divine strength, in the eternity of Israel, and in the salvation which must come." Moshe Bernstein ends the conference with the wish:

> that the second regional conference will be called in Eretz Israel, for free citizens of the Jewish sovereignty. Go home immediatley, distinguished delegates, and take the flame you received in this glorious Conference with you to light the hearts of the weakened Jew. Inspire the Shearith Hapleitah with our ideals. Tell the great news to our heroic brothers and sisters, that the day is near when the phrase "next year in rebuilt Jerusalem" will be realized.23

NEW YORK CITY

Among the Orthodox rabbis who gather in New York City from various parts of America, similar "Ani Ma'amim's" emerge.

JUDAISM'S TRANSCENDANT UNIQUENESS

Jewish history is unique. Joseph Isaac Schneersohn condemns American Jews for thinking that Israel, like other nations, can be saved by the democracies of the world.24 Other nations are removed from the stage of history after the respective cycle of ascent and decline is complete, while Israel survives repeated ascents and declines. Indeed, Israel endures while its persecutors suffer in proportion to the extent they attack her.25 Israel Halevi Rosenberg of the Agudas Harabbonim distinguishes the world of Jewry from that of the sword. Prohibition against murder, except in self-defense, is in Judaism's very soul, and Jews are incapable of the barbarities perpetrated by the Nazis.26

The unique history is explained by and rooted in divine providence. Joseph Isaac Schneersohn connects all major events in Jewish history to God's direction.27 Eliezer Silver of the Agudas Harabbonim tells Queen Wilhelmina of Holland in 1946 that while he is grateful for her offer of help, his confidence remains in God.28 Rosenberg's faith is unaffected by the continuity of persecution even after the war and the world's failure to recognize its sins and provide a Jewish homeland, because his faith is tied to God and not to nations.29 Schneersohn stresses that nothing is in the control of Jews alone, that everything -- especially exile and redemption -- is a matter of God's power.30 The Lubavitcher Chassidim stress that redemption and restoration are not political matters, but of "Ve'al Hanissim Ve'al Hapurkan" ("We thank thee for the miracles and for the redemption") of the Eighteen Benedictions prayer. Involvement with political means, indeed, divert from repentant return (Teshuvah) and catalyze Chevlay Moshiach.31 They are anyhow impotent:

> You can expect peace from the cannon shots [at the opening of the United Nations Conference on International Organization, April 1945] in San Francisco, as much as you can expect bananas to grow from onion seeds at the north pole.32

The Holocaust is under divine aegis as well. As such, there is precedence for it and the redemption-to-come in the Egyptian experience.33 Hamessiloh, published by the Greater New York Va'ad Harabbonim, aligns the Holocaust with earlier attempts to annihilate the Jews.34

Insofar as God determines historical events, their meaning is ultimately beyond human comprehension. Jacob Rosenheim of Agudas Israel asks, "Why did the Holocaust happen?":

> To what purpose? To ask this is to delve into God's wisdom. . . Who gave us the right to measure world-historical events with a human measure of time? If possibly thousands of years are for the Creator no more than one day or even a third part of a night, what is the importance of five or ten or thirty years -- from 1914 to 1944 -- to the final evaluation of world history?35

The sole response to the question "Where is God, why is salvation delayed?" is Teshuvah.36 Schneersohn refers to the Aggadah about Moses' asking about Akiva's reward for all his sacrifice for Torah. He is shown Akiva's butchered flesh being sold at market. Moses protests, and God commands silence. (Menachoth 29b). Since man exists in a universe of change, Schneersohn explains, God's ways are necessarily beyond human comprehension. God is revealed in descending degrees in the worlds of Atziluth (emanation), Beriyyah (creation), Yetzirah (formation) and Assiyah (activity). Man's perception of God is necessarily incomplete and changing, while God does not change. There is no common area between God and man that allows for man's knowledge of Him.37

EXPLANATION

Yet there are attempts to discern God's rationale, as if the assertion of inquiry in itself begins to express and explain the mystery between divine providence and human knowledge. Conversely, a failure to inquire would acknowledge implicitly that God is severed from history. Our rabbis try to understand. They thereby delineate and express a simultaneity and common ground of transcendence and immanence, of incomprehensible and comprehensible.

The Hurban is Chevlay Moshiach, Asschalta Degeulah. If there is darkness, there must be light ahead (see Sanhedrin 99).38 The Bobover Rav Shlomo Halberstamm states:

> I lost my father and my children. I tremble when I recall how we survivors existed. At night we jumped out of bed, full of fear, thinking we heard our children being killed. . . We knew that all the sufferings we endured were

> for the purpose of bringing redemption closer. Once, Israel stood in the sea with water up to her neck. Then redemption came.39

The Lubavitcher Chassidim are absolutely sure that "the contemporary destruction of diaspora Jewry, the uprooting of thousands of Jewish communities, must and will bring salvation."40 Hurban provides specific means for the transformation of the universe into its eschatological redemption. Hurban cleanses the world of filth -- when, tragically, good people are also dragged down by the evil ones being removed.41 Hurban presents the choice between belief with Teshuvah which lead to life, and disbelief which leads to ashes.42 It is the Shofar of Elijah, warning of the end and signalling the opportunity for return.43

The Nazis play a role in the apocalyptic process. While they are to be punished for their evil,44 they are also servants of God. When Jews exchanged divine Torah for idols, Nebuchadnezzar lay siege to Jerusalem or there was a Spanish Inquisition or ghettos were built -- all under divine direction. Now there is Maidanek and Lublin.45 The punishment, which evokes Teshuvah, is appropriate. The attempt by Jews to ignore the uniqueness of Jewish history is

> a perverse Jewish Nazism, preaching the invalidity of Jewish chosenness. . . It is precisely against this shameless Jewish nullification of our own nobility that the punishment by German Nazism is designed. It is measure-for-measure, proclaiming its own chosenness, claiming to be so noble and holy that it cannot live on one planet with the degraded Jewish people and must therefore exterminate them.46

Hitler is the contemporary Amalek and Hamann, an instrument of divine punishment.47 The tyrants crystallize the purpose of exile, which is to refine the belief in God following the sins in ancient Eretz Israel. Thus:

> Jews were not sent into exile to enjoy themselves on a vacation. They were sent to become martyrs, to be beaten and to hurt until they recognized the immorality of false civilizations and they turned to God to save them from horrible imprisonment.

The tyranny intensifies in proportion to the Jews' surrender to the influences of exile.48

RESPONSE

How may man respond? As failure to perform Teshuvah brought about the current situation, so Teshuvah can turn it around. Moreover, failure to do so could bring on something "far more unbearable and incomprehensible than the unparallelled wickedness and absurd falsehoods of the barbaric Nazis."49 It is not impossible that American Jews will be abandoned as were those of Europe,50 or that Germany could reassert itself and Hitler return to power:

> If our merciful and compassionate God wishes to bring the Jewish people within [the range of] His mercy, He can do nothing other than contract His punishment to a portion of Jews so as to awaken the remaining portion to avoid punishment. Would it be better for the Hurban to come all at once to the entire Jewish people? And if God shows us mercy by punishing a portion of the Jews in order to warn the rest, does not this prove that the sin of the rest in refusing Teshuvah even after warning is greater than that of those punished without it?51

The Teshuvah of man will ultimately "explode" into the Teshuvah of God's redemption. Schneersohn proclaims:

> "Redemption now!" For the days of redemption of Israel are now coming. [Redemption] is the only authentic Teshuvah for the [contemporary] Hurban of the world and for all the troubles which have come upon Israel. . . "Redemption now!" means redemption soon. It comes in quick strides, even though we do not see it. Indeed, it stands behind a wall [around us]. The righteous redeemer is already behind our wall. The time to prepare to meet him is very short.52

The Torah provides the foundation for Teshuvah's transformation of Hurban into redemption. Torah has ultimate being, and history must ultimately come around to it. The world was created for Torah, and historical traumas of history are really alignments with Torah and man's recognition of it.53 In the Hurban the proponents of Torah were lost -- they were eighty percent of the six million.54 Yet the Torah survives, it has ontological roots, and through it the Torah-people survive as well. They live and die together. Thus, when Rabbi Chananiah ben Teradyon was being killed he told his daughter "If I were burned by myself the judgment would be difficult for me. But I am burning with the Torah, so that anyone who bemoans the Torah bemoans me as well" (Avodah Zorah 18a).55 The status of the Torah is to be reinforced by its perpetuation within the community. In essence, Torah-education responds to Maidanek. It is a "triumph from the grave, the posthumous victory of each Jew who sacrificed himself for Torah and became a victim."56 The perpetuation, in turn, is anchored in hope. To hope is in itself a response to Hurban:

> Strengthen yourself and strengthen your heart to be as steel. Do not let the terrible thoughts [of Hurban] take over your soul. Place the bitter food inside the Matzoh. This olive-sized Matzoh taken from your platter is [like] a tractate on faith, which contains sparks of light. It will bring light to your dark eyes. When you taste it your bitterness will turn sweet.57

ERETZ ISRAEL

At first, Orthodox Jews see America as the new location for Torah on the road to redemption.58 Instead, it is in the process of bringing about a Hurban of its own. Torah is dying. As the body of Israel is burned in Europe, the Jewish soul is devoured in America.59 European Jews are displaced physically, and those in America are displaced spiritually.60 Shemirat Shabbath, Kashruth, the longing for Zion, are all openly defied.61 American Jews even abandon their European brethren. During the war they ignored the convulsions of the holy ones being buried alive and went to parties. Perhaps they did not know what was really happening. Now they do know and they still hesitate.62 While the victims of Shearith Hapleitah suffer, American Jews go to banquets and get involved in political intrigues.63 Eretz Israel is the last hope.

The rabbis agree that the land is to be restored on the basis of Torah. Israel Rosenberg states:

> Without Torah foundations it is impossible to build our land. Insofar as there is an Eretz Israel it means there is a God of Israel. If there is a nation of Israel it must exist according to Torath Israel.64

But they differ on the weight of autonomous and heteronomous forces. Rosenheim stresses the metahistorical claim to the land, that the State is to be based on Torah and under God. Political sovereignty would be a surrender to assimilation and a denial of values of Jewish history. Indeed, sovereignty precipitated the Holocaust catastrophe, and could do so again.65 Eliezer Silver and Hillel Zaidmann retain the ideal of Torah-Israel, while recognizing the need for immediate refuge in the wake of Hurban.66 The Lubavitcher reject any active precipitation of restoration. Attempts at settlement so far have failed and the world will rightly oppose it until the messianic coming. Redemption will come soon but the preparation for it is Teshuvah.67

SHANGHAI 1947

CHAOS AND FAITH

Our inquiry into the reflections of Jews in Shanghai is limited to the treatise entitled The Akedah of Treblinka.68 Its author is Simcha Elberg, who arrives there in 1941 from Warsaw via Vilna, Slobodka and Kovno. Elberg begins with the awareness of the destruction of the world and the return to pre-historical chaos. Creation is erased by the satanic Hitler, and now a new creation is needed for the world to exist. For now, life remains in a vacuum. Even the language and emotion to relate to the Hurban have been destroyed.

Nevertheless, Elberg assumes that the God of the covenant remains and that ultimately meaning can be found for the catastrophe. He asserts his faith, which contains its own understanding, and thereby begins the path towards meaning. The path is filled with contradiction -- as if on an existential level, Elberg must go through chaos to uncover the truth. For example, while the Hurban is the apocalyptic battle between satan and holiness, Israel which is the instrument of holiness must sacrifice itself to atone for its sins. Hitler is God's instrument for educating the Jews, yet Hitler is absolutely evil. The history of Judaism is characteristically Akedah in nature, yet Treblinka is without comparison.

EXPLANATIONS

Meaning begins with a question which is eternally new in Jewish history: "Why do the righteous suffer? This query sets Elberg's faith in the traditional Jewish context. A first explanation is that the Akedah of Mt. Moriah is inherent to Jewish historical existence.

> Treblinka is the most difficult philosophical book. Abraham began to write it in Ur-kasdim a thousand years ago. Even today, the book remains unfinished. It still Treblinka's in the world.69

There are, however, gigantic differences between Akedath Yitzchak and Akedath Treblinka. Isaac is led to the altar by Abraham in joy. Then he is removed from it. There is an angel of mercy to stop the murder. As the founder of his people, Abraham would never allow a Jew to be killed. He alleviates Isaac's pain with his voice of mercy. At Treblinka, all is reversed.

A second explanation is that Hurban is an ontological battle between satan and holiness, between hatred and love. Hitler slaughters Jews as a "Mitzvah," in God's name. He wants to destroy exilic history by killing those who make it. If there can be the total evil of a Hitler there can be the total good of a messiah. Holiness will win out. Even from the graves, Jewish bones will overcome:

> The chemical material manufactured from Jewish bones and skin contains power greater than that of the atom bomb. In each little piece of soap there are a hundred Jews of sorrow. Someday the pieces will explode and rip the world apart. Against such a metaphysical power there is no protection.70

The dead Jew is like Holy Scripture which ultimately cannot be defied. In this battle there is no neutral ground. The nations which stand by passively are by default within the satanic realm, and this includes the democratic nations.

A third explanation is that the catastrophe is a sacrifice. This includes testing, which the Akedath-Yitzchak people pass with a Shema-Yisroel declaration which splits the heavens. The sacrifice atones for sins of assimilation:

> We have made too much peace with exile. We have not come to terms with the fact that we sit accused for generations of sin, and that at any moment exile can [punish us] for our guilt. We have not properly understood the deep tragedy of exile.71 . . . We did not want to learn [about exile] from our [internally developed] world when there were six million in the congregation. So we needed to learn from the Tohu Vovohu.72

The sacrifice also atones for the sins of man. Indeed, Judaism has the mission to atone for the world with its blood. Finally, the sacrifice manifests divine wrath for sin (Ezekiel 20), a wrath which precedes the sounding of the horn of redemption. Because they are uniquely holy, the Jews of Poland and Lithuania are appropriate to the holy sacrifice. "Through those near to Me I shall make Myself holy" (Leviticus 10/3). In the holy suffering al Kiddush Hashem, Elberg believes, there is an inner spiritual contentment, a special strength provided by God where the sacred assumes physical reality. Thus, the mother entering a gas chamber can endure the suffering because she already lives in a heavenly atmosphere.

In all its aspects, the sacrifice is under divine direction:

> Just as Isaac was led to the Akedah solely by God's command, so also God's will was effective at the Akedah of Treblinka.73

Accordingly Hitler, the "deep translation of exile,"74 is an instrument of God. While of the strain of all Amaleks, Hitler also surpasses all others. He pulverizes

Jews, builds gas chambers in God's name, makes slaughtering Jews a Mitzvah, and attacks not only the living Jew but the dead as well.

ERETZ ISRAEL

For Elberg, exile is the worst punishment for a people and a homeland is the only solution. But the act of return itself is not enough. There could be exile in Eretz Israel itself, unless return involves piety. The outer transformation must result from inner change. This, tragically, is not taking place:

> The contemporary Hurban has not evoked the deep, inner [resurgence] which we have the right to expect. Amidst the surviving Jewish camp we do not see the signs of an inner spiritual surge [of life in reaction to] the extraordinary spiritual shocks.75

THE UNIVERSALITY OF RESPONSE

Orthodox Jewry which survives the Holocaust also endures the consequent geographical dispersion theologically intact. There is a universal spiritual community which spreads from the Far East to the West, with its center in Germany.

ONTOLOGICAL PRINCIPLES

The first Ani Ma'amim of this community of faith is the ontic stability of God and Torah, and the historical durability of the principles of holiness, Jewish uniqueness, self-sacrifice and covenant. In Munich, the senselessness of the attack on the Jews is interpreted as evidence of Judaism's exceptional character and divine ties.76 Emunah, self-sacrifice up to Kiddush Hashem, and the indestructibility of the messianic process of redemption are real. Torah-education is a reality which can turn back persecution and even overcome death. Emunah which rises to Messirath Nefesh is an eternal stream which runs through the generations. In New York, the failure by American Jewry to recognize the uniqueness of Jewish existence is considered a destruction of the American Jewish soul parallel to the destruction of the body in Europe. God, not man, is seen to control history. Torah has ultimate being, to which history itself must adapt:

> The world was created for the sake of Torah. Only when the Torah and its spirit, with its laws is recognized by all peoples, will the sinful world receive its Tikkun (mending). The shock [of history] will not end until the world recognizes Sinai and the Jewish people.77

Accordingly, Torah-education is a path of life which penetrates even the barrier between death at Maidanek and the life of the survivors. In Shanghai, Simcha Elberg continues to assume the existence of God even while the world itself is destroyed. He speaks of the continuity of Messirath Nefesh as Akedah, and of the indestructibility of Jewish holiness. The difference between chaos and creation is Torah:

> The world has descended to the deepest depths, into the abyss of mass murder, into Tohu Vovohu. A new creation of six days must take place. This new creation (Bereshith-Yetzirah) can come about only when Torah becomes a light to the nations, when the time arrives that "many nations shall walk by your light." [Isaiah 60/3].78

Later in America, Elberg explains that Israel has been able to survive millenia of dispersion, lawlessness and barbarism because she shares a trans-natural reality in which "Israel, Torah and God are one" (Zohar III/73a) in Torah.79

Ritual observance is the daily counterpart to these lasting principles. In Germany, desperate pleas for ritual articles point to their indispensability to participating in the principles. Mitzvah is the key factor in survival itself. In New York, Teshuvah, the immediate expression of Torah reality, includes religious observance. Indeed, failure to observe is tantamount to another Hurban.

THE SOURCE OF FAITH

The principles may be drawn upon to rebuild Jewish life in history. There is a caesura between empirical reality and God, but a spark in the abyss is possible with the act of faith and hope. In Germany, Y.L. Thorn distinguishes between the transcendental and human realms of understanding. Jacob Rosenheim in New York states that it is impossible to comprehend God's ways. Elberg states that there are no words available to speak of the tragedy. The act of faith enters in between, placing itself between known and unknown, between the reality of God and the abandonment of man. It is given life by the ultimate principles. By its internal force, faith overcomes the terrible disjunction between God and world. It creates a path of meaning anew. Each enunciation of continuing Jewish belief bears this message. The vehicle for this faith must simultaneously be of history and outside it. This is midrash.

FROM HURBAN TO REDEMPTION

A first midrashic theme is that the Hurban is a cosmic battle between the Nazi satan and Jewish holiness. In Germany, Galuth is seen as catastrophic history and the idea of continuing it after the war must be fought like an enemy. In New York, ontic Torah which is pure and good is described as being in combat with evil which necessarily tries to destroy it.80 Exilic civilizations are out to torture Jews, albeit as instruments of divine providence teaching the radical difference between Jews and other nations. For Elberg, Hurban is an ontic battle between satanic hatred and holy love. Throughout, it is believed that Israel will win the struggle. At the Foehrenwald conference, Moshe Bernstein declares:

> We Revisionists do not begin with Dr. Herzl, [Max] Nordau or [Ze'ev] Jabotinsky! We begin with our teacher Moses and with Joshua ben Nun. [Our history] does not end with the Jewish sovereignty. It reaches further, into the times of the end of days and the days of the messiah.81

The Lubavitcher urge Teshuvah so all Jews may survive to participate in messianic redemption -- as the filth of the world is swept into the sea.82 Elberg assures that holiness is indestructible, ontologically and even in terms of individual dead Jews.

In the ontological battle, God's presence is evident. In Germany, Hurban is described as the pain preceding the redemption in which history under God culminates. In New York, the Hurban is aligned with previous catastrophes, but in addition preludes redemption. The Nazis serve God, as does Hitler himself. Elberg speaks of the Hurban as an outpouring of divine wrath, as a holy sacrifice before God. The martyrs are filled with a special strength to endure by God. Hitler is God's ultimate definition of what exile is for the Jews. Our rabbis do not speak of God's hiddenness, of His departure from the world. To the contrary, the Hurban is God's aggressive manifestation in history.

Under God, the Hurban is a positive stage in history's development towards its messianic culmination. In Germany, it is the necessary pain of messianic birth. In New York, it precipitates redemption by forcing the choice between absolute good and absolute evil and imposing Teshuvah. As the worst disaster, it is the immediate precondition for redemption.83 Elberg speaks of the Hurban sacrifice as test and atonement which enhance holiness.

Our rabbis share the hope that the restoration of Eretz Israel for the Jews is imminent. They insist that restoration be based upon Torah; if Torah is endangered the idea of a Jewish sovereignty becomes questionable. In Germany, it is believed that a state not based upon Torah would remove the meaning to Jewish exilic history, that Judaism survives because of Torah. The sovereignty of Israel is achieved only through the Torah of Israel. In New York, the failure of American Jewry to re-establish the spirit of Judaism intensifies the thrust towards Eretz Israel. Still, without Torah foundations the land may not be rebuilt. Political sovereignty is dangerous because it compromises God's Torah.

THE ETERNALITY OF JUDAISM

Collectively, our Orthodox Jewish thinkers bring foward their traditional beliefs -- which were enunciated before the catastrophe by the Chofetz Chaim and by Jehudah Meir Shkapiro of Lublin and after Kristallnacht by Wassermann, Grodzensky and Spira.84 The Hurban does not undermine the nature of their faith -- by itself a de facto declaration of the eternality of God and Torah. Nor does geographical distance, nor the shattering of the communal context. In turn, this collective declaration of faith is testimony to the eternality of God, Torah, and God's covenantal tie to Israel through history.

NOTES

1. Ben Tziyyon Firer (May 1948), Netzach Israel (NI) 1, 15 [Yiddish]. Idem. (June 1948), NI 1, 13 [Yiddish]. Idem. (September 1948), NI 1, 10 [Yiddish]. Idem. (June 1948), NI 2, 14 [Yiddish]. Idem. (August 1948), Yeshurun 6, 8 [Yiddish].

2. Chananiah Lippa Goldmann (May 1948), NI 1, 11-12 [Hebrew].

3. Y.L. Thorn (August 1948), Yeshurun 6, 6 [Yiddish]. Idem. (May 1947), Yeshurun 1, 3 [Yiddish]. Idem. (November 1947), Yeshurun 5, 4 [Yiddish].

4. Moshe Halpern (August 1948), Yeshurun 6, 26-27 [Yiddish].

5. Yitzchak Zemba (May 1948), NI 1, 14 [Yiddish]. Idem. (June 1948), NI 2, 9 [Yiddish].

6. Thorn, supra.

7. Firer, supra.

8. Naftali Baruch (June 1948), NI 1, 1 [Yiddish]. Idem. (May 1948), NI 1, 1 [Yiddish].

9. Cf. Pirke Aboth 5/8, Abraham Aharon Braude, Bayyit Haggadol on Pirke de Rabbi Eliezer 31. Moshe Alscheich, Torath Moshe on Vayyere part 13, p. 60. Menachem Mendel Kasher, Torah Shelameh no. 159, pp. 904-905. I am grateful to my student Yishai Chazit of Haifa University for these references.

10. Mordechai Perlov (September 1948), NI 4, 17-18 [Hebrews].

11. Goldmann, supra.

12. Agudas Israel Archives, NYC. File 2-6 [Hebrew], FF19 [Hebrew].

13. Eliezer Silver Archives, Cincinnati, Ohio.

14. Agudas Israel Archives, New York City. AZ-2 Box 9, folder 17. Published in Kol Israel 24 no. 47 (August 30, 1945).

15. Shlomo Baumgarten (October 1945), The Jewish Spectator 10, no. 12, 26.

16. Y.Y. Bistritzer (May 1948), NI 1, 17 [Yiddish]. Idem. (April 1948), Hemshech, 52-59 [Yiddish]. Idem. (June 1948), NI 1, 24 [Yiddish].

17. Aaron Potashnik (August 1948), NI 3, 16 [Yiddish].

18. Firer, supra. Ya'ackov Zerubavel, Barg Hurban (Buenos Aires 1946)62, 132.

19. Y.Y. Bistritzer, supra.

20. Moshe Bernstein (August 1948), Yeshurun 6, 15-16 [Yiddish].

21. Aviezer Burstein (May 1948), NI 1, 1 [Yiddish]. Idem. (September 1948), NI 4, 1 [Yiddish]. Idem. (June 1948), NI 2, 1 [Yiddish].

22. Yitzchak Zemba, supra.

23. Protocol of the First Regional Conference of the German Brith Yeshurun in Foehrenwald, June 2 & 3 [1947] [Yiddish].

24. Joseph Isaac Schneersohn (August 1948), NI 3, 6-7 [Hebrew].

25. Anonymous (February 1945), Hakeriyyah Vehakedushah (HK) 5 no. 53, 1-2 [Yiddish].

26. Israel Halevi Rosenberg (April 1949), Hapardes 23 no. 7, 2-9 [Hebrew].

27. Joseph Isaac Schneersohn (April 1945), HK 5 no. 56, 2-3 [Yiddish].

28. Eliezer Silver, Report on a Mission to the Remnants of Jewry in Sixteen Countries and a Visit to the Holy Land, ed. Z.H. Wachsman. Reprinted from Daily Hebrew Journal (Toronto 1947)5-6 [Yiddish].

29. Israel Halevi Rosenberg (June 1947), Hapardes 21 no. 9, 3-4 [Hebrew].

30. Joseph Isaac Schneersohn (April 1945), HK 5 no. 56, 2-3 [Yiddish].

31. The editor (January 1945), HK 5 no. 52, 4-5 [Yiddish].

32. Anonymous (April 1945), HK 5 no. 56, 1-2 [Yiddish].

33. Joseph Isaac Schneersohn (April 1945), HK 5 no. 56, 2-3 [Yiddish].

34. Anonymous (February 1945, March 1945, April 1945), Hamessiloh 10 nos. 1-3, 1-2 [Hebrew].

35. Jacob Rosenheim, "Between Despair and Hope," reprinted from The Jewish Voice in idem., Comfort My People: A Collection of Essays and Speeches (New York 1984)198-206.

36. Anonymous (June 1945), HK 5 no. 58, 1 [Yiddish].

37. Joseph Isaac Schneersohn (March 1945), HK 5 no. 54, 2-3 [Yiddish].

38. Israel Halevi Rosenberg (June 1947), Hapardes 21 no. 9, 3-4 [Hebrew].

39. Shlomo Halberstamm (September 1946), Hapardes 20 no. 6, 11 [Hebrew].

40. Anonymous (February 1945), HV 5 no. 53, 8 [Yiddish].

41. The editor (March 1945), HK 5 no. 53, 8 [Yiddish].

42. Anonymous (September 1945), HK 5 no. 61, 8 [Yiddish]. Anonymous (June 1945), HK 5 no. 58, 1 [Yiddish]. Joseph Isaac Schneersohn (August 1948), NI 3, 6-7 [Hebrew].

43. Anonymous (September 1945), HK 5 no. 61, 1-2 [Yiddish].

44. Anonymous (January 1945), HK 5 no. 2, 8.

45. Anonymous (February 1945), HK 5 no. 53, 1 [Yiddish].

46. Anonymous (March 1945), HK 5 no. 54, 8.

47. Anonymous (April 1945), HK 5 no. 55, 1 [Yiddish]. The editor (April 1945), HK 5 no. 55, 4-5 [Yiddish]. Anonymous (April 1945), HK 5 no. 55, 8.

48. The editor (April 1945), HK 5 no. 56, 4-5 [Yiddish].

49. Anonymous (March 1945), HK 5 no. 54, 8.

50. Anonymous (April 1945), HK 5 no. 55, 1-2 [Yiddish].

51. Anonymous (July 1945), HK 5 no. 54, 1 [Yiddish].

52. Joseph Isaac Schneersohn (August 1948), NI 3, 6-7 [Hebrew].

53. The editor (June 1945), HK 5 no. 58, 4-5 [Yiddish].

54. Israel Dushavitz (September 1946), Hapardes 20 no. 6, 13 [Hebrew].

55. Moshe Shatzkes (June 1947), Hapardes 21 no. 9, 7 [Hebrew]. Shatzkes was at Chaim Ozer Grodzensky's bedside in Vilna when he died. Cf. Shmuel Rothstein, Achiezer (Tel Aviv 1948)59.

56. Hillel Zaidmann (April 1947), Ortodoxishe Tribuna, 21-19 [Yiddish].

57. Anonymous (February-April 1946), Hamessiloh 11 nos. 1-3, 1.

58. For example, Anonymous (March 1948), Or Hameir 1 no. 3, 30-31 [Yiddish]. Anonymous (May 1945), Der Yiddisher Veg 1 no. 1, 3 [Yiddish]. In his last words, Elchonon Wassermann of Baranowitch (1875-1941) expresses this belief. Efraim Oshry, Churban Litta (New York 1951)48-50.

59. Joseph Isaac Schneersohn (August 1948), NI 3, 6-7 [Hebrew].

60. Hillel Zaidmann (April 1947), Ortodoxisha Tribuna, 21-19.

61. For example Chaim Liebermann (May 1946), Der Yiddisher Veg 1 no. 1, 4-7 [Yiddish].

62. Yisroel Gustmann (September 1946), Hapardes 20 no. 6, 14-15 [Hebrew].

63. Anonymous (November 1944, December 1944, January 1945), Hamessiloh 9 nos. 10-12, 1-4 [Hebrew].

64. Israel Halevi Rosenberg (April 1949), Hapardes 23 no. 7, 2-9 [Hebrew].

65. Jacob Rosenheim (January 1945), Orthodox Tribune 5 no. 3, 3, 7. Idem. (August-September 1946), Orthodox Tribune Convention Issue, 9-11. Idem., "Between Despair and Hope," reprinted from The Jewish Voice in idem., Comfort My People: A Collection of Essays and Speeches (New York 1984) 198-206. Idem. (June 1947), Orthodox Tribune, 5-7, 9-11. Idem., Agudas Israel Faces The World Scene. New York 1947.

66. Anonymous, "Rabbi Silver's Rescue Trip Through Europe," Hurbn in Rettung (New York 1957)417-448 [Yiddish]. Hillel Zaidmann (October 1946), Ortodoxishe Tribuna, 11-13 [Yiddish].

67. Anonymous (July 1945), HK 5 no. 59, 8 [Yiddish]. The editor (August 1945, HK 5 no. 60, 4-5 [Yiddish].

68. Simcha Elberg, Akedas Treblinka. Shanghai 1946 [Yiddish].

69. Ibid., p. 3.

70. Ibid., pp. 17-18.

71. Ibid., p. 32.

72. Ibid., p. 36.

73. Ibid., p. 5.

74. Ibid., p. 32.

75. Ibid., p. 35.

76. Cf. Kalonymous Kalman Spira, Esh Kodesh (Jerusalem 1960) 61 [Hebrew] and Jerusalem Talmud Peah 1/1.

77. The editor (June 1945), HK 5 no. 58, 4-5 [Yiddish].

78. Elberg, Akedas Treblinka, supra, p. 12.

79. Simcha Elberg, "Essay on the Power of Torah," The Entire Simchah IV (Brooklyn, N.Y. 1964)25-29 [Hebrew].

80. Anonymous (June 1945), HK 5 no. 58, 6.

81. Protocol. . . , supra.

82. The editor (March 1945), HK 54 no. 5, 4-5 [Yiddish].

83. Cf. "According to the degree of darkness [of Chevlay Moshiach] it is possible to recognize the degree of positive experience which God will provide in the era of redemption." Judah ben Bezalel Loew, Netzach Israel (Prague 1599) ch. 3 [Hebrew].

84. Chofetz Chaim (d. 1933), "Expectation of Salvation," Kol Kitve Chofetz Chaim Hashalem I (N.Y. 1973) [Hebrew]. Jehudah Meir Shapiro, "Redemption of the Soul and Redemption of the Body." Reprinted May 1945, NI 1, 5 [Yiddish]. Elchonon Wassermann, Ma'amar Ikvossoh Demeschicho Vema'amar al Ha'emunah. A Belaychtung fun der yetztiger Tekufa (New York 1939) [Yiddish]. Chaim Ozer Grodzensky, Shealot U'teshuvoth Achiezer III (Vilna 1939) preface [Hebrew]. Kalonymous Kalman Spira, Esh Kodesh (Jerusalem 1960) [Hebrew].

IDEOLOGIES, ATTITUDES AND HOLOCAUST TEACHING IN THE STATE OF ISRAEL - HISTORY AND RECENT DEVELOPMENT

N. KEREN

Teachers State College - Seminar HaKibbutzim, Tel-Aviv, 149 Haifa Road, Israel.

Since the birth of the State of Israel, the impact of the Holocaust on its society and educational policy, has been pronounced.

The Israeli community was comprised of the following groups: The pioneers' families,Holocaust survivors, newcomers coming from Islamic countries and the new generation born in Israel - the 'Sabras'.

Even before the establishment of the State, the leaders of the Jewish community in Palestine, as well as the community itself could not ignore the events of the Holocaust. The Majority of the population immigrated to Palestine from the same communities destroyed by the Nazis, and the victims were their own families and friends. Zionist ideology viewed the members of these communities as the human potential of the future Jewish State. It was the Holocaust which provided the strongest and most convincing argument in support of a sovereign Jewish State. In their vision, the founders of the State wished to offer the remnants of the Jewish people a safe home and a guarrantee that "Massada should never fall again!"

The Zionist Movement has always warned the Jews in the Diaspora from a future disaster, and it has believed that the only possible answer to antisemitism was a sovereign Jewish State in Palestine. One of the main pillars of the Zionist world view was the "Negation of the Diaspora"; a view which lied at the basis of the national education in the pre-state days of the Jewish community in Palestine. What followed was a strong reproach to Jewish existance in the Diaspora, forseeing a future disaster. The only solution to antisemitism was was to be the founding of a Jewish national State.
Thus, for the Zionist Movement the events of the Holocaust were a self-fulfilling prophecy.

Fourty years have elapsed since the Nazi horrors, but its effects in Israeli life have not diminished. Israeli society experienced various changes from every possible aspect. Yet, the Holocaust has always been there. Its presence took different forms at different times, but it became an inseparable part of the Israeli being.
Historical researches provided more information and better explanations, but it had a little effect on the popular attitudes and on the existential anxieties aroused by the Holocaust events, as told and reminded by Holocaust survivors.

Unfortunately, it seems impossible to deal with the history of these processes in a short presentation; therefore this paper will be limitted to one aspect only, which is reflected in the development of the education policy, the educational aims, and in the curriculum: The public debate over the national and universal meanings of the Holocaust events and its influence on the Israeli point of view.

*

Typically, Israeli society viewed the Holocaust in a very decisive and categorical manner. Hence society was divided into three categories: the victims - the Jewish people, the oppressors - the Germans and their allies, and the bystanders - the rest of the free world. This view of the entire world brought about the inevitable conclusion that human society rejected the Jewish people and it still does. Antisemitism led to the Holocaust and it will continue to exist as long as Jews live in Exile. In this respect, the Jews bear part of the guilt for what happened to them.
Historically, this conclusion was wrong. The Jews were victims of a phenomenon they could neither forsee, nor influence or change. But it was also wrong in being so categorical: Not the whole world turned against the Jews or ignored their agony; and although the Jewish solitude was outcrying during the Holocaust, there were people, groups and individuals who offered them help and even saved as many Jews as they could. Unfortunately those 'rightous among people' were quite few, all the more reason not to ignore them.

Yet, the facts were much weaker than the desire to emphasize a most crucial point: The Jews should never rely on anybody but their own capacity to defend themselves. Nothing but a strong Jewish State could guarrantee this need. Therefore the only place for the Jews to live safely is in the State of Israel.

This existential lesson was directed, first, towards the outside world. It had to be reminded time and again that their silence during the Holocaust, and the abandonment of the Jews oblige the world to keep the security of the Jewish State. It is not surprising then, that every high official, or non-official foreign guest of the State are brought, upon their arrival, first of all, to Yad Vashem (the Holocaust Memorial in Jerusalem). This in order to remind them what they ought to bear in mind during their political talks.

The above-mentioned lesson was also directed towards the Jews still living in the Diaspora, relatively safe and tranquille. But not less towards the Israeli young generation, who at times have doubts concerning their life in Israel,and are facing various kinds of difficulties. In their case, this lesson took the shape of a warning: 'Living in the Diaspora is dangerous; what happened once, can happen again!'

This viewpoint was sincere; it was the outcome of anxiety and even fear that the State of Israel was the last fortress of the Jewish existance. Therefore it should be solid, independant and undoubted. It should keep a strong army to defend its people; after all, the history of the Jewish struggles in Palestine proved that the Israelis could overcome their enemies by their own military power.

The militant stands of the Israeli society were based on the same arguments, which led to the development of patronizing attitudes towards the Diaspora Jews. It led to criticism of their passiveness during the Holocaust. Israelis, especially the young generations, believed that the Jewish responses to the Nazi attrocities were expressions of what was percieved as typical Diaspora Jewish behaviour.

These attitudes have already existed prior to the Holocaust, but it was the Holocaust and its results that strengthened the feelings of superiority towards those Jews, even without any solid information of what had really happened. the lack of knowledge on the one hand, and the militant viewpoint on the other hand led to the very unjust conclusion blaming the Jews for what had happened to them. and deriving moral and practical lessons on the Jewish level only. This was, inevitably the ground on which the Holocaust survivors met with the accusation: 'Why did you go like sheep to slaughter?' and to the typical Israeli statement: 'It could have never happened here!'

The chapters in the history of the Holocaust which dealt with the Zionist youth movements and their attempts to uprise against the Nazis, were exaggerated. The survivors who were members of those movements made every possible effort to emphasize this issue and making of it, unproportionally, the major issue of the Holocaust. They had no intention to twist the historical events, but it was the only answer they could possibly give to the above-mentioned accusation. Non of the horrible attrocities that Jews had to face during that period could have been understood by the Israeli society of the 1950's. Even the State grasped their glorious stories as the outcome of their Zionist beliefs, and this trend received official sanction by its decision to hold the Holocaust Memorial Day on the date of the Warsaw Ghetto uprising. It was given the name: "Holocaust and Heroism Day". By 'Heroism' they meant, no doubt, militant acts, which were admired by the old and the young.

During this period the responses of the majority of the Jews - men, women and children - to the Nazi horrors were almost totally ignored, and it was even something to be ashamed of; something that was to be whispered between the attrocities of the Nazis and the heroism of the ghetto-fighters and the partisans. Although there was no school curriculum at all concerning this subject, every boy and girl were familiar with the name of Anielevich and the uprising in the Warsaw Ghetto, but only few heard names like Treblinka and Auschwitz.

It should be emphasized that the Israeli society was not preoccupied with Holocaust events in daily or public life, although there were some events which were emotionally provocative. The first was the public and political debate over the question of the 'Compensations Agreement with West Germany; the second was the decision to sell Israeli arms to the West German army. Generally, it was a personal or family matter. Most victims of the Holocaust, as well as the destroyed communities, were the historical background of the majority of the Israeli population in the pre-state years. But at schools, as stated before, there was no interest in this subject and there was not one textbook available. In the history textbooks the Holocaust could be found in three chapters:

1) The attrocities of the Nazis.
2) The silence of the free world.
3) The heroism of the Zionist youth movement during their attempted uprisings, and the help of the Jewish community of Palestine by sending Hebrew Parashooters and the Jewish Brigade to help the Jews in occupied Europe.

The national meanings of the Holocaust on the one hand and the ignorance of the public, especially the younger generations, on the other hand, were in Ben-Gurion's mind when he decided to bring Adolf Eichmann to trial in the State of Israel.
The trial was, therefore, built in a way that made it possible to describe the chronology of the events from the very beginning to the end.
The Eichmann Trial and its impact on the Israeli public is worthy of a wider discussion than this paper can possibly offer. Yet, it should be pointed out that no radical changes occured either in the public attitudes, or in the public viewpoints concerning the Holocaust. Nor was there any remarkable improvement in the educational arena.

Although the Holocaust did not effect daily life,it existed under the skin of the Israeli society like a wound covered with a thin membrane; and it so happened that every event which caused national tension, especially threats on the national security, scratched this wound and reopened it. It has started in the War of Independance (1948), returned during the Sinai Operation (1956), but reached a climax in the 'Waiting Period', three weeks before the 'Six Days War' (May-June, 1967).
The Jewish solitude was then a fact. The threat of war and the apathy of the United Nations were worrying. Suddenly, it became clear to Jews abroad that their tranquility in the Diaspora resulted from the existance of the Jewish State; and they felt threatened by the idea that Israel could have been attacked.
In Israel, the civilian population as well as the recruited soldiers in their units spoke of the necessity to win the war in order 'to prevent another Holocaust'.The anxiety took various forms; there were people, especially Holocaust survivors, who prepared stocks of food, and Israelis who stayed abroad caught the first available seats in planes and hurried to join their fighting units.

It took only six days to achieve an outstanding victory; the three major Arab armies were totally destroyed, and anxiety was replaced by national euphoria. Once again it was proved that the Jewish State and the Jewish army are the only answer to any threat on the security of the Jewish people.
But there was more: During the war, the whole West Bank, including the Eastern part of Jerusalem (formally in Jordan) was occupied by the Israeli army, and by the unification of Jerusalem - a generations' dream came true. There was now an access to holy places like Hebron, Bethlehem and many others.
The victory in the Six Days War was perceived as a salvation from a disaster and as an unshakable proof of the traditional national viewpoints, to which another component has been added: The divine right to return to the holy places, which were freed, not occupied.
But not only religious Israelis were thrilled with joy; thousands of people travelled in the new areas, about which most of them, especially the young, have read only in history or geography books.

In the general national euphoria, another consequence of the occupied territories was was neglected: In the holy places, around them and all over the West Bank and Gaza Strip there lived hundreds of thousands of civilian population, most of them refugees, who did not take part in the war, but were now **under** a new ruler - the Israeli army.
The future of these territories was, of course, a political matter for the government to discuss. However for the Israeli warriors, it was a new and unpleasant task, contrary to their upbringing and their training: They had to rule over men, women and children.

Many of the Israeli soldiers expresses their mixed feelings facing this population; and this confusion had to do with Holocaust events. On one hand they had to fulfill their military duties and to keep an eye on the nests of terrorism which developped inside the refugee camps, but on the other hand, they tried to behave as 'enlighted conqueror', helping women and old men and embracing children.
But no matter what their feelings were, the Israeli Defence Forces, became, at least, in the eyes of the population, an occupation army; the sons and grandsons of the victims were considered as oppressors. Bearing in mind the three categories of human-society created by the typical Israeli world-view - the status of the oppressors was absolutely confusing.

Initially many people believed that these territories would be the best card Israel had in future negotiations for peace, while others considered it as a fulfillment of the generations dream to return to the fatherland.
For more than twenty years no political decision was reached and the national debate over this matter became worse. Here again the Holocaust played a major role. The extreme national groups believe that the territories belong to the Jewish people and, from a security point of view they are the guarrantee against abother Holocaust. Even Abba Eben, the famous statesman, who belongs to the other side of the political map, used the expression 'Auschwitz Line' to describe the old green line of the border. Others could not live in peace with the images of the Israelis as the oppressors of civilian population, and this restlessness was also rooted in the Holocaust experience.

It must be emphasized though, that any comparison between the Holocaust events and the Israeli situation is, totally misleading, although unti-Israeli propaganda used this comparison in order to expose the Israeli policy as denying human-rights.
It should be remembered that there has never been any racial or ideological hate in the Israeli attitude towards the Arab population. Nor were there intentions to inihilate those men, women and children. On the contrary: Often Israeli soldiers were murdered by Arab terrorists hidden behind innocent women and children, whom the soldiers did not want to harm.

Yet, knowing all this did not ease the bad concience of the Israeli young generation. There developed a new point of view out of the Holocaust experience, which demanded more sensitivity and compassion towards the suffering of others.

The Six Days War, then, created the first cracks in the solid, national lessons of the Holocaust events, suggesting a more universal interpratation.

The gap between the traditional conception of the Holocaust and its lessons, and the doubts resulted from them, became even deeper during and after the October War (1973).
However, it was menifested differently and pointed to other directions.

The Israeli leadership was accused by the public of being indifferent and self-confident concerning a possible threat on the people's security. Public opinion accused the political and military establishment of lack of foresight, which resulted in the disastrous beginning of the war. In spite of the obvious differences, similar accusations were directed towards the Jewish leadership in Eastern Europe concerning its reactions to the events in the 1920's and 1930's. The last were accused, of course by the Israelis of the 1950's and 1960's, blaming them of prefering the Diaspora 'here and now fleshpot' on the Zionist solution, and thus, of being responsible for the fatal consequences. Suddenly, those Israelis realized that their own national leaders did not behave differently.

The October War was the first to have entered to the Israeli household via television.
For the first time in the Israeli experience, the public was exposed to pictures of Israeli warriors as prisoners of war, sitting on the ground, hands above their heads, humiliated, guarded by Syrian, or Egyptian soldiers, and totally incapacitated.
Indeed, these sights were particularly depressing and difficult to absorb, in view of the fact that theses images were previously associated with pictures of Jews in documentary films and pictures about the Holocaust.

During the first weeks of the war, due to the shortage of arms, no one could ignore the enormous aid that was provided by the U.S.A. in the form of an 'air-lift' containing everything the Israeli soldiers needed. This fact contradicted, of course, the inclination to believe that ' the whole world is against us', and that Israel can do without any outside help. Combining this fact with the two previous descriptions, it brought a real confusion into the traditional attitudes of the Israeli public towards itself, towards its history and towards its place among the community of nations.
The memory of the Holocaust was present in all the three aspects.

The self-reassessment was sharpened during other tragic events that occured in Israel. or to Israeli people. One case in point was the hijack of the Air-France aircraft by terrorists and bringing it to Idi Amin's Uganda, in 1976.
The descriptions of the helpless Israeli passengers, separated from all the non-Jewish people by four armed terrorists, terrified and waiting for outside help, were quite shocking.
In Israel itself nobody could forget another terrorist attack, in which a father and his daughter were murdered, and the mother with her baby were hidden in the attic.The mother suffocated her baby to death, out of her fear to be caught.It happened in Naharia, in 1979. These two events reminded the self-confident Israeli, that he was, above all, a human-being.

One consequence of these tragic experiences was the development of a new attitude towards the Jewish responses during the Holocaust. They were not considered any more as typical Diaspora--Jewish, but as a human behavior.
The era of the 'Nagation of the Diaspora" ended then in tne end of the 1970's.

During this period the Israeli public had some opportunities to prove its human compassion and sensitivity towards other peoples' sufferings. It has started in the case of the Ibus in Biafra, and continued during the wars in Vietnam and Cambodia.
The public debate over the question of Israeli involvement in these issues used arguments from the Jewish experience during the Holocaust, and even politicians could not ignore the the resemblance of the hungry black Ibu children to the hungry Jewish children in the ghettos of Poland. Nor could anybody fail to make the association between the T.V. reports showing Vietnamese and Cambodian refugees, looking for rescue ships in the ocean, and Jewish refugees knocking on closed doors, looking for a shelter from the Nazi threat.
It was therefore not surprising that the Israeli government decided to absorb some of those refugees, most of whom became Israeli citizens.

All the above-mentioned events had brought about attitudinal changes on various issues in the public agenda. Among them was the attitude towards the Holocaust and its lessons. Increasingly, this experience was analyzed from a universal point of view as well as from a national one.
The Nazi phenomenon, its ideology, policy and attrocities - was percieved as deeds of human-beings; the behavior of the victims came to be understood as a human response in extreme situations, and not as typically Jewish. And the decision of people to take a position or to remain passive was perceived as a moral choice, of human communities and individuals.

The more these universal lessons has been uprooted within the Israeli society, the more uneasy were the feelings of many Israelis concerning the population in the occupied territories. In this case the clash between the national and the universal lessons from the events of the Holocaust was not only ideological, but very much existential. On the one hand nobody wanted to bring back the security problems of the 1960's, and on the other hand, the role of an oppressor was sensed by many Israelis as a contradiction to their moral attitudes; and both had to do with the Holocaust experience. As it was expressed by A. B. Yehushua:

"...We should always remember that the fact of being victims did not provide us with a moral stand. The victim does not become morally just, merely by being a victim. Although the Holocaust did horrible things to us, it did not provide us with an eternal 'Honesty Certificate'. It made the murderers immoral but it did not make the victim automatically moral. In order to be considered as one, one do things of moral nature; and this should be put to a daily eduring test..."

The education establishment could not ignore the changes in attitudes within the Israeli society concerning the Holocaust.
Since the Eichmann Trial in 1961, the policy and the curricula have remained unchanged. It was unexplainable, especially considering the upgraded level of historical research, the involvement of the universities in promoting the subject, and above all - the growing public interest.
Even after the Six Days War the view of the Holocaust's proper place in educational programs remained the same. The emphasis on the Zionist lessons was expressed by the wide discussion on the 'Heroism' and the minor attention to the 'Shoa' (Holocaust); and again, the issue of the 'Israeli-Jews' responses was presented through the story of the parashooters and the Jewish Brigade, and their actions in occupied Europe.
After the October War (1973) this conception was not accepted any more. An 'earthquake' was created not only in political and social life, but in educational thought as well.
The facts previously provided by the old history textbooks concerning the events of the Holocaust became suspicious in the eyes of teachers, as well as students; what could be easily swallowed under the circumstances of the past, looked anachronistic and doubtful. These developments exerted pressure on the Ministry of Education, demanding changes in policy, attitude and in the curriculum. All of a sudden, people realized that the Holocaust was never an obligatory subject in high schools, and that in elementary and junior-high schools it did not even exist. As an outcome, a whole generation was brought up in Israel without any decent knowledge about this chapter in the Jewish history, but with all the stereotypes inherited from its parents.

Educators and history teachers, members of the academy, Holocaust survivors and politicians urged the educational establishment to reorganize and to provide teachers and students with a new policy, new curriculum and new textbooks which might satisfy their changed needs.
At the basis of the new concept was the awareness of the need to provide the students with the historical facts and explanation of the general processes, covering the entire period. Then came the discussion of the human dilemmas: of the leadership, of the various organizations and of individuals. It followed by various models of resistance to the Nazi attrocities, including armed uprising, moral decisions, etc.
The Ministry of Education turned to young historians and asked them to compose learning programs in this spirit.
As a result, two proframs were written during the 1970's. The first one, "Antisemitism and Holocaust", followed the new concept and included most of the above-mentioned items.
It demanded from the student to be aware of the factual background before he jumps to any conclusion. Didactically, it was a new method of learning which found its course within the scholl system very slowly. Yet, it caused no ideological arguments, because it did not challange the traditional lessons of the Holocaust and it ended with a chapter which made the connection between the Holocaust events and the establishment of the State of Israel.

In the case of the second program things went differently.
"The Holocaust - A Subject for High Schools" - reflected the trend to introduce the universal aspects of the Holocaust. It was done by showing the process of socialization that adolescents have gone through in Nazi Germany, versus the developments of the Jewish traditional community, putting in the center individuals and their moral decisions and moral responsibility. The goal of this program was to provide the student with tools which would enable him to reach moral decisions, based on positive values, realizing that immoral decisions based on negative values caused the destruction of his own people.
The author of this program believed that there should not be an exclusive Jewish concept of teaching the Holocaust. His program was directed to all the adolescents of the world, presuming that the absorption of positive values should become the shield against another Genocide.

The establishment could not cope with this revolutionary educational experiment. It had gone too far from the traditional conception of Holocaust education. People wer not prepared for such point of view. In spite of a call for changes, they still prefered to demand moral attitudes from the outside world, but showed little moral doubts concerning themselves. Even university scholars rejected the idea of 'recruiting the Holocaust' in order to foster values of any kind. They believed that teaching the Holocaust is a goal by itself, and by no means a tool for reaching other purposes.
This attitude did not preclude reaching moral conclusions while studying the Holocaust events. However, its assumption was that education should always deal with values which might assist the scholars to reach moral lessons from every experience, including the Holocaust.

It is not surprising, then, that the discussion concerning Holocaust studies have not reached a valent end.
At the end of the 1970's there was a political inverse in Israel, and the National Right, headed by M. Begin was to rule the State for several years. The public debate over the old issues became even stronger after the achievement of the Peace Treaty with Egypt and the withdrawal from Sinai. Again, the Holocaust memory played a major role. Both sides were convinced that better knowledge of Holocaust events might help its cause. The Right wing saw in the Holocaust experience the most convincing point for keeping the occupied territories under Israeli control for ever. The Left wing learnt from the Holocaust that any people, including the Palestinians has its human rights, and therefore Israel should be ready to withdraw from these territories in return for a Peace Treaty with the Palestinian people. Both sides were combined in their demand to change the Law of State Education, adding the obligation of teaching the Holocaust in every high school in Israel.

Being now a political issue no less than educational one, Holocaust education has only gone through technical- bureaucratical changes.
Nor could the Ministry of Education provide the teachers with a satisfactory curriculum. A decent curriculum should include a declaration of educational aims, suggested tools,list of subjects and a chosen bibliograpgy. The public debate over the aims on one hand, and the inability to offer tools to reach any aim, on the other hand - left the official program with the last two items: A list of subjects and a bibliography.

Each teacher had to draft his own aims according to his moral and educational values, careful not to depart from the concensus, using the material offered by the establishment and preparing his students for the final examinations. Moreover, since the 1970's only one textbook was published and it is the only book on the Holocaust recognized by the Ministry of Education.

Yet, although the programs are not provocative, the students of the 1980's are very much preoccupied with the Holocaust events. Among other reasons, it is the media which has an important role in bringing the Holocaust into the public consciousness. Information, as well as opinions concerning the Holocaust events are now available not only at school.
The American serial "Holocaust", for example, which was shown via television, in every household, made a deeper impression on students than any educational program could possibly have. The grandsons of the Holocaust survivors show sincere interest in those events and they find themselves asking questions and bothered by human dilemmas, born by the facts. After all, the changes in the general attitudes towards Jewish history and especially towards the Holocaust have not gone unnoticed by them.

Some of the major questions are directed towards the Israeli establishment of the pre-State period: 'What have you done in those days? Have you really made every possible effort to help your dying brothers, or were you preoccupied with exploiting the situation for the improvement of the Zionist cause?!'
The students are no longer satisfied with the traditional answers and with the old examples of the parashooters and the Jewish Brigade, with all the respect to their contributions. In some cases the students dare to accuse the old leadership of being bystanders, no less than others in the free world.
Although it was not a black-and-white situation, and even the facts do not help much to ease those feelings, the educational establishment have not yet found the way to meet these challanges. It should be mentioned here, that the historical research on these issues is currently on the 'public agenda' and it is carried out by young, Israeli-born schlars.

The second phenomenon is rather unexpected; it is probably the outcome of a new outlook of Jewish history in the Diaspora, on one hand, and the adoption of a more universal approach to the Holocaust events, on the other hand.
The grandsons of Holocaust-survivors and of immigrants from Arab countries, as well as the descendants of the 'Sabras', manage to look at the events in a wider spectrum, both as human beings and Jews. They cannot accept the premeditated verdict given by the Zionist trends to the Jews in exile, which was known as 'The Negation of the Diaspora'.
They are searching now for their own toots in the Jewish existance in the Diaspora. There is a need to understand the various processes that characterized Jewish life in order to reach a better understanding of the Jewish responses to the Nazi attrocities.
By such explorations of Jewish life before and during the Holocaust, they realize for themselves the enormous loss caused to the Jewish people and to Jewish life by the Holocaust.

A most important result of this exploration is the inclination developped among the third generation to inquire their grandparents about their life in the Diaspora, especially about the Holocaust period. They show true interest and involvement, and their curiosity cause their grandparents, especially the Holocaust survivors, to share their personal experiences with them. Previously, it was a shame to tell stories in which there were no acts of 'Heroism'; The second generation was never interested in the 'Diaspora stories' of their parents which contradicted their upbringing. Many of the survivors shut themselves in because they wished to spare their agony from their children.
But recently, their need to reopen meet with their grandchildren's need to know. As a result, many survivors are writing their memories of the Holocaust period, publish hidden diaries, knowing that they fulfill their duty both towards the past and the future.

This phenomenon is followed by another cosequence: The desire of a growing number of high-school students to visit Poland and to see in their own eyes the ruins of the Jewish community there.
For more than two years already hundreds of Israeli students arrive in Poland, visit the old Jewish quarters and seeking for Jewish remnants. Many of them come to Poland to pay their tribute to their own families, and go to visit their grandparents' hometowns, looking for 'granpa's house or 'granpa's street'.
They walk inside the death camps, watching the horrible sights of the barracks, terryfied by the looks of the gas chambers and the crematoria, and crying over their murdered Jewish people. Although most of them are not religious, some of them are saying the prayers to honour the memory of the dead.
Coming back from Poland they develop a growing identification with their own people's fate, but also a higher sensitivity to human nature.

All these changes, including the "Polish Experience', sharpen the painful question: 'How could it happen?'

This question has been dealt with before, but previously the answers lied within the old lessons. Now the search for better explanations leads the students to further possible answers. A major one is the nature of man. The Holocaust was the outcome of a regime created by human-beings, accepted and even appreciated by human-beings. It happened in the Twentieth Century, in civilized Europe, and it was a product of a human mind and human behavior.

The conclusions of this search are pessimistic in nature; it can happen again if mankind will not stand on guard; it can be done to anyone by anyone under certain circumstances. The threat is always there.

What are the lessons that the Israeli student obtain from the Holocaust events?

He probably realizes the danger of being a hated and haunted minority, and therefore he appreciates the importance of a strong Jewish State. Yet he has bad conscience concerning the Israeli involvement in the suffering of another people.
He sympathizes with the life and destiny of his people in exile, but he ie conclusive that every Jew must live in the State of Israel.
He is sure that any threat on the Jewish State can be disastrous for the Jewish future, and unfortunately it can be safe only by exercising force. Yet, he feels morally bad about this alternative.

For the Israeli public, and especially for the young generations the experience of the Holocaust and the existential anxieties create a vicious circle, which takes enormous political and educational courage to break through.
Political attitudes in Israel are too complicated, especially concerning national vs. universal matters, and therefore one cannot seek revolutionary changes in that area. It leaves the educational system on its own, carrying the responsibility of shaping the attitudes of the generations to come.

Education, then, has a major role, and even a sacred duty.

"... We, as the victims of the Nazi virus, should be the carriers of the antitoxin to this horrible desease, by which every people can be attacked. And being the carriers of this antitoxin, we have to be especially careful in regard to ourselves. But at the same time, we should be cautious not to loose proportions, and not to measure everything in comparison to the Holocaust.

Just because we have gone through such a horrible experience, we could become indifferent to any other suffering which is less strong than ours..."

REFERENCES

Ackerman, W., Carmon, A., Zucker, D, (1985) Education in Evolving Society, HaKibbutz HaMeuhad, 117-185.
Bauer, Y. Moreshet, 17, (1974), Moreshet, 6-10. Lessons of the Holocaust, (1978), Philadelphia, 3-5.
Carmon, A. (1980). The Annals, 227-236. The Holocaust - A Learning Subject in Highschools, (1979). Maalot, Tel-Aviv.
Eilon, A. (1972). The Israelis, Shocken, 121-223.
Firer, R. (1985). The Agents of Zionist Education, Sifriat Poalim, 50-104.
Gutman, I., Schatzker, H. (1983). The Holocaust and Its Meaning, Shazar Center, Jerusalem.
Herman, S. N. (1980) Jewish Identity, Jerusalem, 73-96.
History Curriculum For Highschools - The Holocaust, (1981), Ministry of Education, Jerusalem.
Keren, N. (1986). The Impact of the Public-Opinion Shapers and of the Historical Research on the Development of Educational Thought and Educational Programs Concerning the Holocaust in Highschools and in Informal Education in Israel (1948-1981), The Hebrew University, Jerusalem.
Lieblich, A. (1979). The Soldiers of Jerusalem Beach, Shocken, Tel-Aviv.
Porat, D. (1986). An Entangled Leadership - The Yishuv and the Holocaust 1942-1945, Am Oved, Tel-Aviv.
Schatzker, H. (1980). The Annals, 218-226. (1981). Forum 41, 135-141.
Yehoshua, A. B. (1980). Between Right and Right, Shocken, Tel-Aviv, 9-25.

HISTORICISM, EVIL, AND POST-HOLOCAUST MORAL THOUGHT

Michael L. Morgan

Indiana University, Bloomington, Indiana, U.S.A.

There is an irony about post-Holocaust Jewish thought that is well worth addressing. Like most ironies, it gains in power and surprise by simple formulation. There are two groups of post-Holocaust Jewish thinkers, those who recognize the event's unique, radical evil and those who do not. The latter, while agreeing that Auschwitz was an event of extreme horror and intense suffering, do not believe that it or any other historical episode can alter the theological and moral truths of Judaism. The former, on the other hand, are persuaded that the unprecedented atrocities have altered the very shape of Jewish self- understanding, for Judaism is rooted in history and is always revisable in terms of it. For one group the moral resources of Judaism are decisive and unalterable; for the other they are rich but constantly in flux. The result is irony, for those who take the Holocaust most seriously are without the unconditional moral resources to oppose it absolutely, while those who reject the event's unprecedented character are more able to oppose it unqualifiedly even while they refuse to treat its evil as distinctive. In short, the more transforming the event, the less decisive one's ability to oppose it; the less transforming, the more unconditional one's capacity for opposition.

Perhaps this irony is, like so many, more apparent than real. One would like to think so. For the irony concerns large and important questions about morality and relativism, truth and history, and the very nature of Jewish faith, moral thought, and Jewish life. Let me propose, then, that we use the irony as a way of exposing these problems and examining them. Our goal will be to determine if the particularly powerful <u>moral context</u> of post-Holocaust religious -- here Jewish -- thought may result in an especially profound attempt to resolve the dispute between realism and historicism and to understand the relation between thought and history in the sphere of religious and moral life.

It will be useful to clarify this goal at the outset. Recently philosophers, literary critics, and others have inclined away from some form of objectivism or realism toward what has been called historicism, idealism, or pragmatism. Nietzsche and Heidegger are, among others, the forebearers of this movement, but its current practitioners include analytic as well as continental style philosophers, historians, students of anthropology, science, and religion, literary theorists, and many more. What they share is a refusal to admit invariable standards of value and judgment and a penchant for interpretation and understanding rather than exlanation, truth, and certitude. For them acting, thinking, and writing are context-bound activities, events to be understood against a background of discourse, purpose, and reception. History and community determine thought in the sense that all thinking emerges out of the discourse of historical communities. Transcendence is never totally complete; all thought is moored in and emerges from the individual subject's point of view and is subject to historical alteration, confirmation, and revision.

There are many motivations for holding the views incorporated in this way of thinking -- doubts about the universality of logical principles (like bivalence), about traditional distinctions (like that between *a priori* and *a posteriori* knowledge), about the objectivity of moral principles and judgments, about translation and communication, about skepticism and its presuppositions, and on and on. The results of these motivations and the arguments they generate are a variety of kinds of anti-foundationalism. The question I am raising is this: if the context that gives rise to thoughts about historicism and these issues is profoundly moral and historically particular, as the Holocaust is, then does it yield any hopes for a result that is *historically serious* -- and hence anti-foundationalist or historicist -- and at the same time *morally deep and responsible*? In other words, can we show some reason to think that the irony with which we began is in fact only apparent?

We should begin with a thinker who is sensitive to the moral dimension of human and specifically Jewish existence but who cannot bring himself to think that post-Holocaust Jewish theology is substantially transformed by Auschwitz. Here, I think, Eliezer Berkovits is an excellent example. *Faith after the Holocaust*, published in 1973, is a morally impassioned attempt to confront the event with utter seriousness and honesty, while at the same time identifying and holding to a transcendent, yet historically relevant conception of God, the Jewish people, and their convenantal relationship in history. In the end, for Berkovits, Auschwitz is a psychological, not a theological problem for the Jewish people; it is an event that both represents the nadir of human moral development and threatens the Jewish commitment to moral mission, to spearheading the moral redemption of creation. The theological conception that lies behind this twin judgment is *not* threatened, revised, or destroyed. As an historical event, the Holocaust has an impact on historical creatures, on the Jewish people, and it does *threaten* them and their level of allegiance to their moral-religious post. But it does not threaten the philosophy of history and conception of divine providence which these people hold. What is shaken is not the theory itself but rather their ability to accept it, to believe it, to act in its behalf.

This is what Berkovits says:

> "The question raised by the holocaust that concerns man most directly is not, 'Where was God?', but 'Where was man?' The presence of God in history or his absence from it is a complex theological problem; the presence or absence of man as an ethical and moral agent is a matter of experience. The Jewish experience in the ghettos and death camps made manifest in our days the collapse of man as a moral being....In terms of the spirit...it was a world catastrophe on the widest possible scale."[1]

Berkovits argues, that is, that the event implicates, in addition to the Nazis themselves, the Christian churches, the Allied nations, the Germans, indeed the entire West. "The plight of the Jew became the point for the crystallization of moral direction in history" (36), and it was a point of "disintegration" and failure. For Berkovits, then, the Holocaust is the moment when the moral bankruptcy of Western civilization exposed itself, and at least for this reason it is an event of world-historical significance.

In our post-Holocaust world Christianity is in disarray, and the Jewish people ought to be. But the Jewish thinker must avoid an inauthentic questioning of God. "The inexplicable will not be explained" (70), but it can be endured. "The question of faith for the Jew is ... not to explain why God was silent while the crematoria were consuming a third of the Jewish people. The question is whether within the frame of reference of Judaism it is possible to take cognizance of the tragedy and promise of existence and whether one may hold on to the promise in spite of the tragedy" (85). After Auschwitz, there is every reason for the Jew to give up, to forego his sense of purpose and abandon hope. But, Berkovits argues, a secure self-understanding of history, providence, and the role of the Jewish people, together with a recognition of the significance of the reestablishment of the State of Israel, should enable him to endure.

We need not examine Berkovits' account of a genuine Jewish conception of history and God's involvement in it. Suffice it to say that he takes innocent suffering to be a Biblical and Rabbinic problem and that he uses a notion of paradox in which free will is given, as is moral command, by a divine presence that is also paradoxically a divine absence, and thereby sees God's impact as issuing in a millenial task to bring moral perfection to the created world, a task enabled and hindered by the gift of human freedom.[2] The result of this view of history and the Jewish covenantal responsibility is a distinction between two histories, that of the nations or power history and that of Israel or faith history. It is the twin outcome of Nazism that power history seems to have become overwhelmingly victorious in the modern world and that the Jewish people, witness to faith, has become utterly demoralized. The question of urgency, then, is not God's role; rather it is whether the Jewish people can remain at their covenantal post, witnessing to "God's elusive presence in history" (131).

It is not necessary to complete Berkovits' story, for its relevance to our inquiry should already be clear. Berkovits is willing to give the Holocaust a central role in his understanding of contemporary Jewish life. It is the nemesis of power history, the outcome of nature victorious over faith and moral purpose. But Auschwitz "does not preempt the future course of Jewish history" (134), by which Berkovits means that rabbinic faith must not be consumed by the Shoah. Rather the event must be understood as part of a history whose character is defined by the Biblical and Rabbinic teachings. Theologically speaking, the enormity of the _hurban_ is insignificant.[3] Psychologically speaking, the level of suffering and atrocity is overwhelming. What Berkovits calls the Jewish "philosophy of history" and "concept of divine providence," established in the Biblical text and developed by Rabbinic interpretation, are unconditional and unrevisable in their basic design. It is faith, subjectively rather than objectively speaking, that is at issue, and the Holocaust puts it in jeapordy. Furthermore, the event is the outcome of all those natural forces -- desire, need, power, etc. -- which faith and moral purpose are an effort to control, shape, and direct. In short, Berkovits is a kind of Manichean; in his eyes the Jewish people are mandated by goodness to oppose the sources of evil in nature. Hence, the evil of the Holocaust is rooted in the forces of nature, while goodness is the banner of the divine carried by human freedom. An original irony, then, is mitigated, for the evil, particularized in its object, is reduced to power and its associates, while its motivational effects do, to some degree, influence the career of faith, albeit not in content. In the end, Berkovits cannot submit to any form of theological historicism, nor does he give evil its complete due. He employs powerful moral weapons but against a compromised enemy.[4]

Berkovits incorporates the Holocaust into a pre-existing pattern of Jewish thought. Neither the latter's conception of evil nor its conception of the divine-human relationship are altered by the evil. Yet Berkovits is sensitive to the suffering and the atrocity, to the Holocaust's impact on contemporary Jews, Christians, and others. Hence, in moving away from his position, we seek one that is at least equally sensitive to the event's impact, is respectful of the transcendent character of Jewish self-understanding, but is more responsive to the event's theological significance. This position, I believe, is held by Irving Greenberg in his important essay "Cloud of Smoke, Pillar of Fire: Judaism, Christianity, and Modernity after the Holocaust" (1977).[5]

First, Greenberg is keenly attentive to the historicity of Jewish experience. Judaism applies to history and indeed emerges from history, from the "basic orienting experience" of the Exodus. God cares about human life; in the end human life will be redeemed from suffering, poverty, indignity. The result of these facts is that "events happen in history which change our perception of human fate, events from which we draw the fundamental norms by which we act and interpret what happens to us. One such event is the Holocaust." (8) Greenberg then says that it is impossible to isolate the Exodus from "further revelations " and counter-experiences. In principle, then, for Greenberg the original Jewish understanding of the divine-human encounter and its meaning for Jewish life can be reinterpreted and revised. It is historically exposed.[6]

With respect to the Holocaust, then, how does this exposure occur? Greenberg proposes that Judaism "stand[s] or fall[s] on [the] fundamental claim that the human being is ... of ultimate and absolute value" (9). He then cites a powerful piece of testimony from the Nuremberg trial record, of the burning alive of Jewish children at Auschwitz, purportedly to save the miniscule cost of gassing them, as a "counter-testimony" to this affirmation of human worth and dignity. This pit of burning, screaming children now represents the atrocities, the evil of the Holocaust, and in terms of it Greenberg does two things:

(1) he formulates a criterion of acceptability -- perhaps even of authenticity -- for all statements, theological or otherwise, that deal with post-Holocaust Jewish life (the criterion of the burning children);

(2) he claims that as a result of applying this criterion, all responses to the event will be dialectical (the dialectical criterion).[7]

It is not clear how Greenberg sees the relationship between these two criteria. On the face of it, he seems to be reasoning this way: the Holocaust is incomprehensible; so our existing standards and concepts cannot deal with it fully, simply, or adequately. There is no way of combining sufficient sensitivity to the event's horror and our categories of thought and action, for these latter reflect our sense of human value. Greenberg draws from this fact of <u>incommensurability</u> or <u>incompatibility</u> the conclusion that all attempts to deal with or respond to the Shoah are dialectical, where this seems to mean 'complex', 'partial', torn by "irresolvable tensions." Hence, if one theorizes after the event, one's theory must be dialectical, i.e., without any complete or final resolution, involving a tension of thought that moves from pole to pole. This characteristic, then, is the "verification principle" for post- Holocaust thinking (see (2) above).

Greenberg proceeds to formulate what he calls a "working principle," and what I have called the "criterion of the burning children:" "No statement, theological or otherwise, should be made that would not be credible in the presence of the burning children" (23).[8] Now, this is a bit confusing. Which is the adequacy-criterion for theological thought -- this working principle or the dialectical condition, or both? Let us set aside the objection that the Holocaust is not the only motivation for dialectical thinking. If so, then I think that what Greenberg means is this: authentic post-Holocaust theology -- we omit for convenience other types of thinking -- will be partial, tense, and complex, in a word "dialectical." But this is a result of the fact that no complete solutions and simple answers can be held at the same time that one is sufficiently moved by the horrors of the Holocaust. To check to see if one's thought is dialectical would be formal and insufficient. To check to see if one could affirm a claim while wholly conscious of and receptive to the pain, the horror, the atrocity -- this will not only expose the flaw in one's thinking but also direct one's thinking through the dialectical process of affirmation, denial, qualification, affirmation, and so on. In a sense, then, Greenberg wants the two principles to be coextensive. In effect, the principle of the burning children (see (1) above) actually generates dialectical thinking and does so by never allowing thought to escape the utter concreteness and particularity of the event. The tension between universal categories, principles, and so on and the precise horror of this collection of concrete episodes arises in the mind of the thinker when his thought is not allowed to escape the particular episode.

In terms of profundity of insight, this attempt to insure that the encounter of thought with the Shoah never be permitted to escape the concrete particularity of its episodes of horror marks a highpoint in Greenberg's discussion. His thought quickly becomes less powerful. For example, he asks, what about faith after Auschwitz? His answer, that it must be dialectical and momentary, is riddled with problems. "Neither classical theism nor atheism," he says, "is adequate to incorporate the incommensurability of the Holocaust." This may be true, but his brief, critical comments about and classification of Berkovits, Emil Fackenheim, and Richard Rubenstein fail to understand any of the three. Berkovits may be a classical theist but hardly a self-satisfied one; Fackenheim simply is not, and Rubenstein is too complex to be cast simply as an atheist. Furthermore, as Greenberg turns to describe "dialectical faith," he weakens his own conception, for he treats dialectic as a movement from moment to moment, from belief to skepticism, conviction to doubt (27, 33). But surely a strong view of dialectic would treat every moment as simultaneously a moment of faith and insecurity, of hope and despair. Indeed, his earlier discussion of Wiesel's Sarah, both saint and prostitute, suggests this notion of a simultaneous dialectic, as does his later account of secularity and religiosity (45-52).

In principle, all of Judaism can be revised for Greenberg. In fact, however, much resists revision. He argues against the utter destruction of faith, explores Biblical models for a post-Holocaust understanding of the divine-human relation, and mines traditional texts for testimony in behalf of human worth and dignity. Greenberg derives this multifaceted commitment to Jewish faith and its traditional expressions from a general notion of moral necessity against the "idols of the age," secularism, idolatry, humanism, rationalism, and so forth. If the dialectical character of authentic response is the hallmark of Greenberg's historicism, this unqualified opposition to the failures of modernity signals his moral absolutism.

From a moral point of view, then, Greenberg has a good deal in common with Berkovits. The Holocaust is a signal of the moral bankruptcy of the modern world, of a secular culture framed by "science, philosophy, and social science," "rationalism and human liberation." "Modernity fostered the excessive rationalism and utilitarian relations which created the need for and susceptibility to mass movements and the surrender of moral judgment" (28). Greenberg argues that secular civilization, after Auschwitz, hardly warrants our commitment. We must resist the "absolutization of the secular" (29). To be sure, what Greenberg advocates is no simple-minded return to a spiritual traditionalism. Remember the mandate to dialectical positions -- secular and religious, self-reliant and submissive, and so forth. But nonetheless his doubts about modernity and his respect for the resources of the Jewish tradition do reflect a bias, for to Greenberg the Holocaust is the supreme counter-testimony to the millenial Jewish commitment to human dignity and value.

In the end, Greenberg resists our irony but only with an ungrounded, essentially unconditional act of opposition. Once he has admitted the historical openness of Jewish theological thought to the Holocaust, he can recover so much of Judaism only by an act of allegiance to a way of thinking and acting that has always stood for human dignity and value. By seeing the Holocaust as the nemesis of modernity, Greenberg gives a slightly more subtle, more dialectical version of Berkovits' traditionalism, but it is a traditionalism nonetheless.

To a traditional Jewish reader Greenberg's thought must seem threatening or perhaps utterly misguided. From Berkovits' point of view, the lapse into historicism surely must be seen as an error. Berkovits tried but could not completely treat the Holocaust as an unprecedented case of evil, but he could oppose it and its conditions unconditionally, as the outcome of a timeless divine mandate. Greenberg is more receptive to the Holocaust's concrete particularity, to its theological impact, but he can only call upon the resources of Jewish moral purposes, as if nothing had changed. If he is called upon by them, he must ask, why.

In this context, Emil Fackenheim's articulation of a 614th commandment and his recognition of a Divine Voice that spoke at Auschwitz look like answers. The struggle between historicism and transcendence has been a central theme of Fackenheim's work for thirty years or more. In Metaphysics and Historicity he argued that even an existential account of man as radical self-making in a situation included an element of philosophical transcendence.[9] In the late 1960s he altered that conviction by admitting that even Jewish religious thought, at every level, was not immune to historical alteration.[10] Religious self-understanding is always a matter of an interpretive recovery of the past for and in the present; no doctrines, principles, or even categories are beyond historical impact. In principle, everything is negotiable, and after Auschwitz in particular, everything is on trial.

The question is, when the verdict is in, what resources are still available to oppose the evil? We focus on Judaism: what Midrashic teachings are recoverable? What kind of opposition is there to the "demons of Auschwitz?" What is the ground of that opposition, i.e., what makes it necessary and what makes it possible? How can that ground make the opposition more than arbitrary or subjective or whimsical or temporary or conditional or ...? And how, given the overwhelming nature of the evil, does the ground make it possible, conceivable, humanly will-able?

These are serious questions, and Fackenheim's attention to them has become more and more thematic and self-critical over the years. His first real attempt to deal with them comes, for our purposes, in the third chapter of God's Presence in History.[11] Here he argues for the following conclusions. First, that when religious thought fails to comprehend the Shoah, it turns to the task of identifying a response that can only be understood as the response to an imperative of opposition to Nazi purposes. Secondly, that the ground of that imperative cannot be a humanly created or humanly centered ideal. And finally, that the appropriate Jewish ground for such an imperative is a divine Voice that renders it a Divine Command, complexly human in its interpretation and execution but divine in its origin.[12]

Other moral philosophers and religious thinkers, may have the problem of being sufficiently attentive to the concrete particularlity of the Holocaust and its momentousness. Fackenheim has the problem of showing that obligations generated by such attentiveness are sufficiently rich to frame broad concerns about human dignity, justice, and so on. Indeed, Fackenheim's problem is even deeper. For he explicitly eschews, in his own thinking, any strategy of rational justification for such obligations. What we want to know of Fackenheim's obligations is how secure their grounding is, the grounds that is for the obligation to oppose this evil, the conditions that make such opposition possible and the results that flow from it. For our purposes, we begin where Fackenheim shows us that theological, philosophical thought -- indeed all thought -- reaches an impasse, with a recognition of the depth of the evil, its particularity, and the obligation to oppose that is the result:

> "A Jew at Auschwitz ... was singled out by a demonic power which sought his death absolutely, i.e., as an end in itself. For a Jew today merely to affirm his Jewish existence is to accept his singled-out condition; it is to oppose the demons of Auschwitz: and it is to oppose them in the only way in which they can be opposed -- with an absolute opposition." (81)

Fackenheim takes this to be the situation of religious and secular Jew alike. He focusses on the secular Jew who "knows that the devil, if not God, is alive," who "has relativized all former absolutes," but who "as a Jewish secularist ... opposes the demons of Auschwitz absolutely by his mere commitment to Jewish survival" (82).[13] But alongside this relativistic sort of Jewish secularist, who is confounded by the contradiction of universality and particularity, of relativism and accepting an absolute obligation, there is another Jewish secularist, who tries, albeit unsuccessfully, to oppose "the demons of Auschwitz absolutely -- but in behalf of `free,' autonomous post-religious humanity" (82). Why unsuccessfully? Because, as Fackenheim argues, both "humanly created ideals" and "internalized absolutes" -- those of Reason or Progress, for example, "either cannot single out or else cannot remain absolute" (83). In short, the Jewish secularist cannot respond to principles of either sort, for they cannot do justice to the evil, the victims, or the unconditionality of the opposition. Fackenheim concludes:

> "Jewish opposition to Auschwitz cannot be grasped in terms of humanly created ideals but only as an imposed Commandment. And the Jewish secularist, no less than the believer, is absolutely singled out by a Voice as truly other than man-made ideals -- an imperative as truly given -- as was the Voice of Sinai." (83)

Today, the class of authentic Jews who affirm their Jewishness includes both secular and religious Jews, who "are united by a commanding Voice which speaks from Auschwitz" (84), and what it speaks is -- interpreted as -- the 614th Commandment of opposition to Hitler's purposes.

Fackenheim begins this line of thinking by identifying an imperative of opposition to Nazi purposes. We can ignore how he arrives at it.[14] But then, in the face of attempts to ground that imperative in rational principles or ideals, he argues that such theories fail for lack of particularity or absoluteness or both. Now this claim, made rather quickly, might be denied, but let us accept it, and follow Fackenheim a step further. If such ideals cannot ground the imperative, what can? Fackenheim infers that it must be "an imposed commandment," the singling out revelation of a divine Commanding Voice. Even if we ignore the problems that cloud the secularist's relation to such a Voice, there are others, more serious still, and it is these that Fackenheim himself comes to appreciate. What we seem to have here is a transcendental-style argument for the Divine Presence, an attempt to show that no such imposed commandment is possible without a Divine Commanding Voice. But how can either the believer or the skeptic, especially after Auschwitz, be inclined to accept such an argument? If Divine Command is the ground of the imperative, then in fact there _is_ no ground -- at least not yet. Perhaps Fackenheim is right that the imperative is received as _imposed_, but why as a command? and why as God's command? And if we hold the Divine out of it -- at least until faith can be recovered more slowly and patiently, what makes the imperative _imposed_? And furthermore, what, without Divine grace, makes it possible for us to perform it? What, finally, is its real ground -- once the humanly created ideals are seen to be insufficient?

Fackenheim, in other words, reaches his conclusions too hastily, both the fact that the imperative is imposed and that it is a commandment. Indeed, perhaps even the claim that opposition requires an imperative is already too hasty. Why not a reaction to threat? Or a repugnance to a storied ugliness or hatred? In part, Fackenheim's problem arises because he directs thought, once stopped in its tracks, to turn to subsequent Jewish life in order to seek guidance about a response. Such life is not clearly a response, nor is it based on more than defiance or revulsion or conformity, at least not consciously and intentionally. But in part the problem is deeper, for even once an imperative of opposition is identified, its _ground_ is not so easily got. It may be clear that in order for it to pick out its subjects and in order not to be conditioned by human will it must be _imposed_ from the outside and also enabled from the outside. But if faith is not yet assumed,[15] what grounds its status as imposed? What, in different terms, makes it both possible and necessary? What gives opposition its realism and its authority?

In subsequent essays and books Fackenheim makes it clear that for him moral principles and traditional ideas must be reinterpreted in the light of "epoch-making" events.[16] To be sure, he does not rule out the possibility that some idea or principle might emerge that would transcend history and achieve an objectivity and permanence as yet unrealized. But in terms of the Holocaust, as he sees it, all is called into question. This historicist outcome of the impact of the Holocaust can, for our purposes, be accepted. The central issue concerns not the _content_ of post-Holocaust moral principles but rather their _ground_, i.e., the source of their possibility and their necessity. Does Fackenheim, deferring theological recovery to a future not-yet, nonetheless find a ground sufficiently deep, secure, and rich to support a mandate of opposition?

In _To Mend the World_[17] Fackenheim knows that this problem is _an aspect_ of the "central question" facing him, how thought -- Jewish, Christian, philosophical, and so on -- "can both expose itself to the Holocaust and survive" (24). But what aspect is it? Here Fackenheim focusses on the question of possibility. His earlier treatment, couched in the terms of the 614th commandment, was, he says, either Kantian or neo-orthodox. That is, the possibility of response, of acknowledging and obeying the imperative, was rooted in the Kantian answer, "that we _can_ do what we _ought_ to do," or the neo-orthodox one, "that a Grace that gives commandments also gives the freedom to obey them" (24).[18] His task, in _To Mend the World_, as he sees it, is to rectify the shallowness of these solutions, to show that obedience is only possible _now_ because _during the event itself_ resistance was actual.[19] That is, he will acknowledge the role of those who, in Auschwitz itself, "heard orders not of their making, and found the will and the strength to obey them" (26).[20] In short, Fackenheim seeks to ground both the orders, the imperative of opposition, and the possibility of obedience to them, without inferring the latter from the former or using any glib notion of grace to account for that possibility, a human possibility given at the moment of imposition. For the victims of Nazism it is the very possibility of resistance that surprises, and Fackenheim wants to understand its ground. This, then, is his task as he sees it. Our question, not unconnected with it, is nonetheless different, for it concerns the ground of the imperative's necessity and not its possibility.[21]

First, Fackenheim argues that there is an imperative to live a post-Holocaust life, to recover from "the total rupture."[22] He calls such a life a Tikkun or mending of the rupture and says that it is mandatory: "A Tikkun, here and now, is mandatory for a Tikkun, then and there, was actual" (254). Such a Tikkun, he says, is both impossible and necessary. Impossible, for how could any one, at any time, rectify or repair the murderous slaughter of millions, their souls, their bodies? Necessary, because .... that is our question: why is it necessary?

Fackenheim says this:

> "Authentic thought was actual during the Holocaust among resisting victims; therefore such thought must be possible for us after the event: and, being possible, it is mandatory. Moreover, their resisting thought pointed to and helped make possible a resisting life; our post-Holocaust thought, however authentic in other respects, would still lapse into inauthenticity if it remained in an academically self-enclosed circle -- if it failed to point to, and help make possible, a post- Holocaust life" (249).

He then calls this an "imperative," which must mean that the victims' recognition of the Nazi logic of destruction had given rise to an imperative to resist in life. Hence, both that recognition and that imperative are mandatory, necessary, binding upon us, "resistance in thought and resistance in life" (248).

The derivation of this conclusion includes two stages, one descriptive, the other analytical. First, Fackenheim describes, through memoir and report, different manifestations of resistance during the Holocaust and its phenomenology, how the victims experienced and understood the "logic of destruction" employed against them, how they responded, and what they thought of their murderers, the system, and their responsibility. Crucial to this descriptive account is the report of those who "confronted and grasped this whole-of-horror even while they were in it and trapped by it" and of their self-conscious opposition understood as a response to "orders" to live.[23] There were both believers and non-believers who sensed these "orders," although one but not the other testified to any awareness of their source (218-19).[24] Secondly, Fackenheim argues against explaining away or reducing these experiences by means of psychological or other historical categories. He seeks to show that they, like the evil that engulfed them and gave rise to them, are "ultimate" and foundational experiences, incapable of analysis into general terms. We cannot explain away the "orders" as a mere psychological reaction, but rather the experience of them is sufficient reason to take them as presented. The victims' testimony should be accepted as truth-revealing. Nor can we explain away their testimony of the horror and its murderous logic. Our thought, Fackenheim shows, as it moves from agent to agent, can only grasp so much, as it tries to encompass both the details and then the whole of horror itself. In the end, the philosopher realizes this:

> "On our part...we confront in the Holocaust world a whole of horror. We cannot comprehend it but only comprehend its incomprehensibility. We cannot transcend it but only be struck by the brutal truth that it cannot be transcended....
>
> The philosopher may feel -- he believes that nothing human is alien to him -- that this whole is not unintelligible after all.

> He wants to understand Eichmann and Himmler, for he wants to understand Auschwitz. And he wants to understand Auschwitz, for he wants to understand Eichmann and Himmler. Thus his understanding gets _inside_ them and their world, bold enough not to be stopped even by Eichmann's smirk and Himmler's gloves. To get inside them is to get inside the ideas behind the smirk and the gloves; and whereas this is not necessarily to accept these ideas it is in any case to obtain a kind of empathy. And thus it comes to pass, little by little, that a philosopher's _comprehension_ of the Holocaust whole-of-horror turns into a _surrender_, for which the horror has vanished from the whole and the _Unwelt_ has become a _Welt_ like any other. In this way, one obtains a glimpse of the Ph.D.s among the murderers, and shudders.
>
> The truth disclosed in this shudder is that to grasp the Holocaust whole-of-horror is not to comprehend or transcend it, but rather _to say no to it, or resist it_. The Holocaust whole-of-horror _is_ (for it _has been_); but it _ought not_ to be (and _not_ to have been). It ought _not_ to be (and have been), but it _is_ (for it has been). Thought would lapse into escapism if it held fast to the "ought not" alone; and it would lapse into paralyzed impotence if it confronted, nakedly, the devastating "is" alone. _Only by holding fast at once to the "is" and "ought not" can thought achieve an authentic survival. Thought, that is, must take the form of resistance._" (238-39)

But even this is not sufficient: "_resisting thought must point beyond the sphere of thought altogether, to a resistance which is not in `mere' thought but rather in overt, flesh-and-blood action and life_" (239).

How does this happen, this "ecstatic" shift from resisting thought to a life of resistance? What takes the thinker from horrified amazement to an acknowledged mandate to oppose in life what thought could never comprehend? What makes this movement necessary? What makes it possible?
In order to answer these questions Fackenheim takes us on a tour of the whole-of-horror, from the torturers and murderers to Hoess, to Eichmann, Himmler, and finally Hitler. In each case, the intellect seeks satisfaction, understanding, only to resist, to doubt, be bewildered, dismayed, until finally the thinker acknowledges how utterly impossible it is to place thought and the evil in the same space, as it were, except insofar as thought grasps the evil as a whole.[25] But the grasp, as Fackenheim cautions, is not a comprehension. That is, the grasp of the whole-of-horror includes both surprise at what it has surveyed and horror at it, so that the acceptance cannot abide but must issue, beyond itself, in opposition. We have, in the end, a cognitive state that simply cannot remain passive and reflective but must become active, and its activity cannot merely be cognitive activity, for the object is too horrible, too repelling. It is an object that cannot merely be eliminated in thought; it must be -- it demands to be -- eliminated in reality.

> "It is, rather, at once a _surprised acceptance and a horrified resistance_. It is a horrified surprise and, since the thought that is _in_ this surprise is forced to accept what is yet in all eternity unacceptable, _thought is required to become `ecstatic,' such as to point beyond resistance within its own native sphere, to a resistance that is beyond the sphere of thought altogether, and in the sphere of life_....Resistance-in- thought to the Holocaust would degenerate into academic self-satisfaction unless it climaxed in calling for, praying for, working for, resistance in life." (247)

Furthermore, the ground of the possibility of the thinker's resisting thought and resistance in life is the thinking and living of the resisting victims themselves. "Resistance in that extremity was a way of being. For our thought now, it is an ontological category" (248).[26]

In a sense, then, resistance during the Holocaust both confirms the mandate to opposition, to a Tikkun or mending of life after the rupture, and makes it possible. If Fackenheim is right, then the resistance of the victims exhibits an irreducible courage and capability, without which post-Holocaust resistance would be impossible. The primary locus of the possibility of resistance, then, is the resisting victim. But what of its necessity? Where is the ground of the necessity of resistance for us now? Does it reside in thought itself as it tries to comprehend the evil only to end up in "horrified surprise?" Or does it reside in the victims' resisting thought that issues in a resisting life? In both? Or elsewhere?

The answer, I think, is that there is no single ground. The ground of the necessity to resist in life, to oppose the "demons of Auschwitz," differs for different agents. For victims of faith, the ground resides in Divine command; for non-believers, in the "orders" to live which have no acknowledged or identifiable source at all. For post-Holocaust philosophers and thinkers, the imperative arises out of their thought itself, and it is confirmed by that of the victims, for, Fackenheim argues, the thinking of the victims cannot be explained away psychologically, historically, or in any other way. In the end, to the thinker, the necessity of resistance in life arises out of the very particular encounter of his or her thought, pushed to its greatest capacities, with the Holocaust's special features -- its murderous criminals, its horror, its dehumanized victims, and so on. The results of this encounter are two: a cognitive state that is both passive and active, both receptive and resisting, a "surprised acceptance" that is also a "horrified resistance," and, secondly, a thought- motivated "calling for, praying for, working for, resistance in life" (247) that is a response to an uncompromisable, unavoidable, and to all appearances permanent mandate.[27] That mandate or imperative is imposed by thinking itself in its unique effort to grasp the incomprehensible horrors of Auschwitz.

Such a thinker or philosopher, later, might add to this picture another feature, and then he might revise his understanding of the ground of the imperative's necessity, taking it to be a Divine Commanding Presence. But this addition is just that, a supplement or revision that is neither necessary nor predictable for acknowledging the mandate, its necessity and possibility. Such an addition is wholly contingent, in part on whether he is a Jewish thinker, in part on whether he is capable of recovering an openness to that Presence, in part on historical events. However it turns out, this project of recovery, which he begins with the event itself and a painstaking encounter with it, establishes and confirms a mandate to tikkun or mending that arises out of his exposure to the event and the thought and life of its resisting victims. It is a contingent mandate, arising out of a particular encounter, but it is necessary too, for it arises necessarily out of a cognitive grasping that is neither comprehensive nor acquiescent. That thought and its ecstatic transformation from description to prescription to action are confirmed by a similar occurrence in the lives of victims, as they came to a resisting recognition that led to a life of resistance.

For Fackenheim, then, the Holocaust is a total rupture in history, and it chases all thought into historicism. But, at the same time, those who respond have substantial moral resources out of which to shape an imperative of opposition into a life of tikkun, of mending after the rupture. These resources -- resisting victims and thought confronting them -- yield an unconditional, unavoidable, yet historically situated result, a mandate to oppose the demons of Auschwitz by recovery and repair of a shattered world.

Finally, then, our original irony is dissolved, if, that is, Fackenheim's enterprise succeeds. We have not asked whether it does. That would require a much fuller analysis than we have attempted. For now it is sufficient to have shown that the irony of historicism and evil, with which we began, can be disengaged by a post-Holocaust thought that is both historically serious and morally deep. If Fackenheim succeeds, then his thinking is both, fully exposed to the evils of Auschwitz and yet able to survive that exposure in the form of a deeply grounded mandate to opposition and recovery. We would all along have hoped that a deep sensitivity to the impact of the Holocaust on thought would not have left thought impotent against that evil, and if Fackenheim is right, then our hopes have not been in vain.

ENDNOTES

1. Eliezer Berkovits, Faith after the Holocaust (New York: Ktav Publishing House, 1973), 36; cf.18.

2. Faith after the Holocaust, Ch.IV.

3. Faith after the Holocaust, 128: "As far as our faith in an absolutely just and merciful God is concerned, the suffering of a single innocent child poses no less a problem than the undeserved suffering of millions."

4. One should note that for all of its virtues Berkovits' book has a very uncomfortable tone. He is exceedingly chauvanistic; his writing is inflated and highly rhetorical. And his philosophical categories, which are all traditional (nature and morality, is and ought, fact and value, etc.), are simply appropriated without any critical assessment.

5. Irving Greenberg, "Cloud of Smoke, Pillar of Fire: Judaism, Christianity, and Modernity after the Holocaust," in Eva Fleischner (ed.), Auschwitz: Beginning of a New Era? (New York: Ktav Publishing House, 1977), 7-55.

6. Cf. "Cloud of Smoke," 24-26; the classic Jewish and Christian traditions will resist revision, but Greenberg argues that such resistance is incompatible with their concern for history and their fundamental historicity. But Greenberg associates these revisions, these new "orienting experiences," with "new revelations," although he provides no grounds for so doing. See 24, 35, 41, where Greenberg speaks of Auschwitz as a revelatory event, but without justification.

7. Ibid., 22-27.

8. This principle of course alludes to the testimony of the Polish guard at Auschwitz regarding the burning alive of Jewish babies in order to minimize costs.

9. Emil L. Fackenheim, Metaphysics and Historicity (Milwaukee, Wisc.:Marquette University Press, 1961).

10. For the relevant texts, see the introductions to Quest for Past and Future, Encounters Between Judaism and Modern Philosophy, and To Mend the World; also, my introduction to Part III, Michael L. Morgan (ed.), The Jewish Thought of Emil Fackenheim (Detroit, Mich.: Wayne State University Press, 1987).

11. Emil L. Fackenheim, God's Presence in History (New York: New York University Press, 1970), Ch.3; see also Fackenheim's contribution to the symposium in Judaism, "Jewish Values in a Post-Holocaust Future" reprinted as Ch.2 in The Jewish Return into History (New York: Schocken Books, 1978) and "Jewish Faith and the Holocaust," Commentary (1967), reprinted as Ch.3 in The Jewish Return into History.

12. Fackenheim s argument for these conclusions is complex. See the two essays and the entire chapter referred to in the previous note, my introductions in _The Jewish Thought of Emil Fackenheim: A Reader_, edited with introductions by Michael L. Morgan (Detroit, Mich.: Wayne State University Press, 1987), and my "Jewish Ethics after the Holocaust," _The Journal of Religious Ethics_ 12,2 (Fall, 1984)1,256-77.

13. Fackenheim goes on to point out the problematic for Jewish secularism in our time: "Thus a radical contradiction has appeared in Jewish secularist existence in our time. As secularist the Jewish secularist seeks Jewish normalcy; as Jewish secularist he fragments this normalcy by accepting his singled-out Jewish condition. As secularist, he reduces all absolute to relative affirmations; as Jewish secularist he opposes absolutely the demons of death with his own Jewish life. Throughout the ages the religious Jew was a witness to God. After Auschwitz even the most secularist of Jews bears witness, by the mere affirmation of his Jewishness, against the devil" (82). An excellent portrait of such a Jewish secularist can be found in Jean Amery, _At the Mind's Limit_ (Bloomington: Indiana University Press, 1980), 82-103.

14. Perhaps, we might think, the evil is not so extreme, the victims not so particular, the imperative not so absolute. And indeed what does absolute mean here? unqualifiedly strong or permanent? what?

15. Cf. _God's Presence in History_, 88-89.

16. Fackenhiem shows how this would work for the ideas of martyrdom, messianism, antisemitism, and others. See _Encounters_, Ch.2; JRH, Chs.14, 15, 16, 17; TMW _passim_.

17. Emil Fackenheim, _To Mend the World_ (New York: Schocken Books, 1982), Ch.IV, sections 8-9, 201-50, the core of the book.

18. Fackenheim himself has used this neo-orthodox argument in _Quest for Past and Future_, Ch.14, revised in Ch.2, _Encounters_.

19. Cf. _To Mend the World_, 25: "_To hear and obey the commanding Voice of Auschwitz is an 'ontological' possibility, here and now, because the hearing and obeying was already an 'ontic' reality, then and there_."

20. Cf. Nietzsche's statement, "one takes and does not ask who gives" (_Ecce Homo_, quoted often by Buber).

21. At pp.25-26 Fackenheim calls it a "commanding Voice of Auschwitz" and says that it is theologically neutral. He seems to have had in mind the Nietzsche quote (see previous note), often cited by Buber.

22. _To Mend the World_, 249-50, 250-55.

23. The crucial case is that of Pelagia Lewinska at Auschwitz, TMW, 25, 217; cf. Lewinska, 41ff., 54; Des Pres.

24. TMW, Ch.IV, section 8, 201-225.

25. To Mend the World, 247.

26. Cf. To Mend the World, 25.

27. The direction of the ecstasy of thought is given by the encounter itself and the character of its object. That is, in the case of the Holocaust the ecstasy is resisting and oppositional, for the event is wholly repelling.

Abstract of Paper for Conference

REMEMBERING FOR THE FUTURE

Oxford July 1987

DOES THE SHOAH REQUIRE A RADICALLY NEW JEWISH THEOLOGY?

The paper opens with a discussion of the historical uniqueness of the Shoah.

The second section is a review of the main types of post-Holocaust Jewish theology which have emerged. Traditional views are examined first, commencing with the response of halakha and examining the traditional theology of suffering. The modern critique of traditional responses follows. We then have a range of modern responses, including Narrative Exegesis and Liturgy, the Assertion of Meaning and Value, the Imperative of Survival or Tikkun, the Imperative to Dialogue, and "Beyond Survival".

The third part questions the call for a new theology. Do the terrible experiences of the Shoah add anything qualitative to the age-old problem of evil? The suggestion is made that the forms of response which have emerged apparently in response to the Shoah have arisen as a result of radical differences between modern and medieval intellectual orientations rather than in response to any new problem posed by the Shoah itself. The Shoah has focused, not created nor freshly demanded, the reorientation towards traditional theodicy.

Norman Solomon

1 UNIQUENESS AND THE SHOAH

Was the Shoah unique? If we look at books of logic, we do not find discussions of "uniqueness", but rather of "similarity"[1], of which "truthlikeness" is a special case. Whilst it is easy to say "The Shoah is unique" it is harder to spell that out as "The Shoah is in no way similar to any other event".

There is a *trivial* sense in which every event is unique, tied to a singularity of time and place. However, communication amongst people demands that events be classified, by considering their similarities, into general groups, for otherwise we could have no common language to talk about them. One may classify the Shoah as "an act of mass murder", indicating its similarities with innumerable human atrocities of past and present; however, this broad category fails to draw attention to the most distinctive features of the Shoah. One may narrow the field by classifying it as "an attempted genocide"[2]; there have been other attempted genocides (of the Armenians, for instance) and also actual genocides (for instance, of the indigenous population of Tasmania by the hand of the European settlers). Even this grim classification, however, fails to capture the distinctive horror of the Shoah.

Emil Fackenheim offers the following preliminary list of "basic facts" about the Shoah which, though some may have occurred elsewhere, are in their combination unique[3]:

1. Fully one-third of the Jewish people was murdered; and as this included the most Jewish of Jews - East European Jewry - Jewish survival as a whole is gravely in doubt.

2. This murder was quite literally "extermination"; not a single Jewish man, woman or child was to survive, or - except for a few that were well-hidden or overlooked - would have survived had Hitler won the war.

3. This was because Jewish birth was sufficient cause to merit torture and death; whereas the "crime" of Poles and Russians was that there were too many of them, with the possible exception of Gypsies only Jews had committed the "crime" of existing at all.

4. The "Final Solution" was not a pragmatic project serving such ends as political power or economic greed. Nor was it the negative side of a positive religious or political fanaticism. It was an end in itself. And, at least in the final stage of the dominion of the Third Reich (when Eichmann diverted trains to Auschwitz from the Russian front), it was the only such end that remained.

---

1 See, for instance, Niiliiuoto, Ilkka <u>TRUTHLIKENESS</u> D Reidel, Dordrecht 1987, especially chapter 6.

2 The word "genocide" was coined only in the 1940's, with specific reference to the Holocaust. But it is a general term, and cannot be withheld from any other event it fits.

3 Fackenheim, Emil L <u>TO MEND THE WORLD: Foundations of Future Jewish Thought</u>, Schocken Books, New York 1982, p.12.

5. Only a minority of the perpetrators were sadists or perverts. For the most part, they were ordinary jobholders with an extraordinary job. And the tone-setters were ordinary idealists, except that the ideals were torture and murder.

To this list Fackenheim might well have added a sixth factor, over which he agonizes at length later in his book[4], viz. the studied and perverse manner in which the Nazis and those under their direction sought to humiliate, dehumanize, and induce self-disgust in the Jews even before killing them.

Yet another factor compounds the horror and uniqueness of the Shoah. The attitudes which enabled the Nazis to "demonize" the Jews and thus carry out their programme were already deeply embedded in the popular cultures of the nations amongst whom they operated. For so long had Christians taught that Jews were a despised people, the rejectors and killers of Christ, obdurate in their adherence to a superseded faith, that European culture was saturated with this image of the Jew. It is surely unique that for little short of two thousand years one people has been singled out for constant and *religiously sanctioned* vilification through much of the "civilized" world.

Jews have suffered major tragedies before - the Destruction of the Temple in 70 CE, the Expulsion from Spain in 1492 - and these were accompanied by horrendous sufferings. Fackenheim writes[5]: "The earlier catastrophes were great but not beyond belief, and thus lived on in the memory of the generations until the time was ripe for a response. Our catastrophe, in contrast, is beyond belief and becomes ever more so with the passage of time." Well, this is not quite true. It happened, it must and can be reflected upon. Fackenheim himself reflects upon it volubly. But the tendency to deny is strong, and manifests itself not only in the fringe phenomenon of outright denial by 'revisionist' historians[6], but in the tendency to assimilate the Shoah to general categories of tragedy and cruelty, 'losing' it as 'just an example' of something or other, denying its unique character.

2 THE MAIN TYPES OF JEWISH HOLOCAUST THEOLOGY

2.1 Traditional Responses - Halakhic

The most characteristic expression of traditional Judaism is the halakha, or law. God, in His gracious compassion, granted us the Torah with its many commandments *(mitzvot)* so that we might learn from it to live according to His will.

---

4 See particularly pp. 206 f.

5 *ibid.* p.29

6 See Seidel, Gill, THE HOLOCAUST DENIAL Beyond the Pale Collective, Leeds, England, 1986, for an analysis of the phenomenon of right-wing Holocaust Denial.

The Halakha of *Kiddush Hashem* is specially relevant to the problems faced by victims of the Shoah. Let us listen to the solemn words of Maimonides on this subject in his great Code of Jewish Law, the *Mishneh Torah*[7] - bearing in mind that he is merely codifying a long process of halakhic development reaching back to biblical times:

> All the House of Israel are commanded to sanctify this Great Name (i.e. God), as it is written: 'I shall be sanctified amongst the people of Israel'[8]. Likewise, they are commanded not to profane it, as it is written: 'Do not profane My holy name'[9]. How is this fulfilled? If an idolater arises and forces a Jew to transgress any of the commandments of Torah under pain of death, he should transgress rather than be killed, for it is written of the commandments: 'that a man shall do and live by them'[10] - *live* by them, not *die* by them - if he die rather than transgress he is guilty of taking his own life.
>
> In what circumstances does this apply? With regard to any of the commandments other than three, *viz.* idolatry, adultery/incest and the shedding of blood. With regard to these three, should he (the Jew) be ordered to commit them or face death he should die rather than transgress .....
>
> If the idolaters said to a group of women 'Hand over one of you and we will defile her or else we will defile all of you' they must not hand over even one Jewish soul. Similarly, if the idolaters said (to a group of Jews) 'hand over one of you and we will kill him, or else we will kill all of you', they must not hand over even one Jewish soul .....

Sadly, the halakha of *kiddush Hashem* was the everyday law of the Shoah. Sadly, confessing Christians acted the part of the 'idolaters' of whom that law speaks.

But it was not the only halakha that was applied in facing the horrors. The rabbinic responsum is the *genre* which over the centuries has been the crucible within which the practical expression of Judaism has been forged. *She'elot uTeshuvot* afford us an intimate window into the concerns of ordinary Jewish men and women as they turned for guidance to their spiritual leaders. The process of composing them did not stop in the Shoah - indeed, the careful application of *halakha* in the most extreme circumstances is a supreme expression of Torah; somehow, where theology was inadequate *halakha* survived and made survival possible.

---

7 Maimonides, Moses (1135-1204) *MISHNEH TORAH Hilkhot Yesodey Ha-Torah* Chapter 5. The translation is the present writer's.
8 Leviticus 22:32
9 *ibid.*
10 Leviticus 18:5

"If emotion is evident in a responsum, it is rarely overt. The rabbi's juristic function imposed upon him the discipline of composure and reason. To have yielded entirely to emotion would have been to forfeit the crucial responsibility entrusted to him by his people"[11].

Rabbi Ephraim Oshry survived the Holocaust in the ghetto of Kovno, Lithuania. There, people approached him with their questions. He committed the questions and answers to writing on paper torn surreptitiously from cement sacks, and hid the writing in cans which miraculously survived the war. "The daily life of the ghetto, the food we ate, the crowded quarters we shared, the rags on our feet, the lice in our skin, the relationships between men and women - all this was contained within the specifics of the questions ..."[12] A glance at the range of subjects bears out how ordinary people in the ghetto, with the deep strength born of faith in God, were concerned quietly to walk in the precepts of God: "Jews Forced to Shred a Torah Scroll", "Sabbath Torah Reading for Slave Laborers", "The Blessing for Martyrdom", "Saving Oneself with a Baptismal Certificate", "Contraceptives in the Ghetto", "The Repentant Kapo" - such headings rend the heart of the reader as the answers gave sacred meaning to the lives and deaths of the victims.

"We Jews of the ghetto of Kovno ... were enslaved by the Germans; were worked to the bone night and day without rest; were starved and were paid nothing. The German enemy decreed our total annihilation. We were completely dispensable. Most would die". So was it proper to recite the customary blessing in the morning prayers thanking God "who has not made me a slave"? Oshry's brief answer[13] encapsulates the spirit of this work. "One of the earliest commentators on the prayers points out that this blessing was not formulated in order to praise God for our physical liberty but rather for our spiritual liberty. I therefore ruled that we might not skip or alter this blessing under any circumstances. On the contrary, despite our physical captivity, we were more obligated than ever to recite the blessing to show our enemies that as a people we were spiritually free."

Yet of all the questions submitted by quite "ordinary" people to Oshry and thousands of other rabbis of the *Shoah* period none are so agonising as those involving harm to the life of other victims. The Nazis did their utmost to degrade and dehumanize Jews by forcing them to destroy each other. They failed. And that they failed is due in large part to the spirit engendered by the *halakha* on the sanctity of life.

2.2 Traditional Responses - Theological

It has to be stressed that the traditional interpretations of suffering depend heavily for such cogency as they may have not only on a strong sense

11 Kirschner, Robert, RABBINIC RESPONSA OF THE HOLOCAUST ERA, Schocken Books, New York, 1985 p.11.

12 Oshry, Ephraim RESPONSA FROM THE HOLOCAUST Translated into English by Y. Leiman, Judaica Press, New York 1983, p.ix. The Hebrew volumes (vol. 5 appeared in 1978), under the title *MIN HA-MAAMAQIM*, are published by the Brothers Gross, New York.

13 *ibid.* p.85

of guilt (see section 2.2.2) but also on the belief in life after death. This belief, whether expressed as bodily resurrection, eternal life of the spirit, or some combination, remains central in orthodox teaching. Some of the orthodox, under the influence of Kabbala, have adopted in addition the concept of the transmigration of souls. Such beliefs simplify the theology of suffering, for (a) they diminish the significance of the vicissitudes of 'this world', and (b) they provide an opportunity for 'compensation' for the evils of this world in the next. The transmigration of souls easily explains the suffering of innocent children - either they they are being punished now for sins committed in a previous incarnation, or else they will get compensation for their present sufferings in a later one.

2.2.1 Providence - Individual and General

Fundamental to the traditional Jewish understanding of suffering is the distinction between *hashgacha peratit* and *hashgacha kelalit* - individual and general (collective) Providence. In terms of general Providence the Shoah can be "understood", for it is not hard to rationalize the destruction of part of the people of Israel as part of God's redemptive process, leading ultimately to Israel's restoration, whether or not in terms of the Land. It is the individual Providence which is most problematic. Since everything is subject to God's will, it is legitimate to ask not just why the people of Israel suffered, but why each individual suffered. Maimonides, it is true, denied that God extended Providence to individuals in the sub-lunar sphere other than to those whose spiritual excellence raised them above sub-lunar materiality[14]. But, if spiritual excellence is something we can recognize at all, it certainly characterized many of those who perished.

Unfortunately, the statements we report briefly below do not always distinguish clearly between the individual and general aspects of God's Providence.

2.2.2 God's Judgment

Elchanan Wasserman[15] was one of the leading rabbis of the pre-War generation. His writings, speeches, life and martyrdom offer a paradigm of the orthodox theology of suffering. Wasserman visited the United States in 1938, and was dismayed by the lack of Torah learning and observance amongst the Jews he met. There he completed his pamphlet *Iqvata diMeshicha*[16], in which he predicts that dire destruction will come upon the Jewish people on account of its lack of faith and its

14 Maimonides' views on Providence are worked out in his GUIDE OF THE PERPLEXED III:8-24.

15 1875-1941. He was a disciple of the saintly Chafetz Chayim. The best biography of Wasserman (it is in Hebrew) is Sorsky, A, *OR ELCHANAN*, Israel 1978, 2 vols.

16 Notwithstanding the Aramaic title this was originally written in Yiddish. It has been reissued many times in Hebrew and English versions. An earlier, Hebrew, sketch, was appended to the second (Baranovichi ?1936) edition of the first volume of his halakhic work *KOVETZ HE'AROT*, originally published in Pietrkow in 1922. The development of the small but significant work is explained in Sorsky *op. cit.* chapter 23.

laxity in the observance of God's commandments. Amongst the orthodox there seems to be a broad consensus that his "prophecy" was both justified and fulfilled.

Wasserman was martyred in 1941 - *before* the actual *Endlösung* was put into operation. Those of us today who write with some knowledge of the actual horrors of the Shoah tend angrily to dismiss all talk of "punishment for sin" in this context as gratuitously insulting to those who perished and as demanding an image of God as unforgiving, intolerant of even the smallest lapses, and unready when punishment is unleashed to distinguish between the innocent and the guilty. To understand the rabbis who spoke and even now speak in this way it is necessary to know how deeply they felt the gulf between the ideal demanded by Torah and the reality of modern secular civilization. It was for them, in their piety and faithfulness, as if the modern way of life, adopted by many Jews through assimilation to "the ways of the nations round about", had totally destroyed the holy world of the Jew nurtured over the centuries; not unnaturally they feared, and believed they witnessed, the prophesied chastisement of Israel with but a small and faithful remnant escaping.

2.2.3 *Kiddush Hashem*

"It is clear beyond all doubt that the blessed Holy One is the ruler of the universe, and we must accept the judgment with love ..." These words of the Hungarian Rabbi Shmuel David Ungar[17] exactly express the simple faith of those who entered the gas chambers with *Ani Ma'amin*[18] or *Shema Israel*[19] on their lips. What was happening defied their understanding, but their faith triumphed over evil and they were ready, in the traditional phrase, to "sanctify the name of God" - *kiddush Hashem*. Hence it is normal amongst Jews to refer to those who perished under the Nazis as *kedoshim*, "holy ones, saints".

2.2.4 God's Love

Has not God acted *un*justly towards Israel? Israel has indeed sinned, but surely others, not least Israel's oppressors, have sinned more? The traditional reply to this is that of Amos, that it is precisely God's love for Israel that leads Him to chastise them more than any other nation - "For you alone have I cared among all the nations of the world; therefore will I punish you for all your iniquities"[20].

Suffering is thus received as a token of God's special concern for Israel.

---

17 Cited on pp.98/9 of Kirschner, Robert *op. cit.*, from Eliav, M *ANI MA'AMIN* (Hebrew), Jerusalem 1965 pp.30-31.

18 The declaration of faith as formulated by Maimonides.

19 Deuteronomy 6:4-9, declaring God's unity and the duty to love Him and obey His commandments. It is read daily at the morning and evening Services and forms part of the deathbed confession.

20 Amos 3:2 (NEB translation).

2.2.5 Birth Pangs of the Messiah

The sense of apocalyptic[21], of being part of the events heralding the Messiah and the Final Redemption of Israel and the World, was strong amongst the orthodox victims of the Shoah, and if anything has become stronger since. It was already part of Jewish tradition, receiving its most potent expression in the Lurianic kabbala, according to which every *mitzva* performed by a Jew is part of the cosmic process of *tikkun* (repair), part of the messianic work of redemption. Indeed, precisely the same concept was being developed, before and independently of the Holocaust, by Rav Kook, the first Chief Rabbi of Palestine in modern times, for he understood the Return to Zion as *atchalta di-geulta*, the beginning of redemption[22]. The further step, taken by many religious Zionists, has been to interpret both the Shoah and the strife surrounding the emergence of the State of Israel as "birth pangs" of the Messiah.

2.2.6 Sacrifice and Atonement

Birth pangs of the Messiah, atonement, sacrifice .....

Here is Oshry's eye-witness account of Wasserman's martydom[23]:

> Reb Elchonon spoke in a quiet and relaxed manner as always ..... the same earnest expression on his face ..... he addressed all Jews:
>
> "It seems that in Heaven we are regarded as *tzadikkim*[24], for we are being asked to atone with our bodies for the sins of Israel. Now we really must do *teshuva* (repent) in such a manner - for the time is short and we are not far from the ninth port[25] - we must have in mind that we will be better sacrifices if we do *teshuva*, and we may (?save?) our American brothers and sisters.
>
> "God forbid that anyone should allow any improper thought to enter his head, for the *korban*[26] is invalidated by improper thought. We are about to fulfil the greatest *mitzva* of all - "with fire You destroyed it, with fire You will rebuild it"[27] - the fire which destroys our bodies is the selfsame fire which will restore the Jewish people."

---

21 The general rabbinic tendency is to play down apocalyptic. But see the 'rabbinic Apocalypse' in the versions of Mishnah *Sotah* 9:15 from which Wasserman's above-mentioned essay *Iqvata diMeshicha* takes its name. There are parallels in Christian (eg Mark 13:12) and other literature.

22 See Bokser, Ben Zion ABRAHAM ISAAC KOOK Paulist Press, New York 1978, for an English translation of some of Kook's smaller works.

23 This has been published frequently. I translate the Yiddish version which appears in the introduction to the New York, 1952, edition of the first volume of Wasserman's major halakhic work, KOVETZ HE'AROT.

24 "Righteous". He is not boasting, but expressing mild surprise at the divine compliment of having been selected for a sacred task.

25 The place where the Jews of Slobodka (Kovno) were murdered.

26 Sacrifice

27 This phrase occurs in the liturgy for the Ninth of Ab and is reminiscent of Lamentations 4:11.

2.2.7 The 'Hidden God' and the Negation of Evil

The idea of God being "hidden" features strongly, perhaps because of its full development by the mystics (kabbalists). It links with the common midrashic idea of God, or the *Shekhina* (divine presence), being "in exile" with Israel, for "I am with him in his distress"[28]. Martin Buber asks[29]: "How is a life with God still possible in a time in which there is an Auschwitz? The estrangement has become too cruel, the *hiddenness* too deep?" (our italics) Eliezer Berkevitz seems to go further than anyone else in his attachment to the notion of the "Hidden face of God" [30].

On the other hand, there seems little echo of the idea espoused by Maimonides[31] that evil is merely the absence of good. This may be because the Holocaust gives such a strong sense of the *reality* of evil that any doctrine asserting its non-reality is self-evidently false.

Curiously Hannah Arendt, by no means a traditional Jewess, comes close to the doctrine of *privatio boni*, for to her, only the good has depth, whereas even the most extreme evil is superficial and banal.[32]

2.3 The Critique of Traditional Responses

2.3.1 General Objections

The philosopher W V O Quine has argued that the totality of our beliefs is "a man-made fabric which impinges on experience only along the edges" [33]. Beliefs in the centre are less amenable to modification or refutation than those on the periphery. Indeed, a central belief may sometimes be maintained despite a considerable body of *prima facie* evidence against it; it may become virtually immune to refutation.

Emil Fackenheim[34] in like vein argues that normative Judaism and Christianity act as if they were immune to all future events except Messianic ones, as if there could be no epoch-making event between Sinai and Messiah. He rejects traditional responses as underestimating the radical challenge of the Shoah, equal in its significance to a new Revelation. He cites approvingly Kirkegaard's remark that a single event of inexplicable horror "has the power to make everything inexplicable,

28 Psalm 91:15

29 THE DIALOGUE BETWEEN HEAVEN AND EARTH, originally delivered in 1951.

30 Berkevitz, E, FAITH AFTER THE HOLOCAUST New York, KTAV, 1973.

31 cf GUIDE OF THE PERPLEXED III:10-12. The idea of evil as the *privatio boni* is generally traced back to pseudo-Dionysius, and is represented in Christian tradition from Augustine onwards.

32 Arendt, Hannah EICHMANN IN JERUSALEM: A Report on the Banality of Evil The Viking Press, New York, 1963

33 Quine, W V O, TWO DOGMAS OF EMPIRICISM, in FROM A LOGICAL POINT OF VIEW Harvard University Press, 1980[3] p.42.

34 *op. cit.* p.19

including the most explicable events"[35], and in the light of it condemns Heidegger, Barth, Tillich and others for continuing to teach after the Holocaust "as though nothing had happened". This is a puzzling use of Kirkegaard's remark. Surely there were "single events of inexplicable horror" before the Shoah, and far more horrendous than the crucifixion to which Kirkegaard refers. If so, the Shoah itself would not demand a new way of thinking; the demand for such a way was already there[36].

2.3.2 The Questioning of God

Judaism and its Christian and Muslim offshoots all teach their faithful that God shapes history, on occasion actually intervening even for the sake of individuals. But, as Irving Greenberg has put it: "The Holocaust poses the most radical counter-testimony to both Judaism and Christianity .... The cruelty and the killing raise the question whether even those who believe after such an event dare to talk about God who loves and cares without making a mockery of those who suffered."[37]

Richard Rubinstein[38] is driven by reflection on the Shoah to reject the traditional idea of God as the2.5 "Lord of history". God simply failed to intervene to save his faithful. He urges both Christians and Jews to adopt non-theistic forms of religion, based on pagan or Asian models.

Rubinstein and others who share his views are determined to maintain Jewish identity - in his case a *religious* identity - even if not based, as it was in the past, on theistic faith. Other Jews would express their identity in secular terms, including the secular forms of Zionism, or simply in social terms.

2.4 Narrative Exegesis - Liturgy

I am not sure that Elie Wiesel would care to be described as doing "narrative exegesis"[39], or indeed any kind of theology. Yet Wiesel's achievement is to have enabled people to talk about the Shoah, to enter, so to speak, into its "social and cultural context"[40]. He imposes no systematic structure or interpretation on the reality he places before us, but rather

---

35 *ibid.* p.191. See also p.278. The source of Kirkegaard's remark is Kirkegaard, S EITHER/OR New York, Anchor Press, 1959, II, p.344.

36 See our final section.

37 Greenberg, I, CLOUD OF SMOKE, PILLAR OF FIRE, in Fleischner, E (Ed.), AUSCHWITZ: Beginning of a New Era? New York, KTAV, 1977.

38 See, in particular, Rubinstein, Richard L, AFTER AUSCHWITZ; RADICAL THEOLOGY AND CONTEMPORARY JUDAISM Indianapolis, Bobbs-Merrill, 1966.

39 Walter J Hollenweger has written: "A narrative exegesis therefore does not divorce the theological element from its cultural and social base, but has to argue its theology in its involvement, in its function, in these other fields of conflict."

40 Walter J Hollenweger has written: "A narrative exegesis does not divorce the theological element from its cultural and social base, but has to argue its theology in its involvement, in its function, in these other fields of conflict." (CONFLICT IN CORINTH Paulist Press, NJ, 1982, p.66).

creates a new myth (in the most constructive sense of that term), through which the reader or hearer absorbs the meaning that cannot be said. His stories are indeed a "narrative exegesis" of the Shoah.

Theologians will see in many of Wiesel's stories paradigms of suffering leading to salvation. This is a common enough Jewish concept from Exodus onwards, but Wiesel's closeness to Christian expressions of the theology of suffering verges on the substitution of the six million for Christ on the Cross.[41]

It is not far from story telling to formal liturgy which, ultimately, is the religious means of conveying that for which words are insufficient. Marcia Littell[42] is amongst those responsible for the development of Holocaust Liturgies for use by Christians, Jews or both together, and these have achieved widespread use particularly in North America. YOM HASHOAH, which often atracts joint Christian and Jewish participation, is so far observed by only a minority of Jews, as some prefer to assimilate remembrance of the Holocaust to the existing fast of 9th Ab[43].

2.5 The Assertion of Meaning and Value

The psychiatrist Viktor Frankl developed his "logotherapy" as a victim in Auschwitz and Dachau, and has left us a profoundly moving account of how he discovered meaning and "supra-meaning" precisely there, where the oppressor aimed to deprive the life of the Jew of all meaning and value. Those who were unable to achieve the "will to meaning" soon perished, observed Frankl; those who could somehow find meaning survived wherever survival was physically possible.[44]

Likewise, in religious terms, Rabbi Isaac Nissenbaum declared in the Warsaw Ghetto at the time of the uprising[45]:

> This is a time for *kiddush ha-hayyim*, the sanctification of life, and not for *kiddush ha-Shem*, the holiness of martyrdom. Previously the Jew's enemy sought his soul and the Jew sanctified his body in martyrdom [i.e., he made a point of preserving what the enemy wished to take from him]; now the oppressor demands the Jew's body, and the Jew is obliged therefore to defend it, to preserve his life.

---

41 I have in mind the story in Wiesel's THE GATES OF THE FOREST New York, Avon, 1967 pp.9-12. The same thought is explored in the Christian Franklin H Littell's work THE CRUCIFIXION OF THE JEWS (New York, Harper & Row, 1975).

42 Littell, Marcia Sachs, ed. LITURGIES ON THE HOLOCAUST: AN INTERFAITH ANTHOLOGY New York, Edwin Mellen Press, 1986.

43 Fackenheim *op. cit.* p.310 f. challenges this view. But Chief Rabbi Jakobovitz, in his paper RELIGIOUS RESPONSES TO THE HOLOCAUST (Chief Rabbi's Office, London, 1987) argues strongly against the introduction of new fast days.

44 See Frankl, Viktor E, MAN'S SEARCH FOR MEANING, Touchstone Books, Simon and Schuster, New York, 1959 (and subsequent editions, some revised). The work was first published in Austria under the title EIN PSYCHOLOG ERLEBT DAS KONZENTRATIONSLAGER.

45 Fackenheim *op. cit.*, from Esh, Shaul, THE DIGNITY OF THE DESTROYED, in THE CATASTROPHE OF EUROPEAN JEWRY, ed. Gutman, Y and Rothkirchen, L, Jerusalem, Yad Vashem, 1976 p. 355.

There is an aesthetic version of *kiddush ha-hayyim* also. Much of the visual art produced in the appalling hell of the concentration camps has been rescued, exhibited, published. But what of music? Could the "songs of the Lord" be sung in that dark land?[46] Indeed yes. At Theresienstadt, where Jews of Czechoslovakia were interned prior to being exterminated in Auschwitz, orchestras were formed, operas staged, the composers wrote and the singers sang. This was *truly kiddush ha-hayyim,* to assert the beauty (for beauty is a category of holiness) of life in the face of so much suffering[47].

2.6 The Imperative of Survival - *Tikkun*

Fackenheim grounds his own Holocaust theology in the actual resistance of Shoah victims to whom no realistic hope remained.[48] "A philosophical *Tikkun*[49] is possible after the Holocaust because a philosophical *Tikkun* *already* took place, however fragmentarily, during the Holocaust itself."[50] Before writing his main work Fackenheim had achieved note for his statement that there should be a 614th commandment - to survive as Jews, to remember, never to despair of God, lest we hand Hitler a posthumous victory[51]. What one discerns in his evolving position is, at least, an affirmation of life and of God, and a challenge to Christian, Jew and all mankind to "mend the world". For Fackenheim, Israel (the Jewish State) is the central affirmation of Jewish survival, central in the world process of *Tikkun*; hence, he has now made his home there.

2.7 The Imperative to Dialogue

Dr Gerhart Riegner, in the office of the World Jewish Congress in Geneva in 1942, had the task of relaying to a disbelieving world the news of the "Final Solution". Since then, he has devoted his life to the furtherance of international Jewish-Christian dialogue. I once asked him how it was that his experience in 1942 had not embittered him, had not made him turn away from the "nations of the world" who had been unwilling to help Israel in her hour of need. His answer was illuminating. "It was then that I decided that my task in life was to end the isolation of Jewish people." Though the response of many - Berkevitz for example - has been to declare that dialogue with a Church which failed to warn its followers away from Hitler is simply not possible, Riegner and others have determined otherwise.

---

46 cf Psalm 137.

47 See Karas, Joza MUSIC IN TEREZIN: 1941-1945 New York, Beaufort Books, 1985, p.197, and Josef Bor's novel THE TEREZIN REQUIEM New York, Alfred A Knopf, 1963. In the Warsaw ghetto, an orchestra gave concerts under the baton of Szymon Pullmann (Simon Pulver).

48 Fackenheim *op. cit.* especially IV:8-12.

49 This Hebrew word for mending or restoration is an important term for Fackenheim, and his usage owes something to the Lurianic kabbala. I expect he wishes to avoid anything that sounds like "salvation".

50 *ibid.* p.266.

51 JUDAISM 16 (Summer 1967): 272-3. The popular tradition that the Torah contained 613 commandments originated with a third century rabbi.

2.8 Beyond Survival

The eminent Jewish philosopher Emmanuel Lévinas is not alone is demanding that we go beyond the Holocaust[52], that we do not allow ourselves to be permanently imprisoned in it. The phrase "Beyond Survival" is the title of an important book by Dow Marmur, who expresses the feeling not only of Reform Jews like himself and of many others that the "imperative to survival" which is the end result of Holocaust theology such as that of Fackenheim is a hollow call. Survival is not an end in itself, nor is the proving wrong of Hitler an adequate goal for life in general. One has to ask "survival for what?".

A similar view, refusing to allow Jews to be imprisoned by the Shoah in the Holocaust alternative of "A Cruel God or none", and instead concentrating on the development of Torah in ethics, with special application to ecology and world peace, emerges from Robert Gordis' fine work JUDAIC ETHICS FOR A LAWLESS WORLD[53].

Irving Greenberg divides the history of Judaism into three eras[54]. The first extended from Sinai to the the Destruction of the Second Temple. The second, the rabbinic period, characterized by powerlessness and by the "hiddenness" of God but at the same time by a deep faith in the covenant and redemption, extended from 70 CE until the Shoah. The Shoah shattered the naive faith in the covenant of redemption, inaugurating a third era the shape of which is determined by our response to the crisis of faith. Greenberg insists that this response must involve *all* Jews, not merely those who share his orthodox commitment. Auschwitz was "a call to humans to stop the Holocaust, a call to the people Israel to rise to a new, unprecedented level of covenantal responsibility ... Even as God was in Treblinka, so God went up with Israel to Jerusalem." Jews today, in Israel and elsewhere, have a special responsibility, in fidelity to those who perished, to work for the abolition of that matrix of values that supported genocide.

So, for Greenberg, post-Holocaust Jewish philosophy has to be formulated in terms of empowerment - now that Jews have "taken on power and responsibility to act", how will they use that power? It is but a small step from this

52 His statement is cited without a specific reference in a letter dated 6 November 1987 from Dr. Pierre Duprey to Dr Eugene Fisher and Bishop Keeler in the aftermath of the "Ratzinger affair"

53 Gordis, Robert, JUDAIC ETHICS FOR A LAWLESS WORLD Jewish Theological Seminary of America, New York, 1986. It is worth noting that Gordis has published some of the finest and most original Jewish Bible commentaries, on Ecclesiastes, Job and the Song of Solomon.

54 Greenberg, I. ON THE THIRD ERA IN JEWISH HISTORY: Power and Politics in PERSPECTIVES New York, 1980. See also his 1981 article in the same journal.

(a step Greenberg has resisted) to espousing some form of Jewish "Liberation Theology", and the step has been taken by Dan Cohn-Sherbok[55] and Marc Ellis.[56]

3 DOES THE SHOAH REQUIRE A RADICALLY NEW THEOLOGY?

We are now in a position to address the question of whether, as so many of those whose views we have cited claim, a "new theology" is demanded of Jews (we do not speak here of the special problems for Christians) as a result of the Shoah.

Let us concede that the Shoah is *historically* unique. Is it *theologically* unique?

Consider Irving Greenberg's striking statement that, after the Shoah, "no statement theological or otherwise should be made that could not be made in the presence of burning children" - or Kirkegaard's remark, cited in section 2.3.1, that a single event of inexplicable horror "has the power to make everything inexplicable, including the most explicable events". Then reflect sombrely that children were burned long before the Shoah and continue to be burned, and people, many of them undoubtedly innocent, were crucified long before Jesus and frequently afterwards (not that one crucifixion is an impressive matter where we are talking of the systematic humiliation and extermination of millions).

Both Judaism and Christianity developed at least partly in response to horrible experiences, and in the awareness that such horrible experiences were likely to be the lot of mankind until some transforming event (Messiah, kingdom of God on earth) would come about. Therefore, they both have a "theology of suffering", an attempt to vindicate the ways of God to man[57]. Whereas Deuteronomy presupposes a direct relationship between sin and suffering, obedience and prosperity, Psalms, Job and Ecclesiastes in their different ways try to come to terms with the presence of suffering and injustice in the world. The biblical seeds bear fruit in the writings of theologians, both Jewish and Christian, to the present day.

Holocaust theologians insist that the Shoah was not only quantitatively, but qualitatively, different from previous suffering. It introduced a *novum* (Fackenheim[58]), a *tremendum* (Arthur A Cohen[59]), which invalidates previous responses to suffering.

---

55 Cohn-Sherbok's article JEWS, CHRISTIANS AND LIBERATION THEOLOGY appeared in the journal CHRISTIAN JEWISH RELATIONS Volume 17 No. 1 in March 1984. His book ON EARTH AS IT IS IN HEAVEN was published by Orbis Books, Maryknoll, New York, 1987, shortly before Ellis's work.

CHRISTIAN JEWISH RELATIONS, which is published by the Institute of Jewish Affairs, London, in conjunction with the World Jewish Congress, is due to publish a special issue on the Jewish/Christian Dialogue and Liberation Theology in Spring, 1988.

56 Ellis, Marc H TOWARD A JEWISH LIBERATION THEOLOGY Orbis Books, Maryknoll, New York, 1987.

57 Leibniz' THEODICY sharply expresses an age-old problem.

58 Fackenheim *op. cit.*

59 Cohen, Arthur A THE TREMENDUM: A Theological Interpretation of the Holocaust Crossroad, New York, 1981.

Certainly, it is more horrible for a million to perish than for one to perish, and it is more horrible to be subjected to humiliation and killed than to be killed without humiliation. Also, some of the traditional "answers" are harder to apply to large numbers than small; for instance, if a mere handful of righteous people suffer apparent injustice we can easily convince ourselves that despite all appearances they were not really righteous, whereas if millions suffer it becomes much less reasonable to suggest that *all* of them were really evil. But this is an effect of quantity, not of quality. *If* we could know that an individual was really righteous (as, for instance, Scripture assures us in the case of Job), then the dodge of saying "perhaps appearances were deceptive" cannot be used, any more than it can where the numbers involved are so great that it would be absurd to maintain that none of the sufferers was righteous.

So, even though the Shoah was in significant ways dissimilar from other historical events, it does not appear to have posed radically new questions for theology. The questions were there all the time. The Shoah has focused our attention on them as never before, but they are the same questions.

To a surprising degree the answers given by the Holocaust theologians are *the same answers*. Many of them - those we have described under the headings of Narrative Exegesis, Liturgy, the Assertion of Meaning and Value, the Imperative of Survival, and *tikkun* - are varieties of one of those answers, that of redemption through suffering, worked out with new insights arising from modern psychological and sociological perspectives and applied, often with great sensitivity, to the present situation of the Jewish people. But they are not radically new answers. Even those responses (section 2.3.2) which demand a revision of the traditional concept of God follow in a modern, but certainly pre-Shoah, theological trend which, in Jewish terms, is specially associated with Kaplan's "Reconstructionism".

If this is true, why have so many prominent thinkers felt impelled to distance themselves from traditional Jewish theologies of suffering?

There are two reasons.

First, the answers *never were satisfactory*. In the words of the second century rabbi Yannai: "It is not in our power to explain either the prosperity of the wicked or the afflictions of the righteous"[60]. Yannai's words did not stop rabbis in his own or later generations speculating on the problem of evil. Indeed, though none of the answers is satisfactory they may all *contribute*, if only a little, to the upholding of faith in the face of evil.

Second, the reason that the non-orthodox Holocaust theologians reject "traditional" answers may be something quite other than the intrinsic inadequacy of those answers. In section 2.2 we stressed that the traditional interpretations of suffering depend heavily for such cogency as they may have on the belief in life after death and/or the transmigration of souls. Equally, they depend upon a belief in the inerrancy of Scripture and in the authenticity of its rabbinic interpretation. These beliefs have been under attack in modern times for reasons which have *nothing to do with* the Shoah. Jews, like Christians, have been challenged by, for instance, modern biblical studies, which

60 Mishnah, AVOT (Ethics of the Fathers) 4:19.

tend to undermine the traditional type of scriptural belief and demand a new kind of attitude to the authority of the Bible. Likewise, modern intellectual developments, for instance the radical questioning of Cartesian dualism, have placed new strains on the concept of life after death. These changes have so weakened the traditional arguments justifying the ways of God with man that the Shoah has provided the *coup de grace* to lead the modernist wing of Judaism to abandon altogether traditional theodicy.

Thus it is not a question of a new challenge posed to theology by the Shoah, but rather that the Shoah came at a time when theology was already in a greater ferment than ever before in its history, a ferment occasioned by the intellectual movements of the modern world. This explains why earlier tragedies, for instance the Expulsion from Spain, occasioned not the abandonment but the development of traditional modes of response to suffering.

It is dangerously misleading for Holocaust theologians to base their challenge to traditional beliefs on the fact of the Shoah. The serious intellectual issues of faith in the modern world thereby become submerged in a deep emotional trauma which prevents their being directly faced. It is otherwise for the historian, or for the politician whose first concern is "to work for the abolition of that matrix of values that supported genocide." But even for them it is salutary to remain aware of similarities as well as dissimilarities between the Shoah and other events, for to ignore the similarities would be to fail to encompass the Shoah in human terms at all.

The survivors' challenges and contributions

CHAIRPERSON **Mr Ze'ev Mancowitz**

RAPPORTEUR **Dr Abraham Peck**

EDUCATION TOWARDS THE CULTIVATION OF REMEMBRANCE IN THE THIRD GENERATION AFTER THE HOLOCAUST

N. BARZEL

University of Haifa School of Education of the Kibbutz Movement, Oranim, Oranim Tivon, Israel.

I would like to describe a conception and an educational experiment intended to transfer the memory of the Holocaust to Israeli youngsters. The experiment is based on a programme which has been developed over the last four years in Israel, particularly in the kibbutz movement. The programme focuses on the formation and the instruction of an educational group prior to and during its journey to the concentration camps in Poland and to villages and towns where Jews lived before the Holocaust.
This educational procedure is designed to contribute to the construction of a personal and collective moral system at adolescence, which is a significant age for the crystallization of political and social positions. Although our experience is relatively brief, I believe that the experiment provides at least a partial solution to the dilemma of teaching the Holocaust, provided the educational work in preparing the journey and in accompanying it has been satisfactorily executed.

In the 1980's, teachers in Israel have been faced with the problem of teaching the third generation after the Holocaust. According to official data, the division of the high school student population in Israel according to their, and their fathers' countries of origin is as follows (The Central Bureau of Statistics, 1977): 91.1% of high school students were born in Israel, 3.3% in Asia and Africa, 5.6% in Europe and America. Twenty-one percent of students born in Israel are children of fathers born in Israel, 58.5% of fathers born in Asia and Africa, 20.5% of fathers born in Europe and America.[1] One may assume that the encounter and the acquaintance with the subject of the Holocaust of the majority of high school students could have only partially and limitedly taken place at their homes. Hence, for a great part of the youngsters the Holocaust is a chapter in history. The encounter of the high school student with this chapter most probably occurs at school, when he studies the history of the era and prepares for Holocaust memorial services at school. Under these circumstances, the transmission of the subject is the educational responsibility of teachers born in Israel, and they become the main vessel whereby the students are acquainted with the Holocaust. Presumably, the distance in time from the events of both the educator and the student affects the ability of both parties to create experiential attachment. The contrast between the existential reality of the Holocaust and the reality the student is familiar with, makes it difficult for him to place himself in the historical sequence.

Assuming that in addition to passing on the factual details of the Holocaust one should also aim at the development of the experiential dimension, which is essential for the formation of identification and a sense of belonging, both students and educators are confronted with a complex problem. How should the story of the process of extermination, suffering and pain, humiliation and degradation be presented along with that of endurance and reprisal?
The two existing studies on the subject which deal with the analysis of instructional objectives in textbooks devoted to the Holocaust refer to this problem.[2] The discussion of the textbooks in both analyses is divided into two periods : the first referring to the period prior to the Six Day War; and the second to the weeks of expectation preceding the Six Day War and to the Yom Kippur War. In order to clarify my discussion I would like to present in brief only those definitions taken from the above mentioned studies that refer to the second

period.

Ruth Fuehrer has pointed out two different attitudes in the textbooks published in the Seventies: one postulating an indirect encounter of the student with the subject of suffering and methods of extermination, and the other maintaining that it is necessary and possible to make the students face the direct description of the extermination machinery.[3] From among the concepts one has to cope with, such as dignity or shame, defeat or victory, related to the problematic issue of reaction and the image of a people who "were led like sheep to the slaughter," the textbooks of the Seventies select Jewish endurance as the main focus for study on the individual as well as on the national - Zionist level. The fight in the ghettos[4] and the camps is presented in the above mentioned textbooks as part of Jewish endurance.

On April 1st, 1979, the Ministry of Education announced its intention to turn the instruction of the Holocaust into a compulsory subject in the upper grades of high school. Professor Y. Ben-Shlomo, then chairman of the pedagogical secretariat, was appointed to chair the committee that was to prepare the material. He pointed out that the committee regarded the goal of the instruction of the Holocaust as follows : "We want our students to identify with the victims of the Holocaust. The Holocaust should primarily be felt as an experience, and it must be felt as a fact unto itself, emerging from the events of the Holocaust itself and not from a broad historical context, or studied as scientific research."[5]
In March 1981, the Ministry of Education published the requirements of the curriculum in history, which included the subject of the Holocaust to be studied as a compulsory unit for the matriculation exams. The very establishment of the committee and the educational trends in the curricula testify to the political and public significance attributed to the subject. Undoubtedly, the approach to the subject in the textbooks from the Seventies and even more so in those from the Eighties, testifies to a new way of coping with both the aspects of the instruction of the Holocaust and with the doubts that have been arising in the last years about the fundamental thesis of Zionism, namely, about the assumption that Zionism and the State of Israel are answers to the Holocaust.[6]
However, the basic educational question whether the needs of educators as well as pupils trying to cope with the subject of the Holocaust have been met by the new curricula, is left open by the above mentioned studies.

There is evidence, deriving from educational practice, of a continuous difficulty for both students and teachers in coping with the subject on the individual level.[7]
"Poland is the basis. There occurred the most important event to my people in the twentieth century. Maybe, to a certain extent it is even more important than Zionism. And the personal aspect is not less important. As far as my personal and Jewish identities are concerned, similar to most Israeli-born, the Holocaust has remained an unsolved issue. I have no problem with my being a Jew, a kibbutz member, with being a secular person. This account I have already closed. But I could not feel a sense of belonging to my people who have perished. There was no way I could experience what the Jews in Eastern Europe had experienced, nor could I really mourn for them. I had no way - for me that is essential." (Dany, educator, Be'eri, 1986).
"Previously, when I heard about the Holocaust, it was as remote as science fiction. Certain experiences were capable of shocking me. I wanted to see, to know, not only the one story of a boy that moves us when we see him crying because his mother had to leave him. I wanted to understand the experiences and the stories behind them, to see, to understand and not merely be shaken." (Efrat, Ein Carmel, 1985).

The youngsters testify to their need to see in order to understand, to experience in order to belong, to their incapability to grasp the extent of the loss. They wish to feel and know what happened. Their curiosity makes them transcend the word-by-word explanation of documents about the method of murder. "How could they have done this?"
Nilly Keren, who prepared and accompanied the group from Kibbutz Be'eri in 1986, reports that the first question she asked the group was: "What do you expect to know as a preparation for the journey?" They replied : "No more history, please. We have studied Gutman (a history book), the entire Holocaust, and passed our matriculation exams on the subject in the eleventh grade." (Nilly Keren, escort, Be'eri, 1986).
"Ever since pre-school days we were taken to the Holocaust Monument at Yad Mordechai. I was always angry during those ceremonies and I could not understand why. I always felt that something went wrong. I knew I had to know what was hidden behind the words, behind the things that could not be told. I knew that I would never do it on my own. I am just not strong enough - but together with my classmates - yes."
"I was cynical, completely without feelings. Everything was up in the air,all these figures and symbols." (Students, Be'eri, 1986). Recent programmes of study find it difficult to

supply an answer to these issues.[8]

How then can one build a sense of identification with modes of behaviour and reaction included in the concept of Jewish endurance? How can one connect the issue of the maintenance of human dignity in the Holocaust to the sphere of personal and collective decision-making which is familiar to and identifiable by the student as part of his own reality? All this, in an open society, based on democratic ways of life in a complex political reality. How should one then express the connection to a past which is different in its definitions, sounds, landscapes and names, and still be aware that this past constitutes a part of the identity of a group to which he belongs?

To present this I would like to propose two assumptions.
1) The development of the ability to distinguish between different situations and deal with information about a reality entirely different from the student's one, yet belonging to him acause of his being a Jew who lives in Israel, demands transfer to the realm of experience. The process of constructing a normative system along with the student can be achieved if the acquisition of knowledge is accompanied by the experiential dimension which creates the focus for identification and for a sense of belonging.

2) The memory of the Holocaust is based on the fact and the feeling of absence and loss. Its transmission should, therefore, depend on the development of the ability to face emptiness. In order to create a normative system it is essential to create for the student a transfer from the sphere of the concrete to that of the abstract. I shall expand and clarify this idea later on, but at this stage I would like to present an argument in opposition to the above presented approach. It is characteristic of criticism voiced within the kibbutz movement.
Shneur Kopelevitz, an educator from Kibbutz Sefayim writes: "The visit to concentration camps is the utmost height of our educational attempt in the use of stimulation. Should one personally climb the Himalayas in order to know that they are high? Must one take students to Treblinka in order to make them know how their ancestors were exterminated? What sort of an educational idea is this? To take to a concentration camp in order to understand the Holocaust.. By adopting this method of instruction we impair man's ability to touch upon the abstract. The urge to touch in order to understand prevails in all spheres of life. But what about the soul? Can't it soar unless hands are touching? This is a contageous disease. Next, the entire kibbutz movement will proceed to Treblinka in order to understand the Holocaust! It is sick.
Our children travel all around the world because they are unable to take off to the abstract - yet one can know the entire world without actually travelling. Kafka never went beyond seventy miles from his home, yet was the highest of all. Kant never went further than five kilometres from Koenigsberg, and I don't have to go to Alaska to realize that no Eucaliptus trees grow there. What have we come to?"[9]
Yitzhak Gefen, an educator from Kfar Szold replies: "Everybody has his own credo. I'm from North Africa and had no connection to Poland. Yet, since the age of ten, when I heard that the Jewish people had been hurt, I have felt that I belong to that people. My positions have been formed on the basis of that period. This has also made me introduce the subject of the Holocaust as a project at the school where I teach. I have myself been to Poland with a group of youngsters, and have realized how important the visit is for the increase of awareness and understanding through sight and proximity. Until that moment I had known (underlined in the text - N.B.), but there was no way I could have grasped the dimension of the Holocaust without actually being there."[10]

To complement Yitzhak Gefen's words I would like to substantiate the assumptions I have presented. I'll do that on the basis of conclusions derived from my educational experience, gained by the preparation and accompaniment of a group of students to Poland, and conclusions derived from talks of students who participated in the project, in the course of the years.

The combined operation of preparations and a journey is intended to deal with concepts that belong to the cultivation of remembrance. In the course of learning, prior to the journey and during it, elements from various disciplines have been used. An important part of the preparation is devoted to the construction of a process whereby the mission is conceived as a social interest that unites the individuals into a communal body, which is sent by the community and carries its mission.
The theoretical studies include the history of the Nazi regime and of the "Final Solution". Acquaintance is made with the history of Polish Jewry and with their cultural life before the Holocaust, and with its destruction in the course of the war. The theoretical study relates to the individuals, namely, to the practical meaning of the National Socialist ideology and the operation of the bureaucratic and military system of political organizations

for the individual, on the level of his everyday existence. The integration of documents testifying to the anti-Jewish policy with diaries and memoirs of the victims makes the students face the world of people whose lives had been severely shaken. The student perceives the connection between the administrative language of the documents and of the 'policy', and the lives, anxieties and worries of individuals who are the objects of policies enforced on them. He learns about certain answers people managed to devise for themselves in the midst of the ruins of their previous lives. The student takes the first step within their story, setting out on a voyage even before leaving for Poland. He proceeds with the aid of maps, facts, events and characters from the period of the Holocaust, passing along the intended course of his journey, throughout individual, as well as group studies. Thereby, he builds the contexts of the journey within the general events of that time.

A further, integrated way of preparatory study is the construction of a personal relatedness to general historical events throughout the common creation of a sequential story. The family history of each student, (family in the broad sense), between 1933 and 1945, is put against the context of the historical time-table of events. The young boys and girls themselves reveal the stories and the family connections, and thereby they become partners to the generation of their grandfathers and grandmothers and to direct and distant relatives, both living and deceased, through investigation, verification of facts and the anchoring of the family fragment in the sequence of general historical events. Even if the group includes students of Eastern origin, detailed acquaintance with the family branches, with the story of the era and with the political and anti-Jewish tendencies, create their ties with the concept of "common fate." Then the individual stories are gathered into one single sequence, that gains its meaning from the relatedness of individual fate to the meaning of Jewish history, part of which are the individual family endings that leave the youngster facing the unknown. The ability to create attachment by conversation bridges over the generation gap, and even though indirectly, turns the event into a part of family or community history. Conclusively, the historical event in its context belongs now to the sphere of self inspection into the students' own lives and becomes a constructive factor of their social belonging to the group. They acknowledge the difference between the reality of their lives and that of the object of their investigation and choose which parts are to be documented and told together in a group to their fellow travellers.

At that stage the educator's role is to provide legitimation to their otherness and to the inherence of each individual to the story. Through the creation of the sequence story and the talks of the students with witnesses from the period of the Holocaust, they develop an ability to converse with people about their past, to ask questions more delicately, yet insist on being answered. They also experience the fact that there are not definite, general answers and that ultimately each individual has to face the reality of his own life. The students question the meaning of rule and power, destiny and choice, and the nature and meanings of decision making.

In all the talks held by educators with the pupils who participated in the various groups, when being asked about the process and the structure of the preparation, students, with almost no exception, pointed out the importance of learning and the knowledge of details, especially of those related to the names, landscapes and sites they had met in the course of the journey. Thus, the study of the route becomes an acquaintance with places, people and with their stories, some of which resemble the stories they had heard from the witnesses, and others - the stories that had been entrusted to them by older members of their kibbutz community, which often ended by "We never heard of them ever since," "We lost all touch," "Later we were told that.."

The youngsters set out for Poland equipped with questions and requests of people from their near and more distant environment, feeling as missionaries who have to ask, enquire, add further details to the network of information, say prayers and communicate silently. They take along names, fragments of stories, some ending in the unknown. They are assigned to complete the stories even though they are aware of the fact that the completion of the story would not mean any addition or discovery of facts, but their finding of their own selves within the story that had been suddenly cut off.

The youngsters' first encounter with sites and memories creates a turmoil of shock, pain, loneliness, alienation, anger and loss. "I retreated into myself with a feeling of suffocation. It was a turmoil of feelings that I could not cope with" (Yif'at, Nitzanim, 1985). "I am left alone in one of the buildings.. Once again I am filled with fear." (Nimrod, Sefayim, 1985).

"I could not believe that this piece of land, now covered with soft, green grass, has absorbed so much blood, and this sky.. how could it,, I was filled with fear and anxiety. I felt suffocating." (Anat, Yotveta, 1985).

"Auschwitz hit me with a shock that I had not anticipated. I trembled and broke down. I was helpless." (Lior, Dovrat, 1987).

The first encounter with the death camps and his stay there expose the youngster to the utmost, to the extreme which leaves him with no escape. Thus, the intensity of the pain and his existential fear turn the knowledge of the general loss into a feeling of a personal one. "I had certain fears. I was afraid of being indifferent. I was afraid that everything would pass me by without leaving any trace. I also feared that I would be unable to digest it because my family had not experienced the Holocaust. When I reached the camp, it was as though my family had gone through it all." (Eli, Yaqum, 1985).
"Before the journey, my attitude to the Holocaust had been as to some event that had happened to them, there. It hurt, but I did not belong to it.
In Poland I met the remains of what had happened, and then felt them infiltrating into me and making me feel that I was becoming part of the Jewish people." (Izik, Beit Oren, 1985).
First hand evidence of sight and touch, proving to one that horrors had actually taken place, creates a strong sense of certainty on the one hand, and a feeling of incapability to explain and comprehend, on the other.

The intensity of the emotional confrontation at first leaves the youngsters trapped within themselves. The rest of the journey, the task of collecting details and the identification of sites, build up a feeling of belonging. The previously meaningless sites are gradually filled up with the youngsters' however incomplete knowledge, learning and with their young and free existence. In Birkenau, Nitzan from Gvat, a young boy of ploughsheds, fields, machines and maintenance told me: "Look at the quantity of the iron they put into the construction of those furnaces. Iron, and more iron, more.. Look how taut the barbed wire fences remained after forty years! As though they were put up only yesterday.. I can't grasp it - they built the death camps to last for centuries."
"To come to those gas chambers and to get out alive. I can't explain it. Throughout our journey I felt as though we were attending a march. We, the Israelis, march in the centre and all those who perished are watching us from the side, crying out something to us, telling us to witness, to see all that has happened, to make us understand." (Sharon, Kiryat Anavim, 1985). "Masses of items aren't meaningful, but when you see a single personal object you begin to think and grasp. I have never thought that I would think of the Holocaust in terms of details instead of masses. It is a completely different notion from the one I had before. I started to grasp the details in this vast, mute mass." (Arnon, Ramat Hakovesh, 1987).
"Jewish Warsaw and especially the cemetery told me a story of a strong, prosperous and influential Jewish community. I felt as though I was walking through my city, a city in which a third of the population were my people. I could walk in it just as if I were in Tel Aviv. Kotsk took me back in thought to the Jewish cemetery in Warsaw. Once again I felt the size and the grandeur that had been destroyed. On the way to the cemetery at Kotsk I kept telling myself stories that resembled many others, stories like my grandfather's that always stay with me." (Dany, Ein Gedi, 1985).

The youngsters feel the absence more acutely and emphatically when they compare it with Polish continuity of existence.
"They insisted on showing us their grand past" (Irit, Nezer Sireni, 1987); "When we visited the remains of the Warsaw Ghetto, when we stood at the ramp from where hundreds of thousands of Jews had been sent to Treblinka, when we stood at the very centre of a city of graves, or sat in the small theatre with a few dozen spectators watching a Jewish play, performed in Yiddish by Polish actors, it was then that we realized that in the same century in which the Third Temple had been built and the Jewish State had been established, an entire Jewish world had been destroyed." (Dror, Hulata, 1985).
Hostility towards the Poles is intensified when one becomes aware of the location of the camps and their proximity of Polish cities.
"It is most amazing.. the proximity of the camp to Lublin.. the feeling that the Poles could smell the burning and that they must have known." (Various students, 1984). "They could almost hang their washing on the fence of the camp." (Hagit, Ramat David, 1987).
On leaving Birkenau at sun set, I noticed Einat from Kfar Baruch, far away in the field. She was kicking up earth clods and when I joined her she said, "I am so angry that I just can't get on to the bus. I can't face hearing Polish, facing them." She referred to our escorts, those polite, courteous people from the Korczak House. At that time Einat was incapable of distinguishing between them and others.
"To want us to visit more of their overly-decorated palaces and less of Birkenau and Auschwitz is not to understand what was happening inside us. It must be kept in mind that we had come to experience the Holocaust of our people and to cry, and they (the Polish hosts) had arranged palace tours for us." (Irit, Nezer Sireni, 1987). For the Israeli youngsters there it was a total contradiction.

The sensation of anger at the Poles, the immediate objects of their dejection, often rattles the youngsters during the journey, and is expressed in their words upon their return. The very fact that the Jewish loss is blurred in the explanation they hear at the camps from the Polish guides, by the description of their people's suffering during World War II and by hints at a common fate, confuse the youngsters. This is a situation that requires the educator's sensitive intervention at the time occurrence and on their return home. The involvement of the Poles in the journey has to do with the concept of bystanders. It also has direct implications for the youngsters' various spheres of life. A distinction should be made, therefore, between legitimation to the emotional response in the course of the journey and between the process that analyses the reaction, selects and substantiates the manner in which conclusions are reached upon returning home.

In the presence of the sights and at their very existence, the meaning of the system of murder becomes more keen and distinct. Amazement and wonder remain but they are channelled now to understand the behaviour of individuals. "For a long time I have been trying to understand, but in vain. Evidently from the analysis of processes historical facts can be explained, but when one is actually at the spot and relates to people who did it.. I just can't understand." (Muki, Beit Haemeq, 1987). "In Maidanek there is a small cell next to the gas chamber, from which the German could peep at the victims through the window. This picture sticks in my mind. Just imagine the man, sitting there. How did he dare? What passed through his mind? How could he open the gas taps?" (Sal'it, Cabri, 1985).
Both the crimes and the criminals cease to be parts of a demonic occurrence and become parts of the sphere of human relations.

The acknowledgement that such cruel behaviour did exist and is possible, makes some youngsters adopt a pessimistic attitude, of almost total despair, towards the human race. "Another thing that has come out of me lately is the fear of the Holocaust. In Maidanek I understood and this understanding made me ask many questions and aroused fear and pessimism as regards human society." (Ruthi, Giv'at Brenner, 1985).
Outside the gates of the death camp Birkenau, our coach was waiting for us. No'am from Dovrat got on the bus, shaking and feeling low. Turning to me, he says quietly: "Am I worth anything? Is life worth at all? What is everything really worth?" Alarmed, I just hold him firmly, look straight into his eyes and say, "You are No'am, No'am from the kibbutz, from the Emek, from Israel." He looks back and smiles. Later, while walking in the rain-swept streets of Krakov, we talk about our pain and anxieties, about the probability of a way of life where every step is weighed by the principle of choice between right and wrong. And we continue to search for the difference between the humane and the inhumane.

Holocaust survivors, who had been youngsters at the time of the Holocaust about the age of the students, and who actually stayed in the sites we visit, accompany the group. "Before the journey I'd never told. I knew that nobody would listen." (Yisrael Levin, escort, Yagur, 1987). The common encounter of witnesses and youngsters with the sites turns the memory of horror more concrete and personal. The story of the witnesses at the very sites, quasi the fulfillment of the command "And Thou shall tell your son," builds a bridge among the generations and creates an unsaid commitment of the youngsters to continue the story." I felt a sort of mixture of awe and pride. I felt my eyes fill with tears. This became stronger when Simcha Appelbaum approached the crematorium and said Kaddish for the members of his family who had perished there. Suddenly the horror of the extermination of the Jewish people was no longer abstract. Simcha was standing there, mourning his family at the very site where they had been slaughtered. At once a feeling of deep identification overwhelmed me. We said Yizkor and stayed there for a long time." (Koren, Netzer Sireni, 1987).
Yozek, who escorted the 1984 Takam delegation, reports: "Right after the war I worked with youngsters when I was active in the "Bricha" (illegal escape to Palestine-N.B.) My people left Poland beaten and humiliated. Now I returned to Poland with proud and free youngsters, who grew up in freedom. It is difficult to digest. The identification of the youngsters with me when I visited my native town, Tarnov, meant a lot to me, it relieved me and made me feel as if I had not parted with my childhood but came back to it."
The youngsters share the witness' return to his past, and when they together leave this past behind, he entrusts his story with their memories and their consciousness. A sensation of support and mutual help is created and it is directed towards the more sensitive and fragile in the group. He is their witness, who leads them through the Ghetto and the camp and together they emerge from the story through his pain and torment, into a togetherness, which is formed in order to create support that is mutually transferred to the reality of their lives, and holds them together within the endless nothingness revealed to the young boys and girls. The concrete detail in the personal story of the witness requires a wholeness in their minds.

During the journey, the young people examine every detail, such as the lettering, the meaning of initials and terms on headstones, compare maps that describe what used to be in the past with the apparent present. They attach stories and poems of the lost Jewish culture to the streets of the Polish village. I have chosen to relate our story at Kotsk in order to illustrate the specific nature of this process of attachment, exactly as I put it down in my travel diary.

"It is early morning and freezing cold. Put on warm clothes, kids. On the Lublin-Maidanek road we leave the highway and turn towards Kotsk. Before the journey I had read in Judaica that the tales of the village had been collected in a book that appeared in 1938. Just before the Holocaust over sixty percent of the citizens in Kotsk had been Jewish. According to records, all the Jews of Kotsk had perished and there is no knowledge of Jews who returned to the village after the war.

We enter Kotsk - a dreary, grey square. We try to attach to it a Jewish scene. It is still difficult. We find a Pole to converse with. He used to be a fisherman and sold his catch to the Jews. "The entire square belonged to them, except three shops. On this street they concentrated them and also shot a few hundreds. It was O.K. with the Jews. One merchant I used to work with even returned my ring when I lost it. They set fire to the synagogue, but the Rabbi's house (he used the Hebrew word) and yard are still there." It all comes out in one sequence, life, killing, personal acquaintances and business relations - there is unity of time and place for this old Pole who speaks to us, toothless, giggling, clasping his hands, pointing here and there. "The Rabbi's house? Just turn left at the next corner." We get excited and proceed to look for Menachem Mendel. The vast story becomes definite and specific. We feel odd, walking in the village as Jews once again, even though the people here may not realise wherefrom this strange group has suddenly turned up, and certainly do not relate us to their Jews. Everything is close by. Leaving the Jewish square, we pass two streets and are in the very centre of the Jewish village. The wooden village cottages are close together, almost leaning one against the other, as though emerging straight out of the stories of Bialik, Perez and Sholem Aleichem. Over there, behind that fence, a meadow, the narrow paths where they used to play secretly and across the corner - the Rabbi's house and yard, a large house, surrounded by open porches, with numerous entrances and passages that gradually fill up with sights from then. There was room to gather, aggroup, consult, wait for a meeting with the Rabbi, and discourse about joys and sorrows. And in the street horse driven carriages that unload the produce they brought in from the nearby villages. Along the road, on both sides, there are disorderly piles of apples, pickled cucumbers, salt herring, potatoes, corn, old and new clothing and other village merchandise. We have a feeling that we have found the Jewish village, a feeling of having regained something you thought you had been robbed of forever, a sensation of tasting a forbidden fruit. Is it amazement deriving from nostalgia? Do colourfulness and simplicity replace true roots? Any criticism is legitimate. But at that moment we belonged there very clearly. This village was ours once again and we were the Jews of Kotsk, with our Hebrew, the youth of our boys and girls, with their smiles and joy. There was no gloominess, no mourning, just real relief and Hassidic tunes in our ears. I bought a shabby grey hat. Putting it on, I felt I had found Menachem Mendel. This feeling, which gradually crystallized during the journey, consisted of both a measure of sentiment and of enlightenment.

I had come to Poland also to find emotional relatedness to the great Jewry that lived there and now is gone forever. In our country I have difficulty in belonging to those who claim to be their followers both because of their fanaticism and the dogmatism characteristic of their way of life, and because of political contexts.

In the course of the journey I could actually touch the vanished community that lived there, engaged in the trifles of daily life. In Kotsk and Levov, in the Jewish quarters of Krakov and Lublin, in the cemetries and the Jewish archives I discovered a changing, colourful and heterogenous Jewry. I had learned about them for many years, but here I became belonging, so that in addition to being amazed, I can identify myself as their follower and feel committed to them. This sensation would make it easier for me to present my newly gained sense of being a follower in opposition to the claims and the arguments of the extreme orthodox Jews in Israel. I discovered Menachem Mendel in conversations, in the village cottages, in the complex relations between neighbours, in stories and graveyard inscriptions, in the great pain that united us all, in the stories of escapes and hidings, in the quest on the verge of death to become partners to the shaping of a common future. The villagers tell us about the Jews who had hidden during the massacre but had been discovered, about the handful who had run away to the forest and about the dying out of the opposition there. They do not talk about the continuity of their lives without Jews, and we who just turn up from Eretz Yisrael for a short while, don't ask. I have not seen any point in that. I have no intention to compete with them for Poland.

We proceed to the cemetery. They told us that it was outside the village. We walk, pass houses at the outskirts of the village, a dirt road. Can it be here? We cross a field

towards the distant horizon. What are these boys and girls from Israel doing here on this marsh land? A distant horizon, narrow fields and we are searching for a Jewish cemetery. On our right there is a small duck farm, to the left a birch wood. According to the description we have received, this should be the place. We step inside, onto the layers of fallen leaves. Hesitantly, we begin to grope for something, to scrape the ground with our shoes. We soon reach the remains of ashes and clumps of stones. With unsure hands we remove the leaves and the dust. Our fingers feel broken stones, inscriptions, Hebrew words, broken bits of headstones.. It is here! The youngsters spread all over the wood and start, with inexplicable fever and excitement, to dig with their hands in order to uncover old tombstones. They try to read the script, erect the stones, to locate the dates. The headstones are all beautiful Hebrew and the dates are in Hebrew letters as well. Suddenly all this belongs to us, the Hebrew, the names and the titles that relate to the deceased. Here, the graveyard in Kotsk the Poles had not touched, they did not plough it and did not cut the trees off. It was a piece of land that still belonged to the Jews and to us. A whole story of centuries, three or four centuries of Jewish settlement - they were all here - those who think highly of themselves, and those who are content with pointing out the date and the year. The young, virtuous virgin, the man of deeds. Nearby the tombs we have just uncovered, Menachem Mendel, the Tzaddik's grave with an opening for entreaties so that they would proceed straight upwards, and the heavens would open to receive those who practice what they preach and also to those who put up a petition just in times of trouble.
The sight of boys and girls groping, finding, touching, caressing, performing a rite of love and attachment had a unique beauty. It consisted of both amazement and total submergence, expressed even by their clinging to the ground. The touch of fingers, the effort, the discovery, the joy.

When we held a memorial service for the Jews of Kotsk, there, at the roadside, in the wood, among the smashed and burnt graves, Simcha said Kaddish and we rehearsed Menachem Mendel's sayings and sang for them Hatikva, we established for ourselves a real contact with Jewish past. I know that none of us will ever forget those moments. It was also a kind of victory that we reached them, inspite of all. And I know how much we needed this victory. Consciously, I know that we merely helped ourselves but not them and that we can carry along only the smallest part of their painful, humiliated, senseless and terrible story. That was Kotsk, and we are on our way to Lublin."

At the various sites that the delegations visit during the journey they hold memorial services. It would be almost unnecessary to point out the reserved attitude of Israeli youth towards ceremonies as it appears in the Israeli educational reality. In the journey to Poland the youngster finds the memorial service a proper way to express his personal attachment. "Many of us were surprised when indifference to the traditional Jewish services seemed to have vanished. It was as though the unseen barrier between being an Israeli and a Jew had fallen and integration and joining into a single unity has been formed." (Nira, educator, Netzer Sireni, 1987).
"There wasn't even an argument about eating "hammetz" - it was self understood that we all joined the Jewish culture by symbols and ceremonies among other things. I am willing to admit that there, for the first time, I said to myself : "You are Jewish," and felt proud and belonging in my being a Jew." (Lilach, Netzer Sireni, 1987).
"When we sang Hatikva at Treblinka, I silently shouted the line "Our hope has not been lost, yet," because I felt that that line had strengthened the victims." (Dani, Ein Gedi, 1985).
"I felt alone (at Treblinka). I wanted to give of myself to the place, to give an answer. When I read out a passage I felt I was paying them a special tribute by a young, living Israeli voice, heard in that place of death." (Sharon, Kiryat Anavim, 1985).
"At the ceremony in Auschwitz.. to me religion does not mean a lot, but "El Male Rachamim" and the "Kaddish" you said entered deep into my soul, opening hidden doors of pride, that let out all the pain, anger and dejection." (Sharon, Kiryat Anavim, 1985).
"I felt how erect I was. We stood there, singing the anthem and suddenly I understood the profound meaning of the words 'To be a free people in our country, the land of Zion, Jerusalem.' My Jewish consciousness had become so strong that I felt privileged to have come to that place." (Anat, Yotveta, 1985).

"We had taken with us to Poland almost a whole library. It included songs by Yitzhak Katzenelson, Fogel, Alterman, excerpts from diaries left by Jews at the time of the Holocaust, songs from the Ghetto and from the past of the vanished Jewry, Hassidic sayings as well as modern poems by Amir Gilboa and Wieseltier, passages of prose by A.B. Yehoshua, David Grossman and others. The children prepared the ceremonies with great sensitivity, selecting the pieces very carefully and attentively. After reading them out aloud to the group, the passages would become their own. There was even a kind of covert competition between them for who would participate in the ceremony, who would be the flag bearer. This division of tasks was an additional expression of their ability to be considerate of each other, which they had newly discovered in themselves.

The checking of details, the integration of pieces of information joined together to build a personal commitment which has been translated to the level of Jewish and Zionist identity.
"While I was there (in Poland) I performed my duty as a Jew to remember and remind others of the past, bearing the Holocaust within me, to be proud of the present that our people has come through in the hard way." (Nimrod, Cabri, 1985).
"The visit to synagogues and cemeteries drastically sharpened my Jewish identity. Even though I am not a religous person I made a point of wearing a kippa (headcover) and at the synagogue of the "Rema", (Rabbi Moses Isserles) at Krakov, I even prayed from the siddur (the Jewish prayer book). Nevertheless, I relate to my Jewishness from a national aspect rather than from a religious one." (Gal, Gevim, 1985).
"At the utmost of death, to see the utmost of life, and it is related to Eretz Yisrael, our homeland, and to our life here. Not to live anywhere else, and proceed with what we are expected to proceed, is the most important matter for me now. I believe that it is the most significant message that I carry along from there. For, aside from the emotional experience of being there, of seeing and trying to understand what is understandable, of experiencing pain and death, I felt the importance of our being here, sensed our strength which is here, opposed to weakness anywhere else. Therefore, I believe that our walking together, wearing our shirts with the Israeli badge and carrying the flag, gave me a lot of strength. That is one of the most important things." (Michal, Yiftach, 1987). No doubt these words reflect an obviously declarative dimension and use expressions of belonging as a defence against the mixture of feelings of weakness and strength, strangeness and presence. A controlled intervention of the educator is certainly required. It should include working out the educational procedure and it is to be continued after the group's return home.

Nevertheless, one can sum up and say that in the course of the journey these youngsters ask questions which people rarely ever face throughout their lives. They enquire about the difference between the humane and the inhumane, about how someone can commit murder and adopt it as a way of life. They want to know how and when people cease to think. This clarification is accompanied by the process of choice between acts one should or should not do, between groups one chooses to belong to and others he rejects. The process of choice is then transferred from sensation to consciousness.
"We have to live with it without losing our sanity. We have to create a people, build a land, foster a culture, propagate wisdom and beauty. We should neither be victims nor murderers. We have to be strong in order not to be at the mercy of criminals or bystanders. But that won't be enough. We must be humane, so that nothing of that filth ever sticks to us." (Dror, Hulata, 1985).
"I had a painful and severe crisis in belief on my return. I saw the degenerate and deteriorate state of the country and felt like shouting "It's not fair" We are not a suitable answer to those thousands of eyes that had been watching us in Auschwitz." (Ruthi, Giv'at Brenner, 1985).
In addition, the youngsters learn how to relate to characters, to individuals in the history of the Holocaust not as to one dimensional symbols but as to individuals facing up to their fate. "There I began to understand that the reaction of the Jews had nothing to do at all with what I think, and realised that I had no right to be angry with anyone who had been there, or judge them for having fought or not. In that respect I could relax." (Muki, Beit Haemeq, 1987).

On returning to their respective kibbutzim the youngsters began to talk to survivors who had never talked to their children and grandchildren about the Holocaust.
"I would like to tell you about a conversation I had with a Holocaust survivor. I felt I understood him much better now and that it was much easier for me to absorb and accept what he had told me. I also felt that it was much easier for him to talk to me rather than to anybody else. I really felt that I could understand him and could experience his story. It was an entirely different point of view, totally different from any other testimony I had heard. I think the journey has changed my attitude towards survivors. It has given me a tool to understand them and to accept them the way they are." (Adi, Einat, 1987).
"One of the Holocaust survivors, of whom there is a whole nucleus on our kibbutz, hardly ever speaks to anybody. He has turned into a recluse. He has incomprehensible mannerisms. He did not agree to come to my lecture on the journey to Poland, claiming that he was unable to face those slides. He began to talk to me. I felt that I was getting close to him. When I came home I told my mother : "Do you know, I spoke with N. and he told me". I felt that this is really the climax." (Anat, Nahsolim, 1987).
"I am a neighbour of an old woman. As a child I thought slightly of her, and used to say that she did not speak good Hebrew. Today I don't know - I feel differently towards her. I

think that whoever lived through the Holocaust and then managed to live in this country, is very brave. It is one of the things I have brought along from Poland. This understanding. To understand the people who had gone through the Holocaust." (Nilly, Shefayim, 1987).

By the attachment of Holocaust survivors and the youngsters who return from Poland the memory of the Holocaust is sustained when the youngsters become a vessel whereby their story is transferred after two generations of silence. This feeling of attachment to the story becomes a kind of commitment on the personal level.
"It's a must that more people should know what we went through and what we know. I know this very firmly now, and it is important that every one of us should pass it on to his circle." (Yitzhaki, Kfar Tavor, 1987).
This direct attachment is especially important, since Holocaust survivors will be able to accompany the groups only for a limited time.

On meeting their peers, the overwhelmed messengers succeed in transmitting their impressions and personal conclusions, based on the experience they have compiled, and thereby create an impact on their immediate social circle.

As soon as the story becomes theirs, it's mingled with the flavour of the youngsters' otherness. It would be advisable to legitimize this otherness, since it is almost a condition to the continuation of the story.
However, the legitimation to adopt unconventional ways to interpret reality is problematic especially as regards the way in which youngsters relate to the relations between Arabs and Jews in Israel. The youngsters transfer the conclusion "We have no other place" which they had reached throughout the journey to the Arab-Israeli conflict.
It is therefore, the accompanying educator's responsibility to be precise with distinctions and with the description of implications and of limits to be put and prices to be paid on the personal moral level.

Finally, I would like to point out shortly some of the risks involved in such an educational endeavour.
1) The exhaustion of such an encounter in the sphere of sentiments may result in the omission of the position-building process, and may have a merely short term effect on the emotional aspect.
2) The threat and the feeling of loneliness the youngsters have to face, might result in the creation of a system of defence and the construction of an enclosing wall that would provide a mechanical sense of security, in the form of "A people dwelling alone."
3) The intensity of the experience and the emotional load to which the young people are being exposed may lead to a conceptual confusion. Their urge to vent their anger may cause them to transfer the responsibility from the German ruling system that initiated the planning and the execution of extermination, to the Poles who were strangers, present at the time of the visit. The impiling anger can also be exchanged by hatred, which may be an answer to distress and depression, and which may be expressed by the manifestation of power. This is the most immediate danger of the above mentioned ones, especially against the background of the Israeli experience, which has been a source of growth, especially in the course of the journey.

All this necessitates and emphasizes the intervention of the accompanying educator throughout all the phases of the preparation and the journey itself, in order to turn the participants into an educational group to which one essentially becomes belonging by the acception of the mission. The educator's task is to be a partner, a supporter, to be involved in the intimate talks throughout the journey and in the course of the educational accompaniment that follows and reacts, upon the return of the youngsters to their schools and communities.

NOTES

1 The data is processed by me, based on Special Series No. 629, Tables 6, 7, 25-41, published by the Central Bureau of Statistics. The data refers to elementary and junior high school population in 1977, namely to the age group between 6-12 in 1977.
2 Ruth Fuehrer, Agents of Zionist Education (Tel Aviv : Oranim, Kibbutz Meuchad, Sifriat Poalim, 1985), pp. 65-107.
Nilly Keren, "The Impact of Public Opinion Shaper and of the Historical Research on the Development of Educational Thought and Educational Programmes Concerning the Holocaust in High Schools and in Informal Education in Israel 1948-1981, Diss. Hebrew University 1985. pp. 71-85, 116-140, 166-191, 213-257.
3 Fuehrer, p. 71
4 Fuehrer, pp. 77, 83
5 Keren, p. 239

6 Books and pamphlets devoted to the subject of the Holocaust, issued since the Seventies, are presented here in the chronological order of their appearance.
Ariyeh Carmon and Y. Oron, Textbook : Jewish Vitality in the Holocaust (Jerusalem : Ministry of Culture and Education, 1975).
The Hebrew University and the Minsitry of Culture and Education, Anti-Semitism and the Holocaust (Jerusalem : The Hebrew University and the Ministry of Culture and Education, 1977).
Ariyeh Carmon, The Holocaust: Subject for the Upper Grades in High Schools (Jerusalem : Ministry of Culture and Education, 1980).
The Ministry of Culture and Education, The Department of Religious Education, Sources and Studies on the Holocaust (Jerusalem : Ministry of Culture and Education, 1983).
Yisrael Gutman and Haim Satzker, The Holocaust and its Meaning (Jerusalem : Shazar Centre, 1983).

7 By "testimonies taken from educational practice" I mean words of both pupils and educators who participated in the project of the journey to Poland in the course of the last four years. I have collected the transcripts of the talks held prior to, and after the journey. I have based my work mainly on transcripts gathered in "Beit Lochame Hagetaot" (Ghetto Fighters' Museum), which is the main academic and educational institution involved in the preparation of groups for the journey. I also have a detailed transcript of the students' words in the group which I prepared and accompanied me on the journey to Poland. In most cases the talks were led by the escorts; some - in the respective kibbutzim of the students. Next to the quotation I'll point out the name of the speaker, the settlement he is from, and the year of the journey. If the speaker is not a student, I'll also point out his function in the group.

8 Keren, p. 236
Fuehrer, p. 77.

9 "To Poland and Back," Yachad, 27 June 1986, p.7.

10 "To Poland and Back," Yachad, 27 June 1986, p.7.

REFERENCES

The Central Bureau of Statistics and the Ministry of Culture and Education. Demographic and Social Characteristics of Kindergarten and School Pupils, 1976-1977. Special Series No. 629. Jerusalem : The Central Bureau of Statistics and the Ministry of Culture and Education, 1980.

"To Poland and Back" Yachad, 27 June 1986, p.7.

Fuehrer, Ruth. Agents of Zionist Education. Tel Aviv : Oranim, Kibbutz Meuchad, Sifriat Hapoalim, 1985.

Keren, Nilly. "The Impact of Public Opinion Shapers and of the Historical Research on the Development of Educational Thought and Educational Programmes Concerning the Holocaust in High Schools and in Informal Education in Israel 1948-1981." Diss. Hebrew University 1985.

The Problem of Survivor Discourse: Toward a Poetics of Survivor Testimonies

Sidney M. Bolkosky, Professor of History

University of Michigan-Dearborn

In an impassioned critical attack on a recently published Holocaust curriculum, one survivor angrily denounced the statement that most of the perpetrators had not been "barbarians, but civilized men." The thesis of that curriculum continues the arguments of Hannah Arendt, Raul Hilberg and others who contend that an entire society participated in business as usual even when business elided into the routinized systematic murder of the Jews. Yet, such a suggestion, when it appeared in writing, denying the "barbarian" nature of those perpetrators, not only offended but enraged a victim of that system. While he did not compare an analysis of banal and boring men who produced distinctly extraordinarily evil consequences to specious arguments of the revisionists who deny the history of the Holocaust, this victim who survived nevertheless perceived a threat to the memory or the sanctity of the murdered victims. A historian stands confronted by a "remnant" who demands denunciations that are spiritually and intellectually apposite to those evil consequences.

Michael Marrus has recently warned that submitting the Holocaust to historical, critical scrutiny, might stimulate such reactions (Marrus, 1987). But what can one learn from such an understandable disapprobation as this man's refusal to accept a prospect that attributes normality to those who murdered his family? Recollections full of emotion contend with historical data revealing that the two do not necessarily corroborate each other. To the survivor, meaning emerges from his experience of history. To the historian, data about reality emerges for analysis. The first cannot bow to the second; the second, however, must recognize the active dynamics of the encounter. Data ought not compete with reality; but emotions ought not replace fact. At issue in this meeting are more than just emotionalism which clouds logic and historical data that ignores experiential reality. The admonition of the survivor haunts listeners: "You weren't there. You can't know what it was like." How does a historian, a generation removed from the events, dispute this ground with a living historical resource? And why, after such painstaking examination of documents, biographies, records, bureaucracies, the machinery of destruction and of state, should this particular conclusion still remain problematic?

Language bears at least part of the responsibility for this conflict in perception and interpretation. Emblematic words seem to emit fundamentally different meanings and discourse, dialogue becomes problematic, even impossible. I would like to address a function of such encounters, a phenomenon of survivor alienation that derives, in part, from failings inherent in their forms of discourse. Through such discussions about how Holocaust victims speak, both survivors and listeners might overcome at least some of that linguistically imposed alienation.

In order to help alleviate some of the nearly insurmountable difficulties bound up with questions about how to listen and how to speak, listeners need a poetics of such testimonies, a way of ordering the words so that they may be better assimilated, shared and, consequently, understood. Such a guide to survivor narratives must facilitate not only the listening, but also the speaking: survivors might then gain a measure of trust in their listeners and feel some degree of security in talking. A poetics of survivor narratives would demand not only knowledge of the history of the Holocaust, but of its potentially debilitating and inappropriate questions like the "family of questions" about resistance or flight to which another victim, Primo Levi, referred in The Drowned and the Saved (Levi, 1987).

Because of many victims' sensitivity to the power of language to distort, or the weakness of language to convey reality, not a sentence, not a word about the Holocaust can be taken for granted. In this respect, groping for analogies, some pale comparisons about how to listen to survivor narratives might come to mind. Psychoanalysis, for example, demands acute concentration on individual words, on the "semantic" rather than "syntactic" conveyors of meaning. If the psychological and emotional stakes in discussing neuroses in individual patients are not so high as discussing the annihilation of families, we might nevertheless pay assiduous attention to specific words when considering both Holocaust testimonies and Holocaust history. Each word carries narratives in it and conveys potentially volatile and misleading connotations. Partly for this reason, survivor testimonies, sparse yet full of hidden meanings, weigh heavily on listeners, burdening them with unique demands.

Recognizing, again, the inadequacy of such comparisons when speaking of the Holocaust, narrative techniques of pre-Holocaust literature might offer another analogy. James Joyce struggled most of his life with the problem of multiple meanings of single words. Like Freud or Lewis Carroll, whose term "portmanteau words" capsulized the problem, Joyce perceived what sociologists of language like Karl Mannheim considered among western civilization's most significant challenges: failure to communicate because of loss of community, shared experiences, traditions and values. Bound together with that disappearance of social community, was the concomitant loss of linguistic community which provided self-evident shared meanings. In a fragmented world, where alienation had become the rule, words that had carried portmanteau meanings formerly instantly grasped by interlocutors could no longer call up common associations. In Ulysses, Joyce surprised the unsuspecting reader when a descriptive passage about a walk through Dublin suddenly was jarred by an incomprehensible paragraph that seemed to intrude itself like a typographical error. Paragraphs followed in which description alternated with internal associations—stream of consciousness—as Joyce addressed the impossibility of serial or non-poetic language to convey the simultaneity of internal and external experience, and its failure to replicate the simultaneity of multiple associations that some words elicit. Finnegans Wake was his final, seventeen year attempt to overcome the restrictions of non-poetic language.

Joyce's Holocaust writer-counterpart who addressed the issue in profoundly sadder and deadlier terms was Elie Wiesel. "For the survivor," wrote Wiesel, "every word carries a hundred words" (Wiesel, 1979). Implicit in this statement is the sad fact of loneliness that haunts many survivors. Who can intuit those hundreds of unspoken words? How can they be voiced? Limitations of meaning and communication that caused Karl Mannheim to despair for the linguistically derived alienation of modern man multiply enormously when the abyss between Holocaust and other historical experiences discloses itself. Only one conclusion seems possible, a conclusion which survivors have sensed since the liberation, and which are here voiced by those perhaps less poetic than James Joyce or Elie Wiesel, but as poignant and more depressing:

> If the oceans were ink and the sky was paper, there would not be enough ink or paper to tell of one hour in Auschwitz.
>
> You cannot say in an hour, or a day or a week what it was like during those years. It is not possible to tell you.
>
> There is not enough tape, not enough paper, not enough time and not enough words to make you understand what we went through.
>
> I cannot tell you—I cannot. There are no words to tell you.
> (UM, 53-83-46A, 53-83-38A, 53-84-40A, 53-83-29A)

It has become a commonplace to speak of "unspeakable" memories. They are, of course, unspeakable in the sense that their horror seems to forbid description. "I pulled the shade on the past. Closed my memory in 1946." "In a way, we were ashamed of our experience. And we maybe didn't want to open up old wounds by discussing or telling about it." Primo Levi echoed this second comment in his disturbing final essay: "those remain silent who feel more deeply that sense of malaise which I for simplicity's sake call 'shame,' . . . or whose wounds still burn" (Levi). But for most, memories remained omnipresent as these two men suggest: "It's always with you. Try not to think about it, but it's in the back of your mind." "I don't think about it all the time; but I do think about it all the time. It's somewhere in the back of your head. I don't want to tell you; but I do want to tell you. I can't tell you" (53-87-32V).

If critical analysis of survivor testimonies reveals anything, it is a warning against cliches, a plea to use words cautiously, a fear of trivializing by misusing particular words that embody whole experiences. So even this concept of "unspeakable memories" threatens to become trivialized. Beyond some rather obvious reasons for not speaking about this past, those memories may in fact be unspeakable because of a deeply felt inadequacy to fully communicate meaning; an inadequacy implied by the last comment, "I can't tell you." Frustration, anger, bitterness, despair at that failure plague the survivor who at last wants to truly tell his/her story. If language rests on shared meanings which themselves derive from common histories and common experiences, Holocaust narratives simply cannot portray the whole truth. Yet they offer portions or fragments of the truth. (Both victim narrators and non-victim listeners might recognize this as a blessing.) Fragments imply reduction, and reduction simplifies the contradictions and paradoxical complexities of a tortured past—of individual histories which immure baffling tragedies. Fear of the "terrible simplifiers," at whose hands Holocaust history "slides fatally toward simplification and stereotype," (Levi) must number among those uncountable reasons for silence.

Silent or not, victims of the Holocaust remain victims even after they survived. Their testimonies and often their behaviors attest to that. Like some insatiable monster, the tentacles of that epoch reach beyond its closing date and continue to strangle the innocent. Often those later casualties have tried, have successfully spoken or written of their experiences. Yet bearing witness proved to be no antidote, proved, perhaps, that speaking aggravated the wounds. Thus, Thaddeus Borowski, brilliant young Polish non-Jewish writer died in a gas oven in his kitchen in 1953, a victim of his reminiscences. Thus, Primo Levi, brilliant testifier, indefatigable chronicler and analyst of Auschwitz and survival, died in 1987, a late victim of Auschwitz. Both had recorded their stories, expanded on the stories of others, offered their testimonies, their eyes and ears to the rest of us. To speak, to write, failed to purge their minds just as it fails in so many cases of survivors who testify. For after talking or writing for hours upon hours, the testimony remains incomplete, unsatisfactory, still a mystery which teaches nothing to the listeners and frustrates the narrators.

Those narratives of the Holocaust which have been squeezed from surviving victims remain inchoate. Not only have testifiers like Zoltan R. from Presov, Nathan R. from Beregszacz, Ruth K. from Lodz, Alex E. from Kralovsky Chlumec, convinced us of this, but so, too, Elie Wiesel of Sighet, Primo Levi of Turin, and Thaddeus Borowski of Warsaw. Even to such masters of language, this event reduces linguistic possibilities, defeats attempts at coherent narratives, defies proper syntax and confounds normal semantics. To seek whatever meaning such tales may offer presumes a first step of assimilating the words, understanding their logic. Many victims intuit that such first steps cannot be taken, that listeners are infants in their understanding.

> You're afraid of sounding ridiculous when you tell some of these things . . . [People's] reaction to what you are saying will be totally inadequate . . . After that happens to you, you just don't want to talk any more. What for?
>
> [All of you] are outsiders—including my children and my wife. [Pause] What do you know? You don't understand it anyway . . .There's no belief, no understanding. What's the use [of talking]? It's mine. Only I understand it.
>
> I don't know, I could never decide [if I should tell people]. Especially my children. I didn't believe it [so] how could they believe it? [Quickly digresses, walks around the room, agitated.] Maybe it's a mistake . . . [Weeps] I don't want them to know. [Stops, long pause, weeps again, then digresses and suddenly

exclaims] No! I don't want to tell my kids. I don't want them to know the hell . . . [long pause] When I start to think . . . [pause] Over 70 people murdered for nothing! What good would it do to tell them? [Long digression, returning to earlier experiences and suddenly] I never talked until now. [Weeps, long pauses, thinking, staring.] It was too hard. Just . . . [Long pause] Maybe I don't want my kids to know about it. [Leaves the room; returns.] I come from a big family. I feel I am a strong man and don't want anyone to feel sorry for me—not even my wife or child.

My first son [murdered during the Holocaust] was bright, very attentive—a brilliant child. How he would listen! [Long pause.] My son [now a successful doctor] doesn't want to know about these things [her experiences during the Holocaust] and I don't want to tell him. Maybe he'll listen to the tape. Maybe he shouldn't. I don't know. That child was such a beautiful, smart . . . such an exceptional kid [laughs and cries simultaneously]. My grandson reminds me of him.
(UM, 53-83-32V, 53-85-16V, 53-84-45A, 53-84-28A)

The first speaker, Nathan R., remembers inappropriate responses and remains suspicious about listeners and uncertain why he should talk of what he calls "the missing five years." Alex E., the second speaker, angrily accuses "outsiders" of insincerity and of inability to "understand" his experience finally questioning, like Nathan R., the purpose of talking. It is almost as if Alex E. has suffered the fate of Nathan R. and so many others, reacts with resentment to the insouciant disbelief of listeners who may include his own family. And Zoltan R., confused, ambivalent primarily expresses distrust of potential listeners. All three recognize a deep seated certainty that no one really cares enough to listen thoroughly, sympathetically and with proper understanding of the Holocaust. This fear manifests itself most acutely when it concerns their children. It is perhaps most poignant in the last speaker, Elizabeth S., whose conflicted views about her living son are aggravated by the first son, murdered, and for whom she feels responsible.

These oral testimonies bluntly acknowledge what some of the more literate witnesses revealed. In the first paragraph of that final work, a work which almost pointed to despairing suicide, Levi quoted Simon Wiesenthal's account of an SS guard's cynical admonition to Jewish prisoners that "even if someone were to survive, the world will not believe him" (Levi). Less pointed, but no less devastating was Elie Wiesel's midrash on the prophet Elijah's fiery ascendance to heaven as he predicted the fate of his disciple, the survivor: "You are the survivor . . . You, too, will be alone, you already are. You will speak . . . You will tell people what you have seen, what you have lived . . . few will listen, fewer will understand . . ." (Wiesel, 1981). The survivor-prophet speaks poetically and few, if any, understand—who would believe the story of the fire?

As she calmly revealed her memories about working near one of the crematoria at Auschwitz, Agi R. grew uncharacteristically agitated, almost incredulous herself: "I saw the flames every day because I worked right across from it [the crematorium] and I said to 'No, it's not true. It's not my family. They're not in there.' Because I couldn't believe it. I mean, I knew it was true, I knew it—but I didn't want to know it." Her conclusion, after a prolonged pause: "If you didn't know about this, would you believe it if I told you such tales" (53-85-10V)? Numerous questions lie implicit in her last one. How will you listen? How will I speak so that you will understand?

Let me now return to the survivor who so vehemently objected to abandoning the idea that the perpetrators were barbarians. To a person raised in European civilization, the word barbarian stands in sharp juxtaposition to civilized behavior. One cannot be both barbarian and civilized. The first implies brutality and violence, suffering and non-thinking sadism. Ignorance, hatred, racism, are the hallmarks of barbarism and the grounds of murderous acts. The survivor knows this because he observed it and experienced it. Civilized people might hold anti-Semitic ideas, but civilized men would not carry out barbaric acts. To remove the label is to remove the reasons for mass murder, or, more to the point, for the murder of specific family members, friends, teachers. To remove the label is to remove the simpler answers. Assuming that general scholarship recognizes the complicity in the Holocaust of state, industrial, judicial, educational, medical, scientific and other elements of civilization, how do we react to emphatic denials about barbarians?

One aspect of this question which needs consideration adumbrates the problem of survivor discourse by raising a correlative question about what sorts of information survivors are able to impart to historians. How would the victims know about the timetables, the scientific papers written and delivered by doctors, the priorities appointed to trains by railroad bureaucrats, the profit and loss margins of camps like Treblinka and Auschwitz, the rationale behind adopting Zyklon B, the industrial profits, the railroad cost-accountants, the careers made, the lawyers, technicians, engineers and millions of "cogs" in the death machine? Had they known, would it have mattered to them? Does it now?

Perhaps one glaring example sheds light on this discussion. In almost every account of train transports time seems immeasurable. It is certain that a journey that ought to have taken hours usually took days. Those who suffered the boxcars speak of sadistic German torturers who left carloads of Jews to die of thirst and starvation and disease. Approximately one third of the deportees who arrived at the camps were dead before they reached their horrible destinations. Raul Hilberg has pointed out, however, that during time of war, railroad trains were assigned priority ratings: military trains carrying troops or materiele were given highest priorities, passenger trains next, excursion trains next, and so on. Trains carrying Jews in boxcars were given no priority rating, or the lowest rating. Thus, when two trains needed the same track, the train with the higher priority got the right of way and the other would be shunted aside for an indefinite period (Hilberg, 1978). Itinerary plotters in Berlin or Crakow may have known that Jews were the cargo, but their considerations had little to do with sadism or even anti-Semitism. These were strictly administrative, bureaucratic decisions made by the book, efficiently and dispassionately—indifferently. After watching and listening to Walter Stier, declare emphatically in the film Shoah that he knew nothing about extermination at Treblinka or Auschwitz because "I was strictly a bureaucrat!" one can be dumbfounded by such indifference, but not doubt it. Stier was the former head of Reich Railways Department 33, assigned to Crakow's Head Office of Eastbound Traffic and then to Warsaw where he was chief traffic planner, head of the Traffic Planning Office (Lanzmann, 1985).

The result of such routine behavior was the prolonged, agonizing death of Jewish children in boxcars. Those who observed, smelled, felt and lived with this, experienced and remember starkly sadistic actions. What use, then, trying to convince the victims that their families died of "civilized" procedures, decisions empty of any emotion, sadistic or otherwise; or that to Walter Stier and his ilk Treblinka and Auschwitz were "just a destination" (Lanzmann)?

When they have used testimonies of eye witnesses, historians traditionally have relied upon literate sources—writers, diarists, other historians. They have recognized the limitations and heeded the caveats that accompany such primary sources. Using survivor testimonies falls under the same caveats, yet creates puzzling dilemmas. No one wants to contravene the victim who recounts his/her suffering. These statements simply defy traditional, usually pedantic, historical debates. Yet they offer material to be examined critically as historical evidence.

For example, in 1943, German occupation forces and the SS deported almost all the 63,000 Jews of Salonika to Auschwitz in a matter of weeks. It was an operation carried out with relative ease because of the cooperation of two leaders of the Jewish community. One of those leaders, Rabbi Koretz, became almost equivalent to the infamous Rumkowski of Lodz in his power and authority. Soothing Salonika's Jews with German stories of resettlement in Crakow, Koretz managed to convince them to cooperate in the deportations. He, of course, was among the last to go. Two sources report on his fate: one, Molho, writes that Koretz died en route to Bergen Belsen. The other speculates that he died of typhus at Bergen Belsen shortly after liberation (Nehama, 1948; Roth, 1950).

Here is a survivor from Salonika, among the first to arrive at Auschwitz, commenting on Rabbi Koretz. When asked if he remembered the rabbi, he recoiled in surprise. Presumably he had not heard the name, or thought of the man for forty years.

> Sure I remember him! He was a German Jew. He became the leader of the Jews. Salonik trusted him . . . he ran back and forth to the Germans and told us not to worry.
>
> We killed him.

(Interviewer: "What do you mean? Who killed him?")

> I told you—<u>we</u> killed him. When I met the last train from Salonik [at Auschwitz] the Jews told me. They murdered him on the train. We killed him (UM, 53-83-01A)

It seems clear that the murder of Rabbi Koretz is of some importance to this man. It reclaims some independence, vengeance or justice for the Jews of Salonika in his eyes. Why this is so remains a significant issue. But of interest here are the conflicting historical events. Rabbi Koretz died. Perhaps that remains the most salient historical point. Yet, how did he die and where? By whose hand? Which source is the more trustworthy? Like the issue of "administrative massacres" so adamantly rejected by some survivors, historical questions like this one relate to the sometimes faulty perceptions, partial observations or interpretations of eye witnesses. Forty years have passed; the story of Rabbi Koretz came to the survivor second hand. Mythmaking may have begun—must have begun. Survivors' voices are incomplete in more ways than one, not least of all, because they are sometimes historically uninformed. But students of the Holocaust do not listen to survivors to learn about historical facts.

Beyond the question of survivors' knowledge of the history of the Holocaust lurk suspicions about credibility and intention. On camera, whether in a studio or a home, a speaker transforms into a performer.[1] Lawrence Langer recently commented upon a phenomenon he has witnessed viewing the Yale tapes. Langer has voiced what many commentators feared to express, the impact of the intrusion of the camera, the technician, and/or the interviewer in this artificial, media situation. Survivors prepare for their interviewers in a variety of ways: some write their thoughts down, others bring notes or pictures; some bring tapes they have made on their own and offer them as substitutes. All of them think, remember, try to organize events in their minds for days prior to the interviews. They continue to rehash their testimonies long after their interviews, sometimes calling the interviewers to continue. Their presentations vary in drama; some resolutely eschew all emotion, determined to retell experiences that permitted no emotion while they were happening. Others listen to themselves as if for the first time, pausing to analyze their own sentences:

> [We returned to Plaszow and they started loading us on cattle trains.] My brother . . . both brothers . . . and my father . . . [long pause] Yes. Yes, they were loading us all on the cattle train. Yes. Starting to evacuate Plaszow (53-87-32V)

"Yes. Yes." As if he has confirmed the memory to himself, been reassured of its accuracy, and, remarkable to imagine, he has perhaps realized for the first time what the Germans were doing and how it related to his own experience: "Yes . . . [they were] starting to evacuate Plaszow." I am not suggesting any guile or deliberate dramatics here—the narrative forms usually emerge spontaneously. In this particular case, the interview was conducted on audio tape. Nathan O. intermittently slipped into the past, <u>recalling but not retelling</u> surrounding circumstances perhaps too painful to speak, to reenvision, to hear and observe.

A sense of revelation or discovery intermittently passed over him. He had thought about these events every day, fleetingly—"Not a day goes by when something doesn't remind you of your experience. [Slowly and deliberately] It's always with you, you can never forget it; it's always in the back of your mind"—yet not systematically or historically.

As he unfolded his story for the first time, as incomplete as it may have been, he realized more fully what he and his family had endured. That realization produced a profound sadness in him that transcended any he had felt before. This narrative form of discovery arose spontaneously with some prodding from the interviewer who posed specific questions about specific places and people ("Do you remember Josephinska Street?" or "Had you heard of Dr. Bieberstein?" or "Can you describe the scene at Plasz Szgoda?"). At critical junctures in the narrative, Nathan O. would speak a word or phrase, pause, stare fixedly and continue, often punctuating his comments with "yes, yes." Those affirmations appear as confirmations of his thoughts: first the silent recollection, then the "yes, yes" and then the telling, in rapid bursts of words followed again by pauses.

---

[1] This is less the case in audiotaped interviews which are usually longer, reveal more information, and, because they may continue for several sessions, often produce more straightforward comments.

Similarly, this woman from Lodz spoke with simple eloquence, pausing to measure her memories against her words:

> That journey took probably two or three days. [Pause] And there were no sanitary conditions or anything. It was crying and pushing and screaming and my mother tried to get us together and keep us calm but it was impossible . . . And maybe after a day or two—don't remember how long that journey took—we arrived [pause] and I call it Auschwitz now (UM, 53-85-05V).

There can be no substitute for the listening. Transcriptions of such testimonies do them an injustice—tones, whispers, rhythm, hesitations, strained voices are lost. Ruth K. remained precariously on the brink of tears, yet with persistent control. Time remains problematic here—were they in the cattle car one day or three—and she passes over her mother's failure to keep the children together and calm ("but it was impossible") thereby avoiding discussing separation and perhaps panic, but the conclusion appears most revealing: "I call it Auschwitz now." That sentence reflects premeditation, careful thought. Mrs. K. wanted to make a point about how little she and her family knew about their destination. Auschwitz might have been another world, unheard of then, but "Auschwitz now" conveys the fear and bewilderment of the experience in a distant, adult perception that remains, as she notes, "like an echo" of "Auschwitz then."

Critical tools that might be brought to bear on written texts frequently prove inadequate for critical analysis of oral texts. Voices, tone, pitch, pauses, croaks, whispers, sobs, sighs transform these texts in ways ungraspable for literary criticism. Silences often speak more eloquently than words in many survivor testimonies; pauses convey welters of meanings; whispers signify a broad variety of innuendoes; tone of voice produces multiple referents. The listener must be aware of these peculiarities and able to contextualize them. This contextualization requires historical awareness, a sense of Jewish culture and some prior knowledge of the Holocaust if only because listening without context easily distorts the importance and significance of the testimonies, threatens to reduce those narratives to emotional, non-reflective exercises in pity.

If historical consciousness and context open up some greater appreciation of the testimonies, most central to properly critical listening is the recognition of the polysemy of the language—the multiple meanings of individual words—and the requirement that the listener focus on the semantic level of the narratives, on the words as "jealously independent" conveyors of meaning. In this respect, survivor testimonies resemble poetic narratives, or dream interpretations in which specific words become the critical elements apart from their positions in sentences or paragraphs or the longer narratives.

Those words, like "barbarian," act like emblems, full of emotional and other meanings. Their verbal expression might cause a flood of associative memories; a flood of such magnitude that in order to assimilate it survivors frequently (not always) react in one of two ways: silence or what often appears to be chaotic, rapid and intense discourse. What follows are excerpts from the testimony of Milech from Volovo, in Sub-Carpathian Ruthenia (Hungarian occupied Czechoslovakia after 1939). His audiotaped interview totalled twenty-five hours over eight sessions. Numerous themes emerged from Milech's discursive narrative which, upon reflection, revealed surprising unity despite the apparent rambling, jokes, and digressions.

> [In the ghetto], again, remember, I'm only fourteen . . . And I find out my mother got pregnant with the fifth child. I knew that child would not do us any good [there couldn't be enough] food or care. But I didn't sit her down and say 'Hey, Mother . . .' I just knew, <u>at age 14</u>, the child was there. [There was] no one to discuss it with. I'm all of 14 . . . I'm watching long, long trains; boarded up cattle cars every day go by. I was only 14. I see a few people looking through barbed wire on the windows . . . Keep in mind, <u>I am 14 years old</u>. I understand it at 56. But at 14, nobody explained anything before, during or after.
>
> [They marched us to the train station.] The Germans, in full gear. Angels, God's emissaries would look like those Germans. Again, I look at them at age 14. But their helmets shine, uniforms immaculate, boots, guns, bayonets. They were gods—<u>not</u> messengers of God, they <u>were</u> God.
>
> Shooting, beating, running to the trains.] I didn't think anything. To me—I was watching a movie. Nobody <u>said</u> anything to me. I'm still only 14. I was a grown-up at 14.

I was blank. A 14 year old boy going on a trip. The older people had their apprehensions, I didn't have any apprehensions. I had no fear, no sorrow, no . . . [pause] I was elated, I was part of the package—I happened to be there.

[The doors opened at Birkenau.] Chaos! Chaos! . . . Schnell! Raus! Screaming! Hollering! But, again, I am 14. It was nothing for me to jump down to the ground. [Lowers voice] I don't know if my father helped my mother down to the ground.

I don't remember seeing my mother. But I hear her words. She said to my father: "Los Milech geh mit dir [let Milech go with you] and I'll go with the children."

I'm near my father. Whether I held his hand or I didn't I don't remember. Some guy asks my father "Is this your son? How old is he?" "14." Not like I'm talking to you! Clandestine. He's doing his work, he's not allowed to talk. "Tell him he's 16."

A German officer; white gloves, a beautiful interview [sarcasm]. Most of the people he looked over like a horse; directing traffic—didn't talk. "Wie alt bist du? "16." "Kannst du arbeiten?" Not like a conversation. [Repeats the exchange in sharp, abrupt, loud exclamations.] He wasn't happy to let me through. He figured let the kapo or the Vorarbeiter kill him (UM, 53-85-01-05A).

At the start of Milech's interview, the interviewer asked what he remembered about life in Volovo before the war. Although Milech would return repeatedly to anecdotes about his life before the war, this initial question elicited a brief statement in which he described public schools, cheder, his village, the number of Jewish families and after five minutes concluded with "When they took us away in 1944 I was 14."

Articulate, expansive and thoughtful, Milech cannot escape his preoccupation with his age at the time of his deportation to Auschwitz. Recognizing that he is a rarity, a relatively young survivor of Auschwitz, Buchenwald and Dora, he dwells on this topic throughout the 25 hours. These few excerpts reveal hidden resentment, anger, bitterness, frustration, bewilderment: condensed, compacted into tightly packed anecdotes. His pregnant mother depressed and puzzled him; God had abandoned him and taken the form of SS guards, "angels, God's emissaries . . . not messengers of God, they were God"; his elders abandoned him to the arbitrary whims of some randomized procedure, "Nobody said anything to me." Perhaps he feels some guilt for disregarding not only his parents at critical moments like the arrival at Auschwitz, but his siblings as well; bewilderment and anger first toward his mother who sent him away to be with his father, thus saving his life, and then toward his father who seemed to have quickly lost his reason and will to live. Perhaps most baffling is the coldness with which he describes his "interview" with Mengele, the "angel of God"—a deliberate variation on the usual "angel of death"—who harshly questioned Milech and then spared him. There are, of course, countless other examples of confusion, ambivalence, anger, depression, guilt.

For such a man, who until recently refused to speak or was rejected by others, looms one overwhelming question: how will he speak of such feelings, experiences, memories? There is never enough time, never the proper words, never the right sequence of events, never enough calm or composure. And yet Milech refuses to give up: one more interview, one more tape, one more videotape and the story will be more meaningful as he simultaneously confronts the realization that the story cannot be told more meaningfully.

While Milech's preoccupation with his age reflects a common concern of survivors who were "child survivors," I believe he demonstrates a fundamental principle of survivor testimonies. His age, the word "fourteen" becomes an emblem for all the experiences he remembers. He speaks the number and a flood of memories overtakes him. Those memories tend to stultify most survivors—thus, the long silences, choking the words which rush together. When Milech says "I was only 14," he instantaneously reexperiences that age. Every age is measured against that one: "I'm 57 now. Now I want to be younger. At 14 I wanted to be older." And the word itself carries indelible, tightly bound associations. When asked how he felt as a 14 year old on what he described as "those wooden shelves in the barracks" his response is quick, almost hostile:

> What I felt on those shelves? Remember, I am 14. You could ask me what did I feel any place. How did I feel when I saw people hanging, how did I feel when I saw people being beaten to death, [faster and louder] how did I feel when I saw piles of dead bodies and I knew the pile had to be a certain height until the truck comes to take them? How did I feel when I saw my father in that pile and I maybe would have liked to go and take one more look but I know if I go near him I'll be killed—at 14? There was no time for feelings. No time for all these normal things . . . What did I feel [pauses, exhales and sighs] that I couldn't even say good-bye to my brother and sister and my mother (UM, 53-85-04A)?

All this encapsulated in and decanted from the number, the age fourteen. "I was fourteen" prefaces such lists, such rapid memories; contains them.

Were the transcriptions of these interviews assigned reading to a class studying the history of the Holocaust, they could be read as literary resources and thus with critical skills that apply to other works of literature. Whenever the number fourteen appeared in Milech's transcript, it would signal deep structures at work, subterranean forces that evoke vivid, crowded memories. To listen to this testimony is to recognize that the memories come faster than they can be spoken, and they virtually spill forth from Milech in rapid, often disconnected spurts or bursts not unlike the testimony of Nathan O. Pauses interrupt those bursts or clumps of words; thoughtful hiatuses during which Milech seems to be assessing and reassessing what he has spoken.

This halting, erratic rhythm echoes that of many survivors. Examining oral testimonies means listening to rhythms as well as words; to patterns of silence, to patterns of hesitation and intonation. What lies beneath the surface? Are there signposts in the tones, in the specific words, that might guide a listener to deeper appreciation of the victims' experiences? Why such bursts and such pauses? It ought not be surprising that painful memories are related with painful pauses: there are obvious efforts to maintain control of emotions, to choke back tears, to suppress anger or despair. Yet one cannot help but be struck by the unusual patterns of speech, the rhythms of narrative. I would like to suggest another text that might provide some explanation and direction for a better appreciation of survivor narrative forms.

In her work with pre-civilized cultures, anthropologist Dorothy Lee explored a linguistic phenomenon that had been briefly characterized by her mentor Bronislaw Malinowski. Malinowski had described the speech of the Trobriand Islanders as coming in "bursts or aggregates of words" which were followed by long pauses or silences. Lee pursued this observation further and discovered underlying, structural motifs to Trobriand and other, similar "primitive" languages. First, there appeared to be very few verbs and adjectives and a disproportionately large number of nouns. Second, the pauses served the purpose of allowing both listener and speaker to reflect on the aggregate or burst of words just spoken (Lee, 1959).

Those nouns served as poetic carriers of multiple meanings. When one speaks of "full" words in this context, the reference surpasses an abstract description of poetic symbolism. This form of "poetic diction" implies that each noun conveys several meanings, is full of meanings which have accrued historically, culturally and experientially to the word. Thus a particular tree might simultaneously act as referent for the tree itself, a tribal totem, a grandmother or other ancestor and simultaneously evoke memories of that spot, that tribe, that grandmother. These are historical memories that connect to group and individual acts and thoughts. That tree, then, stimulates a congeries of ideas and associated histories whenever the name is spoken. No need, then, for many verbs or adjectives because the noun embodies the descriptive and active elements contained in the full images.

Such dense language, with each individual word potentially full of meanings (the number increasing through time), demands thoughtful listening, slow listening. At the semantic level, i.e. the consideration of individual words, whole narratives are transmitted in the nouns. It becomes necessary to pause and think of the collection of narratives communicated by only a few words. Were the language to be written, some individual words might express the equivalent of pages of non-poetic diction in which meanings are conveyed through sentences placed into paragraphs which are then arranged into narratives. As in Trobriand and other archaic speech, words contain worlds. Those pauses between the bursts of nouns, between signifiers of holistic experiences, allow all those engaged in listening and speaking to assimilate and ponder, and perhaps expand, the meanings of particular words. It is worth repeating that such words fill up from historical experience that is both individual and collective. The group has the experience and collective memory of its tree, and each individual has his/her specific experience and affective memory of the tree.

I think this model of packed language, of poetic diction, which has been elaborated further by such linguistic analysts as Marvin Bram, Owen Barfield, Gaston Bachelard, Sigmund Freud, and writers like James Joyce and Thomas Mann, provides some direction for a poetics of survivor narratives. Barfield and Bachelard considered enlivening, collective diction. Bachelard's "poetic reveries" function on linguistic planes with words touching off warm and life enhancing associations (similar to Proust's). Barfield's discussions of communal meanings that are exclusive to specific groups rests on shared experiences captured in and denoted by specific words (Bachelard, 19 ; Barfield, 19). None of them anticipated the depth of sadness that poetic emblems could communicate to an unimaginably vast community that shared complete loss and totally debilitating memories. "Fourteen" cannot transmit the collection of meanings that it holds for Milech to anyone else except, perhaps, another child survivor; and uttering that word <u>automatically</u> evokes those meanings which virtually demand thoughtful reconsideration, silence.

That silence is as full as the spoken word. Here is another example in a brief discourse on "Appell":

> The word 'Appell': you heard it a million times. You're a professor, but for me to explain that word . . . [pauses] <u>You</u> didn't stand 3-4 hours in that Appellplatz. You could hear that word a million times, [long pause, nearly a full minute] you'll never know what it means (UM, 53-85-04A).

This categorical denial from a victim of literally hundreds of Appells was followed by a series of memories related in fragments:

> 103 fever next to you . . . raining or freezing or sun . . . I'm always in front . . . the dead in front . . . the Blockaeltester counts and reports to the SS officer [repeats the exact words of the report] . . . those numbers 'Block number eins ein und vierzig is standing' . . . then 'Achtung! Das [sic] ganze Stube stand—Muetzen—auf! Augen rechts!' . . . and lice, lice, lice, lice, lice . . . (UM, 53-85-04A).

What transpired during the silent pauses before this man's accusations that "<u>You</u> didn't stand 3-4 hours" and "you'll never know what it means"? During those pauses he searched for a way to explain the meaning of "Appell." His mind began scanning possible definitions, some means to convey exactly what an Appell entailed. Realizing again that such a search would be futile, he frustratedly acknowledged defeat and in an unmistakably accusatory tone apprises the interviewer of an inability to know. Yet, even having given up the attempt, he pursues a definition of sorts, one composed entirely of exemplary images.

Two words, "fourteen" and "Appell," each defined by a series of examples, not by a dictionary definition, demanding associations that only the survivor can make and which lead to other, more devastating associations which grow more particular and detailed until he/she must stop. What is the point? Who can understand? Here is Milech again on two other words:

> [After the selection we were herded into a huge room and received our uniforms.] They throw your clothes at you. One guy a union suit, another guy a jacket . . . a pair of pants . . . cap . . . shoes and belt. I got everything a human being could want. [Sarcastically] I could belong to eight country clubs . . . No pockets—but—what do you need pockets for? [Pause, thoughtful and quieter] You don't need pockets.
>
> [After the arrival at Auschwitz] they opened those doors . . . It was a <u>sealed car of people</u> [pause] like furniture or mattresses (UM, 53-85-05-06A).

Difficult to imagine, every time Milech reaches in his pocket he reexperiences that "huge room" at Auschwitz-Birkenau, replete with its pandemonium and clothes. And every time he sees a mattress, he returns to the "sealed car of people." Milech sells furniture; specializes in mattresses.

When survivors stop in the middle of a sentence, or speak in incomplete sentences, they frequently become introspective, remembering, even reliving one or more experiences. When they appear to reaffirm their own recollections, as Nathan O. or Ruth K., they are reevaluating those memories. When they are reluctant to speak of their pre-war lives it may be because those memories are immediately cathected by memories of the destruction of their families and the fates of their worlds during the Holocaust. When one survivor after another refers to the memories which remain perpetually "in the back of your mind" they testify to the fragility of the normalcy they have constructed and the persistence of associations triggered by mattresses or fourteen year old boys, by pockets or God—or by words like barbarian and civilized.

A poetics of survivor narratives implies creating meaning in part by creating order from seemingly random series of words or fortuitous events. It implies, too, practicing critical analysis by evaluating the words and placing them within a particular historical and experiential context. Just as readers encounter difficulties in evaluating a text outside of its social and historical context, so, too, with listeners of Holocaust narratives. Gaining historical background and listening to many testimonies remain essential. If Holocaust students, scholars and educators become more aware that a fullness hides beneath the words, become attuned to motifs within poetic emblems, a deeper appreciation of the experiences of the victims might become possible. That demands what any significant text demands of a serious reader/listener: meticulously alert listening, an exacting attentiveness both sympathetic and critical.

ACKNOWLEDGMENT

The author presented a draft of this paper before the Scholars' Forum of the Ecumenical Institute of Detroit. The suggestions from that group, as usual, were constructive and generative.

REFERENCES

Barfield, Owen (1973). Poetic Diction: A Study in Meaning. Wesleyan University Press.

Bachelard, Gaston (1969). The Poetics of Reverie Beacon Press.

Hilberg, Raul (1978). In: Social Education.

Lanzmann, Claude (1985). Shoah: An Oral History of the Holocaust. Pantheon Books.

Lee, Dorothy (1959). In: Freedom and Culture. Prentice-Hall, Inc. 105-120.

Levi, Primo (1987). The Drowned and the Saved. Summit Books.

Nehama, Josef and Molho, Michael, ed. (1948). In Memoriam—Homage aux victimes juives des Nazis en Grece. Salonika.

Roth, Cecil (1950). Commentary 7, 49-55.

University of Michigan-Dearborn "Holocaust Survivor Collection" of Video and Audio Tapes.

Wiesel, Elie (1979). In: A Jew Today. Vintage, 218-247.

Wiesel, Elie (1981). In: Five Biblical Portraits. University of Notre Dame Press, 66-67.

THE SURVIVOR AS LIVING WITNESS

AN APPROACH TO UNDERSTANDING THE SURVIVOR OF SHOAH FREE FROM HER PSYCHIATRIC LABEL, AND THE IMPACT HER ADAPTATION HAS ON THE CONTEMPORARY WORLD

JUDITH HASSAN

Jewish Welfare Board, 221 Golders Green Road, London, NW11 9DW

The most important lesson from the Nazi holocaust is that it should never happen again. To "make" people watch and hear over and over again the atrocities of those in the camps; in hiding; in ghettoes or fleeing, all of whom are survivors, does little to ensure this goal. Yes, people should know what really happened but this tends to preach to the already converted. For most it is just too painful and so best avoided.

The message is that Hitler's Final Solution failed. There are still living amongst us the witnesses, the survivors - those who against all odds are here to tell the world how they survived. They are not from history books, nor psychiatric cases - they are people who have managed to find meaning in their lives, for example, by creating new families.

I would like to show how, through my early work as a caseworker with survivors, I was influenced by the medico/psychiatric classifications of survivor syndrome - working on such issues as loss of basic trust, helplessness, vulnerability, survivor guilt, delayed mourning, and so on.

Important though this individual work has been in giving elderly survivors a feeling of being heard and understood, it overlooked an important dimension in our role of enabling survivors to find meaning in their survival. I am referring to the healing aspect of mutual aid and social support, particularly in relation to concentration camp survivors.

In the concentration camp, individuals stood a far better chance of surviving if they were part of a pair or group. Reference to the literature on this subject will be made in the following paper as the background to the development of a self-help group for survivors. I had failed to reach these survivors through my individual counselling based in an office.

These survivors are members of the group, not clients or patients. Our focus is on their strengths which helped them to adjust to life after the camps. Their aim is for a future though not forgetting the past. They do not want to be seen as pathetic victims, though their suffering has been immense. They have the determination to bear witness and thereby have an enormous impact on the contemporary world.

INTRODUCTION

My first thoughts when writing are how am I going to do justice to this subject, which will be acceptable to those survivors who are alive today, and also honour those who died in the Shoah? Some would say that this is arrogance on my part to even try. Nevertheless it is a determination borne out of a message I hear over and over again in my work with survivors - "we are not psychiatric cases, we are not pathetic victims only worthy of pity ... we have managed against all odds to make lives for ourselves ... we are the living witnesses of what really happened, and we must let the world know, so that it may never happen again."

I hope my Paper will carry their urgent message. It is this which encourages me to proceed. It is my belief that if one only sees the survivor of Shoah in terms of suffering psychiatric symptoms such as those characterised in "Survivor Syndrome", one is in danger of adhering to the inevitability of Hitler's Final Solution. The "sickness" of the survivor completes the work that the death camps began. This view, I feel, gives a distorted picture of the reality of the survivor's strengths, coping mechanisms and adaptations.

1. FROM AN INCARCERATION IN PSYCHO PATHOLOGY...

At the same time as acknowledging the pain, loss, humiliation and degradation that many survivors suffered, and most would agree still scars them today, one must also, I feel, learn from them about how they survived intact at all. Victor Frankl in his book "Man's Search for Meaning"[1] stresses that the survivor's behaviour can be better understood when we recognise that it was the environment under persecution and in the camps which was abnormal - the survivor's reaction to it was normal. It was a mad world, a world turned upside down, in which the stress and trauma were unimaginable.

With very little outside help and support, the survivors after liberation worked hard, raised families, and generally succeeded extremely well. However, the literature tends to concentrate on those who suffered serious emotional/physical repercussions from their incarceration in the camps, or in hiding, or who suffered persecution to a great extent prior to their enforced expulsion as refugees. Much of this literature relates to clinical cases with an emphasis on psychopathology derived from examinations for compensation claims.

This over-emphasis on pathology tends to be compounded by the eyewitness accounts of survivors themselves. They have felt compelled to tell the world about the atrocities which happened to them - the victimisation, brutalisation, degradation and dehumanisation. Des Pres writes, "As a witness the survivor aims above all to convey the otherness of the camp, their specifie inhumanity ... acts of care and decency seem so out of place in the camps that survivors themselves are perplexed .. in the larger picture the image of viciousness and death grows to such an enormous intensity that all else - any sign of elementary humanness - pales to insignificance".[2]

The will to bear witness by the survivor - the going over again and again what happened - has in turn been interpreted as some form of neurotic behaviour. Des Pres points out that psychiatric treatment is directed towards processes of "adjustment, acceptance, forgetting".[3] However, these psychiatric goals are at variance with the survivor's goal to remember so that others will not forget. The survivor's need to hold on to his past to preserve a future, not only for himself but the community, therefore presents problems for the traditional psychiatrist, "To assume that the need to bear witness is rooted in neurosis is to ignore entirely the nature of extreme experience".[4]

This misinterpretation of the survivor's need to bear witness is exposed strongly by Shamai Davidson. There is indeed a conflict, he notes, between the survivor's longing to forget, and a commitment to remember and bear witness. In the world of the survivor bearing witness is an essential part of healing. "He needs to be heard and to be believed within the framework of the social community in order to feel recognition and validity for his experiences and for his having succeeded in the struggle to survive".[5]

This view contrasts strongly with Krystal's argument that self-healing and self-integration is at odds with the necessity for survivors to be "angry witnesses against the outrage of the Holocaust".[6] He felt he had failed to help elderly survivors achieve integration following their massive losses for this could not be done without the completion of mourning. A sense of hopelessness on the part of the survivor, and an inability to help on his part led to a rather pessimistic conclusion. He saw the survivor as locked in his anger unable to accept his past. "The answer is", he writes, "it must be accepted or we must keep waging an internal war against the ghosts of our past".[7] He notes that acceptance by survivors of what happened somehow justifies Nazism and all the evil they had been through.

(1) Frankl, V., Man's Search for Meaning P.18
(2) des Pres, T., The Survivor P.98-99
(3) des Pres, T., The Survivor P.39
(4) des Pres, T., The Survivor P.42
(5) Davidson, S., On Relating to Traumatised/Persecuted People 1980 P.56
(6) Krystal, H., Integration & Self-Healing in Post-Traumatic States P.123
(7) Krystal, H., Integration & Self-Healing in Post-Traumatic States P.115

As a therapist/counsellor, it would be difficult and unrealistic to refute Krystal's arguments on the importance of the mourning process. However, it is perhaps arrogance and omnipotence on the part of the therapist which impedes the possibility of healing when applied to survivors. Krystal almost apologises at the end of his article for using "supportive" measures to help survivors and yet it is in this notion of support and sharing that the survivor perhaps finds a more acceptable way of adapting, through an opportunity to bear witness.[1] This theme will be illustrated later in the paper when looking at its application in practice - notably the case studies.

The survivor's needs are clearly not understood by many professionals because the latter are trying to fit the survivor into a framework which is not meaningful to her experience. This can perhaps be illustrated more fully by the term often associated with survivors, namely, "survivor guilt". The psychiatrist and other professionals use the term survivor guilt as a way of seeming to understand and make sense of the survivor's need to talk - for the world to hear the "scream". However, according to des Pres it has not been recognised that the will to bear witness began early in the traumatic experience, not after the event. The guilt for the survivor would be in not bearing witness. Baron in his article on Surviving the Holocaust supports this view. He writes that, "instead of being plagued by personal guilt, the survivor was motivated by a sense of responsibility to the slaughtered who were silenced forever".[2] He calls this a sense of duty not a "disease".

Dorothy Rabinowitz (1976) adds a further dimension to the issue of survivor guilt when she argues that professional workers presupposed that survivors must have felt guilty about surviving because they could only have done so at the expense of others. The consequence of this assumption she states was that survivors "Pressed to respond in the appropriate manner, ... eventually learned to conceal their real opinions and gave the anticipated replies, thinking that no-one would believe them otherwise".[3] Whether one agrees with this statement or not, it makes us as professionals feel uneasy about our power and control. In this context, it is an essential ingredient to feel this discomfort, and to look again at our attitudes and methods of practice if we are to understand the issues related to survivors.

Not only has the professional world weighed heavily in favour of the survivor's "ill health", but the media too reinforces this view. On the one hand, they provide an opportunity for some survivors to tell the public what happened, but those whom they "select" are not necessarily representative of the survivor population. There is again a heavy emphasis on the atrocities, which tends to be heard by the converted few.

I personally feel that the impact of the Shoah on the contemporary world is weakened by the manner in which it is transmitted. Yes, people should know what really happened, and the best way to learn is to talk to survivors. One survivor told me that what hurt most was the fact that no-one wanted to know what had happened in the camps. The survivors were, as des Pres puts it, "disturbers of the peace".[4] This survivor who had suffered severely from frostbite, the result of which caused her to lose fingers and toes, felt compelled to hide the fact about her disability having been caused through brutalisation by the Nazis. She said people had shied away from her when she told the truth - she had received much more sympathy when she said it had happened as the result of an accident.

On the one hand the survivor needs to talk, but, on the other hand, the message needs to be transmitted in such a way that it <u>can</u> be heard. Not only must the survivor find meaning in her survival, but those who were not there must be helped to identify with what happened in the context of today and tomorrow, so that it is meaningful to them too.

2. ...TO LIBERATION IN THE SEARCH FOR MEANING

Changing from the universal survivor to the particular survivor starts a process of creating a more complete and realistic account of the experience of the Shoah. Survivors are in fact you and I, but our experience is drastically different - a point brought home to me sharply by one survivor I am in contact with. When I was speculating with her how I would behave if I was starving and weak, she said that she thought I would not be different to how I am now. Victor Frankl[5] echoes her view when he writes that there remained to the prisoner a "freedom to bear oneself "This way, or that way", and there <u>was</u> a "this or that".

1. Krystal, H., Integration & Self-Healing in Post-Traumatic States P.130
2. Baron, L., Surviving the Holocaust P.33
3. Baron, L., Surviving the Holocaust P.33
4. des Pres, T., The Survivors
5. Frankl, V., Group, Therapeutic Experiences in a Concentration Camp P.83

Starting to see the survivor as an individual helps us to identify with her rather than seeing her either as an alien being, or as some part of an elite. We see that individual variables affected how the survivor coped with the trauma; whether she had a good experience of early childhood relationships; whether she remained with her family during the trauma; whether there was a history of psychiatric disturbance prior to the trauma and so on - all affected the adaptation after the Shoah.

The survivors of the camps tell us that they survived by pure chance. However, how they coped and adapted, during and after, varied. Herein lies the germ of my thesis - that the survivor who finds meaning in her survival has the greatest impact on the contemporary world - not only does it sustain her and give her strength, but others are affected through her adaptation.

3. RELATING THEORY TO PRACTICE

It is this development in my thinking which helped me to break away from the pathological constraints which influenced me early on in my work with survivors. I was able to progress on from Krystal's influence on the impact of massive psychic trauma with its emphasis on how the traumatic process relates to individual intrapsychic events, to a recognition of the importance of the interpersonal dimension - what Shamai Davidson calls "social bonding".[1]

Shamai Davidson develops this observation when he writes, "social bonding could mitigate the destructive process that led to the overwhelming and paralysis of the coping and recuperative resources of the psyche".[2] He goes further to state that such social support was not only important during the camp experience, but was also an important variable in "preventing or modifying the long-term effects of massive psychic trauma as manifested in the Clinical Concentration Camp Syndrome.[3]

It was in this interpersonal bonding and support that human dignity was in some way sustained, and survivors continued with their struggle to live. It is recognition of this essential yet understated dynamic which gives credence to Victor Frankl's quote from Nietsche that, "he who has a <u>why</u> to live for can bear almost any <u>how</u>".[4]

This is perhaps a very grand and dramatic philosophical statement, but what relevance could it possibly have for me as a social worker? My adherence to it could be seen as a rather naive attempt to make me as a professional feel better,rather than being overwhelmed by the trauma of the survivor's past.

Far from being simplistic, I would like to show that this concept of meaning in survival has enabled my work with survivors to progress, and to think more creatively about therapy. It is certainly neater and tidier to be able to diagnose a syndrome into identifiable behaviour, but it proved to be of little value in the social work setting in which I work. In the survivor's world we are rubbing up against chaos and overwhelming feelings of helplessness - a deskilling process some would call it. The professionals tendency has been either to back away with such comments as - "it is over 40 years, we should not try to dig up the past...". Alternatively, we try to classify survivors medically/psychiatrically and thereby labelling them for all time as victims of mental disturbance.

I am neither a doctor nor a psychiatrist. I have two valuable assets at my disposal. One is that I have ears to <u>hear</u> what is really being said by the survivor. Secondly, I have learned to have the <u>courage</u> to face with the survivor who wishes to, the "unfinished business" she brings from the Shoah, in her current encounter with me.

Firstly I would like to develop this theme of how I adapted my model of working with survivors who have come to me individually. Though the language and terminology I use may be all too familiar to the psycho-therapeutically orientated practitioner, I hope I will be able to convey how it is essential to modify this approach to really be in tune with the survivor and her world.

1. Davidson, S, Human Reciprocity among Jewish Prisoners in the Nazi Concentration Camps P.556
2. Davidson, S, Human Reciprocity among Jewish Prisoners in the Nazi Concentration Camps P.563
3. Davidson, S, Human Reciprocity among Jewish Prisoners in the Nazi Concentration Camps P.565
4. Frankl, V, Man's Search for Meaning

I will then go on to show how this approach was only partially meeting the needs of survivors. Though the individual work acknowledged the importance of the survivor's need to find meaning in her survival, it failed to understand certain dimensions which would be more meaningful to the survivor, and would also have greater impact on those around her. Most particularly I am referring to the group dynamic and the importance of self help and interpersonal bonding as the therapeutic medium. It is this later approach with a non-clinical group of survivors, mostly from concentration camps that I have begun to understand the complexity of survivors and how I relate to them.

4. CASE STUDIES

The JWB is an agency which specialises in work with the elderly and mentally ill. The NW Team covers the area in which there is the highest number of survivors living. Survivors do not come to us for counselling related to their holocaust traumatic past, but for any number of presenting problems, mostly related to being elderly or having experienced a current traumatic event such as a bereavement, retirement, loss of health, etc. Like most elderly people, it is also the time of life when they start to reflect on what has happened in their lives. As their short-term memories tend to diminish and their long-term memories become stronger, events from the past have more chance of returning to consciousness.

The first central component when the elderly survivor comes to the agency, is an <u>awareness</u> by the social worker that, in addition to this person's presenting problem, there are other needs which have brought her at that moment in time. Without this awareness, the elderly survivor is not heard or, as is often the case, diagnosed as a paranoid schizophrenic or a hypochondriac, or suffering from psychosomatic problems, with all the associated negative connotations.

CASE STUDY I

Mrs H. was a refugee in her 80's. Most of her family perished in the war. She came to the JWB asking for a volunteer to help her to move. On first contact it seemed to me that her level of anxiety was excessive for the request she was making. This was conveyed to her and we agreed to meet over a period of time to try and understand what had brought her to me at that moment in time. After all, she said she had managed for over 80 years.

Before our meeting, however, she had a road accident and was admitted to hospital. I continued to see her there. Mrs H. refused to be operated on for a fractured leg and, indeed, refused all treatment for infection. The staff in desperation called in a psychiatrist who diagnosed her as paranoid schizophrenic, without taking into account her background.

During her time in hospital, as she lay helpless and vulnerable and unable to move, she began to talk about her past, particularly her persecution under the Nazis. Her current helplessness seemed to reactivate similar feelings she had about being unable to save her mother from being killed whom she left behind. She began to mourn for her mother, which she said she had never done before.

Though she displayed considerable hostility with paranoid features towards the staff, she allowed me to continue to see her regularly. Our relationship was not without difficulty, and I felt I was always walking a fine line between colluding with her paranoid feelings, and becoming yet another persecuting "Nazi" in her eyes by differentiating myself from her.

However, I seemed to convey to her a sense that she was heard and understood, and some feeling of trust developed.

I continued to see her weekly over one and a half years. The move which had brought her to me initially, turned out to be an eviction - a traumatic enough event at any time, but for her it was also a reminder of her enforced "eviction" from Germany as a refugee. Mrs H. was able to share with me her real fear of breaking down-mentally and being admitted to psychiatric hospital. This did not happen, though she came very close to it. She made a successful move to new accommodation, thereby avoiding the trauma of eviction.

However, once the crisis was over, Mrs H's defences re-emerged. What she found so difficult to acknowledge was that through our relationship I had become significant to her. Once more in control of events, she defended herself against the feelings of vulnerability and helplessness, firstly by trying to use my sessions with her to do practical tasks which the local authority worker was already doing, and secondly by rejecting me altogether. Dr Hillel Klein has noted that this "fear of getting to love someone" is not uncommon in survivors of the holocaust.[1]

Understanding the reality base of her paranoia rather than labelling her as psychiatrically ill, allowed us an opportunity to struggle with the fears and anxieties I had initially felt at our first meeting. Mrs H. was a highly intelligent, articulate woman who internalised something from what transpired in our sessions. Despite a great deal of denial concerning the connections made between current and past trauma, we were able to work through some of the "unfinished business", which had contributed to her vulnerability and sense of aloneness.

Entering into Mrs H's world gave me a unique opportunity to learn how to relate to someone who, in another setting, would be labelled as paranoid, and consequently seen as having impaired ability to relate. Mrs H. had been touched by a "mad" environment under the Nazis. She may have had some disturbance prior to this period, but there is no doubt that the reality of what she experienced affected her ability to trust. Despite her "paranoia" she had amazing support from neighbours and friends as well as social services. There was a warmth that emanated from her and it was these strengths that I tended to build on.

I could have so easily just seen Mrs H. as yet another victim of Nazi persecution perhaps feeling that it is not surprising she is as she is considering what she has been through. Consequently, I might have tried to make reparation to her through practical provision and giving as much emotional comfort as possible. However, it was in the struggle and fight which constituted our work together, which I believe helped Mrs H. to break out from the "victim" category. It may have helped her to experience again a feeling of being in control of events so that her current trauma did not overwhelm her.

Mrs H's other agenda was to tell her "story" so that someone would know what really happened. Interestingly, during the course of our meetings, Mrs H's son came from the USA to visit his mother for the first time in many years. He had written to her that he had wanted to know more about what had happened to her and her family, and wanted to help her to write it down.

The survivor who feels they can tell their story because they believe that it will be heard and thereby transmitted, can sometimes unburden themselves dramatically. This may make great demands on the social worker, who often becomes the sole means for passing this on - it demands availability by the social worker to the survivor to an extent possibly not encountered with other clients.

The second case study will show how when this is empathetically handled, the survivor frees herself from her need to stay alive to maintain the memory of those who perished.

CASE STUDY II

Mrs A. was a woman in her 80's who came to this country on a domestic permit just prior to the war. She managed to make a life for herself, but her health was impoverished through severe attacks of asthma.

The social worker visited her at her request because of her feelings of isolation and depression. In her attempts to understand these feelings, it emerged that this survivor felt increasingly badly about not having done enough to save her family who were killed in concentration camps.

On the surface this seemed like an "ideal case" - the client wishing to talk about what had happened, and feeling helped by the social worker's visits. However, it was not so simple. The social worker was idealised by this client, the latter becoming very dependent on her. The social worker on her part felt this client had suffered so much, but feared she was encouraging the client to be too dependent on her, and perhaps should not see her so often.

1. Klein, Dr.H., Massive Psychic Trauma. P.233

She feared the power the client invested in her for a "cure", and hence her tendency to want to withdraw, rationalising this as the client not really needing her that much - she had after all quite a network of friends.

However, when the countertransference factors were looked at, the social worker could see how she was reacting, and continued seeing Mrs A. Mrs A. was gradually able to tell her story, and the cosy nature of the earlier encounters developed to expressions of anger mixed with love for the social worker, who undertook this journey back with her.

Mrs A. had told the social worker that she had wanted to die but was not able to. The social worker's acceptance of Mrs A's strengths and weaknesses and her belief in her worth and dignity, enabled her to unburden herself of the "secrets" she had carried inside her. The work ended by Mrs A. dying peacefully, knowing that she would live on through her contact with the social worker. Medically, no cause of death could be ascertained - it was certainly not her asthma which directly led to her death. The social worker believed that their work together was a rehearsal for Mrs A's day of judgement - if the worker whom she revered so much could accept her with all her faults, then perhaps G-d would judge her kindly.

Individual and group support for the professional helps to sustain her in a role in which she is neither the persecuting authority figure nor the idealised saviour. Her task is to contain, but also be touched by what the survivor is telling her; to be knowledgeable about the Shoah, and yet to learn from each encounter with a survivor; to project a feeling of humility in not knowing at times while, at the same time, maintaining a sense of confidence in her professional self to sustain the encounter.

5. FROM THE MISSING DIMENSION... INTERPERSONAL BONDING, HUMANITY AND DIGNITY

These two case studies illustrate ways in which survivors can individually be helped to find meaning in their survival. I believe this work is important, but it is also dependent on the survivor's willingness to enter a relationship of being a client, with all its associated feelings of vulnerability. I became increasingly aware that we were only touching the tip of the iceberg. Despite a good deal of publicity about our work, relatively few survivors came to our organisation for help. I was also aware of the fact that those who did, tended to be those who had come as refugees in the 1930's. One would have expected, according to the literature, that the concentration camp survivors would be in greater need of professional help.

This was a grave misunderstanding on my part. I have subsequently learned through my contact with concentration camp survivors why they kept their distance from our professional organisation - anger towards the Jewish community for not having done enough to help them when they needed it after liberation; the indifference of Jews towards their suffering; their feelings towards authority and institutions; their fears of weakness and vulnerability which asking for help would imply. Factors such as these meant that the organisation became for me a fortress, with the survivor outside and myself locked inside.

To escape meant a giant leap for me professionally. The opportunity came when a concentration camp survivor came to see me having been given my name through the Elah organisation in Israel. What I heard from her was that she knew several other survivors who wanted to come together in a group. They did not want therapy, but to help each other mutually. They would not need to explain or justify why they were there. There was an urgency to come together.

As one survivor told me recently, "more than the physical atrocities that were perpetrated towards us, the Nazis wanted to rob us of our dignity. I had to keep my dignity at all costs if I was to survive, and that I decided to do when I entered Auschwitz".

To preserve the survivor's dignity became an essential part of my approach, but I needed to understand what this meant in terms of the camp experience. Instead of the comfort of my usual professional role, I have to face constant role conflicts and paradoxes in trying to enable this survivor's group to get off the ground - being there as a catalyst, but leaving space for the survivors to find their own way; hearing the hidden agendas, but using the survivors to draw these out rather than my interpretating them; acknowledging my own identity as a professional, but allowing the survivors to use my presence in a way acceptable to them - often this includes a more informal/social role.

The camp presented constant paradoxes which my own role was possibly reflecting - not just those of good/evil, victim/oppressor; passive/aggressive, etc, but what Eli Pfefferkorn[1] in his critique of Bettleheim focuses on, namely the individual surviving for himself as proposed by Bettleheim, and the prisoner surviving through mutually supportive relationships with other prisoners. A paradox also observed by Elie Wiesel in "Night".

Through my participation in the group, I was hitting up against my "old" role as an individual "therapist" and my new role as an "honorary member" of the group which had accepted me despite not personally being a survivor. To survive I had to adapt.

What challenges us most I believe, the ones who were not there, is the acknowledgement of the power of human beings to transcend the evil environment through acts of humanity. The importance of human reciprocity tends to get overlooked because what we see on the whole are not great acts of heroism in the camps, but small acts of caring which helped to make life a bit more bearable. The significance of this, however, has tremendous influence on our professional practice and on our understanding of the survivor's adaptation, and consequently deserves to be looked at in more depth. It counteracts the view postulated that survivors must have "done something" in order to survive - the implication being that it was done at the expense of others. Emphasis on the kapos and sonderkommandos is well known - a parallel often being drawn between these prisoners and the Nazi perpetrators. Certainly under extreme conditions human beings can degenerate into cruel monsters. If all the prisoners had reacted in this way, then the Nazis would have done their job very thoroughly. The fact of the matter is that this was not the case - out of evil good deeds can be born, but the choices involved are immense.

One survivor told me how she had been selected to be a kapo. However, she knew what was expected, and yet the people she would have been assigned to were already weak. She could not add to their suffering. She refused to take on this "privilege" but, at the same time, knew she may thereby have been enabled to save her sister from being killed. She had been sustained through the support of her fellow prisoners, and she could not debase herself so far.

"Mutual aid constituted the key to survival in the camps. After overcoming the initial shock of being tossed into such debilitating circumstances, the prisoner gradually realised the struggle was a collective one".[2] One survivor who was a very young child in Theresienstadt remembered how the children he was together with in the camp shared everything. Even after their arrival in England none would eat unless they all had something to eat.

On the other hand, another survivor told me that he survived by fending for himself. However, he quietly also told me how he had helped to keep a fellow prisoner alive during one of the journeys between camps in the cattle trucks. They remained in touch with each other after the war - this man owing him his life.

Yet so little is made of the act of heroism and humanity by this survivor. Terrence des Pres in his enlightened work "The Survivor - An Atonomy of Life in the Death Camps", particularly in his chapter "Life in death", tries to redress the balance, so that these "small gestures of kindness" as Baron[3] calls them are given full credit and importance. Shamai Davidson too devotes a Paper on Human Reciprocity[4] among Jewish prisoners in the camps, to highlight how essential this aspect is to our understanding of survival and adaptation.

Kitty Hart (I Am Alive 1962), Eugene Heimler (Resistance Against Tyranny 1966), Elie Wiesel, Richard Glazer a Treblinka survivor, amongst many others, all maintained that they could not have survived alone. The position of the Greek Jews in the camps adds to this argument. They spoke a different language and came from a very different culture to the majority of those in the camps. It was very difficult for them to be incorporated into groups, and their survival rate was extremely poor.

1. Pfefferkorn, E, The Case of Bruno Bettelheim and Nina Wertmuller's Seven Beauties P.663-668
2. Baron, L., Surviving The Holocaust P.27
3. Baron, L., Surviving The Holocaust P.27
4. Davidson, S, Human Reciprocity Among Jewish Prisoners In The Nazi Concentration Camp

The more prisoners were moved about the more difficult it was to keep these bonds going, though even in the extreme conditions of the death marches "some degree of sharing and cooperation was maintained or re-emerged.[1] "United we stand, divided we fall!",[2] Baron says is the overriding imperative of survival. Des Pres develops this "teamwork"[3] aspect when talking about the importance of "organising" - for example, sharing out clothes and food in order to survive. "In extremity life depends on solidarity for collective action is more effective than individual effort".[4]

S Davidson goes further to say that it was not only the solidarity in the camp which sustained the prisoners, but that, "the memory of the solidarity of mutual support in the Nazi concentration camp, where death was almost inevitable, accompanies the survivor throughout his life cycle as a sustaining and humanising influence".[5]

This was interestingly put into perspective by another survivor I have spoken to who did not go through a concentration camp. She left Germany as a young girl having to leave her family behind. The emotion she felt most strongly, and which stays with her today, was an acute sense of isolation. She told me that in a way she would have been better off in a camp, at least that way she would have been with others like herself.

6. ...TO THE LINK IN THE CHAIN - PAST, PRESENT AND FUTURE

In the current situation, the survivor is now reaching middle to late middle age - retirement, loss of health, divorce, bereavement or some other traumatic experience often brings back a sense of vulnerability - a re-awakening of a feeling prominent during the concentration camp experience. To turn to professional help at that moment would serve to reinforce the survivor's fear of weakness, and in the camp experience, subsequent death. Far better then to return to the "old" experience of mutual help to cope with the trauma.

However, Ruth Jaffe in her article on "Group Activity and a Defence Method in Concentration Camps", questions this view. Whilst supporting the functional nature of groups in the camps, she found them to become dysfunctional in terms of later behaviour, and indeed to have a negative effect on adjustment after liberation. Clinging to the importance of the group in the camp she thought, interfered with the survivor's ability to make new relationships. Thus in her view, it would seem that going back to a group of survivors for support would be an acknowledgement of the current non-coping behaviour of the survivor.

It is not enough for me to say that in my view the case material Ruth Jaffe brings is inadequate to support her theory. The limitations of what she claims stems from the need to return always to the past. For the group to have meaning for the survivor today, it must deal with the current trauma by relating it to a present and a future as well as linking it to the past. In contrast to Ruth Jaffe's view, Shamai Davidson advocates self-help survivor groups as a functional way of helping to free the survivor from her "victim" past, to one of being in control and shaping the future so that it may never happen again.

Eugene Heimler highlights this in an article based on his experience as a camp survivor "Forty Years On" (1985). "And if I reflect: talking about the past only belongs to the past, whilst doing something about the present belongs to the future". Whilst acknowledging the importance of remembering the past and bearing witness, the hate and anger need to be transformed. Heimler is able to conclude that "my memories are alive, but my hate has gone"... If those of us who survived the camps limit ourselves to grieving only over our tragedy, harbouring a continuous depression or anger, then we will not do justice to the magnitude of the tragedy, and will fail even to try and turn it into a healing experience ... we have to speak not only of the pain of yesterday, but of the lessons of tomorrow".[6]

1. Davidson, S, Article on Human Reciprocity P.560 refers to Elmer Luchterhand's Work: Prisoner Behaviour & Social System In The Nazi Camp - Int. J. of Psych., Vol.13 1967 P.245-264
2. Baron, L., Surviving The Holocaust P.27
3. des Pres, T, The Survivor P.22
4. Frankl, V., Man's Search For Meaning P.121
5. Davidson, S, Human Reciprocity Among Jewish Prisoners In The Nazi Concentration Camps P.571
6. Heimler, E., Forty Years On (Manna 1985)

7. THE SURVIVORS OF SHOAH GROUP - RELATING PRACTICE TO THEORY

Self help formed the basis of the "Survivors of Shoah" which I have been privileged to be part of. The naming of the group was an important focus when they began, in giving these heterogeneous survivors a sense of belonging and identity. Their uniting bond was that they had all "been there" - they had all been through something unimaginable, and they were all witnesses. Though the majority were in camps, there was an acceptance of the suffering of those in hiding, living under false papers, or who came in the late 1930's as persecuted refugees.

Through their aims and objectives, we see a mirroring of those described by Shamai Davidson of groups in concentration camps. (See Human reciprocity among Jewish prisoners in the camps). They are as follows:

1. Friendship to be in touch with other survivors with whom they do not have to explain why they are there. A general acceptance of each other. S. Davidson refers to pairing friendships as the most common bonding relationship in the camp, and the most effective, and the value in this of restoring some sense of trust.[1]

2. Help with practical matters particularly related to survivors - for example problems with pensions, medical matters, etc. In the camps, these practical matters were more basic ones of obtaining food, clothing, as well as life-saving acts such as propping up sick inmates during roll call.

3. Self-help - solidarity and mutual aid. Advising each other; supporting each other through informal networks outside of the meetings. Shamai Davidson refers to this as the "helping hand" experience.[2] Collectively the self-help aspect is used to unite the group and give them "power" to realize their goals.

4. Information sharing and cultural activities - to give a sense of community again through cultural interests and social gatherings. Also to put together a book based on their experiences. Shamai Davidson refers to this as a need to preserve links with the destroyed cultural past. Reminiscing, singing, joking were all important for morale in the camps. Similarly the SOS group needs this social, relaxed, informal component, as well as a format or agenda to carry them forward.

5. A place to talk and share experiences and feel understood. Look to the future as well as the past, for example acting as watchdogs against fascism and racism, etc. What Shamai Davidson refers to as "resistance" activities in the camp groups as a way of sustaining hope.[3]

The significance of the group to the survivor today is not just a return to something familiar from his past. The mirroring acknowledges that there is possibly an important connection, but the use of the group is different. Their mission is not only to bear witness through their verbal/written testimonies, but to be active agents in warning others of the dangers of facism and racism today. This they feel they cannot do as individuals- they use the name of the group for example to write letters to the Jewish Chronicle or television. The incident of Le Pen's intended visit was an important example. The anger and rage they felt towards the lack of response and interest from the Jewish community which they originally projected outside the group, gets translated into positive action. The process by which they convey their message is achieved not through a constant return to the atrocities, but by the image they create to those around them which incorporates the paradox of the Auschwitz number branded on the arm, with the well dressed, articulate survivor laughing and joking as I observed at their recent Chanukah party.

1. Davidson, S, Human Reciprocity Among Jewish Prisoners In The Nazi Concentration Camps P.567
2. Davidson, S, Human Reciprocity Among Jewish Prisoners In The Nazi Concentration Camps P.568
3. Davidson, S, Human Reciprocity Among Jewish Prisoners In The Nazi Concentration Camps P.569

It would be naive to say that the group is free of difficulties. The conflicts within are many. The issue of control is a recurring theme. The chaos which is around in the meetings seems at times to threaten their survival. The newly appointed committee will hopefully steer the group. They feel there is an urgency and a need to exist and this will no doubt sustain them.

The group may change and develop. As they start to compile their book, memories may return of what happened to them and their families. However, by producing a book which will live on after them, it may free them from the burden of carrying these memories on their own. It will therefore not only help in their catharsis, but will have an educative function for generations to follow. This in turn may have a positive effect on the children of survivors so that they in turn may be freed from the label of the "second generation" and the problems which have become associated with them.

The nurturing, healing aspect of survivors coming together in a group has had ramifications more recently for survivors of disasters currently - the Zeebrugge ferry disaster and the Bradford fire being the best known. Though it is inappropriate, in my view, to make comparisons between massive trauma of the Shoah and accidents such as those mentioned, the survivors of Shoah give us important leads as to how survivors can be helped to adapt through the buffering effect of the group.

8. CONCLUSIONS

The survivors are the living witnesses of the Shoah. They not only provide testimony of what really happened, but both warn against and act upon signs which may lead to a similar situation happening again.

As individuals they have to a great extent had to hide their identity. They tended to be shunned particularly by the Jewish community and/or labelled by professionals as having some form of psychiatric disturbance. Though many found meaning in their lives through newly created families and/or work, a gap remained between their past, their present and their future.

I have tried through my Paper to balance up the view of survivors as pathetic victims by emphasising their strengths. I hope I have managed to convey that despite the enormity of their suffering, which I in no way underestimate or belittle, there remains a perspective that is too easily overlooked - namely, the survivor's ability to transcend evil and maintain a sense of humanity and dignity. "The experience of the concentration camp survivor, thus echoes the Jewish historical theme of survival, in the manner in which a negative and destructive experience is transformed into a positive and enduring value" - Shamai Davidson.[1]

I have emphasised the importance of the group and the interpersonal dimension as the means of helping to achieve this goal. I have illustrated through the Survivors of Shoah group how this non-clinical self-help setting is perhaps more meaningful and healing for survivors, particularly from the camps, than the traditional counselling/therapy model.

I do not wish to discredit the individual/group therapy approach. Without an understanding and internalisation of this model - as can be seen in the case studies, I would not have been able to progress. However, in this work with survivors, I feel that the theory needs to develop out of practice, rather than trying to fit practice into theory. Human reciprocity, laughter, mutual aid, etc. strengthened the survivor to live day by day, hour by hour, minute by minute. We always need to bear this in mind in our professional work.

The impact of such coping behaviour in extremity has much wider implications than the subject matter. It takes on what J.E. Dimsdale calls an "allegorical meaning". He writes that, "for many the image of man in the camps is quite simply the image of man and his fate, thrown into a world that is hostile, with no chance for escape and no real chance for change. The way that man deals with his feelings about such a condition, the way he goes on to create a world within these confines, may not be dissimilar to the way that millions coped with their immersion in concentration camps".[2] Dimsdale sees the camps and the survivor as symbols of today's world, not just historical factors from the past. In this way he tries to give them meaning for each of us.

1. Davidson, S, Human Reciprocity Among Jewish Prisoners In The Nazi Concentration Camps P.572
2. Dimsdale, J.E, The Coping Behaviour Of Nazi Concentration Camp Survivors P.797

ACKNOWLEDGEMENTS

1. Professor Shamai Davidson who gave me so much support in developing my ideas and practice in my work with survivors.

2. The Survivors of Shoah who both individually and as a group teach me about the meaning of the Shoah.

REFERENCES

Baron, L., Journal of Psychology & Judaism. Vol.I No.2, Spring 1977. Surviving The Holocaust P.25-37

Davidson, S., Human Reciprocity Among the Jewish Prisoners in the Nazi Concentration Camps. In The Nazi Concentration Camps Proceedings of the 4th Yad Vashem Int. Historical Conference Jan.1980. Publ.Yad Vashem Jerusalem 1984 P.555-572

Davidson, S., On Relating to Traumatised Persecuted People. Israel Netherlands Symposium on the Impact of Persecution II. Dalfern - Amsterdam 14-18 April 1980. The Netherlands: Rijsuijk 1981. P.55-63

Des Pres, T., The Survivor - An Anatomy of Life In The Death Camps. Oxford University Press New York 1976.

Dimsdale, J.E., The Coping Behaviour of Nazi Concentration Camp Survivors. Am.J.Psychiatry 131: 7 July 1974. P.792-797

Frankl, V., Group Therapeutic Experiences in Concentration Camps. Group Psychother.(1954)7: P.81-90.

Frankl, V., Man's Search for Meaning. Publ.Hodder & Stoughton 1987 Ed.

Heimler, E., My Memories are Alive but my Hate has gone. Manna, Summer 1985 P.2-3

Jaffe, R., Group Activity as a Defence Method in Concentration Camps. The Isr.Ann.Psychiat.Rel.Disc (1963) 1(2). P.235-245.

Klein, Dr.H., Chapter on Problems in the Psychotherapeutic Treatment of Israeli Survivors of the Holocaust. P.233 in Massive Psychic Trauma - Edited by H.Krystal International Universities Press Inc.1968 Section IV. P.73

Krystal, H., Integration & Self-Healing in Post-Traumatic States. In Luel S.A. & P.Marus (Ed) Psychoanalytic Reflections on the Holocaust: Selected Essays New York. Ktav Publishing House 1984. P.113-134.

Pfefferkorn, E., The Case of Bruno Bettelheim and Nina Wertmuller's Seven Beauties. In The Nazi Concentration Camps Proceedings of the 4th Yad Vashem Int. Historical Conference Jan.1980. Publ.Yad Vashem Jerusalem 1984. P.663-682

Reading Ashes: The Holocaust and the Question of Beginning

Michael Lustigman

Department of Sociology
Bishop's University
Lennoxville, Quebec
J1M 1Z7

Is it possible for the vapours of Zyclone B and the fires of the crematoria to extinguish a tremendous number of human lives without at the same time erasing the forms of life that organized these human beings into socially meaningful collectives? Mothers, daughters, fathers and sons died; yet how can family members burn without at the same time having the very idea of the family go up in smoke? The fires have long subsided, order and certainty rule over the familial realm, but the question persists; given the Holocaust, what sort of family life is possible?

By raising the variability of family life as our question, we do not mean to bring into doubt the circumstantial presence of the family, we mean instead to trace some of the ways that the Holocaust has been brought into the home so as to discern what is other to circumstance about the family. We begin our inquiry at the most recent layer, at what appears first for us even though it may not be first. We begin where **Children of the Holocaust** begins, with the "iron box."[1]

Into the "iron box", Helen Epstein deposits those properties that make children of concentration-camp survivors unique. Their uniqueness is formulated as a peculiar familial tension whose on-going character is experienced by these children as a mutation (mutilation) which they must resist if they are to survive. The "iron box" is thus the insignia of their resistance. As the name suggests, it is intended to contain and thereby arrest the causes of their mutation — the Holocaust. As a structure designed to subordinate the Holocaust to the rule of reason, the "iron box" signals the childrens' resolve to begin a new life by generating an unbridgeable gap between their lives and the lives of the parents whom they come to recognize as the living embodiment of the Holocaust.

The new, it seems, demands the displacement and containment of the old, which, for Helen Epstein, is not unlike the enclosure required for radio-active materials: "I built my iron box carefully, the way we were taught in school the nuclear reactors were built. I conceived lead walls around the dangerous parts, concentric circles of water channels and air ducts that would soften and contain any kind of explosion. I enclosed it all with a metal casing and buried the box far away from my brain toward the small part of the neck, in the part of my body that seemed least alive."[2] The care and attention applied to the construction and fortification of the "iron box" speaks to the perceived potency of the parents -- the survivors of the Holocaust -- to contaminate their childrens' social environment. More precisely, it speaks to this child's fear of being made different from her peers. And yet, the connection between the "iron box" and the nuclear reactor makes apparent that the anxiety regarding contamination i.e., becoming like her parents, cannot be arrested with any degree of finality but merely deferred by instituting a course of conduct wherein that which is most feared is ironically nourished by the very attempts to annul it. The "iron box" thus names a constituency whose members, while sharing in the common project of guarding against possible contamination by the Holocaust, share in the maintenance and thereby in the preservation of the Holocaust through the self-same project. In organizing these children in relation to each other and simultaneously in opposition to their parents, the "iron box" reorganizes all who submit to this order into a relation of subservience to it. Hence, while the child may place the "iron box" in that part of her body that seems least alive, that part becomes by virtue of the box most alive with the determination to rule over all the other parts.

It rules through fear, a fear derived from an unexamined conviction that this and only this artificially constructed box can withstand the corrosive impact of its so-called contents. The heart, the brain, the lungs must, so it is maintained, be isolated from these contents, an insularity which, in guarding these vital organs provides the "iron box" with the power to deprive these organs their inherent vitality. These deprivations constitute Epstein's child. The privation necessary to resist the Holocaust, to resist a parasite whose infiltration serves to paralyze the will and decimate sensibilities, reduces the afflicted into contemporary figures of the **Muselmänn.**[3] Within this state of apprehension the "iron box" is the first and foremost line of defence. And as a line of defence it serves to uphold and sustain the very entity it opposes. The "iron box" thus reachieves the status of a necessary yet "terrible bomb"; terrible because the impossibility of escaping its sphere of destruction combined with the absence of ready-made tools to defuse it, leaves the child inescapably at its mercy -- its hostage. Elsewhere, the "iron box" reappropriates the attribute of a "tomb", one that holds within its impregnable walls the ashes of a shattered genealogy, a family tree that has been burned to the stump; a crypt within which the dead rest restlessly, disturbing and disrupting the life of the living -- threatening to inter the living with the dead. And insofar as the "iron box" is invisible, it is a "vault" disposed to disguise, to hide not only its contents but also its very presence. Always within another, the "iron box" is however rigorously separate from it. In this way it is able to isolate, to protect and shelter the Holocaust from any penetration, from anything that can filter in from the outside. Caulked and padded along its inner partition, the "iron box" protects as well the secret of its inclusion within the self and of its internal exclusion from the self. As an inside that is heterogeneous to the inside of the self, the "iron box" effects a divided self whose parts by virtue of its commanding presence are bound to silence. The "children of the Holocaust" are thus condemned to remain mute. Even though enclosed within the self, this inclusion prevents the "iron box" from becoming the jury box of consciousness. A jury presumes witnesses and henceforth a tribunal preparing the case; summoning the plaintiff for indictment, statements of council, a plurality of opinions called up by **sub-poena** and finally, sentencing. But here the tyranny of silence subverts the very speech that is sought, annuls the very encounter that is desired: "The iron box contained a special room for my mother and father, warm and moist as a greenhouse. They lived there inside me rare and separate from other beings... The door that led to this special room was a secret, the place had to be protected."[4]

Enclosed within the "iron box" as in a "greenhouse", the parents are kept apart from their offspring and are equally partitioned off from the naturalness of the outside world. The artificiality of their enclosure discloses a sterile universe, a world whose ordered character precludes the necessity for parent-child relations. Rather than guide the child through the precarious world of growing up in the natural realm, within the hothouse growth is determined to the exclusion of all else by the "iron box". The contained parents cannot strictly speaking be called parents: their absolute dependency on the "iron box" for whatever life they may have renders them impotent to reproduce themselves **other-wise** i. e., to have children. Deprived of the capacity to moderate their circumstances, these so-called parents are reduced to an abstraction capable of neither life nor death. Against what does the "iron box" keep these parents intact -- safe both from life and from death, allowing death to take no part in life?

Stripped of particularity , these greenhouse parents serve as an image of a life without life, a life not for the living -- the Holocaust -- an image which, if given the opportunity to rule over the child would, so she suspects, rule out the possibility of any other life except for the repetition of this lifeless life. The "iron box" is thus intended to arrest an image in order to allow for the guidance of an alternate image. By segregating and incarcerating undesirable elements of one's history, the "iron box" aims at setting the ground for a new and different, history. "...On the way home, the safe world fell away and I saw things no little girl should see. Blood and shattered glass, piles of skeletons and blackened barbed wire with bits of flesh stuck to it, the way flies stick to walls after they have been swatted dead."[5]

By placing "under arrest" the bloody vista of damaged and dismembered lives, of a universe where flies and men share in the same fate, the "iron box" provides the child with a view of a safe world. A world view however, whose safety is contingent on the policing powers of the "iron box". Conceived as central to the child's survival, the "iron box", in serving the child, turns the child into its service, becoming as it were her tyrannical ruler. While the child would like to have the "iron box" "dredged up into the light, opened, its contents sorted out", any such opening is made conditional on the prior satisfaction of requirements. All of this serves to reproduce the "iron box", no longer as an individual exorcism of an unwanted inheritance, but as a response which in its collective thrust gives rise to a community whose members share in the displacement of what came before them.

If the displacement of parents is the contribution required of each and every member to the community of "children of the Holocaust", then the center of this community is a place of emptiness and silence, into which none venture. For here lies the horror that no-one would pronounce: the recognition that the ritual of displacement, far from erasing the Holocaust, merely reissues it; no longer as an historical fact but from now on as a social and psychological reality. How is one to partake in such a collective and not lose one's mind and not beat one's fists against the walls? Madness and violence belong to this place and what this place gathers through the litany of broken relations is the commitment of the member to the notion that the family is dead; that it died in Auschwitz-Birkenau, that it is no longer.

II

Our project is not intended to lament the "orphaned" child but to salvage the speech of the parent -- not for the sake of some snapshots of a life that is no longer, but for the sake of the **awe** that inspires children to approach the unapproachable. It is for our sake that we inquire into the fabric of this encounter and precisely because of its unfolding within the home, we are concerned with the difference between what belongs to the household (i. e., property/propriety) and what is deeply ours (i.e., desire). In drawing attention to the difference we are in fact drawn to the pulse that enables this difference, the question: **What survives?** By linking what is proper with what is desirable our question passes over the chasm that separates them -- a way of looking into the chasm which would, under conditions of fidelity to either side, remain hidden. The question is thus an unauthorized bridge. Constructed without the permission of either side this bridge, rather than collecting the sides, recalls that these sides are themselves limits to the chasm. So if this bridge is authorized by neither side, it is because as sides they are without authority -- **what then author-izes?**

In moments of profound despair Epstein's child raises the question of authority only to succumb to already established authorities. "Why", she wants to know, "did they go like sheep to the slaughter?" But are those "they" any different from her? Are her shepherds i.e., leaders and teachers, any different from their predecessors? Despite the question mark, the question she asks about those others is no question, because it fails to disclose the ground that moves her to question. Instead, the so-called question occasions speculation on her respective standing in the line to slaughter. Such numerological speculations are, it seems, little more than desperate games of the doomed; the games of those unwilling to resist their link to sheep by resisting the grammar that makes this link possible.

The link is, at least initially, clear; "like sheep to the slaughter"[6] brings up the issue of man's death, specifically of a dying that resembles the slaughter of sheep. "How can any man recall through this way of dying the virtues of living?" At face value, the analogy connects man and sheep by introducing death as their common fate. That we are going to die is self-evident, what is doubtful is the way of death, at which point "like sheep to the slaughter" nominates a way; one that the child is deeply familiar with, for the site of the slaughter is the market-place. It is in the market-place that sheep are slaughtered and it is in response to the demands of the market-place that the sort and the quantity of sheep is assessed and processed. "Like sheep to the slaughter" introduces, by way of analogy, human life which, not unlike the life of sheep, has no value other than use-value; whatever is intrinsic to the life of man is displaced in favour of the "currency" that their slaughter will bring to those who claim to possess them.

If we are to follow the lead, be led by this line of reasoning, then we must conclude that to possess man in the way that one owns sheep speaks to the owner's indifference to the difference between man and sheep. An indifference whose very formulation recasts the proprietress as herself a sheep led by the abstract dictum of the market-place. The meekness which sheep are held to display -- one following in the footprints of the other -- reappears as the sign of the proprietress's own domesticity. "Like sheep to the slaughter" names not the fate of sheep so much as the fate of those who submit to a life not other than the market-place. By bringing to the fore the interchangeability of men and sheep, which at its finest moment (of madness) reclaims the dispensibility of all manner of things, men, women and children not excluded; the slaughter mirrors the lifelessness of a life, according to which everyone has a price. It may indeed be that the recognition of and acquiescence to the notion of a fixed price for all manner of things is the condition necessary for slaughter; at which point the actual slaughter is but the realization of the self-mutilation that the child had already performed on herself.

From every quarter merchants of opinion make their stand, each of which serves in their own fashion to furnish an answer to the child's question — one that we deeply ask of ourselves and for reasons that will be made clear as we proceed, in the guise of an other. Survivor names that other, the one who elects in face of death to live-on (sur-vivre); the one whose very rejection of death threatens the order of things; according to which death is far better than the life of transgression. When called to respond all, without exception, repeat the virtues of death. While some maintain that only a few died like "sheep" and many more died like "lions", still other voices contend that the death of "sheep" was in itself an act of courage, an act of spiritual resistance.[7] Despite substantive disagreements these answers share in the question's presumption; namely, that the slaughter of human beings could be made a topic for moral education without necessarily having to immerse the participants to this lesson in the immediacy of survival. Removed from its context, talk about slaughter appears devoid of violence; figuratively speaking, absent is the boot to the head, the velocity of exploding bullets or the fumes of Zyclone B. And yet in listening to these moral lessons, echoes of receding and approaching slaughters could be heard, for none of these opinion-makers are prepared to transgress the order of things but merely to recite the condition under which the faithful are obliged to submit to the knife's edge rather than engage the life of survival.

III

"At first glance it seems insane, a plea for the survivors?"[8] With these words the survivor's **apology**, the defense of survival begins. But then, what are survivors accused of? What is the charge? They are accused of surviving, of living on; of resisting the slaughter by resisting the logic that made it possible. They are charged with rejecting their status as "sheep", with rejecting the authority of their shepherds, so as to become as it were their own shepherds, caring for what is good for them rather than attending to the price their flesh and blood will bring in the market-place. In bearing witness to the radical alternity that made life possible in the death-camps, their very testimony radicalizes daily life.[9] The survivors are thus charged with bringing on the Holocaust, that is with bringing into daily life a foreign or alien entity whose presence contaminates its surroundings, running the risk of fundamentally transforming mundane life. Accordingly, the Holocaust and those whose speech and conduct embody it have no place in daily life; they are thus condemned to a life of containment.

As the contained struggle to break through the symbolic walls that contain them their guardians, in this instance their children, are busy reinforcing the fortification, struggling as it were to prevent the "iron box" from rupturing. The struggle is truly titanic. And if one listens to the sighs of their respective labours, one may hear through the grunts, the form of life that authorizes their mutual exclusion. In "A Plea for the Survivors", Wiesel invites the children, Epstein's "children of the Holocaust" to suspend their labour, to wait. Wait? For what? For whom? reappears as a corresponding cry: "Wait until the last survivor, the last witness has joined the long procession of silent ghosts whose judgement day will resound and shake the earth and its Creator. Wait..."[10] Here one wait flows into, only to bring about a far more encompassing wait. The former asks the children to defer the "burial" of the Holocaust until those who have had first hand experience with the death-camps are themselves dead. The latter re-gathers the dead and the living in waiting for the messianic moment. Hence, while the parent **qua** survivor is moved to explore the Holocaust as an event warranting the re-union of what is essential about the family, the child in contra-distinction, reappears to treat the Holocaust as an event consistant with the death of the family. The difference in usage registers the logic that propels Wiesel to counsel patience; he knows the child, he knows of her teachers and leaders -- of their accent on busyness, that time is money, an opportunity postponed is an opportunity lost, that to seize the advantage is to advance through the logic of the market-place, one's private interests. He knows as well what the child's teachers are reluctant to teach; namely that the difference between survivor and non-survivor is not the presence or absence of a particular historical event in their lives, rather it is their attitude to life.

Attitudes however are worthless, as such of no real interest to the child whose interests are limited to real interests. For this realist, the Holocaust is seen as an historical catastrophy that befell her parents, European Jews, and those less fortunate than herself. However, not unlike those others, her fortune (as is their misfortune) stems from her accidental presence here rather than there. And what is unique to this sort of fortune is its given, or gift-like property. Outside of human volition, this sense of fortune serves to divide the world and its inhabitants into regions of sameness and difference; enabling the fortunate to envisage the Holocaust as belonging there and then and not here and now. However, if one is to lead a fortunate life, the imperative of fortune demands submission, so that the difference between self and fortune disappears and she becomes nothing more than an examplar of her fortunate environment. Hence, while the logic that fuelled the fires of mass annihilation is displaced by the practical enactment of the fortunate life, the mere presence of survivors casts grave doubts on the effectiveness of this displacement.

What is to be done with the parent whose presence stands as a living exception to the notion of the fortunate life? Within the ranks of mundane transaction this survivor disturbs, shakes loose the supporting grid of daily life by inviting the fortunate sibling to imagine the limitation to her fortune. For instance, if one can survive death can one not then imagine life in death, at which point the clearly demarcated distinction between life and death and the moral interdictions which these distinction make possible collapse into ruins; for here is a life that seems indifferent to the difference between life and death, a life that is seemingly outside the order of things. With this imaginative possibility of a life in mind, the life of quotidian concerns reappears devoid of imagination, representing as it were fortune as misfortune. Although pointing to the survivor, the question returns to point to the realist as one afflicted with a paralysis of the imagination. Wiesel beckons her to wait, to defer her impulse to appropriate, so as to hear through the pause her commitment to an economy that authorizes the slaughter of men as though they were sheep. At the cutting edge of the imagination, the survivor of the Holocaust acts as a reminder of what the child necessarily leaves out in order to live in her world and conversely what must be added to her daily diet if she is to live-on (sur-vivre).[11] Here the Holocaust strikes a rift between "living" and "living-on" by striking out at the incapacity of the "living" to imagine a life worth living for.

The principled quest, the quest for what orients human life gives, according to Wiesel, the survivor's life its orientation. As an orientation it is pregnant with the anticipation of what will "resound and shake the earth and its Creator". Yet what is to come, in the act of anticipation, is already coming, making itself resound on earth. For in counselling Epstein's children to wait, Wiesel invites them to consider the pause of waiting as the only possible response to the Holocaust. The waiting in question is not the same as the conventional waiting; the kind of waiting that is already familiar with what it is waiting for. The waiting that will "resound and shatter" marks its difference by already resounding and shattering not the "designs for living"[12] but the promise inherent to these designs; namely, the promise of continuity.

It is this promise which the survivor is unable to promise. For him, social unfolding is a self-repeating catastrophe which always finds new and more deadly ways of building ruins upon ruins. "Where we perceive a chain of events," the angel of history, according to Walter Benjamin, "sees one single catastrophe which keeps piling wreckage upon wreckage and hurls it in front of his feet".[13] Although "the angel would like to stay, awaken the dead and make whole what has been smashed" he is powerless to do so because a storm blowing from Paradise rushes him backwards into the future, his gaze still fixed on the destructive past. Benjamin's angel is very much Wiesel's survivor whose view of life questions the continuity of life not excluding the continuity of his very own view of life.

"But what of me?" the child wants to know. "How do I make of this view my view, a ground for cognition and re-cognition? How do I bridge the schism that separates me from those who gave life to me?" The questions open the "iron box", releasing the child to wonder at survival. Without doubt wonder(ing) is not survival; it is however a particular hearing of the awe that comes first, that first in-forms the child of what is other. By all accounts the Holocaust is **awe-full**: "How can I possibly say how I survived..."[14]

"The Killer's laughter and the hallucinatory silence of the condemned; the distant look of old men who knew; the dull lament of children afraid to know; the screams, the moaning, the beatings; the thirst inside the sealed wagons; the terror inside the barracks during the selections; the silent, almost solemn processions marching toward the mass graves or flames; the lucidity of some, the delirium of others; ...the little girl undressing her little brother as she tells him gently, so very gently, not to be afraid...for one must not be afraid of death; and the woman who in the edge of hysteria begs the Killer to spare her three children and receives this response: very well, I shall take two, tell me which two; and the father who watches his little girl disappear into the distance, swept away by...How is one to speak of such things and not lose one's mind, and not beat one's fists against the walls?"[15]

The fist is no menace, it is already worn down by the walls. The fist and madness are however related, they have their origin in the same recurring question: **How is one to say SURVIVAL?** "How can I possibly say how I survived...three days before liberation Hessler came into the barracks and I was sick in bed, I could not go to work and the Kapo even told me to stay in bed. And Hessler asks: 'Why are you in bed?' I told him that I was sick and the Kapo said the same. Hessler's response: 'If I see you here tomorrow you're dead, I'll shoot you down like a dog.' Two days later, he was in jail, it was liberation already...

How can I know how I survived?"[16]

The concluding remark turns to haunt the account by repeating the question that originally moved it. The speaker is uncertain, not of events but of their sense and reference; an uncertainty which Wiesel, speaking on behalf of those who refuse to speak, identifies as "chance": "They did not know how they had eluded their enemy and cheated death. They knew that they had nothing to do with it. The choice had not been theirs. Intelligence, education, intuition and courage -- nothing had counted. Everything had been arranged by **chance** only **chance.** A step towards the right or left, a movement begun too early or too late, a change in the mood of a particular overseer and their fate would have been different."[17]

The randomness of conduct, the absence of individual and collective design are within the account regathered as expressions of some sort of play orchestrated by forces other to those coerced into this life. **Chance** is thus beyond individual choice; it resists appropriation either to person, thing or idea, as such it is other than technique. Moreover, in the way that it is inscribed, **chance** is radically different from our customary usages of it. Ordinarily, it is introduced by reintroducing certainty as that against which it may be judged. Here, **chance** reigns without its customary other, it is the law of survival itself. While "everything is arranged by chance", **chance** as law seems unlawful, it offers no affirmative guidance, it proposes no rules of conduct, it abstains from differentiating between proper and improper modes of behaviour; that which it does offer is a methodology of suspicion, a mistrust of sociation to guide and preserve human life. While mistrust is not the same as the absence of trust, it is however a critical position in relation to trust, specifically in relation to the prevailing assumption that enfolded within sociation is a binding ethic that curtails man from annahilating fellow man.

While the law of sociation collects fellow humans, this collective according to the survivor, does not include all humans; the Holocaust names Mankind as a manufactured kind -- the kind that is always already culturally informed. Mankind thus serves to differentiate between kinds; claiming that some merely look like men but are not in fact men, a distinction which under the auspices of National Socialism, laid waste a tremendous number of lives and all for the sake of a valued kind -- the so-called superior kind. Being a survivor from the kind that excluded his kind Wiesel talks about life outside, about a life without the kindness that stems from being of the same kind. To maintain that survival is possible only through **chance** and that **chance** is the phenomena of dwelling outside is to locate the survivor as one who desires to bring into speech that which is "un-kind" about Mankind. By raising as his problem the problem of not knowing how to talk about "such things", the survivor turns to confront the paucity of what men faithful to their kind can talk about; showing through the confrontation that his problem, unlike theirs, is not merely a problem of selecting from an already available pool of knowledge the words that would describe the events which took place -- the problem is the relation between events and their articulation.

To bring survival into speech is to remind Epstein's child, through and throughout the speech, of the battle for the very words with which to speak. What is decisive about such a description is that it cannot be spoken without doubting the very words that make up the description; as though what survival seeks to accomplish is a description of doubt itself. If this ritual of dramaturgical doubt constitutes the speaker's attempt to say SURVIVAL, it must then be acknowledged that the saying of SURVIVAL is, structurally speaking, not so much a saying of something as its un-saying. SURVIVAL, in other words, decontextualizes the context from within which it occurs, so that to SURVIVE is always to survive something and always by transforming it into no-thing. Hence, that SURVIVAL should address the death-camps all the while deconstructing its own speech, serves to paralyze the customary distinction between thought and action and with it the sense of the Holocaust as a purely historical event. For within the deconstructive veils of **awe**, the Holocaust did not happen; it is a happening that resists ending and is in this way endlessly beginning.

The foregoing leads to a double conclusion: first that SURVIVAL cannot be allotted a determined place in the familial realm and second, although outside the family SURVIVAL is nonetheless contained within a well-defined interval -- the interval that collects Wiesel's parent and Epstein's child in relation to what comes first. While SURVIVAL eludes public speech, both parent and child do however know of its place or better yet of its non-place; that it stands along side the familiar and yet is other to it. This, then is the role of capitalized SURVIVAL: instead of presenting the family by representing as its virtues the visible accomplishments of household management, it recalls the familial prior to familiarity.

And what comes prior to familiarity, first appears not as speech already formed and sealed but as an awesome, awe-inspiring silence. The silence of lips forming, trans-forming, stretching apart to release a glimpse of what can only be glimpsed in the figure of the word/the infant as it takes its place in the world of relatives and relations. SURVIVAL names not the world of relatives and relations but the **founding silence** of the new in the eternal cycle of renewal.

Notes

1. Helen Epstein, **Children of the Holocaust**, (New York: Bantam, 1980) 4.

2. **Ibid.**, 4.

3. On their entry into the camp...they are overcome before they can adapt themselves; they are beaten by time, they do not begin to learn German, to disentangle the infernal knot of laws and prohibitions until their body is already in decay and nothing can save them from selection or from death by exhaustion. Their life is short but their number is endless; they, the Muselmänner, the drowned, form the backbone of the camp, an anonymous mass, continuously renewed and always identical, of non-men who march and labour in silence, the divine spark dead within them, already too empty really to suffer. One hesitates to call them living; one hesitates to call their death death.

   Primo Levi, **Survival in Auschwitz**, (New York: Collier, 1961) 82.

4. **Op. cit.**, Epstein, 4.

5. **Ibid.**, 4.

6. "For thy sake are we killed all day; we are accounted as sheep to the slaughter." (**Psalms** 44:23) The analogic character of this fragment and the place of analogy in theological discourse is articulated by David Tracy in **The Analogical Imagination** (New York: Crossroads, 1981).

7. Directly or indirectly the totality of the literature on the Holocaust engages the issue of resistance. Of importance to our analysis however, is not so much instances of resistance as that in the service of which they have been applied; a number of texts may serve as an example. Yehuda Bauer, **They Chose Life: Jewish Resistance in the Holocaust** (New York: The American Jewish Committee, 1973); Yuri Suhl, ed., **They Fought Back: The Story of Jewish Resistance in Nazi Europe** (New York: Crown, 1967).

8. Elie Wiesel, "A Plea for the Survivors", **A Jew Today**, (New York: Vantage, 1978) 218.

9. Emil L. Fackenheim, **The Jewish Return into History: Reflections in the Age of Auschwitz and a New Jerusalem** (New York: Schocken, 1978) 19-24.

10. **Op. cit.**, Weisel, 236.

11. Jacques Derrida, "Living-On -- Border Lines", **Deconstruction and Criticism**, edited by Harold Bloom, et.al., (New York: Seabury Press, 1979) 75-77.

12. Robert K. Merton, "Social Structure and Anomie", in **Social Theory and Social Structure** (Glencoe, Illinois: The Free Press, 1949).

13. Walter Benjamin, **Illuminations**, edited by Hannah Arendt, (New York: Free Press, 1969) 257-258.

14. This and the other segment identified by the name Bernard Laufer constitute parts of a conversation held during the years 1971-72 on the nature of bearing witness. Through and throughout his testimony the account resonates with a tormented wisdom, one which Franz Rosenzweig had detected in the poetry of Yehuda Halevi:

> It begins with a cry from an abyss of suffering, an abyss so terribly deep that He whom the cry is destined to reach is at first merely a target for outcry, doubt and blasphemy.

Franz Rosenzweig, edited by Nahum N. Glatzer, (New York: Schocken, 1961) 349.

15. **Op. cit.**, Wiesel, 221.

16. Bernard Laufer.

17. **Op. cit.**, Wiesel, 234.

THE AFFIRMATION OF LIFE IN SHE'ERITH HAPLEITA

Ze'ev Mankowitz

The Hebrew University
Jerusalem

The Holocaust forces upon us a reconsideration of human possibility. On the one hand we have to face up to idealistic depravity, to a system where murder was elevated to a form of self expression and carried within itself the promise of global redemption. We have to contend with the Commandant of Auschwitz who, in vindicating his essential humanity after the war, wrote:"I also see now that the extermination of the Jews was fundamentally wrong. Precisely because of these mass exterminations, Germany has drawn upon itself the hatred of the entire world. It in no way served the cause of antisemitism, but on the contrary brought the Jews far closer to their ultimate objective."(1)

On the other hand we are equally compelled to rethink our notions of resilience and humanity that somehow survived the impossible world created by the Nazis. Psychological theories that highlighted the complex delicacy of man's inner life do not help us account for the psychic ruggedness of those who did not "drown". We in no way mean to uncritically celebrate "man's search for meaning " in the shadow of the gas chambers nor do we find the notion of biological dignity persuasive.(2) What we have in mind is much closer to Primo Levi's reading of humanity in extremis. "We do not believe...that man is fundamentally brutal, egoistic and stupid in his conduct once every civilized institution is taken away...We believe, rather, that the only conclusion to be drawn is that in the face of driving necessity and physical disabilities many social habits and instincts are reduced to silence."(3) Social instincts were silenced by driving necessity - silenced but not destroyed. A brief respite from the camp regime brought old sensibilities to the surface in the same way as liberation opened the way to a less tentative return to life.

It is with this in mind that we wish to examine some major themes in the brief history of **She'erith Hapleita**, themes which speak to general human concerns while casting light on both the Holocaust and its aftermath. The term **She'erith Hapleita** - the Saved Remnant - refers to all surviving Jews in Europe but designates most particularly the collective identity of the 300,000 survivors who converged on the Occupied Zones of Germany, Austria and Italy between 1945 and 1949. The distinguishing mark of this group of people is their vitality, their inner strength, their affirmation of life. On the morrow of liberation we already witness a flurry of activity amongst the survivors which in due course elaborated itself into a network of representative councils, political movements, youth groups, agricultural training farms, vocational and Hebrew schools and a wide range of of educational and cultural projects.

Despite its obvious importance and the availibility of rich archival sources the inner history of **She'erith Hapleitah** has been sadly neglected and, until a few years ago, all but forgotten. It was perhaps to be expected that this brief moment of history wedged between the Holocaust and the creation of the State of Israel would be overlooked. Moreover the growing volume of research on the years 1945-1948 focuses on Zionist, British and American policies thereby unwittingly casting the the survivors into a subsidiary if not supine role. It seems to us, however, that this implicit image of **She'erith Hapleitah** as objects of history has been compounded by a tenacious negative stereotype of the "survivor".

The image has its genesis in the widely read reports on the "living corpses" and "walking skeletons" uncovered on liberation, it solidifies in the image of the "helpless heap of human wreckage" used to raise money and win world sympathy at that time and turns ugly with accusations of parasitism and blackmarketeering by Occupation authorities who found their dealings with **She'erith Hapleitah** to be both thankless and politically costly. One further factor fed into the negative view of those who had remained alive - the suspicion, fed at times by the survivors themselves, that the worthy went under while the less scrupulous somehow managed to survive. Even the recent spate of interest in survivors and surviving has not really changed this picture for the collective enterprise of the people of **She'erith Hapleitah,** articulated mainly in Yiddish, remains a closed book for most. At best they are still perceived as rather passive, faceless displaced persons; at worst they yet appear to be somewhat tarnished.

Our view, as we have suggested, is rather different and takes the initial organization of **She'erith Hapleitah** as its point of departure. The first steps towards the organization of what came to be known as **She'erith Hapleitah** were taken by survivors of the Lithuanian ghettoes in Germany at the end of 1944. The date, nearly half a year before liberation, is of significance because it underscores the role played by the survivors in organizing themselves long before any help from the outside became available. It also helps account for one of the more surprising features of **She'erith Hapleitah** - the fact that its major institutions came into existence, at least in embryonic form, on the very morrow of liberation. By May 1945 **Techiyat Hametim** - Resurrection,(4) the first survivor newspaper in Germany, had been published in Buchenwald, Kibbutz Buchenwald, a pioneer youth agricultural training farm was in its formative stages, the nucleus of the Central Committee of the Liberated Jews in Bavaria was taking shape in St. Ottilien, the United Zionist Organization started operating in Dachau and committees and Zionist groups had sprung up in a number of camps.

The nuclei of all of these groups were young men who had taken an active part in underground activities prior to their deportation to Germany. Their major task, now that systematic destruction had ceased, was to fight the dehumanization of the camp regime and to prepare as best they could for liberation. In Kaufering, a sub-camp of Dachau, for example, an older group ran clandestine evening seminars on the the Jewish future while a younger group managed, in what appears to be an unprecedented venture in concentration camp life, to put out seven numbers of an underground newspaper **Nizoz** - The Spark.(5) Beyond the courage that informed this daring initiative **Nizoz** represents a remarkable first attempt to sum up the meaning of what the paper called the "catastrophe" and to map out the possible shape of the future.

The Jews, most of the writers agreed, attracted emnity because they were a people apart and, as a landless minority, were unable to protect themselves. The struggle for Jewish statehood represented the central response to the Holocaust and the crucial question was how to achieve this now that the problem of European Jewry, the central dynamic force and resource of Zionist realization, "had already been solved by Adolf Hitler."(6)

The existential centrality of Zionism was stated clearly by Leib Garfunkel, a Zionist leader who had been a member of the Kovno Jewish Council, in April 1945: "While in this Nazi hell one burning question racks our brains and gives us no respite: What was it all for, why the murder of millions and a sea of blood? A vain sacrifice from which nothing good will come? Or will this revolutionize our lives and lead to a fundamental change in the way the world relates to us? Perhaps both they and we will come to the realization that the Jewish people can no longer live without a national centre of its own..."(7) In time, we should add, most of the opinion makers in **She'erith Hapleitah** came to see that the past resisted meaning, that no redeeming purpose could be found in the **churban.** The terrible question "**farwos**?" - why? could not be answered adequately. As they perceived it, then, their task was to redeem the future and the return to Zion came to be the critical first step in this endeavour.

The move to Jewish sovereignty was an act of loyalty to the dead who had made their wishes clear before they met their end: what the Jewish people needed above all else was independence, a country of their own where they could look after themselves and ensure that a catastrophe of this kind would never again be possible. The dead commanded life and the collective life of the Jewish people was bound up with the fulfilment of the Zionist vision. This would give expression to the traditional Jewish affirmation of life, it would serve as a symbolic defiance of the Nazi design to destroy the Jewish people and would hopefully prevent tne descent of **She'erith Hapleitah** into hatred and wanton destructiveness.

The bid for sovereignty represented a self-conscious attempt to shake off the abject status of being the millenial victims of history and allow Jews to take their fate into their own hands. This essentially ideological commitment points up an important feature in the psychological make-up of these survivors. While many descriptions of human behaviour in extreme situations stress the debilitating effect of totalitarian terror we have come to recognize a reverse phenomenon worthy of close study. It is akin to something that Robert Lifton discerned in Hiroshima when he noted that after a protracted immersion in helplessness and death "...the survivor can retain an opposite image of having met death and conquered it, a sense of reinforced invunerability."(8) The leaders of **She'erith Hapleitah** emerged from the Holocaust with a special blend of strength, determination and daring. David Wolpe, a Hebrew poet from Kovno, wrote of this while still in Kaufering:

And the saved remnants of Israel
A small camp
Bold, brave and strong
As reinforced concrete
Tempered by a thousand trials.(9)

It should be noted that this sense of being beyond fear could easily have come to serve destructive ends and this indeed happened on occasion. The young leaders we are concerned with, however, emerged from the Holocaust with their devotion strengthened and their sense of historic responsibilty deepened. Their self-example in caring for others gained them the respect of their fellow prisoners and endowed them with the moral authority to take the lead when liberation came.

The great achievement of this small band of surviors of the ghettos, concentration camps and death marches - there were but 18,000 in Bavaria after the mass repatriation that followed liberation - was that they created both the organizational infrastructure which allowed **She'erith Hapleitah** to successfully absorb the tens of thousands of East European Jews who poured into the American Zone in 1946 and 1947 and standards of conduct which remained normative for the very different population that came to constitute **She'erith Hapleitah.** If in the fall of 1945 there were 55,000 survivors in Germany in two major concentrations - 18,000 in Bavaria and 20,000 in Bergen Belsen - by January 1946 some 40,000 Jews were to be found in American Zone of Occupation and by the end of the year that number had grown to nearly 160,000. Some 70% of this number were from Poland with smaller groups from Hungary, Rumania, Czechoslovakia, Austria and Germany. Those who left Poland in the last months of 1945 were primarily direct survivors of the Holocaust, including a fair number of partisans and resistance fighters, while the remainder that followed in their footsteps in 1946-47 were Polish repatriates who had survived the war in the interior of the Soviet Union. The majority of these Jews were guided across Europe by the **Brichah** rescue organization that was established in Lublin by veteran resistance fighters in the latter half of 1944.

All the Jews who sought refuge in Germany saw their sojourn as a brief stop-off on their way to a future outside of Europe. In the first months of their stay the survivors were persuaded that the world would hasten to recognize their elementary right to a home of their own and expedite their exodus. Their expectations, however, were premature. The bitter irony of their situation did not escape them and as time went by the profound tensions arising from the anomaly of survivors of the Holocaust living on German soil could no longer be contained.

For **She'erith Hapleitah** the collective guilt of the German people was axiomatic.(10) They had experienced the Holocaust as a collective deed and they scornfully thrust aside German attempts to evade responsibility. They pointed to the deep historical and cultural roots of Nazism, they stressed that it was the German people who put Hitler in power, that hundreds of thousands were part of the murder machine, that there were no examples of orders that were disobeyed, that millions kew what was happening and knowingly benefitted from the wholesale spoilation of the Jewish people. Furthermore, and this was decisive, many recalled their cold, cruel reception by the German populace during the murderous death marches. Many survivors were thus convinced that only physical revenge could begin to settle their historical account with the German people. Yet only a few, small groups attempted to translate this conviction into action beyond initial acts of retribution carried out under the aegis of the Red Army in the final stages of the war.

Those survivors who contemplated revenge but ultimately desisted, and they were the vast majority, were moved by a number of motives both psychological and practical. There were those who feared that revenge would reduce them to the level of the Nazis while others attributed their timidity to the long conditioning of life in exile. But for the most part the reasons were eminently practical: planned, systematic revenge required military skills, tight organization, financial support and, above all, a willingness to go underground and surrender that which the survivors wanted more than anything else - a safe refuge and a return to normal life.

In view of this the normative response became one of symbolic as opposed to real revenge. Symbolic revenge refers to all those economic, judicial, political and educational deeds that set out to hurt the Germans without resorting to physical force. An inventory of symbolic revenge would have to encompass the following: visits to destroyed shrines of the Nazi movement and the Nuremberg trials, taking goods and demanding services from Germans without paying, placing Germany under a ban and casting out Jews who consorted with Germans. Life, of course, was far more complicated and there was no way of avoiding daily contact and commercial transactions between Germans and Jews. The rule of the thumb guide in these contacts was that the relations should remain formal and impersonal and strictly devoid of all intimacy. Clearly this whole situation ultimately untenable and the survivors channeled their frustration and anger into two major concerns: doubling their efforts, on the one hand, in the struggle for Jewish sovereignty which for many represented the true victory over the Nazis and making sure, one the other hand, that the deeds of the Nazis would be engraved for all time on the collective memory of humankind.

Equally if not more important for **She'erith Hapleitah** was the integration of the past into the collective memory of the Jewish people. A number of motives came together in this concern: a sense of family obligation sharpened by guilt feelings, a conscious reponse to the Nazi design to cover up their deeds together with an attempt to learn from the past in order to ensure a better future. Memory was a pressing existential concern and was responded to in a variety of ways - there were those who withdrew into themselves, some sought to lose themselves in a life of abandon or frenetic activity while others found that the past obligated them to working for a more human future. The long immersion in death left its mark on the minds and bodies of the survivors. In Landsberg, for example, Dr. Leo Srole, a psychologist, connected some widespread pscho-somatic disorders that he encountered - troubled sleep, excessive sweating, lack of concentration, faulty memory, uncontrollable changes of mood and more - to the extreme trials to which these people had been exposed.(10) It is all the more remarkable to encounter, therefore, early public commemorations that demonstrate human sensitivity and a concern for the future. An example of this can be found in a memorial service held in a temporary DP camp near Stuttgart just after liberation. The chairman ofthe local committee who lost his wife, children and entire family in Radom ended his speech with the following:

"They used...every brutality to wipe us out physically...to still forever our hopes and aspirations, our heritage. Those of us who survive are bleeding still.
There are some among us who say it is too late now for redemption. It is true, it is impossible to bring back our dead. But those of us who remain, those who are the last remnant of our people, must once more have hope...for the revival of all those moral ethical and cultural values which we hold so dear, and without which the world would plunge into barbarism...
We must struggle...we must strive to rise again. We owe that to the memory of our dearly beloved dead...who had the same yearnings. We owe it to them to spend our remaining days in creating...a worthy life once more."(11)

The first attempts to think comprehensively and systematically about the content and form of memorialization begin to appear in Germany with the approach of the first anniversary of liberation. By February-March of 1946 wounds had begun to heal, there was a palpable need to determine a day of memorial for those who did not know when members of their family had perished and to somehow order the endless round of ceremonies which marked the first period of liberation. The whole question was addressed by the Central Committee of the Liberated Jews in Bavaria at the beginning of May when they convened in order to determine a shared day of remembrance for the entire Jewish people. Dr. Zalman Greenberg, the chairman of the Committee, felt that the day should combine the pain of the past with the hope of the future and therefore suggested that it focus on both Holocaust and liberation. Leivik, the Yiddish poet who was part of an American delegation to **She'erith Hapleitah**, argued that this was premature and that mourning alone should mark the day. Various historical models were suggested as a guide to the nature of the day - Purim, Pesach and the Ninth of Av were all considered but in the final analysis it was the survivors who determined that the day would combine both mourning and thanksgiving. Thus the 14th of Iyar which fell on the 15th of May in 1946 was declared as the official Day of Remembrance and Liberation so binding the particular memorial of the Jewish people to the universal celebration of victory over the Nazis.(15)

Telegrams were dispatched to world Jewish organizations around the world informing them of this decision but the declaration failed to elicit any affirmative response. Either the notification was received too late or rabbinic authorities questioned the right of the survivors to legislate for the whole Jewish people while indicating that the 14th of Iyar was set aside by biblical injunction for those who had not managed to celebrate Passover. **She'erith Hapleita** did not really have the time to become a real centre of cultural influence and therefore had little chance of exerting pressure on large and established communities. Besides, in terms of their awareness of the Holocaust, the survivors were far in advance of the rest of the Jewish world and had begun to grappple with questions which those removed from Europe had not even begun to ask.

One such concern was the radical reassessment of the whole process of emancipation which had always been guided by a fervent affirmation of Europe and its culture. Many survivors had lost their faith in the essential humanity of European civilization. Germany which had served as a beacon of progress for many in Eastern Europe, created Auschwitz; many good Christians were able to serve the Nazis or to view the murder of Jews with equanimity; after the war antisemitism did not abate and even the British Labour Party had abandoned **She'erith Hapleitah** through what was perceived as the condemnation of the Yishuv to a slow and painful death. It appeared therefore that the diverse strategies - religious, autonomist and socialist - which sought to secure Jewish survival by binding the Jews to the countries of their Exile had proven to be both futile and dangerous. The promise of a new age, the hope of creating a better future died with the victims of the Holocaust. But one course of action remained - to leave Europe for once and for all and to do so with dignity.

The complex relationship of **She'erith Hapleitah** to European civilization can perhaps best be seen in the person of Samuel Gringauz. Gringauz was born in East Prussia, studied law, served as a judge in Memel and during the war found himself in the Kovno Ghetto. He was deported to Germany in August of 1944, played an active role in the Zionist underground movement in Kaufering and with liberation gravitated to the DP camp in Landsberg. From the outset he took a leading role in the affairs of the survivors both as the chairman of the Jewish Committee in Landsberg and as president of the Council of Liberated Jews in Germany.

Dr. Gringauz was persuaded that the fate of the Jewish people was inextricably bound up up with universal developments and therefore, despite his own ambivalence, he argued against retreating into a shell of bitter parochialism. In the immediate aftermath of the war this was easier said than done for the utopian hopes that the survivors had built up prior to liberation had to be measured against a far less promising reality: the Jewish world was slow in coming forth to extend much needed aid, the Allies refused to recognize the Jewish people as a full partner to the war and thus refused to see them as party to the political fruits of victory while from an internal perspective the spiritual distortions imposed by life in extremity were far greater than had been previously recognized. In truth Gringauz was hard put to hide his own bitter disappointment when he attempted to sum up the major trends of 1945. It was a year, he wrote, in which the assault on Western civilization had not been repulsed from within and the inability of Europe to liberate itself from the evils of antisemitism did not augur well for the future.(16)

The spontaneous Jewish response to what had happpened during the war and after was to take leave of Europe especially when they came to realize that they, the handful of survivors, were seen as a nuisance and that very few Europeans sincerely mourned the annihilation of their Jewish communities. The prevalent tendency was to hold Western civilization as a whole responsible for the Holocaust and to see Nazi Germany as giving expression to attitudes that were widely shared throughout the continent. Gringauz while drawn to this point of view strived to achieve a more balanced perspective that would help heal the psychic wounds left by the war, that would contribute to the achievement of political goals of the Jewish people while leading to the reappropriation of values that the Jewish people had brought to their interaction with the European world.

In this fashion Gringauz's call to take leave of Europe moved from being a primarily moral protest to become an historically necessary step of a more constructive kind. The initial premise which guided this new thinking was the recognition that the European era of Jewish history had drawn to a close and that the Holocaust had created a radically new situation: the Jewish future would of necessity now focus on two new centers - America and Palestine. In consequence the remnants of European Jewry were obligated to carrytheir cultural heritage to the two new centres that would shoulder the burden of shaping the Jewish future. "The renunciation of Europe in no way signifies for us the renunciation of European culture. Quite the contrary. Our resolve to quit Europe is based precisely on the the conviction that Europe itself has betrayed the legacy of European culture and that European culture must be carried forward outside of Europe. We have been too much part of European culture to abandon it now. As we once expressed it: 'We leave Europe because Europe has injured us in our very quality as Europeans.'" (17)

Gringauz located the core of this Jewish - European ethic in what he termed "neo-humanism" which began with a commitment to the sanctity of human life and in the context of the post-Holocaust world sought to translate it into reality by closing the gap between the technological advances of mankind and its moral development. Thus he hoped that Zionism would go beyond the crucial return of the Jewish people to its historic homeland and would also involve a commitment to universal concerns. It was in the cooperative settlements of Eretz Yisrael that these ideals could pass their ultimate test, the test of translation into reality, and thereafter serve as a beacon to people everywhere.

Thus it could be said that **She'erith Hapleitah** went through a dialectical process in its attempt to forge a relationship to the countries and civilization that let them down so badly. The initial response was one of total rejection followed by a process of partial moderation. It would not do, so it was argued, for the Jews to enclose themselves within a wall of hatred and neither was it wise for a small people to turn its back on the constituency of decent people who held out the hand of friendship. Ultimately the most viable synthesis between rejection and accomodation was found in the drive to create a Jewish state. Through Zionism one could leave Europe and recast the Jewish relationship to the world on a new basis of reciprocity: Europe could be left behind while its finest ideals, many of which were of Jewish provenance, could inform the creation of a new society.

The romanticization of **She'erith Hapleita** is a constant temptation and in this context it would only be fair to note that its sharpest critics were the Jewish DP's themselves. They mecilessly exposed their own shortcomings and refused to accept the Holocaust as a blanket excuse for their failings. Given our stress on the constructive and defiant side of **She'erith Hapleitah**, we have to ask whether this is a distortion of the past. The answer is to be found in the recounting of the many and powerful forces that could so easily have cast the survivors into a bottomless pit of nihilistic abandon. Here were a group of people who had lost everything that was dear to them, who had been exposed to unspeakable suffering and now found themselves living on handouts in DP camps, in Germany, with no way out and totally dependent on governments that had very different priorities.

Thus the truth about the survivors emerges when the history of the **She'erith** is seen as a continuous struggle between opposing forces, a struggle wherein, for the most part, the affirmation of life came out on top. In this struggle it was the vitality and defiance of the survivors that set the norm, that found expression in the numerous marriages and high birthrate, in rehabilitation projects, educational concerns and cultural activities. Indeed, the record of **She'erith Hapleitah** compares most favourably with the sad breakdown of dignity and restraint that marked German life under occupation. The sources of this remarkable resilience can be sought in the traditional Jewish commitment to the sanctification of life but its more immediate inspiration is to be found in the Holocaust itself. On numerous occasions survivors held up the sanctification of life in the ghettos - the impossible fight against the cold, hunger, disease and dehumanization - as their model and inspiration. Thus the suffering of the past did not provide a sanction for wild abandon and untrammeled rage.

This conscious tie between the vitality of **She'erith Hapleitah** and spiritual resistance during the Holocaust appears to confirm the view of historians who see the sanctification of life as a key dimension of Jewish behaviour in the face of disaster. From this point of view the Surviving Remnant can serve as a control group in comparing behaviour during and after the Holocaust and in this context the fact that the survivors in Germany became the leaders of European Jewry so soon after liberation raises some interesting questions. It appears to refute, for example, those characterizations of Jewish behaviour during the Holocaust which rest on the notion of a "ghetto mentality". Such conditioned passivity could not be undone by an act of will in such a short space of time, especially in view of the important lines of continuity that begin during the Holocaust and persist into liberation. The initial organization of **She'erith Hapleitah** began, as we saw, many months before liberation and in itself was the product of clandestine activity that had begun two or three years before. Many arguments have been directed against Hilberg and Bettelheim and the historically rooted activism of the Surviving Remnant is another.

The affirmation of life of which we speak was inspired by what came before and has, we suggest, similarly influenced those who come after. A number of thinkers have warned against the obsessive concern with the Holocaust fearing that it will breed alienation and a sovereign disregard for outsiders. While the fear is understandable reality, thus far at least, has followed a different course and the destructive implications of the Holocaust have been kept at bay. **She'erith Hapleitah**, in our view, filled a significant role in shaping this reality. They had every cause to surrender themselves to blind anger and cynical destructiveness. But this, by and large, has not been the case: while the suffering and losses they sustained were their point of departure their best energies were given over to grappling with the fundamental causes of the Jewish catastrophe. In the aftermath of the Holocaust the survivors refused to surrender their humanity and once they turned their backs on nihilistic despair they created a norm which those who were not "there" cannot easily disregard.

Notes.

1. Rudolf Hoess, The Commandant of Auschwitz, New York,1972, p.178.
2. Victor Frankl, Man's Search for Meaning, Boston, 1963. Terrence Des Pres, The Survivor: An Anatomy of Life in the Death Camps, New York, 1976.
3. Primo Levi, Survival in Auschwitz, New York, 1961, p.79.
4. **Techiyat Hametim: A Newspaper for Liberated Jews in the Camps**, Buchenwald, 4.5.1945, (Yiddish), Yad Vashem Archives, Jerusalem.
5. **Nizoz: Organ of the Association of National Youth in the Concentration Camp Dachau-Kaufering**, (Hebrew) Yad Vashem Archives, Jerusalem.
6. Ivri (Shlomo Frankel-Shafir), "At the Crossroads", **Nizoz**, No.3(38), Chanukah, 1944, p.14-15.
7. Aryeh (Leib Garfunkel), "A Hint of Hope", **Nizoz**, No.5(40), Purim 1945, p.72-73.
8. Robert J. Lifton, Death In Life: Survivors of Hiroshima, New York, 1969, p.481.
9. David Wolpe, "The Hope of the Golah", **Nizoz**, No.6(41), Eve of Passover, 1945, p.93.
10. Jean Amery, At the Mind's Limits: Contemplations by a Survivor on Auschwitz, Bloomington, 1980.
11. Moshe Smolar, I Fought for my Life, Tel Aviv, 1978, p.159-160. (Hebrew)
12. Dr. Leo Srole, Submission to the Anglo-American Commission for Palestine, AJDC Archive, File DP's Germany, 1946.
13. Ethel Ostry, After the Holocaust: My Work with UNRRA, ed. Elizabeth Fisher, Private Edition, 1978, Yad Vashem Library, p.127-128.
14. Leo W. Schwarz, "Memorial in Munich", Congress Weekly, Vol.22, No.15, April 18 1955, p.6.
15. Dr. Samuel Gringauz, "1945 in World History", **Landsberger Lager Cajtung**, No.12, 31.12.1945, p.3. (Yiddish)
16. Samuel Gringauz, "Jewish Destiny as the DP's see It: The Ideology of the Surviving Remnant", Commentary, Vo.4, No.6, December 1947, p.505.

THE RETURN OF THE SECRET JEWS
(Jewish children sheltered from the Holocaust by Christians and returned to the Jewish Community)

by Odette Meyers

2627 Fulton St.Berkeley, CA 94704, U.S.

-They jeopardized their own and their family's lives to do what they did, but they also know little or nothing of Jews.

-...after the war, it was just business as usual. No one gave us any kind of pyschological assistance. We smoldered in ourselves.

-...if they had not closed the door on my Christian past, making me feel it had simply been a necessary evil in order to survive. If I could have felt free to talk about it...

-...if it would have been talked about, it would have helped me get over the feeling I had - But my parents had their own struggle with themselves, having come back from their own war experiences, my father from Auschwitz, my mother from hiding.

-Through the needs of my own child I learned of my needs. I better understand the deprivation of those years and the losses I suffered.

This sampling of responses to a questionnaire by adult Jewish child survivors summarizes their unique dilemma. They were spared a Holocaust death by being sheltered in the Christian world, but they were left to resolve their identity conflicts alone and in silence. The sampling brings up a number of important questions: 1) just what was the nature of their experience? 2) how did they live their transition from the Christian world to the post-war Jewish world? 3) how did the silence and repression surrounding their Christian years affect their development into mature adults? 4) why has the breaking of that silence begun to occur only recently? and finally 5) what lessons can we learn that may help us "remember for the future" with lucid honesty?

In the vast amount of literature on the Holocaust, very little appears on the experience of those Jewish children who survived by being placed in a Christian environment during the war and were later returned to the Jewish community. The recent work of Sarah Moskovitz provides an important exception.

In her follow-up interviews of a group of child survivors from concentration camps, orphanages and from hiding who were cared for at the experimental Lingfield Home in England, Moskovitz does include a few adults who had spent their early childhood in a Christian environment. In her concluding chapter, aptly entitled "Reflections", she notes - about all the survivors: "One can hardly turn a page of most of the interviews without sensing the continuing burden of loss the survivors feel for parents whom they may never have known, a hunger for some link with the past through family connections destroyed or distorted, for traces of themselves buried in childhoods they dare not remember." (*Love Despite Hate,* Child Survivors of the Holocaust and their adult lives, Schocken Books, New York, 1983, p.226)

My study is based on a long detailed questionnaire of a sampling of child survivors who were sheltered by Christian individuals or institutions, and now live in the United States. Its results confirm Moskovitz's observations. But what stands out is not only the "hunger...for traces of themselves in buried childhoods they dare not remember", but also the sadness of their painful efforts to satisfy that hunger unaided by the world at large. In the case of the subjects of my study, that quest implied an added level of complexity: the fact that the "self" buried in their Christian childhood was a double self - the open Christian one they had to assume in order to survive, and their previous Jewish self they had to keep secret. Characterizing the nature of that dilemna are the following two survivors' comments: "Christian identity could not be secondary, it had to be primary for survival." and "I associate it with being in hiding, undercover, not being my true self."

Since the formative years of childhood determine the course of an adult's life, how does one manage to reclaim a self that was not only buried in one's past but was never fully a "true self", especially if the message you get as you approach your post-war adolescence, from both your private world and the world at large is to "forget it" and get back to "normalcy"? Normalcy? For a European Jewish child in the aftermath of the Holocaust? Given the unusual childhoods of this group of survivors, it is humbling to see how how they have managed to grow into responsible and compassionate adults, despite an incurable "secret" sadness and a deep sense of difference, of alienation.

My academic training is in the field of French poetry and I belong to the group I study. My approach is consistent with my training: once placed in its historical perspective, I consider the <u>text</u> that I work with (the questionnaire) my major source of information. As an "insider" to the group, I feel that my own experience had two effects: it gave my respondents the trust necessary to answer some very hard questions (or in some cases answer the questionnaire at all) and as someone familiar with juggling more than one identity, it allowed me to be both on the inside and the outside of the "text" so as to better evaluate its meaning.

HISTORICAL AND EDUCATIONAL PERSPECTIVES:

As children, these respondents were suddenly uprooted from their Jewish families, placed in a strange, Christian environment - mostly with families - where they assumed a Christian identity and kept their Jewish identity secret. When the war was over, they were suddenly uprooted from their Christian host families and replaced in a Jewish community that had been so devastated that it bore little resemblance to their original milieu. In most cases, they had been orphaned of one or both parents and so had to adapt to yet a third family setting. Urged to "forget the past" and re-establish "normal lives", they complied. Within the next few years, they would have to make yet another radical transition and leave Europe for the United States, in most cases with yet another family.

Imagine this kind of experience happening to a group of European or American children within the last 20 years. Public acknowledgment of the enormous difficulties they had faced in coping with their multiple and painful transitions would have most likely provided a whole network of psychological help. Sociologists and psychologists would have conducted studies and written books and articles on the subject. The fact that so little of this took place then, brings up several critical points in relation to the group being studied:

1. The enormity of the trauma caused by the Holocaust was such that it has taken us the last 40 years (a biblical generation) to begin to understand and appreciate its long-range effects on all its survivors.

2. Attitudes toward children have changed radically. In the 1940's, children were still trained to unquestioningly obey and respect their parents and guardians. They were believed to be extremely flexible, quick to adapt thoroughly to any new situation. Their "child-size" problems were temporary, would pass with time, as the Jewish saying went: "before they married."

3. Traumatized by the realization that governments and, with rare exceptions, individuals had at best closed their eyes to the fate of the Jews or the fact that centuries of European antisemitism had prepared the ground for the Holocaust, the remnant of the post-war European Jewish community closed in upon itself, counted its losses, including a million and a half of its children, and concentrated on its surviving young who could reclaim a future for its people. Naturally, it was eager to make sure its young had a strong Jewish identity.

It is important to remember those points. They help us place this study in its proper historical perspective. This generation of Jewish children was caught between the Jewish and the Christian worlds, growing up in highly abnormal times and being urged to pursue a "normal life" without even the benefit of a private or public recognition of the abnormalcy of their childhood. As a whole, aside from sad but gently understanding regrets at having had to work out their problems by themselves, the survivors do not blame either their hosts or their families, but rather the over-all war experience and the lack of knowledge of each other's culture between Jews and Christians.

I will first tell you what personal discoveries led me to research this subject. Then, I will describe the methodology I used to gather the data, present the results, and finally discuss my interpretation of those results and draw my conclusions.

I myself fit into that category of survivors. I migrated from France to the United States in 1949, at the age of fourteen. Until I started this study, I had typically known (and not till my thirties) only one other person with a similar experience. Like my peers, I considered myself lucky to have survived. I felt privileged to have had a wonderful Catholic rescuer for part of my rescue story (rarely mentioning the other, more troubling parts of my survival - and its painful aftermath - as a secret Jew in a deeply antisemitic Catholic rural setting.) And like my peers, until very recently, I did not think of myself as a "Holocaust survivor," a term I associated strictly with concentration camp survivors. As a consequence, I felt that the right and responsibility of bearing witness belonged to those camp survivors who were older than I at the time and had suffered the worst.

However, in the last few years, I was called upon to tell the story of my rescuer in public. I did so, at a conference on righteous gentiles in 1984 in Washington, D.C. when I also participated in interviews in both the film "The Courage to Care" and its companion book by the same title. This involvement later led to my being more and more frequently called upon to do presentations on the subject in local schools and other community organizations, to Jewish, Christian, and mixed audiences.

As a teacher by profession (although on a university level), I was especially interested in my class-room experiences. There, my approach was to tell the essence of my story briefly, and then to open myself to whatever questions the children would ask. I figured that this way they would learn what they wanted to learn, not what I, as an adult, assumed they would or should want to know.

Although they were profoundly relieved to learn that there were indeed some good people who helped Jews, they (logically) wanted to know what happened to those children who were not so lucky. I had to tell them; they were stunned. But to my surprise, they also asked me questions no one else had ever asked me. They were very curious about what it was like for me to be a Jewish child (their age) in occupied Paris, and later, hiding in the country, what it felt like to pass as a Catholic and finally, how it felt to be Jewish again after the war and now. They, in effect, were conducting a collective interview from their own child's point of view. They drew out of me many memories that had been buried for decades. Its was startling, upsetting, and revealing. I suddenly realized the value of my particular kind of testimony in educating young people on the Holocaust. Originally, I had thought that what I could offer them was the consolation of the decency of rescuers, but then I saw that aside from that, I could also make them empathize with the over-all fate of the Jews during the Holocaust, through my personal story as a Jewish child in WWII Europe. In the pure cartesian reasoning natural to children, it was easier - and more enriching - for them to proceed from the concrete to the abstract, from the simple to the complex. Their questions followed that line of logical thought. Two aspects of my story also held a special dramatic appeal to them: being rescued from extreme danger and living under false identity.

In order to be able to offer the children a fuller and broader view of the story and place myself in perspective within the group of survivors to which I belonged, I looked for material in print....and found very little. Of the rare printed testimonies of a secret Jewish childhood, *A Touch of Earth, A Wartime Childhood,* by the Polish Jew, Janina David (The Orion Press, New York, 1966) proved to me most thorough (perhaps because it was based on the diary she kept through those years). In it, David confronted and described not only the "before" and "during" parts of her stay in the Catholic world, but also, what I was particularly looking for, the transition between the Catholic and the Jewish-again part of her childhood spiritual journey.

After the war, away from the shelter of the convent, and the new ties she had made there, living with relatives with whom she did not discuss her Catholic past, and waiting in vain for her parents to return from camp, she got discouraged: *Life was impossible. It was too difficult. I didn't know how to live. There was no one to show me, to tell me what to do, how to do it and most important; Why.* (p.184). As an escape, she goes to movies, almost indiscriminately. Once, unaware of what was going to be shown, she sees a film showing the liberation of a concentration camp. In the scenes of horror, she strains in vain to recognize her parents in the living skeletons of survivors. She hears someone say the dead numbered millions. At that point, she suddenly loses both her hope that her parents would return, and her religious faith. She writes: *In the cinema the spectators wept, fainted and prayed aloud. I came out into the cold winter night with clenched teeth and murder in my heart. My last childish dream was dead: There was no God.* (p.193). Eventually, her youth and her stubborn love of life prevailed, and she found out what to do and why: she wrote a fully honest, detailed and beautiful testimony of her complicated childhood and the life and death of her religious faith. (Unfortunately, her book has long been out of print.)

I wondered how typical Janina David's experience and reactions to that experience were. Since I could not find much else in print along that line, when the "Call for papers" came for the "Remembering for the Future" conference, I decided to collect the personal testimonies of a pilot group of twenty ex-children who shared a somewhat similar experience and conduct a formal systematic study. The fact that I was one of them and was personally involved as an educator on the Holocaust was helpful. I was very moved by the degree of honesty and the intelligent sensitivity with which they answered my questionnaire.

METHODOLOGY:

After intensive informal talks and/or telephone interviews with potential research subjects, I designed a comprehensive 13 page questionnaire that called for both yes/no or other objective, factual short answers, and relatively longer subjective or descriptive answers. I did so because I needed both the facts and the feelings, and I wanted to hear (and transmit) the actual words of the respondents, in their own voice and their own tone.

I divided the questionnaire into four major parts: I) Before the War, II) During the War (in two sections: "At point of entry into Christian world" and "During your stay in Christian world"), III) After the War (in two sections: "Immediate post-war" and "As time went on...to the present) and IV) Conclusions.

My goal was to concentrate on the transition between the subjects' stay in the Christian world and their return to the Jewish world - first to the European, then to the American one. I would analyze the effects of that transition on their adult lives and report on their own interpretation of their childhood experience as well as on the generalisations they could draw from it that may be useful to contemporary Jewish-Christian relations.

It was necessary, however, that I place that area of concentration in proper perspective. To do so, I needed to know what variables might affect the nature of the respondents' transition. For part I, the pre-war period, it meant: their date of birth, their family environment, including the degree and kind of Jewish identity and religious education they grew up with in their early years, the family's attitudes toward Christians, etc. For Part II, the war period, I needed to know the circumstances of their ending up in the Christian world, their age at the time, whether they were with a family or an institution, physically confined or at large living under false identity, their external and inner involvement with the Christian religion. I also had to find out how they handled their double identity, what perception of Jews was given them in their new environment, whether or not they formed strong emotional bonds to their Christian hosts. The questions throughout were chronologically and thematically sequenced to elicit that kind of information.

The third part, After the War, is the longest (6½ pp.) and deals with the transition from the Christian years back to the post-war Jewish community, which is at the center of my study. I will refer to the questions I raised and will summarize their answers in the following section detailing the results of my study.

The fourth part, Conclusions. is short, but elicited the longest comments as it asked the respondents how, in retrospect, they thought their transition would have been easier if handled differently by Jews and non-Jews, how their perception of their childhood had changed and what conclusions they could draw from their experience that would be useful to others.

All told, over 80% of the questionnaires I sent out were returned completed. Of the people who did not fill them out, most had been orphaned by the war and had lived their childhood years in a convent. After the war, they had been placed in a Jewish orphanage, and later sent to relatives in the U.S. It seemed evident that they had been most traumatized by their experience, and that their memories were too painful to revive and sort out. I never insisted, but I am convinced that further efforts should be made to study this particular group of people.

RESULTS:

The group of 20 people consisted of 15 females and 5 males. This high proportion of females to males may reflect the fact that hiding circumcised boys put the host families or institutions at greater risk than hiding girls.

Twelve of the children came from two countries: 7 from Holland and 5 from France; there were 2 each from Poland and Austria, and 1 each from Belgium, Germany, Yugoslavia and Hungary. During the war, all of the Dutch children lived in Protestant homes, except for one who lived in a Catholic family. Children from other countries were placed with Catholics (two in convents, two in children's homes, the rest with families). Almost all of the hosts were deeply religious.

When the war ended, 16 of them were between 5 and 13, with the following age distribution: 5-7:6; 8-10:5; 11-13:5. At either extreme, the 2 youngest ones were 3 and under, the 2 oldest were 15 and 19.

Of the 20, only 2 never married, and a total of 3 (including those 2) never had children. Of the 17 who had children, only 1 did not raise them to be conscious Jews, and 1 raised the younger of her two children with Jewish consciousness. Although the question was not asked, one fifth of the parents volunteered the information that their spouse was non-Jewish, which gives yet greater weight to the choice made to encourage children to be Jewish.

The choice of career varied, with one third being teachers, and the others running the gamut of various professional, semi-professional or business positions. None, however, was in a position of great authority or power.

To summarize the mass of details gathered in the questionnaires, I will take the following approach: first outline a typical scenario most representative of the majority of the respondents, then deal separately with the variables.

Most Typical Scenario:

- The children are raised in a close-knit, nuclear family who has a favorable attitude toward Christians in general, and friendly relations with Christian individuals. Although mostly religious at home, the family, especially in Holland and Germany, tends to be assimilated.

- Still young (mostly under 8) they are abruptly separated from their parents who are deported or go underground, and thereafter have no contact, except through occasional correspondence (or rare visits) with one parent.

- The children have been placed in a Christian family who knew they were Jewish but had not known them before. A few are physically confined to their hiding place. The others move around freely under false identiy.

- They miss their parents, but eventually get attached to their foster family, and take to their whole way of life, which includes religion. The younger the child, the more profound the attachment. They realize the danger involved (almost everyone notes the occurence of "close calls" and the pervasiveness of fear of being caught).

- sworn to secrecy (which they faithfully maintain) as to their Jewish origin, they suppress their feelings of sadness, betrayal and inferiority when they see Jews portrayed in a variety of negative ways (ranging from victims to Christ-killers) in their new Christian environment. That is true of most of those placed in Catholic homes or institutions, while those placed in Protestant homes (Holland) are given two major impressions of Jews: that they are "misguided" in not recognizing Christ as savior, or that Jews as the "Chosen People" deserve special protection.

- On their return to the Jewish community, they have many new and confusing problems to confront at once, in the powerless status children held in those days:

1. In the majority of cases, they are orphaned of one or both parents.

2. The death of their parent(s) and close relatives is unnatural - even uncertain, mysterious. The most common explanation they are given is: "they never came back." Death then is associated with both being Jewish and long separation. Many hold fantasies that those who "never came back" are alive somewhere, have amnesia which explains why they have not yet con-

tacted their family, but that they will do so sooner or later.

3. Deaths of parent(s) and/or relatives are not only unnatural (most were young) but are actual, impersonal murders. Knowledge of that comes mostly gradually, but very painfully, and is sometimes associated with a temporary or permanent loss of religious faith (as was the case with Janina David).

4. The foster family to whom they had gotten attached, and who had served as substitute family during time of crisis, is now far away. The "message" is: forget them and their ways, your Christian identity was just a necessary evil; let's get back to business as usual (though that was hard to believe if the family was not intact). Though respect is granted the foster family for their decent behavior, the whole episode is turned into an abstraction and the children kept away from actual contact with their rescuers. The children then suffer a second trauma of separation.

5. The children are given a Jewish education, in which Christians are either not mentioned, or at best are "the others". An exception is made of the respected minority of Righteous Gentiles. The original identity of Jewishness must be regained; the other (the Christian one) forgotten. Often, then, the children feel ashamed of their Christian past, as if somehow it represented a betrayal of their people who had just suffered the worst catastrophe in their history. Adult survivors are the spokespeople of the Holocaust experience. In view of the hierarchy of suffering which prevails, and the mass of documentation that surfaces, no one - least of all the children themselves - acknowledges their trauma and conflicts, except in their status as full or half orphans. A shamed silence covers the rest, particularly their Christian years. On the positive side of the Jewish education they receive, the children enjoy the sense of belonging, of "coming home" to a rich set of traditions, a long history, a great deal of warmth and communal caring. On the negative side, many are oppressed by the history of persecution, the horrors of the Shoah, the ethnocentricity of their community, the "strangeness" of the rituals.

6. Some struggle for a long time with the sense that, on balance, it would have been more desirable for them to have been born Christians. Some feel that their Christianity is so much a part of them that they must continue, somehow, to practice that religion. A number of them (almost half) temporarily - and with a double level of guilt, both toward Jews and toward Christians - become "secret Christians" - from a few months to a few years.

7. The children, used to having a "secret self", a "secret past" accept the situation as given. They do not have outlets for talking about it to anyone, including their peers who had a similar fate, since all are silent, and all are trying to reconstruct a semblance of normalcy with whatever new family configuration or its facsimile they have to deal with.

8. With few exceptions, respondents disclaim suffering psychological problems related to the change-over of religious environment. In retrospect, they claim that they suffered more from the over-all war experience, particularly separation from parents. Few volunteer to say - until almost the end of the questionnaire - that the second separation (from foster family and its world) also caused problems. (Meaningful reunions and contacts with the foster family would be mostly initiated by the children when they became adults, with families of their own. Those reunions were emotionally loaded, mostly marked by immense gratitude and pleasure on both sides.)

Adult life:

- As adults, they have placed great value on their own family life, raised their children to be conscious Jews, giving them either a religious or a secular education involving the home and the community, or both.

- Having children, and the recent emerging of a public interest in their type of story, were major factors in their growing awareness that their own childhood had been highly abnormal. Their answers to the question of how their perception of their particular kind of childhood had changed in recent times, if it had (which it did for 3/4 of them) brought out an impressive number of strong and clear answers. All pointed to the unanimous conclusion that it had been a painfully traumatic, confusing and alienating childhood, fraught with losses not fully mourned, and with unresolved and buried psychological conflicts dealing with security, self-esteem and acceptance.

- Almost all of them had told their story in private, to members of their family and close friends. In a recent development, nearly half of them have started to tell their story in a public forum (schools, youth groups and other community institutions). Their story was received with interest and sympathy - American Jews showing more ambivalent guilt and relief at having been spared, non-Jews showing more shock and surprise and young people reacting with more uncomprehending disbelief that such an event had actually happened - though it seemed to them to be something of rather ancient history.

- To the question as to why they felt it was important that others should know about their kind of story, they gave variations of the following responses: "to know what happened.", "so it never happens again.", "to bear witness that it happened.", "to better understand capabilities of humans for good or evil."

- Their conclusions divided into the following categories:
a) we need more and better understanding - and mutual respect between Jews and Christians. (90%); everyone is basically the same, stress similarities.(5%) and c)be selective in trust of Christians. Respect those who act with respect toward Jews and everyone; ignore the others.(5%)

Important variables:

1. Age:

Two children were orphaned babies when they were placed in host families (1 with a gentile relative, the other through the Red Cross, to an unrelated Protestant family.) Neither learned of their Jewish identity - or of what happened to their parents until much later. Both were uprooted from their second set of parents to yet a new family. In case of the one in the Protestant family, his surviving uncle had to fight a legal battle to get custody of him which he won by a narrow vote. Both have struggled to acquire a sense of belonging. A third was placed with a Catholic family when she was 3, and was not reclaimed from it by her natural mother until she was 12. She has remained torn by conflicts of loyalty to her two mothers and her two religious backgrounds, living her adult life as a Catholic until a recent loss of faith which triggered a serious crisis, but never denying her Jewish identity. She still suffers, as do many of the survivors, from fear of separations. At the other extreme, the two oldest, as was the case with most of the children over 10 when the war was over, had the easiest time dealing with a double identity: their pre-war exposure to Judaism was strong enough that they only went through the necessary motions of acting as Christians without adopting the Christian faith.

2. Institutions:

a. Convents:
The two girls sheltered in convents were the most permanently traumatized - although that became apparent only in recent times. One is recovering from a nervous breakdown, the other, also in therapy, suffers from suicidal tendencies. Neither of them has maintained contacts with their hosts. Both had serious problems related to their double identity. The first tried to resolve them by calling herself a "Catholic Jew", then transcending all religious distinctions. She says: "I figure if there's a God, he would not necessarily be Christian or Jewish-He would be closer to Nature and rather indifferent to our sufferings." The other had troubled relationships - with both Jewish and Christian men - which were marked by her own conflicts over her Jewish identity. She is particularly bitter about the imposition of religious distinctions during her difficult transition.

b. Children's homes:
Two children were placed in homes that were not affiliated with a religious order (in the same countries as the convents, France and Belgium). They were not exposed to anti-Jewish feelings, had happier experiences and have kept contacts with their hosts. Although they did have some lingering sense of unease just under the surface, their transition was not acutely painful as the others.

3. Pride in being Jewish was:

a) always there (that was true almost exclusively of the older children who had a longer pre-war family life).

b) temporarily (and partially or completely) crushed during the Christian exposure years as well as the immediate post-war ones with their revelations about the full nature and extent of the Holocaust. This was followed by a long struggle to gain or regain that pride through involvment in the religious or secular Jewish community.

c) permanently crushed and never regained. This applied particularly to those who felt that they had been saved by Christians not for themselves but for their souls, and later reclaimed by Jews more for their Jewish origins than their child selves. It is hard to say, however, that they managed to acquire a "Christian pride". They seem rather to have suffered from lack of any sort of pride in belonging to any people.

4. The transition to the U.S.:

All indicated that their last uprooting was accompanied by much confusion and alienation, in a society that traditionally discourages immigrants from dwelling on their past, and a Jewish community whose attitude toward the Holocaust was often marked by guilt and ambivalence. Suffering the greatest sense of displacement were those orphans who had already gone through a series of temporary homes after returning from their Christian one(s). Most upsetting were the situations where the new immigrants' Jewish identity was deemed undesirable by their new (Jewish) hosts. In a couple of extreme cases, the new family pressured them not to say that they were Jewish and in one case, the adolescent girl was pressured to convert to the Lutheran religion, but refused and married a Jew. On the level of personal integration into the new family, a couple of adolescent girls fared badly. They were used as housekeepers and baby-sitters by the American aunts and uncles they had expected to welcome them as family members. The confusion and disapointment were horrendous.

5. Attitudes toward Christian hosts took the following shape:

- The greatest number (90%) were very grateful and felt a special bond; they kept or renewed contacts with their hosts. It helped them maintain a "faith in humankind" which sustained them through their adult lives and, I think, contributed to their high degree of tolerance and compassion and their deep concerns with ethical issues, despite the complexities of the conflicts and losses they had suffered.

- Some (especially those who had a series of assorted rescuers) made a clear distinction between them. They were bitter toward those who acted out of greed for money (one tells of her Polish rescuer who put her and her mother back on the streets of Warsaw when their money ran out), or those who mostly valued the "good points" acquired through "saving a soul". They had immense respect, love and gratitude, for those truly righteous gentiles who acted out of conviction that it was the right thing, or the Christian thing to do.

CONCLUSIONS:

More than 40 years have passed since these "secret Jews" returned to the Jewish community. The hopes that came out of the victims' ashes: the creation of a democratic Jewish state that would eventually live at peace with its neighbors, the belief that the devastation of World War II would have taught our society that the horrors of war could not permanently benefit anyone and that war would therefore be wisely abandoned as means of settling conflicts, that knowledge of the Holocaust would forever bar any repetition of genocide - all those hopes have faded through the years, in a world additionally beset by new and grave problems created by both war and peace technologies and persistent greed.

In view of all this, a buried double self in a distant childhood seems a small matter. Still, one has to live out one's life the best one can. And as a whole, our group of survivors has done so quite honorably. It is my belief that they drew their strength principally from close family members and friends and from involvement in the Jewish community for the sake of their family. Such concrete emphasis on individuals is in keeping with their childhood experience. As children everywhere, they did not deal in abstractions: love and safety and even religion were embodied not in generalities but in specific individuals. In their case, however, their own individuality was threatened, diminished or contradicted by their being submerged into an abstraction in relation to the Holocaust and their place in it.

If we can value this group of child-survivors now turned adults and encourage them not only to break out of their long silence but also out of the oppression of abstractions, if we can let them reveal to us their remembered child's view of the Holocaust, in all its concreteness, we could nurture a critical resource of personal information that our young, especially the children, can identify with. With the diminishing number of those camp survivors who were willing to relive their days of horror in order that others may know "what happened", we are left with those survivors who were children. Of those, very few survived concentration camps, so their story is basically that of passing as Christians. Some were returned to the Jewish community, some were not.

Many of those who are conscious of the responsibility of belonging to the last generation of eye-witnesses feel that they have problems clearly remembering their confusing childhoods and because of it are not in a position to speak out in public. There are several ways, though, that would help them retrieve more memories:1) participation in a child-survivor group; 2) reading scholarly books, articles, interviews related to people of similar experience; 3) reading short stories, novels, poetry or seeing plays and films that portray such childhood histories; 4) exposing themselves to audience questions (especially of children) after telling whatever they remember of their story in public and finally 5) being offered advice and support from professional community educators.

All this would encourage them to talk about their experiences and their related feelings - something they were so long denied. It would provide them some relief from isolation, and all of us a fuller understanding of the ramifications of the Holocaust, and of how we can give more rounded educational presentations of the subject. These survivors were spared the gas chamber and so got through life feeling that they had "no story" since they had been lucky enough to survive - or that whatever resembled some kind of "story" had no particular importance and in any case, no one was interested in it. Yet, it is now evident that they were confronted by some of the most complex emotional and spiritual dilemnas ever faced - unaided - by a generation of children, in that they had to maintain their original identity secret, adopt a new one, disadopt it, regain the original one which the Holocaust had irreparably modified...and yet were expected to grow up as normal, decent adults, full Jews and good Americans.

My study shows that, 43 years after their return to the Jewish world and the injunction for them to get back on track to a "normal life", four new developments are occuring: 1) the realization of how traumatic, how abnormal their childhood had been, 2) the long-delayed mourning for their parents, relatives, neighbors and for the peers they have lost 3) a renewed gratitude for the offer of safety, and often love or deep caring of their rescuers and 4) the beginning of their speaking out on all that, in public or among themselves.

Like Hansel and Gretel, they can look for pebbles they had dropped, to help them chart their return to the dwelling of their true selves. Some of the pebbles are memories of how they were the recipients of active and efficient love (or at least caring) from both their Jewish parents or guardians and their Christian hosts - even though it seemed so bumbled at times, through human weakness or group ignorance. Contemporary children, themselves so often torn by conflicting family loyalties, are quite able to identify with such a situation. Some of the pebbles, though, feel heavy as lead. They are memories of the proximity and pervasiveness of abandon, danger, betrayal, death...how does one show those to children?

If there is a death in a child's family, our instinct is not to keep ourselves at arm's length, and give a clinical description of death and dying, but rather to hug them warmly and talk of the person who died, who mattered so much, who hoped and cared and loved. And gradually, we can tell them the clinical facts so they can handle that person's permanent absence. How much more do we need to do that when we have to explain not a simple, individual, natural death, but the mass murder of six million people for a reason that they cannot accept as legitimate!

Still, how do you teach about the Jewish Holocaust of the past when to contemporary children that word echoes the other one, the feared nuclear holocaust for which no yellow star is needed? How do you teach it to the young without risking to turn them to stone from fear, impotence or worse, indifference? The ideal would be if, instead of burying the six million in the mass grave of their collective number, we could recite not only each of their names but portray every one of their lives. Since no one can do that, it is important to remember the popularity of Anne Frank's diary, and the current critical reception of Louis Malle's most recent film "Au Revoir Les Enfants!" Both make us relive a Jewish child's life before it was brutally ended by the Shoah. The concrete, the personalized individual histories give an effective access to the history of the Holocaust. From there, little by little, the reader, viewer or listener can proceed to learn of the terrifying anti-life machinery of the Shoah, fueled by depersonalization and abstraction of human beings. But he must have something positive, life-affirming, not only to contrast it with, but also to use as a raft against being drowned in despair.

We must listen to the children, the ones in our classrooms, the ones in our memory, learn from them to avoid abstractions, of whatever kind, including the "good ones" such as "love". The child survivors I studied suffered as children from an overdose of abstractions and are therefore in a privileged position to know the stifling, paralyzing affect of abstraction, the importance of valuing the concrete, the personal, the individual. If they can be encouraged to contribute, in their personal presence and in their own words, to the study and the teaching of the Holocaust, we will all be enriched.

In a small gesture along that line, I would like to end this paper the way I started it, with the voices of the witnesses, articulating their pains and triumphs:

- (entry into the Christian world) mainly entailed being ripped out of my own environment, wondering about the fate of my father and now also of my mother, being thrown into a totally foreign milieu and having to bury my past while acquiring a new present.

- I knew to be Jewish was undesirable. It meant losing your parents. It meant that to be a Jew was to be in danger and not something to be proud of. It meant that you had to keep your Jewishness secret.

- I don't see it as the "Christian world" since I didn't know a Jewish world to contrast it with. At the age of 8 I "left" Christianity, at the same time a loving family ("my" family, I thought). They risked their lives for me. I later commented on this to them as an adult parent myself; they seemed surprised - "How could we have done otherwise?"

- True Christians never betray Jews.

- I had been given a St. Christopher medal, when leaving Holland, by my Christian family, to come to America and my aunt and uncle (my new Jewish parents whom I did not know) to keep always as a memento - I had promised. It was taken away. They were horrified.

- We are Jewish, we will be Jewish, and we must preserve knowledge of ourselves. We must understand the world and the forces that shape it, to be able to survive and evolve with it, whatever shape our identity will take.

-...the Holocaust happened to real people; ....some good people took responsibilities for others.

Impact of the Holocaust on Second Generation of Survivors: The Differential Socialization of Affirmative Commitment to the Collective

David Mittelberg

The Institute for Research of the Kibbutz and the Cooperative Idea, University of Haifa, Israel.

This paper draws on four distinct sources of data. The first is the professional literature predominantly psychological and psychiatrical which dealt with the effects of the Holocaust on the second generation.(1) It was the clinicians who coined the term, styled the language and described the parameters of the phenomena. I will briefly relate to this data concentrating only on the most recent and indeed more interesting work in the field.

The second is the writings of some of the prominent members of the second generation who discovered the meaning of this phenomena in their own terms and for their own lives. In the third, I will report preliminary findings of my own ongoing though yet incomplete research, which sheds light on some important aspects raised in the most recent literature cited above. Finally, this paper derived its driving force and this needs to be made unequivocably explicit, from my own biography, since I myself am the son of a concentration camp survivor, who grew up in the community of survivors in Melbourne Australia.(2) My family came from Warsaw and my father's experience of the Holocaust took him from the Umschlag Platz in the Warsaw Ghetto in 1943 to Treblinka, Maidanek, Buchenwald and Matthausen. My mother lived through the war in Russia. Both lost their entire large families in the Holocaust, my younger sister Rachel and I are their only children.

The early research on the 'children' of survivors has been reported both in professional journals and in popular literature. A brief summary of this literature written from the stand point of a 'child' of survivors can be found in Epstein (1980), 177-193, as well as Wanderman (1977), 115-123.

The general message that arises from this literature is a view of the survivor as a traumatised individual hampering the natural/normal growth of his offspring. The trauma becomes both mutated and transmitted transgenerationally,emotionally crippling the second generation. Among the authors cited here are Barocas and Barocas (1973) and Kestenberg (1972).

Miriam Rieck (1985), a psychologist, presented recently in an outstanding survey of the professional literature in this field, the major weaknesses of these clinical studies. Amongst those she cites principally "the tendency to generalise from subjective impressions, based on work with clinical groups, to the holocaust survivor offspring at large."(ibid: 6) In addition, Rieck notes that these earlier reports failed to distinguish between different types of holocaust experiences, primarily concentration camps or partisan activity, as well as the role that the contemporary life situations play on the development of second generation members. Both epistemologically and methodologically these results were prematurely closed within their pathogenic clinical paradigms as well as lacking the incorporation of control groups which would allow the comparison of Holocaust offspring with their peers.

Having referred to some of the inherent weaknesses of the clinical work, I wish to move on to the discussion of two non-clinical studies which Rieck reports in her survey. The first was conducted by Kav-Venaki and Nadler (1979). Here, important sociological variables were introduced, the primary one being whether the survivors themselves talked about their Holocaust experience to their offspring. The argument presented is quite simple. Concentration camp survivors talked less about their experiences than did partisans, while it was the silence which was burdensome to the second generation. Mothers were found to talk more than fathers while daughters were more affected by the parents' experiences than sons. Kav-Venaki and Nadler conducted their research in Israel comparing 15 partisan couples with 15 concentration camp couples and their respective offsprings. While this research is more sophisticated than the earlier ones both in epistemology and methodology, there remains one important question unanswered, namely is the silence, the deleterious effects of which are universally recognized, a function of the Holocaust experience itself or of the environment in which the offspring were being brought up, namely Israeli society.

I cannot offer conclusive evidence to contradict the causal hypothesis than that cited, but I do wish to offer an alternative plausible hypothesis the support for which I draw from my own biography. In Israel the Holocaust commemoration is called "The Day of the Holocaust and of Herosim". To the best of my knowledge, in the first two decades after the war, this commemoration did not bear this name anywhere else in the world - I refer, of course, to the appendage 'Herosim;. It would seem to me that the culture of remembering generated by the state memorials served both to legitimate the heroism (and of course, why not?) but also to delegitimize or at least neutralize the status of survival from the concentration camps: Hence the roar of silence, the consequent repression that follows and the need to break that silence which was superbly shown in the documentary made by Eva Fogelman in the United States with the title 'Breaking the Silence'. It would seem that this movie supports the thesis of Kav-Venaki and Nadler and in many ways it does, but what of the alternative hypothesis?

The Jewish community in Melbourne was more than doubled from 9,500 in 1933 to 24,000 in 1954 by Holocaust survivors, many from the concentration camps. I grew up both in a family and a community of survivors of the worst concentration camp experiences, where it was legitimate and prevalent to talk about these experiences. Apart from the formal community memorials which were just that - a collective illusionless mourning, survivor families often met, paradigmatically at the Passover Seder table, but in fact all year round, where they talked almost competitively and compulsively of their suffering and ordeals. It appears to me, that the community in Melbourne itself served as the cathartic agent that elsewhere may have required professional and group attention (see, for an example of the latter, Fogelman and Sarvan, 1980).

Thus, while I agree that it is the talking about the Holocaust experience, both public and private which attenuates the effect it has on the offspring, it is by no means clear to me that this is exclusively a consequence of the survivor's experience itself, but crucially how this experience is mediated by the post war society itself in which the survivor and his family grows up.

Support for the general thesis of the mediating role of the social environment is offered indirectly by another professional, the late Professor Hillel Klein (1971). What is interesting about Klein's work is primarily the context in which his 25 survivor families were interviewed - namely being members of three kibbutzim in Israel.

Klein reported a number of presumed effects of the Holocaust on the offspring with which I do not wish to take issue here. I do, however, wish to relate to two interesting points he raised. The first is that on the one hand like the Israelis reported by Kav-Venaki et al, parents here apparently did not talk about the Holocaust. Epstein directly cites Klein as writing that "The children tend to emphasize the herosim of their parents..." (Klein in Epstein, ibid: 188). On the other hand despite this silence, the kibbutz community nevertheless attenuated the pernicious effects of the silence by providing an additional family both in the adult community and the children's own peer group, so that survivors here seemed to be better socially integrated than elsewhere.

So society or community matters when assessing the effects of Holocaust parenthood on offspring but is the question here one only of the pattern of personality and adjustment. Is that the only outcome relevant, ranging on a continuum from normal to abnormal? It appears not.

Before I turn to this additional theme I wish to close the discussion on the psychiatric and psychological literature. It would appear that the clinical studies have seriously exaggerated and overgeneralized their findings of the pathological consequences of Holocaust parenthood on their offspring. Controlled studies performed by Reick (1987) seem to indicate that "...emotional behavioral and learning problems are not more frequent among Holocaust survivor offspring of the second or third (sic.) generation than among controls" (ibid: 8). Rieck's conclusions are that Holocaust offsprings are able to develop 'coping'mechanisms to deal with possible emotional vulnerability, with the outcome that the variance of the latter within the holocaust offspring population falls within the normal range.

I wish to address now the final item in the literature which will introduce the thesis of this paper. Heller (1982) has argued that second generation of Holocaust survivors generate a stronger, ethnic identification thereby strengthening their personality. That is to say Holocaust offspring tend to be more concerned for the continuity of their culture and heritage than do their peer controls. Heller offers the explanation that the identification with cultural and ethnic roots serves to strengthen the feeling of belonging in generating a broader framework for identification and self development. I would add here that perhaps the fact of being a child of survivor predisposes one to seek out other voluntary frameworks or intentional societies in which identification is the basis of membership, such as social and political youth movements.

Heller's essay which I received only very recently, reveals a refreshing recognition by a clinical psychologist of the weakness of much previous research which ... "involved methodological difficulties such as inadequate sample size, omission of a control group or an adequate campaign group, absence of multiple measuring instruments, and highly selected clinical samples with restricted generalisability." (ibid: 249)

What is very relevant here is that "no investigation sufficiently explained the cultural context in which survivors and children responded to a legacy of massive trauma."(ibid)

I indeed report this empirical finding here, however, his major conclusions are that firstly "Children of concentration camp survivors are more sensitive to traditional Jewish themes than others of similar background."(ibid: 253) While for these children the ..."importance of cultural solidarity and cultural preservation are borne out by the survivors childrens' high degree of participation in cultural activities and by their opposition to intermarriage." (ibid: 253)

Heller's work which was obviously conducted independently from my own, in a different cultural context, from within a different discipline, nevertheless gives strong support to many of the main findings of the paper presented here. It is to these I now turn.

I have argued to this point that previous researchers have not asked all the right questions nor used all the appropriate tools which would uncover a broad spectrum of responses of the second generation to their biographical situation. I wish to argue that the major lacuna here is the absence of a sociological dimension of explanation which will open up the prematurely closed typology of responses, as well as take into account the ongoing process of response which is socially and culturally mediated.

At this stage, I wish to report findings of my own research which is still in progress, but I feel can already at this time shed light on the questions raised by Heller and others. In this research I do not consider in any way the clinical psychological variables discussed above, for the focus of the research is on youth emigration of Israeli-born from Israel, especially the kibbutz. Here a dominant research question concerns the role of value committment (or the lack of it) in determining whether young people leave Israel and the kibbutz. The kibbutz, as a society which is by definition an intentional and value based society is perturbed by the growing rate of young kibbutz-born who seem to be not returning from their extended visits overseas. The data is on a sample of 118 kibbutz born currently in North America more than two years. They left Israel between 1978 and 1986, 80% of them before 1986, young sabras, 50% under the age of 30, 50% under the age of 40. The broader research question addressed was why do they leave and why they do not return? What of their concerns for the continuity of their kibbutz, their country, their ethnicity, their peoplehood. In our terms, we have here an opportunity for a 'worst case analysis'.

I will not report all these findings here, however, we do have an opportunity to compare a group of 16 kibbutz-born second generation of Holocaust survivors with 95 kibbutz-born sabra peers of the same age and gender distribution on a variety of dimensions, comparable to that discussed by Heller.

Why worst case analysis? Emigrants from Israel are often seen as alienated refugees from the Jewish homeland. Holocaust offspring could be suspected, now having left their families and country to have done so as a result of any number of alienating factors, among them a lower ideological commitment to their Jewishness, to Israel, to army service, to their peers, to their parents. Much of the testimony of second generation that Helen Epstein collected in her book would encourage one to look in this direction of individualistic alienation from the commitment to the collective. After all, they have left Israel haven't they?

First of all I wish to comment on the demographic characteristics of both groups, the 2nd generation emigrants and their emigre peers. First the obvious: they are all young, born on an Israeli kibbutz, after the war. Both groups consist of 2/3 male and one third female. In both groups 75% are now married, 50% were married at the time of departure from Israel. In both groups exactly 2/3 of the spouses were foreign born, again in both groups, 80% of these spouses were Jewish. One important difference between them was reflected in the fact that the Holocaust group had a higher percentage of those who had only completed high school, only 54% compared to 38% of controls, a fact which matches previous research. Similarly, as will be seen, both parents of second generation, perhaps quite understandably, were less educated than the parents of controls. (I would stress here that in the sampling process no steps whatsover were taken to purposively include the Holocaust survivor offspring - this is a truly random outcome).

What differences then were found between these otherwise remarkably similar groups of young kibbutz-born emigres to America? One field in which there was no difference was in the relationship to parents, 61% of second generation, as well as controls, reported that their relationship with parents was warm and close. It is of note, that amongst the children of survivors 62% reported that their mothers spoke of the Holocaust experiences, while only 44% reported that their fathers did so, a finding which matches with previous research, cited above. The differences between the two groups will be presented in a series of tables, which report the significant differences between them on a series of variables. I will discuss each in turn.

1. Background characteristics

I have already reported that overall, the demographic characteristics of the two groups are uniform however the differences between them can be seen in Table 1.

First, as already stated, parents education of Holocaust survivor offspring (HSO) is lower than controls, while father's less frequently held central positions in the kibbutz. Second, conflict resolution between father and child was participative in both groups, that is to say the father was likely to take into account the views of the child; there was no difference alienating or otherwise between the groups here. Third, with respect to the content of the education they received HSO regarded as more meaningful Holocaust studies than did controls, but considered studies on land of Israel to have been less meaningful for them than controls reported. On the level of satisfaction with different areas of school life, HSO reported higher satisfaction from relations with peer group and teachers as well as from the 'preparation of life' that they received in school. Hardly an alienating etiology.

Table 1

	Mean	S.D.	N	T	D.F	Sign.
Background Factors						
a) Fathers years of education	a1.7	0.96	15	-2.1	109	*
(1 = low)	b2.4	.66	96			
b) Mothers years of education	a1.9	0.77	15	-2.0	100	
(1 = low)	b2.3	1.99	97			
Background						
c) Executive role of father on kibbutz (1 = no executive position, 7 = senior executive)	a1.1	1.2	14	-3.55	93	***
	b3.8	1.9	81			
Conflict resolution with father (1 = participating, 5 = rejecting)	a2.9	0.7	15	-1.5	107	N.S.
	b3.2	0.6	94			
School Activities that were meaningful to you						
a) Holocaust studies	a4.6	0.5	16	4.8	4.29+	***
b) Personal projects concerning the Land of Israel	a3.1	1.1	16	-4.0	50.5	**
	b4.6	2.5	92			
(1 = not meaningful 5 = meaningful)	b3.8	1.1	96			
Retrospective satisfaction with school in following areas						
1) relations with peer group	a4.4	0.6	16	3.1	34.5+	***
	b3.8	1.1	93			
2) relationships with teachers	a4.2	0.75	16	2.3	107	***
	b3.6	0.99	93			
3) Preparation for life that you received (5 = very satisfied)	a3.6	0.9	16			
	b2.8	1.2	93	2.5	107	***

+ unequal variance, *** $p < 0.001$, ** $p < .01$, * $p < .05$ (one-tailed)
a = Holocaust Survivor Offspring (HSO), b = peer controls

I now move to the question of Jewish identity and ethnicity. Heller reported survivors as having a fiercer opposition to intermarriage, could we expect such a difference between secular educated kibbutz- born? The answer is to be found in Table 2.

Table 2

	Mean	S.D.	N	T	D.F.	Sign.
Jewish identity						
Is your fate and future bound with fate and future of Jewish people? (1 = no, 5 = definitely yes)	a4.6 b3.8	0.63 1.13	15 96	3.78	30.6+	***
Attitude to assimilation (1 = negative)	a2.0 b2.4	0.63 0.69	16 95	-2.2	109	*
Synagogue participation (1 = none)	a1.8 b1.4	0.8 0.5	16 95	2.1	17.1+	*
Israel is the only place in the world where one can live a full Jewish life (1 = not agree, 4 = full agreement)	a2.6 b2.0	1.2 1.1	15 90	1.8	103	*

+ unequal variance, *** $p < 0.001$, ** $p < .01$, * $p < .05$ (one-tailed)
a = Holocaust Survivor Offspring (HSO), b = peer controls

From here we can see that the attitude to assimilation of HSO is more negative than their peers. Heller reported that 71% of HSO opposed intermarriage as compared to 46% of controls (Heller (1982):252), here we found that 81% of HSO opposed intermarriage compared to 51% of controls. This is all the more remarkable since in the present study 2/3 of respondents are male, the gender which according to Heller and Kav-Vaneki et al is supposed to be less affected by parents. In addition, HSO's identify their fate and future with the fate and future of the Jewish people, as well as being in a fuller agreement with the statement that "Israel is the only place in the world where one can live a full Jewish life."

These attitudes have expression in ritual behavior so that we find HSO attending synagogue more frequently than do controls. Thus the HSO seem to have higher scores on indicators of Jewish identity. What about identification with Israel, will this be the domain in which the controls will compensate for the lower scores on Jewish identity? The answer is found in Table 3.

Table 3

	Mean	S.D.	N	T	D.F.	Sign.
Identification with Israel						
Are you personally threatened by attitudes on Israel in press?	a4.5 b3.9	0.51 1.16	15 95	3.25	41.6+	***
Commitment to Israel conditional on its democratic character (1 = No)	a2.9 b3.9	1.6 1.4	16 97	-2.7	111	**
Responsibility to the collective (State of Israel)						
(1 = personal interest prevails 5 = will take interests of state into account)	a3.0 b2.7	0.8 0.6	15 92	1.75	105	*

+ unequal variance, *** $p < 0.001$, ** $p < .01$, * $p < .05$ (one-tailed)
a = Holocaust Survivor Offspring (HSO), b = peer controls

There are three separate dimensions here. First, straight out identification with Israel. HSO are more threatened by criticism of Israel in the foreign press than are controls. At the same time, they to a lesser degree make their commitment to Israel conditional on it having a democratic character or more accurately they are less likely to revise their commitment to Israel if it did not have a democratic character. The third dimension relates to balance of obligations and mutual responsibilities between the individual and the state of Israel. The respondents were asked if there were a clash between their personal interests and those of the state to what extent would they take into account the interests of the state at the expense of their own. HSO are more likely to take into account the interests of the state than controls. Thus both in the domain of Jewish identity and commitment to Israel, the HSO consistently score higher on indices of affirmative commitment to the collective than do their peers.

What about universal values, pacifism, egalitarinism, kibbutz socialism? The answer is found in Table 4.

Table 4

	Mean	S.D.	N	T	D.F	Sign.
Universal values						
Attitude to war	a2.4	0.63	16	1.9	108	*
(1 = pacifist)	b2.1	0.73	94			
Egalitarianism = rewards should be distributed equally to workers						
a) in general society	a3.14	1.6	14			
	b2.14	1.4	94	2.49	106	**
b) in kibbutz	a4.3	0.80	15	2.38	31.4+	**
	b3.7	1.46	94			
(5 = agree, 1 = no)						
Values in decision making concerning ones future on kibbutz						
Fidelity of the kibbutz to its values	a3.8	1.2	12	2.68	92	***
(5 = very important)	b2.8	1.3	82			

+ unequal variance, *** $p < 0.001$, ** $p < .01$, * $p < .05$ (one-tailed)
a = Holocaust Survivor Offspring (HSO), b = peer controls

On the question of pacifism, we find for the first time a value that the controls are slightly more committed to than the HSO, but there it ends. On the question of the propriety of the egalitarian distribution of rewards both in the kibbutz and outside of it, HSO are more supportive of the position. Finally, respondents were asked a series of questions concerning dimensions that would be important for them in the event that they would reconsider rejoining kibbutz. The criteria that differentiated significantly between the groups was the fidelity of the kibbutz to its values.

All our respondents are nevertheless emigrants to North America, what were their personal ambitions that brought them there, what were they seeking? The answer is found in Table 5.

Table 5

	Mean	S.D.	N	T	D.F	Sign.
Ambition in life						
1.a) achieve executive position	a3.8	0.8	16	3.4	30.3+	***
	b2.9	1.3	94			
b) to feel that you are living according to values you believe in (1 = not meaningful)	a4.4	0.7	16	-1.9	17.2+	*
	b4.7	0.5	97			
What you are looking for in your stay overseas						
2.a) to reexamine my connection with the kibbutz	a2.6	1.4	14	2.4	105	**
	b1.8	1.2	93			
b) Adventure and danger	a2.6	1.4	14	2.2	105	**
	b1.9	1.1	93			
c) Pleasure and entertainment	a3.1	1.6	14	1.6	105	*
	b2.5	1.2	93			
d) to test my ability to reach economic independence	a3.9	1.5	14	1.7	106	*
	b3.1	1.5	94			
e) to achieve personal economic success (1 = to a small degree)	a3.8	1.4	14	1.8	105	*
	b3.0	1.4	93			

+ unequal variance, *** $p < 0.001$, ** $p < .01$, * $p < .05$ (one-tailed)
a = Holocaust Survivor Offspring (HSO), b = peer controls

Here an interesting picture emerges, perhaps in contrast somewhat to the one presented above. HSO are clearly far more ambitious than controls yearning for executive position. HSO's also saw their stay in the US as an opportunity to test their ability to become economically independent and to achieve personal economic success in a higher degree than did controls. At the same time we find that the controls yearn to live according to values they believe in, slightly more so than do HSO, though both score very highly on this dimension. On a more specific level, HSO's sought to use their stay in the US as a period of reexamination of their connection with their kibbutz, the controls were less concerned with this goal. HSO's also sought pleasure and entertainment even adventure and danger to a greater degree than did the controls.

Finally, what has become of all these kibbutz-born offspring? Is there any difference between them,in their degree of social integration, in the society of destination or the degree of associational ties within the local Jewish or Israeli emigre community that might reflect their value responses cited above? The answer is to be found in the final table, Table 6.

Table 6

	Mean	S.D.	N	T	D.F	Sign.
Social integration in Country of destination						
1) with local Jews	a3.5	0.9	15	1.8	108	*
	b3.5	1.0	15			
2) with local non-Jews	a2.9	1.1	95	1.8	108	*
Jewish associational ties	b2.4	1.2	15			
1) Jewish Community Centre	a1.8	1.1	94	1.8	107	*
	b1.3	0.7	94			
2) Israeli organizations	a2.1	1.3	15	2.1	15.5+	*
	b2.9	1.2	95			
(5 = frequent social ties, 1 = none)						

+ unequal variance, *** $p < 0.001$, ** $p < .01$, * $p < .05$ (one-tailed)
a = Holocaust Survivor Offspring (HSO), b = peer controls

First, HSO report more social ties both with local Jewish community as well as with the local non-Jewish community. Community participation per se, might well be a goal of these HSO.

As for Jewish associational ties, once again the frequency of these both in the local Jewish community centre as well as even with Israeli organizations is higher with HSO than with controls.

Each and every test item in the data above cannot on its own (this despite the actual statistical significance of the difference) tell a story. Moreover, caution is well advised in reading these data considering the small number of cases involved. However, it is the overall consistency of the findings which are stunning, which serve to give prima facie evidence at least, of the major thesis of this paper namely that in the socialization process of HSO, there are generated forces pushing for community and commitment to that community, over time and even space.

I would like to then summarize the principal findings of the data presented here. First, that in this admittedly small but non-clinical random sample of kibbutz-born children of concentration camp survivors, there were not found any indicators of parent-child alienation in comparison to their peers. Second, that despite the similarity of the education that all the subjects in the study received, children of concentration camp survivors systematically scored higher on indicators of Jewish identity, both in positive terms and in the negation of intermarriage, identification with Israel and commitment to the State of Israel. These findings seem to give quite considerable though provisional support for Heller's thesis reported above. Third, the children of Holocaust survivors seem to nevertheless express more personal ambition both for executive position and economic independence and success. They are achievers who have come to America primarily for individualistic fulfillment, a factor which has undoubtedly more to do with their identity as kibbutzniks than as Jews. Despite their emigration from Israel, or perhaps because of it, their Jewish identity has become more salient for them, while collective or cultural continuity is more important for them than their otherwise similar kibbutz emigre peers. Fourth, these observed differences in attitude and value scores is also reflected in behavioral indices such as frequency of attendance at Synagogue as well as involvement in Jewish community and Israeli organizations in America.

What emerges from this data is a lesson no less important for the sociology of the kibbutz than for an understanding of children of Holocaust survivors. The lesson is this - that while in kibbutz individualistic aspirations and ambitions are sometimes perceived as being antagonistic to commitment to the collective they need not necessarily be so. Thus kibbutz-born can be both ambitious and individualistic in their personal ambitions, while retaining an altruistic attitude to the goals of the collective - the kibbutz or the community, the State of Israel, the Jewish people or mankind at large.

Put the other way round, I would argue that discrimination of factors of individual achievement that has indeed often been observed in the early literature on children of Holocaust survivors, should not obscure the equally powerful additional dimensions which generate simultaneously individual commitment to the collective, its values, its past, its present and its future. It is in this sense that I have argued for opening up the typology of responses of Holocaust survivors' children by making it less exclusive, unidimensional and hypostatised but instead more inclusive, multidimensional and dynamic both in time and in the cultural space of survivors' children ongoing life-worlds.

Commonality, Community and Commitment

I have argued in this paper that children of survivors share a commonality of experience that derived from their specific process of socialization. This commonality cuts across many of the primary cultural distinctions within the contemporary Jewish world. These include the manifest differences between different diaspora Jewish communities, but more critically between Israel and the diaspora itself, as well as between secular, traditional and religious Jews. While this commonality is certainly not overwhelming nor overriding, it continuously persists in generating both a heightened awareness of the precariousness of human civilisation in general and Jewish survival within it in particular.

This commonality has been for the most part directly unarticulated by the generation itself, despite the growth of national and international networks of members of the second generation, since the late 70's and their maturity into adulthood. It is partly reflected however in the Arts and their engagement in community activism on a wide spectrum of issues related to their specific biographies and ideologies.

The research evidence I have offered here while consistent with recent findings of other scholars does not reflect a direct articulation of the second generation themselves in the issues raised. Before concluding this paper, I wish to refer to a select number of such articulated responses by the second generation, with special reference to the structural commonality yet to the differing contents of that ongoing process of articulation.

1. Commonality

The structural precondition of commonality is the shared recognition of being different from others. Hannah Levinsky Koevary (1977) has written that compared to other Jews in her community "My parents were different and I knew now ... to be a stranger among Jews was worse than being hated by Gentiles" (ibid: 140). After encountering disparaging comments about refugees from her fellow Jews who belittled the burden of the Holocaust by comparing it with the material 'suffering' of the Depression, she went on to write that if between them ..."there was no common present, it was because there was no shared past." (ibid: 141).

Lilly Brett the child of survivors of Auschwitz, encountered the same belittling of survivors' suffering. In an interview in the Melbourne Age, on the publication of her book "The Auschwitz Poems" she reported "One man said to my father: 'We didn't have it so easy here, either, during the war. We couldn't get herrings in Melbourne'" (Melbourne Age: 30.8.86). Epstein (1980) reports the panoramic responses of children of survivors. 'Aviva' a sabra complained that Holocaust wasn't taught in her school, while Hebrew literature "looked down on survivors" (ibid: 107), both in the portrait painted of them and in the inevitable comparison with the pioneers of Israel. "The Israelis were so glorified that behind them the survivors were shameful" (ibid: 108).

What all the children of survivors seem to share then is a profound appreciation of the difference in their life situation and its courses. Their responses are not uniform. Lilly Brett, wrote a powerful poetic personalized memorialization of her mother's experiences. Hannah Levinsky Koevary and Yehuda whom Epstein reported, sought out the option of Jewish sovereignity in Israel. Helen Epstein hereself, the chronicler, after spending three years in Israel after the Six Day War (like Hannah and Yehuda) concluded that for her "In Israel, I saw a future of limited possibilities".

Community

Epstein had sought community everywhere and had not found it except amongst the children of Holocaust survivors, on her return for Israel. Community had been a common theme for all her interviewees and the continuity of that community their common goal even when expressd in different cultural parameters within differing biographies.

Community would seem to be a goal of many children of Holocaust survivors while the primary motif of that community was often that of Jewish survival.

3. Commitment

Menachem Rosensaft (1985) the founder of the International Network of children of Jewish Holocaust survivors has attested "Second Generation groups are a way station, not the ultimate goal" (ibid:14). The survivor groups that were sprouting up in the late 70's and the international Network that was founded in 1981 were borne on the basis of that commonality seeking continuity and community. However this same institutional articulation led to the advancement of other issues beyond the memorialisation of the Holocaust, namely support for Ethiopian and Soviet Jewry as well as mobilising support in the US Senate to ratify the Genocide Convention Treaty (Rosensaft, 1985:15).

In conclusion, I argue here not for any determinism, on the contrary, it is precisely the psychiatric determinism that needs to be rejected. There are many responses to the Holocaust, even by children of concentration camp survivors. The range of the responses are however far more open than has hitherto been widely acknowledged, being affected in a complex way both by the experience of the parents, the response of the host society to the survivors and their children as well as the cultural milieu in which the children grew up.

The evidence seems to suggest that even such disparate groups of young Jews, whether college students in Boston, kibbutz-born emigres in America, American immigrants to Israel, artists, intellectuals, poets and lawyers, from Israel, America, Australia, the world over, share a common burden which in many cases generates a powerful commitment to the meaning of their collective past and to the importance of the collective future of the culture to which they belong.

The coming decade may well witness a more stable and balanced articulation of this commonality which could have far reaching consequences for the memory of the Holocaust itself, as well as for the articulation and then affirmation of the implications of the Holocaust for future generations with their commitment in turn, to a more Jewish and humane future.

(1) I wish to record here my special indebtedness to Mrs. Miriam Rieck, of the Ray D. Wolfe Centre for the Study of Psychological Stress, University of Haifa, for her very helpful bibliographic guidance in this area.
(2) A systematic account of the biographical component is currently in preparation to be published together with the translation of my later father's concentration camp experiences and survival (forthcoming)

Bibliography

Barocas, H.A. & Barocas, C.B. (1973) "Manifestations of concentration camp effects on the second-generation", American Journal of Psychiatry, 130, 7, 820-821.

Brett, L. (1986) The Auschwitz Poems, Scribe: Melbourne.

Brett, L. (1986) Interview with Anna Murdoch, Melbourne Age, August 30, 1986.

Epstein, H. (1980) Children of the Holocaust: Conversations with Sons and Daughters of Survivors. New York: Bantam Books.

Fogelman, E. & Sarvan, B. (1980) "Brief group therapy with offspring of holocaust survivors". American Journal of Orthospcyhiatry, 50(1): 96-108.

Heller, D. (1982) "Themes of culture and ancestry among children of concentration camp survivors". Psychiatry, 45, 247-261.

Kav-Venaki, S. and Nadler, A. (1979) "Sharing the Holocaust Experience: Comparison between Two Groups of Survivors and their Children". Presented at the conference on the "Second generation": Children of holocaust survivors, NYC. USA

Kestenberg, J. "Psychianalytic contributions to the problem of children of survivors from Nazi persecution". The Israel Annals of Psychiatry and Related Disciplines, Vol. 10, No. 4, pp. 311-325.

Klein, H. (1971) "Families of Survivors in the Kibbutz: Psychological Studies" in H. Krystal and W. Niederland, eds. Psychic Traumatization (Vol. 8 of International Psychiatry Clinics), Boston: Little Brown & Co., pp. 67-92.

Koevary Levinsky, H. "A Search for Home, The Road to Israel" in Living After the Holocaust, edited by Lucy Y Steinitz with David M. Szoni, Bloch, New York,

Rieck, M. (1985) "Psychological Investigations of Holocaust Survivors' Offspring: A Literature Survey". Paper presented at the 8th Biennial Meeting of the ISSBD Tours, 6-10 July, 1985.

Rieck, M. (1987) "The Emotional State of Holocaust Survivors Offspring". Paper presented at the 10th International Colloquium on School Psychology, Interlaken, Switzerland, August 9th-13th.

Rosensaft, M. (1985) "Children of Survivors" Interview by Aron Hirt Manheimer, Reform Judaism, Spring.

Wanderman, E. (1977) "Children and Families of Holocaust Survivors: A Psychological Overview", in Living After the Holocaust, edited by Lucy Y Steinitz with David M. Szoni, Bloch, New York,

SPECIAL LIVES: SURVIVORS OF THE HOLOCAUST AND THE AMERICAN DREAM

Abraham J. Peck

American Jewish Archives
Hebrew Union College-Jewish Institute of Religion
Cincinnati, Ohio U.S.A.

On May 8, 1945, the S. S. Brand Whitlock, bearing the very first survivors of Auschwitz to the United States, slipped into the harbor at Newport News, Virginia.

Three of the passengers were sisters, Hungarian Jewish women named Katz. They had gone through the hell-hole of Auschwitz and survived the whistle and thumb flick of Dr. Josef Mengele, the devastatingly simple means he had employed to decide who would live and who would die.

Forty years later, one of the sisters would, as the novelist Isabella Leitner, write about that sea voyage and what she had felt escaping from one universe into another:

"Dr. Mengele, we are on our way to America," she wrote, "and we are going to forget every brutal German word you forced us to learn. We are going to learn a new language. We are going to ask for bread and milk in Shaekespeare's tongue. We will learn how to live speaking English and forget how people die speaking German.

"The ship," she continued, "detaches itself from land and plunges into the waves of the Black Sea. I search the sky to see if I can conjure my mother and my little sister, Potyo. I look in desperate sorrow but can discern no human form. The smoke has vanished. There is not a trace. No grave, nothing. Absolutely nothing.

Our sailor friend Jack talks to us about this new world we are about to encounter: skyscrapers, buildings that rise to the clouds in New York; the world's tallest building, the Empire State, Times Square and 42nd Street, the crossroads of the world.

He speaks of Ellis Island and New York harbor, where millions of immigrants have been greeted by a 'lady' holding high a torch of liberty.

He describes a land where the color of people's skin can vary from white to black, from yellow to red; where people can be Protestant, Baptist, Buddhist, or Catholic - even Jewish or atheist - and they all live together in that melting pot called democracy; where people ride in huge automobiles or sweat in the belly of the earth; where there are slums and estates with private tennis courts, tall Texans and short Mexicans, the very rich and the very poor, and a great many people who are neither rich nor poor, just citizens of a free country, a country very different from those we have known."[1]

Isabella Leitner and her fellow survivors came to America, the goldene medina, with the same hopes and dreams that symbolized other Jews from other places who had preceded them to these shores. The same hopes and dreams, but yet different.

I

In April of 1945, the late American Jewish novelist Meyer Levin was a war correspondent traveling with the Fourth Armored Division as it made its way east around the German town of Gotha. He and his companions came upon some "cadaverous refugees" along the road. "They were like none we have ever seen; Levin wrote later: "Skeletal with feverish sunken eyes, shaven skulls." They identified themselves as Poles and asked Levin and the others to come to the site where they had been held prisoner. They spoke of "People buried in a Big Hold" and "Death Commando." They described a camp but the Americans did not want to go there during the oncoming darkness for fear of enemy attack. They would wait for light.

What they found the next morning at a camp called Ohrdruf, named for and just outside a small town near Gotha were scenes that had not been seen before - not in the quantity, not in the form of death, not in the manner of killing.

As Levin drove through the gate he saw piles of dead prisoners, all in striped uniforms. The corpses were fleshless, and at the back of each skull was a bullet hole. A shack held a stack of stiff and naked men, "The bodies were flat and yellow as lumber" Levin remembered.[2]

This was only the beginning. During the next several weeks, camp after camp was liberated by Americans, English and Russians. We know best what the American liberators felt at the moment of liberation of such camps as Nordhausen, Buchenwald, Dachau, and Mauthausen in Austria:

"Oh, the odors," wrote one, "well there is no way to describe the odors .... Many of the boys I am talking about - those were tough soldiers, there were combat men who had been all the way through on the invasion - were ill and vomiting, throwing up, just the sight of this...."[3]

Another wrote: "These Jewish people were like animals, they were so degraded, there was no goodness, no kindness, nothing of that nature, there was no sharing. If they got a piece of something to eat, they grabbed it and ran away in a corner and fought off anyone who came near them."[4]

Finally a third wrote: "the prisoners were so thin, they didn't have anything, didn't have any buttocks to lie on; there wasn't any flesh on their arms to rest their skulls on... one man that I saw there who had died on his knees, with his arms and head in a praying position, and he was still there, apparently had been for days."[5] These were some of the physical reactions and impressions of tough American GI's, farm boys from Iowa, street-wise New Yorkers and mountain men from Appalachia. But it took the sensitivity of a literary imagination like Meyer Levin's to give it the perspective, the meaning, which defines the Holocaust for our time; Levin wrote:

"We had known. The world had vaguely heard. But until now no one of us had looked on this. Even this morning we had not imagined we would look on this. It was as though we had penetrated at last to the center of the black heart, to the very crawling inside of the vicious heart."[6]

The gulf of experience and expectations that lay between liberators and survivors, the different world that made battle weary Americans innocent by comparison, disoriented and disturbed even those most ready to embrace the victims of Nazi terror. Speaking to an international conference of liberators in 1981, Elie Wiesel spoke of the American soldiers who liberated him from Buchenwald on April 11, 1945. "You were our liberators," Wiesel said, but we, "the diseased, emaciated, barely human survivors were your teachers. We taught you to understand the Kingdom of Night." What the liberators learned and what the survivors already knew would force both to confront a world which suffered from what Robert Abzug has called a case of "Double Vision," of seeing the reality of newsreel films which showed a pile of bodies stacked as they were described "like cordwood" at Dachau, hundreds of corpses laid out in rows before the ruins of buildings at Buchenwald, bulldozers filling mass graves at Bergen-Belsen, but at the same time of not seeing these things, of not believing that they were possible.[7] The result was a world which shut it all out, a world which was silent.

But not entirely. The New York intellectual, Dwight MacDonald, writing in 1945, reflected on the events in Europe from 1933 to 1945. "Something has happened to Europe he wrote. What is it? Who or what is responsible? What does it mean about our civilization, our whole system of values?"[8] For MacDonald, indeed for the major portion of American and European liberals, a great catastrophe had taken place. Their world view of rationality and progress toward international peace had been smashed to pieces, victims of the "belief that humanity had set limits to the degredation and persecution of one's fellow man."[9] Those inside the vicious heart, even for a short time, already knew this much earlier. The Viennese Jewish writer, Stefan Zweig writing about the new order of things as a refugee from Nazism in Brasil, knew: "We of the new generation," Zweig wrote, in opposition to "that idealistically blinded generation (prior to World War I)...have learned not to be surprised by any outbreak of bestiality; we who each new day expect things worse than the day before, are markedly more skeptical about a possible moral improvement of mankind."[10] Zweig's skepticism drove him and his wife into suicide a few short months later.

But such despair was not evident for the Jewish survivors of the Holocaust at the moment of liberation. Simon Schochet was a prisoner in Dachau:

"When I awoke, morning had finally come and the pains subsided. At the window Alexis and another man suddenly began to shout that they saw some vehicles which did not look German. We crawled to the window and peeked out. A long column of tanks moved slowly down the road below us. They were marked with white stars. We stared at each other in disbelief. Was it true? Were we suffering a collective hallucination brought on by events of the previous day? Perhaps the Germans had captured those tanks... but against these fears, a single thought, hope, belief overwhelmed us, a single unvoiced thought sounded and echoed in our confused and tortured minds: We are free: I saw this in Alexis' eyes and in the eyes of all the men. And so, clutching our aching stomachs, we turned toward the door and began to climb down the attic steps.

They were waiting for us in front of the villa, where Alexis said we should turn in our uniforms to the proper side. And so, having undressed and dressed again, we walked down the middle of the open road on this cool May morning to meet our liberators."[11]

And on that cool morning in May, a group of perhaps as many as 100,000 Jewish survivors found themselves among the eleven million uprooted and homeless people wandering throughout Germany and Central Europe. Many of these Displaced Persons (DPs) sought to return home to rebuild their lives and their nations.[12]

Not so the Jews. As one Jewish survivor wrote: "The Jews suddenly faced themselves. Where now? Where to? For them things were not so simple. To go back to Poland? To Hungary? To streets empty of Jews. To wander in those lands, lonely, homeless, always with the tragedy before one's eyes... and to meet again, a former Gentile neighbor who would open his eyes wide and smile; remarking with double meaning, "What Yankel: You still alive?"[13]

These Jews, later to be joined by 150,000 others from Russia and Poland, formed the She'erit Hapletah (Hebrew for the Saved Remnant). We are not even certain when the term came to be applied to those who survived Hitler's war against the Jews. It is a biblical term which appears in 1 Chronicles 5, referring to the Jewish remnant that survived the Assyrian conquest. It reappears in the list of survivors which was published in July 1945. More importantly the term was both a description and a source of identity for those surviving the death camps, those who were partisans in the forests and those who took refuge from Hitler in the deepest reaches of Russian Siberia. It was an identity which would give birth to a revolutionary ideology created from the inner being and experience of the She'erit Hapletah.

We know little about the hopes and aims of the Jewish DPs beyond their need to leave Galut (exile) for the land of Eretz Israel and other nations. Marie Syrkin has recently written that "Displaced Person is a savage euphemism." "By now," she contends, "a DP is an almost forgotten term as is DP camp." Yet the period between liberation and the establishment of Israel during which survivors of the Nazi death camps became DPs represents for Syrkin, a grim epilogue to the Holocaust and a coda to its meaning.[14]

Marie Syrkin is surely correct: DP is an almost forgotten term. Indeed, when we think or read of the Jewish DP's they are inevitably portrayed as the passive objects of history, awaiting with resignation and despair, the acting out of a drama in which they could play little if any role.

Yet this is simply not true. From the very beginning of their liberation, Jewish DP's sought to recapture their sense of humanity and their sense of Jewishness, aspects of an identity which had been systematically taken away by the Nazis. "The Jews who have been liberated in the camp want to catch up," wrote one observer.... "They are starving for a word of Judaism."[15]

But this was not an easy task. The American and British military authorities, in their efforts to bring order to the chaos of post-war Europe, set up DP camps in Germany and Austria. In those camps Jews were thrown together with their former persecutors. Often, ex-Nazis were put in charge of the DP camps, which were patrolled by armed guards. One American report noted that the "hard core" of the non-Jewish DP's "have been proved to be a criminal and fascist group, many of whom left their countries voluntarily to work for Hitler."[16]

Perhaps most shocking was the attitude of General George S. Patton who led the Third Army in Southern Germany, which contained most of the DPs in the US zone. Patton insisted that every camp be surrounded by barbed wire and manned by armed guards to watch the survivors as if they were the vanquished enemy. Patton wrote in his diary on September 15, 1945 that others "believe that the Displaced Person is a human being, which he is not, and this applies particularly to the Jews who are lower than animals."[17]

Word of these conditions soon reached American government authorities. Jewish leaders in America and abroad asked President Harry Truman to investigate the situation. Truman approved an investigation headed by Earl G. Harrison, the dean of the University of Pennsylvania Law School.

Harrison's subsequent report on the conditions of the Jewish DPs shocked officials at the highest levels of the American government and military. A portion of his report stated that "as matters now stand, we appear to be treating the Jews as the Nazis treated them except that we do not exterminate them. They are in concentration camps in large numbers under our own military guards instead of the SS troops. One is led to wonder whether the German people seeing this, are not supposing that we are following or at least condoning Nazi policy."[18]

Within months Jewish DP camps were created in both the American and British zones of Germany and Austria. In addition, an advisor for Jewish affairs, Chaplain Judah P. Nadich, was added to the staff of General Dwight D. Eisenhower, the commander of the Supreme Headquarters of the Allied Expeditionary Forces in Europe.[19]

Jewish DP camps were established on or near the sites of former concentration camps. By May of 1947 there were at least sixty of these camps. Among the most important were Bergen-Belsen in the British zone of Germany and Landsberg, Feldafing and Foehrenwald in the American zone.[20] There were also numerous Jewish children's centers, hospitals and agricultural training centers. The latter prepared Jewish survivors for eventual immigration to Palestine. Ironically, two of these centers were located on estates once belonging to the notorious Julius Streicher, the editor of the fanatically anti-Semitic newspaper, Der Stuermer, and to Hermann Goering, one of Hitler's most important lieutenants.

Perhaps even more ironic, the nucleus of the Jewish DP community in the American sector of Berlin lived in an empty pavillion in the district of Wannsee. It was there in 1942 that the "Final Solution" to the "Jewish Problem" in Europe, the total destruction of the Jewish people, had been planned.

These tragic ironies only underscored the incredible dilemma of the Jewish DPs. It was as if they were living in one vast Jewish cemetery with no hope of leaving its confines. Entry to Palestine was blocked by British fears of Arab hostility; emigration to the United States and other nations was made almost impossible by unyielding quota systems. Few Jews wished to return to their former homes in Eastern

Europe. Indeed, after a tragic pogrom on July 4, 1946 in the Polish city of Kielce, in which at least forty Jews were killed, thousands of Jews from Poland and later Rumania, fled to the American zone of Germany.[21]

Yet despair was never an issue in the camps. Instead of allowing themselves to be overwhelmed by blocked immigration, overcrowded housing and the continuing anti-Semitism surrounding them, the Jewish DPs resolved to create a new beginning. With the support of Jewish and international relief associations, the Jewish camps became centers of Jewish cultural life.

Mir szeinen doh (We are here), was the phrase which best expressed the resolution of the Jewish DPs to rebuild their shattered lives. It was the unshakable belief of a group of survivors who felt that they had seen in the Holocaust, as one survivor stated, "the end of creation - not only an indelible memory of horror - but a permanent warning," that what he and others had experienced was a pilot project for the destruction of humanity.

"We are here" was expressed in a number of ways. By the end of 1946 the Jewish DP camps had the distinction of having the highest birthrate of any Jewish community in the world. This resolve to say yes to a Jewish future, surprised American Jewish visitors to the camps, who had come there expecting to find a despair-ridden and essentially pessimistic community.[22]

Even more pronounced than the birthrate was the resolve of the She'erit Hapletah to develop a philosophy of survival which would never again allow Jews to experience such a tragedy as the Holocaust.

Writing in April 1946 in the Jewish DP newspapers, J. Nemenczyk related a concentration camp fantasy which he had experienced lying on lice-filled straw in hunger and in pain. "I had a vision, he wrote, "that if the world could not give us back our dead brothers and sisters then it could give us a moral world."[23] Even earlier, speaking at the first ceremony, in June 1945, marking the liberation from Nazism, Dr. Zalman Grinberg, one of the earliest acknowledged spokespersons of the She'erit Hapletah, stressed the moral aspect of its existence:

"Hitler won the war against the European Jews. If we took revenge, we would descend into the lowest depths... which the German nation has fallen during the past ten years. We are not able to slaughter women and children. We are not able to burn millions of people."[24]

The Free Word, the journal of the Feldafing camp, echoed Grinsberg's message in an article entitled, "We Jews and the World." It stated that "what we, the She'erit Hapletah must do is, show that we, the victims of Nazism, have always been and will always be the carriers of humanity."[25]

Thus the nucleus of a philosophy of Jewish survival was being formed. But it would not develop on European soil. Despite the expectations of many, the survivors would not, as had other previous generations of European Jews struck by the sword of hatred, cast off its tragedy and rebuild on European soil." Should we help in the rebuilding of Europe," Grinberg asked in early 1946, "so that Europe will in time erect new crematoria for us?"[26] Instead, they would journey back to the Jewish homeland, Eretz Israel, and rebuild their shattered remnants as other nations were doing in the aftermath of Nazism.

There was an anticipation, a nervous level of activity among the survivors in the months following liberation. The need for Palestine was clear but so was the need for another source of purpose. In Zalman Grinberg's opening remarks at the first Congress of Liberated Jews in the American Zone, he echoed this need: "This is a conference of surviving Kaddish-sayers who will not satisfy themselves with merely saying Kaddish."[27] A short time later, the journalist Menahem Sztajer grappled with the ultimate role and purpose of the She'rith Hapletah. In October 1946 he challenged the survivors to decide for themselves. "Will the She'erit Hapletah simply mean an accidental term for survivors of a destroyed people," he asked "or will it mean a revolution in Jewish history - a renaissance in Jewish life."[28]

The ideology of the She'erit Hapletah was crystallized in a series of brilliant essays by Samuel Gringauz in the years 1947 and 1948.

Gringauz reiterated the need for European Jews to say farewell to the discredited continent. "Our place is no longer in Europe. We carry with us the legacy of our millenial history to Palestine and America so that the secular continuity of our ethical and cultural values may be assured." It was the survivors, he maintained, who were the victims of civilization and it was they "who have been called upon to discover the positive basis on which we can unite with it... Our tragedy must become the starting point of a new humanism." This ideal for Gringauz was no less than a neo-humanism, the ideal of the moral and social perfection of humanity.[29]

Thus the ideology of the She'erit Hapletah was formulated and the conditions for its implementation were set. Emissaries spoke to gatherings of Jewish organizations in America, expecting to become the vehicle for revolutionary change within the Jewish people and within the world. But the encounter with the world was only now beginning and it was not a positive one. As early as June 1945, Grinberg had expressed the fear that "mankind does not comprehend what we have gone through and what we experienced during this period of time and it seems to us," he speculated, "neither shall we be understood in the future."[30]

Grinberg's fear was well founded. Even those who were sent to aid the survivors, to assist them in recovering their humanity did not understand. The administrator of the Landsberg camp, an American Jew in the employ of the United Nations, told a group of visiting Americans that the camp inhabitants did not deserve too much sympathy. "One must not remind them of their frightful yesterdays - they must forget this and work instead. They must realize that work means freedom."[31]

A psychologist writing in Commentary Magazine in 1948 commented on the lack of psychiatric understanding of what the survivors had experienced.

Indeed, he wrote, "a number of observers who went to Europe in the early days of relief organizations found the DPs, especially those who had come out of the concentration camps in a state of elation and enthusiasm bordering on euphoria. Uninformed in matters of psychology these observers reported that the state of mind of the people in the DP camps was almost miraculously unaffected by their recent terrible experiences. But one could have anticipated that it would not take long for the first euphoric reaction to vanish and be replaced by a deep depression. This happened."[32]

And even though the activity associated with the survivor's ideology was an important source of hope, by 1950 a deep sense of disillusion and disappointment was already evident. In one of the last issues of Undser Veg, Pesach Pekatsch expressed a sense of that disappointment. "We believed that it was time to conquer evil and inhumanity," he wrote, "that it would be a long time before bestiality would again be able to conquer the idea of freedom." Instead, Pekatsch found a different picture, one in which the "Spectre of Hatred" and the forces advocating the call to destruction and murder emerged freely and openly to attack the democracies they so hated.[33]

II

Slowly but surely, in the late 1940's and early 1950's, the survivors left Germany and left Europe. A quarter of a million went to Eretz Israel and over a hundred thousand to the United States. Those coming to America, for the most part, came penniless, physically and emotionally drained, with personal losses that words and numbers could not describe.

Yet they were coming to America, where millions of European Jews before them had found new lives and transformed their existence into the freest and most tolerant of any Jewish society in history.

But survivors were different. These were special lives, because these lives had been participants in history, both Jewish and world. And it was the sense of that history that opened their mouths not only about the specific tragic experiences they had survived but about human experience in general. The Holocaust was the central illumination and the authority for that which they knew about life, a sum of knowledge that was, in their eyes, considerable. The Holocaust had tested them, and taught them, taught them to know the nature of men, as they believed, and to know it in a way and a degree it was not given other people to know. Not even in America.

Pesach Pekatsch had realized, even in the DP camps that the She'erit Hapletah's call for change within the human condition and within the Jewish condition was not being heard. The "Double Vision" inherent in the human condition took precedence over what the survivors felt was a sacred mission.

Elie Wiesel has put it best: "What the survivors wanted was to transmit a message to the world, a message of which they were the sole bearers. Having gained an insight into man that will forever remain unequalled, they tried to share a knowledge with that world."[34]

But the survivors, according to Wiesel, found themselves in another kind of exile, another kind of prison. People welcomed them with tears and sobs when they stepped off the boats, then turned away.[35] And why not. As one survivor recounted of her first years in this country: "My cousins were American-born Jews -- kind, generous, people who also shrank from me a little. You understand, the concentration camp experience is nothing that endears you to people."[36]

Shortly after her arrival in America in 1951, one survivor had the experience of being told by her American-born Jewish neighbor in Brooklyn that she should write stories. "You have a terrific imagination," the neighbor told her on hearing a tale about selections and gas chambers.[37]

In New Orleans a truck driver told a survivor: "Don't try to tell people here what happened in Europe: forget about it. I was in the American army. I walked into those camps and I saw all the things the

Germans did and people here don't believe it when you tell them." The truck driver had given up mentioning the sights he had seen in the camps to anyone but people who had been there.[38]

In many respects, these attitudes were the beginning of a "conspiracy of silence" between Holocaust survivors and society,[39] a silence that would characterize the lives of most survivors even 25 years after their arrival in America. For many Americans, they would still be the "refugees" who had come with amazing tales to tell, but who soon stopped talking and interacting with the native American community.

Helen Epstein, whose book on the children of survivors has become the Bible of the Second Generation, remembers her mother's tatoo as being "like a mysterious flag. It made some people blush, turn their eyes aside, mumble odd, garbled things."[40]

So the survivors retreated, convinced that tales about starvation, the ghetto, Auschwitz selections, or any other such experiences, could not be accepted as the truth or as lessons to change the nature of our world.

Instead, the survivors remained different. They were not like Americans, indeed the connection between American Jews and themselves was only slightly less remote than the connection between themselves and American Gentiles.

They worked hard, bore children, and found a place for themselves in their adopted homeland. Many became professionally successful, steeled by the experience of survival to endure the slings and arrows of the difficult and uncertain world of trade and commerce.[41]

Yet with a determined consistency certain feelings emerged from within the survivor communities which reflected a long lost echo of that early sense of idealism, of the revolutionary fervor which shook the DP camps. There were those survivors who believed that, for many in their group, material well being became an end rather than a means. They felt that, because survivors saw and suffered, "there should have come forward from among them a better sort of person, less selfish than the ordinary, perhaps; one more sensitive to humankind, one with spiritual goals that were a little higher than those of most people - otherwise, for what had they survived?"[42]

Not more than a decade ago, the conspiracy of silence - a scrupulously kept taboo which lasted for decades — broke apart. The genius of the American soul allowed both the survivor and his and her children to occupy a unique role in the evolution of the Jewish presence in history. The Holocaust and its observance became, in its rites and rituals, an American obsession: from the President of the United States who issued a mandate that its rememberance become a full national memorial museum in our nation's capital to annual observances of its meaning for Christians and Jews in every state of the Union. The children of the survivors have opened, in the words of Helen Epstein, their "iron boxes," that internal sense of being different, of having grown up in a home with survivors, but without grandparents or aunts and uncles. What it has meant for their development as Americans, as Jews, as members of a community of the Second Generation is still being evaluated.[43]

Indeed, to some observers, the American Jewish return to Judaism is comprised of the rites and rituals of identification with and fascination about the Holocaust which allows "ready access to deep feelings and a direct encounter with transcendental experience."

All of this is too much to grasp, almost too unbelievable to accept.

The "in" status of the Holocaust has not found acceptance within the entire range of the survivor community. Its most persistent voice, Elie Wiesel, remains its most persistent critic. As early as the 1970's he wrote that "suddenly everyone began calling himself a survivor. One consequence is that an international symposium on the Holocaust was held recently in New York without the participation of any Holocaust survivors. The survivors didn't count. They never did. They are best forgotten.... They are an embarrassment. If only they weren't there, it would be so much easier."[44]

And even in this "decade of the survivor," when they are asked to speak in the classrooms and into the cassette recorder they are, in the words of Terence Des Pres, "both sought and shunned: the desire to hear the survivor's truth is countered by the need to ignore him. Insofar as we feel compelled to defend a comforting view of life, we tend to deny the survivor's voice."[45]

Despite all of the surface success, the world has not really listened to the voice of the She'erit

Hapletah. We have not listened to the prophetic voice that sought to change the direction of Jewish identity and of human destiny, to steer a course towards the moral and social perfection of humanity. We have not listened to a voice that could tell us that the consequences of the Holocaust are all around us in what we see and what we are.

Where is the voice of the She'erit Hapletah? Perhaps it is in the voice of Jacob Felberbaum who talks about the memories and feelings which haunt the aging survivor:

"To no surprise we take our memorabilia. The fragments saved from the abyss of our tragedy. Photographs of our dear ones grace the walls. And we try to read those sometimes yellowing faces and to recreate their past and with it our own past. Somehow it is not possible. The time blurred our memory and we stare in the empty space. So when we are talking about loneliness, we are talking about feelings in different dimensions than in the usual meaning of this word.

This is simply the result of absence of generations that are gone and also those generations that were denied to come into being. We are condemned never to see our dear ones, never to listen to our friends, or for that matter to those we did not like so much.

So we lost the world of our fathers. In the smokestacks of devilish camps, in the ravines in the outskirts of cities, within the ravished ghettos, a deep-rooted credence in the justice of the Higher Power was fundamentally shaken. We remained with the hidden pain of indescribable loneliness."[46]

But perhaps the voice of the She'erit Hapletah belongs to another time, a century or more from now, when Jews will talk of the Holocaust in the same distant, almost metaphysical way in which they describe the Exodus from Egypt, or the revolt of the Macabees. One day, the Holocaust will simply be a child's memory, a parent's recounting of a tale that will give meaning to Jewish identity and bring special meaning to being a Jew. But that, after all, is what lay at the very center of the voice of the She'erit Hapletah and all the other prophetic voices that have spoken to the Jewish people and to the world--and which will, we pray, continue to do so.

Notes

This paper is dedicated to the memory of my mother, Anna Peck, of blessed memory, a part of the voice of the She'erit Hapletah, whose spirit is scattered to the winds. Research for the paper was made possible by support from the Memorial Foundation for Jewish Culture.

1. Isabella Leitner: Saving the Fragments. New York, 1985, pp. 77 ff.

2. Quoted in Robert H. Abzug, Inside the Vicious Heart. Americans and the Liberation of Nazi Concentration Camps. New York, p. 21.

3. C. W. Doughty, quoted in Abzug, p. 31.

4. Samuel Glasshow, quoted in Abzug, p. 63.

5. William B. Lovelady, quoted in Abzug, p. 33.

6. Meyer Levin, quoted in Abzug, p. 19.

7. Abzug, Chapter 7: "Telling the Story."

8. Quoted in Alfred Gottschalk, "Religion in a Post Holocaust World," in Abraham J. Peck, Jews and Christians After the Holocaust, Philadelphia, 1982, p. 2.

9. Alexander Donat quoted in Henry L. Feingold, "Who Shall Bear Guilt for the Holocaust: The Human Dilemma," in American Jewish History 68, (March, 1979), p. 281.

10. Stefan Zweig, Die Welt von Gestern. Frankfurt, 1981, p. 17.

11. Simon Schochet, Feldafing. Vancouver, 1983, pp. 14-15.

12. See Wolfgang Jacobmeyer, Vom Zwangsarbeiter zum Heimatlosen Auslaender, Goettingen, 1985; as well as his illuminating essay, "Juedische Ueberlebende als "Displaced Persons," Untersuchungen zur Besatzungspolitik in den deutschen Westzonen und zur Zuwanderung osteuropaeischer Juden, 1945-1947," in Geschichte und Gesellschaft, vol. 9, 1983, pp. 421-452.

13. Quoted in "Homecoming in Israel," in Leo W. Schwarz, The Root and the Bough. New York, 1949, p. 310.

14. Marie Syrkin, The State of the Jews. Washington, D.C. 1980, p. 11.

15. H. Leivick, Mit der She'erit Hapletah. Toronto, 1947 (Yiddish).

16. Ira Hirschmann, quoted in Leonard Dinnerstein, America and the Survivors of the Holocaust. New York, 1982, p. 22.

17. Quoted in ibid., pp. 16-17.

18. Quoted in ibid., p. 43.

19. See Judah Nadich, Eisenhower and the Jews, New York, 1953.

20. See Leo W. Schwartz. The Redeemers. New York, 1953; Ursula Buettner, "Not nach der Befreiung. Die Situation der deutschen Juden in der britischen Bezatzungszone, 1945-1948," in Ursula Buettner (editor), Das Unrechtsregime (volume 2) Hamburg, 1986, pp. 373-406; Irving Heymont, Among the Survivors of the Holocaust: 1945. The Landsberg DP Camp Letters of Major Irving Heymont, U.S. Army. Cincinnati, 1982.

21. See Dinnerstein, America and the Survivors of the Holocaust; Yehudah Bauer, Flight and Rescue: Brichah. New York, 1970; Michael Checinski, "The Kielce Pogrom: Some Unanswered Questions," in Soviet Jewish Affairs, (Vol. 5, 1, 1975): 57-72.

22. See the statistics in Jacobmeyer, "Juedische Ueberlebende," which show that the DP birthrate in 1946 of 29 per 1,000 was nearly four times the German one, p. 437.

23. J. Nemenczyk in the Landsberger Lager-Caytung (15.4. 1946), p. 3 (Yiddish).

24. "Mir Yidn un die Velt," in Dos Fraye Vort (28:6. 1946), P. 5 (Yiddish).

26. Quoted in Undzer Veg 17, Munich (15.1.1946), p. 2 (Yiddish).

27. Quoted in "Die Problematische Stellung der Juden in Deutschland," in Der Weg, Berlin (1.3.1946), p.2.

28. Menachem Sztajer, "Szerit Hapleita," in DP Express - Fun Jidiszn leben, Munich, (October, 1946), p. 2 ff.

29. Samuel Gringauz, "Die Zukunft der Jeudischen Kultur," in Juedische Rundschau, Marburg, (May-June 1946) pp. 22-24.

30. Grinberg, "We are Living Corpses," p. 7; One month later, in July, 1945, Abba Kovner in a meeting of Jewish Brigade members and partisan fighters in Italy, spoke in a familiar vein: "But how does one instill it in the hearts of a generation that did not live through all this... For such people, all this will represent mere abstractions." Abba Kovner, The Mission of the Survivors," in Yisrael Gutman and Livia Rothkirchen, (eds.), The Catastrophe of European Jewry, Jerusalem, 1976, p. 681.

31. Quoted in Israel Efros, Heimlose Yidn. Buenos Aires/Sao Paulo, 1947, p. 44. (Yiddish)

32. Paul Friedman, "The Road Back for the DPs, in Commentary, (vol. 6, 1948), p. 502.

33. Pesach Pekatsch in Undzer Veg, (28.9.1950) p. 2.

34. Elie Wiesel, A Jew Today. New York, 1978, pp. 185-208.

35. Ibid.

36. Quoted in Dorothy Rabinowitz, New Lives. Survivors of the Holocaust Living in America. New York, 1976, p. 43.

37. Ibid., p. 196.

38. Ibid.

39. For a comprehensive analysis of the "Conspiracy of Silence," see Yael Danieli, "Therapists' Difficulties in Treating Survivors of the Nazi Holocaust and their Children," unpublished Ph.D. dissertation (New York University, 1981).

40. Helen Epstein, Children of the Holocaust. New York, 1979, p. 43.

41. Abraham J. Peck, "The Children of Holocaust Survivors," in Allon Schoener, The American Jewish Album, 1654 to the Present. New York, 1983, pp. 309-310.

42. Rabinowitz, New Lives, p. 220 ff.

43. The children of survivors have formed an international network of communication and have staged a number of conferences, the most recent being in Los Angeles in early 1988.

44. Wiesel, A Jew Today, pp. 185 ff.

45. Terence Des Pres, The Survivor. An Anatomy of Life in the Death Camps. New York, 1976, p. 43.

46. Jacob Felberbaum, "The Loneliness of a Survivor," in Together. American Gathering/Federation of Jewish Holocaust Survivors, vol. 1, no. 3., p. 15.

THE PROBLEMATICAL ROLE OF THE SURVIVOR AS WITNESS

Nelly Wilson

Department of French
University of Bristol
BS8 1TE

One aspect of camp behaviour which has never ceased to amaze me, is the exhausting battle fought relentlessly to stay alive when death would have been such a merciful release. Suicide may have been common in Berlin in 1933 or in Vienna in 1938 but it was not in Auschwitz-Birkenau. And yet dying in that hell required infinitely less effort than hanging on to life; it was the natural process which, moreover, could be speeded up relatively painlessly.

What stood between me and the electified barbed wires were the almost daily letters I wrote to the outside world, in my mind for I possessed nothing so precious as pen and paper, informing it of what was happening. The passion to testify, to bear witness, was a not uncommon response to the Apocalypse. "Write and record", Simon Dubnov's alleged last words to inmates of the Riga ghetto, sum up a distinct form of Jewish resistance, as evidenced by the diaries and chronicles hidden or buried in the ground in tins in the hope that the testimonies at least would survive. What is remarkable about these "scrolls of agony", Kaplan's Warsaw Diary for example, is the purity of the historical motive. Kaplan recorded for the world and posterity without any of my certainty that the civilised world cared and that, caring, it would come to our help if only it knew. For the Warsaw diarist testifying was an end in itself.

This brings me to some misgivings I have, which may turn out to be wholly unjustified, about the purpose of this gathering or at least about its choice of title.

I am not at all sure that the view of man, history and the holocaust implicit in "Remembering for the Future" is valid or altogether desirable. Does mankind draw lessons from the past? There is considerable historical evidence to suggest that this is not the case. One might go on to argue that this is to be expected since no two events or situations are ever alike; we need to respond to the specificity of each, grasp as best we can the particular combination of forces operative at a given moment in time. Continuity should not be confused with repetition. If history does not repeat itself then historical lessons are not automatically transferable and we cannot make up or atone for yesterday's unheeded lessons by applying them to today, and still less to tomorrow. The morally unbearable corollary to all this is that "remembering for the future" and "it must not happen again" may be no more than expressions of remorse, wishful thinking, vital lies which help the world to survive the holocaust, to live with its memory. So be it. However, there is still something to be said for the pure historical imperative, for remembering the holocaust because it happened, for its own sake, without looking for ethical silver linings or God's will in a senseless and futile massacre of the innocents.

Today, in the face of revisionist denials, misleading analogies, widespread exploitation, speculation as to how it could have happened, the reality of the extermination camps needs to be rescued. And who better to restore a note of sanity and sanctity than the former insider who has made it to the outside? And yet, from a documentary point of view, the position of the eyewitness is even more problematical today than it was forty years ago when the first wave of fact-and-figure historians made us, the living documents, largely redundant. We knew what hell was like but they knew its precise location, size, capacity, how it functioned. However much we may have resented such measuring of our Leidensgechichte, there can be little doubt that it conveyed the enormity of the crime, or at least one kind of enormity, more comprehensively and coherently than most eyewitness accounts based on necessarily limited perception and comprehension. What did the majority of ordinary Auschwitz inmates, as distinct from the Sonderkommandos condemned to death by their very knowledge, see or know of the camp, its purpose and organisation? To those spared the sight of gaschambers and crematoria, even the ominous chimneys, flames and smoke did not add up to the murder of one's family, let alone mass extermination. These are facts which did not become clear until much later, through reading. The luck "not to have been in the know", inability to make sense of the clues made both dying and surviving a little easier. We lived through what we saw as an incomprehensible nightmare, absurd acts of atrocity devised by a Herrenvolk gone mad, without perceiving that it was all part and parcel of an organised system called the Final Solution. When I came to learn of the full history, after the liberation, my own story dwindled into insignificance and my passion to bear witness abruptly stopped. Historically, the ordinary survivors' testimony is of limited value, even more uncertain forty years on. They are rarely in a position to provide the "clear and incontrovertible statements" required in courts of law, by historians and even, it seems, by the organisers of Remembering for the Future.

They have the right, however, and even the duty, to protest against theories and interpretations which distort their experiences and dishonour the dead. One such view, made fashionable some twenty years ago by Raul Hilberg, Hugh Trevor-Roper and most questionably by Bruno Bettelheim, was that European Jewry, for long accustomed to passivity and resignation, trotted to the gaschambers like sheep to the slaughter, rounded up and shepherded by their own leaders. What these "explanations", which incidentally are not without raising some important questions about general and not only Jewish behaviour in extreme situations, demonstrated above all was the gulf between theory and reality, between outsider and insider. Justifiable insider anger (Alexander Donat's Jewish Resistance, for example) provoked a "They fought back" reaction which tended to heroize or martyrize all victims on the example of the genuinely heroic resistance of the few, as if the will to stay alive and remain human and all the basic imperatives this implied, a sort of camp decalogue, were not daily acts of moral resistance (e.g. don't steal from a fellow-inmate, fight for every extra scrap of food but not at the expense of somebody else's ration; keep clean; don't cry, etc.,etc.)

This daily struggle is part of the wider historical canvas which only survivors can fill in. They have done so in numerous memoirs and autobiographical writings without, for the most part, displaying the emotionalism and "spirit of martyrology" against which Philip Friedman, doyen of holocaust historians, warned researchers.[1] It is in this sphere perhaps, let us call it mind over body under stress, that survivors have made and are still able to make the most valuable contributions, if they can bear to remember and provided they can overcome the distortions of time and the inadequacy of language. Whether words can convey in the deepest sense what "it was like" is questionable. However, holocaust aesthetics and the poet's dilemma in particular are a different story. Let us stay for the moment with historical interpretations and misinterpretations.

For some time past attention has been shifting from the victims' complicity in and resistance to their own destruction to the policy of extermination pursued by the Third Reich. Here, the most spectacular distortion evidently comes from revisionism. Yet I fear that neither the historian with massive evidence at his fingertips nor the insider with direct but limited knowledge is in a position to deny the denial, a particularly excruciating impotence for those who were there and yet not there. The eyewitnesses who came closest are the Nazi officials directly concerned, such as the deputy commandant of Treblinka who in a recent press interview[2] declared the denial of the existence of the gaschambers to be "stupid", and the handful of surviving Sonderkommandos and gravediggers. They have testified, most recently in Richard Rashke's Escape from Sobibor and, more directly, in Claude Lanzmann's Shoah. We owe a debt of gratitude to them for publicly remembering the most painful experiences as well as to the sensitive artists who presented the testimony, a good example of history and Leidensgechichte intermingling and complementing each other. Will these accounts or any others have any effect on so-called historical revisionism? Probably not. "Six million did not die" is not an historical conclusion open to discussion or challenge but an ideological statement, an article of faith.

More serious because more widespread and respectable is the tendency to relativize Nazi atrocities by means of analogies: Stalin's Russia; Algerians tortured by the French; the Vietnamese maimed or killed by American bombs, etc.,etc. What is objectionable about these comparisons is not the fact that the Jewish tragedy is scaled down or deprived of its uniqueness but the banalisation of Nazi ideology. When liberal intellectuals prove their broadminded humanitarianism and sense of justice by comparing Treblinka to Cambodia, one is baffled by their confusion or else by a display of absurdist ethics: one massacre being like any other. It is more worrying when German academics use such _analogetics_ - if I may coin a term - to elaborate their apologetics. For whose benefit? That of their guilty fathers or their innocent children? I am inclined to say about the former, possibly comprising an SS guard or two, that they must learn to live with their guilt as we have learnt to live with our grief. As for the young, they need to understand the past rather than be taught how to analogise it out of its awesome significance.

Serious holocaust historiography has reached the stage of speculation, debate, rival approaches and explanations. Why did it happen, who exactly was responsible, was the extermination policy a predetermined plan or an unplanned process growing out of control, some Golem-like machine? As one historian put it at the recent Paris conference on Nazi extermination policy at which these and other questions were discussed (December 1987)[3] Now that the facts are known the field is wide open to interpretation. To which Lanzmann retorted: The facts are not known, they have disappeared; eternally absent. Who could write a meaningful history of Treblinka? We were back with the real "shoah". Rescuing it from abstraction and intellectualisation is a useful - and urgent - task. But how is it to be achieved?

Lanzmann's film _Shoah_ suggests an answer. It embodies much of what, in my view, a holocaust work of art should be: a work of terrible beauty and haunting images not of atrocities but of faces and places. Its impact is such that no one with any sensitivity who has seen it will ever speak or think of Treblinka as he had done before. Ideally, this should be the aim of holocaust art: not to explain, accuse, excuse, moralise, describe atrocities or transform them, but to turn the incredulous outsider into an insider, to make him feel the unimaginable as part of his experience, make him feel, for example, the presence of the burnt corpses below the luscious grass. Only such art can preserve the holocaust from the desecration to which it is so frequently and mindlessly subjected by the mass media, the press and, most nauseatingly, by our spiritual leaders given to drawing parallels between the extermination of Jewry and the threat posed to Judaism by marrying out of the faith. The survivor must protest against such exploitations but if he or she were a genius that protest might take the form of an undegradable image, symbol or inscription which would impose itself on man's consciousness in the way certain legendary figures have imposed themselves. Judas and Shylock are, alas, such figures.

Primo Levi once remarked that survivors fall into two groups: those who cannot bear to write about their experiences and those who feel compelled to do so. I belong to what is perhaps a not inconsiderable third group: those whom a feeling of artistic impotence condemns to silence.

Notes

1 "Problems of Research on the Holocaust", 1957, in Philip Friedman: _Roads to Extinction: Essays on the Holocaust_, The Jewish Publication Society of America, New York 1980,p.559.

2 In _Le Monde Diplomatique_, quoted in _Jewish Chronicle_, 18 March 1988.

3 For a report on this conference see: N. Wilson: "Variations on the theme of mass murder", _Patterns of Prejudice_ Vol. 22, spring 1988 p.43.

